THE NEW YORK *Chronology*

ALSO BY JAMES TRAGER

∷

The People's Chronology

The Women's Chronology

The Food Chronology

West of Fifth

Park Avenue: City of Dreams

❖ THE ❖
NEW YORK
Chronology

The ULTIMATE COMPENDIUM *of* EVENTS, PEOPLE, *and* ANECDOTES *from the* DUTCH *to the* PRESENT

JAMES TRAGER

HarperResource
An Imprint of HarperCollins*Publishers*

HarperCollins books may be purchased for educational, business, or sales promotional use. For information, please write: Special Markets Department, HarperCollins Publishers Inc., 10 East 53rd Street, New York, NY 10022.

FIRST EDITION

Designed by Leah Carlson-Stanisic

Library of Congress Cataloging-in-Publication Data is available upon request.

ISBN 0-06-052341-7

03 04 05 06 07 WBC/RRD 10 9 8 7 6 5 4 3 2 1

Acknowledgments

Nobody but nobody loves New York (or books) more than my wise and capable wife, Chie Nishio, whose photographic eye is just one of the many talents she has brought to bear on this project. Others whose advice, information, and suggestions helped bring the effort to fruition include Anthony F. Bandelato of the Madison Square Boys' and Girls' Club; Norman Brouwer and Gretchen McKenzie of the South Street Seaport Museum; Jean B. Butner of Value Line; my editor Greg Chaput and his capable HarperCollins colleagues Diane Aronson, Leah Carlson-Stanisic, Mary Ellen Curley, Karen Lumley, Donna Ruvituso, and Shelby Meizlik; Linda Corcoran of the Wildlife Conservation Society; Lawrence Creshkoff; Osborn Elliott of Citizens Union; Victor Elmaleh of World Wide Holdings; Jennifer L. Freer of The Conference Board; William Lee Frost; Burt and Elena Glinn; Dale Jennings of John Jay College of Criminal Justice; Jim Lebenthal; archivist Adele Lerner of the New York Hospital-Cornell Medical Center; Gerald and Larry Maslon; Doris Palca; Fred Papert; Joseph Petta of Consolidated Edison; Ellen and James Stewart Polshek; Dan Schoenberg of Madison Square Garden; Betsy Sosland; William Soto, Ron Mohamed, and James Vaval of the Department of Buildings; John and Judith Stonehill; Gay Talese; my son Oliver Trager; and Eunice Weed. My sincere thanks to them all.

Preface

How New York grew to be the center of the financial world, art world, fashion, theater, music, publishing, architecture, and so much else is a story that begs to be told chronologically.

Actors' Equity, Polly Adler, Stella Adler, anti-Semitism, Arnold Constable, Nick Arnstein, Chester A. Arthur, Astors, Auden, Audubon—they all deserve inclusion in the story of this incredible city. Presented in alphabetical order, out of context, they simply do not interact the way they actually did as events unfolded year by year.

Wall Street, the Westminster Kennel Club, Stanford White, Winchell, Woodhull, Woolworth—they all went into making New York New York. How to place them all in perspective has been the problem, and its solution is here in *The New York Chronology*.

Hundreds, perhaps thousands, of books have been written about the many aspects of the world's foremost metropolis, and this is not the first attempt to pull together in one volume the various facets of its colorful history. The purpose of this book is not only to provide an accurate, concise desk reference but also to entertain readers with details of the less familiar characters and happenings that figured in the city's rise to prominence.

In these pages the reader will find radicals, Radio City, Rauschenberg, Renwick, Jacob Riis, Jackie Robinson, Rockefellers, Rodgers, Roeblings, Roosevelts, Roseland, Rosenwach, Emery Roth, Rothko, Helena Rubinstein, Jacob Ruppert, Babe Ruth, and Morrie Ryskind, not in alphabetical order but as they appeared, along with some of the things that originated in New York—baseball rules, elevators, vaudeville, hot dog, brassieres, Xerox copies, bebop and many more.

Love it or hate it, New York over the years has unquestionably been a magnetic force that attracted more capital, more immigrants (Asians, Germans, Haitians, Irish, Italians, Jews, Latinos, Poles, you name it), more talent, more wannabes from every part of America and elsewhere in the world, more of everything than any other city in modern times. An alphabetical index makes it easy to find entries covering a wide range of specific subjects; casual browsing will turn up illuminating surprises on every page.

Key to Symbols

political events

human rights, social justice

philanthropy

exploration, colonization

commerce

retailing

energy

transportation

technology

science

medicine

religion

education

communications, media

literature

art

photography

theater, film

music

sports

everyday life

tobacco

crime

real estate

environment

marine resources

agriculture

food availability

consumer protection

food and drink

restaurants

population

The Early Years

1524 Florentine navigator Giovanni da Verrazano, 39, explores the North American coast with a 49-man crew. Master of the 100-ton French vessel *Dauphine*, he comes upon a "beautiful" harbor in April and gives the name Angoulême to the island that later will be called Manhattan (Angoulême is the home province of Verrazano's employer, France's François I). "At the end of a hundred leagues," Verrazano will write to the king, "we found a very agreeable location situated within two prominent hills, in the midst of which flowed to the sea a very great river which was deep at the mouth." He notes in his diary that "steep little hills" rose up on both sides of his ship, and that coming into the body of water where he lies at anchor is a "great stream of water" (*see* Hudson, 1609).

1609 French explorer Samuel de Champlain, 41, travels south from the St. Lawrence River with a party of Huron and two fellow Frenchmen, proceeding down a large lake that will later bear his name. The group encounters a party of Iroquois July 30, a scuffle ensues, Champlain fires his arquebus, two Iroquois chiefs fall dead, their tribesmen flee, and the resulting animosity will lead to an alliance between the Iroquois and the English.

English navigator and Arctic explorer Henry Hudson, 59, makes a third voyage to America, this time in the employ of Dutch interests (the 7-year-old United East India Company). Commissioned March 25, Hudson's 80-ton ship *Halve Maen* (*Half Moon*) has sailed out of Amsterdam in early April with a mixed Dutch-English crew of 18 or 20. Hudson drops anchor September 2 in the lower bay of what will become New York Harbor, and finally, on September 3, enters a 154-mile tidal estuary that will be called the Hudson River (it will later be found to rise in Lake Tear of the Clouds, 4,923 feet high in the Adirondack Mountains, and to be 315 miles long). Hudson sails off October 4 with nothing to show for his efforts, but the Hudson Valley that will bear his name is destined to become a source of wealth much greater than the spice islands of the East Indies.

Henry Hudson's second mate Robert Juet writes the name "Manhattan" to denote the land that lies to the starboard as they ascend the estuary. But Hudson's maps will not show Manhattan to be an island, and historians will debate the origin of the word, some of them tracing it to the Munsee word *manahactanienk* ("place of general inebriation"), others to the Munsee word *manahatouh* ("place where timber may be procured for bows and arrows"), still others simply to the Munsee word *menatay*, meaning island.

English authorities detain Henry Hudson's ship after he lands at Dartmouth (Dutch seamen will return her to Amsterdam next year), but Hudson himself reaches Amsterdam and shows his Dutch employers some beaver pelts he has obtained from the natives in return for beads, hatchets, and knives. Amsterdam merchants see the possibility of a new source of furs, which they have been buying from Russia for sale to both men and women for wear indoors and out (*see* 1610).

1610 A sporadic fur trade begins to develop between Dutch merchants and the Native Americans encountered last year by Henry Hudson.

1614 The Nieuw Nederland colony is founded in the area between the Connecticut and Delaware rivers (*see* 1623).

The United Nieuw Nederland Company formed by 13 merchants of Amsterdam and Hoorn receives a charter that gives it a virtual monopoly in the fur trade and other trade that will continue until 1617.

1623 The Dutch make Nieuw Nederland a formally organized province and organize a group of families to settle there (*see* 1614). The Dutch West India Company draws up Provisional Regulations for Colonists under whose terms they are to be provided with

1

clothing and supplies from the Company's store-houses, these to be paid for at modest prices in installments, but they may not produce any handicrafts and may engage in trade only if they sell their wares to the Company. They must promise to stay for at least 6 years and to settle wherever the Company locates them (see 1624).

1624 Some 34 Dutch families land in May on Manhattan Island (see 1623). Sent by the 2-year-old Dutch West India Company under the command of Cornelis Jacobsen May, the 110 men, women, and children have come by way of the Canary Islands and the West Indies, taking nearly 2 months to make the voyage aboard the 260-ton vessel *Nieuw Nederland*. Most are French-speaking Protestant Walloons from the Spanish Netherlands under the leadership of Jesse De Forest of Avesnes, Hainaut, and most settle on a 65-acre piece of land off the southern tip of Manhattan (later to be called Governors Island), but in order to cover as much territory as possible Capt. May sends some to the Connecticut River Valley and a few upriver to Fort Nassau, where they find that the stockade has been ruined by spring flood waters and build a new one, naming it Fort Orange (the House of Orange is Holland's ruling family) (see 1625).

$ Fort Orange becomes the headquarters of the Dutch West India Company's fur trade. The Walloon colonists on Manhattan Island export 4,000 beaver pelts and 700 otter skins worth a total of 27,125 guilders—slightly more than the value of the goods supplied by the Company to the colonists (the name Beaver Street will bear witness through the centuries to the city's first great source of income). Having profited hugely from the sugar and slave trade, the Company has spent 20,000 guilders to establish the Nieuw Amsterdam colony; the first shipload of furs that it sends back to Holland is by some accounts worth 45,000 guilders.

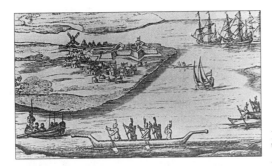

Export of beaver pelts acquired from the natives provided Dutch settlers with the basis of their earliest commerce.

∞ A *ziekentrooster* (comforter of the sick) arrives on Manhattan Island as the colony's first preacher.

1625 Fort Amsterdam is founded April 22 on the lower tip of Manhattan Island by the Dutch West India Company (see 1624). The Company builds a few houses near the fort that it is constructing (see 1635) and lays out some streets.

Fort Amsterdam gets its first slaves—some Angolan men taken by a Dutch privateer from a Portuguese ship bound for Brazil. The men are put to work building the fort; loading Dutch West India Company ships with beaver, mink, otter, rat, and wildcat pelts; and tending the colonists' fields of barley, buckwheat, oats, rye, wheat, canary seed, and flax (see 1626).

The Dutch ship *Oranjeboom* (*Orange Tree*) arrives in late March or early April from Plymouth, England, with an unrecorded number of additional colonists, but 11 passengers have died and 20 fallen ill while waiting for the weather to lift at Plymouth, where plague was raging. A convoy of four Dutch ships sets sail for Fort Amsterdam April 25, but pirates capture one of them—*De Makereel*—off Dunkirk April 27.

Fort Amsterdam's first jail is opened to confine those convicted of crimes. It will also be used to hold Native Americans.

Dutch engineer-surveyor Cryn Fredericksz arrives at Fort Amsterdam with diagrams that he made before leaving the Netherlands. Engaged by the Dutch West India Company to lay out a settlement, Fredericksz has plans for a church, hospital, houses, a school, a mill, streets, and fortifications (see 1635).

Three Dutch ships (the *Paert* [*Horse*], the *Koe* [*Cow*], and the *Schaep* [*Sheep*]) arrive at Fort Amsterdam with 45 more colonists and the colony's first livestock—100 stallions, mares, Holstein bulls and cows, sheep, and hogs. Amsterdam brewer Pieter Evertsen Hulst has paid for their passage, and although three animals have died on the voyage the rest have been kept alive en route in individual stalls. They are put ashore at Nutten (later Governors) Island to keep them from wandering into Manhattan's forests, but a lack of pasturage and water on the island forces their quick removal to Manhattan, where 20 will die in the next few months from eating poisonous weeds.

1626 Pieter Minuit arrives at Fort Amsterdam May 4, replacing director Willem Verhulst, who succeeded Cornelius May but has been found guilty of mismanagement and recalled by the Dutch West India Company. Minuit later in the year buys Manhattan Island from Lenape tribal chiefs of the Wappinger Confederacy for cloth, beads, fish hooks, hatchets, and trinkets valued by the Dutch at 60 guilders. Details of the transaction will remain sketchy, and by some accounts the sale is not concluded until November 25, although a document dated November 7 by one Peter Schlager at Amsterdam informs the States General that the ship *The Arms of Amsterdam* has arrived with a cargo of furs and timber. Reports Schlager, "They have bought the Island Manhattes from the wildmen for the value of 60 guilders; 'tis 11,000 morgens [22,000 acres] in size" (the letter will be found in the national archives at The Hague in 1839); historians will base their accounts on this one brief mention, and although it gives no details of what the colonists gave the "wildmen" or where exactly the transaction took place, some will conclude that the deal was made near what later will be the corner of South and Whitehall streets. Minuit assigns large tracts of Manhattan land to members of the Company (patroons) on condition that they bring over stipulated numbers of settlers to the new town of Nieuw Amsterdam founded by Minuit.

More black slaves from Angola are put ashore at Fort Amsterdam, bringing the total to about a dozen men (*see* 1625; women, 1628).

$ The 60 guilders paid for Manhattan is by some accounts $24 and by others $39 (roughly 0.2¢ per acre), but 20th century economists will reckon the purchasing power of 60 guilders at somewhere between $345 and several thousand dollars in modern terms (and the recipients have sold land that does not belong to them).

1627 Pieter Minuit relocates Dutch colonists living near the Delaware River to Manhattan in June to protect them from attacks by Native Americans.

Pieter Minuit bought Manhattan Island from the "wildmen" for 60 guilders' worth of trinkets. It wasn't theirs to sell.

Shad ascend the Hudson River March 11 with such regularity each year that Dutch colonists at Nieuw Amsterdam will call the herring *elft* (the 11 fish). In other colonies it will be called the May Fish because it comes up the rivers to spawn in that month. Shad is considered the poor man's fish; most are dried and smoked for later use in stews.

Dutch colonists at Nieuw Amsterdam will enrich the American cuisine in the next 37 years with cookies (*koekjes*), coleslaw, and waffles.

1628 The first female slaves arrive at Fort Amsterdam (*see* 1626). The three Angolan women quickly find husbands, free blacks will soon join the fort's workforce, and virtually all of the slaves will eventually be freed and given land (*see* 1634).

The Rev. Jonas Michaëlius arrives at Fort Amsterdam in April as first minister of the Dutch Reformed Church in America and holds services on the second floor of a mill until a wooden church can be built.

Rev. Michaëlius writes a letter August 28 describing his efforts to teach catechism to Native American children in a town that still has no more than a few hundred settlers (*see* Collegiate School, 1638).

1630 Natives of what the colonists call Staten Island sell their land for "kittles, axes, Hoos, wampum, drilling awles, Jews Harps, and diverse small wares," according to an undated translation of recollections by Cornelius Meylin, the island's patroon, that will be recorded in 1659 (exchanged to mark ceremonies or celebrate past events, "wampum" is made from clam and whelk shells that are turned into stringed patterns of purple and off-white). The island is named for the States General of the Netherlands, and its natives soon demand more. Unfamiliar with European ideas of land ownership, the natives believe they are being paid for allowing the settlers to *use* the land.

Agents of Amsterdam pearl merchant Kiliaen van Rensselaer buy a tract of land for him on the west bank of the Hudson River. They give the Indians "certain quantities of duffels, axes, knives and wampum" for a territory 24 miles in length, 48 in breadth. Van Rensselaer's nephew Arendt van Corlaer (or van Curler), 30, makes a settlement at what will be called Rensselaerwyck, where he has jurisdiction over nearly 1,000 square miles, and will make his patroonship far more prosperous than Nieuw Amsterdam (*see* 1642).

1631 Amsterdam recalls Pieter Minuit from New Netherland for granting undue privileges to patroons (landowners) and concentrating economic and political power in the hands of an elite few (see 1626). Minuit will enter the service of Sweden (see 1638).

1633 The new director general of New Netherland arrives at Nieuw Amsterdam in April and wastes no time in turning his office to his own profit. A former clerk at the Amsterdam warehouse of the Dutch West India Company who has married a niece of Kiliaen van Rensselaer, Wouter van Twiller deeds himself several hundred acres of tobacco-growing land in what later will be Greenwich Village—land that Peter Minuit had set aside for the Company. Not satisfied, van Twiller goes on to acquire Nutten (later Governors) Island and will also acquire a share in the Brooklyn Flatlands (see 1636; dismissal, 1637).

1634 A meeting of Dutch West India Company directors at Amsterdam hears a petition from "five Negroes arrived from New Netherland, claiming to have earned eight guilders a month, requesting settlement" (see 1629). The petition is referred back to the administrators of New Netherland (see 1644).

1635 Fort Amsterdam is completed at the tip of Manhattan Island (see 1625). It has four bastions—brick walls covered with battered earth and sod on the outside. Engineer-surveyor Cryn Fredericksz's plan calls for about 12 streets, with Pearl Street marking the eastern boundary and Greenwich Street the western, but the principal street is *Heere Wegh*, or "Broad Way," running roughly a mile in length to the northern edge of a settlement at what later will be Wall Street.

1636 Dutch settlers acquire 15,000 acres of Canarsee tribal lands in southeastern Breuckelen (later Brooklyn), known to the natives as *Keskachauge*. Close to the marshes of Jamaica Bay, the Flatland acreage is rich in agricultural potential (see 1647). The buyers include Jacob van Corlaer, Wolfert Gerritsen van Couwenhoven, Andries Hudde, and New Netherland's director general Wouter van Twiller (see 1633; 1637).

1637 The Dutch West India Company's New Netherland director general Wouter van Twiller acquires two small islands in the East River that the natives have called Tenkenas and Minnahanonck but later will be called Wards and Randalls (see 1669; Randel, 1784). He also buys what the natives have called Minnehanonck; the Dutch call it Varcken Eylandt and it ultimately will be called Roosevelt Island.

The Dutch West India Company dismisses Wouter van Twiller and replaces him with Willem Kieft. Van Twiller has fired the public prosecutor Lubertus van Dincklagen and sent him back to Amsterdam without giving him the 3 years' pay that was owed him,

Wouter van Twiller succeeded Pieter Minuit as governor of Nieuw Amsterdam and proved even more corrupt.

van Dincklagen has complained to the Company about van Twiller's corruption, the Company sends the former prosecutor back to New Netherland as assistant director, and it will take back much of the land that van Twiller has acquired. Van Twiller remains in New Netherland, where he enjoys his status as the colony's richest citizen.

Dutch soldier Oloff Stevensen van Cortlandt arrives at Nieuw Amsterdam, where he will amass a fortune as a brewer.

1638 Willem Kieft arrives at Nieuw Amsterdam March 28 aboard the Dutch West India Company ship *Harinck* (Herring) to take the place of Wouter van Twiller as director general of New Netherland. Former director general Pieter Minuit dies at sea in June at age 57 (approximate), having set out on a trading expedition to the West Indies only to have a storm destroy his ship.

The city's first ferry begins operating across the East River between Fulton Street, in Brooklyn, and Dover and Pearl streets, in Manhattan. Ferryman Cornelis Dircksen has started the service, but will sell it in 1643 (see 1654).

Collegiate School is founded by the Rev. Jonas Michaëlius, who starts classes under the direction of Friesland schoolmaster Adam Roelantsen, 32. The Dutch West India Company has brought Roelantsen over at the request of Dominie Everardus Bogardus and he has arrived aboard the *Harinck* along with the new director general Willem Kieft (*see* 1628; 1824).

1639 Swedish-born sea captain Jonas Jonassen Bronck, 39, settles with his wife and indentured servants on a farmstead in New Netherland. He left his father's farm in his youth, moved to Amsterdam, taught himself navigation, arrived last year at Nieuw Amsterdam, and now acquires a 500-acre piece of land from the Dutch at what later will be 132nd Street and Lincoln Avenue (*see* 1642).

1640 New Netherland director general Willem Kieft sends some men to Staten Island to investigate the theft of a pig; they attack a Raritan Indian community, inciting what will be called Governor Kieft's War.

Gardiner's Island at the eastern end of Long Island Sound gets its name as English colonist Lion Gardiner, 41, buys Manchouake Island from the Shinnecock a year after being given the property in a land grant from Charles I. Seven miles from the nearest point of land, the island is seven miles long and up to three miles wide. Gardiner is a military engineer who arrived at Boston in 1635, has befriended the natives, and will ingratiate himself with the most powerful of the Long Island chiefs, Wyandanch, by ransoming the man's daughter and returning her to the chief on her wedding day. He will acquire 78,000 acres, permitting him to travel on his own land from Montauk to Flushing, and although he will move in 1653 to what later will become East Hampton, the island will remain in the Gardiner family for more than 3½-centuries.

Malaria, measles, and smallpox epidemics continue to wreak havoc on Native American communities, as does alcohol abuse, and the tribes have good reason to resent the presence of the colonists.

1641 Dutch colonist Claes Smit is killed by a 28-year-old Wiechquaesgeck brave. Smit has been a wheelwright living in a remote house on the East River at what later will be 45th Street. The Indian saw his uncle killed by colonists near the Collect when he was 12 and has waited to take his revenge. Gov. Kieft sends a message ordering the sachem to turn over the murderer, the sachem refuses, Kieft threatens to eliminate the tribe by force of arms, but the colonists balk at escalating hostilities with the tribesmen.

1642 New Netherland colonist Jonassen Bronck makes his stone house available for a peace conference with Wiechquaesgeck chiefs and braves, who have blocked settlement to the north (*see* 1641; 1643;

Bronck, 1639). Bronck's house contains the largest library in the colonies.

Arendt van Corlaer resigns his position as colonial secretary (*see* 1630). Now 42, he will marry Jonassen Bronck's widow in 1646 (*see* 1661).

Dutch colonist Rem Jansen Vanderbeeck marries the daughter of Joris Jansen de Rapalje, who owns what will be called Brooklyn's Wallabout district. Vanderbeeck settled 2 years ago at Fort Orange (later Albany); by the end of the next century his descendants, the Remsens, will own most of the land from Red Hook Point north to what will become Livingston Street.

English Anabaptist John Throckmorton arrives from the Rhode Island colony and establishes a tiny settlement on a peninsula in the southeastern corner of what will come to be known as the Bronx (after Jonassen Bronck; *see* Throgs Neck Bridge, 1961).

The Stadt Huys is erected at what later will be the corner of Pearl Street and Coenties Slip; the first city hall, it contains courtrooms, a school, a tavern, and a jail.

1643 Dutch forces launch a surprise attack on the night of February 23 against Wiechquaesgeck and Hackensack tribespeople who have taken refuge at Corlaer's Hook and Pavonia (later Jersey City). The Amsterdam chamber of the Dutch West India Company has ordered Gov. Kieft to avoid an open break with the natives but he has chosen to ignore it. Some 80 men, women, and children are killed and mutilated in the Pavonia Massacre, several of the soldiers return with the severed heads of slain tribesmen, and stories circulate in Nieuw Amsterdam of cruel Dutch soldiers grabbing children from their mothers' breasts and hacking them to death or throwing them into the river. A Mahican attack in the winter eliminates almost all of the survivors as 11 Algonquin tribes rise up to avenge the massacre, killing and scalping colonists over a wide area and burning their farmsteads.

Colonist Jonassen Bronck dies childless in the region of what later will be Westchester County; his younger brother Pieter signs the estate inventory and moves to the area around Fort Orange (later Albany), and his indentured servants scatter to various other parts of the Dutch colony. The Bronx River (originally the Aquehung, later the Bronck's) will be named after Jonassen Bronck, as will the borough of that name.

Colonist Anne Hutchinson (*née* Marbury), 53, is killed by Munsee warriors in August or September at what later will become Pelham Bay. Her husband died last year, she moved from the Rhode Island colony to a new settlement in what later will be called Throgs Neck, in the Bronx, and all but one of the 15 members of her family are also killed in a war between the Dutch and the Wiechquaesgeck. The Hutchinson River will be named in her memory.

1644 The first American emancipation proclamation is read out February 25, liberating 11 blacks "from their servitude and set at liberty, especially as they have been many years in the service of the Honble West India Company here, and have been long since promised their freedom; also, that they are burdened with many children, so that it is impossible for them to support their wives and children, as they have been accustomed to do, if they must continue in the Company's service." The lands given to the former slaves are in what later will be Greenwich Village, but each freed black is obliged to pay an annual rent of "thirty skepels [baskets] of Maize, or Wheat, Pease or Beans, and one Fat hog, valued at thirty guilders" or return to slavery. Any child, born or unborn, is to be a slave (*see* 1646). The former slaves settle in a Manhattan area south of what later will be Houston Street (it will be called SoHo), bounded on its south by a polluted canal (city planners fill it in to create new farmland).

Gov. Kieft conscripts every male colonist in Manhattan to resist the hostile tribes, finds only about 200 fit to bear arms, presses four or five dozen Englishmen into service before they can leave the colony, and orders a massacre of the Wappinger, who have sought Dutch protection from attacks by Mohawk raiders. Some 1,500 of the 15,000 Wappinger are treacherously wiped out.

Nieuw Amsterdam's colonists build a wall to prevent cattle from leaving their pastures near the foot of Manhattan Island (herds have proliferated since the introduction of milk cows in 1625). The wall is near what later will be Wall Street (*see* 1653).

1645 A treaty signed August 29 brings temporary peace between Dutch colonists and Munsee tribal chiefs, following another massacre of tribesmen, this one on the Connecticut side of Long Island Sound in which English mercenaries have been helped by a fresh contingent of soldiers sent from the Netherlands, but the Munsee continue to resent Dutch encroachments in and about Manhattan (*see* 1655).

Gravesend is founded in Brooklyn by English-born widow Deborah, Lady Moody (*née* Dunch), 62, and some other English residents of Nieuw Amsterdam. Widowed in 1629, she inherited her husband's baronetcy, emigrated to New England 10 years later, came to Nieuw Amsterdam 2 years ago after antagonizing Puritan authorities with her radical Protestantism, and now organizes an English colony under a Dutch patent providing for self-government and freedom of religion (it will become a sanctuary for persecuted Quakers).

1646 Authorities at Amsterdam summon Gov. Kieft home to face complaints lodged against him by colonists that he behaved in a blundering and cowardly manner. Kieft's ship sinks on the return voyage and he is drowned (*see* Stuyvesant, 1647).

The ship *Tamandara* arrives at Fort Amsterdam in May with slaves from Brazil; they are sold for peas and pork (*see* 1644; 1655).

Dutch colonist Adriaen van der Donck forms a patroonship in an area that includes what later will be Riverdale and part of Westchester County. Van der Donck has attracted 50 families to the area and been rewarded with a huge land grant (*see* 1655).

1647 The Dutch States-General gives former Curaçao governor Peter (originally Petrus) Stuyvesant, 37, a commission as director general of New Netherland, replacing the late Willem Kieft, whose policies have led to bloody encounters between natives and colonists. Stuyvesant sails into the port of Nieuw Amsterdam May 11 aboard the ship *Princess* with a fleet of four vessels, takes up residence in the governor's house at Fort Amsterdam; he issues ordinances with regard to Sunday religious observance and the sale of intoxicating beverages, but public reaction against his autocratic rule is so strong that he is obliged to appoint a nine-man advisory board to assist him.

Peter Stuyvesant endeavors to impose social and religious uniformity on the province but meets with strong opposition from a population that speaks at least 18 different foreign languages and espouses a variety of religious faiths.

The new director general of New Netherland grants a deed to Dutch colonist Anthony Jansen van Salee covering an area that will become Brooklyn's New Utrecht (*see* 1652). Still inhabited by Nyack tribespeople, it will become one of the first six towns in a section that will include Bensonhurst (*see* 1661), Bath Beach, Dyker Heights, Mapleton, and Bay Ridge.

Peter Stuyvesant finds New Netherland nearly bankrupt, but his highhanded efforts to raise taxes

Peter Stuyvesant found colonists would pay no taxes except those levied on liquor. One out of four houses was a tavern.

meet with little success, and when he raises customs duties it drives away trade. Revenues to support Nieuw Amsterdam will come largely from levies imposed on the sale of liquor; colonists balk at paying any other kind of tax.

The hog and cattle market that has occupied Bowling Green is cleared away to provide a place of recreation.

1648 A law enacted September 18 tries to protect merchants against price-cutting peddlers. Singling out "several of the Scotch Merchants and Petty Traders who from time to time come over in the ships from Fatherland, do and aim at nothing else than solely to spoil trade and business by their underselling; they dispose of their goods with the utmost speed; give 11 @ 12 guilders in loose Wampum for one Beaver, and when sold out, go back again in the ships of that same year in which they come, without bestowing or conferring any benefit on the Country, all the burthens whereof, on the contrary, the Inhabitants who own property must bear." The law forbids "those Merchants, Scots and Petty traders" to "carry on any business in the least on shore here unless they take up their abode here in New Netherland three consecutive years, and in addition build in this city Nieuw Amsterdam a decent citizen dwelling, each according to his circumstances and means . . ."

Dutch colonists build the first pier on the East River, which will vie with the North (Hudson) River as a commercial port (*see* ferry, 1638). The landing at Schreyers' Hook (Weepers' Point) will be the city's only wharf until 1659.

Peter Stuyvesant complains that 25 percent of Nieuw Amsterdam's houses are taverns (*see* 1641). He

imposes strict regulations on the hours when such establishments may be open.

1651 Peter Stuyvesant buys a Manhattan farm in what later will be an area bounded by 5th and 17th streets between the East River and Fourth Avenue.

1652 The Dutch West India Company buys a tract of land from Nyack tribal chiefs. Included are parts of Brooklyn that include Yellow Hook (later Bay Ridge; *see* 1853).

The town of Flatbush is settled in the center of an area known as Midwout (middle woods). The word is derived from the Dutch *vlackebos*, meaning wooden plain, and the area will remain largely rural for 230 years.

Elmhurst, Queens, has its beginnings in Newtown, which will be the administrative seat of the town of Newtown as it grows into a large county from 1683 to 1898 (*see* 1896).

The land deeded to Anthony Jansen van Salee 5 years ago in what later will be New Utrecht gets its first European settlement: colonist Cornelius van Werckhoven has served as a *schepen* (alderman) in the Dutch city of Utrecht and erects a mill and a house for his wife, his two children, and their tutor Jacques Cortelyou (*see* 1655).

Wyckoff House goes up in Brooklyn on what later will be Clarendon Road near Ralph Avenue (year approximate). The house will take its name from Pieter Claesen Wyckoff, who came to America from the Netherlands as an indentured servant in 1637 and has become a successful farmer and magistrate. Wyckoff will be one of the richest men in New Netherland, and his descendants will occupy the house until 1902.

Nieuw Amsterdam's first Latin school is established.

1653 A grant of municipal government proclaimed by Peter Stuyvesant February 2 incorporates Nieuw Amsterdam as a city, distinct from the surrounding province. A charter granted under pressure by the Dutch West India Company establishes the offices of *schout* (mayor), two burgomasters (who are charged with nominating church wardens, fire inspectors, and surveyors, subject to approval by the director general), and five *schepens* (aldermen), all to be appointed by the director general. Less democratic than the government of the homeland, it is at least less autocratic than what has existed heretofore. The Stadt Huys tavern is converted into the first city hall, and Nicasius de Sille arrives in November after a 73-day voyage from the Netherlands; he will serve as *schout* before removing to New Utrecht on Long Island.

Colonists build a log wall across Manhattan from the North River to the East River for protection against English (and Indian) attacks. Peter Stuyvesant has borrowed 6,000 guilders from local merchants and ordered every able-bodied male to help build the wall, whose 16-foot logs are sunk 4 feet into the earth and sharpened at the top. The newly appointed City Council refuses to pay for the wall, saying that defending the colony is the Dutch West India Company's responsibility, but finally agrees when Gov. Stuyvesant agrees to turn over revenues from a tax on liquor. Wall Street will get its name from a wagon road that runs beside the defensive wall, extending 2,340 feet between Pearl Street and what later will be the western edge of Trinity Churchyard; it will stand until nearly the end of the century (*see* City Hall, 1700).

Nieuw Amsterdam's first poorhouse is completed at 21–23 Beaver Street. "The women of the neighborhood entertain each other with a pipe and a brazier," writes Nicasius de Sille; "young and old, they all smoke."

The city fathers inaugurate a night watch and build the city's first prison inside Fort Amsterdam.

Colonists throw their garbage over the new wall at what later will be Wall Street; the area to the north of that wall will for some years be used as a dump.

1654 Connecticut colony physician Thomas Pell purchases 9,000 acres of land from the Siwanoy tribe in what later will be the eastern Bronx; a brother of English mathematician John Pell, 34, he invites 16 families to form the village of Westchester, near what will become Westchester Square (*see* Pelham Manor, 1666).

An ordinance passed by the Council of New Netherland July 1 has a preamble that begins, "That very great confusion and disorder prevail more and more among the Ferrymen on both sides of the Ferry of the *Manhattan* to the serious inconvenience of the Passengers and Inhabitants of this Province, so that those under the necessity of going over, are frequently obliged to wait whole days and nights, and then again are constrained to give up their journey not without gross extortion of double and higher fare, disputes and other unmannerly practices . . ." (*see* Dircksen, 1638).

Nieuw Amsterdam's first recorded Jewish colonist—an Ashkenazi named Jacob bar Simon—arrives from Amsterdam August 22 on the Dutch ship *Pereboom*

(*Pear Tree*) after a 6–week voyage. Some 23 Sephardic Jews from Pernambuco (later Recife), Brazil, arrive at Nieuw Amsterdam in September, celebrate Rosh Hashanah in private September 12 and 13, and establish congregation Shearith Israel (Remnant of Israel), despite efforts by Peter Stuyvesant to exclude them (*see* 1642). The city will have 20 Jewish families by 1695, with a synagogue on the north side of Mill Street (later called South William Street), and Saul Brown (originally Pardo) as rabbi (*see* synagogue, 1730).

1655 The Wiechquaesgeck renew hostilities against New Netherland's colonists after one of their women has allegedly been murdered by a Dutch farmer who found her picking peaches in his orchard. They destroy the settlement made by patroon Adriaen van der Donck 9 years ago plus one made by former Rhode Island colony farmer Thomas Cornell at what will become Clason Point in a conflict that will continue for several years.

The ship *Witte Paert* (*White Horse*) arrives at Nieuw Amsterdam with the colony's first slaves to come directly from Africa (*see* 1646). Directors of the Dutch West India Company at Amsterdam have authorized Jan de Sweerts and Dirck Pieterson Wittepaert to import the slaves, reasoning that such importation to New Netherland will lead "to the increase of population and the advancement of said place" (*see* slave revolt, 1712).

Colonist Wilhelmus Beekman receives a patent June 20 for Manhattan property beyond the freshwater pond (the Collect). An officer of the Dutch West India Company, Beekman arrived with Peter Stuyvesant aboard the ship *Princess* in 1647 and builds a fine house at what later will be the intersection of Beekman and Cliff streets.

New Utrecht colonist Cornelius van Werckhoven dies; his children's tutor Jacques Cortelyou, now 30, assumes leadership of his little community, secures patents for lands that will later be occupied by Fort Hamilton, and divides the area into 20 50-acre plots, one of which he reserves for the poor (*see* 1657; church, 1677).

Peter Stuyvesant uses his director general's salary of 250 guilders per month to build White Hall, a large Manhattan house at what later will be the intersection of State and Whitehall streets. He will buy the property in 1658 and make the house his official residence.

1656 Dutch colonist Jan Jansen Bleecker, 17, arrives at Nieuw Amsterdam but will soon weary of Manhattan and move upriver to Albany, where his children and descendants will marry sons and daughters of prominent families.

Douglaston, Queens, has its beginnings in a settlement founded by colonist Thomas Hicks on a peninsula called Little Madman's Neck (see 1735).

∞ Nieuw Amsterdam's population includes not only Calvinists of the Dutch Reformed Church (the official religious denomination) but also Anabaptists, Catholics, English Independents, Jews, Lutherans, and Quakers.

A law approved by Peter Stuyvesant and his council October 26 forbids dancing, drinking, going for a ride in a cart, or playing tennis on Sundays.

✗ A price-fixing law approved October 26 does "hereby Ordain and command that all Bakers and all other Inhabitants who make a business of baking or selling Bread, whether for Christians or Barbarians, shall be obliged, as well for the accommodation of Christians as to derive profit thereby from Indians, to bake at least once or twice a week both coarse and white Bread, as well for Christians as Indians, of the stated weight and at the price, as follows . . ." Bakers have heretofore been forbidden by law to sell white bread because only Native Americans had sufficient wampum to buy it.

👫 The city's first census survey shows Nieuw Amsterdam to have a population of about 1,000 living in 120 houses (most of them one-room hovels). Orphans and children from Dutch poorhouses have been sent to the town since last year to increase its population, and these transportations will continue until 1659 along with those of indentured servants.

1657 The Flushing Remonstrance written to Nieuw Amsterdam's Gov. Peter Stuyvesant December 27 is probably the first declaration of religious tolerance by any group of ordinary citizens in America. Gov. Stuyvesant has imposed restrictions on Quakers because they were not members of the Dutch Reformed Church, but about 30 freeholders of the Long Island settlement of Vlissingen (later Flushing) tell Stuyvesant that they will not accept his command. The town sheriff, town clerk, and two magistrate present the Remonstrance to Stuyvesant's colonial government December 29, they are promptly arrested, but although they are soon released five Quakers who have arrived at Nieuw Amsterdam are shipped off to Rhode Island (see Bowne, 1662; Friends Seminary, 1786).

$ The granting of great and small burgher rights in the city restricts trade to burghers, giving privileges and monopolies to local citizens, as is customary in European municipalities, but it sets Nieuw Amsterdam apart from the pioneer fur-trading and agricultural economy in which it has been a participant.

⚡ Tutor Jacques Cortelyou is appointed surveyor general of New Netherland January 23 and becomes the city's first commuter, traveling daily between his home overlooking the Narrows at New Utrecht and the Manhattan engineering office that he rents in Marketfield, near Bowling Green (see 1655).

● The city establishes refuse dumps, forbids disposal of animal carcasses, dirt, and other offensive material in city streets, and makes residents responsible for cleaning the streets in front of their homes and shops.

1658 New Netherland colonists go to war with Esopus
✗ tribesmen living far up the Hudson. The new hostilities will weaken the colony, making it vulnerable to takeover by the English (see 1664).

◐ Dutch colonists receive permission in March to establish the village of Nieuw Haarlem north of Nieuw Amsterdam on Manhattan Island; they name it after a town near Antwerp.

⚡ Nieuw Amsterdam's first paved streets are laid with cobblestones along what later will be Stone Street between Whitehall and Broad streets. Local residents have requested the paving, which cuts down on dust but also contributes to noise. By 1661 all the main thoroughfares will be paved with cobblestones (see 1684).

☤ The city's first hospital opens in Bridge Street and is the first in North America. A surgeon to the Dutch West India Company named Varravanger attends patients in a clean house, supervised by a Dutch matron, with plenty of firewood and a fire, but it will be abandoned in 1674 and the city will have no hospital thereafter until 1776 (see 1769).

● The city tries to ban emptying of chamber pots and privies in the streets, but most residents ignore the prohibition, and sewers remain either open or closed ditches, designed for draining surface water and often becoming clogged with solid waste that causes them to overflow with the contents of cesspools, privies, and sinks connected illegally to the sewers.

1659 Inflation depresses the value of the wampum used
$ by Nieuw Amsterdam's colonists to trade with the natives. It takes 16 white beads or eight black beads to equal a Dutch stuiver (1/20 of a guilder), up from six white beads (or three black beads) in 1650. The cost of furs soars as a result, and when Gov.

Stuyvesant imposes price controls they are generally ignored (*see* Philipse, 1666).

The city's first (volunteer) fire department is established (*see* 1731).

1660 The town of Bushwick is founded in Brooklyn between Bushwick and Newtown creeks. Originally *Boswijck* (Dutch for heavy woods), it will be a farming community for nearly 2 centuries before becoming better known as a brewing district (*see* 1854; Williamsburgh, 1800).

Nieuw Amsterdam gets its first post office, and the first city directory is published.

1661 Gov. Stuyvesant grants home rule to residents of southeastern Brooklyn's Flatlands, where he himself acquired a large plot 10 years ago. Bensonhurst has its beginnings as part of the Brooklyn town of New Utrecht (*see* 1915).

Staten Island gets its first permanent settlement. It will be known as Oude Dorp (Old Town). The island's wooded ridges are the highest on the eastern seaboard south of Mount Desert Island on the Maine coast.

Colonist Jan Dyckman settles on a farm in upper Manhattan.

A system of unemployment relief is inaugurated in the colony, and the city enacts its first legislation against loan sharking (*see* inflation, 1659).

The New Netherland Council grants a charter to William Jansen to operate a ferry service between Manhattan and Communipaw (later part of Jersey City) (*see* 1654). Charters for other routes will soon follow, the ferries being scows propelled by oars and sails (*see* 1811).

Nonfiction: *Description of the Towne of Mannadens, 1661* by an English visitor says, "The town is seated . . . commodiously for trades, and that is their chief employment for they plant and sow little." He reports that "beaver, otter, musk, and other skins" come from the natives and settlers in the back country. The "gut" (canal), built between 1657 and 1659 along what soon will be Broad Street, extends "almost through the towne," he says, permitting the entrance of boats at high water and giving the town a feature reminiscent of old Amsterdam.

Long Island farmers provide Nieuw Amsterdam with beef, pork, wheat, butter, and some tobacco, writes the English visitor. New England sends additional food supplies, including "flower" and "bisket," malt, fish, and cider apples, plus iron and tar, while shipments from the Virginia colony bring in "store of tobacco, oxhides, dried, some beef, pork and fruit."

1662 Nieuw Amsterdam authorities arrest colonist John Bowne for permitting Quakers to hold meetings in his Flushing house, completed last year at what will become 37-01 Bowne Street, Queens (*see* Flushing Remonstrance, 1657). Bowne is convicted of having violated Gov. Peter Stuyvesant's ban on Quaker assemblies, jailed, and banished, but when he reaches Holland and appeals to the Dutch West India Company it acquits him of all charges, frees him, and rebukes Gov. Stuyvesant, thereby establishing the right to free practice of religious worship.

Colonist Richard Morris settles on a 2,000-acre estate in the southeastern Bronx, an area that will come to be called Morrisania (*see* 1675).

Dutch colonist Frederick Philipse (originally Felypse or Felypsen), 36, marries Margaret Hardenbroek, widow of the rich merchant Pietrus Rudolphus De Vries; she continues the business of her first husband, making frequent voyages to Holland as supercargo aboard her own ships. Philipse came to Nieuw Amsterdam in 1647 at age 21, found work as a carpenter to Peter Stuyvesant, traded with the Five Nations (Iroquois), and has engaged in commerce with the East and West Indies, profiting from the slave trade and as silent partner to privateering expeditions. Gov. Stuyvesant has given him some city lots, and he adopts Margaret's only child, a daughter who becomes Eva Philipse (*see* 1666).

1663 A Navigation Act passed by Parliament July 27 forbids English colonists to trade with other European countries. European goods bound for America must be unloaded at English ports and reshipped, even though English export duties and profits to middlemen may make prices prohibitive in America. A similar act passed by Parliament in October 1660 declared that certain "enumerated articles" from England's American colonies could be exported only to the British Isles. Included were tobacco, sugar, wool, indigo, and apples. The list was amended to include rice, molasses, and other articles, producing widespread economic distress in some colonies (*see* 1672).

Nieuw Amsterdam has its first recorded earthquake, but the tremor is mild. Standing for the most part on solid rock, the city will never be prone to earthquake damage (*see* 1884).

1664 Nieuw Amsterdam becomes New York August 27 as 300 English soldiers under Col. Richard Nicolls, 40, take the town from the Dutch under orders from

Charles II. Charles has granted his brother James, duke of York, the territory of New Netherland, including eastern Maine and islands to the south and west of Cape Cod. Col. Nicolls has sailed from Portsmouth in May with a squadron of four vessels, stopped at Boston (where the colonists gave him little help), and blockaded Nieuw Amsterdam. Gov. Stuyvesant receives assurances that Dutch settlers will be allowed free settlement and free trade, he decides not to fire on the English, and the town is renamed upon its surrender September 8. Richard Nicolls takes over as first governor of the Province of New York, and Thomas Willett is appointed first mayor of New York City (although English by birth, Willett has lived in Leyden, speaks Dutch, and has owned property and traded in Nieuw Amsterdam, where he has been on friendly terms with Gov. Stuyvesant, who is known as "Old Silver Nails"). Jurist Mathias Nicolls, 34, is probably no relation to Gov. Nicolls but has served as a captain in the colonel's command and been appointed secretary to the commission. Hudson Valley Dutch patroons become English landlords (see Treaties of Breda, 1667).

Gov. Stuyvesant withdraws from public life and retires to the farm that he bought in 1651, occupying a manor house in what later will be called Stuyvesant Street on a property that extends from what later will be 5th Street to 17th Street between the East River and what later will be Fourth Avenue.

Canarsee chiefs sell an area they call Equandito (broken lands) to colonists John Tilton, Jr., and Samuel Spicer. It will be acquired in 1675 by Jan Martense Schenck, become part of Flatlands, have several tidal mills on it, and be called Mill Basin.

Public education has flourished under Dutch rule but will virtually disappear under the English, although churches will occasionally establish elementary and secondary schools.

1665 New York's English governor Richard Nicolls replaces the form of city government set up by the Dutch charter of 1653 with a new administration February 2. A mayor, five aldermen, and a sheriff are to run the town, all of them appointed by the royal governor to 1-year terms, but Nicolls allows Dutch municipal officers to remain in office and even to name their own successors. In response to local petition, as required under English law, a corporation is founded in June that will come to be called "the Mayor Aldermen and Commonality of the city of New York," and Nicolls establishes a county (he calls it Yorkshire) consisting of three "ridings:" Long Island, Staten Island, and the Bronx peninsula

known as Westchester; he leaves New York City to be governed by its seven new officers, four of whom are Dutch.

The Duke's Laws issued by Gov. Richard Nicolls in the name of the duke of York will serve as the city's first legal code and remain in force until 1683. Largely the work of jurist Mathias Nicolls, it is basically a liberal, just, and sensible set of laws based on English law, Roman-Dutch law, and the laws and regulations of the New England colonies, listing among a number of capital offenses the crime of sodomy, defined as "unnatural lusts of men with men and women with women." The death penalty for sodomy and other such offenses will remain in effect until 1797. Submitted to the duke of York and his council in England, the document is approved, printed, and sent out by the duke with orders that it be promulgated and established as the law of New York; delegates to a meeting held at Hempstead in Queens County for that purpose follow the duke's orders and establish a court of assizes under the new law.

The mayor is given power to grant licenses to would-be tavernkeepers.

The city's population reaches about 1,470, but of the 254 persons listed for purposes of taxation only 16 have English names.

1666 England's Charles II grants colonist Thomas Pell a charter to create the Manor of Pelham (see 1654). Pell will die childless, leaving his estate to his nephew, John Pell (see 1675).

Colonist Frederick Philipse begins buying up wampum and removing it from circulation in an effort to dampen the inflation that has depressed the value of beads (see 1659; Philipse, 1662). Now 40, he buries the wampum in hogsheads and within a few weeks it takes only three white beads to equal a stuiver. Philipse will soon become the city's richest citizen.

1667 The Treaties of Breda signed July 21 end the second Anglo-Dutch war after a Dutch fleet under the command of Admiral Michiel de Ruyter, now 60, has broken the chain in England's Medway River, reached Chatham, and captured the flagship Royal Charles. The Dutch councillor pensionary Johan de Witt has gone to sea with the fleet and used his organizational skills and diplomacy to gain terms favorable to the United Provinces, a Dutch fleet has seized the English colony of Surinam in South America (see 1651), England cedes that sugar-rich country plus the Indian Ocean spice island of Pulau

Run in the Bandas to the Dutch in exchange for Nieuw Amsterdam.

Col. Sir Francis Lovelace, 46, is appointed August 17 to succeed Richard Nicolls as governor of the New York province (see 1668).

Brooklyn is chartered under the name Brueckelen October 18 by the provincial governor Richard Nicolls. The new town includes "all the lots and plantations lying and being at the Gowanus, Bedford, Walle Bocht and Ferry."

$ Dutch Huguenot colonist Francis Goelet arrives at New York with his son Jacobus. The Goelets and their descendants will build one of Manhattan's greatest real-estate empires.

1668 Col. Francis Lovelace arrives from England in March and takes office in August as royal governor of the New York province following the resignation of Gov. Richard Nicolls, who returns to England. Lovelace will extend commerce, regulate trade, open the first mercantile exchange, promote shipbuilding, and improve roads and ferry service.

Capt. John Manning purchases an island in the East River that will later be called Blackwell's, Welfare, and ultimately Roosevelt Island (see 1637).

1670 The royal governor Sir Francis Lovelace organizes New York's first merchants' exchange. Dutch and English craftsmen, importers, merchants, and traders meet at 11 o'clock on Friday mornings and do business for 1 hour on a bridge spanning the canal at Brugh Street (later Bridge Street).

1671 The royal governor Sir Francis Lovelace grants the Manor of Fordham to colonist John Archer (see 1787; Fordham University, 1841).

1672 Peter Stuyvesant dies at New York in February at age 61 and is buried beneath the chapel of his manor house, which fronts on what later will be the site of St. Mark's Church in-the-Bouwerie; former governor Richard Nicolls is killed May 28 at age 47 while fighting Dutch naval forces in the Battle of Soleway off the coast of Suffolk in the North Sea.

Jurist Mathias Nicolls is chosen third mayor of New York, having sat as presiding judge of the court of assizes established at Hempstead in the county of Queens.

$ New York merchant Frederick Philipse, now 46, begins acquiring a manorial estate of 205,000 acres in what later will be upper Yonkers (some say by altering a phrase in a contract with the Indians) (see 1666). The English have granted him some tracts of land, and Philipse wants to enlarge his holdings (see 1674; King's Bridge, 1693).

England imposes customs duties on goods carried from one of her American colonies to another, thus putting a crimp in New York's economy (see Navigation Acts, 1663; 1696).

The New York to Boston Post Road is laid out to speed coach travel between the second and third largest American cities (see 1673).

1673 A Dutch squadron retakes New York and Delaware (see 1655; 1664). Gov. Lovelace has left the city to supervise construction of a post road to Boston and is recalled to London, where he will be imprisoned in the Tower. Capt. John Manning has surrendered the New York province to the Dutch and retires in disgrace to the East River island that he purchased 5 years ago (see 1674). Manning's daughter Mary will marry Robert Blackwell, he will use the East River island as a farm, and it will come to be called Blackwell's Island (see 1668; 1828).

The Boston Post Road is formally established at the behest of England's Charles II as the first official post road in North America. Beginning near the Battery, it runs past the manor house of the late Peter Stuyvesant and up through Harlem, crosses to the mainland via the Kingsbridge, cuts diagonally across the Bronx, proceeds through Westchester, and will promote the growth of towns in eastern New York, Connecticut, Rhode Island, and Massachusetts.

1674 The Treaty of Westminster February 9 ends the 2-year war between England and the Dutch. New York and Delaware are returned to England (see 1673), freeing the English to expand their trade and grow prosperous while Europe becomes embroiled in depleting warfare. Parliament has cut off funds, forcing Charles II to cease hostilities. The Crown appoints court favorite Major Edmund Andros, 36, royal governor of the New York province November 10 in place of Gov. Lovelace.

$ Frederick Philipse, now 48 and the richest man in New York City, has assets worth 80,000 guilders (see 1672); 94 burghers have estates valued at 1,000 guilders or more, and 22 have estates worth between 5,000 and 10,000. A planter worth 500 guilders is considered rich.

1675 Morrisania has its beginnings in a tract of land north of Manhattan Island granted by New York's provincial governor Edmund Andros to Col. Lewis Morris, son of the late landowner Richard Morris (see 1662; annexation, 1874).

Sir John Pell builds a manor house that will survive for a century. His late uncle Thomas created the Manor of Pelham in 1666 but died childless. Sir John will encourage settlement of the village of Eastchester in the northeastern Bronx. The village of Westchester will be a county seat from 1683 to 1714, and the county will include the Bronx until late in the 19th century.

1676 The Great Dock is built along Water Street from Whitehall Slip to Coenties Slip; it will be the city's only commercial wharf for 77 years.

The city prohibits slaughterhouses to be located within city limits, but population is growing so rapidly that abbatoirs built on the outskirts soon find themselves within the city limits.

1677 Anthony Brockholles is appointed commander in chief November 16 and will for a brief period hold superior power to Gov. Andros. Merchant Stephanus Van Cortlandt, 34, is appointed mayor, becoming the city's first chief officer not born in Europe. Born in Nieuw Amsterdam, Van Cortlandt had made his fortune by age 21 and has been a colonel in the militia and a member of the governor's council.

City carters stage a strike to block a threatened stop to their monopoly. New Yorkers have been accustomed for decades to move each May 1, paying the carters handsomely to transport their effects from one address to another. Having pledged themselves to obey municipal ordinances derived from Dutch and English law, the carters have refused to employ juveniles, blacks, or nonresidents.

Gov. Andros commissions construction of the first insane asylum to be built in the province of New York.

The Reformed Protestant Dutch Church is founded by members of the New Utrecht community and will survive for centuries (see building, 1828).

1678 Sir Edmund Andros is appointed governor of the New York province for a second time August 7.

The city's first Anglican preacher to be assigned to the province arrives at New York: Charles Wolley serves as chaplain to Gov. Andros.

1679 Scots-born colonist Robert Livingston, 24, is married July 9 to Alida Schuyler Van Rensselaer, widow of the late Nicholas Van Rensselaer (see 1630). Livingston arrived in New England 6 years ago and moved a year later to the New York colony, and his marriage extends his landholdings in the Albany area; he and his wife will have 10 children (see 1683).

Gov. Andros gives orders that every seventh house in a street must display a lighted candle in a lantern on nights when there is no moon. The seven property owners in the adjacent houses are to share the cost of the "streetlights."

A city ordinance restricts the number of oyster boats on Long Island's Great South Bay, but although only 10 such boats may legally remove bivalves from the bay other oystermen will defy the regulation and continue to deplete the oyster beds.

1681 Anthony Brockholles is appointed commander in chief for a second time January 13; Gov. Andros is temporarily superseded.

1682 James, duke of York, appoints Irish-born military commander Thomas Dongan, 48, governor of the New York province August 27, replacing Gov. Andros. The duke is a convert to Roman Catholicism, and Dongan will be the province's first Catholic governor (see 1683).

1683 The New York province's new governor Thomas Dongan arrives at the city April 25 together with a Jesuit priest, arousing initial suspicions among a populace that is overwhelmingly Protestant. He attends the first Mass ever to be celebrated in the city October 30, but Gov. Dongan will surround himself with Protestant advisers and resist the duke's orders to extend Catholic influence in the colony.

The New York province is divided into 10 counties that include Kings (Brooklyn) and Richmond (Staten Island, Shooters Island, and the Island of Meadows), named for the Yorkshire estate of James, duke of York, brother of England's Charles II.

Colonist Robert Livingston, now 28, purchases 2,000 acres of land on the eastern bank of the Hudson River from the Native Americans who have lived on it; the land is about halfway between New York and Albany (see 1679; 1686).

The new colonial governor Thomas Dongan issues a "Charter of Liberties" providing for religious toleration.

1684 Canarsie tribal chiefs sell the last of their lands in Brooklyn in the 22nd and final deed to be executed since 1636. Dispossessed tribespeople will in many cases live as tenant farmers or relocate to remote swamplands.

The city issues an order in May requiring that owners of adjacent properties pay to have principal streets paved with cobblestones (see 1658; 1708).

1685 England's Charles II dies February 6 at age 54 and is
succeeded by his Catholic brother James, duke of
York, who will reign until 1688 as James II. Gov.
Dongan owes his appointment to the new king and
appoints Dutch-born politician Nicholas Bayard,
41, mayor of New York. A nephew of the late Peter
Stuyvesant, Bayard was provincial secretary before
and after Nieuw Amsterdam became New York in
1664, the Dutch appointed him receiver general
when they returned to power briefly 12 years ago, but
he was imprisoned for a while by the English on
Governors Island.

1686 Gov. Dongan grants a new city charter April 27,
establishing six wards and giving freemen in each
ward the right to elect one alderman and one assistant plus constables, tax collectors, and other local
officials. The aldermen, the mayor (who is to be
appointed annually), and the recorder comprise the
Common Council, which is empowered to regulate
markets, access to docks, and transportation of
goods, but any law it enacts will expire after 3
months unless confirmed by the royal governor and
council. England's James II writes to the governor
May 29 ordering that the Assembly be disallowed
along with the recently granted "Charter of Liber-
tyes and priviledges" (see 1730).

William (originally Wilhelmus) Beekman is
appointed mayor under the rule of the English commander and aldermen (see Beekman, 1655).

Albany becomes a city under terms of a charter
obtained by colonist Robert Livingston and his
brother-in-law Peter Schuyler, who receive the
charter from Gov. Dongan (see 1683). Colonist Jan
Jansen Bleecker, now 45, has prospered in commercial activities and is appointed city treasurer.

$ Robert Livingston creates a manor under a patent
from the colony, which extends to him privileges
that include holding a court-leet and a court baron,
and properly receiving fines which belong to the lord
of a manor; Livingstone will make additional purchases, and by 1714 his landholdings will embrace
160,000 acres with nearly 12 miles of shorefront
along the Hudson and 19 miles back to the Massachusetts boundary that it will border for 20 miles.

Colonist Etienne de Lancy, 22, arrives with his family jewels at New York and uses his capital to start a
mercantile business that will produce a fortune of
$500,000. Son of a rich Huguenot family, he left
France last year following the revocation of the Edict
of Nantes that forbade the practice of any religion
but Roman Catholicism. De Lancy will change his

name to Stephen de Lancey and marry into the Van
Cortlandt family.

● The last wolves in Manhattan are killed, ridding the
still mostly rural island of an animal that many have
feared.

1687 Nicholas Bayard becomes a member of the governor's council (see 1685).

Former mayor Mathias Nicolls dies at his 2,000-
acre Plandome, Long Island, estate December 22 at
age 57 (approximate), having distinguished himself
as a jurist and served as speaker of the Assembly.

1688 England's "Glorious Revolution" ends nearly 4 years
of Roman Catholic rule. The birth of a son to James
II's wife June 10 has suggested the likelihood of a
Catholic succession, the nation's Whig leaders have
sent an invitation to the king's son-in-law Willem of
Orange June 30, Willem lands in England November
5, and moves to assume the throne with his wife,
Mary. James II flees to France December 23.

New York's Gov. Dongan is nominally replaced by
Sir Edmund Andros, now 50, who has been governor
of the Dominion since 1686. Dongan has pursued a
policy of cooperation with the Iroquois Confederation against the French, encouraged religious tolerance, tried to set up postal services between Nova
Scotia and the Carolinas, and approved representative government; he retires to his 5,100-acre Staten
Island estate, granted to him when he was appointed
by James, then duke of York, 6 years ago (see 1689),
and will enlarge his estate to 25,000 acres before
returning to England in 1691.

1689 The failure of Gov. Andros to announce the acces-
sion of William and Mary to the English throne in
January sparks rumors that the province will be
turned over to the French. New York City's militia
revolts, seizing Fort James May 31. A committee of
public safety is organized, and a convention of representatives from East Jersey and all New York
counties except Albany governs the province beginning June 27. The convention chooses German-
born merchant and militia captain Jacob Leisler, 49,
to be "captain of the fort" June 28, and it makes him
chief military commander August 16. Leisler's
opponents include Stephanus Van Cortlandt, now
47, and the late Mathias Nicoll's son William, but
they fail to challenge his actions and are obliged to
leave the city (Van Cortlandt has associated himself
too closely with the widely disliked Andros and the
deposed Catholic king James II). Leisler leads an
anti-Catholic faction that has strongly opposed the
claims of Willem of Orange to the English throne,
former governor Dongan flees to New England along

with the city's Catholic priests (he will inherit his brother's title in 1698, becoming 2nd earl of Limerick), and appointees of James II retain control of New York City's government until September, when Peter Delanoy becomes the city's first elected mayor under provisions laid down by the provincial convention.

William and Mary apppoint Col. Henry Sloughter governor of New York September 2, but he will not arrive until next year. Jacob Leisler assumes the title lieutenant governor and dissolves the convention December 16, arresting alleged "papists" and instituting tax policies that alienate many of his supporters (*see* 1690).

1690 Lieut. Gov. Jacob Leisler's followers imprison former mayor Nicholas Bayard early in the year. Opponents of Leisler meet at the King's Arms tavern in Cedar Street, but America's first intercolonial congress meets in May at Leisler's initiative to address issues of defending the colonies against possible attacks by the French and Indians.

1691 Three English ships arrive at New York in January with a force of regular troops under the command of former mayor Richard Ingoldsby, who has been named lieutenant governor of the province, but his papers are aboard the frigate *Archangel*, carrying Gov. Sloughter. Jacob Leisler refuses to surrender Fort James, Ingoldsby quarters his men in City Hall, Leisler gives him 2 hours to disband his forces, Ingoldsby does not comply, Leisler has his own troops open fire, and a brief but bloody clash ensues. The new royal governor Henry Sloughter arrives 2 days later and gains control of the city March 17 with help from Scots-born sea captain and privateer William Kidd, 45, who settled at New York last year; Gov. Sloughter issues writs for the election of a representative assembly that meets in a Pearl Street tavern April 9 and appoints Nieuw Amsterdam-born merchant's son Abraham De Peyster, 34, mayor (he will serve until 1693). The governor releases political prisoners who include Nicholas Bayard and, at the urging of Bayard and others, orders that Leisler be tried for treason. Vigorously prosecuted at the urging of Stephanus Van Cortlandt and found guilty after a 1-week trial, Leisler is hanged May 16 along with his son-in-law Jacob Milborne (his opponents have persuaded Gov. Sloughter to sign the death warrants by plying him with liquor). The state confiscates the estates of Leisler and Milborne (*but see* 1695).

Gov. Sloughter dies suddenly in June (an autopsy reveals that he suffered from delirium tremens before his death and he is judged to have died after a

Jacob Leisler seized power, defied the English authorities, and went to the gallows for his treachery.

drunken spree). Sloughter is succeeded on an interim basis by Richard Ingoldsby pending arrival of a new royal governor.

The New York State Supreme Court has its beginnings in the Supreme Court of Judicature adopted by the New York Assembly. Given jurisdiction over criminal and civil pleas, it is also empowered to hear appeals from local courts and will survive as the oldest continuing court of general jurisdiction in America, but appeals for the next 80 years and more will be taken to the royal governor and his council, and from there to the Privy Council at London. The Assembly and the royal governors meanwhile will wrangle over who has authority to regulate the jurisdiction and authority of the court, with many New Yorkers insisting that the acts of the Assembly and English common law define that authority, and statute law will not be codified until the 19th century.

$ The city establishes set fees for carters and sets standardized rules governing ownership of carts, measurement of loads, etc. (*see* strike, 1677). The new law requires cartmen to serve any orderly person who seeks their assistance and will remain essentially unchanged until 1844 (*see* 1789).

1692 Benjamin Fletcher arrives in August to take office as the new royal governor, replacing the late Gov. Sloughter. Citizens who opposed the late Jacob Leisler welcome Fletcher with a parade (they include Capt. William Kidd and Robert Livingston).

$ Capt. Kidd receives £150 from the city council for chasing a hostile privateer off the New York coast. He purchases a large lot on the north side of Wall Street, marries the twice-widowed Sara Bradley Cox Oort, thus increasing his holdings by £155 14s, and settles with his bride in a tall brick-and-stone house with gabled windows east of Hanover Square at 119–121 Pearl Street, corner of Hanover Street, furnishing it with fine furniture, Turkish carpets, an abundance of silver plate, and casks of Madeira in his cellar. In addition to his town house, Kidd will soon have a 38–acre country estate near what later will be East 73rd Street (see 1695).

Frederick Philipse marries for a second time November 30 (his first wife, Margaret, has died), this time to Catherine, daughter of Oloff Stevenson Van Cortlandt and widow of the rich merchant John Derval. Now 66, Philipse has befriended every royal governor since Edmund Andros, avoiding political controversies.

∞ Gov. Fletcher confiscates the Congregational churches in Elmhurst and Jamaica and turns their property over to the Church of England, which next year will become the province's official religion, but Congregational churches elsewhere on Long Island are too strong (most will later become Presbyterian churches).

1693 Gov. Fletcher mounts artillery at the lower tip of Manhattan Island to defend the city by commanding the approach to the Hudson River with 92 cannon. The Battery will take its name from the emplacement (see 1734).

Colonist Caleb Heathcote, 28, is appointed to the governor's council. Heathcote's brother Gilbert is lord mayor of London; he arrived at New York last year possessed of a considerable fortune (see 1701).

Merchant Frederick Philipse builds a bridge across Spuyten Duyvil Creek—the first bridge connecting the Bronx with Manhattan (see Philipse, 1674; ferry, 1699). It will be called the King's Bridge, and the Kingsbridge section in the Bronx will get its name from the new span. Philipse is in possession of a strip of land extending from Spuyten Duyvil to the Croton River and is manager of Philipseboro, including what later will be Yonkers. He has founded Fredericksboro, or Sleepy Hollow, covering 240 square miles.

New York's first printing press begins operating April 10 at 81 Pearl Street, where William Bradford, formerly official printer for the Pennsylvania colony, prints city laws, lawbooks, and volumes that will soon include a 51-page booklet entitled, "A Letter of Advice to a Young Gentleman Leaving the University, Concerning His Conversation and Behavior in the World" (see newspaper, 1725).

1694 Sandy Hook pilots begin guiding ships into New York Harbor, which will grow to rival Sag Harbor as the province's leading port of entry.

∞ A Friends Meeting House is completed in Flushing, Queens, and will survive as New York's oldest structure to remain in continuous use as a house of worship (see Bowne, 1662; additions will be built between 1716 and 1719).

1695 England's William II determines to replace Gov. Fletcher with Richard Coote, earl of Bellomont, who has told him that New York is infested with pirates. Parliament reverses the attainder that deprived the late Jacob Leisler and his son-in-law of their civil and legal rights (see 1691); it restores the confiscated estates to their heirs (see 1702).

A city ordinance enacted early in the year provides "that an Oath be drawn up & Administered to all Such as Shall be made Free or are Already Free According to the Usage & Practice of Corporations in England." Used in England since the 14th century, the oath will be administered to freed slaves and servants released from indentures.

$ Capt. William Kidd visits London, as does New York landowner Robert Livingston, now 41, who hears from the impecunious Lord Bellomont that King William has proposed to outfit a frigate and send her to the Indian Ocean with orders to protect English merchantmen from pirates. Bellomont's real intention is to have Kidd hijack pirate cargoes and bring them to New York, where they can be sold to his own benefit. Livingston recommends Capt. Kidd as a "bold and honest man," and the earl signs an agreement with Kidd and Livingston at London October 10, giving the king half of all profits that may be reaped in the Indian Ocean venture, the other half to be divided between Lord Bellomont, Kidd, and Livingston (see 1696).

1696 A new Navigation Act passed by Parliament April 10 forbids New Yorkers and other colonists to export directly to Scotland or Ireland (see 1663; 1699).

Capt. William Kidd sails from New York harbor September 6, bound for the Indian Ocean in the 34-ton galley Adventure with a crew of more than 100 (including desperadoes and oarsmen) to attack pirate ships that are preying on honest merchantmen (see 1695; 1697).

∞ Gov. Fletcher grants approval for the city's Anglican community to buy land for a new church (see Trinity, 1697).

Manhattan's first coffeehouse opens under the direction of English colonist John Hutchins.

Coffeehouses will become community meeting places.

1697 Nicholas Bayard is dismissed from his position as a member of the governor's council.

Mayor Stephanus Van Cortlandt is granted a royal patent for the manor of Cortlandt.

$ Capt. William Kidd reaches Madagascar after a fruitless year at sea in which a third of his crew has died of cholera (*see* 1696). He shoots one of his gunners dead in the course of quelling a mutiny (*see* 1698).

Broad Street is created by covering over the short-lived *Heere Gracht* (Gentlemen's Canal) and combining it with the wide serviceways on each side of it.

∞ Trinity Church receives its charter and a land grant from Britain's William III; the Crown is to receive an annual rent of "one peppercorn."

1698 Trinity Church holds its first religious services
∞ March 13 (*see* 1697). Its Church of England status gives the institution a quasi-public character, and a modest rectangular structure with a gambrel roof and small porch has been built at the head of Wall Street, on the west side of Broadway, with contributions from virtually every prosperous citizen, including Catholics, Jews (who are listed on a separate page), and Capt. William Kidd (who has lent ship's tackle and other marine equipment for hoisting its stones into place). The city has given the church permission to claim stranded whales for conversion into oil and whalebone (*see* 1705).

Capt. William Kidd seizes the Armenian merchantman *Auedagh Merchant* in the Indian Ocean January 30 and divides her rich cargo among his crewmen (*see* 1697). He has balked at attacking pirate ships as being too dangerous and, instead, has turned to piracy himself, going on to take other prizes. News of his criminality reaches India's aged Mughal emperor Aurangzeb, who threatens the East India Company; its officers communicate with London, where the Admiralty declares Kidd a pirate and dispatches a fleet to apprehend him. Scuttling his leaky 34-ton galley *Adventure* off Madagascar, Kidd sails in the *Auedagh Merchant* for the West Indies, where he will find that he has been proclaimed a pirate (*see* 1700).

The population of the New York province reaches 18,067, with two-thirds of it on Long Island and near the mouth of the Hudson as the Iroquois and other hostile tribes block expansion to the north and west. New York City has 4,937, 14 percent of it black slaves (no other northern colony has a large slave population). The first Brooklyn census shows a population of 2,017, including Dutch and English settlers, blacks, and Native Americans, who are outnumbered by their cows, goats, pigs, dogs, and chickens.

1699 The Woolens Act passed by Parliament under pres-
$ sure from the English wool lobby forbids New York or any other of England's American colonies to export wool, wool yarn, or wool cloth "to any place whatsoever."

A ferry across the eight-mile-long Harlem River tidal strait is established at Spuyten Duyvil (*see* bridge; ship canal, 1895).

● English authorities take down the wall that was erected by Dutch colonists in 1644.

1700 Stephanus Van Cortlandt becomes chief judge of the province but dies at New York November 25 at age 57, leaving a manor that totals more than 87,000 acres, most of it along the Hudson north of Manhattan.

Capt. William Kidd arrives at London in chains (*see* 1698). After hearing that he had been branded a pirate, Kidd sailed from the West Indies to New England with the intent of declaring his innocence, but he was tricked into coming ashore at Boston on the promise of a pardon, and the Board of the Admiralty examines him in private, fearing that Lord Bellomont and his other backers will defend Kidd in a public trial (*see* 1701).

A new City Hall is completed at the northeast corner of Wall and Nassau streets to replace the structure at 71–73 Pearl Street that has served as City Hall since 1653. Merchant Abraham De Peyster and Col. Nicholas Bayard own nearly all of the north side of Wall Street in alternating sections, and De Peyster has donated a strip of his land large enough to accommodate the City Hall, constructed in large part with stones taken from the wall built in 1653 and demolished because it has fallen into decay (*see* 1811).

England's American colonies have an estimated population of 262,000, with 5,250 (including 750 blacks and about 300 Irish) in New York; Boston and Philadelphia have 12,000 each (*see* 1765).

18th CENTURY

1701 Caleb Heathcote acquires a tract of Westchester land
$ that includes what later will be Larchmont, Orienta
Point, Scarsdale, and White Plains, partly by purchasing it from the Native American inhabitants.
Now 36, he will obtain a royal charter to the vast
manor of Scarsdale but exclude White Plains in deference to the people of Rye, who have a prior claim.

The Society for the Propagation of the Gospel is
established as a missionary arm of the Church of
England and immediately sets to work converting
Native Americans and blacks in New York and the
other English colonies, distributing Anglican prayer
books in languages other than English, establishing
Anglican churches where none exist, and strength-
ening weaker ones (*see* Bartow, 1702).

English authorities bring Capt. Kidd from London's
Newgate Prison March 27 for examination before
the House of Commons; unwilling to accuse his
backers, who include Lord Bellomont and Robert
Livingston, he protests his innocence. He is tried
May 8 on charges of having murdered his gunner in
1697, found guilty, convicted also on three counts of
piracy, and hanged at Execution Dock, Wapping,
May 23 at age 55.

1702 Edward Hyde, Viscount Cornbury, 40, arrives at
New York to take up his duties as provincial governor of New York and New Jersey, replacing Lord
Bellomont, who has died of natural causes. A first
cousin of Queen Anne, Lord Cornbury supports
opponents of the late Jacob Leisler and wins favor
with the provincial assembly, which will give him a
gift of £2,000, but he antagonizes some formerly
influential politicians by merging the proprietary
colonies of East and West Jersey into the royal
colony of New Jersey (*see* 1703).

Col. Nicholas Bayard, now 58, is convicted of treason
and sentenced to death. He will be pardoned before
the sentence is carried out and survive until 1709.

The New York Assembly appropriates money to pay a
large indemnity to the heirs of the late Jacob Leisler
and his son-in-law, Jacob Milborne (*see* 1695).

$ Landowner Frederick Philipse dies at New York
November 6 at age 76, leaving to his daughter Anna
(Mrs. Philip French) all of his New York City and
New Jersey properties; his son Adolphus and
Barbados-born grandson Frederick (orphan son of
the late Philip and Maria Philipse), now 7, inherit
the manor of Philipseborough—some 90,000 acres
of fertile Hudson River Valley land operated by 200
tenant farmers. The younger Frederick, whose
maternal grandfather is governor of Barbados, has
been sent to England for his education and will
remain there until early manhood (*see* 1751).

A yellow fever epidemic kills 570 New Yorkers; many
others die in a smallpox epidemic.

English missionary John Bartow of the Society for
the Propagation of the Gospel arrives in the town of
Westchester and becomes the first resident minister
of any faith in the Bronx. Bartow supervises construction of St. Peter's Church and will establish the
first school to teach arithmetic and reading to local
children.

Lord Cornbury devotes his speech at his welcoming
ceremony to praising his wife's ears and invites
every male guest to feel for himself. He has married
Katherine, Baroness Clifton of Leighton Bromwold,
a daughter of Lord O'Brien and heiress to Charles,
duke of Richmond and Lenox, but his critics say he
is a transvestite with a penchant for appearing in
public dressed like the queen, a flouting of convention that puzzles most New Yorkers.

1703 The eccentric Lord Cornbury raises eyebrows by
$ borrowing money from colonists and not repaying it
(*see* 1702). When he cuts the allowance of his wife,
Katherine, she borrows gowns from the aristocratic
women in town and does not return them. When

women hear her carriage approaching they have their servants hide the silver and china lest Lady Cornbury appropriate them, or so it will be alleged.

Dutch colonist Jacobus Van Cortlandt purchases 500 acres from the Indian sachem Katonah.

The Bloomingdale Road (later Broadway) opens from what one day will be 23rd Street through Manhattan farmland to the northern edge of Bloomingdale Village, near what later will be 114th Street (*see* 1795).

The Assembly passes "an Act to bring the weights and measures of this place, which hitherto have been according to the Standards of Holland, to that of England." *Schepels* become pecks, *morgens* become acres, and the like.

A new city census shows a population of 4,375, down from a reported 4,937 in 1698. Fewer than half of the 818 heads of households are of Dutch origin.

1704 Boston boardinghouse manager-schoolteacher Sarah Kemble Knight, 38, sets out on horseback for New York in December, securing guides and stopping at various post houses, inns, and homes in the towns through which she passes en route to settle a relative's estate. "The city of New York," she will note, "is a pleasant, well-compacted place, situated on a commodius river which is a fine harbor for shipping. The buildings brick generally, very stately and high, though not altogether like ours in Boston. They are not strict in keeping the sabbath as in Boston and other places where I have been, but seem to deal with great exactness as far as I see or deal with." Knight will return to Boston early next year, the first woman ever to accomplish the journey on her own (the journal that she keeps will be published in 1865).

1705 England's Queen Anne donates the "Queen's Farm" to Trinity Church, increasing its holdings to 215 acres (*see* 1698). The large tract of land heretofore leased by the queen to the Crown extends from what later will be Fulton Street to the south, Broadway to the east, Washington Street to the west, and although the church will give away 97 percent of the land the remaining acreage will produce huge rental incomes to Trinity in centuries to come (*see* 1789; Trinity School, 1709).

1706 Lord Cornbury's wife, Katherine, dies in August at age 34 after having given birth to seven children and receives a splendid funeral at Trinity Church, in whose churchyard she is buried (*see* 1703). Lord Cornbury charges the cost of the funeral to the taxpayers and has the funeral sermon printed up in

London and sold "for the benefit of the poor" (it runs to 16 pages of small type; *see* 1708).

1707 The creation of the United Kingdom of Great Britain May 1 makes New York and other English colonies, strictly speaking, British colonies. The Act of Union joins England and Scotland under the Union Jack.

Presbyterian minister Francis Makemie preaches a sermon entitled "A Good Conversation" January 20 in the Pearl Street home of William Jackson and is arrested by order of the colonial governor, Lord Cornbury, on charges of preaching without a license. Born in northern Ireland, Makemie has been refused permission to preach from the pulpit of the Dutch Reformed Church, and Lord Cornbury writes to the London Board of Trade, "I entreat your Lordship's protection against this malicious man." After being held in jail for 6 weeks awaiting trial, Makemie wins acquittal, pleading protection under Britain's Toleration Act of 1689, but is obliged to pay all court costs (*see* Cornbury, 1708; First Presbyterian Church, 1716).

1708 The provincial assembly condemns the administration of New York's (and New Jersey's) royal governor Lord Cornbury, who has allegedly used tax revenues for his own purposes and whose arrest of the Presbyterian minister Francis Makemie last year has antagonized many citizens (*see* 1703). New Jersey Chief Justice Lewis Morris, 37, wrote to England last year saying that Cornbury "rarely fails of being dresst in Womens's Cloaths every day, and almost half his time is spent that way and seldom misses it on Sacrament day, as in that Garb when his dead Lady was carried out of the Fort and this not privately but in face of the Sun and sight of the Town." Colonist Robert Livingston has asked a friend in London to use this information for "our advantage." Cornbury is recalled by Queen Anne, but as he is about to board ship in December his creditors have him arrested and the sheriff puts him in the common jail in Wall Street, where he will continue for nearly a year by some accounts to affect women's garb (he owes £8,000 to New York merchants and shopkeepers alone). Cornbury's successor, John Lovelace, baron of Hurley, arrives at New York in a snowstorm December 18 after a 9-week passage and is so weak from the bitter cold he will not be well enough to take up his duties until spring. "This Coast is so terrible in Winter," he writes home, "[that] I think no Ship ought to be sent hither from England after August."

The Common Council notes that regulations with regard to street paving have been ignored and passes legislation May 20 requiring stricter enforcement of paving laws (*see* 1684; 1748).

1709 Lord Cornbury's father, 2nd earl of Clarendon, dies, leaving him enough money to pay off most of his debts (*see* 1708). A letter back to England says, "My Lord Cornbury has and dos still make use of an unfortunate Custom of dressing himself in Womens Cloaths and of exposing himself in that Garb upon the Ramparts to the view of the public; in that dress he draws a World of Spectators about him and consequently as many Censures" (like the one in 1707, the letter was written by a political enemy and will not be made readily available until the 20th century). Inheriting also the title earl of Clarendon, Cornbury returns to England, leaving the New York and New Jersey province to be governed briefly by the Assembly, headed by Council President Richard Ingoldesby, until Lord Lovelace is strong enough to assume office, but Col. Peter Schuyler, 51, is appointed president of the Council May 6, the new governor-general, Lord Lovelace, dies May 7, Richard Ingoldsby is appointed lieutenant governor May 9, Peter Schuyler is reappointed president of the Council May 25, Ingoldsby is reappointed lieutenant governor June 1, and news of Lord Lovelace's death reaches London August 17; Sidney, 1st earl of Godolphin, recommends to the duke of Marlborough that Queen Anne appoint Scottish soldier Robert Hunter, 42, as Lovelace's replacement (*see* 1710).

$ The Assembly enacts appropriation laws that give a provincial treasurer direct control of all monies and specifies the purposes for which they are to be spent.

New York's first paper money is issued November 1. William Bradford has printed the notes, generally called Lyon dollars.

The Charity School of Trinity Parish opens in Trinity Churchyard; founded under terms of a royal charter granted by Britain's Queen Anne, it has been started under the auspices of the London-based Society for the Propagation of the Gospel in Foreign Parts with help from church wardens of Trinity Parish, will be coeducational for nearly 140 years, and will commonly be called the Free School for 129 years (*see* 1838; King's College, 1754).

1710 Gerardus Beekman, 56, is appointed president of the Council April 10. Robert Hunter arrives at New York June 14 with refugees from the German Palatine to take over the duties of provincial governor of New York and New Jersey. Hunter will be governor

until 1720, insisting on parliamentary legislation for colonial finance.

1711 Westchester landowner Caleb Heathcote is appointed mayor of New York (*see* 1701). Now 46, he inherited some land in the city last year from a cousin, has speculated in real estate, profited from his position as collector of taxes in Westchester, raised flax and hemp, and built gristmills, a linseed oil mill, and sawmill while engaged in trade as a merchant and contractor. Heathcote will serve until 1713, during which time the city will complete a large bridge next to the customhouse to facilitate landing and shipping cargos, repair a market building at the foot of Broad Street, and set up a new one near the north end.

The city's first slave market opens as such; the buying and selling of slaves has been going on for some years (*see* revolt, 1712).

1712 A slave revolt at New York ends with six whites killed before the militia can restore order; 12 blacks are hanged July 4 (six have hanged themselves). The revolt leaves whites suspicious of all blacks, whose treatment becomes harsher as a result. If three slaves are seen talking together in the street they may be tied to whipping posts and given 40 lashes. One citizen, John Van Zandt, horsewhips his slave to death after the man is picked up by city watchmen (the coroner's jury acquits him, saying that "correction given by the master was not the cause of his death, but that it was by the Visitation of God") (*see* 1741).

1713 The Treaty of Utrecht signed April 11 ends Queen Anne's War (called the War of the Spanish Succession in Europe), terminating hostilities between Britain and France.

1714 Former governor Edmund Andros dies in February at age 76. Gov. Hunter describes his predecessor, Lord Cornbury, as "a Devotee to Long Robes of both Gendres." Baron von Bothmer, a German diplomat, writes of Cornbury that he "thought it necessary for him, in order to represent Her Majesty [the gouty Queen Anne, who dies August 1 at age 48], to dress himself as a woman."

Manhattan merchant Henrick Van Brevoort pays £400 to acquire land that covers what later will be part of lower Fifth Avenue, running eastward to the Bowery, and extending northward for some distance (*see* Smith, 1762).

1715 The death of France's Louis XIV September 1 at age 76 after a 72-year reign has political repercussions in Britain and her colonies.

Jacobite supporters of Britain's James II gather at New York taverns, as do loyalist supporters of the Hanoverian succession, the taverns become known as mug-house clubs, and when both groups occupy the same alehouse October 31 a confrontation results in a fight that spills out into the streets, spawning violent brawls that continue for days (the mug-house riots).

Former New York governor Thomas Dongan, 2nd earl of Limerick, dies at London December 14 at age 81.

1716 New York's Common Council passes an ordinance requiring midwives to take out licenses and swear a version of the traditional midwives' oath.

∞ The city's first Presbyterian congregation is formed in Manhattan by Francis Makemie (see 1707). Being too poor to build a church, members of the group apply for funds to the College of Glasgow, the Synod of Philadelphia, and the Congregational Legislature of Connecticut (see 1719).

1717 A bill enacted by New York's provincial assembly calls for issuing £32,000 in paper money, a sum to be raised by imposing a tax on retailers and a duty on imported liquors. The province has debts of £12,000, and the assembly proposes to loan out the balance at 5 percent interest. The grand jury of New York, whose members are mostly merchants, protests to Governor-General Hunter November 29, asking him to veto the bill, but he gives it his approval and sends it to London for royal confirmation.

1718 Colonist Robert Livingston is elected speaker of the provincial assembly and will preside over its sessions for the next 7 years.

1719 Governor-General Hunter, now 52 and crippled with arthritis, turns the government of New York over to Peter Schuyler July 13, and the government of New Jersey to Chief Justice Lewis Morris, now 48. Schuyler is appointed president of the Council July 21.

∞ Manhattan's First Presbyterian Church holds services in a Wall Street house of worship constructed for its use with money contributed by supporters in Scotland, Philadelphia, and Connecticut (see 1716; real estate, 1846).

The first great New York mansion is completed for merchant Stephen de Lancey, 55, at 115 Broadway (it will be converted into the Queen's Head Tavern in 1762).

1720 William Burnet, 32, is appointed provincial governor September 17 and arrives shortly afterward to take up his position, vowing to suppress trading of furs with the Iroquois (see 1713).

1721 Former New York mayor Caleb Heathcote dies at Mamaroneck February 28 at age 55, leaving the manor of Scarsdale to his daughter Anne, who has married James de Lancey, 18.

1722 The Beekman Slip on Manhattan's East River waterfront is opened by merchant Gerardus Beekman, now 69.

1723 Irish-born Scottish colonial scientist-philosopher Cadwallader Colden, 34, submits a report on the province's commerce: "The Trade of New York is chiefly to Britain and the British Plantations in the West Indies besides which we have our Wines from Madeira and a considerable Trade with Curaçao; some with Surinam & some little private Trade with the French Islands—The Trade to the West Indies is wholly to the advantage of this Province the Balance being every where in our favor so that we have money remitted from every place we trade with, but cheifly [sic] from Curaçao and Jamaica, these places taking off great quantitys [sic] of Flower [flour] for the Spanish trade." Cadwallader moved to New York 4 years ago after an 8-year sojourn at Philadelphia, was appointed by the royal governor in 1720 to the posts of surveyor general and master in chancery, and since 1721 has been a member of the governor's council.

Merchant and former Council president Gerardus Beekman dies at New York October 10 at age 70. He has acquired substantial properties in downtown Manhattan and in Brooklyn.

Scottish farmer John Murray acquires a piece of Manhattan land on high land lying to the west of Kipsborough (the Jacobus Kips farm on the East River) between the Middle Road and the Eastern Post Road. The area will come to be known as Murray Hill.

1725 The *New-York Gazette* that begins publication November 1 (October 16 by some accounts) is the city's first newspaper. Royal printer William Bradford's shop at 1 Hanover Square (see 1695) gives whatever news the colonial government wishes to disseminate—out-of-date reports from Europe and customhouse items for the most part—and includes a few advertisements, mostly for runaway slaves (see 1728).

1727 The first American smelting furnace is built at New York, where manufacture of lampblack begins.

Smallpox strikes the city, killing 500 people within a few weeks.

Nonfiction: *A History of the Five Indian Nations, Depending on the Province of New York* by Cadwallader Colden.

1728 John Montgomerie is appointed April 15 to succeed the ailing William Burnet as governor of the New York province. Burnet will die in September of next year at age 41.

Former mayor Abraham De Peyster dies at New York August 3 at age 71, having become one of the city's richest merchants.

Politician-entrepreneur Robert Livingston dies at Boston October 1 at age 73, leaving his four sons a vast estate whose size they and *their* sons will increase.

New-York Gazette publisher William Bradford complains in his June 17 issue that his venture is losing money: "... the first of May last it was two years and a half that we have continued its Publication; but having calculated the Charge of Printing and Paper for the Same, as also how much will arise to defray that Charge (when all those who take this *Gazette* have paid in what is due to the first of May last) do find that we shall loose [sic] Thirty-five pounds in the two years and a half, by Publishing this Paper" (*see* 1725; 1744; Zenger, 1733).

1730 Gov. Montgomerie issues a new city charter that creates a seventh ward (it will be called the Montgomerie Ward until wards are assigned numbers in 1791), thus raising the number of aldermen in the Common Council to seven, plus seven assistants. Laws passed by the Common Council are to expire after 1 year, rather than just 3 months as has been the case since 1686, unless confirmed by the royal governor and his council. The governor retains the authority to appoint a new mayor each year.

The mayor appointed by the province's royal governor is to be a justice of the peace under Gov. Montgomerie's charter and he, or the recorder, and two other men qualify as a court of common pleas.

A slave market opens on the East River at the foot of Wall Street.

Congregation Shearith Israel erects its first synagogue in Mill Street at what later will be 18 South William Street (*see* 1654). The congregation has for the past 2 years been paying a yearly rental of £8 to shoemaker John Heperding (from whom John Street will get its name) for use of his house and has paid him £100, a loaf of sugar, and a pound of Bohea tea for the lot that accomodates its synagogue (*see* 1834).

Entrepreneur William Bayard opens the city's first sugar refinery, in Liberty Street between Wall and King streets. Most customers buy sugar in tall, conical loaves that weigh roughly a pound and can be sawed into cubes to make lump sugar or pounded into a powder and stored in a sugar castor, which resembles a giant salt shaker. New York refiners receive raw sugar, not cane, from West Indies plantations (cane must be processed quickly after cutting before it spoils) (*see* 1763).

Nearly 40 percent of the city's population is still Dutch, and people of Dutch descent probably remain the largest single nationality.

1731 Provincial governor John Montgomerie dies at New York June 30, probably of smallpox. Albany-born merchant-shipowner Rip Van Dam, a man of about 71 who has never quite mastered English, is appointed president of the Council July 1 and will serve as provincial governor until next year.

New York jurist James de Lancey, now 28, is appointed to the colony's Supreme Court. The eldest son of merchant Stephen de Lancey, now 67, young James has studied law in England (*see* 1686; 1744).

A smallpox epidemic kills 478 whites and 71 blacks in the city. The epidemic brings the city almost to a standstill: the Assembly adjourns, farmers in many cases fail to bring produce into town, and the ferryman asks the Common Council for a rent reduction on grounds that his business has completely ceased.

The city's first public library opens in the City Hall with 1,642 books owned by the Society for the Propagation of the Gospel in Foreign Parts.

Fire engines ordered from London arrive at the Battery December 3 (*see* 1659). Each is 13 feet long and requires 20 men to operate, 40 volunteers drag the contraptions to City Hall, Mayor Robert Lurting accepts them ceremoniously, and they are installed in sheds behind City Hall to mark the start of the city's fire department. Most of the city's houses are wooden, fire is an ever-present danger, and two public officials, known as viewers, make regular inspection rounds to make sure that chimneys and hearths are kept clean. A homeowner with three fireplaces is obliged by law to keep two leather buckets filled with water and handy at all times. Landlords of rented premises must pay for such buckets, but only one bucket is required where a house has only one or two fireplaces. The new fire engines have large tanks, piston rods, pipes, and a rear nozzle, but they are mounted on large wooden block wheels, must be lifted off the ground to turn corners, and are more impressive to look at than effective in the event of a fire.

New York City's population reaches 9,000, up from 5,250 in 1700.

1732 Col. William Cosby, 42, is appointed August 1 to succeed Rip Van Dam as governor of the New York province. Sent out from England, he soon demands that the assembly make him a large gift of cash in addition to his excessive salary. Gov. Cosby takes bribes, sells government positions, tries to seize rich properties in the Mohawk Valley, sneers at critics, and finally demands half the salary received by Van Dam during his 13 months as acting governor. Van Dam objects, the new governor creates a special court consisting of supreme court justices who will sit as barons of the exchequer, and the attorney general is ordered to bring an action before this court in the king's name. Lewis Morris II, 60, chief justice of the supreme court, agrees with Van Dam's lawyers that the governor has exceeded his powers in creating the special equity court, justices James de Lancey and Frederick Philipse II, 36, side with the governor, but the case is dropped, and Gov. Cosby receives none of Van Dam's money.

Colonist Jan Jansen Bleecker dies at Albany in November at age 91 (approximate), survived by his Albany-born sons John, now 64, and Rutger, now 57, who has married Catalina Schuyler, daughter of David Pieterse Schuyler. Jan's daughter Catherine has married the socially prominent Abraham Cuyler.

The New Theater opens December 6 at the corner of Maiden Lane and Pearl Street, where a warehouse owned by former acting governor Rip Van Dam has been converted into the city's first playhouse. Members of the audience huddle on benches that accommodate about 300; they have brought along foot warmers normally used at church, candles illuminate the stage, a barrel hoop hangs from the ceiling with more candles to shed additional light, a sign urges playgoers not to spit, and what they see are plays from the London stage, notably works by Colley Cibber, Richard Steele, and the late George Farquhar.

Gov. William Cosby stocks Governors Island with six pairs of English pheasants that will multiply and migrate to Long Island.

1733 The *New-York Weekly Journal* begins publication under the direction of German-born printer John Peter Zenger, 36, who worked as an apprentice in William Bradford's printing shop at 81 Pearl Street from 1711 to 1719. Zenger reports November 5 that

Bowling on the green near the southern tip of Manhattan provided diversion for early settlers.

an election held at St. Paul's Church village green in the village of Eastchester (later Mount Vernon) was rigged by supporters of the autocratic and corrupt colonial governor William Cosby. Authorities seize Zenger and hold him on charges of printing false and seditious information (*see* 1735).

The Common Council passes a resolution March 12 ordering that "the piece of land lying at the lower end of Broadway fronting the fort, be leased to some of the inhabitants of Broadway, in order to be inclosed to make a Bowling Green, with walks therein, for the beauty and ornamentation of the said street, as well as for the recreation and delight of the inhabitants of this city, leaving the street on each side fifty feet wide" (*see* 1734). Bowling Green will survive as the city's oldest park.

1734 New York's provincial assembly enacts legislation providing for the erection of a battery on Capsey Rocks and forbidding anyone to build a house that could interfere with the fire of its guns "on the river, or on parts which overflow with water, between the west part of the Battery, or Capsey Rocks, to Ells Corner on the Hudson River" (*see* 1693; 1869).

Bowling Green is leased in October for a period of 10 years to Frederick Philipse, John Chambers, and John Roosevelt, who agree to keep it in repair at their own expense (*see* 1733; 1741).

1735 The area of Queens that will become Douglaston begins to develop as the Van Wyck family builds a house on the west side of the peninsula that was first settled by Thomas Hicks in 1656 (*see* 1819).

John Peter Zenger wins a landmark victory for freedom of the press (*see* 1733). The provincial governor

John Peter Zenger printed the truth, served time in prison for it, and won fame for championing freedom of the press.

Col. William Cosby controls the courts, has forbidden the legislature to meet, and has made it hard to get permission to hold elections. He has brought libel charges against the printer, but friends of former acting governor Rip Van Dam and Supreme Court Chief Justice Lewis Morris II have hired Zenger to print and edit a newspaper that will counter the lies reported in William Bradford's *New-York Gazette*, controlled by Col. Cosby. Zenger's trial opens August 4 in the courtroom on the second floor of City Hall, Philadelphia lawyer Andrew Hamilton admits that his client printed the report in his *New-York Weekly Journal* as charged, but he persuades the jury that Zenger printed only the truth and wins acquittal with his argument that if the information published was true it could not have been seditious.

1736 Provincial governor Col. William Cosby dies March 10 at age 45; George Clarke, 59, is appointed president of the Council to succeed Cosby and will serve until 1743.

The New York Poorhouse opens as the city's first public institution to provide care for neglected children, many of whom live in various almshouses.

Bellevue Hospital has its beginnings in a municipal almshouse (the city's first), with a six-bed infirmary built at a cost of £122 (£80 plus 70 gallons of rum, 70 pounds of sugar, and small beer for the construction workers; (the carpenter receives £60 plus 50 gallons of rum given at the time of "laying the beams and raising the roof"). Opened by the Public Work House and Home of Correction, it stands on a site that will later be occupied by City Hall on lower Broadway (*see* 1794).

1737 New York's first dancing master arrives from England; the citizenry begins to entertain itself with public balls.

1739 Dutch-born merchant John Cruger, 59, is appointed mayor, a post that he will hold for five consecutive terms. Having gained fortune and prominence as a shipper and slave trader, he won election as alderman from the dock district in 1712 and retained that position until 1735.

Irish-born British colonist William Johnson, 24, purchases property of his own, beginning a series of acquisitions that will make him one of the largest landowners in the colonies. He has been managing the Mohawk Valley estate of his uncle Sir Peter Warren and cultivates friendships with members of the Six Nations, chiefly the Mohawk, as he works to develop a fur-trading business (*see* politics, 1745).

New York City's first Masonic Lodge is organized (it is also the first in North America). The secret fraternal order of Freemasons formed in the 17th century by English stonemasons' guilds has roots as old as the Egyptian pyramids; the English Grand Lodge appointed a provincial grand master of New York, New Jersey, and Pennsylvania 9 years ago (*see* 1787).

1741 A fire at Fort George March 18 destroys the provincial governor's house, barracks, and a chapel. More conflagrations break out later in March and in early April. New Yorkers charge a "conspiracy" of Spanish blacks with having started the blazes, blacks are seized at random, even some who have helped to put out fires, and the Council meets April 11 to discuss the situation (*see* 1712). The city's population of 10,000 includes 2,000 slaves, some of whom have been called "Spanish Negroes" since they arrived at New York aboard a Spanish ship that had been captured by a British warship in West Indian waters and were sold as slaves. Fears are raised that the Spaniards, who last year attacked Florida, intend to attack New York. Roman Catholic priests are inciting slaves to burn the town on orders from Spain, say the rumormongers, other fantastic stories are told, and Mayor Cruger, whose fortune was derived in part from slave trading, ruthlessly suppresses the uprising: two slaves are hanged May 11 on a little island in the Collect despite the lack of any real evidence against them. Two more blacks are burnt alive, six are hanged June 7, more hangings and burnings ensue, and three white "conspirators" are hanged June 12. By August 29, when the racist and anti-papist paranoia subsides after the last hanging, 154 blacks have been jailed, 18 hanged, 14 burnt alive, and 71 banished to the West Indies; 24 whites have been imprisoned, and four of them have been hanged.

Slaves played important roles in the life of the British colony; some were put to death for "conspiracy."

New York's journeymen bakers go out on strike for higher pay and better working conditions. Obliged to start before dawn and work in hot basements, they are among the most ill-used workers in the colonial food industry.

$ Merchant Stephen de Lancey (originally Etienne de Lancy) dies at New York November 18 at age 78 (*see* Fraunces Tavern, 1763).

A yellow fever epidemic rages through the summer, exacerbating the woes of the city, and those who can afford it move out of town to escape either the fever or accusations of involvement in the "Negro Conspiracy."

The destruction by fire of Fort George allows for improvement of the area adjacent to Bowling Green that will soon be surrounded by substantial houses (*see* 1734; statue, 1771).

1743 Adm. George Clinton, 57, is appointed to succeed George Clarke as governor of the New York province September 2 and will serve in that capacity until 1753.

● The secret marriage of Oliver de Lancey to Phila Franks scandalizes the city: the bride is the daughter of a prominent Jewish family.

1744 James de Lancey, now 38, is named chief justice of the New York State Supreme Court, a position that he will hold until his death in 1760.

$ James de Lancey's pretty young sister Susannah marries Admiral Sir Peter Warren, 40, a bewigged Irishman whose 16-ship squadron has captured 24 French and Spanish prizes off Martinique between February 12 and June 24. One of his vessels has landed at New York carrying a fortune in plate (silver), and its cargo is advertised in the *Weekly Post-Boy* June 30 as being for sale through "Messieurs Stephen de Lancey & Company." Warren will buy a 300-acre estate in Greenwich Village, erect a house that will stand until 1865, but return to London and win election to Parliament in 1747.

The *New-York Gazette* publishes its final issue November 19 (*see* 1728). William Bradford's apprentice Henry de Forrest launches a new paper, the *New-York Evening Post*, that will continue until 1752.

1745 Landowner-fur trader William Johnson in the Mohawk Valley persuades chiefs of the Six Nations not to ally themselves with the French in King George's War.

$ Merchant-landowner Adolph Philipse retires at age 80, having increased his tenant population from 200 to 1,100 and his slave ownership to about 23. His mills along the Pocantico River process the barley, wheat, and corn produced by his tenant farmers and slaves, his coopering shop produces barrel staves, the flour from his mills is sent to New York City, shipped abroad, or baked at the Upper Mills (later North Tarrytown) into ship biscuit for sale in the city's maritime market.

1746 Provincial governor George Clinton rewards William Johnson for keeping the Six Nations out of King George's War last year by making him a colonel of the Six Nations, responsible for their affairs (*see* 1745; 1750).

Printer-editor John Peter Zenger dies at New York July 28 at age 49. His widow and son will carry on his anti-government *New-York Weekly Journal* until 1751.

1748 Visitors to New York report that its streets are wide and well paved (*see* 1708; 1787).

Van Cortlandt Mansion goes up for Frederick Van Cortlandt, a grandson of Oloff Van Cortlandt. The large stone house will stand for more than 250 years near what later will be the corner of Broadway and

242nd Street, and members of the Van Cortlandt family will continue to occupy it for 141 years (another Van Cortlandt mansion will be built at 9–11 Broadway; see Van Cortlandt Park, 1889).

1749 Former acting governor Rip Van Dam dies at New York June 10 at age 89.

1750 Landowner-fur trader William Johnson, now 35, is appointed a member of the Council of New York, a position he will hold until his death in 1774.

More than 20 percent of the city's population is made up of blacks, half of them slaves; no other city except Charleston has more slaves and slave owners.

New Jersey-born New York physician John Bard, 34, and John Middleton perform the first recorded dissection of a human body for the instruction of medical students in America. Bard moved to New York 4 years ago on the advice of his friend Benjamin Franklin, persuaded the authorities to establish a quarantine station on Bedloe's Island, and won appointment as the city's first health officer.

1751 Landowner Frederick Philipse II dies at New York at age 56 (see 1702). Renowned for his courtly good manners and lavish entertainments, he has expanded his grandfather's manor house and leaves it to his son.

New Yorkers defeat Londoners May 1 in the city's first cricket match.

1753 Sir Danvers Osborne, 37, Baronet, is appointed October 10 to succeed Adm. George Clinton as governor of the New York province but dies October 12. Lieut. Gov. James de Lancey, 49, is appointed to succeed him and will serve for nearly 2 years.

Theater: a company of London comedians brought over by actor Lewis Hallam begins the city's season September 17 at The Play House in Nassau Street and will continue until March 25 of next year with performances of plays such as Richard Steele's *The Conscious Lovers* of 1722. The company includes Hallam's wife and his 13-year-old son and namesake. Box seats sell for 8 shillings, places in the pit for 6s, and places in the gallery for 3s (a bushel of wheat sells for 5 shillings sixpence, a hundredweight of flour for 15s, a cwt of butter for 45s, a pound of Bohea tea for 5s 6p).

Fire destroys the steeple of the 55-year-old Trinity Church that was enlarged in 1737. The church's Charity School is also destroyed, and all records of parish baptisms, marriages, and burials are lost (see 1776).

1754 The Albany Convention that meets June 19 is the first colonial congress of its kind in America. Supreme Court Chief Justice (and provincial governor) James de Lancey presides over discussions of methods of common defense against the French and ways to conciliate the Indians, but the delegates spurn the advice of Boston-born Philadelphia printer Benjamin Franklin, now 48, who has drawn a cartoon in May suggesting that the colonies unite by act of Parliament.

Columbia University has its beginnings in a charter granted October 31 by Supreme Court Chief Justice James de Lancey to the King's College (see 1709). The charter will not be delivered until May of next year because of Presbyterian opposition (Albany-born lawyer William Livingston, 30, opposes its governance by trustees associated with the Anglican Church), but classes begin in a room of the Trinity School under the auspices of Trinity Church, and the college will have a library by 1757 (see 1784; lottery, 1756; Columbia Grammar, 1764).

The New York Society Library is founded April 8 in the City Hall. Modeled on Benjamin Franklin's 23-year-old Library Company of Philadelphia, it is open only to those who pay a subscription fee and is the city's first library of any real significance (see 1795; lending library, 1763).

Theater: *The Gamester, a Tragedy* 3/25 at the New Play House in Nassau Street with Lewis Hallam.

1755 Sir Charles Hardy, 39, is appointed September 3 to succeed James de Lancey as governor of the New York province; he will serve only until 1757.

The Battle of Lake George September 8 ends in victory for British colonial troops over the French in a resumption of the French and Indian Wars. French and Indian forces led by Baron Ludwig August Dieskau have attacked William Johnson's men, Johnson routs them, and although he fails to reach Crown Point he erects Fort William Henry at the head of Lake George; Britain's George II makes him a baronet in November.

1756 Sir William Johnson is named sole agent and superintendent of the affairs of the Six Nations (see 1755; 1759).

Alderman John Cruger, Jr., now 46, is appointed mayor, a position he will retain until 1765.

The first known use of the term *New Yorker* appears in a letter written by Virginia planter George Washington, 24, who has been engaged in defending his colony's western frontier against raids by the

French and Indians. He makes a brief visit to New York in February.

The first lottery ever seen in the city is held to raise money for King's College (later Columbia; *see* 1754; 1784).

1757 Former governor James de Lancey is reappointed governor of the New York province June 3, succeeding Sir Charles Hardy. He will serve until 1760.

Nonfiction: *A History of New York* by English author William Smith is published at London.

1758 A new city jail is built in a field north of Broad Street to relieve crowding in the facility that has housed prisoners in the basement of City Hall since 1704 (*see* Bridewell, 1775).

1759 British colonial troops under the command of Sir William Johnson take Niagara from the French July 25 (*see* 1756; Treaty of Fort Stanwix, 1768).

1760 Supreme Court Chief Justice and provincial governor James de Lancey dies at New York July 30 at age 56. He is survived by his wife, Anne, a daughter of the late Caleb Heathcote. Scientist Cadwallader Colden, now 72, is appointed president of the Council August 4 and becomes acting lieutenant governor of the New York province (*see* 1761).

The city enacts its first laws requiring the examination and licensing of medical practitioners.

1761 Former royal governor Admiral George Clinton dies July 10 at age 75. Maj. Gen. Robert Monckton, 35, is appointed governor of the New York province October 26, but Cadwallader Colden is reappointed president of the Council, is named lieutenant governor November 18, and remains the ultimate authority in the province. He will continue to have such authority as governors come and go, taking strict measures to enforce the law and enjoying little popularity (*see* 1760; 1765).

Irish-born teacher Robert Harpur, 30, arrives at New York September 1 and within 3 days has accepted a position at King's College (later Columbia) as professor of mathematics and natural philosophy at a salary (fixed later) of £80 per year. He will be appointed the college's first librarian next year (*see* 1784).

Theater: a new theater opens in Chapel Street 11/18 under the direction of actor David Douglass.

1762 The city's first St. Patrick's Day parade steps off March 17 as Irish contingents of the British Army celebrate a man whom historians will agree was not named Patrick, was not Irish, did not drive the snakes from Ireland, did not bring Christianity to Ireland, and was not born March 17. Irish-Americans will grow in number until New York has a larger Irish population than that of Dublin, the parade will grow to become an annual Fifth Avenue event of paralyzing proportions, and it will never be canceled on account of inclement weather (*see* Society of the Friendly Sons, 1784; Fifth Avenue, 1852).

The Brevoort family sells a piece of its land north of what later will be 14th Street to merchant John Smith, who has made a fortune in the slave trade (*see* 1714). Smith builds a country house just west of what later will be Fifth Avenue.

1763 The Treaty of Paris signed February 10 ends Europe's Seven Years' War and brings peace between New York's British colonists and the French, whose Native American allies have kept many of the city's 12,000 residents fearful of attack.

The city's first for-profit lending library and reading room opens under the aegis of bookseller Garret Noel.

The Rhinelander family puts up a sugar refinery near Rose, Duane, and William streets as growing use of tea and coffee increases demand for sugar (*see* Bayard, 1730). The industry has attracted investment by such prominent families as the Cuylers, Livingstons, Roosevelts, Stewarts, and Van Cortlandts.

Fraunces Tavern has its beginnings in the Queen's Head Tavern named in honor of George III's wife, Charlotte. Jamaican-born entrepreneur Samuel Fraunces has taken over a house built in 1719 by colonist Stephen de Lancey at the corner of Broad and Pearl streets and turned it into a public house (*see* Chamber of Commerce, 1768; Washington, 1783).

1764 Monthly transatlantic packet service is inaugurated between New York and London; crossings sometimes take 2 months and more.

Columbia Grammar School has its beginnings in a school founded to prepare boys for the new King's College (*see* 1754; 1907). English-born clergyman (William) Samuel Johnson, 68, has headed the college since last year, when he became assistant minister of Trinity Church on Broadway facing Wall Street.

A country house is completed for colonist Charles Ward Apthorp (or Apthorpe) at what later will be 91st Street between Amsterdam and Columbus avenues. Apthorp's farm occupies much of the surrounding area (*see* 1783).

1765 ✗ The Stamp Act passed by Parliament March 22 is the first measure to impose direct taxes on Britain's American colonies. New York City has levied minor property taxes to fund public works, relief, and other municipal functions, but the purpose of the Stamp Act is to increase the revenues of the British government. Intended to raise £60,000 per year, the act requires revenue stamps on all newspapers, pamphlets, playing cards, dice, almanacs, and legal documents. Sons of Liberty Clubs spring up at several colonial towns to resist the new measure, a Declaration of the Rights and Grievances of the Colonists in America is sent to London, and a Stamp Act Congress convenes at New York in October with delegates from nine colonies under the leadership of Mayor John Cruger, Jr., who is removed from office by the colonial governor. Delegates include New York's largest landowner Robert R. Livingston, now 47, who has married Margaret Beekman, daughter of Col. Henry Beekman, and lives on Broadway near Bowling Green when not at his country seat, Clermont, up the Hudson. The Congress produces a set of resolutions protesting taxation without representation but rejecting the idea of sending American representatives to Parliament. Some 200 New York merchants sign an agreement October 31 to purchase no European goods, nor welcome any British ship, nor send any cargo to Britain, until the Stamp Act is repealed, and when the law goes into effect November 1 no stamp commissioner is in business in New York or anywhere else in the colonies. The royal lieutenant governor Cadwallader Colden has refused to condemn the measure, New York mobs demonstrate against the Stamp Act November 1, burn Colden in effigy right under the guns of the city fort, burn his carriages as well, and will control the streets until the act is repealed next spring (*see* 1769).

Sir Henry Moore, 52, Baronet, is appointed governor of the New York province November 13 but Cadwallader Colden continues to hold the real power.

$ Colonial American shipping interests have 28,000 tons of shipping and employ some 4,000 seamen. Exports of tobacco are nearly double in value the exports of bread and flour, with fish, rice, indigo, and wheat next in order of value. The major shippers include Thomas Francis Lewis of New York.

🏠 The Morris (later Morris-Jumel) mansion is completed as a summer villa for Col. Roger Morris, whose father in England is a prominent Palladian architect and who is himself a member of the British Executive Council of the Province of New York, married to heiress Mary Philipse. His Georgian frame

Demonstrations against the Stamp Act excited patriots, but most New Yorkers opposed separation from Britain.

and-shingle house on the highest point in Manhattan (later 165th Street and Edgecombe Avenue), will survive for more than 2 centuries (*see* 1810; Washington, 1776).

🍳 The Ranelagh Garden tavern opened by John Jones at the corner of Broadway and Thomas Street takes its name from a London establishment of the same kind, with illuminated grounds that are used at night for concerts, fireworks, and other entertainments. The tavern will continue in operation to 1769; it occupies the former homestead of the late Anthony Rutgers, who died in 1746 and whose heirs will sell the property in 1790.

👫 New York's population reaches 12,500, up from 5,000 in 1700 but far behind that of Philadelphia (*see* 1793).

1766 ✗ Parliament repeals last year's Stamp Act and New York's mobs disperse in the spring when news of the repeal reaches the city, but a Liberty Pole erected by the Sons of Liberty brings a clash with colonial troops August 10, and similar confrontations will continue until 1770 (*see* 1767). Founders of the Sons of Liberty include retired merchant Francis Lewis, 53.

∞ New York-born rabbinical student Gershon Mendes Seixas becomes a rabbi at age 21 to begin a notable career.

The John Street Methodist Church has its beginnings in the Wesley Chapel congregation established by Irish-born clergyman Philip Embury and his first cousin Barbara Heck between Dutch and Nassau streets. Embury and his cousin are among the so-called "Irish Palatines." Their chapel will be destroyed by fire but will be rebuilt in 1812 (*see* 1841, real estate, 1768).

🏠 St. Paul's Chapel opens on the west side of Broadway between what later will be Fulton and Vesey streets, extending with its churchyard to Church Street. Designed by Thomas McBean, it will get a tower and steeple designed by James Crommelin Lawrence in 1796 (*see* 1789).

1767 The Townshend Revenue Act passed by Parliament
$ June 29 imposes duties on tea, glass, paint, oil, lead, and paper imported into Britain's American colonies in hopes of raising £40,000 per year, but when news of the legislation reaches the colonies there are fresh protests (*see* 1768).

🎭 Theater: *The Beaux' Stratagem* 12/7 at the new John Street Theater in a production of the 1706 London comedy by George Farquhar. The theater has opened under the direction of actor David Douglass, who has married the widow of Lewis Hallam (she gives an epilogue).

1768 The Treaty of Fort Stanwix signed November 5
✗ between the Iroquois Nation and British colonial authorities bars colonists from settling west of a line drawn between Fort Stanwix (later Rome, N.Y.) and what will become Deposit, N.Y. Negotiated by Sir William Johnson, it is the first treaty under whose terms the white man begins to obtain land from Native Americans.

New Yorkers demonstrate November 14 in protest against Britain's Townshend duties, carrying effigies of colonial government officials as they did in 1765 when they protested the Stamp Act (*see* 1769; Battle of Golden Hill, 1770).

$ The Chamber of Commerce of the State of New York has its beginnings in the New York Chamber of Commerce, organized April 5 by 20 merchants meeting at the 5-year-old Fraunces Tavern. They form a civic association, possibly the first of its kind,

and elect merchant-ship owner and former mayor John Cruger, Jr. as their first president. Now 58, he leads their campaign against the Townshend Acts (*see* 1770).

🏠 The John Street Methodist Church dedicated October 30 stands on the former site of the Wesley Chapel at 44 John Street.

1769 Gov. Sir Henry Moore dies September 11 at age 56
✗ and is succeeded the next day by Cadwallader Colden, now 81.

$ New York merchants sign a new agreement not only to buy no more of what they consider heavily taxed goods but also to trade with no merchant who does not honor the agreement (*see* 1765; Townshend duties protest, 1768). The value of British imports into the city falls to £75,930, down from $490,673 last year (*see* Battle of Golden Hill, 1770).

⚕ Philadelphia-born New York physician Samuel Bard, 28, delivers an address in Trinity Church May 16 at the first graduation exercises (for two students) of the King's College Medical College, saying, "It is truly a reproach that a city like this should want a public hospital, one of the most useful and necessary charitable institutions that can be imagined." Son of Dr. John Bard, the younger Bard was graduated from King's College in 1760, sailed for England to study medicine, was imprisoned for 5 months when his ship was captured by a French privateer, gained release through the intercession of his father's friend Benjamin Franklin, and obtained his medical degree at Edinburgh 4 years ago. He helped to establish the medical school at King's College (Columbia) in 1767 and he has his remarks published in a pamphlet entitled, "A Discourse upon the Duties of a Physician, with Some Sentiments on the Usefulness and Necessity of a Public Hospital." The provincial governor Sir Henry Moore is in attendance at the exercises and addresses a special message to the provincial assembly May 17, noting that a subscription has "very lately been set on foot for building an hospital in this City" (*see* 1771).

1770 The Battle of Golden Hill at New York January 19 and
✗ 20 brings the first bloodshed between British troops and American colonists. The Sons of Liberty have put up a series of Liberty poles with pennants bearing slogans, the redcoats have torn them down, and when they tear down the fourth pole on the common west of Golden Hill two Sons of Liberty seize two soldiers. The soldiers resist, more citizens arrive with clubs, the officer in charge orders his men back to quarters, but a second skirmish occurs the following day. Crowds harass officers of the Crown, who are

The Battle of Golden Hill moved colonists closer to outright rebellion. Loyalists still outnumbered patriots.

sometimes tarred and feathered, and demonstrators May 10 carry effigies of British officials to protest what they call colonial oppression.

John Murray, 38, earl of Dunmore is appointed governor of the New York province October 19 but a demonstration similar to that of May 10 takes place in the city November 5 and Murray will be replaced next year.

$ The 2-year-old New York Chamber of Commerce is granted a charter March 13 by Britain's George III. The Chamber has no relation to any governmental body; it promotes business and serves as a mediator in business disputes (*see* building, 1902).

New York imports only 25,000 tons of cargo, as compared with Philadelphia's 47,000 tons, Boston's 38,000, and Charleston's 27,000. British law has forbidden the establishment of any banks in the American colonies, British banknotes are not readily available, nor are British coins, so merchants conduct trade using foreign coins (chiefly the Spanish real), paper money issued by colonial governments, warehouse receipts, and such. The silver real is often cut into halves, quarters, and eighths (pieces of eight, with two bits [or pieces] making a quarter).

1771 Provincial New York authorities erect an iron fence around Bowling Green to protect a gilded equestrian statue of Britain's George III and keep the bowling field from being used as a dump (*see* 1741). Purchased in England, the leaden statue has already become a symbol of tyranny, and the fence, built at a cost of £843, is considered necessary to preserve it (*see* 1776).

William Tryon, 42, is appointed governor of the New York province July 9.

The Society of the Hospital of the City of New York and its board of governors are created under terms of a charter granted June 13 by George III, "by the grace of God of Great Britain, France, and Ireland king, defender of the faith . . ." (*see* 1769). Provincial Governor John Murray, 4th earl of Dunmore, affixes the seal of the good samaritan to the charter and urges the colonial assembly to vote the hospital an annual appropriation of £800 for 20 years, offering it a three-quarter-acre tract. The Society's board of governors holds its first meeting July 24, opts to acquire a five-acre site on the west side of Broadway, opposite Pearl Street, and will build its first facility in Pearl Street, where a cornerstone will be laid September 3, 1773 (*see* 1776).

The city's population reaches 21,800, up from 12,000 in 1763, but New York remains rural north of Grand Street. Staten Island's population reaches 2,847, up from 727 in 1698.

1773 Parliament enacts a Tea Act to help the East India Company, whose debts of £1.3 million are owed in large part to the British government. Some 18 million pounds of unsold tea have piled up in the Company's London warehouses, and the Bank of England has refused to loan it any more money. New York and Philadelphia send tea-laden ships back to Britain, but men of "sense and property" such as Virginia planter-flour miller George Washington deplore the "Boston Tea Party" of December 16.

Alexander Hamilton, 18, enters King's College (later Columbia), having been sent to school earlier in New Jersey. Born on Nevis in the Caribbean, Hamilton is the illegitimate son of a Scottish nobleman, who abandoned the youth's mother and siblings; he went to work at age 9 in the St. Croix office of New York merchant Nicholas Cruger, who operated a trading post on the island and found Hamilton so intelligent that when he returned to New York for reasons of health he left the ambitious Hamilton, then 13, in charge. Hamilton lost his mother 5 years ago, continued working, and so impressed relatives and friends with his intellect that they have financed his education. Cruger paid for the youth's passage to New York 4 years ago (*see* politics, 1774).

The *New-York Gazeteer* begins publication April 22 under the direction of London-born Loyalist James Rivington, 48, who arrived at the city 12 years ago from Philadelphia (*see* 1775).

1774 The British ship *London* docks at New York April 22, and the Sons of Liberty prepare to follow the example set at Boston 4 months earlier, but while they are making themselves up as Mohawks an impatient crowd on the pier boards the vessel and heaves its cargo of tea into the Hudson.

King's College student Alexander Hamilton interrupts his studies to join in the public debate about British rule of the colonies and publishes the first of several pamphlets that he will write in behalf of the patriot cause (see 1777).

Colonial Indian agent Sir William Johnson gives a long speech in response to Iroquois complaints about trade and white encroachments but is suddenly taken ill and dies July 11 at age 59.

A Massachusetts delegation to the Continental Congress stops off at New York in August en route to Philadelphia and visits the City Hall, the college, and the gilded equestrian statue of George III at Bowling Green. Lawyer John Adams, 38, writes about New Yorkers in his diary: "They talk very loud, very fast, and altogether. If they ask you a question, before you can utter three words of your answer, they will break out upon you again—and talk away."

Theatrical activities throughout the colonies are abolished in October by resolution of the Continental Congress, whose members recommend that all places of amusement be closed.

Scottish visitor Patrick M'Robert visits New York and notes that the entrance to King's College "is thro' one of the streets where the most noted prostitutes live," and there are "above 500 ladies of pleasure [who] keep lodgings contiguous within the consecrated liberties of St. Paul's."

Kingsland House is completed at Flushing in the New York colony.

New Yorkers continue to drink tea, but most of it is smuggled in from the Dutch and Danish West Indies to avoid paying the tax that was imposed by the Tea Act of 1773.

1775 News of a skirmish between British troops and colonists at Lexington, Mass., reaches New York April 23 via post rider Israel Bissel, 23, who carries a note penned at 10 o'clock in the morning of April 19. The intelligence from Boston causes New Yorkers to close the port, distribute arms, and burn two sloops bound for the British garrison at Boston. The New York colony's provincial congress has made Albany-born patroon Philip Livingston, 59, president April 20, and he is succeeded May 23 by Peter V. Livingston.

"There never was a more total revolution at any place than at New York," Virginian Richard Henry Lee, 43, of the Continental Congress writes home to his brother Francis from Philadelphia May 21; "the Tories have been obliged to fly" and "the governor dares not call his prostituted Assembly to receive Lord North's foolish plan," but New York's royal governor is a Loyalist, as are the governors of New Jersey and Pennsylvania, and the majority of citizens in all three still oppose independence.

George Washington visits New York in June before taking command of the Continental Army. The provincial assembly creates a Committee of Public Safety, headed by the president of the assembly, in July, and the province's royal governor, William Tryon, who has been reappointed June 28, moves aboard a British ship in New York harbor in August to avoid being arrested by the assembly.

The provincial assembly makes Long Island-born patriot Nathaniel Woodhull, 52, president pro tem August 28; he is succeeded as president November 2 by Albany-born patriot Abraham Yates, Jr., 51, and John Haring takes over as president pro tem December 16.

Patroon Robert R. Livingston dies December 9 at age 57, leaving his New York-born son and namesake, now 29, to carry on his huge estates. The younger Livingston was appointed New York City recorder 2 years ago but has been dismissed from that post this year because of his sympathies for the colonial cause and been elected to the Continental Congress.

Bowne & Co. has its beginnings in a shop opened by Flushing-born stationer-printer Robert Bowne, 31, to sell quill pens, powder, account books, furs, and nails. He will have a balance of $23,000 by 1787 and his firm will grow to become the largest American printer of bond and stock certificates and other financial instruments.

Connecticut militiamen under the command of Capt. I. Sears seize the office of James Rivington's 2-year-old Loyalist newspaper the *New-York Gazette*, break up his presses, and melt his lead type down for bullets. Rivington flees home to England (see 1777).

Nonfiction: *Tour Through Part of the North Provinces of America* (Volume I) by Scottish traveler Patrick M'Robert, who writes of New York, "The inhabitants are in general brisk and lively, kind to strangers, dress very gay; the fair sex are in general handsome, and said to be very obliging."

▥ The Bridewell is constructed to serve as the city's prison, supplementing the jail built in 1758 (*see* 1816; prison, 1797).

1776 Nathaniel Woodhull resumes the presidency of New
✗ York's provincial assembly February 12 as agitation for independence continues to embroil the colony. Rebel forces in Queens County seize more than 1,000 weapons from known Loyalists early in the year but only with the help of New Jersey militiamen.

A Loyalist plot to kidnap George Washington, blow up patriot magazines, and trap the Continental Army on Manhattan by blowing up Kings Bridge at the northern end of the island comes to light in late June. More than 700 men are implicated, according to evidence presented in court, and they include not only one Thomas Hickey, a member of Washington's personal guard, but also David Matthews, mayor of the city.

Vice Admiral Lord Richard Howe, 50, Royal Navy, sails into New York Harbor in June; he has been given command of the North American station and hopes to conciliate the colonists. His brother, Gen. William Howe, 46, lands on Staten Island June 30, and the tents of his men cover the island's hills in plain sight of Manhattan.

The Continental Congress meeting at Philadelphia votes July 2 to declare independence from Britain, but New York delegates abstain on orders from home, and they do not sign the Declaration of Independence July 4. The New York colony probably has more Loyalists than any of the other 12.

News reaches the city July 9 that a Declaration of Independence has been signed at Philadelphia. Gen. Washington has the declaration read to his troops, who return to their barracks and campgrounds, whereupon a crowd rampages through town, break-

Patriots pulled down George III's statue at Bowling Green, They remained in a minority, opposed by staunch Tories.

Fire reduced much of the city to ruins in 1776, but British redcoats retained control until late in 1783.

ing the windows of prominent Loyalists. The Sons of Liberty and other civilians pull down and destroy the 4,000-pound equestrian statue of Britain's George III in Bowling Green; its head is sawed off and its lead taken away by some accounts to be melted down and molded into 42,000 bullets by the wife and daughter of the governor of Connecticut; the iron fence surrounding the statue is partly destroyed as the mob tears off its ornaments, but much, if not most, of the city remains staunchly loyal to the Crown and regards the bid for independence as ill-advised, ill-conceived, and certain to fail.

The Provincial Congress of New York convenes at White Plains, ratifies the Declaration of Independence July 9, renames itself the Convention of the Representatives of the State of New York July 10 (*see* Constitution, 1777).

Gen. Washington sets up headquarters in what later will be Charlton Street between Varick and Mac-Dougal streets. He will soon relocate to the 11-year-old Morris mansion uptown.

Lord Howe joins his brother on Staten Island July 12. Gen. Howe sends the British warships *Rose* and *Phoenix* up the Hudson in July to open communications with his troops to the north, but colonial militiamen follow along the shore and prevent a landing of British troops in Haverstraw Bay. Five American ships—the *Crown*, *Lady Washington*, *Shark*, *Spitfire*, and *Whiting*—engage the British ships August 3 in the Tappan Zee; smaller but heavily armed, they exchange fire for 90 minutes, and although the Battle of the Tappan Zee is indecisive the Americans give a good account of themselves. Colonists install a *chevaux-de-frise* (an underwater fence of sharpened logs) in the Hudson River north of West Point, but the British are not fooled and no Royal Navy ship is sunk.

Britain's royal governor William Tryon returns to his old office in August and tries to restore order in the rebellious colony. Gen. Henry Clinton and eight British regiments have returned to New York August 1 after a failed effort to take Charleston, S.C., and by mid-August some 400 transports and men-of-war are in New York Harbor along with close to 25,000 troops, including 8,000 German mercenaries—the largest armada and largest army ever sent out from Britain.

The Battle of Brooklyn August 27 pits 11,000 Colonial militiamen against nearly 32,000 British troops, including 20,000 regulars, who have come ashore from 75 flatboats with planked-up sides beginning August 22 at Gravesend Bay and Denyse Ferry (later Fort Hamilton). Gen. Howe fires off two shots at 9 o'clock in the morning at Bedford, signalling some 4,000 British soldiers to attack; Gen. Israel Putnam's Colonials contain them briefly, but about 8,000 additional redcoats arrive an hour later, gain support from local Loyalists who know the terrain, and come up from behind to surround the 1,200 Americans, most of whom surrender (although many are massacred) in part of the larger Battle of Long Island (still called Nassau Island). A band of 400 Marylanders launches an assault on the 10,000 surrounding British and German forces; forced back, 250 survivors put up stout resistance at the old stone Vechte-Cortelyou house and give the routed Colonial forces time to retreat across a bridge over Gowanus Creek before seeking refuge in the forts on Brooklyn Heights, having lost 1,407 men killed, wounded, or missing (the British have sustained relatively few casualties). Gen. Washington sets up headquarters at the Cornell house on Brooklyn Heights and brings over reinforcements from New York, but his aides persuade him that Manhattan offers better opportunities for defensive action, so he moves his 9,300 men across the East River from Fulton Landing under cover of fog and rain on the night of August 29. Admiral Howe has somehow failed to block the East River crossing.

Gen. Washington realizes that he cannot hold the city; Rhode Island-born Gen. Nathanael Greene, 34, urges that nothing be left behind that the enemy can use, two-thirds of New York property belongs to Loyalists, and Washington writes to the Continental Congress at Philadelphia September 2, asking whether he should have his departing troops torch the city or let the British have it for use as winter quarters. "They would derive great convenience from it on the one hand; and much property would be destroyed on the other." Congress still hopes that New York can be recaptured and opposes any scorched-earth policy.

Gen. Howe and his secretary Sir Henry Starchey meet September 11 at the 86-year-old Christopher Billopp house in Staten Island's Tottenville section with John Adams, Benjamin Franklin, and Edward Rutledge in an effort to end the war by negotiation. Howe has captured two major generals, including New Hampshire-born soldier John Sullivan, 36, and learns for the first time that the Declaration of Independence has been signed. He offers "clemency and full pardon to all repentant rebels" if they will lay down their arms. Sullivan gains Gen. Washington's grudging consent to carry Gen. Howe's peace overtures to the Continental Congress at Philadelphia (where he is freed in exchange for a British general), but Franklin, Adams, and Rutledge demur, Congress refuses to retract the declaration, and negotiations break off. Gen. Washington sends the Congress a letter urging that a regular army be enlisted to serve for the duration of the war (many regiments have voted to disband and return home in the wake of the defeat in Brooklyn), he warns that he may not be able to obey his orders to defend Manhattan, whose environs the British clearly intend to use as their winter quarters, and he devises a new strategy of evasive actions that will exhaust the British without directly engaging them. Washington positions 9,500 men on the heights of Harlem and at Kings Bridge, deploys 5,000 along the shore of the East River above New York, and leaves only 5,000 in Manhattan.

Royal Navy vessels on the East River open fire September 15 on Horn's Hook, where the Americans have appropriated the country house of Loyalist merchant Jacob Walton and set up a fort with nine guns. The bombardment reduces the structure to ruins (see Gracie, 1798).

Gen. Howe arrives at Kips Bay on Manhattan September 15 with five frigates, his cannon fire disperses defenders ashore, his infantry clambers up the steep rocks at what later will be the foot of East 34th Street, and—by some accounts—he stops for lunch at the Murray Hill home of Mary Murray (née Lindley), 50, whose husband, Robert, has built a house that he calls Inclenberg on property acquired by his late father, James, in 1723. She entertains the general and his officers with help from her beautiful daughters. Howe has been carrying on an affair with the wife of a subordinate; he narrowly misses catching Gen. Washington, who has galloped down from the Jumel Mansion to hold off the British until Gen. Putnam can withdraw troops trapped at the Battery;

Washington retreats to Harlem Heights and repulses a British attack September 16 with help from his sharpshooters. Armed with Pennsylvania long rifles, the Continental Army can fire accurately at 200 to 400 yards, while musket balls carry effectively only 80 to 100 yards (the British will complain that American sharpshooters are unsportsmanlike in concentrating their fire on officers).

The British capture Continental Army Captain Nathan Hale, 21, September 21 as he returns to Manhattan from an espionage mission to gather intelligence on Long Island. Having set numerous fires to harry the British in New York, Hale has disguised himself as a Dutch schoolmaster to avoid arrest, but incriminating documents are found in his shoes and he is hanged September 22 by order of Gen. Howe on a site near what later will be First Avenue near 63rd Street. His last words will be reported as "I only regret that I have but one life to lose for my country," a paraphrase of a line from the Joseph Addison play *Cato* that has enjoyed great popularity in New York.

Polish-born merchant Haym Salomon, 36, is arrested as a spy but released on parole after serving his British captors as interpreter with their Hessian mercenaries (whom he encouraged to desert). Having been given responsibility for provisioning the Continental Army in upstate New York, Salomon returned to the city in early September and has collaborated with other patriots in a scheme to fire British ships in the harbor (*see* 1778).

Former lieutenant governor Cadwallader Colden dies September 28 at age 88. He retired to his Long Island estate last year after 15 years of controlling the colony's government, and that is where he dies.

The Battle of White Plains October 28 gives Gen. Howe a narrow victory over Gen. Washington.

The Maryland and Virginia Regiment holds Fort Washington against Hessian troops but a turncoat American officer has supplied the British with detailed plans of the fort and its outworks; it falls to the British November 16 and is renamed Fort Tryon (*see* Tryon Park, 1935). British and Hessian forces also take Cock-Hill Fort on Inwood Hill and Fort George.

Gen. Howe occupies Manhattan; the British will hold it until 1783.

Gen. Nathanael Greene surrenders Fort Lee to the British November 20, giving up 2,811 trained Continental troops along with 43 cannon and tons of gunpowder and supplies; Washington has taken 2,500 men into New Jersey and begins a retreat across that colony the next day, with Gen. Charles Cornwallis, 38, in hot pursuit. He has left 11,000 men under the command of English-born Gen. Charles Lee, 45, in Westchester to discourage a British advance into New England; he takes refuge in Pennsylvania but crosses the ice-choked Delaware River Christmas night, surprises a garrison of Hessians at Trenton with help from Gen. John Sullivan, and takes 868 officers and men prisoners (only 300 to 400 escape). But Washington this year has lost 218 cannon and thousands of tents, blankets, and entrenching tools; the British have captured 329 Continental officers and 4,100 men, another 600 have been killed or wounded, several thousand have died of disease, more thousands have simply gone home, convinced that the cause is hopeless, and Washington has scarcely 3,000 men left to resist a British army of 27,000.

New York lawyer Gouverneur Morris, 24, attends the New York constitutional convention and succeeds in having it adopt a provision allowing religious freedom. He has been a delegate to the Continental Congress since last year but has delayed signing the Declaration of Independence for some weeks.

Bushnell's "Connecticut Turtle" goes into action the night of September 6 in New York Harbor, pioneering the use of the submarine in warfare. Built by Yale graduate David Bushnell, 34, the pear-shaped seven-foot vessel is made of oak staves held together with pitch and iron hoops. It has ballast tanks operated by foot pumps, its conning tower has windows level with the head of the operator (Sgt. Ezra Lee), who uses two air tubes for intake and exhaustion of air (automatic valves close them for diving), is propelled horizontally and vertically by hand-cranked propellers and guided by a flexible rudder, carries a powder magazine with a clock timer. An auger mounted on its top is designed to bore a hole into the wooden hull of an enemy vessel so that it may plant its powder magazine, but many of the British vessels have copperclad bottoms to protect them against shipworms, and several attempts to plant charges prove fruitless.

Merchant John Broome, 38, abandons his business and retires to Connecticut, where he will fit out privateers for attacks on British commerce.

New York Hospital opens its first facility, in Pearl Street (an earlier building was gutted by fire February 28 of last year before it was quite finished; *see* 1771). The colonial assembly has granted £4,000 for use in erecting a new building. The first patients treated are two Continental Army soldiers wounded

July 12 in an engagement between shore batteries and two British men-of-war trying to force their way up the Hudson (*see* 1788).

A great fire September 21 affects one third of the city, beginning at the foot of Broad Street and destroying 493 houses including more than 100 along the Hudson River before it dies out. By British accounts, colonial officers have sent in arsonists to set the city ablaze and thus make it harder for the British to find winter quarters. The first Trinity Church is burned down along with the entire west side of Broadway between Whitehall and Barclay streets (*see* 1778).

New York's population reaches 24,000, but Philadelphia has 40,000, making it larger than Boston and New York combined.

1777 Gen. Washington deploys his small force throughout the area surrounding Morristown, New Jersey, to make it appear that he has more men, tricks the British into thinking he has 12,000 instead of 3,000, harrasses British foraging parties with skirmishers and snipers, and uses the same methods against the enemy near Kings Bridge in northern Manhattan. New Yorker Alexander Hamilton, now 22, organized a company at the outbreak of hostilities 2 years ago; Washington makes him his aide-de-camp and personal secretary (*see* 1781).

Robert R. Livingston becomes the first chancellor of New York under terms of the state Constitution that he helped to draft last year and will continue in the position until 1781. The first New York State Constitution is signed April 20 at Kingston, having been framed largely by New York-born lawyer John Jay, 31, upstate New York-born Brig. Gen. George Clinton, 37, and Alexander Hamilton with help from patriot Gouverneur Morris, former city recorder Robert R. Livingston, and other members of the Fourth Provincial Congress who include former King's College professor Robert Harpur.

A British fleet commanded by Gen. John Burgoyne, 54, sails down Lake Champlain and appears before Fort Ticonderoga June 30 with 7,586 soldiers and 400 sailors of the Royal Navy. By July 5 the British have succeeded in mounting two 12-pound cannon atop a 750-foot-high crest overlooking the fort, whose commander, Gen. Arthur St. Clair, 40, has scarcely 3,500 men and officers. When the guns start firing on vessels in the narrows between Ticonderoga and Fort Independence, St. Clair takes his forces out of harm's way, leaving four artillerymen with orders to fire grapeshot on a bridge between the two forts. British and Hessian troops rout St. Clair,

who gains support from Albany-born Gen. Philip John Schuyler, 42, who is dismissed along with St. Clair by the Continental Congress; that body places English-born Continental Army general Horatio Gates, 50, in charge of all forces north of Albany.

Gen. Gates sets out September 8 with a 6,200-man Continental Army toward Bemis Heights, 28 miles north of Albany, where Polish engineering officer Thaddeus Kosciuszko, 31, has built fortifications on the 300-foot-high bluffs and on a 500-foot strip of level ground along the Hudson. Gen. Burgoyne has spent his nights carousing with his mistress, his army has diminished to 4,600 regulars plus about 800 Canadians but only 50 Iroquois, and without his Iroquois scouts he is unable to determine the location of the Americans. Worse, Burgoyne divides his force into three parts, commanding the center himself at the head of four regiments numbering about 1,100 men; New Jersey-born veteran soldier Col. Daniel Morgan, 41, comes to Gates's aid with 400 frontier riflemen, Connecticut-born Gen. Benedict Arnold, 35, sends in seven Continental regiments plus a regiment of New York militia September 19, political squabbling breaks out between Arnold and Gates, who orders Arnold to remain in his tent within the fortifications; deprived of Arnold's bold leadership, the Americans fall back to escape the grapeshot from British field guns, Col. Philip Van Cortlandt orders his Second New York Regiment to aim "below the flash" of the enemy guns, and the Americans win the day, sustaining 319 casualties as compared to more than 600 for the British in this first Battle of Saratoga.

A combined force of 16,000 British and German troops heads down Lake Champlain from Canada October 5 aboard 640 flatboats. A Continental fleet commanded by Gen. Benedict Arnold aboard the flagship *Congress* opens fire on the smaller craft at the rear of the British armada October 10; the British prevail, but Arnold escapes, burns his ships, and the British get bogged down building a 23-mile road from Lake Champlain through the dense woods and bogs to the south. A thousand axmen, engaged by Gen. Schuyler (who has enlisted 300 Oneida and Tuscarora allies), set to work felling trees in the path of the enemy; they destroy more than 40 bridges over creeks and ravines, impeding the British progress.

Gen. Burgoyne orders a second attack at Saratoga October 6 but his 5,000 redcoats are outnumbered four to one. Gen. Arnold joins the fray in defiance of Gates's orders, a German musket ball shatters his thighbone, but he sees Burgoyne's second-in-command (Brig. Gen. Simon Fraser, 48) on horseback encouraging his men, orders New Jersey-born sharpshooter Timothy Murphy, 26, to "Get Fraser," and Murphy fires his long rifle from a distance of 300 yards, mortally wounding Fraser, demoralizing the British, and inspiring Gates's men to defeat them; Gen. Burgoyne surrenders with his entire force, marches his troops to Boston, signs a peace convention October 16, and embarks for England. The first great triumph of Continental arms in the war will persuade France to support the cause of American independence.

British forces under Gen. Henry Clinton attack and burn Kingston October 16. The New York state government has been meeting at Kingston, a small town near the old Hudson River Dutch settlement of Rondout (from the Dutch word *reduyt*, or redoubt, meaning fort).

Brig. Gen. George Clinton is elected governor and also lieutenant governor; having served in New York's provincial assembly from 1768 until 1775, when he was elected to the Continental Congress, he declines the latter office but will serve as governor for all but 4 of the next 27 years.

British occupation forces use Livingston's Sugar House in Liberty Street as a prison for captured Continental Army soldiers. Cuyler's Sugar House in Rose Street and other such buildings are also used for the purpose, being five-story stone structures with low ceilings and small windows, but many prisoners will be confined aboard ships anchored in the East River.

The new state Constitution signed at Kingston excludes all priests and ministers from the legislature and political office, requiring a religious test for foreign-born Roman Catholics who apply for citizenship. John Jay has been outspoken in his efforts to impose such restraints on his fellow Catholics, but the Constitution otherwise proclaims general religious liberty.

The *Rivington New-York Gazette* begins publication in December under protection from the British. Publisher James Rivington has returned to the city; local Whigs call his paper the *Lying Gazette*.

1778 Sir Henry Clinton returns to New York in July, having given up his occupation of Philadelphia and retreated across New Jersey with Continental forces in pursuit of his 12-mile-long baggage train. A French fleet arrives off the American coast July 9 under the command of Charles Hector Theodat, Comte d'Estaing, but although the French have 850 guns to Admiral Howe's 534, Howe blocks the narrow entrance to New York Harbor with his men-of-war.

Patriot Haym Salomon is arrested again (*see* 1776). Confined in the Provost Prison and condemned to death, he bribes a jailer, escapes to the American lines, and flees to Philadelphia, where he will help local banker Robert Morris sell government bonds to finance the war and give much of his own money to support that cause.

Fire breaks out August 3 in the British-occupied city, destroying 64 buildings in Cruger's Wharf plus nearly 240 other structures on the East River, thus adding to the desolation created by the great fire of 1776.

1779 British troops under Sir Henry Clinton take Stony Point and Verplanck May 31 but lose Stony Point July 16 to Pennsylvania-born Gen. Anthony Wayne, 34, who has attacked "Little Gibralter" at midnight on orders from Gen. Washington and is knocked unconscious by grapeshot. The entire 700-man British garrison is captured, Gen. Washington orders the post evacuated, the Americans raze its fortifications, and Sir Henry abandons all hope of offensive operations in northern New York.

The British confiscate Philipse Manor on the Hudson but compensate the great-grandson of Frederick Philipse with £62,000 for his property (*see* 1867).

James Rivington's *Gazette* in British-occupied New York carries an advertisement April 21: "To the GOLF PLAYERS. The Season for this pleasant and healthy Exercise now advancing, Gentlemen may be furnished with excellent CLUBS and the veritable Caledonian BALLS by enquiring at the Printer's."

1780 The Hudson River freezes over for 5 weeks at New York, enabling British forces to cross on the ice from Manhattan to Staten Island with heavy gear that includes cannon. Eighty sleighs loaded with provisions cross on the ice to Staten Island with a large body of troops. It is the coldest winter ever known on the North American continent; the British erect blockhouses on the ice to prevent Americans from crossing, and the ice remains strong enough to bear a man riding a horse as late as March 17.

The British Army at New York decides June 8 to launch a surprise attack on Gen. Washington's 3,500-man Continental Army at Morristown, New Jersey, where the demoralized Connecticut brigade has mutinied May 26 and attempted to march home, stopped only by the leveled muskets of regiments from other states. Baron Wilhelm von Knyphausen has been persuaded that he could end the war, and he tries to take 5,000 men through passes in the Watchung Mountains in hopes of falling on Washington's headquarters, but he is forced to retreat back to New York.

British spy Major John André, 29, falls into American hands at Tarrytown September 23 with papers revealing a plot by Benedict Arnold to surrender West Point to Gen. Sir Henry Clinton, 42 (the papers are actually found in the major's boots by three men, possibly brigands intent on robbing him; they order him to strip, find the papers, and the one man among them who can read recognizes their significance). Now 39 and a widower, Arnold has recently married the beautiful 20-year-old Philadelphia coquette Peggy Shippen; the captured papers show that he has accepted an offer of £30,000 for the plans and inventory of West Point, whose capture would give the British control of the vital Hudson River waterway, and Arnold escapes downriver from Dobb's Ferry to the British sloop *Vulture* that is waiting for André; attempts to exchange André for Arnold come to naught, Gen. Washington appoints a board of military officers to hear evidence against him, they find him guilty of espionage, and André is hanged October 2 despite pleas on his behalf by Washington's aide Alexander Hamilton.

1781 Gen. Washington meets in May at Wethersfield, Connecticut, with the French marshal Jean Baptiste Donatien de Vimeur, Comte de Rochambeau, 55, but Rochambeau has received only 600 men instead of the 6,000 he was promised, and even with help from the French fleet in the West Indies he doubts that the small combined French and American force can take New York from the British. One of Rochambeau's officers writes a letter to the French ambassador, accusing Rochambeau of having insulted Gen. Washington; the messenger is captured, and the letter he was carrying is published in the *New York Royal Gazette*.

Brigadier Gen. Benedict Arnold now serves in the British Army at New York and begs Sir Henry Clinton to let him have 6,000 men, promising that he can destroy the 5,500 French and 2,500 American troops headed south for Virginia. Superintendent of Finance Gouverneur Morris has obtained the funds needed to transport Gen. Washington's army to Virginia. Convinced that the American cause is losing steam, Clinton resists Arnold's exhortations, and the allied army marches through Philadelphia September 2.

The American Revolution ends October 19 with the surrender of Gen. George Cornwallis at Yorktown, Virginia, but New York City will remain in British hands until November 1783. Col. Alexander Hamilton has impetuously resigned from Gen. Washington's staff and led a 400-man nighttime assault on a key British redoubt at Yorktown while French infantrymen seized another redoubt nearby. The British Army and Royal Navy at New York have argued too long over the issue of whether or not to send reinforcements to Cornwallis, and on October 13, when the fleet was supposed to sail, a thunderstorm sent such strong gusts of wind across New York Harbor that one ship of the line snapped her anchor cable and was driven into another, damaging both. New York State has seen 228 engagements during the war, second only to New Jersey's 238, and more than 90 have been fought in the Hudson River Valley.

Alexander Hamilton moves to Albany to study law and publishes newspaper essays advocating a strong federal government; he will be admitted to the bar next year and elected to Congress.

 Former British midshipman Robert Lenox returns to the city, marries, and buys a tract of elevated land, once part of the city's common lands, just west of the Boston Post Road in the remote village of Yorkville. A Scotsman who came to New York with the Royal Navy in 1779, Lenox starts a farm that will grow to cover 30 acres and the area will come to be known as Lenox Hill (*see* 1840).

1783 The Treaty of Paris signed September 3 recognizes the independence of the 13 colonies, and the last British troops finally leave New York November 25. Gen. Guy Carleton leads his forces onto ships at 1 o'clock in the afternoon, and American forces march south from the Bronx within the hour, crossing a bridge over Spuyten Duyvil Creek from McGowan's Pass and proceeding down the Bowery through Chatham and Pearl streets to the Battery under the command of Generals Washington and Clinton. Lieutenant Governor Pierre Van Cortlandt, 62, accompanies Gen. Washington on his triumphant entry into the city (his son Philip, 34, is made responsible for breaking up and selling confiscated Loyalist holdings in the city and surrounding counties). The new American flag is run up at the Battery to replace the Union Jack, and celebrations continue for 10 days until Gen. Washington bids farewell to his troops December 4 in a speech delivered at Fraunces Tavern. The last British troopship leaves for England from Staten Island December 5, and New Yorkers will observe Evacuation Day (as it will be called) on November 25 every year for nearly 140 years (see 1983).

Thousands of fugitive slaves leave New York aboard departing British vessels; some of them have been promised freedom and land in Nova Scotia, but most will wind up as slaves in the Caribbean and elsewhere (see 1741). Many have come to New York from other colonies in hopes that a British victory would enable them to escape from bondage (see 1784).

Captured Continental Army soldiers struggle to survive: some 16,000 American prisoners of war (11,500 by some accounts) have died of disease, flogging, and starvation at the hands of the sadistic British provost marshal William Cunningham in the Sugar House Prison and in 25 prison ships such as H.M.S. *Jersey* anchored in Brooklyn's Wallabout Bay (where four out of five prisoners died) and in the Hudson and East rivers.

New Yorkers returning to the city find that it has sustained more damage than any other American community, most of it from the 1776 and 1778 fires that destroyed houses, churches, and business establishments, most of them still in ruins.

English merchant John Delafield, 35, arrives at New York in the spring with the first copy of the provisional peace treaty between Britain and her former colonies. Son of a prosperous cheese dealer whose family has been in Britain since the Norman Conquest in the 12th century, Delafield has booked passage on a British vessel that carried letters of marque; she seized a French merchantman en route, and Delafield's £100 share of the prize money has enhanced his already substantial patrimony. He goes into trade and will be one of the city's richest men before he turns 50.

The *Rivington New-York Royal Gazette* resumes November 22 under the name *New-York Gazette & Universal Advertiser* but soon ceases publication (see 1777). Printer John Holt begins publishing The *Independent New-York Gazette*.

The 192,000-acre Philipse manor is broken up, as are other estates held by former Loyalists. The de Lancey manor is sold to 275 individuals under the direction of Philip Van Cortlandt in his capacity as commissioner of forfeiture for the Southern District.

Former patroon Stephen Van Rensselaer, 18, marries a daughter of Gen. Philip Schuyler. A graduate of Harvard College, Van Rensselaer inherited his father's enormous upstate manor at age 5 and will do more than any other landowner (or any of his predecessors) to improve and settle his estates.

Charles W. Apthorp is among the Tories who have vacated the city (see 1764); part of his large farm is acquired by one Gerrit Stryker, whose family will retain the property until 1856 (his name will be memorialized for years after in Stryker's Bay in the Hudson River at what later will be 96th Street). A 200-acre portion is acquired by one William Jauncey, a rich landowner who lives in Wall Street and will rename the property Elmwood. The southern section of the farm has been conveyed to Apthorp's daughter and her husband, John Cornelius Vandenheuvel, who will erect a mansion on the property in 1792 (it will become Burnham's Hotel in 1833 and survive until 1905; see Astor, 1860).

New York's population remains under 25,000 but will rise sharply in the next 7 years.

1784 Prussian-born Revolutionary War hero Baron Friedrich Wilhelm Ludolf Gerhard Augustin von Steuben, 53, is discharged from the Continental Army March 24 and takes up residence in New York City. He reported to Gen. Washington at Valley Forge, Pa., in February 1778, went on to command a division at Yorktown, served without pay, and was granted American citizenship last year by the Pennsylvania legislature.

French-born Revolutionary War hero M. J. P. Y. R. G. Du Motier, marquis de Lafayette, 26, visits New York for the first time from August 4 to 8, returns September 11, and is given a banquet at Capes Tavern by former officers of the Continental Army. Receptions September 12 include one at which Mayor James Duane presents the French nobleman with a gold box containing the "freedom of the city." Orphaned at age 13 and left with a princely fortune, Lafayette joined the American cause in 1777 and distinguished himself in battle. He remains in the city for a few days, returns 3 months later, and is escorted to his frigate December 21 with a parade, artillery salute, and farewell ode (see 1824).

The Manumission Society is founded by New York humanitarians to free slaves (see 1783). Its organizers include stationer-printer Robert Bowne, now 40.

The Society of the Friendly Sons of St. Patrick in the City of New York is founded as a charitable and fraternal order to help needy Irish immigrants. It will assist both Catholic and Protestant immigrants, and the society will hold annual St. Patrick's Day dinners for more than 200 years (see 1762).

The Bank of New York is organized February 24 at the Merchant's Coffee House, where merchants (including Robert Bowne) have met in response to an advertisement placed in the *New York Packet* February 23 by local attorney Alexander Hamilton, now 27, who calls on the "Gentlemen of this City to establish a Bank on liberal principles." English-born speculator William Duer, 36, has been the prime mover behind establishing the new bank; son of a prosperous West Indian planter, he himself prospered before the Revolution by supplying the Royal Navy with masts and spars made from timber harvested on a large tract that he had acquired outside Saratoga Springs at the urging of Philip J. Schuyler, and he made a fortune supplying the Continental Army, enabling him to marry the daughter of the rich American general William Alexander. The bank opens for business at the Wanton House June 9 with a capital of $500,000, will move in 1791 to the McEvers mansion across the street from Hamilton's residence at the corner of Wall and William streets (Hamilton will have sold his interest in the bank), and will erect its own building in 1797 at 48 Wall Street (*see* Bank of the Manhattan, 1799).

German-born entrepreneur John Jacob Astor (originally John [or Johannes] Jakob Asdour), 21, arrives at the city in March to join his brother Henry, receives a shipment of flutes from England, sells them at a profit, and begins buying furs in western New York. He has worked for 2 years at London, learned English, saved his money, and will soon marry one Sarah Todd, whose $300 dowry will help him expand his fur business. By 1786 he will have his own small shop in Water Street selling musical instruments as well as furs, and by 1800 he will have amassed a fortune of $250,000 (*see* 1801).

Economic depression continues in America.

Rabbi Gershon Mendes Seixas, now 39, returns to the city from Philadelphia, where he has lived since the British occupation of New York in 1776 (*see* 1766; Columbia, 1787).

St. Ann's Protestant Episcopal Church is founded at Brooklyn. It will survive as the oldest Episcopal parish in Brooklyn (*see* real estate, 1867).

The New York Board of Regents is founded to establish standards and policies for the state's public and private schools without consideration of partisan politics. Members of the appointed, unpaid Board include Alexander Hamilton and John Jay.

Columbia College opens as such. The King's College founded 30 years ago has been closed for 6 years, and the war has obliged King's College students such as Alexander Hamilton to educate themselves while the college's buildings were used as a hospital. Former professor Robert Harpur resigned in February 1767 but continued as a tutor, imposing such severe discipline that there were frequent student rebellions (*see* 1761). He serves now as secretary of the Regents of the University of the State of New York, whose members govern Columbia, and will continue as such until 1787, when he becomes trustee and clerk of the college's board of trustees (*see* 1857; 1890).

New York farmer Jonathan Randel buys an island in the East River that will be acquired by the city in 1835 and come to be called Randalls. It has heretofore been called Little Barn after its previous owner, a man named Barendt.

1785 The first Federal Congress convenes January 11 in the City Hall at the corner of Wall and Nassau streets, having met previously at Philadelphia and then at Princeton, Annapolis, and Trenton. Each state has one vote, regardless of size or population.

The *New-York Daily Advertiser* begins publication: it is the city's first daily newspaper.

Theater: The John Street Theater reopens with a lecture by actor Lewis Hallam the younger entitled "Monody to the Memory of the Chiefs Who Have Fallen in the Cause of American Liberty."

The fieldstone and white clapboard Dyckman House is completed at what later will be the corner of Broadway and 204th Street in Manhattan's Inwood section. William Dyckman is a grandson of Jan Dyckman, a Westphalian immigrant who settled in the area in 1661.

The Lefferts Homestead is completed on what later will be Flatbush Avenue near Maple Avenue in Brooklyn. Former Continental Army lieutenant Peter Lefferts has built his farmhouse in Dutch style, with gambrel roof, front and back porches, and rooms arranged symmetrically. It will be moved in time to Flatbush Avenue near Empire Boulevard.

1786 New York-born merchant William Bayard, 25, forms a partnership December 1 with Herman Le Roy that will grow in the next 40 years to become the city's leading commercial trading company. Bayard's landowner merchant father raised a Loyalist regiment at the start of the Revolution and his property was confiscated. The younger Bayard and his partner each invest $2,000 to import liquor from Tenerife in the Canary Islands, and they will later take Bayard's cousin James McEvers into the business to create Le Roy, Bayard & McEvers, but Bayard will play the dominant role in making the firm prosper as New York's commerce recovers.

∞ The Episcopal diocese of New York is created; Trinity Church's rector Samuel Provoost is consecrated as the first bishop of the diocese.

The Friends Seminary has its beginnings in the Friends Institute opened by Quakers (the New York Monthly Meeting of the Religious Society of Friends) in Pearl Street (*see* 1657); the seminary will become a leading elementary and secondary coeducational private school (*see* 1826).

1787 "Federalist Papers" explaining the new U.S. Constitution appear under the name "Publius" in the *New York Independent Journal* beginning October 27 and will run for 7 months. New York lawyer Alexander Hamilton, now 32, Scottish-born jurist James Wilson, 45, Virginian James Madison, 36, and U.S. foreign affairs secretary John Jay, now 41, have written the papers.

A Northwest Ordinance adopted by Congress, sitting at New York, provides for a government of the Northwest Territory. The region is to gain ultimate statehood, and no slavery is to be permitted.

$ New Yorker Robert Watts acquires the Manor of Fordham and renames it Rose Hill after his father's residence (*see* 1671). The property will change hands several times in the next few decades (*see* Fordham University, 1841).

The United Insurance Company of the City of New York is organized under a deed of settlement dated April 3. The city's first insurance firm, it will receive a charter from the state in 1798 to write fire, marine, and life insurance policies as well as property insurance policies, and it will continue under other names (Mutual Assurance Company, Knickerbocker Fire Insurance) until 1890.

∞ Rabbi Gershon Mendes Seixas wins appointment as a trustee of Columbia College, a position that he will hold until 1815 (*see* 1784). The college is largely an Episcopalian institution, but Rabbi Seixas has developed a reputation for wise counsel.

Erasmus Hall High School has its beginnings in a private school erected at what will be 911 Flatbush Avenue for the children of Brooklyn's Dutch farmers. It will be the first school chartered by New York State and survive as the second-oldest public school in the United States (*see* 1896).

The African Free School founded by the Manumission Society is the city's first school for blacks.

Theater: *The Contrast* by Boston-born playwright Royall Tyler, 29, 4/6 at the John Street Theater is a reworking of Richard Brinsley Sheridan's 1777 London success *The School for Scandal*. The first comedy of any real merit by an American, it is one of the first to introduce the "stage Yankee," a shrewd and realistic rustic who will be a fixture in many plays.

● New York City and New York State Freemason lodges declare independence from any obligations to the British (*see* 1739; 1789).

● The state legislature at Albany grants the Common Council power April 6 to pave the city's streets, most of them reportedly filthy and often even impassable (*see* 1748; 1789).

1788 New York State ratifies the Constitution July 26, becoming the 11th state to join the union, but only by a vote of 30 to 27. The state has an area of 49,170 square miles, of which 1,500 are water surface, measuring 300 miles long on the line of the Hudson River and 326.46 miles wide, from the Atlantic Ocean to Lake Erie and the Niagara River. Alexander Hamilton stages a big parade in the city to celebrate ratification. No mention is made of city government in the Constitution, and cities will have only such powers as the separate states grant them: although the state of New York will have overall jurisdiction of New York City's governance—including control of parks, schools, etc.—the city will often balk at having legislators from upstate counties determine city taxes and the like, and the extent of the state's jurisdiction in city matters will for more than 2 centuries be disputed, sometimes in court.

New York physicians go into hiding for 3 days in April as a mob riots in protest against grave robbers, who in years past have taken remains from the Negro Burying Ground and the cemetery of the almshouse but, more recently, have begun digging up the bodies of "respectable" people (the city has appointed a night watchman to guard graves on the common). Pathologist Richard Bayley has set up a laboratory at the 17-year-old Society of the Hospital of the City of New York on Broadway at Pearl Street, and surgeon Wright Post has been giving anatomy lessons, using cadavers to illustrate his points. Boys playing on Sunday afternoon, April 13, outside the hospital see an arm that a young doctor has left near an open window to dry, one of them climbs a ladder that painters have left against the hospital's wall, and when he peers in the window he discovers medical students and physicians dissecting a cadaver for study. He runs home, by some accounts, and tells his father, who takes some friends and visits the grave of his recently buried wife; finding the casket open and the corpse gone, the men rush to the hospital. By other accounts the boy tells his companions what he has seen and they shout the news to passersby in the street. An angry mob gathers, tears down the hospital's iron fence, smashes windows, and batters at the oak doors. Mayor Duane calls for civilian volunteers to help stop the violence; the mob pelts the men with dirt and bricks, and a second, larger, group of volunteers receives similar treatment. The mayor sends most of the doctors to the country but Dr. Samuel Bard, now 46, stands up to the mob, throwing open his windows and placing himself in full view while most other physicians hide for fear of their lives. Bard was a Loyalist during the Revolution but remained in the city after the British evacuated late in 1783. Ransacking offices and laboratories in search of incriminating evidence, the mob buries (or reburies) every cadaver it can find and seizes four doctors, but the sheriff rescues them and puts them in jail overnight to protect them. A mob of 5,000 storms the jail Monday afternoon, injuring Alexander Hamilton, John Jay, Baron von Steuben, Mayor Duane, and Gov. Clinton. A brigade of artillery is called in to protect the jailhouse, and when the mob continues to menace the peace the infantry is ordered to fire into the mob, three citizens are killed, and the riot continues through Tuesday, but the state will pass a law next year enabling physicians to obtain cadavers without robbing graves (see New York Hospital, 1791).

Supporters of the Constitution trash the New York City printing office of anti-Federalist Thomas Greenleaf July 26.

Cruger's Wharf goes up in flames August 3 and the fire spreads, destroying 64 houses.

1789 George Washington assumes office as president of the United States April 30 at New York's Federal Hall (the city's second city hall before being remodeled by French architect Pierre L'Enfant, 34, it will revert to use as city hall next year and continue as such until 1812). Washington has been rowed to the city from Elizabethtown Point by a crew of 13 ships' captains, he is sworn in by diplomat Robert R. Livingston, now 42, and begins the first of two terms as the nation's first president, taking care not to set any unfortunate precedents. He rejected suggestions made 2 years ago at the Constitutional Convention in Philadelphia that he be king, but he does not shake hands with visitors, choosing instead merely to bow. The president has taken up residence in the four-story house of importer Walter Franklin at 1 Cherry Street (a cherry orchard once grew in the vicinity, and the area will later be called Franklin Square). His five-man staff shares a house nearby at 39 Broadway. City recorder Richard Varick, 36, served as Gen. Washington's secretary in 1781 and is

appointed mayor by Gov. George Clinton. (A "recorder" is a judge, and a judge's duties have traditionally included keeping a record of various happenings in the city.) Like Clinton, Varick is a Federalist.

Tammany Hall (the Society of St. Tammany, or Columbian Order) is organized officially May 12, alleged birth date of the legendary Delaware Algonquin chief Tamanend, who is reputed to have been wise and devoted to freedom (other Tammany societies have been started in Pennsylvania, New Jersey, and Virginia). New York's Tammany began 2 years ago as a charitable, social, and patriotic order, mostly by craftsmen as an alternative to the city's more exclusive clubs; its members call themselves a "fraternity of patriots," protest rule by the aristocracy, and adopt pseudo-Native American titles and symbols (council members are called "sachems," ordinary members "braves"), but the organization will evolve into a powerful political machine. Upholsterer-paperhanger William Mooney appeared on a float in last year's parade to celebrate ratification of the Constitution and is Tammany's first Grand Sachem, but the power behind the club is evidently merchant-philanthropist John Pintard. Initiation fees are $2 to $8, depending on ability to pay, quarterly dues are 24¢, and by the autumn of 1791 Tammany will have more than 300 members (see 1812).

James Madison rises in the House of Representatives in what later will be called Federal Hall June 8

George Washington took his oath of office at New York and became America's first president. LIBRARY OF CONGRESS

to propose a number of amendments to the Constitution. Both houses pass 12 of them and submit them to the states for ratification September 25 (*see* Bill of Rights, 1791).

The United States Supreme Court is formed in September under terms of the Constitution. President Washington nominates New Yorker John Jay, now 43, as the court's first chief justice (all nominations are subject to confirmation by the Senate), and he will preside until his resignation in 1795.

Maine-born New York lawyer Rufus King, 34, is elected to the state legislature, whose members elect him one of the state's two U.S. senators. King moved to the city last year.

$ Mayor Varick ends the practice of awarding licensed carters the status of freeman, denying suffrage to the less prosperous carters who fail to meet requirements of property ownership (*see* 1691). His action antagonizes the cartmen, who throw their support to the emerging Democratic Republican Party (*see* politics, 1795).

Congress establishes a U.S. Customs Service under terms of the Tariff Act adopted July 4 passed at what later will be called Federal Hall. The second piece of federal legislation, it creates a source of revenue that will be the nation's major source until 1913. A customs house that will evolve into the Treasury Department opens at New York and levies duties of $145,329 its first year as revenue cutters put to sea and meet incoming ships; the figure will grow to more than $8.3 billion in 165 years as New York becomes the nation's major port of entry, but in New York State the city still lags behind Sag Harbor as a port of entry.

New York-born New Jersey landowner Col. John Stevens III, 39, petitions the state legislature at Albany February 9 to grant him exclusive rights to build steamboats. A King's College (later Columbia) graduate who served as treasurer for New Jersey during the Revolution, Stevens has seen such a boat operated on the Delaware River by Maryland-born inventor James Rumsey, now 45, and worked out designs of boilers and engines, but Rumsey has submitted a similar petition and the legislature awards him the grant (*see* patent law, 1790).

∞ Trinity Church donates land to help the war-ravaged city and in return is given the right to name any streets laid out on the land: Rector, Church, Chapel, Vesey, Barclay, Chambers, Reade, and Vandam.

The Alexander Robertson School opens at the corner of Broadway and King's Street (later Pine Street); it will survive into the 21st century as the city's oldest co-educational school. Started by the Second Presbyterian Church, it has been named for a local Scotsman who raised money after the Revolution to repair the church, used as a Hessian barracks; the school will relocate in 1813 to West 14th Street.

Theater: *The Father, or American Shandyism* by Perth Amboy-born playwright William Dunlap, 23, 9/7 at the John Street Theater, with Maria Storer.

The Bible used for President Washington's swearing-in belongs to the St. John's Lodge No. 1. Washington has been a Freemason since 1752, Robert R. Livingston has been grand master of New York State's Freemasons since 1784, and by 1800 the city will have 10 lodges (*see* 1739; 1826).

The first known American advertisement for tobacco appears with a picture of an Indian smoking a long clay pipe while leaning against a hogshead marked "Best Virginia." The advertisement has been placed by Peter and George Lorillard, whose Huguenot French immigrant father, Pierre, then 18, opened a shop in 1760 on the High Road between New York and Boston at a point that will later be called Park Row but was killed by Hessian troops in the Revolution.

The Common Council passes legislation in April imposing strict penalties for violations of the city's paving regulations (*see* 1787; 1876).

1790 President Washington moves into larger quarters in February, taking up residence at 39 Broadway with his wife, Martha, and a staff of 21, including seven slaves. Virginia planter-diplomat Thomas Jefferson, 46, arrives at New York March 21 to take up his duties as first U.S. secretary of state; unable to find a house, he finds temporary lodgings at the City Tavern on the west side of Broadway between Cedar and Thames streets but moves in June to a small house at 17 Maiden Lane.

$ Congress meets for the last time at New York August 12, and the Washingtons leave in October, as does Jefferson, for the new capital at Philadelphia. Wives of Southern congressmen have pushed their husbands to move away from the temptations of New York and closer to home.

Congress grants Gen. von Steuben a pension of $2,800 per year, enabling him to escape bankruptcy; he will divide his time hereafter between New York City and the farm granted to him by the state at Remsen, N.Y.

Secretary of the Treasury Alexander Hamilton presents his first report on the public credit to Congress in January. Charged with creating a financial system for the new government, Hamilton draws sharp criticism from Southerners by proposing that the national debt be funded, with the federal government assuming the unpaid debts incurred by the states during the Revolution. Speculators from New York and New Jersey have bought up depreciated securities; James Madison and other Southern delegates oppose paying off these securities at par value plus accrued interest lest the speculators be allowed to make huge profits. The Southern states have already paid their war debts; Secretary of State Jefferson works out a compromise that leads to congressional passage of Hamilton's debt-assumption act combined with a relocation of the nation's capital to Washington, D.C., after a stopover in Philadelphia (see Bank of the United States, 1791).

New York remains a comparatively minor commercial center as compared to Philadelphia and Boston; even Sag Harbor near the eastern end of Long Island clears more square-riggers than New York.

Congress votes April 10 to establish a patent office that will protect inventors and give them an incentive to develop new machines and methods; denied a grant of exclusivity by the state legislature at Albany, steamboat designer John Stevens has petitioned his friends in the federal government to give him patent protection (see 1789; transportation, 1791).

The second Trinity Church is consecrated, replacing the structure that was burned in 1776. It will stand until 1839.

Washington Market is established in lower Manhattan, taking its name from the nation's first president. The site will later be expanded through a gift of land from Trinity Church, whose elders want to move peddlers from the front of St. Mark's Church on lower Broadway.

The first U.S. decennial census shows the population to be 3,929,000, 95 percent of it rural; population density is four to five people per square mile. New York has 32,328 (with another 19,000 or so on surrounding farms and settlements that will later be incorporated into the city). Philadelphia has 28,522, Boston 18,320, Baltimore 13,503, Providence, R.I., 6,830. Staten Island's population reaches 3,835, up from 2,847 in 1771 (the estates of its two most prominent Loyalists, who fled to Canada in 1783, have been subdivided and sold).

About 14 percent of New York's population is black, and the census makes a distinction between free blacks (and all other free persons who are neither white nor slave) and slaves. Nearly one third of Kings County's population is black, including slaves, and blacks comprise 25 percent of what will become the Bronx, 25 percent of what will become Queens County, 23.1 percent of Richmond County, and 10.5 percent of New York County (Manhattan).

1791 New York's political wards are assigned numbers to replace the original names (North, East, West, South, Dock, and Out) used since 1683 and Montgomerie, used since 1731.

Ten of the 12 amendments to the federal Constitution approved by Congress at New York in September 1789 are ratified by the states in mid-December and will be known as the Bill of Rights.

Former mayor (and Chamber of Commerce president) John Cruger, Jr. dies at New York December 27 at age 81.

The first Bank of the United States is established February 25 at the insistence of Secretary of the Treasury Alexander Hamilton. The new bank receives a 20-year charter from Congress, succeeding the Bank of North America chartered at the end of 1781; it has an initial capital of $10 million, 80 percent of it provided by private investors who buy stock with bonds acquired under a funding plan devised by Hamilton.

New York has its first financial panic as the U.S. government files suit against former assistant secretary of the treasury William Duer for alleged malfeasance during his 6 months in office; the speculator floats a rumor that his bank is about to be acquired, shares in the bank soar in value, and prices collapse when the story proves unfounded (see 1792).

Engineer John Stevens receives a U.S. patent in August on a vertical steam boiler and improved engine for steamboats plus one for the application of steam to bellows (see 1789; patent office, 1790). One of the first 12 Americans to receive a U.S. patent, Stevens continues his steam-engine experiments (see 1803).

New York Hospital reopens February 1 on Broadway between what later will be Worth and Duane streets with two wings, a theater for surgery, and separate wards for surgical and other patients (see 1788). President Washington's personal physician, Samuel Bard, now 49, heads the institution, whose large two-story greystone building in the shape of a letter "H" is set back about 90 feet from the street and has windows that look down on the Hudson River, about

600 yards away. Medical students are, for a small fee, allowed to accompany surgeons on their rounds, and private patients are afforded what is generally considered the best medical care available in the city, being treated with far more skill than the barber-surgeons who ply their trade.

A yellow fever epidemic causes a panic in the city.

1792 New York's gubernatorial contest is marked by bitter charges and countercharges that bring the city to the verge of violence. Gov. Clinton runs for reelection against a challenge by Supreme Court Chief Justice John Jay, whose supporters claim that Clinton has awarded state offices and given away large land tracts to political favorites; Clinton's supporters call Jay a captive of the aristocracy who would subvert the principles of republican government; the vote tally gives Clinton the victory, Jay's supporters say their man would have been elected had the votes been counted correctly (the anti-Federalists on the board of election canvassers have invalidated ballots from Otsego, Tioga, and Clinton counties on various technicalities), but while it is clear that the will of the voters has not prevailed, Jay does not press the point and restrains his more ardent supporters (*see* 1795).

U.S. money markets collapse in March following the failure of some land companies organized by New York speculator William Duer (*see* 1791). He has sought European capital for the settlement of lands in the Ohio Valley, his scheme fails, he is imprisoned for debt, and New York investors and speculators lose some $5 million, an amount equal to the value of all the buildings in the city (Boston and Philadelphia sustain losses of $1 million each). Secretary of the Treasury Alexander Hamilton averts a U.S. economic depression by supporting the government's 6 percent bonds at par value. Duer has overplayed his hand, falls hopelessly into debt, is arrested March 23, and will die in debtor's prison in May 1799 at age 52.

The New York Stock Exchange has its origin May 17 in an agreement signed by 21 local brokers who have been buying and selling government bonds and other securities in good weather under an ancient buttonwood (sycamore) tree at 62 Wall Street. Pushed by Secretary of the Treasury Alexander Hamilton, they have met March 21 at Corre's Hotel and agreed to form a new auction market beginning April 21. Some brokers have organized a central auction earlier in the year at 22 Wall Street, but many outside brokers have attended this Stock Exchange Office only to discover the latest prices and have then traded the same securities on the side at lower

commissions. The signers of the agreement formalize rules of conduct, pledging themselves to trade with each other before trading with any outsider and not to charge commissions lower than .25 percent. Prices are quoted in eighths because the most commonly circulated coins are Spanish reals which are frequently cut into eight parts, called "pieces of eight." The new exchange meets initially at the Merchant's Coffee House but members soon build their own Tontine Coffee House at the corner of Wall and Water streets, close to the East River piers where captains of oceangoing vessels prefer to dock because of prevailing winds (*see* 1817).

Yellow fever strikes the city on repeated occasions in July and August, claiming thousands of victims (who are buried in yellow sheets symbolic of the disease). Hypnosis is tried as a remedy but to no avail.

The New York Hospital that opened last year on Broadway becomes the first institution in the state to care for patients with mental disorders, who heretofore have been placed in prisons or almshouses. The hospital pioneers in treating lunacy as a medical rather than a social problem (*see* 1808).

New York entrepreneur Nicholas Denise opens a "very convenient Bathing House, having eight rooms, in every one of which Baths may be had with either fresh, salt, or warm water . . . prices fixed at 4s per person." But most New Yorkers simply sponge themselves off, as they have since colonial times; only people of some means can afford Denise's public bathhouse (*see* 1849; Croton water, 1842).

Duncan Phyfe, 25, sets up a New York joiner's shop that he will continue until his retirement in 1847. The Scots-born cabinetmaker begins producing mahogany chairs, tables, and couches that will make the name Duncan Phyfe as famous as the names Hepplewhite, Sheraton, and Chippendale.

1793 The Fugitive Slave Act voted by Congress at Philadelphia February 12 shocks New Yorkers opposed to slavery by making it illegal for anyone to help a slave escape to freedom or give a runaway slave refuge (*see* 1850).

French émigré engineer and inventor Marc Isambard Brunel, 24, flees the Reign of Terror at Paris and arrives at New York, where he will soon gain appointment to the city post of chief engineer. He will remain until 1799, improving the defenses of the channel between Staten Island and Long Island, constructing an arsenal and a cannon factory, and putting up many other buildings of his own design.

♠ Painting: *View of New York from Le Jupiter* (watercolor drawing) by English-born painter Archibald Robertson, who came to the city 2 years ago. He and his brother Alexander open the Academy of Painting at 89 William Street in the fall, and a colored engraving of his drawing will published a few years hence.

● A New York mob riots from October 14 to 15 in connection with what it considers immoral behavior in the city's houses of prostitution.

🏠 New York's houses are numbered for the first time on a systematic basis.

1794 Federalist candidates win a majority in the state legislature at Albany. Supporters of Gov. Clinton end their attempts to impeach Judge William Cooper on charges that he used illegal means to obtain votes for Supreme Court Chief Justice John Jay in the 1792 gubernatorial election.

⚕ Yellow fever devastates New Orleans, Boston, and other cities, and although New York has relatively few cases its almshouse hospital is soon overflowing with patients. Only two of the city's physicians have ever seen a case. The Board of Aldermen prepare for a possible epidemic by purchasing Belle Vue, a country place about three miles out of town on Kips Bay (see 1736). It has been offered for sale by its owner, who was a Tory during the Revolution, and the two-story building on the property will be converted into a hospital (see 1795).

✒ Fiction: *Charlotte—A Tale of Truth* by English-born New York novelist Susanna Rowson (*née* Haswell), 29, whose heroine is an English schoolgirl who is seduced by a British officer and taken to New York, where she is abandoned when the young officer wants to marry a rich society woman, is driven from their farmhouse on the Bowery, wanders the snowy streets sick and penniless, gives birth in a hovel in Chatham Street, dies, and is buried in a churchyard. Retitled *Charlotte Temple—A Tale of Truth* in later editions, it becomes the first U.S. best seller (about 200 editions will be published between 1797 and 1903).

1795 Gov. Clinton announces January 22 that he will not seek reelection. The Republicans nominate New York State Chief Justice Robert Yates to succeed him, the Federalists nominate Supreme Court Chief Justice John Jay, who is still in England, where in December he signed a treaty settling outstanding disputes between the United States and Britain. Jay learns of the nomination May 28, when his ship *Severn* docks at Akerly's Wharf; Robert R. Livingston, now 48, has become an anti-Federalist and opposes Jay in the gubernatorial election, but Jay is elected

June 5, resigns his office as chief justice June 29, and is sworn in July 1. The text of Jay's Treaty is published July 2, and the governor is denounced by political opponents. Secretary of the Treasury Alexander Hamilton resigns his $3,500 position and returns to New York, where he resumes his law practice and earns $12,000 per year to support his family of eight. The "Camillus Papers" written by Hamilton and Rufus King with help from Jay defend the treaty, whose terms require the British to evacuate their posts in the Northwest between the Great Lakes and Ohio River while permitting U.S. ships to carry cocoa, coffee, cotton, molasses, and sugar from the British West Indies to any part of the world.

$ Business comes almost to a standstill from July to October as people who can afford it flee the city to escape a yellow fever epidemic. Streets are practically deserted.

🖎 The Bloomingdale Road that opened in 1703 is extended north to what will be 147th Street and linked to the Kingsbridge Road (see King's Bridge, 1693; Western Boulevard, 1869).

⚕ The ship *Antoinette* docks at Whitehall in May with two of its crew suffering from yellow fever (see 1794). Pathologist Richard Bayley is the city's health officer and isolates the sailors on Staten Island, but although he quarantines the ship a yellow fever epidemic begins in July, when the brig *Zephyr* arrives from the West Indies carrying the body of a boy who has died aboard ship. An outbreak follows among the crew of a British ship from Liverpool docked at Fitch's Wharf on the East River at Dover Street. Tar is burned in the streets, but prominent families leave the city and Columbia College is deserted. Those who remain in town drink vinegar, sniff sponges saturated with camphor, wear bags of asefetida around their necks, and carry bits of charred rope in their hands to disinfect them when they touch a doorknob or railing. The Committee of Health issues an optimistic report August 18, but 20 people have died in the preceding 4 days, and at month's end the governor of Pennsylvania bans all traffic between New York and Philadelphia. The epidemic spreads in September up the East River to the Seventh Ward, Gov. Jay issues a proclamation September 14 requiring health certificates from all ships arriving at New York from the West Indies, but 71 victims die during the month at the new Belle Vue hospital near Kips Bay, where Dr. Bayley and two assistants struggle to keep up with the patient load (Bayley says the disease is infectious but not contagious; bodies at Belle Vue are buried in unmarked graves on the nearby potter's field). The governor and his family remain in Government House (later the site of the customhouse) lest their removal "increase the alarm which is already too great," but the northeast quarter of the city empties out, with more than 20,000 people taking temporary refuge in the nearby countryside until frost brings an end to the fever in October after it has killed 732 people (*see* 1798; Bellevue, 1811).

The 41-year-old New York Society Library moves into a building of its own in Nassau Street—the first structure in the city designed specifically to be a library. Its members include Aaron Burr, Alexander Hamilton, and John Jay (*see* 1937).

Opera: *Tammany, or The Indian Chief* 3/3 at the John Street Theater with John Hodgkinson in the title role, Lewis Hallam as Christopher Columbus, John Martin as King Ferdinand, and a cast that includes also the two leading actors' wives.

The city's first underground sewer pipes are laid at the persuasion of Dr. Richard Bayley, the city's health officer. Open ditches and cesspools have served until now to carry off storm water and collect waste, although now the Dutch did pave over a canal to create Broadway and, beneath it, a common sewer. Unfinished docks near Coenties slip have been filled in with refuse, the carcasses of dead horses, and whatnot to create some 51 acres to the east of the Battery and 10 acres to the west. The new ground is a little above the high-water mark, but there are no drains, and the cellars of buildings on Front Street, Water Street, and even Pearl Street are frequently flooded, and the backyards of Water Street houses are filled with accumulations of filth and stagnant water, creating such a stench that windows of many houses cannot be opened. Encouraged by protests from angry citizens, the city has agreed to put the sewer pipes underground (*see* 1849).

1796 John Adams of Massachusetts is elected to succeed George Washington as president of the United States, defeating Thomas Jefferson with help from the voters of New York.

Federalist alderman Gabriel Furman accuses two New York ferrymen of insolence and orders that they be whipped and imprisoned without any right to counsel or even to testify in their own defense. Republican lawyer William Keteltas demands that the state assembly at Albany strip Furman of his office, the assembly absolves Furman, Keteltas calls it a "flagrant abuse of rights," he is jailed for contempt, and Jeffersonians (who include many laborers and craftsmen) protest what they call typical Federalist disregard for the working classes.

Treatise on the Improvement of Canal Navigation by Pennsylvania-born engineer Robert Fulton, 32, launches its author on a career. Now living at Birmingham, England, he will travel to Paris next year to work on his submarine, *Nautilus*, and in 1803 will develop a small ship propelled by steam power (*see* 1807).

The city improvises a pest house on Bedloe Island and has the beds and bedding from Belle Vue moved to the new facility, but the linens are so filthy that, according to one doctor, the porters who move them all come down with fever inside of 8 days, as do the nurses and stewards on Bedloe Island.

A new Flatbush Reformed Church is completed at the corner of Flatbush Avenue and Church Lane for Brooklyn's oldest parish. Organized in 1654, it put up its first church the following year; its new church will survive for 2 centuries.

Fire destroys the Coffee House Slip below Front Street between Murray Wharf and Pearl Street December 9; the conflagration spreads, destroying 50 houses.

1797 The state legislature reassembles at Albany January 3 and shortly thereafter chooses that city as the state capital.

The New York City Ladies' Society for the Relief of Poor Widows with Small Children is founded by philanthropic volunteers who include Isabella Graham and Elizabeth Seton. In its first year it assists 98 widows and 223 children with a budget of $4,000, and it will help widows gain economic security by employing them in the Society's own sewing and laundry businesses and as teachers in its own schools (*see* 1802); the society's child-care service will be reorganized as the Orphan Asylum Society (*see* 1806; Poorhouse, 1736).

The city rents Belle Vue for use as a hospital following a yellow fever outbreak in the spring. The place is soon overflowing with patients, some lying in the Chinese summer houses, some in the basement, some in the bathhouses. Belle Vue has as many as 60 funerals per day through the summer as 329 people, including 16 physicians, succumb to the fever. Following instructions from Dr. Richard Bayley, the jailer of the debtor's prison has his walls scrubbed, disinfected, and whitewashed once a week, but the number of debtors in his care falls to 39 in October, down from 163 at the start of the epidemic. The Board of Aldermen holds a lottery to raise $10,000 to build a new almshouse, it issues 18,000 tickets at $10 each, a free black wins the high ticket, and the city's 15 percent take gives it the means to build the new almshouse—a three-story structure facing on Chambers Street.

A state prison opens in Greenwich Village to house convicts sentenced to terms of 3 years or more, relieving pressure on the city's jails (*see* 1775; 1816).

An act passed by the Common Council February 10 provides that after July 1 "no person shall dress sheep or lamb skins, or manufacture glue, nor shall any soap-boiler, or tallow-chandler, or starch-maker, or maker or dresser of vellum, carry on any of their processes or operations of their said trades, which produce impure air, or offensive smells . . . at any place within the city of New-York, south of the south side of Grant [Grand] Street." The new law meets such strong protests from candle- and soap-makers that the Council will exempt them on condition that they keep their operations inoffensive.

The city acquires what later will be Washington Square Park for use as a potter's field and for public hangings (*see* 1827).

1798 The U.S. customs collector at New York is removed from office on charges of embezzlement (*see* 1789). Revolutionary War general John Lamb had served as collector since March 22, 1784, and was appointed by President Washington in 1792 at an annual salary of $1,900 (*see* 1872).

Yellow fever strikes the city again in July (*see* 1795). Heavy rains have filled cellars and choked drains, causing water to collect in pools that give off foul vapors. Dr. Richard Bayley of New York Hospital blames the epidemic on the noxious vapors rising from the putrid pools of water that have collected in the lower parts of the city. Carters go through the streets crying, "Bring out your dead." By early October the death list has reached 1,400 or more, and at least two-thirds of the city has fled to the countryside to escape the epidemic that continues until the first frost in late October.

Theater: a production of Shakespeare's 1600 comedy *As You Like It* 1/29 at the new Park Theater on Park Row north of Ann Street and east of City Hall Park. Designed by French architects Joseph and Charles Mangin, who have fled the Reign of Terror at Paris, the elegant theater seats 1,200 and has cost $130,000. Gentlemen wear their hats during the premier performance, as is the custom (*see* 1808).

Scottish-born commission merchant-shipowner Archibald Gracie, 43, pays $5,652 to purchase an 11-acre site at Horn's Hook on the East River for a country house (*see* politics, 1776). The property is just south of John Jacob Astor's Hell Gate Farm, and

Gracie will use the foundations of the old Jacob Walton house to put up a modest house that will be enlarged in the early 1800s to create what will be called Gracie Mansion (*see* 1829).

A paper submitted to the Common Council in June under the title "Memoir on the Utility and Means of Furnishing the City with Water From the River Bronx" calls for construction of dams on the Bronx and Harlem rivers with a series of pumps and pipes to divert a flow of water into a reservoir at a high point in the hilly north end of Manhattan Island. Physician-scientist-engineer Joseph Browne, a brother-in-law of State Assemblyman Aaron Burr, has written the "memoir" proposing a $200,000 system to be privately operated. Some opponents say the Collect (a spring-fed pond in the upper part of the city) could be cleared of dead animals and putrid garbage to make it a source of pure and wholesome water, others that the $200,000 cost estimate is far too low. A special committee reports to the Council in December, rejecting the idea of private ownership (*see* Manhattan Co., 1799).

1799 The Manhattan Company is chartered in March following passage of a "water bill" introduced by Aaron Burr in the state assembly near the end of its session, but the chief justice warns Gov. Jay before he signs the measure that there is more than "pure and wholesome water" in the bill's final paragraph. The words in question state, "That it shall and may be lawful for the said company to employ all such surplus capital as may belong or accrue to the said company in the purchase of public or other stock or any other monied transactions not inconsistent with the Constitution and laws of this state or of the United States, for the sole benefit of said Company." Directors of the Manhattan Company hold their first meeting April 15 and invite those who would like to buy stock in the company to meet the following Monday at the Tontine City Tavern on Broadway. The Common Council buys 2,000 shares at $2.50 per share, but the *Gazette and General Advertiser* charges Burr and his friends with "scandalous duplicity," and Burr is defeated along with the entire Republican slate by 900 votes in the April Assembly elections that come 4 weeks after the charter has been granted. Burr has persuaded the legislature to adopt a measure making it legal for aliens to hold real estate, and the Holland Land Co. has canceled a bond agreement that had obligated Burr to pay $20,000 (details of the deal will not come to light until after Burr's death in 1836). The 15-year-old Bank of New York and a branch of the Bank of the United States have been the only two banks in town, the Federalists have blocked creation of any rivals, and Burr is accused of chicanery by Alexander Hamilton and other Federalists, especially after the Bank of the Manhattan Company opens its doors in September on a site that will later be 40 Wall Street (*see* building, 1930; Chase Manhattan, 1955).

Merchant William Duer dies in debtor's prison at New York May 7 at age 52 (*see* 1792). The first American millionaire, he made most of his money by trading on inside information while serving as assistant secretary of the treasury in President Washington's second term, using fronts and secret understandings.

New York Hospital enters into an agreement with the U.S. Treasury Department to receive "sick and disabled seamen" of the Port of New York at a rate of $3 per week to be paid by the Collector of the Port, who will assess the pay of sailors arriving from foreign ports at a rate of 20¢ per month.

Fiction: *Ormond* and *Wieland* by Philadelphia-born New York novelist Charles Brockden Brown, 28.

A New York mob riots from July 17 to 20 over alleged immoral behavior in the city's houses of ill repute.

St. Mark's Church in-the-Bouwerie is dedicated on what was once part of Peter Stuyvesant's farm at what later will be the corner of Second Avenue and 10th Street. A Greek revival steeple will be added in 1828, a clock will be added following a disastrous fire in 1978, and the church will survive as the second oldest in the city (St. Paul's Chapel on lower Broadway, built in 1766, will be the oldest).

Alexander Hamilton buys 30 acres of land in upper Manhattan for a country house (the Hamilton Grange) at what later will be the corner of 143rd Street and Convent Avenue (*see* 1802).

The Manhattan Company digs a well in lower Manhattan during the summer and lays nearly a mile of wooden pipes to convey water to pumps in various blocks (*see* 1798). The pipes are made by boring holes lengthwise in logs that are then fastened together by fitting the tapered end of one through the widened hole of the next. Drawing water also from other spring-fed wells near Collect Pond, the company will build 25 miles of such pipes to help satisfy the demand for drinking water, much of it sold by vendors from giant casks pushed up and down the streets (*see* Croton water, 1842).

1800 Washington, D.C., replaces New York and Philadelphia as the U.S. capital, 123 federal government clerks are moved to the new city during the summer, and Congress convenes there for the first time November 17.

Secretary of the Navy Benjamin Stoddart authorizes purchase of Brooklyn property on the East River at Wallabout Bay for what will become the New York Naval Shipyard (Brooklyn Navy Yard; *see* commandant's house, 1806).

New York-born merchant Philip Hone, 19, becomes a partner with his older brother John in the auction business that has employed him since he was 16. The firm will enjoy a rapid growth, net profits will reach $159,000 by 1815, and by 1821 Hone will have an individual net worth of at least $500,000.

Developer John Jackson purchases a large tract of land on Wallabout Bay from the Sands brothers (year approximate) and names a small part of it "Vinegar Hill" after the battle 2 years ago that saw British forces breaking Irish resistance. Jackson's idea is to attract Irish immigrants.

Ferryboat operator Richard M. Woodhull buys a 13-acre parcel of land in the Bushwick section near his landing on the Brooklyn side of the East River; his intention is to develop a town for people who will commute to work in Manhattan aboard his ferry, landing at Corlaer's Hook. He names the site Williamsburgh after surveyor Jonathan Williams but will sell only a few lots before going bankrupt in 1806 (*see* 1854).

Brooklyn's population reaches 2,378, up from 1,603 in 1790, with another 656 in Bushwick, 946 in Flatbush, 493 in Flatlands, 489 in Gravesend, and 778 in New Utrecht. Staten Island's population reaches 4,564, up from 3,835 in 1790.

19th CENTURY

1801 Gov. John Jay resigns his office at age 55 and retires to his farm near Bedford, N.Y. Former governor George Clinton, now 61, regains his old office July 1 and inaugurates what later will be called the "spoils system," giving the victor in any election power to reward his supporters with government jobs (*see* 1832). Mayor Varick loses office after a bitterly fought contest, but mayors have limited powers at best, wielding no more influence than other members of the Common Council.

Sailors' Snug Harbor is founded with a bequest from the late New York merchant Robert Richard Randall, son of the late Thomas Randall. The father made a fortune as a pirate in the Caribbean before retiring to life as a Manhattan merchant and property owner, he left son Robert well off, and Robert had lawyer Alexander Hamilton draw up a will making bequests to relatives and servants and bequeathing his 21-acre estate to provide for "aged, decrepit and worn out sailors." Now worth $25,000, the land extends up to what soon will be 8th Street on Fifth Avenue and will produce a large income as the area becomes filled with houses (*see* 1831).

The office of city comptroller is initiated, making it easier to collect city taxes, but no important tax legislation will be enacted until 1859.

Fur trader John Jacob Astor, now 38, travels through upstate New York bartering "firewater" (whiskey) and flannel with the Iroquois and Seneca to obtain animal pelts, chiefly beaver for use in hats (*see* 1784). Some he sells in the Albany market, but the best go to his wife, Sarah, who has borne eight children, three of whom died soon after birth. A better judge of furs than her husband, Sarah beats the smelly pelts and does her best to sell them to customers of her successful music store. Distantly related to the Brevoorts, she will help her husband make profitable connections (*see* 1834).

The Elgin Botanic Garden is established by Manhattan physician David Hosack on land that will later be the site of Rockefeller Center. A professor of botany and materia medica at Columbia College, Dr. Hosack grows plants for study by his medical students in the city's first botanical garden; he has bought 245 lots (20 acres) for $4,807.36, plus an annual rent of 16 bushels of wheat (*see* 1810).

Physician Richard Bayley dies of yellow fever on Staten Island August 17 at age 56.

The *New-York Evening Post* begins publication November 16 with four five-column pages printed on one large sheet that has been folded to create pages measuring 19 inches by 14 (14 or 15 of the 20 columns are filled with advertisements placed by merchants). Alexander Hamilton has put up $1,000 of the $10,000 needed to found the Federalist newspaper (other investors include former mayor Richard Varick and merchant-shipowner Archibald Gracie), its editor is William Coleman, its type is set in four different fonts at a time when most papers use only two, and it will survive into the 21st century as the city's oldest daily.

The Zion English Lutheran Church opens at 25 Mott Street on the Lower East Side. Designed in Georgian-Gothic style and constructed of locally quarried Manhattan Schist, it will become a Roman Catholic church in 1853. (The glittery, mica-bearing rock that comprises the church's exterior is known as Manhattan Schist but is found throughout Long Island and Westchester as well.)

New York City's population rises to 60,000 (Philadelphia has about 70,000, Boston 25,000, Charleston, S.C., 18,000, Baltimore 13,000).

1802 New York politician De Witt Clinton, 33, wins appointment to the U.S. Senate. Born in Little Britain, N.Y., and a son of Revolutionary War general James Clinton, he has been serving for more than a decade as personal secretary to his uncle, Gov. George Clinton.

New York's journeymen cabinetmakers strike to protest a list of piecework rates that an organization of master cabinetmakers has sought to impose.

The city gives $15,000 to the 5-year-old Society for the Relief of Poor Widows with Small Children as a yellow fever epidemic leaves thousands of women widowed and destitute.

Jacob Hays, 30, of Bedford, N.Y., is appointed to the city post of High Constable and will be reappointed by every incoming mayor for nearly 48 years. Hays will personally suppress riots, apprehend criminals, and organize a detective force (*see* Police Department, 1845).

Hamilton Grange is completed for Alexander Hamilton at what later will be 287 Convent Avenue, corner 143rd Street, in upper Manhattan (*see* 1800). New York-born architect John McComb, Jr., 38, has designed the country house, named for Hamilton's grandfather Alexander Hamilton, Laird of the Grange, in Ayrshire, Scotland. McComb has earlier designed the Montauk Lighthouse and other lighthouses; his Hamilton Grange has sweeping views of the Harlem and Hudson rivers, and 13 gum-tree saplings from the late George Washington's Mount Vernon plantation are planted on the property that will remain in the Hamilton family until 1833.

1803 Gen. Morgan Lewis is elected to succeed George Clinton as state governor. Now 48, Lewis will hold office until 1807.

U.S. Sen. De Witt Clinton returns to New York City, is appointed mayor, and will be reappointed every year until 1815 with the exceptions of 1807 and 1810, when his political opponents will control the state's Council of Appointment.

The Merchants Bank begins operating June 2 with $1.25 million in capital, but it runs into opposition from other banks and will not obtain a corporate charter until March 1805.

Steamboat pioneer John Stevens obtains a patent April 11 for a multitubular boiler (*see* 1791). Col. Stevens paid about $90,000 in 1784 for a New Jersey island separated from the mainland by marshes, renamed it Hoboken from an amalgamation of the Dutch and Indian words for it, hopes to develop it as a resort, and sees possibilitiies in a steamboat ferry service that will make it easily accessible from Manhattan (*see* Little Juliana, 1804).

1804 Former U.S. Treasury Secretary Alexander Hamilton is mortally wounded July 11 at age 49 in a duel at Weehawken, N.J., with Vice President Aaron Burr, now 48, who has heard of insults directed at him by Hamilton and demanded satisfaction (*see* 1799). Later historians will suggest that Burr shrugged off earlier attacks but has been infuriated by Hamilton's suggestions that he, Burr, has had an incestuous relationship with his only legitimate daughter, Theodosia, whom he has had educated as if she were his son. The two men have been law partners and personal friends. Hamilton has very possibly invited the contest with the intent of committing assisted suicide and at the same time ruining the career of his political adversary. Dr. David Hosack of 1801 botanical garden fame treats Hamilton's wounds but cannot save him. Hamilton's body is interred in the Trinity Church cemetery and Burr, indicted for murder in New York and New Jersey, flees to Philadelphia, whence he will proceed to the South (*see* 1812). A group headed by merchant-shipowner Archibald Gracie buys Hamilton's 2-year-old Hamilton Grange country house and sells it to his widow, Elizabeth, at half price. Hamilton's father-in-law, Gen. Philip J. Schuyler, dies at Albany November 18 at age 71.

The steamboat *Little Juliana* built by Col. John Stevens steams back and forth across the Hudson between the Battery and Hoboken (*see* 1803). Two of Stevens's sons operate the vessel; the first to have twin screw propellers, she is successful enough to encourage Stevens, now 54, in his ambition to introduce a steam-ferry service (*see* Fulton, 1807; *Phoenix*, 1809).

Alexander Hamilton was killed in a duel with his erstwhile friend Aaron Burr. LIBRARY OF CONGRESS

The New-York Historical Society is founded to collect and preserve materials related to U.S. and New York State history. Prominent among the founders is city inspector John Pintard of Tammany Hall, a veteran of the War of Independence who worries that his generation is dying off and gains support from business and government leaders who include Mayor De Witt Clinton. Headed initially by jurist Egbert Benson, the society takes rooms in a Wall Street building formerly used for federal government offices (see 1827).

The Stuyvesant-Fish mansion is completed at 21 Stuyvesant Street, between Second and Third Avenues, as a wedding gift from a great-grandson of Peter Stuyvesant to his daughter, who is to marry Nicholas Fish.

A second Coffee House Fire December 18 destroys 40 houses in the area surrounding Wall and Pearl streets.

1805 The Orphan Asylum Society is founded at New York by Canadian-born schoolteacher Joanne Bethune, 36, with help from her mother, Isabella Graham; they gain support from Alexander Hamilton's widow, Elizabeth, and Sarah Hoffman.

Painting: *Edward Livingston* by Connecticut-born painter Jonathan Trumbull, 49, who has lived at New York since last year after painting portraits of men who served as members of the claims commission set up under Jay's Treaty in 1794. His subject, now 41, is a younger brother of Robert R. Livingston who has been a prominent lawyer in the city and has served as U.S. attorney for the state of New York.

Former Edmund Seaman & Co. employee William Havemeyer, 35, and his brother Frederick open a sugar refinery in Vandam Street (see 1857).

1806 Former Continental Army general Horatio Gates dies on his Manhattan farm April 10 at age 77. Triumphant at Saratoga in 1777, he suffered a calamitous loss at Camden, S.C., 3 years later and was relieved of his command.

The Seventh Regiment of the U.S. National Guard is organized at New York, where it will play an important role in the city's history.

The city cedes to the federal government a potter's field at what later will be Madison Square. An arsenal is erected on the site for use by the U.S. Army (see juvenile delinquent home, 1824).

The Orphan Asylum Society rents a small house in Raisin Street and uses it to look after, and instruct, six recently orphaned children (see 1805). The society's numbers will grow rapidly, it will buy land next year for a new building in Bank Street, and in 1808 the state legislature at Albany will conduct a lottery to raise $5,000 for the orphanage (see 1836).

The city's first fire insurance company is incorporated April 4 with a capital stock of $100,000. Eagle Insurance is a stock company; in 1815 it will make a reinsurance agreement, the first such in America to anyone's knowledge, and it will eventually become the National Reinsurance Co.

Colgate-Palmolive has its beginnings in a tallow chandlery and soap manufactory opened at 6 Dutch Street by English-born candlemaker William Colgate, 23.

A house for the commandant of the New York Naval Shipyard (Brooklyn Navy Yard) is completed to designs by Boston architect Charles Bulfinch, 43, in association with John McComb, Jr.

1807 New York City jurist Daniel D. Tompkins, 33, is elected governor in a victory engineered by Mayor De Witt Clinton. Born in the Westchester hamlet of Fox Meadows (later Scarsdale), Tompkins will be reelected three times and serve until 1817.

Imports entering the city reach a value of $7.6 million, up from $1.4 million in 1790, and are nearly double the value of imports arriving at Philadelphia; exports from the city have a value of $26 million, up from a mere $1.4 million in 1790, but an Embargo Act signed by President Jefferson December 22 prohibits all ships from leaving U.S. ports for foreign ports. Designed to force French and British withdrawal of restrictions on trade in the ongoing Napoleonic wars, the new law will effectively block overseas sales of farm surpluses and cripple the port of New York.

Robert Fulton's steamboat began a new era in water travel, but most Hudson journeys continued to be on giant sloops.

The first commercially successful steamboat travels up the Hudson River August 17 and arrives in 32 hours at Albany to begin regular service between New York and Albany. Designed by engineer Robert Fulton, now 42, and backed by U.S. Minister to France Robert R. Livingston, now 60, the *Clermont* (initially called simply the *North River Steamboat*) has paddle wheels (suggested by New York-born engineer-inventor Nicholas J. Roosevelt, now 39) powered by an English Boulton and Watt engine with a cylinder 24 inches in diameter and a four-foot stroke. The vessel is 133 feet long, 18 feet wide in the beam, with a seven-foot draft and a stack 30 feet high. The *Clermont* (she will get that name only after Fulton's death in 1815) completes her round trip in 62 hours of steaming time, but travel on the Hudson will continue for decades to be mostly in large sloops.

Papers satirizing the city's genteel society begin appearing under the title *Salmagundi, or, the Whim-whams and Opinions of Launcelot Langstaff and Others*. Written by men who include James Kirke Paulding, 29, and Washington Irving, 23, it sardonically calls the city "Gotham," originally the name of a town near Nottingham, England, whose citizens in medieval times pretended to be insane in order to avoid taxation by King John. The word was Anglo-Saxon for "goat town"; Irving uses it to suggest that New York is a town of self-important but foolish people (residents of the English Gotham were said to be "foolishly wise").

The publishing house John Wiley & Sons has its beginnings in a print shop opened at 6 Reade Street by Charles Wiley, 25, who will work with Isaac Riley and other printers to produce law books and by 1814 will be publishing pirated reprints of works by European authors. Wiley's son John, then 18, will take over upon Charles's death in 1826 and move the firm to Nassau Street (*see* 1836).

The Park Theater reopens August 27 after a thorough refurbishing by London architect John Holland. It has 2,372 seats—1,292 in the boxes, 392 in the lower tier, 360 in each of the second and third tiers, 160 in the slip tier, 500 in the pit, and 600 in the gallery.

St. John's Chapel is completed in Varick Street to Georgian-Federal designs by John McComb, Jr. at what will be called St. John's Park. The chapel will survive until 1918.

1808 Thomas Jefferson declines a third term as president and supports his secretary of state James Madison, who wins the fall election, receiving 122 electoral votes to 47 for Federalist Charles C. Pinckney.

Dire economic depression grips the city as a result of the Embargo Act signed into law by President Jefferson near the end of last year. One-third of all U.S. trade has passed through New York, and the complete suspension of that trade brings many in the city close to ruin. Merchant-shipowner Archibald Gracie, now 52, claims he has lost $1 million and files suit against the federal government to recover his property.

The S.S. *Phoenix* launched by engineer John Stevens is the first steamboat with an American-built engine (*see* Fulton, 1807). Col. Stevens learns that his brother-in-law Robert R. Livingston and Robert Fulton have obtained a 20-year monopoly on steamboat operations in New York State waters; he prepares to have his son take the new sidewheeler to Philadelphia (*see* 1809).

The Medical Society of the State of New York is founded with Massachusetts-born Saratoga County physician John Stearns, 37, as secretary.

New York Hospital erects a separate building on its grounds for the humane treatment of mental patients (*see* 1792; 1821).

Pope Pius VII establishes the Diocese of New York April 8 and appoints Richard Luke Concanen, 60, first bishop of the diocese that embraces all of New York State and northern New Jersey. Archbishop Carroll of Baltimore appoints Alsatian-born Jesuit Anthony Kohlmann, 36, administrator of the diocese pending Father Concanen's arrival (*see* 1809; *but see also* 1810).

The Fifth Avenue Presbyterian Church has its beginnings June 28 in a meeting of the Presbytery of New York. The Presbytery receives a new congregation, whose members propose to worship in Cedar Street. Rev. John Brodhead Romeyn, 31, of Albany, son of a Dutch Reformed minister, is installed as pastor of the congregation November 9 (*see* 1875).

Stephen Price buys a controlling interest in the 10-year-old Park Theater; he will make it a policy to import actors from abroad, casting a celebrated player in every production and thereby inaugurating the star system that will begin the decline of stock companies.

The city's commissioners engage John Randel, Jr., 23, to survey all of Manhattan Island's 11,400 acres (22 square miles) with a view to determining the optimum siting of streets and avenues. Using a house at the corner of Christopher and Herring streets as their field headquarters, Randel and his assistants tramp through the countryside each day with measuring instruments, despite opposition from farmers and other property owners (*see* Commissioners' Plan, 1811).

1809 Former colonial governor John Murray, earl of Dunmore, dies March 5 at age 76; political theorist Thomas Paine dies at New York June 8 at age 72. He has lived in the city since 1802 but society has virtually ostracized him for his alleged atheism, and his remains are returned for burial in his native England by William Cobbett.

A new U.S. law removes restrictions against blacks' inheriting land, but most of New York's (and the nation's) blacks are slaves with no prospects of such legacies (*see* 1821).

President Madison withdraws the embargo on trade with Britain imposed late in 1807 following assurances from the British minister that Britain will repeal her 1807 Orders in Council. Some 1,200 ships sail from New York and other U.S. ports, but London says its ambassador has exceeded his authority and trade halts once again.

The New York State Assembly at Albany receives a report January 20 from Pennsylvania-born civil engineer and assemblyman James Geddes, 45, who has had no technical training but who last year surveyed a possible route for a canal that would connect the Hudson River to Lake Erie. Geneva, N.Y., miller Jesse Hawley has proposed building the canal (*see* Clinton, 1811).

Mariner Moses Rogers, 30, makes the first ocean voyage by steamboat in the *Phoenix*, launched last year by Col. John Stevens. He steams from New York around Sandy Hook and Cape May to the Delaware River (*see* 1819; *Juliana*, 1811).

Father Anthony Kohlmann purchases an old house and a large block of land for the new diocese of New York at what later will be Fifth Avenue at 50th Street (*see* 1808; St. Patrick's Cathedral, 1879).

The New York Bible Society is founded December 4 at the home of Theodorus Van Wyck with the avowed purpose of distributing English-language Bibles throughout the city (*see* American Bible Society, 1816).

Nonfiction: *A History of New York from the Beginning of the World to the End of the Dutch Dynasty* by Washington Irving is published on St. Nicholas Day, December 6. Irving dedicates his comic history derisively to the 5-year-old New-York Historical Society and makes references to an impish, pipesmoking St. Nicholas who brings gifts down chimneys, thus beginning a legend that will travel around the world

(*see* Moore, 1823). *Compendious Lexicon of the Hebrew Language* by New York landowner and scholar Clement Clarke Moore, 30.

Theater: East Hampton-born New York actor-playwright John Howard Payne, 17, makes his stage debut 2/24 at the Park Theater. He wrote an anonymous eight-page critique of the New York theater at age 14, his play *Julia, or The Wanderer*, was a failure when it was produced 3 years ago, and he has had no dramatic training, but his acting in the mid-18th century play *Douglas* by English playwright John Home wins immediate success.

1810 Bishop Richard Luke Concanen dies in Italy June 10 at age 62 (*see* 1808). The Napoleonic wars have prevented him from reaching the New York diocese to which he was appointed 2 years ago (*see* Connolly, 1814).

The Shamrock, or Hibernian Chronicle begins publication at New York, whose Irish population has been growing through an influx of indentured workers.

French merchant Stephen Jumel acquires the Morris mansion built in 1765 on Manhattan's highest point of land (*see* 1765). Jumel's wife, Betsy, will bear an illegitimate son who will be named George Washington Bowen, her husband will leave her, and after his death she will marry Aaron Burr, who will die a few months later at age 79. She will survive until 1865 before dying in the New York house that the city will buy in 1903 and preserve as a museum.

New York passes Philadelphia in population to become the largest U.S. city.

1811 The Southwest Battery is completed along with four other forts to repel a potential British attack and fires its first salute November 25 to mark the 28th anniversary of Evacuation Day. It is 200 feet from the shore, and a drawbridge across 35-foot-deep water connects it to the mainland; it will become the headquarters of the Third Military District in 1815 and renamed Castle Clinton (*see* 1821).

U.S. customs duties fall to $6 million as loss of trade with Britain and France reduces duties to half their 1806 level (*see* embargo, 1807). New York suffers more than any other city as foreign trade continues to be crippled.

Mayor De Witt Clinton proposes construction of a canal that would link the Hudson River to Buffalo on Lake Erie, bring the produce of America's agricultural heartland into New York City, and make the city prosper (*see* Geddes, 1809). Most canals in the country are no more than two miles long, the longest is 27 miles, and the idea of a 360-mile "ditch"

A new City Hall gave New York its first great architectural masterpiece. LIBRARY OF CONGRESS

strikes most people as preposterous. The state legislature opposes his idea, as do most of the city's merchants, but Clinton will rally public support by holding huge rallies for the great Erie Canal. He appoints a commission whose members hire Weathersfield, Conn.-born civil engineer Benjamin Wright, 40, to survey a possible route between Rome (formerly Fort Stanwix) on the Mohawk River to Waterford on the Hudson (*see* 1815).

The steam ferry *Juliana* goes into service between Vesey Street and Hoboken under the direction of Col. John Stevens. She is the first steamboat to be used for a ferry service that heretofore has been based on small paddle-wheelers whose motive power came from four horses plodding around shafts (*see* 1809; 1812).

The city purchases a 150-acre site on the East River for an almshouse that will open in 1816 under the name Bellevue Establishment (*see* 1794). Its grounds extend to what is laid out this year as Second Avenue between 23rd and 28th streets, and the Establishment will take the name Bellevue Hospital beginning in 1825 (*see* 1831).

New York adopts a Commissioners' Plan marking off future Manhattan streets and avenues in a grid pattern employed earlier for Spanish colonial towns on Caribbean islands and by William Penn at Philadelphia (*see* 1808). Commissioned by Mayor De Witt Clinton and issued March 22, the plan is more than eight feet long and provides for 12 numbered avenues, extending to the north. Hills are to be leveled, ponds filled in, and 155 numbered cross streets, extending from the North (Hudson) River to the East River, are to be 60 feet wide, except for 14th, 23rd, 34th, 42nd, 57th, 72nd, 86th, and eight others, each to be 100 feet wide. Devised with the purpose of imposing some order on future development with an eye to facilitating taxation, the plan has been adopted following a 4-year survey conducted by the Commissioners after seeing the city's population rise to 83,503, with streets laid out in haphazard fashion. Surveyor John Randel, Jr. says his plan will be helpful in the "buying, selling, and developing of real estate." It plots a grid pattern for Manhattan Island all the way up to 110th Street, even though the city remains mostly farmland above Canal Street, and although other thoroughfares are drawn in straight lines the plan calls for bending Broadway to connect with the Bowery at 11th Street. Landowner Henry Brevoort, 64, a descendant of Henrich Van Brevoort, prevails upon the city not to cut 11th Street across his farm from Broadway to Fourth Avenue (*see* 1832; Grace Church, 1846).

A new City Hall nears completion just north of the City Common at Broadway and Park Row after 9 years of construction on a site used since 1736 variously for a poorhouse, powderhouse, burying ground, jail, whipping post, and demonstrations that preceded the American Revolution (its closest neighbors as it receives its first occupants remain the bridewell to its west, the almshouse behind it, and the jail that will be turned into a Hall of Records). Designed in a combination of Federal and French Renaissance styles with a Georgian interior, the handsome new $500,000 building has been designed mainly by French émigré Joseph François Mangin, who has been assisted by the first American-born architect, John McComb, Jr., now 47 (a plan submitted by the two in 1802 won a competition). City Hall's front and sides are faced with $35,000 worth of white marble from West Stockbridge, Mass., but when it is finished next year its north side will be left in undecorated New Jersey brownstone to save $15,000 (a statue of Justice will be installed in a cupola atop the building in 1887).

The new Commissioners' Plan for laying out Manhattan streets and avenues provides for Tompkins Square Park and Union Place (later Union Square) but makes little other provision for parks, it being thought that the banks of the Hudson and East rivers allow ample space for strolling and other outdoor recreation. Union Place is so named because it unites Fourth Avenue and Broadway; its gated park will make it an attractive residential area for the affluent.

1812 The War of 1812 begins June 18 as the United States declares war on Britain. The British have rescinded their January 1807 Order in Council prohibiting neutral nations from trading with Napoleon's France or her allies, but news of that rescinding has not yet reached Washington, D.C. Former governor George Clinton has died at Washington April 20 at age 72, having served as president of the U.S. Senate. Gov. Daniel D. Tompkins is commander in chief of the New York militia and must see to the defense of the state and perform various military duties; he pledges his own credit to equip and arm the militia and surround the city with some 25,000 troops (*see* 1814).

Eastern shipping interests support the candidacy of Mayor De Witt Clinton for president; he has strengthened the defenses of New York Harbor in preparation for war with Britain, and he carries every northern state except Pennsylvania and Vermont in the November elections, but President Madison wins reelection, receiving 129 electoral votes to Clinton's 89.

Tammany Hall leaves the building in Spruce Street where it has met since 1798 and relocates to a large new "Wigwam" at the corner of Nassau and Frankfort streets, one block from the new City Hall, where it will remain until 1868 (*see* 1789; 1835).

$ Citibank has its beginnings in the City Bank of New York that opens June 16 at 52 Wall Street (*see* 1865).

Manufacturers Trust has its beginnings in the New York Manufacturing Co., a textile firm whose charter permits it to engage in banking activities (*see* 1853). The company's bank will evolve into the Chatham and Phenix (*see* 1932).

Aaron Burr returns to New York and resumes his law practice; now 55, he will remain in obscurity until he dies in 1836 (*see* 1804).

Robert Fulton and Robert R. Livingston establish a Hudson River ferry service connecting Cortlandt Street and Powles Hook with the steamboats *Jersey* and *York* (*see* 1811).

The state legislature at Albany enacts a law providing for popular education. It has previously given Union College $10,000 and a grant of public lands.

New York's first City Hall at 28 Wall Street is demolished and sold as salvage for $425 (*see* 1811). It is where George Washington took his oath of office in 1789 (*see* 1842).

Schermerhorn Row is completed near the East River. Merchant and ship owner Peter Schermerhorn operates his own ship chandlery at 243 Water Street and has erected the 12 four-story buildings

with red Flemish bond brickwork, stone lintels, arched brownstone entrances, brick chimneys, and slate hip roofs to house his and various other chandleries (ship provisioners), rope lofts, sail lofts, and warehouses for naval supplies (*see* ferry, 1816).

1813 Former diplomat and steamboat financier Robert R. Livingston dies suddenly at Clermont in Columbia County February 26 at age 66.

New Jersey-born Capt. James Lawrence, 31, U.S. Navy, engages the British frigate *Shannon* outside of Boston Harbor in early June, is wounded, and shouts, "Tell the men to fire faster and not to give up the ship; fight her till she sinks." His ship *Chesapeake* is captured, he dies of his wounds aboard ship, and he is buried in New York's Trinity Churchyard.

The Battle of Lake Erie September 10 ends in victory for an improvised U.S. squadron commanded by Rhode Island-born Capt. Oliver Hazard Perry, 28.

Poetry: verses published anonymously in Charles Holt's *Columbian* December 22 are by Connecticut-born poet Fitz-Greene Halleck, 23: "When the bright star of peace from our country was clouded,/ Hope fondly presaged it would still reappear." The war has forced Halleck's New York mercantile firm Halleck & Barker to suspend payments.

1814 Former governor Morgan Lewis is given the rank of major general; now 59, he is awarded command of forces defending New York City in the continuing War of 1812.

A British army of 11,000 men under the command of Gen. Sir George Prevost marches south from the St. Lawrence River beginning August 31 and proceeds down the west side of Lake Champlain. Delaware-born Lieut. Thomas Macdonough, 31, U.S. Navy, has long seen that control of the lake was essential to the defense of New York City and has built up a fleet of four ships and 10 gunboats. When Capt. George Downie's fleet enters the lake MacDonough deploys his vessels in a narrow channel across the bay from Plattsburgh and drops anchor; when the British round Cumberland Head September 11 the Americans open fire at a range of 500 yards, force Downie to strike his colors, seize or destroy the four British warships, and leave 168 crewmen killed, 220 wounded (U.S. casualties: 104 killed, 116 wounded, no ships lost). The Battle of Plattsburgh ends the threat to New York; Gen. Prevost retires to Canada and is relieved of his command as the War of 1812 winds down. Gov. Tompkins has been obliged to borrow large sums, often on his own personal credit, to field and supply the state militia.

The Treaty of Ghent signed December 24 ends the War of 1812, enabling New York merchants to resume trade with Britain.

♥ The Association for the Relief of Respectable Aged Indigent Females is chartered by socially prominent New York women to aid poor Protestant women who have been widowed by the War of 1812 or the American Revolution and have never worked as domestic servants (see building, 1838).

$ Robert Fulton and William Cutting start an East River ferry service to connect Beekman's Slip with Brooklyn via steamboat.

A U.S. patent is awarded December 1 to steamboat pioneer Nicholas J. Roosevelt for use of vertical paddle wheels, but when Roosevelt applies to the New Jersey legislature in January of next year for protection the legislature will turn him down, partly because Robert Fulton will object that it is "inexpedient to make any special provision in connection with the matter in controversy . . ."

∞ The Vatican appoints its Irish-born Dominican librarian John Connolly, 64, bishop of the diocese of New York October 14 (see 1815).

The State of New York grants land to Columbia College that it acquired from Dr. David Hosack in 1810 (see 1985; Rockefeller Center, 1928).

1815 Steamboat pioneer Robert Fulton dies at New York February 24 at age 49, just 2 months after the launching of his steam-powered warship *Fulton the First*, or *Demologus*—a mobile floating fort that he has designed for the defense of New York Harbor.

Former New Bedford, Mass., whaling captain and merchant Preserved Fish, 49, goes into partnership at New York with his cousin Joseph Grinnell, 27, also from New Bedford, to sell whale oil. The two will acquire ships and organize packet lines connecting the city with London and Liverpool (see Tradesmen's Bank, 1829).

The New York State legislature approves a plan to finance an Erie Canal with state bonds pursuant to the proposal made by Mayor De Witt Clinton in 1811. Former president Thomas Jefferson has opposed the plan, calling it "little short of madness," other detractors call it "Clinton's Ditch" and even "Clinton's Folly," but Clinton has persuaded New York bankers that the canal will be profitable and bring an economic boom to the city (see 1817).

∞ Bishop John Connolly arrives at the city from Rome November 25 to take up his duties (see 1814). In the next 9 years he will approve new parishes, open an orphanage, welcome the Sisters of Charity, and negotiate with lay trustees who claim ownership of church properties.

St. Patrick's Cathedral is completed at 260 Mulberry Street. Designed by Joseph F. Mangin, it is the largest church in the city, and although it will be destroyed by fire in 1866 it will be rebuilt 2 years later (see 1879).

Fur merchant Adam Treadwell purchases the Van Zandt Farm in an area that later will be bounded by Second and Third avenues between 61st and 62nd streets in an area that has been farmed by Peter Van Zandt and William Beekman. Treadwell's daughter Elizabeth will inherit the property upon his death in 1852 and buy the Beekman portion of the land.

1816 Brooklyn's built-up area near the 2-year-old ferry landing in Brooklyn Heights is incorporated as a village in April (see 1834; Brooklyn Museum, 1823).

Former U.S. senator (and U.S. Constitution drafter) Gouverneur Morris dies at his family manor of Morrisania in the Bronx November 6 at age 64.

$ Congress imposes a 25 percent duty on all imports to protect America's infant industry from foreign competition and make the nation self-sufficient, but even with the tariff wall British manufacturers will find ways to undersell the Americans. Rep. Daniel Webster, 34 (N.H.), has opposed the tariff as a representative of New England shipping interests, and many New Yorkers have also opposed it.

The New York merchant trading house G. G. & S. Howland is established by Connecticut-born shipowner's sons Gardiner Greene Howland, 28, and his brother Samuel (Shaw), 25, who use their one schooner to begin trade with the Cuban port of Matanzas. Gardiner has worked for Le Roy, Bayard & McEvers; his marriage in mid-December 1812 to the daughter of William Edgar has given him the wherewithal and access to credit needed to start his own firm, which competes with Bayard and will overtake it (see 1825).

The Black Ball Line begins regular Baltimore clipper ship service between New York and Liverpool, but the full flowering of the clipper ship will not come for three decades (see 1790; 1832).

The Brooklyn Ferry Co. builds a landing at Peter Schermerhorn's wharf at the foot of Fulton Street on the East River.

The Albany Post Road (or Bloomingdale Road, later Broadway) is laid out on Manhattan's West Side, going through an area of swamps and huge rocks that discourage construction. The new road carries far less traffic than the Boston Post Road (later Fourth Avenue) to the east.

 The first formulary (pharmacopoeia) for a civilian hospital is established at New York Hospital (*see U.S. Pharmacopoeia*, 1820).

∞ The American Bible Society is founded by philanthropists who include soap maker William Colgate, now 33 (*see* New York Bible Society, 1809).

Rabbi Gershon Mendes Seixas dies at New York July 2 at age 71.

An almshouse at the corner of First Avenue and 26th Street is turned into a city penitentiary. It is the first prison whose inmates are put to work on a "stepping wheel" that powers a mill and serves as punishment. The bridewell built in 1775 is converted into a debtor's jail and will become the Hall of Records in 1838.

1817 Gov. Tompkins resigns February 24 to take office (March 4) as U.S. vice president. New York City-born Lieut. Gov. John Tayler, 74, assumes the office on a pro tem basis.

Men purporting to represent the city's Irish Catholics interrupt a meeting of Tammany Hall's General Committee April 24. They have asked Tammany's sachems to back Irish-born lawyer and orator Thomas Addis Emmett, a brother of Ireland's revolutionary leader Robert Emmett, for Congress; Tammany has refused, partly because Emmett is a friend of Mayor Clinton but perhaps more because Tammany's leaders have doubts about the American patriotism of Irish immigrants. The insurgents break up furniture and use it as weapons, beating committee members and leaving most bruised or even bloodied before reinforcements arrive to drive them out.

Mayor De Witt Clinton is elected to replace John Tayler in the governor's chair. Now 48, Clinton wins 43,310 votes as compared to 1,479 for his Tammany-supported opponent and takes office July 1.

Irish-born fur trader Cornelius Heeney, 63, is elected to the state legislature at Albany, becoming only the second Roman Catholic to serve. Heeney came to America in 1784, made a fortune selling furs in the city, is well known for his philanthropies, and will serve in the legislature until 1822.

$ The New York Stock and Exchange Board is established February 25 to bring order to securities trading (*see* Buttonwood agreement, 1792). New York remains a financial backwater as compared to Philadelphia or London (*see* 1825).

Unskilled workers break ground at Rome, N.Y., July 4 for construction of a 363-mile Erie Canal that will connect Buffalo on Lake Erie with Troy on the Hudson River, where the river becomes navigable for 151 miles to the Atlantic Ocean (*see* 1815). The state legislature authorized a state bond issue for the canal 2 years ago, and last year it gave civil engineers James Geddes, Benjamin Wright, and Charles C. Broadhead responsibility for the western, middle, and eastern sections, respectively (Wright will soon be made chief engineer for the project). Gov. Clinton has ordered work to begin without further delay, the starting point has been selected because work can proceed from there for about 80 miles with no need for locks or aqueducts that would slow progress and encourage the project's detractors, but the state has expropriated farmland along the canal route, which in many cases cuts through farms, and thousands of farmers remain opposed to the project (*see* 1819).

The first steam ferry between Manhattan and Staten Island goes into service. The *Nautilus* is owned by Vice President Tompkins.

 The New York Academy of Sciences has its beginnings in the Lyceum of Natural History founded by a group of interested citizens whose *Annals* will be published beginning in 1823. Founders include New York-born medical student and botanist John Torrey, 21 (*see* 1961).

∞ The General Convention of the Episcopal Church is held at New York and establishes a "general Theological Seminary, which may have the united support of the whole church" rather that of any particular state or diocese. Chelsea landowner Clement Clarke Moore next year will offer a full city block of his estate—extending from Ninth to Tenth avenues between 20th and 21st streets—as a gift to the church for construction of the seminary that will begin classes in 1819 with six students (*see* 1826).

The mayor's office issues regulations requiring strict observance of Sunday as a day of rest: no work is to be performed, there is to be no buying or selling (except of fish and milk that may otherwise spoil), no hunting, and no sport of any kind. Churches are permitted to hang chains across streets to block the passage of noisy carriages and stagecoaches.

 Harper and Brothers has its origin in a New York print shop opened in Dover Street by former printing apprentice James Harper, 22, with his younger brother John under the name J & J Harper. Their brothers Wesley and Fletcher will join them in 1825, and they will revolutionize book publishing with the first volumes bound in cloth over boards and the first to be published in series as "libraries." Harper and Brothers will be the first to make stereotyping a regular procedure and the first to employ editors (*see* 1850; Harper & Row, 1962).

P. Maverick-Durand, Engravers opens in October at the corner of Pine Street and Broadway. New Jersey-born artist Asher Brown Durand, 21, has been apprenticed since 1812 to engraver Peter Maverick, now 37, near Newark, N.J., and becomes his partner as the two set up shop in Manhattan.

1818 New York-born hatter's son Peter Cooper, 17, is
$ apprenticed to a coachmaker for $25 per year plus board. His maternal grandfather, John Campbell, served briefly as mayor of the city, and although young Cooper has had no more than 2 or 3 months' formal education he has learned all the complexities of the hat trade and will use his inventive genius and hard work to make his mark.

Brooks Brothers has its beginnings in a New York menswear shop opened April 7 at the corner of Catharine and Cherry Streets by merchant Henry Sands Brooks, 46, who invests $17,000 in a stock of imported British woolens and adopts the golden fleece symbol of a dead lamb cradled by a ribbon, the symbol used in the 15th century for a knighthood established by the duke of Burgundy Philippe le Bon. Brooks Brothers will clothe generations of bankers, lawyers, military officers, statesmen, and upwardly mobile Americans (*see* 1850; seersucker suit, 1830).

The Essex Street Market opens in Grand Street between Ludlow and Essex streets. Local laborers and mechanics have requested that the city build a market on the site, but it will create congestion in the narrow streets nearby and officials will close it in 1836 (*see* 1940).

Staten Island ferry operator Cornelius van Derbilt, now 24, persuades Thomas Gibbons to build a large steamboat that will enable him to carry cargo between New Jersey ports and New York in defiance of the monopoly granted by the state of New York to the late Robert Fulton and Robert Livingston. Gibbons is a former partner of Aaron Ogden, who obtained a steam navigation license from Fulton and Livingston; van Derbilt enrages Ogden by underbidding him and landing cargoes at New York (*see* Supreme Court decision, 1824).

Mayor Marinus Willett ends an acrimonious dispute by dividing the city's waste-disposal business into two parts—general carting and dirt carting, with the latter to be performed by Irish contractors against whom the regular carters have been fighting (*see* 1789; 1825).

1819 The Bank for Savings in the City of New York
$ receives a charter 3 years after it was proposed to the state legislature by John Pintard, Thomas Eddy, and other city officials and businessmen desirous of instilling "provident habits" among working-class residents. The legislature at Albany has been strongly opposed to banks of any kind, but banks have opened in other cities and the Society for the Prevention of Pauperism has supported the proposal for a new savings bank modeled on English banks of its kind (*see* Greenwich, 1833).

The first stretch of the Erie Canal opens after 2 years of construction to connect Utica and Rome (*see* 1817). Yankee engineers have devised an endless screw linked to a roller, a cable, and a crank to pull down tall trees. They have improvised a horse-drawn crane to lift rock debris out of the cut, but most of the work is done by Irish immigrants who receive 37.5¢ per day (plus as much as a quart of whiskey per day in periodic work breaks) and die by the thousands of malaria, pneumonia, and snakebite (*see* 1825).

The Market Street Church (later the Sea and Land Church) is completed at 61 Henry Street, northwest corner Market Street.

Merchant and alderman Wyant Van Zandt purchases the farm established 84 years ago by the Van Wyck family on the Queens peninsula that will become known as Douglaston. Van Zandt builds a large square farmhouse on the property to house his wife and 15 children (*see* Douglas, 1835).

1820 Gov. Clinton wins reelection, defeating a bid by Vice President Tompkins to regain the position that he held from 1808 to 1817. The state comptroller announced after the War of 1812 that the state's military accounts showed a shortage of $120,000, and although an investigation showed that the state actually owed Tompkins $90,000 there has remained some question in many voters' minds as to the truth of the matter.

The U.S. Pharmaeopoeia established by New York physician Lyman Spalding, 45, is a government-approved list of medical drugs with their formulas, methods for preparing medicines, and requirements and tests for purity.

The New York Eye and Ear Infirmary founded in Manhattan will survive into the 21st century as the oldest specialty hospital in the Western Hemisphere.

Washington Irving created a mythology for the Hudson River Valley. LIBRARY OF CONGRESS

The Mercantile Library Association is founded by merchants' clerks who will open a circulating library next year in rented rooms at 49 Fulton Street (*see* 1830).

Fiction: *The Sketch Book* by Geoffrey Crayon (Washington Irving) contains "The Legend of Sleepy Hollow."

Bronx pioneer Rachel Eden buys a hilly farm in the Tremont section, an area that will remain agricultural for close to 100 years and be known even thereafter as Mount Eden.

Sugar refining is New York City's second most important industry, surpassed only by ironworks and followed closely by brewing. Hogsheads of sugar containing 1,000 pounds each leave the city's refineries every day for shipment to inland cities and towns.

The city's population reaches 123,706, making New York the largest metropolis in America. A family of 14 can live comfortably on $3,000 per year.

1821 Federal authorities close down the 10-year-old Castle Clinton at the Battery and move the Third Military District's heaquarters to Governors Island.

The facility will be ceded to the city in 1823 (*see* Theater [Castle Garden], 1824).

A state constitutional convention is held through the efforts of political leaders such as Martin Van Buren, 38, who has served as a Democratic Republican in the state senate since his election in 1812, when he won office by opposing the Bank of the United States. Head of his party's "Bucktail" faction, Van Buren has locked horns on frequent occasion with Gov. Clinton. A native of Kinderhook, he is elected to the U.S. Senate and leaves behind him the "Albany Regency," a group of associates bent on maintaining his power of patronage in the state.

The new state constitution makes ownership of at least $250 worth of property a requisite for black voters (*see* 1825).

Bloomingdale Insane Asylum opens on Morningside Heights at what later will be 116th Street and Broadway (*see* 1808). The state's first fully dedicated mental hospital, it has been started as a branch of New York Hospital at the urging of reformer Thomas Eddy, charity cases make up the bulk of its patients, and for its first 20 years it will be subsidized by the state, caring for many indigent patients with a combination of traditional medical interventions and "moral treatment" (a form of reeducation) (*see* 1894).

The African Methodist Episcopal Zion Church is founded by blacks whose African Chapel has been within the jurisdiction of the Methodist Episcopal Church but who have been unable to win independence within the white church. They will elect James Varick as their first bishop; now 71, he was ordained only last year, will be reelected in 1827, and will serve until his death in July 1827.

Fiction: *The Spy* by Burlington, N.J.-born New York novelist James Fenimore Cooper, 32. Set in Westchester during the American Revolution, it brings Cooper fame and fortune.

The Union Course racetrack opens in what later will be Woodhaven, Queens, where for nearly 50 years it will be the scene of horseraces—often between horses of rich Southern plantation owners and those from Northern stables (*see* 1823).

The Crane's Wharf fire on Front Street January 24 destroys 31 houses and buildings that include a market at the end of Fulton Street. The land there was donated to the city by the Beekman Estate in 1807 on condition that a market on the site since the middle of the last century remain a market (*see* 1822).

The Hudson River freezes over so solidly that taverns spring up on the ice in the middle of the stream to provide pedestrians with warmth and refreshment. Daring Manhattanites walk over to Brooklyn, Jersey City, and Staten Island.

1822 Gov. Clinton declines to seek another term in the face of strong opposition from Sen. Van Buren's "Bucktail" faction. He is succeeded by Schenectady-born state supreme court justice Joseph C. Yates, now 53, who is besieged by office seekers in the wake of a new law that has changed the tenure of many appointed offices.

The Jewish Child Care Association has its beginnings in the Hebrew Benevolent Society, founded by New York philanthropists to care for orphans and other needy Jews (*see* 1942; real estate, 1884).

Yellow fever strikes the city; thousands flee to Greenwich Village, whose growth is spurred by the influx. A 300-guest hotel goes up in just 2 days at the corner of Hammond (later West 11th) and 4th streets. The Village remains a rural Manhattan area whose streets will never conform to the grid pattern employed north of Washington Square under the Commissioners' Plan of 1811.

A Grammar of Botany compiled by Henry Muhlenberg is published at 23 Lumber Street (later Trinity Place) by Barnet and Doolittle—the first U.S. lithography company. It was founded last year by French-trained lithographers William Armand Barnet and Isaac Doolittle, 37, who also publish illustrations for the *American Journal of Science* before the yellow fever epidemic and a shortage of work oblige them to close. Lithography will become a major New York industry.

Poetry: "Marco Bozzaris" by Fitz-Greene Halleck is published in the *New-York Review*.

The Fulton Market reopens on the East River (*see* 1821). In addition to fresh catches from the fishing fleet, it receives produce from Long Island farms; new structures will be erected in 1831 and 1848, but the butchers' and greengrocers' stalls will move westward to the Hudson (North) River by the middle of the century, leaving the Fulton Market to fishmongers (*see* 1869; 1880).

1823 Customs duties collected at the port of New York are enough to fund the entire federal government with the exception of interest on the national debt. The port accounts for one-third of America's exports and half the nation's imports.

The A. T. Stewart Department Store has its beginnings in a small dry-goods shop opened September

Clement Clark Moore was Chelsea's biggest landowner. And he created the immortal verses about St. Nicholas.

1 at 283 Broadway by Irish-born merchant Alexander Turney Stewart, 21, who will create the world's first true department store (*see* 1846).

The New York Gas Light Co. is incorporated March 26 to manufacture methane gas from coal and supply it for street lights and home use from the Battery to Canal Street; although many New Yorkers are fearful of possible explosions and initially resist having gas piped into their homes, its economy and efficiency will soon make gas lighting irresistible; by 1847 there will be gas lamps up Fifth Avenue as far north as 18th Street and many homes will be lighted by gas (*see* 1830; Brooklyn, 1825).

The Brooklyn Institute of Arts and Sciences has its beginnings in the Apprentice Library, created "to shield young men from evil associations, and to encourage improvement during leisure hours by reading and conversation." The library rents rooms at 143 Fulton Street and opens with 724 books and 150 pamphlets contributed by donors who have carted them in wheelbarrows (*see* 1825).

Fiction: *The Pioneers* by James Fenimore Cooper begins a series of *Leatherstocking Tales*.

Poetry: "A Visit from St. Nicholas" is published anonymously December 23 in the *Troy Sentinel* (*see* food, 1822). Clement Clark Moore has written the verses, bringing to life the elfin figure depicted by Washington Irving in 1809 (Moore will not acknowledge authorship until 1837): " 'Twas the night before Christmas . . . Now, Dasher! now, Dancer! now, Prancer and Vixen! On, Comet, on, Cupid! on, Donder and Blitzen!" (*see* Nast drawing, 1862).

The first U.S. horserace to attract worldwide attention takes place at the 2-year-old Union Course in what later will be Woodhaven, Queens, where American Eclipse beats a thoroughbred named Henry in a match that draws a crowd of 60,000.

Clement Clarke Moore writes his verses about St. Nicholas (it will become known to many as "The Night Before Christmas") in reaction to the lawlessness that has long attended Christmas celebrations in the city; indigent New Yorkers have often pushed their way into more prosperous citizens' homes, demanding food, drink, and money; more respectable citizens have had little or no police protection against break-ins, vandalism, and even sexual assaults by drunken beggars. New York children of Dutch descent have traditionally been visited on St. Nicholas Day Eve, December 5, by a figure dressed like a bishop and riding a white horse; Moore's poem will help change the way Christmas is celebrated (*see* police, 1828).

Bryant Park has its beginnings in a potter's field laid out on a remote piece of property bounded by 41st and 42nd streets between what soon will be Fifth and Sixth avenues (*see* 1847).

1824 The marquis de Lafayette returns to New York August 14 for a 6-day visit (*see* 1784). Now 66, he is given a triumphal procession to City Hall, the mayor gives him a grand reception, and he is honored with a state banquet 2 days later. Lafayette returns for a 9-day visit beginning September 5.

The presidential election in November ends with no candidate having a majority in the Electoral College, although John Calhoun is elected vice president. Andrew Jackson receives 90 electoral votes, John Quincy Adams 81, William H. Crawford 41, Henry Clay 37 (*see* 1825).

Former governor De Witt Clinton is reelected to his old office. Supporters have been angered by Sen. Van Buren's "Bucktail" faction, whose members have ousted Clinton from his job as unsalaried canal commissioner.

Tarrytown-born state adjutant general William Paulding, Jr., 54, is elected mayor. A Democrat who has served in Congress, he is an older brother of the poet James Kirke Paulding, will be replaced next year by Philip Hone, but will be reelected and hold office from 1826 to 1829.

Chemical Bank opens at 216 Broadway, opposite St. Paul's Church, as a subsidiary of the New York Chemical Manufacturing Co., a Greenwich Village concern. New York's 12 banks are clustered about Wall Street, and Chemical's remote location puts it at a competitive disadvantage (*see* 1850).

The landmark U.S. Supreme Court decision handed down March 2 in the case of *Gibbons v. Ogden* frees rivers from monopoly control (*see* 1818). New Jersey steamboat operator Aaron Ogden, now 68, has been running a ferry service between New York and Elizabethtown; steamboat operator Thomas Gibbons holds a monopoly originally granted by the New York State legislature to the late Robert Fulton and Robert Livingston and has sued Ogden and retained Daniel Webster to plead his case. Chief Justice John Marshall writes the majority opinion, holding that the monopoly granted by New York violates the interstate commerce clause in the Constitution, and the ruling opens waterways to all steamboats that can comply with regulations designed to keep boilers from exploding (*see* van Derbilt, 1829).

Fifth Avenue has its beginnings. The city acquires title August 2 to seven blocks on the middle route between the Albany Post Road (Broadway) and the Boston Post Road (Third Avenue). Work begins in November on a 100-foot wide thoroughfare from 6th Street (or Art Street; later Waverly Place) north to 13th Street; it will reach 21st Street by 1830, 42nd by 1837, 120th by 1838 (*see* Brevoort mansion, 1834).

The 187-year-old Collegiate School reopens after a 38-year hiatus that began in 1776 (*see* 1892).

Theater: the city leases Castle Clinton (formerly Fort Clinton), has it remodeled to plans by architect John McComb, Jr., now 60, renames it Castle Garden, makes it available as a place for band concerts, fireworks, demonstrations of scientific achievements, and other public events, and opens it 7/3 (it will be roofed over in 1845; *see* immigration, 1855).

The Society for the Reformation of Juvenile Delinquents headed by John H. Griscom and Thomas Eddy acquires the grounds of the 17-year-old U.S. Arsenal at the junction of Broadway and Fifth

Avenue and erects another large stone building that will open at the start of next year as the House of Refuge—the first U.S. institution to separate youthful offenders from adult criminals. It will initially hold six girls and three boys, its founders hope to rehabilitate such offenders with progressive methods, but the four-acre grounds of the House of Refuge are enclosed by a stone wall 17 feet in height and the house will become a harsh penal institution (see 1838).

A building to house the Branch Bank of the United States is completed on the north side of Wall Street, between Nassau and William streets, to Greek Revival designs by Martin E. Thompson. It will later become the U.S. Assay Office.

The Church of St. Luke-in-the-Fields (initially St. Luke's Episcopal Chapel of Trinity Parish) is completed in a rural area at what later will be 485 Hudson Street, near Barrow Street, to designs by carpenter-builder James N. Wells, who will become a friend of scholar and landowner Clement Clarke Moore (see fire, 1981). Moore is the church's first warden and will hire Wells to manage his family estate, seeking his advice in developing the area that will come to be known as Chelsea (see 1833).

A seven-story walkup building goes up at 65 Mott Street, near Pell Street (date approximate). The first of what will be called "tenant houses" (later tenements), it towers above its two-story wooden neighbors and provides housing for unrelated families in apartments, each typically comprising a 12' × 12' front room that serves as living room, dining room, and kitchen plus an unventilated 8' × 10' "sleeping closet" in the rear where as many as 12 people may live. The building will stand for more than 60 years (see 1850).

Builders put up some 3,000 new houses to accommodate the city's swelling population, but there are still housing shortages. Real estate values soar, and rents for shops and stores will soon double.

1825 John Quincy Adams is elected president February 9 in the House of Representatives at Washington, D.C., where Kentucky's Henry Clay controls the deciding block of votes. Stephen Van Rensselaer of New York casts the deciding vote.

Vice President Daniel D. Tompkins leaves office March 4 and dies at his Staten Island home June 11 at age 50.

Retired merchant Philip Hone is elected mayor as a Whig for 1 year when the Democratic Common Council splits over two rival candidates. Hone and

The Erie Canal fulfilled De Witt Clinton's dream of opening up trade. Clinton's "folly" became a great success.

his wife, Catherine (née Dunscomb), live with their six children in a Broadway house overlooking City Hall Park.

Property qualifications for white male voters are removed, but black males must still have property worth at least $250 (see 1821). Federalist Party chancellor James Kent warns, "The growth of the city of New York is enough to startle and awaken those who are pursuing the *ignis fatuus* [foolish fire] of universal suffrage . . . It is rapidly swelling into the unwieldy population . . . and with the burdensome pauperism of an European metropolis . . ."

A new city waste-disposal law restricts general carting licenses to citizens, barring blacks from participating in the trade, despite protests, and limiting Irish carters to dirt hauling (see 1818; 1829).

The New York Stock Board and Exchange trades mostly in securities issued by canal, turnpike, mining, and gaslighting companies (see 1817). The new Erie Canal is making New York a boomtown like none ever before seen, and although promoters will soon be promoting shares in fledgling railroad ventures no shares in industrial corporations will appear until 1831; the Boston exchange is closer to the nation's manufacturing center, but even there no industrial shares will be traded until 1827. Few will appear on the New York, Philadelphia, or Boston exchange for another 40 years (see NYSE, 1863).

Brown Brothers & Co. is established at New York November 11 with an office at 191 Pearl Street. James Brown, 34, heads the New York office (his Irish-born father, Alexander Brown, 61, has built up a Baltimore linen-importing and banking house with worldwide connections). Brown's brother William, now 40, started the Liverpool firm Brown, Shipley & Co. in 1810, and his brother John A., now 37, founded Brown Brothers at Philadelphia 7 years ago (*see* 1835).

⚡ Gas street lights are introduced below Canal Street on Manhattan Island (*see* 1823). Candles remain the only source of artificial light elsewhere in the city.

Brooklyn Gas Light Co. receives a charter from the New York State legislature, but the village refuses to sign a contract with the new company, whose officers buy back its stock and stop producing methane gas from coal. Brooklyn will not have gas lighting until 1847.

⚡ The Erie Canal opens October 26 to link the Great Lakes with the Hudson River and the Atlantic (*see* 1819). The greatest engineering feat of the day, it has been completed ahead of schedule. Gov. De Witt Clinton and Mayor Philip Hone preside over the ceremonies that greet the first canal boat on the $8 million state-owned canal; dug by hand at a cost of more than $20,000 per mile, it is 363 miles long, 40 feet wide, and four feet deep, with tow paths for the mules that pull barges up and down its length at 1½ miles per hour. It has cost more to ship a ton of grain 30 miles in America than to ship it across the Atlantic, but the time required to move freight from the Midwest to the Atlantic now falls to 8 or 10 days, down from between 20 and 30, freight rates drop immediately from $100 per ton to less than $6, New York City becomes the Atlantic port for the Midwest and the economic capital of America. The canal boat *Seneca Chief* arrives at New York November 4 carrying Gov. Clinton, distinguished guests, and a barrel of Lake Erie water, having gone through 83 locks to complete the first voyage from Buffalo. By year's end some 13,110 boats have passed from Buffalo to Albany and paid $500,000 in tolls, more than enough to fund the debt incurred by the state to build it, but the canal freezes over in winter and is out of service for weeks and months at a time (*see* 1882; Erie Railroad, 1832).

∞ Bishop John Connolly dies at New York February 6 at age 74 and is buried beneath St. Patrick's Cathedral in Mulberry Street at the corner of Prince and Mott streets. The Roman Catholic diocese has grown to have two churches in the city, one at Albany, another at Auburn, and one at Carthage on the Black River, all served by one bishop and eight priests. Catholic and Protestant churchgoers agitate for an abolition of pew rents.

The conservative synagogue B'nai Jeshurum is organized following a dispute among members of the 171-year-old Shearith Israel congregation over how communal honors are to be distributed. Most of the city's 400-odd Jews are of Dutch, German, English, or Polish descent, but the overcrowded Shearith Israel synagogue in Mill Street has alienated newcomers by insisting on Sephardic ritual and charging a fee of two shillings (for charity) to anyone wanting to read from the Torah. The departing Ashkenazic faction takes over a former Elm Street church, near Canal Street, where it will remain until the 1870s (*see* Anshe Chesed, 1828; Shearith Israel, 1834).

🪶 Former Columbia professor and Regents secretary Robert Harpur dies at his upstate home in Harpursville April 15 at age 94, having spent his final 30 years developing more than 30,000 acres of land on the Susquehanna River that he purchased from the state in 1795. Some historians will credit Harpur with having given classical names (Attica, Carthage, Corinth, Delphi, Ithaca, Palmyra, Phoenicia, Rome, Syracuse, Troy, Utica) to various upstate towns and cities.

The visiting marquis de Lafayette lays the cornerstone July 24 of a building at the corner of Henry and Cranberry streets for the 2-year-old Apprentice Library that will become the Brooklyn Institute of Arts and Sciences and evolve into the Brooklyn Museum. The Library will broaden its activities to include a variety of interests, ranging from art, French lessons, and music to chemistry and machinery (*see* 1838).

Columbia College appoints Italian immigrant Lorenzo da Ponte (originally Emanuele Conagliano) in September as its first professor of Italian literature, probably through the influence of his friend Clement Clarke Moore, a Columbia trustee. Now 76, Ponte lost his Jewish mother at an early age, was renamed as a child when his Jewish father converted to Roman Catholicism in order to marry a young woman whose family insisted on such a conversion, was librettist for the late Wolfgang Amadeus Mozart's operas *Le Nozze di Figaro* (1785), *Don Giovanni* (1787), and *Cosi fan Tutti* (1791), had a reputation in Europe as a libertine, but came to this country in 1805 at age 56 to join his wife, Nancy, and their children, bringing with him only $40 or $50, a box of violin strings, and some books. He has few pupils initially (modern language is not much studied; French and Spanish are more popular than Italian), but da Ponte sells a considerable number of

Italian books to the college library and will do so again in 1829.

Painting: *General Lafayette* by New York-born painter Samuel F. B. (Finley Breese) Morse, 34; *Lake with Dead Trees (Catskill)* by Lancashire-born artist-poet Thomas Cole, 24, who has worked as an engraver and portrait painter at Philadelphia, Pittsburgh, and Steubenville, Ohio, since 1818, came to New York City, and moves now to a Catskill, N.Y., house where he founds the Hudson River school of American painting.

Opera: *Il Barbieri di Siviglia* 11/29 at the Park Theater with Spanish singer Manuel García singing the role of Almaviva in the first New York performance of any Italian opera. Columbia College Italian literature professor Lorenzo da Ponte acts as impresario for the 1816 work by Gioacchino Rossini, which has created a furor in Europe, and the evening is the most brilliant social occasion New York has had in many years (newspapers have received many letters asking how one should dress "in the European manner" for an evening at the opera and what was the proper etiquette during performances). García's daughter Maria Felicità, 17, sings the mezzo-soprano role of Rosina (she will marry Eugène Malibran, a French merchant, next year in order to free herself from her despotic father's demands and will become famous as Maria Malibran) (see 1826; first opera house, 1833).

The city's first organized street gang appears on the Lower East Side.

The first organized group of Norwegian immigrants to the United States arrives at New York October 9 from Stavenger, where 52 emigrants, many of them Quakers fleeing a hostile state church, boarded the sloop *Restauration* July 4 (a baby has been born aboard ship). The Norwegians who arrive October 9 begin a movement that will take hundreds of thousands to the Midwest and Northwest in the next 100 years, but many will settle in Brooklyn, notably near Red Hook (see relief society, 1883).

1826 The city celebrates the 50th anniversary of the Declaration of Independence July 4. The horse artillery fires a salute at 7 o'clock in the morning; Gov. Clinton and a group of "Honorables" with names like Bogardus, Fish, Van Rensselaer, and Van Courtland march up from the Battery to the Washington Parade Ground, newly created atop a potter's field containing 10,000 bodies (see 1797; Washington Square Park, 1828).

Lord & Taylor has its beginnings in a shop opened at 47 Catherine Street by English-born merchant Samuel Lord, 23, who has borrowed $1,000 from his wife's uncle, John Taylor, to start. By year's end Lord has taken into partnership his wife's cousin George Washington Taylor, and by 1832 their business will have an annex in an adjoining building.

The city has fewer than eight miles of lighted streets, with 2,478 lampposts for its gaslights (see 1823).

The 632-ton New York-built sailing packet *Britannia* goes into service for the Black Ball line and will continue transatlantic voyages between the city and Liverpool through 1835, averaging 38 days on her westbound trips. Measuring nearly 133 feet in length, 32 feet wide in the beam, and 16 feet deep, she will make her shortest passage in 28 days, her longest in 59.

Paris-born Maryland cleric John DuBois, 62, is named bishop of the New York archdiocese October 29, succeeding the late John Connolly, and although parishioners charge that he has used undue influence to obtain the position he will refute their allegations, collect contributions, build a seminary (it will burn down in 1834), have his pay cut off by the trustees of St. Patrick's Cathedral, and serve until he is disabled by a stroke in 1838 (see Hughes, 1842).

The Friends Seminary founded in 1786 moves to Elizabeth Street after 40 years in Pearl Street (see 1860).

The first building of the General Theological Seminary opens on the Chelsea Square block donated by Clement Clarke Moore in 1818 (see 1817). A second, matching stone structure will be completed to its west in 1836, and further construction toward the end of the century will further enlarge the seminary.

Fiction: *The Last of the Mohicans* by James Fenimore Cooper.

Painting: *The Falls of Kaaterskill* by Thomas Cole.

Theater: New York-born comedian James H. (Henry) Hackett, 25, makes his stage debut 3/1 at the Park Theater as Justus Woodcock, and although he is hardly a success he scores big a few weeks later in the role of Sylvester Daggenwood.

The Great Bowery Theater dedicated 10/23 is the largest theater in North America. It will burn down and be rebuilt several times as the Bowery becomes the center of the city's theatrical life from the 1850s to the 1870s.

Opera: *Don Giovanni* 5/23 at the Park Theater, in the first U.S. performance of the Mozart opera whose libretto Lorenzo da Ponte wrote in 1787 (the greatest ambition of his old age has been realized; see 1825).

Da Ponte's son Lorenzo, Jr. has made an English translation, the Park Theater gives da Ponte permission to print and sell the libretti in both English and Italian for his personal benefit, and although this does not produce much profit he is persuaded by a bookseller to buy a lottery ticket and he wins $500, which he uses to import some rare and important Italian books that he will eventually give to the library of Columbia College (see Opera, 1833).

Sing Sing State Prison (initially called Mt. Pleasant) opens its first cell block some 30 miles north of New York on the Hudson River at a small town facing the Tappan Zee bluffs that was named by an early Dutch trader after the Chinese city of Tsing-sing. Its first warden is a former Army captain, Elam Lynds, who has come down by barge on the new Erie Canal and then by Hudson freight steamer with some inmates and "keepers" from the Auburn State Prison, where he has established a reputation for cruel but innovative disciplinary measures. The inmates have quarried local stone for the cell block, they wear striped uniforms, make combs, furniture, and other goods as well as cutting stone, are beaten if they are heard speaking, and march in lockstep, but their treatment is considered humane as compared with that at other prisons. Lynds will remain warden until 1844, when floggings and other abuses will lead a legislative committee chargd with examining conditions at Sing Sing to order his dismissal. Use of the cat-o'-nine-tails will be eliminated in 1848, but where unruly slaves in the South may be "sold down the river" wrongdoers in New York may be "sent up the river."

1827 Former U.S. senator (and three-time Federalist Party presidential candidate) Rufus King dies at Jamaica, Queens, April 29 at age 72, having favored an orderly emancipation of slaves, with the proceeds of public-land sales being used to compensate slaveholders. He declined to run again in 1825, was appointed (for a second time) U.S. ambassador to Britain, but returned in June 1825 and retired.

New York State abolishes slavery July 4. The Hudson River Valley at one time had more slaves per capita than North Carolina, and slaves have accounted for as much as 20 percent of the population in parts of Brooklyn, where they have been used to produce corn, squash, beans, and tobacco.

Arnold Constable has its beginnings in a dry-goods shop opened at the corner of Canal and Mercer streets by merchant Aaron Arnold (see 1842).

The city's first public transit facility begins operations. Local entrepreneur Abraham Bower runs a horse-drawn bus with seats for 12, calling it an "accommodation," but New York's population of 200,000 depends chiefly on private carts, carriages, saddle horses, and ferries for transportation (see 1832).

Christ Church moves its services March 23 to Christ Protestant Episcopal Church at 41 Ann Street. Cuban political refugee Felix Varela, 38, came to New York 3 years ago and held services in the basement of the Church of St. Peter after becoming pastor of Christ Church in 1825 (see 1836).

The first free school for infants opens at New York under the direction of Joanne Bethune to free working-class parents from some of the burdens of child care. Now 57, Bethune is a disciple of Swiss educator Johann Heinrich Pestalozzi, her school is open to children 18 months to 5 years of age, and is soon followed by eight others.

The state legislature at Albany appropriates $8,000 to save the 23-year-old New-York Historical Society from having to sell its library in order to pay off its debts (see 1908; art, 1863).

The *Freeman's Journal* begins publication March 16 at 5 Varick Street—the first U.S. black newspaper. The city's white press has largely favored slavery, but the new black paper denounces slavery (the legislature at Albany abolishes it in the state July 4) and urges free blacks to seek education and practice thrift. It has been started by local clergyman Samuel E. Cornish, who has founded the first U.S. black Presbyterian church, and Jamaican-born college graduate John B. Russworm, who will move to Liberia after 1847 and publish the *Liberia Herald* at Monrovia.

The Journal of Commerce begins publication September 1 at New York. The semi-religious publication has been started by silk importer and textile merchant Arthur Tappan (see 1826) with portrait artist Samuel F. B. Morse (see telegraph, 1832). Tappan's brother Lewis will take over the paper next year and sell it in 1831.

The National Academy of Design founded January 14 at New York aims to promote artistic design by exhibiting only works by living artists. Samuel F. B. Morse and the other founders have tried without success to merge the American Academy of the Fine Arts and the New York Association of Artists (the Drawing Association) (see 1863).

Painting: *Scene from "Last of the Mohicans": Cora Kneeling at the Feet of Tamenund* and *The Close, Catskills* by Thomas Cole (year approximate).

Delmonico's Restaurant has its beginnings in a café and pastry shop opened in lower Manhattan by Swiss wine merchant Giovanni Del-Monico and his older brother Pietro, who has run a pastry shop at Bern. Giovanni came to America aboard a trading ship from the West Indies and opened a small wine shop near the Battery 2 years ago, buying by the cask and selling by the bottle. Patrons of the new shop purchase cakes, ices, and wine, either taking it home or consuming it on the premises, sitting at plain pine tables where they are impressed by the clean aprons and good manners of the brothers Del-Monico (*see* 1832).

1828 Gov. De Witt Clinton dies at Albany February 11 at age 58 and is succeeded by his Connecticut-born lieutenant governor Nathaniel Pitcher, 50. Sen. Martin Van Buren is elected governor in November to succeed Gov. Pitcher.

An anti-Catholic mob burns down St. Mary's Church in Grand Street as agitation against Irish immigrants increases (*see* real estate, 1833; Ancient Order of Hibernians, 1836).

New York acquires Blackwell's Island in the East River from descendants of Robert Blackwell (*see* 1673). In the next 30 years the city will use it to build an almshouse, prison, workhouse, and three hospitals (*see* Lunatic Asylum, 1839).

The first barges to navigate the new Delaware & Hudson Canal arrive at the city in October with anthracite coal in time for the heating season, and 7,000 tons are delivered before the canal freezes over. Completed in less than 3 years, the waterway is four feet deep and accommodates boats that carry up to 30,000 tons of coal each. Two mules or horses pulling a canal boat can haul 100 tons faster than they could haul one ton in a wagon on land; the canal company requires that each boat have a captain, a bowman (often the captain's wife), and a driver or muleteer (usually a young boy or girl, often a homeless orphan from New York City, who must feed, water, and otherwise tend to the horses or mules, walking 15 to 20 miles per day on the towpaths, 6 days per week, in all kinds of weather from April to December, receiving perhaps $4.50 per month plus room and board). The project still lacks a rail link to the coal mines at Carbondale.

New York's Common Council institutes the city's first professional police force following an especially violent Christmastime riot (*see* "A Visit From St. Nicholas," 1823).

Washington Square Park is created on the site of a potter's field cemetery, originally a swamp fed by Minetta Brook near a Sappokanican Indian settlement (*see* politics, 1826). The potter's field cemetery has been removed to a 42nd Street site acquired by the city in 1823 (*see* Bryant, 1844), and the city treasury this year spends $2,876.28 to surround the square with a wooden fence. The new park will spur residential development in the area.

1829 Gov. Van Buren resigns March 12 to assume office as U.S. secretary of state and is succeeded by his lieutenant governor Enos Thompson Throop, now 49. Former governor John Jay dies following a stroke at his Bedford, N.Y., home May 17 at age 83.

The Workingman's Movement attacks the monopoly in waste disposal enjoyed by licensed carters (*see* 1825; 1844; General Trades Union, 1833).

The Tradesmen's Bank engages whale-oil merchant Preserved Fish to succeed Stephan Allen as president (*see* 1815). Now 63, Fish retired in 1826 and will be a leader in the city's free trade movement.

Merchant Archibald Gracie dies at New York April 11 at age 73. Once one of the richest men in town, he has filed for bankruptcy, having been ruined by shipping losses suffered in the Napoleonic wars and delays in collecting spoliation claims. While he was in England trying to collect on those claims his son and one of his sons-in-law lost heavily in cotton speculations and put up his country house at Horn's Hook on the East River as collateral on their debts, which they were unable to pay. The house has been purchased by merchant-shipowner Joseph Foulkes, whose heirs will sell it in 1857 to Connecticut-born builder Noah Wheaton, whose family will retain ownership until 1896.

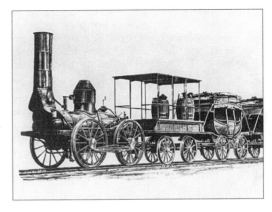

Early railroads like the De Witt Clinton *had passenger carriages that were basically stagecoaches on rails.*

Cornelius van Derbilt starts building steamboats with $30,000 he has amassed skippering for Thomas Gibbons and in his own coastal schooner ventures (*see* 1824). Now 35, van Derbilt goes into business for himself, establishing a steamboat line on the Delaware River and is soon undercutting competitors on the Hudson River and Atlantic coast until they agree to pay him off (*see* 1834).

Congregation Anshe Chesed is founded by Ashkenazic Jews who have split off from the B'nai Jeshurun congregation founded in 1820.

Niblo's Garden opens May 18 at the corner of Broadway and Prince Street. Irish-born impresario William Niblo bought the site 5 years ago, added the Sans Souci Theater to what formerly was called the Columbian Gardens, landscaped the grounds, and has added a saloon and hotel.

Theater: *Metamora, or the Last of the Wampanoags; a Tragedy of Indian Life* by U.S. playwright John Augustus Stone, 29, 12/15 at the Park Theater, with Philadelphia-born actor Edwin Forrest, 23, who last year offered a $500 prize for the best five-act tragedy whose "hero, or principal character, shall be an aboriginal of this country." Forrest subtly suggests in a prologue that the audience not condemn the play simply because it is American; Stone will find that playwrights do not make much money and will commit suicide in 1834.

1830 The first Fifth Avenue parade celebrates France's revolutionists, who have deposed the king (Charles X) July 29 after a 6-year reign and replaced him with the 56-year-old Bourbon duc d'Orléans, who will reign until 1848 as Louis Philippe. Mounted Frenchmen lead the parade down to Washington Square, and the thousands of onlookers include former president James Monroe, but some of the enthusiasm may be based on the hope, soon to be dashed, that the marquis de Lafayette will become president of a French republic.

Acting governor Enos T. Throop is elected governor in his own right, having taken over Gov. Van Buren's duties last year.

Upstate New York lawyer William Henry Seward, 29, wins election to the state senate with support from Anti-Masonic Party leader Thurlow Weed, 32, a prominent member of the "Albany Regency." When anti-Masonic fervor dies down and opponents of Jacksonian democracy form the Whig party, Seward will become a Whig (*see* 1838).

Landholder-philanthropist Henry Rutgers dies at New York February 17 at age 84. His estate in Chatham Square is valued at more than $900,000.

The New York Stock Exchange has its slowest day ever March 16: only 31 shares are traded (*see* 1825; 1865).

New York Life Insurance and Trust Co. is founded by Philadelphia-born businessman William Bard, 52, whose late father, Dr. Samuel Bard, died in 1821. It is the first company to make life insurance its primary concern rather than a sideline, and Bard will use advertising and pamphleteering to overcome initial public apathy and distrust, devising an agency system to sell policies (*see* later New York Life, 1845).

The Manhattan Gas Light Co. is incorporated February 26 to provide coal gas for streetlights and home use south of 14th Street (*see* 1823; 1826; 1855).

The Mercantile Library moves into Clinton Hall, a new building put up to house the association's growing collection (*see* 1820). The library opens to the public at the corner of Nassau and Beekman streets (*see* 1854).

Retailer Henry Sands Brooks introduces a cotton seersucker suit for summer wear (*see* 1818). The new fashion will gain wide popularity (*see* Brooks Brothers, 1850).

Connecticut-born dry-goods merchant and developer Don Alonzo Cushman, 37, purchases a large parcel of land in Chelsea and builds a house at what later will be 172 Ninth Avenue. Cushman is a friend of landowner and scholar Clement Clark Moore.

"Woodman, Spare That Tree" by newspaper editor George Pope Morris, now 28, is published in Morris's 7-year-old *New-York Mirror and Ladies' Literary Gazette*: "Woodman spare that tree./ Touch not a single bough; in youth it sheltered me,/ And I'll protect it now" (*see* Kilmer, 1913).

New York's Irish population reaches nearly 17,775, with the heaviest concentration in the Sixth Ward (what later will be Chinatown) on the Lower East Side and in the area near City Hall.

1831 Former mayor Richard Varick dies at Jersey City July 30 at age 78, having served from 1789 to 1801; former congressman Philip Van Cortlandt dies at Croton-on-Hudson November 5 at age 80.

New York has its first labor demonstrations as stone-cutters riot in protest against the use of stone cut at Sing Sing Prison (*see* 1827) for buildings of the new University of the City of New York (*see* General Trades Union, 1833).

$ The National Bank of the City of New York opens for business with Swiss-born banker Albert (Abraham Alfonse) Gallatin, 70, as its first president. Fur trader John Jacob Astor has been the chief source of the bank's capital, Gallatin has served as secretary of the treasury under Presidents Jefferson and Madison, and Astor has persuaded him to head the bank that was chartered 2 years ago (*see* Hanover, 1912).

The New York & Harlem Railroad receives an exclusive franchise to use Fourth Avenue for its operations and is chartered to run horsecars on tracks from Prince Street north along Fourth Avenue as far as Harlem. Alderman George Sharp has protested granting the franchise without charge, but Tammany Hall members have evidently received payoffs and Sharp is warned to hold his tongue. The avenue has not been developed for residential or commercial use because it has been too costly to blast away the rocks (Manhattan Schist) that line its path (*see* 1832).

A European cholera epidemic reaches New York in June as the city's shortage of uncontaminated drinking water makes residents vulnerable (although nobody yet knows the cause). Bellevue Hospital (it adopted that name 6 years ago) receives 556 cases between June 27 and July 7, and 334 have died by August 8. People stricken with the disease beg for water, Bellevue cares for some 2,000 cases—one-sixth of all victims—and registers about 600 deaths in all. The epidemic takes 3,513 lives (4,000 according to some accounts) by October, and spreads south and west.

Kings County Medical Center has its beginnings in a one-room infirmary opened in the town of Flatbush; it will be expanded in 1837 (*see* 1931).

New York University (NYU) has its beginnings in the University of the City of New York founded by some eminent private citizens in response to the example set 3 years ago with the founding of London University. Banker Albert Gallatin serves as president of the new university's governing council, whose members declare that theirs will be a "national university" offering a "rational and practical education for all" (*see* 1832; stonemason riot, 1834).

Fiction: *The Dutchman's Fireside* by James Kirke Paulding.

Theater: *The Gladiator* by U.S. playwright Robert Montgomery Bird, 25, 9/26 at the Park Theater, with Edwin Forrest as Spartacus.

The *Spirit of the Times* begins publication at New York December 10 as the city begins its career as a national center for sport. Founded by William T. Porter, it is the first comprehensive U.S. sporting journal and will continue until 1902.

A burglary March 20 at the City Bank, 52 Wall Street, northeast corner William Street, nets $200,000 in bills and Spanish doubloons for one Edward Smith, who is apprehended a week later, convicted, and sentenced to 5 years' hard labor; $175,738 of the loot is recovered.

Sailors' Snug Harbor buys 80 acres on Staten Island to provide a retirement home for seamen (*see* 1801). Morristown, N.J.-born architect Minard Lafever, 33, designs a building for the men, four other buildings plus a Veterans Memorial Hall and gatehouse will be added, and by 1900 the complex will house 900 men (the estate left by Robert Randall in 1801 will by that time be worth $50 million).

Gramercy Park is deeded by real-estate developer Samuel B. Ruggles December 17 to five trustees who are pledged to hold 42 lots between Third and Fourth avenues as parkland. The property has been part of Gramercy Farm, established in the 18th century by James Duane and still owned for the most part by his heirs, who have sold Ruggles 22 acres, minus some land that has been used for city streets (*see* 1832).

1832 The spoils system in politics gets its name January 21 in a speech delivered in the U.S. Senate by William Learned Marcy, 46 (N.Y.). Marcy speaks out in defense of former governor Martin Van Buren, who has been appointed U.S. minister to the Court of St. James; Sen. Henry Clay, 54 (Ky.), has cast aspersions on Van Buren's appointment, but Marcy has close ties to the "Albany Regency" and says, "It may be that the politicians of New York are not so fastidious as some gentlemen are. They boldly preach what they practice. When they are contending for victory, they avow their intention of enjoying the fruits of it. If they fail, they will not murmur. If they win, they expect to reap all the advantages. They see nothing wrong in the rule, that to the victor belong the spoils of the enemy." New York politicians continue as they have since at least 1801 to name cronies to government jobs and dispense favors that will enrich their friends (*see* Pendleton Civil Service Reform Act, 1883).

"A Treatise on the Practice of the Supreme Court of the State of New York" by English-born New York lawyer David Graham, 24, gains quick acceptance in the profession and will soon be the standard work on the tortuous system of pleading cases in the courts (*see* Code of Procedure, 1848). Graham is selected to serve on a committee drafting a new charter for New York City.

Sen. Marcy is elected governor. He enjoys the support of anti-Masonic voters and will twice be reelected to 2-year terms.

The city establishes a Department of Charities and Corrections to supervise conditions in its jails (*see* 1816; Blackwell's Island, 1836).

$ New York-born G. G. & S. Howland Co. clerk Moses Taylor, 26, quits his job with the South Street shipping firm that he joined at age 15, marries Catherine A. Wilson, and goes into business for himself, having amassed $15,000 in capital. He contracts with Cuban planters for the sale of their sugar and soon has a business so prosperous that it will continue to do well even after a fire in December 1835 destroys his South Street offices and nearly all his earthly possessions.

The Hudson River Day Line has its beginnings in the Hudson River Steamboat Association, a quasi-monopoly that begins night-boat service with the *James Kent* (*see* 1851).

The Erie Rail Road is chartered April 24 under the name New York and Erie Rail Road Co. by a special act of the state legislature at Albany. Legislators from counties bordering on the 7-year-old Erie Canal have opposed building a railroad south of that canal; they have approved the charter measure only on terms requiring that the railroad not connect with any out-of-state road (it is to run from the small town of Piermont on the west bank of the Hudson to the small town of Dunkirk on the shore of Lake Erie), that the new company raise $10 million, and that it not organize on a formal basis until half its stock is subscribed to (*see* 1851).

The Long Island Rail Road has its beginnings in the Brooklyn & Jamaica Railroad Co. Incorporated April 25; it begins construction of a 10-mile line along Atlantic Avenue from the East River to Jamaica with the ultimate purpose of creating a rail-ferry-rail link from New York to Boston via Long Island's North Fork (*see* 1836).

Manhattan's grid plan of 1811 is modified by law to permit cutting through of Lexington Avenue and will be modified next year to permit cutting through of Madison Avenue (*see* 1836). The Commissioners' Plan assumed that most of Manhattan's traffic would flow from river to river and has included many more streets than avenues per mile.

The New York and Harlem Railroad goes into service November 14—the first New York City street railway (*see* 1831). Two horse-drawn cars travel up and down the Bowery between Prince and 14th Streets on tracks slotted deep into the pavement. Built by coachmaker John Stephenson, the horsecars that replace Abraham Bower's 5-year-old "accommodation" have a capacity of 40 passengers each, attain speeds of 12 miles per hour, run every 15 minutes, charge a 25¢ fare, and will soon move up and down Fourth Avenue (*see* 1834).

New York inventor Walter Hunt, 36, devises a modern sewing machine whose needle has an eye in its point that pushes thread through cloth to interlock with a second thread carried by a shuttle. Hunt does not obtain a patent, and when he suggests in 1838 that his daughter Caroline, then 15, go into business making corsets with his machine, she will protest that it would put needy seamstresses out of work (*see* Singer, 1851; Hunt's safety pin, 1849).

The first buildings of New York University (University of the City of New York) are completed in the vicinity of Washington Square Park (*see* 1831). Construction will continue until 1835 (*see* 1894; stonemason riot, 1834).

New York University art professor Samuel F. B. Morse begins development of an electric telegraph that will speed communication (*see* 1827; 1837).

Nonfiction: *Domestic Manners of the Americans* by English novelist Frances Milton Trollope, 52, who came to America with her barrister husband 5 years ago to open a business at Cincinnati: "On the first of May the city of New York has the appearance of sending off a population flying from the plague, or of a town which has surrendered on condition of carrying away all their goods and chattels. Rich furniture and ragged furniture, carts, waggons, and drays, ropes, canvas, and straw, packers, porters, and draymen, white, yellow, and black, occupy the streets from east to west, from north to south, on this day. Every one I spoke to on the subject complained of this custom as the most annoying, but all assured me it was unavoidable, if you inhabit a rented house." Leases have been signed on May 1 (or, sometimes, October 1) since colonial days, and tenants will continue to move May 1 in an effort to find cheaper rents until housing shortages are alleviated.

Poet Fitz-Greene Halleck enters John Jacob Astor's counting house May 15 and will continue in Astor's employ until 1848, when he will receive an annuity of $200 under the terms of Astor's will.

New York-born minstrel-show pioneer Thomas Dartmouth "Daddy" Rice, 24, introduces the city to "Jim Crow," a blackface song-and-dance act that won 20 encores when he presented it at Louisville, Ky., 4 years ago. Having seen an elderly, deformed slave named Jim Crow perform a little jump while working in a livery stable near Louisville's City Theater, Rice reproduced the young man's hop and song: "Wheelabout, turn about,/ Do jes so/ An' every time I wheel about/ I jump Jim Crow."

Union Square gets its name through a renaming of the 3.48-acre field that was indicated in the commissioners' plan of 1811 as Union Place (because it unites Broadway and Fourth Avenue). A gated park has made the square attractive to affluent homeowners.

The Board of Aldermen agrees February 13 to grant tax exemption to Gramercy Park (see 1831). Developer Samuel Ruggles has argued that the tax exemption will actually boost the city's tax revenues by increasing the value of the 66 lots surrounding the park, and he obtains the Board's promise to levy no taxes on the property as long as the property is maintained purely as an ornamental square. Ruggles also obtains a 30-year lease on all the lots along Fourth Avenue from 15th Street to just north of 19th, with rights to renew the leases for another 50 years (see 1833).

A second Delmonico's Restaurant opens at 494 Pearl Street to augment the one at 23 and 25 William Street, New York (see 1827). John and Peter Delmonico have anglicized their names and bring over their nephew Lorenzo to help them in their enterprise (see 1837).

1833 Massachusetts-born leather merchant and city alderman Gideon Lee wins appointment as mayor; now 55, he has received help from Tammany Hall (but see 1834).

The General Trades' Union of the City of New York (GTU) is founded August 14 to unite several trade societies and obtains wage increases; trade unionism begins to supersede workingmen's political parties, but the movement will collapse in the financial panic and economic depression 4 years from now (see 1834; 1864).

The American Anti-Slavery Society founded by abolitionists at Philadelphia December 4 names New Yorker Arthur Tappan as its first president. Parliament has voted August 23 to abolish slavery in the British colonies as of August 1, 1834; agitation increases at New York and other northern cities to follow suit (see 1834).

Columbia College graduate James William Beekman, 17, inherits a fortune upon the death of his uncle James Beekman. Included is the family estate on the East River where the Beekman mansion has stood since before the Revolution.

Phelps, Dodge & Co. is founded by New York metals trader Anson Greene Phelps, 51, whose warehouse at Clift and Fulton streets collapsed last year. He takes into partnership his 27-year-old son-in-law William Earl Dodge, a dry-goods merchant who last year married Phelps's daughter Melissa; Dodge will acquire timberlands in Georgia, Canada, and Wisconsin and buy copper mines on Lake Superior (see 1872).

The Greenwich Savings Bank opens as the success of the 14-year-old Bank for Savings inspires others to follow its lead. The population of Greenwich Village has expanded rapidly since the yellow fever epidemic of 1822, and the new bank, like others that will open hereafter, departs from the "philanthropic" objectives previously espoused by savings banks to focus on making profits.

The Bowery Savings Bank is founded by New York businessmen whose "bank of the little people" will grow to become the nation's largest savings bank.

Brooks Brothers takes the name H. and D. H. Brooks & Co. upon the death of founder Henry Sands Brooks at age 61 (see 1850; seersucker suit, 1830).

The shipping firm Grinnell, Minturn & Co. is founded by Henry Grinnell, 34, his brother Moses Hicks Grinnell, 31, and their brother-in-law Robert Bowne Minturn, 28, who have reorganized the firm started by Joseph Grinnell with Preserved Fish in 1815. Their swallowtail flag will fly over more than 50 vessels as they develop regular packet-line service to London and Liverpool (see Flying Cloud, 1851).

McKesson & Robbins has its beginnings in the wholesale pharmaceutical drug firm McKesson & Olcott opened in Maiden Lane by New York-born pharmacist John McKesson, 26, and Charles M. Olcott. D. C. Robbins will be admitted to the partnership, the firm will become McKesson & Robbins when Olcott dies in 1853, and by the time McKesson retires in 1884 the firm will have a nationwide drug-distribution business. It will be incorporated at New York in 1916 and McKesson's family will retain an interest in it until 1925 (see commerce, 1938).

St. Nicholas Kirche is founded in East 2nd Street by Austrian priest Johann Stephen Raffeiner, who establishes the city's first German Catholic congregation (see 1842).

The *New-York Sun* begins publication September 3. Launched by printer Benjamin H. (Henry) Day, 23, at 222 William Street, it is the city's (and the world's) first successful penny daily (the competition charges 6¢). Day seeks to expand the field for his one-man press; he puts together a four-page inaugural issue with the help of one journeyman printer and a "devil," prints 1,000 copies, and soon hires George W. Wismer, an unemployed printer, as his first reporter. Circulation of the 8¼" × 11" paper will rise to 8,000 within a year, it will get a boost in 1835 when its chief reporter perpetrates a hoax telling of the discovery by a British astronomer of orangutan-like creatures hopping about on the moon, and Day will acquire an abolitionist writer whose views on slavery do not quite jibe with his own, although he himself is opposed to slavery (see 1838). Day's son and namesake will invent the Ben Day process for shading in printed illustrations.

Painting: *Catskill Scenery* by Thomas Cole.

Opera: The Italian Opera House opens 11/18 at the corner of Church and Leonard streets with a performance of Gioacchino Rossini's *La Gazza Ladra* (see 1825). Backed by investors who include Philip Hone, Dominick Lynch, and Lorenzo da Ponte, now 84, and built on the European plan at a cost of $150,000, the white, blue, and gold auditorium of the city's first opera house is composed entirely of boxes and boasts fine acoustics, and it has a magnificent chandelier; its company has a season of 80 performances that will continue until 7/21 of next year, but the house will end with a deficit of $29,275, be turned into an ordinary legitimate theater (the National) in 1836, and burn down in 1839. Neither New York nor any other city in America will have a comparable venue for opera until 1883 (see 1844).

A new St. Mary's Church is completed at 438 Grand Street, west of Pitt Street, to replace the previous Roman Catholic Church on the site that was burned down in 1828 by bigots fearful of the Catholic Church's "dangerous interests." The congregation is largely Irish but may sometimes include some Germans and Poles; its gray ashlar stone building will be enlarged in 1871 with a new red-brick façade and twin spires designed by church architect Patrick Charles Keely, and it will survive as the city's oldest Roman Catholic Church.

La Grange Terrace (Colonnade Row) is completed in Lafayette Street south of Astor Place. Probably designed by developer Seth Greer and named for the marquis de Lafayette's estate in France, the nine Greek Revival residences have marble fronts that are unified by a two-store colonnade of 27 Corinthian columns cut by Sing Sing prisoners at Ossining from gleaming Westchester marble.

Gramercy Park developer Samuel B. Ruggles obtains approval from the Board of Aldermen January 28 to open Fourth Avenue to something besides rail traffic (see 1832). Ruggles saw as early as 1825 that the city's growing population would have to expand north of 14th Street and began investing in land that other developers had spurned because it was too far north; borrowing from banks and individuals, he has not only been developing the 66 lots surrounding Gramercy Park but also a collection of vacant lots from 14th Street to 17th between Broadway and Fourth Avenue (see Lexington Avenue, 1836).

A fire in Greenwich Village April 30 destroys 90 to 100 buildings in an area surrounding Hudson and Greenwich streets.

1834 New York voters elect their first mayor by popular vote in April (mayors up to now have been appointed, not elected, and have had little power): Tammany Hall has rejected incumbent Gideon Lee because he has shown partiality to the Bank of United States, and in place of that banker (and Tammany sachem) has nominated Jacksonian Democrat Cornelius Van Wyck Lawrence, 43, a congressman who narrowly defeats former congressman Gulian Crommelin Verplanck, 48, a Whig. The 3-day election begins with heavy rain, but one observer notes, "To such a fever heat had the public feeling been carried, that no one seemed to heed the storm . . . The stores were closed, business of all kinds suspended . . . Men stood in long lines, extending clear out into the streets, patiently enduring the pelting rain, waiting till their turn came to vote." Tammany Hall has posted beefy guards at the polls, and they bar entry to all except those with Tammany approval, who are admitted through back doors. Riots rage from April 8 to 11, with as many as 10,000 to 15,000 Whigs and Democrats fighting in various parts of the city (most notably in the racially mixed Sixth Ward), and at one point some Tammany toughs break into the Whig command post, attack those inside with clubs and knives, severely wound a considerable number, stab one to death, smash furniture, tear down banners, and destroy ballots. The mob attacks the state arsenal, and the military is finally brought in to suppress the disorders.

Brooklynites elect painter-glazier George Hall, 39, for a 1-year term as the city's first mayor following adoption of a municipal charter (see 1816).

John Jacob Astor's fur business made him a fortune that he multiplied in real estate. LIBRARY OF CONGRESS

Mexico, Britain, and the Mediterranean countries, has a capitalization of $200,000, and will soon have a virtual monopoly on trade with Venezuela (*see* transportation [Pacific Railroad & Panama Steamship Co.], 1848).

John Jacob Astor sells his fur interests as pelts threaten to become scarce (*see* 1801). Beaver pelts have sold for $6 apiece in peak years, enabling trappers to make $1,000 per season, but the fur companies have charged enormous prices for supplies hauled from St. Louis to summer rendezvous points, so while the beaver has been nearly exterminated none of the trappers have made fortunes. Now 71, Astor has monopolized the upper Missouri Valley fur trade, made himself the richest man in America, and will now devote his efforts to administering his fortune, much of which he will invest in New York real estate (*see* hotel, 1836).

The New York & Harlem Railroad extends its horse-car route up Fourth Avenue to 84th Street (*see* 1832). The railroad's engineers have dug a cut through Murray Hill to spare draft horses from having to pull loads up the slope, but the rocky promontory of Mount Pleasant blocks further progress between 92nd and 94th streets (*see* 1837).

Cornelius van Derbilt begins to multiply the $500,000 he has amassed in the steamboat trade (*see* 1829; 1850).

Brooklyn-born seminary graduate John McCloskey, 23, is ordained a Roman Catholic secular priest January 12, becoming the first man born in the metropolitan area to be so ordained. He will tour Europe before taking up his duties in 1837 as pastor of St. Joseph's Church (*see* 1864; Fordham University, 1841).

The *New Yorker Staats-Zeitung* has its beginnings in the German-language weekly *Der Freischuetz* that starts publication at New York under the direction of Wilhelm Newmann (*see* 1845).

Poetry: "Bronx" by Joseph Rodman Drake sings the praises of his boyhood home: "Yes, I will look upon thy face again,/ My own romantic Bronx, and it will be/ A face more pleasant than the face of men."

Painting: *The Course of Empire: The Savage State* by Thomas Cole.

Unskilled New York workers demonstrate against abolitionists, fearing that they will be displaced by black freedmen (*see* 1833). Rioters break up an anti-slavery society meeting at the Chatham Street Chapel July 4, protesting the presence of some blacks in the audience; the rioting continues for more than a week, Lewis Tappan's house is sacked, and the mob destroys other houses and churches (*see* 1840; Cinqué, 1839).

New York's General Trades Union organizes a National Trades Union that takes in all crafts (*see* 1833; 1850).

Merchants Gardiner G. and Samuel Howland turn over their 18-year-old New York mercantile house to William E. (Edgar) Howland and their sister Susan's son William H. (Henry) Aspinwall, 26, whose sea-captain father died before he was born. Largest general trading, exporting, and importing firm in the city, it has built up a heavy trade with

Utica-born portrait painter Henry Inman, 32, returns from a 3-year stay in Philadelphia and completes four mayoral portraits for City Hall; Inman opened a studio in Vesey Street at age 20.

St. Joseph's Church is completed for a Roman Catholic congregation at 365 Sixth Avenue, northwest corner Washington Place, to designs by John Doran.

Congregation Shearith Israel consecrates a new, gas-lit synagogue in Crosby Street (*see* 1820). It sold off its old Mill Street synagogue last year (*see* 1897).

The first Fifth Avenue mansion goes up at the northeast corner of 9th Street for landowner's son Henry Brevoort, Jr., who has profited on Wall Street from investments based on real-estate sales. His almost square house at No. 24 is of neo-classical design, has spacious rooms, boasts a garden surrounded by a wrought-iron fence, will stand until 1925 (its stable will survive only until 1903), and will lead within the year to more such houses erected by a dozen other rich families. They call it "the Fifth Avenue" and will make it the city's most desirable residential address; by 1836 lots fronting on Fifth Avenue at Union Square will be fetching as much as $57,000 each (lots in the block between 16th and 17th streets, from Union Square to Fifth Avenue, will bring as much as $197,000).

Tompkins Square Park has its beginnings as the city condemns and buys property on the Lower East Side that has belonged to John Jacob Astor and other landowners. The park will serve nearby residents, who now include mostly lower-middle-class immigrants, including many Irish shipbuilders (*see* riot, 1874).

Farms and gardens still occupy five-sixths of Manhattan's land area.

1835 *New-York Evening Post* editor William Leggett, 33, calls for political reforms that will abolish the legal favoritism accorded economic monopolists against the interests of working people. Leggett's biting editorials lead to the formation of the Equal Rights Party, an egalitarian faction of the Democrats who dissent from Tammany Hall's pro-business positions. Tammany's official nominating committee calls a meeting for October 29 to ratify its slate of candidates, but when Equal Rights supporters arrive at the Wigwam they find right-wing officials already there and endorsing the ticket. Demanding to be heard, the insurgents are declared out of order but charge the dais and eject the right-wingers, who repair to a nearby tavern to complete their nominating process. One of them steals back into the Wigwam's basement and turns off the gas, leaving the Long Room in darkness, but the Equal Rights men have come prepared with candles and self-lighting matches, called "loco-focos," they nominate their

own slate of candidates, opposing the election of alderman Isaac Leggett Varian, 43, as grand sachem (chairman), and they adopt a platform calling for an end to chartered monopolies and exclusive privileges, endorsing President Jackson's denunciations of "shinplaster" paper money and his actions against the Bank of the United States. Members of the Equal Rights Party will be called, derisively, Loco-Focos.

Mayor Cornelius W. Lawrence wins easy reelection, with 17,696 of the total 20,196 votes cast (down from a total of 34,989 last year).

A great fire that rages out of control December 16 to 17 forces banks to suspend payments. Insurance companies cannot pay claims, business firms are unable to rebuild, hundreds of people are thrown out of work, and prices rise, but the Tammany Hall-dominated Common Council authorizes loans totalling only $6 million at 5 percent to banks and insurance companies, and nothing is done to relieve distress among the poor whose lives have been shattered by the fire (*see* 1837).

The Merchants' Exchange is virtually destroyed by the fire that guts many buildings. Brown Brothers founder James Brown sold the dry-goods part of his business last year following the death of his father and moved earlier this year from Pine Street to 46 (later 58) Wall Street, opposite the Merchants' Exchange (*see* 1825; 1843).

The *New-York Herald* begins publication May 6 under the direction of Scots-born journalist James Gordon Bennett, 40, as a rival to the *Morning Sun*. Bennett has started the 1¢ newspaper with $500, two wooden chairs, and an old dry goods box in a cellar office; he announces in his first issue that the *Herald* will be a "saucy" paper with "good taste,

Fire destroyed much of downtown New York, but a new city rose from the ashes. HARPER'S WEEKLY

brevity, variety, point, and piquancy" intended for "the great masses of the community." His four-column pages include the first financial page (Bennett covers Wall Street himself), but will also be the first to give full coverage to murder trials, including questions and answers from court proceedings. Pandering to the lowest tastes, giving emphasis to crime, scandal, and sex, the *Herald* quickly gains a wide circulation.

Scottish merchant-horticulturist George Douglas acquires the Queens estate of Wyant Van Zandt at what later will be called Douglaston (*see* 1819; 1866).

A fire in Fulton, Nassau, and Ann streets August 12 kills five people and destroys 35 houses; a much worse fire breaks out December 16, and although fire chief James "Handsome Jim" Gulick and his men receive help from organized bucket brigades to keep it from spreading north of Wall Street the fire rages out of control in the commercial, pier, and warehouse area of Wall, Broad, and South streets, destroying a marble statue of Alexander Hamilton. It ignites turpentine inside warehouses along the East River, the river itself becomes a blazing sea, and gale-force winds blow debris over Brooklyn. Manhattan's Dutch Riverside Church catches fire and burns down while an organist inside plays a funeral dirge until he is consumed by the flames. Mobs come down from the Five Points to loot, and a man caught setting fire to a house at the corner of Stone and Broad streets is lynched from a tree. Rioters fight over French hats, Manchester woollens, and baskets of Champagne, but one merchant saves his goods by stopping the driver of a horse cart and paying the man $500 to haul away the contents of his store. The conflagration is visible for miles, volunteer firefighters arrive by ferry from Brooklyn, Newark, and Jersey City, 400 come from Philadelphia, the mercury plunges to 3° F., pumping engines freeze, water freezes in cisterns, in hydrants, and in the leather hoses, and although covered with ice some of the 1,900 firemen are singed while others nearby suffer frostbite. The fire continues well into the next day, destroying the Merchants' Exchange, the Post Office, and the Stock Exchange until explosives are finally used to create fire stops following a consultation with Mayor Lawrence. The flames have leveled 13 acres in the heart of the city's commercial and financial district, destroyed 674 buildings, many of them in Hanover and Pearl Streets, caused damage estimated at between $20 million and $40 million (*see* insurance companies, 1836), reduced one-quarter of Manhattan to cinders, and left many hundreds of people homeless (but only two dead) and more than 4,000 out of work. Lack of water

pressure needed to fight the flames is blamed for much of the damage (*see* Croton aqueduct, 1837). Tammany Hall ward leaders distribute Christmas food baskets, firewood, clothing, and money to the needy in their neighborhoods.

1836 Former U.S. minister to France Edward Livingston dies on his Dutchess County estate May 23 at age 71; former president James Monroe at New York July 4 at age 73. His New York-born wife, Elizabeth (*née* Kortwright), died 6 years ago and he came to the city in October of that year to live with his daughter and son-in-law Samuel Gouverneur in their home at the northeast corner of Lafayette and Prince streets. Monroe's funeral service at St. Paul's Episcopal Church July 7 is the most elaborate held up to now in the city, and he is buried after a funeral procession up Broadway to the walled-in New York Marble Cemetery, completed 4 years ago in East 2nd Street between First and Second avenues (a slightly older Marble Cemetery is in the block bounded by 2nd and 3rd streets between Second Avenue and the Bowery; Monroe's remains will be reinterred at Richmond, Va., in 1858).

Vice President Martin Van Buren is elected to the presidency with support from outgoing President Jackson. Now 53, the New Yorker receives more popular votes than his four opponents combined,

Ferries across the East River and North River connected New Yorkers with Brooklyn and New Jersey.

winning 170 electoral votes to 124 for all the others, but his margin of victory in New York City is only 1,124.

Mayor Cornelius W. Lawrence wins reelection to a third term, defeating Whig Seth Geer, Equal Rights (Loco-Foco) Party candidate Alexander Ming, Jr., and Native Party candidate Samuel F. B. Morse.

The Ancient Order of Hibernians is chartered in May on the Lower East Side as Irish Catholic parishioners organize a fraternal order to protect the Church of St. James, the Mass, and the priest from persecution (*see* 1831). The AOH will become a nationwide organization.

The Orphan Asylum Society founded in 1806 moves its orphanage to a large new building overlooking the Hudson River at 73rd Street, where it has room to accommodate 200 children (*see* 1899).

The Colored Orphan Asylum opens on Fifth Avenue between 43rd and 44th streets. Started by Mary Murray and Anna Shotwell, it will be managed entirely by women for more than a century as a shelter for black children, fewer than a third of whom will actually be orphans. Most of the children are returned to their parents at age 12 or given positions as domestic servants or farm workers (*see* 1867; draft riots, 1863).

Twenty-three of the city's 26 fire-insurance companies file for bankruptcy protection as claims mount for losses sustained in last year's disastrous fire in downtown Manhattan. Some banks also fail, the insurance companies cannot pay what they owe, but textile merchant Arthur Tappan collects $300,000 from a Boston company that insures abolitionists whereas New York companies will not. Prices rise further in the wake of the fire. By autumn the price of flour has risen to $7 per barrel; it then goes to $12, and bread has become scarce (*see* 1837).

The South Ferry begins service across the East River to link Whitehall Street with Brooklyn's Atlantic Street (*see* 1814; 1846).

New York-born naval architect William Henry Webb, 20, opens a shipyard that he will continue in the city until 1869 (*see* 1869).

Lexington Avenue opens north from Gramercy Park to 42nd Street, cutting in between Fourth Avenue (formerly the Boston Post Road) and Third Avenue (*see* 1832). Developer Samuel Ruggles has petitioned the city's Street Committee to create the thoroughfare that runs in part through land he owns; named after the first battle of the American Revolution, it will be extended next year to the Harlem River.

Madison Avenue opens north from 26th Street to 42nd Street, cutting between Fourth and Fifth avenues (Madison Square); it will be extended to 124th Street by 1869. Begun 10 years ago as Madison Street, it is renamed Madison Avenue following the death of former President James Madison at his Montpelier estate in Virginia June 28 at age 85.

The Bellevue jail on First Avenue at 26th Street has an epidemic of puerperal peritonitis. Massachusetts-born physician Alonzo Clark, 43, prescribes large doses of opium and brandy, reducing the death rate to zero (*see* 1847).

The former Reformed Scots Presbyterian Church in Chambers and Park streets is rededicated March 31 by Cuban-born religious and political reformer Felix Varela, 48, who heads one of two branches of the former Christ Church and has renamed the Scots church the Church of the Transfiguration. Since most of his parishioners are poor residents of the Five Points area, Father Varela finances the church out of his own income, gained from publishing ventures, and with money obtained from family and friends.

Union Theological Seminary has its beginnings in the New York Theological Seminary, established in a house at 8 Bond Street in May by Presbyterians who embrace revivalism, eschewing strict adherence to confessional standards and attracting some notable New Yorkers (*see* 1884; Lenox, 1840).

Publisher John Wiley hires George P. Putnam, 22, as junior partner (*see* 1807). Now 28, he and Putnam will prosper together until Putnam leaves in 1848, gaining prominence with works by major American and European novelists (*see* 1891; Putnam, 1866).

Painting: *The Course of Empire: The Consummation of Empire* and *The Course of Empire: Destruction* by Thomas Cole, who is creating a series for his Coxsackie, N.Y.-born patron Luman Reed, a merchant with a private gallery at 61 Bleecker Street in New York City; *The Wrath of Peter Stuyvesant*, *The Pedlar Displaying His Wares*, *Boys Playing Marbles*, *School Let Out*, and *Blind Man's Buff* by Asher Durand.

The Union Club is founded by a group of socially prominent New York men who may have taken the name from that of a London club. The socialites include Philip Hone, begin with rooms at 343 Broadway, and will move farther uptown by stages (*see* 1903).

The Jewett murder April 10 excites New Yorkers, who read accounts of the case written personally by James Gordon Bennett in his 11-month-old *New-*

York Herald. Circumstantial evidence is brought forward to show that shop clerk Richard P. Robinson, 19, took an axe into a house of assignation at 41 Thomas Street late at night and shattered the skull of Maine-born prostitute Helen Jewett (originally Dorcas Doyen), 22, lest she betray the fact that he has embezzled funds from a trusting employer. The murderer has set fire to the body of a woman famed as much for her wit, independence, learning (she has been fond of novels by Sir Walter Scott), and green silk dress as for her charm and beauty. Bennett sets out to prove that Robinson was innocent of her murder, former district attorney Ogden Hoffman mounts a brilliant defense, and a jury finds Robinson not guilty after a sensational trial at City Hall that has seen spectators fight to get in; *Herald* readers have been appalled to learn the extent of the prostitution trade that flourishes quite openly in the city. Formerly concentrated in a few areas such as the "holy ground" beside St. Paul's Church, on what later will be City Hall Park, the prostitutes may now be found in many other neighborhoods (*see* 1850). Robinson soon makes his way to Texas, where the "Great Unhung" will spend most of his remaining years under an assumed name.

The 4-year-old Department of Charities and Corrections opens a penitentiary on Blackwell's Island. The 20-year-old Bellevue jail on First Avenue at 26th Street is turned over to use as a jail for female inmates (*see* Tombs, 1838).

 The Astor House opens June 1 at the northwest corner of Broadway and Vesey Streets and sets new standards of hotel luxury. Financed by fur merchant-turned-developer John Jacob Astor, now 73, and built of Quincy granite with a central courtyard, the five-story structure has a vast rotunda that will be a popular luncheon spot for the city's merchants. The hotel will stand until 1926.

The Eastern Pearl Street House opens at the southwest corner of the junction of Pearl Street, Ferry Street, and Peck Slip, where it will remain in operation for well over a century (the five-story hostelry will be renamed the Hartford in the late 1860s when it receives guests coming off steamboats from Hartford and other New England ports that dock at Peck Slip).

Developers rebuild the area devastated by last year's fire in lower Manhattan. Appeals from Boston, Philadelphia, and other cities have persuaded Congress for the first time to appropriate funds for such a purpose, and by year's end the total value of city real estate has climbed to $233 million, up from $143 million before the fire.

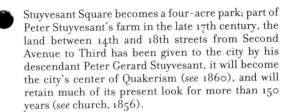 Stuyvesant Square becomes a four-acre park; part of Peter Stuyvesant's farm in the late 17th century, the land between 14th and 18th streets from Second Avenue to Third has been given to the city by his descendant Peter Gerard Stuyvesant; it will become the city's center of Quakerism (*see* 1860), and will retain much of its present look for more than 150 years (*see* church, 1856).

Delmonico's reopens in temporary quarters at 494 Pearl Street following destruction of its William Street premises in last year's fire. The menu issued by the 5-year-old establishment calls itself a "bill of fare;" the first American restaurant menu (a word that will not be coined until next year), it offers a "regular dinner" at 12¢ and charges 10¢ for hamburger steak (the same price as roast chicken or ham and eggs; regular beef steak is only 4¢, as are pork chops, corn beef and cabbage, pigs head and cabbage, and fried fish. Roast beef or veal, roast mutton, veal cutlet, or chicken stew is 5¢) (*see* 1837).

1837 Massachusetts-born New York State comptroller Silas Wright, 41, wins a special January 4 election for the unexpired U.S. Senate seat of Gov. William L. Marcy. Wright supported former governor Martin Van Buren's presidential bid last year.

A mass meeting in City Hall Park called by the Equal Rights (Loco-Foco) Party in February protests undue profits made by bankers and merchants at the expense of workingmen and shopkeepers. The large crowd becomes restless during a speech about hard and soft money, but when another speaker accuses local flour merchants of hoarding a mob of some 200 leaves the park and advances on the Washington Street warehouse of Eli Hart & Co. a few blocks away; the mob batters down the doors, seizes nearly 500 barrels of flour and 1,000 bushels of wheat, throws or rolls them out of the building, and empties the barrels in the street, where the flour and wheat are grabbed by others. Another such merchant is similarly ransacked until constables can restore order.

Whig lawyer Aaron Clark, 53, becomes the city's second directly elected mayor, defeating Democrat John I. Morgan and Equal Rights (Loco-Foco) Party candidate Moses Jacques with 16,140 votes to 12,974 for Morgan, 3,911 for Jacques as New York's economy falters.

Economic depression begins nationwide following the failure in March of a New Orleans cotton brokerage. Inflated land values, speculation, and wildcat banking have contributed to the crisis, the Wall Street firm J. L. & S. Joseph & Co. fails March 17 (it represents the Rothschilds in Europe, and a large granite building under construction for the firm has collapsed 3 days earlier), New York banks suspend specie payments May 10, financial panic ensues, at least 800 U.S. banks suspend specie payment, 618 banks fail before the year is out (many have deceived bank inspectors as to the amount of gold backing their banknotes), specie disappears from circulation, and employers pay workers in paper "shinplasters" of dubious value and often counterfeit until New York banker Albert Gallatin, now 76, uses his influence to persuade his colleagues to resume specie payment. Philip Hone has signed a good deal of paper to get two sons started in business and loses a substantial part of his fortune (he will go back to work as head of the American Mutual Insurance Co. but it will go bankrupt) (see 1839).

The financial crisis leaves one-third of New Yorkers who subsist by manual labor unemployed, at least 10,000 become dependent on almshouses, but those institutions are unable to prevent many from starving to death. The depression wipes out the more than 50 confederated unions whose members have included two-thirds of the city's workingmen.

Frankfurt banker August Schönberg, 20, hears of the financial panic in New York while en route to Havana to transact business for the younger Meyer Rothschild. Schönberg completes his Cuban business, sends in his resignation to Frankfurt but offers to act as agent for the Rothschilds, sails for New York, rents a small office in Wall Street, changes his name to Belmont (the French version of Schönberg, meaning "beautiful mountain"), becomes an Episcopalian, and although virtually without capital is able to take over bankrupt firms and begin a business that will grow into a powerful banking house.

Retail merchant James McCreery opens a Canal Street dry-goods store selling silk and other imported fabrics and dress materials. McCreery's will move uptown to Broadway and 11th Street and thereafter to the southeast corner of Sixth Avenue and West 23rd Street, where it will continue for more than 20 years before moving to 34th Street (see Ohrbachs, 1954).

Tiffany & Co. has its beginnings in a "Stationery and Fancy Goods Store" opened September 18 near City Hall. Merchant Charles Lewis Tiffany, 25, began as a Yankee peddler and knows nothing about gemstones; he has borrowed $1,000 from his father in Connecticut, he and his partner John B. Young stock Chinese bric-a-brac, pottery, and umbrellas as well as stationery, total receipts for the first 3 days are $4.98, and profits after a full week total only 33¢, but the firm will grow to be one of the world's most prestigious jewelry retailers (see 1847).

The New York & Harlem Railroad reaches suburban Harlem with its horsecars and buys its first steam locomotive, making it the world's first urban steam transit line (see 1834). The company's engineers have succeeded in blasting a 596-foot tunnel deep below Observatory Place, permitting the two-track line to reach the Harlem flats. A station built at 86th Street will facilitate development of Yorkville, a village in upper Manhattan that has been connected only by stagecoach to the city several miles south (see Fordham, 1841).

White Plains-born entrepreneur Thomas Cornell, 23, begins carrying coal on his Hudson River sloop from Rondout (later part of Kingston) to New York City, beginning an enterprise that will develop into the Cornell Steamboat Co., with a virtual monopoly in the business of towing barges up and down the Hudson. By buying out or forcing out competition, the company will become the largest organization of its kind in America, with 60 steam towboats and tugs pulling barges laden not only with coal but also baled hay for the city's thousands of horses, wheat for its millers, ice harvested from upstate lakes and rivers for its iceboxes, Ulster County bluestone for its sidewalks, brick from the Hudson River Valley and Rosendale cement for its buildings.

Samuel F. B. Morse gives a public demonstration at New York of a magnetic telegraph he invented 5 years ago and is granted a U.S. patent September 23. New Jersey-born mechanic Alfred Lewis Vail, 29, sees the demonstration, persuades Morse to take him into partnership making telegraphic instruments, and devises a "Morse code" using dots and dashes to represent letters in place of an earlier system that assigned numbers to letters (see 1842).

Real estate developer John Jacob Astor takes advantage of the financial panic to buy up distressed properties in midtown Manhattan and elsewhere, foreclosing on hundreds of properties whose mortgages he holds or obtains. Astor's summer home "Astoria" (or "Hell Gate Farm") is at what later will be 87th Street between York and East End avenues.

Work begins in May on an aqueduct to carry water 41 miles to the city from the Croton River in northern Westchester (see fire, 1835). Farmers have resisted, but the state legislature at Albany has given the city the right to condemn land for the acqueduct, West Point engineering professor Major David B. Douglass has initiated its design and placement, bankers who include the Rothschilds in Europe have raised

$12 million to finance the project, and by next year some 4,000 men will be working on the project. The City Water Commission will replace Douglass in 1839 with Erie Canal veteran John B. Jervis, and he will see the project through to completion, paying laborers—most of them Irish immigrants—75¢ to $1 per 10-hour day to build a 270-foot-long, 50-foot-high dam that creates a 400-acre lake six miles above the junction of the Croton and Hudson rivers with a storage capacity of about 660 million gallons. By January 1841 Jervis will have completed about 32 miles of the waterway, including a massive 88-foot-long double stone arch bridge across the Sing Sing Kill in downtown Ossining and a brick-lined tube consisting of 12 tunnels, each 8-feet high and 7-feet wide, with an aggregate length of 4,406 feet (*see* 1842).

Delmonico's Restaurant reopens at the corner of William and Beaver Streets (*see* 1836). The new place is far more splendid, with marble columns from Pompeii, a main dining room with a three-story ceiling, private dining rooms, lounge, and ballroom. John and Peter's nephew Lorenzo Delmonico, now 24, goes to the market early each morning to select the freshest produce, freshest seafood, and best cuts of meat; the European cooks and recipes he imports for the establishment will popularize green vegetables, salads, and ices (*see* 1845).

1838 State Senator William H. Seward wins election as governor on the Whig ticket with support from party leader Thurlow Weed. Now 38, Seward defeats Gov. William Learned Marcy's bid for a fourth term.

New York City's mayor Aaron Clark narrowly wins reelection, securing 19,723 votes to 19,204 for his Democratic rival Isaac L. Varian of Tammany Hall.

The 24-year-old Association for the Relief of Respectable Aged Indigent Females moves into its first residence at 226 East 20th Street (*see* 1883).

Lord & Taylor moves into a four-story building at 61–63 Catherine Street, offering "Irish linens, sheeting, diapers, shawls, laces, gloves, silk and cotton hosiery, &c. &c. &c." (*see* 1826; 1853).

Knox Hat Co. is founded at 110 Fulton Street by merchant Charles Knox, whose firm will become the best known of its kind (*see* 1902).

Manhattan's numbered streets are divided into east and west numbers according to which side of Fifth Avenue they are on.

Two British steamers arrive at New York April 23 after the first transatlantic crossings by ships pow-

ered entirely by steam. The 703-ton paddle wheeler S.S. *Sirius*, 19 days out of Cork, arrives in the morning, the 1,440-ton paddle wheeler S.S. *Great Western*, 15 days out of Bristol, in the afternoon. Used until now only for English Channel crossings, the *Sirius* has been chartered by Connecticut-born London lawyer and promoter Junius Smith, 57, who in 1832 was on a British sailing ship that took 54 days to reach New York and 4 years later organized the British & American Steam Navigation Co. in 1836 with backing from British shipbuilder and explorer Macgregor Laird, 30 (New York investors scoffed at his idea for a transatlantic steamship company). Smith and Laird's little ship averaged 8.03 knots on the crossing but is considered too small for such service and will be used between Cork and Dublin (*see British Queen*, 1839); the *Great Western* has averaged 9.52 knots and goes into service for Britain's Great Western Railway Co. English engineer Isambard Kingdom Brunel, 32, has designed both ships.

Steamboat and railroad pioneer John Stevens dies at Hoboken March 6 at age 88; Erie Canal planner James Geddes at Geddes, N.Y., August 19 at age 75.

Irish-born Jesuit priest John Joseph Hughes, 40, is consecrated coadjutor bishop of New York January 7 under the ailing John DuBois. Hughes came to the city as a laborer from the north of Ireland and has championed the interests of working people, but his traditional views will not appeal to most working-class Irish immigrants.

Bishop Hughes demands state aid for Catholic schools, calling for a return to the system that prevailed before 1826, when the state stopped funding denominational schools. The Public School Society controls public education in the city, allocating state funds on the basis of a "common" understanding of Protestant Christianity (*see* 1840; Maclay Bill, 1842).

The Apprentice Library that will become the Brooklyn Institute of Arts and Sciences and later the Brooklyn Museum moves to the Lyceum Building in Washington Street (*see* 1825; Brooklyn Institute, 1843).

Trinity School loses its city and state support, starts charging tuition, becomes an all-boys school, and changes its name from the Charity School (*see* 1709; 1895).

The *New-York Sun* is acquired from founder Benjamin Day by his son-in-law Moses Y. (Yale) Beach, 38 (*see* 1833). An inventor who has become manager of the paper's mechanical department, Beach will own the *Sun* through 1852, making it one of the nation's leading "penny" newspapers before control passes to his sons Alfred E. and, later, Moses S. Beach (see Dana, 1868; Crédit Mobilier exposé, 1872).

D. Appleton & Co. publishers is founded at New York by former dry-goods merchant Daniel Appleton, 53, who was running a general store at 16 Exchange Place in 1831 when he put out his first book—a volume of inspirational biblical texts. He takes his son William Henry, 24, into partnership and they will prosper with a line of Spanish-language and children's books. W. H. Appleton will open a London branch next year, and by the time Daniel dies in 1849 his five sons will be running the firm that by 1865 will be second only to Harper Bros. (see 1817). The Appleton family will control it until 1900 (see Appleton-Century, 1933).

Painting: *The Dance on the Battery in the Presence of Peter Stuyvesant* by Asher Durand; *Dream of Arcadia* by Thomas Cole.

Lorenzo da Ponte dies penniless in his home at 91 Spring Street August 17 at age 89 and is buried, like Mozart, in an unmarked grave, this one at the Catholic Cemetery in East 11th Street. Da Ponte's wife, Nancy, died in 1831 after a short illness, and his own passing brings genuine grief to his best friend Clement Clarke Moore, now 59, and his Columbia College students.

The Halls of Justice (popularly known as The Tombs) are completed in Egyptian style on a low, damp site bounded by Centre, Elm, Leonard, and Franklin streets, formerly occupied by the Collect Pond. The building has been designed to hold 200 prisoners awaiting trial, sentencing, or execution; in less than 30 years it will be housing an average of 400 prisoners.

Fire destroys the House of Refuge erected in 1824 by the Society for the Reformation of Juvenile Delinquents. The facility will move next year to the site of the Bellevue Fever Hospital (see 1850).

St. Peter's Protestant Episcopal Church is consecrated February 2 at 344 West 20th Street, between Eighth and Ninth avenues in Chelsea. Designed by Clement Clark Moore in Greek Revival style and built by James W. Smith with buttressed fieldstone walls, it will survive into the 21st century.

Madison Square will be laid out in the next few years, occupying about 10 acres at the junction of Broadway and Fifth Avenue between 23rd and 26th streets, formerly the site of the House of Refuge.

Lyndhurst Castle at Tarrytown has its beginnings in a Gothic Revival mansion built on a knoll overlooking the Hudson for former mayor William Paulding, Jr. to designs by Newburgh-born architect Alexander Jackson Davis, 22. Neighbors call it "Paulding's Folly."

1839 The Collector of the Port of New York is found to have misappropriated more than $1 million in public funds. Samuel Swartwout has fled to England.

Tammany Hall's Isaac L. Varian wins election as mayor, defeating the Whig incumbent Aaron Clark with 21,072 votes to Clark's 20,005. Tammany Democrats will control the city's government for most of the next 100 years with a growingly powerful political machine whose ward heelers command loyalty by dispensing jobs, contracts, money for funerals, and coal and food for cold and hungry constituents. Upstate Democrat Horatio Seymour, 29, moves to Utica, having served since 1833 as military secretary to former governor William L. Marcy and aligned himself with the right-wing "Hunker" faction at Albany.

Stephen Van Rensselaer dies at Albany January 26 at age 74 (see education, 1824). Last of the Dutch patroons who once controlled so much of New York's land, he has done nothing to amend the cumbersome system of land tenures on his vast estates, which have some 3,000 farms on 436,000 acres, or to mitigate the grievances of its tenants except to be careless about collecting rents and charitable toward the more unfortunate. His tenant farmers are said to be $400,000 in arrears on their rents, they have expected these debts to be remitted, and violence breaks out when this is not done.

The Crouch and Fitzgerald leatherware shop has its beginnings in a firm founded by harness and luggage maker George Crouch, who will produce wood-framed leather trunks for traveling salesmen. By 1892 the company will have a factory in West 41st Street, three Manhattan retail shops, and 200 employees.

The 1,862-ton British & American Steam Navigation Co. paddle wheeler *British Queen* arrives from England July 27 (see 1838); 254 feet in length, she is the world's largest passenger ship thus far, and company founder Junius Smith will be hailed as the "father of the Atlantic liner," but the 2,366-ton, 267-foot-long paddle wheeler *President* launched by Smith and Macgregor Laird in December will come to grief (see Cunard, 1840).

From New York to Boston is an overnight steamer trip or a 6-hour train journey and costs $7. From New York to Philadelphia by train and ferry takes 6 hours, down from 3 days in 1817, but it takes longer when the Delaware River freezes over, halting train-ferry service and forcing passengers to walk across the ice.

Adams Express Co. has its beginnings in an express service started by William Frederick Harnden, 27, who carries packages in a carpetbag on the railroad between New York and Boston.

A New York & Harlem Railroad train is nearly wrecked near 58th Street when it collides with a herd of cows that have strayed onto its tracks.

The New York City Inebriate Asylum (later Metropolitan Hospital) is completed on Blackwell's Island to designs by Alexander Jackson Davis (*see* 1828). Its octagonal tower will survive for more than 150 years (*see* smallpox hospital, 1859).

The University of the City of New York's medical school is organized by men who include English-born chemist-physicist and physician John W. (William) Draper, 27, who will become president of the school in 1850 (*see* photography, 1840).

The *Morning Telegraph* has its beginnings in the *Sunday Morning Visitor* published at New York starting May 12, and the *Sunday Mercury Weekly* that begins publication October 27. They will be merged into a daily—the city's first daily theatrical and horseracing newspaper.

Painting: *Sunday Morning* by Asher Durand.

The National Theater fire at Leonard and Church streets September 23 destroys the theater, a school, and three churches; entire blocks go up in flames in a worse fire October 5 at Water, Pearl, and Fletcher streets, destroying at least 90 buildings (*see* Croton water, 1842).

The second Trinity Church is demolished (*see* 1790). It has been weakened by heavy snows and will be replaced (*see* 1846; cemetery, 1842).

Mt. Morris Park (it will be renamed Marcus Garvey Memorial Park in 1973) has its beginnings in rocky land purchased by the city in Central Harlem on Fifth Avenue between 120th and 124th streets (*see* watch tower, 1855).

1840 President Van Buren loses his bid for reelection, receiving only 60 electoral votes to 234 for Virginia-born Indian fighter William Henry Harrison, 67. Gov. Seward wins reelection as a Whig, again with support from Thurlow Weed, defeating candidates who include abolitionist Gerrit Smith, 43, who has been active in the Underground Railway and in starting an anti-slavery Liberal Party.

Mayor Varian gains reelection, securing 21,243 votes to 19,622 for his Whig rival J. P. Phoenix. City recorder and former assistant district attorney Robert H. Morris, 38, uncovers an election scandal involving the Whigs and gains prominence in the Democratic Party.

The American and Foreign Anti-Slavery Society is founded at New York by Arthur and Lewis Tappan, who have broken with Massachusetts-born abolitionist William Lloyd Garrison, 34, because of his insistence that women be allowed to participate in the movement (*see* 1834). Arthur Tappan is president of the new organization and will be active in starting abolitionist journals at New York and Washington, D.C., but it is Lewis Tappan who leads the struggle for the release of the *Amistad* slaves.

Manhattan farmer Robert Lenox dies, leaving his estate to his son James, who will donate some Lenox Hill property on Fourth Avenue between 69th and 71st streets to the Union Theological Seminary founded 4 years ago (*see* 1884). Lenox is buried in the New York Marble Cemetery in 2nd Street; his will, dated April 27, notes that the farm "at the five-mile stone, purchased in part from the corporation of the City of New York, containing about 30 acres," is worth less than he paid for it (values have declined since the panic of 1837). But although his father has expressly asked that the property not be sold, James Lenox begins selling off lots, perhaps because the noisy steam engines of the New York & Harlem Railroad do nothing to enhance land values in the pastoral reaches north of 42nd Street, frightening carriage and dray horses by belching coal smoke. (The younger Lenox lives in a house at 53 Fifth Avenue, northeast corner 12th Street.)

Salem, Mass.-born Brooklyn merchant Abiel Abbot Low, 29, returns from a 7-year sojourn at Guangzhou (Canton), where he went to work as a clerk for the mercantile firm Russell & Co., was admitted as a partner 3 years ago, and has profited handsomely in a joint venture with a Chinese merchant. One of 12 children, Low moved from Salem to Brooklyn with his father, Seth, at age 18 and worked in the latter's business of importing drugs and Indian ware. He determines to build fast clipper ships that will dominate the China trade, and the firm A. A. Low & Brothers will soon gain prominence in the import of Chinese tea and Japanese silk (*see* 1844).

The wooden paddle wheeler *Britannia* arrives at Boston July 18 on the first voyage by a ship of the British and North America Royal Mail Steam Packet Co., established last year by Nova Scotia-born shipper Samuel Cunard, 43, in association with George and James Burns of Glasgow and David M'Iver of Liverpool. Cunard risked his entire fortune to start the company, destroyed the short-lived British & American Steam Navigation Co. by obtaining the lucrative British mail subsidy, and is aboard the *Britannia*, whose maiden voyage has taken 14 days, 8 hours. Measuring 200 feet in length, 32 feet wide at the beam, and 21 feet deep, she carries 120 passengers and 12 crewmen, will come to New York in July of next year, and will be followed by three sister ships—*Acadia*, *Caledonia*, and *Columbia* (the latter will set a new transatlantic speed record by averaging 9.78 knots on the westward passage). Cunard will introduce iron steamers in 1855 and in 1862 will replace paddle wheels with screw propellers to break the Black Ball line's dominance of the transatlantic packet trade (*see* 1848).

Gov. Seward delivers a message to the state legislature at Albany in January recommending the "establishment of schools in which [immigrants] may be instructed by teachers speaking the same language with themselves and professing the same faith" (*see* Hughes, 1838). About 5,000 children attend eight Catholic schools in New York City, but at least 12,000 Catholic children either attend no school or are enrolled in public schools where Protestantism is taught. Seward continues to advocate the employment of foreign-born and Roman Catholic teachers in New York City's public schools, but the Catholic schools petition the Common Council for a share of the state school fund distributed through the Public School Society, whose members argue that funding Catholic schools would dissipate the moneys at their disposal and would mean replacing the common schools with "sectarian" schools. The Common Council agrees and denies the Catholic petition; Bishop Hughes blasts the Public School Society for "corrupting" Catholic children and submits a new petition, demanding that Catholics be given a share of the state funds for education, and he represents Catholic schools in a debate before the Common Council in late October, with the Protestants responding in 2 days of rhetoric consisting largely of anti-Catholic diatribes (*see* 1841; Board of Education, 1842).

Fiction: *The Pathfinder* by James Fenimore Cooper.

English-born portrait painter John Jarvis dies at New York January 12 at age 59. He has painted full-length portraits of some War of 1812 heroes for City Hall.

The first successful portrait daguerreotype is produced at New York by chemist-physicist-physician John W. Draper, who last year heard from his friend Samuel F. B. Morse of Louis Daguerre's invention and has developed an improved plate, adding bromine to the silver iodide to create a coating material with much greater sensitivity than Daguerre's. Draper makes a daguerreotype of the moon in the first application of a photographic method to astronomy.

Developer Don Alonzo Cushman completes a row of Greek Revival houses at 406 to 418 West 20th Street, between Ninth and Tenth avenues, in Chelsea. They will be named Cushman Row, and the DONAC apartment building at 402 West 20th Street will commemorate his name, as will the real estate firm Cushman-Wakefield.

Green-Wood Cemetery opens in rural southwestern Brooklyn, where the 478-acre burial ground has been modeled on the Mount Auburn Cemetery at Cambridge, Mass. Cemeteries are privately landscaped with trees, flowers, and winding paths; in the absence of public parks they provide places of refuge and recreation for the living as well as final resting places for the dead (*see* Manhattan Grid Plan, 1811). Green-Wood, however, is far removed from any urban center.

New York is a city of more than 312,000, up from fewer than 124,000 in 1820, with nearly 50,000 passing through each year; the number of blacks reaches 16,358, up from 3,262 in 1790, but blacks now represent only 5 percent of the population, down from 10 percent.

1841 President Harrison takes office March 4 but catches pneumonia and dies at Washington, D.C., April 4 at age 67. His Virginia-born vice president John Tyler, 51, becomes president despite efforts to deny him the succession, becoming the first vice president to assume office as president.

Democrat Robert H. Morris narrowly wins election as New York's mayor, defeating Whig candidate J. P. Phoenix (who receives 18,206 votes to Morris's 18,605; Native Party candidate Samuel F. B. Morse gets only 77).

R. G. Dun & Co. has its beginnings in the Mercantile Agency, founded at New York under the name Lewis Tappan & Co. by former *Journal of Commerce* copublisher Lewis Tappan as the world's first agency whose purpose is to determine the creditworthiness of prospective customers in remote locations. Now 53, Tappan was credit manager of Arthur Tappan & Co. and helped make it a success before the panic of 1837; he will run the new enterprise until he retires in 1849 to pursue his humanitarian interests, whereupon his older brother Arthur will take over the firm (*see* Douglass, 1854; Dun & Bradstreet, 1933).

The New York & Harlem Railroad reaches Fordham in the Bronx (*see* 1837; White Plains, 1844).

The New York Hospital that opened in 1791 grows with the opening of a new building with 115 beds just north of the main building (*see* 1861).

The Common Council votes overwhelmingly in January to reject last year's petition that Catholic schools in the city be given a share of the state funds administered by the Public School Society. Says one opponent, "They demand of Republicans to give them funds to train up their children to worship a ghostly monarch of vicars, bishops, archbishops, cardinals, and Popes! They demand of us to take away our children's funds and bestow them on subjects of Rome, the creatures of a foreign hiearchy," but Bishop Hughes continues to press the issue (*see* 1842).

Fordham University has its beginnings in St. John's College, Fordham, that opens with six students June 24—44th birthday of Bishop Hughes, the Jesuit priest who will become New York's first Catholic archbishop and who purchased the Rose Hill estate 2 years ago (*see* 1787). Father John McCloskey is the college's first president (*see* 1905; McCloskey, 1864).

Manhattanville College of the Sacred Heart is founded at New York.

The *New-York Tribune* begins publication April 10. The city's first Whig daily paper, it has been founded by New Hampshire-born printer Horace Greeley, 30, who has come to New York with idealistic ideas of abolishing slavery, uplifting labor, establishing utopian socialism, and prohibiting liquor. Started with $2,000 (half of it borrowed), his 1¢ paper will grow to have a circulation of nearly 300,000 by 1860, making it the largest in the country, and will have great influence on popular opinion as Greeley sends weekly and semi-weekly editions (condensed versions of the daily) to rural areas from Maine to California.

James Gordon Bennett gets the *New-York Sunday Herald* off to a successful start after two abortive efforts (in 1835 and 1838).

The *Brooklyn Eagle* begins publication October 26 under the name *Brooklyn Daily Eagle and Kings County Democrat*. Isaac Van Anden has founded the daily that will continue until 1955.

Fiction: "The Murders in the Rue Morgue" by Boston-born poet-author Edgar Allan Poe, 32, in the April issue of *Graham's Magazine* at Philadelphia is the world's first detective story. Poe is editor of the new magazine and his story is about events in New York; *The Deerslayer* by James Fenimore Cooper, now 52.

Connecticut-born showman P. T. (Phineas Taylor) Barnum, 30, pays $12,000 to acquire the 31-year-old Scudder's New York Museum at the corner of Broadway and Ann Street from the estate of its founder and opens a freak show under the name Barnum's American Museum. He will enlarge it twice by 1850 as he turns the Museum into a center of popular entertainment (*see* "Tom Thumb," 1842).

A new John Street Methodist Church is completed in Italianate style just east of Nassau Street on the site of the first American Methodist church (*see* 1766).

The Church of the Ascension (Episcopal) is consecrated at 36–38 Fifth Avenue, northwest corner 10th Street. English-born architect Richard Upjohn, 39, has designed the brownstone structure.

Haitian-born naturalist-painter John James Audubon, 56, acquires a 24-acre parcel of land in northern Manhattan, calls it Minnie's Land (it will later be known as Audubon Park), and builds an estate there. Audubon settled in New York with his family 5 years ago, taking up residence at 5 White Street, and is given permission this year by Mayor Varian to shoot rats on the Battery at dawn for use as specimens (his paintings of them will appear in his book *Viviparous Quadrupeds of North America*, to be published beginning in 1845) (*see* 1842).

A Treatise on the Theory and Practice of Landscape Gardening by architect-nurseryman Andrew Jackson Downing, now 25, establishes its author as an authority (*see* 1851).

The Irish Emigrant Society of New York is founded to help newcomers find work and protect them from swindlers. The society will protest conditions aboard ships from the old country (*see* Emigrant Savings Bank, 1850).

1842 Former Erie Canal commissioner William C. Bouck, 56, wins election as governor, running on the Democratic ticket. New York lawyer Hamilton Fish, 34, a grandson of the late Peter Stuyvesant, is elected lieutenant governor.

Mayor Morris wins reelection with 20,633 votes. The Whigs have nominated J. P. Phoenix for the third time, but he receives only 18,755 votes and abolitionist Thomas F. Field gets a mere 136. Horatio Seymour wins election as mayor of Utica and also serves his first term in the state legislature.

$ A city directory lists 51 exchange offices whose chief business is buying and selling banknotes issued by state-chartered banks. The federal government is empowered only to mint coins, and a $1 banknote from Planters Bank in Nashville, Tenn., is worth only 80¢ at New York, while one from the State Bank of Illinois fetches only 50¢, making it difficult to transact interstate business. There will be no universal U.S. currency until 1863.

Atlantic Mutual Insurance Co. receives a charter from the state legislature April 11 and opens offices at the corner of Wall and William streets, taking over the business of a former maritime insurer. A reinsurance agreement with the Insurance Company of North America will allow it to insure single vessels with larger amounts of insurance, and profits will accrue to policyholders rather than stockholders.

Stockbridge, Mass.-born paper merchant Cyrus W. (West) Field, 22, goes into partnership at New York with his brother-in-law Joseph F. Stone under the name Cyrus W. Field & Co. Young Field came to the city at age 15 with $8 given to him by his father, took a job as errand boy at the dry-goods store A. T. Stewart & Co. on Broadway between Murray and Warren streets, returned to Stockbridge, took a job as bookkeeper for his brother Matthew at a paper mill in Lee, Mass., bought an interest in a small paper mill at Westfield, Mass., and early last year became a junior partner in a wholesale paper dealership with offices in Maiden Lane. The firm soon failed, Field was somehow stuck with its debts, he settled with its creditors, wound up the business, and has set up his own firm. It will be so prosperous that Field will retire in 1853 at age 33 with a fortune of more than $250,000 (see communications [Atlantic Cable], 1852).

Hearn's opens at 425 Broadway, near Canal Street. English-born retail merchant George A. (Arnold)

Clean water from the Catskills filled the city's reservoirs, providing health benefits and making it easier to fight fires.

Hearn, Jr. from the Isle of Wight has been in business with his uncle Aaron Arnold (see 1827). His son James will move the dry-goods store to West 14th Street between Fifth and Sixth avenues (see 1902). James Mansell Constable comes in to join Arnold in place of Hearn, and the Arnold store in Canal Street becomes Arnold Constable (see 1856).

Gas tanks go up near the East River north of 14th Street, an area that will soon be populated largely by poor Irish working-class families, to hold methane gas for lighting and cookstoves. The tanks will become leaky before long, and a foul stench will pervade the area.

Bishop John DuBois dies December 20 at age 78 (he has been incapacitated by a stroke since February 1838). Coadjutor Bishop Hughes, now 45, is immediately appointed to succeed him. The city's Roman Catholic population has increased to 200,000 (most of them poor Irish immigrants), up from 15,000 in 1815, creating a severe shortage of priests.

St. Nicholas Kirche priest Johann Stephen Raffeiner abandons his parish following a dispute with the congregation, whose members gain formal recognition from the Roman Catholic archdiocese (see 1833). Bishop Hughes appoints Gabriel Rumpler to succeed Father Raffeiner as pastor of St. Nicholas Kirche (but see 1844).

The city's first Board of Education is established following political and religious controversies over the role of the Public School Society, the private organization that has managed the public schools up to now with state funding (see Hughes, 1841). The Maclay Bill bars all religious instruction from public schools (in accordance with the establishment clause in the U.S. Constitution's First Amendment) and provides no money for parochial schools, the Board has 34 commissioners—two from each of the city's 17 wards—elected by popular vote, and a board of five trustees, popularly elected in each ward; it has powers to appoint teachers and manage most affairs of the public schools in that ward. Two inspectors are to be elected in each ward to inspect the schools and certify the teachers' qualifications (see 1843). The new Board will gradually eliminate the Bible from school curricula in response to complaints that the King James Version is anti-Catholic and therefore "sectarian;" the city's new bishop John Hughes will build a system of parochial schools while still continuing to insist that such schools be given public financial support, but he will have no success, nor will any of his successors.

Samuel F. B. Morse lays an insulated copper telegraph wire under New York Harbor from Governor's Island to the Battery October 18 (*see* 1837), but although messages are transmitted and received a ship soon pulls up its anchor and hauls the wire with it, breaking the connection (*see* 1843).

English novelist Charles Dickens, 30, arrives at New York (he will call his Cunard steamship cabin "a hearse with windows") and meets with Washington Irving, William Cullen Bryant, and other leading literary figures. The Boz Ball held in his honor February 14 at the Park Theater draws a crowd of 3,000 prominent New Yorkers, and Dickens gives lectures to raise support for copyright laws, whose lack permits U.S. publishers to pirate his works. His *American Notes* published some months after his return to London criticize the cultural crudeness, materialism, and dirty streets he encountered in a New York that he characterizes as a city where "a vast amount of good and evil is intermixed and jumbled up together" (*see* 1867).

Fiction: "The Mystery of Marie Roget" by Edgar Allan Poe begins in the November issue of *Snowden's Lady's Companion*. It is based on the case of New York prostitute Mary Roger, a sales clerk at Anderson's Tobacco Shop, 26 Nassau Street, who was patronized by James Fenimore Cooper and Washington Irving, among others. Rogers disappeared, her disfigured body was later found floating in the Hudson River, and it turned out that she had become pregnant, sought out an abortionist, and was accidentally killed by the woman who performed the procedure; the woman and her young lover had panicked, and together they had disposed of the body.

"Tom Thumb" is exhibited at Barnum's American Museum by P. T. Barnum, who has discovered the midget Charles Sherwood Stratton at Bridgeport, Conn., and will use him to gain world prominence (*see* Barnum, 1841). Now 4, Stratton will stand no taller than 25 inches until he is in his teens, at maturity he will be no more than 40 inches tall with a weight of 70 pounds, and Queen Victoria will give him the title General Tom Thumb (*see* 1863). Barnum's American Museum will attract 82 million visitors in the next 16 years.

The New York Philharmonic gives its first concert December 7 at the Apollo Rooms on lower Broadway, with all musicians except the cellist standing up as they play in the manner of the Leipzig Gewandhaus concerts, a practice they will continue until 1855. Connecticut-born violinist Ureli Corelli Hill, 40, went to Europe 6 years ago to study under a prominent teacher at Cassel (he paid $1 each for 43 les-

Showman P. T. Barnum produced extravaganzas that entertained credulous New Yorkers. HARPER'S WEEKLY

sons) and has organized the cooperative, which will give four concerts each year until 1863 when the number will be increased to five (*see* Carnegie Hall, 1893).

The three-story Merchant's Exchange is completed at 55 Wall Street to Greek Revival designs by architect Isaiah Rogers to replace the exchange that was destroyed in the great fire of 1835. Occupying the block bounded by Wall, Williams, and Hanover Streets and Exchange Place, it has a portico with 32-foot high granite Ionic columns supporting a simple pediment, and its 13,000-square foot marble-walled trading hall has a 72-foot-high paneled rotunda dome that measures 60 feet in diameter. The building will be turned into a customhouse in 1863 and be enlarged in 1907 to serve as headquarters of the National City Bank.

A new customshouse is completed at 26 Wall Street, northeast corner Nassau Street, on the site of the City Hall that was razed in 1812. Designed in classical revival style by architects Ithiel Town and Alexander Jackson Davis, it has eight Doric columns at each end, a low triangular pediment like that of the Parthenon at Athens, and an ornamental interior by sculptor John Frazee with a dome (*see* commerce, 1862).

John James Audubon sells 23 of his 24 acres in Minnie's Land to Richard F. Carmen, who will use the land beginning next year for Trinity Cemetery (*see* 1841).

Some 10,000 stray hogs run wild in the streets of the city, a fact that is not lost on visitor Charles Dickens. But although the animals defecate at random they consume so much garbage and provide so much food for the poor that political considerations prevent their removal.

Croton River water enters the new 41-mile aqueduct at 5 o'clock in the morning of June 22, emerges at the Harlem River end of the line 22 hours later, crosses the 1,450-foot-long High Bridge, is admitted June 27 into the Yorkville receiving reservoir in what will become Central Park (later the Great Lawn) (*see* 1862), and on July 4 reaches the Murray Hill Distributing Reservoir (it will be popularly called the Croton Reservoir) on the west side of Fifth Avenue between 40th and 42nd streets via cast-iron pipes to give Manhattan its first good municipal reservoir system (*see* 1837). The High Bridge has cost $963,000 and sits 114 feet above the river at high tide (engineer John B. Jervis favored a lower structure but was overruled). "Nothing is talked of or thought of in New York but Croton water," writes Philip Hone in his diary. "It is astonishing how popular the introduction of water is among all classes of our citizens, and how cheerfully they acquiesce in the enormous expense which will burden them and their posterity with taxes to the later generation. Water! Water! is the universal note which is sounded through every part of the city, and infuses joy and exultation into the masses." The system's great 36-inch pipes have been cast by the Phoenix Foundry, owned by Rhinebeck-born engineer Cornelius H. (Henry) Delamater, 20, in partnership with Peter Hogg. Stone ventilating towers every mile keep the air fresh inside the tunnels, waste weirs allow diversion of the water for repairs, and Horace Greeley's *New-York Tribune* finds it "surpassing ancient Rome in one of her proudest boasts." Construction will continue until 1848, and total cost, including the purchase of land, will amount to between $12 and $13 million. The first aqueduct of its kind ever built in America, it uses an inverted siphon of two 36-inch iron pipes, covered with five feet of earth, to put the water under pressure, and it not only provides safe and reliable drinking water but will also make it easier to put out fires like the conflagration of 1835. Built in Egyptian mausolesum style and destined to remain until 1899, the Croton Reservoir on Fifth Avenue rises six stories high, and the eight-foot-wide promenade atop its walls affords panoramic views of the city (*see* 1892; High Bridge Water Tower, 1872).

Few households can afford to install running water; most of the city's population relies for bathing on public bathhouses or hydrants.

The city receives its first shipment of milk by rail as the New York & Erie Rail Road line is completed to Goshen in Orange County. New Yorkers are unaccustomed to milk rich in butterfat and complain of the light yellow scum atop the milk, but 3 million quarts of the upstate milk comes into town, a figure that will increase to 9 million by 1849.

F. and M. Schaefer Brewing Co. is founded at New York in September by Prussian-born brewery worker Frederick Schaefer, 25, of Wetzlar and his younger brother Maximilian, who pool their savings to purchase the small brewery on Broadway between 18th and 19th streets that has employed Frederick since he arrived at New York in October 1838 with just $1. Maximilian arrived in June 1839 with a formula for lager beer, the brothers buy out Frederick's employer Sebastian Sommers, and they are among the first U.S. brewers to produce lager, an effervescent beverage whose aging permits unremoved bottom-fermenting yeast to settle and allows the beer to store longer without going bad. Schaefer will move in 1845 to larger premises at Seventh Avenue and 17th Street, move again in 1849 to Fourth Avenue and 51st Street, and remain there for 67 years, expanding through the purchase of adjacent lots between 50th and 52nd streets before moving in 1916 to Brooklyn (*see* bottled beer, 1891).

1843 Mayor Morris wins election to a third term, receiving 24,395 votes to Whig rival Robert Smith's 19,516. Brooklyn voters elect Massachusetts-born businessman Joseph Sprague, 60, who was instrumental in obtaining the city charter for Brooklyn 9 years ago, will be reelected next year, and will introduce municipal street cleaning.

The Association for Improving the Condition of the Poor is founded by New York philanthropists, notably English-born merchant Robert M. (Milham) Hartley, 47, who will head the organization as general agent until 1876. Hartley and his colleagues will introduce a system of district visitors to provide the poor with moral and spiritual advice (*see* bathhouse, 1849).

The B'nai B'rith secular Jewish fraternal order is founded as a mutual-aid society by German immigrants meeting at Sinsheimer's Saloon in Essex Street on the Lower East Side (Bavarian-born rabbi Leo Merzbacher, 33, will be credited with originating the name B'nai B'rith). As its founders begin to gain financial security, the order will sponsor hospitals, old-age homes, and orphanages; by 1882 it will have chapters in 30 countries.

Banker James Brown, now 52, buys a banking house at 47 and 49 (later 59 and 61) Wall Street, southeast corner Hanover Street, for his family firm Brown

Brothers & Co., paying $130,000 for the property and building (*see* 1835; transportation, 1854).

W. and J. Sloane has its beginnings in a store opened at 245 Broadway by newly arrived Scottish-born merchant William Sloane, who at age 19 discovered a way to shoot a shuttle across the entire width of a carpet to produce the world's first piece of tapestry carpet. His establishment will grow tenfold in the next 39 years, and the enterprise will expand to have more than 44 stores nationwide, with W. and J. Sloane furniture, carpets, and home furnishings being sold at other furniture and department stores as well.

The New York and New Haven Railroad reaches New Haven, Conn., opening the coast of Long Island Sound to suburban living (in Europe, rich people live in cities while suburban areas are used for undesirable industries and housing developments for the poor; in America, the suburbs will become bedroom communities for affluent residents who derive their wealth for the most part from the cities).

The 1-year-old Board of Education opens New York's first public school.

Congress appropriates $30,000 to enable Samuel F. B. Morse to construct an experimental telegraph line between Washington, D.C., and Baltimore (*see* 1842). Obtaining further financial help from Ithaca miller Ezra Cornell, 36, and Rochester banker-businessman Hiram Sibley, 36, Morse proceeds to build the world's first long-distance telegraph line (*see* 1844).

The Brooklyn Institute of Arts and Sciences (formerly the Library Association and Brooklyn Lyceum) is incorporated under the direction of Augustus Graham, a rich distiller who proposed the library 20 years ago (*see* 1838). The Institute will establish a permanent art collection in 1846, and when Graham dies in 1851 he will bequeath funds to endow an art school and acquire works of art (*see* Brooklyn Museum, 1890).

Painting: *Farmyard on the Hudson* by Asher Durand. Jonathan Trumbull dies at New York November 10 at age 87.

The Virginia Minstrels give the first full-scale minstrel show 2/6 at the Bowery Amphitheater—the first of the Negro minstrel troupes that will dominate U.S. musical entertainment for most of the century. Directed by Ohio-born performer Daniel Decatur Emmet, 28, the minstrels are gaudily costumed blackfaced white performers who sit in a semicircle of chairs, exchange jokes based on the popular white imagination of southern black folklore, and sing songs that include Emmet's "Old Dan Tucker." The minstrel show will be the one form of American entertainment with any direct relation to American life (*see* "Dixie," 1859).

The 27-room Admiral's House (initially the Commanding General's quarters) is completed on Governors Island. The brick manor house has two-story Doric columns.

Riverdale's Wave Hill estate has its beginnings in a gray stone mansion built for lawyer William Lewis Morris on a site overlooking the Hudson. Future owners will add greenhouses and exotic gardens, acquire adjoining woodlands, install a basement bowling alley, and build a connecting museum to house an armor collection (*see* 1960).

1844 Publisher James Harper of 4 Gramercy Park West runs as the Native ("Know Nothing") Party candidate and wins election as mayor in April, securing 24,606 votes as compared with 20,726 for Equal Rights (Loco-Foco) Party candidate Jonathan I. Coddington. Morris Franklin receives 5,207 votes on the Whig ticket, but Harper owes his victory to intimidation of Irish voters by his supporters, who have stormed 1,500 strong through the 6th and 14th wards on election eve, carrying brickbats, clubs, and an assortment of anti-Roman Catholic, anti-Pope banners while daring the Irish to come out and fight. Rumors that they intended to burn down St. Patrick's Cathedral in Mulberry Street have motivated Bishop Hughes to assemble between 3,000 and 4,000 Catholic men armed with swords and derringer pistols to defend the church.

An anti-rent struggle breaks out in the manorial lands of upstate New York, tenants seize official papers from the sheriff of Columbia County and burn them, similar violence occurs in Rensselaer County, and although the offenders are arrested and will be punished following court proceedings, the turmoil embarrasses Gov. Bouck. Former state comptroller Silas Wright, now 49, is elected governor and resigns from the U.S. Senate in December in order to take office at Albany.

The National Reform Association is founded by English-born New York editor George Henry Evans, 39, who has taken part in the Equal Rights (Loco-Foco) Party revolt within the Democratic Party. Evans became a spokesman for the Working Man's Party in 1829, defended the city's labor union movement, and for the past 4 years has concentrated on land reform as the only practicable solution to class injustice. Irish-born labor leaders Mike Walsh and John Commerford join Evans in starting the new association, whose slogan is, "Vote Yourself a Farm," and although they will have little success their ideas will eventually prove influential.

The clipper ship *Houqua* launched by Brooklyn merchant A. A. Low bears the name of the Chinese merchant with whom Low profited in a joint enterprise 7 years ago (*see* 1840). It will soon be followed by the *Samuel Russell*, the *Oriental*, and the *Surprise*—a fleet that will enable A. A. Low & Brothers to buy fresh Chinese tea at Guangzhou (Canton), acquiring it at low prices after competitors have filled their requirements, and sell it at U.S. ports earlier than the competition, receiving high prices for his cargoes (*see* 1849; *Rainbow*, 1845).

The New York & Harlem Railroad reaches White Plains in suburban Westchester County (*see* 1841; Van Derbilt, 1862). Rail travel will make it possible for people to commute to work in Manhattan from communities such as Mount Vernon, Bronxville, Greenburgh, Hartsdale, and Scarsdale.

The New York and New Haven Railroad is founded by entrepreneurs who will try next year to establish their own entry into Manhattan. The Harlem will block them from obtaining trackage rights (*see* 1848; New York, New Haven & Hartford, 1872).

The Board of Aldermen votes to abolish the licensing requirement that has required every driver to own his own cart (*see* 1825). The carters' monopoly will collapse in the next 2 decades as the needs of the growing metropolis for larger carts make the old rules impossible to enforce.

Samuel F. B. Morse transmits the first telegraph message ("What hath God wrought?") May 24 from the U.S. Supreme Court room in the Capitol at Washington, D.C., to his associate Alfred L. Vail at the Mount Clare Station of the B&O Railroad at Baltimore, and Vail transmits it back (*see* 1837; 1843).

Nonfiction: *Wealth and Biography of Wealthy Citizens of the City of New York* by *New-York Sun* owner Moses Y. (Yale) Beach, now 44, lists some 850 New Yorkers worth $100,000 or more, including 25 with net worth of at least $1 million. Included are John Jacob Astor ($44 million), Stephen Van Rensselaer ($10 million, all of it in land [one son owns Albany County, the other Van Rensselaer County]), William B. Astor ($5 million), Cornelius van Derbilt ($1.2 million), Peter Cooper, merchant A. T. Stewart, and importer Moses Taylor, now 38.

Poet Edgar Allan Poe moves with his wife (and cousin), Virginia Clemm, now 21, into the garret of a Bloomingdale Village farmhouse at what later will be 84th Street between Amsterdam Avenue and the Bloomingdale Road (Broadway). Now 35, Poe works in a spacious study on the floor below on his poem "The Raven" (*see* 1845).

Painting: *Catskill Mountain House: The Four Elements* by Thomas Cole.

Theater: *The Drunkard, or The Fallen Saved* by U.S. playwright William H. Smith (originally Sedley), 37, and an anonymous "Gentleman" 2/12 at the Boston Museum. P. T. Barnum picks up the morality play about the evils of drink and presents it at New York and other cities, where it attracts many women whose husbands have drinking problems (it will have frequent revivals).

The polka is introduced to New York in May at the Chatham Theater by dancers Mary Ann Gannon, 15, and L. de G. Brockes after 14 years of growing popularity in Europe.

The New York Yacht Club is organized by sportsman John Cox Stevens and eight other sailing enthusiasts aboard the schooner *Gimcrack* anchored off the Battery. They will build a clubhouse on Stevens's Elysian Fields property at Hoboken, N.J., but will move several times in the next half century. Their organization will survive as the nation's oldest club of its kind (*see* 1901).

President John Tyler, now 55, is married at the 3-year-old Church of the Ascension June 26 to Julia Gardiner, 22. Philip Hone writes in his diary that Tyler "flew on the wings of love—the old fool—to the arms of his expectant bride . . . The illustrious bridegroom is said to be 55 years of age and looks 10 years older . . ."

The Municipal Police Act adopted by the city provides for the creation of a regular police force to replace the 1,132 community protection force and constables who have been overwhelmed by the growing chaos, drunkenness, and violence in a metropolis with little law and order (*see* 1845).

William Cullen Bryant proposes a public park for Manhattan. Visits to London's Kensington Gardens and Regent's Park have inspired him, as has New England essayist Henry David Thoreau, and Bryant's editorial "A New Park" in the July 3 issue of the 44-year-old *New-York Evening Post* says, "Commerce is devouring inch by inch the coast of the island, and if we rescue any part of it for health and recreation, it must be done now . . . All large cities have their extensive public grounds and gardens, Madrid and Mexico their Alamedas, London its Regent's Park, Paris its Champs Elysées, and Vienna its Prater."

The poet-journalist is co-editor and co-owner of the paper; he makes no specific recommendation as to the location of the park, and one candidate is Jones' Wood, an extensive area between Third Avenue and the East River (see 1853; Downing, 1851; Olmsted, 1857).

1845 New York gets its first professional police force under terms of the Municipal Police Law enacted last year, but the 800 men who replace the watch system are all political appointees, are not required to pass any mental or physical tests, serve for only 1 year, and are not uniformed (see 1853).

Former sugar refiner William F. (Friedrich) Havemeyer, 41, defeats Mayor Harper's bid for reelection. The Tammany Hall Democrat quit business 4 years ago to enter politics; he wins 24,183 votes, Harper 17,472, Whig candidate Dudley Selden 7,082. Horatio Seymour is elected speaker of the state assembly at Albany.

$ New York Life Insurance Co. has its beginnings in the Nautilus Insurance Co. that holds its first meeting April 12. Chartered by the state legislature May 21, 1841, the new mutual company has been founded by Pliny Freeman, who has persuaded 56 prominent New Yorkers to pledge a total of $55,815 to start the firm, whose name will be changed to New York Life under terms of a legislative act April 5, 1849. Other founders include New York-born lawyer and financier Thomas W. (William) Ludlow, 50, who has long served as counsel to a Dutch banking house and promoted the New York Life Insurance and Trust Co. established in 1830. Freeman becomes the firm's first actuary and will direct company operations for years.

Johnson & Higgins has its beginnings in the marine insurance brokerage Jones & Johnson, founded by Walter Restored Jones, Jr. and Henry W. Johnson (see 1854).

The 3,270-ton Great Western Steamship Co. S.S. *Great Britain* arrives from Liverpool to begin a career of transatlantic service that will continue until 1854; 322 feet in length, she is the world's largest passenger ship thus far and will remain the largest on the Atlantic until 1860.

The Rainbow begins a new era of improved clipper ships that will compete with the new screw-propelled iron steamships (see 1832). First of the "extreme" clipper ships that will for years be the fastest vessels afloat, it is narrow in the bow, high in the stern, and has aft-displaced beams. New York-born naval architect John Willis Griffiths, 36, has

designed the vessel for the China trade (see *Oriental*, 1850).

The paddle wheeler *Hendrick Hudson* steams up the Hudson from New York to Albany in just 7 hours. She incorporates suggestions made by Troy iron manufacturer and inventor Henry Burden, 54, who will be credited with such innovations as locating sleeping berths on the upper decks.

Brooklyn railroad investor and developer Edwin Litchfield buys most of the land around the Gowanus Creek and turns the creek (called Gouwane's Creek by the Dutch) into a canal that will become not only an important shipping route but also a repository for the local sewer system (see flushing tunnel, 1911).

∞ The Reform Jewish congregation Temple Emanu-El has its beginnings in a German literary society, or *cultus verein*, founded by Rabbi Leo Merzbacher, who came to New York 4 years ago as a teacher for the German Orthodox congregation Rodeph Shalom and for the German Reform congregation Anshe Chesed (see B'nai B'rith, 1843). The city's first professionally trained rabbi, he has had a falling out with the congregation of Rodeph Shalom (see architecture, 1868).

James Gordon Bennett's *New-York Herald* publishes a full-page illustration of former president Andrew Jackson's funeral in June. It has taken 2 weeks to produce the plate, so the picture appears long after the event.

Scientific American begins publication August 28 at New York in a newspaper format (see 1946).

The *New York National Police Gazette* begins publication with lurid illustrations. Founded by Richard Kyle Fox and George Wilkes, the weekly scandal sheet will gain wide readership.

The 11-year-old German-language newspaper *Der Freischuetz* is acquired by German-born printer Jakob Uhl, 39, and his German-born wife, Anna (née Behr), 30, who rename it the *New Yorker Staats-Zeitung*. They will make it a daily beginning in 1849, Mrs. Uhl will run it herself after her husband's death in April 1852, and 7 years later she will marry her Moravian-born assistant Oswald Ottendorfer, 11 years her junior. By 1860 the *Staats-Zeitung* will claim to have the largest circulation of any German-language paper in the world (see Ridder, 1901; German Hospital, 1861).

Poetry: *The Raven and Other Poems* by Edgar Allan Poe, whose title poem has appeared in the January 29 *New-York Evening Mirror*, where Poe is assistant editor (see 1844): "... And his eyes have all the seeming of a demon's that is dreaming,/ And the lamplight o'er him streaming throws his shadow on the floor;/ And my soul from out that shadow that lies floating on the floor,/ Shall be lifted—nevermore!"

Theater: *Fashion, or Life in New York* by French-born novelist-playwright Anna Cora Mowatt (*née* Ogden), 26, 3/24 at New York's Park Theater. The playwright married New York lawyer James Mowatt when she was 15, his business failure in 1841 forced her to earn a living, a friend suggested that she write a play, her 1841 play *Gulzara* met with indifferent success, but her witty satire on New York society enjoys an unprecedented 3-week run, ridiculing parvenu women who fawn obsequiously over what they think of as titled foreigners (in this case a former barber and cook).

The five-story Stuyvesant Fish house is completed at 19 Gramercy Park South, southeast corner Irving Place, with more than 37 rooms that include six bedroom suites, a drawing room, a penthouse ballroom, and 13 fireplaces (the red brick mansion will not be acquired by Fish and his wife until 1888) (*see* Sonnenberg, 1935).

The four-story London Terrace row houses are completed for developer Clement Clarke Moore on the north side of 23rd Street between Ninth and Tenth avenues; built with the participation of Presbyterian minister Cyrus Mason and his partner William Torrey, they will be replaced by town houses in 1889 (*see* London Terrace apartment houses, 1930).

A patent is granted for small glass circles that can be built into sidewalks and permit natural light to enter vaulted basement spaces used by merchants for storage under commercial buildings. The glass circles will find wide use in New York.

The Broad Street fire July 19 rages out of control despite the availability of water from the 3-year-old Croton Aqueduct; the conflagration kills 30, destroys 300 buildings, and causes so much damage in lower Manhattan that practically every New York casualty insurance company is wiped out (*see* Home Insurance, 1853).

Potato crops fail in Ireland and throughout Europe as the fungus disease *Phytophthora infestans*, brought inadvertently from America in the holds of ships, rots potatoes in the ground as well as those in storage. The resulting famine spurs a massive emigration from Ireland, much of it to New York (*see* population, 1847).

Fire destroys Delmonico's Restaurant in Broad Street July 19 (*see* 1832). Lorenzo Delmonico replaces it with a new establishment across from Bowling Green where he will play host not only to New York society but also to visiting dignitaries and celebrities. He imports more European cooks and recipes for the large new hotel and restaurant (*see* 1861).

1846 The Mexican War that begins January 13 excites New Yorkers, who read accounts of the conflict sent back by correspondents of James Gordon Bennett's *New-York Herald* and Horace Greeley's *New-York Tribune*. Anti-slavery factions oppose the war on grounds that it has been fomented by the Southern "slavocracy," whose aim is to obtain new lands for planting slave-grown cotton.

Gov. Wright loses his bid for reelection, being defeated by Vermont-born Whig congressman John Young, 44. Wright has suppressed the anti-rent riots in Delaware County; Young disapproves of the tenures that enable tenants to hold manorial lands in the state, and he will pardon the anti-renters on grounds that their offenses were political, not criminal.

Editor Horace Greeley won readers for his New-York Tribune *throughout America.* LIBRARY OF CONGRESS

Democrat Andrew H. Mickle wins the city's mayoralty election, securing 21,675 votes. His Whig rival Robert Taylor receives only 15,111, Native Party candidate William B. Cozzens 8,301.

West Farms (initially Ten Farms) is incorporated as a town west of the Bronx River near the village of Westchester. The section has grown since about 1812 to have bleaching factories, coal yards, flour mills, glass, paint, and pottery factories, and other industries (see annexation, 1874).

The "Marble Palace" (so called by the *New-York Herald* September 18) opens September 21 at 280 Broadway, between Reade and Chambers streets, where retail merchant A. T. Stewart has commissioned London-born architect John Butler Snook, 31, of Trench & Snook to design the first commercial building with a marble façade (see 1823). The brilliant white structure houses an emporium stocked with the costliest satins, silks, and brocades. Stewart, now 44, lets his carriage-trade customers browse at will throughout his new dry-goods store, whose mahogany cabinets and elaborate fixtures under a domed atrium offer a wide variety of goods at fixed prices, attracting such crowds that he will outgrow his new establishment; he will expand it in 4 years to fill the entire block but it will still be too small (see 1862).

The Hamilton Ferry goes into service across the East River, linking the Battery to Brooklyn's Hamilton Avenue (see 1836; 1854).

St. Luke's Hospital has its beginnings in an appeal made October 18 to the congregation of the new Episcopal Church of the Holy Communion by its Philadelphia-born pastor William Augustus Muhlenberg, 50, who collects a fund of $30 that will grow in 10 years to $20,000 (see 1858).

The Sisters of Charity of Mount St. Vincent is founded with help from Bishop Hughes's Irish-born sister Ellen (Mother Mary Angela), 40 (see St. Vincent's Hospital, 1849).

The rotary "lightning press" patented by New York printing press manufacturer Richard March Hoe, 34, can run 10,000 sheets per hour, a rate far faster than that of traditional flatbed presses. The type form of Hoe's press is attached to a central cylinder rather than to a flatbed and from four to 10 impression cylinders revolve about the central cylinder (see 1847).

Town & Country magazine has its beginnings in the *Home Journal*, edited by George Pope Morris and Nathaniel Parker Willis and published at New York to report the doings of America's growing moneyed class.

A telegraph line opens July 3 to link New York and Buffalo (see 1844).

Fiction: *Typee: A Peep at Polynesian Life* by New York–born novelist Herman Melville, 27, whose father died bankrupt and insane 16 years ago. The young man shipped out of New York as a cabin boy aboard the Liverpool-bound packet *St. Lawrence* at age 19 and left Fairhaven, Mass., January 3, 1841, for a voyage of nearly 4 years on the whaler *Acushnet*. He jumped ship with fellow deserter Richard Tobias Greene after 18 months and found refuge on a jungle island of the Marquesas, whose friendly but cannibal Taipi tribe he describes in a first novel that gains wide readership with its spicy tale of adventure and romance based in part on his experiences in the South Pacific; *The Old Continental* by James Kirke Paulding, whose novels gain wide popularity by avoiding romanticism and florid prose.

Charles Scribner's Sons has its beginnings in the New York publishing house Baker and Scribner. New York–born College of New Jersey (Princeton) graduate Charles Scribner, 25, has given up a budding law practice for reasons of health and gone into partnership with Isaac D. Baker, with whom he opens a small office in the old Brick Meeting House at the corner of Nassau Street and Park Row, specializing in theological and philosophical works. Baker will die in 1850 and Scribner will carry on under his own name (see magazine, 1870).

Painter Henry Inman dies at New York January 17 at age 44.

M. Knoedler & Co. opens at Broadway and 9th Street. French-born art dealer Michel Knoedler has bought the business started by Goupil et Cie of Paris and starts a gallery under his own name. It will be one of the nation's leading art dealers by the 1880s (see 1912).

Fourteen baseball rules are codified by bank clerk Alexander J. Cartwright, Jr. and three other members of the Knickerbocker Base Ball Club, whose clubhouse is in the Murray Hill area. The club has been playing the "New York game" since 1842 in an open area near Broadway at 22nd Street (or by some accounts on a vacant lot at the corner of Madison Avenue and 27th Street). Bases are laid out in a diamond pattern rather than a square, distances between them are set at 90 feet, each team has nine players, each player is allowed three strikes, and the team is allowed three outs per inning. Cartwright's team is defeated 23 to 1 by the New York Nine in its first game June 19 at the Elysian Fields in Hoboken (*see* 1867).

The Century Association is founded by *New-York Evening Post* editor-owner William Cullen Bryant, now 51, and others with the purpose of promoting interest in literature and the fine arts; membership is initially limited to 100 and includes former members of the Sketch Club, founded in 1829 (*see* 1869).

A third Trinity Church is consecrated May 21 (Ascension Day) on Broadway at the head of Wall Street. Designed in Gothic revival style by Richard Upjohn, it is 166 feet long and 79 feet wide; its buttresses are merely decorative, doing nothing to support the structure of the nave, and the ceiling is made of plaster rather than of real stone vaults, but its exterior use of brownstone (a chocolate-colored

A new Trinity Church with a brownstone exterior went up at the head of Wall Street. HARPER'S WEEKLY

New Jersey sandstone composed of sheets that will eventually separate) begins a revolution in New York construction (*see* 1700). The 280-foot spire of the new church rises to a height equivalent to that of a 22-story building, can be seen throughout the city, nothing else being taller, and will remain the city's tallest structure until 1890; as at most churches, parishioners pay for their pews and will continue to do so until 1919.

Grace Episcopal Church is completed on Broadway at East 10th Street to plans by Scottish-born engineer James Renwick, Jr., 28, who has won an architectural competition for the design of what soon becomes the ecclesiastical center of New York society. Occupying 12 city lots that have been purchased from the Brevoort family for $58,600 (Renwick is a grandson of the late Henry Brevoort, who died 5 years ago at age 94), the church replaces a structure built nearly 50 years ago at the corner of Broadway and Rector streets, just below Trinity Church, on a site that was once part of the old Randall Farm.

The Church of the Holy Communion is completed at the corner of 20th Street and Sixth Avenue. Richard Upjohn has designed the structure in Gothic revival style.

Calvary Church is completed on the east side of Fourth Avenue at 21st Street to designs by James Renwick.

The Clarendon Hotel opens at the southeast corner of Fourth Avenue and 18th Street. Financed by William B. Astor and designed by James Renwick, the five-story structure of yellow brick and brownstone has ornate terra-cotta window heads and cast-iron balconies, but critics observe that it is too far north of Union Square, the heart of the city's hotel district, and it soon goes bankrupt. A new owner will acquire the Clarendon and enlarge it to have 300 rooms (*see* 1853).

1847 The New York State Court of Appeals begins hearings in September with a calendar dominated by private disputes over land and money; it will survive as the state's highest court and perhaps the nation's leading interpreter of legal principles, often showing the way for other states' courts and even the U.S. Supreme Court.

Whig politician William Vermilye Brady, 36, wins election as mayor, receiving 21,310 votes. His Tammany Hall rival J. Sherman Brownell gets 19,877, Native Party candidate E. G. Drake 2,078. The Common Council will reject Brady's proposal that the new police department be eliminated to save money.

New York jeweler Charles Tiffany moves north to 271 Broadway on Union Square and next year will start manufacturing his own wares, adding gold jewelry to his line (*see* 1837); he will open a Paris branch in 1850, adopt the firm name Tiffany & Co. in 1853 (*see* 1905; Tiffany Diamond, Louis Comfort Tiffany, 1878).

The village of Brooklyn signs a street-lighting contract with the revived Brooklyn Gas Light Co. (*see* 1825), which builds a manufacturing plant near the Brooklyn Navy Yard where it heats coal until it becomes coke, capturing the methane released in the process. By 1849 methane gas will be coursing through 6½ miles of Brooklyn mains and lighting the village's most prosperous area.

The German shipping firm Hamburg-Amerikanische Paketfahrt Aktien Gesellschaft (HAPAG) founded at Hamburg launches three copper-bottomed sailing ships: one of them, the 220-passenger *Deutschland*, sails for New York October 15 to begin monthly transatlantic service (the passage takes an average of 41 days). The Hamburg-Amerika line will commission its first steamship, the *Borussia*, in 1856, and by 1897 will be the largest steamship company in the world.

The New York Academy of Medicine is founded by physicians who include Samuel Smith Purple, 25, of the New York Dispensary, who will start the Academy's library by donating 4,000 volumes that he will augment with thousands of other books and pamphlets before he dies a bachelor in 1900 (*see* 1926).

The Emigrant Refuge and Hospital opens on Wards Island; by 1860 it will be the world's largest medical complex.

Bellevue Hospital is revitalized by a city-appointed committee whose members include Valentine Mott, John Wakefield Francis, and Mamaroneck-born physician James Rushmore Wood, 33 (*see* 1836; operating amphitheater, 1849).

The American Medical Association is founded under the leadership of upstate New York physician Nathan Smith Davis, 30, following a Philadelphia convention attended by representatives of medical societies and medical schools.

New York has 16 daily newspapers—including the *Evening Post*, *Sun*, *Herald*, and *Tribune*—to serve a population that has grown to 400,000 (*see Times*, 1851).

Fiction: *Omoo* by Herman Melville, who arouses controversy by revealing the hypocrisy and venality of Christian missionaries in the South Pacific.

Melville is married at Boston in August to Elizabeth Shaw, the only daughter of the chief justice of the Massachusetts Supreme Court, and takes up residence at New York with his bride, his brother Allan, his brother's bride, his mother, Maria Gansevoort Melville, and four unmarried sisters in a house at 103 Fourth Avenue, close to that of his publisher Evert Augustus Duyckinck, 30, of Wiley & Putnam.

Painting: *July Sunset* by Hartford, Conn.-born painter Frederick E. (Edwin) Church, 21, whose father agreed in May 1844 to pay Thomas Cole $300 per year for the young man's instruction plus $3 per week for room and board, an arrangement that continued until June of last year; *Autumn—On the Hudson River* and *Pontine Marshes* by Staten Island-born painter and architect Jaspar Francis Cropsey, 24, who visits England, France, Switzerland, and Italy.

Connecticut-born landscape painter John Frederick Kensett, 31, returns home to New York after a 6-year tour of Europe and discovers that paintings he sent back from Europe have established his reputation.

Theater: *Used Up* 9/27 at Wallack's Theater, with New York actor Lester (originally John Johnstone) Wallack, 27, making his local debut in the role of Sir Charles Coldstream (he will not adopt the name Lester until 1861). His London-born father, James William Wallack, now 52, managed the city's National Theater from 1837 to 1839, went on tour thereafter, returned to the city in 1852 as manager of Brougham's Lyceum, and has renamed it (*see* 1861).

Opera: The Astor Place Opera House opens 11/22 with a performance of the 1844 Giuseppe Verdi opera *Ernani*. Financed by 150 rich New Yorkers, its seats are upholstered in red damask and are sold only by subscription, there is no open seating, women are admitted only in the company of men in order to exclude women of dubious reputation, and men are expected to conform to a dress code that requires evening clothes, a fresh vest, and kid gloves to exclude working-class opera lovers; the new house will close in 1852 after five seasons (*see* riot, 1849; Academy of Music, 1854).

John Jacob Astor III marries South Carolina belle Charlotte Augusta Gibbes, whose quick wit and imagination will do little to help her in New York society (*see* 1861). She will give birth next year to a son, William Waldorf Astor, who will be the couple's only child.

A builder completes a row of modest frame houses in West 40th Street between Sixth Avenue and Broadway, renting them for less than $11 per month, but Manhattan's West Side north of Chelsea has few other dwellings, and even Chelsea remains more than half rural.

Reservoir Square (later Bryant Park) opens to the public just west of the holding reservoir built in 1842. It occupies part of the potter's field laid out in 1823 (see 1884; Crystal Palace, 1853).

More than 200,000 emigrants leave Ireland, up from 60,000 in 1842, and most of them head for New York (see potato famine, 1845). Irish landlords pay fares of about £4 ($20) per head to clear their lands of tenants who cannot pay their rents, and the ousted emigrés leave aboard small sailing vessels, few of them inspected and many not seaworthy. Passengers provide their own food, which is often inadequate when adverse winds make the passage a long one, and by some estimates some 100,000 will die of disease en route in what will come to be called "coffin ships" (although the dead are often dumped overboard without benefit of coffins). The "famine Irish" who arrive at New York are mostly half-starved rural folk who have never before lived in a city, cannot read or write, may speak only Gaelic, have few skills, and often have trouble finding work.

The New York Commissioners of Emigration begin to keep accurate records for the first time and to regulate reception of new arrivals, who heretofore have been subjected to exploitation by boarding-house runners, confidence men, tavern keepers, and other waterfront sharpies, who have been allowed to board arriving ships and make deals with the confused passengers, often cheating them in money exchange, selling them tickets to unintended destinations at inflated prices, and luring them to fleabag boarding houses without interference by the police. Between now and 1860 some 2.5 million immigrants will enter the United States through the port of New York alone, and more than a million of these will be Irish (see Castle Garden, 1855).

New York's first Chinese immigrants arrive July 10 aboard the seagoing junk Kee Ying, 212 days under sail out of Guangzhou (Canton), with 35 passengers and crewmen (some of whom jump ship). Their arrival marks the beginning of the city's Chinatown, which will have 1,000 residents by 1887 (see 1868; general store, 1875).

1848 The Treaty of Guadalupe Hidalgo February 2 ends the Mexican War that began in 1846. Virginia-born Gen. Winfield Scott, 62, arrives at New York and is given a rousing reception (see 1852).

The state legislature at Albany enacts a Code of Civil Procedure that will be adopted or used as a model by many states and foreign countries, including Britain and Ireland. Haddam, Conn.-born New York lawyer and legal reformer David Dudley Field, 43, and Winchester, Conn.-born Little Falls, N.Y., lawyer Arphaxed Loomis, 50, induced the state constitutional convention 2 years ago to announce its support of the reformed legal system, which goes into effect July 1 and will be amended next year.

Whigs nominate Virginia-born Mexican War hero Zachary Taylor, 63, for the presidency in preference to the controversial party leaders Henry Clay and Daniel Webster. Democrats nominate Lewis Cass of Michigan, who receives only 127 electoral votes to Taylor's 163 and loses New York State because Martin Van Buren, now 65, has run as a Free Soil candidate and taken the state's Democratic votes.

Former state adjutant general John Adams Dix, 50, runs for governor as a Democrat. He served as President Madison's secretary of the treasury but loses to former lieutenant governor Hamilton Fish, now 40.

Former governor William H. Seward, now 47, is elected U.S. senator from New York with support from his longtime political ally Thurlow Weed of the Albany Regency; Seward will oppose compromising anti-slavery positions.

New York City voters narrowly defeat Mayor Brady's bid for reelection, giving him 22,227 votes as compared to 23,155 for former mayor William F. Havemeyer, who is elected to a second term.

The state legislature at Albany passes a Married Women's Property Act that allows divorced women to retain at least some of their possessions. Polish-born feminist Ernestine L. Rose (née Potowski), 38, has addressed the legislature at least five times to urge passage of the measure. Enacted in April (the State Senate has voted for it 21 to 1, the Assembly 93 to 9), the New York law will be amended repeatedly as male legislators weaken it.

The first Woman's Rights Convention opens July 19 at Wesleyan Methodist Chapel in Seneca Falls, N.Y., under the leadership of Elizabeth Cady Stanton, 32, and Lucretia Coffin Mott of 1833 Anti-Slavery Society fame. The convention launches a women's rights movement (see 1850).

Philanthropist Cornelius Heeney dies at Brooklyn May 3 at age 93, leaving a bequest that will permit his 3-year-old Brooklyn Benevolent Society to distribute $2 million among the city's poor and homeless.

Gold is discovered in California January 24 by New Jersey-born prospector James Marshall, 38, while working to free the wheel in the millrace for a sawmill he is building on the American River for Swiss-born settler Johann Sutter. Sutter tries to keep Marshall's discovery a secret in order to avoid disruption of his farm, but the news appears August 19 in James Gordon Bennett's *New-York Herald*, and by year's end some 6,000 men are working in the goldfields (*see* transportation, 1849).

John Jacob Astor dies at New York March 28 at age 84, leaving a fortune of $20 million acquired in the fur trade and New York real estate. The richest man in America, Astor has lived at 362 Pearl Street, and his income for the past decade has been more than $1.25 million from rents alone.

Dry Dock Savings Bank opens at 619 4th Street, corner of Avenue C, near the East River to serve seamen, dockworkers, and mechanics (*see* Dollar Dry Dock, 1983).

The East River Savings Bank is founded.

The 4-year-old New York and New Haven Railroad buys a perpetual right to operate on the New York & Harlem's right-of-way into Manhattan, enabling people to commute to work in Manhattan from suburban communities such as Mount Vernon, New Rochelle, Portchester, Rye, Larchmont, Mamaroneck, Greenwich, and Westport (*see* 1844; depots, 1857).

Samuel Cunard's 9-year-old Royal Mail Steamship Line makes New York its base for transatlantic operations (*see* 1839). Cunard's 1,422-ton wooden-hulled S.S. *Hibernia* arrived at New York in December of last year; it has a service speed of 9.5 knots.

The Pacific Railroad & Panama Steamship Co. is founded at New York to build a rail link across the Isthmus of Panama and thereby facilitate transportation between Atlantic Coast ports and San Francisco. New York financier and lawyer Thomas W. (William) Ludlow, now 54, helps local merchant William H. Aspinwall, his brother Lloyd, his uncles Gardiner G. and Samuel Howland, Richard Alsop, Edwin Bartlett, Henry Chauncey, and former transatlantic steamship operator John Lloyd Stephens establish the company with a capitalization of $400,000 (*see* 1849).

The Five Points Mission opens in a former saloon at the corner of Cross and Little Water Streets. Founded by the Ladies Home Missionary Society of the Methodist Episcopal Church, it has support from the church and from rich businessmen intent on cleaning up the squalid and dangerous neighborhood. The Mission will sponsor temperance meet-

ings, a charity day school, and a chapel (*see* House of Industry, 1854).

A telegraph line opens between New York and Chicago (*see* Morse, 1844; Western Union, 1856).

The Associated Press has its beginnings in the New York News Agency formed in May by a group of six New York newspapers to save money in using the new telegraph connection. Each newspaper has its own political and social views, the neutral news agency is intended to report only the facts without bias, and the need to wire information economically (and allow for transmission problems) dictates an "inverted pyramid" style of reporting that calls for the most important facts to come first. The name Associated Press will be adopted in 1851 (*see* 1900).

The Astor Library is founded with a $400,000 bequest from the late John Jacob Astor. His son William Backhouse Astor, now 56, will add another $550,000 to the library's endowment (*see* 1854).

Painter Thomas Cole attends church February 6, complains of lassitude, and dies of pleurisy and lung congestion in the west bedroom of his house at Catskill, N.Y., February 11 at age 47, having gained an international following for his landscapes of the Hudson River Valley.

Brooklyn's City Hall (later Borough Hall) opens at 209 Joralemon Street. Designed originally by architect Calvin Pollard, who won a design competition with his Greek Revival drawings, its construction began in 1836 but was interrupted by the financial panic of 1837. The state legislature at Albany voted in 1845 to authorize a $50,000 bond issue to finance the structure, Brooklyn architect Gamaliel King was commissioned to design a building for the existing foundations, and he has simplified Pollard's design.

Manhattan's Arsenal is completed at 821 Fifth Avenue, opposite 64th Street. Designed by Martin E. Thompson to serve as the state's primary cache of military explosives, it will be turned over to the city in 1857 (*see* Museum of Natural History, 1869).

A Brooklyn fire September 9 rages through Henry, Pineapple, Sands, and Washington streets, destroying seven blocks of buildings that include a post office, three churches, and two newspapers. Some 300 houses on Brooklyn Heights are lost to the flames.

Failure of the liberal movement in the German states forces hundreds of young men to flee for their lives. Many will emigrate to New York.

1849 President Taylor removes former governor Bouck from his position as New York City assistant treasurer in May and replaces him with former governor Young, now 46, who supported Taylor in last year's presidential election.

City voters defeat Democratic mayoral candidate Myndert Van Schaick and elect Whig candidate Caleb S. Woodhull, 57, who receives 21,656 votes (Van Schaick gets 17,435), as the Democrats fail to reconcile internal party differences. The mayor's term is extended to 2 years, the change to take effect beginning next year.

$ More than 3,000 ships from 150 foreign ports arrive at the New York Harbor, up from about 1,000 in 1835, carrying half of all America's imports and departing with nearly one-third of her exports as the city becomes more than ever the leading U.S. center of commerce. By next year there will be 60 docks, piers, slips, and wharves on the East River below 14th Street and at least 50 on the Hudson. Ship tonnages going through the port will rise by another 60 percent in the next 10 years.

Former National Bank of New York president Albert Gallatin dies at the Astoria home of his daughter Frances Stevens August 12 at age 88 and is buried in Trinity Church Yard.

Railroad construction begins across the Isthmus of Panama to facilitate passage to California (see 1848). John Lloyd Stephens of the Pacific Railroad & Panama Steamship Co. has handled negotiations with New Granada officials at Bogotá, and he will soon succeed Thomas W. Ludlow as the company's president (see 1850).

Brooklyn merchant-shipowner A. A. Low moves his headquarters to Manhattan, occupying offices at Burling Slip (see 1844). One of his clipper ships will beat British competitors in the annual tea race from China to London next year, and by the time he retires in 1887 Low will have built up a considerable fortune.

The Hudson River Railroad's line to East Albany opens with several stops along Manhattan's West Side. The Common Council enacts a law requiring that trains moving down Eleventh Avenue from the yards north of 60th Street must be preceded by a man on horseback carrying a red flag or, at night, a lantern, but the trains will nevertheless kill children and some adults each year until 1934, when a "High Line" will replace the street-level tracks.

The Harlem River line reaches Peekskill, opening up more of Westchester to suburban living as railroad commuters begin to play a significant role.

A cholera epidemic takes about 5,000 lives in the city as crowding and lack of good sanitation encourage spread of the disease (see 1831; 1854). Drinking water from contaminated wells is responsible for many if not most of the cases; Manhattan still has a shortage of pure water (see environment, 1842).

Pfizer Inc. has its beginnings in a Williamsburgh, Brooklyn, shop opened by Swabian-born chemist Charles Pfizer, 25, in partnership with his cousin Charles Erhart. They establish a laboratory in a modest red-brick house and gain quick success with an oral antiparisitic preparation that they sell under the name Santonin (they have blended the bitter active ingredient with almond-toffee flavoring).

St. Vincent's Hospital opens in 13th Street between Third and Fourth avenues with 30 patients and will have 70 patients by 1852. Sister Angela Hughes of the 3-year-old Roman Catholic order Sisters of Charity of Mount St. Vincent has opened the hospital, whose president is Valentine Mott, now 64, and whose attending surgeon is Mott's Philadelphia-born son-in-law William H. (Holme) Van Buren, 30. Sister Angela becomes a role model for the city's Irish women (see 1856).

Bellevue Hospital's operating amphitheater opens with great ceremony (see 1847). William H. Van Buren is the amphitheater's star practitioner (see pathology department, 1857).

The first U.S. woman M.D. graduates at the head of her class at Geneva Medical College at Syracuse, having been ostracized by other students. English-born, New York-raised physician Elizabeth Blackwell, 28, will play an important role in U.S. medicine (see New York Infirmary, 1857).

The College of the City of New York (CCNY) has its beginnings in the Free Academy that opens on Lexington Avenue at 23rd Street (the CCNY name will be used beginning in 1866). Most New Yorkers receive no more than 3 years of primary-school education, followed by 4 years of grammar school; they are finished with school by age 14, although grammar-school principals give supplementary classes for those who want to continue their schooling. Local merchant and autodidact Townsend Harris, 42, has played a leading role in planning the college as a member of the board of education. Established under a charter signed May 7, 1847, the tuition-free institution of higher learning has a mission to educate the "children of the whole people" and occupies a building that accommodates 1,000 students, its full course of studies initially takes 5 years, and it will enable thousands of poor immigrants and children of immigrants to attain prominent positions in life, but admission in some years will require a high school average of close to 85 (*see* 1907; 1976; City University of New York [CUNY], 1961).

Eberhard Faber pencils have their beginnings as German-born pencil manufacturer John Eberhard Faber, 26, sets up a New York office at 133 William Street to import and market pencils from his family's Bavarian factory, established by his great-grandfather Kasper Faber in 1761 (*see* 1861).

Painting: *Kindred Spirits* by Asher Durand, who has been commissioned by his patron Jonathan Sturges to paint the work in memory of the late Thomas Cole.

Theater: English actor William Charles Macready, 56, plays the title role in *Macbeth* 5/10 at the Astor Place Opera House, managed by onetime comedian James H. Hackett, now 49; partisans of actor Edwin Forrest, now 43, gather outside, possibly at the instigation of Forrest, who was mistreated at London in 1845. The mob grows to number more than 20,000 working-class men, who rage against William Backhouse Astor, the city's largest landlord and owner of the Opera House. "Burn the damned den of aristocracy," the crowd shouts; it interrupts the performance, proceeds to wreck the 18-month-old theater, and vandalizes the home of Mayor Woodhull. The police are unable to disperse the rioters, the Seventh Regiment of the National Guard commanded by mahogany merchant Abram Duryée, 34, is called in, Duryée is wounded twice, and militia men fire into the mob that surrounds the Opera House, killing 22 (as many as nine more will die later of their wounds), and injuring 48. Some men in the crowd retaliate, and the Astor Place riots end the next day with 50 to 70 policemen injured. Stamford, N.Y.-born adventurer Edward Zane Carroll "Ned Buntline" Judson, 26, is convicted of having led the riots and sentenced to a year in prison (*see* 1854). Judson earned a U.S. Navy midshipman's commission at age 15, and his action stories have appeared in *Knickerbocker Magazine* under the name Ned Buntline; he tracked down and captured two fugitive murderers in Kentucky in 1845, was arrested in 1846 for shooting to death the husband of his alleged mistress, somehow survived an actual lynching, and has recently been publishing his sensational periodical *Ned Buntline's Own* at New York. A newspaper editorial observes after the riots that they left behind "a feeling to which this community had hitherto been a stranger, . . . that there is now in our country, in New York City, what every good patriot has hitherto considered it his duty to deny—a *high* and a *low* class."

Sewing machine inventor Walter Hunt patents a safety pin (*see* 1832); now 53, he sells the patent rights for $400 in order to raise money to discharge a small debt (*see* paper collar, 1854).

The People's Bathing and Washing Establishment opened at 141 Mott Street is the city's first public bath (*see* 1792; Croton Water, 1842). The 5-year-old Association for Improving the Condition of the Poor has built the bathhouse; it is open only during the summer months, has separate baths for men and women, provides laundry facilities, and has a swimming pool. Some 60,000 persons will soon be availing themselves of the establishment, but relatively few can afford to pay 3¢ per hour to use the laundry or 5¢ to 10¢ for a bath, and the bath will close in 1861 for lack of business (*see* tenements, 1850).

Anshe Chesed synagogue is completed on the Lower East Side at 172-176 Norfolk Street, between Stanton and East Houston streets, to designs by Alexander Saeltzer. The first synagogue built as such (converted churches have been used up to now for Jewish congregations), it will survive as the city's oldest synagogue long after the Anshe Chesed congregation has moved to the upper West Side and will for years be its largest.

Plymouth Church is completed in Orange Street, between Hicks and Henry streets, for the Brooklyn Heights congregation of Connecticut-born Congregationalist pastor Henry Ward Beecher, 36, whose writings, abolitionist views, unorthodox manner, and original style of preaching, sermonizing, and attire have won him a wide following. The large brick meeting house replaces a 2-year-old structure that has burned down; designed by English architect James C. Wells, it has no steeple, and it looks more like an assembly hall than a house of worship, but its theater-like interior can accommodate 2,800, including standees (*see* human rights, 1856).

The first modular prefabricated cast iron and glass "curtain wall" buildings are erected at the corner of Washington and Murray streets in Manhattan by former watchmaker and inventor James Bogardus, 49, who has designed them on commission from local merchant Edgar H. Laing. The columns and spandrels that make up the façades are simply bolted together with the bolt heads covered by cast iron rosettes and other decorative ornaments. Born at Catskill, N.Y., Bogardus began by making iron parts for buildings, he will obtain a patent in early May of next year to cover his revolutionary invention, and prefabricated buildings will soon go up all over Manhattan, and in other cities as well (*see* department store, 1862).

The Croton Aqueduct Department is reorganized and charged with building a comprehensive brick sewer system for the city (*see* 1842). Increased water supplies now permit transporting waste through underground pipes, and cholera epidemics have highlighted the need for better sewage disposal, but the Association for Improving the Condition of the Poor will estimate nearly a decade hence that three-quarters of the city's 500 miles of streets still have no sewers (*see* 1902).

1850 Sen. Seward gains national recognition by his outspoken opposition to the compromise resolutions proposed January 29 by Kentucky's Whig Party senator Henry Clay, who is trying to reduce the growing polarity between North and South with regard to slavery in the various states, but Clay prevails.

Vice president (and former University of Buffalo chancellor) Millard Fillmore is sworn in as president of the United States July 10 following the death of President Zachary Taylor at Washington, D.C.

Italian independence fighter Giuseppe Garibaldi, 43, flees Austrian authorities and arrives at New York, where he is given shelter by inventor Antonio Meucci on Staten Island. The latter has just rented a four-room cottage in the Rosebank section, and Garibaldi will remain at the house until next year, making candles and teaching Meucci's parrot to say, "*Viva l'Italia—Fuori lo straniero*" ("Long live Italy—out with the foreigner").

Assembly speaker Horatio Seymour, now 40, runs for governor on the Democratic Party ticket but loses to Washington Hunt, 39, a Whig who has served as a congressman and state controller.

City voters elect Whig candidate Ambrose Cornelius Kingsland, 46, in the mayoralty race, defeating former congressman Fernando Wood, 38, who has been convicted of defrauding investors during the gold rush but nevertheless receives 17,973 votes to the 22,656 piled up by Kingsland (who will serve until 1852).

Real estate heir James William Beekman, now 34, is elected to the state senate at Albany (he will be reelected in 1862).

The American Antislavery Society's annual meeting opens at the Broadway Tabernacle May 7 with an address by Boston abolitionist William Lloyd Garrison, now 44. Also scheduled to speak is former Maryland slave Frederick Douglass, whose freedom was purchased by public subscription 2 years ago. Incensed at the presence of a black in the Tabernacle, Isaiah Rynders, leader of the Bowery B'hoys, jumps up at the start of Garrison's speech and heckles him, an abolitionist choir begins to sing, but the Bowery B'hoys make such a disturbance that the meeting cannot continue. When *Evening Post* editor Parke Godwin denounces the demonstrations May 8 the Bowery B'hoys decide to kill him, Godwin hears of it just in time, and he manages to escape.

A new Fugitive Slave Act passed by Congress September 18 strengthens the 1793 act by substituting federal jurisdiction for state jurisdiction. A deputy U.S. marshal at New York arrests local freedman James Hamlet as a fugitive from Baltimore in the first recorded action under the new act, but the arrest arouses so much public indignation that Hamlet is redeemed and freed. The Chicago City Council moves October 21 not to sustain the new act, but a mass meeting at New York October 30 resolves that the act *should* be sustained (*see* Syracuse, 1851).

Some 2,000 striking New York tailors found the Cooperative Union of Tailoring Estates July 15; a worker is killed in a trade dispute for the first time in U.S. history.

An estimated 50,000 Irish prostitutes work the city's streets and parks; many have been forced into the trade in order to support themselves and families or coerced into it by pimps (*see* 1870).

Chemical Bank moves to new premises at 270 Broadway, near Chambers Street (*see* 1824). Owners Isaac and John Jones dissolved the company's chemical works several years ago to concentrate on banking, renewed the bank's charter in 1844, and last year declared Chemical's first dividend—a 6 percent dividend that will increase to 18 percent in 1855 and 24 percent in 1856 (*see* Clearing House, 1853; panic, 1857).

Marine Midland Bank is founded by eight New York City and Buffalo businessmen to finance shipping operations on the Great Lakes.

The Manhattan Savings Institution is founded April 10 with offices at 648 Broadway. Mayor Ambrose C. Kingsland and former mayor Caleb S. Woodhull have organized the bank to serve working-class New Yorkers (*see* 1942).

Independence Savings Bank has its beginnings in the South Brooklyn Savings Institution that opens June 1 at 118 Atlantic Avenue; by day's end it has 12 accounts whose balances total $249. Open Mondays,

Wednesdays, and Saturdays from 5 o'clock until 7 (Wednesdays are for women depositors only), the bank will relocate its headquarters to Montague Street and change its name in 1975.

The Emigrant Industrial Savings Bank opens September 30 as an offshoot of the 33-year-old Irish Emigrant Society and takes in $3,009 from 20 depositors. Archbishop John Hughes has urged creation of the bank to protect immigrants' savings from sharpies, and many of the 18 businessmen who open the bank in a rented building at 51 Chambers Street are members of the society. Depositors will use the good offices of the bank to send $30 million in cash and prepaid tickets back to Ireland in the next 30 years as they use their earnings to finance the passage of family and friends to America (*see* 1967).

Manhattan Life Insurance Co. is founded February 28, its charter gains approval May 29, and it opens for business August 1 at 108 Broadway (it will move in 1865 to 156-158 Broadway). Ambrose C. Kingsland, Edwin D. Morgan, and Caleb S. Woodhull are among its 30 founders, and by 1870 it will have assets of $6.9 million (*see* building, 1894).

United States Life Insurance Co. is founded with $100,000 as New York emerges from a cholera epidemic (*see* medicine, 1849). Headed by Frederick Sheldon, it starts out with offices at 27 Wall Street, will move in 1852 to larger premises at 40 Wall Street, and by 1900 will have policies in force worth $20 million.

Brooks Brothers becomes Brooks Brothers as founder Henry Sands Brooks's sons Daniel, John, and Elisha take over the menswear store that he opened in 1818 (*see* 1833; 1874).

A visitor to the city reports that the "continuous chain" of omnibuses [horsecars] on Broadway creates such a "crush of traffic" that "you often have to wait 10 minutes before you are able to cross the street." The horsecars have pot-bellied stoves at one end to provide warmth in winter but are otherwise unheated.

The S.S. *Atlantic* goes into service for the New York & Liverpool United States Mail Steamship Co. (Collins Line), beginning the most audacious challenge mounted thus far to Samuel Cunard's Royal Mail Steam Packet Co. Truro, Mass.-born New York shipowner E. K. (Edward Knight) Collins, 47, came to New York at age 15 and has operated sailing packets since 1837; Brown Brothers has backed him in building the 2,856-ton 200-passenger paddle-wheeler, 282 feet in length overall, and although she

damages her side-wheels on ice off Sandy Hook after leaving her Hudson River pier at the foot of Canal Street April 27 she breaks the Royal Mail's speed record on her return voyage from Liverpool, crossing in 10 days, 16 hours (*see* 1852).

Surgeon James Marion Sims, 37, moves to New York from his native Montgomery, Ala., following publication in the *American Journal of the Medical Sciences* of a paper describing his success in repairing a vesico-vaginal fistula, an unpleasant and not uncommon tear between the bladder and vagina causing urine to leak into the vagina. Sims has developed a special speculum for use in the procedure, and his breakthrough establishes his reputation.

The archdiocese of New York is created July 19 and Bishop Hughes, now 53, is appointed the city's first archbishop, a position he will hold until his death in 1864. The Vatican's move incenses many Protestants, as does Archbishop Hughes's sermon "The Decline of Protestantism," in which he vows that the "true" church will "convert all pagan nations—including the inhabitants of the United States."

The Episcopal Church of the Transfiguration holds its first service in a structure erected at 1 East 29th Street to designs by architect Frederick Clarke Withers. The Rev. George H. Houghton founded the congregation 2 years ago and the size of his brick church will double in the next few decades (*see* "Little Church Around the Corner," 1870).

The city has nearly 50,000 Jews and 15 synagogues, most of them for immigrants on the Lower East Side.

Xavier High School takes over a building at 30 West 16th Street. Founded 3 years ago, it renames itself the College of St. Francis Xavier (it will offer college-level courses for many years) and will remain at its new location for the next 150 years, growing to have a student body of about 1,000.

Harper's Monthly (initally *Harper's New Monthly Magazine*) begins publication at New York in June and will continue into the 21st century (*see* publishers, 1817). The four Harper brothers have started the periodical to occupy the downtime of new steam presses they have installed in their Franklin Square plant and to promote their books (*see* Harper's Weekly, 1856).

Nonfiction: *New York by Gaslight* by *New-York Tribune* reporter George G. Foster, who writes about patrons of the city's oyster cellars, "The women, of course, are of the usual kind; but among the men, you would find, if you looked curiously, reverend judges and juvenile delinquents, pious and devout hypocrites, and undisguised libertines and debauchees."

Gallery of Illustrious Americans by upstate New York-born portrait photographer Matthew B. Brady, 27 (approximate), gains national prominence for Brady, who learned to make daguerrotypes from Samuel F. B. Morse in 1840 and set up a commercial studio in the city 6 years ago (*see* 1856).

Coloratura soprano Johanna Maria "Jenny" Lind, 30, signs a contract in January with showman P. T. Barnum, who guarantees "the Swedish nightingale" $1,000 per night plus all expenses, allows her to select her own concert repertory, and frees her to perform for charity. Barnum uses handbills, broadsides, and newspaper advertisements to make her name known; a crowd of more than 30,000 is on hand to greet Lind when she arrives at New York September 1, she opens at Castle Garden September 11 in a concert that attracts a crowd of more than 6,000, grosses $17,864.05, donates nearly $15,000 (her share of the receipts from her first two concerts) to charity, and departs November 25 on a 2-year tour that will earn $130,000, of which $100,000 will go to charities. The contract is revised to give Lind a share in the profits when it becomes clear that proceeds will exceed Barnum's original projections.

The Society for the Reformation of Juvenile Delinquents relocates its House of Refuge to a 10-acre site on Wards Island; it will exchange the property next year for a 30-acre site on Randalls Island, where it will have separate buildings for boys and girls (*see* 1838; 1884).

Mott Haven in the southwestern Bronx is developed by Manhasset-born ironworks owner Jordan L. Mott, 52, as an industrial village with suburban housing for workers holding jobs in Manhattan. Having invented the first stove that can burn anthracite coal, Mott purchased property from Gouverneur Morris 9 years ago and built a foundry in an area bounded by East 149th Street and St. Mary's Park to the north and the Harlem River to the south and west. He has encouraged the Harlem River Railroad to extend its line to his property by granting it a right-of-way over his land so long as it maintains a station there, built the Mott Haven Canal to provide access by boat and barge, encouraged other businessmen to locate factories in the area, and is soon joined by another foundry and a bakery (*see* 1888).

A 50-year period of large-scale tenement construction begins. The city has had tenements since 1824, the term having no pejorative connotations (it is simply another word for a multi-family house), but property in choice locations has become so expensive that only the rich can afford to use a standard 25-by-100-foot lot for a single-family house when the same lot can accommodate a five- or six-story tenement with four families per floor (*see* 1824). The new tenements have rudimentary plumbing facilities on each floor, if only because backyard outhouses take up valuable space that can be used to better advantage. Private houses and older tenements continue to rely on outhouses, but a national movement has been growing to promote personal cleanliness (*see* 1849; floating baths, 1870).

An explosion in Queens February 5 kills 64 people at 5-7 Hague Street.

Canal Street oyster cellars offer patrons all they can eat for 6¢ and along with vendors elsewhere in the city sell $6 million worth of the mollusks that are generally eaten raw with pepper, salt, lemon juice, or vinegar.

Poet Walt Whitman wrote for the Brooklyn Eagle *and sang of a city whose dynamism stirred the imagination.*

The population of New York City reaches 700,000, with 20 percent of it foreign-born, mostly German and Irish (the latter account for 69 percent of the city's indigent and 55 percent of its arrests). Brooklyn's population is scarcely 200,000.

1851 The 69th New York State Volunteer Regiment gains official acceptance October 12 as part of the state militia and is designated the 69th Regiment. Known locally as the Second Regiment of Irish Volunteers, it includes a company whose original members fought in the American Revolution and War of 1812, but the 69th is now made up mostly of immigrants from the city's Lower East Side (*see* 1861).

Former New York lieutenant governor Hamilton Fish is elected to the U.S. Senate with support from state party leaders William H. Seward and Thurlow Weed. He will be a loyal Whig until that party is dissolved in 1854, whereupon he will become a Republican.

Former chair maker and volunteer fire company foreman William M. (Magear) Tweed, 28, wins election to the city's Board of Aldermen, whose members are mostly Democrats with reputations for corruption (they will come to be known as "the forty thieves"). Tweed's middle name will come down through history as *Marcy*, but Magear was his mother's maiden name, he will never use the middle name *Marcy*, and it will later be concluded that *Marcy* was introduced by writers to associate Tweed with former U.S. Senator William L. Marcy, now 64, who made his famous "spoils system" speech in 1832.

Abolitionists at Syracuse rescue a fugitive slave October 1, but New Yorkers generally support last year's Fugitive Slave Law.

The U.S. Treasury turns out nearly 4 million $1 gold pieces—tiny coins authorized by Congress in 1849. Congress votes March 3 to authorize minting of 3¢ silver coins to reduce the demand for large copper pennies.

The Williamsburgh Savings Bank opens in a corner of the basement of a Greek Revival church at the corner of Old Fourth and South Third streets in Brooklyn. The bank will have a building of its own by 1854 (*see* "Tower of Strength," 1929).

Hanover Bank is founded in Manhattan (*see* 1912; real estate [India House], 1854; Manufacturers Hanover Trust, 1961).

Irving Trust Co. has its beginnings in a bank founded at New York; it will go through various name changes to become New York and London Trust, Columbia Trust, Knickerbocker Trust, Columbia-Knickerbocker Trust, etc. (*see* real estate, 1932; Bank of New York, 1988).

Businessman Philip Hone dies at his home near City Hall May 5 at age 70, having made a fortune from his auction business and, later, his investment in Pennsylvania coalfields and the Delaware & Hudson Canal but lost much of it in the panic of 1837; merchant Gardiner G. Howland hears of a friend's death and dies himself of a sudden heart attack at his Washington Square home November 9 at age 64, leaving a fortune estimated at $1 million.

The New York & Erie Rail Road reaches Dunkirk on Lake Erie May 15—the first line linking New York City with the Great Lakes, providing competition for the 26-year-old Erie Canal. President Millard Fillmore and other notables celebrate the occasion by traveling 20 miles upriver on a steamboat from the foot of Duane Street to Piedmont on the west bank of the Hudson and then riding 447 miles to Dunkirk. Begun in 1832 with state and county money, the Erie is now controlled by New York financier Daniel Drew, 53, who began his fortune as an upstate livestock dealer (he gained notoriety for "watering" his stock—feeding the animals salt and letting them drink their fill to put on weight before selling them). Drew has operated steamboats on the Hudson and on Long Island Sound in competition with Commodore van Derbilt (*see* 1852).

The New York and Hudson River Rail Road opens to link New York City with East Albany. Engineers and laborers have laid 144 miles of track along the riverbank, and the Hudson Line tracks—unlike those of the Erie—extend right into Manhattan, carrying steam locomotives and their cars south on Eleventh Avenue to a large depot between 30th and 32nd streets, whence horsecars carry passengers and freight down Tenth Avenue, West Street, and Hudson Street, with stops at 23rd, 14th, Christopher, and Chambers streets (*see* van Derbilt, 1858).

Completion of the Hudson River Railroad line to East Albany reduces demand for travel on Hudson River steamboats like the *Isaac Newton*, *Alida*, *New World*, and other ships except for recreation (*see* 1832). The rail journey takes only 4 hours as compared with 7½ by water, but steamboats will continue to play an important role in freight movement (*see Mary Powell*, 1861).

The *Flying Cloud* is launched by Nova Scotia-born Boston shipbuilder Donald McKay, 40, whose 229-foot clipper ship is the greatest of some 40 that will be built this year and next. Forty-one feet wide, 22 feet deep, and displacing 1,783 tons, she is bought by

New York merchant Moses H. Grinnell, now 48, of Grinnell, Minturn & Co. (*see* 1833), sails from Pier 20 on New York's East River under the command of Marblehead master Josiah Creasy and sets a new record by reaching San Francisco in just under 90 days (*see* 1852).

The Singer Sewing Machine patented August 12 by Rensselaer County-born itinerant actor-mechanic Isaac Merrit Singer, 39, will soon go into production with help from New York lawyer Edward Clark, 41, who will defend Singer against patent suits brought by Elias Howe of Boston, Walter Hunt, and others (*see* Hunt, 1832). After a boiler explosion destroyed his patented wood-carving machine, Singer watched some Boston mechanics try to repair a primitive sewing machine and was inspired to devise a better one; his machine will make him (and Clark) millionaires by turning unskilled workers into expert seamstresses and be the basis of a New York garment industry whose working conditions will often be deplorable. Howe will eventually win a Massachusetts court decision and make a fortune from royalties that Singer will pay as the sewing machine gains worldwide distribution (*see* 1856).

The city has a typhus epidemic that is traced to Irish immigrants. Bellevue Hospital is overrun with cases, and all other hospitals are filled to capacity. Twelve of Bellevue's medical staff come down with the fever; two die.

Kiehl's apothecary is founded by German-born entrepreneur John Kiehl, whose shop at 103 Third Avenue will sell medicinal ointments, baldness remedies, virility creams, and other such nostrums into the 21st century.

New York-born Roman Catholic convert Isaac T. Hecker, 31, returns home after studies in Europe to work as a missionary in the Redemptorist order, but he will become impatient with the order's (mainly German) hierarchy and together with four fellow priests will develop a plan for an English-speaking missionary order that will minister to the city's quickly Americanizing immigrant population (*see* Paulist Fathers, 1858).

The *New-York Times* (initially the *New-York Daily Times*) begins publication September 18 in candlelit fifth-floor loft offices at 113 Nassau Street with Henry J. (Jarvis) Raymond, 31, as editor. Raymond has worked for Horace Greeley's *Tribune* and James Watson Webb's *Courier and Enquirer*; elected to the State Assembly at Albany 2 years ago, he was named speaker this year and has gained backing from Albany bankers, who have raised $110,000 to start a paper that will be centrist in its style and political views. Windows in the building have not yet been fitted, nor have gaslight fixtures, the floors are unfinished, there are not enough desks, but Raymond has bought a steam-driven Hoe Lightning Press, hired a large staff, and achieves quick success, doubling his circulation to 10,000 in 10 days by offering more comprehensive reporting than the competition. The first edition of his six-column, 1¢ paper reports on three steamships that have just arrived, an ice-cart accident, and two fires (including a forest fire in Flatbush); it misses a fire in an iron foundry at 288 Stanton Street but covers the possible poisoning of a woman by her estranged husband. The *Times* doubles its circulation to 20,000 by year's end, supports the Whigs, and will support the new Republican Party beginning in 1854; its price will be 2¢ by 1858, 4¢ by 1865, 2¢ by 1873, 3¢ by 1891 (*see* 1889).

Irish-born printer-journalist Robert Bonner, 27, buys the *New-York Merchant's Ledger*, drops the word *Merchant's*, turns the *Ledger* into a family newspaper, fills its pages with fiction as well as reportage, pays well for contributions from popular writers, accepts no advertising, depends entirely on circulation for his profits, advertises in other papers to attract readers, and will see circulation grow to nearly 500,000 in the next 48 years.

Fiction: *Moby-Dick* by Herman Melville, who has based it in part on the 1823 William Scoresby book *Journal of a Voyage to the Northern Whale Fishery*, borrowed (for 13 months) from the 97-year-old New York Society Library. The book is published at London October 18 simply as *The Whale*, appears in a U.S. edition at New York November 14 as *Moby-Dick, or The Whale*, but will have sales of barely 50 copies in the author's lifetime and will not be recognized as a masterwork for another 70 years. Melville's narrator Ishmael walks along New York's waterfront early in the novel and decides on a "damp, drizzly November in [his] soul" to go to sea: "There now is your insular city of the Manhattoes, belted round by wharves as Indian isles by coral reefs—commerce surrounds it with her surf. Right and left, the streets take you waterward. Its extreme down-town is the battery, where that noble mole is washed by waves, and cooled by breezes, which a few hours previous were out of sight of land. Look at the crowds of water-gazers there. Circumambulate the city of a dreamy Sabbath afternoon. Go from Corlears Hook to Coenties Slip, and from thence, by Whitehall, northward. What do you see?—Posted like silent sentinels all around the town, stand thousands upon thousands of mortal men fixed in ocean reveries.

Some leaning against the spiles; some seated upon the pier-heads; some looking over the bulwarks of ships from China; some high aloft in the rigging, as if striving to get a still better seaward peep. But these are all landsmen; of week days pent up in lath and plaster—tied to counters, nailed to benches, clinched to desks . . ."

Novelist James Fenimore Cooper dies at Cooperstown September 14 on the eve of his 62nd birthday.

Painter John James Audubon dies at his northern Manhattan estate Minnie's Land January 27 at age 65 and is buried under a 16-foot runic cross in Trinity Cemetery (*see* 1842; New-York Historical Society, 1863).

The city outlaws gambling under strict terms imposed by the new Green Law, named for reformer Jonathan F. Green, but New York will remain wide open to betting parlors of various kinds as casino operators pay off patrol officers, ward politicians, and political bosses (*see* 1872).

George Templeton Strong notes in his diary in May that "half the city is being pulled down. The north corner of Wall and Broadway, an old landmark, is falling amid the execrations of pedestrians whom its ruins and rubbish drive off the sidewalk. The building on the north side of Trinity churchyard is to follow."

William Backhouse Astor begins construction of 200 brownstones in the blocks between Broadway and Ninth Avenue from 44th to 47th streets, using land that once belonged to the 70-acre Medcef Eden farm but was acquired by his late father, John Jacob Astor, and William Cutting in 1803 for $25,000 (Astor got the eastern half of the property, Cutting the western). Each brownstone house is three to five stories in height, and addresses in the West 40s between Tenth and Eleventh avenues will by 1855 be considered quite respectable for families of moderate means.

William Astor's contractors clear away rocky outcroppings along Sixth Avenue, putting up tenements and row houses on the avenue and in side streets as each block is graded.

The August issue of the *Horticulturist* magazine contains an article by Newburgh, N.Y., architect-horticulturist Andrew Jackson Downing, now 35, outlining the virtues of a large, centrally located park for Manhattan (*see* 1853; Bryant, 1844).

Norwich, N.Y.-born inventor Gail Borden, 48, returns from last year's London Great Exhibition with the Great Council Gold Medal for a dried-meat biscuit he developed as a surveyor in Texas. His ship encounters rough seas on the Atlantic, the two cows in the ship's hold become too seasick to be milked, an immigrant infant dies, and the hungry cries of the other infants determine Borden to find a way to produce a portable condensed milk that can keep without spoiling (*see* 1853).

Better-class New York restaurants offer their patrons turtle soup, calves'-head soup, planked shad, boiled chicken with oyster sauce, boiled mutton with capers, and roast partridge. A bottle of Mumm's Champagne in a silver bucket generally goes for $2, and $1 buys a bottle of imported Sauternes, while $2 will buy a bottle of Hochheimer or 1811 Rudesheimer. One restaurant advertises strawberries in January and prices the berries that have been shipped from southern Europe at 50¢ each.

The United States will receive 2.5 million immigrants in this decade, up from 1.7 million in the 1840s, and a large percentage will be Irish.

1852 Mexican War hero Gen. Winfield Scott, now 66, settles in the city. Friends who include Sen. Hamilton Fish present him with a four-story brownstone at 24 West 12th Street and he makes a bid for the presidency as a Whig candidate, winning only 42 electoral votes as compared to 254 for Democratic "dark horse" Franklin Pierce, 47, of New Hampshire.

Horatio Seymour is elected governor of New York, defeating the reelection bid of Washington Hunt. Now 42, Seymour will serve only one term before being ousted because he vetoed a prohibition measure.

Democrat Jacob A. Westervelt wins easy election in New York City's mayoralty contest, defeating his Whig rival Morgan Morgans with 33,251 votes (Morgans receives 23,719).

Wells, Fargo & Co. is founded at New York to "forward Gold Dust, Bullion, Specie, Packages, Parcels & Freight of all kinds, to and from New York and San Francisco . . . and all the principal towns of California and Oregon." Henry Wells, then 38, started an express service in 1844 between Buffalo and Detroit in partnership with William G. Fargo, then 26, and another partner. Fargo will consolidate with rival stagecoach companies in 1866 and become president of American Express in 1868 after a larger merger.

The S.S. *Pacific* goes into transatlantic service for the Collins Line (New York and Liverpool United States Mail Steamship Co.). A sister ship to the S.S. *Atlantic* that began service in 1850, the 2,856-ton *Pacific* is the first ship to cross from New York to Liverpool in less than 10 days (*see* 1854).

The *Sovereign of the Seas* launched by Donald McKay of last year's *Flying Cloud* fame confounds skeptics by showing that a 2,421-ton clipper ship can be practical (*but see* 1853).

 Mount Sinai Hospital has its beginnings in the Jews' Hospital in the city of New York (*see* 1855).

The death rate among Irish families in this decade will be 21 percent, as compared with 3 percent among the city's non-Irish.

The city's first YMCA has its beginnings in a reading room established at 659 Broadway by merchant George H. Petrie, who attended the London Great Exhibition 3 years ago and learned about the interdenominational Christian organization begun as a prayer group in 1844 by a 23-year-old dry-goods clerk. Petrie's YMCA, like the one at London, emphasizes Bible classes, missionary efforts, relief for the poor and sick, street-corner evangelism, and Sunday schools, but it will soon offer temporary boarding facilities as well (*see* education, 1857).

The Beth Hamedrash Hagodol congregation established on the Lower East Side will survive into the 21st century as the nation's oldest Orthodox Jewish congregation of Russians (*see* 1885).

Fiction: *Pierre, or The Ambiguities* by Herman Melville, whose hero moves from upstate New York into the city, where he is horrified by "the thieves' quarters, and all the brothels, Lock-and-Sin hospitals for incurables, and infirmaries and infernos of hell [that] seemed to have made one combined sortie, and poured out upon earth through the vile vomitory of some unmentionable cellar;" *A Peep at "Number 5;" or, a Chapter in the Life of a City Pastor* and *The Angel Over the Right Shoulder; or, The Beginning of a New Year* by Elizabeth Wooster Phelps, who gives birth to her third child in August and dies of "brain disease" November 30 at age 37.

 Theater: *Uncle Tom's Cabin* by George L. Aiken, 22, 9/27 at the Troy Museum. Adapted from the new Harriet Beecher Stowe novel, the play is performed at Purdy's National Theater on the Bowery, where "respectable colored people" are for the first time admitted, albeit through a special entrance, and seated in a parquet apart from the rest of the audience.

The 90-year-old St. Patrick's Day Parade marches up Fifth Avenue for the first time March 17.

The Harmonie Club has its beginnings in the Harmonie Gesellschaft, founded by German Jews who cannot gain admission to the city's other clubs. Members speak German as the club's official language, will hang a portrait of the kaiser in their hall after 1871, and will not adopt the name Harmonie Club until 1893 (*see* real estate, 1906).

The Metropolitan Hotel opens at the corner of Broadway and Prince Street. Designed in Italian palazzo style by John Butler Snook of Trench & Snook, the six-story hostelry is the city's first luxury hotel since the Astor House opened in 1836, with lavish furnishings in the public rooms and some 500 guest rooms boasting hot and cold running water, with steam heat in every room. The hotel and its garden will survive until 1895.

The safety elevator invented in a Yonkers foundry by Vermont-born master mechanic Elisha G. (Graves) Otis, 41, will lead to the development of the high-rise buildings that will transform New York by permitting population density without overcrowding. Otis sets up ratchets along each side of an elevator shaft at the Yonkers Bedstead Manufacturing Co., he attaches teeth to the sides of the cage, the hoisting rope that holds up the cage keeps the teeth clear of the ratchets as long as the rope remains under tension, and when the tension is released the teeth grip the ratchets in the shaft and hold the cage securely in place. Otis has been about to join the gold rush to California but changes his mind when he receives two unsolicited orders for his "safety hoister" (*see* 1854).

 Horticulturist, architect, and landscape designer Andrew Jackson Downing drowns July 28 at age 36 while trying to save fellow passengers aboard the steamboat *Henry Clay* that has caught fire and exploded while proceeding down the Hudson toward New York (*see* 1851). His English-born assistant Calvert Vaux, 27, carries on Downing's work, having gained a reputation with his 1841 "Treatise on the Theory and Practice of Landscape Gardening" and his 1842 work *Cottage Residences* (*see* Central Park, 1853).

1853 A new city charter adopted by the electorate in June replaces wards with newly drawn voting districts. The number of wards in the city has grown to 22, up from just six in 1686 (Brooklyn has 19), and ward boundaries will be continued until the end of the century for purposes of census taking and school administration, but although wards may vary in size from a few blocks to several square miles, they have since 1800 been defined as much by their cultural characteristics, economic status, ethnic makeup, and population density as by geography, and they have become centers of political power and political corruption. Most of New York's wards have been below 14th Street; ward bosses have often been saloonkeepers, and they have dispensed patronage to the workingmen of their districts in return for support at the polls, relaying opinions and complaints to political leaders higher up the ladder while stumping for votes. A City Reform League headed by Peter Cooper has persuaded members of the state legislature at Albany to propose the new charter, whose measures have the support of League members who include merchants Henry Aspinwall and Henry Grinnell, Merchants Exchange president Simeon Baldwin, *New-York Times* editor Henry Raymond, capitalist Moses Taylor, shipbuilder William Webb, publisher James Harper, and other prominent citizens. Under the new charter, aldermen may suggest amendments but have little power beyond that; the charter entrusts a 60-man Board of Councilmen, elected annually, to handle all legislation with regard to expenditure and to award any contract worth more than $250 to the lowest bidder. The city's "Forty Thieves" are swept out of office in the November elections as nativist agitators turn public sentiment against immigrants.

The city's police force wears uniforms for the first time (*see* 1845), but police officers remain political appointees, they will not have to pass civil-service examinations until 1884, and many if not most of them depend on illegal payoffs to supplement their salaries (*see* 1857).

The Children's Aid Society is founded by Connecticut-born social worker Charles Loring Brace, 27 (Yale '46), who has studied at Yale Divinity School and Union Theological Seminary, worked with homeless, illiterate, immigrant boys in the city (the police call them "street rats"), and gained support from prominent philanthropists who include Howard Potter and Theodore Roosevelt. Preaching the gospel of self-help, opposing charitable aid that will encourage dependence, Brace goes into "crime nests" with "moral disinfectants," beginning with mission classes (religious meetings). He will move on to open a reading room and an industrial school, or workshop, and although the Society's aim is to return as many of the boys as possible to their own families, if such exist, it will more often ship them out of the city to adoptive families in Ohio, Illinois, and beyond (*see* Newsboys' Lodging House, 1854).

The Society for the Protection of Destitute Catholic Children (the Catholic Protectory) is established with encouragement from Archbishop Hughes and attempts to deal with as many as 60,000 Irish children who wander the city. Headed by Levi Ives, who believes that "by proper religious instruction and the teaching of useful trades" it can "raise the children above their slum environment," the Protectory will acquire a 114-acre farm in Westchester.

Corn Exchange Bank is founded February 1 with initial capitalization of $500,000. A group of merchants who trade in grain, cotton, and coffee at the Corn Exchange (predecessor of the Produce Exchange) have subscribed funds to start the bank that in 1899 will be the city's first to establish a branch.

United States Trust is chartered with offices at 45 Wall Street. The bank will specialize in trusts for individuals and corporations and survive as the oldest financial institution of its kind.

Manufacturers Trust is founded at Brooklyn (*see* 1812; 1950; Manufacturers Hanover Trust, 1961).

President Franklin Pierce opens the first U.S. world's fair July 14 in a Crystal Palace modeled on the one used for the 1851 London Great Exhibition. Located to the west of the holding reservoir on Fifth Avenue between 40th and 42nd streets, the structure designed by architects Georg J. B. Carstensen and Charles Gildemeister is in the shape of a Greek cross with a dome in the center. It houses an "Exhibition of the Industry of All Nations" with more than 4,000 exhibitors, most of them American, but temperatures reach 100°, as many as 230 New Yorkers die of heat in one day, and although paid attendance increases in September as the weather cools and eventually exceeds 1 million, its sponsors are stuck with debts of about $300,000 when the fair closes November 1. Space will be leased out for various events in the next few years (*but see* fire, 1858).

The New York Clearing House that opens October 11 at 14 Wall Street is the first U.S. bank clearinghouse; 52 commercial banks have created the nonprofit entity to facilitate daily settling of demand obligations such as checks in the first U.S. organization of its kind; 38 banks use the facility on its first day, and total clearings for the day amount to nearly $2 million.

The Home Insurance Co. is founded with an initial subscription of $500,000 by New York entrepreneurs who defy warnings that their venture is "a desperate undertaking" in light of the 1845 Broad Street fire. The New York state comptroller warned in his annual report last year that mutual companies should not go outside the bounds of their own counties or, at most, beyond an adjoining county, but the

Home proceeds to underwrite protection on a national scale through local agents, and within 18 months the company has 140 agents.

The Continental Insurance Co. is founded by a group of 12 New Yorkers who open offices in the basement of 6 Wall Street to offer fire insurance. Its initial capital is $500,000 and its first president is former mayor William V. Brady.

Merchant Samuel S. Howland dies at New York February 9 at age 62, leaving a fortune estimated at $1 million; businessman and insurance pioneer William Bard dies on Staten Island October 17 at age 75; metals-trading magnate Anson Greene Phelps of Phelps, Dodge dies at New York November 30 at age 72.

New York has 683 horse-drawn omnibuses, up from 255 in 1846, and they carry more than 100,000 passengers per day. The city begins to replace its circular cobblestones with so-called Belgian blocks that provide better footing for horses and stand up better to the wear of iron-rimmed wagon wheels (*see* 1876).

The New York Central Railroad is created by a consolidation of 10 short-line railroads between Albany and Buffalo. It is the first major U.S. rail combine, but gauge standards change at the New York, Pennsylvania, and Ohio state borders, and the city of Erie, Pa., tears up rails of identical gauge in order to force trains to stop at Erie (*see* van Derbilt, 1867).

Transatlantic steamship pioneer Junius Smith dies at the Bloomingdale Asylum January 22 at age 72 after some months' illness in a nephew's home in Astoria. He returned to America in 1843, bought a plantation outside Greenville, S.C., tried to grow tea, but was beaten senseless in December 1851 by neighbors who took offense at his antislavery sentiments.

The *Great Republic* launched by Donald McKay is the world's largest sailing ship but is too big to be a commercial success (*see* 1852). The 4,555-ton four-masted barque has patent double topsails and a 15-horsepower steam engine on deck to handle her yards and work her pumps.

New York shipping magnate Cornelius van Derbilt acknowledges that he is worth $11 million and that his fortune brings him an annual return of 25 percent (*see* 1850; 1858).

The Catholic diocese of Brooklyn is established, the first Bishop of Brooklyn being one John Loughlin.

Manhattan College has its beginnings in the Academy of Holy Infancy, opened by the Brothers of the Christian Schools on the Bloomingdale Road (later Broadway) at 131st Street (*see* 1923).

Fiction: "Bartleby, the Scrivener: A Story of Wall Street" by Herman Melville is published in *Putnam's* magazine. It has been inspired by Charles Dickens's novel *Bleak House.*

The world's fair in New York's Crystal Palace is the first to exhibit paintings in a picture gallery; it also includes the best and largest sculpture collection exhibited thus far in America.

New York post-debutante Caroline Webster Schermerhorn, 23, marries local real estate baron William Backhouse Astor, Jr., whose brother lives next door to her family's house in Lafayette Place (she will drop William's middle name and become queen of society as the Mrs. Astor; *see* 1872).

Bay Ridge, Brooklyn, gets its name (*see* 1652). Until now it has been called Yellow Hook because of the yellow clay found in the region, but associations with recent yellow fever epidemics have made that name undesirable.

The Rodeph Sholom synagogue is completed on the Lower East Side at 8-10 Clinton Street, between Stanton and East Houston streets, where it will survive as the city's second-oldest synagogue long after 1886, when its congregation will move uptown.

A cast-iron-clad office building designed by James Bogardus is completed for Tatham & Brothers at 82 Beekman Street in Lower Manhattan; it will survive until 1967.

Architect John McComb, Jr. dies at New York May 25 at age 89.

The St. Nicholas Hotel opens in January on Broadway between Spring and Broome streets. Built of white marble with 600 rooms, it has a staff of 322, soon fills up with guests attracted by the Crystal Palace Exhibition, and is considered more luxurious than the Astor House, although neither has private baths.

The Everett House opens on the northwest corner of 17th Street and Fourth Avenue, fronting on Union Square. A five-story building, it will be enlarged in a few years and stand until 1908 with a portrait of orator Edward Everett in its reading room.

Lord Ellsmere arrives as Britain's representative at the world's fair and is greeted by the enterprising manager of the 7-year-old Clarendon Hotel on Fourth Avenue at 18th Street, who sends a boat down the harbor to receive his lordship, who takes rooms for himself and his entourage at the Clarendon, bringing it instant success. The hotel has no private baths (no hotel does), but its wine rooms are extensive and it offers privacy comparable to that found in a high-class club. The Clarendon will close in 1898, but the building at 215 Fourth Avenue will survive until 1909.

The state legislature at Albany votes July 21 to let the city use its power of eminent domain to acquire more than 700 acres of land for use as a great "public space" (*see* Bryant, 1844; Downing, 1851; 1852). The Commissioners' Plan of 1811 provided for parade grounds, squares, and "places" that totaled about 450 acres, but subsequent development has shrunk that area to about 117 acres. Assemblyman Daniel E. (Edgar) Sickles, 33, of New York City has sponsored the legislation, which for the first time employs the term "Central Park;" son of a local real estate speculator, Sickles claims to be only 27, partly because he was married in September of last year to 16-year-old Teresa Bagilio, whom he had seduced while living, as was she, in the home of the late librettist Lorenzo Da Ponte (Archbishop Hughes married them). Sickles was indicted in 1837 for stealing $100 entrusted to him by philanthropist Peter Cooper but later studied law, became involved in Tammany politics, is appointed first secretary to the U.S. legation at London, and embarks August 6, leaving his wife and infant daughter behind. The city appropriates some 624 acres of rocky, swampy real estate that runs from 59th Street north to 106th Street between Fifth and Eighth avenues; the land has been left undeveloped because it is too remote from the city's population center and because its tremendous rock outcroppings make it too difficult and costly to develop for any other purpose. The rock is Manhattan Schist dating to the time of the dinosaurs; 20,000 years ago it was covered with glacial ice hundreds of feet thick (*see* Olmsted, 1857).

A fire December 10 in Franklin Square destroys 16 buildings, including the offices of Harper and Brothers.

Gail Borden succeeds in his efforts to produce condensed milk (*see* 1852). Now 52, he has lost between $60,000 and $100,000 in his meat-biscuit venture, but he has used vacuum pans borrowed from Shakers at New Lebanon, N.Y., to develop a process for making a product that has no burnt taste or discoloration and lasts for nearly 3 days without souring. (He believes its keeping properties are due to the fact that it is condensed; only later will he learn that his heating process has destroyed microorganisms that cause milk to spoil.) Borden travels to Washington to file a patent claim (*see* 1856).

1854 The new Republican Party organized February 28 at Ripon, Wis., attracts New York Whigs, who follow the lead of Sen. Seward. He strongly opposes the Kansas-Nebraska Bill that would open Nebraska to settlement on the basis of popular sovereignty, but Congress passes the legislation May 20, it undoes the sectional truce of 1850, and it effectively destroys the Whig Party.

Bushwick and Williamsburgh are incorporated into the growing city of Brooklyn (*see* 1660; 1800).

Republican Myron Holley Clark, 48, wins election to the state governorship by just 305 votes out of a 370,000 total. An ardent Prohibitionist, he will succeed in obtaining passage of a bill banning sale of alcoholic beverages, but it will be in force for less than 1 year before being declared unconstitutional.

Fernando Wood wins election to office as mayor, running on the Soft Shells-Hard Shells ticket and receiving 19,993 votes as compared with 18,553 for the nativist American Party candidate James W. Barker and 15,386 for the Reform Party candidate Wilson G. Hunt. A racist who defends slavery, citing the importance of the cotton trade to the city's economy, Wood will make himself a political "boss" and gain wide support from poor immigrants.

New York Democrat John Kelly, 32, wins election to the House of Representatives with support from Tammany Hall. The only Roman Catholic in Congress, Kelly will speak out vigorously against the new nativist American Party, whose members hold their first national convention in November at Cincinnati after launching attacks against immigration, persecuting Irish Catholics in particular. New York publisher E. Z. C. "Ned Buntline" Judson calls it the "Know-Nothing" Party because its members, when asked about it, say, "I know nothing" (*see* Kelly, 1868).

Daniel E. Sickles leaves his post as first secretary of the U.S. legation at London December 16, having introduced a notorious New York prostitute and madam to Queen Victoria. Now 35, he returns to his native New York and next year will win election to the state senate at Albany (*see* 1861).

Scots-born journalist James Redpath, 21, of Horace Greeley's *New-York Tribune* travels through the slave states urging slaves to run away.

The Newsboys' Lodging House opens at the corner of Fulton and Nassau streets. Founded by philanthropist Charles Loring Brace of the Children's Aid Society for orphaned newsboys, it charges 6¢ per night for a bed and breakfast (*see* 1853; strike, 1899).

$ Johnson & Higgins insurance brokers takes that name following the departure of Walter Restored Jones, Jr., who is succeeded by A. Foster Higgins (*see* 1845).

The credit-rating service B. Douglass and Co. is founded by Benjamin Douglass, 38, who 5 years ago joined with Lewis Tappan's brother Arthur to buy the Mercantile Agency started by Lewis in 1841. Douglass has purchased Arthur's interest and will, in turn, sell his agency to R. G. Dun in 1858 (*see* Bradstreet, 1855; Dun and Bradstreet, 1933).

German-born entrepreneur Conrad Poppenhusen, 36, arrives at what later will be College Point, Queens, and sets up a rubber factory on cheap waterfront land. He began his career at age 10, doing accounts in English and German for his textile-trader father at Hamburg, worked to support his mother and pay off debts after his father died in 1832, came to Brooklyn at age 25 to manage a small business in the Williamsburg section, became a partner in firm of Meyer & Poppenhusen making buttons, brushes, combs, and corset stays from whalebone, met Charles Goodyear, and obtained exclusive rights to the vulcanizing process that has made hard rubber a cheap replacement for whalebone in everything from combs to telescopes. In the next few years Poppenhusen will drain the surrounding marshes, erect houses for his workers, bring in clean running water, and build a cobblestone causeway. His Enterprise Rubber Works will acquire other firms to become the American Hard Rubber Co., Poppenhusen will recruit immigrant workers on their arrival, and College Point will become the "rubber capital of the Northeast" (*see* iron mines, education [Poppenhusen Institute], 1868).

The 949-ton emigrant ship *Bremen* arrives under sail May 18 from Bremerhaven, having carried 418 passengers on her 37-day maiden voyage. She will be rerigged as a bark in 1868 and used on various routes for various purposes until she goes missing in November 1888 (*see* S.S. *Bremen*, 1858).

Steamboat pioneer Nicholas J. Roosevelt dies at Skaneateles in Onondaga County July 30 at age 86.

The Union Ferry Company consolidates a dozen competing East River ferry lines and makes 1,250 crossings per day at a standard 2¢ fare, with Williamsburg ferries leaving Peck's Slip every 10 minutes and Grand Street every 5 minutes during working hours. By 1870 the city will have more than two dozen ferry lines, 16 of them on the East River, 10 on the North (Hudson) River; there will be 10 between Manhattan and Brooklyn, two to Hunter's Point, two to Green Point, one to Mott Haven, and one to Harlem; on the Hudson there will be five to Jersey City, one to Weehawken, one to Fort Lee, two to Staten Island, and one to Elizabethport. Fares on the big, comfortable side-wheelers will vary from 2¢ to Brooklyn, 3¢ to New Jersey, and 10¢ to Harlem or Staten Island, and while ferry travel is pleasant in fine weather it can be hazardous when fog, rain, or snow limits visibility, collisions on the crowded waterways are all too common, and safety inspection is lax (*see Westfield* explosion, 1871).

The side-wheeler S.S. *Arctic* sinks off Cape Race, Newfoundland, September 27 after colliding with the 250-ton French iron propeller ship S.S. *Vesta*. A sister ship to the S.S. *Pacific* that went into service in 1852, the 3,000-ton S.S. *Arctic* has been the largest and most splendid of the Collins Line steamships (*see* 1850), her casualties include 92 of her 153 officers and men, and all her women and children are lost, including the wife, only daughter, and youngest son of E. K. Collins, Brown Brothers partner William Benedict Brown, 29, his French-born wife Clara (*née* Moulton), their infant child, the child's nurse, and Brown's sister Maria Miller "Millie" Brown, 21, favorite daughter of New York banker James Brown of Brown Brothers, who also loses his daughter Grace Davison Brown Allen and her infant son in the tragedy. George Templeton Strong writes in his diary that Brown, now 63, is "so crushed and shattered" that he is "hardly expected to live."

A cholera epidemic takes 2,509 lives in the city despite the availability of pure water since 1842 (*see* 1849; 1866).

∞ The Five Points House of Industry operated by clergyman Lewis M. Pease at 155 Worth Street separates from the Five Points Mission founded 7 years ago.

Polytechnic University has its beginnings in the Brooklyn Collegiate and Polytechnic Institute, chartered with financial help from Mrs. William S. Packer. The college preparatory school will hold its first classes next year under the presidency of John H. Raymond and gain prominence as Brooklyn Polyprep (*see* 1869).

Frank Leslie's Ladies' Gazette of Paris, London, and New York Fashions begins publication at New York in January. English-born engraver-publisher Frank Leslie, 32, changed his name from Henry Carter, gained experience as an engraver for the *Illustrated London News*, and has been a poster artist for P. T. Barnum (*see* 1842; *Leslie's Illustrated Newspaper*, 1855).

The Academy of Music catered to the Old Guard of the upper crust, staging operatic productions that rivaled Europe's.

The Astor Library opens February 1 just below Astor Place in Lafayette Street (*see* 1848). None of the library's 80,000 volumes may be taken from the building, nor can a book even be removed from the shelf unless the visitor is accompanied by a library officer, but by 1873 the library will be averaging 86 visitors per day, 5 percent of them women (*see* New York Public Library, 1895).

The Mercantile Library moves into Clinton Hall at 13 Astor Place (*see* 1830). The building was formerly the Italian Opera House, before that the Astor Place Opera House (*see* 1870).

Franconi's Hippodrome opens in March on the west side of Broadway opposite Madison Square between 23rd and 24th streets with a spectacular chariot race. Built at a cost of $200,000, the Hippodrome has a two-story outer wall, a canvas roof 80 feet high, can accommodate 10,000 spectators for exhibitions of gymnastics, horsemanship, and the like, but it will be razed in less than 2 years to make way for the Fifth Avenue Hotel.

Opera: The New York Academy of Music opens 10/2 at the northeast corner of 14th Street and Irving Place with a performance of the 1831 Vincenzo Bellini opera *Norma*, featuring Italian soprano Giulia Grisi, 43 (she has appeared earlier in the year at Castle Garden in the title role of the 1833 Donizetti opera *Lucrezia Borgia*) with her paramour, tenor Giovanni Matteo Mario, 43, backed by a 24-piece orchestra (*see* Astor Place Opera House, 1847). Built at a cost of $335,000, the new house has private and stage boxes for the city's Old Guard social families, 4,600 seats upholstered in crimson velvet, and an interior painted in white and gold with thousands of gaslights to provide illumination. Its first season will consist of 79 or 80 performances

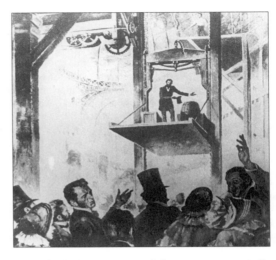

Elisha Otis's elevator permitted the city to rise vertically instead of sprawling over vast distances. OTIS ELEVATOR CO.

(*see* Metropolitan Opera House, 1883; Carnegie Hall, 1891).

Cabinetmaker Duncan Phyfe dies at New York August 16 at age 86 (approximate). He sold his business and retired 7 years ago.

New York socialite Robert Schuyler absconds to Canada. President of both the New Haven and New York & Harlem railroads, he turns out to have counterfeited 20,000 shares of New Haven stock and sold them for $2 million; just as shocking, it develops that he has for years been living a double life, keeping a second family under the name Spicer.

The Otis safety elevator invented 2 years ago impresses visitors to the world's fair that opens for a second season on Fifth Avenue. The eight-sided, 350-foot Latting Observatory erected by Warren Latting just north of the Crystal Palace provides spectacular city views for visitors to the fair, and a steam-powered elevator gets them to the top. Elisha G. Otis has thus far sold only three of his devices, but he has himself hoisted aloft in the cage, orders the hoisting rope to be cut, and plunges melodramatically earthward as spectators gasp and scream; safety ratchets engage to halt his descent, and Otis emerges from his elevator cage saying, "All safe. All safe, ladies and gentlemen" as he sweeps the stovepipe hat from his head and takes a bow. His stop is abrupt because his design is still crude, but he works on improvements and next year will invent a new steam engine drive (*see* 1857). Latting's

$100,000 venture fails: the walls of the reservoir just to the east of the Crystal Palace afford views just as sweeping and at no cost whatever.

St. Stephen's Church is completed at 149 East 28th Street, between Lexington and Third avenues. James Renwick, Jr. has designed the structure in red-brick and brownstone Romanesque Revival style for a Roman Catholic congregation that has engaged Italian-born painter Constantino Brumidi to paint a 22-by-44-foot Crucifixion scene behind the altar as well as murals of the Immaculate Conception, the Sacred Heart, St. Cecilia, a Madonna, and King David (an exile who arrived in 1852 after having sided with revolutionaries against the Pope, Brumidi may also have designed the church's 100 stained-glass windows); a brick-and-stone extension to 29th Street will be completed in 1865 to designs by P. C. Keely.

The Marble Collegiate Church has its beginnings in the Fifth Avenue Church consecrated at 272 Fifth Avenue (29th Street). Built to Gothic Revival designs by Samuel A. Warner, it is part of the Collegiate Reformed Protestant Dutch Church whose origins date to 1628 and it will be designated the Marble Collegiate Church in 1906.

The five-story Hotel Brevoort opens on Fifth Avenue at 10th Street. Created by joining together three existing structures on property owned by the Brevoort family, it caters to English sea captains who may advise passengers to stay at the new hostelry.

Corona, Queens, has its beginnings in the community of West Flushing developed by New York City real-estate speculators on land adjoining Flushing Bay.

Architect Minard Lafever dies at Williamsburg, L.I., September 26 at age 56.

The Jennings Building fire April 25 at 231 Broadway in Manhattan kills 11 firefighters.

The Brooklyn Institute introduces house sparrows to North America, releasing eight pairs inside Green-Wood Cemetery in hopes of limiting the growth of the canker-worm, whose caterpillars are eating the cemetery's shade trees, but instead of eating the worms the birds (a species of wood finch) will eat fruits, grains, insects, and seeds (plentiful where horses congregate), displacing native species and carrying diseases (see starlings, 1890).

McSorley's Ale-House opens in the ground floor of a five-story red-brick tenement at 15 East 7th Street, off Cooper Square, under the proprietorship of Irish-born publican John McSorley, 31, who opens each morning at 7 o'clock, sweeps out, covers the floor with fresh sawdust, serves ale in pewter mugs at 5¢ per mug to the German and Irish brewers, bricklayers, carpenters, slaughterhouse workers, tanners, and teamsters who frequent the neighborhood, serves a free lunch of cheese, soda crackers, and raw onions, lives above the place (he will buy the building in 1864), heats his rooms with a pot-bellied stove, does not serve women, and will own the saloon until his death in 1910 at age 87, whereupon his son will take over.

1855 Alderman William M. Tweed, now 32, loses a bid for reelection but has so strengthened his position in Tammany Hall that he will rival Mayor Fernando Wood as leader of the Democratic Party organization. Tweed has served in the House of Representatives at Washington without giving up his aldermanic seat.

The Cincinnati credit-rating agency John M. Bradstreet & Co. moves to New York, where Bradstreet, 40, will compete with B. Douglass & Co. (see R. G. Dun, 1859; Dun and Bradstreet, 1933).

Importer Moses Taylor quits the business to become president of the City Bank. Now 49, he has long since become a millionaire.

The Harlem Gas Light Co. is founded February 8 to produce and distribute methane gas. The Metropolitan Gas Light Co. of the city of New York is founded April 17 for the same purpose as more New Yorkers demand modern illumination to replace candles. The Flushing Gas Light Co. is founded October 11 to provide service beyond Manhattan.

Kerosene gets its name from Long Island physician Abraham Gestner of Newtown Creek, who makes kerosene from raw petroleum, promotes it as a patent medicine (in the absence of any lamp or stove that can burn it efficiently as a fuel), and coins a word from the Greek keros (wax) (see 1859).

German-born engineer John A. (Augustus) Roebling, 48, completes a suspension bridge across Niagara Gorge after another engineer has quit in a dispute over finances. A 368-ton train traverses the 821-foot single-span Roebling bridge March 6 and is the first train to cross a bridge sustained by wire cables.

An accident on the Camden and Amboy Railroad near Burlington, N.J., August 29 kills 21, injures 75.

Directors of the Hudson River Railroad make Irish-born Brooklyn commission merchant Samuel Sloan, 37, a director and will soon elect him president, a position that he will hold for the next 9 years, during which time shares in the company will rise in value from $17 to $140 (*see* Delaware, Lackawanna, 1864).

Woman's Hospital opens May 4 at 29th Street and Madison Avenue. The world's first institution established by women "for the treatment of diseases peculiar to women and for the maintenance of a lying-in hospital," it is a charity institution with a capacity of 40 beds, one surgeon (the now famous gynecologist J. Marion Sims; *see* 1850), a nurse, and two matrons—one to administer to the sick, one to supervise domestic arrangements. Created with financial support from civic-minded New York women and a $2,500 grant from the Board of Aldermen, it will later move to 49th Street, between Park and Lexington avenues, and then to 114th Street, between Columbus and Amsterdam avenues, where it will become part of St. Luke's Hospital in 1952.

New York Hospital grows with the addition of South House, erected to replace the marine department (*see* 1841; 1865).

Mount Sinai Hospital (still called The Jews' Hospital) opens a facility in West 28th Street between Seventh and Eighth avenues (*see* 1852; 1866).

Frank Leslie's Illustrated Newspaper begins publication at New York December 15 with the announced intention of "seizing promptly and illustrating the passing events of the day" (*see* 1854; 1871).

Fiction: *Ruth Hall* by Maine-born writer Sara Payson Willis, 44, satirizes her brother Nathaniel, 49, who co-publishes and edits the *New York Home Journal*, and his social life (she will marry English-born biographer James Parton, now 33, next year, move to New York, and go to work for Robert Bonner's *New York Ledger*, with which she will maintain a relationship until her death in 1872).

Poetry: *Leaves of Grass* by former *Brooklyn Eagle* editor Walt (Walter) Whitman, 36, whose volume of 12 poems has been published at his own expense, receives mixed reviews, and sells few copies. Included are poems that will later be titled "Song of Myself," "I Sing the Body Electric," and "There Was a Child Went Forth" (*see* 1856).

London-born actress-theatrical producer Laura Keene (originally Mary Moss), 35 (approximate), opens her own theater in New York under the name Laura Keene's Varieties. She made her New York debut 3 years ago with James W. Wallack's company and has enjoyed great success at San Francisco.

The Union Club moves into a $300,000 brownstone at the corner of Fifth Avenue and 21st Street; it has grown since 1836 to have between 400 and 500 members (*see* 1932).

One of every four New York families has at least one domestic servant (the city has 31,000 domestics, more women are thus employed than in any other occupation, and being able to afford a cook, maid, or nurse defines one's status as middle class).

Street tough William "Butcher Boy" Poole, 25, is shot to death March 8 by Welshman Lewis Baker following his dispute with Irish-born heavyweight boxer John Morrissey. Poole has fought the Bowery Boys and other immigrant gangs, more than 50,000 attend his funeral, nativist newspapers report that his last words were, "Goodbye, boys, I die a true American," and Baker's murder trial exacerbates animosities between native-born Americans and Irish immigrants. So widespread is crime among the city's Irish population that incidents of mob violence in the streets are called "donnybrooks" after the town in Ireland, and police vans sent to carry arrested individuals to jail are called "paddy wagons."

The Workingmen's Home is completed north of Canal Street between Mott and Elizabeth streets. Financed for black tenants by the 10-year-old New York Association for Improving the Conditions of the Poor and designed by John W. Ritch, the six-story structure has gas-lighted exterior galleries to provide access to the upper floors, each tenant has running water and a toilet; although interior bedrooms receive no light, the standards for natural light and ventilation are slightly superior to those at the Gotham Court built in 1850. Two large rooms at the top are used for concerts, moral indoctrination, and religious services, and while there is initially "much disorder, disquiet, and even great indecencies of conduct" (as the 1858 annual report will state), a superintendent is charged with enforcing a strict code of morals and hygiene (*see* 1867).

A three-sided cast-iron fire watchtower designed by architect Julius Kroehl is erected at the southwest corner of Madison Avenue and 121st Street in Harlem's Mount Morris Park (*see* 1839). The three-tiered structure with spiral staircase and octagonal lookout will serve until 1878 as a fire tower and survive as the only such tower.

The Knickerbocker Ice Co. is founded to supply local residents with ice harvested from lakes and ponds up the Hudson River or in New England. Most New York households preserve large blocks of ice through the warm-weather months, keeping them in deep wells insulated by hay and sawdust to minimize melting (*see* 1882).

Rheingold Beer has its beginnings in a large Brooklyn plant opened by German-born brewer Samuel Liebmann, 56, who left his native Würtemberg last year with his sons Joseph, Henry, and Charles. They will carry on the business after Samuel's death in 1872 and give it over to their six sons in 1905; the brewery will continue production in Brooklyn until 1976.

New York and other states adopt Prohibition laws as widespread drunkenness raises alarms (see 1849).

Gail Borden obtains a patent for his condensed milk containing sugar to inhibit bacterial growth (see 1853; 1856). Unsweetened condensed milk will not be canned satisfactorily until 1885.

The city's Irish population reaches 244,886, up from 17,773 just 15 years ago, as the after-effects of Ireland's potato famine in the 1840s continue to encourage emigration (see 1900).

The New York State Immigration Commission leases Castle Garden at the foot of Manhattan August 3 to receive immigrants and connects it to the mainland with landfill, fencing it off from the surrounding area (see 1847). Some 400,000 people arrive in the course of the year; by 1889 Castle Garden will process more than 8 million arrivals (two out of every three U.S. immigrants) after medical inspection at Staten Island. Passengers not held in quarantine at Staten Island now dock at piers on the Hudson or East River, first- and second-class passengers are discharged after going through Customs, and steerage passengers are taken by barge to Castle Garden, where they are registered (meaning simply that their names are recorded) and where translators are available to help them change money, buy rail tickets, deposit valuables for brief periods, send letters or telegrams, receive visitors or messages, and perhaps make use of the employment agency just outside. A restaurant operated under contract provides food and beverages at reasonable prices (a large sandwich for 13¢, beer 10¢/bottle, coffee 5¢/cup), runners are not allowed inside, and an immigrant can finally arrive at New York without being bilked and abused (see Ellis Island, 1892).

1856 Pennsylvania Democrat James Buchanan, 65, wins the presidential election, but Georgia-born Republican John C. Frémont, 43, carries New York State with help from Albany district attorney Roscoe Conkling, 27, whose father has served in Congress and been a federal judge.

New York-born congressman John Alsop King, 68, is elected governor to succeed Prohibitionist Myron Holley Clark.

Mayor Fernando Wood wins easy reelection, this time as a Democrat, with 35,860 votes. American ("Know-Nothing") Party candidate Isaac O. Backer receives 25,209, Republican Anthony J. Bleecker 9,654, Bog Democrat James S. Libby 4,764, Municipal Reform candidate James R. Whiting 3,646.

Congregationalist preacher Henry Ward Beecher of Brooklyn's 7-year-old Plymouth Church raises money in the spring to send rifles and Bibles to antislavery settlers in Kansas. Now 42, Beecher has made his church a "station" (safe house) for the Underground Railway that defies the Fugitive Slave Law of 1793 and astonishes his congregation June 1 by letting them ransom the 22-year-old slave daughter of a white Virginia planter, who has sold the young woman to a slave trader for resale in the Deep South. "This is a remarkable commodity. Such as she are put into one balance and silver into the other," Beecher declaims. "What will you do now? May she read liberty in your eyes? Will you stretch forth your hands?" Plates passed around the church come back containing $50 bills, rings, a diamond cross, and other valuables worth a total of $783, and the young woman is liberated forthwith.

I. M. Singer & Co. offers a $50 allowance on old sewing machines turned in for new Singer machines—the first trade-in allowances (see 1851). Edward Clark has established 14 branch stores with pretty demonstrators, he follows his trade-in offer with a pioneer installment-buying (hire-purchase) plan that allows $5 monthly rental fees to be applied toward ultimate purchase price, and Singer sales will increase by 200 percent within the year (see 1861).

Arnold Constable & Co. dry goods store moves into a new building at 307-311 Canal Street, northeast corner Mercer Street (see 1842). It will add a fifth story in 1862 as it expands (see 1869; 1914).

A yellow fever epidemic in Brooklyn's Bay Ridge and Fort Hamilton sections rouses Virginia-born physician Agrippa Nelson Bell, 36, to press for improved quarantine measures. He writes vigorous articles to attack the existing system (see 1858).

St. Vincent's Hospital moves to the corner of Seventh Avenue and 11th Street, taking over a building formerly occupied by the St. Joseph's Half Orphan Asylum (see 1849; nursing school, 1892).

Smallpox Hospital is completed on Blackwell's Island to designs of architect James Renwick, Jr. (*see* 1839; City Hospital, 1856).

Western Union is chartered as an amalgamation of small U.S. telegraph companies by Ezra Cornell and Hiram Sibley, who financed Samuel F. B. Morse in 1844. Sibley organized the New York and Mississippi Valley Printing Telegraph Co. in 1851, and he becomes president of the new Western Union, whose facilities will be greatly expanded (*see* 1859).

The *Albany Times Union* has its beginnings in the *Morning Times* published April 21 by *Albany Morning Express* founder Alfred Stone in partnership with David M. Barnes and Edward H. Boyd. The paper will become the *Evening Times* September 25, 1865. The *Evening Union* will begin publication May 29, 1882, and the two will merge November 19, 1891, to create the *Times Union*, which will be the leading paper in the region into the 21st century.

Harper's Weekly begins publication at New York, where it will continue until 1915 (*see* Thomas Nast, 1869). *Harper's Monthly*, published since 1850, asks, "Why should [New York] be loved as a city? It is never the same city for a dozen years together. A man born in New York 40 years ago finds nothing of the New York he knew."

Fiction: *The Piazza Tales* (stories) by Herman Melville is a collection of short works that have appeared in magazines. Included are "Bartleby the Scrivener" (set entirely in New York), "Benito Cereno," and "The Encantadas."

Poetry: *Leaves of Grass* (second edition) by Walt Whitman, who includes his poem "Crossing Brooklyn Ferry:" "Ah, what can ever be more stately and admirable to me than mast-hemm'd Manhattan?/ River and sunset and scallop-edg'd waves of flood-tide? The sea-gulls oscillating their bodies, the hay-boat in twilight, and the belated lighter?" Whitman describes New York as the "City of the World (for all races are here, all the lands make contributions here:) City of the sea! City of hurried and glittering tides! City whose gleeful tides continually rush and recede, whirling in and out with eddies and foam! City of wharves and stores—city of tall façades of marble and iron! Proud and passionate city—met-tlesome, mad, extravagant city!" A larger (third) edition will appear in 1860.

Sculpture: an equestrian statue of George Washington is unveiled July 4 at the southern end of Union Square Park. Created by Massachusetts-born artist Henry Kirke Brown, 42, the heroic bronze figure dominates the square.

Portrait photographer Matthew B. Brady introduces what he calls "Imperial Photographs"—paper prints nearly 16" × 19" in size, enlarged from wet-plate negatives and "tinted" or painted by artists in his studio (*see* 1850). One newspaper calls them "the ne plus ultra of art," and rich clients pay as much as $700 each for them.

U.S. playwrights get their first legal copyright protection under a new law that releases a flood of dramatic productions.

Laura Keene moves into a new New York theater—Laura Keene's Theater—as manager and leading lady (*see* 1855). The first major woman theatrical manager in America, she will be prominent for the next 8 years, presenting works by a company whose members will include Dion Boucicault, Joseph Jefferson, and Edward H. Sothern.

The cage crinoline patented by a French-born American inventor named Tavernier consists of lightweight, flexible, "watchspring" steel hoops, protected by rubber inserts riveted to vertical tapes. Easier to wear and much more efficient to produce, it will eventually bring an end to the fashion of hoopskirts now worn by so many New York women (*see* 1875).

The city's first marble house is completed at 8 Fifth Avenue for railroad magnate John Taylor Johnson, who will convert a stable into the city's first art gallery, opening it to the public on Thursday afternoons.

St. George's Episcopal Church is completed on the west side of Stuyvesant Square at 16th Street. Created in 1752 as a chapel of Trinity Church, the congregation has been independent since 1811 and has engaged Blesch & Eidlitz to design its solid brownstone church in Byzantine-Romanesque Revival style. Prague-born architect Leopold Eidlitz, now 33, will receive some major commissions in the city, as will his son Cyrus, born at New York July 27.

Gail Borden receives a patent for his condensed milk (*see* 1853). The product gets a cold shoulder from New York customers accustomed to watered milk doctored with chalk to make it white and molasses to make it seem creamy (*see* 1841; 1855). The condensed milk is made from skim milk devoid of all fats and of certain necessary food factors; it will contribute to rickets in young working-class children. Borden abandons the factory he has set up with two partners at Wolcottville, Conn., and sells a half-share in his patent to one of his partners (*but see* 1857).

1857 The state legislature at Albany establishes a new police district that combines forces from the counties of New York, Kings (Brooklyn), Richmond (Staten Island), and Westchester (including the Bronx) (see 1853). Gov. King appoints five commissioners to run the new Metropolitan Police district, with the mayors of New York and Brooklyn to serve as ex officio members, appoints Frederick Talmadge police superintendent, and orders New York City to disband its Municipal Police force, whose record is one of flagrant corruption.

Mayor Wood refuses to disband his police force, says the legislature's act is unconstitutional, and gains support from 800 of the 1,100 members of his police force, all of them Democrats. The other 300 men, led by Capt. George W. Walling, resign to join the new Metropolitan Police force that opens headquarters in White Street and recruits new men. Having two rival police forces leaves the city without any real police protection; when the street commissioner dies, and the Republican governor appoints Daniel D. Conover to succeed him, Mayor Wood's police beat up Conover and his friends June 16. Conover gets a judge to issue warrants charging the mayor with assault and inciting to riot, the mayor posts 500 of his Municipal Police outside City Hall with a reserve force inside, Capt. Walling tries to arrest the mayor, 20 of the mayor's Municipal Police throw him out, 50 Metropolitan Police rescue Capt. Walling, a riot ensues, most of Walling's men sustain injuries, 12 of them serious, and one man is left crippled for life. Capt. Walling persuades the city recorder to have Sheriff J. J. V. Westervelt arrest the mayor, the sheriff's lawyer tells him he is obliged to do his duty, but Mayor Wood shouts, "I will never let you arrest me!" The Seventh Regiment of the National Guard marches down Broadway just then to board a ship for Boston, Metropolitan Police

officers persuade Maj. Gen. Charles W. Sanford to intervene, he has his men surround City Hall, and he takes Mayor Wood into custody. The mayor is released on bond, a civil court holds that the governor has no right to appoint a city street commissioner, Wood never stands trial, and the state supreme court upholds the law creating the state police force. An appeals court upholds the ruling in early fall, and Mayor Wood disbands the Municipal Police force, throwing 1,100 men out of work. A new law provides for retirement of police officers at half pay after 20 years of service.

Former governor William Learned Marcy dies at Ballston Spa, N.Y., July 4 at age 70.

The Republican-controlled state assembly at Albany strips Mayor Wood of his power and calls for a new election in December. Independent Party candidate Daniel Fawcett Tiemann, 52, calls attention to Wood's excesses; a former paint dealer who belongs to Tammany Hall, he wins 43,216 votes to Wood's 40,889 (but see 1859).

The Communist Club of New York is founded by followers of German socialist Karl Marx, 39, who has been writing weekly letters for the *New-York Tribune* about European economics and politics.

Fort Totten is completed by the U.S. Army at Willets Point on the edge of Bayside, Queens, to protect the city from enemy attack. It will continue for 110 years to be used mainly as a training base for recruits.

New York seamstresses stage a demonstration March 8 to demand higher pay and better working conditions (see 1908).

Soap maker-philanthropist William Colgate dies at New York March 25 at age 74.

Financial panic strikes New York in October following failure of the Ohio Life Insurance and Trust Co. and news that the S.S. *Central America* bound from Aspinwall on the Isthmus of Panama has gone down September 12 in a hurricane off the coast of South Carolina with 21 tons of gold from California. A cashier in the New York office of Ohio Life is revealed October 24 to have embezzled nearly all the company's assets to cover his stock-market operations. A consequence in part of overextending credit after a period of speculation, the economic downturn quickly spreads nationwide. Chemical Bank continues to pay specie on demand, a policy that will give it the nickname "Old Bullion," but some 30,000 New Yorkers are thrown out of work in the severe depression; 4,932 business firms will fail, and having 1,100 unemployed police officers con-

The panic that swept Wall Street was the worst in 20 years. The ensuing business recession put thousands out of work.

tributes to the economic woes. Mayor Wood proposes a large work-relief program that will pay the workers in food, but the Common Council balks when he adds, "Truly may it be said that in New York those who produce everything get nothing, and those who produce nothing get everything." Says an editorial in the *New-York Times*, "Mr. Wood raises the banner of the most fiery communism" (*see* 1858).

 A nationwide celebration marks the linking by rail of New York and St. Louis.

The New York & Harlem Railroad and the New York and New Haven build depots side by side in the block between Fourth and Madison avenues from 26th Street to 27th. More than 30 trains per day, carrying 8,000 passengers, chug in and out of the depots on 12 tracks, but the city will ban locomotives within built-up sections of the city next year after two engines blow up and a third engine burns in the crowded area below 14th Street, creating a public outcry. Trains coming into the city will be obliged to stop at 42nd Street and be pulled by horses from there to the depots at 27th Street; stables will be built on the east side of Fourth Avenue between 32nd and 33rd streets. Stock in the New York & Harlem has a par value of $100 but falls to just $3 (*see* van Derbilt, 1862; Grand Central, 1871).

Delaware, Lackawanna & Western Railroad stock falls to $5 per share in the October panic, enabling banker Moses Taylor to buy up shares in the open market and obtain a controlling interest. The price will rebound to $240 per share within 7 years and Taylor will retain control until his death in 1882.

New York to San Francisco ocean freight rates drop to $10 per ton, down from as high as $60 in gold rush days, as an excess of shipping intensifies competition, making the industry unprofitable. Some clipper ships can cover more than 400 miles on a good day, a speed no steamship can match, but the day of the clipper ship is ending.

Lenox Hill Hospital has its beginnings in the German Dispensary, founded January 19 by immigrant German physicians and opened May 28 at 132 Canal Street to serve the needs of fellow Germans, most of whom live east of the Bowery and south of 9th Street and few of whom speak much English. The dispensary has received 2,374 indigent patients by year's end and written 4,547 prescriptions (*see* 1862).

The New York Infirmary for Indigent Women and Children opens on Florence Nightingale's birthday, May 12, under the direction of Elizabeth Blackwell, her younger sister Emily, 30, and Polish-born physician Marie E. Zackrzewska, 27, who has been head midwife at Berlin's Royal Maternity Hospital (*see* 1849). The loss of an eye has prevented Blackwell from achieving her ambition to practice as a surgeon, she has been unable to find a place on any other hospital staff because of her sex, and has started the first U.S. hospital to be staffed entirely by women, partly for the benefit of the poor, partly to give women physicians opportunities to gain clinical experience. Located on Stuyvesant Square at 15th Street, the Infirmary will move in November 1875 to 321 East 15th Street and remain there until 1981 (*see* 1979; Christmas Cotillion, 1935; New York Hospital, 1991).

Bellevue Hospital's pathology building is completed (*see* operating amphitheater, 1849). Physician James R. Wood, now 40, has persuaded the city to appropriate $3,000 for the new structure, whose dedication ceremony is held in a lecture room crowded with physicians, professors, and 300 students from Physicians and Surgeons, New York University College of Medicine, and Brooklyn's Long Island College Hospital. Dr. Valentine Mott performs a hernia operation on a cadaver (*see* nurses' training school, 1873).

U.S. cities have higher death rates than any other places in the world. Tuberculosis is the big killer, causing roughly 400 deaths per 100,000 population (the disease is not considered contagious), and while New York has the highest death rate, Philadelphia and Boston are not far behind. More than half of New York's children die before reaching age 5, 70 percent die before age 2, the death rate exceeds the birth rate, and by the end of the decade New York's death rate will be 50 percent higher than that of Philadelphia (or of London).

 The Cooper Institute is founded in Astor Place by inventor-industrialist Peter Cooper, who is himself barely literate. His institute will develop into the Cooper Union for the Moral, Mental and the Physical Improvement of the Youth of the City, the Country, and the World, carrying on extensive programs of adult education (*see* 1859).

Young Men's Christian Association (YMCA) branches in Manhattan and Brooklyn begin offering classes in foreign languages, gymnastics, and music (*see* 1852; 1866).

Columbia College moves uptown to a new campus at 49th Street between Fourth and Madison avenues, where it will remain for 40 years (*see* 1784). It has used buildings since 1754 on a site bounded by Murray, Barclay, and Church streets and West Broadway, but last year acquired property on Madison Avenue and also purchased the Deaf and Dumb Asylum on the west side of Fourth Avenue between 49th and 50th streets. The new site has a lawn that slopes southward down to 49th Street and, as the *Evening Post* says May 11, is "on a comanding eminence affording an extensive and pleasant view. That part of the city is still quite new and the hand of improvement is visible in all directions." Columbia's president Charles King has headed the college since 1849 and oversees the move; the college's downtown buildings are sold and demolished (*see* 1890; law school, 1858).

The *New-York Tribune* sacks all but two of its foreign correspondents in an economy move. One of the two retained is German socialist Karl Marx.

Nonfiction: *Young America in Wall Street* and *An American Merchant in Europe, Asia, and Australia* by Boston-born New York merchant George Francis Train, 28, who calls New York "the locomotive of these United States." A former partner in his father's Boston ship-owning firm Enoch Train & Co., the handsome, charming, and abstemious young Train has enjoyed financial success at Liverpool and in Australia while developing a reputation for eccentricity and reckless behavior.

Fiction: *The Confidence Man* by Herman Melville is a dense allegory of American materialism.

Painting: *Niagara Falls* by Frederic E. Church, now 31; *Wall Street, Half Past 2 O'Clock, October 13, 1857* by New York painters James Cafferty and Charles G. Rosenberg.

The 10th Street Studio Building that opens at 15 10th Street (it will be renumbered 51 West 10th Street in 1866) is the first U.S. structure built specifically to house artists' studios. Designed in Beaux Arts style by Vermont-born architect Richard Morris Hunt, 30, for banker-art patron James Boorman Johnston, the three-story structure's 25 double-height studios are each 300 to 600 square feet in size (the larger ones have adjoining bedrooms) and surround a two-story, gaslit, communal exhibition gallery with glass ceiling. Architect Hunt is a younger brother of portrait artist William Morris Hunt, 33. Initial tenants of his building, some of whom actually live in it, include Frederick E. Church and John LaFarge and will soon include also Albert Bierstadt, William Merritt Chase (who will take over the communal gallery for himself in 1879 and remain until 1895), and Winslow Homer. The building will stand until 1956.

The first Currier & Ives prints are issued as Roxbury, Mass.-born New York lithographer Nathaniel Currier, 44, takes into partnership his New York-born bookkeeper of 5 years James Merritt Ives, 33, and begins signing all his prints with the new firm name. Currier has been issuing lithographs since 1835, when he struck one called *The Burning of the Merchants' Exchange* in the great fire of that year, he has been famous since 1840 for his prints of W. K. Hewitt's lurid depiction of a fire aboard the steamship *Lexington*, and since then he has illustrated U.S. manners, personages, and notable events. His most prolific talent since 1849 has been English-born artist Frances Fanny Bond Palmer, now 45, who draws directly on the stones used to make her lithographs. Her views of Manhattan, one from Brooklyn Heights and the other from Weehawken, N.J., have been among Currier's best sellers. Priced at 15¢ to $3, Currier & Ives prints will be sold all over the United States and distributed through branch offices in European cities.

The Worth Monument is erected at the intersection of Broadway and Fifth Avenue to commemorate the memory of the late Mexican War hero Gen. William Jenkins Worth, who distinguished himself in battle but died of cholera at San Antonio, Texas, in May 1849 at age 55.

Theater: *The Poor of New York* by Irish-born actor-playwright Dion Boucicault (originally Dionysius Lardner Boursiquot), 36, 1/8 at Wallack's Theater. Boucicault emigrated from London to New York in 1853 and has adapted *Les pauvres de Paris* by Edouard-Louis-Alexandre Brisebarre and Eugène Nus.; Paterson, N.J.,-born actor Lawrence Barrett, 18, makes his New York debut 1/20 at Burton's Chambers Street Theater in the role of Sir Thomas Clifford in James Sheridan Knowles's 1832 play *The Hunchback* to begin a notable career (he will excel as a Shakespearean actor).

The first American Chess Congress opens at New York in the fall. Top honors go to New Orleans player Paul C. (Charles) Morphy, 20, who taught himself the game in childhood by watching his father play, won two out of three games (the third was a draw) against a visiting Hungarian chess master before he was 13, and will tour Europe in the next 2 years, defeating all challengers and winning the unofficial world title.

New York's criminal element has a field day as the standoff between the Metropolitan Police and Municipal Police leaves a law-enforcement vaccum. Burglaries, robberies, and murders increase while lawyers debate the legitimacy of the respective police forces in courtrooms. Rival gangs on the Lower East Side try to settle their grudges July 4 and 5 in a fracas that involves 800 to 1,000 hooligans; two regiments of state militia are needed to quell the disorder that leaves 10 men dead and more than 100 injured. George Templeton Strong notes in his diary July 5, "It seems to have been a battle between Irish Blackguardism and Native Bowery Blackguardism, the belligerents afterwards making common cause against the police and uniting to resist their common enemy."

The American Institute of Architects (AIA) is founded February 23 by 13 men who include Leopold Eidlitz, Richard Morris Hunt, English-born architect Jacob Wrey Mould, 32, and Richard Upjohn. Its constitution, signed May 18, states its purpose to be the promotion of "the scientific and practical perfection of its members and to elevate the standing of the profession."

The Cary Building is completed at 105-107 Chambers Street, northwest corner of Church Street. John Kellum of King & Kellum has designed the loft building in Anglo-Italianate style with a cast-iron façade from D. D. Badger's Architectural Ironworks.

A cast-iron building completed at the southwest corner of Canal and Lafayette streets will survive into the 21st century as a prime example of the construction style pioneered by James Bogardus (*see* 1849). Designed by King & Kellum in a Venetian palazzo style to give it the illusion of being a solid masonry structure, it has been erected for printing-industry magnate George Bruce.

The world's first commercial passenger elevator is installed in the five-story china-and-glass emporium of E. G. Haughwout, a new building designed by Irish-born architect John Plant Gaynor, 30 (with a prefabricated iron front designed by Daniel Badger), at 488 (later 490) Broadway, northeast corner Broome Street. Installed by Elisha G. Otis, the elevator does not yet have a completely enclosed cab (*see* 1854; 1861; Fifth Avenue Hotel, 1859).

Construction of a new St. Patrick's Cathedral begins on the east side of Fifth Avenue between 50th and 51st streets, where the Roman Catholic archdiocese owns a full block of property that was been given to it by the late Brooklyn philanthropist Cornelius Heeney and soap maker Andrew Morris. Architect James Renwick, Jr. has designed the structure in Gothic Revival style, and the cornerstone is laid in August at the northeast corner of 50th Street (*see* 1879).

"The Adaption of Houses à la Française to This Country" by architect Calvert Vaux, now 33, is published in June. Vaux has lectured members of the newly revived American Institute of Architects on the benefits of a "Continental Plan of Housing," and his paper states that the structures he has in mind shall be no more than four stories high: "Two or three flights of easy stairs may be readily surmounted and the freedom from dust and noise obtained by those who might live in the third or fourth stories would be found to compensate, in a great measure, for the trouble of traversing an extra flight or two of stairs; and thus people of about the same standing in society could, in all probability, be readily induced to occupy comfortable apartments as high as the fourth floor . . . To be suitable to New York needs, the public staircase, which is the unusual feature to which we have to be accustomed, must be made light, airy, and elegant, and if possible lighter, airier, and more elegant than other parts of the house, or a prejudice will be likely to be excited on entering the premises against the whole effect, and this it is all-important to avoid" (*see* Stuyvesant apartments, 1870).

Connecticut-born landscape architect Frederick Law Olmsted, 35, wins appointment as superintendent of the new Central Park, whose construction has begun but whose name belies the fact that it is far to the north of the city's present population center (*see* 1844). The city has acquired some 7,500 lots since 1853, paying a total of $5,169,369.90 for land, most of it unoccupied, between Fifth and Eighth avenues from 59th Street north to 106th (the area will later be extended to 110th to make the park two and a half miles long and half a mile wide). Calvert Vaux has collaborated with Olmsted on the park design that won a competition (held at his urging), and architect Jacob Wrey Mould has also contributed substantially to the design. William Cullen Bryant, *Tribune* publisher Horace Greeley, botanist Asa Gray, financier August Belmont, and author Washington Irving, now 74, have endorsed Olmsted's application, but he finds the park site filled with hog farms, bone-boiling works, and squatters' "shacks"—"a pestilential spot where rank vegetation and miasmatic odors taint every breath of air." Olmsted engages Pound Ridge-born sanitary engineer George Edwin Waring, Jr., 24, to design a drainage system for the park. The largest and best-established of the so-called shantytowns, sometimes called Seneca Village, is near 85th Street and boasts three churches, a school for "colored children," and two cemeteries; it has provided housing for many poor arrivals from the German states and Ireland, as well as for blacks, but police clear the area of its 1,600 residents to make way for a reservoir; work on the visionary park project becomes a relief project for 3,800 men who have been thrown out of jobs as city politicians struggle to cope with the economic depression (*see* 1858).

The sugar-refining firm Havemeyer, Townsend and Co. is founded with a refinery in South 3rd Street in the northwestern Brooklyn area known as Williamsburg (*see* 1805). The area's deep-water docking facilities, undeveloped land, and cheap labor will soon attract other refiners (*see* 1872).

Commercial production of Borden's condensed milk begins at Burrville, Conn., where Borden has opened a condensing plant with financial backing from New York grocery wholesaler Jeremiah Milbank, 39, whom he has met by chance on a train (*see* 1856). *Leslie's Illustrated Newspaper* helps Borden's sales by crusading against "swill milk" from Brooklyn cows fed on distillery mash. Samples of Borden's product are carried through the streets of New York and now meet with more success (*see* New York Condensed Milk Co., 1858).

1858 Admiral Matthew Calbraith Perry, U.S. Navy, dies at New York March 4 at age 63. His daughter has married banker August Belmont, and the man credited with having opened Japan to the western world 5 years ago is buried in the churchyard of the 59-year-old St. Mark's-in-the-Bouwerie at the corner of Second Avenue and 10th Street.

Former state senator Edwin Denison Morgan is elected governor of New York with support from Thurlow Weed. A prominent wholesale grocer, banker, and broker, Morgan was elected to the senate as a Whig in 1850 and introduced the bill providing for the creation of Central Park. Now 47, he will increase canal revenues and reduce the state debt.

The Association for Improving the Condition of the Poor laments the fact that "our city, operating like a sieve, lets through the enterprising and industrious, while it retains the indolent, the aged, and infirm, who can earn this subsistence nowhere."

Some 25,000 men are unemployed in the economic recession that began in the city last year; together with their families, there are about 100,000 in need, and the 13-year-old Association for Improving the Condition of the Poor will report suffering heretofore unknown in the city's history.

American Bank Note Co. is created at New York by a merger of the seven independent engraving-printing firms that have printed paper currency since the Revolution. The company will print U.S. currency until 1879, U.S. postage stamps until 1894, and currency and stamps for scores of foreign nations thereafter.

Lehman Brothers of Montgomery, Ala., opens a New York office at 119 Liberty Street. Founder Henry Lehman was a German-born merchant who opened a dry goods store in 1845. He prospered in cotton trading, extending long-term credit to planters, but died of yellow fever late in 1855 at age 33. His brother Emmanuel, 31, settles in New York (*see* Cotton Exchange, 1870).

R. H. Macy Company opens October 27 with an 11-foot storefront on Sixth Avenue, just south of 14th Street and close to the city's fashionable Fifth Avenue residential area but well north of the busy shopping district near City Hall. Nantucket-born merchant Rowland Hussey Macy, 36, went to sea on a whaling ship at age 15, returned with a red star tattooed on his arm, opened a dry goods store at Boston in 1843 and failed, joined the gold rush to California, opened another store in 1851 at Haverhill, Mass., selling only for cash and never deviating from a fixed price, failed after 3 years, but has made enough money in Wisconsin real estate speculation to try again. The first day's sales of ribbons, trimmings, hosiery, and gloves at his 660-square-foot fancy dry-goods shop total only $11.06, his rent is $150 per month, but he begins advertising in the *New-York Tribune* November 25 ("Cheap Ribbons!!! You want them, of course. Go to Macy's"). Macy will use flamboyant advertising, repeating phrases ("Our goods shall be sold cheap! Our goods shall be sold cheap!") to make his new store successful, and gross sales next year will be $90,000 despite the

The Crystal Palace went up in flames that could be seen for miles. HARPER'S WEEKLY

economic depression that continues to grip the city (*see* 1860).

Citizen Gas Light Co. begins serving the Brooklyn public, competing with companies established earlier (*see* 1847). It will become common practice for a new company to buy the rights to some unserved territory from a competitor and, once established, to send salesmen door to door in an attempt to win away customers in more prosperous areas, often laying parallel gas lines (*see* Brooklyn Union Gas, 1895).

The first practical sleeping car is perfected for the Chicago & Alton Railroad by Brocton, N.Y., cabinetmaker George M. (Mortimer) Pullman, 27, whose retractable upper berth doubles the sleeping car's payload.

The 2,674-ton North German Lloyd (Norddeutscher Lloyd) Line passenger vessel S.S. *Bremen* arrives July 4 with 115 passengers and 150 tons of cargo (*see* 1854). Built in Scotland at a cost of 1,281,000 gold marks, the single-funnel iron ship has a clipper bow, three masts, screw propulsion, a service speed of 11 knots per hour, a crew of more than 102, and accommodations for 570 passengers (60 in first class, 110 second, 400 in steerage). She will be converted to a sailing ship in 1874.

"Commodore" van Derbilt sells his New York-to-California shipping line to rivals who will operate via Panama rather than Nicaragua (*see* 1857; railroad investment, 1862).

St. Luke's Hospital opens May 13 on Fifth Avenue at 54th Street with enough beds for 200 patients (*see* 1846). The Fifth Avenue site had belonged to the St. George's Society, whose members failed in their attempt to establish a hospital there for British emigrants, and St. Luke's has a 20-bed ward reserved for such patients. Rev. W. A. Muhlenberg's London-born associate Sister Anne Ayres, 42, has organized the enterprise; he resigns from the Church of the Holy Communion to devote all his time to the new hospital (*see* 1896).

Yellow fever reappears in the city (*see* 1856); the Castleton board of health on Staten Island says, "The board recommends the citizens of the county to protect themselves by abating the abominable nuisance without delay," a reference to the state quarantine hospital for contagious diseases at Tompkinsville in the northeastern corner of the island. Staten Islanders have petitioned the state legislature for years to remove the facility, saying that it depresses property values. Led by 30 prominent men of means and social position, a crowd meets under a tree on Fort Hill the night of September 1, when Metropolitan Police are in Manhattan for a celebration. Each conspirator (some wear masks) is given a bit of straw, a bottle of camphene, and a box of matches, others join the crowd as it marches toward the quarantine station, and they use wooden beams as battering rams against the high brick outer wall. Several structures are set afire, and only the heroism of some nurses saves smallpox patients from incineration. The mob returns the following night and sets fire to the main building, which survived the first attack, a regiment of militia and a boatload of marines arrives late the next day, but although some arrests are made no one is convicted. The state closes the quarantine station, allowing Staten Island to become a summer resort; Dr. Agrippa Nelson Bell advocates establishing a new quarantine station on the west bank in the lower bay, and it will be erected a few years hence (*see* floating hospital, 1861).

E. R. Squibb & Sons has its beginnings in a Brooklyn laboratory established by Delaware-born physician Edward Robinson Squibb, 39, who discovered while working as an assistant surgeon in the U.S. Navy that many of the drugs supplied to him were impure or of inferior quality. He gained permission 7 years ago to establish a laboratory in the naval hospital at Brooklyn, but the military cut off his funding and he resigned. His new lab is soon destroyed by fire, but he will have new premises built to his specifications next year, obtain massive orders from the military beginning in 1861, and become a leading opponent of unlicensed medical practitioners, medical advertising, and the ineffective patent medicines on which so many people rely.

The Paulist Fathers (the order of Missionary Priests of St. Paul the Apostle) is organized at New York in July with Isaac Thomas Hecker, now 38, as its superior (*see* 1851). Father Hecker traveled to Rome last year to present a plan for a new order, was expelled from the Redemptorist order for having made the trip without permission, but gained approval from Pope Pius IX, who released him and his colleagues from their vows (*see Catholic World*, 1865).

Columbia College establishes a School of Law (*see* 1857; Mines, 1864).

Queen Victoria and President Buchanan exchange messages August 16 over the first transatlantic cable, whose completion makes it possible to communicate in minutes what heretofore has taken weeks. New York paper merchant Cyrus W. Field, now 39 (a younger brother of legal reformer David Dudley Field), has promoted the project first proposed by Frederick Newton Gisborne, 39, consulted with

Samuel F. B. Morse, and founded the New York, Newfoundland, and London Telegraph Co. with backing from Peter Cooper, clipper-ship magnate A. A. Low, and others. Queen Victoria cables, "Glory to God in the Highest, peace on earth, good will to men," and the first commercial cable message follows (at $5 per word). London merchant John Cash wires his New York representative, "Go to Chicago" (his firm J. and J. Cash makes woven name labels), but the cable's faulty electrical insulation fails September 4, making further transmission of messages impossible (*see* 1866).

Street & Smith Publications, Inc. has its beginnings in the *New-York Weekly* published by former *Sunday Dispatch* bookkeeper Francis S. Street and former *Sunday Dispatch* reporter Francis Shubael Smith, 38, who buy out the *New-York Weekly Dispatch* for $40,000 and rename it. Begun in 1843 as the *Weekly Universe*, the fiction magazine has a small circulation and Street and Smith have less than $100 between them, but founder Amos J. Williamson agrees to wait for his money until the new owners have earned it, they boost circulation by attracting well-known writers with enormous sums, and by 1861 their *Weekly* will have a circulation of 100,000 (*see* Nick Carter, 1886).

Maine-born painter (Jonathan) Eastman Johnson, 34, returns to America after 9 years of study in Europe and opens a New York studio, bringing with him his painting *The Old Kentucky Home.* He quickly gains a reputation for his portraits and within 2 years will gain election to the National Academy of Design.

Theater: *Jessie Brown, or The Relief of Lucknow* by Dion Boucicault 2/22 at Wallack's Theater; *Our American Cousin* by Tom Taylor 10/18 at Laura Keene's Theater.

The New York Police Department's Harbor Patrol has its beginnings in the Marine Division, a fleet of 12 rowboats with five-man crews that goes into service starting March 15 to combat piracy aboard merchant ships anchored in the harbor and thugs who terrorize the docks. The patrol's first steamboat will be launched in 1863 and steamers will have replaced rowboats by 1901.

Johns Manville Corp. has its beginnings in the H. W. Johns Manufacturing Co., started by New York entrepreneur Johns to produce paint and roofing materials.

An office building with a cast-iron façade is completed at 75 Murray Street for glass dealer Francis James Hopkins, formerly of 61 Barclay Street.

Designed by James Bogardus, the structure has 11,375 square feet of office space.

A loft building designed by architect John Butler Snook is completed at 620 Broadway, between East Houston and Bleecker streets, with Corinthian cast-iron window frames.

Fireworks set off from the roof of City Hall to celebrate the new Atlantic Cable on the night of August 17 ignite the roof of the building, destroying the cupola and part of the roof (they are quickly rebuilt).

The Crystal Palace erected in 1853 for the world's fair burns to the ground October 5. Reputed to be fireproof, it is destroyed by some accounts in just 15 minutes.

Central Park opens to the public in the autumn, although it is still 5 years short of completion (*see* 1857). Architect Calvert Vaux has designed cast-iron bridges, boat houses, and other structures while working with Frederick Law Olmsted to develop the recreation area, workers have moved more than 10 million cartloads—5 million cubic yards—of dirt in and out of the park under their direction, created seven man-made bodies of water, installed 95 miles of drainage pipes, dug sunken transverse roads, and planted more than 4 million trees of 632 different species along with 815 varieties of flowers, plants, and vines; the project has cost $5 million, but the high cost of horsecar and elevated railway transportation will for years keep the sylvan retreat beyond the reach of most New Yorkers, and bone boilers still occupy shacks in the southern part of the park near 59th Street. Ice skating becomes fashionable on the pond at the park's southeast corner, with men skaters separated from women (they will remain officially segregated until 1870), and an estimated 60,000 pairs of skates will be sold in the city next year, some of them expensive imports (*see* transverse, 1859; Wollman Rink, 1952).

New York Condensed Milk Co. is established by Gail Borden (*see* 1857; 1861).

The Mason jar patented November 30 by New York metalworker John Landis Mason, 26, is a glass container with a thread molded into its top and a zinc lid with a threaded ring sealer. "Be it known that I, JOHN L. MASON . . . have invented Improvements in the Necks of Bottles, Jars, &c., Especially such as are intended to air and water tight, such as are used for sweetmeats &c. . . ." Mason's reusable screw-cap jar is far superior to earlier jars that were sealed with corks and wax; it will free farm families from having to rely on pickle barrels, root cellars, and smokehouses to get through the winter. Urban families, too, will use Mason jars to put up excess fruits and vegetables, especially tomatoes, sweet corn, berries, peaches, relish, and pickles, and the jars will soon be sealed with paraffin wax. Mason's patent will run out before he can capitalize on it, and he will die in the poorhouse.

1859 Congressman Daniel E. Sickles murders the son of "Star Spangled Banner" composer Francis Scott Key at Washington, D.C., February 27 for what he calls "improper attentions" to his beautiful young wife, Teresa. Sickles has been notoriously unfaithful, Teresa has begun an affair with the handsome widower Philip Barton Key, who serves as U.S. Attorney for Washington, he has been pointed out to Sickles across the street from the congressman's house in Lafayette Square, Sickles shoots him three times at point-blank range, but he wins acquittal in late April on grounds of temporary insanity, a novel defense at the time.

Former mayor Fernando Wood regains office, running as a Mozart Democrat (he has founded Mozart Hall after a quarrel with Tammany Hall) to defeat former mayor William F. Havemeyer, who has Tammany's support, and Republican George Opdyke, 53, a onetime clothing merchant. Despite his mishandling of the 1857 police riot, Wood remains popular with immigrants for facilitating their naturalization, and with workingmen (as well as many businessmen who have customers in the South) for supporting slavery. Wood receives 29,940 votes to Havemeyer's 26,913 and Opdyke's 21,417.

$ The city establishes its first comprehensive system for assessing property values and collecting taxes based on such values. Under the new law the mayor appoints three commissioners of taxes and assessments; the commissioners in turn appoint deputies

Currier & Ives depicted the recreation to be enjoyed in Central Park, which was far from the center of town.

who will go out every September to appraise property—including not only land and buildings but also personal property such as financial assets and jewelry. A citizen has 4 months to challenge his or her assessment; after that the Board of Aldermen will set a tax rate based on the city's needs for the year, but the tax rate on real estate will always be much higher than that on personal property.

The city has 4,375 factories, employing 90,204 workers, and leads the nation in industrial output. Its 539 ironworks employ more than 10,000. The availability of cheap labor attracts manufacturers, as does the proximity to port facilities that handle imports of raw materials, including metals, textiles, and foodstuffs.

Equitable Life Assurance Society is founded by Catskill, N.Y.-born entrepreneur Henry B. (Baldwin) Hyde, 25, who hangs a 30-foot sign across the front of a building where he has rented a one-room office with borrowed desks and chairs. Formerly a cashier for Mutual Life Insurance, Hyde has been sacked for proposing the establishment of a company that will insure lives for more than $10,000 and 2 days later has rented space above his former employer's offices, whose sign is completely dwarfed by the new Equitable sign. By January of next year Hyde will have raised the $100,000 deposit required by the state comptroller for life insurance companies and will have installed as president of Equitable the brother of his pastor at the Fifth Avenue Presbyterian Church. By the end of next year he will have 229 agents, all of whom he has personally selected and trained (see 1862).

R. G. Dun Co. is founded at New York by Robert Graham Dun, 33, who purchases the financial rating service B. Douglass and Co. (see 1854) and begins

Peter Cooper's philanthropy endowed Cooper Union in Astor Place to provide education for the working class.

publishing the *Mercantile Agency's Reference Book* (*see* Bradstreet, 1855; Dun and Bradstreet, 1933).

Petroleum production begins at Titusville, Penn., giving the world a new source of energy and reducing demand for the whale oil, coal gas, and lard now used in lamps. Unemployed New Haven & Hartford Railroad conductor "Colonel" Edwin Laurentine Drake, 40, has been sent to Titusville in Pennsylvania's Venange County by New York banker James Townsend. Using salt-well drilling equipment to dig into oil-bearing strata, Drake strikes oil August 28 and his 70-foot well is soon producing 400 gallons per day (2,000 barrels per year) to begin the first commercial exploitation of petroleum in the United States and inaugurate a new era of kerosene lamps and stoves (*see* Gestner, 1855; Rockefeller, 1861).

New York-born entrepreneur John H. (Henry) Starin, 34, finds it difficult to ship the toilet articles he has been manufacturing and organizes a general freight agency under the name Starin City River and Harbor Transportation Lines; it soon gains support from Cornelius van Derbilt and other railroad officials who recognize the need for a centralized system that will address the chaos produced by having so many railroads start on the New Jersey side of the Hudson (*see* car float, 1866).

The first Central Park transverse road opens, connecting Fifth Avenue at 79th Street to Eighth Avenue (later Central Park West) at 81st (*see* 1858). The plan submitted by F. L. Olmsted and Calvert Vaux called for sunken transverse roads at 65th, 79th, 85th, and 97th streets, and the deliberately winding 79th Street transverse, blasted out of solid rock, has sidewalks for pedestrians running parallel to carriage drives and bridle paths.

Inventor Walter Hunt dies at New York June 8 at age 62 before receiving the first of five annual $10,000 payments owed to him by Isaac M. Singer. His patented paper collar, Globe stove, fountain pen, safety pin, and sewing machine will come into common use in the next few decades.

City Hospital is completed on Blackwell's Island (*see* Smallpox Hospital, 1856). Architect James Renwick, Jr. has designed the charity institution, built of stones quarried on the island by convicts confined to the prison there.

The Cooper Union for the Advancement of Science and Art opens its first building, designed by Frederick A. Peterson, at Astor Place and Fourth Avenue (*see* Cooper Institute, 1857). The institution provides free education for young working-class men and women (*see* Lincoln speech, 1860).

Telegraph promoter Samuel F. B. Morse agrees to the formation of the North American Telegraph Association as a near-monopoly (*see* 1844). His former associate Alfred L. Vail has died at his native Morristown, N.J., January 18 at age 51 (*see* Western Union, 1856, 1866).

Author Washington Irving dies at his Sunnyside home near Tarrytown November 28 at age 76.

Sculpture: a bronze bust of the late German playwright Friedrich von Schiller is unveiled near Central Park's Mall. The first portrait statue to be erected in the new park, it is the work of C. L. Richter.

Theater: *The Octaroon, or Life in Louisiana* by Dion Boucicault 12/5 at New York's Winter Garden Theater. Boucicault has adapted the 1856 novel *The Quadroon* by Mayne Reid to create his melodrama.

Opera: Spanish-born Italian soprano Adelina (*née* Adela Juana Maria) Patti, 16, makes her debut 11/24 at the Academy of Music singing the title role in Donizetti's 1835 opera *Lucia di Lammermoor*.

Popular songs: "Dixie" ("I Wish I Was in Dixie's Land") by performer Daniel Decatur Emmet, formerly of the Virginia Minstrels, now of the blackface troupe Bryant's Minstrels, is performed for the first time 4/4 at Mechanics Hall, 472 Broadway. The song meets with immediate success among lower Manhattan's working-class audiences, most of whom support the Southern cause. Emmet may well have learned the song from Ben and Lew Snowden, the sons of freed slaves who have been performing with their family in rural Ohio.

The Steinway Piano developed by German-born New York piano maker Henry Steinway, Jr. is the first piano with a single cast-metal plate. Steinway is the son of Heinrich Engelhard Steinweg, now 62, a cabinetmaker and instrument maker who started making pianos at the small town of Seesen in 1835 and 15 years later came to New York with his wife to escape political agitation and restrictive trade regulations (their son Charles had come earlier). The men of the family apprenticed themselves to various piano makers, one of whom, Henry Pirsson, had produced a double-grand pianoforte with keyboards facing each other, and they established a New York piano factory of their own in 1853 (the elder Steinweg will not call himself Steinway until 1865). The Steinways will take pride in their workmanship, shaping and fitting hundreds of pieces by hand for each instrument and following a precise and patient procedure that involves drying wood for a year and applying several coats of varnish to the case, with long intervals between each coat, but what will make Steinway & Sons world famous is the fuller, warmer tone of their pianos, made possible by the cast-metal plate, strong enough to withstand the pull of strings that have been combined with an overstrung scale both to save space and to produce a much larger tone than that of earlier grand pianos (see 1860; Steinway Hall, 1866).

Manhattan's Fifth Avenue Hotel opens in August at the northwest corner of Fifth and 23rd streets, on a site opposite Madison Square that was formerly occupied by Franconi's Hippodrome (see 1853), where it will stand until 1908. Designed by William Washburn for financier Amos R. Eno (who leases it to New Hampshire-born hotel operator Col. Paran Stevens), the new six-story, white marble hostelry has accommodations for 800 guests, a "screw-type" passenger elevator (the first elevator in any hotel), and a room rate of $2.50 per day, including four meals (a late evening supper is served at large tables that seat 12 or more each). It is an immediate success, eclipsing the 6-year-old St. Nicholas a mile to the south and attracting royal visitors as well as Wall Street figures who congregate in its public rooms after the markets close. Boston civil engineer Otis Tufts has installed the hotel's experimental "perpendicular railway," made of iron cylinders joined together from the cellar to the attic; it is the first elevator to have a completely enclosed car (see Otis, 1857). A belt from a steam engine turns the vertical screw, and the elevator car rises or falls depending on which way the screw is turned, but the device is costly, clumsy, and slow; it will be replaced in 1875.

A tenement fire in Elm Street February 2 kills 20 people.

The state legislature at Albany authorizes acquisition of land for Brooklyn's Prospect Park (see Central Park, 1858).

George Templeton Strong speculates in his diary June 1 that Manhattan's Central Park "will be a feature of the city within 5 years and a lovely place in A.D. 1900, when its trees will have acquired dignity and appreciable diameters" (see 1858). Journalists cheer as police use force to dislodge bone boilers from the southern part of the park (see 1863).

The A&P retail food chain has its beginnings in the Great American Tea Co. store opened at 31 Vesey Street by local merchant George Huntington Hartford, 26, who has persuaded his employer George P. Gilman to give up his hide and leather business and go partners in buying Chinese and Japanese tea directly from ships in New York Harbor. Both originally from Maine, the two men buy whole clipper-ship cargoes at one fell swoop, sell the tea at less than one-third the price charged by other merchants, identify their store with flaked gold letters on a Chinese vermilion background, and start a business that will grow into the first chain store operation (see 1863; A&P, 1869).

1860 Illinois lawyer Abraham Lincoln, 51, arrives at New York February 26, stays at the Astor House, attends services at Brooklyn's Plymouth Church to hear a sermon preached by Henry Ward Beecher, now 46, and visits the Five Points on the Lower East Side. Campaigning for the Republican Party presidential nomination February 27, he receives a new silk hat from Knox's Great Hat and Cap Establishment at Broadway and Fulton Street, has his photograph taken at Matthew B. Brady's studio (643 Broadway), is introduced by William Cullen Bryant that evening to an audience of about 1,500 in the Great Hall of the Cooper Union (admission: 25¢), and gives an address that ends, "Let us have faith that right makes might, and in that faith let us to the end dare to do our duty as we understand it." Some of the city's richest families—including Astors, Delanos, and van Derbilts—live in the Astor Place area outside Cooper Union, but warehousing companies will soon move into the area.

A huge crowd gathers in Union Square in October to watch a torchlight parade of demonstrators expressing opposition to Republican Lincoln's presidential candidacy. Bands play "Dixie" while rockets explode in the air and Roman candles turn night into day.

The United States becomes less united following the election of Abraham Lincoln as president in November with 40 percent of the popular vote (Lincoln receives only about one-third of New York City's vote). South Carolina adopts an Ordinance of Secession December 20 to protest the election.

Gov. Edwin D. Morgan wins reelection by the widest margin thus far recorded in any New York state gubernatorial contest.

Elizabeth Cady Stanton urges woman suffrage in an address to a joint session of the New York State Legislature (see 1848; Equal Rights Association, 1866).

The city reportedly has 500 brothels, many of whose madames advertise their houses of prostitution quite openly (see 1850). The city's first "red light" district has developed in the area north of Canal Street that will later be called SoHo (see crime, 1867).

Abraham Lincoln posed for Matthew Brady when he visited before winning election. LIBRARY OF CONGRESS

$ The East Brooklyn Savings Bank (later Cross Land Savings) opens on Myrtle Avenue in Bedford under the management of Samuel C. Barnes (see 1922).

Home Life Insurance Co. opens its first office May 1 at the corner of Court and Joralemon streets in Brooklyn. Founded by backers who include former congressman John T. Stranahan, 51, and merchant A. A. Low, now 49, it will move its headquarters to Manhattan in 1870 (see building, 1892).

Guardian Life Insurance Co. has its beginnings in the Germania Life Insurance Co., founded at New York in July by German-born entrepreneur Hugo Wesendonck, 43, who was a member of the Frankfurt Parliament, participated in its rump session, was sentenced to death, and fled to New York as a political refugee in December 1849. He has enlisted the support of German-born banker-diplomat August Belmont, publisher Oswald Ottendorfer, brewer Maximilian Schaefer, and financier Joseph

Seligman to back a company that will sell life insurance to German-speaking Americans.

Nantucket schoolteacher Margaret Getchell, 19, travels to New York, where a distant cousin, R. H. Macy, opened a dry goods store 2 years ago on Sixth Avenue near 14th Street. A childhood injury has forced her to wear a glass eye, and she has resigned to seek a less demanding job. Macy hires her as a cashier; she takes a room across the street and works late to help balance accounts. At her suggestion Macy will expand his line of ribbons, laces, and other accessories to include toiletries, hats, specialty clothing, and, later, books, china, silver, home furnishings, jewelry, and—most successfully—groceries (see 1863).

Lord & Taylor moves from its Catherine Street location of 1826 to a new five-story building at the corner of Broadway and Grand Street, where its staircase is lighted by a huge $500 gas chandelier made by the 23-year-old firm Tiffany & Co. (see 1873).

Mme. Demorest's Emporium opens on Broadway to sell dry goods. Schuylerville-born entrepreneur Ellen (Louise) "Nell" Demorest (née Curtis), 35, has operated millinery shops at Philadelphia and Troy, married dry goods merchant William Jennings Demorest in New York 2 years ago, has watched her maid cut out a dress pattern from pieces of wrapping paper, and has come up with the idea of creating accurate patterns that can be copied and used for dressmaking at home. The idea is not new: a 13th century French tailor devised a pattern made of thin wood, the Master Tailors' Guild initially suppressed the invention lest it put them out of business, Germans have produced full-scale paper patterns earlier in this century, Demorest's husband has suggested a fashion quarterly that would incorporate her idea, and they begin publishing *Mme. Demorest's Mirror of Fashions*, with a tissue-paper dressmaking pattern stapled to each copy. The magazine will develop into a monthly and by 1876 will be selling 3 million patterns per year. Demorest will hire large numbers of women to help her in her enterprise, urging them to seek employment in such "unladylike" occupations as bookkeeping, typesetting, and telegraphy, but sales will drop off after 1876 and Demorest will fail to patent her idea (see Butterick, 1869).

The British passenger liner S.S. *Great Eastern* arrives from Liverpool June 28 on her first transatlantic voyage. Designed by the late English engineer-inventor Isambard Kingdom Brunel, who died last year at age 53, the 680-foot, 22,500-ton iron paddle steamer has made the voyage in just 11 days but has barely cleared the shoals of Sandy Hook. She will prove too costly to operate, her owners will break her up for scrap in 1877, and no larger ship will be built until 1899.

Moran Towing & Transportation Co. has its beginnings as Irish-born entrepreneur Michael Moran, 26, takes the $2,700 he has earned working on the Erie Canal, rides a grain boat down the Hudson, and opens a towing brokerage office at 14 South Street. Brought to the United States by his parents at age 3, Moran went to work driving canal-boat horses and mules at age 9. "Build boats capable of doing the work," Moran tells tugboat operators, "and the work will seek you out" (see 1863).

Vulcanized-rubber inventor Charles Goodyear dies at New York July 1 at age 59, leaving his family with debts of some $200,000. Goodyear perfected his product in 1839 at Woburn, Mass., but paid more in legal fees to Daniel Webster for patent defense than he ever made in profits.

Botanist John Torrey turns his library and herbarium over to Columbia College, whose trustees will later give them to the New York Botanical Garden. Now 64, Torrey was appointed chief assayer of the U.S. Assay Office at New York 7 years ago and has prepared botanical reports based on specimens sent back from the West by explorers such as Joseph N. Nicollet and John C. Frémont, and his position with the Assay Office has permitted him to travel on occasion to see the plants in their native habitats.

A wave of gangrene cases sweeps the city July 4 following explosions of gunpowder to celebrate Independence Day. Doctors treat wounds with permangenate of potash, but many patients lose their limbs.

German-born political refugee-physician Abraham Jacobi, 30, is appointed professor of children's diseases at the New York Medical College and establishes the first U.S. pediatric clinic.

The Friends Meeting House and Seminary is completed for the Society of Friends (Quakers) at 221 East 15th Street, northwest corner Rutherford Place, facing Stuyvesant Square (see 1826; Stuyvesant Square, 1836). Architect Charles T. Bunting has designed the austere red-brick structure, Friends Seminary moves to the new building after 34 years in Elizabeth Street, and Rutherford Place will become the center of Quakerism in New York.

The New-York World begins publication in June through the efforts of Vermont-born entrepreneur

James Reed Spalding, 38, who sees to it that the paper is conducted "on Christian principles, independent of church, sects, and political parties," but financial problems will force a change of management next year (see World Almanac, 1868; Pulitzer, 1883).

Theater: The Colleen Bawn, or The Brides of Garryowen by Dion Boucicault 3/29 at Laura Keene's Theater, with John Drew in a melodrama based on the 1829 novel The Collegians by Gerald Griffin; Rip Van Winkle 12/24 at New York, with Philadelphia-born actor Joseph Jefferson, 31, playing the title role in his own dramatization of the Washington Irving story.

Steinway & Sons opens a large piano factory on Fourth Avenue at 53rd Street (see 1859). The factory will remain in production until 1910 (see Steinway Hall, 1866).

Minstrel-show pioneer Thomas Dartmouth Rice dies at his native New York September 19 at age 42, having earned a fortune but lived above his means.

New York society turns out June 25 to honor a group of Japanese ambassadors at a ball given by banker August Belmont at the Metropolitan Hotel. Belmont's late father-in-law, Admiral Matthew C. Perry, opened Japan to the West, and he has engaged five orchestras to provide music for the affair.

James Gordon Bennett's New-York Herald reports that Manhattan's West Side, meaning mostly Chelsea and sections to the south, has "a superior class of residents than those on the East Side of town;" Frank Leslie's Illustrated Newspaper says of the same area that it has "a good English or rather American population." Seventh Avenue, reports the Herald, is "very wide and well paved . . . [with] a number of fine edifices . . . in course of erection, under the pressure of the Central Park excitement."

Real estate mogul William B. Astor buys the southern part of the old Apthorp farm at the fringe of the village of Bloomingdale, paying $16,875 for the acreage and for Burnham's Hotel (formerly the mansion of Apthorp's daughter and her husband, J. C. Vandenheuvel) (see Apthorp apartment house, 1908).

Only nine U.S. cities have populations of more than 100,000: New York has 805,651, Philadelphia 562,529, Brooklyn 266,661, Baltimore 212,418, Boston 177,812, New Orleans 168,675, Cincinnati 161,044, St. Louis 160,773, Chicago 109,260. New York and Brooklyn combined have 1,072,312, up from a mere 123,700 in 1820 before the Erie Canal was opened.

1861 ✗ Mayor Fernando Wood proposes in his inaugural address to the Common Council January 7 that New York secede from the Union. As a free city, he declares, New York could trade with anyone, even with "our aggrieved brethren of the Slave States." But most New Yorkers believe the Union must be preserved; says the *New-York Sun*, "Mayor Wood's secessionist message has sounded the bathos of absurdity." (Wood is actually as much concerned with freeing the city from interference by Albany Republicans as with breaking away from the Union.) The state assembly at Albany adopts a resolution January 11 stating (in part) that it "is profoundly impressed with the value of the Union, and determined to preserve it unimpaired . . ."

President-elect Lincoln arrives at New York from his Springfield, Ill., home February 19 en route to Washington, D.C. He stays at the Astor House, gives a brief speech there, has breakfast the next morning at the mansion of merchant Moses Hicks Grinnell on Fifth Avenue at 14th Street, attends a reception given by Mayor Wood at City Hall, and hears the 1859 Verdi opera *Un Ballo in Maschera* at the Academy of Music before retiring. Lincoln leaves the next day for Washington and will not see New York again.

The Civil War begins April 12 as Fort Sumter on an island in Charleston harbor is bombarded by Gen. Pierre Gustave Toutant de Beauregard, 42, who has resigned as superintendent of the U.S. Military Academy at West Point to assume command of the Confederate Army. New York's socially elite Seventh Regiment leaves its new armory on Third Avenue between 6th and 7th streets April 19 and sets out for Washington (the New York Stock and Exchange Board has allocated $1,000 to help pay its expenses).

Thousands of New Yorkers volunteered to fight the rebels, but sympathy for the South was strong.

Gen. John Adams Dix presides over a Union Square meeting of 50,000 citizens April 24 and organizes 17 regiments of volunteers, who are soon bivouacked in tents behind the seawall at the Battery and in wooden barracks hastily erected in City Hall Park, Central Park, and elsewhere. Now 62, Gen. Dix fought as an ensign in the War of 1812.

Daniel E. Sickles has resigned from Congress in March, organizes the Excelsior Brigade of Volunteers at New York, and at age 41 is commissioned colonel of one of the five brigades, beginning a military career in which he will rise to the rank of major general (*see* Gettysburg, 1863).

Duryée's Zouaves (Fifth Regiment, New York State Volunteers) is raised in less than a week by mahogany merchant Abram Duryée to fight the rebels.

The Fire Zouaves (11th Regiment, New York State Volunteers) leaves for Annapolis April 29 aboard the steamship *Baltic*, full of enthusiasm but practically untrained. Former second lieutenant Elmer Ephraim Ellsworth, 24, has resigned his commission after the firing on Fort Sumter, returned to the city, enlisted more than 1,000 volunteers—mostly from the city's firefighters—and been elected colonel—by his men in a meeting at Palace Garden. Merchant A. T. Stewart has persuaded other well-to-do citizens to contribute $60,000 to arm the regiment with Sharp's rifles (in 10 different models) and 16-inch knives and outfit them in "Zouave" uniforms consisting of gry jackets, baggy gry breeches, red shirts, and red fezzes. Ellsworth becomes the first major Union casualty.

The Garibaldi Guard leaves for Washington May 28. Its members are mostly Italian-born officers and men who have seen combat fighting the Austrians, and they display the flag carried by onetime Staten Islander Giuseppe Garibaldi. Together with the 750-man Italian Legion, the Netherlands Legion, the Hungarian Legion, the First Foreign Rifles, and the Polish Legion (18th New York Volunteer Infantry, raised by Col. Wladimir Krzyzanowski among Germans, Poles, and other immigrants), the Garibaldi Guard forms the 39th Regiment, New York State Volunteer Infantry, and will see action in many engagements. The 69th Regiment of New York Volunteers is Irish (regiments are given numbers rather than names at the recommendation of Archbishop Hughes) and will distinguish itself in combat over the next 4 years.

Delphi, N.Y.-born West Point graduate Henry Warner Slocum, 33, receives a commission May 21 as colonel of the 27th New York Infantry, sustains severe wounds at the Battle of Bull Run (First Manassas) July 21, but wins promotion as brigadier-general of volunteers August 9 and will rise to the rank of major general.

The Knickerbocker Grays is organized to instill qualities of leadership in New York boys aged 8 to 15. It is composed of about 100 boys from socially prominent families, and its officers will wear uniforms modeled on West Point dress grays.

Irish-born *Irish News* editor Thomas F. (Francis) Meagher, 37, has joined the New York Volunteers as a captain and fights July 21 at the Battle of Bull Run that turns into a rout of the Union Army. The 69th Regiment serves with distinction in the rear guard of the federal withdrawal, but it was organized as a 90-day unit, returns to New York after Bull Run, and is mustered out; it is then reorganized as two separate volunteer regiments, one of them forming the nucleus of the Irish Brigade formed by Capt. Meagher, who was exiled to Tasmania earlier in life for his actions in behalf of Irish independence and will be promoted to brigadier general next year. The other part of the 69th is joined by the 63rd and 88th New York regiments, both made up primarily of Irishmen, and will form the nucleus of the Irish Legion under the command of Col. Michael Corcoran after he is released from a Confederate prison.

Mayor Wood fails in his bid for reelection as New Yorkers reject his defense of slavery and racist views. They give Republican George Opdyke 25,380 votes, but fur merchant Charles Godfrey Gunther, 39, running as a Tammany Democrat, receives nearly as many (24,767), and Fernando Wood (who has run again as a Mozart Democrat) 24,417. Wood's critics say that some of his statements border on treason. Tammany Hall has elevated James Conner to the post of Grand Sachem on the recommendation of council member William M. Tweed, Conner has become the society's first Irish and first Roman Catholic leader, and the "Wigwam" has enrolled vast numbers of immigrants and Catholics in its effort to unseat Mayor Wood, but it is the rich banker and merchant Opdyke who will be the city's mayor through the end of 1863.

 The Children's Aid Society founded in 1853 tries to help the children of Union Army volunteers, hundreds of whom roam the city's streets, and suggestions are made that impoverished adults be shipped out west the way Children's Aid ships children. The Union Defense Committee opens a center in a vacant store at 14 Fourth Avenue to provide help for families of volunteers; the city gives needy families $3 per week, plus $1 for the first child and 50¢ for each additional child, but relief for the head of a family is reduced to $2 by June 10 (critics complain that this is more than many husbands earned before they enlisted). Women demonstrate at City Hall, saying they will ask their husbands to desert.

A Woman's Central Association of Relief is founded by society leaders who include New York-born Louisa Lee Schuyler, 23, a great-granddaughter of Alexander Hamilton who also works to help sick and wounded soldiers.

$ A business downturn early in the year bankrupts scores of New York firms, throws thousands of men out of work, and gives employers an excuse to cut wages from an average of $1.25 per day to just 85¢ (women are lucky to earn $1 to $3 per week; seamstresses who lost their jobs before the war have not yet been rehired, and some have been forced into prostitution for lack of other means of support).

J. P. Morgan & Co. has its beginnings at New York, where Hartford-born banker's son John Pierpont Morgan, 24, becomes the local agent for his father, Junius Spencer Morgan, 48; educated at Boston and at the University of Göttingen, the younger Morgan started his career 4 years ago as an accountant for the New York firm Duncan, Sherman & Co. that has represented the London firm George Peabody & Co. Morgan will be a partner in Dabney, Morgan & Co. from 1864 to 1871 and come to be the most powerful financier in America (*see* transportation [steamships], 1869; Drexel, Morgan, 1871).

Prices on the New York Stock Board & Exchange drop after the firing on Fort Sumter and plunge after the Battle of Bull Run July 21. Secretary of the Treasury Salmon Portland Chase, 53, comes to New York seeking more robust support from the city's financial district, which has been ambivalent about the war lest it antagonize Southern customers (banks continue to pay drafts against funds deposited by Southerners). Specifically, Chase wants to borrow $50 million by issuing treasury notes paying 7.3 percent interest with the option of converting them into 20-year bonds; James Gallatin of the National Bank of New York opposes the plan, as does John A. Stevens of the Bank of Commerce, and it is only with great difficulty that Chase obtains the money from a consortium of New York, Boston, and Philadelphia banks organized by Moses Taylor of the City Bank, who is known as a "hard money Democrat" but supports the Lincoln administration and acts as chairman of the committee that makes the first federal loan.

New York State factories work night and day to produce ordnance, uniforms, shoes, tents, and other supplies for the Union Army. The arsenal at Watervliet employs 1,000 men, the Brooklyn Navy Yard more than 2,500. New York shipbuilder John Englis launches the *Unadilla* in just 58 days and delivers it 12 days ahead of schedule—the first gunboat built for the navy after the firing on Fort Sumter. New York industrialist Abram Stevens Hewitt, 39, of Cooper, Hewitt (he is Peter Cooper's son-in-law) develops a reputation for being able to deliver iron deck beams for warships on short notice; he and his partner, Edward Cooper, 37, produce mortar beds and gun carriages, and Hewitt learns how to make gunbarrel iron as good as any from Britain.

Congressman William M. Tweed's chair business fails and he files for bankruptcy, listing as his worldly assets "Three Hats, Two Caps, Two Thick Overcoats, One Thin Overcoat, Three Pair Pants, Six Vests, Two Dress Coats, One Business Coat, Three Pair Boots, Two Pair Shoes, Ten Pair Socks, Thirty Collars, Twelve Linen Shirts, Twelve Cotton Shirts, Ten Handkerchiefs." But in 5 years Tweed will own a Manhattan brownstone and a country home in Greenwich, Conn. (*see* politics, 1863).

The recession that began in the fall of 1857 ends by autumn as railroads, foundries, textile factories, and other concerns make large profits from war contracts granted by the federal government, whose expenses soar from $172,000 per day to more than $1 million per day, but wages lag behind prices, which begin a sharp ascent; property owner William B. Astor raises rents by 30 percent.

I. M. Singer sells more sewing machines abroad than in America and has profits of nearly $200,000 on assets of little more than $1 million (*see* 1856; 1862).

Cash reserves in New York banks fall in December to just over $29 million, down from more than $60 million in January. All U.S. banks suspend payments in gold December 30; specie payment will not resume until 1879.

The New York State Military Board learns that Washington will not clothe the troops and advertises April 23 for bids on 12,000 uniforms. Brooks Brothers assures the board that it has enough suitable cloth and receives a contract to produce blue uniforms at $19.50 each, only to find 2 days after signing the contract that it cannot fill the order without using something other than standard army cloth. The state treasurer inspects the alternative material, the military board approves its use, but it turns out to be "shoddy"—made up of scraps that can fall apart in wet weather or rough use. The newspapers expose what they call a "scandal," but Daniel, Elisha, John, and Edward Brooks negotiate a new contract with Gov. Morgan, agreeing to replace the shoddy uniforms with suits made of the best-quality cloth without charge to the state. Other contractors are less scrupulous, and some will reap large fortunes supplying the government with shoddy goods of all sorts.

John D. (Davison) Rockefeller enters the kerosene business at age 24. Having prospered as a Cleveland produce merchant, the upstate New York-born Rockefeller and his English-born partner Maurice B. Clark pool their $4,000 in savings to buy a half interest in the lard-oil refinery of Samuel Andrews and build a petroleum refinery at Cleveland (*see* 1865).

The sleek passenger ship S.S. *City of New York* begins transatlantic service for the Inman Line with engines that develop 1,500 horsepower.

The side-wheeler *Mary Powell* goes into service on the Hudson River, beginning a career that will continue until 1917 despite competition from railroads (*see* 1851). Built at Jersey City for Capt. Absalom L. Anderson of Kingston, N.Y., the "speed queen of the Hudson is 288 feet in length after modification, is powered by vertical-beam steam engine and provides daily round-trip service between New York and Kingston" (*see* Morse, 1902).

Bellevue Hospital loses many surgeons and physicians to the Union Army, and when a typhus epidemic breaks out, 14 of the hospital's staff of 21 come down with the disease; six of them die. Bellevue Hospital Medical College is established at New York with Lewis Albert Sayre, 41, as the first U.S. professor of orthopedic surgery. Sayre is joined in founding the college by Massachusetts-born physician Austin Flint, 48, who becomes professor of internal medicine at the new Bellevue College.

The German Hospital that will become Lenox Hill in 1901 receives a charter and is incorporated by men who include German-language newspaper publisher Oswald Ottendorfer, 35, who 2 years ago married the widow of the *New Yorker Staats-Zeitung* publisher Jakob Uhl (*see* 1845; German Dispensary, 1857). Anna Uhl Ottendorfer (*née* Behr), now 50, becomes treasurer of a Ladies' Auxiliary (*see* 1868).

James Gordon Bennett's *New-York Herald* sends correspondents to cover the Battle of Bull Run and other engagements. Pro-slavery before the firing on Fort Sumter, Bennett had his plant stormed by an angry mob. He has become a supporter of the Union, and the *Herald*'s war correspondents will grow to number about 40.

The *New-York Times* publishes its first Sunday edition to capitalize on interest in the war. *New-York World* founder James Reed Spalding joins the *Times*, edited by his University of Vermont classmate Henry J. Raymond, and will be the paper's responsible editor during Raymond's service as U.S. congressman.

A federal grand jury finds the 34-year-old *Journal of Commerce* to be "disloyal." Editor Gerard Hallock has been critical of President Lincoln's war on the South, he has on one occasion printed details of Union military strategy, and the government will refuse to distribute the paper by mail until Hallock resigns.

The city has 20 advertising agencies.

The first U.S. pencil factory opens on the East River near 42nd Street under the direction of John Eberhard Faber, now 38 (*see* 1849). He continues to import graphite and clay from abroad but has bought tracts of cedar forest in Florida, built a sawmill at Cedar Keys, and opted to eliminate shipping and tariff costs by launching his own manufacturing operation; it prospers despite the problems created by the war (*see* Mongol pencil, 1893).

Painting: *Departure of the Seventh on the 19th of April, 1861* by German-born New York painter-caricaturist Thomas Nast, 20, who went to work at age 15 as a draftsman for *Frank Leslie's Illustrated Weekly* and has been with the *New-York Illustrated News* since 1859, learning by trial and error how to transfer his drawings to wooden blocks for accurate reproduction (he will become a regular staff artist for *Harper's Weekly* next year); *St. John* by New York-born painter John La Farge, 26.

Photographer Matthew B. Brady records the Battle of Bull Run in July with help from assistants who include Irish-born, Staten Island-raised photographer Timothy O'Sullivan, 21. Brady switched to the new wet-plate process 6 years ago and has poured all his money into training assistants who will help him make photographic records of the war (his own eyesight has been so poor since 1851 that he can scarcely focus). He will travel through the war-torn South with a wagonful of equipment to record scenes of the conflict.

Theater: *The New President* in September at an elegant new theater built by Lester Wallack and his father, James, at the northeast corner of Broadway and 13th Street. Now 41, Lester Wallack has put up

the theater on land leased from William B. Astor at $8,000 per year, he pays some of the actors in his stock company as much as $100 per week, and audiences pay $1 for orchestra seats, $7 for a private box that seats seven, 25¢ for seats in the family circle.

Dancer Lola Montez dies in obscurity at Astoria, Queens, January 17 at age 42 and is buried in Green-Wood Cemetery under the name Mrs. Eliza Gilbert. Born Marie Dolores Eliza Rosanna Gilbert in Ireland, she became mistress to Bavaria's Ludwig I but settled at New York in 1856 after an Australian lecture tour and gained a reputation for helping women in distress with money earned lecturing on fashion, gallantry, and feminine beauty.

G. Schirmer Co. has its beginnings in the New York firm Beer & Schirmer founded (with a partner) by German-born music publisher Gustav Schirmer, 32, who will gain an international reputation by encouraging young musicians and uncovering new talents.

Popular songs: "Dixie" is played at the inaugural of Confederate president Jefferson Davis and quickly becomes the marching song of the Confederate Army, much to the chagrin of New Yorker Daniel Decatur Emmett (*see* 1859).

Elisha G. Otis patents a steam-powered elevator but dies at Yonkers April 8 at age 50, leaving Otis Elevator Co. to his sons (*see* 1857). The Otis elevator together with cheaper steel will permit development of tall buildings without thick masonry walls and lead to the rise of the modern city, with offices and apartments on upper floors fetching higher rentals than those on lower floors whereas tenants up to now have paid more for space that required fewer stairs to climb (*see* 1884).

New York hotels reduce their rates as unemployment persists through the summer. The St. Nicholas lowers its American Plan (meals included) rate from $2.50 per day to $2.

The New-York Produce Exchange has its beginnings in the New-York Commercial Association (it will change its name in 1868; *see* building, 1884).

Gail Borden licenses more factories to produce his condensed milk, which the Union Army is purchasing for use in field rations. Borden's son John Gail fights for the Union, his son Lee with the Texas Cavalry for the Confederacy (*see* 1858; 1866).

1862 The Union gains its first major success in February as Fort Henry on the Tennessee River and Fort Donelson on the Cumberland fall to U.S. forces under Brig. Gen. Ulysses S. Grant, 39, who wins promotion to major general of volunteers.

The first naval battle between ironclad ships takes place March 8. The Union ironclad *Monitor* forces the Confederate ironclad *Merrimack* to withdraw from Hampton Roads; she has been built by Swedish-born New York naval engineer John Ericsson, 58, with help from the Delamater Iron Works of Cornelius H. Delamater, now 39, and the victory brings Ericsson orders for more such vessels. He came to New York in 1839 and oversaw the design and construction of a single-screw warship.

Former president Martin Van Buren dies at his native Kinderhook, N.Y., July 24 at age 79.

Democrat Horatio Seymour wins the New York gubernatorial election, defeating Gen. James S. Wadsworth, who distinguished himself last year at the disastrous Battle of Bull Run (First Manassas) and has been military governor of Washington, D.C. Now 52, Seymour has supported the Union cause despite his opposition to Abraham Lincoln's election (and to emancipation) and his fierce attacks on Lincoln's extraconstitutional war powers; although he opposes any federal conscription law on the grounds that troops should be raised by the individual states, the new governor will work effectively to fill New York's army quotas (*see* draft riots, 1863).

"My paramount object in this struggle is to save the Union," writes President Lincoln August 22 in a letter to Horace Greeley of the *New-York Tribune*, "and is not either to save or to destroy slavery. If I could save the Union without freeing any slave, I would do it; and if I could do it by freeing all the slaves, I would do it; and if I could save it by freeing some and leaving others alone, I would also do that." An Emancipation Proclamation issued by President Lincoln September 22 declares that "persons held as slaves" within areas "in rebellion against the United States" will be free on and after January 1, 1863. Lincoln makes emancipation a war aim.

New York workers stage walkouts to demand higher pay as prices rise. Bakers, boatbuilders, journeymen shipjoiners, journeymen house painters (who receive 17¢ per hour), journeymen coppersmiths (who get $1.75 per day at best), hack drivers (who get $9 per week), and sign painters all feel squeezed, as do longshoremen, but when Irish laborers employed by the Manhattan Gas Co. at the foot of 14th Street and the East River refuse to return to work after a few days unless some of their discharged colleagues are rehired they are simply replaced by German laborers.

The federal government converts the Customs House completed 20 years ago at 26 Wall Street into a subtreasury building that soon contains 70 percent of the nation's revenues (which have provided virtually all federal income). The gold and bank notes are initially stored in a large safe, but vaults will be built in the basement; the building will remain a subtreasury until 1920. It will become the Federal Hall National Memorial in 1939 (*see* Washington statue, 1886).

A revised federal income tax act is signed into law by President Lincoln July 1 (*see* 1861). Drafted to raise funds for pursuit of the war, it levies 3 percent on incomes from $600 to $10,000 and 5 percent on incomes above $10,000, but the law exempts dividends on railroad company stock to encourage railway development.

Singer Manufacturing Co. is incorporated by sewing machine inventor I. M. Singer and Edward Clark, who split 4,100 of the 5,000 shares between them (*see* 1861). Family incomes in America average only $500 per year, and a new Singer sewing machine sells for $100, but Clark's $5-per-month installment plan persuades customers to buy Singer machines that cost perhaps $40 to make including all overhead (*see* 1877).

Henry B. Hyde's 3-year-old Equitable Life Assurance Society employs hundreds of agents and writes nearly $2 million in new policies as the Civil War makes Americans more aware of life's jeopardies. All New York life insurance companies enjoy nearly twice the business seen in any previous year, but Equitable grows much faster than its rivals (Hyde himself will avoid the draft quite legally by hiring a substitute for $800) and will pay its first dividend to policy holders in 1865.

Department store king A. T. Stewart contributes $100,000 to the Union cause and sells uniforms at cost to the Union Army (*see* 1846). Stewart has introduced a revolutionary one-price system with each item carrying a price tag, an innovation that permits him to employ women sales clerks, who can be hired more cheaply than men. Having amassed a fortune of $50 million, Stewart gives a 10 percent discount to wives and children of clergymen and schoolteachers.

The world's largest department store opens in 10th Street at Astor Place where merchant A. T. Stewart has employed James Bogardus, now 62, to design the eight-story structure that is also the world's largest building with a cast-iron front (*see* 1849). An uptown counterpart of the Marble Palace, the cavernous store is at the east end of the old Randall Farm; it has a central court, a huge skylight, a grand stairway leading up from the spacious ground floor, and elevators to make the upper floors accessible (*see* Otis, 1861; Wanamaker, 1896).

Coal prices reach $7.50 per ton in September, up from $4.50 earlier in the year. Heating one's house becomes far costlier, and coal dealers warn that prices may rise to $10 or even $12 as winter wears on.

The Common Council passes an ordinance on the evening of April 21 authorizing the New York & Harlem Railroad to build a street railway down Broadway to the Battery. The news reaches Wall Street April 22 and stock in the company, heretofore under pressure, shoots up to 75. Cornelius van Derbilt, now 67, has used some of the $20 million he has acquired in shipping and war profiteering to buy stock in the New York & Harlem; he owns 55,000 shares, has more than $2.5 million invested in the company, and has been bribing members of the Common Council to secure their votes. The stock keeps rising until it reaches par before backing off; van Derbilt gains support from his rival Daniel Drew, now 64, to win election in May to the presidency of the New York & Harlem, but Drew then suggests to the councilmen that they can all get rich if they join him in selling the stock short, and then revoking permission for the street railway. Van Derbilt's crew begins tearing up the street June 25 pursuant to the Council's ordinance and the company's stock hits 110, but the councilmen vote to revoke the franchise and the stock promptly drops to 72. Waiting for the price to fall further, the councilmen are shocked to see it rising. Van Derbilt buys stock, squeezing the short sellers as the price rises to 80, to 95, to 108, and then to 125 and 150. As the warrants come due, the short sellers have to produce stock or go to jail, and they are obliged to buy at the Commodore's price: $180 per share. By July 4 they are out of pocket as much as $70 for every share they have pledged, and van Derbilt will have unchallenged control of the New York & Harlem by next year.

Commodore van Derbilt uses some of his profits to buy stock in the nearly bankrupt Hudson River Railroad that runs parallel to the Harlem line before branching off to follow the river up to East Albany (*see* 1864).

The Medical College for Women and Hospital for Women and Children opens at 724 Broadway, near 8th Street; founded with help from Elizabeth Cady Stanton, it is a homeopathic institution.

The German Dispensary that opened in 1857 moves from Canal Street to larger quarters at 8 East 3rd Street, where next year it will install six beds. The dispensary has been treating 10,000 patients per year and crowding has become intolerable (*see* 1868).

The city's Board of Commissioners of Health conclude that smallpox can be eliminated by compulsory vaccination, but a bill that would require such vaccination is stalled in the legislature at Albany; smallpox goes unchecked in much of the city (*see* 1865).

New York women scrape lint and roll bandages for the wounded, mostly in haphazard fashion, and raise money for the Sanitary Commission.

Nonfiction: *North America* by English novelist Anthony Trollope, 47, who writes, "Speaking of New York as a traveler, I have two faults to find with it. In the first place, there is nothing to see; and, in the second place, there is no mode of getting about to see anything. . . . I own that I have enjoyed the vistas as I have walked up and down Fifth Avenue, and have felt that the city had a right to be proud of its wealth. But . . . I have known no great man, no celebrated statesman, no philanthropist of peculiar note who has lived on Fifth Avenue. That gentleman on the right made a million dollars by inventing a shirt collar; this one on the left electrified the world by a lotion; as to the gentleman at the corner there,—there are rumours about him and the Cuban slave trade; . . . Such are the aristocracy of Fifth Avenue. I can only say that if I could make a million dollars by a lotion, I should certainly be right to live in such a house as one of these. . . . Every man worships the dollar, and is down before his shrine from morning till night." The women of the city, Trollope says, have never been taught good manners or behavior.

Two illustrations by Thomas Nast in *Harper's Weekly* at year's end attract nationwide attention: "Christmas Eve" shows a young mother praying over her two sleeping children while her husband, wearing the uniform of the Army of the Potomac, looks at a tintype of his family by the light of a campfire (a twilight image of the graves of Union dead appears at the bottom of the page); "Santa Claus in Camp" depicts a rotund, white-bearded man clad in a fur-trimmed American flag and passing out gifts in a Union Army camp (*see* Moore poem, 1823). Transforming Clement Clark Moore's elf into a full-size man, Nast will produce Santa Claus illustrations next year and in 1864.

Theater: Niblo's Garden opens in April on Broadway at Prince Street under the direction of New York-born London actor-manager William Wheatley, 45, who appeared at age 10 at the Park Theater and will continue to direct productions at Niblo's Garden until his retirement in August 1868; *Mazeppa* 6/16 at the New Bowery Theater, with Louisiana-born poet-actress Adah Isaacs Menken, 27, creating a sensation strapped half naked to a horse in a melodramatic adaptation of the 1819 Byron poem.

Retired minstrel-show entertainer Edwin P. Christy jumps from a New York window in a fit of depression May 21 and dies at age 46.

The state legislature at Albany establishes a Department of Survey and Inspection of Buildings independent of the Fire Department that has had the responsibility for the past 2 years of enforcing compliance with structural safety laws. The solons make it mandatory for architectural plans to be submitted to the department for review, with appeals from its decisions to be referred directly to the state supreme court (they will be referred to the Board of Examiners beginning in 1874).

The 20-year-old Yorkville receiving reservoir in Central Park is enlarged to cover 106 acres and made 40 feet deep with a capacity of 1 billion gallons. It will remain part of the city's water system until late 1993.

The state legislature at Albany votes in April to ban the sale of alcohol and employment of waitresses in saloons that have come under attack for encouraging drunkenness and prostitution. Saloonkeepers quickly find political protection and devise ways to evade the law.

Lorenzo Delmonico opens a third café-restaurant at Fifth Avenue and 14th Street, where he has acquired shipowner Moses Hicks Grinnell's mansion to keep up with society's move uptown (*see* 1845). Delmonico's ballroom has windows facing on Fifth Avenue, and chef Charles Ranhofer will contribute to Delmonico's reputation (*see* 1868).

1863 William M. Tweed has himself elected chairman of Tammany Hall's general committee January 1 and has himself elected Grand Sachem in April, thus combining two positions that heretofore have been separate and thwarting any challenge to his power as the city's political boss. He also wins appointment as deputy street commissioner and by 1867 will have quadrupled the street department's payroll as he gives jobs to political cronies.

Draft riots brought unprecedented violence to the city amidst widespread opposition to the war.

Gen. John A. Dix is given command of the Union Army's Department of the East with headquarters at New York City. When Confederate forces invade Pennsylvania in March, Gov. Seymour orders every available regiment sent to the front for 30 days' service.

Union forces suffer defeat at Chancellorsville, Va., from May 1 to May 5. Gen. Thomas F. Meagher's Irish Brigade is decimated and he resigns his commission, but Union troops triumph at the Battle of Gettysburg July 1 to 3, ending the danger to Philadelphia. Gen. Daniel E. Sickles has put his men forward of the line ordered by the commanding general George Meade July 2, most of the officers and one-third of the men in his Third Corps fall in the battle, and a shell fragment shatters Sickles's right leg below the knee, requiring its amputation in the field.

Conscription for the Union Army begins July 11 under legislation passed March 3 giving exemption to any man who pays $300 to hire a substitute. Union victories at Gettysburg and Vicksburg earlier in July have sealed the fate of the Confederacy, many Northerners see no point in joining the army, only the rich can afford $300 for a substitute, and many workingmen resent having to fight for the emancipation of slaves who may come north and take away the unskilled jobs on which their families depend. Tammany Grand Sachem William M. Tweed institutes a low-interest loan program intended to enable poor New Yorkers to hire substitutes, but draft riots break out in several cities, and the worst riot in U.S. history begins at New York on the night of Sunday, July 12. An angry crowd armed with iron bars, bludgeons, and brickbats mills about the door of the recruiting office on Third Avenue early July

13, and before more than 40 or 50 names have been drawn from the drum a paving stone crashes through the window; ragged Irish immigrants pour out of the infamous Sixth Ward east of Broadway shouting, "Kill the rich!" and "Down with the Black Republican nigger lovers!" Angry mobs cut telegraph lines and attack various targets, notably houses of the rich near Gramercy Park and elsewhere, the New York Times building, and streetcars. City officials and well-dressed citizens are assaulted, and by Tuesday the mob has begun to attack blacks, many of whom are dragged from their houses, beaten up, chased to the docks, thrown into the river, or hanged. Courageous neighbors evacuate more than 200 children through the back doors of the 27-year-old Colored Orphan Asylum on Fifth Avenue between 43rd and 44th streets before they can be harmed, but the building is burned and blacks throughout the city are set upon and killed or maimed.

Mayor Opdyke refuses to make any deals with the rioters, who come out of the Five Points bent on violence; he abandons City Hall to the mob and takes refuge in the St. Nicholas Hotel as the city verges on anarchy. Police Superintendent John Kennedy tries to stop the mob single-handedly and is lucky to escape with no worse than a severe beating. Rioters tear up railroad tracks and burn 43 buildings, including hotels, between 46th Street and the Cooper Union in Astor Place; gangs from the Five Points join with their traditional rivals to prevent firemen from reaching the blazes. They sack stores such as Brooks Brothers and create general chaos in their battles with police before the secretary of war orders the Seventh Regiment home to protect the city (recalled from Gettysburg, troops of the 56th New York Regiment begin arriving by ferry and march down Third Avenue, scattering the rioters and shooting those who resist, even though many of the soldiers are themselves Irish and German). By the time the disturbance is suppressed July 17 at least 18 blacks (and possibly 50) have been lynched, nearly that number maimed, many more are reported missing, and a total of at least 100 (and possibly as many as 1,200) people have been killed and thousands injured (the Bowery toughs take care of their own dead and wounded, so the official counts may be understated). Archbishop Hughes, now 66, addresses the riot participants July 17 at the request of Gov. Seymour, who helps put down the disorders but is widely (if falsely) suspected of having encouraged them. Now a city of 800,000 with some 200,000 of its inhabitants Irish, New York suffers more than $2 million (and possibly $5 million) in property dam-

age, some 3,000 people are left homeless and destitute, but the war is creating an economic boom and the city will soon be rebuilt.

Conscription resumes quietly August 19, with a blind man drawing names out of a wooden box at the office of the provost marshal, Sixth District, at 185 Sixth Avenue, and although men of means find it easy to avoid the draft by paying for substitutes, New York State will have contributed 475,000 men to the Union Army by 1865—more than any other state (New Yorkers constitute one-sixth of the army), and New York City alone will have contributed 116,000 at a cost of $14.5 million.

Many of the hoodlums who participated in the July draft riots escape conviction through the efforts of London-born lawyer William F. Howe, 35, who has resigned the position he acquired last year as judge advocate of the New York Cavalry Brigade. Howe evidently arrived in America as a ticket-of-leave man (paroled convict) 5 years ago after serving time for an illegal act performed as a physician; he hires as office boy Abraham Henry Hummel, 13, who will later become his partner (see 1869), and succeeds in having Union soldiers discharged on writs of habeas corpus, deposing in court that they were drunk when they volunteered, or that they were conscripted contrary to law owing to circumstances in their family or business affairs. Howe secures the discharge of an entire 70-man company, and President Lincoln suspends the writ of habeas corpus throughout the country September 15, antagonizing many of his supporters.

Gov. Seymour loses his bid for reelection. "We say most clearly that we are the party for stopping the war at the earliest possible period," he declares at a mass meeting held in the Great Hall of the Cooper Union, but many still blame him for the draft riots, and Republican congressman Reuben Eaton Fenton, 45, runs far ahead of his ticket in defeating the governor, securing 368,557 votes to Seymour's 361,264.

Former New York governor Edwin D. Morgan is elected to the U.S. Senate as a Republican (he left politics last year to direct the fortification of New York Harbor), but without the support of former Republican Party boss Thurlow Weed, now 66, whose Albany Regency was responsible for William H. Seward's rise from Whig lawyer to New York governor to U.S. senator and U.S. secretary of state. Weed has moved to New York City, holds sway from his suite at the Astor House, but has had a falling out with the radical wing of the party.

Independent Democrat C. Godfrey Gunther wins the mayoralty election in December, receiving 29,121 votes (Mayor Opdyke has declined to run for reelection). Tammany Democrat Francis I. A. Boole gets 22,597 votes (a city inspector backed by Grand Sachem William M. Tweed, he has antagonized Irishmen with placating statements about blacks), Republican Orison Blunt (who supports President Lincoln) only 19,383. Now 41, Gunther is a pacifist who has adopted the name of his German stepfather (his real father was French Alsatian), most people think he is German, the German Union Democratic Party has backed him, and it has organized a reform coalition to back its underdog candidate.

♥ A newly founded Citizens' Association of New York addresses issues of inadequate housing, public health, and other such issues that have contributed to the misery that culminated in the July draft riots (*see* medicine, 1865).

$ The price of gold reaches 160 by January 31, up from 100½ in April of last year, but falls to about 139 in March as speculators sell in anticipation of Confederate reversals.

Clipper-ship magnate A. A. Low is elected president of the city's Chamber of Commerce, a position that he will retain until he resigns in 1866. Confederate privateers have destroyed his speedy ships *The Contest* and *Jacob Bell* while he has headed the Union Defence Committee of New York and other war-financing groups.

A Russian fleet sails into New York Harbor in September on a goodwill mission, Adm. Lisovski and his officers receive a warm welcome, and before they leave they donate $4,760 to the city to buy fuel for the poor who have not participated in the city's wartime economic boom and are being squeezed by inflation.

Some 72 ships from New York arrive at Metamoros, Mexico, carrying wagons, medical supplies, uniforms, and other cargo that will be transshipped to Confederate ports; some New Yorkers reap large profits by such trade.

Wall Street hears about the Union victory at Gettysburg even before the news reaches President Lincoln, New York becomes second only to London as a financial center, and new after-hours exchanges open in uptown hotels and elsewhere amidst a frenzy to speculate. The New York Stock Exchange takes that name, having operated since 1817 as the New York Stock Board & Exchange. Prices on the exchange (and in unofficial trading) plummet on news of Union victories and rise when Confederate troops prevail; speculators act on the premise that a longer war will benefit industry and railroads.

First National Bank of New York is founded in the basement of a building at the corner of Broadway and Wall Street by local entrepreneur John Thompson, 61, who publishes the *Thompson Bank Note Detector* (*see* Chase, 1877; First National City, 1955). The bank has a capital of $100,000 and is soon followed by the Second National Bank, under the Fifth Avenue Hotel, with a capital of $200,000, and the Third National Bank, with a capital of $300,000.

The Apple Bank for Savings has its beginnings in the Harlem Savings Bank (*see* 1983).

Merchant A. T. Stewart pays taxes on an income of $1,843,637, slightly more than William B. Astor or Cornelius van Derbilt, and even though the income tax rate is low the revenue produced is considerable (*see* 1862). War profits and speculations have enabled some people to create large fortunes almost overnight: several hundred New Yorkers are estimated to be worth at least $1 million, and some as much as $20 million.

R. H. Macy holds his first clearance sale (*see* 1860). Macy has acquired the leases of neighboring stores, expanded his wares to include clothing, jewelry, dolls, toys, plants, and toiletries in a maze of salesrooms, has accepted mail orders since 1861, and promises free delivery to customers in Brooklyn, Hoboken, and Jersey City (*see* 1866).

The Anthracite Gas Lighting and Heating Co. of New York is founded May 26.

South Street tugboat broker Michael Moran, now 29, buys a half interest in the 42-ton, 60-foot tugboat *Ida Miller* (*see* 1860; 1906; McAllister Brothers, 1864).

Onandaigua-born financier Leonard W. (Walter) Jerome, 44, builds Jerome Avenue in the Bronx to provide access to the park that he has acquired (*see* sports [race track], 1866).

Ground is broken at Sacramento, Calif., February 22 for the Central Pacific Railroad. Chief engineer Theodore D. Judah has laid out the route, the first Central Pacific rails are spiked to ties October 23, Judah arrives with his wife, Anna, that day at New York, but he has contracted yellow fever crossing the Isthmus of Panama and dies in a Wall Street hotel November 2 at age 37, having done more than anyone to make the transcontinental railroad a reality (*see* 1869).

The New York & Erie Rail Road has earnings of $10 million, up from $5 million in 1860, as the war fuels demand for railcars (and for railroad securities on what is now officially known as the New York Stock Exchange).

Investors, who include former mayor Henry Havemeyer, assume control of the bankrupt Long Island Rail Road and install former police chief Oliver Charlick as the company's president (see 1850). Brooklyn banned the LIRR's smoky steam locomotives 2 years ago, it has been forced to move its terminal from Brooklyn to Hunter's Point in what later will be Long Island City, the move has cost it some passenger traffic, competition from the New York & New Haven's all-rail link to Boston has taken away riders as well as freight, and while Charlick will remain president until 1875 he will fail to rebuild the line's customer base, rejecting appeals that he build branches to the south shore.

The Brooklyn Historical Society has its beginnings in the Long Island Historical Society that will initially have offices in the Hamilton Building at the corner of Joralemon Street (see 1880).

Novelist Herman Melville moves back to his native Manhattan in October, having derived little from his 1851 masterpiece *Moby-Dick* (he has never made a living from his writings and has survived, as his father did, by scraping by on loans). Now 45, he manages to buy a house from his brother Allan at 104 East 26th Street (60 East by later numbering), where he will live until his death in 1891.

Poet-scholar (and Chelsea real estate developer) Clement Clark Moore dies at Newport, R.I., July 10 just 5 days short of his 84th birthday.

The National Academy of Design founded in 1827 moves into a building designed by P. B. Wright at 23rd Street and Fourth Avenue.

The 55-year-old New-York Historical Society raises $4,000 by public subscription to purchase the 464 original watercolors by the late John James Audubon from his widow, Lucy (née Bakewell), who had received an offer from a foreign buyer but said, "It was always the wish of Mr. Audubon that his 40 years of labor should remain in this country."

General Tom Thumb is married February 10 at Grace Church on Broadway and 10th Street to Lavinia Warren (Mercy Bunn), who stands two feet eight inches in height (see 1842). Heavily promoted by showman P. T. Barnum, the wedding attracts huge crowds that jam the streets (the wedding party stands on a grand piano to receive guests at the Metropolitan Hotel).

The first four-wheeled roller skates are patented by New York inventor James L. Plimpton, whose small boxwood wheels are arranged in pairs and cushioned by rubber pads, making it possible to maintain balance while executing intricate maneuvers. Plimpton's roller skates will lead to a widespread roller-skating fad later in this decade.

Home building comes almost to a total halt in the city, leaving the poor in dark, squalid tenements (see 1864). Rents continue to rise as housing shortages develop, and the draft riots are motivated in part by experience with absentee landlords in Ireland whose New York counterparts gouge immigrants with high rents and permit overcrowding.

The Riverdale Presbyterian Church and its manse (Duff House) are completed in 249th Street, the Bronx, to designs by James Renwick, Jr.

St. James Church (Episcopal) is completed at 2500 Jerome Avenue, northeast corner 190th Street, in the Bronx, to Gothic Revival designs by Dudley & Diaper.

Woodlawn Cemetery is laid out by James C. Sidney in the north central Bronx, where its easy accessibility by rail will help make it a popular burying place for prominent Americans.

Central Park is extended north to 110th Street, giving it a total of 843 acres that will now include the Harlem Meer and other bucolic features. The Central Park Commission reports, "If all the applications for the erection and maintenance of towers, houses, drinking fountains, telescopes, mineral water fountains, cottages, Eolian harps, gymnasiums, observatories, and weighing scales, for the sale of eatables, velocipedes, perambulators, indian work, tobacco and segars, iceboats and the use of the ice for fancy dress carnivals were granted, they would occupy a large portion of the surface of the park, establish a very extensive and very various business, and give to it the appearance of the grounds of a country fair, or of a militia training ground" (see carousel, 1871).

The 4-year-old Great American Tea Co. grows to have six stores and begins selling a line of groceries in addition to tea (see A&P, 1869).

Lamb sells in the city for 23¢/lb., up from 10¢ in 1861; mutton 15¢, up from 6¢; beef 18¢, up from 8¢; coffee 50¢, up from 10¢; sugar 20¢, up from 5¢. Unscrupulous merchants adulterate their coffee and wheat, and some bakers shrink the size of their loaves.

The Cunard Line enters the immigrant trade with low rates for passengers aboard its new screw-propeller transatlantic ships as potato rot hits Ireland once again, restimulating the exodus to America (see 1846).

1864 A Board of Estimate and Apportionment is established to estimate the annual cost of operating the city's police force. Made up of Metropolitan Police commissioners and the comptrollers of New York and Brooklyn, the board will grow to have as much political power as the mayor (see 1901).

News that the Union cruiser *Kearsarge* has sunk the Confederate raider *Alabama* off Cherbourg June 19 thrills New York supporters of what some opponents still call "Mr. Lincoln's war." The New York Chamber of Commerce raises a $25,000 purse for distribution to Capt. John Winslow of the *Kearsarge* and his officers and men (Winslow receives $10,000, his officers $10,000, his crew $5,000). But the Confederate steamer *Tallahassee* commanded by cavalry colonel John Taylor Wood captures two Sandy Hook pilot boats in August, destroys or damages dozens of merchant ships, threatens to set fire to ships in New York Harbor, blast the Brooklyn Navy Yard, and escape into Long Island Sound. Wood's presence off Sandy Hook forces other ships to remain in port until he leaves for Nova Scotia.

Former mayor Isaac L. Varian dies at suburban Peekskill August 10 at age 71 and is buried at the New York Marble Cemetery in 2nd Street.

Gov. Seymour presides over the Democratic national convention that nominates Gen. George B. McClellan, who lives in a West 31st Street house given to him by friends. McClellan wins New York City's 22 wards in November by a margin of 73,734 votes to 36,737, but President Lincoln gains reelection despite his disfavor in the city as Union forces score victories. Lincoln has the support of New York Republican Party boss Thurlow Weed, who can be relied upon to come up with money for emergencies when Congress will not appropriate it (a telegram to Weed at the Astor House produces the cash within 48 hours, a list of the contributors' names attached). Mary Todd Lincoln has gone to New York behind the president's back, run up debts totaling $27,000 at dry goods stores, and then tried to get Republican politicians to pay them, arguing that they grew rich from her husband's patronage. A. T. Stewart and other merchants have offered her unlimited credit, and she has feared that news of her profligacy would be used to defeat her husband's effort to gain reelection.

Alfred M. Wood, 36, returns to Brooklyn and is elected mayor, an office that he will hold until 1866. Wood commanded the 14th Regiment of the New York State Militia, was wounded and captured 3 years ago in the first Battle of Bull Run, but has been discharged from prison and allowed to go home.

Flames are discovered Friday evening, November 25, at the St. James Hotel, Barnum's Museum, St. Nicholas Hotel, Lafarge House, Metropolitan Hotel, and Lovejoy's Hotel but are extinguished with relatively little damage (although repairs to the St. Nicholas will cost $10,000). "REMARKABLE INCENDIARISM—Several Hotels Set on Fire," headlines Horace Greeley's *New-York Tribune* Saturday morning, going on to say, "A concentrated and skillful attempt was made last night by Secessionist thieves, conspirators, and incendiaries to set on fire our principal hotels, though, fortunately—at the time of this writing, 12:15 A.M.—without success in any instance, the efforts of the conspirators being in each case foiled by the early discovery of the fire before the flames had gathered any dangerous strength." "THE REBEL PLOT—Attempt to Burn the City—All the Principal Hotels Simultaneously Set on Fire—The Fires Promptly Extinguished—Prompt Arrests of Rebel Emissaries—The Police on the Track of Others," headlines the *New-York Times*, but while police catch Robert Kennedy, 20, he is the only one of the Confederate agents who have set the fires to be apprehended (see 1865).

The Brooklyn Sanitary Fair held February 22 raises $440,000—four times what was anticipated—to supply front-line hospitals, physicians, nurses, clothing, and extra food for men serving in the Union Army and provide care for their widows and orphans.

The Metropolitan Fair that opens April 4 in a specially erected building at the corner of Sixth Avenue and 14th Street raises more than $1 million for the U.S. Sanitary Commission, headed by All Souls Unitarian Church pastor Henry W. Bellows (Central Park's designer Frederick Law Olmsted gives up his park job to become general secretary). Gifts have come into the city from all parts of the country to be sold at the fair (a receiving station has been set up in Great Jones Street), a second building—called Union Square on 17th Street—has been put up to house the children's department, music hall, and colonial "Knickerbocker Kitchen," opening ceremonies include a parade of some 10,000 troops led by Gen. Dix, lawyer Joseph Choate gives a speech to launch the 3-week event, choirs from several churches sing an "Army Hymn" written by Oliver Wendell Holmes of Boston, and some 30,000 visitors attend the fair, whose booths are operated by fashionable belles of the city.

$ Bavarian-born financier Joseph Seligman, 45, helps the Union cause with clothing supplies and by marketing U.S. Treasury bonds abroad. The banking house J. & W. Seligman that he establishes May 1 at 59 Exchange Place soon has offices at San Francisco, New Orleans, London, Paris, and Frankfurt-am-Main, managed by Seligman's seven brothers, who emigrated to America between 1837 and 1842 to work as peddlers, shopkeepers, and importers.

The second-largest underwriter of U.S. government bonds is English-born New York financier Henry Clews, 30, who cofounded the firm Stout, Clews and Mason 5 years ago.

Speculation in gold and securities increases along with inflation. Gold approaches 175 April 4; Treasury Secretary Salmon P. Chase arrives in mid-April to confer with Philadelphia financier Jay Cooke and Assistant Treasurer John J. Cisco, who is in charge of the subtreasury in New York, and by that time gold has risen to 188. Chase gives Cooke approval to start selling some of the $6 to $7 million in gold stored by Cisco, and the price drops to 174. By April 21 Cooke has sold about $7 million in gold and the price has fallen to 160; it rebounds to a high of 285 in July as Confederate forces under Gen. Jubal Early march through Maryland, falls again in early November as Cisco receives authority to resume selling, rises about $12\frac{1}{2}$ percent to $259\frac{1}{2}$ at news of President Lincoln's reelection, but drops soon thereafter to 252. Stock and bond prices have similar wild swings, with frequent—albeit short-lived—panics.

Guaranty Trust Co. has its beginnings in the New York Guaranty and Indemnity Co. founded with a capital of $100,000. The bank will be renamed Guaranty Trust Co. of New York in 1895, and by the end of 1928 it will have resources of more than $1 billion with a staff of 4,000 (see Morgan Guaranty, 1959).

Business booms before Christmas as New Yorkers gain confidence in Union victory. Arnold Constable sells lace at $1,000 per yard, shawls at $1,500 each, lace parasols at $500 (merchant Aaron Arnold pleases patrons with services that include a message book where notes may be left for friends).

Cornelius Vanderbilt (he has changed his name from van Derbilt) decides to merge his New York & Harlem line with the New York and Hudson River line in order to end their ruinous competition (see 1862). Now 70, he travels to Albany and begins bribing legislators to support a consolidation bill. New York & Erie Rail Road president Daniel Drew persuades the legislators to sell Hudson River Railroad stock short, promising to make them rich. Vanderbilt is out of the city when he hears that Drew and his confederates are trying to drive down the price of the stock, he gives orders to buy, and he acquires all the stock there is plus another 27,000 shares that Drew's confederates James Fisk and Jay Gould have had printed. When Drew and the Albany legislators cannot deliver the stock they have sold there is chaos. Vanderbilt raises money by mortgaging other properties and winds up owning 137,000 shares—27,000 more than actually exist. The short sellers come to him for stock, Vanderbilt demands $1,000 per share, many brokerage houses face bankruptcy, but Vanderbilt's ally Leonard W. Jerome, now 45, persuades him to accept $285 per share so that they may deliver, many are driven to bankruptcy nevertheless, and Vanderbilt winds up not only with a profit of more than $3 million (he would have made $25 million had all the legislators been able to deliver) but also with control of the New York and Hudson. Hudson River Railroad president Samuel Sloan resigns; now 46, he becomes a director of the Delaware, Lackawanna & Western, whose other directors will elect him president in 1867 (he will hold that position until 1899). The Commodore makes his son William Henry Vanderbilt chief operating officer of the Hudson River line and he will become president of the railroad in 1865 (see 1867).

The French Line paddle wheeler S.S. *Washington* arrives at New York in June to begin 110 years of service between New York and the Channel ports by the Compagnie Génerale Transatlantique. Her engines develop only 900 horsepower but she will later become the first twin-screw liner on the Atlantic.

McAllister Brothers has its beginnings as Irish-born entrepreneur James McAlllister of County Antrim uses his small savings to buy a part interest in the sail lighter *Hard Tack* and with one employee goes into competition with hundreds of other such work vessels in New York Harbor, working against currents and tides to move 80 to 100 tons of cargo at a time from ships docked at East River piers to piers at Newark and elsewhere along New York's 750 miles of waterfront. McAllister will soon bring over his three brothers, all will become skippers, they will start operating flat-bottomed, square-ended scows, install steam winches and derricks on some of them, and by the mid-1870s will have their first steam tugboat, competing with Michael Moran (see 1924).

The Medical College for Women and Children is founded at 724 Broadway, near 8th Street, by Dr. Elizabeth Blackwell and her sister Emily at their New York Infirmary for Women and Children. The college has America's first professorship of hygiene, or preventive medicine (Elizabeth Blackwell holds the chair).

The city's first archbishop John Hughes dies at New York January 3 at age 66, having established parochial schools, erected seminaries, and worked to protect the Irish in his diocese from attacks by the "Know Nothings." Bishop John McCloskey resigns his Albany bishopric and succeeds Hughes as archbishop of New York May 6 (see 1875).

Tammany Hall Grand Sachem William M. Tweed purchases a controlling interest in a local printing company; it soon becomes the city's chief supplier of stationery and vouchers.

Nonfiction: French traveler Ernest Duvergier de Hauranne, 21, arrives at the city in June and will write, "The first impression of New York is that it is repulsive and vulgar. The broken pavements, the muddy streets, the squares overrun with grass and underbrush, the disreputable horse cars, and the irregular houses plastered with huge handbills have the careless ugliness of an open-air bazaar. The old cities of Europe all have character; this has nothing but commonplaceness . . . Everybody is obsessed with business . . . Advertising is the indispensable adjunct of this great village fair. On every hand are floating banners, monstrous signs, flamboyant decoration . . . New York is primarily a city without a country. It is the cosmopolitan market, the vast hostelry which America opens to all people. But here sacrifice occurs without devotion. Last year, in connection with conscription, the money of the rich Copperheads fomented a riot among the Irish which even their Archbishop could not quell. This was perpetuated at a moment when the city was stripped of troops and deprived of its militia and so could not resist the insurgents. The riot . . . was a savage one. The mob killed, pillaged, hung Negroes to lampposts, and mutilated and tortured their prisoners. Its cruelty was ungovernable."

A picture gallery opened in the main hall of the Metropolitan Fair attracts large crowds to see Albert Bierstadt's painting *Rocky Mountains*, Frederick E. Church's *Heart of the Andes*, Emanuel Leutze's *Washington Crossing the Delaware*, and other works. Merchant William H. Aspinwall, now 56, opens his mansion at University Place and 10th Street to display his collection of old masters, said to be the largest in the country, that includes works by Leonardo da Vinci, Rembrandt, Sir Joshua Reynolds, Rubens, and Van Dyke.

Theater: a benefit performance of *Julius Caesar* featuring the Booth brothers (Edwin, 31, and John Wilkes, 26) 11/25 for the Shakespeare Monument Fund at the Winter Garden Theater, next door to the La Farge Hotel, is interrupted by someone spreading word of the fire set at the hotel. The *New-York Times* reports 11/26 that the audience paid double price for seats, that Confederate incendiaries set the theater ablaze, but that Edwin Booth avoided panic by assuring everyone that all was safe and the show would go on.

Actor-theater manager James W. Wallack dies at New York December 25 at age 69, leaving his son Lester, now 44, to carry on the family's 3-year-old Wallack's Theater on Broadway.

Composer Stephen C. Foster dies at Bellevue Hospital January 13 at age 37. He moved to the city in 1860 and has gone deeper and deeper into debt and dissolution.

Massachusetts-born inventor Ebenezer Butterick, 41, opens offices with his wife, Ellen, at 192 Broadway to market paper patterns for men's shirts and children's clothing (see Mrs. Demorest, 1860). A tailor and shirtmaker, Butterick devised a paper pattern for a man's shirt about 8 years ago, he or Ellen saw a need for graded patterns that would permit shirts to be reproduced in vast quantities, they began marketing cardboard-template patterns in mid-June 1863, soon diversified into patterns for boys' suits (known as "Garibaldi suits"), and have given up cardboard in favor of tissue paper (see 1867).

The city appropriates an additional $800,000 to the initial appropriation of $250,000 made in 1858 to build a new county courthouse between City Hall and Chambers Street. Architect John Kellum has designed the structure, and $250,000 should have been enough to pay for it, but Tammany Hall's Boss Tweed has seen an opportunity to profit from the project, and work proceeds at a snail's pace (see 1865).

A report by the city inspector shows that New York's 15,000 tenements house some 500,000 people—an average of eight families to a house, although some have many more, and a family can easily include 10 people (see 1863; 1867).

The country house Greyston is completed on the Riverdale estate of metals magnate William Earl Dodge of Phelps, Dodge. Designed by James Renwick, Jr. at what later will be 690 West 247th Street, southwest corner Independence Avenue, the gabled, chimneyed mansion will remain in the family until 1961. Now 58, Dodge has landholdings that extend from the Hudson River to the Westchester County border.

Central Park's first zoo opens: the menagerie behind the Arsenal contains a bear and some other animals received as gifts by park workers (a camel from the menagerie will be used to pull a lawn mower; see 1934; Prospect Park, 1893).

The state legislature at Albany enacts a law late in the year forbidding use of New York's Central Park for military drills, clearing the way for use of a 22-acre field between 66th and 69th streets as a sheep meadow. A sheepfold is built to the west of the meadow, a shepherd is installed with a flock of 150 sheep, and the sheep meadow will continue as such until 1934.

Pete's Tavern has its beginnings in Healy's Café, opened at the northeast corner of Irving Place and 18th Street, near Gramercy Park. It will soon become a favorite meeting place of Tammany Hall politicians, whose grand lodge is a few blocks to the south, and initially offers rooms for the night and stables for horses in addition to food and drink.

1865 New York stages a mammoth victory parade March 6 as the Civil War nears its end. A court martial has rendered a guilty verdict in February against Robert Kennedy, the Confederate agent charged with having set fire to some buildings in November of last year, and he goes to the gallows March 25.

Gen. Grant takes Richmond April 2, and the city goes wild when news of the victory arrives April 3.

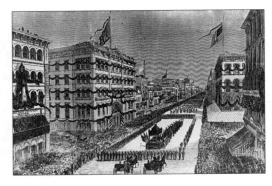

President Lincoln's death brought mourning to the city in the wake of the Civil War. HARPER'S WEEKLY

The war ends April 9, and President Lincoln is assassinated at Washington, D.C., April 14. The president's embalmed body arrives at New York April 24 in the course of its train journey back to Lincoln's native Illinois. The casket is transferred to a hearse drawn by 16 gray horses and travels slowly up Broadway past Astor Place to Union Square, where an appropriate ceremony is held with an oration by Worcester, Mass.-born historian George Bancroft, 65, and two poems by William Cullen Bryant read by a clergyman; taken from there to City Hall, the body lies in state atop the staircase until noon of the following day as 100,000 mourners file past. A large procession accompanies the coffin as it is drawn in a hearse up Broadway to the Hudson River Railroad depot for its trip west, and a 12-year Era of Reconstruction begins in the South with state legislatures run by "carpetbaggers" and "scalawags."

New York-born Tammany Democrat John Thompson Hoffman, 37, wins the mayoralty election, receiving 32,820 votes. Formerly city recorder, Hoffman gained a reputation for ability, diligence, and judgment 2 years ago when he tried and sentenced men involved in the Draft Riots. Republican Marshall O. Roberts gets 31,657, Mozart Democrat John Hecker 10,390, former mayor C. Godfrey Gunther 6,718.

The New York Infant Asylum moves into a large L-shaped wooden building at the corner of Tenth Avenue and 61st Street.

The price of gold reaches 149 March 30 and 151 the next day, but it drops 9 percent April 3 at the news that Grant has taken Richmond, and the securities market strengthens, although investors worry that peace will have an adverse effect on commerce. Prices rise as sentiment changes to one of expectation that the end of hostilities will begin a period of enduring prosperity, and Wall Street exults at news of Lee's surrender April 10.

The New York Stock Exchange moves to 8 Broad Street, between Wall Street and Exchange Place, where it will remain for more than 134 years. Transactions have taken place up to now in taverns; the old buttonwood tree at 68 Wall Street, under whose limbs trading began in 1792, is toppled this year in a storm (see ticker, 1867; real estate, 1903).

The Bank of New York founded in 1784 obtains a federal charter and is reorganized as the Bank of New York National Banking Association.

City Bank obtains a federal charter and becomes National City Bank (see First National, 1812; First National City, 1961).

The National Bank of New York is reorganized as the Gallatin National Bank, taking its name from its president James Gallatin (*see* 1868).

The Stabile Bank is established to serve the city's small Italian community that numbers fewer than 5,000. Nearly three out of four Italians who come to New York have had their tickets prepaid by someone who lives in the city, and about one-third of the arrivals will return to Italy at least once, either to visit or to live. The bank will help immigrants who do not speak English to send money home, buy ship tickets, and the like.

Deering, Milliken is founded at Portland, Me., by local fabric salesmen William Deering, 39, and Seth M. Milliken, 29, who will soon move to New York. Deering will quit to start a farm machinery company; Milliken and his heirs will prosper by buying up financially troubled New England and Southern textile mills; being quick to adopt advanced technology, Milliken will make his mills the largest U.S. textile manufacturers.

B. Altman & Co. is founded by New York milliner's son Benjamin Altman, 25, who has worked at the Newark, N.J., department store Beetlebeck's. Located initially on Sixth Avenue between 18th and 19th streets, his dry-goods store will grow to become a giant department store (*see* 1876).

The Citizens Mutual Gas Co. of New York is incorporated May 27.

A smallpox epidemic breaks out in the spring and spreads throughout the city's poorer districts despite the availability of vaccination (*see* 1862). John Jacob Astor II, August Belmont, Hamilton Fish, New Hampshire-born Bellevue Hospital physician Willard Parker, 58, and other leading members of the 2-year-old Citizens' Association of New York divide the city into 29 districts, send in inspectors, and appropriate funds for insecticides. The Association's Council of Hygiene and Public Health publishes a "Sanitary Survey" report that includes a Sanitary and Social Chart of the Fourth Ward that describes overcrowding in the 30 blocks south of Chatham Square; smallpox and typhus are found in the area where 78 people reportedly share one privy. In Mulberry Street and other tenement areas, typhus causes nearly as many deaths as smallpox. In 40th Street between Broadway and Seventh Avenue three latrines are found within 30 feet of each other, creating a stench that makes the houses unlivable (*see* 1866).

Dr. Valentine Mott dies at New York April 26 at age 79.

The New York Infant Asylum is founded for women who nurse their own infants, requiring them also to nurse foundlings (*see* 1869). Pregnant women are also accepted.

The New York College of Dentistry is founded in rented rooms at the corner of 22nd Street and Fifth Avenue with 10 faculty members and 31 students (*see* 1925).

Catholic World begins publication at New York under the aegis of Paulist Fathers superior Isaac Thomas Hecker (*see* 1858). He will organize the Catholic Publication Society next year and begin the *Young Catholic* in 1870.

Cornell University is founded at Ithaca, N.Y., by Andrew Jackson White, 32, a state senator who last year helped codify the state's school laws and create a system of training schools for teachers. White has persuaded Ezra Cornell of Western Union to provide large sums of working capital that will make use of land granted to the state under the Morrill Act of 1862, the private university will open in 1868, and its faculty of nonresident professors will include Louis Agassiz and James Russell Lowell. New York State does not avail itself of federal land for any public university, and although it will operate some institutions of higher learning it will not establish a state university system until 1948.

An improved rotary press devised by Philadelphia inventor William A. Bullock, 52, draws on a continuous roll of paper and cuts the sheets before they are printed. The Hoes at New York (*see* 1846) will evolve a true web press, but only after U.S. paper manufacturers develop paper strong enough to form a long web that will run over many cylinders without tearing, and only after the perfection of quick-drying inks that will permit presses to print newspapers first and cut them afterward (*see* 1870).

The *Nation* begins publication at New York July 12 under the direction of Irish-born journalist E. L. (Edwin Lawrence) Godkin, 34, whose weekly journal of liberal opinion supports the cause of former slaves and will continue for more than 130 years to support civil rights, civil liberties, and freedom of expression.

The 23-year-old New York Philharmonic cancels its April 15 concert as it joins the city in mourning the death of President Lincoln.

Tony Pastor's Opera House opens August 14 at 201 Bowery under the management of New York-born actor-clown-comedian-balladeer Antonio Pastor, 28, who will move to 14th Street in 1881.

The New York Turkish Bath Establishment opens in February at 13 Laight Street, near St. John's Park.

The University Club has its beginnings as New York college graduates begin meeting for dinner. Mainly Yale men, they will organize themselves into the University Club in 1879, opening their membership to men holding degrees, including honorary degrees, from any college, university, or U.S. military or naval academy (see real estate, 1899).

The Harvard Club of New York is founded in late October by a small group of graduates who meet in an upstairs room of the Mercantile Library at 13 Astor Place. The Rev. Samuel Osgood, Class of 1832, agrees to serve as president beginning in January of next year, having read the two William Cullen Bryant poems at the Union Square ceremonies honoring the late President Lincoln (see real estate, 1894).

 The state legislature at Albany orders the Central Park Commission to correct defects in the city's 1811 grid plan, which was drawn up without regard to topography. The grades of upper West Side streets are so steep as to make traffic virtually impossible. Central Park's comptroller Andrew Haskell Green, 45, will work for the next 10 years to improve the West Side grade, but the project will be delayed for 3 years while city planners agonize over whether to keep Riverside Avenue (later Riverside Drive) and Morningside Heights for parkland or use it for housing (see West Side Association, 1866; Boulevard, 1869).

Housing construction resumes in the city after a 4-year wartime hiatus. Brownstones on Fifth and Madison avenues rent for $320 to $500 per month—twice the prewar level; working-class houses that rented for $40 to $50 per month in 1860 now go for $58 to $83 per month, and the New-York Times reports that would-be tenants "have to go begging to get them for that." The city has 15,309 tenements, and few of them have even tiny air shafts for ventilation (see 1864; 1867); middle-class families live mostly in boarding houses, and those who can afford it have houses of their own, but private indoor toilets remain few and far between.

The city appropriates another $300,000 for the New York County Courthouse under construction north of City Hall (see 1864). Still another $300,000 is soon added, and the slow-moving project will receive another $500,000 next year. Contractors who include plasterer Andrew Garvey, carpenter George S. Miller, and plumber John H. Keyser are submitting inflated bills and kicking back large sums to members of the Tweed Ring, who have no interest in seeing the building completed when it is providing them with such large amounts of money. The cut taken by the Tweed Ring has climbed to 55 percent, up from 10 percent in the beginning, and by next year will be 65 percent, but the graft will not come to light for several more years (see 1876; politics, 1868).

 The city's first professional fire department is created by the state legislature at Albany to replace the volunteer companies whose ties to Tammany Hall have been related to increasing losses of life and property. The new Metropolitan Fire Department (MFD) is a paid force of 700 men in Manhattan and Brooklyn directed by the Republican-controlled board of commissioners. By early next year steam engines, horses, and a fairly reliable telegraph system will be operating in downtown Manhattan, and efficiency will improve under the direction of Gen. Alexander T. Shaler, who will reorganize the department along military lines, with officer ranks, battalions, discipline, specialization, and trials for disobedience (see 1870).

 The city's black population falls to 9,945, down from about 12,450 in 1860, but many white Southerners flock to New York, leaving their ruined homes and fields behind.

1866 Gov. Fenton wins reelection, piling up 366,315 votes as compared to 352,526 for New York City's mayor John T. Hoffman—an even larger plurality than the governor managed to get 2 years ago.

Clipper-ship magnate A. A. Low delivers an address May 3 expressing fierce opposition to labor organizations.

Compassion for overworked horses led to the establishment of a Society for the Prevention of Cruelty to Animals.

The American Equal Rights Association is founded May 10 at New York as an outgrowth of the Woman's Rights Society (*see* 1860; Anthony, 1869).

New York State has 60 orphanages, up from two in 1825, and there are still far too few. Homeless children roam the city's streets.

The Brooklyn Howard Orphan Asylum opens at the corner of Dean Street and Troy Avenue. Minister's widow Sarah A. Tillman has found that 20 children of emancipated slaves cannot be accommodated at the 30-year-old Colored Orphan Asylum; Maine-born Gen. Oliver Otis Howard, 35, has helped her, and she has started the first orphanage (and first philanthropic institution) in the New York area to be controlled and operated entirely by blacks.

The Society for the Prevention of Cruelty to Animals (SPCA) is founded by shipbuilder's son Henry Bergh, 43, of 17 Fifth Avenue, who has seen overworked horses savagely beaten without interference by police or passersby. Bergh serves as first president of the society, whose chief object is to stop the abuse of working horses and riding horses (*see* SPCC, 1875).

Postwar economic depression begins in the United States as prices begin a rapid decline following the Civil War's inflation (*see* Black Friday, 1869).

W. R. Grace and Co. is founded by Irish-born merchant William Russell Grace, 35, who moves into offices at 110 Wall Street after 15 years in Peru's guano trade. Grace made his way to Callao, Peru, at age 18, joined a local chandlery, and with help from a brother took over the business a few years later. They established the Grace Line 10 years ago to link Callao and other South American ports with U.S. ports such as New York. In the next decade Grace will amass a considerable fortune in trade with the western coast of South America (*see* politics, 1880).

The brokerage firm Fisk & Belden opens under the direction of Vermont-born speculator James "Jim" Fisk, now 32, who has represented Daniel Drew in the latter's sale of Stonington steamboats to a Boston group and has obtained backing from Drew in his venture.

R. H. Macy makes Margaret Getchell superintendent of his store (*see* 1863). Promoted to bookkeeper 3 years ago, she is the first woman in the city to have charge of what is becoming a major department store (*see* 1867).

Cleveland petroleum refiner John D. Rockefeller sends his brother William to New York to oversee exports of kerosene and other products of their refineries (*see* 1861). Setting up a simple office at 181 Pearl Street, William is in a position to obtain credit from Wall Street banks on better terms than those available at Cleveland, and to advise the partnership's buyers in the Pennsylvania oil fields of sudden price drops (*see* 1868).

The New York Mutual Gas Light Co. is founded April 17 and the College Point Gas Co. July 2 as more entrepreneurs seek profits from the growing market for gas lighting.

A car float invented by Starin City River and Harbor Transportation Lines founder John H. Starin permits a freight train to be broken into parts and its cars carried across New York Harbor (*see* 1859). Now 41, Starin served the Union cause during the Civil War by moving men, munitions, and supplies quickly, and he has been expanding his fleet of lighters and tugs. Modifications of his car-float system will remain in use into the 21st century.

New York halts the use of cobblestones for paving streets. Pavements for the rest of this century and beyond will be of concrete, asphalt, and other materials.

The 3-year-old Citizens Committee of New York's Council on Public Health shocks the city with more reports of its investigations into tenements on the East Side, where filthy dark alleys and dead ends breed disease (*see* 1865). Slaughterhouses are in the most populated districts. Bellevue Hospital's Stephen Smith and Vermont-born activist Elisha Harris, 42, present the state legislature at Albany with a basic sanitary code (*see* Board of Health, 1870).

Cholera strikes the city as it did in 1854. Writes George Templeton Strong in his diary July 26, "It is severe in certain districts of New York and Brooklyn, inhabited by the unwashed, and very severe, indeed, among soldiers at Governors Island and Hart's Island, and among paupers at Bellevue Hospital and Ward's Island . . ." (New York Hospital does not accept cholera cases). Bellevue sends wagons through the streets carrying tanks of disinfectant but New York still has 1,091 cholera fatalities between June and November (the disease kills some 48,000 other Americans). The city has had recurring epidemics of cholera, scarlet fever, smallpox, typhoid fever, typhus, and yellow fever, and they will grow more severe in the next 7 years (*see* 1865).

Mount Sinai Hospital adopts that name after 14 years as the Jews' Hospital (*see* 1855). It has treated large numbers of Union soldiers regardless of their religious faith during the Civil War but still has only 45 beds (*see* 1872).

The 19-year-old Free Academy becomes the College of the City of New York (CCNY) and opens an Evening High School for men (*see* 1905).

One of the first black YMCAs opens at New York (*see* 1857). The Young Men's Christian Association has not admitted blacks to membership in its other branches but has encouraged them to open their own. Segregation will continue until 1919, long after it has ended in the city's public schools (*see* everyday life, 1869).

Telegraph service over a new Atlantic cable begins July 27 with the message, "A treaty of peace has been signed between Austria and Prussia" (*see* 1858). Cyrus W. Field and John Pender of the Atlantic Telegraph Co. have financed the new line, with backing from Peter Cooper and other investors, but only the very rich can afford to send messages at $1 per letter, payable in gold (a workingman typically earns $20 per month); Field receives a unanimous vote of thanks from Congress (*see* 1869).

Western Union Telegraph Co. absorbs two smaller telegraph companies to gain control of 75,000 miles of wire and become the first great U.S. industrial monopoly (*see* 1856; 1881).

Henry Holt and Co. has its beginnings in Leypoldt and Holt, founded at New York by German-born bibliographer and onetime bookstore owner Frederick Leypoldt, 30, and Baltimore-born Yale graduate Henry Holt, 26. Holt rejected a manuscript submitted by Leypoldt to another publisher for whom Holt worked as an editor, but the two have become fast friends. Leypoldt will quit book publishing by 1868 and leave the business to Holt, who will change the firm name to Henry Holt by 1873. He will introduce U.S. readers to the daring works of English novelist Thomas Hardy and, later, to the tales of Robert Louis Stevenson (*see* Publishers' *Weekly*, 1872).

G. P. Putnam and Sons is founded at New York by former John Wiley partner George P. Putnam, now 52, who began campaigning at age 23 for international copyright agreements, moved to London 4 years later to open a bookshop specializing in American books, and has returned to go into the book publishing business with his son.

Nonfiction: *Miller's New York As It Is, or Stranger's Guide-Book* says, "If we glance prospectively, how shall we venture to limit its progressive march in opulence and greatness? In less than half a century hence, it will doubtless double its present numerical importance. As illustrations of the enormous increase in the value of real estate, it may be mentioned that a lot on the northwest corner of Chambers Street and Broadway was purchased by a gentleman who died in 1858 for $1,000. Its present value is now estimated at no less than $125,000. The lots lately sold at auction, by Ludlow & Co., under the direction of the executors of Judge Jay, were a part of the fifteen acres of the late John Jay, at $500 per acre. One lot out of said purchased, situated on Broadway, we are informed has been sold within the past month for $80,000. Fabulous as is the advance from $500 per acre to $80,000 per lot, it is fully justified, as the present owner—who is now erecting a store on the lot—has refused a rent of $16,000 per year for the same. A little more than two centuries since, the entire site of this noble city was purchased of the Indians for what was equivalent to the nominal sum of $24. Now the total amount of its assessed property is $10.5 million. If such vast accessions of wealth have characterized the history of the past, who shall compute the constantly augmenting resources of its onward course?"

Poetry: *Battle-Pieces and Aspects of War* by Herman Melville, now 47, who is appointed a deputy Customs Office inspector of cargoes at the port of New York (he will retain the position until the end of 1885, working at $4 per day on Hudson River piers); "O Captain! My Captain!" by Walt Whitman, whose elegiac ode commemorates Lincoln.

Painting: *Bird Catchers* by Winslow Homer.

Harper's Weekly publishes a two-page Christmas illustration by Thomas Nast showing Santa Claus decorating a tree, making toys in his workshop, sewing clothes, studying his account books, and spying through a telescope "for good children" (*see* 1862).

Steinway Hall opens at 71-73 East 14th Street with fine acoustics, lavish appointments, and seating for 2,500. Built by the 13-year-old piano company as an adjunct to its showrooms, it will be the city's leading concert hall for more than 2 decades (*see* 1859; Chickering Hall, 1875).

Broadway musicals: *The Black Crook* 9/12 at Niblo's Garden, with a Faustian plot by U.S. playwright Charles M. Barras, 40, a cast of 100 dancing girls, including Italian-born dancer Marie Bonfanti, 19, in pink tights (clergymen denounce their costumes and indelicate postures as does James Gordon Bennett in his *New-York Herald*), music adapted from various sources, 474 perfs. The first true Broadway musical, it runs 5 hours on opening night, will see many revivals, and will tour for more than 40 years.

The New York Athletic Club is founded June 17 by John G. Babcock (who has invented the sliding seat for rowers), Henry E. Buermeyer, and William B. Curtis (*see* spiked shoes, 1868; building, 1928).

The Jerome Park Racetrack opens September 25 on the 230-acre Bathgate estate in Fordham. It has a 650-foot grandstand, boasts a clubhouse whose dining room, bars, and bedrooms make it as luxurious as any hotel, and will introduce claiming races, handicapping, races for 2-year-olds, and parimutuel betting. Financier-sportsman Leonard W. Jerome, now 48, owes much of his fortune to his relationship with Commodore Vanderbilt and has financed the 1.5-mile track with support from the new American Jockey Club that he has organized with help from August Belmont and William R. Travers, and the races on opening day attract sportsmen from all over the country, to say nothing of actresses, bankers, brothel keepers, gamblers, pickpockets, society figures, speculator Jim Fisk, Civil War hero Gen. Ulysses S. Grant, and Tammany Hall boss William M. Tweed, now 42. The racetrack will continue in use until it is closed in 1889 to make way for a reservoir, being opened only temporarily in 1891 for the Monmouth Park (N.J.) Racing Association (*see* Belmont Stakes, 1867).

Methodist Bishop Matthew Simpson gives an address at the Cooper Union claiming that the city has more prostitutes than Methodists (*see* human rights, 1860). Preaching later at St. Paul's Methodist Episcopal Church, he says there are 20,000 prostitutes, 30,000 thieves, 2,000 gambling houses, and 3,000 saloons. The police say he has exaggerated: there are only 2,670 prostitutes, or possibly 3,300, at 621 brothels and 99 houses of assignation (which are advertised discreetly in the classified section of respectable newspapers), but they do not include 747 waiter girls at the dozens of concert saloons, the pre-adolescent girls available near the Bowery and Chatham Square, or the many women who ply their trade mostly in the Washington Square, Union Square, and Madison Square parks. Whatever the exact figures, prostitution has grown by quantum leaps during the Civil War and its aftermath, spreading from its former concentration along the waterfront, Cherry and Water streets, the Five Points, and the Bowery to the side streets west of Broadway, where a red light designates what used to be called a bagnio or disorderly house but may now rank as a "parlor house," with a piano player ("the

Professor") to provide background music and liquor to be had by the drink.

The city's first French Ball attracts a crowd of libertines to begin an annual event that will continue until 1901 despite objections from reformers. Sponsored by the Cercle Français de l'Harmonie, it enjoys the protection of high-ranking police officials, many of whom attend its unfettered revels (*see* 1893).

Douglaston, Queens, gets its name as the Long Island Rail Road builds a station on right-of-way granted to it by William P. Douglas, a vice-commodore of the New York Yacht Club whose Scottish-born father, George, acquired much of the land in the area in 1835 (*see* 1656).

The Rosenwach Tank Co. has its beginnings in a company started by New York entrepreneur William Dalton to produce rooftop water tanks, vats for brewers and vintners, and other large containers of juniper or white cedar. Dalton's widow will sell the business for $55 in 1896 to Polish immigrant Harris Rosenwach, whose son Julius, grandson Wallace, and great-grandson Andrew will carry it on. Wood conserves heat 10 times better than concrete, and since a wooden rooftop tank can last 60 years and more, thousands of New York buildings will have Rosenwach tanks on their roofs well into the 21st century.

The West Side Association is organized by real estate investors to promote development of the area north of 59th Street, where the Jacob Harsen Farm has been subdivided into 500 lots to be sold strictly for residential use, but the upper West Side remains a remote bucolic region (*see* East Side Association, 1868; Boulevard, 1869).

Christ Church (Episcopal) is completed at 252nd Street in the Riverdale section of the Bronx to designs by architect Richard Upjohn.

Prospect Park construction begins in Brooklyn on a site at Mount Prospect selected by a commission established in 1859. The location is endowed with good soil, plenty of trees, and an abundance of water; Frederick Law Olmsted and Calvert Vaux have devised a plan for the park, it is officially accepted in May, and workers use machinery invented by Olsted and Vaux to transplant trees and move soil for the creation of berms, meadows, ponds, and streams. Acreage of Cortelyou Farm owned by lawyer-real estate speculator Edwin Clark Litchfield, 51, lies in the central part of Park Slope, he has taken an active role in planning the new park, and his country residence Litchfield Villa, built by his father in 1857 between 4th and 5th streets, is incorporated into the park; it will become Brooklyn Parks Department headquarters in 1892 (see Camperdown Elm, 1872; Eastern Parkway, 1874).

German-born brewer George Ehret opens the Hell-Gate Brewery; in 10 years it will be the largest U.S. beer producer, and as Ehret prospers he will move into an imposing Manhattan mansion atop a hill on Fourth Avenue.

1867 Mayor (and Tammany Hall Grand Sachem) John T. Hoffman wins reelection by a landslide in November, defeating former mayor Fernando Wood and Republican William A. Darling with 63,061 votes as compared with 22,837 for Wood (who has founded Mozart Hall to compete with Tammany), 18,483 for Darling. Former governor John Alsop King has died at Jamaica, Queens, July 7 at age 79. Hoffman has turned a blind eye to the fraudulent machinations of the Tweed Ring, he has even appointed Tweed Ring insider Peter B. Sweeney to the position of comptroller, and Boss Tweed has rallied the electorate.

Former Utica mayor and congressman Roscoe Conkling is elected to the U.S. Senate. Regarded by many as arrogant, the 38-year-old Conkling avoided military service during the Civil War and although politically ambitious is ridiculed by opponents as "invincible in peace and invisible in war."

Elizabeth Cady Stanton addresses the New York State Senate Judiciary Committee at Albany January 23, urging that women be permitted to vote for delegates to a convention that will rewrite the state constitution of 1777. Stanton and Susan B. Anthony launch an effort in August to have the legislature give women the right to vote. Stanton's husband, Henry Brewster Stanton, now 61, enjoys the profitable position of Collector of the Port of New York and does not back her, but the women receive support from George Francis Train, now 38, who has made a fortune in foreign ventures, harbors presidential aspirations, and supports women's rights (along with Irish independence, free trade, monetary inflation, and central banking) while opposing extension of the franchise to the illiterate. Attired always in purple gloves and full dress, Train pleads the case of woman suffrage to the New York State constitutional convention and finances Anthony and Stanton, who speak in favor of the measure (see The *Revolution*, 1868).

The Colored Orphan Asylum that was burned down in the draft riots of 1863 is rebuilt at 143rd Street and Amsterdam Avenue (see 1907).

Kuhn, Loeb & Co. is founded at New York February 1 by German-born banker Abraham Kuhn and his 38-year-old brother-in-law Solomon Loeb, who came to America in 1849, went into partnership at Lafayette, Ind., in 1850 to sell clothing, moved to Cincinnati, retired in 1865, moved to New York to lead lives of leisure, and now open a commercial banking house; capitalized with $500,000, it will soon make a market for U.S. government bonds and railway bonds. Kuhn will retire shortly to live in Germany; Loeb will head the firm until he retires in 1885 (see Schiff, 1875).

The Gold and Stock Telegraph Co. is incorporated in August with offices at 18 New Street and promotes the first stock ticker, adapted from a printing telegraph invented by Edward Callahan. The clacking ticker will be installed next year on the New York Stock Exchange, will initially serve only brokers on that exchange, but will soon be used on other exchanges throughout the country, printing stock quotes on strips of paper and eliminating the need to have runners carry quotes from one office to another (see Western Union, 1871).

Standard and Poor's has its beginnings in Poor's Publishing Co., a corporation founded by Maine-born New York historian-economist Henry Varnum Poor, 55, to publish his annual "Manual of the Railroads and Canals of the United States." Poor's *History of Railroads and Canals of the United States* appeared in 1860, pioneering U.S. publication of financial and investment information (see 1941; Standard Statistics Co., 1913).

German lawyer's son August Heckscher, 19, arrives from his native Hamburg with $500 in gold borrowed from his mother, rents a small room, joins the Mercantile Library in Astor Place, and spends 12 hours per day reading English books and practicing diction; within 3 months he has made himself proficient in reading and writing English, calls on his cousin Richard Heckscher, and is hired to help run the family company that owns some 20,000 acres of anthracite coal fields in Pennsylvania's Schuylkill County, near Shenandoah. Richard falls ill 2 weeks later, August takes over complete management, he makes the mines prosper, and he will go on to become general manager of a New Jersey zinc mine whose deposits are the richest in America (see 1884).

The Metropolitan Savings Bank opens at 6 East 7th Street in an iron-frame building designed by Carl Pfeiffer with a masonry sheath in Second Empire style.

Stern Brothers opens at 367 Sixth Avenue to sell dress material, laces, and silk. German-born retail merchants Louis, Bernard, and Benjamin Stern will do so well that they will outgrow their premises by 1877 (see 1878).

Lord & Taylor runs the first double-column newspaper advertisements.

Tiffany & Co. wins the gold medal for silver craftsmanship at the Paris Exposition Universelle, becoming the first U.S. design house to be thus honored (see 1847). Tiffany is the first U.S. company to employ the 925/1000 standard of silver purity, it will open a London office next year, and Congress will adopt 925/1000 as the U.S. sterling silver standard, thanks largely to the efforts of Charles L. Tiffany (see Preakness Woodlawn Vase, 1873; Tiffany Diamond, Louis Comfort Tiffany, 1878).

R. H. Macy Company remains open Christmas Eve until midnight and has record 1-day receipts of $6,000 (see 1866; 1869).

Cornelius Vanderbilt issues an order January 14 that all trains on his New York & Hudson River Railroad must terminate at East Albany, two miles from the Albany depot (see 1864). Vanderbilt built a 2,000-foot wooden truss bridge across the Hudson at Albany last year, allowing both Harlem and Hudson River railroad trains to come into the New York Central's Albany station, but hostile interests gained control of the Central in December. When legislators protest he shows them an old law specifically forbidding the New York & Hudson River to run trains across the Hudson River; stock in the Central drops sharply, and Vanderbilt, now 73, buys enough to secure control by December (see 1869).

The Wagner Drawing Room Car designed by New York wagon maker Webster Wagner, 50, goes into service on the New York Central. Wagner will soon contract to use George Pullman's folding upper berth and hinged seats, but when he uses the Pullman-designed equipment on Vanderbilt's Lake Shore and Michigan Southern line after 1873, Pullman will sue and the lawsuit will not yet have been settled when Wagner dies in a New York Central train collision in 1882.

Directors of the Union Pacific Railroad let congressmen have shares in their 3-year-old Crédit Mobilier company in an effort to stave off investigation into the high personal profits they are making on the line under construction in the West. The company will pay dividends of 200 percent to its shareholders in one year while its workers go unpaid. Oneonta-born Central Pacific vice president Collis P. (Potter)

Huntington, now 45, joined the gold rush to California in 1849, made money as a storekeeper, has been trying to sell Central Pacific stock to Wall Street investors, and comes down from his New York office to bribe congressmen, offering cash for their votes (see 1869; communications [Sun exposé], 1872).

The South Side Railroad of Long Island opens a line October 28 from Jamaica to Babylon to carry passengers ignored by the Long Island Rail Road (see 1863). The line has stops at South Oyster Bay (later Massapequa) and will be extended within 9 months to Islip, but the South Side has no western terminus with access to the East River, and Long Island Rail Road president Oliver Charlick refuses to let it share the LIRR terminal in what later will be Long Island City (see 1868).

East River ferries stop running January 23 as the world's busiest waterway freezes over, bringing traffic between Manhattan and Brooklyn to a standstill and crippling it for weeks. The state legislature at Albany appropriates funds in April for construction of a bridge that will connect the two cities (see Roebling, 1869).

Clipper-ship magnate A. A. Low returns from a round-the-world voyage and delivers a speech to the Chamber of Commerce October 8 favoring federal subsidies for the U.S. merchant marine.

Inventor Elias Howe dies at Brooklyn October 3 at age 48. His sewing machine patent on which Isaac M. Singer infringed has recently expired.

Bellevue Hospital opens its first outpatient department to relieve the hospital of cases that can be treated successfully without taking up bed room. The Bureau of Medical and Surgical Relief for the Out Door Poor is the first such department in any U.S. hospital, and in its first year it handles 437 patients, setting bones and treating eye, ear, skin, and chest complaints to begin what will become one of the most important services of the hospital (next year it will treat more than 15,000). Bellevue gets its first ambulance in the spring: the lightweight carriage, open at the back, has a removable floor that can serve as a stretcher, and beneath the driver's seat are a quart flask of brandy, two tourniquets, six bandages, splints, pieces of old blankets for padding, strips of various lengths with buckles, and a two-ounce vial of persulphate of iron. It takes between 30 seconds and 2 minutes to harness its horses, it jingles a bell as it races about the streets, and the two surgeons who man it work exclusively for the ambulance service. Within 3 years it will be joined by five additional ambulances, but it will be some time before the regular training of interns includes ambulance service.

∞ A letter from Missouri-born writer Mark Twain (Samuel Langhorne Clemens), 31, to San Francisco's *Alta Californian* February 18 says, "You cannot imagine what an infatuation church-going has become in New York. Youths and young misses, young gentlemen and ladies, the middle-aged and the old, all swarm to church, morning and night, every Sunday."

The state legislature at Albany votes to establish a free public school system.

Brooklyn Friends School has its beginnings in the basement of the Quaker Meeting House in Schermerhorn Street. It will develop into a coeducational elementary and secondary school promoting ethnic and racial diversity, with emphasis on academic excellence combined with community service, compassion, equality, pacifism, and tolerance in the Quaker tradition (*see* 1972).

The Lexington School for the Deaf has its beginnings in the private New York Institution for the Improved Instruction of Deaf-mutes opened for hearing-impaired children of German-speaking immigrants on the west side of Lexington Avenue between 67th and 68th streets. Bernhard Engelsman, its director, has taught in Vienna and employs the traditional German oral method of teaching that relies on lip reading and eschews sign language (*see* 1967).

The George P. Rowell Co. founded at New York April 1 by Vermont-born advertising-space salesman George Presbury Rowell, 28, is a pioneer advertising agency and gains immediate success. Rowell has established a reputation for prompt payment to publishers, they are happy to give him the responsibility of collecting from advertisers, and although he will later campaign for "truth in advertising" his initial clients are for the most part promoters of lotteries and patent medicines, notably an expensive dry form of rhubarb and soda sold under the name Ripans Tabules (*see* 1869).

The *New-York Evening Telegram* begins publication. Started by *New-York Herald* managing editor James Gordon Bennett, 26, with help from his father, James Gordon senior, now 72, the new paper will not show a profit for some years (*see World-Telegram*, 1931; *World-Telegram & Sun*, 1966).

Charles Dickens pays a second visit to New York (*see* 1842). Now 55, he attracts large audiences to his readings at the new Steinway Hall in East 14th Street, where he appears for the first time December 9 and 21 times thereafter (*see* 1868).

Poetry: *Poems and Translations* by New York poet-essayist Emma Lazarus, 18, whose work wins praise from Ralph Waldo Emerson.

Juvenile: *Ragged Dick, or Street Life in New York* is serialized in the periodical *Student and Schoolmate*, published at New York under the name "Oliver Optic" by William Taylor Adams, 45. Author of the novel is former Unitarian minister Horatio Alger, 35, who was born at Revere, Mass., and was dismissed from his ministry at Brewster, Mass., on charges of having had homosexual encounters with boys. His more than 100 rags-to-riches novels in the next 30 years will dramatize virtues of pluck, honesty, hard work, and marrying the boss's daughter (*see* 1871).

Sculpture: *Tigress and Cubs* (bronze) by French sculptor Auguste Cain, 45, is erected near the south end of Central Park.

Theater: *Under the Gaslight* by North Carolina-born playwright-producer (John) Augustin Daly, 29, opens at the New York Theater with the hero being tied to railroad tracks and being rescued melodramatically, at the last moment, from certain death.

Baseball's curveball pitch is invented by Brooklyn pitcher William Arthur Cummings.

New York's Knickerbocker Base Ball Club establishes the last Tuesday of each month in the season as "Ladies' Day," offering free admission to wives, daughters, and girlfriends with "suitable seats or settees" (*see* 1846). Cofounder Alexander Cartwright went to California in the gold rush of 1849 and has wound up at Honolulu in the Sandwich Islands, where he will die in 1892, having started an insurance company and founded that city's first fire department.

The Belmont Stakes has its first running at the Jerome Park Racetrack, opened last year; the 1.5-mile test for 3-year-old thoroughbreds is won by a horse named Ruthless. Banker August Belmont, now 60, helped to organize the Jockey Club last year to oversee U.S. horse racing and has inaugurated the stakes race.

Pattern manufacturer Ebenezer Butterick hears from his agent J. W. Wilder that a demand exists for paper patterns that can be used to make women's clothing (*see* 1864). Wilder and A. W. Pollard go into business with Butterick, and under Wilder's direction they compete aggressively with Mrs. Demorest, whose patterns come only in size 36 and must be enlarged or reduced by a seamstress (see 1860). Most women make new dresses by taking apart their old ones and using them as guides, but the new Butterick patterns are available in different sizes, need not be cut from magazines, come folded in envelopes with instruction sheets, and enable women of modest means to make garments with their sewing machines that are almost indistinguishable from the tailored clothing worn by society women (see 1869).

 A new Tenement House law enacted by the state legislature at Albany defines a "tenement" as "any house, building, or portion thereof, which is rented, leased, let or hired out to be occupied or is occupied, as the home or residence of more than three families living independently of one another and doing their own cooking upon the premises, or by more than two families upon a floor, so living and cooking and having a common right in the halls, stairways, yards, water-closets, or privies, or some of them" (see 1865). The state's first comprehensive housing law, it sets new standards for building construction and marks the start of a long effort to raise the quality of low-cost housing design, but developers will continue to put up tenements without fire escapes, or only rear fire escapes (see 1879).

The 12-year-old Workingmen's Home north of Canal Street is sold to a private investor. The Association for Improving the Conditions of the Poor has been unable to find white tenants who would rent quarters previously occupied by blacks in what is now known as the Big Flat; by 1879 the structure will be occupied mostly by Polish Jews.

Developer Benjamin W. Hitchcock lays out the streets of Woodside, Queens, next to what later will be Long Island City and sells lots in the area (see railroad, 1861). His success will encourage other developers, and the population of Woodside will reach 1,355 by 1875 (see 1900).

Manhattan lawyer Albon P. Man of the firm Man and Parsons employs landscape architect Edward Richmond to buy farmland and lay out a community that will later be called Richmond Hill in east central Queens. By 1874 the community will have a church, a school, streets, and trees; a railroad station will go into service that year, and the village will be incorporated in 1894 (see Kew Gardens, 1910).

The Philipse Manor house is acquired by the city fathers of Tarrytown, who will use it for offices (it will later become a museum) (see 1779).

A new church for Brooklyn's 83-year-old St. Ann's Episcopal parish is completed in northern Gothic style at the corner of Clinton and Livingston streets.

● Brooklyn's mayor Samuel Booth initiates a plan in January for a comprehensive city park system and engages landscape architects Frederick Law Olmsted and Calvert Vaux to design four new parks while redesigning the Fort Greene Park that is incorporated into the new system. Originally a cemetery for 11,500 men killed in the 1776 Battle of Brooklyn, the park was begun in 1848 through the efforts of *Brooklyn Daily Eagle* editor Walt Whitman on the ruins of Fort Greene, which was hastily constructed in 1812, and has been the city's first successful public park. The redesigned park will open in 1869 (see politics, 1908).

 Ruppert's Brewery has its beginnings as Baltimore-born brewer Jacob Ruppert, 25, buys a tract of timberland on Third Avenue between 91st and 92nd streets to build his own plant after 4 years of managing his father's Turtle Bay malt business. Ruppert's own son and namesake is born at New York August 5 as he clears the timber and erects a three-story building that will grow to become the world's largest lager brewery (see 1874).

German-born entrepreneur Charles Feltman, 25, has a wheelwright build a burner in the back of the pie-wagon he has been driving up and down the beach at Coney Island in Brooklyn. His customers have asked for hot sandwiches, and the burner enables him to keep warm sausages on hand (see 1874).

1868 President Johnson dismisses Secretary of War Stanton February 18, allegedly violating a law passed over Johnson's veto less than a year ago forbidding removal of certain officials without the Senate's consent. Congress restores Stanton to office and the House votes February 25 to impeach the president for "high crimes and misdemeanors." Although Johnson enjoys little popularity in the country, seven Republicans join with Democrats May 16 and May 26 to acquit him; the 35-to-19 decision fails by one vote to achieve the necessary two-thirds majority. Boston-born New York lawyer William Maxwell Evarts, 50, defends the president, and Johnson rewards him by appointing him U.S. attorney general.

Central Park comptroller Andrew Haskell Green proposes that Manhattan, the Bronx, Brooklyn, Queens, and Staten Island be amalgamated into Greater New York (see 1897; Bronx, 1874).

Gambling houses and prostitution flourished in a corrupt city grown fat from war profits. HARPER'S WEEKLY

The Democratic Party convention held in Tammany Hall's long room July 4 nominates former New York governor Horatio Seymour, now 58, for the presidency, but the Republicans have nominated Civil War hero Ulysses S. Grant, now 46; they "wave the bloody shirt," labeling the Democratic Party the party of treason, and although Seymour carries New York State, Grant wins 53 percent of the popular vote nationwide with 214 electoral votes to Seymour's 80.

Gov. Fenton loses his bid for a third term. The Republicans nominate Rensselaer Iron Co. owner John Augustus Griswold, 49, but his 411,355-vote total falls short of the 439,301 polled by New York City's tall, imposing mayor John T. Hoffman, now 40. Boss Tweed has used his political muscle to win Hoffman's election and is himself elected to the state senate; he will assume leadership of the legislature.

Boss Tweed brings out voters to elect former district attorney A. (Abraham) Oakey Hall, 42, as mayor. Hall rolls up a whopping 75,109 votes as compared with 20,835 for Republican Frederick A. Conkling. A Democratic reform group nominated former congressman John Kelly, now 46, but he withdrew 9 days later and took his two daughters to Europe (his wife and son died of tuberculosis 2 years ago and he has been suffering from a bronchial ailment); a congressional investigating committee reports that gangs of men "supplied abundantly with intoxicating drinks" voted "early and often" to give Tammany Hall its victory at the polls; Kelly quits Tammany in protest against the Tweed Ring's corruption and vote manipulation, winning the soubriquet "Honest John," although some will question his probity (rumor had it that he withdrew for fear that irregularities might come to light with regard to his tenure as sheriff, and he will remain in Europe and the Holy

Land until the autumn of 1871, studying religious antiquities) (*see* 1871).

Women hired for factory, office, and retail-store jobs during the Civil War continue in such work (New York City alone has nearly 30,000 working women) but are almost universally relegated to menial positions or are paid less than men doing the same work. Elizabeth Cady Stanton founds the Working Woman's Association September 17 with help from militant trades union women attracted by the pro-labor position of her newspaper. Those attending the first meeting include printer Augusta Lewis, who is famous for having set the entire text of Washington Irving's "Rip Van Winkle" in 6½ hours (*see* 1869).

Long Island industrialist Conrad Poppenhusen agrees January 10 to pay $100,000 for an iron mine in Morris County, N.J. Now 49, Poppenhusen prospered with his College Point, Queens, rubber factory by supplying the Union Army during the Civil War with cups, flasks, and uniform buttons; he paid $70,000 in 1865 to acquire another iron mine in the area.

Former Chamber of Commerce president A. A. Low delivers an address April 6 at the Chamber's centennial celebration and voices demands by New York merchants for a prompt resumption of specie payments.

New York-born banker Frederick Dobbs Tappen, 43, succeeds James Gallatin in July as president of the Gallatin National Bank (*see* 1865).

Metropolitan Life Insurance Co. is founded at New York by a reorganization of National Travelers Insurance Co., started 5 years ago as National Life & Limb Insurance Co. (*see* 1879).

Chinese immigrant Wah Kee opens a Pell Street store selling curios, dried fruit, and vegetables (*see* population, 1847). He keeps a room upstairs for gambling and opium smoking (U.S. opium imports approach 500,000 pounds per year, up from an estimated 24,000 in 1840, with customs officials collecting duties of $2.50 per pound) (*see* general store, 1875).

Roxbury, N.Y.-born financier Jay Gould, 32, concludes a secret deal with Cleveland petroleum refiner John D. Rockefeller and Rockefeller's partner Henry M. Flagler whereby they receive a 75 percent rebate on oil shipped through the New York & Erie Rail Road or one of its subsidaries (*see* 1866); Rockefeller and Flagler then persuade the new Lake Shore Railroad vice president Gen. J. H. Devereux to let them ship crude oil to Cleveland and refined oil to New York at a rate of $1.65 per barrel—75¢ less than the official rate—by promising 60 carloads of refined oil per day, enabling the New York Central subsidiary to operate trains made up exclusively of tank cars and reduce its tank-car fleet from 1,800 cars to 600 by cutting the average round-trip time of trains between New York and Cleveland from 30 days to 10. Rockefeller, Andrews & Flagler does not yet have enough refining capacity to make good on its promise, but it soon will have (*see* Standard Oil, 1870).

English shipbuilder's son Thomas Henry Ismay, 31, acquires the name White Star Line for £1,000 January 18, salvaging a 23-year-old sailing and steam-packet line that began with the clipper ships *Red Jacket*, *Ellen*, and *Blue Jacket* in 1845, launched its first steamship (the 2,000-ton *Royal Standard*) in 1863 for the Liverpool-to-Melbourne run, but has gone bankrupt. Ismay goes into partnership with Wall Street banker J. P. Morgan and promptly contracts with the Belfast shipbuilding firm Harland and Wolff to construct four new ships for the Oceanic Steam Navigation Co. (White Star's official name) (*see* R.M.S. *Oceanic*, 1871).

Shipbuilder-inventor-financier Edwin A. Stevens dies at Paris August 7 at age 83 (*see* education [Stevens Institute], 1870).

Jay Gould wrests control of the New York & Erie Rail Road from Commodore Vanderbilt (*see* 1864). Vanderbilt has conspired with a judge to gain control of the Erie, the judge has issued an injunction against issuing any more stock in the company, Gould's fellow Erie director James Fisk, now 34, seizes 50,000 shares that have already been signed, Vanderbilt's judge issues an order for the arrest of Gould and Fisk, they flee to Jersey City, and Daniel Drew, now 71, helps them inflate the value of their stock, bringing Tammany boss William M. Tweed into their plot and bribing state legislators to block Vanderbilt. Working out of Taylor's Hotel at Jersey City over the summer, they boost the stock by October 24 from $34,265,000 to $57,766,000, sell off watered stock to break Vanderbilt's corner, and make millions of dollars in net profit after using some of the proceeds to expand the half-ruined railroad (*see* 1872; commerce, 1869).

The Westinghouse air brake devised by upstate New York inventor George Westinghouse, 22, will permit development of modern rail travel, although Cornelius Vanderbilt dismisses it as a "fool idea" and other railroad barons will resist adopting it until Congress passes legislation in 1893 requiring its use. Brakemen continue to jump from car to car and set brakes manually in all kinds of weather, few of them live long, they are easily replaced if killed or injured, and it is much cheaper to pay men $1.50 per day than to invest millions of dollars in equipment, but Americans have been horrified at the deaths and injuries caused by train wrecks. Westinghouse invented a device for rerailing derailed cars 3 years ago, has seen compressed air used in European mining operations, and has devised a system that employs a hose running the full length of a train, with each car having its own tank of compressed air. He will make his air brake automatic in 1872, and it will permit an engineer to set the brakes simultaneously throughout a whole train by means of a steam-driven air pump (*see* Union Switch and Signal, 1882).

America's first commercial cable railway begins operating on an experimental basis July 3 along a single track between Battery Place and 30th Street above Greenwich Street (Ninth Avenue). Built by Charles Harvey's West Side and Yonkers Patent Railway Co., its track has been laid atop an iron superstructure 30 feet above the street, and a steam-powered generator at the terminus powers the cables that pull the cars along. The cables frequently break, ladders have to be fetched to enable passengers to climb down, and the venture will fail in 1871 (*see* 1872).

The South Side Railroad of Long Island opens a line July 18 extending west from Jamaica to Fresh Pond and thence southwest to the Bushwick Terminal at Bushwick Avenue near Montrose Avenue, where horsecars pick up passengers and carry them along Broadway to East River ferries (*see* 1867). Small steam locomotives (steam dummies) will replace the horsecars by next year. The company opens depots at Amityville, Wellwood (Lindhurst), Seaside (Babylon), Penataquit (Bayshore), Islip, Oakdale, Sayville, and Bayport (*see* 1869).

The Long Island Rail Road completes a branch line to Northport but continues to slight the South Shore and remains in financial distress (*see* 1863; Sag Harbor, 1870).

The German Dispensary joins with the German Hospital of New York and moves from East 3rd Street to a new facility completed in October at the southeast corner of 77th Street and Fourth Avenue on land, leased from the city at $1 per year, that once was once part of the Robert Lenox Farm (*see* 1861; 1862). A corporation headed by Carl Gottfried Gunther and a membership that includes pediatrician Abraham Jacobi, gynecologist Emil Noeggerath, ophthalmologist Herman Althof, and newspaper editor Carl Schurz have combined their efforts to relocate the hospital, whose patients will now come mostly from Yorkville, but the New York & Harlem Railroad runs up and down Fourth Avenue, a thoroughfare that has no sewers and is lined with shanties that lack amenities (*see* 1875).

Caswell Massey moves to New York after 112 years at Newport, R.I. The chemist and perfumers shop will continue to fill prescriptions and supply customers with imported soaps, perfumes, and other goods into the 21st century.

Poppenhusen Institute opens at 114-04 14th Road in College Point, Queens, where industrialist Conrad Poppenhusen has endowed a vocational school with $100,000 plus land to train workers for his hard-rubber plant (*see* commerce, 1854). Designed in French Second Empire style by Mundell & Teckritz, the five-story institute with its tall arched windows is open to people of all races and creeds, giving working people a place to learn English, acquire a trade, and study history, literature, art, theater, and music. It has a grand ballroom and houses the public library, bank, village hall, and two jail cells in the basement; now 50, Poppenhusen will put up another $100,000 for teachers' salaries and operating costs, and in 1870 the institute will open America's first free kindergarten for working mothers.

The newspaper *Revolution* begins publication at New York under the direction of suffragists Susan B. Anthony and Elizabeth Cady Stanton with financial backing from George Francis Train (*see* 1867). Its slogan is, "Men, their rights and nothing more; women, their rights and nothing less." The paper publishes reports that thousands of infants are being abandoned each year on New York doorsteps and in alleys.

New Hampshire-born journalist Charles A. (Anderson) Dana, 49, acquires ownership of the 35-year-old *New-York Sun* for $175,000. Dana was made city editor of Horace Greeley's *Tribune* in 1847 and remained with that paper for 15 years before resigning to take a position as front-line observer for Secretary of War Edwin M. Stanton and, thereafter, as assisant secretary of war in the Lincoln Cabinet. The *Sun* now sells for 2¢ per copy at a time when other papers cost 4¢, it will employ the new "interview" technique, Dana will oppose labor organizations and income taxes, and the *Sun* will more than double its circulation (*see* Crédit Mobilier exposé, 1872; evening edition, 1887).

The *World Almanac* is published for the first time. The *New-York World* has compiled a 108-page compendium of facts (mostly political, with notes on Southern Reconstruction, the impeachment of President Johnson, and the extension of suffrage to blacks in the North), the *Almanac* has 12 pages of advertising, annual publication will end in 1876, but publisher Joseph Pulitzer will take over the *World* and revive the *Almanac* in 1886, and it will appear every year thereafter, going to press after the November elections, becoming the *World Almanac and Encyclopedia* in 1894, the *World Almanac and Book of Facts* in 1923.

J. Walter Thompson has its beginnings as New York advertising pioneer James Walter Thompson, 20, persuades publishers of magazines such as *Godey's Ladies Book* to let him sell space in all the magazines as if they were one unit. Thompson persuades merchants to buy space in a group of magazines rather than in one at a time; the influx of new advertising enables the publishers to improve the quality of their printing, their paper, and their illustrations and to pay authors and artists better rates while selling their publications at 10¢ or 15¢ as advertising revenues increase their profits (*see* 1878).

Charles Dickens gives four readings at Plymouth Congregational Church in Brooklyn Heights from January 16 to 21, says that since his 1842 visit, "Everything . . . looks as if the order of nature were reversed, and everything grew newer every day instead of older," and promises at a banquet given in his honor at Delmonico's April 18 that he will never speak ill of America again. He gives his final reading at Steinway Hall April 20 and embarks for England April 23, narrowly avoiding capture by federal tax agents who want a share of the proceeds he has earned from his lectures.

Sculpture: a bronze statue of the late Abraham Lincoln by Henry Kirke Brown is erected at the north end of Union Square. The newly organized Union League Club has sponsored a popular subscription to raise funds for the work; it depicts Lincoln wearing baggy trousers and a cloak as he addressed an unseen audience.

Opera: Pike's Opera House opens in January at the northwest corner of 23rd Street and 8th Avenue with 2,600 seats and 33 boxes. Built by financier Samuel N. Pike in hopes of supplanting the 15-year-old Academy of Music in Irving Place, the elegant white-marble and iron hall is in a less fashionable part of town and will be sold next year to railroad speculators Jim Fisk and Jay Gould, who will rename it the Grand Opera House and use the top floors for their

New York & Erie Rail Road offices (*see* commerce, 1872).

Popular song: "The Fifth Avenue Galop" (the "galop" is a fast polka-like dance).

 The New York Athletic Club introduces the world's first spiked shoes at its first open indoor competition November 11 at the Empire Skating Rink (*see* 1866; 1928).

Three schooners race from Sandy Hook, N.J., to Cowes on the Isle of Wight in the first transatlantic yacht race. Ranging in length from 32 to 32.6 meters, the *Fleetwing*, *Vesta*, and *Henrietta* compete under rules established by the New York Yacht Club; newspaper publishing heir apparent James Gordon Bennett sails his *Henrietta* to victory after a 13-day voyage (*see* 1905).

 The Union League Club is founded either as an outgrowth of the U.S. Sanitary Commission started in June 1861 or by Republican members of the Union Club, which had 70 Southern members, including Judah P. Benjamin of New Orleans, when the Civil War began (the club's governors ruled against those who wanted the Southerners expelled, saying that they were gentlemen first, traitors and rebels second). Founders of the new club include merchant William H. Aspinwall and engineer Horatio Allen, now 66, who has headed the New York & Erie Rail Road since 1842; its stated goal is "to discountenance disloyalty to the United States," and it moves into the former Leonard W. Jerome house at 26th Street and Madison Avenue; card playing and similar games are forbidden (*see* 1881).

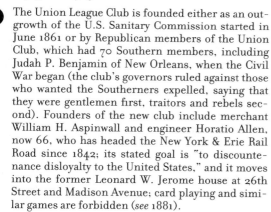 The East Side Association is organized by property owners to develop the area east of Fifth Avenue, where land south of the Harlem Flats (which begin at 110th Street) is relatively easy to grade and can be acquired at prices cheaper than those prevailing on the West Side (*see* West Side Association, 1866).

Temple Emanu-El is completed at the northeast corner of Fifth Avenue and 43rd Street (*see* religion, 1845); designed by Leopold Eidlitz and built at a cost of $800,000, the Moorish structure holds 1,800, with another 500 seats in the gallery, and will be the Reform congregation's house of worship until 1927 (*see* 1930).

The Grand Hotel opens at 1232-1238 Broadway, between Madison and Herald squares, in an area that is becoming fashionable because of its proximity to smart shops and a growing entertainment district.

The Ashland House opens at the southeast corner of 24th Street and Fourth Avenue, where its barroom does a large business at intermissions and after performances at the Lyceum Theater across the street. Built by Horace Brockway, the seven-story hotel will develop a reputation for comfortable accommodations, cleanliness, and good food, remaining open until the 1890s.

 The hottest summer since 1824 brings a heightened demand for trains that will take more affluent New Yorkers to the mountains and seashore; heat is blamed for 246 deaths in 6 days in July.

 The Old Homestead Steak House opens on the site of a trading post established in 1760 at what later will be 56 Ninth Avenue. The restaurant with its stained-glass skylight is near the city's Gansevoort wholesale meat market and is patronized by the same butchers who supply it; the place will serve sirloin steaks and prime ribs for more than 125 years.

The Landmark Tavern opens in October at 626 Eleventh Avenue, southeast corner 46th Street, serving roast beef and mashed potatoes for 35¢, fish and chips for 20¢, corned beef and cabbage for 45¢, beer for 5¢/pint, whiskey for 10¢/shot. Its initial patrons are mostly dockworkers, merchant seamen, and the like, but the place will continue in operation for more than 130 years, long after Eleventh Avenue has ceased to be a major dock area.

 The *Revolution* runs stories about New York's thinly disguised abortionist offices and the easy availability of abortifacients, including patent medicines that, it points out, are often highly alcoholic or laced with laudanum.

1869 President Grant takes office March 4 and former 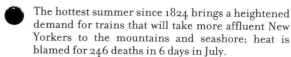 U.S. senator Hamilton Fish reluctantly accepts appointment as secretary of state. He will play a major role in keeping Grant from getting personally involved in the corrupt schemes of the president's associates and will eventually secure the dismissal of the worst of them.

Tammany's mayor A. Oakey Hall wins reelection almost unopposed, receiving all but 1,051 of the total 66,619 votes cast. New Lebanon, N.Y.-born Democrat Samuel Jones Tilden, 55, has spoken out against Tammany boss William M. Tweed, but Tweed says of him, "Sam Tilden wants to throw out Tammany Hall. He wants to drive me out of politics. He wants to stop the pickings, starve out the bugs, and run the government of the city as if it was a blanked little country store up in New Lebanon. He wants to bring the hayloft and the cheese-press down to the city and crush out the machine. He wants to get a crowd of city reformers in the legislature . . . And then, when he gets everything well fixed to suit him, he wants to go to the U.S. Senate."

Susan B. Anthony breaks with the 3-year-old American Equal Rights Association to campaign and lecture on the need for a constitutional amendment that would give all women the right to vote, but she antagonizes Frederick Douglass and many others in May by saying at the American Equal Rights Association meeting at New York that "Sambo" is not yet ready for voting rights. Douglass acknowledges the good treatment that he has received from Anthony and Stanton but declares that the cause of equality for former slaves must be paramount for this generation and that the issue of woman suffrage can be postponed (see 1872).

The Women's Typographical Union Local #1 is founded by Augusta Lewis as an outgrowth of the Working Women's Association (see 1868). The president of the international union says, "Though most liberal inducements were offered to women compositors to take the place of men on strike, not a single member of the union could be induced to do so" (see 1871).

$ Green Point Savings Bank opens January 11 at the corner of Franklin and Oak streets (see 1907).

The Goldman, Sachs investment bank has its beginnings in an office opened at 30 Pine Street by German-born entrepreneur Marcus Goldman, who came to America in 1848 and has given up his Philadelphia retail establishment to start a New York "note-shaving" firm that buys promissory notes from retail jewelers and resells them to commercial banks and other investors (see 1882).

Wall Street has a financial panic September 24, ruining small speculators who went short on gold and had to cover their positions. Financiers Jay Gould, James Fisk, and other freebooters try to corner all the gold available in New York, driving the price up to $162 per ounce by noon. President Grant's brother-in-law is among those who have joined Gould and Fisk in the scheme, which comes close to destroying half the banks and businesses in New York on "Black Friday" before Secretary of the Treasury George S. Boutwell begins selling government gold, bringing the price down to $133 within 15 minutes (see 1873). Commodore Vanderbilt by some accounts has made a profit of $1.3 million by withdrawing from the market just before the September 24 crash; Ohio-born spiritualist Victoria Claflin Woodhull, 32, has advised Vanderbilt to get out, using information from a well-connected friend to counsel the railroad tycoon while pretending to conduct a séance (see 1870).

Railroad executive-turned-financier Henry Clark Stimson of 8 Wall Street is wiped out by the market collapse and withdraws from business, supporting his family on his own small savings and his wife's modest inheritance. His son Louis Atterbury Stimson, now 25, will follow his example in 1871, selling his seat on the exchange to take his wife and two young children to Europe, where he will study medicine.

R. H. Macy Co. enjoys sales of more than $1 million and employs 200 people (see 1867). Store superintendent Margaret Getchell has attracted crowds with stunts such as dressing a pair of cats in dolls' clothing and letting them sleep in twin cribs placed in a show window. She has moved in with Macy's family and marries Abiel LaForge, who served as a captain in the Union Army and is a friend of Macy's son (Macy hires him as a lace buyer). The couple takes up residence in a five-room apartment right over the store where in the next 8 years Margaret will give birth to six children, including twins (see 1870).

Arnold Constable moves uptown from Canal Street to a new store at 881-887 Broadway, southwest corner 19th Street, where it will specialize for nearly half a century in dry goods, carpets, and upholstery (see 1856). Architect Griffith Thomas has designed the building with a marble façade and mansard roofs; he will design extensions in the 1870s that will bring it through to 115 Fifth Avenue (see 1914).

Merchant Morris A. Modell opens a sporting-goods store in Cortlandt Street that will grow into a chain of about 90 owned and affiliated stores in New York, Long Island, Rockland and Westchester counties, and throughout New Jersey and Pennsylvania. Modell's will continue into the 21st century as the oldest family-owned and -operated sporting-goods retailer in America.

Brooklyn's Frederick Loeser & Co. department store has its beginnings in a store opened by merchant Loeser at the intersection of Fulton, Tillary, and Washington streets (see 1887).

The Bloomingdale Road that opened in 1703 and was extended in 1795 is overlaid north of 59th Street by the Western Boulevard, a name that will soon be shortened simply to the Boulevard. Originally 33 feet wide, it has been 75 feet wide for more than 20 years and for a time was called Broadway, like its continuation to the south. Andrew H. Green's Central Park Commission, which is working to improve the upper West Side between 59th and 155th streets, will rename it the Boulevard and make it 160 feet wide, separating its two 50-foot-wide carriageways with a 30-foot-wide planted median and laying out broad sidewalks (*see* Broadway, 1899).

The state legislature at Albany passes a law May 11 giving Brooklyn Park Commissioners authority to "lay out, open, and improve a public highway or avenue from Prospect Park, in the City of Brooklyn, towards Coney Island." The law will be amended in 1873 (*see* Eastern Parkway, 1874; Ocean Parkway, 1876).

The transcontinental railroad created May 10 by a linking up of Union Pacific and Central Pacific tracks in Utah Territory will enable New York and other eastern markets to receive shipments of California grain, fruit, and vegetables in less than a week (*see* 1867). Shipping 15,660 nautical miles via Cape Horn (13,436 miles via the Straits of Magellan) took up to 120 days.

Cornelius Vanderbilt consolidates the Hudson River and New York Central railroads to gain a monopoly in rail transport between New York and Buffalo (*see* 1867; Lake Shore and Michigan, 1873).

Engineer John Augustus Roebling wins approval for a bridge that will span the East River to connect New York and Brooklyn (*see* 1867), but he sustains a relatively minor injury when his leg is crushed by a ferryboat while working on the project and dies of a tetanus infection July 22 at age 63. His Pennsylvania-born son Washington Augustus, 32, served as an engineer in the Union Army and takes charge of the operation, which will involve sinking underwater chambers 44 feet deep on the Brooklyn side and 78 feet on the Manhattan side and is projected to cost $4 million (*see* 1883).

The South Side Railroad of Long Island opens its first branch July 29, having built a line to Far Rockaway (*see* 1868). The line branches off from the railroad's main line at Valley Stream and has stops at Cedar Grove, Hewlitts, Woodsburgh (Woodmere), Ocean Point (Cedarhurst), and Lawrence, extending south almost to the boardwalk (*see* 1870).

The Flushing and North Side Railroad is incorporated by industrialist and philanthropist Conrad Poppenhusen to run parallel with the Long Island Rail Road between what later will be Long Island City and Woodside, where it is to branch south to Great Neck and where its Woodside & Flushing Railroad subsidiary branches north to provide a more direct route to Flushing. The Whitestone & Westchester Railroad is to provide a branch through College Point (*see* 1871).

New York shipbuilder William H. Webb closes the shipyard he started in 1836, having built more ves-sels than any other American, including warships for France, Italy, and Russia. His clippers, schooners, packets, side-wheelers, and steamships have been innovative and varied in design, and he has built ironclads as well as wooden ships, but although he will continue his shipping interests until 1872 the shift from wood to iron has discouraged him from continuing the yard.

The New York Foundling Hospital is established by the Sisters of Charity through the efforts of Bellevue physician J. Lewis Smith in response to rising infant mortality rates among illegitimate babies (*see* Infant Asylum, 1865). Foundlings committed to the almshouse on Blackwell's Island seldom survive for more than 2 months. The new institution, which will be reorganized in 1872, will preserve the reputation of women and their families. The publicly supported Randalls Island Infant Hospital also opens to care for foundlings; it will continue in that role until 1905.

Hunter College has its beginnings in the Female Normal College established on Fourth Avenue. The college will change its name next year to the Normal College of the City of New York and by 1874 its president, Thomas Hunter, will have put up two neo-Gothic structures on the east side of Fourth Avenue between 68th and 69th streets. The college will train countless teachers for the city's public-school system (*see* 1914; Lexington Avenue building, 1913).

The State Board of Regents authorizes Brooklyn Collegiate and Polytechnic Institute to confer bachelor degrees (*see* 1854). Now headed by David H. Cochran, who will be president until 1900, it will confer its first two degrees in 1871, establish bachelor of science degrees in chemistry and engineering in 1886, and change its name to Polytechnic Institute of Brooklyn in 1889 (*see* 1890).

Hunter College High School has its beginnings in a school opened as part of the new Female Normal College; the city's first free secondary school for girls, it takes pupils beyond the eight grammar-school grades (*see* 1903).

The American Museum of Natural History opens at the 21-year-old Arsenal on the west side of Fifth Avenue at 64th Street. Founded last year at the instigation of scientist Albert Bickmore, the new museum displays exhibitions of specimens (*see* 1877).

 Harper's Weekly cartoonist Thomas Nast draws the first of many caricatures attacking New York's Tweed Ring—a group headed by state senator and

Tammany Hall boss William M. Tweed and his cronies pocketed vast sums in graft. THOMAS NAST, HARPER'S WEEKLY

Tammany boss William M. Tweed that includes the city comptroller, city chamberlain, and Mayor A. Oakey Hall—that has been bilking the city treasury out of millions of dollars. Now 29, Nast has been with the *Weekly* since 1862, and his drawings infuriate Tweed, who says his supporters may not be able to read but they can understand pictures. Circulation of *Harper's Weekly* soars, the *New-York Times* will join in the attack on the Tweed Ring, and its ringleaders will be arrested late in 1871 (*see* donkey symbol for Democratic Party, 1870; "Tweed" Courthouse, 1876).

George P. Rowell stabilizes the U.S. advertising business by publishing the first open, accurate list of space rates in American newspapers (*see* 1867), but agents continue to set space rates in the country's 5,411 papers (*see Printer's Ink,* 1888).

New-York Times editor (and former congressman) Henry J. Raymond dies at New York June 18 at age 49.

Cyrus Field completes an Atlantic cable connection between France and Duxbury, Mass., with links to New York (*see* 1866). The new cable embodies technical improvements that will make it a great success.

Nonfiction: *The Great Metropolis: A Mirror of New York* by former *New-York Tribune* Civil War correspondent Junius Henri Browne, 35, who writes, "No thoroughfare in the country so completely represents its wealth, its enterprise, its fluctuations, and its progress. Broadway is always being built, but it is never finished. The structures that were deemed stately and magnificent a few years ago are constantly disappearing and new, more splendid ones are rising in their places. Wood has yielded to brick, brick to stone, and stone to marble. Before the next decade has passed, Broadway is likely to glitter in continuous marble from the Battery to Madison Square; and, ere the century is ended, it promises to be the most splendid street, architecturally, on either side of the Atlantic."

Juvenile: *Luck and Pluck* by Horatio Alger; *Little Women: Or Meg, Jo, Beth and Amy* by Pennsylvania-born New York novelist Louisa May Alcott, 37, who served as a nurse during the Civil War. Proceeds of the book will give her and her family financial security.

The 27-year-old English publishing house Macmillan & Co. opens a New York bookshop at 53 Bleecker Street under the direction of English bookseller George Edward Brett. Macmillan will start its own U.S. publishing operation in 1886 (*see* Collier, 1898).

Harper Brothers partner James Harper dies at New York March 27 at age 75.

Sculpture: *The Indian Hunter* (bronze) by Ohio-born sculptor John Quincy Adams Ward, 39, is installed in Central Park; Ward's bronze memorial to the Seventh Regiment is installed near 68th Street facing the park's West Drive; a bust of German explorer Alexander von Humboldt by German sculptor Gustav Blaeser, 56, is installed near the Plaza entrance to Central Park.

Theater: *The Red Scarf* by Augustin Daly opens at the Broadway Theater (its hero, tied to a log, is rescued melodramatically, at the last moment, from a buzz saw). Daly leases the Fifth Avenue Theater and begins assembling a company of repertory players. Actor Edwin Booth opens Booth's Theater at the corner of Sixth Avenue and 23rd Street, beginning a movement of the city's theater district to the north and west; although his brother John Wilkes Booth shot President Lincoln 4 years ago, he remains a favorite with audiences, but his theater will survive for only 5 years (*see* Wallack's, 1882).

Popular songs: "Listening to the Music Up in Central Park" by New York songwriter George Leyborne.

The McBurney Young Men's Christian Assocation (YMCA) opens on Fourth Avenue (*see* education,

1866). It will move in 1904 to West 23rd Street, offering low-priced rooms, meals, and recreational facilities to youths who move into the city from rural areas.

Pattern maker Ebenezer Butterick relocates his factory from Fitchburg, Mass., to Brooklyn, and his partner J. W. Wilder starts a magazine to compete with that of Mrs. Demorest and stimulate pattern sales (see 1867). The *Metropolitan* (later the *Delineator*) will be so successful that E. Butterick & Co. will sell 6 million patterns in 1871 and by 1876 will have branches at London, Paris, Berlin, and Vienna.

Railroad tycoon Cornelius Vanderbilt, now 75, is married in Ontario August 21 to Frances "Frank" Crawford, 31, whose great-grandfather was Vanderbilt's maternal uncle. Deeply religious, she receives $500,000 worth of first-mortgage bonds on Vanderbilt's Hudson River Railroad Co. under terms of a prenuptial agreement, persuades him to give up his whist games at the Manhattan Club, but cannot make him conform to her standards of Victorian morality. A 150-foot frieze by sculptor Eric Plassman that includes a bronze statue of the commodore is unveiled November 10 in Hudson Square, or St. John's Park—a four-acre parcel bounded by Varick, Beach, Hudson, and Leight streets, which Vanderbilt has bought and covered with train sidings in order to load and discharge freight on his Hudson River line. Vanderbilt and Mayor A. Oakey Hall are in the crowd assembled for the unveiling.

The New York Genealogical and Biographical Society is founded by residents who include Dr. Samuel Smith Purple.

The 23-year-old Century Association moves into a new clubhouse at 109-111 East 15th Street, overlooking Union Square. Designed by Louisiana-born New York architect Henry Hobson Richardson, 32, of Gambrill & Richardson, it will survive as the city's oldest clubhouse building (see 1891).

The law offices of Howe & Hummel open at 89 Centre Street, opposite the Tombs, where the two criminal lawyers occupy the ground floor of a three-story red-brick mansard-roofed building at the corner of Leonard Street; cable address: LENIENT (see 1863). Ignoring the convention that forbids lawyers to advertise, they will display a banner 30 to 40 feet long and four feet high, illuminated at night and bearing enormous block letters: "HOWE AND HUMMELL LAW OFFICES." William F. Howe, now 41, is a large, imposing man of ruddy complexion with a walrus moustache and wavy locks of hair (James Gordon Bennett's *New-York Herald* carries

advertisements for brothels and will describe Howe as "the Nestor of the criminal bar"); his partner Abe Hummel, now 20, is barely five feet tall; together they will defend more than 1,000 people indicted for murder or manslaughter, with Howe himself appearing in behalf of more than 650 of them.

The city gets its first luxury apartment building (the term *apartment house* will not come into use until about 1880) at 142 East 18th Street, between Third Avenue and Irving Place, close to fashionable Stuyvesant Square. Developer Rutherfurd Stuyvesant (originally Stuyvesant Rutherfurd), 29, changed his name in order to comply with the will of his mother's great-uncle Peter Girard Stuyvesant and thereby inherit large real estate holdings; he met architect Richard Morris Hunt, now 43, in Paris last year, and Hunt has designed the new five-story walk-up Stuyvesant apartment house, which is modeled on Parisian apartment buildings, complete with concierge, a red-brick exterior, and a high, sloping mansard roof. Its apartment layouts are poorly planned: two of the bedrooms are at opposite ends of the apartment from its one bathroom, considerable distances separate kitchen from dining room from service entrance from dumbwaiter, the long and narrow inner hall has quite a few right-angle turns, and closet space is inadequate, but ceilings are high, and the two mahogany staircases (one for each section), brass doorknobs, an abundance of cupboards and closets, and the plentitude of wood-burning fireplaces (four in each apartment, including one in the big square kitchen) are deemed highly desirable. Rents for six to seven rooms with bath range from $83.50 to $125 per month ($1,000 to $1,500 per year), depending on size and location, which is far beyond the means of New York's boarding-house and tenement-dwelling masses. The four artists' studios on the top floor go for $76 per month, and the owner's annual income from the building, which has cost $100,000 to build, is $23,000. Early tenants include publisher G. P. Putnam and architect Calvert Vaux (see 1857). Most respectable families live in brownstone row houses, and one New Yorker says, "Gentlemen will never consent to live on mere shelves under a common roof," but within 50 years few New Yorkers, even among the rich, will still live in private houses. The Stuyvesant family will own the building until 1954, and it will stand until late 1957.

The $3 million A. T. Stewart mansion is completed for the retail merchant on six lots at the northwest corner of Fifth Avenue and 34th Street. *Harper's Weekly* editors marvel at the palatial marble structure, saying, "New York is a series of experiments, and every thing which has lived its life and played its part is held to be dead, and is buried, and over it grows a new world . . . But there is one edifice in New York that if not swallowed up by an earthquake will stand as long as the city remains." The Stewart house, designed by John Kellum, will stand for only 32 years before being demolished to make way for a bank building.

The German United Cabinet Workers purchase four farms between 35th and 50th streets in Astoria, Queens, to develop a community (see Long Island City, 1870).

Garden City, Long Island, is founded by department store magnate A. T. Stewart as a planned community for families of moderate income.

Whitestone in north central Queens is incorporated as a village in April. Brooklyn tin- and copperware manufacturer John D. Locke built a large stamping works in the area 16 years ago, many of his men moved with him, and the population reached 800 by 1860.

Glendale in west central Queens has its beginnings as Ohio-born developer John C. Schooley of Jamaica buys up farms and lays out streets south of the Long Island Rail Road tracks (the South Side Railroad was extended to the area 2 years ago). Schooley sells 100' × 15' lots for $300 each.

The Battery is extended to meet a seawall completed by the federal government to protect the land at the foot of Manhattan Island. Rubbish is removed and street stands leveled to restore the tree-shaded Battery as lower Manhattan's favorite park.

Belvedere Castle is completed in Central Park to designs by Calvert Vaux and Jacob Wrey Mould. Begun in 1865, it stands on Vista Rock, the park's highest natural elevation, and overlooks the reservoir that will be replaced by the Great Lawn, but the "castle" is initially an empty shell with open window frames and no actual doors (see Weather Bureau, 1919).

Central Park's Ramble is completed to designs by Frederick Law Olmsted, who has shoved boulders aside to create a Gothic arch and false waterfall (the cascade will be replaced in the 1930s by a 1,000-foot artificial stream, the Gill), chosen shrubs for the painterly effects of their various shades of green, and otherwise made the 38-acre area look as much as possible like a comparable area in the Adirondacks. His original plan called for black oaks, red maples, and native azaleas, but a recent trip to Panama has persuaded Olmsted to introduce Chinese *Ailanthus glandulosa* and *Ailanthus altissima*

(trees of heaven) that would give the effect of a tropical jungle. (*Ailanthus* trees thrive in poor soil with little moisture, grow as tall as 60 feet, tolerate dust and noxious gases, grow like weeds, and will become among the most common trees in the metropolitan area. The first to grow in America was planted at Philadelphia in 1784, a Flushing nurseryman brought the fast-growing, pollution-resistant tree to Long Island in 1820, and by 1850 it was common in the streets of New York, admired by some, scorned by others because of the unpleasant odor given off by its male flowers in the spring.) Olmsted has planted Japanese knotweed in the belief that it would help prevent erosion (it will actually have the opposite effect by shading undergrowth).

The new transcontinental railroad increases demand for Fulton Market oysters; by 1892 the market will be shipping thousands of barrels of saddle rocks and bluepoints to Denver and other western cities each Christmas, and every steamer leaving New York after the first week in December will be carrying shipments of U.S. oysters for holiday tables abroad. The Fulton market tempts retail buyers, some of whom come from Brooklyn by ferry, with displays of crayfish, lobsters (many of them bright red from the steaming pots), prawns, shrimp, salmon, and Southern red snapper.

The A&P gets its name as the 10-year-old Great American Tea Company is renamed the Great Atlantic and Pacific Tea Company to capitalize on the national excitement about the new transcontinental rail link. Proprietors George Huntington Hartford and George F. Gilman attract customers by offering premiums to lucky winners, use cashier cages in the form of Chinese pagodas, offer band music on Saturdays, and they employ other promotional efforts while broadening their line of grocery items to include coffee, spices, baking powder, condensed milk, and soap as well as tea (see 1912).

Dr. Brown's Çel-Ray celery tonic is introduced by a Brooklyn company that will broaden its line to include Dr. Brown's Black Cherry, Cream Soda, Ginger Ale, and other flavors.

1870 Long Island City is created May 4 by a consolidation of Astoria, Dutch Kills, Hunter's Point, Steinway, and Ravenswood. Piano maker William Steinway has acquired a large tract for factories on both sides of Steinway Street from Astoria Boulevard to the East River, and Scheutzen Park has been laid out at the corner of Broadway and Steinway Street.

Nearly 600 Roman Catholic Irish attack a gathering of 2,500 Orangemen picnicking with their wives and children in Elm Park July 12. Celebrating the victory of England's William III over the Catholic pretender James II at the Battle of the Boyne in July 1690, the Protestants (Orangemen) have held a parade up Eighth Avenue to the park at 19th Street, about 200 Catholics have harrassed the marchers, and more than 300 Irish laborers who were working near the park join in the assault. They seek revenge for the death of a Roman Catholic alderman some months earlier, and before police can break up the fracas a total of eight men on both sides have been killed, many others wounded (*see* 1871).

Irish Republican activist Jeremiah O'Donovan Rossa, 38, arrives at New York after being released from a British prison on condition that he go into exile. Given a rousing reception by fellow émigrés at the Cooper Union, he will continue to agitate for Irish independence (*see United Irishman*, 1881).

Gov. Hoffman wins reelection in statewide balloting, running up a total of 399,490 as compared with 366,424 for New York City-born Civil War general Stewart Lyndon Woodford, 35. Many predict confidently that Hoffman will be nominated for president, but public indignation about the abuses of Tammany Hall is increasing, and Boss Tweed and Mayor A. Oakey Hall will later admit that they deliberately miscounted Republican votes in the city to ensure victory for the governor.

Mayor Hall again wins easy reelection, piling up 71,037 votes to his anti-Tammany Democrat opponent Thomas A. Ledwith's 46,392, but the scandals of the Tweed Ring have tainted Hall's reputation.

Secretary of State Hamilton Fish, now 61, proclaims ratification of the Fifteenth Amendment to the Constitution March 30. The amendment forbids denial of the right to vote "on account of race, color, or previous condition of servitude."

A New York City jury acquits sometime lawyer Albert McFarland of the murder in the *Tribune* office of reporter James Richardson. The prosecution has contended that McFarland was an alcoholic who could not hold a job and periodically beat his wife, Abby Sage. She took up dramatic reading and moved the family into a boarding house, met Richardson there, obtained a divorce in Indiana, and was planning to marry Richardson when he was attacked (*Tribune* editor Horace Greeley performed the ceremony before Richardson died). The defense has contended that Abby Sage was a loose woman, that her divorce was not valid, and that she could not therefore testify against her husband even though she was the key witness to his alleged alcoholism and

violence. The all-male jury rules that McFarland is innocent by reason of temporary insanity. He is released and given custody of the couple's child, but the *Tribune* publishes Abby Sage's account of their marriage, which she was not allowed to present in court.

Elizabeth Cady Stanton and Susan B. Anthony call a public meeting in the spring to protest the outcome of the McFarland-Richardson case, attracting 1,000 women—the largest crowd ever assembled in the city. Stanton calls it "the Dred Scott decision of the woman's movement," comparing it to the 1857 Supreme Court ruling that supported the rights of slaveowners to recover runaways. She asserts that it will bring a new phase to women's rights: "As personal liberty, in the true order, comes before political freedom, woman must first be emancipated from the old bondage of a divinely ordained allegiance to man before her pride of sex can be so aroused as to demand the rights of citizenship." Stanton attacks the 14th Amendment (ratified 2 years ago) and 15th Amendment (ratified March 30) because they do not extend voting rights to women, and she promises to work toward the "alteration and modification of our divorce laws."

The State Charities Aid Association is founded by Louisa Lee Schuyler and other philanthropists to improve public institutions.

The first woman's brokerage firm opens February 4 in two elegantly furnished rooms at 44 Broad Street, attracting some 4,000 curious visitors (it takes 100 police officers to keep the crowd in check). Railroad magnate Cornelius Vanderbilt has backed the firm, which is operated by spiritualist Victoria Claflin Woodhull and her "magnetic healer" sister Tennessee Celeste Claflin, 24 (Vanderbilt reportedly profited last year from Victoria's advice to get out of the gold market and once told Tennessee he would marry her); within a few months the young women have raked in some $700,000, profiting from inside information supplied by the commodore in a bull market (his portrait is on prominent display). Daughters of an itinerant Ohio peddler and his spiritualist wife, the Claflin sisters have grown up with their eight siblings in a world of medicine shows and theatrical troupes. Victoria was married twice before age 30 and scandalous stories have circulated about the sisters, but socially prominent wives and widows, teachers, actresses, small-business owners, and high-priced prostitutes seek out their investment advice and that of Victoria's current husband, Col. James Harvey Blood, producing so much money in commissions that they are able to rent an expensive apartment in Murray Hill (*see* human rights, 1871; politics, 1872).

Investment banker Spencer Trask, 25, acquires a seat on the New York Stock Exchange, takes over the interests of Henry G. Marquand, whose office he joined after graduation from the College of New Jersey at Princeton in 1866, and organizes the firm Trask & Stone, which will become Spencer Trask & Co. in 1881 with offices at Philadelphia, Albany, Providence, and Saratoga Springs (*see New-York Times*, 1897).

The New York Cotton Exchange is founded by 100 firms that include the 25-year-old partnership Lehman Brothers of Montgomery, Ala., whose Mayer Lehman is on the board of governors. The Exchange rents quarters at 142 Pearl Street but will move in 1872 to 1 Hanover Square, occupying what later will be called India House. The U.S. cotton crop is 4.03 million bales, up from 3.48 in 1860.

The Association of the Bar of the City of New York is founded by 500 of the city's 4,000 lawyers; William M. Evarts, now 52, will serve as president until 1880 (*see* 1871; real estate, 1896).

The city has an estimated 115 millionaires, and fortunes made during the Civil War have created a substantial class of affluent New Yorkers.

The Port of New York handles 57 percent of U.S. foreign trade, up from 37 percent in 1830, as the 45-year-old Erie Canal continues along with the new railroads to make the city a hub of commerce.

The F. A. O. Schwarz toy shop opens at 745 Broadway, corner 9th Street. German-born merchant Frederick August Otto Schwarz, 34, has worked in the Baltimore shop of his brother Henry, he will relocate to much larger premises in West 23rd Street, the store will net nearly $100,000 per year by 1900 selling dolls, dollhouses, Kiddie Kars, rocking horses, Swiss music boxes, and the like, and it will go on to become the world's leading toy emporium (*see* 1930).

Suffragist Elizabeth B. Phelps shops for Christmas gifts at R. H. Macy & Co. December 24 and drops a box of bonbons on the floor of the store at the corner of Sixth Avenue and 14th Street (*see* Macy's, 1969). Salesclerk Margaret Grotty says she was trying to steal the candy and summons a store detective, Phelps says the box fell while she was juggling packages in an effort to get coins out of her purse, a judge dismisses the case, the newspapers give the story a big play, it turns out that other affluent women were arrested at Macy's that day, and New Yorkers begin

chanting, "Oh, I won't go to Macy's any more, more, more/ There's a big fat policeman at the door, door, door/ He'll pull you by the collar/ And make you pay a dollar/ Oh, I won't go to Macy's any more, more more" (*see* 1874).

The Suburban Gas Light Co. is founded June 11. It will buy the mains, meters, and services of the Westchester County Gas Light Co. early next year to supply the area lying north of the town of Morrisania.

Chesebrough Manufacturing Co. is founded at Brooklyn by English-born oil refiner Robert A. (Augustus) Chesebrough, 33, who has pioneered in using crude oil under burners and stills for refining oil. He will make kerosene and lubricating oils until 1881 (*see* everyday life [Vaseline petroleum jelly], 1875).

Lower Manhattan streets are so congested that teamsters often have to fight their way across intersections, which have no traffic signals, but the Beach Pneumatic Transit Co. organized by visionary *Scientific American* publisher Alfred Ely Beach, 43, gives a public demonstration February 25 of a pneumatic subway that runs for 312 feet under Broadway from Warren Street to Murray Street near City Hall. The state legislature at Albany chartered Beach's project 2 years ago as a pneumatic tube for shipping parcels (after the Tammany-controlled governor John T. Hoffman vetoed a bill authorizing construction of a subway for humans), and Beach has defied the Tweed Ring by clandestinely boring the one-block tunnel 21 feet below street level in 58 nights of work, renting the bottom floor of a clothing factory as a cover, using an improved hydraulic shield to prevent cave-ins, and removing the earth by dumping bags of it into wagons whose wheels were muffled to keep them quiet. Beach's small gang of workers has bricked in the tunnel, whose inside diameter of eight feet is just large enough to accommodate the diameter of the car. Powered by a steam-driven, high-velocity fan that produces compressed air, Beach's 22-passenger car has upholstered seats; his underground station is decorated with frescoed walls, paintings, zircon chandeliers, a grandfather clock, a grand piano, and a fountain with goldfish. By year's end some 400,000 people will have paid 25¢ each to ride on Beach's pneumatic subway, but the Tweed Ring blocks his efforts to extend it (*see* 1873; Gilbert, 1872).

The first through railway cars from the Pacific Coast reach New York City July 24 (*see* 1869).

The Long Island Rail Road reaches Sag Harbor on the island's South Fork (*see* 1868). Company president Oliver Charlick has probably extended his line to counter any move to extend the South Side Railroad to Patchogue; the LIRR will complete a branch line to Port Jefferson in 1873 and gain a virtual monopoly in freight and passenger service to and from the east end of Long Island, with a branch line having stops at Moriches Station (later Eastport), Quogue, Watermill, Southampton, and Amagansett.

The South Side Railroad builds a branch north from Valley Stream to Hempstead (see 1869; 1872).

Rubber-goods manufacturer and philanthropist Conrad Poppenhusen acquires control of the North Shore Railroad, which runs between Long Island City and Flushing; he extends it to College Point (see LIRR, 1875).

Fugazy Steamship Co. is founded by Italian-born New York entrepreneur Louis V. Fugazy (originally Luigi Fugazzi), who arrived from his native Piedmont last year with a good command of English and a substantial patrimony, which he will increase by expediting immigration of Italians to America (see immigration, 1892).

The Cunard Line's S.S. *Parthia* arrives in late December on her maiden voyage from Liverpool and Queenstown. Built at Dumbarton and launched in September, the 3,167-ton iron vessel has a two-cylinder compound engine to drive her propellor and operates at about 12 knots per hour; she can accommodate 150 passengers in first class, 1,031 in steerage, and will continue in the transatlantic service until November 1883.

The *Bulletin of the Torrey Botanical Club* begins publication at New York. Columbia College trustee John Torrey, now 74, was a student of the late David Hosack, pioneered botanical field work, published a catalogue in 1817 listing the plants that grow within 30 miles of the city, received a house from Columbia in exchange for opening his library and herbarium to the college, organized the Torrey Botanical Club 3 years ago, and now launches the first U.S. periodical devoted to botany (see Botanical Garden, 1891).

The state legislature at Albany enacts a law creating a Metropolitan Board of Health. The first such U.S. municipal entity, its mission is to enforce the city health code drawn up 4 years ago by Stephen Smith and Elisha Harris; Dr. Smith is appointed the city's first commissioner of health, Harris is appointed the first registrar of records for the new board, he organizes the first free public vaccination program for smallpox, and he is named sanitary superintendent of the city (see real estate, 1879).

The New York Hospital that opened in 1791 closes temporarily (see 1841). State support ended with an appropriation of $10,000 for 1865, and the institution has been operating at a deficit, but it will maintain the Chambers Street House of Relief as a small facility for emergency care (see 1877; 1884).

The Bellevue Hospital Visiting Committee established by Louisa Lee Schuyler is a group of 60 women chosen for their ability and social position. A branch of the new State Charities Aid Association, it is headed by Mrs. Joseph Hobson, and its members find that most of the nurses at Bellevue are drunks, and most of the doctors oppose a nurses' training school. Patients have no nurses at night, only three watchmen (who give morphine pills to troublesome cases), no dishes on which to eat the salt fish that an attendant brings to the ward in a bag, and no knives, forks, or other implements—only their dirty fingers (staff members say they are afraid the patients might cut themselves); the cook in the kitchen prepares both coffee and soup in the same greasy kettle, and the scraps of food that fall to the floor are taken away at night by scavenger rats. The elderly man responsible for doing the whole hospital's laundry single-handed has had no soap for 6 weeks because the funds appropriated for soap have given out. Mrs. Hobson's women are made to feel that they are making nuisances of themselves, and clergymen tell them that hospitals are not fit places for ladies, but they renovate the kitchen and laundries, and the State Charities Aid Association sets out to raise $20,000 to buy a house for a nurses' training school (see 1873).

The Church of the Transfiguration that opened in 1850 gets its nickname "The Little Church Around the Corner" in December. Actor George Holland has died at age 79, his friend Joseph Jefferson has approached the Rev. William T. Sabine of the more prestigious Church of the Atonement at the corner of Madison Avenue and 28th Street to make funeral arrangements for December 21, Sabine has not recognized the names of either actor, and although he agreed at first he has changed his mind upon learning that Holland was an actor (he has warned his congregation to keep away from theaters, saying, "They don't teach moral lessons," and by some accounts he has told Jefferson, "God bless that little church around the corner"). He will later claim that he offered to perform the funeral service at Holland's home, but the *Commercial Advertiser* condemns Father Sabine's "insolence, bigotry, and ignorance"; Samuel L. Clemens (Mark Twain) calls the minister's action a "ludicrous satire upon Christian charity," and the incident brings prominence to the little church, which will be enlarged, gain many actor parishioners, and become popular for weddings.

St. John's University has its beginnings in a Roman Catholic college founded at Brooklyn by the Vincentian Fathers at the request of Brooklyn's first bishop John Loughlin. Headed by John T. Landry, it moves into a new building at the corner of Willoughby Street and Lewis Avenue. St. John's will award its first baccalaureate degrees in 1881 and add a seminary building 10 years later at the corner of Lewis Avenue and Hart Street (see 1906).

A rotary press built by Richard Hoe incorporates advances patented by William Bullock, printing both sides of a page in a single operation (see 1846; 1865). The *New-York Tribune* will install the new press in its pressroom (see folding apparatus, 1875).

The donkey symbol that will identify the Democratic Party in the United States for more than a century appears January 15 in *Harper's Weekly*, where cartoonist Thomas Nast continues to caricature Boss Tweed and his cronies (see 1869). No Democrat will gain the presidency until 1884, but Nast will create the elephant symbol for the Republican Party in 1874.

The Revolution suspends publication at New York with outstanding debts of $10,000 (George F. Train withdrew his support last year and the paper has refused to accept patent medicine advertising, which is the mainstay of most newspapers). Susan B. Anthony is stuck with the bills; Elizabeth Cady Stanton disclaims any obligation and advises Anthony to ignore the debt, give up feminist activity for a while, and amass some personal savings.

Woodhull & Claflin's Weekly begins publication May 14 at New York. "Progress! Free Thought! Untrammeled Lives! Breaking the Way for Future Generations!" shouts its masthead; backed by Commodore Vanderbilt, the paper published by Victoria Woodhull and her sister Tennessee Claflin exposes stock and bond frauds and political corruption, advocates women's rights, and promotes clairvoyant healing and free love.

The *Irish World* begins publication at New York under the aegis of Patrick Ford. The weekly will be renamed the *Irish World and Industrial Liberator* in 1878, reach a national circulation of 35,000 in the 1880s, and continue until 1951.

Century Illustrated Monthly magazine has its beginnings in *Scribner's Monthly*, which starts publication at New York in November under the aegis of Charles Scribner, now 49, with Massachusetts-born poet-essayist Josiah G. (Gilbert) Holland, 51, as editor (see 1881).

The *New-York Sun* proposes December 12 that a monument be raised to Boss Tweed, showing him on his steam yacht repairing lines during a hurricane. The paper has opposed Tweed and its suggestion may well be a joke, but Tammany Hall forms a Tweed Testimonial Association and prints a circular at taxpayers' expense to solicit funds for a statue of Tweed "in consideration of his services to the Commonwealth of New York."

The Lenox Library opens on Fifth Avenue between 70th and 71st streets, where bibliophile James Lenox has had architect Richard Morris Hunt design a building for his Gutenberg Bible and other treasures, which he has given to a trust after years of permitting only scholars to use the works, and then only with strict limitations (see Public Library, 1895).

Dodd and Mead publishers is founded at New York by Frank H. (Howard) Dodd, 28, and his cousin Edward S. Mead. Dodd's father, Moses W. Dodd, has just retired after achieving great success with *Elsie Dinsmore* novels, and the firm will become Dodd, Mead & Co.

Harper Brothers partner Wesley Harper dies at New York February 14 at age 68.

Membership in the Mercantile Library Association reaches its peak of more than 12,000, with as many as 1,000 persons using it each day to consult the 3,000 reference books and 400-odd newspapers and periodicals in its Astor Place reading room or to borrow from its collection of 120,000 books (see 1854; 1933).

Painting: *Storm over Lake George* by John Frederick Kensett.

The Metropolitan Museum of Art is chartered April 13. Local real estate investor William T. Blodgett buys up three important private collections at Paris in the summer, paying $116,180 for 174 pictures (see 1872).

The Salmagundi Club is founded by artists who include John La Farge, taking their name from a journal published by the late Washington Irving. The club will acquire a 17-year-old brownstone next year at 47 Fifth Avenue, between 11th and 12th streets.

Sculpture: a bronze statue of William Shakespeare is installed at the south end of Central Park's Mall. John Quincy Adams Ward receives $20,000 for his work.

Theater: Wallack's Theater reopens 9/26 with a revival of the 1775 Sheridan play *The Rivals* starring George Clarke as Captain Absolute, Ellen Tracy (to 10/8); *Saratoga* by New York newspaper reporter-turned-playwright Bronson Howard, 28, 12/27 at Daly's Theater (formerly the Fifth Avenue Theater), with James Lewis, Daniel H. Hoskins, Fanny Davenport, Kate Claxton.

The Cincinnati Red Stockings lose June 14 to the Brooklyn Athletics. Baseball's first professional team, it sustains its first defeat (*see* 1846; National League, 1876).

The first English bid to regain the America's Cup in ocean racing, won by the schooner *America* in 1851, ends in failure; the *Cambria* loses 1 to 0 to the U.S. defender *Magic* in New York Bay.

The Department of Public Works builds large floating baths and installs them in the Hudson and East rivers for free bathing from June to October. Open to the public without charge, the large wooden structures are designed to promote cleanliness among inhabitants of the city's increasingly crowded slums, and by 1888 there will be 15 such baths, attracting 2.5 million men and 1.5 million children each year—so many that the city will impose a 20-minute limit on use of a bath (*see* 1914).

One in every four New York families has a live-in servant, as compared with one in three Boston families, one in four San Francisco families, and one in five Philadelphia and Chicago families.

The Lotos Club is founded with rooms at 2 Irving Place. The literary club will move in 6 years to 21st Street and make several other moves thereafter (*see* 1947).

German-born New York designer-decorator Christian Herter, 31, buys out his brother Gustav and establishes his own firm to produce carpets and textiles for the new homes of the city's growing plutocracy. Herter came to America from his native Stuttgart in 1860 to join his brother, who had arrived earlier; he married in 1864, went to Paris that year to study, and returned in 1868.

The seven-story Equitable Life Assurance Society Building completed at the corner of Broadway and Cedar Street is the city's first high-rise, takes in rentals of $136,000 in its first year, and will prompt other companies to add floors to their buildings. Designed by Arthur Delavan Gilman and Edward Hale Kendall on an 8,000-square-foot lot, the gray granite structure has a 26-foot-high galleried hall illuminated by skylights, extensive iron framing, large windows, and elevators that the *New-York Post* calls "The New Way of Getting Up Stairs:" "If you call on a lawyer—instead (as now) of throwing away time, rupturing blood vessels, and losing your wind by clambering up dark staircases—you walk directly from the street into one of the vertical steam cars (which will always be in readiness, one ascending while the other descends), and taking a seat on the comfortably cushioned seats, will be almost instantaneously lifted to the sixth floor." (The seventh floor is used by the janitor.) (*see* fire, 1912).

The Faith Chapel of the West Presbyterian Church (later St. Cornelius Church, then St. Clement's Church) is completed at 423 West 46th Street, between Ninth and Tenth avenues, to Gothic Revival designs by Edward D. Lindsey.

Architects incorporate rear entrances, back stairways, and servants' quarters in designing middle-class houses so that domestics can perform their chores without disturbing the family.

The 5-year-old Metropolitan Fire Department extends service to "suburban districts" north of 86th Street and sets up locked-door fire alarm boxes in the streets. Boss Tweed's "home rule" charter replaces the MFD with a second Fire Department of the City of New York (FDNY), which continues most of the reforms introduced by Gen. Alexander T. Shaler, who has headed the department for the past 3 years.

Flatbush potato production exceeds 133,000 bushels, up from 25,000 in 1842, but rising land values in the next few decades will induce many farmers to sell their acreages to developers.

The city has at least 7,000 establishments licensed to sell liquor by the drink, and countless illegal "blind tigers," dives, needled-beer cellars, and such, most of them in the slums.

An engraving of immigrants aboard ship published in the April 9 issue of *Harper's Weekly* is captioned "Steerage Bunks." "The discomforts of a long ocean voyage are sufficiently trying to the nerves, even when alleviated by all the luxuries and comforts of the first-cabin. To be sure, the first-cabin, or saloon, as it is now generally called, is small and cramped, and the state-rooms are narrow, dark, and close; but these accommodations are palatial in comparison with the steerage—the quarters where the poor emigrants are huddled together like beasts in pens." Passage aboard a steamship takes only 10 to 14 days, but a sailing ship can take anywhere from 5 weeks to 2 months, and a ship delayed by storms may take as much as 100 days, during which time food and water inevitably run short and people die.

1871 Boss Tweed's daughter Mary Amelia marries Arthur Ambrose Maginnis of New Orleans at Trinity Chapel on the evening of May 31 and guests at a full-dress reception that follows at the Tweed mansion on Fifth Avenue marvel at the gifts displayed in a second-floor room: 40 complete sterling dinner services, an enormous frosted silver iceberg (for serving ice cream) from Jim Fisk, diamond bracelets from city comptroller Peter Sweeney, and countless other treasures. James Gordon Bennett of the *New-York Herald* places the total value of the gifts at $700,000 and writes, "What a testimony of the loyalty, the royalty, and the abounding East Indian resources of Tammany Hall!" The *New-York Times* begins running articles by Louis Jennings July 8 exposing the corruption of Boss Tweed and his Tammany Hall ring, whose members have brazenly cheated the citizenry of an estimated $200 million.

Police Commissioner James J. Kelso acts on orders from Tammany Hall to prohibit the Orangemen from repeating the march they held in July of last year lest it provoke fresh violence; Gov. Hoffman defies Tammany, overrules Kelso, and calls out five regiments of militia to escort the marchers July 12. Roman Catholics rush the parade at the corner of 24th Street and Eighth Avenue, and some of the guardsmen, acting without orders, open fire, killing 51 of the attackers (the total body count is 67, including militiamen and police officers; 110 are wounded). The incident embarrasses Tammany Hall, which has claimed to be able to keep order among the people, and it will spur efforts to improve the National Guard.

Anti-Tweed Democrats organize the Young Men's Democratic Club of New York. Founders include Massachusetts-born lawyer William C. (Collins) Whitney, 31 (married 2 years ago to Flora Payne, daughter of U.S. Senator Harry Payne of Ohio, he will be appointed state inspector of New York schools next year).

Boss Tweed begins in August to transfer ownership of his investments to other members of his family. A mass meeting at Cooper Union September 4 hears speeches designed to galvanize public sentiment against the Tweed Ring. Former mayor William F. Havemeyer once relied on Tammany Hall for political support but presides over the rally. Supported by financier Joseph Seligman among others, Havemeyer helps Samuel J. Tilden persuade Richard B. "Slippery Dick" Connolly to appoint Andrew H. Green deputy city comptroller. Salem, Mass.-born lawyer Joseph H. (Hodges) Choate, 39, presents a resolution calling for a Committee of Seventy to investigate charges against Tweed and his cronies, lawyers from the new Association of the Bar of the City of New York City organize the committee, its members include William Maxwell Evarts; Samuel J. Tilden, now 57; and Joseph H. Choate, it submits a report November 3, and Choate delivers an address that rouses the public to action.

Boss Tweed is reelected chairman of Tammany's general committee and wins reelection as state senator in November, despite the fact that he has been served with an arrest warrant October 26 and openly repudiated by Gov. Hoffman, whose own political career has been ruined. Tweed's New York real estate holdings are exceeded only by those of the Astors and merchant A. T. Stewart; he is indicted on criminal charges in December, rearrested, and at year's end deposed as grand sachem and expelled from Tammany Hall (*see* 1873).

"Honest John" Kelly replaces William M. Tweed as boss of Tammany Hall (*see* 1868). The first Roman Catholic to head the "Wigwam," he will gain mastery over the city's Democratic Party by eliminating other party factions, control patronage with an iron fist, and transform Tammany Hall from a gang of cronies into a powerful political machine, with 23 assembly-district leaders appointing precinct captains who gain support by helping men find work, providing aid to families in emergencies, assisting them in any problems they may have with the law, and—above all—making sure they vote. But comptroller Connolly yields his office to Andrew H. Green November 20, and Green will work to clean up the city's corrupt administration (*see* 1876).

 Victoria Woodhull electrifies the convention of the National Woman Suffrage Association at Washington in January by arranging through her congressional connections to speak in support of woman suffrage before the House Committee on the Judiciary (*see* commerce, 1870). She meets in May with Elizabeth Cady Stanton, who confirms what she has heard about an alleged adulterous affair between Brooklyn clergyman Henry Ward Beecher and his parishioner Elizabeth Tilton. Beecher's sisters (Catharine, Harriet Beecher Stowe, and Isabella Beecher Hooker) have taken conservative positions on women's issues, and Stowe's recent novel *My Wife and I* has parodied both Woodhull and Stanton. Stanton has privately characterized Catharine Beecher as a "narrow, bigoted, arrogant" woman who might have become humane if she had ever "loved with sufficient devotion, passion, & abandon;" she cautions Susan B. Anthony against any involvement with Woodhull.

Typographical Union corresponding secretary Augusta Lewis issues a statement to the union's annual convention: "We refuse to take the men's situations when they are on strike, and when there is no strike if we ask for work in union offices we are told by union foremen that 'there are no conveniences for us.' We are ostracized in many offices because we are members of the union, and although the principle is right, disadvantages are so many that we cannot much longer hold together . . . It is the general opinion of female compositors that they are more justly treated by what is termed 'rat' foremen, printers, and employers than they are by union men." Lewis is the first woman to hold office in an international union (*see* 1869; 1878).

$ Drexel, Morgan & Co. is organized with offices at Philadelphia and on Wall Street; banker J. P. Morgan, now 34, joins with Anthony J. Drexel, now 44, and other members of Philadelphia's Drexel family to create a powerful new banking house (*see* 1861; energy [Edison], 1882).

The national bond market collapses following the great Chicago fire in October. Philadelphia banker Charles Tyson Yerkes, 34, has specialized in the sale of federal, state, and city bonds but finds himself unable to pay the city what he owes in monthly interest; he loses his fortune, is convicted officially of having embezzled $400,000 in city funds (but actually of giving preference in his payments to someone other than the city), and is sentenced to a 33-month prison term. Yerkes will serve only 7 before some prominent Philadelphians persuade the governor to grant him a pardon, and he will recoup by the mid-1870s before going on to make a career in Chicago and London transit ventures.

The Bank of the Metropolis is founded to serve the needs of businesses in the Union Square area (*see* 1918; real estate, 1903).

⚡ The Empire Gas Light Co. is founded March 31.

Brooklyn oilman Henry Huttleston Rogers, 31, patents machinery for separating naphtha from crude petroleum. He went into the Pennsylvania oil fields in 1861 and has been operating a Brooklyn refinery for the past 4 years with New England-born Charles Pratt, 41, whose Astral Oil in the Greenpoint section has become a major producer of lamp oil. Both will join Rockefeller's Standard Oil Co. in 1874 and Rogers will push the idea of pipeline transportation that he has originated (*see* 1864).

The 3,807-ton White Star passenger liner R.M.S. *Oceanic* arrives off Sandy Hook from Liverpool on her maiden voyage March 31 after a 15-day crossing in which she has averaged 13.5 knots per day and docks at the foot of Pavonia Avenue in Jersey City (*see* Ismay, Morgan, 1868). Some 50,000 New Yorkers take ferries across the Hudson to view the great 420-foot-long ship. Her grand saloon and great square parlor are placed squarely amidships, instead of high in the stern as has been the practice heretofore, and span the full 41-foot width of the ship. The saloon has coal-burning fireplaces at each end with marble mantlepieces, the ship has 1,200 berths, she even has bathtubs, and she is joined within the year by identical sister ships—the *Atlantic*, *Baltic*, and *Republic*, with the slightly larger *Adriatic* and *Celtic* soon to follow.

The Staten Island ferry *Westfield* explodes July 30 as she prepares to leave her slip at the foot of Whitehall Street, tossing some passengers and crewmen into the air, scalding some with steam and boiling water, pinning others under parts of the ship: 104 of the 400 people on board are killed (although the pilot, whose pilothouse is blown sky high and then shattered when it falls back to the deck, survives without a scratch). The ferry's boiler is found to be so corroded that "a knife blade could cut through the metal," but steamboat inspection remains lax and there are no rigorous design or maintenance codes (*see* 1854).

The 22-year-old Pennsylvania Railroad establishes a connection to New York 2 years after gaining entry to Chicago and St. Louis (*see* Long Island Rail Road, 1900).

Trains of the New York & Harlem Railroad begin operating from the new Grand Central Depot October 9. Designed in French Second Empire style by John Butler Snook, the new L-shaped, red brick station has taken 2 years to build and cost $6.5 million, its glass-roofed train shed rises 90 feet in height, it extends 249 feet in width along 42nd Street, and it runs 698 feet in length along the newly created Vanderbilt Avenue, between Fourth and Madison. Its marshaling yards extend north to 48th Street, 10 of its 12 tracks are stub-ended, and the two eastern-most tracks extend through the station, continuing south on Fourth Avenue to the depot built in 1857 at 27th Street. The New York & Harlem, New York Central & Hudson River, and New York and New Haven each has its own waiting room and ticket counter. Because of a dispute with the Harlem over rental charges at the new depot, the New Haven uses the two easternmost tracks and will continue until November 21 of next year to have horses tow its trains between 27th and 42nd streets. Through trains of the New York Central & Hudson River Railroad begin using the new station November 14, although some local trains continue to use the old Hudson River station at 30th Street and Ninth Avenue that will remain in existence until 1931 (*see* 1885; track lowering, 1875).

 The Roosevelt Hospital opens November 2 in 59th Street between Ninth and Tenth Avenues with a benediction given by Rev. William Augustus Muhlenberg, now 75. The hospital is named for the late James Henry Roosevelt, a Columbia- and Harvard-educated lawyer who died unmarried in 1863 at age 62 after amassing nearly $1 million from real estate investments (and living frugally in a cold-water flat); he left his fortune to trustees who acquired a parcel of land that was once part of the Somarindyck Farm that reached from the Bloomingdale Road (later Broadway) to the Hudson River. The institution for the indigent poor is located just south of the Manhattan Brewery, east of a varnish and sealing wax factory, and opposite the Roman Catholic Convent of St. Paul in an area filled otherwise with vacant lots, shanties, goats, and an occasional cow or pig, but it is one of the few U.S. hospitals to offer private rooms (at $3 to $4 per day) at a time when Bellevue and most other hospitals have only wards, many of them crawling with rats. Its own ward buildings accommodate about 180 patients (each high-ceilinged ward has 14 beds on opposite walls, with a nurse's desk in the middle). The 12 members of the medical staff, selected by the trustees, are all graduates of Columbia's College of Physicians and Surgeons (*see* Syms operating theater, 1892).

 Western Union Telegraph Co. acquires the 4-year-old Gold and Stock Telegraph Co. in May and will operate it as a subsidiary until 1962, controlling

Cornelius Vanderbilt built the first Grand Central railroad station. HARPER'S WEEKLY

most of the major printing telegraph patents that cover communications that connect courthouses, law offices, factories, business offices, and homes.

Frank Leslie's Lady's Journal begins publication at New York with New Orleans-born writer Miriam Florence Folline, 35, as editor (*see* 1855; 1876).

Fiction: *The Hoosier Schoolmaster* by Indiana-born New York writer-editor Edward Eggleston, 34, is serialized in *Hearth and Home*; Street & Smith's *New-York Weekly* serializes *Birth of the Sewing-Machine Girl, or Death at the Wheel*, a melodramatic story.

Publisher Charles Scribner dies at Lucerne, Switzerland, August 26 at age 50 (his sons will incorporate as Charles Scribner's Sons in 1878).

Juvenile: *Tattered Tom* by Horatio Alger, who begins a new series. He will live at 26 West 34th Street from 1872 to 1876, but his books will have only modest success in his lifetime.

Sculpture: a statue of Samuel F. B. Morse is installed near the north end of Central Park's Mall, parallel with 69th Street. Sculptor Byron M. Pickett has depicted Morse with his left hand resting on a telegraph key (funds contributed by telegraph operators have paid for the work, which is dedicated with an address by William Cullen Bryant); a bust of Washington Irving by sculptor James Wilson MacDonald is installed in Brooklyn's Prospect Park.

French sculptor Frédéric Auguste Bartholdi, 37, visits New York in search of a suitable site for a statue he is creating in response to an appeal from historian Edouard-René Lefebvre de Laboulaye, 60, who 6 years ago invited a group to his country house near Versailles and discussed with them his dream of ridding the world of slavery. It has been suggested to Bartholdi that Central Park would be an ideal location for his work, and he writes home to his mother June 24 after visiting Central Park, "It is cheerful, elegant, well cared for, and clean; it is the pet pride of the city, but here and there are some rather mediocre statues" (*see* immigration [Statue of Liberty], 1885).

 Barnum's Circus opens at Brooklyn, and "The Greatest Show on Earth" grosses $400,000 in its first season. Showman P. T. Barnum has made a fortune promoting Jenny Lind (*see* 1850), will enlarge his show next year to two rings and make it the first circus to travel the country by rail (using 65 railcars), and by 1874 will be playing to 20,000 people per day, charging 50¢ and taking in twice his huge

$5,100-per-day operating cost (*see* 1873; Barnum & Bailey, 1881).

Theater: *Horizon* and *Divorce* by Augustin Daly at Daly's Theater. Comedian-theater manager James H. Hackett dies at Jamaica, L.I., December 28 at age 78.

♪♪ Piano manufacturer Henry E. Steinway dies at New York February 7 at age 73. His oldest surviving son, Theodore, 45, and fourth son, William, 35, take over the family concern.

● Central Park gets its first carousel. Pulled by a blind horse and a blind mule, it will continue for years to provide entertainment for the children (*see* 1923).

The Knickerbocker Club is founded on Fifth Avenue by 18 socially prominent New York men who are frustrated by the fact the waiting list of the Union Club is so long that it takes 10 years for a prospective member to reach the top. Old New York families are called "Knickerbockers" in the same way that old Boston families are called "Brahmins." Among the first members are John Jacob Astor II, August Belmont, the grandson and namesake of Alexander Hamilton, and Moses Lazarus (*see* real estate, 1915).

The National Rifle Association is founded at New York November 24 by some former Union Army officers to encourage marksmanship and gun safety (Civil War soldiers were often poorly trained and barely able to use their weapons). The N.R.A. will become a potent political lobby for "sportsmen."

Black Jack chewing gum (initially called Adams New York Gum No. 1) is the first chewing gum to be made from chicle and the first to be sold in stick form. Former Mexican president Antonio de Santa Anna, now 77, talked Staten Island photographer Thomas Adams, Jr., now 26, into buying a ton of chicle in 1869. Adams experimented fruitlessly with a project to make a substitute rubber for carriage tires from the latex of tropical trees such as the sapodilla. He recalled that Indians used to chew chicle, and adding licorice flavor to the gray gum, he has begun production at a Front Street warehouse, and goes into competition with State of Maine Pure Spruce gum magnate John B. Curtis, who has been selling his gum for 20 years. Adams will sell his Tutti-Frutti gum on elevated railway station platforms beginning in 1888, employing the first vending machines for chewing gum (*see* American Chicle Co., 1899).

▥ The New York Police Department's Mounted Unit has its beginnings in the Mounted District founded July 10 with 20 mounted officers deployed, mainly around Central Park, in response to reckless galloping and runaway carriages. Public contributions will help the unit grow to number 136 officers and 96 horses, divided into seven troops for use in controlling crowds during demonstrations and on other occasions when pedestrian or vehicular traffic is especially dense.

The city's homicide rate will rise to 6.5 per 100,000 in the next 5 years, up from 4.0 per 100,000 in the last 5 (*see* 1876).

⌂ The Gilsey House hotel opens in April at 1200 Broadway, northeast corner 29th Street. Designed by Stephen Decatur Hatch in an elaborate Second Empire style for Danish-born merchant-real estate investor Peter Gilsey and constructed of marble and cast iron, the eight-story structure has an Otis elevator, a ballroom, a bar made of silver dollars, and will continue as a grand hotel until 1911 before being turned to other uses.

✗ Pittsburgh-born inventor and coffee merchant John Arbuckle, 32, arrives at New York with his younger brother Charles to open a coffee roasting and grinding business that will grow to have nationwide distribution. A draftsman and machinist have helped the elder Arbuckle devise a machine that fills, weighs, seals, and labels paper packages of coffee that will be sold as Arbuckle Ariosa and make Arbuckle Brothers not only the world's largest importers of coffee but also the largest U.S. shipowners, since the firm will own virtually every merchant vessel engaged in the South American trade (*see* 1896).

👫 A movement to outlaw abortion gains impetus from the discovery August 26 of a nude female corpse crammed into a trunk measuring three feet by three feet by two feet at the Hudson River Depot. An investigation reveals that an unmarried, 19-year-old Patterson, N.J., woman named Alice Augusta Bowlsby was impregnated by one Walter Conklin, procured the services of Jacob Rosenszweig, and was accidentally killed by him in his efforts to abort her fetus; he has tried to conceal the evidence by shipping her remains to Chicago and after being sentenced to 7 years' imprisonment will commit suicide (*see* Comstock law, 1872; Mme. Restell, 1878).

1872 Radical Republicans renominate President Grant despite the corruption of his administration; liberal Republicans nominate New York publisher Horace Greeley of the *Tribune*. Greeley gains vigorous support from civil service reformer Carl Schurz, who has been the chief organizer of the liberal Republicans, from Republican malcontents who have not shared in the spoils of war and of politics, and from Democrats.

Former secretary of state William H. Seward has died at his Auburn, N.Y., home October 10 at age 71.

Victoria Woodhull announces that she will be a candidate for the presidency on the People's Party ticket, with freedman Frederick Douglass as her running mate. She calls on all activist women to register and vote, contending that the Fourteenth Amendment, ratified in 1868, actually enfranchised women, since it made no mention of gender in its provision asserting the rights of citizenship, and there is therefore no necessity for a Sixteenth Amendment that would grant woman suffrage. Woodhull has made a fortune in Wall Street but is unable to get on the ballot. Susan B. Anthony and other women's rights advocates are arrested at Rochester for attempting to vote in the November 5 election (Anthony is tried for breaking the law). President Grant wins reelection with 56 percent of the popular vote (and 286 electoral votes to Greeley's 66).

Gen. John A. Dix, now 73, wins the New York governorship, running on the Republican ticket and receiving a 53,000 plurality. His opponent has been Democrat Francis Kernan, 56, a member of the so-called "Utica trio" (the other two are Roscoe Conkling and Horatio Seymour) who succeeded to Reuben Fenton's U.S. Senate seat but secures only 392,350 votes to Dix's 445,801.

Ithaca-born Republican Alonzo B. Cornell, 40, has resigned his post as surveyor of Customs at New York and wins election to the state assembly at Albany. A son of Cornell University founder Ezra Cornell, now 65, he is named speaker of the assembly by the 96-member Republican caucus.

Former New York City mayor William F. Havemeyer, now 68, is returned to his old office on the Republican ticket, winning 53,806 votes. Liberal-Republican candidate A. R. Lawrence receives 45,398, Apollo Hall Democrat James O'Brien 31,121.

Victoria Woodhull demands that women be given the right to vote, but *Woodhull & Claflin's Weekly* damages the cause of women's rights by exposing the Beecher-Tilton affair in its October 28 issue. It goes on to advocate free love and socialism, publishing the first English translation of *The Communist Manifesto*. The weekly recommends licensing and medical inspection of prostitutes.

$ The Erie Ring of Wall Street speculators James Fisk and Jay Gould collapses following the January 6 murder of Fisk by Edward S. (Stiles) Stokes, a business partner and a rival for the favors of Fisk's favorite mistress, the actress Josie Mansfield. Fisk and Gould have been looting the New York & Erie Rail Road's treasury with the complicity of Tammany Hall's Boss Tweed, and Fisk's death at age 37 draws attention to the corruption that has flourished under the Grant administration (he has coyly told a congressional committee investigating the disappearance of some money that it had "gone where the woodbine twineth"). Stokes shoots Fisk in the lobby of the Grand Central Hotel as he is coming down the stairway, Fisk dies the next day, and his body is laid out in the railroad company offices atop the 4-year-old Grand Opera House at the corner of Eighth Avenue and 23rd Street. A member of a rich Brooklyn family, Stokes retains trial lawyer John R. Dos Passos to represent him, no eyewitness to the shooting is ever presented (a physician is by some accounts paid to leave the country and winds up at Yokohama), and Stokes gets off with a 4-year term in the penitentiary.

A special agent of the New York Customs House summons William E. Dodge of Phelps, Dodge & Co. to his office, informs him that the firm has been defrauding the government by undervaluing certain imports of copper, lead, zinc, and other metals, advises him that the amount in question is $271,017.23, and says he can either settle out of court or face a lawsuit that might cost as much as five times that amount and cause bad publicity. Dodge has been a vocal critic of Customs House practices but pays the money and then discovers that it is he who has been defrauded: any undervaluations by his firm have been more than outweighed by overvaluations. It has been common practice for Customs House employees—including the Collector, the Naval Officer, the Surveyor of the Port, and the Appraiser—to share in whatever fines and forfeitures, legal or not, that the Custom House obtains. Dodge demands an investigation, but by the time Congress ends the practice his money will have disappeared and Sen. Roscoe Conkling will have received a handsome fee for legal services. The Collector of the Port of New York is Vermont-born Conkling ally Chester Alan Arthur, 42, who was appointed to the plum job last year and receives about $22,000 from the extortion of Phelps, Dodge, but he will deny any knowledge of the details in the case and survive the investigation. (Arthur's salary is $12,000, but his income from the job really comes to about $55,000—more than most men earn in 10 or 12 years.)

The New York Mercantile Exchange has its beginnings in the Butter and Cheese Exchange organized by wholesale grocery merchants on Manhattan's West Side (see 1882).

Congress abolishes the federal income tax imposed in 1861 during the Civil War (see 1881).

Charles A. Dana's *New-York Sun* begins an exposure of the Crédit Mobilier September 4: "THE KING OF FRAUDS/ How the Credit Mobilier Bought Its Way Through Congress/ COLOSSAL BRIBERY/ Congressmen who Have Robbed the/ People, and who now Support/ The National Robber/ HOW SOME MEN GET FORTUNES." Congress votes December 2 to appoint a committee to investigate the Crédit Mobilier set up by Union Pacific Railroad directors in 1864 (*see* 1873).

Bloomingdale's has its beginnings in the Great East Side Store opened April 17 at 938 Third Avenue, near 56th Street, by New York-born merchant Lyman G. Bloomingdale, 31, with help from his brothers Joseph B. (Bernard), 29, and Gustave. Like Benjamin Altman, Lyman has worked as a salesman at the Newark department store Beetlebeck & Co. His small "bazaar" is located far to the north of the city's main shopping district, its surrounding population is made up largely of immigrants and working-class people, sales for the first day amount to only $3.68, but Lyman is convinced that the new Central Park and Metropolitan Museum of Art will attract more people to live uptown (*see* 1886).

Directors of the New York & Erie Rail Road remove Jay Gould March 10 and replace him with Gen. John A. Dix (who is elected governor in November). The diminutive Gould is generally despised but continues to use his great wealth to buy large blocks of railroad stock. The Erie this year reaches Buffalo from Jamestown via the Buffalo & Southwestern Railroad (*see* Erie, 1875).

The New York Elevated Railroad Co. is created by a reorganization of the West Side and Yonkers Patent Railway Co. (*see* 1868). The new company extends the line from South Ferry north to 9th Street, adding stations and introducing steam locomotives ("dummies") in place of cables to pull the wooden cars (*see* 1878).

The Gilbert Electric Railway Co. is incorporated June 17 by Guilford, N.Y.-born surgeon and transit expert Rufus H. (Henry) Gilbert, 40, to build elevated lines using cars that are to be propelled by air pressure from pneumatic tubes mounted on elevated structures (*see* 1878; Beach, 1870).

The New York, New Haven and Hartford Railroad Co. grows to have 188 miles of track that will increase to 1,800 miles (*see* Grand Central, 1871). The 28-year-old New York and New Haven has merged with the 38-year-old Hartford and New Haven to create the new company and end a competitive struggle that has continued for nearly 20 years.

The South Side Railroad takes over the former New York & Flushing's right of way to Hunter's Point and builds a connection from Fresh Pond to complete the Long Island City branch from Jamaica (*see* 1870). Ridership on the South Side rises to more than 600,000 (*see* Poppenhusen, 1874).

Steam ferries between Brooklyn and Manhattan make 1,200 crossings per day.

The Netherlands-America Steamship Co. (Holland-America Line) passenger ship *Rotterdam* arrives at New York on her maiden voyage October 30 after a 15-day crossing. The company will own a fleet of six cargo and passenger vessels by 1897; within a few years after that it will have carried 850,000 immigrants to New York.

The 103-foot, 282-ton, Canadian-built, New York-registered brigantine *Mary Celeste* leaves her berth on the East River November 5 under the command of Captain Benjamin S. (Spooner) Briggs, 37, whose wife, Sarah, and 2-year-old daughter Sophia Matilda accompany him along with a crew of seven. Bound for Genoa, her cargo consists of 1,701 barrels of alcohol used for fortifying Italian wines (Meissner Ackermann & Co. has valued the shipment at about $35,000 and insured it in Europe). A friend of Briggs leaves New York November 15 in command of the sailing vessel *Dei Gratia* with 1,735 barrels of petroleum in her hold. Capt. Morehouse of the *Dei Gratia* sights the *Mary Celeste* off the Azores December 5, observes that she is sailing erratically on a starboard tack, boards her, and finds her cargo and stores intact but without a soul aboard, a "ghost" ship whose mystery will never be solved.

Presbyterian Hospital opens on the west side of Fourth (later Park) Avenue between 69th and 70th streets on a block donated 4 years ago by James Lenox, who has become a real estate investor and philanthropist well known for the book collection in his mansion at 53 Fifth Avenue (*see* 1840). The hospital, he says, is "For the Poor of New York without Regard to Race, Creed or Color;" designed by Richard Morris Hunt, its first building faces 70th Street, other buildings will be added, there will be 330 beds by 1889, and the hospital will stand until 1928 (*see* Columbia Presbyterian, 1925).

Mount Sinai Hospital moves to much larger quarters on Lexington Avenue between 66th and 67th streets, where it has 125 beds (*see* 1867). It will soon have a modern laboratory, inaugurate the first pediatric department in any general hospital in 1878 and have other specialty departments, open a nurses' training school in 1881, have a house staff system, an outpatient department, and—beginning in 1900—the city's first hospital neurological service as it expands its capacity to 225 beds (*see* 1904).

The Women's Medical Association of New York City is founded by New York-born physician and publisher's daughter Mary Jacobi (*née* Putnam), 30, who has married pediatrician Abraham Jacobi and teaches at the Women's Medical College of the New York Infirmary for Women and Children.

Fletcher's Castoria is introduced by New York entrepreneur Charles H. Fletcher, 34, who has purchased a physician's formula for a root-beer-flavored children's laxative, opens a shop at 80 Varick Street, and starts advertising the elixir that will make him a fortune, using slogans that will include, "Children Cry for Castoria."

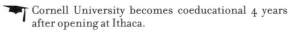 Cornell University becomes coeducational 4 years after opening at Ithaca.

Telegraph pioneer Samuel F. B. Morse dies at New York April 2 at age 80.

New-York Herald publisher James Gordon Bennett dies at New York June 1 at age 77. His son and namesake, now 31, has been chief executive officer of the paper since Bennett senior's retirement at the end of 1866 but is more interested in polo playing, womanizing, yachting, and other pursuits than in the paper. When told that 12 men on the staff are "indispensable," he will autocratically sack them, and beginning in 1877 he will live in Europe.

New-York Tribune publisher Horace Greeley dies at suburban Pleasantville November 29 at age 61, exhausted and depressed by his crushing defeat in the presidential election (he will be memorialized in Manhattan's Greeley Square, between Broadway and Sixth Avenue from 31st Street to 33rd). Greeley is succeeded by his scholarly, well-educated Ohio-born editor Whitelaw Reid, 35, who is named editor by the stockholders after a struggle, obtains an option to buy control of what has become the nation's most powerful newspaper (financier Jay Gould will help him in the purchase), and will retain editorial control of the paper until 1905; a bitter foe of organized labor, Reid will marry Elizabeth Mills, a daughter of banker Darius Ogden Mills, he will turn the *Tribune* into the leading voice of the Republican Party, and his family will retain ownership until 1958 (*see* 1912).

Publishers Weekly (initially *Publishers' and Stationers' Weekly Trade Circular*) begins publication at New York under the direction of Frederick Leypoldt, now 36, who split with Henry Holt in 1868 to take over the firm's *Literary Bulletin*, a forerunner of the periodical whose name he will shorten next year to focus exclusively on book publishing (*see* 1879).

 Nonfiction: *Lights and Shadows of New York Life; or, The Sights and Sensations of The Great City* by New York journalist James D. McCabe, Jr., whose title page promises "full and graphic accounts of its splendors and wretchedness; its high and low life; its marble palaces and dark dens; its attractions and dangers; its rings and frauds; its leading men and politicians; its adventurers; its charities; its mysteries, and its crimes;" *The Dangerous Classes of New York and Twenty Years' Work Among Them* by Children's Aid Society founder Charles Loring Brace, who has headed the Society since 1853 and will remain its executive director until his death in 1890.

 The Metropolitan Museum of Art opens at 681 Fifth Avenue (*see* 1870). Hamilton Square—a 15-acre, city-owned tract half again as large as Washington Square that extends from Fifth Avenue to Fourth between 66th and 68th streets—would make an ideal site, but the museum will move next year to a mansion in 14th Street (*see* 1880).

Painting: *Snap the Whip* by Winslow Homer, who depicts a popular children's game. John Frederick Kensett dies at New York December 14 at age 56.

Sculpture: a full-length bronze statue of Benjamin Franklin holding a copy of his *Pennsylvania Gazette* is installed opposite the east side of City Hall. Created by German-born sculptor Ernst Plassman, 49, it is a gift to the city's press and printers from Benjamin de Groot.

 Theater: *Life's Peril, or The Drunkard's Wife* by S. G. Maedere and E. Z. C. "Ned Buntline" Judson 9/28 at Brooklyn's Park Theater, with J. B. Studley as Fred Kelly (Judson gives an opening address).

 Carl Fischer is established by German-born New York music publisher Fisher, 22, to compete with G. Schirmer (*see* 1861; 1923).

 Columbia loses to Rutgers 6 to 3 in the first football game between the two. Rutgers defeated Princeton 3 years ago in the first intercollegiate game, but football remains a form of soccer with 25 men on a team; not until 1874 will a variation on rugby, played at Boston between Harvard and McGill, begin to establish the American game of football.

New York society matron Caroline (Mrs. William) Astor, now 41, meets Savannah-born promoter

Ward McAllister, 45, who failed in a San Francisco law practice, traveled east to Newport, R.I., at age 22 to marry the heiress to a steamboat fortune, and aspires to be a social arbiter. Mrs. Astor's mother-in-law, Margaret Armstrong Astor, has just died, her sister-in-law Charlotte Augusta Astor has refused to follow the convention of letting wealth and lineage determine who shall receive invitations, Caroline wants to bring her elder daughter into society, and she backs McAllister in starting a series of exclusive subscription dances under the auspices of The Patriarchs, a group composed of the heads of the city's oldest families on whose approval social aspirants depend (see 1853; 1883).

The New York Society for the Suppression of Vice is founded by moralists whose most prominent member is New England-born dry-goods clerk Anthony Comstock, 28, who arrived in the city in the 1860s, found what he considered widespread moral decay, filed charges against publishers for printing what he considered indecent material, and reported saloons that were open on Sundays to the police. Comstock has railed against poet Walt Whitman and insisted that department stores remove "naked" mannequins; the society will continue in existence until 1950.

Woodhull & Claflin's Weekly's November 12 issue carries a fuller account of the alleged affair between Congregationalist minister Henry Ward Beecher of Brooklyn's Plymouth Church and one of his parishioners, a Mrs. Theodore Tilton (see 1871; 1875). The paper also reports the alleged seduction of two underaged young women at the French Ball by Luther B. Challis, a well-known (and married) securities dealer. Neither Beecher nor Challis wants to sue the paper for slander, so moralist Anthony Comstock has Victoria Woodhull and her sister Tennessee indicted for obscenity (the "obscene" words in question being *token* and *virginity*). The sisters are incarcerated at the Ludlow Street Jail and retain the law firm Howe & Hummel to represent them (see 1873).

Abraham Hummel of the law firm Howe & Hummel helps to obtain the release of 240 prisoners from Blackwell's Island.

A gambling casino opened at 818 Broadway by Irish-born entrepreneur John Morrissey, 38, will be the most prominent gaming house in the city for several years. Despite their illegality under the 1851 Green Law, New York has by one account as many as 200 gambling houses, plus 350 to 400 lottery offices, policy shops, and the like. Morrissey is a onetime gang leader and lower West Side politician who has gained a reputation for honesty; he is now so respectable that he will be elected twice to Congress but will die in 1878 after losing most of his fortune in the stock market (see Daly, 1885).

Central Synagogue is completed at 625 Lexington Avenue, southwest corner 55th Street, for Ahawath Chesed, a Reform congregation begun in Ludlum Street on the Lower East Side 26 years ago. Architect Henry Fernbach has employed a Moorish-Islamic revival style, modeling the structure after a synagogue at Budapest with twin minarets.

The High Bridge Water Tower is completed on the Manhattan bluffs overlooking the Harlem River at 174th Street (see high bridge, 1848). Authorized as part of a new city waterworks by the state legislature at Albany 9 years ago in response to growing demand for more water pressure (the introduction of flush toilets has helped fuel the demand), the tower pumps water nearly 100 feet up to a seven-acre reservoir and to a 47,000-gallon tank in a 200-foot tower. Engineer John B. Jervis supervised construction of the Croton Aqueduct 30 years ago and has designed the new system, but its capacity will be outstripped by 1875 (see 1890).

Brooklyn's Prospect Park receives a tree that will stand for more than a century: the Camperdown Elm is a gift from A. G. Burgess.

Sugar refining continues to be New York City's most profitable industry and will remain so for the next 45 years (see 1857). Fully 59 percent of the raw sugar imported into the United States is refined at New York, and the percentage will increase to 68 by 1887. Competing with the Havemeyers are firms such as Wintjen, Dick and Schumacher, headed by William Dick, 49; Dick and Meyer; DeCastro and Donner with its two Brooklyn refineries; Greenpoint Sugar Refining; and Brooklyn Sugar Refining (see Havemeyer, 1887).

The "Comstock Law" enacted by Congress November 1 makes it a criminal offense to import, mail, or transport in interstate commerce "any article of medicine for the prevention of conception or for causing abortion." The law takes its name from New York moralist Anthony Comstock of the Society for the Suppression of Vice (see 1871; Mme. Restell, 1878).

1873 Boss Tweed goes on trial January 7, the proceedings end in a hung jury, but a second trial on fraud charges begins November 19 and this time Tweed is convicted on 204 of 220 counts, sentenced to 12 years' imprisonment, and ordered to pay a fine of $12,750. Judge Noah Davis chastises the defendant:

"Holding high public office, honored and respected by large classes of the community in which you lived, and, I have no doubt, beloved by your associates, you, with all these trusts devolved upon you, with all the opportunity you had, by the faithful discharge of your duty, to win the honor and respect of the whole community, you saw fit to pervert the powers with which you were clothed in a manner more infamous, more outrageous, than any instance of like character which the history of the civilized world contains," but respectable businessmen in the city are at least as guilty as Tweed for the crimes committed (see 1874).

Former mahogany merchant and Civil War officer Abram Duryée, now 58, is appointed police commissioner, a post that he will hold for some years.

New York workers agitate for an 8-hour day. The German Cabinetmakers' Association leads the movement (its 4,000 members make it the city's largest German labor union), but competition from furniture makers at Cincinnati and Grand Rapids, Mich., is taking midwestern markets away from New York firms, most of whom have small shops in what later will be called SoHo, although they remain the dominant U.S. makers of high-grade "imperial" and custom furniture.

Susan B. Anthony goes on trial for voting in last year's election and tells a Rochester court June 18, "As when the slaves who got their freedom had to take it over or under or through the unjust forms of the law, precisely so now must women take it to get their right to a voice in this government." Fined $100, she says, "I shall never pay a penny of this unjust claim."

Merchant-philanthropist-social reformer Lewis Tappan dies of a stroke at Brooklyn June 21 at age 85; his older brother Arthur died at New Haven in 1865.

Nearly 40 New York banks and brokerage houses fail September 18 following news that the Philadelphia banking house Jay Cooke & Co. has closed its doors just before 11 o'clock in the morning. Heavy borrowing to meet the costs of the Civil War, Europe's Franco-Prussian War, and the rebuilding of Chicago following that city's disastrous 1871 fire have combined with worldwide inflation, overspeculation in railroads, and other factors to oblige European investors to withdraw capital from the United States. Jay Cooke & Co. has been financial agent for the Northern Pacific Railway; Black Friday on the New York Stock Exchange sends prices tumbling September 19, and the exchange closes September 20; it remains closed for 10 days, well-established Wall Street firms go under.

"Wall Street continues in feverish, nervous malaise," writes George Templeton Strong in his diary October 27. "Its pulse keeps going up to 120 under hourly rumors of defalcation in this or that great corporation, railroad, or others. Faith in financial agents is gone. Every treasurer and cashier is 'suspect,' and no wonder after the recent epidemic of fraud." By year's end some 5,000 business firms have failed nationwide, millions of working Americans are obliged to depend on soup kitchens and other charities, tens of thousands come close to starvation.

A textile house that employs Augustus D. Juilliard, 37, files for bankruptcy as the recession deepens. Born at sea while his parents were en route from their native Burgundy to America, Juilliard grew up in Ohio, left home at an early age, came to New York, and takes over his employer's business as receiver. He will conserve its assets and when trade revives will establish his own dry-goods commission company, a firm that will prosper to the extent that Juilliard will be able to obtain large interests in woolen, silk, and cotton mills at Providence, R.I.; Phillipsburg, N.J.; Aragon, Ga.; and Brookford, N.C., as well as in the New York Mills Corp. (see 1919; music [Juilliard School], 1920).

Lord & Taylor moves uptown from its Grand Street and Broadway location to a new building at the corner of Broadway and 20th Street, the city's first iron-frame building with steam elevators (see 1860). The five-story (including attic) store, designed by James H. Giles with mansard roof, dormer windows, and display windows, is lighted with gas chandeliers, will be extended to Fifth Avenue, and will house the growing fashion emporium until 1914.

R. H. Macy permits Bavarian-born merchant Isidor Straus, 28, and his brother Nathan, 25, to rent 2,500 square feet of space in the store's basement for a china and crockery department (see 1870). The Straus brothers' father, Lazarus, emigrated in 1852, worked as a peddler in backwoods Georgia, sent home for his wife, Sara, and their four children in 1854, moved with his family to New York after the Civil War to escape anti-Semitism in Talbotton, Ga., and bought a small china and crockery wholesale firm in lower Manhattan (see 1874).

Cornelius Vanderbilt of the New York Central gains control of the rail line between New York and

Chicago by leasing the Lake Shore & Michigan Southern (*see* 1869; 1877).

The state legislature at Albany gives approval to a third bill authorizing subway inventor Alfred E. Beach to proceed with his project (*see* 1870). Gov. Dix signs the measure, but the city's straitened circumstances make it impossible for Beach to raise enough capital to continue, and Gov. Dix withdraws the charter with "the greatest reluctance" late in the year. Beach has sunk $70,000 of his own money into the project plus more than $100,000 of investors' money, he will rent his tunnel for use as a shooting gallery and then for storage, it will then be sealed up, and the city will have no subway until 1904 (*see* 1894).

Botanist John Torrey dies at his native New York March 10 at age 76.

Bellevue Hospital establishes the Nightingale System of nurses' training (*see* 1870). The first regular nurses' training school in the United States, it has been started with support from philanthropist Louisa Lee Schuyler, now 35, and opens with six students May 1 in a house bought and furnished by Mrs. William H. Osborne in 23rd Street, opposite the hospital. Dr. Valentine Seaman has given a class earlier at New York Hospital, for which he wrote *The Midwives' Monitor and the Mothers' Mirror*. Bellevue engages three nurses who have worked in hospitals before and makes them night nurses, responsible for six wards.

Columbia College chemist and New York College of Pharmacy president Charles F. Chandler is appointed president of the city's Metropolitan Board of Health. Now 36, he will head the board until 1884, investigating a variety of public-health problems, promoting compulsory vaccination of schoolchildren, inventing a new type of toilet-flushing mechanism, and pioneering efforts to reduce the hazards arising from milk adulteration, kerosene-lamp explosions, and the operations of gas companies and slaughterhouses. Chandler continues to head Columbia's chemistry department, and will do so until his retirement in 1910.

Millionaire George Francis Train retains William F. Howe of the law firm Howe & Hummel to represent him after having himself arrested on charges brought by Anthony Comstock for making speeches in Wall Street defending Victoria Woodhull and her sister and reprinting their articles in pamphlets. Train was in Paris as a member of the Commune in 1870. Howe uses an argument based on the First Amendment's guarantee of a free press in his Janu-

ary defense of *Woodhull & Claflin's Weekly* against Anthony Comstock's obscenity charges and wins acquittal (*see* 1872). Wearing plaid pantaloons and a purple vest with a large diamond stickpin in his white satin scarf, he thunders, "Intolerance is on the march! If we lose this battle, who knows but what the Holy Bible, Shakespeare, and Lord Byron will share the fate of this suppressed journal." Howe asks whether Deuteronomy and the works of Henry Fielding are obscene, and why the court has not ordered the seizure of all writings by Lord Byron and Tobias Smollett. Instead of defending Train on First Amendment grounds, he uses an insanity defense to win the case; Train stands up in court and says, "I would rather rot in jail than take such a hypocritical way out." He is returned to the Tombs, where he will remain for almost a year, writing poetry and having himself elected president of the Murderers Club.

Barnes & Noble has its beginnings in a second-hand book retailing operation started at Wheaton, Ill., by Charles Montgomery Barnes, whose son William R. Barnes will go into partnership at New York with G. Clifford Noble to supply new and used volumes to book dealers, colleges, schools, and libraries (*see* 1917).

Sculpture: *Angel of the Waters* by sculptress Emma Stebbins, 58, is installed atop Central Park's Bethesda Fountain at the northern end of the Mall. Designed in 1865 as a memorial to the Civil War dead and cast in bronze at Munich, it evokes the New Testament story of Jerusalem's pool of Bethesda with its healing powers and surmounts four allegorical figures representing health, peace, purity, and temperance. New York's largest fountain, Bethesda is 96 feet in diameter, holds 52,000 gallons of water, and rises 26 feet high.

Theater: Irish-born Brooklyn-raised actress Ada Rehan (originally Crehan), 13, makes her stage debut at Newark, N.J., in *Across the Continent*. Her name will be misspelled when she appears at Louisa Lane Drew's Arch Street Theater in Philadelphia and she will retain Rehan as her stage name; *Roughing It* by Augustin Daly at Daly's Theater. Daly's New Fifth Avenue Theater opens and will be successful until 1877.

Actress-producer Laura Keene dies at Montclair, N.J., November 4 at age 53 (approximate).

The Oratorio Society of New York is founded by Prussian-born violinist-orchestra conductor Leopold Damrosch, 40, who arrived in the city 2 years ago to become director of the Arion Society (*Männers-*

gesängverein Arion), a German group. His amateur chorus will celebrate Christmas each year with performances of the 1742 George Frideric Handel oratario *The Messiah* (*see* Symphony Society, 1878).

The bay colt Survivor wins the first Preakness at Baltimore's Pimlico racetrack and its owner gains possession for 1 year of the Woodlawn Vase created in 1860 by Tiffany and Co. (*see* Belmont Stakes, 1867).

Woodhull & Claflin's Weekly reports in January that 23 of the 25 prisoners awaiting trial in the Tombs for murder or manslaughter are clients of the law firm Howe & Hummel (*see* 1869; 1874).

The village of Woodlawn (or Woodlawn Heights) is founded in the north central Bronx near the 10-year-old cemetery and beside the railroad. George Updyke establishes the village on what formerly was the farm of Gilbert Valentine.

The Bennett Building is completed with a cast-iron façade for *New-York Herald* publishers James Gordon Bennett and his namesake son at 139 Fulton Street (99 Nassau Street), fronting on Fulton, Nassau, and Ann streets. Arthur D. Gilman has designed the six-story loft building (four upper floors will be added in the 1890s).

The six-story cast-iron Hitchcock Silk Building is completed at 453 Broome Street to designs by Griffith Thomas.

The six-story Windsor Hotel opens at 565 Fifth Avenue, between 46th and 47th streets (*see* fire, 1899).

German-born Maspeth entrepreneur Cord Meyer, 49, founds the Acme Fertilizer Co. with a factory on Newtown Creek, burning animal bones to produce the raw material used for fertilizer (and also for sugar refining; Meyer will become part-owner of a profitable sugar refinery).

Delmonico's restaurant is the scene of a $10,000 dinner given by one Henry Lukemeyer, for whom the restaurant has arranged a 30-foot oval pond as a centerpiece. Four swans taken out of Brooklyn's Prospect Park under heavy sedation float on the pond, and when the drugs wear off the swans begin pecking furiously at each other, creating bedlam.

 1874 Morrisania (*see* 1675), Kingsbridge (*see* 1693), and West Farms (*see* 1846) in the Bronx are annexed to New York City; placed under the jurisdiction of the Parks Department, this "Annexed District" will become the city's 23rd and 24th wards.

Former Tammany Hall boss William M. Tweed is incarcerated in the Tombs prison to begin serving his 12-year term (*see* 1873; 1875).

Gov. Dix, now 75, loses his bid for reelection to reform Democrat Samuel J. Tilden, who receives 416,391 votes to Dix's 366,674. Now 60, Tilden will use his office to expose and break up the "Canal Ring"—a conspiracy of contractors and politicians that has been defrauding the state in connection with canal repairs (*see* Tilden, 1876).

Democrat William C. Wickham wins easy election in the New York City mayoralty race, garnering 70,071 votes as compared with 36,953 for Republican Salem H. Wales, 24,226 for Independent Oswald Ottendorfer.

Former mayor William F. Havemeyer dies at New York November 30 at age 70.

 German socialists hold a mass meeting of workers in the 40-year-old Tompkins Square Park January 13 to bring public attention to widespread poverty following last year's Wall Street collapse; a small force of mounted police headed by Commissioner Abram Duryée charges the crowd of some 7,000 people agitating for work relief and drives it from the square, capturing its flags; hundreds are injured, some of them severely, and although no one is killed the incident will be remembered as the Tompkins Square "Massacre."

 United Hebrew Charities is created through a confederation of five German Jewish philanthropic groups to assist Jews from eastern Europe to adjust to American life. Its leaders include German-born banker Jacob Henry Schiff, 26, and German-born importer Adolph Lewisohn, 24.

Social worker Etta Angel Wheeler finds a little girl crying in the slums of West 43rd Street after having been beaten and slashed by her drunken foster mother. Getting no satisfaction from the police, Wheeler appeals to Henry Bergh, president of the 8-year-old SPCA, and the Society for the Prevention of Cruelty to Animals decides that the child is deserving of shelter. The SPCA prosecutes the foster mother for starving and abusing the 9-year-old girl, and Bergh persuades Elbridge T. Gerry to establish the New York Society for the Prevention of Cruelty to Children (SPCC) (*see* Children's Law, 1875; Heckscher Foundation, 1921).

Philanthropist Gerrit Smith dies at his native New York December 28 at age 77.

$ The economic depression that began last year continues, leaving tens of thousands of city dwellers without means of support.

Brooks Brothers builds a red brick and granite store at 670 Broadway, northeast corner Bond Street, to supplement its other store (see 1850). George E. Harney has designed the structure (see 1909; button-down collar, 1896).

L. Straus & Sons opens a china department in Macy's basement in March and within a few months advertises that it has the "most extensive assortment" of its kind every displayed in America—majolica, plates, saucers, tureens, glassware of every size and shape, cut-glass vases, and the like (see 1873). R. H. Macy follows Margaret Getchell LaForge's suggestion and displays its doll collection in the world's first Christmas windows, beginning a tradition that other stores will follow (see 1877).

New York gets its first electric streetcars, but the system invented by Stephen Dudley Field, 28, is hazardous and presents no immediate threat to the horsecar. One wheel of Field's streetcars—the first car to be run successfully with current generated by a stationary dynamo—picks up electric power carried by one of the rails. Conveyed to the car's motor, it flows back to the other rail via a second wheel, insulated from the first, and is returned to the dynamo (see 1888).

Brooklyn's Eastern Parkway is completed after 4 years' construction to plans drawn up by landscape architect Frederick Law Olmsted of Olmsted & Vaux (see 1869). The world's first six-lane parkway, it has been designed for "pleasure riding and driving" as an extension of Prospect Park, and it stretches through Crown Heights from Grand Army Plaza to Ralph Avenue with broad median strips to be used as promenades and equestrian paths, side lanes as service roads for carriages (see Ocean Parkway, 1876).

Bellevue Hospital has an outbreak of puerperal fever; peritonitis mortality soars, with 31 deaths between January and June, and some newspapers demand that the hospital be torn down. Maternity cases are attended by nurses and surgeons who have come from surgical wards and operating rooms on the floor below without washing their hands or disinfecting their clothes; the hospital board orders that maternity cases be moved to Blackwell's Island, but the facility there has no provision for complications. Expectant mothers who come to Bellevue for their deliveries usually do so at the last moment, an average of 11 per month go into labor on the street, and babies are not infrequently born in the waiting room of the East River ferry landing or on the boat itself. The hospital's medical board will obtain an old, dismantled engine house between Second and Third avenues, Mrs. William H. Osborne will fit it out as a lying-in hospital, and nurses will be put in charge.

The 92nd Street Y has its beginnings in the Young Men's Hebrew Association, founded as a social and literary center that will grow to promote Americanization through educational and social activities (see Educational Alliance, 1889; YWHA, 1902).

Cornell University benefactor and telegraph consolidator Ezra Cornell dies at Ithaca December 9 at age 77. The school has derived more than $3 million from land transactions he has made on its behalf.

The Remington typewriter introduced by E. Remington & Sons Fire Arms Co. begins a revolution in written communication. Philo Remington, 68, has headed his late father's company since 1868 and has acquired sole rights to the Sholes typewriter of 1868 for $12,000, but the $125 price of his machine is more than a month's rent for many substantial business firms and Remington produces only eight (see 1876).

The Lambs Club is founded by five theatrical men at Delmonico's restaurant. The group will meet in Union Square area restaurants until it rents accommodations of its own at 34 West 26th Street (see 1904; Players Club, 1888; Friars Club, 1904).

Lawn tennis is patented under the name *Spharistike* (Greek for playing ball) by British sportsman Walter Clopton Wingfield, 41, who has codified rules for a game played indoors for at least 5 centuries. The new game is introduced in Bermuda and from there into the United States, but more vigorous sportsmen dismiss it as suitable only for ladies (see West Side Tennis Club, 1892).

Madison Square Garden opens in April under the name Barnum's Great Roman Hippodrome (Monster Classical and Geological Hippodrome, by some accounts) at the northeast corner of the city's 38-year-old Madison Square Park on Madison Avenue. Showman P. T. Barnum has taken over a shed used until 1871 as a freight depot for the New York and Harlem Railroad and spent $35,000 to remodel the roofless structure, surrounding it with a 28-foot brick wall and building an elliptical arena ringed by tiers of wooden seats for extravaganzas that include chariot races, mock battles, prancing Arabian horses, waltzing elephants, and the like. He will sell his lease in the winter to Irish-born bandmaster-composer Patrick Sarsfield Gilmore, now 44;

Gilmore will rename it Gilmore's Garden, install fountains, potted flowers, and statues, and use it for flower shows, policemen's balls, America's first beauty contest, religious and temperance meetings, and a dog show; Barnum will pitch his circus tent at Gilmore's Garden each spring (*see* 1879; Barnum, 1871; Westminster Kennel Club, 1877).

Jennie Jerome, 20, daughter of Wall Street speculator Leonard Jerome, is married April 15 at the British Embassy in Paris to Lord Randolph Henry Churchill, 24, third son of the seventh Duke of Marlborough and newly elected member of Parliament. The father of the dark-eyed bride has suffered financial reverses but provides the couple with an income of £3,000 per year.

A man and wife who have retained Howe & Hummel to defend them against charges of white slavery file suit against the partners, claiming to have been cheated by them. Former mayor A. Oakey Hall represents Howe, who is asked to tell the jury why he left England; Hall objects on the ground that the question is immaterial, his objection is sustained and he is sustained again when objecting to a question asking whether Howe's license to practice medicine in England was suspended; Howe denies being the William Frederick Howe wanted for murder in England, and he denies being the William Frederick Howe convicted of forgery in Brooklyn a few years ago, but he does not deny having been a witness in a London murder trial when he was 12 and in another when he was 16. Howe has sometimes claimed that he was born in Boston, as was Hummell, his cockney accent betrays him, but he continues to enjoy great success representing the likes of counterfeiter Charles O. Brockway, a fence known as Mother Mandelbaum, madams, and procuresses as well as the accused felons indicted for capital offenses.

The Grand Union Hotel (initially the Westchester House) opens at the southeast corner of Fourth Avenue and 42nd Street, opposite the 3-year-old Grand Central Depot (sometimes called the Grand Union). Operated on the European plan (the room rate does not include meals), it has marble floors, walls, and lavatory; although few of its 350 elegant rooms have running water and the baths are all on the first floor (50¢ extra), it has one of the best restaurants in town and quickly gains a following among politicians, many of whom make frequent trips to Albany. It will be called the Grand Union beginning in early 1882 and survive for 40 years.

Topographical Atlas by civil engineer Gen. Egbert L. Viele shows all of Manhattan's streams, ponds, and rivers, most of them now running, entirely or in part, underground.

Restaurateur Lorenzo Delmonico's chef Charles Ranhofer supervises the preparation of free meals for the hungry as economic depression continues in the city; *New-York Herald* publisher James Gordon Bennett has donated $30,000 to fund soup kitchens, and Delmonico reports that in one city ward alone 71,892 persons were fed between February 18 and April 7.

Condensed milk pioneer Gail Borden dies at Borden, Tex. (named for him), January 11 at age 72. He campaigned in recent years for sanitary dairying practices, and his son John Gail continues that effort, devoting his time to educating dairy farmers in how to produce better—and cleaner—milk. Borden has selected a gravesite in Woodlawn Cemetery and his tombstone is engraved with the words, "I tried and failed, I tried again and again and succeeded."

Coney Island sandwich vendor Charles Feltman, now 32, opens a shorefront shack where he sells frankfurters wrapped in a roll or bun (*see* 1867); adapted from a Nuremberg custom, they gain quick popularity (*see* 1875).

Jacob Ruppert builds a new brewery with a capacity of 50,000 barrels and turns his old brewery into an ice-house (*see* 1867). His operation pales beside that of George Ehret's 8-year-old Hell Gate Brewery, soon to be the largest in the country, but real estate investments will make Ruppert one of the city's leading financiers. By 1879 Manhattan will have 78 breweries, Brooklyn 43 (*see* 1910).

U.S. postal inspectors seize more than 60,000 "rubber articles" and 3,000 boxes of pills under terms of the 1872 Comstock Law.

Nearly 400,000 immigrants arrive at New York, with more and more of them beginning to come from Italy and other parts of southern Europe along with some Polish and Russian Jews from eastern Europe, whereas arrivals until now have been almost entirely from England, Ireland, Germany, and Scandinavia.

1875 Lawyer William C. Whitney, now 34, is appointed city corporation counsel and draws up plans for the city and the courts that will effect notable economies through reorganization of departments and reforms within bureaus.

An appellate court rules that former Tammany Hall boss William M. Tweed was given too harsh a sentence, his sentence is reduced to time served plus a fine of $250, and Boss Tweed is released from prison

Preacher Henry Ward Beecher enjoyed a great following until scandal raised questions about his morality.

in November after serving 1 year of his original 12-year term for larceny and forgery (*see* 1873). Authorities rearrest Tweed in a civil action brought by the state to recover his loot, he gives his warden and keeper the slip December 4 while visiting his home at 647 Madison Avenue, corner of 60th Street, makes his way to the Hudson River, and is rowed across to New Jersey (*see* 1876).

The Children's Law enacted by the state legislature at Albany prohibits keeping children between the ages of 3 and 16 in an almshouse anywhere in the state (*see* SPCC, 1874). The first U.S. law of its kind, it will close the nurseries on Randalls Island and lead to the formation of many private child-care agencies. The Society for the Prevention of Cruelty to Children founded last year receives thousands of complaints that lead it to prosecute offenders and remove children from unfit homes, but the city teems with abused and neglected children.

Kuhn, Loeb & Co. admits German-born banker Jacob Schiff, now 27, to partnership January 1 (*see* 1867), and Schiff marries cofounder Solomon Loeb's eldest daughter Therese May 6. He will move the firm into railroad financing in 1877, underwriting a loan to the Chicago and North Western, head Kuhn, Loeb after Loeb's retirement in 1885, and with help from partner Abraham Wolff and others make the banking house a powerful force in U.S. and international finance (*see* Kahn, 1897).

Merchant William H. Aspinwall dies at his native New York January 18 at age 67, having become one of the city's richest men through his clipper-ship fleet and his monopoly of travel across the Isthmus of Panama before completion of the transcontinental railroad in 1869.

Chemical Bank stock reaches $1,500 per share, up from $425 in 1860 and the highest of any New York bank, as its reputation grows (*see* 1850; 1888; panic, 1857).

Prudential Insurance Co. of America is founded at Newark, N.J., under the name Prudential Friendly Society by Maine-born insurance agent John Fairfield Dryden, 36, with backing from local investors. It will grow by selling sickness and accident insurance and will sell ordinary life insurance beginning in 1886 (*see* Rock of Gibraltar advertisement, 1896).

Hugh O'Neill's Dry Goods Store opens on Sixth Avenue between 20th and 21st streets. "Ladies' Mile" is still on Broadway, but it will soon be on Sixth Avenue as more and more stores relocate to that thoroughfare (*see* Altman's, 1877).

The city's first Chinese general store opens at 8 Mott Street. Named for butcher-innkeeper James Mott, it sells groceries, herbs, and medicines (including opium) to serve a Chinatown population that has grown as more and more Chinese have arrived in the city to escape mistreatment in the western states (*see* Wah Kee, 1868). The area bounded by Baxter Street, the Bowery, Canal Street, and Chatham Square will become a Chinese enclave whose restaurants will include some of the best in the city (*see* immigration [Chinese Exclusion Act], 1882).

The bankrupt Erie Railway (formerly the New York & Erie Rail Road) is sold April 24 for $6 million and transferred to the New York, Lake Erie and Western Railway (*see* 1872; 1893).

The New York Central completes a 3-year, $6 million program of excavation to lower its tracks down Fourth (Park) Avenue into a giant ditch after years of complaints about accidents (*see* 1871). The ditch will soon be covered over for most of its length from 96th Street south to 56th with 40-foot-wide planted medians dividing the north- and southbound sides of the avenue, engineer Isaac C. Buckhout has designed beam tunnels (iron beams span the tracks directly above the trains) where the land is too low to permit conventional brick and stone arch tunnels, but hot cinders from the tracks below continue to present a hazard, and the train whistles continue to annoy residents and pedestrians aboveground (*see* electricity, 1903; Grand Central Terminal, 1913).

The Brooklyn City Railroad Co. inaugurates horsecar service along Flatbush Avenue to Kings Highway, making downtown Brooklyn accessible from the Flatlands area and encouraging development of that area (*see* electrification, 1893).

Health Commissioner Stephen Smith acts to prevent an epidemic of cholera like one that has broken out at Memphis. Advised that the city's public markets are filthy, he finds that butchers at Washington Market have built out to the middle of the street, where bones and scraps of trimmings drop and putrefy, tainting the rest of the meat, but when he orders that they remove the parts of their stalls that extend beyond the curb he runs into resistance. The Department of Public Works ignores his request that its men remove the stalls, so he organizes several hundred inspectors, mechanics, laborers, and symphathetic policemen, who tear down and cart off the offending stalls, thereby enabling street cleaners to clear pavements that have moldered untouched for more than 40 years. Butchers at the Fulton and Center markets co-operate, and when the Washington Market butchers sue the city for $59,000 the courts rule that they have been trespassing on the highway. In all, strenuous actions by the Board of Health produce lawsuits against the city amounting to some $6 million, the courts uphold the city in every case, and there is no cholera epidemic.

German Hospital and Dispensary (later Lenox Hill) adds a new building—the Krackowizer Pavilion, named for Dr. Ernst Krackowizer, one of the hospital's incorporators in 1861 (see 1868; women's wing, 1882).

Phillips Milk of Magnesia is introduced by New York entrepreneur Charles H. Phillips, whose antacid and laxative product will be sold for well over a century.

Some 3,000 New Yorkers come down with smallpox in December, the death toll reaches 1,200 in a few weeks, and Health Commissioner Stephen Smith sends squads from house to house giving vaccinations. Since the hospital on Blackwell's Island has such a foul reputation, the people in tenement houses conceal their cases lest any family member be taken off to die at the Smallpox Hospital, administered by the Department of Charities and Corrections. Smith visits Cardinal McCloskey to request that the Sisters of Charity run the facility in place of the alcoholic women who work there, the cardinal sends over 14 nuns, and the name of the place is changed to Riverside Hospital. Since many tenement dwellers are afraid of ambulances, Smith buys a second-hand coupé with four grey horses, and families take pride in having their loved ones taken to the hospital in such style.

New York's death rate climbs to 15 percent, up from 9.5 percent in 1869, as immigrants crowd into the city, living under unsanitary conditions that breed tuberculosis and other disease (see 1892).

Archbishop McCloskey, now 65, is elected cardinal March 15, becoming the first American cardinal. As archbishop, he has authorized the city's first permanent parishes for Poles and for blacks.

The Theosophical Society is founded by charismatic Ukraine-born mystic Helena Blavatsky (née Helena Petrovna Hahn), 44, who arrived at New York in steerage 2 years ago, claims to have received knowledge from "masters" on a trip to Tibet, and has charmed millionaire Col. Henry Steel Olcott into abandoning his family to devote all his time (and money) to his spiritualist studies with her. Chaired by Olcott, the Society's avowed purpose is to encourage the "universal Brotherhood of Humanity" and to reveal "unexplained laws of Nature and the psychical powers latent in man" (see 1884).

Flushing High School is incorporated in Queens. It will survive as New York's oldest public secondary school.

Richard Hoe invents a high-speed newspaper folding apparatus (see 1870).

Ohio-born New York inventor Thomas Alva Edison, 28, perfects the first duplicating process to employ a wax stencil. He has developed quadruplex telegraphy, is experimenting with paraffin paper for possible use as telegraph tape, and will receive a patent next year for "a method of preparing autographic stencils for printing." Edison will improve the process, obtain a second patent in 1880, and license Chicago lumberman Albert B. (Blake) Dick, now 19, to use his invention.

"Mere girls are now earning from $10 to $20 a week with the 'Type-Writer,'" says an advertisement placed by Remington Fire Arms Co. in The Nation December 15, "and we can secure good situations for 100 expert writers on it in counting-rooms in this City" (see 1874; 1876).

Fiction: Roderick Hudson by New York novelist Henry James, 31, is serialized in the Atlantic Monthly, which pays him $100 per month. The Nation pays him a like amount for the critical reviews he writes. James has two rooms in a house at 111 East 25th Street but will soon opt to live abroad, initially in Paris.

Harper Brothers partner John Harper dies at New York April 22 at age 78, leaving only his brother Fletcher to carry on the family firm; lawyer-diarist George Templeton Strong dies of liver disease at New York July 21 at age 55.

The Art Students League is founded by members of the 49-year-old National Academy of Design. Indiana-born still-life painter William Merritt

Chase, 26, will join the League's teaching staff (*see* building, 1898).

German-born New York photographer David Bachrach, Jr., 30, and Edward Levy, 29, patent a photoengraving process that will be the basis of an industry. Bachrach will establish the portrait photography firm Bachrach, Inc. Levy and his brother Max will patent an etched glass grating or screen for making halftone engravings (*see* 1880; Ives, 1886).

New York Philharmonic founder Ureli Corelli Hill dies at Paterson, N.J., September 2 at age 73, having given his daughter a final music lesson and then taken a lethal dose of morphine. A suicide note to his second wife says, "Why should or how can a man exist and be powerless to earn means for his family?"

Chickering Hall opens in November at the northwest corner of Fifth Avenue and 18th Street in competition with Steinway Hall in East 14th Street. Built for the Boston piano company started by cabinet maker Jonas Chickering in 1829, the new concert hall gains quick popularity with a series of recitals by German pianist Hans von Bülow, 45.

Alabama-born New York belle Alva Ertskin Smith, 22, is married April 20 to William Kissam Vanderbilt, 26, a grandson of railroad tycoon Cornelius Vanderbilt, now 80. She is a daughter of Mobile planter Murray Forbes Smith (*see* 1883).

Hoopskirts go out of fashion after nearly half a century as bustles come in to replace them (although not all women have worn hoopskirts and nobody has ever worn them all the time) (*see* crinoline cage, 1856). The hoops have become so large as to require at least 25 yards of material for a single dress, and the weight of so much fabric has so taxed the strength of a young woman with the 18-inch waist mandated by fashion that she has often worn supporting pads to relieve her back by throwing some of the weight onto the backs of her hips. The gathers of the skirt have gradually been pushed forward, and the "back pannier" that has bunched the skirt over the rear of the hoops has evolved into the bustle.

Men and women both wear high black shoes; Congress gaiters—shoes with elastic gores on the sides—are more popular than Oxford Ties. Men generally wear derbies in the winter (silk hats are only for rich gentlemen to wear on special occasions), stiff straw boaters in summer; their white shirts have detachable collars (of linen, cotton, paper, or celluloid) and cuffs, and are fastened in front with studs, being open in the back.

Vaseline petroleum jelly is introduced by the 5-year-old Chesebrough Manufacturing Co. of Brooklyn. Robert Chesebrough will turn his oil-refining business over to John D. Rockefeller's Standard Oil trust in 1881 and build headquarters in Manhattan's State Street (*see* Chesebrough-Pond's, 1955).

Brooklyn Congregational minister Henry Ward Beecher, now 62, wins acquittal July 2 when a sensational 5-month adultery trial ends with the jury voting nine to three in Beecher's favor (*see* 1872). The jurors have heard 25 days of testimony and argument over the months, with postponements when ice in the East River prevented ferries from crossing to Brooklyn, and the Associated Press alone has had 30 reporters covering the story. Thomas G. Shearman of Shearman and Sterling has masterminded the arguments of William M. Evarts in his defense of Beecher, who is clearly guilty of having had sex with a parishioner's wife in the late 1860s, and while his older sisters, Catharine and Harriet, have staunchly defended his innocence in the affair, his younger half-sister Isabella Beecher Hooker has publicly questioned it.

Chelsea developer Don Alonzo Cushman of Cushman-Wakefield dies at New York May 1 at age 82 (*see* 1830).

The Western Union Building is completed at the corner of Broadway and Dey Street to designs by New York-born architect George B. (Browne) Post, 37. The 11-story masonry structure rises 230 feet.

The Tribune Building is completed at the corner of Nassau and Spruce streets facing Printing House Square. The 11-story structure has a 260-foot spire nearly as tall as the spire on Trinity Church. The Tribune tower and Western Union Building are the world's two tallest buildings.

Masonic Hall is completed at the corner of Sixth Avenue and 23rd Street for the secret order of Freemasons, whose members have formed a corporation to build and own a temple, the "funds derived from the rent or income thereof" to be used to establish educational and charitable programs (*see* 1905; human rights, 1828).

The Fifth Avenue Presbyterian Church opens in the spring at the northwest corner of the avenue at 55th Street (*see* 1808). Architect Carl Pfeiffer has designed the neo-Gothic brownstone structure.

Coney Island sausage vendor Charles Feltman opens the Ocean Pavilion—a huge restaurant extending from Surf Avenue to the beach along West 10th Street, where it will remain for upwards of 75 years (*see* 1874). By 1882 Coney Island will have 80 frank-furter vendors, most of them immigrants, and by the turn of the century Feltman's place on the board-walk will have 1,200 waiters serving 10¢ frankfurters turned out by seven grills (*see* "hot dog," 1906; Handwerker, 1916).

1876 President Grant appoints Assembly Speaker Alonzo B. Cornell, now 44, naval officer of the Port of New York Customs House, where Moses H. Grinnell serves as collector. Cornell's father, Ezra, died at Ithaca late in 1874 and he has been acting president of Western Union Telegraph Co. in the absence of William Orton.

Another trial of former Tammany Hall boss William M. Tweed begins in February while Tweed is holed up in New Jersey (*see* 1875); judged guilty in March and ordered to pay more than $6 million, Tweed takes refuge on Staten Island, flees from there to Florida aboard a small schooner, reaches Cuba, and—believing, mistakenly, that Spain has no extra-dition treaty with the United States—proceeds to Spain disguised as a sailor; but the U.S. consul at Cuba has recognized him from a Thomas Nast car-toon that has been circulated throughout Europe as a

William Cullen Bryant carried a lot of weight in city affairs well into his 80s. LIBRARY OF CONGRESS

"Wanted" poster, Spanish authorities apprehend him and hand him over to U.S. authorities, a U.S. warship returns him to New York after nearly a year's freedom, and he is locked up again November 23 in the Ludlow Street Jail (*see* 1877).

President Grant lets it be known that he will not seek a third term, Sen. Roscoe Conkling (R. N.Y.) lets it be known that he wants to succeed Grant, whom he has staunchly supported, but the news arouses fierce opposition; aghast at the corruption of an adminis-tration that has allowed the Whiskey Ring to rob the Treasury of an estimated $4 million, permitted a secretary of the navy somehow to profit by $300,000 above what he earns, and countenanced widescale petty corruption and thievery while the nation struggles with economic depression, former senator Carl Schurz, now 47, joins with Providence-born *Harper's Weekly* editor George William Curtis, now 52, in organizing a Republican Reform Club at the Union League Club. A conference at the Fifth Avenue Hotel beginning May 15 assembles some 200 like-minded men, including Peter Cooper, now 85; William Cullen Bryant, now 81; E. L. Godkin of The *Nation* magazine, and Frederick Law Olmsted. Schurz declares forcefully that no machine politi-cian, however brilliant he may be, should ever be the Republican standard-bearer, and a 60-man reform delegation headed by businessman Theodore Roo-sevelt, now 44, goes to the Republican Convention determined to stop Conkling. A brass band tries to drown him out when he speaks June 12, but Roose-velt tells the delegates that they have just witnessed a demonstration of how the forces of political corrup-tion try to suppress any respectable expression of opinion. The convention rejects Conkling, it also rejects James G. Blaine, 46, of Maine, the speaker of the House, who has been called the "plumed knight" in a rousing speech by Col. Robert G. Ingersoll, 42, a prominent lecturer. It nominates Gov. Rutherford B. (Birchard) Hayes, 54, of Ohio.

The Democrats meet in convention at St. Louis and nominate New York's governor Samuel J. Tilden of 15 Gramercy Park following a rousing speech by for-mer New York gubernatorial candidate Frank Ker-nan, who has said, "The taxes collected in New York in 1874 were $15 million. Mr. Tilden has been in office 18 months, and the taxes to be collected next year will be $8 million."

The presidential election in November ends in a dispute when neither Democrat Tilden nor Republi-can Hayes wins the necessary 185 electoral votes (Gov. Tilden falls one vote short): two sets of returns leave 20 votes from Florida, Louisiana, Oregon, and

South Carolina in dispute and there is no constitutional provision to cover the situation (*see* 1877). Civil service reformer Carl Schurz has returned to the ranks of regular Republicans and supports Hayes.

Democrat Lucius Robinson, 66, wins election to a 3-year term as governor of New York State, securing 519,831 votes as compared with the 489,371 polled by his Republican opponent, former governor Edwin D. Morgan.

New Jersey-born merchant and congressman Smith Ely, Jr., 51, wins handily in the New York mayoralty election, running on the Democratic Party ticket and receiving 111,880 of the 170,243 votes cast. Tammany boss John Kelly gets himself elected city comptroller.

The Legal Aid Society has its beginnings in the Deutscher Rechtesschutz Verein, founded in March to provide legal advice to German immigrants. Charles K. Lexow, Columbia Law School '75, is hired March 31 at a salary of $1,000 per year and begins work, initially on cases involving child labor, citizenship, and seamen's rights. German sponsorship will end in 1896, and by 1916 the Society will be handling 40 percent of all legal-aid cases in America, providing help to any New Yorker who cannot afford legal counsel.

The Boys' Club of New York is founded by Hempstead-born New York Stock Exchange member Edward H. (Henry) Harriman, 28, who left school at age 14 to work as a broker's clerk in Wall Street and had made enough money by age 20 to buy a seat on the exchange. The club starts in the base-

The Metropolitan Museum of Art on Fifth Avenue grew with bequests from millionaires. LIBRARY OF CONGRESS

ment of the Wilson Mission School at the corner of Avenue A and 8th Street near Tompkins Square Park, welcoming any boy aged 6 to 17, and in the next 33 years it will receive about $500,000 in help from Harriman (*see* 1901).

The New York State Charities Commission appoints its first woman commissioner: Massachusetts-born charity worker Josephine Lowell (*née* Shaw), 32, was married in 1863 to a nephew of James Russell Lowell, he was wounded at Cedar Creek, Va., and died in 1864, and she became active after the war in the Freedmen's Relief Association of New York. She will hold the position until 1889 (*see* 1882).

Merchant A. T. Stewart dies at New York April 10 at age 72 (he is buried in the 77-year-old graveyard of St. Marks in-the-Bowery, where body snatchers will steal his remains in 2 years and hold them for ransom that will eventually be paid). Philadelphia merchant John Wanamaker will acquire Stewart's department store holdings (*see* 1862; 1896).

B. Altman & Co. enlarges its premises on Sixth Avenue between 18th and 19th streets (*see* 1865; 1877; O'Neill's, 1875; Stern's, 1878).

Brooklyn's Ocean Parkway opens after 2 years of construction with six miles of roadway connecting Coney Island with a point just south of Prospect Park (*see* Eastern Parkway, 1874). Influenced by boulevards in Paris and Berlin, Frederick Law Olmsted and Calvert Vaux have designed the 210-foot-wide, tree-lined thoroughfare with a central roadway, two malls, two side roads, two sidewalks, a bicycle path, benches, and playing tables, and its cost has been borne by property owners whose lots lie within 1,050 feet of the parkway (they will be reimbursed beginning in 1882).

New York has 299 miles of paved streets, with Belgian blocks and traprock stones accounting for 146 miles, cobblestones 86, other materials (concrete, wood, macadam, gravel) 67 (*see* 1789). Rectangular trap stones have been widely used since the 1830s, so-called Belgian blocks (square granite stones) since 1853 (*see* asphalt, 1884).

Bellevue Hospital nurses wear caps and uniforms for the first time. Designer of the cap and striped uniform is Euphemia Van Rensselaer, a tall, dignified, beautiful young woman who has graduated with the first class of the hospital's nurses' training school and become the first nurse to enter an operating room. Her classmate Frances Root will pioneer social service nursing.

The Tweed Courthouse just north of City Hall was an architectural triumph and a monument to graft.

∞ The nonsectarian Society for Ethical Culture is founded at New York in May by German-born educator Felix Adler, 24, who has found it impossible to reconcile his critical views of the modern world into the framework of his Jewish religion. Brought to New York at age 6 when his father became rabbi of Temple Emanu-El, Adler has taught Hebrew and Oriental literature for 2 years at Cornell University in Ithaca; he joins with some friends to start a society dedicated to realizing the moral potential in humans, taking as its motto, "Deed not creed." Adler will direct it toward practical, rather than ideological, concerns (*see* kindergarten, 1877).

Temple Ansche Chesed (initially Chebra Ansche Chesed) is founded by German-speaking Conservative Jews at the corner of Third Avenue and 86th Street in Yorkville. It will move in the 1890s to East 112th Street in Harlem (*see* 1907).

Stenotypy begins to facilitate courtroom reporting and make records of legal proceedings more accurate. New York inventor John Colinergos Zachos patents a "typewriter and phonotypic notation" device with type fixed on 18 shuttle bars, two or more of which may be placed in position simultaneously; the device has a plunger common to all the bars for making impressions, and it permits printing a legible text at a high reporting speed.

McCall's magazine begins publication at New York in April under the name *The Queen*. Scots-born tailor James McCall started McCall Pattern Co. in 1870 with a small shop at 543 Broadway and uses the eight-page pattern and fashion periodical to promote his dress patterns, but it will grow to become a major magazine for women, retaining the name *McCall's* until 2002.

Puck magazine begins publication (in German) in September at New York (an English-language edition will be launched next year). Started by caricaturist Joseph Keppler and printer Adolph Schwarmann, the periodical has been inspired by the 35-year-old English magazine *Punch* and will continue until 1918 (*see* building, 1886).

Frank Leslie's Illustrated Monthly begins publication at New York (*see* 1871; 1880; *American* magazine, 1906).

Thomas Y. Crowell Co. publishers is founded at New York by Thomas Young Crowell, 40, who last year bought the plates, bound books, and sheet stock of a bankrupt publisher of religious books for less than $6,000. A former bookbinder for the 9-year-old Boston textbook firm Ginn Brothers, Crowell is an ex-seaman who learned his craft from Benjamin Bradley at Boston (*see* Crowell-Collier, 1934; Harper & Row, 1977).

Sculpture: a bronze statue of the marquis de Lafayette standing at the prow of his ship by Frédéric Bartholdi is installed on Fourth Avenue near 15th Street (French residents have presented the work to the city in gratitude for the sympathy shown to the French cause in the Franco-Prussian War of 1870 to 1871); a bronze statue of the late William H. Seward by Randolph Rogers is installed at the southwest corner of Madison Square, corner of 23rd Street and Broadway. Critics charge that Rogers has taken a statue of Abraham Lincoln and replaced the head with that of Seward; a bronze statue of the late Daniel Webster is unveiled on Central Park's West Drive near 72nd Street. Created by Massachusetts-born sculptor Thomas Ball, 57, it has a base inscribed with Webster's words, "Liberty and Justice, Now and Forever, One and Indivisible."

Theater: fire breaks out backstage in the Brooklyn Theater at 313 Washington Street 12/5 as an audience of 1,000 watches Kate Claxton wind up her performance in *The Two Orphans*. Members of the cast do their best to calm the audience, but there is no time to evacuate the building, 500 balcony patrons block the stairs in their stampede for the exits, and the 295 people killed (they include actors Claude Burroughs and Harry Murdoch) are so badly burned that they must be buried in a common grave at Green-Wood Cemetery. Five more people die, the tragedy will kill the theatrical business for nearly a year throughout America, and it will force Brooklyn and New York to institute stricter theater inspections.

The National Baseball League is organized at the Broadway Central Hotel as more professional ball clubs come into being (*see* 1870; 1884).

The Polo Grounds opens in an area bounded by Fifth and Sixth Avenues between 110th and 112th streets. The field will be used for baseball by the New York Giants and New York Metropolitans beginning in 1883 but will be abandoned in 1889 when streets are cut through it (*see* 1891).

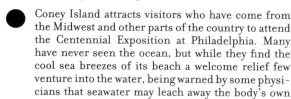

Coney Island attracts visitors who have come from the Midwest and other parts of the country to attend the Centennial Exposition at Philadelphia. Many have never seen the ocean, but while they find the cool sea breezes of its beach a welcome relief few venture into the water, being warned by some physicians that seawater may leach away the body's own essential salts.

B.V.D. underwear for men is introduced by Bradley, Voorhees, and Day of New York, whose one-piece B.V.D.s will be called "Babies' Ventilated Diapers" but B.V.D. will become almost a generic term.

Manhattan's "Tenderloin" section gets its name by one account from a remark by newly appointed police precinct captain Alexander S. "Clubber" Williams to a newspaper reporter. Williams is infamous for using his nightstick on suspects to impose order on the Gashouse Gang that for some years terrorized the neighborhood between Fourth Avenue and the East River from 27th Street south to 14th. His new precinct covers the large area, sometimes called "Satan's Circus," from Madison Square north to 48th Street between Fifth and Seventh avenues, an area notorious for prostitution, gambling, white slavery, opium dens, illegal saloons, and criminality—and a prime source of extortion from legitimate and not-so-legitimate enterprises to benefit police officers and Tammany Hall Democrats. No more chuck or rump steak for him, says Williams; henceforth he will eat only tenderloin. By another account, "Whisker" Williams has taken over the West 30th Street station, come into Delmonico's for dinner, seen Abraham Hummel of the law firm Howe & Hummel, and said, "You'd better behave yourself, Mr. Hummel, or you won't be coming in here for any more of them juicy beefsteaks you're always eating," prompting Hummel to reply, "Speaking of that, Inspector, that's a pretty juicy tenderloin they just handed you" (*see* Hell's Kitchen, 1881).

The city's homicide rate will fall to 4.8 per 100,000 in the next 5 years, down from 6.5 per 100,000 in the last 5 (*see* 1891).

 The "Tweed" Courthouse completed north of City Hall on a site formerly occupied by an almshouse has cost at least $13 million—far more than the United States paid Russia for Alaska. At least three-quarters of the money has gone into graft: the state legislature at Albany appropriated $250,000 for the county courthouse in 1858, but its stone has come from a Massachusetts quarry acquired earlier by a Tweed-organized company and has been sold to the city at exorbitant prices; Boss Tweed's cronies have run up huge and fraudulent bills, including $179,729 for three tables and 40 chairs, nearly $361,000 for a month's work by a single, solitary carpenter; and they have taken so long to build the structure that *Harper's Weekly* commented, "The process seemed like the gradual upheaval of a continent, perceptible only by measurements separated by cycles. People who saw it every day forgot when it began, and at length came to regard it as something which had never had a beginning, and, probably, would never have an ending." But for all the corruption involved in its construction the building has a skylighted five-story rotunda, granite columns, and ornate cage elevators, contains 30 splendid, high-ceilinged courtrooms, and will stand as an architectural masterpiece into the 21st century.

The Church of St. Paul the Apostle is completed at the southwest corner of Ninth Avenue and 70th Street. Designed for the Paulist Fathers by the late Jeremiah O'Rourke, who modeled it on Florence's 13th century Cathedral of Santa Croce, the huge structure has been built with stone salvaged from the old Croton Aqueduct. Its 60-foot wide nave is flanked by giant round and octagonal columns of blue limestone, it will be expanded and reopen in January 1885, after which it will be decorated by prominent artists, and it will be the largest church in America after St. Patrick's Cathedral, now being built on Fifth Avenue (*see* 1879).

 Work on Central Park is completed after 17 years: the 843-acre park extends from 59th Street to 110th between Fifth and Eighth avenues (*see* Olmsted, 1878).

The U.S. Army Corps of Engineers uses nitroglycerin to blast away sunken rock off Horn's Hook near Gracie Mansion. The city will take over the property in 1891 and add it to a picnic ground to the south, creating East End Park (to be renamed Carl Schurz Park in 1911).

 Lorenzo Delmonico sells his Fifth Avenue restaurant at 14th Street and moves farther uptown (*see* 1868). The city has more than 6,000 restaurants, but none can match the new Delmonico's, where dinner for two can cost an extravagant $4 to $5 and a more elaborate meal even more. No reservations are accepted except for the private rooms, and even the richest patrons must wait in line for tables. His new establishment faces Madison Square at 26th Street and is even more elegant than any previous Delmonico's (see Ranhofer, 1894; Delmonico's, 1897).

1877 An electoral commission decides last year's disputed presidential election. Appointed January 29 and composed of five senators, five representatives, and five Supreme Court justices, it decides all questions along partisan lines (eight members are Republicans, seven Democrats), denying Gov. Tilden of New York his marginal victory at the polls. Tilden has been represented by David Dudley Field, now nearly 72; he has by some accounts been less than vigorous in advancing his own cause and says, "I can retire to private life with the consciousness that I shall receive from posterity the credit of having been elected to the highest position in the gift of the people, without any of the cares and responsibilities of the office." Rutherford B. Hayes is sworn in as president March 4, having named a cabinet whose members were chosen on the basis of ability rather than cronyism; "Party leaders should have no more influence in appointments than other equally respectable citizens," he declares, but many people consider the election to have been stolen and call him "Rutherford B. Fraud." Tilden resumes his New York City law practice and will remain a power in the Democratic Party.

The Board of Aldermen appoints a committee to hold hearings on alleged frauds committed by the Tweed Ring. Former Tammany Hall boss William M. Tweed is taken from the Ludlow Street Jail late in the year and gives extensive testimony, but although the Tweed Ring has cost taxpayers at least $50 million, tripling the city's debt and raising taxes by approximately the same multiple, the amount recovered from Ring members and their estates amounts to less than $876,500.

 Victoria Woodhull and her sister Tennessee Claflin move to England to escape puritanical criticism of their views and behavior (see 1872). William H. Vanderbilt, son of the late Commodore, sets Woodhull up abroad, she will marry a British banker and peer, deny ever having favored free love, and live until 1927.

London-born New York cigarmaker Samuel Gompers, 27, reorganizes the Cigarmakers' Union, establishing the supremacy of the international union over locals and introducing high dues to finance strike and pension funds. Gompers will use the leverage of strikes and boycotts to gain higher wages, better working conditions, and more job security, but will avoid political alignments (see politics, 1882).

President Hayes appoints reformer Carl Schurz, now 48, secretary of the interior. Schurz will use the post to support more enlightened treatment of Native Americans.

 The Fresh Air Fund brings 60 needy New York children for a visit to the rural community of Sherman, Pa. Most have never seen a cow. Sherman clergyman Willard Parsons has started the fund in June; he will turn management of the 2-week program over to the New-York Tribune in 1881, and the newspaper will appeal to the public for funds to continue it (see 1962).

 The New York Central, Erie, Pennsylvania, and Baltimore & Ohio call off a long-standing rate war in April and announce a 10 percent wage cut. When the B&O announces a further 10 percent cut in mid-July its workers begin a strike at Martinsburg, W. Va., that is soon joined by Pennsylvania Railroad workers. Strikers set the Pittsburgh roundhouse ablaze, the strike spreads across the nation, the railroads are shut down for a week, and the strike is not ended until federal troops are called in, firing on the workers, killing some, wounding many (both sides claim victory).

Chase National Bank is founded September 12 by New York banker John Thompson, now 75, who founded First National Bank in 1863 but sold his controlling interest in that institution 4 years ago. The new bank opens offices at 104 Broadway, taking its name from the late chief justice of the U.S. Supreme Court, Salmon P. Chase, who originated the national banking system in 1863 but died at New York 4 years ago. The bank's first balance sheet, published December 27, shows total resources of $1,042,009.25 (see 1930; building, 1928; Chase Manhattan, 1955).

Banker James Brown of Brown Brothers dies November 1 at age 86; his fourth son, John Crosby Brown, 39, was admitted to partnership in 1864 and takes over as senior partner (see transportation, 1854; Brown Brothers Harriman, 1931).

 Merchant B. Altman moves into a new building at 621 Sixth Avenue, between 18th and 19th streets, where the store will remain until 1906. Designed by D. and J. Jardine, the structure will be enlarged in 1887 with an addition designed by William H. Hume.

R. H. Macy founder Rowland H. Macy dies at Paris March 29 at age 54, having pioneered such innovations as cash-only sales, money-back guarantees, and an on-premise factory to sew made-to-measure garments. His only son ran away at age 16 to join the Union Army and deserted after 10 days; Macy's will leave his interest in the department store to a nephew (*see* Straus brothers, 1888).

Cornelius Vanderbilt dies at New York January 4 at age 82, having laid new steel rails and built new bridges to cut running time on the New York Central between New York and Chicago from 50 hours to 24 (*see* 1873; 1902). He leaves a fortune of $105 million to his 38-year-old widow and the children who survive him (relatively little goes to the widow and eight daughters, but his 55-year-old son William Henry receives $90 million and *his* four sons receive $11.5 million among them, all in stock). Vanderbilt is buried in a mausoleum designed by Richard Morris Hunt in Staten Island's Moravian Cemetery.

William H. Vanderbilt's daughter Florence Adele is married at New York November 21 to Boston-born railroad director Hamilton McKown Twombly, 28, who joins the management of the New York Central & Hudson River Railroad. Twombly will for many years be the sole representative of the Vanderbilt interests, when other members of the family are abroad, and—unlike the husbands of the Commodore's other four granddaughters—will multiply his wife's inheritance, enabling her to maintain a mansion at 684 Fifth Avenue, a 50-room Newport cottage ("Vinland"), and a 1,000-acre estate ("Florham") near Madison, N.J.

Freight trains come into the large Vanderbilt terminal between 60th and 71st streets from the New York Central's main line, crossing the Harlem River at Spuyten Duyvil and moving along the Hudson. Other freight arrives by barge. To facilitate berthing of barges and lighters against the current, the terminal has floating bridges plus finger piers pointing downstream rather than at right angles to the bulkhead line. From the terminal yards, trains carry produce to the perishable-food yard at 33rd Street and carry cattle by elevated tracks from there to a stockyard at West Houston Street, whence they are moved to slaughterhouses.

The New York and Sea Beach Railway begins operating July 18 on a four-and-a-half-mile stretch of private track between Brooklyn's New Utrecht Avenue and Coney Island's Sea Beach Palace, a structure built for last year's Centennial Exposition at Philadelphia. The new passenger line will be extended in 1879 from New Utrecht Avenue to the ferry terminal at 65th Street (*see* 1897).

The Coney Island Concourse opens as a mile-and-a-half extension of the King's Highway that links the so-called "island" to the rest of Brooklyn (actually a slip of sand and marsh with a shoreline that extends for nearly four miles from Sheepshead Bay to the Lower Bay, Coney Island is separated from the southernmost promontory of Brooklyn only by a narrow creek). The concrete roadway for carriages is 250 feet wide and helps attract summer visitors to the resort.

Staten Island-born clerk Rudolph Kunhardt, 16, enters the employ of the Atlas Steamship Co., agents for the Hamburg-Amerika Line. He will introduce the use of through bills of lading for the shipment of goods from one country to another via New York.

The New York Hospital that was closed temporarily in 1870 reopens March 16 on a site between Fifth and Sixth avenues from 15th Street to 16th, with the former Thorn mansion in 16th Street as its administrative center (it will be rebuilt in 1901 to house the outpatient department, records room, and meeting room for the board of governors). Designed by architect George B. Post, the new facility has 163 beds, 10 of them for private patients in separate rooms "luxuriously furnished" by the Society that was chartered in 1771, and newly developed systems of hygiene are employed, including heating and ventilation provided by forced air from fan blowers in the basement and attic through outlets along windowsills. The hospital's governors establish a training school for nurses to ensure quality care for patients, and the hospital will remain under the mansard roof of the red-brick and wrought-iron structure until 1932, acquiring adjacent properties to provide a nurses' residence and a "helps" dormitory.

Harlem Hospital has its beginnings in a municipal hospital opened in an East 120th Street house to house patients awaiting transfer to hospitals on Wards and Randalls islands. Bellevue Hospital will soon use it as an emergency-treatment branch, sparing patients a long ambulance ride (*see* 1907).

The Roosevelt, St. Luke's, and two other local hospitals inaugurate the first ambulance service for emergency and critical care.

Felix Adler's Society for Ethical Culture opens a free kindergarten (*see* 1876; 1880).

The American Museum of Natural History opens its first building December 22 in ceremonies attended by President Hayes, Harvard president Charles W.

Eliot, and other notables (*see* 1869). President Grant took part in the groundbreaking ceremonies 3 years ago on what heretofore has been Manhattan Square—a 10-acre, city-owned site across from Central Park at West 77th Street—where the museum will add more buildings in years to come. Its board has been headed since 1872 by former sugar refiner Robert L. Stuart, now 71, who will continue as president of the museum until 1881 (*see* food, 1828). His house at 154 Fifth Avenue boasts an extensive library and a large collection of American and European art (*see* 1881). The 29-year-old Arsenal in Central Park has housed the museum's collection up to now; it will become the headquarters of the city's parks department.

The first Bell telephone is sold in May; 778 are in use by August, and the American Bell Telephone Co. grants its first New York licenses August 27, but the devices remain crude. Scottish-born Boston inventor Alexander Graham Bell invented the telephone in 1875, was granted a patent on his 29th birthday March 3 of last year (Patent No. 174,465 for "improvements in telegraphy" will often be called the most valuable patent ever issued), and has used the instrument to speak with his assistant Thomas A. Watson at what later will be computed as 2,000 "bits" per second (the telegraph of 1844 transmits five bits per second).

The Bell Telephone Association is organized with headquarters at New York. Founder Gardiner Hubbard gives himself and his son-in-law Alexander Graham Bell each a 30 percent interest in the Bell patent, gives Bell's assistant Thomas A. Watson a 10 percent interest, and gives a 30 percent interest to investor Thomas Sanders, 38, who put up more than $100,000 to back Bell's early experiments. Western Union Telegraph Co.'s American Speaking-Telephone Co. competes with Bell, but the new Bell firm is deluged with applications for telephone agencies, and Hubbard starts leasing telephones at the rate of 1,000 per month.

German-born inventor Emile Berliner, 26, develops a loose-contact telephone transmitter superior to Bell's telephone (*see* 1878).

The central branch of New York's YMCA offers the world's first typing course—a 6-month program for women.

The *Columbia Spectator* begins publication July 1 with a pledge to avoid "class politics." Its undergraduate editors promise in their first editorial, "The *Spectator* seeks to be nothing more than an interesting an instructive University paper, more 'newsy' and

lighter in tone than the periodicals which have hitherto flourished at Columbia." The paper will continue for more than 125 years as Columbia moves uptown from Park Avenue to Morningside Heights.

Funk & Wagnalls Co. has its beginnings in the I. K. Funk & Co. publishing house founded at New York by local clergyman-bookseller Isaac Kauffman Funk, 38, and Adams Willis Wagnalls, 34. The firm will publish *A Standard Dictionary of the English Language* in 1890 and take the name Funk & Wagnalls in 1891.

Harper Brothers partner Fletcher Harper dies at New York May 29 at age 71, the last of the brothers who became partners in 1825, but the firm will remain in family hands until 1900 (*see* Harper & Row, 1961).

The New York Etching Club is founded by local artists who include English-born landscape painter Thomas Moran, 40, an illustrator for *Scribner's Monthly* who will gain prominence with huge paintings of Rocky Mountain peaks.

Sculpture: a bronze statue of the late poet Fitz-Greene Halleck by Ohio-born sculptor J. Wilson MacDonald, 53, is installed at the south entrance to Central Park's Mall.

The cakewalk is introduced into minstrel shows by the New York team Harrigan and Hart, whose "Walking for Dat Cake" number imitates antebellum plantation "cakewalks."

The Westminster Kennel Club dog show inaugurated in May at the 3-year-old Gilmore's Garden attracts 1,201 entries in the "first annual N.Y. Bench Show." Dogs compete for silver trophies produced by Tiffany & Co. Fanciers have organized the club at the Westminster Hotel on Irving Place at 16th Street, the founding members have adopted as the club's symbol the head of their pointer Sensation, whose stud services they offer at $35. While no "best of show" award will be made until 1907 the first show is so popular that its scheduled 3-day run is extended for an extra day with proceeds from the fourth session going to the ASPCA.

The Jefferson Market Courthouse (Third Judicial District Courthouse) is completed at 425 Sixth Avenue in Greenwich Village to Victorian Gothic designs by Frederick Clarke Withers and Calvert Vaux. Part of a civic center that includes a jail and a public market, its tall belfry has a clock and serves as a fire-warning tower (*see* food market, 1929).

The first low-rent U.S. housing "project" opens in Brooklyn Heights, where businessman Alfred Tredway White, 31, has financed construction of cottages for middle-class workingmen at Hicks Street and Baltic, each 11.5 feet wide with six rooms. By 1880 White will have built 44 of the cottages for $1,150 each, exclusive of land, and be renting them at $14 per month, netting investors a 7 percent profit. He also builds the Tower Apartments—226 four-room units, each with a balcony gallery and indoor toilet, in six-story "sun-lighted tenements" around a central court with communal bathing facilities in their basement, renting them for $1.90 to $2.50 per week. White's Improved Dwellings Association in Manhattan will build a block of tenements in East 71st Street that will provide housing for 208 families and produce a return of 5 percent on investment.

The Manhattan Beach Hotel opens July 19 at the eastern end of Coney Island, where banker-developer Austin Corbin's Manhattan Beach Improvement Co. is turning a 600-acre salt marsh into a self-contained resort community. Designed by architect J. Pickering Putnam, the four-story Queen Anne structure has 350 rooms and soon attracts an upscale clientele that includes financiers August Belmont and Leonard W. Jerome (who enjoy its proximity to the Sheepshead Bay racetrack). Corbin will open the more opulent Oriental Hotel in 1880 and in 1882 will open the Argyle at Babylon; a notorious bigot, he bars blacks and Jews.

The *Real Estate Record and Builders' Guide* for October 13 carries a piece entitled "East Side West Side," saying that Manhattan's West Side seems destined to become "the cheap side of the city," being isolated from the main line of city development and cut off from the East Side by Central Park (*but see* Clark, 1879).

The New York Central Railroad erects a grain elevator on the Hudson River at the foot of 60th Street to receive wheat, corn, and other grain coming in by rail or barge from the Midwest for loading aboard ships to be sent abroad. New York remains a major port for shipping grain.

1878 Former Tammany Hall boss William M. Tweed dies of pleurisy and other ailments in the Ludlow Street Jail April 12 at age 65 (his offer to tell the whole truth if only he were allowed to die outside the jail was refused, and he has been paying $75 per week to occupy the warden's parlor) (*see* 1876). Editor E. L. Godkin of The *Nation* writes that this "villain" found "the seizure of the government and the malversation of its funds so easy at the outset that he was thrown off his guard. His successors here and elsewhere will not imitate him in this, but that he will have successors there is no doubt."

Elevated railways relieved street congestion with an alternative to horsecars and carriages. HARPER'S WEEKLY

Former mayor Ambrose C. Kingsland dies at New York October 13 at age 74.

Republican Edward Cooper, 54, wins election in the mayoralty race. Son of inventor-philanthropist Peter Cooper, now 87, he receives 79,986 votes as compared with 60,485 for Democrat August Schell.

Augusta Lewis's Women's Local #1 collapses after 9 years, and women are accepted into the printer's union on the same basis as men (*see* 1871). No other U.S. trade union except the Cigarmakers, headed by Samuel Gompers, admits women equally with men, and women are accepted only begrudgingly in both unions.

Philanthropist Theodore Roosevelt dies in agony of colon cancer at his new 6 East 57th Street house February 9 at age 46. His 19-year old son and namesake is summoned home from Harvard for the funeral at the Fifth Avenue Presbyterian Church, and the body is taken by ferry to Brooklyn for interment in Green-Wood Cemetery. E. L. Godkin, writing in The *Nation*, says of the deceased, "We believe, the mere fact that New York could even in these later, evil years produce him, and hold his love and devotion, has been to hundreds of those who knew him and watched his career a reason for not despairing of the future of the city."

Merchant (and onetime U.S. consul general in Japan) Townsend Harris dies at New York February 25 at age 73; financier and society leader Thomas W. Ludlow at Yonkers July 17 at age 78.

Nearly 10,500 U.S. business firms, including many at New York, go bankrupt as the economic depression that began in 1873 continues.

Stern's dry goods store moves to 110 West 23rd Street, between Fifth and Sixth avenues, near what is becoming a new Ladies' Mile (see 1867; Altman's, 1876). Stern's will be the city's largest department store until 1910 (see 1911).

Tiffany & Co. purchases what will be called the Tiffany Diamond—the largest and finest yellow diamond ever discovered. Found in South Africa's Kimberley Mine, it weighs 287.42 carats, Tiffany gemologist George Frederic Kunz will study it for a year before touching it, cutters at Paris next year will turn it into a 128.51-carat stone with 90 facets (most brilliant-cuts have only 58), and it will lead to a Tiffany tradition of cutting stones for brilliance rather than size (see Tiffany setting, 1886).

The newly founded United States Electric Lighting Co. places arc lights on an experimental basis in the main post office at the tip of City Hall Park, in the Park Avenue Hotel, and in the corridors of the Equitable Building, but the lights are too bright for indoor use and considered hazardous (see 1879). Electric street lights are installed on Broadway between 14th and 26th streets.

Thomas A. Edison works out methods for cheap production and transmission of electrical current and succeeds in subdividing current to make it adaptable to household use. Gas company shares plummet as news of Edison's work reaches Wall Street; he obtains $50,000 in financing from J. Pierpont Morgan, the Vanderbilt interests, and other investors. The Edison Electric Light Co. is founded October 15, and Edison receives half the stock in the company, incorporated later in the month with $300,000 in capital. Johns Hopkins professor Henry Rowland, 30, and Harvard professor John Trowbridge, 35, have helped Edison, who experiments with molybdenum, nickel, and platinum filaments as he searches for a lamp filament that will burn for extended periods of time in a high vacuum (see 1879).

Shipowner Edward Knight Collins dies at his Madison Avenue home January 22 at age 75, having sold his country seat at Larchmont 2 years ago and bought the house in town.

The Ninth Avenue Elevated begins running June 6 from Trinity Church to 58th Street. Its mahogany cars are equipped with brass rails, big silver-plated lamps whose acetylene gaslights are covered with white china shades, linoleum-covered floors, and comfortable cane seats that are replaced in winter by cushioned seats. Steam trains of the Metropolitan Elevated Railway (formerly the Gilbert Electric Railway Co.) provide much quicker transportation than do the horsecars below, and the new line will hook up within a decade to the Third Avenue El, opened in August by the New York Elevated Railway Co. between City Hall Park and 42nd Street. The financial recession that began in 1873 delayed construction of Rufus H. Gilbert's projected elevated line (see 1872), financiers forced him out of the company, and the Metropolitan Elevated Railway uses conventional steam locomotives. Architect-painter Jaspar Francis Cropsey, now 55, designs and supervises construction of the Sixth Avenue El stations; by next year the Ninth Avenue El will be a double-track road extending 6½ miles from Morris Street up Sixth to 53rd Street, west to Ninth Avenue (a spur continues up Sixth to 59th Street), and on to 155th Street, with a 63-foot high trestle, known as the suicide curve, carrying it from 109th Street and Columbus Avenue across 110th Street to Eighth Avenue, where it resumes its south-north course; apartment houses will rise up quickly along the route of the El, whose tracks by year's end have reached 129th Street (see 1880).

The Brooklyn, Flatbush & Coney Island Railroad begins running July 2, opening up Flatbush and other sections of Brooklyn to residential and commercial development (see Germania Land and Improvement Co., 1892).

An elevated railway begins running along the Bowery August 26; hot coals and oil drippings from its small steam engines shower down on the street below, and the Bowery, once a popular commercial and residential thoroughfare, begins its descent as respectable pedestrians avoid it.

Norolk, Conn.-born New York physician William Henry Welch, 28, at Bellevue Hospital opens the first U.S. pathology laboratory.

Brooklyn's Boys and Girls High School has its beginnings in the Central Grammar School, opened at the corner of Court and Livingston streets. The girls' division will move in 8 years to a new building at Norstrand Avenue between Macon and Halsey streets, where it will remain until it closes in 1964; the two divisions will be formally separated in 1891, and Boys High will move in 1892 to Madison Street between Marcy and Putnam avenues (see 1976).

The Metropolitan Telephone and Telegraph Co. is organized at New York with a central switching office in Manhattan to serve 271 subscribers (see 1877). New York's first telephone directory is published, and the city's telephone system will have 2,800 subscribers by 1880, 15,000 by 1896 (see 1896).

Remington Arms Co. improves the Remington typewriter of 1876 by adding a shift key system that employs upper- and lower-case letters on the same type bar. Wyckoff, Seamens, and Benedict buy Remington's typewriter business and found Remington Typewriter Co. (see Underwood, 1895).

J. Walter Thompson takes over the 14-year-old advertising firm Carlton and Smith that he joined in 1868 and begins representing general magazines (see 1868). Commodore Thompson's first advertisement will be for Prudential Insurance Co. (see commerce, 1875), and in 15 years he will control the advertising in 30 publications, mostly women's magazines (see Curtis, 1901).

Editor-poet William Cullen Bryant unveils a bust of Giuseppe Mazzini in Central Park in April, strikes his head in a fall as he enters a friend's home after the ceremonies, suffers a brain concussion, lapses into a coma, and dies June 12 at age 83 (see Bryant Park, 1884).

Painting: *Music and Literature* by Irish-born New York painter William Michael Harnett, 30, who gave up his work as a jewelry engraver 3 years ago and began exhibiting his still-life works, modeled on those of the 17th century Dutch *trompe l'oeil* painters.

Tiffany glass has its beginnings in a factory established by New York painter-craftsman Louis Comfort Tiffany, 30, son of the jeweler, who has studied with Venetian glassmaker Andrea Boldoni (see 1894).

Sculpture: a bust of the late Italian patriot Giuseppe Mazzini by Italian-born sculptor Giovanni Turini is unveiled in April beside Central Park's West Drive at 67th Street.

Theater: *Old Love Letters* by Detroit-born New York journalist-turned-playwright Bronson (Crocker) Howard, 35, 8/31 at the Park Theater, with Agnes Booth, Joseph Whiting; *The Banker's Daughter* by Bronson Howard 11/30 at the Union Square Theater, 137 perfs. (an extraordinary run for the times; Howard is the first U.S. playwright to deal seriously with the strains of business and home life).

The New York Symphony Society is founded by Leopold Damrosch, who invites New York-born violinist David Mannes, 12, to join (see 1885; Oratorio Society, 1873; Carnegie Hall, 1891; Mannes, 1899).

Bank robbers hold up the Manhattan Savings Institution October 27 and make off with a record $3 million. Police indict one George Leonidas Leslie, alias Western George; Howe & Hummel defends him and receives $90,000—the largest fee thus far collected

by any criminal law firm (see 1869). Howe & Hummel has built a thriving practice representing arsonists, brothel keepers, bucket-shop proprietors, confidence men, forgers, safecrackers, and other members of the city's underworld. The pair will continue to serve as the mouthpieces of New York's organized crime until 1907 (see 1884), becoming prominent also in divorce cases and representing such clients as P. T. Barnum, John Barrymore, Edwin Booth, John Drew, Ned Harrigan, Sir Henry Irving, Lillie Langtree, Tony Pastor, and Lester Wallach.

The Society for the Prevention of Crime is founded to help police arrest gamblers, prostitutes, and saloonkeepers who violate the Sunday closing laws. It will be led until his death in 1891 by Howard Crosby.

Manhattan investor Charles H. Cheever and some associates buy an 80-acre section of upland in the southwestern part of Far Rockaway, Queens; they will enclose it as an exclusive park, complete with lodges and gate entrances, and call it "Wavecrest" (construction will begin in 1880). Bordered on the south by the Atlantic Ocean, the development will have "cottages" that insurance executives, railroad presidents, and Wall Street investors will buy for prices ranging between $5,000 and $30,000; the estates will not be broken up, streets laid down, and apartment houses erected for more than 40 years.

The Brooklyn-based iron contracting firm Post & McCord Co. uses steam-powered derricks for the first time to raise iron beams in constructing the Morse Building in lower Manhattan that will be completed in 1880.

The Woman's Home opens in April on the west side of Fourth Avenue between 32nd and 33rd streets. Built with funds provided by the late merchant prince A. T. Stewart, who died 2 years ago, the residential hotel for working women is a seven-story structure with penthouse, has 502 sleeping rooms, a large interior garden graced with ornate fountains, amd eight reception rooms, parlors, and dining rooms, but rates are $6 to $10 per week at a time when working girls earn only $5 to $15 per week. Residents may not bring in pets, sewing machines, pianos, memorabilia, or other expressions of individuality, and they are not permitted to entertain gentlemen callers. The *Daily Tribune* announces in late May that the Woman's Home will be converted into the Park Avenue Hotel, open to both sexes, and it will continue as such until it is razed in 1927.

Architect Richard Upjohn dies at Garrison, N.Y., August 17 at age 76; his son Richard M. (Mitchell), 50, carries on his practice.

Frederick Law Olmsted, now 55, sails for Europe in January to begin a 3-month leave of absence on his doctor's orders. Central Park's board of commissioners dismissed him in late December, it receives a long letter signed by such prominent men as August Belmont, Henry Havemeyer, Henry Holt, and Whitelaw Reid "requesting reconsideration in depriving the city of Mr. Olmsted's services," but Olmsted himself has given up hope of resisting Tammany Hall and does not join in the protest. The great park that has occupied his efforts for 21 years is essentially complete, awaiting only the finishing touches of nature to bring its plantings to maturity.

Fire alarm boxes are installed throughout Manhattan, making it unnecessary to maintain fire lookout towers.

The 18th century manor house of Castleton in northern Staten Island is destroyed by fire December 25.

Anti-vice crusader Anthony Comstock of 1872 Comstock Law fame approaches a reputed abortionist who has a luxurious mansion at 657 Fifth Avenue (52nd Street). Hiding his identity, he says he is desperately poor and will be ruined if his wife has another child. English-born brothel-keeper Anna A. Trow Somers Lohman, 65, alias Mme. Restell, supplies Comstock with drugs and contraceptives. He has her indicted and refuses a $40,000 offer to drop his charges, Mme. Restell posts bail and returns to her house, newspaper stories convince her that she will be convicted, and she slits her throat in her bathtub April 1.

1879 Former state assembly speaker Alonzo B. Cornell, now 47, is elected governor, succeeding Lucius Robinson; he secures 418,567 votes to Robinson's 375,790. Gov. Cornell's 3-year administration will be notable for a bill providing for a public restaurant in Central Park.

Abolitionist-reformer William Lloyd Garrison dies at New York May 24 at age 73. He has worked since 1865 for woman suffrage and better treatment of Native Americans.

U.S. specie payments resume January 1 for the first time since the end of 1861. An era of finance capitalism that will last for more than half a century begins in the United States.

Progress and Poverty by Philadelpia-born economist Henry George, 40, points out that while America has

Spires of a new St. Patrick's Cathedral soared above Fifth Avenue, replacing the old St. Pat's in Mulberry Street.

become richer and richer most Americans have become poorer and poorer. Appointed New York State inspector of gas meters 3 years ago, George remembers the poverty he saw on a visit to the city a decade ago. He has sought to explain the anomalies of capitalistic economics, analyzed wealth in terms of land ownership, and determined that landlords who demand rents on their land violate economic law to the detriment of general prosperity. Since land values represent monopoly power, says George, replacing all other forms of taxation with a "single tax" on land, a tax equal to the land's rental, would yield enough revenue to fund ordinary government operations, produce surplus revenues for public-works projects, prevent speculative land investment, free industry from taxation, allow economic laws to operate freely, and lead to a more equitable distribution of wealth.

Financier Daniel Drew dies in obscurity at New York September 18 at age 82, having gone bankrupt in 1876 after contributing handsomely to the Methodist

Church and establishing the Drew Theological Seminary at Madison, N.J., and the Drew Seminary for Young Ladies at his native Carmel, N.Y.

Metropolitan Life Insurance Co. of New York begins offering small policies for wage-earners and pioneers mass insurance coverage in an age of high mortality (see 1868). Agents collect small weekly premiums in cash from the working classes who most need insurance protection. The company will attract 554 English agents, who will emigrate with their families, and within 3 years Metropolitan Life will have increased the number of its district offices from 3 to 50 (see architecture, 1893).

Best & Co. has its beginnings in the Lilliputian Bazaar, opened at 315 Sixth Avenue by retail merchants Albert Best and James A. Smith (see 1947).

F. W. Woolworth Co. has its beginnings at Watertown, N.Y., where store clerk Frank Winfield Woolworth, 27, persuades his employer to install a counter whose goods are all priced at 5¢. He then induces one of the firm's principals to lend him $400 with which to open a Utica store at which all items are priced at 5¢. The store fails in 3 months because it is badly located, but the same partner stakes Woolworth to try a five-and-dime store that opens at Lancaster, Pa., June 21 and proves successful as Woolworth pioneers in displaying merchandise where customers can examine it and selling it at fixed prices. Stores at Philadelphia, Harrisburg, and York, Pa., and at Newark, N.J., will have indifferent success, but when he opens five-and-dimes at Buffalo, Erie, Scranton, and some other cities Woolworth will tap the low-income market and begin to build a worldwide chain of open-shelf, self-service stores that will employ thousands of women (see 1896).

The Fulton Municipal Gas Co. is founded in Brooklyn but does not start in the usual way by buying a small territory for itself. Instead, it lays long mains in the most populous and prosperous areas of the city and offers to sell gas wholesale to the smaller companies. The competing companies will soon be engaged in a debilitating price war (see Brooklyn Union Gas, 1895).

The Board of Aldermen asks the municipal gas commission to investigate the feasibility of using arc lights to illuminate city streets (see 1878).

The incandescent bulb that Edison demonstrates October 21 has a loop of cotton thread impregnated with lampblack and baked for hours in a carbonizing oven. This "evacuated glass globe" is much like one pioneered by German chemist Herman Sprengel in 1865 (see Edison, 1878). After it has burned for 45 hours Edison is sure it will burn for at least 100. His bulb is announced December 21, Edison Electric Co. stock soars, and the inventor says electricity will make lighting so cheap that only the rich will be able to afford candles. But coal gas, coal oil, kerosene, candlewax, and whale oil will continue to light the world until the development of dynamos, fuses, and sockets (see 1880; 1882).

The Third Avenue El reaches 129th Street only 1 year after reaching 67th Street.

The United Hospital Fund has its beginnings in the Hospital Saturday and Sunday Association, established to promote economy in hospital management and to collect alms for treating patients unable to pay. It will take the name United Hospital Fund in 1916 and expand throughout the city.

Index Medicus is founded at New York by *Publishers' Weekly* editor Frederick Leypoldt, whose Index will lose money but be continued because of its great value and become the *Quarterly Cumulative Index Medicus* in 1927.

Pencil manufacturer John Eberhard Faber dies at his Staten Island home March 2 at age 56. He has introduced machinery to reduce the need for manual labor, attached rubber erasers to his pencils, and built a second factory at Newark, N.J., to produce erasers and rubber bands.

The Union School of Stenography and Typewriting opened at New York by schoolteacher Mary Foot Seymour, 33, is the first U.S. secretarial school whose students are all women. Only 5 percent of copyists, bookkeepers, accountants, and office clerks are women, but Seymour has taught herself shorthand and become a court reporter. She has hired women to transcribe her notes into longhand, but sees that it will save time if they can be transcribed directly on a typewriter. By the end of the century women office workers will far outnumber men.

New York merchants urge Bell Telephone Co. to open its exchange for calls at 5 o'clock in the morning rather than 8 and to remain open later than 6 o'clock in the evening (Fulton Fish Market dealers lead the appeal).The multiple switchboard invented by U.S. engineer Leroy B. Firman will make the telephone a commercial success and help increase the number of U.S. telephone subscribers from 50,000 in 1880 to 250,000 in 1890.

Frederick Leypoldt sells his *Publishers Weekly* to Massachusetts-born CCNY graduate Richard Rogers

Bowker, 30, who retains Leypoldt as editor (*see* 1872; *Library Journal*, 1880).

 Painting: *The Bulls and Bears in the Market* by New York painter William Holbrook Beard.

 Theater: *Hearts of Oak* by actor-playwright James A. Herne (originally James Ahern), 40, and San Francisco-born playwright-producer David Belasco, 25 (they have rewritten the play *Chums* adapted from Henry J. Leslie's English drama *The Mariner Compass*), 3/29 at the Fifth Avenue Theater, with Herne, Katharine Corcoran Herne, 22 (James's wife in her New York debut). Herne has made his reputation playing with his sister-in-law Lucille Western in the tear jerker *East Lynne*; the composite cast represents a departure from the stock-company system that will be obsolete by the end of the century (to 4/24, but the mawkish drama will be a perennial favorite); Ada Rehan, now 19, makes her New York debut in May in *L'Assomoir* and soon becomes the leading lady for Augustin Daly's repertory company, playing opposite John Drew; Massachusetts-born actor Otis Skinner, 21, makes his New York debut at Niblo's Gardens. He will play more than 325 parts in addition to many Shakespearean roles in the course of a notable career; *Wives* by Bronson Howard (an adaptation of a 17th century play by Molière) 10/18 at Daly's Theater (Augustin Daly has converted the old Broadway Theater into a new house bearing his name).

Stage musical: *The Mulligan Guards' Ball* 1/13 at the Théâtre Comique, with Ed Harrigan and Tony Hart, who opened in a variety show at Chicago's Academy of Music in mid-July of 1873 and have toured the country mocking the pretensions of men who wear military uniforms. Harrigan and Hart will dominate vaudeville (*see* 1881) until Hart dies in 1891, Dan Collyer will replace Hart, and the new team will continue for another 5 years.

Opera: *The Pirates of Penzance* (or *The Slave of Duty*) 12/31 at the Fifth Avenue Theater, with Gilbert and Sullivan arias that include "Model of a Modern Major-General" and "A Policeman's Lot Is Not a Happy One." Lyricist William Schwenck Gilbert, now 43, and composer-conductor Arthur S. Sullivan, now 37, have come to the city to direct and conduct a production of *H.M.S. Pinafore* (it opened last year in London) and have been staying in a room at 45 East 20th Street.

Madison Square Garden gets its name May 30 as railroad heir William K. Vanderbilt, 30, acquires the 5-year-old Gilmore's Garden, renames it, and announces that it will be used primarily as an ath-letic center. The Garden will be the scene of the National Horse Show beginning in 1884 (*see* 1887).

 The new St. Patrick's Cathedral is dedicated by John Cardinal McCloskey May 25 after 26 years of planning and construction. Designed in the shape of a Latin cross by James Renwick, the white marble structure is 332 feet long and 174 feet wide; it occupies a full block at the outskirts of the city on the east side of Fifth Avenue (50th Street to 51st) on land purchased in 1809 by the late Father Anthony Kohlmann. St. Patrick's will remain the largest Roman Catholic church in the United States and the seat of the Archdiocese of New York; the circular rose window above its entrance is 26 feet in diameter, its nave is 108 feet long and 48 feet wide, its sanctuary has a bronze baldachin 57 feet high, its spires will not be completed until 1888 (the north tower will hold the cathedral's 19 bells and the spires will dominate Manhattan's skyline until the 1930s), its Lady Chapel will be added in 1906 (*see* entrance doors, 1949).

The state legislature at Albany enacts a Tenement House Law that requires every apartment bedroom to have a window (*see* 1867). The legislature expands the authority of New York City's 9-year-old Board of Health to oversee construction of tenement housing. The trade journal *Plumber and Sanitary Engineer* sponsored a competition last year for the best design of a tenement to fit a standard building lot measuring 100 feet by 25, the winner was New York-born architect James E. Ware, and his model "dumbbell" tenement design will quickly become the standard. Five to seven stories high, the tenements will have 14 rooms per floor, with two four-room apartments in front, two three-room apartments in back, and two toilets near the center of each floor to be shared by the tenants. The bedrooms all have windows, but 10 of the 14 rooms open onto air shafts only three to five feet wide, created by indenting the hallway sections of abutting tenements; little light or air reaches the apartments, the air shafts often become filled with refuse, and they become fire hazards (*see* 1901).

The Benedick apartment house is completed at 80 Washington Square to designs by McKim, Mead & Bigelow. Iron merchant Lucius Tuckerman has commissioned the six-story structure that opens in the fall with 33 bachelor apartments (rents: $28 to $45.50 per month), and has named it for the confirmed bachelor in Shakespeare's *Much Ado About Nothing* (boarding-house operators and apartment-house owners look askance at bachelors). An elevator runs night and day, maid and bootblack services are available, a janitor in the basement provides breakfast, and the four studios on Benedick's top floor soon attract painters Winslow Homer, Albert Pinkham Ryder, and J. Alden Weir along with artist John LaFarge, whose glass factory is nearby at 39 West Fourth Street.

Civil engineer Gen. Egbert L. Viele writes that Murray Hill, for so long "regarded as a synonym of fashion," will in time "be more strictly synonymous with shabby gentility." The upper West Side, says the former Civil War general, is "the section of the city that has been held in reserve until the time when the progress of wealth and refinement shall have attained that period of development when our citizens can appreciate and are ready to take advantage of the situation . . . Moreover, the entire region combines in its general aspect all that is magnificent in the leading capitals of Europe. In our Central Park, we have the fine Prater of Vienna, in our grand Boulevard [Broadway] the rival of the finest avenues of the gay capital of France, in our Riverside Avenue the equivalent of the Chiara of Naples and the Corso of Rome, while the beautiful 'Unter den Linden' of Berlin and the finest portions of the West End of London are reproduced again and again" (see 1880).

McKim, Mead & White is established in September by New York architects Charles Follen McKim, 32, William Rutherford Mead, 33, and Stanford White, 26. The firm will become famous for such buildings as the Century, Harvard, Metropolitan, Players, and University clubs in midtown Manhattan, some Columbia University buildings, railroad stations, bridges, and at least one municipal government building. By 1892 it will be the world's largest architectural firm, employing 120 draftsmen.

The Van Corlear apartment house goes up on the blockfront occupying the west side of Seventh Avenue between 55th and 56th streets. Built at a cost of $300,000 by Singer Manufacturing Co. magnate Edward S. Clark, it has been designed by New Brunswick, N.J.-born architect Henry Janeway Hardenbergh, 29.

Edward S. Clark reads a paper at a meeting of the West Side Association December 20, extolling the merits of diversity and predicting that the West Side will combine apartment buildings with single-family dwellings to house rich and poor, "some splendidly, many elegantly, and all comfortably . . . the architecture should be ornate, solid and permanent . . . the principle of economic combination should be employed to the greatest extent possible" (see 1877; Dakota, 1884).

Real estate developer William H. DeForest purchases the 30-acre Hamilton Grange property in upper Manhattan and divides it into 300 lots (see 1833); developer Amos Cotting buys the lot occupied by the Grange itself (see 1889).

The first milk bottles appear in Brooklyn, where the Echo Farms Dairy delivers milk in glass bottles instead of measuring it into the pitchers of housewives and serving-maids from barrels carried in milk wagons. Some competitors will soon follow suit.

Gage & Tollner's opens at Brooklyn. The seafood house of restaurateurs Charles M. Gage and Eugene Tollner attracts New York notables who cross the East River by ferry to enjoy oysters, clams, lobster bisque, crabmeat Virginia, scallops, lobster, terrapin, and other aquatic dishes. "Our Cooking Strictly to Order," its menus will proclaim for more than a century (it will move in 1892 to 374 Fulton Street, opposite Borough Hall).

1880 Former mayor George Opdyke dies at New York June 12 at age 74. As mayor during the draft riots of 1863, he stood firm against the rioters.

Sen. Roscoe Conkling (R. N.Y.) goes to the Republican convention at Chicago in hopes of gaining the presidential nomination for former president Grant, who is in Chicago with his wife, Julia; she urges her husband to appear on the convention floor, he declines, Conkling bungles some matters of protocol, the delegates are reluctant to depart from the precedent set by George Washington, President Hayes is widely unpopular, and after more than 100 ballots the nomination goes to Civil War general James Abram Garfield, 48, of Ohio. With former Collector of the City of New York Chester A. Arthur as his running mate, Garfield wins a narrow victory over the Democratic candidate Winfield Scott, another Civil War general, who loses by fewer than 100,000 votes. New York's votes make the difference: Brooklyn's Organization of Young Republicans has campaigned for Garfield and Arthur with prominent support from Palmyra, N.Y.-born lawyer Horace Edward Deming, 30, who seeks to establish an organization for the betterment of local government in Brooklyn (see 1882).

Merchant William R. Grace wins election as mayor with support from Tammany Hall, narrowly defeating his Republican rival William Dowd, who receives 98,715 votes to Grace's 101,760 (see commerce, 1866). Now 49, Grace becomes the city's first Irish-born Catholic mayor.

Former New York congressman Thomas C. (Collier) Platt, 47, wins election to the U.S. Senate with help from his friend and longtime political ally Sen. Roscoe Conkling, who is the state's Republican Party leader. The two will become leaders of the "Stalwart" faction of the Republican Party (*see* 1881).

The Salvation Army opens its first New York mission. Founded at London under that name 2 years ago, it had its beginnings 15 years ago in a Whitechapel, London, mission started by itinerant English religious revivalist William Booth, then 36, who said, "A man may be down but he's never out" (*see* Volunteers of America, 1896).

Lazard Frères opens a New York office under the direction of Alexander Weill, a cousin of the French-born Lazard brothers who began it in 1848 as a New Orleans dry-goods store; the Paris-based firm moved to San Francisco in 1849, established itself at Paris in 1852, opened a London branch in 1877, and will grow to be a major investment bank (*see* 1926).

Financier and reformer Joseph Seligman dies at New Orleans April 25 at age 60. His New York-born son Edwin (Robert Anderson) Seligman turns 19 April 25, graduated from Columbia last year, and will become a leading economist.

Thomas Edison obtains a patent on his 1879 incandescent bulb. Legal technicalities force the creation of an Edison Electric Co. subsidiary, Edison Electric Illuminating Co., and Edison Electric Light will remain a holding company that controls Edison's patents. A mile of Broadway is illuminated by Brush electric arc lights December 20, and although arc lights are glary, emit dangerous gases, and are suitable only for outdoor lighting in public spaces, it is clear that electricity rather than gas will be the illuminant of the future (*see* 1881).

The Manhattan Elevated Railway Co. opens its Second Avenue line March 1, having gained control of all Manhattan El lines last year; initially connecting Chatham Square with 65th Street, it reaches 129th Street August 16. The Third Avenue El that opened in 1878 is extended to connect with the Grand Central Depot and with the Long Island Rail Road's ferry terminal on the East River at 34th Street. The Ninth Avenue El reaches 155th Street, with stops at 66th, 72nd, 81st, 93rd, and 104th. Four-car elevated steam trains rumble up and down Second, Third, Sixth, and Ninth avenues from 5:30 o'clock until midnight, carrying 60.8 million revenue passengers in light green cars whose seats are upholstered in dark brown (horsedrawn surface carriers carry 148.6 million). The fare is 10¢ (5¢ during rush hours), the Els create a good deal of noise and vibra-

tion, they drop ashes, sparks, oil, and cinders on pedestrians below, but they provide much quicker transportation than horsecars or other surface conveyances (*see* 1886; politics, 1882).

The Suburban Rapid Transit Co. organized in March proposes to connect the Bronx with Manhattan via an elevated railway line (*see* 1891).

Columbia College establishes a graduate school of political science (*see* 1857; philosophy, 1890).

The 17-year-old Brooklyn Historical Society (still called the Long Island Historical Society) moves into a new building at 128 Pierrepont Street designed by architect George B. Post (who has studied under Richard Morris Hunt) with an auditorium, offices, a handsome second-story library, and a fourth-story museum. (The LIHS will not take the name BHS until 1985.)

The Society of Ethical Culture adds elementary grades to the free kindergarten it started last year. It will admit tuition-paying pupils beginning in 1890 (*see* 1895).

Publisher Frank Leslie of *Leslie's Illustrated Weekly* dies at New York January 10 at age 58, leaving debts amounting to more than $250,000 (his business, begun in 1854, was forced into receivership in 1877). New York-born editor (and athlete) James Edward Sullivan, 19, joined Leslie 2 years ago and will continue with the publishing house until 1889. Leslie's second wife, Miriam Florence Felline Leslie, now 43, who had had three previous husbands before marrying Leslie in 1874, will have her name legally changed to Frank Leslie in 1882, and will head the publication until she sells it to a syndicate in 1895 (*see* human rights, 1914); *New York Tribune* literary editor and social reformer George Ripley dies at New York July 4 at age 77. He has held the position since 1849.

The *Dial* begins publication, taking its name from the transcendalist journal published at Boston. It will absorb a Chicago literary review in 1898 and become a prominent literary journal (*see* 1929).

The Century Co. is founded at New York by former Scribner & Co. editor Roswell Smith, 51, who buys out Charles Scribner, Jr. with $100,000 of the $110,000 he has received from a railroad company for some land he owned out West. Smith will begin publishing The *Century Magazine* late next year.

The *Library Journal* is founded at New York by Richard R. Bowker and Frederick Leypoldt of *Publishers' Weekly* in partnership with former Amherst College librarian Melvil Dewey (originally Melville

Louis Kossuth Dewey), 28, who 4 years ago published *A Classification and Subject Index for Cataloguing and Arranging the Books and Pamphlets of a Library* (the Dewey Decimal System) (*see* 1879). They also help organize the American Library Association (ALA). Dewey will work for a few years as an editor of the new publication that Bowker will edit for more than 50 years.

The Metropolitan Museum of Art opens March 30 in a red-brick building put up a few years ago at the eastern edge of Central Park at 82nd Street for the now defunct American Academy of Music and Art (*see* 1872). The New-York Historical Society was offered the Central Park site by the city in 1868 but rejected it, saying that its commitment to private-sector support precluded acceptance. Hamilton Square would have been a preferable site for the Met but has been divided into lots for private houses and is now on the city's tax rolls. Calvert Vaux and Jacob Wrey Mould will make some changes in the building, whose masonry will be embedded in the museum as it grows (*see* 1888).

"Cleopatra's Needle" arrives from Egypt July 20 aboard the S.S. *Dessoug* as a gift from the khedive to the United States. The 69-foot, red granite obelisk (it has no connection with the Egyptian queen of antiquity) weighs between 193 and 220 tons and was erected by Thutmose III at Heliopolis in about 1471 B.C. Roman soldiers moved it to Alexandria in 12 B.C., the U.S. consul to Egypt acquired it by extortion from the country's reluctant khedive 2 years ago, and former U.S. naval commander Henry Honeychurch Gorringe, 39, backed by railroad magnate William H. Vanderbilt, has masterminded the stupendous feat of transporting the monolith to New York. Moored in the Hudson off 23rd Street, the *Dessoug* moves at the end of the month to a pier at the end of 51st Street, anchors at the foot of 96th Street, and discharges the Alexandrian obelisk September 16 for its trip to Central Park. A parade of 9,000 Freemasons marches up Fifth Avenue October 9 for a cornerstone ceremony on Graywacke Knoll near the new Metropolitan Museum of Art (Gorringe and Vanderbilt are both Masons, as are Mayor Cooper, the police commissioner, and many other local politicians); the obelisk inches along, reaching the West Boulevard (Broadway) October 27, Central Park November 25, Fifth Avenue December 16, and 82nd Street December 22 (*see* 1881).

Sculpture: a statue of Robert Burns by Scottish sculptor Sir John Steell, 76, is installed near the south end of Central Park's Mall, close to a marble statue of Sir Walter Scott that Steell created in 1872 to win a competition. Steell has made the new work expressly for New York, and resident Scots have presented the works to the city.

The first photographic reproduction in a newspaper appears March 4 in the *New-York Daily Graphic*. "A Scene in Shantytown, New York" is printed from a halftone produced by photographing through a fine screen with dots in the photograph representing shadows (*see* press halftones, 1897).

Theater: *Hazel Kirke* by Buffalo-born playwright (James Morrison) Steele Mackaye, 37, 2/4 at the Madison Square Theater, 486 perfs. (a new record). Fire destroys the drop curtain 2/26 as the audience is taking its seats, but firemen extinguish the blaze and the performance goes on as scheduled.

Publisher Whitelaw Reid of the *New-York Tribune* invites Michigan-born Cincinnati music critic Henry Edward Krehbiel, 26, to join the paper as music critic. Krehbiel will retain the position for 43 years, writing books and showing appreciation for black spirituals as well as for younger classical composers.

Clinton, Iowa-born soprano Lillian Russell (originally Helen Louise Leonard), 18, makes her debut as "the English Ballad Singer" 11/22 at Tony Pastor's Opera House to begin a career that will continue until 1912.

The Cosmopolitan Club has its beginnings in an organization founded by New York women to provide their female domestic help with a gathering place. The organization will evolve into a women's club whose members will for the most part be professionals and businesswomen.

Chinatown's first tong begins operations, although the area probably has no more than 800 residents. The tong is a criminal organization that controls gambling (especially fan-tan and lotteries), promotes opium use, settles local disputes, and deals with the police and politicians (*see* 1875). The On Leong Tong and Hip Sing Tong will battle until 1926 for control of opium traffic and gambling in Chinatown (*see* 1924).

The 10-story Morse Building (later the Nassau-Beekman Building) is completed at 12 Beekman Street, northeast corner Nassau Street, where the late Samuel F. B. Morse first experimented with his electric telegraph. Designed by Silliman & Farnsworth and built on speculation by Morse's nephew Sidney E. Morse and his cousin G. Livingston Morse, the building is 85 feet wide, 70 feet deep, and rises 165 feet high. Its bearing walls are of unusually thick brick, and some observers say the fireproof masonry and terra-cotta structure is the tallest straight-walled building in the world (it will be increased to 12 stories in 1901).

The Seventh Regiment Armory opens April 26 on Fourth Avenue between 66th and 67th streets, extending east to Lexington Avenue, with a 187- by 290-foot drill hall. New York-born architect Charles W. Clinton, 42, studied under the late Richard Upjohn and has designed the structure for the regiment that protected Washington, D.C., in 1861 when it was cut off by rebel forces in Maryland; members of the Astor, Morgan, Stewart, Vanderbilt, and other families were alarmed by the nationwide rail strike of 1877 and raised more than $500,000 for the armory's construction.

Gen. Egbert L. Viele proposes to the West Side Association that Eleventh Avenue be called West End Avenue north of 63rd Street, where it is clear of railroad tracks (see 1879). The name is changed officially February 10, but Viele's "West End" remains largely a wasteland of asylums, athletic fields, breweries, grain elevators, rocky promontories, swamps, and slaughterhouses.

The Sherwood Studios completed at the southeast corner of 57th Street and Sixth Avenue is a seven-story brick apartment house with 44 units designed specifically for artists. Bootmaker-banker-turned real estate developer John H. Sherwood has designed and put up the building at the urging of painter Frederick Church, the ceilings in its rooms are 15 feet high, and it is equipped with an oversize elevator (to accommodate large canvases and pieces of sculpture), electric bell signals, speaking tubes, and gas service. The Sherwood will become a center of the city's artistic community and stand for 80 years.

The Rembrandt Studios open on the south side of 57th Street between Sixth and Seventh avenues. Designed by French-born architect Philip Gengembre Hubert, 50, the co-operative apartment house for artists is a great success, despite the fact that it has only one bath for as many as four bedrooms. Hubert (he has adopted his English grandmother's surname) received a patent in his 20s for a self-fastening button, sold it for $120,000, went abroad after the Civil War to study architecture after a career teaching French, and 10 years ago started a New York architectural firm in partnership with James L. Pirsson (see Spanish Flats, 1883).

A Manhattan apartment house completed at the corner of Second Avenue and 86th Street will stand for more than 120 years.

Half the city's population is packed into tenements on the Lower East Side, an area that accounts for a disproportionate 70 percent of the city's deaths. Most affluent New Yorkers live in row houses (an ostentatious brownstone is typically five or six stories high, has 16 to 20 rooms, and occupies more than 90 percent of its lot); less affluent middle-class residents occupy multiple-dwelling houses that include boarding houses.

Riverside Park is completed in May along the Hudson River between 72nd and 153rd streets after 10 years of lawsuits and 7 years of changes in the design submitted by Frederick Law Olmsted in 1873. Claiming that the city still owes him money, the contractor blocks off cross streets with derricks and timbers to deny access to the new park, but a crowd breaks through the barricade at night and enjoys the promenade, disturbed only by the noise and odors coming from trains on the New York Central tracks along the river's edge.

The city's 40,000 horses produce 400 tons of manure per day, to say nothing of 20,000 gallons of urine (and nearly 200 carcasses). The odor of horse droppings is everywhere, carried into houses in the form of dried manure that blows into the cuffs of trousers and the folds of skirts (see Waring's "white wings," 1895).

The Fulton Market is torn down and replaced (see 1822; 1907).

Thomas' English Muffins are introduced by English-born baker Samuel Bath Thomas, who opens a retail bakery in 20th Street between Ninth and Tenth avenues and delivers to hotels and restaurants by pushcart.

P. J. Clarke's opens at the northeast corner of Third Avenue and 55th Street, where the saloon will continue into the 21st century (see 1945).

The White Horse Tavern opens in a wood-frame building at the corner of Hudson and West 11th streets in Greenwich Village.

Nearly 550,000 English and 440,000 Irish immigrants enter the United States; most arrive through New York, whose population has risen to 1,206,299—up from 942,292 in 1870. It is the first U.S. city to have a population of more than 1 million.

1881 Sen. Roscoe Conkling (R. N.Y.) and Sen. Thomas C. Platt (R. N.Y) resign their Senate seats in May when

President Garfield refuses to follow Conkling's advice with regard to the appointment of a new Collector of the Port of New York and sends federal appointees instead. Now 51, Conkling fought Garfield's nomination and refused to support the party ticket last year; he retires from politics. President Garfield is shot by a disappointed office seeker at a Washington, D.C., railroad station July 2, and Vice President Chester A. Arthur, now 51, is sworn in as president by Judge John Brady of the state supreme court September 19 at the vice president's 123 Lexington Avenue town house following Garfield's death at Elberon, N.J. Arthur is the first president since George Washington to take the oath of office at New York (see Pendleton Act, 1883).

Theodore Roosevelt, now 23, wins election to the state assembly at Albany, running in Manhattan's 21st ("brownstone") district and defeating his Democratic opponent, a former director of the lunatic asylum on Blackwell's Island who has been sacked for incompetence.

The United Brotherhood of Carpenters union is founded at New York by Peter McGuire to fight for an 8-hour day and other benefits. An outgrowth of earlier carpenters' unions, it will grow to represent architectural woodworkers, general carpenters, machine operators, millwrights, and stair builders.

Anti-Semitism appears in America; German Jews have mixed on equal terms with other German immigrants for generations, New York's Jewish community has reached 80,000, most of it German, but it still represents only 4 percent of the city's total population and by 1910 an influx of Jews from eastern Europe will have raised the percentage to 25.

Former president Ulysses S. Grant becomes a silent partner in the new Wall Street brokerage firm Grant & Ward started by his son Buck (Ulysses, Jr.) with financial "genius" Ferdinand Ward, each of whom (by Ward's account) has invested $100,000. Grant borrows $50,000 from his friend Cornelius Kingsland Garrison, now nearly 72, to acquire a seventh share in the business and then puts in another $50,000 obtained from his wife, Julia, and younger son Jesse; the firm prospers, almost entirely because most people believe the "Grant" in its name is that of the war hero (who actually plays little part in it except to sign papers he has not read). Ward will turn out to be a manipulator and confidence man who talks about huge profits and keeps his investors happy by paying interest out of principal while using incoming funds to finance personal extravagances

that include a lavish Manhattan town house and a country estate at Stamford, Conn. (see 1884).

Fahnestock & Co. is founded by New York banker's son William Fahnestock, 24, whose father, Horace C. Fahnestock, 46, is a former Jay Cooke partner and now serves as a director of First National Bank of New York.

The American Horse Exchange opens on Long Acre Square, extending from Broadway to Seventh Avenue between 50th and 51st streets. Built by William K. Vanderbilt and a group of millionaire horsemen who include Frederic Bronson, William Jay, and George Wetmore, the two-story brick building provides a center for trading thoroughbred horses.

Thomas Edison's Edison Electric Light Co. creates a subsidiary (The Edison Co. for Isolated Lighting) to furnish factories and large department stores with individual power plants (see 1880). Edison moves in the summer to 24 Gramercy Park South and will remain there until he relocates to New Jersey in 1883 (see 1882).

Henry Villard gains control of the Northern Pacific by means of a pool he has formed to monopolize Pacific Northwest transportation. Now 46, Villard came to New York from his native Bavaria at age 18, changed his name from Ferdinand Heinrich Gustav Hilgard to avoid being returned and drafted into the army, and worked for years as a journalist for the New-Yorker Staats-Zeitung, James Gordon Bennett's Herald, and Horace Greeley's Tribune (see 1883; 1901).

Brooklyn's Methodist Episcopal Hospital is founded by George I. Seney. The nonsectarian hospital will erect buildings on Seventh Avenue at 6th Street in the Park Slope section, establish a dispensary in 1895, and soon be caring for 18,000 indigent patients per year.

The American Museum of Natural History's new (third) president engages a taxidermist to create dramatic new displays that will attract far more interest than the specimens displayed heretofore (see 1877). Railroad securities broker Morris Ketchum Jesup, 51, supports Albert Bickmore's idea of having lectures on nature for schoolteachers, will keep the museum open on Sundays, and will appoint zoologist Joel E. Allen as curator of mammalogy and ornithology (see Osborn, 1891).

Western Union Telegraph is created at New York by a consolidation of Western Union Co. with two smaller telegraph companies to form a giant monopoly (*see* 1866). Financier Jay Gould and railroad magnate William H. Vanderbilt have effected the consolidation (*see* Postal Telegraph, 1886).

Financier Henry Villard acquires a controlling interest in the 80-year-old *New-York Evening Post*; he hires Carl Schurz and Horace White as editors (*see* 1883; 1900).

The *United Irishman* begins publication at New York under the direction of Jeremiah O'Donovan Rossa, now 49, who has taken up residence at 194 Richmond Terrace, Brighton (*see* politics, 1870). His fiery editorials urge the use of assassination and dynamite as the only way to obtain Irish independence (*see* 1915).

The *Nation* becomes the weekly edition of the *New-York Evening Post* and its editor, E. L. Godkin, now 49, becomes associate editor of the *Post* (*see* 1865; 1883).

Scribner's Monthly editor Josiah G. Holland dies at New York October 12 at age 62. His publication becomes independent of publisher Charles Scribner's Sons, changes its name to the *Century Illustrated Magazine*, employs a new engraving process that will give it more visual appeal, runs a series of memoirs by Civil War veterans from both sides of that bloody conflict, and raises circulation to 250,000 (*see* 1930).

The Judge magazine begins publication October 29. *Puck* cartoonists who include James A. Wales have started the new 10¢ magazine of humor, politics, and satire, attacking corruption but lampooning immigrants with anti-Semitic slurs. Publisher Isaac M. Gregory will support the Republican Party and increase circulation to 85,000 by the turn of the century (*see* 1922).

Il Progresso Italo-Americano begins publication at New York, whose Italian population remains small. Pisa-born *padrone* Carlo Barsotti has founded the paper that will grow to become the largest-circulation foreign-language daily in the city (*see* Columbus Day, 1892).

 Fiction: *Washington Square* by émigré novelist Henry James, now 38.

Poetry: *The Puritan's Guest and Other Poems* by Scribner's Monthly editor Josiah G. Holland.

Sculpture: *Admiral Farragut* by Irish-born sculptor Augustus Saint-Gaudens, 33, who opened studios at New York in 1873 but will move to Cornish, N.H., in 1885. Saint-Gaudens shows a style of dramatic simplicity that has made him popular with architects such as Stanford White, who has designed a pedestal for the full-length statue of the late naval hero in Madison Square.

"Cleopatra's Needle" reaches its destination at Graywacke Knoll in Central Park January 5, is turned into position January 22 on a mechanism imported from Egypt, and is given an official reception February 22 in the Great Hall of the Metropolitan Museum of Art (*see* 1880). The huge crowd on hand for the ceremony includes 100 honor students chosen from the city's public schools (each is given a commemorative bronze medal bearing the inscription, *"Discipulus est priori posterior dies"* ("Let the future profit by lessons of the past").

Theater: *The Professor* by Hartford-born actor-playwright William Hooker Gillette, 27, 6/1 at the Madison Square Theater, with Gillette in the title role; *Esmeralda* by William H. Gillette and English-born novelist Frances (Eliza) Burnett (*née* Hodgson), 31, 10/29 at the Madison Square Theater, with Annie Russell in the title role, Alabama-born actress Viola (Emily) Allen, 14, in a supporting role.

Barnum & Bailey's Circus is created through a merger that joins the 10-year-old P. T. Barnum circus with the Hutchinson & Bailey Circus of Detroit-born showman John Anthony Bailey (originally James McGinnis), 34, who has purchased the Great London Circus, gone on tour in competition with Barnum, and will gain control in 1888 (*see* Jumbo, 1882; Ringling brothers, 1907). Lawyer Abraham Hummel of Howe & Hummel has negotiated the deal; he will be credited with persuading U.S. courts that theatrical contracts are just as valid as any other contracts and their provisions enforceable. Courts have been inclined to view actors and managers as irresponsible and engaged in a business so dependent on such intangibles as artistry that they could not be considered bound by the rules, formulated by laws of equity, that governed other businesses.

Tony Pastor's Opera House on Union Square stages the first vaudeville show 10/24, putting on a variety of acts that include actors, dancers, singers, and other entertainers. Vaudeville (the word will soon be introduced by B. F. Keith; *see* 1883) will be the leading entertainment for working-class Americans for the next 50 years, with animal acts, bird acts, adagio dancers, apache dancers, flamenco dancers, tap dancers, and other "hoofers," as well as comedians, impersonators, jugglers, magicians, brother acts, sister acts, family acts, ventriloquists, accordionists, banjo players, harpists, mandolin players, ukelele players, xylophonists, whistlers, and every other kind of act imaginable.

Broadway musical: *The Great Mogul; or The Snake Charmer* 10/29 with Lillian Russell, now 19, as D'Jemma, music by French composer Edmond Audran, 39. Russell has toured California in the new comic opera that she will follow with roles in *Patience* and other Gilbert and Sullivan operettas; by 1883 she will be earning $150 per week with the McCaull Opera Co. and will be popular for more than 20 years for her clear soprano voice and well-upholstered beauty.

The Union League Club moves March 5 into a clubhouse that it has had built on Fifth Avenue at 39th Street, where it will remain for 50 years (*see* 1868; 1930). It has outgrown its house on Madison Avenue at 26th Street, and some of its members—Albert Bierstadt, Francis B. Carpenter, Jaspar F. Cropsey, and Thomas Nast—are artists who pay their dues by contributing paintings to the club's collection.

"Hell's Kitchen" gets its name in September when a *New-York Times* reporter goes into Manhattan's West 40s with a police guide to get the details of a story about a man who has killed his daughter and fatally wounded his hired man while "defending himself from a gang of ruffians" (*see* Tenderloin, 1876). Street gangs have flourished since the Civil War in the area from Ninth Avenue west to the Hudson between 36th and 59th streets, where tenements are intermingled with tenements and crime is rampant. There are 7,500 licensed grog shops plus many more unlicensed ones, and thousands of sailors are robbed each year. Constables patrol the area in pairs. The reporter uses the term "Hell's Kitchen" in reference to a single building, but he says the entire section is "probably the lowest and filthiest in the city." By one account, the term was coined by a veteran policeman as he and a rookie watched a small riot in West 39th Street. The rookie turned to the older man and said, "This place is hell itself," causing the veteran to reply, "Hell's mild climate. This is hell's kitchen" (*see* real estate, 1959).

Author Sarah Gilman Young writes in her book *European Modes of Living, or The Question of Apartment Houses (French Flats)* that Americans are always trying to appear better than they are. "Especially do we seek an exterior air of respectability and wealth in our homes. The desire to live in a fine house is peculiarly American. There are no objections to apartment houses in American cities except prejudice, and this is stronger in the United States than elsewhere. To Americans it is a matter of rank. Anything which resembles what we term a tenement is tabooed. There being no fixed caste in America, as in the foreign states, we have established a certain style of living and expenditure, as a distinctive mark of social position."

Drought strikes the eastern United States. New York City runs out of water (only 2 percent of city houses have water connections anyway) and people die of heat exhaustion. Tenement builders have installed rudimentary plumbing facilities (communal toilets at the ends of floors) in order to save space; private houses and the boarding houses in which most New Yorkers live have privies in their basements or, sometimes, in their backyards.

Restaurateur Lorenzo Delmonico dies of a stroke at Sharon Springs, N.Y., September 3 at age 68.

Some 669,431 immigrants enter the United States, up from 91,918 in 1861, as a decade begins that will see the arrival of 5.25 million immigrants. The U.S. population reaches 53 million.

Some 500,000 Romanian Jews will emigrate to America in the next few decades and be joined by other Eastern European Jews plus 1.5 million Russian Jews, adding new diversity to the population. Most will settle at least initially in New York.

1882 Former U.S. senator Roscoe Conkling declines President Arthur's offer of a U.S. Supreme Court seat. He has resumed a lucrative law practice at New York.

Lawyer Theodore Roosevelt calls March 29 for the investigation and impeachment of State Supreme Court Justice T. R. Westbrook, whose involvement with—and favoritism toward—financier Jay Gould has been detailed in the *New-York Times* and other newspapers (but not, of course, in Gould's *New-York World*). In addition to controlling perhaps 10 percent of the nation's railroads, Gould now also controls the Associated Press through his holdings in Western Union Telegraph Co. and has recently gained power over the Manhattan Elevated Railway Co., driving down the price of its stock with misleading articles in the *World* and then snapping up shares. Other legislators balk at taking steps against the judge, but young "Teddy" perseveres despite all odds. He turns 24 October 28 and is elected to the state assembly at Albany by a margin of 3,490 to 1,989, becoming the youngest man ever elected.

New Jersey-born Buffalo reform mayor (Stephen) Grover Cleveland, 45, wins election to the governorship, running on the Democratic Party ticket; he secures 535,718 votes to 342,464 for his Republican opponent, Nantucket-born lawyer Charles James Folger, 64, but Cleveland has really won by default: more than 300,000 Republicans in the state have stayed away from the polls to protest interference in state affairs by party officials at Washington, D.C. The Brooklyn Young Republican Club led by Horace E. Deming has opposed the machine candidate and supported Cleveland for governor.

Franklin Edson gains an easy victory in New York City's mayoralty election, receiving 97,802 votes as compared to 76,385 for his Republican rival Allan Campbell.

Brooklyn-born shipping heir Seth Low, 32, is elected mayor of his native city, running on the Republican ticket. Valedictorian of Columbia College's Class of 1870, Low has campaigned for civic reform; in his two terms as mayor he will institute civil-service reform, eliminate the city debt, and reorganize Brooklyn's public-school system, opening its schools to blacks for the first time (see education [Columbia College], 1889).

A wave of strikes for higher wages in the United States is touched off by higher prices that have resulted from last year's poor crops. New York's first Labor Day parade September 5 brings out 30,000 marchers.

The Charity Organization Society is founded by philanthropist Josephine Shaw Lowell, now 38, in an effort to bring order to the city's fragmented charitable organizations (see 1876). She will be the society's guiding spirit for 25 years, working to achieve cooperation among the various groups (see Nonfiction, 1884).

The New York Mercantile Exchange adopts that name after a decade as the Butter and Cheese Exchange (see 1872). It now trades in eggs and other foodstuffs as well as butter and cheese, mostly in cash, and will move in 1886 to the corner of Hudson and Harrison streets. By 1903 it will be trading butter and egg futures as well as the actual commodities (see potatoes, 1941).

Financier Moses Taylor dies at New York May 23 at age 76, leaving an estate estimated at $40 million.

Electric current from generators at 255-257 Pearl Street begins to flow at 3 o'clock in the afternoon of September 4 as Thomas Edison throws a switch in the offices of financier J. Pierpont Morgan to light the offices and inaugurate commercial transmission of electric power from the Morgan-financed Edison Illuminating Co. power plant, but the company can supply power for only one mile before its direct-current electricity begins to lose voltage (see 1881). Gas companies have tried to block Edison, arguing that digging up the streets to install electric mains

would bring traffic to a standstill, Edison has insisted that electric lighting would be much safer than alternatives, the city has given the Edison Illuminating Co. only 6 months to lay down its mains, Edison has built large new dynamos to generate the necessary power, the company will soon supply current to all of Manhattan, and it will develop into the Consolidated Edison Co., prototype of all central-station U.S. power companies. By the spring of next year there will be 334 Edison plants in operation, most of them much smaller than the one in Pearl Street, and by 1884 Edison's London-born private secretary Samuel Insull, now 22, will have helped him gain control of Edison Light Co. as well as Edison Illuminating Co. (see Villard, 1884; Westinghouse, 1885).

The world's first electric fan is devised by the chief engineer of New York's Crocker and Curtis Electric Motor Co. The two-bladed desk fan is the work of Schuyler Skaats Wheeler, 22.

The world's first electrically lighted Christmas tree is installed in December in the rear parlor of Thomas Edison associate Edward H. Johnson's New York house. Its 80 hand-wired, hand-blown glass bulbs are wrapped in red, white, and blue crepe paper and twinkle as the tree revolves six times per minute in a little pine box. Tree lights will not be sold commercially until early in the next century, and most people will continue for years to feel safer with candles, but mass production of strings of lights will begin in 1903 and by 1930 the use of candles for Christmas trees will be fading fast.

The Standard Oil trust incorporated by John D. Rockefeller and his associates to circumvent state corporation laws brings 95 percent of the U.S. petroleum industry under the control of a nine-man directorate. Pennsylvania lawyer Samuel C. T. Dodd has shown Rockefeller how the idea of a trust employed in personal estate law can be applied to industry and the oil trust will soon be followed by other trusts. The richest company of any kind in the world, the Standard Oil trust controls 14,000 miles of underground pipeline and all the oil cars of the Pennsylvania Railroad (see 1877; 1883).

The New York Steam Co. is founded to provide steam for heating homes and office buildings through subterranean steam pipes (see Con Edison, 1936).

Clipper-ship architect John W. Griffiths dies at Brooklyn March 30 at age 72.

The Erie Canal that opened in 1825 becomes toll-free, having earned $42 million over and above its

P. T. Barnum brought over an elephant so large it introduced a new word to the language. HARPER'S WEEKLY

initial cost and the cost of enlarging, maintaining, and operating it for 57 years (*see* Barge Canal, 1918).

Eighth Avenue north of 59th Street in Manhattan is officially renamed Central Park West April 22. Ninth Avenue north of 59th becomes Columbus Avenue that day, and Tenth Avenue becomes Amsterdam Avenue.

"The public be damned," says New York railroad magnate William H. Vanderbilt October 8 to *Chicago Daily News* reporter Clarence Dresser, who has asked, "Don't you run it for the public benefit?" when told that the fast *Chicago Limited* extra-fare mail train was being eliminated. "I am working for my stockholders," Vanderbilt says. "If the public want the train, why don't they pay for it?"

The German Hospital that will become Lenox Hill in 1918 opens a women's wing for 50 patients May 27 (*see* 1868). Anna Ottendorfer, now 70, has contributed $68,000 to help finance construction and furnishing of the new facility (*see* 1861; Poliklinik, 1884; Lenox Hill, 1918).

Former Western Union telegraph operator Frank (Andrew) Munsey, 28, leaves his Maine home, arrives at New York, and launches a weekly children's magazine, the *Golden Argosy*. He has a suitcase full of manuscripts (they have cost him $450) plus about $40 in cash, he buys an $8 table, and his first issue appears December 2. It will fail in 5 months, but Munsey will buy paper on time, obtain credit for everything else he needs, and his 6,000-word story, "Afloat in a Great City," will revive the magazine's fortunes next year, bailing its author out of a $10,000 debt; by 1887 he will be netting $100 per week (*see Munsey's Magazine*, 1891; *Argosy*, 1896).

"When a dog bites a man that is not news, but when a man bites a dog that is news," says *New-York Evening Sun* city editor John B. Bogart.

Dow Jones & Co. (initially Dow, Jones & Co.) is founded in November by Connecticut-born former *Providence Journal* reporter Charles H. Dow, 31, and Edward D. Jones, 26, who open offices in a small, unpainted room at the bottom of some wooden stairs at 15 Wall Street, where former Drexel, Morgan employee Charles Milford Bergstrasser helps them go into business distributing handwritten news bulletins reproduced with carbon paper and tissue (they will not get a hand-cranked printing press until 1884) (*see Wall Street Journal*, 1889; commerce [Dow Jones Average], 1884).

The Hoffman House on Madison Square at 25th Street and Broadway installs the titillating 1873 work *Nymphs and Satyr* by French painter William Adolphe Bouguereau, 56, opposite the long mahogany bar in its splendid barroom where the 8.5 × 5.8-foot picture can be seen not only on the wall but also reflected in the mirror behind the bar. Proprietor Edward S. Stokes (who shot financier Jim Fiske to death in 1871) has bought the painting at auction, uses a brass railing to keep viewers four feet away from it, puts up a plaque informing them how much he paid for it, illuminates it with a crystal chandelier, and attracts crowds of prurient male patrons.

Theater: *La Belle Russe* by David Belasco, now 28, 5/8 at the new Wallack's Theater, opened by Lester Wallack, now 62, on Broadway at 30th Street; *Fogg's Ferry* 5/15 at the Park Theater with New Orleans-born actress Minnie Maddern (originally Marie Augusta Davey), 16, whose talent wins praise despite the mediocrity of the play; *The Witch* by Abraham Goldfaden 8/12 at the Turnverein (Gymnastic Club) at 66 East 4th Street with an amateur-group cast that includes Russian-born ingénu Boris Thomashevsky, 16, in the first U.S. performance of a Yiddish play (Russia's Czar Alexander II will outlaw that country's Yiddish theater next year and many actors and playwrights will come to New York); the Casino Theater designed by Kennebunk, Me.-born architect Francis H. (Hatch) Kimball, 37, opens in October on Broadway at 39th Street; *Young Mrs. Winthrop* by Bronson Howard 10/9 at the Union Square Theater; *The Squire* by London playwright Arthur Wing Pinero, 27, 10/9 at Daly's Theater, with John Drew as Lieut. Thorndyke, Ada Rehan as Kate Verity, William Gilbert as Izzod Hagerstone in a play that has opened earlier at London; *An Unequal Match* by the late English playwright Tom Taylor 11/6 at Wallack's Theater introduces U.S. audiences to the "Jersey Lilly" Lillie Langtry (Emily Charlotte Le Breton Langtry), 30, who made her London stage debut last year. Mrs. Langtry gained her soubriquet from the painting "The Jersey Lilly" by Sir John Everett Millais, for whom she posed.

Jumbo the elephant appears at Madison Square Garden beginning April 10 in performances of Barnum & Bailey's Circus, which expands from two rings to three. P. T. Barnum has imported the "largest elephant in or out of captivity" (its name has introduced the word *jumbo* to the English language), the animal stands 11 feet tall at the shoulders and weighs 6 tons. Barnum claims it stands 12 feet tall at the shoulders, measures 26 feet in length if the trunk is included, and weighs 10 tons. Captured 20 years ago as a baby, Jumbo has been a prime attraction at London's 56-year-old Royal Zoological Gardens since 1865, when he was acquired from the Jardin des Plantes at Paris in exchange for a rhinoceros, the London zoo has sold him to Barnum for $10,000 because he has become difficult to handle, his sale has raised a storm of protest in England, and there will be general mourning when Jumbo is killed by a freight train on the Grand Trunk Railway at St. Thomas, Ontario, in mid-September 1885.

Popular song: "She Lives on Murray Hill" by New York composer David Braham, lyrics by Ned Harrigan of Harrigan & Hart.

The world's first electric flatiron is patented June 6 by New York inventor Henry W. Weely, but his iron heats up only when plugged into its stand and quickly cools down when in use. Since few homes have electricity anyway, Weely's iron is not a success.

The eight-story Windermere apartment house is completed at 400-406 West 57th Street, southwest corner Ninth Avenue, to Romanesque Revival designs by architect Theophilus G. Smith. Lawyer Nathaniel McBride, then 34, went into business 3 years ago with his 24-year-old clerk William E. Stewart and 25-year-old builder William F. Burroughs to buy the 100' × 125' plot for $30,000 and they have spent another $350,000 to erect the massive structure, whose 39 "French flats" have five or six bedrooms each and rent for between $50 and $91.66 per month at a time when incomes of middle-class New Yorkers average about $2,500. Amenities include a staff of liveried servants, three hydraulic elevators that operate on a 24-hour basis and dumbwaiters to bring up food from a basement kitchen to apartments that have engraved marble fireplaces, glossy parquet floors, carved hazelwood moldings, mirrored parlor walls, and telephone service.

Henderson Place is completed at the northwest corner of East End Avenue and 86th Street, where an enclave of 32 red-brick row houses has been commissioned by hatmaker John C. Henderson. Designed by Lamb & Rich in an elegant Queen Anne style with chimneys, dormer windows, parapets, pediments, and gray slate roof gables, they form a self-contained cul-de-sac (six of the houses will later be razed to make way for an apartment house).

The New-York World Building at 53 Park Row, corner Nassau Street, goes up in flames January 31, killing 12 people (*see* 1890).

New Yorkers consume an estimated 1,885,000 tons of ice per year, and icemen—many of them Italian immigrants—sell the product from some 1,500 horse-drawn wagons. The Knickerbocker Ice Co., founded in 1855, has become the largest such firm in the city, with icehouses in Delancey Street, at 432 Canal Street, in Bank Street, West 20th Street, East 33rd Street, West 43rd Street, East 92nd Street, and East 128th Street (*see* Morse, 1896).

Luchow's restaurant opens at 110 East 14th Street. German restaurateur August Luchow has obtained help from piano maker William Steinway, 47, to buy a small beer hall that he will enlarge by acquiring a livery stable, a museum, and other adjacent structures. Songwriter Harry von Tilzer will write "Down where the Würzburger Flows" at one of his tables, he will pay Victor Herbert to conduct a Viennese string ensemble on the premises for nearly 4 years, and when Luchow dies a bachelor in 1926 he will leave the gigantic eating place (accommodating nearly 1,000 diners) to the Eckstein family, whose staff will continue serving such delicacies as smoked freshwater eel, homemade head cheese (a jellied loaf of pig parts from head, feet, etc.) vinaigrette, *Bauernwurst*, knackwurst, bratwurst, and *gespickter Hasenrücken* (larded saddle of Canadian hare with sour-cream sauce, red cabbage, and *Spätzle*) (*see* 1933).

The Chinese Exclusion Act of 1880 takes effect but will have little effect on New York's Chinatown restaurants (the law excludes laborers but permits entry of merchants, students, teachers, and temporary visitors).

U.S. immigration from Germany reaches its peak, with most of the arrivals coming through Castle Garden.

Congress passes the first act restricting general immigration (*see* 1875). It excludes "any convict, lunatic, idiot, or any person unable to take care of himself or herself without becoming a public charge" and "all foreign convicts except those convicted of political offenses;" it imposes a 50¢ head tax on any immigrant arriving by water to defray the costs of examining immigrants and helping those in need (*see* 1885; 1890).

1883 The Pendleton Civil Service Reform Act passed by Congress January 16 and signed into law by President Arthur provides for competitive examinations for positions in the federal government and establishes a Civil Service Commission to end the abuses that culminated in the assassination of President Garfield 2 years ago. The act sharply reduces the number of federal appointees who get their jobs from elected officials under the "spoils system," it establishes a merit system for appointment and promotion based on competitive examinations, and the number of "classified" civil service workers employed on the basis of merit will be expanded by Congress, with such workers protected from loss of job through change in political administration. Many find it ironic that the former Collector of the Port of New York—a onetime lieutenant of New York party boss Roscoe Conkling—should have signed the measure.

Former governor Edwin D. Morgan dies at New York February 14 at age 71, leaving a fortune of $8 to $10 million; he has bequeathed most of it to charities such as the Eye and Ear Hospital, Woman's Hospital, and Presbyterian Hospital.

Republican Theodore Roosevelt wins reelection to the state assembly, carrying his district by a two-to-one margin. Having won by the widest margin of any legislator in the state, he becomes minority leader and follows Republican Party policy, opposing a $2 daily minimum wage for municipal workers, voting against salary increases for New York City police and firemen, but supporting a measure that would improve the city's water supply. He opposes a bill introduced by the Cigarmakers' Union that would ban the manufacture of cigars in tenement apartments, but English-born union president Samuel Gompers, now 33, shows him how bad conditions are in the tenements, and Roosevelt is so horrified that he supports the measure and works for its passage.

The Working Girls' Vacation Society founded by philanthropists at New York is one of the first such organizations.

The Voluntary Relief Society for the Sick and Poor among Norwegians in Brooklyn and New York is founded by Lutheran deaconess Sister Elizabeth Fedde, 33, and eight clergymen (*see* hospital, 1892).

Merchant William Earl Dodge of Phelps, Dodge dies at New York February 9 at age 77; inventor-philanthropist Peter Cooper at New York April 4 at age 92; rubber-goods manufacturer-philanthropist Conrad Poppenhusen in his College Point mansion at age 65 (approximate).

Retail merchant James T. McCreery opens at the southeast corner of Sixth Avenue and 23rd Street, where Booth's Theater (built for actor Edwin Booth in 1869 at a cost of more than $1 million) has been converted into a department store.

The Brooklyn Bridge (Great East River Bridge) opens to traffic May 24, linking America's two largest cities. President Arthur, Gov. Cleveland, New York's mayor Edson, and Brooklyn's mayor Low officiate at the opening ceremonies, and Emily Roebling is the first person to cross the bridge, using a parasol to shade her from the sun (she has mastered enough mathematics and engineering to superintend the final phases of construction). "It so happens that the work which is likely to be our most durable monument, and which is likely to convey some knowledge of us to the most remote posterity, is a work of bare utility," writes Montgomery Schuyler in *Harper's Weekly*, "not a shrine, nor a fortress, not a palace, but a bridge." Designed by the late John A. Roebling (*see* 1869), financed in large part by the Brooklyn Trust Co., and built in 13 years at a cost of more than $16 million (and 20 lives), the 1,595.5-foot span has a steel web truss to keep it from swaying in the wind; it has been completed by Roebling's son Washington Augustus, now 45, who

Bridging the East River brought America's two largest cities closer together. LIBRARY OF CONGRESS

has been crippled, half-paralyzed, and made partially blind by caisson disease (the "bends") but observes the dedication ceremony from the bedroom window of his house on Columbia Heights and sees his wife, Emily, cross to Manhattan. The great bridge rises 276 feet into the air (only the spire of Trinity Church is higher), its overall length is 5,989 feet, its center span is 85 feet wide, each of its four main cables is 15¼ inches in diameter and contains 5,434 galvanized steel wires, each 3,515 feet long and able to sustain a load of 12,000 tons (there are 14,357 miles of wire overall); its 86-foot-wide surface accommodates two outer roadways for horse-drawn vehicles, two tracks for trains, and a center walk for foot traffic. Showman P. T. Barnum leads 21 of his elephants across the span on opening day to assure spectators of its safety (and publicize his circus), but a panic May 30 produces a stampede and 12 pedestrians are trampled to death on the bridge's promenade.

The Brooklyn Elevated Railroad runs its first train September 24, bringing elevated railway service for the first time to America's second largest city.

The New York and Brooklyn Bridge Railway operates cable-powered trains between Manhattan's Park Row and Brooklyn's Sands Street, but cable cars will be involved in so many accidents that they will soon be given up as an unsuccessful experiment (see elevated trains, 1885).

Commercial Cable Co. is founded by Comstock Lode millionaire John W. Mackay, now 52, and *New-York Herald* publisher James Gordon Bennett, who challenge Jay Gould's control of transatlantic cable communications. Mackay and Bennett will lay two submarine cables to Europe next year and break the Gould monopoly (see 1869; 1886).

Hungarian-born newspaper publisher Joseph Pulitzer, 36, of the *St. Louis Post-Dispatch* visits Jay Gould at his offices in the Western Union Buiding May 8 and agrees to buy Gould's *New-York World* for $240,000, the money to be paid in installments. Pulitzer arrived at Boston in 1864, served in the First New York Cavalry in the Civil War, worked as a reporter for a German-language newspaper in St. Louis, won election to the legislature in 1869, studied law, and was admitted to the bar in 1876. Gould has owned the *World* since 1879 and used it to mislead the public about his activities; it has a circulation of 15,000 and has been losing $40,000 per year, but Pulitzer will raise circulation and make the paper profitable (see 1886).

Carl Schurz resigns as editor of the *New-York Evening Post* and is succeeded by his associate editor E. L. Godkin.

Life magazine begins publication at New York. Edward Sandford Martin, 27, helped start the *Harvard Lampoon* in 1876 and joins with New York-born illustrator, architect, and writer John Ames Mitchell, 38, in starting the new humor magazine that will continue as such for more than half a century (see Gibson Girl, 1890; Luce, 1936).

More than 3,000 Remington typewriters are sold, up from about 2,350 last year. By 1885 sales will reach 5,000 per year (see 1878; Underwood, 1895).

Sculpture: a full-length bronze figure of philanthropist Robert R. Randall by Augustus Saint-Gaudens is installed on the lawn of Sailors' Snug Harbor on Staten Island; *Still Hunt* (a bronze panther) by Georgia-born sculptor Edward Kemys, 40, is erected on Central Park's East Drive at 76th Street (the first U.S. sculptor to specialize in animal representations, Kemys served as an axman with the engineer corps that laid out Central Park and then as an artillery captain in the Civil War).

The Herald Square Theater that will survive until 1914 has its beginnings in the New Park Theater, opened on Broadway at 35th Street with an interior taken from the short-lived Booth's Theater of 1869. The vaudeville team Harrigan and Hart (Ned Harrigan and Tony Hart) leases the new house for several years.

New York song-and-dance comedians Joe Weber and Lew Fields (Shanfield), both 16, go on eight times a day for $40 per week at Keith & Batchelder's Dime Museum, opened at 585 Washington Street, Boston, by former circus promoters Benjamin Franklin Keith, 37, and George H. Batchelder (see Tony Pastor, 1881). The proprietors employ Edward F. Albee, 26, to manage a second-floor vaudeville theater that opens at 10 in the morning (see 1886).

The Metropolitan Opera House opens 10/22 with a performance of the 1859 Gounod opera *Faust* sung in Italian with soprano Christine Nilsson, 40, of Sweden as Marguerite. The 3,700-seat Met, occupying the block bounded by Broadway, Seventh Avenue, 39th Street, and 40th Street, replaces the smaller Academy of Music that opened in Irving Place in 1854; it has three tiers of boxes, and the Old Guard of the Academy contemptuously calls the yellow-brick Early Renaissance structure "that yellow brewery uptown" (*but see* 1886).

Broadway musical: *Cordelia's Aspirations* 11/5 at the Theatre-Comique, with Ned Harrigan and Tony Hart, songs by Harrigan and Hart that include "My Dad's Dinner Pail."

The New York Gothams baseball team holds the first Ladies' Day in professional ball June 16, allowing women into its ballpark at a reduced rate (*see* 1867). Spectators at public sporting events have been virtually all men up to now.

The most lavish party yet held in America is staged March 26 to celebrate the official opening of the new $2 million Gothic mansion of railroad magnate William K. Vanderbilt, now 34 (*see* 1875). The *New York World* estimates that Vanderbilt's wife, Alva, now 29, has spent $155,730 for costumes alone. Ward McAllister has persuaded Mrs. Astor, now 52, to end her hostility toward the Vanderbilts, and she has deigned to call on Alva Vanderbilt in order to secure an invitation for her unmarried daughter Carrie (who next year will marry Orme Wilson, Jr.).

Box 6 of the new Metropolitan Opera House is reserved for Alva (Mrs. William K.) Vanderbilt, who could not obtain one of the Academy of Music's 18 boxes because they were blocked by the Old Guard (Astors, Bayards, Beekmans, Belmonts, Cuttings, and Schuylers). The city's new millionaires have been unable to buy or lease desirable boxes, and the Met's opening is a social event as much as a musical one. The new opera house has 70 boxes for patrons such as George F. Baker, James Gordon Bennett, J. R. Drexel, Cyrus Field, Elbridge T. Gerry, Ogden Goelet, Jay Gould, William Rhinelander, Collis P. Huntington, Adrian Iselin, D. Ogden Mills, William Rhinelander, William Rockefeller, and William C. Whitney as well as for the Vanderbilts. The lower tier of boxes, or parterre, at the Met make up what will be called the "Diamond Horseshoe," with Box 7 for Mrs. Astor, who comes each evening (arriving at 9 o'clock, after the first act) except the Monday in January when she gives her annual ball (*see* 1888).

Dublin-born detective Thomas F. Byrnes, 41, persuades the state legislature at Albany to give him command of all New York City precinct detectives, whose chief concern up to now has been collecting payoffs for precinct captains. Byrnes has solved a case that involved a $3 million robbery from the Manhattan Bank; he will be elevated to the rank of chief inspector in 1888 and made superintendent of the force 4 years later, despite the fact that he hobnobs with underworld figures and does not shrink from using brutality (some will say he invented the "third degree").

The Temple Court office building is completed at the southwest corner of Nassau and Beekman streets to designs by Silliman & Farnsworth. The red-painted structure has a full-height atrium and a tall steeple; it will be joined in 1892 by a northern counterpart designed by Benjamin Silliman, Jr.

The Gorham Building is completed at the northwest corner of Broadway and 19th Street to designs by McKim, Mead & White, whose client will move its jewelry and silverware workshops and emporium uptown in 1906.

The Hampshire apartment house is completed at 46–50 West 9th Street, between Fifth and Sixth avenues, to Victorian designs by New York-born architect-developer Ralph S. Townsend, 29, who last year completed the Portsmouth apartment house in similar style at 38–44 West 9th Street.

The Albert Hotel (later the Albert Apartments) is completed at the southeast corner of University Place and 11th Street to designs by Henry Janeway Hardenbergh, who has given its dark red-brick exterior a black-painted wrought-iron trim.

The Gramercy apartment house (initially the Gramercy Park Hotel) is completed at 34 Gramercy Park East (northeast corner 20th Street) with three cable-controlled "birdcage" elevators, one of them for passengers. Designed in Queen Anne style by architect G. W. da Cunha, the red-brick and red terra-cotta structure is a pioneer co-operative but has only one bath per apartment, even for the largest units. A Louis Sherry's restaurant is on the eighth floor and delivers to tenants' apartments but closes within a year for lack of patronage.

The 10-story 121 Madison Avenue co-operative apartment is completed at 31st Street to designs by Hubert, Pirrson. The red-brick structure has five duplex apartments for every two floors.

The Lisbon apartment house goes up at the northeast corner of 58th Street and Seventh Avenue. Designed by Philip G. Hubert and built by José de Navarro, the first of the Central Park Apartments (generally called the Spanish Flats) will be followed by the Barcelona, Salamanca, and Tolosa in 58th Street and the Madrid, Cordova, Grenada, and Valencia in 59th—all eight-story buildings. Constructed of granite, stone, brownstone, and brick to give the appearance of one large block, they will occupy a plot of land 200 feet wide by 425 feet long. Each will contain 12 eight- to 16-room apartments, three of them duplexes, with drawing rooms measuring 30 feet by 16, libraries 22 by 17, dining rooms 20 by 18, chambers (bedrooms) 15 by 11, and kitchens

15 by 16. Maids' rooms and storage space are in the basement, reached by a vehicular tunnel in which delivery wagons can be unloaded under cover and off the street, and the long common courtyard will have flowerbeds and fountains. Half the apartments are sold as co-operatives, but the rental apartments do not find a ready market, since the area is now filled almost entirely by private houses and stables. The Spanish Flats will survive until 1927 (see Sevillia Hotel, 1893; Athletic Club, 1928; Essex House, 1930).

The imposing new 58-room Indiana limestone mansion completed for William K. Vanderbilt and his wife, Alva, at 640 Fifth Avenue, northwest corner 53rd Street, stands out from its brownstone neighbors with an elaborate entrance porch and a gabled mansard roof. Architect Richard Morris Hunt has modeled it on a French château at Blois.

Designer-decorator Christian Herter dies of tuberculosis at his New York home November 2 at age 44. He has produced carpets and textiles for the home of banker J. Pierpont Morgan and, most recently, that of railroad magnate William H. Vanderbilt.

A new building for the Association for the Relief of Respectable Aged Indigent Females is completed on the east side of Amsterdam Avenue between 103rd and 104th streets to Victorian Gothic designs by Richard Morris Hunt (see 1838). An addition will be built between 1907 and 1908, it will be remodeled in the 1960s, renamed the Association Residence for Women, and continue as such until 1974.

The state legislature at Albany appoints a commission to select appropriate park sites for the Bronx, most of which is still bucolic. Headed by John Mullaly, the commission will designate and lay out three large areas—soon to be Van Cortlandt, Bronx, and Pelham Bay parks—that will be connected to each other, and to Woodlawn Cemetery, by broad avenues that will create a greenbelt, plus three smaller, unconnected areas that will become Crotona, St. Mary's, and Claremont parks. Largest of the parks is Pelham Bay, which will eventually have 2,764 acres of woodlands on property acquired by Thomas Pelham in 1654 (23 percent of the property is set aside for a park this year) (see Mosholu Parkway, 1888; Botanical Garden, 1891).

1884 Assemblyman Theodore Roosevelt receives word at Albany February 13 that his 22-year-old wife, Alice (Hathaway) Lee, has been delivered of a baby girl in the family's town house at 6 West 57th Street, but a second telegram arrives within hours advising him that his mother is dying and Alice as well. Heavy fog slows his train, and by the time he reaches her side Alice is comatose with Bright's disease (chronic kidney failure); his mother, Martha Bulloch Roosevelt, dies of pneumonia in the small hours of February 14 at age 48, and Alice dies in his arms at 2 o'clock that afternoon, leaving Roosevelt in despair. The Assembly votes to adjourn in an unprecedented show of respect. Roosevelt's baby daughter is given the name Alice Lee after her mother's funeral, but Roosevelt, now 25, pays the infant little heed, plunging himself into a frenzy of political activity, shuttling back and forth between New York and Albany by night train, speaking out for his Reform Charter Bill, inspecting the city's infamous Ludlow Street Jail, interviewing witnesses who come before his City Affairs Committee, and making speeches.

The Republican convention at Chicago nominates former secretary of state James G. (Gillespie) Blaine, now 54, who was denied the nomination 8 years ago by Sen. Roscoe Conkling but has won the support of Thomas C. Platt over opposition from

Wall Street panicked when the brokerage house Grant & Ward collapsed in a fraud. HARPER'S WEEKLY

New York reformers led by *Harper's Weekly* editor George William Curtis and including, among others, *New-York Evening Post* editor E. L. Godkin, *New-York Times* editor George Jones, Theodore Roosevelt, Carl Schurz, Brooklyn lawyer Horace E. Deming, and Cornell University president Andrew D. White. Roosevelt, disgusted, leaves for the Bad Lands of northern Dakota Territory to pursue his ranching interests (he invested in a cattle operation there several years ago) (*see* Sagamore Hill, 1885).

The political slogan "Rum, Romanism, and Rebellion" defeats presidential candidate Blaine and helps elect New York's Gov. Grover Cleveland, now 47, to the presidency in the first Democratic Party national victory since James Buchanan won in 1856. Republicans have tried to make capital of Cleveland's having fathered a child out of wedlock nearly 10 years ago; as sheriff of Buffalo, he met widow Maria Halpin (*née* Crofts), a woman 2 years his junior with two grown children, who worked in a fancy dress shop and was musical and fluent in French, but he has honorably agreed to support her and the child she bore him. Democrats have captured the crucial Catholic vote as a result of remarks made October 29 at the Fifth Avenue Hotel by local clergyman Samuel D. Burchard ("We are Republicans, and don't propose to have our party identify ourselves with the party whose antecedents have been Rum, Romanism, and Rebellion"), New York City voters—many of them Irishmen—have taken exception, and they give Cleveland a narrow 1,149-vote edge in the state that gives him a plurality of 20,000 votes out of nearly 10 million total, 219 electoral votes to 189 for Blaine (Wall Street lawyer and financier William C. Whitney, now 43, has led the Cleveland forces at the Democratic National Convention and outsmarted older politicians, New York State's electoral votes provide the margin of victory, and President Cleveland will make Whitney his secretary of the navy).

William R. Grace runs as an Independent and regains the New York City mayorship, receiving 96,288 votes as compared with 85,361 for his Tammany Hall Democrat rival Hugh J. Grant, 44,386 for Republican Frederick S. Gibbs.

♥ The first branch of the New York City Young Men's Christian Association (YMCA) is completed at 222 Bowery, between Prince and Spring streets, to Queen Anne-style designs by architect Bradford Lee Gilbert, who has secured the commission for the five-story structure with help from YMCA board member Cornelius Vanderbilt 2nd (it will be used by the YMCA until 1932). Initially called the Young Men's Institute and intended to serve as a counter-weight to evil influences, it is in a street lined with beer gardens and saloons and surrounded by lodging houses and tenements. The Institute offers classes in architectural drawing, bookkeeping, electricity, engineering, mechanical drawing, penmanship, typing, vocal music, and other subjects; members pay dues of $4 per year to enjoy use of the building's bowling alleys, gymnasium, library, and reading room, and membership will grow to 659 by 1891.

The Madison Square Boys' Club is founded in a vacant First Avenue store at 37th Street to provide recreation for disadvantaged youth in a district dominated by street gangs. Massachusetts-born pastor Charles Henry Parkhurst, 42, of the Madison Square Presbyterian Church has persuaded two rich young parishioners—William Morgan Kingsley, 20, and Arthur Curtiss James, 17—to start the club as a mission of the church.

$ *History of New York City* by Benson J. Lossing says, "New York, unfortunately, is becoming in large degree a city of only two conspicuous classes, the rich and the poor. The great middle classes, which constitute the bone and sinew of the social structure, have been squeezed out, as it were, by the continually increasing pressure of the burden of the cost of living in the city."

The London, Paris & American Bank Ltd. of Great Britain is founded with offices at New York by a silk importing and exchange firm that began in 1847 as a New Orleans dry-goods business opened by émigré French merchant Alexandre Lazard. He took two of his brothers into partnership in 1848, a fire wiped them out in 1849, one brother returned to Sarrequemines, in Lorraine, but Alexandre and Simon Lazard moved to San Francisco, bought an interest in a fabric house making woolen yard goods, took their youngest brother Elie and their cousin Alexandre Weill into partnership, and now have offices in Paris and London as well as the one in New York, opened in 1880 by Simon Lazard and Alexandre Weill (*see* 1940).

The Knickerbocker Trust Co. is founded by bankers who include Cleveland-born Charles Tracy Barney, 33, a brother-in-law of William C. Whitney. Barney will be elected president of the bank in 1898 (*see* 1907).

New York coal merchant August Heckscher, now 36, and his cousin Richard sell their company to the Philadelphia & Reading Railroad, go into the zinc business, and will later enter the copper business. Hecksher will build a fortune and invest much of it in New York real estate (*see* real estate, 1904).

Former president Ulysses S. Grant visits the offices of Grant & Ward May 5 and learns from his son Buck (Ulysses, Jr.) that Ferdinand Ward has absconded and the firm has no funds (see 1881). Assets total $57,000; liabilities exceed $16 million. Having persuaded his Union Army comrades and everyone in his family to invest in the firm, Grant is left almost penniless. Wall Street panics May 14 following the sudden collapse of Marine Bank as well as Grant & Ward, the downturn is short lived, and Ward is convicted of fraud and sentenced to 10 years' imprisonment at Sing Sing (he will serve more than 6 years). Grant has borrowed $100,000 from railroad magnate William H. Vanderbilt, pledging his medals and honors as collateral (Vanderbilt turns them over to the Smithsonian Institution at Washington, D.C.). Grant consults a physician about his throat pain, asks if it is cancer, is told that it is an "epithelial condition" that is sometimes curable, and contracts with Mark Twain to publish his memoirs (see politics, 1885).

The first Dow Jones Average appears July 3 in the *Afternoon News Letter* published since 1882 by Charles H. Dow and Edward Jones. Activity on the New York Stock Exchange averages 250,000 shares per day, Dow's average is intended to provide an overall measure of how the active shares performed, and his list gives the closing prices of shares in 11 companies, nine railroads and two industrials (see 1896; communications [*Wall Street Journal*], 1889).

⚡ Cleveland-born oil mogul Oliver Hazard Payne, 45, moves to New York and becomes treasurer of John D. Rockefeller's Standard Oil Co., a position that he will hold until 1911. Payne joined with Cleveland industrialists Maurice and James Clark in 1866 to found Clark, Payne & Co., Rockefeller's chief rival until it consolidated with Standard Oil in 1872 (see medicine, 1887).

German financiers led by Henry Villard propose creation of a new electric combination that will include all of Thomas Edison's manufacturing companies and control the stock of Edison Electric Light Co., whose largest block is held by the J. P. Morgan interests. Complex negotiations ensue, resulting in the creation of Edison General Electric, whose stock is 40 percent owned by J. Pierpont Morgan while Edison has to settle for 10 percent and enough cash to make him rich (see General Electric, 1892). Some 500 buildings now have 11,272 lamps lighted by electricity, but most large hotels and office buildings have their own generating plants.

Consolidated Gas Co. of New York is created November 10 by a merger of the city's six largest gaslight companies—New York Gas Light, Manhattan Gas Light, Harlem Gas Light, Metropolitan Gas Light, Knickerbocker Gas Light, Municipal Gas Light. The consolidation of competing companies begins a long process that will see scores of small electricity, gas, and steam companies combined into one entity (see 1890; Consolidated Edison, 1936).

⚡ Asphalt paving is introduced for New York streets, providing a smoother, quieter surface for carriages and wagons than the cobblestones and other paving stones used up to now (see 1876; 1890).

⚕ The Deutsches (German) Poliklinik opens at 137 Second Avenue, between St. Mark's Place and East Ninth Street. A dispensary of German Hospital (later Lenox Hill; see 1882), it has been designed by architect William Schickel for *New Yorker Staats-Zeitung* publisher Oswald Ottendorfer and his wife, Anna, and will later become Stuyvesant Polyclinic Hospital.

Montefiore Medical Center has its beginnings in the Montefiore Home for Chronic Individuals opened by Jewish philanthropists (notably Jacob Schiff, now 36, of Kuhn, Loeb) at 84th Street and Avenue A (later to be called York Avenue). Named for English philanthropist Moses Montefiore, the 25-bed facility employs Polish-born physician Simon Baruch, 44, as chief of its medical staff and provides permanent care for poor, incurably ill patients. The home will become nonsectarian in 1887 and move 2 years later to Broadway between 138th and 139th streets (see 1913).

Memorial Hospital has its beginnings in the New York Cancer Hospital, opened at Central Park West and 106th Street by local gynecologist J. Marion Sims with support from John Jacob Astor, 62, who administers the estate of his late grandfather and namesake. The first U.S. hospital to specialize in cancer in an age when the disease is considered incurable, it will be renamed the General Memorial Hospital for the Treatment of Cancer and Allied Diseases in 1899 and innovate use of circular wards to avoid corners that are thought to accumulate dirt and stagnant air (see 1886).

New York surgeon William S. (Stewart) Halsted, 31, injects a patient with cocaine, pioneering the practice of local anaesthesia. He introduced the use of rubber gloves in surgery at Roosevelt Hospital 2 years ago, but he becomes addicted to the drug derived from leaves of a South American Andes shrub, and although he will recover in 2 years he will require morphine in order to function.

New York ophthalmologist Carl Killer, 27, introduces cocaine as a local anaesthetic in eye surgery, obtaining it from the 10-year-old Brooklyn firm Lehn & Fink, founded by entrepreneur Louis Lehn and German-born drug wholesaler Frederick W. (William) Fink, now 38.

∞ The Church of Our Lady of Mount Carmel in East 116th Street holds a procession in July to celebrate Italian culture, beginning a tradition that will continue for more than a century.

Spiritualist Helena Blavatsky is summoned to England to face challenges to her authority (see 1875). A report labels her a fraud, describing her as "one of the most accomplished, ingenious, and interesting imposters in history," but by the time of her death in 1891 Blavatsky will have 100,000 followers.

The Union Theological Seminary, founded in 1836, moves uptown from University Place to the west side of Fourth Avenue between 69th and 70th streets (see Lenox, 1840). Former New York governor Edwin D. Morgan offered the institution $300,000 for a new library 4 years ago and agreed to sell it 10 lots. A chapel, library, and lecture hall have been put up on the Fourth Avenue frontage, a dormitory for 160 students in the rear (see 1910).

The Brearley School opens with 50 girls in a brownstone house at 6 East 45th Street under the direction of educator Samuel Brearley, Jr., 33, who studied at Philips Andover, received his bachelor's degree from Harvard in 1871, attended Oxford's Balliol College for 3 years, and has been persuaded by Mrs. Joseph H. Choate to start a good private school for girls. Brearley has announced the creation of "A Day School for Girls" in the *New-York Times*, specifying an annual tuition of $250 or $300, depending on whether the pupil is under or over age 15, spelling out the course of study in detail, and even naming the sanitary engineer responsible for plumbing and drainage. He has borrowed a few thousand dollars from his Harvard classmate Charles Bonaparte, a great-nephew of the emperor, and although he will die late in 1886, his school will grow to have 550 girls (see 1929).

The Linotype typesetting machine patented by German-born mechanic Ottmar Mergenthaler, 30, will revolutionize newspaper composing rooms. (*see New-York Tribune*, 1886).

The Grolier Club is founded by nine New York business and cultural leaders who collect fine books and prints as an avocation and want to encourage high standards in all phases of printing. Founders include Connecticut-born printer Theodore Low De Vinne, 55, whose firm produces *Scribner's Monthly*, *St. Nicholas Magazine*, the *Century Illustrated Magazine*, and other periodicals in addition to books. Taking its name from the French bibliophile Jean Grolier, Vicomte d'Aguisy (1479–1565), the club will grow in the next 100 years to have more than 3,000 members (*see* architecture, 1917).

The *Press* begins publication under the direction of former U.S. assistant postmaster Frank Hatton, who uses the paper to favor a protective tariff (*see* Munsey, 1912).

The Waterman pen is the first practical fountain pen with a capillary feed. New York insurance man Lewis E. (Edson) Waterman, 47, has lost a sale because his pen leaked on an important document, he has developed a revolutionary ink filling system, and he has 200 of the pens made by hand, but the end of the pen must be removed and ink squirted in with an eye dropper (the lever-fill pen will not be introduced until 1904).

Nonfiction: *Public Relief and Private Charity* by New York State Board of Charities commissioner Josephine Shaw Lowell, now 40, advocates a state-administered philanthropy; *History of New York City* by Benson J. Lossing.

The New York Free Circulating Library opens at 135 Second Avenue beside the new German Dispensary. The private library has been built and endowed by *New Yorker Staats-Zeitung* publisher Oswald Ottendorfer and his wife, Anna, to help other German immigrants; its building has been designed by William Schickel; and it will survive as the oldest operating branch of the New York Public Library (*see* 1895).

Publishers Weekly founder Frederick Leypoldt dies at New York March 31 at age 48. He sold the publication to *Library Journal* editor Richard R. Bowker in 1879, and Bowker handles both positions (*see* 1911).

Sculpture: a bust of Ludwig von Beethoven by German-born sculptor Henry Baerer, 47, is installed northwest of Central Park's Mall, having been presented to the city by a local singing society.

Theater: *May Blossom* by David Belasco 4/12 at the Madison Square Theater, with Georgia Cayvan in the title role, Walden Ramsay, Joseph Wheelock, W. J. LeMoyne, Angela Logans (to 9/27). New York theaters—most of them vaudeville houses—have a combined seating capacity of 41,000.

The Playbill has its beginnings in the *New-York Dramatic Chronicle*, a one-page flyer started by local printer Frank V. Strauss. It will evolve into a slick magazine with editions in every major U.S. city (*see* Storrs, 1895).

The American Academy of Dramatic Arts is founded at New York and will survive as the oldest acting school in the English-speaking world.

First performances: Piano Suite No. 2 by New York-born composer Edward (Alexander) MacDowell, 22, 3/8 at New York. A child prodigy, MacDowell has studied at the Conservatoire in Paris and at the Frankfurt Conservatory in Germany.

Broadway musical: *Adonis* 9/24 at the Bijoux Theater, with Henry E. Dixey, music by Edward E. Rice, book and lyrics by William F. Gill and Henry Dixey, 603 perfs.

Popular song: "The Aldermanic March" by David Braham, lyrics by Ned Harrigan.

Boston-born heavyweight prizefight champion John L. Sullivan, 25, and his challenger Alf Greenfield, the British champion, are indicted for "fighting without weapons" at Madison Square Garden, where they have drawn a near-record crowd. Defended by Howe & Hummel, the two boxers win acquittal, but Sullivan will later claim that his legal fees equalled his winnings.

The National Horse Show opens in October at Madison Square Garden in East 27th Street with 352 animals in 105 classes including hunters, jumpers, harness horses, ponies, Arabians, police and fire horses, mules, and donkeys in an event that will be held annually the first week of November.

The first roller coaster opens at Coney Island. It has been put up by former Elkhart, Ind., Sunday school

The Dakota was in the middle of nowhere when it first opened. MUSEUM OF THE CITY OF NEW YORK

teacher Lemarcus A. Thompson, who will soon be making improved models for amusement parks throughout America and Japan (*see* Steeplechase Park, 1897).

Durham, N.C., tobacco grower's son James Buchanan Duke, 27, arrives at New York in April with good financial resources and determines to become a dominant force in the growing tobacco business, by whatever means are necessary. Virginia tobacco grower's son James Bonsack has invented a machine that produces 200 cigarettes per minute and replaces 200 workers. Duke has four of the Bonsack machines installed in a factory on the Bowery, they make cigarettes the cheapest, most accessible, most easily distributed form of tobacco (albeit the deadliest), and Duke begins opening tobacco shops, some of them alongside existent shops whose prices he then undercuts, forcing the proprietors to sell him their businesses and hiring them as managers. He will distribute his cigarettes free to immigrants arriving from Europe and turn them into loyal customers (*see* 1888).

Police round up 74 brothel keepers in a "purity" drive. Every madam names Howe & Hummel as her counsel (Howe is well known for his ability to burst into tears at will in court at the slightest mention of women and children, thus winning over many juries).

The city acquires Riker's Island, an 87-acre parcel of land in the East River that has been owned by the Ryker family, for use as a prison farm (*see* House of Refuge, 1850). It will utilize the land for prisons, whose numbers will grow in the next century to 11 with a combined capacity of more than 16,000 inmates (*see* 1987).

The architectural firm Carrère & Hastings is founded in the spring by John Merven Carrère, 26, and Thomas Hastings, 25, who met while studying at the Ecole des Beaux-Arts in Paris and have both worked for McKim, Mead & White.

A new Produce Exchange Building designed by George B. Post is completed in Beaver Street at Bowling Green, where the massive red-brick structure rises the equivalent of 10 stories high exclusive of its tall square tower (*see* 1861). Chartered in 1862, the Exchange has outgrown an earlier building on the site, designed by Leopold Eidlitz, and the new building with its 220 × 144-foot trading floor will stand until 1957.

The brownstone St. James Episcopal Church is completed for a 74-year-old congregation at 861-863

Madison Avenue, northeast corner 71st Street, to designs by R. H. Robertson (it will be rebuilt in 1924 to designs by Boston architect Ralph Adams Cram).

The 15 Gramercy Park South house of former governor Samuel J. Tilden is merged with an adjoining brownstone house and given a new Gothic façade designed by Calvert Vaux; it has two entrances, one for political or literary guests, and contains Tilden's vast library. Rolling steel doors behind the windows on the Gramercy Park side afford protection in case of a riot, and a tunnel to 19th Street provides an escape route.

The Chelsea Hotel (initially called the Chelsea Home Club) opens at 222 West 23rd Street between Seventh and Eight avenues. Designed by Philip G. Hubert, the 11-story brick structure has about 100 three- to nine-room suites; shareholders pay $7,000 to $12,000 for 70 of the suites, owned on a co-operative basis, and the other 30 are rented at $50 to $100 per month (the projected $10,000 annual income is expected to ensure the financial stability of the club, easing the burden on shareholders). Few of the flats have full kitchen facilities, so the ground floor contains a restaurant and several private dining rooms along with a ladies' reception room. A large skylight illuminates the open stairwell and its elaborate iron railing. Artists' studios occupy the top floor, and there is a roof garden. Other amenities include carved marble fireplaces, ceiling murals, maid service, and a barbershop. The Chelsea will become a combination residential and transient hotel in 1905.

The Villard houses are completed on Madison Avenue between 50th and 51st streets (behind St. Patrick's Cathedral). They have been designed by McKim, Mead & White based on Rome's Canceleria for Henry Villard of the Northern Pacific, who loses control of the railroad and suffers a nervous breakdown. Villard occupies the mansion on the southerly corner but will soon sell it to New-York Tribune publisher Whitelaw Reid, now 49. A fifth house will be built on the northeast corner of the property in 1886 and a sixth house thereafter.

An article in the New-York Tribune May 6 extols the upper West Side: "That this section is possessed of natural advantages superior to any other part of Manhattan Island is no new discovery." The piece goes on to talk of the "unequalled views, pure air, solid foundations and proximity to the city's pleasure grounds . . . substantial inducements for residential settlement." But columns in the Tribune, Herald, and World about the social life of what is often called the West End are segregated from the social columns relating the goings-on in more fashionable parts of town.

The Dakota apartment house opens October 27 at 72nd Street and Central Park West (so called since 1882) and is fully rented by opening day. Financed by the late Singer Sewing Machine magnate Edward S. Clark and designed by Henry J. Hardenbergh, the $2 million, eight-story, yellow-brick building is the city's first true luxury apartment hotel. It has a steep-pitched slate roof, a two-story arched gateway to its inner-courtyard entrance, a large central courtyard, a large wine cellar, two ground-floor dining rooms, one of them overlooking Central Park, and nine hydraulic Otis elevators (operated by Irish women dressed in black bombazine) to serve its 85 four- to five-room marble-floored, mahogany-paneled apartments, some with 15-foot ceilings (each elevator serves just two apartments per floor). Walls are two feet thick, floors 18 inches thick (including nine inches of dirt for soundproofing), and the building has its own electrical generator. Drawing rooms in many cases measure 48×20 feet ($40' \times 20'$ is more typical), bedrooms 20×20, and the 18-room, sixth-floor flat planned originally for owner Clark, who has left it to his grandson and namesake, has a drawing room 49 feet long and 24 feet wide. Tenants soon include two bank presidents, a member of the governing board of the New York Stock Exchange, piano maker Theodor Steinway and several other substantial business owners, music publisher Gustav Schirmer, and sugar refiner William Arbuckle Jamison. Clark's son Alfred Corning Clark has taken over his real estate activities; the elder Clark named his building the Dakota when construction began in 1881 (other buildings have been given names that symbolize the wealth gained through the hazard of fortunes out west) and gambled that the advent of the new Ninth Avenue El would make the location attractive to prospective tenants.

The city has an earthquake August 10 but it does little damage (see 1663). New York has had quakes in 1757 and 1785 but its underpinnings of Manhattan Schist, Fordham gneiss, and other rock formations will make it largely immune from earth tremors.

Bryant Park is given that name to honor the late poet, editor, and civic leader who died in 1878 (see 1847; Crystal Palace fire, 1858). Located between

41st and 42nd streets east of Sixth Avenue, the former potter's field is immediately to the west of the reservoir on Fifth Avenue (*see* 1934).

1885 Former president Ulysses S. Grant dies at his Mount McGregor retreat in the Adirondacks July 23 at age 63, having completed his memoirs about 4 days earlier after using tea laced with cocaine to dull the excruciating pain of his throat cancer while he saw the work through to completion. His funeral procession is the largest yet seen in the city, pallbearers include his wartime comrade Gen. William T. Sherman, now 65, and former Confederate general Simon Bolivar Buckner, now 62 (who has been editor of the *Louisville Courier* since 1868), and Grant is buried in Riverside Park pending construction of a mausoleum (the largest in America) that will be built as a national memorial on Riverside Avenue (later Riverside Drive) at 122nd Street. Mayor Grace has donated the land for Grant's Tomb (*see* real estate, 1897).

Former governor (now President) Cleveland's lieutenant governor Daniel Bennett Hill, 42, of Elmira is elected governor in his own right, winning 501,465 votes to 490,331 for his Republican opponent I. Davenport.

The first U.S. custodial asylum for feebleminded women is established at New York following investigations by Josephine Shaw Lowell of the New York Charities Commission (*see* 1886).

London-born New York seamstress Jeanette De Pinna (*née* Prince) finds it impossible to obtain the sailor suits popular in England for her son Leo Safati

De Pinna, now 12. She begins making copies of English children's clothing, opens a shop on Fifth Avenue at 36th Street, and is soon joined by her husband, Alfred, who gives up the feather trade that he entered upon the family's arrival in America 4 years ago. When his wife dies next year, Alfred will take over the business, manufacturing and selling boys' and girls' outfits (*see* 1911).

Westinghouse Electrical & Manufacturing Co. is founded by George Westinghouse, who buys up rights to the European Gaulard-Gibbs transformer and will buy patents to the Nikola Tesla induction motor and Tesla polyphase alternator that will make it economically feasible to transmit alternating-current (AC) power over long distances (*see* 1883; 1888).

Gas lighting gets a new lease on life from Austrian chemist Carl Auer von Welsbach, 27, who isolates the element praseodymium and patents a gas mantle of woven cotton mesh impregnated with thorium and cerium oxides, rare earths obtained from India's Travencore sands. The Wellsbach mantle is fitted over a gas jet to increase its brilliance, and gas lighting will continue to illuminate much of New York for decades before giving way entirely to electricity.

Brooklyn's first elevated railway begins service on Lexington Avenue, with branch lines connecting the downtown area with ferries to and from Manhattan (*see* cable cars, 1883). By 1893 there will be elevated lines on Myrtle Avenue, Fulton Street, Broadway, and Fifth Avenue, with connections to surfce lines running south of the city to suburban, semirural, and resort areas, and by 1898 there will be large terminals at Sands Street and Manhattan's Park Row (*see* 1899).

Elevated railway pioneer Rufus H. Gilbert dies at New York July 10 at age 53.

A grand jury investigates the Broadway "railroad frauds" and indicts the so-called "boodle aldermen." Merchant Charles B. Fosdick, 61, is chairman of the jury.

Fifth Avenue Transportation Co., Ltd., is founded by New York entrepreneurs determined to forestall the introduction of trolley cars. The company's horsecars will remain in service until 1907 (*see* Fifth Avenue Coach Co., 1896).

The New York Central begins rearranging and enlarging its Grand Central yards and providing them with improved interlocking switches and signals (*see* 1871; track lowering, 1875). A new annex with a seven-track, 100-foot train shed will be built

Former president Grant's death produced a parade of mourners. NATIONAL ARCHIVE

on the east side of the original depot and used to receive incoming trains (*see* Mott Haven, 1888).

Former New York Central president William H. Vanderbilt dies suddenly at New York December 8 at age 64, leaving a fortune of $200 million in securities that he bequeaths to his eight children. He has paid only $500,000 in taxes during his lifetime, and it is estimated that only $40 million of his personal estate is taxable. His eldest son, Cornelius Vanderbilt II, 42, becomes chairman of the board of various corporations that have been owned by W. H., takes charge of the family's investments.

∞ John Cardinal McCloskey dies at Mount St. Vincent-on-Hudson (later part of the Bronx) October 10 at age 75 and is buried beneath St. Patrick's Cathedral. The Vatican elevates Newark-born New York prelate Michael Augustine Bishop Corrigan, 46, to the archbishopric. Bishop Corrigan has opened 75 parochial schools to serve the city's growing population of Catholic immigrants, built St. Joseph's Seminary at Yonkers, and organized a number of charitable organizations (*see* politics, 1886).

The world's first Yiddish-language daily begins publication at 185-197 East Broadway. Kasriel H. Sarasohn's *Yiddishe Tageblatt* will support Orthodox and Zionist causes and merge in 1928 with *Der Morgen Zhornal* (*see* 1901).

Nonfiction: *The Personal Memoirs of U. S. Grant* (first volume) by the nation's 18th president, whose exceptional work has been published posthumously with help from Mark Twain and will restore the Grant and Clemens families to financial solvency (the second volume will appear next year; *see* 1886); *The Science of Revolutionary Warfare* by German-born anarchist Johann Joseph Most, 39, who arrived at New York from London 3 years ago and has been publishing his newspaper *Freiheit* from an office at 167 William Street. Most's manual of terrorism favors the use of dynamite in waging war for the rights of the working classes.

Sculpture: a bronze bust of Washington Irving by German-born sculptor Frederick Beer, 39, is unveiled outside the Washington Irving High School on Irving Place between 16th and 17th streets; a bronze figure of the late merchant William Earl Dodge by John Quincy Adams Ward, now 55, is installed on the north side of Bryant Park near 42nd Street; *Pilgrim* (bronze) by J. Q. A. Ward is erected by the New England Society near Central Park's East Drive at 72nd Street.

Theater: *One of Our Girls* by Bronson Howard 11/10 at the Lyceum Theater, with Helen Dauvray, New Orleans-born actor Edward Hugh Sothern, 25.

Opera: conductor Leopold Damrosch dies at New York February 15 at age 52. He has recently given the first U.S. performances of Wagner's *Die Ring des Niebelungen* and *Tristan und Isolde*, and his son Walter (Johannes), 23, becomes a director of the Metropolitan Opera with German-born conductor Anton Seidl, 32 (who will conduct the New York Philharmonic until 1898).

Dexter Park opens on a 10-acre site formerly occupied by the Union Course racetrack just north of Jamaica Avenue in Woodhaven, Queens. Named for a champion trotter, it will be used by semiprofessional, working-class baseball teams by the turn of the century (*see* Bushwicks, 1918).

A gambling establishment opens at 39 West 29th Street under the management of John Daly, whose lavish house serves food and wine that some claim is a match for Delmonico's and whose gaming tables are considered relatively honest (*see* 1872). Daly's will remain the city's leading casino until 1895 (*see* Canfield, 1899).

The 15-year-old Cotton Exchange moves into a new nine-story building, designed by George B. Post, in Hanover Square at Beaver Street.

Jewelry retailer Charles L. Tiffany moves into a large Romanesque-style mansion at 19 East 72nd Street, northwest corner Madison Avenue. Designed by architect Stanford White (who last year married heiress Bessie Smith of the Smithtown, L.I., Smiths), the Tiffany house will stand until 1936.

A new city building law forbids construction of residential buildings taller than 70 feet (80 if they face on avenues). Owners of three- and four-story East Side town houses have complained that nine- and 10-story apartment houses will block their light and air, reducing their property values. Except for some hotels, no high-rise residential buildings will be erected until the law is repealed in 1901.

The Osborne Apartments are completed at 205 West 57th Street, northwest corner Seventh Avenue. Designed by James E. Ware with a rusticated redstone exterior, the 11-story Renaissance palazzo is, briefly, the tallest building in the city. It was started by stone contractor Thomas Osborne, who went bankrupt, and has been completed by hotel man John Taylor, who has not stinted on luxury. The Osborne has an elaborate front porch, a billiard room, and, on the roof, a croquet ground and gardens. Some of the 40 suites are duplexes, major rooms have 15-foot ceilings (sleeping rooms, in the rear, have eight-foot ceilings), mahogany woodwork is used extensively, the parquet flooring is elaborate, there are bronze mantels, crystal chandeliers, a marble-and-stone lobby designed by Tiffany Studios with mosaic-encrusted walls, and two sweeping staircases. A narrow extension will be added in 1910 to provide more bedrooms for the westernmost apartments.

Brooklyn land speculator and Prospect Park planner Edwin C. Litchfield dies at Aix-les-Bains, France, at age 70. He and his older brother Electus have created the 1,700-foot-long, 100-foot-wide Gowanus Canal between Hamilton Avenue and Douglass Street, contributing to the development of Brooklyn's Red Hook section.

Brooklyn's St. George Hotel has its beginnings in a single 30-room building that will be joined by seven more structures to fill the entire block bounded by Clark, Hicks, Pineapple, and Henry streets (see 1929).

New York City's (and America's) first incinerator is erected on Governors Island. Within 80 years the city will be burning nearly one-third of its trash in 22 municipal incinerators and 2,500 apartment-building incinerators (see 1990).

Mayor Grace appoints lawyer Henry Rutgers Beekman park commissioner to fill the term of the late William M. Oliffe. Now 39, Beekman will be reappointed for a term of 5 years and draw up extensive plans for establishing small parks as "breathing places" for the tenement districts (see 1887); he will also arrange for public baths to be warmed in wintertime and propose buildings where the children of the poor can play, where their mothers can sit on rainy days, and where concerts and other public entertainment can be provided on winter evenings at municipal expense.

Keen's English Chop House opens. It will move in 1903 to 72 West 36th Street, where it will remain for more than 90 years, serving loin mutton chops under ceilings hung with clay churchwarden pipes.

The Exchange Buffet opens September 4 across from the New York Stock Exchange at 7 New Street; it is the world's first self-service restaurant (see Horn & Hardart, 1902).

Joseph Pulitzer's *New-York World* launches a campaign March 13 to raise funds needed to complete the pedestal of the Statue of Liberty on Bedloe's Island (see sculpture, 1871). Pulitzer himself contributes $1,000, promises to publish the names of all contributors, and some 120,000 Americans respond, donating $101,091, mostly in small coins. Gen. Charles Pomeroy Stone, U.S. Army (Ret.), has solved the engineering problems of erecting the huge statue, but only 15 feet of its 150-foot pedestal have been built. Stone boards the French freighter *Isère* in New York Harbor June 17 and receives the documents of transfer for 139 crates containing Frédéric A. Bartholdi's 225-ton statue (see 1886).

Congress passes the first alien contract labor law, making it illegal to import foreign workers in return for work or service, or assist in such importation. Exempted from the new law are foreigners and their employees now living temporarily in the United States, skilled workers for any new industry not yet established here, and professional performing artists along with their relatives and personal friends already here. The Secretary of the Treasury is charged with administering the law and assigns federal contract labor inspectors to New York's Castle Garden (see 1882; 1887).

1886 Tammany Hall boss John Kelly dies at New York June 1 at age 64, leaving a relatively modest fortune said to be about $500,000. Irish-born politician Richard Croker, 44, takes over Kelly's desk at the "Wigwam" June 2 and will use the position to enrich himself by selling city jobs (men will be charged as much as $250 for a job that pays only $1,000 per year) and collecting protection money from brothels, gambling dens, saloons, and other business establishments. Croker has fought his way up from leader of the Fourth Avenue Tunnel Gang to election as alderman and subsequent appointment and election to a series of city administrative positions.

Former governor Samuel J. Tilden dies at Yonkers August 4 at age 72. His home at 15 Gramercy Park South will be turned into a boarding house (see National Arts Club, 1905).

The Commonwealth Club is founded by reformers who include Brooklyn lawyer Horace E. Deming. It will pioneer in substituting the Australian secret ballot for the open ballot that is held responsible for much of the corruption in politics (see 1889).

Industrialist Abram S. Hewitt obtains backing from Tammany Hall and wins election in the mayoralty race; he defeats economist-reformer Henry George, now 47, the "single tax" advocate, who has run on the Union Labor ticket, and Republican Theodore Roosevelt, who has returned to New York after sustaining horrific losses from the blizzards that killed most of his cattle in the Dakota Territory (now 28, he

The Statue of Liberty would become a symbol of welcome for immigrants. HARPER'S WEEKLY

has been the youngest mayoralty candidate in the city's history). Henry George argues that a heavy tax on land would force the speculators who hold land off the market to release that property for construction of housing, alleviate overcrowding of tenements, expand educational and recreational facilities, and generate enough revenue for the city to take over the elevated railroads and operate them without charge to passengers. Now 64, Hewitt receives 90,552 votes, George 68,110, Roosevelt 60,435 after a strongly contested battle in which many Republicans have cast their votes for Hewitt out of fear that George might prevail (his speeches have attracted large street-corner crowds and rattled property owners). Archbishop Corrigan excommunicates priest Edward McGlynn for having supported George, but the Vatican will reinstate Father McGlynn in 1892 over the archbishop's protests. Roosevelt remarries December 2 at London, taking Norwich, Conn.-born Edith Kermit Carow, 25, as his second wife (she will bear him three sons and a second daughter).

Park commissioner Henry Rutgers Beekman is elected president of the board of aldermen, running on the United Democratic ticket (*see* parks, 1885; 1887).

Labor agitation for an 8-hour day and better working conditions makes this the peak year for strikes in 19th-century America. Some 610,000 workers go out on strike, and monetary losses exceed $33.5 million, but many New York workers do win 8- or 10-hour days.

A new American Federation of Labor (AF of L) is founded under the leadership of cigar maker Samuel Gompers, now 35, who 5 years ago founded the Federation of Organized Trades and Labor unions at Pittsburgh; he will be AF of L president for 37 of the next 38 years (*see* 1902).

A brief streetcar strike in March ties up Manhattan's public transit completely until the city's 15,000 horsecar drivers, conductors, and stablemen settle for $2 for a 12-hour day with a half hour off for dinner.

The U.S. settlement house movement has its beginnings in two small rooms at 146 Forsythe Street, rented by ethical culture leader Stanton Coit, 29, who has returned from a visit to London's 2-year-old Toynbee Hall. An assistant to Felix Adler in the 10-year-old Society for Ethical Culture, Coit begins forming neighborhood clubs to help organize the poor to work for social improvement, and he will establish the Neighborhood Guild next year (*see* University Settlement, 1891).

The House of Refuge for Women (later the State Training School for Girls) is established at New York through the effort of Charities Commissioner Josephine Shaw Lowell (*see* 1885).

A model Bloomingdale's department store opens October 5 at the corner of Third Avenue at 59th Street near a station of the Third Avenue El that opened 8 years ago (*see* 1872). The elevated line built beginning in 1879 has contributed to an uptown movement of the city's middle class, helping the Bloomingdale brothers Lyman, Joseph, and Gustave to build up a thriving enterprise, specializing in whalebone for corsets, yard goods, ladies' notions, and hoopskirts. By the turn of the century Bloomingdale's will cover 80 percent of the block from 59th to 60th Street between Third and Lexington avenues, and by 1927 it will occupy the entire block (*see* 1931; Federated, 1929).

Tiffany & Co. introduces a six-prong setting for diamonds that will be called the "Tiffany" setting (*see* 1877). Set away from the band by six platinum prongs, the positioning maximizes brilliance by allowing a more complete return of light from the stone. Tiffany redesigned the Great Seal of the United States last year.

The Second and Ninth Avenue Elevated Railways drop their fares June 1 to 5¢ at all hours; the Third and Sixth Avenue Els follow suit October 1 (*see* 1880). Fares up to now have been 10¢ except during rush hours (5:30 o'clock to 8:30 in the morning, 4:30 o'clock to 7:30 in the evening), when they were

5¢, but a fare payer has been guaranteed a seat. By 1890 El ridership will have increased to 190 million (*see* 1902).

The Metropolitan Traction Co., organized by local financier Thomas Fortune Ryan, 35, is the nation's first holding company. Orphaned at age 14, Ryan moved to New York from Baltimore in 1872, married his boss's daughter, started a brokerage house at age 21, had his own seat on the New York Stock Exchange 2 years later, has been buying up street railway franchises, and calls his company "the great tin box." By 1900 he will have beaten his rival William C. Whitney for control of the Broadway surface line and will control nearly all other streetcar lines in the city.

The New York Cancer Hospital (later the Towers Nursing Home) opens its first building on Central Park West at 106th Street (*see* Memorial, 1884). Founded 2 years ago to advance the study and treatment of a disease that has almost always proved fatal, the building has been funded by real estate heir John Jacob Astor IV, 22, and houses female patients. It is called the Astor Pavilion and has been designed in French château style by New York-born architect Charles C. (Coolidge) Haight, 45; a pavilion for male patients will be added in 1890 on the adjoining lots at 105th Street.

New York Hospital's Bloomingdale Asylum for mental patients opens on the Boulevard (formerly the Bloomingdale Road, later Broadway) at 114th Street on Morningside Heights, where it will remain until 1894 (*see* 1808; Columbia, 1891).

Otsego County-born lawyer and New York State Normal School board member Andrew S. (Sloan) Draper, 38, is elected state superintendent of public education, despite opposition from educational leaders who protest that he is just another politician. An ardent Republican, he will lose his post in 1892 when Democrats gain control of the state legislature at Albany, but meanwhile he will get the legislature to increase appropriations for education, allocate funds raised by school taxes more equitably, license teachers on the basis of uniform examinations rather than on political recommendations, and provide for more regularity and security in teachers' contracts and salaries.

Girls' High School opens on the east side of Brooklyn's Nostrand Avenue between Macon and Halsey streets, set back on a large grassy plot. It is one of Brooklyn's first public secondary schools.

Yeshiva University has its beginnings in Yeshiva Etz Chaim, a boys' elementary school founded by Orthodox Jews on the Lower East Side to give their sons a traditional Eastern European education and discourage them from being Americanized (*see* 1897).

Postal Telegraph breaks Western Union's telegraph monopoly. Commercial Cable's J. W. Mackay starts the company that will be headed by his son Clarence Hungerford Mackay beginning in 1902 (*see* 1881; 1883; 1928).

The *New-York World* reaches a circulation of 100,000 and earns $500,000 (*see* 1883); Joseph Pulitzer's office is lined with cork to keep out sound, he often edits the paper from his yacht in the harbor, and he celebrates by having guns fired in City Hall Park and giving each employee a new silk hat (*see* 1888).

The *New-York Tribune* installs linotype machines, the first newspaper to do so (*see* Merganthaler, 1884; Fotosetter, 1949).

Author-publisher Mark Twain gives former first lady Julia Grant a royalty check for $200,000 February 27 (*see Memoirs*, 1885). It is the largest such check thus far in history, Mrs. Grant will receive more than $220,000 more in royalties, and the money will enable her to live comfortably until her death in 1902 at age 76.

The will of the late Samuel J. Tilden leaves most of his $5 million fortune to establish a free library for the city. He never married, but his heirs will break the will and donate a much smaller amount for the purpose intended by Tilden (*see* Public Library, 1895).

Paris art dealer Paul Durand-Ruel visits New York to exhibit the works of Impressionist painters at the National Academy of Design. Now 55, he has been championing those works since the early 1870s, and his show is so well received that he will open a New York branch of his gallery next year.

Painter-engraver Asher B. Durand dies at his South Orange, N.J., homestead September 17 at age 90.

Sculpture: a full-length bronze statue of George Washington by John Quincy Adams Ward is dedicated November 26 and installed on a limestone pedestal in front of the 44-year-old Customs House at 26 Wall Street. The Chamber of Commerce has raised $33,000 in voluntary contributions to pay Ward for the statue, whose pedestal has been designed by architect Richard Morris Hunt.

Theater: *Held by the Enemy* by William H. Gillette 8/16 at the Madison Square Theater, with Gillette, Kathryn Kidder, Louise Dillon, George R. Parks, in a Civil War drama.

Theater managers B. F. Keith and Edward F. Albee found the Keith-Albee Vaudeville Circuit (*see* 1885; Orpheum Circuit, 1897).

Playwright-author-adventurer E. Z. C. "Ned Bunt-line" Judson dies at Stamford, N.Y., July 16 at age 63.

The Academy of Music at Irving Place closes after nearly 32 years, forced out of business by the new Metropolitan Opera House that opened in 1883 and will survive until 1966. The Academy's manager Col. James Mapelson says he cannot "fight Wall Street," but boxholders at the new Met commonly carry on such noisy conversations during performances as to make it difficult for audiences to hear the recitatives.

Popular songs: "Mulberry Springs" and "On Union Square" by David Braham, lyrics by Ned Harrigan.

New Yorker Steve Brodie is found in the water beneath the 3-year-old Great East River (Brooklyn) Bridge July 23 and claims to have jumped. Nobody has witnessed it, and Brodie's claim is suspect since previous jumpers have fallen to their deaths, but any suicide leap—especially one from a bridge—will in many circles be called hereafter a "brodie."

Avon Products Co. has its beginnings in the California Perfume Co., founded by Brooklyn door-to-door book salesman David H. McConnell, 28, whose firm will become the world's largest cosmetic company. He hires Mrs. P. F. E. Albee of Winchester, N.H., who has sold books for him, to develop a door-to-door selling strategy. Believing that women are more likely to trust other women, she creates an all-woman sales force and by 1897 will have 12 women selling 18 fragrances (*see* 1898).

Brooklyn's Astral Apartments are completed at 184 Franklin Street, in Greenpoint, to house workers in the area. Oilman-philanthropist Charles Pratt, now 56, has retained architects Lamb & Rich to design the six-story, Queen Anne-style structure that occupies an entire block between India and Java streets; it has a kitchen in each apartment, dumbwaiters in the halls, a lecture hall in the basement, and a large rear courtyard to provide light and air.

The Puck Building is completed for the 10-year-old comic weekly in a block bounded by East Houston, Lafayette, Mulberry, and Jersey streets on the edge of the printing district. Architects Albert and Herman Wagner have designed the seven-story structure to house also the J. Ottman Lithography Co. (which prints *Puck*'s illustrations).

Gen. William Tecumseh Sherman of Civil War fame moves into a house at 75 West 71st Street as that area develops into an attractive residential section. Real estate values are climbing so fast that only people of some means can think of buying there.

Mott Haven in the Bronx becomes a fashionable residential area following completion of the Third Avenue El (*see* 1850). It has become a center of piano manufacturing and now attracts Irish immigrants (mostly on Alexander Avenue), Italians in the northwestern section, and Germans, including Jews, throughout (*see* railroad, 1888).

The Statue of Liberty is dedicated by President Cleveland October 28 on Bedloe's Island in New York Harbor, and the city's first ticker-tape parade celebrates the dedication October 29 (*see* 1885). Designed by sculptor Frédéric A. Bartholdi, now 52, the statue *Liberty Enlightening the World* (*Liberté Eclairant le Monde*) stands 152 feet tall, its right arm and torch measure 45 feet (the hand alone extends 16 feet, the index finger eight feet), and the interior of its crown can accommodate 30 people; built in 11 years at a cost of $400,000 with a steel skeletal frame engineered by Alexandre Gustave Eiffel, it has 300 copper sheets riveted to its steel-and-iron framework and has been presented by the people of France in response to an idea by the late Edouard-René Lefebvre de Laboulaye, who died 3 years ago, as a symbol of the common quest by the two countries for liberty and freedom. Joseph Pulitzer's *New-York World* has raised more than $100,000 for a 154-foot-high Stony Creek granite and concrete pedestal that Congress refused to fund (*see* 1885). Nothing is said at the dedication about immigration, but the base of the statue will be inscribed in 1903 with words written in 1883 under the title "The New Colossus" by poet-philanthropist Emma Lazarus, now 37: "Give me your tired, your poor,/ Your huddled masses, yearning to breathe free,/ The wretched refuse of your teeming shore./ Send these, the homeless, tempest tossed, to me:/ I lift my lamp beside the golden door."

1887 The New York Reform Club is founded by political activists who include Horace E. Deming to oppose corruption and support measures designed to make life in the city not only better but closer to perfection.

Longshoremen strike in January following cuts in wages and benefits. The work stoppage will continue for a full year, and by the time it ends the Port of New York will not have a single longshoremen's association. The Knights of Labor (Assembly 49) stage a strike February 11.

New York stationer Julius Blumberg, 16, starts a firm whose standardized legal forms will be used for wills, contracts, and other documents long after he dies at his Brooklyn home in May 1955 at age 84.

Brooklyn's 18-year-old Frederick Loeser & Co. department store relocates to larger premises beside the El on Fulton Street at the junction of De Kalb Avenue. The premises will be expanded 10 times until it covers two city blocks, between Elm Place and Bond Street, with 15 acres of floor space. Loeser's pioneers in guaranteeing prices as low or lower than any offered for the same merchandise elsewhere.

Fares on Cunard Line steamships bound for Liverpool via Queenstown: $60, $80, and $100 in cabin class, $35 in intermediate class, much lower in steerage. The ships leave from Pier 40 on the North River and include the S.S. *Aurania*, S.S. *Etruria*, S.S. *Servia*, and S.S. *Umbria*. White Star Line ships (S.S. *Arabic*, S.S. *Celtic*, S.S. *Germania*, and S.S. *Republic*) have identical fare structures (steerage is $20) and leave from the foot of West 10th Street. These lines compete for passengers with the Inman Line, Anchor Line, State Steamship Line, North German Lloyd (Norddeutscher Lloyd) Mail Line, Hamburg-Amerika Line, French Line (Compagnie Générale Transatlantique), Guion Line, National Line, and Red Star Line.

Harlem Hospital opens April 18 with 54 beds in three leased wooden buildings at the foot of East 120th Street and the East River. It initially serves as an emergency branch of Bellevue and a reception center for patients awaiting transfer to facilities on Ward's and Randall's islands, but its three-story buildings are soon overcrowded and its dispensary is moved to a fourth wooden structure built on a nearby vacant lot (*see* 1907).

"INSIDE THE MADHOUSE," says a *New-York World* front-page headline October 16. "Nellie Bly's Experience in the Blackwell's Island Asylum." "Continuation of the Story of Ten Days With Lunatics." "How the City's Unfortunate Wards Are Fed and Treated." "The Terrors of Cold Baths and Cruel, Unsympathetic Nurses." "Attendants Who Harass and Abuse Patients and Laugh at Their Miseries." The *World* has run editorials July 3 and July 9 demanding a probe of alleged mistreatment of patients at the charitable and penal institutions on Ward's Island, just north of Blackwell's Island, and two keepers on Ward Island have been indicted for manslaughter following the killing of a "lunatic." Former *Pittsburgh Dispatch* reporter Nellie Bly (Elizabeth Cochrane), 20, has persuaded the *World*'s managing editor Col. John Cockerill to hire her (no paper in the city has any female reporters) by accepting his dare and feigning madness in order to gain admission for 10 days to the asylum on Blackwell's Island, other papers have been taken in by her ruse, and it required the *World*'s lawyer, Peter A. Hendricks, to obtain her release October 4. "Pink" Cochrane adopted her *nom de plume* (taken from a Stephen Foster song) while working on the *Dispatch*, and her articles exposing conditions at the "madhouse" create a sensation, launching their author on a career of "stunt" journalism (*see* transportation, 1889). They will also lead to significant reforms.

Henry Ward Beecher dies at Brooklyn March 8 at age 73. He preached at the Plymouth Church for 40 years and will be succeeded in 1890 by Massachusetts-born journalist Lyman Abbott, now 51.

Teachers College receives a temporary charter and opens at 9 University Place under the direction of Elizabeth, N.J.-born Industrial Education Association president Nicholas Murray Butler, 25, with a Model School for boys that beginning in the early 1890s will be called Horace Mann (although Mann, who died in 1859 at age 65, championed *public* coeducation). Railroad heir George W. Vanderbilt has provided the funds for Butler's salary, and Butler has accepted the post on condition that his school be allowed to train teachers not only in the domestic and industrial arts but in every discipline. The Model School will have 64 pupils by next year and enroll 1,250 children from public elementary schools in special afternoon and Saturday classes (*see* 1889).

Pratt Institute opens at Brooklyn to provide training for artisans and draftsmen. Charles Pratt sold his oil refinery to John D. Rockefeller in 1874; the school he has funded is four blocks east of his brownstone mansion at 232 Clinton Avenue, between DeKalb and Willoughby avenues. Its main building at 123 Ryerson Street is a brownstone-and-red-brick structure designed in Romanesque Revival style by Lamb & Rich (it can be converted to a factory if it fails as a vocational school). It is supported primarily with rents from the Astral apartment house completed last year. Courses include bricklaying, cooking, drawing, painting, photography, plastering, soap making, and "typewriting;" Pratt will have 1,000 students by next year (*see* 1927; library, 1896).

Charles A. Dana launches an evening edition of his *New-York Sun* in March at the persuasion of his publisher William M. Leffan (*see* 1868). The four-page *Evening Sun*, whose managing editor is Buffalo-born journalist Arthur Brisbane, 22, sells for 1¢ and is an immediate success.

Cosmopolitan magazine begins publication at Rochester and soon moves operations to New York, where iron and real estate mogul John Brisben Walker, a onetime newspaperman, will develop it into a journal focusing on domestic and foreign policy (*see* 1895).

Theater: *Met by Chance* by Bronson Howard 1/11 at the Lyceum Theater; *The Henrietta* by Bronson Howard 9/23 at the Union Square Theater, with comedians Stuart Robson and William H. Crane.

The first U.S. social register is published by New York golf promoter Louis Keller, 30, the son of a patent lawyer who has founded the Baltusro Golf Club on a farm he owns at Springfield, N.J. Keller has earlier helped start the scandal sheet *Town Topics*. His 100-page book sells for $1.75, contains roughly 3,600 names based largely on telephone listings printed in larger type than that used in the phone company directory, draws on the membership list of the Calumet Club at 29th Street and Fifth Avenue, and will be followed by social registers published in most major cities, with preference given to white, non-Jewish, non-divorced residents considered respectable by the arbiters who compile the books.

Madison Square Garden is acquired by a syndicate of horse show sponsors, including financier J. Pierpont Morgan (*see* 1874; 1890).

 The city's 2,232-man police force makes 81,176 arrests, 20,000 of them for drunkenness.

 The Eldridge Street Synagogue (Kahal Adas Jeshurun Anshe Lubz) opens on the Lower East Side to serve an Orthodox congregation whose members include banker Sandor Jarmulowsky and frankfurter maker Isaac Gellis. Intended to rival the elegant Reform temples uptown, it is the city's first synagogue to be erected by Eastern European Jews. The architectural firm Herter Brothers has designed the elegant $100,000 structure, whose opulent interior has a false sky and stars painted on its high ceiling, an upstairs gallery for women, Moorish windows of stained glass, brass chandeliers, and—on its western façade—a huge rose window constructed of 12 interlocking circles.

Brooklyn's Emmanuel Baptist Church is completed at 279 Lafayette Avenue in the Clinton Hills section for a congregation founded 3 years ago by members of the Washington Avenue Baptist Church, notably Standard Oil partner Charles Pratt, who took offense at a novel by that church's minister Emory J. Haynes satirizing monopoly power. Designed by Francis H. Kimball and financed by Pratt (some people call it

the Astral Church or the Standard Oil Church), it has a sanctuary with 900 seats.

The Goelet Building is completed at the southeast corner of Broadway and 20th Street to designs by McKim, Mead & White for socialite developers Robert and Ogden Goelet, whose family has prospered as hardware merchants. The Goelet town house is close by, and the Goelets move their office from 9 West 17th Street into the new nine-story structure, whose façade is intricately patterned in brick and terra cotta (a 10th story will be added in 1905).

Ten row houses are completed for developer William Rhinelander at 146-156 East 89th Street, in Yorkville, to Queen Anne-style designs by Hubert, Pirrson & Co.

 Board of Aldermen president Henry Rutgers Beekman secures passage of a bill providing for the extension of the people's parks: Manhattan's Mulberry Street Park, East River Park, Corlear's Hook Park, and others are pushed toward completion.

Sugar refiner Henry Osborne Havemeyer, 40, founds Sugar Refineries Co. (*see* 1857). Son of former mayor William F. Havemeyer, he has taken over most of his competitors in Brooklyn in an effort to eliminate cutthroat competition, control prices, and control the available labor pool, and his 17 refineries account for 78 percent of U.S. refining capacity (*see* American Sugar Refining, 1891).

 German-born restaurateur Peter Luger, 22, opens a Brooklyn steakhouse at 178 Broadway, corner Driggs Avenue, where it will attract patrons into the 21st century with prime porterhouse steaks (served for two, three, or four persons), lamb chops, German fried potatoes, creamed spinach, apple strudel, and beer.

The *New-York World* leads an attack on the cooperative state and federal management of the immigrant receiving station at Castle Garden (*see* 1885). A committee appointed by the secretary of the treasury conducts public hearings into charges that officials have failed to enforce immigration laws, especially the 3-year-old contract labor law and subsequent measures of that kind, and that the officials have personally been taking advantage of immigrants (371,619 steerage passengers disembark at Castle Garden this year). The committee concludes that Castle Garden's administration has been a "perfect farce" and recommends that the federal government take sole responsibility for regulating immigration (*see* 1889).

1888 Mayor Hewitt appoints Henry Rutgers Beekman corporation counsel to the city in January (*see* parks, 1887). Beekman gives up his position as president of the Board of Aldermen.

Former governor (and mayor) John T. Hoffman dies at Wiesbaden, Germany, March 24 at age 60, having gone abroad in an effort to regain his health; former Republican Party boss Roscoe Conkling dies of pneumonia at New York April 18 at age 58 after suffering hypothermia in the great blizzard that has hit the city in March. He was found near Union Square, overcome by the storm.

President Cleveland receives a 100,000-vote plurality in the popular vote but loses his bid for reelection to Republican Benjamin Harrison, who gets 233 electoral votes to Cleveland's 166. Cleveland has refused to campaign, New York State's vote helps to make the difference as it did in 1884, and again it is the Irish vote that swings the state, this time in reaction to a statement by the British minister to Washington that Cleveland would be friendlier to Britain than Harrison. New York Republican boss Thomas C. Platt claims credit for swinging the state to Harrison, but by some accounts the president-elect owes his victory to Democratic Party boss John Y. McKane of Gravesend, who has had a falling out with the state party leaders at Albany and sees to it that not a single vote in his district goes to Cleveland (McKane is notorious for recording the names of guests staying at Coney Island's summer hotels and casting them in the November elections, giving Gravesend four times as many votes as it has registered voters; Tammany Hall does not support Cleveland because he is perceived as an opponent of political patronage).

The Blizzard of '88 would be remembered as the most crippling storm ever to hit the city.

Gov. Hill wins reelection despite opposition from the Knights of Labor. He secures 650,464 votes to 631,293 for his Republican challenger Sen. Warner Miller, 48, who succeeded the late Roscoe Conkling in the U.S. Senate but whose political career will now decline.

Mayor Hewitt loses his bid for reelection, coming in third in a race won by Democrat Hugh J. (John) Grant, 36, who scores an easy victory over Republican Joel B. Erhardt, a former police commissioner who was chosen October 11 at the suggestion of merchant Cornelius N. (Newton) Bliss, 55 (Bliss declined the nomination himself at the convention in Saratoga). Rejected by Tammany Hall, Hewitt runs as a Citizens Democrat and receives 71,979 votes as compared with 73,037 for Erhardt, 114,111 for Grant.

Danish-born *New-York Tribune* police reporter Jacob A. (August) Riis, 39, establishes a settlement house in the infamous Mulberry Bend section of the Lower East Side. It will be named the Jacob A. Riis Neighborhood House next year (*see* Nonfiction, 1890).

The Police Department inaugurates the practice of employing matrons at station houses following efforts by Charities Commission member Josephine Shaw Lowell.

ASPCA founder and social reformer Henry Bergh dies at his native New York March 12 at age 76.

Astoria Federal Savings and Loan has its beginnings in the Central Permanent Building and Loan Association founded at Long Island City (*see* 1937).

Chemical Bank declares a dividend of 150 percent, a level that will be maintained for nearly 20 years (*see* 1875; 1920).

R. H. Macy executives Isidor Straus, now 43, and his brother Nathan, now 40, buy Jerome Wheeler's 45 percent interest in the store in January (*see* 1874). The founder sold his shares to relatives rather than leaving it to his only son and namesake, who drank himself to death at age 31 a year after his father's demise, and the 14th Street store's ownership has changed hands several times (*see* 1896; Abraham & Straus, 1893; *Titanic* sinking, 1912).

An alternating-current (AC) electric motor developed by Croatian-born inventor Nikola Tesla, 31, applies a variation of the rotary magnetic field principle discovered 3 years ago by the Italian Galileo Ferraris to a practical induction motor that will largely supplant direct-current (DC) motors for most uses. A former Edison Co. employee at West Orange, N.J., Tesla will make possible the production and distribution of alternating current with his induction, synchronous, and split-phase motors (he will also develop systems for polyphase transmission of power over long distances and pioneer the invention of radio), but the Tesla Electric Co. he organized last year is unsuccessful and he will never derive much material success from his inventions (see 1893).

The *Florida Special* leaves Jersey City in January on H. M. Flagler's Florida East Coast Railway. Flagler has contracted with George M. Pullman to build the fully vestibuled, electrically lighted train, and its 70 passengers include Pullman.

The New York Central opens Mott Haven yards in the Bronx, five miles north of Grand Central, to repair, clean, and house the Central's trains (see 1885; real estate, 1886). Smoke and cinders from steam engines choke the tunnels leading into the train shed at Grand Central, and there are frequent accidents, but the first electric trolley cars have gone into service February 2 at Richmond, Va., and their success raises hopes that railroad lines may someday be electrified (see 1902).

The Board of Aldermen resolves March 1 that "Fourth Avenue from 43rd to 96th Street hereafter be known as Park Avenue." The stretch north to the Harlem River is similarly renamed 2 weeks later in an effort to raise property values.

Mosholu Parkway is laid out in the northwestern Bronx near the Albany Post Road (see parks, 1883). The new road will lead to a population increase in the area, still largely rural except for a general store, wagon shop, and Methodist Church. (Mosholu is an Algonquin word, probably meaning smooth or small stones.)

The blizzard that hits the city in March brings street traffic to a standstill, passengers stranded on elevated trains must be rescued by men on ladders, and the storm gives impetus to the idea of a rapid-transit system that will run underground (see subways, 1873; 1900). The city's xenophobic mayor Abram S. Hewitt pushes for mass transit as the only means by which New York's population can escape the encroachment of foreigners.

Police officers establish "frostbite patrols" and rub pedestrians' ears to keep them from freezing in the great blizzard that hits the city in March.

Schenectady-born Episcopal clergyman Henry Codman Potter, 44, is elevated to bishop of the Diocese of New York (see St. John the Divine, 1892).

Paulist Fathers founder Isaac Thomas Hecker dies at New York December 22 at age 69.

New York and New England telephone linemen work through the blizzard that strikes the Atlantic Coast in March to restore service on the new line that connects Boston with New York, but the storm disrupts communications and many communities are isolated for days. New York City's maze of overhead telephone and electric wires comes crashing down in the strong winds that sweep through the streets, snapping some of the poles in two, sending others smashing through windows. Work begins following the storm to lay the wires underground, and laws forbidding overhead wires will be enforced.

Once a Week magazine begins publication under the direction of Irish-born New York publisher Peter Fenelon Collier, 42, who emigrated to America with his parents in 1862, came to New York in 1875, and with $300 in capital pioneered the subscription-book business from a basement store in Vandewater Street. The magazine is designed to promote Collier's book business (see *Collier's*, 1895).

Printer's Ink begins publication July 15 at New York under the direction of advertising agent George P. Rowell, now 50 (see 1869); his trade magazine will demand equitable rates for advertisers and publishers in opposition to the post office department and campaign for honest advertising.

McGraw-Hill Co. has its beginnings as Panama, N.Y., schoolteacher James H. McGraw, 28, quits teaching and buys control of the *American Journal of Railway Appliances*. Vermont-born railroad man John A. Hill, 30, quits the Denver & Rio Grande to become editor of *Locomotive Engineer*, having written for that publication (see 1909).

Nonfiction: *In Danger, or, Life in New York: A True History of the Great City's Wiles and Temptations* by William F. Howe and Abraham Hummel of the law firm Howe & Hummel contains several chapters on the city's nightlife. It includes plugs for Harry Hill's Dance House, Billy McGlory's, and the French Madame's in 34th Street, where "the performances are of such a nature as to horrify any but the most blasé roué" (all are Howe & Hummel clients).

The Metropolitan Museum of Art opens its first addition and begins an expansion that will continue until the museum occupies 20 acres of Central Park (see 1880; environment, 1914).

Lithographer Nathaniel Currier of Currier & Ives dies at New York November 20 at age 75. He retired in 1880, his partner James M. Ives, now 64, will live until 1895, and his son Edward West Currier will sell out in 1902 to Ives's son Chauncey, whose firm will continue until 1907.

Sculpture: a full-length figure of the late Italian patriot Giuseppe Garibaldi by Giovanni Turini is unveiled on the east side of Washington Square. Completed in 3 weeks, it depicts Garibaldi drawing his sword and has been presented to the city by Italian residents.

 Theater: the Broadway Theater opens 5/3 at the southeast corner of Broadway and 41st Street; *Drifting Apart* by James A. Herne 5/7 at the People's Theater on the Bowery, with Herne, Katharine Corcoran Herne; *A Legal Wreck* by William H. Gillette 8/14 at the Madison Square Theater with Nina Boucicault, Sidney Drew, Ida Vernon (to 11/10; a special matinée performance is given 10/18 to benefit yellow fever sufferers in the South).

The Players Club is incorporated for men active in the theater, music, and literature. Actor Edwin Booth, now 55, has donated his home at 16 Gramercy Park, retaining an apartment for his own use, and architect Stanford White remodels the Gothic Revival-style house, erected in 1845, to give it the look of a Renaissance Italian palace.

The Klaw & Erlanger theatrical-booking agency founded by Paducah, Ky.-born lawyer Marc Klaw, 30, and Buffalo-born booking agent Abraham Lincoln Erlanger, 28, will dominate the New York (and U.S.) theater world for decades. Klaw has represented Charles and Daniel Frohman, he joins with Erlanger to take over New York's Taylor Theatrical Exchange, and within 7 years their connections with southern theater managers will make them the second-largest booking agency, controlling nearly 200 theaters, most of them in the South (*see* Theatrical Syndicate, 1896).

Actor-playwright-theater manager Lester Wallack dies near Stamford, Conn., September 6 at age 68.

 The Amateur Athletic Union of the United States (AAU) is founded at New York by *Leslie's Illustrated Weekly* editor James E. Sullivan, now 27, who has accused the National Association of Amateur Athletics of failing to make proper distinctions between amateurs and professionals (*see Sporting Times*, 1889).

"There are only about four hundred people in New York Society," says social arbiter (and climber) Ward McAllister, now 60, in a *New-York Tribune* interview (*see* 1872; social register, 1887). The ballroom of his patron Mrs. Astor's Fifth Avenue mansion can accommodate 400 people (but, please, no clergymen, physicians, Jews, blacks, musicians, or actors).

 A factory in Rivington Street owned by Durham, N.C., tobacco merchant Washington B. Duke, 67, produces cigarettes in vast volume, using machines leased from their Virginia inventor, James Bonsack (*see* James B. Duke, 1884). A Confederate army veteran, Duke turns out 744 million cigarettes at New York and Durham, a figure that will reach 1 billion by next year; W. Duke & Sons grosses $600,000 (*see* American Tobacco Trust, 1890).

 Convicted cop killer "Handsome Harry" Carlton comes up for sentencing in December. The state legislature at Albany has voted June 4 to use electrocution rather than hanging for capital crimes beginning January 1 of next year, and it has carelessly neglected to specify terms of punishment for such crimes until that time. Carlton has murdered patrolman Joseph Brennan, but trial lawyer William F. Howe of Howe & Hummel argues that a crime for which no penalty is prescribed by law cannot properly be called a crime; he is upheld by the Court of General Sessions, but a higher court rules that the legislature, whatever its failings in legal language, certainly did not intend that a convicted murderer go free; Carlton is hanged at the Tombs shortly after Christmas.

 A turreted limestone mansion for circus owner James A. Bailey is completed at St. Nicholas Place and 150th Street to designs by S. B. Reed. It has an art gallery and billiard room on the third floor, stained glass, and costly interiors, but Bailey will sell the place in 1904, having moved to Mount Vernon.

The state legislature acts at the urging of the New York Park Association to acquire a 2,764-acre parcel of land—three times the size of Manhattan's Central Park—that will become Pelham Bay Park (*see* 1883). It has more than nine miles of shoreline and will become a major recreational area (*see* golf course, 1914; Orchard Beach, 1935).

The blizzard that strikes the northeast in March comes on the heels of a warm spell that has seen buds open on trees in Central Park. New York's temperature drops to 10.7° F. on Monday, March 12, and winds off the Atlantic build up to 48 miles per hour, bringing unpredicted snow that continues off and on into the early morning of Wednesday, March 14. The 3-day accumulation totals 20.9 inches in the city (some places upstate get as much as 60 inches), snowdrifts 15 to 20 feet high bring city traffic to a standstill, pedestrians and horses freeze to death in the streets, food in warehouses cannot be delivered to grocery stores, grocers double prices, and at least 400 die, including malt-and-hops merchant George D. Baremore, who wakes up in his suite at the 3-year-old Osborne Apartments March 12, trudges off into the snow en route to his office downtown, finds the Sixth Avenue El station at 59th Street closed, and tries to reach the Ninth Avenue El; police later find his body in a snowdrift. Even the husky six-foot-three-inch Roscoe Conkling is no match for the storm. Havana-born poet and independence leader José (Julián) Martí y Pérez, 35, writes that the city, "like the victim of an outrage, goes about freeing itself of its shroud." Martí moved to New York in January 1880 after escaping from prison in Spain; he notes that the blizzard brought out "a sense of great humility and a sudden rush of kindness, as though the dread hand had touched the shoulders of all men."

✗ Levy's Bakery opens at the corner of Moore Street and Graham Avenue, Brooklyn, with a stone hearth making heavily textured rye and pumpernickel breads with the thick, chewy crust popular among immigrants from Russia and the Balkans. Proprietor Henry F. Levy will relocate to 413 Park Avenue, retaining his original "sour" (starter yeast) whose bacteria are kept constantly alive to provide the bread's essential taste.

A small dairy store opens at 135 Madison Street on the Lower East Side under the direction of Lithuanian-born merchant Isaac Breakstone, 24, and his brother Joseph. Isaac, who has been in the ice cream business after several years of peddling, arrived in New York 6 years ago and was greeted at the pier by Joseph, who had arrived 6 months earlier; their Madison Street shop will continue until 1895, and in 1896 they will start a wholesale butter business under the name Breakstone Brothers at 29 Jay Street, Brooklyn (see 1899).

Katz's Delicatessen opens at 205 East Houston Street, corner Ludlow Street, to provide the area's fast-growing immigrant population with corned beef, hand-cut pastrami (a Yiddish word), salami, and other European specialties (see 1942).

The first Childs restaurant opens at New York and is soon followed by four others. Samuel S. (Shannon) Childs, 25, and his brother William, Jr. invest $1,600 to start the chain that will grow to have 107 restaurants in 29 U.S. cities by the time Samuel S. dies in 1925—the largest restaurant chain of its kind, serving nearly 1 million patrons each week. The Childs brothers use all-white furnishings and equipment, dress their young waitresses in white uniforms, obtain the best food available at reasonable prices, insist on absolute cleanliness in the preparation of that food, and maintain the lowest

prices for their buttercakes and other Childs favorites (see 1925).

1889 New York celebrates the centenary of George Washington's inauguration April 29 with the city's second ticker-tape parade and a naval parade that attracts spectators to witness steamships proceed from Castle William on Governors Island to a point far beyond the Statute of Liberty, following in the wake of the U.S.S. *Despatch* that carries President Benjamin Harrison and other notables. Architect Stanford White has designed a temporary arch for the ticker-tape parade at the foot of Fifth Avenue, and the festivities continue for 3 days (see Washington Arch, 1895).

New York State adopts the paper Australian ballot for statewide elections, becoming the first U.S. state to do so. First used in South Australia and Victoria in 1858, it was adopted by Parliament for British elections in 1872 (see voting machine, 1892).

"The man who dies rich dies disgraced," writes steel magnate Andrew Carnegie in his essay "Wealth" in the *North American Review*. The very rich should live without extravagance, he says, provide moderately for their dependents, leave little to their male heirs, and give the rest away in their own lifetime, doing for the poor "better than they would or could do for themselves." Oil magnate John D. Rockefeller praises Carnegie for his philanthropies, whose purpose is to help the poor help themselves.

Camden, S.C.-born physician's son Bernard Mannes Baruch, 17, receives his bachelor's degree from City College and goes to work as a clerk in a Wall Street brokerage house at a salary of $3 per week. By the time he is 30 he will have made and lost more than $1 million (see 1903).

Horsecars carried passengers past Fifth Avenue mansions. Most New Yorkers lived in boarding houses or tenements.

I. M. Singer Co. introduces the first electric sewing machines, based on a patent issued January 25, 1887, for a motor developed by Philip Diehl, head of Singer's experimental department at Elizabethport, N.J. The company sells a million machines (many of them to New York sweatshop operators), up from 539,000 in 1880.

The Boulevard north of Columbus Circle is renamed Broadway under a law that takes effect February 14 as the entire 15-mile stretch north to 157th Street is given a single name (it will not be paved north of 92nd Street until after 1891).

The Claremont Stables go up in West 89th Street between Columbus and Amsterdam avenues (date approximate). Stables, blacksmith shops, farriers, and the like continue to occupy an inordinate amount of city real estate, sometimes in relatively high-rise structures such as the four-story Claremont. A cable railway line was completed 3 years ago along 125th Street, and more are in prospect, but most people travel about the city either on horsecars, in hansom cabs, or in their own private carriages.

The Glasgow-built Inman Line ship S.S. *City of Paris* leaves Liverpool for New York on her maiden voyage April 3 and sets a speed record in May, averaging 20.01 knots on the westbound passage. Built at a cost of more than £350,000, the 10,500-ton vessel is 580 feet long, 63 feet wide in the beam, boasts two complete sets of triple-expansion engines that generate about 20,000 horsepower, and has three stacks (although she has a clipper bow and three masts rigged for sails). Burning an average of 350 tons of coal per day, she has 1,000 electric light bulbs, carries a crew of 370, can accommodate 1,450 passengers, and will repeatedly cross the Atlantic in less than 6 days.

Nellie Bly leaves Hoboken, N.J., November 14 aboard the Hamburg-Amerika Line ship S.S. *Augusta Victoria* in an attempt to outdo the hero of the 1873 Jules Verne novel *Le Tour du Monde en Quatre-Vingt Jours* (see medicine, 1887). Having persuaded her editor to give her a bold new assignment, *New-York World* reporter Elizabeth "Nellie Bly" Cochrane, now 22, leaves at just after 9:40 in the morning to begin her bid to break the fictional record of Phileas Fogg. At Calais, she boards a mail train for Brindisi, Italy, where she arrives November 24. Cabled stories in the *World* keep readers apprised of her progress (circulation soars) as she boards the British ship *Victoria* November 25 for the Egyptian port of Ismailia, reaches Aden December 2, and Colombo December 8, where she is delayed for 5 days before proceeding aboard the S.S. *Oriental* to Colombo and thence to Hong Kong, leaving there December 28 aboard the S.S. *Oceanic* for Yokohama (see 1890).

 Columbia College trustees elect former Brooklyn mayor Seth Low president. He will add graduate schools, end compulsory attendance at chapel (which has offended Jewish students), and persuade the board to move uptown from Columbia's campus on Fourth Avenue (see 1891).

Barnard College opens in October after 3 years of effort by Annie Nathan Meyer, 24, who has charmed and cajoled Columbia College trustees and alumni. Columbia has had a Collegiate Course for Women that let members of the opposite sex study independently for the same examinations as men; Meyer passed the entrance exam for the Collegiate Course in 1885, and when her father discovered what she had done he warned her that she would never marry, since "men hate intelligent wives." The new woman's college is named for Columbia's late president Frederick August Porter Barnard, who has died at New York April 27 at age 80, having favored extending the university's educational opportunities to women. Nicholas Murray Butler's Model School at 9 University Place expands to include a high school (see 1887). *New-York World* publisher Joseph Pulitzer sponsors a competition in city grammar schools with the winners receiving scholarships for study at the new school (tuition for high school is $50 per year), which will soon be called Horace Mann (see 1891).

Trinity School moves uptown to 627 Madison Avenue, southeast corner 59th Street, but will move again next year to 108 West 45th Street (see 1895).

The New York Educational Alliance is organized by German Jewish groups with rooms on East Broadway to provide education and recreation for residents of the Lower East Side, most of them from eastern Europe. The left-wing Yiddish press decries the Alliance as a scheme by uptown Jews to make bourgeois Americans out of the slum dwellers (see 1895).

The *Wall-Street Journal* begins publication July 8 as an outgrowth of the *Customer's Afternoon Letter*, a daily financial news summary distributed since 1882 by financial reporters Charles H. Dow, now 38, Edward D. Jones, now 33, and Charles Bergtresser (see commerce [Dow Jones Average], 1884). Dow has been a member of the New York Stock Exchange since 1885 and a partner in the brokerage firm Goodbody, Glyn & Dow. Initially a four-page sheet giving railroad and crop conditions plus Dow's index of leading stock prices, the 2¢ *Journal* will have 7,000 readers by the late 1890s and grow to become the second largest U.S. newspaper in terms of circulation, with regional and foreign editions (*see* commerce [Dow Jones Industrial Average], 1896).

The 38-year-old *New-York Times* moves into a new 10-story building at 41 Park Row between Beekman and Spruce streets, near City Hall Park. Designed by George B. Post, it has a mansard roof and a façade of stone arches carved from Maine granite and Indiana limestone. Three more stories will be added with a commodious oak-paneled newsroom on the 12th floor, the composing room on the top floor (so that typesetters may work by sunlight), and the five presses below street level, where they they will have the capacity to print 12,000 papers per hour (*see* 1904; Ochs, 1896).

Former *New-York Sun* publisher Benjamin H. Day dies at New York December 21 at age 79.

Painting: *Ascension of Our Lord* (mural) by John La Farge, now 54, for Manhattan's 48-year-old Church of the Ascension.

The Harlem Opera House opens in 125th Street. German-born cigar maker-theatrical magnate Oscar Hammerstein, 42, has built the hall for the area's growing German population.

Leslie's Illustrated Weekly editor James E. Sullivan resigns to become editor and manager of the *Sporting Times*, whose ownership he will acquire in 1891 (*see* 1888). Sullivan's 1-year-old AAU claims jurisdiction over 17 sports.

The city's first real skyscraper opens September 27 at 50 Broadway, between Exchange Place and Morris Street. Designed by architect Bradford L. Gilbert, the 11-story Tower Building rises on a lot that is less than 22 feet wide, with a Chicago-style steel skeleton supporting its thin exterior walls. The architect has climbed a scaffold to the top during construction and let down a plumb line during a hurricane to show crowds gathered to watch the building collapse that it is as steady as a rock.

Otis Co. installs the world's first electric elevators in the Demarest building on Fifth Avenue at 33rd Street.

The Endicott Hotel opens at the northwest corner of Columbus Avenue and 81st Street, north of the American Museum of Natural History, in an area containing mostly one-family houses. Designed by architect Edward L. Angell, the six-story red-brick and terra-cotta structure has a central skylit palm court.

Van Cortlandt Park is donated to the city for use by the public. The 1,122-acre expanse of land includes the family's 141-year-old mansion, its Parade Ground opened last year for use by the National Guard, and it will be used for baseball, cricket, football, hurling, and other sports, becoming the park's most popular section, but many New Yorkers will value it more for its bird sanctuary, bridle path, cross-country track, nature walkways, picnic grounds, and tree and shrub nursery (*see* golf course, 1895).

The Hudson River shad catch reaches 4.33 million pounds. The catch begins to decline, and although it will climb back up to 4.25 million pounds in 1942, it will then fall off drastically, and water pollution will spoil its taste.

The immigrant receiving station at Castle Garden prepares to shut down (*see* 1887); it has received nearly 7.7 million immigrants since it opened in 1855 (*see* 1890).

1890 Mayor Grant wins reelection, receiving 116,581 votes as compared with 93,382 for his Republican rival Francis M. Scott. Former police commissioner Abram Duryée has died at New York September 27 at age 75. Grant has favored low taxes and a limited role for government but has supported investment in sewer lines, streets, water lines, and fire stations in parts of the city being developed by real estate interests.

The Consumers League of New York is founded by former State Board of Charities commissioner Josephine Shaw Lowell, now 46, and Maud Nathan, 27, whose reformer sister Annie was largely responsible for the founding of Barnard College last year. The league is the first organization of its kind (*see* National Consumers League, 1900).

Children's Aid Society founder Charles Loring Brace dies at Campfèr, Switzerland, August 11 at age 64. The Society has opened five lodging houses for boys and one for girls, operated 21 tuition-free industrial schools where children can learn carpentry, dressmaking, laundry work, printing, typing, and woodworking, and—more controversially—it has found foster homes for about 90,000 New York slum children, mostly with farm families in Illinois, Iowa, Michigan, and Wisconsin. Brace is succeeded as executive director of the organization by his son, Charles, Jr., 35.

Dollar Savings Bank opens at 2771 Third Avenue in Mott Haven, the Bronx. It will merge with the Fordham Savings Bank in 1932, open branches throughout the borough, and fund many of its building projects (see Dollar Dry Dock, 1983).

The U.S. Census Bureau determines that Brooklyn's Park Slope section has the highest per-capita income of any place in the country.

The Sherman Anti-Trust Act adopted by Congress July 2 curtails the powers of U.S. business monopolies, but it will have little initial effect; legally or illegally, railroads, petroleum refiners, sugar refiners, meat packers, margarine makers, distillers, and others will continue to make price-fixing agreements and block efforts by newcomers to enter their industries (see Clayton Act, 1914).

The McKinley Tariff Act passed by Congress October 1 increases the average import duty to its highest level yet, but while the average is roughly 50 percent the act does provide for reciprocal tariff-lowering agreements with other countries.

Wall Street has a panic in November as the London banking house Baring Brothers fails and English investors dump U.S. securities.

Financier August Belmont dies at New York November 24 at age 73. His financial acumen and his marriage to the socially prominent daughter of Commodore Matthew C. Perry have long since made him a member of city's elite, a position that is inherited by his son and namesake, now 37.

Consolidated Gas Co. absorbs United Electric Light and Power (see 1884; 1899; Consolidated Edison, 1936).

A measure adopted by the Common Council January 6 makes asphalt the official paving surface for all city streets except those used primarily for business purposes (see 1884). Belgian blocks, cobblestones, and other surfaces will continue to be found on Third Avenue and some other thoroughfares for more than 65 years, but within a century such pavements will have become rare.

Nellie Bly leaves Yokohama aboard the S.S. *Oceanic* January 7 and sails for San Francisco after having crossed the Atlantic, Europe, and Asia in her well-publicized attempt to girdle the earth in less than 80 days (see 1889). The *New-York World* reporter is advised outside San Francisco January 20 that the purser has left the ship's bill of health behind at Yokohama and that nobody may leave the ship for 2 weeks, she threatens to jump overboard and swim but is put on a tug and taken ashore; a special train, chartered by Joseph Pulitzer to take her across the continent, detours in order to avoid blizzards and is almost derailed when it hits a handcar, but the intrepid Nellie Bly pulls into Jersey City at 3:41 o'clock in the afternoon of January 25 after a journey of more than 24,000 miles in 72 days, 6 hours, 11 minutes, 14 seconds (see Mears, 1913).

The White Star passenger liner R.M.S. *Majestic* arrives from Liverpool on her maiden voyage April 8 to begin nearly 24 years' service on the transatlantic run. Built by Harland and Wolff's of Belfast, the 10,150-ton vessel will make the crossing in as little as 5 days, 18 hours, 8 minutes at an average speed of just over 20 knots per day, winning the Blue Riband speed record.

Staten Island gets its first rail link to New Jersey as the Baltimore & Ohio Railroad completes the $500,000 Arthur Kill Bridge (see 1959; Goethals Bridge, 1928).

The National Florence Crittenden Missions of the United States and Abroad is founded by New York patent medicine dealer Charles N. Crittenden with help from Frances Willard of the Women's Christian Temperance Union.

Nearly one-third of the city's schoolteachers are Irish women, and literacy among Irish children exceeds 90 percent, thanks to free public education.

Polytechnic Institute of Brooklyn obtains a new charter and moves into a building at 85 Livingston Street (see 1869). It will award its first bachelor of science degree (in engineering) next year and establish separate courses in mechanical engineering in 1899 (see 1901). Only 3 percent of Americans age 18 to 21 attend college. The figure will rise to 8 percent by 1930, but male students will still far outnumber females.

Daily papers in New York City include the *Commercial Advertiser*, the *Daily News* (not the tabloid that will be started under that name in 1919), the *Evening News*, the *Evening Sun*, the *Evening World*, the *Gazette*, the *Herald*, the *Mail & Express*, the *Morning Journal*, the *Morning Sun*, the *Morning World*, the *Post*, the *Press*, the *Star*, the *Telegram*, the *Times*, and the *Tribune*.

Nonfiction: *How the Other Half Lives: Studies Among the Tenements of New York* by *New-York Evening Sun* police reporter Jacob Riis, now 41, portrays slum life and the conditions that make for crime, vice, and disease: "When the houses were filled, the crowds overflowed into the yards. In winter [there were] tenants living in sheds built of old boards and roof tin, paying a dollar a week for herding with the rats." Riis worked as a police reporter for the *Tribune* from 1877 to 1888, when he joined the *Sun*, built a house for himself in 1887 at 84-41 120th Street in Richmond Hill, and says the most dangerous place in the city is Mulberry Bend, on the Lower East Side near the Five Points, along Mulberry Street between Bayard and Park streets; the city will soon condemn the buildings on Mulberry Bend, and they will be replaced in 1894 by Mulberry Bend Park, which will become Columbus Park in 1911 (see Small Parks Act, 1895; Steffens, 1904).

Fiction: *A Hazard of New Fortunes* by Ohio-born former *Atlantic Monthly* editor William Dean Howells, 53, who moved to New York from Boston 2 years ago and shows the conflict between striking workers and capitalist interests. Howells revels in his success and moves from the Chelsea Hotel to a house in West 57th Street (he will soon relocate to 59th Street).

The Brooklyn Institute loses books and works of art in a fire that destroys part of the Lyceum Building that it has occupied in Washington Street since 1838 and remodeled in 1867. Works saved from the fire are stored in nearby buildings, the Institute's name is changed to the Brooklyn Institute of Arts and Sciences, and the trustees lay plans to erect a new building (see 1843; 1891).

The "Gibson Girl" makes her first appearance in the humor weekly *Life*, which since 1886 has been buying drawings (initially at $4 each) by Roxbury, Mass.-born New York illustrator Charles Dana Gibson, now 22. Apprenticed briefly to sculptor Augustus Saint-Gaudens, Gibson has studied at the Art Students League; millions will share his conception of the ideal American girl whose looks are modeled on those of Southern belle Irene Langhorne, now 17 and at finishing school in New York. She will marry Gibson in 1895 (see 1902; Theater, 1896).

Sculpture: a bronze statue of onetime assembly speaker John Watts by Connecticut-born sculptor George Bissell, 51, is installed in Trinity Churchyard by Watts's grandson John Watts De Peyster, a descendant of Abraham De Peyster; a bronze statue of the late *New-York Tribune* publisher Horace Greeley holding a folded newspaper is completed by Ohio-born, Italian-trained sculptor Alexander Doyle and installed in Greeley Square (32nd Street near the intersection of Broadway and Sixth Avenue). A second statue of Greeley, this one by John Quincy Adams Ward and also with a newspaper, is installed between Broadway and Park Row in lower Manhattan.

The April 12 issue of the *New York Dramatic Mirror* carries an article by actress Minnie Maddern Fiske deploring the triviality of most theatrical publicity.

Now 24, Mrs. Fiske has been married since March 19 to the journal's editor, Harrison, N.Y.-born Harrison Grey Fiske, 28, and retired from the stage, but she will return in 1893.

Theater: *Beau Brummel* by Elmira-born playwright (William) Clyde Fitch, 25, 5/17 at Madison Square Garden, with English-born actor Richard Mansfield, 36, who has commissioned the play; *Margaret Fleming* by James A. Herne 12/9 at Palmer's Theater (previously Wallack's), diagonally across from Daly's Theater at Broadway and 30th Street, with Katharine Corcoran Herne in a pioneering effort at realism.

The Garrick Theater has its beginnings in a playhouse built for himself by vaudevillian Ned Harrigan on the north side of 35th Street just east of Sixth Avenue. Actor Richard Mansfield will acquire the house in 1895 and rename it the Garrick.

Actor-playwright Dion Boucicault dies at New York September 18 at age 69 (or 67). London-born actor-director Henry John Miller, 30, takes over as principal actor of the Empire Theater Stock Company.

Popular song: "The Great Four Hundred" by David Braham, lyrics by Ned Harrigan.

Banker J. P. Morgan buys Madison Square Garden for $400,000 and commissions architect Stanford White to design a replacement for it (see 1887; 1892).

The Racquet & Tennis Club is founded with the stated purpose of "encouraging all many sports" among its members; it is an outgrowth of the Racquet Court Club, founded in 1875, which absorbed the Racquet Club, started in 1868—before lawn tennis was invented. Its first clubhouse is at 27 West 43rd Street (see real estate, 1918), and its members include Evander Berry Wall of 43 Park Avenue, a dandy with a reputation for changing his costume numerous times in the course of a day.

The Preakness Stakes that had its first running at Baltimore's Pimlico racetrack in 1873 moves to New York's Morris Park. It will be run at Brooklyn's Gravesend track beginning next year and not return to Baltimore until 1909.

American Tobacco Co. is founded by James Buchanan "Buck" Duke, now 33, who creates a colossal trust by merging his father Washington Duke's Durham, N.C., company with four other major plug tobacco firms (see 1888). Helped by New York and Philadelphia financiers who include Peter A. B. Widener, Grant B. Schley, 45, William C. Whitney, and Thomas Fortune Ryan, Duke is joined by tobacco magnate R. J. Reynolds and will pyramid a group of holdings to include American Snuff, American Cigar, American Stogie, and United Cigar Stores (*see* 1911).

New York State introduces the electric chair for capital punishment on the grounds that it is more modern and humane than hanging, but its first application proves anything but humane. Buffalo grocer William Kessler confesses March 29 to having murdered his wife and says he expects to be hanged; George Westinghouse installed an alternating-current (AC) generator at Buffalo in November 1886, and his rival Thomas Edison sees an opportunity to associate executions with alternating current so he recommends using a chair wired for alternating current. Kemmler is seated in the chair at Buffalo August 6; his head has been shaved, openings for electrodes have been cut in his shirt and trousers, the executioner closes the circuit, a 1,450-volt current passes through Kemmler's body, but death is not instantaneous, and the current has to be turned on again. The *New-York Sun* suggests that "civilization find other ways with which to manifest progress," the *New-York World* says, "The single quick pull of the rope around the neck is doubtless better than this passing through the tortures of hell to the relief of death," but while most other states will eventually adopt lethal injection for executions, capital punishment in New York will continue to be by electrocution.

Brooklyn's Bush Terminal has its beginnings in a single warehouse put up by developer Irving T. Bush, 21, on the city's waterfront, where the structure provides jobs for many of the Polish, Norwegian, and Finnish immigrants who have begun settling in the Sunset Park area. Using funds produced by the sale of his father's oil refinery to John D. Rockefeller, Bush will pursue his vision of organizing New York's chaotic port facilities that now require ships to wait for dock space to become available. He will put up new buildings beginning in 1902, and the terminal will grow to become a 200-acre industrial park with 18 deep-water piers, its own rail system with a capacity of handling 50,000 freight cars, its own fire and police forces, 16 buildings (mostly factory lofts and warehouses) containing 6.5 million square feet of floor space, and 150 tenants employing 25,000 workers.

The 16-story Pulitzer Building (or World Building) is completed at 53 Park Row, near the Manhattan end of the Brooklyn Bridge, for Joseph Pulitzer's *New-York World*, replacing the building that burned down in 1882. Designed by George B. Post, now 52, and erected at a cost of $2.5 million, the new steel-skeleton office tower with its gilded dome stands on the site where Jacob Leisler was hanged in 1691; soaring 309 feet into the sky, it is the first building to reach higher than the spire of Trinity Church, completed in 1846, and will be the city's tallest structure until 1909 (it will be demolished in 1925).

The New York Loan & Improvement Co. syndicate is founded by men who include banker Charles T. Barney of Knickerbocker Trust Co., his brother-in-law William C. Whitney, Francis M. Jencks, and W. E. D. Stokes to develop land purchased in the Washington Heights section and on the upper West Side.

Brooklyn's Alhambra Apartments are completed at 500-518 Nostrand Avenue and 29-33 Macon Street in Bedford-Stuyvesant. Designed in a combination of Romanesque Revival and Queen Anne styles by architect Montrose W. Morris and developer Louis F. Seitz, 30, the two identical five-story buildings of brick, brownstone, iron, terra cotta, and red tile have 30 three- and four-bedroom apartments, oak floors, stained-glass windows, frescos, and slate mansard roofs; they are set back 15 feet from the street line to provide space for croquet grounds and a tennis court.

The Imperial Hotel opens at the southeast corner of Broadway and 32nd Street with a Palm Room in green marble, a luxurious lobby, and a dining room that attracts the city's parvenus.

The New Croton Aqueduct supplements the 1842 aqueduct and 1872 High Bridge Water Tower, whose capacity has become insufficient to meet the growing city's need for water. Use of the Murray Hill Distributing Reservoir on Fifth Avenue between 40th and 42nd streets is discontinued after 48 years (*see* new dam, 1907; Public Library, 1911).

Starlings are released in Central Park by local drug manufacturer Eugene Schieffelin, who has failed in efforts to introduce skylarks, song thrushes, and nightingales from his native Germany with the romantic notion of introducing to North America every bird mentioned by Shakespeare. Schieffelin releases some 60 starlings, he will release another 20 pairs next year, the birds will prey upon the English sparrows that have overrun Central Park since their introduction in 1854, and there will be jubilation when starlings are seen nesting in the eaves of the American Museum of Natural History, but by 1928 they will be seen as pests.

Delmonico's moves into an eight-story building whose dining and banquet rooms keep it the city's most splendid dining establishment.

Louis Sherry's opens at Fifth Avenue and 37th Street with an elegance that rivals Delmonico's. French-born caterer Sherry has operated a four-story confectionery shop and catering establishment on Sixth Avenue near the Metropolitan Opera House since 1881 to serve the city's carriage trade, he has purchased a house owned by the Goelet family, and his restaurant will continue on Fifth Avenue until 1919 (*see* 1898).

The Café Martin operated by Jean Baptiste Martin in University Place hires 20-year-old French-born restaurateur Raymond Orteig as manager. Orteig arrived at New York a few years ago with 13 francs sewn into his clothes, began work as a bar porter at Winkler's Restaurant, 3 William Street, at $2 per week, and has risen from bus boy at Fortwengler's Restaurant to become headwaiter at that establishment (*see* 1902).

The last immigrants to be processed at Castle Garden pass through April 18, and the facility closes after 35 years as control of immigration passes to a new U.S. Superintendent of Immigration (*see* 1889). Processing of immigrants moves up the Battery to the Barge Office, a small, cramped facility used heretofore by the Customs Bureau for inspecting first- and second-class passengers but hardly adequate for handling masses of steerage passengers. Its inspectors are in many cases former Castle Garden employees, and in the next 20 months they will process 525,000 arrivals—80 percent of all immigrants (*see* Ellis Island, 1892).

1891 Manhattan's Sherman Square receives that name March 3 in honor of Gen. William Tecumseh Sherman, who has died at New York February 14 at age 71. Former U.S. senator (and onetime *New-York Times* proprietor) Leonard W. Jerome dies at Brighton, England, March 3 at age 73.

Former banker and congressman Roswell Pettibone Flower, 57, wins election as governor, running as a Democrat against Elmira-born Republican state senator Jacob Sloat Fassett, 37, who secures 534,956 votes to Flower's 582,893.

The Baron de Hirsch Fund is incorporated in February by German-born New York philanthropist Baron Maurice de Hirsch, 60, with $2.4 million; it is dedicated to helping fellow Jewish immigrants.

The University Settlement is founded by philanthropists to take over the work begun 5 years ago by Stanton Coit. He has gone to England as Ethical Culture minister to London and will head the West London Ethical Culture Society while Felix Adler's society in New York urges university students to vol-unteer as settlers in the city slums, helping immigrants learn English, acquire job skills, and avoid illness (*see* 1897; Ethical Culture, 1895).

Brooklyn oil baron Charles Pratt dies at his Manhattan office in the Standard Oil Building, 26 Broadway, May 4 at age 60 with John D. Rockefeller at his side, leaving an estate valued at between $15 million and $20 million (*see* Pratt Institute, 1887; library, 1896).

The city's tax commissioner acknowledges that while his office can collect property taxes it is able to collect taxes on personal property only from "the widows and orphans," because their personal property is documented by the surrogate court (*see* 1859; 1896).

The American Express Travelers Cheque copyrighted July 7 by the 41-year-old American Express Co. will become an important means of protecting travelers' funds from theft and loss. American Express guarantees checks countersigned by the purchaser, pays banks a commission for selling the checks, receives a 1 percent commission from the purchaser, and enjoys the use of vast sums of money interest free (*see* credit card, 1958).

National Lead Co. is created at New York by a merger of some 25 firms that supply white lead to U.S. paint makers. The company will grow to become a leading producer of paint (Dutch Boy), and its products, along with those of other paint makers, will be used to cover the interior walls of some 2 million New York apartments before lead-based paint is banned in 1960 to protect children.

The city's first hansom cabs are introduced from London, where they have been in use since 1834. (Architect Joseph Aloysius Hansom, then 31, obtained a patent that year on the safety cab that Londoners came to call "gondolas.")

The Manhattan Railway Co. gains control of the 11-year-old Suburban Rapid Transit Co. that is building an elevated railway to link the Bronx with Manhattan (*see* 1896).

The New York Central's *Empire State Express* travels 436 miles from New York to East Buffalo in a record-breaking 7 hours, 6 minutes (*see* 1893).

 New York Hospital opens negotiations with Columbia College to sell four blocks of Morningside Heights property lying from 116th Street to 120th between 10th (later Amsterdam) Avenue and the Boulevard (later Broadway) (*see* Bloomingdale Asylum, 1886). The entire property will be disposed of in the next 20 years, some of it to the city for use as crosstown streets, with the hospital receiving a total of $5,883,550, of which $5 million will be paid by Columbia and Barnard College (see 1894).

Hackensack-born bacteriologist Anna W. (Wessels) Williams, 28, obtains her M.D. from the Women's Medical of New York and accepts a position in the newly created diagnostic laboratory of the city's Health Department, the first such lab in America. New York is in the grip of a diphtheria epidemic; an antitoxin has been developed but is too weak to be effective and impossible to manufacture in the massive quantities needed (see 1894).

Beth Israel Medical Center has its beginnings in a 20-bed facility opened at 196 East Broadway by Orthodox Jews who opened a dispensary 2 years ago at 97 Henry Street. It has a Yiddish-speaking staff, serves kosher food, relies heavily on donations, and will provide free medical care to almost all of its patients for the next 20 years, during which time it will move to 206 East Broadway and then to 195 Division Street (see Federation, 1917).

Jamaica Hospital has its beginnings in a nonprofit facility opened in a small house by a group of women to provide emergency care for Queens residents. It will add an operating room and some more wards in 1899 (see 1916).

Nicholas Murray Butler resigns from Teachers College and the Horace Mann school to accept a position at Columbia College, whose trustees agree to relocate north to a four-block site bounded by Broadway and Amsterdam avenues between 116th and 120th streets. Horace Mann has continued to teach industrial arts while adding Greek and Latin; it created a College Preparatory Section last year, charging an annual tuition of $150 for students in that section, and total enrollment has swelled to more than 250 since the high school was added 2 years ago. Now 29, Butler is succeeded by Walter Hervey (see 1894; Butler, 1902).

New York Law School is founded by former Columbia Law School professor George Chase, who resigns from Columbia after a dispute with its president Seth Low, who has opposed the practical approach to legal education espoused by Theodore Dwight and others. Several other professors join Chase, who rents space in the Equitable Life Assurance Building and by 1906 will have 1,000 students, making it the largest law school in the country; it will move in 1919 to the McBurney YMCA in West 23rd Street (see 1947).

The American Museum of Natural History opens a new wing in 77th Street (see 1878). Designed by Providence-born New York architect Josiah Cleve-land Cady, 54, of J. C. Cady and Co., it harmonizes with the original structure. Museum president Morris K. Jesup invites Connecticut-born paleontologist Henry Fairfield Osborn, 33, to become curator of vertebrate paleontology and develop a new program in that area. Osborn has just joined the faculty of Columbia College as professor of biology (see 1908; Bronx Zoo, 1899).

The first full-service advertising agency opens March 15 in Park Row. New Jersey-born copywriter George Batten, 36, has worked for N. W. Ayer at Philadelphia and offers "service contracts," handling copy, art, production, and placement, thereby relieving clients of any need to maintain their own elaborate advertising departments. Newspapers, magazines, and billboard companies pay Batten commissions on space rates (see ANPA, 1893; BBDO, 1928).

Munsey's Magazine begins publication under the name *Munsey's Weekly* and enjoys an initial circulation of 40,000 (see 1882). Publisher Frank A. Munsey, now 37, will combine his *Golden Argosy* magazine into the new periodical, charge 25¢ per copy, be ridiculed by other publishers when he cuts the price to 10¢, and make *Munsey's* the world's largest-selling periodical by 1907. *Argosy* will be earning him $300,000 per year by then, and he will later build *Munsey's* circulation to 1 million (see *Argosy*, 1896).

Nonfiction: *History of New York* by Theodore Roosevelt, who 2 years ago was appointed U.S. Civil Service Commissioner at Washington, D.C.

Brooklyn's city government enacts legislation providing funds for the construction of a new building for the Brooklyn Institute of Arts and Sciences (later the Brooklyn Museum) and authorizes the Institute to lease land on Prospect Hills for the structure (see 1890). The Institute will be given a 100-year lease at $1 per year in 1893, its collection will be housed temporarily in the Adams mansion in Bedford Park, and construction of its own building will begin in 1895 (see 1897).

Sculpture: a full-length bronze statue of former congressman Samuel Sullivan Cox by sculptress Louise Lawson is installed in Tompkins Square Park at the southwest corner of 7th Street and Avenue A (letter carriers have funded the work as a memorial to the legislator who sponsored legislation raising salaries for postmen and giving them paid vacations); a bronze bust of the late Civil War general Winfield Scott by J. Wilson MacDonald is installed on Morningside Avenue at 123rd Street.

Showman P. T. Barnum dies at Philadelphia April 7 at age 80.

Carnegie Hall opens May 5 at the southeast corner of 57th Street and Seventh Avenue with a concert conducted in part by Petr Ilich Tchaikovsky (he leads the orchestra in a performance of his *Marche Solennelle*). Tchaikovsky has come from Russia at the persuasion of Oratorio Society director Walter Damrosch, now 29, who has left the Metropolitan Opera after 6 years and urged steel magnate Andrew Carnegie to contribute funds for construction of what is initially called simply "The Music Hall." Several hundred standees swell the audience of 3,000 that fills the new Music Hall, built with private contributions that included a $2 million gift from Carnegie, whose income for the year is $4.3 million and who 3 years ago became president of the Oratorio Society. Designed by architect William B. (Burnet) Tuthill, the auditorium has marvelous acoustics and will be New York's (and probably America's) preeminent concert hall for more than a century (*see* 1924).

A new Polo Grounds stadium goes up for the New York Giants baseball club to replace a small 6,000-seat polo stadium first used by the Giants in 1883 (*see* 1876). The Giants have taken over Brotherhood Park, established last year on Coogan's Bluff (named for real estate developer James Jay Coogan, 46), overlooking the Harlem River at 157th Street. In 3 years the Giants will set a league attendance record of 400,000 (*see* 1911; Yankee Stadium, 1923).

The Metropolitan Club holds its first meeting February 20. Banker J. Pierpont Morgan and some 24 other Union Club members who include Goelets, Vanderbilts, and Whitneys have started the new club after the Union's board of governors declined to admit one of Morgan's associates (Morgan retains his Union Club membership and will later return, conceding ruefully that his associate was every bit as obnoxious as the governors judged him). The dissidents are motivated also by a feeling that the location of the Union Club, now on the west side of Fifth Avenue at 21st Street, is too far downtown. They agree to pay $420,000 for a parcel of land at the northeast corner of Fifth Avenue and 60th Street (*see* real estate, 1893).

The Century Association moves into a large new clubhouse at 7 West 43rd Street designed by Stanford White. Founded in 1846 with the idea of having only 100 members, it has grown to have about 800.

Brooklyn's Montauk Club moves into a clubhouse designed by architect Francis H. Kimball in Venetian Gothic palazzo style in Park Slope at 25 Eighth Avenue, northeast corner Lincoln Place, with exterior friezes evocative of the Native American tribe, with depictions of indigenous plants and animals, at the third- and fourth-floor levels on the Eighth Avenue side. Founded 2 years ago for members of Brooklyn's social elite, its membership is limited to 500, and the club soon has a long waiting list.

The city's homicide rate will fall to 3.5 per 100,000 in the next 5 years after 15 years of varying between 4.5 and 4.9 per 100,000 (*see* 1896).

The 71st Regiment Armory is completed except for its tower at the southeast corner of Fourth Avenue and 33rd Street. Designed by Clinton & Russell, it will be damaged by fire in 1902, whereupon the same architects will repair it, adding a 250-foot tower modeled on the town hall of Siena, Italy, and it will survive until the 1970s.

Brooklyn's Wechsler Brothers Block (later the Offerman Building) is completed at 503 Fulton Street, between Bridge and Duffield streets, to Romanesque Revival designs by Lauritzen & Voss.

Harlem row houses and apartment houses that will come to be called Strivers' Row in the 1920s and '30s are completed for developer David H. King, Jr. at 138th and 139th streets between Seventh and Eighth avenues. The 130 row houses have rear alleys with entrances from the side streets; their designers include James Brown Lord (south side of 138th Street), Bruce Price and Clarence S. Luce (north side of 138th Street and south side of 139th Street), and McKim, Mead & White (north side of 139th Street).

The Empire City Subway Co. obtains a city contract to bury low-tension wires below street level. The blizzard 3 years ago knocked down electric, telegraph, and telephone wires strung on wooden poles, Empire digs up streets to install ducts for the wires, and it will grow in the next century to own or lease (and maintain) 12,000 miles of underground four-inch conduits, with 10,000 manholes to allow access to the conduits.

The New York Botanical Garden is created by an act of the state legislature at Albany April 28. Columbia College botany professor Nathaniel Lord Britton, 32, studied under the late John Torrey and has campaigned with his wife, Elizabeth (*née* Knight), 33, for the establishment of the garden; a site has been chosen at the northern end of Bronx Park; and a committee whose members include Calvert Vaux has designed the garden, retaining structures from the old Lorillard estate that include a stone snuff mill built in 1840 (*see* conservatory, 1902).

The Taylor Building on Park Row burns down August 22, killing 61 people.

American Sugar Refining is incorporated in New Jersey by H. O. Havemeyer, whose 4-year-old Sugar Refineries Co. is dissolved by the New York courts. The new company begins taking over the entire U.S. sugar industry in one colossal trust (*see* 1892).

The Gristede Brothers grocery chain begins with a carriage-trade store opened by Diedrich and Charles Gristede at 42nd Street and Second Avenue.

The first bottled beer is introduced by F. & M. Schaefer Brewing Co. president Rudolph Jay Schaefer, 28, who joined the family-owned firm 9 years ago (*see* 1842). Most beer continues to be sold in kegs to restaurants or saloons, where it may be purchased by the glass, stein, or schooner. New York has more soda fountains than saloons.

The $1.2 million Holland House opens on Fifth Avenue, a few blocks north of Madison Square, with a dining room rivaling that of the Imperial Hotel opened last year. The city's luxury hotels encourage lavish wining and dining.

Congress votes March 3 to establish a U.S. Office of Superintendent of Immigration (*see* 1894).

1892 Madison Square Presbyterian Church minister Charles H. Parkhurst delivers a sermon February 14 charging that "every step that we take looking to the moral betterment of this city has to be taken directly in the teeth of the damnable pack of administrative bloodhounds that are fattening themselves on the ethical flesh and blood of our citizenship . . ." Now 50, Parkhurst took over the presidency last year of the Society for the Prevention of Crime that he will head until 1908. Calling New York thoroughly rotten ("polluted by harpies that, under the pretense of governing this city, are feeding day and night on its quivering vitals"), the scholarly clergyman rouses his congregation, whose members include state Republican Party boss Thomas C. Platt, now 58; he blames Mayor Grant, District Attorney De Lancy Nicoll, and the police commissioners ("They are a lying, perjured, rum-soaked, and libidinous lot") for the city's moral decay. *New-York Sun* editor-publisher Charles A. Dana, now 72, urges that Parkhurst be driven from his pulpit, Nicoll orders him to appear before a grand jury, and when he appears in court February 23 and is asked to substantiate his allegations he is obliged to admit that

he has based them only on what he has read in the papers. To gain evidence, Parkhurst hires detective Charles W. Gardner to show him the evils reported in the press; Gardner charges $6 per night, disguises the minister's appearance, takes him to a saloon in Cherry Street where small children buy whiskey at 10¢/pint to take home to their parents, and moves on with him to the Golden Rule Pleasure Club, a brothel in West 3rd Street where the "girls" are transvestites who speak in falsetto voices. When Parkhurst on a subsequent evening asks for "something worse," Gardner escorts him to Hattie Adams's brothel in the Tenderloin, where five girls take off their Mother Hubbard gowns and dance the cancan stark naked while a blindfolded man plays the piano. (Other centers of vice include the Artistic Club on the Bowery and Paresis Hall on Fourth Avenue.) Parkhurst returns to the pulpit March 13 and delivers a sermon that backs up his charges; his exposés will lead to creation of the Lexow Commission and to the election of a reform mayor.

The City Club is founded to promote interest in efficient government and encourage election of appropriate candidates to public office. The club will publish books and pamphlets dealing with bridges, public charities, the city charter, the police department, rapid transit, the school calendar, the water supply, and similar issues.

Irish-born Tammany Hall Grand Sachem Thomas F. (Francis) Gilroy, 53, wins easy election in the mayoralty race, receiving 173,510 votes as compared with 97,923 for his Republican rival Edwin Einstein (Mayor Grant has declined to run for reelection). One election district in the Bowery shows a suspicious return of 388 Democratic votes to four Republican: state assemblyman Timothy Daniel "Big Tim" Sullivan, 29, grew up in the tenements of the Five

Castle Garden had received most immigrants to America from 1855 to 1892; Ellis Island took over until 1932.

Columbus Circle was still far uptown when the column was erected 400 years after the great navigator's discovery.

Points, controls that district, and has employed various ruses to have his constituents vote two, three, and even four times while keeping other prospective voters away from the polls. Former congressman Gen. Daniel E. Sickles, now 67, wins election to the House of Representatives, where he will serve a final term before being defeated for reelection.

President Harrison loses his bid for reelection as the Democrats campaign on a platform opposing the McKinley Tariff Act of 1890 and reelect Grover Cleveland with 277 electoral votes to Harrison's 145. Democrat Cleveland wins 46 percent of the popular vote, Harrison 43 percent, the Populist candidate 11 percent.

The "Myers Automatic Booth" employed by voters at Lockport, N.Y., is the first lever-type voting machine used in an election (*see* Australian ballot, 1889). Such machines will be used on a large scale at Rochester in 1896, and by 1930 they will have been installed at voting places in virtually every major U.S. city, but they provide no paper trail in case of malfunction, and most precincts will continue to use cheaper punchcard systems or other paper-ballot systems.

The 24-year-old Union League Club blackballs prospective member Theodore Seligman, whose father resigns (so do all of the club's remaining Jewish members).

Economic depression begins in the United States, but the *New-York Tribune* publishes a list of the country's 4,047 millionaires, a number that has grown from fewer than 20 in 1840. Most are in the northeast and live in cities, 27 percent in New York (Chicago ranks second but has only 7 percent). New York's 1,103 millionaires include people with fortunes based on real estate (Astors, Beekmans, Cuttings, DePeysters, Fishes, Gerrys, Goelets, Hamiltons, Livingstons, Morrises, Rhinelanders, Roosevelts, Schermerhorns, Stuyvesants), the fortunes of nearly 40 percent are at least partially inherited, 17 percent of the millionaires are women, and the list includes bankers George F. Baker and J. P. Morgan, jeweler Charles L. Tiffany, oil baron John D. Rockefeller and his brother William, financier Jay Gould, inventor Thomas A. Edison, retail merchants Benjamin Altman and Isidor Straus, dry goods wholesaler and woollen manufacturer Augustus D. Juilliard, publishers Charles A. Dana and Joseph Pulitzer, and brewer Jacob Ruppert.

Bache & Co. is created by a reorganization of the 13-year-old New York brokerage house Leopold Cahn under the direction of financier Jules S. Bache, now 30, who joined the firm as a cashier in 1880, became a partner in 1886, and will expand the firm from a one-room operation with 15 employees to a house with 37 branches and 800 employees.

Financier Cyrus W. Field dies at New York July 12 at age 72, having lost most of his fortune; financier Jay Gould dies of tuberculosis at New York December 2 at age 56, leaving an estate valued officially at more than $73 million but generally believed to be more like $145 million. His eldest son George, 28, takes over the Gould business interests, moves into his late father's house at 579 Fifth Avenue with his wife, Edith (*née* Kingdon), and will build a new house at 857 Fifth Avenue, northeast corner 67th Street (next door to the 50-room Thomas Fortune Ryan mansion).

Abercrombie & Fitch has its beginnings in the small, waterfront sporting-goods shop and factory opened in South Street by Baltimore-born merchant-inventor David T. Abercrombie, who has worked as a trapper, prospector, and railroad surveyor. Most of the customers for his camping, fishing, and hunting gear are professional hunters, explorers, and trappers, but they will soon include Kingston, N.Y., lawyer and outdoorsman Ezra Fitch (*see* 1904).

General Electric Co. is created through a merger engineered by financier J. P. Morgan, who combines Henry Villard's Edison General Electric with Charles A. Coffin's Thomson-Houston (see 1883; 1884), eliminating the Edison name because it has lost prestige since the electric chair fiasco 2 years ago and because Thomas Edison still favors direct current, not alternating current (see Langmuir, 1912).

The Grand Concourse (Grand Boulevard and Concourse) in the Bronx has its beginnings in the Speedway Concourse laid out by Louis Risse to provide easy access from Manhattan to the large parks of the so-called "Annexed District," with separate paths for cyclists, horse-drawn vehicles, and pedestrians.

Cholera arrives in America August 30 with steerage passengers from the Hamburg-Amerika Line ship S.S. *Moravia*. New York-born physician Hermann M. (Michael) Biggs, 34, imposes measures to fight the cholera epidemic. A member of the Board of Health since last year, Biggs received his medical degree from Bellevue Hospital Medical College in 1883—1 year after his graduation from Cornell. He studied in Germany for 2 years and has been a professor of pathology at Bellevue since 1889.

The William J. Syms Operating Theater opens November 3 for the 21-year-old Roosevelt Hospital at the southwest corner of 59th Street and Ninth Avenue; planned and directed by surgeon Charles McBurney, the skylit operating theater seats 185 observers. A one-story outpatient clinic was added in 1885, and an operating room specifically for gynecological patients opened 2 years ago.

The first tuberculosis diagnostic community laboratory opens December 12 under the direction of physician Hermann M. Biggs, who will set up clinics for treating consumption (TB). His laboratory administers sputum examinations, reports and registers those who test positive (registration is compulsory for institutions but voluntary on the part of physicians), supervises the disinfection of premises, isolates TB patients and arranges visits by nurses, provides for hospitalization, and works to educate the public on detection and prevention.

New York City's death rate falls to 5.5 percent, down from 15 percent in 1875, as a result of better drainage, new sewers, and the introduction of antiseptic surgery.

The Sacred Heart of Jesus School opens in four West 51st Street brownstone houses purchased by Father Joseph Mooney of the church by that name. Staffed by the Sisters of Charity and headed by Sister Marie Austin (who keeps clothing in a closet for needy girls and goes from house to house Sunday mornings to rouse children for mass), the school for daughters of working-class families will move to a large building in West 52nd Street and accept boys as well as girls (keeping them separated until the 1970s) as it grows into the largest school on the West Side, with nearly 3,000 pupils, before shrinking with demographic changes to fewer than 300.

The Spence School has its beginnings in Miss Spence's School, opened at 6 West 48th Street by educator Clara Beebe Spence, 30, who will resist efforts by parents to influence school policies, putting emphasis on charity (see nursery, 1895), formal etiquette, and moral as well as intellectual development (see 1929).

Collegiate School moves to new premises at 241 West 77th Street near West End Avenue (see 1824). Coeducational up to now, it will become an all-boys school beginning in the fall of next year.

Telephone service between New York and Chicago begins October 18.

Vogue magazine begins publication late in the year at New York as a society weekly, devoting its first issues largely to coming-out parties, galas, betrothals, marriages, travel itineraries, golf, theater, concerts, and art. Editor Josephine Redding is never without a hat but does not wear corsets (see Condé Nast, 1909; Chase, 1914).

Still-life *trompe l'oeil* painter William M. Harnett dies at New York October 29 at age 44.

Sculpture: *Diana* by Augustus Saint-Gaudens for the new Madison Square Garden. The enormous copper statue of the naked goddess glitters from atop the building's 320-foot-tall square spire.

Theater: *Koldunya (The Witch)* by Yiddish playwright Avram Goldfadn at Turn Hall in the Bowery marks the start of Yiddish theater in America (see 1882). Most of the audience has never seen a Yiddish-language play, even in eastern Europe, but the Lower East Side will grow to have America's largest Yiddish-speaking population, and a theater district will grow up in the area.

Popular songs: "The Bowery" by English-born composer Percy Gaunt, 40, lyrics by Charles H. Hoyt.

The West Side Tennis Club is founded April 22 and rents ground for three courts on Central Park West between 88th and 89th streets (see 1874). Its initial membership of 13 grows to 43 by the end of the season and the club builds additional courts (*see* 1902).

Madison Square Garden reopens with an auditorium that seats 8,000, making it the largest indoor space of its kind in America (with the city's largest restaurant). Architect Stanford White has designed the splendid structure of yellow brick and Pompeiian terra cotta (*see* 1890; 1925).

Columbia College medical student Carlyle Harris uses morphine to murder his child bride, Helen Potts. Harris's rich parents retain William F. Howe of the celebrated law firm Howe & Hummel to defend their son; dressed in purple and using oratory of a matching hue, Howe wins acquittal.

The Reno Inclined Elevator patented March 15 by U.S. mining engineer Jesse Wilford Reno, 30, is the world's first escalator. It will be installed in the fall of 1896 at Coney Island's Old Iron Pier, but the flat-step moving staircase patented by U.S. inventor Charles A. Wheeler August 2 is the first practical escalator. It will never be built; inventor Charles D. Seeberger will buy Wheeler's patent, incorporate its basic feature in his own improved design, and have Otis Elevator produce it.

The term *skeleton construction* is introduced by the *Real Estate Record and Builders' Guide* for what hitherto has been called *steel cage construction* and is used in the city building code adopted in April.

Columbus Circle gets its name as a memorial to the Great Navigator is unveiled October 12—the 400th anniversary of his discovery of America (*see* 1792). *Il Progresso Italo-Americano* publisher Carlo Barsotti started his paper 11 years ago and has run editorials urging that the discovery be celebrated, although not all historians agree that Christopher Columbus was Genoese. Donated by Italians in the city, the 80-foot column of Carrera marble will be surmounted in 1894 with a statue by sculptor Gaetano Russo (*see* parade, 1909).

"New York Flats and French Flats" by architect Philip Hubert and his colleagues at Hubert, Pirsson and Hoddick is published in the *Architectural Record*. "Are we wasting millions in the building up of a city so radically defective in plan and construction," they ask, "that a few decades will find it honeycombed with squalid tenement districts, ever spreading and ever tending to lower depths in fetid degradation?" What is needed, they say, is a "radical change in our division of our land, our mode of building, and a study of yet unsolved and most intricate social questions."

The Bushwick Democratic Club building is completed at 719 Bushwick Avenue, northwest corner Hart Street, to innovative designs by Frank Freeman.

Brooklyn grocer Henry A. Meyer's Germania Land and Improvement Co. lays a grid across 65 acres of Flatbush potato fields, formerly owned by the Vanderveer family, and puts up rows of cottages designed in Queen Anne style (*see* railroad, 1878).

The Sea Gate Association is organized as an exclusive residential community at the western end of Coney Island and a 12-foot-high fence is erected to keep out visitors to the growingly popular Brooklyn resort. Sea Beach Railroad president Alrick Man has proposed the gated community on a site purchased 4 years ago by Royal Baking Powder Co. president William K. Ziegler, gates are installed at Surf and Mermaid avenues with round-the-clock guards, and Sea Gate will soon have scores of houses, including two designed by Stanford White, with its own police force.

Judson Memorial Church is completed on Washington Square to designs by architect Stanford White.

The cornerstone of St. John the Divine is laid by Bishop Potter December 27 (St. John's Day) on an 11.5-acre site acquired last year on Morningside Heights by the Episcopal diocese of New York for $850,000. Planned as the world's largest cathedral, it has been designed by architects George Lewis Heins, 32, and Christopher Grant La Farge, 30, who studied under Henry H. Richardson at Boston before going into partnership 6 years ago; Heins will die in 1907, and the firm of Heins and La Farge will be replaced in 1911. Construction will begin next year but will be halted when soft stone is discovered where bedrock was supposed to be; work will not resume for 3-years, by which time more than $500,000 will have been spent on excavating the soft stone and pouring concrete (*see* 1909).

The Hotel Royal on Sixth Avenue at 40th Street burns down February 5, killing 28 people.

New York City receives new torrents of clean Catskill Mountain drinking water as the $24 million New Croton Aqueduct is completed after 7 years of construction further inland from the original aqueduct (*see* 1842; 1848). That first aqueduct will continue to provide water to the city until 1955 (*see* Catskill system, 1917).

R. H. Macy partner Nathan Straus launches a campaign for pasteurized milk; he will establish milk stations in New York and other large cities.

American Sugar Refining controls 98 percent of the U.S. sugar industry; H. O. Havemeyer's New York-based Sugar Trust uses political influence to suppress foreign competition with tariff walls and the company saves itself millions of dollars per year in duties by having its raw sugar imports shortweighted (*see* 1891; 1895).

Caffe A. Ferrara opens at 195 Grand Street, between Mulberry and Mott streets. Neapolitan-born opera lover Antonio Ferrara, 32, has started what will soon be a *pasticceria* in a building that houses the Order of the Sons of Italy in America; within a few years he will be serving customers who include Enrico Caruso with cakes, cookies, cannoli, sfogliatelle, and coffee that is roasted daily and ground as needed, his daughter Eleanor will marry stowaway immigrant Peter Lepore in 1932, and Lepore will transform the café into a neighborhood landmark where patrons play a Neapolitan card game called scopa; Pasticceria Ferrara will continue in the same location into the 21st century.

New York's immigrant receiving station moves to Ellis Island, a piece of land in the Upper Bay of New York Harbor (*see* 1890). Known since late in the 18th century as Ellis Island after a butcher, Samuel Ellis, who was one of several people to own it, the island was deeded to the federal government by Gov. Daniel Tompkins earlier in this century. A powder magazine was removed in April 1890 after safety concerns were raised, construction of the new 12-building facility began shortly thereafter, the island is being enlarged to 27 acres, its buildings have cost about $500,000 (nearly twice the original estimate), it opens January 1, and the first immigrant processed is one Annie Moore of Cork (*see* 1897). Ellis Island will process immigrants until 1932.

1893 Russian-born anarchist Emma Goldman, 24, makes a speech in Union Square August 21 urging striking clockmakers to steal bread if they cannot afford to buy food for their families in the economic depression. There is little practical difference, she says, between the cruelties of the U.S. plutocracy and those of czarist Russia. Police arrest her for inciting to riot and she is sentenced to 1 year's imprisonment (*see* 1901). Emma Goldman will define anarchism as "the philosophy of a new social order based on liberty unrestricted by man-made law; the theory that all forms of government rest on violence and are therefore wrong and harmful."

Former New York governor and U.S. secretary of state Hamilton Fish dies at Garrison, N.Y., September 6 at age 75.

The Henry Street Settlement House has its beginnings in the Nurses' Settlement founded by Rochester-born trained nurse and social worker Lillian D. Wald, 26, to help immigrants on the city's Lower East Side, most of them poor Jews. Backed by the Schiff and Loeb families, she will soon add a nurses' training program, community educational programs, and youth clubs.

Philanthropist Louisa Lee Schuyler appoints Michigan-born reformer Homer Folks, 26, secretary of the privately operated State Charities Aid Association, a watchdog group that oversees the work of public welfare institutions.

Economic recession continues as European investors withdraw funds. The average worker earns $9.42 per week, and immigrants often receive less than $1 per day. Unemployed workers roam New York streets, begging for help, and abandoned children are often left to live by their wits.

Wall Street stock prices take a sudden drop May 5. Business is paralyzed by mid-June as liabilities of major corporations, banks, railroads, and other business firms reach nearly $2 billion, and gold reserves in the U.S. Treasury are so low that the redemption of Treasury notes in silver seems inevitable; the market collapses June 27, the Clearing-House Association decides that the banks can maintain the volume of their loans and avert serious disaster by extending their credit, but 600 U.S. banks close their doors, more than 15,000 business firms fail, and 74 railroads go into receivership in a depression that will continue for 4 more years.

Brooklyn's Abraham & Straus department store is founded as Joseph Wechsler of Wechsler & Abraham sells his interest to Macy's Isidor and Nathan Straus and their partner Charles B. Webster (*see* 1888). Like Benjamin Altman and Lyman Bloomingdale, 59-year-old merchant Abraham Abraham began as a salesman at the Newark department store Beetlebeck's; he will brings his sons-in-law Simon F. Rothschild, now 32, and Edward C. (Charles) Blum, now 30, into the store to counter control by the Macy interests, and by the turn of the century A&S will have entrances on four sides of the block that it will largely occupy (*see* Federated, 1929).

Retired clipper-ship magnate A. A. Low dies at Brooklyn January 7 at age 81. His son Seth, now nearly 43, has served as mayor of Brooklyn and is president of Columbia College.

Thousands of New Yorkers crowd the seawall at the Battery February 22 to watch President Harrison run up the U.S. flag on the new White Star passenger liner S.S. *City of New York* (an Inman Line ship of the same name foundered outside Queenstown, Ireland, in late March 1864 but with no reported loss of life). Her grand saloon can seat 400 at a single meal; her library boasts stained-glass windows and 800 volumes bound with gold-stamped leather; her smoking room is paneled in American walnut, decorated with scarlet-dyed leather couches, and can accommodate 130.

The New York Central & Hudson River Railroad's 2-year-old *Empire State Express* hits a record speed of 112 miles per hour May 10 pulling four heavy Wagner cars down a 0.28 percent grade and averages 102.8 miles per hour over five miles (see 1891). Locomotive #999 has been built for speed with 86-inch driver wheels and is exhibited at the Columbian Exposition in Chicago but will later be fitted with more normal 78-inch wheels.

The New York, Lake Erie and Western Railway files for bankruptcy in May and will be reorganized in 1895 as the Erie Railroad Co. (see 1875). Its entire main line was narrowed to standard gauge in 1 day June 23, 1880 (see Erie Lackawanna, 1961).

The Myrtle Avenue trolley line in Queens improves service May 23 with a steam dummy (a car powered by a small steam engine), attracting more settlement of west central neighborhoods such as Glendale (see 1869).

The Brooklyn City Railroad Co. electrifies its line along Flatbush Avenue (see 1875). Lowell, Mass.-born engineer Fred S. (Stark) Pearson, 32, has designed and erected the largest and most modern electric power station to date, and the trolleys are so much more efficient than horsecars that they encourage development of suburban housing in the Flatlands (see Pearson, 1896).

Brooklyn's "J" line El opens along Fulton Street in East New York between Alabama Avenue and Crescent Street, where it will continue to operate for more than a century.

Lebanon Hospital opens with 50 beds in a former Ursuline convent in the Bronx at the corner of Westchester Avenue and 151st Street. Initially for Jewish immigrants, it will add a school of nursing next year (see 1932; Bronx-Lebanon, 1962).

Lillian D. Wald of the Henry Street Settlement develops a visiting nurse program that within 13 years will have 100 nurses making 227,000 house calls per year (see 1944).

New York City's Woman Teachers' Association petitions the state legislature at Albany to place them "on an equal financial footing with men," who receive $3,000 per year as compared to $1,700 for the women.

A survey of Brooklyn schools reveals that 18 classes have 90 to 100 students each, while one classroom is jammed with 158 (see 1867). Despite the state's 19-year-old compulsory-education legislation, schools in Manhattan and Brooklyn turn away thousands of children for lack of seats, and many have half-day sessions so that the same classroom may be used for two shifts of pupils.

Joseph Pulitzer marks the 10th anniversary of his *New-York World* purchase from Jay Gould May 7 by putting out a 100-page edition that has sales of 400,000 copies (see 1883). Pulitzer installs a four-color rotary press in hopes of reproducing great works of art in the *World*'s Sunday supplement. Designed by the city's Hoe Co. of 1875 folding apparatus fame, the new press will be used to produce the first colored cartoon (see 1896).

The American Newspaper Publishers Association (ANPA) founded in 1886 adopts a resolution agreeing to pay commission in the form of discounts to recognized independent advertising agencies and to give no discounts on space sold directly to advertisers. The resolution establishes the modern advertising agency system (see Batten, 1891).

McClure's magazine begins publication at New York under the direction of Irish-born publisher S. S. (Samuel Sidney) McClure, 36, who created the first U.S. newspaper syndicate in 1884. His partner is Iowa-born editor John Sanborn Phillips, 32, and their 15¢ monthly will be one of the first mass-circulation magazines (most magazines sell for 25¢ or 35¢). John Brisben Walker acquired *Cosmopolitan* magazine 4 years ago and cuts its price to 12¢; Frank A. Munsey cuts the price of *Munsey's* magazine to 10¢ and will later estimate that "the ten-cent magazine increased the magazine-buying public from 250,000 to 750,000" from 1893 to 1899; higher circulation will lead to more advertising revenue, enabling publishers to sell magazines for less than their production costs.

Nonfiction: *Children of the Poor* by Jacob Riis; *Hell Up to Date* by Illinois-born cartoonist Arthur Henry "Art" Young, 23, satirizes capitalism, militarism, and the middle class. Young came to New York 5 years ago and enrolled at the Art Students League.

Fiction: *Maggie: A Girl of the Streets* by Newark, N.J.-born New York newspaper reporter Stephen Crane,

21, who has the naturalistic portrayal of slum life published at his own expense with money borrowed from his brother.

Booksellers Row has its beginnings in a used book shop opened by Polish-born bookseller Jacob Abrahams at 80 Fourth Avenue. He will move in 1898 to 145 Fourth Avenue, where he will remain until his death in the late 1930s (*see* Stammer, 1900).

 The Municipal Art Society is founded by New York artists whose initial mission is to paint murals and carve monuments for the city's public spaces.

Sculpture: a statue of shipbuilder John Ericsson by upstate New York-born sculptor Jonathan Scott Hartley, 48, is unveiled in Battery Park with bronze tablets on its stone pedestal depicting Ericsson's ironclad *Monitor* in action; a statue of Nathan Hale by Brooklyn-born sculptor Frederick W. (William) MacMonnies, 33, is completed for City Hall Park; a statue of the late Roscoe Conkling by John Quincy Adams Ward is dedicated at the southeast corner of Madison Square near 23rd Street.

Theater: *The Girl I Left Behind Me* by David Belasco and *New-York Sun* critic Franklin Fyler 1/25 at the new Empire Theater, 208 perfs. Charles Frohman, now 32, has placed actor John Drew under contract, assembled the Empire Theater Stock Company to support him, and built the Empire opposite the 10-year-old Metropolitan Opera House on Broadway just south of 40th Street, where it will remain for more than 60 years; *Ninety Days* by William H. Gillette 2/6 at the Broadway Theater, with a cast of 50 (to 3/18; the costly failure takes all of Gillette's savings); Oscar Hammerstein's 5,200-seat Victoria Theater opens 2/20 at the corner of 42nd Street and Seventh Avenue, having been built from used materials in 3 months for $80,000; *Shore Acres* by James A. Herne 10/3 at Minor's Fifth Avenue Theater, with Herne, Charles Craig, Katharine Corcoran Herne (it has opened earlier at the Boston Museum and moves to Daly's Theater 12/25), 180 perfs.

Actor Edwin Booth dies in his rooms at the Players Club June 7 at age 59. A heavy smoker (at least 10 cigars per day, plus pipes and cigarettes), he has been suffering mild strokes since 1889, sometimes forgetting his lines, and has been losing his eyesight and hearing.

Thomas A. Edison demonstrates his Kinetoscope at the Columbian Exposition in Chicago, having filed a caveat with the Patent Office 10/17/1888 describing his idea for a device that would "do for the eye what the phonograph does for the ear." He filed for a patent 8/24/1891 (*see* 1894).

 First performances: Symphony No. 9 (*From the New World*) by Czech composer Antonin Dvorák 12/15 at Carnegie Hall in a performance by the New York Philharmonic, which has moved into the 2-year-old hall in West 57th Street where it will remain until 1962.

Music publisher Gustav Schirmer dies at Eisenach, Germany, August 6 at age 63. His New York firm is incorporated and taken over by his sons Rudolph and Gustave.

Stage musicals: *A Trip to Chinatown* 8/7 at the Madison Square Theater, with book by Charles Hoyt, music and lyrics by Percy Gaunt, songs that include "The Bowery," "Reuben, Reuben," "Push the Clouds Away," and "After the Ball" by songwriter Chester K. Harris, 26, whose song will be the first to have sheet music sales of more than 5 million copies, 650 perfs.

 Newspaper reporters don formal attire February 11 to attend the annual French Ball held since 1866. Dancing begins at midnight, having been preceded for some hours by what the *New-York Herald* describes as "a blizzard of passion" and "a riot of debauchery" in which carriages blocked the streets outside Madison Square Garden while old men "crazy with wine" committed sex acts in the Garden's family boxes. The *Times* headline reads, "Jezebel Holds Carnival—an orgy winds up the big French ball." Police have turned a blind eye to the proceedings but respond to public outrage February 20 with a midnight raid on the annual (and far more sedate) Mardi Gras ball held at Lenox Lyceum in West 59th Street and sponsored in part by the French consul.

Singer Lillian Russell, now 31, obtains an annulment at New York November 16 of her 1884 marriage at Hoboken to English comic-opera writer Edward Solomon, who was not legally separated from an earlier wife when he married her. He was her second husband, she has borne his daughter, Abe Hummel has represented her in the proceedings, and she will remarry at Hoboken in January of next year.

 Howe & Hummel takes in so much money representing accused criminals and other clients that its two partners earn an estimated $300,000 or more each (*see* 1884; 1897). The firm employs detectives, process servers (often disguised as milkmen, scrubwomen, Western Union messengers, or simply men looking for directions or a drink of water), and other agents to help it in its work, the partners meet at the end of each day in the back room of a Franklin Street restaurant to empty their pockets on a table and divide the day's takings on an equal basis (the other table in the room is reserved for judges of the Court of General Sessions). The two men keep no records, doing all their bookkeeping on the restaurant's tablecloths.

The 14-story Havemeyer Building is completed in Church Street between Dey and Cortlandt streets. George B. Post has designed the structure for sugar heir Theodore A. Havemeyer, who has built it as a speculative venture, and its six Otis hydraulic elevators ascend and descend at 25 feet per minute (it is the first building in New York to have express elevators; two such elevators rise non-stop to the seventh floor).

Mayor Gilroy tries to have City Hall replaced with a building more suited "for office purposes for the departments of a great city." The *New-York Times* says January 29, "Here Tweed and his fellow-bandits despoiled the city. Here foul-mouthed, illiterate, be-diamonded Aldermen divided plunder wrested from the taxpayers . . . In this hall corrupt Aldermen and officials of higher station laughingly discussed their indictments." Citizens who appreciate good architecture thwart Gilroy's plan.

The U.S. Supreme Court rules March 27 in *Monongahela Navigation Co. v. United States* that property may not be condemned except for clear public use. In an opinion written by Justice David Josiah Brewer, 55, the court rules that the Fifteenth Amendment prohibits the taking of private property without "just compensation," and the profit-making potential of a property is a matter for the courts, not any legislative body, to decide. Construction of low-rent municipal housing is "class legislation," the court declares, and its decision will hamper the city's slum-clearance efforts.

The nine-story Cable Building is completed at 621 Broadway, northwest corner Houston Street, to Beaux-Arts designs by Stanford White. Its all-steel frame is designed to muffle the noise from its basement, where 100-ton wheels, each 32 feet in diameter, provide power to the Broadway Cable and Seventh Avenue Railway Co. The company's cable cars move up and down Broadway between Bowling Green and West 36th Street.

The first Metropolitan Life Insurance Co. building is completed at the northeast corner of Madison Avenue and 23rd Street (*see* commerce, 1879). Napoleon LeBrun & Sons has designed the 11-story white marble structure that will be expanded by the addition of five matching buildings, extending north to 24th Street and farther east on 23rd. The company will buy the southeast corner of Madison Avenue and 24th Street in 1905 for the erection of a skyscraper (*see* 1909).

The West End Collegiate Church is completed at the northeast corner of West End Avenue and 77th Street to designs by Robert W. Gibson, whose Dutch stepped-gable façade reflects the Dutch Reformed Church origins of his client.

"The New York Tenement House Evil and Its Cure" by Brooklyn-born architect Ernest Flagg, 36, is published in *Scribner's* magazine and says that the city's tenement apartments are dark and airless because their buildings were put up on such small lots. Strung end to end like railroad cars, the old six-story tenements have only tiny air shafts to provide light and air between their 90-foot ends, they crowd 10 families into 25-by-100-foot lots, and their minimal communal plumbing is indoors only because outhouses would consume land used for building. Flagg urges that lots be combined in the future to allow for buildings at least 100 feet square (*see* 1850; tenement law, 1901).

The 13-story Waldorf Hotel opens March 14 on Fifth Avenue at 33rd Street, where the residence of William B. Astor has been torn down to make room for the hotel, designed in German Renaissance style by architect Henry Janeway Hardenbergh with 530 rooms and 350 private baths (*see* Astor House, 1836; Astoria, 1897).

The 17-story Hotel New Netherland is completed at the northeast corner of Fifth Avenue and 59th Street. Designed in neo-Romanesque style by William Hume, the 234-foot tower is called "the tallest hotel structure in the world" (*see* Savoy, 1892; Sherry-Netherland, 1926).

The Sevillia Hotel (later the Park Wald Hotel, subsequently the Central Park Mews apartment house) opens at 117 West 58th Street (*see* Spanish Flats, 1883). Designed by Philip Hubert, the 12-story brownstone structure is the city's first hotel with stone floors (Hubert and his associates have maintained that it is no more expensive to build a fireproof brick-and-iron building than to put up the firetraps that most hotels continue to be).

A clubhouse for the 2-year-old Metropolitan Club is completed at Fifth Avenue and 60th Street to designs by Stanford White. J. Pierpont Morgan and his friends have commissioned the Italian Renaissance palazzo, whose English carriage entrance has a courtyard; its interior is marked by Corinthian columns, oversized rooms, marble coffers, scarlet carpeting, and gilt.

The Gowanus Canal has become an open cesspool, says the *Brooklyn Daily Eagle* July 14 (*see* Litchfield, 1885; flushing tunnel, 1911).

A hurricane moves up from Norfolk, Va., in 12 hours and hits the city on the evening of August 23, ripping off roofs, knocking down chimneys, felling telephone and telegraph lines, flooding lower Manhattan, uprooting more than 100 trees in Central Park, and smashing bathing pavilions on Hog Island, a popular resort—sometimes called Far Rockaway Beach—off the Far Rockaway Peninsula in Queens (the island will have disappeared by 1902).

Brooklyn's Prospect Park gets its first zoo (*see* Central Park, 1864). Bears, deer, sheep, and peafowl go on exhibit, and the facility will grow to encompass 12 acres, with 261 animals of 61 species (*see* 1993).

Joseph Pulitzer's *New-York World* establishes a Free Bread Fund and sends wagons through tenement districts, handing out bread (and promoting the newspaper) to long lines of hungry people as the economic recession tightens its grip. Nathan Straus of R. H. Macy Co. establishes restaurants that serve 5¢ meals and opens three apartment buildings that charge 5¢ for a night's lodging. He establishes depots where bundles of food and fuel can be obtained at 5¢ each.

The new Waldorf Hotel engages Swiss-born chef Oscar Tschirky, 26, as maître d'hôtel. Formerly in charge of private dining rooms at Delmonico's, Oscar of the Waldorf arrived at New York with his mother May 14, 1883, and went to work the next day as a busboy at the Hoffman House on Broadway at 24th Street; he will be credited with creating eggs Benedict and the Waldorf salad, made from bits of apple, lettuce, and mayonnaise (*see* 1931). A respectable New York woman can now eat in the public rooms of restaurants without causing gossip.

The *padrone* system that prevails in Italian immigration to the United States encounters resistance from Roman Catholic missionaries. They open the Church of Our Lady of Pompeii in a storefront at 113 Waverly Place to help immigrants whose passage has been paid by *padroni*, who receive kickbacks from steamship companies and to whom the immigrants are bound almost as indentured servants. The most prominent *padrone* is Louis V. Fugazy, who has operated the Fugazy Steamship Co. since 1870 and increased his wealth by acting as a travel agent for a steamship company, labor negotiator, and bank owner. Fugazy has a service company that provides

translators and letter writers (many immigrants are illiterate), issues loans, and notarizes documents such as licenses, mortgages, and wills. The clergymen will open a church at 25 Carmine Street in 1925.

Immigration falls to 25,000, down from 65,000 last year, and among some foreign-born groups more people leave New York than arrive.

1894 City firefighters win the same retirement benefits given to police officers in 1857: retirement at half pay after 20 years' service.

Republican William Lafayette Strong, 67, obtains reluctant support from party boss Thomas C. Platt and unseats Tammany Hall in the city's mayoralty race. A millionaire merchant turned banker, Strong receives 154,094 votes to 108,907 for former mayor Hugh J. Grant, who has sought a return to office but will quit politics in 1897. University Settlement workers have carried the message of good government into immigrant neighborhoods considered safe Tammany districts, and Josephine Shaw Lowell has (at the Rev. Parkhurst's suggestion) organized a Women's Municipal League that attracts the wives of some prominent reformers. Preliminary findings by the Lexow Committee help bring down Tammany Hall with revelations that the police have not only participated in election rigging and vice operations but also have behaved arrogantly and even engaged in physical brutality, routinely using clubs and brass knuckles to attack Italian and Jewish immigrants who have not committed any crimes (*see* 1895).

Former vice president Levi P. Morton wins election in the New York gubernatorial contest, securing 673,818 votes to 517,710 for former governor D. B. Hill, who has run on the Democratic Party ticket in an effort to regain his old position. Now 70, Morton will reform the state's civil service.

The Provident Loan Society of New York is founded by the Charity Organization in response to a plea from local philanthropist Alfred Bishop Mason. Cornelius Vanderbilt III and 30 other philanthropists have responded to form the society "for the purpose of aiding such persons as said Society shall deem in need of pecuniary assistance, by loans of money at interest, upon the pledge or mortgage of personal property." Society employees will become expert gem appraisers (*see* building, 1908).

The Wilson-Gorman Tariff Act that becomes law August 27 without President Cleveland's signature reduces duties by roughly 20 percent, but lobbyists keep most of the 1890 McKinley Act's protective features intact (*see* Dingley Act, 1897). The new law includes an income tax on incomes above $4,000 per year. New York lawyer Joseph H. Choate, now 62, calls the 2 percent tax "communistic, socialistic" (*see* 1895).

The Rapid Transit Act approved by the state legislature at Albany authorizes New York City to let a private company build and operate a subway system (*see* 1873). The Chamber of Commerce supports the idea, but many object that vibrations from an underground railroad will weaken the support of buildings and the work of construction will disrupt the life of the city for years (*see* 1900).

Some 879 passenger vessels arrive at New York from Europe, down from 972 last year; 92,561 passengers have come in cabin class, 188,164 in steerage. Fares to Europe have risen since 1887: the Cunard Line charges $90, $100, $125, and $150 one way for cabin class on its S.S. *Campania* and S.S. *Lucania*, $75, $90, and up to $175 on S.S. *Etruria* and S.S. *Umbria*, $75 to $175 on S.S. *Aurania*, S.S. *Servia*, and S.S. *Gallia*. Steerage fare is $15 (on White Star Line and other ships it is $10). Round-trip fares are lower, clergymen and their families get a 10 percent discount, but competition is so fierce that not one of the seven companies in the transatlantic trade paid a dividend last year, and four have not paid dividends in the last 3 years.

Physician Hermann M. Biggs introduces the diphtheria antitoxin developed by German bacteriologist Emil von Behring into U.S. medical practice (*see* tuberculosis diagnostic clinic, 1893). He obtains the legislation and appropriation needed for the Board of Health to produce, employ, and sell biological products. Anna W. Williams isolates an unusually powerful and prolific strain of diphtheria toxin and produces an antitoxin that will bear her name and continue in production for at least a century (*see* 1891). The antitoxin will make diphtheria a rare disease in most of the world (*see* rabies, 1905).

Bloomingdale Insane Asylum moves from Morningside Heights to a site acquired in 1868 at White Plains (*see* 1886; 1891). Virtually the sole treatment for mental illness has for some 20 years been the administering of chloral hydrate to keep patients subdued, real estate developers have been pushing for years to have the asylum relocated, and some 300 patients are transferred in groups beginning in the fall.

New York University (the University of the City of New York) moves some of its departments from Washington Square to University Heights in the Bronx, where McKim, Mead & White has designed a group of buildings that occupy a campus on a site

bounded by Sedgwick and Aqueduct avenues between 179th and 181st streets on what will be called University Heights (*see* 1832; 1896).

Teachers College and the Horace Mann School move uptown from 9 University Place to a building they share in 120th Street near the Boulevard (later Broadway) (*see* 1891). Board chairman Spencer Trask suggested the location, across the street from the former Bloomingdale Insane Asylum (one wing of the asylum has been adapted for use as a dormitory for Teachers College students), and benefactor George W. Vanderbilt donated $100,000 to purchase the lots (whose price doubled the next day when Columbia College purchased the Bloomingdale property). The school hires Virgil Prettyman, 20, as an instructor, and he is appointed principal at the end of his first year; by 1900 Horace Mann alone will have 639 students (*see* 1901).

The Public Education Association of New York is founded to provide visiting teachers and other assistance to the city's public schools.

The Greek-language weekly *Atlantis* begins publication for the city's growing Greek population. Lamp-oil merchant Solon J. Vlasto immigrated to New York in 1880 and was one of the first tenants of the Dakota apartment house when it opened 4 years later; he has founded the paper, and it gains a reputation by handing out dictionaries imprinted with its name to immigrants debarking from ships from Greece. *Atlantis* will become a daily in 1905 and continue until 1973 (*see* Ethnikos Kerus, 1915).

New-York World Sunday editor Morril Goddard asks Ohio-born cartoonist Richard F. (Felton) Outcault, 31, to submit some drawings. The *World* has developed a process for printing colored pictures, Outcault has attracted Goddard's attention with his work for the *Electrical World* and the *Street Railway Journal*, his drawing "The Origin of a New Species" is published in the *World* November 18, and it marks the beginning of what will become known as the "funny papers," or "funnies" (*see* "Yellow Kid," 1896).

Nonfiction: *Shepp's New York City Illustrated: Scene and Story of the Metropolis of the Western World* by English authors James W. and Daniel B. Shepp says, "Fourth Avenue and Park Avenue, which form one continuous street, is devoted to business as far up as Thirty-third street, with a group of notably fine buildings at Twenty-third, including the Bank for Savings, the United Charities Building, the Society for the Prevention of Cruelty to Animals, the Young Men's Christian Association, and the Academy of

Design. At Thirty-third street are the Park Avenue Hotel and the Seventy-first Regiment Armory."

Louis Comfort Tiffany trademarks Favrile glass (*see* 1878). He has invented a process for staining glass by adding pigments to molten glass while it is being made, instead of applying stain or burning pigments into hardened glass, and achieves incomparable iridescences that he employs in free-form "art nouveau" shapes. By 1897 he will have 40 to 50 young women artisans producing brilliant lamps, chandeliers, vases, jewelry, and other objects in his studio at the southeast corner of Fourth Avenue and 25th Street.

Photograph: *The Terminal (New York)* by Hoboken-born photographer Alfred Stieglitz, 29.

Billboard magazine has its beginnings in an eight-page monthly begun by Cincinnati publishers James Hennegan and W. H. Donaldson as *Billboard Advertising*. Theater notes will be introduced beginning in late 1901, a motion picture section will be added in 1907, and *Billboard* will become a show business weekly (*see Variety*, 1905).

Theater: *Too Much Johnson* by William H. Gillette 11/26 at the Standard Theater with Gillette, Kate Meek in an adaptation of Maurice Ordonneau's *La Plantation Thomasin*, 216 perfs.

Actor-playwright-theater manager Steele Mackaye dies February 25 at age 51 in Colorado while en route to California.

The first Kinetoscope parlor opens 4/14 at 1155 Broadway with peephole devices showing brief films made with Thomas Edison's equipment (*see* 1893; 1895).

Wisconsin-born illusionist-escape artist Harry Houdini (originally Ehrich Weiss), 20, entertains audiences at Huber's Opera House, next door to Lüchow's Restaurant in 14th Street, with his wife, Bess, in an act billed as "The Metamorphosis Miracle." He has himself tied inside a sack with his hands bound behind his back and locked into a wooden trunk; Bess stands atop the trunk, hidden by a screen; on the count of three, the screen is removed, revealing Houdini himself standing atop the trunk, and when the trunk is opened Bess is found to be inside the tied sack with her hands bound behind her back (*see* 1912).

Broadway musicals: *The Passing Show* 5/12 at the Casino Theater, with music by Vienna-born composer Ludwig Englander, 35, book and lyrics by Sydney Rosenberg. The production introduces the revue to the musical theater; *Little Christopher*

Columbus 10/15 at the Garden Theater, with a cast of more than 65, music by Belgian-born composer Ivan Caryll (originally Felix Tilken) and Gustave Kerker, libretto by George R. Simon and Cecil Raleigh, 208 perfs.

Popular songs: "The Sidewalks of New York" by Irish-born composer Charles B. Lawlor, 42, lyrics by native New Yorker James W. Blake, 32 ("East side, West side, all around the town,/The tots sang 'Ring-a-rosie,' 'London Bridge is falling down;'/Boys and girls together, me and Mamie O'Rourke,/Tripped the light fantastic on the sidewalks of New York"); "Only a Bowery Boy" by New York songwriters Charles B. Ward and Gussie L. Davis; "My Pearl's a Bowery Girl" by New York composer Andrew Mack, lyrics by William Jerome.

The first U.S. Open golf tournament is held at St. Andrew Golf Club in Yonkers at the initiative of Scots-born golfer John Reid, who helps to organize the U.S. Golf Association (USGA).

Lawyer Abraham Hummel of Howe & Hummel writes a signed article on divorce for the *New-York Herald*, saying, "Journey Dakotaward to have the chains quickly severed. Matrimonial fetters are easily shaken there. They have the greatest bargains ever offered in civilized communities. They have 14 separate and distinct grounds for divorce. Step up quickly and make your own selection. If you like the community you can remain. If not, 90 days is sufficient." New York, like most states, has laws making adultery almost the only ground for divorce and will not change until 1966. Hummel has split-fee arrangements with lawyers in Sioux Falls and other South Dakota communities.

A gambling den allegedly operated by Tammany Hall state senator Timothy D. "Big Tim" Sullivan (known to his intimates as "Dry Dollar") at 99 Bowery is raided Saturday evening, March 4, by Anthony Comstock and a party of detectives from the Eldridge Street Station, who arrest some 20 men and seize $210 from the crap tables, where gamblers have been playing a Russian game called "Stutz" and other variations. The place has a restaurant in front, a billiard and pool establishment in the next room, and the gambling operation in the rear. Comstock is secretary of the New-York Society for the Suppression of Vice (*see* 1899).

The Lexow Committee hears testimony from witnesses who include most notably Alsatian-born brothel keeper Matilda Hermann, known widely as "the French Madam," whose bagnio at 133 West 3rd street has been paying off the police for years.

Electric streetcars reach the Ridgewood section of Queens, where a building boom in the next 25 years will bring some 5,000 row houses, first of wood, later of yellow brick, for working-class German immigrants, many of them brewery workers. Some of the houses in Bleecker, Menaham, and Stockholm streets between Onderdonk and Woodward avenues will survive for a century and more (*see* Myrtle Avenue Line, 1906).

The 44-year-old Manhattan Life Insurance Co. moves into a new headquarters building at 66 Broadway, just south of Wall Street. Rising 348 feet, it is the tallest building in the United States and will remain such until completion of the Park Row Building in 1900. It will be demolished in 1930 and the company will relocate in 1936 to 111 West 57th Street.

Home Life Insurance Co. moves into a 15-story skyscraper at 256 Broadway, between Murray and Warren streets (*see* 1860). Designed by Napoleon LeBrun & Sons, the steel-walled structure rises 287 feet, has four elevators, and contains 56,456 square feet of floor space, but it is so tall that some tenants in nearby buildings move to "safer" neighborhoods (*see* fire, 1898).

The six-story Church Missions House is completed for the 73-year-old Episcopal Domestic and Foreign Missionary Society at the southeast corner of Fourth Avenue and 22nd Street. Designed by architects Robert W. Gibson and Edward J. Neville Stent to resemble a Flemish or Belgian town hall or guildhall, the steel-framed structure rises immediately to the north of Calvary Church and has been financed by contributions from prominent businessmen who include Cornelius Vanderbilt II.

The Harvard Club of New York leaves its first clubhouse at 11 West 22nd Street and moves June 12 into a new building at 27 West 44th Street, designed in Georgian style by Charles Follen McKim of McKim, Mead and White (*see* 1865). The firm will design additions that will be made in 1903, 1915, and 1946, and another addition will be completed in 2003.

Eight five-story "black-and-white" walk-up tenements are completed at 527 to 541 East 72nd Street, near the East River, in an area dominated by malt houses and cigar factories. The exteriors are of brick painted black (actually grayish brown) with white doorways and window frames (*see* Snow, 1938).

Some 6,576 New York slum dwellers live in windowless inside rooms (*see* 1879). Landlords have installed air shafts that circumvent the 1879 law passed to ban such inside rooms, but the shafts are used in many cases as garbage chutes.

The Hotel Girard (later the 1-2-3 Hotel) is completed at 123 West 44th Street, between Sixth Avenue and Broadway, to designs by George Keister.

English-born sports concessionaire Harry M. (Mozley) Stevens, 39, moves to New York and wins exclusive rights to sell snack foods at the Polo Grounds. A onetime iron peddler who became a bookseller, Stevens began a new career at Columbus, Ohio, 7 years ago, selling baseball scorecards with advertising printed on their backs. Granted a concession by Columbus Park, he was soon selling his scorecards at ballparks all over the country. Stevens begins catering events at hotels and exhibitions, but will concentrate on sporting events (*see* 1901).

Congress creates a Bureau of Immigration to regulate the growing influx of foreigners.

1895 The Lexow Committee report issued in mid-January details the corruption that permeates the city's administration, showing that politicians, police, and judges work hand-in-glove with abortionists, bawdyhouse keepers, gamblers, prostitutes, robbers, saloonkeepers, swindlers, and thieves (*see* 1894). Police Commissioner James J. Martin has admitted under questioning that in 5 years he has promoted only five men on merit alone, and that 85 percent of his appointments to the force have been on recommendations from Tammany Hall leaders.

Mayor Strong appoints Theodore Roosevelt president of a new, bipartisan, four-man Board of Police Commissioners following release of the Lexow

Hansom cabs remained common in the absence of more modern means of getting about. LIBRARY OF CONGRESS

Committee's report. Now 37, Roosevelt resigns his Civil Service Commissioner job at Washington, D.C. May 6; he makes "midnight rambles" in search of patrolmen not at their posts, will enlarge the force by about 1,500 men (it has been recruiting no more than 75 per year), open it to Jews and women, issue pistols to patrolmen (who have been allowed to carry firearms since 1888 but have had to pay for them), train them in marksmanship, and effectively establish the first modern police department; his new position will boost TR's reputation as a reformer (so will his friendship with journalist Jacob Riis).

The Civil Service Reform Association of New York State is founded by reformers who include Josephine Shaw Lowell.

Cuban insurgents stage an abortive revolution. Poet and independence leader José (Julián) Martí y Pérez leaves for the Caribbean January 31; now 42, he has been editing the weekly newspaper *Patria* from an office at 120 Front Street while working to end slavery and Spanish rule on the island. *Cosmopolitan* publisher John Brisben Walker uses his magazine to offer Spain $100 million for Cuban independence, but Martí invades Cuba with a small expeditionary force April 11 and is killed while fighting the Spaniards May 19 at Dos Rios. Madrid takes ruthless measures to suppress the revolt, leaving the island in turmoil (*see* 1898).

Brooklyn elects its last mayor: North Carolina-born businessman Frederick W. Wurster, 45, will serve until January 1, 1898, when Brooklyn becomes part of Greater New York.

"White wings" struggled to keep streets clean of horse droppings. MUNICIPAL ARCHIVE

The Spence Nursery is started by Spence School founder Clara Spence to care for crippled and tubercular children. It will evolve by 1915 into the Spence Alumnae Society, an adoption agency (*see* 1910).

The Hudson Guild settlement house opens in Chelsea, offering services that include basic access to food and milk, obstetrical services, funeral arrangements, and education. The Guild will open the state's first free kindergarten.

The U.S. Supreme Court emasculates the 1890 Sherman Anti-Trust Act January 21 in the case of *U.S. v. E. C. Knight Co.* The court upholds H. O. Havemeyer's 3-year-old Sugar Trust, dismissing an antitrust case on the ground that control of the manufacturing process affects interstate commerce only incidentally and indirectly (*see* Clayton Act, 1914).

U.S. Treasury gold reserves fall to $41,393,000 as economic depression continues, but the banking houses of J. P. Morgan and August Belmont join forces to loan the Treasury $65 million in gold to be paid for at a stiff price in government bonds. Morgan has made a fortune reorganizing and consolidating railroads.

The New York Stock Exchange orders companies to issue annual reports as a condition for being listed on the exchange.

The U.S. Supreme Court rules May 20 that the income tax provision in last year's Wilson-Gorman Tariff Act was unconstitutional, handing down the 5-to-4 decision in the case of *Pollock v. Farmers' Loan and Trust Co.* (*see* 1913). New York lawyer Joseph H. Choate has argued against the law before the high court and will be credited with saying, "There are two kinds of lawyers—those who know the law and those who know the judge," but Abraham Hummel of the law firm Howe & Hummel will claim next year that it was he, not Choate, who first said it, and that he made the comment many years ago when he was first admitted to the bar ("I was very observant," he will add).

Brooklyn Union Gas Co. is created by a merger of the Brooklyn Gas Light Co., founded in 1825, with Fulton Municipal Gas, Citizens Gas Light, Metropolitan Gas Light, Peoples Gas Light, Nassau Gas Light, and Williamsburg Gas Light. The merger ends a period of cutthroat competition that has seen rival companies employ "gas-house" gangs to lay pipes in competitors' territories and engage in price wars to drive each other out of business. The new company recasts itself as a supplier of gas for cooking and heating rather than lighting; serving 106,650 customers in Brooklyn and 1,400 in Queens, it manufactures its own gas at a huge plant on Newtown Creek in Greenpoint, and it will acquire some smaller companies as it expands further into Queens, tripling its manufacturing capacity and quadrupling storage (*see* 1906).

The first section of the Harlem River Ship Canal opens between the East River and Spuyten Duyvil Creek (*see* ferry, 1699). Cut through rock outcroppings between Inwood and Marble Hill in upper Manhattan, the waterway connects the Harlem and Hudson rivers, making it possible for the first time for ships to circumnavigate Manhattan (Marble Hill remains attached to the Bronx). A final section will be completed in 1923 (*see* Henry Hudson Bridge, 1936).

The city's last cable-car line opens on Lexington Avenue with a 43,700-foot line, the longest in America.

Trinity School moves uptown to 139 West 91st Street after 14 or 15 changes of venue since 1838 (*see* 1889). A physician left his estate to the school in the 1790s and it has taken nearly a century for it to obtain use of the funds. Enrollment in the all-boys school will increase by 85 to 90 percent in the next few years.

The Ethical Culture School adopts that name after some years as The Workingman's School (*see* 1880). It will buy an entire blockfront on Central Park West between 63rd and 64th streets in 1899 and expand in 1900 to include a high school (*see* 1904).

Underwood Typewriter Co. is founded by New York ribbon and carbon merchant John Thomas Underwood, 38, to develop and market a machine patented 2 years ago by Brooklyn inventors Franz X. and Herman L. Wagner, whose typewriter enables the typist to see what is being typed.

William Randolph Hearst moves to New York from his native San Francisco and acquires the 13-year-old *New-York Morning Journal*, founded by Albert Pulitzer, from John R. McLean for $180,000 (Hearst's mining magnate father died in early 1891 at age 70, leaving a vast fortune to his son). Now 32, Hearst will call the paper's morning edition the *New-York American* beginning in 1902 after acquiring papers in other cities and will go on to publish magazines that will include *Good Housekeeping*, *Harper's Bazaar*, *Town and Country*, and *Hearst's International-Cosmopolitan* (*see* 1905; "The Yellow Kid," 1896; *Journal-American*, 1937).

Collier's: The National Weekly magazine begins publication at New York (*see* 1888). Publisher Peter F. Collier, now 49, has changed the name of his *Once a Week* magazine and challenges the *Saturday Evening Post* with a 5¢ periodical that accepts no advertisements for patent medicines or alcoholic beverages and rejects articles that make claims about medicinal effects or investments that promise extraordinary results. *Collier's* will have a circulation of 200,000 by 1900 and continue until mid-December 1956 (*see* Macmillan, 1898; Nast, 1900).

The original Alexander Graham Bell telephone patent expires after 19 years of monopoly control, opening the market to competition (*see* 1877; New York Telephone Co., 1896).

The New York Public Library is created May 23 with the signing of a consolidation agreement that merges the 41-year-old Astor Library, the 25-year-old Lenox Library, and the Tilden Library to "establish and maintain a free public library and reading-room in the City of New York." Medical bibliographer John Shaw Billings, 57, is named director December 11 (*see* 1911; Carnegie, 1901).

Poetry: *Majors and Minors* by Dayton, Ohio, poet Paul Laurence Dunbar, 23, whose first collection was privately printed as *Oak and Ivory* late in 1893. The son of former slaves, Dunbar will come to New York next year for a series of poetry readings; William Dean Howells warmly praises his work in *Harper's* magazine.

Theater: *The Heart of Maryland* by David Belasco 10/22 at the Herald Square Theater, with Kentucky-born actress Mrs. Leslie Carter (*née* Caroline Louise Dudley), now 33, who was married at age 18 and divorced by her husband 9 years later for infidelity, 229 perfs.

The New York Theater Program Corp. is founded by Ohio-born advertising executive Frank Vance Storrs, 22, who will secure a monopoly on the publications of all legitimate theaters in the city (*see* *Playbill*, 1884).

Impresario Oscar Hammerstein, now 48, opens the Olympia—a blocklong structure housing a concert hall, music hall, and theater—on Broadway between 44th and 45th streets. The Criterion Theater (initially called the Lyric and designed for musicals) opens 11/2; the Music Hall, intended for spectacles, opens 12/17.

The first commercial presentation of a film on a screen takes place May 20 in a converted store at 153 Broadway, where an audience views a 4-minute film of a boxing match (*see* 1896).

Biograph Co. is founded at New York to compete with Thomas A. Edison's motion-picture company (*see* studios, 1912).

♪♪ Popular songs: "The Band Played On" by New York actor-composer John F. Palmer, lyrics by English-born actor Charles B. Ward: "Casey would waltz with a strawberry blonde . . . ;" "My Best Girl's a Corker" by New York-born songwriter John "Honey" Stromberg, 42, whose lyric wins him a commission from showmen Weber & Fields to compose and direct burlesques for the music hall they propose to build; "The Belle of Avenoo A" by New York songwriter Safford Waters.

● Cat fanciers exhibit their pets at Madison Square Garden May 8 in the first cat show ever to be held in North America. English cat lover James T. Hyde has sponsored the event.

▥ The murder trial of Italian-born New York seamstress Maria Barbella, 27, opens July 11 and attracts worldwide attention. Barbella (many newspapers persist in calling her Marie Barberi) came to the city 3 years ago, sewed until midnight each day to earn $8 per week doing piecework for a cloakmaker, was seduced with promises of marriage by one Domenico Cataldo, slit his throat with a razor April 25 when he told her, "Only pigs marry," was taken to the Essex Street prison, and has been confined to the Tombs awaiting trial. She claims to be 22 (her true age will not be discovered for nearly a century), is found guilty, sentenced to death July 18, and transported up the river to Sing Sing, where she is scheduled to be the first woman ever electrocuted. But her case has come to the attention of New Orleans-born Italian writer Cora, Countess di Brazza (née Slocomb), 33, who comes to New York, pleads Barbella's case, and gains support from Italians and Americans who protest the death penalty for a crime of passion (see 1896).

🏠 The Washington Arch dedicated April 30 at the foot of Fifth Avenue has been completed at a cost of $128,000. William Rhinelander Stewart has raised $2,765 for his project from Washington Square residents, and Stanford White has created a permanent version of the ornamental wood-and-stucco arch he designed for the 1889 centenary of President Washington's inauguration. The new structure rises 77 feet high (a frieze surmounts the coffered ceiling of the 47-foot-high arch), 30 feet wide, 10 feet deep, and dominates the entrance to the 68-year-old Washington Square Park. The two piers are decorated with sculptures by Alexander Stirling Calder (west) and Herman A. MacNeil (east).

A firehouse for Engine Company No. 31 is completed in the style of a Loire Valley château at 87 Lafayette Street, northeast corner White Street, to designs by Napoleon Le Brun & Sons. Firehouses include stables for the horses that pull pumping engines to conflagrations.

A 23-story office tower is completed at 150 Nassau Street to Romanesque and Renaissance Revival designs by architect Robert H. Robertson.

The 26-story American Surety Co. building (later the Bank of Tokyo Trust building) is completed at 100 Broadway, southeast corner Pine Street, to designs by Bruce Price. Statues of eight Athenian women by sculptor J. Massey Rhind stand in niches on the third-floor façade above the two-story Ionic columns.

Herald Square gets its name from a building completed for the *New-York Herald* to designs by McKim, Mead & White.

The Squadron A Armory is completed for the Eighth Regiment of the New York National Guard in the block bounded by Park and Madison avenues between 94th and 95th streets. Gentlemen equestrians organized the squadron 11 years ago as the New York Hussars, or First Dragoons (Squadron A is its new name), and it is mostly a social club. Designed by Rochester architect John R. Thomas with a plethora of arches, corbels, and crenellations that make it look like a medieval castle, the brick structure contains an indoor polo field that will be used by members for the next 70 years, sometimes attracting as many as 2,000 spectators to Saturday evening games.

Architect James Renwick dies at New York June 23 at age 76; Richard Morris Hunt at Newport, R.I., July 31 at age 67; Calvert Vaux drowns under mysterious

Stanford White's Washington Arch replaced a temporary 1889 structure. LIBRARY OF CONGRESS

circumstances in Brooklyn's Gravesend Bay November 18 at age 71.

The state legislature at Albany authorizes New York City's Board of Health to pull down tenements that present a health hazard (*see* 1894). The Small Parks Act permits leveling of tenements and lodging houses in the infamous Mulberry Bend section of the Lower East Side (*see* Riis, 1890), displacing 1,200 people to make way for what will become Columbus Park in 1911.

Mayor Strong's new commissioner of street cleaning George E. Waring, Jr. reorganizes his department along military lines, assembles a squadron of street sweepers in January, outfits the men in white-duck uniforms (they are quickly dubbed "white wings"), trains them in hand sweeping and discipline, equips them with brooms, buckets, and hand-carts, and sends them out to keep the streets and gutters clear of horse droppings (*see* 1880), garbage, and trash. Now 61, Waring also organizes juvenile street-cleaning leagues that will grow to include 5,000 youngsters.

The first U.S. pizzeria opens at 53½ Spring Street in Manhattan, baking pies with thick crusts, mozzarella cheese, and tomato sauce. Factory workers who put in 14-hour days buy cold pizza pies in the morning and heat them on radiators for their lunches and evening meals (*see* 1905).

The population of Manhattan's Lower East Side has a population density second only to that of Bombay.

1896 Ohio's Republican governor William McKinley, 53, wins his party's presidential nomination with help from Cleveland industrialist Marcus Alonzo "Mark" Hanna, 58. Democrats nominate Nebraska religious Fundamentalist William Jennings Bryan, 36, who says in a speech at his party's convention July 8, "You shall not press down upon the brow of labor this crown of thorns, you shall not crucify mankind on a cross of gold." Joseph Pulitzer's *New-York World* favors Bryan. Writer Charles E. Farrell asks in the *World* October 11, "What is the difference between Mark Hanna and a silver-mine owner? One is a shining Mark and the other is a mining shark."

William Randolph Hearst's *New-York Journal* asks editorially October 13, "Can Mr. Hanna buy the voters of the Midwest? The Standard Oil Company, the great railroad corporations, the big manufacturing trusts, the bond syndicates, Mr. Carnegie, Mr. Pierpont Morgan, Mr. Huntington, and all the rest of the high-minded patriots who are furnishing Mr. Hanna with the means to defend the national honor,

think he can." But Bryan loses both New York and Brooklyn—the first Democratic nominee since 1848 to do so—and his failure to capture urban voters costs him the election. McKinley wins 271 electoral votes to Bryan's 176.

Maine-born Republican Frank S. Black, 43, wins the New York gubernatorial election, securing 787,516 votes as compared with 574,524 cast for Democrat William Porter. Black will oversee the consolidation of the five boroughs into Greater New York (*see* 1897).

Volunteers of America is founded by a grandson of the Salvation Army's founder William Booth, now 67 (*see* 1880). Ballington Booth has been in charge of the army's American operation but has had a falling out with his father; helped by his wife, Maud, he organizes a rival group that will work to help relieve poverty in New York and other cities.

New York narrows the differential between real estate taxes and personal property taxes, but the tax on real property (land and buildings) is still 22 percent higher, and only 21,000 of the city's 2 million residents pay taxes on personal property (*see* 1891; 1933).

The Dow Jones Industrial Average is published for the first time May 26 (*see* *Wall Street Journal*, 1889). Charles H. Dow has added up the closing prices of 12 stocks listed on the New York Stock Exchange, divided the number by 12, and come up with figure of 40.94. The 12 stocks include General Electric Co., American Leather Co., and Tennessee Coal & Iron; industrial stocks are considered speculative, railroad stocks being regarded as much safer. The number of stocks used for the average will be increased to 20 in 1916 and 30 in 1928 (*see* 1906).

Wanamaker's New York opens in East 10th Street as merchant John Wanamaker takes over the cast-iron A. T. Stewart retail palace built in 1862. Now 58, Wanamaker opened a Philadelphia menswear shop with his brother-in-law Nathan Brown in 1861, pioneered in selling all items at fixed prices with none of the haggling that had been customary between customer and clerk, became the largest U.S. menswear retailer, and has long since expanded his menswear shop into a department store. He lures customers with bargain prices, good service, and concerts in the great Wanamaker Auditorium (*see* 1903).

Siegel-Cooper opens at the northeast corner of Sixth Avenue and 18th Street in the heart of what is known as "Ladies' Mile." Built for German-born merchant Henry Siegel and his partner Frank

Cooper, the largest department store in the city has been designed by De Lemos & Cordes, who have embellished it with glazed terra cotta, and its 18 acres of floor space include an art gallery, nursery, theater, dental parlor, and post office. It will advertise itself as the city's only fireproof store (see 1915).

Nathan and Isidore Straus pay Charles Webster $1.2 million for the remaining 55 percent of Macy's, whose annual profits now exceed $250,000, and become sole owners (see 1888). Nathan Straus has introduced the practice of pricing merchandise at $4.98, $9.98, and so forth instead of $5 or $10, and this has helped boost sales, enabling the Strauses to build a wide nine-story building at 55 West 13th Street, east of Sixth Avenue, and a narrow nine-story building at 56 West 14th Street, both designed by William Schickel & Co. (see 1902).

Brooks Brothers executive John E. Brooks introduces the button-down collar for dress shirts (see 1874). A grandson of founder Henry Sands Brooks, he has seen such collars on athletic shirts worn by polo players and adapted the idea (see 1909).

The first F. W. Woolworth five-and-dime store in New York City opens on Sixth Avenue at 17th Street, near Macy's on "Ladies' Mile" (see 1879). Woolworth's suppliers give him good prices because he buys candy and other items in such large quantities, they are mostly in New York. He moved to the city himself 10 years ago and has been living with his family in a modest town house in Brooklyn's Bedford-Stuyvesant section, and his chain had sales of more than $1 million last year (see 1911; real estate, 1901). The richest New York retailers by a wide margin are carpet and furniture merchants William D. and John Sloane, whose W. & J. Sloane stores have made each of them worth an estimated $15 million.

Henri Bendel opens at 10 Bond Street. Louisiana-born merchant Bendel, 38, will move his millinery shop next year to 67 East 9th Street, move in 1906 to Fifth Avenue, and relocate in 1917 or 1918 to 10 West 57th Street, where he will sell clothing, cosmetics, and perfume as well as hats (see 1985).

 Through service by elevated railway begins between the Bronx and Manhattan (see 1891). The Manhattan Railway Co. uses the line built by the Suburban Rapid Transit Co. on an iron bridge across the Harlem River between 129th and 145th streets via a private right of way, and north of the Fordham Road via Third Avenue. Transfers between all four Els are available at South Ferry, and a single 5¢ fare permits a passenger to travel all the way from lower Manhattan to the Bronx.

Brooklyn's Franklin Avenue El shuttle opens between Prospect Park and Fulton Street, where it will continue for more than a century.

Engineer Fred S. Pearson designs and erects the 96th Street Power House for Manhattan's Metropolitan Street Railway Co. with which he has been associated since 1894 (see 1893). He has devised an underground conduit, or trolley, for the company's streetcars, his power house has a generating capacity of 70,000 horsepower and is the largest in the country; it will survive for more than a century.

The Fifth Avenue Coach Co. is incorporated to purchase the franchise of the 11-year-old Fifth Avenue Transportation Co. and continues to operate horse-drawn coaches (see 1907).

 St. Luke's Hospital reopens January 24 in the Vanderbilt Building at the corner of 113th Street and Amsterdam Avenue, where 45 city lots were purchased 4 years ago (see 1858). Morningside Park, just east of the new hospital, lies at the foot of a steep cliff; a water pumping station, firehouse, and some wooden outbuildings have been built on the land to the north and west, but those properties remain otherwise unoccupied. Horse-drawn ambulances transport 38 patients from Madison Avenue at 54th Street to the new Vanderbilt Building, designed by Ernest Flagg; it will be followed next year by the Muhlenberg Chapel and the Norrie and Minturn pavilions, but Sister Anne Ayres dies at New York February 9 at age 80, having played a leading role in founding the hospital (see St. Luke's-Roosevelt Hospital, 1979).

Columbia College changes its name to Columbia University, having added graduate schools of law, mines, political science, architecture, library service, philosophy, pure science, and nursing. Columbia will change its name again in 1912 to Columbia University in the City of New York (see library, 1897).

New York University assumes that name 65 years after being chartered as the University of the City of New York (see 1894). It will grow within a century to have 13 schools, colleges, and divisions at five major centers in Manhattan, with branch campus programs in Westchester and Rockland counties, offering more than 2,500 courses leading to more than 25 different degrees (see Gould Memorial Library, 1899).

A bill signed into law by Mayor Strong April 22 centralizes control over the city's public schools, including those in Brooklyn, with the Board of Education to have authority over the business side of the school system and a Board of Superintendents authority over education. Trustees selected by ward bosses have run the existing decentralized system, and critics say they have rewarded political allies, handicapped planning, and resisted new theories that would extend education for the city's growing immigrant population beyond mere literacy and rote drills. Manhattan educators favor the appointment of former superintendent of instruction Andrew S. Draper to head the new Board of Superintendents (see 1886), Brooklyn educators favor Ulster-born Presbyterian minister's son William H. (Henry) Maxwell, 44, who has been superintendent of Brooklyn schools since 1887, and Draper will recommend Maxwell (see 1898; 1916).

The 109-year-old Erasmus Hall High School at 911 Flatbush Avenue is deeded to the City of Brooklyn. Its neo-Gothic building will be augmented in the next century by four adjoining structures around a central courtyard.

The New York Aquarium opens December 10 in what used to be the Castle Garden immigrant receiving station at the Battery (see population, 1892). It has two gilded seahorses over its main doorway, charges no admission, initially contains only specimens from waters around the city, attracts 30,000 people on opening day, and will draw more than 2 million visitors its first year. Contributions of more exotic specimens from local yachtsmen and sea captains will soon make it the world's largest aquarium in terms of number and variety of species; the New York Zoological Society will assume control in 1902, and the aquarium will remain open until 1941 (see 1957).

New York Telephone Co. is organized to absorb Bell operations in the city that now has 15,000 subscribers, each with a simple four-digit number. As the system grows in the next few years, so many business firms and residences in Manhattan will have telephones that the company will have to assign names as well as numbers: New Yorkers will soon be asking operators to ring numbers preceded by ACAdemy, ALGonquin, APPlegate, ASHland, ASToria, ATWater, AUDubon, BARclay, BEEkman, BOWling Green, BRYant, BUTterfield, CALedonia, CANal, CAThedral, CHElsea, CHIckering, CIRcle, COLumbus, CORtlandt, DIGby, DRYdock, EDGcombe, ELDorado, ENDicott, EVErgreen, EXChange, FAIrbanks, FORdham, GRAmercy, HANover, HARlem, HAVemeyer, INTervale, IROn-sides, JERome, JOHn, LACkawanna, LEHigh, LEXington, LONgacre, LORraine, MEDallion, MOHawk, MONument, MURray Hill, ORChard, PENnsylvania, PLAza, RECtor, REGent, RHInelander, RIVerside, SACramento, SCHuyler, SPRuce, STUyvesant, SUSquehanna, TRAfalgar, UNIversity, VANderbilt, VOLunteer, WADsworth, WALker, WAShington Heights, WATkins, WHItehall, WICkersham, WISconsin, or WORth (by the 1930s, the zones will be subdivided, with the names followed by five digits instead of four, and by the 1970s the names will be discarded altogether).

"The Yellow Kid" appears in Joseph Pulitzer's New-York World in March. The one-panel cartoon by Richard F. Outcault, now 33, boosts the paper's circulation (see 1897).

The 45-year-old New-York Times gets a face-lift from Cincinnati-born publisher Adolph S. Ochs, 38, who has made his Chattanooga Times prosper, been married since 1883 to the daughter of Cincinnati's Rabbi Isaac Wise, and acquires control of the New-York Times August 18 for $75,000, having received a $100,000 loan from Marcellus Hartley, founder of the Union Metallic Cartridge Co. The paper's circulation has dropped to 9,000 and its other owners assure Ochs a stock majority if he can make it profitable for 3 consecutive years; he throws out the paper's romantic fiction and tiny typefaces, improves neglected areas such as financial news, starts a weekly book-review section and Sunday magazine, and beginning December 1 drops the hyphen in the paper's name (see "All the News That's Fit to Print," 1897).

Argosy magazine begins publication at New York, specializing in adventure stories. Publisher Frank Munsey, now 42, has tried a variety of formats with his 14-year-old children's magazine Golden Argosy and developed what will be the first successful pulp magazine. By the time circulation peaks in 1910 it will have newsstand sales of about 500,000 copies per issue.

The Pratt Institute Free Library of Brooklyn's 9-year-old Pratt Institute is the first free library in New York State. Designed by William Tubby, it is across Ryerson Street from the main building but set back from the street and surrounded by grass.

The first New-York Times Book Review (initially called the Saturday Book Review Supplement) is published October 10.

Fiction: Yekl: A Tale of New York by Lithuanian-born novelist-journalist Abraham Cahan, 36, whose revolutionist views forced him to flee czarist Russia. He has been invited to William Dean Howell's 59th Street house overlooking Central Park and advised to change his original title, *Yankele the Yankee*: "Suffolk Street is in the very thick of the battle for breath. For it lies in the heart of that part of the East Side which has within the last two or three decades become the Ghetto of the American metropolis, and, indeed, the Ghetto of the world. It is one of the most densely populated spots on the face of the earth—a seething human sea fed by streams, streamlets, and rills of immigration flowing from all the Yiddish-speaking centers of Europe."

Poetry: *Lyrics of Lowly Life* by Paul Laurence Dunbar, whose book has a sympathetic introduction by William Dean Howells that helps make the young man fashionable; *The Torrent and the Night Before* by Maine-born New York poet Edwin Arlington Robinson, 26, whose work is privately printed.

The Parsons School of Design has its beginnings in the Chase School of Art, founded by painter-art teacher William Merritt Chase, now 46 (*see* Art Students League, 1875). Frank Alvah Parsons, now 30, will head the school from 1905 until his death in 1930, and it will take the name Parsons beginning in 1940 (*see* 1970).

Sculpture: *Abraham de Peyster* by George Bissell is installed in Bowling Green (it will be moved to a site three blocks east of Bowling Green late in the next century).

Photographer Matthew B. Brady dies in the charity ward of a city hospital January 15 at age 72 (approximate). He was wiped out by the financial panic of 1873 and in recent years has lived alone in obscurity.

King's New York Views is a photographic supplement to *King's Handbook of New York City*, compiled by local publisher Moses King with 130 "views" of bridges, monuments, office buildings, hotels, piers, ships, and the like. Says King, "New York is the foremost city of the Western Hemisphere, and in some respects the foremost city of the world, ranking with London and Paris. In great lofty structures; in commercial activity; in financial affairs; in international relations; in polyglotical representation; in gigantic enterprises; in notable scientific and engineering achievements; in colossal individual aggrandizements; in mammoth corporate wealth; in maritime commerce; in absolute freedom of citizens; and in the aggregation of civil, social, philanthropic, and religious associations, New York stands unsurpassed anywhere on the globe . . . Less than a century ago New York was only a quaint little provincial city, covering the lower part of Manhattan Island.

The hundred and forty pictures in this paper tell an unmistakable story of her present gigantic magnitude." New editions will appear in 1903, 1905, 1908, 1911, and 1915.

Theater: *Rosemary* by French-born English playwright Louis Napoleon Parker, 44, and Murray Carson 8/31 at the Empire Theater, with Salt Lake City–born actress Maude Adams (originally Maude Ewing Adams Kiskadden), 23, who has adopted her mother's maiden name, Philadelphia-born ingénue Ethel Barrymore (originally Ethel Mae Blythe), 17, John Drew, Jr., illustrator-actor Charles (Dana) Gibson, now 28, Barnesville, Ohio-born actor Arthur Byron, 20, 136 perfs.; *Secret Service* by William H. Gillette 10/5 at the Garrick Theatre, with Gillette as Captain Thorne, a secret agent for the Union Army, 176 perfs.

French comedienne Anna Held, 23, makes her U.S. debut 9/21 at the Herald Square Theater in a lavish production of the 1884 Charles H. Hoyt play *A Parlor Match* mounted by Florenz Ziegfeld with help from 28-year-old Hartford-born *New-York Sun* drama critic Charles (Bancroft) Dillingham, 48 perfs.

The 8-year-old Klaw & Erlanger booking agency joins with Charles Frohman, Al Hayman, Samuel F. Nixon, and J. Frederick Zimmerman to create what will be called the Theatrical Syndicate. The six men control more than 500 theaters nationwide, supplying vaudeville acts and other attractions only to theaters that agree to let them be exclusive agents; Charles Frohman heads the Syndicate, but Marc Klaw and A. L. Erlanger are responsible for booking all attractions and they arrange bookings only for performers who agree to be represented exclusively by the Syndicate (*see* Shubert brothers, 1900).

The first U.S. public showing of motion pictures April 20 at Koster and Bial's Music Hall in 23rd Street west of Sixth Avenue employs Thomas Edison's Vitascope, an improvement over his 1893 Kinetoscope, and a projector made by Thomas Armat (*see* 1895). Introduced as part of a vaudeville show, the hand-tinted black-and-white films begin with *Sea Waves* (so real that patrons with front-row seats scatter in alarm) and include also *Burlesque Boxers*, *The Butterfly Dance*, *Kaiser Wilhelm Reviewing His Troops*, and eight other subjects (*see* 1903).

Canadian-born music hall comedienne May Irwin, now 34, is filmed in a brief episode from *The Widow Jones*, a farce in which she has been starring opposite actor John Rice. A long close-up of their kiss in the film *The Kiss* scandalizes audiences and brings the first demands for screen censorship.

Broadway musicals: *El Capitán* 4/20 at the Broadway Theater, with New York-born comedian De Wolf Hopper, 38, music by John Philip Sousa, 112 perfs.; *The Art of Maryland* 9/5 at the new Weber and Fields Music Hall, with Joe Weber and Lew Fields in a parody of David Belasco's legitimate stage hit *The Heart of Maryland* (*see* 1895), music by John Stromberg, lyrics by Edgar Smith.

Popular song: "Sweet Rosie O'Grady" by New York songwriter Maude Nugent, 19, who has been unable to find a publisher and introduces the song herself at Tony Pastor's Opera House.

Piano maker Henry Engelhard Steinway dies at New York November 30 at age 99.

March: "Stars and Stripes Forever" by John Philip Sousa, who writes down the notes on Christmas Day in his apartment in the Carnegie Hall building.

The world's first public golf course opens in Van Cortlandt Park (*see* 1889).

The first U.S. indoor ice-skating rink opens at 57 West 66th Street in a structure designed by Walter B. Chambers with help from architect Ernest Flagg (the St. Nicholas Rink will later become the St. Nicholas Arena and be used for boxing matches).

Harry Payne Whitney, 24, son of New York financier William C. Whitney, is married at Newport, R.I., August 25 to railroad heiress Gertrude Vanderbilt, daughter of Cornelius Vanderbilt II (*see* art museum, 1930).

"Little Egypt" dances on the table at a December 19 dinner for 20 male guests in a private room at Louis Sherry's by New York playboy Herbert Barnum Seeley, a nephew of the late circus promoter P. T. Barnum who wants to celebrate the forthcoming marriage of his brother Clinton Barnum Seeley. The young woman wears only lace stockings and high-heeled slippers, but while Fahrida Mahszar is widely thought to have performed the *danse du ventre*, or hootchy-kootchy, on the Midway Plaisance of Chicago's 1893 Columbian Exposition under the name "Little Egypt," she never in fact appeared there. Police raid the restaurant just after midnight and halt the proceedings.

An appellate court at Albany reviews the case of convicted murderess Maria Barbella April 7 and grants her a retrial April 16 on grounds that Dublin-born Judge John W. Goff last year showed flagrant bias in addressing the jury (*see* 1894). The new trial begins November 20, creating sensational newspaper stories, and the jury returns a verdict of not guilty December 10, the countess di Brazza arrives at New York that day aboard the S.S. *Fulda*, she telephones Barbella's lawyers, and Barbella gets on the phone to tell her the good news.

The city's homicide rate will fall to just 2.5 per 100,000 in the next 5 years, down from 3.5 in the last 5 (*see* 1901).

The New York Chamber of Commerce announces early in the year that it opposes construction of skyscrapers, widely criticized for being unsafe and for blocking light from streets and other buildings, but there are no legal restrictions on the height of commercial buildings (*see* zoning resolution, 1916).

The Real Estate Board of New York is organized by brokers, builders, managers, property owners, and executives of related industries who will emphasize commercial rather than residential real estate (the board will be incorporated in 1908).

The Bar Association Building is completed at 42 West 44th Street (and 37 West 43rd Street) between Fifth and Sixth avenues for the 26-year-old lawyers' organization. Designed by Cyrus L. W. (Lazelle Warner) Eidlitz, now 44, it has a classic limestone exterior.

The Edward J. Berwind town house (later an apartment building) is completed for the world's largest coal-mine owner at 2 East 64th Street, southeast corner Fifth Avenue, to designs by Nicholas Clark Mellen.

The Henry T. Sloane town house is completed in limestone at 9 East 72nd Street to French Empire designs by Carrère & Hastings. It will later be the James Stillman residence, the John Sanford residence, and from 1964 to 2001 the Lycée de Français de New York.

The Nathaniel L. McCready town house is completed at 5 East 75th Street with a 22-foot-by-28-foot front hall, a 28-foot-by-46-foot salon, and a 25-foot-by-26-foot drawing room. It will later be the Thomas J. Watson, Jr. residence, later still the Harkness House for Ballet Arts. The house has been designed by the firm Trowbridge, Colt & Livingston organized by New York-born architect (Samuel) Breck (Parkman) Trowbridge, 34, Stockton B. Colt, 31 (who will leave the firm in 1899), and Goodhue Livingston, also 31, who is descended from the Hudson River landowner Robert R. Livingston. All three have studied with George B. Post.

Newtown is renamed Elmhurst to distinguish it from the foul-smelling Newtown Creek (*see* 1652). The Cord Meyer Development Co. is developing the area north of the railroad station with houses for commuters and has pushed for the renaming.

✗ The American Ice Co. is founded by Maine-born ice dealer Charles W. (Wyman) Morse, 40, who has gained control of the Knickerbocker Ice Co. and most of the city's other large-scale ice operations (*see* 1882; politics, 1900).

New York coffee merchant and shipowner John Arbuckle challenges the Havemeyer sugar trust, building a large Brooklyn refinery and cutting prices so low that he sells almost at cost (*see* 1871). Having used machinery developed by Arbuckle to weigh and package their sugar, the Havemeyers have cancelled their sales agreement with his company, and he is determined not to let them get away with it. The Havemeyers retaliate by entering the coffee business, but Arbuckle, now 57, will not be intimidated (*see* 1901).

Brewer Jacob Ruppert retires; his 29-year-old son and namesake takes over (*see* sports, 1915).

1897 Former Brooklyn mayor James Howell dies at ✗ Brooklyn January 27 at age 69 amidst activity at Albany to combine his city—the third largest in America—with Queens and New York.

Grant's Tomb became a popular destination for outings and sightseerers. LIBRARY OF CONGRESS

Citizens' Union is founded February 22 to oppose Tammany Hall. Lawyer Elihu Root and 164 other prominent citizens announce their intention to separate muncipal elections from state and national contests; the citizens include bankers, lawyers, merchants, and physicians, and they choose R. Fulton Cutting, 44, as chairman (he will serve until 1908), but although they form clubs in various parts of the city they reject bids to join with Republicans in nominating fusion candidates for office.

President McKinley appoints New York Police Commission president Theodore Roosevelt assistant secretary of the navy April 19.

A giant parade April 27 marks the dedication of Grant's Tomb on Riverside Avenue (later Riverside Drive) at 122nd Street (*see* politics, 1885). More than a million spectators turn out to watch Civil War veterans, city officials, and dignitaries who include Chief Joseph of the Nez Perce tribe march in the parade, beginning at 24th Street, going up Madison Avenue to 55th Street, turning west to Fifth Avenue, moving up Fifth to 59th Street, turning west to Columbus Circle, proceeding up the Boulevard (Broadway) to 72nd Street, turning west to Riverside Avenue, continuing up to Clermont Avenue, and turning back to 119th Street where the marchers pass in review.

The state legislature at Albany votes to consolidate Brooklyn, Queens, and Staten Island with Manhattan and the Bronx (both parts of New York County) to create the City of Greater New York. Congregationalist minister Richard Salter Storrs has opposed the bill, saying, "We don't need the political sewage of Europe," Mayor Strong of New York has vetoed a consolidation measure, and the opposition includes also Brooklyn's former mayor Seth Low and *Brooklyn Daily Eagle* editor St. Clair McKelway, but Republican boss Thomas C. Platt sees it as a way to dilute the power of Manhattan's Democrats; Brooklynites approve the consolidation by a margin of only 277 votes (out of more than 129,000 cast), and Gov. Black signs the new charter (Chapter 378 of the Laws of 1897) May 4, fulfilling the dream of Andrew Haskell Green (*see* 1898).

The new Citizens' Union launches its mayoralty campaign for Seth Low October 6 with a rally at the Cooper Union that attracts a crowd of about 4,000 mostly well-to-do men and 500 women.

Reformer Henry George makes another attempt to gain the mayor's office but dies in his campaign headquarters at the Union Square Hotel October 29 at age 58. His funeral procession is the longest seen in the city since Abraham Lincoln died in 1865.

Judge Robert A. Van Wyck, 48, campaigns on the slogan "To Hell with Reform" and wins the mayoralty election, receiving 233,997 votes to become the first mayor elected by voters in all five boroughs (Tammany leader Richard Croker, now 55, returned to New York September 7 after more than 3 years abroad and picked Van Wyck to head the Democratic Party ticket). Columbia University president Seth Low, now 47, has run on the Citizens Union' ticket and gets 151,540 votes, Republican Benjamin Tracy receives 101,863.

The 6-year-old University Settlement moves to 184 Eldridge Street, southeast corner Rivington Street, where a $200,000 "castle" is nearing completion to designs by Howells & Stokes (Cambridge, Mass.-born architect John Mead Howells, 29 [son of editor-novelist William Dean Howells and a nephew of William Rutherford Mead of McKim, Mead & White], and New York-born architect I. N. [Isaac Newton] Phelps Stokes, 30, son of banker Anson Phelps Stokes). The settlement house started by Stanton Coit in 1886 has built public baths that will serve as models for municipal baths and leads the fight for a city subway system (see Rapid Transit Act, 1894).

Christodora House has its beginnings in a settlement house opened by philanthropists Sara Libby Carson and Christina MacColl in the basement and ground floor of a tenement at 163 7 Avenue B. Within a few years it will be providing education, food, health services, and shelter to nearly 5,000 Russian, Polish, and Ukrainian immigrants each week (see 1928).

Kuhn, Loeb & Co. admits German-born banker Otto Hermann Kahn, 29, to membership January 1. A naturalized British subject, Kahn joined the New York banking firm Speyer & Co. in 1893, stayed for 2 years, traveled in Europe for a year, has married the daughter of partner Abraham Wolff, and joins with Kuhn, Loeb partner Jacob Schiff and with speculator Edward Henry Harriman, 49, in reorganizing the bankrupt Union Pacific (see 1901).

Goldman, Sachs adds a brokerage operation after 28 years of dealing in commercial paper and begins underwriting securities (see 1869).

The Greater New York Savings Bank is founded in May at Brooklyn by Charles J. Obermayer and other businessmen. The bank opens offices in Park Slope at the corner of Seventh Avenue and 1st Street; it will grow by acquiring other thrifts.

The Dingley Tariff Act passed by Congress July 24 raises living costs by increasing duties to an average of 57 percent (see Wilson-Gorman Act, 1894). The measure hikes rates on sugar, salt, tin cans, glassware, and tobacco, as well as on iron and steel, steel rails, petroleum, lead, copper, locomotives, matches, whiskey, and leather goods, but the influx of gold from the Klondike helps end the 4-year economic depression and begin a decade of prosperity.

New York has more than 2,000 street vendors selling cheaply priced fruits, vegetables, household goods, and clothing. Their pushcarts are to be found mostly on the Lower East Side but also in Greek and Italian neighborhoods of Greenwich Village, Jewish and Italian sections of Brooklyn, and on Saturdays in the black and Irish neighborhoods of Hell's Kitchen. The vendors buy wholesale lots of factory seconds, surplus or damaged food items, and the like; customers buy rotting pears for almost nothing and salvage the edible portions; they buy second- and third-hand shoes, even complete wedding outfits (for as little as $10). Peddlers often pool their money and delegate one of their colleagues to buy from wholesalers at midnight, arranging to have the goods delivered to their carts. A pushcart can be bought outright for $5 to $10, but most of the vendors rent their carts for 10¢ to 25¢ per day; with an initial investment of $5, a peddler can earn $8 to $10 per week, enough to support a family of five (see 1906).

ABC Carpet & Home has its beginnings as entrepreneur Sam Weinrib starts selling used carpet and linoleum from a pushcart on the Lower East Side.

Trolley service begins across the 14-year-old Brooklyn Bridge.

The 20-year-old New York and Sea Beach Railway leases its tracks to the Brooklyn Rapid Transit System, which will electrify them and link them to elevated lines. The tracks will be used by trolleys until 1907 (see 1915).

The Electric Carriage and Wagon Co. founded at New York introduces 12 electric-powered vehicles to the city streets. By 1899 about 90 percent of such vehicles will be electric, providing virtually silent transportation, and by 1900 the Electric Vehicle Co. will have hundreds of its electric hansom cabs on the streets; modeled along the lines of horse-drawn hansom cabs, they will have separate motors and axles for each rear wheel, thereby eliminating the need for a differential gear, but batteries for the vehicles weigh at least 800 pounds each (see 1907).

The North German Lloyd steamship S.S. *Friedrich der Grosse* arrives at her Hoboken pier April 20 after a maiden voyage from Bremen. First of six North German Lloyd vessels, the 10,000-ton ship is 550 feet long overall, is designed to have a speed of 14 knots, and has accommodations for 200 first-class passengers, 78 in second class, and a large steerage. Passenger quarters are all above the main deck, with space below given over entirely to cargo.

The Hamburg-Amerika Line (*Hamburg-Amerikanische Paketfahrt Aktien Gesellschaft*) celebrates its 50th anniversary at New York May 22. It has become the world's largest passenger-ship line.

 Canadian-born Brooklyn dental-school graduate Edgar Rudolph Randolph Parker, 24, puts up a sign reading, "Painless Parker/Dentist/He Won't Hurt You." Parker opened a dental office over a German saloon on Flatbush Avenue last year, charging 50¢ to remove a tooth. He had trouble attracting patients, but his new sign brings in so many that he is soon extracting 30 teeth per day and taking in $90 per week, all in cash. Since his office rental is only $15 per month (sirloin steak sells at 20¢/lb., and good whiskey sells at 90¢/fifth), Parker is soon prosperous enough to have two men tramping the streets of Brooklyn with signs promoting his services, and his practice doubles in short order. Brooklyn's ethical dentists oppose him, not only because he advertises but also because they know his claims are false. But Parker will have two assistants by the end of next year, and by 1900 he will have half a floor of a Flatbush office building, eight dentists to help him, and a goatee (*see* 1900).

 De Witt Clinton High School has its beginnings in the Boys' High School opened at 60 West 13th Street. Manhattan's first public high school for boys, it will adopt the name De Witt Clinton in 1900 (*see* 1906; 1929).

The Rabbi Isaac Elchanan Theological Seminary (RIETS) is founded at New York to give Orthodox Jewish youths advanced Talmudic education (*see* Yeshiva Etz Chaim, 1886). Within 6 years it will graduate the first rabbis trained in the United States to the standards of eastern European Orthodoxy (*see* Talmudical Academy, 1915).

"All the News That's Fit to Print" appears February 10 in a box to the left of the title of the *New York Times*, where it will remain for more than a century (*see* 1896). Adolph S. Ochs has offered a $100 prize to anyone who could think up a better slogan, but the motto devised by Ochs and his editors in October of last year and placed originally on the editorial page

has not been topped. Investment banker Spencer Trask, now 52, is the largest owner of the *Times* and president of the company that controls it.

The *Jewish Daily Forward* (*Vorwert*) begins publication in April at 175 East Broadway under a sign that reads, "*Arbeiter Ring*" ("Workmen's Circle") (the Yiddish-language paper takes its name from that of a Berlin paper and has close ties to the Socialist Party). Novelist Abraham Cahan has started the paper with help from Russian-born journalist William H. Leaf, 22, and will hold the position of editor until his death in 1951, gaining readership with his advice column "*Bintel Brief*" ("packet of letters") that allows readers and editors to exchange views on ethics, love, money, and getting along in America as he works to assimilate immigrants. Newsboys will buy the papers at two for a penny and sell them for 1¢ per copy, hawking them at meeting halls and on the streets (*see* The *Day*, 1914).

The *New-York Tribune* prints halftones on a power press and on newsprint for the first time, employing techniques developed by Frederick E. Ives and Stephen Horgan (*see* 1880).

New-York Evening Sun reader (Laura) Virginia O'Hanlon of 115 West 95th Street writes to the paper's editor saying, "I am 8 years old. Some of my little friends say there is no Santa Claus. Papa says, 'If you see it in The Sun it's so.' Please tell me the truth; is there a Santa Claus?" Former *New-York Times* Civil War correspondent Francis P. (Parcellus) Church, 58, childless himself, replies in an unsigned front page editorial published September 21: "Virginia, your little friends are wrong. They have been affected by the skepticism of a skeptical age. They do not believe except they see . . . Yes, Virginia, there is a Santa Claus. He exists as certainly as love and generosity and devotion exist . . . Not believe in Santa Claus? You might as well not believe in fairies . . . No Santa Claus! Thank God, he lives, and he lives forever." The *Sun* will reprint the editorial each year until it is merged with the *World-Telegram* in January 1950.

New-York Evening Sun editor-publisher Charles A. Dana dies at Glen Cove, L.I., October 17 at age 78 and is succeeded at the *Sun* by his son Paul (*see* 1887). His name will be commemorated in the Charles A. Dana Foundation that beginning in 1986 will confer awards "for pioneering achievements in health and education" (*see* Sun, 1916).

"The Yellow Kid" appears in strip form in the color supplement of William Randolph Hearst's *New-York Journal* beginning October 24 (*see* 1896). Circulation of Joseph Pulitzer's *New-York World* has reached 360,000 as compared to 309,000 for Hearst's *Journal* (the *Evening Sun* and *Evening Telegram* each has 100,000, Henry Villard's *Evening Post* 25,000), Hearst has hired *Sunday World* editor Arthur Brisbane, now 32, who uses what will be called "yellow journalism" techniques to build *Journal* circulation from 40,000 to 325,000 in 6 weeks (*see* 1895). Hearst and Pulitzer battle over rights to the cartoon, and the contest for readership between the two will be marked by sensationalism.(*see* 1898).

"The Katzenjammer Kids" by German-born cartoonist Rudolph Dirks, 21, begins appearing in the *New-York Journal* December 12. The antics of Hans und Fritz (who torment der Captain, der Inspector, und Momma) ape those of the German cartoon characters Max und Moritz by Wilhelm Busch (*see* 1917).

Artkraft Strauss has its beginnings in the Strauss Signs firm founded by New York craftsman Benjamin Strauss to supply the city's retailers with meticulously painted showcards. He will send teams of artisans across the country to apply gold-leaf lettering to windows, office doors, storefronts (*see* 1935).

Columbia University's Low Memorial Library is completed on a high terrace north of 116th Street, between Broadway and Amsterdam avenues. Designed by Charles F. McKim of McKim, Mead & White and built as a memorial to president Seth Low's late father, A. A. Low, it has two giant green columns of Connemara marble inside its front entrance, a domed central reading room, and stacks for a million books. It will be superseded in 1934 by the much larger Butler Library.

Doubleday & Co. has its beginnings in the New York publishing house Doubleday & McClure, started by Frank Nelson Doubleday, 35, with S. S. McClure of *McClure's* magazine (*see* communications, 1893). Doubleday began at age 15 with Charles Scribner's Sons, and his new firm will become the most prolific U.S. publishing house (*see* Doran, 1908; Literary Guild, 1934).

Brooklyn's first public library opens December 20 in a clapboard house located in a cornfield next to Bedford Avenue in the Bedford-Stuyvesant section (*see* 1905; main branch, 1941).

Nonfiction: *The American Metropolis* (three volumes) by Lexow Committee counsel and man about town Frank Moss; "Merry Christmas in the Tenements" by Jacob Riis appears in the December issue of *Century* magazine: "It is evening in Grand Street. The

shops east and west are pouring forth their swarms of workers. Street and sidewalk and filled with an eager throng of young men and women, chatting gaily, and elbowing the jam of holiday shoppers that linger about the big stores. The street-cars labor along, loaded down to the steps with passengers carrying bundles of every size and odd shape. Along the curb a string of peddlers hawk penny toys in push-carts with noisy clamor, fearless for once of being moved on by the police . . . At the corner, where two opposing tides of travel form an eddy, the line of push-carts debouches down the darker side-street. In its gloom their torches burn with a fitful glare that wakes black shadows among the trusses of the railroad structure overhead. A woman, with worn shawl drawn tightly about head and shoulders, bargains with a peddler for a monkey on a stick and two cents' worth of flittergold."

Novelist Herman Melville dies at his native New York September 28 at age 72 and is buried at Woodlawn Cemetery. Many of his works are still in manuscript, and he received his final royalty statement from Harper Brothers more than 4 years ago. *Omoo*, *White-Jacket*, and *Moby-Dick* are all out of print, and lifetime earnings from his books have totaled only $5,900 from U.S. publishers, $4,500 from British; Melville's writings will not gain widespread recognition in America for another 30 years.

Poetry: *The Children of the Night* by Edwin Arlington Robinson.

The Brooklyn Museum opens its west wing to the public at 200 Eastern Parkway, where an imposing granite building designed by McKim, Mead & White is under construction (*see* 1891); its central section will be completed in 1905, its front steps and central approach in 1906, its east wing in 1907, and the rest in 1924; more wings will be added in 1978 and 1987.

The Cooper-Hewitt National Design Museum has its beginnings in the Cooper Union Museum, a collection opened on the fourth floor of the Cooper Union at Astor Place. Former mayor Abram S. Hewitt's slightly eccentric daughters Sarah Hewitt, 39, and Eleanor Gurnee Hewitt, 33, are granddaughters of the late Peter Cooper; they have made annual visits to Europe, studied the exhibits at the Musée des Arts Décoratifs in Paris and at London's Victoria and Albert Museum, and assembled the collection of decorative arts ranging from furniture to wallpapers (*see* 1976).

Sculpture: a bronze statue of Peter Cooper by Augustus Saint-Gaudens is installed in a shrine-like niche on a white marble pedestal designed by Stanford

White south of the Cooper Union on Third Avenue and Bowery Street.

Theater: *The Little Minister* by English playwright James M. (Matthew) Barrie, 37, 9/27 at the Empire Theater, with Maude Adams, 300 perfs.; *The Devil's Disciple* by Irish playwright George Bernard Shaw, 41, 10/4 at the Fifth Avenue Theater, with Richard Mansfield, 64 perfs.

Broadway musicals: *The Good Mr. Best* 8/3 at the Garrick Theatre, with book by John J. McNally and a demonstration in the third act of the new cinematograph (*see* 1895); *The Belle of New York* 9/18 at the Casino Theater, with Edna May, 17, as the Salvation Army girl Violet Gray, Harry Davenport, music by Gustave A. Kecker, book and lyrics by Hugh Martin, songs that include "She Is the Belle of New York," "The Anti-Cigarette Society," "You and I," 56 perfs.

The Brooklyn Conservatory of Music is founded by Edward Adolf Whitelaw, who will head the institution until his death in 1944. Modeled on European conservatories, it requires prospective students to audition for admission and will grow to have an enrollment of 1,400, including 500 at a school in Flushing, Queens, that will be established in 1955.

Congress broadens copyright laws to give copyright owners exclusive rights to public performances of their works, but the new law will be widely flouted (*see* 1909; ASCAP, 1914; Victor Herbert, 1917).

Popular song: "Take Back Your Gold" by New York composer Monroe H. Rosenfeld, lyrics by Louis W. Pritzkow.

Aqueduct Racetrack opens September 27 in Ozone Park, Queens, under the direction of the Queens County Jockey Club but will not gain prominence for nearly 50 years.

Steeplechase Park opens in the spring at Coney Island under the management of local real estate operator George C. (Cornelius) Tilyou, 35, who at age 17 laid out the "Bowery" amusement area and built a theater. The ambience of Coney Island has improved somewhat since former Tammany Hall crony John Y. McKane went to prison in 1894, Brooklyn trolleys have been bringing out visitors since 1895 to enjoy the beach and cool ocean breezes, Tilyou has acquired more property at the corner of Ocean and Surf avenues and West 16th Street, and he names his amusement park after the eight mechanical, gravity-powered wooden racehorses that take passengers on a 35-second ride along a curving half-mile track that ends on a dark indoor stage, where jets of air blow up women's skirts. Tilyou has purchased the U.S. and Canadian patents on a carousel designed by inventor William Cawdery, and within 2 years a million visitors will be visiting Steeplchase Park, many of whose rides and fun houses Tilyou will invent himself, among them the Aerial Thrill, Barrel of Love, the Electric Seat, and the Human Roulette Wheel. Capt. Paul Boyton pioneered the idea of an amusement park 3 years ago, when he opened a Water Chutes ride at Chicago, and he has just opened Coney Island's Sea Lion Park, enclosing his rides within walls to keep out the gamblers, prostitutes, and other undesirables who still frequent the area. Competing attractions will spring up in the next decade to make Coney Island the greatest amusement area in the world (*see* 1907; Luna Park, 1903; Dreamland, 1904).

The city has 62 commercial bathhouses, including Russian (steam) baths (notably one on 10th Street between Avenue A and First Avenue), Turkish (hot air) baths, medicated baths, and vapor baths, most of them operated by orthodox Jews from eastern Europe who maintain *mikvas* (ritual baths) to preserve religious and social traditions (*see* public baths, 1906).

The Yale Club of New York is founded in an old brownstone at 17 East 26th Street; by next year it will have nearly 1,000 members and a surplus of $20,000, and by 1902 it will have a seemingly capacious 11-story clubhouse with six floors of bachelor apartments at 30 West 44th Street, opposite the Harvard Club, but Yale architectural graduates Evarts Tracy and Egerton Swartwout will leave McKim, Mead & White to start their own concern and design the building in such a way that if the club should fail the entire building can be turned into bachelor apartments like those at the nearby Royalton Hotel (Plainfield, N.J.-born Tracy is now 37, Fort Wayne, Ind.-born Swartwout 27; *see* 1915).

The Riverside Funeral Home has its beginnings in the Meyers Livery Stable horse-drawn funeral livery business founded in Norfolk Street on the Lower East Side by stableman Louis Meyers, 35. His eldest daughter Sarah will marry Charles Rosenthal, she will open a formal funeral business as Meyers Undertakers at 54 East 109th Street in 1905, and it will relocate in 1916 to 228 Lenox Avenue, corner 122nd Street, under the name Meyers & Co. (*see* 1926).

A complex of buildings for Bell Laboratories opens at 155 Bank Street in a block bounded by Bank, West, Bethune, and Washington streets. Cyrus L. W. Eidlitz and others have designed the structures that will later be converted to residential use for artists (*see* Westbeth, 1969).

A four-story clubhouse for the 45-year-old American Society of Civil Engineers is completed at 220 West 57th Street. Designed by Cyrus L. W. Eidlitz with a delicate French Gothic façade, its first floor has a lounge at the rear, its second floor a reading room in front, and a triple-height auditorium in the rear seats 400.

Grant's Tomb is completed to house the remains of the late president and his wife, Julia (*née* Dent). Some 90,000 subscribers from around the country and worldwide have contributed $650,000 to finance the limestone and marble structure, New Orleans-born architect John H. (Hemenway) Duncan, 42, has modeled it on the 350 B.C. tomb of Mausoleus at Halicarnassus, one of the Seven Wonders of the ancient world, and it rises 150 feet high above Riverside Avenue (later Riverside Drive) at 122nd Street, the largest mausoleum in North America. A mural in its rotunda shows Robert E. Lee surrendering to Grant at Appomattox Courthouse in 1865, and its two eight-and-a-half-ton sarcophagi are made of polished red Wisconsin granite. Outside the tomb, between the two sculptures over the entrance, are the words, "Let us have peace," taken from Grant's letter accepting the Republican Party's nomination for president in 1868.

The Board of Street Opening and Improvements votes December 31 to redraw the 116th Street corners of Riverside Avenue to give them a curved configuration for "the public interest" as completion of Grant's Tomb attracts developers to the area (*see* Colosseum and Paterno apartment houses, 1910).

The Hotel Greenwich opens under the name Mills Hotel No. 1 at 160 Bleecker Street, between Sullivan and Thompson streets. Funded by former San Francisco banker Darius Ogden Mills, now 71, who lives in a Fifth Avenue mansion, the $1.25 million, 11-story structure has been designed by architect Ernest Flagg with 1,560 tiny (five-by-seven-foot) bedrooms whose walls come within a foot of the ceiling. Each has a window overlooking either the street or one of two 50-by-50-foot grassy inner courts, each is furnished with an iron bedstead, a hair mattress, a chair, and a clothes rack, there are four toilets and six washbasins for the 182 men on each floor, bathrooms are on the ground floor, lodgings are available at 20¢ per night to poor "gentlemen" (about half the going rate at decent boarding-houses) and the dining room serves meals at 10¢ to 15¢ each that allow the hotel to make a small profit. Mills will put up two more such hotels, one at the corner of Chrystie and Rivington streets, one on Seventh Avenue at 36th Street.

The Waldorf-Astoria Hotel opens November 1 with 1,000 rooms and 765 private baths, making it the largest, most luxurious hotel in the world. Real estate heir John Jacob Astor IV, 30, has had his mother's mansion at 34th Street and Fifth Avenue demolished, engaged architect Henry Janeway Hardenbergh to design a 17-story Astoria Hotel, and combined it with the 13-story Hardenbergh-designed Waldorf Hotel opened by his estranged cousin William Waldorf Astor, now 46, in 1893. The three floors of public rooms include a ballroom, barbershop, galleries, theater, and Palm Court restaurant (*see* new Waldorf-Astoria, 1931).

The Hotel Martinique opens at 32nd Street and Broadway. Designed by Henry J. Hardenbergh in French Renaissance style with a mansard roof, it will be enlarged in 1910 to 1911, and its ornate public rooms and dining room will for years attract the city's *beau monde*.

Bellerose, Queens, has its beginnings as Massachusetts-born real estate agent Helen Marsh buys five parcels of land in neighboring Nassau County and lays out a village. She will form the United Holding Co. in 1906, it will supervise development for the next 21 years, opening a residential area across the line in Queens in 1910, with streets in a semicircular arrangement around a Long Island Rail Road station, and its population will grow by 1980 to 22,880.

Fishermen land more than 1.2 million pounds of sturgeon in New York and New Jersey, but pollution begins to reduce the Hudson River's "Albany beef" industry.

William F. Schrafft Co. of Boston engages confectionery salesman Frank G. (Garrett) Shattuck, 35, who disposes of the factory's output for the balance of the year within 3 months (*see* 1898).

Some 900 guests wearing Louis XV period costumes consume more than 60 cases of champagne at a ball given February 10 by Mrs. Bradley Martin, daughter of steel magnate Henry Phipps, who has had a huge Waldorf Hotel suite decorated in the manner of Versailles despite the national economic depression that has persisted since 1893. August Belmont II arrives in a $10,000 suit of gold-inlaid armor. The Martins boast afterward that the affair has cost them $370,000.

The new Waldorf-Astoria Hotel has an Empire Dining Room modeled after the grand salon of a royal palace at Munich and a Palm Court restaurant whose waiters speak French and German as well as English. Guests must wear full formal attire (white tie and tails for men); the chef earns $10,000 per year. There is also a large Palm Garden for tea, and a Turkish salon where a Turk pours coffee.

A new Delmonico's restaurant that will survive until 1923 opens November 15 at the northeast corner of Fifth Avenue and 44th Street (see 1876). Charles Crist Delmonico (he has received permission from the state legislature to add his great-uncle's name) plays host to more than 1,000 patrons, who dine in the Ladies' Restaurant, the Palm Garden, the Gentlemen's Elizabethan Café, the private dining and banquet rooms, the ballroom, and the Roof Conservatory.

Ellis Island's large two-story main processing building burns down soon after midnight June 14, having processed nearly 1,644,000 immigrants (see 1892). All immigration records from 1855 to 1897 have recently been transferred to a vault on the island and are completely destroyed (see 1900). Immigration falls to 13,000, down from 25,000 in 1893 and 65,000 in 1892, as unemployment remains high.

1898 New York City becomes Greater New York January 1 under terms of last year's state law uniting Kings County (Brooklyn), Richmond County (Staten Island), Queens County, and Manhattan to create a 359-square-mile metropolis with 578 miles of waterfront and 3,388,834 inhabitants—the largest city in the Western Hemisphere, with a population that includes 900,000 Brooklynites and is second in size only to that of London. Kings County includes the towns of Flatbush, Flatlands, Gravesend, New Lots, and New Utrecht; Richmond County the towns of Castleton, Middletown, Northfield, Southfield, and Westfield; Queens County the towns of Flushing, Hempstead, Jamaica, Long Island City, and Newtown. Also included are the towns of Eastchester and Westchester (see Bronx County, 1914).

The city's first board of aldermen takes office; full of sinecures, including 11 sergeants-at-arms, it will be called "the forty thieves."

The battleship U.S.S. *Maine* blows up in Havana harbor February 15 in an explosion that kills 258 sailors and two officers, precipitating a Spanish-American War that lasts for 112 days (see Sagasta, 1897). The sinking of the *Maine* follows by 6 days the publication in William Randolph Hearst's *New-York Journal* of a letter stolen from the mails at Havana, a private letter from the Spanish minister to the United States

Brooklyn's Grand Army Plaza honored Civil War dead. MUNICIPAL ARCHIVE

calling President McKinley a spineless politician (Madrid has recalled the minister).

Assistant secretary of the navy Theodore Roosevelt resigns his position May 6 to join with New Hampshire-born Col. Leonard Wood, 37, in organizing the 1st U.S. Volunteer Cavalry. He buys a uniform at Brooks Brothers and cuts a fine figure leading his "Rough Riders" up Kettle Hill near Santiago de Cuba in early July, a peace protocol is signed with Spain August 12, the Rough Riders return to Montauk Point, L.I., August 14 to begin a 6-week quarantine, and Roosevelt then returns to New York, having served from May 15 to September 16.

Former mayor A. Oakey Hall dies at New York October 7 at age 72, and Republican Party boss Thomas C. Platt proposes that Teddy Roosevelt be nominated for governor because he needs a strong soldier candidate to offset the effects of the Erie Canal scandals that have tainted the party. Roosevelt's opponents within the party find an affidavit he executed March 21 swearing he had been a resident of Washington, D.C., since June 1897 (TR has been struggling financially and sought to avoid payment of $1,005 in personal property taxes lodged against the row house at 689 Madison Avenue acquired by his sister Anna in 1886), another affidavit (made in August 1897 to the Town of Oyster Bay) is found in which TR stated that he resided and voted in New York City, the district attorney of Syracuse threatens to file perjury charges, but Elihu Root persuades the party leaders to let Roosevelt's nomination go forward, TR wins the delegate vote by 753 to 218, he campaigns from one end of the state to the other, and at age 40 wins the gubernatorial election, securing 661,707 votes to 643,921 for Democratic Party candidate Augustus Van Wyck, 49, brother of New York City's mayor (who is generally considered a tool of Tammany boss Richard Croker).

Bonwit Teller Co. is founded by New York merchant Edmund G. Teller, who has absorbed the fashion tailoring establishment started by Paul J. Bonwit 3 years ago on Sixth Avenue at 18th Street. The partners will open a new store on Fifth Avenue at 38th Street in 1911 (see 1930). The city's most elegant fashion retailer remains James McCreery, founded in 1837.

The New York Gas and Electric Light, Heat, and Power Co. (NYGLH&P) is created by a merger that combines most of the companies supplying Manhattan with electricity and quickly gains a controlling interest in Edison Electric Illuminating Co. (see Consolidated Gas, 1899).

The 27-year-old Grand Central Depot at 42nd Street is expanded into a six-story Renaissance-style structure of stucco and artificial stone designed by Bradford Lee Gilbert (see Wilgus plan, 1899).

Cornell University Medical College is established April 14 at Ithaca, with six professors. Most of the faculty is from New York University plus some from Bellevue Hospital, where the new college opens in temporary quarters in the fall. It receives a gift of $750,000 from Standard Oil executive Oliver Hazard Payne, now 57, to finance construction of its own building, to be designed by Stanford White and erected on First Avenue between 27th and 28th streets (see 1900).

Educator William H. Maxwell takes office as superintendent of schools March 15 (see 1896). Now 46, he supervises teachers who are in large part Irish Catholics. "New York is the largest and wealthiest city on the continent," he says. "But if New York is to be and remain a truly great city, it can only be through the education given to her children in the public schools. If public education is to do its perfect work for its community, it must be the best education that modern civilization can afford" (but see 1914).

The New York Times drops its price from 3¢ to 1¢ and circulation triples to 75,000 within a year (see 1897). By 1901 its circulation will be over 100,000, and its price will remain 1¢ (5¢ on Sundays) until it is doubled in 1917.

William Randolph Hearst publishes special editions of his New-York Evening Journal from his private yacht anchored in Havana Harbor. He has earlier sent 36-year-old Canton, N.Y.-born cowboy painter Frederic Remington to Cuba, Journal stories have inflamed opinion ("Remember the Maine!"), and the paper's circulation reaches 1.6 million May 2.

Cosmopolitan magazine publisher John Brisben Walker sends two reporters to cover the Spanish-American War (see 1895; 1902).

Fiction: David Harum: A Story of American Life by the late Syracuse-born New York banker-novelist Edward Noyes Westcott, who has died of tuberculosis March 31 at age 51: "Them that has gits;" The Imported Bridegroom and Other Stories of the New York Ghetto by Abraham Cahan.

The American Macmillan publishing house incorporates under the name P. F. Collier & Son (see 1869; Collier's Weekly, 1895). Revenues reached $50,000 in 1890 and will soar under the management of George E. Brett's son George Platt Brett, whose school and college textbooks will account for half the firm's sales as it grows to become the nation's largest publisher, a position it will retain until 1942 (see Crowell-Collier, 1934).

The Ten American Painters group is organized at New York by artists who include Dorchester, Mass.-born painter (Frederick) Childe Hassam, 38, who settled in the city 9 years ago, opened a studio on Fifth Avenue at 17th Street, and began creating impressionistic paintings of the city.

The Fine Arts Building is completed on the north side of West 57th Street between Seventh Avenue and Broadway to house three oganizations that include the Art Students League founded in 1875. Henry J. Hardenbergh has designed the structure in French style.

Sculpture: a memorial to the late architect Richard Morris Hunt created by sculptor Daniel Chester French is installed on the west side of Fifth Avenue between 70th and 71st streets.

American Vitagraph opens an outdoor film studio on the roof of the Morse Building at 140 Nassau

Street and uses the premises to produce a film called *Burglar on the Roof*. J. Stuart Blackton, Albert E. Smith, and William Rock have developed a superior motion-picture camera, will move their offices in 1900 to 110-116 Nassau Street, and in 1906 will relocate to a glass-enclosed Flatbush studio at the corner of 13th Street and Locust Avenue, facilities that they will expand quickly in the following 9 years.

New York Philharmonic and Metropolitan Opera conductor Anton Seidl dies of liver and gallstone ailments at New York March 28 at age 47. He has lived in an East 62nd Street brownstone, spent his afternoons smoking cigars at Fleischmann's Café near Union Square, and is celebrated for his summer concerts at Coney Island that have attracted huge crowds at 25¢ per ticket; some 4,000 mourners attend his funeral at the Metropolitan Opera House.

Broadway musicals: *Hurly-Burly* at the Weber & Fields Music Hall, with Joe Weber, Lew Fields, Little Rock-born singer-actress Fay Templeton, 32, Peter F. Dailey singing the John Stromberg-Edgar Smith song "Dinah" (or "Kiss Me Honey Do"); *The Fortune Teller* 9/26 at Wallack's Theater, with music by Dublin-born conductor-composer Victor Herbert, 30, book and lyrics by Harry B. Smith, songs that include "Gypsy Love Song," 40 perfs.

Brooklyn brewer Charles Ebbets persuades local trolley line owners to help build a stadium in Washington Park near Fourth Avenue and Third Street in the Park Slope section for the "Trolley Dodgers" baseball team that has been playing on a field opposite the new stadium. Ebbets began his career by selling scorecards for the Dodgers and 4 years ago bought a brownstone in First Street between Fifth and Sixth avenues (*see* 1899; Ebbets Field, 1913).

The Harlem Speedway opens for trotting races July 2 along the Harlem River between 155th Street and Dyckman Street. Built at a cost of $5 million (five times the amount originally projected), the 2.3-mile Speedway will attract competitors from eastern and midwestern cities, and rich New Yorkers will use it to show off their carriages and horses, but by 1918 it will be used by fewer than 20 carriages per day, and it will be opened in 1919 to automobile pleasure drivers as well as horse-drawn vehicles.

The Century Road Club is founded by New York cyclists. Bicycle races are major sporting events, and the CRC will become the largest racing club of its kind.

 The Frank E. Campbell Funeral Home has its beginnings in The Funeral Church opened in April at 241 West 23rd Street by undertaker Campbell, 25. He will move his establishment in 1915 to the northeast corner of Broadway and 67th Street.

The French Institute/Alliance Française is founded to encourage cultural exchange.

The 13-year-old California Perfume Co. has 5,000 door-to-door saleswomen offering not only perfume but also cologne, Sweet Sixteen Face Powder, Rose Lip Pomade, headache cures, shaving soap, tooth-cleaning tablets, shoe cleaner, furniture polish, spot remover, moth-proofer, food flavorings, and cookbooks (*see* 1929).

Dress-pattern manufacturer Ellen Curtis Demorest dies at New York August 10 at age 73.

The Chemists' Club is founded November 29 with offices at 108 West 55th Street and begins putting together a large library. The club will have 140 resident and 119 non-resident members by 1901, will move a decade later into a large new clubhouse at 50-54 East 41st Street, and within a century will have a staff of 90 to serve 2,500 members, businessmen as well as scientists.

The 113-year-old General Society of Mechanics and Tradesmen moves into a large classical brick-and-limestone building at 20 West 44th Street, where it will remain into the 21st century, conducting free technical classes for plumbers, electricians, and other construction workers. It has a library in its basement, and its collections will include the John H. Mossman lock museum.

A Long Island Rail Road station opens July 1 on Linden Boulevard in St. Albans, in southeastern Queens, where a syndicate of Manhattan developers bought the Francis farm 6 years ago and laid out streets and building lots. A post office will open next year, and St. Albans will grow into a middle-class suburban community (*see* Cambria Heights, 1923).

Brooklyn's Grand Army Plaza is graced with an 80-foot-high Soldiers' and Sailors' Memorial Arch designed by architect John H. Duncan to commemorate Union Army forces who died in the Civil War. Stanford White has created four tall Doric columns to mark the entrance to Prospect Park, the top of the arch may be reached via a winding staircase of 103 steps, and sculptor Frederick MacMonnies works there to complete *Quadriga*, a statue of Victory in a two-wheeled chariot drawn by four horses abreast.

The 26-story St. Paul Building is completed on a site bounded by Broadway, Park Row, and Ann Street, across Broadway from St. Paul's Chapel, where it replaces the old New York Herald Building. Designed by George B. Post without cupolas, pointed roofs, or flagpoles, the structure rises 315 feet; it is the tallest skyscraper yet built and will stand for more than a century (its 26th floor contains the water tank and other utilities).

The 22-story Empire Building is completed at 71 Broadway, southwest corner of Broadway and Rector Street, overlooking Trinity Church graveyard. Designed in neo-classical style by Kimball & Thompson and built by Marc Eidlitz & Son, it has 300,000 square feet of office space and 10 high-speed hydraulic elevators (the skyscraper will be turned into a luxury rental apartment house in 1997).

A brick and terra-cotta mansion is completed at 23 Park Avenue, northeast corner 35th Street for retired banker, cotton trader, and New York City Parks Commissioner James Hampden Robb and his wife, Cornelia (née Van Rensselaer). Stanford White has designed the five-story house in Italian Renaissance style.

The Gertrude Rhinelander Waldo mansion is completed at 867 Madison Avenue, southeast corner 72nd Street, where Kimball & Thompson has designed a limestone fantasy in neo-French Renaissance style (see retailers, 1986).

The Universalist Church is completed on Central Park West at 76th Street to designs by William A. Potter. Church spires are the city's tallest structures, visible for miles.

Sanitary engineer Col. George E. Waring, Jr. dies of yellow fever at New York October 29 at age 65, having turned trash collecting into a professionally managed municipal service and cleaned up the city's streets. Sent to Cuba by President McKinley to study ways of reducing yellow fever on the island, he contracted the disease himself. He is hailed as the "apostle of cleanliness," and some 5,000 people crowd into his memorial service.

Giovanni Esposito and Sons Pork Shop opens in Mulberry Street. Founded by immigrants from Naples, the butcher shop will continue for more than a century, moving to 500 Ninth Avenue, corner 39th Street, in 1932 and supplying patrons with specialties such as fegatelli (pork liver wrapped with bay leaves in caul fat).

Entenmann's baked goods are introduced by Brooklyn entrepreneur William Entenmann, who starts a home-delivery bakery service.

Martinson's Coffee is founded near the docks at New York by Latvian-born entrepreneur Joseph Martinson, 18, who specializes in supplying hotels and restaurants. When vacuum-packing of coffee is introduced in 1900, Martinson will be one of the first to market his coffee in the new way.

 Schrafft's salesman Frank G. Shattuck opens a retail candy shop at 1345 Broadway in Herald Square where crowds stop to watch the presses of the *New-York Herald* at work (see 1897). The shop soon begins serving lunch, becoming the first Schrafft's restaurant (see 1906).

Louis Sherry's reopens October 10 in a 12-story apartment-hotel at the northwest corner of Fifth Avenue and 44th Street, diagonally across from Delmonico's (see 1890; Delmonico's, 1897). Stanford White has designed the building, whose new restaurant will be among the city's finest for nearly 21 years.

The Salvation Army organizes its first annual dinner for the needy at Madison Square Garden, providing thousands with hot meals at tables set up on the arena floor while rich New Yorkers pay admission to sit in the Garden's box seats and galleries to watch. The event opens with the singing of the hymn "Praise God From Whom All Blessings Flow," a *New York Times* reporter writes that "position and fortune [were] forgotten for one brief moment," and he quotes the Salvation Army's commander as saying, "It means the dawning of a new era, the bridging of the gulf between the rich and poor."

 Greater New York's population of nearly 3.4 million includes more than 1.8 million in Manhattan (Chinatown's population reaches about 4,000, up from no more than 800 in 1880), 1.1 million in Brooklyn (whose numbers have been eclipsed by those of Chicago and other metropolitan areas), 150,000 in Queens, 135,000 in the Bronx, and 70,000 in Staten Island.

1899 Theodore Roosevelt takes office as governor January 1 but will serve only 2 years before becoming U.S. vice president. His administration will be marked by an insistence on competence and a vigorous push for reform measures. An amendment to the Municipal Corporation Act approved by the state legislature at Albany April 4 prohibits any elected official of a city, during his term of office, from holding any appointive position whose salary is paid by the city.

Irish-born political leader John Y. McKane dies at Brooklyn September 5 at age 58. After growing up in Sheepshead Bay, McKane became chief of police at Coney Island, allowed it to become a center of unrestricted prostitution and gambling, and has served 5 years' imprisonment for election fraud.

The Mazet Committee appointed by the state legislature at Albany as a counterpart to the city's Lexow Committee of 1894 finds evidence of wrongdoing on the part of the city's police chief William Devery, who is dismissed.

Admiral George Dewey, U.S. Navy, returns from his victory at Manila Bay in last year's Spanish-American War and receives a New York ticker-tape parade September 30.

Col. Jacob Ruppert is elected to Congress from Manhattan's 15th district, running on the Democratic ticket and winning by a majority of 10,000 even though the district is predominantly Republican. Now 32, the popular brewer was made a colonel in the 7th Regiment of the National Guard 10 years ago; he will be reelected three times before retiring from Congress in 1907.

The Costello Anti-Sweatshop Act approved by the state legislature at Albany April 1 provides for the inspection and regulation of work done in tenements. The state's labor law is amended to increase the number and scope of safety laws, limit working hours of women and children, and increase the authority of factory inspectors.

The 63-year-old Orphan Asylum Society orphanage on Riverside Avenue (later Riverside Drive) at 73rd Street gets its first professional superintendent and soon receives a legacy for scholarship support from the wife of R. G. Dun, whose husband, now 73, purchased a credit-rating firm in 1858. The orphanage will be among the leaders in establishing a "cottage system" whose houseparents take care of about 20 boys or girls under age 12. At age 11 or 12 a child is indentured to a Protestant family, which initially pays the child $25 and another $25 when the child turns 18. The orphanage will be moved to Hastings-on-Hudson in 1902 and be renamed the Graham School in 1929.

J. P. Stevens & Co. is founded at New York by Massachusetts-born textile merchant John P. (Peter) Stevens, 31, whose grandfather Nathaniel started a business at North Andover in 1812. Young Stevens has earned enough money working at the Boston dry-goods commission house Faulkner, Page & Co. to start his own business, he sells the products of the North Andover mill now operated by his uncle Moses, and will go on not only to to buy interests in many New England mills but also to invest heavily in Southern mills.

An amendment to the Greater New York charter approved by the state legislature at Albany March 14 consolidates in a general fund all of the city's county funds and authorizes the comptroller to borrow in anticipation of municipal revenues, the amounts borrowed not to exceed such revenues.

Wall Street's Dow Jones Industrial Average plummets 5.57 points (8.7 percent) December 18 as interest rates rise. British losses in the Boer War and U.S. losses in the Philippines are contributing factors.

The Astoria Light, Heat, and Power Co. is founded January 20 to provide service in part of Queens. The New York and Queens Gas and Electric Co. is founded June 12 and merges June 17 with the 2-year-old Flushing Gas and Electric Light Co. Consolidated Gas Co. buys the year-old New York Gas and Electric Light, Heat, and Power Co. and acquires as many electricity companies as it can (see 1901).

Buffalo-born New York Central chief engineer W. J. (William John) Wilgus, 33, receives a visit early in the year from engineer-inventor Frank J. Sprague, 42, who in 1888 operated the first successful electric trolley car system, at Richmond, Va. Sprague submits a plan for electrifying the Yonkers branch of the railroad. Elevated railways are converting from steam power to electric, says Sprague; why not electrify commuter railroads? More than 500 trains now operate on a daily basis out of Grand Central Station—three times the 1871 volume—and it is a struggle to keep the smoky station running smoothly. Wilgus completes his own plan in June for electrifying not only the Central's suburban trains but also the two tunnels under Park Avenue; the plan calls for new tracks in a widened open cut south of 56th Street, a loop station beneath Grand Central and adjacent property, and a new multilevel terminal that will provide additional capacity without requiring substantial enlargement of the existing site (see 1900).

New York Central chairman Cornelius Vanderbilt II dies at New York September 12 at age 55; his younger brother William Kissam Vanderbilt, now 50, assumes control of the various family enterprises, and although Chauncey Depew and other Central directors give enthusiastic approval to the Wilgus electrification plan they defer implementing it (see accident, 1902).

The Brooklyn Rapid Transit Co. (BRT) begins unifying the borough's various elevated railway companies and will soon replace steam engines with multiple-unit electric trains.

Real estate agent Henry H. Bliss of 235 West 75th Street alights from a southbound Central Park West trolley at 74th Street September 13, turns to help the woman behind him, and is struck by an electric taxi-cab operated by one Arthur Smith of 151 West 62nd Street, who is driving a physician back from a house call in Harlem; Bliss has his head and chest crushed, becoming the first American to be killed in an automobile accident (his wife was poisoned a few years ago, possibly by their daughter).

Former naval architect and shipbuilder William Henry Webb dies at his native New York October 30 at age 83.

The J. Leon Lascoff & Son apothecary shop opens at 1209 Lexington Avenue, southeast corner 81st Street, dispensing remedies that include leeches (for black eyes and bloodletting). It will continue at the same location for more than century, filling prescriptions and purveying sundries.

P.S. 157 opens in the fall at the northwest corner of 126th Street and St. Nicholas Avenue in an area of old factories and recently built flats and tenements. The Board of Education had a budget of only $5 million and a school population of 240,000 when it hired Charles B. Snyder as the replacement for its architect George Debevoise, and Snyder will save millions of dollars by siting schools mid-block instead of on expensive corners. He has revised his plans for P.S. 157 after studying school design in England and France late in 1896, and his H-shaped Renaissance structure of limestone, terra cotta, and light grey brick has 45 classrooms on its second, third, and fourth floors to accommodate 1,974 pupils. The top floor has classrooms for carpentry, cooking, drafting, sewing, and other specialized instruction; the ground floor contains four large playrooms, and the H-shape design allows for courtyards facing on 126th and 127th streets. The school will remain open until 1975.

New York University's Gould Memorial Library is completed on Sedgwick Avenue in the Bronx to designs by Stanford White of McKim, Mead & White (see 1896). The university's trustees voted in 1892 to move its undergraduate school from Washington Square to the Bronx, and White has laid out a new campus in the more rural area with Renaissance-inspired yellow brick buildings. NYU will retain the Bronx campus until 1973.

The Brooklyn Children's Museum opens in two Victorian mansions at the southeast corner of Brooklyn Avenue and St. Mark's Avenue (see 1976).

The New-York Ledger ceases publication after 48 years upon the demise of founder Robert Bonner, who dies at New York July 6 at age 75 after a colorful career in which he has publicized his idiosyncratic personal life while indulging a passion for race-horses.

New York newsboys and bootblacks strike July 20. Joseph Pulitzer's New-York World and William Randolph Hearst's New-York Journal have announced plans to raise the wholesale prices of their papers, the street urchins who deliver and hawk newspapers protest, they remain out for nearly 2 weeks before the papers agree to scale back their plans, and circulation managers begin to increase their use of news-stands and adult deliverymen (see newsstand licensing, 1913).

Nonfiction: The New Metropolis edited by German author E. Idell Zeisloft, who marvels that "the poorest man living in or visiting New York, provided he is well dressed, may sit about these corridors [in the 2-year-old Waldorf-Astoria Hotel] night after night, spending never a cent, speaking to no one, and he will be allowed to stay."

Painting: Fifth Avenue in Winter by Childe Hassam; A Winter's Night on Broadway (sketch) by New Jersey-born illustrator Everett Shinn, 22, who has wangled an interview with the editor of Harper's Weekly, been told the magazine needed a color drawing of the Metropolitan Opera House in a snowstorm, replied that he had one in his studio, quickly bought pastels, produced the work overnight, and saw it featured as a center spread; Self-Portrait by Eastman Johnson, now 75, whose portrait subjects have included the late John Quincy Adams, Chester A. Arthur, Edwin Booth, and William H. Vanderbilt, as well as Grover Cleveland and Benjamin Harrison, but who now outdoes any of his previous work in technical achievement.

Sculpture: a bronze statue of the late Chester A. Arthur by George E. Bissell is installed at the northeast corner of Madison Square near Madison Avenue and 26th Street.

Theater: Griffith Davenport (initially, The Reverend Griffith Davenport) by James A. Herne 1/16 at the Herald Square Theater, with Katharine Corcoran Herne, her daughters Julia A. and Chrystal, Sidney Booth (a nephew of Edwin Booth); Miss Hobbs by Jerome K. Jerome 9/7 at the Lyceum Theater, with Chicago-born actor Charles Richman, 34, 158 perfs.; Barbara Frietchie by Clyde Fitch 10/23 at the Criterion Theater, with Julia Marlowe, 83 perfs.; Sherlock Holmes by William H. Gillette (who has adapted some A. Conan Doyle detective stories) 11/6 at the Garrick Theater, with Gillette in a role that he will play hundreds of times.

Playwright-theater owner Augustin Daly dies at Paris June 7 at age 60 while on a business trip. His death effectively ends the career of actress Ada Rehan, now 39, although she will continue to perform at New York until 1905.

♪ Violinist David Mannes becomes concertmaster of the 21-year-old New York Symphony Society. Now 33, he was married last year to pianist Clara Damrosch, daughter of the late Leopold Damrosch, with whom he has given recitals since 1896, and has organized a small violin class at the Music Settlement on the Lower East Side (see 1910). Mannes will remain with the Symphony Society until 1912, becoming assistant conductor.

Broadway musicals: *The Rounders* 7/12 at the Casino Theater, with New York-born actor Joseph Cawthorn, 30, music and lyrics by Ludwig Englander, book by Buffalo-born writer Harry B. Smith, 38, 97 perfs.; *Whirl-i-gig* 9/21 at Weber and Fields' Broadway Music Hall, with Lilian Russell, with book by Edgar Smith, lyrics by Harry B. Smith, 264 perfs.; *The Singing Girl* 10/23 at the Casino Theater, with Joseph Cawthorn, music by Victor Herbert, lyrics by Harry B. Smith, 80 perfs.

Popular songs: "In Good Old New York Town" by Indiana-born New York songwriter Paul Dresser (originally Dreiser), 42, who gained success 2 years ago with his song, "On the Banks of the Wabash Far Away" and has written the new song with help from his brother Theodore, 28, who was sleeping in Bowery flophouses before Paul helped him get a job as editor of *Ev'ry Month* (see Fiction, 1900); "My Wild Irish Rose" by New York songwriter Chauncey Olcott, 41; "Hello, Ma Baby" by New York composer Joseph E. Howard, lyrics by Ida Emerson that begin, "Hello, ma baby,/ Hello, ma honey,/ Hello, ma ragtime gal . . ."

"Lift Every Voice and Sing" by Florida songwriters John Rosamond Johnson, 26, and his brother James Weldon Johnson, 28, will be called the black national anthem. James Weldon became the first black to be elected to the Florida bar 2 years ago, the Johnson brothers will move to New York in 1901 to begin a brief career as a songwriting team, but James Weldon will soon go back to school to prepare for a larger career (see Fiction, 1912).

🚶 Ohio-born prizefighter James J. "Jim" Jeffries, 24, wins the world heavyweight title from Bob Fitzsimmons June 9 with an 11th-round knockout in a match held at Coney Island. Jeffries will retire undefeated in March 1905 and be succeeded by Marvin Hart.

The Brooklyn Trolley Dodgers win their first National League pennant, playing home games at Washington Park and winning 101 of all 148 (see 1898). California-born pitcher James Michael "Jim" Hughes, 25, wins 28 games, loses six, and has an earned run average of 2.68; Brooklyn-born outfielder William Henry "Wee Willie" Keeler, 27, stands less than five feet, five inches tall and weighs only 140 pounds but ends the season with a batting average of .377 (he has explained his success as a matter of "hitting 'em where they ain't;" see 1900).

● American Chicle Co. is created at New York by a merger of seven chewing-gum manufacturers, including Thomas Adams (see 1871). The new company will have its factory and headquarters in 44th Street, Manhattan, until 1923, when it will move to Thomson Avenue in Long Island City, producing Chiclets, Black Jack, and Dentyne brands.

Dentyne chewing gum is introduced by New York drugstore manager Franklin V. Canning and a neighborhood dentist who have developed a cinnamon-flavored gum designed to promote dental hygiene (the brand name is a contraction of the two words). The flavor actually comes from oil of cassia, esteemed for its antiseptic value, and the product will gain a reputation for freshening the breath.

The Princeton Club of New York is incorporated December 12 under laws of the state and occupies quarters in the former Vanderbilt house at the corner of 34th Street and Park Avenue, where it will remain until 1907.

▥ "New York is Wide Open" (to gambling), says a *New York Times* headline April 7 (see 1894; Daly, 1885). Joseph J. Britton is chief agent of the 9-year-old New-York Society for the Enforcement of Criminal Law, 108 Fulton Street, whose members have collected evidence that has never been used, says the *Times*, and reports of the Society's activities have never been filed (the Society's counsel says no such filing is required by law). Poolrooms and other gambling establishments have continued to do business, taking mostly $1 and $2 bets, but various citizens have put pressure on the police and they have raided gambling houses all week. The *Times* runs the names and addresses of several dozen such places in downtown Manhattan, reporting that they are filled day and night with white and black patrons. One, on the Bowery, is run by a former police captain and is only a stone's throw from police headquarters; one of the largest is the Arcade, at St. Mark's Place, where sometimes as many as 2,000 persons gather, some of them police officers in uniform, who want to bet on horse races. Richard Canfield's club at 5 East 44th Street is popular with more affluent men of the city. Col. Asa Bird Gardiner tells the *Times* that never since becoming Manhattan district attorney has he ever received any money from the New York Society for the Enforcement of Criminal Law, but the *Times* reports that the First Precinct alone has 15 slot machines installed in barrooms, and Gardiner says saloon keepers must remove them or face prosecution (*see* Jerome, 1901).

The city inaugurates Family and Juvenile courts; reformers have pushed for a segregation of youthful offenders from adults.

The 29-story Park Row Building is completed at 15 Park Row to designs by Robert H. Robertson. Three stories taller than the St. Paul Building put up last year, with additional three-story cupolas, it rises 386 feet into the air and will remain the world's tallest building until 1909, but an article entitled "American Architecture from a Foreign Point of View" by French critic Jean Schopfer in *Architectural Review* calls the Park Row Building "detestable." A syndicate headed by August Belmont has financed the structure, which provides office space for about 4,000 workers, using 10 elevators set in a semicircular bay.

The Charles Broadway Rouss loft building is completed at 555 Broadway, between Prince and Spring streets. Designed by architect Alfred Zucker, it has been built for a Virginian whose construction sign has read, "He who builds, owns, and will occupy this marvel of brick, iron, and granite, thirteen years ago walked these streets penniless and $50,000 in debt."

The 12-story Bayard Building is completed at 65 Bleecker Street; designed by Chicago architect Louis Henri Sullivan, 42, the radical loft structure will soon be acquired by Silas Alden Condict and renamed the Condict Building. "Form follows function," Sullivan has said, and in his 1895 essay "The Tall Office Building Artistically Considered" he has written that the steel-framed office building should not ape the forms of older, masonry structures but must, rather, "be every inch a proud and soaring thing . . . without a single dissenting line."

The 33-year-old University Club moves into a seven-story Renaissance palazzo at 1 West 54th Street, northwest corner Fifth Avenue. Charles Follen McKim of McKim, Mead & White has designed the structure, and sculptor Daniel Chester French has decorated its frieze with the seals of 18 universities.

Investment banker Jules S. Bache moves into an 18-year-old house at 10 East 67th Street. Originally designed by James E. Ware, it has been altered for Bache by New York-born architect C. P. H. (Charles Pierrepont Henry) Gilbert, 39, who has studied at the Ecole des Beaux-Arts in Paris.

The Oliver Gould Jennings town house (later the Lycée Français de New York) is completed at 7 East 72nd Street. Flagg & Chambers has designed the mansion in French Empire style.

A limestone château for banker and broker Isaac Dudley Fletcher, 53, is completed at 2 East 79th Street, opposite the 8-year-old Isaac Brokaw mansion at 1 East 79th Street. C. P. H. Gilbert has designed the house in French Gothic style for Fletcher, his wife, Mary, and their eight servants.

The Pabst Hotel opens in November at the south end of Long Acre Square. A nine-story structure built for $225,000 by Milwaukee's Pabst Brewing Co., which has opened a brewery at 606 West 49th Street, the new limestone building has a restaurant, bar, and basement rathskeller but will survive only 3 years (*see* Times Tower, 1904).

The elegant 16-year-old, six-story Windsor Hotel on Fifth Avenue between 46th and 47th streets burns down March 17, killing 33 people and injuring 52. A guest lighting a cigar in a second-story sitting room has thrown his match out the window, it has set some lace curtains ablaze, shouts of "fire" have been drowned out by the din of the St. Patrick's Day parade outside, firefighters are handicapped by low water pressure, and 25 people are killed as guests leap from upper-floor windows.

The Bronx Zoo opens November 8 under the auspices of the 4-year-old New York Zoological Society that will become the Wildlife Conservation Society in 1993. Henry Fairfield Osborn has persuaded Columbia University undergraduate Charles William Beebe, 22, to drop out at the end of his junior year and become the zoo's assistant curator of birds, and he has talked Newark, N.J.-born *New York Times* reporter Raymond L. (Lee) Ditmars, 23, into becoming assistant curator of reptiles. Indiana-born taxidermist William Temple Hornaday, 44, designed the National Zoo at Washington, D.C., has overseen the design of the new zoo, and is in charge of its day-to-day operations, working to save wildlife that are being destroyed faster than they can multiply. His initial collection of 843 animals, representing 157 different species, will grow as Zoological Society expeditions bring back specimens from farflung parts of the earth, and within 48 years the zoo will have received 100 million visitors.

✗ The American Sugar Refining trust has almost a 100 percent monopoly in the U.S. industry (see 1907). The American Beet Sugar Co. is founded by New York lawyer William Bayard Cutting, 49, his brother Robert Fulton Cutting, now 47, and Robert H. T. Oxnard.

Breakstone Brothers relocates to 300 Greenwich Street, where it specializes in sweet and sour cream (see 1888). The business prospers, it will soon move to larger quarters at 344 Greenwich Street as it expands to become a wholesaler of butter, soft cheeses, and sour cream, and by 1912 it will have manufacturing plants in upstate New York (see 1918).

Rector's Lobster Palace opens one block north of Shanley Brothers on the west side of Broadway between 43rd and 44th streets in New York. Restaurateur Charles Rector's father, George, runs Rector's Oyster Palace in Chicago, and George will attract some of New York's more notable trencher-men (see Brady, 1902).

1900 Gov. Roosevelt writes in a letter January 26, "I have
✗ always been fond of the West African proverb, 'Speak softly and carry a big stick; you will go far.'"

Joseph Pulitzer's *New-York World* reports on its front page April 4 that the price of block ice will soon double from 30¢ to 60¢ per 100-pound block. Virtually every household in the city depends on regular deliveries of ice to keep food and medicines from spoiling, the weather is turning warmer, and news of the price hike creates a brouhaha. The State of New York institutes antitrust action against ice baron Charles W. Morse and his 4-year-old American Ice Co., but Mayor Van Wyck and Tammany leader Richard Croker have been given hundreds of thousands of dollars worth of stock in the company; the mayor's dock commissioner Charles Francis Murphy, 43, allows no other company to land ice on the city's few Hudson River docks, and although the mayor is cleared of any wrongdoing by Gov. Roosevelt, the charges will cost Tammany Hall the next mayoralty election. Morse moves his business to Chicago rather than contest the action in court (see 1901).

Gov. Roosevelt holds lengthy hearings September 1 on Col. Asa Bird Gardiner, a Democrat who was elected to the post of district attorney in 1898. Charges have been preferred against Col. Gardiner, a court decides that the charges were "not proven," Col. Gardiner writes the governor a saucy letter, and

Roosevelt removes him from office, replacing him with another Democrat, Stephen A. Philbin, to fill the vacancy until next year's election.

Republican party boss Thomas C. Platt works to obtain the nomination of Gov. Roosevelt as vice president in order to get the reformer out of New York State; Roosevelt wins election in November, running with President McKinley, who is reelected (see 1901). The Democratic ticket headed by William Jennings Bryan and former vice president Adlai E. Stevenson receives 6,358,071 votes (155 electoral votes), the Republican ticket 7,219,530 votes (292 electoral votes).

Newburgh-born Republican Benjamin B. Odell, Jr., 46, succeeds Theodore Roosevelt as governor of New York. Odell's father has served as mayor of Newburgh, he knows something about politics, and he wins 804,859 votes, as compared with 693,733 for his Democratic rival John Barry Stanchfield, 45, a former Elmira mayor and state assemblyman who was ex-governor D. B. Hill's law partner.

✊ The International Ladies' Garment Workers' Union is founded June 3 by cloakmakers who meet in a small hall on the Lower East Side. The union's seven locals represent 2,310 workers in New York, Newark, Philadelphia, and Baltimore. By 1904 the ILGWU will have 5,400 members in 66 locals in 27 cities (see 1909 strike), and by 1913 it will be the American Federation of Labor's third largest affiliate. Only 3.5 percent of the U.S. work force is organized; employers are free to hire and fire at will and at whim.

The National Consumers League has its beginnings in the Consumers League for Fair Labor Standards founded by Philadelphia-born New York social worker Florence Kelley, 41, who last year joined the Henry Street Settlement after 8 years at Chicago's Hull-House (see New York Consumers League, 1890). Conscientious consumers, says Kelley, will not want to buy goods made in substandard factories, or by child labor, or finished in tenements. She is joined by Josephine Goldmark and others in a campaign against child labor and tenement sweatshops. The League will work for minimum wage laws, shorter hours, improved working conditions, occupational safety, better conditions for migrant farm labor, and consumer protection in the form of pure food and drug laws.

$ *Moody's Manual of Railroads and Corporation Securities* begins publication under the direction of Jersey City-born New York financial analyst John Moody, 31, who has worked for 10 years in the banking house Spencer Trask & Co. Moody will establish the investor's monthly *Moody's* magazine in 1905, and his annual *Moody's Analyses of Investments* will appear beginning in 1909.

The Wall Street area has about 200 "bucket shops"—fly-by-night operations that solicit business through direct-mail and Sunday newspaper advertisements aimed at low-end clients with promises of quick speculative profits.

The Port of New York handles about 47 percent of U.S. foreign trade, down from 57 percent in 1870, as other ports grow to handle more coal, crude oil, ore, grain, and other commodities, but manufactured and processed goods continue to be exported mostly through New York, whose docks will account for more than half of all imports through the next decade and beyond.

Pennsylvania-born Carnegie Steel Co. president Charles M. (Michael) Schwab, 38, sits beside J. Pierpont Morgan at a dinner given December 12 at the University Club on Fifth Avenue, delivers a speech on the history of the steel industry, and a week or two later hears from Morgan that the financier would like to talk with him. Schwab travels to New York and visits with Morgan at 23 Wall Street (*see* United States Steel, 1901).

Macy's advertises a sale of corsets and petticoats in January, pricing corsets at 49¢ and up, petticoats at 99¢ and up. Lord & Taylor holds a linen sale with tablecloths for $1.45.

Pennsylvania-born merchant Samuel H. (Henry) Kress, 37, moves to New York and by 1907 will have 51 variety stores in operation. Inspired by the success of F. W. Woolworth, he decided to start a similar chain-store business in the South, opened his first 5-, 10-, and 25-cent store at Memphis in 1896, found immediate success, and opened stores in other Southern cities (*see* 1955).

The South Brooklyn Railway inaugurated January 13 by the Brooklyn Rapid Transit Co. provides freight service between Bush Terminal and Coney Island (*see* 1907; Bush Terminal, 1890).

Excavation begins March 24 at the corner of Bleecker and Greene streets on a subway system that will grow to become the largest in the world (*see* Rapid Transit Act, 1894). City planners have predicted that Manhattan traffic will soon come to a standstill, there being too many horses and too many tons of manure for anyone to be able to move, but the city has refused to accept defeat. It has required contractor John B. Macdonald to deposit $1 million in cash or securities plus two bonds, amounting to $5 million and $1 million each. Since no other financier has been willing to take the risk, some private investors led by August Belmont & Co. with backing from the English Rothschilds have come to Macdonald's aid, financing the Rapid Transit Subway Construction Co., headed by August Belmont II. He has hired engineer William Barclay Parsons, 35, to work out the formidable problems presented by underground streams, quicksand, varying depths of bedrock, and river tunneling (Parsons has helped build a railroad in China; Belmont has sent him to study the London underground and the Paris Métro now under construction). Contractor Mcdonald hires more than 7,700 laborers, most of them Italian, Irish, and Polish from the tenement districts or brought over from Italy by *padrones* who receive part of the men's wages; they begin digging up the streets for 10 hours per day at wages of 20¢ per hour, sometimes blasting through solid rock although most of the work is digging relatively shallow trenches (Parsons fears that too many steps will discourage passengers from using the stations), using the cut-and-cover method employed in building the Budapest subway rather than the deep-tunnel method used in London. The project will involve relocating miles of gas mains, water mains, steam pipes, electric conduits, telephone lines, and the like; the Rapid Transit Commission Contract specifies that the subway and its equipment shall "constitute a great public work," so station walls will be lined with ceramic tiles that are fireproof, lightweight, durable, and easily cleaned. Poet Edwin Arlington Robinson, now 30, obtains a job checking stone weights during the removal of debris (*see* IRT, 1902).

Electric trolley cars that take their power from overhead wires provide transportation in much of Brooklyn and Queens (but not in Manhattan, where aerial wires are forbidden). Introduced at Richmond, Va., only 12 years ago, trolleys are used in every other major U.S. city (*see* 1917).

The city's elevated trains can go no faster than 20 miles per hour without causing their supporting structures to shake ominously.

New York Central engineer William J. Wilgus improves the interior of the 29-year-old Grand Central Depot with help from architect Samuel Huckel, Jr. (*see* 1899). Instead of having separate waiting rooms for New York Central, Hudson River Line, and New Haven Line commuters, the station is given a single waiting room that measures 200 by 100 feet, with an arched roof 50 feet high, open fireplaces, armchairs, rocking chairs, and writing desks. Long-distance passengers use a new "emigrants' waiting room" in the basement (see accident, 1902; Grand Central Terminal, 1913).

The 51-year-old Pennsylvania Railroad acquires control of the Long Island Rail Road in exchange for providing the company with tunnels into Manhattan. The Pennsy has plans to build tunnels under both the East River and the Hudson; the LIRR will soon be the nation's largest passenger carrier (see 1905).

The first National Automobile Show opens November 10 at Madison Square Garden with 31 exhibitors displaying 159 vehicles, most of them steam or electric. Contestants compete in starting and braking, and exhibitors demonstrate hill-climbing ability on a specially built ramp, but horseless carriages are forbidden to park on the city's streets and even stables refuse to take them in.

 Brooklyn dentist "Painless Parker" opens his first Manhattan office on Lower Broadway (see 1897). To attract patients he hires a clown, an Irish tenor, a three-piece brass band, and two chorus girls wearing tights, drives the troupe about town in a horse-drawn wagon, and gives free shows at street corners; when he has gathered a crowd he goes into his sales pitch, and soon has more Manhattanites standing in line to have their teeth pulled than he has in his Brooklyn office. By 1905 Parker will have a Vandyke beard and be employing 26 dentists in Manhattan and Brooklyn, charging $1 per extraction, and acquiring a 50-acre Long Island estate for his wife and four children, but his obsession with tooth extraction will take its toll, he will have a breakdown, and after nearly a year in bed will be persuaded by his wife to sell out (for $3 million) and move to California, where, before too long, he will resume his practice, eventually (when ethical dentists threaten to sue him for misrepresentation) having his name legally changed from Edgar Rudolph Randolph Parker to Painless Parker.

Physician and pharmaceutical manufacturer E. R. Squibb dies at Brooklyn October 25 at age 81.

Cornell University Medical College opens its new building December 29 on First Avenue between 27th and 28th streets (see 1898). Cornell's Canadian-born president Jacob Gould Schurman, 46, surgeon Lewis A. (Atterbury) Stimson, 56, and the new college's Tennessee-born dean William M. (Mecklenburg) Polk, 56, are among those making speeches. The Medical College conferred its first doctor of medicine degrees last year (to students who had entered in 1898 with advanced standing). Qualifications for entrance are minimal; Cornell will occupy the building until 1932 (see 1904).

 Gov. Roosevelt signs into law April 18 a measure providing that no person shall be excluded from any public school in the state on account of race or color and repealing an earlier law that provided for the establishment of separate schools for black children at the discretion of local authorities.

Loyola High School has its beginnings in a boys' school founded by the Society of Jesus, whose directors will put up a building at 980 Park Avenue, between 83rd and 84th streets (the school will be coeducational starting in 1973, and Loyola will be the only coeducational Jesuit school in the metropolitan area).

The U.S. College Entrance Examination Board is founded at New York to screen applicants to colleges (see S.A.T.s, 1926).

Collier's Weekly publisher's son Robert F. Collier, 23, invites his New York-born Georgetown University classmate Condé Nast, 26, to return to the city and join *Collier's* as advertising manager (see 1895). Nast accepts, begins to raise circulation from its present 200,000 level, will become business manager of Collier publications in 1905, and will soon be earning $50,000 per year (see *Vogue*, 1909).

The Associated Press leaves Chicago in the wake of an adverse 1898 court decision and is reorganized at New York April 20 with objectives that include eliminating bias and partisanship from the collecting and disseminating of news (see 1848). *Chicago Daily News* cofounder Melville Elijah Stone, 51, will head the AP until 1921, making it a worldwide news-gathering service (see International News Service, 1906).

New-York Evening Post publisher and financier Henry Villard dies at suburban Dobbs Ferry November 12 at age 65, leaving the broadsheet paper to his German-born journalist son Oswald Garrison Villard, 28. A grandson of the late abolitionist and women's rights advocate William Lloyd Garrison, young Villard will make the *Post* a leading organ of liberal thought with a nationwide readership (see 1918).

Nonfiction: *History of Public Franchise in New York City* by Trenton, N.J.-born writer Gustavus Myers, 28; *Wounds in the Rain* by Stephen Crane, who dies of tuberculosis at Badenweiler, Germany, June 5 at age 28. He served as a correspondent for the *New-York World* in the Spanish-American War 2 years ago and his book is a collection of war sketches.

Fiction: *Sister Carrie* by Indiana-born New York novelist Theodore Dreiser, now 29, of 6 West 102nd Street, whose poor heroine arrives in the city and is taken to Louis Sherry's: "Here was the place where the matter of expense limited the patrons to the moneyed or pleasure loving-class . . . Incandescent lights, the reflection of their glow in polished glasses, and the shine of gilt upon the walls combined into one tone of light which it requires minutes of complacent observation to separate and take particular note of . . . The floor was of reddish hue, waxed and polished, and in every direction were mirrors—tall, brilliant, bevel-edge mirrors—reflecting and re-reflecting forms, faces, and candelabras a score and a hundred times." Publisher Frank N. Doubleday hastily withdraws the book when his wife says it is too sordid, the small edition goes almost unnoticed, and Dreiser suffers a nervous breakdown; *The Touchstone* by New York novelist Edith Newbold Wharton (*née* Jones), 38, who portrays what she sees as the evil lying beneath New York society's show of manners.

 Painter Frederick E. Church dies at his Oleana home overlooking the Hudson River April 7 at age 73; Jaspar Francis Cropsey at Hastings-on-Hudson June 22 at age 77.

 Theater: *Sag Harbor* by James A. Herne 9/27 at the new Republic Theater, 207 West 42nd Street, with William T. Hodge, Herne's daughters Julia A. and Chrystal, Philadelphia-born actor Lionel Barrymore (originally Blythe), 22, 76 perfs. Herne himself appears on stage in the third entr'acte and calls the Republic "the finest building in New York." Its exterior (unfinished on opening night) is of dark brownstone and grey Powhattan brick, and Doric columns, and it has a 35-foot proscenium arch, excellent acoustics, and a dome patterned after the capitol at Washington, D.C. Hot and cold air circulate through floor ducts to ventilate the house (the system does not work opening night); curtain and scenery are operated by an electric motor controlled by one man at an onstage switchboard. Twelve musicians play at each performance. Auditoriums of the city's earlier theaters have been ringed with tiers of shallow balconies in the tradition of Baroque European auditoriums; the new ones will have just two big balconies, eliminating the upper tiers whose seats were cheap enough for poorer patrons. Theater operators will be under pressure to have long-running hits in order to make their houses pay. Unable to secure stars for his new house, Oscar Hammerstein leases it to producer David Belasco for $30,000 per year plus 10 percent of gross

Christy Mathewson pitched for the Giants at the Polo Grounds and became legendary for his prowess.

receipts and will soon be receiving $60,000 to $72,000 per year on the deal.

The Shubert brothers of Syracuse lease the Herald Square Theater, challenging the 4-year-old Theatrical Syndicate headed by booking agent Charles Frohman, now 40. Lithuanian-born theatrical manager Sam S. Shubert (originally Szemanski), 24, and his brothers Lee, 25, and J. J. (Jacob J.), 20, begin a 10-year battle with Frohman, Marc Klaw, and A. L. Erlanger by renting theaters to producers against whom the Syndicate discriminates. The Shuberts will soon become producers themselves (*see* 1905).

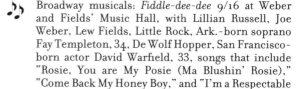 Broadway musicals: *Fiddle-dee-dee* 9/16 at Weber and Fields' Music Hall, with Lillian Russell, Joe Weber, Lew Fields, Little Rock, Ark.-born soprano Fay Templeton, 34, De Wolf Hopper, San Francisco-born actor David Warfield, 33, songs that include "Rosie, You are My Posie (Ma Blushin' Rosie)," "Come Back My Honey Boy," and "I'm a Respectable Working Girl" by John Stromberg, book and lyrics by Edgar Smith, 262 perfs.

Popular song: "A Bird in a Gilded Cage" by New York composer Harry Von Tilzer (Harry Gumm), 28, lyrics by Arthur J. Lamb.

 Christy Matthewson leaves Bucknell University to join the New York Giants, but pitches so poorly that New York sells him to the Cincinnati Red Stockings. Right-hander Christopher Matthewson, 20, will be bought back (see 1903).

The Brooklyn Trolley Dodgers win their second National League pennant, playing home games at Washington Park and winning 82 of all 136 games (see 1899). Illinois-born pitcher Joseph Jerome "Joe" McGinnity, 36, wins 28 games, loses 17, and has an earned-run average of 2.90; Willie Keeler hits four home runs in the season and ends it with a batting average of .368 (see Ebbets Field, 1913).

Prague-born chess player William (originally Wilhelm) Steinetz dies a pauper in the Manhattan State Hospital on Ward's Island August 12 at age 64. Having held the world title since 1872, his defeat for the championship by Emanuel Lasker in 1894 upset his mental balance and he has had several breakdowns.

The Junior League of the New York College Settlement is founded by post-debutante Barnard College undergraduate Mary Harriman, 19. Eldest of financier Edward Harriman's six children, she organizes a group to aid a local settlement house; debutantes flock to join the league that Harriman will head as chairman until 1904 and that will be followed by Junior Leagues of Baltimore, Brooklyn, Philadelphia, and Boston. By 1920 there will be 39 Junior Leagues engaged in civic improvement projects, and Mrs. Willard Straight (née Dorothy Whitney) will organize them into the Association of Junior Leagues of America.

Lionel Train Co. is founded by New York inventor-entrepreneur Joshua Lionel Cowan, 23, who grew up on the Lower East Side. The eighth of nine children, he has created a little wooden railcar, placed it on a battery-powered two-rail track, and persuaded local shopkeeper Robert Ingersoll to use it in an eye-catching window display. It fails to move the other merchandise in the window, but Ingersoll sells the toy in his display and Cowan is encouraged to make hundreds of such toys, going into competition with German imports.

The Hamilton Fish Park Gymnasium and Public Baths designed in Beaux-Arts style by Carrère & Hastings open on the Lower East Side in Hamilton Fish Park at 130 Pitt Street, between Stanton and Houston streets. One U.S. home in seven has a bathtub; showers are even rarer, and on New York's crowded Lower East Side hardly any family has access to a private bath.

The Appellate Division of the New York State Supreme Court's First Department moves from rented quarters on Fifth Avenue and 19th Street into a $700,000 white marble courthouse completed at the northeast corner of Madison Avenue and 25th Street opposite Madison Square. Designed by James Brown Lord, the dome-topped structure has an elaborate entrance hall, gilding, paneling, stained glass, painted friezes, and sculptures that include *Justice* by Daniel Chester French, *Peace* by Karl Bitter, and figures by others representing such lawgivers as Confucius and Moses.

Euclid Hall is completed at 2349 Broadway between 85th and 86th streets. The seven-story apartment house is one of more than 50 upper West Side residential buildings put up this year by developers anticipating that the new subway under construction on Broadway will boost demand for housing in the area (see Euclid Hall, 1995).

The nine-story Turrets is completed at 125 Riverside Avenue (later Riverside Drive). Designed by S. B. Ogden, the first apartment house on the Drive has apartments ranging in size from 10 rooms with three baths to 20 with six baths. It boasts a white marble swimming pool, gymnasium, billiard room, basketball court, bowling alleys, banquet hall, and a large ballroom, and is soon followed by comparable structures. A six-room apartment in West 98th Street rents typically for between $22 and $28 per month.

The New York State Tenement House Commission samples 2,877 of the city's tenements and finds that 98 have no fire escapes at all, while 653 have fire escapes only in the rear. Housing reformers Lawrence Veiller and Hugh Bonner write, "There is no reason why fire escapes should be omitted on the front of such buildings except the pride of the architect and the owner, who dislike seeing cheap iron balconies upon their front of their buildings. If these balconies offend their artistic sensibilities, they have two remedies: one to make balconies artistic; the other to build their buildings fireproof. We believe that the protection of human life is of much greater importance than anything else."

The Army & Navy Club of America building (later Touro College) is completed at 30 West 44th Street, between Fifth and Sixth avenues, to designs by Tracy & Swartwout.

The Hotel Renaissance (later the Columbia University Club, later still the Unification Church headquarters) is completed at 4 West 43rd Street to Renaissance Revival designs by Howard, Cauldwell & Morgan.

Hamilton Fish Park opens on the Lower East Side with structures designed by Carrère & Hastings, but the formal park is soon in ruins, owing, it is said, "to the radical defects of the original plan and to the strenuous nature of the youth of the neighborhood." It will be redone in 3 years, and a swimming pool will be added in 1936.

The 15-year-old National Audubon Society conducts its first annual Christmas bird count as an alternative to the custom of going out after Christmas dinner, choosing sides, and vying to see which side could shoot the most birds. Volunteer bird lovers throughout the next century will take different parts of Central Park and other New York areas, count the number of birds in each species, and look for rare and unusual species.

The city's five boroughs still contain more than 2,000 farms, and there are even some in Manhattan, but the average size of a farm has shrunk to 25 acres.

Missouri-born publisher Bernarr Macfadden, 32, opens a restaurant at 487 Pearl Street with prices that undercut the competition to help promote *Physical Culture*, the magazine he has published since 1898. Most items on the menu are priced at 1¢ at a time when other restaurants charge 15¢ for a full meal (saloon-bars offer "free" lunches for a nickel or less, depending for their profits on alcohol sales).

The population of Woodside, Queens, reaches 3,878, up from 1,355 in 1875, thanks in part to the installation of trolley lines 5 years ago (*see* real estate, 1867; elevated, 1917). Other Queens communities served by trolleys show similar gains.

The population of Greater New York reaches 3,437,202, making it twice as large as Chicago. Well over a third of the city is foreign born, and Manhattan's population is even more so, with Germans and Irish predominating although the numbers of immigrants from Italy and Eastern Europe are fast increasing (the city has 220,000 Italians, up from fewer than 20,000 in 1880, and 748,882 Germans, up from about half that number in 1880, plus nearly 134,000 Austrians). Irish immigrants and their children number 275,102, up from 244,886 in 1855, and account for 22 percent of the total, but the city has fewer than 60,000 blacks, many having left after the 1863 draft riots (*see* 1960).

A new fireproof main building dedicated on Ellis Island December 17 will be the main U.S. immigrant reception depot until 1924 (*see* 1897). French-educated architects William A. (Alciphron) Boring and Edward L. (Lippincott) Tilton have competed with others for the contract to rebuild the receiving station and been paid $26,000 for their plan. Completed at a cost of $1.5 million, the new Immigrant Receiving Station is in Beaux Arts style, its copper-capped rusticated limestone and red-brick towers rise 134 feet above New York Harbor, its huge Registry Hall is on the second floor, and its 50-foot vaulted ceiling is decorated with interlocking terra-cotta tiles. The new facility processes 2,251 arrivals on its opening day; immigration has been declining and the structure is considered large enough to handle the load (*but see* 1907).

20th CENTURY

1901 President McKinley visits the Pan-American Exposition at Buffalo and is shot at point-blank range September 6 with a .32 caliber Ivor Johnson revolver fired by mentally defective, Polish-born anarchist Leon Czolgosz, 28. His wounds are not properly dressed, McKinley dies of gangrene September 14 at age 58, and former New York governor Theodore Roosevelt at age 42 becomes the youngest chief executive in the nation's history.

Police accuse anarchist Emma Goldman of having had a hand in the assassination of President McKinley (see 1893). President Roosevelt blames the tragedy on editorials in William Randolph Hearst's *New York Journal*; Goldman has actually renounced the use of violence as a tactic but is deprived of her U.S. citizenship (see 1917).

A Board of Estimate created to set the city's budget has "residual powers" that will make it a political force rivaling the mayor's office (see 1804). Its members are the mayor, the president of the Board of Aldermen, the comptroller, and the presidents of the five boroughs; it will consider proposals prepared by subordinate agencies that will make recommendations as to who shall receive building permits, utility lines, and transporatation franchises; its deliberations will for the most part be private; and Democrats will have a dominant influence on its decisions for nearly 90 years (see 1990).

Park Slope, Brooklyn, rooming-house keeper Mrs. Charles F. Dodge marries ice baron Charles W. Morse, now 45 and a widower with four children (see 1900). She obtained an uncontested divorce 4 years ago on grounds of adultery from her previous husband, then a desk clerk at the Everett House on Madison Avenue at 22nd Street, but her new husband's monopoly in ice has widespread political ramifications (see crime, 1903).

Seth Low wins the mayoralty election, having resigned his presidency of Columbia to run on a Fusion Party ticket. Tammany Hall boss Richard Croker has denied Mayor Van Wyck the Democratic nomination and chosen lawyer Edward Shephard in his place, but Democrat Shephard secures only 265,177 votes to Low's 296,813, Croker loses all credibility, and he retires with his wealth to his native Ireland.

Republican William Travers Jerome, 42, is elected district attorney of New York County, having campaigned with the slogan, "Jerome on the Square" (he has distributed square black buttons with JEROME printed diagonally across them in square white letters); he actually owes his victory to the fact that so many ballots have been invalidated by voters scribbling invectives beside the name Van Wyck. (Van Wyck lives at 135 East 46th Street and is alleged to have ties to C. W. Morse's Ice Trust, whose directors have gained control of all ice entering the city and used their monopoly position to raise prices.)

The south end of Long Acre Square at 42nd Street has more than 90 brothels; young women arriving in the city in search of work are often forced into prostitution, and the center of the sex industry has moved uptown.

United States Steel Co. is created March 2 by financier J. P. Morgan, who underwrites a successful public offering of bonds in the world's first $1 billion corporation, nets millions for himself in a few weeks of hard work, and pays $492 million to Andrew Carnegie for about $80 million in actual assets in order to eliminate the steel industry's major price cutter (see 1900). Charles M. Schwab has contrived to play golf with Carnegie at a course outside New York, told him that Morgan wanted to buy him out, returned to Morgan with a paper bearing a figure scrawled by Carnegie, and obtained Morgan's acceptance. Carnegie's steel works are far more efficient than Morgan's and Carnegie personally receives $225 million ($300 million by some accounts) in 5 percent gold bonds; Morgan congratulates him on being "the richest man in the world" and merges Carnegie's properties with other steel properties to create a company that controls 65 percent of U.S. steelmaking capacity. Carnegie divorces himself from steelmaking to pursue his philanthropic interests.

The "Pig Market" in Seward Park on the Lower East Side attracts immigrant workmen, who stand about with symbols of their trades—panes of window glass, a hammer and saw, sewing machines—waiting for casual employers who may hire them for a day's work.

Wall Street panics May 9 as brokerage houses sell off stock to raise funds to cover their short positions in Northern Pacific Railroad stock. Financiers Edward H. Harriman, Jacob H. Schiff of Kuhn, Loeb & Co., and James Stillman, 51, of National City Bank vie for control of the railroad controlled by J. P. Morgan and by James J. Hill of Canadian Pacific. Stillman's City Bank is the repository of John D. Rockefeller's Standard Oil Co. money, Harriman and Schiff have acquired control of the Union Pacific, the Southern Pacific, and the SP's subsidiary Central Pacific, they seek control of the Chicago, Burlington & Quincy to gain access to Chicago, the rivals for the Northern Pacific bid up the price of its stock from about 110 to 1,000 in 4 days, but they grow frightened when other stock prices collapse in the panic, let short-sellers cover their positions at $150 per share, and join forces to form Northern Securities, a holding company that controls not only the Northern Pacific but also the Great Northern and the Chicago, Burlington & Quincy (see Supreme Court ruling, 1904).

Wall Street's Dow Jones Industrial Average closes December 31 at 64.56, down from 70.71 at the end of 1900.

Consolidated Gas Co. merges the electric companies it controls into a subsidiary, the New York Edison Co. (see 1899). Included are the Edison Electric Illuminating Co. and NYGHL&P. By 1910 electricity will have largely replaced gas as the standard choice for power and illumination; New York Edison will control most of the electricity generated in Manhattan and the western part of the Bronx, and the company will gradually have replaced most of its small direct-current generating stations (see 1906; Consolidated Edison, 1936).

The Willis Avenue Bridge across the Harlem River opens August 23 to link Manhattan's First Avenue at 125th Street with Willis Avenue and 132nd Street in the Bronx. Designed by engineer Thomas C. Clark, it is 3,212 feet in length, including its approaches, and is intended to relieve traffic congestion on Clark's Third Avenue Bridge.

St. Nicholas Avenue is given that name (originally an Indian trail that became the road between the town of Harlem and the Spuyten Duyvil ferry established in 1699, it has been called at various times the Kings Way, the Great Post Road, the Albany Post Road, the Queens Road, and Kingsbridge Road).

Manhattan Railway Co. extends the Third Avenue El to Fordham Road and begins converting its elevated trains to electric power (see 1886; 1903), but horsecars continue to move up and down Fifth Avenue (see 1885; 1907).

Pennsylvania Railroad president Alexander Cassatt announces December 12 that his company will build tunnels beneath the Hudson so that his trains can enter Manhattan. The world's first electrified railway terminal, the Gare d'Orsay, has recently opened at Paris, and Cassatt intends to use electric locomotives to pull his trains through the tunnels (see 1904).

Rockefeller University has its beginnings in the Rockefeller Institute for Medical Research, incorporated June 14 by John D. Rockefeller on the advice of Louisville-born physician Simon Flexner, 38, who will head the Institute from 1903 to 1935, receiving a high salary to keep him from being tempted by a university professorship. Rockefeller's first grandchild John Rockefeller McCormick has died of scarlet fever January 2, and he pledges an average of up to $20,000 per year for 10 years to support the new Institute. His son John D., Jr. acquires a site just east of Avenue A between 63rd and 68th streets that has belonged since 1818 to the Schermerhorn family. Unlike European laboratories such as the 13-year-old Pasteur Institute, built around individuals, the Rockefeller Institute will offer facilities to groups of collaborating investigators and establish a new pattern that others will follow (see 1906; milk contamination report, 1902).

Japanese-born biochemist Jokichi Takamine, 46, isolates the chemical adrenalin (later to be called epinephrine) from the suprarenal gland; it is the first pure hormone to be isolated from natural sources. After making a small fortune with an artificial fertilizer company he had founded, Takamine was invited to New York in 1890 and asked to find a practical application for the distilling industry of a starch-digesting enzyme he had developed from a rice fungus; he set up a laboratory at Clifton, N.J., and has been associated with Parke-Davis Co., doing research in applied chemistry (*see* everyday life [Nippon Club], 1905).

The New York Lung Association has its beginnings in the New York Society for the Prevention of Tuberculosis that opens offices in West 43rd Street. One in 10 New Yorkers can expect to die of TB, endemic in many neighborhoods where it kills well over half the residents.

The German Hospital and Dispensary opens its first private pavilion (*see* 1882; Lenox Hill, 1918).

Poughkeepsie-born New York physician Sara Josephine Baker, 28, gives up her private practice after 1 year and obtains a position as a city medical inspector at an annual salary that is double the $185 she earned last year (although her patients included actress Lillian Russell). Baker graduated second in her class of 18 from the Women's Medical College of New York 3 years ago and works in the West Side slum known as Hell's Kitchen, where she looks for cases of contagious diseases such as influenza, dysentery, smallpox, and typhoid fever (*see* 1903).

Brooklyn Law School opens in Brooklyn Heights. William Payne Richardson, 37, has started the private academy that he will head as dean until his death in 1945 (*see* 1968).

The 117-year-old New York State Board of Regents approves Polytechnic Institute of Brooklyn's application to award masters degrees (*see* 1890). While its preparatory school will continue to flourish as Brooklyn Polyprep, Polytech will award its first master of science degrees next year, inaugurate undergraduate evening courses in 1904, and drop its liberal arts program in 1908 to focus exclusively on science and engineering (*see* 1935).

The Chapin School has its beginnings in Miss Chapin's School for Girls and Kindergarten for Boys and Girls, opened in the fall by former Brearley primary classes director Maria Bowen Chapin, 38, in a town house at 12 East 47th Street. Her primary school for 75 pupils will move to 48-50 East 58th Street in 1905, add an upper school in 1909, move into two brownstones at 32-54 East 57th Street in 1910, become a girls-only school in 1918, and have 318 students by 1925 (*see* 1928).

Horace Mann School moves half a block west into a splendid new building donated by Teachers College trustees Mr. and Mrs. V. Everitt Macy at the corner of 120th Street and Broadway (*see* 1894; 1914).

 Publisher Herman Ridder, 49, acquires the *New Yorker Staats-Zeitung* published since 1834. Born in a house at 400 Greenwich Street, Ridder had only a few years of public schooling before becoming, successively, an errand boy, a clerk for a Wall Street brokerage house, an insurance company clerk, and, in 1879, publisher of the German-language *Katholisches Volksblatte*. He acquired stock in the *New Yorker Staats-Zeitung* in 1880, became active in New York politics, and founded the *Catholic News* in 1889 (*see* 1920).

The Yiddish-language daily *Der Morgen Zhornal* begins publication at 75-79 Bowery. Started by Jacob Sapirstein, it is the only daily morning paper of its kind, and its large help-wanted section wins it quick popularity among the fast-growing immigrant population of the Lower East Side. Circulation will peak at 111,000 in 1916, the *Morgen Zhornal* will merge with *Der Yiddishe Tageblatt* in 1928 (*see* 1885), and a 1953 merger with *Der Tog* (*see* 1914) will create the *Tog-Morgen Zhornal*.

J. Walter Thompson Co. receives a letter from the Curtis Publishing Co. of Philadelphia announcing that Curtis will apply the ANPA rules of 1893 to its *Ladies' Home Journal*, *Saturday Evening Post*, and *Country Gentleman* magazines (*see* 1878). The 10 percent agency commission for placing advertisements in Curtis magazines will be followed by other magazines and rise in time to 15 percent.

Advertising man O. J. Gude gives Long Acre Square (later Times Square) the name "The Great White Way," by some accounts to suggest the possibilities of electric signs for advertising in the area (*see* 1904; 1909).

Fountain pen inventor Lewis E. Waterman dies at Brooklyn May 1 at age 63.

Andrew Carnegie writes a letter March 12 to the New York Public Library's director John Shaw Billings, saying, "If New York will furnish sites for these branches for the special benefit of the masses of the people, as it has done for the Central Library, and also agree in satisfactory form to provide for their maintenance as built, I should esteem it a rare privilege to be permitted to furnish the money as needed for the buildings, say $5.2 million" (*see* 1895).

The 11 existing branches of the 21-year-old Free Circulating Library are incorporated into the NYPL March 15. The Carnegie Corporation of New York awards $2 million in June to the New York Public Library and $1 million each to the Brooklyn Public Library and the Queens Borough Public Library. Between 1902 and 1909 the city will build 67 Carnegie libraries, most of them with arched windows (more will be built thereafter); within 55 years the library will have 75 branches in Manhattan, the

Bronx, and Staten Island (Brooklyn and Queens will have their own systems). By 1998 there will be 85 branches (plus four research libraries), the staff size will grow to 1,240 (409 of them hourly employees), and the total annual budget to $191,121,000, of which $106,217,000 will be for the branches (*see* main branch, 1911).

Nonfiction: *History of Tammany Hall* by Gustavus Myers; *Richard Croker* by New York author Alfred Henry Lewis, whose subject is the onetime "Master of Manhattan."

Theater: *The Climbers* by Clyde Fitch 1/21 at the Bijou Theater, with Ohio-born actress Amelia Bingham (*née* Smiley), 31, who made her New York debut in 1893, decided last year to become a producer, and has taken over the Bijou, 163 perfs.; *Under Two Flags* by Paul M. Potter (who has adapted the Ouida Bergère novel) 2/5 at the Garden Theater, with Portland, Ore.-born actress Blanche Bates, 27, St. Louis-born actor Edward Abeles, 31, 135 perfs.; *On the Quiet* by St. Louis-born playwright Augustus Thomas, 44, 2/11 at the Madison Square Theater, with New York-born actor William Collier, 36, 160 perfs.; *Miranda of the Balcony* by playwright Ann Crawford Flexner, 27, 9/24 with Minnie Maddern Fiske, to open Harrison Grey Fiske's Manhattan Theater, 62 perfs. (the Fiskes have rented the theater because the Theatrical Syndicate has refused to give Mrs. Fiske any road bookings, and they will operate the house for 6 years with a talented acting company); *The Way of the World* by Fitch 11/4 at Hammerstein's Victoria Theater, with New York-born actress Elsie (originally Ella Anderson) de Wolfe, 35, 35 perfs.; *The Girl and the Judge* by Fitch 12/4 at the Lyceum Theater, with Anne Russell, 125 perfs.

Actor-playwright James A. Herne dies of pleuro-pneumonia at New York June 2 at age 62, leaving only $29,500 (he has given away many times that much to needy actors and friends).

Films: Edwin S. (Stratton) Porter's *It Happened on 23rd Street*.

Broadway musicals: *The Girl from Up There* 1/7 at the Herald Square Theater, with St. Joseph, Mo.-born vaudeville veteran Dave Montgomery, 30, his Longmont, Colo.-born partner Fred Stone, 36, music by Gustav Kerker, 96 perfs.; *Captain Jinks of the Horse Marines* 2/4 at the Garrick Theatre, with H. Reeves Smith, Ethel Barrymore, book by Clyde Fitch, music by T. Maclaglen, lyrics by female impersonator William H. Lingard, and a song that begins "I'm Captain Jinks of the Horse Marines,/ I feed my horse on pork and beans,/ And often live beyond my means,/ I'm a captain in the army," 168 perfs.; *My Lady* (extravaganza) 2/11 at the Victoria Theater, with Quebec-born ingénue Eva Tanguay, 22, 93 perfs.; *The Governor's Son* 2/25 at the Savoy Theatre, with music, book, and lyrics by Providence, R.I.-born song-and-dance man George M. (Michael) Cohan, 23, who began touring in vaudeville with his parents as a child, wrote songs for the act beginning in his teens, gained his first popular success at age 17 with "Hot Tamale Alley," and followed it 3 years later with "I Guess I'll Have to Telegraph My Baby," 32 perfs.

Baseball's American League is organized at New York by Ohio-born promoter Byron Bancroft "Ban" Johnson, 37, a onetime Cincinnati sportswriter who 7 years ago took over the reorganized Western Association, a minor league, changed its name to the American League, got nowhere in talks with National League officials about moving his teams east, and now deserts the National Agreement under whose terms organized baseball has operated up to now. The towering, flamboyant Johnson signs up so many National League players that his new league starts the season as a "major" league (*see* 1903).

Christy Mathewson pitches a no-hit game for the New York Giants July 15 at St. Louis (*see* 1900; 1903).

Pennsylvania-born model and Floradora showgirl Evelyn Nesbit, 16, meets architect Stanford White, who is notoriously unfaithful to his wife, Bessie, and has a penchant for adolescent girls. Now 47, he invites Evelyn to lunch at his 22 West 24th Street hideaway, a studio with a huge green velvet sofa and a velvet swing suspended from its high ceiling by red velvet ropes; the luncheon *à deux* is soon followed by an intimate champagne dinner, and White deflowers Evelyn, who will be his mistress until 1904 (*see* crime, 1906).

Manhattan's newly-elected district attorney William Travers Jerome begins almost nightly raids on gambling establishments where games such as faro, red and black, and klondike attract some of the town's richest men, including the scion of a prominent American family who has lost $500,000 in 5 nights (*see* 1899). The raids will continue through much of next year, Richard Canfield's club will be closed, and the mahogany tables in the gambling dens will be given to the poor for use as firewood.

The city's homicide rate will rise to 3.8 per 100,000 in the next 5 years, up from 2.5 per 100,000 in the last 5 (*see* 1906).

The 12-story Textile Building is completed at 66 Leonard Street, southeast corner Church Street, to plans by Henry Janeway Hardenbergh, who has designed the steel-frame structure for the Importer's Building Company.

The Lower East Side's first elevator building is completed at the corner of Grand and Chrystie streets for developers Jacob and Nathan Levy.

A new tenement house law takes effect in January, requiring that each apartment have a toilet and more than token amounts of light and fresh air. The 83,000 pre-law and "old law" masonry and wood tenements that house 70 percent of the city's population are mostly of dumbbell design (see 1879), generally have wooden staircases, and their air shafts are only three feet wide (see Flagg, 1893). Many builders have put up such structures in the past year or two, anticipating the new law that has been enacted at the urging of journalist Jacob Riis, the Charity Organization Society, and others. Since they require lots 35 to 50 feet wide in order to provide a decent economic return, most of the "new law" tenements will go up in the outer boroughs, where speculative builders can find such lots, and the "old law" tenements will continue to dominate Manhattan neighborhoods.

The 12-story Beaux Arts Studios (later the Bryant Park Studios) is completed at 80 West 40th Street, southeast corner Sixth Avenue. Designed by Charles A. Rich, its double-height units have two-story windows to catch the north light from across the park.

Harlem begins its rise as a black enclave following the start of construction of a Lenox Avenue subway line that triggers a real estate boom (see transportation, 1904). The uptown Manhattan area will be overbuilt with apartment houses, many buildings will be unoccupied, and the razing of structures for a new Macy's department store, for Pennsylvania Station, and for large hotels, office buildings, and lofts in the Tenderloin area west of Herald Square is forcing blacks to seek new homes (see Payton, 1904).

The eight-story Graham Court apartment house is completed at the southwest corner of 116th Street and Seventh Avenue. Designed by Clinton & Russell for the Astor family, it has a large inner courtyard.

The 57-year-old New York Yacht Club moves into a new clubhouse at 37 West 44th Street, designed with a nautical motif by New York-born architect Whitney Warren, 38, of Warren & Wetmore (his Elmira-born partner Charles Delavan Wetmore is 35). Financier J. P. Morgan has donated the property to the club, whose commodores have included Astors, Morgans, and Vanderbilts (members of the club own 47 yachts more than 200 feet in length, the largest being a 352-foot schooner owned by Anthony J. Drexel and manned by a professional crew of 90 men). The America's Cup won in 1851 will be on display at the club until 1983 (see sport [transatlantic race], 1905).

A town house for banker Harry B. Hollins is completed at 10 West 56th Street to neo-Georgian designs by Stanford White. The Calumet Club will purchase the house after Hollins's firm fails in 1913, the club will close in 1935, and the Argentine government will acquire the house in 1947 for use as a consulate.

F. W. Woolworth moves his family into a 30-room mansion at 990 Fifth Avenue, northeast corner 80th Street (see commerce, 1896). Now 49, Woolworth has seen his dime-store chain grow to have 120 stores nationwide.

The Villa Julia is completed on Riverside Avenue (later Riverside Drive) at 89th Street by electric storage-battery pioneer Isaac L. Rice for his wife. The brick house will be sold in December 1907 for $600,000 to Turkish-born cigarette manufacturer Solomon Schinasi, whose brother Morris will have a house built for him that year on the Drive at 107th Street.

The Carnegie mansion for philanthropist Andrew Carnegie is completed on Fifth Avenue between 91st and 92nd streets, an area used up to now mainly for stables, riding academies, and small farms. Designed by Babb, Cook and Willard, the six-story, 64-room, neo-Georgian house has wood panels carved by Scottish and Indian craftsmen, a utilities basement fitted like a steamship engine room, a conservatory, and a large garden fronting on 91st Street opposite Central Park (see Cooper-Hewitt Museum, 1976).

Architect Napoleon Le Brun dies at New York July 9 at age 80; John Butler Snook at his Brooklyn home November 1 at age 86.

Auburndale is laid out in north central Queens by the New England Development and Improvement Co., whose directors have acquired 90 acres of farmland previously owned by Thomas Willet. A Long Island Rail Road station opens in May, and the area south of Crocheton Avenue will soon be a suburb marked by fine houses and well-kept streets.

 Governors Island grows as the city begins dumping dirt excavated for the construction of Manhattan's subway line to create landfill; by the time 4,787,000

cubic feet of fill has been added the island's size will have grown from 60 acres to 172.

Madison Square Garden has a fire November 2 that kills 15 people.

Harry M. Stevens introduces frankfurters, bottled soda, and peanuts as the basic stock for his vendors at the Polo Grounds (see 1894; "hot dog," 1906).

Coffee and sugar merchant John Arbuckle prevails in his 5-year-old battle with the Sugar Trust (see 1896); the Havemeyer family exits the coffee trade and Arbuckle continues to build his business, importing coffee and sugar in his own ships and towing canal boats between New York and Albany at rates that undercut the competition.

New York's population reaches 3.44 million, while London has 6.6 million, Chicago 1.7, Philadelphia 1.3, Los Angeles 103,000, Houston 45,000, Dallas 43,000. Manhattan's Lower East Side is the most densely populated place on earth, surpassing in squalor even the slums of Budapest, Calcutta, Glasgow, and London. Some 9 million immigrants will enter the United States in this decade, most of them through Ellis Island.

1902 Gov. Odell narrowly wins reelection, securing 665,150 votes to 656,347 for his Illinois-born Democratic challenger, New York banker Bird Sim Coler, 35.

Publisher William Randolph Hearst wins election to Congress representing a Greenwich Village district, he celebrates with a fireworks display at Madison Square November 4, a mortar containing 10,000 shells topples over and catches fire, the resulting explosion blows out doors and windows on the square, 17 people are killed, 100 injured.

United Mine Workers leader John Mitchell leads his 147,000 anthracite coal workers out of the pits May 12 to begin a 5-month strike. Mine operators and railroad presidents have rejected an invitation from Mitchell to attend a conference, they continue to oppose unionization, and by September the price of anthracite at New York has climbed from $5 per ton to $14. The poor buy by the bucket or bushel, paying a penny per pound—$20 per ton. Schools close to conserve fuel, people buy oil, coke, and gas stoves, and by October New Yorkers are paying $30 per ton (and much more if they buy in smaller quantities).

Montana copper magnate William Andrews Clark, 63, heats his 121-room Fifth Avenue mansion with a furnace that consumes 17 tons of coal per day. He resigned his U.S. Senate seat in 1900 after charges of election fraud were supported by a Senate com-

mittee that reported him "not duly and legally elected," but Clark will move to an even larger house (see real estate, 1911).

President Roosevelt brings about a settlement of the coal strike that one writer hails as "the greatest single event affecting the relations of capital and labor in the history of America." The strike ends October 21, but while the strikers gain pay raises, they do not win recognition of their union as bargaining agent for their rights.

Rabbi Jacob Joseph dies at New York July 28 at age 54. The Vilna-born rabbi has headed the American Orthodox Congregations since soon after its founding in 1887; his funeral procession is proceeding toward Grand Street Ferry July 31 (the Williamsburg Bridge is under construction) when it passes the R. Hoe Co. plant, some of whose employees throw discarded type metal on the heads of mourners. A hose from one of the plant's windows spatters scalding water on the crowd, dozens of mourners are hospitalized, and although a police riot squad runs into the building it cannot identify the miscreants. Before the day is over every window in the factory has been shattered, Irish cops having helped to smash out the front entrance in the neighborhood's first anti-Semitic disturbance. Lawsuits filed against R. Hoe cause the company to sustain heavy losses. Mayor Low appoints lawyer and Educational Alliance director Louis Marshall to head a commission whose recommendations will result in city officials reducing harrassment of Jews and affording them better housing opportunities.

Feminists mourn the loss of suffragist Elizabeth Cady Stanton, who dies at New York October 26 at age 87, but many condemn her racist views.

Greenwich House has its beginnings in the Cooperative Social Settlement Society founded in Jones Street, Greenwich Village, by social reformers who include Citizens' Union chairman R. Fulton Cutting, Felix Adler, and Boston heiress Mary Simkovitch (née Kingsbury), 35, who 3 years ago married a Russian-born Columbia University professor of economic history whom she had met in Berlin. She will be head resident until 1946 (see 1917; City Housing Authority, 1934).

A large new home for abandoned and needy children is completed at 936 Woodycrest Avenue in the Bronx. Architect William B. Tuthill has designed the building in Beaux Arts style for the 68-year-old American Female Guardian Society and Home for the Friendless, which has given up its 50-year-old Manhattan offices and home just north of Madison

Square and moved to suburban Highbridge. The society will merge with another charitable organization later in the century and move in 1974 to Rockland County.

$ President Roosevelt works through his attorney general Philander C. Knox, 49, to institute antitrust proceedings against various U.S. corporations. Roosevelt departs from the policies of the late President McKinley that he had pledged himself to continue, provoking the ire of financier J. P. Morgan.

Carl H. Pforzheimer & Co. is founded by New York-born investment banker Carl Howard Pforzheimer, 23, who will marry Lily M. Oppenheimer early in 1906 and make his firm a powerful force in Wall Street.

Boston-born *Philadelphia Financial News* publisher Clarence W. (Walker) Barron, 46, buys out Dow Jones & Co. in March for $130,000 and becomes the publisher of its 12-year-old daily *Wall Street Journal*. Economist Charles H. Dow of Dow Jones & Co. dies at Brooklyn December 4 at age 51; the Scots-born journalist William Peter Hamilton whom he hired as a reporter in 1899 will take over as editor of the *Wall Street Journal* next year and write virtually every editorial until his death in December 1929.

Wall Street's Dow Jones Industrial Average ends the year at 64.29, down from 64.56 at the end of 1901.

S Tiffany & Co. founder Charles Lewis Tiffany dies at suburban Yonkers February 18 at age 90, leaving an estate of $35 million.

The 60-year-old James A. Hearn & Son store in West 14th Street engages in a price war with nearby Macy's, each trying to undercut the other on the price of silk. From 41¢ a yard at the start of the day, the price drops to a penny by closing time (*see* 1955).

Macy's lays the cornerstone of a new building close to the Sixth Avenue El on Broadway just north of 34th Street, on Herald Square (*see* 1896). Merchants Isidor and Nathan Straus have expanded the late R. H. Macy's store into a complex of 11 buildings in 13th and 14th streets, which they sell to merchant Henry Siegel of Siegel & Cooper (who has architects Cady, Berg & See design a new 10-story blockfront on Sixth Avenue to unite the properties). Although the Strauses have been unable to obtain a small parcel of land at the corner of Broadway and 34th Street they have engaged De Lemos & Cordes to design a nine-story red-brick-and-limestone structure measuring 700 feet by 200 with bay windows and four-story-high Corinthian columns on the Broadway side; when they move from Ladies' Mile in the fall into the larger store, the Strauses operate a steam wagonette to transport customers uptown to what will later become the world's largest department store building, with more than 2 million square feet of floor space (*see* 1912; Gimbels, 1910).

Saks & Co. opens on a site just south of the new Macy's store under the management of former Siegel, Cooper department store executive Andrew Saks, 55, and two other Siegel, Cooper men (*see* Saks Fifth Avenue, 1924).

Franklin Simon opens at 414 Fifth Avenue, between 37th and 38th streets, to sell women's clothing. Retail merchant Simon, 38, started as a $2.50 per week clerk at Stern Brothers at age 13. His fashion shop is the first important Fifth Avenue store north of 34th Street, it offers made-to-order children's clothes, made-to-order underwear and hats, and a wide selection of riding habits, has a special department for "big women," and will remain in business until 1977 (*see* 1962).

The 64-year-old Knox Hat Co. headed by Col. Edward M. Knox moves its headquarters into a new building at 452 Fifth Avenue, southwest corner 40th Street. Architect John H. Duncan has designed the 11-story structure.

⚡ The new Central Power House for the 21-mile Manhattan subway now under construction uses Westinghouse generators to produce alternating-current electricity that is then put through rotary converters to produce direct current for the subway's third rails.

A rear-end railroad collision January 8 in the dimly lit smoke-filled Park Avenue tunnel at 56th Street kills 15 passengers and crewmen, severely injuring 40 others (two more die within a few days). Pedestrians on the street above hear the cries of people being burned and scalded alive, and the *New York Times* calls it "the worst railroad disaster that ever occurred on Manhattan Island." A New York Central (Harlem Division) train from White Plains has plowed into a New Haven commuter train from Danbury, whose last two cars were reserved for New Rochelle passengers, and all those killed are among the 60 who boarded the rear car at New Rochelle. Sen. Chauncey Depew, now 67, arrives from Europe with his bride January 11 (he has remarried after losing his first wife) and blames the accident on human error, saying, "Money is of no earthly value to the New York Central as compared with the safety of its passengers." The Central contracts with Consolidated Gas Co.'s New York Edison Co. subsidiary to install electric lights in the tunnel and facilitate preparations for a change in motive power (*see* 1903; Wilgus plan, 1899).

The *Twentieth Century Limited* goes into service June 15 to begin a 65-year career on the route between New York and Chicago. The New York Central's new luxury express has two buffet, smoking, and library cars, two observation cars, and 12 drawing-room and stateroom cars. It reduces running time on the 980-mile "water-level route" to 20 hours—down from 24 in 1877—but the *Limited*'s 49-mile-per-hour average is well below the 61.3 miles per hour averaged on the 184-mile route of the *Paris-Calais Express*.

The *Broadway Limited* (initially the *Pennsylvania Special*) goes into service June 16 for the Pennsylvania Railroad to begin a career of 93 years on the route between New York and Chicago. Staffed with barbers, maids, valets, and secretaries to rival the Central's *Twentieth Century Limited*, the new luxury express makes the 907-mile run in 20 hours, but the ride is less comfortable than that of the Central's train.

New York Els convert to electric operation after 35 years of showering sparks, ashes, and oil on pedestrians in the streets below them (*see* 1886; 1903).

The Interborough Rapid Transit Co. (IRT) is founded July 10 by financier August Belmont II to acquire the 2-year-old Rapid Transit Subway Construction Co. and equip the subway (*see* 1900). Belmont's IRT also acquires the New York and Long Island Railroad Co. with the idea of completing its Steinway Tunnel and equipping it for electric streetcars (*see* 1892; New York & Queens County Railway, 1903). Civil engineer William B. Parsons oversees the Manhattan subway project, ripping out utility lines where they get in the way and reinstalling them, avoiding building foundations, and dealing with myriad problems of soil composition and the like (*see* 1904).

The Hudson Navigation Co. is founded by ice king Charles W. Morse, who combines night-boat services on the river, using the 41-year-old *Mary Powell* and other steamboats. The *C. W. Morse* will be launched next year, the *Hendrick Hudson* in 1906, and the *Robert Fulton* in 1909 (*see* Washington Irving, Berkshire, 1913).

Sensational articles in the *New York Herald*, *New York Journal*, and *New York Sun* January 19 report findings by Rockefeller Institute experts: "FIND GERMS SWARMING IN CITY'S PUREST MILK." Uncleanliness prevails in most of the dairies that supply New York, the experts have found; they trace 130 epi-

demics to this cause and urge more rigorous inspection.

Michael Augustine Archbishop Corrigan dies at New York May 2 at age 72. Papal encyclicals have supported his reactionary positions, and the various charitable organizations he founded are consolidated into the Association of Catholic Charities. Irish-born bishop John Murphy Farley, 60, is named archbishop September 15 (*see* 1911).

The Young Women's Hebrew Association (YWHA) is founded as a female counterpart of the YMHA (*see* 1874; 1957).

Nicholas Murray Butler becomes president of Columbia University, a position he will hold until his retirement in 1945 (*see* Teacher's College, 1887). Now 40, he has been dean of Columbia's faculty of philosophy since 1890 and demonstrated talents as a speechmaker and fund-raiser. The school's endowment will grow by leaps and bounds under Butler's administration, as will the size of its student body, faculty, campus buildings, and international reputation as a leader in advanced studies and research.

Washington Irving High School has its beginnings in the Commercial High School for Girls opened at 36 East 12th Street. The public high school will take its new name in 1906 and move 7 years later to 40 Irving Place (*see* 1986).

"Buster Brown" debuts May 4 in the *New York Herald*. Richard F. Outcault's comic-strip adventures of the middle-class boy and his dog Tige will be far more successful than his "Yellow Kid" strip (*see* 1896; "Mutt and Jeff," 1908).

Journalist E. L. Godkin dies in England May 21 at age 70. He founded The *Nation* in 1865 and became chief editor of the *New-York Evening Post* in 1882.

Former Kansas lawman William Barclay "Bat" Masterson, 48, moves to New York and becomes a sports writer for the *Morning Telegraph*.

Former *Harper's Weekly* cartoonist Thomas Nast dies of yellow fever at Guayaquil, Ecuador, December 7 at age 62 (President Roosevelt had given him an appointment as consul general at Guayaquil, a sinecure that paid a handsome $4,000 per year, but Nast has survived a scant 6 months in the fever-plagued post).

Nonfiction: *The Battle with the Slum* by Jacob Riis; *The Spirit of the Ghetto* by Chicago-born author Hutchins Hapgood, 33, who writes of his lifelong interest in "how individuals and groups who represent what might be called the underdog, when they are endowed with energy and life, exert pressure towards modification of our cast-iron habits and lay rich deposits of cultural enhancement, if we are able to take advantage of them."

Poetry: *Captain Craig* by Edwin Arlington Robinson, whose work so impresses President Roosevelt that he will use his influence to procure a position for Robinson as a clerk at the New York Custom House.

Juvenile: *Adrift in New York* by the late Horatio Alger, who died in July 1899 at age 67; *Just So Stories* by English poet-novelist Rudyard Kipling, 36, who has written most of the stories at the suggestion of New York publisher's son Nelson Doubleday, 13. Young Doubleday read Kipling's story "How the Whale Got Its Tiny Throat" in *St. Nicholas* magazine and wrote a letter to its author, asking why he did not write about how the leopard got its spots, how the elephant acquired its trunk, and so forth. The book has sales of more than 500,000 copies in America alone, and Doubleday will receive a royalty of 1¢ per copy until the day he dies in 1963.

Minnesota-born sculptor James Earle Fraser, 25, opens a New York studio on the strength of his fame as the creator of the 1896 work *The End of the Trail*, depicting an exhausted Plains Indian on horseback. He is promptly flooded with commissions including one for a bust of President Roosevelt. Fraser will teach at the Art Students League from 1906 to 1911 and design the "buffalo head" nickel of 1913, using a likeness of Blackfoot chief Two-Gun Davis on its obverse side.

Painter Albert Bierstadt dies at New York February 18 at age 72. Actor-turned-illustrator Charles Dana Gibson, now 35, signs an agreement October 23 accepting an offer from *Collier's Weekly* to draw only for *Life* and *Collier's* for the next 4 years and do 100 double-page drawings for *Collier's* for $100,000 (see 1890).

ARTnews has its beginnings in *Hyde's Weekly Art News*, published at New York starting November 29 by former *New York World* and *New York Tribune* art writer James Clarence Hyde. His 17-by-13-inch broadside appears on Wednesdays during the art season, targets collectors and art editors, contains no advertisements or illustrations, and devotes its five columns of type to reporting on exhibitions, museum acquisitions, and the activities of notable figures in the art world (see 1904).

The Soldiers and Sailors Monument installed on the west side of Riverside Avenue (later Riverside Drive) at 89th Street has been designed by architects Arthur A. Stoughton, 35, and Paul Duboy.

Theater: *The Darling of the Gods: A Drama of Japan* by David Belasco and John Luther Long 12/3 at the Belasco Theater, with Blanche Bates as Yo-San, 182 perfs.; *The Girl with the Green Eyes* by Clyde Fitch 12/25 at the Savoy Theatre, with Canadian-born actress Lucile Watson, 23, 108 perfs.

Film: Edwin S. Porter's *How They Do Things on the Bowery*.

The Barnum & Bailey Circus entertains children outdoors at Bellevue Hospital, beginning an annual tradition. Nurses bring stretcher and wheelchair patients out to 26th Street to watch the clowns and elephants.

Broadway musicals: *The Wild Rose* 5/5 at the Knickerbocker Theater, with Brooklyn-born vaudeville veteran Marie Cahill, 28, singing "Nancy Brown," Toledo, Ohio-born actor-lyricist Junie McCree, 36, music and lyrics by Ludwig Englander, book by Harry B. Smith and Nova Scotia-born playwright-lyricist George V. Hobart, 35, 136 perfs; *A Chinese Honeymoon* 6/22 at the Casino Theater, with music by New York-born composer Howard Talbot (originally Munkitrick), 37, additional music by Hungarian-born composer Jean Schwartz, 23, lyrics by William Jerome, songs that include "Mr. Dooley," 376 perfs.; *Twirly Whirly* 9/11 at the Weber and Fields Music Hall, with Lillian Russell, Fay Templeton, William Collier, music by John Stromberg, lyrics by Robert B. Smith, songs that include "Come Down Ma Evenin' Star," 244 perfs.

Popular songs: "Fifth Avenue" by George V. Hobart, lyrics by A. B. Sloane.

The West Side Tennis Club relocates from Central Park West to Morningside Heights, renting eight courts from Mrs. John Drexel for $20 each (see 1892). The club has for the past 5 years sponsored the Metropolitan Matches of the United States National Lawn Tennis Association (later the USLTA, then the USTA), and membership has grown to 102 (see 1908).

Former Baltimore Oriole baseball player John J. (Joseph) McGraw, 29, is named manager of the New York Giants in July and will continue as player-manager until 1906, when he will retire with a lifetime batting average of .334, having helped the Giants win two National League pennants and a World Series victory; he will continue as manager of the Giants until June 1932.

The Teddy Bear creates a sensation with its movable legs and head. Russian-born Brooklyn candy store operator Morris Michtom, 32, and his wife, Rose, have seen a cartoon ("Drawing the Line in Mississippi") by Clifford K. Berryman in the November 16 *Washington Evening Star* showing President "Teddy" Roosevelt refusing to shoot a mother bear while hunting in Mississippi. The Michtoms have obtained the president's permission to use his nickname for their brown plush toy. It will encounter a challenge next year from the German firm Steiff Co., but the New York wholesale firm Butler Brothers will take Michtom's entire output of Teddy Bears (it will call itself Ideal Novelty and Toy Co. beginning in 1938, shorten it later to Ideal Toy Co., and become the world's largest manufacturer of dolls).

New York Philip Morris Corp. is founded with help from local tobacco importer Gustav Eckmeyer, who has been exclusive agent for English Ovals, Marlboros, and other cigarettes produced by Philip Morris of London (*see* 1933).

Defense attorney William F. Howe dies in his sleep September 2 at age 74 in his home on the Boston Post Road in the Bronx. His partner Abraham Hummel, now 53, continues under the name Howe & Hummel but will soon come under attack from District Attorney William Travers Jerome and have to give up the firm's Centre Street offices when the city takes the property for municipal buildings (he will move to the New York Life Insurance Building at 346 Broadway).

The 18-story 170 Broadway office tower is completed at the southeast corner of Maiden Lane to designs by Clinton & Russell.

The 21-story "Flatiron" Building opens October 1 southwest of Madison Square at 23rd Street to designs by Chicago architect Daniel Burnham, 55, whose steel-frame Fuller Building (named for its developer) soars 285 feet high and brings people from far and near to ascend to its top for the panoramic view. Constructed in Renaissance Revival style at the intersection of Broadway and Fifth Avenue, the rusticated limestone and molded terra-cotta building has no setbacks, its shape inspires viewers to call it something other than the Fuller Building, and its downdrafts whip up young women's skirts to expose their ankles, inspiring young men to say, "23-Skidoo" (other derivations for the expression will be advanced).

Turner Construction Co. is founded by Maryland-born contractor Henry Chandlee Turner, 30, with DeForest H. Dixon and Gordon B. Horton to carry out Turner's vision of using reinforced concrete in place of timber and brick for factories and warehouses. The firm will become the nation's largest builder of commercial, industrial, institutional, health-care, and governmental buildings; its revenues will reach $6.5 million by 1916 and more than $35 million 2 years later.

The New York Chamber of Commerce Building is dedicated November 11 at 65 Cedar (later Liberty) Street, between Nassau Street and Broadway, with ceremonies attended by President Roosevelt and former president Cleveland (*see* 1770). Designed in Beaux Arts style by architect James Barnes Baker, it has rusticated Ionic columns, a copper-crested mansard roof, and oval porthole windows. Statues of Alexander Hamilton, DeWitt Clinton, and John Jay rise between the columns.

More than 10 percent of Manhattan's 3 million people still live in private houses that have no inside toilets, and at least another 10 percent have accommodations only slightly better, but 77.5 percent of Manhattanites live in tenements, and while the basic rent in 20 percent of tenement houses is $10 per month for three rooms and $12 for four, the average rent in 30 percent of Manhattan's 38,732 tenements is $4 or more (in 24 percent it is under $3, and only in 20 percent is it $5 or more). Some 4,425 Manhattan apartment houses will be completed between now and 1910, many of them on the upper West Side where the Broadway subway line is under construction.

The Dorilton apartment house is completed at 171 West 71st Street, northeast corner of Broadway. The firm of Janes and Leo has designed the 12-story luxury building, widely considered an architectural aberration.

The Jonathan Thorne house is completed at 1028 Fifth Avenue, southeast corner 84th Street, to designs by C. P. H. Gilbert. It will later become the Marymount School.

Architect James Brown Lord dies at New York June 1 at age 42.

The Algonquin Hotel opens at 59 West 44th Street, between Fifth and Sixth avenues, with 143 suites and 192 rooms to begin a career as gathering place for actors, painters, musicians, and literati. Goldwin Starrett has designed the structure, and desk clerk Frank Case, 32, has persuaded owner Albert Foster to name it the Algonquin rather than the Puritan. A room and bath rent for $2 per day, a three-bedroom, three-bath suite with private hall, sitting room, dining room, and library goes for $10. Case will himself acquire ownership for $717,000 in 1927 and operate the hotel until his death in 1946 (*see* Round Table, 1919).

A fire spreads from the 71st Regiment Armory to the Park Avenue Hotel February 22, killing 18 persons.

Angola, N.Y.-born engineer Willis Haviland Carrier, 25, designs a humidity control process to accompany a new air-cooling system for Brooklyn's Sackett-Wilhelms Lithographic and Publishing Co. printing plant and pioneers modern air conditioning. High humidity has been making it difficult to print color with any accuracy. Carrier received his degree from Cornell last year; he uses ammonia gas to chill coils that cool the air and lower the humidity to 55 percent (or any other level desired) with precision (*see* 1911; Dielene, 1922).

The city has more than 1,400 miles of sewers, up from 70 in 1855 and 464 just 10 years ago (*see* 1849). Most newly constructed tenements are equipped with private flush toilets, but the vast majority of New Yorkers live in old-law tenements and raw sewage continues to flow directly into the harbor (*see* 1937).

The New York Botanical Garden's Conservatory Range (later the Enid Annenberg Haupt Conservatory) is completed in Victorian greenhouse style to designs by William R. Cobb for the greenhouse manufacturing firm Lord & Burnham (*see* 1891). Modeled on the greenhouse of England's Royal Botanic Garden at Kew, and the largest structure of its kind in America, it will be altered in 1938 and 1953, restored in 1978, and restored again in 1997.

"Prices That Stagger Humanity," headlines Joseph Pulitzer's *New York World* in a campaign against the "beef trust" (24¢/lb. for sirloin steak, 18¢ for lamb chops, pork chops, or ham).

The Café Martin in University Place moves to Fifth Avenue opposite Madison Square; manager Raymond Orteig, now 32, takes over the old location and turns it into the Café Lafayette (*see* 1890). He and his friend Emil Daution lease the Hotel Brevoort on Fifth Avenue that Daution manages. Another Martin manager, Louis Bustanoby, opens the Café des Beaux Arts that rivals Martin's, Rector's (*see* 1899), Sherry's (*see* 1890), the Lafayette, and Delmonico's among gastronomes such as New York-born railroad-equipment salesman and financial manipulator James Buchanan Brady, 46, who has amassed a fortune of nearly $12 million. The flamboyant Broadway sport "Diamond Jim" Brady has a legendary appetite that has endeared him to restaurant proprietors (Charles Rector calls him "the best 25 customers I have").

Angelo's opens at 46 Mulberry Street in "Little Italy" to serve the city's Italian population with Florentine, Milanese, and Livornese dishes.

Immigration to the United States sets new records. Most of the arrivals are from Italy, Austro-Hungary, and Russia and come through Ellis Island.

1903 Gunboat diplomacy expedites construction of a Panama Canal. The Hay-Herran Treaty signed January 22 by Secretary of State John Hay and the foreign minister of Colombia provides for a six-mile strip across the Isthmus of Panama to be leased to the United States for $10 million plus annual payments of $250,000. Washington had favored a route across Nicaragua, but French engineer-promoter Philippe Jean Bunau-Varilla, 42, has cut a deal with New York lawyer William Nelson Cromwell, 49, who has made a $60,000 contribution to the Republican Party. The Senate votes its consent March 17 to the treaty, under whose terms $40 million goes to stockholders in the French canal company, many of whom are now U.S. speculators, while stipulating that Colombia is to give up all rights to sue for any portion of the $40 million and give up all police powers in the contemplated canal zone.

Bunau-Varilla has his wife stitch up a flag for a new Panamanian republic, meets in room 1162 of the Waldorf-Astoria Hotel at 34th Street with a physician who works for the cross-isthmus railroad represented by William Cromwell, and provides him with a secret code, a declaration of independence, the flag, the draft of a Panamanian constitution, and transportation back to Panama. Financier J. P. Morgan receives $40 million for transfer to French

Coney Island's attractions vied with its beaches to make it a popular summer resort for swells and the hoi polloi.

canal company stockholders, whose names lawyer Cromwell refuses to divulge to a Senate committee. Cromwell receives $800,000 for his legal services.

Mayor Seth Low loses his bid for reelection, securing 252,086 votes as compared with 314,782 for Congressman George B. McClellan, Jr., 37, son of the late Civil War general. Charles F. Murphy, now 45, has succeeded Richard Croker as Tammany Hall boss and persuaded McClellan to accept the Democratic Party nomination (Murphy is a onetime horsecar driver who was dismissed from his job and is alleged to have said, "If I can't drive horses I'll drive men.")

Tammany Hall ward heeler Alfred Emmanuel "Al" Smith, 29, wins election to the state assembly at Albany. Smith grew up in a Lower East Side neighborhood near the Brooklyn Bridge piers, close to where his grandfather arrived by ship from Ireland; he dropped out of school when he was barely 13 to support his widowed mother and sister, has never been away from home, began his political career 8 years ago as a process server for the commissioner

The Flatiron Building at 23rd Street rose 21 stories high, providing panoramic views from its top floor.

of jurors (a patronage job), is quite unprepared for his new job, but is possessed of a common touch that has won the support of saloon keeper and Tammany leader Thomas "Big Tom" Foley. Smith will rise to the heights of political achievement (*see* 1911).

"Everybody is talking about Tammany men growing rich on 'graft,'" says onetime political boss George Washington Plunkitt, now 61, "but nobody thinks of drawing the distinction between honest graft and dishonest graft. There's an honest graft, and I'm an example of how it works. I would sum up the whole thing by saying, I seen my opportunities and I took 'em." A long-time opponent of civil service reforms who has bought up land he knew the city would want and then resold it to the city at a profit, Plunkitt lives at 323 West 51st Street.

Tammany Hall piles up its majorities in part by buying votes, in part by registering names from graveyards, and in part by having men vote more than once, but mostly by doing favors for needy constituents. Tammany continues to keep voters loyal as it has for years by having ward bosses at Tammany clubs throughout the city hold court Friday evenings, giving instructions on how to obtain citizenship and get free English lessons; helping constituents obtain peddlers' licenses, working papers, jobs, and—if there are no jobs—welfare; handing out wedding presents, money for funerals, turkeys at Thanksgiving, coal in winter, and matzohs at Passover.

Former city comptroller Andrew Haskell Green is shot dead November 13 at age 83 while sitting on the front stoop of his house at 91 Park Avenue (or by some accounts, while entering his front door). A jealous suitor has waited in ambush for his rival (a different white-haired octogenarian) and shot the wrong man. Hailed as the father of Greater New York, Green is memorialized with a service at City Hall.

Agnes Nestor and Elizabeth Christman lead female glove makers out of the International Glove Workers Union and form their own women's local (*see* 1902); Nestor, now 23, is elected president. Sweatshop workers are obliged to accept whatever treatment they receive and have no means of redress. Not only are they penalized if their stitches are crooked or if they stain goods with machine oil but also if they talk or laugh while at work. They may be charged 50¢ per week for the use of a machine and electricity, 5¢ per week for the use of a mirror and towel, 5¢ per week for drinking water.

President Roosevelt names his New York-born secretary George B. (Bruce) Cortelyou, 40, the nation's first secretary of commerce and labor. Cortelyou distinguished himself in the negotiations that settled last year's coal strike.

National Cash Register president J. H. Patterson gives his upstate New York-born executive Thomas J. (John) Watson, 29, a budget of $1 million to start a company that will pose as a rival to NCR but will actually take control of the U.S. used-cash-register business. Watson's Cash Register and Second Hand Exchange opens in 14th Street, undersells competitors, and drives them out of business or forces them to sell out. Watson will set up similar illegal operations in Philadelphia and Chicago (see THINK, 1908).

Bankers Trust Co. is incorporated March 24 with $1.5 million in capital and surplus. The company will acquire Mercantile Trust (founded 1868) in 1911 and Manhattan Trust (founded 1871) in 1912, Astor Trust (formerly Sixth National Bank) in 1917, and by 1928 will have assets of more than $734 million (see 1998).

The New York Stock Exchange building is completed at 8 Broad Street between Wall Street and Exchange Plaza, where the Exchange has been located since 1865. It opens April 23 with an enunciator board for paging brokers and 500 telephones at the sides of the trading floor to connect traders with their offices.

Speculator Bernard M. Baruch leaves A. A. Housman and Co. and establishes a firm under his own name (see 1889). Now 33, tall, and good looking, he suffered some early setbacks after joining Housman in 1891 but has prospered as a bond salesman and customers' man, playing his hunches, winning big by going short before bear markets; he will now speculate on his own account. Baruch will add to his fortune in the next decade by buying and selling raw materials—copper, gold, iron, tungsten, zinc, rubber, and sulfur—in America and abroad, often in alliance with the Guggenheim brothers. In 1905 he will buy the Hobcaw Barony estate near his native Camden, S.C. (see politics, 1917).

Wall Street's Dow Jones Industrial Average ends the year at 49.11, down from 64.29 at the end of 1902.

A new Wanamaker Department Store replaces the A. T. Stewart store of 1862, operated by Wanamaker since 1896. Designed by Chicago's Daniel H. Burnham and Co., the enormous 15-story department store fills the block between Broadway and Fourth Avenue from 9th Street to 10th and has no inner courtyards.

Bergdorf Goodman has its beginnings in a tailoring firm for affluent women founded by Rochester-born tailor Edwin Goodman, 26. He buys out his elderly Alsatian-born partner for $15,000, moves from a private house in 19th Street to a building in West 32nd Street, and will move in 1914 to 616 Fifth Avenue (see 1928).

The Peck & Peck retail chain has its beginnings in a hosiery shop opened near the new Flatiron Building by merchants George F. and Edgar Wallace Peck to sell imported, colorfast black stockings, hand-embroidered with clocking made by German firefighters waiting for blazes and dyed in the United States (year approximate). The Peck brothers will move to Fifth Avenue at 27th Street as they attract customers who include architect Stanford White and Pittsburgh millionaire Harry K. Thaw (see 1910).

The January 17 issue of *Scientific American* shows some features of a plan devised in December of last year by New York Central chief engineer William J. Wilgus for connecting Grand Central's suburban-level tracks with the new IRT subway now under construction under Park Avenue to the south of the station (see 1899; accident, 1902). The plan calls for building new viaducts for crosstown streets on steel girders above the tracks between 45th and 55th streets, extending Park Avenue through the train shed, and building an elevated driveway for carriages within the shed.

The state legislature at Albany passes legislation in response to last year's Park Avenue tunnel accident requiring that the railroad convert to electricity by 1908. Wilgus presents a new plan in March that calls for a 57-track, all-electric, double-level terminal. From a single level north of 50th Street, tracks would fan out and occupy two levels under the area between Lexington and Madison avenues. Trains would discharge passengers under 44th Street, and a loop extending to 41st Street would permit them to be turned about and backed into gates to take on passengers, thus avoiding the costly and time-consuming process of reassembling them. An elevated north-south roadway, circumscribing the terminal structure and bridging over 42nd Street, would link upper and lower Park Avenue. Preliminary estimates place the cost of such a project at more than $43 million—a staggering figure but, Wilgus insists, an investment, not an expense. The Central begins buying up property on Park Avenue and presents its plans June 3 to a special committee of the city's Board of Estimate and Apportionment. The Central has solicited suggestions from a number of architectural firms, but it has given engineering priority over architecture and awarded the contract to Reed & Stem, a small St. Paul, Minn., firm whose Charles Reed is married to Wilgus's sister May. Reed has devised an "elevated circumferential plaza" that takes traffic by ramp around the terminal's periphery, while a system of interior ramps obviates any need to climb stairs. The Board of Estimate gives its formal approval June 19, and contractors are excavating the site by mid-August (see 1911).

The Interborough Rapid Transit Co. (IRT) acquires the Manhattan Railway Co. to coordinate service on the Els and the new subway it is building (see 1902). August Belmont also acquires the 41-mile electric network of the New York & Queens County Railway. The city's crowded surface and elevated railroads carry more paying passengers than do all the steam railroads of North and South America combined, but the cars are bitter cold in winter, steaming hot in summer, the Els are slow, and traffic congestion impedes the progress of the surface cars (see subway, 1904).

The Williamsburg Bridge opens to traffic December 19, providing a second link between Brooklyn and Manhattan to supplement the 20-year-old Brooklyn Bridge. The new $24.1 million 488-meter span is the first major suspension bridge with steel towers instead of masonry, and it puts an end to the Grand Street ferry, whose vessels brought generations of Brooklynites to and from the Lower East Side. Delancey Street has been widened to facilitate access to the new bridge and begins to eclipse Grand Street as the Lower East Side's main east-west thoroughfare (see 1908; Queensboro, Manhattan bridges, 1909).

The Rockefeller Institute for Medical Research (later Rockefeller University) moves May 11 into its first building on the west side of Avenue A (later York Avenue) near East 66th Street in April (see 1901). Designed by York & Sawyer, the structure has its own powerhouse and a building to house experimental animals.

"Typhoid Mary" gets her name as New York has an outbreak of typhoid fever, with 1,300 cases reported. City medical inspector Sara Josephine Baker helps trace the epidemic to one Mary Mallon, 33, an Irish-born carrier of the disease (but not a victim), who has taken jobs that involve handling food. By all accounts an excellent cook, Typhoid Mary refuses to stop (see 1907).

Sara Josephine Baker is appointed assistant health commissioner (see 1901). Her all-male staff resigns en masse, but Baker will license midwives, stan-dardize the inspection of schoolchildren for contagious diseases, teach mothers hygiene, proper ventilation, and nutrition, establish "milk stations" where mothers can obtain free pasteurized milk, distribute baby formula of lime water and milk sugar that any woman can make at home, and start a "Little Mothers League" that teaches infant care to children whose mothers leave them in charge of their siblings. Within 15 years her efforts will help cut the death rate in New York's slums from 1,500 per week to 300, enabling the city to claim the lowest infant mortality rate of any in the Western world (see 1916).

The opening of the Williamsburg Bridge encourages a move to Brooklyn's Williamsburg section by Jews from Manhattan's overcrowded Lower East Side. Many will walk across the bridge to attend Sabbath and holiday religious services in their old Manhattan synagogues.

The New York State Board of Regents grants a charter to the 34-year-old girls' high school of Hunter College (still called the Female Normal School), whose directors change its name to Normal College High School. It will take the name Hunter College High School in 1914 (see 1955).

The city acquires the Morris-Jumel mansion of 1765 and turns it into a museum.

Pulitzer prizes have their beginning in an agreement signed April 10 by New York World publisher Joseph Pulitzer to endow a school of journalism at Columbia University. Pulitzer has made a fortune since acquiring the World in 1883 and specifies that $500,000 of his $2 million gift shall be allotted for "prizes or scholarships for the encouragement of public service, public morale, American literature, and the advancement of education."

Nonfiction: Children of the Tenements by Jacob Riis; The Souls of Black Folk (essays and sketches) by Great Barrington, Mass.-born Atlanta University professor W. E. B. (William Edward Burghardt) Du Bois, 35, who began to understand racial prejudice when he attended Fisk University. It awarded him a B.A. in 1888, and he deliberately segregated himself from white students at Harvard, where he received a B.A. cum laude in 1890 (see NAACP, 1909).

The Wildenstein Gallery opens at 647 Fifth Avenue under the direction of Alsatian-born Paris art dealer Nathan Wildenstein, 51, and his associate René Gimpel with a storefront sign that reads, "Old Paintings." Wildenstein founded his Paris gallery in 1875 and has come to realize that his best market is in America (see 1932).

Steuben Glass Works is founded by British-born designer Frederick Carder, 35, who will head the firm until 1932 and not retire until he is 96. Carder's lustrous Aurene technique will produce glass rivaling in its iridescent color the Favrile designs of Louis Comfort Tiffany, now 55 (see 1878).

Sculpture: a full-length bronze statue of Nathan Hale by Frederick MacMonnies is erected in City Hall Park at the corner of Broadway and Murray Street on a pedestal designed by architect Stanford White; a gilded bronze statue of Alma Mater by New Hampshire-born sculptor Daniel Chester French, now 53, is installed on the Columbia University campus in front of the 6-year-old Low Memorial Library.

Theater: the Lyric Theater opens 10/12 at 213 West 42nd Street, the Hudson 10/19 at 139 West 44th Street, the New Amsterdam (an Art Nouveau gem designed by Herts & Tallant for the theatrical booking firm Klaw and Erlanger) 11/2 at 214 West 42nd Street; *The Proud Prince* 11/2 at the new Lyceum Theater at 149-157 West 45th Street (designed by Herts & Tallant for theater impresario Daniel Frohman; the Long Acre Square area has become a new theater district); *The County Chairman* by Indiana-born

New theaters like the Lyceum opened near Broadway as it became the new Rialto. MUSEUM OF THE CITY OF NEW YORK

humorist-playwright George Ade, 37, 11/24 at Wallack's Theater, 222 perfs.; *Glad of It* by Clyde Fitch 12/28 at the Savoy Theater, with Brockway, Minn.-born actress Zelda Sears, 30, Philadelphia-born actor John Barrymore (originally Blyth), 21, 32 perfs. A nephew of actor John Drew, Barrymore is the younger brother of Lionel and Ethel, who have been on the stage since ages 6 and 14, respectively. "The Great Profile" will become a matinée idol, famous beginning in 1924 for his Hamlet; *The Other Girl* by Augustus Thomas 12/29 at the Criterion Theater, with Lionel Barrymore, Elsie de Wolfe, Indiana-born actor Richard Bennett, 31, (to Empire Theater 1/25/1904, Lyceum Theater 5/2/1904), 160 perfs.

Film: Edwin S. Porter's *The Great Train Robbery* is the first motion picture to tell a complete story (see 1896). Produced by Edison Studios and photographed at the Paterson, N.J., freight yards of the Delaware & Lackawanna Railroad, the 12-minute epic establishes a pattern of suspense drama that future moviemakers will follow; Scottish-born director Porter also creates the first U.S. documentary film, *The Life of an American Fireman*, interpolating scenes of actors into stock footage of actual fire scenes.

Opera: Adelina Patti begins her final American tour 11/4 at Carnegie Hall; Italian tenor Enrico Caruso, 30, makes his American debut 11/21 singing in *Rigoletto* at the 20-year-old Metropolitan Opera House. He has gained a worldwide reputation since his debut at Milan's Teatro alla Scala in 1899, will be the Met's leading tenor for years, and will have a repertoire of more than 40 operatic roles.

Broadway musicals *The Wizard of Oz* 1/21 at the new Majestic Theater (put up by publisher William Randolph Hearst at 5 Columbus Circle), with Fred Stone and Dave Montgomery in a musical extravaganza based on the L. Frank Baum novel of 1900, 293 perfs.; *Mr. Bluebeard* 1/21 at the Knickerbocker Theater, with veteran vaudeville soft-shoe dancer and comedian Edwin Fitzgerald "Eddie" Foy, 46, music by Frederick Solomon and C. Herbert Kerr, lyrics by J. Cheever Goodwin, 134 perfs.; *Nancy Brown* 2/16 at the Bijou Theater, with Marie Cahill, music by Henry K. Hadley, lyrics by George H. Broadhurst and Frederic Ranken, songs that include "Navajo" by Chicago-born composer Egbert (Anson) Van Alstyne, 20, lyrics by Harry H. Williams, 104 perfs.; *In Dahomey* 2/18 at the New York Theater, with an all-black 15-member cast, music by Marion Cook, lyrics by poet Paul Laurence Dunbar, 106 perfs.; *Whoop-Dee-Doo* 9/24 at the Weber & Fields Music

Hall, with Weber and Fields, music by W. T. Francis, book and lyrics by Edgar Smith, 151 perfs.; *Babette* 11/16 at the Broadway Theater, with Fritzi Scheff, now 21, music by Victor Herbert, book and lyrics by Harry B. Smith, 59 perfs.; *Babes in Toyland* 10/13 at the Majestic Theater, with music by Victor Herbert, lyrics by Glenn MacDonough, songs that include "March of the Toys" and the title song (lyrics by Glen MacDonough), 192 perfs.; *The Office Boy* 11/2 at the Victoria Theater, with Eva Tanguay, Missouri-born actor Sidney Toler, 29, music by Ludwig Englander, book by Harry B. Smith, 66 perfs.; *The Girl from Kay's* 11/2 at the Herald Square Theater, with a cast that includes Winchell Smith, music by Ivan Caryll, additional music and lyrics by Clare Kummer, 31, 205 perfs.

Popular songs: "(You're the Flower of My Heart) Sweet Adeline" by New York composer Henry W. Armstrong, 24, lyrics by Richard H. Gerard (R. G. Husch), 27, whose words, inspired by the farewell tour of Italian diva Adelina Patti, will be sung by generations of barbershop quartets (the publishing firm Witmark buys the tune outright for $5,000 and Armstrong receives only $1,000).

"Tin Pan Alley" gets its name from songwriter-publisher Harry Von Tilzer. He receives a visit from songwriter-journalist Monroe H. Rosenfeld, who has earned little from his 1897 song "Take Back Your Gold" and other hits. Von Tilzer's piano has a peculiarly muffled tone; he explains that other tenants of the building in East 14th Street have demanded that piano players make less noise and he has used newspapers to reduce volume. Rosenfeld says, "It sounds like a tin pan," Von Tilzer says, "Yes, I guess this is tin pan alley," and Rosenfeld repeats the phrase in his *New York Herald* music columns.

 The New York Public School Athletic League is founded by Luther Halsey Gulick, 38, who helped James Naismith invent basketball 12 years ago and has become director of physical education for the city's public schools.

Jamaica Racetrack opens April 27 under the auspices of the Metropolitan Jockey Club. A raucous crowd of 15,000 turns out for the opening, coming on the Long Island Rail Road or by trolley, but the grandstand has only 9,000 seats (admission: $2; the field seats go for 75¢) (see 1945).

Ban Johnson's 2-year-old American League gains recognition under baseball's new National Agreement. Fronting for William Devery and pool-hall owner-bookie Frank Farrell, Tammany Hall politician Joseph Gordon tells Johnson in March that he has some lots at 165th Street and Broadway on Washington Heights that could be used for a stadium provided that he can buy a franchise; Johnson sells him the franchise for $18,000; Gordon rents the lots for $10,000 per year, and he awards local district leader Thomas McAvoy a $200,000 contract to excavate the site and a $75,000 contract to build a stadium. McAvoy puts up Hilltop Park, a flimsy wooden stadium with 16,000 seats (1,500 of them go for 25¢ each). The New York Highlanders have moved from Baltimore and play their opening game April 3 before a capacity crowd, everyone going through the turnstile has received an American flag, and the Highlanders win, defeating the Washington Senators 8 to 6. Managed by Clark Griffith, the team ends the season with a 72-62 won-lost record, placing it fourth in the league, helped by "Wee Willie" Keeler, now 31, who hits .318, and Massachusetts-born pitcher John Dwight "Jack" Chesbro, 29 (see Yankees, 1913). The American League's annual pennant winner is to compete in World Series playoffs with the top team of the 27-year-old National League under the new National Agreement, but no New York team wins the pennant in either league this year and the first World Series is between the Boston Red Sox and Pittsburgh Pirates.

Christy Mathewson pitches his first full season for the New York Giants, winning 30 games with a 267-strikeout record that will stand for 50 years (see 1900). He will be nicknamed "Big Six" after a famous fire engine and will have a lifetime record of 372 wins, 187 losses, and 2,499 strikeouts.

● Paper clothing pattern pioneer Ebenezer Butterick dies at New York March 31 at age 76 as a new factory for his E. Butterick & Co. goes up in Brooklyn.

Railroad heir William K. Vanderbilt, now 53, is married at New York April 25 to divorcée Ann Rutherfurd (*née* Harriman), daughter of financier Oliver Harriman. Vanderbilt's first wife divorced him in 1895.

Former ice baron Charles W. Morse tries to have his 1901 marriage to Mrs. Dodge annulled in order that he may marry a Roman Catholic heiress who cannot marry a divorced man for religious reasons. Abraham Hummel of the law firm Howe & Hummel persuades Mrs. Dodge's previous husband to perjure himself by claiming that he was not served divorce papers at the Everett House on the night of October 3, 1897, as was claimed, but a letter written to his lawyer at the time shows that he was indeed served notice that his wife intended to sue for divorce. Hummel has known about the letter but banked on the fact that the lawyer was dead and decided to ignore the matter. District Attorney William Travers Jerome uses the case to hound Hummel and advance his own lofty political ambitions (*see* 1905).

Luna Park opens May 16 on Coney Island with a permanent array of entertainments on a 38-acre West Brighton site illuminated with spectacular electrical displays. Ironton, Ohio-born fairground concessionaire Frederic "Fred" Thompson, 29, and Omaha-born concessionaire Elmer "Skip" Dundy met 2 years ago at Buffalo's Pan American Exposition, they operated some rides at George C. Tilyou's Steeplechase Park last year, Tilyou offered them a lower share of the take at the end of the season, they declined, and they have acquired the 6-year-old Sea Lion Park for the site of their own amusement park. Its City of Delhi features natives with elephants, zebras, and camels; a "Trip to the Moon" illusion ride originally used by Thompson and Dundy at the Pan American Exposition, a "Submarine Ride," a renactment of the Civil War battle between the ironclads *Monitor* and *Merrimac*, an ascending merry-go-round, centrifugal swings, and other attractions will attract so many visitors that by 1907 Luna Park will have some 1,700 employees, 1.3 million light bulbs (the electric bill will be $4,000 to $5,000 per week), and its own telegraph office, radio office, and long-distance telephone service (*see* Dreamland, 1904; Hippodrome, 1905).

The Union Club moves uptown into a magnificent new clubhouse at the northeast corner of Fifth Avenue and 51st Street, just north of St. Patrick's Cathedral (*see* 1836). A survey of members has shown that only 17 percent lived below 23rd Street and only 7 percent between 23rd and 34th streets, and the club has taken over the site of the Catholic Orphanage (*see* 1927).

The Colony Club is founded by women who include society matron Mrs. J. (Jefferson) Borden Harriman (*née* Florence Jaffray Jones), 32, who was obliged to leave Newport last summer to run some errands in the city and found the Harriman town house full of painters and plasterers. It is unheard of for a proper woman to check into a hotel alone, and the city has no women's club with a proper clubhouse. She has persuaded Mrs. John Jacob Astor, Mrs. Payne Whitney (*née* Helen Hay), and some other women to join her in building a clubhouse with all the comforts of the Union Club. They fix an initiation fee of $150 and annual dues at $100, placing the Colony Club on the same level as the most expensive men's clubs, and set exclusive admission standards. J. P. Morgan, whose three daughters all join, agrees to subscribe $10,000 toward building the clubhouse if

nine other men will do the same, William C. Whitney offers to put up $25,000 if the clubhouse is as large as the new Metropolitan Club, and Stanford White is commissioned to design the building at 120 Madison Avenue, between 30th and 31st streets (*see* real estate, 1907).

Barnard College holds its first Greek Games, beginning an annual competition between freshmen and sophomores: the young women will vie for laurel wreaths in discus throwing, hurdling, chariot racing, hoop relay races, torch relay races, choreography, lyrics, costume design, and other events.

The body of a man who has been stabbed and nearly decapitated is discovered April 14 in an ash barrel on a corner of East 11th Street. Police identify the body as that of one Benedetto Madonia, his murder raises fears that a Sicilian-based crime syndicate is about to make attacks on non-Italian Americans, but a police investigation led by Italian-born detective Joseph Petrosino, 43, determines that the murder was simply the result of an internecine dispute (*see* Petrosino, 1909).

The 20-story Whitehall Building is completed at 17 Battery Place, northeast corner West Street. Henry J. Hardenbergh has designed the structure; another 14 floors will be added in 1911 to give the office tower 550,000 square feet of rentable floor space.

The New York Stock Exchange building is completed at 8 Broad Street, between Wall Street and Exchange Plaza. Designed in Greek Revival style by George B. Post, it has a four-story glass curtain wall to admit light to the trading floor, whose walls are of marble and whose ceiling is gilded. The building will be augmented in 1920 with an addition designed by Trowbridge & Livingston. Its 52-foot Corinthian columns support a classic Greek pediment bearing sculptures by J. Q. A. Ward and Paul Bartlett (air pollution will destroy the original marbles and they will be replaced in 1936 by copper and lead figures coated to resemble stone).

Architect Richard M. Upjohn dies at New York March 3 at age 74; architect Hugh Lamb of typhoid fever at his East Orange, N.J., home April 3 at age 84.

The Bank of the Metropolis building is completed at 31 Union Square West for the 32-year-old commercial bank. Architect Bruce Price has designed the limestone structure in a neo-Renaissance style, but Price has voyaged to Europe in an effort to recover his health and dies at Paris May 29 at age 59.

The architectural firm Delano and Aldrich is founded in November by New York-born Ecole des

Beaux-Arts graduate William Adams Delano, 29, and Providence, R.I.-born architect Chester Holmes Aldrich, 32, who has studied at the Ecole and worked for Carrère & Hastings.

Land values at Broadway and Wall Street are the highest in the city, ranging from $350 to $400 per square foot (versus $25 per square foot just two blocks away).

The 14-story 67th Street Studios building is completed at 27 West 67th Street, between Central Park West and Columbus Avenue, with enormous duplex apartments whose living rooms have two-story ceilings.

The Marshall Orme Wilson town house is completed at 3 East 64th Street, between Fifth and Madison avenues, for Mrs. Astor's daughter Caroline Astor Wilson, whose mother lives around the corner on Fifth Avenue. Warren & Wetmore has designed the limestone house with a slate and copper mansard roof, dormers, and oval windows (it will later become New India House).

A limestone-faced town house for John Henry Hammond Sloane and his wife, Emily (*née* Vanderbilt), is completed at 9 East 91st Street to 16th-century Roman designs by Carrère & Hastings. The Sloanes have purchased the site from Andrew Carnegie.

The 12—story Woodward Hotel opens at 1724 Broadway, southeast corner 55th Street. Designed by George F. Pelham, it will expand to fill the block-front between Broadway and Seventh Avenue.

The 10-story Belleclaire Hotel is completed in Art Nouveau style at 250 West 77th Street, southwest corner Broadway, to designs by Czech-born architect Emery Roth, 32, of Stein, Cohen & Roth. Orphaned at age 13, Roth came to Chicago in search of an uncle whose street address he did not know, never found the uncle, obtained work as an office boy in an architect's office, worked at Burnham & Root from 1890 to 1893, came to New York to work for Richard Morris Hunt, and joined with Theodore G. Stein and Alfred N. Cohen in 1898.

Landscape architect Frederick Law Olmsted dies at Brookline, Mass., August 28 at age 81. His creations included Central Park and Prospect Park plus parks in cities other than New York, but in recent years he has been insane.

Millionaire C. K. G. (Cornelius Kingsley Garrison) Billings, 42, celebrates the completion of his 25,000-square-foot, $200,000 trotting-horse stable near the Speedway on the Harlem River by giving a March 29 dinner in the grand ballroom of Louis Sherry's. Billings retired 2 years ago from the presidency of Chicago's People's Gas Light & Coke Co., moved with his family into a Fifth Avenue house at 53rd Street, and acquired a hilltop country estate near 190th Street where his stable, designed by architect Guy Lowell, includes rooms for entertaining guests. He had originally planned to have the party at the stable but has decided to hold it in Sherry's ballroom, transformed into a woodland scene for the occasion; saddle horses have been hired from local riding academies and taken to the ballroom in freight elevators, miniature tables have been attached to the pommels of the saddles, and waiters dressed as grooms at a hunting party serve Billings and his 36 guests. Oat-filled feeding troughs are then set before the mounts, whose hooves are padded to spare the sodded floor.

1904 Former mayor W. R. Grace dies at New York March 21 at age 71 after a distinguished mercantile and political career that began when he ran away to sea from his native Ireland at age 14.

President Roosevelt wins election in his own right with 336 electoral votes to 140 for the Democratic Party's candidate, Judge Alton Brooks Parker, 52, of New York, who has been nominated in preference to William Jennings Bryan. Financier August Belmont II headed the New York delegation to the convention at St. Louis and opposed Bryan's candidacy. Secretary of Commerce and Labor George B. Cortelyou has been elected chairman of the Republican

Unnumbered subway stations like Astor Place had visual symbols for foreigners. MUNICIPAL ARCHIVE

National Committee and managed the president's reelection campaign; he is named postmaster general in December, beginning a 27-month stint in which he will reorganize the postal service, insisting that appointments and promotions be based on merit whenever possible.

Republican Frank W. Higgins, 48, wins the New York State gubernatorial contest, defeating Democrat D. Cady Herrick, 58, a state supreme court justice who receives 732,704 votes to Higgins's 813,264.

The Amalgamated Association of Street and Electric Railway Employees, Brotherhood of Locomotive Firemen, and Brotherhood of Locomotive Engineers strike from March 7 to March 11 but fail to gain their demands.

Polish-born garment worker Rose (originally Rachel) Schneiderman, 22, is elected to the executive board of the United Cloth Hat and Cap Makers Union and involves herself in a strike against a "runaway" shop that has relocated to New Jersey in order to avoid paying union wages. Brought to America at age 6, Schneiderman is a tailor's daughter from the Lower East Side who became interested in labor problems when she saw that her co-workers

Long Acre Square became Times Square when the New York Times tower rose at 42nd Street. LIBRARY OF CONGRESS

in a department store were getting the same weekly $2.75 wage that she earned despite 14 years of service; she learned to be a capmaker and went to work at age 16 lining caps at $6 per week, out of which she had to pay $25 in cash plus $45 in installments for her sewing machine, plus paying for power and thread, lunches, and transportation. Her mother warned her that "men don't want a woman with a big mouth," but she and two other women obtained a UCHCU charter by stationing themselves outside factories as workers came off their shifts and getting 25 signatures on membership blanks for their own local of the Jewish Socialist United Cloth Hat and Cap-makers' Union (*see* 1906).

The 92-year-old City Bank of New York issues travelers checks that compete with the American Express Travelers' Cheque copyrighted in 1891.

Financier and former U.S. secretary of the navy William C. Whitney dies at New York February 2 at age 62, leaving a vast fortune that enabled him to maintain racing stables and ten homes, including a Fifth Avenue mansion at 68th Street. In addition to his Manhattan residence he has owned 5,000 acres in the Wheatley Hills near Jamaica, L.I., a house at Sheepshead Bay with 300 acres and a private racetrack, a mansion with 700 acres in the Berkshire Hills, an Adirondack game preserve of 16,000 acres, a bluegrass horse farm of 3,000 acres in Kentucky, another horse farm in New York State, an estate at Aiken, S.C., that includes a mansion, a racecourse, and 2,000 acres of hunting land, and a palazzo at Venice. His survivors include his sons Harry Payne, 31, and Payne, 27, and two daughters; Goldman, Sachs founder Marcus Goldman dies at Elberon, N.J., July 20. His son-in-law Samuel Sachs takes over as senior partner.

E. F. Hutton and Co. is founded by New York stockbroker Edward Francis Hutton, 28, whose brokerage house will be the first to serve California by wire service.

Wall Street's Dow Jones Industrial Average closes December 31 at 69.61, up from 49.11 at the end of 1903.

Russian-born lingerie seamstress Lane Bryant (originally Lena Himmelstein), 24, opens a New York store in a one-room flat in Governeur Street selling maternity clothes. The first merchant to sell ready-to-wear clothing for stout and pregnant women, she will build a chain of Lane Bryant stores.

Abercrombie & Fitch is incorporated under that name, having opened a new sporting-goods store at 314 Broadway (*see* 1892). Ezra Fitch persuaded

David T. Abercrombie 4 years ago to let him buy into the business and become a partner, he insists that merchandise be displayed realistically rather than kept in glass cabinets, the store sets up a tent and equips it as if it were in the Adirondacks, employing an experienced guide to answer questions, but Abercrombie will balk at Fitch's insistence that they expand and will quit in 1907, the store will begin publishing a catalog soon afterward, and by 1913 it will have moved to a midtown location just off Fifth Avenue, selling women's outdoor clothing as well as men's (see 1917).

Merchant Joseph B. Bloomingdale dies at his native New York November 21 at age 61. He has instituted a 10-hour work day at Bloomingdale's with a half-day off each week.

⚡ The Municipal Ownership League of Greater New York is founded December 22 at an Albany conference of reformers dissatisfied with the high rates charged and poor service delivered by privately owned gas, electric, and mass transit companies. The League favors public, nonprofit ownership of the utilities, and its membership includes Groton, Conn.-born muncipal judge Samuel Seabury, 32 (who has prepared a 200-page study of abuses by the Consolidated Gas and New York Edison Co. monopolies), and publisher William Randolph Hearst, who has been advocating muncipal ownership for several years.

⚡ The first tunnel under the Hudson River connects Jersey City with Manhattan March 8 but will not open officially until February 25, 1908 (see 1906). The Pennsylvania Railroad's Hudson & Manhattan Railroad Co. has built two single-track tubes, each more than a mile long. Georgia-born William G. (Gibbs) McAdoo, 41, heads the Hudson & Manhattan, whose Manhattan tunnel entrance will lead to a gentrification of the Tenderloin area (see 1876), home for years to dance halls, bars, and brothels but an area that will soon be attracting crowds to middle-class department stores (see commerce [Macy's], 1902).

The 264-foot wooden excursion boat S.S. *General Slocum* catches fire in the East River off Astoria, Queens, June 15 while carrying 1,400 German-Americans from the Lower East Side to Locust Grove on Long Island Sound for a Wednesday picnic sponsored by St. Mark's Lutheran Church of Sixth Street. Passengers leap into the river with their clothes on fire, more than 1,020 die within 50 yards of shore, most are women and children, the tragedy shatters the German community in the Lower East Side, a court finds the paddle-wheeler's captain guilty of criminal negligence and sentences him to 10 years at hard labor in Sing Sing Prison, and more Germans move uptown to settle in Yorkville on the upper East Side.

The first New York City subway line of any importance opens to the public October 27 after more than 4 years of construction that has cost the lives of at least 44 men and seen thousands injured. A crowd of 25,000 hears speeches marking the occasion in City Hall Park as ships in the harbor blow their whistles and a 21-gun salute is fired (see 1900). The Interborough Rapid Transit (IRT) line runs from Brooklyn Bridge north under Lafayette Street, Fourth Avenue, and Park Avenue to 42nd Street, west to Broadway, and north to 145th Street, reaching a top speed of 45 miles per hour (more than twice the safe speed of an elevated train). Wearing a top hat, Mayor McClellan mans the controls for the inaugural run, completing it in 26 minutes with a train of five copper-sheathed wooden cars, each seating 56 passengers, with red-painted roofs. Mosaic tiles bearing visual symbols identify unnumbered stations to aid the city's polyglot population, and there are 133 handsome metal and glass kiosks—modeled on those used for the Budapest subway—to cover entranceways to the gleaming tiled stations (architects George L. Heins and Christoper J. La Farge have designed the interiors and many of the kiosks, including the Battery Park Control House at Bowling Green—so called because a passenger is under the control of the subway once he or she enters the building). Tickets cost 5¢ each, 111,000 people ride the first day, 319,000 the second, and 350,000 the third as New York inaugurates a system that alleviates congestion on trolley cars and elevated trains (see 1903). Ridership on surface transit immediately drops 75 percent, but it operates initially only in Manhattan, and above 42nd Street only on the West Side. The world's first subway system to have separate express and local tracks in each direction, its express trains go 35 miles per hour (three times the speed of an El), and the system that starts with just over nine miles and 26 stations is soon extended to 157th Street at the southern end of Washington Heights, with six-car trains requiring platforms at least 310 feet long. Going 180 feet below street level (its greatest depth by far) under a hill at 191st Street and St. Nicholas Avenue, it will cross the Harlem and East rivers to reach the Bronx next year, Brooklyn in 1908, Queens in 1915, and grow to cover more than 842 miles (443 of them underground)—the largest rapid-transit complex in the world—with the world's largest and most complex power system, having a capacity of 1,100 megawatts of 650-volt direct current supplied via "third rails" through 216 substations by means of 2,500 miles of cable and 2,900 circuit breakers. Financier August Belmont II has his own private car equipped with commissary and plumbing facilities. Engineer Parsons predicted from the outset that demand for rapid transit would be insatiable, and work proceeds on a tunnel that will carry the subway to Borough Hall, Brooklyn (see 1911).

The Westchester Avenue elevated line is completed between 149th Street and Bronx Park (180th Street) for use not only by the new IRT subway (whose tracks are elevated in some places to maintain consistent grade levels) but also by the Second Avenue El.

Mount Sinai Hospital moves into a new 10-building facility with 456 beds on upper Fifth Avenue at 100th Street, where it purchased land in 1898 (see 1872). It will grow to become one of the city's major teaching hospitals beginning in 1910, when it starts post-graduate physician training in conjunction with Columbia University (see Columbia-Presbyterian, 1928; medical school, 1963).

Cornell University Medical School requires that every member of its Class of 1908 have a college education or its equivalent, a daring innovation (see 1900). Only 10 students are admitted under the new policy, but there will be 24 next year and by 1920 the college will be turning away applicants for lack of space. Beginning in 1908 medical students will receive only their first year of instruction on the campus at Ithaca, it being deemed preferable that they should come earlier under the influence of teachings centered about the various New York City hospitals (see 1912).

The state legislature at Albany consolidates the educational system of the state under the Board of Regents. Former superintendent of instruction Andrew W. Draper has revitalized schools at Cleveland as superintendent there from 1892 to 1894, served as president of the University of Illinois for 2 years thereafter, and is elected by the legislature to fill the new office of commissioner of education, a post that he will hold until his death in 1913. Now 56, Draper has received awards and medals at the St. Louis International Exposition.

Stuyvesant High School opens in East 23rd Street, where it will remain until 1907. Superintendent of Schools William H. Maxwell has developed the idea of a school that will prepare children of immigrants for careers in science (see 1907).

Curtis High School opens at Hamilton Avenue at St. Mark's Place in St. George on Staten Island, taking its name from the late editor-writer-reformer George William Curtis. The first public secondary school on Staten Island, it will grow to have 1,600 students.

St. Bernard's School opens at 510 Fifth Avenue. Educator John Jenkins has started the private boys' school that will move in 1910 to 111 East 60th Street and 5 years later take possession of a building at 5 East 98th Street, where it will admit boys of 6 to 15. Enrollment will grow to 334 by 1994, and St. Bernard's will start a kindergarten in 1997.

A five-story brick-and-limestone schoolhouse for the 28-year-old Ethical Culture Society is completed at the northwest corner of Central Park West and 63rd Street to designs by Carrère & Hastings (see 1895). The school will graduate its first seniors next year (see 1910).

The New York Association for the Blind is established in November by social worker Winifred Holt, 33, and her sister Edith to educate the public on the possibilities of rehabilitation and vocational training to make sightless people self-supporting. A daughter of publisher Henry Holt, Winifred last year established a New York bureau to provide concert and theater tickets for the blind and has returned from England, where she attended London's Royal Normal College and Academy of Music for the Blind (see Lighthouse, 1913).

Nonfiction: The Shame of the Cities by San Francisco-born McClure's magazine managing editor (Joseph) Lincoln Steffens, 38, whose exposé of squalor in America's urban centers creates a sensation (a long-time friend of Theodore Roosevelt, Steffens worked as a reporter for the New-York Evening Post from 1892 to 1897, became city editor of the New-York Commercial Advertiser, and joined McClure's as managing editor in 1901).

Fiction: Cabbages and Kings by North Carolina-born short story writer O. Henry (William Sydney Porter), 42, who calls New York "Baghdad on the Hudson." Porter was indicted by federal bank examiners 8 years ago on charges of having embezzled funds from the Austin, Tex., bank that employed him as a teller from 1891 to 1894. (He was the bank's only bonded employee and had little means; it will later be suggested that owners of the First National Bank were helping themselves and friends to loans that were often not repaid, that any losses ascribable to Porter were covered by insurance, and that he was made to pay for wrongdoing by others.) Porter fled to Honduras to escape prosecution, returned in 1897 when he heard his young wife, Athol (née Estes), was dying of tuberculosis, was convicted after a 3-day trial at Austin February 17, 1898, served 3 years of a 5-year prison term at Ohio State Penitentiary in Columbus, and came to New York; "The Maxmilian Diamond" by assistant New York district attorney Arthur (Cheney) Train, 29, is published in the July issue of *Leslie's* magazine, launching its author on a writing career.

 Sculpture: *General Sherman Memorial* by Augustus Saint-Gaudens for the southeast entrance to Central Park. The gilded equestrian statue shows the late general being led on his horse by a woman.

American Art News begins publication November 5. *New York Herald* art critic James Bliss Townsend, 47, has bought the 2-year-old *Hyde's Weekly Art News*, renamed it, increases its size to four pages, and starts to include photogravure illustrations, adding advertisements to help defray his higher production costs. By February 1912 Townsend will be putting out a 12-page weekly, and he will continue to enlarge the magazine until his death (*see* 1921; *Art in America*, 1913).

 Theater: *The Superstition of Sue* by Missouri-born playwright Paul Armstrong, 34, 4/4 at the Savoy Theater, with William Friend, Eddie Heron, 8 perfs.; *The College Widow* by George Ade 9/20 at the Garden Theater, 278 perfs.; *The Music Master* by Charles Klein 9/26 at the Belasco Theater, with David Warfield, 288 perfs.; the Liberty Theater opens 10/10 at 234 West 42nd Street; *Leah Kleschna* by C. M. S. McClellan 12/12 at the Manhattan Theater, rented since 1901 by Mrs. Fiske and her husband, playwright Harrison Grey Fiske, in order to be independent of Charles Frohman's Theatrical Syndicate, with Mrs. Fiske, Charles Cartwright, George Arliss, 631 perfs.

Abraham Hummel of the law firm Howe & Hummel wins a court decision upholding the rights of theater managers not to honor tickets bought from speculators. A combine of ticket scalpers has engaged lawyer Max Steuer to represent its members, but Hummel prevails.

The Friars Club is founded by New York press agents for vaudeville and burlesque performers who in many cases cannot gain membership in the more exclusive Players or Lambs clubs.

The 30-year-old Lambs Club moves into a new building at 134 West 44th Street, completed in the city's new theater district in time for its annual Christmas Gambol. Architect Stanford White (a member of "the Flock" who has altered the previous clubhouse at 70 West 36th Street) has designed the new structure that will be the organization's home until it moves to 3 West 51st Street.

 Opera: *Madama Butterfly* 2/17 at Milan's Teatra alla Scala, with music by Giacomo Puccini, who has seen John Luther Long's play *Madame Butterfly* at London. Staged originally by David Belasco in New York, the play about the opening of Japan is based on the short story "Madame Butterfly" that appeared in the January 1900 issue of *Century* magazine (the new opera is a fiasco in its initial production).

Broadway musicals: *Piff! Paff! Pouff!* 4/2 at the Casino Theater, with Eddie Foy, music by Jean Schwartz, lyrics by William Jerome, 264 perfs. (plus a week at the Majestic Theater beginning 12/26); *Higgledy-Piggledy* 10/12 at the Weber Music Hall, with Anna Held, Canadian actress Marie Dressler (Leila von Koerber), 34, Fred M. Weber, music by Maurice Levy, lyrics by Edgar Smith, 185 perfs.; *Little Johnny Jones* 11/17 at the Liberty Theater, with George M. Cohan, his parents (Jerry J. and Helen F.), book, music, and lyrics by Cohan, songs that include "Give My Regards to Broadway" and "Yankee Doodle Boy," 52 perfs.

Broadway composer John "Honey" Stromberg is found dead in his apartment at his native New York in July at age 49, an apparent suicide.

 No World Series is played because John McGraw of the New York Giants refuses to have his team face the Boston Red Sox.

Coney Island's Dreamland amusement park opens to compete with Luna Park, opened last year by Fred Thompson and Elmer "Skip" Dundy. Promoted by Republican State Senator William H. Reynolds and built at a cost of $3.5 million, Dreamland replaces various pavilions and tawdry shows with a 300-foot tower, exhibitions transported from the St. Louis world's fair, restaurants, a ballroom on a pier that extends out to sea, illusionist attractions that include the "Canals of Venice" and "Coasting in Switzerland," long-distance chute-the-chutes, a miniature railroad, and morality plays but is less imaginative than Luna Park. Washington, D.C.-born circus veteran Samuel Gumpertz, 36, has been operating a chain of 17 theaters for a business acquaintance of William "Buffalo Bill" Cody and makes a hit at Dreamland with a miniature replica of 15th century Nuremberg peopled by midgets, but one of the greatest successes is a realistic fire exhibition called "Fighting the Flames" (*see* 1911; Popular songs, 1909).

The Explorers Club is founded by two New Yorkers who take over the short-lived Arctic Club and attract members who include mountain climbers, physicists, war correspondents, outdoorsmen, and the American Museum of Natural History's curator of birds and mammals. The club will later occupy a mansion at 46 East 70th Street and grow to have 3,000 members, of whom 400 will live in the New York area.

Cosmetics manufacturer Harriet Hubbard Ayer dies at New York November 23 at age 54.

August Heckscher begins a new career as New York real estate developer (see commerce, 1867). Now 56, he resigns as general manager of the zinc company he has headed since 1897, intending to retire with the fortune he has made from Pennsylvania coal and New Jersey zinc, but sees the potential of Manhattan real estate and begins to acquire land and buildings in midtown, especially around 42nd Street (see Heckscher Building, 1916).

The 11-story, L-shaped Singer Manufacturing Co. loft building is completed at 561 Broadway, between Prince and Spring streets, to designs by architect Ernest Flagg. Its façade of curlicued steel, recessed glass, and textured terra cotta anticipates the metal-and-glass curtain wall that will sheath the city's skyscrapers later in the century.

The 24-story Times Tower completed for the *New York Times* opens at Broadway and 42nd Street December 31 with an eight-story tower atop a 16-story base (floor space on the upper eight floors is so small that most of the newspaper's offices will be moved to an annex around the corner in 43rd Street by 1913). Designed for publisher Adolph S. Ochs in Italian Renaissance style by Eidlitz and McKenzie (who have modeled it on Giotto's 14th century Campanile at Florence), the city's second-tallest skyscraper replaces Pabst's Hotel and Restaurant (see 1899); dominated for years by saddle and carriage shops (the Brewster Carriage Works still occupies its north end), Long Acre Square becomes Times Square. The midnight fireworks display that marks the building's opening will become in modified form a New Year's Eve tradition (see everyday life, 1907; communications [Zipper], 1928).

The Chatsworth apartment house is completed at 346 West 72nd Street, southeast corner of Riverside Avenue (later Riverside Drive). Designed by John E. Schlarsmith, its upper-floor apartments range in size from a one-bedroom flat (with maid's room, living room, dining room, and kitchen) at $83 per month to a 15-room suite with five large bedrooms, four and a half baths, two maids' rooms, laundry, kitchen, butler's pantry, dining room, library, and

living room at $380 per month. A sun parlor runs across the entire top (13th) floor, complete with conservatory and potted plants; the basement contains a café, billiard room, barbershop, hairdresser, valet, and tailor, and the management maintains an electric bus service along 72nd Street to Central Park West.

The Ansonia Hotel (actually an apartment hotel) opens on the west side of Broadway between 73rd and 74th streets. Phelps, Dodge copper heir William Earl Dodge Stokes, 52, has named the Ansonia in honor of his maternal grandfather, Anson Greene Phelps, founder of Ansonia Brass & Copper Co. at Ansonia, Conn. Stokes put up more than 50 row houses west of Broadway (then called the Boulevard) in 1886. Architect Paul E. M. Duboy has helped him design a gleaming white 16-story structure, whose turrets and balconies give it the look of a 19th century French resort hotel, and its floor plans are based on models that Stokes has studied in France. Stokes and his young son Weddy live in a sprawling apartment on the 16th floor that also houses the Ansonia's banquet hall and English Grille. An orchestra plays in the roof garden to entertain guests on summer evenings, and the roof garden is used also to keep goats, hogs, a pet bear, chickens, ducks, and geese (the Health Department forces him to get rid of the hogs and geese, but Stokes will sell chicken and duck eggs to tenants at half price until stopped by a lawsuit, and whatever goatsmilk he and his son do not drink he uses to make cheese). The main dining room, on the lobby floor, seats 550, and the lobby also has a fountain containing live seals. A swimming pool is in the basement, and a sub-basement contains electric blowers that circulate air over coils that are steam-heated in winter and cooled by freezing brine in summer to keep the Ansonia's interior at a constant 70° F. It has 400 baths plus 600 toilets and washbasins. A single room rents for $50 per month, a suite of 18 rooms with three baths and four toilets for $625 per month. High ceilings and large rooms give the suites a manorial air.

The six-story Red House apartment building is completed at 350 West 85th Street, between West End Avenue and Riverside Avenue (soon to be Riverside Drive). Designed by Harde & Short in the style of an Elizabethan manor house, it rises to the west of some 9-year-old English-style red-brick row houses.

The 12-story St. Urban apartment house is completed at 285 Central Park West, southwest corner 89th Street, to designs by Robert L. Lyons, who has given it a port-cochère entrance and a single tower crowned by a dome and cupola. Its 47 apartments have 11 rooms and three baths each and rent for between $250 and $333 per month.

The Afro-American Realty Company is founded by black real estate operator Philip A. Payton, Jr., 28, who guarantees premium rates to Harlem landlords and thus makes good housing available for the first time to black New Yorkers (see 1901). Harlem will become America's largest black community—a model community until overcrowding in the 1920s turns it into a ghetto.

Harlem's Kortwright apartments open on Sugar Hill at 1990 Seventh Avenue with 29 luxury units. The first black residents will move into the building in 1926.

The 12-story Astor Hotel opens on Broadway between 44th and 45th streets in what soon will be called Times Square. Designed by Henry J. Hardenbergh for William Waldorf Astor and constructed in classic French style, the 660-room hostelry has cost $7 million and will be enlarged in 1909 to have 900 suites with baths, meeting rooms, a banquet hall that seats 1,200, a roof garden, a restaurant on the main floor, and private dining rooms. It will remain a popular gathering place for more than 50 years.

The 19-story St. Regis Hotel opens at the southeast corner of Fifth Avenue and 55th Street and tries to outswank the Waldorf-Astoria at 34th Street as the city's most elegant hostelry. Designed by Trowbridge & Livingston in a beaux-arts style for John Jacob Astor IV, the skyscraper contains 316 rooms and is one of the first hotels in a neighborhood known until now only for mansions and churches. Its public rooms are smaller than those at the Waldorf, its guest rooms larger (their number will later be expanded to 322, including 86 suites; see 1929).

The 12-story Lucerne Hotel opens at 201 West 79th Street, northwest corner Amsterdam Avenue, with apartments in addition to transient rooms. Architect Harry B. Mulliken has given the building a rich exterior of brick and brownstone with terra-cotta ornamentation manufactured by the New York Architecture Terra Cotta Co. of Long Island City (the hotel's dining room will have what many will call the best free lunch in town, with choices that include lobster salad).

The Wales Hotel opens on Madison Avenue at the corner of 92nd Street on what is becoming known as Carnegie Hill (see Carnegie mansion, 1901).

Publisher Joseph Pulitzer moves into a huge Italian Renaissance mansion at 11 East 73rd Street. Designed by architect Stanford White, the fireproof structure replaces a house in East 55th Street that was destroyed by fire in 1900.

Artist-illustrator Charles Dana Gibson and his wife, Irene, move into a five-story house at 127 East 73rd Street. Stanford White has designed the house in neo-Federal style.

A New York Zoological Park forester observes that the park's native chestnut trees, Castanea dentata, are dying of a strange fungus disease that will later be identified as Endothia parasitica, a bark blight. A Japanese exhibit has introduced the blight that begins to wipe out the trees, whose nuts have been an important food source.

Charles C. Weisz of the New York department of charities urges that immigration of people over 50 be restricted, arguing that most of the city's almshouse residents are foreign born and new arrivals of a certain age are likely to become public charges.

1905 Mayor McClellan narrowly wins reelection, this time to a 4-year term, defeating publisher William Randolph Hearst and Republican candidate William M. Ivins. Hearst has run as an Independent, having moved with his family 5 years ago into the house at 123 Lexington Avenue where President Arthur was sworn into office in 1881. The mayor receives 228,397 votes, Hearst 224,929, Ivins 137,193, and the election results are beamed for the first time from the roof of the 10-month-old Times Tower on Times Square (see Zipper, 1928).

The Harlem Equal Rights League is founded by Irish-born public librarian Maud Malone as part of the city's division of the National Women's Suffrage League.

Bethlehem Steel Co. is founded by Charles M. Schwab to compete with United States Steel Corp., whose presidency he resigned in 1903 (see 1901). Bethlehem begins as the parent company of Schwab's United States Shipbuilding Co.

A scandal over the management of the Equitable Life Assurance Society of New York depresses the company's stock; traction king Thomas Fortune Ryan, now 53, gains virtual control of its $400 million in assets by investing a mere $2.5 million.

North Fork Bank has its beginnings in the Mattituck Bank founded on Long Island under a charter granted April 26. It will adopt the name North Fork Bank and Trust Co. in 1950 and merge in the following 10 years with three other banks on the north fork of eastern Long Island (*see* 1988).

North Side Savings Bank is founded in the Bronx with offices at 3196 Third Avenue, near 161st Street. Headed by Irish-born banker John J. Barry, it will move in 1910 to 3230 Third Avenue, near 163rd Street, and grow as the borough's population increases (*see* 1951).

Swiss-born copper magnate Meyer Guggenheim dies at Palm Beach, Fla., March 15 at age 77; former Chicago traction magnate Charles Tyson Yerkes at New York December 29 at age 68, leaving an estate valued at $4 million. His will provides that his widow, Mary Adelaide, receive one-third of that amount, and she objects to a decision by his executor to sell $4.5 million in Chicago City Railway bonds at 30¢ on the dollar, beginning a dispute that will not be settled before her death in 1911 (*see* everyday life [Mizner], 1906).

Wall Street's Dow Jones Industrial Average closes December 30 at 96.20, up from 69.61 at the end of 1904.

Gorham Manufacturing Co. moves uptown in September from the Queen Anne-style building it has occupied since 1884 at the northwest corner of Broadway and 19th Street into a new Florentine Renaissance-style palazzo designed by Stanford White of McKim, Mead & White at 390 Fifth Avenue, southwest corner 36th Street. Gorham's president Edward Holbrook has headed the firm since 1894 and expanded by acquiring other silver companies to rival Tiffany & Co.

Tiffany & Co. moves uptown in September from Union Square to a new building at the southeast corner of Fifth Avenue and 37th Street, where Stanford White has designed a structure modeled on Venice's 16th century Palazzo Grimani. Tiffany's has been at 271 Broadway since 1847 and will remain at 37th Street until it moves to 57th Street in 1940. The store sells a pearl necklace for $1 million—the largest single sale in the store's 68-year history and one that will not be surpassed in this century if ever.

The New York auto show opens January 20 at Madison Square Garden with more than 100 motor cars on display ranging in size from runabouts that sell for as little as $450 to 20- to 40-horsepower limousines costing up to $8,000.

One-way rotary traffic is imposed on Columbus Circle, and some one-way regulations are instituted later in the year on Times Square as the growing popularity of motor vehicles creates congestion (*see* 1916).

The Long Island Rail Road installs a low-voltage third rail system, becoming the first U.S. road completely to abandon steam locomotion. The LIRR has been controlled since 1900 by the Pennsylvania, but the Pennsy will not exert much voice in its management until the 1920s.

A rush-hour Ninth Avenue El leaves the track at 7 o'clock in the morning of September 11 while going more than three times the regulation nine miles per hour on the 53rd Street curve; the second car in the train plunges to the street below, killing 12 passengers and seriously injuring 48 (one of whom soon dies). Few in the crowded car escape injury in the accident; police say the switch at the curve was improperly set and arrest the motorman and towerman on charges of manslaughter, but elevated trains continue to carry far more people than the new subway, whose ridership will not overtake that of the Els until 1913 (*see* 1921).

The 22,225-ton Hamburg-Amerika Line passenger ship S.S. *Amerika* arrives from Hamburg October 7 to begin more than 50 years of transatlantic service. Equipped with a Marconi wireless system, an automatic fire-extinguishing system, electrically controlled watertight doors that can be controlled from her bridge, and the first passenger elevator ever seen on an ocean liner, the 668-foot-long vessel has accommodations for 2,662 passengers (410 in first class, 254 in second, 223 in third, 1,765 in steerage), and nine kitchens, including two for steerage passengers, a kosher kitchen for Orthodox Jews, and a special one for the 120-seat Ritz-Carlton restaurant on board.

Bacteriologist Anna W. Williams wins appointment as assistant director of the laboratory at the Department of Health and publishes an improved method for diagnosing rabies based on a technique of analyzing brain-tissue samples (*see* diphtheria, 1894). Instead of taking 10 days, her method takes only minutes and will remain the standard for more than 30 years.

The Bialystoker congregation founded in 1878 takes over the 79-year-old Willett Street Methodist Episcopal Church on the Lower East Side for use as a synagogue as thousands of Eastern European Jews continue to pour into the area.

TIAA-CREF has its beginnings in the Carnegie Foundation for the Advancement of Teaching (CFAT) established at New York with $10 million by philanthropist Andrew Carnegie to fund a pension system for teachers. Shocked to discover how little professors were paid, Carnegie engaged Missouri-born former MIT president Henry S. (Smith) Pritchett, 48, to set up a system of free, portable retirement annuities for teachers at nonsectarian colleges, universities, and other education and research institutions in the United States and Canada, requiring no contributions from either employers or employees (*see* 1918).

Fordham University adopts that name after 64 years as St. John's College (*see* 1841).

¶¶ The last issue of the *New York Times* to be printed in its 1889 building at 41 Park Row comes off the presses January 1, whereupon the presses are moved uptown to the new Times Tower on Times Square (formerly Long Acre Square), along with 27 Merganthaler Linotype machines (11 new Linotype machines are added). The editorial offices are moved uptown from Broadway and 32nd Street, and Ohio-born *New York Sun* editor Carr (Vattel) Van Anda, 39, joins the *Times* as managing editor, beginning a 21-year relationship.

Joseph Pulitzer's *New York World* launches an exposé of the insurance industry, showing how leading companies have used agents to keep their eyes on state legislatures, bribing lawmakers to suppress bills that would be against their interests. Pulitzer himself gave up his editorship in 1890 because of failing eyesight but has resumed direct control since the days of "yellow journalist" sensationalism near the turn of the century and returned to the paper's more responsible format while continuing a politically independent posture of hard-hitting, accurate reporting. The *New York Times* launches its own exposé; publisher Adolph S. Ochs borrows $300,000 from Remington Arms heir Marcellus Hartley Dodge, 24, to pay off a debt to the Equitable Life Assurance Society in order to avoid any embarrassment, pledging his controlling interest in the paper as collateral (he will repay the loan in 1916 and regain his shares).

William Randolph Hearst pays John Brisben Walker $400,000 to acquire *Cosmopolitan* magazine (*see* politics, 1902). The magazine runs an article headed "The Treason of the Senate" alleging that an alliance exists between several U.S. senators and big business interests (*see* 1925).

L. C. Smith & Brothers sells its first typewriter to the *New York Tribune* for the paper's newsroom. The Syracuse firm will for years be the largest producer of typewriters.

Royal Typewriter Co. is founded by financier Thomas Fortune Ryan, who puts up $220,000 to back inventors Edward B. Hess and Lewis C. Meyers. Their machine has innovations that include a friction-free ball-bearing one-track rail to support the weight of the carriage as it moves back and forth, a new paper feed, a shield to keep erasure crumbs from falling into the nest of type bars, a lighter and faster type bar action, and complete visibility of words as they are typed.

"Little Nemo in Slumberland" by Spring Lake, Mich.-born cartoonist (Zenas) Winsor McCay, 34, debuts October 15 in the *New York Herald*. McKay eloped at age 21 with a 12-year-old girl (Maude DuFour), she gave birth to their son Robert at age 16, the boy has inspired McCay's work, which has appeared in the *Cincinnati Commercial Tribune* since 1898 under the nom de plume Silas, James Gordon Bennett has invited McCay to New York, and his pioneer strip will continue in the *Trib* until July 23, 1911.

The Brooklyn Public Library collection that opened late in 1897 is moved to a new two-story building in Hancock Street near Franklin Avenue, built—as are 19 other Brooklyn libraries—with a $1.6 million gift from Andrew Carnegie.

Nonfiction: *Plunkitt of Tammany Hall* by Irish-born journalist William L. Riordon of the *New York Evening Post*, who calls the Tammany Hall Grand Sachem "perhaps the most thoroughly practical politician of the day" (*see* politics, 1903).

Fiction: *The House of Mirth* by Edith Wharton, now 43, who gains her first popularity with a fictional analysis of the stratified New York society that she knows so well as the wife of a rich banker and of this society's reaction to change.

Painting: *Central Park, Winter* by Philadelphia-born New York painter William James Glackens, 35.

The 291 Gallery at 291 Fifth Avenue opens under the direction of photographer Alfred Stieglitz, now 41, with a group of other photographers (Steiglitz calls them "photo-secessionists" and they include Luxembourg-born photographer Edward [Jean] Steichen, 26, who opened a studio at 291 Fifth in 1902 after 2 years of study in Europe with sculptor Auguste Rodin). The new gallery will show only photographs until 1908 but will then begin to give Americans their first look at work by Henri Matisse, Pablo Picasso, and the late Henri de Toulouse-Lautrec, among others.

The Hippodrome opens April 12, occupying the entire blockfront on the east side of Sixth Avenue between 43rd and 44th streets. Financed in large part by financier John W. "Bet a Million" Gates and built by Coney Island amusement park developers Fred Thompson and Elmer "Skip" Dundy of 1903 Luna Park fame, the world's largest theater has 5,200 seats that range in price from 25¢ to $1; it will survive until 1939, presenting spectaculars that compete with those of Marc Klaw and A. L. Erlanger's Theater Syndicate (*see* Shubert brothers, 1906).

Theater: *Cousin Billy* by Clyde Fitch 1/2 at the Criterion Theater, with Melbourne-born actress May Robson, 46, Zelda Sears, Edward Abeles, Columbus, Ohio-born actor Grant Mitchell, 30, 76 perfs.; *The Heir to the Hoorah* by Paul Armstrong 4/10 at the Hudson Theater, 59 perfs.; *The Squaw Man* by Edward Milton Royle 10/23 at Wallack's Theater, with Newburgh-born actor William S. (Surrey) Hart, 34, 722 perfs.; *Mrs. Warren's Profession* by George Bernard Shaw 10/30 at the Garrick Theater, with Mary Shaw, Arnold Daly, 14 perfs. (London's Lord Chamberlain has refused to license the play about a woman whose income is derived from houses of prostitution, moralist Anthony Comstock has tried to block the New York production, the actors are prosecuted for performing in an "immoral" play, Shaw coins the term *Comstockery* for such strict censorship, London will not see a production until 1926); *The Girl of the Golden West* by David Belasco 11/14 at the Belasco Theater, with Blanche Bates, 224 perfs.

Onetime matinée idol Maurice Barrymore (originally Herbert Blyth) dies at Amityville, L.I., March 26 at age 56, survived by his children Lionel, now 26, Ethel, now 25, and John, now 23, who have begun acting careers of their own; actor Joseph Jefferson dies at Palm Beach, Fla., April 23 at age 76, and a memorial service is held for him at the Church of the Transfiguration ("the Little Church Around the Corner") with "almost every well known actor and acress in New York" in attendance (as the *New York Times* reports); producer Sam Shubert is killed in a Pennsylvania train wreck May 11 at age 28. Rival A. L. Erlanger refuses to adhere to an agreement with "a dead man" and Shubert's brothers Lee and Jacob begin a feud with the Klaw-Erlanger syndicate, triumphing over what is essentially a theatrical trust to develop the most far-flung privately controlled organization of its kind in the world.

Variety begins weekly publication at New York December 16 under the direction of former *Morning Telegraph* editor Sime Silverman, 32 (*see* 1935).

The Juilliard School of Music has its beginnings in the Institute of Musical Art founded by Frank Damrosch and James Loeb (*see* 1920).

The 42-year-old Musical Mutual Protective Union fines New York Symphony Orchestra conductor Walter Damrosch $1,000 for hiring five French musicians without obtaining prior approval from the union (*see* 1916).

Broadway musicals: *Fontana* 1/14 at the Lyric Theater, with music by Urbana, Ohio-born composer Raymond Hubbell, 25, book by S. S. Shubert and Robert B. Smith, lyrics by Smith, 298 perfs.; *Fritz in Tammany Hall* 10/16 at the Herald Square Theater, with Joseph Cawthorn, music and lyrics by William Jerome and Jean Schwartz, book by John J. McNally, 48 perfs.; *Mlle. Modiste* 12/25 at the Knickerbocker Theater, with Fritzi Scheff, music by Victor Herbert, book and lyrics by Henry Blossom, songs that include "Kiss Me Again" and "I Want What I Want When I Want It," 262 perfs.

Popular songs: "Tammany" by German-born vaudeville composer Gus Edwards (originally Gustave Simon), 26, lyrics by Vincent P. Bryan, 22 (brought to Brooklyn's Williamsburg section at age 7, Edwards worked in the family cigar store as a youth, later was a song plugger, sang at lodge halls, in ferry boat lodges, and at age 17 was spotted at Johnny Palmer's Gaiety Saloon in Brooklyn and booked by a vaudeville agent with four other boys to tour as The Newsboys Quintet. Written in 1 hour, his song is interpolated into the Broadway musical *Fontana* and will be the political club's theme song); "Will You Love Me in December as You Do in May?" by Ernest R. Ball, lyrics by New York law student James J. Walker, 24, who obtains a $500 advance from his publisher and uses it to buy three custom-made suits with peg-top trousers (no cuffs), a dozen silk shirts, four pairs of shoes with sharply pointed toes, three fedora hats, a new walking stick, and gifts for his mother and girlfriend.

 Germany's Kaiser Wilhelm II challenges yachtsmen to compete in a transatlantic race that he expects will prove the superiority of German seamanship and ship construction, the winner to receive a solid gold cup (the Kaiser's Cup) (*see* 1868). Eight U.S. and two British millionaires accept the challenge, the 11 ships that assemble in New York Harbor in May include an eccentric British nobleman's 245-foot ship *Valhalla* that displaces 645 tons, another British peer's yacht, and the comparatively tiny (108-foot, 86-ton) *Fleur de Lys* owned by surgeon Lewis A. Stimson. Heavy weather forces all but two contenders to drop out, and the 185-foot (56-

meter) schooner *Atlantic* owned by New York traction heir and playboy Wilson Marshall embarrasses the kaiser, beating his schooner *Hamburg* by crossing 3,013 miles from Sandy Hook off the New Jersey coast to the Lizard off the English coast in 12 days, 4 hours, 1 minute, 19 seconds—22 hours ahead of *Hamburg* and a record that will stand into the 21st century for displacement sailing yachts. Marshall's steel-hulled, 206-ton ship has marble floors and a grand saloon with three Tiffany skylights, she can carry more than 20,000 square feet of sail, but Marshall remains below while five-foot-three-inch Scottish-born U.S. skipper Charles Barr, 40, averages 10.31 knots per hour to win the cup. (Barr has won three America's Cup races.)

Christy Mathewson pitches a no-hitter for John McGraw's New York Giants June 13 at Chicago. The Giants win the World Series, defeating Connie Mack's Philadelphia Athletics 4 games to 1. Mathewson shuts out the Athletics in the first, third, and fifth games, a feat that will never be equalled.

Louis Sherry's 7-year-old Fifth Avenue restaurant at New York is the scene of a ball given January 31 by Equitable Life Assurance Society heir and chief stockholder James Hazen Hyde, 28, who has had architect Stanford White decorate a banquet room in the style of Louis XIV. Hyde denies reports that the affair cost $100,000 (he says it cost only $20,000), but the extravaganza triggers a congressional investigation into insurance industry practices.

The Nippon Club is founded by chemist Jokichi Takamine (*see* real estate, 1912).

President Roosevelt gives away the bride March 5 in a ceremony at the Ludlow-Parish family houses, 6 and 8 East 76th Street, when his cousin Anna Eleanor Roosevelt, 20, marries Columbia Law School student Franklin Delano Roosevelt, 23, her fifth cousin once removed. Orphaned since age 10, she has been raised by a grandmother and is considered an ugly duckling, while Franklin (Harvard '04) is one of the handsomest men in America. He has been living with his widowed mother, Sara, in the family's old rowhouse at 200 Madison Avenue, at 35th Street, but moves with his bride into a brownstone at 125 East 36th Street; at year's end Sara promises the couple a new home as a Christmas present (*see* real estate, 1908; medicine, 1921).

The Dodge-Morse marriage scandal that began in 1901 continues to titillate New Yorkers (*see* 1903). District Attorney William Travers Jerome indicts Abraham Hummel of the law firm Howe & Hummel, whom he has been trying to prosecute since 1903,

subpoenas the firm's records, but finds to his dismay that Hummel and his late partner never kept records. Hummel goes on trial for criminal conspiracy in January and is convicted in 2 days, the jury having deliberated for only 18 minutes (*see* 1907).

The 21-story Trinity Building opens in May at 111 Broadway, replacing an older building of the same name directly north of the Trinity Church churchyard. Designed in neo-Gothic style by architect Francis H. Kimball for the 4-year-old U.S. Realty and Construction Co., the office tower has 166,000 square feet of rentable floor space behind a serene stone façade that harmonizes with the church (*see* 1907).

The Joseph Raphael De Lamar mansion is completed at 233 Madison Avenue, northeast corner 37th Street, for a Dutch-born merchant seaman who made a fortune in the California Gold Rush. The Beaux Arts Parisian town house designed by architect C. P. H. Gilbert will become the headquarters of the National Democratic Club and, later, the Polish Consulate General's building.

The James A. Burden, Jr. mansion is completed at 7 East 91st Street to Beaux Arts designs by Warren & Wetmore for Burden and his wife, Florence (*née* Sloane). Her parents, William and Emily Sloane, have purchased the site from Andrew Carnegie, who lives across the street. Architect Whitney Warren studied at the Ecole des Beaux Arts in Paris from 1885 to 1894, having attended Columbia only briefly; an avowed Francophile, he deplores New York's lack of a promenade such as the Champs Elysées at Paris.

The 12-story Astor Apartments are completed at 2141-2157 Broadway, between 74th and 75th streets with an entrance at 245 West 75th Street. Designed by Clinton & Russell for William Waldorf Astor, they will be given an addition (by Peabody, Wilson & Brown) to the north in 1914.

The Gotham Hotel (later the Peninsular) opens October 2 in West 55th Street off Fifth Avenue. Designed in neo-Italian Renaissance style by H. Hobart Weekes of Hiss & Weekes, the 23-story, 400-room Gotham is a near mate to the ornate St. Regis that opened last year across the avenue. Arranged in the shape of a C, with its inner court facing south over the University Club, its main dining room faces on Fifth Avenue, with large French doors that open onto an enclosed terrace for use as a summer restaurant. But the Fifth Avenue Presbyterian Church is directly across 55th Street, a law prohibits sale of alcoholic beverages within 200 feet of any church, and although the St. Regis was somehow able to obtain a liquor license the Gotham cannot and it will go into foreclosure in 1908. Built at a cost of $4 million, it will be sold for $2.45 million (*see* Peninsular, 1988).

The Utopia Land Co. acquires a 50-acre tract between Jamaica and Flushing in central Queens, announces plans to build a co-operative town for Jews from the Lower East Side, receives a $9,000 loan from the New York Mortgage and Security Co. to grade streets (with names like Division, Essex, Hester, and Ludlow, taken from their counterparts on the Lower East Side), and stakes out lots, but the plans will never be brought to fruition and the land will be sold in 1911.

Brooklyn-born landscape architect Richard Schermerhorn, Jr., 27, opens a Manhattan office and will soon win a competition to design Jacob Riis Park.

The National Audubon Society is founded (*see* Grinnell, 1885). It will move in the early 1920s to the red-brick Willard Straight mansion at 1130 Fifth Avenue, northeast corner 94th Street, that it will outgrow in the 1970s (*see* 1993; International Center of Photography, 1975).

Hebrew National Foods has its beginnings at New York, where Isadore Pinkowitz starts producing kosher frankfurters. His son Leonard Pines will take over the business after Pinkowitz's death in 1936, and the enterprise will grow to have a line that includes salami, sauerkraut, mustard, and other kosher products.

The dairy restaurant Ratner's opens in April in Pitt Street, serving soup, gefilte fish, whitefish, and a few other kosher dishes under sanitary conditions for the city's large and growing Jewish population concentrated on Manhattan's Lower East Side. Jacob Harmatz, 21, and Morris Ratner, 22, have flipped a coin to decide whose name would be on the front, and Harmatz has lost (*see* 1918).

The pizzeria opened in Spring Street in 1895 is acquired for $200 by Naples-born grocer Gennaro Lombardi, who has seen a way to use his day-old bread. His coal-fired brick oven in Little Italy bakes pizza pies at temperatures of 800° to 900° F.—twice as hot as any gas oven—and his success will spawn a number of other pizzerias in the city, all operated by immigrants whom Lombardi has trained to use fresh mozzarella cheese (*see* 1924).

The state legislature at Albany enacts the Raines Law, forbidding the sale of alcohol except in establishments with at least 10 rooms. Named for a Republican upstate assemblyman, its object is to shut down the saloons that serve working-class New Yorkers and provide much of the revenue for Tammany Hall, but its effect will be to encourage saloonkeepers to add rooms (that will commonly be used for immoral purposes) and create what will be called "Raines Hotels" even long after the law is repealed.

A New York State census reveals that the population of the crowded Lower East Side has increased by 14 percent since 1900, but construction of bridge approaches, parks, and schools in the area since 1895 has removed nearly 700 tenements that provided cheap housing for some 50,000 people.

1906 City magistrate Charles S. (Seymour) Whitman, 37, dismisses charges against a minor offender and works to break up the corrupt system that has allowed arresting police officers to split fees with bail bondsmen. He orders raids of after-hours saloons that have been paying off New York's Finest and inaugurates night courts to hear some cases (*see* 1909).

Former National Civil Service Reform League president Carl Schurz dies at New York May 14 at age 77, leaving behind three volumes of reminiscences that are published beginning later in the year (*see* Carl Schurz Park, 1911).

Publisher William Randolph Hearst wins the Democratic nomination for governor with support from Tammany Hall boss Charles F. Murphy, the Republicans nominate Manhattan lawyer Charles Evans Hughes, now 44 (Gov. Frank W. Higgins has decided not to seek reelection and will die early next year at age 50). Thousands jam Times Square to await the election results on the night of November 6, the first edition of the *New York American* November 7 says Hearst has won by at least 20,000 votes, but Hearst concedes defeat at 2:30 o'clock that morning. Final returns (749,602 versus 691,105) show that Hughes has won with a comfortable plurality, despite the fact that Hearst, now 43, has won every New York City borough, piling up a plurality of 71,644 votes in the city.

Mother Earth is founded at New York by Emma Goldman, now 37, and Alexander Berkman, who has just been released from prison after serving time for an attempt on the life of Henry Clay Frick in the Homestead Strike of 1892. Goldman has lived since 1903 in a sixth-floor apartment at 210 East 13th Street, near Third Avenue, and made it a gathering place for Greenwich Village intellectuals and radicals (*see* 1909).

The National Urban League has its beginnings in the Committee for Improving the Industrial Conditions of Negroes in New York and the National League for the Protection of Colored Women (*see* 1911).

The American Jewish Committee is founded by New Yorkers to protect civil and religious rights and fight prejudice. The founders are mostly of German descent and include Syracuse-born lawyer Louis Marshall, now 48.

The New York Zoological Society puts a 23-year-old pygmy from the Belgian Congo on display during afternoons at the Bronx Zoo for 2 weeks in September until public outcry forces it to stop.

Massachusetts-born speculator Jesse (Lauriston) Livermore, 29, arrives at New York with $2,500 he has made working in Boston, Chicago, and Denver bucket shops (crooked investment houses that find various ways to bilk their customers) (*see* 1907).

The 14-year-old Boston investment banking house Hayden Stone moves to New York and opens offices at 25 Broad Street. Boston-born banker Charles Hayden, 36, started as a broker's clerk at age 21 and went into a partnership with a fellow clerk 1 year later to start the firm (*see* 1979; science, 1935).

The National Exchange Bank merges with the Irving National Bank under the name Irving National Exchange Bank, headed by New Jersey-born banker Lewis E. (Eugene) Pierson, 36, who will be the first to issue monthly statements to customers instead of just balancing passbooks. The bank will become Irving Trust Co.

Wall Street's Dow Jones Industrial Average closes above 100 for the first time January 12 but closes December 31 at 94.35, down from 96.20 at the end of 1905.

B. Altman & Co. moves from its Sixth Avenue and 18th Street premises of 1865 to Fifth Avenue at 34th Street, a residential area of fine homes and mansions where the arrival of a commercial establishment is not welcomed (*see* 1876). Merchant Altman, now 66, has engaged Trowbridge & Livingston to design a gracious emporium that caters to the city's rising middle class (*see* 1914).

A special Mayor's Pushcart Commission convenes to study the proliferation of street vendors (*see* 1897). Merchants complain that the street congestion caused by the vendors impedes delivery of goods and increases their costs. Commission members include housing reformer Lawrence Veiller and settlement house founder Lillian Wald; by 1912 the pushcarts will be banned in most parts of the city

and crammed almost entirely into the Lower East Side (*see* 1938).

The Public Service Commission establishes an 80¢ gas law, reducing the price of 1,000 cubic feet of gas by 20 percent. Consolidated Gas, Brooklyn Union Gas, and other companies will fight the new law all the way to the U.S. Supreme Court, which will rule that while governmental bodies have a clear right to oversee the operations of utilities they may not set rates so low as to prevent the utilities from earning a reasonable rate of return on investment, but the court will rule that 80¢ per 1,000 cubic feet of gas is not too low (*see* 1895; 1923).

The Hamburg Amerika Line's 24,581-ton S.S. *Kaiserin Auguste Victoria* arrives on her maiden voyage from Hamburg via Dover and Cherbourg May 15 to begin service on the transatlantic run. The largest passenger ship thus far, the twin-screw vessel has two funnels, a maximum speed of 18 knots per hour, is 677 feet in length overall, 77.3 feet wide in the beam, 50.2 feet deep, carries a crew of 593, has five decks, and can accommodate 2,466 passengers (472 in first class, 174 second, 212 third, 1,608 in steerage).

Tugboat mogul Capt. Michael Moran dies at his 10 First Place, Brooklyn, home June 28 at age 72 and is succeeded as head of Moran Towing Co. by his son Eugene F., who will run the company until 1961 (*see* 1863). The family business will continue into the 21st century, becoming the largest of the Port of New York's towing companies (whose number will grow to 30 before declining to no more than a dozen) (*see* 1917).

The Interborough Rapid Transit Co. (IRT) and Brooklyn Rapid Transit Co. (BRT) subway systems are consolidated by a merger completed March 6. The 2-year-old IRT reaches the northern part of Washington Heights; by 1908 the entire system will be in operation.

Traction king Thomas Fortune Ryan withdraws from the Interborough Metropolitan Traction Co., the company fails, and the city has to take over. An investigation will show that "the Ryan crowd" got away with at least $100 million, but no indictments will be handed up.

Justice (later Mayor) William Jay Gaynor rules in August that the Brooklyn Rapid Transit Co. cannot collect a double fare on El trains to and from Coney Island, but the BRT hires 250 special police officers to enforce the policy. Disturbances break out August 12 (a Sunday) at various Brooklyn El stations, more than 1,000 passengers are ejected from BRT trains and trolleys, a car full of passengers who have refused to pay the extra nickel on a Coney Island-bound train is uncoupled and left on a siding, a young girl's body is found floating in Coney Island Creek, and a BRT lawyer actually suggests that the company has a clear right to kill anyone who refuses to pay the extra fare. One of the passengers ejected is Borough President Bird S. Coler, who will be a strong advocate of municipal ownership of transit properties (see Dual Contracts, 1913).

An electrically powered New York Central locomotive pulls a train out of Grand Central September 30, and the Central begins running electrically powered multiple-unit suburban trains in December (see 1903; 1907). Electrifying the tracks beneath Park Avenue not only makes the tunnel to Grand Central safer but also puts an end to the sparks, smoke, and soot that have emanated through grilles to the avenue above.

The first tunnels under the Hudson River come together October 6 to permit commuter trains to operate between Hoboken, N.J., and Morton Street in Greenwich Village (see 1904). Col. DeWitt Clinton Haskins first broke ground for the project at Hoboken in 1874, a blowout 6 years later killed 20 men, work was abandoned in 1892 after completion of 2,000 feet of tunnel beneath the river, William G. McAdoo took over in 1902, organized the New York & New Jersey Railroad (later the Hudson & Manhattan), and has overseen completion of the original tunnel plus a parallel tunnel (see 1908; Hudson Terminal Building, 1909; Penn Station, 1910).

A trolley tunnel financed by August Belmont II is completed in December under the East River to link Bowling Green with Brooklyn's Joralemon Street and reduce the need for ferries.

 The 5-year-old Rockefeller Institute for Medical Research moves to 1270 Avenue A (later York Avenue) between 63rd and 68th streets, a site acquired in 1901. John D. Rockefeller originally pledged himself to contribute $20,000 per year for 10 years, but he will give the Institute $2.6 million next year and another $3.8 million in 1910. York & Sawyer designed its first building, which opened on the campus 3 years ago, and the Institute will remain on the site into the 21st century, initially providing financial grants to support private and public scientific studies, mostly of infectious diseases (see 1959; Caspary Auditorium, 1957).

The 2-year-old Hispanic Society of America opens a museum on Audubon Terrace, on the west side of Broadway between 155th and 156th streets. Philan-thropist Archer Huntington (originally Worsham), 36, bought a 200-by-550-foot parcel of land (once part of the old John James Audubon estate) 2 years ago and inaugurated a program of building institutions on the site. His mother, Arabella, married the late railroad builder Collis P. Huntington in 1884, and he lives with his wife, Helen, and 14 servants in a town house at 1083 Fifth Avenue, near 89th Street. The Hispanic Museum will be joined next year by the American Numismatic Society, in 1909 by the Church of Our Lady of Esperanza and the American Geographical Society, in 1922 by the Museum of the American Indian, and in 1930 by the National Institute of Arts and Letters, most of them designed by Huntington's architect cousin Charles Pratt Huntington.

St. John's College in Brooklyn receives a charter as a university (see 1870). It will add a law school in 1925, a college of pharmacy in 1929, and a downtown division in Schermerhorn Street that same year (see 1936).

Pace University has its beginnings in a school of accountancy opened at the New York Tribune Building in lower Manhattan by Homer St. Clair Pace and his brother Charles Ashford Pace to tutor candidates for the state examinations given to would-be certified public accountants. The Pace brothers also conduct classes in accounting at YMCAs in Manhattan, Brooklyn, and New Jersey; they will increase enrollment to more than 300 by 1909 and by 1919 will have over 4,000 (see 1951).

A new building for the 9-year-old De Witt Clinton High School is completed at 899 Tenth Avenue, between 58th and 59th streets, just east of the 2-year-old IRT subway powerhouse (later to be a Consolidated Edison powerhouse). Schools superintendent Charles B. J. Snyder has designed the structure in Flemish Renaissance Revival style with overscaled double-hung windows that admit lots of light and air (glass accounts for more of the exterior than brick), 78 high-ceilinged classrooms, 14 labs, four study halls, two gyms, and an auditorium. Snyder's H-plan gives the school a long, elevated forecourt and a shallow rear court, but De Witt Clinton will remain in the building only until 1927 (see 1929; John Jay College, 1988).

The Nightingale Bamford School has its beginnings in Miss Nightingale's Classes, given at girls' homes by educator Frances Nightingale, a Georgia-born spinster who has never been to college but has been encouraged by her New York cousins, the Delafields, to teach girls in the city (see 1920).

William Randolph Hearst establishes International News Service (INS), a wire service to compete with the Associated Press founded in 1848 (*see* Brisbane, 1897; United Press, 1907).

The *American Magazine* begins publication at New York, where "muckrakers" Lincoln Steffens, Ida Tarbell, Ray Stannard Baker, and others have acquired the 30-year-old *Frank Leslie's Popular Monthly*, changed its name, and begun a periodical that will continue for 50 years, reaching a circulation of 2.2 million (*see* Crowell, 1911).

Oneida-born "muckraker" William Henry "Will" Irwin, 32, quits his job as reporter for the *New York Sun*, becomes writing editor for *McClure's* magazine, but continues to turn out pieces for the *Sun*, including one about this year's San Francisco earthquake entitled "The City That Was."

New York lithographer Joseph F. (Fairchild) Knapp, 42, pays $750,000 to acquire Crowell Publishing Co. of Springfield, Ohio; Crowell has been publishing the *Women's Home Companion* since 1897 and also publishes *Farm & Fireside* (Knapp will retitle it *Country Home; see* 1911).

New York Telephone Co. advertises in September that the city has 269,364 phones—two and a half times as many as London.

 The Pierpont Morgan Library is completed in Italianate marble style by McKim, Mead & White adjacent to J. P. Morgan's brownstone in East 36th Street to house the banker's prodigious collection of rare books, manuscripts, documents, and incunabula (books printed before 1501). Imported works of art are subject to a 20 percent duty under terms of the 1897 Revenue Act (books and manuscripts are exempt if they are intended for educational, philosophical, religious, or scientific purposes), so most of Morgan's paintings and sculpture remain in England.

Nonfiction: *The Devil's Dictionary* by Ohio-born journalist Ambrose Bierce, now 64, who is the Hearst correspondent at Washington, D.C.: "Mammon: the god of the world's leading religion. His chief temple is in the holy city of New York;" *A Prisoner at the Bar: Sidelights on the Administration of Criminal Justice* by Arthur Train, now 31, who has worked as press agent for District Attorney William Travers Jerome.

Fiction: *The Four Million* (stories) by O. Henry, who gains renown for "The Furnished Room" and "The Gift of the Magi" (indigent New Yorkers Della and Jim exchange gifts—combs for the hair she has cut off and sold to buy him a fob for the watch he has sold to buy her the combs. O. Henry has written it in the second booth of Pete's Tavern at the northeast corner of 18th Street and Irving Place).

 The 13-year-old National Arts Club acquires the 15 Gramercy Park South boarding house that was Samuel J. Tilden's home from 1865 until his death in 1886. Founded by *New York Times* critic Charles de Kay as a gathering place for artists, writers, and collectors, the club accepted women on an equal basis with men from its inception and now has a board of governors headed by investment banker Spencer Trask.

Portrait painter Eastman Johnson dies at New York April 5 at age 81, having painted likenesses of such notables as presidents Cleveland, Arthur, and Harrison, oil magnate John D. Rockefeller, lawyer William M. Evarts, Bishop Potter, and Columbia's President Barnard.

Theater: Lee and J. J. Shubert take over the huge Hippodrome on Sixth Avenue at the start of the season and use the world's largest theater to mount a three-part spectacle that includes a large band of genuine Sioux in war paint performing a Ghost Dance, a two-ring circus with clowns and a procession of elephants, and a three-scene romantic extravaganza featuring a giant water tank and hundreds of chorines costumed to represent every variety of fish; *The Hypocrites* by Henry Arthur Jones 8/30 at the Hudson Theater, with Richard Bennett, Doris Keane, 209 perfs.; the Astor Theater opens 9/21 at 1537 Broadway (corner of 45th Street) with a revival of Shakespeare's *A Midsummer Night's Dream* (it will become a movie house in 1925); *The Great Divide* by Indiana-born poet-playwright William Vaughn Moody, 37, 10/3 at the Princess Theater, with Henry Miller (who also directs and makes the play a success), 238 perfs.; *The Three of Us* by Illinois-born playwright Rachel Crothers, 28, 10/17 at the Madison Square Theater; *The New York Idea* by Philadelphia-born playwright Langdon (Elwyn) Mitchell (who uses the pen name John Philip Varley), 44, 11/19 at the 3-year-old Lyric Theater, with Mrs. Fiske, London-born actor George Arliss (originally Augustus George Andrews), 38, 66 perfs.; *Brewster's Millions* by New York playwrights Winchell Smith, 35, and Byron Ongley (who have adapted a 1902 novel by Indiana-born New York novelist George Barr McCutcheon, now 40) 12/31 at the New Amsterdam Theater, with a cast that includes Edward Abeles and "George Spelvin," a name Smith has invented to designate a player who doubles in another role, 163 perfs.

Abraham Hummel of the law firm Howe & Hummel has an assistant file suit against David Belasco for what he claims is an unauthorized production of the French play *Zaza* (Hummel is at liberty pending appeal of his criminal conspiracy conviction). He buys a front-row seat for one of his process servers, and when the leading lady appears his man leaps onto the stage and thrusts his paper into the outstretched hand of Mrs. Leslie Carter, who has to retire for a few moments and begin all over again.

Circus magnate James Bailey of Barnum & Bailey dies of acute erysipelas at his home near suburban Mount Vernon April 11 at age 59.

Cameraman Frank A. Dobson begins filming *The Skyscrapers of New York* November 8 atop the framework of an office tower going up at the corner of Broadway and 12th Street. The melodrama about a construction foreman who dismisses a worker for fighting and the disgruntled worker's subsequent act of theft is interwoven with scenes of brick masons at work, men descending a crane line, other men maneuvering a steel girder into place.

 The Manhattan Opera House designed and financed by Oscar Hammerstein opens 12/3 at 315 West 34th Street with a performance of the 1835 Bellini opera *I Puritani*.

Broadway musicals: *Forty-Five Minutes from Broadway* 1/1 at the New Amsterdam Theater, with Fay Templeton, Hammonton, N.J.-born actor Victor Moore, 29, music and lyrics by George M. Cohan, songs that include "Mary's a Grand Old Name" and the title song, 90 perfs. (Templeton plays a housemaid who scorns a fortune to marry the man she loves, but in real life she marries an industrialist and becomes one of the richest women in America); *The Vanderbilt Cup* 1/16 at the Broadway Theater, with Columbus, Ohio-born ingénue Elsie Janis (originally Elsie Jane Bierbower), 16, music by Robert Hood Bowers, 143 perfs.; *George Washington, Jr.* 2/12 at the Knickerbocker Theater, with George M. Cohan, songs by Cohan that include "You're a Grand Old Flag," 81 perfs.; *His Honor the Mayor* 5/28 at the New York Theater, with songs that include "Waltz Me Around Again, Willie (Around, Around, Around)," by Ren Shields, lyrics by Will D. Cobb, 30, 104 perfs.; *About Town* 8/30 at the Herald Square Theater, with English-born dancer Vernon Castle (originally Vernon Blythe), 19, Louise Dresser, Lew Fields, Jack Norworth, music by Melville Ellis and Raymond Hubbell, book and lyrics by Joseph Herbert, 138 perfs.; *The Red Mill* 9/24 at the Knickerbocker Theater, with Dave Montgomery, Fred Stone, music by Victor Herbert, book and lyrics by Henry Blossom, songs that include "In Old New York," "Every Day Is Ladies Day with Me," 274 perfs.

Popular songs: "China Town, My China Town" by Jean Schwartz, lyrics by William Jerome.

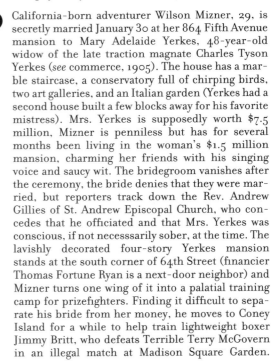 The International Collegiate Athletic Association founded at New York January 12 works to make football safer after a 1905 season that saw 19 boys killed playing the game and 154 seriously injured. Some have been paralyzed from the waist down, but 33 boys will die playing football in 1909 and 246 will sustain major injuries as the sport grows in popularity. The ICAA shortens the game from 70 minutes to 60, legalizes the forward pass, makes a 10-yard gain rather than five the standard for a first down, and requires leather helmets. The ICAA will be renamed the National Collegiate Athletic Association (NCAA) in 1910.

The New York Highlanders of baseball's American League, managed by Clark Griffith, finish the year with a won-lost record of 90-61, second only to the Chicago White Sox's record of 93-58 (*see* 1903). Despite a pledge by the owners to keep the outfield fences of their Hilltop Park clear of commercial signs, the walls will be covered with unsightly advertising by next year (*see* Yankees, 1913).

California-born adventurer Wilson Mizner, 29, is secretly married January 30 at her 864 Fifth Avenue mansion to Mary Adelaide Yerkes, 48-year-old widow of the late traction magnate Charles Tyson Yerkes (*see* commerce, 1905). The house has a marble staircase, a conservatory full of chirping birds, two art galleries, and an Italian garden (Yerkes had a second house built a few blocks away for his favorite mistress). Mrs. Yerkes is supposedly worth $7.5 million, Mizner is penniless but has for several months been living in the woman's $1.5 million mansion, charming her friends with his singing voice and saucy wit. The bridegroom vanishes after the ceremony, the bride denies that they were married, but reporters track down the Rev. Andrew Gillies of St. Andrew Episcopal Church, who concedes that he officiated and that Mrs. Yerkes was conscious, if not necesssarily sober, at the time. The lavishly decorated four-story Yerkes mansion stands at the south corner of 64th Street (financier Thomas Fortune Ryan is a next-door neighbor) and Mizner turns one wing of it into a palatial training camp for prizefighters. Finding it difficult to separate his bride from her money, he moves to Coney Island for a while to help train lightweight boxer Jimmy Britt, who defeats Terrible Terry McGovern in an illegal match at Madison Square Garden.

Mizner patches things up with Mary but then decamps in the summer for Goldfield, Nev., where Mizner's old friend George Lewis "Tex" Rickard, now 35, has staged a world's lightweight championship bout between Joe Gans and Battling Nelson. Left fatherless at age 10, Rickard worked as a cowboy to help support his family, was elected marshal of Henrietta, Texas, at age 23, opened gambling houses that made him a fortune, but lost it in land speculation when he went to the Klondike in 1897 with Addison and Wilson Mizner and a few other men (*see* Mizner, 1907; sports, 1916).

President Roosevelt's 21-year-old daughter Alice Lee is married February 17 in the East Room of the White House to Congressman Nicholas Longworth (R. Ohio), 39. The bride's father gives the couple a spacious four-story Manhattan brownstone with a large garden at 217 East 61st Street, between Second and Third avenues.

Public baths designed in Roman style by Arnold W. Brunner and William Martin Aiken are completed in 23rd Street east of First Avenue. Most of the area's population has no access to private baths, few can afford commercial baths (*see* 1897), and the city-sponsored baths soon have long waiting lines. The 54th Street Public Bath and Gymnasium is completed at 348 East 54th Street, between First and Second avenues, to designs by Werner & Windolph.

General Cigar Co. is created by financier Henry Goldman of the 37-year-old firm Goldman, Sachs. The new company will gain wide distribution for its Robert Burns, William Penn, Shakespeare, Van Dyck, and White Owl brands.

Architect Stanford White is shot dead June 25 at 52 in the roof-garden supper-club theater atop the Madison Square Garden that he designed in 1889. His murderer is Pittsburgh millionaire Harry K. (Kendall) Thaw, 36, who in April of last year married White's mistress Evelyn Nesbit, now 21 (an apartment house at 101 West 78th Street, built by Thaw's family, has been named for her). Thaw has learned of their relationship, secreted a pistol under a heavy coat, followed White to the supper club where he has gone for the opening of the musical revue *Mam'zelle Champagne*, crosses the room to White's table, and shoots him in the face three times at point-blank range; Nesbit purchases $2,000 worth of silver on credit this year from the new Gorham store on Fifth Avenue and gives it away, and when Gorham sues for payment in 1913 she will claim to have less than $250 to her name (*see* 1907).

The city's homicide rate will rise to 5.5 per 100,000 in the next 5 years, up from 3.8 per 100,000 in the last 5 (*see* 1916).

The *Real Estate Record and Builders' Guide* says January 30, "Many fine private houses are now being built on the upper East Side from Madison to Third between 60th and 73rd, now fast emerging into what may be called an aristocratic residential section." Electrification of the railroad beneath Park Avenue initiates a new building boom on the thoroughfare, which has had seven-story apartment buildings since the 1890s.

Bethlehem Steel president Charles M. Schwab moves into a 75-room château that occupies the full block between Riverside Avenue (later Riverside Drive) and West End Avenue from 73rd Street to 74th. Under construction since 1901, the Schwab mansion has turrets 116 feet high, a private chapel, a state drawing room copied from the Petit Trianon outside Paris, a banquet hall that seats 1,500, and air conditioning. Now 44, Schwab has paid $865,000 for the site of the former New York Orphan Asylum, owned by Jacob Schiff of Kuhn, Loeb & Co., who sold the property to Schwab after his wife complained tearfully that if she moved so far west she would never see her Fifth Avenue friends again. Architect Maurice Hebert has designed the mansion, adapting the façades of three French châteaux—Blois, Chenonceaux, and Azay-le Rideau (*see* 1948).

A town house for Long Island sportsman Payne Whitney, now 30, and his wife, Helen (*née* Hay), is completed at 972 Fifth Avenue, between 78th and 79th streets, with a mirrored Venetian-style reception room designed by Stanford White. The Whitneys were married in 1902 and last year went with White on a European shopping spree, buying the wood paneling from a Gonzaga palace in Italy, a Louis XV ormolu and Meissen mantel clock at Paris, and other treasures. Whitney's uncle Oliver Hazard Payne has paid for the house as a wedding gift.

An 11-story co-operative apartment house is completed at 131-135 East 66th Street and another soon afterward at 130-134 East 67th Street, southeast corner Lexington Avenue. Both contain mostly duplex units with double-height living rooms, and both have been designed by Connecticut-born architect Charles A. (Adams) Platt, 44, of Pollard & Steinam, whose own town apartment is in the 66th Street building, but people of means who live on the East Side virtually all occupy private houses.

The 69th Regiment Armory is completed for the New York National Guard unit at 68 Lexington

Avenue, between 25th and 26th streets. Hunt & Hunt has designed the brick, mansard-roofed structure (*see* art show, 1913).

The 13-story Wyoming apartment house is completed at 166 West 55th Street, northeast corner Seventh Avenue, with an enclosed port-cochère entrance. Designed in French Renaissance style by Rouse & Sloan for developer Eugene C. Potter, it replaces a building of the same name with a more elegant structure whose seven- to 13-room flats rent for between $166 and $466 per month. The larger units face front and have their dining rooms, drawing rooms, and libraries arranged en suite so that their connecting doors may be opened to create a 42-foot-long space for entertaining.

The Board of Aldermen approves a resolution giving the name Lincoln Square to an area bounded by Columbus and Amsterdam avenues between 63rd and 66th streets (*see* music, 1962).

Polish-born Harlem apartment developer Sol Simon, 50, buys the entire block bounded by Broadway and Amsterdam avenues between 143rd and 144th streeets, razes the Colored Orphan Asylum that has occupied the block, and replaces it with six-story elevator apartment houses.

The Myrtle Avenue streetcar line reaches the Ridgewood section of Queens, giving new impetus to construction in the area (*see* 1894).

The 22-story Belmont Hotel opens May 6 at the southeast corner of Park Avenue and 42nd Street, opposite the Grand Central Depot and just north of the 22-year-old Murray Hill Hotel, whose manager B. L. M. Bates manages the new Belmont. He has persuaded August Belmont II, John McEntee Bowman, and other investors to join him in putting up the $7 million hotel, designed by Warren & Wetmore and furnished by W. and J. Sloane. The main restaurant can seat 300, and there are also private dining rooms, five cafés, and grillrooms. Far and away the tallest building in the area, it has more than 1,000 guest rooms, each located near a high-speed elevator and decorated with pictures, etchings, and rotogravures from Paris. Rates range from $2 per night for a single room to $1,000 per night for a suite, and the hotel has 1,000 employees. The Belmont enjoys immediate success but will close in just 24 years.

The 15-story Knickerbocker Hotel opens in October at 1466 Broadway (southeast corner 42nd Street). Designed in French Renaissance style by Marvin & Davis with an assist from the late Bruce Price and interiors by Trowbridge & Livingston, the elaborate red-brick, limestone, and terra-cotta caravansary has a copper roof, its own subway entrance, 556 rooms, and three floors of dining and entertainment rooms that soon attract a following among opera stars such as Enrico Caruso (it is only two blocks from the 23-year-old Metropolitan Opera House), show business people such as George M. Cohan, and businessmen. Completed at a cost of $3.3 million for John Jacob Astor IV, the Knickerbocker boasts pneumatic tubes to deliver messages to each floor of guest rooms, a gold dinner service for 48, and a public display of artworks that include works by Frederick MacMonnies, Frederic Remington, and Maxfield Parrish, whose saucy mural *Old King Cole and His Fiddlers Three* hangs in the hotel's main barroom (it will later be moved to Astor's St. Regis, opened 2 years ago on Fifth Avenue). The Knickerbocker will close in 1921 and be converted into an office building.

The Harmonie Club building is completed at 4 East 60th Street to designs by architect Stanford White of McKim, Mead & White for the 54-year-old German-Jewish social group. The Harmonie dining room will be the first in any men's club to admit women for dinner.

Brooklyn's Crescent Athletic Club building is completed for the 22-year-old club at at the corner of Pierrepont and Clinton streets, opposite the Long Island Historical Society (later the Brooklyn Historical Society). Designed in neo-classical style by Frank Freeman, the structure has 12 levels, with a swimming pool, bowling alley, and rifle range in the basement, a grand hall on the second floor, a double-height oak-paneled dining room on the third, a gym on the top, handball and squash courts, a billiard room, a library, and sleeping rooms on the other floors, and double-height window frames to give it the outward appearance of a much lower building. Membership will reach 2,650 by 1912 (*see* education [St. Anne's], 1966).

Forest Hills is founded in Queens by lawyer-developer Cord Meyer II, who has bought six large farms, totaling about 600 acres. Its proximity to Forest Park and its high rolling terrain have inspired the name (*see* tennis stadium, 1924).

The "hot dog" gets its name by some accounts from a cartoon by Chicago cartoonist Thomas Aloysius "Tad" Dorgan, 29, who shows a dachshund inside a frankfurter bun (*see* Feldman, 1867), but New Haven vendors have reportedly been selling frankfurters from "dog wagons" to students at Yale dorms since 1894. Vendors employed by Harry M. Stevens have been selling frankfurters at the Polo Grounds since

1901, his franks have been called "pigs-in-a-blanket," but Stevens will soon be known as the "hot dog king," and he will eventually gain rights to operate Madison Square Garden's dining room, employing vendors to serve sports fans in the Garden itself.

The Bronx cocktail created at the Waldorf-Astoria Hotel by bartender Johnny Solon is a mixture of gin, sweet and dry vermouth, and orange juice.

Frank G. Shattuck Co. is founded by Schrafft Candy salesman Shattuck to operate retail stores (see 1898). Backed by George Frederick Schrafft and his brother William Frederick, Shattuck has opened a second Herald Square store and restaurant near the southeast corner of 34th Street and will open more; by 1928 there will be 29 Schrafft's restaurants in New York, four in Boston, and one in Syracuse, each with uniformed waitresses—many of them Irish immigrants—serving luncheon and dinner at reasonable prices (see 1925).

1907 The Bureau of Municipal Research founded at New York by sugar baron R. Fulton Cutting aims to inform the public on the facts of government and methods of administration. The Bureau will become the Institute of Public Administration in 1932 and will, among other things, establish a Bureau of Child Hygiene in the city's Department of Health.

The Women's Political Union has its beginnings in the Equality League of Self-Supporting Women founded at New York by suffragist Harriet Eaton Blatch (née Stanton), 51, daughter of the late Elizabeth Cady Stanton. Seeing that more genteel approaches are ineffective, the group (it will change its name next year) stages street parades and uses other means to recruit wage-earning women.

The Colored Orphan Asylum moves to new facilities in Riverdale, where children are housed in small cottages on a campus (see 1867). Founded in 1836, the asylum will be renamed the Riverdale Children's Association in 1944 and be abolished 2 years later in favor of placing the children in foster care.

$ A U.S. economic crisis looms as a result of drains on the money supply by the Russo-Japanese War of 1905, the demands imposed by the rebuilding of San Francisco following last year's earthquake and fire, several large railroad expansion programs, and the fact that a late harvest has tied up farmers' cash. New York Stock Exchange prices suddenly collapse March 14, falling 6.89 points (8.29 percent) in the worst plunge since 1899; President Roosevelt names his postmaster general George B. Cortelyou secretary of the treasury in March; a July 4th address by Princeton University president Woodrow Wilson urges an attack on the illegal manipulations of financiers rather than on corporations, and President Roosevelt attacks "malefactors of great wealth" in a speech August 20.

The Green Point Savings Bank moves into the first building of its own at the corner of Manhattan Avenue and Calyer Street (see 1869; 1931).

Failure of the American Ice Co. in October contributes to giving Wall Street a bad scare (other factors include the failure of the Alexandria Stock Exchange, a run on the British pound following shipment of gold to Egypt, bank failures in Japan, and an antiquated U.S. banking system). Financier J. P. Morgan is called back to New York from an Episcopal church conference in Virginia and acts singlehandedly to avert financial panic following a rush by depositors October 23 to withdraw their money from the city's 23-year-old Knickerbocker Trust and other bank runs that follow. Banker Charles T. Barney has built up deposits at the Knickerbocker Trust from $11 million to $65 million since becoming president in 1898 (see 1884), and reserves have increased from $14 million to $72 million, but Barney resigns and asks that operations be suspended until March of next year; he dies at New York November 14 at age 56 (see 1908).

J. P. Morgan obtains a pledge of $10 million in John D. Rockefeller money from National City Bank president James Stillman, obtains $10 million in specie from the Bank of England (it arrives in October via the new Cunard liner Lusitania), receives support from First National Bank president George Baker and from financiers Edward H. Harriman and Thomas Fortune Ryan, promises Mayor McClellan $30 million at 6 percent interest to keep the city from having to default on some short-term bonds, and locks up leading New York trust company presidents, including Baker, overnight in his new library in East 36th Street until 5 o'clock in the morning of November 4.

President Roosevelt commends J. P. Morgan for his action and permits United States Steel Co. to acquire the financially troubled Tennessee Coal, Iron and Railroad Co. for $35.3 million in U.S. Steel bonds, despite questions as to the legality of the acquisition under the 1890 Sherman Anti-Trust Act (Morgan and John W. "Bet a Million" Gates agreed last year to buy the company, whose iron-ore deposits are second in size only to those of United States Steel). Standard Oil Co. treasurer Oliver Hazard Payne has recommended the acquisition, the president's action November 4 saves the Wall Street brokerage firm of Moore & Schley from collapse, faith is restored, and the stock market recovers to some extent.

Speculator Jesse L. Livermore emerges from Wall Street's financial panic with $3 million (*see* 1906). Now 30, he shorted Union Pacific stock, invested his profits in Anaconda Copper, sold Anaconda short to make another killing, and is hailed as "The Boy Plunger" (*see* 1908).

Wall Street's Dow Jones Industrial Average closes December 31 at 58.75, down from 94.35 at the end of 1906.

The Steinway Tunnel opens to trolley traffic beneath the East River between 42nd Street in Manhattan and Long Island City. Financed originally by piano executive William Steinway, it will be converted to use by subway trains in 1915.

Taximeter cabs appear at New York in May, giving the United States her first successors to hansom cabs (their meters compute fares based on distance traveled and time elapsed; *see* 1897). Local motor enthusiast Harry Nathaniel Allen, 30, has obtained $3 million in backing from friends in Europe and from some of his father's associates in New York, brought bright red Darracq landaulets over from Paris, coined the term *taxicab* (the word combines the taximeter invented in 1891 and the horse-drawn carriage called a cabriolet), founded the New York Taxicab Co., and obtained a license from the city to open taxi stands at hotels, restaurants, railroad stations, steamship piers, and ferry terminals. Other drivers substitute meter-equipped cars for their previously horse-drawn cabs and appropriate the term *taxicab*, but Allen is obliged to open a school for drivers, since there are so few qualified applicants available, and establishes a school for auto mechanics to keep his fleet in repair. The Darracqs have been built for smooth European boulevards and do not stand up to the rough, cobblestoned New York streets; Allen is soon obliged to abandon them in favor of four-cylinder, 14-horsepower gasoline cars, and by the spring of next year he will be operating more than 700 taxicabs, having built a four-story garage, reputedly the first to have floors connected by ramps (*see* 1908).

Manhattan's Fifth Avenue horsecars give way July 30 to double-decker, gasoline-powered motorbuses (*see* Fifth Avenue Transportation Co., 1885); the rest of the city has long since turned to electric trolley cars, Els, and subway cars (*see* 1904; 1932).

The S.S. *Yale* leaves New York for Boston in June and the S.S. *Harvard* leaves September 18 to begin service that will continue making overnight voyages until 1917 (the ships will be moved to the West Coast in the 1920s). The steamship *Commonwealth* goes into service on the Fall River Line (*see* 1894; Cape Cod Canal, 1914).

The Cunard Line's S.S. *Lusitania* arrives from Liverpool at Pier 54 on the North River September 13 on her maiden voyage, leaves for home September 21, and returns in October with specie from the Bank of England to relieve the U.S. financial crisis. Built by John Brown & Co. at Clydebank and named for the Roman province that has long since become Portugal, the 31,550 ton *Lusitania* is 700 feet in length overall with four screws. She can carry 2,000 passengers, a crew of 600, and although slowed by fog on her first voyage averages 23.99 knots per day on her second westward passage, regaining the Blue Riband for Britain (she will soon be averaging 25.65 knots).

The Cunard Line's R.M.S. *Mauretania* arrives from Liverpool at Pier 54 on the North River November 22 on her maiden voyage and averages 26.06 knots per day on her return trip (she clocked 27.04 knots on her trials). Slightly larger than her sister ship *Lusitania*, the 31,938-ton, four-screw liner is 790 feet in length overall, 88 feet wide, 61 feet deep, has six decks, can accommodate 2,335 passengers (560 in first class, 475 in second, 1,300 in third), carries 812 officers and crew, burns 1,000 tons of coal per day, and requires a "black squad" of 324 firemen and trimmers to feed her furnaces (*see* 1910). She will remain in service until 1935, making her final crossing in 1934.

New York is the world's third largest shipping port, surpassed only by London and Liverpool. Cargo valued at roughly $780 million arrives at the port, exports worth $600 million leave.

 Sanitary engineer George Soper tracks down Typhoid Mary in the spring as new cases of the disease appear (*see* 1903). The young daughter of Lincoln Bank president Charles Henry Warren has fallen ill with typhoid fever at the family's Long Island summer home, Soper finds that Mallon has recently left the Warrens' employ, he discovers that cases have cropped up in other households that had employed Mary Mallon, and he confronts her in the kitchen of her newest employers on Park Avenue, demanding a feces sample. She chases him away with a carving fork, the Board of Health sends out five police officers who wrestle her to the floor, she says the Board of Health is just trying to "get credit for protecting the rich," some newspapers take up her cause, but she is placed under quarantine detention on North Brother Island in the East River, and although she will be released in 1910 and employed in other food-preparation jobs, often using assumed names, she will be confined again in 1915 and remain behind bars until her death in 1938.

Harlem Hospital opens April 13 at 506 Lenox Avenue, between 136th and 137th streets, having moved from its original 1887 location in East 120th Street to larger premises with 150 beds. It will develop a full range of medical services, but when it hires some black nurses in 1917 many of its white nurses will resign.

∞ The Glad Tidings Tabernacle is founded by Pentecostal pastor Marie Burgess, 27, who will be joined in 1909 by her husband, Robert Brown, now 35. The tabernacle will become affiliated with the Assemblies of God Church in 1916 and move 6 years later to 325 West 33rd Street, where it will become a Pentecostal center for the entire Northeast, sponsoring missions through various parts of the city. It will later relocate to 416 West 42nd Street.

The College of the City of New York (CCNY) moves some of its offices and classes from its original 1849 location on Lexington Avenue at 23rd Street to a new campus on Hamilton Heights, where a group of fieldstone and terra-cotta buildings has been completed at a cost of $4 million to designs by George B. Post in an area bounded by St. Nicholas Terrace and Amsterdam Avenue between 138th and 140th streets. The campus is at the end of the West Side IRT subway, and stones for its buildings have been taken from the cut excavated for the new subway. The tuition-free, 4-year college has grown to have 1,045 students, and its 3-year preparatory department, with 2,896 pupils and 207 instructors, occupies Townsend Harris Hall on the new campus as well as the college's previous building.

Fire destroys Stuyvesant High School, which will move from East 23rd Street to a Victorian building in East 15th Street on Stuyvesant Square (see 1904). It will admit only boys until 1969, limiting admission to those boys who can pass demanding entrance examinations (see 1992).

Columbia Grammar School moves into a new building at 5 West 93rd Street (see 1764; 1937).

Riverdale Country School opens on a rented country estate above Van Cortlandt Park with four teachers and 12 boys. Albany-born Trinity School and Columbia graduate Frank S. (Sutcliff) Hackett, 30, and his wife, Frances (née Allen), have used $500 in savings to start the school, and it will grow to have 630 students in grades from kindergarten through 12th grade (see 1935).

The *Bronx Home News* begins publication. Born on the Lower East Side, James O'Flaherty, 34, has started the four-page weekly in a wooden shack at the corner of Third Avenue and East 148th Street, mentioning as many Bronxites as he can in every issue and relying on home delivery to boost circulation. The paper will appear twice a week beginning in 1912, thrice beginning in 1914 (see 1919; politics, 1917).

The United Press is founded to compete with the Associated Press started in 1848 and the Hearst International News Service (INS) started last year. The new wire service is created by a merger of Publishers' Press, owned since 1904 by newspaper publisher E. W. Scripps, now 53, and the Scripps-McRae Press Association in which Scripps has been a partner since 1897. Ohio-born journalist Roy (Wilson) Howard, 24, heads UP's New York office and will be UP president in 5 years.

Rube Goldberg starts work with William Randolph Hearst's *New York Evening Journal* to begin a career as cartoonist. San Francisco-born graduate engineer Reuben (Lucius) Goldberg, 24, will have his cartoons syndicated beginning in 1915, he will often show elaborate machines he has devised to perform simple tasks, and his ludicrous inventions will appear for nearly 60 years.

Bell Telephone Laboratories begins operations at 463 West Street as part of Western Electric Co., the Chicago-based manufacturing division of American Telephone & Telegraph Co. In addition to making significant contributions to telephony, its researchers will score major breakthroughs in other forms of communication.

Fiction: *The Trimmed Lamp* and *Heart of the West* (stories) by O. Henry.

Painting: *Forty-Two Kids* by Ohio-born New York painter-lithographer George Wesley Bellows, 25, who gains his first success with a picture of urchins tumbling, swimming, diving, and playing around a New York dock and follows it with *Stag at Sharkey's* inspired by retired prizefighter Tom Sharkey's boxing arena at 127 Columbus Avenue (boxing is still illegal in the city but patrons circumvent the law by joining Sharkey's "club" for the evening, and every handbill promoting a fight bears the words, "Both Members of This Club"); *Laughing Child* by Cincinnati-born New York painter Robert Henri (originally Robert Henry Cozad), 42; *Election Night* by Pennsylvania-born New York painter John French Sloan, 36.

The National Academy of Design rejects paintings by artists William Glackens, cartoonist George Luks (who has worked on "The Yellow Kid"), and realist Everett Shinn, now 31. Influenced by Thomas Eakins of Philadelphia, they have revolted against academicism with encouragement from their mentor Robert Henri, who resigns his membership in the Academy (see 1908).

Sculpture: two heroic granite groups representing New York in Revolutionary War days and New York in its infancy by French-born sculptor Philip Martiny, 49, are installed at the entrance to the Surrogate Court House and Hall of Records at 31 Chambers Street.

 Theater: *The Witching Hour* by Augustus Thomas 4/18 at Hackett's Theater, 212 perfs.; *A Grand Army Man* by David Belasco and others 10/16 at the new Stuyvesant Theater, designed by George Keister at 111-121 West 44th Street, with David Warfield, William Elliott, Denver-born actress Antoinette Perry, 19, 149 perfs. (Perry has been performing since before she was 17 but will give up the stage for 15 years beginning in 1909; the theater will be renamed the Belasco in September 1910).

Actor Richard Mansfield dies at New London, Conn., August 30 at age 53.

The Barnum & Bailey Circus created in 1881 becomes the Ringling Bros. Barnum & Bailey Circus. Albert C. Ringling, 55, and his brothers Otto, 49, Alfred T., 45, Charles, 44, and John, 41, have purchased The Greatest Show on Earth from the widow of the late James A. Bailey and will continue touring it around the country. Abraham Hummel of the law firm Howe & Hummel has lobbied for the circus (and vaudeville producers) against a bill that would have banned wearing tights in public.

Film: Edwin S. Porter's *Rescued from an Eagle's Nest* with Kentucky-born actor D. W. (David Llewlyn Wark) Griffith, 32, who works briefly for the Thomas A. Edison studio at Orange, N.J., but will become a director himself next year.

 Broadway musicals: *The Honeymooners* 6/3 at the Aerial Gardens, with George M. Cohan and his parents (Jerry J. and Helen F.), music and lyrics by Cohan, 72 perfs.; *The Follies of 1907* 7/18 at the Jardin de Paris on the roof of the New York Theater, with 50 "Anna Held Girls" in an extravaganza staged by Florenz Ziegfeld, now 38, who married comedienne Anna Held 10 years ago. She writes lyrics to Vincent Scotto's song "It's Delightful to Be Married (The Parisian Model)," show girls appear in a swimming pool in a simulated motion picture sequence, and opulent new editions will appear each year until 1931

(with the exceptions of 1926, 1928, and 1929) featuring chorus lines composed of beautiful *Follies* girls chosen with an eye to slenderness of figure as Ziegfeld creates a new ideal to replace the ample figure now in vogue, 70 perfs.; *A Yankee Tourist* 8/12 at the Astor Theater, with Kansas City-born comedian Wallace Beery, 22, Auburn, N.Y.-born singer Raymond Hitchcock, 40, music by Alfred G. Robyn, William Jerome, and Jean Schwartz, lyrics by Wallace Irwin based on Richard Harding Davis's novel *The Galloper*, 103 perfs.; *The Girl Behind the Counter* 10/1 at the Herald Square Theater, with Connie Ediss, Louise Dresser, Lew Fields, Vernon Castle, music and lyrics by Howard Talbot and Arthur Anderson, 260 perfs.; *The Talk of the Town* 12/3 at the Knickerbocker Theater, with Victor Moore, music and lyrics by George M. Cohan, songs that include "When a Fellow's on the Level with a Girl That's on the Square," 157 perfs.

Popular songs: "Marie of Sunny Italy" by New York pianist M. "Nick" Nicholson, lyrics by Siberian-born New York singing waiter-songwriter Irving Berlin (originally Israel Baline), whose last name has been misprinted on the sheet music that will earn Berlin 37¢ in royalties. He went to work 5 years ago as a waiter at the Pelham Café, 12 Pell Street, in Chinatown (his compatriot Mike Sutter ran the place), making $7 per week plus whatever tips he could pick up from the sawdust on the floor, and turns 19 just 3 days after the song is published; "Take Me Back to New York Town" by Harry Von Tilzer, lyrics by Andrew B. Sterling.

Texas-born ragtime pioneer Scott Joplin, 38, opens an office at 128 West 29th Street to compose and arrange music.

 The April 18 marriage of Standard Oil partner William Rockefeller's daughter Geraldine, 23, to Remington Arms heir Marcellus Hartley Dodge, now 26, unites two of America's richest families. Young Dodge has inherited $60 million; his bride is even richer (see real estate, 1923).

Wilson Mizner's wife, Mary, obtains a divorce and receives court permission to adopt her former name, Mrs. Charles T. Yerkes (see 1906). Mizner returns from Nevada and for a few months takes over the management of a shady Times Square hotel, the Rand, in West 49th Street, where gongs ring on all floors at 3 o'clock in the morning to alert guests (mostly chorus girls, gigolos, and the like) that they may wish to return to their own rooms. Wilson's older brother Addison, now 35, designs a fancy bar for the hotel, whose lobby has a fountain. A newspaper reports October 8 that Wilson Mizner has left: "The change in the management of the hotel was such an interesting topic," it continues, "that half the chorus girls missed their cues last night."

Coney Island's Drop the Dips roller coaster opens June 6. Carpenter Christopher Feucht has built it from a design he saw in his dentist's office, its steep drops and sharp curves delight riders, and the first roller-coaster lap bar gives them more protection than the chains or straps used on earlier rides.

Fire damages Coney Island's 10-year-old Steeplechase Park, but founder George C. Tilyou rebuilds, adding a steel-and-glass structure covering 2.83 acres that enables him to stay open even on rainy days. He will also build the world's largest outdoor saltwater swimming pool—90 feet wide, 270 feet long—and although another fire will destroy part of his amusement park it will continue operating until 1964, outliving all other Coney Island attractions.

The 8-year-old Princeton Club gives up its quarters at 34th Street and Fifth Avenue and takes over the former Stanford White residence at the corner of Gramercy Park North and Lexington Avenue (see 1922).

Times Square's New Year's Eve celebration includes for the first time a lighted ball that drops at midnight from the top of the 3-year-old Times Tower, beginning a tradition that will continue even after the *Times* moves to larger quarters in West 43rd Street in 1913 and the Tower changes hands (see real estate, 1913).

Lawyer Abraham Hummel loses his appeal and is disbarred and sentenced to a 1-year prison term on Blackwell's Island (the firm of Howe & Hummel is terminated; see 1905). He has made a deal with District Attorney William Travers Jerome by helping him in his case against millionaire murderer Harry K. Thaw, producing an affidavit signed by Evelyn Nesbit stating that her husband once told her in Paris that he intended to kill Stanford White someday; Jerome has used the document to prove intent and premeditation on Thaw's part, and Hummel has testified to the document's authenticity. Bachelor Hummel has a box at the Metropolitan Opera, front-row seats for every Broadway opening, and summer homes at Saratoga and Long Branch, N.J.; widely known as "Little Abe, light of the Tenderloin, first lord of the racetrack, and friend to all Broadway," he throws the biggest party of his life at his West 73rd Street brownstone on the evening of March 7 (a cordon of police surrounds the block to prevent his escape) and goes to Blackwell's Island the next morning. His assistants David May and Isaac Jacobson start the firm of May and Jacobson that will prosper until the early 1930s.

The trial of architect Stanford White's murderer Harry K. Thaw ends in a mistrial April 13 after a 2-month court battle in which he has testified, among other things, that the walls of his law firm Howe & Hummel are covered with pictures of stage beauties affectionately inscribed to the late William F. Howe (Hummel's office contains an iron brazier used chiefly to burn legal papers in the presence of blackmail victims, who have come to the office to make payoffs) (see 1906). Thaw awaited trial for 9 months, imprisoned in the Tombs but having his meals catered by Delmonico's. New York-born lawyer Charles A. (Anderson) Dana, 25, has gained national attention in his role as assistant prosecutor, but the court has defined insanity as being "unable to know the nature and quality of the act" or "unable to know that it was wrong," Thaw's behavior in the courtroom has raised doubts about his mental state, and the jury has voted seven to five for conviction after 47 hours of deliberation, some of the jurors being impressed by the "unwritten law" favoring a husband who defends his wife's honor (see 1909).

A new Customs House is completed on the south side of Bowling Green to designs by Ohio-born architect Cass Gilbert, 47.

The 22-story, $2 million West Street Building is completed at 90 West Street, between Albany and Cedar streets, to designs by Cass Gilbert, who remarked in 1900 that a skyscraper was "a machine that makes the land pay;" his structure has an exterior sheath of limestone and cast terra cotta with a six-story mansard roof and dormered pinnacle.

The Colony Club building opens formally March 11 at 120 Madison Avenue (see 1903). Designed by the late Stanford White, it has been brightly and cheerfully decorated by socialite Elsie de Wolfe, now 41, who ended her stage career 2 years ago after playing against such actors as John Drew (Jr.). A trendsetter who has presided since 1887 over a salon in the 62-year-old house at 122 East 17th Street that she shares with playwright's agent Elizabeth Marbury, de Wolfe will inaugurate the fashion of wearing little white gloves. The club now has 498 members, and by next year will have 819 (see 1923).

The Edward S. Harkness town house is completed for the Standard Oil heir and his wife, Rebekah, at 1 East 75th Street, southeast corner Fifth Avenue, to designs by Hale & Rogers.

The Fifth Avenue Association is founded to keep loft and factory buildings from being built uptown and limit construction of other buildings on the avenue to clubs, hotels, private residences, luxury shops, and fine restaurants.

The Henry Phipps houses go up west of Amsterdam Avenue between 63rd and 64th streets, where Philadelphia-born steel magnate-philanthropist Phipps has financed construction of model six-story walk-up working-class apartments in the area known as San Juan Hill. Now 67, Phipps is a former scale manufacturer who founded Union Iron Mills in partnership with Andrew Carnegie in 1867; his nonprofit foundation has also financed an East 31st Street tenement designed by Grosvenor Atterbury (*see* 1911).

The Prasada apartment house is completed at 50 Central Park West, southwest corner 65th Street. Designed for developer Samuel B. Haines by architect Charles Romeyn in a version of Second Empire style, the 12-story building has an inside central court, three stained-glass skylights over the lobby, and three apartments per floor, each with eight to 12 rooms and a long interior hall. None of the bedrooms has a private bath, and many rooms have sinks inside closets; rents range between $190 and $300 per month.

The Langham apartment house is completed at 135 Central Park West, between 73rd and 74th streets, just north of the 21-year-old Dakota. Clinton & Russell has designed the 12-story building, whose four apartments per floor rent for $375 per month and more. Each flat has a built-in wall safe, a built-in vacuum system with connections in the wall, but no refrigerator (a central refrigeration system is used instead). The lobby is ornate, and a conveyor system carries mail directly to each apartment.

The Hendrik Hudson apartment house is completed at 380 Riverside Avenue (later Riverside Drive), between Cathedral Parkway and 111th Street (a Broadway wing will be added next year). Designed by William L. Rouse in Italianate style, the eight-story, L-shaped structure has 72 eight-room/two-bath apartments (rents: $125 to $250 per month), billiard room, barber, hairdresser, and basement café.

Saint Paul's Chapel is completed at Columbia University to Northern Italian Renaissance designs by architects John Mead Howells and I. N. Phelps Stokes (Stokes's aunts Olivia and Caroline Phelps Stokes have donated the chapel in memory of their parents).

Architect William Hamilton Russell of Clinton & Russell dies at Lyons, France, July 23 at age 51.

The Plaza Hotel opens October 1 on the Grand Army Plaza just south of Central Park, a site formerly occupied by the Alfred Gwynne Vanderbilt mansion. Henry Janeway Hardenbergh has designed the 18-story, $12 million "home hotel" in the French Renaissance Beaux-Arts style he used for the Waldorf of 1893, the Astor House of 1897, and the Astor of 1904, giving it a three-story marble base, ten stories sheathed in white-brick, balustrade balconies, a massive cornice, and a five-story mansard slate roof with dormers, gables, and a copper crest that has already begun to turn green. Single rooms fetch as much as $25 per night. The 753-room hotel's main entrance will be moved in 1921 from Central Park South to the east side of the building.

Cornelius Vanderbilt II and his wife, Alice, occupy a colossal red-brick and white stone château just south of the new Plaza Hotel; staffed with 30 servants, their mansion will survive until 1927 (*see* retailers [Bergdorf Goodman], 1928).

The New Croton Dam (Cornell Dam) is completed to enlarge the capacity of the lake created by the dam used since 1842 (*see* 1890). Built of granite from the Cornell Quarry east of Peekskill, its waters cover the old dam except at times when reservoir levels are low and the old dam's ramparts are visible.

The Bronx River Commission established by the state legislature at Albany will try to clean up the polluted river (whose waters are killing animals in

The Plaza Hotel was an architectural marvel with Edwardian charms. LIBRARY OF CONGRESS

the Bronx Zoo), acquire 797 acres for Westchester's first parkland, and in a joint undertaking between New York City and Westchester County build the Bronx River Parkway through the Parkland (*see* transportation, 1925).

 The Fulton Fish Market moves into a new building on the East River (*see* 1880; 1939).

 The American Sugar Refining trust is found to have defrauded the government out of import duties (*see* 1899). Several company officials are convicted, and more than $4 million is recovered. American Sugar Co. president H. O. Havemeyer goes out pheasant hunting with his son Horace on his private shooting preserves after Thanksgiving dinner at his Commack, L.I., estate, comes down with acute indigestion, and dies in the large house December 4 at age 60.

 The new Plaza Hotel has a large kitchen, a bakery, and dining rooms that will remain popular for more than 90 years. Most of the city's luxury apartment houses have their own dining rooms.

The Sons of the American Revolution restore Fraunces Tavern at 54 Pearl Street, southeast corner Broad Street, to designs by architect William H. (Howard) Mesereau, a member of the society who has rebuilt the place almost from scratch with a museum upstairs.

An immigration act passed by Congress February 20 excludes undesirables, raises the head tax on arrivals to $4, and creates a commission to investigate. Nearly 1.29 million immigrants enter the United States, a new record that will not be surpassed. The nation has 70 immigrant receiving stations, but 90 percent of arrivals come through Ellis Island, built to accommodate fewer than 250,000 per year and now woefully overcrowded.

1908 President Roosevelt adheres to the tradition against a third term. Republicans nominate Roosevelt's secretary of war William Howard Taft, 50, of Cincinnati, who has served as governor of the Philippines, quelled a potential rebellion in Cuba, and organized construction of the Panama Canal. He easily defeats his Democratic rival, William Jennings Bryan (who runs for the third and last time), winning 321 electoral votes to 162 for the "Great Commoner," but Taft has little interest in being president and will antagonize Roosevelt by allowing Wall Street and business interests to control his administration (*see* 1912).

Gov. Hughes wins reelection, defeating Lt. Gov. Lewis Stuyvesant Chanler, 41 (who has had his brother John Armstrong Chanler committed to an insane asylum). The final tally shows 804,651 votes for Hughes, 735,189 for Democrat Chanler.

President-elect Taft arrives at Brooklyn's Fort Greene Park November 14 to dedicate the 145-foot fluted granite Prison Ship Martyrs' Monument, designed by the late Stanford White to honor the 11,000 patriots who died on overcrowded British prison ships anchored in Wallabout Bay for 6 years during the American Revolution.

 New York women socialists demonstrate for equal rights and better working conditions March 8 to commemorate the demonstration of March 8, 1857. They demand voting rights and an end to sweatshops and child labor.

Triangle Waist Co. owners Max Blanck and Isaac Harris establish a company union in a move to stymie organizing efforts by the 8-year-old International Ladies' Garment Workers' Union. Blanck and Harris charge their employees for needles and other supplies, for their clothing lockers, even for the chairs they use. About 100 Triangle workers meet in secret with officers of the ILGWU and the United Hebrew Trades union, some of them are sacked a few days later (Blanck and Harris say poor business has obliged them to lay off the workers, but they quickly advertise for more seamstresses), Local 25 of the ILGWU calls a strike against the company, Blanck and Harris employ thugs to beat up male strikers and hire prostitutes to join with the young women on the picket line, a magistrate tells the workers, "You are on strike against God!" but some society women and enlightened clergymen lend support, and Triangle reaches a compromise with the workers while remaining a nonunion shop (*see* fire, 1911).

An account of a Springfield, Ill., race riot by Louisville, Ky.-born New York journalist William English Walling, 30, is published September 3 in the liberal weekly The *Independent* under the title "Race War in the North." Eight people have been left dead, the populace shows no remorse, some whites go so far as to demand disenfranchisement as a way to keep blacks "in their place," and Walling's article calls for a revival of abolitionist fervor to resist any repetition of the incident. He describes the plight of U.S. blacks, asks, "What large and powerful body of citizens is ready to come to their aid?" He receives a response from Brooklyn-born social worker Mary White Ovington, 43 (*see* NAACP, 1909).

The 4-year-old National Child Labor Committee hires Oshkosh, Wis.-born Ethical Culture Society botany and nature teacher Lewis W. (Wickes) Hine,

34, as an investigative photographer to document working conditions of children nationwide. The 1900 census estimated that more than 2 million children between the ages of 10 and 15 were working in factories, mines, and in the streets; Hine photographed immigrants arriving at Ellis Island 3 years ago, he quits his teaching job, and he will be the committee's staff photographer until 1921, taking hundreds of pictures and obtaining information about his subjects.

$ Retired securities broker-philanthropist Morris K. Jesup dies at New York January 12 at age 77 (see Museum of Natural History, 1877). President of the city's Chamber of Commerce from 1899 until last year, Jesup has lived at 197 Madison Avenue.

U.S. banks close as the economic depression continues. Westinghouse Electric Co. goes bankrupt, but Knickerbocker Trust Co. reopens in March (see 1907), it pays its depositors in full with 6 percent interest for the time that the bank was closed, and no irregularities are revealed.

Thomas J. Watson makes an easel presentation to National Cash Register salesmen and writes the word "THINK" at the head of every sheet of paper (see 1903). NCR president J. H. Patterson sees the presentation and orders "THINK" signs to be made up for every NCR office (see IBM, 1924).

Speculator Jesse L. Livermore tries to corner the cotton market, loses $900,000, but racks up $1 million in stock market profits within a few days (see 1907). Livermore will file for bankruptcy in 1915 but repay all his creditors in full 2 years later (see 1925).

New York City's Progress Toward Bankruptcy by a former official of the comptroller's office notes that the city's population has increased by 35 percent since 1898 from 3.27 to 4.42 million while the cost of servicing the city's debt has risen 189 percent, and the cost of running the Board of City Records by 207 percent. The College of the City of New York requires an appropriation 182 percent higher than in 1898, and library appropriations have climbed by 425 percent.

Wall Street's Dow Jones Industrial Average closes December 30 at 86.15, up from 58.75 at the end of 1907.

An aerial walkway bridge is completed across East 9th Street to connect John Wanamaker's massive 2-year-old department store with the old cast-iron A. T. Stewart store that Wanamaker took over in 1896. He calls it "the bridge of progress."

The Dobbs hat-store chain founded by New York merchant John J. Cavanaugh, 45, will grow to have 28 shops. Cavanaugh will merge with the Knox Co. in 1932 to create Hat Corp. of America.

The New York Police Department takes over jurisdiction of city traffic from the Board of Aldermen. Police officers control traffic with whistles (one blast of the whistle indicates that north-south traffic may proceed, two blasts that east-west traffic may go, and three blasts that everyone must stop). North-south traffic has the right of way (see 1909).

Riverside Avenue is renamed Riverside Drive. Extending northward from 72nd Street, it has become lined with private houses and apartment buildings, but icy winds off the river can make the Drive uncomfortable in winter, trains carrying cattle and hogs move down the New York Central tracks near the river, and animal smells waft into Riverside Drive windows on warm days and nights.

Taxicab pioneer Harry Nathaniel Allen gives a Christmas Day party for his taxi drivers, mechanics, and other employees, whose total number has grown to number 1,500, and hands out gold watches to all who have remained with him from the start (see 1907); he announces that he has inaugurated a generous pension plan, but he is notified within a few hours that the employees have decided to strike over the issue of organizing a local cabdrivers' union, opposed by Allen lest it be dominated by horse hackmen who have fought the introduction of taxicabs (see 1909).

Ferry traffic reaches its peak, with dozens of ferries making 201 million passenger trips across the East and North (Hudson) rivers (see East River bridges, 1909).

Two subway tunnels open to rail traffic February 25. The Hudson and Manhattan Railway Co.'s McAdoo Tunnel goes under the Hudson River to Hoboken (see 1906), another tunnel connects Bowling Green in lower Manhattan with Brooklyn's Joralemon Street across the East River. President Roosevelt at Washington, D.C., presses a button that turns on the electric power for the line at midnight, hundreds of people have been waiting to board the train at Manhattan's 19th Street station, the 100,000 passengers who ride the train on its first day include financier Edward Harriman and railroad magnate Cornelius Vanderbilt II, and they appreciate the fact that the 10-minute trip is three times faster than the Hoboken Ferry.

The 4-year-old IRT Broadway subway line is extended to Kingsbridge in the Bronx.

The Brooklyn Rapid Transit Co. (BRT) opens an elevated railway line across the 5-year-old Williamsburg Bridge as an alternative to the line over the Brooklyn Bridge. By the 1920s the bridge will be carrying 500,000 people per day to Manhattan, but it will later be converted to use primarily for motorcars and will be able to carry only half that many people per day by car and rail combined.

Episcopal Bishop Henry Codman Potter dies at Cooperstown July 21 at age 74.

Henry Fairfield Osborn becomes the fourth president of the American Museum of Natural History following the death of Morris K. Jesup (see 1891). Osborn is also president of the New York Zoological Society; now 50, he will head the museum until 1933, promoting expeditions to the farthest reaches of the world in search of fossil remains that can be shown in the massive exhibition halls whose construction he will oversee.

The 105-year-old New-York Historical Society moves into a blocklong building on Central Park West between 76th and 77th streets (see 1827; art, 1863). The New York Herald deplored the neglect and inaccessibility of much of the Society's holdings in an editorial published 9 years ago. Designed by York & Sawyer to resemble a Parisian bibliothèque, and built in part with a gift of about $225,000 from West Cambridge, Mass.-born American News Co. cofounder Henry Dexter, 95, the Society's elegant new home houses a museum, library, and auditorium. Dexter has had a pamphlet distributed stating that he has had the building erected in memory of his only son Orrando Perry Dexter, but trustees halt distribution, claiming that the society had supplied the site and put some $171,000 into construction of the building, so Dexter had no right to claim full credit. The auditorium will be named Henry Dexter Hall, and a member will speak out at a meeting in 1917 to say that the Society has become an "old men's club" with little appeal or service to the public (see 1938).

The New York Chinese Public School (Niuye Huaqiao Gongh Xuexio) opens to teach Chinese children the basics of their native language and culture.

Canadian book publisher George H. Doran, 39, moves to New York. He founded a company at Toronto last year (see Doubleday, Doran, 1927).

Nonfiction: Old Chinatown by Will Irwin; Fifty Years in Wall Street by financier Henry Clews, now 74, whose brokerage house failed on the second day of the panic of 1873; True Stories of Crime from the District Attorney's Office by Arthur Train.

Fiction: The Gentle Grafter and The Voice of the City: Further Stories of the Four Million by O. Henry, who has his young reporter protagonist say in the title story of his latter book, "Other cities have voices, and New York . . . had better not hand me a cigar and say, 'Old man, I can't talk for publication.'"

Painting: North River by George Bellows; Harmony in Red by French painter Henri Matisse, whose work is exhibited at New York's Stieglitz-Photo-Secession 291 Gallery.

The Ashcan School of U.S. realist art has its beginnings in a February exhibition at New York's Macbeth Galleries of work by William Glackens, George Luks, John Sloan, and Everett Shinn, who are joined by symbolist Arthur B. Davies, impressionist Ernest Lawson, and Postimpressionist Maurice Prendergast. Their works make lavish use of black and create a sensation, drawing such crowds that the police are called in to maintain order. Critic James Gibbons Huneker labels them "The Eight," less sympathetic critics call them "the apostles of ugliness" or "the revolutionary black gang;" a critic in the 1930s will label them the Ashcan School.

Sculpture: a bronze statue of Alexander Hamilton by William Ordway Partridge, 47, is installed in front of Hamilton Hall on the campus of Columbia University.

Theater: Salomy Jane by Paul Armstrong (who has adapted the Bret Harte story "Salomy Jane's Kiss") 1/19 at the Liberty Theater, 122 perfs.; The Man from Home by Indiana-born novelist-playwright Booth Tarkington, 39, and Harry Leon Wilson 8/17 at the Astor Theater, with William Hodge, 496 perfs.; Wildfire 9/7 at the Liberty Theater, with Lillian Russell, Kansas City-born actor Ernest Truex, 18, in a racetrack melodrama, 64 perfs.; Via Wireless by Paul Armstrong and Winchell Smith 11/2 at the Liberty Theater, 88 perfs.; Salvation Nell by Chicago-born playwright Edward (Brewster) Sheldon, 22, 11/17 at the Hackett Theater, with Minnie Maddern Fiske, 71 perfs. (Sheldon was George Pierce Baker's star student at Harvard's 47 Workshop); The Patriot by J. Hartley Manners and William Collier 11/23 at the Garrick Theater, with Collier, 160 perfs.; The Nigger by Edward Sheldon 12/4 at the New Theater, in repertory; What Every Woman Knows by English playwright James M. Barrie, 48, 12/23 at the Empire Theater, with Maude Adams in the U.S. premiere of a comedy that opened earlier in the year at London, 198 perfs.

Broadway musicals: The Three Twins 6/15 at the Herald Square Theater, with music by Karl Hoschna, book and lyrics by Cleveland-born playwright Otto (Abels) Hauerbach (later Harbach), 35, songs that include "Cuddle Up a Little Closer," 288 perfs.; *The* (Ziegfeld) *Follies* 6/15 at the Jardin de Paris, with Joliet, Ill.-born contralto Nora Bayes (originally Dora Goldberg), 28, book and lyrics mostly by Harry B. Smith, music by Maurice Levi and others, songs that include "Shine On, Harvest Moon" by Nora Bayes, lyrics by her husband, Jack Norworth, 120 perfs.; *The Man Who Owns Broadway* 10/11 at the New York Theater, with Raymond Hitchcock, book by George M. Cohan, 128 perfs.

Vaudevillian Tony Pastor dies at his Elmhurst, L.I., home August 26 at age 76. The theater he has owned in 14th Street since 1881 will not survive.

Opera: impresario Oscar Hammerstein announces March 30 that he has signed Italian coloratura soprano Luisa Tettrazini, 36, to a 5-year contract. She had her first big success last year singing the role of Violetta in the 1853 Verdi opera *La Traviata*.

The Metropolitan Opera House hires Giulio Gatti-Casazza, 40, from Milan's Teatro alla Scala. He will mastermind the Met until 1935, raising it to new heights of artistic and financial success.

The Brooklyn Academy of Music opens November 4 on Lafayette Avenue between Ashland Place and St. Felix Street, replacing a structure that opened in 1861.

Chicago-born violin prodigy Albert Spalding, 19, makes his New York debut at Carnegie Hall with the New York Symphony Orchestra under the direction of Walter Damrosch. Son of sporting-goods manufacturer Albert Goodwill Spalding, now 57, the younger Spalding began his violin studies at age 7 and has pursued his studies in Europe.

Popular songs: "The City Where Nobody Cares" by Charles K. Harris; "Take Me Out to the Ball Game" by Indianapolis-born composer Albert von Tilzer, 30 (younger brother of Harry), lyrics by Jack Norworth that will make it the national anthem of baseball (and help popularize the confection Cracker Jack introduced in 1896).

The West Side Tennis Club moves from Morningside Heights to 238th Street and Broadway, renting two full city blocks (*see* 1902). The club installs 12 grass courts, 15 clay courts, and erects a two-story clubhouse (*see* Forest Hills, 1924).

A bathhouse designed by Stoughton & Stoughton opens in John Jay Park, on the east side of Avenue A (later York Avenue) between 76th and 78th streets.

Mrs. Astor dies of heart disease at New York October 30 at age 78. "Many people think I could have done a great deal in making New York society as democratic as it is in London and open to anyone of intellectual attainments, as it is over there," she has told a reporter, "but one can only do one's best under the conditions. We have to be more exclusive in New York because in America there is no authority in society. Each woman is for herself in trying to outdo the others in lavish display and mad extravagance."

The Sullivan Ordinance enacted by the Board of Aldermen January 21 forbids women to smoke in any public place. One Katie Mulcahey is arrested for lighting up a cigarette January 22 and says in night court, "I've got as much right to smoke as you have. I never heard of this new law and I don't want to hear about it. No man shall dictate to me." But when she cannot pay a $5 fine she is sent to jail. A Columbia University professor declares February 28 that the deleterious effects of tobacco are greatly exaggerated.

Lawyer Abraham Hummel is released from Blackwell's Island in early March after his 1-year incarceration (*see* 1907), sails for London a week later on the S.S. *Lusitania*, and will live abroad in luxury for the rest of his life.

Slovak-born lawyer Max (David) Steuer, 37, gains prominence by winning acquittal for New York-born comic actor Raymond Hitchcock, 42, who has been indicted for a statutory offense. Steuer has previously secured the conviction of a city police inspector charged with brutality and defended by Howe & Hummell.

Architect Leopold Eidlitz dies at his 309 West 89th Street home March 22 at age 84.

The 46-story Singer Tower is completed at 149 Broadway to designs by Ernest Flagg. Built for the Singer Manufacturing Co. on a site bounded by Liberty, Church, and Cortlandt streets and Broadway, it has 312,440 square feet of floor space, rises 612 feet, and will be the world's tallest office building in terms of usable floor space until 1913 (visitors pay 50¢ to ride to the observation balcony until the owners close it to thwart would-be suicides). The structure towers over the financial district and draws harsh criticism from people who say that buildings this high will reduce the availability of light and air (*see* 1915), but by the time the tower is demolished in 1968 it will seem relatively small.

The 14-year-old Provident Loan Society of New York moves into a new headquarters building at 346 Fourth Avenue, northwest corner 25th Street. Renwick, Aspinwall & Tucker has designed the two-story structure for the nonprofit corporation's growing pawnshop operation.

Two 14-story co-operative studio apartment buildings are completed at 130 and 140 West 57th Street, between Sixth and Seventh avenues. Designed by Pollard & Steinem for a syndicate of artists, the units have double-height rooms; residents soon include novelist William Dean Howells and painter Childe Hassam (some of whose oils will feature the building's trapezoidal windows).

The Gainsborough Studios open at 222 Central Park South, between Seventh Avenue and Columbus Circle. Designed by architect Charles W. Buckham, ostensibly for artists and would-be artists, its 14 duplex co-op apartments face north, overlooking Central Park (its 25 simplex apartments face south and rent initially for $125 per month). A ladies' reception room is available to tenants.

An elaborately façaded apartment building is completed at 45 East 66th Stret, northeast corner Madison Avenue, on a site formerly occupied by All Souls Church. Designed by Harde & Short for developer Charles F. Rogers, the 10-story structure has just two 12- to 13-room wood-paneled apartments per floor; a central court provides air and light, its multipaned windows are framed in white terra cotta and overhung with Gothic ornamentation, and its entrance at 777 Madison Avenue will be moved in 1929 to 45 East 66th Street as ground-floor Madison Avenue apartments are turned into retail shops.

The Kenilworth apartment house is completed at 151 Central Park West, northwest corner 75th Street, to designs by Ralph S. Townsend of Townsend, Steinle & Haskell.

The 12-story 863 Park Avenue co-operative apartment house is completed at the northwest corner of 77th Street. Designed by Pollard & Steinam for developer William J. Taylor, it has six duplexes on its Park Avenue side, 12 simplexes on the end toward Lexington Avenue.

The Apthorp apartment house opens in the fall on the west side of Broadway between 78th and 79th streets with rents ranging up to $460 per month (two-thirds of the apartments have been rented by opening day). Designed by Clinton & Russell, it stands on the site of the old Vandenheuvel mansion, erected in 1792 and converted into a hotel in 1833 (see 1783). Landowner William Waldorf Astor has had the Apthorp constructed with a subterranean carriage drive (his late father's 1860 investment of $16,875 has grown to have a value of about $10 mil-

lion). The building has a bank, pharmacy, and several doctors' offices on its ground floor, and five duplex apartments to provide living quarters and professional offices for physicians. Apartments open off four elevator halls and have glass-paneled French doors throughout, and the building has its own refrigeration system. On the third floor are 12 apartments ranging in size from six rooms with bath up to nine rooms with three baths; the fourth to eleventh floors have 11 apartments each, making a total of 104. Servants' quarters and guest rooms occupy the 12th floor, which has a laundry room with 140 tubs, two large drying rooms with steam dryers, and an open area for clotheslines. On the 78th and 79th street sides there are shaded promenades above the 12th floor, and the formal garden in the courtyard has exotic plants, two fountains, benches, and lighting fixtures.

The 12-story Clarendon apartment house opens at 137 Riverside Drive (southeast corner 86th Street). Designed by Charles E. Birge, its top three floors have been leased by publisher William Randolph Hearst, whose triplex contains more than 30 rooms and occupies nearly three-quarters of an acre, not counting its roof garden (see 1913).

The Graham Court apartment house erected by William Waldorf Astor at Seventh Avenue and 116th Street will be called "the Apthorp of Harlem." Designed by Clinton & Russell with huge rooms, 14-foot ceilings, and fireplaces, the Italian Renaissance building has a large inner courtyard like that of the Apthorp 37 blocks to the south.

Franklin and Eleanor Roosevelt move into a new house at 47 East 65th Street, between Madison and Park avenues (see everyday life, 1905). Franklin's mother bought and demolished two houses last year, hired architect Charles A. Platt, and arranged with him to have two houses, one for herself (at 49 East 65th Street), with connections between the two so that the dining and drawing rooms on the first and second floors may be combined for entertaining. (Eleanor will later recall that she was "never quite sure" when her mother-in-law "would appear, day or night." Sara Roosevelt will live until 1941; her son will sell the twin houses in 1942.)

A mansion for German-born Kuhn, Loeb & Co. banker Felix M. (Moritz) Warburg, 37, and his wife, Frieda, is completed in Renaissance château style at 1109 Fifth Avenue, northeast corner 92nd Street. Architect C. P. H. Gilbert has designed the residence that will become the Jewish Museum in 1947.

A fire in a picture-frame factory at 215 Canal Street February 14 brings out the crew of Truck 8, Deputy Chief Charles W. "Big-Hearted Charley" Kruger leads his men through the building's smoke-filled cellar, a rotten floor gives way, and the 300-pound Kruger drowns in eight feet of water at age 54 (*see* memorial, 1913).

1909 The centennial of Abraham Lincoln's birth February 12 produces a New York celebration that brings out a million participants; ceremonies are held at the Cooper Union in Astor Place, where Lincoln made a memorable speech in 1860, and the Republican Club hears an address by Tuskegee Institute founder Booker T. Washington, who was born a slave in April 1856.

Albany lawyer Learned Hand, 37, is appointed U.S. judge for the Southern District of New York, a position he will hold until 1924, when he will be named to the Federal Court of Appeals for the Second District.

The city celebrates the 300th anniversary of Henry Hudson's discovery of the river that bears his name September 25 with a parade of 1,595 merchant, war, and pleasure vessels up the river—the largest multinational fleet ever assembled in one place. Ships of Argentina, Britain, France, Germany, Italy, Mexico, the Netherlands, and the United States are represented in tercentenary festivities that continue until October 11 with a series of Army and Navy parades, historical pageants, carnivals, and a display of fireworks larger than any before seen in New York.

Workers and humanitarians demonstrated against use of child labor. LIBRARY OF CONGRESS

Light bulbs illuminate bridges, prominent buildings, and monuments such as the Washington Arch to mark the occasion.

The city's first Columbus Day parade steps off October 12 (*see* 1892). The state legislature at Albany has made the day a legal holiday, and the Italian government has sent two cruisers to New York Harbor to join in the festivities, but Spaniards will insist that Christopher Columbus was not Italian and will hold their own parades.

State supreme court justice William Jay Gaynor, 61, wins the mayoralty election on the Democratic Party ticket, defeating Fusion Party candidate Otto T. Bannard and Independent Party candidate William Randolph Hearst, whose second attempt fares worse than his first. Supported by Tammany Hall boss Charles F. Murphy and Wall Street speculator Bernard M. Baruch, Judge Gaynor garners 250,378 votes as compared to Bannard's 177,929, and Hearst's 154,187 (Hearst will not make another try). Charles S. Whitman, now 41, is elected Manhattan district attorney.

The Honest Ballot Association is founded by civic leaders who include former president Theodore Roosevelt in response to reports of widespread election fraud. The association will work to have voting machines used in place of paper ballots and support other measures to ensure honest elections, supervising balloting for corporations, unions, and other organizations as well as political vote counting.

The NAACP (National Association for the Advancement of Colored People) is founded at New York following a January meeting attended by social worker Mary White Ovington (*see* 1908). She joins with W. E. Walling; union leader Leonora O'Reilly, now 38; social worker Henry Moskowitz, now 29; Columbia University comparative language teacher Joel E. Spingarn, now 34; *New York Evening Post* publisher Oswald Garrison Villard, now 36; Unitarian minister John Haynes Holmes, 29; and others in "a revival of the Abolitionist spirit," and the association holds its first conference May 30. The new organization is headed by W. E. B. Du Bois and supported by Chicago social worker Jane Addams, educator John Dewey, journalist Lincoln Steffens, Rabbi Stephen Wise, 35, and 49 others, including six blacks (*see* 1910).

Police break up a lecture by Emma Goldman May 23 (*see* 1906). A police detective has tried to stop her, charging that she has "wandered away" from her announced subject ("Modern Drama, the Strongest Disseminator of Radical Thought") by talking about

Joan of Arc and other martyrs, members of the audience have knocked over tables and chairs, the detective has rounded up reinforcements, but Goldman denies that she has advocated violence. The authorities will suppress her anarchist journal in 1917 (*see* 1919).

A Committee of Amusement Resources for Working Girls is founded by the Women's City Club at the instigation of social worker Belle Israels (*née* Lindner) of the Educational Alliance and launches an investigation of the city's "dancing academies." The only readily accessible places of weekday recreation for girls employed in the sweatshops of the Lower East Side, the "academies" have tables on the dance floor where liquor is served, rooms for rent down adjacent corridors, and easy opportunities for unsophisticated teenage girls to be lured into prostitution. Belle Lindner married architect Charles Israels 6 years ago; when she discovers by checking incorporation papers that the owners of the academies include Tammany Hall leaders and other fairly prominent members of the community she advises them that she will keep their names secret provided that they make sure to have legislation passed to regulate the "academies" and take responsibility to have the regulations strictly enforced. The new laws, the *New York Times* will later say, "did more to improve the moral surroundings of young girls" than any other single reform at the time (*see* 1911).

The Men's League for Woman Suffrage is founded by Canandaigua-born Columbia University doctoral candidate Max F. (Forrester) Eastman, 26, at the instigation of his Marlboro, Mass.-born sister Crystal, 28, with whom he moves into an apartment at 118 Waverly Place, between Sixth Avenue and MacDougal Street. Their mother, Annis Eastman (*née* Ford), is a self-taught minister (she preaches from Thomas K. Beecher's old pulpit at Elmira).

Mayor-elect Gaynor rails against a ruling by the New York Court of Appeals that an 1899 law banning nightwork for women is unconstitutional because it deprives women of the "liberty" to work in factories.

New York garment workers assemble at the Cooper Union in Astor Place on the night of November 22 to hear speeches by Samuel Gompers of the AF of L and others about a proposed strike. The speakers caution against a strike, fearing reprisals, but most of the workers in attendance are immigrant women under age 25 who work at piece rates in dark, unheated lofts, where sanitation is poor, special permission is needed to go to the washroom, and a girl may lose her job if she is absent for reasons of health or speaks to another girl. Clara Lemlich, 19, is recovering from a beating on a picket line but stands up on the floor, asks to be heard, makes her way to the platform, and says in Yiddish, "I am a working girl, one of those who are on strike against intolerable conditions. I am tired of listening to speakers who talk in general terms. What we are here for is to decide whether we shall or shall not strike. I offer a resolution that a general strike be declared—now." Lemlich's words are translated into English and Italian, her resolution is adopted, and a strike begins that will last more than 9 weeks and involve some 20,000 women wage-earners. The strikers belong to the Ladies' Waist Makers' Union Local 25 of the 9-year-old International Ladies' Garment Workers' Union (ILGWU) and heed the exhortations of Rose Schneiderman, now 27, who walks the picket lines, harangues the crowds, and attends countless meetings, braving cold, hunger, police brutality, and attacks by company-hired thugs. Society women who include Alva Ertskin Belmont (*née* Smith), now 56, and Anne Morgan (daughter of financier J. P. Morgan) join the picket lines in December to avert further violence, getting more press coverage for the strikers and contributions to their strike fund. The sight of rich suffragists on the picket lines persuades thousands of working-class women to join the suffrage movement, whose success will help them in their struggle for improved working conditions (*see* 1910).

$ Banker John Crosby Brown of Brown Brothers dies at Brighthurst, N.J., June 25 at age 70; financier Edward H. Harriman at his Arden, N.Y., estate September 9 at age 61; investment banker Spencer Trask is killed December 31 at age 65 when a freight train crashes into the midnight Montreal Express on which he is traveling. His body is taken to his Yaddo estate at Saratoga Springs, cremated at Troy, and interred in the family plot at Brooklyn's Green-Wood Cemetery, where four of his children lie buried.

Wall Street's Dow Jones Industrial Average closes December 31 at 99.05, up from 86.15 at the end of 1908.

$ Shoppers riot at Williamsburg April 24 as the Adler department store and F. W. Woolworth on Broadway advertise bargains that bring out huge crowds, most of them women. A few men are in the crowd, one of them tries to choke a woman, and police are called in to restore order.

Brooks Brothers closes its two downtown stores and reopens at Broadway and 22nd Street, near the city's most fashionable residential district (*see* 1874; 1915).

Secretary of the Treasury George B. Cortelyou, now 46, resigns in March to become president of the nearly 25-year-old New York Consolidated Gas Co., a position he will hold until 1935.

Standard Oil Co. chief executive officer (and Amalgamated Copper Co. president) Henry H. Rogers dies of apoplexy at New York May 19 at age 68, leaving a fortune estimated to be as much as $75 million.

The taxicab strike that began at Christmas of last year is settled in February with the creation of a union dominated by horse hackmen. Harry Nathaniel Allen arranges to dispose of his interests in the New York Taxicab Co. he founded 2 years ago, but motorized taxicabs will remain a permanent part of the New York scene (see 1923).

U.S. automobile production reaches 127,731, up from 63,500 last year, but while most of America will become dependent upon the motorcar, and cities will spread horizontally as more and more people acquire motorcars, New York will rise vertically and the vast majority of residents will live comfortably without owning cars.

The New York Police Department establishes a "Broadway Squad" to direct traffic (see 1908). Every officer on the squad must be at least six feet tall (see 1910).

Aviation pioneer Wilbur Wright flies from Governors Island up the Hudson to Grant's Tomb and back in 33 minutes October 4, making the first successful flight ever seen in New York. His flying machine is equipped with a red canoe for emergency water landings.

A second tunnel for William G. McAdoo's Hudson & Manhattan Railroad opens between Cortlandt Street and Jersey City's Exchange Place (see 1908). A below-ground terminal is completed to serve passengers (see 1910).

Railroad and shipping magnate John H. Starin dies at his native New York March 22 at age 83, having made himself one of the richest men in America.

The Queensboro Bridge opens March 30 to carry traffic across the East River between Manhattan's East 59th Street and Long Island City. Designed by Austrian-born civil engineer Gustav Lindenthal, 58, and built at a cost of $12 million primarily for trolley cars, the cantilevered span is the first important double-deck bridge and is 3,724 feet long (7,450 feet, counting its approaches). Copper-roofed kiosks of terra-cotta panels with glazed tile interiors, designed by Lindenthal and architect Henry Hornbostel, shelter passengers on the Manhattan side as they descend stairways from Second Avenue to an underground streetcar terminal (on the Queens side, three trolley lines fan out to Jamaica, College Point, Corona, and Queens Plaza, and there are two stops on the bridge where passengers may descend by elevator or stairway to Welfare Island) (see 1957); the toll for motor vehicles will be removed in 1911, and within 80 years the bridge will be carrying 140,000 motor vehicles per day.

The Manhattan Bridge opens December 31 to carry traffic between the Bowery at Canal Street and an extension of Flatbush Avenue in Brooklyn (the third such link across the East River). Designed by Leon Moisseff and built of nickel steel in 8 years at a cost of $31 million, its main span is 1,470 feet long, its total length is 6,855 feet, its width is 120 feet, and it is the first important double-deck suspension bridge, with four trolley tracks, four El tracks, a 35-foot roadway, and two 11-foot promenades. Carrère and Hastings has designed its grand arch and flanking colonnades (see 1915).

The National Kindergarten Association (National Association for the Promotion of Kindergarten Education) is founded at New York by Massachusetts-born educator Bessie Locke, 44, who herself attended a private kindergarten in 1870 at Boston. She has reportedly seen the success of a friend's kindergarten in a city slum area, quit the business world, and in the next 30 years will help to open more than 3,260 kindergartens serving 1.6 million U.S. children.

Times Square's first large electric sign appears following a court order overturning a regulation against such signs (see Gude, 1901). A 50-foot display put up by Heatherbloom Petticoats carries the slogan, "Silk's Only Rival" and shows a girl's skirt fluttering in simulated gusts of wind and rain. Within 3 years the square will be aglow in such advertising signs, one for chewing gum (with a winking girl), a second with a fountain spouting effervescent water, a third showing a 30-foot kitten playing with a spool of thread, others with chariot races and bareback riders (see Artkraft-Strauss, 1935).

Condé Nast takes over Vogue magazine (see 1892; Collier's, 1900). Now 35, he married the daughter of lawyer Charles H. Coudert of Coudert Brothers in 1902 (the marriage will end in divorce, as will a second marriage) and in 1904 organized the Home Pattern Co. with Tagron McCampbell to make and sell dress patterns under an arrangement with Cyrus Curtis's Ladies' Home Journal; he left Collier's in 1907, Vogue has a circulation of only 22,500, but

Nast will make it a monthly and in 1914 will name managing editor Edna Woolman Chase, now 32, as editor-in-chief; she will build circulation to more than 130,000, launching British and French editions, and training a generation of fashion editors, including Carmel Snow, now 19, who will become editor-in-chief of Hearst's *Harper's Bazaar*.

Collier's magazine founder, book publisher, and fox hunter Peter F. Collier dies in New Jersey April 24 at age 59. His New York book manufacturing plant employs 700 people and has modern presses that can produce 20,000 volumes per day. Collier's son Robert J., now 32, takes over his enterprises and will continue until his own death in 1918.

The weekly *Amsterdam News* begins publication at Harlem in December. The paper's circulation will peak at 100,000, making it the nation's largest non-religious black weekly.

McGraw-Hill Book Publishing Co. is created by a merger of rival publishers James McGraw and John Hill (*see* 1888), each of whom has developed a group of magazines, McGraw's in the electrical and transportation industries, Hill's in the mechanical and engineering fields. After Hill's death in 1916 his five magazines will be merged with those of McGraw (in 1917) to create McGraw-Hill Publishing Co. (*see Business Week*, 1929).

Nonfiction: *The Government of American Cities* by Brooklyn lawyer-reformer Horace E. Deming, now 59.

Fiction: *Roads of Destiny* (stories) by O. Henry; *The Butler's Story* by Arthur Train; *The Hungry Heart* by David Graham Phillips.

Painting: *Both Members of This Club* (prizefighters) by George Bellows; *Salomé* by Robert Henri. Alfred Stieglitz introduces Rutherford, N.J.-born watercolorist John Marin, 38, to New York, including him in a show at his Photo-Secession 291 Gallery.

Sculpture: a bronze bust of Giovanni da Verrazano by sculptor Ettore Ximenes is installed in Battery Park with a bronze female figure holding a sword. The city's Italian community has provided the funds for the statue in response to a drive conducted by the daily paper *Il Progresso*.

Theater: *The Easiest Way* by Cleveland-born playwright Eugene Walter, 35, 1/19 at the Stuyvesant (Belasco) Theater, with Joseph Kilgour, 157 perfs.; *The Goddess of Reason* by Mary Johnston 2/15 at Daly's Theater, with Julia Marlowe, 48 perfs.; *Going Some* by Paul Armstrong and Rex Beach 4/12 at the Belasco Theater (to Maxine Elliott's Theater 6/21),

96 perfs.; *The Only Law* by Wilson Mizner and George Bronson Howard 8/2 at the Hackett Theater (the plot concerns a broker who keeps a chorus girl who keeps a gigolo, the title comes from the line, "Being on the square with a pal is the only law we know"), *New York World* critic Louis De Foe calls it a drama of "tenderloinized life," *New York Tribune* critic William Winter says, "The play, it will be seen, invited an audience to observe the proceedings of sluts, scoundrels, and boobies," "a dishonor to the amusement profession," "vulgar and reprehensible to the last degree" (it moves to the American Music Hall 8/30), 48 perfs.; *The Fortune Hunter* by Winchell Smith 9/4 at the new Gaiety Theater on Broadway between 45th and 46th streets, with John Barrymore, 345 perfs.; *The Melting Pot* by Israel Zangwill 9/17 at the Artef Theater after a year on the road, with Walker Whiteside as David Quixano, a Russian-born Jewish immigrant who marries a Christian woman and, looking out from the roof garden of a settlement house, says, "There she lies, the great Melting Pot—listen! Can't you hear the roaring and the bubbling? Ah, what a stirring and seething! Celt and Latin, Slav and Teuton, Greek and Syrian,—black and yellow," 136 perfs. The play introduces the term *melting pot* to describe America's (and especially New York's) amalgam of nationalities and races; *The Man Who Owns Broadway* by George M. Cohan 10/11 at the New York Theater, with Raymond Hitchcock, 128 perfs.; *Seven Days* by Mary Roberts Rinehart and Avery Hopwood 11/11 at the Astor Theater, with Hope Latham, Florence Reed, Lucille La Verne, 397 perfs.; *The City* by the late Clyde Fitch 12/21 at the Lyric Theater, with 29-year-old Brooklyn-born actor Walter Hampden (originally Walter Hampden Dougherty), 190 perfs.

Playwright Clyde Fitch dies at Châlons-sur-Marne, France, August 4 at age 44.

German-born film producer Carl Laemmle, 42, opens a studio on Eleventh Avenue. Laemmle arrived at New York with $50 at age 17 after his mother died, joined an elder brother at Chicago, worked as a bookkeeper for an Oshkosh, Wis., clothing firm, saw a Chicago nickelodeon 3 years ago and recognized its potential, used his meager savings to convert a clothing store into a theater, painted its exterior a brilliant white, equipped it with 120 folding chairs, rented from an undertaker, and by year's end had opened two theaters, acquired a partner, and begun distributing films to other theaters in the area. Demand having outpaced supply, he has moved back to New York, established IMP (Independent Motion Pictures), whose acting troupe includes Canadian-born beauty Mary Pickford (Gladys Mary Smith), 16, and produces a 1,988-foot-long film version of the Henry Wadsworth Longfellow classic "Hiawatha" that appears October 25 starring Florence Lawrence, who is paid an unheard-of $1,000 per week. Laemmle next year will produce 100 short films, challenging the virtual monopoly held by the General Film Co. coalition that holds the patents on operating machines and forces exhibitors to show its films, charging steep fees (*see* Universal Pictures, 1912).

♪ Broadway musicals: *The Fair Co-Ed* 2/1 at the Knickerbocker Theater, with Elsie Janis, Gustav Laders-George Ade songs, 136 perfs.; *The Beauty Spot* 4/10 at the Herald Square Theater, with music by Reginald De Koven, book by Joseph V. Herbert, 137 perfs.; *The* (Ziegfeld) *Follies* 6/14 at the Jardin de Paris, with Nora Bayes, Jack Norworth, Eva Tanguay, Russian-born actress-singer Sophie Tucker (originally Sonia Kalish), 25, San Francisco-born ingénue Lillian Lorraine (*née* Eulallean de Jacques), 17, music by Maurice Levi and others, book and lyrics chiefly by Harry B. Smith, songs that include "By the Light of the Silvery Moon" by Gus Edwards, lyrics by Edward Madden, 64 perfs.; *Old Dutch* 11/22 at the Herald Square Theater, with Lew Fields, dancer Vernon Castle, and Washington, D.C.-born actress Helen Hayes (Brown), 9, in her first New York appearance (she has been acting professionally since age 5), book by Edgar Smith, music by Victor Herbert, lyrics by George V. Hobart, 88 perfs.

Popular song: "Meet Me Tonight in Dreamland" by Leo Friedman, 40, lyrics by Beth Slater Whitson, 30, whose song quickly becomes the theme of the Coney Island amusement park opened in 1904.

🚶 A U.S. polo team organized and captained by millionaire New York sportsman Harry Payne Whitney defeats a British team July 5 at Hurlingham, England, to win the International Polo Cup, the first American team to do so. Now 37, Whitney married Gertrude Vanderbilt in 1896, inherited about $24 million when his father died in 1904, and owns extensive racing stables at Westbury, Brookdale, N.J., and Lexington, Ky. Daniel Guggenheim has helped him increase his family fortune with investments in silver, lead, and copper mines and oil ventures in the West, Southwest, and Mexico.

● Vienna-born milliner Hattie Carnegie (originally Henrietta Königeiser), 23, goes into partnership with her seamstress neighbor Ruth Rose Roth at New York. Carnegie (she has borrowed her name from the steel magnate) left school at age 13 when her father died and went to work at Macy's. In 4 years she and Roth will have their own shop near Riverside Drive, with Roth designing clothes that Carnegie (who makes the hats) will model and sell (*see* 1919).

The "kewpie" (short for cupid) figure with a cherubic head that comes to a point is patented by Pennsylvania-born New York author-illustrator Rose Cecil O'Neill, 35, whose creation is soon translated into buttons, cutouts, salt-and-pepper shakers, soap, curtain fabric, and birthday cards. Kewpie will be the basis of a mold that will be made in 1913 by Pratt Institute art student Joseph L. Kallus and manufactured as a doll, initially in Germany from bisque. Mass-produced in America from celluloid and other materials, the Kewpie Doll and other kewpie renditions will earn $1.5 million for O'Neill, who wears a toga at her Greenwich Village salon.

Florenz Ziegfeld installs his 17-year-old mistress Lillian Lorraine in a 13th-floor apartment at the Ansonia Hotel just like the 10th-floor suite he occupies with his wife, Anna Held, who is vacationing in Europe, having been forced by her husband to undergo an illegal abortion (13 rooms with four baths at the Ansonia rent for about $400 per month). Some regard young Lillian as the most beautiful girl in the world but she has a drinking problem.

The New York Bureau of Charities issues a report August 13 claiming that as many as 3,000 local men have deserted their wives in the past year, up 33 percent from the previous year. Most were poor men, aged 20 to 24, who left for economic reasons, unable to support their wives and two or more children and unable to afford divorces. Desertion is a misdemeanor, subject to a 6-month prison term; the Bureau blames drinking along with meddlesome neighbors and relatives, but changes in marital roles may also be responsible.

▥ New York police detective Joseph Petrosino is murdered March 12 at Palermo, Sicily, while checking criminal records for a deportation proceeding (*see* "barrel murder," 1903). Petrosino was appointed in December to lead an effort whose purpose was to eliminate the secret criminal organization known as the Black Hand, but his investigations found no evidence to support the belief that a Sicilian-based international crime syndicate had a branch at New York. His murder at age 48 will remain unsolved, and a small plaza just north of 240 Centre Street will be dedicated to his memory.

Stanford White's murderer Harry K. Thaw begins an appeal July 12 to prove his sanity and gain release from the asylum where he has been confined, but he is found August 12 still to be criminally insane and returned to his mental asylum (*see* 1907; 1913).

 The 33-story City Investing Co. Building (Broadway-Cortlandt Building) is completed at 165 Broadway on a site bounded by Broadway, Church Street, and Trinity Place. Designed by Francis H. Kimball, it has 550,000 square feet of floor space and is the largest office building yet erected.

The Hudson Terminal Building is completed for William G. McAdoo's Hudson & Manhattan Railroad Co. on a site bounded by Church, Cortlandt, Fulton, and Dey streets. George A. Fuller Co. has constructed the two 22-story steel-frame towers, designed by James Hollis Wells of Clinton & Russell, and together they comprise the largest office complex yet constructed. Offices in the floors above the new underground passenger terminal have been occupied since the middle of last year.

The 42-story Metropolitan Life Insurance Tower is completed January 29 with a 40th-story observation floor on the east side of Madison Square at 23rd Street (*see* 1893). Designed by Napoleon Le Brun & Sons in a style based on St. Mark's Campanile in Venice, the 700-foot tower of white Tuckahoe marble rises to nearly twice the height of the 386-foot Park Row Building completed in 1899. It has a giant clock on each of its four sides, with each clock measuring 26-feet in diameter, and a beacon at the top that can be seen for miles. While in terms of usable floor space it is surpassed in height by the Singer Tower completed last year, it will remain the world's tallest building until 1913.

The Grand Central Post Office opens at the southwest corner of Lexington Avenue and 45th Street with a long, open truck bay along Depew Place. Designed in Roman Doric style by Warren & Wetmore with Reed & Stem, it is part of the Grand Central Terminal complex being built above the tracks of the New York Central and New Haven railroads. The project has required clearing 48 acres of prime midtown real estate, demolition of some 200 buildings, and moving 25 miles of sewer pipes without affecting the schedules of 600 trains that move in and out of Grand Central Station each day (*see* transportation, 1913).

The first Municipal Lodging House opens at 438 West 25th Street with nearly 1,000 beds, some in a separate dormitory for women and children. It is soon overcrowded and many of the homeless revert to sleeping in churches, on park benches, under bridges, and in public toilets, saloons, subways, and waiting rooms.

The 12-story Alwyn Court apartment house opens at the southeast corner of Seventh Avenue and 58th Street with two 14-room, five-bath apartments per floor (rent: a little more than $500 per month) and a 32-room duplex with nine baths (rent: just over $1,800 per month) whose first tenant is United Cigar Stores chairman Jacob Wertheim. Designed by Harde & Short, the building's limestone exterior is lavishly decorated with terra-cotta ornamentation and its apartments have wood-paneled walls, fitted closets, marble mantelpieces, and other luxury features (*see* 1938; fire, 1910).

The Verona apartment house is completed at 32 East 64th Street, southeast corner Madison Avenue. William E. Mowbray has designed the 10-story structure in Venetian Renaissance palazzo style with an entrance flanked by bronze lamp standars.

A 14-story co-operative apartment house is completed at 50 West 77th Street, facing the American Museum of Natural History, with two apartments per floor. Designed by Harde & Short, it resembles a Gothic cathedral from the outside, its lobby has a groined, vaulted ceiling, its foyers are of stone, and its apartments have 11 or 12 rooms each, including an elaborately paneled dining room. Most apartments have extra-height studios, and those on the top floor have 18-foot ceilings.

The 13-story Belnord apartment house opens in the fall, occupying an entire block between Amsterdam Avenue and Broadway from 86th Street to 87th. Designed by architect H. Hobart Weekes of Hiss and Weekes to resemble the Dakota that opened in 1884, the structure has an inner courtyard more than 231 feet long and 90 feet wide, with walls of terra-cotta-trimmed limestone (the Italian Renaissance streetside exterior uses 6 million ordinary bricks). The Belnord's 175 apartments open off six elevator halls and have seven to 11 rooms each, with one to four baths and one to three servants' rooms, but the upper floors for the most part have sixteen two- to four-bedroom apartments each, and four of the upper floors have apartments with double-size living and dining rooms. Doors connecting parlor to library to dining room can be thrown open in some suites to create a space spanning the entire 58 feet between inner court and avenue. Each flat has a built-in vacuum-cleaning system, a wall safe, and an electric refrigerator that makes ice (almost every other apartment house and private dwelling in the city receives regular visits from the iceman). The Belnord's boilers and generating plant make it independent of city power sources; they are placed beneath the courtyard so as not to create disturbing vibrations. Rents range from $167 to $583 per month (tenement accommodations may be had in the city for between $7 and $20 per month while luxury apartments can rent for as much as $2,000).

A mansion of white Vermont marble is completed at the northeast corner of Riverside Drive and 107th Street for Turkish-born tobacco merchant Morris Schinasi, who has joined with his brother Solomon to corner the market for strong Turkish cigarettes. Solomon has acquired the former Isaac Rice mansion on Riverside Drive at 89th Street, nearly a mile to the south, and Morris outdoes him. His new house, designed by William Tuthill, is a larger version of a 6-year-old Tuthill house at the northeast corner of West End Avenue and 93rd Street, and has a plethora of outdoor water faucets to facilitate frequent cleaning of the exterior.

Architect Russell Sturgis dies at his New York home February 11 at age 72; Charles F. McKim at St. James, L.I., September 4 at age 62.

The *Real Estate Record and Builders' Guide* observes November 6 that "apartments are coming to be so preferred over the private dwelling for one reason, because a private dwelling may not be obtainable in a particular neighborhood where the family wishes to reside when in town."

A "temporary" dome is completed over the crossing of the Cathedral of St. John the Divine under construction at 110th Street (*see* 1893). A company headed by Spanish-born architect-craftsman Rafael Guastavino y Esposito, 38, has created special tiles and finished the job in 15 weeks without using a support structure (Guastavino's architect father, Rafael Guastavino y Morano, emigrated to America with his 9-year-old son in 1881 at age 39 and died at Baltimore last year at age 66, having introduced centuries-old Catalan-style methods of tile-and-mortar construction to America) (*see* 1911).

The Hebrew Immigrant Aid Society (HIAS) is created at New York March 16 by a merger of the Hebrew Sheltering Society, founded in 1889 to help Jews from Eastern Europe, and a Hebrew Immigrant Aid Society founded 7 years ago to provide traditional burial for Jews who die on Ellis Island. Started with a budget of less than $10,000, HIAS will help immigrants gain legal entry, find relatives, and obtain work and schooling.

1910 Former Republican party boss Thomas C. Platt dies of Bright's disease at New York March 6 at age 76. He masterminded the consolidation of Greater New York in the 1890s and has lived at 2 Rector Street.

Penn Station's grandeur was destined to last only 53 years before it fell to the wrecking ball. MUNICIPAL ARCHIVE

Gov. Hughes appoints lawyer-author Arthur Train as special deputy attorney general to investigate political offenses in Queens County. Train will obtain 100 indictments but will be thrown out of office early next year, when the state administration changes, and given no opportunity to try the cases.

A would-be assassin narrowly misses killing Mayor Gaynor August 9. The mayor has appointed officials with no ties to Tammany Hall, eliminated "no-show" jobs, and instituted other fiscal reforms, but as he boards the S.S. *Kaiser Wilhelm der Grosse* at Hoboken with his son Rufus for a vacation in Europe a *New York World* photographer lifts his camera to take a picture, and a short man who has been dismissed from his job in the docks department fires a handgun at Gaynor's head. The bullet enters behind the mayor's right ear, blood gushes down his beard and onto his suit (the *World* photographer captures the image clearly), the ship's doctor bandages the wound, and Gaynor does not return to his City Hall office until October 3. The surgeons have not been able to extricate the bullet, and the mayor will suffer its effects for the rest of his short life; he turns irascible and becomes involved in political feuds (after quarreling with the police commissioner, he will replace him with socialite Rhinelander Waldo, who will prove too naïve for the post).

Gov. Hughes resigns October 6, having been appointed to the U.S. Supreme Court by President Taft. His two terms in office have seen major reforms in the state government, and he is succeeded by his lieutenant governor Horace White, who will serve until the new governor takes office in January of next year.

Former mayor Hugh J. Grant dies at New York November 3 at age 58.

Former pulp and paper manufacturer John Alden Dix, 49, is elected governor, defeating a bid by U.S. District Attorney Henry L. (Lewis) Stimson, 43, whose father is a well-known New York physician (Stimson has been persuaded to run as a Republican and will be appointed secretary of war by President Taft next year). Dix receives 689,700 votes to Stimson's 622,299, and the Democrats win control of both houses of the state assembly for the first time in 18 years following revelations that Republican legislators have accepted payoffs from insurance companies (see Smith, 1911).

The International Ladies' Garment Workers' Union (ILGWU) wins its 9-week strike for New York cloakmakers with help from Rose Schneiderman (see 1909). The strike ends February 15 after arbitration proceedings mediated by lawyer Louis Marshall, now 53; the strikers win higher wages (although data collected 2 years ago by the U.S. Immigration Service showed that garment workers actually received 8 percent *more* than the average in 21 industries), better working conditions (although some sweatshops still remain), and a 52-hour work week, but 60,000 ILGWU workers strike from July 7 to September 2, demanding a "Protocol of Peace" that will give them a 50-hour work week, overtime pay, 10 legal holidays, compulsory arbitration of disputes, and a joint labor-management board. The strike will be followed in the next few years by similar job actions in Brooklyn and elsewhere, but its success paves the way for a long period of labor stability (see Dubinsky, 1932).

The state legislature at Albany enacts a workers' compensation insurance system that increases financial incentives for employers to improve workplace safety. *Work Accidents and the Law* by suffragist Crystal Eastman will contribute to the passage of worker-safety legislation. Most employers have taken measures to make their factories safer, if only to avoid lawsuits and attract workers who would demand higher wages to work under dangerous conditions (*but see* Triangle Shirtwaist Factory fire, 1911).

A Manhattan race riot breaks out August 15 when black resident Arthur Harris sees his wife accosted by a white man, Robert Thorpe, at the corner of Eighth Avenue and 41st Street. Fighting to rescue her, he stabs Thorpe, who turns out to be a plain-clothes police officer. Thorpe dies August 16, having claimed he was about to arrest Mrs. Harris for soliciting, and white gangs riot all over the Tenderloin section, beating up blacks; police do not intervene.

The National Association for the Advancement of Colored People (NAACP) is formally established at New York (see 1909). Eight out of 10 U.S. blacks still live in the 11 states of the Old Confederacy, but a "great migration" begins that will bring more than 2 million blacks to the North (see 1917; census, 1940).

Some 3,000 Brooklyn Boot and Shoe Workers strike in November but obtain no concessions. The average U.S. workingman earns less than $15 per week, working hours range from 54 to 60 hours, and there is wide irregularity of employment.

The Chapin Nursery has its beginnings in a service started by Chapin School founder Alice Chapin and her pediatrician husband, who take in abandoned infants and try to find homes for them (see Spence, 1895; Spence-Chapin, 1943).

The Wall Street banking house Salomon Brothers (initially Salomon Brothers and Hutzler) opens at 80 Broadway. German-born broker Ferdinand Salomon opened a small money-brokerage firm in Exchange Place in the 1880s, his sons Arthur K., now 33; Percy S., 28; and Herbert, 26, went into business together 2 years ago and have now gone into partnership with Morton Hutzler to trade in short-term securities and conduct a money-brokerage business; the firm will grow to be the largest partnership in the financial district (see 1919).

Wall Street's Dow Jones Industrial Average closes December 31 at 81.36, down from 99.05 at the end of 1909.

Gimbel Brothers Department Store opens September 29 on Greeley Square between 32nd and 33rd streets, one block south of the Macy's store that opened in the fall of 1902 (people will soon be asking, "Does Macy's tell Gimbels?"). Begun in 1842 as a trading post at Vincennes, Ind., by Bavarian-born peddler Adam Gimbel, Gimbels has grown to have stores at Milwaukee (1887) and Philadelphia (1894). Vincennes-born former University of Pennsylvania heavyweight champion Bernard F. (Feustmann) Gimbel, 25, a grandson of the late Adam, overcame the strenuous objections of his father, Isaac, and his uncle Louis last year and paid $9 million for the Greeley Square site, convenient to the Hudson-Manhattan tube, the new Pennsylvania Station (which serves the Long Island Rail Road as well as the Pennsy), two (later three) subway lines, and the

Sixth Avenue El. Designed by the Chicago firm Daniel Burnham & Co., the new store has 1 million square feet of floor space, two acres of window glass, 7,000 employees, and 164 departments. Opening day advertisements attract a crowd of 300,000, and Gimbel will enlarge the store by acquiring adjacent buildings and adding three upper floors (see Saks Fifth Avenue, 1924).

Peck & Peck moves to a new location at 501 Fifth Avenue, becoming one of the first merchants to move north of 42nd Street (see 1903). The Peck brothers now stock neckties for men who like to match their stockings to their ties, have begun stocking shirts and sweaters as well, and when they find to their surprise that women like the silk sweaters and want skirts to match they will start to carry women's apparel.

New York Central railroad baron Hamilton McK. Twombly dies at Convent, N.J., January 11 at age 60. A son predeceased him in 1906, but he is survived by his widow, Florence Adele (née Vanderbilt), and three daughters, one of whom, Florence, has married William (Armestead Moale) Burden.

Service on William G. McAdoo's Hudson & Manhattan Railroad is extended to Newark, N.J., and to West 33rd Street in Manhattan (see 1909).

Pennsylvania Station opens to Long Island Rail Road commuter traffic September 8 via a new rail tunnel under the East River that connects Long Island with Manhattan and New Jersey (LIRR passengers up to now have had to take ferries across the river). Built in the heart of the old Tenderloin area, the station opens to long-distance trains from Chicago and points west beginning November 27, with 46 Pennsylvania trains heading west and 43 LIRR trains heading east. Tunnels from the New Jersey meadowlands permit Pennsylvania Railroad passengers to come directly into Manhattan instead of having to be transferred by ferry across the Hudson River, the Pennsy uses its Manhattan Transfer in New Jersey to switch passengers between steam trains and the electric lines that go through the tunnels (the entire main line will be electrified in 1933), and it is finally able to compete on equal terms with the New York Central. The Pennsy's late president Alexander Johnston Cassatt died at Philadelphia in 1906 at age 67, having proposed putting up a hotel on the terminal's air rights, but he was persuaded to create a monumental gateway to New York as a matter of obligation. Covering two square blocks between Seventh and Eighth avenues from 31st Street north to 33rd, the $112 million granite and travertine depot has been modeled by McKim, Mead, & White

on the warm room of Rome's ancient Baths of Caracalla with 84 doric columns each 35 feet high; great steel girders support the 150-foot coffered ceiling of its vast waiting room, whose skylights allow it to be bathed in natural light by day. (There are also separate men's and women's waiting rooms, and a changing room where a traveler may rent a small chamber with toilet facilities enclosed by glass partitions and supplied with soap, towels, and a silver-handled whiskbroom. A man can change into formal wear for dinner or theater, check his bag, and emerge feeling like a gentleman.) A lunchroom and formal dining room flank the station's grand staircase. Penn Station has three levels below the street— one for tracks and platforms, one for subway lines and for the LIRR concourse and ticket offices, and a third for the general concourse and main waiting room. The world's first station designed to separate incoming and outgoing pedestrian traffic, its exit concourse is located between the main concourse and the train platforms, ensuring uninterrupted movement; the LIRR has its own waiting room and ticket offices at the northern end of the station, below 33rd Street (see 1961; Connecting Bridge, 1917).

The Police Department installs the city's first hand-operated semaphore signals to direct traffic at major intersections (see 1909). They will continue to be used to some extent until 1933 (see 1919).

The Cunard liner R.M.S. *Mauretania* sails from Cobb to New York in 4 days, 20 hours, 41 minutes, winning the Blue Riband as she sets a new transatlantic speed record that will stand until 1929 (see 1907).

Hammondsport, N.Y.-born aviator Glenn H. (Hammond) Curtiss, 32, flies 150 miles from Albany to New York May 29 in 2 hours, 51 minutes, to set a new long-distance speed record and win a $10,000 prize put up by Joseph Pulitzer's *New York World* (see Wright, 1909). He lands at Poughkeepsie and at Spuyten Duyvil before finally reaching Governors Island.

San Francisco-born rabbi Judah Leon Magnes, 33, quits Temple Emanu-El after a dispute with the trustees. He served as rabbi at a reform temple in Brooklyn from 1904 to 1906 become coming to Manhattan and will be rabbi of Congregation B'nai Jeshurun from 1911 to 1912 before becoming leader of the Society for the Advancement of Judaism.

The Society of Ethical Culture's Meeting House is completed at the southwest corner of Central Park West and 64th Street to Art Nouveau designs by architect (and society member) Robert D. Kohn, who has used Bedford limestone for the building's exterior (see education, 1904, 1928 [Fieldston School]).

The 74-year-old Union Theological Seminary moves from Lenox Hill to Morningside Heights, where Allen & Collens has designed buildings that will grow in the next 20 years to occupy a Gothic quadrangle on a site just north of Columbia University bounded by Broadway and Claremont avenues and 120th and 122nd streets (see Lenox, 1840). Liverpool-born philanthropist Daniel Willis James, now 78, has provided the wherewithal for the move at the urging of his late friend John Crosby Brown (see real estate, 1911).

Brooklyn College opens as an extension division of City College for Teachers. It will be enlarged in 1917 to include freshman evening classes for high school graduates, but only for males (see 1926).

American Telephone and Telegraph chief Theodore N. (Newton) Vail, 65, has himself elected president of Western Union and abolishes the 40¢ to 50¢ charge for placing telegraph messages by telephone. Vail has acquired a controlling interest in Western Union from the Jay Gould estate for $30 million in AT&T stock, and while the courts will force AT&T to sell its Western Union stock in 1914, free placement of telegraph messages by telephone will continue even after Vail resigns (see 1913).

American News Co. cofounder and New-York Historical Society benefactor Henry Dexter dies at New York July 11 at age 97.

Women's Wear Daily begins publication at New York July 13 under the direction of journalist Edmund Fairchild, now 44, whose new trade paper is an outgrowth of the Daily News Record, a menswear journal that had a different name and was failing when he took it over in 1892.

The Crisis begins monthly publication at Harlem under the direction of W. E. B. Du Bois and will become the official organ of the new NAACP, covering activities of the organization and incidents of discrimination against blacks. Du Bois will run the periodical until 1934.

Nonfiction: History of the Great American Fortunes by Gustavus Myers; Diary of a Shirtwaist Striker by Russian-born feminist Theresa Serber Malkiel, 36.

Fiction: Whirligigs (stories) by O. Henry. In his story "Strictly Business" he has written, "Not only by blows does [New York City] seek to subdue you. It woos you to its heart with the subtlety of a siren." "Far below and around lay the city like a ragged pur-

ple dream . . . There below him lay all things, good and bad, that can be brought from the four corners of the earth to instruct, please, thrill, enrich, despoil, elevate, cast down, nurture, or kill."

O. Henry (William Sidney Porter) dies penniless at New York June 5 at age 47. An alcoholic who preferred Scotch, he has published 381 short stories that have virtually defined the form.

Canandaigua-born painter Arthur Garfield Dove, 30, meets Alfred Stieglitz, whose 291 Gallery will hereafter show his work on a regular basis. Dove will be widely regarded as the first U.S. abstract artist. Sculptor J. Q. A. Ward dies at New York May 1 at age 79; painter John La Farge at Providence, R.I., November 14 at age 75.

Theater: Alias Jimmy Valentine by Paul Armstrong 1/21 at Wallack's Theater, 115 perfs. (Armstrong has written it in the warden's office of the Tombs, adapting the O. Henry story "A Retrieved Reformation," and, possibly with help from his friend Wilson Mizner, introducing terms such as "stir" to mean prison, and "the big house" to mean Sing Sing Prison up the river at Ossining); Get-Rich-Quick Wallingford by George M. Cohan 9/19 at the Gaiety Theater, with Hale Hamilton as J. Rufus Wallingford (Wilson Mizner has turned down the role, telling Cohan that regular stage appearances would spoil his evenings) in a comedy based on a novel by George Randolph Chet, 424 perfs.; English comedian Charles Chaplin, 21, arrives in late September, rents a back room above a drycleaning shop in a dirty and malodorous brownstone in West 43rd Street, and initially finds the city unfriendly and intimidating although he will later be stimulated by the energy of American life and its apparent classlessness. He appears in an English farce The Wow-Wows, or A Night in a London Secret Society at the Colonial Theater, and Sime Silverman says in Variety, "Chaplin will do all right for America, but it is too bad that he didn't first appear in New York with something more in it than this piece." Although audience response is not encouraging, the show goes on tour to Chicago and points west; A Night in an English Music Hall 10/3 at the Colonial Theater with Charles Chaplin as an inebriate in a farce that had been called Mummingbirds in London; Nobody's Widow by Cleveland-born playwright Avery Hopwood, 28, 11/15 at the Hudson Theater, with Blanche Bates, 215 perfs.; Pomander Walk by Louis N. Parker 12/20 at the Wallack Theater, 143 perfs.

Brooklyn Eagle cartoonist John Randolph Bray, 31, pioneers animated motion picture cartoons, using a "cel" system he has invented and that will be used by all future animators. Each cartoon frame is a photograph of several layers of celluloid transparencies, the only layers that change from frame to frame being those that involve movements of figures; backgrounds (and some figures) remain constant, a technique that avoids the distracting moves seen when each frame was drawn entirely by hand (it also reduces production costs enormously). Pathé acquires Bray's cartoon "The Dachshund and the Sausage," Bray develops a "Colonel Heeza Liar" cartoon based roughly on Theodore Roosevelt, and he will employ animators Max and David Fleischer, who will create "Betty Boop" and "Popeye" cartoons (see 1929), Paul Terry, who will produce "Terry Toons," and Walter Lantz, who will create "Bugs Bunny" and "Woody Woodpecker" (see Culhane, 1925).

David Mannes founds the Music Settlement for Colored People in Harlem (see 1899). He will serve as its director for 5 years while serving also as director of the East Side House (see 1916).

Broadway musicals: *The Old Town* 1/10 at the new 1,192-seat Globe Theater (it will be the Lunt-Fontanne beginning in 1958), put up by producer (and onetime *Evening Sun* drama critic) Charles B. Dillingham, now 41, at 205 West 46th Street with a façade designed by Carrère & Hastings; *The Arcadians* 1/17 at the Liberty Theater, with English-born actor Lawrence Grant, 39, music by English composer Lionel Monckton, now 48, and Howard Talbot (the show opened at London in late April of last year), 136 perfs.; *Tillie's Nightmare* 5/5 at the Herald Square Theater, with Marie Dressler, music by A. Baldwin Sloane, lyrics by Edgar Smith, songs that include "Heaven Will Protect the Working Girl" based on the 1898 song "She Was Bred in Old Kentucky," 77 perfs.; *Girlies* 6/13 at the New Amsterdam Theater, with Joseph Cawthorn, Boston-born actor Jed Prouty, 31, music by Egbert Van Alstyne, lyrics by Harry Williams, book by George V. Hobart, 88 perfs; *The* (Ziegfeld) *Follies* 6/20 at the Jardin de Paris, with Lillian Lorraine, singer Fannie Brice (originally Fannie Borach), 18, who won a Brooklyn talent contest 5 years ago singing "When You Know You're Not Forgotten by the Girl You Can't Forget," left school to start a theatrical career, and has been hired at $75 per week by Florenz Ziegfeld. Music by Gus Edwards and others, book and lyrics by Harry B. Smith, 88 perfs.; *Madame Sherry* 8/30 at the New Amsterdam Theater, with songs that include "Every Little Movement Has a Meaning All Its Own" by Karl Hoschna and Otto Harbach, "Put Your Arms Around Me, Honey" by Albert von Tilzer, lyrics by Junie McCree, 231 perfs.; *Naughty Marietta* 11/7 at the New

York Theater, with music by Victor Herbert, book and lyrics by Baltimore-born actress manqué and songwriter Rida Young (*née* Johnson), 35, songs that include "Tramp! Tramp! Tramp!," "I'm Falling in Love with Someone," "Ah, Sweet Mystery of Life," 136 perfs.; *The Spring Maid* 12/28 at the Liberty Theater, with English entertainer Tom McNaughton, 43, music by Henrich Reinhardt, book by Harry B. Smith, lyrics by Harry B. and Robert B. Smith, 192 perfs.

Popular song: "Come, Josephine, in My Flying Machine" by German-born New York composer Fred Fisher, 35, lyrics by Canadian-born writer Alfred Bryan, 39.

English-born actress Eleanor Robson retires from the stage at age 30 (she has been starring since 1908 in *The Dawn of Tomorrow*) and is married February 26 to financier August Belmont II, now 53, whose first wife died in 1898.

The Elizabeth Arden beauty-salon chain has its beginnings in a New York parlor started by Canadian-born beauty-shop secretary Florence Nightingale Graham, 25, who first goes into business with Elizabeth Hubbard, has a falling out with her partner, borrows $6,000 from a cousin, and opens a Fifth Avenue shop under the name Elizabeth Arden inspired by the 1864 Tennyson poem "Enoch Arden." Graham repays the loan within 4 months, will move farther uptown in 1915, and open a Washington, D.C., branch. By 1938 there will be 29 Elizabeth Arden salons, 10 of them in foreign countries, while Graham's Maine vacation home will be operating as a health resort under the name Maine Chance Farm. Elizabeth Arden beauty products will by that time be selling at major department stores.

U.S. federal district attorney Henry L. Stimson indicts former ice baron Charles W. Morse, now 54, for making false entries in the Bank of North America. Stimson's Vienna-born assistant Felix Frankfurter, 27, helps him prosecute the case; convicted, Morse is sentenced to a term of 30 years, but he will simulate the symptoms of Bright's disease by drinking a mixture of soap suds and other chemicals, a board of physicians will advise President Taft that he is ill, and Taft will pardon him in 1912.

Former superintendent of New York police detectives Thomas F. Byrnes dies May 7 at age 67 (see 1883). Hardly a pillar of justice, he is said to have amassed a fortune of $350,000 by the time he retired.

Heiress Dorothy (Harriet Camille) Arnold, 25, leaves her family home at 108 East 79th Street to go shopping December 12, runs into a friend at the corner of Fifth Avenue and 27th Street, and disappears. Her family will keep the news from the press until late January of next year, a long search will ensue, but she will never be found.

 The 32-story Liberty Tower (initially the Bryant Building) is completed at 55 Cedar (later Liberty) Street, northwest corner Nassau Street, to designs by Henry Ives Cobb. It replaces an earlier Bryant Building, completed in 1882 to replace the Evening Post Building, and is constructed on caissons that go down 95 feet to bedrock.

The 12-story 1 Lexington Avenue apartment house is completed at Gramercy Park. Designed by Herbert Lucas, it rises next door to former mayor Abram Hewitt's house and faces the former Stanford White residence.

The 12-story 563 Park Avenue co-operative apartment house is completed at the northeast corner of 62nd Street, where it replaces five row houses that had faced onto 62nd Street. Designed by Walter B. Chambers, it will be called upper Park Avenue's "first luxury apartment house," with duplex apartments facing on the avenue, simplexes in the rear. A duplex typically has on its first floor a 26' × 18'6" drawing room, a 25' × 16' dining room, a private hall, a servants' dining room, butler's pantry, and kitchen; on its second floor are four bedrooms ranging in size from 18' × 16' to 14' × 9', with three baths, plus two servants' rooms with sink.

The nine-story Lucania apartment house is completed at 235 West 71st Street, between Broadway and West End Avenue, with circulating hot water and filters to screen out any impurities in the city water supply. Designed on an H plan by architect Gaetano Ajello and built by Anthony Campagna, it has four asymmetrical, six-room apartments per floor, two of them with quarters for sleep-in maids, three with formal dining rooms. Rents range from $75 to $167 per month.

The 12-story Colosseum apartment house is completed at 435 Riverside Drive, southeast corner 116th Street. Designed by Schwartz & Gross for Charles and Joseph Paterno, it curves around the corner and has just 16 apartments, some of them duplexes, some full-floor simplexes. The building boasts mahogany dining rooms, wall safes, and a ground-floor lounge for chauffeurs.

The 14-story Paterno apartment house is completed at 440 Riverside Drive, northeast corner 116th Street. Designed by Schwartz & Gross, it has a curved façade and two square light courts separated by a

glassed-in elevator core. An eight-room apartment rents for between $150 and $175 per month.

Kew Gardens property in Queens goes on sale from the estate of the late Albon Platt Man, a developer who acquired the hilly land in 1868. A Long Island Rail Road station was built last year on Lefferts Boulevard; Man's sons Alrick Hubbell Man and Albon P. Man, Jr. have laid out a new community, and they have engaged architects to design some 300 $8,000 and $20,000 English and neo-Tudor houses for the area that they name after the English botanical gardens outside London. The land will be graded in the next few years, streets extended, and water and sewer pipes installed (*see* 1915).

The Katharine House residence opens at 118 West 13th Street, Manhattan, under the auspices of the 50-year-old Ladies' Christian Union to provide "respectable" housing for 80 poor "young ladies," aged 18 to 35, who "are supporting themselves" after having come to the city from all parts of America. Modest rentals for the single-room accommodations include breakfast and dinner; residents must remain for at least 3 months and may stay for as long as 3 years. Dozens of such long-term hotels for young women will eventually dot the city, but most will have vanished before the end of the century.

Architect Charles W. Clinton of Clinton & Russell dies at his native New York December 1 at age 72.

The Ritz-Carlton Hotel opens December 15 on the west side of Madison Avenue between 46th and 47th streets. Architect Charles Wetmore and Ritz Hotels syndicator William Harris have persuaded real estate heir Robert Walton Goelet, 27, to build the 12-story luxury hotel, whose inner garden has a duck pond (Goelet's family has for generations owned vast holdings in midtown Manhattan). To quiet street noises, the new hotel will have Madison Avenue's cobblestones replaced between 42nd to 48th streets with wood blocks, paying for work that the city has refused to finance, but switching engines in the nearby Grand Central yards will continue to disturb guests for some years to come. Harris was a hotel accountant 8 years ago when he organized the Ritz Hotel Development Corp. to build Ritz hotels all over the world, and Goelet in the next 17 years will buy up most of the shares in that concern.

 The 4-month-old Alwyn Court apartment house has a fire the night of March 4 that attracts a crowd of 10,000. The building has no fire escapes, fire doors, or central standpipe, the blaze starts in a vacant flat on the ninth floor, it is difficult to contain, but only five of its luxurious apartments have been rented, no one is seriously hurt, and the damage is soon repaired.

The Brooklyn Botanic Garden opens alongside the Brooklyn Museum on Washington and Flatbush avenues, replacing a Parks Department ash dump. Initially part of the Brooklyn Institute of Arts and Sciences, it is directed by C. Stuart Gager, 38.

Yonah Shimmel's Knish Bakery opens at the corner of Forsyth and Houston streets on Manhattan's Lower East Side. The *shammes* (beadle) of the neighboring Romanian Synagogue, Shimmel grates baked potato or *kasha* (buckwheat groats), mixes it with flour, eggs, and onion, and encases it in a baked crust to create the knishes that his descendants will produce for more than 85 years.

Di Palo's opens at 206 Grand Street in Little Italy as a latteria, selling only fresh cheeses, milk, and butter. It will expand to carry also aged pecorino, dry-cured sausages, dried figs, and other fancy foods.

Coney Island frankfurter king Charles Feltman dies at Kassel, Germany, September 20 at age 68.

The city has 39 breweries, down from 121 (43 of them in Brooklyn) in 1879. Cheap rail transportation and mechanical refrigeration have enabled Cincinnati, Milwaukee, and St. Louis brewers to compete with the local breweries, which have had to either merge or go out of business.

New York's population reaches 4,766,883, up from 3,437,202 in 1900; Manhattan alone has 2,331,542, up from 1,850,093 (and up from 515,000 in 1850), but the Manhattan numbers will never again be so high, nor will the percentage of foreign-born New Yorkers—40.8 percent, up from an estimated 37 percent in 1900 (another 38 percent have at least one foreign-born parent). Half of all New Yorkers live in Manhattan, and some 530,000—one in every eight—live in tenements south of 14th Street.

1911 Tammany leader Charles F. "Silent Charlie" Murphy persuades the Democratic caucus in the state assembly to make Alfred E. Smith, now 37, majority leader (*see* 1910; Smith, 1903). The Citizens Union is outraged, calling Smith "the Tammany man," "one of the most dangerous men in Albany," but Al Smith conscientiously studies every bill that comes before the assembly and will distinguish himself as a reformer. His trademark brown derby hat and cigar have made him a familiar figure in New York and Albany (*see* 1912).

New York members of the Industrial Workers of the World (Local 168) strike March 18 to protest low pay and unsafe working conditions.

Sweatshop working conditions culminated in the horror of the infamous Triangle Shirtwaist Factory fire.

The Triangle Shirtwaist Co. factory on the top three floors of the 10-story Asch Building at Washington Place and Greene Street has a four-alarm fire March 25 that kills 146 people, 125 of them Italian and Jewish seamstresses aged 13 to 23 who are unable to escape (*see* 1908). The factory has employed some 500 women and 50 men, working them from 7:30 o'clock in the morning until 6 at night, mostly for $6 to $8 per week, under conditions so crowded that their chairs are dovetailed. Factory owners Max Blanck and Isaac Harris have locked all exits to the roof lest employees steal the shirtwaists, take them to the roof, and drop them to accomplices in the street below. Oil-soaked rags and lint lie ankle deep on the floor beneath each sewing machine, and someone has apparently lighted a cigar or cigarette and carelessly thrown the burning match onto the floor. The rags have burst into flames, there is no sprinkler system, a fire escape collapses under the weight of 30 girls, fire truck extension ladders reach only to the sixth floor, water from fire hoses reaches only to the seventh floor, executives on the top floor get away across neighboring rooftops, all except one of the workers on the eighth floor make their way to safety, but screaming young women leap from the loft building's ninth floor to escape the flames and almost none on that floor survive. The corpses are removed to the 26th Street Pier, where it takes a week to identify the dead; seven never are identified. The bodies are buried in a common grave at

The U.S. Supreme Court broke up John D. Rockefeller's Standard Oil Trust. LIBRARY OF CONGRESS

tee comprising two state senators, three assemblymen, and four citizens appointed by the state government. Assembly majority leader Al Smith is vice-chairman; Belle Israels (*née* Lindner) becomes a widow this year at age 33 and sits on the committee, whose members will work for 16 months to revise the state labor code, making it the best of any state in the country (*see* 1914; "dancing academies," 1909).

The state legislature at Albany enacts a law limiting to 54 the number of hours per week that a woman can work in any factory in the state. The measure has been drafted by State Senator Timothy Daniel "Big Tim" Sullivan, now 48, at the behest of Boston-born reformer Frances (originally Fannie Coralie) Perkins, 29, who since last year has been executive secretary of the Consumers' League of New York.

Max Blanck and Isaac Harris of the Triangle Shirtwaist Co. are indicted on charges of manslaughter, their trial begins at the Tombs December 4, lawyer Max Steuer represents the defendants, the prosecution presents more than 150 witnesses, but Tammany-appointed judge Thomas C. T. Crain essentially directs the verdict December 27, saying the case depends on whether the defendants knew the door was locked; the all-male jury debates for scarcely an hour and 40 minutes before pronouncing the defendants not guilty, and the court denies the prosecution's request for a retrial. Relatives of the Triangle fire victims have gathered outside the Tombs, and when the verdict is announced there is a pandemonium of rage that will fuel strikes for years to come.

The New York Police Department gets its first black patrolman August 12: Samuel Battle's appointment breaks the color barrier, but it will be decades before the force includes any appreciable number of blacks.

 The National League of Urban Conditions is founded at New York in October to ameliorate the economic situation of blacks. Created by a merger of the 5-year-old Committee for Improving the Industrial Conditions of Negroes in New York and National League for the Protection of Colored Women with the 1-year-old Committee on Urban Conditions Among Negroes, the interracial organization will shorten its name by 1919 to National Urban League, and as thousands of blacks migrate later in the century from the South to northern cities, the League will help them find jobs and housing, establishing affiliates in other cities to broaden its scope.

Mount Zion Cemetery in Maspeth, Queens, and the tragedy brings new demands for better working conditions: a protest meeting at the Metropolitan Opera House in early April is marked by shouts of, "Down with the capitalist legislature!" and the like. Rabbi Stephen S. Wise calls "the life of the lowliest worker . . . sacred and inviolable," Rose Schneiderman says, "I would be a traitor to these poor, burned bodies if I came here to talk good fellowship . . . Every year thousands of us are maimed. The life of men and women is so cheap and property is so sacred." Settlement-house worker Henry Moskowitz introduces a resolution calling on the legislature to make a thorough investigation of safety conditions and pass tough new laws.

German-born state senator Robert F. (Ferdinand) Wagner, 33, heads a Factory Investigation Commit-

New York Times publisher Adolph S. Ochs launches the Neediest Cases Fund. Approached on Christmas Day by a New Yorker who was down on his luck, he gave the man a few dollars, offered him work, and had his editors send a reporter to some of the city's private welfare agencies; Ochs publishes 100 brief accounts portraying the poor of the city and raises nearly $4,000. By 1997 the fund will be raising nearly $5 million each year and giving it to organizations that will include the Children's Aid Society, the Community Service Society of New York, the Brooklyn Bureau of Community Services, the Catholic Charities of the Archdiocese of New York, UJA-Federation of Jewish Philanthropies, and the Federation of Protestant Welfare Agencies.

$ Financier John W. "Bet-a-Million" Gates dies at Paris August 9 at age 56. His body is returned to New York and interred at Woodlawn Cemetery. Wall Street's Dow Jones Industrial Average closes December 30 at 81.68, up from 81.36 at the end of 1910.

Stern's department store vacates its West 23rd Street location and moves into a building with a cast-iron façade on the north side of 42nd Street just east of Sixth Avenue. Having prospered since 1878 by serving working-class customers as well as the carriage trade, the store will remain at its new site until 1969.

Merchant Alfred De Pinna retires from the store started by his late wife in 1885 and turns over management to his son Leo S., now 38, who has been working for De Pinna since graduation from CCNY in 1895 and will run the store until his own retirement in 1939. As its customers grew up, De Pinna has added departments to cater to their needs (*see* 1916).

Abraham & Straus cofounder Abraham Abraham suffers an acute attack of indigestion and dies at his Thousand Islands summer home on the St. Lawrence River June 28 at age 67.

The U.S. Supreme Court breaks up John D. Rockefeller's Standard Oil Company trust May 15, ruling in the case of *Standard Oil Co. of N.J. v. United States*, but the court rules only against "unreasonable" restraints of trade, where a company has "purpose or intent" to exercise monopoly power in violation of the Sherman Act of 1890. The trust is reorganized into five separate corporations plus some smaller ones—Standard Oil of New Jersey will later be called Esso and then Exxon, Standard of New York (later Socony-Vacuum, then Mobil), etc. Rockefeller is unfazed by the decision; now 71 and worth about

$300 million, he will have a net worth of about $900 million by the end of 1913.

Tolls on the 8-year-old Williamsburg Bridge are removed at midnight July 19.

The Bronx and Pelham Bay Parkway is laid out with one lane to connect 661-acre Bronx Park with 1,756-acre Pelham Bay Park. Lined with trees on both sides, the parkway is protected by strict codes that prevent anyone from building within 150 feet of its center and from putting up bars or hotels anywhere alongside it; railroads are barred from crossing over it, and it will eventually be widened to 400 feet as its name is shortened to Pelham Parkway.

The New York Central begins buying property in the area of 42nd Street between Madison and Lexington avenues as construction proceeds on a new Grand Central Terminal between 42nd and 45th streets (*see* 1903). The purpose of the program is to secure subsurface rights in order to build track loops under the terminal in accordance with plans devised by the railroad's chief engineer William J. Wilgus and to enjoy air rights for putting up hotels and other revenue-producing structures (*see* Grand Central, 1913; Commodore Hotel, 1919).

The White Star passenger liner S.S. *Olympic* arrives from Liverpool June 21 to begin service that will continue until 1935. Built by Harland & Wolff at Belfast with an overall length of 852 feet, the 45,324-ton, triple-screw, four-funnel "greyhound of the sea" is by far the largest liner yet built—92 feet wide in the beam, five decks amidships, five to seven decks elsewhere, with a bridge deck 540 feet long, a 495-foot promenade deck; she carries 2,510 passengers (735 in first class, 675 in second, 1,300 in steerage), her 114-foot-long Louis XVI dining salon can seat 532 persons at once, and she is the first ship to have a swimming pool (called a "plunge bath"). H.M.S. *Hawke* rams her in a fog September 20 as she heads west on another voyage to New York, her watertight doors close, she is in no danger of sinking, but her passengers have to be disembarked.

The 140-year-old New York Hospital begins receiving regular support from the city in amounts that will range from $20,000 to $40,000 for the care of indigent patients.

Bronx Hospital opens with six beds. Designed to serve Jewish immigrants, it will move in 1918 to the Eichler estate at the corner of 169th Street and Fulton Avenue (*see* 1932).

Archbishop Farley welcomes the new motherhouse of the Catholic Foreign Mission Society of America at Maryknoll into his archdiocese; now 69, he is named to the college of cardinals at Rome November 27.

The Carnegie Corporation of New York is created with a $125 million gift from Andrew Carnegie to encourage education (see 1905). The state legislature has passed an enabling law June 9, and the corporation's trustees meet for the first time at Carnegie's house on Fifth Avenue at 91st Street, where the philanthropist makes an initial gift of $25 million in first-mortgage 50-year bonds of the United States Steel Corp. Two more gifts follow in short order until $125 million has been transferred to the new entity—the largest sum deeded thus far to the cause of human betterment (see medicine, 1910).

The *Masses* begins monthly publication in January from offices in Nassau Street. Max Eastman and others have founded the literary and political journal, whose ownership is on a co-operative basis and whose powerful graphics advance the cause of class warfare, satirizing bourgeois values. Contributors from the start include author-cartoonist Art Young, now 45, who established residence in Washington Square 15 years ago and produced comic drawings for *Judge, Life,* and *Puck* before being invited by Arthur Brisbane to draw cartoon illustrations for editorials in Hearst's *New York Evening Journal* and *Sunday American*. Once a Republican, he has refused since last year to draw cartoons for ideas that did not coincide with his own anti-capitalist views (see 1913).

The Typographers Association of New York is founded to represent Linotype operators in dealings with management (see 1884). The union will continue for 87 years as its members hammer hot molten lead from the machines into place in giant 40-pound blocks to create plates for printing presses.

J. F. Knapp's Crowell Publishing Co. pays $40,000 in cash and $396,000 in Crowell preferred stock to acquire the *American Magazine*, founded 5 years ago (see *Collier's*, 1919).

New York World publisher Joseph Pulitzer dies at Charleston, S.C., October 29 at age 64 (see 1905). His will provides for the endowment of a Columbia School of Journalism and for Pulitzer prizes (see 1913; *World-Telegram*, 1931).

McCann-Erickson has its beginnings in the H. K. McCann advertising agency founded at New York by former Standard Oil Co. employee Harrison King McCann, 31, who sets up a shop to serve the various divisions of the company that has been split up by the Supreme Court (see McCann-Erickson, 1930).

The *New York Times Book Review* is renamed the *Review of Books* and appears on Sundays beginning January 29 instead of in the Saturday edition as it has since October 1896.

The New York Public Library main branch on Fifth Avenue between 40th and 42nd streets opens to the public May 24 (between 30,000 and 50,000 people come through its doors that day). Dedicated May 23 with ceremonies attended by dignitaries who include President Taft, the library's board president John Bigelow, 93, and its director, Dr. John Shaw Billings, who sketched a plan for the building on a postcard in 1897 (see 1895), it has been built in 9 years at a cost of $29 million, it is one of the first large buildings to be fully equipped with electric lights; its main reading room (Room 315) on the third floor, created at the suggestion of Dr. Billings, is 297 feet long and 78 feet wide, its 17-foot-high windows overlook Bryant Park, and its long tables have 676 seats lighted not only from the windows but also by bronze chandeliers and table lamps. Five subterranean floors of stacks house catalogued books that readers can order by means of an innovative delivery system employing pneumatic tubes (within 55 years the public catalogue will contain some 10 million cards, requiring 419,228 cubic feet of space; they will be photographed and bound into an 800-volume dictionary catalogue that takes up only 13,095 cubic feet). Stone lions sculpted by Edward Clark Potter, 53, guard the entrance to the $9 million Vermont white marble palace, designed in Beaux-Arts style by Thomas Hastings of Carrère and Hastings (Carrère has died at Presbyterian Hospital on Park Avenue March 1 at age 52, never having gained full consciousness after his taxicab was struck on the night of February 12 by a motorcar at the corner of 74th Street and Madison Avenue, throwing him 10 feet and causing him to suffer a scalp wound and a fatal concussion of the brain). The Fifth Avenue entrance to the magnificent new library has wide terraces and three arched bays flanked by Corinthian columns; the building replaces the Croton Aqueduct Distributing Reservoir that stood on the spot from 1842 to 1902 (some 500 workers took 2 years to dismantle it). Frederick MacMonnies has designed the statues *Beauty* and *Truth* on either side of the Fifth Avenue entrance, and the 11-foot-high figures (*History, Drama, Poetry, Religion,* and *Romance*) on the frieze have been designed by Paul Bartlett.

Nonfiction: "Some Picture Show Audiences" by Greenwich Village reformer Mary Heaton Vorse appears in *The Outlook* June 24: "Houston Street, on the East Side, of an afternoon is always more crowded than Broadway. Push-carts line the street. The faces that you see are almost all Jewish—Jews of many different types; swarthy little men, most of them, looking undersized according to the Anglo-Saxon standard. Here and there a deep-chested mother of Israel sails along, majestic in her *shietel* and shawl. These are the toilers—garment-makers, a great many of them—people who work 'by pants,' as they say. A long and terrible workday they have to keep body and soul together."

Painting: Polish-born painter Max Weber, 30, has his work exhibited at Alfred Stieglitz's 6-year-old 291 Gallery but the modernist paintings attract almost no favorable interest (no museum will buy any of Weber's works until 1926).

Sculpture: a bronze statue of William Cullen Bryant by Vermont-born sculptor Herbert Adams, 53, is unveiled in Bryant Park, directly behind the new central branch of the New York Public Library, in a marble setting designed by the library's architect Thomas Hastings.

Theater: *The Deep Purple* by Paul Armstrong and Wilson Mizner 1/9 at the Lyric Theater, with Richard Bennett, Catherine Calvert, 152 perfs. (the play makes Mizner a lot of money, and he calls his new profession "telling lies at two dollars per head"); George M. Cohan's Theater opens 2/12 at 1482 Broadway with its main entrance in 43rd Street; *Everywoman* by Walter Brown 2/27 at the Herald Square Theater, with Dublin-born actress Patricia Collinge, 18, 144 perfs.; *Mrs. Bumpsted-Leigh* by Connecticut-born playwright Harry J. (James) Smith, 31, 4/3 at the Lyceum Theater, with Mrs. Minnie Maddern Fiske, 64 perfs.; The Playhouse opens 4/15 at 137 West 48th Street, where it has been put up by San Francisco-born actor-producer-prizefight manager William Aloysius Brady, 47; the Folies Bergère Theater (later the Fulton, then the Helen Hayes) opens 5/1 at 210 West 46th Street (initially a theater-restaurant, it becomes a legitimate theater in October); *Disraeli* by Louis Napoleon Parker 9/18 at Wallack's Theater, with George Arliss, 280 perfs.; *The Return of Peter Grimm* by David Belasco 10/17 at the Belasco Theater, with David Warfield, 231 perfs.; *The Garden of Allah* by English novelist Robert Smythe Hichens, 47, and Mary Hudson 10/21 at the Century Theater, is based on Hichens's 1905 novel, 241 perfs.; *Kismet* by English-born playwright Edward Knoblock, 37, 12/25 at the Knickerbocker Theater, with Otis Skinner, now 53, 184 perfs.

Keystone Co. is founded by Canadian-born motion picture pioneer Mack Sennett, 27, who changed his name from Michael Sinnott when he came to New York in 1904 to begin a stage career in burlesque and the circus. Sennett has been working with D. W. Griffith at Biograph Studios (*see* Chaplin, 1913).

Broadway musicals: *The Pink Lady* 3/13 at the New Amsterdam Theater with Ogden, Utah-born entertainer Hazel Dawn, 19, music by Ivan Caryll, 312 perfs. (the hit makes pink the year's fashion color); *La Belle Parée* and *Bow Sing* (a twin bill) 3/20 at Lee Shubert's new Winter Garden Theater on Broadway between 50th and 51st streets, with Russian-born blackface minstrel singer Al Jolson (originally Asa Yoelson), 24, New York- (or Toronto-) born vaudeville entertainer George White (originally Weitz), 21, music by New York-born composer Jerome (David) Kern, 26, and others, lyrics by Edward Madden and others, 104 perfs.; *The Ziegfeld Follies* 6/26 at the Jardin de Paris with the 18-year-old Dolly Sisters (Viennese dancers Jennie [Jan Szieka Deutsch] and Rosie [Roszika Deutsch]), Australian-born comedian Leon Errol, 30, Oklahoma-born humorist and vaudeville star William Penn Adair "Will" Rogers, now 35 (who made his New York debut 10 years ago at Hammerstein's Roof Garden), Antigua, BVI-born blackface comedian Bert Williams (originally Egbert Austin), 36, the first black man to star in an all-white show on Broadway), music by Hungarian-born composer Sigmund Romberg, 23, and others, 80 perfs.; *The Fascinating Widow* 9/11 at the Liberty Theater, with Massachusetts-born female impersonator Julian Eltinge (originally William Dalton), 28, music by F. A. Mills and Jean Schwartz, book by Otto Hauerbach, 56 perfs.

The New York Military Band is founded by Louisville, Ky.-born bandmaster Edwin Franko Goldman, 33, who was solo cornetist with the Metropolitan Opera from 1895 to 1905 (*see* 1922).

Popular songs: "Alexander's Ragtime Band" by Irving Berlin popularizes the ragtime music pioneered by Scott Joplin in 1899 (Berlin has adapted his unsuccessful song "Alexander and His Clarinet," George M. Cohan sings the improved version at a *Frolics* of the 7-year-old Friars Club, more than 2 million copies of the sheet music have been sold by year's end, and Berlin's earnings next year will be a phenomenal $100,000); "Everybody's Doin' It" by Irving Berlin popularizes the Turkey Trot dance invented by dancer Vernon Castle and his 18-year-old bride Irene Foote Castle.

Fire destroys the Polo Grounds stadium of John McGraw's New York Giants April 13; a new structure completed June 28 is of steel and concrete construction with a seating capacity of 38,000 (it will be expanded in time to seat nearly 56,000) (*see* 1958). The Giants win the National League pennant, but Connie Mack's Philadelphia Athletics win the World Series, defeating the Giants 4 games to 2, despite the best efforts of pitcher Christy Mathewson, now 31, and Cleveland-born pitcher Richard William "Rube" Marquard, 22.

Coney Island's 7-year-old Dreamland Park goes up in flames May 27, consuming the Pike's Peak scenic railway and 50 other attractions, destroying Feltman's hot-dog stand, and killing one of six infants on display in incubators. Water pressure fails at a critical time, damage is estimated to be about $4 million, and insurance coverage amounts to only $343,500. A lioness escapes to Surf Avenue but will be found under the Boardwalk at Luna Park June 11. Concessionaires, police, fire, and water departments all blame each other for the disaster, the ruins attract a crowd of 350,000 May 28, Steeplechase Park is left with only one pier, Samuel Gumpertz immediately organizes the Dreamland Circus Sideshow in a tent on Surf Avenue (it will continue to 1929), some Dreamland attractions reopen, a record crowd of 400,000 comes out July 2, but 2,500 workers are left without jobs. The Board of Estimate votes July 27 to buy the site of Dreamland for $1,225,000 to use as a seaside park.

The Giant Racer roller coaster at Coney Island flies off its tracks September 4, killing two women and injuring three other persons. Built at a cost of $180,000, the 900-foot-long two-track racing coaster has a steel superstructure that enabled it to survive the Dreamland fire in late May, but the train has left the tracks on a curve 50 feet above Surf Avenue (*see* Cyclone, 1927).

Fire destroys part of Coney Island's Luna Park December 11; the loss is placed at $150,000 (*see* 1912).

The U.S. Supreme Court breaks up James B. Duke's 21-year-old American Tobacco Co. Trust May 29, ruling in the case of *United States v. American Tobacco Co.* Emerging from the trust are American Tobacco (controlled by 10 major investors who include Oliver Hazard Payne and Thomas Fortune Ryan), P. Lorillard (*see* 1789), Liggett & Myers, R. J. Reynolds, and British-American Tobacco Co.

The Sullivan Law enacted by the legislature at Albany is the state's first effort to control possession of handguns. State Senator "Big Tim" Sullivan grew up in the infamous Five Points section of the Lower East Side and is well acquainted with the uses of handguns in committing violent crimes (his Sullivan-Considine vaudeville theaters and nickelodeon and racetrack investments are making him a fortune).

The Hall of Records (later Surrogate's Court) is completed at 31 Chambers Street after 12 years of work and used for records that date in some cases to 1653. Architect John R. Thomas has designed the granite structure in an elaborate French Renaissance style, using Siena marble for a lobby that apes the foyer of the Paris Opéra and English oak and mahogany for the fifth-floor courtrooms.

The 21-story Germania Life (later Guardian Life) Building is completed at the northeast corner of Fourth Avenue and 17th Street for the 51-year-old insurance company. Designed by D'Oench & Yost in French Renaissance Revival style with an ornamented four-story copper and terra-cotta roof, it towers 281 feet above Union Square and will be converted to use as a hotel at the end of the century.

Grand Central Palace opens at 480 Lexington Avenue, between 46th and 47th streets, with offices and showrooms and (on its first four floors) exhibition areas used at the opening for an architecture and building-trades show. Designed by Warren & Wetmore in Roman Renaissance style, it rises above the New York Central's railyards (its steel underpinnings are an integral part of the railroad tunnel below), replaces an earlier Grand Central Palace exposition hall that stood just two blocks to the south, will house the annual Automobile Show, Boat Show, Chemical Show, Flower Show (*see* 1914), Sportsmen's Show, and other events until 1956, and will also contain a dance hall ("Clover Gardens"), a home-making center, and an indoor golf course (*see* 245 Park Avenue, 1966).

The Jonathan Bulkley house is completed at 600 Park Avenue, northwest corner 64th Street, for the head of Bulkley Dunton & Co., a New York paper-making firm founded as Cross, Bulkley & Gookin by Bulkley's Connecticut-born father, Edwin, in 1838. Park Avenue remains a thoroughfare lined for the most part with row houses, small apartment houses, and shops selling everything from beer, ice, coal, and groceries, but Kentucky-born architect James Gamble Rogers, 44, has designed Bulkley's palatial white Modern Renaissance house, which replaces a row house and a small apartment building built in 1879 (*see* 1947).

An Italian Renaissance mansion for German-born investment banker George Blumenthal, 53, of Lazard Frères is completed in East 70th Street off Park Avenue to designs by Trowbridge & Livingston. Blumenthal's French Renaissance town house in West 53rd Street, between Fifth and Sixth avenues, was finished at the turn of the century; he joined last year with Susan Vanderpoel Clark, Arthur Curtiss James, Anna Louise Poor, and Elisha Walker to buy the grounds of the Union Theological Seminary, whose trustees moved it in 1908 to Morningside Heights. Blumenthal is building a collection of Renaissance enamels and canvases; his is the city's first private residence to have its own swimming pool.

The six-story Henry Phipps Houses are completed in 63rd and 64th streets west of Amsterdam Avenue (see 1907). Designed by Whitfield and King, the sanitary new flats contain nearly 1,100 units (the first opened 4 years ago with white tenants, but efforts have been made to integrate the project; blacks and Hispanics will soon predominate).

Fifth Avenue gets its first luxury apartment house as 998 Fifth Avenue opens opposite the Metropolitan Museum of Art at 81st Street. The *New York Times* has run an editorial March 31 saying that the building may be beautiful but is "another instance of the persistent defiance of all plan and purpose in building up Manhattan . . . an act of deliberate incivicism, and as such honestly to be condemned." Subway builder August Belmont II has paid $215,000 for the empty lot, and the structure that fills it has been designed in Italian Renaissance style by W. S. Richardson of McKim, Mead & White with one flat per floor. Each apartment has 22 rooms—eight master bedrooms, 10 baths, nine maids' rooms, an octagonal salon, large living and dining rooms, and a reception room 36 feet long. But 998 Fifth has trouble attracting tenants (90 percent of the fashionable rich still live in private houses) until real estate agent Douglas L. Elliman, 29, persuades Sen. Elihu Root to give up his big brick town house at 71st Street and Park and take an apartment that would normally rent at more than $2,000 per month for just $1,250.

The 12-story Evanston apartment house is completed at 610 West End Avenue (272 West 90th Street). Designed by George and Edward Blum, it has four apartments per floor, two of them duplexed with sleeping rooms on the floor higher than the rooms used for entertaining but not directly above them. A music room adjoins each living room, and throwing open the connecting doors creates a space that in some cases is 80 feet long. The largest room in each unit is a windowless reception room, complete with fireplace, for entertaining guests without disturbing the everyday living room.

The apse, choir, crossing, and first two chapels of the Cathedral of St. John the Divine are consecrated April 19 at 110th Street and Amsterdam Avenue (see 1909). The trustees replace Heins & La Farge in May with Boston architects Ralph Adams Cram, now 46, and Frank William Ferguson, now 48, whose plan calls for removing all traces of Byzantine, or Romanesque, design and replacing it with a Gothic design, but the cathedral's building fund runs of out money and construction will not resume until 1916.

The Gowanus Flushing Tunnel is completed beneath South Brooklyn with a large propeller to pump water from New York Harbor into the 66-year-old Gowanus Canal and force its waste into the harbor (see 1893).

A paper presented to the American Society of Mechanical Engineers by Willis H. Carrier will be the basis of modern air conditioning (see 1902). "Rational Psychometric Formulae" is based on 10 years' work that have initiated a scientific approach to air conditioning; its author will help start Carrier Corp. in 1915.

Manhattan's Carl Schurz Park gets that name as the East End Park extending north from 86th Street on the East River is renamed to honor the late U.S. secretary of the interior and political reformer.

Ellis Island has a record 1-day influx of 11,745 immigrants April 17 (see 1892). Having given many immigrants their first bananas, oranges, and prunes, the facility's kitchen is enlarged to enable it to prepare kosher meals (many Orthodox Jews from Eastern Europe have refused to eat anything while they awaited processing).

1912 The cornerstone of the *Maine* Memorial is laid at Columbus Circle May 30 before a crowd that includes onetime city corporation counsel, Civil War general, U.S. ambassador to Spain, and congressman Daniel E. Sickles, now 92. The marble-and-brass sculpture completed by Attilio Piccirilli in April contains metal salvaged from the U.S. battleship in Havana's harbor and commemorates the men who died when she exploded in February 1898. Influential artists protest that the work is militaristic, gaudy, tasteless, and a waste of the taxpayers' money.

The murder of Lower East Side gambling-house operator Herman "Beansie" Rosenthal at midnight July 16 leads to revelations of widespread corruption in the city government. A 1909 Packard touring car

R.M.S. Titanic *never reached New York; her sinking in the icy North Atlantic dismayed the world.*

pulls up to the curb, four gangsters step out, and Rosenthal is gunned down as he emerges from the Metropole Café (later Rosoff's Restaurant) in West 43rd Street, near Broadway. He has accused police lieutenant Charles Becker, 46, of graft in a *New York World* story July 14 (Becker's "strong-arm squad" has supposedly been trying to eradicate gambling, but Rosenthal has claimed that Becker was his partner in a West 45th Street gambling house), Mayor Gaynor defends Becker and attacks "lawless foreigners," Jewish leaders criticize the mayor, *New York World* reporter Herbert Bayard Swope, 30, helps make the case a cause célèbre, District Attorney Charles S. Whitman launches an investigation with support from leading citizens bent on exposing police corruption and reforming city government; the Board of Aldermen appoints lawyer Henry H. Curran head of a committee to look into the matter of police corruption, professional stool pigeon "Bald Jack" Rose (originally Jacob Rosenzweig) turns state's evidence, and Becker's trial creates a sensation by revealing police collusion with mobsters. Becker is found guilty October 22 of having ordered Rosenthal's murder, and he will go to the electric chair at Sing Sing in July 1915 along with the four gunmen who shot Rosenthal.

Financier Thomas Fortune Ryan tries to gain control of the Democratic Party convention (he has been buying politicians for years) but is formally banned from the proceedings by a group of delegates who include William Jennings Bryan; the convention nominates Virginia-born Gov. Woodrow Wilson, now 55, of New Jersey as its presidential candidate. Wilson has received help from Texas-born politician Edward Mandell House, 54, who briefly favored the candidacy of New York's Mayor Gaynor. Col. House (the "colonel" is a Texas honorary title) has taken up residence with his wife in a Murray Hill apartment at 145 East 35th Street.

Former president Theodore Roosevelt wins all the Republican presidential primaries but the party convention refuses to nominate him because he has dared to oppose J. P. Morgan and other Wall Street interests. Roosevelt runs as an independent on the Progressive (Bull Moose) Party, and although he wins 88 electoral votes to President Taft's eight, Gov. Wilson receives 435 electoral votes with 42 percent of the popular vote to put a Democrat in the White House for the first time since Grover Cleveland left it in 1897. The Democratic National Committee's finance chairman has been German-born businessman Henry Morgenthau, 56, who has made a fortune developing real estate in northern Manhattan and the Bronx.

Former congressman William Sulzer, 49, is elected governor with support from Tammany Hall boss Charles F. Murphy. His New Jersey-born Republican challenger, Job Elmer Hedges, 50, secures only 444,105 votes to Sulzer's 649,559, Progressive Party candidate Oscar S. Straus fares even worse, and the Democrats regain control of both houses of the state legislature at Albany, having lost it briefly to the Republicans (*but see* 1913).

A mass meeting of the Wage Earner's League and the Collegiate Equal Suffrage League in the Great Hall of the People at the Cooper Union April 22 protests the state legislature's failure to pass a resolution endorsing woman suffrage. Labor leader Rose Schneiderman attacks a state senator who has said that if women were to get "into the arena of politics with its alliances and distressing contests—the delicacy is gone, the charm is gone, and you emasculate woman;" rising to her full four feet nine inches, she says, "I wonder if it will add to my height when I get the vote. I might work for it all the harder if it did." She speaks of women in laundries standing 13 to 14 hours each day in terrible steam and heat with their hands in hot starch. "Certainly these women won't lose any more of their beauty and charm by putting a ballot in a ballot box once a year than they are likely to standing in the . . . laundries all year round."

A New York suffrage parade marches up Fifth Avenue from Washington Square beginning at sundown May 4. The 10,000 marchers reverently carry huge banners bearing the names of the late Susan B. Anthony, Elizabeth Cady Stanton, and Julia Ward Howe, 1,000 sympathetic men join them, as does a contingent led by feminist Inez Milholland, 25 (Vassar '09), wearing Grecian robes and mounted on a white horse. An overflow crowd that includes women of all ages, occupations, and professions packs Carnegie Hall to hear speeches urging that women be given the vote. "Ladies," Inez Milholland urges, "think for yourselves and see just how independent you really are."

The Hotel Workers Industrial Union brings 18,000 employees out on strike May 7 and obtains signature of several contracts. The United Hebrew Trades union strikes June 21, bringing out 9,000 workers in a demand for union recognition, a 49-hour week, 10 paid holidays, a ban on home work, a permanent arbitration board, and a joint sanitary control board; the action brings almost complete unionization of the fur industry. The Industrial Workers of the World (IWW) strikes June 28.

The International Ladies' Garment Workers' Union (ILGWU) calls a strike in December (but see 1913).

$ The Hanover Bank merges with the National Bank of the City of New York, chartered in 1829 (see 1831). Founded in 1851, the Hanover prospered in the last third of the 19th century through loans and investments in the South during Reconstruction and in the opening of the West (see Manufacturers Hanover, 1961).

Wall Street's Dow Jones Industrial Average closes December 31 at 87.87, up from 81.68 at the end of 1911.

[s] S. Klein opens on Union Square, where real estate values have plummeted as the city's commercial center moved north. Russian-born merchant Samuel Klein, 25, has taken over a small building that is said to have housed the saloon where "The Face on the Barroom Floor" was written. Klein's idea is to sell clothing as cheaply and quickly as possible, and in the greatest volume; he will buy 5,000 dresses at a time on average—and often 20,000 or 30,000—and by paying spot cash obtain a price advantage of 5 to 10 percent over other buyers. Anything not sold at the end of 2 weeks will be marked down, and drastic reductions will be made until the merchandise is gone. Klein will take over additional ramshackle buildings and put up a huge sign that stretches from 14th Street to beyond 15th. He will

stop advertising sales in the 1920s after some of his ads bring out women shoppers in such hordes that subway service is disrupted, Union Square is jammed, windows are broken, and mounted police have to be rushed in to keep order (see 1931).

Retail merchant Henri Bendel moves his 20-year-old women's specialty shop from 520 Fifth Avenue to larger premises at 10 West 57th Street, where it will prosper for the next 70 years (see 1986).

Vehicles cross Park Avenue at 51st Street April 1 for the first time in 40 years as barriers come down to open the street across the covered railroad yards.

The 46,328-ton White Star liner R.M.S. *Titanic* scrapes an iceberg in the North Atlantic on her maiden voyage late in the night of April 14, her hold is punctured, and she sinks in 2 hours early Monday morning, April 15. The largest passenger liner built to date (882 feet in length overall), she was bound for Pier 59 at West 20th Street. A White Star vice president in the company's offices at 11 Broadway insists that the ship will be fine: "She is absolutely unsinkable," Philip A. S. Franklin tells a *New York Tribune* reporter April 15. A small crowd gathers outside the building to await further news, a representative of J. P. Morgan drops by to get the latest report (Morgan's company helped finance the three-screw ship), and soon after 7 o'clock in the evening Franklin calls reporters into his office to say, "We have reason to believe that the *Titanic* went down at 2:20 o'clock this morning." The Cunard liner R.M.S. *Carpathia* arrives at Pier 54, at the foot of 14th Street, April 18 with 675 survivors, mostly women and children, and the *New York Times* will report April 19 that the pier "echoed with the shrieks of women and even of men." Most of the injured are rushed to St. Vincent's and St. Luke's hospitals, the White Star company puts second cabin class survivors up at the Chelsea Hotel in West 23rd Street, and some survivors are taken to a seamen's lodge at the corner of Jane and West streets (crew members are detained under guard aboard R.M.S. *Celtic* with orders not to talk to the press). Flags in the city are lowered to half mast in honor of the dead: only 711 of the 2,224 aboard have survived, and the 1,513 lost include prominent millionaires, among them R. H. Macy's Isidor Straus, 67; copper heir Benjamin Guggenheim, 47; and Col. John Jacob Astor IV, 47, whose New York real estate holdings have been exceeded only by those of his expatriate cousin William Waldorf Astor, now 63, of London.

Ida Straus drowns along with her husband, Isidor, having refused to join other women from the first-class section in the lifeboats (she gave her fur coat and her seat in the lifeboat to her maid). The body of Isidor Straus is recovered and buried in a ship-shaped mausoleum at Woodlawn Cemetery in the Bronx; a plaque memorializing the couple will be placed above the 34th Street entrance to the store (*see* environment [Straus Park], 1915).

Lewis A. Stimson of the Cornell University Medical College writes to New York Hospital's board of governors that the sum of $250,000 (received from banker-philanthropist George F. Baker) has been placed in an account "for the purpose of effecting an affiliation" between New York Hospital and Cornell "with the object of promoting medical research, aiding the care of patients in the hospital, and furthering the education of students in the college" by allowing them to obtain clinical instruction in the hospital's ward (*see* 1904). Philanthropist Oliver Hazard Payne's endowment to the medical school will total $4,850,000 by next year and will ultimately total more than $8 million (*see* 1917).

Lysol production begins at New York, where the 38-year-old firm Lehn & Fink manufactures the household disinfectant it has been importing from Germany.

Creedmore Psychiatric Center has its beginnings in a "farm colony" for mental patients opened for the Brooklyn Psychiatric Hospital on a tract of land one mile north of Queens Village used until 4 years ago by the National Guard for a barracks and firing range. New buildings will be erected in 1926, 1929, and 1933 to give it a nominal capacity of 3,300 patients, but overcrowding will be common until the mid-1950s, when the introduction of tranquilizing drugs will reduce the need for confinement.

The wireless message "SS *TITANIC* RAN INTO ICE-BERG. SINKING FAST" is picked up accidentally by Russian-born wireless operator David Sarnoff, 20, who will later say he was manning a station set up by John Wanamaker in his New York store window ostensibly to keep in touch with the Philadelphia Wanamaker's but actually as a publicity stunt (doubts will be raised about the story, since the store is closed at night, certainly on Sunday). Sarnoff relays the message from the *Titanic* to another steamer, whose wireless man reports that the liner has sunk but that some survivors have been picked up. President Taft orders other stations to remain silent and Sarnoff remains at his post for 72 hours, taking the names of survivors and making his own name familiar to millions of newspaper readers.

The S. I. Newhouse publishing empire has its beginnings at Bayonne, N.J., where a local lawyer has acquired controlling interest in the foundering *Bayonne Times* as payment for a legal fee and sends his office boy Samuel Irving Newhouse, 17, to take charge, offering him half the paper's profits in lieu of salary. By the time he is 21 Newhouse will have earned a law degree at night school and be earning $30,000 per year from the newspaper. He will persuade his employer to join him in buying the *Staten Island Advance* in 1922, and by 1955 the Newhouse chain will include the *Long Island Press*, *Newark Star-Ledger*, *Syracuse Post-Standard*, *Herald-Journal*, and *Herald-American*, and papers as far away as Portland, Ore. (*see* 1967).

Circulation of the 15-year-old *Jewish Daily Forward* reaches 120,000 and the paper moves its offices into a new building at 175 East Broadway, between Rutgers and Jefferson streets. Designed by architect George Boehm, the 11-story building has a cream-and-tan exterior and towers above the three- to five-story houses and tenements of the area.

Buffalo heiress Mabel (Ganson) Dodge, 33, returns from Europe, leases the second floor of a Greenwich Village brownstone at 23 Fifth Avenue (northeast corner 9th Street), and journalist Lincoln Steffens persuades her to open her home to the local intelligentsia because "you have a centralizing, magnetic, social faculty." Gen. Daniel E. Sickles has rented the space, and before she leaves in 1916 her "Salon Dodge" in New York will flourish on Wednesday evenings for 3 years, attracting such notables as Max Eastman, Elizabeth Gurley Flynn, Emma Goldman, Walter Lippmann, John Reed, Margaret Sanger, Gertrude Stein, Alfred Stieglitz, and Carl Van Vechten.

Iowa-born Columbia Law School graduate Carl Byoir, 24, goes to work at New York as an advertising salesman for Hearst magazines. Byoir began his career at age 14 as a reporter for the *Des Moines State Register*, entered the University of Iowa 6 years ago with only $30, worked his way through college by publishing yearbooks, came out with savings of $6,500, and last year bought the U.S. rights to the Montessori system of education (*see* 1932).

Publisher Frank A. Munsey buys The *Press* September 5 and uses its editorial voice to support "Bull Moose" candidate Theodore Roosevelt (*see Sun*, 1916).

New York Tribune publisher and U.S. ambassador to Britain Whitelaw Reid dies at London December 15 at age 75 (*see* 1872). His son Ogden Mills Reid, 30, last year married his mother's social secretary Helen Rogers (*née* Miles), now 29, and will take over management of the paper; its circulation and advertising have declined, young Ogden will not be able to rebuild it even with the help of his capable wife, but they will reject Frank A. Munsey's offers to buy it (*see Herald Tribune*, 1924).

Fiction: *The Autobiography of an Ex-Colored Man* by poet-essayist James Weldon Johnson of 1899 "Lift Every Voice and Sing" fame (he will not acknowledge authorship until 1927); *The Financier* by Theodore Dreiser is based on the life of the late Charles T. Yerkes.

M. Knoedler & Co. opens in January at 556 Fifth Avenue, southwest corner 46th Street, with an exhibition of works by Gainsborough, Romney, Van Dyke, and other Old Masters (*see* 1846). Founder's son Roland Knoedler has commissioned architects Carrère & Hastings to design the five-story limestone mansionlike gallery and moves his business uptown from 34th Street, where it has been since 1910 (*see* 1925).

Painting: *McSorley's Bar* and *Sunday, Women Drying Their Hair* by John Sloan; *Team of Horses* by Arthur Dove; *Woolworth Building* and *Movement, Fifth Avenue* by water-colorist John Marin (*see* real estate, 1913).

Theater: *The Greyhound* by Paul Armstrong and Wilson Mizner 2/29 at the Astor Theater, with David Burton in a melodrama about oceangoing confidence men (Armstrong has taken Mizner on a transatlantic voyage and pumped him for stories of larceny on the high seas), 108 perfs. (the sinking of the *Titanic* April 15 horrifies prospective playgoers, forcing the show to close); the 299-seat Little Theater (later to be a second Helen Hayes Theater) opens 3/12 at 238 West 44th Street (designed by Ingalls & Hoffman, it has been commissioned by producer Winthrop Ames), the 48th Street Theater 8/12 at 157 West 48th Street (built by William A. Brady), the Eltinge Theater (named for female impersonator Julian Eltinge and later to be a second Empire Theater) 9/11 at 236 West 42nd Street; *The Yellow Jacket* by George C. Hazelton and San Francisco-born actor-turned-playwright J. (Joseph) Harry Benrimo, 38 (who have written it at the 80-year-old Stuyvesant apartment house in East 18th Street) 11/4 at the Fulton Theater (formerly the Folies Bèrgere), 80 perfs.; *Peg O' My Heart* by J. Hartley Manners 12/20 at the new Cort Theater (designed by Thomas W. Lamb for producer John Cort) at 138-146 West 48th Street, with the playwright's bride, Laurette Taylor, 605 perfs.; *Years of Discretion* by Frederick and Fanny Hatton 12/25 at the Belasco Theater with Grant Mitchell, Cam-

bridge, Mass.-born actress Effie Shannon, 45, 190 perfs.

The Minsky brothers—Abe, 31, Billy (Michael William), 21, Herbert Kay, 20, and Morton, 10—take over their father's National Winter Garden Theater in East Houston Street for bawdy burlesque productions, beginning a chain that will continue until 1937 (*see* 1922).

Illusionist Harry Houdini charters a tugboat from McAllister Brothers, is told it is illegal under New York law to hold a public performance on a Sunday, instructs Capt. J. P. McAllister July 7 to make for Governors Island, where New York laws do not apply, has himself shackled, nailed into a pine crate that is sealed with steel bands, weighted down with two sewer pipes, and dropped into the harbor (*see* 1894). Within 1 minute he is spotted bobbing up and down in the water. Now 38, he repeats the "miraculous escape" nightly in a 5,500-gallon tank on Hammerstein's Roof, earning $1,000 per week (*see* 1914).

Harlem's Lafayette Theater opens in November on Seventh Avenue between 131st and 132nd streets. Financed by Canal Street banker Meyer Jarmulovsky and designed by architect V. Hugo Koehler, the 1,500-seat house has a white director, A. C. Winn (although buildings in 132nd Street are now occupied by blacks, those in 131st Street are still mostly white). Winn will begin admitting blacks to the orchestra in August of next year, making the Lafayette the first theater to integrate, but he will initially charge blacks twice the normal admission price of 10¢ (5¢ for children). Actor Charles Gilpin will found the Lafayette Players—Harlem's first black legitimate theater group—in 1916, and the house will become an important venue for black stock companies presenting one-act plays and adaptations of Broadway hits.

Film: *Queen Elizabeth* with Sarah Bernhardt, now 57, 7/12 at the Lyceum Theater—the first feature-length motion picture seen in America. Hungarian-born furrier turned nickelodeon-chain operator Adolph Zukor, 39, has persuaded theatrical producer Charles Frohman to join him in investing $35,000 to acquire U.S. rights to the 40-minute French film, the two earn $200,000 showing it on a reserved-seat basis in theaters across the country, and they form Famous Players Co. to produce films of their own (*see* Lasky, 1913).

The Biograph Co. studios are completed in the East Tremont section of the Bronx at 807 East 175th Street and 790 East 176th Street, between Marmion and Prospect avenues (*see* 1895); D. W. Griffith is Biograph's leading director, but filmmakers need bright outdoor light on a more consistent basis than New York can offer and most of the film industry will soon move to Hollywood, Calif.

Universal Pictures Corp. is created at New York by a merger of independent film producers who include cinema pioneer Carl Laemmle, now 45 (*see* 1909). He will move to Hollywood, have sole control of Universal from 1920 to 1936, and be the first to promote the personalities of his film performers as "movie stars," hiring Mary Pickford from the Biograph Studios.

The Audubon Theater on Broadway at 165th Street opens to show films produced by Hungarian-born motion-picture pioneer William Fox, 33, who has had Thomas W. Lamb design the 2,368-seat house with a line of three-dimensional fox heads adorning its terra-cotta façade (*see* Regent, 1913).

Broadway musicals: *Over the River* 1/8 at the Globe Theater, with Eddie Foy, Jr., Lillian Lorraine, music by John Golden, book by George V. Hobart and H. A. Du Souchet, 120 perfs.; *The Isle o' Dreams* 1/27 at the Grand Opera House, with Chauncey Olcott, music by Ernest R. Ball, lyrics by Olcott and George Graf, Jr., 26 (who has never been to Ireland), songs that include "When Irish Eyes Are Smiling," 32 perfs.; *Hokey-pokey/Bunting, Bulls and Strings* 2/8 at the Broadway Theater, with Lillian Russell, Fay Templeton, Joe Weber, Lew Fields, William Collier, music by John Stromberg and others, lyrics by Edgar Smith and E. Ray Goetz, 108 perfs.; *The Passing Show* 7/22 at the Winter Garden Theater, with Willie and Eugene Howard, Philadelphia-born ingénue (Frances) Charlotte Greenwood, 22, music by Louis A. Hirsch, lyrics by Lake Forest, Ill.-born writer-composer Harold (Richard) Atteridge, 26, 136 perfs.; *The Ziegfeld Follies* 10/21 at the Moulin Rouge, with Leon Errol, Vera Maxwell, 77 perfs.; *The Lady of the Slipper* 10/28 at the Globe Theater, with Elsie Janis, dancer Vernon Castle, Dave Montgomery, Fred Stone, music by Victor Herbert, 232 perfs.; *The Firefly* 12/12 at the Lyric Theater, with music by Prague-born composer Rudolf Friml, 32, lyrics by Otto Harbach, songs that include "Giannina Mia," 120 perfs.

The Clef Club Orchestra organized in Harlem 2 years ago by Mobile, Ala.-born bandleader James Reese Europe, 31, gives a concert at Carnegie Hall May 2, becoming the first black ensemble and first jazz band to play there. So warmly is its program received that the management will book return engagements next year and in 1914.

Popular songs: "When the Midnight Choo Choo Leaves for Alabam" by Irving Berlin; "Bulldog" and "Bingo Eli Yale" by Peru, Ind.-born Yale sophomore Cole Porter, 20.

The New York Giants win the National League pennant, but the Boston Red Sox win the World Series, defeating the Giants 4 games to 3 (the Sox changed their name from Red Stockings 5 years ago and earlier this year completed Fenway Park with 33,487 seats). The second game has been called on account of darkness with the score tied 6 to 6. Rube Marquard wins the third and sixth games, but Christy Mathewson loses the fifth and eighth.

Creditors take over Coney Island's 9-year-old Luna Park from its cofounder Fred Thompson April 2. His partner Elmer "Skip" Dundy died early in 1907, a fire in December of last year destroyed some of the amusement park's rides, Thompson himself suffered a stroke just before Christmas of last year, the Luna Park Co. is in debt to the tune of nearly $2.7 million, Thompson files for personal bankruptcy in June, but the Sea Beach Land Co. and other leaseholders form the Luna Amusement Co., whose directors will keep the park going until 1944.

An actress arriving at New York poses for newspaper photographers at the ship's rail and exposes an unconventional expanse of leg; reporters call it "cheesecake."

Vincent Astor, 20, inherits $87 million and becomes head of his family's New York real estate empire following the loss of his father, Col. John Jacob IV, in the sinking of R.M.S. *Titanic*.

The 37-story Bankers Trust Building opens in May at 16 Wall Street, northwest corner Nassau Street. Designed by Trowbridge & Livingston, it has six storage floors inside its steeply pitched, copper-clad pyramid roof.

The 27-story 80 Maiden Lane (27 Cedar Street) building is completed between William and Pearl streets to designs by Chicago architects D. H. Burnham & Co. Thompson Starrett has erected the structure whose floor space totals 354,000 square feet.

The 24-story Candler Building is completed at 220 West 42nd Street, between Broadway and Seventh Avenue, for Coca-Cola president Asa Candler. Designed in Spanish Renaissance style by Willauer, Shape & Bready, it has 230,000 square feet of floor space and features a fire-stair tower sealed off from the rest of the building (to isolate it from smoke and flames) and accessible only through exterior balconies.

The 20-story U.S. Rubber Co. Building is completed at 1790 Broadway, southeast corner 58th Street. Designed by Carrère & Hastings in Modern French style, it has 142,000 square feet of floor space, and its exterior is sheathed entirely in Vermont marble with fire escapes in the rear.

A luxury apartment house is completed at 635 Park Avenue, northeast corner 66th Street, to neo-Renaissance designs by Tennessee-born architect J. E. R. (John Edwin Ruethven) Carpenter, 45, who has studied at MIT and at the Ecole des Beaux Arts in Paris. Rising 13 stories high, the building just south of the Seventh Regiment Armory replaces a far more modest one put up in 1887 to designs by Henry Janeway Hardenbergh and has only one 13-room, four-bath apartment per floor. Living rooms measure 30'6" × 18'6", dining rooms 27' × 18'6", circular foyers 13'6" in diameter, and these public rooms are divided from the private quarters and service rooms. The four bedrooms include two that measure 20'6" × 14'6" each, the other two are only slightly smaller, and there are four servants' rooms, a servants' hall, and a kitchen.

The 13-story 960 Park Avenue apartment house is completed at the northwest corner of 82nd Street. Designed for Bing & Bing by J. E. R. Carpenter with D. Everett Waid, the co-operative has two apartments on some floors, four on others.

A mansion for publisher Charles Scribner, Jr., now 57, is completed at 9 East 66th Street to designs by Ernest Flagg, whose sister Louisa married Scribner in 1899; he gives the house a façade containing large expanses of glass. The Scribners move from their old house at 10 East 38th Street and occupy the new house with six servants.

A town house for tobacco magnate James B. Duke is completed at 1 East 78th Street, northeast corner Fifth Avenue, to Bordeaux château designs by Horace Trumbauer. It will be remodeled in 1958 for conversion to use by the NYU Institute of Fine Arts.

A private house for composer Reginald DeKoven is completed at 1025 Park Avenue, between 85th and 86th streets, to designs by New York-born architect John Russell Pope, 38, who has studied at the Ecole des Beaux Arts in Paris and this year marries the daughter of a Newport, R.I., society queen.

The South Reformed Church (later called the Park Avenue Christian Church) is completed at the southwest corner of Park and 85th Street. Cram, Goodhue & Ferguson of Boston has designed the new house of worship.

The 7-year-old Nippon Club erects its first building at 101 West 93rd Street, between Columbus and Amsterdam avenues. Founder Jokichi Takamine has a town house at 334 Riverside Drive, between 105th and 106th streets, and has been instrumental in hiring architect John Vredenburgh Van Pelt to design the structure, whose façade is of light brown brick (see human rights, 1942).

The McAlpin Hotel opens on the east side of Broadway at 34th Street. Designed by F. M. Andrews and built by David H. McAlpin at a cost of $7.1 million on a site acquired from the late Jay Gould in 1877, the 24-story structure with its 1,515 rooms is the world's largest hotel, and McAlpin will add a 185-room annex in 1919. Backed by E. I. DuPont de Nemours president Thomas Coleman du Pont, 48, Pougkeepsie-born hotelman Lucius M. (Messenger) Boomer, 34, has supervised the furnishings and installs a cost-accounting system that eliminates much of the waste incidental to the operation of most U.S. hotels. Boomer will run the McAlpin until 1922, managing at the same time the Claridge, Woodstock, and other hotels.

The Vanderbilt Hotel opens at the southwest corner of lower Park Avenue and 34th Street. Railroad heir Alfred Gwynne Vanderbilt inherited the property (along with $42 million) from his late father, Cornelius Vanderbilt II, and saw the potential of a site equidistant from Penn Station and the new Grand Central Terminal now nearing completion at 42nd Street. A great-grandson of the commodore, he has engaged Warren & Wetmore to design the 21-story structure, whose 600 rooms with baths have 11-foot ceilings, and a 15-room penthouse is reserved as a town home for Vanderbilt and his family (see 1965).

The Equitable Life Assurance Society Building completed in 1870 at the corner of Broadway and Cedar Street catches fire January 6; six people are killed, and the tragedy points up the need for better ways to fight conflagrations in buildings more than 10 stories high (see 1914).

The Ashokan Reservoir completed near Phoenicia in the Catskills is the largest of the city's 34 reservoirs. More than 15,000 acres of land have been acquired for its construction, seven villages razed, and 2,800 bodies removed from 32 cemeteries to create a 12-mile-long body of water with an estimated capacity of 130 billion gallons.

The state legislature at Albany bans the sale of oysters in state restaurants and fish houses from May 15 through August 31 as a conservation measure. The idea that it is safe to eat oysters only in "R" months is based solely on the lack of refrigeration to keep shellfish from spoiling in warm weather, and oysters from New York waters will continue to be shipped to buyers in states where the myth is disregarded, but New York's ban will remain in effect until 1971.

 Coffee and sugar magnate John Arbuckle dies at Brooklyn March 27 at age 74, leaving an estate valued at $20 million.

The Jack Rose cocktail (made with applejack, grenadine, and lime juice) is created in honor of gambler "Bald Jack" Rose, who has hired gunmen to kill gambler Herman Rosenthal at the behest of police lieutenant Charles Becker.

Hellmann's Blue Ribbon Mayonnaise is introduced by German-born delicatessen owner Richard Hellmann, 35, who has operated Hellmann's Delicatessen at 490 Columbus Avenue since 1905, ladling out portions of mayonnaise from big glass jars into wooden boats for sale by weight. He now packs the product in individual glass jars and enjoys such success that he will build a three-story factory in Astoria, Queens, next year and by 1915 will have given up the delicatessen to concentrate on manufacturing. Hellman will erect a larger Astoria plant in 1922, and by 1927 will have plants at Chicago, San Francisco, Atlanta, Dallas, and Tampa.

The Grand Central Oyster Bar opens at the new railroad terminal, whose lower level begins commuter-train service in October (its upper level, for long-distance trains, will be inaugurated early next year). The restaurant has tiled walls and ceilings that make it noisy but it will continue into the 21st century serving bluepoints, Cape Cods, Chincoteagues from Maryland's Eastern Shore, Gardiners Bays from eastern Long Island Sound, Lynnhavens, Mattitucks, Saddle Rocks, and other varieties plus all manner of seafood.

Entrepeneur Arnold Reuben opens a modest sandwich shop on upper Broadway and soon uses his magnetic personality to attract theatrical luminaries (who will persuade him to move closer to Times Square). He will become famous for the Reuben sandwich, containing eight ounces of corned beef on thinly sliced rye toast covered with melted Swiss cheese.

The first New York Horn & Hardart Automat opens at 1557 Broadway, between 46th and 47th streets (see Exchange Buffet, 1885). Joseph B. Horn and Frank Hardart met in 1888 and soon thereafter opened a small basement lunch counter at Philadelphia. Hardart toured Europe in 1900, saw an automatic restaurant at Berlin, and paid a German importer

$30,000 for the mechanism that permitted patrons to drop nickels into slots to open glass doors and obtain food from compartments that are refilled by employees behind the scenes. The company's engineer John Fritsche made improvements in the mechanism, and the Automat opened in Philadelphia's Chestnut Street 10 years ago became so popular that the city soon had scores of them. The Automat has tiled floors, patrons sit at plain, circular tables, each with four chairs, the surrounding banks of food compartments are set in Victorian-style wooden frames surmounted by cut-glass mirrors. A second Automat will open in 1914 at 250 West 42nd Street, and by 1922 there will be 21 Horn & Hardart Automats, but they will not gain the height of their success until the 1920s, when steam tables will be introduced to provide hot food (see 1991).

1913 William Sulzer is inaugurated as governor at Albany January 1, calls the executive mansion the People's House, and soon finds himself at odds with Tammany Hall boss Charles F. Murphy, launching investigations into some state administrative departments, finding evidence of waste and fraud that involve contractors with Tammany connections, dismissing the state highways superintendent and several other department heads, rejecting all of Murphy's suggestions for high-level appointments, and introducing a direct-primary bill that would eliminate nominating conventions for all candidates for state offices. When Tammany-controlled legislators pass another election reform bill that does not apply to top state officials, Gov. Sulzer vetoes it, and when they pass it again in May he begins replacing party regulars with his own men. The governor maintains his residence at 118 Washington Place in Manhattan and continues his law practice at 115 Broadway.

Charles F. Murphy has the Democratic caucus in the state assembly make Alfred E. Smith the assembly speaker (see 1912; Smith, 1911). Smith bellows out parliamentary rulings in his hoarse roar, sometimes eats lunch at the podium and talks with food in his mouth, fights for Tammany bills that extend the "Wigwam's" power and patronage, pounds his gavel vigorously to keep order, and moves bills through swiftly and smoothly, going to bat for measures that improve the lot of working people, including a workmen's compensation law that many consider radical.

"Big Tim" Sullivan is killed by a train August 13 while visiting his brother Patrick at Eastchester (see

Grand Central Terminal dwarfed Penn Station, giving midtown Manhattan a landmark. MUNICIPAL ARCHIVE

Sullivan Law, 1911). A longtime champion of the poor, he has represented the Bowery in the state legislature at Albany beginning in his early 20s, served in the U.S. Congress from 1902 to 1906, but tertiary syphilis has resulted in his being declared insane. He leaves a fortune estimated at $2 million, and his funeral on the Bowery brings out a crowd of 75,000.

Tammany Hall refuses to renominate Mayor Gaynor, whose final years in office have seen growing corruption in the police department, unsuccessful efforts to end private ownership of the subways, and failed attempts to obtain a new city charter. Encouraged by support from reform groups, the mayor declares his candidacy but falls ill and dies aboard a ship September 12 at age 65. Alderman Adolph L. (Loges) Kline, 55, is appointed interim mayor. John Purroy Mitchel, 34, acted as mayor while Mayor Gaynor was recuperating from his 1910 bullet wound and has been appointed Collector of the Port of New York by President Wilson.

The state legislature impeaches Gov. Sulzer and a 4-week trial begins September 18 before a high court made up of the state senate and judges of the Court of Appeals. He is found guilty October 17 of having "willfully, knowingly and corruptly" falsified records of campaign contributions and expenditures last year and is removed from office (*see* Whitman, 1914).

Fusion Party candidate John Purroy Mitchel easily defeats Tammany's Democratic Party mayoralty candidate Edward E. McCall in the November 4 election, racking up 358,217 votes to McCall's 233,919. Strongly supported by progressives,

Mitchel is at age 34 the youngest man thus far elected mayor, but although he will make good appointments and institute significant reforms his relief program for the unemployed will have little success and he will antagonize the working classes—especially the Germans and Irish—by revealing mismanagement in the Catholic Charities and supporting a plan for vocational education.

Former governor William Sulzer runs as an independent and wins reelection to the Assembly, despite the allegations against him. Democrats who voted for his impeachment all go down to defeat, including nine from Manhattan. "I was impeached," Sulzer has said in an interview, "not because of the offenses with which I was charged, but because I refused to do Charles F. Murphy's bidding, and because, as the records show, I have relentlessly pursued Mr. Murphy's corrupt henchmen in office." Murphy has said Sulzer's failure to testify in his own behalf amounted to a confession of guilt; giving his first (and last) statement to the press, he has said that "the only man responsible for the disgrace and downfall of Gov. Sulzer is William Sulzer himself."

A general strike of lingerie makers in Brooklyn and Manhattan brings out 35,000 young women, many still in their early teens, who march in picket lines organized by Rose Schneiderman. But the ILGWU strike that began last December is called off March 15 after 13 weeks.

The Rockefeller Foundation chartered by John D. Rockefeller, Sr. will be a major force in improving world health, world agriculture, and education and will work toward world peace (*see* 1914).

The Salvation Army takes title to Booth House 2 at 225 Bowery, southeast corner 3rd Street, and provides food and shelter for railroad and merchant marine retirees, a function that the 10-story brick tenement will continue until 1978.

The Sixteenth Amendment to the Constitution proclaimed in force February 25 by Secretary of State Philander C. (Chase) Knox, 59, empowers Congress to levy graduated income taxes on incomes above $3,000 per year. The income tax will bring drastic changes to the lifestyles of some rich New Yorkers, but the very rich will find ways to avoid taxes.

A sensational report published February 28 by the House Committee on Banking and Currency exposes the "money trust" that controls U.S. financial power. Rep. Arsene P. Pujo of Louisiana heads the committee, and it has called witnesses who included financier J. P. Morgan; the Pujo Report reveals that

Morgan, George F. Baker, and James Stillman have between them controlled at least nine banks or trust companies with assets of about $1.5 billion and had a voice in the management of most U.S. railroads, industries, and public utilities. Their representatives have held 341 directorships in 112 concerns with resources exceeding $22 billion.

J. P. Morgan dies at Rome March 31 at age 75 leaving a vast estate; banker-philanthropist Anson Phelps Stokes dies at his native New York June 28 at age 75, having lost a leg 15 years ago in a riding accident near his Lenox, Mass., country home.

The Bank of the United States opens at the corner of Orchard and Delancey streets. Founded by former garment maker Joseph Marcus, its customers are chiefly recent immigrants, most of them Jews from Eastern Europe and Italians; it will move its head office in 5 years to Fifth Avenue at 32nd Street (*see* 1930).

Standard Statistics Co. has its beginnings in Standard Statistic Service, founded by New York entrepreneur Luther Blake; the financial publication house will compete with the one set up by Henry Varnum Poor in 1867 (*see* Standard and Poor's, 1941).

The Federal Reserve System created under terms of a measure signed into law by President Wilson December 23 will reform U.S. banking and currency. Drafted to prevent panics such as the one in 1907, the Glass-Owen Currency Act establishes Federal Reserve banks at New York and 11 other major cities, requiring member banks to maintain cash reserves proportionate to their deposits with the Fed, which loans money to the banks at low rates of interest relative to the rates the banks charge customers. The Fed's Board of Governors determines the amount of money in circulation at any given time; it provides elasticity to the supply of currency and can act to control inflation (*see* Banking Act, 1935).

Wall Street's Dow Jones Industrial Average closes December 31 at 78.78, down from 87.87 at the end of 1912.

R. H. Macy's Nathan Straus is so shaken by the loss of his brother Isidor in last year's sinking of R.M.S. *Titanic* that he sells his interest in the store to Isidor's sons Jesse Isidor Straus, now 41, Percy Seldon Straus, 37, and Herbert N. Straus, 31 (*see* Thanksgiving Day parade, 1924).

Merchant Benjamin Altman of B. Altman & Co. dies at New York October 7 at age 73, having created a vast art collection (*see* store, 1914).

Grand Central Terminal opens February 1 at 42nd Street and Park Avenue, replacing a 41-year-old New York Central and New Haven train shed with the world's largest railway station. Trains under Park Avenue have been electrified since December 1906, and the new $80 million terminal provides a luxurious point of entry to and departure from the city. Far bigger than Penn Station, Grand Central has 31 tracks on its upper level, 17 on the lower level that opened for commuter service in October 1912. Separate men's and women's waiting rooms and lavatories are at either end of the main waiting room off 42nd Street; the women's waiting room, at the east end, has amenities that include a hairdressing salon. Ramps (rather than stairways as at Penn Station) slope gently down from the street level to the main concourse, and other ramps slope down to the station platforms inside the 48 gates.

The subway and elevated railway Dual Contracts signed in March have required an amendment to the New York State Constitution, new legislation, the creation of new regulatory agencies, and the abolition of old ones. Manhattan borough president George McAneny, State Public Service Commission head William R. Wilcox, PSC chief engineer Alfred Craven, and two former mayors have persuaded or outmaneuvered those advocating total municipal control to accept a combination of private and public ownership. The double fare on El trains to and from Coney Island is eliminated (*see* 1906; 1940).

The Interborough Rapid Transit Co. (IRT) and Brooklyn Rapid Transit Co. (BRT) agree to equip and operate new city-built elevated railway lines and improve service by rebuilding old lines to reduce running times. The IRT installs center tracks for express trains on its Second, Third, and Ninth avenue lines, and in many cases builds two-level "hump" stations with one level for express trains, the other for locals.

The city enacts its first law against jaywalking (crossing the street against the light or between intersections) but it is almost universally ignored and will soon be repealed.

The steamboats *Washington Irving* and *Berkshire* go into night-boat service on the Hudson River (*see* 1902). Built by the New York Shipbuilding Co. of Camden, N.J., the elegantly appointed *Berkshire* is 422 feet in length and 50 in width, making her the largest passenger vessel on the river, and she will remain in service between New York and Albany until 1937 (*see Alexander Hamilton*, 1924).

The Hamburg-Amerika Line passenger ship S.S. *Imperator* that will later become the S.S. *Berengaria* leaves Cuxhaven for New York on her maiden voyage June 20. Built at Hamburg's Vulcan Werft Shipyard, the 52,022-ton vessel is 919 feet in length overall, has four screws, and can reach a maximum speed of 24 knots (*but see* 1914).

The Titanic Memorial Lighthouse is erected atop the Seaman's Church Institute building near the Brooklyn Bridge to honor the crew of the ship that went down in mid-April of last year. A black ball on the mast of the lighthouse is activated by a telegraphic signal from the U.S. Naval Observatory at Washington, D.C.; it will for many years be lowered at noon each day for ships in the harbor to see. Other memorials will be erected on corners from Chelsea to the Bronx (*see* sculpture, 1915).

The Montefiore Home for Chronic Individuals moves to the northern Bronx on a site between Gun Hill Road and 210th Street, where it opens its first private pavilion (*see* 1884). It bought a suburban Bedford farm for tuberculosis patients in 1897, will become a teaching hospital in 1916, and open a nursing school in 1922.

The American Cancer Society has its beginnings in the American Society for the Control of Cancer, founded at New York with support from philanthropist John D. Rockefeller, Jr. Nine out of 10 cancer patients die of the disease; the mortality rate will fall sharply but the incidence of cancer will increase.

The Lighthouse opens in February as a permanent home for the New York Association for the Blind founded late in 1905. Cofounder Winifred Holt has given speeches and fund raisers to help the association grow from a small group that met at her home to a large welfare organization with its own rented loft space; it gives courses in broommaking, piano tuning, sewing, stenography, typing, and other marketable skills. Now 42, Holt will found *Searchlight* magazine for children, work with the Board of Education to end segregation of blind children in New York public schools, and introduce Braille reading materials.

A new building for the 44-year-old Normal College of the City of New York (to be called Hunter College beginning next year) is completed at 930 Lexington Avenue, between 68th and 69th streets, to English Gothic designs by C. B. J. Snyder.

The Columbia School of Journalism is founded with a bequest from the late *New York World* publisher Joseph Pulitzer, who died in 1911.

The *New York Times* adopts an eight-column configuration that it will continue until September 7, 1976. Begun April 1, the new format expands the seven-column measure used since December 4, 1865.

"Bringing Up Father" by St. Louis-born *New York American* cartoonist George McManus, 29, introduces readers to the comic-strip characters Maggie and Jiggs. Publisher William Randolph Hearst last year lured McManus away from the *New York World*, where he had been producing "The Newlyweds and Their Baby." His will be the first strip to gain an international following, and when he has his nouveau-riche Jiggs steal off to Dinty Moore's for corned beef and cabbage he has him eat tamales and tortillas in Mexico, beef stew in Argentina and France, tripe and onions in British versions, rice and fish in China and Japan (*see* 1938).

La Prensa begins publication on a weekly basis to provide the city's Spanish-speaking population with a newspaper of general interest. Daily publication will begin in 1918 as the Hispanic community grows (*see El Diario*, 1948).

The city inaugurates a licensing system for newsstands, giving preference to war veterans, the blind, and the disabled (in that order).

Harper's Bazar is purchased by William Randolph Hearst, who will change its name to *Harper's Bazaar* in 1929. The magazine for women has been published at New York since 1867 by Harper Bros.

Condé Nast launches *Dress & Vanity Fair*, a new fashion magazine whose name is shortened after four issues simply to *Vanity Fair*; edited by Frank Crowninshield, it will be merged with *Vogue* in 1936 and not re-emerge under its own name until the 1980s.

Illinois-born editor-author Floyd (James) Dell, 26, quits the *Chicago Evening Post* in September, moves to New York in November, settles in Greenwich Village, and joins the *Masses* as managing editor, adopting a Bohemian life. The Associated Press brings charges of criminal libel against the *Masses*, whose editor Max Eastman and cartoonist Art Young are indicted in November (*see* 1911). Young's cartoon "Poisoned at the Source" has shown a man personifying the AP pouring the contents of bottles labeled "Lies," "Suppressed Facts," "Prejudice," "Slander," and "Hatred of Labor Organizations" into a reservoir labeled "The News." The suit will be dropped late next year (*but see* 1917).

The first U.S. crossword puzzle appears December 21 in the weekend supplement of the *New York World*.

English-born journalist Arthur Wynne has seen similar puzzles in 19th century English periodicals for children and in the *London Graphic* and has arranged squares in a diamond pattern with 31 clues, most of them simple word definitions: "What bargain hunters enjoy," five letters; "A boy," three letters; "An animal of prey," four letters (sales, lad, lion).

Prentice-Hall is founded by New York University economics teacher Charles W. Gerstenberg, 31, and his colleague Richard Prentice Ettinger, 20, who use their mothers' maiden names and publish Gerstenberg's *Methods of Corporation Finance*. The new publishing house will establish a mail-order department in 1923 and a trade division in 1937.

New York Public Library director John Shaw Billings, M.D., dies at New York March 11 at age 74.

Fiction: *O Pioneers* by former *McClure's* magazine managing editor Willa Sibert Cather, 39, who grew up on the Nebraska frontier. S. S. McClure brought her to New York from Pittsburgh in 1906, she met Edith Lewis, they occupied a studio apartment together at 60 Washington Square, Cather quit *McClure's* 2 years ago, and she moves with Lewis this year to 5 Bank Street; *The Custom of the Country* by Edith Wharton (the custom being for a man to keep his wife totally in the dark about "the real business of life").

The Scribner Book Store opens at 597 Fifth Avenue, just north of 48th Street, in a new 10-story building designed by architect Ernest Flagg. The triple-height selling floor of the 13,000-square foot store has a vaulted ceiling, and balconies run along each side (the publisher's offices are upstairs). Scribner's will regild the storefront in the 1970s and occupy the space until 1984 (*see* 1988).

Art in America begins publication at New York in January. Art dealer Frederic Fairchild Sherman has founded the black-and-white quarterly of art history and specializes in works by Massachusetts-born painter Albert Pinkham Ryder, now 65; he targets an elite audience that can afford $1 per issue when most magazines sell for 5¢ and will raise the price to $1.50 in 1932 (*see* 1941).

The Armory Show that opens February 17 at the huge 7-year-old 69th Regiment Armory on Lexington Avenue between 24th and 25th streets gives Americans their first look at cubism in an International Exhibition of Modern Art organized by Arthur Davies. Represented are the late Paul Cézanne, Paul Gauguin, Vincent van Gogh, and other French impressionists, but what shocks most of the 100,000 visitors are works by Paris-born sculptor Gaston Lachaise, 31, Philadelphia-born cubist (and photographer) Charles R. Sheeler, Jr., 30, Nyack-born realist Edward Hopper, 31, Philadelphia-born water-colorist Stuart Davis, 18, impressionist Childe Hassam, now 53, water-colorist John Marin, and the canvas *Nude Descending Staircase* by French Dadaist Marcel Duchamp, 26 (who will say that the two American achievements he most admires are its bridges and its plumbing; Theodore Roosevelt describes his painting as "an explosion in a shingle factory"). Although it upsets most of the roughly 250,000 who see it at New York, Chicago, and Boston, the Armory Show ushers in a new era of acceptance for unromantic art expression.

Other paintings: *Coney Island, Battle of Lights* by Italian-born New York painter Joseph Stella, 36; *Sentimental Music* (pastel drawing) by Arthur Dove.

Anthony Comstock of the New York Society for the Suppression of Vice sees a print of last year's Paul Chabas painting *September Morn* May 13 in the window of an art dealer at 13 West 46th Street (*see* Comstock Law, 1872). Publicity agent Harry Reichenback has persuaded Braun & Co. to place the print in its window, hired urchins to stand in front of the building and make remarks about the picture, and then complained to Comstock. Now 69, Comstock falls for the bait and demands that the picture be removed from the window because it shows "too little morning and too much maid," Chicago alderman "Bathhouse John" Coughlin vows that the picture will not be displayed publicly in Chicago, but oilman Calouste Gulbenkian will acquire the oil and it will wind up at the Metropolitan Museum of Art.

Sculpture: *Firemen's Memorial* by Attilio Piccirilli is unveiled September 4 on Riverside Drive at 100th Street with a base by architect H. Van Buren Magonigle inscribed with the words, "To the Heroic Dead of the Fire Department;" R. H. Macy executive Jesse Isidor Straus makes a little speech, saying, "We erect monuments to our war heroes, and it is fitting that we should erect them to the men who fight the war that never ends." The late Episcopal bishop Henry Codman Potter came up with the idea for the $50,000 memorial 5 years ago after the death of Deputy Chief Charles W. Kruger; a statue of the late Carl Schurz by Karl T. F. Bitter is installed on the east side of Morningside Drive at 116th Street. Architect Henry Bacon has designed the base.

Theater: *Romance* by Edward Sheldon, now 26, 2/10 at Maxine Elliott's Theater, New York, with Doris Keane, 160 perfs. (it will open at London in 1915 and run for 1,099 perfs.); the Palace Theater opens 3/24 at Broadway and 47th Street. Other vaudeville houses have a top price of 50¢, the Palace (designed by Kirchhoff & Rose for producer Martin Beck) charges $2, and B. F. Keith of Boston and his partner Edward F. Albee in the Keith Circuit's United Booking Office present a bill that includes a wire act, a Spanish violinist, a one-act play by George Ade, and Philadelphia-born comedian Ed Wynn (originally Isaiah Edwin Leopold), 26. The Palace has no success, however, until May 5, when Sarah Bernhardt opens for a 2-week engagement that is extended for another week and a half. Philadelphia-born pantomime juggler W. C. Fields (originally William Claude Dukenfield), 33, joins the act in May, having begun his career at age 14; *Are You a Crook?* 5/1 at the new Longacre Theater, designed by Henry B. Herts and put up by producer (and baseball magnate) Harry H. Frazee at 234 West 48th Street; *Hamlet* 10/2 at the new Shubert Theater, 225 West 44th Street, with J. Forbes Robertson (designed by Henry B. Herts and built as a memorial to the late Sam Shubert, the new house will be used mostly for musicals); *The Seven Keys to Baldpate* by George M. Cohan (who has adapted a novel by Earl Derr Biggers, 29)

The Woolworth Building gave new meaning to the word skyscraper. LIBRARY OF CONGRESS

9/22 at the 7-year-old Astor Theater, with Wallace Eddinger, 320 perfs.; *The Great Adventure* by English novelist-playwright Arnold Bennett 10/15 at the new Booth Theater, designed by Henry B. Herts at 222 West 45th Street, with a cast that includes Seattle-born actor Guthrie McClintic, 30, 52 perfs.

Actors' Equity Association is founded by 112 actors May 26 at the Pabst Grand Circle Hotel with Francis Wilson as president, actor-director-producer Henry Miller, now 43, as vice president. Actors have been victimized by arbitrary work rules and low wages, but Actors' Equity will set up contracts under whose terms actors are employed and maintain a benefit system for its membership (see 1919).

Illusionist Harry Houdini has himself locked in irons July 15 and thrown into a small cell in the prison ship *Success* docked at the 79th Street Hudson River boat basin (see 1912). Houdini has lived since 1904 at 278 West 113th Street, where he practices his tricks in an oversize bathtub and where he will continue to reside until his death in 1926. Staging his "challenge to death" close to shore so more people can see, he escapes within an hour, climbs out of a porthole, and swims ashore.

Films: D. W. Griffith's *Judith of Bethulia* with Chicago-born actress Blanche Sweet (originally Daphne Wayne), 17, Alabama-born actor Henry B. Walthall, 33, New Mexico-born actress Mae (originally Mary) Marsh, 18, in the first American-made four-reel film; Colin Campbell's *The Spoilers* with William Farnum; Mack Sennett's *Barney Oldfield's Race for Life* with Sennett, Staten Island-born actress Mabel Normand (originally Fortescue), 19.

Charlie Chaplin, now 24, signs a $150 per week contract with the Keystone Film Co.

The Jesse L. Lasky Feature Play Co. is founded by San Jose, Calif.-born New York vaudeville producer Jesse Louis Lasky, 32, his brother-in-law Samuel Goldwyn, 30, and Ashville, Mass.-born playwright Cecil B. (Blount) De Mille, 31, who has selected Hollywood for making *The Squaw Man* because California has an abundance of sunshine (but every studio back lot will have a New York set that faithfully reproduces stoops and streets and storefronts). Goldwyn (originally Schmuel Gelbfisz) is a Polish-born glove maker whose business has been ruined by the new Underwood-Simmons Tariff Act that has lowered duties on imported gloves. The Lasky firm will merge with Adolph Zukor's Famous Players to create Famous Players-Lasky and become Paramount Pictures in 1932 (see Loews, 1919; M-G-M, 1924).

The Regent Theater opens at the southwest corner of Seventh Avenue and 116th Street. Designed by architect Thomas W. Lamb, whose Audubon Theater opened last year farther north, it is the city's first true movie palace (*see* Strand, 1914).

Broadway musicals: *The Sunshine Girl* 2/3 at the Knickerbocker Theater, with Vernon and Irene Castle doing the Turkey Trot, music by John L. Golden, lyrics by Joseph Cawthorne, 160 perfs.; *The Passing Show* 6/10 at the Winter Garden Theater, with Charlotte Greenwood, a runway to bring the show's scantily clad chorus girls close to the audience, music chiefly by Sigmund Romberg, lyrics chiefly by Harold Atteridge, 116 perfs.; *The Ziegfeld Follies* 6/16 at the New Amsterdam Theater, with petite Wilmington, Del.-born dancer Ann (originally Anna) Pennington, 19, comedienne-singer Fanny Brice, Leon Errol, 96 perfs.; *Sweethearts* 9/8 at the New Amsterdam Theater, with music by Victor Herbert, lyrics by Robert B. Smith, 136 perfs.; *High Jinks* 12/10 at the Lyric Theater, with music by Rudolf Friml, book and lyrics by Otto Hauerbach (later Harbach) and Leo Ditrichstein, songs that include "Something Seems Tingle-angeling," 213 perfs.

Popular song: "Up on the Hudson Shore" by Jean Schwartz, lyrics by Joseph W. Herbert and Harold Atteridge.

Ebbets Field opens in Brooklyn April 9 (*see* 1898). Brewer Charles Ebbets has kept the Dodgers from moving to Baltimore by paying about $100,000 for a piece of property bordered by Bedford Avenue, Belmont Avenue, Sackman Street, and Sullivan Place, and the owners of the Dodgers have spent $650,000 to put up a steel-and-concrete stadium seating 18,000 (it will be expanded to seat nearly 31,500) that will survive until 1957.

The New York Yankees (formerly the American League's Highlanders) give up their wooden Hilltop Stadium, become tenants of the Giants at the Polo Grounds, and adopt a new name (*see* 1903; Ruppert, 1915; Yankee Stadium, 1923).

The New York Giants win the National League pennant, but Connie Mack's Philadelphia Athletics win the World Series, defeating the Giants 4 games to 1. Christy Mathewson's pitching wins the second game 3 to 0 and he hits an RBI single.

Gen. Daniel E. Sickles faces imprisonment in the Ludlow Street Jail at age 93 after the disappearance of $28,000 from the New York State Monuments Commission that he has chaired but he wins acquittal.

Stanford White's millionaire murderer Harry K. Thaw escapes from the Matteawan State Hospital for the Criminally Insane August 17 in a carefully arranged scheme. He makes it to Canada but is deported and arrested at Colebrook, N.H., September 10 (*see* 1909; 1915).

 The 57-story Woolworth Building opens April 24 at 233 Broadway, between Barclay Street and Park Place, near City Hall (*see* commerce, 1911). President Wilson at Washington, D.C., presses a telegraph signal button that illuminates the skyscraper's 80,000 lights. Designed in Gothic Revival style by Cass Gilbert and built at a cost of $13.5 million (Woolworth has paid cash), the 792-foot "Cathedral of Commerce" has a lobby that features glass mosaic vaultings, stained-glass ceilings, and terra-cotta reliefs that include caricatures of Woolworth counting his nickels and dimes and architect Gilbert studying a model of the structure; the basement contains a 15-by-55-foot swimming pool, the building's steel skeleton is sheathed in cream-colored terra cotta from the fourth floor to the top, its detailing includes flying buttresses, pinnacles, and sculptured gargoyles, it contains 932,000 square feet of floor space, and it will be the world's tallest habitable structure until 1930. Visitors pay 50¢ to ride an elevator to the 54th floor, where they take a shuttle elevator encased in a cylindrical glass shaft and encircled by a spiral staircase; ascending to the top, they find themselves on an octagonal outdoor deck, 65 feet around and so far above the street that the loudest noise is the wind.

A new Equitable Life Assurance Society Building nears completion on lower Broadway (*see* fire, 1912). The world's largest office building thus far, it has been financed by a syndicate that includes T. Coleman du Pont, who has put up $30 million (*see* 1915).

The 26-story Consolidated Gas Building is completed on the site once occupied by the Academy of Music on Irving Place between 14th and 15th streets. Designed by Henry Janeway Hardenbergh, it has about 1 million square feet of available floor space for the 7,000 employees of the Consolidated Gas and New York Edison companies, and the Westminster chimes and bells in its clock tower are the second largest in America.

The General Post Office building opens on the west side of Eighth Avenue between 31st and 33rd streets across from the 3-year-old Pennsylvania Station. Designed by McKim, Mead & White with two blocks of Corinthian columns, the building's front is inscribed with lines written by the Greek historian Herodotus about the couriers of Xerxes in the 5th

Century B.C.: "Neither snow, nor rain, nor heat, nor gloom of night stays these couriers from the swift completion of their appointed rounds."

The new Grand Central Terminal designed by Warren & Wetmore has cost $80 million. Stony Creek granite and Bedford limestone sheath its steel frame, and pairs of Doric columns flank each of the three great arches on its Beaux Arts 42nd Street façade, surmounted by a 13-foot clock surrounded by Jules A. Coutan's sculptures *Mercury*, *Hercules*, and *Minerva*. (Albert De Groot's 1869 statue of the late Commodore Vanderbilt is set in front of the middle arch.) The three-story waiting room inside its 42nd Street entrance opens onto ramps that slope down to a mammoth main concourse—470 feet long, 160 wide, 125 high—that is paved with Tennessee marble and lighted by three gigantic windows at each end, facing Depew Place and Vanderbilt Avenue, plus five clerestory lunettes set in the curve on each side of the 12-story-high vaulted ceiling (illumination at night is from huge bronze chandeliers and from indirect lighting fixtures). French society artist Paul Helleu has been commissioned to create a painting for the ceiling (his astronomical mural, painted in gold on cerulean blue tempera, is supposed to depict the Mediterranean sky in winter, with the 60 largest of his 2,500 stars lighted from behind by 10-watt bulbs, but Helleu has got the celestial map backward). Walls are covered in Caen stone, with wainscots and trimmings of Botticino marble. A circular information booth surmounted by a four-faced golden clock is in the center of the concourse at what once was the exact center of the intersection of Park Avenue and 43rd Street. The grand staircase diverges between the west balcony (Vanderbilt Avenue) and main concourse levels, comes together again, and diverges once more as it descends to the suburban passenger concourse on the lower level.

The *New York Times* moves its headquarters from its tower in Times Square into a larger building in West 43rd Street and begins transferring its operations to the new building, but it will continue to own the Times Tower until 1961 (*see* communications, 1928).

Carrère and Hastings completes a three-story limestone Fifth Avenue mansion for steel magnate Henry Clay Frick between 70th and 71st streets. Replacing the empty Lenox Library of 1870, whose books were moved in 1911 to the new New York Public Library at 42nd Street, the $5 million house requires a staff of 27 (first and second butlers; first, second, and third footmen; first, second, third, and fourth chambermaids; chef, second cook, two vegetable cooks; three laundresses; and servants' hall girl) to serve Frick, his wife, Adelaide, and their daughter Helen. Frick came to New York from Pittsburgh about 10 years ago and rented the old Vanderbilt mansion at 640 Fifth Avenue to house his family and his growing art collection, amassed with help from London dealer Joseph Duveen (*see* art, 1935).

A large complex of model tenements is completed after 13 years of construction at 1470-1492 Avenue A (later York Avenue), 501-555 East 78th Street, and 502-540 East 79th Street. Designed by Harde & Short, Percy Griffin, and Philip H. Ohm, the buildings have been financed by the City and Suburban Homes Co. that put up the First Avenue Estate (designed by different architects altogether) in 1898. Prominent residents have invested in the company, agreeing to limit their returns to 5 percent.

Architect George B. Post dies at his Bernardsville, N.J., summer home November 28 at age 75.

The 13-story Hotel Theresa opens at the corner of Seventh Avenue and 125th Street. Designed by George and Edward Blum with an exterior of white brick and terra cotta, it is the tallest structure in Harlem and has a two-story penthouse dining room with sweeping views of the Palisades and Long Island Sound, but it will not admit blacks until 1937 and will be turned into an office building in 1966.

The Queensboro Corp. begins development of Jackson Heights in northwestern Queens. Encouraged by the construction of the Queensboro Bridge that opened in 1909, the investors (a syndicate of bankers and real estate agents who called themselves the Queensboro Real Estate Co.) began buying elevated farmland in 1908 and by 1910 had acquired 350 acres. They have persuaded the city to close Trains Meadow Road and now lay out consecutively numbered streets in a grid pattern. John C. Jackson laid out Northern Boulevard and his name will be memorialized in the area (*see* 1914; elevated railroad, 1917).

The city's first Nedick's orange drink and frankfurter stand opens. Entrepreneurs Robert T. Neely and Orville Dickinson start an enterprise that will blossom into a $12 million chain.

1914 Mayor Mitchel takes office January 1 as Bronx County (the county of Bronx) becomes New York State's 62nd county by an act of the state legislature at Albany. Mitchel comes close to being assassinated April 17 as he starts to leave City Hall for lunch but the shot fired point-blank by an elderly psychotic only grazes the mayor's cheek.

Gen. Daniel E. Sickles suffers a cerebral hemorrhage and dies at his 23 Fifth Avenue home May 3 at age 94 (the *New York Times* gives his age as 90).

The *New York Times* runs a front-page headline June 28: "Heir to Austria's Throne Is Slain With His Wife [at Sarajevo] By a Bosnian Youth to Avenge Seizure of His Country." Some 300 demonstrators led by emigré Italian anarchist Carlo Tresca, 40, try to take over a celebration of the 107th birthday of the late Giuseppe Garibaldi July 4 by putting up a red flag on the Garibaldi Memorial on Staten Island; police arrest them. The Police Department responds to anarchist threats by forming a bomb squad.

A World War that will continue until 1918 begins in Europe July 28. Crystal Eastman brings together the first meeting of the Woman's Peace Party at New York in November.

Former Manhattan district attorney Charles S. Whitman, now 48, is elected governor of New York. Tammany Hall has secured the Democratic Party nomination for former state comptroller Morton H. Glynn, 43, but Glynn gets only 541,194 votes as compared with 686,701 for Republican Whitman. His party regains control of the state legislature at Albany, and high-paid insurance-company lobbyists descend upon the capitol once again (*see* 1910).

Former assembly speaker Al Smith blasts legislators who tack on amendments crippling his workmen's compensation act, reformers stand up in the gallery to cheer the speaker, and although he does not prevail in the case of workmen's compensation he blocks further efforts to worsen working conditions (*see* 1915).

John D. Rockefeller, Jr. comes under attack for his anti-labor policies, but the death of his mother prevents him from traveling west following the April 20 Ludlow Massacre of Colorado coal miners struggling for recognition of their United Mine Workers union (he will go next year). A battle with state militia near Trinidad has ended with at least 24 dead, including two women and 11 children who hid to escape the flying bullets and were caught in tents that were set ablaze.

Former social worker Belle Lindner Israels Moskowitz heads the labor department of the Dress & Waist Manufacturers Association; she has just been remarried, this time to Municipal Civil Service Commission president Henry Moskowitz, and by 1916 she will have helped to settle more than 10,000 labor-management disputes (*see* 1921).

The Spingarn Medal established by NAACP co-founder Joel E. Spingarn will be awarded annually to recognize an African-American who has been of special service to his race.

The Japanese American Association has its beginnings in the Japanese Association of New York, founded to fight racism and advance the welfare of the city's small Japanese population, whose numbers will reach 4,652 by 1920, 75 percent of them domestic servants.

The Police Athletic League (P.A.L.) has its beginnings in the Junior Police founded by Police Commissioner Arthur Woods and NYPD Capt. John Sweeney to give tenement children recreational opportunities when school lets out for the summer. Run by volunteer police officers, the nonprofit organization will initially sponsor boxing matches and other athletic events but will grow to offer job training, remedial reading courses, educational summer day camps, creative writing contests, and other programs to help disadvantaged youths, while closing off streets and maintaining 132 play-area sites for some 60,000 children.

Delegates to a conference on safety and sanitation in industry convene at Buffalo March 23 under the direction of New York-born engineer Magnus (Washington) Alexander, 43. A tobacco dealer's son who has studied in Europe and is a member of the Commission on Industrial Relations appointed last year by President Wilson, Alexander urges the delegates to address grievances and hazards revealed since last year at hearings held by the commission's chairman Frank P. Walsh. The delegates represent companies that employ some 5 million workers, and the conference gives rise to the Conference Board on Safety and Sanitation, whose initial focus is exclusively on preventive measures. Alexander soon urges that factories and other workplaces be equipped with a "uniform set of first aid instructions," together with "medicaments, bandages, and other paraphernalia" so as "to attend promptly and effectively to the injured employee in order to restore him as quickly as possible to health and industrial usefulness." He organizes a Conference Board of Physicians in Industrial Practice, and it develops standards for physical examinations required under newly enacted workers' compensation laws. The various conference boards pioneer in the area of scientific management (*see* 1915).

Montreal, Toronto, and Madrid stock exchanges close July 28 at news of the outbreak of hostilities, half a dozen other European bourses close July 29, the London exchange closes July 31, and the New York Stock Exchange immediately follows suit (it does not reopen until December 12). Secretary of the Treasury William G. McAdoo (President Wilson's son-in-law) meets with Wall Street bankers, who are concerned among other things that $77 million worth of the city's bonds and notes are in European hands.

New York lawyer Dwight W. (Whitney) Morrow, 41, becomes a partner in the J. P. Morgan & Co. private banking house, which moves into its new five-story building at 23 Wall Street and involves itself in arranging for financial and material aid to the Allied powers in Europe (see 1915).

Republican lawyer and assemblyman Charles A. Dana leaves Albany, having represented Manhattan's 27th district for three consecutive terms but angered suffragists by opposing a revision of the state constitution that would permit women to vote. Now 33, Dana joins the Spencer Trask investment banking firm and refinances Spicer Manufacturing Co., a struggling producer of drive shafts and universal joints for motorcars and trucks. Mechanic Clarence Spicer will turn over the company's presidency to Dana in 1916, Dana will acquire other companies related to the automotive industry, and his Dana Corp. conglomerate will make him a fortune.

Two New York banks with large numbers of foreign-born depositors go out of business as immigrants try to withdraw funds to send to relatives caught in the European war. The 41-year-old S. Jarmulovsky's Bank at 54-58 Canal Street, southwest corner Orchard Street, and another bank are ordered closed August 4 as being "in an unsound and unsatisfactory condition," and thousands lose their savings. Runs on these and other banks have led to riots; the Jarmulovskys are convicted but given suspended sentences.

The outbreak of war increases unemployment at New York. Iowa-born social worker Harry L. (Lloyd) Hopkins, 24, is appointed executive secretary of the city's Board of Civil Welfare.

The Clayton Anti-Trust Act adopted by Congress October 15 toughens the federal government's power against combinations in restraint of trade as outlawed by the Sherman Act of 1890.

Merrill Lynch has its beginnings in a New York brokerage firm started by former semipro baseball player Charles (Edward) Merrill, 28, who will team up next year with Johns Hopkins graduate Edmund C. Lynch, 29. Merrill is among the first to recognize the mass-market potential of "bringing Wall Street to Main Street" by selling stocks and bonds to small investors, providing them with simple, sound, conservative financial advice (see 1941).

Wall Street's Dow Jones Industrial Average closes December 31 at 54.58, down from 78.78 at the end of 1913.

The 8-year-old B. Altman & Co. store on Fifth Avenue at 34th Street is enlarged to designs by Trowbridge & Livingston filling the entire block east to Madison Avenue. Altman's staff includes people who can speak with customers in 32 languages; it will offer free knitting instructions to customers who bring their materials to the store on Wednesdays and Thursdays from 11 o'clock to 4, open suburban stores, and thrive as a merchant to the carriage trade.

Lord & Taylor moves into a large new store at 424-434 Fifth Avenue, between 38th and 39th streets, after 41 years at Broadway and 20th Street, and begins a tradition of animated Christmas windows that attract customers. Starrett & Van Vleck has designed the structure (see Shaver, 1931).

Arnold Constable moves into a large new Fifth Avenue building at the southeast corner of 40th Street, taking over a site previously occupied by the Frederick W. Vanderbilt house (see 1856; Mid-Manhattan Library, 1970).

Electric-power and railroad air-brake pioneer George Westinghouse dies at New York March 12 at age 67.

The Hamburg-Amerika Line's S.S. Vaterland that will become the S.S. Leviathan in 1919 arrives at New York from Cherbourg May 21 on her maiden voyage to begin a 24-year career on the North Atlantic. The 54,282-ton ship is 950 feet in length overall, has four screws, and can accommodate 4,000 passengers plus 1,134 in crew (see 1917).

The S.S. Bismarck that will become the S.S. Majestic in 1919 begins a 26-year career on the North Atlantic. The 56,621-ton German passenger liner is 954 feet in length overall and has four screws.

The Cunard Line's R.M.S. Aquitania arrives from Liverpool on her maiden voyage June 15. Built by John Brown & Co. at Clydesbank and powered by four direct-action Parson steam turbines, the 45,647-ton passenger liner is 901 feet in length overall, 97 feet wide, 55 feet deep, has six decks, accommodates 3,250 passengers, 550 officers and crew, has a normal speed of 24 knots, and is double-skinned with an average of 15 feet between her inner and outer shells. She will be the last of the four-funneled ships.

The Panama Canal opens to traffic August 3 just as Germany declares war on France. The canal uses a system of locks to carry ships 50.7 miles between deep water in the Atlantic and deep water in the Pacific.

The Cape Cod Ship Canal opens to link Buzzards Bay with Cape Cod Bay. Financed by August Belmont II, the $12 million, 17.4-mile waterway enables coastal shipping to avoid the 70-mile voyage around the Cape, and a railroad bridge decreases the need for the Fall River Line, whose vessels have carried freight and passengers since 1847 (see 1907). Its *Commonwealth* and other steamships will continue nevertheless to operate until 1937.

Hunter College adopts that name following the death of its president, Thomas Hunter (see 1869; building, 1913; Brooklyn Collegiate Center, 1926).

Regis High School opens at 55 East 84th Street, although its building (designed by Maginnis and Walsh) will not be completed until 1917. Enrollment at the Jesuit day school for boys will grow to 500, with boys from the entire metropolitan area, including Connecticut and New Jersey, receiving full scholarships (except for activity and laboratory fees). Admission will be by competitive examination, and the school will maintain rigorous academic standards long after public high schools have relaxed theirs.

Horace Mann School for Boys moves uptown again, this time from 120th Street in Manhattan to 246th Street in Riverdale's Fieldston section, with Virgil Prettyman, now 30, as headmaster (see 1901). Prettyman found a 13-acre parcel of land north of Van Cortlandt Park 5 years ago, Teachers College purchased it for $20,000 with a view to building dormitories on the property but gave up on the idea, Prettyman acquired an adjacent lot, Horace Mann boys have been using the land for athletics since 1912, and facilities have now been completed for teaching there. Horace Mann High School for Girls, headed by Henry Carr Pearson, remains at 120th Street and Broadway.

The Professional Children's School is founded by Mrs. Franklin W. Robinson and Deaconess Jane Harris Hall, who have gone backstage at the Gaiety Theater where the hit play *Daddy Long-Legs* opened September 28 and discovered five young actors playing poker instead of studying. They saw a need for stage children to have some formal education, and their first students are all performing onstage as actors, comedians, dancers, jugglers, musicians, and singers.

The city has only 38 more public schools than in 1899 despite an increase of more than 300,000 in enrollment. Overcrowded schools turn away 60,000 to 75,000 children each year for lack of space.

The *New Republic* begins publication from offices in West 21st Street. New York-born author Herbert D. Croly, now 45, influenced the thinking of Theodore Roosevelt and Woodrow Wilson with his 1909 book *The Promise of American Life* and has obtained backing from Willard Straight to cofound the "journal of opinion" that will compete with The *Nation* founded in 1865.

Georgia-born New York public relations pioneer Ivy (Ledbetter) Lee, 36, advises John D. Rockefeller to visit Colorado following the Ludlow Massacre and speak personally to the miners, hoping to improve relations between the Rockefeller family and outraged strikers. An advocate of frank and open dealing with the public, Lee will help make the Rockefellers famous for their philanthropies—partly by having John D. Sr. hand out dimes to schoolchildren.

Journalist-reformer Jacob Riis dies at Barre, Mass., May 26 at age 66.

The German newspaper *New Yorker Herold* runs a headline August 1: "All German Hearts Beat Higher Today." Some New Yorkers are reservists in the German army and parade in the streets carrying German flags, sometimes exchanging blows with men carrying British or French flags until Mayor Mitchel bans all foreign flags. William Randolph Hearst owns the German-language *Deutsches Journal*, opposes aid to the Allies, and wins praise from the Berlin paper *Vossische Zeitung*, whose editorial writer says of Hearst, "He has exposed the selfishness of England and her campaign of abuse against Germany, and has preached justice for the Central Powers."

The *Day* begins publication at New York to compete with The *Forward* founded in 1897. The new Yiddish newspaper incorporates a section in English.

U.S. newspapers, magazines, advertisers, and advertising agencies set up the Audit Bureau of Circulation to produce accurate data.

Nonfiction: *A Preface to Politics* by New York-born journalist Walter Lippmann, 25.

Painting: *Backyards, Greenwich Village* by John Sloan.

Sculpture: the Pulitzer Fountain with a statue of Pomona by sculptor Karl T. F. Bitter is unveiled in front of the Plaza Hotel in the Grand Army Plaza now being completed to designs by architect Thomas Hastings (the late publisher Joseph Pulitzer left $50,000 in his will to fund the fountain, and the 1903 St. Gaudens statue of Gen. Sherman is being moved to align it with the new fountain; a heroic bronze statue of Thomas Jefferson by William Ordway Partridge is completed on commission from the late Pulitzer and placed before Columbia University's School of Journalism that Pulitzer endowed.

Theater: *Too Many Cooks* by Boston-born playwright-actor Frank Craven, 33, 2/24 at the 39th Street Theater, with Craven, 223 perfs.; *On Trial* by New York-born playwright Elmer Rice (originally Elmer Leopold Reizenstein), 21, 8/19 at the new Candler Theater at 226 West 42nd Street, 365 perfs. (initially a movie house, the Candler has been turned into a legitimate theater that will later be called the Harris); *Daddy Long-Legs* by Jean Webster 9/28 at the Gaiety Theater, with Boots Wooster, New York-born actress Ruth Chatterton, 20, Lillian Ross, Gladys Smith; *The Song of Songs* by Edward Sheldon (who has adapted a novel by Hermann Sudermann) 12/22 at the Eltinge Theater, with Dorothy Donnelly, 191 perfs. (now 28, Sheldon will experience a stiffening of the knees next summer, his ankylosing spondylitis [a severe form of arthritis] will grow progressively worse, and by the 1920s he will be almost completely paralyzed and able to travel only by having a window removed from a sleeping car to accommodate his stretcher); *The Show Shop* by U.S. playright James Forbes, 43, 12/31 at the Hudson Theater, with Douglas Fairbanks, Patricia Collinge, Zelda Sears, 156 perfs.

Films: Mack Sennett's *Tillie's Punctured Romance* with Charles Chaplin, Marie Dressler, Mabel Normand, Chester Conklin, Mack Swain, Charles Bennett, and the Keystone Kops in the first U.S. feature-length comedy; Donald MacKenzie's *The Perils of Pauline* with Pearl Fay White, 22, and Crane Wilbur. Produced by a Hearst-controlled company, it is a "cliff-hanger" serial ("To be continued . . .") designed to bring audiences back each week to see "The Lady Daredevil of the Fillums."

The Strand movie theater opens with 3,300 seats on Times Square at the northwest corner of Broadway and 47th Street (see Regent, 1913). Buffalo-born nickelodeon operator Mitchell L. "Moe" Marks has acquired the property and given architect Thomas Lamb and Minnesota-born impresario Samuel Lionel "Roxy" Rothafel, now 32, free reign to create a theater—the largest such house in the country to date—that will "stand for all time as the model of Moving Picture Palaces." In addition to showing films, the so-called "dream palace" makes moviegoing respectable for middle-class audiences by offering a ballet troupe, opera selections, and a symphony orchestra (see Rialto, 1916).

Broadway musicals: *Sari* 1/3 at the Liberty Theater, with music by Emmanuel Kelman, lyrics by C. C. S. Cushing and Eric Heath, 151 perfs.; *The Whirl of the World* (revue) 1/10 at the Winter Garden Theater, with Rozsika Dolly, Eugene and Willie Howard, Lillian Lorraine, Lawrence Grant, music by Sigmund Romberg, book and lyrics by Harold Atteridge, 161 perfs.; *The Crinoline Girl* 3/16 at the Knickerbocker Theater, with Julian Eltinge, music by Percy Wenrich, book by Otto Hauerbach, lyrics by Eltinge, 88 perfs.; *The Ziegfeld Follies* 6/1 at the New Amsterdam Theater, with Ed Wynn, Ann Pennington, Leon Errol, music by Dave Stamper, Raymond Hubbell, and others, lyrics by Gene Buck and others, 112 perfs.; *The Passing Show* 6/10 at the Winter Garden Theater, with Evansville, Ind.-born comedy actress Marilyn Miller (Mary Ellen Reynolds) making her debut at age 15, barelegged chorus girls, music chiefly by Sigmund Romberg, lyrics chiefly by Harold Atteridge, 133 perfs.; *The Girl From Utah* 8/24 at the Knickerbocker Theater, with a cast of 16, music by Paul Rubens and Sidney Jones, songs that include "They Didn't Believe Me" by Jerome Kern, lyrics by English writer Michael E. Rourke, 47, 120 perfs.; *Wars of the World* (extravaganza) 9/5 at the Hippodrome, with Lawrence Grant, music by Manuel Klein, 229 perfs.; *Chin-Chin* 10/20 at the Globe Theater, with music by Ivan Caryll, book by Boston-born writer Anne Caldwell, 38, and R. H. Burnside, lyrics by Caldwell and James O'Dea, songs that include "It's a Long Way to Tipperary," 295 perfs.; *The Only Girl* 11/2 at the 39th Street Theater, with Jed Prouty, music by Victor Herbert, lyrics by Henry Blossom, songs that include "You're the Only Girl for Me," 240 perfs.; *Watch Your Step* 12/8 at the New Amsterdam Theater, with Vernon and Irene Castle doing the Castle Walk, Fanny Brice, music and lyrics by Irving Berlin, songs that include "Play a Simple Melody," 175 perfs.; *Hello Broadway* 12/25 at the Astor Theater, with George M. Cohan, William Collier, Brooklyn-born ingénue Peggy Wood, 22, Louise Dresser, music and book by Cohan, 123 perfs.

Harlem's Apollo Theater has its beginnings in Hurtig & Seamon's New (Burlesque) Theater, opened at 253 West 125th Street between Seventh and Eighth avenues. Designed by George Keister, it is intended for white audiences only (Harlem's population remains predominantly Jewish) and will bar blacks for 20 years (*see* 1934).

The American Society of Composers, Authors, and Publishers (ASCAP) is founded by nine songwriters at New York to protect the interests of music writers, lyricists, and publishers (*see* 1909 copyright law). Conceived over dinner at Lüchow's Restaurant by Irving Berlin, Victor Herbert, Jerome Kern, John Philip Sousa, and five others, ASCAP will defend its members against illegal public performances for profit of copyrighted musical compositions, protect them against other forms of infringement, and collect license fees for authorized performances (*see* Victor Herbert, 1917; BMI, 1939).

The Millrose Games are held for the first time January 28 at Madison Square Garden. Named for the country estate of department store executive Lewis Rodman Wanamaker, 50, the Millrose Athletic Association (initially the Wahna Athletic Association) is composed of Wanamaker's department store employees, and its indoor track meet includes as a major event the Wanamaker Mile footrace.

The Gaelic Athletic Association of New York is founded to arrange and supervise championship matches in Irish football, hurling, and camogie (a woman's version of hurling). The Association will grow to have representatives from 62 clubs (*see* Gaelic Park, 1926).

Pelham Bay Golf Course opens in Pelham Bay Park in the Bronx (*see* 1888). The public course will be followed by a second such course as the sport gains popularity (*see* 1936).

Helena Rubinstein challenges Elizabeth Arden for leadership in the fledgling U.S. cosmetics industry (*see* 1910). Now 44 (she claims to be 54 so that her products will seem more effective), Rubinstein left her native Poland after an unhappy love affair at age 19 to seek a husband in Australia, made $100,000 in 3 years near Melbourne selling to sunburned Australian women a skin cream she formulated from ingredients that included almonds and tree bark, has opened England's first beauty salon in London, opened another one in Paris, and is the reigning beauty adviser to French and British society. The four-foot-eleven-inch cosmetician gains quick popularity with her Maison de Beauté in Manhattan's 49th Street. Rubinstein will introduce medicated face creams and waterproof mascara and pioneer in sending saleswomen out on road tours to demonstrate proper makeup application as she builds a chain of beauty salons (*see* 1928).

The elastic brassiere that will supplant the corset now in common use is patented in November by New York inventor Mary Phelps "Polly" Jacob, 21, who as a debutante found that her bulky corset hampered her freedom of movement and that its cover showed over her decolletage. Dressing for a dance, she asked her French maid, Marie, for two silk pocket handkerchiefs, some pink ribbon, needle and thread, and the two devised a prototype bra that flattens the bustline against the chest. She engaged a designer to make drawings, borrowed $100, rented two sewing machines, and hired two immigrant girls to stitch up a few hundred Backless Brassieres. Through a family friend she will sell her patent to the corset maker Warner Brothers Corset Co. of Bridgeport, Conn., whose management will pay $1,500 to acquire all rights to a patent that will later be estimated to be worth $15 million (*see* Maiden Form, 1923).

Coney Island's Steeplechase Park owner George C. Tilyou dies at Brooklyn November 30 at age 52.

Pollution of the Hudson and East rivers forces New York to require that floating baths be made water-

The Municipal Building provided offices for everything from archives to marriages. MUNICIPAL ARCHIVE

tight and filled with purified water (see 1870). The city has built 17 public bathhouses in Manhattan since 1895, plus seven in Brooklyn, and one each in the Bronx and Queens, most of them in areas with large immigrant populations, to create the nation's most elaborate and costly bath system (bathhouses built since 1904 generally include gymnasiums and swimming pools). Men and women have separate waiting rooms, each is given 20 minutes to shower in a small cubicle (divided into a changing area and shower stall), and the time and water temperature are controlled by an attendant. But use of public bathhouses has been declining and no more will be built after this year.

The J. P. Morgan & Co. Building is completed in pink Tennessee marble at 23 Wall Street, southeast corner Broad Street, to designs by Trowbridge & Livingston (see commerce, 1920).

The Municipal Building is completed near the Manhattan end of the Brooklyn Bridge at the intersection of Chambers and Centre streets. Designed by architect William Mitchell Kendall, 57, of McKim, Mead & White with classical details, the 24-story complex houses city administrative offices. It is topped by Adolf A. Weinman's $300,000, 25-foot-high sculpture Civic Fame, made from 500 pieces of hammered copper over a steel frame.

St. Thomas Episcopal Church at Fifth Avenue and 53rd Street is completed to designs by Connecticut-born architect Bertram (Grosvenor) Goodhue, 45, who leaves the Boston firm Cram, Goodhue & Ferguson to open his own office at New York.

The Church of the Intercession (Episcopal) is completed with a vicarage at 550 West 155th Street, southeast corner Broadway, to designs by Bertram Goodhue.

The 17-story 903 Park Avenue apartment house is completed at the northeast corner of 79th Street. Hailed as the world's tallest residential structure, it has been erected by lawyer-developers Alexander M. and Leo S. Bing to designs by architect Robert L. Lyons with Warren & Wetmore and has units that occupy full floors, having as many as 18 rooms with circular foyers 13 feet wide, living rooms measuring 26' × 20', bedrooms 23' × 20', and six baths, each with tub, shower, and bidet. Each unit has its own laundry, six servants' rooms, and a servants' dining room. Tenants pay as much as $800 per month in rent (those on the top five floors pay the most).

The 12-story Umbria apartment house is completed at 465 West End Avenue, northwest corner 82nd Street; the 12-story 600 West End Avenue apart-ment house at the northeast corner of 89th Street; the 12-story 838 West End Avenue apartment house at the southeast corner of 101st street to designs by George and Edward Blum. The prohibition against building anything other than private houses on the avenue has been removed for about a decade, and builders on West End Avenue claim that the thoroughfare is far less damp and windy than Riverside Drive.

The Biltmore Hotel opens January 1 (after a gala New Year's Eve dinner) at the southwest corner of Vanderbilt Avenue and 44th Street, across from the new Grand Central Terminal and directly above the Terminal's new room for incoming long-distance trains (the so-called "kissing gallery"). John McEntee Bowman heads the syndicate that has financed it and has engaged architects Warren & Wetmore to design the 26-story hotel that stands on land leased from the New York Central. Of its 1,000 rooms, 900 have private baths. A guest from Chicago can go from his Pullman car to his room, take the subway downtown to transact business, and return to his home town without ever going outdoors. The main dining room and men's café (later called the Men's Bar) are on the Madison Avenue blockfront, there is a Turkish bath and plunge for the men, a men's writing room and a women's writing room, and the hotel's north entrance, on Vanderbilt Avenue, leads into a women's corridor, designed so that ladies may come and go without passing through the main lobby. The Biltmore's lobby clock will become a favorite meeting place for generations of preppies, college students, and young lovers until the hotel closes in 1981.

The Grand Union Hotel closes May 2 (see 1874). Its hodgepodge of five- to seven-story masonry buildings has been condemned, and the city has paid more than $3.5 million for the hotel. It will spend another $644,000 to demolish it in order to obtain land needed for a link between the new Lexington Avenue IRT subway and the Fourth Avenue line of the original subway.

The Arthur Curtiss James mansion is completed at the northwest corner of Park Avenue and 69th Street to designs by Allen & Collens. Railroad magnate James, now 47, is a grandson of Daniel James, who established the family fortune with mining ventures in the southwest, and a son of D. Willis James, who helped finance James J. Hill's Great Northern and Canadian Pacific railroad ventures. A. C. James has created his own rail network, extending from Chicago to California and accounting for nearly 15 percent of all the track in the United

States. Covered in Knoxville gray marble, his new house will be his home until he dies in 1941 (*see* 700 Park Avenue, 1959).

A five-story town house is completed at 1015 Park Avenue, southeast corner 85th Street, for Wall Street broker Lewis Gouverneur Morris, 32, and his wife, Natalie Lawlor Bailey, who have been living at 77 Madison Avenue. Ernest Flagg has designed the gabled red-brick neo-Federal house, built on property acquired from Amos Pinchot, and it replaces a five-story tenement.

The palatial William Starr Miller house is completed in limestone and brick at 1048 Fifth Avenue, southeast corner 86th Street, to designs by Carrère & Hastings. Commissioned by industrialist Miller, the six-story mansion will later be acquired by Mrs. Cornelius Vanderbilt III (*see* religion [YIVO Institute], 1940).

An article in the February issue of *Harper's* magazine calls the rear of the Metropolitan Museum of Art "a harsh assault on the landscape and the eye. It is a horrible example of starting any kind of building not necessary to a park within a park enclosure (*see* 1880). It is a formidable intruder, vast, heavy, addicted to excessive growth and reproachful of the greeneries it pushes into."

The city's first International Flower Show opens at the 3-year-old Grand Central Palace under the auspices of the 15-year-old Horticultural Society of New York and the New York Florists Club.

The Department of Health closes Jamaica Bay to shellfishing. The 148 square miles of water surrounding New York City from the Inwood Peninsula to Little Neck Bay contain fertile clam beds, but a sewer in Canarsie has drained new lots into the bay since 1886, another has begun draining Jamaica, and the beds have become so contaminated with pathogens and heavy metals that mollusks taken from them are toxic. Poachers will continue to harvest the clam beds, elude the Coast Guard and other authorities, and mislabel their catches, claiming they came from legal areas (*see* medicine, 1916).

Dinty Moore's opens at 216 West 46th Street serving corned beef and cabbage, Irish stew, and a few other dishes that will attract a clientele of publishing and theater people. Having run a bar in West 39th Street, Tenth Avenue-born proprietor James C. Moore, 45, has bought three brownstones, converted the ground floor of one into a restaurant with an open kitchen, given it a white exterior, and decorated its interior with polished brass and mirrors; he will operate the establishment until his death in 1952.

Mama Leone's has its beginnings in a restaurant opened in a brownstone at 239 West 48th Street. Leone's wine shop has been near the back of the Metropolitan Opera house since 1906, Leone's wife has run a little restaurant above the shop, and the 48th Street establishment will prosper with the help of Mama's sons Gene and Celestine, taking over two adjacent houses.

Corning-born New York feminist Margaret Louise Sanger (*née* Higgins), 31, introduces the term *birth control* in her radical feminist magazine *The Woman Rebel*. Sanger has seen her mother worn out by having more than a dozen babies, and as a nurse she has seen the effects of self-induced abortions. She exiles herself to England to escape federal prosecution for publishing and mailing *Family Limitation*, a brochure that describes the benefits to working-class couples of using douches, condoms, and pessaries for contraception (*see* Brooklyn clinic, 1916).

1915 The Great War in Europe intensifies. Casualty lists mount for both sides on the eastern and western fronts and a German U-boat (submarine) blockade of Britain begins February 18. A torpedo from the German submarine U-20 hits the forward cargo hold of the Cunard Line passenger ship S.S. *Lusitania* at 2:10 o'clock in the afternoon of May 7 off the coast of Ireland, a second explosion occurs, and the huge vessel sinks in 18 minutes, killing 1,201 men, women, and children who include 128 U.S. citizens, among them railroad magnate Alfred Gwynne Vanderbilt, 38, and New York theatrical magnate Charles Frohman, 75.

Irish-born political activist Jeremiah O'Donovan Rossa dies at New York June 19 at age 83 after 45 years in the city. His body is returned to Ireland, where patriots call him the personification of the Fenian movement that will inspire freedom from British rule (*see* Easter rebellion, 1916).

A constitutional convention at Albany agrees in late August to adopt a Municipal Research Bureau's recommendation for reorganizing the inefficient state government. Tammany Hall has opposed the new constitution, and Al Smith has reluctantly followed orders from the "Wigwam" in 14th Street, but when he attends Tammany's Friday night dinners at Delmonico's he begins efforts to persuade the older sachems that times are changing, that working-class voters need something more than civil service jobs, holiday gift baskets, and outings if the Democrats are to retain their allegiance, that they want government to play a more active role in protecting them from rapacious employers, and that the uptown reformers are on the right track.

The Women's City Club of New York is founded by suffragists who include Katharine Bement Davis, Mary E. Dreier, Genevieve Earle, Mary Garrett Hay, Dorothy Kenyon, Belle Moskowitz, Frances Perkins, and Eleanor Roosevelt.

The New York State Department of Charities launches an investigation into New York City charitable organizations.

The Conference Board has its beginnings in the first Yama Conference on National Industrial Efficiency held June 5 to 7 at the Yama Farms Inn 100 miles northwest of New York in the foothills of the Catskills (see 1914). Commission on Industrial Relations member Magnus Alexander has been urging such a conference since last year's Ludlow Massacre, and the 23 attendees include 12 presidents of major corporations and presidents of six leading industry associations; their deliberations address the causes of increasing conflict between management and labor, the effect on business of growingly restrictive labor and social legislation, and the decline in public respect for big business. A second Yama Conference September 18 considers a plan developed by Alexander and a committee that he has headed to deal with the "unsympathetic, often unfriendly public attitude toward industry and its leaders" (see 1916).

A joint English-French commission arrives at New York September 10 in hopes of floating an Allied war loan. The State Department has placed no limit on sales of munitions to belligerents and non-belligerents, and it now lets the J. P. Morgan bank head up a $500 billion loan by a consortium of 61 New York banks. By 1918 the House of Morgan will have purchased $3 billion in war supplies for the Allies, earning a commission of 1 percent ($30 million).

Wall Street's Dow Jones Industrial Average rises a record 81 percent for the year and closes December 31 at 98.81, up from 54.58 at the end of 1914, having been closed for more than 4 months last year.

Brooks Brothers moves from Broadway and 22nd Street into a large new Madison Avenue store at 44th Street (see 1909; 1946).

Siegel-Cooper on Sixth Avenue goes bankrupt after 19 years as a high-volume department store that was also a retail fashion leader. Merchant Henry Siegel has been convicted of falsifying data in order to obtain further credit, his store closes, so does a related bank, many of his 900 employees lose their savings, and Siegel is sentenced to a 10-month prison term for fraud.

The Fifth Avenue Coach Co. starts designing and assembling its own buses to replace the French DeDions and English Daimlers imported since 1907. The new 34-seat double-decker coaches are powered by 40-horsepower four-cylinder Knight sleeve-valve engines (see 1936).

The Interborough (IRT) subway opens the Steinway Tunnels under the East River June 22 (see 1907).

The National Committee for the Prevention of Blindness is founded at New York by philanthropist Louisa Lee Schuyler, now 77, with help from Winifred Holt and others.

Long-distance telephone service between New York and San Francisco begins January 25. Alexander Graham Bell, now 68, repeats the words that he allegedly spoke in 1876 ("Mr. Watson, come here . . .") to Thomas Watson in San Francisco, the call takes 23 minutes to go through and costs $20.70.

The Greek-language newspaper *Ethnikos Kerus* (*National Herald*) begins publication, giving the city's growing Greek community (it now numbers more than 22,000) a liberal alternative to the 21-year-old *Atlantis* that has appeared on a daily basis since 1905 (see *Proini*, 1976).

Newspaper publisher Herman Ridder dies of arteriosclerosis at his 11 West 81st Street home November 1 at age 63 (see 1901). He has not visited his office at the *Staats-Zeitung* Building, 182 William Street, since mid-December of last year but has directed the paper's editorial policy from his sickroom. Ridder has lost all his personal assets in the failure of the International Typesetting Machine Co. and he is practically penniless; his son Bernard H. takes over management of the paper (see 1920).

Condé Nast acquires *House and Garden* magazine, whose circulation is only about 10,000 and whose pages carry little advertising (see *Vogue*, 1909).

Alfred A. Knopf is founded at New York with $5,000 in capital. New York-born Doubleday, Page veteran Alfred Abraham Knopf, 23, will marry his assistant Blanche Wolf, now 21, next year, they will choose a Russian wolfhound (borzoi) as their colophon, and they will achieve their first success with an American edition of the 1904 romance *Green Mansions* by W. H. Hudson (see 1960).

Nonfiction: *The House on Henry Street* by Lillian Wald (see philanthropy, 1893).

Fiction: *The "Genius"* by Theodore Dreiser, who makes failure in the big city seem inevitable; *The Titan* by Dreiser is another work based on the life of the late Charles T. Yerkes; *Just Around the Corner* (stories) by Ohio-born New York writer Fannie Hurst, 24.

Poetry: *Rivers to the Sea* by St. Louis-born New York poet Sara Teasdale, 33.

Sculpture: a bronze bust of Peter Stuyvesant is presented to New York by Wilhelmina of the Netherlands and placed opposite the entrance to St. Mark's-in-the-Bouwerie, in whose churchyard Stuyvesant was buried. It was sculpted at the Hague 4 years ago by Dutch artist Toom Depuis; the Wireless Operators Memorial is erected in Battery Park to honor men who include Jack Phillips, the operator on R.M.S. *Titanic*, who was one of the first to use the new SOS distress signal; a bronze statue of Joan of Arc by New York sculptor Anna Vaughn Hyatt is installed on a 1.578-acre site on Riverside Drive at 93rd Street.

Sculptor Karl T. F. Bitter is struck by a motorcar and dies of his injuries at New York April 10 at age 47.

Theater: *The Boomerang* by Winchell Smith and Victor Mapes 8/10 at the Belasco Theater, with Wallace Eddinger, 522 perfs.; *Common Clay* by Cleves Kinkead 8/26 at the Republic Theater, with Jane Cowl, 316 perfs.; *Young America* by Fred Ballard 8/28 at the Astor Theater, with Toledo-born actor Otto Kruger, 29, Peggy Wood, 105 perfs.; *The House of Glass* by Max Marcin 9/1 at the Candler Theater, with Barry Ryan, 245 perfs.; *The Unchastened Woman* by Louis Kaufman Anspacher 10/9 at the 39th Street Theater, 193 perfs.

The Neighborhood Playhouse of the Henry Street Settlement is founded at 466 Grand Street by Irene and Alice Lewisohn, daughters of the late copper baron-philanthropist Leonard Lewisohn, who died at London in 1902. The playhouse will continue until 1927, presenting works by Shaw, O'Neill, and Leonid Andreyev for immigrant audiences (*see* Neighborhood School of Theater, 1928).

Playwright Paul Armstrong dies of a heart attack at his 829 Park Avenue apartment August 31 at age 46.

Film: D. W. Griffith's *The Birth of a Nation* with Lillian Gish, Mae Marsh, Henry B. Walthall has such cinematic innovations as the close-up, pan (panoramic shot), flashback, and use of a moving camera in addition to its element of racism.

Fox Film Corp. is created by William Fox, now 36, who started his career as a New York penny arcade manager in 1904, added nickelodeons, joined with Sol Brill and B. S. Moss in 1908 to start an exhibition firm, and 2 years ago founded Box Office

Attraction Co. to produce his own films. He is soon employing such stars as Theda Bara, William Farnum, and Annette Kellerman. Fox will merge with Twentieth Century Pictures in 1935 to form Twentieth Century Fox.

Broadway musicals: *The Passing Show* 5/29 at the Winter Garden Theater, with Marilyn Miller, baritone John Charles Thomas in his Broadway debut, music chiefly by Leo Edwards and W. F. Peter, lyrics by Harold Atteridge, 145 perfs.; *The Ziegfeld Follies* 6/21 at the New Amsterdam Theater, with W. C. Fields, Ed Wynn, George White, Ann Pennington, music by Louis A. Hirsch, Dave Stamper, and others, songs that include "Hello, Frisco" by Hirsch and Gene Buck, 104 perfs.; *The Blue Paradise* 8/5 at the Casino Theater, with Vivienne Segal, music by Edmund Eysler, book by Edgar Smith based on a Viennese opera, lyrics by M. E. Rourke, 356 perfs.; *The Princess Pat* 9/29 at the Cort Theater, with Al Shean, Syracuse-born ingénue Doris Kenyon, 18, music by Victor Herbert, book and lyrics by Henry Blossom, 158 perfs.; *Hip-Hip-Hooray* 9/30 at the Hippodrome, with music by Raymond Hubbell, lyrics by John L. Golden, 425 perfs.; *Very Good Eddie* 12/23 at the Princess Theater, with music by Jerome Kern, lyrics by Schuyler Greene, 341 perfs.; *Stop! Look! Listen!* 12/25 at the Globe Theater, with music and lyrics by Irving Berlin, book by Harry B. Smith, 105 perfs.

Popular song: "There's a Broken Heart for Every Light on Broadway" by Fred Fisher, lyrics by Howard Johnson.

The New York Yankees and the American League franchise change hands January 11 for $450,000. Purchased in 1903 for $18,000 by Frank Farrell and William Devery through Tammany front man Joseph Gordon, they are acquired by brewer Col. Jacob Ruppert, now 47, and engineer Tillinghast l'Hommidieu Houston (each man puts up $225,000); the 12-year-old Hilltop Park stadium used by the Yankees from 1903 to 1912 is near collapse and Ruppert will later say, "For $450,000 we got an orphan ball club without a home of its own, without players of outstanding ability, without prestige" (*see* Babe Ruth, 1920; Yankee Stadium, 1923).

A New York judge declares Stanford White's millionaire murderer Harry K. Thaw sane July 16, and Thaw is freed from the mental asylum where he has been confined since 1907 (*see* 1913). He shows no interest in his wife, Evelyn, or their child and tells intimates he will cut Evelyn out of his will.

The Equitable Life Assurance Society Building is completed at 120 Broadway between Pine and Cedar Streets (*see* 1913; fire, 1912). Designed by Ernest R. Graham of Graham, Anderson, Probst & White (successors to D. H. Burnham & Co.), the new 36-story office building contains 1.2 million square feet of floor space on a plot of just under one acre, has nearly 30 times as much floor space as was contained in its site, exploits its site as no building has ever done before, puts the financial district in shadow, and fuels demand for a zoning law that will prohibit such buildings (*see* 1916; Singer Tower, 1908).

The 18-year-old Yale Club moves into a 21-story building at 50 Vanderbilt Avenue, northwest corner 44th Street, with an underground entrance from the subway and from that part of Grand Central Terminal extending below the avenue (the underground entrance will be closed in the early 1960s). The New York Central has approved the height of the structure, and because it has been built atop two stories of railroad tracks architect James Gamble Rogers has had to locate his supporting columns where they would not interfere with the clearance needed for trains. He has placed a three-quarter-inch space of mastic material just a few inches above the sidewalk to compensate for vibration and allow for movement caused by the expansion and contraction of steel. An office, large cloakroom, telephone booths and elevators are on the low-ceilinged entrance hall; the second floor, reached by a short flight of stairs (or by elevator) contains a high-ceilinged lounge with nine windows and deep embrasures. The Grill Room is on the second mezzanine, the billiard room on the third floor, the library on the fourth; Turkish baths are on the fifth floor, along with a small swimming pool (or plunge) and lockers; the gymnasium and squash courts are on the sixth, and bedrooms occupy all floors from the seventh to the 17th, inclusive; the 18th floor has private dining rooms, the kitchen is on the 19th, the 20th contains the main dining room, a wine "cellar" is on the 21st together with storage rooms, and a roof garden provides commanding views of Manhattan and the country beyond the rivers.

The 44-year-old Knickberbocker Club moves from its clubhouse on Fifth Avenue and 32nd Street into a handsome new red-brick building at the southeast corner of Fifth Avenue and 62nd Street designed by William Adams Delano of Delano & Aldrich.

The 1155 Park Avenue apartment house is completed at the southeast corner of 92nd Street. Designed by Robert L. Lyons, it has an inner courtyard measuring 34' × 32' (Bing & Bing has acquired two three-story houses at 109 and 111 East 91st Street to keep anyone from putting up a tall building that would block the light of 1155; the houses are razed and replaced with a 30-foot town house, designed by S. Edson Gage for I. Townsend Burden). Apartments at 1155 are as large as 12 rooms, four baths, and have living rooms as large as 25' × 20', dining rooms 24' × 14'9", bedrooms 20' × 13' (one tenant puts together two units to create an apartment with 18 rooms, six baths).

The Willard Straight mansion is completed for diplomat Willard Straight, now 35, and his wife, Dorothy (*née* Whitney), at 1130 Fifth Avenue, northeast corner 94th Street. Delano & Aldrich has designed the red-brick-and-marble Georgian-style house, Straight will die of influenza at Paris in December 1918, his widow will remarry and move to England, utilties lawyer Harrison Williams will take over the place in 1928, it will become the headquarters of the Audubon Society in the early 1950s, the International Center of Photography will acquire it in 1974, and it will be sold to a private investor for $17.5 million in the summer of 2000.

Queens begins to adopt the Philadelphia system of building numbers and street names under the direction of engineer Charles Underhill Powell, 39, who is appointed chief engineer of the borough's Topographical Bureau and given responsibility for laying out some 2,500 miles of streets covering 75,000 acres of what remains mostly farmland in the city's fastest-growing section. Each building number includes the number of the nearest intersecting avenue or street, considered an advantage when trying to find an address. Powell will continue in the position until 1942.

The Kew Bolmer completed in Queens at 80-45 Kew Gardens Road is the first Kew Gardens apartment house (*see* 1910). By 1936 the community will have more than 20 such buildings.

Straus Park is dedicated April 15, occupying the triangle (formerly Bloomingdale Square) at the intersection of Broadway, West End Avenue, and 106th Street. Created by architect Evarts Tracy and sculptor Augustus Lukeman as a memorial to the late R. H. Macy partner Isidor Straus and his wife, Ida, it features a bronze entitled *Memory*.

The Japanese Hill and Pond Garden opens in Brooklyn's Prospect Park with antique lanterns, cherry and pine trees, shrubbery, flowers, and waterfalls that will make it the centerpiece of the park's Botanic Garden.

A fire at 66 North 6th Street in Williamsburg November 2 and another 4 days later at 285-287 North 6th Street take a combined toll of 25 lives.

Birth control opponent and self-appointed moralist Anthony Comstock dies at New York September 21 at age 71.

Ellis Island receives only 178,416 immigrants, down nearly 80 percent from the 878,052 who arrived last year as the war in Europe and the threat of attacks by German U-boats discourages emigration (*see* 1918). President Wilson has appointed Frederick C. Howe commissioner of immigration; formerly director of the People's Institute at the Cooper Union, Howe has reformed conditions on the island, recruiting teachers to give instruction in English, child care, hygiene, and the like, setting up a kindergarten for younger children, arranging classes where women and older children can learn sewing and knitting, and organizing athletic programs for men.

1916 The Great War in Europe takes a heavy toll, the United States remains neutral, marchers in the city's annual St. Patrick's Day parade on Fifth Avenue carry banners and placards demanding a free Ireland, and the Irish rise against the British in a great Easter rebellion, led in part by New York-born activist Eamon de Valera, 33, who is caught by the British but spared execution because he holds both U.S. and British citizenship (*see* O'Donovan Rossa, 1915); de Valera solicits contributions from the city's Irish population to support recognition of Irish independence.

The Black Tom explosions early in the morning of July 31 blow up 1 million tons of munitions stored in railcars and on piers and barges at the docks of Jersey City's Black Tom River, killing seven men, injuring 35, and destroying $40 million worth of property within a 25-mile radius. Shells and shrapnel that had been awaiting transfer to Allied ships continue to burst for 3 hours, shaking apartment houses and skyscrapers, smashing half the windows in the Custom House, breaking panes throughout the Wall Street area, and shattering plate glass as far away as Times Square. German saboteurs are generally considered responsible, and although no clear evidence will ever be produced that sabotage was involved the city has become a center for German agents, financed in part by the German ambassador Count Johann von Bernstorff, who has deposited $150 million in German treasury notes in the Chase National Bank.

Former Brooklyn and, later, New York mayor (and Columbia University president) Seth Low dies at suburban Bedford Hills September 17 at age 66.

President Wilson wins reelection on a platform that includes the slogan, "He kept us out of war," but he believes he has lost until late returns from California give him 23 more electoral votes than his Republican opponent, Justice Charles Evans Hughes of the U.S. Supreme Court, who receives 46 percent of the popular vote to Wilson's 49 percent. New York newspapers have published extras proclaiming Hughes the president-elect, and Hughes has fallen asleep at the Astor Hotel in Times Square believing the headlines. Tammany Hall has not supported Wilson, who has angered Tammany sachems by not helping the Irish rebels.

Gov. Whitman wins reelection, defeating his Democratic opponent Judge Samuel Seabury, now 43, who receives 686,862 votes as compared with 835,820 for Republican Whitman.

Jamaican-born social reformer Marcus (Moziah) Garvey (,Jr.), 28, arrives at New York March 23 and begins a 5-month speaking tour to raise money for the Universal Negro Improvement Association he founded 3 years ago in the British West Indies. He will open branches throughout America and the Caribbean in the next few years, begin publishing the newspaper *Negro World* in English, Spanish, and French at Harlem in 1918, encourage blacks to return to Africa and build a new nation there, urge them to start their own businesses, and establish the Black Star Line shipping company at New York in 1919 (*see* 1920).

The International Ladies' Garment Workers' Union (ILGWU) strikes April 16, bringing 60,000 workers off the job. The union wins full representation, binding 2-year contracts, and standard collective bargaining agreements.

The Amalgamated Association of Street and Electric Railway Employees Union returns to work September 27 after a 54-day strike that has won the workers nothing.

The National Industrial Conference Board (later simply the Conference Board) comes into formal existence May 5 at Bronxville's Hotel Gramatan, where delegates from 11 employers' associations have assembled for a private meeting (*see* 1915). It is agreed that the NICB can best serve the country (and employers' interests) by encouraging employers to maintain working conditions and methods that will foster good employee relations. The 21-year-old

National Association of Manufacturers is one of the Conference Board's charter members, holds a meeting in Manhattan May 16, and is reported by the *New York Times* to be "progressing toward an association of all American employers of labor to represent capital in dealings with the American Federation of Labor" (*see* Baruch, 1919).

Hetty Green dies in her son's home at 7 West 90th Street July 3 at age 80, leaving an estate of more than $100 million that has made her the richest woman in America. Henrietta Howland Green (*née* Robinson) inherited $10 million at age 29 from her father and a maternal aunt, members of a New Bedford, Mass., whaling-ship family, and kept her finances separate from those of her late husband, Edward H. Green, whom she married in 1867. She multiplied her fortune with investments in railroad stocks, government bonds, mortgages, and Chicago real estate while living penuriously; her son lost a leg because she would not hire a physician to treat him, and the eccentric "witch of Wall Street" has kept a small fourth-floor apartment at 1203 Washington St. in Hoboken (a quick ferry ride from Wall Street) that she has occupied since 1895, paying less than $20 per month.

De Pinna moves from its original 1885 store at Fifth Avenue and 36th Street to new, larger premises on Fifth Avenue at 50th Street (*see* 1911; 1928).

Howard Stores have their beginnings in the apparel manufacturing firm Kappel & Marks opened by Russian-born entrepreneurs Samuel Kappel, 27, and Henry C. Marks.

The *New York Times* reports that 27 Manhattan streets have been designated one-way as the city tries "to find a solution to the vexing traffic problem" created by increased numbers of motor vehicles (*see* 1905); included are Cortlandt, Thomas, and Dey streets, which have been particularly congested (*see* 1918).

New York shipbuilder William H. Todd, 42, founds Todd Shipyards following passage by Congress August 29 of legislation appropriating $313 million for a 3-year naval construction program. The Battle of Jutland (Skagerrak) May 31 to June 1 has demonstrated the value of dreadnoughts and light cruisers.

A U.S. poliomyelitis epidemic strikes 28,767 in midsummer and fall. Some 6,000 people die, 2,000 of them in New York, and thousands more are crippled. Jamaica Hospital in Queens opens an orthopaedic clinic in response to the epidemic (*see* 1891), and it will build a new facility in 1924 as the area's population grows.

The Board of Health closes Jamaica Bay to bathers as well as clammers (*see* 1914). Beach resorts on the bay shut down.

"Peace, it's wonderful," says "Father Divine," and he organizes the Peace Mission movement. Savannah-born New York evangelist George Baker, 42, will garner a substantial following in the next 45 years preaching a renunciation of personal property, complete racial equality, and a strict moral code in the more than 170 Peace Mission settlements, or "heavens," that he will open. Tobacco, cosmetics, liquor, motion pictures, and sex will be totally banned.

St. Joseph's College opens at 286 Washington Avenue, Brooklyn. Started by the Sisters of St. Joseph, the women's college will move in 2 years to 245 Clinton Avenue (*see* 1970).

City Comptroller William Prendergast addresses problems of overcrowding in public schools, part-time classes, high dropout rates, inadequate equipment, an outmoded curriculum, and a dearth of practical education (*see* 1896). Prendergast issues a report calling for a longer school day and school year, with no corresponding increase in pay for teachers (he calls their long summer vacations "a public scandal" and proposes a 10 percent cut in the teaching staff). Double sessions would maximize school use, he says, and he favors a moratorium on school construction, except in new districts or for replacing obsolete buildings, but not to relieve overcrowding. Tammany Hall opposes the plan, as do many other critics, and it will never be fully implemented.

The Bank Street School has its beginnings in the Bureau of Educational Experiment, Bank Street opened in the Greenwich Village brownstone of Chicago-born retailing heiress Lucy Sprague Mitchell, 38, who has studied with John Dweey at Teachers College and obtained a $50,000 pledge from her cousin Elizabeth Sprague Coolidge. Bureau teachers work with progressive schools in the Village to study children and learn more about how to develop programs based on how they really behave rather than on how educators want them to behave. The wife of a Columbia University economist, Mitchell is horrified at the idea, now standard in public schools, of having desks screwed firmly in place, but will disown early ideas of progressive education that children can manage themselves, and will insist that children need to learn proper spelling and memorize multiplication tables (*see* School for Children, 1919).

"Krazy Kat" by New Orleans-born *New York Journal* cartoonist George (Joseph) Herriman, 35, appears in full-page color form for the first time April 23. Hermann created the surrealistic strip 5 years ago, it features an androgynous love triangle that involves brick-throwing Ignatz Mouse, Krazy Kat, and Offissa B. Pupp (a dog disguised as a Keystone Kop), and Herriman will continue it until his death in 1944.

Publisher Frank A. Munsey buys the *New York Evening Sun* June 30 from William Reick and merges it with the *Press*, which he acquired in 1912, giving the *Sun* membership in the Associated Press (*see* 1897; *Herald* and *Evening Telegram*, 1920).

Author-playwright Sholom Aleichem (Solomon Rabinowitz) dies at his Kelly Street home in the Bronx May 13 at age 57 and is memorialized as the "Jewish Mark Twain."

Poetry: *The Man Against the Sky* by Edwin Arlington Robinson, who gains wide recognition at age 46 for his narrative poem.

Painting: *Gertrude Vanderbilt Whitney* by Robert Henri.

The *Saturday Evening Post* buys its first Norman Rockwell illustration from *Boys' Life* illustrator Norman Rockwell, 22, who dropped out of Mamaroneck High School 6 years ago to work for the monthly magazine of the Boy Scouts of America. Rockwell has been art director of *Boys' Life* since 1913, but he will now draw mostly for the *Post*, which will buy an average of 10 Norman Rockwell covers per year until it ceases weekly publication in 1969.

Sculpture: a statue of the late actor Edwin Booth by Edmond T. Quinn is erected in Gramercy Park (Booth lived at 16 Gramercy Park South).

Massachusetts-born photographer James Augustus VanDerZee, 30, opens his own portrait studio in 113th Street near Lenox Avenue. It will relocate to 2069-2077 Seventh Avenue and then to 272 Lenox Avenue as it becomes Harlem's most fashionable photo studio, and VanDerZee will become official photographer to Universal Negro Improvement Society founder Marcus Garvey.

Theater: *Upstairs and Down* by Frederick Hatton, 36, and his wife, Fanny, 9/25 at the Cort Theater, with Los Angeles-born actor Leo Carillo, 35, 320 perfs.; *Good Gracious Annabelle* by playwright-composer-lyricist Clare Kummer, now 45, 10/31 at the Republic Theater, with Lola Fisher, Roland Young, Walter Hampden, 111 perfs.; *Bound East for Cardiff*, a one-act play by playwright Eugene (Gladstone) O'Neill, 27, 11/16 at the rectangular, 150-seat Provincetown

Playhouse in Greenwich Village, a converted brownstone stable and bottling plant with pewlike benches at 133 MacDougal Street (son of the actor James O'Neill, now 66, the playwright was born in a Broadway hotel room in October 1888; his play is produced later in the year at the Playwrights Theater).

Actress Ada Rehan dies at New York January 8 at age 55. She gave her final performance in the city in 1905.

The Provincetown Players is founded in a converted fish warehouse at Provincetown, Mass., by Iowa-born novelist-playwright Susan Glaspell, now 33, and her novelist-poet-playwright husband, George Cram Cook, now 41, who have started the theater group to stage their one-act play *Suppressed Desires*, which satirizes psychoanalysis. They stage their productions in the homes of friends such as Hutchins Hapgood, Robert Edmond Jones, Wilbur Steele, and Mary Heaton Vorse but will move the company to New York next year.

The Rialto Theater opens at the northwest corner of Seventh Avenue and 42nd Street, replacing Hammerstein's Victoria Theater of 1898 (*see* Strand, 1914). The Strand, says the *New York Times*, was "built so that at very short notice, it could be converted to the uses of opera or drama," but the Rialto, with its short proscenium, "is a motion picture house pure and simple . . . built in the conviction that the American passion for movies is here to stay." Designed by Thomas W. Lamb for S. L. "Roxy" Rothafel, the new 2,020-seat house has a huge electric sign out front that dazzles passersby with vari-colored lights that give an illusion of showering sparks. Lights inside the auditorium are synchronized to the action on screen (*see* Rivoli, 1917).

The David Mannes Music School of New York City opens under the direction of violinist-conductor Mannes, now 50, who will remain codirector until 1947. Raising money from contributors, he rents a large private house on the Upper East Side (*see* 1919; Metropolitan Opera concerts, 1918).

Musical Mutual Protective Union president D. Edward Porter threatens legal action against the city if nonprofessional musicians are allowed to continue playing in fire, police, sanitation, and other department parade bands (*see* 1905; Local 802, 1921).

Broadway musicals: *Robinson Crusoe, Jr.* 2/17 at the Winter Garden Theater, with Al Jolson, music by Sigmund Romberg and James Hanley, book and lyrics by Harold Atteridge and Edgar Smith, 139 perfs.; *Pom-pom* 2/28 at George M. Cohan's Theater, with music by Hugo Felix, book and lyrics by Anne

Caldwell, 128 perfs; *The Ziegfeld Follies* 6/12 at the New Amsterdam Theater, with W. C. Fields, Fanny Brice, Washington, D.C.-born comic Ina Claire (originally Ina Fagan), 23, Ann Pennington, music by Louis Hirsch, Jerome Kern, and Dave Stamper, 112 perfs. Brooklyn-born *Follies* girl Marion Davies (originally Marion Cecilia Douras), 19, meets publisher William Randolph Hearst, now 53 and the father of five (he married another chorus girl, Millicent Wilson, in 1903), with whom she will remain until his death in 1951; *The Passing Show* 6/22 at the Winter Garden Theater, with Ed Wynn, music chiefly by Sigmund Romberg, lyrics chiefly by Harold Atteridge, songs that include "Pretty Baby" by Tony Jackson and Egbert van Alstyne, lyrics by German-born songwriter Gus Kahn, 30, 140 perf.; *Miss Springtime* 9/25 at the New Amsterdam Theater, with Indiana-born performer Wayne Nunn, 35, Jed Prouty, music by Emmerich Kalman, book by English writer Guy Bolton, 31, 224 perfs.; *The Century Girl* 11/16 at the Century Theater, with Hazel Dawn, Marie Dressler, Elsie Janis, Leon Errol, music by Irving Berlin and Victor Herbert, lyrics by Berlin and Henry Blossom, songs that include Berlin's "You Belong to Me," 200 perfs.

 Heavyweight champion Jess Willard retains his title March 25 at Madison Square Garden, defeating challenger Frank Moran in the city's first heavyweight title match since 1900. Promoter Tex Rickard, now 45, has arranged the bout, but boxing remains technically illegal in New York State (*see* Walker Law, 1920).

The Brooklyn Dodgers win the National League pennant but lose the World Series to the Boston Red Sox, who win 4 games to 1. The Dodgers win the third game 4 to 3 with help from a two-run fifth-inning triple by Kansas City-born shortstop Ivy (Ivan Massie) Olson, 28, but Olson also commits four errors, and although Iowa-born pitcher Jack (John Wesley) Coombs, 33, is credited with the win, he and Rube Marquard and the rest of the pitching staff are no match for Boston pitchers Ernie Shore, Babe Ruth, and Dutch Leonard.

 Lucky Strike cigarettes are introduced by American Tobacco Co. (*see* 1911). The new brand will soon outsell the company's Sweet Caporal and Pall Mall brands and challenge the Camels brand launched 3 years ago by R. J. Reynolds (*see* 1918; 1925).

The Harrison Drug Act signed into law by President Wilson May 2 requires that all persons licensed to sell narcotic drugs file inventories of their stocks with the Internal Revenue Service. The U.S. Supreme Court rules June 5 that users and unlicensed sellers of opium are liable to prosecution.

The city's homicide rate will fall to 4.9 per 100,000 in the next 5 years, down from 5.8 per 100,000 in the last 5 (*see* 1926).

 The 27-story Heckscher Building is completed at 50 East 42nd Street, southeast corner Madison Avenue, to designs by Jardine, Hill & Murdock. Millionaire developer August Heckscher, now 68, initially favored the German side in the Great War (*see* 1904). Replacing five row houses that have faced on Madison Avenue, the skyscraper is set back 23 feet from its 42nd Street side (thereby giving up close to half its potential floor space) and has a squash court on its 23rd floor. Terraces at its top are available to tenants.

The comprehensive zoning ordinance adopted by the Board of Estimate is the first U.S. law of its kind. The state legislature empowered the city 2 years ago to adopt a zoning resolution, and the Equitable Life Assurance Society Building completed last year at 120 Broadway has given impetus to concerns by reformers that such massive structures are robbing the city of light and air. Merchants who include B. Altman, Arnold Constable, Gimbel Brothers, Lord & Taylor, Macy's, and Saks have run a full-page newspaper advertisement headlined, "Shall We Save New York?" The Board of Estimate's Building Heights and Restrictions Commission issues a final report July 2, and while the ordinance adopted by the board at the end of the year does not set absolute limits on the height of buildings it does require that a tower occupy no more than 25 percent of the area of a building's lot and specifies the portion of the lot that can be built up (*see* set-back law, 1923).

The 12-story 820 Fifth Avenue apartment house is completed at the northeast corner of 63rd Street. Designed in Italian Renaissance palazzo style by Starrett & Van Vleck for the Fred T. Ley Co., it has one 18-room, 7,000-square-foot apartment per floor, each with a 12-foot by 43-foot entrance gallery, four rooms overlooking Central Park, five bedrooms, six-and-a-half baths, seven servants' rooms, and five fireplaces. Each kitchen has four sinks.

The 13-story-plus-penthouse 570 Park Avenue apartment house is completed at the southwest corner of 63rd Street, where it replaces eight row houses. Commissioned by Bing & Bing and designed in neo-Renaissance style by architect Emery Roth, it has a wide white marble base, white terra-cotta ornamentation, and an inner courtyard 30 feet square.

The 12-story 630 Park Avenue apartment house is completed at the southwest corner of 66th Street, where it replaces five row houses that faced onto the street. Designed by J. E. R. Carpenter, it has apartments as large as 17 rooms, six baths, with five master bedrooms and eight servants' rooms.

The 12-story 907 Fifth Avenue apartment house is completed at the southeast corner of 72nd Street, replacing the Burden family mansion. Designed by J. E. R. Carpenter, it has no more than two apartments per floor (the largest has 28 rooms and rents for $2,500 per month).

The 13-story Astor Court apartment house is completed on the east side of Broadway between 89th and 90th streets to designs by Charles Platt. Built for real estate heir Vincent Astor at a cost of $1 million, it has apartments of six to nine rooms each that rent for between $133 and $266 per month, its two lobbies have coffered ceilings, and its inner courtyard is a landscaped garden.

The 12-story 1000 Park Avenue apartment house is completed at the northwest corner of 84th Street. Commissioned by Bing & Bing, it has been designed, like 570 Park, by Emery Roth, who this time uses a neo-Gothic style with terra-cotta ornaments that include Masonic symbols and figures modeled (legend will have it) on Roth's clients Leo and Alexander Bing.

The 12-story Cliff Dwelling apartment-hotel is completed at 243 Riverside Drive, northeast corner 96th Street, to designs by Herman Lee Meader, who has worked for Ernest Flagg and become fascinated with Mayan and Aztec architecture.

Construction resumes on the Cathedral of St. John the Divine in May but is discontinued in November when funds run out once again (see 1911). Work will not resume this time until 1924.

The Links Club is completed at 36 East 62nd Street for a new organization created by bankers, financiers, and others (including writer Finley Peter Dunne) "to promote and conserve throughout the United States the best and true spirit of the game of golf as embodied in its ancient and honorable tradition." Cross & Cross has remodeled a 1902 Georgian-style town house, giving it a large ground-floor dressing room for members to change into sporting attire before motoring off to suburban golf courses.

The National Park Service created in the Department of the Interior by an act of Congress signed into law by President Wilson August 25 will be responsible for maintaining Castle Clinton, Federal Hall, Grant's Tomb, Hamilton Grange, Ellis Island, the Statue of Liberty, and some other federally owned New York sites.

The F. & M. Schaefer Brewing Co. relocates from Manhattan to a large new plant on Brooklyn's East River waterfront bounded by Kent Avenue and South 9th and 10th streets, having operated its brewery on Fourth (now Park) Avenue at 51st Street for 67 years. The late Maximilian Schaefer's son Rudolph, now 53, sold that site 2 years ago to St. Bartholomew's Church for a reputed $1.5 million (see 1919; real estate, 1918).

Nathan's Famous frankfurters have their beginning in a Coney Island hot dog stand at the corner of Stillwell and Surf Avenues opened by Polish-born merchant Nathan Handwerker, 25, who sells his franks at 5¢ each (half the price charged by Feltman's German Gardens on Surf Avenue, where Handwerker has worked weekends as a counterman while making $4.50 per week as a delivery boy on Manhattan's Lower East Side). Handwerker charges 5¢/bottle for soda pop, 6¢ for a malted milk, and 10¢ for an ice-cream soda, nothing for sauerkraut, mustard, and onions. He has invested his life savings of $300 in the hot dog stand and works 18 to 20 hours per day with his 19-year-old bride Ida, who laces the franks with her secret spice recipe, but although they use only good beef in their hot dogs they meet initial resistance because their low price raises suspicions that they may be using inferior (and possibly unhealthful) ingredients (see 1917).

The first birth control clinic outside Holland opens at 46 Amboy Street, Brooklyn. Margaret Sanger distributes circulars printed in English, Italian, and Yiddish to announce the opening (see 1914). Police raid the clinic, Sanger is jailed for 30 days, founds the New York Birth Control League after her release, and begins publication of the Birth Control Review (see 1921).

1917 President Wilson summons Congress into special session April 1 and Congress declares war on Germany April 6. Germany has 18 ships in the port of New York, five of them anchored in the Hudson off 135th Street; Dudley Field Malone, collector of the port, sends 600 customs agents to board the vessels and seize them in the name of the United States Government. Malone himself is in the boarding party that takes over the giant S.S. Vaterland and runs up the U.S. flag in the first act of war. The 22nd

1917

U.S. Infantry boards army tugboats at Governors Island, steams out to ships anchored offshore or tied up at docks, and arrests 1,200 German soldiers along with 325 officers; all are taken to Ellis Island for internment. A company of troops marches through the Hudson tubes to Hoboken, seizes the piers of the North German Lloyd and Hamburg-Amerika lines, and rounds up about 200 Germans in dock-area saloons and boarding houses for internment on Ellis Island. A steel net is sunk in the waters across the Narrows to block any U-boat trying to sneak into the Upper Bay, and New York becomes the nation's chief port of embarkation for shipping cargo and troops overseas. Gen. John J. "Blackjack" Pershing, 56, has been recalled from his pursuit of Pancho Villa and named to head an American Expeditionary Force as the French and British sustain enormous losses on the western front.

The Selective Service Act passed by Congress May 18 provides for the draft of all able-bodied American men between the ages of 21 and 31. Mayor Mitchel gives vigorous support to the Allied war effort but observes that only 900 men from the city have enlisted in the navy, falling far short of the 2,000-man quota. The Mayor's Committee on National Defense raises funds to build a 200-foot by 40-foot mock battleship of wood and tin in Union Square, and Mitchel's wife, Olive, breaks a bottle of Champagne across her bow May 30 (Memorial Day), christening her the *Recruit*. Equipped with a searchlight, semaphore signals, and one-pound gun, the *Recruit* will remain in the square until 1920 and be credited with securing 25,000 Navy enlistments. The first U.S. Army unit

to embark for France goes through Fort Totten at Willets Point in Queens.

Emma Goldman is arrested along with Alexander Berkman, their journal *Mother Earth* is suppressed, and they are sentenced to 2 years' imprisonment for leading opposition to military conscription (*see* 1906; 1919).

New York's National Guard is drafted into federal service July 15; the 69th Regiment has been mustered out of service in March after serving on the Mexican border, discharges and furloughs have reduced its strength from 783 officers and men to about 490, it begins a recruitment campaign to bring the number up to 2,000, and it soon accomplishes that goal, using the slogan, "Don't join the 69th unless you want to be among the first to go to France." More than 90 percent of the men are Irish born or of Irish descent, the regiment is soon joined by the 7th Regiment and members of other New York regiments, it is renamed the 165th Infantry of the 42nd "Rainbow" Division, and by the time it leaves Camp Mills for France October 25 under the command of Buffalo-born Major William J. (Joseph) Donovan, 34, its strength has grown to 3,500.

The city's fusion movement collapses and Mayor Mitchel loses his bid for reelection, having been outspoken in support of the Allies since the start of the war. Tammany Hall nominates John F. (Francis) Hylan, 48, a coarse and clumsy jurist known as "Red Mike" because of his red hair and moustache; he has gained the support of publisher William Randolph Hearst, who agrees with Hylan's position supporting public ownership and operation of the city's rapid transit system and believes he can control the man. To the dismay of President Wilson and many others, Hylan receives 313,956 votes, easily defeating Mayor Mitchel (who gets 155,497) and Socialist candidate Morris Hillquit (145,332). Mitchel joins the army, is commissioned a major in the air service, will be killed next July at Lake Charles, La., when he falls out of the cockpit of his single-seat scout plane at 500 feet, and will be buried in Woodlawn Cemetery.

The Jones Act passed by Congress March 2 makes Puerto Rico a U.S. territory and Puerto Ricans U.S. citizens. The law makes voting compulsory and applies the Selective Service Act to Puerto Rico at the request of the San Juan government; Puerto Rico drafts 18,000 men into the U.S. Army.

A Bolshevik revolution begins in Russia at Petrograd the night of November 6. Revolutionist Leon Trotsky (originally Lev Davidovich Bronstein), 38, has

The Hell Gate Bridge across the East River let trains from Penn Station reach New England. LIBRARY OF CONGRESS

been printing the newspaper *Novy Mir* in the basement of a New York apartment building at 77 St. Mark's Place, near First Avenue, but has returned to his native land to join with V. I. Lenin in overthrowing the czarist government and become commissar of foreign affairs. He formerly lived in the Bronx, and the *Bronx Home News* runs a headline that reads, "Bronx Man Leads Russian Revolution" (publisher James O'Flaherty starts Harlem, Washington Heights, and Yorkville editions).

The 69th Regiment in France begins a march December 26 down an ancient Roman road en route to its assigned area at Longeau. The men are ill fed, ill shod, and not warmly clothed, but they make their way through a blizzard over mountain passes, traveling on foot for 4 days and nights; not a single man falls out except those who drop from exhaustion and are picked up by ambulances (*see* 1919).

New York blacks led by W. E. B. DuBois and James Weldon Johnson of the NAACP walk in silence 15,000 strong down Fifth Avenue to protest an outbreak of racial violence that has left 39 dead and hundreds injured at East St. Louis July 2 (*see* 1910; 1948).

President Wilson endorses equal suffrage October 25 when he speaks at the White House before a group from the New York State Woman Suffrage Party; 20,000 women march in a New York suffrage parade October 27. New York adopts a constitutional amendment November 6, becoming the first state to grant equal voting rights to women (*see* 1918). Labor leader Rose Schneiderman has made regular trips to Albany and continues to lobby the legislature for passage of a 48-hour week law for women, and a minimum wage that would benefit men as well as women, since employers would be less likely to replace male workers with lower-paid female workers.

Federation of Jewish Philanthropies is founded to consolidate the fund-raising activities of 54 New York charitable organizations, including hospital groups such as Beth Israel (*see* 1891). Philanthropists Joseph Buttenwieser, Arthur Lehman, and Felix Warburg have organized the consolidation; Federation will become the world's largest philanthropic organization, with counterparts in Jewish communities across the country.

The 15-year-old Greenwich House settlement moves into a handsome new headquarters building at 27 Barrow Street. Designed by Delano & Aldrich with murals by Arthur Crisp, it has an auditorium,

art studio, gymnasium, running track, and rooms for social workers.

An embargo proclamation issued by President Wilson July 9 places exports of U.S. foodstuffs, fuel, iron, steel, and war matériel under government control. Wilson sends U.S. destroyers to help blockade German ports and convoy merchant ships bound for Britain. Bernard M. Baruch becomes commissioner for raw materials in the newly created War Industries Board (WIB). A Democrat and admirer of the president, he has been using his former business contacts since spring to negotiate a series of raw material purchases for the military and administer them on an informal basis (*see* 1918).

Wall Street's Dow Jones Industrial Average falls 6.91 points (7.24 percent) February 1 in the worst drop since 1907.

Goldman, Sachs partner Henry Goldman withdraws from the firm in a disagreement over the purchase of U.S. Government War Bonds, severing connections between the Goldman family (which has supported the German cause in the war) and the Sachs family (*see* 1906; 1926).

Millionaire railroad equipment salesman and trencherman James Buchanan "Diamond Jim" Brady dies in his $1,000-per-week ocean-view suite at Atlantic City's Shelburne Hotel April 13 at age 60, leaving a large bequest to New York Hospital for research on urology; lawyer-diplomat Joseph H. Choate dies at New York May 14 at age 85; former Standard Oil Co. treasurer Oliver Hazard Payne at New York June 27 at age 77, leaving a fortune of more than $178 million, the largest U.S. estate appraised to date.

Wall Street's Dow Jones Industrial Average closes December 31 at 74.38, down from 95 at the end of 1916.

A full-page advertisement appears in the *New York Times* April 2: "Whatever Congress Decides! Franklin Simon & Co. are ready to take immediate orders for Hand-Tailored Khaki Army Uniforms for officers and privates. $16.00"

Paris jeweler Pierre Cartier gives financier Morton F. Plant a two-strand Oriental pearl necklace in exchange for Plant's Renaissance-style mansion at Fifth Avenue and 52nd Street. Cartier opened his family's first New York Cartier salon in 1908 on a Fifth Avenue mezzanine; he will introduce the Tank watch next year as a tribute to the men of the American Tank Corps, and the Plant mansion will remain New York Cartier headquarters into the 21st century.

The Lerner Stores chain of women's apparel shops has its beginnings in the Lorraine Store opened by Philadelphia-born Brooklyn merchant Michael Lerner, 25, and a partner.

Abercrombie & Fitch opens at the northwest corner of Madison Avenue and 45th Street (see 1904). Abercrombie left the firm in 1907, Fitch provided President Roosevelt with African safari equipment in 1908, and he has moved his establishment to larger and more fashionably located premises, installing a fly-casting pond on the roof (where a log cabin serves as his town house) and a shooting range in the basement (see 1977).

U.S. Fuel Administrator Harry A. Garfield restricts use of electric signs November 16 to conserve coal. "New York responded with such howls and denunciations as can hardly be described," Secretary of the Navy Josephus Daniels will later write. ". . . Smaller cities obeyed the order to do without the White Way at night because of the exigency of war. Not New York. It raised such a row that coal operators doubled their energies to furnish enough coal so that the White Way could again blaze brightly and let New York City turn night into day."

The Astoria Elevated Railway begins running February 1 on 31st Street to serve the thousands of families that have moved into homes built in Long Island City, Woodside, and other communities in the area since the 1890s. Extending out Roosevelt Avenue, it has four stations in Jackson Heights—at 74th Street, 82nd Street, Elmhurst Avenue, and Junction Boulevard.

The Hell Gate Bridge (the New York Connecting Railroad Bridge) opens April 1 over the East River to give Pennsylvania Railroad trains access to New England. Designed by engineer Gustav Lindenthal with help from New York-born engineer David B. (Barnard) Steinman, 30, it is the longest steel arch bridge built up to now, its massive arch extends for 977 feet, it carries four tracks, and it is part of a two-and-a-half-mile system that includes viaducts, overpasses, and two smaller bridges. Not only does it shorten the trip between Boston and Washington from 15 hours to about 12, but it also reduces traffic at Grand Central Terminal and increases traffic at Penn Station. Says the *New York Times* in an editorial, "The Grand Central Terminal is overworked, and the Pennsylvania terminal [sic] has capacity to spare. The change in their relations marks the difference in their conception."

The Corona extension of the Dual Subway System opens April 21 as a train from Grand Central carries a party of officials and businessmen along a mostly elevated route that has 11 Queens stations after Bridge Plaza: Rawson Street, Lowery Street, Bliss Street, Lincoln Avenue, Fiske Avenue, Broadway, 25th Street, Elmhurst Avenue, Junction Avenue, and Alburtis Avenue, with a connection to the Long Island Rail Road at Woodside. The entire borough of Queens celebrates the inauguration of rapid-transit, which will spur commercial and residential development of the area.

New York's last two-horse streetcar moves down Broadway July 26 and disappears into oblivion. The city for the first time has more motor vehicles than horses—147,727 motorcars, taxis, and trucks versus 108,743 horses.

Assistant Secretary of the Navy Franklin D. Roosevelt appoints a three-man committee to assemble in short order a fleet of small craft for the embattled British, who are in urgent need of patrol vessels (see 1906). Members include Moran Co. head Eugene F. Moran, who has already sold some of his tugboats to the Admiralty, and other companies contribute to the pool of nearly 40 towboats for British use (see 1942).

Railroad and shipping congestion in the New York area reaches alarming proportions by November as lighters, cargo vessels, and troop transports in New York Harbor, freight cars in New Jersey railyards, and trucks struggle through a series of transfers to handle 20 percent of U.S. transportation needs. Shortages of rolling stock, ships, and manpower exacerbate the problem, the Arthur Kill Bridge that opened in 1890 is hard put to carry all the trains loaded with aircraft, ordinance, tanks, troops, and trucks between Staten Island and New Jersey, 180,000 railcars are trapped in Eastern ports, and although 1.3 million troops will embark from the port of New York through severe weather in the next few months, the congestion dramatizes the need for new highways and tunnels.

New York Hospital mobilizes and staffs the 2,250-bed Base Hospital No. 9 at Châteauroux, France. Roosevelt Hospital supplies equipment and personnel for Base Hospital No. 15 to treat battle casualties in France. Two of its physicians and six nurses will be killed this year and next.

Canadian-born Roman Catholic priest Francis Patrick Duffy, 46, embarks for France with New York's 69th Regiment to which he was appointed chaplain 3 years ago. He has been serving with the regiment at the Mexican border.

Most of the city's Jewish population worships in some 800 small synagogues built by immigrants.

The Katharine Gibbs School opens at New York and will soon be at 247 Park Avenue. For most women the only job opportunities are as nurses, secretaries, receptionists, and schoolteachers; Rhode Island widow Gibbs, then 46, sold her jewelry 6 years ago to raise the funds and joined with her sister Mary M. Ryan, then 51, to start the Providence School for Secretaries. Lacking any experience but with two sons to support, she recognized the need for a school that she will develop to include not only stenography and typing courses but also some in business law and liberal arts, with classes at various East Coast cities (the schools will later teach hotel and restaurant management; they will accept male students beginning in the late 1990s).

New York-born socialist Dorothy Day, 19, quits her job on the IWW newspaper *The Call* and joins The *Masses*, which is suppressed in December for its opposition to U.S. participation in the war. Day began her career with the *New Orleans Item* by working on assignment as a taxi dancer in a cheap Canal Street dance hall; she will abruptly become a Catholic in 1927 after years of Bohemian Greenwich Village life in which she will rally "the masses," go to jail, drink all night with her radical friends, marry on the rebound, write a novel, fall in love, and bear a child (*see* 1933).

The "Katzenjammer Kids" launched in 1897 is renamed "The Captain and the Kids" as German names become unpopular. The comic strip moved 5 years ago from Hearst's *New York Journal* to the late Joseph Pulitzer's *New York World*.

"I Want You," says Uncle Sam in a recruitment poster painted by Pelham Manor-born illustrator James Montgomery Flagg, 40, who has used his own face as a model for the stern-visaged Uncle Sam. Army recruitment officers distribute 4 million copies.

Grey Advertising has its beginnings in Grey Studios, a direct-mail agency opened August 1 at 309 Fifth Avenue by New York entrepreneur Lawrence Valenstein, 18, who has borrowed $100 from his mother to lease space in an office whose walls are grey. He produces folders in which local furriers buy space and will soon turn the folders into the slick magazine *Furs & Fashion* (*see* 1925).

Advertising man Milton Biow, 25, opens a one-man agency on lower Fifth Avenue that will continue until 1956, becoming one of the top 10 U.S. agencies.

Forbes magazine begins publication at New York September 15 under the management of Scots-born Hearst financial columnist B. C. (Bertie Charles) Forbes, 37, with *Magazine of Wall Street* general manager Walter Drey. One of 10 children, Forbes worked on Aberdeenshire farms as a youth, shined shoes, taught himself shorthand, worked as a printer's devil, became a reporter for a Dundee newspaper at age 16, worked his way up to subeditor and editorial writer, joined with English author Edgar Wallace to start the *Rand Daily Mail* at Johannesburg in 1901, came to New York 3 years later and joined the staff of the *Journal of Commerce*, soon became financial editor, and since 1912 has been business and financial editor of the *New York American*, writing a syndicated daily column that will continue in the Hearst papers until 1942. Forbes will claim that he gave up a salary higher than that of the governor (Gov. Whitman's salary is $10,000 per year) to start the 15¢ fortnightly.

H. W. Wilson Co. moves from White Plains to 950-972 University Avenue in the Bronx, where one of its buildings will be surmounted by a 30-foot-high lighthouse resting on a huge bronze book. Vermont-born publisher Halsey William Wilson, now 49, was orphaned in childhood and raised on an uncle's Iowa farm. After running a bookstore briefly with a fellow student at the University of Minnesota he put out the first issue of his *Cumulative Book Index* February 1, 1898, issued the *Essay and General Literature Index* beginning in 1900, *Book Review Digest* in 1905, *International Index to Periodicals* in 1907, the *Index to Legal Periodicals* in 1908, *Industrial Arts Index* in 1913, and *Agricultural Index* in 1916. He moved to White Plains in 1913, and by the time Wilson dies in March 1954 his firm will be publishing on a cumulative basis indices to the contents of 118 periodicals but will be best known for its *Readers' Guide to Periodical Literature*, which will be found in virtually every U.S. library.

Fiction: *The Rise of David Levinsky* by Abraham Cahan, now 57, who has based his novel on "The Autobiography of an American Jew," a series of articles he wrote for *McClure's* magazine 4 years ago.

The first Barnes & Noble retail book shop opens at 31 West 15th Street (*see* 1873; 1931).

Painting: *John D. Rockefeller* by Italian-born U.S. painter John Singer Sargent, 61, who has spent most of his life abroad. Albert Pinkham Ryder dies at the Elmhurst, L.I., home of a friend March 28 at age 70.

The Independents exhibition that opens at Grand Central Palace April 10 is the largest art show ever held in America—twice as large as the Armory Show 4 years ago. Financed by Vanderbilts, Whitneys, Archer M. Huntington, and other philanthropists, it displays 2,125 works by some 1,200 artists, but a "sculpture" entitled *Fountain* and signed "R. Mutt" is narrowly rejected just before the opening by the exhibition's committee (the *New York Herald* reveals that Marcel Duchamps submitted the urinal, either as a prank or a Dadaist gesture).

Alfred Stieglitz devotes an entire issue of his 14-year-old magazine *Camera Work* to New York-born photographer Paul Strand, 27, who was raised on the upper West Side, received a Brownie camera on his 12th birthday, and was introduced to Stieglitz's Fifth Avenue gallery by photographer-sociologist Lewis W. Hine, now 43, who gave a hobby course in photography at the Ethical Culture School. Strand had his first one-man show last year and has won distinction by breaking away from the soft focus romanticism of the 19th century, using an 8" × 10" Deardorff view camera or a 5" × 7" Graflex. Says Stieglitz, "His work is rooted in the best tradition of photography. His vision is potential, his work is pure. It is direct. It does not rely upon tricks or the process" (*see* film, 1921).

Theater: *A Successful Calamity* by Clare Kummer 2/5 at the Booth Theater, with William H. Gillette (moved 10/16 to the new Plymouth Theater, designed by Herbert J. Krapp, at 234-240 West 45th Street), 144 perfs.; *The Knife* by Eugene Walter 4/12 at the Shubert brothers' new Bijou Theater at 209 West 45th Street, with Lowell Sherman, Olive Wyndham, Caroline Newcombe, 84 perfs.; *Lombardi, Ltd.* by Frederick and Fanny Hatton 9/24 at the Morosco Theater, with Columbus, Ohio-born actor Warner Baxter, 28, Leo Carillo, 296 perfs.; *Misalliance* by George Bernard Shaw 9/27 at the new Broadhurst Theater at 235 West 44th Street, designed by Herbert J. Krapp, built by Lee Shubert, and named for playwright George Broadhurst, 51, 52 perfs.; *In the Zone* by Eugene O'Neill 10/31 at the Provincetown Playhouse (one-act play); *The Long Voyage Home* by O'Neill 11/2 at the Provincetown Playhouse (one-act play); *Why Marry?* by Illinois-born playwright Jesse Lynch Williams, 46, 12/25 at the Astor Theater, with English actress Estelle Winwood, 34, 120 perfs.

Film: Charles Chaplin's *The Immigrant* with Chaplin.

The Rivoli movie theater opens at 1620 Broadway in Times Square. Designed by Thomas W. Lamb and S. L. "Roxy" Rothafel for the Rialto Theater Corp., it has 2,206 seats and fills the east side of Broadway between 49th and 50th streets with an austere

façade resembling that of a Greek Doric temple, precluding the need for an extravagant electrical sign such as the one used on the Rialto that opened last year (*see* Capitol, 1919; air conditioning, 1925).

Lithuanian (Vilna)-born violin prodigy Jascha Heifetz, 16, makes his Carnegie Hall debut 10/27; he has been playing the Mendolssohn Violin Concerto since age 7.

The Manhattan School of Music has its beginnings in the Neighborhood Music School, opened on the upper East Side by philanthropist Janet D. Schenck, who will be its director until 1956. It will change its name in 1939 (*see* 1969).

Broadway musicals: *Have a Heart* 1/11 at the Liberty Theater, with Evansville, Ind.-born actress Louise Dresser (originally Louise Josephine Kerlin), 38, Thurston Hall, book and lyrics by Guy Bolton and P. G. Wodehouse, music by Jerome Kern, 76 perfs.; *Love o' Mike* 1/15 at the Shubert Theater, with Peggy Wood, Indiana-born dancer Clifton Webb (originally Webb Parmelee Hallenbeck), 20, book by Thomas Sydney, music by Jerome Kern, lyrics by Harry B. Smith, 192 perfs.; *Canary Cottage* 2/5 at the new Morosco Theater at 217 West 45th Street, with Dublin-born singer Hugh Cameron, 37, Los Angeles-born actor Charles Ruggles, 30, book by Elmer Harris and Oliver Morosco, music and lyrics by Earl Carroll, 112 perfs.; *Oh, Boy!* 2/20 at the Princess Theater, with Marion Davies, Edna May Oliver, Kansas City-born dancer Dorothy Dickson, 24, and her husband, Carl Hyson, music by Jerome Kern, book and lyrics by Guy Bolton and P. G. Wodehouse, songs that include "Till the Clouds Roll By," 463 perfs.; *The Passing Show* 4/26 at the Winter Garden Theater, with De Wolf Hopper, music chiefly by Sigmund Romberg, lyrics chiefly by Harold Atteridge, songs that include "Goodbye Broadway, Hello France" by Billy Baskette, lyrics by C. Francis Reisner and Benny Davis, 196 perfs.; *Hitchy-Koo* 6/7 at the Cohan and Harris Theater, with French-born singer Irene Bordoni, 22, Raymond Hitchcock, Leon Errol, music by E. Ray Goetz, lyrics by Goetz, Glen MacDonough, and Harry Grattan, 220 perfs.; *The Ziegfeld Follies* 6/12 at the New Amsterdam Theater, with Lower East Side-born blackface comedian Eddie Cantor (originally Edward Israel Iskowitz), 25 (who grew up at 19 Eldridge Street and sang in the Eldridge Street Synagogue choir), W. C. Fields, Will Rogers, Fanny Brice, dancer Dorothy Dickson, music by Raymond Hubbell and Dave Stamper with a patriotic finale by Victor Herbert, 111 perfs.; *Maytime* 8/17 at the Shubert Theater, with Peggy Wood, Charles Purcell, music by Sigmund Romberg, book and lyrics by Rida Johnson Young, songs that include "Will You Remember (Sweetheart)," 492 perfs.; *Leave It to Jane* 9/28 at the Longacre Theater, with music by Jerome Kern, book and lyrics by Guy Bolton based on George Ade's 1904 play *The College Widow*, 167 perfs.; *Over the Top* (revue) 11/28 at the 44th Street Roof Theater, with comedian Joe Laurie, Omaha-born dancer Fred Astaire (originally Austerlitz), 18, and his sister Adele, music by Sigmund Romberg and others, 78 perfs.; *Going Up* 12/25 at the Liberty Theater, with Frank Craven, Donald Meek, music by Louis A. Hirsch, book and lyrics by Otto Harbach based on the 1910 play *The Aviator*, 351 perfs.

Popular songs: "Over There" by George M. Cohan, who writes it for the American Expeditionary Force embarking for the war in Europe; "You're in the Army Now" by Isham Jones, lyrics by Tell Taylor and Ole Olssen; "It's a Windy Day on the Bowery" by Sigmund Romberg, lyrics by Rida Johnson Young.

The Original Dixieland Jazz Band opens in January at Reisenweber's beer garden on Eighth Avenue near Columbus Circle; another New Orleans jazz group has appeared in the city earlier, but this one uses showmanship and publicity to attract wide attention. "The Darktown Strutters' Ball" by Shelton Brooks, recorded for Columbia Records at New York in January, is by some accounts the first jazz record and has sales of 1 million copies by year's end, but other jazz historians will give the honor of being first to D. J. "Nick" LaRocca's Original Dixieland Jazz Band, which records a one-step and "Livery Stable Blue" February 26 at New York's Victor Studio; released March 5, it has sales of 250,000 copies at 75¢ each, outselling any record ever made by Enrico Caruso or John Philip Sousa. "Tiger Rag" is published as a one-step with music by D. J. LaRocca of the Original Dixieland Jazz Band, lyrics by LaRocca's clarinetist Lawrence (James) Shields, 24.

Ragtime composer Scott Joplin dies at New York April 1 at age 49. He has lived in the city since the summer of 1907, and although many of his songs have been published, and some put on mechanical piano rolls, not one has been recorded.

The U.S. Supreme Court upholds composer Victor Herbert in his suit against Shanley's Café for using his songs without permission. The decision supports ASCAP, which licenses hotels, restaurants, dance halls, cabarets, motion picture theaters, and other establishments to play music controlled by ASCAP members.

 Lower East Side prizefighter Benny Leonard (originally Benjamin Leiner), 21, wins the world lightweight championship May 28 by knocking out titleholder Freddy Welsh in a bout at New York.

The New York Giants win the National League pennant, but the Chicago White Sox win the World Series, defeating the Giants 4 games to 2. New York shuts out the Sox in the third and fourth games with help from Virginia-born Dave (Davis Aydelotte) Robertson, 28, who gets 11 hits, and Ohio-born Benjamin Michael "Benny" Kauff, 27, who hits two home runs, but are edged out in the fifth and lose the sixth entirely on errors, two of them by New York–born third baseman Henry "Heinie" Zimmerman, 30, who will be suspended in 1919 on charges of attempting to throw games.

The National Hockey League (NHL) is organized November 22 at Montreal with teams from Montreal (the Canadians and the Wanderers), Quebec, Ottawa, and Toronto. The first U.S. team to join will be the Boston Bruins in 1924, followed by the Pittsburgh Pirates in 1925 and the New York Rangers, Chicago Black Hawks, and Detroit Cougars (later Red Wings) in 1926, but the U.S. teams will be composed almost solely of Canadian-born players.

Everlast Sports Manufacturing Co. is founded by New York entrepreneur Jacob Golomb, 24, who at age 17 invented a durable bathing suit for men and sold it on the Lower East Side. Everlast will specialize in making boxing gloves, trunks, and other equipment for prizefighters, earning a reputation for quality (*see* Dempsey, 1921).

 F. W. Woolworth's daughter Edna (Mrs. Franklyn Laws) Hutton, 33, is found dead May 2 in her apartment at the Plaza Hotel (she has committed suicide but an attending physician says she has suffered from a chronic disease that has caused a hardening of bones in her ears and caused suffocation). She leaves her 5-year-old daughter Barbara $2 million. Mrs. Hutton and her stockbroker husband have until recently maintained a town house at 2 West 80th Street; Woolworth takes his granddaughter to live with him in his mansion at 990 Fifth Avenue, near 80th Street (*see* 1924).

 General Cigar Co. introduces a new machine-rolled cigar and names it White Owl. The moderately priced cigar will gain wide popularity.

 Former ice baron Charles W. Morse, now 61, becomes one of the first war profiteers, obtaining contracts to build ships in nonexistent shipyards.

🏠 Architect Charles C. Haight dies at his Garrison-on-Hudson home February 8 at age 75.

The American Telephone & Telegraph building completed at 195 Broadway between Dey and Fulton streets has eight Ionic columns on a Doric order—more columns than any other building in the world. Designed by architect Welles Bosworth, the 29-story structure's first section opened in 1915 and a third section will open in 1922, but the section that opens this year is surmounted by a gold-leafed, 10-ton statue by sculptor Evelyn Beatrice Longman, whose *Genius of Telegraphy* will be renamed *Genius of Electricity* after AT&T is forced to sell Western Union, but most people will call the 24-foot-tall winged statue "Golden Boy." Cast at the Roman Bronze Works in Brooklyn's Greenpoint section last year, the figure holds a quiver of thunderbolts in one hand and an electrical cable in the other.

The 29-story Bush Terminal Building is completed at 130 West 42nd Street, between Sixth Avenue and Broadway. Designed by architect Harvey Wiley Corbett, now 44, for Brooklyn's Bush Terminal developer Irving T. Bush, now 48, the Gothic-style tower occupies a site only 25 feet wide.

The Postal Life Insurance Co. building is completed at 511 Fifth Avenue, southeast corner 43rd Street, to designs by York & Sawyer for Russian-born developer Henry Mandel, 33.

A building with a large ballroom is completed for Russian-born dancing teacher Louis Chalif at 163 West 57th Street to designs by George and Henry Boehm. Chalif deplores modern music as "barbarians banging on human skulls in a cannabilistic orgy;" his building will become the headquarters of Columbia Artists Management and be known as CAMI Hall.

A new clubhouse for the Grolier Club is completed at 47 East 60th Street to designs by Bertram Goodhue, a member of the club (*see* 1884). It replaces the club's second home, at 29 East 32nd Street.

The Kingsbridge Armory (Eighth Coastal Artillery Armory) is completed in the Bronx to Romanesque designs by Pilcher & Tachau. Replete with vaults and turrets, it occupies five acres, covering the entire block bounded by Kingsbridge Road, 195th Street, and Reservoir and Jerome avenues; its drill hall measures 300 by 600 feet, its earthen floor permits pitching of tents (it will be paved over in the 1920s), and its ceiling rises to a pointed arch 121 feet high. The armory's gallery accommodates 4,000 spectators, and the place will be used for bicycle races, boat shows, stockholders' meetings, and a wide range of other events in addition to its original military and law-enforcement function.

A six-story neo-Federal-style mansion for Pennsylvania-born banker and Red Cross executive Henry Pomeroy Davison, 50, is completed at 690 Park Avenue to designs by Walker & Gillette on property acquired from Arthur Curtiss James. Replacing three row houses in 69th Street and one on Park Avenue, it has 10 master bedrooms, nine baths, 16 servants' rooms, a large library, living, dining, and reception rooms, two elevators, and an attached garage. The Italian government will buy the mansion and its neighbor at 52 East 69th Street in the summer of 1955 for use as a consulate.

A mansion for manufacturer John Sherman Hoyt, 48, and his wife, Ethel Valentine (*née* Stokes), is completed at the northwest corner of Park Avenue and 79th Street to designs by I. N. Phelps Stokes. Hoyt married Stokes's sister in 1895.

A mansion for New York-born lawyer John Shillito Rogers, 40, and his copper heiress wife, Catherine (*née* Dodge), is completed at 53 East 79th Street, between Madison and Park avenues, to designs by Trowbridge & Livingston (*see* Miss Hewitt's Classes, 1919; Society Library, 1937).

The 13-story-plus-penthouse 417 Park Avenue apartment house is completed at the southeast corner of 55th Street, where it will remain long after the 12 other residential buildings on the avenue south of 57th Street have been replaced by office towers (it will be a rental building until 1947). Commissioned by Bing & Bing and designed by Emery Roth, the limestone-faced structure has two elevators, one for each line of apartments; the 28 units include four penthouses, two of them duplexes of three and seven rooms, respectively. Simplexes range in size mostly from six to 10 rooms.

The Rodin Studios apartment house (later an office building) is completed at 200 West 57th Street to French Gothic designs by Cass Gilbert, providing double-height studios and residential space for artists.

The nine-story 140 West 58th Street apartment house is completed to designs by Schwartz & Gross. The red-brick building has four units per floor, each four to five rooms, renting at $113.50 to $162.50 per month. Optional maid service is available.

The 17-story 550 Park Avenue apartment house is completed at the southeast corner of 62nd Street with two apartments per floor, each with 12 rooms, three baths, renting for between $375 and $500 per month. Corner apartments with 14 rooms and four baths rent for between $542 and $665. Designed by J. E. R. Carpenter, it replaces the Yosemite, a seven-story apartment house by McKim Mead & White that opened in 1891.

The Hotel des Artistes opens at 1 West 67th Street, just to the west of a town house that faces on Central Park. Designed by architect George Mort Pollard, the 20-floor co-operative apartment house (it is not a hotel in the American sense of that word) boasts a swimming pool, squash courts, theater, ballroom, and apartments as large as a triplex with 30-foot ceilings for tenants who will include dancer Isadora Duncan, screen idol Rudolph Valentino, and—for 3 decades beginning in 1932—novelist Fannie Hurst (who will occupy the big triplex).

The 12-story 927 Fifth Avenue apartment house is completed at the corner of 74th Street to designs by Warren & Wetmore with one apartment per floor. Monthly rentals for a flat with 14 rooms, five baths range from $950 to $1,416.50; 10 rooms with three baths go for as little as $708.

The 12-story Edgecombe Avenue Apartments (initially called the Colonial Parkway Apartments) are completed at 409 Edgecombe Avenue on a ridge overlooking Harlem. Designed by Schwartz & Gross, the units will attract a roster of prominent black tenants beginning in the 1930s.

A new Catskill water-system aqueduct opens to provide the city with 250 million gallons daily of the purest, best-tasting water of any major American metropolis (see 1892). The city's First Water Tunnel is dedicated October 12 at the reservoir in Central Park (see 1936).

Riots break out in February in areas where rising food prices have made it difficult for poor people to feed their families. The rioters attack food shops and burn peddlers' pushcarts on the Lower East Side and in Brooklyn's Brownsville and Williamsburg sections, rejecting suggestions that they substitute rice for potatoes and milk for eggs and meat. Some 6,000 kosher poultry shops and 150 kosher poultry slaughterhouses close down just before Passover to protest wholesalers accused of cornering the market.

Brooklyn-born fur trader Clarence Birdseye, 31, returns home to pursue the commercial exploitation of his food-freezing discoveries. He has spent 3 years in Labrador, where obtaining fresh food for his young family has been an urgent problem. Birdseye has learned after much experimentation how to freeze cabbages in barrels of seawater, and he has found that frozen foods remain fresh when kept refrigerated at low temperatures.

A&P cofounder George Huntington Hartford dies at Spring Lake, N.J., August 29 at age 83.

 The new Hotel des Artistes in West 67th Street has a communal kitchen for tenants and a restaurant, the Café des Artistes (see Christy murals, 1932).

Nathan Handwerker counters rumors spread by Coney Island rivals who say 5¢ hot dogs cannot be of the best quality (see 1916). He offers nurses and residents at Coney Island Hospital free meals if they will stand at his counters wearing white jackets with stethoscopes hanging out of their pockets, and word spreads that doctors from the hospital are eating Nathan's hot dogs.

A U.S. immigration bill enacted January 29 over a second veto by President Wilson requires that a would-be immigrant pass a literacy test in any language. Inspired by the Immigration Restriction League founded in 1894, it becomes law February 5, excluding immigrants from most of Asia and the Pacific Islands, but to relieve the distress of Russian Jews it exempts refugees from religious persecution (see 1921). The U.S. population passes 100 million.

1918 Mayor Hylan appoints former patrolman Richard E. Enright, 47, police commissioner, the first man to rise from pounding a beat to head the department. "Horse rooms [gambling establishments] were running wide open all over town," he will tell a reporter in 1950. "Western Union was feeding them track information." The police inspector in charge of the vice and gambling squad receives orders to clean up the gambling mess within 15 days or face dismissal: Daniel "Honest Dan" Costigan is soon forced to retire, his successor John F. McDonald is more successful at closing the gambling joints, but they will come back to flourish under future administrations.

Gen. Pershing makes his first major offensive in mid-September at Saint-Mihiel and forces the Germans to give up salients they have held since 1914. Some 1,656,000 doughboys have left New York for France.

Allied troops rescue the "Lost Battalion" in the Argonne Forest October 7. Commanded by Wisconsin-born New York lawyer Maj. Charles W. (White) Whittlesey, 34, and made up mostly of volunteers and enlistees from the streets of New York, the 308th Battalion of the U.S. 77th Division crashed through the German line with about 800 men Octo-

Broadway musicals entertained doughboys and officers about to go "over there." LIBRARY OF CONGRESS

ber 1 but was soon isolated and surrounded. By October 2 it numbered only 463 men, well-supplied German troops kept it under almost constant machine-gun and mortar fire, its only means of communication were homing pigeons, its position came under "friendly fire" from Allied artillery, rations were reduced almost to nothing, ammunition ran low, but Whittlesey refused a German demand that he surrender. Only 194 survivors of the battalion are able to walk, Maj. Whittlesey is promoted to lieutenant colonel and awarded the Congressional Medal of Honor, but he will commit suicide in November 1921, jumping overboard from a United Fruit Co. ship bound for Havana.

New York-born Congressman Fiorello (Raffaele) Henry La Guardia, 35, returns from Europe, where he has commanded U.S. bombing squadrons on the Italian-Austrian front. A Republican who was elected from the 14th congressional district 2 years ago, La Guardia launches a campaign for reelection November 2, debating Pennsylvania-born Socialist candidate Scott Nearing, 34, in the Great Hall of the Cooper Union; he wears his uniform and wins the hearts of the audience, which has more in common with him than with his opponent, who inherited a small fortune from an aunt 4 years ago.

Tammany Hall boss Charles F. Murphy secures the Democratic gubernatorial nomination for Alfred E. Smith, now 44, who last year became president of the city's Board of Aldermen and narrowly wins election, securing 1,009,936 votes to Gov. Whitman's 995,094. Murphy summons Smith to his Long Island estate Good Ground, tells him how proud he is that an Irishman from the Lower East

Side has become the state's first Irish Catholic governor, and relieves him of any obligation to serve Tammany if it interferes with his being a great governor (*see* 1919).

Congressman La Guardia wins easy reelection to the House of Representatives from the 14th congressional district, receiving 14,208 votes to 6,168 for Scott Nearing, who has campaigned on a platform of pacifism.

New York goes wild November 7 following a false report by the United Press that an armistice has been signed. Germany's Wilhelm II abdicates November 8 and hostilities on the western front do end November 11 in a bona fide armistice signed at Compiègne outside Paris. La Guardia resigns his U.S. Army commission November 12.

The 9-year-old National Association for the Advancement of Colored People calls Atlanta NAACP organizer Walter (Francis) White, 25, to New York and asks him to report on racial incidents in the South. With his light skin, blond hair, and blue eyes that make him indistinguishable from any Caucasian, he can cross the color line whenever he likes and will pass as a white reporter in the next 10 years to investigate some 40 lynchings and eight race riots, interviewing members of lynch mobs and state officials.

Governor-elect Al Smith puts in a phone call to Belle Moskowitz, now 41. He asks her to bring her assistants to his office to help plan social legislation as called for in the Democratic Party platform, and she will put together a comprehensive program to relieve housing shortages, with emphasis on public health and food markets.

National City Bank chairman James Stillman dies at his 9 East 72nd Street home March 15 at age 67, leaving a personal fortune estimated at more than $50 million.

The 119-year-old Bank of Manhattan absorbs the Bank of the Metropolis established in 1871 (*see* Chase Manhattan, 1955).

Wall Street's Dow Jones Industrial Average closes December 31 at 82.20, up from 74.38 at the end of 1917.

The New York Barge Canal that opens to traffic May 15 replaces the 93-year-old Erie Canal while using some of the same natural waterways. Steam power has long since made the old canal obsolete (*see* St. Lawrence Seaway, 1959).

The Police Department makes all Manhattan side streets one-way thoroughfares (*see* 1916): with some exceptions, even-numbered streets will be eastbound, odd-numbered streets westbound.

The IRT elevated railway line reaches Woodlawn in the Bronx via two new drawbridges over the Harlem River that bring trains to Jerome Avenue (*see* 1913; 1920).

The Lexington Avenue IRT subway line opens in July, giving East Side New Yorkers a rapid-transit alternative to the "Els" on Second and Third avenues, but the distance between Fifth Avenue and the East River is much larger than that between Central Park West and the Hudson, and most of the East Side will remain without any other subway service until at least the next century, whereas the narrower West Side will have two subway lines by 1940 (*see* 1932).

The worst subway accident in the city's history kills 93 persons and severely injures 103 others, nine of them fatally. A train running at 30 miles per hour on a sharp curve approaching the Malbone Street Tunnel of the Brighton Beach line that runs along Fulton Street and Franklin Avenue to Coney Island jumps the track just before 7 o'clock on the evening of November 2. Manned by inexperienced supervisors in the absence of striking motormen, who belong to the Brotherhood of Locomotive Engineers, the train is traveling at five times the speed limit allowed on the treacherous S curve, many of its cars are wooden, and they are smashed to smithereens when hurled against a concrete barrier separating the north- and southbound tracks near the new Prospect Park station of the Brooklyn Rapid Transit Service (later the BMT).

The German Hospital and Dispensary renames itself Lenox Hill Hospital as wartime hysteria mounts against everything German (*see* 1901). It has been on Park Avenue and 77th Street since 1868.

Booth Memorial Hospital is licensed as a general hospital. Opened by the Salvation Army in 1892 as a rescue home for battered women, it went on to provide medical treatment and shelter for mothers and women addicted to alcohol and drugs, moved after several relocations to a building in East 15th Street, and changed its name to Booth Memorial 4 years ago (*see* 1957).

The Maternity Center Association of New York is founded to provide prenatal care and education for pregnant women in poor neighborhoods.

A mysterious form of influenza kills 19,000 at New York beginning in September, with as many as 851 fatalities in a single day; schools are closed, parades and Liberty Loan rallies banned, hospitals jammed as the worst pandemic to afflict mankind since the Black Death of the mid-14th century sweeps through Europe, America, and the Orient. Hermann M. Biggs, now 58, has been New York's state health commissioner since 1914 and works to contain the epidemic of "Spanish" flu. The worst of the epidemic is over by December.

John Cardinal Farley dies at New York September 17 at age 76 and is buried beneath St. Patrick's Cathedral (*see* 1919).

The board of Teachers Insurance and Annuity Association (later TIAA-CREF) holds its first meeting May 17 at New York and elects Henry S. Pritchett president (*see* 1905). Chartered by New York State as a nonprofit company, its stock is all held by the Carnegie Corporation and it will enjoy tax exemption until 1997.

Wagner College opens on an 86-acre campus (the former Cunard estate) on Staten Island. Founded originally at Rochester as a Lutheran seminary, it took the name Wagner Memorial Lutheran College in 1884 and is now rededicated in honor of George Wagner, whose father helped finance the first campus. The 6-year German Gymnasium has only 16 students, with just one professor to prepare them for a bilingual ministry, but it will begin accepting women in 1933 and grow to have 1,300 undergraduates plus 450 enrolled in graduate programs in bacteriology, business, education, and nursing.

New York Evening Post publisher Oswald Garrison Villard sells the 117-year-old paper (pacifist Villard opposed U.S. entry into the war and the *Post*'s circulation declined as a result) but retains control of The *Nation*, some of whose issues have been temporarily impounded by postal authorities because of Villard's controversial editorials.

New York Herald publisher James Gordon Bennett dies at his Beaulieu estate in France May 14 at age 77. He has lived abroad since 1877 and, always eccentric, has become more so in his later years, spending tens of millions of dollars from his newspapers; although the *Herald* has been losing money, the *Telegram* that he started in 1867 became highly profitable beginning in 1910 and has saved him and his publishing empire from bankruptcy (*see* Munsey, 1920; *Herald Tribune*, 1924).

"Believe It or Not!" is published for the first time by Santa Rosa, Calif.-born *New York Globe* sports cartoonist Robert L. (LeRoy) Ripley, 24, who sketches figures of men who have set records for such unlikely events as running backward and broad jumping on ice. Encouraged by reader response to pursue his quest for oddities, Ripley will move to the *New York Post* in 1923, syndication of his cartoons will begin soon after, and "Believe It or Not!" will eventually be carried by 326 newspapers in 38 countries.

Managing editor Floyd Dell, cartoonist Art Young, and other members of The *Masses* staff are indicted in April under the Espionage Act of 1917 on charges of having conspired to obstruct military recruitment and enlistment (*see* Day, 1917); Young's cartoon "Having Their Fling" has depicted an editor, a capitalist, a politician, and a clergyman performing a wild dance in front of a war-munitions orchestra led by Satan. Asked in court why he draws anti-war cartoons, Young replies, "For the public good." Now 30, Dell is inducted into the army in June but discharged because he is still under indictment, and two trials will end in hung juries before the government abandons prosecution of the case. Young, now 52, joins with others in starting The *Liberator* and draws cartoons that include one lampooning the Supreme Court's ruling with regard to the Owen-Keating Child Labor Act (a fat, cigar-smoking boss leads a crowd of underage workers in a factory yard and says, "Now children, all together, three cheers for the Supreme Court").

Collier's magazine publisher Robert J. Collier returns home November 8 from a long tour of the front, sits down to dinner at his 1067 Fifth Avenue town house, and dies of a heart attack at age 42, leaving his widow an estate of only $2,194 (*see* Crowell-Collier, 1919).

Nonfiction: *The Green Book* (initially the *New York City Directory*, it will be renamed in 1984) is published for the first time, giving the names, salaries, office (and home) addresses, and telephone numbers of city officials from the mayor on down (Mayor Hylan lives at 959 Bushwick Avenue, Brooklyn). Priced at 30¢ (leather bound) and 15¢ (paperback), the directory has 112 pages and lists agencies that include the Board of Inebriety, the Board of Hazardous Trades, and the Tenement House Department (*see* 1932); *The Elements of Style* by Cornell University English professor William Strunk, Jr., 49.

Fiction: *Dere Mabel* by New York humorist-banker Edward Streeter, 26, whose "letters" from "Bill Smith" appeared originally last year in the magazine *Gas Attack*, published at Camp Wadsworth, Spartanburg, S.C., where Streeter was an army lieutenant; *Gaslight Sonatas* (stories) by Fannie Hurst.

Poetry: *The Ghetto and Other Poems* by Dublin-born Brooklyn poet Lola Ridge, 35, who was raised in Australia and New Zealand; *Minna and Myself* by Mississippi-born Greenwich Village poet Maxwell Bodenheim, 25.

Sculpture: a bronze statue of the late actor Edwin Booth by sculptor Edmond Quinn is unveiled in Gramercy Park opposite the Players Club, whose members have given the work to the Gramercy Park Commission (Quinn is a member); a statue of Gen. Daniel Butterfield by Idaho-born architect Gutzon Borglum, 51, is unveiled at the northwest corner of 122nd Street and Claremont Avenue. The Civil War general died in 1901, having composed "Taps" in 1862.

Theater: *The Off Chance* by R. C. Carton 2/14 at the Empire Theater, with Ethel Barrymore, London-born actress Eva Le Gallienne, 19, Charles (Dana) Gibson, 92 perfs.; Henry Miller's Theater opens 4/1 at 124–130 West 43rd Street (Allen, Ingalls & Hoffman has designed it for director-producer Miller, now 48, who has enjoyed dazzling success); *Lightnin'* by Winchell Smith and Frank Bacon 8/26 at the Gaiety Theater, with Bacon as Lightnin' Bill Jones, 1,291 perfs.; *The Betrothal* by Belgian poet-playwright Maurice Maeterlinck 11/18 at the Shubert Theater, with Henry Travers, Brooklyn-born ingénue Winifred Lenihan, 18, Chicago-born ingénue June Walker, 18, Boston-born ingénue Lillian Roth, 7, 120 perfs.; the Selwyn Theater opens 10/2 at 229 West 42nd Street; *The Moon of the Caribbees* by Eugene O'Neill 12/20 at the Playwrights Theater; *A Kiss for Cinderella* by James M. Barrie 12/25 at the Empire Theater, with Maude Adams, 152 perfs.

The first Pulitzer prize for drama is awarded to Jesse Lynch Williams for his 1917 comedy *Why Marry?* which continues at the Astor Theater.

Illusionist Harry Houdini amazes audiences at the Hippodrome by making a 10,000-pound elephant vanish into thin air. Said to be a daughter of P. T. Barnum's Jumbo, Jenny is placed with her trainer in a wooden cabinet, and when Houdini fires a pistol both animal and trainer disappear.

Lewisohn Stadium opens between West 136th and 138th streets and Convent and Amsterdam avenues with 6,000 seats and standing room for 1,500 to hear summertime orchestral concerts sponsored by German-born copper baron-philanthropist Adolph Lewisohn, now 69, and financed by philanthropist Minna Guggenheimer (*née* Schafer), who will continue her support until 1964, attending most of the concerts and making uninhibited intermission speeches. Former City College president John H. Finley urged construction of the stadium, Lewisohn donated $50,000 for it in May 1915, its concerts will continue through 1966, and it will be demolished in 1975.

Michigan-born Los Angeles designer Norman Bel Geddes (originally Norman Geddes), 25, comes to New York on a grant from his patron Otto Kahn of Kuhn, Loeb & Co. to present his ideas about stage design and is commissioned to design several sets for the Metropolitan Opera. He substitutes clean, functional backgrounds for the cluttered, ornamental backgrounds that have distracted the eye.

Broadway musicals: *Oh, Lady! Lady!* 2/1 at the Princess Theater, with Philadelphia-born singer Vivienne Segal, 20, New York-born actress Constance Binney, 21, Edward Abeles, music by Jerome Kern, book and lyrics by Guy Bolton and P. G. Wodehouse, songs that include "Greenwich Village," 219 perfs.; *Sinbad* 2/14 at the Winter Garden Theater, with Al Jolson, book by Harold Atteridge, music by Sigmund Romberg and others, songs that include "My Mammy" by Brooklyn-born composer Walter Donaldson, 25, lyrics by Joe Young (originally Youdavich), 20, and New York-born writer Sam M. Lewis, 33, "Rock-a-by Your Baby with a Dixie Melody" by Jean Schwartz, lyrics by Joe Young and Sam M. Lewis, 164 perfs.; *Oh, Look!* 3/7 at the new Vanderbilt Theater, 148 West 48th Street, with Swiss-born actor Alfred Kappeler, 41, songs that include "I'm Always Chasing Rainbows" by Harry Caroll, who has adapted Chopin's Fantaisie Impromptu in C sharp minor, lyrics by Joseph McCarthy, 68 perfs.; *The Rainbow Girl* 4/1 at the New Amsterdam Theater, with music by Louis A. Hirsch, book and lyrics by Rennold Wolf from a comedy by Jerome K. Jerome; *Hitchy-Koo of 1918* (revue) 6/6 at the Globe Theater, with comedian Raymond Hitchcock, now 52, Leon Errol, Irene Bordoni, songs that include "You-oo Just You" by New York-born Tin Pan Alley song plugger-composer George Gershwin, 20, lyrics by Irving Caesar, now 23 (the two have met at the offices of the music publisher Remick's), 68 perfs.; *The Passing Show* 7/25 at the Winter Garden Theater, with Marilyn Miller, Fred and Adele Astaire, Eugene and Willie Howard, Charles Ruggles, Frank Fay, music chiefly by Sigmund Romberg and Jean Schwartz, lyrics chiefly by Harold Atteridge, songs that include "Smiles" by J. Will Callahan and Lee G. Robert, and with June Caprice, 19, singing "I'm Forever Blowing Bubbles" by John William Kellette, lyrics by Jean Kenbrovin (James Kendis, James Brockman, Nat Vincent), 124 perfs.; *The Ziegfeld Follies* 6/18 at the New Amsterdam Theater with Eddie Cantor, Will Rogers, Marilyn Miller, W. C. Fields, dancer Dorothy Dickson, music by Louis A. Hirsch, 151 perfs.; *Yip Yip Yaphank* 8/19 at the Century Theater with a cast of 350 recruits from Camp Upton at Yaphank, L.I., music and lyrics by Private Irving Berlin, songs that include "Oh, How I Hate to Get Up in the Morning," "Mandy," "Soldier Boy," 32 perfs.; *Sometime* 10/4 at the Shubert Theater, with Brooklyn-born vaudeville trooper Mae West, 26, singing numbers that include "Any Kind of Man" by Rudolf Friml, 283 perfs.

Lyricist Junie McCree dies at New York January 13 at age 52; dancer Vernon Castle is killed in an airplane accident while training at Newport News, Va., February 15 at age 30 and is buried at Woodlawn Cemetery; Anna Held dies of pernicious anemia and bronchial pneumonia at the Plaza Hotel August 12 at age 45.

The semiprofessional Brooklyn Bushwicks start playing at the 33-year-old Dexter Park in Woodside, Queens, whose grandstand holds 15,500 spectators and where the team will continue to play until the 1950s, often outdrawing the Brooklyn Dodgers. Dexter Park will play host to barnstorming baseball teams, whose players will include Babe Ruth and Lou Gehrig, as well as Negro League teams such as the Brooklyn Royal Giants, Homestead Grays, and Kansas City Monarchs, whose players will include Satchel Paige and Jackie Robinson.

Russian-born Lower East Side street tough Meyer Lansky (originally Maier Suchowizansky), 16, is arrested on charges of felonious assault in Ludlow Street April 24, charges are dismissed, but he is convicted of disorderly conduct November 18 and fined $2. Lansky came through Ellis Island 7 years ago (*see* 1928; Prohibition, 1919).

Architect Henry Janeway Hardenbergh dies at New York March 13 at age 71.

Managers of the 10-year-old Singer Tower at 149 Broadway report in June that they are using 21 female elevator operators and four starters. Automatic leveling and push-button controls have reduced the amount of physical effort required to operate elevators, but their heavy metal gates must still be opened and closed by hand.

The St. Vincent Ferrer Church is completed on the east side of Lexington Avenue at 68th Street to designs by Bertram Goodhue.

St. Bartholomew's Episcopal Church (St. Bart's) opens for services in October on the easterly blockfront of Park Avenue between 51st and 52nd streets, a site formerly occupied by the F. & M. Schaefer brewery and seven old dwellings. Designed in neo-Byzantine style by Bertram Goodhue, it is the city's third St. Bart's; the second, designed by James Renwick, Jr., opened in 1872 at the corner of Madison Avenue and 44th Street, where the late William Henry Vanderbilt offered the land to the church at a concessionary price, but the land under the church turned out to be soft clay rather than good Manhattan Schist, the church was sinking by 1914, and its ornamental porch designed in 1899 by the late Stanford White with a seated figure of Christ by sculptor Daniel Chester French will be moved to the new church (*see* 1923).

The Racquet & Tennis Club on the west side of Park Avenue between 52nd and 53rd streets is completed in brick and limestone to Florentine Renaissance palazzo-style designs by McKim, Mead & White. Real estate heir Robert W. Goelet owns the property and has persuaded the other members of the 28-year-old club to let him put up the building and then lease it from him. The two lower floors contain a lounge, library, billiard room, 60-foot bar ("Old Mahogany," moved from the club's previous building at 27 West 43rd Street), restaurant, and loggia; the third floor has a gymnasium, steam room, swimming pool, and changing room; the fourth and fifth floors contain squash courts and one of the few courts in America designed for the game of court tennis, or Louis Quatorze.

A mansion for Emily Thorn Sloane (*née* Vanderbilt) is completed at 686 Park Avenue with interior detailing taken in part from the 17th century Belton House in Grantham, England, designed by Christopher Wren. Widow of the carpet and furniture retailer William Douglas Sloane, who died 3 years ago, Mrs. Sloane spends most of her time at her Berkshire estate, Elm Court; her New York house will be sold in 1941 to engineer Thomas E. Murray and his wife, Marie, and in 1959 will become the Italian Cultural Institute.

A Fifth Avenue mansion for financier Otto Kahn is completed at 1 East 91st Street. Designed in the style of Rome's Palazzo della Cancelleria by architect J. Armstrong Stenhouse with help from C. P. H. Gilbert, it resembles the Villard Houses designed by McKim, Mead & White in the 1880s (*see* education, 1934).

✗ Italian-born pasta maker Emanuele Ronzoni, 48, acquires American-made macaroni machinery and incorporates under his own name. Brought to New York at age 11, he worked as a helper at $2 per week in a Lower East Side macaroni factory, opened his own factory in 1892 on the lower West Side near Canal Street, and as production manager for the past 12 years of a Brooklyn macaroni factory has seen the growing demand for U.S.-made pasta products.

Breakstone Brothers moves to a larger building at 195 Franklin Street (*see* 1899). It has become a large producer of condensed milk for the armed forces and will soon begin manufacturing cream cheese at Downsville, N.Y.

New Yorkers call sauerkraut "liberty cabbage;" German toast becomes "French toast."

👨‍🍳 The dairy restaurant Ratner's moves to larger premises at 138 Delancey Street near the Brooklyn Bridge (*see* 1905). Jacob Harmatz will buy out Morris Ratner's interest in 1920 and the place will grow with help from Max and Louis Zankel (and crowds from the neighboring Loew's Delancey vaudeville theater) to serve onion rolls, bagels, challah, matzoh brie, chopped liver, lox, Nova Scotia salmon, vegetarian dishes, pastries, and blintzes, in addition to borscht, matzoh-ball soup, and gefilte fish.

👫 Ellis Island receives only 28,867 immigrants, down from 178,416 in 1915 and 878,052 in 1914. Nearly half the staff—clerks, cooks, inspectors, interpreters, janitors, watchmen, but not doctors or nurses—has been dismissed or furloughed. The island is turned over to the army and navy, and most of the 2,200 foreign crewmen and persons of "suspected loyalty" who have been detained on the island are sent to camps in Georgia and North Carolina. Wounded doughboys—amputees and shell-shock victims—begin arriving in March. The Immigration Service transfers its own patients to mainland hospitals, retaining only a small area for aliens held for special inquiry and immigrants waiting to be released to relatives, but Immigration continues to administer the entire facility (*see* 1919).

1919 Gov. Al Smith is inaugurated January 1 with a parade up Albany's State Street led by survivors of the 69th Regiment of the National Guard—New York's "Fighting 69th" (*see* 1917). The predominantly Irish unit was in contact with the enemy for 180 days from 1917 to 1918 and suffered 3,501 casualties—644 killed, 2,857 wounded. Major William J. Donovan has been promoted to colonel, having been wounded three times in combat.

Former president Theodore Roosevelt dies in his sleep January 6 at his Sagamore Hill home near Oyster Bay, L.I., at age 60. His youngest son, Quentin, was killed last year while flying over enemy lines in France and TR has never recovered from the loss. The house where he was born at 28 West 20th Street

James Reese Europe's jazz band led the 369th Infantry up Fifth Avenue to Harlem. NATIONAL ARCHIVE

was torn down in 1916; a double house will be built on the site in 1923 and be operated as a National Historic Site, becoming known (somewhat erroneously) as Roosevelt's birthplace.

The 369th Regiment marches up Fifth Avenue from Lower Manhattan to Harlem February 17 led by James Reese Europe's jazz band. Formerly the 15th Infantry National Guard unit, the "Harlem Hellfighters" served 191 days in combat—longer than any other U.S. unit—and its members won 170 Croix de Guerre medals for bravery. More than 1 million New Yorkers turn out for the parade, and when the troops turn off 110th Street onto Lenox Avenue Europe's band strikes up "Here Comes My Daddy Now."

Thousands in Brooklyn's Brownsville section parade in the rain May 1 with banners of protest, singing revolutionary songs. Crowds of shouting and jeering U.S. soldiers, sailors, and marines led by a Canadian veteran threaten to break up May Day celebrations at Madison Square Garden and other venues in the city, where speakers demand the release of San Francisco labor leader Thomas F. Mooney (who has been convicted of throwing a bomb in a Preparedness Day parade and sentenced to life imprisonment) and Socialist labor organizer Eugene V. Debs (who has been convicted of sedition under a 1917 Espionage Act and given a 10-year sentence), but 1,700 mounted police wearing rubber coats in a heavy rain throw up a cordon around the Garden and keep the "anti-Bolshevik" demonstrators at a two-block distance from what newspapers will call the most closely guarded mass meeting ever held in the city. While the meeting in Madison Square Garden is peaceful, police detectives in plain clothes attend most of the meetings and make notes of the speakers' remarks. Soldiers and sailors armed with sticks and clubs do break up some gatherings, including a reception for 700 men, women, and children held at the new offices of The *Call* in a five-story building at 112 Fourth Avenue, where posters hung in the windows are removed, literature destroyed, and people beaten as they leave (17 are treated for injuries); more than 40 arrests are reported.

Gen. John J. "Black Jack" Pershing returns from France and New York gives him a ticker-tape parade September 8. Mayor Hylan has appointed New York-born Wanamaker's executive Grover (Aloysius) Whalen, 33, chairman of his reception committee, and Whalen will remain the city's official greeter until 1953. Pershing commanded the American Expeditionary Force in the Great War, he turns 59 September 13, and the street opposite Grand Central Terminal is named Pershing Square in his honor.

The first Feminist Congress opens at New York March 1 with a statement by Crystal Eastman, who reminds her audience that four-fifths of the women in America are "still denied the elementary political right of voting" (*see* 1918). A "lame duck" House of Representatives has failed by one vote February 16 to pass a woman's suffrage bill, but the U.S. Senate votes 56 to 25 June 4 to submit a woman's suffrage amendment to the states for ratification (*see* 1920).

The cost of living in New York City is 79 percent higher than it was in 1914, says the Bureau of Labor Statistics. The average U.S. worker earns only $1,144 per year, and many New York dressmakers, cloak- and suitmakers, cigarmakers, printers, subway workers, longshoremen, and actors earn less than the average. They all strike for higher pay, and large numbers of middle-class New Yorkers move to the outer boroughs and suburbs in order to escape congestion and high housing costs.

Capitalist Augustus D. Juilliard attends the opera April 19, catches pneumonia, and dies at New York April 25 at age 83, having become a leading figure in the city's banking and investment worlds. He bequeaths the great bulk of his vast fortune to establish music departments at U.S. colleges, provide education for promising music students, encourage musical composition, and finance operas deemed to have merit (*see* music [Juilliard School], 1920); Andrew Carnegie dies August 11 at age 83 in his Berkshire Hills mansion at Lenox, Mass., having by some estimates given away all but $11.8 million of his $475 million fortune in contributions that inspired other U.S. millionaires to be philanthropic (*see* 1889). His widow, Louise (*née* Whitfield), will continue until her death in 1946 to occupy the great mansion completed in 1901 at 2 East 91st Street; former Carnegie Steel boss Henry Clay Frick dies at New York December 2 at age 69, leaving an estate of more than $92 million, including his Fifth Avenue house and art collection (*see* art, 1935). His erstwhile business partner Andrew Carnegie had invited him to come a mile up Fifth Avenue for a visit to make their peace, but Frick allegedly replied, "We'll meet in hell, which is where we're both going to go."

The 9-year-old house of Salomon Brothers and Hutzler goes into the business of trading U.S. Government securities (they will be its mainstay for the next 50 years). The firm will move to 60 Wall Street in 1922 as Arthur Salomon becomes one of the city's leading financiers (*see* 1935).

A Wall Street boom in "war baby" stocks sends prices to new highs. The Dow Jones Industrial Average closes December 31 at 107.23, up from 82.20 at the end of 1918.

Merchant F. W. Woolworth dies at his Glen Cove, L.I., estate April 8 at age 67 and is buried at Woodlawn Cemetery. He leaves a fortune of $67 million, none of it to charity: there are 1,000 Woolworth stores in the United States plus many in Britain, and the chain has annual sales of $107 million.

The Grand Central Viaduct opens to carry Park Avenue traffic between 40th and 46th streets, easing somewhat the congestion that has clogged Vanderbilt, Park, and Fifth avenues (when a young auto salesman demonstrating a new Stutz was stopped 4 years ago for going 25 miles per hour on Park Avenue, the traffic cop was riding a bicycle). The Fifth Avenue Association has agitated for years to have the city relieve its thoroughfare's heavy volume of traffic by opening up Park Avenue. Nearly 600 feet long, the viaduct takes two-way traffic around the west side of the terminal but deposits it at the corner of 45th Street and Vanderbilt Avenue (a spur runs along the east side of the terminal, providing parking space and forming an entrance to the new Commodore Hotel, but southbound motorists encounter a bottleneck at 45th Street: diverted to Vanderbilt, they can either go south three blocks to 42nd Street and then back onto Park, or they can go up the viaduct at 45th and Vanderbilt (where congestion is probably the worst in the city) and onto Park again at 40th. Northbound cars can take one of three routes: they can turn right on 40th Street to Lexington Avenue, go up to 45th Street, and then go west onto Park; they can use the viaduct at 45th and Vanderbilt; or they can go up Park to 42nd

Street, west to Vanderbilt, and up Vanderbilt to 45th (Vanderbilt is a private thoroughfare above 45th Street) (*see* 1920).

The city's first electric traffic signal is installed at the intersection of Fifth Avenue and 42nd Street (*see* semaphore, 1910). Borrowed from railroad signals, the green, amber, and red light is operated by a police officer (traffic lights will be hand operated until the 1930s); traffic moves on 42nd Street when the light is green, on Fifth Avenue when it is amber, and when it is red all traffic must stop (*see* 1924).

The 5-year-old German passenger liners S.S. *Vaterland* and S.S. *Bismarck* are handed over to the British as war reparations and renamed the S.S. *Leviathan* and S.S. *Majestic*. They will soon be arriving at New York as regular transatlantic passenger traffic resumes.

Restaurateur-hotel proprietor Raymond Orteig speaks at the Aero Club of America March 22 and offers a $25,000 prize for the first nonstop flight, in either direction, between New York and Paris. Now 49, Orteig operates the Brevoort and Lafayette hotels; his prize will not be claimed for 8 years (*see* Lindbergh, 1927).

New York-born Roman Catholic priest Patrick (Joseph) Hayes, 51, is appointed archbishop March 10, taking over the duties of the late John Cardinal Farley. Concerned with social welfare, Hayes served as bishop ordinary to the chaplain of the army and navy in the Great War and signs the Bishops' Program of Social Reconstruction, but he has opposed a U.S. constitutional amendment forbidding child labor on grounds that it interfered with parental authority (*see* 1920).

Buffalo-born Union Theological Seminary professor Harry Emerson Fosdick, 41, accepts a position as assistant pastor of the city's First Presbyterian Church, whose elders have decided to experiment with an interdenominational ministry. Fosdick has been outspoken in opposing credal restrictions (*see* 1922).

Trinity Church abolishes the common practice of having parishioners pay for their pews.

The New School for Social Research is founded in Greenwich Village by Columbia University historians Charles A. Beard, now 44; Bloomington, Ill.-born historian James Harvey Robinson, 56; Vermont-born educator John Dewey, 59; Nebraska-born economist Alvin Saunders Johnson, 44; Wisconsin-born social scientist Thorstein Veblen,

62; and others as an alternative to the "academic authoritarianism" of Columbia.

The Dalton School has its beginnings in the Children's University School opened in West 74th Street by Wisconsin-born educator Helen Parkhurst, 32, who studied at Rome with Maria Montessori early in 1914. The girls' school will move in 1922 to a building in West 72nd Street and take its name from the Dalton Plan applied to the Dalton, Mass., high school 3 years ago with encouragement from the wife of paper company heir W. Murray Crane (see 1929).

Lucy Sprague Mitchell opens a nursery school (see 1916). It will move in 1930 with its sponsor, the Bureau of Educational Experiments, into an abandoned Fleischmann's Yeast factory at 69 Bank Street, where it will expand into a full elementary school. The Bureau will become the Bank Street College of Education in the 1950s so that it can grant master's degrees in teaching (see 1970).

 Radio Corp. of America (RCA) is founded at New York by Owen D. Young, who loans Ernst Alexanderson to RCA, where he will be employed as chief engineer for 5 years (see 1906). RCA will acquire the Victor Co. and become a radio-phonograph colossus, but antitrust court actions will separate RCA from GE (see NBC, 1926).

The *New York Daily News* (initially the *New York Illustrated Daily News*) begins publication June 26 under the direction of *Chicago Tribune* veteran Joseph Medill Patterson, 40, a socialist who tells his editors, "Tell it to Sweeney—the Stuyvesants will take care of themselves." A war correspondent before 1917, Patterson won a captaincy and commanded a field artillery unit in the Rainbow Division; he got the idea for his paper from British publisher A. C. W. Harmsworth, Lord Northcliffe, 54, a family friend whose *London Mirror* is selling 800,000 copies per day. Capt. Patterson will remain in Chicago until 1925 but has rented offices in the Evening Mail Building and uses the slogan "See New York's Most Beautiful Girls Every Morning;" he begins with a print-run of only 57,000 copies, fills his paper with suggestive pictures, comic strips, sports coverage, beauty and limerick contests with cash prizes, and stories of sex and crime that attract readers who never before read any newspaper on a regular basis. The *News* will show a profit beginning next year and will go on to become the first successful U.S. tabloid, the most widely read U.S. newspaper of any kind (see 1921).

Frank A. Munsey moves his *New York Sun* to the former A. T. Stewart Marble Emporium of 1846 at 280 Broadway; a four-sided bronze clock bearing the motto "The Sun, it shines for all" will be installed at its Chambers Street corner in 1930 (but see 1950).

J. F. Knapp's Crowell Publishing Co. pays $1.75 million for a majority stock interest in P. F. Collier & Son and becomes Crowell-Collier (see 1911; Collier, 1918). Competing with the *Saturday Evening Post*, Crowell will pour $15 million into the 5¢ magazine over the next 15 years before *Collier's* becomes profitable, but by 1950 it will have a circulation of 3.5 million (see 1925).

True Story magazine is started by New York physical culture enthusiast Bernarr Macfadden, now 51, who has been publishing *Physical Culture* magazine since 1898. *True Story* will reach a peak circulation of more than a million as it titillates readers with suggestive morality stories while Macfadden goes on to publish a host of movie, romance, and detective story magazines plus 10 daily newspapers including the *New York Evening Graphic*.

Vienna-born public relations pioneer Edward L. Bernays, 27, opens a New York publicity office in partnership with Doris E. Fleischman, also 27, whom he will soon marry. A nephew of psychoanalyst Sigmund Freud, Bernays was brought to New York as an infant, became a Broadway press agent before the war, and worked for the Committee of Public Information from 1917 until last year. He will teach the first course on public relations in 1923 at New York University (see tobacco, 1929).

Tennessee-born preacher's son Bruce (Fairchild) Barton, 33, opens a New York advertising agency that will grow to be one of the city's largest (see BBDO, 1928). Barton came to the city 7 years ago as assistant sales manager for P. F. Collier & Son, has managed publicity for the United War Work Campaign that raised funds to help the troops during the Great War, and has joined with other members of the campaign to open the shop; as copy chief and creative director, he will develop successful campaigns that will attract clients such as United States Steel, General Electric, General Mills, and General Motors.

Harcourt, Brace is founded at New York by former Henry Holt publishing-house editor Alfred Harcourt, 38, after a dispute with Holt over a manuscript that Harcourt has bought from English philosopher-mathematician Bertrand Russell. Helped by author and social reformer Joel E. Spingarn, Harcourt takes with him Holt's production chief Donald Brace and Holt's most promising novelist, Sinclair Lewis.

W. E. B. DuBois invites New Jersey-born Washington, D.C., schoolteacher Jessie Redmon Fauset, 35, to become literary editor of his magazine *The Crisis*. The first black woman to graduate from Cornell, she will publish works of her own in the magazine, plus works by such Harlem Renaissance writers as Countee Cullen, Langston Hughes, Claude McKay, George Schuyler, and Jean Toomer.

The Algonquin Round Table is founded in June at a luncheon given in honor of New Jersey-born *New York Times* theater critic Alexander Woollcott, 32, in the 17-year-old West 44th Street hotel. In the next 10 years manager Frank Case will attract a literary crowd whose members will on different occasions include playwrights Marc Connelly, Ben Hecht, George S. Kaufman, Charles MacArthur, and Robert Sherwood (who is initially a film critic), actor Alfred Lunt, journalists Heywood Broun and Franklin P. Adams, novelist-playwright Edna Ferber, wit and writer Dorothy Parker, *Vanity Fair* magazine editor Frank Crowninshield, humorists Robert Benchley and James Thurber, essayist-screenwriter Donald Ogden Stewart, and others whose various quips, malicious ripostes, and repartee will become legendary. (When challenged to use the word *horticulture* in a sentence, Parker will respond, "You can lead a horticulture but you can't make her think," but while Benchley will say, "I've got to get out of these wet clothes and into a dry martini" it is doubtful that he will say it at the Algonquin.)

Nonfiction: *Parnassus on Wheels* by Pennsylvania-born Doubleday, Page editor Christopher (Darlington) Morley, 29, is the odyssey of a horse-drawn library. Says Morley, "New York is Babylon; Brooklyn is the truly holy city. New York is the city of office work, and hustle: Brooklyn is the region of home and happiness . . . There is no hope for New Yorkers, for they glory in their skyscraping sins; but in Brooklyn there is the wisdom of the lowly."

Poetry: *In Nyu-york* by Galician-born New York Yiddish poet Moyshe-Leyb Halpern, 33.

 Theater: *Up in Mabel's Room* by Ohio-born playwright Wilson Collison, 26, and Otto Harbach 1/15 at the Eltinge Theater, with Hazel Dawn, Colorado-born ingénue Enid Markey, 22, 229 perfs.; *Augustus Does His Bit* by George Bernard Shaw 3/12 at the Guild Theater, with Norman Trevor, Herbert Druce, Merle Maddern, 111 perfs.; *The Fall and Rise of Susan Lenox* by George V. Hobart 6/9 at the 44th Street Theater, with Alma Tell, 27, Harry Southard, Perce

Benton; *Adam and Eva* by Guy Bolton and George Middleton 9/13 at the Longacre Theater, with Otto Kruger, Ruth Shepley, Berton Churchill, 312 perfs.; *The Gold Diggers* by Avery Hopwood 9/30 at the Lyceum Theater, with Ina Claire, Ruth Terry, 282 perfs.; *Clarence* by Indianapolis-born playwright Booth Tarkington, 50, 9/20 at the Hudson Theater, with Helen Hayes, Milwaukee-born actor Alfred Lunt, 27, Mary Boland, 306 perfs.; *The Girl in the Limousine* by Wilson Collison and Avery Hopwood 10/6 at the Eltinge 42nd Street Theater, with Doris Kenyon, Charles Ruggles, 137 perfs.; *Déclassée* by Zoë Akins 10/6 at the Empire Theater, with Ethel Barrymore, Hartford, Conn.-born actress Clare Eames, 23, 257 perfs.; *The Son-Daughter* by George Scarborough and David Belasco 11/19 at the Belasco Theater, with New Ulm, Minn.-born actress Lenore Ulric (originally Ulrich), 22, San Francisco-born actor John Willard, 33, 223 perfs.; *Aria Da Capo* by Maine-born poet-playwright Edna St. Vincent Millay, 27, 12/15 at the Provincetown Playhouse in Greenwich Village (Millay has moved with her mother and two sisters in January into a cheap tenement apartment at 449 West 19th Street, between Ninth and Tenth avenues, where she will remain until September of next year).

The Theatre Guild is organized by a group of directors, actors, and stage designers who have belonged to the recently disbanded Washington Square Players. Among them is New York-born set designer Lee Simonson, 31.

Hippodrome Theater builder and Coney Island amusement-park developer Fred Thompson dies at St. Vincent's Hospital June 6 at age 45 following surgery for appendicitis, gallstones, and a hernia. He is buried beside his mother on the edge of Woodlawn Cemetery; actor Edward Abeles dies at New York July 10 at age 49.

Actors' Equity Association goes on strike from August 7 to September 6, demanding recognition as the labor union of the acting profession (*see* 1913). The actors win a closed shop, an eight-performance week, and unpaid rehearsal time. Members of the 31-year-old Hebrew Actors Union pass out coffee and doughnuts to the strikers. Equity membership increases to upwards of 8,000 (14,000 by some accounts), and the 6-year-old union will obtain a 5-year contract with the Producing Managers' Association. By 1990 it will have more than 15,000 members in New York plus nearly 26,000 elsewhere in the country.

Loews Corp. is founded by New York-born vaudeville theater owner Marcus Loew, 49, and his

Russian-born partners Joseph and Nicholas Schenck, 40 and 37, respectively who own and operate Palisades Park in New Jersey. Loew has purchased a film production company called Metro Pictures Corp., and Loews will soon turn many of its theaters into movie houses (*see* M-G-M, 1924).

The Capitol movie theater opens on Times Square at the southwest corner of Broadway and 51st Street (*see* Rivoli, 1917). Designed by Thomas W. Lamb for Michigan-born lawyer Messmore Kendall, 46, and other prominent investors, its 5,320 seats have views unobstructed by columns. Wartime restrictions have forced its builders to use recycled structural beams, its interior includes apartments for Kendall and Major Edward J. Bowes (who owns some legitimate theaters), and reserved seats cost a steep $2.20 (*see* 1920).

Paramount-Famous Players-Lasky Corp. opens the first studio of a six-acre Astoria complex on 35th Avenue between 34th and 37th streets. About 110 of its 440 films will be produced in the Queens studios between now and 1927 (the rest will be made in Hollywood), using a stage 225 feet by 126 by 60 (*see* 1942).

The 3-year-old David Mannes Music School purchases three buildings in East 74th Street to house its expanding enrollment of students, whose teachers will soon include composer Ernest Bloch (*see* 1953).

The Choir School of St. Thomas Church is founded by the Rev. T. Tertius Noble with an endowment from Charles Steele. An organist and choirmaster at England's York Minster, Noble has accepted a similar position at St. Thomas on condition that a residential choir school be established. Boys aged 8 to 14 will study at the facility, and enrollment will rise to 41, including some men as well as youngsters whose soprano voices have changed (*see* 1989).

Opera impresario Oscar Hammerstein dies at New York August 1 at age 73. His grandson Oscar II, now 24, has attended Columbia University and will become famous as a Broadway librettist and lyricist.

Broadway musicals: *The Velvet Lady* 2/3 at the New Amsterdam Theater, with ingénue Fay Marbe, 20, Woonsocket, R.I.-born actor Eddie Dowling (originally Joseph Nelson Goucher), 29, Jed Prouty, music by Victor Herbert, lyrics by Henry Blossom, 136 perfs.; *The Royal Vagabond* 2/17 at the Cohan and Harris Theater, with English-born singer Winifred Harris, 38, dancer Dorothy Dickson, music by Anselm Goetzi, additional numbers by George M. Cohan, 208 perfs.; *The Whirl of Society* 3/5 at the

Winter Garden Theater, with Al Jolson, George White, Blossom Seeley (who runs up and down the aisles via a runway across the pit that also gives audiences a closer look at the chorus girls), music by Louis A. Hirsch, lyrics by Harold Atteridge, 136 perfs.; (George White's) *Scandals* 6/2 at the Liberty Theater, with White, "dimple-kneed" Ann Pennington (White has stolen her from Florenz Ziegfeld, who is irate), music by Richard Whiting, book and lyrics by White, Arthur Jackson, 128 perfs.; *The Ziegfeld Follies* 6/16 at the New Amsterdam Theater, with Marilyn Miller, Eddie Cantor, Bert Williams, Eddie Dowling, Van and Schenck, music and lyrics by Irving Berlin, Dave Stamper, Gene Buck, songs that include "A Pretty Girl Is Like a Melody" by Berlin, whose song will be the *Follies* theme, 171 perfs.; *The Ziegfeld Midnight Frolic* 10/2 at the New Amsterdam Roof, with Fanny Brice, Ohioborn clarinetist, bandleader, and comedian Ted Lewis (Theodore Leopold Friedman), 27, Will Rogers, W. C. Fields, Chic Sale, music and lyrics chiefly by Dave Stamper and Gene Buck, songs that include "Rose of Washington Square" by James F. Hanley, lyrics by Ballard MacDonald; *Apple Blossoms* 10/7 at the Globe Theater, with Fred and Adele Astaire, music by Austrian-born violinist Fritz Kreisler, 44, and Hungarian-born composer Victor Jacobi, 28, book and lyrics by William Le Baron, songs that include "I'm in Love," "Who Can Tell," 259 perfs.; *The Passing Show* 10/23 at the Winter Garden Theater, with Charles Winninger, James Barton, Reginald Denny, music chiefly by Sigmund Romberg, lyrics chiefly by Harold Atteridge, 280 perfs.; *Buddies* 10/27 at the Selwyn Theater, with Peggy Wood, Roland Young, book by George V. Hobart, music and lyrics by B. C. Hilliam, 256 perfs.; *The Magic Melody* 11/11 at the Shubert Theater, with Bertee Beaumont, 30, Fay Marbe, music by Sigmund Romberg, book and lyrics by Frederic Arnold Krummer, 143 perfs.; *Irene* 11/18 at the Vanderbilt Theater, with Edith Day, music by Harry Tierney, lyrics by Joseph McCarthy, songs that include "In My Sweet Little Alice Blue Gown," 670 perfs.

Composer-writer-lyricist Henry Blossom dies at New York March 23 at age 51 (approximate).

Popular song: "Swanee" by George Gershwin, lyrics by Irving Caesar (who will later say that he and Gershwin were lunching at Dinty Moore's restaurant when he suggested they write a one-step in the style of the popular song "Hindustani" but with an American locale such as that in the 1851 Stephen Foster song "Old Folks at Home." Gershwin agreed, they boarded a bus for the Gershwin family home in

Washington Heights, and by the time they arrived the song was written). Introduced at the Capitol Theater with 60 chorus girls wearing electric light bulbs attached to their slippers, the song receives a tepid reception, but Al Jolson will introduce it early next year in a Sunday night concert at the Winter Garden Theater, insert it into his hit Broadway musical *Sinbad*, record it, and make it a hit.

Irving Berlin incorporates the Irving Berlin Music Corp. and will hereafter publish his own works, which have been producing enormous royalties.

Jazz pioneer James Reese Europe dies at Boston May 14 at age 38 when a deranged drummer slits his jugular vein with a penknife while Reese is preparing for a show at Mechanics Hall.

Roseland Ballroom opens December 31 at 1658 Broadway (51st Street), where it will remain (one flight up) until 1956, when it will move to 239 West 52nd Street. Proprietor Louis J. Brecker, 21, opened a Philadelphia Roseland 3 years ago while attending the Wharton School and has moved to New York to escape Philadelphia's blue laws.

The Steuben Society is founded by New Yorkers of German descent to improve German-American relations in the wake of the Great War. Its name honors the Prussian military hero Baron Friedrich Wilhelm von Steuben, who helped Gen. Washington train Continental Army troops in the American Revolution (*see* parade, 1958).

Hattie Carnegie, Inc. is incorporated by designer Carnegie, who has dissolved her partnership and begun making trips to Paris (*see* 1909). She brings back sample fashions, redesigning them to satisfy American tastes, and in 10 years will have annual sales of $3.5 million (*see* 1942).

Beauty cream millionairess Mme. C. J. Walker dies at her suburban Irvington villa May 25 at age 51. Her daughter A'lelia Walker, 34, takes over the business and will be the richest woman in Harlem, sponsoring grand functions for actors, musicians, and writers at her 80 Edgecombe Avenue home on Sugar Hill and at her Westchester villa.

Gov. Smith appoints Elmira-born prison reformer Lewis E. (Edward) Lawes, 35, warden of the 92-year-old state correctional facility at Sing Sing. Lawes has been superintendent of the New York City Reformatory and will remain at Sing Sing for 21 years, opposing capital punishment while advancing his ideas that prisons should try to rehabilitate inmates.

Prohibition of alcoholic beverage sales provides new opportunities for the city's criminal class; gambler Arnold Rothstein, 37, starts a Manhattan trucking company as a cover for bootlegging operations, hires men who include Meyer Lansky and New York-born gangster Benjamin Hyman "Bugsy" Siegel, loads his trucks with beer and hard liquor, runs them day and night, and makes a fortune. Rothstein has fixed the World Series by bribing Chicago White Sox players to throw games to the Cincinnati Reds.

Police arrest Lower East Side-born burglar Dutch Schultz (Arthur Simon Flegenheimer), 17, December 12 for burglarizing a Bronx apartment; sent to Blackwell's Island, he will soon gain release, involve himself in the illicit beer trade, and wipe out rivals to make himself beer baron of the Bronx.

An apartment house begun in 1916 is completed at 2 West 67th Street with about 24 double-height studios and many regular flats. Designed by Rich & Mathesius, the building is the seventh in a series of structures put up in West 67th Street since 1902 by a group headed by painter-illustrator Penrhyn Stanlaws. They sell half the 2 West 67th Street units at prices ranging from $5,000 to $30,000 and rent the other half, thus producing enough revenue to pay all costs (owners of the co-op apartments, whose ceilings can be 19 feet in height, pay no maintenance fees). Only two of the initial tenants are artists.

Wartime demand for structural steel delayed completion of many New York buildings, but the end of hostilities in Europe has brought a resumption in building.

The 33-story Commodore Hotel opens beside Grand Central Terminal January 28 with 2,000 rooms. Designed by Warren & Wetmore and built by John McEntee Bowman of 1914 Biltmore fame, it occupies a site formerly used by the Hospital for Ruptured and Crippled, purchased by the New York Central in 1911 as part of its program to acquire property in the neighborhood of its new terminal, giving hotel guests easy access; the hotel's name commemmorates that of the late New York Central Railroad magnate Cornelius Vanderbilt (*see* 1958).

The 20-story Hotel Pennsylvania opens at 401 Seventh Avenue, between 32nd and 33rd streets. Designed by McKim, Mead & White, the new hostelry faces the 8-year-old Pennsylvania Station and is the largest in the world, with 2,200 rooms and 1.5 million square feet of floor space, including 70,000 square feet of banquet and ballroom space. E. M. Statler, now 58, has built the hotel with funds supplied by the Pennsylvania Railroad.

A monument to the late architect John M. Carrère is unveiled October 16 on Riverside Drive at 98th Street (see Public Library, 1911). Designed by Carrère's partner Thomas Hastings, the exedra of pink granite has a stairway of the same material that leads down to the park below.

New York-born expatriate landowner William Waldorf Astor, 1st Viscount Astor, dies of heart disease at his home in Brighton, England, October 18 at age 71, having established residence abroad in 1892 and become a British subject in 1899 (the United States, he said, was no place for a gentleman to live). His New York real estate holdings alone are worth $60 million (he transferred ownership in 1916 to his sons Waldorf and John Jacob in order to avoid paying British taxes on the property); architect Francis H. Kimball dies at New York December 25 at age 74, remembered by some as the "father of New York skyscrapers."

The United States Weather Bureau installs meterological equipment in Central Park's 50-year-old Belvedere Castle to record temperatures.

An 18th amendment to the Constitution prohibiting the sale, transportation, importation, and exportation of intoxicating beverages is proclaimed January 16 to take effect January 16, 1920; a War Prohibition Act passed last year goes into effect at the end of June to continue resistance until demobilization. The Prohibition Enforcement Act (Volstead Act) drafted by Minnesota congressman Andrew J. Volstead and passed over President Wilson's veto October 28 defines as "intoxicating" any beverage containing 0.5 percent alcohol or more but makes a few exceptions, such as wine for sacramental purposes (see 1920).

The 3-year-old F. & M. Schaefer Brewing Co. plant in Brooklyn converts its facilities to producing "near beer." It will also manufacture dyes and artificial ice until the Prohibition law is repealed in 1933. Other New York breweries will find similar ways to survive or will go out of business.

Louis Sherry's restaurant closes May 17 after 21 years on Fifth Avenue (see 1921).

The city's first Longchamps restaurant opens, taking its name from the racetrack in Paris's Bois de Boulogne; by the 1950s there will be 10 Manhattan Longchamps, most of them in midtown, serving specialties such as oxtail soup, crabmeat à la Dewey, Nesselrode pie, baked apple, and "21 percent butterfat" ice cream (see Riese brothers, 1973).

Ellis Island is returned to the U.S. Immigration Service in July (see 1918). The service is soon ready to receive what is expected to be a torrent of immigrants from the shambles that the Great War has left Europe; it quickly finds that the island is being used to detain suspected communists and anarchists who are being deported (see 1920).

1920 British reinforcements arrive in Ireland May 15 to support His Majesty's forces against attacks by Sinn Fein political militants, who have received financial assistance by New York's more affluent Irish population to continue resistance to British regulars and to the new "Black and Tans"—Royal Irish Constabulary recruits, whose khaki tunics and trousers and dark green caps are almost black. Irish New Yorkers wil continue to fund the resistance.

Democrats nominate former assistant Navy secretary Franklin D. Roosevelt of New York to run for vice president on a ticket headed by Ohio's governor James M. Cox, 50, but Republicans nominate Sen. Warren Gamaliel Harding, 54, of Ohio and Harding wins 404 electoral votes to 127 for the Cox-Roosevelt ticket.

Gov. Smith loses his bid for reelection. Republican challenger Nathan L. Miller, 52, wins 1,261,812 votes to Smith's 1,235,878, but Smith runs far ahead of the Democratic ticket and will regain the governorship in 1922.

The American Civil Liberties Union is founded by social reformers who include former War Labor Policies Board chairman Felix Frankfurter, now 37; New York lawyer Arthur Garfield Hays, 38; and Ohio-born New York Socialist Norman (Mattoon) Thomas, 35, a former clergyman who will staunchly oppose both communism and fascism but advocate such radical ideas as low-cost public housing, a 5-day work week, minimum wage laws, and the abolition of child labor (Congress will ultimately legislate them all). Thomas will be a quadrennial Socialist Party candidate for president from 1928 through 1948. FBI agents soon infiltrate the ACLU.

The first Universal Negro Improvement Association international convention opens at Madison Square Garden in August with some 25,000 delegates from 25 nations (see 1916). Marcus Garvey opens offices at Liberty Hall in Harlem, having founded UNIA branches in nearly every U.S. city with a sizeable black population; he begins to exalt African beauty and promote a "back to Africa" movement with a plan for resettlement in Liberia. Within a few years his UNIA will have branches in nearly 40 states and in more than 40 countries worldwide, with as many as 11 million members by some estimates (see 1924).

Woman suffrage is proclaimed in effect August 26 following Tennessee's ratification of the 19th amendment to the Constitution.

The Amalgamated Clothing Workers of America begins a 6-month strike in December against sweat-shops and nonunion shops. Now 100,000 strong, the union workers find themselves locked out by New York, Boston, and Baltimore clothing manufacturers who charge the union leadership with "Sovietism" and demand a return to piecework pay. The manufacturers will lose an estimated $10 million before the strike ends in June of next year, the workers will accept a 15 percent wage cut while promising to increase productivity by 15 percent, but clothing makers will agree to a union shop and a continuation of the 44-hour week (see 1937).

$ Chemical Bank acquires Citizens National Bank (see 1888). It will open its first branch office in 1923 on Fifth Avenue at 29th Street (see 1929).

Anarchist Thomas W. Simpson sets out to assassinate banker J. P. Morgan, Jr. April 18 during services at St. George's Church in Stuyvesant Square, where Morgan has been a vestryman, but he shoots the wrong man (Morgan family physician James Markoe), who is rushed around the corner to the Lying-in Hospital on Second Avenue at 17th Street, donated by Morgan's father to the city in 1902 at Markoe's urging. Physicians are unable to save the doctor's life.

Banker (and former New York governor and U.S. vice president) Levi P. Morton dies at Rhinebeck May 16 on his 96th birthday; investment banker-philanthropist Jacob Schiff of Kuhn, Loeb & Co. dies at New York September 25 at age 73.

A bomb explosion September 16 scars the J. P. Morgan bank building, kills 35, injures 130, and causes between $2 million and $3 million in property damage. A brown wagon covered with canvas and pulled by an old bay horse stops at the corner of Wall and Nassau streets, the driver walks away, the clock on Trinity Church finishes striking the noon hour, and the horse and wagon disappear in a blast that sends iron fragments flying through the air and starts fires. Windowpanes are knocked out for 10 blocks around; clerks in offices as high as the sixth floor suffer severe burns; pedestrians hit by metal shards suffer crushed skulls, smashed legs, and gashed arms, and the dead include millionaire Edward Sweet, who once owned Sweet's restaurant at Fulton

and South streets. The perpetrators will never be discovered.

Wall Street's Dow Jones Industrial Average plummets to 43.12 November 19, rebounds to 74.63 the next day, and closes December 31 at 71.95, down from 107.23 at the end of 1919 amidst concerns about labor unrest.

Ⓢ Former A. T. Stewart & Co. coat buyer Frieda Loehmann (née Muller), 47, and her son Charles invest $800 to open a specialty shop in her Brooklyn home. They soon open a shop on Bedford Avenue but will have little success until they make it a discount store. Loehmann pays cash to buy overstocked dresses at a fraction of their wholesale prices from garment makers in Manhattan's cash-short Seventh Avenue, resells them in season, passing the savings on to her customers, will shift entirely to discounting in 1922, and will shop for bargains until 2 weeks before her death in 1962, and by that time Loehmann's will have annual sales of $3 million. (Son Charles will open a Bronx store in 1930 that will develop into a 13-state chain of 34 stores, each with plain pipe racks, open areas with mirrors that will evolve into communal dressing rooms, and a cash only, no-returns policy; see 1996).

⚡ The city tries making Park Avenue one-way northbound and Fifth Avenue one-way southbound from 10 o'clock in the morning until 5 in the afternoon (see 1919). Police predict that a vehicle will be able to travel from 57th Street to 34th in less than 10 minutes instead of the 40 sometimes required, but the experiment begun in mid-February is abandoned after a month. The Fifth Avenue Association petitions Mayor Hylan to accept its plan for permanent relief; the plan provides for an easterly roadway to take northbound traffic around Grand Central Terminal into 45th Street at Depew Place, leaving the existing, westerly viaduct a one-way road for southbound traffic (see 1921).

The IRT's elevated railway line reaches Gun Hill Road and White Plains Road in the Bronx via Webster Avenue (see 1918). The new line north of 149th Street will continue to operate until April 1973.

Former New York Central railroad chairman William Kissam Vanderbilt dies at Paris July 22 at age 70.

∞ The Catholic Charities launches its first fundraising drive May 1 at the instigation of Archbishop Hayes (see 1919; 1924).

The New York Korean Church is founded by members of the city's tiny Korean population, many of them Protestants.

Former school superintendent William H. Maxwell dies at New York May 3 at age 68, having made merit rather than political connections the basis for teacher appointments and promotions. When he fell ill in 1917 the city charter was amended to permit his retirement with full pay.

Miss Nightingale's School opens with 50 girls in an East 92nd Street brownstone (see 1906). Frances Nightingale was joined last year by university-educated Northern Irish teacher Maya Bamford, who came to the United States during the Great War and has taught at the Bryn Mawr School in Baltimore, and their school now includes a high school (see 1929).

The Hewitt School has its beginnings in Miss Hewitt's Classes, begun with one class on the top floor of John Shillito Rogers's 2-year-old East 79th Street town house by English-born actress manqué and former Tuxedo Park tutor Caroline Danella Hewitt, 48, who is backed by loans from members of the Astor, Biddle, Harriman, Pulitzer, Vanderbilt, and Whitney families who will soon be repaid with interest. "Miss Hew" will move, first, to the David Mannes Music School in East 74th Street, then—as the school grows—to 68 East 79th Street, and will acquire 72 and 74 East 79th until she has classes from kindergarten through 12th grade. The school will move in 1951 to two spacious brownstones at 45 East 75th Street, "Miss Hew" will die in the summer of 1961 at age 89, and her school will grow to have 325 girls, aged 5 to 18, from all neighborhoods of the city (see 2001).

Publisher Frank A. Munsey agrees January 4 to pay $4 million for the New York Herald, its Paris edition, and the Evening Telegram (see 1918). Now 66, Munsey has been buying up newspapers on speculation and effects a merger of the Sun that he bought 4 years ago with the Herald, calls his paper the Sun and New York Herald for a while, and makes the Evening Sun simply the Sun, a name that will survive until 1950 (see 1924).

The Staats Herold Corp. is organized to publish a German-language evening paper under the name New Yorker Herold (see Ridder, 1901; 1915). The new company will put up a building at 22 North William Street, publishing also the illustrated weekly Deutsch-American and—most successfully—the (Sunday) Sonntagsblatt Staats-Zeitung & Herold, whose circulation will soon exceed 100,000.

"Winnie Winkle the Breadwinner" by cartoonist Martin Michael Branner, 31, begins in September in the 15-month-old New York Daily News.

Dell Publishing Co. is founded by Brooklyn-born publisher George T. (Thomas) Delacorte, Jr., 26, and former New York World Sunday editor William A. Johnston, who initially publish 10¢ pamphlets offering horoscopes. New Fiction Publishing Co. put Delacorte in charge of promoting circulation 7 years ago, he gave newsstand owners cigars to have them give the company's publications prominent placement, New Fiction has fired him for failing to predict and provide for an economic recession, but it has given him $15,000 to compensate for the time remaining on his contract. His partner will die after Dell's first year, and Delacorte's magazine Sweetheart Stories will gain a wide circulation among low-brow readers. In 10 years Dell will be publishing 14 magazines, most of them pulp, confession, and movie-fan periodicals that will include Modern Screen and Modern Romances, and by 1945 Delacorte will have upwards of 200 magazines, including comic books (see Delacorte Press, 1921).

Fiction: This Side of Paradise by Minnesota-born New York advertising agency copywriter F. (Francis) Scott (Key) Fitzgerald, 23, who came to the city last year and took a run-down apartment at 200 Claremont Avenue. He relocated February 11 to a room at the new Allerton Hotel in 39th Street, but the success of his novel, published in March, gives him the wherewithal to marry Alabama-born writer Zelda Sayre, 20, in the rectory of St. Patrick's Cathedral and move with her in May into the 6-year-old Biltmore Hotel; The Age of Innocence by Edith Wharton; Hungry Hearts (stories) by Polish-born New York writer Anzia Yezierska, 35, who arrived in the city in 1901 at age 16, lived with her family in a Lower East Side tenement, found work as a servant, got jobs in a sweatshop and factory, learned English at night school, and has taken courses at Columbia; Tutt and Mr. Tutt by Arthur Train.

Novelist-critic-editor William Dean Howells dies at New York May 10 at age 83.

Poetry: A Few Figs from Thistles by Edna St. Vincent Millay: "My candle burns at both ends;/ It will not last the night;/ But, ah, my foes, and, oh, my friends—/ It gives a lovely light." Millay moves in September to a large room at 77 West 12th Street, corner of Sixth Avenue, but will live there only until January of next year, when she will leave for Europe; Sunup by Lola Ridge; Advice by Maxwell Bodenheim; Spring in New Hampshire, and Other Poems by Jamaica, BWI-born poet Claude (originally Festus Claudius)

McKay, 30, who came to New York 6 years ago, left last year for Europe, but will return briefly in 1921. His poem "Harlem Shadows" uses the plight of black prostitutes to symbolize the degradation of his entire race in the urban environment.

The Gotham Book Mart opens in a brownstone at 41 West 47th Street, between Fifth and Sixth avenues and soon has customers that include Charles Chaplin, Eugene O'Neill, George and Ira Gershwin, and Ina Claire. Saratoga Springs-born proprietor (Ida) Frances "Fanny" Steloff, 32, never got beyond seventh grade in school, came to New York at age 19 and got a job selling corsets at Loeser's department store in Brooklyn before being transferred to the book department in the Christmas rush and going on to work for a series of bookstores (*see Ulysses*, 1933).

 The Société Anonyme is founded by Marcel Duchamp, Brooklyn-born reformer and arts patron Katherine S. Dreier, now 42, and Philadelphia-born Dadaist photographer-painter-sculptor Man Ray (originally Emmanuel Radinski), 30, who will open the city's first modern art museum (*see* MOMA, 1929).

Painting: *Elsie de Wolfe* and *Miss Natalie Barney*, *"L'Amazone"* by Romare Bearden.

Sculpture: a bronze statue of Minerva is completed as part of the Altar to Liberty erected at the top of Battle Hill in Brooklyn's Green-Wood Cemetery. Designed by Frederick W. Ruckstull, it has been financed by India-ink inventor Charles M. Higgins and erected to commemorate the Battle of Long Island.

 Theater: *Beyond the Horizon* by Eugene O'Neill 2/2 at the Morosco Theater, with Richard Bennett in O'Neill's first full-length play, 111 perfs.; *The Bat* by Mary Roberts Rinehart and Avery Hopwood 8/23 at the Morosco Theater, with Effie Ellsler in a dramatization of Rinehart's 1908 novel *The Circular Staircase*, 867 perfs.; *Little Old New York* by Rida Johnson Young 9/8 at the Plymouth Theater, with Frank Charlton as Washington Irving, Douglas J. Ward as 1810 ferry-boat operator Cornelius van Derbilt, Albert Anders as John Jacob Astor, Wiliam J. McClure as Peter Delmonico, John Randall as Fitz Green Halleck, 308 perfs.; *Ladies Night* by Avery Hopwood and Charlton Andrews 8/9 at the Eltinge 42nd Street Theater, with Canadian-born actress Mrs. Stuart Robson (*née* May Waldron), Charles Ruggles, 360 perfs.; the Times Square Theater opens 9/30 at 219 West 42nd Street; *The First Year* by Frank Craven 10/20 at the Little Theater, with Craven, 760 perfs.; *The Emperor Jones* by Eugene

O'Neill 11/1 at the Provincetown Playhouse in Greenwich Village, with Richmond, Va.-born actor Charles S. Gilpin, 42, as the Pullman porter who becomes dictator of a tropical island and disintegrates morally (vaudevillian Gilpin has been working as an elevator operator at Macy's, he will be received at the White House and be awarded the NAACP's Spingarn Medal for his performance, O'Neill's play is the first to star a black in an all-white theater, and it moves uptown 12/27), 204 perfs.; *Just Suppose* by A. E. Thomas 11/1 at Henry Miller's Theater, with Patricia Collinge, London-born actor Leslie Howard (originally Stainer), 27, 88 perfs.; *Heartbreak House* by George Bernard Shaw 11/10 at the Garrick Theater, with Helen Westley, Dublin-born actor Dudley Digges, 41, 125 perfs.; *Miss Lulu Bett* by Zona Gale 12/27 at the Biltmore Theater, with Carroll McComas as the abused spinster who rebels against her dense brother-in-law, Richmond, Va.-born actress Catherine Calhoun Doucet, 45 (Gale rewrites the last act after a week to give the play a happy ending and wits say it should now be called *Miss Lulu Better*), 178 perfs.

Actor James O'Neill, father of the playwright, dies at New London, Conn., August 10 at age 70.

The Loews State movie theater opens on Times Square at the northeast corner of Broadway and 45th Street. Designed by Thomas Lamb, it has a 16-story office tower above its ornate lobby (the auditorium, farther down the block, extends to 46th Street).

Goldwyn Pictures takes over the Capitol movie theater that opened on Times Square last year and makes S. L. "Roxy" Rothafel manager; he abandons the reserved-seat policy, charges a top price of $1, and introduces stage presentations (ballet, opera, instrumental soloists, and the like) to supplement the Goldwyn film shows.

The Juilliard Foundation is established with a $20 million bequest left by the late capitalist Augustus D. Juilliard, who stipulated in his will that income from the legacy be used to further music in America. The Juilliard Graduate School will be founded in 1924, the foundation's trustees 2 years later will take over the Institute of Musical Art opened in 1905, and in 1946 the two schools will be combined under the name Juilliard School of Music.

Broadway musicals: (George White's) *Scandals* 6/7 at the 10-year-old Globe Theater with Ann Pennington, San Francisco-born comic Lou Holtz, 22, music by George Gershwin, lyrics by Arthur Jackson, 134 perfs.; *The Ziegfeld Follies* 6/22 at the New Amsterdam Theater with Fanny Brice, W. C. Fields,

Moran and Mack, Van and Schenck, music and lyrics by Irving Berlin, Victor Herbert, Joseph McCarthy, Harry Tierney, Gene Buck, and others, 123 perfs. (Brice's husband, gambler Nicky Arnstein, has been charged with stealing $5 million in securities and passing bad checks and Brice has made headlines in February by refusing to turn him over to authorities unless he is given immunity from questioning and released on $50,000 bail); *The Greenwich Village Follies* (revue) 8/30 at the Greenwich Village Theater, with Boston-born female impersonator Bert Savoy (originally Everett McKenzie), 32, music by A. Baldwin Sloane, lyrics by St. John's, Newfoundland-born writer-producer John Murray Anderson, 33, 192 perfs.; *Hitchy-Koo* 10/19 at the New Amsterdam Theater, with Raymond Hitchcock, Slabtown, Tenn.-born soprano Grace Moore, 18, music by Jerome Kern, lyrics by Glen MacDonough and Anne Caldwell, 71 perfs.; *Sally* 12/21 at the New Amsterdam Theater with Marilyn Miller (who receives 10 percent of the gross), Leon Errol, music by Jerome Kern, lyrics by New York-born songwriter B. G. "Buddy" DeSylva (originally George Gard DeSylva), 25, songs that include "Look for the Silver Lining," 570 perfs.; *The Passing Show* 12/29 at the Winter Garden Theater, with Eugene and Willie Howard, Marie Dressler, Janet Adair, music by Jean Schwartz, lyrics by Harold Atteridge, songs that include "In Little Old New York," 200 perfs.

Georgia-born jazz pianist (James) Fletcher Henderson, 23, arrives at New York with the idea of going to graduate school but begins playing piano on a Hudson riverboat and gets a job as song plugger for a sheet-music company; he will organize a band under his own name in 1924.

Denver-born jazz conductor Paul Whiteman, 28, opens the Palais Royale on Broadway with a style that will be hailed as the start of the Jazz Age. He organizes bands to play in clubs nationwide, and by the time he gives the first formal jazz concert at New York's Aeolian Hall in 1924 there will more than 50 Paul Whiteman orchestras.

Babe Ruth signs with the New York Yankees January 3 to begin a 14-year career as "Sultan of Swat" for New York. Yankee co-owner Col. Jacob Ruppert has acquired Baltimore-born Boston Red Sox pitcher George Herman Ruth, 24, for $100,000 plus a personal loan of $300,000 to Red Sox owner (and Broadway show backer) Harry Frazee, his new left-hander sets a slugging average record of .847 in his first season with New York, hitting 54 home runs (homers will become more common in the next decade as baseball owners introduce a harder, livelier

ball), batting .376, scoring 158 runs, and making the Yankees the first team in any sport to draw more than a million spectators, nearly double the team's 1919 gate. Kentucky-born Cleveland Indians shortstop Ray Chapman dies at Caledonian Hospital August 16 at age 29 after being hit by fastball thrown by Yankee right-hander Carl Mays (he will remain the only player ever killed in a major-league game). The Giants tell the Yankees at the end of the season that they will have to move out of the Polo Grounds, and Col. Ruppert closes a deal with the Astor estate to acquire some property across the river in the Bronx for construction of a new ballpark (he will buy out Tillinghast l'Hommidieu Houston for $1.2 million in 1922 and become sole owner; *see* Yankee Stadium, 1923).

The Brooklyn Dodgers win the National League pennant but lose the World Series to the Cleveland Indians, who win 5 games to 2 in the last Series that will require 5 victories.

The Walker Law enacted by the state legislature at Albany is the first significant U.S. legislation related to boxing. Sponsored by senate speaker James J. Walker, it legalizes professional boxing in the state and establishes the New York State Athletic Commission, which will remain independent of other boxing commissions. Its code of rules has been written for the most part by English-born promoter William Gavin, and the new law will serve as the basis for similar laws in other states.

The ratio of domestic servants to the city's general population is half what it was in 1890. Middle-class women employ mostly day workers, who tend to be blacks rather than immigrants or native-born whites and who return to their own families at night; only relatively affluent households can afford live-in help. Architects design middle-class houses and apartments with "servant-less" kitchens in response to decreased employment of domestic help.

The state legislature at Albany enacts a real estate tax-abatement law that will stimulate construction of more than $1 billion worth of housing in New York City alone. Gov. Smith has warned that the state has a serious housing shortage (as does Britain, most of Europe, and much of America). The state legislature establishes rent regulations in April to prevent landlords from taking advantage of housing shortages (war priorities brought new housing construction virtually to a standstill). What a landlord may charge is based on how much he can fairly earn on his property; the new law bars excess profits, and there is means testing of landlords to guide the courts in deciding how much a landlord may raise rents (*see* Rosenman Act, 1923).

A five-story neo-Georgian (or neo-Federal) red-brick town house is completed at 603 Park Avenue, northeast corner 64th Street, for sugar wholesaler Thomas A. Howell and his wife, Emilia (the Howells will sell it in 1923 to retired coal-mining magnate James W. Ellsworth, he will die of pneumonia in 1925, and his explorer son Lincoln will inherit the place). Designed by Lund & Gayler (Walter Lund, Julius F. Gayler) and built at a cost of $65,000, the house is only 20 feet deep but extends 100 feet along Park Avenue. Its interior rooms cluster about a skylit stone staircase.

An English Renaissance limestone palace is completed on the west side of Park Avenue at 68th Street for Standard Oil heir Harold I. Pratt, youngest son of the late Brooklyn kerosene magnate and Standard Oil stockholder Charles Pratt, whose other three sons have built houses on Brooklyn's Clinton Avenue. Designed by Delano & Aldrich, the mansion will later house the Council on Foreign Relations (*see* politics, 1921).

A co-operative apartment house opens at 4 East 66th Street and 845 Fifth Avenue to designs by J. E. R. Carpenter. Built by William Henry Barnum, it has one apartment per floor, each with 18 rooms—including six bedrooms and two large rooms overlooking Central Park for entertaining.

Apartment houses go up along Brooklyn's Ocean Avenue as far south as King's Highway in Flatbush as the new Brighton Beach subway line makes the area accessible to New York commuters.

Manhattan's Dante Park opens between Broadway and Columbus Avenue from 63rd to 64th streets with a statue of the Italian poet by Ettore Ximines (the neighborhood has a large Italian population).

National Prohibition of sales of alcoholic beverages goes into effect at midnight January 16 (*see* 1919). Col. Jacob Ruppert has increased the capacity of his brewery to 1.3 million barrels per year, up from 350,000 in 1890, but will not produce any more beer until 1933. New York bars, cafés, saloons, restaurants, and nightclubs stop serving liquor, but only after a few have sent out black-bordered invitations to "Last rites and ceremonies attending the departure of our spirited friend, John Barleycorn." Bartenders at some such establishments dress as pallbearers and carry coffins. Consumption of alcoholic beverages will continue in the city through illegal sales of bootleg beer and distilled spirits, legally permissible home-brewed wine, and home-

made "bathtub gin," but fewer people will imbibe such beverages even though the number of places where liquor can be purchased will more than double, from 15,000 legal spots to 32,000 illegal ones.

New York hotels begin in many instances to convert their bars into soda fountains and lunch counters, with soda jerks replacing bartenders, in order to comply with Prohibition rules.

The advent of Prohibition brings an end to the "free lunch" that has been a fixture at virtually every city bar and saloon (most did not give it away free but generally offered it at a nominal price of a nickel or so while charging 30¢ for a five-course businessman's lunch). The free luncheon buffet at Delmonico's has included hard-boiled eggs with caviar, half a lobster, cold cuts, lobster aspic, pickled walnuts, hot roast beef, and Kentucky hams. Other fashionable restaurants have had similar spreads. Prohibition will force the closing of such gastronomic palaces as Shanley's on the west side of Broadway (it will be replaced by the Paramount Building).

Lundy's seafood restaurant and clam bar opens at the corner of Ocean and Emmons avenues in Sheepshead Bay, Brooklyn. Restaurateur (Frederick William) Irving Lundy will expand into a two-story stucco building, his 220 waiters will serve up to 5,000 patrons per day, and he will continue to operate the place until it closes in 1979 (it will reopen in 1996).

New York's population reaches 5,620,048, up from 4,766,883 in 1910, but the growth has been entirely in the outer boroughs (Manhattan's population has actually decreased).

Ellis Island receives 225,206 immigrants, up from 26,731 last year, as deportations of suspected anarchists and communists drop off in response to protests from church, social, and legal groups. Inspectors scrutinize eyes of arrivals for signs of trachoma and examine hair for lice, medical devices probe for evidence of tuberculosis, heart disease, and nervous disorders, and anyone suspected of ill health has the back of his or her coat chalked with white letters indicating a need for further examination and possible deportation. Destitute arrivals (those without at least $10 in foreign coins or currency) are also subject to deportation (*see* 1921).

1921 The Council on Foreign Relations is founded at New York to offer advice on the direction of U.S. foreign policy. A group of elite bankers and lawyers who accompanied President Wilson to Versailles 2 years ago has received an endowment from John D. Rockefeller, Jr. to start the Council, whose trustees will obtain the Pratt mansion completed last year on Park Avenue to use as its headquarters.

Mayor Hylan wins easy reelection, defeating Republican candidate Henry H. Curran and Socialist candidate Jacob Panken. The mayor's abilities command little respect but he has the support of publisher William Randolph Hearst and receives 750,247 votes to Curran's 332,846 and Panken's 82,607. Irish-born state assemblyman Edward J. (Joseph) Flynn, 30, has had his supporters organize the Pondiac Democratic Club (the registrar misspelled Pontiac when the club was registered), with offices at 809 Westchester Avenue. Headed by Albert Cohn with a dues-paying membership that is largely Irish and Jewish, the club has produced a huge voter turnout and succeeded in having its man elected sheriff, defeating district leader Patrick Kane (*see* 1932).

The Jewish Board of Guardians is founded April 23 to combat juvenile delinquency. The board represents a merger of the 28-year-old Jewish Prisoners Aid Society, the 19-year-old Jewish Protectory and Aid, the 14-year-old Jewish Big Brothers, and the 8-year-old Jewish Big Sisters.

The Heckscher Foundation for Children is founded by developer and philanthropist August Heckscher, now 73, who has become concerned for the welfare of delinquent, homeless, and neglected children. The foundation constructs a five-story building on upper Fifth Avenue to serve as a neighborhood center for the 47-year-old New York Society for the Prevention of Cruelty to Children; built at a cost of $4 million (the largest charitable contribution to benefit children thus far in the city's history), it contains dormitories for several hundred children committed by the courts to the SPCC, a large indoor swimming pool, and an 800-seat theater.

Blackwell's Island in the East River is renamed Welfare Island and will remain such until 1971, when it will become Roosevelt Island.

An economic recession hits New York business firms.

The New York Curb Exchange moves into a new building of its own in Trinity Place; members have for decades transacted business in all kinds of weather by signaling from curbstone street positions to clerks located in windows of surrounding buildings (*see* American Stock Exchange, 1953).

Dillon Read adopts that name (*see* 1905). Texas-born financier Clarence Dillon, 37, has adopted his mother's maiden name (his father, Samuel Lapowski, came to Texas from Poland after the Civil War and sent Clarence to Harvard). Dillon has been a leading partner in Read & Co., now at 28 Nassau Street (*see* 1997).

Wall Street's Dow Jones Industrial Average closes December 31 at 81.10, up from 71.95 at the end of 1920.

The Port of New York Authority is created April 30 by New York State and New Jersey to prevent mutually ruinous competition between the two states and enable them to work on a cooperative basis. Eugenius H. Outerbridge, now 61, has campaigned for years to have the waterways of the metropolitan area treated as a single entity rather than in piecemeal fashion; the Port Authority will administer marine terminals, tunnels, bridges, and other facilities that will include airports, helicopter pads, rail and bus terminals, and office buildings (*see* Bridge and Tunnel Commission, 1930; bus terminal, 1950; World Trade Center, 1972).

The city's elevated railway volume peaks at 374.3 million revenue passengers (*see* 1905; 1938).

Mayor Hylan owes his reelection in part to his championing of the city's 5¢ transit fare, having called it a "property right" of the people, but prices of steel, coal, brake shoes, and the like have soared since 1916, the subways and Els receive no municipal subsidies, and they maintain the 5¢ fare only by deferring maintenance, keeping wages low, and installing labor-saving devices (e.g., turnstiles and automatic door openers).

City engineers propose extending the east and west viaducts around Grand Central Terminal to 45th Street and having them converge at 45th and Park Avenue (*see* 1920). New York Central engineers counter with a proposal that Park Avenue be closed to all vehicular traffic at the 45th Street grade, and that new roadways be built to carry traffic around both sides of Grand Central Terminal between 45th and 47th streets (*see* 1923).

Shipping companies carrying immigrants to New York suffer losses as a new immigration law sets national quotas and requires the companies to return would-be immigrants whose numbers exceed those quotas.

A lighthouse erected at Sandy Hook, N.J., in 1880 is reconstructed at Jeffrey's Hook on the Hudson River, where it will become famous as the Little Red Lighthouse (*see* Juvenile fiction, 1942).

Poliomyelitis (infantile paralysis) strikes former assistant secretary of the navy Franklin Delano Roosevelt August 10 at his vacation home on Campobello Island, New Brunswick. Now 39, he is brought back to his house at 47 East 65th Street to recuperate but will never again be able to walk unaided.

The East Harlem Health Center opens with support from reformers who include Homer Folks, now 54. The city's first neighborhood health center, it will meet with such success that the public health department will take it over; by 1944 the department will have opened centers in 14 other neighborhoods.

∞ English-born, Nebraska-raised Trinity Church rector William Thomas Manning, 55, is elected Episcopal bishop of New York, an office he will hold until 1946.

The Little Red School House opens as an experimental school for first-graders in the red-painted annex of P.S. 61 at 535 East 16th Street, a structure built in 1897 for the Children's Aid Society. Started by Elisabeth Irwin, now 40, it emphasizes learning by doing (academic work does not begin until the middle of the second grade) and will be supported by the Board of Education until 1932 (see 1932; Irwin, 1916; high school, 1941).

The *Sunday News* is launched by New York's 2-year-old *Daily News*; the paper has shown a small profit since last year and moves to larger quarters at 25 Park Place (see 1925).

New York Morning Telegraph sports editor and one-time Kansas lawman William Barclay "Bat" Masterson dies at New York October 25 at age 67 and is buried at Woodlawn Cemetery.

The Delacorte Press is founded by publisher George T. Delacorte, Jr., whose 5-year-old magazine company Dell Publishing Co. shows signs of prospering (see 1916). He attracts a mass audience with his new magazines *I Confess* and *Cupid's Diary* (see Dell Books, 1942).

Nonfiction: *History of the New York Times, 1851–1921* by journalist Elmer Davis; *New York: The Nation's Metropolis* by New York author Peter Marcus, 32.

Fiction: *By Advice of Counsel, Being Adventures of the Celebrated Firm of Tutt & Tutt, Attorneys and Counselors at Law* by Arthur Train.

Poetry: *Second April* by Edna St. Vincent Millay; *Collected Poems* by Edwin Arlington Robinson.

Painting: *Thunderstorm* and *Mowing Machine* (charcoal on paper) by Arthur Dove.

Sculpture: a bronze figure of a U.S. soldier by sculptor Philip Martiny is unveiled on Abingdon Square in West 12th Street at the corner of Eighth Avenue and Hudson Street.

American Art News founder James Bliss Townsend dies and the magazine is sold to St. Louis-born publicist Samuel W. Frankel, who came to New York at an early age, found work as a compositor on the *New York Herald*, later became an advertising solicitor, specializing in the art field, and 6 years ago established an agency to advertise and publicize art. He hires Peyton Boswell as editor, they will call it simply *The Art News* beginning February 17, 1923, and publish it weekly from October to mid-June and monthly from July to September; Frankel will replace Boswell and acquire his interest in 1925, and by October 1929 the weekly cover price will be 25¢ (see 1935; Art Digest, 1926).

Theater: *Diff'rent* by Eugene O'Neill 1/4 at the Provincetown Playhouse, 100 perfs.; *The Green Goddess* by Scottish playwright William Archer, 65, 1/18 at the Booth Theater with George Arliss, 440 perfs.; *Nice People* by Rachel Crothers 3/2 at the new Klaw Theater (later to be called the Avon) at 251 West 45th Street, with German-born actress Katherine Cornell, 28, Alabama-born ingénue Tallulah (Brockman) Bankhead, 18, and Francine Larrimore; *Mary Stuart/Man About Town* by English poet-playwright John Drinkwater, 38, 3/21 at the new Ritz Theater (the Walter Kerr beginning in 1983), opened by the Shubert brothers at 219 West 48th Street, with Clare Eames, 40 perfs.; *A Punch for Judy* (initially *Oh Promise Me*) by New York-born playwright Philip (James Quinn) Barry, 24, 4/18 at the Morosco Theater; *Clair de Lune* by New York-born poet-playwright Michael Strange (née Blanche Oelrichs, now Mrs. John Barrymore), 30, 4/18 at the Empire Theater, with Ethel Barrymore, 64 perfs.; *Dulcy* by Pittsburgh-born playwright George S. (Simon) Kaufman, 31, and his McKeesport, Pa.-born collaborator Marc (Marcus Cook) Connelly, 30, 8/13 at the Frazee Theater, 246 perfs.; *Getting Gertie's Garter* by Wilson Collison and Avery Hopwood 8/21 at the Republic Theater, with Hazel Dawn, 120 perfs.; *Swords* by Sidney Howard 9/1 at the new National Theater (later to be called the Billy Rose, then the Nederlander) at 208 West 41st Street; *A Bill of Divorcement* by Clemence Dane 10/10 at the George M. Cohan Theater (after a March opening at London), with Katherine Cornell as Sidney, Charles Waldron, 173 perfs.; *Anna Christie* by Eugene O'Neill 11/2 at the Vanderbilt Theater, with Pauline Lord as Anna Christopherson in the story of a prostitute's fight for redemption, 177 perfs.

Town Hall opens at 113-123 West 43rd Street, between Sixth Avenue and Broadway. Designed in Georgian Revival style by McKim, Mead & White for the League of Political Education, the 1,498-seat auditorium will be used for lectures, concerts, and theatrical productions.

Film: Charles Sheeler and Paul Strand's documentary *Manhattan* (initially entitled *New York the Magnificent*). Painter Sheeler, now 38, has produced the avant-garde film in collaboration with photographer Strand, now 31.

New York musicians organize Local 802 of the American Federation of Musicians. The powerful local replaces the Musical Mutual Protective Union, that group having lost its charter (*see* 1916), and will negotiate contracts with the Metropolitan Opera, the League of New York Theaters, and recording companies.

Broadway musicals: *The Rose Girl* 2/11 at the new Ambassador Theater, 215-223 West 42nd Street (designed by Herbert J. Krapp for the Shubert brothers), with Mabel Withee, Charles Purcell, music by Anselm Goetzl, book and lyrics by William Carey Duncan; *The Right Girl* 3/15 at the Times Square Theater, with music by Percy Wenrich, book and lyrics by Raymond Peck; *Shuffle Along* 5/23 at the 63rd Street Music Hall, with Florence Mills, 25, and teenager Josephine Baker in an all-black revue, songs that include "Love Will Find a Way" and "I'm Just Wild About Harry" by Eubie (James Hubert) Blake, 38, and Noble Sissle, 32, 504 perfs.; *Two Little Girls in Blue* 5/31 at the George M. Cohan Theater, with music by Vincent Youmans, 23, and P. Lannin, lyrics by Arthur Francis (Ira Gershwin), songs that include "Oh Me! Oh My!" 134 perfs.; *The Ziegfeld Follies* 6/21 at the Globe Theater, with Raymond Hitchcock, Fanny Brice singing the torch song "My Man," published at Paris last year under the title "Mon Homme" and made poignant by the fact that Brice is married to gambler Nick Arnstein (English lyrics by Alfred Willametz). "Second Hand Rose (From Second Avenue)" by James F. Hanley, lyrics by Grant Clarke, is another *Follies* hit, 119 perfs.; (George White's) *Scandals* 7/11 at the Liberty Theater, with White, Ann Pennington, Lou Holtz, music by George Gershwin, lyrics by Arthur Jackson, 97 perfs.; *Tangerine* 8/9 at the Casino Theater, with book by Philip Bartholomae and Guy Bolton, music by Carlo Sanders, lyrics by Howard Johnson, 337 perfs.; *The Greenwich Village Follies* (revue) 8/31 at the Shubert Theater, with Ted Lewis, songs that include "Three O'Clock in the Morning" by Spanish composer Julian Robledo, 34, lyrics by New York lyricist Dolly

Morse (Dorothy Terrio), 31, 167 perfs.; *Blossom Time* 9/21 at the Ambassador Theater, with book and lyrics by Dorothy Donnelly, who has adapted the German operetta *Das Dreimädelhaus* based on the life of composer Franz Schubert, music by Sigmund Romberg, 592 perfs.; *The Music Box Revue* 9/22 at the new Music Box Theater at 239-247 West 45th Street (designed by C. Howard Crane and E. George Kiehler), with Irving Berlin songs that include "Say It with Music," 440 perfs.; *Bombo* 10/6 at the new Jolson Theater (later to be called the Century) at 932 Seventh Avenue, between 58th and 59th streets, with Al Jolson singing numbers by Sigmund Romberg, book and lyrics by B. G. DeSylva. Jolson soon interpolates "My Mammy," "Toot, Toot, Tootsie" by Dan Russo, lyrics by Gus Kahn and Ernie Erdman, "April Showers" by Louis Silvers, 32, lyrics by Jack Yellen, "California, Here I Come" by Joseph Meyer, lyrics by Jolson and B. G. DeSylva, 219 perfs.; *The Perfect Fool* 11/7 at the George M. Cohan Theater, with Ed Wynn, book, music, and lyrics by Wynn; *Kiki* 11/29 at the Belasco Theater, with Lenore Ulric, songs that include "Some Day I'll Find You" by Zoel Parenteau, lyrics by Schuyler Green, 600 perfs.

Boxing has its first $1 million gate July 2 at Boyle's Thirty Acres in Jersey City, where Colorado-born heavyweight champion Jack Dempsey, 26, defeats French challenger Georges Carpentier by a fourth-round knockout. The handsome Carpentier won the world light-heavyweight title by defeating Battling Levinsky in a Jersey City bout held October 20 of last year and Tex Rickard of Madison Square Garden has promoted the bout with Dempsey. Dempsey won the title 2 years ago wearing Everlast boxing gloves manufactured at New York by the Everlast Sports Manufacturing Co., whose factory begins mass production of boxing equipment (*see* 1917; 1938).

Stillman's Gymnasium opens on the west side of Eighth Avenue between 54th and 55th streets. Founder Lou Stillman will sell the place in 1959 and it will be razed 2 years later to make way for a 17-story apartment house, but not before it has been used as a training arena for prizefighters (and as a source of material for writers such as Damon Runyon).

Bill Tilden and Mrs. Mallory win the U.S. singles titles at the West Side Tennis Club courts in Forest Hills.

Babe Ruth hits 59 home runs in the regular season, up from 54 last year, and the Yankees win their first pennant as they continue to play at the Polo Grounds (*see* 1920), but the New York Giants win the World Series (the first "Subway Series"), defeating the Yankees 5 games to 3 in the last eight-game series.

The Yankees win the first two games behind the pitching of Carl Mays, 29, and Brooklyn-born Waite "Schoolboy" Hoyt, 22 (whose Series ERA is 0.00), but the Giants come back in the third, winning it 13 to 5, and go on to take four more in the first Series ever to be aired on radio. Newark, N.J.-based radio station WJZ receives play-by-play telephone reports from a *Newark Star* reporter and relays them to listeners who pick up the signals on their crystal sets.

Gangster Carlo Gambino, 19, comes to New York in December after arriving by freighter at Norfolk, Va., from his native Palermo. The family of the Mafioso's mother has smuggled him out of Italy and he is welcomed by her relatives, the Castellanos, in Brooklyn, where he will begin a career of shrewd and ruthless criminality (*see* 1931).

The Building Congress organized by New York mortgage bankers and builders works to get the city's construction industry through the economic recession by campaigning against seasonal unemployment, unsound investment, and waste. Construction workers generally get $9 per day, helpers $7, up from $5.50 and $3.50, respectively, in 1913; pay cuts introduced July 6 by the Builidng Trades Employers Association reduce these rates by $1 per day, affecting 100,000 workers.

The Cunard Building is completed on Bowling Green across from Cass Gilbert's Customs House of 1907. The 21-story office tower has been designed by Portland, Ore.-born architect Benjamin Wistar Morris, 50, with an assist from Thomas Hastings of Carrère and Hastings; it stands on a site once occupied by Delmonico's Hotel (it later became Stevens House but was demolished in 1919), and has a Great Hall with elaborately decorated domed vaults designed by Ezra Winter.

The 24-story Fisk Building opens October 1 at 250 West 57th Street, southwest corner Broadway. Designed by Carrère & Hastings with Shreve, Lamb & Harmon, it has 343,000 square feet of floor space.

Brooklyn's $500,000 Temple Beth El is completed at the corner of Thirteenth Avenue and 48th Street. Designed by Shampan & Shampan, it has seats for 1,872 worshipers.

A six-story limestone mansion for theater magnate Martin Beck is completed at 13 East 67th Street to neo-classical designs by Harry Allan Jacobs. The first two floors resemble a miniature Broadway theater, and a wide marble stairway leads from a formal reception room on the first floor to a double-height 21' × 30' living room. The master bedroom is 22 by 17 feet, and a 9' × 20' interior light-well provides light to the central upstairs rooms.

A mansion for J. P. Morgan senior partner Thomas W. Lamont and his wife, Florence, is completed at 107 East 70th (Lamont has been renting the Franklin D. Roosevelt house in East 65th Street). Designed by Walker & Gillette, the English Gothic house will provide headquarters for the Visiting Nurse Service of New York after Lamont's death in 1948.

Housing reformer Alfred Tredway White dies at Harriman State Park in Orange County June 29 at age 75; architect Cyrus L. W. Eidlitz of heart disease at his Southampton, L.I., summer home October 5 at age 73.

Lindy's restaurant has its beginnings in a delicatessen opened August 20 at 1626 Broadway, near 50th Street, under the management of Leo "Lindy" Lindeman, 33, a linen salesman's son who came to New York from his native Germany in 1913, worked as a busboy, graduated to waiting on tables at the Marie Antoinette Hotel on Broadway, and in 1915 married Clara Gertner after working as a waiter in the restaurant at 1446 Broadway that she ran with her brother. Three customers have backed them in their new venture; Lindemann slices meat and pumpernickel bread behind the counter while Clara works in the kitchen, she also serves as a cashier, and her recipes will help the place evolve into a popular restaurant; Lindy's coffee, crullers, cheesecake, and notoriously rude waiters will be favored by newspapermen, politicians, gamblers, con artists, music publishers, and theater people until 1957 (*see* 1929).

Sardi's restaurant opens in West 44th Street under the direction of Italian-born restaurateur Vincent Sardi, 35, and his wife, Eugenia, whose *cannelloni* and other dishes will attract the Broadway theater world for more than 80 years. Sardi's will move to 234 West 44th Street in 1927 when the first building is razed to make way for construction of the Erlanger Theater (later to be called the St. James); Vincent Jr. will take over in 1946, and he will build a following.

Louis Sherry's reopens under the direction of August Weisbrod on the ground floor of a new apartment house at 300 Park Avenue, where it will continue until the 1950s, but the glory days it knew as a restaurant for New York's conservative *haut monde* at Fifth Avenue and 44th Street are over. It will continue for close to 30 years, and the Louis Sherry name will survive as a brand name for ice cream and chocolates.

Ellis Island receives 560,971 immigrants, up more than 100 percent from last year. Some 900,000 immigrants enter the United States in the fiscal year ending June 30.

The Dillingham Bill (Emergency Quota Act) enacted by Congress May 19 establishes a quota system to restrict immigration. Vetoed earlier by President Wilson but signed by President Harding, it permits entry only to 3 percent of the people of any nationality who lived in the United States in 1910 (see 1917). Shipping companies with immigrant ships in New York Harbor are in many cases obliged to return their passengers to Europe at their own expense (see 1924; Ellis Island, 1922).

Margaret Sanger and Mary Ware Dennett found the American Birth Control League November 2 at 104 Fifth Avenue. Sanger tries to give a lecture on contraception at the new Town Hall in West 43rd Street November 13, police remove her from the stage, and a riot nearly ensues (see 1916; 1923).

1922 Bronx Democratic Party political boss Arthur H. Murphy dies at New York February 6; Tammany Hall grand sachem Charles F. Murphy replaces him with a triumvirate that includes Bronx County Sheriff Edward J. Flynn, who arranges a vote May 15 that leaves him sole chairman of the county executive committee.

Former Tammany Hall boss Richard Croker dies at his native Dublin April 29 at age 80; he retired with his wealth to England after 1901 and became known for his philanthropy and horse breeding.

Former governor Alfred E. Smith wins election to the governorship, securing 1,397,657 votes to Gov. Miller's 1,011,725. Smith has refused to accept publisher William Randolph Hearst as the Democratic Party's candidate for U.S. senator, physician and health commissioner Royal S. Copeland runs for the senate, the scandals of the Harding administration have raised public animus against Republicans, and Copeland outpolls incumbent William M. Calder by about 281,000 votes, winning the seat to which he will be reelected in 1928 and 1934.

 The East Brooklyn Savings Bank founded in 1860 moves its headquarters to Bedford Avenue (see 1962).

Wall Street's Dow Jones Industrial Average closes December 30 at 98.73, up from 81.10 at the end of 1921, as a U.S. business revival led by the automobile industry begins 7 years of prosperity.

 R. H. Macy Co. sells shares to the public for the first time after 64 years of private ownership (see 1913).

Gov. Al Smith did not let Tammany Hall stand in the way of his reforms. LAURENCE MASLON

The Jazz Age gave New York a reputation as the place to go for fun. Speakeasies flourished. ESTATE OF MRS. JOHN HELD, J.

The Fortunoff's retail chain has its beginnings in a small store selling pots and pans under the IRT elevated railroad tracks on Livonia Avenue in Brooklyn's East New York section. Entrepreneur Max Fortunoff, 25, and his wife, Clara, 20, open what later will be described as the first discount retail establishment in the New York area (*see* 1964).

The Fifth Avenue Association presents the city with seven bronze signal towers as an act of "civic statesmanship" to help control traffic on the avenue; the towers have cost $125,000. Taxis are not permitted to cruise on Fifth Avenue for more than one block; taxi drivers must wear caps, jackets, and ties.

Globe-circling journalist "Nellie Bly" (Elizabeth Cochrane Seaman) dies of pneumonia at New York January 27 at age 54 (*see* Kilgallen, 1936).

Gas sweeps through a northbound Jerome Avenue express subway July 6 after it has been stalled just north of 59th Street under Lexington Avenue. About 150 passengers are partly asphyxiated.

The Veterans Administration Medical Center has its beginnings in a facility opened by the federal government at 130 West Kingsbridge Road in the Bronx to treat sick and wounded veterans of the Great War. It will grow to have 775 beds (*see* Brooklyn center, 1947).

Patent medicine magnate Charles H. Fletcher of Fletcher's Castoria fame dies at his daughter's Orange, N.J., home April 9 at age 84, having made a fortune from the formula he purchased from a physician and promoted as a remedy for children; biochemist (and Nippon Club founder) Jokichi Takamine dies at New York July 22 at age 67.

First Presbyterian Church assistant pastor Harry Emerson Fosdick triggers a split in the Presbyterian general assembly with his sermon, "Shall the Fundamentalists Win?" (*see* 1919; 1925).

The Museum of the American Indian opens on Audubon Terrace (*see* 1906). Oil heir George Gustav Heye, 48, developed an interest in Native American culture while working as an engineer in Arizona and began 6 years ago to amass a collection that will grow to have nearly a million pieces (*see* 1994).

Economist Alvin S. Johnson takes over the foundering 2-year-old New School for Social Research, replaces its faculty with visiting lecturers, expands its curriculum beyond the social sciences, and allows anyone to enroll in non-credit evening courses at modest fees. Within a few years the school will be offering courses in art, literature, music, philosophy, and psychology given by such experts as composer Aaron Copland, architectural historian Lewis Mumford, painters Stuart Davis and Thomas Hart Benton, sculptor William Zorach, art historian Leo Stein, and dancers Doris Humphrey and Charles Weidman.

Brooklyn Technical High School opens September 11 with nearly 2,500 students in a renovated factory loft at 49 Flatbush Avenue. Former Manual Training High School mathematics department chairman Albert L. Colston serves as principal, having won approval from the Board of Superintendents in November 1918 for an innovative engineering program; he has developed an advanced science, mathematics, and engineering curriculum (*see* 1933).

David Sarnoff acquires a half interest in the Westinghouse radio station WJZ at Newark, N.J., and will acquire the other half with some associates next year. The station has studios at the Waldorf-Astoria Hotel on Fifth Avenue at 34th Street (*see* NBC, 1926).

Station WEAF (later WNBC) begins broadcasting August 16 from a studio at 463 West Street, where it has been set up as a subsidiary of AT&T with offices in that company's Walker Street headquarters; Indiana-born advertising executive William H. Rankin, 44, creates the first sponsored radio program with commercials for the Queensboro Corp. apartments, and WEAF airs the first paid radio commercials August 28, setting a pattern of private control of U.S. public airwaves. Sales of crystal-set radio sets do not provide a large enough revenue stream to support broadcast stations, the 10-minute commercial has cost the real estate developer $100, it produces $127,000 in sales within a few months, and while taxes and fees will support broadcasting in Britain and the European continent it will be advertising that supports it in America. "What have you done with my child?" radio pioneer Lee De Forest, now 48, will ask. "You have sent him out on the street in rags of ragtime to collect money from all and sundry. You have made of him a laughingstock of intelligence, surely a stench in the nostrils of the gods of the ionosphere." The station's 360-meter frequency is changed October 2 to 400 meters (*see* 1924; NBC, 1926).

Emerson Radio & Phonograph Co. is founded by New York entrepreneur Benjamin Abrams, 29, and his two brothers.

The *Bronx Home News* begins daily publication after 15 years as a weekly (*see* 1907). Circulation will reach 110,000 by the time founder James O'Flaherty dies in 1939 (*see* 1945).

The *Reader's Digest* begins publication at New York with a February issue that appears January 20. Canadian-born social worker Lila Bell Acheson, 32, was married in October of last year to former St. Paul, Minn., book salesman De Witt Wallace, also

32, and has helped him condense articles "of lasting interest" found at the New York Public Library and collected in a pocket-size magazine that they edit in a basement apartment under a speakeasy at 1 Minetta Street, corner of Sixth Avenue. The *Digest* contains no advertising, its cover will carry its table of contents until 1998, bar girls hired from the speakeasy help the Wallaces wrap and address the first 1,500 copies that arrive from the printer, and circulation will grow to more than 200,000 by 1929 as the *Digest* plants some of its articles in other magazines and then condenses them. The magazine will accept no advertising until 1955 and by the 1970s will be publishing 29 million copies per month in 13 languages. Although its readership will be overwhelmingly female, the *Digest* will not be averse to publishing off-color stories; for years to come it will show a marked bias in favor of Europe's rising totalitarian governments and against both Jews and Roman Catholics (*see* 1955).

Humorist and *Follies* star Will Rogers begins a weekly column for the *New York Times* that is soon syndicated nationally.

Hearst circulation director Moses L. (Louis) Annenberg, 44, and two colleagues pay $500,000 to acquire the *Racing Form*, a daily tip-sheet established a few years ago by Chicago newspaperman Frank Buenell. Annenberg will buy the competing *Morning Telegraph*, quit Hearst in 1926, go into partnership with Chicago gambler Monte Tennes to control bookie joints with leased wires to racetracks, and force his *Racing Form* partners to sell their interests to him for more than $2 million (*see* 1936).

The *New York Times Book Review* appears for the first time as a separate section of the newspaper (*see* Markel, 1923).

Nonfiction: *Etiquette in Society, in Business, in Politics, and at Home—The Blue Book of Social Usage* by New York writer Emily Post (*née* Price), 48, a daughter of the late architect Bruce Price who has found the manners of Americans far inferior to those of their social counterparts in Europe. Divorced at the turn of the century from her banker husband, Edwin Post, the author moved to Tuxedo Park, designed in part by her father, and has been writing fiction with only moderate success. *Vanity Fair* editor Frank Crowninshield told Post that most books on etiquette were full of misinformation and suggested she write an accurate one. The resulting work is 650 pages long (revisions will soon bring it to more than 700 pages), is peopled with fictitious characters (e.g., Mr. and Mrs. Gotham Toplofty, Mr. and Mrs. Richan Vulgar), and contains pragmatic advice.

Post's book becomes a best-seller and she is offered advertising-endorsement contracts and a contract to write a monthly column for *McCall's* magazine.

Fiction: *The Beautiful and Damned* by F. Scott Fitzgerald; *Tales of the Jazz Age* (stories) by F. Scott Fitzgerald with illustrations by Salt Lake City-born New York cartoonist John Held, Jr., 32, whose work for *Judge, Life,* and *College Humor* is capturing the essence of "flaming youth;" "The Diamond as Big as the Ritz" by Scott Fitzgerald; *The Vertical City* (stories) by Fannie Hurst; *Salome of the Tenements* by Anzia Yezierska; *The Confessions of Artemas Quibble, Being the Ingenuous and Unvarnished History of Artemas Quibble, Esquire, a Onetime Practitioner in the New York Criminal Courts, Together with an Account of the Divers Wiles, Tricks, Sophistries, Technicalities, and Sundry Artifices of Himself and Others of the Fraternity Commonly Yclept "Shysters" or "Shyster Lawyers"* by Arthur Train, who has followed the career of former Howe & Hummel partner Abe Hummel. His works are serialized in the *Saturday Evening Post*.

Poetry: *The Book of American Negro Poetry*, edited by James Weldon Johnson, will be hailed as the start of the New Negro Movement, or Harlem Renaissance (the term will be coined in 1947 by historian John Hope Franklin), as blacks pour out of the rural South into Manhattan north of Central Park and assert a new pride of idealistic independence; *Harlem Shadows: The Poems of Claude McKay* (with an introduction by Max Eastman, who accompanied McKay on a visit to Soviet Russia in 1920; the book includes McKay's poem "If We Must Die"); *Introducing Irony* by Maxwell Bodenheim.

Sculpture: *Civic Virtue* by Frederick MacMonnies, now 58, whose monumental fountain for City Hall Park includes a male nude trampling on two women who are supposed to personify Vice. The work will be moved in 1941 to the grounds of the Queens Municipal Hall in response to objections from women's groups; a bronze war memorial depicting three soldiers is unveiled on a small "island" between Broadway and St. Nicholas Avenue. Gertrude Vanderbilt Whitney has created the work.

Theater: *The Cat and the Canary* by actor-playwright John Willard 2/7 at the National Theater with New York-born actress Florence Eldridge (*née* McKechnie), 20, Louisville, Ky.-born actor Henry Hull, 30, John Willard; *To the Ladies* by Marc Connelly and George S. Kaufman 2/20 at the Liberty Theater, 128 perfs.; *Back to Methuselah* by George Bernard Shaw 2/27 at the Garrick Theater (Parts I and II) with Dennis King, 24, English actress Margaret Wycherley, Edinburgh-born actor Moffat Johnston, 35,

(Parts III and IV) 3/6, (Part V) 3/13, 72 perfs. total; *The Hairy Ape* by Eugene O'Neill 3/9 at the Province-town Playhouse (and then uptown at the Plymouth Theater) with Louis Wolheim, 127 perfs.; *Abie's Irish Rose* by Georgia-born playwright Anne Nichols, 30, 5/23 at the Fulton Theater, a play about a mixed marriage, 2,327 perfs. (a new record); *The Awful Truth* by New York-born playwright Arthur Richman, 36, 9/18 at the Henry Miller Theater, with Ina Claire, 144 perfs.; *The Fool* by Washington, D.C.-born playwright Channing Pollock, 42, 10/23 at the Times Square Theater with James Kirkwood, Lowell Sherman, 773 perfs.; *The World We Live In* (*The Insect Comedy*) by Czech playwrights Karel and Josef Capek 10/31 at the Al Jolson Theater, with Mary Blair as a butterfly, Vinton Freedley as a male cricket, 112 perfs.; *Rain* by U.S. playwrights John Colton and Clemence Randolph 11/7 at the Maxine Elliott Theater, with Kansas City, Mo.-born actress Jeanne Eagels (Aguilar), 30, as Somerset Maugham's Sadie Thompson, 321 perfs.; *The Texas Nightingale* by Missouri-born playwright Zoë Akins, 36, 11/20 at the Empire Theater, with Jobyna Howland as soprano Hollyhock Jones who becomes the Wagnerian diva "Brasa Canava," Cyril Keightly, 31 perfs.; *Why Not?* by Monckton Hoffe 12/25 at the Broadhurst Theater, with Arthur Byron, Lawrence Grant, Leslie Howard, 120 perfs.

The Minsky brothers take over the Park Theater on Columbus Circle for a year and use it to put on burlesque shows (*see* 1912; 1923).

Life magazine drama critic Robert (Charles) Benchley, 33, presents *The Treasurer's Report* at an amateur revue; his comedy monologue launches Benchley on a new career as humorist.

 Broadway musicals: *The Ziegfeld Follies* 6/5 at the New Amsterdam Theater, with Will Rogers, Ed Gallagher, Al Shean, Olsen and Johnson, music by Dave Stamper, Louis A. Hirsch, Victor Herbert, and others, book and lyrics by Ring Lardner, Gene Buck, and others, songs that include "Mister Gallagher and Mister Shean," 541 perfs.; *George White's Scandals* 8/22 at the Globe Theater, with W. C. Fields, Paul Whiteman and His Orchestra, music by George Gershwin, lyrics by E. Ray Goetz, B. G. DeSylva, and Fields, songs that include "I'll Build a Stairway to Paradise" with lyrics by B. G. DeSylva and Arthur Francis (Ira Gershwin), 88 perfs.; *The Gingham Girl* 8/28 at the Earl Carroll Theater, with music by Albert von Tilzer, lyrics by Neville Fleeson, songs that include "As Long as I Have You," "Down Greenwich Village Way," "42nd Street and Broadway," 322 perfs.; *The Greenwich Village Follies* (revue) 9/12 at

the Shubert Theater, with Bert Savoy, music by Louis A. Hirsch, lyrics by George V. Hobart, John Murray Anderson, and Irving Caesar, 216 perfs.; *The Passing Show* (revue) 9/20 at the Winter Garden Theater, with Eugene and Willie Howard, Janet Adair, Fred Allen, music largely by Alfred Goodman, lyrics mainly by Harold Atteridge, songs that include "Carolina in the Morning" by Walter Donaldson, lyrics by Gus Kahn, 95 perfs.; *The Music Box Revue* 10/23 at the Music Box Theater, with Bobby Clark, William Gaxton, Charlotte Greenwood, music, book, and lyrics by Irving Berlin, 272 perfs.; *Little Nellie Kelly* 11/13 at the Liberty Theater, with Georgia Caine, Elizabeth Hines, music and lyrics by George M. Cohan, songs that include "The Great New York Police," 276 perfs.

Edwin Franko Goldman's New York Military Band moves its summer outdoor concerts to the Central Park Mall that leads up to the Terrace and Bethesda Fountain (*see* 1918; new construction at Columbia University has forced the change). Beginning in 1924 the concerts will be completely underwritten by the Daniel and Florence Guggenheim Foundation, and beginning in 1926 the band will perform also in Brooklyn's Prospect Park (*see* Naumburg Bandshell, 1923).

Comedian-singer-dancer Bert Williams of 2309 Seventh Avenue opens in *Underneath the Bamboo Tree* but falls ill with pneumonia and dies at New York March 4 at age 47 (49 by some accounts). He has gained international fame with his sad song "Nobody," and despite his being black has been obliged to perform in blackface so he will look like other performers made up to conform to a racial stereotype.

Popular song: "Times Square" by Jerome Kern, lyrics by Anne Caldwell.

The New York Renaissance basketball team is organized by Bob Douglas, whose team plays its home games at Harlem's Renaissance Center. Within 15 years the Rens will be the city's leading team and will continue to play until the late 1940s, sometimes against the Chicago-based Harlem Globetrotters.

Bill Tilden wins in U.S. men's singles at Forest Hills, Mrs. Mallory in women's singles.

Mah-jongg is introduced in America, where a nationwide craze begins for the ancient Chinese game. In New York the 144-tile sets will outsell radios within a year.

Ring magazine begins publication at New York. Lower East Side-born sportswriter Nathaniel S. (Stanley)

"Nat" Fleischer, 34, stands only five feet two, was knocked out in the first round of an amateur match at age 15, has created the only publication devoted exclusively to fisticuffs, and will continue to publish it until his death in 1972, working to improve the image of prizefighting and encouraging equal treatment for black pugilists.

The New York Yankees win their second pennant, but the New York Giants win the World Series, defeating the Yankees 4 games to 0 with standout performances by first baseman George Kelly, third baseman Heinie Groh, and outfielder Frankie Frisch. The second game ended in a 3-to-3 tie (umpires stopped it "on account of darkness" even though the sun was still high in the sky, a decision that infuriated Judge Kenesaw Mountain Landis, 36, the first baseball commissioner; he ordered that the receipts for that game be donated to charity).

"Texas" Guinan begins her career as Prohibition-era New York nightclub hostess. Mary Louise Cecilia Guinan, 38, goes to work as mistress of ceremonies at the Café des Beaux Arts and is soon hired away by Larry Fay of El Fey from whose club she will move to the Rendezvous, 300 Club, Argonaut, Century, Salon Royal, Club Intime, and to several Texas Guinan Clubs that will serve bootleg Scotch at $25 a fifth, bootleg Champagne at $25 a bottle, plain water at $2 a pitcher. The clubs will charge from $5 to $25 cover to the "butter-and-egg men;" Texas Guinan ("give the little girl a great big hand") will welcome customers from her seat atop a piano with the cry, "Hello, sucker!"

The Princeton Club of New York moves into the former residence of Harvard graduate Austen G. Fox (Class of 1869) at 39 East 39th Street, northwest corner of Park Avenue on Murray Hill (see 1907). The Yale Club has taken in Princeton graduates since 1917, when most younger members were at war; the Victorian brownstone with its 10-story annex will remain the club's home until early 1963, sharing quarters at times with the Brown and Dartmouth clubs (see 1960).

The general contracting firm Starrett Brothers is founded by builders Paul Starrett, 56, and William A. Starrett, 45, who will specialize in putting up large buildings.

The 26-story Pershing Square Building is completed at 100 East 42nd Street, opposite Grand Central Terminal, on a site occupied until 1914 by the old Grand Union Hotel. After the Victory Hall Association tried without success to raise $20 million for an amphitheater on the site to memorialize America's war dead, developer Henry Mandel took over, he engaged architect John Sloan, and he has put up the new skyscraper.

The 26-story Heckscher Building (later the Crown Building) is completed for developer August Heckscher at 730 Fifth Avenue, southwest corner 57th Street. Designed by Warren & Wetmore, it has nearly 260,000 square feet of rentable floor space and will for some years be the tallest building north of 42nd Street.

St. Louis-born New York draftsman and architectural visionary Hugh Ferriss, 33, collaborates with architect Harvey Wiley Corbett, now 49, on a series of carbon-pencil "zoning envelope" studies that show how architects and developers can create buildings with the maximum amount of rentable space consistent with the setback zoning law of 1916.

The Central Presbyterian Church (initially called the Fifth Avenue Baptist Church) is completed at 593 Park Avenue, southeast corner 64th Street. Designed by Henry C. Pelton with Allen & Collens and built with matching contributions from the Rockefeller family (John D., Jr. holds Bible classes in the basement), it replaces five row houses that had faced on 64th Street.

The Park Avenue Association is founded by English-born socialite H. Gordon Duval, 29, who will publish the *Park Avenue Social Review* and work to keep the avenue free of commercialism and unwanted motor traffic.

Russian-born plumbing contractor-builder Sam Minskoff, 27, puts up the Muriel Arms apartment house at the northwest corner of Kingsbridge Road and the Grand Concourse in the Bronx. The New York chapter of the American Institute of Architects awards the building first prize as the finest fireproof apartment house of the year (see 1924).

Manhattan's 15-story Empire Hotel is completed on the south side of 63rd Street between Broadway and Columbus Avenue, replacing an 1894 hotel of the same name.

Carrier Corp. engineers replace the ammonia gas in their air conditioner coils with dielene, a coolant that poses no hazards, and introduce a central compressor that makes the cooling units far more compact (see 1915; Rivoli Theater, 1925).

Horse-drawn fire apparatus makes its final appearance in New York December 22 as equipment from Brooklyn's Engine Company 205 at 160 Pierrepont Street races to put out a fire.

The Colony restaurant opens in 63rd Street off Madison Avenue under the direction of restaurateur Gene Cavallero, who serves liquor in demitasse cups (he keeps his liquor bottles in an elevator that is sent up to the top floor and left there when Prohibition inspectors arrive). The Colony will develop a reputation for fine cuisine.

Bootlegger Matt Winkle advertises his "Kinvara Cafe" at 381 Park Avenue, across from the Racquet and Tennis Club, in the *Yale Daily News* and *Daily Princetonian* (the ads show the proprietor, wearing a raccoon coat, leaning against a Stutz Bearcat roadster and bear the caption, "Matt Winkle himself"). Most of the speakeasy's "wet goods" are kept in the pockets of an enormous overcoat that is worn summer and winter by a man who stands on the customers' side of the bar and hands bottles across to the barman as demand requires. In the event of a raid he simply walks out with the customers. After Winkle surrenders to the law his collegiate trade will shift to Dan Moriarty's at 216 East 58th Street, to the Puncheon Club at 21 West 52nd Street (*see* "21," 1930), and other watering holes that pay off the police or in other ways evade Prohibition laws.

Prohibition agents receive reports of a bachelor party at the Racquet & Tennis Club and arrest club member René LaMontagne, a prominent polo player who is charged with having sold 16,000 gallons of rye, 316 cases of Scotch, 500 cases of gin, and 9,000 gallons of wine. LaMontagne is given a 4-year prison sentence, and the club's bar will be removed in January of next year.

Ellis Island receives only 209,778 immigrants, down from 560,971 last year as the Dillingham Bill takes effect; the total number of U.S. immigrants falls to 309,556, down from 805,228 last year.

1923 Former British prime minister David Lloyd George receives a ticker-tape parade October 5 as the city continues to honor the statesmen and military leaders who helped win the Great War.

$ Amalgamated Bank of New York is founded by the Amalgamated Clothing Workers to provide low-interest loans, unsecured personal loans, free checking with no minimum balance, and other banking services not generally available to workers. Muncie, Ind.-born lawyer Benjamin V. (Victor) Cohen, 28, has helped the union organize the bank, which opens offices on Union Square. The only bank owned by a labor union, it will grow in 75 years to have assets of nearly $2 billion, with six branch offices offering personal and commercial loans, mortgage loans, health-care financial services, and pension-trust and custodial services.

Bear, Stearns is founded by stockbrokers Harold C. Mayer, Joseph Ainslie Bear, and Robert B. Stearns with offices at 100 Broadway. The firm will open an investment banking division in 1943 and in later years move to midtown.

Wall Street's Dow Jones Industrial Average closes December 31 at 95.52, down from 98.73 at the end of 1922.

Ohrbach's opens October 4 in 14th Street on a site occupied until last year by a penny arcade that Adolph Zukor opened in 1903 (the arcade has burned down). Vienna-born merchant Nathan M. Ohrbach, 38, has acquired the property and put up a dress shop in partnership with Max Wiesen, his advertised bargains attract such large crowds that windows are broken, and 20 people suffer minor injuries. The store will have sales of more than $15 million next year, and when partner Wiesen sells out in 1928 for $625,000 he will have increased his initial investment tenfold (*see* 1954).

A new $1 gas law replaces the 80¢ gas law of 1906. Other regulated rates will follow in years to come as the Public Service Commission resists efforts by utility companies to raise the price of cooking gas.

An enabling act signed into law by Gov. Smith permits the city to carry out a plan for building vehicular roadways around Grand Central Terminal and letting Park Avenue carry more traffic (*see* 1921). (The new law also allows the New York Central to obtain air rights that will let it construct high buildings on the site bounded by 45th and 46th streets between Vanderbilt Avenue and Depew Place.) The Board of Estimate appropriates $1,661,000 in the summer to cut 18 feet from each side of the 56-foot-wide grass plots in the center of Park Avenue, thereby widening the roadways in the blocks between 46th and 57th streets (*see* 1925).

The Police Department takes control of licensing taxicabs, charging that the cabs are often used in burglaries, bootlegging, and holdups. The city has 16,000 licensed taxis, but virtually anyone can get a license (*see* 1925).

The bankrupt Brooklyn Rapid Transit Co. (BRT) is reorganized as the Brooklyn-Manhattan Transit Corp. (BMT).

Pan American World Airways has its beginnings in a New York City plane taxi service started by local bond salesman Juan Terry Trippe, 24, who quits his job and joins his friend John Hambleton in buying nine flying boats the U.S. Navy was about to scrap (*see* 1925).

Former state commissioner of health Hermann M. Biggs dies at New York June 28 at age 63, having pioneered in fighting cholera, diphtheria, and tuberculosis.

The Abyssynian Baptist Church opens in June at 132 West 138th Street, between Lenox and Seventh avenues, on a site purchased 3 years ago by the congregation, formerly in West 40th Street and headed since 1908 by Virginia-born pastor Adam Clayton Powell, now 58. Rev. Powell has raised large sums of money for the new church, designed by Charles W. Bolton and built at a cost of $550,000 (*see* politics, 1941).

The Museum of the City of New York opens in Gracie Mansion with a mission to preserve artifacts related to local history. Amateur historian Mrs. John King Van Rensselaer denounced the New-York Historical Society in 1917 as "a deformed monstrosity filled with curiosities, ill-arranged and badly assorted," her efforts to take control of the Society's board of directors came to nought, and she founded the Society of Patriotic New Yorkers to "teach the inhabitants of the city and state just what New York really is." Her short-lived society has restored the 1799 country house of Archibald Gracie (used most recently as a concession stand and comfort station for Carl Schurz Park) and loaned it a small collection of furniture and prints (*see* 1932).

Manhattan College moves to Riverdale in the Bronx after 70 years in Manhattan (*see* 1853). Now a liberal arts college for men, it will add schools of engineering, business, education, and human services, become coeducational in 1973, and grow within the next 70 years to have 3,100 undergraduates, 600 graduate students, and roughly 300 faculty members.

Time magazine begins publication March 3 from a 39th Street loft office that was earlier the headquarters for Hupfel's Brewery. Based on rewrites of wire service stories with little additional reporting, the 32-page newsweekly is put out by China-born missionary's son Henry R. (Robinson) Luce, 24, and his Brooklyn-born Yale classmate Briton Hadden, also 24, who came up with the idea for the magazine while serving in the army, resigned last year from their jobs as reporters for the *Baltimore News*, wrote the prospectus for their enterprise in a $55-per-month upstairs room at 141 East 17th Street, and have assembled a staff of 33 to help them start a venture that will mushroom into a vast publishing empire. Hadden will die of a streptoccal infection at age 31 in 1929 after establishing a distinctive Timestyle by inverting sentences, inventing such words as "socialite," "GOPolitician," "cinemaddict," and "tycoon" (meaning a business magnate), and using the code phrase "great and good friend" to mean something more than just a good friend (*see* *Fortune*, 1930; *Newsweek*, 1933).

Publisher Frank A. Munsey buys the *Globe & Commercial Advertiser* May 26 and merges one of the nation's oldest surviving dailies with the afternoon *New York Sun* that he acquired in 1916 (*see* 1917).

The *New York Times* hires the *Tribune*'s New York-born assistant managing editor Lester Markel, 29, as Sunday editor; he will hold the position until 1965, inaugurating the News of the Week, Magazine, Entertainment, Travel, and other sections (*see* Book Review, 1922), eliminating the rotogravure pages, and making the Sunday edition virtually a separate entity with a national circulation much larger than that of the daily *Times*.

W. W. Norton Co. has its beginnings in the People's Institute Publishing Co. founded by Ohio-born New York editor William Warder Norton, 31, who hires a stenographer to transcribe lectures given by the People's Institute at the Cooper Union Forum (*see* education, 1859). He sells "Lectures in Print" pamphlets week by week to subscribers, his friends will persuade him to combine the pamphlets into books, and the first five will enjoy such success that Norton will go into business under his own name (*see* 1926).

Nonfiction: *The Color of a Great City* (memoir) by Theodore Dreiser: "The glory of the city is its variety. The drama of it lies in its extremes;" *My Forty Years in New York, and Our Fight with Tammany* by the Rev. Charles H. Parkhurst, now 81.

Poetry: *The Harp-Weaver and Other Poems* by Edna St. Vincent Millay, who marries Dutch coffee importer Eugen Boissevain, 12 years her senior, and moves with him in November to 75 Bedford Street, corner of Commerce Street (built in 1873, it is less than 10 feet wide): "Euclid alone has looked on Beauty bare" (Sonnet 22, II, 11-12); *The Sardonic Arm* by Maxwell Bodenheim.

Painting: *Skyscraper: New York Interpreted* by Joseph Stella; *Church Street El* by Charles Sheeler.

Theater: *Icebound* by Portland, Me.-born playwright Owen (Gould) Davis, 49, 2/10 at the Sam Harris Theater (originally the Candler), with Boots Wooster, 171 perfs.; *You and I* by Philip Barry 2/19 at the Belmont Theater with Lucile Watson, 140 perfs.; *The Adding Machine* by Elmer Rice 3/9 at the Garrick

Theater, with Dudley Digges as Mr. Zero, Edward G. Robinson as Shrdlu, Helen Westley, 72 perfs.; *Poppy* by playwright-lyricist Dorothy Donnelly 9/3 at the Apollo Theater, with former *Ziegfeld Follies* juggler W. C. Fields, who has been helped by showman Philip Goodman to develop the fraudulent character Eustace McGargle that Fields will portray for 20 years, 346 perfs.; *White Cargo* by English-born actor-turned-playwright Leon Gordon, 29, 11/5 at the Greenwich Village Theater, with Richard Stevenson, Annette Margules as Tondeleyo, 678 perfs.; *Saint Joan* by George Bernard Shaw 12/28 at the Garrick Theater, with Winifred Lenihan, Morris Carnovsky, 214 perfs.

The Minsky brothers return to the National Winter Garden Theater in East Houston Street, near Second Avenue, where Billy Minsky installs a runway to give patrons a closer look at his slim, shapely chorus girls (*see* 1922; 1924).

New York Tribune music critic Henry E. Krehbiel dies at New York March 20 at age 69 after a 43-year career with the paper.

Broadway musicals: *The Passing Show* (revue) 6/14 at the Winter Garden Theater, with New York-born vaudeville entertainer George Albert "Georgie" Jessel, 25, music by Sigmund Romberg and Jean Schwartz, book and lyrics by Harold Atteridge, 118 perfs.; *George White's Scandals* 6/18 at the Globe Theater, with music by George Gershwin, lyrics by E. Ray Goetz, B. G. DeSylva, Portland, Ore.-born songwriter Ballard MacDonald, 40, 168 perfs.; *Helen of Troy, N. Y.* 6/19 at the 5-year-old Selwyn Theater, with Helen Ford, music and lyrics by Bert Kalmar and Harry Ruby, book by George S. Kaufman and Marc Connelly, 191 perfs.; *Artists and Models* 8/20 at

the Shubert Theater, with Frank Fay, seminude showgirls, music by Jean Schwartz, book and lyrics by Harold Atteridge, 312 perfs.; *The Greenwich Village Follies* (revue) 9/20 at the Winter Garden Theater, with Allegheny, Pa.-born dancer Martha Graham, 29, Bert Savoy, music by Louis A. Hirsch and Con Conrad, lyrics by Irving Caesar and John Murray Anderson, 140 perfs.; *The Music Box Revue* 9/22 at the Music Box Theater, with Springfield, Ohio-born comedian Robert Edwin "Bobby" Clark, 34, Tennessee-born soprano Grace Moore, 21, music and lyrics by Irving Berlin, 273 perfs.; *Battling Butler* 10/8 at the Selwyn Theater, with St. Paul, Minn.-born actor William Kent, 37, Charles Ruggles, music by Walter Rosemont, book adapted by Ballard MacDonald, 288 perfs.; *The Ziegfeld Follies* 10/20 at the New Amsterdam Theater, with Fanny Brice, Paul Whiteman and his Orchestra, music by Dave Stamper, Rudolf Friml, Victor Herbert, and others, songs that include "Little Old New York" by Victor Herbert, lyrics by Gene Buck, 233 perfs.; *Runnin' Wild* (revue) 10/29 at the Colonial Theater, with an all-black cast, title song by A. Harrington Gibbs, lyrics by Joe Grey and Leo Wood, "Charleston" by Cecil Mack (Richard C. McPherson), 40, and Jimmy Johnson, 29, whose song launches a national dance craze, 213 perfs.; *Topics of 1923* (revue) 11/20 at the Broadhurst Theater, with Fay Marbe, Harry McNaughton, music by Jean Schwartz and Alfred Goodman, lyrics by Harold Atteridge, 143 perfs.; *Mary Jane McKane* 12/25 at the new Imperial Theater at 239 West 45th Street, with New York-born ingénue Kitty Kelly, 21, music by Herbert P. Stothart and Vincent Youmans, book by William Cary Duncan and Oscar Hammerstein II, 28, 151 perfs.; *Kid Boots* 12/31 at the Earl Carroll Theater, with Eddie Cantor, music by Harry Tierney, lyrics by Joseph McCarthy, songs that include "Polly Put the Kettle On," 479 perfs.; *The Song and Dance Man* 12/31 at the George M. Cohan Theater, with Cohan, Robert Cummings, music and lyrics by Cohan, songs that include "Born and Bred in Brooklyn," 96 perfs.

Music publisher Carl Fischer dies at New York February 4 at age 73. The firm he started in 1872 moves into a 12-story building across Fourth Avenue from Cooper Union and will continue until 1999 to sell sheet music on the premises; female impersonator Bert Savoy is killed by a bolt of lightning on a Long Island beach June 26 at age 35.

Popular songs: "Barney Google" and "You Gotta See Mama Ev'ry Night, Or You Can't See Mama At All" by Con Conrad and New York-born songwriter Billy Rose (originally William Samuel Rosenberg), 23, who studied shorthand at high school under John R.

Yankee Stadium opened in the Bronx, where Babe Ruth and Lou Gehrig brought out huge crowds.

Gregg, became world champion of Gregg-method notation, learned to write shorthand with both hands simultaneously at a speed of 200 words per minute, worked as a secretary to financier Bernard Baruch, became head of the War Industries Board's clerical staff, spent more than 5 months analyzing hit songs at the New York Public Library while he lived on coffee and doughnuts in a $5-per-week room, and has become a lyricist for Leo Feist, Inc. Sophie Tucker sings "You Gotta See Mama" with great success; "Down Hearted Blues" by Memphis-born blues singer Alberta Hunter, 28 (a niece of the late Bert Williams who moved from Chicago to New York 2 years ago and has been recording with Fletcher Henderson's Novelty Orchestra on the Black Swan label), lyrics by Lovie Austin (Philadelphia-born blues singer Bessie Smith, 23, records the song and it has sales of 2 million copies).

The Cotton Club opens on the second floor of a building at 644 Lexington Avenue at the corner of 142nd Street, where English-born bootlegger Owen "Owney" Madden, 31, has taken over the Club Deluxe run by former heavyweight champion Jack Johnson and gained backing from other mobsters. Madden is released on parole from Sing Sing, where he has been serving time for manslaughter, and pays off police to look the other way; bandleader Andy Preer conducts the nightclub's house orchestra, black chorus girls entertain the white-only patrons, and the club's musical revue features comedians and variety acts as well as dancers and singers (see 1936).

The Club Durant opens under the direction of New York-born entertainer James Francis "Jimmy" Durante, 30, singer Eddie Jackson, and dancer Lou Clayton who have drawn crowds with their raucous act at Harlem's Club Alamo. The new enterprise lasts only 6 months but establishes the reputations of Durante, Jackson, and Clayton.

Central Park's Naumburg Bandshell is completed on the Mall (see Goldman, 1922). Retired merchant and banker Elkan Naumburg has given the city $100,000 to build the Indiana limestone structure, and his nephew William Tachau (who helped design the Kingsbridge Armory completed 6 years ago) has designed it. Backing into a hill that will be planted with wisteria, it has a coffered half-dome that echoes through the summer with five concerts per week. Naumburg's son Walter will endow free concerts by the Naumburg Orchestra, and it will continue to play for more than 5 decades.

 Bill Tilden wins in men's singles at Forest Hills, California-born Helen (Newington) Wills, 17, in women's singles (reporters call the unsmiling Wills "Miss Pokerface").

Baseball legend William H. "Wee Willie" Keeler dies at his native Brooklyn January 1 at age 50.

Yankee Stadium opens in the Bronx April 18, draws a sellout crowd of 74,217, and turns away 25,000 for lack of seats (bleacher-seat tickets go for 25¢). With help from Tillinghast l'Hommedieu Houston (who sold his share in the club to brewer Ruppert last year), Col. Jacob Ruppert has built the $2.5 million stadium—largest in the country—west of the Grand Concourse at the southwest corner of River Avenue and 161st Street. Helped by a short right field, Babe Ruth hits a three-run homer into the right-field bleacher seats in the third inning of the inaugural game, and the Yankees beat the Boston Red Sox 4 to 1.

The New York Yankees win their first World Series, defeating the Giants 4 games to 2 in the second "Subway Series." An inside-the-park Giant home run by Kansas City-born outfielder Charles Dillon "Casey" Stengel, now 33, in the ninth inning has decided the first game, but Yankee pitchers Herb Pennock, 29, Joe Bush, 30, and Bob Shawkey, 32, have overpowered the Giant batting order.

The Dempsey-Firpo fight at the Polo Grounds September 14 sees Argentine fighter Luis Angel Firpo, 29, knock Jack Dempsey out of the ring and into the laps of ringside sportswriters, but Dempsey knocks the "Wild Bull of the Pampas" down nine times, wins in two rounds, and retains his title.

Winged Foot Country Club is founded by the New York Athletic Club at suburban Mamaroneck.

Golf enthusiasts lay out a course in Queens at the intersection of Fresh Meadow Lane and Nassau Boulevard. Planned by Benjamin C. Ribman of Brooklyn, the Fresh Meadows course will be the site of some major tournaments (see real estate, 1946).

Central Park gets its first mechanical carousel (see 1871; 1920).

A new Coney Island Boardwalk is completed in late May for the Atlantic Ocean beach resort; also called the Riegelmann Boardwalk in honor of Brooklyn Borough President Edward Riegelmann, it stands 15 feet above sea level and stretches from Brighton Beach through Coney Island to Sea Gate, making Coney Island a rival to Atlantic City.

Maiden Form brassieres are introduced by four-foot-11-inch Russian-born entrepreneur Ida Rosenthal (née Kagonovich), 36, who last year bought a half-interest in a fashionable dress shop in West 57th Street (*see* 1914). She and her English-born partner Enid Bissett have given away sample brassieres with a little uplift because they did not like the fit of their dresses on flat-chested "flappers." Rosenthal, whose family changed its name to Cohen when it came to America in 1904, married William Rosenthal in 1906 and together they invest $4,500 to incorporate the Maiden Form Brassiere Co. He is an amateur sculptor, and as head of production he designs a precursor to cup sizing. The new company will move its operations to Bayonne, N.J., and by 1928 will be doing a volume of nearly $500,000 per year, despite the flapper look that deemphasizes breasts. By 1938 it will have revenues of $4.5 million and by the 1960s will be grossing $40 million.

New York fashion designers introduce new styles in November that emphasize corduroy, flannel, and knitted fabrics, with hemlines 10 inches from the floor.

The Colony Club moves from 120 Madison Avenue to a lavish new clubhouse at the northwest corner of Park Avenue and 63rd Street (*see* 1907). Membership has grown to more than 2,000, with a waiting list of more than 1,000. Designed in Georgian style by Delano & Aldrich but delayed by the war, the red-brick and marble structure has a round entrance hall lined with Caen stone and a one-and-a-half-story ballroom. A 20-foot-by-60-foot marble-and-tile swimming pool is in the basement, together with massage baths, mud baths, and sulfur baths similar to those found at European spas; a special elevator links the basement to the fully equipped oak-paneled gymnasium on the fifth floor and the squash courts above. The second floor has two dining rooms, library, card room, and a 70-foot lounge paneled in American butternut. There are 40 bedrooms and a kennel where members can leave their dogs.

The Bowery Savings Bank Building is completed across 42nd Street from the Grand Central Terminal with a banking room whose massive counters are almost dwarfed by the immense ceiling height, marble columns, mosaics, and chandeliers. York & Sawyer has designed the palatial paean to capitalism.

The Third Church of Christ Scientist is completed at 554 Park Avenue, northeast corner 63rd Street to neo-Georgian designs by Delano & Aldrich.

A mansion for Marcellus Hartley Dodge and his wife, Geraldine (*née* Rockefeller), is completed at 800 Fifth Avenue, northeast corner 61st Street, to

designs by R. S. Shapter. It will survive until the mid-1970s (*see* apartment house, 1978).

The 369th Regiment Armory for the National Guard is completed at 2366 Fifth Avenue, between 142nd and 143rd streets. Van Wart & Wein has designed the brick structure in a Moderne style.

The city adopts a new setback law that limits the height and configuration of buildings as luxury apartment houses and hotels go up on Park Avenue (*see* Grand Central, 1913; zoning laws, 1916; 1961).

The 14-story 580 Park Avenue apartment house is completed between 63rd and 64th streets. Designed by J. E. R. Carpenter, the co-operative structure occupies the entire blockfront with a four-story colonnaded base of variegated limestone, doctors' offices with separate entrances flank its monumental doorway, and all of its 52 eight- and nine-room apartments (two of each per floor) have separate laundry-and-storage rooms in the basement (there are 30 servants' rooms in the penthouse).

The 14-story 956 Fifth Avenue apartment house is completed at the southeast corner of 77th Street. I. N. Phelps Stokes has designed the structure in Italian Renaissance style with one apartment per floor.

The 14-story-plus-penthouse 1050 Park Avenue apartment house is completed at the southwest corner of 87th Street to designs by J. E. R. Carpenter.

The 14-story 1105 Park Avenue apartment house is completed at the northeast corner of 89th Street to designs by Sicilian-born architect Rosario Candela, 33, who will rival J. E. R. Carpenter in creating luxury apartment houses.

The Rosenman Act adopted by the state legislature at Albany strengthens rent-control laws (*see* 1920). San Antonio-born Democratic assemblyman Samuel (Irving) Rosenman, 27, has written the measure; a skilled legislative technician, jurist, and poltical operative, he has supported Gov. Smith's progressive efforts in the areas of housing, labor, and public works, will leave elective office in 1926 to serve on the Legislative Bill Drafting Commission, and will play a major role in the state and national Democratic Party (*but see* rent de-control, 1926).

Rego Park in east central Queens is so named by developers Henry Schloh and Charles I. Hausmann. The Real Good Construction Co. has been buying up farms in the area, many of them operated by Chinese to grow vegetables for sale in Chinatown, and erecting one-family row houses (eight-room houses designed to sell at $8,000 each), multi-family houses, and small apartment buildings (*see* railroad station, 1928).

Cambria Heights is developed in southeastern Queens by East New York real estate agent Oliver B. LaFreniere, who has acquired 163 acres of farmland within St. Albans near Belmont Racetrack. Once known as "Kerosene Hill" because it did not have piped-in gas, the area has a 50-foot elevation above sea level, one of the highest in Queens.

✕ New York State gives up trying to administer the Volstead Act and turns the job of policing the illegal alcoholic beverage trade over to the federal government. The law is widely evaded in New York City: "cordial" shops pay off local patrolmen to close their eyes to the fact that liquor is being sold, physicians write prescriptions wholesale for "medicinal" spirits, and bootleggers do a thriving business.

🍳 Delmonico's restaurant serves its last dinner May 21 to a gathering of invited guests and closes after 96 years. It has been the city's foremost eating place, rivalled only by Louis Sherry's (*see* 1921), but has been unprofitable since the Volstead Act prohibited sale of wines and liquors.

The American Birth Control League opens the Birth Control Clinical Research Bureau (later called the Margaret Sanger Bureau) January 2 with a birth control clinic in Margaret Sanger's house at 17 West 16th Street, where it will remain for 50 years (*see* 1921). Sanger last year married millionaire J. Noah Slee, who supports her work (*see* 1929).

1924 The city gains home rule under terms of an amendment to the state constitution establishing a new Municipal Assembly with two chambers: the upper chamber is the Board of Estimate and Apportionment, established in 1864 (*see* 1901), and the lower chamber is the Board of Aldermen, comprising a president (to be elected at large), the five borough presidents, and representatives of 65 districts, each to be elected for a 2-year term.

Tammany boss Charles F. Murphy dies at New York April 25 at age 65, leaving an estate valued at more than $5 million. His funeral is held at St. Patrick's Cathedral and an estimated 50,000 people line nearby streets to honor a man whom few have ever known. Tammany Hall is left without any real leadership, the job of developing new talent will be given to district leaders, and they will not find people who can compare with Al Smith, James A. Farley, Robert F. Wagner, and the other men whom Murphy brought to the fore.

Gov. Smith wins reelection to a fourth term, endearing himself to city voters with his New Yawkese (a "poisun" goes to "woik" and performs a "soivice") and securing 1,627,111 votes to 1,518,552 for his 37-year-old Republican challenger Col. Theodore Roosevelt, Jr.

Onetime Tammany Hall sachem George Washington Plunkitt dies at New York November 19 at age 82, leaving an estate of between $500,000 and $1.5 million obtained through what he called "honest graft."

Liberia rejects Marcus Garvey's plan for resettlement of U.S. blacks, fearing that his motive is to foment revolution (*see* 1920). A court will convict Garvey next year of fraudulent dealings in the now-bankrupt Black Star Steamship Co. he has founded; President Coolidge will commute his 5-year sentence, but Garvey will be deported back to Jamaica in 1927 (*see* 1940).

$ International Business Machines Corp. (IBM) is reorganized at New York by former National Cash Register executive Thomas J. Watson, who has headed the Elmira-based Computer-Tabulating-Recording Co. (C-T-R) since 1915, increased sales of its various punched-card tabulating machines, and merges C-T-R with a firm that has been using the IBM name; Watson adopts it as that of the new company (*see* typewriters, 1933).

Financier August Belmont II dies of blood poisoning in his Park Avenue apartment December 11 at age 71.

Wall Street's Dow Jones Industrial Average closes December 31 at a new high of 120.51, up from 95.52 at the end of 1923.

Barney's opens on Seventh Avenue at 17th Street, where it will continue for 74 years. Merchant Barney Pressman, 28, started his career by pressing pants at 3¢ per pair in his father's Elizabeth Street clothing store on the Lower East Side. His wife has handed him her engagement ring to be pawned for the $500 he needed to take over the lease on his new store, it has 200 feet of frontage, and he buys 40 name-brand suits to stock the 500-square-foot establishment, whose sign over the door reads, "No Bunk. No Junk. No Imitation." Women wearing barrels will hand out matchbooks stamped with the store's name and address, and Pressman will be one of the first retailers to use radio for advertising ("Calling All Men to Barney's"), hiring Irish bands to play jigs and reels, and offering free alterations. Manufacturers who control the distribution of their suits and coats have no interest in Pressman's small shop, so he will buy at auctions and bankruptcy sales of Southern retailers, offering Hickey-Freeman and Oxxford suits at prices well below those advertised elsewhere (some customers will ask him to take out the Barney's label so their friends will think they paid full price); Pressman's son Fred, born this year, will turn the discount store into America's largest menswear retailer (see women's apparel, 1977).

Saks Fifth Avenue opens September 15 just south of St. Patrick's Cathedral with window displays featuring $1,000 raccoon coats, chauffeurs' livery, and a $3,000 pigskin trunk. Merchant Bernard F. Gimbel, now 39, bought out Horace Saks, 42, son of the late Andrew Saks, last year and merged their stores at Greeley Square (see Gimbels, 1910); the new store (designed by Ernest A. Van Vleck of Starrett & Van Vleck) is the first large specialty shop north of 42nd Street, and it sells out its stock of silver pocket flasks the first day. Horace Saks will die next year and Gimbel will become president of the business that he will expand in accordance with Saks's plans (see 1927).

R. H. Macy Co. opens a new building west of its existing store on Herald Square (see 1901; 1912). Two further additions in 1928 and 1931 will make Macy's the world's largest department store under one roof, with 45 acres—more than 2 million square feet—of floor space.

Macy's first Thanksgiving Day parade moves two miles from Central Park West down Broadway to Herald Square, with volunteers from the store's huge staff wearing costumes and driving floats to begin an annual promotion event designed to boost Christmas sales (see balloons, 1927).

The city installs automatically controlled electric traffic lights at 50 intersections (see 1919). New Yorkers call them "peach baskets on stilts," and to save money the signals have only red and green lights, no amber. Three-color lights will be used beginning in 1952 after studies show that New York leads the nation in traffic accidents.

Manhattan's one-way street system is extended to nearly all narrow cross streets south of 57th Street (see 1916; 1927).

The steamboat *Alexander Hamilton* goes into service for the Hudson River Day Line and will survive as the last operating sidewheeler on the river (see *Berkshire*, 1913). Shorter but wider than the 11-year-old *Berkshire*, she is 349 feet in length, 77 in width, and has a triple-expansion inclined engine.

J. P. McAllister joins the tugboat firm McAllister Brothers started by his grandfather in 1864 as the lighterage business booms in New York Harbor. Within 5 years more than 50 other independent lighter companies will be competing with McAllister Brothers at 17 State Street and the 64-year-old Moran Towing Co. to move passenger ships, freighters, railroad barges, and other vessels in the harbor, while carrying break-bulk cargoes of coffee, fruit, sugar, lead, lumber, sulphur, and other commodities between ships and waterside refineries or warehouses.

The Sixth Avenue El north of 53rd Street is demolished, encouraging real estate development in the area. The El south of 53rd Street will continue to operate until December 1938.

Gov. Smith appoints Justice John V. McAvoy December 7 to conduct a "summary investigation" of what the governor calls "intolerable" conditions on the subways. A new Board of Transportation appointed by Mayor Hylan also looks into the conditions, and one of its members, Gen. John F. O'Ryan, says, "Had I treated German prisoners during the war as passengers on the transit lines are here being treated, I would have been court-martialed." The McAvoy Commission hears testimony through the month and will continue into January.

Philanthropist Payne Whitney pays $2.75 million to purchase land along the East River between 68th and 70th streets for New York Hospital (see 1916). The property has been used mostly for mule stables (see 1927).

The Genovese drugstore chain has its beginnings in an Astoria, Queens, establishment opened by pharmacist Joseph Genovese, whose enterprise will grow to have 141 stores in New York, New Jersey, and Connecticut.

Archbishop Hayes, now 56, is elected cardinal at Rome March 24 and continues his involvement in workers' issues, encouraging the work of Dorothy Day and Peter Maurin (see 1919; Catholic Industrial Conference, 1933).

Publisher Frank A. Munsey buys the *New York Evening Mail* January 24 and merges it with the *Evening Telegram* that he acquired in 1920. "The New York evening newspaper field is now in good shape," he says, "through the elimination of an oversupply of evening newspapers. These evening newspapers have been eliminated as individual entitities from New York journalism by myself alone" (see 1925; *World Telegram and Sun*, 1950).

The *New York Evening Graphic* begins publication under the aegis of Bernarr MacFadden. The tabloid will continue until 1932, illustrating stories that emphasize scandal, sex, and violence with "cosmographs"—faked photographs made by stripping celebrities' faces onto pictures of models (including staff members) who pose for them.

The *New York Herald Tribune* is created by a merger March 15. *Tribune* editor Ogden Mills Reid, now 42, has purchased the 89-year-old *Herald* and its Paris edition from Frank A. Munsey for $5 million in order to kill it, combines it with his own 83-year old paper, and heads the new daily that begins publication March 18 at its new building, 225 West 40th Street. The Venetian palazzo in West 35th Street that has housed the *Herald* on Herald Square will be torn down, and the *Herald Tribune* will give the *New York Times* healthy competition until 1966.

The *New York Daily Mirror* begins publication June 24 as a tabloid competitor to the *Daily News*. Its publisher is William Randolph Hearst, who has bought papers at Rochester, Syracuse, Los Angeles, Oakland, and Washington, D.C.; he has tried putting a tabloid section in his *New York American* but the experiment did not work. San Francisco-born editor John Russel Hastings, 50, runs the *Mirror* and announces that it will be 90 percent entertainment and 10 percent news (*see Brisbane, 1934*).

"Little Orphan Annie" appears October 5 in the *New York Daily News*, which in 5 years has become the most widely read paper in America, with a circulation of 750,000 (*see 1925*). *Chicago Tribune* staff cartoonist Harold Lincoln Gray, 30, who has helped Sidney Smith draw "The Gumps," has developed a blank-eyed, 12-year-old character together with her dog Sandy, her guardian Oliver "Daddy" Warbucks, and his manservant Punjab. The comic strip will campaign against communism, blind liberalism, and other threats to free enterprise and rugged individualism, continuing beyond Gray's death in 1968.

A gala dinner March 21 at the Civic Club in 12th Street brings together black and white intellectuals from Greenwich Village and Harlem. Charles S. Johnson, editor of the National Urban League's 1-year-old magazine *Opportunity*, plays host to the affair, and Howard University philosopher Alain Locke is the keynote speaker. Illinois-born *Century* magazine editor Carl Van Doren, 38, says, "What American literature decidedly needs at this moment is color, music, gusto, the free expression of gay or desperate moods." The NAACP announces the establishment of *Crisis* literary prizes, and the *Herald Tribune* predicts a week later that America is "on the edge, if not already in the midst of, what might not improperly be called a Negro renaissance."

Station WNYC begins broadcasting July 17—the first municipally owned U.S. radio station (*see 1925*).

Station WINS has its beginnings in WGBS, which goes on the air from studios in the 14-year-old Gimbel Brothers department store in Greeley Square; publisher William Randolph Hearst will acquire the station in the 1930s and change the call letters to correspond with those of his International News Service, and it will later be acquired by Westinghouse Broadcasting (*see 1965*).

Station WEAF begins network broadcasting October 14 from a new studio at 195 Broadway (*see 1922; NBC, 1926*). U.S. radio set ownership reaches 3 million, but most listeners use crystal sets with earphones to pick up signals from the growing number of stations.

Simon & Schuster is founded at New York by Boni & Liveright sales manager Richard Leo Simon, 25, and local journalist Max Lincoln Schuster, 27, who have pooled $8,000 in savings to start the firm with pledges of help from friends and relatives. *New York World* editor Margaret Petheridge Farrar, 27, and two colleagues have created the world's first crossword-puzzle book; it is the first S&S book, and it has sales of 400,000 its first year. The success of that and two other books enables the firm to end its first year with a profit of $100,000.

The Dial Press is founded by former Henry Holt editor Lincoln MacVeagh, 33, with backing from his Harvard classmate Scofield Thayer, who publishes *The Dial*.

The 18-year-old Pierpont Morgan Library becomes a public institution; a north wing will enlarge the marble Renaissance palazzo in 1962 and it will be further enlarged in 1976.

Nonfiction: *The Seven Lively Arts* by New Jersey-born *Dial* critic Gilbert (Vivian) Seldes, 31, who has finished the book at Paris, married Alice Hall there, received a drawing as a gift from his friend Pablo Picasso, and traveled to the Riviera to visit with his and Alice's friends Scott and Zelda Fitzgerald; *Sticks and Stones* by Flushing-born *Dial* editor and architectural critic Lewis Mumford, 28; *Manhattan: Now and Long Ago* by Lucy Sprague Mitchell and Clara D. Lambert.

Fiction: *Old New York* by Edith Wharton, now 62, is a collection of four novellas. Her first memory, she has recalled in her memoir *A Backward Glance*, is of walking up Fifth Avenue with her father: "the old

Fifth Avenue with its double line of low brown-stone houses, of a desperate uniformity of style, broken only—and surprisingly—by two equally unexpected features: the fenced-in plot of ground where the old Miss Kennedys' cows were pastured, and the truncated Egyptian pyramid [between 40th and 42nd streets] which so strangely served as a reservoir for New York's water supply;" *So Big* by Michigan-born New York novelist Edna Ferber, 37, who has been churning out novels and magazine stories since age 24, moved last year into an apartment in the Prasada at 50 Central Park West, wins the Pulitzer prize, and is emboldened to take a 5-year lease on a larger apartment in the building, with eight windows overlooking Central Park; *Crazy Man* by Maxwell Bodenheim; *There Is Confusion* by Jessie Redmon Fauset, who will continue until 1926 as literary editor of The *Crisis*.

Poetry: *The Man Who Died Twice* by Edwin Arlington Robinson; *Observations* by St. Louis-born poet Marianne (Craig) Moore, 36, who has lived with her mother in a ground-floor apartment at 15 St. Luke's Place since 1918 and will edit the *Dial* beginning in 1925.

The Argosy Book Store opens on Fourth Avenue (Booksellers Row); proprietor Louis Cohen deals in secondhand books (*see* 1931).

Painting: *The Dempsey-Firpo Fight* by George Bellows (*see* sports, 1923); *Penetration* and *Sunrise* by Arthur Dove.

New York-born painter Alfred H. Maurer has his first one-man show at New York's Weyhe Gallery (dealer Erhard Weyhe has paid $2,000 to acquire the entire contents of the artist's studio). Now 56, Maurer returned home from Paris 10 years ago and moved in with his father, a representational painter who had little use for his son's abstract works, which have been virtually ignored up to now.

Sculpture: *Rain* (assemblage of twigs and rubber cement on metal and glass) by Arthur Dove.

The Eternal Light Memorial commemorating U.S. soldiers who died in France from 1917 to 1918 is illuminated for the first time in Madison Square Park June 7; designed by sculptor Paul Bartlett and architect Thomas Hastings, the 120-foot flagpole topped by a multisided glass star will be removed in 1973, its star rebuilt, and its Oregon pine pole replaced by a steel pole that will be reinstalled in 1976.

Theater: *Hell-Bent fer Heaven* by North Carolina-born playwright Hatcher Hughes, 42, 1/4 at the Klaw Theater, with George Abbott, John Hamilton, Los Angeles-born actor Glenn Anders, 34, 122 perfs.; *Outward Bound* by English playwright Sutton Vane, 35, at the Ritz Theater (it opened at London's Garrick Theatre in mid-October of last year) with English actress Margalo Gilmore, 22, Dublin-born actor J. M. (Joseph Michael) Kerrigan, 39, Alfred Lunt, Leslie Howard, Dudley Digges, 144 perfs.; *The Show-Off* by Pennsylvania-born actor-turned-playwright George (E.) Kelly, 37, 2/4 at The Playhouse, with Louis John Bartels, Atlanta-born actor (William) Lee Tracy, 25, 575 perfs.; *Beggar on Horseback* by George S. Kaufman and Marc Connelly 2/12 at the Broadhurst Theater, with West Newton, Mass.-born actor (James Ripley) Osgood Perkins, 29, Colorado Springs-born actress Spring Byington, 30, 164 perfs.; *Welded* by Eugene O'Neill 3/17 at the 39th Street Theater, with Minsk-born actor Jacob Ben-Ami, 33, Doris Keane, 24 perfs.; *All God's Chillun Got Wings* by O'Neill 5/15 at the Provincetown Playhouse in Greenwich Village, with former Rutgers football star Paul (Bustill) Robeson, 26, playing a black man married to a white woman (Mary Blair). The Ku Klux Klan threatens reprisals, the Salvation Army and the Society for the Suppression of Vice warn that "such a play might easily lead to racial riots or disorder," but there are no disturbances; *The Best People* by David Gray and Avery Hopwood 8/19 at the Lyceum Theater, 143 perfs.; *What Price Glory?* by New York playwright Laurence Stallings, 28, and his Pennsylvania-born collaborator Maxwell Anderson, 35, 9/3 at the Plymouth Theater, with Louis Wolheim as Captain Flagg, Irish-born actor Brian Donlevy, 23, as Corporal Gowdy, 299 perfs.; *The Saint* by Mississippi-born playwright-critic-painter Stark Young, 43, 10/11 at the Greenwich Village Theater, with Leo Carillo and extras who include New York-born Sorbonne graduate Harold (Edgar) Clurman, 22, who will become a major director, producer, and drama critic, 17 perfs. (Young gives up his job as drama critic of the *New Republic* but will continue with *Theatre Arts* magazine as associate editor until 1940); *Desire Under the Elms* by Eugene O'Neill 11/11 at the Greenwich Village Theater, with Walter Huston, 208 perfs. (the play moves uptown after 2 months); *They Knew What They Wanted* by California-born playwright Sidney (Coe) Howard, 33, 11/24 at the Garrick Theater, with Pauline Lord, Glenn Anders, Richard Bennett, Brooklyn-born actor Sanford Meisner, 19, 414 perfs.; *The Harem* by Avery Hopwood (who has adapted a book by Ernest Vajda) 12/2 at the Belasco Theater, with Lenore Ulric, 183 perfs.; *The Youngest* by Philip Barry 12/22 at the Gaiety Theater, with Henry Hull, 104 perfs.; the Colony Theater (later to be called the Broadway) opens 12/25 at 1681 Broadway (53rd Street), initially as a movie house showing a Douglas Fairbanks film (it will reopen as a legitimate theater 12/8/1930).

The *New York Times* publishes a caricature January 29 of a Scottish music-hall star by local poster artist Al Hirschfeld, 20, who has received a telegram reading, "WOULD LIKE A DRAWING OF A HARRY LAUDER TWO COLS DEEP DELIVERY NO LATER THAN TUESDAY. SAM ZOLOTOW NEW YORK TIMES." Hirschfeld began his career as an office boy at Goldwyn Pictures in 1920, became art director at Selznick Pictures 2 years ago, and will now rent a studio in West 42nd Street, sharing it with Mexican artist Miguel Covarrubias. His eloquent theatrical cartoons will continue for more than 75 years (see Nina, 1943).

Film: James Cruze's *The City That Never Sleeps* with Louise Dresser, Ricardo Cortez, Virginia Lee Corbin.

Metro-Goldwyn-Mayer (M-G-M) is founded by New York vaudeville theater magnate Marcus Loew, now 54, who has absorbed Louis B. Mayer Pictures Corp. and buys Goldwyn Pictures Corp., Samuel Goldwyn having resigned (see 1913).

First performances: *Rhapsody in Blue* by George Gershwin 2/12 at Aeolian Hall with Paul Whiteman's Palais Royale Orchestra accompanying the pianist-composer, who completed the piano score January 7 after 3 weeks' work. New York-born composer Ferde (originally Ferdinand) Grofé, 31, has orchestrated the *Rhapsody* for piano and jazz ensemble.

Andrew Carnegie's widow, Louise, sells Carnegie Hall to real estate developer Robert E. Simon (see 1891). The hall has been operating at a deficit, but terms of the sale preclude demolishing it or using it for anything less than an auditorium before 1930; Simon will be tempted to turn the place into a movie theater after inaugurating a series of free noontime organ recitals; after his sudden death in September 1935 his son Robert E. Jr. will maintain the building until 1960 (see 1960).

Broadway musicals: *André Charlot's Revue of 1924* 1/9 at the Times Square Theater, with Glasgow-born comedian Jack Buchanan, 30, English comedienne Beatrice Lillie (originally Constance Sylvia Munston), 29, Douglas Furber, music by Philip Braham, lyrics by Furber, songs that include "Limehouse Blues," 138 perfs.; *The Ziegfeld Follies* 6/24 at the New Amsterdam Theater, with Will Rogers, Vivienne Segal (W. C. Fields and Ray Dooley will join next spring), music by Raymond Hubbell, Dave Stamper, Harry Tierney, Victor Herbert, and others, 520 perfs.; *George White's Scandals* 6/30 at the Apollo Theater, with music by George Gershwin, lyrics by B. G. DeSylva, 192 perfs.;

Rose Marie 9/2 at the Imperial Theater, with Mary Ellis, Dennis King, music by Rudolf Friml, lyrics by Otto Harbach and Oscar Hammerstein II, songs that include "Indian Love Call" and the title song, 557 perfs.; *The Passing Show* 9/3 at the Winter Garden Theater, with James Barton, English-born entertainer Harry McNaughton, 28, music by Sigmund Romberg and Jean Schwartz, lyrics by Harold Atteridge, 104 perfs.; *Earl Carroll's Vanities* (revue) 9/10 at the Earl Carroll Theater, with Sophie Tucker, Joe Cook, Russian-born entertainer Dave Chasen, 26, music and lyrics by Carroll, 440 perfs.; *The Greenwich Village Follies* (revue) 9/16 at the Shubert Theater, with comedians Charles Mack and George Moran, the Dolly sisters Jennie and Rozsika, Vincent Lopez, music by Cole Porter, lyrics by Porter, Irving Caesar, and John Murray Anderson, songs that include "I'm in Love Again," "Babes in the Woods," 127 perfs.; *Mme. Pompadour* 11/11 at the new Martin Beck Theater (designed in Moorish style by C. Albert Lansburgh), 302-314 West 45th Street, with Wilda Bennett, music by Leo Fall, book and lyrics by Rudolph Schanger and Ernst Welisch, 80 perfs.; *Dixie to Broadway* 11/22 at the Broadhurst Theater, with Florence Mills in an all-black revue, music by George Meyer and Arthur Johnston, lyrics by Grant Clarke and Roy Turk, 77 perfs.; *Lady Be Good* 12/1 at the Liberty Theater, with Fred Astaire and his sister Adele dancing to music by George Gershwin, lyrics by Ira Gershwin, songs that include "Somebody Loves Me," "The Man I Love," "Fascinating Rhythm," 184 perfs.; *The Student Prince of Heidelberg* 12/2 at the Jolson Theater, with music by Sigmund Romberg, lyrics by Dorothy Donnelly, songs that include "Deep in My Heart, Dear," "Welcome to Heidelberg," "Student Life," 608 perfs.; *Greenwich Follies* 12/24 at the new 46th Street Theater (the Richard Rodgers beginning in March 1990), designed by Herbert J. Krapp and built by the Chanins at 226-236 West 46th Street.

Composer Victor Herbert dies at New York May 26 at age 65.

The Minsky brothers take over the Apollo Theater for their risqué burlesque shows (see 1923; 1931).

Popular songs: "What'll I Do" and "Where Is My Little Old New York?" by Irving Berlin, whose earnings have climbed to about $500,000 per year (asked about Berlin's place in American music, Jerome Kern replies, "Irving Berlin has no place in American music—he *is* American Music").

Forest Hills, L.I., completes a tennis stadium for the West Side Tennis Club that held USLTA championship matches from 1915 to 1920 at the Queens community. The matches that began in 1881 have been held for the past 3 years at Philadelphia's Germantown Cricket Club but will be held until 1980 at Forest Hills.

Bill Tilden wins in men's singles at Forest Hills, Helen Wills in women's singles.

The New York Giants win the National League pennant but lose the World Series to the Washington Senators 4 games to 3. Queens-born second baseman Frankie Frisch, 26, gets 10 hits, including a triple; Atlanta-born first baseman Bill Terry, 25, gets a home run, as do San Francisco-born first baseman George Kelly, 29, who has played in what will be his only major-league season; Maryland-born pitcher John Needles "Jack" Bentley, 29; and Worcester-born pitcher Wilfred Patrick "Rosy" Ryan, 26, but the Senators win the deciding game in 12 innings.

● Paris milliner Lilly Daché, 32, arrives at New York, sells hats for R. H. Macy's, works for 10 weeks in a small Broadway hat shop, saves her money, and then opens her own shop with a $100 down payment, selling American-made hats molded to the head in the latest fashion. Working for Riboud last year, she introduced the cloche, a new shape to go with women's short hair.

Polly's Apparel Shop at 2719 Broadway closes down as Polish-born New York retailer Polly (originally Pearl) Adler, 24, goes back into business as a madam with a large apartment off Riverside Drive, paying heavy bribes to corrupt law-enforcement officials to keep her establishment open. She arrived in steerage at Ellis Island in 1914; raped at age 17 by her supervisor in a Brooklyn shirt factory, she had an abortion, moved to Manhattan, worked in a corset factory, met a young actress who introduced her to gangsters and bootleggers on the upper West Side, met one who offered to pay her rent if he and his girlfriend could use her apartment as a meeting place, and began procuring for him and his friends. Soprano Rosa Ponselle was among the customers at her lingerie shop, whereas Adler's brothel clients soon include actor Wallace Beery, playwright George S. Kaufman (who has a charge account), humorist Robert Benchley, business magnates, socialites, gambler Arnold Rothstein, and gangsters Al Capone, Jack "Legs" Diamond, and Dutch Schulz (Arthur Flegenheimer). Dark-haired, tall (five feet eleven), plump, flamboyantly dressed, and surrounded by her "girls," Polly is soon a familiar figure at the city's popular speakeasies, moving her operation to Saratoga Springs each summer as she builds her business with houses that always have paneled French-gray walls and are furnished with jade and rose quartz lamps, Gobelin tapestries, and Louis XVI furniture (see 1935).

▥ Sicilian-born mobster Joseph Bonanno, 19, goes to work for underworld bootleggers who are profiting from the opportunities offered by Prohibition. Bonanno grew up in Brooklyn's Williamsburg section before his parents moved back to Italy, he has slipped ashore illegally at Tampa, Fla., becomes an enforcer for a gang run by Salvatore Maranzano, and will rise to become the leader of his own Mafia "family," competing with Vito Genovese (who uses the trucks of a Queens bakery to transport alcohol at night) and others (see 1931).

Chinatown's bloodiest Tong War breaks out October 7 when the On Leongs try to storm the headquarters of the rival Hip Sings in Pell Street (see 1880). Lem Hing of the Hip Sings is shot to death a few hours later in a Delancey Street restaurant, five more Hip Sings are killed within the week, and the hostilities will continue for more than 5 months (see 1925).

🏠 The Federal Reserve Bank of New York building is completed at 35 Liberty Street in the style of a massive Florentine palazzo of Indiana limestone, Ohio sandstone, and ironwork. Designed by York & Sawyer, it has a vast vault five stories underground and accessible only by a well-guarded elevator. Other nations have been placing their gold bullion in the care of the New York branch of the Fed since 1916, and the vaults will ultimately hold about 40 percent of all the monetary gold in the world.

The 24-story Westinghouse Building is completed at 150 Broadway, northeast corner Liberty Street, to designs by Starrett & Van Vleck.

Architect Bertram G. Goodhue dies at New York April 23 at age 54.

The 36-story American Radiator Building (later the American Standard Building, later the Bryant Park Hotel) is completed at 40 West 40th Street, between Fifth and Sixth avenues, to Gothic-inspired designs by Hood & Fouilhoux. It has one of the city's first pyramidal silhouettes, Pawtucket, R.I.-born architect Raymond M. (Mathewson) Hood, 43, has created its black brick and gold terra-cotta façade, an addition by his partner André Fouilhoux will be completed in 1937.

A 10-story luxury apartment house is completed at 40 West 55th Street, just west of Fifth Avenue, to designs by Rosario Candela.

Doormen and elevator men in even the best New York apartment houses typically earn $20 per week.

The Hudson View Gardens apartment complex is completed in upper Manhattan between Pinehurst

Avenue and Cabrini Boulevard from 183rd Street to 185th. Designed by George F. Pelham, Jr. for Dr. Charles V. Paterno, 50, the enclave contains six-story elevator buildings and four-story walk-ups with a total of 354 co-op apartments, the most expensive one having two bedrooms and selling for $10,000, with monthly maintenance of $94. Kitchens have automatic dishwashers, living rooms are equipped with built-in Murphy beds, a rooftop technician monitors incoming signals for the central radio service, and tenants have their own post office, community rooms, barbershop, children's nursery, grocery store, and restaurant, but restrictive covenants bar sales to blacks and Jews.

Builder Sam Minskoff builds two more apartment houses in the Bronx and completes the Nathan Hale Memorial apartments on the west blockfront of Amsterdam Avenue between 89th and 90th streets in Manhattan (see 1924).

A Long Island City housing project is completed with six five-story buildings; financed by Metropolitan Life Insurance Co., it has been designed by architect Andrew Thomas.

The City Housing Corp. is founded by members of the Regional Planning Association of America to implement their theories of planning and housing design. Sponsored by the new limited-profit corporation, Rochester-born architect Clarence S. Stein, 42, and Henry Wright lay out the design of Sunnyside Gardens in northwestern Queens—a mix of single-, double-, and multi-family attached brick structures, with garages, porches, gables, and slate roofs. A planned community whose purpose is to provide middle-income families with "health, open space, greenery, and idyllic community living for all," the project will be completed in the next 5 years with help from architect Frederick Lee Ackerman, now 48, and occupy 12 contiguous blocks on 77 acres, its dwellings interspersed with shade trees, center courts, lawns, and flower gardens, some private, some communal, laid out by landscape architect Marjorie Cautley. Sunnyside's 1,202 families will enjoy common ownership of the shaded courtyards, and residents will include jazz cornetist Bix Beiderbecke, singer Perry Como, actress Judy Holliday, architectural critic Lewis Mumford, painter Raphael Soyer, and singer-actor Rudy Vallée.

The 15-story Hotel Times Square opens at the northeast corner of Eighth Avenue and 43rd Street with 1,000 rooms.

The 22-story Roosevelt Hotel opens September 22 across from Grand Central Terminal, occupying the full block bounded by 45th and 46th streets between Vanderbilt and Madison avenues. Designed by George B. Post & Sons and built at a cost of $10 million, it has 1,100 rooms and is inaugurated with a dinner where Mayor Hylan, millionaire Cornelius Vanderbilt IV, and explorer Carl Akeley, a friend of the late Theodore Roosevelt, sit on the dais. On its Madison Avenue side it replaces the Tiffany Studios, an old red-brick structure built by the Vanderbilt family to serve as the Railroad YMCA, and by 1929 the hotel will be paying the New York Central $285,000 per year in rentals on the real estate it occupies (see 1995; Guy Lombardo, 1929).

The Shelton Towers hotel (later Marriott East; see 1991) opens on Lexington Avenue between 48th and 49th streets. Designed by Arthur Loomis Harmon for developer James T. Lee, the 1,200-room structure looms 34 stories above midtown, making it the world's tallest hotel, with swimming pool, lounges, solaria, a bowling alley, three squash courts, and a reading room.

The 13-story Park Lane Hotel opens on a block of unused New York Central property facing Park Avenue between 48th and 49th streets. Designed by Schultze & Weaver, the H-shaped structure has 600 rooms, in suites of one to six rooms, with maids' quarters in the larger suites. A two-room suite comprises a living room 27' × 14', a bedroom 21' × 14', a bath, two closets, a foyer hall, and a serving pantry equipped with refrigerator and china closet. The Park Lane's Louis XVI-style restaurant, ballroom, and private dining rooms are on the ground floors; maid, valet, and lighting are included in the rent; and the kitchen, located between the ballroom and restaurant, provides room service at no additional charge. Single rooms are set aside on each floor to accommodate tenants' guests. The hotel will survive until 1965.

International House is completed at 500 Riverside Drive, north of 122nd Street, as a residence for students who attend Barnard, Columbia, Teachers College, and other nearby institutions of higher education. Lindsay & Warren has designed the structure.

Bankers George F. Baker and J. P. Morgan, Jr. purchase the Hamilton Grange for $50,000 and donate it to the American Scenic and Historic Preservation Society on condition that it be moved to a more "suitable location." The National Park Service will take over the building in 1964 and propose in 1991 that it be moved to St. Nicholas Park, but fiscal constraints and other considerations will delay any such move for years thereafter.

Department-store heir Rodman Wanamaker tells the Board of Estimate March 31 that Central Park as a recreation ground is "doomed if not already a thing of the past," the automobile having "killed it" as a resort where people might go for fresh air, and that a war memorial should be built on the site of the reservoir. Wanamaker chairs the Mayor's Committee on a Permanent War Memorial.

Gov. Smith appoints New York lawyer Robert Moses, 35, president of the Long Island State Park Commission April 18. Long Island has just one state park, a 200-acre tract on Fire Island; by the end of the 1928 summer season it will have 14, embracing 9,700 acres—6,775 of them acquired as gifts from the towns of Babylon, Hempstead, and Oyster Bay, the city of New York, private individuals, and the U.S. Department of Commerce.

Totonno's pizzeria opens in Coney Island. Anthony "Totonno" Pero has trained under Gennaro Lombardi in Manhattan (see 1905); Pero's descendants will continue the operation for more than 75 years (see John's, 1929).

The Johnson-Reed Immigration Act passed by Congress May 26 limits the annual quota from any country to 2 percent of U.S. residents of that nationality in 1890 (see Dillingham Act, 1921). The Ku Klux Klan founded in 1915 raises $5 million to change the U.S. immigration law in ways that will keep the nation white and Protestant. Sometimes called the National Origins Act, the new law bars Africans and Asians from entry (New York's Japanese population will fall in the next few decades to between 2,500 and 2,900—down from more than 4,600 in 1920 (see 1948; Japanese Association, 1914) and Japanese will not be admitted until 1965. The law limits immigration from southern and Eastern Europe to 20 percent of the total, but it permits close relatives of U.S. citizens to enter as non-quota immigrants and places no restrictions on immigration from Canada or Latin America. Ellis Island has processed more than 70 percent of all U.S. immigrants since it opened in 1892; henceforth most legal immigrants will be issued visas by consulates abroad, Ellis Island's function as a processing center will disappear, and the flood of immigrants into New York will slow to a trickle (see 1932).

1925 State senate floor leader James J. Walker gains the support of Tammany Hall, defeats Mayor Hylan in the Democratic Party primary, and goes on to win the mayoralty election, stacking up 748,687 votes and carrying every borough, including Hylan's Brooklyn. Fountain-pen manufacturer Frank D. Waterman receives only 346,564 votes running as a Republican, Socialist Norman Thomas gets 39,574 (Thomas 2 years ago bought a four-story house at 206 East 18th Street for his family of five children and will live there until 1939). Now 44, the slim, elegant mayor-elect was persuaded by his father to give up his songwriting career in 1909 and still lives in the house where he was born at 6 St. Luke's Place, between Hudson Street and Seventh Avenue; he has promoted bills to legalize prizefighting and Sunday baseball, pushed through Gov. Alfred E. Smith's progressive legislation, received key support from Bronx political boss Edward J. Flynn, and will champion the interests of the people in his first term as mayor.

The Brotherhood of Sleeping Car Porters is organized at Harlem August 25 by Florida-born minister's son A. (Asa) Philip Randolph, 36, who publishes the *Messenger*, a New York monthly devoted to black politics and culture. Wages for porters have risen in the past year to $67.50 per month, up from a minimum of $27.50 in 1915; Randolph will work to raise them further.

Speculator Jesse L. Livermore makes $10 million in wheat futures (see 1908). He has made "bear raids" on the market, and when "Black Friday" hits the Chicago trading pits the plunge in prices redounds to Livermore's profit. His profitable dealings have enabled him to buy the Locust Lawn estate at King's Point, L.I., and a large yacht (see 1929).

Lebenthal & Co. is founded by New York lawyer Louis S. Lebenthal, 27, and his lawyer wife, Sayra (née Fischer), 30, who entered Wall Street 3 years ago as employees of Stephens & Co. Pioneering in the retail sale of tax-exempt and taxable municipal bonds in odd-lots at a time when only major financial institutions and very high net-worth individuals buy such securities, their office at 135 Broadway will open the municipal-bond market to the average investor and prosper with help from daily advertisements on newspaper financial pages and a regular column by Louis Lebenthal in the *New York World Telegram* (see 1951).

Wall Street's Dow Jones Industrial average closes December 31 at 156.66, up from 120.51 at the end of 1924.

Brooklyn Union Gas sells its electric franchises and the distribution system of its Flatbush Gas Co. to Brooklyn Edison Co. (see 1895). Newly constructed New York apartment houses still have gaslight fixtures, but only in stair halls for use in emergencies. Most city buildings are wired for electricity.

Mayor Hylan breaks ground with a silver-plated shovel March 14 at the intersection of St. Nicholas Avenue and West 123rd Street for a municipal subway system that will compete with the BMT and IRT. Addressing a crowd of some 2,000 at Hancock Square in Washington Heights, the mayor tears into the Transit Commission (whose new members have been appointed by Gov. Smith) and the "million dollar traction conspiracy" of the "railroad corporations."

The Fifth Avenue Association releases the results of a study showing that traffic on all the city's central avenues has increased by 20 percent in just one year. Parks Department landscape gardener Julius Burgevin has designed 24-foot-wide center malls in place of Park Avenue's 40-foot-wide median, but despite its narrow, 27-foot roadways and despite its continuing Vanderbilt Avenue bottleneck Park Avenue has overtaken Fifth as a traffic artery (see 1923); the Fifth Avenue Association presses to have Park Avenue's roadways widened so they can relieve the burden on Fifth (see 1927).

The city's taxi fleets lower fares by as much as 50 percent in a savage rate war, New York gets its first women licensed taxi drivers, and the Police Department establishes a Taxicab Commission to gain tighter control of licensing (see 1923; 1933).

The 15-mile-long Bronx River Parkway is completed from the Bronx north into Westchester. Considered the most beautiful highway in America, it winds along the small river, over and under bridges, and through woods, with no traffic lights to impede traffic.

Colonial Air Transport Co. starts carrying mail between New York and Boston (see 1923). The company has been created by a merger of Boston's Colonial Airways with Eastern Air Transport, a line organized by Juan Trippe and John Hambleton with backing from Cornelius Vanderbilt Whitney and William H. Vanderbilt (see Cuba, 1927).

Columbia Presbyterian Hospital is created as a joint effort by Columbia University and Presbyterian Hospital (see 1868). It acquires property on upper Broadway at 168th Street, where it will expand to become one of the city's most prestigious medical centers (see 1928).

The New York College of Dentistry merges with New York University. Founded in 1865, it will establish an affiliation with the dental department of Bellevue Hospital next year, enabling students to receive instruction in surgery and treat patients in the hospital's dental clinic (see 1957).

Clergyman Harry Emerson Fosdick, now 46, resigns from the First Presbyterian Church early in the year and later becomes pastor of the Park Avenue Baptist Church, but only on condition that the church offer interdenominational ministry and open membership (see 1922; Riverside Church, 1931).

Mayor Hylan tries to use the 3-year-old municipal radio station WNYC to attack his political opponents but is stopped by a judge.

The Scripps-Howard newspaper chain is created as New York newspaperman Roy Howard moves up to co-directorship of the Scripps-McRae chain. Howard broke the news of the 1918 World War armistice 4 days early by acting on a tip and will bring new dynamism to the newspapers in the chain.

The 4-year-old New York Sunday News outsells all other Sunday papers with help from its comic strips and stories that focus on sex and crime. Circulation of the Daily News passes the million mark, and publisher Joseph M. Patterson will say, "The Daily News was built on legs, but when we got enough circulation we draped them." (He runs few stories dealing with foreign or even U.S. national politics and competitors call his paper "the shopgirls' Bible.") Capt. Patterson moves to New York to take sole charge of the News, bringing with him his favorite daughter Alicia, 18, who will go to work as a cub reporter (see Newsday, 1940); Patterson makes the Bowery his favorite slumming ground, eating and drinking with the down-and-outers he finds there and panhandling for coins; his wife will soon return to Chicago and divorce him.

The New Yorker begins publication February 19 at 25 West 45th Street with $25,000 in backing from Fleischmann's Yeast heir Raoul (Herbert) Fleischmann, 39, a racetrack aficionado and poker player who has a 20-room house on an 11-acre Port Washington, L.I., estate in addition to a Fifth Avenue apartment but is bored with running a General Baking Co. plant. Aspen, Colo.-born, Salt Lake City-raised high-school dropout Harold (Wallace) Ross, 33, was de facto editor of Stars and Stripes in 1918 and has often played poker with Fleischmann at the Algonquin Hotel (both are members of the "Thanatopsis Literary and Inside Straight Club"); he and his New York Times reporter wife, Jane (née Grant), have pooled their own $25,000 in savings to start the 36-page, 15¢ weekly magazine of "gaiety, wit, and satire," fiction, social commentary, and criticism; their prospectus says, "The New Yorker will be the magazine which is not edited for the old lady in Dubuque. It will be what is commonly called sophisticated, in that it will assume a reasonable degree of enlightenment on the part of its readers. It will hate bunk." The magazine's first employee

February 21, 1925 · THE · Price 15 cents

NEW YORKER

A new weekly introduced readers not from Dubuque to sophisticated editorial content. THE NEW YORKER

is San Francisco-born artist-cartoonist Rea Irvin, 43, whose drawing of a Regency dandy (who will be named Eustace Tilley) contemplating a butterfly through a magnifying glass adorns its first cover. The first issue sells only 15,000 copies but it quickly attracts the talents of New York-born cartoonist Peter Arno (Curtis Arnoux Peters), 21, Indianapolis-born cartoonist Helen Hokinson, 26, and Mount Vernon-born advertising writer E. B. (Elwyn Brooks) White, 25, who will write most of the "Talk of the Town" items that begin each issue. Katherine S. White, 32, is the first fiction editor, but circulation falls to 8,009 by late spring, Ross is soon borrowing from Fleischmann at the rate of $5,000 per week, and the directors decide at a meeting in May at the Princeton Club to suspend publication. Walking up Madison Avenue, Fleischmann overhears magazine consultant and director John Hanrahan say to Ross (or to director H. Holly Truax) at the corner of 42nd Street, "I can't blame Raoul for a moment for refusing to go on, but it's like killing something that's alive." The remark gets under Fleischmann's skin, and he decides to persevere; by 1927 he will have poured more than $700,000 into the venture, sometimes at the rate of

$20,000 per week. In October The *New Yorker* begins publishing a "Letter from Paris," signed Genêt but written by Illinois-born journalist Janet Flanner, 33, who will continue writing the "Letters" for nearly 50 years. Ohio-born humorist James (Grover) Thurber, 30, will become a *New Yorker* regular after receiving rejection slips for his first 20 submissions. When the magazine is criticized for running advertisements promoting "restricted" hotels and resorts, Ross will consult Fleischmann, who will say, "That's a good thing, because then the Jewish clientele knows forthrightly where they will not be made comfortable." The magazine will turn the corner next year, show a net profit of $287,000 on a gross of $1.8 million in 1928, and remain profitable for more than 40 years.

A new *Cosmopolitan* magazine is created by a merger of *Hearst's International Magazine* with an earlier *Cosmopolitan* under the editorship of Raymond Land, 47 (*see* 1905). He will publish works by Louis Bromfield, Edna Ferber, Fannie Hurst, Rupert Hughes, Sinclair Lewis, Somerset Maugham, Dorothy Parker, O. O. McIntyre, Booth Tarkington, and P. G. Wodehouse (*see* Helen Gurley Brown, 1965).

Collier's editor William Ludlow Chenery sends three staff writers on a nationwide tour to report on Prohibition. They find a breakdown in law enforcement of all kinds and *Collier's* becomes the first major magazine to call for a repeal of the 18th Amendment that has been in effect since January 1920. The magazine loses 3,000 readers but gains 400,000 new ones.

Il Nuovo Mondo begins publication at New York November 21 to give the city its first anti-fascist Italian-language daily.

Publisher Frank A. Munsey undergoes surgery for appendicitis at Lenox Hill Hospital December 12 but dies there of peritonitis December 22 at age 71, having built up the circulation of his two major magazines and acquired an empire of newspapers in New York and other cities (*see* 1889; *Argosy*, 1896). A bachelor, he leaves an estate valued at upwards of $20 million and perhaps as much as $40 million (*see* Scripps-Howard, 1927).

Grey Advertising takes that name after 8 years as Grey Studios (*see* 1917). Founder Lawrence Valenstein placed a help-wanted ad in the *New York Times* 4 years ago, he hired Arthur (Cornell) Fatt, now 21, as an office boy, and Fatt has become equal partner. Grey's accounts are mostly garment-trade companies, but Fatt will bring in clients such as Chock full 'o Nuts, Ford Motor Company, Procter & Gamble, and Greyhound Bus Lines. Following Valenstein's philosophy (devise a product to fill a need, something that does not exist, and use pre-selling to build a market), Grey will be billing $1 million per year by the 1930s and grow to become the fifth largest U.S. agency.

The Viking Press is founded by New York law graduate Harold K. Guinzburg, 26, and former Alfred E. Knopf promotion man George S. Oppenheimer, 27, who start out at 30 Irving Place with $50,000 in capital (Guinzburg's family has prospered in the Kleinert dress shield business). The partners obtain a backlist to carry their overhead by acquiring the 20-year-old firm R. W. Huebsch, whose authors include Sherwood Anderson, James Joyce, D. H. Lawrence, and Thorstein Veblen; they persuade Huebsch to join them as editor-in-chief and open with a list that includes *The Book of American Spirituals* by James Weldon Johnson, arrangements by his brother Rosamond (*see* Literary Guild, 1927).

The Modern Library is acquired from Boni and Liveright by the firm's vice president Bennett Alfred Cerf, 27, with Donald S. Klopfer, 23. They begin building the clothbound reprints into a low-priced line that will grow to have 400 titles in the next 50 years with sales of more than 50 million copies (*see* Random House, 1927).

Nonfiction: *The Tragedy of Waste* by New Hampshire-born New York economist Stuart Chase, 37, who 3 years ago joined with George Soule to establish the Labor Bureau, a research agency for labor unions and co-operatives; *Skyline Promenades: A Potpourri* by Massachusetts-born writer (Justin) Brooks Atkinson, 31, who is named drama critic of the *New York Times*, a position he will hold until 1942.

Fiction: *The Great Gatsby* by F. Scott Fitzgerald, who says of the Corona Dumps on Flushing Bay, "this is a valley of ashes . . ." The novella has only modest sales but will later be hailed as Fitzgerald's greatest work; *Manhattan Transfer* by Chicago-born New York novelist John Dos Passos (originally John Randolph Madison), 29, the illegitimate son of New York lawyer John R. Dos Passos, who railed as a Harvard undergraduate against "the cossack tactics of the New York police force" but will later become a staunch defender of traditional American values: "Crammed on the narrow island the millionwindowed buildings will jut glittering, pyramid on pyramid like the white cloudhead above the thunderstorm." Dos Passos moves to an apartment at 106-110 Columbia Heights in Brooklyn (poet Hart Crane is in the same building), having lived at 11 Bank Street and, before that, at 3 Washington Square North; *Bread Givers* by Anzia Yezierska, who bitterly describes public school teachers "just peddling their little bit of education for a living, the same as any pushcart peddler."

Poetry: *Color* by Louisville, Ky.-born Harlem poet Countee Cullen (originally Countee LeRoy Porter), 22, includes "Heritage," "Near White," "Brown Boy to Brown Girl," "To a Brown Boy," "The Shroud of Color," "Yet Do I Marvel," "Pagan Prayer," and "Oh, for a Little While to Be Kind;" *Against This Age* by Maxwell Bodenheim.

Harlem's Schomburg Center for Research in Black Culture branch of the New York Public Library has its beginnings May 8 (*see* 1926).

Construction of the Brooklyn Museum (still called the Institute of Arts and Sciences) ceases after 30 years of work even though not much more than the north façade has been completed (*see* 1897). Its grand stairway is surmounted by 28 giant statues, its north façade resembles an Ionic temple, but its neo-classic McKim, Mead & White design is already considered outmoded, the grand stairs and statuary hall will be removed, and new architects will be brought in to give it a more modern look.

M. Knoedler & Co. moves its art gallery from Fifth Avenue and 46th Street to a new building at 14 East 57th Street (*see* 1912). It will remain at the new location for decades before moving uptown to 19 East 70th Street.

Painting: *New York Street with Moon* by Wisconsin-born painter Georgia O'Keeffe, 37, who first came to the city in 1907, has lived here off and on ever since, and was married last year to photographer and gallery owner Alfred Stieglitz; *Golden Storm, Sea II*, and *The Critic* by Arthur Dove. George Bellows dies of a ruptured appendix at New York January 8 at age 42. He has been living at 146 East 19th Street, between Irving Place and Third Avenue.

Sculpture: a bronze statue of the sled dog Balto created by Brooklyn-born artist Frederick Roth, 53, is installed near Central Park's East Drive parallel with 66th Street to honor the Alaskan dog teams that covered 655 miles in 5 days and 7 hours (the previous record was 9 days) to carry antitoxin that prevented an epidemic of malignant diphtheria at icebound Nome, Alaska, in early February.

Theater: *Is Zat So?* by New York-born playwright-actor James Gleason, 38, and Richard Taber 1/5 at the 39th Street Theater, with Gleason and Robert Armstrong in a prizefight comedy, 618 perfs.; *Processional* by New York-born playwright John Howard Lawson, 29, 1/12 at the Garrick Theater, with George

Abbott, June Walker, New York-born actor Ben Grauer, 16, 96 perfs.; *Caesar and Cleopatra* by George Bernard Shaw 4/13 at the new Guild Theater (later to be called ANTA, and beginning in 1981 the Virginia) at 245 West 52nd Street; *The Jazz Singer* by New York-born playwright Samson Raphaelson, 23, 9/14 at the Fulton Theater, with George Jessel as Jack Robbins (formerly Jakie Rabinowitz), the son of a fourth-generation cantor who has declined to follow the family tradition, run off at age 15 to sing jazz, been discovered singing in a Chicago movie theater and signed to appear in a big Broadway revue, but quits after a struggle when told that his father's dying request is that he become a cantor, 303 perfs. (a close friend of Mayor Walker, Jessel will for years be the city's unofficial toastmaster); *The Green Hat* by Bulgarian-born English writer Michael Arlen (originally Dikran Kouyoumdjian), 29 (he has adapted his 1924 novel), 9/15 at the Broadhurst Theater, with Katherine Cornell, Leslie Howard, 231 perfs.; *The Butter and Egg Man* by George S. Kaufman 9/23 at the Longacre Theater, with London-born actor George Alison, 60 (the title comes from nightclub hostess Texas Guinan, who used it for a big spender from the midwest at her El Fey Club who would not give his real name), 243 perfs.; *Craig's Wife* by George Kelly 10/12 at the Morosco Theater, with Chrystal Herne, 289 perfs.; *Lucky Sam McGarver* by Sidney Howard 10/21 at The Playhouse, with John Cromwell, Clare Eames, 29 perfs.; *Naughty Cinderella* by Avery Hopwood (who has adapted a French work by René Peter and Henri Falk) 11/9 at the Lyceum Theater, with Irene Bordoni, 121 perfs.; *In a Garden* by Philip Barry 11/16 at the Plymouth Theater, with Laurette Taylor, New York-born actor Louis Calhern (originally Carl Henry Vogt), 30, 73 perfs.; *Mayflowers* 11/24 at the new Forrest Theater (later the Coronet, and beginning in 1959 the Eugene O'Neill, it has been designed by architect Herbert J. Krapp for the Shubert brothers); *Easy Come, Easy Go* by Owen Davis 12/7 at the new Biltmore Theater, 261-265 West 47th Street (designed for developer Irwin S. Chanin by Herbert J. Krapp), with Otto Kruger, Victor Moore, 180 perfs.; *Easy Virtue* by English actor-playwright Noël (Pierce) Coward, 25, 12/7 at the Empire Theater, with Boston-born actress Jane Cowl, 35, and Joyce Carey (*née* Lawrence [Lilian Braithwaite's daughter]), 26, 147 perfs.

Swedish film actress Greta Garbo (originally Greta Lovisa Gustafsson), 19, arrives at New York aboard the S.S. *Drottningholm* July 5 with director Mauritz Stiller.

J. R. Bray office boy Shamus Culhane, 17, animates his first scene—a monkey with a hot towel—while covering for a drunken animator and begins a notable career (*see* Bray, 1910). Culhane's father deserted the family last year, young Shamus won medals for his artwork as a student at P.S. 82 in Yorkville, took commercial art courses at Boy's High School in Harlem, and has obtained his office-boy job because Walter Lantz, head of animation at J. R. Bray, is his best friend's brother.

Air conditioning is introduced at the 8-year-old Rivoli movie theater on Broadway, ushering in a new era of comfortable theater-going.

First performances: Symphony for Organ and Orchestra by Brooklyn-born composer Aaron Copland, 24, 1/11 at New York, with Nadia Boulanger.

Broadway musicals: *Big Boy* 1/7 at the Winter Garden Theater, with Al Jolson, songs that include "It All Depends on You" by Ray Henderson, lyrics by B. G. DeSylva and Lew Brown (Russian-born writer Lewis Bronstein, 31), "If You Knew Susie Like I Know Susie" by Joseph Meyer, lyrics by B. G. DeSylva, 188 perfs.; *Puzzles of 1925* (revue) 2/2 at the Fulton Theater, with Elsie Janis, Philadelphia-born Ziegfeld Follies veteran Helen Broderick, 33, Saint John, N.B.-born actor Walter Pidgeon, 26, Sydney, Australia-born dancer-singer-actor Cyril Ritchard (originally Trimnell-Ritchard), 26, book by Janis (who directs), 104 perfs.; *The Garrick Gaieties* 6/8 at the Garrick Theater, with Sterling Holloway, Mexican-born actor Romney Brent (originally Romulo Larraide), 23, music by local composer Richard Rodgers, 23, lyrics by Lorenz (Milton) Hart, 27, songs that include "Sentimental Me," 14 perfs. (plus 43 beginning 5/10/26); *Artists and Models* 6/24 at the Winter Garden Theater, with music by J. Fred Coots, Alfred Goodman, Maurice Rubens, lyrics by Clifford Grey, 411 perfs.; *Dearest Enemy* 9/18 at the Knickerbocker Theater, with Helen Ford, music by Richard Rodgers, lyrics by Lorenz Hart, book by Herbert Fields based on the Revolutionary War legend about Mrs. Robert Murray delaying General Howe, songs that include "Here in My Arms," "Where the Hudson River Flows," 286 perfs.; *The Vagabond King* 9/21 at the Casino Theater, with Dennis King, music by Rudolf Friml, lyrics by Bryan Hooker, songs that include "Only a Rose," 511 perfs.; *Sunny* 9/22 at the New Amsterdam Theater, with Marilyn Miller (who receives 10 percent of the gross), Jack Donahue, Clifton Webb, music by Jerome Kern, lyrics by Otto Harbach and Oscar Hammerstein II, songs that include "Who," 517 perfs.; *The Charlot Revue* 11/10 at the Selwyn Theater, with Beatrice Lillie, Gertrude Lawrence, Jack Buchanan, London-born ingénue Anna Neagle (originally Marjorie Robertson), 21, songs that include "Poor Little Rich Girl" by Noël Coward, "A Cup of Coffee, a Sandwich, and You" by Joseph Meyer, lyrics by Billy Rose and Swiss-born writer Al Dubin, 34, 138 perfs.; *The Cocoanuts* 12/8 at the Lyric Theater, with the Four Marx Brothers, Margaret Dumont, book by George S. Kaufman, music and lyrics by Irving Berlin, 377 perfs. Vaudeville monologist Art Fisher has given the New York-born Marx Brothers their nicknames and has helped develop their characters: Groucho (Julius Henry), 30, is a moustached wit, Harpo (Arthur), 32, an idiotic kleptomaniacal mute harpist, Chico (Leonard), 34, a pianist and confidence man who serves as Harpo's interpreter, Zeppo (Herbert) is straight man; *Tip-Toes* 12/28 at the Liberty Theater, with Queenie Smith, Philadelphia-born soprano Jeanette MacDonald, 24, Robert Halliday, music by George Gershwin, lyrics by Ira Gershwin, book by Guy Bolton and Fred Thompson, songs that include "Sweet and Low-Down," 194 perfs.

Popular songs: "I'm Something on Avenue A" by George Gershwin; "Don't Bring Lulu" by Henderson, lyrics by Billy Rose and Lew Brown (Rose opened the Backstage Club speakeasy last year in a loft over a garage with Joe Frisco as MC and Danville, Ohio-born torch singer Helen Morgan (originally Helen Riggins), 24, sitting atop the piano, where by some accounts she had been put by writer Ring Lardner because she was too drunk to stand up; "My Yiddishe Momme" by Jack Yellen and Lew Pollack, lyrics by Yellen (for Sophie Tucker).

"They Laughed When I Sat Down at the Piano but When I Started to Play!—" is the headline for a U.S. School of Music advertisement written by New York copywriter John Caples, 25, who has quit the engineering department of New York Telephone Co. to join the Ruthrauff & Ryan agency.

The Arthur Murray Correspondence School of Dancing moves to New York, where local baker's son Arthur Murray (Teichmann), 30, marries his partner Kathryn (*née* Kohnfelder) and will soon set up a midtown Manhattan studio to teach ballroom dancing. Born in East Harlem, Murray learned to dance from a girlfriend and from lessons at the Educational Alliance, took further lessons at a school started by Vernon and Irene Castle, joined the school's faculty, taught dancing at an Asheville, N.C., resort hotel, and started his correspondence school at Atlanta 4 years ago after studying at Georgia Tech. His enterprise will grow in the next 40 years to have more than 350 franchised dance studios, including nearly 50 in foreign countries.

Smalls' Paradise opens October 22 at 2294½ Seventh Avenue on the corner of 135th Street. Ed Smalls's jazz club seats about 1,500 patrons, most of them white (few blacks can afford the prices), who enjoy Chinese food, elaborate floor shows, singing waiters (who wear roller skates or dance the Charleston), and performances by instrumentalists who include Fletcher Henderson, James P. Johnson, and Newark, N.J.-born stride pianist Willie "the Lion" Smith (William Henry Joseph Berthol Bonaparte Bertholoff Smith), 31. "Harlem's House of Mirth and Music" will continue to draw crowds until its closing in 1986.

The Wood Memorial at Belmont Park in April is a new test for 3-year-old thoroughbreds prior to the Kentucky Derby in May.

New York-born swimmer Gertrude Ederle, 17, swims 21 miles from the Battery to Sandy Hook June 15, breaking the record set earlier by a man and becoming the first woman to make the swim (*see* English Channel, 1926).

Bill Tilden wins in men's singles at Forest Hills, Helen Wills in women's singles.

New York-born Columbia graduate Henry Louis "Lou" Gehrig, 22, joins the New York Yankees as a first baseman and begins a 14-year career of 2,130 consecutive games, in which he will have a batting average of .341. He has been signed by Yankee chief scout Paul B. Krichell, 42, who saw Gehrig play in a game between Columbia and Rutgers 3 years ago and pays him a $1,500 signing bonus. Krichell was a coach for the Boston Red Sox in 1920, was asked by Yankee general manager Ed Barrow to join the Yankee organization as a scout, and will continue in that position until his death in 1957 (*see* Gehrig, 1939).

Former Giants pitcher Christy Mathewson dies of tuberculosis at a Saranac Lake sanatorium October 7 at age 45.

The New York Giants professional football team is founded by former bookmaker Timothy (James) Mara, 38, who obtains a franchise from the new National Football League. The Mara family will own the Giants for more than 70 years.

Madison Square Garden is demolished after 35 years of providing a venue for prizefights, 6-day bicycle races, rodeos (beginning in 1923), horse shows, and last year's Democratic National Convention. Architect Thomas W. Lamb has designed a new $5.6 million Garden for Tex Rickard and it opens November 28 on Eighth Avenue between 49th and 50th streets;

it will be used for circuses, hockey games, horse shows, basketball games, ice shows, political rallies, and track meets until February 1968, but it has been designed chiefly for boxing and wrestling matches, has poor sightlines for other events, and will for decades be a hangout for gamblers and other underworld figures.

Contract bridge begins to replace auction bridge. Railroad heir and yachtsman Harold S. Vanderbilt, 41, invents the variation while on a Caribbean cruise; it will eclipse auction bridge and whist beginning in 1930 when Romanian-born expert Ely Culbertson defeats Lieut. Col. W. T. M. Butler in a challenge match at London's Almack's Club that will bring the game wide publicity. The Cavendish Club organized this year by Wilbur E. Whitehead will meet for the next 8 years at the new Mayfair House hotel on Park Avenue (it will later have other venues) and beginning in 1928 will sponsor the Cavendish Trophy.

Swingline Inc. has its beginnings in a distributing operation launched on the Lower East Side by Russian-born entrepreneur Jack Linsky, 28, who was brought to New York as a child, went to work at age 14 for a stationery company, has learned from some importer friends about German-made stapling machines, gone to Germany, and become exclusive agent for the company that makes the machines. The Germans have not taken up his suggestion that they streamline their staplers, so Linsky establishes a Long Island City company under the name Speed Fastener Corp. and by 1930 will be manufacturing easy-loading, open-channel staplers of his own design under the name Parrot. Stapler users have had to load staples individually or buy them in sheets of metal that did not break away cleanly, but Linsky will soon introduce "Frozen Wire" staples that are glued together in strips and "stroke control" to reduce jamming (see 1946).

Old Gold cigarettes are introduced by P. Lorillard. The firm is well known for its Murad cigarettes and their slogan "Be nonchalant—light a Murad," and Old Golds will gain popularity with the slogan "Not a cough in a carload" (see 1911; Kent, 1952).

"Blow some my way," says a woman to a man lighting a cigarette in billboards put up by Liggett & Myers for its 12-year-old Chesterfield brand. The advertisement breaks a taboo by suggesting that women smoke.

Lucky Strike cigarettes are promoted by George Washington Hill, 41, who succeeds his father, Percival, as head of American Tobacco (see 1918; 1928).

Tobacco magnate James Buchanan "Buck" Duke dies of pernicious anemia and pneumonia at New York October 10 at age 68, leaving his daughter Doris more than $30 million of his $100 million estate; nearly 14 and an A student at the Brearley School, she is more than four times richer than Woolworth heiress Barbara Hutton.

The Chinatown Tong War that began last year ends March 26 after as many as 70 men have been killed; the Tongs will continue to fight from time to time, but the violence will end before the mid-1930s.

Architect S. B. P. Trowbridge of Trowbridge & Livingston dies of pneumonia at his 123 East 70th Street home January 29 at age 62. His partner Goodhue Livingston, now 59, will survive until 1951.

The 31-story Standard Oil Building is completed at 26 Broadway, across Beaver Street from the Produce Exchange that opened in 1884. Designed by Carrère & Hastings and Shreve & Lamb, it replaces the Adelphi Hotel with 505,000 square feet of rental space and has 24 elevators.

The 20-story 1 Park Avenue office building is completed between 32nd and 33rd streets for developer Henry Mandel.

The 16-story 181 Madison Avenue office building is completed at the southeast corner of 34th Street to Art Deco designs by Warren & Wetmore.

The Postum Building is completed at 250 Park Avenue (between 46th and 47th streets). Cross & Cross has designed the 21-story office tower.

Steinway Hall opens October 18 at 109 West 57th Street (between Sixth and Seventh avenues) to designs by Warren & Wetmore. Busts of Bach, Beethoven, Haydn, and other composers decorate the façade of the 16-story limestone office building; it has showrooms for Steinway & Sons pianos on its ground floor and a boardroom for the company's directors on the second floor facing 58th Street.

The 14-story 817 Fifth Avenue apartment house is completed at the southeast corner of 63rd Street; designed in Italian Renaissance style by George B. Post & Sons, it replaces two mansions.

The 14-story 860 Park Avenue apartment house is completed at the northwest corner of 77th Street. Designed by York & Sawyer, it replaces a tenement and stable; some of its apartments occupy entire floors, with 12 rooms, five baths.

The 1020 Fifth Avenue co-operative apartment house is completed at the northeast corner of 83rd

Street to designs by Warren & Wetmore. Built by Michael E. Paterno, its 13 stories are topped by a duplex penthouse with 17 rooms, seven-and-a-half baths. Initial offering prices range from $40,000 to $150,000; maintenance charges are between $410 and $1,540 per month.

The 13-story 1030 Fifth Avenue co-operative apartment house is completed at the northeast corner of 84th Street to designs by J. E. R. Carpenter. L. Gordon Hamersley, now 32, was 6 years old when his late father, J. Hooker Hamersley, bought the property and had it remodeled into a town house in 1898; he has engaged Carpenter to design the new building, and it has a 23-room penthouse for Hamersley. The other apartments all occupy full floors and are offered at prices ranging from $54,000 to $112,000, with monthly maintenance charges of between $500 and $1,000.

The 14-story 1111 Park Avenue apartment house is completed at the southeast corner of 90th Street. Designed by Schwartz & Gross, it extends deep into the block toward Lexington Avenue and has six apartments per floor renting for $285 to $600 per month. Each unit has six to nine rooms, three to four baths, with drawing rooms measuring 27' × 16', reception halls 16' × 16', and woodburning fireplaces.

Construction of the Cathedral of St. John the Divine's baptistry, nave, Women's Transept, and west façade begins with money raised in a campaign headed by lawyer Franklin D. Roosevelt (see 1916; 1941).

The Mother African Methodist Episcopal Zion Church is completed for the city's oldest black congregation at 140 West 137th Street to neo-Gothic designs by George W. Foster, Jr.

The Gramercy Park Hotel (initially the 52 Gramercy Park North residential hotel) opens at 2 Lexington Avenue, formerly the site of architect Stanford White's house.

The 17-story Buckingham Hotel opens at 101 West 57th Street, northwest corner Sixth Avenue. Designed by Emery Roth and an associate, it has 312 guest rooms.

Mayfair House (later the Mayfair Regent) opens November 9 at 610 Park Avenue, southwest corner 65th Street. Designed by J. E. R. Carpenter with 450 guest rooms, it has some unfurnished suites as well as some luxuriously furnished ones (see Le Cirque restaurant, 1974).

The 19-story Alamac Hotel is completed at 160 West 71st Street, southeast corner Broadway. Designed by Maynicke & Franke, it has more than 600 rooms and replaces the Church of the Blessed Sacrament school.

 Restaurateur Samuel S. Childs dies at New York March 17 at age 61, but a new Childs restaurant opens in a modernistic five-story limestone building designed for it by Brooklyn-born architect William Van Alen, 44, at 604 Fifth Avenue (see 1888). William Childs has leased the Russell Sage residence on the west side of the avenue between 48th and 49th streets and replaced it with the new building. Despite opposition from the 18-year-old Fifth Avenue Association, the avenue will soon have nine Childs restaurants (see 1981; Riese, 1961).

A large new Schrafft's restaurant opens for Frank G. Shattuck Co. at 556 Fifth Avenue, occupying the building put up in 1912 for the art gallery M. Knoedler & Co., which has moved uptown to 57th Street (see Schrafft's, 1906; 1929).

 Census figures made public December 22 show that the city's population has reached 5,873,356, up by 253,308 since 1920. Queens has grown by 245,605, mostly at the expense of Manhattan, whose population has declined.

1926 Mayor Jimmy Walker keeps the city happy with a latter-day equivalent of bread and circuses. He breaks out of the line of march in the St. Patrick's Day parade March 17 to bound up the front steps of St. Patrick's Cathedral, kneel, and kiss the cardinal's ring. A ticker-tape parade June 23 honors Commander Richard E. Byrd and pilot Floyd Bennett, 36, who have flown over the North Pole.

Gov. Smith wins reelection, piling up 1,523,813 votes to 1,276,137 for Newport, R.I.-born Congressman Ogden Livingston Mills, 42, a grandson of the late Darius Ogden Mills, who has headed the state Republican slate. Smith has proposed a constitutional amendment authorizing a $100 million bond issue for state improvements, Mills has favored a pay-as-you-go policy, the two have debated the issue October 25 at Buffalo's Elmwood Music Hall, and Mills has been unable to sway the crowd.

 State Charities Aid Association founder and pioneer welfare worker Louisa Lee Schuyler dies at her Highland Falls, N.Y., home October 10 at age 88.

$ AIG (American International Group) has its U.S. beginnings in the American International Underwriters Co. established at New York by California-born entrepreneur Cornelius Vander Starr, 34, who

7 years ago founded American Asiatic Underwriters at Shanghai to sell burial-plot life insurance. By 1929 he will have offices throughout much of East Asia, and AIG will grow to become the world's largest insurance company (*see* medicine, 1986).

Wall Street's Dow Jones Industrial Average closes September 7 at 166.10 and closes December 31 at 157.20, up from 156.66 at the end of 1925.

Hammacher Schlemmer completes an office building-showroom at 145 East 57th Street, between Park and Lexington avenues. Headed by William F. Schlemmer, the store sells paint, varnish, and garden implements as well as more exotic housewares, renting out the upper floors of its building.

A new Public Service Commission ruling sets the price of methane gas at $1.15 per 1,000 cubic feet but allows price adjustments for volume users (*see* 1923). Brooklyn Union Gas and Consolidated Gas have virtually doubled their business in the past 15 years and the PSC ruling lets them pursue large accounts that heretofore found gas uneconomical. By 1932 Consolidated Gas will be the largest company in the world providing electrical service (*see* Con Edison, 1936; Brooklyn Union Gas, 1928).

Jimmy Walker flouted the Volstead Act with insouciance, keeping the electorate happy. LAURENCE MASLON

Brooklyn Bridge engineer Washington A. Roebling dies at Trenton, N.J., July 21 at age 89.

Some 55 million passengers use the 16-year-old Pennsylvania Station, 44 million use the 13-year-old Grand Central Terminal, 27 million the Flatbush Avenue Station. Rail travel has enabled many New Yorkers to move from heavily congested parts of the city to various communities in Long Island, Westchester, Connecticut, and New Jersey. Roughly 80 percent of commuters on the Long Island Rail Road live within 25 miles of Manhattan.

The New York Academy of Medicine moves out of the large building it has occupied since 1890 at 119 West 43rd Street into a Fifth Avenue palazzo designed by York & Sawyer at the southeast corner of 103rd Street. The Academy has campaigned for improved public hygiene and sanitation, it has developed a reputation for expertise on municipal health, and its library will grow to have nearly 700,000 catalogued works occupying more than 14 miles of shelf space (the second largest such collection in America, it includes many volumes received from New York Hospital).

The College Entrance Examination Board created in 1900 administers its first Scholastic Aptitude Test (S.A.T.). The S.A.T.s will be graded on a scale of 200 to 800, and colleges will use S.A.T. scores as a supplement to secondary-school records and other relevant information in judging qualifications of applicants, but the scores will never be more than approximate and will have a standard error of measurement in the area of 32 points (*see* Kaplan, 1946).

A newly created New York State Board of Higher Education opens the Brooklyn Collegiate Center of City College to offer 2 years of college in an office building at the corner of Willoughby and Bridge streets (*see* Brooklyn College, 1910). Classes are for men only (*see* 1930).

Hunter College opens a Brooklyn Collegiate Center in the Chamber of Commerce building at the corner of Court and Livingston streets as enrollment in the women's college nears 4,000 (*see* 1914; Bronx, 1931).

Long Island University (LIU) is created at Brooklyn November 2 by a merger of two groups who take over an old electric company building. Starting with fewer than 200 students, the institution will grow in 60 years to have 19,000 on campuses in Brooklyn, Southampton, L.I., and Greenvale, N.Y.

Amazing Stories magazine begins publication at New York under the direction of Luxembourg-born inventor and science-fiction enthusiast Hugo Gernsback, 42, who came to America at age 20 to promote an improved dry cell battery he had invented.

Fire!! magazine begins publication in Harlem in November with an editorial board whose members include Gwendolyn Bennett, John Davis, Aaron Douglas, and Zora Neale Hurston. Poet Langston Hughes and graphic artist Richard Nugent have come up with the idea at Washington, D.C., for the experimental, apolitical black literary journal, its editor is Salt Lake City-born author Wallace (Henry) Thurman, 24, he obtains submissions from Arna Bontemps, Countee Cullen, and other leaders of the New Negro movement, but the first issue meets with a mixture of apathy and scorn, financial support is not forthcoming, the venture fails, and a fire destroys the building where several hundred unsold copies are stored.

Young and Rubicam moves to New York, where it will grow to become the largest U.S. advertising agency. Former Lord and Thomas copywriter John Orr Young, now 39, teamed up at Philadelphia 3 years ago with Raymond Rubicam, now 35, who had recently coined the slogan "The Priceless Ingredient" for E. R. Squibb. Taking offices in the new 25-story building at 285 Madison Avenue, Y&R will pioneer in market research and counseling as part of its service to clients, building a nationwide research staff to gather marketing data and study newspaper and magazine reading habits.

John Powers inaugurates a fashion-model agency industry that will grow to gross upwards of $1 billion per year. New York actor John Robert Powers, 30, has overheard a businessman saying he wanted a group of attractive people to pose for a magazine advertisement; he rounded up some friends, delivered the photograph, bound up a catalogue of pictures, and distributed them to advertising agencies. Powers has gained backing from Sir Herbert Beerbohm Tree to open the world's first model agency.

The National Broadcasting Company (NBC) is founded November 11 by David Sarnoff, who has bought station WEAF from AT&T October 29 and makes it the flagship of a 19-station Red Network that soon has 31 affiliates (*see* 1922). The station goes on the air November 15 with entertainment from the Waldorf-Astoria Hotel at 34th Street, and the company's first president Merlin H. Aylesworth gushes, "Think of it! Ten or maybe 12 million persons may be hearing what takes place in this ballroom tonight" (*see* 1927).

The New York Public Library acquires the black-history collection of Puerto Rican-born Harlem collector Arthur Alphonzo Schomburg, who will work as curator of the library's 135th Street branch from 1932 until his death in 1938 (*see* 1925; 1948).

Publisher Henry Holt dies at his 57 East 72nd Street home February 13 at age 86.

W. W. Norton & Co. is incorporated at New York with a capital of $7,500 (*see* 1923). Having read works by the late English biologist Thomas H. Huxley, Norton will adhere to the principle that experts in their fields should have their ideas expressed directly wherever possible rather than having them interpreted by popularizers.

The Book-Of-The-Month Club is founded by New York advertising men Maxwell (Byron) Sackheim, 35, and Harry Scherman, 39, who left the Ruthrauff & Ryan agency in 1919 to start Sackheim & Scherman. They are joined by Charles and Albert Boni, whose Little Leather Library provides the basis of their enterprise, and Robert Haas to start a cut-rate mail-order company that will market some 300 million hardcover books in the next 50 years. Titles are chosen by an editorial board consisting initially of *New York World* columnist Heywood Broun, 37, Henry Seidel Canby of Yale, author Dorothea Canfield Fisher, 48, author Christopher Morley, now 36, and Kansas publisher William Allen White, 58; the first selection (*Lolly Willowes* by English novelist Sylvia Townsend Warner, 33) goes out April 16 to 4,750 members (*see* Literary Guild, 1927).

Nonfiction: *New York: Not So Little and Not So Old* by New York author Sarah M. Lockwood; *Through Many Windows* by New York advertising executive Helen Woodward (*née* Rosen), 44, who has worked as an agency account executive, helped develop a number of campaigns, and quit 2 years ago to write this critique of the advertising business; *Public Speaking: A Practical Course for Business Men* by Missouri-born New York lecturer-author Dale Carnegie, 37, whose book will be retitled *Public Speaking and Influencing Men in Business* in 1931.

Fiction: *Love in Greenwich Village* (stories) by Floyd Dell; *Ninth Avenue* by Maxwell Bodenheim.

Poetry: *White Buildings* by Ohio-born New York poet Hart Crane, 27 (son of Life Savers creator Clarence Crane); *The Weary Blues* by Missouri-born New York poet (James Mercer) Langston Hughes, 24, who has been encouraged by Vachel Lindsay; *Enough Rope* by New York poet-author Dorothy Parker (*née* Rothschild), 33, who grew up in her family's house at 57 West 68th Street. She is well-known for her 1920 advertising line "Brevity is the soul of lingerie" and will be better known for "Men seldom make passes/

At girls who wear glasses," for putting down an actress with the line, "She ran the whole gamut of emotions from A to B," and for her verse about suicide, "Guns aren't lawful;/ Nooses give;/ Gas smells awful;/ You might as well live."

The *New York Herald Tribune* appoints Irita Bradford (Mrs. Carl) Van Doren, 35, head of its *Book Review* section following the death of *Book Review* editor Stuart Sherman. Her stewardship over the next 37 years will have a powerful influence on what America reads.

 Painting: *The Shelton with Sunspots, N.Y.* by Georgia O'Keeffe.

Sculpture: the Murphy Memorial dedicated July 4 (150th anniversary of the Declaration of Independence) is installed in Union Square. Created by Italian-born sculptor Anthony De Francisi, 39, it honors the late Tammany Hall boss Charles Francis Murphy.

Art Digest magazine begins publication at New York under the direction of Peyton Boswell (*see Art News*, 1921).

Poet Langston Hughes played a significant role in the Harlem Renaissance. LIBRARY OF CONGRESS

 Theater: *The Great God Brown* by Eugene O'Neill 1/23 at the Greenwich Village Theater, with William Harrigan, 171 perfs.; the Mansfield Theater (designed by Herbert J. Krapp for the Chanin Organization) opens 2/15 at 256 West 47th Street (it will be called the Brooks Atkinson beginning in 1960); *Broadway* by U.S. playwright Philip Dunning and Forestville, N.Y.-born playwright-producer-director George Abbott, 39, 9/16 at the Broadhurst Theater, with Lee Tracy, 332 perfs.; *Caponsacchi* by U.S. playwright Arthur F. (Frederick) Goodrich, 48, 10/26 at Hampden's Theater, with Goodrich's brother-in-law Walter Hampden as the canon Giuseppe Gaposacchi, from Robert Browning's dramatic monologues *The Ring and the Book* of 1868 and 1869, 269 perfs.; *The Tenth Commandment* by the late Abraham Goldfaden, founder of New York's Yiddish theater, 11/18 at the new Yiddish Art Theater, southwest corner Second Avenue and 12th Street; *The Constant Wife* by English novelist-playwright W. Somerset Maugham, 52, 11/29 at the Maxine Elliott Theater, with English-born actor Thomas Braiden, 56, English-born actor Frank Conroy, 36, New Orleans-born actress Cora Witherspoon, 36, 295 perfs.; *The Silver Cord* by Sidney Howard 12/20 at the Theater Masque, with comedienne Laura Hope Crews, 46, Margalo Gilmore, Oregon-born actor Earle Larimore, 27, in a play about mother-son love, 112 perfs.; *In Abraham's Bosom* by North Carolina-born playwright Paul Eliot Green, 32, 12/30 at the Provincetown Playhouse, with Waco, Texas-born actor-singer Julius K. "Jules" Bledsoe, 27, 123 perfs. (many after it moves uptown).

English actress Eva Le Gallienne, 27, gives up a Broadway acting career to found the Civic Repertory Theater of New York with a view to giving audiences quality plays at modest prices. Every program displays her slogan, "The theater should be an instrument for giving, not a machinery for getting." But shaky finances will force her to close the repertory theater in 1936.

Savannah-born theater critic Ward Morehouse, 26, quits the *New York Herald Tribune* and begins a "Broadway After Dark" column that will continue in the *New York Sun* for 25 years.

Playwright-lyricist George V. Hobart dies at Cumberland, Md., February 1 at age 59; Yiddish Art Theater actor Jacob P. Adler at New York April 1 at age 70. Hundreds of thousands gather to view his body at the Hebrew Actors Union on Second Avenue; director-producer Henry Miller dies at New York April 9 at age 66 on the eve of another opening at the theater he built in 1918 (his son Gilbert takes over the theater in West 43rd Street and will operate it until his own death in 1966).

Illusionist and escape artist Harry Houdini sustains an abdominal injury and dies of peritonitis at Detroit October 31 at age 52. The Society of American Magicians holds a funeral service at the Elks Club (later the Hotel Diplomat), 108 West 43rd Street, a block from the Hippodrome; 2,000 people attend, and an official of the society breaks a wand in half, inaugurating a ritual that will become traditional. Houdini's body is buried at Machpelah Cemetery in Queens.

Films: Alan Crosland's *Don Juan* with John Barrymore 8/6 at the Manhattan Opera House, accompanied by sound electrically recorded on disks in the Warner Brothers Vitaphone process developed by Western Electric engineers. Film czar Will H. Hays, 47, has headed the Motion Picture Producers and Distributors of America (MPPDA) since 1922 and appears on screen to predict that Vitaphone will revolutionize the industry, but few exhibitors are willing to install the costly equipment needed, and better established film studios will have no part of it (*see* 1927).

Other films: Sam Taylor's *For Heaven's Sake* with comedian Harold Lloyd, 33, as a young millionaire whose crush on Jobyna Ralston inspires him to attract "customers" to her father's Bowery mission; George Fitzmaurice's *Son of the Sheik* with Rudolph Valentino, who dies of peritonitis at New York August 23 at age 31 after surgery for an inflamed appendix and two perforated gastric ulcers. Press agents hired by Joseph Schenck of United Artists have the matinee idol's body placed in an ornate coffin at Frank E. Campbell's 11-year-old funeral parlor on Broadway at 67th Street. Close to 100,000 mourners line up for 11 blocks to view the remains, and Bernarr MacFadden's *Evening Graphic* publishes a "composograph" depicting Valentino in heaven.

The Paramount movie theater opens on Times Square behind the new Paramount Building completed on the west side of Broadway between 43rd and 44th streets. Chicago architects C. W. and George L. Rapp have specialized in designing elegant movie palaces; this one has a 3,900-seat auditorium whose ceiling is the equivalent of 10 stories high, and it will continue until 1964 to attract large audiences.

The ornate Savoy Ballroom opens March 12 at 596 Lenox Avenue, between 140th and 141 streets, where "the world's most beautiful ballroom" will continue until 1958 to provide dance music for upwards of 3,000 patrons per night. Georgia-born bandleader Fletcher Henderson, 28, conducts his group on opening night and will be followed by other great jazz ensembles, including those of Duke Ellington, Benny Goodman, Chick Webb, and hundreds of others who will play for dance contests, band battles, and other events that dance enthusiasts of all races will attend.

Ballet: dancer-choreographer Martha Graham makes her first solo appearance 4/18 at the 48th Street Theater. Now 31, Graham studied at Los Angeles with Ruth St. Denis, now 49, and Ted Shawn, 35; she performed as lead dancer in the ballet *Xochitl* in 1920, joined the *Greenwich Village Follies* in 1923, will form her own dance troupe, and will improvise a highly individual choreography. Graham will continue dancing until 1970.

Broadway musicals: *The Girl Friend* 3/17 at the Vanderbilt Theater, with Eva Puck, Sammy White, Roy Royston, music by Richard Rodgers, lyrics by Lorenz Hart, songs that include "The Blue Room," "The Simple Life," "Why Do I," 301 perfs.; *The Garrick Gaieties* 5/10 at the Garrick Theater, with Sterling Holloway, Romney Brent, music by Richard Rodgers, lyrics by Lorenz Hart, songs that include "Mountain Greenery," 174 perfs.; *George White's Scandals* 6/14 at the Apollo Theater, with Ann Pennington introducing the Black Bottom dance step that will rival the Charleston, songs that include "The Birth of the Blues" by Ray Henderson, lyrics by B. G. DeSylva and Lew Brown, 424 perfs.; *Americana* (revue) 7/26 at the Belmont Theater, with South Bend, Ind.-born actor Charles Butterworth, 29, English-born ingénue Betty Compton (originally Violet Halling Compton), 19, music by Con Conrad and Henry Souvaine, 224 perfs.; *Countess Maritza* 9/18 at the Shubert Theater, with Yvonne D'Arle, music by Viennese composer Emmerich Kalman, book and lyrics by Harry B. Smith, who has adapted a Viennese operetta, 318 perfs.; *Honeymoon Lane* 9/20 at the Knickerbocker Theater, with Eddie Dowling, Pauline Mason, Kate Smith, music by James F. Hanley, lyrics by Dowling, songs that include "The Little White House (At the End of Honeymoon Lane)," 317 perfs.; *Oh, Kay* 11/8 at the Imperial Theater, with Gertrude Lawrence, Victor Moore, Betty Compton, music by George Gershwin, songs that include "Do, Do, Do" and "Someone to Watch over Me" with lyrics by Ira Gershwin, "Heaven on Earth" and the title song with lyrics by Ira Gershwin and New York-born writer Howard Dietz, 30 (who has designed the M-G-M lion logotype), 256 perfs.; *The Desert Song* 11/30 at the Casino Theater, with Vivienne Segal, Robert Halliday, music by Sigmund Romberg, lyrics by Oscar Hammerstein II and Otto Harbach, songs that include "Blue Heaven" and "One Alone," 471 perfs.; *Peggy-Ann* 12/27 at the Vanderbilt Theater, with Helen Ford, music by Richard Rodgers, lyrics by Lorenz Hart, songs that include "Where's that Rainbow?" 333 perfs.; *Betsy* 12/28 at the New Amsterdam

Theater, with Al Shean, Belle Baker, music by Richard Rodgers, lyrics by Lorenz Hart, songs that include "Blue Skies" by Irving Berlin, now 38, who eloped in January with New York society girl Ellin Mackay, 22, daughter of Postal Telegraph president Clarence Mackay, 39 perfs.

 (Jean) René LaCoste, 21, (France) wins in men's singles at Forest Hills, Mrs. Mallory in women's singles.

Members of the 12-year-old Gaelic Athletic Association acquire property in the Bronx at 240th Street and Broadway, where, beginning in 1928, the Association will sponsor Irish football and hurling matches. The owners will go bankrupt a decade later, and the city will take over the land (see 1941).

The New York Lawn Bowling Club is founded by enthusiasts who have a green built near the West 69th Street entrance to Central Park. Members dress in white to play a game that has been enjoyed in the city since its first green opened in 1664 on the parade grounds of Fort Amsterdam. The Central Park green is divided into lanes, or "rinks," and eight games can go on simultaneously, with players tossing the jack at least 60 feet down the rink and then taking turns bowling from the opposite end, trying to get their balls as close as possible to the jack.

Olympic champion Gertrude Ederle becomes the first woman to swim the English Channel, arriving at Dover August 6 after 14.5 hours in the water (see 1925). Now 19, she receives a ticker-tape parade August 27 from the Battery to a reception at City Hall and thence to her home on Amsterdam Avenue at 63rd Street.

The Downtown Athletic Club is organized September 10 by a group headed by financier Schuyler Van Vechten Hoffman, occupying rooms in the Singer Building at 149 Broadway (see 1930).

Gene Tunney wins the world heavyweight boxing championship held by Jack Dempsey since 1919. New York-born prizefighter James Joseph Tunney, 28, gains a 10-round decision September 23 at Philadelphia (see 1927).

The New York Yankees win the American League pennant, but the St. Louis Cardinals win the World Series, defeating the Yankees 4 games to 3 despite the efforts of Babe Ruth, whose six hits include four home runs, and Lou Gehrig, whose eight hits include two doubles. St. Louis pitcher Grover Cleveland Alexander, now 39, wins the sixth game 10 to 2 and saves the final game, relieving Jesse Haines, 33, with two out and the bases loaded, and striking out

San Franciso-born rookie Yankee second baseman Anthony Michael "Push 'Em Up Tony" Lazzeri, 22.

 Society decorator Elsie de Wolfe is married March 10 to British diplomat Sir Charles Mendl, whose wealth will enable her to throw lavish parties at their homes in New York, Beverly Hills, and Versailles, decorated by the new Lady Mendl with delicate 18th century furniture and her usual glazed cotton chintz fabrics. Now 60, de Wolfe in 1924 became the first woman to tint her gray hair blue.

The first electric steam irons go on sale at New York department stores, but although their moisture helps prevent scorching they find few buyers at $10 when regular electric irons cost only $6.

Coney Island's Thunderbolt roller coaster begins operation; it will carry passengers until 1983 and be torn down in November 2000 (see accident, 1911; Cyclone, 1927).

The Riverside Funeral Home (initially Meyers & Co.) is completed at 180 West 76th Street, southeast corner Amsterdam Avenue, for Charles Rosenthal and his wife, Sarah (née Meyers) (see 1897). Funeral ceremonies have traditionally been held in the homes of the deceased, but demand has increased for more central public facilities that can accommodate large groups of people (see 1934).

 Former criminal lawyer Abraham Hummel of the old Howe & Hummel firm dies in his Baker Street, London, flat January 21 at age 75; his body is returned to his native New York, where it lies in state at Frank E. Campell's Funeral Home before being interred in the Salem Fields Cemetery, Queens.

The city's homicide rate will rise to an unprecedented 6.0 per 100,000 in the next 5 years, up from 5.4 per 100,000 in the last 5 (see 1931).

 The 28-story Bank of America Building is completed at 44 Wall Street, northwest corner William Street, to designs by Trowbridge & Livingston.

The New York County Court House is completed at 60 Centre Street on the east side of Foley Square, named for the late saloon keeper and Tammany Hall politician Thomas F. Foley, who died last year at age 73. Designed by architect Guy Lowell, the hexagonal building with its Corinthian portico occupies a site bounded by Pearl Street, Hamill Place, and Worth Street. It will generally be called the Manhattan Supreme Court Building.

The Brooklyn Municipal Building is completed opposite Borough Hall at 210 Joralemon Street, southeast corner Court Street, to designs by McKenzie, Voorhees & Gmelin.

Otis Elevator faces a challenge from Westinghouse Co., which acquires the patents and engineering skills of several sizeable companies that include Otis's chief competitors. Westinghouse will vie with Otis in supplying elevators for the city's proliferating skyscrapers, while smaller companies will produce elevators for apartment houses and other lower-rise buildings. Virtually all elevators will for more than 25 years continue to be operated manually, giving employment to tens of thousands.

The 34-story New York Telephone Co. Building (Barclay-Vesey Building) is completed at 140 West Street, covering a block bounded by West, Barclay, Washington, and Vesey streets. Designed in Art Deco style by Ralph Walker of McKenzie, Voorhees & Gmelin, the massive brick-faced skyscraper has 851,300 square feet of rental space and is the first building to exploit the requirements of the zoning code adopted in 1916. Its lobby has walls of veined marble, floors of travertine with bronze medallions, ornamentation that repeats the Mayan-inspired exterior ornaments, and a vaulted ceiling with a mural tracing the evolution of human communication. Guastavino-vaulted pedestrian arcades make up for the fact that Vesey Street has been widened and its sidewalks narrowed.

A 25-story masonry office building for developer Isaac Harby is completed at 285 Madison Avenue, northeast corner 40th Street, to designs by William L. Rouse and Lafayette A. Goldstone of Rouse & Goldstone. Its chief occupant will be the Young & Rubicam advertising agency.

The Paramount Building opens in Times Square with a Paramount Theater for Adolph Zukor's Paramount-Publix Corp. Designed by C. W. and George L. Rapp of Chicago, the 33-story skyscraper rises directly south of the Astor Hotel on a site formerly occupied by Shanley's restaurant and is the tallest Broadway structure north of the Woolworth Building. Its clock tower adds another six stories to its height, its clock face is 25 feet in diameter, and the 24,000-watt glow of its 19-foot copper-and-glass globe can be seen for miles at night.

A Limited Dividend Housing Companies Law passed by the state legislature at Albany permits condemnation of land for housing sites, abatement of local taxes, and other measures to encourage housing construction. The law sets limits on what landlords may charge in rent, limits their profits, and sets limits on how much income tenants of subsidized housing may have.

The U.S. Supreme Court upholds municipal zoning ordinances authorized by state governments on the ground that "states are the legal repository of police power" (see 1916). The decision handed down November 22 in the case of *Euclid v. Ambler Realty Company* establishes the principle, and the Department of Commerce publishes a "Standard State Zoning Enabling Act" to serve as a model for state legislatures (see 1961).

The Amalgamated Housing Corp. established by the Amalgamated Clothing Workers union takes advantage of the new state law to pursue plans for a low-cost housing project near Jerome Park Reservoir and Van Cortlandt Park in the Bronx yet close to a subway station. Metropolitan Life Insurance Co. and publishers of the *Jewish Daily Forward* provide credit to help the union finance its project, the corporation engages architects George W. Springsteen and Albert Goldhammer to design it, and ground is broken in November (see 1927).

The state legislature decontrols rents on vacated apartments (see Rosenman Act, 1923). Rapid resumption of housing construction since 1920 has produced high vacancy rates, market pressures keep rents low, and vacancy decontrol excites little interest (see 1928).

The Ritz Tower is completed for Hearst editor Arthur Brisbane at the northeast corner of Park Avenue and 57th Street to designs by Emery Roth with Carrère & Hastings. A 42-story luxury residential hotel that provides full service to tenants, its 18-room duplex apartment for Brisbane on the 19th and 20th floors has a 62' × 30' living room with a 24' ceiling.

The 13-story-plus-penthouse 810 Fifth Avenue apartment house is completed at the northeast corner of 62nd Street to designs by J. E. R. Carpenter.

The 14-story 820 Park Avenue apartment house is completed at the northwest corner of 75th Street, where it replaces a costly private house built only 6 years ago plus three 75th Street row houses. Designed by Harry Allan Jacobs for Vienna-born Hearst executive Albert J. Kobler, 40, it has just nine apartments; ranging in size from 15 to 20 rooms, the duplexes and triplexes command rents of between $2,088 and $3,333 per month (Kobler's 4,000-square-foot triplex occupies the top three floors).

The 14-story 39 East 79th Street apartment house is completed at the northeast corner of Madison

Avenue to designs by Kenneth Murchison, who has been engaged by author-socialite Emily Post, now 53 (her father was architect Bruce Price and her son works in Murchison's office). Apartments are priced at between $25,000 and $60,000, every buyer is in the Social Register, the building's simplex and duplex co-op units have two to eight servants' rooms each, with servants' dining rooms (Post's own apartment, 9B, has two bedrooms with a 19' × 25' living room).

The 14-story 1040 Park Avenue apartment house is completed at the northwest corner of 86th Street. Designed in a mixture of Georgian and Art Deco styles by Delano & Aldrich, the co-op replaces some frame houses dating to 1870 or earlier and has apartments as large as 12 rooms, four baths, with five master bedrooms and three servants' rooms (publisher Condé Nast has a glassed-in penthouse).

The 15-story 1088 Park Avenue apartment house is complete at the southwest corner of 89th Street. Designed by Middletown, N.Y.-born architect Mott B. Schmidt, 36, for Funk & Wagnalls publisher Robert J. Cuddihy, 63, its apartments (most are six to nine rooms) all overlook a central garden courtyard, nearly a quarter acre in size, with fountains and Italian loggia. Rents range from $433 to $617 per month.

The 14-story 1172 Park Avenue apartment house is completed at the southwest corner of 93rd Street. Designed by Rosario Candela for Michael E. Paterno, its high-ceilinged units for the most part have 11 or 12 rooms with five baths each; living rooms measure 30' × 20', bedrooms 18' × 17', and each living room and library has a woodburning fireplace. The 12-room penthouse has 14-foot ceilings and a 32-foot-long living room.

Postum Cereal boss Marjorie Merriweather Post (Hutton) moves into a 54-room apartment—the largest in New York—at 1107 Fifth Avenue, completed at the end of last year to designs by Rouse & Goldstone. Now 39, she sold her town house at the southeast corner of 92nd Street on condition that the builder George A. Fuller Co. replicate it atop the 14-story apartment house erected on the site. Entered by a private porte-cochère, the triplex has a private foyer on the building's ground floor with two private elevators. Upstairs are separate men's and women's guest closets, a ballroom, a gown room for hanging ball gowns, a cold-storage room for flowers and furs, a silver room, a wine room, a bakery, a sun porch, swimming pool, gymnasium, and separate laundry rooms for household and servants. Mrs.

Hutton pays $6,250 per month rent on a 15-year lease.

The 14-story-plus-penthouse 1115 Fifth Avenue (2 East 93rd Street) apartment house is completed by builder Anthony Campagna at the southeast corner to designs by J. E. R. Carpenter with co-operative units ranging in size from eight to 15 rooms (a 12-room flat sells for $45,000 with monthly maintenance of $409).

A new Fifth Avenue Hotel opens at the northwest corner of Fifth Avenue and 9th Street. The 18-story structure replaces the Henry Brevoort, Jr. house of 1834 and has 630 guest rooms (the de Rham family purchased the house in 1850 and occupied it until 1921).

The Sherry-Netherland Hotel opens on the east side of Fifth Avenue at 59th Street. Designed by Schultze & Weaver with Buchman & Kahn primarily as a residential hotel, the 37-story structure has 550 rooms, lavishly appointed to attract a clientele seeking luxury. It replaces the 34-year-old New Netherland Hotel, one of the city's first steel-framed structures.

The Mayflower Hotel opens on Central Park West between 60th and 61st streets. Emery Roth has designed the 18-story structure with 600 guest rooms.

The Barbizon Hotel for Women opens at the southeast corner of Lexington Avenue and 63rd Street. Designed in neo-Gothic style by Murgatroyd & Ogden, it has a swimming pool, health club, library, music studios, an 18th-floor terrace with lounge, daily maid service, and will attract an exclusive tenancy, despite its small rooms. Prospective residents must provide references, including one from a clergyman, and men are not allowed on the premises except in certain lounges and semi-private "beau rooms" (see 1973).

The 15-story Park Royal Hotel opens at 23 West 73rd Street, half a block west of Central Park. George F. Pelham has designed the 510-room structure.

The Stanhope Hotel opens at 997 Fifth Avenue, southeast corner 81st Street, just south of the 15-year-old 998 Fifth apartment house and opposite the Metropolitan Museum of Art. Rosario Candela has designed the structure.

The Hotel Alden is completed at 225 Central Park West, north of 82nd Street. Designed by Emery Roth (who will live in the building until his death in 1948), the 17-story structure contains more than 600 rooms.

The Barclay Hotel (later the Inter-Continental) opens November 4 with a dinner dance. A syndicate headed by J. Seward Webb, Jr. (a grandson of the late William Henry Vanderbilt) and architect Eliot Cross has leased a 205-by-200-square-foot block bounded by Lexington Avenue and Park Lane between 48th and 49th streets for the 14-story structure, whose top floor has a 17-room apartment for yachtsman and contract bridge inventor Harold S. Vanderbilt. A circular onyx-and-marble stairway from his entrance hall ascends to the roof, equipped with a gymnasium and squash court. Portraits of Vanderbilt ancestors hang on the drawing room walls, paneled—like those in the library, dining room, and bedchambers—in antique French oak. Michigan-born socialite hostess Perle Mesta (née Skirvin), 37, soon takes an entire floor, giving her even more space than Vanderbilt. Only 505 rooms are designed for transient guests, but within a few weeks another 100 are being furnished for that clientele.

The Taft Hotel (initially the Manger) opens November 15 on the east side of Seventh Avenue between 50th and 51st streets in Times Square. Designed by H. Craig Severance, it has been built at a cost of $10 million by Julius and William Manger, 33 and 27, respectively, who will soon be operating 17 smaller New York hotels (including the Great Northern, Navarro, Endicott, Wolcott, Woodstock, and Martha Washington). The 20-story hostelry has 1,250 rooms; it will be enlarged in 1931 to give it 2,000 rooms and renamed the Taft.

The city takes over Staten Island's 200-acre Clove Lakes Park in West New Brighton and gives it that name. Its Brooks Pond was the island's water source earlier in the century, as it was in the 19th century, and it will be the island's most popular recreation area, with facilities for boating, fishing, hiking, and horseback riding.

Citarella opens at the corner of 178th Street and Broadway, selling fresh seafood (year approximate). Started by an Italian-born fishmonger, it will move in the 1930s to 109th Street and Broadway (see 1940).

Congressman Fiorello La Guardia demonstrates the absurdity of the Volstead Act June 17 at Kaufman's Drugstore, 95 Lenox Avenue. Wearing a business suit and fedora hat, he shows that by mixing malt extract and near beer he can produce an illegal beverage that he proceeds to drink (the publicity triggers a boom in sales of malt extract and malt tonic). It would take 250,000 police officers to enforce the law, La Guardia has said, and another 200,000 to keep the cops honest.

Entrepreneur William Black (originally Schwarz), 22, obtains a bachelor's degree in engineering from Columbia, cannot find a job, and opens a nut stand under the name Chock full 'o Nuts in a basement at Broadway and 46th Street. By 1932 he will own a chain of 18 Manhattan Chock full o' Nuts stands (see luncheonettes, 1932).

The Central Park Casino in the park near 66th Street gets an ornate redesign by architect Joseph Urban and reopens, serving liquor covertly to guests who frequently include Mayor Walker. Designed by Calvert Vaux in 1924 as the Ladies Refreshment Salon, it has been used as a small nightclub for the past few years and will remain until 1934.

Christ Cella opens as a speakeasy on the ground floor of a brownstone boarding house in East 45th Street. Italian-born restaurateur Christopher Cella, 29, serves liquor in coffee cups, saying that any society that denies a man a glass of wine at the end of the day is not worthy of the name, and attracts patrons with French cuisine that will give way in time to hearty portions of T-bone and sirloin steak; thick lamb chops; softshell crabs in season; rice pudding; and apple pie (see 1947).

The Palm opens at 837 Second Avenue, between 44th and 45th streets. Italian-born restaurateurs Pio Bozzi and John Ganzi from the province of Emilia intended to name their speakeasy Parma but have been frustrated by a city clerk who has licensed the place as a chophouse under the name Palm.

1927 The American Communist Party moves its national headquarters from Chicago to New York, renting offices a block south of Union Square on the ninth floor of a building at 35 East 12th Street, close to the offices of the *Daily Worker* published since 1924 and the literary magazine *New Masses* that started last year (see 1930).

Former New York social reformer Victoria C. Woodhull dies at Norton Park, Worcestershire, England, June 10 at age 88.

The New York Stock Exchange seats a woman member for the first time January 13.

The private banking firm W. A. Harriman & Co. creates the first banker's acceptance October 24, extending $29,689.66 in credit to the New York exporting firm C. Tennant Sons at the request of a German metal refining company to which Harriman has offered a line of credit facilities up to a specified sum. Banker's acceptances will be used primarily to

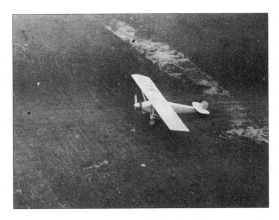

They called him "Lucky Lindy." His solo flight was a milestone in aviation history. LIBRARY OF CONGRESS

finance exports and imports by substituting a bank's credit for that of its customer (*see* Brown Brothers Harriman, 1931).

Wall Street's Dow Jones Industrial Average closes December 31 at 202.40, its high for the year, up from 157.20 at the end of 1926.

Bernard F. Gimbel, now 42, becomes head of the family business, which takes in $122 million, up from $15 million in 1907 when Gimbel got out of the University of Pennsylvania and went to work (*see* 1953; Saks Fifth Avenue, 1924).

The Macy's Thanksgiving Day parade that began 3 years ago uses balloons for the first time (*see* 1924). Puppeteer Tony Sarg has designed a helium-filled turkey, crocodile, and dog, more characters will soon be added as Walt Disney lends his efforts to the enterprise, and for a few years the balloons will be released after each parade, with rewards given to those who find them.

Detroit-born pilot Charles A. Lindbergh, 25, takes off in the rain from a muddy runway at Roosevelt Field on Long Island at 7:55 o'clock on the morning of May 20 with his 2,100-pound plane so heavily laden with 2,500 pounds (451 gallons) of gasoline that he clears some telephone wires by a scant 20 feet, navigates by dead reckoning to cover 3,600 miles (1,000 of it through snow and sleet) in 33 hours, 29 minutes, drops a flag over the Place de la Concorde (where it is picked up by New York restaurateur Raymond Orteig, who has been told where it would drop and has been waiting for it), and lands his single-engine monoplane *Spirit of St. Louis* at Le Bourget Airfield, Paris, May 21 at 10:24 in the eve-

ning after completing the first non-stop solo transatlantic flight. A New York ticker-tape parade honors the "Lone Eagle" June 13, bringing out a record crowd of 4 million and leaving Broadway littered with an estimated 1,750 tons of confetti, ticker tape, and other paper; Orteig gives a dinner at the Brevoort Hotel to award Lindbergh the $25,000 prize he offered in 1919.

Juan Trippe founds Pan American Airways and obtains exclusive rights from Cuban president Gerardo Machado y Morales to land at Havana (*see* 1925); he begins mail service between Key West, Fla., and Havana with Fokker F-7 single-engine monoplanes (*see* 1929).

The S.S. *Ile de France* arrives from Le Havre on her maiden voyage June 28. Built at St. Nazaire, the 43,153-ton French Line "Boulevard of the Atlantic" can accommodate 1,586 passengers (670 in first class, 408 in cabin class, 508 in third class), shows remarkable stability at sea (her motion is sometimes imperceptible), has an Art Deco dining salon that seats 700, and sets a transatlantic speed record on her return voyage, averaging 23.1 knots per hour. Passengers gather August 28 to witness the plane-launching catapult on her afterdeck hurl a mail plane aloft while she is still 400 miles northeast of Sandy Hook. By 1935 the new luxury liner will have carried more first-class passengers than any other on the transatlantic run (*see* 1947).

The easterly roadway of the Grand Central Viaduct opens to traffic in January (*see* 1925), and contracts are let for widening Park Avenue from 46th Street (the northern end of the new viaduct) to 57th Street. The avenue's central promenade, formerly 56 feet wide, is to be narrowed to 20 feet, to make room for two roadways, each 45 feet wide, on either side (the two viaducts that carry traffic around Grand Central are each 33'10" wide). Park Avenue gets its first traffic signals in May, but only north of 59th Street. The roadway south of 59th is still too narrow to accommodate heavy traffic, but it is widened by year's end (*see* 1928).

All Manhattan cross streets up to 110th Street are made one way thoroughfares in February as increased motor-vehicle traffic congests traffic flow (*see* 1924; avenues, 1951).

The Holland Tunnel opens November 12 to connect Canal Street in Manhattan with Jersey City, giving motor vehicles a road link under the Hudson River, the first alternative to New York-New Jersey ferry boats. Speaking at a dinner at the Manhattan Club, Gov. Smith says, "When the Brooklyn Bridge was built everybody thought it would be the last bridge across the East River from Manhattan but it proved to be but the beginning. I predict the same will be true of the Holland Tunnel. There will be more tunnels. They have got to come. They will be the only answer to the pressure that will be felt by the Holland Tunnel immediately." Smith recalls that when he was chairman of the board of the United States Trucking Corp. there were sometimes such great delays in ferries that it was impossible to take two loads of freight between New York and New Jersey in 8 hours. "Such conditions add considerably to the cost of transportation by truck and, in turn, to the cost of living." Within an hour some 20,000 people have walked the 9,250 feet from entrance to exit; the tunnel is closed at 7 o'clock, and regular paid vehicular traffic begins just after midnight with a toll of 50¢. The tunnel's chief engineer Clifton Milburn Holland died in the fall of 1924—just 2 days before diggers from east and west met below the Hudson—and the Hudson River Vehicular Tunnel has been renamed in his memory; his successor Milton H. Freeman has also died before the project could be completed, and 13 men lost their lives in the 7-year effort to build the tunnel, whose design and ventilating system are credited to Norwegian-born engineer Ole Singstad, 45 (see Lincoln Tunnel, 1940).

New York Hospital benefactor and sportsman Payne Whitney drops dead of a heart attack on a tennis court at his Manhasset, L.I., estate May 25 on the eve of his 50th birthday, leaving a will that bequeaths most of his very large fortune to his son John Hay "Jock" Whitney, 22, and daughter Joan (Mrs. Charles S. Payson), 24, but provides bountifully for the hospital (see 1924). New York Hospital and Cornell University enter into an agreement of "organic association" June 14 that will create The New York University-Cornell Medical Center, a facility dedicated to patient care, research in the health sciences, and the education of health professionals. Its new buildings and site (when totally acquired) will cost an estimated $15 million (see 1932).

Pratt Institute's Memorial Hall is completed beside the 40-year-old Main Building (architect John Mead Howells has designed the structure in Byzantine style). Pratt's curriculum will grow to include courses in architecture, art and design, information and library sciences, and the liberal arts; within 70 years it will have more than 3,800 students.

Transatlantic telephone service begins January 7 between London and New York: 3 minutes of conversation cost $75, or £15.

The Scripps-Howard newspaper chain buys the *New York Evening Telegram* in February from the estate of the late Frank A. Munsey (see 1925; *World Telegram and Sun*, 1950).

Ziff-Davis publishers is founded at New York by William B. Ziff, 29, of the 7-year-old Park Avenue advertising agency W. B. Ziff & Co. The new company will gain success with *Modern Bride*, *Car and Driver*, and more than a dozen other magazines (see 1994).

Television gets its first public U.S. demonstration April 7 in the Manhattan auditorium of Bell Telephone Laboratories. AT&T president Walter S. Gifford lets a large group of viewers see a fuzzy picture of Commerce Secretary Herbert C. Hoover in his office at Washington while hearing his voice over telephone wires. The mechanical TV system demonstrated will be superseded by the far clearer electronic system pioneered this year at San Francisco by Utah-born engineer Philo T. Farnsworth, 22, but development of the new medium is thwarted by the fact that it takes a frequency band of 4 million cycles, versus only 400 for an ordinary radio band, to transmit the 250,000 elements needed for a clear picture (see 1930).

David Sarnoff's year-old National Broadcasting Co. has so many radio stations that it splits up into a Blue Network and a Red Network (see American Broadcasting, 1943; CBS, 1928).

WEVD begins broadcasting in October with most of its programming in Yiddish. Its socialist founders have chosen their call letters to memorialize the late labor organizer and political leader Eugene V. Debs, who died in October of last year at age 70.

The Literary Guild of America sends out its first selection in March to 5,732 subscribers. Incorporated last year by Samuel W. Craig with support from Harold Guinzburg of Viking Press, the new book club has been inspired by the success of the Book-Of-The-Month Club (see 1926); it offers 12 books per year, each averaging $3 in price, for $18 paid in advance or $19 in installments, and its first book is a biography of the late anti-vice crusader Anthony Comstock by Heywood Broun and Margaret Leech. The Guild will have 70,000 subscribers by January 1929 as its editor-in-chief, Carl Van Doren, selects titles that attract demand (see 1934).

Random House publishers is founded by Bennett Cerf and Donald S. Klopfer, who 2 years ago purchased Boni and Liveright's Modern Library for $225,000. Starting with a tiny ninth-floor office at 73 West 45th Street, the new publishing house produces elegant limited editions but within a few years will be a trade publisher (*see* Knopf, Vintage Books, 1960).

Doubleday, Doran is created by Frank Nelson Doubleday, now 65 (*see* 1897), and George H. Doran (*see* 1908; Literary Guild, 1934). The publishing house will shorten its name to Doubleday & Co. in 1945 (*see* Literary Guild, 1934).

Nonfiction: *"Boss" Tweed—The Story of a Grim Generation* by New York author Denis Tilden Lynch; *The Gangs of New York* by Missouri-born *Herald Tribune* writer Herbert Asbury, 37, who has taken much of his material from the old *Police Gazette*; *Highlights of Manhattan* by Will Irwin.

Fiction: *archy and mehitabel* by Illinois-born *Herald Tribune* humorist Donald Robert Perry "Don" Marquis, 44, whose cockroach archy is the reincarnation of a poet and whose alley cat mehitabel has rowdy misadventures (a sequel will be published in 1940 under the title *The Lives and Times of Archy and Mehitabel* with illustrations by "Krazy Kat" creator George Herriman); *Page Mr. Tutt* and *When Tutt Meets Tutt* by Arthur Train.

Poetry: "American Names" by Pennsylvania-born New York poet Stephen Vincent Benét, 29; *Tristram* by Edwin Arlington Robinson; *Copper Sun* by Countee Cullen includes "Threnody for a Brown Girl," "The Love Tree," "Nocturne," "If Love Be Staunch," and "To Lovers of Earth: Fair Warning;" *Fine Clothes to the Jew* by Langston Hughes.

 Painting: *Manhattan Bridge*, *Automat*, and *Drug Store* by Nyack-born painter Edward Hopper, 45, who has a studio at 3 Washington Square North; *Radiator Building—Night, New York* and *Calla Lily—White With Black* by Georgia O'Keeffe, who has been spending more and more time in the Southwest while her husband, Alfred Stieglitz, now 63, devotes his attentions to Philadelphia-born photographer Dorothy Norman (*née* Sticker), 22, whose husband, Edward A., is the son of a Sears, Roebuck founder; *The Park*, *Something in Brown, Carmine, and Blue*, and *George Gershwin—"Rhapsody in Blue," Part II* by Arthur Dove.

Paris-born fashion illustrator Raymond (Fernand) Loewy, 31, organizes an industrial-design firm at New York and begins a new career. Loewy has designed displays for some of the city's best department stores and will redesign the interiors of stores such as Gimbels and Lord & Taylor.

Sculpture: *Seventh Regiment Monument, New York National Guard* (bronze) by sculptor Karl Illava on the west side of Fifth Avenue at 67th Street. The work memorializes the valor of the regiment in the Great War that ended 9 years ago; a bust of the late composer Victor Herbert by Philadelphia-born sculptor Edmond T. Quinn, 59, is installed near Central Park's Mall.

Theater: *Saturday's Children* by Maxwell Anderson 1/26 at the Booth Theater, with New York-born actor Humphrey Bogart, 27, Wollaston, Mass.-born actress Ruth Gordon (Jones), 30, Chicago-born actress Beulah Bondi (originally Bondy), 34, Ruth Hammond, New York-born actor Roger Pryor, 25 (to Forrest Theater 4/9/28), 310 perfs.; *Puppets of Passion* by Rosso di San Secondo (adapted by Ernest Boyd and Eduardo Cravell) 2/24 at the new Masque Theater, 252 West 45th Street (designed by Herbert J. Krapp and built by Irwin S. Chanin, the house will be renamed for producer John Golden in 1937), with New York-born actor Frank Morgan (Francis Phillip Wupperman), 35, Rose Hobart, 12 perfs.; *The Second Man* by New York playwright S. N. (Samuel Nathan) Behrman, 34, 4/11 at the 2-year-old Guild Theater, with Alfred Lunt, English-born actress Lynn (*née* Lillie Louise) Fontanne (Lunt), 39, Margalo Gilmore, Earle Larimore, 178 perfs.; *The Merry Malones* by George M. Cohan 9/26 at the new Erlanger Theater (designed by Warren & Wetmore and later to be called the St. James) at 246-256 West 44th Street (formerly the site of Sardi's restaurant), with Alan Edwards, Polly Walker, 192 perfs.; *The 19th Hole* by Frank Craven 10/11 at George M. Cohan's Theater, with Craven, Kitty Kelly, 119 perfs.; *Porgy* by Charleston-born novelist-playwright DuBose Heyward, 42, and his wife, Dorothy, 10/27 at the Guild Theater, 367 perfs. (*see* Gershwin opera, 1935); the New Yorker Theater (initially the Gallo, later the San Carlos Opera House) opens 11/7 at 245 West 54th Street; *The Road to Rome* by New Rochelle-born playwright Robert (Emmet) Sherwood, 31, 11/31 at The Playhouse, with Jane Cowl, 440 perfs.; *Paris Bound* by Philip Barry 12/27 at the Music Box Theater, with Hope Williams, 234 perfs.; *The Royal Family* by George S. Kaufman and New York-born playwright Moss Hart, 23, 12/28 at the Selwyn Theater, with Otto Kruger, Catherine Calhoun Doucet, Roger Pryor in a story based on the Barrymores, 345 perfs.

Annals of the New York Stage by Columbia University drama professor George Clinton Denamore Odell, 61, appears in its first two volumes. Odell's older brother Benjamin served as governor of New York from 1900 to 1904, he joined the teaching staff at Columbia in 1895, and 3 years ago he succeeded Brander Matthews as professor of dramatic literature. He began compiling his *Annals* in 1920 and will work on it for 25 years, producing a 15-volume work that will catalog and describe every play, actor, director, producer, and dramatic author, every opera, concert, vaudeville, and minstrel show from 1700 to 1894, never employing an assistant even to read proof. Columbia University Press will issue the *Annals* two volumes at a time through 1947.

Actress-producer Amelia Bingham dies at New York September 1 at age 58.

The Roxy movie theater opens 3/11 on Times Square at the northeast corner of Seventh Avenue and 50th Street. Chicago architect Walter Ahlschlager has designed the 4,000-seat house for William Fox, Irwin Chanin, and other investors, who provide showman S. L. "Roxy" Rothafel with an orchestra pit that can accommodate 110 musicians, private projection rooms, a broadcasting studio, club rooms, rehearsal rooms, a music library, and a lavish apartment for Roxy's personal use.

Films: Alan Crosland's *The Jazz Singer* is the first full-length talking picture to achieve success. Executive producer Darryl F. (Francis) Zanuck, 25, has given Al Jolson his movie debut, the film opens at New York 10/6, it contains only brief sequences of dialogue and singing, but the sound-on-disk Warner Brothers Vitaphone system introduces a new era of "the talkies" that will end the careers of some movie stars (*see* 1926).

Famous Players-Lasky changes its name to Paramount Pictures (*see* Paramount Building, 1926). The company will have Western Electric adapt its 7-year-old Astoria Studio in Queens to sound in 1929 and rename it Eastern Studios, Inc.

Theater owner Marcus Loew dies at his native New York September 5 at age 57, having amassed a large fortune. He is succeeded as president of Loews Inc. and its motion-picture subsidiary by film executive Nicholas Schenck, now 45.

New York-born prodigy Yehudi Menuhin, 11, makes his Carnegie Hall debut 11/25. He has played the Mendolssohn Violin Concerto since age 7, performed with the San Francisco Symphony Orchestra at age 8 (he grew up in the Bay Area), and will make international concert tours, often with his pianist sister, Hephzibah.

Broadway musicals: *Piggy* 1/11 at the new Royale Theater (designed by Herbert J. Krapp and built by Irwin S. Chanin), 242 West 45th Street, with Harry McNaughton, music and lyrics by Harry B. Smith (the show is renamed *I Told You So* in midrun), 83 perfs.; *Rio Rita* 2/2 at the new Ziegfeld Theater on Sixth Avenue at 54th Street, with music and lyrics by Harry Tierney and Joseph McCarthy, songs that include the title song, 494 perfs. Now 58, Florenz Ziegfeld has

hired *Follies* set designer Joseph Urban, a Vienna-born sculptor-painter-architect, to design the modern theater (it will stand for 40 years); *Rufus LeMaire's Affairs* (revue) 3/28 at the new 1,629-seat Majestic Theater at 247 West 44th Street (designed by Herbert J. Krapp and built by Irwin S. Chanin), with Charlotte Greenwood, Ted Lewis, music by Greenwood's New York-born husband, Martin Broones, 34, book and lyrics by Ballard MacDonald, 56 perfs.; *Hit the Deck* 4/25 at the Belasco Theater, with Brian Donlevy, music by Vincent Youmans, lyrics by Pittsburgh-born writer Leo Robin, 27, and Clifford Grey, songs that include "Join the Navy," "Hallelujah," 352 perfs.; *Merry-Go-Round* 5/31 at the Klaw Theater, with Marie Cahill, William Collier, Ohio-born torch singer Libby Holman (originally Holtzman), 23, music by Henry Souvaine and Jay Gorney, book and lyrics by Brooklyn-born comedy writer Morrie Ryskind, 31, and Howard Dietz, 136 perfs.; *Allez-Oop* 8/2 at the Earl Carroll Theater, with Charles Butterworth, Victor Moore, music by Charig and Richard Myers, lyrics by Leo Robin, 120 perfs.; *The Ziegfeld Follies* 8/16 at the Ziegfeld Theater, with Eddie Cantor, Nebraska-born torch singer Ruth Etting, 28, dancer Claire Luce, 24, music and lyrics entirely by Irving Berlin, songs that include "Shakin' the Blues Away," 167 perfs.; *Good News* 9/6 at the 46th Street Theater, with book by B. G. DeSylva, music by Ray Henderson, lyrics by DeSylva and Lew Brown, songs that include "The Best Things in Life Are Free," "Lucky in Love," "Flaming Youth," 551 perfs.; *My Maryland* 9/12 at the Jolson Theater, with a book based on the 1899 Clyde Fitch play *Barbara Frietchie*, music by Sigmund Romberg, 312 perfs.; *A Connecticut Yankee* 11/3 at the Vanderbilt Theater, with San Francisco-born actor William Gaxton, 33, Constance Carpenter, dance routines by Los Angeles-born choreographer Busby Berkeley (originally William Berkeley Enos), 31, music by Richard Rodgers, lyrics by Lorenz Hart, songs that include "My Heart Stood Still," "Thou Swell," 418 perfs.; *Funny Face* 11/22 at the new Alvin Theater at 250 West 52nd Street (named for producers Alex A. Aarons and Vinton Freedley, later to be called the Neil Simon), with Victor Moore, William Kent, Betty Compton, music by George Gershwin, lyrics by Ira Gershwin, songs that include "The Babbitt and the Bromide," 244 perfs.; *Delmar's Revels* 11/28 at the Shubert Theater, with Frank Fay, New York-born comedian Bert Lahr (originally Irving Lahrheim), 32, ingénue Patsy (originally Sarah Veronica Rose) Kelly, 17, music by Jimmy McHugh, lyrics by Dorothy Fields, 112 perfs.; *Golden Dawn* 11/30 at Hammerstein's Theater, with Australian-born performer Robert Chisholm, music by Emmerich Kalman and Herbert B. Stothart, book by Otto Harbach and Oscar Hammerstein II, 184 perfs.;

Show Boat 12/27 at the Ziegfeld Theater, with bass Paul Robeson singing "Ol Man River," torch singer Helen Morgan, now 27, as Julie LaVerne, baritone Jules Bledsoe in the first stage musical to deal with subjects such as miscegenation, the first to depict blacks as real people, book by Edna Ferber, music by Jerome Kern, lyrics by Oscar Hammerstein II, songs that include also "Bill," "Can't Help Lovin' that Man," "Only Make Believe," "Life on the Wicked Stage," "Why Do I Love You," 527 perfs.

Popular songs: "Black and Tan Fantasy" by Washington, D.C.-born composer Edward Kennedy "Duke" Ellington, 28 (who succeeds Andy Preer December 4 as bandleader at mobster Owen "Owney" Madden's Cotton Club in Harlem), lyrics by Ellington's plunger-muted trumpet player "Bubber" Miller; "In Central Park" by Harold Orlob, lyrics by Irving Caesar; "Headin' for Harlem" by New York composer James Hawley, lyrics by Eddie Dowling; "Let a Smile Be Your Umbrella" by New York-born composer Sammy Fain (originally Samuel Feinberg), 25, lyrics by Irving Kahal, Francis Wheeler.

The first Golden Gloves boxing tournament for amateur fighters opens March 11 at the Knights of Columbus center and at Brooklyn's Knights of St. Anthony's center; the finals are held March 28 at Tex Rickard's new Madison Square Garden, witnessed by a record crowd of 21,954, with an estimated 10,000 turned away for lack of space. Proposed by New York-born *Daily News* sportswriter Paul (William) Gallico, 29, in a February 14 back-page headline and feature story, the event will continue for more than 50 years, attracting thousands of contenders who will include Emile Griffith, Gus Lesnevich, Floyd Patterson, Ray Robinson, and José Torres.

A professional heavyweight bout at Yankee Stadium May 20 pits Binghamton-born boxer Jack Sharkey (originally Josef Paul Cakoschay), 24, against Jim Maloney. Fight announcer Joe Humphries asks the crowd of 40,000 to rise for a moment of silent prayer for Charles A. Lindbergh, who is attempting to fly the Atlantic, Sharkey knocks out Maloney in five rounds, and he goes on to administer punishing blows to former champion Jack Dempsey, now 32, for six rounds at the Stadium July 21 before being decked by a left hook in the seventh. Spectators shout, "Foul!" (Sharkey has signaled the referee that the Manassa Mauler landed a low blow), but Dempsey wins a rematch with Gene Tunney, only to be beaten by Tunney once again September 22 at Chicago. Tunney will retire undefeated next year.

René LaCoste wins in men's singles at Forest Hills, Helen Wills in women's singles.

Babe Ruth hits his 60th home run of the season at Yankee Stadium September 30 off an eighth-inning pitch by Washington left-hander Tom Zachary to break a 2–2 tie and set a record that will stand for 30 years, but only 10,000 fans are on hand to witness the event.

The New York Yankees win a record-breaking 110 games to take the American League pennant, finishing 19 games ahead of the Philadelphia Athletics in a banner year. Helped by pitcher Waite Hoyt, they go on to win the World Series, defeating the Pittsburgh Pirates 4 games to 0. Babe Ruth gets six hits, including two home runs; Lou Gehrig four hits, including two doubles and two triples.

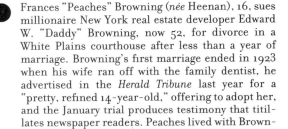

Frances "Peaches" Browning (*née* Heenan), 16, sues millionaire New York real estate developer Edward W. "Daddy" Browning, now 52, for divorce in a White Plains courthouse after less than a year of marriage. Browning's first marriage ended in 1923 when his wife ran off with the family dentist, he advertised in the *Herald Tribune* last year for a "pretty, refined 14-year-old," offering to adopt her, and the January trial produces testimony that titillates newspaper readers. Peaches lived with Browning for only 10 months before leaving to pursue a stage career; she will sue for divorce again in 1931 but lose.

The Cyclone roller coaster opens June 26 at Coney Island with a 100-second ride that takes screaming passengers up and down nine 85-foot hills at 60 miles per hour and over connecting tilted curves for the price of a 25¢ ticket (*see* Thunderbolt, 1926). It will continue running into the 21st century.

Simplicity Pattern Co. is founded at New York by entrepreneur James J. Shapiro, whose simple dress designs will propel his company past Butterick, McCall's, Vogue, and other competitors.

The Snyder-Gray murder trial makes world headlines. Queens Village, L.I., housewife Ruth Snyder met her corset-salesman lover Henry Judd Gray in 1925 in a restaurant at the northeast corner of Sixth Avenue and 36th Street; they kill New York magazine art editor Albert Snyder with a sashweight on the night of March 19 in a suburban sex triangle, a jury convicts the pair, and they will die in the electric chair at Sing Sing early next year.

Bootlegger Frankie Yale (originally Frank Uele) dies in a hail of machine-gun bullets on a street in his native Brooklyn July 1 at age 42 as another car pulls up alongside. Allegedly killed on orders from Al Capone on suspicion of having hijacked a truckload of liquor, Yale is buried in a $12,000 casket after a funeral procession that includes 28 trucks decorated with flowers.

The U.S. Supreme Court rules that illegal income is taxable, thus giving the federal government a powerful new weapon against the underworld.

Architect Evarts Tracy of Tracy & Swartwout dies in the American Hospital at Neuilly outside Paris January 30 at age 53. A camouflage officer during the Great War, Col. Tracy has been doing reconstruction work in Europe.

The six-story New York American and Evening Journal Building is completed at 210 South Street, facing the East River, to designs by Ludlow & Peabody and New York-born architect Ely Jacques Kahn, 44.

The 36-story 50 Broadway office tower opens between Exchange Place and Morris Street. H. Craig Severance has designed the structure that replaces the pioneer 11-story "skyscraper" opened in 1889.

Office towers go up on Park Avenue South (386 at the northwest corner of 27th Street, with 20 floors; 419 at the southeast corner of 29th Street, with 18 floors; 425 at the northeast corner of 29th Street, with 20 floors) and at 2 Park Avenue (northwest corner 32nd Street), with 25 floors. Designed by Ely Jacques Kahn and initially called the Park Avenue Building, 2 Park Avenue will win high praise from critic Lewis Mumford.

The 31-story Graybar Building opens at 420 Lexington Avenue with a passage connecting it to Grand Central Terminal. Named for the Graybar Electric Co., spun off from Western Electric Co., the $21 million tower designed by Sloan & Robertson has 1.2 million square feet of rentable floor space—more than any other office building in the world.

The Fred F. French Building is completed at 551 Fifth Avenue (northeast corner on 45th Street) for real estate investor French, 43, to designs by H. Douglas Ives and Sloan & Robertson. The 38-story structure has 312,000 square feet of rentable floor space.

The Durst Organization is founded by real estate investor Joseph Durst, a former garment maker who arrived from his native Austria in 1902. He will buy up commercial office-building mortgages and leases on Manhattan's East Side in the 1930s; his son Seymour, now 13, will join the firm in 1940 and develop office buildings on Third and Sixth avenues.

A new East River Savings Bank branch is completed at the northeast corner of Amsterdam Avenue and 96th Street, opposite the 26-year-old Church of the Holy Name of Jesus. Designed by Walker & Gillette and opened March 5, the limestone building with its tall Ionic columns attracts so many depositors that it will have to be enlarged in the early 1930s.

Union Club members vote June 13 to accept lawyer Jeremiah Milbank's offer to buy their palatial clubhouse on Fifth Avenue for $4 million and build a new one on lower-taxed land (see 1903). A building committee has made a survey of every available corner on Fifth and Park Avenues and taken a 20-day option on the Redmond house at the northeast corner of Park Avenue and 69th Street (see 1933).

The Pythian Temple is completed at 135 West 70th Street to serve as a clubhouse for the fraternal, nonsectarian Order of the Knights of Pythias founded during the Civil War at Washington, D.C. Designed in neo-Egyptian style by Thomas W. Lamb, it contains lodge halls, meeting rooms, a columnless auditorium, but virtually no windows (fenestration will be added in 1982, when the structure is turned into condominium apartments; the two 10-foot seated pharaohs will remain in place).

The 13-story 1 Sutton Place South apartment house is completed at the southeast corner of 57th Street and Avenue A (soon to be renamed York Avenue) to designs by Cross & Cross and Rosario Candela. Former Carnegie Steel partner Henry Phipps has developed the property in an area heretofore a slum, and his daughter Amy occupies the 17-room, 6,400-square-foot penthouse; it has two 40-foot drawing rooms (one with a coffered ceiling and skylight), one at each end, white marble floors, 18th century gold-and-ivory door frames, four bedrooms, four maids' rooms, a servants' hall, and 6,000 square feet of wraparound terrace overlooking the East River.

The New York Building Congress confers awards for exceptional craftsmanship on eight mechanics who have worked on 660 Park Avenue, completed by Starrett Brothers at the northwest corner of 67th Street to designs by York & Sawyer. Each of the 13-story building's top nine floors has a single apartment; its 27-room maisonette has its own separate entrance at 666, just west of the main entrance in 67th Street, and takes up the entire first, second, and third floors, with each floor measuring 100 by 60 feet, permitting as many as 13 rooms per floor. A flight of marble steps leads from the street entrance to a foyer whose walls are of carved Caen stone. On this level are a double-height living room measuring 22 by 49 feet, a double-height library, a study, the kitchen, service pantries, and servants' hall. The second level has separate men's and women's coat rooms and six servants' rooms. On the third level are the master suite (bedroom, sitting room, dressing room, and bath) plus two other master bedrooms, each with bath, as well as a sewing room, endless closets, and five more servants' rooms.

The 13-story 765-775 Park Avenue co-operative apartment house is completed in the blockfront between 72nd and 73rd streets. Designed by Rosario Candela for builder Michael E. Paterno, it has only 40 rooms per floor instead of the usual 45, its 47 luxury apartments range in size from nine to 16 rooms, each apartment has between two and six woodburning fireplaces, ceilings are between 10'4" and 13 feet high, each of the four duplex maisonettes has its own private entrance and address, four of the five roof-garden penthouses are duplexes and the other is a 16-room triplex with its own private, automatic elevator. Duplex and triplex apartments have separate stairways for servants. Paterno has razed 10 buildings to make way for his new co-op.

The New York chapter of the A.I.A. (American Institute of Architects) gives its gold medal for the year's best-designed large residential building to 812 Park Avenue, a neo-Renaissance structure designed by J. E. R. Carpenter with co-operative duplex and triplex apartments for 36 families. The duplexes typically have 13 rooms, five baths.

Economist Stuart Chase writes in *The New Republic*, "Park Avenue on the island of Manhattan is the end of the American ladder of success. Higher one cannot go . . . The spoil of a continent, ay of the seven seas, is massed along this harsh stone canyon—the winnings from oil, steel, railroads, mining, lumber, motorcars, banking, real estate, moving pictures, foreign trade, speculating, the manufacturing of widgets, the marketing of toothpaste, the distribution of the assets of button kings . . . There are no more worlds to conquer. If America has a heaven this is it . . . The last ducal families are leaving Fifth—save for a strip opposite Central Park—and the palaces that they reared in the nineties are, after solemn public exhibition, being ignominiously destroyed . . . to give way to department stores, skyscraper office buildings, shops developed to the ultra-exquisite. It is to the social vacuum left by this desecration that Park Avenue has moved, but never, in its palmiest days, did Fifth Avenue boast such surried phalanxes of millionaires. More fashion it may have had, more individuality, more resplendent names bursting above the rooftops of an adolescent nation—Vanderbilts, Goulds, Astors . . . but never such solid, crushing and cascading wealth . . . It is a broad and noble street, lined like an arrow from north to south from the Grand Central to Fifty-seventh Street. The park space in its center, under which rumble the trains of the New York Central, burns its dull stone pavement without a touch of green, but from Fifty-seventh north it blossoms into a strip of formal garden with grass and shrubs."

The 173-175 Riverside Drive apartment house opens between 89th and 90th streets on a site formerly occupied by the Hamilton School for Girls. Italian-born law-school graduate and builder Anthony Campagna, now 40, visited Joseph and Dr. Charles V. Paterno in his 20s, was offered a construction job, gave up his law career, built the Rialto Theater on 42nd Street in 1916 among other commercial structures, and has put up the twin 16-story residential buildings, designed by J. E. R. Carpenter with a curving façade.

A town house for real estate heir Vincent Astor is completed at 130 East 80th Street to designs by Mott B. Schmidt (Astor will sell the house in 1947 to the New York Junior League). The Buildings Department reports in December that it has not received a single application for construction of a private house in the previous 12 months.

The six-story Alhambra Gardens apartment house is completed in the Bronx at 750-760 Pelham Parkway, between Holland and Wallace avenues, to Spanish designs by Springsteen & Goldhammer.

The Amalgamated Cooperative Apartments open in the Bronx north of Sedgwick Street between Saxon and Dickinson avenues (*see* 1926). The 305 families that move in pay $500 per month to buy in plus $11 per month per room, the rooms are large and airy, and there are inner garden courtyards; initial occupants include ILGWU president David Dubinsky, tenants receive ice on a co-operative basis, the corporation provides dental, medical, and children's services, it oversees cultural activities and publishes the *Community News*, and by 1937 there will be more such housing in the neighborhood built under the aegis of the Amalgamated Housing Corp.

Brooklyn Heights's 17-story Leverich Towers apartment-hotel is completed on a site bounded by Clark, Willow, and Pineapple streets. Designed by Starrett & Van Vleck, it has six elevators and 585 rooms.

The 31-story Park Central Hotel opens on the west side of Seventh Avenue between 55th and 56th streets. Designed by Gronenberg & Leuchtag, it has 1,600 guest rooms.

The 21-story Drake Hotel opens at 440 Park Avenue, northwest corner 56th Street. Built by Bing & Bing at a cost of $5.5 million to designs by Emery Roth, the structure has 477 rooms laid out in units of one to three rooms each, with serving pantries in the two- and three-room suites. Suites on the 10th, 12th, 15th, 17th, and 20th floors have roof terraces, and living rooms on the 17th to 19th floors are as large as 26'5" × 20', bedrooms as large as 20' × 14'; on the 20th and 21st floors, living rooms are as large as 25' × 17' and 27'7" × 16'4", with open fireplaces, dining rooms measuring 18'8" × 12', and bedrooms 16' × 16'. The largest suite has 28 rooms.

The 21-story Lombardy Hotel opens at 111 East 56th Street, between Park and Lexington avenues. Designed in North Italian Renaissance style by Farrar & Watmaugh for developer-builder Henry Mandel, the apartment-hotel has 175 units—330 rooms, singles and in suites, some with terraces. There are two three-bedroom triplex penthouses and a two-bedroom, two-bath flat.

The Delmonico Hotel opens in September at 502 Park Avenue, northwest corner 58th Street. Designed by Goldner & Goldner, the $5 million, 32-story structure has 525 guest rooms and a three-story ballroom; it is intended primarily as a residential hotel for tenants who will occupy suites, but it will soon go bankrupt.

The 29-story Savoy-Plaza apartment hotel opens on the east side of Fifth Avenue between 58th and 59th streets. Designed by McKim, Mead & White for a syndicate that includes T. Coleman du Pont and Lucius M. Boomer, the French Renaissance structure with its white marble base, white brick facing, and green tiled roof rises directly south of the 1-year-old Sherry-Netherland, replacing the 35-year-old Hotel Savoy and the 32-year-old Bolkenhayn apartment house at 763 Fifth Avenue that Plaza Hotel owner Harry S. Black purchased 2 years ago (*see* General Motors Building, 1968).

 Mayor Walker engages landscape architect Herman W. Merkel to devise a plan for improving Central Park, which has had problems of vandalism, litter, and vegetation failure. Merkel deplores the tennis courts built below the 96th Street transverse and the 17 acres that have been converted into the Heckscher Playground; he presents a plan calling for eight other playgrounds, all at entrances to the park; a special force of park police; and an underground sprinkler system that is installed at a cost of $1 million (*see* Moses, 1934).

 The Russian Tea Room opens at 150 West 57th Street, a 51-year-old five-story brownstone built by a tea and coffee merchant, used briefly for a girls' school, and more recently for studio apartments. Members of the Russian Imperial Ballet who fled the Revolution of 1917 have started the tea room as a meeting place for other emigrés, decorating it with wicker furniture and serving tea, homemade pastries, and ice cream (it will not serve vodka until after Repeal late in 1933, when its soda fountain will give way to a bar stocked with 20 varieties) (*see* 1945).

1928 Police make two dozen arrests July 3 when that many men, women, and children demonstrate in front of J. P. Morgan & Co. headquarters at the corner of Broad and Wall streets carrying placards that denounce U.S. Marine rule in Nicaragua with sentiments such as "Freedom for Black Haiti," "Support the Strike of Nicaraguan People Against American Imperialism," "Why Not Relieve Farmers Instead of Supporting the Banks?" and "Down With Wall Street Imperialism."

Allegations of Queens sewage-construction kickbacks elicit a response from Gov. Al Smith, who appoints Emory R. Buckner as special prosecutor. Buckner names John M. Harlan as his assistant, and Harlan hires Harlem-born lawyer J. Edward Lumbard, 27, to help him.

Gov. Smith wins the Democratic nomination for president but loses five states of the "Solid South" as well as his home state and obtains only 41 percent of the popular vote as compared with 58 percent for Iowa-born Republican candidate Herbert C. Hoover, who receives 444 electoral votes to 87 for Smith. Now 54, Smith has misguidedly followed the advice of business friends and come out for high tariffs and restrictions on immigration; he is named president of a company that is financing what will soon be the world's tallest skyscraper and moves into a penthouse apartment at 51 Fifth Avenue, southeast corner 12th Street.

Former vice presidential nominee Franklin D. Roosevelt attends the Democratic Party convention, as he did 4 years ago, despite the fact that his bout with poliomyelitis in 1921 has left him almost totally without the use of his legs; helped by Bronx political boss Edward J. Flynn to overcome opposition from Tammany leader John Francis Curry, he wins the New York State gubernatorial primary, outpolling Al Smith, and with help from speeches written by Samuel Rosenman gains the governorship, winning 2,130,193 votes as compared with 2,104,629 for Republican attorney general Albert Ottinger, 50. Roosevelt appoints Rosenman counsel later in

November and Rosenman will play an essential role in promoting the governor's program for developing the state's hydroelectric resources.

Crystal Eastman dies of nephritis at Erie, Pa., July 8 at age 47 after writing in The *Nation* magazine, "No self-respecting feminist would accept alimony. It would be her own confession that she could not take care of herself" (she has been married and divorced twice).

The National Conference of Christians and Jews is founded to fight U.S. bigotry following the defeat of presidential candidate Al Smith. No Roman Catholic will win election to the presidency until 1960.

Christodora House moves into a 17-story building at 147 Avenue B, corner 9th Street, where it will become known as "the skyscraper settlement house" (*see* 1897). Railroad magnate Arthur Curtiss James has provided the wherewithal to put up the structure containing a gymnasium, swimming pool, dining room with river view, music school, poets' guild, and playhouse (*see* 1975).

$ "We in America today are nearer the final triumph over poverty than ever before in the history of any land," says presidential candidate Herbert Hoover. Now 54, he hails "the American system of rugged individualism" October 22 in a speech at New York. It will later turn out that his opponent Al Smith has since 1923 been secretly receiving cash and stocks totalling about $400,000 from Michigan-born New York lawyer and national Democratic Party fundraiser Thomas Lincoln Chadbourne, 57, to supplement his salary as governor.

Real estate taxes provide about 80 percent of New York City's revenue. Land values have increased by nearly 75 percent since 1919, and apartments on Park Avenue rent for as much as $40,000 per year.

National City Bank of New York goes into competition with the Morris Plan started in 1910, offering loans to employed borrowers on terms similar to those offered by Morris Plan banks.

Goldman, Sachs forms the Goldman, Sachs Trading Corp. to sell shares to the public. Tennessee-born partner Waddill Catchings has dreamed up the leveraged investment trust that is marked up and sold to the public as barbers, housewives, shoeshine boys, and waiters clamor to buy on margin in the galloping stock-market mania (*see* 1926; 1929).

New York Central lawyer (and two-term U.S. senator from New York) Chauncey M. Depew dies at New York April 5 at age 93. He has once said, "I get my exercise acting as pallbearer to my friends who exercise;" Salomon Brothers and Hutzler cofounder

Arthur K. Salomon dies childless of peritonitis following surgery at Post Graduate Hospital July 3 at age 51. One of the city's most prominent financiers, he and his wife, Edna (*née* Heller), have been living at 1016 Fifth Avenue; financier Thomas Fortune Ryan dies at New York November 23 at age 77, leaving an estate valued by some accounts at $130 million and by others at more than $200 million. His grandson Clendenin J. Ryan, 23, inherits a large portion.

Wall Street's Dow Jones Industrial Average closes at 300 December 31, up from 202.40 at the end of 1927 after a spectacular year that has seen Radio Corporation of America (RCA) stock soar from 85 to 428 (although it has never paid a dividend), DuPont from 310 to 525, Montgomery Ward from 117 to 440, and Wright Aeronautic from 69 to 289. Corporations and investment trusts lend money to stockbrokers for speculative purposes, and much of the country is growing accustomed to installment buying of consumer goods (*but see* 1929).

De Pinna moves two blocks north from 50th Street to a new nine-story building at the southwest corner of Fifth Ave and 52nd Street, where it will remain for 41 years (*see* 1916). The Rockefeller family has taken over its premises for construction of Rockefeller Center (*see* 1939).

Bergdorf Goodman moves north from 616 Fifth Avenue to occupy a new marble-clad building at 58th Street opposite the Plaza Hotel on the site of the former Cornelius Vanderbilt 2nd mansion that was built 45 years ago (Vanderbilt's widow, Alice, has been paying $130,000 per year in taxes on the house; a deal to replace it with a 52-story apartment hotel collapsed in 1926) (*see* Bergdorf, 1901). Designed by Kahn & Jacobs for real estate agent Frederick Brown, the new, mansion-like structure combines seven- and nine-story buildings that contain various other retailers, including the jeweler Van Cleef & Arpels, the linen store Grande Maison de Blanc, and the hatter Dobbs (at the northeast corner). Merchant Edwin Goodman sells his brownstone at 320 West 71st Street and takes over the ninth floor of the northernmost part of the store for use as an apartment.

Alexander's department store opens in the Bronx at Third Avenue and 152nd Street. Merchant George Farkas, 26, names the store for his father and will build a following by selling fashion at discount prices to customers who cannot begin to afford Bergdorf Goodman or choose not to pay such fancy prices (*see* 1965).

 Brooklyn Union Gas completes a large new gasification plant on a 115-acre site on Newtown Creek at

Greenpoint to meet the growing demand (*see* 1926). It replaces five older plants and produces methane gas at 60 percent of the cost, using both the coke-oven method and water-gas method (*see* 1935).

Pilot Floyd Bennett rises from a sickbed and flies with Bernt Balchen to rescue three transatlantic fly-ers whose Junkers plane, the *Bremen*, has landed on an island in Labrador. Bennett contracts pneumonia and dies April 25 at age 37 in a Quebec hospital, his coffin arrives at New York April 27 en route to Arlington Cemetery at Washington, and the pilots he rescued receive a ticker-tape parade April 29 (*see* Floyd Bennett Field, 1931).

The Board of Estimate holds hearings April 11 on the question of widening Park Avenue north of 57th Street to accommodate more traffic, thus relieving Fifth Avenue (*see* 1927). Borough President Julius Miller issues orders in the spring that Park Avenue property owners between 57th and 72nd streets remove stoops, railings, and other projections preparatory to work that would narrow sidewalks and widen roadways; he announces June 6 that the New York Central has agreed to close its center-mall vents between 57th and 72nd streets at a cost to the railroad of $162,000. The Park Avenue Association opposes any widening, but its founder H. Gordon Duval opens the door to the ele-vator shaft in the corridor of his 570 Park Avenue penthouse apartment June 29 just before 5 o'clock in the morning and plunges to his death. The new west-erly roadway around Grand Central Terminal opens to traffic September 6 with a parade of motorcars. Crosstown traffic in the highly congested Grand Cen-tral area is now eliminated, and the Grand Central Viaduct at long last carries north- and southbound traffic unimpeded by cross streets or stoplights between 40th and 46th streets.

Central Park West is widened to 100 feet, giving it the same width as Fifth and Sixth avenues, as con-struction proceeds on an Independent subway line just west of Central Park.

The Goethals Bridge and Outerbridge Crossing open simultaneously June 29 to carry vehicular traffic between Charleston and Tottenvillle on Staten Island and Perth Amboy, N.J. (*see* Arthur Kill Bridge, 1890). Designed by engineer Shortridge Hardesty, 42, both have been built by the Port of New York Authority; the first has been built on the site of the 1890 rail-road bridge, is 8,600 feet long, has cost more than $7 million, and is named for the late Gen. George Washington Goethals, chief engineer of the 14-year-old Panama Canal and the Port Authority's first con-sulting engineer (Goethals has died at New York January 21 at age 69); the second is 10,200 feet long,

has cost just over $10 million, and is named for Staten Island importer-exporter Eugenius H. Outer-bridge, who was chairman of the Port Authority from 1921 to 1924 (*see* Bayonne Bridge, 1931).

York Avenue (formerly Avenue A) is renamed to honor Tennessee-born Great War hero Alvin C. York, now 40. York's petition for draft exemption as a conscientious objector was rejected in 1917, and in the Battle of the Argonne Forest October 8, 1918, he led an attack on a German machine-gun nest, killing 25 enemy soldiers and almost single-handedly tak-ing 132 prisoners and 35 machine guns, but he has refused to capitalize on his fame.

A subway accident in the tunnel south of Times Square August 24 kills 13 (the death toll soon rises to 16) and leaves 100 injured after a train jumps the track. A faulty switch has derailed the last two cars of a rush-hour IRT express, they are crushed against a wall and twisted like paper, and the roadbed is littered with the possessions of the ill-fated straphangers. Mayor Walker rushes to the scene, and a maintenance worker is arrested on charges of homicide. Traffic on all lines is snarled for hours.

Columbia Presbyterian Hospital opens on a 20-acre site west of Broadway at 168th Street (*see* 1925). Headed by philanthropist John Sherman Hoyt, now 49, the institution has grown to include Babies Hos-pital, Sloane Hospital, the Vanderbilt Clinic, and the Neurological Institute.

The Fieldston School opens in the Bronx on an 18-acre Riverdale campus, incorporating the high-school grades of the Ethical Culture School (*see* 1895; 1933).

Miss Chapin's School for Girls moves from two brownstone houses in East 57th Street into its own building at East End Avenue and 84th Street (*see* 1901). It will become simply the Chapin School in 1934, take girls of 5 to 18, and grow to have an enrollment of nearly 600.

The world's first Motogram (it will later be called the Zipper) begins relating headlines on the Times Tower November 6 (election day), flashing five-foot-high news messages with 14,800 electric lights along a 368-foot track that runs continously around the 24-year-old tower in Times Square at the rate of four or five letters per second. It will continue with-out interruption for 4,971 consecutive days (*see* 1997; dim-out, 1942).

The world's first combined radio, cable, and tele-graph service company is created by a merger of Clarence Mackay's Commercial Cable-Postal Telegraph with International Telephone and Telegraph (ITT). Mackay's father broke Western Union's telegraph monopoly in 1886, Clarence inherited the J. W. Mackay communications empire in 1902, and he has expanded it.

The New York Telephone Co. issues the city's first classified telephone directory, listing business establishments, clubs, corporations, hotels, restaurants, theaters, and the like.

Columbia Broadcasting System (CBS) is founded by Chicago-born Congress Cigar Co. advertising manager William S. Paley, 27, who has been receiving $50,000 per year from his father's firm and last year committed the company to an advertising contract of $50 per week with Philadelphia's 225-watt radio station WCAU while his father was away on vacation. Young Paley was criticized for making the contract but has seen sales of La Palina cigars soar in response to radio advertising; he sells some of his stock in Congress Cigar to raise upwards of $275,000, buys into financially ailing United Independent Broadcasters that controls Columbia Phonograph, is elected president of the 22-station network September 26, and keeps CBS solvent by selling a 49 percent interest to Adolph Zukor's Paramount-Publix motion picture firm (broadcasting 16 hours per day over long-line telephone wires costs $1 million per year). Paley's network includes the 4-year-old New York station WABC (it will become WCBS in 1943); he will move CBS to New York next year and make it a rival to David Sarnoff's NBC (see ABC, 1943).

The *Irish Echo* begins weekly publication at New York, competing with John C. O'Connor's 35-year-old *Irish Advocate*. Printer-publisher Charles Connolly covers some events in Ireland but focuses on the activities of the city's Irish community. He will sell the paper in 1955 to Patrick Grimes, now 38.

Naples-born businessman Generoso Pope, 37, buys *Il Progresso Italo-Americano*, the city's leading Italian-language daily. Owner of the Colonial Sand and Gravel Co. that has been involved in tunnel excavations, Pope will buy the weekly *Il Corriere d'America* next year and use the papers to support Italy's fascist dictator Benito Mussolini, who gave him a medal 2 years ago, gives him another, and will give him a third in 1930.

Batten, Barton, Durstine & Osborn (BBDO) is created at New York September 15 by the merger of the 37-year-old George Batten Co. (whose founder died in 1918 but which has billings of $8 million) with the 9-year-old firm Barton, Durstine, & Osborn, which has $23 million in billings and is headed by Bruce

Barton, now 42, Roy S. Durstine, 42, and Alex Osborn, 40. Both companies have been at 383 Madison Avenue since 1923, BDO has been using radio commercials for its client Atwater Kent since 1925, and the new agency has 113 clients, 600 employees, with branch offices at Boston, Buffalo, and Chicago.

Cartoonist Richard F. Outcault dies at Flushing, Queens, September 25 at age 65, having devoted his time in recent years to the advertising agency he set up for the purpose of licensing companies to use his Buster Brown figure; advertising pioneer J. Walter Thompson dies at New York October 16 at age 80.

The Strand Bookshop is founded by bookseller Ben Bass in 8th Street. The store will move to larger quarters at 81 Fourth Avenue and, in 1956, to the northeast corner of Broadway and 12th Street, where it will grow to have 50,000 square feet of space, a stock of more than 2 million books, and a staff of 150.

Nonfiction: *The Iconography of Manhattan Island, 1498-1909* by architect I. N. Phelps Stokes, now 61, whose first volume (this is the sixth and final one) appeared 13 years ago; *Tammany Hall* by New York author Morris R. Werner.

Fiction: *Home to Harlem* by Claude McKay, now 38, who writes, "The lovely trees of Seventh Avenue were a vivid flame-green. Children, lightly clad, skipped on the pavement. Light open coats prevailed and the smooth bare throats of brown girls were a token as charming as the first pussy-willows. Far and high above all, the sky was a grand blue benediction, and beneath it the wonderful air of New York tasted like dry Champagne" (McKay has lived abroad since 1922 and will not return to America until 1934); *Dark Princess: A Romance* by W. E. B. Du Bois; *She Walks in Beauty* by Ohio-born New York novelist Dawn Powell, 30; *Nothing Is Sacred* by Sioux City-born novelist Josephine Herbst, 36, who came to New York late in 1919 and early in 1920 began an adulterous affair with playwright Maxwell Anderson, then an editorial writer for the *New York Globe* (his wife will die in 1931, and he will marry two other women, but not Josie Herbst); *Quicksand* by Chicago-born Harlem novelist Nella Larsen, 37; *The Walls of Jericho* by Washington, D.C.-born Harlem novelist Rudolph Fisher, 32, whose short stories have been appearing in major magazines since February 1925.

Novelist George Barr McCutcheon dies suddenly October 23 at age 62 while attending a luncheon of the Dutch Treat Club in the Hotel Martinique.

Poetry: *Buck in the Snow* by Edna St. Vincent Millay.

Painting: *Manhattan Bridge Loop* and *Night Windows* by Edward Hopper; *Sixth Avenue and Third Street* by John Sloan; *Houses on a Barge* by Arthur Dove.

Theater: *Marco Millions* by Eugene O'Neill 1/9 at the Garrick Theater, with New York-born actor Robert Barrat, 38, Margalo Gilmore, Alfred Lunt, St. Louis-born actor Morris Carnovsky, 30, Sanford Meisner, 92 perfs.; *Cock Robin* by Philip Barry and Elmer Rice 1/12 at the 48th Street Theater, with Yonkers-born actress Muriel Kirkland, 24, Moffat Johnston, 100 perfs.; *Strange Interlude* by O'Neill 1/30 at John Golden's Theater, with Lynn Fontanne, Glenn Anders, Earle Larimore, Australian actress Judith (originally Frances Margaret) Anderson, 29, and Tom Powers in a Freudian study of women with Elizabethan monologistic asides (the curtain rises at 5:30, descends at 7 for an 80-minute dinner interval, rises again at 8:20, and does not fall until after 11), 426 perfs.; *Skidding* by U.S. playwright Aurania Rouverol (Aurania Ellerbeck Rouveyrol) 5/21 at the Bijou Theater, with Marguerite Churchill, 448 perfs.; *The Front Page* by New York-born former *Chicago Daily News* staff writer Ben Hecht, 34, and Scranton, Pa.-born former *Hearst's International Magazine* staff writer Charles MacArthur, 33, 8/14 at the Times Square Theater, with Lee Tracy, Osgood Perkins, North Dakota-born actress Dorothy Stickney, 28, 276 perfs. (MacArthur marries actress Helen Hayes 8/17); *Machinal* by Sophie Treadwell 9/7 at the Plymouth Theater, with Jean Adair, Ohio-born actor Clark Gable, 27, Zita Johann in an expressionist drama based on last year's Snyder-Gray murder case, 91 perfs.; *Elmer the Great* by George M. Cohan and Ring Lardner 9/24 at the Lyceum Theater, with Walter Huston, 40 perfs.; *Holiday* by Philip Barry 11/26 at the Plymouth Theater, with Columbus, Ohio-born actor-writer Donald Ogden Stewart, 33, New York-born actress Hope Williams, 31, 229 perfs.; *The Kingdom of God* by Madrid playwright Gregorio Martinez Sierra, 47 (or his wife, Maria; translated by Helen and Granville Barker) 12/20 at the new Ethel Barrymore Theater, 243 West 47th Street, with Ethel Barrymore as Sister Gracia (she is 19 in Act I, 29 in Act II, 70 in Act III), 92 perfs.

Playwright-lyricist Avery Hopwood dies at Juan-les-Pins, France, July 1 at age 46.

The Neighborhood School of Theater opens on the Lower East Side (*see* Meisner, 1935).

Films: King Vidor's *The Crowd* with Eleanor Boardman (silent but breathtaking); Josef von Sternberg's *The Docks of New York* with George Bancroft, Betty Compson; *The Lights of New York* opens July 6 at New York—the first all-sound, full-length feature. Also:

Edward Sedgwick Jr.'s *The Cameraman* with John Francis "Buster" Keaton; Ted Wilde's *Speedy* with Harold Lloyd.

The Beacon Theater opens on the upper West Side at 2124 Broadway (between 74th and 75th streets). Designed by Walter Ahlschlager with stained glass and murals in its lobby, a rotunda, carved wood, intricate ceilings, and brass ornaments, it has 2,600 seats and is initially a movie house, a replica of the Ahlschlager-designed Roxy at 49th Street and Seventh Avenue.

Russian-born virtuoso pianist Vladimir Horowitz, 23, makes his Carnegie Hall debut 1/12; Philadelphia-born contralto Marian Anderson, 31, her Carnegie Hall debut 12/30.

Broadway musicals: *Rosalie* 1/10 at the New Amsterdam Theater, with Marilyn Miller, Frank Morgan, Jack Donahue, music by George Gershwin and Sigmund Romberg, lyrics by Ira Gershwin and P. G. Wodehouse, book by Guy Bolton and William Anthony McGuire, 335 perfs.; *Sunny Days* 2/8 at the Imperial Theater, with Jeanette MacDonald, music by Jean Schwartz, book and lyrics by Clifford Grey and William Carey Duncan (from the French version by Maurice Hennequin and Pierre Veber), 101 perfs.; *The Three Musketeers* 3/13 at the Lyric Theater, with Dennis King as D'Artagnan, Vivienne Segal, Reginald Owen as Cardinal Richelieu, Clarence Derwent as Louis XIII, music by Rudolf Friml, songs that include "March of the Musketeers," 318 perfs.; *Present Arms* 4/26 at the Mansfield Theater, with English-born performer Joyce Barbour, 27, Charles King, choreography by Busby Berkeley, music by Richard Rodgers, lyrics by Lorenz Hart, songs that include "You Took Advantage of Me," 155 perfs.; *Blackbirds of 1928* 5/9 at the Liberty Theater, with Richmond, Va.-born dancer Bill "Bojangles" Robinson, 39, songs that include "Digga Digga Do" and "I Can't Give You Anything but Love" by Jimmy McHugh, lyrics by Dorothy Fields, 518 perfs.; *George White's Scandals* 7/2 at the Apollo Theater, with vaudevillian Harry Richman (originally Reichman), 33, Ann Pennington, Willie and Eugene Howard, music by Ray Henderson, lyrics by B. G. DeSylva and Lew Brown, 240 perfs.; *Good Boy* 9/15 at the Hammerstein Theater, with Eddie Buzzell, Charles Butterworth, songs that include "I Wanna Be Loved by You" by Herbert Stothart, Bert Kalmar, and Harry Ruby (Bronx-born singer Helen Kane, 24, inserts some "boop-boop-a-doops," becomes known as the "boop-boop-a-doop" girl, and is booked into the Palace Theater to sing her specialty), 253 perfs.; *The New Moon* 9/10 at the Imperial Theater, with Robert Halliday, Evelyn Herbert, music by Sigmund

Romberg, lyrics by Oscar Hammerstein II and others, songs that include "One Kiss," "Lover, Come Back to Me," "Softly, as in a Morning Sunrise," "Wanting You," "Stout-Hearted Men," 509 perfs.; *Paris* 10/8 at the Music Box Theater, with Irene Bordoni, music and lyrics by Cole Porter, now 36, and E. Ray Goetz, songs that include "Let's Fall in Love" with lyrics that begin, "Let's do it . . ." 195 perfs.; *Hold Everything* 10/10 at the Broadhurst Theater, with Bert Lahr, Jack Whiting, Victor Moore, Betty Compton, Portland, Ore.-born actress Ona Munson, 23, book by B. G. DeSylva, music by Ray Henderson, lyrics by DeSylva and Lew Brown, songs that include "You're the Cream in My Coffee," 413 perfs.; *Animal Crackers* 10/23 at the 44th Street Theater, with the Four Marx Brothers, New York-born actress Margaret Dumont, 39, book by George S. Kaufman and Morrie Ryskind, music and lyrics by Bert Kalmar and Harry Ruby, 191 perfs.; *Treasure Girl* 11/8 at the Alvin Theater, with Gertrude Lawrence, Clifton Webb, music by George Gershwin, lyrics by Ira Gershwin, songs that include "I've Got a Crush on You," "I've Got a Feeling I'm Falling," "Oh, So Nice," 68 perfs.; *Whoopee* 12/4 at the New Amsterdam Theater, with Eddie Cantor, music and lyrics by Walter Donaldson and Gus Kahn, songs that include "Love Me or Leave Me," "Makin' Whoopee," 379 perfs.

Vaudevillian Eddie Foy Sr. dies on a farewell tour at Kansas City, Mo., February 16 at age 71; comedienne-songwriter Nora Bayes of cancer at Brooklyn March 19 at age 48; composer Howard Talbot at London September 12 at age 63.

First performances: *An American in Paris* by George Gershwin 12/13 at Carnegie Hall with Gershwin at the piano, Walter Damrosch conducting.

Rudy Vallée forms his own band and opens at New York's Heigh-Ho Club with a megaphone to amplify his voice. The first "crooner," Vermont-born Hubert Prior Vallée, 27, Yale '27, is a self-taught saxophonist who worked his way through a year at the University of Maine and 3 years at Yale with interruptions for musical engagements, sings the Maine "Stein Song," and makes his theme song "My Time Is Your Time."

Nashville-born trumpeter Adolphus Anthony "Doc" Cheatham, 23, comes to New York from Philadelphia, where he played second trumpet behind Sidney De Paris in Wilbur De Paris's band, and lends his talents to drummer and bandleader Chick Webb (*see* 1931).

Popular songs: "Puttin' On the Ritz" by Irving Berlin, who writes about "the well-to-do, up and down Park Avenue" with their noses in the air;

"Harlem Drag" by New York songwriters R. Arthur Booker and Walter Bishop.

 Tex Rickard dies January 6 at age 58 while promoting a prizefight at Miami Beach, Fla.

The 3-year-old New York Rangers win their first National Hockey League championship. Coached by Lester Patrick, they beat the Montreal Canadiens to take possession of the Stanley Cup, North America's professional hockey trophy since 1910.

Henri Cochet wins in men's singles at Forest Hills, Helen Wills in women's singles.

The New York Yankees win the World Series, defeating the St. Louis Cardinals 4 games to 0. Babe Ruth gets 10 hits, including three doubles and three home runs, Lou Gehrig six hits, including a double and four home runs.

Notre Dame beats Army at Yankee Stadium November 11 after Norwegian-born coach Knute Rockne, now 40, gives a halftime locker-room speech urging his team to "Win one for the Gipper" (a reference to George Gipp, who has died of a football injury). Notre Dame has played Army at the Stadium since 1925 and will do so through 1946.

 Mayor Walker leaves his wife, Janet, and moves with his showgirl mistress, Betty Compton, into a suite at the Mayfair House on Park Avenue at 65th Street.

 American Tobacco Co. boss George Washington Hill, now 44, promotes Lucky Strike cigarettes to women with the slogan "Reach for a Lucky instead of a sweet" in an effort to persuade women that candy is fattening while smoking is not (*see* 1929).

Gangster Meyer Lansky, now 25, is arrested on murder charges March 7 but the case is dropped and Lansky obtains U.S. citizenship later in the year (*see* 1918; 1942).

Gambler Arnold Rothstein receives a message at Lindy's November 4 to come to Room 349 of the Park Central Hotel at 870 Seventh Avenue, between 55th and 56th streets, and is shot in the stomach when he arrives, probably because he has welshed on a bet, perhaps to fellow gambler George C. McManus. He dies 2 days later at age 46 and his killer will not be found. Rothstein has been living with his wife, Carolyn, at 912 Fifth Avenue, between 72nd and 73rd streets, and his death tempts his one-time bodyguard Jack "Legs" Diamond, now a bootlegger, to attempt a takeover of the Rothstein crime syndicate (*see* Diamond, 1931).

 The 19-story New York Evening Post Building is completed at 75 West Street to designs by Horace

Trumbauer. It extends through the block to Washington Street.

The 37-story Chase National Bank Building is completed at 20 Pine Street, northeast corner Nassau Street, with a bank entrance at 18 Pine and a rear entrance at 60 Cedar Street; the 32-story Bank of New York Building at 48 Wall Street, northeast corner William Street, to Renaissance Revival (neo-Georgian) designs by Benjamin Wistar Morris; the 34-story National City Co. Building at 52 Wall Street, just east of William Street, to designs by McKim, Mead & White; the 33-story 67 Broad Street office building in Art Deco style between South William and Beaver streets with 650,000 square feet of space; the 37-story 39 Broadway office building between Morris Street and Exchange Place with 447,000 square feet of space; the 44-story Transportation Building at 225 Broadway, southwest corner Barclay Street, to designs by York & Sawyer.

New York Life Insurance Co. moves from its 346 Broadway offices into a pyramid-topped tower completed on the west side of Park Avenue South between 26th and 27th streets. Designed in neo-Gothic style by Cass Gilbert (based on work by builder Paul Starrett's young Japanese-born architect Yasuo Matsui) the 39-story tower has been erected by Starrett Brothers and stands on a site formerly occupied by Madison Square Garden and—before that—the old New York & Harlem Railroad terminal. The $25 million "Cathedral of Insurance" has an imposing three-story lobby, 38 elevators, 925,000 square feet of floor space, and 2,180 windows, its golden pinnacle is six stories high, 72 gargoyles decorate its exterior.

The 54-story Lincoln Building is completed at 60 East 42nd Street. Designed by J. E. R. Carpenter, it has 1.1 million square feet of floor space, towers above the Belmont Hotel to its east, and wraps around the 12-year-old building put up by August Heckscher at 50 East 42nd Street.

The 40-story Lefcourt National Building is completed at 521 Fifth Avenue (northeast corner 43rd Street) for Abraham E. Lefcourt, 50, replacing Temple Emmanu-El (see 1868). Shreve, Lamb & Harmon has designed the structure with 260,000 square feet of rentable floor space.

John D. Rockefeller, Jr. leases a three-block area extending from 48th Street to 51st between Fifth and Sixth avenues with a view to relocating the Metropolitan Opera House to the area and replacing its brothels, speakeasies, and tenements with modern office buildings. Columbia University has owned the land since 1814; paying Columbia rent and providing for utilities costs Rockefeller $5 million per year, and when the Met decides not to move he will be stuck with large expenses (see Rockefeller Center, 1931).

A new 25-story General Motors Building is completed at 1775 Broadway on a site bounded by Broadway and Eighth Avenue between 57th and 58th streets. Architects Shreve & Lamb have added 22 floors to an existing three-story structure.

The International Magazine Building (later the Hearst Magazine Building) is completed at 959 Eighth Avenue, between 56th and 57th streets, to designs by Joseph Urban; William Randolph Hearst has convinced himself that a bridge will be built across the Hudson at 57th Street, and he intends to top the six-story Moorish structure with a seven-story office tower, but Hearst moved to California last year (he will return in 1935 to avoid high California taxes) and the tower will not be built in this century.

A new building for the Central Savings Bank (originally the German Savings Bank, later to be the Apple Bank for Savings) goes up at 2100 Broadway, northeast corner 73rd Street, to occupy the entire block north of Sherman Square opposite the Ansonia Hotel. York & Sawyer has designed the structure in a Florentine palazzo style that makes it look like a miniature of their Federal Reserve Bank building, completed 4 years ago in Liberty Street.

Architect William Rutherford Mead of McKim, Mead & White dies at Paris June 30 at age 81.

Tudor City is completed east of Second Avenue between 40th and 43rd streets. Designed by Fred F. French and H. Douglas Ives and built at a cost of $25 million, its 12 buildings range in height from 12 to 32 stories, contain 3,000 apartments (plus 600 hotel rooms), and face on a private park.

The 15-story 30 Sutton Place South co-operative apartment house is completed to plans by Rosario Candela. Built by Joseph Paterno, it has units of six, seven, and eight rooms plus two special duplexes of 13 rooms each and two 15-room duplex penthouses.

Harlem's Paul Lawrence Dunbar Apartments are completed between 149th and 150th streets. Designed by architect Andrew J. Thomas and built with financing from John D. Rockefeller, Jr., the six co-operative garden apartment buildings represent the first development of its kind built for blacks. The Dunbar National Bank on the premises is the first large bank in Harlem to have a black manager and black staff. An initial down payment of $150 plus $50 per room buys a four-, five-, or six-room apartment, and tenants (who will soon include poet Countee Cullen, writer W. E. B. Du Bois, polar explorer Matthew A. Henson, labor leader A. Philip Randolph, actor Paul Robeson, and tap dancer Bill "Bojangles" Robinson) have their own nursery, kindergarten, retail shops, men's and women's clubs, a club for older boys, a playground, an athletic field, and a vocational guidance center (see 1936).

The Long Island Rail Road opens a station at Rego Park, where apartment houses such as Jupiter Court, Marion Court, and Remo Hall have been going up to supplement the one- and multi-family houses and small apartment buildings erected since 1920 (see 1923).

The Phipps Garden Apartments are completed in Sunnyside Gardens, Queens (see 1924). Financed by the Phipps Foundation, the complex of four- to six-story buildings surround a courtyard and have been designed by Isador Rosenfeld of the Clarence Stein firm, who has been inspired by Harlem's Dunbar Apartments.

The block-square five-story Thomas Garden apartment houses are completed in the Bronx at 840 Grand Concourse, between 158th and 159th streets. Architect Andrew J. Thomas has grouped the buildings around a westernized Japanese garden in a sunken courtyard, and the walk-up units are reached by walking over bridges that span an artificial stream.

The rent regulation law enacted in April 1920 is repealed (see 1926). New York builders have put up so much housing for middle-class tenants that the city has some 83,000 vacant apartments, but more people live in old-law tenements than in 1909 (see 1942).

The 27-story Lincoln Hotel (later the Milford Plaza) opens on the east side of Eighth Avenue between 44th and 45th streets. Designed by Schwartz & Gross and erected by the Chanin Construction Co., it has 1,400 rooms.

The 22-story Hotel Paramount opens at 235 West 46th Street, just west of Broadway. Designed by Thomas W. Lamb, it has 700 guest rooms.

The 27-story Panhellenic Hotel (later the Beekman Tower apartment house) is completed at 3 Mitchell Place, northeast corner First Avenue and 49th Street. Designed by John Mead Howells, its initial purpose is to provide quarters for sorority (Greek letter society) members.

The 35-story Warwick Hotel is completed at the northeast corner of Sixth Avenue and 54th Street with 512 guest rooms and a penthouse suite for actress Marion Davies, who has been William Randolph Hearst's mistress since 1917. Hearst and his chief editor Arthur Brisbane have financed the new hotel, designed by George B. Post Co., and Brisbane will briefly make it his home.

The Oliver Cromwell hotel is completed at 12 West 72nd Street, opposite the 43-year-old Dakota. Designed by Emery Roth, the 1,000-room structure towers over Central Park West (it will become almost entirely a residential hotel).

1929 The city's police force marches 5,300-strong in uniform from 74th Street to the Battery May 18 as Mayor Walker, former governor Al Smith, and Lieutenant Governor Herbert H. Lehman watch from the reviewing stand. Protesters charging police brutality unfurl a large communist banner at Union Square, sparking a disorder that is quelled in 20 minutes with the arrest of 27 people, nine of them under age 16.

The Communist Party of America celebrates International Red Day August 1 in Union Square with speeches and banners opposing imperialist war and defending the Soviet Union; the party has been torn by internal dissension since Josef Stalin's expulsion of Leon Trotsky in mid-January (see 1930).

Mayor Jimmy Walker wins reelection by a wide margin, receiving 867,522 votes. Republican Congressman Fiorello H. La Guardia, now 46, gets 367,675, Socialist Norman Thomas 175,697. A popular bon

The collapse of prices on the New York Stock Exchange did not start the Great Depression. It did end an era. VARIETY

vivant often seen in the city's speakeasies, Walker has appointed an honest police commissioner, unified city hospitals, and argued successfully before the U.S. Supreme Court in favor of preserving the city's 5¢ subway fare, but he has also been accepting under-the-table political contributions from businessmen in exchange for municipal contracts, and he has made little or no effort to conceal his extramarital affair with actress Betty Compton. The Republican keynote address August 1 has ridiculed Walker as "Jimmy the Jester," and the party's platform has said, "James J. Walker, when candidate for mayor, promised stern suppression of all corruption in public office as mayor; he has not only tolerated but jested at such corruption in city departments. He promised strict economy in city finance, yet his administration has indulged in an orgy of spending surpassing by hundreds of millions that of any previous administration" (see 1932).

Irish-born commissioner of records John Francis Curry, 55, wins election as Grand Sachem of Tammany Hall with support from Mayor Walker and uptown political leader James J. Hines, 53, who opposed the late Charles F. Murphy.

$ New York reports February 3 that business girls average $33.50 for a 50-hour week, but wages will soon drop. Seventy-one percent of U.S. families have incomes below $2,500, generally considered the minimum necessary for a decent standard of living. The average weekly wage is $28 (see 1932).

Chemical Bank opens its first international office, at London, and converts to a state charter that permits it to merge with the United States Mortgage Trust Co. (see 1920). Chemical has grown to have 12 branches in Manhattan and Brooklyn (see Corn Exchange, 1954).

Financier Paul Warburg, now 59, issues a warning in January that sharply criticizes the "present orgies of unrestrained speculation" on Wall Street. Few people listen.

Wall Street's Dow Jones Industrial Average reaches 381.17 September 3, up from a low of 88 in 1924, and a seat on the New York Stock Exchange sells for a high of $625,000. "Stocks have reached what looks like a permanently high plateau," writes Yale economist Irving Fisher October 17. "I expect to see the stock market a good deal higher than it is today within a few months." But trading is dominated by pools whose managers rig the market, and prices soon begin to break. U.S. iron and steel production has fallen, and a rise in British interest rates to 6.5 percent pulls European capital out of the U.S. money market. *Wall Street Journal* editor William Peter Hamilton's edito-

rial "The Turn in the Tide" appears October 21. Hamilton has predicted impending doom in January 1927, June 1928, and July 28 of this year, but sell orders pour in from Europe that Monday evening and Wall Street panics October 22. Irving Fisher calls the weakness "a shaking out of the lunatic fringe," but October 24 ("Black Thursday") brings a total collapse. Beverly, Mass.-born New York Stock Exchange president Richard Whitney, 41, moves onto the floor of the exchange and tries to stem the tide, placing an order for 10,000 shares of U.S. Steel at 205—40 points above the market price. Acting on behalf of the exchange's "old guard," he places orders totaling more than $20 million in a single afternoon, but the Dow falls 38.88 points (12.82 percent) October 28, and a record 16.4 million shares (twice the March 29 volume) trade October 29 as the Dow plummets another 30.57 points (11.73 percent); liquidation continues despite assurances by leading economists that no business recession is imminent. The Dow closes November 13 at 198.69, and $30 billion has disappeared from the U.S. economy, a sum almost equal to what the 1914-1918 war cost America; no reports of speculators jumping out of windows will be substantiated. While more than 99 percent of Americans own no stock (only 1.3 million people do), speculators who have bought on 10 percent margin have to sell (Charles E. Merrill of Merrill, Lynch has anticipated the crash and saves his customers $6 million, but Irving Fisher in the next few years will lose most of his considerable fortune, some of it acquired from a rich wife, some from his Index Visible filing system). The Dow recovers enough to close December 31 at 248.48, down from 300 at the end of 1928, but much worse is to come.

Many investors blame the Wall Street crash on speculator Jesse L. Livermore, who has 30 telephone lines linking him to brokerage houses (see 1925). Now 52, Livermore actually went short in the market during the summer, several months too early, and has gone broke (see 1934).

The Goldman, Sachs Trading Corp. created last year fails in one of the more spectacular financial disasters related to the collapse of stock prices; shares that sold for $326 each in early October fall to $1.75 within a few weeks, but the parent company founded 60 years ago continues as a private partnership.

Federated Department Stores is created by a loose confederation of three stores put together by Columbus, Ohio, retail merchant Fred Lazarus, Jr., 44, of Lazarus Brothers. Brooklyn's Abraham & Straus and Filene's at Boston join with Lazarus Brothers in the holding company of family-owned department-store chains that will be joined next year by Bloomingdale's and others to make Federated the largest U.S. chain.

Indiana-born Ohio utilities company lawyer Wendell L. (Lewis) Willkie, 41, moves to New York to become legal counsel to the new Commonwealth & Southern Corp., a giant holding company put together by Bernard C. Cobb but owned for the most part by Wall Street operator Alfred Lee Loomis, 41, a cousin of Henry L. Stimson who has made a fortune from utilities investments and pursues scientific experiments at his Tuxedo Park mansion (see 1933).

Newark Metropolitan Airport opens February 16 near Elizabeth, N.J., and will soon be the eastern terminus for American Airlines, TWA, and United Airlines (see 1930). New Jersey authorities have built a highway across the meadows to their end of the Holland Tunnel that opened in 1927 and filled in marshland to create the 68-acre, $1.75 million field that will serve 20,557 passengers next year, 90,177 in 1931, 123,329 by 1934, and although it will not have a central terminal building until early in 1936 it will eventually grow to cover 2,300 acres (see Floyd Bennett Field, 1931; La Guardia, 1939).

The Southern State Parkway opens in July to speed auto traffic to the beaches opened by Parks Commissioner Robert Moses (who has never learned to drive but has a chauffeur). Forty feet wide and shaded by trees, the new Long Island road has no grade crossings and comes into heavier use beginning August 4, when the Wantagh Causeway opens to the new Jones Beach State Park (25,000 motorcars cross the causeway on its first day).

Robert Moses opened Jones Beach but he favored motorists over straphangers. MUNICIPAL ARCHIVE

"A Regional Plan of New York and Its Environs" envisions such things as a Broome Street Expressway that would cut across lower Manhattan and a Cross-Brooklyn Expressway for that borough. Made public August 3 by Robert Moses and others after a 5-year study, the report states, "It is planned that arterial highways must necessarily run in every direction and turn the street system into a network, and that residential life must occupy the interstitial spaces . . . as the inevitable product of an automobile age." The Regional Plan Association of New York will sponsor the plan, and landlords will abandon warehouses and other structures along the proposed Broome Street right of way, anticipating the destruction of those buildings, but neither of the proposed expressways will be built (see 1961).

The S.S. *Bremen* arrives at New York July 22 after setting a new transatlantic speed record of 27.91 knots per hour. Built with welded plates and a bulbous prow that will be widely copied, the North German-Lloyd Line's floating palace has crossed from Cherbourg on her maiden voyage from Bremerhaven in 4 days, 17 hours, 42 minutes, cutting 3 hours off the record set by the S.S. *Mauretania* in 1910.

City health groups meet in October at the YMCA, 179 West 137th Street, to find ways to reduce the high death rate in Harlem, whose population has doubled in the last 10 years and where rates are 40 percent higher than in the city as whole. Payton F. Anderson of the Harlem Tuberculosis and Health Committee says conditions in what has now become the city's most heavily congested area are better than those in the black sections of other large cities, but disease resulting from overcrowded conditions and unsanitary housing has created undeniable problems, including high infant mortality: the infant mortality rate last year was 124 per 1,000 persons as compared with 62 per 1,000 in white sections, and the maternity death rate 10 per 1,000 cases versus five per 1,000 in white neighborhoods; the death rate from tuberculosis was 300 per 100,000 as compared with 75 among the white population; from pneumonia 360 as compared with 150. The New York Tuberculosis and Health Association says that biologically there is no such thing as racial susceptibility to disease.

De Witt Clinton High School moves after 23 years at 899 Tenth Avenue to a new campus in the Bronx on Moshulu Parkway at 205th Street (see coeducation, 1983). The Tenth Avenue building will become Haaren High School and, later, John Jay College of Criminal Justice.

The 10-year-old Dalton School moves from West 72nd Street into a new building at 108 East 89th Street, between Park and Lexington avenues (*see* 1939).

The Spence School moves to 22 East 91st Street (*see* 1892). It will merge with the Chandor School in 1932 and grow to have an enrollment of 350 girls in kindergarten through 12th grade.

The 45-year-old Brearley School prepares to leave its nine-story building on the southwest corner of Park Avenue and 61st Street for a larger structure at 610 East 83rd Street, near Carl Schurz Park (*see* 1947).

The Nightingale-Bamford School takes that name after 9 years as Miss Nightingale's School. It will grow to have 500 girls in grades kindergarten through 12th grade.

The Roerich Museum is completed at 310 Riverside Drive, northeast corner 103rd Street. Designed for artist Nicholas Roerich by Helmle, Corbett & Harrison with Sugarman & Berger, the 29-story structure is intended to be a residential hotel with a restaurant as well as a school, museum, and auditorium. It will later become the Master Institute of United Arts and Riverside Museum; later still simply the Master Apartments.

Lucius (Morris) Beebe, 27, goes to work for the *New York Tribune*, whose editor Stanley Walker hires the six-foot-four-inch Massachusetts gas company executive's son at $35 per week. Expelled from Yale, Beebe was in the Class of '27 at Harvard, went on to graduate school to study poetry, and has worked for the *Boston Transcript* (*see* 1933).

Former Associated Press president Melville E. Stone dies at New York February 15 at age 80; *Wall Street Journal* editor William Peter Hamilton of pneumonia at his 1 Pierrepont Street, Brooklyn, home December 9 at age 62.

New Yorkers begin to use French phones with mouthpiece and receiver in one unit. The United States has 20 million telephones, up from 10 million in 1918 and twice as many as all the rest of the world combined. Most are wooden boxes hung on walls with cranks to ring Central, but many tall tube-like phones are in use with hooks to hold their receivers.

Milwaukee-born *Brooklyn Eagle* associate editor H. V. (Hans von) Kaltenborn, 51, joins the 1-year-old Columbia Broadcasting System (CBS) as chief news commentator (he will switch to NBC in 1940). Kaltenborn joined the *Eagle* in 1910 and 12 years later began an *Eagle*-sponsored radio commentary over local stations.

Benton & Bowles is founded at New York July 15 by Minneapolis-born advertising agency executive William Benton, 29, and Massachusetts-born copywriter Chester (Bliss) Bowles, 28, whose friend Charles Mortimer works in the advertising department of Postum Co. The Yale alumni will pioneer in radio advertising, making themselves millionaires within 6 years.

The *Dial* suspends operations after 49 years of publication.

Business Week magazine begins publication September 7 at New York. The new McGraw-Hill publication will have lost $1.5 million by the end of 1935 but will turn the corner to become the leading magazine of its kind. In many years it will be the leading magazine of any kind in terms of advertising pages.

Farrar and Rinehart is founded by Doubleday, Doran editors John C. (Chipman) Farrar, 33, and Stanley M. Rinehart, Jr., 32, with Stanley's brother Frederick R., 27. The Rineharts are sons of mystery novelist Mary Roberts Rinehart (*see* Farrar Straus, 1946; Rinehart and Winston, 1960).

Fiction: *Look Homeward, Angel* by NYU English instructor Thomas Wolfe, 29, who has written his semi-autobiographical novel in his apartments, first at 263 West 11th Street and then at 17 West 15th Street (Scribner's New York-born editor [William] Maxwell [Evarts] Perkins, 45, has also been F. Scott Fitzgerald's mentor. He organizes and edits Wolfe's inchoate typescript about the Gant [Wolfe] family of Asheville, N.C.); *I Thought of Daisy* by New Jersey-born *New Republic* critic-novelist Edmund Wilson, 34, who moves into a new apartment at 224 West 13th Street; *The Wings of the Eagle* by critic-novelist-playwright Gilbert Seldes; *Dawn Ginsbergh's Revenge* (magazine pieces) by New York humorist S. J. (Sidney Joseph) Perelman, 25; *Hudson River Bracketed* by Edith Wharton, now 67; *Passing* by Nella Larsen; *The Blacker the Berry: A Novel of Negro Life* by Salt Lake City-born Harlem novelist Wallace Thurman; *Banjo: A Story without a Plot* by Claude McKay; *Sixty Seconds* by Maxwell Bodenheim; *Red Harvest* and *The Dain Curse* by former Pinkerton detective (Samuel) Dashiell Hammett, 35, who comes to New York from San Francisco in the fall and lives in an apartment at 155 East 30th Street, between Lexington and Third avenues.

Poetry: *Angel Arms* by Illinois-born New York poet Kenneth Fearing, 27; *The Black Christ, and Other Poems* by Countee Cullen, who married a daughter of W. E. B. DuBois last year but will be divorced next year.

Painting: *Chop Suey* by Edward Hopper; *New York Night* by Georgia O'Keeffe, who moved with her husband, Alfred Stieglitz, into a 30th-floor apartment at the Shelton Hotel on Lexington Avenue in November 1925 and since then has completed more than 20 drawings, paintings, and pastels of skyscrapers and other views as seen from the living room of that apartment; *Upper Deck* by Charles Sheeler; *Fog Horns*, *Sun on the Water*, *Silver Sun*, and *Alfie's Delight* by Arthur Dove. Robert Henri dies at New York July 12 at age 64.

The Museum of Modern Art (MoMA) opens November 8 on the 12th floor of the Heckscher Building at 730 Fifth Avenue with an exhibition of works by the late French impressionists Paul Cézanne, Paul Gauguin, Georges Seurat, and Vincent Van Gogh. Its four founders are rich patrons for whom the collapse of the stock market has meant very little: John D. Rockefeller, Jr.'s wife, Abby (née Aldrich), Lizzie Plummer Bliss, 65 (who has been collecting modern art since the 1913 Armory show), Joan Whitney Payson, and Mrs. Cornelius J. Sullivan, who has studied at London's Slade School of Art and taught at Pratt Institute. Trustees include New York-born banker and power-company consolidator Chester Dale, 46, who since the Great War has been traveling on a regular basis to Europe with his wife, Maud, to buy works by the Impressionists and modern French painters. Director of the museum is Detroit-born scholar Alfred H. (Hamilton) Barr, Jr., 27, who has been recommended by Harvard fine-arts scholar Paul Sachs, 51, and will be MoMA's guiding spirit for some 38 years (see d'Harnoncourt, 1949); its first president is lumber baron Anson Conger Goodyear, 42, of Buffalo, who served briefly as president of that city's Albright Gallery until he antagonized his fellow trustees by paying $5,000 for a "pink period" Picasso and whose own collection includes works by Maillol, Renoir, Seurat, and Van Gogh (see 1932).

Theater: *Street Scene* by Elmer Rice 1/10 at The Playhouse, with a cast of more than 40 that includes London-born actor Horace Braham, 36, Russian-born actor Leo Bulgakov, 30, Los Angeles-born actress Erin O'Brien-Moore, 26, Chicago-born actress Beulah Bondi (originally Bondy), 36, 601 perfs.; *Dynamo* by Eugene O'Neill 2/11 at the Martin Beck Theater, with Dudley Digges, Glenn Anders, Helen Wylie, French-born actress Claudette Colbert (Lily Claudette Chauchoin), 23, 50 perfs.; *Harlem: A Melodrama of Negro Life in Harlem* by Wallace Thurman and his white collaborator William Jourdan Rapp 2/20 at the Apollo Theater; *It's a Wise Child* by Lawrence E. Johnson 8/6 at the Belasco Theater, with Humphrey Bogart, Sidney Toler, 378 perfs.; *Strictly Dishonorable* by Chicago-born playwright Preston Sturges (originally Edmund Preston Biden), 31, 9/18 at the Alvin Theater with Ed McNamara, a former police officer who plays the role of a cop, and Muriel Kirkland, who falls ill in December and is replaced by Antoinette Perry's 17-year-old daughter Marguerite, 557 perfs.; *Berkeley Square* by John L. Balderston 11/4 at the Lyceum Theater, with Leslie Howard, Margalo Gilmore, 229 perfs.; *It Never Rains* by Aurania Rouverol 11/19 at the Republic Theater, with Sidney Fox as Dorothy Donovan, 185 perfs.

Actress Jeanne Eagels dies of alcohol and a sleeping-pill overdose at the Park Avenue Hospital October 3 at age 35.

Radio: *The Goldbergs* (initially, *The Rise of the Goldbergs*) 11/20 on NBC's Blue Network, with Harlem-born actress Gertrude Berg (née Edelstein), 30, in the role of Molly Goldberg in a series whose backup cast will include Menasha Skulnik, Everett Sloane, Arnold Stang, and Joan Tetzel (see television, 1949).

Broadway musicals: *Follow Thru* 1/9 at the 46th Street Theater, with Boston-born actor Jack Haley, 28, Irene Delroy, Springfield, Mass.-born tap dancer Eleanor Powell (originally Torrey), 18, book by B. G. DeSylva, music by Ray Henderson, lyrics by DeSylva and Lew Brown, songs that include "Button up Your Overcoat," 403 perfs.; *Spring Is Here* 3/11 at the Alvin Theater, with Joyce Barbour, Glenn Hunter, music by Richard Rodgers, lyrics by Lorenz Hart, songs that include "With a Song in My Heart," 104 perfs.; *Sing for Your Supper* 4/24 at the Adelphi Theater, with Earl Robinson, music by Lee Warner and Ned Lieber, lyrics by Robert Sous, songs that include "Ballad for Americans," 60 perfs.; *The Little Show* 4/30 at the Music Box Theater, with Clifton Webb, Romney Brent, Cambridge, Mass.-born former vaudeville juggler Fred Allen (originally John Florence Sullivan), 34, Portland Hoffa, Libby Holman, Bettina Hall, Peggy Conklin, music by Arthur Schwartz and others, lyrics by Howard Dietz, songs that include "I Guess I'll Have to Change My Plan," "Moanin' Low" (music by New York-born composer Ralph Rainger, 27), "Caught in the Rain" (music by Henry Sullivan), "Can't We Be Friends" (music by New York-born composer-lyricist Kay Swift, 26), 321 perfs.; *Hot Chocolates* 6/20 at the Hudson Theater, with Louis Armstrong in an all-black revue, songs that include "Ain't Misbehavin' " by New York-born composer Thomas Wright "Fats" Waller, 25, and Henry Brooks, lyrics by Washington, D.C.-born writer Andy Razaf (Paul Andreamenentania Razafinkeriefo), 33, 219 perfs.; *Show Girl* 7/2 at the Ziegfeld Theater, with Canadian-born dancer-actress Ruby (originally

Ethel) Keeler, 18, Jimmy Durante, Duke Ellington and his Orchestra, music by George Gershwin that includes the ballet "An American in Paris," lyrics by Ira Gershwin and Gus Kahn, songs that include "Liza" sung by Al Jolson, now 42, in the audience to his wife, Ruby Keeler, onstage, 111 perfs.; *Sweet Adeline* 9/3 at the Hammerstein Theater, with Helen Morgan as Addie Schmidt, Charles Butterworth, music by Jerome Kern, book and lyrics by Oscar Hammerstein II, songs that include "Why Was I Born," "Don't Ever Leave Me," "Here Am I," 234 perfs.; *George White's Scandals* 9/23 at the Apollo Theater, with Willie Howard, songs by Irving Caesar, George White, and Cliff Friend, 161 perfs.; *June Moon* 10/9 at the Broadhurst Theater, with book by George S. Kaufman (who last year moved into a penthouse at 158 East 63rd Street with his wife, Beatrice) and Ring Lardner, music and lyrics by Lardner, 273 perfs.; *Fifty Million Frenchmen* 11/27 at the Lyric Theater, with William Gaxton, Betty Compton, music and lyrics by Cole Porter, songs that include "You Do Something to Me," 254 perfs.; *Wake Up and Dream* 12/30 at the Selwyn Theater, with Jack Buchanan, music and lyrics by Cole Porter, songs that include "I'm a Gigolo," "What Is This Thing Called Love?," 136 perfs.

Comedian Edward Gallagher of Gallagher and Shean fame dies May 28 at age 56 in a Queens sanitarium where he has remained since suffering a nervous breakdown 2 years ago.

Alabama-born New York trumpet player Charles Melvin "Cootie" Williams, 21, joins the Duke Ellington band as a replacement for Ellington's plunger-muted trumpet player "Bubber" Miller.

Guy Lombardo and his Royal Canadians open at the Roosevelt Hotel, where the group directed by Canadian-born bandleader Guy Albert Lombardo, 27, will play dance music each winter for decades. A December 31 radio broadcast begins a national New Year's Eve tradition.

The New York Yankees become the first team to wear numbers on the backs of their uniforms, but a rainstorm at the stadium May 19 creates a stampede as bleacher-seat patrons rush for the exit; a 60-year old man and a 17-year-old Hunter College freshman are killed, 20 people injured. The Yankees win only 88 of their 154 games.

Bill Tilden wins in men's singles at Forest Hills, Helen Wills in women's singles.

The 4-year-old New York Giants win the National Football League championship with a 10-3 won-lost record.

Bridge World magazine begins publication at New York in October as Ely Culbertson gains backing from contract bridge creator Harold S. Vanderbilt to publicize his bidding system.

Songwriter Billy Rose is married in February to *Ziegfeld Follies* star Fanny Brice, who has divorced her second husband, gambler Nick Arnstein, and moves with Rose and her children into an apartment at 15 East 69th Street.

California Perfume Co. chief David McConnell, now 72, introduces a new line of products under the name Avon, inspired by Shakespeare's hometown Stratford-upon-Avon (*see* 1898). The door-to-door cosmetic company will rename itself Avon Products in 1939 and its saleswomen will be called Avon Ladies. It will grow to have 1.5 million Avon Ladies (plus 2,000 Avon Men) and become the world's largest employer of women.

Crawfordsville, Ind.-born reporter and department-store advertising artist Eleanor Lambert, 25, arrives at New York with $100 and finds two part-time jobs, one doing consumer research and one designing book jackets. A publisher asks her to write a publicity release, and as the daughter of a Ringling Brothers and Barnum & Bailey circus advance man she sets up her own small 57th Street public-relations business for creative artists. Lambert will make herself the city's (and country's) leading fashion publicist, a role she will continue to play into the 21st century.

Public-relations pioneer Edward L. Bernays engages 10 carefully selected women, provides them with Lucky Strike cigarettes, gives them detailed instructions on how and when they are to light up, and sends them down Fifth Avenue on Easter Sunday in a "Torches of Freedom" march calculated to counter objections to women smoking in public (*see* 1928). Newspapers across the country run front-page photographs of the event, making no mention of the fact that Bernays has been employed by the American Tobacco Co. (He has seen reports about the health hazards of cigarettes and has been trying to get his wife to stop smoking.)

The Police Department strengthens its Chinatown details in early August as incidents in other cities raise fears that warfare may resume between the Hip Sing Tong and the Wong Luan Tong.

Caresse Crosby (Polly Jacob), now 35, is widowed December 10 when her husband, Harry, kills his mistress Josephine Bigelow (*née* Rotch), 22, and then takes his own life in an apparent suicide pact. She and Harry have lived in France since 1922, she has been attending theater with poet Hart Crane, and she emerges to learn that Harry has killed himself in a friend's duplex apartment at the Hotel des Artistes in West 67th Street.

New York has 401 reported murders, Chicago 498, Detroit 228, Philadelphia 182, Cleveland 134, Birmingham 122, Atlanta and Memphis 115 each, New Orleans 111.

Brooklyn's 34-story Williamsburgh Savings Bank Tower opens May 1 at 1 Hanson Place, behind the Brooklyn Academy of Music, and will remain the borough's tallest structure into the 21st century. Designed in a Classical Revival style by Halsey, McCormack and Helmer, the 512-foot skyscraper supplements the bank's Manhattan building, put up in 1875 at 175 Broadway. Clocks on each of its four sides are 27 feet in diameter, its banking room has a vaulted ceiling 63 feet high decorated with gold leaf mosaic figures, and the doors of the ornate lobby that lead into the banking hall are ornamented with metal figures designed to represent the workingmen who will deposit their savings in the thrift institution.

Tammany Hall dedicates a new clubhouse July 4 at the southeast corner of Fourth Avenue and 17th Street facing Union Square, but Manhattan Democrats will lose the "wigwam" in 1945 for failure to keep up mortgage payments.

The 47-story 295 Madison Avenue skyscraper is completed at the southeast corner of 41st Street to Art Deco designs by Charles F. Moyer for developer Abraham E. Lefcourt.

The 56-story Chanin Building is completed at 122 East 42nd Street, where it towers above Grand Central Terminal. Sloan & Robertson has designed it for real estate developer Irwin S. Chanin, now 37, who has employed designer Jacques Delamarre to make its lobby an Art Deco extravaganza (the Art Deco façades are by designer Edward Trumbull); it has a two-story off-Broadway theater on its 50th and 51st floors, and the Baltimore & Ohio Railroad uses its basement as a terminal.

The Metropolis of Tomorrow by architectural visionary Hugh Ferriss envisions an ideal city that is divided into business, science, and art zones, with giant pyramidal structures rising from bases that cover four to eight blocks each and are surrounded by low-rise buildings laid out on geometric grids, with a large park in the center. Now 40, Ferris praises the new Chanin Building and the Chrysler Building nearing completion nearby; he fails to include factories, hospitals, schools, and other institutional buildings, but his work stimulates discussion about what a city should be.

The 34-story New York Central Building (later the Helmsley Building) is completed north of Grand Central at 230 Park Avenue, between 45th and 46th streets. Warren & Wetmore has designed a structure that rises on stilts above the railroad tracks below, contains 1.3 million square feet of floor space, and has pedestrian walkways connecting Park Avenue with 45th Street.

The 21-story 400 Madison Avenue office tower is completed between 47th and 48th streets; designed by H. Craig Severance, it has been erected by George A. Fuller Construction Co.

The 40-story Fuller Building is completed at 597 Madison Avenue (northeast corner 57th Street) to provide headquarters for the George A. Fuller Construction Co. Walker & Gillette has designed a structure that rises to a height of 491 feet.

The New York Junior League clubhouse is completed at 221 East 71st Street, between Second and Third avenues, to designs by John Russell Pope.

Architect Thomas Hastings of Carrère and Hastings dies after an appendectomy at Nassau Hospital in Mineola, L.I, October 22 at age 69.

The Church of the Heavenly Rest is completed for an Episcopalian congregation at the southeast corner of Fifth Avenue and 90th Street to designs by Hardie Philip of Mayers, Murray & Philip with a pulpit Madonna by sculptor Malvina Hoffman.

The Multiple Dwellings Law signed into law by Gov. Roosevelt April 19 places all high-rise housing under the legal jurisdiction of the Tenement House Commission. Mayor Walker has opposed the measure on grounds that it violated the home-rule principle, but New York City reformer Stanley M. Isaacs, 46, has led the fight for passage of the law, whose terms mandate improvements in tenement housing but compromise the 1901 Tenement Law by allowing interior public corridors and stairs that have no opening to the exterior, not even to air shafts or courtyards ("mechanical ventilation" may be substituted). The new law also reduces the practicality of 50-by-100-foot lots by increasing minimum courtyard sizes; it mandates bulk and height restrictions, permitting apartment towers on lots measuring 30,000 square feet or more to rise three times the width of the streets they are on, provided they do not exceed one-fifth of the area of the lot (heights are fixed in most cases to 300 feet, with a cap of 19 floors but extra floors are permitted if the building site is large enough and the tower portion occupies no more than 20 percent of the site). A state supreme court judge rules June 25 that the new law is unconstitutional, and it will be amended. A *New York Times* editorial December 26 notes that the new law "traveled a rocky road, both in the legislature and in the courts. It was criticized for going too far and not going far enough. The city fought the measure all the way up to the court of appeals on the ground that it infringed the principle of home rule. Many settlement workers, on the other hand, had no use for it because it did not definitely doom the 'old-law' tenements . . . At a public hearing last week errors or omissions in the measure were reported as 'gratifyingly few.' Social workers, however, urged an amendment which would make life in some of the ancient rookeries on the East Side less dismal and unhealthy by requiring that every bedroom should have an opening either on the street or on a court. Real estate interests sharply opposed any such change in the law, crying 'confiscation' " (*see* 1930).

The 18-story 720 Park Avenue apartment house is completed at the northwest corner of 70th Street, replacing some of Presbyterian Hospital's medical pavilions. Designed by Cross & Cross with Rosario Candela, the luxury co-operative has apartments ranging in size from nine to 14 rooms. Macy's boss Jesse Straus takes two floors.

The 19-story 730 Park Avenue apartment house is completed at the southwest corner of 71st Street, occupying another part of the former Presbyterian Hospital property. Designed by F. Burrall Hoffman, Jr. and Lafayette A. Goldstone, its apartments include a 16-room duplex with six master bedrooms, six baths, and five servants' rooms. Each of its duplex maisonettes has 13 rooms, five baths, and a lavatory.

The Beresford apartment house is completed just north of the Museum of Natural History at the northwest corner of Central Park West and 81st Street, replacing a 40-year-old six-story apartment-hotel of the same name, its slightly younger annex, and a private house at 3 West 81st Street. Emery Roth has designed the 21-story, 1,300-room building, whose 179 units range in size from five to 15 rooms (its three stubby towers are used to house mechanical equipment and water tanks).

The 1175 Park Avenue apartment house is completed at the southeast corner of 93rd Street with 14 floors plus penthouse. Emery Roth has designed the building, put up by the George Backer Construction Co. (Backer is married to a granddaughter of the late Kuhn, Loeb & Co. banker Jacob H. Schiff).

The luxury apartment house 1185 Park Avenue is completed on the east side of the avenue between 92nd and 93rd streets, where the 15-story-plus-penthouse structure occupies almost the entire block, extending to within 100 feet of Lexington Avenue. Designed by Schwartz & Gross to accommodate 180 families, the 1,300-room building on Carnegie Hill has a large inner courtyard and rises on a site formerly occupied by the mansion of brewer George Ehret, who died in January 1927 after amassing a fortune estimated at $40 million. The duplex penthouse has a living room measuring 32' × 20'6", a dining room 24' × 14', a library 27'8" × 16'8", master bedroom 26' × 13'7", three other bedrooms, a sun parlor, two maids' rooms, and five baths upstairs; downstairs are a servants' hall, two maids' rooms, and a lavatory off a circular staircase that connects the two floors. Bricken Construction Co. has had 300 masons and about 700 other workmen rushing to complete the job before August 24, when a new 5-day work week went into effect (instead of 5½), raising wages by 10 percent. At the time the company bought the property in April of last year for nearly $3 million its president Abraham Bricken told the press, "We have designed what we believe will be the sunniest apartment building in the city." But there is no air conditioning, and the canvas awnings used to keep apartments cool in summer will eventually be banned as a fire hazard.

The Buildings Department gives approval to its 391st penthouse, and an 11-room penthouse at 480 Park rents for $1,788 per month, but most penthouses fetch less than $100 per room per month and are used chiefly for servants' quarters or laundry rooms (with open-air rooftop drying facilities).

The 15-story luxury apartment house 1192 Park Avenue is completed at the southwest corner of 94th Street to plans by Rosario Candela.

The 31-story-plus-penthouse Hotel Governor Clinton opens August 19 at the southeast corner of Seventh Avenue and 31st Street with a dinner for Gov. Roosevelt (guests include former governor Al Smith and Mayor Walker). Designed by Murgatroyd & Ogden in collaboration with George B. Post and erected by Thompson Starrett Co., it has 1,200 rooms, each with bath, servidor, running ice water, French phone, full-length mirror, and radio.

The St. Regis Hotel that opened in 1905 gets a 21-story annex. Designed by Sloan & Robertson and financed by real estate heir Vincent Astor, it increases the number of rooms to 650.

Brooklyn's St. George Hotel gets a 31-story tower, giving it a total of 2,600 rooms and the world's largest swimming pool (120 by 140 feet, with slightly salty water).

New York land values have increased by 75 percent since 1919, and real estate taxes provide about 80 percent of the city's revenues.

Heckscher State Park opens June 2 at East Islip, L.I., with formal ceremonies on the steps of the George C. Taylor mansion that was once the center of a 1,500-acre estate. Former governor Al Smith is acclaimed, but developer-philanthropist August Heckscher, now 80, has contributed $250,000 for its construction and tells the crowd of 15,000, "You owe this park . . . to the amazing public spirit of Robert Moses."

Jones Beach State Park and Causeway open August 4 with speeches by Gov. Roosevelt, former governor Al Smith, Parks Commissioner Robert Moses, and others (the ceremonies are disrupted by a sudden windstorm that drives sand into people's eyes and fouls automobile carburetors). Occupying 1,200 acres, the new park has four miles of clean, white, sandy ocean beaches, a boardwalk with mahogany railings, parking for 12,000 automobiles, a 200-foot-high, 300,000-gallon water tower built to resemble Venice's Campanile de San Marco, two saltwater swimming pools, east and west bathhouses that accommodate 10,000 visitors, an Indian Village, playgrounds, shuffleboard courts, and other recreational facilities. Attendants wear nautical uniforms, and the well-policed Jones Beach attracts more than 325,000 people in its first month, despite predictions that New Yorkers would not drive 40 miles to a park located on a sandbar (only two sections of Jones Beach are completed, and Coney Island and Rockaway Beach remain far more popular: Coney Island has 600,000 visitors August 4 and the Rockaways 200,000, despite biting winds that keep temperatures below 70° F. most of the day).

The Jefferson Market food store opens in the 52-year-old Third Judicial Courthouse at 425 Sixth Avenue, where it will remain until it moves across the street in 1995.

New York grocer Barney Greengrass opens a shop at 541 Amsterdam Avenue, near 79th Street, that will continue into the 21st century with sawdust on its floor and groceries on its shelves. Greengrass started in 1908 at 1403 Fifth Avenue, near 115th Street, specializing in lox and whitefish; he moved soon after to the corner of 113th Street and St. Nicholas Avenue, and has followed his largely Jewish clientele out of Harlem to the upper West Side, where such notables as Franklin D. Roosevelt, Ir-

ving Berlin, and the Marx Brothers will come to buy the "sturgeon king's" borscht, bagels, sable, whitefish, kippered salmon, smoked salmon, and—above all—smoked lake sturgeon.

A second, larger Lindy's restaurant opens on Broadway at 51st Street (*see* 1921). The original Lindy's will continue to operate at 1626 Broadway until 1957; Al Jolson, Damon Runyon, and other entertainment-world figures have built up a following for Leo Lindemann, and his new restaurant introduces more patrons to Lindy's matzoh-ball soup, sturgeon, and cheesecake.

John's Pizzeria opens at 278 Bleecker Street under the direction of John Sasso, who has trained under Gennaro Lombardi in Spring Street (*see* 1905). Sasso's descendants will continue his operation for at least 70 years (*see* Patsy's, 1933).

The Stork Club speakeasy opens at 132 West 58th Street under the management of former Oklahoma bootlegger Sherman Billingsley, 29, who has received backing from three gangsters (Cotton Club owner Owney Madden and Oklahoma gamblers Carl Henninger and John Patton) and encouraged to open the little hole in the wall (*see* 1933).

New York police raid Sanger's Clinic, but Margaret Sanger continues to campaign for birth control (*see* 1923; 1951).

1930 The Communist Party stages a demonstration in Union Square March 6 that brings out a crowd estimated by the *New York Times* to number 35,000 (the *Daily Worker* estimates 100,000). Mounted police ride into the crowd swinging clubs to prevent it from marching on City Hall. "Those who had come to see [a Communist rally] had their fill," writes the *New York World*. "Women struck in the face with blackjacks, boys beaten by gangs of seven and eight policemen, and an old man backed into a doorway and knocked down time after time, only to be dragged to his feet and struck down with fist and club. Detectives, many wearing badges, running wildly through the crowd, screaming as they beat and kicked those who looked to them like Communists." Communists throughout the city organize unemployed workers into councils as the year wears on, gathering crowds to resist evictions, and leading protest marches on city relief offices. Attracting U.S.-born children of immigrants and building a following among blacks, the party will have about 58,000 members in New York State by 1938.

Brooklyn lawyer-reformer Horace E. Deming dies at New York June 11 at age 80.

Gov. Roosevelt wins easy reelection, defeating his Republican challenger, lawyer Charles Henry Tuttle, 53. The Franklin D. Roosevelt administration has brought about the creation of a state power authority, reduced public utility rates, and given tax relief to the state's hard-pressed farmers. Nearly 175,000 of the governor's 725,000-vote plurality come from outside New York City, a triumph without precedent.

$ Wall Street prices break again in May and June after an early spring rally that has seen leading stocks regain between one-third and one-half the losses they sustained last year. As more investors realize the economic realities of the business depression, stock prices begin a long decline that will carry them to new depths (see 1932).

The Smoot-Hawley Tariff Bill signed into law by President Hoover June 17 raises tariffs to their highest levels in history—higher even than under the Payne-Aldrich Act of 1909. Congress has approved the measure in a special session called by Hoover despite a petition signed by 1,028 economists. Other countries raise tariffs in response to the Smoot-Hawley Tariff Act and a general world economic depression sets in as world trade declines, production drops, and unemployment increases.

Industrialist-philanthropist Henry Phipps dies at his Great Neck, L.I., estate September 22 at age 90; copper magnate and philanthropist Daniel Guggenheim at his Port Washington, L.I., home September 28 at age 74; financier-sportsman Harry Payne Whitney of pneumonia at his 871 Fifth Avenue home October 26 at age 58, survived by his wife, Gertrude (née Vanderbilt), and three children.

The 55-year-old Chase National Bank acquires the Equitable Trust Co. and the Interstate Trust Co. in May, becoming the world's largest banking institution. Rhode Island-born banker Winthrop W. Aldrich, 44, is elected president of Chase.

More than 1,300 banks close during the year. New York's Bank of the United States has grown since its founding in 1913 to become the nation's largest, with 62 branches (up from five in 1925) and 440,000 depositors, but it closes December 11 (some members of the New York Clearing House will be accused of anti-Semitism for having let the bank fail, but even those who make the charges will admit that the bank was guilty of dubious practices; founder's son Bernard Marcus and his partner Saul Singer will go to prison in March of next year after trial lawyer Max Steuer obtains their conviction).

More people ate at Automats in the Great Depression.
BERNICE ABBOTT, MUSEUM OF THE CITY OF NEW YORK

Wall Street's Dow Jones Industrial Average closes December 31 at 164.50, down from 248.48 at the end of 1929, as U.S. unemployment passes 4 million and national income falls from $81 billion to less than $68 billion.

Bonwit Teller moves into a new Fifth Avenue building at 56th Street acquired from Stewart & Co. (see 1898). Paul Bonwit will retire in 1934 and sell the company that will start a new 12-story addition in 1939 (see real estate [Trump Tower], 1983).

F. A. O. Schwarz moves uptown from 31st Street to open a large store in the new Squibb Building at the southeast corner of Fifth Avenue and 58th Street (see 1870; 1985).

The Park Association holds its annual dinner February 25 in the Grand Ballroom of the Commodore Hotel. Park Commissioner Robert Moses unveils a huge map of the city before a crowd of 500 civic leaders, with red lines marking limited-access arterial routes within the city, plus bridges and tunnels, some of them already built, and green ink marking the tens of thousands of acres he wants to acquire for new parks. Among the planned routes is a 36-mile road he calls the Marginal Boulevard (it will later be named the Circumferential Parkway and finally the Belt Parkway; see 1940).

The West Side Highway (Miller Elevated Highway) opens to speed vehicular traffic along West Street and Twelfth Avenue between Rector and 72nd streets. It will be extended farther north and heavily used but not well maintained (see collapse, 1973; Henry Hudson Parkway, 1937).

The New York State Bridge and Tunnel Commission is merged into the 9-year-old Port of New York Authority. Brooklyn-born lawyer Paul Windels, 44, has been counsel to the commission since 1918.

Mayor Walker vetoes a bill April 21 that would have raised taxi fares. The Board of Aldermen has voted April 8 to fix a minimum fare of 15¢ for the first quarter mile and 5¢ for each additional mile, increasing charges for waiting time from $1.50 per hour to $2.40. The taxi industry has had no system or standards, and the mayor calls the measure "an earnest effort to improve these conditions," but he finds it inadequate.

The Park Avenue Baptist Church moves to 490 Riverside Drive, between 120th and 122nd Streets, becomes the nondenominational Riverside Church (its congregation is still led by Harry Emerson Fosdick), and holds its first Sunday service October 5. Designed in pure Gothic style by the Boston architectural firm Allen & Collens with Henry C. Pelton to resemble France's Chartres Cathedral and built with $8 milllion from philanthropist John D. Rockefeller, Jr., the steel-framed structure rises 21 stories high, its 392-foot tower is topped by the world's largest carillon—74 bells, including a 20-ton tuned bass bell, but one critic calls it "a late example of bewildered eclecticism." A south wing designed in Modern Gothic style will be added in 1959.

The New York State Board of Higher Education authorizes formation of a new 4-year Brooklyn College that will be open to women as well as men (see 1926; 1937).

A television image produced at NBC's Fifth Avenue studio is transmitted January 16 to the RKO Proctor Theater on Third Avenue at 58th Street and projected on a six-foot screen (see 1927). NBC acquires control July 30 of General Electric's 2-year-old experimental station W2XBS and its transmitter in Van Cortlandt Park (see 1931).

Fortune magazine begins publication in February at New York. The new Henry Luce business monthly has 182 pages in its first issue and sells at newsstands for $1 ($10 per year by subscription) (see 1936; *Time*, 1923; *Fortune* "500," 1954).

Century Illustrated Monthly magazine (originally *Scribner's*) ceases after 60 years. Competition from *McClure's* and other mass-market periodicals has reduced its readership.

McCann-Erickson is created at New York by a merger of the 19-year-old H. K. McCann advertising agency with the 28-year-old Alfred W. Erickson agency (see Harper, 1948; Interpublic, 1961).

Nonfiction: *Park Avenue* by New York-born author Cornelius Vanderbilt, Jr. (IV), 32.

Poetry: *The Bridge* by Hart Crane, who began the 15-poem book in 1923 while living in Cleveland and moved the following year into a room at 110 Columbia Heights, where John Augustus Roebling and his son Washington lived during the construction of the Brooklyn Bridge. Helped with financing from banker Otto Kahn, Crane has taken the 47-year-old bridge as a symbol of man's creative power; his book's many poems explore the essence of the American destiny, but its mixed reception contributes to the poet's growing insecurity; "Spring Comes to Murray Hill" by Rye-born New York poet Ogden Nash, 28, appears in The *New Yorker* May 3. Nash will soon join the magazine's staff and be celebrated for such verses as "Candy is dandy/ But liquor is quicker" that will often be falsely attributed to Dorothy Parker; *Laments For the Living* by Dorothy Parker.

Painting: *Early Sunday Morning* by Edward Hopper; *Why Not Use the "L"* by Reginald Marsh; *Fishboat* by Arthur Dove; *Self-Portrait* by New York painter Lee Krasner (Lena Krassner), 22. The 1-year-old Museum of Modern Art has a retrospective exhibition of paintings by Max Weber, now 49, who has taught at the Art Students League.

Theater: *Children of Darkness* by New York playwright Edwin Justus Mayer, 33, 1/7 at the Biltmore Theater, with New York-born actress Mary Ellis, 32, 79 perfs.; *The Green Pastures* by Marc Connelly 2/21 at the Mansfield Theater is an adaptation of a 1928 collection of racially stereotyped tales by Tennessee-born author Roark Bradford, 34, depicting heaven, the angels, and the Lord as envisioned by a black country preacher for a Louisiana congregation, 640 perfs.; the Mark Hellinger Theater opens 4/22 at 237 West 51st Street (named for a *Daily News* columnist, author, and film producer, it is initially a movie house but will reopen as a legitimate theater 12/13/1934); *Once in a Lifetime* by George S. Kaufman and Moss Hart 9/24 at the Music Box Theater, with Kaufman and Spring Byington, 401 perfs.; *The Greeks Had a Word for It* by Zoë Akins 9/25 at the Sam H. Harris Theater, with Dorothy Hall, Verree Teasdale, and Muriel Kirkland as three ex-Follies girls on the make, 253 perfs.; *Grand Hotel* by W. A. Drake, who has adapted the Vicki Baum novel, 11/13 at the National Theater, with Henry Hull, New York-born actor Sam Jaffe, 37, Russian-born actress Eugenie Leontovich, 30, as the dancer Grusinskaya, 459 perfs.

Theater owner Abraham Lincoln Erlanger dies of cancer at New York March 7 at age 69; showman Edward F. Albee of heart failure at the Breakers Hotel in Palm Beach, Fla., March 11 at age 72; actor Charles S. Gilpin at Eldridge Park, N.J., near Trenton May 6 at age 50.

Radio: *The First Nighter Program* 12/4 on NBC (the show emanates not from Broadway but rather from NBC studios in Chicago's new Merchandise Mart).

Films: Clarence Brown's *Anna Christie* with Greta Garbo, Charles Bickford, Marie Dressler, Lee Phelps; George Cukor and Cyril Gardner's *The Royal Family of Broadway* with Frederic March, Ina Claire.

The Loews Valencia movie theater opens January 12 at 165-11 Jamaica Avenue in Queens with 3,500 seats. Designed by Austrian-born architect John Eberson, it has a 40-foot-wide façade inspired by Spanish and Mexican baroque designs, with rows of cherub heads, half shells, swirls, and other complex flourishes that are echoed throughout the theater's interior. Stars such as Ginger Rogers and Kate Smith will appear on the Valencia's stage to promote their pictures.

The Loews 175th Street movie theater opens in Washington Heights. Designed by Thomas W. Lamb, its double-height lobby with mezzanines evokes the style of a Moorish seraglio, while its domed auditorium is decorated in Byzantine and Romanesque styles.

The Loews Pitkin movie theater opens at 1501 Pitkin Avenue, northwest corner Saratoga Avenue, in Brooklyn's Brownsville section. Thomas W. Lamb has designed the brick and terra-cotta structure, whose auditorium has a ceiling-sky adorned with moving clouds and twinkling stars.

Loews Paradise opens on the Grand Concourse at 188th Street in the Bronx. Designed in Italian Baroque style by architect John Eberson, the $4 million movie theater has a 4,200-seat auditorium whose ceiling has twinkling stars and clouds that move across it and a lobby that looks like a Spanish patio.

The Brooklyn Paramount movie theater opens at the southeast corner of Flatbush and DeKalb avenues. Designed by Rapp & Rapp, it has atmospherics similar to those at the Loews Paradise.

The Loews Kings movie theater that opens on Brooklyn's Flatbush Avenue September 7 has 3,692 seats and a huge, ornate lobby, with a sweeping staircase, walnut columns, marble fountains, gilded ceilings, and two Art Deco chandeliers, where patrons play mah-jongg and canasta while waiting for the next vaudeville performance or movie showing to begin. Located between Tilden Avenue and Beverly Road, the Kings will be the flagship of the Loews chain for years, with Milton Berle, Cab Calloway, Eddie Cantor, Joan Crawford, Bette Davis, Jimmy Durante, Bill "Bojangles" Robinson, and other stars making personal appearances to promote their films, and will remain open until 1978.

Moviegoing increases as all studios rush to make "talkies" and a new Vitascope widens theater screens.

The Hebrew Actors Union forbids its members to appear in Yiddish talking pictures, fearing damage to the integrity of the Yiddish theater, but it soon removes the ban.

Film musicals: Harry Beaumont's *The Broadway Melody* with Bessie Love, Anita Page, Charles King, Jed Prouty, music and lyrics by Arthur Freed and Nacio Herb Brown, songs that include "You Were Meant for Me," "The Wedding of the Painted Doll;" Edward Sloman's *Puttin' On the Ritz* with Harry Richman as a vaudevillian with a drinking problem, Joan Bennett, James Gleason.

Broadway musicals: *Strike Up the Band* 1/14 at the Times Square Theater, with comedian Bobby Clark, Red Nichols's Band (members include Benny Goodman, Glenn Miller, Jimmy Dorsey, and Jack Teagarden), music by George Gershwin, lyrics by Ira Gershwin, book by George S. Kaufman, songs that include "I've Got a Crush on You," and the title song, 191 perfs.; *Nine-Fifteen Revue* 2/11 at the George M. Cohan Theater, with Ruth Etting, music by Buffalo-born cantor's son Harold Arlen (originally Hyman Arluck), 24, lyrics by Ted Koehler, songs that include "Get Happy," 7 perfs.; *Lew Leslie's International Revue* 2/15 at the Majestic Theater, with Gertrude Lawrence, Harry Richman, English-born dancer Anton Dolin, 25, music by Jimmy McHugh, lyrics by Dorothy Fields, songs that include "Exactly Like You," "On the Sunny Side of the Street," 96 perfs.; *Simple Simon* 2/18 at the Ziegfeld Theater, with Ed Wynn, Ruth Etting, music by Richard Rodgers, lyrics by Lorenz Hart, songs that include "Ten Cents a Dance," "I Still Believe in You," 135 perfs.; *Fine and Dandy* 9/23 at the Erlanger Theater, with Joe Cook, dancer Eleanor Powell, Dave Chasen, music by Kay Swift, lyrics by Paul James (Swift's husband, James Warburg), book by Donald Ogden Stewart, songs that include "Can This Be Love?" 255 perfs.; *Girl Crazy* 10/14 at the Alvin Theater, with William Kent, Astoria-born vocalist Ethel Merman (originally Zimmerman), 21, who has had no formal musical training but knocks 'em dead with her rendition of "I Got Rhythm," music by George Gershwin, lyrics by Walter Donaldson and Ira Gershwin, a pit orchestra whose members include Benny Goodman and Jack Teagarden, songs that include also "Embraceable You," "Little White Lies," "But Not for Me," "Bidin' My Time," 272 perfs.; *Three's a Crowd* 10/15 at the Selwyn Theater, with Libby Holman, Fred Allen, Clifton Webb, songs that include "Body and Soul" by Johnny Green, lyrics by Robert Sour, 25, and Edward Heyman, 23, plus "Something to Remember You By" and "The Moment I Saw You" by Arthur Schwartz, lyrics by Howard Dietz, 272 perfs.; *The Garrick Gaieties* 10/16 at the Guild Theater, with Sterling Holloway, Waterbury, Conn.-born ingénue Rosalind Russell, 19, Imogene Coca, songs that include "I'm Only Human After All" by Russian-born composer Vernon Duke (Vladimir Dukelsky), 27, lyrics by E. Y. Harburg and Ira Gershwin, "Out of Breath and Scared to Death of You" by Johnny Mercer and Everett Miller, 158 perfs.; *Lew Leslie's Blackbirds of 1930* 10/22 at the Royale Theater, with Chester, Pa.-born actress-jazz singer Ethel Waters (*née* Howard), 34, Cecil Mack's Choir, songs that include "Memories of You" by Eubie Blake, lyrics by Andy Razaf, 57 perfs.; *Sweet and Low* 11/17 at the 46th Street Theater, with George Jessel, Fanny Brice, songs that include "Outside Looking In" by Harry Archer and Edward Ellison, "Cheerful Little Earful" by Harry Warren, Ira Gershwin, and Billy Rose, 184 perfs.; *Smiles* 11/18 at the Ziegfeld Theater, with Marilyn Miller, English-born comedian Bob Hope (originally Leslie Townes), 27, New Rochelle-born comedian Eddie Foy, Jr., 25, Fred and Adele Astaire, songs that include "Time on My Hands" by Vincent Youmans, lyrics by Harold Adamson and Polish-born writer Mack Gordon, 26, "You're Driving Me Crazy" by Walter Donaldson, 63 perfs.; *The New Yorkers* 12/8 at B. S. Moss's Broadway Theater, with Hope Williams, dancer Ann Pennington, comedian Jimmy Durante, dancer Lew Clayton, singer Eddie Jackson, book from a story by songwriter E. Ray Goetz and *New Yorker* magazine cartoonist Peter Arno, music and lyrics by Cole Porter, songs that include "Take Me Back to Manhattan," "I Happen to Like New York," "Love for Sale," 168 perfs.

Popular songs: "I Happen to Like New York" by Cole Porter ("I happen to like this town. I like the city air. I like to drink of it. The more I know New York, the more I think of it. I like the sight and sound and even the stink of it"); "Wall Street Wail" by Duke Ellington; "Down Where the East River Flows" by Vincent Youmans, lyrics by Harold Adamson and Clifford Grey.

German prizefighter Max Schmeling, 24, is fouled by world heavyweight champion Jack Sharkey, now 27, in the fourth round of a title bout at New York June 12. Schmeling wins the title but will lose it back to Sharkey in 1932.

John H. Doeg, 21, wins in men's singles at Forest Hills, Betty Nuthall, 19, (Br) in women's singles (the first non-American U.S. champion).

The Harlem social club Gay Northeasterners founded by Agatha Scott Davis will change its name to The Northeasterners in 1979. Its founder is the wife of Brig. Gen. Benjamin O. Davis, Jr.; it will organize community-help projects, contribute to the NAACP, Urban League, United Negro College Fund, American Cancer Society, Tuskegee Institute Infantile Paralysis Library Project, and endow annual scholarships to Howard University.

Chicago-born fashion designer Mainbocher (Main [Rousseau] Bocher), 37, quits his editorial job at *Harper's Bazaar* magazine and opens a New York house of haute couture.

Woolworth heiress Barbara Hutton turns 18 in November and makes her debut December 21 at a $60,000 ball in the Ritz-Carlton Hotel, whose first floor has been transformed with white birches, eucalyptus trees from California, mountain heather, scarlet poinsettias, and 10,000 American Beauty roses (workmen have labored for 2 days and nights to create the opulent bower). The 1,000 guests (they include Brooke Astor, Doris Duke, Virginia Thaw, and Louise Van Alen) are greeted by Maurice Chevalier, dressed as Santa Claus, and helpers who hand out party favors—pocket-size gold jewelry cases containing unmounted diamonds, emeralds, rubies, and sapphires—while unemployed men sell apples on the sidewalks outside. Hutton's aunt Marjorie Merriweather Post (Mrs. E. F. Hutton) has arranged the affair, which goes on in the face of worsening economic problems. Despite Prohibition, 200 waiters serve 2,000 bottles of Champagne plus 1,000 seven-course midnight suppers and 1,000 breakfasts (*see* 1924; 1931).

Judge Crater disappears August 6. Appointed to administer the affairs of the bankrupt Libby Hotel on the Lower East Side, which was appraised at $1.2 million, Tammany lawyer Joseph Force Crater, then 40, arranged for its sale in June of last year for only $75,000 to American Bond and Mortgage Co., whose officers sold it to the city in August for $2.85 million to be used as the site of a proposed Chrystie-Forsyth housing project. Gov. Roosevelt appointed Crater in April to fill an unexpired term on the New York Supreme Court; he has interrupted his summer vacation to return to the city, withdrawn all the cash in his bank account (just over $5,000), sold $16,000 worth of stock, dined with friends, stepped into a taxi outside the restaurant, and will never be heard of again (the case will be officially closed in July 1937). Crater has lived with his wife, Stella, in an apartment at 40 Fifth Avenue (he also has kept a mistress in a midtown hotel), and he has left Stella a note saying that American Bond and Mortgage Co. owed him "a very large sum" that she will never be able to collect.

 The 70-story Bank of the Manhattan Co. Building at 40 Wall Street is completed between William and Nassau streets to designs by H. Craig Severance and Yasuo Matsui with a pyramidal crown that gives it a height of 927 feet, making it briefly the world's tallest building (*see* plane crash, 1946).

The 34-story 120 Wall Street office building is completed at the northwest corner of Wall and South Street. The office of Ely Jacques Kahn has designed the structure, which extends to Pine Street.

The 37-story 19 Rector Building is completed at the southeast corner of Rector and Washington streets to designs by L. A. Goldstone.

The 46-story Navarre Building is completed in the garment district at 512 Seventh Avenue, southwest corner 38th Street, to designs by Sugarman & Berger.

The 77-story Chrysler Building opens May 27 at the northeast corner of Lexington Avenue and 42nd Street and will be the tallest building in the world until the spring of next year. Designed by William Van Alen, now 46, for automaker Walter P. Chrysler, the 1,048-foot Art Deco tower of steel and concrete is the first structure to rise higher than the Eiffel Tower erected at Paris in 1889. It has eight stainless steel American eagles that extend like gargoyles from its 61st-floor level, and the 185-foot spire that caps it is of highly polished nickel-chrome stainless steel produced by Nirosta Metalldach of Netphen, Germany, and brought by ship to America; the nickel-chrome steel is also used for lobby decorations designed by Oscar Bach. Former state senator William J. Reynolds leased the site a few years ago from Cooper Union and hired Van Alen, who had been a partner of H. Craig Severance and designed the 1925 Childs restaurant at 604 Fifth Avenue; determined to make his skyscraper taller than the tower going up at 40 Wall Street, Van Alen secretly assembled a 185-foot spire in five pieces inside the building's crown and had it hoisted into place in about 90 minutes 6 months ago. The soaring structure contains 20,961 tons of structural steel, 391,881 rivets, more than 3.8 million bricks, 10,000 light bulbs, and 3,862 windows; Chrysler refuses to pay

The Chrysler Building was the world's tallest skyscraper only briefly. LIBRARY OF CONGRESS

Van Alen his fee, suggesting that he was guilty of some improper arrangement with the contractor, but although Van Alen puts a mechanic's lien on the building he will drop the matter.

The 38-story New York Daily News Building opens June 25 at 220 East 42nd Street, southwest corner Second Avenue, with 718,000 square feet of floor space. Rising 467 feet high and clad in white brick, the $10 million skyscraper has been designed by John Mead Howells, Raymond M. Hood, and J. André Fouilhoux. *News* owner Capt. J. M. Patterson has ordered that the words, "God must have loved the common people, he made so many of them—Lincoln," be inscribed on the building that will house the tabloid paper's offices until 1995, but he has not quoted the 16th president exactly.

The 24-story Columbia Broadcasting Building is completed for the 2-year-old CBS radio network at 485 Madison Avenue, southeast corner 52nd Street, to designs by J. E. R. Carpenter (*see* 1965).

The 37-story Squibb Building is completed at 745 Fifth Avenue, southeast corner 58th Street. Designed by Ely Jacques Kahn for developer Abe N.

Adelson (who will lose the property in a 1933 foreclosure sale), it towers over the Grand Army Plaza, with E. R. Squibb offices on the top 12 floors; its lower façade is marble, the rest of the façade is of white brick, and the lobby has a ceiling mural by Arthur Covey depicting stylized airplanes flying over a map of Manhattan.

A new Temple Emanu-El is dedicated at the northeast corner of Fifth Avenue and 65th Street (see 1868). The congregation sold its building in 1927 for $7 million to developer Joseph Durst and merged last year with another Reform congregation (Beth-El). Designed in Art Deco style by Robert D. Kohn, Charles Butler, Clarence Stein, and the late Bertram G. Goodhue, the limestone structure has a sanctuary that seats 2,500—more, even, than St. Patrick's Cathedral—and replaces the twin houses of John Jacob Astor and his mother, Mrs. William B. Astor.

The Union League Club lays the cornerstone June 4 of a new building at the southwest corner of Park Avenue and 37th Street (see 1881).

The 24-story American Woman's Club Association Clubhouse is completed at 353 West 57th Street, near the northeast corner of Ninth Avenue. Designed by Benjamin Wistar Morris, the boxy, unadorned structure has 1,200 rooms (sleeping rooms are decorated in 128 different color combinations), a swimming pool, gymnasium, meeting rooms, music rooms, a restaurant, and wide terraces on the upper setbacks for use by members of the club, headed by philanthropist Anne Morgan (see hotel, 1941).

The New York Athletic Club moves from its former location at the southeast corner of Central Park South and Sixth Avenue into a new building on Central Park South at Seventh Avenue. Designed by York & Sawyer, the 21-story clubhouse extends south to 58th Street, replacing the Madrid and Lisbon apartment houses put up by José de Navarro in the 1880s, and it has 300 bedrooms in addition to its baths, billiard room, bowling alleys, boxing ring, card room, chess room, squash courts, indoor and outdoor handball courts, 42' × 62' rooftop solarium, running track, 30' × 75' fourth-floor swimming pool, 11th floor dining room with open-air loggia, and grillroom (the taproom will come later).

The West Side YMCA moves in March from 318 West 57th Street into a new building at 5 West 63rd Street modeled on the Davanzati Palace in Florence with exterior walls comprised of special bricks from South Carolina. Designed by Dwight J. Baum, 43, and extending north to 64th Street, the 14-story neo-Romanesque structure contains a Log Cabin Room with rustic furniture, a Pirates Den with curved walls, ship's wheel, and a parrot, a Farm House Attic, a Totem Room, a "little theater," a 10-table billiard room, six handball courts, three gymnasiums, two swimming pools (one for boys, one for men), 8,000 lockers, a cafeteria, and 600 sleeping rooms that rent for as little as $5.50 per month. Within 10 years the Y will have 2,000 young men enrolled in trade courses.

The 4-year-old Downtown Athletic Club moves October 1 into a 38-story building at 19 West Street, just south of Morris Street. Designed by Starrett & Van Vleck, the 531-foot-high building has Art Deco interiors, 143 bedrooms (from the 20th to 35th floors), billiard and card rooms on the third floor, handball and squash courts on the fourth and sixth floors, bowling alleys on the fifth, a miniature golf course that occupies the entire seventh floor, a gym on the eighth, and a swimming pool on the 12th, but while the club's membership has grown to 3,826 it will default on its real estate taxes beginning in 1932, have only 3,500 members by 1936, file for bankruptcy that year, and not recover possession of its building until 1963 (see sports, 1935).

Last year's Multiple Dwellings Law comes under further attack for alleged injustices to rooming-house keepers by requiring that rooms have open air and prohibiting further erection of so-called "cold-water" tenements. There are proposals to allow construction of garages in apartment-house basements, to prohibit occupancy of basements in old-law tenements, and so forth. The state legislature at Albany amends the law, Stanley Isaacs calls the amendments "unprogressive," but Gov. Roosevelt approves them April 28, pleasing real estate interests. City inspectors fan out across the city in August, find thousands of violations in Queens alone, and criticize judges for being too lenient toward violators.

The London Terrace apartment complex opens in Chelsea between Ninth and Tenth avenues from 23rd Street north to 24th. Designed by Farrar & Watmaugh for developer Henry Mandel and described as the greatest single residential development the world has ever seen, the 1,670-unit facility comprises 14 buildings, ranging in height from 16 to 20 stories, and replaces the brownstone town houses with deep front lawns built in 23rd Street in 1880 and the Chelsea Cottages put up by Clement Clark Moore in 1845 in 24th Street (Mandel has acquired a long leasehold from Moore's heirs; a Mrs. Tilly Hart of 429 West 23rd Street refused for weeks to leave her house and defied efforts by the police, wrecking crews, and the Manhattan Bureau of Buildings to dislodge her). The complex boasts a blocklong private garden, a rooftop deck designed to look like part of an ocean liner, a solarium, swimming pool, and doormen dressed as London "Bobbies." A three-and-a-half-room apartment rents for $100 to $110 per month, and leases are staggered, a departure from the long-prevailing norm of having all leases run from May to May or October to October, sparking large-scale migrations each spring and autumn as upwardly (and downwardly) mobile New Yorkers move bag and baggage from one apartment to another. The steady pace of new construction has maintained a downward pressure on rental prices.

The twin Beaux-Arts Apartments open early in the year at 307 and 310 East 44th Street, between First and Second avenues, where 310 adjoins the 2-year-old Beaux-Arts Institute of Design at 304. Former Institute president Kenneth Murchison has designed the 16-story structures with Raymond M. Hood of Hood, Godley & Fouilhoux, they have cost $5.2 milion, upper floors include some duplexes with double-height rooms and cork floors, but most of the 648 units are 286-square-foot studios with tiny kitchens (the ultramodern Cafe Bonaparte serves as a central restaurant for the buildings) and beds that fold into the walls. Rents include twice-a-day maid service, and there is dining-room and room service until 11:30 o'clock each night.

The 322 East 57th Street luxury apartment house completed between First and Second avenues to designs of Harry M. Clawson of Caughey & Evans has duplex living rooms with 18-foot ceilings.

The luxury apartment house 740 Park Avenue is completed at the northwest corner of 71st Street with an immense four-floor apartment for John D. Rockefeller, Jr. with gymasium, billiard room, and accommodations for five live-in servants. Designed by Rosario Candela with Arthur Loomis Harmon, the limestone-sheathed 17-story structure replaces three buildings that had faced on the avenue and a nurses' residence in 71st Street. Most of its 31 apartments are duplexes with living rooms nearly 40 feet long, and its tenants will include some of the richest people in the world.

The twin-towered San Remo apartment house is completed at 145-146 Central Park West, between 74th and 75th streets with 27-story square towers rising above a 17-story base. Designed by Emery Roth, built by contractor Saul Ravitch, and financed by the Bank of the United States, it has 122 apartments and replaces the 1891 apartment-hotel of the same name plus a private house, whose owner has

been compensated with a 10-year lease on a 14-room duplex in the Beresford. The south tower has five 13-room duplexes with 32- to 35-foot living rooms (rental: $1,667 per month; a nine-room apartment with two baths rents for $200 per month).

The 12-story 960 Fifth Avenue apartment house is completed at the northeast corner of 77th Street, replacing the 130-room mansion built for the Montana copper baron Sen. William A. Clark in 1911. Rosario Candela and Warren & Wetmore have designed the structure for Anthony Campagna; its duplex apartments range in size from 8,000 to 10,000 square feet, and the 17 rooms of its largest apartment include a ballroom with a 16-foot ceiling and floor-to-ceiling windows. An in-house chef prepares meals to be served in the private Georgian Suite behind the lobby and will also prepare picnic baskets and casseroles to tide residents over weekends when he does not work. Maid service is available, as is laundry service (shirts are washed, ironed, and returned within 2 hours). A separate 12-story section of the building, containing rental units, faces on 77th Street.

The 15-story-plus-penthouse 1040 Fifth Avenue apartment house is completed in October at the northeast corner of 85th Street to designs by Rosario Candela.

The 13-story 2 East 88th Street apartment house is completed at the southeast corner of Fifth Avenue to designs by Pennington & Lewis. It replaces the mansion that was completed in 1902 at 1069 Fifth Avenue.

The 15-story-plus-penthouse 1215 Fifth Avenue apartment house is completed at the northeast corner of 102nd Street. It has been designed by Schultze & Weaver with Thompson Starrett Co. for Hearst publisher Arthur Brisbane, whose huge apartment on the 14th, 15th, and penthouse floors contains a two-story living room 60 feet long with fireplaces at each end and a two-story dining hall 33 feet long, making it larger even than his previous apartment at the Ritz Tower.

Lefrak City raises the first of 20 18-story apartment towers that the Lefrak Corp. will erect on 32 acres of the old Astor estate in the Corona, Queens, section. Russian-born developer-builder Harry Lefrak, now 45, came to New York from Palestine at the turn of the century with $4, went to work shoveling snow and running errands, began building one-family houses in Brooklyn, bought a 2,000-acre Brooklyn farm, and built entire blocks of homes before turning to apartment-house construction for middle-income families (*see* 1963).

Model co-operative apartments open in Grand Street on Manhattan's Lower East Side in November. Built by the State Board of Housing, the 231 units replace the old Hoe factory in an area bounded by Grand, Broome, Sheriff, and Columbia streets; for many of the tenants they are the first homes with steam heat, ample hot water, a quiet courtyard, and a rooftop play area.

The 41-story New Yorker Hotel opens at 481 Eighth Avenue, between 34th and 35th streets, with 23 elevators, a private subterranean power plant that is the largest in America, a private tunnel to Pennsylvania Station, a 42-chair barbershop with 20 manicurists, and 41st-floor switchboards manned by 92 "telephone girls." Designed by Sugarman & Berger, it has 2,503 guest rooms, including 100 one- and two-bedroom suites (*see* religion, 1976).

The Belmont Hotel that opened in 1906 closes in early May.

The 23-story Hotel Dixie (later the Hotel Carter) opens at 251 West 42nd Street, just west of Broadway. Designed by Emery Roth, it has 650 guest rooms.

The 27-story Hotel Wellington is completed at 871 Seventh Avenue, northeast corner 55th Street, with 750 rooms.

The 121-room Salisbury Hotel is completed at 123-141 West 57th Street, between Sixth and Seventh avenues, and houses the Calvary Baptist Church that will take over the hotel's lease in February 1932.

The 24-story Manhattan Towers Hotel opens in April on a site that wraps itself around a low building at the northeast corner of Broadway and 76th Street. Tillion and Tillion, the architects, have tried to preserve the Gothic style of the Manhattan Congregational Church that formerly occupied the site and takes the first three floors of the new building. The structure includes also an auditorium (later the Promenade Theater), gymnasium, banquet hall, two penthouses, and 626 rooms.

The 42-story Barbizon-Plaza Hotel (later Trump Parc) opens May 12 at the corner of Sixth Avenue and 58th Street. Designed by Murgatroyd and Ogden, the $10 million hotel has 1,400 rooms, three separate halls for concerts, musicals, recitals, and amateur dance and dramatic offerings, a glass-enclosed roof for indoor and outdoor athletics, art galleries, club rooms, a fully equipped library, numerous duplex studios for artists and sculptors, and immediate financial troubles (*see* 1933).

The St. Moritz Hotel opens October 1 at Sixth Avenue and Central Park South (59th Street) on a site formerly occupied by the New York Athletic Club that has moved into a new, larger building one block to the west. Designed by Emery Roth for developers Harris H. and Percy Uris of the Harper organization with a sky-room restaurant, the 35-story, 1,000-room hotel has financial problems from the start. The Bowery Savings Bank will foreclose on its mortgage in mid-March 1932 and the hotel will be acquired soon afterward by private buyers for $4 million (*see* 2002).

The 44-story Hotel Pierre opens in October on Fifth Avenue at 61st Street, replacing the mansion of Commodore Elbridge T. Gerry. Designed by Schultze & Weaver for Corsican-born restaurateur Charles Pierre (originally C. P. Casalesco), who has had a restaurant at 230 Park Avenue, the tower boasts a splendid ballroom and banquet halls, contains more than 700 rooms, and will become recognized as the city's most luxurious hotel (in later years most of its rooms and suites will be leased on a year-round basis).

The 40-story Carlyle Hotel opens in the fall at the northeast corner of Madison Avenue and 76th Street. Developer Moses Ginsberg has engaged architect Sylvan Bien of Bien & Prince to design the Art Deco structure that combines an apartment hotel to the south and a 17-story apartment house to the north, with 40 terraces, a roof garden, a gymnasium, a playroom, and its own kindergarten. Apartments in the hotel range in size from one room to nine and rent for as much as $161.50 per month. The hotel and apartment house will fetch $7 million combined at a foreclosure sale in 1932.

A 43-room Manhattan mansion is completed at 60 East 93rd Street for silver-mine heiress Virginia Graham Fair Vanderbilt, divorced wife of railroad heir William K. Vanderbilt, Jr. Architect John Russell Pope has designed the house; it will later house a Romanian diplomatic mission before being used by the Lycée Français de New York.

The last Manhattan farm ceases operations at the corner of Broadway and 213th Street but there are still farms in the Bronx, Brooklyn, and Queens.

The International Apple Shippers Association offers its fruit on credit to jobless men who will peddle apples on street corners and help the association dispose of its vast surplus. By November some 6,000 men are selling apples on New York sidewalks, but by the spring of next year the apple sellers will be called a nuisance and City Hall will order them off the streets.

New York has 82 breadlines by year's end.

Stella D'Oro Biscuit Co. has its beginnings in a Bronx bakery opened on Bailey Avenue by Italian-born baker Joseph Kresevich and his wife, Angela, who produce anisette toast biscuits, egg biscuits, and breadsticks. They adopt the Stella D'Oro name within a year and will move in 1947 to Kingsbridge, where they will open a factory in 237th Street as their products gain widespread popularity.

The first true supermarket opens in August at 171-06 Jamaica Avenue, Queens, where former Kroger Grocery and Baking Co. store manager Michael S. Cullen, 46, has acquired an abandoned garage and started the King Kullen Market. Cullen has written Kroger president William H. Albers suggesting a plan for "monstrous stores . . . away from the high-rent districts" that will attract customers with aggressive price cutting. "I could afford to sell a can of milk at cost if I could sell a can of peas and make two cents," Cullen has written, but another Kroger executive has intercepted the letter. Cullen's advertising says, "King Kullen, the world's greatest price wrecker—how does he do it?" and he meets with instant success.

Jack & Charlie's "21" Club opens in January at 21 West 52nd Street. Restaurateur John Karl "Jack" Kriendler, 31, and his accountant cousin Charles "Charlie" Berns, 28, have been operating speakeasy saloons since 1922, beginning with the Red Head in Greenwich Village, lightly disguised as a tearoom, and most recently the Puncheon Club (or Puncheon Grotto). They have in effect been subsidized by the Rockefellers, who have purchased their lease at 42 West 49th Street in order to clear the block for construction of Rockefeller Center, and they have been joined by Kriendler's brother H. Peter "Pete," 24, who last year sold the Curb Exchange seat Jack had bought him for 10 times the $20,000 Jack paid. The Kriendlers and Berns store their illicit liquor behind secret walls and devise an arrangement that permits the bartender to push a button at the first sign of a raid by federal Prohibition enforcement agents, tilting the shelves of the bar to send all bottles down a chute to smash in the cellar and thus destroy evidence needed for a conviction. They will prosper at the new location and acquire the building at 19 West 52nd Street in 1935 as they attract patrons with crème andalouse, green turtle, and petite marmite soups; duckling à l'orange; prime ribs; and chicken hash, all served in a club-like atmosphere.

Prohibition agents raid the Ritz-Carlton Hotel and Central Park Casino June 24, making 27 arrests, eight at the Ritz.

New York's population reaches 6,930,446, up from 5,620,048 in 1920, but Manhattan's population has dropped to 1,867,312, down from 2,284,103 in 1920. The population of Manhattan's Lower East Side has fallen to 250,000, down from some 530,000 in 1910, thanks to subsidized garden apartments near Brooklyn, Bronx, and Queens transit lines. Emigration for the first time in history exceeds immigration; arrivals at Ellis Island dwindle to a small fraction of their peak numbers (see 1932).

1931 Gov. Roosevelt releases a report by the City Affairs Committee March 18 accusing Mayor Walker of inefficiency, neglect, and incompetency. The mayor has gone to Palm Springs, Calif., for his health, and makes no comment. Tammany Hall sweeps the November elections, but a legislative committee investigating possible diversion of federal unemployment relief funds to political campaign use reveals November 30 that former Tammany leader George W. Olvany had an income of more than $2 million in the 4½ years that the Madison Avenue lawyer headed the Wigwam. Republicans in the state legislature at Albany have put through a joint resolution appointing Sen. Samuel H. Hofstadter, 37, to chair the investigating committee, whose counsel is former court of appeals judge Samuel Seabury, an anti-Tammany Democrat appointed by Gov. Roosevelt in the fall of last year to sit on a committee looking into charges that the Tammany-sponsored district attorney for New York County Thomas C. T. Crain had been derelict in his duties (the committee has censured the administration of the D.A.'s office but has not recommended Crain's dismissal; see 1932).

The "Swope Plan" for economic recovery outlined by General Electric president Gerard Swope, 58, says, in effect, leave the problem to business and let trade associations develop national economic plans to revive the economy. New York City spends nearly $1.5 billion to fund its operations and relieve economic distress—upwards of $32.5 million more than it takes in.

Landlords evict some 100,000 New Yorkers from their homes because they cannot pay the rent (22 men are arrested for vagrancy in July following complaints by Fifth Avenue residents that "hobos" are sleeping in Central Park, but a sympathetic judge suspends their sentences, gives each one $2, and sends them all back to the park, which by autumn has 17 chimneyed shacks, all furnished with chairs and beds). Men and women in Harlem and elsewhere wait for garbage trucks to arrive at city dumps and scavenge for food; they compete with dogs and cats for the contents of garbage cans. Brooklyn clothing factories pay 15-year-old girls 6¢ per hour—$2.78 per week—for sponging pants. President Hoover was U.S. Food Administrator from 1917 to 1918 but opposes suggestions that the federal government distribute food to the needy, insisting that charitable organizations will provide what is needed, but while Red Cross dietitians offer advice on how to eat economically, the Red Cross refuses to use its funds to help the unemployed.

Brown Brothers Harriman & Co. is created January 1 by a merger of the venerable New York banking house Brown Brothers & Co., opened in 1825, with Harriman Brothers and W. A. Harriman (see banker's acceptance, 1927). Son of the late railroad securities speculator Edward H. Harriman, New York-born banker W. (William) Averell Harriman, 40, founded his own firm in 1919 and has more recently organized Harriman Brothers with his brother Edward Roland Noel Harriman, now 35. (Averell will head the Union Pacific Railroad beginning next year.) Brown Brothers' underwriting department sustained such huge losses in the 1929 market crash that the firm was obliged to seek additional capital. Rivaled in size and influence only by J. P. Morgan & Co., Kuhn, Loeb & Co., and Lee Higginson of Boston, the newly organized firm has its main office at 59 Wall Street (see 1843).

Carl M. Loeb Co. opens January 1 with 12 employees in a 2,500-square foot office at 50 Broad Street. Now 55, Loeb is the former head of American Metal Co.; his son John Langeloth Loeb, 28 (Harvard '24), has worked for Wertheim & Co., purchased a seat on the New York Stock Exchange late last year for $250,000, and has brought some former Wertheim people with him (see Loeb, Rhoades, 1938).

Reynolds Securities (later Dean Witter Reynolds) is founded at New York by tobacco heir Richard S. Reynolds, 22, with John D. Baker and Thomas F. Staley, 27.

Value Line Investment Survey has its beginnings in the *Value Line Ratings* put out by New York-born securities analyst Arnold Bernhard, 29, a onetime *New York Post* theater critic who took a job with speculator Jesse Livermore in the fall of 1928, switched to Moody's Investors Services, and became convinced after the market plunge of 1929 that there must be a way to establish a stock's intrinsic value without emotionalism. Bernhard's first issue of *Value Line Ratings of Normal Value* goes out to subscribers who pay $200 per year; it offers buy-sell advice on more than 120 companies based on the principle that a stock is undervalued if its current price-to-earnings and price-to-book ratios are markedly below their 20-year averages and overvalued if the opposite is true. Bernhard determines the normal value of a stock by visually fitting its annual earnings curve to its price history. Multiplying a projection of the company's earnings by its appropriate multiple produces a "normal value;" stocks below normal value are candidates for purchase, those above, for sale. Having thus come up with an individual formula and price goal for each company's stock, he has drawn graphs by hand, written editorials, and used a mimeograph machine at his Pelham home to turn out copies of his ratings, initially selling them door to door (see 1937).

First National Bank chairman George F. Baker dies at New York May 2 at age 91, leaving $60 million to his son George F., Jr. Philanthropist Baker has endowed Harvard's Graduate School of Business Administration and his name survives in Columbia University's Baker Field; former J. P. Morgan & Co. partner Dwight W. Morrow dies at Englewood, N.J., October 5 at age 58.

Green Point Savings Bank acquires the Home Savings Bank as it grows to become one of the city's largest thrift institutions (see 1907).

Fiduciary Trust Co. is founded by New York lawyers Grenville Clark and Elihu Root. Concerned about recent excesses in banking practices, Clark and Root have determined to make no commercial loans, underwrite no securities, and advertise their money-management firm only on a limited basis.

Wall Street's Dow Jones Industrial Average drops to 52.46 December 10, rebounds to 79.63 the next day, but closes December 31 at 77.90, down a record 52 percent from 164.50 at the end of 1930.

Bloomingdale's completes a $3 million building on Lexington Avenue between 59th and 60th streets, occupying the full block between Lexington and Third avenues (see 1886; Federated, 1929).

Lord & Taylor makes its fashion and interior decoration director Dorothy Shaver vice president in charge of advertising and publicity. Now 34, Shaver will bring to prominence such fashion designers as Ann Fogarty, Lilly Daché, Claire McCardell, Rose Marie Reid, and Pauline Trigère (see 1945).

S. Klein on Union Square sells 3 million dresses, 1.5 million coats, and 750,000 women's tailored suits, taking in about $25 million (Bloomingdale's, including all departments, grosses only $22 million) despite the Depression (*see* 1912). Never advertising except to announce that the store will be closed for a legal or Jewish holiday, Klein does not deliver, sells only for cash, but attracts customers from Park Avenue and the suburbs as well as from poor neighborhoods. Women cram their purses down the fronts of their blouses to free both hands to pluck dresses off the racks, there are practically no dressing rooms, the floors are bare, and girls at 12 IBM duplicating keypunch machines punch holes in tabulating cards according to data on merchandise tags. If a shoplifter is apprehended she is immediately placed on display in one of the store's glass-enclosed "crying" rooms upstairs, but an honest customer can easily return merchandise and get her money back, even a moth-eaten garment purchased 8 months earlier. The customer is always right (*see* 1975).

Merchant-philanthropist Nathan Straus of R. H. Macy Co. dies at New York January 11 at age 82; Patrick F. Murphy of the Fifth Avenue haberdashery and luggage shop Mark Cross & Co. dies of pneumonia at New York November 23 at age 73 and is given an enormous funeral at St. Patrick's Cathedral. Business at Mark Cross has dwindled since the 1929 Wall Street crash, with reduced demand for such items as steamer trunks.

Incandescent-bulb inventor Thomas Alva Edison dies at West Orange, N.J., October 18 at age 84, having pioneered in the creation of professional research laboratories, created industries that now employ millions of people, and received a record 1,093 U.S. patents (he leaves an estate valued at $12 million).

Floyd Bennett Field is dedicated May 23 on the coast at Jamaica Bay with Mayor Walker presiding over ceremonies attended by a crowd of 15,000 (*see* Bennett, 1928). The city has pumped 6 million cubic yards of sand from the bay to connect 33 small islands, reclaim marshland, and create a 1,500-acre facility that will be enlarged in 1936, but New York lags far behind the rest of the country in establishing a passenger air terminal, New Jersey led the way (*see* Newark Airport, 1929), and attempts to make Floyd Bennett Field the designated eastern mail terminus for New York will fail (*see* La Guardia, 1939).

Texas-born pilot Wiley Post, 32, and Harold Gatty land at Roosevelt Field on Long Island July 1 after completing a 15,474-mile round-the-world flight in a record 8 days, 15 hours, 51 minutes. They receive a New York ticker-tape parade the next day.

The George Washington Bridge opens to traffic October 24, spanning the Hudson River between Manhattan and New Jersey. Designed by Swiss-born engineer Othmar H. Ammann, 52, with an assist from David B. Steinman, built by the Port of New York Authority, and completed below budget 8 months ahead of schedule, the 3,502-foot (1,067-meter) structure is the world's largest suspension bridge thus far; its 90,000 tons of deadweight are suspended from four cables, each three feet in diameter, made by John A. Roebling's Sons of Trenton, N.J. (*see* Brooklyn Bridge, 1883). Each cable contains 26,474 steel wires, and although each wire is drawn to just 0.196 inches in diameter it is strong enough to hold at least 240,000 pounds per square inch, more than one and a half times the strength of the cable wires supporting the Brooklyn Bridge. The toll on the new bridge is 50¢ each way.

The Bayonne (Kill Van Kull) Bridge opens to vehicular traffic November 15, providing another link between Staten Island and New Jersey (*see* Goethal, Outerbridge Crossing bridges, 1928); designed by Othmar H. Ammann with architect Cass Gilbert and built by the Port of New York Authority at a cost of more than $13 million, the 1,675-foot span is the world's longest steel arch bridge thus far. Financial constraints prevent implementation of a plan to sheath the steel arch abutments in granite (*see* Arthur Kill Bridge, 1959).

Kings County Hospital opens in Brooklyn (*see* 1831). Built with city funds, the municipal hospital will grow to cover an area bounded by New York Avenue, Winthrop Street, Albany Avenue, and Clarkson Avenue.

Hunter College expands to a 45-acre Bronx campus built on what formerly was the Jerome Avenue reservoir (*see* Brooklyn, 1926). Enrollment has topped 23,000, up from fewer than 4,000 in 1926; Hunter has opened extension centers in Queens as well as the new Bronx satellite campus; and it is now the world's largest institution of learning exclusively for women (*see* Lehman College, 1968).

The *New York World-Telegram* begins publication February 27. Roy Howard of the 25-paper Scripps-Howard chain has paid $5 million—$8.69 per reader—to obtain the Associated Press franchise and goodwill of Pulitzer's *New York World* and *Evening World* and merged them with the 64-year-old *Telegram* to create the new evening paper. The late Joseph Pulitzer's will stipulated that the *World* not be sold, but his sons Herbert, Ralph, and Joseph, Jr. have sustained losses averaging $811,000 per year since 1926, lost nearly $2 million last year, and have obtained court permission to violate the terms of the will (*see* 1966; *Sun*, 1950).

The city still has 10 major daily papers, including the *American*, the *Graphic*, the *Herald Tribune*, the *Journal*, the *Mirror*, the *News*, the *Post*, the *Sun*, the *Times*, and the new *World-Telegram*.

NBC begins experimental television-signal transmissions from atop the new Empire State Building (*see* 1930; 1939).

Nonfiction: *The Autobiography of Lincoln Steffens* by journalist Steffens, now 66; *Living My Life* by Emma Goldman, now 62; *The Brown Decades* by Lewis Mumford; *Nuova York* by Italian-born *New York World-Telegram* writer and *Corriere della Sera* (Milan) correspondent Luigi (Giorgio) Barzini, 22; *New York City During the War of Independence* by Oscar T. Barck; *Old Bowery Days* by Alvin F. Harlow; *The New York Money Market: Origins and Development* by Margaret G. Myers.

Barnes & Noble launches its first publishing venture—a College Outline Series for students too preoccupied to do the reading required for their coursework (*see* 1917; 1969).

Fiction: *Guys and Dolls* (stories) by Manhattan, Kansas-born *New York American* writer Damon Runyon, now 50, who has recorded (and sometimes invented) the argot of New York's streets, calling money *potatoes*, Lindy's restaurant *Mindy's*, and complimentary tickets *Chinee* (because they are punched with holes like Chinese coins). When he became a sportswriter at the *American* in 1911 his editor dropped Runyon's first name, Alfred; *The Dream Life of Balso Snell* by New York novelist Nathanael West (Nathan Wallenstein Weinstein), 27, who has developed a style derived from dadaism and surrealism in the arts.

Poetry: *Death and Taxes* by Dorothy Parker.

The Argosy Book Store founded by Louis Cohen in 1923 moves from Fourth Avenue (Booksellers Row) to 114 East 59th Street, where it will remain until it moves next door to 116 in 1964. In addition to selling secondhand books, the store will deal in first editions, antique prints, and other rare printed items, expanding to occupy all six floors of its 19th century building.

The Whitney Museum of American Art opens at 8-12 West 8th Street in Greenwich Village to display works by young artists. Sculptor (and railroad heiress) Gertrude Vanderbilt Whitney's husband, Harry, died last year, she has offered the Metropolitan Museum of Art $3 million and some 700 works of U.S. art if it will open a gallery for such art, but the Met has declined her offer. Now 56, she displays works by her friends Edward Hopper, Charles Sheeler, and John Sloan but will modestly wait 8 years before displaying any of her own (*see* 1966).

Painting: *Chatham Square* by Reginald Marsh; *Ferry Boat Wreck*, *Pine Tree*, and *Fields of Grain as Seen From Train* by Arthur Dove; *Forms in Space: No. 1* and *House and Street* by Stuart Davis.

Photograph: *Icarus Atop Empire State Building* by Lewis W. Hine, now 56, whose camera has recorded conditions in the city's tenements and sweatshops.

Theater: *Tomorrow and Tomorrow* by Philip Barry 1/13 at the Henry Miller Theater, with Zita Johann, Osgood Perkins, London-born actor Herbert Marshall, 30, 206 perfs.; *Green Grow the Lilacs* by Cherokee Nation Indian Territory (later Oklahoma)-born playwright (Rolla) Lynn Riggs, 30, 1/26 at the Guild Theater, with Helen Westley, Lee Strasberg, June Walker, Niagara Falls-born actor (Stanislas Pascal) Franchot Tone, 25, 64 perfs.; *As Husbands Go* by Rachel Crothers, now 59, 3/15 at the John Golden Theater, with Lily Cahill, Catherine Calhoun Doucet, 148 perfs.; *The House of Connelly* by Paul Green 10/5 at the Martin Beck Theater, with Stella Adler, Franchot Tone, Philadelphia-born actor Clifford Odets, 25, Rose McClendon, 81 perfs.; *The Left Bank* by Elmer Rice 10/5 at the Little Theater, with Katherine Alexander, Horace Braham, Cledge Roberts, 242 perfs.; *Mourning Becomes Electra* by Eugene O'Neill 10/26 at the Guild Theater, with Alla Nazimova, Alice Brady in a play based on 5th Century B.C. Greek tragedies, 150 perfs.; *Counsellor-at-Law* by Elmer Rice 11/6 at the Plymouth Theater, with Austrian-born actor Paul Muni (originally Muni Weisenfreund), 37, 292 perfs.; *Springtime for Henry* by English playwright Benn W. Levy, 31, 12/9 at the Bijou Theater, with English actor Leslie Banks, 41, Mexican-born actor Nigel Bruce, 36, 199 perfs.

Playwright-producer David Belasco dies at New York May 14 at age 77.

The Group Theater is established at New York by admirers of Russian acting teacher Stanislavsky (Konstantin Sergeivitch Alexeyev), now 66. Founders of the socially conscious left-wing experimental enterprise include producers Harold Clurman and Cheryl Crawford, actor-playwright Clifford Odets, and actors Stella Adler, John Garfield, Elia Kazan, Brooklyn-born Robert "Bobby" Lewis, 22, and Franchot Tone. The Group will continue until 1941 with productions that will tend to glorify the workingman and demonize the capitalist system (*see* Actors Studio, 1947).

Radio: *The March of Time* 3/6 on CBS with announcers Harry Von Zell and Ted Husing, who will soon be joined by Westbrook Van Voorhis in a show produced by *Time* magazine (to 1945). The series is also produced on film by Louis de Rochemont, whose theatrical presentations depart from the newsreels of the day by focusing on labor unrest, foreign dictators, and other controversial subjects that newsreel producers avoid lest audiences find them unpleasant; *Little Orphan Annie* 4/6 on NBC Blue Network stations (to 1943); *The Easy Aces* in October on CBS with Kansas City-born comedian-columnist Goodman Ace, 32, and his wife, Jane (*née* Epstein), 26, who have been offered $500 per week to move to Chicago and go nationwide. NBC will offer them more next year to move to New York, where they will gain a reputation for witticisms such as "Time wounds all heels." *The Easy Aces* will continue until 1945, *Mr. Ace and Jane* until 1955; *The Story of Myrt and Marge* 11/1 on CBS with Donna Damarel and Gene Kretzinger as Broadway chorus girls in a show written by vaudeville veteran Myrtle Vail, 43, (to 1946).

Films: Jules White and Zion Myers's *Sidewalks of New York* with Buster Keaton, Anita Page, Cliff Edwards; King Vidor's *Street Scene* with Sylvia Sidney (originally Sophia Koslow), William Collier, Jr., David Landau, Estelle Taylor; Robert Z. Leonard's *Susan Lenox: Her Fall and Rise* with Greta Garbo, Clark Gable, Jean Hersholt.

Movie theaters show double features to boost business as attendance drops. Many former executives, now unemployed, spend their afternoons at the movies.

Kate Smith makes her CBS radio debut May 1 singing "When the Moon Comes over the Mountain." Having played comic fat-girl roles in Broadway shows, Virginia-born Kathryn Elizabeth Smith, 22, has finally won a singing role at the Palace Theater, Columbia Phonograph Co. recording manager Ted Collins has caught her act and signed her to a contract, and she begins a radio career that will continue for nearly half a century (*see* 1937; Hennie Youngman, 1937).

Broadway musicals: *America's Sweetheart* 2/10 at the Broadhurst Theater, with music by Richard Rodgers, lyrics by Lorenz Hart, songs that include "I've Got Five Dollars," 135 perfs.; *Billy Rose's Crazy Quilt* 5/19 at the 44th Street Theater, with Fanny Brice (Rose's wife), music by Harry Warren, lyrics by Rose and Mort Dixon, songs that include "I Found a Million Dollar Baby—in a Five and Ten Cent Store," 79 perfs.; *The Little Show* 6/1 at the Music Box Theater, with Beatrice Lillie, Ernest Truex, music and lyrics by Noël

Coward, songs that include "Mad Dogs and Englishmen," written by Coward last year while motoring between Hanoi and Saigon, 136 perfs.; *The Band Wagon* 6/3 at the New Amsterdam Theater, with Fred and Adele Astaire in their last appearance together on the first revolving stage to be used in a musical, music by Arthur Schwartz, lyrics by Howard Dietz, songs that include "Dancing in the Dark," "I Love Louisa," 260 perfs.; *The Ziegfeld Follies* 7/1 at the Ziegfeld Theater, with torch singer Helen Morgan, Ruth Etting, Harry Richman, music by Walter Donaldson, Dave Stamper, and others, lyrics by E. Y. Harburg and others, 165 perfs.; *Earl Carroll's Vanities* (revue) 7/27 at the new 3,000-seat Earl Carroll Theater, designed by George Keister, on Seventh Avenue at 50th Street, with William Demarest, Lillian Roth, naked chorus girls, music mostly by New York-born composer Burton Lane (originally Morris Hyman Kushner), 19, plus Ravel's "Bolero," lyrics by Harold Adamson, songs that include "Goodnight, Sweetheart" by English songwriters Ray Noble, James Campbell, and Reg Connelly, 278 perfs.; *George White's Scandals* (revue) 9/14 at the Apollo Theater, with Willie Howard, Rudy Vallée, Ray Bolger, Ethel Merman, music and lyrics by Ray Henderson and Lew Brown, songs that include "Life Is Just a Bowl of Cherries," 202 perfs.; *Everybody's Welcome* 10/13 at the Shubert Theater, with Tommy and Jimmy Dorsey, Ann Pennington, Harriet Lake (Ann Sothern), songs that include "As Time Goes By" by Montclair, N.J.-born composer Herman Hupfeld, 36, 139 perfs.; *The Cat and the Fiddle* 10/15 at the Globe Theater, with Bettina Hall, Georges Metaxa, 32, Eddie Foy, Jr., music by Jerome Kern, lyrics by Otto Harbach, songs that include "She Didn't Say 'Yes'," "The Night Was Made for Love", 395 perfs.; *The Laugh Parade* 11/2 at the Imperial Theater, with Ed Wynn, music by Harry Warren, lyrics by Mort Dixon and Joe Young, songs that include "You're My Everything," 231 perfs.; *Of Thee I Sing* 12/26 at the Music Box Theater, with Victor Moore as Alexander Throttlebottom, William Gaxton as John P. Wintergreen, music by George Gershwin, lyrics by Ira Gershwin, songs that include "Love Is Sweeping the Country," "Wintergreen for President," "Who Cares?" and the title song, 441 perfs.

The Minsky brothers stage one of the first burlesque shows on Broadway, at the Republic Theater in 42nd Street, while continuing to mount shows at the Apollo (*see* 1924). Their productions will have suggestive titles such as *Panty's Inferno* and *Mind Over Mattress* (*see* 1937).

Popular songs: "Mood Indigo" by Duke Ellington, lyrics by New Orleans-born clarinetist Barney (originally Alban Leon) Bigard, 25, Irving Mills;

Workers finished the Empire State Building ahead of schedule. LEWIS HINE, MUSEUM OF THE CITY OF NEW YORK

"(Potatoes Are Cheaper—Tomatoes are Cheaper) Now's the Time to Fall in Love" by Al Sherman, lyrics by Al Lewis.

The Brill Building opens at 1619 Broadway with 11 stories, all of them soon occupied by Tin Pan Alley publishers and bandleaders. Victor Bark, Jr. has designed the white brick Art Deco structure for developer Abraham E. Lefcourt.

Trumpeter Adolphus A. "Doc" Cheatham returns from 3 years in Europe and later in the year joins Cab Calloway's orchestra at the Cotton Club in Harlem (*see* 1928). He will remain with Calloway until 1939, when a mysterious disease will interrupt his career.

Iowa-born cornetist-pianist-composer Leon Bismarck "Bix" Beiderbecke dies of chronic alcoholism at New York August 6 at age 28. He had recently moved into an apartment at 43-30 46th Street in Sunnyside, Queens.

 H. Ellsworth Vines, Jr., 19, wins in men's singles at Forest Hills, Helen Wills Moody in women's singles.

 The El Morocco nightclub has its beginnings in a speakeasy opened by Italian-born entrepreneur John Perona at 154 East 54th Street, where Perona will preside nightly at his "round table," attracting café society types, entertainers, and politicians with its blue-and-white zebra-striped decor until January 1961 (*see* 1960).

Fashion Group International is founded by professional women in the city's fashion industry and related fields. Initial members include *Vogue* magazine's Edna Woolman Chase and Carmel Snow, *New York Times* fashion editor Virginia Pope, designers Lilly Daché, Edith Head, Claire McCardell, and Adele Simpson, and cosmetics queens Elizabeth Arden and Helena Rubinstein.

Construction workers at Rockefeller Center put up a Christmas tree, beginning a tradition.

 Underworld boss Joe Masseria is shot dead April 15 by gunmen Joe Adonis, Umberto "Albert" Anastasia (originally Anastasio), 28, Vito Genovese, and Bugsy Siegel at Gerardo Scarpato's Restaurant in Coney Island (one of Anastasia's two brothers, Salvatore, is a priest, and Umberto changed his name "to save the family's honor" when he was arrested for the first time in 1921). Masseria and his archrival Salvatore Maranzano have been battling in what police call the Castellammarese War (both come from the Castellammare del Golfo region of Sicily (also the birthplace of mobster Joseph Bonanno, now 26); five New York children are hit in a beer-war shootout July 28, and one of them dies; Salvatore Maranzano is assassinated September 10 at his offices in the New York Central Building in a murder engineered, as was Masseria's, by Italian-born New York mobster Charles "Lucky" Luciano (originally Salvatore Lucania), 34, who has been Masseria's trusted lieutenant and who now restructures the New York Mafia into a federation of five "families"—Bonanno, Genovese, Gotti, Luchesi, and Luciano—all of them engaging in bootlegging, extortion, and other operations (*see* 1936).

The city's homicide rate will rise to 7.4 per 100,000 in the next 5 years, up from 6.0 per 100,000 in the last 5 (*see* 1936).

"Beer Baron of the Catskills" Jack "Legs" Diamond dies at Albany December 18 at age 35 of a bullet wound in the head. He has been shot on 13 previous occasions; authorities suspect that his assailants this time were friends of a henchman who took the rap for a murder Diamond himself committed.

 The 31-story 21 West Street building is completed for developer Alfred Rheintein to Art Deco designs by Starrett & Van Vleck. Running from West Street to Washington Street along Morris Street, it overlooks Battery Park.

The 31-story 60 John Street building is completed at the southwest corner of William Street (150 William Street) for the New Amsterdam Casualty Co. Designed by Clinton & Russell with Holten & George, it has 320,000 square feet of rental space.

The 38-story 116 John Street skyscraper is completed with an entrance on Pearl Street and extending to Platt Street. Designed by Louis Abramson, it has 300,000 square feet of rental space.

The 53-story City Bank Farmers Trust Building is completed at 22 William Street, covering a site bounded by William, Beaver, and Hanover streets and Exchange Place. Designed by Cross & Cross and erected by the George A. Fuller Construction Co., it has 30 elevators and 533,000 square feet of rental space.

The 19-story Starrett-Lehigh loft building is completed at 602 West 26th Street in an area bounded by Eleventh and Twelfth avenues between 26th and 27th streets. Designed by Russell G. and Walter M. Cory with Yasuo Matsui, it rises above the former Lehigh Valley Railroad freight terminal with perhaps nine miles of strip windows.

The 45-story Nelson Tower office building is completed at 450 Seventh Avenue, northwest corner 34th Street, to designs by H. Craig Severance. It has 400,000 square feet of rental space.

The 102-story Empire State Building opens with formal ceremonies May 1 on Fifth Avenue between 33rd and 34th streets, where the Waldorf-Astoria Hotel of 1897 was torn down beginning in May 1929 to make way for the steel-framed skyscraper that will remain the world's tallest building until 1973. Former General Motors executive John Jakob Raskob has helped raise the money for the 1,250-foot structure, former governor Alfred E. Smith heads the company that financed its construction, and he joins with President Hoover, Gov. Roosevelt, and Mayor Walker in making appropriate speeches. Shreve, Lamb & Harmon has designed the office tower, built in only 18 months at a cost of $41 million (the budget called for $60 million, but windows, stone and steel spandrels, and other basic components have been fabricated off-site and installed on an assembly-line basis to permit the building to rise at a rate of four stories per week), 14 workers have fallen to their deaths during its construction, its steel frame is clad in granite, limestone, aluminum, nickel, and upwards of 10 million bricks, its three-story Art Deco lobby is lined with European marble, stainless steel, and glass in geometric patterns, but the interiors of only its first 22 floors are complete, its initial occupancy rate is

only 23 percent, and while its 2,158,000 square feet of rentable space go begging for tenants most of its income will come from admissions to the building's 86th-floor observation deck ($1 per head), that will pay off 2 percent of its total cost. Visitors on a clear day can see for 80 miles.

Rockefeller Center construction begins on a 12-acre, three-block midtown Manhattan site bounded by Fifth and Sixth avenues between 49th and 52nd streets, where 14 buildings will replace more than 200 smaller structures on a site whose tenants will employ more than 75,000 people (see 1928). John D. Rockefeller, Jr. has been paying $5 million per year to lease the land and pay for utilities, he has decided to invest nearly $100 million in a program to develop the property and make it pay, the 23-year lease given by Columbia University will be renewed periodically, and the university will continue to receive rent on the land until 1985. Architect Raymond M. Hood has laid out the design for the office-building complex, including a street and gardens to separate the structures with light and air (see Radio City, 1932; RCA [GE] Building, 1934).

The 50-story RCA-Victor Building is completed on the west side of Lexington Avenue at 51st Street. Designed by Schultze & Weaver, the 570-foot Art Deco tower will soon be acquired by General Electric and become the General Electric Building (see 1993).

The 59-story 500 Fifth Avenue office tower is completed at the northwest corner of Fifth Avenue and 42nd Street, formerly the site of the Bristol Hotel. Designed by Shreve, Lamb & Harmon, it looms over the 20-year-old New York Public Library.

The 35-story McGraw-Hill Building at 330 West 42nd Street is completed in October west of Eighth Avenue with 550,000 square feet of floor space. Designed in modernistic style by Raymond M. Hood, its exterior has horizontal bands of blue-green terra cotta and factory-style windows, its interior plain concrete walls and ceilings; the bindery is on the fifth floor, the composing room on the sixth, and editorial offices on the seventh. McGraw-Hill rents out floors nine through 15.

The 28-story 10 Park Avenue apartment hotel is completed at the northwest corner of 34th Street to designs by Helmle, Corbett & Harrison.

River House opens at 435 East 52nd Street on the East River, replacing tenement houses in what has been a slum area. Designed by Bottomley, Wagner & White, the lower floors of the palatial 26-story co-operative apartment house contain the River Club, with its swimming pool, tennis courts, squash courts, and ballroom. A dock on the river provides mooring for yachts but will be destroyed to make way for the East River Drive that will open in 1942.

The 20-story Parc Vendome apartments open with 570 units in four buildings just east of Ninth Avenue in 57th Street and opposite the 2-year-old American Women's Association Clubhouse. Banker-philanthropist-art patron Otto Kahn, now 64, had assembled the property to provide a new home for the Metropolitan Opera, and the clubhouse was built with the idea that it would be opposite the new Met (the Rockefellers leased more than 11 acres west of Fifth Avenue for the same purpose, but the Met did not accept either offer). Built by developer Henry Mandel, the Parc Vendome lures prospective tenants with a gymnasium, swimming pool, solarium, terraced gardens, and dining hall.

The 32-story Century apartment house opens on Central Park West between 62nd and 63rd streets. Designed in Art Deco style by developer Irwin S. Chanin and his architect Jacques Delamarre, it occupies much of the block west to Broadway and replaces the Century Theater built in 1909. Initial tenants include playwright Marc Connelly.

The 13-story 625 Park Avenue apartment house is completed at the northeast corner of 65th Street with a 26-room triplex penthouse whose occupants will include cosmetics queen Helena Rubinstein (for 30 years) and, later, Charles Revson. Designed by J. E. R. Carpenter, the building's apartments are all luxurious, but none can match the penthouse, whose three floors are connected by a circular staircase. The living room, dining room, and library all have woodburning fireplaces, terraces surround them and the gallery and kitchen; other terraces surround the 68' × 17' salon; the bedroom floor has six bedrooms, one of them measuring 33'6" × 18'2" and another 29'8" × 20'6", plus a maid's room.

The 11-story Milan House apartment houses are completed at 115 East 67th and 116 East 68th streets, between Park and Lexington avenues. Architect Andrew J. Thomas has designed them in neo-Romanesque style with an Italian garden courtyard between them.

A new Majestic apartment house is completed on Central Park West between 71st and 72nd streets. The 29-story structure replaces not only an 1894 Majestic Hotel but also two rows of brownstones that had extended west from the old hotel on both streets. A study of apartment accomodations in the late 1920s indicated a demand for apartments of 11 to 24 rooms each, Irwin S. Chanin had originally planned a 45-story building for the site, he was obliged by the 1929 Wall Street crash to revise his plans, so the largest apartment in the Majestic is 14 rooms (there are also some one-room studios). Architect Jacques Delamarre is responsible for the cantilevered construction on the side facing Central Park that permits small solaria to be placed at each corner (the twin-towered, Art Deco-style Majestic has wide banks of windows, streamlined around its corners) and there is a large solarium on the 19th floor for use by all tenants, although the sun-worshiping fad has only just begun.

The 17-story 120 East End Avenue co-operative apartment house is completed at the northeast corner of 85th Street to designs by Charles A. Platt. Real estate heir Vincent Astor has engaged the George A. Fuller Co. to build the limestone-faced structure, whose top floor is occupied entirely by Astor's own apartment (seven bedrooms, six servants' rooms). More typically, floors have three apartments of 10, 11, and 14 rooms each, while apartments on the upper floors can be as small as three rooms or as large as 19, with five duplexes.

The 30-story, 1,300-room Eldorado apartment house is completed at 300 Central Park West, between 90th and 91st streets. Designed in Art Deco style by Margon & Holder (with help from Emery Roth), it replaces the turreted eight-story El Dorado of 1902; like the avenue's other twin-towered buildings, its design has been strongly influenced by the Multiple Dwellings Law of 1929.

The 21-story Ardsley apartment house is completed at 320 Central Park West, southwest corner 92nd Street, to Art Deco ("Mayan") designs by Emery Roth.

Two groups of three six-story apartment houses designed by Henry Atterbury Smith are completed in Jackson Heights, Queens, at 34-19 to 34-47 90th Street and 34-48 91st Street, between 34th and 35th avenues. Only the middle building in each group has an elevator: tenants on upper floors of the other buildings must use roof bridges to reach their apartments.

A mansion designed by Delano & Aldrich is completed at 67 East 93rd Street for former banker George F. Baker, who has died in May before its completion. Along with its courtyard, it adjoins the residence of his son George F., Jr., who acquired the former Francis F. Palmer house at the northwest corner of Park Avenue and 2 years ago added to it with a Delano & Aldrich house at 69 East 93rd.

The 45-story Essex House hotel (initially the Seville Towers) opens January 29 on Central Park South just east of the new Athletic Club building on Seventh

Avenue. Designed by Newark architect Frank Grad, the 1,286-room hotel is already in the hands of the Reconstruction Finance Corp. that will retain possession until 1946, when private owners will acquire it for $6 million.

The 26-story Edison Hotel opens with 1,000 guest rooms at 228 West 47th Street, just west of Broadway. Herbert J. Knapp has designed the hotel, whose 8,000-square-foot ballroom has a splendid domed ceiling. Room rates begin at $2.50 per day.

The 24-story Paris Hotel opens at the southeast corner of West End Avenue and 97th Street with 900 rooms, each with bath, shower, and radio speaker, plus suites of up to four rooms each, many with terraces. Amenities include a swimming pool and gymnasium (free to tenants every morning), billiard room, large dining room, grillroom, lounge, mezzanine with library and card rooms, and rooftop solaria (open and closed).

A new Waldorf-Astoria Hotel opens October 1 on a full-block site leased for 63 years from the New York Central Railroad from 49th to 50th Street between Park and Lexington avenues, where it replaces the American Express Building on Lexington Avenue, the Central YMCA on Park. Designed by Schultze & Weaver and built at a cost of about $25 million in just two years by Thompson Starrett Co., the hotel has 2,000 rooms, including 300 residential suites, each having a foyer, living room, dining room, three or four bedrooms and baths, and furnished in early American, 18th century English, Adam Brothers, Chippendale, Sheraton, Hepplewhite, Louis XV, or Louis XVI styles by decorators from America, England, France, and Sweden. Living and dining rooms have open fireplaces with Louis XV or XVI antique marble mantles. A private railroad siding enables guests with their own railcars to have them routed to the hotel's special elevator on Track 61, whence they can be whisked directly to their suites or to the lobby. Two subbasement levels extend far below the tracks to accommodate service facilities. There are 31 elevators, counting service lifts. Public rooms are air-conditioned and kept at an even temperature year-round by Carrier equipment. Terraces extend to the 19th floor. The Towers go from the 28th floor to the 42nd and have four 24-hour-per-day elevators for their 115 suites, many of them leased to private tenants (who will sometimes have their own chefs, butlers, and telephone systems). The hotel retains many of the old Waldorf's traditional features, including Peacock Alley, the Empire Room, and the Astor Gallery, but the new Waldorf-Astoria will lose money for 12 years before turning a profit (*see* 1932).

 The new Waldorf-Astoria has its own butcher shop, bakery, and ice plant (it will soon have a fifth-floor wine cellar large enough to cradle 37,000 gallons of wine). It employs the old Waldorf's maître d'hôtel Oscar Tschirky, now 65, who is paid $30,000 per year at a time when doctors and lawyers are lucky to make $5,000. He has been so heavily promoted as Oscar of the Waldorf that his calling cards are so inscribed (*see* Men's Bar, Palm Bar, 1934).

1932 A state legislative commission headed by Judge Samuel Seabury, now 58, issues a 198-page report January 24 stating that the "financial condition in which the city of New York finds itself is due to the waste, the graft, and the corruption with which the city is infested. The mayor of the City of New York has not by a single public utterance or act made any attempt to induce his fugitive agent [who has been missing since August] to return . . ." "It is perfectly apparent that what these men did was part of the system upon which Tammany Hall exists and expands, that Tammany Hall approves it and is ready to extend its arms to the utmost to protect and perpetuate its sordid traffic [in jobs] and political influence." "The evidence with respect to the administration of the Unemployment Relief Fund in Richmond and Manhattan establishes the shocking abuse of a sacred trust. It shows that the money of the taxpayers intended to prevent starvation and privation was used instead to take care of faithful Democrats." The commission's report favors a city-manager form of government, and its revelations will bring down Tammany Hall boss John Francis Curry in 1934.

"I pledge you, I pledge myself, to a new deal for the American people," says Gov. Roosevelt as he accepts the Democratic Party nomination for president at Chicago. The first nominee of either party to accept at a convention, he has broken all precedent by flying to Chicago with his wife, Eleanor, and in his acceptance speech he speaks out in defense of the "common man," taking a cue from former presidential candidate Al Smith, who has had more support at the convention than anyone but FDR in a bitterly contested floor fight. Roosevelt has followed the suggestion of his counsel Samuel Rosenman and created a "Brain Trust" headed by Ohio-born Columbia University professor Raymond (Charles) Moley, 45, who has suggested the term *New Deal* (Moley writes many of the governor's campaign speeches, having recruited fellow Columbia professors Adolph A. [Augustus] Berle, 38, and Rexford Guy Tugwell, 41, to join the Brain Trust, whose members advise the nominee on national issues and include also Roosevelt's close associate Louis Howe, who has come up with term *Brain Trust*). New York labor organizer Rose Schneiderman, now 48, soon joins the group.

The Hofstadter Committee appointed by the state legislature last year hears evidence after Gov. Roosevelt's nomination that New York's playboy mayor Jimmy Walker received $246,692 from a joint brokerage account opened with newspaper publisher and advertising representative Paul Bloch, now 54; Walker did not invest a dime, and the committee learns that Bloch has been interested in a company that hopes to sell tile to contractors building the new city subway line. The governor's counsel Samuel Rosenman advises Roosevelt with regard to political aspects of the investigation into Walker's corruption and Mayor Walker resigns September 1 as investigations of corruption by the Seabury Commission continue. Now 51, he has testified before the commission May 25 in a Foley Square courtroom, the Roman Catholic hierarchy has blocked Walker's effort to get Tammany Hall's support, the mayor denies reports that he received $964,000 in cash payoffs but leaves for Europe to join his mistress.

Democrats nominate city corporation counsel and surrogate John P. "Boo Boo" O'Brien, 59, to run in a special election for someone to fill out former mayor Walker's unexpired term, and O'Brien wins easy victory with 1,056,115 votes. Republican Lewis H. Pounds receives 443,901, Socialist Morris Hillquit 249,887, write-in candidate Joseph V. McKee, 43, an impressive 234,372 (he was president of the Board of Aldermen when Walker resigned, reduced the mayoralty salary from $40,000 to $25,000, and has been serving as acting mayor; see 1933).

Gov. Roosevelt wins the presidential election by a landslide, gaining 472 electoral votes and 57 percent of the popular vote versus 59 electoral votes and 40 percent of the popular vote for President Hoover, who carries only six states as economic depression worsens. The governor has been guided to some extent by the advice of Bronx party leader Edward J. Flynn, now 41, who served as sheriff of Bronx County from 1922 to 1925 and has developed a reputation for integrity and liberal outlook. Judge Seabury has recommended the removal of Bronx borough president Henry Bruckner, 62, a Tammany stalwart who has held office since 1917 (and developed Bruckner Beverages, the city's largest soda-water bottler; its best-known brand is labeled U-No-Us); Bruckner resists Boss Flynn's pressure to resign but will not be nominated for reelection and will retire only because of illness. President-

elect Roosevelt appoints Samuel Rosenman to the State Supreme Court but Rosenman has so antagonized Tammany Hall with his role in the investigations into city corruption that it will refuse to nominate him for election to a regular term (*but see* 1933).

Voters elect Lieut. Gov. Herbert H. (Henry) Lehman, 54, to succeed Gov. Roosevelt, despite opposition from Tammany leader John F. Curry. Lehman wins 2,659,519 votes to 1,812,090 for his Republican opponent William J. Donovan. Now 49, Donovan is the New York lawyer and war hero who led the 69th Regiment in the Great War; Lehman's older brother Irving is a judge on the State Court of Appeals.

The New York County Republican machine and Tammany Hall both nominate State Senator Samuel H. Hofstadter and Tammany protégé Aron Steuer for vacancies on the New York Supreme Court, the Bar Association pronounces both men unfit, the *World-Telegram* publishes a cartoon October 10 by Illinois-born staff cartoonist Rollin Kirby, 57, opposing their election, but both win nevertheless.

The Norris-La Guardia Act passed by Congress March 23 prohibits the use of injunctions in labor disputes except under defined conditions and outlaws "yellow-dog contracts" that make workers promise not to join any labor union. Sponsored by George William Norris (R. Neb.) and Fiorello H. La Guardia (R. N.Y.), now 39, the bill helps establish labor's right to strike, picket, and conduct boycotts.

The Amalgamated Clothing and Textile Workers union pulls 30,000 workers off the job in July and 15,000 in August. David Dubinsky (originally Dobnievski) becomes president of the International Ladies' Garment Workers' Union (ILGWU) at age 40; the Polish-born organizer launches a membership drive that will triple the union's rolls in 3 years.

Financier Paul M. Warburg dies of pneumonia at his 17 East 80th Street home January 24 at age 63; Conference Board president and cofounder Magnus W. Alexander of a heart attack at his Park Avenue home September 10 at age 62.

Manufacturers Trust, founded at Brooklyn in 1853, absorbs the Chatham and Phenix Bank, whose origins date to 1812 (*see* Manufacturers Hanover Trust, 1961).

Wall Street's Dow Jones Industrial Average plummets to 41.22 by July 7, down from its high of 381.17

September 3, 1929. The average U.S. weekly wage falls to $17, down from $28 in 1929. Some 1,616 U.S. banks fail, nearly 20,000 business firms go bankrupt, there are 21,000 suicides, and expenditures for food and tobacco fall $10 billion below 1929 levels. The Dow rallies somewhat before falling 5.79 points (8.40 percent) August 12, its fourth worst plunge yet, but remains above its July 7 low. Stock prices have lost 85 to 90 percent of their pre-Crash values and will never again fall so low, but they will not reach their 1929 heights until 1954 (when adjusted for inflation, not until the 1990s). The Dow struggles back to close December 31 at 59.93, down from 77.90 at the end of 1931.

Harry Winston, Inc. is founded by New York-born diamond dealer Winston, 36, who quit school at age 15 to go into business with his father; they opened a small store on St. Nicholas Avenue in 1914, the son served an apprenticeship at the New York Diamond Exchange, started Premier Diamond Co. with $2,000 in capital, obtained bank financing (he engaged a distinguished-looking older man to front for him after being mistaken by the bank for a messenger boy), and has developed a reputation for recognizing the potential value of estate jewelry; his father died 3 years ago, and the younger Winston will borrow money to buy collections that he will refurbish and resell.

An investigation by New York's Taxicab Commission uncovers evidence that the Checker Cab Manufacturing Co. owns the city's largest taxi fleet (Parmalee) and has paid bribes to Mayor Walker. Based in Kalamazoo, Mich., the company was started 10 years ago by Russian-born entrepreneur Morris Markin, now 39; its cabs compete with Chrysler-made DeSoto Skyview taxis, Hudson Terraplanes, and Packards, all with leather upholstery and jump seats.

A section of the Cross-County Parkway opens May 2 to connect the Hutchinson River and Saw Mill River parkways in Westchester.

The Pulaski Skyway opens September 1, relieving congestion at the New Jersey end of the Holland Tunnel that opened in 1927 and speeding access to the Newark Metropolitan Airport that opened in 1929. Built at a cost of $20 million and 15 lives (plus a labor-related murder), it is part of a $40 million, 13.2-mile Route 1 extension across the marshy meadowlands that was supposed to open 6 years ago but was delayed by disputes over where and how to cross the Hackensack and Passaic rivers; the can-

tilever and truss bridge has two main spans totaling 550 feet in length and will help make Route 1 a major truck route.

The Independent subway system opens September 10, extending service into areas not served by the BMT or IRT and encouraging development in some areas of the Bronx, Brooklyn, and Queens with trains designated by letter rather than number. By the time it is completed in 1940 the IND will have 59 miles of track, including trunk lines under Sixth and Eighth avenues in Manhattan that link up with lines in lower Manhattan and across 53rd Street; feeder lines will extend to northern Manhattan, under the Grand Concourse in the Bronx, under Queens Boulevard, and to Flatbush, replacing elevated lines and connecting Brooklyn and Queens for the first time without requiring a transfer in Manhattan. Begun in the Hylan administration for the express purpose of siphoning passengers away from the BMT, IRT, and elevated lines in order to ruin them and make them vulnerable to takeover by the city, the new subway has taken far longer to build than was intended, its cost has been twice what was called for, and its long station platforms are purely functional with none of the mosaic tiling that has distinguished earlier stations. Hylan had to be dissuaded from tearing up Central Park to put in the Central Park West trunk line, and the *Herald Tribune* was moved to editorialize 7 years ago, "New subways . . . have been obstructed for no other reason save that Mr. Hylan neither knew how to build them nor was willing to allow anyone else to build them" (*see* 1933; 1936).

New York Hospital begins receiving patients September 1 at a huge new facility on the east side of York Avenue between 68th and 70th streets with nearly 1,000 beds (*see* 1924). Its buildings include the Payne Whitney Neurological and Psychiatric Clinic (financed with money set aside in the late Payne Whitney's will) and an 11-story Lying-In Hospital with accomodations for 192 patients (132 ward beds, 36 beds for semi-private patients, 26 rooms for private patients). Canby Robinson and Henry R. Shepley of the Boston architectural firm Coolidge, Shepley, Bulfinch & Abbott have designed the buildings put up by Marc Eidlitz & Son, their arched windows are modeled on the Gothic-style Palais des Papes in Avignon, the 27-story central tower has operating rooms on its 10th and 11th floors, private patients' rooms and intern residents are on the floors above (the 24th to 27th floors contain squash, tennis, and handball courts and a bowling alley) while lower floors have separate men's and women's wards with a glass-enclosed solarium at the end of each floor, but the architects have failed to provide for enough elevators in the main buildings, patient rooms are not air-conditioned, and the rooms will be used for nearly 65 years—long after other, newer hospitals have adopted more modern patient facilities. Governors of the New York Hospital-Cornell Medical Center soon pay nearly $3 million to acquire the block between 70th and 71st streets; the complex will grow in 40 years to have 21 buildings, 1,160 beds, 1,200 doctors, 900 nurses, a staff of 4,200, and remain the city's largest private voluntary hospital, acquiring other hospitals while expanding its own capacity.

Bronx Hospital moves into a new building (see 1911). Its old one becomes a nursing home (see Bronx-Lebanon, 1962). Lebanon Hospital moves into a new building on the Grand Concourse (see 1893; Bronx-Lebanon, 1962).

Former 69th Regiment chaplain Francis P. Duffy dies at New York June 26 at age 61. He has served since 1920 as pastor of the Church of the Holy Cross near Times Square (see Sculpture, 1937).

The Museum of the City of New York reopens January 11 in a neo-Georgian red brick building, designed by Joseph H. Friedlander, on the east side of Fifth Avenue between 103rd and 104th streets (see 1923). The city has donated the site, and 1,500 subscribers have raised $2 million to build and endow the museum, but it will be some years before the institution has a collection that even begins to approach that of the New-York Historical Society.

The Board of Education announces that it will stop supporting the Little Red School House begun by Elisabeth Irwin in 1921 and housed most recently in P.S. 41 on Greenwich Avenue between 10th and 11th streets. In an article written for the New York Times, Irwin says field trips (to the Coney Island lighthouse keeper, fishermen in Sheepshead Bay, the Fulton Market, a milk plant, storekeepers, streetsweepers, and the like) take precedence over classroom work at the school, and that "grades and marks, merits and demerits . . . have no part at all in the progressive scheme." She takes over a 12-year-old building at 196 Bleecker Street, corner Sixth Avenue, that was built as a mission church (the First Presbyterian Church will sell it to the school in 1937), and turns her institution into a private school, opened in September with 138 students whose parents pay tuitions of $150 per year (other private schools typically charge $600) (see 1941).

Irish-born Vogue fashion editor Carmel Snow resigns at age 41 to become fashion editor of Hearst's Harper's Bazaar and will head that magazine from 1934 until her retirement in 1958. Condé Nast has been grooming her to succeed Edna Woolman Chase and will never speak to her again.

The Family Circle begins publication at Newark, N.J., early in September with 24 pages. The first magazine to be distributed exclusively through grocery stores, the weekly is given free to shoppers at two eastern chains and will have a circulation of 1.44 million by 1939 (see 1946; Woman's Day, 1937).

Public relations pioneer Carl Byoir, now 44, directs an effort sponsored by the American Legion, the American Federation of Labor, and the Association of National Advertisers to fight the Depression by persuading employers to create new jobs (see 1912; medicine, 1934).

Nonfiction: "In America Today" (essay) by English lecturer Mary Agnes Hamilton, 48, who writes, "I landed in New York on December 24th, 1931 . . . I looked about me . . . Yes: those grey-faced, shambling men, standing about in serried rows and groups, had never been there, looking like that, before. More of them: masses, indeed, as we drove along and across the high-numbered avenues: listlessly parked against the walls, blocking the sidewalks . . . Every day, one sees the degrading misery of bread lines. Every day one is told that this great industry and that, from railroads to publishing, is collapsing. The building slump spreads . . . [The] most salient structure, the magnificent Empire State, stands unlet and can only pay its taxes by collecting dollars from the sightseers who ascend to its eyrie for the stupendous view . . . Stories of failing banks, turned in motor-cars, despairing suicides, are dinned into one's ears . . . ;" New York the Wonder City by local author W. Parker Chase of 301 East 21st Street, who says, "At the time this is written, a new legislative investigation of New York City's administration has Tammany under fire on charges of various misdeeds . . . But Tammany history reveals the names of many of America's most prominent and respected sons, who are or have been enrolled as members . . . Those who can see no good in Tammany insist that Tammany is an agency of Satan, and that policy prompts these benefactions. They claim that all this is merely a part for a price paid for votes and popularity . . . New York politics are so intimately identified with Tammany Hall it is said that the Democratic Party in New York City is so completely controlled by this powerful organization that no nominee has even a fighting chance for victory unless endorsed by Tammany;" God and My Father by former New York stockbroker Clarence (Shephard) Day, Jr., 57, who was forced by crippling arthritis to retire in 1903 from his late father's firm and has contributed prose and drawings to various magazines; the 15th annual edition of the *New York City Directory* (later to be called *The Green Book*) sells at the same price it did when it first appeared in 1918 but now runs to 359 pages, giving Mayor Walker's home address (6 St. Luke's Place, Greenwich Village) and salary ($40,000), and listing the floating public baths at the 79th Street Boat Basin ("only white, grey, or natural colored suits are allowed") as well as the Institution for Male Delinquents and farm colonies for paupers on Staten Island.

Poetry: *The Dream Keeper* and *Scottsboro Limited* by Langston Hughes, now 30, who will be called the "Poet Laureate of Harlem."

Poet Hart Crane jumps or falls from a ship bound for the United States from Mexico and drowns April 27 at age 32.

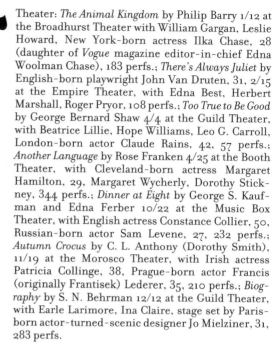

Painting: *New York Mural* by Stuart Davis; *Room in New York* by Edward Hopper; *Man at the Crossroads* (fresco for the new RCA Building) and *Sacco and Vanzetti* by Lithuanian-born New York painter Ben (Benjamin) Shahn, 33, who produces 23 gouaches inspired by the execution of two alleged murderers in 1927; *The Bowery* by Paris-born New York painter Reginald Marsh, 34. Painter Alfred H. Maurer dies at his native New York August 4 at age 64.

Sculpture: a bronze bust of Johann Wolfgang von Goethe by Karl Fischer is unveiled behind the south end of the New York Public Library's central branch in 40th Street, having been erected by the Goethe Society to mark the centennial of the poet-playwright's death; Flushing, Queens, sculptor Joseph Cornell, 28, exhibits his first boxes containing found objects.

The Museum of Modern Art (MoMA) that opened 3 years ago moves into a limestone town house at 11 East 52nd Street, where it backs up on property owned by the Rockefeller family. The museum exhibits not only painting and sculpture but also architectural works, films, and photographs (*see* 1939).

The Wildenstein Gallery that opened in 1903 moves from Fifth Avenue to an elegant new five-story building designed by Horace Trumbauer at 19 East 64th Street (*see* PaceWildenstein, 1993).

Photographs: *Men at Work* by Lewis Hine, whose book records the construction of the Empire State Building last year.

Theater: *The Animal Kingdom* by Philip Barry 1/12 at the Broadhurst Theater with William Gargan, Leslie Howard, New York-born actress Ilka Chase, 28 (daughter of *Vogue* magazine editor-in-chief Edna Woolman Chase), 183 perfs.; *There's Always Juliet* by English-born playwright John Van Druten, 31, 2/15 at the Empire Theater, with Edna Best, Herbert Marshall, Roger Pryor, 108 perfs.; *Too True to Be Good* by George Bernard Shaw 4/4 at the Guild Theater, with Beatrice Lillie, Hope Williams, Leo G. Carroll, London-born actor Claude Rains, 42, 57 perfs.; *Another Language* by Rose Franken 4/25 at the Booth Theater, with Cleveland-born actress Margaret Hamilton, 29, Margaret Wycherly, Dorothy Stickney, 344 perfs.; *Dinner at Eight* by George S. Kaufman and Edna Ferber 10/22 at the Music Box Theater, with English actress Constance Collier, 50, Russian-born actor Sam Levene, 27, 232 perfs.; *Autumn Crocus* by C. L. Anthony (Dorothy Smith), 11/19 at the Morosco Theater, with Irish actress Patricia Collinge, 38, Prague-born actor Francis (originally Frantisek) Lederer, 35, 210 perfs.; *Biography* by S. N. Behrman 12/12 at the Guild Theater, with Earle Larimore, Ina Claire, stage set by Paris-born actor-turned-scenic designer Jo Mielziner, 31, 283 perfs.

Minnie Maddern Fiske dies of heart failure at Hollis, Queens, February 15 at age 66; theatrical booking agent William Morris sits down to a game of pinochle with three vaudevillians at the Friars' Club, 110 West 48th Street, begins playing at 12:15 o'clock in the morning of November 2, and drops dead of a heart attack 15 minutes later at age 59.

Radio: *The Walter Winchell Show* 12/4 on the NBC Blue Network with New York-born *Daily Mirror* columnist Walter Winchell, 35, who moved his column from the *Graphic* to the *Mirror* in 1929 and now syndicates it to more than 1,000 newspapers nationwide: "Good evening, Mr. and Mrs. North and South America and all the ships at sea—let's go to press!"

More New Yorkers have radios than have telephones, and millions depend on radio for news and virtually free entertainment.

Films: Mervyn LeRoy's *Big City Blues* with Joan Blondell, Eric Linden; Roy Del Ruth's *Blessed Event* with Lee Tracy, Mary Brian, Dick Powell; John Adolfi's *Central Park* with Joan Blondell, Guy Kibbee, Wallace Ford, Henry B. Walthall; William Dieterle's *The Crash* with George Brent, Ruth Chatterton, Victor Schertzinger's *Uptown New York* with Jack Oakie, Shirley Grey.

Loews 72nd Street movie theater opens at the southwest corner of Third Avenue. Thomas Lamb has designed its exterior and lobby, John Eberson its auditorium, whose orchestra pit is covered over after Loews decides to abandon plans to combine live entertainment with films.

The Thalia movie theater opens at 250 West 95th Street, just west of Broadway. Designed by Schlanger & Irrera, it has no soundproofing, its floor slopes up toward the screen (partially obstructed by a column), its red-plush upright seats are uncomfortable, but the small house will continue until 1993 to be a favorite venue for foreign films and revivals of Hollywood classics, always double features, with no intermission (see 2002).

♪♪ Broadway musicals: *Face the Music* 2/17 at the New Amsterdam Theater, with comedienne Mary Boland, now 52, music and lyrics by Irving Berlin, songs that include "Let's Have Another Cup of Coffee," 165 perfs.; *Flying Colors* (revue) 9/15 at the Imperial Theater, with Clifton Webb, Philadelphia-born comedienne Imogene Coca, 23, Petrograd-born dancer Tamara Geva (originally Gevergeyeva), 24, Baltimore-born dancer Larry Adler, 18, Belleville, Ohio-born comedian Christian Rudolf "Buddy" Ebsen, 24, Charles Butterworth, music by Arthur Schwartz, lyrics by Howard Dietz, 188 perfs.; *Earl Carroll's Vanities* (revue) 9/27 at the Broadway Theater, with Milton Berle, Helen Broderick, now 41, music by Harold Arlen and Richard Myers, lyrics by Ted Koehler and Edward Heyman, songs that include "I Gotta Right to Sing the Blues," 87 perfs.; *Americana* 10/5 at the Shubert Theater, with music by Jay Gorney, Harold Arlen, Richard Myers, Herman Hupfeld, lyrics by E. Y. Harburg, songs that include "Brother, Can You Spare a Dime" (music by Gorney), 77 perfs.; *Music in the Air* 11/8 at the Alvin Theater, with Al Shean, Vienna-born actor Walter Slezak, 30, music by Jerome Kern, lyrics by Oscar Hammerstein II, songs that include "I've Told Every Little Star," 334 perfs.; *Take a Chance* 11/26 at the Apollo Theater, with Jack Haley, Ethel Merman, Brooklyn-born comedian Sid Silvers, 33, book by B. G. DeSylva, music by Nacio Herb Brown, Vincent Youmans, and Richard Whiting, lyrics by DeSylva, songs that include "You're an Old Smoothie," 243 perfs.; *Gay Divorce* 11/29 at the Ethel Barrymore Theater, with Fred Astaire, Claire Luce, music and lyrics by Cole Porter, songs that include "Night and Day," 248 perfs.; *Walk a Little Faster* 12/7 at the St. James Theater, with Beatrice Lillie, Bobby Clark, music by Vernon Duke, lyrics by E. Y. Harburg, songs that include "April in Paris," "That's Life," 119 perfs.

Florenz Ziegfeld dies of a heart attack at Hollywood July 22 at age 63. He lost his fortune in the 1929 Wall Street crash, has never recovered, and leaves his widow, Billie Burke, now 46, with a mountain of debts (see Broadway musicals, 1934).

Radio City Music Hall opens December 27 at 160 Sixth Avenue in Rockefeller Center with 6,200 seats (the number will later be reduced to 5,874). Designed by Art Deco interior designer Donald Deskey and initially called the International Music Hall, its grand foyer is covered from floor to ceiling in mirrors and draperies, extends fully a city block long (60 feet long, 60 feet wide), boasts a grand staircase, has a 24-carat gold leaf ceiling, and is lighted by two 29-foot-long chandeliers. A 100-piece orchestra and the mighty Wurlitzer organ accompany vaudeville acts on a 144-foot-wide stage that has a turntable 43 feet in diameter and three cross sections that can be raised or lowered independently with an innovative hydraulic system (naval architects will use it as the model for systems on aircraft carriers). The organ built by Rudolf Wurlitzer is the largest and most versatile ever made, with steel and wood pipes ranging in size from 32 feet high to half the size of a pencil, and experts say it would take 3,000 musicians to duplicate all the instrumental sounds and tones generated from its console keyboards. Staff pianist is Richmond Hill-born prodigy Morton Gould, 19. Showman S. L. "Roxy" Rothafel has hired acts that include Martha Graham's ballet troupe, but much of the capacity crowd that attends the opening night of the world's largest indoor theater leaves long before the show ends at 2 o'clock in the morning (by that time Rothafel has collapsed backstage and been taken to the hospital); at $2.75 per ticket the Music Hall fails to attract crowds (see films, 1933).

Popular songs: "On a Roof in Manhattan," "Say It Isn't So," and "How Deep Is the Ocean" by Irving Berlin.

Jack Sharkey regains the world heavyweight boxing title June 21 by a 15-round decision over Max Schmeling at the new Garden Bowl in Long Island City. "We wuz robbed!" cries Schmeling's manager Joe Jacobs.

Ellsworth Vines wins in men's singles at Forest Hills, Helen Hull Jacobs, 23, in women's singles.

The New York Yankees win the World Series, defeating the Chicago Cubs 4 to 0. With the third game tied 4 to 4 October 1 and two strikes against him, Babe Ruth leers at his hecklers, allegedly points to the flagpole at the right of the scoreboard in center field, and hits the next pitch out of Wrigley Field. Ruth gets five hits in the series, including two home runs; Lou Gehrig nine hits, including a double and three home runs; second baseman Tony Lazzeri five hits, including two home runs.

Revlon is founded March 1 by New York cosmetics salesman Charles Revson, 26, with his brother Joseph, 28, and chemist Charles Lachman, 35. His employer Elka Cosmetics has rejected the younger Revson's ultimatum that he be made national distributor, he has rented a loft in the New York garment district, borrowed $300 at 2 percent interest per month, and with Lachman's help develops a superior opaque nail enamel that he promotes with exotic names such as Tropic Sky rather than with the descriptive identifications dark red, medium red, pink, etc., that have been traditional. Focusing on beauty salons, Revlon uses intimidation to obtain distribution. Volume for the first 10 months is only $4,055.09, but Revson will start selling through drugstores in 1937, employing salesmen who "accidentally" destroy displays set up by the competition; by 1941 Revlon will have a virtual monopoly on beauty salon sales.

Hartz Mountain Industries is founded by German-born entrepreneur Max Stern, 33, who arrived at New York 6 years ago with 5,000 singing canaries. His company will grow to supply millions of canaries, parakeets, hamsters, tropical fish, and goldfish, becoming the world's largest manufacturer of pet foods and pet supplies.

Gangster Vincent "Mad Dog" Coll is gunned down at 12:45 o'clock in the morning of February 8 while making a telephone call from a drugstore in 23rd Street near Eighth Avenue (rival gang leaders have reportedly offered $50,000 for Coll's death). *Daily Mirror* gossip columnist Walter Winchell has been predicting the murder of Coll, who has challenged his former employer Dutch Schultz for control of the uptown beer business and has accidentally killed a 5-year-old boy in East 107th Street and wounded four other children in a failed attempt on Schultz's life. Winchell gets protection from gunmen employed by speakeasy owner Owney Madden but asks for police protection February 12 (the police at the West 47th Street precinct house say he appears "nervous and in genuine fear for his life"), and the *Mirror* hires someone else for a few months to report gossip; his radio sponsor hires Louis Sobol to pinch-hit for him in Winchell's absence.

Brooklyn-born bank robber William Francis "Willie the Actor" Sutton, Jr., 31, escapes from prison. He embarked on his criminal career 5 years ago and

quickly acquired the nickname "the actor," a reference to his many costumes and disguises (*see* 1948).

The 67-story Cities Service Building (later the American International Building) is completed at 70 Pine Street, between Pearl and Cedar streets, for oil-and-gas baron Henry L. Doherty, now 62. Designed in Art Deco style by Clinton & Russell, Holton & George with a glass-enclosed observation room and tiny outside balconies at its top, the building rises 952 feet high, has an aerial bridge that connects it to 60 Wall Street, and at the outset uses the name 60 Wall Tower. Instead of having 11 elevator shafts, it has only eight, employing double-deck cabs to save $200,000 in construction costs and free up an extra 40,000 square feet of floor space that can be rented for $3.50 per square foot.

The 28-story Insurance Company of North America Building is completed at 99 John Street, between Gold and Cliff streets, to Art Deco designs by Lamb & Harmon. It will later house the AIG Group.

The 50-story Irving Trust Co. Building is completed at 1 Wall Street, southeast corner Broadway. Designed in Art Deco style by Ralph Walker of Voorhees, Gmelin & Walker, the limestone-sheathed structure occupies the most expensive piece of real estate in the world and replaces an 18-story Irving Trust Co. building with one having 500,000 square feet of rentable floor space. The banking room off Wall Street has gold, red, and orange mosaics by Hildreth Meière. Some $3 billion in deposits have been shuttled to the new building's three-story-high vault, whose chemical coating is designed to emit a paralyzing gas should it be attacked by a safecracker's blowtorch.

The 28-story American Telephone & Telegraph Co. Long Distance Building is completed at 32 Sixth Avenue, south of Canal Street, to designs by Ralph Walker of Voorhees, Gmelin & Walker. Built in stages over the course of 20 years, the skyscraper has an Art Deco lobby with a mural showing a map with allegorical female figures linked by bundles of golden rays that pass through North America, symbolic of the fact that every telephone call to or from the North American continent is routed through this building. "Telephone wires and radio unite to make neighbors of nations," reads the mural's legend, and a ceiling mural has mosaic rays linking Notre Dame Cathedral with pyramids, a kangaroo, and a pagoda.

The Port Authority Building opens at 111 Eighth Avenue, between Eighth and Ninth avenues from 15th to 16th streets in Chelsea. Cass Gilbert, now 73, has designed the 15-story structure with 2.3 million square feet of rentable floor space. It will house the Port Authority's offices until 1973.

The Knickerbocker Laundry Building opens in Long Island City on 37th Avenue between 43rd and 48th streets, facing the Long Island Rail Road tracks. Mechanical refrigeration has reduced demand for ice delivery and Knickerbocker Ice Co. has diversified into the laundry business; it has engaged Irving Fenischel to design the modernistic two-story structure.

Wage agreements of most unions in the building trades expire May 1; canny builders wait until after that date to award contracts, knowing they can be negotiated at lower rates.

The 52-year-old Cosmopolitan Club moves into a new building at 122 East 66th Street designed by Thomas Harlan Elett with a cast-iron balcony reminiscent of New Orleans.

The city's last great mansion is completed at 56 East 93rd Street with 40 rooms for William G. Loew. Designed by Walker & Gillette, it will be acquired by showman Billy Rose, will later become the Smithers Alcoholism Center of St. Luke's-Roosevelt Hospital, and still later will house the Spence School.

Homeless New Yorkers establish a "Hoover Village" on the Hudson River at 74th Street.

The New York Central allows the Waldorf-Astoria to stop its amortization payments until business improves, with the amounts to be paid at that time with interest. The Central will make the same arrangement next year (see 1931). The Central also agrees to a modification of the hotel's land lease that calls for the railroad to receive hotel revenues (after payment of taxes but before payment of interest and other charges) and apply whatever rentals there are up to the amount of the lease rentals as part payment of the rentals. It gives similar leniency to other hotels built on Central-owned property (see 1949).

Architect J. E. R. Carpenter dies at New York June 11 at age 65; real estate developer-banker Abraham E. Lefcourt at New York November 13 at age 55. His properties were worth more than $10 million 8 years ago, but many of his enterprises have filed for bankruptcy.

 Flushing Meadow Park is dedicated in Corona, Queens, on a site used for decades as a dumping ground (the Corona Dump). F. Scott Fitzgerald described it in his 1925 novel *The Great Gatsby* as "a valley of ashes—a fantastic farm where ashes grow like wheat into ridges and hills and grotesque gardens, where ashes take the form of houses and chimneys and rising smoke and finally, with a transcendent effort, of men who move dimly and already crumbling through the powdery air." One ash heap has risen nearly 100 feet high and been called "Mount Corona," but Parks Commissioner Robert Moses envisions a green belt that will connect Flushing Meadow with Kissena, Cunningham, and Alley Pond parks (see World's Fair, 1939).

 More Americans are hungry or ill-fed than ever before in the nation's history. The usual weekly relief check in May is $6 for a New York family of five.

 Prohibition administrator Andrew McCampbell reports February 5 that Bronx "cordial" shops are selling gin for as little as 50¢/quart, whiskey for $2/quart. Agents take the liquor to a government warehouse at 641 Washington Street, where it is found to be of inferior quality.

Col. Jacob Ruppert builds a $500,000 warehouse on Third Avenue at 91st Street with storage capacity of 500,000 barrels in anticipation of the repeal of Prohibition (see 1933).

Italian-born New York entrepreneur Nicholas D'Agostino, 21, marries Josephine Tucciarone at St. Raymond Church in the Bronx, pools his savings with those of his brother Pasquale, 27, and opens a small grocery store on Manhattan's East Side, launching an enterprise that will grow into a chain of more than two dozen supermarkets.

 The city's first Chock full o' Nuts coffee shops open as William Black, now 36, finds that Depression-strapped consumers can no longer afford shelled nuts and converts his 18 Manhattan nut stands to quick-order luncheonettes (see 1926). He offers 5¢ coffee, whole-wheat-raisin-bread-and-cream-cheese sandwiches for another nickel, does not permit tipping, and will build a chain of 110 units that will continue until 1983, selling soup, frankfurters, pie, and orange drink as well as whole-wheat doughnuts and coffee (see Riese brothers, 1973).

The Algonquin Hotel has labor troubles; when waiters walk off the job at 1 o'clock as the three dining rooms are filling up with luncheon patrons, men at the Algonquin's Round Table, including playwright George S. Kaufman, don waiters' white jackets, the women (including actress Ina Claire) put on frilly aprons, and they all go to work serving lunch to the other patrons, but most of the Round Table's members have left for Hollywood (see 1919).

Ellis Island is turned into a detention center for deportees after 40 years as the nation's chief entry point for immigrants (see 1930). Agents will process immigrants and other arrivals hereafter at piers, border crossings, and, later, airports.

1933 Gov. Lehman is sworn into office at Albany January 1 but omits the traditional reception at the governor's mansion (his sister has just died and the family is in mourning). Bronx party boss Edward J. Flynn celebrates with a party at the De Witt Clinton Hotel, and President-elect Roosevelt, who preceded Lehman as governor, attends; former governor Al Smith leaves early to catch a train for New York. Lehman faces the daunting task of erasing a deficit of more than $100 million in the state treasury; he reappoints Samuel Rosenman to the State Supreme Court, Rosenman wins election to a 14-year term, and he will serve until his resignation in September 1943, adhering to principles of judicial restraint.

Belle Moskowitz dies of heart disease January 2 at age 55 in her apartment at 147 West 94th Street. The newspapers note that as Al Smith's strong right arm she wielded more power than any other woman in the nation, but America's new first lady Eleanor Roosevelt (who was close to Mrs. Moskowitz) will be credited by some with wielding even more.

Rep. Fiorello H. La Guardia of 1932 Norris-La Guardia Act fame unseats Tammany Hall in a special

Fiorello La Guardia became mayor on a Fusion ticket and ran the city for 12 colorful years. LIBRARY OF CONGRESS

mayoralty election that produces a record turnout. Tammany goon squads receive support from toughs working for mobster Dutch Schultz, who has paid $15,000 to get William C. Dodge elected Manhattan district attorney (Dodge wins by 12,000 votes), flying squads of college athletes and Golden Glove boxers recruited by traction heir Clendenin J. Ryan, now 28, mix it up with the Tammany thugs, police make arrests, but the violence is widespread. Running on a Republican-City Fusion ticket, "the little flower" has obtained support from Bronx political boss Edward J. Flynn and receives 868,522 votes as compared with 609,053 for his Recovery Party challenger Joseph McKee. Mayor O'Brien runs third, with 586,672, but the Democrats retain control of the Board of Aldermen.

Leather-goods and shoe salesman James Joseph Lyons, 43, wins election as Bronx borough president on the Democratic Party ticket. Party boss Ed Flynn picked him because he was untainted by past political connections, and Lyons will be reelected six times before retiring in 1961.

Raymond V. (Vail) Ingersoll, 58, wins election as Brooklyn borough president on the Fusion ticket.

President Roosevelt takes office March 4. "All the ills of democracy can be cured by more democracy," says former governor Al Smith in a speech delivered June 27. Smith has not reconciled himself to Roosevelt's victory.

President Roosevelt's secretary of labor is Frances Perkins, now 50, who directed studies of female and child labor as executive secretary of the Consumers League of New York from 1910 to 1912. She is the first woman Cabinet member and for the next 12 years will oversee an unprecedented program of government interest in labor while the trade-union movement gains power and political influence.

The Chinese Hand Laundry Alliance of New York is founded April 23 to protest a new ordinance requiring that the city's Chinese hand laundries shut down. It forces revocation of the ordinance and will be the leading force in the fight to obtain civil, economic, and political rights for laundry workers.

President Roosevelt establishes a National Labor Board August 5 under the NRA to enforce the right of collective bargaining under the chairmanship of German-born U.S. Sen. Robert F. Wagner, 56 (D. N.Y.) (*see* NLRB, 1934; Wagner Act, 1935).

The International Rescue Committee opens its first office July 24 at 11 West 42nd Street. Bavarian-born physicist Albert Einstein, 54, has fled to New York from Nazi Germany and founded the Committee, whose volunteers work in a room at the Marseilles Hotel to bring out refugees from German-occupied France. Theologian Reinhold Niebuhr will soon head the IRC (see Cherne, 1951).

$ "The only thing we have to fear is fear itself," says President Roosevelt in his inaugural address March 4, but more than 15 million Americans are out of work and even those with jobs have had their wages and hours reduced. Wage-earner incomes are 40 percent below 1929 levels.

New York banks close following President Roosevelt's March 5 proclamation of a nationwide bank holiday. The Emergency Banking Act passed by Congress March 6 gives the president control over banking transactions and foreign exchange, forbids hoarding or export of gold, and authorizes banks to open as soon as examiners determine them solvent. Banks begin to reopen March 13; about 75 percent are open by March 16.

New York financial institutions come to an agreement (the "Bankers' Agreement") with a city verging on bankruptcy. Property owners account for more than 80 percent of the city's tax revenues and have in many cases been unable to meet their tax obligations, forcing the city to borrow from banks in order to pay its bills. Under the agreement, the city will commit its tax revenues to pay off its bank loans, and will levy a new tax on utilities to provide unemployment benefits (see 1896; 1934).

Patrick Cardinal Hayes of New York sponsors a Catholic Industrial Conference to seek solutions to the problem of mass unemployment.

The Glass-Steagall Act signed into law by President Roosevelt June 16 forbids banks to deal in stocks and bonds (J. P. Morgan & Co. will split off Morgan Stanley in 1935 to comply) and insures bank deposits. Most bankers denounce the new law.

A National Industrial Recovery Act (NIRA) passed by Congress June 16 provides for "codes of fair competition" in industries and for collective bargaining with labor, whose unions have dropped in membership from 3.5 million to less than 3 million. Industrial companies agree to shorten working hours and in some cases limit production and fix prices.

Wall Street's Dow Jones Industrial Average drops 7.55 points (7.84 percent) July 21, its seventh worst day yet.

The first NRA Blue Eagle signs of co-operation with the National Recovery Administration appear in store and factory windows August 1: "We Do Our Part." President Roosevelt has appointed Edward J. Flynn regional administrator of NRA public works, and Grover Whalen unfurls an NRA (National Recovery Administration) flag over the RCA Building in Rockefeller Center September 11. Communists hold an anti-NRA rally September 12, but Mayor O'Brien declares September 13 a half holiday (President's NRA Day), stores close, and traffic is paralyzed as 250,000 New Yorkers march in support of the NRA while 73 airplanes fly over the parade route; 1.5 million watch the parade (but see court decision, 1935).

Dun & Bradstreet is created by a merger of New York's 92-year-old R. G. Dun & Co. and 84-year-old Bradstreet Co. (taken over in 1859 by Robert Graham Dun, Dun has published Dun's Review since 1893). The new mercantile agency will provide financial data and credit ratings of U.S. business firms and business executives, many of them now in dire straits.

Allen & Co. is founded by Wall Street speculator-turned-investment banker Charles Allen, Jr., 30, who buys up securities at bargain prices and will become known as the shy Midas of Wall Street. Raised in a Manhattan tenement, Allen dropped out of Commerce High School at age 15 to become a runner on the New York Stock Exchange; by age 19 he had a stake of $1,000 and was using two telephones to trade bonds. His brother Herbert, now 25, joined him in 1928, they reportedly made $1 million in 1929, promptly lost it, and will finance a number of major company startups.

Wall Street's Dow Jones Industrial Average closes December 30 at 99.90, up from 59.93 at the end of 1932.

Commonwealth & Southern Co. lawyer Wendell L. Willkie succeeds founder Bernard C. Cobb as president of the giant utilities holding company (see 1929). Now 44, Willkie will guide the company effectively through the Depression, but he begins attacking President Roosevelt's New Deal policies on grounds that they represent unwarranted federal intrusion into private enterprise.

The S.S. Europa of the North German-Lloyd Line crosses from Cherbourg to New York in 4 days, 16 hours, 48 minutes, averaging 27.92 knots to break the transatlantic speed record set by her sister ship S.S. Bremen in 1929.

The Italian Line's new passenger liner S.S. Rex averages 28.92 knots to set a new transatlantic speed record, crossing from Cherbourg to New York in 4 days, 13 hours, 58 minutes. Built at Genoa on orders from Benito Mussolini, she carries 2,100 passengers.

Grand Central Parkway and its Northern State Parkway extension open July 15 with dedication ceremonies; Gov. Lehman says, "The day is now in sight when the borough of Queens will no longer be the bottleneck choking the traffic which leads from the city to eastern Long Island. What we are doing here today, my friends, is to celebrate the beginning of the end of the isolation of Long Island . . . When the parkway system is completed, Queens will have 30 miles of express parkways. The entire project will amount to an assessment of more than $32 million. I don't know of any other community in the world with a population of more than a million where you can motor at a speed of 40 miles an hour without stopping for one red light." The Grand Central Parkway extends from Kew Gardens to the boundary of Nassau County and will be extended in 1935 via the Interborough Parkway to Pennsylvania Avenue in East New York, using federal funds obtained as part of the national Public Works Program. The Northern State Parkway has been under construction since 1931; extending initially to Willis Avenue it, along with the Grand Central Parkway, has thus far cost $11 million, much of it ($4.5 million) for construction (land for Grand Central Parkway alone has cost $6 million, twice the original estimate). Grand Central Parkway has been built without destroying any houses since it uses part of the old Union Turnpike roadbed, but Commissioner Robert Moses has built the 12-mile Northern State Parkway through Long Island estates and farms, rejecting suggestions for alternate routes (and, as it will later turn out, making deals with some millionaire estate owners, accepting a $10,000 political campaign contribution from financier Otto Kahn [who has married one of his nieces], to find a route that will not interfere with the private 18-hole golf course Kahn has had built on his Cold Spring Harbor estate).

The A train goes into service on the city's new IND (Independent) subway line. The express will be extended from 207th Street in Manhattan to Far Rockaway or Lefferts Boulevard—a journey of 100 minutes for 5¢ (see 1932; song, 1941). The Independent begins service also on trains that will later be called the D and the F, the D going between 205th Street in the Bronx and Coney Island's Stillwell Avenue, the F between 179th Street in Jamaica and Manhattan and thence to Coney Island's Stillwell Avenue, both 85-minute journeys for 5¢. IND trains are faster than those of the BMT or IRT because the city was able to use its power of eminent domain to

tunnel straight through property that builders of the BMT and IRT were obliged to skirt.

The Rev. Charles H. Parkhurst dies at New York September 8 at age 91 (walking in his sleep, as he has all his life, he has fallen from the roof of a second-story porch). He retired from the Madison Square Presbyterian Church in 1918 and married his secretary at age 85.

Prussian-born Evangelical Lutheran minister and philosopher Paul (Johannes) Tillich flees Nazi Germany at age 47 and joins the faculty of the Union Theological Seminary as professor of philosophy and theology. The first non-Jew to be dismissed from a German university, he will remain at UTS until 1954.

Educator and religious leader Felix Adler of the Ethical Culture Society dies at New York April 24 at age 81. The Society's Fieldston Lower School opens on the 5-year-old Riverdale campus for preschoolers through sixth grade, while the Ethical Culture School continues to operate at the Society's building on Central Park West.

Brooklyn Technical High School reopens in September at 29 Fort Greene Place (see 1922). Built at a cost of $5 million (no other U.S. school building has ever cost so much), the nine-story structure occupies the block between South Eliot Place and Fort Greene Place. Only students who have passed a strict entrance examination are admitted, and Brooklyn Tech will vie with Stuyvesant and Bronx Science to be the best public school in the city.

IBM enters the typewriter business by acquiring a firm that has been trying for 10 years to perfect an electric office typewriter (see 1924). Once part of Northeast Electric Co., Electromatic Typewriters has become independent (see IBM Selectric, 1961).

The Tribune syndicate sells its weekly "So This Is New York" column by Herald Tribune writer Lucius M. Beebe to about eight out-of-town papers (see 1929). The Trib will begin running the column itself under a different name next year.

Newsweek magazine has its beginnings in a weekly newsmagazine published at New York February 17 under the name News-Week by English-born journalist Thomas J. C. (John Cardel) Martyn, who has created the magazine to rival Henry Luce's 10-year-old Time (see 1937; 1961).

The New Yorker publishes its first Whitney Darrow, Jr. cartoon March 18. Now 23, Darrow in the next 49 years will produce more than 1,500 witty drawings for the magazine, many of them related to the negotiations between black-tied sugar daddies and their wide-eyed mistresses.

The *Catholic Worker* begins publication at New York in May with the aim of uniting workers and intellectuals in joint, non-violent efforts to improve farming, education, and social conditions. Founder Dorothy Day, now 36, has since 1922 supervised Maryhouse, a shelter at 55 East 3rd Street, and published a penny newspaper that expresses her religious commitment to human rights. (Day retreats in summer to a beach bungalow on Staten Island where she has lived with her common-law husband, Forster Batterham.) She receives support from Patrick Cardinal Hayes and from French-born editor Peter Maurin, a self-styled "apostle on the bum" who has developed a program of social reconstruction he calls "the green revolution," opening shelters to house and feed the poor in "houses of hospitality" as the monks did after the fall of the Roman Empire, inducing the poor to return to the land (on Staten Island, at Tivoli, N.Y., and elsewhere) and farm communally. The new 1¢ monthly will be a voice for pacifism, social justice, and personal responsibility to help the poor; it will grow within 3 years to have a circulation of 150,000.

Esquire magazine begins publication at New York in October. Editor-publisher Arnold Gingrich, 29, is a former advertising copywriter who has been editing *Apparel Arts* at Chicago since 1931. Intended initially as a men's fashion quarterly to be distributed through retail stores, *Esquire* publishes a story by Ernest Hemingway in its first issue, features risqué cartoons and drawings by George Petty of scantily clad women, quickly sells out on newsstands despite its high 50¢ cover price, begins monthly publication, and in its first 3 years will sell 10 million copies with help from good writing by prominent authors.

Russian-born public-relations man Benjamin Sonnenberg, 32, acquires the 88-year-old Stuyvesant Fish mansion at 19 Gramercy Park South, southeast corner Irving Place, and it will serve as his main place of business (although he also has offices at 247 Park Avenue, with a chauffeur-driven Rolls-Royce outside—a Packard touring car in summer months). Brought to America by his family in 1910, he attended Columbia for a year and worked briefly as a newspaperman at Flint, Mich., before setting himself up as a freelance New York press agent for nightclubs and hotels; given an opportunity to solicit the business of an industrial client, Sonnenberg borrowed enough money to hire a chauffeured limousine to drive him to the prospect's office, and

has added major companies and individuals to his client list.

A billboard for the new St. Moritz Hotel goes up at Fordham Road and Corona Avenue in the Bronx. Alabama-born sign creator Douglas Leigh, 26, has persuaded the owners to advertise on the site, he is paid $50 per month and a room at the hotel (the Central Park South address looks good on his letterhead), and by year's end he has sold the A&P on the idea of putting up a sign with a steaming cup of coffee 15 feet wide at the southeast corner of Seventh Avenue and 47th Street. Leigh will soon have a giant penguin blinking its eyes to promote Kool cigarettes, an animated cartoon for Old Gold cigarettes, a clown tossing quoits in the shape of the three-ring Ballantine Beer logotype, and by 1941 will have created 32 large signs with more than 75,000 light bulbs for Times Square, Columbus Circle, and other venues (*see* 1941).

The American Newspaper Guild is founded at Washington, D.C., in December to protect city room employees. *World-Telegram* reporter Heywood C. Broun, now 45, is elected president.

The 113-year-old Mercantile Library Association gives up the Astor Place location it has occupied since 1854 and moves to a new building at 17 West 47th Street, where it will remain into the 21st century (*see* 1870). Competition from free libraries has shrunk membership to 3,000, but the Association's collection has grown to 230,000 volumes, a number that will be reduced to 150,000.

Nonfiction: *Tammany at Bay* by New York author James E. Finegan; *My Life and Hard Times* by *New Yorker* magazine writer-cartoonist James Thurber.

Fiction: *Miss Lonelyhearts* by Nathanael West; *New York Madness* by Maxwell Bodenheim; *Union Square* by Chicago-born New York novelist Albert Halper, 29, who writes, "Traffic swept around the square. Long before the doors of Klein's Dress Shop opened, crowds of women and girls had gathered. Private policemen in gray uniforms tried to keep order at about nine-thirty, because at that time all the doors were unlocked and the women swept forward in a powerful surge, grabbing at the dresses on the racks, searching and clawing for bargains. It was cash down here, 'on the Square,' each woman held her money in her fist."

The 1922 novel *Ulysses* by Irish writer James Joyce is acceptable for publication in the United States, rules Aiken, S.C.-born Justice John M. (Munro) Woolsey, 56, of the U.S. District Court at New York December 6 (*United States v. One Book Called*

"Ulysses"). The book was serialized in The *Little Review* beginning in 1918 but challenged in a New York court following seizure of the serialized form in 1921. All reputable publishers refused the stream-of-consciousness account of a day (June 16) in the lives of Dubliner Leopold Bloom and his wife Molly (it was judged obscene in Britain as well as in America). Lawyer John Sumner has headed the New York Society for the Suppression of Vice since 1915; less flamboyant than the late Anthony Comstock, whom he considered a religious fanatic, he has assailed Joyce's novel. Postal officials at New York seized and burned 500 copies of the book after it was published as such in 1922, customs officials at New York seized a copy of the book last year as it was being sent to Random House, the press has raised an outcry, and Judge Woolsey decides that the "dirty" words in the book are appropriate in context, not gratuitous. The federal government will lose on appeal in August of next year, and Random House will then publish the first authorized U.S. edition, but the Post Office continues to seize copies of the 1928 D. H. Lawrence novel *Lady Chatterley's Lover* (see 1959). Gotham Book Store proprietor Fanny Steloff imported copies of the banned novel *Lady Chatterley's Lover* directly from its author in the late 1920s (see 1920), will have copies of Henry Miller's banned novel *Tropic of Cancer* smuggled in during the 1930s, ship books as late as 1940 to fill mail orders from James Joyce (she has cofounded the James Joyce Society), sell her store in 1967 to Andreas Brown, but continue to live in a third-floor apartment over the store and preside over the place, making it a rendezvous for bibliophiles (see 1989).

 Painting: *Sun Drawing Water* by Arthur Dove, who has moved to Geneva, N.Y., to settle an estate and will remain there for 5 years.

Mural: *Man at the Crossroads* by Mexican artist Diego Rivera, 46, for the lobby of 30 Rockefeller Center. When officials notice that the 63-by-17-foot mural incorporates a small portrait of V. I. Lenin, Nelson A. Rockefeller asks that it be removed, Rivera refuses, the incident creates a furor in the art world, Rivera is paid in full ($20,000) and dismissed, his mural is destroyed the night of February 10 and its pieces carted away, Rivera uses his fee to pay for the expenses of frescoes that he executes gratis for New York's New Workers School.

Painter-decorator-craftsman Louis Comfort Tiffany dies at New York January 17 at age 84 (his Tiffany Studios filed for bankruptcy last year); painter George Luks dies at New York October 29 at age 66.

Theater: *Design for Living* by Noël Coward 1/24 at the Ethel Barrymore Theater, with Coward, Alfred Lunt, Lynn Fontanne, 135 perfs.; *Alien Corn* by Sidney Howard 2/20 at the Belasco Theater, with Katherine Cornell, 98 perfs.; *Both Your Houses* by Maxwell Anderson 3/6 at the Royale Theater, with Morris Carnovsky, Walter C. Kelly, Mary Phillips, New York-born actor Jerome Cowan, 35, Shepperd Strudwick in a polemic against political corruption, 120 perfs.; *Men in White* by New York playwright Sidney Kingsley (originally Kieschner), 27, 9/26 at the Broadhurst Theater, with Morris Carnovsky, Luther Adler, Elia Kazan, Clifford Odets, 367 perfs.; *Ah, Wilderness* by Eugene O'Neill (his only comedy) 10/2 at the Guild Theater, with George M. Cohan as Nat Miller, William Post, Jr., Elisha Cook, Jr., Gene Lockhart, Philip Moeller, Ruth Gilbert, 289 perfs.; *Mulatto* by Langston Hughes 10/24 at the Vanderbilt Theater, with Rose McClendon, 270 perfs.; *Tobacco Road* by playwright Jack Kirkland, 31, (he has adapted last year's Erskine Caldwell novel) 12/4 at the Masque Theater, with Henry Hull as Jeeter Lester, 3,182 perfs.; *Twentieth Century* by Ben Hecht and Charles MacArthur 12/29 at the Broadhurst Theater, with Eugenie Leontovich as Lilly Garland, Moffat Johnston as Oscar Jaffe, 152 perfs.

Playwright Wilson Mizner dies of a heart ailment at age 56 April 3 in his apartment at Hollywood's Ambassador Hotel (he turned to writing screenplays 6 years ago with the advent of sound films); playwright Winchell Smith dies of cancer at Farmington, Conn., June 10 at age 62; theater architect and scenic designer Joseph Urban of a heart attack in his suite at the St. Regis Hotel July 10 at age 61; playwright-story writer Ring Lardner at East Hampton September 25 at age 48; actor Edward H. Sothern at New York October 28 at age 73.

Radio: *The Manhattan Merry-go-Round* on NBC's Blue Network is a 30-minute Sunday-evening musical show created by Chicago soap-opera writers Frank Hummert and his wife, Ann. It will take listeners to nightspots such as Billy Rose's Diamond Horseshoe and the Stork Club with guests who will include Jimmy Durante and Beatrice Lillie (to 1949).

Films: George Cukor's *Dinner at Eight* with Marie Dressler, John Barrymore, Wallace Beery, Jean Harlow; Frank Capra's *Lady for a Day* with Warren Williams, May Robson, based on the Damon Runyon story "Madame La Glimp;" Lowell Sherman's *Morning Glory* with Katharine Hepburn, Adolphe Menjou, Douglas Fairbanks, Jr. (originally Douglas Elton Ulman, Jr.). Also: Alfred E. Green's *Baby Face* with

Barbara Stanwyck (as an Erie, Pa., speakeasy bartender's daughter who sleeps her way to the top of a New York bank and then says, "What could I do? He's my boss, and I had to earn my living"), George Brent, Donald Cook; Raoul Walsh's *The Bowery* with Wallace Beery, George Raft, Jackie Cooper, Fay Wray; Lewis Milestone's *Hallelujah, I'm a Bum* with Al Jolson, Madge Evans, Frank Morgan, Harry Langdon, songs by Rodgers and Hart, script by Ben Hecht and S. N. Behrman; Mervin C. Cooper and Ernest B. Schoedsack's *King Kong* with Fay Wray, Robert Armstrong, Bruce Cabot, and a final sequence showing a monster ape swatting at fighter planes from atop the 2-year-old Empire State Building.

Actor Fatty Arbuckle dies of a heart attack at New York's Park Central Hotel June 29 at age 46 (three juries acquitted him of any wrongdoing in connection with a 1921 San Francisco scandal but bad publicity ended his career). Frank E. Campbell handles Arbuckle's funeral.

John D. Rockefeller, Jr. hires Broadway producer-songwriter John Murray Anderson, now 46, as director of Radio City Music Hall and then hires Kansas City-born vaudeville and movie-house treasurer Gustav S. "Gus" Eyssell, now 33, who transforms the Music Hall from a vaudeville house to a movie palace (*see* 1932). Frank Capra's *The Bitter Tea of General Yen* with Barbara Stanwyck opens December 17, tickets are 35¢ until 1 o'clock, 50¢ in the afternoon, and 75¢ in the evening, with films supplementing the stage shows (two per day). The Music Hall will start booming next year, when Roxy brings over his high-kicking "Roxyette" chorus girls from the Roxy Theater (the first such chorus line, they were organized in 1925 at St. Louis by Russell Markert, now 34, as the Sixteen Missouri Rockets) and renames them "Rockettes" (*see* 1978).

Film musical: Lloyd Bacon's *42nd Street* with Warner Baxter, Bebe Daniels, Dick Powell, dancer Ruby Keeler, George Brent, music and lyrics by Al Dubin and Harry Warren, songs that include "Shuffle Off to Buffalo" and "You're Getting to Be a Habit with Me."

Broadway musicals: *Strike Me Pink* 3/4 at the Majestic Theater, with Mexican-born singer Lupe (originally Maria Guadalupe Villalobos) Velez, 24, Jimmy Durante, Hope Williams, music by Ray Henderson, lyrics by B. G. DeSylva and Lew Brown, 105 perfs.; *As Thousands Cheer* 9/30 at the Music Box Theater, with Marilyn Miller, Clifton Webb, Ethel Waters, book by Irving Berlin and Moss Hart, music and lyrics by Berlin, Edward Heyman, and Richard Myers, songs that include "Easter Parade," 400 perfs.; *Let 'Em Eat Cake* by George S. Kaufman and Morrie Ryskind

10/21 at the Imperial Theater, with William Gaxton as John P. Wintergreen, Victor Moore as Alexander Throttlebottom, music by George Gershwin, lyrics by Ira Gershwin (George moves into a 14-room apartment with art studio and gymnasium at 125 East 72nd Street, Ira lives across the street and a direct telephone line connects the two apartments to facilitate their collaboration), 90 perfs.; *Roberta* (initially *Gowns by Roberta*) 11/18 at the New Ambassadors Theater, with Ray Middleton, 25, New Haven, Conn.-born comedian George Murphy, 31, Bob Hope, vaudeville veteran Fay Templeton, now 67 (who introduces the song "Yesterdays"), dancer Tamara Geva, English-born actor Sydney Greenstreet, 53, music by Jerome Kern, lyrics by Otto Harbach, songs that include "Smoke Gets in Your Eyes," "The Touch of Your Hand," ("Lovely to Look At" will be added for a 1935 film version), 295 perfs.

Popular songs: "Sophisticated Lady" by Duke Ellington, lyrics by Irving Mills, Mitchell Parish; "Minnie the Moocher" by Rochester-born bandleader Cabell "Cab" Calloway, 26, who plays at gangster Owney Madden's Cotton Club in Harlem (where only white patrons are admitted), lyrics by Irving Mills (when Calloway forgets the lyrics, he "scat" sings "Hi-de-hi-hi" and gets an enthusiastic audience response); "I Gotta Get Back to New York" by Richard Rodgers, lyrics by Lorenz Hart.

Lousiana-born jazz trumpeter Henry James "Red" Allen, Jr., 25, joins the Fletcher Henderson Orchestra in June as the group's lead soloist. He will play with various other ensembles in the next few decades, playing with Cab Calloway, Duke Ellington, Eddie Condon, Coleman Hawkins, Kid Ory, Joe Bushkin, Joe Marsala, Teddy Wilson, James P. Johnson, Louis Armstrong, Benny Goodman, Jelly Roll Morton, Art Tatum, Jack Teagarden, J. C. Higginbotham, and other prominent musicians.

The New York Rangers win their second National Hockey League (NHL) championship. Still coached by Lester Patrick, they take the Stanley Cup away from the Toronto Maple Leafs.

Former world heavyweight boxing champion James J. Corbett dies at Bayside, Queens, February 18 at age 66.

Italian-born prizefighter Primo Carnera, 26, of Argentina wins the world heavyweight title June 29. The 260-pound fighter knocks out Jack Sharkey in the sixth round of a championship bout at Long Island City.

Frederick J. "Fred" Perry, 24, (Br) wins in men's singles at Forest Hills, Helen Hull Jacobs in women's singles (Helen Wills Moody, her opponent, retires with a back injury while trailing by 8-6, 3-6, 3-0, her first loss on any court since 1926).

The New York Giants win the World Series, defeating the Washington Senators 4 games to 1. First baseman Bill Terry, 34, gets six hits, including a double and a 10th-inning home run in the final game; outfielder Melvin Thomas "Mel" Ott, 24, seven hits, including two home runs. Pitcher Carl Hubbell, 30, wins the first and fourth games with an ERA of 0.00.

Philip Morris cigarettes are introduced in the United States. Hired by the 16-year-old Milton Biow advertising agency, four-foot page boy Johnny Roventini, 22, of the 3-year-old Hotel New Yorker delivers the "Call for Phil-lip Mor-ris" slogan over a portion of Ferde Grofé's 2-year-old *Grand Canyon Suite* on radio stations April 17 and will continue to promote the brand for 20 years.

Bootlegger Waxey Gordon (Irving Wexler), 42, is convicted of tax evasion December 1 in a Manhattan federal court. A onetime pickpocket who got his nickname because he could remove a wallet as if it were coated with wax (his first arrest for the felony was in 1905 when he was 17), Gordon allied himself with the late racketeer Arnold Rothstein in narcotics dealing and prostitution as well as bootlegging, has owned large distilleries and breweries in New York and Philadelphia, and has been living high off the hog although his reported net income for 1930 was only $8,100. He has paid off police to avoid arrest while violating laws right and left, former New York County district attorney Thomas C. T. Crain announced he was starting an investigation of Gordon but then reported that no witnesses could be found to testify against him. Owosso, Mich.-born Manhattan district attorney Thomas E. (Edmund) Dewey, 31, has pursued the case, and his detectives have arrested Gordon at his summer cottage in the Catskills, possibly on information supplied by his underworld rivals Meyer Lansky and Charles "Lucky" Luciano. It was stated in his indictment that Gordon's actual income for 1930 was $1,338,000 and for 1931 $1,026,000. U.S. Attorney George Z. Medalie was to have prosecuted the case but resigned November 1, Dewey has taken over, and he has presented 131 witnesses over the course of 9 days with more than 900 exhibits. The jury finds Gordon guilty on four counts, Judge Frank J. Coleman fines him $80,000 and sentences him to 10 years' imprisonment in the federal penitentiary at Atlanta, and he will be released from Leavenworth Prison in 1940 after serving 7 (see 1951).

The 70-story RCA Building (GE Building beginning in 1990) opens in May at 30 Rockefeller Plaza as Rockefeller Center construction proceeds under the direction of Reinhard and Hofmeister, Corbett Harrison and MacMurray, and Hood and Fouilhoux, who will design all the Center buildings put up in this decade. Rising from a four-foot granite base with 2.3 million square feet of office space, the Art Deco, aluminum-trimmed limestone tower has been designed by architect John B. Sanger, 41, it soars 850 feet into the air, and it will be the largest commercial office building in the world until 1963, but the work on it is still short of completion. The small British building opens in May, La Maison Française in September, both on Fifth Avenue.

The 97-year-old Union Club closes its Fifth Avenue palazzo May 19 and moves in August into a Georgian granite-and-limestone air-conditioned clubhouse, designed by Delano & Aldrich, at the northeast corner of Park Avenue and 69th Street (see 1927). The club's members number roughly 900, averaging 50 years of age (22 percent live out of town); it added an adjacent, smaller plot of land next to the Redmond house and after paying off the mortgage on its old building had roughly $1.5 million to build a new one. Unlike its former premises, the new clubhouse has squash courts (three of them), and the chairs in the main lounge face away from the windows. The main floor also has a backgammon room; the banquet and dining rooms are on the second floor, along with a lounge and assembly rooms; the third floor has a balcony and houses a 16,000-volume library along with the club's "eternal light" memorial to its war dead; bedrooms occupy the fourth floor; the fifth contains the squash courts, dressing-room cubicles, and a wicker-furnished lounge; billiard and pool rooms, a barbershop, and the bar (an oyster bar until Prohibition is repealed in December); the Otis elevators have telephones in order that a member en route to or from the fifth-floor squash courts may take a call and transact business on the spot. Only a discreet "UC" over the door identifies the building for what it is.

Vogue magazine runs an article entitled, "The Rise of the Walkup." People who once lived in Fifth Avenue town houses or Park Avenue apartments have moved into tenements, says *Vogue*, and praises them for "living gallantly in simplicity and liking it."

"Hard Luck Town" on the East River at 9th Street is a shantytown that houses 450 people, mostly men, in what has been called a "Hooverville." Even more of the city's homeless live in the Hooverville of jerry-built shacks set up in what used to be Central Park's

Lower Reservoir (soon to be the Great Lawn), drained in 1929 and turned over to the Parks Department.

Architect and painter Charles A. Platt dies at Cornish, N.Y., September 12 at age 71.

The 3-year-old Barbizon-Plaza Hotel in West 58th Street off Sixth Avenue files for bankruptcy and is sold for $2,500 in cash to a buyer who assumes its debts of nearly $6 million (it is actually worth $10 million). A room and bath go for as little as $3 per night, or $17 per week, including a Continental breakfast delivered to the room; weekly rates for a living room-bedroom-bath-serving pantry suite begin at $45. The Barbizon will remain a hotel until 1985 before being converted into a luxury apartment building.

 Lowell, Mass.-born New York entrepreneur Jacob M. Kaplan, 40, acquires a small winery at Brocton, N.Y., and sets out to revive the upstate grape industry, establishing a floor price of $50/ton and guaranteeing the price before the grapes are picked. Having prospered in West Indian sugar and rum ventures during Prohibition, Kaplan hires chemists and mechanical engineers to produce a uniform beverage efficiently and economically and encourages growers to improve their vineyards, concentrating on Concord grapes. Kaplan will acquire Welch Grape Juice Co. in 1945, modernize it, and later sell it to the farmers (see philanthropy, 1947).

Sales of 3.2 beer (3.2 percent alcohol) are legalized after 14 years of Prohibition and the world's longest beer bar opens with an outdoor beer garden in September just south of Grand Central Terminal on the site of the old Belmont Hotel that was torn down 2 years ago. Manhattan's Ruppert Brewery has obtained a license May 25 to resume production, the first license granted in the state by the Alcoholic Beverage Control Board. Rudolph Schaefer, Jr. of F. & M. Schaefer Brewing Co. has anticipated Repeal by launching an advertising campaign with the slogan, "Our hand has never lost its skill" (see 1935).

The prohibition against sale of alcoholic beverages that began early in 1920 ends December 5 as Utah becomes the 36th state to ratify the Twenty-First Amendment repealing the 18th Amendment after an estimated 1.4 billion gallons of hard liquor have been sold illegally. "Texas" Guinan has died of an internal infection at Vancouver, B.C., November 5 at age 49, leaving an estate of only $28,173, although she is known to have banked well over $1 million in the mid-1920s (see 1922).

 Gallagher's Steak House opens in May at 228 West 52nd Street, with steak, a baked potato, and salad for $1.75 but with nothing stronger than 3.2 beer until December. The proprietors are former *Ziegfeld Follies* girl Helen Gallagher, widow of vaudevillian Ed Gallager of Gallagher and Shean fame, and her second husband, Jack Solomon, who has persuaded her to leave the stage and open the restaurant with him. It will be famous for its sawdust floor and for serving just five appetizers, two soups, five entrées (sirloin steak, broiled lobster, roast beef, hamburger, and chicken), a few cold meats, five vegetables, two salads, homemade pies, and four or five other desserts (including rice pudding) and cheeses.

Patsy's pizzeria opens in East Harlem under the direction of Pasquale "Patsy" Lancieri, who may have trained under Gennaro Lombardi in Spring Street.

Luchow's in 14th Street is the first New York restaurant to obtain a liquor license after Repeal of Prohibition (see 1882). Patrons resume their enjoyment of *wienerschnitzel* and *hasenpfeffer* at Bock Beer festivals, May wine festivals, Somerfests, and Oktoberfests.

The Stork Club reopens with a liquor license in a five-story town house at 53½ East 51st Street (see 1929). A union controlled by mob boss Dutch Schultz runs Sherman Billingsley's dining room and harrasses him for payoffs, but Billingsley gets police protection, fires the employees, recruits new people, and will move next year to larger premises at 3 East 53rd Street, where his exclusive Cub Room will attract celebrities such as Walter Winchell and Damon Runyon (who will frequently sit together at Table 50 with host Billingsley) (see 1965).

1934 Mayor La Guardia assumes office January 1 with the city bankrupt and more than 400,000 families on one form of relief or another—one sixth of the city's population, a number greater than the entire population of Los Angeles. Having taken his oath of office just after midnight in the library of Judge Samuel Seabury's town house, La Guardia appoints former State Bridge and Tunnel Commission counsel Paul Windels corporation counsel for the city.

Former Manhattan district attorney William Travers Jerome dies of pneumonia at his 125 East 36th Street town house February 13 at age 74.

Gov. Lehman wins reelection, defeating his Republican challenger Robert Moses, who has antagonized Jewish voters by denying his roots at a time when they are agonizing about the fate of fellow Jews in Nazi Germany. Lehman receives 2,201,729 votes, Parks Commissioner Moses 1,393,638 (35 percent

Fifth Avenue's double-decker buses went up Riverside Drive, charging 10¢ instead of a nickel. LIBRARY OF CONGRESS

of all votes cast—the lowest percentage for any major-party gubernatorial candidate in the state's 157-year history). Moses has never been elected to public office and never will be, but he is appointed to 6-year terms and will wield more power in his 44-year career than any governor or mayor.

$ Last year's "Bankers' Agreement" takes effect January 1, putting the city under sharp restraints with regard to taxation and discretionary spending (it will remain in effect through 1937). Mayor La Guardia goes to Albany with his aides January 10 to present detailed reports on the city's financial condition. The city has technically been in default since mid-December on revenue bills totaling $4.5 million, security holders are pressing for payment, and unless the city receives help the bankers may renege on their 4-year agreement, and Washington will withhold vital loans. La Guardia has the backing of the Citizens Union and of the City Club, headed by John Haynes Holmes and Rabbi Stephen S. Wise. The mayor embarks on a cost-cutting crusade, slashing salaries and dismissing Tammany Hall hacks from sinecures despite objections from lobbyist Frank J. Prial and pressure from higher-ups.

The city establishes a business tax of less than 1 percent and a sales tax of 2 percent. The sales tax is intended as a temporary measure but will in fact be raised eventually to 4 percent and remain permanent, despite objections that it is regressive (people with low incomes have to spend a far greater percentage of their incomes on items subject to sales tax; suburbanites will escape sales taxes by having purchases made in the city delivered without charge to their out-of-town addresses) (*see* city income tax, 1966).

Speculator Jesse L. Livermore files for bankruptcy in March (*see* 1929). His lawyer tells a congressional investigating committee that Livermore has been bankrupt four times but has always repaid his creditors 100 cents on the dollar (*see* 1940).

Banker Otto Kahn suffers a heart attack as he sits down to lunch at the Kuhn, Loeb & Co. offices in Manhattan March 29 and dies at age 67.

A Securities and Exchange Commission (SEC) created by Congress June 6 limits bank credit for speculators as it polices the securities industry. Boston-born Wall Street speculator Joseph P. (Patrick) Kennedy, 45, campaigned for Roosevelt in 1932 and is named in July to head the new commission despite opposition from New Dealers and from leading newspapers. (Father of nine, Kennedy moved with his family to Riverdale 7 years ago and to Bronxville the following year; he will hold the SEC post for 431 days before being appoiinted head of the U.S. Maritime Commission.)

The Liberty League formed in August to oppose New Deal economic measures is a bipartisan group whose members include businessmen and politicians such as New York Democrats Alfred E. Smith and John Jacob Raskob.

CS First Boston has its beginnings in the First Boston Corp. founded at New York in June as a joint venture of First National Bank of Boston and Chase National Bank, who are required under the terms of last year's Glass-Steagall Act to separate their investment-banking functions (*see* 1993).

Security Analysis by London-born New York investor Benjamin Graham (originally Grossbaum), 40, and his Columbia University colleague David J. Dodd pioneers modern security analysis; it will remain the standard text for more than 55 years and have sales of more than 100,000 copies. Starting out at $12 per week with a job writing stock and bond prices on a Wall Street brokerage house blackboard, Graham became a partner at Newberger, Henderson & Loeb at age 26, left 2 years later to manage money for private investors (initial capital: $250,000), was a millionaire before age 35, began teaching an investment class at Columbia in 1928, had 150 students by 1929, and declined a partnership that year with Bernard Baruch, having built up the portfolio that he managed to $2.5 million. Emphasizing the importance of a stock's book value—the physical assets of the company issuing the stock—the book aims in part to revive investing in the moribund equities market and enjoys wide popularity.

Wall Street's Dow Jones Industrial Average closes December 31 at 104.04, up from 99.90 at the end of 1933.

Taxi drivers strike from February 6 to March 12. The city has 75,000 drivers operating 19,000 taxis, up from 16,000 in 1923, and the average driver earns only $15 per week, down from $26 in 1929. Various unions try with limited success to organize the drivers in an industry plagued by corruption (see 1932), loan sharks, and racketeers. The Walker administration granted owners a 5¢ fare increase, the drivers have demanded a share of the take, Mayor La Guardia feels the drivers are underpaid, and he invites the pickets to City Hall; warning them against hiring strongmen or gangsters, he advises them to seek leadership from the American Federation of Labor (La Guardia favors the growth of unions in the private sector but opposes them in the public sector). The mayor appoints lawyer Morris L. Ernst as mediator, the strikers meet with Ernst in his office at 285 Madison Avenue, and the drivers complain that a new 5¢ tax on rides has caused meters to be calibrated with a 20¢ minimum fare instead of the previous 15¢, cutting down on their tips and causing former riders to use cheaper forms of transportation. The courts have ruled the new tax unconstitutional, but the city has received $500,000 in taxes; the drivers want it distributed among them, fleet owners demand that they receive 60 percent of it, Ernst rules that it be split 50-50 between drivers and owners, the strikers reject his plan, the mayor says the drivers must know there are "10,000 others waiting to take their places," the strike leaders accept a new plan, the rank-and-file continues to reject settlements, and the strike gets violent, with serious rioting on the nights of March 20 and 21. Drivers manhandle scabs and their passengers, overturn and dismantle taxis, and strew streets with auto parts. A grand jury finds that the mayor has "imposed upon the police department a special obligation of consideration for the striking drivers," La Guardia rebukes the grand jury April 11 and blames fleet owners for the violence, calling them "arbitrary and cruel." The drivers will eventually win a pay increase (see medallions, 1937).

The New York Central stops running freight trains down Tenth Avenue below 30th Street in March after 85 years that have seen Eleventh Avenue and then Tenth called "Death Alley" because of pedestrian fatalities. The West Side Improvement ("High Line") opens in August, with freight trains that carry raw materials for city factories and slaughterhouses rolling from city piers and other sources through an open cut north of 30th Street and on an elevated viaduct to the south, running at the second-floor level atop and through buildings to alleviate congestion on the streets and carrying finished products to the piers for export (see 1980).

Electric traction pioneer Frank J. Sprague dies of pneumonia at New York October 25 at age 77, having developed not only the first trolley cars but also electric elevators and the multiple-unit system for subways and suburban train lines.

The S.S. *Morro Castle* catches fire off Asbury Park, N.J., September 8; the crew cannot put out the flames, the ship sinks, and 134 lives are lost (see education [Merchant Marine Academy], 1943).

The Cunard Line that began in 1839 as the Royal Mail Steam Packet Co. becomes the Cunard-White Star Line by merging with the White Star Line that it acquired in 1927 (see *Queen Mary*, 1936).

A Franklin D. Roosevelt birthday ball staged by public-relations pioneer Carl Byoir January 30 raises $1,029,000 to fight infantile paralysis (poliomyelitis). Byoir will put on such fund-raisers in 3,600 U.S. communities.

Brooklyn's Plymouth Church merges with the Congregational Church of the Pilgrims at the corner of Henry and Remsen streets, ending a rift that occurred 90 years ago.

Columbia University's Butler Library has its beginnings in South Hall, completed to designs by James Gamble Rogers at 114th Street, between Amsterdam Avenue and Broadway. It will become the university's main library, replacing the Seth Low Library of 1897.

The Convent of the Sacred Heart moves to the mansion at 1 East 91st Street formerly occupied by the late financier Otto Kahn. Founded in 1881, the school will expand in 1966, taking over the adjacent Burden house built in 1905, and by 1992 will have an enrollment of 470 girls in classes from kindergarten through high school.

The Mutual Broadcasting Network is created by an amalgamation of New York's WOR, Chicago's WGN, and Detroit's WXYZ (whose *Lone Ranger* is the network's chief early-evening attraction).

Mayor La Guardia threatens to sell the city's 11-year-old municipal radio station WNYC but uses it instead for a weekly broadcast that by 1944 will have an audience of 1.8 million (see 1938; 1945).

Hearst executive Arthur Brisbane takes over the 10-year-old *New York Daily Mirror*, whose columns begin to emphasize news and reportorial "stars" rather than entertainment. Circulation has reached 600,000 (the *Daily News* has more than 1 million).

Comic-strip pioneer Winsor McCay of "Little Nemo" fame dies of a cerebral hemorrhage at Sheepshead Bay July 26 at age 62.

Hill & Knowlton is founded by Indiana-born Cleveland public-relations counsel John Wiley Hill, 43, who moves to New York and takes Don Knowlton into partnership. The new firm will make a reputation in the next few years by counseling large steelmakers faced with labor problems and grow to become the world's largest PR firm.

Public-relations pioneer Ivy Lee dies of a brain tumor at New York November 9 at age 57, having reshaped the public perception of John D. Rockefeller, taught AT&T how to give its monopoly the appearance of a public service, and done more than anyone else to make PR a respected profession.

Challenge magazine begins publication at New York under the direction of Boston-born Harlem writer Dorothy West, 27, who visited the Soviet Union with poet Langston Hughes and 19 other black Americans in 1932 and remained for a year. The quarterly is intended to be a showcase for younger black writers who hope to rekindle the vitality of the Harlem Renaissance, but it will survive only until 1937.

Publisher Frank Nelson Doubleday dies at Coconut Grove, Fla., January 30 at age 72 and his son Nelson, now 44, becomes board chairman of Doubleday, Doran. The Literary Guild is acquired by Doubleday, Doran, which has had a minority interest since 1929. Founded in 1927, the Guild has changed its membership terms and is selling new hardcover books at a flat rate of $2 each plus a few cents' carrying charge. Its new owners will make the Literary Guild and its 5-year-old Junior Guild the basis of an empire that will include two dozen mail-order book clubs.

Crowell-Collier publishers is created by a merger of the 58-year-old Crowell Publishers with the 36-year-old P. F. Collier & Son, whose parent firm is Macmillan. American Macmillan will become publicly owned in 1950, gaining independence from the British firm (*see* Free Press, 1961).

Nonfiction: *The Tin Box Parade: A Handbook for Larceny* by Iowa-born author Milton Mackaye, 33, who has worked as a *New York Evening News* reporter; *City Editor* by Texas-born *Herald Tribune* city editor Stanley Walker, 35; *This Is New York* by Gilbert Seldes, with photographs by Berenice Abbott; *South Street: A Maritime History of New York* by Richard C. McKay;

Exile's Return by Pennsylvania-born New York writer-editor (David) Malcolm Cowley, 36, who lives at 360 West 22nd Street in Chelsea and has put together a chronicle of the 1920s; *A Backward Glance* by Edith Wharton, who says New York is becoming "as much a vanished city as Atlantis or the lowest layer of Schliemann's Troy."

Fiction: *Tender Is the Night* by F. Scott Fitzgerald, whose central character Dick Diver is modeled on former émigré Gerald Murphy, 46, a painter of considerable talent who returned to New York in 1932 to take over management of his late father's Mark Cross luggage and haberdashery shop and save it from bankruptcy; *Appointment in Samarra* by Pennsylvania-born *New Yorker* magazine writer John (Henry) O'Hara, 29; *Summer in Williamsburg* by Brooklyn novelist Daniel Fuchs, 25; *Call It Sleep* by New York novelist Henry Roth, 28, whose book will not gain popularity until the 1960s; *So Red the Rose* by Stark Young; *The Ways of White Folks* (stories) by Langston Hughes; *I Can Get It for You Wholesale* by New York novelist Jerome Weidman, 22, whose comic novel is about the garment district (*see* Broadway musical, 1962); *The Story of a Country Boy* by Dawn Powell; *Tutt for Tutt* by Arthur Train; *The Thin Man* by Dashiell Hammett.

Poetry: *Wine From These Grapes* by Edna St. Vincent Millay.

Sculptor Paul Manship's bronze statue *Prometheus* is installed at the west end of Rockefeller Center's sunken plaza between 49th and 50th streets (*see* ice-skating rink, 1936). It is covered with gold leafing and detractors call it "Leaping Louie." A bronze statue of *Atlas* supporting an armillary globe, by sculptor Lee Lawrie, is installed in front of the International Building at 630 Fifth Avenue, between 50th and 51st streets.

A fine arts exhibition opens in November at Rockefeller Center, where it has been organized by *Art News* publisher Samuel W. Frankel.

Kentucky-born photographers Marvin and Morgan Smith, both 24, open a portrait studio on the second floor of a building a few doors down from Harlem's new Apollo Theater in 125th Street. The identical twin brothers are a sharecropper's sons who arrived by bus at Times Square in September of last year with less than $100 between them and took jobs initially with the Parks Department, cleaning cobblestones taken from Riverside Drive for re-use. In the next 30 years they will make a photographic record of—and socialize with—Harlem celebrities from all walks of life.

Theater: *Days Without End* by Eugene O'Neill 1/18 at Henry Miller's Theater, with Earle Larimore, English actor Stanley Ridges, 32, Ilka Chase, 57 perfs.; *Yellow Jack* by Sidney Howard and Michigan-born bacteriologist-author Paul (Henry) deKruif, 44, 3/6 at the Martin Beck Theater, with Pennsylvania-born actor James (Maitland) Stewart, 25, Sam Levene in a play about the conquest of yellow fever, 79 perfs.; *Merrily We Roll Along* by George S. Kaufman and Moss Hart 9/9 at the Music Box Theater, with Kenneth McKenna, Jessie Royce Landis, Mary Philips, 155 perfs.; *The Distaff Side* by John Van Druten 9/25 at the Booth Theater, with Baltimore-born actress Mildred Natwick, 26, English actress Sybil Thorndike, 51, English actress Estelle Winwood (originally Goodwin), 51, 177 perfs.; *The Children's Hour* by New Orleans-born New York playwright Lillian Hellman, 29, 11/20 at Maxine Elliott's Theater, with Eugenia Rawls. The plot has been suggested by Hellman's lover, Dashiell Hammett, and hints at sexual abnormalities, 691 perfs. (the play's New York-born set designer Aline Bernstein [née Frankau], now 52, ended her affair with novelist Thomas Wolfe several years ago but will figure in the person of Esther Jack in his posthumous 1939 novel *The Web and the Rock*); *Rain From Heaven* by S. N. Behrman 11/24 at the Golden Theater, with Jane Cowl protests Nazi treatment of German Jews, 99 perfs.; *Valley Forge* by Bucharest-born grain merchant-turned-producer John Houseman (originally Jacques Haussmann), 32, 12/10 at the Guild Theater, with choreography by Martha Graham and a cast that includes English-born actor George Coulouris, 34, 58 perfs.; *Accent on Youth* by Samson Raphaelson 12/25 at the Plymouth Theater, with Seattle-born ingénue Constance Cummings (originally Constance Halverstadt), 24, 229 perfs.

Films: Howard Hawks's *Twentieth Century* with John Barrymore, Carole Lombard. Also: Philip Moeller's *The Age of Innocence* with Irene Dunne, John Boles, Lionel Atwill; W. S. Van Dyke's *Forsaking All Others* with Clark Gable, Joan Crawford, Robert Montgomery, Charles Butterworth, Billie Burke, Rosalind Russell; Alexander Hall's *Little Miss Marker* with Adolphe Menjou, 6-year-old Shirley Temple, screenplay based on a Damon Runyon story; W. S. Van Dyke's *Manhattan Melodrama* with Clark Gable, William Powell, Myrna Loy, Leo Carrillo, Mickey Rooney (originally Joe Yule, Jr.); Mitchell Leisen's *Murder at the Vanities* with Jack Oakie, Kitty Carlisle (originally Catherine Holzman), Carl Brisson; Stephen Rubens's *Romance in Manhattan* with Francis Lederer, Ginger Rogers.

Film musical: George White's *George White's Scandals* with Thornton Freeland, Mary Lachman, Rudy Vallee, Jimmy Durante, New York-born singer-actress Alice Faye (originally Alice Leppert), 22.

Broadway musicals: *The New Ziegfeld Follies* 1/4 at the Winter Garden Theater, with Fanny Brice, St. Louis-born singer Jane Froman, 23, Buddy Ebsen, Eugene and Willie Howard, Mill Valley, Calif.-born ingénue Eve Arden (originally Eunice Quedens), 21, in a production staged by Ziegfeld's widow, Billie Burke, music by Vernon Duke and others, lyrics by E. Y. Harburg and others, songs that include "I Like the Looks of You" by Billy Hill, 182 perfs.; *Life Begins at 8:40* 8/27 at the Winter Garden Theater, with comedian Bert Lahr, Dorchester, Mass.-born dancer Ray Bolger, 30, Irish-born actor Brian Donlevy, 31, music by Harold Arlen, lyrics by Ira Gershwin and E. Y. Harburg, songs that include "You're a Builder Upper," "Let's Take a Walk Around the Block," 237 perfs.; *Anything Goes* 11/21 at the Alvin Theater, with William Gaxton, Ethel Merman, Victor Moore, book by Guy Bolton, P. G. Wodehouse, New York-born playwright Howard Lindsay, 45, and Findlay, Ohio-born playwright-author Russel Crouse, 41, choreography by Bennington, Vt.-born dancer Robert Alton (originally Robert Alton Hart), 36, music and lyrics by Cole Porter, songs that include "The Gypsy in Me," "I Get a Kick Out of You," "You're the Top," "Blow, Gabriel, Blow," "All Through the Night," and the title song, 420 perfs.; *Thumbs Up* 12/27 at the St. James Theater, with Bobby Clark, Ray Dooley, Sheila Barrett, scenic design by Staten Islander Raoul Pène Du Bois, 22, songs that include "Autumn in New York" by Vernon Duke, "Zing! Went the Strings of My Heart" by James Hanley, 156 perfs.

The School of American Ballet is founded at New York by Boston-born Filene's department store heir Lincoln Kirstein, 27, an aesthete who has persuaded Russian choreographer George Balanchine (Georgy Melitonovich Balanchivadze), 30, to come to America. Charter members of the new American Ballet Company include San Diego-born, Italian-trained ballerina Gisella Caccialanza, 19 (see New York City Ballet, 1946).

Sammy's Bowery Follies opens under the direction of Sammy Fuchs, 30, who will run the place until his death in 1969, attracting tourists to skid row.

Harlem's Apollo Theater opens under that name as a showcase for black performing artists at a time when they can find few other venues anywhere in the country (see 1913). Real estate investor Sidney Cohen has bought the old Hertig & Seaman Theater at 253 West 125th Street, between Seventh and Eighth avenues, and leased it to showmen Leo Brecher and Frank Schiffman, who replace its vaudeville show with black entertainers, open it to black as well as white audiences, and inaugurate the place with a show called *Jazz a la Carte*, featuring Benny Carter's big band. Performers in the Apollo's first year include blues singer Bessie Smith, who will be followed in short order by Billie Holiday, Dinah Washington, Huddie "Leadbelly" Ledbetter, Duke Ellington, and Count Basie.

Newport News, Va.-born jazz singer Ella Fitzgerald, 16, lands a job with the Chick Webb Orchestra and begins a notable career after winning first prize in an amateur contest November 21 at Harlem's Apollo Theater singing "The Object of My Affection" and another song in the style of Connee Boswell.

Birmingham, Ala.-born jazz trumpeter Erskine Hawkins, 20, arrives at New York with his Alabama State Teachers College 'Bama State Band, turns it into the Erskine Hawkins Orchestra, and starts making records.

 Columbia upsets Stanford 7 to 0 in the Rose Bowl football game January 1 before a rain-reduced crowd of 40,000. Coached by Lou Little, the Columbia eleven gains only 114 yards as compared with 272 for Stanford, but left halfback Al Barabas carries on a hidden-ball ruse in the second period and races 17 yards for the game's only touchdown.

Former New York Giants baseball star and manager John J. McGraw dies at New Rochelle February 25 at age 60. He retired as manager in June 1932.

CCNY and NYU basketball teams both end their seasons undefeated and play against each other in March at the 168th Street Armory in a tournament mounted by sportswriter Ned Irish, 28, to benefit the city relief fund. The games draw a crowd of 16,000 (see NIT, 1938).

Omaha-born prizefighter Maximilian Adelbert "Max" Baer, 25, knocks out Primo Carnera June 14 in the 11th round of a title bout at Long Island City, winning the world heavyweight championship that he will hold for exactly 1 year.

Fred Perry wins in men's singles at Forest Hills, Helen Jacobs in women's singles.

The New York Giants football team beats the Chicago Bears 30 to 13 December 9 in the Sneakers Game at the Polo Grounds. The Giants beat the Green Bay Packers December 17 at the same venue.

● Undertaker Frank E. Campbell dies January 19 at age 61, having made funeral homes a respectable alternative to home funerals. His remains are interred in a vault in New Jersey, where they will remain with those of his late mother until their transfer to Woodlawn Cemetery in 2001; his widow, Amelia (*née* Klutz), will move the funeral parlor in 1939 to 1076 Madison Avenue, northwest corner 81st Street, where it will remain into the 21st century.

Park West Chapels is founded at the corner of 79th Street and Columbus Avenue by funeral directors Barnet and Simon Alpert with 10 employees in partnership with Herman Meyers. The 8-year-old Meyers & Co. funeral home on Amsterdam Avenue at 76th Street is renamed Riverside Memorial Chapel; it will open a Florida branch next year and a Bronx branch on the Grand Concourse at 179th Street in 1940. Sarah Rosenthal will live until 1946, and the Riverside will be expanded in 1949 with the addition of a building just to the east (*see* Kinney, 1961).

Mayor La Guardia persuades the Board of Aldermen to pass a bill describing slot machines as gambling devices that can be seized on sight, whether or not they are in use, and dumped into the Atlantic Ocean. The city has 25,000 to 30,000 of the "one-armed bandits," whose take is collected by gangsters, with a tiny percentage going to proprietors of stores where the machines have been installed. Makers of the machines try to evade the law by placing an obscure knob that releases a cheap (and almost inedible) candy bar and claiming that their devices are vending machines, the mayor wages a vigorous battle to remove them, posing for cameramen with a sledgehammer and a pile of junked slot machines.

Thieves make off with $427,050 from an armored truck at Bath Beach, Brooklyn, August 21 in the biggest daylight robbery thus far in U.S. history. The truck pulls up just after noon outside the 90-foot loading platform of the Rubel Coal & Ice Co. at the corner of Bay 19th Street and Cropsey Avenue to collect $450 for transfer to a nearby bank. A small-time hoodlum posing as an ice peddler reaches into his cart and grabs a submachine gun, whose snout he jams into the driver's compartment, whereupon four other men appear with weapons; they order the truck guards, branch manager, and more than 12 icemen to lie flat on their faces beneath the platform, two getaway cars arrive, and the robbers speed off with 20 canvas sacks containing the money. Police seal off every road out of Brooklyn, but the perpetrators have two speedboats waiting at the foot of Bay 35th Street and race out into Gravesend Bay, landing at a beach on the Rockaway Peninsula. One man has been mortally wounded in the leg by an accidental shotgun discharge, the nine survivors meet the next day to divvy up the loot, and although police quickly learn from informers the identity of every man involved only three of them will serve any time for the robbery and none of the money will ever be recovered.

New York police arrest German-born Bronx furrier Bruno Richard Hauptmann, 35, September 20 for possession of ransom money paid to recover Charles A. Lindbergh, Jr. in 1932. Hauptmann says he received the gold certificates from a former partner in the fur business and denies any connection with the Lindbergh baby kidnapping and death (see 1936).

Mayor La Guardia appoints Lewis J. (Joseph) Valentine, 52, police commissioner September 25. Valentine joined the force as a patrolman in 1903 and made captain 10 years later.

 The 10-story Bronx County Building is completed at 851 Grand Concourse, southwest corner 161st Street, to designs by Joseph H. Friedlander and Max Hausle. They have decorated the limestone exterior with friezes, and provided for sculptures at the four entrances.

The municipal authority bill passed by the state legislature at Albany February 4 establishes a new City Housing Authority, headed by Langdon W. Post; it holds its first meeting February 20 with members who include Greenwich House founder Mary Simkovitch, now 68, who will serve until 1948 (see 1936).

Knickerbocker Village is completed on the Lower East Side in an area bounded by Catherine, Market, Monroe, and Cherry streets. Designed by Van Wart & Ackerman for developer Fred F. French and built with some public financing, the three-acre complex has 1,600 units and central courtyards reached through gated tunnels.

Swiss-born architect William Lescaze, 38, completes a modern residence for himself at 211 East 48th Street, between Second and Third avenues, with glass-block walls, air conditioning, and an office on the ground floor. Lescaze pioneered International Style architecture in America 2 years ago with his 36-story Philadelphia Saving Fund Society building and has used the commission he received to buy a brownstone in East 48th Street, demolish it, and insert a narrow modern structure in its place. He designs a similar house for client Raymond Kramer at 32 East 74th Street.

Architect Cass Gilbert dies at Brockenhurst, England, May 17 at age 74; Raymond M. Hood at Stamford, Conn., August 14 at age 53.

 Mayor La Guardia appoints Robert Moses the first citywide parks commissioner and he is sworn in January 18 following passage of enabling legislation at Albany. Municipal parks have in many cases degenerated into weed-filled dumps, some of them occupied by squatters, but the Depression has put so many skilled men in public works programs that by February Moses has as many as 64,000 such men supplementing regular park employees. Now 45, he begins turning the site of Central Park's lower reservoir (now a Hooverville) into what will be called the Great Lawn. His exterminators kill 200,000 Central Park rats in 1 week, and he will soon have as many as 100,000 WPA workers in the Parks Department to help him expand the 119 existing playgrounds to more than 600 while building public golf courses, ice rinks, recreation centers, swimming pools, zoos, and other park facilities.

Manhattan's 50-year-old Bryant Park receives new Sixth Avenue entrances, a sunken central lawn with promenades lined by London plane trees along its sides, and a granite balustrade around its perimeter. Designed by Gilmore D. Clarke and financed by Works Progress Administration money, the formal landscaping conforms to a prizewinning overall design by Lusby Simpson, but raising the park's ground level by three or four feet and adding a great many bushes and shrubs around the perimeter makes it difficult for police department patrolmen to look into the park from surrounding sidewalks, creating a situation that invites crime (see 1980).

The city opens 90 garbage-disposal dumps in all the boroughs following a U.S. Supreme Court ruling that bans ocean dumping of waste (see 1944).

A new Central Park Zoo opens December 2 after 9 months' construction, with 25,000 spectators lining Fifth Avenue at 64th Street to watch the fife and drum corps of P.S. 71 escorting the daughter of the Park superintendent in a pony-drawn barouche (see 1864). Decrepit animal cages known as the Menagerie have been torn down to make way for the new facility, and the delicately detailed cast-iron Spur Rock Arch built in 1862 to span the bridle path at the southern end of the park has been destroyed as well. Zookeepers open two decorated boxes at the inaugural ceremony to reveal a gorilla in one and a lion in the other (when ground was broken for the project in February the lion cages of the old Menagerie were so flimsy that keepers carried shotguns in case an animal escaped); brick buildings containing monkeys, snakes, birds, a hippopotamus, and other wildlife surround a pool that is home to seals (see 1980).

The 3-year-old Waldorf-Astoria Hotel on Park Avenue opens a Men's Bar with a standup bar 60 feet long and seating facilities for 200. A man ordering a whiskey has a bottle placed on his table. Women are not admitted. A dry martini costs 35¢, Champagne $1 per glass. The Palm Bar opens in early summer on the 18th floor; it will serve during winter months in connection with dinners and other functions held in the Starlight Roof ballroom.

The Rainbow Room opens October 2 on the 65th floor of the still unfinished RCA (later GE) Building in Rockefeller Center with backing from Standard Oil millionaire-philanthropist John D. Rockefeller, Jr., now 60, who wants the club to serve as an attraction for prospective tenants. Initially called the Stratosphere Room (an organ that displays colored lights on the ceiling will lead to a change in the name of the 40,000-square-foot space), it has been designed by architect Mott B. Schmidt's wife, Elena, with a revolving dance floor. Jolly Coburn's Orchestra provides dance music for women in evening gowns and men in white tie and tails (less formal attire is not permitted). French chanteuse Lucienne Boyer makes her U.S. debut that evening, and guests at the inaugural dance (a benefit for the Lenox Hill Neighborhood Association) include Georgia-born Hollywood star Miriam Hopkins, 32, along with socialites from some of the city's richest families (*see* 1942).

1935 Italian-Americans and blacks clash in Harlem October 3 following reports that Italian troops have invaded Ethiopia. Police are ordered on special duty. Benito Mussolini calls for volunteers, a black congressman advises blacks not to demonstrate against the Italians, the Italian ambassador says U.S. citizens will not be accepted as volunteers, applications of Italian citizens are sent to Rome, and 117 reservist volunteers sail October 19 aboard the S.S. *Rex* for service in Ethiopia. A rally held in Brooklyn December 18 under the auspices of the Italian-American Community succeeds in obtaining contributions of gold for the war effort.

A Harlem race riot March 19 leaves one person killed, 100 injured, and 100 in police custody. Crowds throw stones at police officers and at shop windows in 125th Street (known in Harlem as "the Great White Way" because none of its stores are owned by blacks or employ black clerks) following rumors that a cop has badly beaten (and by some accounts killed) a 12-year-old Puerto Rican youth caught stealing a penknife from an S. H. Kress dime store (the lad later turns up unhurt). Police are unable to control the crowd, hundreds rampage through the streets, the offices of the 4-year-old Domestic Workers' Union are demolished, and property damage amounts to $12 million. Harlem community leaders say the disturbance grew out of suppression of blacks, Mayor La Guardia and Manhattan District Attorney William C. Dodge say that a few radicals initiated the incident, others will label the disturbances "hunger riots," the mayor appoints an investigating commitee but will suppress a report next year that blames discrimination for the disturbance, the *Amsterdam News* will publish the report, and the riots will lead to the construction of public housing in Harlem.

The National Industrial Recovery Act (NIRA) of 1933 is unconstitutional, the Supreme Court rules May 27 in *Schechter Poultry Corp. v. United States*. The "sick chicken" case involves some New York wholesale kosher slaughterhouse operators (called "market men") who have been found guilty of violating the NIRA's "live poultry code" (promulgated under Section 3 of the NIRA), fined $5,000, and given 3-month jail sentences. Manhattan's Terminal Market, the nation's largest live-poultry market, receives birds from 35 states (only 4 percent from New York State), and it is easy for a diseased bird in the West Washington Market to be sold unwittingly, especially at a time when people in the trade have long workweeks and are sadly underpaid. The defense counsel explains that "straight killing means you have got to put your hand into the coop and take out whichever chicken comes to you. You hand the chicken to the rabbi, who slaughters it." The Court concedes that "extraordinary conditions may call for extraordinary remedies" but rules unanimously that in setting maximum hours and minimum wages the code violates not only the commerce clause in the Constitution but also the separation of powers clause, since Congress may not delegate legislative power to the president and give him "an unfettered discretion to make whatever laws he thinks may be needed or advisable for the rehabilitation and expansion of trade or industry." The ruling is a setback for organized labor, whose leaders have been pushing for a 30-hour week to ease unemployment.

The National Labor Relations Act (Wagner-Connery Act) passed by Congress July 5 creates a new National Labor Relations Board and reasserts the right of collective bargaining (*see* 1934). The right was contained in a section of the NRA code of 1933 that the U.S. Supreme Court has struck down.

The Social Security Act signed into law August 14 provides a system of old-age annuities and unemployment insurance benefits, but domestic workers are not included, and 80 percent of black women in Harlem are employed as domestic servants.

Research Institute of America has its beginnings in a New York company founded by Kansas-born Bible salesman Carl Hovgard and New York-born lawyer-economist Leo Cherne, 23, to publish and distribute Cherne's book of advice to businessmen on how to deal with the new Social Security law.

Wall Street's investment bankers refuse to underwrite securities in protest against the New Deal's regulations, but Salomon Brothers and Hutzler breaks the "Wall Street Strike" by underwriting an issue of bonds for Swift & Co. (*see* 1970).

Morgan Stanley is founded at New York by J. P. Morgan's grandson Henry Sturgis Morgan, 34, his fellow Morgan partner Harold Stanley, 49, and four other Morgan bankers (*see* Glass-Steagall Act, 1933).

Wall Street's Dow Jones Industrial Average closes December 31 at 144.13, up from 104.04 at the end of 1934.

Allied Stores Corp. is created by a reorganization of Hahn Department Stores, whose stock plummeted from $57 per share in 1929 to less than $1 in 1932. Headed since 1933 by B. Earl Puckett, 37, Allied's profits have increased from their 1933 low of $25,000 and will be up to $20 million by 1948 as Puckett decentralizes management responsibility to let stores like Lord & Taylor operate more freely.

Brooklyn Union Gas revenues fall to $19 million, down from $25 million in 1929, as more customers convert to electricity, but the board of directors names a new president, Clifford Paige, who will woo business firms back to gas by offering promotional rates to industrial users, giving special deals to those who use gas for water heaters, refrigerators, and other gas appliances (*see* 1928). By 1941 the company will have more than regained the volume of sales it lost in the first half of the Depression (*see* 1945).

Irish-born labor leader Michael J. (Joseph) Quill, 28, is elected president of the Transport Workers Union (TWU); founded last year with his help, it contains a strong Communist Party element.

The French Line passenger ship S.S. *Normandie* arrives at New York June 3 after crossing from Southampton in a record 4 days, 11 hours, 42 minutes, having averaged 29.6 knots per hour, beating the record set last year by the *Rex*, and winning the Hales Trophy. Built at a cost of $60 million, the sleek 79,280-ton luxury liner with four screws is 1,029 feet in length overall, 119 feet in width, and has an 80-foot swimming pool, 23 elevators, a 380-seat movie theater, and a dining room modeled after the Hall of Mirrors at Versailles, but she will never turn a profit. After being viewed by 9,200 visitors, she leaves on her return voyage June 7, sets a new eastbound speed record June 10 by sailing 711 miles in 24 hours, averages 30.31 knots per hour, and reaches port in 4 days, 3 hours, 28 seconds (*see* 1942). R.M.S. *Mauretania* has become too costly to operate and goes to the scrap heap in July after 27 years on the transatlantic run.

American Airlines inaugurates non-stop DC-3 passenger service between New York and Chicago June 25, using the Newark Metropolitan Airport that opened in 1929. Newark's central terminal is nearing completion, with a restaurant and sleeping rooms for passengers, but even without such amenities it has become the world's biggest airport, handling more passengers than London's Croydon, Berlin's Templehof, and Le Bourget at Paris combined. At least 90 percent of arriving passengers head for New York City via the Pulaski Skyway that opened in 1932; flights from Newark can reach Los Angeles in 16 hours, Florida in just 8.

Bridge engineer Gustav Lindenthal dies at Metuchen, N.J., July 31 at age 85.

The American Museum of Natural History's Hayden Planetarium opens October 2 just north of the museum. Architect Goodhue Livingston of Trowbridge & Livingston has designed the building, built largely with federal funds; bachelor investment banker Charles Hayden, now 64, of Hayden Stone has contributed $150,000 to buy the Zeiss projector for the planetarium's simulated star show (*see* 1980).

Polytechnic Institute of Brooklyn awards its first doctorate degree—a Ph.D. in chemistry (*see* 1901). It extended its evening-course program to graduate studies in 1925, offered graduate courses 3 years later in chemistry and in chemical, electrical, and mechanical engineering, its faculty has been strengthened by an influx of refugees from Europe's fascist and Nazi regimes, and in 1939 it will begin offering courses in aeronautical engineering (*see* 1958).

The Lycée Français de New York opens at 3 East 95th Street, where it will remain until early in the next century in a town house with wood-paneled rooms, marble fireplaces, and grand staircases. Initially for French-speaking students, it will grow in 30 years to have an enrollment of more than 1,000 students aged 3 to 18, including Americans and children from more than 50 countries as well as those of French parentage. Backers who include French consulate general Count Charles de Feri de Fontnouvelle, 59, New York-born lawyer-art collector (and *Columbia Law Review* cofounder) Forsyth Wickes, 58, and the city's corporation counsel Paul Windels (a trustee of the French Institute) have started the school, whose graduates will prepare for both foreign and U.S. institutions of higher learning and receive the French Baccalaureate as well as high-school diplomas.

Riverdale Country School for Girls opens on an estate near the boys' school that opened in 1907. The schools will occupy 40 acres by the time founder Frank Sutcliff dies in 1952, and the two will be combined in 1972 to create a private coeducational institution whose elementary grades will be in the girls' school; total enrollment will grow in the next 60 years to 981.

This Week is launched by Crowell-Collier, whose Sunday newspaper supplement will be carried by scores of metropolitan papers (*see Collier's*, 1919).

Vanity Fair magazine is merged with *Vogue* by Condé Nast, who has controlled *Vogue* since 1909 and now acquires *Vanity Fair*, edited since 1914 by Frank Crowninshield (who resigns).

Artkraft Strauss Sign Corp. is created by a merger of the Lima, Ohio-based Artkraft Co. with New York's 38-year-old Strauss Sign Co. Russian-born electrician Jacob Starr helped Strauss become Times Square's leading creator of theater marquees and entertainment displays in the 1920s before quitting to start his own engineering firm, made a connection with Artkraft (a leader in neon lighting), opened a New York branch of Artkraft, and has merged it with his former employer (*see* 1909; Leigh, 1933). The company is among the first to use electric signs for the promotion of motion pictures in Times Square and will be the leading marketer, designer, and builder of outdoor advertising on the Great White Way.

New York Times publisher Adolph S. Ochs dies at Chattanooga, Tenn., April 8 at age 77. His New York-born son-in-law Arthur Hays Sulzberger, 45, married Ochs's daughter Iphigene in 1917 and lives with her at 5 East 80th Street; Sulzberger becomes publisher, and Iphigene inherits a controlling interest in the paper.

Nonfiction: *Life with Father* by Clarence Day; *The Lords of Creation* by Boston-born *Harper's* magazine associate editor Frederick Lewis Allen, 45; *The New York Merchant on the Eve of the Revolution* by Virginia D. Harrington; *The Golden Earth: The Story of Manhattan's Landed Wealth* by Michigan-born author Arthur Pound, 51; *Farewell to Fifth Avenue* by Cornelius Vanderbilt, Jr. (IV), who is dropped from the Social Register.

Author Clarence Day dies at New York December 28 at age 61.

Fiction: *Of Time and the River* and *From Death to Morning* (stories) by Thomas Wolfe, who moves in September from 5 Montague Terrace in Brooklyn Heights to 865 First Avenue in Manhattan. Wolfe writes in his story "Only the Dead Know Brooklyn:" "Dere's no guy livin' dat know Brooklyn t'ree an' t'roo, because it'd take a guy a lifetime just to find his way aroun' duh f— town;" *Flowering Judas and Other Stories* by Texas-born writer Katherine Ann Porter, 45; *The Adventures of Ephraim Tutt, Attorney and Counselor at Law* by Arthur Train, now 70.

Poetry: *Dance of Fire* by Lola Ridge; *Poems* by Kenneth Fearing; *King Jasper* by Edwin Arlington Robinson, who dies at New York April 6 at age 65.

Brooklyn-born graphic designer Paul Rand (originally Peretz Rosenbaum) opens a tiny design study in East 38th Street. The 20-year-old son of an Orthodox Jewish grocer in East New York, Rand persuaded his father to put up a $25 entrance fee for night-school classes at Pratt Institute while he attended Harren High School in Manhattan, he has worked for the George Switzer advertising agency designing packages and lettering for clients that included E. R. Squibb, and beginning next year will design pages for *Apparel Arts* magazine before being hired by its parent company, Esquire-Coronet, where he will develop his own graphic style.

The WPA makes jobs for artists in a program to decorate post offices and other federal buildings.

Painting: *Moon* and *Summer* by Arthur Dove. Childe Hassam dies at East Hampton August 27 at age 75; sculptor Gaston Lachaise at New York October 18 at age 53.

The Bettmann Archive opens at New York with pictures collected by refugee Otto L. Bettmann, 32, who will fill up two basement rooms in East 57th Street before moving in 1961 to 215 East 57th. Formerly curator of rare books in the Prussian State Art Library at Berlin, Bettmann received a doctorate of philosophy from the University of Leipzig in 1927 but has fled Nazi persecution with little except some 25,000 images, many on film negatives, in two trunks. He catalogues his collection, cross-indexing it for easy retrieval, and begins to expand it, obtaining many of his images for less than $1 each from the Library of Congress and receiving rental fees—initially $25 but later much more—for allowing publications, book publishers, and advertisers to use them. The Archive will grow to have 16 million images, making it the world's largest collection of historical photographs and other illustrations (*see* 1981).

Art News publisher Samuel W. Frankel suffers a nervous breakdown in September and dies of double pneumonia at his 17 East 89th Street home October 22 at age 59 (*see* 1921). His widow, Elfreda (*née* Kober), takes over with help from Chicago-born art historian Alfred Moritz Frankfurter, now 29, who has been editor of The *Antiquarian* and The *Fine Arts*, both published at New York. Frankfurter will become editor of *Art News* next year and introduce a bolder format, changing the magazine's typeface, adding more pages, giving more emphasis to U.S. artists, and singlehandedly making the periodical an influential force in the art world (*see* 1941).

The Frick Collection opens to the public December 16 at 1 East 71st Street in the 21-year-old Fifth Avenue mansion of the late steel magnate Henry Clay Frick following the death of his widow, Adelaide. Architect John Russell Pope has remodeled the house, and it attracts 5,000 people in its first week to view its collections. Frick's daughter Helen has purchased two adjacent town houses, demolished them, and had Pope design the Frick Art Reference Library as a memorial to her late father; it is housed in a limestone building at 10 East 71st Street. Admission will be free until 1977 (*see* 1977).

Eastman Kodak introduces Kodachrome for 16-millimeter movie cameras. It has acquired production rights from New York concert violinist Leopold Godowsky, Jr., 35, and his pianist co-inventor Leopold Damrosch Mannes, 35, who have devised a three-color dye-coupling process with a grant from New York banker Lewis L. Strauss and help from a team of Eastman scientists. Godowsky and Mannes met as students at Riverdale Country School in 1916 and have studied physics and chemistry at university while continuing their music careers; Mannes won a Pulitzer prize for musical composition 10 years ago and will use much of the profits from Kodachrome to develop the David Mannes School of Music founded by his father. Godowsky married George and Ira Gershwin's sister Frances in 1931, and the two men have been working at Rochester since July 1931 (*see* 1936).

Theater: *Waiting for Lefty* by Clifford Odets, now 28, 1/5 at the Civic Repertory Theater on 14th Street, 168 perfs.; *The Old Maid* by Zöe Akins 1/7 at the Empire Theater, with Judith Anderson, Helen Mencken, 305 perfs.; *The Petrified Forest* by Robert Sherwood 1/7 at the Broadhurst Theater, with Humphrey Bogart, Peggy Conklin, Leslie Howard, Blanche Sweet, 197 perfs.; *Point Valaine* by Noël Coward 1/16 at the Ethel Barrymore Theater, with Alfred Lunt, Lynn Fontanne, Philadelphia-born actor Broderick Crawford, 23, 55 perfs.; *Three Men on a Horse* by George Abbott and Philadelphia-born writer John Cecil Holm, 30, 1/30 at the Playhouse Theater, with Sam Levene, Rochester-born actor Garson Kanin, 22, New York-born actress Shirley Booth (originally Thelma Booth Ford), 27 (to Fulton Theater 11/10/1936), 835 perfs.; *Awake and Sing* by Clifford Odets 2/19 at the Belasco Theater, with Morris Carnovsky, Stella Adler, New York-born actor Jules Garfinkle (later John Garfield), 21, 209 perfs. (Odets and his Group Theater colleague Harold Clurman have left their tiny apartment in Horatio Street and leased a large 19th-floor flat at 1 University Place but lack the funds to furnish it properly); *Till the Day I Die* and *Waiting for Lefty* by Odets 3/26 at the Longacre Theater with a top price of $1.50 per seat in a production by the Group Theater founded 4 years ago by Odets and director Lee Strasberg, now 33, 136 perfs.; Kenosha, Wis.-born actor-radio announcer-*March of Time* film narrator (George) Orson Welles, 21, directs an all-black cast in a production of *Macbeth* for the WPA-financed Federal Theater Project's Negro People's Theater with help from John Houseman, who has helped Welles organize the Negro Theater Project for the Theater Project established in April by Harry L. Hopkins to provide jobs for out-of-work theater people and managed since May by South Dakota-born Vassar College Experimental Theater director Hallie Flanagan (*née* Ferguson), 45; *Winterset* by Maxwell Anderson 9/25 at the Martin Beck Theater, with Cleveland-born actor Burgess Meredith, 26, Richard Bennett, Margo (Mexican-born ingénue Maria Marguerita Guadelupe Boldao y Castilla, 17) is based on the Sacco-Vanzetti case, 195 perfs.; *Dead End* by Sidney Kingsley 10/28 at the Belasco Theater, with Joseph Dowling, Sheila Trent, 268 perfs.; *Boy Meets Girl* by Bucharest-born playwright Bella Spewack (*née* Cohen) and her Ukraine-born husband Samuel, both 36, 11/27 at the Cort Theater, with Jerome Cowan, Garson Kanin, New York-born actor Everett Sloane, 26, 669 perfs.

The New York Drama Critics Circle confers its first award in May, calling Maxwell Anderson's *Winterset* the best play of the 1934-1935 season. Broadway reviewers have organized the group in reaction to the Pulitzer Prize Committee giving its award to Zöe Akins's *The Old Maid* in preference to what they deemed superior works by Lilian Hellman, John Houseman, Clifford Odets, and Robert Sherwood.

Actor Sanford Meisner, now 30, begins teaching at the Neighborhood Playhouse. He will take over next year and head it until 1959, resuming from 1964 to 1990 (*see* 1928). Originally a member of the Group Theater, he turned against Method acting 2 years ago and his classroom in the playhouse's school in a 54th Street brownstone off First Avenue will be papered with signs urging students to "Act Before You Think," remember that "An Ounce of Behavior Is Worth a Pound of Words," and so forth. His students will include actors Robert Duvall, Diane Keaton, Grace Kelly, Gregory Peck, Tony Randall, Jon Voight, and Joanne Woodward, and Meisner will also teach playwright David Mamet and directors Sidney Lumet, Vivian Matalon, and Sydney Pollack (who has co-directed the Odets plays with Odets).

Former drama teacher-historian George Pierce Baker dies at New York January 6 at age 68; playwright Augustus Thomas of a heart attack at a Nyack golf club August 2 at age 77; onetime Broadway theater tycoon Charles B. Dillingham of arteriosclerosis in his suite at the Astor Hotel August 30 at age 66 (he filed for bankruptcy last year with debts of $7.3 million, including $2,000 owed to Irving Berlin).

Radio: *Major Bowes Amateur Hour* 3/24 on NBC with onetime U.S. intelligence officer Major Edward J. Bowes, now 60, as emcee in a program that will continue until Bowes's death in June 1946. By mid-1936 he will be auditioning 500 to 700 amateur entertainers per week (out of some 10,000 weekly applicants), many of whom will wind up on New York City's relief rolls; *Your Hit Parade* 4/20 on NBC with the Lucky Strike Orchestra playing the week's top 15 tunes (to 4/1959).

Films: Edward Sutherland's *Diamond Jim* with Edward Arnold as the late Diamond Jim Brady, Jean Arthur (originally Gladys Greene), Cesar Romero; Wesley Ruggles's *The Gilded Lily* with Claudette Colbert, Fred MacMurray, Ray Milland; Alfred E. Green's *The Girl from 10th Avenue* with Bette Davis; William A. Seiter's *If You Could Only Cook* with Herbert Marshall, Jean Arthur, Leo Carillo, Lionel Stander; Jack Conway's *One New York Night*.

Air-conditioned movie theaters showing continuous films provide escape for Depression-beleaguered New Yorkers, whose 15¢ tickets (5¢ at matinees) let them see double features, newsreels, cartoons, short subjects, travelogues, and coming attractions (exhibitors sometimes offer free dishes and machine-made glassware to attract patrons). Ushers with flashlights show patrons to their seats in ornate picture palaces.

"STICKS NIX HICK PIX" headlines *Variety* July 17. The 30-year-old show business newspaper reports that rural audiences reject motion pictures with bucolic stories and characters.

The Rialto Theater opens at Christmas on Times Square at 1481 Broadway, between 42nd and 43rd streets, with Texas-born big-game hunter Frank Buck, 51, starring in the film *Fang and Claw*. Designed by architects Rosario Candela and Thomas Lamb with S. L. "Roxy" Rothafel as a showcase for the Mutual Film Corp., it is a remodeled version of the Victoria Theater put up by Oscar Hammerstein in 1893 and calls itself the "temple of the motion picture and shrine of music and the allied arts" (*see* Rivoli, 1917). The Rialto will show first-run Hollywood films for 25 years before turning to pornographic movies and will survive in various ways until 1998 (*see* Cineplex-Odeon, 1986).

Film musicals: George White's *George White's Scandals* with Alice Faye, James Dunn, Ned Sparks, White, dancer Eleanor Powell.

Broadway musicals: *At Home Abroad* 9/19 at the Winter Garden Theater, with Beatrice Lillie, dancer Eleanor Powell, Ethel Waters, Eddie Foy, Jr., music by Arthur Schwartz, lyrics by Howard Dietz, songs that include "Hottentot Potentate," 198 perfs.; *Jubilee* 10/12 at the Imperial Theater, with English-born actor Melville Cooper, 39, Mary Boland, Omaha-born ingénu Montgomery Clift, 15, music and lyrics by Cole Porter, songs that include "Begin the Beguine," "Just One of Those Things," 169 perfs.; *Jumbo* 11/16 at the Hippodrome, with Jimmy Durante and a live elephant in a show produced by Billy Rose and directed by John Murray Anderson, music by Richard Rodgers, lyrics by Lorenz Hart, songs that include "Little Girl Blue," "The Most Beautiful Girl in the World," 233 perfs.; *George White's Scandals* 12/24 at the New Amsterdam Theater, with Bert Lahr, Willie and Eugene Howard, Rudy Vallée, music by Ray Henderson, lyrics by Jack Yellen, 110 perfs.

Charles E. Mack of Moran and Mack vaudeville fame is killed January 11 at age 46 near Mesa, Ariz., when a car driven by his wife overturns en route to New York. His partner, Moran, is not hurt; Broadway lyricist Ballard MacDonald dies at Queens November 17 at age 53.

Former Broadway musical star Elsie Janis suffers a serious automobile injury; now 46, she has extraordinary medical expenses that force her to auction off her historic Philipse Manor estate in Tarrytown.

Opera: *Porgy and Bess* 10/10 at the Alvin Theater, with soprano Anne Wiggins Brown, 20, as Bess, Indianapolis-born baritone Todd Duncan, 32, as Porgy, music by George Gershwin (who calls Duncan "a colored Lawrence Tibbett"), lyrics by Ira Gershwin and DuBose Heyward (whose 1927 stage play *Porgy* has provided the libretto), choral direction by Eva Jessye, 40, of the Eva Jessye Singers, songs that include "Bess, You Is My Woman Now" and "It Ain't Necessarily So," 124 perfs.

The Metropolitan Opera Guild is founded by Eleanor Robson (Mrs. August) Belmont, now 57, to raise funds for the Met. The Guild will begin publishing *Opera News* in December 1936 and grow to have 100,000 members nationwide as it expands its educational and publishing efforts.

Popular songs: "Lullaby of Broadway" by Harry Warren, lyrics by Al Dubin (for the Busby Berkeley film musical *Gold Diggers of 1935*); "About a Quarter to Nine" and "She's a Latin from Manhattan" by Al Dubin, lyrics by Harry Warren (for the film *Go Into Your Dance*).

The Village Vanguard opens in February at 178 Seventh Avenue South (between Waverly Place and West 11th Street), where it will remain into the 21st century. Lithuanian-born nightclub operator Max Gordon, 32, has relocated the Greenwich Village jazz club that he opened last year in a former basement speakeasy in Charles Street (police promptly plastered the original place with violations). The club will provide a venue for avant-garde jazz musicians who will include John Coltrane, Charles Mingus, Thelonius Sphere Monk, Gerry Mulligan, and Max Roach, providing opportunities also for comedians Woody Allen, Lenny Bruce, Wally Cox, and Mort Sahl, guitarist-folk singer Huddie "Leadbelly" Ledbetter, and soul singer Aretha Franklin.

Billy Rose's Diamond Horseshoe nightclub opens under the direction of *Jumbo* producer Rose, whose lavish club will hire John Murray Anderson in 1938 and continue until 1960.

College football's Heisman Memorial Trophy (initially called the Downtown Athletic Club Trophy) is awarded for the first time by the Downtown Athletic Club, whose first athletic director is former University of Pennsylvania football coach John Heisman, 58. He has started the Touchdown Club of New York to honor all college players who have scored on the gridiron, and the trophy will be awarded annually after Heisman's death next year to honor not only the recipient but also the man who introduced the center snap, the vocal "hike" as a signal for starting play, the hidden-ball play, the scoreboard listing downs and yardage, etc., and who was a leader in the fight to legalize the forward pass and to reduce games into quarters instead of halves.

New York-born prizefighter James J. Braddock, 29, wins the world heavyweight title from Max Baer June 13 in an upset at Long Island City. Nicknamed "The Cinderella Man," Braddock gains a 15-round decision over Baer.

Wilmer Lawson Allison, 30, wins in men's singles at Forest Hills, Helen Jacobs in women's singles.

The New York Convention & Visitors Bureau is founded.

Former mayor Jimmy Walker and his second wife, showgirl Betty Compton, move into an apartment at 132 East 72nd Street, where they will live until their divorce in 1941. Another tenant is composer George Gershwin, who is spending more and more of his time in Hollywood.

The first Debutante Cotillion and Christmas Ball is held in December at the 4-year-old Waldorf-Astoria Hotel to benefit the 82-year-old New York Infirmary. The ball honors the commitment of the debutantes' families to helping others through their support of the Infirmary, the only full-service medical facility serving the financial district and the multicultural communities south of Houston Street (it will be renamed New York Downtown Hospital) (*see* International Ball, 1954)

Manhattan district attorney Thomas E. Dewey raids Polly Adler's brothel as part of a crackdown on an alleged prostitution syndicate (*see* 1924). Adler is convicted on charges of possessing pornographic films and serves 24 days under the alias "Joan Martin" (*see* 1943).

Gunmen from the newly organized New York crime syndicate Murder Inc. walk into the Newark, N.J., headquarters of mobster Dutch Schultz (Arthur Flegenheimer) in the Palace Chop House October 23 and open fire, shooting Schultz down along with his three companions. Mortally wounded at age 33, Schultz was a major figure in bootlegging during Prohibition and has twice in the last 2 years been tried and acquitted for evading income taxes on the proceeds of his various rackets; he has killed his lawyer Dixie Walker and threatened to have Manhattan D.A. Dewey assassinated. Meyer Lansky and Charles "Lucky" Luciano have hired the gunmen who rub him out, and they will now dominate New York's National Crime Syndicate. One of their gunmen enters the Hollywood Barber Shop at the corner of Seventh Avenue and 47th Street and murders Marty Krompier, Schultz's chief enforcer of the Harlem numbers racket.

A federal office building is completed at 90 Church Street, between Vesey and Barclay streets. Cross & Cross has designed the structure in co-operation with Pennington, Lewis & Mills and Lewis A. Simon under the supervision of the Architect of the U.S. Treasury.

A new East River Savings Bank branch is completed at 26 Cortlandt Street, northeast corner Church Street and extending north to Dey Street. Walker & Gillette has designed the neo-classical Art Deco structure with stainless steel winged eagles over both entrances.

The 41-story International Building at 630 Fifth Avenue opens in Rockefeller Center in May.

Gov. Lehman, first lady Eleanor Roosevelt, and Mayor La Guardia attend groundbreaking ceremonies on the Lower East Side December 3 for the first U.S. public housing project, an eight-building complex to be built by the City Housing Authority founded in February of last year with a promised grant of $25 million. Every third tenement in a row owned by Vincent Astor in 3rd Street between First Avenue and Avenue A has been demolished to provide light and air, with the remaining ones to be rebuilt to designs by architect Frederick L. Ackerman (*see* 1936).

Fort Tryon Park opens on 67 acres donated to the city by John D. Rockefeller, Jr., who in 1909 acquired the old C. K. G. Billings estate and in 1917 acquired other properties on the rocky bluff north of 190th Street, keeping the old Billings gallery, gatehouse, and double switchback driveway. Landscaped by the sons of the late Frederick Law Olmsted with help from 300 workmen, the park includes Linden Terrace, built on a precipice 268 feet above the Hudson (the highest point in Manhattan) and an outpost of Fort Washington in the American Revolution (*see* politics, 1776; food, 1903). The park's three-acre Heather Garden provides a 600-foot-long overlook purchased by Rockefeller to preserve the view of the New Jersey Palisades (*see* art [Cloisters], 1938).

Pelham Bay Park's Orchard Beach opens on Long Island Sound in the North Bronx, where Parks Commissioner Robert Moses has overseen the development of the 115-acre crescent-shaped facility with a strip of sand just over a mile long (year approximate). More sand will be added from time to time until 1964, but none after that until early in the next century.

Alcoholics Anonymous has its beginnings June 10 at New York, where Vermont-born recovering alcoholic William Griffith "Bill" Wilson, 39, watches his surgeon friend Dr. Robert H. "Bob" Smith take his last drink and works with Smith to share with other alcoholics the experience of shaking the disease. A onetime Wall Street stockbroker, Wilson and his wife, Lois (*née* Burnham), have been living with her family in their Clinton Street, Brooklyn, house since he became unemployable because of his drinking, he underwent the standard barbiturate-and-belladonna purge to cure him of his habit 6 months ago, met Smith in the lobby of the Mayflower Hotel at Akron, Ohio, in early May, and has helped Smith overcome his addiction. Wilson invites alcoholics to the Burnham house in Clinton Street, begins meetings with the statement, "My name is Bill W., and I'm an alcoholic" (the anonymity of "Bill W." will not be broken until his death in 1971) (*see* 1941).

Col. Jacob Ruppert buys the old George Ehret brewery adjoining his own plant to the north on Manhattan's upper East Side (*see* 1933).

1936 Italian forces take Addis Ababa May 5, Rome proclaims the annexation of Ethiopia May 9, but New York publisher Generoso Pope has urged U.S. neutrality in his newspapers *Il Progresso Italo-Americano* and *Il Corriere d'America*, using his political power to support the fascist aggression (*see* 1928; 1941).

President Roosevelt wins reelection by a landslide, with a heavy turnout of 2.8 million voters in New York City, where his success is considered a blow to Tammany Hall (he wins an unprecedented majority of 1,356,458 out of a total vote of 2,016,204; Republican Alf Landon of Kansas wins only 659,796 votes in the city, and FDR's victory is credited in part to work by James A. Farley, Bronx party boss Ed Flynn, and Brooklyn party boss Frank V. Reilly). Judge Samuel Rosenman, now 40, has been FDR's chief speechwriter; Pawtucket, R.I.-born presidential adviser Thomas G. "Tommy the Cork" Corcoran, a former New York lawyer, has written a speech containing the phrase, "This generation has a rendezvous with destiny;" Gov. Lehman runs far behind Roosevelt in the city but wins election to a third term, securing 2,970,595 votes to 2,450,104 for his Republican opponent William F. Bleakley of

Yonkers, a State Supreme Court judge who has promised to cut state taxes, rebuked FDR for refusing to supply Italy with war matériel, and drawn more votes than Lehman outside New York City, although he has done surprisingly well in the city.

Voters adopt a new city charter whose provisions include abolishing the Board of Aldermen in favor of a City Council, a City Planning Commission, and a deputy mayor to be appointed by the mayor, such changes to become effective in 1938. The city's charter was amended in 1901 but has remained essentially unchanged since 1897. The plan for a new frame of government for the city was made public in April after a year of work by a charter revision committee, headed by former U.S. solicitor-general Thomas D. Thacher.

The U.S. Supreme Court rules June 1 that a New York minimum wage law for women passed in 1933 is unconstitutional. The Court hands down the decision in the case of *Morehead v. New York ex. rel. Tipaldo* (see Fair Labor Standards Act, 1938).

Corporation lawyer and onetime U.S. attorney general George W. Wickersham dies at New York January 25 at age 77.

Wall Street's Dow Jones Industrial Average closes December 31 at 179.90, up from 144.13 at the end of 1935, but 38 percent of U.S. families (11.7 million families) have incomes of less than $1,000 per year. The Bureau of Labor Statistics places the "poverty line" at $1,330.

The Robinson-Patman Act passed by Congress June 20 to supplement the Clayton Anti-Trust Act of 1914 forbids manufacturers to practice price discrimination including use of advertising allowances to favored customers such as chain stores. It requires retailers to sell at prices fixed by manufacturers, making it illegal for them to sell at discount.

Consolidated Edison Co. of New York is created March 23 by a merger of the 52-year-old Consolidated Gas Co. with its 35-year-old subsidiary Edison Electric Co. Hudson R. Searing heads the new Con Ed and will improve the heretofore cool relations between its gas and electric divisions. Mayor La Guardia will threaten to create a municipal power company to provide some competition, but Con Ed employs more construction workers and pays more taxes than any other single entity in the city (it has more underground pipes and electrical wire than all the rest of the nation's public utilities combined), and it will stave off La Guardia's threat, largely through the efforts of Charles Eble, who will become the company's chief executive officer.

Con Edison takes over the 54-year-old New York Steam Co. and will inspect its subterranean steam pipes on an annual basis, but no one will ever be able to predict exactly when and where a pipe will burst.

Coal operator Edward J. Berwind of Berwind-White Co. dies at his 2 East 64th Street town house August 18 at age 88, having been the largest individual owner of coal properties in America.

National Bulk Carriers is founded at New York by Michigan-born shipbuilder Daniel K. (Keith) Ludwig, 39, who has pioneered in developing a technique for side-launching newly built ships and a welding process to replace riveting in shipyards (see 1941).

The Cunard White Star Line's S.S. *Queen Mary* arrives at New York June 1, docking at a special Hudson River pier built to accommodate her (a line of taxicabs six blocks long awaits her passengers). The 80,774-ton liner has four screws and measures 1,019.5 feet overall; delayed by fog, she has set no speed record (she will soon do so by averaging 30.14 knots on a westbound passage), but more than 10,000 visitors tour her facilities while she is in port, and when she departs on her return voyage June 5 it is announced that devices will be installed in her funnels to keep them from spewing soot onto her decks.

New York Evening Journal reporter Dorothy Kilgallen, 23, sets out in September to beat Nelly Bly's 1889–1890 round-the-world speed record. She crosses the Atlantic in the German dirigible *Hindenburg*, makes her way across Europe and Asia, and returns via Manila, where she catches a Pan American China Clipper bound for San Francisco via Guam, Wake, Midway, and Honolulu, but she loses out to *New York World-Telegram* reporter Bud Ekins, who breaks the record by circling the earth in 18 days, 14 hours, 56 minutes—all by air over new passenger routes. Kilgallen returns to New York, where she launches a newspaper gossip column, "The Voice of Broadway."

New York City's electric streetcar system is converted in part to a system employing GM buses. General Motors has obtained control of the city's surface transit lines through stock purchases (see 1932; 1949).

The Fifth Avenue Coach Co. replaces its open-air, double-decker omnibuses with closed double-deckers (quickly nicknamed "Queen Marys") that will remain in operation until 1953 (some open-air double-deckers will continue until late in 1948) (see 1907). The fare on Fifth Avenue is 10¢; subways and other bus lines continue to charge 5¢ (*see* higher fares, 1948).

The Grand Central, Interborough, and Laurelton parkways open on Long Island in early summer, bringing to 100 miles the total length of parkways built under programs instituted by Parks Commissioner Robert Moses since 1924. The new roadways are expected to ease traffic on the Southern and Northern State parkways, but they are quickly as jammed as the older roadways.

Mayor La Guardia creates a Tunnel Authority to build an underwater connection between Queens and midtown Manhattan; he excludes Robert Moses from the authority's board, and Moses—who prefers bridges—will try to block tunnel construction (*see* 1946).

The Triborough Bridge opens July 11 to link Manhattan, Queens, and the Bronx. Secretary of the Interior Harold L. Ickes, 62, Mayor La Guardia, Robert Moses, and President Roosevelt all make speeches at the ribbon-cutting ceremony despite sweltering heat (the temperature July 10 hit 102.3° F. to set a new record). When he appointed Moses chairman of the Triborough Bridge Authority, La Guardia told reporters, "We are going to build a bridge instead of patronage. We are going to pile up stone and steel instead of expenses. We are going to build a bridge of steel and spell steel 's-t-e-e-l' instead of 's-t-e-a-l.' The people of the City of New York are going to pay for that bridge, and they are going to pay for it in tolls after its completion." The East River Drive approach to the bridge opens October 31, but only one-and-a-half miles of southbound roadway from 92nd Street and York Avenue to 122nd Street.

FDR, Gov. Lehman, and Mayor La Guardia dedicated the Triborough Bridge. MUSEUM OF THE CITY OF NEW YORK

New York piers are idled beginning October 31 as the International Seamen's Union tries to shut down East and West Coast shipping. Shipping companies hire seamen off the docks or from crimp joints—cheap hotels known to shipping masters who get kickbacks or otherwise exploit seafaring men.

The Henry Hudson Bridge opens December 12 to link Manhattan's West Side and Henry Hudson highways north of 72nd Street with the Riverdale section of the Bronx and the Westchester parkways beyond. The 800-foot steel arch bridge across the Harlem River and Ship Canal has a 10¢ toll.

The Board of Aldermen votes in December to approve a new traffic code that forbids right-hand turns on red lights, but Mayor La Guardia refuses to sign the bill until a provision is deleted that would authorize the police to arrest jaywalkers. "I prefer the happiness of our unorganized imperfection to the organized perfection of other countries," says the mayor. "Broadway is not Unter den Linden."

The Independent subway line opens December 31 along Queens Boulevard to Union Turnpike, making communities such as Rego Park, Forest Hills, and Kew Gardens just a nickel ride away from Manhattan (*see* 1932; 1937).

The American Museum of Natural History on Central Park West opens a Memorial Hall dedicated to the late Theodore Roosevelt. Sculptor James E. Fraser has created an equestrian statue of the president and conservationist.

Marymount Manhattan College is founded by Mother Marie Joseph Butler, now 76, who opened the first Marymount school at Tarrytown in 1907.

St. John's University in Brooklyn buys the Hillcrest Golf Club in Jamaica for use as a future campus (*see* 1906; 1956).

Times Square gets its largest electric advertising sign thus far: designed by artist Dorothy Shepard and erected by General Outdoor Advertising atop a two-story building that houses the International Casino nightclub, it promotes Wrigley's Spearmint chewing gum with fish blowing bubbles (*see* Leigh, 1933; Bond waterfall, 1948).

The *New York American* gives Damon Runyon his own column, "Both Barrels." It will be renamed "As I See It" next year and syndicated to all the Hearst papers.

LIFE magazine appears November 23, beginning weekly publication that will continue through 1972. The initial cover illustration is by New York-born photographer Margaret Bourke-White, 32, and the new 10¢ picture magazine gains enormous success from the start for *Time-Fortune* publisher Henry Luce, who has acquired the name from the publishers of the now-defunct humor magazine begun in 1883.

Hearst newspaper executive Arthur Brisbane dies at New York December 25 at age 72. The mortgage on his building at 1215 Fifth Avenue will be foreclosed in 1939 and his huge triplex apartment will be broken up into smaller units.

Nonfiction: *How to Win Friends and Influence People* by Dale Carnegie, whose best-seller is full of such homilies as, "Believe that you will succeed and you will."

Fiction: *U.S.A.* by John Dos Passos, whose novel *The Forty-Second Parallel* completes a trilogy about post-war America that began with *The Big Money* in 1930 and *1919* in 1932. Dos Passos blames Wall Street and men like his father for much of what has gone wrong in America: "Listen businessmen collegepresidents judges America will not forget her betrayers;" *Nightwood* by New York-born novelist-playwright Djuna Barnes, 44, who started out as a reporter for the *Brooklyn Eagle* before the Great War, has moved from Greenwich Village to Paris, but will return to the city in 1940 and live in a tiny one-and-half-room apartment in Patchin Place; *Turn, Magic World* by Dawn Powell.

Painting: *George C. Tilyou's Steeplechase Park*, *Twenty Cent Movie*, and *End of the 14th Street Crosstown Line* by Reginald Marsh; *Sunrise I, II,* and *III* by Arthur Dove.

Sculpture: a bust of engineer John Wolfe Ambrose by Massachusetts-born sculptor Andrew O'Connor, 62, is installed near the Staten Island and Liberty Island Ferry ticket office at Battery Park; a bronze statue of Peter Stuyvesant by Gertrude Vanderbilt Whitney is unveiled in Stuyvesant Square at Second Avenue and 16th Street; a full-length figure of Civil War general Philip Sheridan by Italian-born sculptor Joseph Pollia, 43, is unveiled two blocks west of Washington Square in Christopher Street at the corner of Seventh Avenue and West 4th Street, where it occupies the northeast end of Sheridan Square. Survivors of the Grand Army of the Republic have presented the work to the city.

Eastman Kodak introduces Kodachrome in 35-millimeter cartridges and a paper-backed roll film (*see* 1935). The 18-exposure 35-millimeter cartridge goes on sale in August for $3.50, processing included, and makes color photography as easy for an amateur as black-and-white.

Theater: *End of Summer* by S. N. Behrman 2/17 at the Guild Theater, with Ina Claire, Osgood Perkins, Mildred Natwick, Oklahoma-born actor Van Heflin, 25, Shepperd Strudwick, 121 perfs.; *Conjur' Man Dies* by the late Rudolph Fisher in March at Harlem's Lafayette Theater; *Idiot's Delight* by Robert Sherwood 3/29 at the Shubert Theater, with Alfred Lunt and Lynn Fontanne (who lease a luxurious seven-room apartment at 130 East 75th Street) in an anti-war drama, 300 perfs.; *Bury the Dead* by Brooklyn-born playwright Irwin Shaw (originally Irwin Gilbert Shamforoff), 23, 4/18 at the Ethel Barrymore Theater, with Philadelphia-born actor Joseph Kramm, 28, Jay Adler, Indiana-born actor Will Geer, 32, Rose Keane in a one-act anti-war drama, 65 perfs.; *The Women* by New York-born playwright Clare Boothe Luce, 33, 7/9 at the Ethel Barrymore Theater, with Ilka Chase, Jane Seymour, Margalo Gilmore, Enid Markey, Boston-born actress Arlene Francis (originally Arlene Kazanjian), 27, Chicago-born actress Audrey Christie, 29, Cincinnati-born actress Doris Day (originally Doris von Kappelhoff), 22, Fort Wayne, Ind.-born actress Marjorie Main, 46, 657 perfs. (the playwright divorced her alcoholic and abusive first husband in May 1929 and went to work for Condé Nast's *Vanity Fair* magazine, became managing editor in 1933, resigned in 1934, and married millionaire publisher Henry R. Luce in November of last year after critics panned her autobiographical first play); *Reflected Glory* by George Kelly 9/21 at the Morosco Theater, with Alabama-born actress Tallulah Bankhead, 34, 127 perfs.; *Stage Door* by George S. Kaufman and Edna Ferber 10/22 at the Music Box Theater, with Norfolk, Va.-born actress Margaret Sullavan (originally Margaret Brooke), 25, Kentucky-born actor Tom Ewell (originally Yewell Tompkins), 27, set design by Harrisburg, Pa.-born Harvard graduate Donald (Mitchell) Oenslager, 34, 169 perfs.; *Tonight at 8:30* (*Hands Across the Sea*, *The Astonished Heart*, and *Red Peppers*) by Noël Coward 11/24 at the National Theater, with Coward, Gertrude Lawrence, Mississippi-born actress Moya Nugent, 36, Joyce Carey, Alan Webb, Anthony Pelissier, 118 perfs.; *You Can't Take It With You* by George S. Kaufman and Moss Hart 12/14 at the Booth Theater with Frank Wilcox, Newtonville, Mass.-born actress Josephine Hull (*née* Sherwood), 50, Ruth Attaway, New York-born actor George Tobias, 35, 837 perfs.; *Brother Rat* by V.M.I. graduates John Monks, Jr. and Fred F. Finklehoff 12/16 at the Biltmore Theater, with Rock Island, Ill.-born actor Eddie Albert (originally Edward Albert Heimberger), 28, Minnesota-born actor Frank Albertson, 27, New Bedford, Mass.-born actor Ezra Stone, 19, Puerto Rico-born actor José Ferrer, 24, 577 perfs.

Films: Gregory LaCava's *5th Ave. Girl* with Ginger Rogers, Walter Connolly, Verree Teasdale, James Ellison, Tim Holt; Robert Z. Leonard's *The Great Ziegfeld* with William Powell, Myrna Loy, Luise Rainer (as Anna Held), Frank Morgan, Fanny Brice; Gregory LaCava's *My Man Godfrey* with William Powell, Carole Lombard, Gail Patrick, Mischa Auer; Richard Boleslawski's *Theodora Goes Wild* with Irene Dunne, Melvyn Douglas. Also: Edward Ludwig's *Adventure in Manhattan* with Jean Arthur, Joel McCrea, Reginald Owen, Thomas Mitchell; William Keighley's *Bullets or Ballots* with Edward G. Robinson, Joan Blondell, Barton MacLane, Humphrey Bogart.

Film musicals: George Stevens's *Swing Time* with Fred Astaire, Ginger Rogers, Victor Moore, Helen Broderick.

Broadway musicals: *The Ziegfeld Follies* 1/30 at the Winter Garden Theater, with Bob Hope, Bobby Clark, Eve Arden, Josephine Baker, Jacksonville, Fla.-born singer Judy Canova, 22, Fanny Brice, Mobile-born tap dancer Fayard Nicholas, 21, and his Winston-Salem, N.C.-born brother Harold, 14, New York-born entertainer Gertrude Niesen, 24, music by Vernon Duke, George Gershwin and others, lyrics by David Freedman, Ira Gershwin, and others, songs that include "I Can't Get Started" by Vernon Duke, lyrics by Ira Gershwin, 227 perfs. (after an interruption due to Fanny Brice's illness); *On Your Toes* 4/11 at the Imperial Theater with Ray Bolger, actress-ballerina Tamara Geva and George Church dancing in the ballet *Slaughter on Tenth Avenue*, music by Richard Rodgers, lyrics by Oscar Hammerstein II, 315 perfs.; *Red, Hot and Blue* 10/29 at the Alvin Theater with Ethel Merman, Jimmy Durante, Grace and Paul Hartman, Bob Hope, book by Howard Lindsay and Russel Crouse, set design by Donald Oenslager, music and lyrics by Cole Porter, songs that include "De-Lovely," "Down in the Depths on the 90th Floor," 183 perfs.; *The Show Is On* 12/25 at the Ethel Barrymore Theater with the same cast as *The Women*, songs that include "By Strauss" by George Gershwin, lyrics by Ira Gershwin, "Little Old Lady" by Indiana-born composer Hoagland "Hoagy" Carmichael, 37, lyrics by Stanley Adams, 202 perfs.

Marilyn Miller dies of toxemia from an acute sinus infection at Doctors Hospital April 7 at age 37; one-time theatrical booking agency and Broadway magnate Marc Klaw of Klaw & Erlanger at his home in England June 14 at age 78. He financed the late Florenz Ziegfeld and received half of Ziegfeld's profits, married a young English woman 11 years ago, and has lived in seclusion.

Billboard magazine publishes the first pop music chart based on record sales January 4. The chart will become a weekly feature beginning in 1940, listing the 10 most popular records of the previous week, and beginning in August 1958 will become the "Hot 100" chart.

The Cotton Club that opened 13 years ago in Harlem reopens September 24 at 200 West 48th Street, off Times Square, where it will remain until early 1942 (*see* Latin Quarter, 1942).

Nick's opens in Greenwich Village. Nick Rogetti's place on Seventh Avenue at 10th Street will for 27 years attract jazz lovers to hear Sidney Bechet, George Bruno, Eddie Condon, "Wild Bill" Davison, Bud Freeman, Bobby Hackett, Max Kaminsky, Pee Wee Russell, Zutty Singleton, Willie "the Lion" Smith, Johnny Windhurst, and others.

Austrian-born pianist Rudolf Serkin, 32, makes his Carnegie Hall debut 2/20.

WQXR begins broadcasting December 3 as the first U.S. classical music station. Started by former women's hosiery merchant Elliot Sanger, 39, and engineer John V. L. Hogan, Interstate Broadcasting Co. is an outgrowth of W2XR, a low-wattage frequency at the end of the commercial band that Hogan has been using for audio transmissions, with an antenna atop a Ford agency and garage at Maspeth, Queens, while pursuing experiments with television (a former assistant to radio pioneer Lee DeForest, Hogan has used his own classical records to generate the music used to test reception of his audio signals). The station initially airs each evening at 5 o'clock because its signal is too weak to be heard in daylight hours; the *New York Times* will acquire it in 1944 and retain Sanger as manager while expanding its news coverage, continuing the station's original policy of limiting commercials.

A rally to raise funds for the Olympic Games at Berlin attracts a crowd of about 1,000 in June to the former Musical Mutual Protective Union Building at 209 East 85th Street in Yorkville. German vice-consul Friedhelm Draeger says the Berlin Olympics will show that Germany under Adolf Hitler is "a country united for peace," but about 100 protesters demonstrate outside, shouting, "Boycott the Nazi Olympics!"

Alabama-born contender Joe Louis (originally Joseph Louis Barrow), 22, fights former world heavyweight champion Max Schmeling, now 30, at Yankee Stadium June 19 and loses by a technical knockout in the 12th round. Germany's Nazi bosses

Rockefeller Center's skating rink attracted the relatively few who could afford it. MUNICIPAL ARCHIVE

have objected to Schmeling's "demeaning" himself by fighting a black, but they hail his victory, fly him home in the *Graf Zeppelin*, and lionize him. Louis will win the championship from James J. Braddock at Chicago in June of next year and hold it for 12 years (*see* 1938).

Fred Perry wins in men's singles at Forest Hills, Alice Marble, 22, in women's singles.

Split Rock golf course opens in Pelham Bay Park, supplementing the public course used since 1914. Named for a boulder and Indian trail, it has a clubhouse designed to resemble a southern plantation mansion.

Joe DiMaggio signs with the New York Yankees and begins a 13-year career in which his batting average will average .325, peak at .381 in 1938, and never fall below .300. San Francisco-born Joseph Paul DiMaggio, Jr., 21, will play until 1952, with a 3-year hiatus from 1943 to 1945.

The New York Yankees win the World Series, defeating the Giants 4 games to 2. Carl Hubbell outpitches Charles Herbert "Red" Ruffing, 32, of the Yankees to win the first game 6 to 1, but Joe DiMaggio gets nine hits in the series, including three doubles; Lou Gehrig seven hits, including a double and two home runs; outfielder George "Twinkletoes" Selkirk, 28, eight hits, including a triple and two home runs; catcher Bill Dickey, 29, three hits, including a home run; and second baseman Tony Lazzeri five hits, including a home run. Mel Ott gets seven hits for the Giants, including two doubles and a home run; shortstop Dick Bartell, 28, eight hits, including three doubles and a home run.

Brooklyn-born Columbia sophomore Sid Luckman, 19, begins a 3-year collegiate football career, having led Erasmus Hall High to two city championships. One of the first high-school players to be the subject of a major national recruiting effort, he had originally intended to go to Annapolis but has visited the Columbia locker room after a game in which the Lions lost 28 to 7 and been so impressed by coach Lou Little that even though Columbia has no athletic scholarships he has opted for Columbia, working his way through school by painting walls and washing dishes for meals at his Zeta Beta Tau fraternity house. Luckman will star in the Lions' backfield, playing 60 minutes per game (*see* 1938).

The first of 10 "million-dollar" public swimming pools is dedicated June 20 in Manhattan's Hamilton Fish Park, the second a week later in Harlem's Thomas Jefferson Park, the third in Astoria, Queens, in time for July 4, and the fifth (the McCarran Pool) July 31 in Brooklyn.

Rockefeller Center's ice-skating rink opens for its first season Christmas Day. It occupies most of a sunken plaza originally intended as a subway entrance to the IND, which was slow to establish a connection. A roller rink attracted undesirable elements from nearby Hell's Kitchen, so the management has opted to build a rink for figure skaters.

Bruno Richard Hauptmann dies in the electric chair at the New Jersey State Prison in Trenton April 3. Hauptmann protests his innocence of having kidnapped and killed Charles A. Lindbergh, Jr. in 1932, the evidence against him is far from conclusive, but anti-German sentiment has helped to seal his fate.

Charles "Lucky" Luciano draws a 30- to 50-year prison sentence after a New York jury convicts him of compulsory prostitution June 7 (*see* 1931; 1935). Luciano has been living under the name Charles Ross in Suite 39D of the Waldorf Towers, rented for $800 per month, but he enters Dannemora Prison upstate June 18 and will remain there until May 12, 1942, when he will be transferred to Great Meadow Prison, closer to the city (*see* 1946).

The city's homicide rate will fall to 4.5 per 100,000 in the next 5 years, down from 7.4 per 100,000 in the last 5 and its lowest level since the 1901-1905 period (*see* 1941).

The U.S. Courthouse is completed at 40 Centre Street. The late Cass Gilbert designed the 31-story neo-classical structure, whose plans have been finished by his son Cass, Jr. It is capped with a gold pyramid.

Greenwich House founder and City Housing Authority member Mary Simkovitch appeals January 30 for better housing for those earning less than $1,500 per year.

Bronx-raised real estate agent Harry B. (Brakmann) Helmsley, 27, buys his first building with a down payment of $1,000. He began his career in the mail room of a real estate firm, started collecting rents, and has reinvested his commissions to raise the $1,000. Enforcing city laws, Helmsley says February 7, will bring foreclosures, creating a shortage of cheaper apartments (see Helmsley-Spear, 1955).

Pressure grows to amend the Multiple Dwellings Law of 1929 and give landlords a moratorium on the requirement to install fire-retardant hallways and a toilet for every family, but the Brownell bill passed by the assembly at Albany February 17 amends the law to require installation of sprinkler systems. While efforts continue to outlaw occupancy of windowless rooms by 1939, at least one real estate expert says February 27 that literal enforcement of current laws would dispossess 1.5 million tenants.

The new city charter creates a City Planning Commission to advise on land-use decisions by the Board of Estimate. Rexford Guy Tugwell heads the commission (see 1938).

The U.S. Supreme Court ruling in *New York City Housing Authority v. Muller* establishes the authority's right to employ the power of eminent domain for slum-clearing purposes. The decision gives a broader meaning to the term *public use* and represents a victory for the Housing Authority's first counsel, Lithuanian-born lawyer Charles Abrams, 34.

First Houses open June 22 on the Lower East Side with 122 units built to provide decent low-cost housing (see 1935). Social workers from local settlement houses have selected the tenants from 15,000 applicants. The city still has 40,000 old-law tenements, and owners of multiple dwellings are ordered to vacate them July 21 unless they are kept fit for habitation. In the next 40 years the City Housing Authority will build 228 projects with 167,000 apartments to house 560,000 persons, and within 60 years New York will have 342 public housing projects; they will generally be considered the best in the country, but while 50 percent of all tenants will for some years be working people that percentage will decline to 33 percent as residents on public assistance come to dominate tenancy.

John D. Rockefeller, Jr. forecloses on the mortgage of Harlem's Dunbar Apartments. Many of the co-op's tenants have defaulted on their maintenance payments; all get back their equity but are allowed to remain on a rental basis.

Former governor Alfred E. Smith accuses the Roosevelt administration October 30 of refusing to cooperate with private capital on state and city housing projects despite promises of aid. Congress has failed to pass the Wagner-Ellenbogen Housing Bill despite urging by Mayor La Guardia and others to enact the slum-clearance and low-cost-housing measure. La Guardia says December 3 that slum clearance can help eliminate tuberculosis in the city.

The Rockefeller Apartments are completed at 17 West 54th Street and 24 West 55th Street. Designed by Harrison & Fouilhoux, the 12-story-plus-penthouse building has cylindrical bay windows.

More than 90 percent of the city's fashionable rich now live in apartments, up from 10 percent 25 years ago. Apartment house owners begin upgrading their buildings in a bid to keep old tenants and attract new ones: 400 Park Avenue becomes the city's (and the nation's) first apartment house to have every room air-conditioned (it also has its 11- and 12-room suites converted into apartments of five and six rooms). Other apartment houses have slashed rents, many co-operative apartments have been sold at sacrifice prices, some co-op buildings have become rental buildings, construction of new buildings has come almost to a halt as vacancy rates soar, and some owners have demolished their buildings and replaced them with "taxpayers"—one-story rows of shops—to reduce their tax burdens.

The 422-unit Flagg Court housing development is completed at 7200 Ridge Road, between 72nd and 73rd streets, in Bay Ridge, Brooklyn, to designs by Ernest Flagg.

The city's second water tunnel comes onstream to supplement the tunnel completed in 1917, feeding water from Catskill and Delaware reservoirs into trunk mains. Both tunnels are required to supply the city's growing needs, and although a third tunnel is needed in order for either of the first two to be shut down for inspection and repairs, the third tunnel will not be completed until the 21st century.

The temperature in Central Park reaches a record 106° July 9 and virtually nobody in the city has air conditioning. People go to air-conditioned movie theaters to cool off, sleeping on fire escapes and in the park to escape stifling indoor temperatures.

Goya Foods has its beginnings in a New York concern started by Puerto Rican entrepreneur Provenzio Unanue Ortiz and his wife, Carolina (*née* Casa), to import olives and olive oil. Sponsoring floats at almost every Puerto Rican Day parade and giving support to Spanish dance and theater groups, their business will grow—despite occasional quality and delivery glitches—to distribute some 750 items of beans, rice, flour, spices, and frozen foods, with close to 80 percent of the market for Hispanic foods in the U.S. Northeast. After Unanue's death in 1976 his sons Joseph (now 10), Francisco (now 3), Charles, and Anthony will take over (Anthony will also die in 1976), and they—along with *their* children—will work to increase sales among the city's (and nation's) rapidly growing Puerto Rican, Cuban, Mexican, and other Hispanic populations.

The A&P begins opening supermarkets, as do other major food chains (*see* King Kullen, 1930). Three or four smaller stores are closed down for every A&P supermarket opened, but most New York City A&Ps remain small (*see* 1912; 1957).

1937 Spanish insurgent forces advance with Italian support, taking Malaga February 8. German bombers annihilate the defenseless Basque town of Guernica April 26 while Heinkel fighter planes strafe civilians who have fled into the fields, but stories by William Carney of the *New York Times* show support for Gen. Francisco Franco's fascist insurgents, as do stories in the Hearst papers, the *Daily News*, the Scripps-Howard papers, and the *Brooklyn Tablet*, a diocesan weekly. They depict all Spanish Loyalists as "communists."

Japanese forces invade China July 7 in an undeclared war that will continue until 1945. The New York Overseas Chinese Anti-Japanese Salvation General Committee for Military Funds is organized to collect money and sponsors programs that expose Japanese atrocities against Chinese civilians, but the *Daily News* says editorially November 5 that China is "licked" and the United States should do "all the business we can [with Japan], regardless of disapproval of the way the land [in China] was acquired."

The German-American Bund holds a parade in Yorkville October 30 and Mayor La Guardia comes under fire for allowing it. The mayor says its effect was to exacerbate racial hatreds and claims it was staged by his opponents to embarrass him: "So they had a Nazi parade. If a permit had been refused they had statements saying that La Guardia was a Jew and if granted La Guardia was a Nazi and the parade was held in Yorkville and I was sorry to see some splen-

did people fall for it." The event was conducted under the supervision of Jewish policemen. Told that a sound truck had been found in the Bronx bearing the emblem of the Communist Party and a sign urging people to "Vote for La Guardia," the mayor says it was financed by Tammany politicians in that borough.

Mayor La Guardia wins reelection with support from the City Fusion, Progressive, American Labor, and Republican parties, receiving 1,344,630 votes as compared with 890,756 for his Democratic opponent, former state supreme court justice Jeremiah Titus Mahoney, 58, who has criticized the mayor for not repudiating communist support and has himself received support from the Trades Union and Anti-Communist parties. Sen. Royal S. Copeland won reelection 3 years ago by a resounding margin of 629,000, he has opposed many New Deal proposals, Tammany Hall has entered him in the Democratic Party's primary for mayor in hopes of breaking the Flynn-Kelly-Farley domination of state politics, and Copeland has also entered the Republican primary on former governor Al Smith's advice, but he has lost both primary races, ending Smith's hope for a political comeback. Fusion's strength is limited to New York County (Manhattan). The American Labor Party formed last year by labor leaders David Dubinsky and Sidney Hillman polls 481,779 votes and holds the balance of power in the city and state. (Augustus) Newbold Morris, 35, is elected president of the City Council that will replace the Board of Aldermen next year. Special Prosecutor Thomas E. Dewey wins election as district attorney in New York County, defeating William C. Dodge and ending Tammany control of the prosecutor's office in Manhattan, but Tammany officials continue to rule in the city's other counties.

Amalgamated Clothing Workers president Sidney Hillman obtains a settlement with the Clothing Manufacturers Association and establishes a bargaining pattern that will be used throughout the industry (*see* 1918). Hillman has organized all but a handful of men's clothing workers.

Mayor La Guardia receives a letter from a Mr. A. W. Brown of the Bombay Oil Co., Rochester: "Did you know the Jews, plus the bankers through Gov. Lehman and Morgenthau, who is United States Treasurer and nephew of Gov. Lehman by marriage, have had this Country by the throat for the last four years and won't let go? What are you going to do about that, Mayor?" La Guardia replies, "Should you come to New York City I would suggest that you contact Dr. Earl Bowman. I think he might understand your case. He is in charge of the psychopathic department of Bellevue Hospital, 29th Street and First Avenue."

$ The U.S. economic recovery that has progressed for 4 years falters beginning in midyear. Business activity suffers a sharp drop; Wall Street's Dow Jones Industrial Average falls from its post-1929 high of 194.40.

Investment banker Charles Hayden of Hayden Stone (and Hayden Planetarium fame) dies at the Savoy-Plaza Hotel January 8 at age 66; lawyer-diplomat Elihu Root at New York February 7—just 8 days before his 92nd birthday; former secretary of the treasury (and 1926 New York gubernatorial candidate) Ogden L. Mills dies of a coronary thrombosis at New York October 11 at age 53; banker Felix M. Warburg suffers a heart attack October 18, dies at New York October 20 at age 66, and is buried in Brooklyn's Salem Fields Cemetery.

The ABC of Municipal Bonds by Louis Lebenthal of Lebenthal & Co. enjoys a wide sale and will become a standard work, explaining to readers how tax-exempt bonds finance city projects (*see* 1925).

Astoria Federal Savings and Loan Association adopts that name and builds a headquarters building at 37-16 30th Avenue, Long Island City (*see* 1888). It has become a major lender of home mortgages throughout Queens, and although the Depression is making it hard for many homeowners to keep up their mortgage payments the loan company will survive and prosper (*see* 1989).

The Value Line Investment Survey is established by Arnold Bernhard of 1931 *Value Line Ratings* fame; let go by Moody's in 1934 because his ideas of portfolio management were considered too revolutionary, he started a firm under his own name in 1935 (*see* mutual funds, 1950).

Wall Street's Dow Jones Industrial Average closes November 24 at 113.64, rallies somewhat, but closes December 31 at 120.85, down from 179.90 at the end of 1936.

Lord & Taylor promotes Dorothy Shaver to president (*see* 1931), but while the press proclaims her $110,000 salary as the highest on record for any woman, LIFE magazine notes that men in comparable jobs earn four times that much. Shaver will boost sales from their current level of $30 million up to $50 million by 1951 and they will reach $100 million by the time of her death in 1959.

Abraham & Straus, Macy's, and other major retailers have disappointing Christmas sales; efforts increase to unionize salesclerks.

Oil baron-philanthropist John D. Rockefeller dies at Ormond Beach, Fla., May 23 at age 97, leaving an estate of just $26.4 million, most of it in U.S. Treasury notes (he has long since given away most of his vast fortune).

The Independent subway line opened in Queens at the end of last year reaches Jamaica April 24, enabling residents to reach Manhattan or Brooklyn 24 hours per day for a 5¢ fare. By 1940 Jamaica will have five theaters and a nightclub as population in the area grows.

The West Side Highway that opened in 1930 as the Miller Elevated Highway becomes an elevated six-lane motorcar and truck route along the Hudson River from the Battery to 72nd Street (where it becomes the Henry Hudson Parkway) (*see* collapse, 1973).

The Chauffeurs Union obtains a CIO contract May 7; the Greater New York Taxicab Chauffeurs and Servicemen union is organized May 22 to seek AF of L membership; alderman Newbold Morris proposes May 25 that an ordinance be passed giving drivers a 10-hour day and a minimum wage; the Transport Workers Union (TWU) issues a strike ultimatum May 29 to the Parmalee Transportation Co., demanding a collective-bargaining referendum in the city; the Terminal Taxicab System ousts its union June 19; the Bell Transportation Co. signs a closed-shop agreement with the TWU October 9 and asks for police protection against labor racketeering; some 300 Sunshine Radio System taxi drivers walk out October 13 to protest a closed-shop contract with the TWU; the strike continues to October 17 but a more widespread one begins in mid-December and scabs are beaten up. The Haas Act signed by Mayor La Guardia at year's end establishes a system of medallions for the city's taxis (*see* strike, 1934). Available for $10 but limited in number to 13,566, these metal tags are official licenses that represent a compromise between independent owners and the owners of large taxicab fleets, but they give medallion owners a monopoly that will work to restrict the number of operating taxis. The city has close to 12,000 licensed cabs, and the market price for a medallion will escalate in the next 60 years to a figure well in excess of $100,000, encouraging the growth of "gypsy" (private livery company) cabs (*see* strike, 1938).

The Lincoln Tunnel between Manhattan and Weehawken, N.J., opens to vehicular traffic under the Hudson River December 22. More than 1,790,000 50¢ tolls will be collected in the 8,000-foot tunnel's first year of operation, a second tube will open in

December 1940, and within 60 years the tunnel will be collecting some 20 million tolls per year.

Brooklyn College moves to a new campus on Avenue H in Flatbush with neo-Georgian buildings (*see* 1930; Gideonse, 1939).

Queens College is founded with a campus off Kissena Boulevard in Flushing used up to now as a school for juvenile delinquents. Originally a group of extension centers set up by Hunter and City colleges in the 1920s, Queens now becomes an autonomous entity that will grow in 30 years to have 17,500 students from 120 countries and a faculty of 1,300.

Xerography is pioneered by Seattle-born New York pre-law student and physicist Chester (Floyd) Carlson, 31, a California Institute of Technology graduate whose dry-copying process will revolutionize duplication of papers in offices, schools, and libraries (*see* 1938).

William Randolph Hearst merges his evening *New York Journal* with his morning *New York American* to create the *New York Journal-American*, an afternoon paper (*see* 1895; 1966).

Newsweek magazine begins publication at New York to compete with Henry Luce's *Time*. Real estate heir Vincent Astor, now 42, and railroad heir W. Averell Harriman, now 45, merge their newsweekly *Today* with Thomas J. C. Martyn's 4-year-old *News-Week*, and bring in as editor former assistant secretary of state Raymond Moley, now 51, installing McGraw-Hill president Malcolm Muir as publisher (*see* 1961).

Look magazine begins publication at Des Moines to compete with Henry Luce's LIFE. *Des Moines Register* publisher Gardner "Mike" Cowles, Jr., 34, launches the biweekly picture magazine that he will move to New York in 1941 and continue until 1971.

Harper's Bazaar promotes columnist Diana Vreeland (*née* Dalziel), 37, to fashion editor. Born in Paris of a U.S. mother and Scottish father, banker's wife Vreeland came to New York in 1914, made her debut in 1922, and last year began writing a *Bazaar* column under the heading "Why Don't You?" with Depression-blind suggestions such as "Why don't you put all your dogs in bright yellow collars and leads like all the dogs in Paris?" and "Why don't you have a furry elk-hide trunk for the back of your car?" (*see* 1962).

Woman's Day appears in October as the A&P launches a 3¢ monthly women's service magazine for distribution in A&P stores. The food chain will sell the magazine to Fawcett Publications in 1958.

Nonfiction: *Life with Mother* by the late Clarence Day.

Fiction: *Their Eyes Were Watching God* by Florida-born Harlem novelist Zora Neale Hurston, 46 (who wrote it in 7 weeks in Haiti, where she studied voodoo practices on a Guggenheim grant); *They Came Like Swallows* by Lincoln, Ill.-born New York novelist William (Keepers) Maxwell (, Jr.), 29, who joined the staff of The *New Yorker* last year and will continue until 1976; *The Education of H*y*m*a*n K*a*p*l*a*n* by New York humorist sociologist Leonard Q. Ross (Leo [Calvin] Rosten), 29, who came to America from Poland as an infant and finds poignant humor in the efforts of immigrants to gain education in the city's free adult education classes; *Strictly from Hunger* by S. J. Perelman.

Juvenile: *And to Think That I Saw It on Mulberry Street* by Massachusetts-born New York writer-illustrator Dr. Seuss (Theodor Seuss Geisel), 33, who has been working in the art department of the McCann-Erickson advertising agency.

The 183-year-old New York Society Library takes over the 20-year-old Rogers house at 53 East 79th Street, between Madison and Park avenues. Having occupied a number of different premises since 1795 (*see* Melville, 1851), it provides working space for writers who will include Willa Cather and Lillian Hellman, pleasing members with services that include lending them books to keep over long summer vacations.

Painting: *Me and the Moon* by Arthur Dove.

The Metropolitan Museum of Art's Costume Institute has its beginnings in the Museum of Costume Art opened at 16 West 46th Street. Philanthropist Irene Lewisohn and a group of her theater friends have been collecting costumes since the 1920s for their Neighborhood Playhouse in Grand Street (*see* 1946).

Sculpture: a bronze statue of 69th Division chaplain Father Francis P. Duffy by Charles Keck is unveiled near the 47th Street end of Times Square. Sculptor Frederick W. MacMonnies dies at Doctors Hospital March 22 at age 73.

Photographs: *Changing New York* by Berenice Abbott, 39, records scenes of the city at whose New School for Social Research she has taught. Born in Maine, Abbott returned to the United States in 1929 after studying sculpture in Paris and photographing well-known artists and writers of the decade. Her undertaking has been financed by the Museum of the City of New York and financed by the Federal Arts Project of the Works Progress Administration (WPA), which has paid her $145 per week at a time when most photographers are lucky to make half that much, provided her with a car to carry the 60 pounds of equipment she used, and furnished her with a secretary, technical assistant, and five part-time researchers (text by Elizabeth McCausland).

 Theater: *High Tor* by Maxwell Anderson 1/9 at the Martin Beck Theater, with Burgess Meredith, Peggy Ashcroft, 171 perfs.; *The Masque of Kings* by Maxwell Anderson 2/8 at the Shubert Theater, with Dudley Digges, Henry Hull, Margo, 89 perfs.; *Yes, My Darling Daughter* by U.S. playwright Mark Reed 2/9 at The Playhouse, with Peggy Conklin, Lucile Watson, 405 perfs.; *"Having Wonderful Time"* by Austrian-born playwright Arthur Kober, 36, 2/20 at the Lyceum Theater, with Katherine Locke, Jules (John) Garfield, New York-born actor Cornel Wilde, 18, 132 perfs.; *Room Service* by John Murray and Allen Boretz 5/19 at the Cort Theater, with Russian-born actor Sam Levene, 31, Eddie Albert, Boston-born actress Betty Field, 19, 500 perfs.; *Susan and God* by Rachel Crothers, now 66, 10/7 at the Plymouth Theater, with Gertrude Lawrence, Douglas Gilmore, Vera Allen, Lowell, Mass.-born actress Nancy Kelly, 16; *Golden Boy* by Clifford Odets 11/23 at the Belasco Theater, with John Garfield, New York-born actor Lee J. Cobb (originally Leo Jacoby), 25, Gary, Ind.-born actor Karl Malden (originally Malden Sekulovich), 24, Turkish-born actor Elia Kazan (originally Elia Kazanjoglous), 28, in a play about prizefighting, 250 perfs.; *Of Mice and Men* by Salinas, Calif.-born novelist-playwright John (Ernst) Steinbeck, 35, 11/23 at the Music Box Theater, with Art Lund as Lennie, 207 perfs. (director George S. Kaufman has polished Steinbeck's efforts to present his story on the stage while Steinbeck gathers material for his novel *The Grapes of Wrath*).

Mayor La Guardia tries to ban burlesque shows in the city. The shows have been featuring such entertainers as Abbott and Costello, Red Buttons, Gypsy Rose Lee, and Phil Silvers, theater critics who include Brooks Atkinson and A. J. Liebling have expressed admiration for burlesque as good fun, but the mayor issues an order April 30 that the Minsky theater licenses are not to be renewed, forbids the use of the words *burlesque* and *Minsky* from theatrical advertising, and forces the closing of 13 theaters; the Minsky brothers have charged 35¢ admission and suffer a blow, the Eltinge Theater that opened in 1912 becomes a movie theater, and exhibitors take over other West 42nd Street houses, showing films 24 hours per day (*see* 1942).

Radio: *Grand Central Station* on NBC Blue Network stations: "As a bullet seeks its target, shining rails in every part of our great country are aimed at Grand Central Station, heart of the nation's greatest city. Drawn by the magnetic force of the fantastic metropolis, day and night great trains rush toward the Hudson River, sweep down its eastern bank for 140 miles, flash briefly by the long red row of tenement houses south of 125th Street, dive with a roar into the two-and-a-half-mile tunnel which burrows beneath the glitter and swank of Park Avenue, and then—EEEEESSSSHHHhhh—Grand Central Station! Crossroads of a million private lives! Gigantic stage on which are placed a thousand dramas daily" (the show will move to CBS in 1944 and to ABC in 1956).

CBS signs London-born New York comic Henny (originally Henry) Youngman, 31, for a 6-minute spot on its 6-year-old Kate Smith radio show, sponsored by A&P, and he gets so many laughs that he is kept on for 10 minutes, receives $250, and will be a regular on the show until 1947. Youngman grew up in the Bay Ridge section of Brooklyn, was thrown out of Manual Training High School for truancy, has worked as a *tummler* (social director) in the Catskills, won the accolade "King of the One-Liners" from columnist Walter Winchell, will play a violin (badly) between jokes (he calls his fiddle a "Stradivaricose"), and will gain a reputation with cracks he makes at the expense of his wife, Sadie (*née* Cohen), the chief examples being, "How's your wife?" "Compared to what?" and "Take my wife—please." .

Films: Leo McCarey's *The Awful Truth* with Irene Dunne, Cary Grant, Ralph Bellamy; William Wellman's *Nothing Sacred* with Carole Lombard, Fredric March; Gregory La Cava's *Stage Door* with Katharine Hepburn, Ginger Rogers, Lucille Ball, Adolphe Menjou. Also: Frank Borzage's *The Big City* with Spencer Tracy, Luise Rainer; Eugene Forde's *Charlie Chan on Broadway* with Warner Oland; Mitchell Leisen's *Easy Living* with Jean Arthur, Edward Arnold, Ray Milland; Harold Young's *52nd Street* with Ian Hunter, Leo Carillo, Kenny Baker, Ella Logan, ZaSu Pitts; Michael Curtiz's *Kid Galahad* with Edward G. Robinson, Bette Davis, Humphrey Bogart; Lloyd Bacon's *Marked Woman* with Bette Davis, Humphrey Bogart; Albert S. Rogell's *Murder in Greenwich Village* with Richard Arlen, Fay Wray; Rowland V. Lee's *The Toast of New York* with Edward Arnold (as Jim Fisk), Cary Grant, Frances Farmer, Jack Oakie.

Film musicals: Mark Sandrich's *Shall We Dance* with Ginger Rogers, Fred Astaire, music by George Gershwin, lyrics by Ira Gershwin, songs that include

"They Can't Take That Away from Me," "They All Laughed," "Slap That Bass," "Let's Call the Whole Thing Off," and the title song. Also: Roy Del Ruth's *On the Avenue* with Dick Powell, Madeleine Carroll, Alice Faye, the Ritz Brothers, music and lyrics by Irving Berlin, songs that include "I've Got My Love to Keep Me Warm," "This Year's Kisses," "The Girl on the Police Gazette," "Let's Go Slumming;" Irving Cummings's *Vogues of 1938* with Warner Baxter, Joan Bennett, songs that include "That Old Feeling" by Sammy Fain, lyrics by Lew Brown.

Broadway and off-Broadway musicals: *The Eternal Road* 1/7 at the Manhattan Opera House with Sam Jaffe, 11-year-old Sidney Lumet, 8-year old Dick Van Patten, Lotte Lenya, music by Lenya's husband, Kurt Weill, based on Hebraic melodies learned from his cantor father, book by Franz Werfel, whose biblical drama is directed by Max Reinhardt (Weill, a non-practicing Jew, has written the music outside Paris), 152 perfs. (the house sells out every performance, but set designer Norman Bel Geddes has removed 300 choice seats to make room for a larger stage and the producers lose $7,000 per performance); *Babes in Arms* 4/14 at the Shubert Theater, with Ray Heatherton, New York-born singer-actor Alfred Drake (originally Alfredo Capurro), 23, New York-born ingénu Dan Dailey, 23, New York-born ingénue Mitzi Green (originally Elizabeth Keno), 18, ingénu Robert Rounseville, 23, music by Richard Rodgers, lyrics by Lorenz Hart, songs that include "My Funny Valentine," "The Lady Is a Tramp," "Johnny One Note," "I Wish I Were in Love Again," "Where or When," 289 perfs.; *The Cradle Will Rock* 6/16 at the Venice Theater, with Cleveland-born actor Howard da Silva (originally Silverblatt), 27, Philadelphia-born singer-composer Marc Blitzstein, 32, a 28-piece orchestra, a 44-member chorus, book and music by Blitzstein, direction by Orson Welles, production by John Houseman, songs that include "Croon Spoon," "Honolulu," "I'm Checkin' Home Now," "Nickel Under the Foot." The show was supposed to open at Maxine Elliott's Theater in West 38th Street, but the Federal Theater Project sent word June 12 that budget cuts and a reorganization dictated a postponement (after 14,000 tickets had been sold), a theatrical agent has offered a theater 21 blocks uptown for $100, the audience, cast, musicians, and crew make their way north to Seventh Avenue and 59th Street, lighting director Abe Feder sets up a spotlight, conductor Lehman Engel strikes up the orchestra, and because Actors Equity has barred them from singing on stage the singers perform from the audience, continuing for 2 weeks of sold-out performances before going on tour; *I'd*

Rather Be Right 11/2 at the Alvin Theater, with George M. Cohan as President Roosevelt, book by George S. Kaufman, music by Richard Rodgers, lyrics by Lorenz Hart, songs that include "Have You Met Miss Jones?" 290 perfs.; *Pins and Needles* 11/27 at the Labor Stage Theater, with music and lyrics by Hartford-born songwriter Harold (originally Jacob) Rome, 29, songs that include "Nobody Makes a Pass at Me," 1,108 perfs. (the International Ladies' Garment Workers' Union [ILGWU] sponsors the production and no cast member receives more than $55 per week); *Between the Devil* 12/22 at the Imperial Theater, with Jack Buchanan, Evelyn Laye, music by Arthur Schwartz, lyrics by Howard Dietz, songs that include "By Myself," 93 perfs.

Songwriter George Gershwin dies of a brain tumor at Hollywood July 11 at age 38. His remains are shipped to New York for a funeral at Frank E. Campbell's.

The National Broadcasting Co. starts the NBC Symphony with Arturo Toscanini as conductor. Now 70, Toscanini has been replaced as conductor of the New York Philharmonic after 8 years but has accepted the new post at the urging of his wife, Carla, who married him in 1897; he will conduct the NBC Symphony until his retirement in 1954.

Brooklyn-born publishing industry graphic artist, amateur violinist, and radio hobbyist Avery Fisher, 31, founds Philharmonic Radio Co. with a $354 investment to market improvements he has made in audio design. He rents a small loft in West 21st Street, buys RCA Photophone amplifiers that are being used in movie theaters, adds Western Electric speakers, an FM tuner, and a turntable, and creates some of the world's first component systems. He will sell the company, found Fisher Radio, and by the early 1960s will account for 50 percent of U.S. high-fidelity component sales. Along with Herman Hosner Scott, Paul Klipsch, Frank McIntosh, and others, Fisher will break new ground in raising the quality of musical sound reproduction (*see* 1969).

Popular songs: "New York After Dark" by Vernon Duke; "When New York Was New York" by George M. Cohan; "Way Out West (on West End Avenue)" by Richard Rodgers, lyrics by Lorenz Hart.

Oakland, Calif.-born player John Donald "Don" Budge, 22, wins in men's singles at Forest Hills, Anita Lizana in women's singles.

The New York Yankees win the World Series, defeating the Giants 4 games to 1. Yankee pitcher Vernon Louis "Lefty" Gomez, 27, wins the first and fifth games, Carl Hubbell of the Giants the fourth. Joe DiMaggio gets six hits, including one home run; Lou

Gehrig five hits, including a double, a triple, and a home run; third baseman Robert Abial "Red" Rolfe, 28, six hits, including two doubles and a triple. Mel Ott hits the only Giant home run.

● Paris-born fashion designer Pauline Trigère, 29, stops at New York en route to Chile with her Russian-born husband, Lazar Radley, and decides to remain. "New York captured my heart," she will later say. The two open a small tailoring shop with Trigère's brother Robert, Radley will quit in 1942 and file for divorce, Trigère will not remarry, and the collections at her Seventh Avenue showrooms will gain a wide following among fashion-conscious women until she retires in 1994, becoming famous for the understated look of her long wool dinner sheaths, short-sleeved coats, and jumpsuits.

The Custom Shop Shirtmakers is founded by New York entrepreneur Mortimer Levitt, 31, whose skinny neck and broad shoulders make it impossible for him to fit into ready-made shirts. He figures out a way to make custom shirts at almost the same price and starts a business that he will still be running in his 90s, producing tailor-made men's shirts and suits in 63 stores nationwide.

The city's first Pulaski Day parade steps off in October on Fifth Avenue, honoring the Revolutionary War hero Count Kazimierz Pulaski, who performed so well at the Battle of Brandywine in 1777 but was mortally wounded in the siege of Savannah in 1779. Lawyer Francis J. Wazeter, 30, saw the St. Patrick's Day parade in March and has persuaded Polish New Yorkers to organize a parade of their own.

The Marijuana Traffic Act signed into law by President Roosevelt August 2 outlaws possession and sale of *Cannabis sativa*.

Major crimes in New York have declined by 19 percent in Mayor La Guardia's first administration; the city has had only four bank robberies, as compared with 15 in the previous (Tammany) administration; there have been 30 percent fewer payroll robberies, and only half as many cases of grand larceny, with 19,958 fewer automobiles stolen, down from 40,785.

The Time-Life Building opens in September at 1 Rockefeller Plaza with 36 floors (*see* 1959).

The Harlem River Houses open in May between 151st and 153rd streets on the Harlem River Drive, where seven four- to five-story red-brick buildings have been built as the city's first federally financed and federally constructed public housing. Graced with trees and spacious plazas, the projects have been erected following 1935 Harlem riots demanding decent low-cost housing; rents are low, and the carefully screened tenants are provided with a nursery, a health clinic, and social rooms; 14,000 black families apply for the project's 577 apartments. Archibald Manning Brown has designed the development with help from Charles F. Fuller, Horace Ginsbern, Frank J. Forster, Will Rice Amon, Richard W. Buckley, John L. Wilson, Michael Rapuano and some landscape architects.

Some 25,000 apartment units are demolished in the five boroughs, 15,000 of them in Manhattan and Brooklyn, as slum-clearance projects go forward.

The U.S. Housing Authority (USHA) created by Congress September 1 in the Wagner-Steagall Act promises to provide financial assistance (grants and long-term loans) to the states in an effort to remedy the nation's housing shortage (and to provide work in the construction trades). Mayor La Guardia obtains agreements for USHA-financed projects in Red Hook, Queensbridge, and Corlears Hook.

The 37-story Hampshire House is completed in October at 150 Central Park South (59th Street), between Sixth and Seventh avenues. Designed by Caughey & Evans with a façade of white brick, two tall chimneys, and a steeply pitched copper roof echoing that of the Savoy Plaza Hotel to its east, it was begun in January 1931 but work on it was stopped after 6 months when its developer failed. The structure opens as a co-operative with 150 units, 550 rooms.

A 16-story apartment house is completed at the northwest corner of Madison Avenue and 72nd Street. Designed by Rosario Candela and Mott B. Schmidt, it replaces the Tiffany mansion.

Millicent (Mrs. William Randolph) Hearst gives up the 30-room apartment at the Clarendon on Riverside Drive at 86th Street that she has occupied since 1908. Insurance company regulators will relax restrictions on where such companies may invest their money, Metropolitan Life Insurance Co. will take over the building from Hearst in 1939, foreclose on its mortgage in 1940, gut the place, and break its 24 units into 60 (it will be converted to co-op ownership in 1985).

The 18-story 565 West End Avenue apartment house is completed at the northwest corner of 87th Street to Art Deco designs by Austrian-born architect H. I. (Hyman Isaac) Feldman, 41.

Architect George F. Pelham dies at Verbank, N.Y., February 7 at age 70; John Russell Pope of cancer at his native New York August 27 at age 63.

Jacob Riis Park opens with a mile of sandy ocean beach stretching to Rockaway Inlet. Designed by Frank Wallis with simple WPA-built locker rooms, it extends from Beach 149th to Beach 169th streets with handball courts, platform tennis courts, shuffleboard courts, and a boardwalk.

The city's first sewage treatment plant is constructed on Coney Island (see 1902). New York has been pouring nearly 1.5 million gallons of raw sewage into the harbor each day, it will build six more treatment plants in the next 5 years, and three more in 1952; by 1962 three-quarters of the city's sewage will be treated before discharge into the environment (see 1987).

Ragú spaghetti sauce has its beginnings in a spicy tomato-and-cheese sauce put up in mason jars at New York and distributed to friends and neighbors by Italian-born pasta, wine, and cheese importer Giovanni Cantisano and his wife, Assunta.

Key Food is organized as a co-operative supermarket chain by a group of independent Brooklyn grocers who join forces to open a Sunset Park store at the corner of Second Avenue and 45th Street and challenge the growing dominance of the A&P and other national chains. Key will grow in 60 years to have nearly 160 stores in the metropolitan area, most of them in the five boroughs, with a warehouse in the Brooklyn Terminal Market in East Flatbush.

Restaurateur Frank G. Shattuck dies of pneumonia at his home in the Hotel Pierre March 13 at age 76. The Schrafft's chain now has 43 stores in New York, Boston, and other eastern cities and will continue for more than 30 years to enjoy wide popularity.

1938 Mayor La Guardia is sworn in just after midnight January 1 to begin a second term, and the City Council that has succeeded the Board of Aldermen meets for the first time January 3, with Newbold Morris presiding. A grandson of former mayor Ambrose C. Kingsland, Republican Morris must deal with the fact that 13 of the 26 Council members are Tammany Hall Democrats; Tammany has lost control of the Board of Estimate and is determined to regain its power and patronage in the city.

Britain and France protest Adolf Hitler's takeover of Austria in April but are unprepared for war and appease *der führer* at Munich September 29, permitting him to take Czechoslovakia's Sudetenland.

Newsman H. V. Kaltenborn, now 60, moves a cot into the CBS studio at 485 Madison Avenue and works for 18 days, giving instant translations of speeches by Hitler and French premier Edouard Daladier plus his own analyses of the Munich Conference. Mayor La Guardia announces that he will not allow Germany to mount an exhibit at the World's Fair next year, and if somehow Germany is able to have an exhibit that he will put a wax effigy of Adolf Hitler in a Museum of Horrors; he calls Hermann Goering a "perverted maniac," Secretary of State Cordell Hull submits a formal apology, another insult and apology ensue, Goering vows to bomb New York from Governors Island to Rockefeller Center "to stop somewhat the mouths of the arrogant people over there," the German consulate in Manhattan demands police protection against possible attacks from angered Jews, and La Guardia sends Jewish cops to stand guard. When the mayor visits the White House to keep an appointment, President Roosevelt extends his right arm and says, "Heil, Fiorello;" La Guardia, also extending his right arm, replies, "Heil, Franklin." (the mayor has persuaded the president to grant the city millions of dollars for construction of an airport, bridges, tunnels, highways, health-care centers, hospitals, parks, schools, and sewer systems).

Gov. Lehman wins election for the fourth time, this time to a 4-year term, securing 2,391,286 votes to 2,326,892 for his Republican opponent, Manhattan District Attorney Thomas E. Dewey, now 40.

Mayor La Guardia receives a small package December 8 containing a live .22-caliber long cartridge and a note, signed with a crayoned swastika, reading, "You will get this if you continue to attack the German Nazi Party." The mayor is punched in the face and knocked down on the steps of City Hall December 20 by a deranged stonemason who has lost his WPA job and blames the mayor for his misfortunes. Hizzoner, unhurt, says, "It's all in a day's work." The German newspaper *Lokal-Anceiger* at Berlin says in a front-page editorial, "Not his victim should be sympathized with but the attacker himself." The incident shows "how well the half-Jew is liked by his closest fellow citizens."

The Fair Labor Standards Act (wage and hour law) passed by Congress June 15 limits working hours of some 12.5 million workers in the first national effort to place a floor under wages and a ceiling on hours. Working hours for the first year after the new law takes effect are limited to 44 per week with the limit to be reduced to 42 for the second year and 40 for every year thereafter. Longer work weeks are permitted only if overtime work is paid for at 1½-times the regular rate. Minimum wage is to be 25¢ per hour for the first year, 30¢ for the next 6 years, but domestic servants will not be included under the law until 1974 and live-in maids continue typically to earn $30 per month or less plus meals (see Minimum Wage Act, 1949).

The new minimum wage law wipes out Puerto Rico's 40,000-worker needlework industry, where 25¢ has been the hourly rate for *skilled* workers. Many Puerto Ricans will move to New York in search of better-paying work.

Abyssinian Baptist Church pastor Adam Clayton Powell, Jr., 29, hails the hiring of black bus drivers for the first time in New York City. Handsome as any matinée idol and perennially attired in an immaculate white suit, Powell has headed the Harlem church since last year.

A Citizens' Rally Against Oppression at Carnegie Hall December 9 protests racial and religious persecution in Europe. Mayor La Guardia has called the rally, whose program has no Jewish speaker but includes remarks by *New Yorker Staats-Zeitung* publisher Victor F. Ritter, who pledges that Americans of German descent will do their full share to prevent the spread of race hatred. High church and government officials denounce in strong language the anti-Semitic violence in Germany and condemn those in America who misuse their freedom to endanger the lives of people abroad.

$ Carl M. Loeb, Rhoades & Co. is created February 1 by a takeover of the Wall Street brokerage house Rhoades and Co. by Carl M. Loeb & Co. (see 1931; Loeb Rhoades, Hornblower, 1978).

Former New York Stock Exchange president Richard Whitney is indicted March 10 on embezzlement charges (see 1929). Now 49, he borrowed more than $30 million from friends, family, and accounts in his trust, taken $1 million worth of bonds from clients' accounts to pledge as collateral for personal bank loans, and declared bankruptcy with debts of about $6.5 million. Says the *New York Daily News*, "Not in our time, in our fathers' time nor in our grandfathers' time has there been such a social debacle . . ." Whitney pleads guilty, enters Sing Sing Prison in handcuffs April 13 to begin a 5- to 10-year sentence; authorities have moved to sell his Manhattan town house, New Jersey hunt-country estate, and thoroughbred horses to satisfy creditors, who include widows and orphans of former NYSE employees. His wife, Gertrude (*née* Sands), begs a bankruptcy referee to return a few

items of her personal jewelry taken for the same purpose (she will sell them to support their three children); he will be released for good behavior in August 1941 after his brother pays all he has borrowed or stolen. The conviction weakens NYSE resistance to reform, and the new Securities and Exchange Commission is soon able to impose new rules on the exchange.

Copper baron-philanthropist Adolph Lewisohn dies at New York August 17 at age 89. He has lived for years in a mansion at 881 Fifth Avenue, near the southeast corner of 70th Street.

The New York Stock Exchange halts trading December 2 in the 105-year-old pharmaceutical firm McKesson & Robbins upon hearing charges of mismanagement and falsification brought by a stockholder. The company had sales last year estimated to have been $174.5 million, but it admits that it overvalued its assets in its latest report; its president, F. (Frank) Donald Coster, is arrested December 14 for violating the Securities Exchange Act and charged in connection with $18 million apparently missing from the assets of the crude drug department, whose operations have been under the exclusive direction of Coster and his assistant George S. Dietrich, who is a neighbor of Coster and is also arrested. Coster and Dietrich are released on $5,000 bail each and remain at their homes in Fairfield, Conn., but an FBI investigation reveals that "Coster" is in reality former convict Frank Musica, now 61, who borrowed $1 million to buy a controlling interest in McKesson 2 years ago. When police come to arrest him again he goes to the bathroom, shoots himself in the head, and is buried in Brooklyn's Cypress Hills Cemetery. It turns out that Musica and his three brothers have set up five dummy Canadian suppliers from whom they pretended to purchase crude drugs, pretended to sell them to foreign dealers, drew up false documents to support the scam, hired secretaries in Canada to receive mail and reroute it with Canadian postmarks, and thereby duped auditors to steal about $3 million over the course of 12 years.

Wall Street's Dow Jones Industrial Average closes December 31 at 154.76, up from 120.85 at the end of 1937, having rebounded from a close of 131.33 August 24.

The Paul Stuart menswear shop opens to compete with the 120-year-old Brooks Brothers on Madison Avenue, selling classic styles.

The city opens a new enclosed market December 1 at the corner of First Avenue and 10th Street to clear the avenue of pushcarts. Constructed by the WPA at a cost of $225,000, the market provides space for 163 vendors of dry goods and novelties as well as fruits and vegetables (*see* Essex Street market, 1940).

General Electric introduces fluorescent lighting April 21. In addition to being far more energy-efficient than incandescent bulbs, the new fluorescent lamps are so bright that they will revolutionize office-building construction, having an impact as important in many ways as the elevator by making interior spaces as bright as offices with windows (although a windowed office will remain a coveted status symbol).

Texas-born industrialist-aviator-filmmaker Howard R. Hughes, 32, sets a round-the-world flight record of 3 days, 19 hours, 8 minutes, and 10 seconds in a twin-engine Lockheed plane and is given a ticker-tape parade at New York July 15. Sanitation Department officials estimate that 1,800 tons of paper have been thrown from office windows.

"Wrong-Way" Corrigan makes headlines July 19. Douglas Gorce Corrigan, 31, has flown nonstop from Los Angeles to New York July 10 and took off from Floyd Bennett Field July 16 in his 1929 $900 Curtiss Robin, presumably on a return flight (although his intention was certainly to fly the Atlantic). When he lands at Dublin's Baldonnel Airport after a 28-hour, 13-minute flight without elaborate instruments, maps, radio (or a passport), he insists that he intended to fly west but had compass trouble. Authorities say his flight and landing were illegal, but Corrigan is lionized, Mayor La Guardia welcomes him to City Hall and hails his "deliberate impetuosity" and "Pickwickian impulsiveness," and New York gives him a ticker-tape parade August 5 that leaves Broadway littered with 1,700 tons of paper. Former mayor Jimmy Walker introduces Corrigan that evening at a gala reception at Yankee Stadium.

Cabrini Boulevard in upper Manhattan is so named for the Italian-born nun Frances Xavier Cabrini, who died at Chicago in December 1917 at age 67 and will be canonized in 1946.

The Greater New York Hackmen's and Taxi Drivers' Union calls a strike January 15 to protest what it calls inequities in contracts with the Transport Workers' Union and fleet operators (*see* 1937). Fleet owners agree March 8 to reinstate locked-out drivers if the union will end the strike, but the TWU refuses to negotiate while owners continue to employ strikebreakers. Mayor La Guardia signs a bill April 6

extending license expiration dates, but a grand jury investigates charges that Parmalee Transportation Co. and Terminal Taxicab System have bribed aldermen, 700 Parmalee drivers strike August 2, some violence ensues, and the year ends without a settlement (*see* 1939).

The Sixth Avenue El ceases operations December 4 after 60 years of operation, leaving 700 workers unemployed after the last northbound train from Rector Street arrives at 53rd Street and Eighth Avenue (*see* 1878). Revelers strip the cars for souvenirs, taking electric bulbs, destination signs, and straps, throwing seat cushions out of windows, pulling safety cords to bring the train to a series of jolting stops, and smoking in defiance of the No Smoking signs. Hundreds pay their nickels simply to stand on station platforms and watch the last trains pass into history. Ridership has declined sharply during the Depression, and Mayor La Guardia wants the elevated train structures eliminated to increase property values along their rights of way (*see* 1939).

The legislature at Albany votes April 12 to enact the first U.S. state law requiring medical tests for marriage license applicants.

The National Foundation for Infantile Paralysis is founded at New York under the leadership of President Roosevelt's former law partner Basil O'Connor, 46, to finance research into poliomyelitis. It takes offices in the Equitable Life Assurance Building at 120 Broadway and is soon renamed the March of Dimes Foundation following a nationwide broadcast by comedian Eddie Cantor, who has asked listeners to send dimes to the White House to support the new foundation (it will be renamed the March of Dimes Birth Defects Foundation in 1979).

Memorial Sloan-Kettering Cancer Center moves into a building at 444 West 68th Street designed by James Gamble Rogers, Inc.

Flower Fifth Avenue Hospital is created by a merger of the Fifth Avenue Hospital at 105th Street with the New York Medical College and Flower Hospital (*see* 1890). The college will move to Westchester County in 1972 (*see* 1978).

"Typhoid Mary" Mallon dies at New York November 11 at age 68 (*see* 1907). She has been confined at Riverside Hospital on North Brother Island since 1915.

∞ Patrick Cardinal Hayes dies at Monticello, N.Y., September 4 at age 70, having given clergymen in his diocese seminars on the subject of labor ethics but denounced the idea of giving contraceptives to welfare recipients, insisting instead that the government should eliminate poverty (*see* Spellman, 1939).

Mayor La Guardia appoints Manhattan-born Board of Estimate secretary Pearl Bernstein (Mrs. Louis Max), 34, as first chief administrator of the city's Board of Higher Education (the title of the office will later be changed to schools chancellor).

Bronx High School of Science opens at the corner of 184th Street and Creston Avenue and admits 300 gifted boys, chosen on the basis of a written examination in science and mathematics. The brainchild of educator Morris Meister, the public secondary school will begin admitting girls in 1946 and Meister will remain principal until 1958 (*see* 1957).

The New-York Historical Society's 30-year-old building on Central Park West between 76th and 77th streets grows with the addition of north and south wings designed by Walker & Gillette (*see* 1956).

Mayor La Guardia swears in Russian-born American Labor Party official Morris S. Novik, 34, as director of the municipal radio station WNYC February 9 (*see* 1933). In the next 8 years Novik will support civic and educational programming while he increases the presentation of classical music, championing the works of American composers (*see* 1940).

Mayor La Guardia celebrates the 25th anniversary of George McManus's comic strip "Bringing Up Father" with a "growler" and corned beef and cabbage party at City Hall. McManus lost $1.5 million in the stock-market crash of 1929 but still has a considerable fortune and earns about $100,000 per year.

Philadelphia-born *New York Post* journalist I. F. (Isidor Feinstein) Stone, 30, joins the staff of The *Nation* and will later be its Washington editor. He will be with the magazine until 1946 before leaving to work on various newspapers, and beginning in 1953 will write and publish his own four-page newsletter *I. F. Stone's Weekly*, gleefully quoting official government statements and comparing them with contradictory statements issued only a week, or perhaps a month or year, earlier.

The first true Xerox image appears October 22 at Astoria, Queens (*see* 1937). The electrophoto-graphic image "10-22-38 Astoria" is imprinted on wax paper which has been pressed against an electrostatically charged two- by three-inch sulfur-coated zinc plate that has been dusted with lycopodium powder. Chester Carlson has been helped by a German refugee physicist; he attends New York Law School night classes, will be admitted to the bar in 1940, and will receive his first patent that year for the process that he will call "xerography," using the Greek word *xeros* for dry, but Carlson will fail in his initial attempts to get financial backing (*see* 1946).

Former Postal Telegraph head and philanthropist Clarence H. Mackay dies at Doctors Hospital November 12 at age 64; Postal Telegraph filed for bankruptcy in 1935 and companies associated with it now also go into bankruptcy.

Nonfiction: *The Culture of Cities* by Lewis Mumford, who writes, "The city fosters art and is art. The city creates the theater and is the theater;" *Philosopher's Holiday* by New York-born Columbia University philosophy professor Irwin Edman, 44, who writes, "My family lived most of the time I went to school and high school on Morningside Avenue, just below Morningside Park. It was a quiet, bourgeois neighbourhood, though neither I nor anybody else knew the word much then. Harlem meant not the world of Negroes or of 'swing' but of middle-class domesticity. Indeed, some of the pleasantest streets in the city were, and are, those up in the One Hundred and Thirties;" *This Man La Guardia* by veteran *New York Daily News* writer Lowell L. Limpus, 41; *The Puerto Rican Migrant in New York City* by Texas-born educator Lawrence R. Chenault, 41; *New York: An American City, 1783–1803* by Sidney I. (Irving) Pomerantz, 29; "A Little Girl's New York" by Edith Wharton appears in the March issue of *Harper's* magazine; *Back Where I Came From* by New York-born journalist-author A. J. (Abbott Joseph) Liebling, 33.

Painting: *Swing Landscape* by Stuart Davis; *The Upstairs* by Charles Sheeler, whose talent will gain wide recognition next year when his works are exhibited at the Museum of Modern Art (MoMA); *Sunday Painting* by Ben Shahn; *Flour Mill* and *Swing Music (Louis Armstrong)* by Arthur Dove. William Glackens dies at Westport, Conn., May 22 at age 68.

The Cloisters opens in Fort Tryon Park (*see* 1935). A gift from the Rockefeller family to the Metropolitan Museum of Art, the medieval European nunnery is filled with art treasures that include a unicorn tapestry and the collection of early Gothic and medieval works acquired by John D. Rockefeller, Jr. in 1925 from Pennsylvania-born sculptor George Grey

Barnard, who dies at New York April 24 at age 74, leaving unfinished his *Memorial Arch* intended for the art center overlooking the Hudson River.

Photography: *Subway Passengers, New York* by St. Louis-born photographer Walker Evans, 34, whose picture will not be published until 1966 out of deference to the subjects revealed by his lens. The Museum of Modern Art (MoMA) gave Walker its first one-man photographic show 4 years ago, exhibiting pictures he had taken beginning in 1930 of 19th century New England architecture.

Theater: *Bachelor Born* by Scottish novelist-playwright Ian Hay (John Hay Beith), 61, 1/25 at the Morosco Theater, with Peggy Simpson, Helen Trenholme, 400 perfs.; *Shadow and Substance* by Irish playwright Paul Vincent Carroll, 38, 1/26 at the Golden Theater, with English actor Cedric Hardwicke, 42, Dublin-born actress Sara Allgood, 53, Oak Park, Ill.-born actress Julie Haydon, 27, 274 perfs.; *On Borrowed Time* by Evansville, Ind.-born playwright Paul Osborn, 36, 2/3 at the Longacre Theater, with Dudley Digges, Dorothy Stickney, Dickie Van Patten, 321 perfs.; *Our Town* by Thornton Wilder 2/4 at the Henry Miller Theater, with Missouri-born actress Martha Scott, 23, Frank Craven, now 62, Philip Coolidge, 29, 336 perfs.; *What a Life* by Clifford Goldsmith 4/13 at the Biltmore Theater, with Ezra Stone as Henry Aldrich, New York-born ingénu Eddie Bracken, 18, Betty Field, 538 perfs.; *Kiss the Boys Goodbye* by Clare Boothe Luce 9/28 at Henry Miller's Theater, with Millard Mitchell, San Francisco-born actress-singer Benay Venuta (originally Venuta Rose Crooke), 27, 286 perfs.; *The Fabulous Invalid* by George S. Kaufman and Moss Hart 10/8 at the Broadhurst Theater, with Jack Norworth, Doris Dalton (as Ethel Barrymore) and more than 72 other actors playing nearly 250 roles, 165 perfs. (the "invalid" is the still relatively healthy legitimate theater); *Abe Lincoln in Illinois* by Robert Sherwood 10/15 at the Plymouth Theater, with Toronto-born actor Raymond Massey, 42, in the title role, 472 perfs.; *Rocket to the Moon* by Clifford Odets 11/24 at the Belasco Theater, with Morris Carnovsky, 131 perfs.; *Here Come the Clowns* by Philip Barry 12/7 at the Booth Theater, with Eddie Dowling, Madge Evans, Russell Collins, 88 perfs.

Radio: *Information, Please!* 5/17 on NBC with former Simon & Schuster editor Clifton (Paul) Fadiman, now 54, as moderator and a panel (selected by NBC producer Dan Golenpaul, 37) whose members include *New York Times* sportswriter John Kieran, 46, Pittsburgh-born pianist-composer Oscar Levant,

32, *New York Post* columnist Franklin P. Adams, and guests. Any listener who sends in a question that stumps the experts receives a 24-volume set of the *Encyclopaedia Britannica* (to 1951); *Mercury Theatre on the Air* 7/11 on CBS with Orson Welles, now 22, as Dracula in the Bram Stoker story (Welles is star, narrator, writer, producer, and director); *The War of the Worlds* 10/30 gives a dramatic demonstration of the power of radio. Orson Welles's *Mercury Theater on the Air* presents a radio version of the 1898 H. G. Wells novel, and its "news" reports of Martian landings in New Jersey are so realistic that near-panics occur in many areas despite occasional announcements by CBS that the program is merely a dramatization (by New York-born lawyer-turned-playwright Howard Koch, 35).

The 450-seat Guild Theater in Rockefeller Center opens as an Embassy Newsreel house offering the "World Around in Sight and Sound," "One Hour of World-Wide News Events" plus short subjects (its lease with Rockefeller Center stipulates that tickets never be sold for less than 25¢ to keep out riffraff). The competing Trans-Lux chain will take it over in 1949 just as television begins to make newsreels obsolete, reopen it as the Guild, and show feature films, as it will continue to do until it closes in September 1999.

Films: Michael Curtiz's *Angels With Dirty Faces* with James Cagney, Pat O'Brien, Humphrey Bogart, Ann Sheridan; George Cukor's *Holiday* with Katharine Hepburn, Cary Grant; Frank Capra's *You Can't Take It With You* with Jean Arthur, Lionel Barrymore, James Stewart, Edward Arnold. Also: Busby Berkeley's *Comet Over Broadway* with Kay Francis, Ian Hunter; Lloyd Bacon's *The Cowboy from Brooklyn* with Dick Powell, Pat O'Brien, Priscilla Lane; Leigh Jason's *The Mad Miss Manton* with Barbara Stanwyck, Henry Fonda, Sam Levene; Richard Thorpe's *Three Loves Has Nancy* with Janet Gaynor, Robert Montgomery, Franchot Tone.

Film musicals: Irving Cummings's *Little Miss Broadway* with Shirley Temple, George Murphy, Jimmy Durante, Edna May Oliver.

Broadway musicals: *I Married an Angel* 5/11 at the Shubert Theater, with Dennis King, Berlin-born Norwegian ballet dancer Vera Zorina (Brigitta Hartwig), 21, Vivienne Segal, music by Richard Rodgers, lyrics by Lorenz Hart, songs that include "Spring Is Here" and the title song, 338 perfs.; *Helzapoppin* 9/22 at the 46th Street Theater, with Peru, Ind.-born comedian Ole Olsen, 45, and Chicago-born comic Chic Johnson, 44, who delight audiences with their slapstick and sight gags, music by Sammy Fain, lyrics by Irving Kahal and Charles Tobias, songs that include "I'll Be Seeing You," 1,404 perfs.; *Knickerbocker Holiday* 10/19 at the Ethel Barrymore Theater, with Walter Huston, Ridgewood, N.J.-born actor-baritone Richard Kollmar, 27, music by Kurt Weill, book and lyrics by Maxwell Anderson, songs that include "September Song," 168 perfs.; *Leave It to Me* 11/9 at the Imperial Theater, with Sophie Tucker, Texas-born ingénue Mary Martin, 24, doing a simulated striptease to Cole Porter's song "My Heart Belongs to Daddy" (other songs include "Most Gentlemen Don't Like Love"), choreography by Robert Alton, costumes by Raoul Pène Du Bois, 307 perfs. (Porter was injured last year in a fall from a horse and will be crippled for the rest of his life); *The Boys from Syracuse* 11/23 at the Alvin Theater, with vaudeville veteran Jimmy Savo, 43, Eddie Albert is about the Shubert brothers, music by Richard Rodgers, lyrics by Lorenz Hart, songs that include "Falling in Love with Love," "Sing for Your Supper," "This Can't Be Love," 235 perfs.

Benny Goodman and His Orchestra give the first Carnegie Hall big-band jazz concert 1/16 with guest performers who include Count Basie and members of the Basie and Duke Ellington orchestras (*see* 1935). Pianist Jess Stacy plays "Sing Sing Sing."

Iowa-born trombonist and bandleader Glenn Miller begins touring with a big band of his own after years of playing for Tommy and Jimmy Dorsey and for Ray Noble, arranging as well as performing. Now 39, Miller will achieve enormous success next year with his recordings of "In the Mood," "Sunrise Serenade," and "Moonlight Serenade" (which will become his theme song) (*see* 1942).

Minton's Playhouse opens at 208 West 18th Street. The jazz club started by tenor saxophonist Henry Minton has seating for just over 100 patrons, most of them black, and will become well known beginning in the early 1940s for its Monday evening jam sessions featuring pianist Thelonious Sphere Monk and the house band with guest saxophonists Charlie Parker and Eddie "Lockjaw" Davis plus trumpet players Miles Davis and Dizzy Gillespie, most of whom will perform until the club closes in 1956.

Kate Smith sings Irving Berlin's "God Bless America" in an Armistice Day broadcast of her 7½-year-old CBS radio show and will acquire exclusive air rights to the song Berlin wrote originally for his 1918 show *Yip-Yip Yaphank* but laid aside.

Café Society opens in December at 2 Sheridan Square in Greenwich Village. Owner Barney Josephson, 36, will introduce New Yorkers to boogie-woogie pianists Pete Johnson, Meade Lux Lewis, and Albert Ammons at his racially integrated club (*see* 1940).

The first National Invitation Tournament (NIT) for college basketball teams is held at Madison Square Garden, sponsored by the Metropolitan Basketball Writers Association.

Don Budge wins in men's singles at Forest Hills (he also wins at Wimbledon and in France and Australia, the first "grand slam" and one not to be duplicated for 24 years); Alice Marble wins in U.S. women's singles.

John J. Downing Stadium is completed on Randalls Island in the East River for the Black Yankees of the National Negro League.

Yankee Stadium sets an attendance record May 30 as 81,841 pay to see the team play a Memorial Day doubleheader against Boston.

The Brooklyn Dodgers lose to the Cincinnati Reds 6 to 0 at Ebbets Field June 15 in the first major-league night game to be played at New York. New Jersey-born Reds left-hander Johnny Vander Meer, 23, signed with the Dodgers' farm system in 1932, wound up with Cincinnati, played in his first major-league game last year, and disappoints a Brooklyn crowd of nearly 39,000 by pitching his second consecutive no-hitter (the first was against the Boston Braves 4 days earlier at Cincinnati's Crosley Field; Yankee Stadium will not have night games until 1946).

The New York Yankees win the American League pennant (they lose a double-header to the St. Louis Browns but the Boston Red Sox are rained out, losing their "mathematical chance" to clinch the flag) and go on to win the World Series, defeating the Chicago Cubs 4 games to 0 behind the pitching of Red Ruffing, Montgomery Marcellus "Monte" Pearson, 29, and Lefty Gomez. Rookie second baseman Joe Gordon, 23, gets six hits, including two doubles and a home run; shortstop Frankie Crosetti, 28, four hits, including two doubles, a triple, and a home run; Joe DiMaggio four hits, including one home run.

Joe Louis retains his world heavyweight title at Yankee Stadium June 22, defeating former champion Max Schmeling in the first round, avenging his loss to Schmeling 2 years ago, and delighting most New Yorkers by puncturing Adolf Hitler's ideas of white supremacy.

Everlast Sports Manufacturing Co. moves to a large factory at 750 East 132nd Street in the South Bronx (*see* 1921). Founder Jacob Golomb, now 45, will continue to run the company until his death in 1951, and his son Daniel will build annual sales to $20 million.

Gerry Cosby & Co. is founded by former New York hockey goaltender Finton Gerard David Cosby, 29, who will supply hockey equipment to amateur and professional hockey teams throughout North America as his firm grows to become a major sporting-goods company.

Columbia wins upset victories over Yale and Army as Sid Luckman plays his final season and enables his otherwise mediocre team to complete a 3-year record of 10 victories, 14 defeats, and two ties (see 1936). Luckman's picture is on the cover of LIFE magazine October 24, and he ends his collegiate career in November, having completed 47.9 percent of his forward passes and scoring 20 touchdowns. Chicago Bears owner-coach George Halas offers the five-foot-ten, 175-pound Luckman an unprecedented $5,500 salary to play for Chicago, Luckman follows Columbia coach Lou Little's advice and signs a contract with Halas, and with coaching from Halas will become an outstanding T-formation quarterback (see 1943).

Hattie Carnegie fashion designer Claire McCardell, 33, creates a tent dress based on an Algerian (or Moroccan) robe, it is included in the fall collection of Townley Sportswear, most buyers reject it, but a Best & Co. buyer orders 100, advertises it in the city's Sunday papers, and promptly orders 200 more. Seventh Avenue garment makers copy the "monastic" design, and McCardell soon finds herself famous as the designer of the "American Look" (see 1941).

Fashion Is Spinach by Ridgewood, N.J.-born New York author Elizabeth Hawes, 35 (Vassar '25), pokes fun at the business she entered 12 years ago after studying at Paris but has recently quit. Her autobiography challenges the prevailing notion that a handful of Paris salons have a monopoly on originating stylish clothing and accessories. Style, she says, changes only in accordance with a true change in public taste or need, whereas fashions change because the industry must meet payrolls, magazines must be published, and a myth must be perpetuated.

A report by the 2-year-old City Planning Commission charges that New York is overbuilt and over-mortgaged.

Brooklyn's Williamsburg Houses open on 10 square blocks in an area bounded by Maujer, Scholes, and Leonard streets and Bushwick Avenue. William Lescaze and a staff of Public Works Administration architects headed by Richmond H. Shreve of Shreve,

Lamb & Harmon have designed the four-story houses, built of reinforced concrete and brick in a project that has pedestrian paths and connected courtyards. Apartments open directly off stair landings, rather than corridors, and although the project will be hailed for decades as the best public housing ever built in New York it is also the most expensive.

The huge apartments of the Alwyn Court at the southwest corner of Seventh Avenue and 58th Street are broken up into 75 units of three to five rooms each as the Great Depression dampens demand for luxury flats and duplexes (see 1909). The location is no longer considered highly desirable, the building has been vacant since last year, and the Dry Dock Savings Institution has foreclosed on its mortgage.

Lawyer-investor George Palen Snow purchases the eight tenements put up in 1894 at 527 to 541 East 72nd Street. Architects Sacchetti & Siegel gut the tenements and combine them to create four buildings with apartments of from two to four bedrooms each, some with wood-burning fireplaces. Snow's Irish-born wife, Carmel (*née* White), now 48, is editor of *Harper's Bazaar* and the two move from their apartment in the Ritz Tower to the easternmost building. By next year five of the nine tenants in the building will be listed in the Social Register.

The city's first centrally air-conditioned apartment house is completed at 23 East 83rd Street to designs by Frederick L. Ackerman and Ramsey & Sleeper. Air is drawn in at the roof and circulated through interior ductwork.

The Castle Village apartment complex completed at 120-200 Cabrini Boulevard, between 181st and 186th streets, has nine apartments per floor, eight of them with views of the George Washington Bridge. Many have extra-height ceilings, sunken living rooms measuring 21' × 13'8", bedrooms 15' × 12', and walk-in closets. Designed by George F. Pelham II, the cruciform buildings rise from the cliffs above the Hudson on what once was the Paterno estate.

Manhattan's (Presbyterian) Brick Church is completed at 1140-1144 Park Avenue, northwest corner 91st Street, to neo-Georgian designs by York & Sawyer.

Minneapolis-born oilman Jean Paul Getty, 45, buys the 8-year-old Hotel Pierre, which has been losing money; Getty builds up its clientele by popularizing it with his society friends.

1939 The New York World's Fair opens April 30 in Flushing Meadow, Queens, with pavilions representing some 60 foreign nations, the League of

Nations, 33 states and territories (including Puerto Rico), the City of New York, and federal agencies (including the Works Progress Administration) as well as exhibits by private companies. The brainchild of Luxembourg-born businessman Joseph Shadgren, who has gained support from former Manhattan borough president George McAneny, the fair celebrates the 150th anniversary of George Washington's inauguration. A Trylon and Perisphere designed by Harrison & Fouilhoux serve as the fair's symbol (the Trylon is a three-sided obelisk rising 610 feet high, the Perisphere a 180-foot spherical exhibit building that rests on five steel pillars above a reflecting pool). President Roosevelt, Gov. Lehman, Mayor La Guardia, and World's Fair Corp. president Grover Whalen officiate at opening ceremonies.

Manhattan District Attorney Thomas E. Dewey wins a conviction against Democratic Party leader James J. Hines, 63, for protecting a numbers racket controlled by the late Dutch Schultz. A onetime black-

The city's second World's Fair opened with the world on the brink of its second World War.

smith who has become friendly with many judges as well as with organized crime figures, Hines has for more than 36 years been the leader of the 11th Assembly District (Morningside Heights and southwestern Harlem), using his position to grant favors and become a notorious Tammany Hall "fixer;" he has received an estimated $200,000 for protecting members of Schultz's policy ring; criminal lawyer Lloyd Paul Stryker, 54, has been unsuccessful in his defense, and the conviction propels Dewey into the national political spotlight.

City garment workers jeer at Jewish communists with shouts of "Heil, Hitler!" beginning August 24 after news arrives that German foreign minister Joachim von Ribbentrop, 46, has signed a mutual non-aggression treaty August 23 with Josef Stalin's new commissar of foreign affairs V. M. Molotov. New York members of the Communist Party leave the party by the thousands.

World War II starts September 1. Having occupied Bohemia and Moravia and annexed Memel, Adolf Hitler sends his troops and aircraft into Poland, beginning a conflict that will have serious effects on New Yorkers.

The United Jewish Appeal (UJA) is founded at New York to raise funds for the rescue of distressed Jews and their resettlement in Palestine (*see* Federation, 1974).

Social reformer Joel E. Spingarn dies of cancer at his 110 East 78th Street home July 26 at age 64. He has been president of the NAACP since 1930 (*see* Spingarn Medal, 1914).

The Community Service Society is created by a merger of the 96-year-old Association for Improving the Condition of the Poor and the 58-year-old Charity Organization Society. It will gradually close those groups' clinics and summer camps to concentrate on family casework but will eliminate that in the 1970s to focus on antipoverty programs designed to help the poor obtain better public housing and welfare through political empowerment.

Onetime steel mogul Charles M. Schwab dies of heart disease at New York September 18 at age 77. Once worth an estimated $200 million, he has lost his fortune in ventures outside of the steel industry and is insolvent.

The World's Fair reduces its admission price from 75¢ to 50¢ (40¢ after 8 o'clock in the evening) as of October 1 (admission has been 50¢ on weekends and attendance has surged, partly because of the lower price).

A seat on the New York Stock Exchange sells for $85,000, well below its peak of $625,000 but higher than in recent years (see 1990).

Wall Street's Dow Jones Industrial Average closes at 131.33 August 24 on concerns about the approaching war but rebounds to close December 30 at 150.24, down from 154.76 at the end of 1938.

Thanksgiving Day is celebrated November 23—the fourth Thursday in the month rather than the last. Federated Department Stores chief Fred Lazarus, Jr. has persuaded President Roosevelt that a longer Christmas shopping season will help the economy, the president has issued a proclamation, and within a few years most states will pass laws changing the date of Thanksgiving to November's fourth Thursday (see Federated, 1929).

Retail merchant Leo S. De Pinna retires for reasons of health and dies at New York December 23 at age 66 (see 1928). De Pinna's son-in-law Roy Foster takes over the 54-year-old firm (see 1969).

Cities Service Co. founder Henry L. "Harry" Doherty dies of bronchial pneumonia at a Philadelphia hospital December 26 at age 69, having been a semi-invalid for the past 3 years. He is buried at Woodlawn Cemetery.

The Transport Workers Union calls for a new taxi strike January 3 (see 1938). Mayor La Guardia invites fleet owners and the union to a City Hall conference, the dispute is referred to the State Mediation Board January 28, fleet owners lock out drivers and bring in scabs (replacements), the drivers hold a rally in Times Square and on Fifth Avenue, they block traffic, and there are altercations between the regular fleet drivers and scabs. A meeting between the TWU and owners April 25 ends in deadlock. Former assemblyman Edward S. Moran, 38, of Brooklyn's Park Slope section goes on trial May 31, having been indicted last year on charges that he accepted $36,000 in bribes from officials of two taxicab companies to use his influence to obtain passage of legislation favorable to the taxi industry. He is convicted by a General Sessions jury in June and given a stiff sentence.

The 60-year-old Sixth Avenue El comes down (see 1938) but the avenue remains a dingy thoroughfare of low buildings with shops, restaurants, some apartment houses, and a few hotels (see Avenue of the Americas, 1945).

The Bronx-Whitestone Bridge opens April 30 to connect the Bronx with Queens; designed by Othmar H. Ammann, the bridge is 2,300 feet (701 meters) in length (the world's fourth longest suspension bridge) and has been built in 23 months at a cost of nearly $18 million; it facilitates access from Westchester County to the World's Fair and to the new La Guardia Airport (see Throgs Neck Bridge, 1961).

The Kosciuszko Bridge (initially the Meeker Avenue Bridge) opens August 23 to span Newtown Creek between Brooklyn and Queens, where the Penny Bridge once stood (it will be renamed in July of next year to honor the Polish patriot who helped win the American War of Independence). Part of the Brooklyn-Queens Connecting Highway, the 300-foot steel and reinforced concrete truss bridge will later be part of the Brooklyn-Queens Expressway, providing access between the Queens-Midtown Tunnel (see 1940) and the Williamsburg Bridge that opened in December 1903.

The General Motors Futurama at the World's Fair in Flushing Meadow is a diorama that depicts the city of 1960. Designed by Norman Bel Geddes, the futuristic display shows crosstown traffic moving smoothly on underpasses; crowds wait in long lines to ride on moving chairs through the fair's most popular exhibit and get what for most of them is the first "aerial" view of the world, but while the vision of a world dominated by automobiles reflects that of Robert Moses and is appealing to some visitors, it appalls many New Yorkers, especially Manhattanites, and bodes ill for cities whose transportation needs are best met by mass transit. More than 40 percent of Americans do not own automobiles; that figure will decline in the next 25 years to about 20 percent, but all except a small fraction of New Yorkers will continue to rely on public transportation, car ownership for most will be prohibitively expensive, and New York will remain one of the few U.S. cities in which a private car is not only unnecessary but actually more a burden than a boon.

Connecticut's Merritt Parkway opens June 22 with 38 miles of landscaped road winding through Fairfield County to link New York's Hutchinson River Parkway with Milford. Industrialist-banker Schuyler Merritt, now 85, represented the state in Congress for nine terms and has headed the state commission that began building the toll road in 1934.

The first commercial transatlantic passenger air service begins June 28 as 22 passengers and 12 crew members take off from Port Washington, L.I., for Marseilles via the Azores and Lisbon aboard the Pan

American Airways *Yankee Clipper*, a Boeing aircraft powered by four 1,550-horsepower Wright Cyclone engines (*see* 1935). Pan Am has been providing air service to the Caribbean, South America, and the Pacific, but Anglo-American disputes over airport landing rights have delayed the start of transatlantic service. The plane has separate passenger cabins, a dining salon, ladies' dressing room, recreation lounge, sleeping berths, and a bridal suite, the flight takes 26.5 hours, and the one-way fare is $375 (*see* 1940).

La Guardia Airport (initially the North Beach Airport) opens with an advanced lighting system December 2 on the east shore of Flushing Bay near the World's Fair grounds (*see* Newark, 1928). The facility has cost more than any other WPA project, formal dedication ceremonies October 15 have brought out a crowd of 325,000, the Board of Estimate has voted in November to name the $40 million facility after the mayor, it replaces the North Beach amusement park, and it will officially be called La Guardia beginning in August of next year. By 1942 it will be the world's busiest commercial airport, with more than 75 flights taking off and arriving each day (*see* Idlewild, 1948).

The German passenger liner *Bremen* arrives at her West 46th Street pier August 29 and is allowed to depart August 30 with a band playing German songs. Every light has been extinguished except for running lights, she returns home on a route far to the north to avoid being taken by Allied warships, and flies the Russian hammer-and-sickle flag when she steams into Murmansk. Allied bombers find her in the Norwegian fjords and set her afire, making her useful only as scrap metal.

The *Pacemaker* goes into service on the New York Central for the Chicago run with a round-trip fare of just over $30 in fancy coaches. The *Trail Blazer* goes into service on the Pennsylvania Railroad to compete with the Central's train.

Boston auxiliary bishop Francis Joseph Spellman, 50, becomes Archbishop Spellman of New York and takes up residence at 452 Madison Avenue, behind St. Patrick's Cathedral. A close friend of the newly elected Pope Pius XII at Rome, Spellman succeeds the late Cardinal Hayes and begins modernizing the structure of the archdiocese (*see* 1946).

Dutch-born Columbia University economics professor Harry D. Gideonse, 38, is elected president of Brooklyn College June 8 (*see* 1937). He will continue in the post until 1966, and by 1990 the college will have a distinguished faculty and more than 16,600 full- and part-time students.

The Dalton School merges with the Todhunter School at the urging of first lady Eleanor Roosevelt, who attended Todhunter and has admired the work of Dalton's founder Helen Parkhurst (*see* 1916; 1929). Parkhurst, now 47, will retire in 1942, and although its preschool and elementary grades are coeducational the progressive school will not accept boys in its high school until 1969 (*see* Barr, 1964).

Glamour magazine begins publication at New York in April. Street & Smith has launched the monthly to reach working women above the age of its 4-year-old *Mademoiselle*'s readership.

Fortune magazine devotes its entire July issue to New York City, whose World's Fair is failing to attract the crowds originally anticipated.

Conover Cover Girls begin to grace magazine covers. Chicago-born radio performer and former model Harry Sayles Conover, 28, has opened his own New York modeling agency in competition with the 16-year-old John Robert Powers agency and will continue for 20 years until a financial scandal closes the business (*see* Candy Jones, 1960).

Real estate magnate George Backer and his heiress wife Dorothy Schiff, 36, buy the *New York Post* from J. David Stern. Schiff has had almost no business experience but becomes vice president, pushes scandal and human-interest stories to boost circulation (it ranks third among the city's afternoon papers), and will change the *Post*'s format from broadsheet to tabloid in 1942 (*see* Murdoch, 1976).

Jewish Daily Forward circulation falls to 170,000, down from its peak of 275,000 in the 1920s. Immigration laws enacted in 1924 and 1929 have tended to restrict the influx of European Jews.

NBC televises opening ceremonies of the New York World's Fair at Flushing Meadow April 30 on its experimental station W2XBS (*see* 1931). Somewhere between 100 and 200 experimental receivers have been set up in the metropolitan area, and close to 1,000 viewers see the telecast (*see* 1941). "Sooner than you realize it, television will play a vital part in the life of the average American," say advertisements for the World's Fair telecast. The ads have been placed by Du Mont Television Receivers, a division of Allen B. Du Mont Laboratories at Clifton, N.J., founded in 1931 by former De Forest Radio chief engineer Allen B. (Balcom) Du Mont, now 38 (*see* 1944).

"This is London," says Greensboro, N.C.-born CBS correspondent Edward R. Murrow, 31, who ends his broadcasts with the tagline "Goodnight and good luck." Murrow's will become the best-known voice on U.S. radio in the next 7 years.

Journalist Heywood Broun dies of pneumonia and cardiac complications at New York December 18 at age 51.

Pocket Books, Inc. Americanizes the paperback revolution in publishing begun by Britain's Penguin Books in 1936. Having sent out 1,000 paperback copies of Pearl Buck's *The Good Earth* and 49,000 questionnaires to determine public interest, the new company founded at New York by Robert F. (Fair) de Graff in partnership with Simon & Schuster puts out its first 10 reprints June 19, pricing them at 25¢ each. Using enormous and fast new rubber-plate rotary presses that permit printing of paperbacks in large, economical quantities at a unit cost of pennies, the company pays artist Frank J. Lieberman $25 to create a bespectacled wallaby to use as a trademark, names it Gertrude, and goes on to turn out reprints of major and minor literary classics. Most authors, agents, and hardcover publishers agree to permit paperback reprints (*see* Avon, 1941).

Nonfiction: *New York City Guide* by the WPA's Federal Writers' Project (whose writers include John Cheever, 27); *New York Past and Present* by I. N. Phelps Stokes; *The Rise of New York Port, 1815–1860* by Robert G. Albion; *Master of Manhattan: The Life of Richard Croker* by Lothrop Stoddard; *Honest Cop: The Dramatic Life Story of Lewis J. Valentine* by Lowell Limpus.

Fiction: "The Secret Life of Walter Mitty" by James Thurber in the March 18 *New Yorker*; *The Web and the Rock* by the late Thomas Wolfe, who died in mid-September of last year at age 37 (Harper Bros. editor Edward Aswell will work his surviving manuscripts into two further novels).

Poetry: *Here Lies* by Dorothy Parker; "September 1, 1939" by W. H. Auden, who has returned August 30 from a transcontinental tour with his lover Chester Kallman and writes, "I sit in one of the dives/ On Fifty-second street/ Uncertain and afraid/ As the clever hopes expire/ Of a low dishonest decade;/ Waves of anger and fear/ Circulate over the bright/ And darkened lands of the earth,/ Obsessing our private lives;/ The unmentionable odour of death/ Offends the September night."

Juvenile: *Madeline* by Austrian-born New York illustrator-novelist Ludwig Bemelmans, 41, who illustrates his own work (it will outlive his new novel *Hotel Splendide*).

Painting: *New York Movie* by Edward Hopper; *The Brooklyn Bridge: Variation on an Old Theme* by Joseph Stella; *Myself Among the Churchgoers* by Ben Shahn.

The Museum of Modern Art (MoMA) reopens May 10 in a handsome new $2 million glass and concrete building at 11 West 53rd Street with an exhibition entitled "Art in Our Time" (*see* 1932). Designed by Philip S. Goodwin and Fayetteville, Ark.-born architect Edward Durrell Stone, 37, the building stands out from its town house neighbors. The museum's trustees have announced May 8 that Nelson A. Rockefeller was replacing A. Conger Goodyear as president and Stephen C. Clark was to become chairman. MoMA is free to members but charges nonmembers an admission fee of 25¢ plus tax (10¢ plus tax for children under age 16) at a time when virtually every other museum in the city charges nothing, movie-theater tickets generally cost 25¢, and most everyday things (subways, hot dogs, soft drinks, candy bars, many weekly magazines, telephone calls) still cost a nickel.

Sculpture: a full-length standing figure of Norse explorer Leif Ericsson by sculptor August Weiner is installed with bronze relief tablets at the corner of Fourth Avenue and 66th Street in Brooklyn.

Theater: *The White Steed* by Paul Vincent Carroll 1/10 at the Cort Theater, with Irish-born actor Barry Fitzgerald (originally William Joseph Shields), 50, Jessica Tandy, George Coulouris, 136 perfs.; *The American Way* by George S. Kaufman and Moss Hart 1/21 at the Center Theater in Rockefeller Center, with Fredric March, Florence Eldridge, 164 perfs.; *The Little Foxes* by Lillian Hellman 2/15 at the National Theater, with Tallulah Bankhead, Carl Benton Reid, Dan Duryea, Patricia Collinge, sets and costumes by Aline Bernstein, 191 perfs.; *Family Portrait* by Lenore Coffee and William Joyce Cowan 3/8 at the Morosco Theater, with Judith Anderson, Philip Truex, 111 perfs.; *The Philadelphia Story* by Philip Barry 3/28 at the Shubert Theater, with Katherine Hepburn, Lenore Lonergan, Shirley Booth, Van Heflin, Joseph Cotten, 96 perfs.; *My Heart's in the Highlands* by Fresno, Calif.-born author-playwright William Saroyan, 30, 4/13 at the Guild Theater, 43 perfs.; *No Time for Comedy* by S. N. Behrman 4/17 at the Ethel Barrymore Theater, with Katherine Cornell, Laurence Olivier, Margalo Gilmore, 185 perfs.; *Skylark* by Samson Raphaelson 10/11 at the Belasco Theater, with Gertrude Lawrence, 250 perfs.; *The Man Who Came to Dinner* by George S. Kaufman and Moss Hart 10/25 at the

Music Box Theater, with New York-born actor Monty (originally Edgar Montillion) Wooley, 50, as Sheridan Whiteside (a lampoon of theater critic Alexander Woollcott) and with Cole Porter's song "What Am I to Do," 739 perfs.; *The Time of Your Life* by William Saroyan 10/25 at the Booth Theater, with Eddie Dowling, Julie Haydon, Pittsburgh-born dancer Gene (Curran) Kelly, 26, New York-born actress Celeste Holm, 20, New York-born actor William Bendix, 32, Reginald Beane, 185 perfs.; *Margin for Error* by Clare Boothe Luce 11/3 at the Plymouth Theater, with Vienna-born actor Otto Preminger, 31, 264 perfs.; *Life with Father* by Howard Lindsay and Russel Crouse 11/8 at the Empire Theater, with Lindsay and Dorothy Stickney in a comedy based on the 1935 book by the late Clarence Day, 3,244 perfs.; *Key Largo* by Maxwell Anderson 11/27 at the Ethel Barrymore Theater, with José Ferrer, Paul Muni, Uta Hagen, 30, 105 perfs.; *Mornings at Seven* by Paul Osborn 11/30 at the Longacre Theater, with Dorothy Gish, Russell Collins, Enid Markey, 44 perfs.

German playwright Ernst Toller hangs himself in his New York hotel room May 22 at age 45 (he has been depressed by the defeat of Spain's Loyalists); Kiev-born Yiddish theater actor-playwright-producer Boris Thomashefsky dies of a heart attack at New York July 9 at age 71; actress Alice Brady at her native New York October 28 at age 46.

The Hippodrome that has stood on the east side of Sixth Avenue between 43rd and 44th streets since 1905 comes down to make way for an office building and parking garage (billed as the world's largest).

Films: Garson Kanin's *Bachelor Mother* with Ginger Rogers, David Niven, Charles Coburn; Leo McCarey's *Love Affair* with Myrna Loy, Charles Boyer. Also: William McGann's *Blackwell's Island* with John Garfield, Rosemary Lane; William Keighley's *Each Dawn I Die* with James Cagney, George Raft; Andrew L. Stone's *The Great Victor Herbert* with Allan Jones, Mary Martin, Walter Connolly; Lewis Seiler and E.A. Dupont's *Hell's Kitchen* with Ronald Reagan, Stanley Fields; Joe May's *House of Fear* with William Gargan, Irene Hervey; John Cromwell's *Made for Each Other* with Carole Lombard, James Stewart, Lucile Watson; Dudley Murphy's *One Third of a Nation* with Sylvia Sidney, Leif Erickson, Myron McCormick; H. C. Potter's *The Story of Vernon and Irene Castle* with Fred Astaire, Ginger Rogers, Walter Brennan, Lew Fields; William Neigh's *The Streets of New York* with Jackie Cooper.

Film musicals: Gregory Ratoff's *Rose of Washington Square* with Tyrone Power, Alice Faye, Al Jolson; Roy

Del Ruth's *The Star Maker* with Bing Crosby (as Tin Pan Alley composer Gus Edwards, now 60); Victor Fleming's *The Wizard of Oz* opens August 17 at the Capitol Theater on Times Square and 15,000 people are lined up outside by 8 o'clock in the morning to see and hear Judy Garland (Frances Gumm, 17), Ray Bolger, Bert Lahr, Jack Haley, Frank Morgan, Margaret Hamilton, music by Harold Arlen, lyrics by E. Y. Harburg.

Broadcast Music, Inc. (BMI) is founded at New York October 14 by radio networks determined to build "an alternative source of music suitable for broadcasting" in competition with the ASCAP monopoly founded in 1914. ASCAP has boosted its license fees, and the networks balk at paying the higher fees (*see* 1940).

Broadway musicals: *The Hot Mikado* 3/23 at the Broadhurst Theater, with Bill "Bojangles" Robinson (who celebrates his 61st birthday 5/25 by dancing down Broadway from Columbus Circle to 44th Street), 125 black performers who include Hell's Kitchen-born chorus girl Rosetta LeNoire (originally Rosetta Burton), 27, music and lyrics adapted in jazz form from the Gilbert & Sullivan operetta (the show moves in June to the World's Fair at Flushing Meadow); *The Streets of Paris* 6/19 at the Broadhurst Theater, with Bobby Clark, Portuguese-born Brazilian entertainer Carmen Miranda (Maria Carno da Cunha), 26, singing "South American Way," music by Jimmy McHugh and others, lyrics by Al Dubin and others, 274 perfs.; *George White's Scandals* (revue) 8/28 at the Alvin Theater, with Willie and Eugene Howard, Montreal-born comedian Ben Blue, 37, Ann Miller, Glasgow-born singer Ella Logan, 26, the Three Stooges in the 13th and final edition of the *Scandals*, music by Sammy Fain, lyrics by Jack Yellen, songs that include "Are You Having Any Fun," 120 perfs.; *Too Many Girls* 10/18 at the Imperial Theater, with Cuban-born entertainer Desi Arnaz (Desiderio Alberto Arnaz y de Acha 3rd), 22, Eddie Bracken, Newport, R.I.-born actor Van Johnson, 23, Richard Kollmar, Marcy Wescott, choreography by Robert Alton, music by Richard Rodgers, lyrics by Lorenz Hart, songs that include "I Didn't Know What Time It Was," costumes by Raoul Pène Du Bois, 249 perfs.; *Very Warm for May* 11/17 at the Alvin Theater, with Grace McDonald, Philadelphia-born actor Jack Whiting, 38, Eve Arden, Lucerne, N.Y.-born ingénue June Allyson (Ella Geisman), 16, Cincinnati-born dancer Vera-Ellen (Vera-Ellen Westmyer), 18, music by Jerome Kern, lyrics by Oscar Hammerstein II, songs that include "All the Things You Are," 59 perfs.; *Du Barry Was a Lady* 12/6 at the 46th Street Theater, with Bert

Lahr, Ethel Merman, St. Louis-born actress Betty Grable (originally Elizabeth Grasle), 22, book by B. G. DeSylva, scenic design and costumes by Raoul Pène Du Bois, choreography by Robert Alton, music and lyrics by Cole Porter, songs that include "Friendship," "Do I Love You?," 408 perfs.

Dancer-choreographer Martha Graham sees Centralia, Wash.-born dancer Merce Cunningham, 20, performing at Oakland, Calif., and invites him to join her New York company. He creates the role of the acrobat in her ballet *Every Soul Is a Clown* and will remain with Graham for 6 years, creating top roles in many of her dances (*see* 1953).

Blue Note Records is founded at New York by German-born jazz fans Alfred Lion, 30, and Francis Wolff, who have come to America to escape Nazi persecution and hold their first jam session January 9 with boogie-woogie and blues pianists Albert Ammons and Meade Lux Lewis. After Lion completes his service with the U.S. Army the pair will record musicians ranging from Sidney Bechet and Art Blakey to John Coltrane, Miles Davis, Thelonious Monk, Bud Powell, Sonny Rollins, Horace Silver, and Cecil Taylor, continuing through the 1960s. Wolff will record alto saxophonist Ornette Colman after Lion's retirement in 1967 and continue the company until his death in 1971.

Frank Sinatra joins bandleader Harry James at age 23 to sing with a new band James is assembling. The Hoboken-born roadhouse singer will leave within a year to join the Tommy Dorsey band and perfect a technique of breath control based on Dorsey's trombone playing (*see* 1942).

Popular songs: "Strange Fruit" by left-wing New York schoolteacher Lewis Allan (Abel Meeropol), 36, who will follow his song about lynching with "The House I Live In;" "And the Angels Sing" by trumpet player Ziggy Elman (Harry Finkelman), who has adapted a Jewish folk tune, lyrics by Savannah-born songwriter John Herndon "Johnny" Mercer, 29.

A season of outdoor dancing in the city's public parks begins June 1, courtesy of the Works Progress Administration (WPA) and the Parks Department. Monday dancing is at Prospect Park, Tuesday and Wednesday on the Mall at Central Park, etc. Rules require hats off, jackets on, no smoking.

California-born heavyweight contender Lou Nova, 24, beats the former "Livermore Larruper" Max Baer at Yankee Stadium June 1 in the 11th round of a scheduled 15-round fight. Joe Louis defeats challenger Tony Galento at Yankee Stadium June 20 to retain his heavyweight title.

Los Angeles-born Robert Larimore "Bobby" Riggs, 21, wins in men's singles at Forest Hills, Alice Marble in women's singles.

Brewing veteran and New York Yankees owner Col. Jacob Ruppert dies in his 12-room apartment at 1120 Fifth Avenue January 13 at age 71 (he has been suffering from phlebitis and other ailments since April of last year). A bachelor, he has shared the apartment with a butler, valet, maid, and laundress, and the last person to see him before his death was Babe Ruth, now 45, who received $80,000 per year to hit home runs for the team. Former Red Sox manager Ed Barrow, now 70, remains general manager of the Yankees, a post he has held since Ruppert hired him at the end of the 1920 season (*see* 1945).

Yankee "Iron Horse" Lou Gehrig is stricken with a rare and fatal form of paralysis (amyotropic lateral sclerosis), takes himself out of the lineup April 30, retires with a lifetime batting average of .340, and bids a tearful farewell to Yankee fans July 4, saying, "I'm the luckiest man on the face of the earth." Appointed parole commissioner by Mayor La Guardia, he will serve until his death in June 1941.

Mississippi-born sportscaster Walter Lanier "Red" Barber, 31, leaves his job at Cincinnati to broadcast games for the Brooklyn Dodgers. He will remain with the Dodgers until 1953, making Brooklyn fans familiar with Southern expressions such as "havin' a rhubarb," "sittin' in the catbird seat," "tearin' up the pea patch," and "walkin' in tall cotton."

A major-league baseball game is telecast for the first time August 26 from Brooklyn's Ebbets Field.

The New York Yankees win the World Series, defeating the Cincinnati Reds 4 games to 0 with help from pitching by Monte Pearson, Red Ruffing, and Irving Darius "Bump" Hadley, 35. Rookie outfielder Charlie Keller, 23, gets seven hits, including a double, a triple, and three home runs; Joe DiMaggio five hits, including one home run; catcher Bill Dickey four hits, including two home runs.

The Parachute Jump at the World's Fair is a 250-foot-high version of a tower patented by Comdr. James H. Strong to train paratroopers and built at a cost of $750,000. Fairgoers pay 40¢ each to be strapped two abreast into any of 22 seats suspended from 11 gaily colored parachutes, hoisted aloft, and then dropped for a 10- or 15-second ride, guided by guy wires and cushioned on landing by shock absorbers. It takes 30 employees to operate the ride, and it is shut down when winds are even of moderate strength. Sponsored by Life Savers, the lakeside attraction shares its site with rides that include the Bunny Hug, the Drive-a-Drome, and the Stratoship (*see* 1941).

Manhattan District Attorney Thomas E. Dewey announces July 28 that he will ask the city to offer a $25,000 reward for the apprehension of mobster Louis "Lepke" Buchalter dead or alive in hopes that the offer will end the "war of extermination" that has been going on since January. Police bodyguards, he says, will be placed around at least 100 members, or former members, of the gangster organization that Lepke and Jacob Gurrah (Shapiro) headed in the heyday of their operations in the garment industry and other industrial fields (*see* 1941).

The World of Tomorrow at the World's Fair has been designed by New York–born architect Harmon H. (Hendricks) Goldstone, 28, of the firm Harrison & Fouilhoux. A great-great-grandson of early 19th century copper merchant Harmon Hendricks, Goldstone has worked out of a makeshift office at the Hotel Marguery on Park Avenue and based the fair's abstract Trylon and Perisphere on a pair of gas storage tanks at the corner of York Avenue and 62nd Street.

The 19-story Normandy apartment house is completed at 140 Riverside Drive, northeast corner 86th Street. Designed in Art Deco style by Emery Roth, it contains 250 apartments and is far less luxurious than Roth's Central Park West buildings.

The Public Housing Act signed into law by Gov. Lehman launches America's first state-subsidized public housing program. Funded by general-obligation bonds, it will finance construction of 66,123 apartments for low-income families statewide, and unlike federal programs its developments will admit elderly single persons and bar discrimination based on "race, color, creed, or religion" (*see* Mitchell-Lama, 1955).

The Red Hook Houses open in a Brooklyn area bounded by Dwight, Clinton, Lorraine, and West 9th streets. A design team headed by Alfred Easton Poor has designed the 20 six-story buildings, they contain 2,545 units, but a 25 percent slash in the original $16 million U.S. Housing Authority budget for the project has forced cost-cutting steps that include reducing the floor area per room from 221 square feet to 172, allowing only one closet with a door per apartment, and eliminating doors to kitchens. The cost per room has been cut to $1,137 (at the Harlem River Houses of 1935 it was $2,103). Elevators (these are the first public housing structures to have them) stop only on the first, third, and fifth floors.

The Queensbridge Houses open in a Ravenswood area bounded by Vernon Boulevard, 21st Street, 40th Avenue, and Bridge Plaza North. Architects Henry Churchill, Frederick G. Frost, and Burnett C. Turner have designed the 26 six-story buildings, they contain 3,149 units (cost per room: $1,044), have been built with federal funds under the U.S. Housing Authority Act, and occupy six superblocks.

Fortune magazine reports that only a handful of the city's super-rich still live in private houses on Fifth Avenue, where property taxes are $42 per square foot as compared with $27 on side streets. Financial wizard Bernard Baruch (who has moved from West 70th Street), National City Bank president Gordon Rentschler, oilman Joseph Feder, Standard Oil heir Edward S. Harkness (at 1 East 75th Street), former U.S. ambassador to Germany James W. Gerard, sculptor and museum donor Gertrude Vanderbilt Whitney, and Mrs. Cornelius Vanderbilt III all have Fifth Avenue mansions. The 58-room Vanderbilt home at the corner of 51st Street has an assessed value of $2.45 million (Mrs. Vanderbilt pays $197 per day in property taxes, *Fortune* declares; *see* 1940). The Baruch home near 87th Street has 32 rooms (including an oval dining room, a large ballroom, and a solarium), 10 baths. Even a house assessed at $250,000 generally supports a staff of 10 servants—butler, chef, valet, lady's maid, footman, parlormaid, chambermaid, two kitchen maids, and a laundress, who are paid a combined $14,000 per year in wages and consume $4,000 worth of food.

The World's Fair at Flushing Meadow rises atop what used to be a 1,216-acre Corona, Queens, ash dump (*see* 1932). The fairgrounds will become a park after the fair closes next year (*see* Flushing Meadows–Corona Park, 1967).

The Fulton Fish Market reopens in a new building put up to replace the 1907 structure that fell into the East River 3 years ago. Fishmongers in the new market handle some 250 million pounds of seafood in the first year.

1940 Brooklyn borough president Raymond V. Ingersoll dies at Brooklyn February 24 at age 64, having played a major role in city politics.

The Alien Registration Act (Smith Act) passed by Congress June 28 requires that aliens be fingerprinted and makes it unlawful to advocate overthrow of the U.S. government or belong to any group advocating such overthrow. Rep. Wright Patman, 46, (D. Tex.) attacks New York public-relations pioneer

Carl Byoir, now 52, on the floor of the House of Representatives, calling him a Nazi sympathizer and accusing him of espionage. Having done publicity for the German Information Office in the United States 6 years ago, Byoir asks for an investigation May 24 and is cleared by the FBI July 16. Patman says the bureau has acted hastily, but the House Un-American Affairs Committee exonerates Byoir September 10.

The first peacetime military draft in U.S. history begins October 29 following passage by Congress of a Selective Service Act. Unprepared for combat, the U.S. Army is surpassed in size by the armies of more than 15 other nations, including those of Greece, Portugal, and Peru. New Yorkers aged 18 to 35 from Canarsie to Park Avenue receive draft notices in November and December.

The Popular Democratic Party that will control Puerto Rico until 1977 comes to power with the election of party founder Luis Muñoz Marin, 42, who started the PDP in 1938. President Roosevelt next year will appoint former Columbia University economics professor Rexford Guy Tugwell governor of Puerto Rico, and Tugwell, now 48, will work with Muñoz Marin to improve the island's economy.

The Republican National Convention at Madison Square Garden nominates New York lawyer Wendell L. Willkie, now 48, to oppose President Roosevelt's bid for a third term. Willkie has attacked the Tennessee Valley Authority as head of the Commonwealth & Southern Corp. utilities holding company, but his internationalist views make him a more attractive candidate than isolationists Robert A. Taft of Ohio, Arthur Vandenberg of Michigan, or New York District Attorney Thomas E. Dewey. Few people know that Willkie was a registered Democrat until last year and considered himself a liberal, having spoken out in support of the League of Nations and fought the Ku Klux Klan. Speakers who include playwright Clare Boothe Luce support Willkie, Republicans play up his Indiana roots, distribute buttons that say, "No Third Term" but disclaim responsibility for buttons that say, "No Triple for a Cripple;" Democrats call Willkie "the barefoot boy from Wall Street." Bronx political boss Edward J. Flynn helps engineer a draft movement to nominate President Roosevelt, who wins reelection with 54 percent of the popular vote, but postmaster general and state Democratic Party committee chairman James A. Farley has refused to withdraw his own candidacy and quits public life. Willkie wins 44 percent of the popular vote but only 82 electoral votes to FDR's 449 and does not carry New York.

Marcus Garvey dies in obscurity and poverty at London June 10 at age 52 (see 1924). He will be memorialized at New York in 1973 by a renaming of Harlem's Mt. Morris Park.

Standard Oil heir and philanthropist Edward Stephen Harkness dies at his 1 East 75th Street town house January 29 at age 66, having given at least $100 million to Yale, Harvard, the Metropolitan Museum of Art, the Commonwealth Fund that his mother started in 1918, and other public institutions (Harkness Pavilion at Columbia Presbyterian Hospital bears his name, and his widow, Mary E. [née Stillman], will carry on his benefactions); social worker Lillian Wald dies at Westport, Conn., September 1 at age 73.

The first Social Security checks go out January 30 and total $75,844, a figure that will rise into the billions as more pensioners become eligible for benefits and the program is broadened to include people other than retirees (see 1935). U.S. unemployment remains above 8 million, with 14.6 percent of the workforce idle.

Lawyer Samuel Untermyer dies of pneumonia at his Palm Springs, Calif., winter home March 16 at age 81 and is buried at Woodlawn Cemetery; lawyer Max Steuer dies of a heart attack at Jackson, N.H., August 21 at age 69. Both have been unofficial attorneys general of the City of New York.

The New York World's Fair closes its second season October 26 with a record one-day attendance of 550,962, but the overall attendance of 44,931,681 for the 2-year exposition has not reached even half the projected total of 100 million, and the fair has lost more than half of the $65 million contributed for its building, including $26.7 million from the city, $6.2 million from the state, $3 million from the federal government, and about $30 million from foreign governments. While showman Billy Rose has attracted sell-out crowds to his Aquacade, almost no one else has made money.

Paris-born financier André (Benoit Mathieu) Meyer, 42, joins the New York office of the 93-year-old banking firm Lazard Frères & Cie., and will be senior partner from 1943 until his death in 1979 (see 1884). Meyer received his secondary-school education in America, Lazard was still small but prestigious when he joined it in 1926, having caught the eye of its senior partner David David-Weill (the family hyphenated its name in the 1920s to make it sound more aristocratic), and with the help of Meyer's acumen Lazard will become a major presence in the financial world (see 1961).

Former Wall Street speculator Jesse L. Livermore, now 63, has lunch alone at the Sherry-Netherland Hotel on Fifth Avenue November 28, goes back to the Squibb Building office that he opened last year, returns to the hotel's bar at 4:30 o'clock, has a couple of drinks, goes into the men's room at about 5:25, pulls out a Colt .32 revolver, and shoots himself (see 1934). Livermore has had an apartment at 550 Park Avenue but has been unable to recover from his 1934 bankruptcy because of Securities and Exchange Commission rules against stock manipulation. He leaves his (third) wife a suicide note in which he says, "My life has been a failure."

Wall Street's Dow Jones Industrial Average closes June 10 at 111.84 but rebounds to close December 31 at 131.13, down from 150.24 at the end of 1939.

The municipally owned Essex Street Retail Market opens January 6 in Grand Street between Ludlow and Essex streets (see 1836; First Avenue market, 1938). Mayor La Guardia has had the structure built to replace the area's open-air markets, moving itinerant peddlers and pushcarts off Lower East Side streets into a facility that will come to be run by the merchants on a co-operative basis (see 1986). The mayor orders food markets (later to be called La Marqueta) built in East Harlem under the New York Central and New Haven railroad tracks on Park Avenue between 111th and 116th streets. His purpose, as on the Lower East Side, is to get pushcart peddlers off the streets, put a roof over their heads, and eliminate many traffic fatalities.

Tiffany & Co. moves uptown into a large new building at 727 Fifth Avenue, southeast corner 57th Street, after 34 years at 37th Street. Designed by Cross & Cross, the polished granite structure is the first fully air-conditioned store of any kind.

Gov. Lehman signs a bill March 31 placing expenditures of the State Transit Commission under the control of the city's Board of Estimate.

The privately owned part of New York's subway and elevated systems becomes publicly owned on the night of June 1 with a ceremony at City Hall as the city turns over $175 million in 3 percent municipal bonds to the Brooklyn-Manhattan Transit Corp. (BMT) for all its tangible assets (see Dual Contracts, 1913). Brooklyn's Third Avenue and Fifth Avenue Els have stopped running at midnight after nearly 50 years of service. The Fulton Street El ends its downtown service but will continue service between East New York and Richmond Hill until April 1956, and the BMT's Myrtle Avenue El line continues to run across the Brooklyn Bridge.

The Ninth Avenue El ceases operations June 11, and the Second Avenue El stops running north of 57th Street; the city hands over $151 million in municipal bonds June 12 to acquire the Interborough Rapid Transit Co. (IRT) in order to expedite removal of elevated railway lines. The last sections of the Sixth Avenue El come down beginning December 20, with Mayor La Guardia using an acetylene torch to start the process (see 1938), and the scrap metal is sold to Japan before passage of an Export Control Act. Only one of Manhattan's four elevated railways remains: the Third Avenue El will continue to operate until 1955 on the premise that it will be needed until a Second Avenue subway can be built. That subway was first proposed in 1929 to ease traffic congestion on the East Side but will not be built in this century, leaving the widest part of Manhattan with no rapid transit except for the Lexington Avenue subway that began service in 1918 (see 1972).

The Belt Parkway is dedicated June 29; Mayor La Guardia announces at the ceremony that the Reconstruction Finance Corp. will lend the city enough money to build a Brooklyn-Battery tunnel (see 1950). The New York Times calls the $30 million Belt Parkway-Cross Island Parkway route "the greatest municipal highway venture ever attempted in an urban setting;" local property owners have blocked construction for two miles between Sheepshead Bay and Marine Park, saying it would cut them off from beaches, but Robert Moses will have his way, the missing link will open in May of next year, and the entire 36-mile roadway (including the 11-mile Cross Island Parkway) will provide quick access from the shorefront to southern Brooklyn and Queens, initially with four 12-foot-wide lanes, a wide grassy median, 47 road bridges (including a 2,740-foot viaduct over the Coney Island subway yards), six pedestrian overpasses, five railroad bridges, and six over-water crossings. The undertaking has employed some 5,000 men since work began in 1934 (see Gowanus Parkway, 1941).

Automobile pioneer Walter P. Chrysler dies at his Great Neck, L.I., estate August 18 at age 65.

The Queens-Midtown Tunnel opens November 15 to link Long Island City with East 36th Street in Manhattan. Designed by Ole Singstad, financed by the federal Public Works Administration and the Reconstruction Finance Corp., and built under the East River in just 4 years, it has two 6,300-foot-long tubes for cars and trucks. The 200,000th car goes through December 1, the 500,000th December 25. So many cars pour into Manhattan that Borough President Stanley M. Isaacs bewails the lack of an underground connection between the new tunnel and the Lincoln Tunnel whose second tube opens in December.

∞ The Lubavitcher Rebbe Joseph Isaac Schneersohn of Warsaw arrives at New York from Riga March 19 aboard the Swedish American Line ship S.S. *Drottningholm*. Now 59, the Rebbe visited the city in 1929 and was received by President Hoover at the White House; he will stay in Manhattan only briefly before settling in Brooklyn's Crown Heights section (*see* 1945).

The 15-year-old YIVO Institute for Jewish Research (*Yiddisher visnshaftlekher institut*) relocates from Vilna, Lithuania, to its branch office at 425 Lafayette Street in Manhattan. It will give instruction in Yiddish, offer graduate courses in Jewish studies, issue scholarly publications, and maintain a multilingual library with the world's largest collection of Yiddish publications. YIVO will later acquire the mansion at 1048 Fifth Avenue, southeast corner 86th Street, built in 1914 (*see* 1994).

A new building for Hunter College is completed at 695 Park Avenue, between 68th and 69th streets, to designs by Shreve, Lamb & Harmon with an assist from Harrison & Fouilhoux.

The Board of Education adopts rules November 13 governing a released-time program for religious classes of public-school students. Such classes are to be voluntary and held outside of school buildings, religious institutions are to provide parents with cards to be filled out and returned to the schools, whose principals will arrange for release times; the religious institutions are to have responsibility for discipline.

The City Council votes to ban broadcasts of its proceedings on the municipal radio station WNYC (*see* 1938). Some listeners have been so amused by what they heard that they rushed to City Hall to witness the goings-on.

Hungarian-born CBS engineer Peter C. (Carl) Goldmark, 34, pioneers color television, but his system requires special receivers. It will give way in the 1950s to an RCA system whose signals will be compatible with conventional black and white TV signals (*see* 1939; long-playing records, 1948).

In fact begins weekly publication May 20 at New York. Former *Chicago Tribune* foreign correspondent George Seldes, 50 (older brother of Gilbert), quit the *Trib* in the late 1920s when publisher Robert R. McCormick suppressed a story he had filed from Mexico, his 31-year career in journalism has been notable for its exposés of conditions in Soviet Russia, fascist Italy, and Nazi Germany, but Seldes has been frustrated by the publishing establishment. His 1938 book *Freedom of the Press* charged that more censorship was caused by advertising pressures than by government, and he calls his four-page 9" × 12" paper "The Antidote for Falsehood in the Daily Press" (he accepts no advertising and receives more stories than he can use each week from reporters on papers throughout the country who cannot get their pieces past their editors). Startup money has come from the Communist Party, and Party member Bruce Minton has helped start the sheet, but Minton soon finds that Seldes will not parrot the party line and quits. Daring to tell the truth in a shrill voice when the mainstream press is all too ready to bow to pressure from advertisers, *In fact* has an initial list of 6,000 subscribers (all C.I.O. members) that will soon grow to include first lady Eleanor Roosevelt, Vice President Henry A. Wallace, Sen. Harry S. Truman (D. Mo.), Supreme Court justices, Secretary of the Interior Harold M. Ickes, and Newspaper Guild members (*see* 1950).

PM begins publication June 18 at New York. Started by Chicago department store heir Marshall Field III, 46, and others, the evening tabloid carries no advertising and will gain a following with its outspoken editorials (and its comic strip "Barnaby and Mr. O'Malley" by Crockett Johnson) (*see* 1948).

Newsday begins publication September 3 at Hempstead, L.I., where copper heir Harry F. Guggenheim, now 50, and his third wife, Alicia (*née* Patterson), have converted a garage into a printing plant and start a daily paper with a name culled from contest submissions. Now 33, publishing heiress Patterson divorced her second husband last year to marry Guggenheim. They have found the equipment of a publication that failed last year for sale at a reasonable price, and their 40-page tabloid rolls off the press with large columns that make it unlike any other tabloid in the country (Capt. Joseph M. Patterson, Alicia's father, has advised against making it a tabloid). The Guggenheims aim to have a circulation of 15,000, will invest $750,000 in the next 6 years before *Newsday* begins to show a profit, build a plant on a five-acre tract in Long Island City, and make their paper politically independent, backing some Democratic candidates in a strongly Republican county; by mid-1963 *Newsday* will have a circulation of 375,000.

The Ted Bates advertising agency is founded by New Haven, Conn.-born Yale graduate Theodore Lewis Bates, 38, who was a vice president at BBD&O before becoming a v.p. at Benton & Bowles in 1935. His shop will specialize in hard-sell ads for package goods and cigarettes (*see* politics, 1952).

"Captain Marvel" makes his debut in biweekly Whiz comic books produced by Fawcett Comics from offices on the 22nd floor of the Paramount Building in Times Square. Rivaling "Superman" in Action Comics, the hero from "Fawcett City, S.D." will make Whiz Comics more popular than Action Comics, with sales of 1.5 million copies per issue; publishers of Action Comics will sue Fawcett next year, the case will be settled out of court, and Captain Marvel will be terminated in 1953 (although he will occasionally be revived by DC Comics).

Nonfiction: *Where Are the Customers' Yachts? Or, a Good Hard Look at Wall Street* by onetime Wall Street trader Fred Schwed, Jr. (who lost his shirt in the 1929 crash and got out of the market), illustrations by *New Yorker* magazine cartoonist Peter Arno; *Father and I* by the late Clarence Day; *Harlem: Negro Metropolis* by poet-novelist Claude McKay; *Let There Be Sculpture* by Lower East Side-born London sculptor Jacob Epstein, 60, who became a British subject 30 years ago: "My earliest recollections are of the teeming East Side where I was born. This Hester Street and its surrounding streets were the most densely populated of any city on earth; and looking back at it, I realized what I owe to its unique and crowded humanity. Its swarms of Russians, Poles, Italians, Greeks, and Chinese lived as much in the streets as in the crowded tenements; and the sights, sounds, and smells had the vividness of an Oriental city. From one end to the other Hester Street was an open-air market. The streets were lined with pushcarts and peddlers, and the crowd that packed the sidewalk and roadway compelled one to move slowly;" *Gossip: The Life and Times of Walter Winchell* by North Carolina-born *New Yorker* magazine editor-writer St. Clair McKelway, 35, who questions the accuracy of Winchell's reporting.

Fiction: *Native Son* by Mississippi-born novelist Richard Wright, 31, who moved to New York in 1937 to edit the *Daily Worker*; *Angels on Toast* by Dawn Powell.

Poetry: *A Poet in New York* (*Poeta en Nueva York*) by the late Spanish poet-playwright Federico García Lorca, who spent the better part of a year at Columbia University from 1929 to 1930 but was killed by Francisco Franco's Falangists in 1936 at age 37.

The Anchor Book Shop opens at 114 Fourth Avenue, The Fourth Avenue Book Store (started by George Rubinowitz and his wife, Jean) at 138 Fourth, and the Corner Bookshop, formerly at 120, moves to new quarters at 102 (not a corner but across the street from the store's old premises). Rents have dropped to a level that even sellers of used books can afford.

Painting: *T. B. Harlem* by "bohemian" New York painter Alice Neel, 40; *Garden in Sochi* by Turkish Armenian-born New York painter Arshile Gorky (originally Vostanig Adoian), 35; *Long Island* and *Thunder Shower* by Arthur Dove; *Three White Squares* (paint on glass) by New York abstractionist I. (Irene) Pereira (*née* Rice), 38, who married Humberto Pereira in 1929, divorced him 1938, and next year will marry George W. Brown; *Seated Nude* by Lee Krasner.

German-born photographer Ilse Bing, 40, and her pianist-musicologist husband, Konrad Wolff, arrive at New York, where they will remain for the rest of their lives. The only photographer to work in Paris exclusively with the Leica, Bing was offered a job by LIFE 4 years ago but turned it down because Wolf, whom she married a year later, was in Paris, but she has accepted assignments from *Harper's Bazaar*.

Photographs: *Promenade des Anglais* by Vienna-born documentary photographer Lisette Model (*née* Seyberg), 33, contains photos taken in 1937 on the French Riviera. She has applied for a darkroom job with the new afternoon paper *PM*, whose picture editor Ralph Steiner has recognized the quality of her work and arranged for publication of the book, which brings her immediate acclaim. Photographer Lewis W. Hine dies at Hastings-on-Hudson November 3 at age 66.

Theater: *The Male Animal* by James Thurber and Ohio-born playwright-actor Elliott (John) Nugent, 40, 1/9 at the Cort Theater, with Nugent, Brooklyn-born ingénue Gene (originally Gene Eliza Taylor) Tierney, 19, 243 perfs. (St. Louis-born New York lawyer David Merrick [originally Margulois], 27, has invested $5,000 in the show, makes a handsome profit, and will give up his law practice in 1949 to become a full-time theatrical producer); *My Dear Children* by Chicago-born playwright Catherine Turney, 33, and Jerry Horwin 1/31 at the Belasco Theater, with John Barrymore, 117 perfs.; *The Fifth Column* by Ernest Hemingway and Belfast-born playwright Benjamin Glazer 3/26 at the Alvin Theater, with Lenore Ulric, Lee J. Cobb, Franchot Tone, 87 perfs.; *There Shall Be No Night* by Robert Sherwood 4/29 at the Alvin Theater, with Alfred Lunt, Lynn Fontanne, English-born actor Sydney Greenstreet, 60, Richard Whorf, Omaha-born ingénu Montgomery Clift, 19, 115 perfs.; *Johnny Belinda* by U.S. playwright Elmer Harris, 62, 9/18 at the Belasco

Theater, with Helen Craig, Horace McNally, 321 perfs.; *George Washington Slept Here* by George S. Kaufman and Moss Hart 10/18 at the Lyceum Theater, with Ernest Truex, Mississippi-born comedienne Jean Dixon, 44, 173 perfs.; *Old Acquaintance* by John Van Druten 12/23 at the Morosco Theater, with Jane Cowl, Kent Smith, 170 perfs.; *My Sister Eileen* by New York playwrights Joseph A. Fields, 45, and Jerome Chodorov, 29, 12/26 at the Biltmore Theater, with Shirley Booth, Washington, D.C.-born actress Jo Ann Sayers, 39, Morris Carnovsky in a play based on Ruth McKinney's book, 865 perfs.

Actress Maxine Elliott dies of a heart ailment at her French Riviera home March 5 at age 69; theater magnate Martin Beck of a cerebral blood clot after surgery at New York November 16 at age 73.

Films: George B. Seitz's *Andy Hardy Meets Debutante* with Mickey Rooney, Judy Garland; Anatole Litvak's *Castle on the Hudson* with John Garfield as a Sing Sing prisoner, Pat O'Brien as the warden; Anatole Litvak's *City for Conquest* with James Cagney, Ann Sheridan; Alfred E. Green's *East of the River* with John Garfield, Brenda Marshall; Sam Wood's *Kitty Foyle* with Ginger Rogers, Dennis Morgan; Henry King's *Little Old New York* with Alice Faye, Brenda Joyce, Fred MacMurray; Harry Lachman's *Murder Over New York* with Sidney Toler as Charlie Chan; William Keighly's *No Time for Comedy* with James Stewart, Rosalind Russell; Ben Holmes's *The Saint in New York* with Louis Hayward, Kay Sutton; Lloyd Bacon's *Three Cheers for the Irish* with Thomas Mitchell, Dennis Morgan, Priscilla Lane.

Film musicals: A. Edward Sutherland's *The Boys from Syracuse* with Allan Jones, Joe Penner, Martha Raye, Rosemary Lane, Rodgers & Hammerstein songs from the 1938 Broadway musical; Norman Taurog's *Little Nellie Kelly* with Judy Garland, George Murphy, Charles Winninger, songs that include "It's a Great Day for the Irish" and "Singin' in the Rain;" Walter Lang's *Tin Pan Alley* with Alice Faye, Betty Grable, Jack Oakie, John Payne; S. Sylvan Simon's *Two Girls on Broadway* with Lana Turner, George Murphy, Joan Blondell.

Broadway musicals: *Two for the Show* 2/8 at the Booth Theater, with Eve Arden, Battle Creek, Mich.-born comedienne Betty Hutton (Betty Jane Thornburg), 18, New York-born comedian Francis Xavier Aloysius "Keenan" Wynn, 23 (son of comedian Ed Wynn), Alfred Drake, songs that include "How High the Moon" by Morgan Lewis, lyrics by Nancy Hamilton, 124 perfs.; *Higher and Higher* 4/4 at the Shubert Theater, with Jack Haley, Marta Eggert, music by Richard Rodgers, lyrics by Lorenz

Hart, songs that include "It Never Entered My Mind," 84 perfs.; *Louisiana Purchase* 5/28 at the Imperial Theater, with William Gaxton, Victor Moore, Vera Zorina, Irene Bordoni, Great Neck-born ingénue Carol Bruce, 20, book from a story by B. G. DeSylva, music and lyrics by Irving Berlin, songs that include "It's a Lovely Day Tomorrow," 444 perfs.; *Cabin in the Sky* 10/25 at the Martin Beck Theater, with Ethel Waters, Chicago-born dancer-choreographer Katherine Dunham, 28, Todd Duncan, Dooley Wilson, Illinois-born actor Rex Ingram, 45, J. Rosamond Johnson, music by Vernon Duke, book and lyrics by Richmond, Va.-born writer John LaTouche, 22, and Ted Felter, songs that include "Taking a Chance on Love," 156 perfs.; *Panama Hattie* 10/30 at the 46th Street Theater, with Ethel Merman, English actor Arthur Treacher, 46, Betty Hutton, Montreal-born comedian Pat Harrington, 39, dancer Vera-Ellen, book by B. G. DeSylva, choreography by Robert Alton, music and lyrics by Cole Porter, songs that include "Let's Be Buddies," 501 perfs.; *Pal Joey* 12/25 at the Ethel Barrymore Theater, with Gene Kelly, Vivienne Segal, Canadian-born actress June Havoc (June Hovick), 30, choreography by Robert Alton, music by Richard Rodgers, lyrics by Lorenz Hart, book based on the new collection of stories by John O'Hara, songs that include "Bewitched," "I Could Write a Book," "Zip," 344 perfs.

The Ballet Theater gives its first performance at New York January 11. An outgrowth of the Mordkin Ballet started by choreographers and dancers who include Monte Carlo-born dancer Vladimir Dokoudovsky, 21, the company was founded last year by Lucia Chase and Richard Pleasant (it will be renamed the American Ballet Theater in 1957).

The Metropolitan Opera of the Air sponsored by the Texas Company (later Texaco Inc.) begins Saturday afternoon broadcasts December 7 with Ezio Pinza, Licia Albanese, and others singing Mozart's *Nozze di Figaro.*

Popular songs: "Times Square Dance" by Sammy Fain, lyrics by Jack Yellen; "Meet Me in Times Square" by Irving Gellers, lyrics by Gladys Shelley; "Tuxedo Junction" by bandleader Erskine Hawkins, William Johnson, and Julian Dash, lyrics by Buddy Feyne.

Terre Haute, Ind.-born arranger and pianist Claude Thornhill, 31, forms his own dance band, having worked with big bands such as Hal Kemp, Benny Goodman, Ray Noble, Artie Shaw, and Freddie Martin.

Café Society Uptown opens in East 58th Street to supplement the downtown nightclub opened by Barney Josephson late in 1938. Performers at the new club will include singers Billie Holiday, Lena Horne, and Sarah Vaughan and comedian Zero Mostel (see 1947).

The Copacabana nightclub opens at 10 East 60th Street, an outgrowth of the Villa Vallee at the same location that has provided a venue for singer Rudy Vallée. Gambler Frank Costello has bankrolled the new place, and entertainers who include Nat King Cole, Jimmy Durante, Ella Fitzgerald, and Frank Sinatra will help the Copa attract patrons until it closes in 1973 for conversion into a discothèque (it will also be used for various private functions).

Radio networks continue to resist ASCAP demands for higher fees (see BMI, 1939). ASCAP has withdrawn music controlled by its members and does not permit the networks even to use birds trained to sing the music. The boycott will not end until the parties reach a compromise late next year.

Muzak is acquired by former New York advertising man William Benton, who pays $135,000 to take over a small company that pipes "background music" into restaurants and bars on leased telephone wires under a system originated in World War I by Brig. Gen. George O. Squire and put into operation in 1925 by a public utility holding company. Now 40, Benton will expand Muzak by piping it into factories, retail stores, offices, and even elevators before selling the company at a $4.2 million profit.

A basketball game is telecast for the first time February 28 from Madison Square Garden.

The New York Rangers win their third National Hockey League (NHL) championship. Coached by Frank Boucher, they take the Stanley Cup away from the Toronto Maple Leafs.

Mel Allen becomes the lead radio announcer for the New York Yankees baseball team and the New York Giants football team. Alabama-born law graduate Melvin Allen Israel, 26, passed his state's bar exam in 1936, took a vacation in New York, was interviewed by Ted Husing of CBS, and accepted a job as sports and special events announcer. He will be the voice of the Yankees for 19 years.

Joe Louis retains his world heavyweight title, defeating challenger Arturo Godoy at Yankee Stadium June 28.

W. Donald McNeil, 22, wins in men's singles at Forest Hills, Alice Marble in women's singles.

 Cornelius Vanderbilt III and his wife, Grace, sell their 58-room 640 Fifth Avenue house at the corner of 51st Street to the William Waldorf Astor estate and move into a 28-room house at 1048 Fifth Avenue, southeast corner 86th Street (the larger house will be replaced by an office tower).

A 16-story apartment house with two penthouse floors is completed at 40 Central Park South to designs by Mayer, Whittlesey and Glass. The stark white-brick structure rises just east of the St. Moritz Hotel.

The Parkchester housing project opens in the Bronx in an area bounded by East Tremont Avenue, Purdy Street, McGraw Avenue, Hugh J. Grant Circle, and White Plains Road. The complex is landscaped with lawns, flower beds, trees, and shrubbery, and by the time it is finished in 1942 the 40,000 tenants of its fireproof, six-story, elevator apartment buildings will be able to enjoy a large movie theater, more than 100 stores (including the first Macy's branch), a bowling alley, and parking garages for 3,000 cars. Only 400 of its 12,000 apartments have more than two bedrooms, and it has a population density of 62 families per acre. Metropolitan Life Insurance Co. has financed the project, whose buildings have replaced scores of tenements (see Stuyvesant Town, 1947; Helmsley-Spear, 1968).

Architect Chester H. Aldrich of Delano and Aldrich dies a bachelor at Rome December 26 at age 69.

 U.S. Fish and Wildlife Agency agents raid Brooklyn pet shops and oblige them to release birds held in violation of a 1913 law (and a more recent treaty with Mexico) that forbids keeping indigenous wild birds in captivity. A songbird of the canary family, the house finch (Carpodacus purpureus) has been taken illegally by nets in the Sierras and sold through the 1930s to dealers at a few dollars per hundred; it will propagate itself throughout New York (and then throughout much of the Northeast), entertaining the city with arguably the most musical call of any wild bird.

 Citarella relocates from 107th Street and Broadway to a new site on the west side of Broadway south of 75th Street (see 1926). Still selling only seafood, it will expand in the 1980s (see Gurrera, 1982).

 Cookbook: Hors d'Oeuvre and Canapes: With a Key to the Cocktail Party by Oregon-born New York caterer James (Andrews) Beard, 37, launches its author on a career that will make his name a household word. A onetime actor and radio announcer, Beard has until recently taught English and French but is now co-owner of Hors d'Oeuvre Inc.

Toots Shor's restaurant opens at 51 West 51st Street. Philadelphia-born saloon keeper Bernard "Toots" Shor, 35, is a onetime B. V. D. salesman who stands six feet two, weighs 250 pounds, and was a speakeasy bouncer for mobster Owney Madden during Prohibition. He will make his place popular among hard-drinking sports fans, sell his lease in 1958 for $1.5 million, open a new place at 33 West 52nd Street, and relocate thereafter to other locations.

The Riese brothers restaurant empire has its beginnings in Paul's Luncheonette, a run-down delicatessen in 40th Street between Fifth and Madison avenues. Irving Riese, 21, has a diploma from DeWitt Clinton High School, he and his high-school dropout brother Murray, 18, have been selling Russian delicacies in a small Harlem deli, they put up $400 in cash to buy the luncheonette for $10,000, work 18-hour days 6 days per week making sandwiches, delivering them, and renovating the place that they will sell in 1942 for $35,000. By the 1950s they will have bought, renovated, and sold hundreds of luncheonettes, coffee shops, and Chinese, Italian, and Mediterranean restaurants (see 1953).

New York's population reaches 7,454,995, up from 6,930,446 in 1930; Manhattan's population has risen, but only by 22,612. Immigration has fallen in recent years, and only 28.7 percent of the population is foreign-born, down from 34.3 percent in 1930. Some 375,000 blacks will move into the city in the next 20 years, the number of Puerto Ricans will more than quadruple, East Harlem between 90th and 125th streets will become known as "El Barrio," and Spanish will become the city's second language.

1941 A patriotic rally in Central Park's Sheep Meadow May 17 brings out a crowd that by some estimates exceeds 650,000—the biggest thus far in New York history. Mayor La Guardia gives a speech, exchanges jokes with comedian Eddie Cantor, twice takes up the baton to conduct a 250-piece band of musicians from the fire, parks, police, and sanitation departments, and listens with the rest of the crowd to performances by violinist Albert Spalding, contralto Marian Anderson, and radio singer-entertainer Kate Smith (who sings "God Bless America").

An America First rally at Madison Square Garden May 23 draws a capacity crowd of 22,000 to hear speeches by Charles A. Lindbergh, Sen. Burton K. Wheeler (R. Mont.), Norman Thomas, novelist Kathleen Norris, and others; they protest President Roosevelt's foreign policy and urge him to keep America out of the war. Crowds estimated to number between 8,000 and 14,000 crowd 49th Street between Eighth and Ninth avenues to hear the speeches over loudspeakers while 800 police officers stand by to prevent violence between America Firsters and anti-Nazi pickets.

German troops invade Soviet Russia June 22, producing consternation among New York's Russian-immigrant population.

Il Progresso Italo-Americano publisher Generoso Pope repudiates fascism in an editorial (see 1936) and supports Mayor La Guardia, whom he had initially opposed.

Mayor La Guardia wins election to an unprecedented third term after a close race against his Irish-born Democratic Party challenger William O'Dwyer, 51, who has gained renown as Brooklyn district attorney by convicting members of the national crime syndicate Murder Inc., originally a Brownsville-based "troop" recruited by Louis "Lepke" Buchalter. Supported by labor, leading Republican figures, and President Roosevelt, La Guardia carries Manhattan, the Bronx, and Brooklyn, receiving 1,186,630 votes to O'Dwyer's 1,054,175. O'Dwyer carries some Jewish and Italian districts and does not sweep the Irish vote by any means.

Abyssinian Baptist Church pastor Adam Clayton Powell, Jr. is elected to the City Council, becoming its first black member. Now 32, he has helped organize the Equal Employment Coordinating Committee in his energetic career and led boycotts of companies that refused to hire black workers (see 1944; bus drivers, 1938).

Japanese planes attack the U.S. naval base at Pearl Harbor in the Hawaiian Islands December 7. In his regular Sunday radio talk on WNYC that day (the talk is also carried on NBC) Mayor La Guardia says, "I want to assure all persons who have been sneering and jeering at defense activities, and even those who have been objecting to them and placing obstacles in their path, that we will protect them now. But we expect their co-operation and there will be no fooling." (Isolationists who include publisher Joseph M. Patterson of the *Daily News* have bitterly opposed President Roosevelt's foreign policies, calling him a "warmonger.") The FBI sends out agents to guard the Kensico and Croton dams and the Brooklyn Navy Yard, where the battleships *Iowa* and *Missouri* are under construction, and by midnight the city has placed air-raid wardens on duty and instituted precautions against sabotage. Men trying to enlist swamp the recruiting office in the U.S. Post Office at Church and Vesey Street Monday morning, and nearly 6,000 people sign up for air-raid warden duty, bringing the city's total to 125,006. The Port of New York Authority cancels leaves and vacations, placing guards at bridges and tunnels. Other guards keep watch at power plants, railroad stations, and reservoirs. Germany declares war on the United States December 11, thus making it possible for President Roosevelt to end U.S. neutrality in the European war. Italy echoes the German declaration, and Congress declares war on Germany and Italy.

Mayor La Guardia returns to the city December 13 from a trip to the West Coast as civil defense coordinator. An antiaircraft battery is stationed on Central Park's Great Hill, others are set up in Prospect Park, Fort Totten, and at other locations; a blackout is imposed on the city and its suburbs, with air-raid wardens enforcing the regulation that lighted windows be covered at night. The U.S. Army installs the East Coast's first radar devices at Fort Totten on Willets Point, Queens.

President Roosevelt appoints a Fair Employment Practice Committee (FEPC) June 25. Brotherhood of Sleeping Car Porters founder A. Philip Randolph has threatened a march by 50,000 blacks on Washington to protest unfair employment practices in war industry and the government (see Randolph, 1925).

The Office of Price Administration and Civilian Supply (OPA) created by the president April 11 has New Deal economist Leon Henderson, 45, as its head, but wartime inflation increases the general price level by 10 percent for the year.

Nearly 40 percent of New York City's workforce is engaged in manufacturing, and the city is far and away the nation's largest manufacturing center, but war contracts will not be awarded for some time to any New York company (see 1942).

Tax rates rise sharply in nearly all categories September 20 in an effort to raise more than $3.5 billion for war-related expenditures.

The U.S. Treasury issues war bonds to help reduce the amount of money in circulation. Priced to yield 2.9 percent return on investment, the Series E savings bonds come in denominations of $25 to $10,000. Hollywood starlet Linda Darnell, 20, appears on the floor of the New York Curb Exchange November 18 in a fund-raising effort to sell U.S. bonds and savings stamps. The 69-year-old New York Mercantile Exchange begins trading in potato futures; they quickly become more important than its other commodities (see heating-oil futures, 1978).

The 10-year-old Diamond Dealers Club moves to West 47th Street between Fifth and Sixth avenues as the diamond district relocates from Canal Street and the corner of Fulton and Nassau streets. Refugees from Amsterdam and Antwerp swell the district that is soon dominated by Orthodox Jews.

Merrill Lynch Pierce Fenner & Beane is created by a merger of New York investment banks (see 1914). Charles Merrill, now 58, transferred his brokerage business and much of his staff to Pierce & Co. to enter investment banking in 1930, merged with Pierce and E.A. Cassatt last year, and now merges with Fenner & Beane. Winthrop Hiram Smith, now 48, will join the firm in 1958 and it will become Merrill Lynch Pierce Fenner & Smith, the world's largest investment banking house.

Standard and Poor's is created at New York by a merger of the 28-year-old Standard Statistics Co. with the 74-year-old publisher Poor's. In addition to issuing dozens of financial publications, S&P will give ratings to bonds and commercial paper, and the S&P average will vie with the Dow Jones Industrial Average as an index of the New York Stock Exchange's ups and downs (see McGraw-Hill, 1966).

Former Lazard Frères senior partner George Blumenthal dies of cancer at his New York home June 26 at age 83. President of the Metropolitan Museum of Art at his death, he leaves the museum his Park Avenue mansion and art collection.

Wall Street's Dow Jones Industrial Average closes December 31 at 110.96, down from 131.13 at the end of 1940.

The Transport Workers Union strikes from March 20 to 21 under the leadership of Michael J. Quill and obtains a wage increase (but the 5¢ transit fare will remain unchanged until 1948).

The Gowanus Parkway opens November 1 to link the 1-year-old Belt Parkway with the Brooklyn-Battery Tunnel now under construction. Robert Moses has had the new parkway built in part atop the pillars of the former BMT Elevated Line above Third Avenue in Brooklyn's Sunset Park section, and he has had Third Avenue widened to 10 lanes.

The Cardinal Hayes Memorial High School for Boys opens on the Grand Concourse in the Bronx. Designed by Eggers & Higgins, the Art Deco structure at the southeast corner of 153rd Street will be the educational flagship of the Archdiocese of New York.

The 20-year-old Little Red School House establishes a high school under the name Elisabeth Irwin at 196 Bleecker Street in Greenwich Village (see 1932). The school will buy a building next year at 40 Charlton Street for its four upper classes, and enrollment of the combined schools will climb to 415 as tuitions ascend.

WNBT goes on the air at 1:29 o'clock in the afternoon of July 1, marking the start of commercial television in America. The National Broadcasting Co. station has evolved from the experimental W2XBS station started in 1928, but only 4,000 TV sets are tuned to its airing of the Dodgers-Phillies game at Ebbets Field.

Radio news broadcasting gets a boost from the attack on Pearl Harbor December 7 since no newspapers have Sunday afternoon editions and people are eager to hear more details.

A giant smoker in a Times Square spectacular put up by Artkraft Straus begins blowing five-foot-wide smoke rings (created by steam from Consolidated Edison Co.) every 4 seconds to promote Camel cigarettes. Designed by Douglas Leigh, the sign requires no lighting (lights might outline merchant ships in peril of U-boat attacks off the coast) and will continue until 1966, attracting attention as the figure is changed from time to time (see 1942; Leigh, 1933).

The Brooklyn Pubic Library's central branch opens in April on Grand Army Plaza (see 1897). Construction began in 1912 but was interrupted for lack of funds; a second floor will open in 1955 and there will be further expansions in 1972 and 1989.

Avon Books is founded at New York by local publisher Joseph Meyers, 43, with backing from William Randolph Hearst. American News Co. has been distributing Pocket Books, but that publisher has switched to using independent distributors so ANC has turned to Meyers, whose elegantly bound reprints have earned him a reputation. He pays between $25 and $500 each to obtain reprint rights to various titles and the new paperback publishing house releases its first Avon Pocket Size Books November 11 (see Bantam, 1945).

Dover Publications has its beginnings in a mail-order business for remaindered books started by former Crown Publishing salesman Hayward Cirker, 24, and his wife, Blanche, who take the name *Dover* from their Forest Hills, Queens, apartment house, start with an operating budget of less than $200, and will put out a line of paperback editions of eclectic titles in the public domain, hiring experts in children's books, art and architecture, music scores, and the like. In the next 40 years Dover will grow to

have catalogues offering thousands of titles as it becomes a $15 million-per-year business.

Nonfiction: *A Maritime History of New York* by the WPA Writers Project; *On Native Grounds* by Brownsville (Brooklyn)-born critic Alfred Kazin, 26, who becomes an editor of The *New Republic* and moves with his wife to a Manhattan apartment at the corner of 24th Street and Lexington Avenue (he has researched his study of U.S. literature and society at the Public Library at 42nd Street and will later write, "Even the spacious twin reading rooms, each two blocks long [an exaggeration], gave me a sense of the powerful amenity that I craved for my own life, a world of American power in which my own people had moved about as strangers"); *The Vanderbilt Legend: The Story of the Vanderbilt Family, 1794–1940* by Illinois-born author Wayne Andrews, 28, who will later work as curator of manuscripts at the New-York Historical Society.

Poet Lola Ridge dies at her Montague Street, Brooklyn, home May 19 at age 57.

Painting: *New York Under Gaslight* by Stuart Davis; *Indian Summer* by Arthur Dove; *Migration of the Negro No. 23: And the Immigration Spread* (tempera on hardboard) by Atlantic City-born Harlem painter Jacob Lawrence, 24, a Pennsylvania coal miner's son whose series of tempera and gouache works on black history (*Toussaint L'Ouverture, Frederick Douglass, Harriet Tubman*) have been gaining attention and respect.

The Art News editor Alfred Frankfurter persuades IBM head Thomas J. Watson, former *Vanity Fair* publisher Frank Crowninshield, publisher Marshall Field III, and others to form a nonprofit corporation, The Art Foundation, that buys out Elfreda Frankel's interest and changes the magazine's name to *ART News* (see 1935). It will appear on a regular monthly basis beginning in March 1947, and editor Thomas Hess will help Frankfurter guide its policy until Frankfurter's death in 1965. By the time it becomes *ARTnews* through a typographical change in 1969 it will be running nearly 90 pages per month.

Art in America gets a new editor who will change it from a quarterly to a bi-monthly (see 1913). Founder Frederic Fairchild Sherman died at the end of last year, Wellesley graduate Jean Lipman, 27, was his assistant, and she will run the magazine for 30 years, adopting color for some illustrations and for the cover in the 1950s as she gradually introduces coverage of the contemporary art scene, increasing circulation from just 199 subscribers, most of them institutions, to reach a wider market. The per-copy price will remain at $1.50 until 1954, when she will raise it (*see* 1970).

The October 25 issue of The *New Yorker* magazine carries a drawing by Romanian-born, Italian-trained architect-artist-cartoonist Saul Steinberg, 27, who fled Italy earlier in the year, reached Ellis Island, was deported to Santo Domingo (the small immigration quota for Romanians had been filled), but will reach New York next year and have his first U.S. one-man show at Manhattan's Wakefield Gallery. He will serve in the U.S. Navy and work for the Office of Strategic Services during the war, sending drawings home to The *New Yorker* from places in Asia, North Africa, and Europe.

Theater: *Arsenic and Old Lace* by New York-born playwright Joseph (Otto) Kesselring, 39, 1/10 at the Fulton Theater with Josephine Hull, Canadian-born actress Jean Adair, 67, London-born actor Boris Karloff (originally William Henry Pratt), 53, New York-born actor Anthony Ross, 31, 1,437 perfs.; *Native Son* by Richard Wright and Paul Green 3/24 at the St. James Theater, with New York-born actor Canada Lee (originally Leonard Cornelius Canegata), 38, 114 perfs. (*see* 1942; 1940 novel); *Watch on the Rhine* by Lillian Hellman 4/1 at the Music Box Theater, with Budapest-born actor Paul Lukas (originally Pal Lukacs), 46, German-born actress Mady (originally Marguerite Maria) Christians, 41, Mount Kisco-born ingénue Ann Blyth, 12, George Coulouris, 378 perfs.; *Candle in the Wind* by Maxwell Anderson 10/22 at the Shubert Theater, with Helen Hayes, Lotte Lenya, 95 perfs.; *Junior Miss* by Jerome Chodorov and Joseph Fields 11/18 at the Lyceum Theater, with Patricia (Cameron) Peardon, 16, as Judy Graves, Lenore Lonergan as Fuffy Adams, 710 perfs.; *Angel Street* by playwright Patrick Hamilton 12/5 at the Golden Theater, with South Dakota-born actress Judith Evelyn, 28, St. Louis-born actor Vincent Price, 30, 1,295 perfs.; *In Time to Come* by Howard Koch and Missouri-born actor-director-playwright John Huston, 35, 12/8 at the Mansfield Theater, with Richard Gaines as Woodrow Wilson, Nedda Harrigan as Wilson's wife, Edith, House Jameson as Sen. Lodge, Russell Collins as Col. House, 40 perfs.

Brooklyn-born comedian Joey Adams (originally Joe Abromowitz), 30, gets his first big break with a gig at Leon & Eddie's nightclub in West 52nd Street. Having cut many classes at CCNY to make vaudeville appearances, he dropped out of college 10 years ago just 3 months short of graduation and supported himself by selling hats at Namm's department store, performing at Catskills resorts, and working in between at dishwashing and bookkeeping jobs.

Female impersonator Julian Eltinge dies at his New York apartment March 7 at age 57; playwright Wilson Collison at Beverly Hills, Calif., May 25 at age 47; Broadway showman Sam H. Harris of liver cancer in his Ritz Tower apartment July 2 at age 69; playwright-screenwriter Eugene Walter of cancer in his Hollywood apartment September 26 at age 66; actress Blanche Bates at San Francisco December 25 at age 68.

Radio: *Duffy's Tavern* 3/1 on CBS with Ed Gardner (originally Edward Poggenberg), 35, as the Brooklyn bartender Archie (to 1951).

Films: Orson Welles's *Citizen Kane* with Welles, Joseph Cotten, Everett Sloane, Agnes Moorehead, Evelyn Keyes, George Coulouris opens May 1 at the Palace Theater, converted to a picture house for the occasion since no other theater will book the film. Publisher William Randolph Hearst has tried to block showing of Welles's allegory on the theme of idealism corrupted by power, threatening to bar any theater that shows it from advertising in his papers (the film is not reviewed or advertised in any Hearst newspaper, and RKO will shelve it for more than a decade); Preston Sturges's *Unfaithfully Yours* with Rex Harrison, Linda Darnell, Rudy Vallée. Also: Robert Stevenson's *Back Street* with Charles Boyer, Margaret Sullavan, John Gavin; Howard Hawks's *Ball of Fire* with Gary Cooper, Barbara Stanwyck; Alfred Hitchcock's *Mr. and Mrs. Smith* with Carol Lombard, Robert Montgomery, Gene Raymond, Jack Carson; Charles Vidor's *New York Town* with Fred MacMurray, Mary Martin, Robert Preston; Anatole Litvak's *Out of the Fog* with Ida Lupino, John Garfield, Thomas Mitchell; Joseph H. Lewis's *Pride of the Bowery* with Leo Gorcey, Bobby Jordan, Donald Haines; Leigh Jason's *Three Girls About Town* with Joan Blondell, Binnie Barnes, Janet Blair.

Director Edwin S. Porter dies of cancer at New York April 30 at age 71.

Film musicals: Busby Berkeley's *Babes on Broadway* with Mickey Rooney, Judy Garland, Fay Bainter, Virginia Weidler, Richard Quine, Donna Reed, Margaret O'Brien; Robert Z. Leonard's *Ziegfeld Girl* with James Stewart, Lana Turner, Judy Garland, Hedy Lamarr.

Broadway musicals: *Lady in the Dark* 1/23 at the Alvin Theater with Gertrude Lawrence, New York-born comedian Danny Kaye (originally David Daniel Kaminsky), 28, music by Kurt Weill, lyrics by Ira Gershwin, songs that include "Jenny (the Saga of),"

"My Ship," "Tchaikovsky," 162 perfs. (Kaye has married Sylvia Fine while working in the Catskill Mountain "borscht circuit" and she has helped him with her witty songs). The show's book is about a fashion-magazine editor who gets psychoanalyzed, and its costumes have been designed by Indiana-born couturier Norman Norell (originally Norman David Levinson), 40, who has worked since 1928 for Hattie Carnegie (see everyday life, 1943); *Best Foot Forward* 10/1 at the Ethel Barrymore Theater, with Iowa-born actress Rosemary Lane (originally Rosemary Mullian), 27, Philadelphia-born ingénue Nancy Walker (originally Ann Myrtle Swoyer), 20, June Allyson, songs by Hugh Martin and Ralph Blane that include "Buckle Down, Winsocki," 326 perfs.; *Let's Face It* 10/29 at the Imperial Theater with Danny Kaye, Eve Arden, San Diego-born ingénue Nanette Fabray (originally Nanette Fabares), 21, music and lyrics by Cole Porter, songs that include "You Irritate Me So," and Danny Kaye patter songs with lyrics by Sylvia Fine, 547 perfs.; *Sons O'Fun* 12/1 at the Winter Garden Theater with Olsen and Johnson, Carmen Miranda, Ella Logan, music by Sammy Fain and Will Irwin, lyrics by Jack Yellen and Irving Kahal, songs that include "Happy in Love," 742 perfs.

Minstrel-show veteran Eddie Leonard (originally Lemuel Gordon Tonay) is found dead at New York's Imperial Hotel August 29 at age 70; alcoholic torch singer Helen Morgan dies of a liver ailment at Chicago October 4 at age 41.

The Collegiate Chorale is founded at the Marble Collegiate Church by California-born choral director-conductor Robert (Lawson) Shaw, 25, who has been reorganizing and directing the Fred Waring Glee Club (see Robert Shaw Chorale, 1948).

Popular songs: "Take the A Train" by Billy Strayhorn (see subway, 1933); "(I Like New York in June) How About You?" by Burton Lane, lyrics by Ralph Freed; "Let's Get Away from It All" by Tommy Dorsey protégé Matt Dennis, lyrics by Tom Adair.

California-born singer Jo Stafford, 23, joins the Tommy Dorsey band after several years' singing with the Stafford Sisters.

Songwriter Howard E. Johnson dies at New York May 1 at age 53.

 Bobby Riggs wins in men's singles at Forest Hills, Sarah Palfrey Cooke, 18, in women's singles.

Bronx community leader John O'Donnell leases Gaelic Park from the city in behalf of the Gaelic Athletic Association (see 1926). O'Donnell and his family will maintain the park's playing field, stadium, ballroom, and bar for 50 years (see 1991).

Yankee great Lou Gehrig dies at New York June 3 at age 37 (see 1939).

Yankee outfielder Joe DiMaggio sets a record 56 consecutive game hitting streak, surpassing Willie Keeler's major league mark of 44, before finally going 0 for 4 July 17 in a night game at Cleveland, where Indian third baseman Ken Keltner makes two outstanding catches that rob the Yankee Clipper of what otherwise would have been solid hits. (DiMaggio's salary for the year is $32,000.)

The Brooklyn Dodgers win their first pennant under the direction of Massachusetts-born manager Leo Ernest "the Lip" Durocher, 35, and the borough celebrates its heroes Adolf Louis "Dolf" Camilli, 34 (who has set National League records for the season, hitting 34 home runs, driving in 120 runs, and fielding superbly); William Jennings (Bryan) "Billy" Herman, 32; Kirby Higbe, 26; Harry Arthur "Cookie" Lavagetto, 27; Joe Medwick, 29; Arnold Malcolm "Mickey" Owen, 25; five-foot, nine-inch, 140-pound Harold Henry "Pee Wee" Reese, 23; Harold Patrick "Pete" Reiser, 22; Fred "Dixie" Walker, 31; and pitcher John Whitlow "Whit" Wyatt, 34, but the New York Yankees win the World Series, defeating the Dodgers 4 games to 1. While pitcher Wyatt ekes out a 3-to-1 victory in the second game, the rest of the Dodger pitching staff cannot stop the Yankees, as Joe Gordon gets seven hits, including a double, a triple, and a home run; outfielder Tommy Henrich, 27, three hits, including a double and a home run. Brooklyn leads 4 to 3 at Ebbets Field in the ninth inning of the fourth game, Georgia-born Dodger pitcher Hugh Casey, 28, apparently strikes out Henrich to win the game, but catcher Mickey Owen drops the ball, Henrich races to first base, the Yankees score four runs in that final inning to win the game 7 to 4, and they win 3 to 1 the next day.

● The Parachute Jump used at the World's Fair from 1939 to 1940 opens at Coney Island's Steeplechase Park, competing with the 150-foot-high Wonder Wheel nearby and the 14-year-old Cyclone roller coaster. The Tilyou family has purchased the 170-ton structure for $150,000 and will continue to operate it until 1968, several years after the rest of the amusement park has closed, halting operations only when its cables turn out upon inspection to be unsafe.

Claire McCardell quits Hattie Carnegie, takes her designs to a reorganized Townley Co., and will remain there with her name on the firm's label (as a partner beginning in 1951) until her death in 1958 (*see* 1938; 1942).

Lower Manhattan's Syrian community scatters as buildings along Washington Street between Battery Place and Rector Street come down to provide access for the Brooklyn-Battery Tunnel now under construction. The community dates to the 1870s and has included a bustling retail section as well as residences.

A New York plainclothesman tells small-time, Flatbush-born gambler-bookmaker Harry Gross, 25, that paying "ice" (protection money) could keep him safe from arrest. Gross sets up his own "horse room," a place where players can place bets and get race results by radio and telephone. Gross begins paying as much as $1,000 per month for police protection (*see* politics, 1950).

Gangster Abe "Kid Twist" Reles "falls" to his death November 12 from a fifth-story window of Coney Island's Half Moon Hotel while in the custody of a six-man police bodyguard. Reles last year informed to Brooklyn district attorney William O'Dwyer, his testimony attributed 130 hired killings between 1930 and 1940 to the national crime syndicate Murder Inc., whose members have been accused of 63 murders for racketeers since 1934, and the testimony will lead to the execution of mob figures who include Louis "Lepke" Buchalter; police say Reles was trying to escape but there are suspicions that he was pushed to keep him from implicating the police. O'Dwyer says the death of Reles ruins the state's "perfect" case against mobster Umberto "Albert" Anastasia, now 39, but a King's County grand jury will severely censure O'Dwyer in 1945 for not having prosecuted Anastasia anyway.

The city's homicide rate will fall to 3.5 per 100,000 in the next 5 years, down from 4.5 per 100,000 in the last 5 and its lowest level of this century (*see* 1946).

The Queens Borough Hall is completed on Queens Boulevard, between Union Turnpike and 82nd Avenue in Forest Hills, to designs by William Gehron & Andrew J. Thomas.

A modern 28-story apartment house with 325 units opens at 240 Central Park South (corner of Broadway and Columbus Circle). Designed by Albert Mayer and Julian Whittlesey of Mayer Whittlesey and Glass, it backs up on 58th Street.

A modern house for Sears, Roebuck heir Edward A. Norman and his wife, Dorothy, is completed at 124

East 70th Street, between Park and Lexington avenues, to designs by William Lescaze.

Marjorie Merriwether Post Hutton gives up her 54-room triplex at 1107 Fifth Avenue upon expiration of its 15-year lease. It will remain vacant for a decade before being chopped up into six units.

The East River Houses are completed in East Harlem as the city's fifth USHA-financed slum-clearance housing project. Designed by Voorhees, Walker, Foley and Smith, Alfred Easton Poor, and C. W. Schlusing under the direction of Perry Coke Smith, the 28 buildings include six 10- and 11-story structures, containing 1,170 units, and rise on a superblock bounded by 102nd and 105th streets and the East River Drive (103rd and 104th streets have been eliminated).

Real estate developer-philanthropist August Heckscher dies at his winter home near Lake Wales, Fla., April 26 at age 92 and is buried in Woodlawn Cemetery. He has been living in the penthouse of his office building at 52 Vanderbilt Avenue with his second wife, Virginia, whom he married in 1930; real estate heir Robert W. Goelet dies at New York May 2 at age 81, leaving an estate that includes the Racquet & Tennis Club building on Park Avenue (the club will buy it from the Goelet estate next year) and the Ritz-Carlton Hotel (Goelet devises it to his alma mater Harvard University, expressing the wish that it be held in a fund to bear his name, with the income to be devoted to the general purposes of the university; *but see* 1951); architect Charles D. Wetmore dies at his 800 Park Avenue apartment May 8 at age 74; architect H. Craig Severance at Neptune, N.J., September 2 at age 62.

The American Women's Association verges on bankruptcy and gives up its West 57th Street clubhouse, completed in 1929. The building is converted into the Henry Hudson Hotel, open to men as well as women.

The expanded Cathedral of St. John the Divine at 110th Street is consecrated November 30 but construction work is suspended in December and will not be resumed until 1979 (*see* 1925; 1978).

The Bronx Zoo opens an African Plains exhibit May 1. The first large-scale U.S. re-creation of a wildlife habitat depicting natural predators and their prey, it draws a record crowd of 83,000 its first Sunday.

Gourmet magazine begins publication at New York in January under the direction of former *National Parent-Teachers* magazine publisher Earle (Rutherford) MacAusland, 51. By the end of 1945 the magazine will have grown from 48 pages to 112 and be headquartered in luxurious penthouse offices atop the Plaza Hotel.

Buitoni Foods is founded at New York by Italian pasta maker Giovanni Buitoni, who has sung at Carnegie Hall to publicize his products. Isolated in the United States since the outbreak of war in Europe late in 1939, he will make his new U.S. company a major producer of pasta and related canned and frozen foods.

The *Saturday Evening Post* runs a story in March about Alcoholics Anonymous (*see* 1935). A local bank foreclosed on the mortgage of the Clinton Street, Brooklyn, house of cofounder Bill W.'s in-laws 2 years ago, he and his wife have been living in borrowed rooms or in temporary quarters above A.A.'s 24th Street clubhouse in Manhattan, but John D. Rockefeller, Jr. last year gave a dinner for A.A. and was impressed enough to establish a small trust that provides Bill W. with $30 per week at a time when many families are living on less. Rockefeller rejected initial appeals to fund A.A., saying that money would spoil its spirit, and the organization has spread through church groups; the magazine article produces a flood of letters, and attendance at meetings begins to soar. English novelist Aldous Huxley will call Bill W. "the greatest social architect of our time."

Le Pavillon opens October 15 at 5 East 55th Street under the direction of Henri Soulé, 38, a Basque from Biarritz who managed the Café de Paris before coming to New York in March 1939 with 30 kitchen workers and 33 maîtres d'hotel, captains, waiters, and wine stewards to run the restaurant at the World's Fair's French Pavilion (some of the 40 employees of his new restaurant worked with Soulé at the fair). He charges $1.75 for a table d'hôte luncheon of hors d'oeuvre, plat du jour, dessert, and coffee but will soon charge a lot more (*see* 1957).

1942 U-boat activity off the U.S. Atlantic Coast takes a heavy toll of merchant ships bound for British and Russian ports with war matériel, foodstuffs, and men. Says the *New York Times* April 1, "The cloud of manmade darkness that has hovered over various parts of the metropolitan area during the last few weeks settled last night upon eight square miles of the lower Bronx, where 935,000 persons co-operated in the latest blackout drill. In a night so bright that the moon coated countless apartment house windows with silvery luster, nearly one-fifth of the borough showed what it could do in case the dread drone of enemy planes sounded overhead." Washington orders a "dim-out" extending 15 miles

from the coast April 28 to make it harder for U-boats to sight their quarry at night. At the navy's request, Times Square signs, including the 13-year-old news "Zipper" on the Times Tower, are extinguished at night above street level beginning May 18 (although the man in the Camel cigarette sign that went up last year will continue throughout the war to emit rings of Con Edison steam as the man dons a uniform, changed periodically to vary his service); volunteer civil defense air-raid wardens make sure that people have drawn blackout curtains to minimize the light that silhouettes merchant ships leaving the port of New York for Europe.

Mayor La Guardia moves into Gracie Mansion on the East River May 14. The Board of Estimate designated the 18th century house as the official home of the city's mayor in November of last year, allocating $20,000 to improve the building and its grounds. Robert Moses had expressed concern about the lack of security at the mayor's modest apartment on Fifth Avenue at 109th Street; the Charles Schwab mansion on Riverside Drive was offered at a price, but the mayor rejected the offer.

The Office of Strategic Services (OSS) created by President Roosevelt's executive order June 13 is headed by World War I hero and former New York State assistant attorney general William J. Donovan, now 59, who has been senior partner in a Wall Street law firm. "Wild Bill" Donovan ran for governor against Herbert Lehman in 1932 and was an outspoken critic of the New Deal, he has become convinced of the need for counterpropaganda and clandestine operations, President Roosevelt asked him in July of last year to head an agency that would collect and

Mayor La Guardia helped persuade FDR to let the city have more war-production contracts. LIBRARY OF CONGRESS

analyze strategic intelligence, and Donovan's OSS military intelligence group will be the basis of the CIA in 1947.

The FBI captures eight German marines June 28 after they have come ashore in civilian clothes from U-boats on Long Island and Florida beaches. One of the Germans has betrayed the mission, his call to the FBI was initially brushed off as a hoax, but he has finally convinced agents that he was on the level; the Coast Guard has apprehended the agents who landed near Amagansett and found them equipped to blow up production and transportation targets. FBI agents arrest 325 Germans (many of them members of the German-American Bund), 65 Italians, seven Japanese, one Hungarian, and two Romanians in the New York area and discover incriminating evidence on some, including maps of U.S. defenses found on a member of the Japanese Association.

Coffins containing the remains of New York servicemen arrive at the city's docks and railroad stations for burial in family plots; gold stars begin to appear among the blue stars displayed on silk banners in household windows as families show that sons, and sometimes daughters, are serving in the armed forces.

Manhattan Distict Attorney Thomas E. Dewey wins election in the gubernatorial race after more than 2 decades of Democratic Party control. Nebraska-born Republican lawyer and former assemblyman Herbert Brownell, Jr., 38, has managed the campaign for Dewey, who receives 2,148,546 votes; Brooklyn-born New York State Attorney General John James Bennett, Jr., 48, receives 1,501,039.

Federal agents round up about 200 of the 2,500 Japanese nationals in New York and its suburbs and take them into custody for temporary confinement on Ellis Island, but persons of Japanese descent in New York and other parts of the eastern United States will not be subjected to internment in "relocation camps" as will West Coast Japanese pursuant to Executive Order 9066 issued by President Roosevelt February 19. U.S. Alien Property Custodian Leo T. Crowley will seize the 30-year-old Nippon Club at 161-165 West 93rd Street next year and invite bids for the property and its contents, the Elks will buy the building and its furniture in 1944, the club for the city's tiny Japanese community will move in 1963 to 145 West 57th Street (see real estate, 1991), and its original clubhouse will become the church of Iglesia Adventista del Septimo Dia.

President Roosevelt appoints former governor Lehman director of the Office of Foreign Relief and Rehabilitation; Lehman will continue to head it without salary after the agency is merged next year into the United Nations Relief and Rehabilitation Agency (UNRRA) and will remain its head until 1946.

The Jewish Child Care Association is created by a merger of 19 organizations that include the 120-year-old Hebrew Benevolent Association, an 82-year-old orphanage, and the 63-year-old Hebrew Sheltering Guardian Society, headed since 1918 by Mary Boretz. The Hebrew Orphan Asylum that opened in 1884 on Amsterdam Avenue between 136th and 138th streets was closed last year (P.S. 192 will be built on part of the site in 1955, the rest will become a park); 30 percent of the 607 children still living in the building were sent to live with family members or dispersed among other Jewish agencies.

An Emergency Price Control Act voted by Congress January 30 gives the Office of Price Administration (OPA) power to control prices (see 1941; 1946).

Congress appropriates more than $150 billion for the war effort, but although the nation is spending $150 million per day by July 1, little of it goes to New York. More than 3.6 million American men remain unemployed, and while the number has fallen from 9.5 million men and women in 1939, New York City still has 400,000 unemployed by early summer. The ranks of the unemployed elsewhere dwindle rapidly as war plants, shipyards, oil fields, and recruiting offices clamor for manpower; 2 million women enter the workforce, but New York's construction industry grinds to a halt for lack of materials, its shipping industry has come virtually to a stop, and ordnance contracts have been awarded to companies in other cities, not New York. War Powers Board chairman Paul McNutt at Washington calls New York "one of the blackest spots in the nation" and suggests that workers looking for jobs go to other parts of the country. Mayor La Guardia begins in late June to visit Washington in quest of war contracts for army uniforms and ships; by August he is able to report that he has received assurances of 200,000 new jobs for the metropolitan area. Women who never worked before take factory and shipyard jobs previously reserved for men; "Rosie the Riveter" becomes a national symbol.

Manhattan Savings Bank is created by a merger of three thrift institutions chartered in the 1850s (see 1850). It sets up headquarters at 744 Broadway but will move in 9 years to 385 Madison Avenue and grow to have 17 branches in New York and Westchester with deposits of $2.8 billion (*see* Republic National, 1990).

Wall Street's Dow Jones Industrial Average closes December 31 at 119.40, up from 110.96 at the end of 1941.

Gasoline rationing begins in May on the East Coast, where U-boat sinkings have reduced tanker shipments, and Washington orders nationwide rationing in September, chiefly to save rubber. All motorists are assigned A, B, or C stickers as of December 1: those with A stickers are allowed four gallons per week, an amount that will later be reduced to three gallons, but nearly half of all motorists obtain B or C stickers, entitling them to supplementary rations because their driving is essential to the war effort, or public health, or for similar reasons. Truckers receive T stickers that allow them unlimited amounts of gasoline or diesel fuel, but pleasure driving is banned and a 35-mile-per-hour speed limit established on highways.

The Port of New York mobilizes its forces to handle the movement of men and war matériel to Europe and other theaters of operation as the nation builds and assembles the largest merchant fleet in history. The Moran Co. alone soon has a fleet of 112 towing vessels, including 49 1,600-ton, 195-foot V-4 tugs assigned to it by the federal government (*see* 1917), and more than half of all the men and war cargo sent abroad will go out from New York (*see* 1944).

The former French Line passenger ship S.S. *Normandie* that went into service in 1935 is gutted by fire and capsizes at her Hudson River pier February 9 while being converted for troop transport service. One person is killed, 128 injured. Renamed the U.S.S. *Lafayette* January 1 after U.S. seizure, she will be righted, towed away, and scrapped, although much of her interior will be saved (some of her doors will wind up on a Brooklyn Heights church).

Railroad heir Cornelius Vanderbilt III dies aboard his yacht off Miami Beach March 1 at age 68, having helped organize the Interborough Rapid Transit Co. (IRT) and acted as a consulting engineer for the construction of the first New York subway.

The Second Avenue El ceases operations south of 57th Street June 13 (*see* 1940). Plans for a Second Avenue subway have been projected, but none will be built in this century and the upper East Side will be left with little in the way of rapid transit (*see* Third Avenue El, 1955).

The East River Drive (FDR Drive) opens from 53rd Street to 92nd Street May 26 with ceremonies led by Mayor La Guardia (*see* 1936). Commissioner of Public Works Walter Binger has been able to make private agreements with most of the residents who own riverfront property to permit construction of the multi-level highway (he has had the home of Lilian Havemeyer at 16 Sutton Square demolished and rebuilt). Northbound lanes are on the lower level, southbound lanes above, with pedestrian and garden decks above that, and a fourth-level play deck for the Brearley School at 83rd Street. The roadbed between 23rd and 34th streets is filled with bricks and rubble left from air raids on London and donated by the British, but the new drive that cuts Manhattan off from the East River is poorly drained and will flood in heavy rains.

Brooklyn Dodgers sportscaster Red Barber cooperates with local hospitals by telling listeners when blood donors are needed for the blood banks being set up to collect plasma for shipment to troops overseas and for surgery at home.

Halloran General Hospital opens on a 375-acre Staten Island site acquired 4 years ago with the intention of using it for the New York State Department of Mental Hygiene. The largest U.S. hospital for wounded soldiers, it will be used by the Veterans Administration from 1947 to 1951 (*see* 1952).

Practice air-raid drills send New York schoolchildren scrambling for cover under their desks with their hands over their heads.

Progressive education pioneer Elisabeth Irwin dies at New York October 16 at age 62, having founded the Little Red School House and written numerous articles on the need to work on a child's social and economic development as well as academics.

Mayor La Guardia gives weekly Sunday radio talks on WNYC beginning January 18; as many as 1.8 million listeners will tune in the mayor's 1 o'clock broadcasts on the 18-year-old municipal station.

The Voice of America makes its first broadcast to Europe February 24 under the auspices of the 8-month-old U.S. Foreign Information Service with announcer William Harlan Hale saying in German, "Here speaks a voice from America" and promising to tell listeners the truth, whether the news is good or bad. FIS director (and playwright) Robert Sherwood has recruited a staff of journalists, hired theatrical producer John Houseman to head up the New York office, and begun producing material for privately owned U.S. shortwave stations to beam to Europe. The FIS made its first broadcast to Asia in December of last year (in Amoy, Cantonese and Mandarin, and Tagalog), the February 24 broadcast

uses medium- and long-range BBC transmitters to relay its signals, the VOA has little trouble in polyglot New York finding newsreaders fluent in foreign languages, and by year's end it is reaching listeners in Afrikaans, Arabic, Bulgarian, Czech, Danish, Farsi, Finnish, Flemish, French, Greek, Hungarian, Indonesian, Italian, Japanese, Korean, Norwegian, Polish, Portuguese, Romanian, Slovak, Thai, and Turkish as well as German and English.

The first *New York Times* Sunday crossword puzzle appears February 15. The *Times* has hired expert Margaret Petheridge Farrar, now 44, to design the puzzles that will appear on a daily basis beginning in 1950. Farrar will continue in the job until she retires in 1968.

"It Happened Last Night" by Ohio-born gossip columnist (Harvey) Earl Wilson, 35, begins in the *New York Post*, where it will appear six times per week for more than 40 years, featuring interviews (and revealing photographs) of Broadway hopefuls and Hollywood starlets. Wilson will refer to his wife, Rosemary (*née* Lyons), as his BW (beautiful wife), eschew criticism of new shows, and eventually syndicate the column to about 200 newspapers.

New York Daily Mirror editor Thomas Russel Hastings dies at New York April 2 at age 68; magazine publisher Condé Nast of a heart attack at his 1040 Park Avenue penthouse September 19 at age 68.

Dell Books is founded by magazine and comic-book publisher George T. Delacorte, Jr., who discussed the idea of paperback books with Richard L. Simon and Max Schuster of Simon & Schuster in 1939 before they decided to help start Pocket Books (*see* 1921). Delacorte uses American News Co. to distribute his 25¢ editions, which will soon have sales of 7 to 11 million copies per year despite wartime shortages of paper and ink.

Popular Library is founded by former newspaper publisher Ned L. Pines, who has prospered with pulp magazines such as *Thrilling Western Stories*, *Future Science Fiction*, *Silver Screen*, and *Screenland*. The new paperback-book line is distributed through American News Company.

Pantheon Books is founded at New York by publisher Kurt Wolff and his Macedonian-born wife, Helen (*née* Mosell), 36.

Nonfiction: *The Eight Million* by New York-born *New York Times* reporter and columnist Meyer "Mike" Berger, 44, whose brother Henry illustrates his collection of human-interest columns.

Fiction: *The Company She Keeps* by Seattle-born New York novelist Mary (Therese) McCarthy, 30; *A Time to Be Born* by Dawn Powell, who has one of her characters say, "I don't know why anyone in New York worries about good neighborhoods. They never see their neighbors anyway so it might as well be a bad neighborhood;" "The Catbird Seat" (story) by James Thurber in the November 14 *New Yorker*.

Juvenile: *The Little Red Lighthouse and the Great Gray Bridge* by New York author Hildegarde Swift (*see* transportation, 1921; 1931).

Painting: *Nighthawks* by Edward Hopper; *Partly Cloudy* by Arthur Dove.

An *Artists in Exile* exhibition opens at New York March 3 with works by André Breton, Marc Chagall, Max Ernst, Fernand Léger (who has an apartment and studio at 222 Bowery), Yves Tanguy, and others; an *Art of This Century* exhibition opens at New York October 20 under the direction of copper heiress Marguerite "Peggy" Guggenheim, 44, who has married German painter Max Ernst.

Sculptress-museum founder Gertrude Vanderbilt Whitney dies of heart disease at New York April 18 at age 67 and is buried at Woodlawn Cemetery. She leaves a bequest that will be used to build a new Whitney Museum of American Art (*see* 1966).

Theater: *Janie* by Herschel Williams and Josephine Bentham 9/10 at the Henry Miller Theater, with Gwen Anderson, Clare Foley, Herbert Evers, Nancy Cushman, 321 perfs.; *The Eve of St. Mark* by Maxwell Anderson 10/7 at the Cort Theater, with Aline MacMahon, William Prince, Matt Crowley, Martin Ritt, 291 perfs.; *Without Love* by Philip Barry 11/10 at the St. James Theater, with Katharine Hepburn, Elliott Nugent, Audrey Christie, 113 perfs.; *The Skin of Our Teeth* by Thornton Wilder 11/18 at the Plymouth Theater, with E. G. Marshall, Florence Eldridge, Fredric March, Tallulah Bankhead, Montgomery Clift, 359 perfs.

Actor Otis Skinner dies at his New York home January 4 at age 83; producer Harrison Grey Fiske at New York September 3 at age 81.

Films: Sam Wood's *Pride of the Yankees* with Gary Cooper (as Lou Gehrig), Teresa Wright, Babe Ruth, Walter Brennan; George Stevens's *Woman of the Year* with Katharine Hepburn, Spencer Tracy. Also: Vincent Sherman's *All Through the Night* with Humphrey Bogart, Conrad Veidt; Irving Reis's *The Big Street* with Henry Fonda, Lucille Ball in a plot based on a Damon Runyon story; Frank Strayer's *Daring Young Man* with Joe E. Brown; S. Sylvan Simon's *Grand*

Central Murder with Van Heflin; Lloyd Bacon's *Larceny, Inc.* with Edward G. Robinson, Jane Wyman, Brodrick Crawford, Jack Carson; Alexander Hall's *My Sister Eileen* with Rosalind Russell, Brian Aherne, Janet Blair; Alfred Hitchcock's *Saboteur* with Robert Cummings, Priscilla Lane; Julien Duvivier's *Tales of Manhattan* with Charles Boyer, Rita Hayworth, Henry Fonda, Ginger Rogers, Charles Laughton, Edward G. Robinson, Ethel Waters, Paul Robeson, Eddie "Rochester" Anderson, Thomas Mitchell, Cesar Romero, George Sanders; Richard Thorpe's *Tarzan's New York Adventure* with Johnny Weissmuller, Maureen O'Hara, Virginia Grey, Charles Bickford, Paul Kelly.

Paramount Pictures sells its Astoria Studio to the army (*see* 1920); renamed the Signal Corps Photographic Center, it is used to produce and edit training films for the war effort.

Film musical: Irving Cummings's *My Gal Sal* with Rita Hayworth, Victor Mature (as 1890s Broadway songwriter Paul Dresser).

Broadway musicals: *Star and Garter* 1/24 at the Music Box Theater, with Bobby Clark, Pat Harrington, Seattle-born striptease dancer Gypsy Rose Lee (Rose Louise Hovick), 18, Georgia Sothern (originally Hazel Eunice Finklestein), 19, in an extravaganza mounted by Minneapolis-born showman Mike Todd (originally Avron Hirsch Golbogen), 34, songs that include Harold Arlen's "Blues in the Night," 609 perfs.; *By Jupiter* 6/2 at the Shubert Theater, with Ray Bolger, Nanette Fabray, choreography by Robert Alton, music by Richard Rodgers, lyrics by Lorenz Hart, 427 perfs.; *This Is the Army* 7/24 at the Broadway Theater, with an all-soldier cast for the benefit of the Army Emergency Relief Fund, music, book, and lyrics by Irving Berlin, songs that include "I Left My Heart at the Stage-Door Canteen," the title song, and songs from Berlin's 1918 musical *Yip-Yip-Yaphank*, 113 perfs.; *Show Time* (vaudeville revue) 9/16 at the Broadhurst Theater (after 20 weeks at Los Angeles and San Francisco), with George Jessel, Jack Haley, Ella Logan, the De Marcos, the Berry Brothers, 342 perfs.; *Rosalinda* 10/28 at the 44th Street Theater, with New York-born singer Dorothy Sarnoff, 25, as Rosalinda von Eisenstein, sets by Wisconsin-born designer Oliver Smith, 24, music from the 1874 Johann Strauss opera *Die Fledermaus*, 611 perfs.

The city license commissioner closes two Manhattan burlesque theaters January 31 for failing to meet decency standards (*see* 1937). The police commissioner threatens to extend the ban to other boroughs, Actors Equity protests the closings on legal grounds, ushers from the closed theaters picket City Hall February 27, Bishop Manning praises Mayor La Guardia for closing the theaters, the Minsky brothers file suit against the license commissioner for his refusal to issue them a license and file for bankruptcy March 12, the New York Theatres League forms a committee to oppose censorship March 17, Archbishop Spellman charges several shows with indecency, and Mike Todd resigns from the Theatres League because its counsel has made "unwarranted" statements about his show *Star and Garter* November 5. The producers of *Wine, Women & Song* go to trial on indecency charges November 30, they are convicted in early December and the show is ordered closed, the license of the Ambassador Theater is revoked on La Guardia's orders December 4, producer Lee Shubert orders the play *Native Son* closed December 4 after the Catholic League labels it objectionable but he rescinds the order December 7 under pressure from the Theatres League, Actors Equity, the Dramatists' Guild, and theatrical managers and agents.

The Latin Quarter nightclub opens April 1 at 200 West 48th Street, off Times Square, where the Cotton Club has been since 1936. Former vaudeville booking agent Lou Walters, 48, opened a Boston club under the same name 5 years ago, will go on to open one under that name at Miami, will keep the New York club open until 1967, and will take his Latin Quarter Revue to Las Vegas.

Joe Weber of Weber and Fields dies at Los Angeles May 10 at age 74 (*see* Fields, 1941); George M. Cohan dies at his Fifth Avenue home November 5 at age 64 (he is buried in Woodlawn Cemetery—just 45 minutes from Broadway); comedienne Laura Hope Crewes dies after a month's illness at New York November 13 at age 62.

Ballet: *Romeo and Juliet* 4/6 at the Metropolitan Opera House, with New York-born dancer Jerome Robbins (originally Rabinowitz), 23, Hugh Laing, Antony Tudor, Alicia Markova, Sono Osato, music by the late Frederick Delius, choreography by Tudor; *Pillar of Fire* 4/8 at the Met, with Hugh Laing, Antony Tudor, Nora Kaye (as Hagar), music by Arnold Schoenberg, choreography by Tudor; *Rodeo* 10/16 at the Met, with Harlem-born dancer-choreographer Agnes (George) de Mille, 37 (a niece of film director Cecil B. de Mille), music by Aaron Copland, choreography by de Mille; *Metamorphoses* 11/25 at the City Center nearing completion in West 55th Street (*see* 1943), with Paris-born ballerina Tanaquil LeClerq, 13, Canton, Ohio-born dancer

Todd Bolender, music by Paul Hindemith, choreography by George Balanchine.

Choreographer Michel Fokine dies at the West Side Hospital and Dispensary August 22 at age 62.

Songwriter Fred Fisher hangs himself at his New York apartment January 14 at age 45, having suffered from an incurable disease; composer Ralph Rainger is killed in an airplane crash outside Palm Springs, Calif., October 23 at age 41.

Frank Sinatra breaks his contract in September with Tommy Dorsey (who holds him to another contract that will give the bandleader more than 40 percent of Sinatra's income for the next 10 years), accepts an 8-week engagement at the Paramount Theater on Times Square, turns 27 December 12, and opens at the Paramount December 30, making his first public appearance in the city (he is billed as an "extra added attraction" on a program headed by Benny Goodman), and draws a huge crowd of squealing teenage "bobby soxers."

 Frederick R. "Ted" Schroeder, 20, wins in men's singles at Forest Hills, Pauline Betz, 22, in women's singles.

The New York Yankees win the American League pennant, but the St. Louis Cardinals win the World Series, defeating the Yankees 4 games to 1. Red Ruffing pitches the Yankees to a 7-to-4 victory in the first game; shortstop Phil "Scooter" Rizzuto, 24, gets eight hits, including a home run, and Charlie Keller gets four hits, including two home runs, but the Bronx Bombers are no match for the Cards.

The WAVES wear uniforms designed by Mainbocher, who moved to New York 2 years ago. The WACS wear uniforms designed by Hattie Carnegie, who has modified her "little Carnegie suit."

Claire McCardell designs stretch leotards to provide an extra layer of warmth for college girls living in dormitories that are chilly because of wartime fuel shortages (see 1941). She will soon design a denim wraparound housedress (the "popover") intended for women whose servants have left for jobs in war plants.

Fashion publicist Eleanor Lambert establishes the Coty American Fashion Critics' Awards, having married *Journal-American* publisher Seymour Berkson in 1936 and founded the International Best Dressed List in 1940; the first award goes to designer Norman Norell, who was fired by Hattie Carnegie after creating the costumes for the 1941 musical *Lady in the Dark* and teamed up with Seventh Avenue garment maker Anthony Traina to create

Traina-Norell; he will work with Traina until 1960 to make the Seventh Avenue garment industry rival pre-war Paris as a fashion center.

 The City Council outlaws pinball machines in a law that takes effect in January. Mayor La Guardia has pushed through the measure, saying that schoolboys are stealing nickels and dimes from their mothers' pocketbooks to feed the machines that are feeding the underworld (slot-machine "king" Frank Costello relocates his activities to New Orleans). The mayor smashes machines with a sledgehammer for news photographers; most of the confiscated machines are dumped into the Atlantic, and the ban will continue until 1976, when a player will demonstrate to the City Council that new flippers and levers have made pinball a game of skill, not chance.

U.S. Naval Intelligence officers approach Charles "Lucky" Luciano at Dannemora Prison in the wake of the S.S. *Normandie* fire, and mobster Meyer Lansky persuades Luciano to have his men co-operate with the government in preventing sabotage on the mob-controlled Manhattan docks (the Brooklyn docks are largely controlled by Carlo Gambino, now 40). Luciano is transferred from Dannemora to a minimum-security facility (see 1946).

Criminal elements associated with the Mafia steal gasoline- and food-ration stamps, selling them on the city's black market and enriching themselves as they did in the Prohibition years before 1933. They also begin to develop a profitable business in blackmailing homosexual men prominent in business, the law, and government.

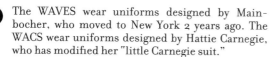 The city has 75,000 vacant apartments by early summer, and many homes in the outer boroughs are put up for sale as the economy of the metropolitan area weakens. The new Office of Price Administration and Civilian Supply (OPA) institutes wartime emergency price controls on virtually everything, but while rent controls are imposed in many cities, New York is initially exempted on grounds that it is a defense rental area rather than a war rental area. New war contracts will soon build demand for more housing and vacancy rates will drop (see rent controls, 1943).

Awnings begin to disappear from city apartment houses as building managers find it hard to find men to put them up in the spring and take them down in the fall.

Real estate operator and builder Henry Mandel dies at Lenox Hill Hospital October 10 at age 58.

Suburban New Yorkers and many in the outer boroughs cultivate "Victory Gardens" in backyards and communal plots as vegetables become scarce.

Sugar rationing begins in May after consumers have created scarcities by hoarding 100-pound bags and commercial users have filled their warehouses. One-sixth of U.S. sugar supplies have come from the Philippines, now in Japanese hands. Householders are asked by ration boards to state how much sugar they have stockpiled and ration stamps are deducted to compensate; the weekly ration averages eight ounces per person but will rise to 12 ounces. Hoarding of coffee leads to coffee rationing, which begins in November with consumers limited to one pound every 5 weeks (enough for one cup per day).

Thousands of New York families change their eating habits as domestic servants leave to take jobs in war plants, shipyards, hospitals, and the like; many housewives take such jobs themselves, and sales of convenience foods increase as women find themselves with less time to spend in the kitchen.

Dannon Yogurt is introduced at New York by Swiss-born Spanish emigré Joe Metzger. He goes into business with Isaac Carasso, who has emigrated from Spain, and employs his own son Juan, 23, at the company's Bronx factory, initially turning out 200 eight-ounce jars per day for sale at 11¢ each, mostly to the ethnic local yogurt market. Dannon will relocate to Long Island City next year and increase production.

The Rainbow Room closes to the public in January as blackout regulations are enforced to protect ships on the Atlantic from German U-boat attacks (*see* 1934; 1950).

Katz's Delicatessen on the Lower East Side puts up a sign that says, "Send a Salami to Your Boy in the Army" (*see* 1888).

1943 German-American Bund leader Fritz Kuhn, 32, leaves a New York courtroom January 4 at the start of hearings on possible subversive activities by his group. Victor Ridder owns the *New Yorker Staats-Herold und Zeitung* and reveals that Nazi Heinz Spunknoebel came to his office at 22 North William Street in July 1933, tried to seize the paper, and then fled the United States with the FBI in hot pursuit. A former Nazi propagandist testifies January 11 that German blood has been considered stronger than any citizenship. FBI agents seize former Bund members and former Nazi Party members throughout the city on suspicion of espionage and possible sabotage. Denaturalization proceedings open in February against 20 former Bund members; among those seized is a Stork Club waiter who wagered his tips on German victories in the European war. Kuhn and 10 other Bund leaders lose their U.S. citizenship March 18; Kuhn is ordered released on parole from prison June 18 after serving a term for theft and is interned as an enemy alien.

Anti-fascist editor Carlo Tresca, now 68, leaves his offices at 2 West 15th Street January 12 and is shot down in the street, apparently on orders from Benito Mussolini, who for decades has been the subject of attacks in Tresca's fortnightly paper *Il Martello* (*The Hammer*). Some local Italian organizations blame the killing on communists, but police trace the getaway car to Mafioso gunman Carmine Galente, 35, and arrest him January 13; he will be convicted of assassinating Tresca.

U.S. troops take Palermo July 23 and Benito Mussolini resigns under pressure July 25 as the tide of war turns against the Axis in North Africa, the Pacific, Italy, and on the Russian front. Mayor La Guardia has been broadcasting regularly in Italian on Armed Forces Radio, telling Italians that the Germans are stealing their food, and the Italian propaganda agency has called him "that false Italian and authenticated Jew, Fiorello H. La Guardia."

Staten Islanders Ernst Fritz Detlev Heinrich Lehmitz and Erwin Harry De Spretter are indicted July 27 on charges of having conspired against the United States since December 1940 under the supervision of a mysterious "Mr. Simon;" both plead guilty September 27 to having provided the German government with defense-related documents, photographs, plans, sketches, and specifica-

Times Square's spectaculars continued to dazzle visitors through the war years. LIBRARY OF CONGRESS

tions to be transmitted via Lisbon, Bilbao, Buenos Aires, and Hamburg; although subject to the death penalty for treason they are sentenced to 30 years' imprisonment each.

The Democratic Judicial Convention of the First District meets at Tammany Hall August 23 and nominates city magistrate Thomas A. Aurelio, 48, for the state supreme court but District Attorney Frank S. Hogan alleges that Aurelio has connections with organized crime. Mayor La Guardia announces August 28 that he may seek Aurelio's ouster if his link with onetime "slot-machine king" Frank Costello is proven. Costello is reputed to have been an associate of the late gambler Arnold Rothstein, Louis "Lepke" Buchalter, former West Harlem Tammany leader (and present Sing Sing Prison inmate) James J. Hines (see 1939), Charles "Lucky" Luciano, Joey Adonis, Nicky Arnstein, Owney Madden, and other underworld figures; he left New York for New Orleans in 1934 after the mayor banned "one-armed bandits" (and Louisiana legalized them). Aurelio took strong public stands against slot machines, calling them "the meanest kind of gambling," but Hogan's detectives have recently recorded incriminating telephone conversations between Aurelio and Costello. A formal complaint is filed August 29, a city Bar Association committee asks Aurelio to attend a hearing on his right to hold office, Aurelio obtains a leave of absence until after election day, the Bar Association asks the appellate division to oust him, and a lawyers' committee asks that a referee be appointed to decide his fitness. Aurelio resigns, the president of the Bar Association announces that the resignation prevents further action on his fitness to hold office, but Aurelio is applauded in the annual Columbus Day march October 12. La Guardia testifies October 27 that Aurelio came to him in August for support but that he had come to recognize "candidate pyschosis" and that Aurelio would do anything he could to get the nomination. Aurelio tearfully denies any wrongdoing, and he wins easy election to the state's highest court, defeating American Labor Party candidate Matthew M. Levy and Republican George Frankenthaler (see Harry Gross, 1950).

The United Nations has its beginnings in a brief congressional resolution drafted by freshman congressman J. William Fulbright, 38 (D. Ark.) (see 1944). The United Nations Relief and Rehabilitation Administration (UNRRA) is established November 9 by an agreement signed at Washington.

A Harlem race riot August 1 and 2 leaves five people dead and at least 400 injured. A black ghetto since at least 1920, Harlem's population has risen to nearly 400,000, unemployment is higher there than elsewhere in the city, and the war has exacerbated social problems that existed there before the war. Patrolman Joseph Collins has arrested a woman for disturbing the peace and using abusive language outside the Hotel Braddock at the corner of Eighth Avenue and 126th Street, Private Robert Bandy has grabbed Collins's nightstick and started beating him on the head and face, Collins goes down but is able to fire a shot at the fleeing soldier, who is taken to Suydenham Hospital with a bullet in his arm. News that a white police officer has shot a black soldier brings a crowd of angry protesters to the 123rd Street precinct house, an army infantry detachment is rushed in to guard the place, and Mayor La Guardia calls for reinforcements; the mayor assigns black policemen to the area and deputizes 1,500 civilian volunteers, most of them black, to patrol the streets; hundreds are booked for violence and vandalism, the hospitals are jammed with injured rioters, and the mayor has the armories opened to hold the rising number of prisoners (along with the food and clothing they have looted); 6,000 policemen, 800 air-raid wardens, and the civilian volunteers keep order, and the blackout in the area is suspended for a week to help the police (fires from vandalized stores have made it the brightest spot in the city anyway). Property damage is estimated at $5 million, and Harlem is ruled by martial law for a few days, with a curfew imposed, liquor sales banned, and traffic cleared from many areas. The mayor draws praise for his handling of the situation but comes in for criticism because he has consistently downplayed crime and delinquency.

The Spence-Chapin Adoption Agency is created by a merger of the Spence Alumnae Society and the Chapin Nursery (see 1895; 1910). The agency will begin placing children from racial minority groups in 1946 (see Harlem-Dowling, 1969).

The Brooklyn Navy Yard works around the clock to build warships, employing 70,000 people. City factories produce uniforms, machine parts, and the like to fill war-related contracts from the U.S. government. Steinway's two Astoria piano factories turn out parts for army air force gliders.

Banker J. P. Morgan, Jr., dies at Boca Grande, Fla., March 13 at age 75 following a cerebral stroke and is cremated at Middle Village, Queens. His death leaves the House of Morgan, now a state corporation, without a Morgan at its head for the first time since Junius Morgan set up his son John Pierpont in 1861. George Whitney is now president, Thomas W.

Lamont vice-chairman, and the bank has assets of $689,361,244 with total resources of $749,725,411.

Ford Motor Company president Edsel Ford dies May 26 at age 49, bequeathing 90 percent of his stock in the company to the Ford Foundation he set up in 1936. He has owned more than 40 percent of the stock and his will employs a tax avoidance scheme created by Wall Street investment banker Sidney Weinberg, 52, of Goldman, Sachs (see 1947). The five-foot-four-inch Weinberg became a Goldman partner at age 35 and has been running the firm since 1930, avoiding risks to the partners' capital and refocusing their efforts in the direction of advising major corporations.

A "Pay-As-You-Go" Current Tax Payment Act voted by Congress June 9 follows a plan proposed by R. H. Macy chairman Beardsley Ruml, 49. The act provides for income taxes on wages and salaries to be withheld by employers from paychecks.

A commission reports that New York is economically outmoded and overextended, a victim of premature obsolescence, with spreading "ghost" neighborhoods deserted by workers who have moved south or west to obtain jobs in booming war plants and middle-class whites who have moved to the suburbs.

Wall Street's Dow Jones Industrial Average closes July 6 at 143.76 on encouraging war news and closes December 31 at 135.89, up from 119.40 at the end of 1942.

Sales at shops on Broadway reach an all-time high as wartime crowds bring a boom to Times Square.

Electrical engineer-inventor Nicola Tesla is found dead in his suite at the Hotel New Yorker January 7 at age 86. Convinced that life exists on other planets, he has been trying to establish wireless communications with extra-terrestrials.

A "brown-out" goes into effect in the city November 1 to save electricity and thereby conserve coal. The news "Zipper" on the Times Tower in Times Square had resumed during daylight hours October 18 (see dim-out, 1942) but it goes dark to comply with the brown-out.

Subway and elevated ridership exceeds 1.9 billion in the city, up from a low of more than 1.7 billion in 1933, thanks in large part to the rubber and gasoline rationing that discourages use of automobiles and to war-fattened paychecks (see unified system, 1940). Complaints about overcrowding on the subways prompt Mayor La Guardia to say, "Any time we don't have crowding during the rush hour, there'll be a receiver sitting in the mayor's chair and New York

will be a ghost town. Why, they talk about the rush hour and the crash and noise. Why, listen, don't you see that's the proof of our life and vitality? Why, why, this is New York City!" The city shows a profit from turnstile receipts, but only because it defers maintenance and improvement costs (see 1947).

The ban on nonessential driving is revoked in September following a dramatic decline in highway traffic deaths.

The French freighter *Wyoming* arrives at New York from Casablanca January 10 with a cargo consisting chiefly of wine and tobacco. Casablanca and other Moroccan cities have had an outbreak of bubonic plague in December, but the *Wyoming*'s crew is apparently healthy, her captain shows Public Health Service inspectors a paper certifying that the ship was free of rats when she left Casablanca, and she is allowed to unload some bags of mail at Brooklyn's Pier 34. When she begins to discharge cargo at Pier 84 on the Hudson River, however, some longshoremen spot rats; health inspectors discover rat droppings, and when they fumigate the *Wyoming* January 18 they find 20 rats that are promptly autopsied. Indications of plague infection show up, tests with guinea pigs confirm that the ship's rats carried the Black Death, but news of the incident is kept from the public to avoid any panic. The ship is refumigated at Staten Island's Pier 25 January 29, crews of trappers are put to work on the Brooklyn, Manhattan, and Staten Island piers, tests on the trapped rats in February prove negative in every case, trapping continues until mid-May, but not until the end of May does the Public Health Service conclude that no rats from the *Wyoming* got ashore.

The 43 churches in the Times Square area attract more worshipers than they have in a generation, pastors report.

The United States Merchant Marine Academy is established at King's Point, N.Y., where the federal government has acquired an estate that once belonged to the late automaker Walter Chrysler, whose white, Greek Revival mansion will serve as the school's administration building. The sinking of the S.S. *Morro Castle* off Asbury Park, N.J., in 1934 was blamed in part on the crew's inability to put out a devastating fire and raised concerns about the lack of formal training for merchant seamen.

The Manhattan Day School (Yeshiva Ohr Torah) is founded at 310 West 75th Street, off West End Avenue, for the children of German Jewish refugees from Hitler's Holocaust.

Public telephones in the Times Square area are the busiest in the city as servicemen from the various branches dial up to 370,000 calls per day from booths in cigar stores, candy stores, hotels, restaurants, and the like.

The Federal Communications Commission votes 5 to 2 May 3 to make NBC divest itself of one of its two radio networks to avoid a monopoly in broadcasting. Life Savers millionaire Edward Noble writes a check for $8 million to acquire the 16-year-old Blue Network, turns it into American Broadcasting Co. (ABC), and sets out to rival NBC and CBS, breaking the duopoly they have enjoyed since the 1920s (see Goldenson, 1953).

Foote, Cone and Belding is founded at New York by former Lord & Thomas advertising agency executives Emerson Foote, 36, Fairfax Mastick Cone, 40, and Don Belding, 45, following the retirement of Lord & Thomas president Albert D. Lasker, now 63, who has made a vast fortune promoting the wares of clients such as American Tobacco Co. (Lasker and his wife, Mary, start giving financial support to cancer research.)

Caricaturist-author Art Young dies of a heart attack at his apartment in the Irving Hotel on Gramercy Park December 29 at age 77. His onetime *Masses* colleague Floyd Dell has said that Young's greatness stemmed from the fact that "his love of humanity is given enough scope to balance his scorn for our failures and follies."

Nonfiction: *Discontent in New York City* by Basil Lee; *McSorley's Wonderful Saloon* by North Carolina-born *New Yorker* magazine staff writer Joseph (Quincy) Mitchell, 35; *Oscar of the Waldorf* by Boston-born historian Karl Schriftgeisser, 39.

Fiction: *A Tree Grows in Brooklyn* by Brooklyn-born novelist Betty (Wehner) Smith, 47, who has been inspired by an *Ailanthus glandulosa*, or tree of heaven. Her protagonist Francie Nolan tells her brother at the end of the novel, "Brooklyn. It's a magic city and it isn't real . . . It's like—yes—a dream . . . but it's like a dream of being poor and fighting;" *Tucker's People* by Brooklyn-born novelist-war correspondent Ira Wolfert, 35, whose novel is about a vicious character in the city's numbers racket.

Poetry: *Western Star* by Stephen Vincent Benét; *Shakespeare in Harlem* by Langston Hughes; *Afternoon of a Pawnbroker* by Kenneth Fearing; *Genesis, Book I* by New York-born poet Delmore (David) Schwartz, 29, is about the life and customs of the city's Jewish immigrants.

Poet Stephen Vincent Benét dies of a heart attack at New York March 13 at age 44. He has been living in a house at 215 East 68th Street, near Third Avenue.

Painting: *Broadway Boogie-Woogie* by Dutch painter Piet Mondrian (originally Pieter Cornelis Mondiaan), 71, who has taken refuge in New York from the war in Europe; *Welders* and *1943 A.D.* by Ben Shahn; *Hotel Lobby* by Edward Hopper; *Queen of Hearts* by Willem de Kooning; *The She-Wolf* by Wyoming-born New York painter Jackson Pollock, 31. Peggy Guggenheim presents the first public display of paintings by Pollock beginning November 9 at her Art of This Century gallery in 57th Street and gains support for his work from Bronx-born critic Clement Greenberg, 34, whose 1939 *Partisan Review* article "Avant-Garde and Kitsch" established his reputation and led to his becoming art critic for the *Nation* last year; *Rain or Snow* by Arthur Dove.

Theater: *Dark Eyes* by Elena Miramova and Eugenie Leontovich 1/14 at the Belasco Theater, with Miramova, Leontovich, and Ludmilla Toretzka as three female Russian refugees trying to survive in New York, 174 perfs.; *The Patriots* by Sidney Kingsley 1/29 at the National Theater, with Madge Evans, Wichita Falls, Texas-born actress Frances Reid, 25, 157 perfs.; *Harriet* by F. Ryerson and Cohn Claues 3/3 at the Henry Miller Theater, with Helen Hayes, 377 perfs.; *Kiss and Tell* by F. Hugh Herbert 3/17 at the Biltmore Theater, with East Orange, N.J.-born ingénue Joan Caulfield, 21, as Corliss Archer, Robert White as Dexter Perkins, 103 perfs.; *Tomorrow the World* by New York playwright James Gow and Los Angeles-born playwright Arnaud d'Usseau, 27, 4/14 at the Ethel Barrymore Theater, with Ralph Bellamy, Shirley Booth, Chicago-born actor Skippy Homeier, 13, 500 perfs.; *The Two Mrs. Carrolls* by Mark Vale 8/3 at the Booth Theater, with émigrée German film star Elisabeth Bergner, 44, Nebraska-born actress Irene Worth (originally Harriet Abrams), 26, 583 perfs.; *Lovers and Friends* by English playwright Dodie Smith 11/29 at the Plymouth Theater, with Katherine Cornell, Raymond Massey, 188 perfs.; *The Voice of the Turtle* by John Van Druten 12/8 at the Morosco Theater, with Margaret Sullavan, Audrey Christie, Elliott Nugent, 1,557 perfs.

Drama critic Alexander Woollcott suffers a heart attack in a CBS studio at New York January 23 and dies at Roosevelt Hospital at age 56 ("All the things I really like to do," he has said, "are either illegal, immoral, or fattening"); actress Katherine Corcoran Herne dies at New York's River Crest Sanitarium February 8 at age 86; showman Max Reinhardt of pneumonia and paralysis at his New York apartment October 31 at age 70.

Theatrical caricaturist Al Hirschfeld, now 40, introduces the name of his newborn daughter, Nina, into a circus sketch that includes a poster with the legend "Nina the Wonder Child," beginning a puzzle game that will continue for more than 50 years (see 1924). Hirschfeld's clean line drawings have been published on the drama pages of the *New York Times* and other papers since 1924 but will henceforth be exclusive to the *Times*.

Films: Richard Wallace's *A Night to Remember* with Loretta Young, Brian Aherne (about the sinking of R.M.S. *Titanic* in 1912). Also: Richard Wallace's *The Fallen Sparrow* with John Garfield, Maureen O'Hara, Walter Slezack, Patricia Morison; William Wellman's *Lady of Burlesque* with Barbara Stanwyck; Frank Borzage's *Stage Door Canteen* with Cheryl Walker, William Terry, Marjorie Riordan, Lon McCallister plus walk-ons by everyone from Edgar Bergen, Count Basie, and Benny Goodman to Helen Hayes, Katharine Hepburn, Harpo Marx, and Paul Muni; S. Sylvan Simon's *Whistling in Brooklyn* with Red Skelton, Ann Rutherford, Sam Levene, and Leo Durocher's Brooklyn Dodgers.

The Broadway Association reports on the basis of a 4-month survey October 27 that Times Square is enjoying the "greatest boom in its history," with record crowds patronizing its hotels, nightclubs, restaurants, shops, picture houses, and legitimate theaters as French sailors, wearing caps with red pom-poms, rub elbows with British tars, wearing bright blue, and the soldiers and sailors of other Allied nations in khaki and olive drab. The 44 movie theaters sell 1,529,408 tickets on average per week, and the 39 legitimate theaters average 220,000. War service agencies such as the United Service Organization (USO) and Stage Door Canteen feed and entertain 93,700 men of the armed forces each week in the Times Square area.

♪♪ Broadway musicals: *Something for the Boys* 1/7 at the Alvin Theater, with Ethel Merman, book by Harold and Dorothy Fields, music and lyrics by Cole Porter, songs that include "Hey, Good Lookin'," 422 perfs.; *Oklahoma!* 3/31 at the St. James Theater, with Alfred Drake, Celeste Holm, Howard da Silva, a book based on the 1931 Broadway play *Green Grow the Lilacs*, choreography by Agnes de Mille, music by Richard Rodgers, lyrics by Oscar Hammerstein II, songs that include "Oh, What a Beautiful Morning," "People Will Say We're in Love," "Kansas City," "I Cain't Say No," "Pore Jud," "The Surrey with the Fringe on Top," and the title song (lyrics by Otto Harbach),

2,212 perfs.; *The Ziegfeld Follies* 4/1 at the Winter Garden Theater, with comedian Milton Berle (originally Berlinger), 34, who was born in a five-story walk-up at 68 West 116th Street, between Fifth and Lenox avenues, made his professional debut as a single at Loew's State Theater in Times Square in December 1924 at age 16, and was paid $600 (his manager gave him $275 and made off with the rest). Music by Ray Henderson and Harold Rome, lyrics by Jack Yellen and others, 553 perfs.; *One Touch of Venus* 10/7 at the Imperial Theater, with Mary Martin, Kenny Baker, music by Kurt Weill, libretto by S. J. Perelman and Ogden Nash, lyrics by Nash, songs that include "Speak Low," "West Wind," 567 perfs.; *Artists and Models* (revue) 11/5 at the Broadway Theater, with Jane Froman, Brooklyn-born comedian Jackie Gleason, 27, 27 perfs.; *Carmen Jones* 12/2 at the Broadway Theater, with Muriel Smith, drummer Cosy Cole, music by the late French composer Georges Bizet, book and lyrics by Oscar Hammerstein II, 503 perfs.

Lyricist Lorenz Hart dies of pneumonia at New York November 22 at age 47 after a final 3-day drinking spree.

Opera: The New York City Opera has its beginnings in the City Center Opera Co. that opens 2/21 with a performance of the 1900 Giacomo Puccini opera *Tosca* (philanthropist Lytle Hull, 48, has helped fund the new company, whose director is Austrian-born conductor-impresario Julius Rudel, 23, who came to America 6 years ago, studied at the Mannes School, joined the company as a rehearsal pianist and coach, makes his conducting debut later in the year with a production of the 1885 Johann Strauss opera *The Gypsy Baron*, and will serve as conductor or director until 1979).

Russian-born violinist Isaac Stern, 22, makes his Carnegie Hill debut 1/8; Duke Ellington his Carnegie Hall debut 1/23; Massachusetts-born conductor-composer Leonard Bernstein, 25, his Carnegie Hall debut 11/14 as conductor of the New York Philharmonic, substituting for Bruno Walter.

The New York City Center of Music and Drama opens formally December 11 (Mayor La Guardia's 61st birthday) in West 55th Street, between Sixth and Seventh avenues, where the city has acquired the Mecca Temple, a Shriners auditorium, for nonpayment of taxes (the structure has stood idle except for occasional use as a venue for Civil Service examinations). The mayor has used WPA musicians to give concerts in Radio City Music Hall, the Metropolitan Opera House, and Carnegie Hall, with tickets priced at 25¢ to $1, Newbold Morris has proposed that the city use the Mecca Temple as a "theater for the people," a "temple for the performing arts" with a top ticket price of $2. Helped by New Jersey-born publicist Jean Dalrymple, 41, Morris has obtained contributions from the Amalgamated Clothing Workers, the Jewish Labor Alliance, Howard Cullman, Marshall Field, Edmund Guggenheim, and John D. Rockefeller, Jr., with the only cost to the city being $65,000 for capital improvements. The hall has acoustical problems but they will be remedied to a large extent and the City Center will become a major venue for ballet, opera, concerts, and theater.

Toledo-born jazz pianist Art Tatum, 32, forms a trio that will continue until 1955. Blind in one eye and nearly so in the other but an acknowledged prodigy from an early age, Tatum has been in New York since 1932, assimilating the influences of Fats Waller, Teddy Wilson, and Earl "Fatha" Hines into a virtuoso style all his own.

Popular songs: "I Have Grown to Love New York" by Vernon Duke; "She Will Be Standing in the Harbor" by Carmen Lombardo, lyrics by John Jacob Loeb.

Thomas "Fats" Waller dies of influenza and bronchial pneumonia in a Pullman car berth en route to New York December 15 at age 39; songwriter Joseph McCarthy of cancer at his New York home December 18 at age 53; George Whiting at his Bronx home December 18 at age 61.

 Count Fleet wins the Kentucky Derby and goes on to win U.S. racing's Triple Crown but injures his leg coming down the stretch at Belmont Park. He is retired to stud.

U.S. Navy Lieut. Joseph R. Hunt, 24, wins in men's singles at Forest Hills, Pauline Betz in women's singles.

The New York Yankees win the World Series, reversing last year's defeat by beating the St. Louis Cardinals 4 games to 1 behind the pitching of Spurgeon Ferdinand "Spud" Chandler, 36, who wins the first and fifth games. Bill Dickey and Joe Gordon hit the only home runs for the Yankees; both teams have lost most of their best players to the armed forces.

Former Columbia football star Sid Luckman leads the Chicago Bears to a 56-to-7 rout of the New York Giants at the Polo Grounds November 14, throwing for 433 yards, becoming the first National Football League quarterback to pass for 400 yards in a single game, and scoring a record seven touchdowns (see 1938). Now nearly 27, Luckman goes off the next day to the Merchant Marine, where he will serve on the

Atlantic until 1945, taking occasional leaves to play football.

 New York madam Polly Adler is arrested in January, but she is ill with pleurisy and charges are dismissed (see 1935). Now 43, Adler retires to the Los Angeles area (see Nonfiction, 1952).

 A U.S. federal rent-control law takes effect in the city November 1 as the Office of Price Administration (OPA) issues regulations freezing rents at their March 1 levels to prevent rent gouging (see 1942). Apartment vacancy rates have fallen below 5 percent, and New York loses its exemption from last year's law. The La Guardia administration has brought pressure on Washington to recognize that what only recently was a glut of available housing has turned into a housing shortage, due in part to a cessation of housing construction and a rise in incomes, but La Guardia says in his radio address October 31 that he has been assured that the system will not be controlled by politicians and pledges cooperation, providing space beginning November 15 for 800,000 or more landlords to register at schools and other buildings in each borough during evening hours. To help the OPA in its task the city makes available 300 inspectors from the Department of Housing and Buildings, 500 inspectors and investigators from the Welfare Department, and 2,500 volunteer workers. Rent controls prevent landlords from raising rents by more than a small percentage each year and by some accounts will be a factor in discouraging new housing construction. Landlords are permitted to ask for voluntary increases, and tenants of East Side buildings will pay higher rents to keep from having services reduced, but many West Siders are European refugees struggling to survive and lack the means to pay more; unable to keep up their properties and pay taxes without rent increases, landlords of West Side buildings will in some cases simply abandon them. The controls will expire in 1950 but New York State and some others will continue them (see 1949).

The 20-year-old Russell Hotel on Murray Hill becomes the Sheraton-Russell (it will later be renamed the Park-Sheraton), the city's first Sheraton hotel. Boston hotel man Ernest Henderson, 46, joined with his Harvard classmate Robert Lowell Moore 10 years ago to start what has now become the Sheraton Hotel chain.

 A lodging house at 437-439 West 42nd Street burns in a spectacular fire December 24, killing 18 people.

 New York housewives wash and flatten tins for recycling: one less tin can per week per family will save

enough tin and steel to build 5,000 tanks or 38 Liberty Ships. They save kitchen fats to be exchanged for red ration points at the butcher's: one jar of kitchen fat contains enough glycerine to make a pound of black powder—enough to fill six 75-mm. shells or 50 32-caliber bullets.

1944 D-Day (June 6) sees 176,000 Allied troops storming ashore at Omaha Beach, Utah Beach, and other Normandy beaches under the supreme command of Abilene, Kansas-born Gen. Dwight D. Eisenhower, 52, whose forces take Cherbourg June 6. News of the landing reaches New York that morning and Mayor La Guardia leads a crowd of 50,000 in prayer at Madison Square Park.

The Liberal Party is founded at New York by former members of the American Labor Party alienated by that party's increasingly left-wing positions. Polish-born labor leaders Alex Rose (originally Olesh Royz), now 45, and David Dubinsky have quit the ALP to start the new party that Rose will build into an effective power in city and state politics.

Former governor Alfred E. Smith dies at New York October 4 at age 70. "His monument," says Mayor La Guardia, "is on the statute books of our state and in the progressive social welfare laws enacted during his term as governor," but although he has lived well in a Fifth Avenue apartment near the Central Park Zoo, the final years of the man whom President Roosevelt called the "Happy Warrior" have been bitter; 1940 presidential candidate Wendell Willkie has suffered a heart attack in August and dies of a coronary thrombosis at Lenox Hill Hospital October 8 at age 52.

President Roosevelt tours Manhattan and the outer boroughs October 21, riding in an open car despite the rain and despite failing health, with Mayor La Guardia at his side; supported by New York's new Liberal Party and the American Labor Party as well as Democrats and many Republicans, he wins reelection to a fourth term with 53 percent of the popular vote and 432 electoral votes. Gov. Dewey, now 42, has defeated Wendell Willkie in the Wisconsin primary and won the Republican nomination, Herbert Brownell, Jr. has managed his campaign, and he receives 46 percent of the popular vote but fails to carry his home state and winds up with only 99 electoral votes. Dewey is a diminutive man with black hair, black moustache, and a faint smile; Washington wit Alice Roosevelt Longworth, now 60, has said of him, "How do you expect people to vote for a man who looks like a bridegroom on a wedding cake?"

City Council member Adam Clayton Powell, Jr., now 35, is elected to Congress after a new 18th congressional district with a black majority is drawn in Harlem (see 1960).

 The Citizen's Committee for Children of New York is created to investigate day-care centers and other modalities set up to look after youngsters whose mothers have taken war industry jobs. The Works Progress Administration (WPA) has opened 27 nursery schools in the city since 1933, and local child welfare agencies have taken control of most of them, but the Citizen's Committee finds conditions in many of the nursery schools and day-care centers to be woefully inadequate (see 1948).

New York manufacturing operations—Bulova (scientific instruments), Ford Instruments, Carl Norden (bombsights), etc.—make it the second largest U.S. military contractor after Los Angeles, with 170,000 people working on war contracts plus thousands more on subcontracts (see 1942). Workers at the Brewster plant in Long Island City who assembled Rolls-Royce motorcars before the war assemble fighter planes; the Brooklyn Navy Yard has 30,000 metal workers building warships and repairing damaged vessels.

The G.I. Bill of Rights (Servicemen's Readjustment Act) that President Roosevelt signs into law June 22 provides war veterans with job training and $20 per week for 52 weeks.

Former National City Bank president James A. Stillman of 900 Park Avenue dies at New York Hospital January 13 at age 70; financier-art collector Jules S. Bache of chronic nephritis at Palm Beach March 24 at age 82 (he is buried in Woodlawn Cemetery).

Cantor Fitzgerald is founded by New York-born financial innovator B. (Bernard) Gerald Cantor, 27, who returns from military service to start a firm that will play an important role in the U.S. Treasury securities market, helping to establish benchmark interest rates for everything from business loans to home mortgages (see 1972).

Wall Street's Dow Jones Industrial Average closes December 30 at 152.32, up from 135.89 at the end of 1943.

 Elevated railway service across the 61-year-old Brooklyn Bridge ends March 5.

New York's 48-year-old Fifth Avenue Coach Co. remains the only company in the country that still operates double-decker buses with conductors as well as drivers (see 1936). Surface Transit Inc., a subsidiary of Fifth Avenue Coach Co., appoints John

E. (Edward) McCarthy, 50, president and converts the buses to one-man operation, eliminating the conductors and thus saving the company about $750,000 per year, overcoming objections from the Transport Workers Union (TWU), with retirement pensions and retraining (see 1953).

New York Harbor carfloats and oil-tank barges facilitate landings of equipment on Normandy beaches June 6 (see 1942). Requisitioned by the navy, they are towed across the Atlantic under the direction of Brooklyn-born tugboat company heir and Navy lieutenant commander Edward J. Moran, 37, a grandson of the late Michael Moran, whose company has developed powerful oceangoing tugs. Allied warships convoy a dozen such tugs, towing 12 carfloats and 12 barges, they reach the English Channel after a 21-day voyage, and Moran commands 160 tugboats on D-Day; New York Central, New Haven, Pennsylvania, and Baltimore & Ohio railcars discharge cargo onto the French beachheads in June while Texaco, Socony, and Bushey barges supply the invasion force with gasoline and diesel fuel.

Roosevelt Hospital and St. Luke's collaborate at the request of the army in planning a 750-bed evacuation hospital that opens June 17 five miles from Omaha Beach in Normandy (see St. Luke's, 1858; Roosevelt, 1864; St. Luke's-Roosevelt, 1979).

The Eye Bank established by the New York Hospital-Cornell Medical Center is the first U.S. facility to store human corneas for transplant operations.

The Health Insurance Plan (HIP) of Greater New York is founded with support from Mayor La Guardia, who responds to a survey showing that city employees go into debt to meet high medical costs more often than for any other reason. The mayor's personal physician Dr. George Baehr has advised him with regard to setting up the health maintenance organization, insuring municipal employees who earn up to $5,000 per year for medical services, surgery, and hospital care, with the city paying half the premiums; HIP will be expanded to cover other middle-income workers and grow to have a network of more than 50 physician groups offering medical and hospital services to nearly 1 million members (see Empire Blue Cross, 1973).

The Visiting Nurse Service of New York is created by a spinoff of the Henry Street Settlement's nursing services (see 1893) into an independent organization that acquires the former Thomas W. Lamont mansion at 107 East 70th Street, just off Park Avenue. It will grow to become the largest voluntary home-care agency in America.

The United Negro College Fund is founded at New York May 13. Tuskegee Institute president Frederick Douglass Patterson has invited representatives of several other private black colleges to meet with him at the Waldorf-Astoria Hotel, and they will raise $100,000 in their first campaign—half of it from the Rosenwald Fund and General Education Board, the other half from various colleges. John D. Rockefeller, Jr. will contribute money and use his influence to have others contribute, and within 50 years the Fund will be raising $50 million per year for 41 member colleges.

The G.I. Bill of Rights signed into law by President Roosevelt June 22 will finance college educations for war veterans, swelling enrollments at CCNY, Columbia, New York University, and the city's other schools of higher learning, opening educational opportunities to many who would not otherwise have been able to attend college; most will major in engineering or science, but the law will also finance tuitions at the city's art schools, drama schools, and the like.

The Fashion Institute of Technology (FIT) opens at the Central Needle Trades High School that will later become the High School of Fashion Industries. It will become a community college in 1951 and a 4-year college in the State University of New York system in 1975.

Columbia Presents Corwin debuts on CBS radio March 7 with Boston-born writer-announcer Norman Corwin, 33.

The Du Mont Television Network has its beginnings in the New York station WABD licensed May 2 (see 1939; 1955).

Seventeen magazine begins publication at New York in September. Publishing heir Walter H. Annenberg, 36, has started the periodical for adolescent girls (see 1939; TV Guide, 1953).

Fiction: The Lost Weekend by Summit, N.J.-born New York novelist Charles (Reginald) Jackson, 41; Crazy Like a Fox by S. J. Perelman.

Painting: Factory Workers by Charlotte, N.C.-born Harlem painter (Fred) Romare (Howard) Bearden, 31; Mother and Child by Sand Bank, N.Y.-born New York painter Milton Avery, 51; Pink Lady by Willem de Kooning; That Red One by Arthur Dove; World in Wax by Reginald Marsh; The Survivor by German-born painter George Grosz, 51, who emigrated to New York in 1932, supported himself by drawing cartoons, nudes, and landscapes, aroused controversy when he was appointed to a teaching position at the Art Students League, and became a U.S. citizen in 1938. Piet Mondrian dies at New York February 1 at age 71; artist-illustrator Charles Dana Gibson at his 127 East 73rd Street town house December 23 at age 76.

Theater: *Decision* by New York-born playwright Edward Chodorov, 39, 2/2 at the Belasco Theater, with Georgia Burke in a melodrama about fascism in America and U.S. race relations, 160 perfs.; *The Searching Wind* by Lillian Hellman 4/12 at the Fulton Theater, with Cornelia Otis Skinner, now 42, Dudley Digges, Montgomery Clift, 318 perfs.; *Anna Lucasta* by Chicago-born playwright Philip Yordan, 31, 8/30 at the Mansfield Theater, with Hilda Simons, Canada Lee, John Tate (Cleveland-born actress Ruby Dee [originally Ruby Ann Wallace], now 16, will join the cast in 1946), 957 perfs.; *I Remember Mama* by John Van Druten (who has adapted Kathryn Forbes's book *Mama's Bank Account*) 10/19 at the Music Box Theater, with Mady Christians, Oklahoma City-born ingénue Frances Heflin, 21, New York-born ingénue Joan (Margaret) Tetzel, 22, Omaha-born actor Marlon Brando, 20, Vienna-born actor Oscar Homolka, 46, 714 perfs.; *Harvey* by Denver newspaperwoman-turned-playwright Mary Coyle Chase, 37, 11/1 at the 48th Street Theater, with San Francisco-born vaudeville veteran Frank Fay, 46, 1,775 perfs.; *Dear Ruth* by Corona, Queens-born playwright-screenwriter Norman Krasna, 35, 12/13 at the Henry Miller Theater, with Lenore Lonergan, 683 perfs.

Films: Otto Preminger's *Laura* with Clifton Webb, Gene Tierney, Dana Andrews; Fritz Lang's *The Woman in the Window* with Joan Bennett, Edward G. Robinson, Dan Duryea, Raymond Massey.

Film musicals: Walter Lang's *Greenwich Village* with Carmen Miranda, Don Ameche, William Bendix; Gregory Ratoff's *Irish Eyes are Smiling* with Monty Wooley as composer Ernest R. Ball, June Haver, Dick Haymes, Anthony Quinn; Tim Whelan's *Step Lively* with Frank Sinatra, George Montgomery, Adolphe Menjou, Gloria DeHaven; Richard Thorpe's *Two Girls and a Sailor* with Van Johnson, June Allyson, Gloria DeHaven, Lena Horne singing "Paper Moon."

Broadway musicals: *Mexican Hayride* 1/28 at the Winter Garden Theater, with Bobby Clark, June Havoc, book by Herbert and Dorothy Fields, music and lyrics by Cole Porter, songs that include "Count Your Blessings," 481 perfs.; *Follow the Girls* 4/8 at the New Century Theater (to 44th Street Theater 6/14,

to Broadhurst Theater 6/5/1945), with Jackie Gleason, Gertrude Niesen, Chicago-born baritone Bill Tabbert, 22, music and lyrics by Dan Shapiro, Milton Pascal, and Phil Chang, book by Guy Bolton and Eddie Davis, 882 perfs; *Hats Off to Ice* 6/22 at the Center Theater, with ice skaters performing to music and lyrics by John Fortis and James Littlefield, 889 perfs.; *The Song of Norway* 8/21 at the Imperial Theater, with music based on works by Edvard Grieg, book and lyrics by Robert Wright and Brooklyn-born writer George Forrest (originally George Forrest Chichester, Jr.), songs that include "Strange Music," 860 perfs.; *Bloomer Girl* 10/5 at the Shubert Theater, with Celeste Holm as Evalina, Nanette Fabray, music by Harold Arlen, lyrics by E. Y. Harburg, songs that include "Evalina," "It Was Good Enough for Grandma," 653 perfs.; *Seven Lively Arts* 12/7 at the Ziegfeld Theater, with Helen Gallagher, Benny Goodman, Bert Lahr, Beatrice Lillie, Bill Tabbert, music and lyrics by Cole Porter, choreography by Anton Dolin, book by Moss Hart, George S. Kaufman, Ben Hecht, 183 perfs.; *On the Town* 12/28 at the Adelphi Theater, with Sono Osato, New York-born comedienne-writer Betty Comden, 25, Adolph Green, Nancy Walker, New York-born comedienne Alice Pearce, 27, sets by Oliver Smith, music by Leonard Bernstein, dances derived from the ballet *Fancy Free*, 563 perfs.

Former Broadway musical star Betty Compton dies at Doctor's Hospital July 12 at age 37. The former Mrs. James J. Walker was divorced in 1941, married Theodore Knaplen, and has been living at 232 East 72nd Street.

Ballet: *Fancy Free* 4/18 at the Metropolitan Opera House, with Jerome Robbins, John Kriza, and Hugh Laing as the Three Sailors, music by Leonard Bernstein, choreography by Robbins.

Frank Sinatra opens at the Paramount Theater October 12 (Columbus Day) to begin a 3-week return engagement (a punctured eardrum has barred the crooner from military service). Hundreds of police officers are called in to control the situation as some 30,000 teenagers crowd Times Square in hopes of attending the concert. A musicians' strike is settled in November and Sinatra begins recording for Columbia Records with help from strings orchestrated by Axel Stordahl, a trombonist who was Tommy Dorsey's lead arranger. Sinatra will continue to record for Columbia until 1953.

Pittsburgh-born New York jazz singer William Clarence "Billy" Eckstine, 30, forms his own band and will soon be proselytizing the new, progressive "bebop" jazz pioneered by instrumentalist Benny

Carter, now 36 (who excels on alto sax, trumpet, trombone, clarinet, and piano), North Carolina-born tenor saxophonist John (William) Coltrane, 18, Alton, Ill.-born trumpeter Miles (Dewey) Davis (III), 18, South Carolina-born trumpeter John Birks "Dizzy" Gillespie, 26, St. Joseph, Mo.-born tenor saxophonist Coleman (Randolph) Hawkins, 39, and alto saxophonist Charles Christopher "Charlie" Parker (Jr)., 24, who moved to Harlem from his native Kansas City in 1939 and has become known as "Yardbird" or simply "Bird" (see Birdland, 1950).

Former Newark Baptist Church choir singer Sarah (Lois) Vaughan, 20, records "I'll Wait and Pray" 12/31 with Billy Eckstine's big band to begin a notable career. Vaughan won an amateur contest at Harlem's Apollo Theater 2 years ago and will come to be known as "the divine Sarah."

The Carter Handicap July 10 at the 50-year-old Aqueduct Racetrack ends in a triple dead heat. Mobster Frank Costello has fixed races at the Big A for years, paying off the police and judges to keep out of jail.

Milwaukee-born Sgt. Frank Parker (originally Franciszek Paikowski), 28, U.S. Army, wins in men's singles at Forest Hills, Pauline Betz in women's singles.

Organized crime leader Louis "Lepke" Buchalter is executed at Sing Sing State Prison March 4 at age 46. He surrendered to police in 1939 and has been convicted of masterminding the murder of a Brooklyn store owner while in prison.

The Roman Catholic archdiocese buys the Villard houses, built on Madison Avenue in 1884 behind St. Patrick's Cathedral and vacant for more than a decade. A restrictive covenant signed in 1919 by all the owners has forbidden any outside alteration of the houses or their conversion into apartments, offices, or museums, but the covenant has expired and Boston businessman Joseph P. Kennedy, now 55, has given financial aid to the archdiocese for their purchase. The Church takes over the south wing, whose rooms were designed by Stanford White and once comprised the Whitelaw Reid house, leasing the plainer north wing to the publishing firm Random House (see Helmsley Palace hotel, 1980).

The G.I. Bill of Rights signed into law June 22 provides for 4 percent home loans to veterans with no down payment required. The law will subsidize a postwar suburban building boom and encourage a mass exodus from New York, depleting the city of middle-income taxpayers (see Levittown, 1947).

The Fort Greene Houses are completed at Brooklyn and will be New York's largest public housing project for years to come. The apartment buildings occupy 38 acres and provide 3,500 flats to house 14,000 people (see Co-Op City, 1968).

The assessed valuation of New York real estate falls to $15,845,991,014, the lowest since 1928, with the largest decrease coming in Manhattan (only Queens real estate shows an increase).

Architect Benjamin Wistar Morris dies at New York December 4 at age 74; architect and housing reformer I. N. Phelps Stokes of a cerebral hemorrhage at the Charleston, S.C., home of a sister December 18 at age 77.

The city imposes stricter regulations on open garbage-disposal dumps (see 1934). Only 15 of the 90 dumps opened in 1934 remain open (see 1945).

Washington Market is "a jumbled mass of antiquated structures and narrow crowded streets," says the Committee on Civic Design of the American Institute of Architects. The wholesale fruit and produce industry is funneled through the market "at a considerable loss reflected in high prices."

Neighborhood candy stores go out of business by the thousands, leaving New York youngsters without the soda fountains that served egg creams and 2¢ plain, and without the public telephones that have made the corner candy store the kids' date bureau and recreation center.

Patsy's opens in 56th Street between Broadway and Eighth Avenue. Restaurateur Patsy Scognamillo specializes in pastas and will attract show-business people such as Frank Sinatra (who will enter by a special entrance and have a special table upstairs in the back, by the windows).

A large-scale migration of Americans from rural to urban areas begins. The shift will create major problems in cities like New York.

1945 The U.S.S. *Alfred E. Smith* launched January 7 has a bit of New York sidewalk fitted into its binnacle for the helmsman to stand on. Legislation signed by Gov. Dewey February 21 calls for a new state office building at Albany to be named in honor of the late governor, who died last year.

President Roosevelt dies of a cerebral hemorrhage at Warm Springs, Ga., April 12 at age 63. Mayor La Guardia speaks for 10 minutes on the city's municipal radio station WNYC and calls the onetime New York governor's death "the greatest loss peace-loving people have suffered in the entire war." FDR

V-J Day brought an end to World War II and delirium to Times Square. ALFRED EISENSTADT/TIMELIFE PICTURES

is succeeded by his Missouri-born vice president Harry S Truman, 60.

World War II ends in Europe May 8; crowds celebrating in Times Square hear the voice of Mayor La Guardia urging in midafternoon that people who have "thoughtlessly left their jobs" go home or return to work, because the war continues in the Pacific and men are dying "at this very moment." Gen. Eisenhower visits New York June 19, City Hall Plaza is packed with a crowd of 250,000, and Mayor La Guardia says, "History has yet to record the achievements of a great commander of a mighty army equal in gallantry, courage, and brilliance." A crowd estimated to number 4 million watches as the mayor and the general ride through Manhattan and the outer boroughs in a ticker-tape parade that is followed by a dinner at the Waldorf-Astoria.

Troopships returning from Europe bring thousands of parents, wives, children, and siblings to New York and New Jersey piers, but many of the veterans bear the marks of combat and some wind up in local hospitals.

The war against Japan ends August 14; thousands cram Times Square August 14 and at 7:03 that evening see the Zipper on the Times Tower flash the words, "OFFICIAL TRUMAN ANNOUNCES JAPANESE SURRENDER." Nearly 900,000 New Yorkers have served in the armed forces, and more than 16,000 have been killed or reported missing in action.

Gen. Jonathan M. Wainwright, 62, receives a ticker-tape parade up Broadway September 30. He was forced to surrender Corregidor in the Philippines in 1942 and taken prisoner but was rescued earlier this year in Manchuria. Admiral Chester W. Nimitz, 60, receives a ticker-tape parade October 10. President Truman reviews the fleet in New York Harbor October 27. Admiral William F. "Bull" Halsey, Jr., 62, receives a ticker-tape parade December 14 despite a 13-inch snowfall (Halsey played a major role in destroying the Japanese fleet last year in the Battle of Leyte Gulf and earlier this year directed final operations of the war around Okinawa).

A San Francisco meeting convenes to discuss the formation of an international body to be called the United Nations (*see* 1944; 1946).

William O'Dwyer wins the mayoralty election, running on the Democrat-American Labor ticket and receiving 1,125,357 votes as compared with 431,601 for Republican-Liberal-Fusion candidate Jonah J. Goldstein (a lifelong Tammany Democrat who has switched parties), 408,348 for City Council president Newbold Morris, now 43, who has run as the No Deal candidate with backing from Mayor La Guardia, Robert Moses, and journalist Dorothy Thompson, but not from Eleanor Roosevelt.

$ The International Longshoremen's Association brings 35,000 men off the job from October 3 to 19, challenging Joseph P. Ryan's control of the union, long a source of underworld bribery and extortion payoffs, and demanding wage gains and better working conditions on the Brooklyn, Manhattan, and Jersey City docks; hiring has been, and continues to be, done at early-morning "shapeups" where pier bosses controlled by Italian-born mobster Anthony "Tough Tony" Anastasia (originally Anastasio) assign work to those who signal how much they will kick back. Mayor La Guardia intervenes in the dispute, as he does in strikes by bus drivers, milk producers, office building workers, and others fighting to regain what they believe they have lost through the sacrifices they were asked to make during the war (*see* crime, 1950).

Wall Street's Dow Jones Industrial Average closes December 31 at 192.91, up from 152.32 at the end of 1944.

Macy's Thanksgiving Day parade resumes after a 3-year hiatus, having been called off in 1942 for lack of helium and to conserve rubber.

Brooklyn Union Gas has more than 20,000 customers heating homes with gas, up from 726 in 1935 (*see* transcontinental pipeline, 1950).

Gasoline and fuel oil rationing ends August 19.

A B-25 light bomber flies into the north side of the Empire State Building during a heavy fog July 28, tearing a hole between the 78th and 79th floors, killing all three men aboard plus 10 office workers and early Saturday morning pedestrians (the offices of Catholic Charities on the 79th floor are closed and nobody is there). Firefighters have to bring hoses up stairways to put out the ensuing blaze; an elevator car falls to the hydraulic bumper at the bottom of its shaft but its operator somehow survives, having been alone in the car.

Manhattan traffic congestion returns by late July to its December 1941 levels, tying up cross streets for hours at a time as cars, taxis, and buses jam intersections. The *Herald Tribune* runs an editorial August 23 demanding to know why nothing has been done since 1941 to address the problem. Robert Moses replies that "we have built and are building wide parkways and expressways, bridges and tunnels, without crossings and lights, with service roads for local use and parking, belt and crosstown systems which take through traffic off ordinary streets and enormously cut down congestion . . . Trolley tracks are being ripped up all over town to promote the flow of traffic." But critics will fault Moses for encouraging private motorcar transportation at the expense of mass transit.

Manhattan's Sixth Avenue becomes the Avenue of the Americas under terms of Local Law 43 signed by Mayor La Guardia October 2, and 800 metal discs representing the nations of the Americas are unveiled October 21 at a parade down the avenue. Its elevated railway structure is long gone but it remains a dingy thoroughfare and most New Yorkers continue to call it Sixth Avenue.

Physician Sara Josephine Baker dies at New York February 22 at age 71.

The Alfred E. Smith Dinner inaugurated at the Waldorf-Astoria Hotel October 4 by Archbishop Spellman raises funds for a memorial wing at St. Vincent's Hospital. Spellman has been Catholic vicar to the armed forces during the war and made himself the best-known Catholic prelate in America. The dinner will become an annual gathering of political figures, and proceeds in future years will go to benefit health care not only at St. Vincent's but at other institutions as well.

Members of the Lubavitcher Hasidic sect who have survived the Holocaust in Poland and elsewhere in Eastern Europe settle in Brooklyn's Crown Heights section under the leadership of Rebbe Joseph I. Schneersohn (*see* 1940; Schneerson, 1950).

New York Post owner Dorothy Schiff and her husband, Theodore O. Thackrey, buy the *Bronx Home News* May 30 (*see* 1922). The paper has been publishing neighborhood editions in upper Manhattan, but circulation has fallen and the paper is losing money (*see* 1948).

Mayor La Guardia reads the Sunday comics over municipal radio station WNYC July 1 during a newspaper truckers' strike (*see* 1933). Sitting before the microphone without a coat or tie (the temperature is 95° F.), he says, "Gather round, children, and I will tell you about Dick Tracy." Saying there is no reason for children to suffer because of "a squabble among grown-ups," he uses different voices to imitate those of "Little Orphan Annie" and other characters, does so again July 8, and the station receives a Peabody Award for public service.

Commentary magazine begins publication at New York in November. Started by the American Jewish Committee and edited by Elliot E. Cohen, the liberal monthly will take on a strongly right-wing tone following Cohen's suicide in 1959 (*see* Podhoretz, 1960).

Ballpoint pens go on sale October 29 at Gimbels on Greeley Square. Chicago promotor Milton Reynolds, 53, has seen such a pen while visiting Buenos Aires on business in June, developed a pen different enough to get around existing patents, gone into production October 6, and is producing 70 pens per day. Gimbels quickly sells out at $12.50 each with the initial promise that the pens will write underwater. Some banks suggest that ballpoint pen signatures may not be legal, but the new pens do not leak at high altitudes and will make it practical to handwrite multicopy business and government forms using carbon paper.

Bantam Books is founded by New York-born publisher Ian (Keith) Ballantine, 29, whose paperback house will compete with Pocket Books, Avon Books, and Popular Library (*see* 1939; 1941; 1942).

Nonfiction: *Portrait of New Netherland* by Ellis L. Raesly; *Black Boy* (autobiography) by Richard Wright.

Fiction: *Mr. Tutt Finds a Way* by Arthur Train, who dies of cancer at Memorial Hospital December 22 at age 70.

Juvenile: *Stuart Little* by E. B. White of The *New Yorker* magazine, whose protagonist is a mouse (illustrations by New York-born artist Garth [Montgomery] Williams, 33).

 Sculpture: *The Hotel Eden* by Joseph Cornell.

 Photographs: *Naked City* by Polish-born New York freelance photographer Weegee (Arthur H. Fellig), 46, whose carefully staged 1943 pictures "The Critic" and "Opening Night at the Opera" (depicting Mrs. George Washington Kavanaugh and Lady Deisch with a ragged woman onlooker) have been widely reprinted. Weegee came to New York with his parents at age 10, began his career on the Lower East Side by purchasing a camera and a pony and photographing youngsters on weekends, later slept in Bryant Park while he worked in the Automat and played a violin at movie houses (before talkies), and eventually opened a studio near Bowling Green. He adopted his nickname (derived phonetically from a Ouija board) about 5 years ago while working for the afternoon tabloid *PM* and since 1938 has been the only press photographer with a permit to have a police radio in his car, enabling him to reach the scenes of accidents, fires, and violent crimes before any of his competitors (he has also taken Peeping Tom shots of lovers in twos and threes on the Coney Island beach at night, transvestites being hustled out of paddy wagons, car crashes, and other scenes of the unsanitary city). Operating out of a $17-per-month room at Centre Street and Market Place in back of police headquarters, Weegee could move quickly in response to teletypes and police radio reports, he has kept his photographic equipment (and savings) in an old Chevrolet and has been using his Speed Graphic to make photographs that he has sold to newspapers and other periodicals. His new book of pictures with text brings him assignments from fashion magazines.

 Theater: *The Hasty Heart* by Louisville, Ky.-born playwright John Patrick (originally John Patrick Goggan), 39, 1/3 at the Hudson Theater, with Rochester-born actor John Lund, 28, Zanesville, Ohio-born actor Richard Basehart, 30, 207 perfs.; *The Glass Menagerie* by Mississippi-born playwright Tennessee (originally Thomas Lanier) Williams, 34, 3/31 at the Plymouth Theater, with Laurette Taylor, Eddie Dowling, Julie Haydon, Anthony Ross (Rosenthal), 561 perfs. (Margo Jones, 31, has directed the play); *State of the Union* by Howard Lindsay and Russel Crouse 11/14 at the Hudson

Theater, with Indiana-born actor Myron McCormick, 38, Ralph Bellamy, 765 perfs.; *Dream Girl* by Elmer Rice 12/14 at the Coronet Theater, with Massachusetts-born actor Wendell Corey, 31, Betty Field (Mrs. Rice), 348 perfs.; *Home of the Brave* by New York-born playwright Arthur Laurents, 27, 12/27 at the Belasco Theater, with Henry Barnard, Alan Baxter in a drama about anti-Semitism in the army, 69 perfs.

Radio: *Arthur Godfrey Time* 4/30 on CBS with New York-born emcee Godfrey, 41, who attracts listeners with his insouciance but offends potential sponsors by not taking their commercials seriously (to 4/30/1972); *The Theatre Guild on the Air* 9/9 on ABC with plays adapted for radio (to 1954); *Meet the Press* 10/5 on WOR-Muutal with New York-born *American Mercury* magazine publisher Lawrence E. (Edmund) Spivak, 44, moderating a "spontaneous, unrehearsed weekly news conference of the air" produced by former *Tampa Tribune* reporter Martha Rountree, 30, who moved to New York in 1938. Journalists interview prominent news figures on the show, which will go on NBC television beginning in November 1947 and be moderated by Spivak until November 1975.

Films: Billy Wilder's *The Lost Weekend* with Ray Milland, Jane Wyman in a grim tale of alcoholism. Also: Wallace Fox's *The Docks of New York* with Leo Gorcey, Huntz Hall in an inferior remake of the 1928 silent classic; Richard Thorpe's *Her Highness and the Bellboy* with Hedy Lamarr, Robert Walker; Henry Hathaway's *The House on 92nd Street* with William Eythe, Lloyd Nolan, Signe Hasso is about Nazi agents operating in New York City; Vincent Sherman's *Mr. Skeffington* with Bette Davis, Claude Rains, Walter Abel; Robert Z. Leonard's *Weekend at the Waldorf* with Ginger Rogers, Lana Turner, Walter Pidgeon, Van Johnson, Edward Arnold, Robert Benchley, Keenan Wynn.

Comedian Robert Benchley dies of complications from cirrhosis of the liver at New York November 21 at age 56.

 Film musicals: Leo McCarey's *Going My Way* with Bing Crosby, Barry Fitzgerald, Risë Stevens. Also: George Seaton's *Billy Rose's Diamond Horseshoe* with Betty Grable, Dick Haymes, Bensonhurst-born comedian Phil Silvers, 34, William Gaxton, music and lyrics by Harry Warren and Mack Gordon, songs that include "The More I See You," "I Wish I Knew;" Felix Feist's *George White's Scandals* with Jean Davis, Jack Haley; George Marshall's *Incendiary Blonde* with Betty Hutton as Prohibition-era nightclub hostess Texas Guinan; Irving Rapper's *Rhapsody in Blue* with

New York-born actor Robert Alda (originally Alphonso d'Abruzzo), 31 (as the late George Gershwin), Joan Leslie, Alexis Smith, Oscar Levant, Charles Coburn, Morris Carnovsky; Hal Walker's *The Stork Club* with Betty Hutton, Barry Fitzgerald.

Broadway musicals: *Up in Central Park* 1/27 at the Century Theater, with music by Sigmund Romberg, book by Dorothy Fields, now 39, and her brother Herbert, lyrics by Dorothy, songs that include "Big Back Yard," "Carousel in the Park," 504 perfs.; *Carousel* 4/19 at the Majestic Theater, with Santa Ana, Calif.-born singer John Raitt, 28, as Billy Bigelow (Liliom), Alamogordo, N.M.-born singer Jan Clayton, 19, as Julie Jordan, music by Richard Rodgers, lyrics by Oscar Hammerstein II, book based on the 1909 Ferenc Molnár play *Liliom*, songs that include "If I Loved You," "June Is Bustin' Out All Over," "Soliloquy," "You'll Never Walk Alone," 890 perfs.; *Billion Dollar Baby* 12/21 at the Alvin Theater, with Philadelphia-born dancer Joan McCracken, 22, New York-born actress Mitzi Green (originally Elizabeth Keno), 25, baritone Bill Tabbert, music by Morton Gould, lyrics by Betty Comden and Adolph Green, choreography by Jerome Robbins, 219 perfs.

Ballet: *Undertow* 4/10 at the Metropolitan Opera House, with Hugh Laing, Havana-born ballerina Alicia Alonso (originally Alicia Ernestina de la Caridad del Cobre Martinez Hoya), 23, music by New York-born composer William Schuman, 34, choreography by Antony Tudor.

The New York Philharmonic cancels its April 13 concert as it joins in mourning the death of the late President Roosevelt. It is the first such cancellation since the death of President Lincoln 80 years ago.

Popular song: "Carnegie Blues" by Duke Ellington.

Songwriter Al Dubin dies of a drug overdose at New York February 11 at age 54; Gus Edwards of a heart attack after 8 years' illness at Hollywood November 7 at age 64; Jerome Kern of a cerebral hemorrhage at Doctors Hospital November 11 at age 60.

 A gambling scheme to have Brooklyn College's basketball team lose to Akron at Madison Square Garden fails in early February (*see* 1949).

Jamaica Racetrack attracts a gate of 64,670 on Memorial Day, setting a state attendance record (*see* 1903; 1959).

Larry McPhail takes over general managership of the New York Yankees in January. McPhail introduced night baseball to the major leagues at Cincinnati and has obtained backing from Del Webb and Dan Topping, who join with him to pay $2.8 million for 97 percent of the stock in the team (McPhail will sell his one-third share to the other two partners for $2 million, about 10 times what he invested, and George Weiss will become general manager) (*see* 1964).

The *New York Herald Tribune* hires Wisconsin-born *Philadelphia Record* sportswriter Walter Wellesley "Red" Smith, 39, to produce a "Views of Sport" column that is soon syndicated nationwide. Smith departs from the tradition of sentiment and hero-worship that has characterized most sportswriting and his column will continue to appear in other papers after the demise of the *Trib* in 1967.

Frank Parker wins in men's singles at Forest Hills, Sarah Cooke in women's singles.

Circle Line sightseeing boats begin circling Manhattan with eight former Coast Guard cutters or landing craft that will remain in use for more than 50 years, starting their counterclockwise route from a Hudson River pier at 42nd Street.

The Park Avenue Association plants 29 cherry trees on the avenue's center islands between 49th and 96th streets as a memorial at Christmas. Mrs. Stephen Clark, the wife of a Singer Sewing Machine Co. heir, has lost a son overseas this year and comes up with the idea; other families who have lost sons or brothers in the war hold a ceremony with caroling at St. Bartholomew's Church. Evergreens will soon supplement the cherry trees, the ceremony will move to the Seventh Regiment Armory before settling at the Brick Presbyterian Church, and the lighted trees will become a holiday tradition.

The Rev. John M. Corridan of the Church of St. Francis Xavier in Chelsea takes up the fight against organized crime on the New York waterfront, starting a mission that will earn him the nickname "the waterfront priest" (*see* Films, 1954).

St. Louis-born Columbia sophomore Lucien Carr parties with his "beatnik" friends William S. Burroughs, 30, Allen Ginsberg, 18, and Jack Kerouac, 22, at the West End bar on Broadway between 113th and 114th streets the night of August 13, drinks too much, and at 3 o'clock the next morning stabs David Kammerer, 33, in the heart with his Boy Scout knife in Riverside Park and rolls the body into the Hudson River. Carr turns himself in, claims self-defense (Kammerer followed him to New York from St. Louis and was allegedly trying to rape him), pleads guilty to manslaughter, and will serve 2 years in an upstate reformatory before being pardoned by Gov. Dewey.

Architect Whitney Warren of Warren & Wetmore dies at New York Hospital January 24 at age 74. He has lived at 280 Park Avenue. Egerton Swartwout dies at New York Hospital February 18 at age 72. He has lived at the Yale Club.

Parks Commissioner Moses proposes turning Staten Island's Fresh Kills wetlands into parkland by using it as a garbage-disposal site to create landfill (*see* 1944; 1948).

Murray's Sturgeon Shop opens at Broadway and 89th Street (it will soon move to 2429 Broadway, at 90th Street) in competition with Barney Greengrass on Amsterdam Avenue (*see* 1929). Polish-born entrepreneur Murray Bernstein, 32, came to New York as a teenager to escape anti-Semitic violence, he has bought the shop from his friend Albert Newman, through whom he met his wife, Nettie (*née* Katz), in 1932, and he begins to build a following among politicians, songwriters, and others who are fond of smoked salmon, smoked sturgeon, sable, whitefish, bagels, ice-cold vodka, and the club-like atmosphere provided by Bernstein, whose family will own the shop until 1974.

P. J. Clarke's 65-year-old saloon on Third Avenue at 55th Street gets a boost from the Hollywood film *The Lost Weekend*, starring Ray Milland as an alcoholic. Except for its hamburger grill, the place is a drinking establishment, not a restaurant (although it does serve beef-barley soup and eggs Benedict), but Clarke will soon retire and his landlord, the Lavezzo family, will take over (*see* 1949).

The Russian Tea Room is acquired by former high-school chemistry teacher Sidney Kaye and other investors (*see* 1927). The RTR has been serving blinis, shashlik, and such since the 1930s, Kaye will buy out his partners in 1955 to become sole owner, and he will leave the restaurant's Christmas decorations up all year round to save labor and because "it looks so Russian." After Kaye's death in 1967 his second wife, Faith, a Broadway and TV actress, will take over, add glitz, and attract celebrities (*see* 1999).

Gino opens before the end of the war at 780 Lexington Avenue near 61st Street. Capri-born Waldorf-Astoria bartender Gino A. Circiello, 33, has enlisted the help of his friends Guy Avventuriero and Emilio Torre, the three have pooled their savings and obtained backing from Naples-born fabric and wallpaper manufacturer Franco Scalamandré to start the unpretentious Italian restaurant, paying a monthly rental of $400 for the premises; Scalamandré's wife, Flora, has designed a tomato-red wallpa-

per with a leaping zebra motif, Circiello buys a second-hand mahogany bar on the Bowery and installs 27 wood-topped tables, his partners will retire in 1980, he himself will retire in 1985, and Gino's (as everyone calls it) will survive into the next century without taking reservations or accepting credit cards (regulars will receive monthly bills in the mail).

1946 The United Nations General Assembly opens its first session January 10 at London with former Belgian premier Paul Henri Spaak, 46, as president (*see* 1945). Norwegian Socialist Trygve Lie, 49, is elected Secretary-General February 1, and the Security Council meets March 25 at Hunter College.

Former British prime minister Winston Churchill visits New York and receives a ticker-tape parade March 15.

An army, navy, and marine corps recruiting office opens in Times Square, where it will remain for more than 50 years.

Manhattan lawyer Jacob K. Javits, 42, wins election to Congress from the upper West Side. He will serve until 1955, supporting civil rights, social welfare, and health benefits. Born on the Lower East Side, Republican Javits will never establish residence in Washington, returning to his family at New York each weekend (*see* 1956).

Gov. Dewey wins reelection, securing 2,825,633 votes as compared with 2,138,482 for Sen. James Michael Mead, 60, of Buffalo, who has run on the Democratic, American Labor, and Liberal party tickets.

Former mayor James J. "Jimmy" Walker dies at New York November 18 at age 65; lawyer-diplomat Henry Morgenthau at New York November 25 at age 90, having remained to the end an outspoken critic of Zionism.

The UN General Assembly selects New York as permanent UN site December 5 (it has met in the city beginning October 23) and 9 days later accepts a gift of $8.5 million offered in December of last year by John D. Rockefeller, Jr. toward purchase of property on the East River for permanent headquarters. Chicago industrialist Henry Crown, 50, had invested $2 million to join with New York investors in buying the property with a view to reselling it; real estate developer William Zeckendorf, 41, and J. Clydesdale Cushman, 59, of Cushman & Wakefield had assembled the land for the site with help from Robert Moses, clearing away the Turtle Bay slaughterhouses and other industrial concerns that have occupied

155 buildings and employed 2,600 workers (*see* real estate [Secretariat Building], 1950).

$ An employment act passed by Congress February 20 declares that maximum employment must be the government's policy goal, but New York City's urban-renewal programs are beginning to drive out businesses that employ blue-collar workers, thereby changing the character of the city's workforce.

Labor leader Sidney Hillman dies at his Long Island home July 10 at age 59. He has been serving as a vice-chairman of the World Federation of Trade Unions since its founding last year.

President Truman issues an executive order November 9 lifting all wage and price controls except those on rents, sugar, and rice. The inflation that will continue for decades begins December 14 as Truman removes curbs on housing priorities and prices by executive order. President Roosevelt's inflation-control order of April 1943 kept prices from climbing more than 29 percent from 1939 to 1945 as compared with a 63 percent jump in the 1914 to 1918 period, but Truman is more worried about a possible postwar depression than about inflation.

Wall Street's 50-year-old Dow Jones Industrial Average reaches a post-1929 high of 212.50, but then falls back to 163.12. It closes December 31 at 172.20, down from 192.91 at the end of 1945.

$ Brooks Brothers is acquired by the Washington, D.C., retailer Garfinckel's, whose management will increase the menswear store's volume in the next 30 years from its present $5.6 million to more than $50 million. The 31-year-old main store at 346 Madison Avenue has opened branches at Boston, Newport, and Palm Beach; it will grow to have branches in many other cities as the Brooks sack suit and button-down (polo) collar become *de rigeur* in the U.S. establishment (*see* Campeau, 1986).

The Staten Island Ferry catches fire at the Battery January 17, killing three, injuring many more, and destroying the ferry house.

The Tunnel Authority created by Mayor La Guardia in 1936 is merged with the Triborough Bridge Authority to create a new agency headed by Robert Moses, who takes a dim view of tunnels.

U.S. troops seize the nation's railroads May 17 in the face of imminent strikes. A brief strike begins May 24, paralyzing New York and other cities; volunteers man commuter trains, service on subways and elevated trains is increased by 40 percent and they handle the increased traffic without difficulty, but

bus facilities are taxed beyond capacity, as are parking lots at outlying subway stations; taxi passengers share cabs, and motorists try to ease the problem by car-pooling; the strike ends when President Truman recommends wage boosts.

Grand Central Terminal reaches its height of volume following the May strike, despite the New York Connecting Bridge that since 1917 has increased traffic at Penn Station. The terminal has 63 million passengers passing through its gates each day to or from the 550 regular trains that arrive or depart 1 minute apart on average during the rush hours. Nearly 3,100 people—dispatchers, trainmasters, car repairmen, gatemen, ticket sellers, parcel room attendants (60), janitors (335), window washers, and cleaning women—are needed to run the terminal, whose 38 reservation clerks handle as many as 2,000 calls per hour; 16 information clerks answer as many as 20,000 questions per day; it has a blacksmith, a clock repairman, two physicians to staff the terminal's emergency hospital, and 285 redcaps. Penn Station handles nearly three times as many passengers, most of them Long Island Rail Road commuters; it has 335 redcaps and 20 information clerks (*see* 1949).

Texas-born stock manipulator Robert (Ralph) Young, 49, attracts attention by running full-page newspaper advertisements headlined, "A Hog Can Cross the Nation without Changing Trains, but You Can't." Young has become board chairman of Allegheny Corp. (*see* New York Central, 1954).

The pilot of a U.S. Army twin-engine C-45 Beechcraft en route to Newark from the South gets lost in a heavy mist May 10 and crashes into the 58th floor of the 70-story Bank of the Manhattan Company Building at 40 Wall Street, killing all five aboard, including a WAC officer. The impact smashes a hole 20 feet wide and 10 feet high, demolishing a window and sending pieces of brick and mortar hurtling down on Pine Street (the building has another entrance at 33 Pine), but even though an estimated 2,000 people are in the building and dozens are in the street below, no one is hurt except the occupants of the aircraft.

The Broadway trolley line of the Third Avenue Transit System makes its final run at midnight December 14 from 42nd Street and Fifth Avenue to the New York Times Tower in Times Square. The line began with horsecar service in 1895 and was soon converted to electric power; the new bus that replaces the trolley leads a procession up Broadway to Columbus Circle and back again to Times Square; regular bus service begins at 5:45 o'clock in the morning of December 15, but a bus takes up more space than a trolley car, creates more air pollution, has a life expectancy one-third as great, and makes more noise.

New York University acquires four blocks of tenements, loft buildings, garages, and lumber yards near the East River with a view toward developing the property into a hospital and medical center.

Archbishop Spellman is elected to the college of cardinals at Rome and becomes Francis Cardinal Spellman.

Xerography wins support from the Rochester firm Haloid Co., whose research director John H. Dessauer has seen an article on "electrophotography" by Chester Carlson in a July 1944 issue of *Radio News* (*see* 1938). Haloid invests $10,000 to acquire production rights, and within 6 years the firm will raise more than $3.5 million to develop what will be called the Xerox copier (*see* 1960).

New York Daily News publisher Capt. Joseph Medill Patterson dies of a liver ailment at Doctors Hospital May 26 at age 67.

The Ford Modeling Agency is founded by New York–born Arnold Constable copywriter Eileen Ford (*née* Otte), 24, who starts with two clients and will have 34 by 1948 as she bargains with advertising agencies and photographers to get better deals for her models, collecting their fees, deducting a 20 percent commission (half of it from whomever hired the model), and setting new standards for the industry. A Barnard College graduate, she eloped in November 1944 with Notre Dame football player Gerard "Jerry" Ford, he works for her family's credit-rating business but will quit in a few years to join her in the agency, and by 1970 it will be representing 180 models and grossing $5 million per year.

Scientific American magazine is acquired after 101 years of publication by former LIFE magazine science editor Gerard Piel, 31, who will be joined by LIFE staffmen Dennis Flanagan, 27, and Donald H. Miller, Jr. in broadening the appeal of the monthly as science grows in its impact on the lives and careers of more Americans.

Family Circle magazine begins monthly publication at New York in September after 14 years as a weekly supermarket giveaway. The cover price is 5¢, the September issue has 96 pages, some chains drop the magazine, others accept it as a profit-making item.

Farrar, Straus is founded at New York by former Farrar & Rinehart partner John C. Farrar, now 50 (*see* 1929), with backing from millionaire Roger W.

Straus, 29. The new publishing house will become, in turn, Farrar, Straus & Young, Farrar, Straus and Cudahy, and Farrar, Straus & Giroux as it develops a reputation for independence and quality (*see* 1994; Giroux, 1963).

Fiction: *Memoirs of Hecate County* (stories) by *New Yorker* book critic-novelist Edmund Wilson, now 51; *Ladders to Fire* by Paris-born New York novelist Anaïs Nin, 43, who came to New York with her mother and brother in 1914 (her father had abandoned the family), lived on the first floor of a rooming house at 158 West 75th Street until 1919, returned to Paris after World War I, gained notoriety in 1934 with her introduction to Henry Miller's novel *Tropic of Cancer*, and has been back in New York since 1940; *The Big Clock* by Kenneth Fearing; *Mr. Blandings Builds His Dream House* by *Fortune* magazine editor Eric Hodgins, 46.

Poetry: *Lord Weary's Castle* by Boston-born former New York publishing house editorial assistant Robert (Traill Spence) Lowell (Jr.), 29.

Painting: *Vessels of Magic* by Russian-born New York abstractionist Mark Rothko (originally Marcus Rothkovich), 42; *Eyes in the Heat* by Jackson Pollock; *Genesis—The Break* by Lower East Side-born abstract expressionist Barnett (originally Baruch) Newman, 41; *Self-Portrait* by Brooklyn-born painter Elaine (Marie) de Kooning (*née* Fried), 27, who at age 19 took private lessons from Dutch-born painter Willem de Kooning, moved into his West 22nd Street studio 2 years later, and married him 3 years ago. Joseph Stella dies at New York November 5 at age 69; Arthur Dove at Huntington, L.I., November 23 at age 66.

The Safani Gallery opens at 960 Madison Avenue, near 75th Street. Persian-born art dealer Edward Safani, 34, is an expert in Islamic art, ancient glass, and Near Eastern art.

Photographer Alfred Stieglitz dies at New York July 13 at age 82, survived by his painter wife, Georgia O'Keeffe, now 58.

Theater: *O Mistress Mine* (*Love in Idleness*) by English playwright Terence Rattigan, 35, 1/28 at the Empire Theater (it opened at London in December 1944), with Alfred Lunt, Lynn Fontanne, Dick Van Patten, 451 perfs.; *Born Yesterday* by Rochester-born playwright-screenwriter-director Garson Kanin, 34, 2/4 at the Lyceum Theater, with New York-born actress Judy Holliday (originally Judith Tuvim), 22, Philadelphia-born actor Paul Douglas, 38, Hartford, Conn.-born actor Gary Merrill, 30, 1,642 perfs.; *Whitman Avenue* by Wisconsin-born playwright Maxine

Wood (originally Maxine Flora Finsterwald), 36, 6/5 at the Cort Theater, with Canada Lee, Vivian Baber in a play about discriminatory housing practices, 148 perfs.; *The Heiress* by Ruth and Augustus Goetz (who have adapted the 1881 Henry James novel *Washington Square*) 9/29 at the Biltmore Theater, with Wendy Hiller, Basil Rathbone, Oregon-born actor Peter Cookson, 34, Patricia Collinge, 410 perfs.; *The Iceman Cometh* by Eugene O'Neill 10/9 at the Martin Beck Theater, with Gloucester City, N.J.-born actor James Barton, 55, Carl Benton Reid, 52, Dudley Digges in a play based on Jimmy-the-Priest's West Side bar and rooming house, "a cheap gin mill of the five-cent whiskey, last resort variety situated on downtown West Side of New York," where O'Neill spent a lot of time in his youth, 136 perfs.; *Joan of Lorraine* by Maxwell Anderson 11/18 at the Alvin Theater, with Stockholm-born actress Ingrid Bergman, 31, Chicago-born actor Sam Wanamaker, 27, as the director of a star playing the role of Joan of Arc (Margo Jones is the real play's director), 201 perfs.; *Another Part of the Forest* by Lillian Hellman 11/20 at the Fulton Theater, with Kentucky-born actress Patricia Neal, 20, Baltimore-born actress Mildred Dunnock, 40, 182 perfs.

The American Repertory Theater is founded by New York-born actress-director-producer Margaret Webster, 41 (daughter of English Shakespearean actor Ben Webster and Dame May Whitty), director-producer Cheryl Crawford, now 44, and Eva Le Gallienne, now 48, but will not survive for long (*see* Shakespeare Theater, 1948).

Playwright Edward Sheldon dies of a heart attack at his 35 East 84th Street home April 1 at age 60 (almost totally paralyzed since 1925 and totally blind since 1931, he has remained cheerful through it all); actress Antoinette Perry dies of a heart attack at her 510 Park Avenue apartment June 28 at age 68 and is buried in Woodlawn Cemetery (*see* Tony Award, 1947); playwright Channing Pollock dies of a cerebral hemorrhage at Shoreham, L.I., August 17 at age 66; actress Laurette Taylor of a coronary thrombosis at her New York home December 7 at age 62; Broadway columnist Damon Runyon of throat cancer at Memorial Hospital December 10 at age 62 (he has been living at the Hotel Buckingham, northwest corner 57th Street and Sixth Avenue, but the cancer has made his speech almost unintelligible for the past year).

Radio talent-show emcee Major Edward L. Bowes dies June 13 at Rumson, N.J., on the eve of his 72nd birthday. He gave up his show in 1943 when earnings dwindled.

Films: Jean Negulesco's *Humoresque* with Joan Crawford, John Garfield, Oscar Levant; Norman Z. McLeod's *The Kid from Brooklyn* with Danny Kaye, Virginia Mayo, Vera-Ellen; David Butler's *Two Guys from Milwaukee* with Dennis Morgan, Jack Carson, Joan Leslie, Janis Paige. Also: Norman Taurog's *The Hoodlum Saint* with William Powell, Esther Williams, Angela Lansbury, James Gleason.

Film musical: Henry Koster's *Two Sisters from Boston* with Kathryn Grayson and June Allyson as singers who go to work in Jimmy Durante's Bowery saloon at the turn of the century.

Broadway musicals: *Lute Song* 2/6 at the Plymouth Theater, with Texas-born singer-actress Mary Martin, 31, Russian-born singer-actor Yul Brynner, 25, music by Brooklyn-born engineer-composer Raymond Scott (originally Harry Warnow), 37, lyrics by Bernard Harrigan, songs that include "Mountain High, Valley Low," 142 perfs.; *St. Louis Woman* 3/30 at the Martin Beck Theater, with Newport News, Va.-born singer Pearl Bailey, 28, heading an all-black cast, book based on an unpublished play by the late Countee Cullen, music by Harold Arlen, lyrics by Johnny Mercer, songs that include "Come Rain or Come Shine," "Any Place I Hang My Hat Is Home," and "I Had Myself a True Love," 113 perfs.; *Call Me Mister* 4/18 at the National Theater, with Betty Garrett, music and lyrics by Harold Rome, book by Arnold Auerbach and Arnold Horwitt, songs that include "South America, Take It Away," 734 perfs.; *Annie Get Your Gun* 5/16 at the Imperial Theater, with Ethel Merman, Ray Middleton, book based on the life of markswoman Phoebe "Annie Oakley" Mozee of Buffalo Bill's Wild West Show, music and lyrics by Irving Berlin, songs that include "Anything You Can Do," "Doin' What Comes Naturally," "The Girl That I Marry," "You Can't Get a Man with a Gun," "I Got the Sun in the Morning," "There's No Business Like Show Business," 1,147 perfs.; *Park Avenue* 11/4 at the Shubert Theater, with Leonora Corbett, Arthur Margetson, music by Arthur Schwartz, lyrics by Ira Gershwin, choreography by Helen Tamiris, book by Nunnally Johnson and George S. Kaufman, sets by Donald Oenslager, 72 perfs.; *Beggar's Holiday* 12/26 at the Broadway Theater, with Alfred Drake, Brooklyn-born comedian Samuel Joel "Zero" Mostel, 31, Baltimore-born dancer Avon Long, 36, Brooklyn-born dancer Herbert Ross, 19, music by Duke Ellington, book and lyrics by John LaTouche, 111 perfs.

Opera: *The Medium* 5/8 at Columbia University's Brander Matthew Theater, with music by Italian-born composer Gian-Carlo Menotti, 34.

Ballet: *The Serpent Heart* 5/10 at Columbia University's McMillin Theater, with Martha Graham, music by Samuel Barber, choreography by Graham; *The Four Temperaments* 11/20 at the Central High School of the Needle Trades, with Gisella Caccialanza, Tanaquil LeClerq, Todd Bolender, music by Paul Hindemith, choreography by George Balanchine.

The New York City Ballet Company has its beginnings in the Ballet Society, founded by George Balanchine and Lincoln Kirstein of 1934 School of American Ballet fame; they will rename the Society in 1948.

The Juilliard Quartet is founded as a resident string group by the Juilliard School's new president William Schuman, now 35.

Popular songs: "New York's My Home" by Gordon Jenkins; "I Wanna Go to City College" by Sammy Fain, lyrics by George Marion, Jr.

Songwriter Harry Von Tilzer dies in his sleep at New York January 10 at age 73, having lived in recent years at the Hotel Woodward.

The National Basketball Associaton (NBA) has its beginnings in the Basketball Association of America, organized by professional teams that include the New York Knickerbockers, but college basketball will continue for years to be what players and fans consider the "big-time" sport (*see* 1948).

The New York Yankees play their first night game at the Stadium May 28, losing to the Washington Senators.

Jack Kramer, 24, wins in men's singles at Forest Hills, Pauline Betz in women's singles.

Joe Louis defeats challenger Billy Conn in a heavyweight title match at Yankee Stadium June 19 and defeats challenger Tami Mauriello at the Stadium September 18. Middleweight Tony Zale defeats Rocky Graziano at the Stadium September 17; former Gary, Ind., steelworker Zale (originally Anthony Florian Zaleski), 32, defends his championship (*see* 1947).

Estée Lauder makes her first sale to Saks Fifth Avenue. Born Josephine Esther Mentzer in Corona, Queens, the 38-year-old beautician has had concessions at beauty salons selling face creams made by an uncle; she and her husband, Joseph, 54, have changed their name from Lauter, their 13-year-old son Leonard has helped them since age 10 collecting cash from the salons, and they open offices at 501 Madison Avenue, converting a West 64th Street restaurant into a factory. Unable even to approach the advertising budgets of older, larger competitors, they distribute free samples. Young Leonard will get a bachelor's degree from the University of Pennsylvania's Wharton School, work for the company full-time beginning in 1958, head it beginning in 1972, and manufacture and market cosmetics whose sales will grow to exceed those of Elizabeth Arden, Helena Rubinstein, or Revlon (*see* Aramis, 1964).

New York fashion designer Ceil Chapman (*née* Mitchell), 32, wins the American Fashion Critics' Award. Her elaborate, feminine styles have attracted customers who include Greer Garson and Mary Martin. The repeal of U.S. order L85 October 19 permits dressmakers to lengthen skirts and ends wartime austerity.

Swingline Co. is incorporated at New York under the name Speed Products Co. (*see* Linsky, 1925). Using the facilities of its 160,000-square-foot plant at Long Island City, the firm made staplers with wooden bases to save metal during World War II but will soon meld its ramheads with its tops to create a moving cover, pioneer in making staplers easier to use and less costly, and in 1956 change its name to Swingline at the suggestion of founder Jack Linsky's Kiev-born wife, Belle. It will remain at Long Island City until 1999, when all production will be moved to Mexico.

Gov. Dewey announces January 2 that Charles "Lucky" Luciano will be released and paroled to his native Sicily (*see* 1941). Luciano has provided help during the war to provide protection from German saboteurs on New York's docks and has sent word to the Mafia in Sicily to help U.S. invasion forces; released from Great Meadow Prison February 2 and taken to Ellis Island, he boards the S.S. *Laura Keene* February 9, receives homage at a bon voyage party, and leaves February 10 with an envelope containing $300,000 to $400,000 in cash collected for him as a going-away gift by fellow mobsters. Back in Italy he obtains two passports and in October boards a freighter that takes him to Caracas, whence he flies to Mexico City, where he books a private plane for a flight to Havana.

The city's homicide rate will rise in the next 5 years to 4.7 per 100,000, up from 3.5 per 100,000 in the last 5 (*see* 1961).

Diesel Construction Co. is founded by New York entrepreneurs Saul Lautenberg and Erwin (Service) Wolfson, 44, who 10 years ago started the Diesel Electric Co. to install generating equipment in office buildings. The firm will develop and build office buildings and hotels, Cincinnati-born Wolfson will succeed to the presidency following Lautenberg's death in 1952, and Diesel will be a major factor in Manhattan development until Wolfson's own death in 1962.

The Fresh Meadows housing development in Queens has its beginnings April 1, when New York Life Insurance Co. buys land near the intersection of Horace Harding Boulevard and 188th Street and engages the architectural firm Voorhees, Walker, Foley and Smith (*see* golf course, 1923). Construction begins July 3 (*see* 1949).

Mayor O'Dwyer announces May 20 that he will not hesitate to take closed buildings away from their owners in condemnation proceedings to push forward the city's program for remodeling tenements to house 10,000 families. Gov. Dewey has initiated a state-sponsored program to convert barracks at Fort Tilden, Queens, into housing for veterans.

Window-unit air conditioners proliferate in the city as Carrier Corp. and a flock of competitors make it possible for New Yorkers to remain in their apartments through July and August without going to summer vacation resorts (*see* Rivoli Theater, 1925). Those who cannot afford the units often go to movie theaters just to escape the heat.

The Knickerbocker Ice Plant at the corner of 184th Street and Amsterdam Avenue burns down December 11, killing 37 people.

Congress votes August 12 to establish Castle Clinton National Monument at the Battery. The immigrant receiving station from 1855 to 1890 (after decades as a fortress and then a theater), later the Aquarium, its upper story and roof have been removed along with some 19th century additions; it will not reopen to the public until the summer of 1975.

1947 A conference of studio executives meeting at the Waldorf-Astoria Hotel compiles a "Hollywood Black List" of alleged communist sympathizers, naming an estimated 300 writers, directors, actors, and others known or suspected to have Communist Party affiliations or of having invoked the Fifth Amendment against self-incrimination when questioned by the House Committee to Investigate Un-American Activities.

Former governor Charles S. Whitman dies of a heart attack at the University Club on Fifth Avenue March 29 at age 78.

Former mayor Fiorello H. La Guardia dies of pancreatic cancer in his $40,000 Riverdale house September 20 at age 64, firehouse gongs sound the 5-5-5-5 signal meaning that a fireman has died, La

Guardia is buried at Woodlawn Cemetery in the Bronx after his body has lain in state at the Cathedral of St. John the Divine, the house and $8,000 in war bonds comprise his entire estate, and President Truman writes the "Little Flower's" widow that her husband was as "incorruptible as the sun."

The Taft-Hartley Act restricts organized labor's power to strike. Enacted June 23 over President Truman's veto, it outlaws the closed shop that requires that employers hire only union members, prohibits use of union funds for political purposes, introduces an 80-day "cooling off" period before a strike or lockout can begin, and empowers the government to obtain injunctions where strikes "will imperil the national health or safety" if allowed to occur or continue. New York City nevertheless has strikes in October that block distribution of bread and milk and halt construction of apartment houses, bridges, and tunnels. The Congdon-Wadlin Act adopted by the state legislature at Albany prohibits strikes by public-sector employees, but police, sanitation workers, teachers, and transit workers will strike nevertheless, and the penalties mandated by the new law are so extreme that they will rarely be applied (*see* politics [Taylor Law], 1967).

The J. M. Kaplan Fund is founded in June by philanthropist Jacob M. Kaplan, whose family foundation will benefit many aspects of New York life (*see* food, 1933).

Henry Ford dies at Dearborn, Mich., April 7 at age 83; his will leaves 90 percent of his Ford Motor Company stock to the Ford Foundation (*see* Edsel Ford, 1943). The federal tax paid by Ford's heirs amounts to only $21 million on a taxable estate of $70 million since the bulk of the $625 million fortune has been placed tax free in the Ford Foundation, making it the richest philanthropic organization in the history of the world. Ford's will provides the foundation with more funds for useful projects in education and other fields.

The East Side Chamber of Commerce weighs the question of changing the name of the Bowery, long since a disreputable thoroughfare noted for down-and-out winos. Sammy Fuchs, now 43, has operated Sammy's Bowery Follies since 1934 and says, "You can put a new suit on a bum but he's still a bum. In the same way, you're not going to improve the Bowery just by changing the name. The only way we can help is to raise funds to send the smoke hounds back to their homes or send them to a farm for a year or so to cure them." Known since last year as the Mayor of the Bowery, Fuchs has handed money out freely, providing free meals (Thanksgiving has long been the occasion for a free turkey dinner at Sammy's), buying clothes, paying for a room at a decent hotel, and providing job leads.

Wall Street's Dow Jones Industrial Average closes December 31 at 181.16, up from 172.20 at the end of 1946.

Best & Co. moves into a 12-story Fifth Avenue building at the northeast corner of 51st Street, just north of St. Patrick's Cathedral, on a site formerly occupied by the Union Club (see 1879). Now a major retailer of women's and girls' clothing for the carriage trade, it has been headed since the death of cofounder Albert Best by Philip LeBoutillier, who continues its famed Lilliputian Bazaar for layettes, children's clothes, perambulators, and the like (see 1970).

Macy's Thanksgiving Day parade November 27 leaves Broadway snowed under with an estimated 12.4 million tons of paper, according to Sanitation Department estimates.

Subway and elevated ridership in the city peaks at more than 2 billion, up from 1.9 billion plus in 1943 (see fare increase, 1948).

The Veterans Administration Medical Center opens at 800 Poly Place, Brooklyn, with 750 beds to treat wounded veterans of World War II.

Members of the 76-year-old Hungarian Hasidic sect known as Satmars settle in Brooklyn's Williamsburg section under the leadership of their Rebbe Joel Teitelbaum, 61, who started his own Hasidic movement 15 years ago in the Carpatho-Russian town of Satmar (Satu Mare) and escaped from the Bergen-Belsen concentration camp, making his way to Switzerland and Palestine. Some of his followers have preceded him, taking up residence on and near Bedford Avenue (see Lubavitchers, 1945). Vehemently opposed to Zionism, the Satmars will grow to become the city's largest Hasidic group. Like the Lubavitchers but unlike earlier Jewish immigrants, they are determined to resist losing their identity and become "Americanized:" their beards, *peyes* (long sidelocks), and broad-brimmed black fur hats will make men of the community conspicuous, their wives will shave their heads and wear wigs, and they will segregate their children by gender beginning at age 3 or 4. Rabbi Teitelbaum will lead the group until his death in 1979 at age 93, and Williamsburg's Hasidic community will grow in the next 50 years to number an estimated 40,000, with Satmars constituting the most sizeable group.

The 43-year-old Jewish Museum moves May 8 into the Fifth Avenue mansion built for banker Felix M. Warburg in 1908. An adjacent building will be added in 1963.

Brooklyn-born CCNY graduate Stanley H. Kaplan, 29, begins preparing high-school students for the College Entrance Examination Board's Scholastic Aptitude Test (S.A.T.) (see 1926). An alumnus of James Madison High School, Kaplan added the H. to his name as a college sophomore when he received a C in biology and showed his professor that the grade was for another Stanley Kaplan whereas he deserved an A. Kaplan began a tutoring service (the Stanley H. Kaplan Educational Center) 8 years ago in the basement of his immigrant parents' Flatbush home on Avenue K, a Coney Island student has come to him with the S.A.T. that is just now coming into wider use for college applicants, and when she aces the exam she tells all her friends about Kaplan, who will marry Rita Gwirtzman in 1951, move to a two-story house on Bedford Avenue, divide its basement into classrooms, and later rent a podiatrist's office near King's Highway at the Brighton Beach subway stop, charging substantial fees for his services. Educators will insist that the S.A.T. is "uncoachable" and disparage Kaplan as the "cram king," but his students will routinely do so well on the tests that he will go national in the 1970s and become a multi-millionaire (see 1984).

New York Law School reopens after a 6-year hiatus (see 1891). Closed in 1941 for reasons related to the Depression and the European war, its administrators are encouraged by the G.I. Bill to take space at 244 William Street and resume classes. It will move in 1962 to 57 Worth Street, take over three adjacent buildings, and by 1991 have 913 full-time and 468 part-time students with a faculty of 50 full-time and 55 adjunct faculty members.

The United Nations International School opens on First Avenue at 51st Street to educate children of UN personnel but will soon accept local boys and girls, aged 5 to 18, as enrollment grows to 1,461, with more than 100 nationalities represented. The school will prepare students for the Baccalaureate as well as for U.S. college entrance exams (see 1973).

Baltimore-born Brearley School headmistress Millicent McIntosh (née Carey), 48, leaves to accept a position as dean at Barnard College, where she replaces Virginia C. Gildersleeve, now 70, who has been dean since 1911; McIntosh has headed Brearley since 1930 and will become Barnard's first woman president (when her title is changed), remaining in the position until 1962.

Nicholas Murray Butler dies at New York December 4 at age 85. He retired from Columbia University 2 years ago after 43 years as its president.

The 28-year-old *Daily News* reaches a circulation peak of 2.4 million. Readership of the tabloid will decline beginning next year but it will remain the most widely read paper in America.

The New American Library publishing house is founded at New York by Kurt Enoch and former Penguin Books executive Victor Weybright, 44, who adopt the slogan "Good Reading for the Millions," adopt the imprint *Mentor* for their line of classic and serious nonfiction books, use *Signet* as the imprint for their fiction and reference books, and break the 25¢ paperback price limit by charging 50¢ for "double volumes."

Nonfiction: *Howe and Hummel: Their True and Scandalous History* by Jersey City-born *New Yorker* staff writer Richard (Halworth) Rovere, 32; *Nightstick: The Autobiography of Lewis J. Valentine* by the former city police commissioner; *You're the Boss* by former Bronx County Democratic Party leader Edward J. Flynn, now 56.

Fiction: *Gentleman's Agreement* by New York-born novelist Laura Zametkin Hobson, 47, examines the covert anti-Semitic practices institutionalized in U.S. society; *Aurora Dawn* by Bronx-born radio scriptwriter Herman Wouk, 32; *Three Rooms in Manhattan (Trois Chambres à Manhattan)* by Belgian novelist Georges (Jacques Christian) Simenon, 43.

Author Willa Cather dies of a cerebral hemorrhage at her 570 Park Avenue apartment April 24 at age 73. Her will stipulates that none of her books may be issued in paperback, and none will be for some decades.

Poet Countee Cullen dies of uremic poisoning at New York January 9 at age 42 and is buried at Woodlawn Cemetery.

Painting: *Y* by North Dakota-born New York painter Clyfford Still, 41; *Full Fathom Five* by Jackson Pollock; *Promenade* (oil on panel) by Lee Krasner, who 2 years ago married Jackson Pollock.

The School of Visual Arts has its beginnings in the School for Cartoonists and Illustrators founded at New York by Silas H. Rhodes and Burne Hogart. The private school will change its name in 1956 and occupy large premises at 209 East 23rd Street, with courses given by working artists, art directors, designers, photographers, and filmmakers. Enrollment will grow to 6,200, making it the nation's largest independent art school.

Sculpture: an equestrian bronze statue of the 14th-15th century Polish king Jagiello (Wladyslaw II) by Polish-born sculptor Stanislaw Ostrowski, 67, is unveiled east of Central Park's Belvedere Lake north of the 79th Street transverse road.

The 9-year-old Museum of Costume Art moves to the Metropolitan Museum of Art and becomes the museum's Costume Institute (*see* benefit party, 1948).

Magnum Photos, Inc. is incorporated May 22 in Manhattan. Hungarian-born photographer Robert Capa (originally André Friedmann), 35; French photographer Henri Cartier-Bresson, 38; Berlin-born Paris photographer Gisèle Freund, 38; George Rodger; Polish-born David "Chim" Seymour, 35; and William Vandivert met in April at the Museum of Modern Art's penthouse restaurant to plan the world's first co-operative of freelance photographers; Eve Arnold, Burton S. Glinn, Erich Hartmann, Erich Lessing, and Dennis Stock will join in 1951.

Theater: *All My Sons* by New York-born playwright Arthur Miller, 32, 1/29 at the Coronet Theater, with Hartford-born actor Ed Begley, 46, 328 perfs.; *Command Decision* by Des Moines-born playwright William Wister Haines, 39, 10/1 at the Fulton Theater, with White Plains-born actor James (Allen) Whitmore, 26, Paul Kelly, 408 perfs.; *Medea* by California poet Robinson Jeffers, 60, 10/20 at the National Theater, with Judith Anderson, Shakespearean actor John Gielgud, 43, Florence Reed, 214 perfs.; *Happy Birthday* by California-born Hollywood scriptwriter Anita Loos, now 50, 11/2 at the Broadhurst Theater, with Helen Hayes as a drab Newark librarian who comes to life in a barroom, 564 perfs.; *A Streetcar Named Desire* by Tennessee Williams 12/3 at the Ethel Barrymore Theater, with Marlon Brando as Stanley Kowalski, Jessica Tandy as Blanche DuBois, Detroit-born actress Kim Hunter (originally Janet Cole), 25, Karl Malden, 855 perfs.

The Actors Studio is founded October 5 in a former Presbyterian church built in 1859 at 432 West 44th Street. Former Group Theater members Cheryl Crawford, Elia Kazan, and Robert "Bobby" Lewis, now 38, have launched the project to help actors develop their craft. Kazan teaches acting fundamentals to a group of 15; Lewis gives an advanced class on the top floor of the Union Methodist Church in West 48th Street to 20 students who include Marlon Brando, Montgomery Clift, Mildred Dunnock, Tom Ewell, John Forsythe, Kim Hunter, Anne Jackson, Sidney Lumet, Karl Malden, E. G. Marshall, Kevin

McCarthy, Patricia Neal, William Redfield, Jerome Robbins, Maureen Stapleton, Eli Wallach, and David Wayne. Beginning in 1951 the Studio will engage actor-director Lee Strasberg, now 46, who will serve as artistic director until his death in 1982.

Tony Awards are established by the American Theatre Wing to honor outstanding Broadway plays, directors, performers, scenic designers, costumers, etc. The name *Tony* honors the late Antoinette Perry, who headed the Theatre Wing during World War II; the awards rival the Oscars given since 1928 by the Motion Picture Academy of Arts and Sciences.

Actor Earle Larimore dies at his New York apartment October 22 at age 48; Dudley Digges of a stroke at his New York home October 24 at age 68.

Television: *Meet the Press* 11/6 on NBC with Lawrence Spivak as moderator (*see* radio, 1945).

Films: Otto Preminger's *Daisy Kenyon* with Joan Crawford, Dana Andrews, Henry Fonda; Irving Rapper's *Deception* with Bette Davis, Claude Rains, Paul Henreid; George Cukor's *A Double Life* with Ronald

Colman, Signe Hasso; Elia Kazan's *Gentleman's Agreement* with Gregory Peck, Dorothy McGuire, John Garfield; Jack Conway's *The Hucksters* with Clark Gable, Deborah Kerr, Sydney Greenstreet, Adolphe Menjou, Ava Gardner, Keenan Wynn, Edward Arnold; Roy Del Ruth's *It Happened on 5th Avenue* with Don DeFore, Ann Harding, Charlie Ruggles, Victor Moore, Gale Storm; Byron Haskin's *I Walk Alone* with Burt Lancaster, Lizabeth Scott; Zoman Z. McLeod's *The Kid from Brooklyn* with Danny Kaye, Virginia Mayo, Vera-Ellen; Henry Hathaway's *Kiss of Death* with Victor Mature, Brian Donlevy, Coleen Gray, Richard Widmark; Michael Curtiz's *Life With Father* with Irene Dunne, William Powell; George Seaton's *Miracle on 34th Street* with Edmund Gwenn, Maureen O'Hara, John Payne, Natalie Wood; Irving Rapper's *The Voice of the Turtle* with Ronald Reagan, Eleanor Parker, Eve Arden; Michael Gordon's *The Web* with Ella Raines, Edmond O'Brien, William Bendix, Vincent Price.

Film musical: Richard Whorf's *It Happened in Brooklyn* with Frank Sinatra, Kathryn Grayson, Jimmy Durante, Peter Lawford.

Broadway musicals: *Finian's Rainbow* 1/10 at the 46th Street Theater, with Ella Logan, now 33, Traverse City, Mich.-born actor David Wayne (originally Wayne James McMeekan), 33, as the leprechaun Og, music by Burton Lane, lyrics by E. Y. Harburg, songs that include "If This Isn't Love," "How Are Things in Glocca Mora," "Old Devil Moon," "Look to the Rainbow," "When I'm Not Near the Girl I Love," "That Great Come-and-Get-It-Day," 725 perfs. The musical breaks new ground with social commentary on subjects ranging from the population explosion to the maldistribution of wealth; *Brigadoon* 3/13 at the Ziegfeld Theater, with James Mitchell, David Brooks, Marion Bell, 27, as Fiona MacLaren, sets by Oliver Smith, music by Vienna-born composer Frederick "Fritz" Loewe, 42 (who will make Bell his second wife), book and lyrics by New York-born writer Alan Jay Lerner, 28 (a son of Lerner Stores founder Joseph J. Lerner), songs that include "The Heather on the Hill," "Come to Me, Bend to Me," "Almost Like Being in Love," "There But for You Go I," 581 perfs.; *High Button Shoes* 10/9 at the Century Theater, with Phil Silvers, Nanette Fabray, Helen Gallagher, Lower East Side-born burlesque comic Joey Faye (originally Joseph Palladino), 38, choreography by Jerome Robbins, music by Jule Styne, lyrics by Sammy Cahn, songs that include "Papa, Won't You Dance with Me," 727 perfs.; *Allegro* 10/10 at the Majestic Theater, with John Battles, John Conte, Pennsylvania-born law school dropout Lisa Kirk, 22, music by Richard

The Brooklyn Dodgers signed Jackie Robinson and broke baseball's color barrier. LIBRARY OF CONGRESS

Rodgers, lyrics by Oscar Hammerstein II, songs that include "A Fellow Needs a Girl," "The Gentleman Is a Dope," 315 perfs.; *Angel in the Wings* 12/11 at the Coronet Theater, with Paul and Grace Hartman, Detroit-born comedienne Elaine Stritch, 21, music by Bob Hilliard, lyrics by Carl Sigman, songs that include "Civilization (Bongo, Bongo, Bongo)," 197 perfs.

Opera: *The Telephone* 2/18 at New York, with music by Gian-Carlo Menotti together with a revised version of his last year's opera *The Medium*; *The Mother of Us All* 5/7 at Columbia University's Brander Matthews Hall with Dorothy Dow as Susan B. Anthony, music by Virgil Thomson, libretto by the late Gertrude Stein, who died at Paris last July at age 72.

Ballet: *The Seasons* 5/17 at New York, with music by Los Angeles-born composer John (Milton) Cage (Jr.), 34.

Mexican-born dancer-choreographer José (Arcadia) Limón, 39, forms his own company at New York. It will be the first to tour abroad with support from the U.S. Department of State.

New York-born musician Tito (originally Ernesto Antonio) Puente, Jr., 24, forms the Tito Puente Orchestra (initially the Piccadilly Boys). Puente's nickname is based on his short stature, coming from Ernestito, the diminutive of Ernesto; he met bandleader Charlie Spivak while serving aboard the U.S.S. *Santee*, has studied at Juilliard, plays at the Palladium dance hall on Broadway, and launches himself on a career that will make him a legend in Latin music.

Brooklyn-born singer Lena Horne, now 30, makes her Carnegie Hall debut 9/29 following years of appearances in nightclubs, black musicals, and Hollywood films; alto saxophonist Charlie Parker, now 27, makes his Carnegie Hall debut the same evening, as does Virginia-born jazz singer Ella Fitzgerald, now 29 (Parker has formed a trio with Max Roach and Miles Davis).

Atlantic Records is founded at the Jefferson Hotel on Broadway at 56th Street by entrepreneurs who include Ahmet Ertegun. The company will do so well beginning in 1949 with recordings by Plymouth, Va.-born rhythm & blues singer Ruth Brown (*née* Weston), now 19, that it will jokingly become known as "the house that Ruth built" (*see* 1987).

Café Society and Café Society Uptown close following savage attacks by newspaper columnists Walter Winchell and Lee Mortimer, who play upon stories that owner Barney Josephson's brother Leon, an avowed communist, has been cited for contempt by the House Un-American Activities Committee (*see* 1938; 1940).

 Jack Kramer wins in men's singles at Forest Hills, Althea Louise Brough, 24, in women's singles.

Former light-heavyweight boxing champion Benny Leonard collapses April 18 while refereeing a bout at the St. Nicholas Arena and dies at age 51.

World middleweight champion Tony Zale knocks out challenger Rocky Graziano at Yankee Stadium September 27 with a left hook to the jaw in the sixth round (*see* 1946). Zale will lose the title to Graziano at Chicago July 16 of next year, Zale will regain it June 10, 1948, with a third-round knockout at Ruppert Stadium in Newark, N.J., he will lose it later that year to Marcel Cerdan, and Cerdan will lose it in 1949.

Middleweight boxer Jake LaMotta throws a fight November 14 at Madison Square Garden. Mobster Frankie Carbo runs the fights at the Garden and has told LaMotta he must take a dive if he wants a crack at the title, but the match is so obviously fixed that the Boxing Commission holds up the purse, makes an investigation, and temporarily suspends LaMotta, who will win a title fight against Marcel Cerdan in 1949 and hold the crown until 1951.

Jackie Robinson signs with the Brooklyn Dodgers and starts the season at first base—the first black baseball player in the major leagues. Georgia-born Kansas City Monarchs shortstop John Roosevelt Robinson, 28, has been recruited by Dodger scout Clyde Sukeworth, 45, and signed by Dodger president Branch Rickey; he will continue through the 1956 season and have a lifetime batting average of .311.

The Brooklyn Dodgers win the National League pennant, but the New York Yankees win the World Series, defeating the Dodgers 4 games to 3 behind the pitching of rookie Frank Joseph "Spec" Shea, 27, Joe Page, 29, and Allie Reynolds, 25. Jackie Robinson and Pee Wee Reese each get seven hits, including one double apiece; Dixie Walker six hits, including a double and a home run; outfielder Carl Furillo, 25, six hits, including two doubles; and rookie third baseman John Donald "Spider" Jorgensen, 27, four hits, including two doubles, but Tommy Henrich of the Yankees gets 10 hits, including two doubles and a home run; Joe DiMaggio six hits, including two home runs; third baseman Billy Johnson, 29, seven hits, including three triples.

Columbia upsets Army 21 to 20 in intercollegiate football October 25, ending a 32-game Cadet winning streak. Army had a 20-7 lead at halftime, but

Columbia has rallied, completing 20 forward passes (mostly by Gene Rossides) to gain 263 yards through the air while Army has gained only 42 yards on four completions and 302 yards rushing versus 100 yards for Columbia, whose team has had 18 first downs as compared with 12 for Army.

● The Collyer brothers make headlines March 21 when police receive an anonymous telephone call saying that recluse Homer Collyer, 71, is dead. Police officers climb ladders to force their way into Collyer's cluttered brownstone at 2078 Fifth Avenue, corner 128th Street, and find Homer, a onetime lawyer, dead of malnutrition in an upstairs room. The rat-gnawed body of his onetime musician brother Langley, 61, is found dead in the house April 8 after searchers have removed 120 tons of rubbish including bicycles, sleds, most of a Model T Ford, a car generator and radiator, the top of a horse-drawn carriage, kerosene stoves, umbrellas, 10 clocks, 14 grand pianos, an organ, a trombone and cornet, three bugles, five violins, 15,000 medical books, thousands of other books, mountains of yellowed newspapers dating to 1918, etc.

The 76-year-old Lotos Club moves after 37 years in West 57th Street to a turn-of-the-century house designed by Richard Howland Hunt at 5 East 66th Street, where it provides lodging and meals for members.

▥ Former Sing Sing Prison warden Lewis E. Lawes dies at Garrison, N.Y., April 23 at age 61.

🏠 The 33-story Esso Building designed by Carson and Lundin opens in Rockefeller Center.

Stuyvesant Town opens with 8,755 units in an area bounded by First Avenue and the East River Drive between 14th and 20th streets (formerly the "gashouse district;" the project has displaced 11,000 working-class tenants). Parks Commissioner Robert Moses obtained support from the late Mayor La Guardia in his efforts to persuade Metropolitan Life Insurance Co. to finance the huge apartment-house complex, whose 35 13- to 14-story buildings have been built under the Redevelopment Companies Law of 1943, a measure that allows the city to grant tax exemptions on the value of a project over and above the land and buildings that were there before the project existed (Met Life will not have to pay full taxes on Stuyvesant Town for 25 years). Most of the more than 11,000 prospective tenants who apply for apartments are World War II veterans, only young, white, married couples are accepted, the units are not wired for air conditioning, tenants will have only electric fans for more than 35 years, and

black veterans will struggle for 10 years, with support from civil-rights groups, to force Metropolitan Life to integrate Stuyvesant Town (see human rights, 1951).

Peter Cooper Village is completed just north of Stuyvesant Town between 20th and 23rd streets. Financed by Metropolitan Life Insurance Co. and designed by the same architects as Stuyvesant Town (Irwin Clavan and Gilmore Clarke), it has roomier and higher-priced apartments. The two projects combined contain 9,000 apartments and are for whites only (the courts will uphold Met Life's rental policy but the company will change its policy voluntarily in August 1950 and the first black families will move in 2 months later). The units are not wired for air-conditioning and the wiring will not be upgraded until the 1960s.

The Elliott Houses—first public housing built since World War II—are completed in West 25th Street between Ninth and Tenth avenues. Architects Archibald Manning Brown and William Lescaze have designed the four 11- and 12-story buildings that occupy a two-block site with 22 percent coverage of the space.

The Swedish government acquires the 36-year-old Jonathan Bulkley house at 600 Park Avenue, northwest corner 64th Street, to use as a residence for its consul general.

Construction workers threaten in October to bring all building to a halt. The city cuts a deal: 39 locals with 185,000 union members agree to a 15-month labor peace with the Building Trades Employers Association in exchange for an immediate wage increase.

Levittown opens at Hempstead, L.I., to help satisfy the booming demand for housing fueled by World War II veterans who no longer want to live in the Bronx and Brooklyn. Brooklyn-born builder William (Jaird) Levitt, 40, and his brother have employed wartime experience gained in the Seabees by building houses for the navy and have used techniques employed earlier by California builders. Rising on what heretofore have been potato fields, their nearly identical 7,500-square-foot Cape Cod-style tract houses (each has a yellow kitchen, two bedrooms, and an unfinished attic) are built on concrete slabs with no basements, non-union crews assemble as many as 36 houses per day using precut materials, and they erect the mass-produced single-family houses on 60-by-100-foot lots around village greens with shops, playgrounds, and community swimming pools. The modest prices

($7,990 with as little as $100 down and mortgage payments of only $65 to $80 per month) include major appliances, and by 1951 there will be 17,447 Levittown houses. Clause 25 of the standard leases bars non-white residents ("The tenant agrees not to permit the premises to be used or occupied by any person other than members of the Caucasian race. But the employment and maintenance of other than Caucasian domestic servants shall be permitted."), and although the courts will strike down that bar next year, and the population of the community will reach 65,440 by 1970, Levittown will remain 97.3 percent white in 1990 (137 blacks, 51,883 whites, 1,266 "other") (*but see* 1957).

The heaviest snowfall since 1888 cripples the city and its environs December 26, continuing for 16 hours, but although it drops 25.8 inches (20.9 inches fell in '88) and stops suburban trains the storm is not accompanied by the savage winds of 1888 and the drifts are not so high.

"21" Club cofounder Jack Kriendler dies of a coronary thrombosis in his apartment above the West 52nd Street restaurant August 13 at age 49. His brothers Bob, Pete (H. Peter), and Mac carry on the tradition of the 17-year-old family-owned place with help from their cousin Jerry, and Pete, now 42, takes over Jack's role as host; restaurateur Christopher Cella dies in a Princeton, N.J., hospital November 10 at age 54 (*see* 1926). His son Richard T., an Air Force Reserve brigadier general and MIT graduate, takes over Christ Cella's, he will move it to 160 East 46th Street when the original brownstone in East 45th Street is torn down, and the place will gain a following not only for its sirloin steak, prime ribs, pot roast, and London broil, but also for seafood (*see* Patroon, 1996).

1948 The State of Israel is proclaimed May 14 and opens her doors to the world's Jews; some New York Jews hail the creation of a Jewish homeland, others deplore the idea, either for political or religious reasons (the Satmars of Brooklyn's Williamsburg section do not recognize Israel's legitimacy).

Alger Hiss supplied Soviet agents with classified U.S. documents while working in the State Department in the 1930s, says *Time* magazine senior editor Whittaker Chambers, 47, in testimony before the House Un-American Activities Committee August 3. Now 43, Hiss lives with his wife, Priscilla, in an apartment at 22 East 8th Street, between University Place and Fifth Avenue; he is president of the Carnegie Endowment for International Peace and when Chambers repeats his allegations on the radio he sues Chambers for slander. Chambers withdrew

from Columbia University in his youth after writing a "blasphemous" play, lost his job at the New York Public Library when stolen books were found in his locker, and joined the infant Communist Party in 1925, when it had barely 7,000 members. A federal jury at New York indicts Hiss for perjury December 15, criminal lawyer Lloyd Paul Stryker, now 63, represents him, and his first trial will end in a hung jury (*but see* 1950).

President Truman wins election in his own right with 303 electoral votes to 189 for his Republican opponent Thomas E. Dewey. The New York governor does better than he did in 1944, receiving 45 percent of the popular vote to Truman's 49.5 percent.

The U.S. Supreme Court rules May 3 that the government may not enforce private acts of discrimination (*Shelley v. Kramer*). Restrictive covenants in deeds have prohibited sales of houses and cooperative apartments to minorities, but such covenants are not legally enforceable, the Court rules, and its decision will have a powerful effect New York and its suburbs.

The Day Care Council of New York opens 97 centers to help working mothers obtain (or retain) their jobs (*see* 1944). The state discontinued aid to day-care centers last year.

Banker-financier Thomas W. Lamont dies at Boca Grande, Fla., February 2 at age 77.

Wall Street's Dow Jones Industrial Average closes December 31 at 177.30, down from 181.6 at the end of 1947. The cost-of-living index has reached a record high of 173 in August but the 80th Congress has resisted President Truman's repeated appeals for anti-inflationary legislation.

Monthly commutation tickets on the Harlem, Hudson, and Putnam divisions of the New York Central Railroad rise 10 percent February 1, having remained at the same levels since 1932 even though wages have increased by 110 percent and the average price of fuel and other supplies by 148 percent.

Subway fares advance to 10¢ March 30, having remained at 5¢ since the I.R.T. opened its first line in 1904 (bus fares rise to 7¢ July 1 and will remain at that level until July 1, 1950; Fifth Avenue buses have charged 10¢ for years, and fares in most other U.S. cities have been 10¢ for some time). Robert Moses has persuaded Mayor O'Dwyer to raise the fare in order to allow the city to float bonds based on revenues from the fares, but former Manhattan borough president Stanley Isaacs, now 65 and a City Council member, writes that the fare was raised "so the city can borrow more money, which will be invested in highways, parkways, etc. . . . for which the motorist will not be asked to contribute a nickel. Why the motorist should be given a free ride and the straphanger asked to pay the full capital cost of the subway investment certainly cannot be explained decently." Transport Workers Union president Michael J. Quill, now 42, has made a deal with Mayor O'Dwyer's labor relations assistant Theodore W. Kheel, 33, to support the 10¢ fare in return for a generous labor contract (see 1953).

President Truman dedicates Idlewild International Airport on Jamaica Bay in southeastern Queens July 1. The world's largest commercial airport to date, it relieves some of the pressure from the city's 9-year-old La Guardia but is much farther (15 miles) from midtown Manhattan (see 1958; JFK, 1963).

A smallpox scare galvanizes the City Health Department in early April after the disease is diagnosed in a businessman just back from Mexico. He is isolated and quarantined but dies in the city's first incidence of smallpox since 1935, the Health Department joins with the U.S. Public Health Service in a search for possible contacts, a second death is reported April 12 but later turns out to be from another cause, New Yorkers line up for free vaccinations, and within 1 month some 6.3 million have received shots; the prompt action limits the number of cases to 12.

The State University of New York (SUNY) is created by an act of the legislature at Albany; every other state has long since had a public university system, using federal land grants provided under the Morrill Act of 1862, but New York designated the private university Cornell as its land-grant university in 1865, and although some of the 29 state-operated but unaffiliated institutions in the initial list date to 1816 New York has gone the route of private colleges and universities. The list will grow to number 75 before being reduced to 64 in 1975 (when the state will enact legislation transfering supervision of eight New York City community colleges to City University [CUNY]), with 35 percent of all New York State high-school graduates enrolled in classes at Albany, Binghamton, Brockport, Buffalo, Canton, Cortland, Farmingdale, Fredonia, Morrisville, New Paltz, New York City, Old Westbury, Oneonta, Oswego, Plattsburgh, Potsdam, Purchase, Stony Brook, Utica, or elsewhere in the system, whose total enrollment will reach nearly 370,000, making it the largest comprehensive system of public education in America, with students from every other state plus four U.S. territories or possessions and from more than 160 foreign countries (see CUNY, 1961).

Gen. Eisenhower accepts the presidency of Columbia University and moves into the presidential mansion at 60 Morningside Heights. He has declined both Democratic and Republican party offers to be a candidate for the U.S. presidency (but see politics, 1952).

 Herald Tribune editor-publisher Ogden Mills Reid dies at New York January 3 at age 64; journalist-editor Will Irwin of a cerebral occlusion at Greenwich Village February 24 at age 74.

The *Bronx Home News* ceases publication February 18 and is absorbed into the *New York Post* after nearly 41 years of reporting the borough's news (see 1945).

The Marshall Field tabloid *PM* ceases publication June 22 after 8 years but the tabloid *New York Star* picks up where *PM* left off.

El Diario begins publication to give the city's fast-growing Hispanic community a daily tabloid newspaper in competition with *La Prensa*, which has been published since 1913. The two will merge in 1968 to create *El Diario/La Prensa* (see 1989).

Ogilvy & Mather has its beginnings in the New York advertising agency Hewitt, Ogilvy, Benson & Mather founded by English-born copywriter and opinion-researcher David (Mackenzie) Ogilvy, 37, with former J. Walter Thompson executive Anderson Fowler Hewitt, 40. The agency gains quick recognition with advertisements for Hathaway shirts featuring Russian-born *Journal-American* society gossip columnist Baron George Wrangell, 44.

A new Times Square sign advertising Bond Stores men's and women's apparel features a waterfall five stories (27 feet) high and 120 feet long. Sign impresario Douglas Leigh, now 41, has persuaded Bond Stores head Barney Ruben to let him put up the most sensational sign ever, and it will continue until October 1954. Running a full 200 feet from 44th Street to 45th, the $350,000 sign has 65-foot-tall male and female figures flanking the waterfall, which recycles 50,000 gallons of water while a zipper flashes the news; a circular sign with a digital clock rises above the word "BOND" with a message reading, "Every Day 3,490 People Buy at Bond."

 The New York Public Library asks Florida-born librarian Jean Blackwell, 34, to take over its 15,000-volume Schomburg collection in Harlem (see 1926). Blackwell noticed while working in a Bronx branch of the library that it had few Spanish-language books and arranged to buy some for the borough's growing Spanish-speaking population. Only the second black woman graduate from Barnard and a friend of such Harlem Renaissance figures as Romare Bearden, W. E. B. DuBois, Dorothy West, and Richard Wright, Blackwell will persuade her childhood friend Langston Hughes to donate some of his papers to the collection, which will grow under her supervision to have 75,000 books plus historical material from Haiti and art from Africa, all housed in the poorly lighted Countee Cullen branch library at 103 West 135th Street (see 1981).

Nonfiction: *The Greater City: New York, 1898–1948* by Illinois-born Columbia University historians Alan Nevins, 52, and John A. Krout (editors); *Politics in the Empire State* by Brooklyn-born *New York Times* writer Warren Moscow, 40; *Father Knickerbocker Rebels: New York City During the Revolution* by Virginia-born author Thomas J. Wertenbaker, 69; *Old Mr. Flood* by Joseph Mitchell.

Fiction: *The World Is a Wedding* (stories) by Delmore Schwartz is about the city's Jewish middle-class life during the Great Depression; *The Naked and the Dead* by New Jersey-born, Brooklyn-raised novelist Norman Mailer, 25, whose novel—based in part on his experiences as an infantryman in World War II—excoriates the hypocrisy of war; *City Boy* by Herman Wouk.

"What a great city New York is!" writes Lowell, Mass.-born "beatnik" poet-novelist Jack (originally Jean-Louis) Kerouac, now 25, to a friend. "We are living at just the right time—Johnson and his London, Balzac and his Paris, Socrates and his Athens—the same thing again."

Poetry: *Fields of Wonder* by Langston Hughes; *Stranger at Coney Island* by Kenneth Fearing.

Poet-novelist Claude McKay dies of heart failure at Chicago May 22 at age 58 and is buried in a Queens cemetery at Woodside.

 Abstract expressionism is pioneered by Jackson Pollock, now 36, whose *Composition No. 1* (tachisma) combines splashes and splotches of multihued paints on canvas to help launch a new school of "action painting" that will radically alter the direction of American art. Pollock says his splashes are controlled by personal moods and unconscious forces, but some critics dismiss him as "Jack the Dripper."

Other paintings: *Elegy to the Spanish Republic* by Aberdeen, Wash.-born New York abstract expressionist Robert Motherwell, 33; *Mailbox* by Willem de Kooning. Arshile Gorky takes his own life at New York July 3 at age 43, having undergone surgery for colon cancer, lost many of his paintings in a studio fire, and found his wife cheating on him with another painter.

Sculpture: a memorial erected in Battery Park honors Coast Guard men and women who gave their lives in World War II. Some 25,000 Coast Guard personnel across the country have contributed $1 each to pay for the work, which has been created by Massachusetts-born sculptor-etcher-mural painter (and Coast Guard veteran) Norman M. Thomas, 32 (the Municipal Art Society has questioned the work's artistic merit but Parks Commissioner Robert Moses has dismissed the Society's objections); a bronze statue of Abraham Lincoln with a black child is completed by Charles Keck, now 73, and installed on the east side of Madison Avenue near 133rd Street.

Photographs: *Brooklyn Bridge in the Fog* by Paris-born LIFE magazine photographer Andreas Feininger, 41, helps build the reputation of a man who trained as an architect in Germany, devoted himself to photography beginning in 1936, and emigrated to America 3 years later; *Little Patriot, American Legion Parade, New York City, Shoeshine Boy, West Village,* and *Rebecca, Harlem* by California-born New York photographer Ruth Orkin, 26, whose work appears regularly in LIFE, *Look,* and other major magazines.

Theater: *Mr. Roberts* by Fort Dodge, Iowa-born playwright Thomas Heggen, 26, and Texarkana, Texas-born playwright Joshua (Lockwood) Logan, 39, 2/18 at the Alvin Theater, with Nebraska-born actor Henry Fonda, 42, David Wayne, Indiana-born actor Robert Keith, 52, 1,157 perfs.; *Summer and Smoke* by Tennessee Williams 10/6 at the Music Box Theater, with Allegheny, Pa.-born actress Anne Jackson, 22, Margaret Phillips, 100 perfs. Williams has taken an apartment in a three-story white-brick building at 235 East 58th Street, between Second and Third avenues; *Anne of the Thousand Days* by Maxwell Anderson 12/8 at the Shubert Theater, with English actress Joyce Redman (originally Joyce Reynolds), 30, as Anne Boleyn, English actor Rex Harrison (originally Reginald Carey), 40, as Henry VIII, 286 perfs.

The Margaret Webster Shakespeare Company is founded at New York by director-producer Webster (see 1947). The group will tour the United States for years, performing in high-school auditoriums, university theaters, and public halls.

New York Daily News drama critic Burns Mantle dies of cancer at his Forest Hills home February 9 at age 74.

Radio: *Our Miss Brooks* 7/19 on CBS with Eve Arden, now 36, as schoolteacher Connie Brooks (*see* television, 1952).

Television: *The Ed Sullivan Show* (initially *The Toast of the Town*) 6/20 with New York-born syndicated *Daily News* columnist Edward (Vincent) Sullivan, 45, as master of ceremonies. CBS program development manager Worthington Miner, 47, has hired the awkward, wooden-faced Sullivan to emcee the Sunday evening variety show, whose first program features comedians Dean Martin and Jerry Lewis, composer Richard Rodgers and lyricist Oscar Hammerstein II, a ballerina, a pianist, a boxing referee, and a troupe of crooning firemen (to 6/6/1971; *see* 1955); *Texaco Star Theater* 9/21 on NBC with comedian Milton Berle, now 40, whose guests include Evelyn Knight and her magic violin, comedian Phil Silvers, and the old vaudeville comedy act Smith and Dale. The Tuesday evening show is soon so popular that NBC does not cancel it for election-night coverage, stores close early for patrons and employees to watch their TV sets, and more people buy sets to watch "Uncle Miltie," whose initial salary is $1,500 per week but will rise to $11,500 by May 3, 1951, when Berle will sign a 30-year contract with NBC for $200,000 per year (to 6/14/1955); *Kukla, Fran and Ollie* 11/12 on NBC with Iowa-born actress Fran Allison, 40, Palm Springs, Calif.-born puppeteer Burr Tillstrom, 35 (to 6/13/1954, and on ABC from 9/6/1954 to 8/30/1957); *Howdy Doody* 12/27 on NBC with Buffalo-born piano player-singer-radio disk jockey-puppeteer "Buffalo Bob" Smith (originally Robert Schmidt), 30, who begins each show by asking the Peanut Gallery of children aged 3 to 8 in his studio at Rockefeller Center what time it is, to which they respond in unison, "It's Howdy Doody Time" (to 9/30/1960).

Films: George Stevens's *I Remember Mama* with Irene Dunne, Barbara Bel Geddes (originally Barbara Geddes Lewis). Also: Roy Del Ruth's *The Babe Ruth Story* with William Bendix, Claire Trevor, Charles Bickford, Sam Levene; Robert Siodmak's *Cry of the City* with Victor Mature, Richard Conte; George Cukor's *A Double Life* with Ronald Colman, Signe Hasso, Edmond O'Brien, Shelley Winters; Abraham Polonsky's *Force of Evil* with John Garfield; Alfred E. Green's *The Girl from Manhattan* with Dorothy Lamour, George Montgomery, Charles Laughton; Henry Hathaway's *Kiss of Death* with Victor Mature, Brian Donlevy, Coleen Gray, Richard Widmark; Jules Dassin's *The Naked City* with Barry Fitzgerald, Howard Duff, Don Taylor, Paul Ford, Molly Picon in a film noir based on photographs by Weegee in his 1945 book; Norman Z. McLeod's *The*

Secret Life of Walter Mitty with Danny Kaye, Virginia Mayo; Roy Rowland's *Tenth Avenue Angel* with Margaret O'Brien, Angela Lansbury, George Murphy; John Gage's *The Velvet Touch* with Rosalind Russell, Leo Genn, Claire Trevor, Sydney Greenstreet.

Film musicals: Charles Walters's *Easter Parade* with Judy Garland, Fred Astaire, Peter Lawford, Ann Miller, music and lyrics by Irving Berlin, songs that include "Stepping Out With My Baby," "Shaking the Blues Away," "A Couple of Swells," and the title song; William A. Seiter's *Up in Central Park* with Deanna Durbin, Dick Haymes, Vincent Price.

Broadway musicals: *Look, Ma, I'm Dancin'!* 1/29 at the Adelphi Theater, with Nancy Walker, Alice Pearce, Daly City, Calif.-born dancer Harold Lang, 24, music and lyrics by Hugh Martin, songs that include "Shauny O'Shay," 188 perfs.; *Where's Charley* 10/11 at the St. James Theater, with Ray Bolger, Brooklyn-born ingénue Doretta Morrow (originally Marano), 20, in an adaptation of the 1892 English comedy *Charley's Aunt*, music and lyrics by Frank Loesser, songs that include "Once in Love with Amy," "My Darling, My Darling," "The New Ashmolean Marching Society and Students' Conservatory Band," 792 perfs.; *As the Girls Go* 11/13 at the Winter Garden Theater, with Bobby Clark, Buffalo-born singer Irene Rich (originally Irene Luther), 51, music by Jimmy McHugh, lyrics by Harold Adamson, songs that include "It Takes a Woman to Make a Man," 420 perfs. (the first Broadway show to charge $7.20 for orchestra seats); *Lend an Ear* 12/16 at the National Theater, with music and lyrics by Charles Gaynor, songs that include "When Someone You Love Loves You," 460 perfs.; *Kiss Me Kate* 12/30 at the New Century Theater, with Alfred Drake, New York-born singer Patricia Morison (originally Eileen Patricia Augusta Fraser), 29, Lisa Kirk, Harold Lang in an adaptation of the 1596 Shakespeare comedy *The Taming of the Shrew*, music and lyrics by Cole Porter, songs that include "We Open in Venice," "I've Come to Wive It Wealthily," "I Hate Men," "Another Opening, Another Show," "Why Can't You Behave," "Were Thine that Special Face," "Too Darn Hot," "Where Is the Life that Late I Led," "Always True to You in My Fashion," "So in Love," "Tom, Dick or Harry," "Wunderbar," "Brush Up Your Shakespeare," 1,077 perfs.

Ballet: *Fall River Legend* 4/22 at the Metropolitan Opera House, with Alicia Alonso, John Kriza, 28, music by Morton Gould, choreography by Agnes de Mille; *Orpheus* 4/28 at the the City Center, with Oklahoma-born dancer Maria Tallchief (Mrs. George Balanchine), 23, as Eurydice, Tanaquil

LeClerq as the leader of the Bacchantes, music by Igor Stravinsky, choreography by George Balanchine.

The New York City Ballet Company gives its first performance 10/11 at the City Center with a program that includes George Balanchine's 1941 ballet *Concerto Barocco* plus *Orpheus* and *Symphony in C* (see 1946). The company will remain at the City Center until 1964.

The Robert Shaw Chorale is founded by former Collegiate Chorale director Robert L. Shaw, now 32 (see 1941). Performing the best known classical and contemporary chorale works, it will develop a reputation as the nation's most professional choral group, giving numerous radio and television concerts, making tours, and issuing recordings.

The Weavers is founded by New York-born folk singer Pete Seeger, 29, Lee Hays, Fred Hellerman, and Ronnie Gilbert. Seeger organized the Almanac Singers in 1940 and toured the country before joining the Office of War Information (OWI), he plays the banjo as well as singing, and he will continue with the group until 1958.

The long-playing 12-inch vinyl plastic phonograph record demonstrated at New York June 18 by CBS engineer Peter Goldmark turns at a rate of 33 revolutions per minute instead of the usual 78, has 250 "Microgrooves" to the inch, plays 45 minutes of music, and begins a revolution in the record industry (see 1946; Goldmark's color television, 1940). Goldmark also unveils a lightweight pickup arm and a silent turntable for his LP records.

 The 17-team National Basketball Association (NBA) is created by a merger of the 2-year-old Basketball Association of America, which includes the New York Knickerbockers, with the National Basketball League (see Clifton, 1950).

Former Yankee slugger Babe Ruth dies of throat cancer at New York August 16 at age 53 and is buried at the Gate of Heaven Cemetery in Hawthorne.

Richard A. "Pancho" Gonzalez, 20, wins in men's singles at Forest Hills, Margaret Osborne duPont in women's singles.

New York fashion designer Anne Klein (*née* Hannah Golofski), 27 (or 43, or somewhere in between), joins with her husband, Ben, to form Junior Sophisticates, a new Seventh Avenue firm for which she creates a dress plus jacket. She began as a freelance design sketcher at age 15 and will go on to design the A-line dress and long, pleated, plaid skirts with blazers (see 1968).

New York fashion designer Hannah Troy (*née* Stern), 47, introduces the short-waisted "petite" size. She has noticed in a California May Company store that women were pulling at their shoulders and waistlines because the dresses they were trying on did not fit properly. After studying measurements of women volunteers for the WACS and WAVES in World War II, she has concluded from the statistics that women are typically short-waisted, whereas most fashions are designed for long-waisted women.

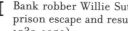 Bank robber Willie Sutton makes good his second prison escape and resumes his criminal career (see 1932; 1950).

The 21-story Universal Pictures Building is completed at 445 Park Avenue, between 56th and 57th streets, to begin Manhattan's postwar building boom. Designed in International Style by Kahn & Jacobs for Tishman Brothers in a "wedding cake" form prescribed by the zoning law, it is the first office building on what heretofore has been a purely residential stretch of the avenue. Architect E. J. Kahn, now 63, formed a partnership some years ago with Robert Allan Jacobs that will continue until Kahn's death in 1972.

Architect Ernest Flagg dies of a heart attack at his home in his native New York April 10 at age 90; Emery Roth at Mount Sinai Hospital August 20 at age 77, having designed more than 500 New York apartment houses and numerous hotels. His sons Julian and Richard became partners with their father 10 years ago and will carry on under the name Emery Roth & Sons, but their work will be distinguished more for efficiency than aesthetics; James Gamble Rogers dies at Columbia Presbyterian Medical Center's Harkness Pavilion October 1 at age 80.

Schwab House is completed at 11 Riverside Drive, between 73rd and 74th streets. Designed by Sylvan Bien, the 17-story red-brick structure occupies the site of the 1906 Charles M. Schwab mansion. Most postwar apartments will have 12 floors in the same space that before the war accommodated only 10, so ceilings will be lower and floors thinner. While a postwar European builder typically installs a concrete floor topped by a layer of sand topped by a layer of cork and overlaid with wood, New York builders lay wood atop concrete and in some cases put fine print in leases requiring tenants to install wall-to-wall carpeting. Walls of new buildings are thinner than before the war, and where old, steel-frame buildings had structural mass that broke up sound and isolated it, sound is easily transmitted through the continuous, monolithic structure of new buildings, 90 percent of which are made of reinforced concrete.

The 19-story 710 Park Avenue apartment house is completed at the southwest corner of 70th Street. Designed by Sylvan Bien for developer Sam Minskoff & Sons, it replaces the George Blumenthal mansion on the corner site used earlier by the Union Theological Seminary.

The state-financed James Weldon Johnson Houses open in December in the East Harlem area from 112th Street to 115th between Third and Park avenues. Designed by Julian Whittlesey, Harry M. Prince, and Robert J. Reilly, the 10 six-, 10-, and 14-story buildings contain a total of 1,310 units, provide housing for eight or nine families per floor, and are occupied initially by poor Italian and Hispanic families (by 1988 tenants will be mostly Puerto Ricans and blacks, with only about 30 whites; gross incomes of tenants will average $10,865).

The Abraham Lincoln Houses open in December in the East Harlem area from 132nd Street to 135th between Fifth and Park avenues. Built as a slum-clearance project, the 14 buildings range in height from six to 14 floors, contain 1,286 units, and replace a section where writer James Baldwin grew up.

Rego Park's eight-story Walden Terrace apartment complex is completed in a two-block area bounded by 98th and 99th streets between 63rd Drive and 64th Road. Architect Leo Stillman has designed the structures with exposed concrete frames.

The Department of Sanitation opens Fresh Kills Landfill on Staten Island following a new ban on dumping raw garbage and ash into the Atlantic Ocean (see 1934; Moses, 1945). Intended initially to be a temporary facility (Mayor O'Dwyer promised last year that it would be closed after 2 years), the 2,200-acre site receives its first scowload of garbage April 16, it will for more than 50 years receive barge- and truckloads of ash from municipal incinerators plus raw household garbage, several layers of cover will be laid atop the waste to keep out rainwater and keep in gases generated by the waste, and soil and sod will be placed atop the covers as mounds grow to exceed 500 feet, the height of a 17-story building, making the landfill the highest point on the Atlantic seaboard and the East Coast's largest gathering place for gulls, attracted by rats, voles, and other prey that feed on the garbage (see 1996).

Balducci's opens as a 24-hour produce market at 1-5 Greenwich Avenue near the Avenue of the Americas. Grocer Louis Balducci, now 48, is an immigrant from Bardi, Italy, who since 1914 has run a similar shop in Brooklyn with his wife, Maria. Their Greenwich Village store will grow to carry caviar, foie gras, smoked fish, cheeses, coffees, fresh seafood, and meats (see 1972).

 Café Nicholson opens before Christmas. Founder John Nicholson, 33, has a kitchen staff headed by Virginia-born chef Edna Lewis, 31, whose menu features chicken and chocolate soufflé. Nicholson will move in 1954 to 148 East 57th Street (formerly the carriage house of Augustus Van Horne Stuyvesant, Jr.), decorating the place with Spanish tiles more than a century old that he will find in a Puerto Rican warehouse and put up on the walls himself; he will also acquire chairs, settees, mirrors, urns, and vases from the old Grand Union Hotel at Saratoga Springs to give his place a Victorian look that many patrons will admire. In the 1960s he will move to 323 East 58th Street (formerly the studio of sculptor Jo Davidson).

1949 Brooklyn-born Judge Harold (Raymond) Medina, 61, presides over the trial of 11 alleged communists in the U.S. District Court for the Southern District of New York. The defendants have been indicted under the 1940 Alien Registration Act (Smith Act) requiring aliens to be fingerprinted and making it unlawful to advocate overthrow of the U.S. government or belong to any group advocating such overthrow.

New York dancer Paul Draper, 39, and harmonica player Larry Adler sue a Greenwich, Conn., woman for libel after Red-baiting columnist Westbrook Pegler has picked up her accusations that they have communist sympathies. The trial will end in a hung jury, but Draper and Adler have been making $100,000 per year and are unable to obtain further bookings (see Red Channels, 1950).

President Truman pledges continued U.S. support of the United Nations October 24 in ceremonies dedicating the new UN site at New York (see 1952; real estate, 1950).

Mayor O'Dwyer wins reelection, defeating Republican-Liberal-Fusion candidate Newbold Morris and Congressman Vito Marcantonio, 46, who has run on the American Labor Party ticket. O'Dwyer receives 1,266,512 votes, Morris 956,069, Marcantonio 356,626 (but see 1950).

$ Wall Street's Dow Jones Industrial Average falls to 161 at midyear, down from 193 a year earlier, but closes December 31 at 200.13, up from 177.30 at the end of 1948. A new Minimum Wage Act passed by Congress October 26 has amended the Fair Labor Standards Act of 1938, raising the minimum hourly wage from 40¢ to 75¢. Unemployment has reached

5.9 percent, up from 3.8 percent last year, but while most consumer prices have dropped, housing and health-care costs have increased. The average American social worker has $3,500 to spend after taxes, a high-school teacher $4,700, a car salesman $8,000, a dentist $10,000. Typical prices include a new Cadillac for $5,000, a gallon of gasoline 25¢, a man's gabardine suit $50, a 10-inch table TV set $250, a pack of cigarettes 21¢. Typical food prices: pork 57¢/lb., lamb chops $1.15/lb., Coca-Cola 5¢ per seven-ounce bottle, milk/21¢ qt., bread 15¢/loaf., eggs 80¢/doz.

Grand Central Terminal tries to boost revenues by broadcasting advertising messages over its public address system, stopping only after a vociferous protest led by *New Yorker* editor Harold Ross (*see* 1946; Kodak Colorama, 1950).

New York taxi drivers go on strike March 31 as they did 10 years ago. Many are World War II veterans who were supposed to get special medallions but ran into opposition from the unions and from other licensed drivers. Mayor O'Dwyer has refused to grant a fare increase until fleet owners improve working conditions, the drivers accuse the police of strikebreaking, the police arrest two union officials and 15 others on charges of violence, but two-thirds of the cabs are rolling after a few days, the strike is called off April 8, and police estimate that 9,000 taxis are on the streets, although drivers in the Bronx continue to strike. The union files 50 complaints of unfair labor practices, and Teamsters Union leader Dave Beck backs a union organizing drive (*see* 1956).

Bishop Manning dies at New York November 18 at age 83. He retired in 1946 as head of the Episcopal diocese, which he headed beginning in 1921, giving foremost attention to the construction of the Cathedral of St. John the Divine, for which he raised $13 million.

Eleanor Roosevelt expresses support in her newspaper column for pending legislation that would give $300 million in federal aid to public schools. Cardinal Spellman, now 60, opposes the measure because it would exclude parochial and other private schools, he calls Mrs. Roosevelt's position "unworthy of an American mother," but the former first lady immediately reiterates her belief in the principle of separating church and state.

Builder Anthony Campagna retires as chairman of the Board of Education's Committee on Building, having served without pay while directing a $100 million school-construction program. Now 64, he

has saved the city millions of dollars in construction costs.

TV station WPIX (Channel 11) goes on the air June 15 under the auspices of the 29-year-old *New York Daily News*.

The Intertype Fotosetter Photographic Line Composing Machine installed by Intertype Corp. of Brooklyn at the Rochester plant of Stecher-Traung Lithograph is the first typesetting machine that dispenses with metal type (*see* Mergenthaler, 1884; Photon process, 1953).

Oklahoma-born Yale graduate Marion Harper, Jr., 32, succeeds McCann-Erickson cofounder H. K. McCann as president of the 18-year-old New York advertising agency that he joined as a mail-room boy in 1939. He became copy-research manager 4 years later, McCann took him under his wing as his assistant, and by focusing on motivation research and pretesting techniques he will attract clients whose business will make the agency a rival in billings to J. Walter Thompson (*see* Interpublic, 1961).

Doyle Dane Bernbach is founded June 1 by Bronx-born former Grey Advertising creative director William Bernbach, 37, who joins with Ned Doyle and Maxwell Dane, 43, to start an agency that will popularize Levy's Jewish rye bread, the Volkswagen, Polaroid Land camera, and other products. Dane has been running an agency whose billings are less than $500,000, Doyle handles finances and promotional work, Bernbach brings along the Ohrbach's department store account. "It's not just what you say that stirs people," he will pronounce, "it's the way that you say it." Treating consumers as intelligent beings, DDB will set new standards of creative, tasteful, "soft-sell" advertising as opposed to the hard-sell, repetitive ads championed by Rosser Reeves of Ted Bates, and within 10 years the agency's billings will rise from about $1 million to more than $40 million.

Shorthand inventor John R. Gregg dies at New York February 23 at age 80; publisher S. S. McClure at New York March 21 at age 92; cartoonist Robert L. "Believe It or Not" Ripley at New York May 27 at age 55; former *New York Evening Post* owner-editor and *Nation* magazine editor Oswald Garrison Villard at New York October 1 at age 77; *New Yorker* magazine cartoonist Helen Hokinson in an airplane crash near Washington, D.C., November 1 at age 50.

Nonfiction: "Here Is New York" by E. B. White, who has been living with his wife, Katherine, in a row house in Turtle Bay Gardens between Second and

Third avenues in the 40s. Published in the April issue of *Holiday* magazine (and, later, as a small book), it says, "No one should come to New York to live unless he is willing to be lucky. New York is the concentrate of art and commerce and sport and religion and entertainment and finance, bringing to a single compact arena the gladiator, the evangelist, the promoter, the actor, the trader and the merchant . . . I am twenty-two blocks from where Rudolph Valentino lay in state, eight blocks from where Nathan Hale was executed, five blocks from the publisher's office where Ernest Hemingway hit Max Eastman on the nose, four miles from where Walt Whitman sat sweating out editorials for the Brooklyn Eagle, thirty-four blocks from the street where Willa Cather lived when she came to New York to write books about Nebraska, . . . thirteen blocks from where Harry Thaw shot Stanford White . . . ;" *The Great Pierpont Morgan* by Frederick Lewis Allen; *The Life and Times of Jimmy Walker* by Denver-born author Eugene Devlan "Gene" Fowler, 57; *Peter Cooper: Citizen of New York* by Edward C. Mack, 44.

Publisher Nelson Doubleday dies of cancer at his Oyster Bay, L.I., home January 11 at age 59.

Fiction: *Other Voices, Other Rooms* by New Orleans-born New York writer Truman Capote, 23, whose work takes the city's literary world by storm.

Painting: *Number 2* by Jackson Pollock; *Onement III* by Barnett Newman; *Woman* and *Two Standing Women* by Willem de Kooning.

The Costume Institute of the Metropolitan Museum of Art holds a benefit party at the Rainbow Room, raising $20,000 from the 400 people who attend (*see* 1946). Fashion consultant and publicist Eleanor Lambert, now 45, has proposed the "Party of the Year," which will be held at the museum beginning in 1960 and become an annual event, with as many as 3,150 guests contributing $1.5 million and more per year.

Photographs: *Sunday at Coney Island Beach* by Andreas Feininger appears as a two-page LIFE magazine photographic spread; *On the Pier* by Ruth Orkin.

Theater: *Death of a Salesman* by Arthur Miller 2/10 at the Morosco Theater, with Lee J. Cobb as salesman Willie Loman, Mildred Dunnock, Winchester, Mass.-born actor (John) Arthur Kennedy, 34, Pennsylvania-born actor Cameron Mitchell, 30, 742 perfs.; *Detective Story* by Sidney Kingsley 3/23 at the Hudson Theater, with Ralph Bellamy, Jean Adair, New York-born ingénue Lee Grant, 21, Brooklyn-born actor Alexander Scourby, 35, Troy-born

actress Maureen Stapleton, 23, New York-born actress Joan Copeland (originally Joan Miller), 26, Montreal-born actor Joseph Wiseman, 30, 581 perfs.

The Stella Adler Conservatory of Acting is founded at New York by veteran actress-teacher Adler, now 48; it will educate players (including Marlon Brando) in the (Stanislavski) Method system of acting that she has studied since 1925.

Theater chronicler George Clinton Denamore Odell dies October 17 at age 83 in his apartment at the Seymour Hotel, 50 West 45th Street (*see* 1927. Odell received the gold medal for achievement in history in 1942 from the New-York Historical Society, but his 15-volume *Annals of the New York Stage* has had relatively few buyers and produced no royalties); playwright Philip Barry dies of a heart attack in his apartment at 510 Park Avenue December 3 at age 53.

Television: *The Goldbergs* 1/17 on CBS is the first TV situation comedy. Derived from the radio show first aired in 1929, it stars Molly Berg, now 50, will continue until late June 1951, and be followed by dozens of "sitcoms."

The National Academy of Television Arts and Sciences confers its first Emmy Awards.

Films: Maxwell Shane's *The City Across the River* with Stephen McNally, Thelma Ritter; Mervyn LeRoy's *East Side, West Side* with Barbara Stanwyck, James Mason, Ava Gardner, Van Heflin, Cyd Charisse; Peter Godfrey's *The Girl from Jones Beach* with Ronald Reagan, Virginia Mayo, Eddie Bracken; Don Hartman's *Holiday Affair* with Robert Mitchum, Janet Leigh, Wendell Corey; Bretaigne Windust's *June Bride* with Bette Davis, Robert Montgomery, Fay Bainter; David Miller's *Love Happy* with the Marx Brothers, Ilona Massey, Vera-Ellen; Ted Tetzlaff's *The Window* with Bobby Driscoll, Barbara Hale, Arthur Kennedy.

Film musicals: Gene Kelly and Stanley Donen's *On the Town* with Kelly, Frank Sinatra, Vera-Ellen, Betty Garrett, Ann Miller, Jules Munshin, Alice Pearce. Shot mostly on location in New York, it has music by Leonard Bernstein, lyrics by Betty Comden and Adolph Green, songs that include "New York, New York" (". . . it's a hell of a town, the Bronx is up and the Battery's down, People ride in a hole in the ground"). Also: Charles Walters's *The Barkleys of Broadway* with Fred Astaire, Ginger Rogers, Oscar Levant, Billie Burke, music and lyrics by Betty Comden and Adolph Green, songs that include "They Can't Take That Away From Me."

Broadway musicals: *Along Fifth Avenue* 1/13 at the Broadhurst Theater (to Imperial Theater 2/21), with Jackie Gleason, Nancy Walker, Carol Bruce, music by Gordon Jenkins, lyrics by Tom Adair, Nat Hiken, and others, 180 perfs.; *South Pacific* 4/7 at the Majestic Theater, with Ezio Pinza, Mary Martin, Myron McCormick, New Jersey-born actress Juanita (Long) Hall, 47, California-born actress Betta St. John, 17, William Tabbert, music by Richard Rodgers, lyrics by Oscar Hammerstein II, book based on James Michener's tales of military personnel in World War II posts, songs that include "Some Enchanted Evening," "Younger Than Springtime," "I'm in Love with a Wonderful Guy," "This Nearly Was Mine," "I'm Gonna Wash that Man Right Out of My Hair," "A Cockeyed Optimist," "Honey Bun," "You've Got to Be Carefully Taught," "Dites-moi Pourquoi," "There Is Nothing Like a Dame," "Happy Talk," "Bali Ha'i," 1,925 perfs.; *Miss Liberty* 6/15 at the Imperial Theater, with actor Phillip Borneuf, 37, choreography by Jerome Robbins, music and lyrics by Irving Berlin, songs that include "Let's Take an Old Fashioned Walk," "Give Me Your Tired, Your Poor," "The Most Expensive Statue in the World," and the title song, 308 perfs.; *Touch and Go* 10/13 at the Broadhurst Theater (to Broadway Theater 2/27/1950), with Boston-born comedienne Peggy Cass, 25, Helen Gallagher, music by Jay Gorney, book and lyrics by Scranton, Pa.-born playwright Jean Kerr (*née* Collins), 25, and Evanston, Ill.-born director and theater critic Walter Kerr, 35, 176 perfs.; *Lost in the Stars* 10/30 at the Music Box Theater, with Todd Duncan, music by Kurt Weill, lyrics by Maxwell Anderson, book based on Alan Paton's 1948 novel *Cry, the Beloved Country*, 273 perfs.; *Gentlemen Prefer Blondes* 12/8 at the Ziegfeld Theater, with Seattle-born actress Carol Channing, 26 (Bennington '45), as Lorelei Lee, Alice Pearce, Philadelphia-born tap dancer Charles "Honi" Coles, 38, sets by Oliver Smith, music by Jule Styne, lyrics by Leo Robin, book based on the 1925 Anita Loos novel, songs that include "A Little Girl from Little Rock," "Diamonds Are a Girl's Best Friend," "Bye Bye Baby," 740 perfs.

Willie Howard dies broke after a brief illness at Paramus, N.J., January 14 at age 62, reportedly having gambled away more than $1 million; George Moran of Moran and Mack fame following a stroke at Oakland, Calif., August 1 at age 67; Al Shean of Gallagher and Shean fame at New York August 12 at age 81; Abraham Minsky of burlesque fame at New York September 5 at age 68; dancer Bill "Bojangles" Robinson of a chronic heart condition at Columbia-Presbyterian Hospital November 25 at age 71 (he has earned more than $2 million but dies penniless; his body lies in state at a Harlem armory, schools are closed, and thousands line the streets to catch a glimpse of his bier).

McKeesport, Pa.-born pianist Byron Janis, 20, makes his Carnegie Hall debut 10/30.

 New York college basketball has another scandal in January (see 1945). Gamblers have tried to bribe George Washington University players to lose their game with Manhattan College in Madison Square Garden, but the plot is aborted (see 1951).

Pancho Gonzalez wins in men's singles at Forest Hills, Mrs. duPont in women's singles.

The New York Yankees win the World Series, defeating the Brooklyn Dodgers 4 games to 1. Pitcher Elwin Charles "Preacher" Roe, 34, shuts out the Yankees in the second game after Allie Reynolds has shut out the Dodgers in the first. Pee Wee Reese gets six hits, including a home run; first baseman Gil Hodges, 25, four hits, including a home run; catcher Roy Campanella, 27, four hits, including a double and a home run; and Puerto Rico-born outfielder Luis Olmo, 30, three hits, including a home run. Joe DiMaggio and Phil Rizzuto hit the only two home runs scored by the Yankees, but Yankee pitchers Reynolds, Vic Raschi, 30, Joe Page, and New York-born Ed Lopat (originally Edmund Walter Lopatynski), 31, wear the Dodgers down.

Evan-Picone is founded at New York by local designer Charles Evans and Sicilian-born tailor Joseph Picone, 31, to manufacture a simple fly-front skirt that Evans has created. Operating out of a storefront on Fifth Avenue at 46th Street, Picone has set up an assembly-line operation, the skirt meets with immediate success, the partners will expand to make women's slacks and sell their sportswear company to Revlon in 1962, Evans will go into real estate, Picone will buy the company back in 1966.

Revlon introduces "Fire and Ice," a new lipstick and nail enamel promoted with a frankly sexual approach in advertisements featuring model Suzy Parker and copy created by advertising agency vice president Kay Daly, 29, who will join Revlon in 1961.

Mayor O'Dwyer marries Texas model Sloan Simpson, 33, of the John Power modeling agency, whom he met last year at a fashion show in the Grand Central Palace convention center held in connection with the Golden Jubilee celebration of the consolidation of the city's five boroughs. The new Mrs. O'Dwyer has obtained an annulment of her first marriage in order to marry the Roman Catholic mayor, now 59 and a widower; she supervises the first significant redecoration of Gracie Mansion.

Four prisoners escape from Rikers Island March 30 but Police Department helicopters equipped with large pontoon floats search the East River and the island perimeter. The escapees surrender March 31 (*see* 1954).

Congress passes a federal Housing Act July 15 to fund slum-clearance and low-rent public housing projects. Sen. Robert Taft (R. Ohio) has sponsored the legislation. Title I of the act encourages municipalities to acquire and resell substandard areas at prices below cost for private redevelopment. Congress ends federal rent regulation and leaves it up to the states either to continue such regulation or drop it (most states abandon it) (*see* 1943). A commission appointed by Gov. Dewey to study the issue decides that New York City is different from other metropolitan areas in having such a large percentage of rental tenants, and the state adopts a two-tiered system, permitting apartments in buildings constructed since 1947 to be rented at rates controlled only by market forces but retaining controls on those in buildings put up in 1947 or earlier (*see* 1965).

The Shore Haven apartments are completed in Bensonhurst, Brooklyn, by New York-born Queens builder Fred C. (Frederick Christ) Trump, 43, whose German-born father died when he was 13. At age 15 he went into business with his mother, Elizabeth, and began a construction business by putting up garages while continuing his high-school education; he went on to build single-family houses, mostly in Queens, for sale at $3,990 each, built a supermarket in Woodhaven, and put up barracks for the navy during World War II (*see* Beach Haven, 1950).

Fresh Meadows Housing Development is completed in Queens (*see* 1946). The 166-acre development contains a mixture of row houses, low- and highrise apartment buildings, schools, a theater, and a regional shopping center. Critic Lewis Mumford calls it "perhaps the most positive and exhilarating example of community planning in the country" (*see* 1972).

A two-bedroom U.S. house sells typically for $10,000 while a five-bedroom New York apartment rents for $110 per month. A four-bedroom duplex co-operative apartment in the East 60s near Park Avenue with two-story living room and wood-burning fireplace in its 16' × 21' library sells for $8,250 with monthly maintenance of $247.50, an eight-room co-op on Fifth Avenue in the 70s with three bedrooms, 30' × 17' living room, and a view of Central Park sells for $7,434 with monthly maintenance of $299.

The Waldorf-Astoria breaks all occupancy records Easter Sunday, and the Hilton Hotel chain acquires the leasehold of the Waldorf in October for $3 million (Conrad Hilton, the Hilton Hotels Corp., and Hilton director Henry Crown of Chicago buy 30 percent of the shares, giving them a controlling interest). Single rooms at the Waldorf now go for $7 to $12 per day with bath, a suite with boudoir fetches $32 to $35, single or double occupancy (*see* 1976).

The Hotel Lafayette and its Café Lafayette restaurant close, ending an era in which the hotel was the equivalent of San Francisco's Palace and its restaurant competed with such now bygone eating places as Bustanoby's, Churchill's, Delmonico's, the Hoffman House, the Holland House, Martin's, Rector's, Shanley's, and Louis Sherry's.

1950 A federal court at New York finds Alger Hiss guilty January 25 of having committed perjury when he denied the allegations made by Whittaker Chambers in 1948. Chambers has supported his charges by producing a microfilm that he kept hidden in a pumpkin at his Westminster, Md., farm; Hiss is sentenced to 5 years' imprisonment January 29 but appeals the verdict (*see* 1951).

Sen. Joseph McCarthy (R. Wis.) launches a campaign against alleged U.S. communists in February, accusing New York lawyer-social reformer Dorothy Kenyon, 64, of being affiliated with at least 28 communist-front organizations. She calls him "an unmitigated liar" and a coward to take shelter in the cloak of congressional immunity. Testifying before a Senate subcommittee, the former municipal judge denies "any connection of any kind with communism or its adherents," but McCarthy's smear campaign will continue.

A Federal jury at New York finds March 7 that former Department of Justice analyst Judith Coplon, 28, and United Nations engineering staff employee Valentin A. Gubitchev, 33, are guilty of espionage charges. FBI agents arrested them a year ago as they were walking on Third Avenue near 16th Street; slips regarding FBI security reports were found in Coplon's handbag, her job involved the study of Soviet espionage, and the jury of six men and six women has rejected her lawyer's arguments that she was collecting material for a book, and that she and Gubitchev acted furtively because they were in love and feared that their liaison would bring down the wrath of Gubitchev's wife or cost Coplon her job.

Communist North Korean forces invade the Republic of South Korea June 25, beginning a 3-year Korean War that will involve 16 nations.

Red Channels makes sweeping accusations of communist subversion in the American entertainment industry (see Hollywood Black List, 1947; Adler and Draper, 1949). Written by former Naval Intelligence officer Vincent Hartnett and published anonymously, the paperback book will lead to hearings before the House Committee on Un-American Activities, scores of actors, choreographers, playwrights, musicians, producers, directors, and screenwriters will be defamed and given no opportunity to defend themselves, dozens will be barred from employment on suspicion of using the films, stage, radio, and television as vehicles for communist propaganda.

FBI director J. Edgar Hoover announces July 17 that his agents have arrested New York-born engineer and businessman Julius Rosenberg, 32, on charges of having played a leading role in a wartime espionage ring. Rosenberg's 34-year-old wife, Ethel (née Greenglass) is also a New York native, her brother David worked at the Los Alamos nuclear research station in New Mexico and allegedly stole some uranium, he has been Rosenberg's business partner, the FBI arrested him June 15, he has admitted involvement in the spy ring and named Julius as the man who recruited him, Julius was hired by the Army Signal Corps in 1940 and dismissed in 1945 for lying about his Communist Party affiliation, the FBI arrests Ethel Rosenberg August 11 (see 1951).

Kings County (Brooklyn) District Attorney Miles F. McDonald notes that lower courts rarely impose prison terms in gambling cases and asks in April for a blue-ribbon grand jury to hear testimony regarding police officers found at the scene of a raid on a "policy bank" (gambling den). A police inspector, a lieutenant, and four plainclothesmen are subpoenaed to testify before Judge Samuel S. Leibowitz. Police raid the Manhattan offices of bookmaker Frank Erickson at 487 Park Avenue May 2 and carry off truckloads of records, which show that Erickson has accepted wagers ranging in size from $200 to $15,000. Manhattan District Attorney Frank Hogan opens his own grand jury inquiry May 5, Senate Crime Committee counsel Rudolph Halley, 36, arrives at New York with Florida data May 29, saying it will aid the city's investigation. Reputed crime family member Vincent Gigante, 22, is sentenced for betting June 13; Frank Erickson changes his plea to guilty June 19 and is given a 2-year jail term plus a $30,000 fine (he enters Riker's Island prison June 27). Brooklyn police captain John G. Flynn attempts suicide July 16 and dies a day later. Arrest records of the Brooklyn police division are subpoenaed, and some 6,000 police march at the Flynn funeral July 20 in a demonstration intended to show disapproval of District Attorney McDonald's probe tactics. Mayor O'Dwyer attends the funeral and calls the probe a "witchhunt."

The White House announces August 16 that Mayor O'Dwyer will resign for what he calls reasons of health August 31 following allegations of ties to organized crime. He accepts an appointment from President Truman as ambassador to Mexico at a salary of $25,000 plus $10,000 per year for entertainment and is granted a city pension of $6,000 per year. City Council President Vincent Richard Impelliteri, 49, becomes acting mayor.

Police arrest bookmaker Harry Gross of Brooklyn's Towers Hotel September 15 and hold him on $100,000 bail as a material witness (see crime, 1941); other raids are made, including one at 69 Joralemon Street, Brooklyn. A wiretap recording played in court on the evening of September 15 in the presence of Police Commissioner William T. O'Brien provides evidence that Gross's gambling ring was paying $350 per week to one policeman for protection. (A first-grade patrolman makes $4,150 per year, a third-grade detective $4,400, a second-grade detective $4,650, a first-grade detective $5,150). Now 34, the flashily dressed, impeccably manicured, five-foot-six-inch, 170-pound Gross earns $75,000 to $100,000 per year from his gambling operations, and when he refuses to disclose the names of policemen who received protection money his bail is raised to $250,000. Commissioner O'Brien orders a probe into allegations that police have been taking bribes from bookmakers, and evidence emerges that Gross has headed a $20 million-per-year gambling ring, operating 27 horse rooms with 400 employees in Brooklyn, Manhattan, and the Bronx plus wire rooms in Nassau County and New Jersey, paying $75,000 per month in police protection, with an extra month's payment at Christmas, plus making lavish gifts (custom-made suits, silk shirts, TV sets, and the like) to police officials. When Gross overreached himself on World Series bets last year and could not (or would not) pay the $40,000 he owed, he fled to Los Angeles, but New York police allegedly persuaded underworld boss Willie Moretti of the Joe Adonis crime family to reinstate Gross so that they could continue receiving payoffs.

Police Commissioner O'Brien resigns September 25 and is succeeded by former U.S. Attorney Thomas F. Murphy, who says he will "start with a clean slate." He issues an order September 29 demoting and transfering to uniform all 336 men in the plainclothes division. Murphy declares that associations with gambling do not pervade entire squads and do not appear to be widespread, but notes that the corruption could not have been limited to lower-level cops; Gov. Dewey appears on television and vows to ferret out all higher-ups who may be involved in gambler-police ties and expects city authorities to go all the way up to find whoever is involved, "and if they don't I will." It is against regulations for a police officer to accept any gift, but raids on policemen's homes October 6 turn up television sets and other items allegedly given to cops by Harry Gross. Former mayor O'Dwyer returns on a visit from Mexico October 9 and apologizes for having called the probe a witch-hunt. Scores of officers submit applications for retirement; those who testify before the grand jury generally refuse to sign waivers of immunity (one says it was "just a coincidence" that he applied for retirement the day that Gross was arrested). If an officer refuses to answer questions fully and truthfully any questions that are put to him he may be prosecuted for contempt of court, and if his answers are not truthful he may be charged with perjury; echoing a demand made 24 hours earlier by Republican mayoralty candidate Edward Corsi, District Attorney McDonald asks the grand jury to recommend to "the proper authorities" a change in the Police Retirement Law, which now states that an officer who refuses to sign a waiver of immunity from criminal acts when brought before a grand jury for questioning as to official conduct forfeits his retirement rights as well as his job, but that if he applies for retirement before being called his retirement rights may not abridged (see 1951).

Former secretary of war Henry L. Stimson dies at his Huntington, L.I., estate October 20 at age 83.

Acting mayor Vincent R. Impelliteri loses the Democratic Party nomination in a special primary election, but he runs on the Experience Party ticket and receives 1,161,171 votes as compared with 935,351 for Italian-born Supreme Court justice Ferdinand Pecora, now 68, who has run on the Democrat-Liberal line, and 382,372 for Republican Edward Corsi. Lawyer Rudolph Halley has made a name for himself as prosecutor for the Senate Crime Commission and is elected president of the City Council; his victory is generally seen as a public protest against links between city government and organized crime, but Mayor Impelliteri questions

Halley's ability to make additional probes into those links.

Gov. Dewey wins election to a third 4-year term, securing 2,819,523 votes to 2,246,738 for his New York City-born Democratic opponent, former congressman Walter A. Lynch, 56, who has called the election a contest between "crime and clean government" because Republican officeholders appointed by "Tom (Chase Bank) Dewey" have refused to prosecute.

$ The Value Line founded in 1931 introduces mutual funds of equities selected on the basis of Arnold Bernhard's quantitative analyses.

The Carver Federal Savings Bank opens in 125th Street. Started by local business and clergymen to serve the black community, it will grow to become the nation's largest black-owned financial institution, prospering by making loans that white-owned banks avoid.

The Celler-Kefauver Amendment to the Clayton Anti-Trust Act of 1914 "puts teeth" into the Clayton Act by curbing mergers of U.S. business firms. Written by Rep. Emmanuel Celler, now 62, (D. N.Y.) and Sen. Estes Kefauver, 47 (D. Tenn.), the new law stops companies from buying up stock in other companies, but large corporations will find other ways to achieve mergers and the number of mergers in years to come will dwarf this year's 219 (see 1960).

Wall Street's Dow Jones Industrial Average closes December 30 at 235.41, up from 200.13 at the end of 1949.

$ The first Pottery Barn store opens on the second floor of a building near the northwest corner of 10th Avenue and 23rd Street. Started by a Philadelphia-born merchant, the chain will grow by 1986 to have 21 stores, all in Manhattan, selling dinnerware, ceramics, and a limited selection of furniture (see Williams-Sonoma, 1986).

⚡ Natural gas from Texas arrives at New York via the transcontinental pipeline. The 1,840-mile "Big Inch" begun 2 years ago will permit Consolidated Edison, Brooklyn Union Gas, and Long Island Lighting Co. to dispense with operations that manufacture methane gas from coal for use in home heating and gas ovens, and the low price of natural gas will allow the utilities to reduce gas rates 27 times between 1952 and 1969.

⚡ The Brooklyn-Battery Tunnel opens May 25 and carries nearly twice the traffic anticipated. Designed by Ole Singstad, the two tubes are lined in cast iron and measure 9,117 feet, making this the longest continuous underwater motor-vehicle tunnel in North America (construction began in 1940 and was interrupted by the war). Material excavated to build the tunnel (and, earlier, to build the Lexington Avenue subway that opened in 1917) has been used as landfill to expand the size of Governors Island from its original 65-acre size to 173 acres. The 1.7-mile tunnel will remain the world's longest for 50 years.

The Port Authority Bus Terminal opens December 15 in Hell's Kitchen on Eighth Avenue between 40th and 41st streets. Built at a cost of $24 million, the facility will grow to handle upwards of 7,000 buses and 188,000 passengers per day and become the world's busiest (it will be enlarged in 1989).

Some 357,000 commuters come into the city every day, up only 19 percent from the weekday average of 301,000 in 1930, but 118,400 now commute by automobile, up from 38,050 in 1930. Only 239,000 commute by rail, down from 263,000 in 1930, and the influx of cars into Manhattan poses major problems of parking and traffic flow. Mayor O'Dwyer says May 26 that he will not approve parking meters until he has proof that their manufacturers are not linked to slot machines. A newly organized traffic department orders in July that the city's traffic signals conform to state and federal standards in order to make New York eligible for federal funds. The city adopts alternate-side-of-the-street parking regulations, beginning at first on the Lower East Side to facilitate street cleaning, which starts using mechanical sweepers in place of hand brooms and water trucks that have sprayed the streets. By 1953 the rules will be imposed on the rest of Manhattan and in the Bronx, Brooklyn, and Queens—more than 10,000 miles of streets—and enforced every day except Sundays and civic holidays or after heavy snowfalls. In many areas parking is allowed on the south sides of streets only for 3-hour periods on Mondays, Wednesdays, and Fridays, and on north sides on Tuesdays, Thursdays, and Saturdays, but the list of days when the regulations are suspended will lengthen to 32, including many religious holidays (see tow-away zone, 1959).

Brooklyn's Lexington Avenue elevated railway ceases operations October 14.

The Eastman Kodak Colorama unveiled in the main concourse of Grand Central Terminal will remain there for 40 years, presenting spectacular scenic views 18 feet high and 60 feet long. Other commercial displays follow, including a Merrill Lynch stockbroker booth, automobile exhibits, and publicity gimmicks and both the main and lower-level concourses. New York Central lawyers have tried for years to have the State of New York refund taxes that the railroad has paid on its right-of-way beneath Park Avenue, but a referee rules against the railroad and is upheld in the courts (see Young, 1954).

Downstate Medical Center (later the SUNY Health Science Center at Brooklyn) is created by the state, which upgrades the Long Island College Hospital to meet a shortage of physicians.

"Sub-human" dwellings in the city are increasing the rate of tuberculosis, says Rudolph Halley September 29 in his campaign to become City Council president.

The Lubavitcher Rebbe Joseph Isaac Schneersohn dies of a heart attack at his Crown Heights, Brooklyn, home January 28 at age 69. A crowd of 3,000 fills the street and sidewalks in front of 770 Eastern Parkway, mourners follow to the yeshiva at 1352 Bedford Avenue, and the leader of the Chabad movement is buried at Montefiore Cemetry, Springfield Gardens, Queens. His second daughter married Russian-born scientist Menachem Mendel Schneerson, now 47, in 1924 (see 1951).

Editor-president Roy W. Howard of the *New York World-Telegram* and Thomas W. Dewart of the *New York Sun* announce January 4 that the *World-Telegram* has acquired the *Sun* to create the *World-Telegram & The Sun*. The 116-year-old *Sun* publishes its last issue January 5, and Dewart attributes the sale to mounting production costs, including rising newsprint costs but particularly "beyond reason" wages enforced on newspapers by labor unions. The *Sun*'s 1,200-1,300 employees take issue, and the Newspaper Guild puts out a statement calling Dewart's remarks "biased," "misleading," and "anti-labor;" the *Sun* is the only New York metropolitan paper whose editorial and commercial workers are not covered by a Guild contract, says the Guild.

Businessman-publisher Generoso Pope dies at New York April 28 at age 59. He has organized Italian relief efforts since 1945 and established a college scholarship fund for graduates of the city's Catholic schools.

George Seldes stops publishing his weekly *In fact* October 3 after 10 years in which he has exposed the tactics of the tobacco industry, Coca-Cola, the National Association of Manufacturers, and other powerful interests that Seldes has regarded as reactionary forces. Public concern about communism has marginalized worries about fascism, the publication has come under attack from the FBI, McCarthyites, and business interests for printing facts that the mainstream media has suppressed, subscribers have been intimidated, and circulation has fallen from its 1947 peak of 176,000 to barely 40,000. Sen. McCarthy's Committee on Un-American Affairs will call Seldes to testify in June 1953 but will clear him of any communist affiliation.

Fiction: "For Esme—With Love and Squalor" (story) by New York-born writer J. D. (Jerome David) Salinger, 31, in The New Yorker April 8; The Injustice Collectors by New York lawyer-novelist Louis (Stanton) Auchincloss, 33; Simple Speaks His Mind (stories) by Langston Hughes, whose columns in the New York Post and Chicago Defender have chronicled the adventures and philosophy of a fictional Jesse B. Simple; The Swiss Family Perelman by S. J. Perelman; The Trouble of One House by Hartford, Conn.-born New Yorker magazine writer Brendan Gill, 35.

Poet-playwright Edna St. Vincent Millay goes up to bed at her Austerlitz, N.Y., farm Steepletop the night of October 18, takes a sleeping pill, goes back to the staircase where she has left a bottle of wine, pitches forward, breaks her neck, and dies at age 58.

The Tibor de Nagy Gallery opens in East 53rd Street with John Bernard Myers as director. English collector Dwight Ripley has agreed to pay the rent for 6 years, and Hungarian-born owner de Nagy, 42, will operate the gallery until his death in 1993, giving prominence to painters such as Fairfield Porter, Larry Rivers, Grace Hartigan, Helen Frankenthaler, and Kenneth Noland.

Trustees of the Museum of Modern Art make its six-foot-six-inch Vienna-born vice president of foreign activities MoMA's director. The trustees ousted Alfred H. Barr, Jr. 6 years ago, Nelson A. Rockefeller brought in René d'Harnoncourt, now 48, the following year, he has personally paid d'Harnoncourt's salary, recognizing that he was a better administrator than Barr, and the courtly, witty new director will remain in his job until he retires in 1968, charming curators, collectors, and trustees, raising funds, and organizing innovative installations that will give MoMA's aesthetics nationwide prominence.

Painting: Chief by Wilkes Barre, Pa.-born New York "action" painter Franz Kline, 40; Subway by Brooklyn-born social realist painter George Tooker, 30; Death of a Miner by Ben Shahn; Number 9: In Praise of Gertrude Stein by Bradley Walker Tomlin; Excavation by Willem de Kooning. Copper heir-art collector Solomon R. Guggenheim dies at Port Washington November 3 at age 88 (see museum, 1959); German-born painter Max Beckmann drops dead at the corner of Central Park West and 61st Street December 27 at age 66.

Sculpture: a full-length bronze statue of former governor Al Smith by Charles Keck is erected on the Lower East Side at the corner of Catherine and Monroe streets with a relief of a Lower East Side scene on the back.

Theater: The Member of the Wedding by Georgia-born novelist-playwright Carson McCullers, 32, 1/5 at the Empire Theater, with Ethel Waters, Grosse Point Park, Mich.-born actress Julie (Julia) Harris, 24, and Brooklyn-born actor (André) Brandon de Wilde, 7, is based on the 1946 McCullers novel and has been mounted by Montreal-born producer Robert (Thomas) Whitehead, 33, and Harold Clurman, 501 perfs.; The Cocktail Party by St. Louis-born English poet-playwright T. S. (Thomas Stearns) Eliot, 61, 1/21 at the Henry Miller Theater, with Alec Guinness, English actress Cathleen Nesbitt, 60, Irene Worth, 409 perfs.; The Happy Time by Chicago-born playwright Samuel (Albert) Taylor, 36 (based on a novel by Robert Fontaine) 1/24 at New York's Plymouth Theater, with Budapest-born actress Eva Gabor, 28, Vienna-born actor Kurt Kasznar (originally Serwicher), 36, scenery and costumes by Aline Bernstein, 614 perfs.; Come Back, Little Sheba by Independence, Kansas-born playwright William (Motter) Inge, 37, 2/15 at the Booth Theater, with Shirley Booth, Sidney Blackmer, Joan Loring, 191 perfs.; Affairs of State by French playwright Louis Verneuil, 57, 9/25 at the Royale Theater, with Reginald Owen, Celeste Holm, Shepperd Strudwick, 610 perfs.; Season in the Sun by New Yorker magazine drama critic-turned-playwright Wolcott Gibbs, now 48, 9/28 at the Cort Theater, with Lowell, Mass.-born actress Nancy Kelly, 29, Winthrop, Mass.-born actor-director Richard Whorf, now 44, Cleveland-born actor Jack Weston (originally Morris Weinstein), 26 (to Booth Theater, 5/14/1951), 284 perfs.; The Country Girl by Clifford Odets 11/10 at the Lyceum Theater, with Paul Kelly, German-born actress Uta Hagen, 31, 235 perfs.; Bell, Book, and Candle by John Van Druten 11/14 at the Ethel Barrymore Theater, with Lili Palmer, Rex Harrison, 233 perfs.

Broadway producer William A. Brady dies at New York January 6 at age 86; Variety publisher Sid Silverman at suburban Harrison March 10 at age 52; Broadway producer Brock Pemberton of a heart attack at New York March 11 at age 64; actress Jane Cowl at Santa Monica, Calif., June 22 at age 66; Elsie de Wolfe (Lady

Mendl) at Versailles July 12 at age 84; Pauline Lord of a heart attack at Alamogordo, New Mexico, October 11 at age 60; poet-playwright Michael Strange (Blanche Oelrichs) of leukemia at Boston November 5 at age 60 (she is buried at Woodlawn Cemetery); Shakespearean actress Julia Marlowe dies in her Plaza Hotel suite November 12 at age 85.

Television: *What's My Line* 2/2 on CBS, with emcee John Charles Daley, Jr., 35, and panelists: Boston-born actress Arlene Francis (*née* Kazanjian), now 41; columnist Dorothy Kilgallen, now 36; and anthologist Louis Untermeyer, 64, who try to guess the occupations of guests. Publisher Bennett A. Cerf, now 51, has lived since 1941 with his wife, Phyllis, in a five-story town house at 132 East 62nd Street and will succeed Untermeyer in 1952 (to 9/3/1967); *Your Show of Shows* 2/25 on NBC with Yonkers-born comedian Sid Caesar, 27, comedienne Imogene Coca, now 41, New York-born comedian Carl Reiner, 27, Howard Morris, and guest stars in a comedy hour developed by Los Angeles-born NBC executive Sylvester (Laflin) "Pat" Weaver, Jr., 41, and written by Gary Belkin, New York-born writer-comedian Mel Brooks (originally Melvin Kaminsky), 24, Caesar, Larry Gelbart, Sheldon Keller, Reiner, Aaron Ruben, New York-born writer (Marvin) Neil Simon, 22, and his brother Danny, Michael Stewart, and Mel Tolkin (160 weekly shows to 6/5/1954; retitled *Caesar's Hour*, to 5/25/1957).

Films: George Cukor's *Adam's Rib* with Spencer Tracy, Katharine Hepburn, Judy Holliday, Tom Ewell, David Wayne; Joseph Mankiewicz's *All About Eve* with Bette Davis, Anne Baxter, George Sanders, Celeste Holm, Gary Merrill, Thelma Ritter; John Huston's *The Asphalt Jungle* with Sterling Hayden, Louis Calhern, Jean Hagen, James Whitmore, Sam Jaffe, Marilyn Monroe. Also: Roy Del Ruth's *Always Leave Them Laughing* with Milton Berle, Virginia Mayo, Ruth Roman, Bert Lahr; Don Hartman's *Holiday Affair* with Robert Mitchum, Janet Leigh, Wendell Corey; Alfred E. Green's *The Jackie Robinson Story* with Robinson, Ruby Dee (see sports, 1947); Earl McAvoy's *The Killer That Stalked New York* with Charles Korvin, Evelyn Keyes, William Bishop, Dorothy Malone, Lola Albright, Jim Backus; Charles Lamont's *Ma and Pa Kettle Go to Town* with Marjorie Main, Percy Kilbride; Edmund Goulding's *Mister 880* with Dorothy McGuire, Burt Lancaster, Edmund Gwenn (based on the true story of an elderly New York City counterfeiter); Henry Levin's *The Petty Girl* with Robert Cummings (as pin-up artist George Petty), Joan Caulfield, Elsa Lanchester; Anthony Mann's *Side Street* with Farley Granger, Cathy O'Donnell; George Sherman's *The Sleeping City* with

Richard Conte, Coleen Gray; Michael Curtiz's *Young Man With a Horn* with Kirk Douglas, Lauren Bacall (originally Betty Joan Perske), Doris Day, Hoagy Carmichael in a plot based on the novel based on the life of Bix Beiderbecke (Harry James dubs the trumpet passages).

Film musicals: David Butler's *Tea for Two* with Doris Day, Gordon MacRae, Gene Nelson, Patrice Wymore, Eve Arden.

Broadway musicals: *Michael Todd's Peep Show* (revue) 6/28 at the Winter Garden Theater, with music and lyrics by Prince Chakrban Bhumibol, book by Bobby Clark, 278 perfs.; *Call Me Madam* 10/12 at the Imperial Theater, with Ethel Merman as U.S. Ambassador to Luxembourg Perle Mesta, Pat Harrington, choreography by Jerome Robbins, music and lyrics by Irving Berlin, songs that include "Hostess With the Mostes' on the Ball," "It's a Lovely Day Today," "The Ocarina," "The Best Thing for You," 644 perfs. (Arizona-born dancer Bill Bradley, 27, has been playing the role of a gypsy in the chorus of *Gentlemen Prefer Blondes* and gives a pale pink robe with white feathers as an opening-night gift to a member of the new show's cast. The "Gypsy Robe" good-luck symbol will become a Broadway tradition); *Guys and Dolls* 11/24 at the 46th Street Theater, with Robert Alda, Newark-born actress Vivian Blaine (originally Vivian S. Stapleton), 29, Sam Levene, Isabel Bigley, rotund Bronx-born comedian Stubby Kaye, 29, as Nicely-Nicely (he sings, "Sit Down, You're Rockin' the Boat"), book by Bensonhurst-born writer Abe Burrows, 39, music and lyrics by Frank Loesser, songs that include also "Luck Be a Lady," "Fugue for Tinhorns," "I've Never Been in Love Before," "A Bushel and a Peck," "Adelaide's Lament," "Sue Me," "If I Were a Bell," "The Oldest Established (Permanent Floating Crap Game in New York)," 1,200 perfs.; *Out of This World* 12/21 at the New Century Theater, with William Eythe, 32, New York-born actor David Burns, 49, Charlotte Greenwood, now 60, music and lyrics by Cole Porter, songs that include "Use Your Imagination," 157 perfs.

Composer Kurt Weill dies of a heart attack at New York April 3 at age 50; softshoe hoofer Lou Clayton of cancer at Hollywood September 12 at age 63 with his old partner Jimmy Durante at his bedside; Al Jolson of a coronary occlusion in his San Francisco hotel suite October 23 at age 64 after returning from Korea, where he had been entertaining U.S. troops.

The Metropolitan Opera appoints Vienna-born impresario Rudolf Bing, 48, general manager. He has managed England's Glyndebourne Opera and the Edinburgh Festival. Former Metropolitan Opera and New York Symphony conductor Walter Damrosch dies at New York December 22 at age 88.

Ballet: *The Age of Anxiety* 2/26 at the City Center, with Jerome Robbins, music by Leonard Bernstein.

New Orleans-born gospel singer Mahalia Jackson, 38, makes her Carnegie Hall debut 10/1.

Birdland opens on Broadway with alto saxophonist Charlie Parker, now 30 (*see* 1944). Parker will be a leading exponent of bebop until his death in 1955.

CCNY wins the National Invitation basketball championship at Madison Square Garden March 18, defeating Bradley University 69 to 61. CCNY goes on to beat Bradley 71 to 68 in the National Collegiate Athletic Association (NCAA) finals at the Garden March 28, becoming the first team ever to win both tournaments the same year (*but see* 1951).

The New York Knickerbockers sign Nat "Sweetwater" Clifton, 28, in the fall, having bought his contract from the Chicago-based Harlem Globetrotters; he plays with the Knicks October 21, becoming one of the first blacks to play in the National Basketball Association (NBA) (Chris Cooper has played a day earlier for the Boston Celtics).

Arthur Larsen, 25, wins in men's singles at Forest Hills, Mrs. duPont in women's singles.

The New York Yankees win the World Series, defeating the Philadelphia Phillies 4 games to 0. The Phillies have won the National League pennant on the last day of the regular season by defeating the Brooklyn Dodgers with a 10th-inning three-run homer by Dick Sisler, 29, but they fail to win a single game from the Yankee pitchers Allie Reynolds, Vic Raschi, rookie Edward Charles "Whitey" Ford, 21, and Tom Ferrick, 35. "Joltin' Joe" DiMaggio gets four hits, including a double and a home run; catcher Lawrence Peter "Yogi" Berra, 25, three hits, including a home run.

A branch of Manufacturers Trust Co. at 47-11 Queens Boulevard in Sunnyside is robbed at gunpoint March 9. Thieves said by many of the bank's employees to include Willie Sutton make off with $64,000 (*see* 1948; 1952).

Theft losses from New York's docks reach an estimated $140 million—three times the amount stolen from all other U.S. ports combined (*see* commerce, 1945). International Longshoremen's Association boss Joseph Ryan has headed the union since 1927 and continues to enforce the waterfront racketeer-ing—which involves embezzlement, extortion, hijacking, kickbacks, payroll padding, and even murder—but corruption at the port has become a national issue (*see* transportation, 1953).

The United Nations Secretariat building is completed in the spring on First Avenue to provide offices for the UN's 3,400 employees on an 18-acre site extending along the East River between 42nd and 48th streets, purchased for $8.5 million by John D. Rockefeller, Jr. and donated to the city in December 1945. The first building in the city with an all-glass curtain wall, the 39-story International Style structure rises 544 feet high, with blue-green Thermopane glass set in an aluminum grid (Vermont white marble covers its north and south elevations, which are both 72 feet wide). The French architect Le Corbusier (Charles-Edouard Jeanneret) contributed the conceptual design in March 1947, ground was broken in mid-September 1948, the cornerstone was laid October 24 of last year, Wallace K. Harrison and consultants have served as construction architects, and the Thermopane glass reduces the need for the degree of air-conditioning ordinarily needed to counter the effect of the sun on so much glass. Foreign governments have been acquiring—

The United Nations Secretariat moved into a new home on the East River. LIBRARY OF CONGRESS

and will continue to acquire—many of the private mansions built in the first decades of the century on or near Fifth, Madison, and Park avenues for use by their UN delegates (*see* politics, 1952).

A 36-story office tower is completed at 100 Park Avenue, between 40th and 41st streets. Designed in International Style by Kahn & Jacobs for developer Samuel Leidesdorf, it replaces the Murray Hill Hotel that opened in 1883.

The 23-story Look Building is completed at 488 Madison Avenue, northwest corner 51st Street (opposite St. Patrick's Cathedral). Designed by Emery Roth & Sons for developers Percy and Harold Uris, the gleaming white-brick structure has two miles of ribbon windows. The picture magazine's offices occupy six floors.

Twelve new Manhattan office buildings are completed with more than 4 million square feet of floor space.

The first Queensview apartment house opens in Long Island City on 34th Avenue at 21st Street. Co-op units of 4- and 5-rooms range in price from $7,350 to $8,400 with monthly maintenance of between $63 and $92. The development is projected to include fourteen 14-story buildings on a 10-acre site with nine acres reserved for landscaped areas.

The Windsor Park apartment development in the Cunningham Park section of Queens opens on a 46-acre tract on Bell Boulevard at 73rd Avenue with 1,638 units, which rent for $79 (three-room suite), $89 (3½ rooms), and $105 (4½) including gas and electricity. The architectural firm Schulman & Soloway has designed the structures, which provide free open-air parking for 990 automobiles on the roof of the sunken garages.

Brooklyn's Beach Haven apartment buildings are completed near Coney Island by builder Fred C. Trump (*see* 1949). Together with the Shore Haven apartments he built last year in Bensonhurst, Trump now has 2,700 units for middle-income tenants (*see* Trump Village, 1963).

Rudolph Halley charges September 29 that unscrupulous city landlords are exploiting lower-income tenants and that 750,000 families in the city "have no proper place in which to live." Running for office as president of the City Council, Halley alleges corruption and incompetence on the part of city officials, who are, he says, allied with crime figures and allow some landlords to charge people with little command of English more than they charge those fluent in the language. The slum-clearance program

has not helped the situation much, Halley claims; it makes sense to tear down slums and put up good housing, he says, but it makes no sense to pull down homes and leave families homeless.

Developer Sam Minskoff dies at New York December 26 at age 66.

The Sanitation Department adds 4,800 new wire trash baskets January 23 to the 2,200 in the Manhattan area between 14th and 72nd streets. The city's new sweepers with mechanical brooms move at two to three miles per hour, clean about 12 miles of curb per day, and will be the standard in all boroughs except Staten Island by 1953.

Air-conditioning pioneer Willis H. Carrier dies at New York October 7 at age 73.

P. J. Clarke's saloon at the northeast corner of Third Avenue and 55th Street is purchased by antiques dealer and real estate owner Daniel H. Lavezzo and his brother John (*see* 1945). The bar remains as it has been, with a small grill cooking hamburgers for patrons who may want food, but Choate-educated Navy veteran Daniel H. (Henry) Lavezzo, Jr., now 32, will put more emphasis on food beginning in 1956, adding a large dining room with checked tablecloths in the back. A sports fan and inveterate horse player, the younger Lavezzo will resist offers to sell the property to developers, choosing instead to negotiate with Tishman Realty and Construction Co., which will pay $1.5 million in a deal that involves cutting off the building's two top floors (never used by Clarke's) so they can trade the space for air rights to permit construction of a higher skyscraper on the adjacent property.

The Rainbow Room reopens as a dining spot in October (*see* 1942), but music will not be revived for another 25 years (*see* 1975).

The Diners Club is founded to give credit-card privileges at a group of 27 New York area restaurants. Local lawyer Frank X. McNamara, 33, starts with 200 cardholders who pay an annual membership fee for the card that will be accepted within a few years at hotels, motels, car rental agencies, airline ticket counters, and retail shops as well as at restaurants in most of the United States and in many foreign countries (*see* 1965).

Junior's restaurant opens November 5 at the intersection of Brooklyn's Fulton Street, DeKalb Avenue, and the Flatbush Avenue extension serving steaks, seafood, corned beef, but not yet cheesecake. Manhattan-born owner Harry Rosen, 46, dropped out of school at age 13 to work as a soda jerk, opened his own Manhattan sandwich shop, built up a chain of four Enduro sandwich shops in Manhattan plus one in Brooklyn, and sold the four Manhattan shops in the 1930s to concentrate on the Brooklyn Enduro, which he had opened in 1929 and developed into a steakhouse with a large bar and nighclub-style entertainers. He closed the place last year, has remodeled it, and reopens under the name Junior's with help from his sons Marvin and Walter. Together with Eigel Petersen, his head baker, he will create Junior's cheesecake (see 1973).

Oscar of the Waldorf (Oscar Tschirky) dies at his New Paltz home November 7 at age 84.

New York's population reaches 7,891,957, up from 7,454,995 in 1940; Manhattan has gained 70,177, the Bronx 56,566, Brooklyn 110,856, Queens 253,215, but Brooklyn's white population has declined by 50,000, the first such decline since the 18th century, and blacks have moved in to take the place of those who have left. East Harlem tenements that once housed a mixed population of Germans, Irish, Italians, and Jews have become *El Barrio* (Spanish for the neighborhood)—a Puerto Rican enclave (see 1940). Smaller Hispanic sections are developing in Washington Heights, the South Bronx, and downtown Brooklyn (see 1970).

1951 The trial of bookmaker Harry Gross opens January 22 and ends abruptly when Gross pleads guilty to 66 counts of criminal information, destroying Brooklyn District Attorney McDonald's months-long graft-conspiracy investigation by refusing to squeal on the police officers whom he has been paying off to the tune of about $1 million per year in "ice" (protection money; see 1950). The U.S. Senate Special Committee on Interstate Crime (Kefauver Committee) hearings at Miami reveal extensive evidence that members of the New York Police Department have received payoffs to protect bookmaking operations; more than 100 officers are either dismissed, resign, or retire. Underworld boss Frank Costello testifies March 19 that he was only an occasional dabbler in politics, giving advice to Tammany Hall but never contributing to political campaigns, although he admits to having recognized Carmine G. De Sapio and more than a dozen Tammany district leaders. Former mayor William O'Dwyer admits to the Kefauver Committee March 20 that he visited Costello's apartment at the Majestic on Central Park West and that he appointed some men with mob connections to political jobs.

FBI agents take convicted communist Alger Hiss in handcuffs to a federal detention center in West Street March 22 to begin serving a 5-year prison term (see 1950). He has exhausted all appeals and will serve 44 months at Lewisburg Penitentiary in Pennsylvania.

Sen. Joseph McCarthy (R. Wis.) carries on what many call a "witch hunt" against alleged "known communists" in the State Department, calling even Secretary of State George C. Marshall, now 70, a communist agent. Sen. Millard E. Tydings, 61, (D. Md.) attacks McCarthy for perpetrating "a fraud and a hoax," but Cardinal Spellman and columnist Walter Winchell (who has embraced the political right since 1945) stoutly defend the McCarthy investigations.

A federal district court sends mystery writer Dashiell Hammett to prison for 22 weeks for refusing to name other members of the Civil Rights Congress, a leftist organization to which he belongs. Now 57, Hammett has been living since 1947 in a duplex apartment at 28 West 10th Street and teaching courses at the Jefferson School of Social Science; he volunteered for military service at age 48 and served for 2 years in the Aleutians.

Federal judge Irving R. (Robert) Kaufman, 40, at New York finds Ethel Rosenberg and her husband, Julius, guilty March 30 of having sold atomic secrets to Soviet agents (see 1950). Also found guilty is Julius's New York-born CCNY classmate Morton Sobell, 33, who fled to Mexico with his family last year but was turned over to the FBI at the Texas border. District Attorney Irving Saypol, 48, has prosecuted all three, the Rosenbergs are sentenced to death April 5 (see 1953), Sobell receives a 30-year prison sentence and will serve 18 (5 of them in Alcatraz). President Truman demands more stringent classification of security information by government agencies September 25.

Gen. Douglas MacArthur receives the largest ticker-tape parade in the city's history April 20. Now 71, he has been relieved of his command in Korea by President Truman April 11, gave a farewell address to a joint session of Congress, and is hailed as a hero at New York, where he rides in an open car with Mayor Impelliteri, Grover Whalen, and his military aides, starting from the Waldorf-Astoria with a motorcade that travels for 19 miles as a crowd estimated to number 7,500,000 (400,000 of them from New England, New Jersey, Long Island, and Westchester) looks on. Cardinal Spellman welcomes the general to St. Patrick's Cathedral; boys and girls from public, parochial, and private schools, many in school uniforms, jam Central Park's eastern and western drives to catch a glimpse of MacArthur; and 10,000 pack Washington Square before the general begins the traditional ticker-tape parade up Broadway, where onlookers shower an estimated 2,850 tons of confetti and torn-up waste paper on the street below. MacArthur and his wife, Jean Marie (*née* Faircloth), met on a cruise to Manila in 1935 and were married at New York's Municipal Building in April 1937; they are fêted with a luncheon for 800 at the Waldorf-Astoria (guests include Spencer W. Aldrich, Bernard Baruch, Brooklyn Borough President John Cashmore, James A. Farley, Bernard F. Gimbel, Bronx Borough President James J. Lyons, Alfred P. Sloan, and Thomas J. Watson). MacArthur retires to private life and will live hereafter in the Waldorf Towers.

The Kefauver Committee reports May 1 that former mayor William O'Dwyer has "contributed to the growth of organized crime, racketeering, and gangsterism in New York City." Convicted bookmaker Gross eludes the two young police officers guarding him at his $30,000 Atlantic Beach home September 11 and spends a day at the races in Atlantic City; he has pleaded guilty January 22 to 12 of 66 counts and Brooklyn's Court of Special Sessions sentences him September 27 to a 12-year prison term (he had expected no more than a 4-year sentence and a fine of perhaps $40,000). He is already serving the first of 60 sentences of 1 month each for contempt of court and has been fined $250 for each count (he wears suits that cost $250 each), with an extra day in prison for each dollar unpaid, so he has thus far racked up sentences totalling 17 years and faces the possibility of serving 10 more.

Former mayor O'Dwyer's brother (Peter) Paul O'Dwyer wins a lawsuit against Metropolitan Life Insurance Co., forcing it to admit blacks to its 4-year-old Stuyvesant Town apartment development (the complex will nevertheless remain predominantly white for more than 50 years). Now 44, lawyer O'Dwyer arrived from his native Ireland in 1925, passed his bar exam 4 years later, and has been championing the cause of the underdog ever since.

NAACP cofounder Mary White Ovington dies at Newton Highlands, Mass., in July at age 86.

Research Institute of America cofounder Leo Cherne succeeds theologian Reinhold Niebuhr as chairman of the 18-year-old International Rescue Committee. Now 38, Cherne worked with Gen. MacArthur's occupation forces in 1945 to help revive Japan's economy; he will turn the IRC into the world's largest agency for the relief and resettlement of refugees, initially in Europe, later in Africa and Asia.

The North Side Savings Bank moves its headquarters to 185 West 231st Street (*see* 1905).

The 3-year-old State of Israel announces its first bond issue May 1 and many New Yorkers eagerly buy interest-bearing bonds with a 3½-percent coupon or capital-appreciation bonds that mature in 12 years. Much of the city's Jewish community remains skeptical, questioning whether it was realistic to establish a Jewish state on the basis of Scripture rather than on realpolitik.

Louis S. Lebenthal of Lebenthal & Co. dies of cancer at his 825 Park Avenue apartment December 16 at age 52. His widow, Sayra, now 56, becomes head of the firm, she will bring her son James, now a U.S. Army corporal, and daughter Eleanor (Bissinger) into the firm and continue working herself until age 93 as Lebenthal & Co. grows to underwrite and sell between $750 million and $1 billion worth of bonds per year (in face value of municipal bonds sold).

Wall Street's Dow Jones Industrial Average closes December 31 at 269.23, up from 235.41 at the end of 1950.

Retail sales come almost to a halt in the city April 20 as clerks and customers desert stores to hail Gen. MacArthur on his visit to the city.

State "fair trade" price-fixing laws are not binding on retailers, the U.S. Supreme Court rules May 21. Price wars begin immediately, and New York department stores are mobbed.

The plastic credit card is pioneered by Brooklyn-born Long Island banker William Boyle, 40, who has devised the Franklin Charge Account Plan for Franklin National Bank to facilitate fuel oil dealers' credit and collections. Banks have typically required anyone borrowing less than $500 to file an application with two co-signatures, but Franklin markets its plan with the slogan, "Just charge it." By October of next year it will have broadened its program to 750 merchants serving 28,000 customers, who will charge $2.5 million per year; the First National Bank of Kalamazoo, Mich., will license the charge-account plan from Franklin next year, signing up 30 merchants and 18,000 customers in its first 3 months, and banks at Rochester, and Plainfield, N.J., will quickly follow suit, receiving small fees in exchange for relieving retail establishments of concerns about creditworthiness, accounting, bookkeeping, billing, and other paperwork as the credit card gains immediate popularity among clothiers, hardware dealers, and specialty stores. The Franklin Charge Account Plan will play a major role in fueling the rise of Long Island suburbs; the *American Banker* magazine will observe in October of next year that the plan is allying merchants and bankers in the same way that car dealers and finance companies allied themselves in the 1920s and 1930s (see American Express, 1958; MasterCard, 1966).

Merchant Lane Bryant dies at her 1056 Fifth Avenue home September 26 at age 72.

Brooklyn's last Flatbush Avenue trolley car goes out of service March 4 after 66 years, leaving the borough that once had about 70 trolley-line routes with only nine (Ralph Avenue-Rockaway, Nostrand Avenue, Utica-Reed Avenue, Rockaway Parkway, Church Avenue, Ocean Avenue, Wilson Avenue, McDonald Avenue, Coney Island Avenue). The first of 66 new diesel-engine buses leaves East 71st Street and Avenue N at 4:53 o'clock in the morning to speed traffic along Flatbush Avenue; it makes the eight-mile run to the Brooklyn Bridge, stopping at various points along Joralemon Street, Court Street, and Fulton Street before reaching Cadmon Plaza, but motorists complain that 150 feet of parking space has been eliminated at each bus stop.

Manhattan's First Avenue becomes one-way northbound and Second Avenue becomes one-way southbound beginning June 4 as the city tries to speed up traffic flow in streets choked with trucks and passenger cars (see 1950). Opponents of the change insist that traffic congestion could be eased if the city stopped providing free parking and allowing double parking along avenues and major crosstown streets. Bus companies say the change will cost them revenues and inconvenience passengers, who must now walk extra blocks to reach their destinations or find other means of transportation (see parking, 1955; Seventh and Eighth Avenues, 1954).

The New Jersey Turnpike opens November 5 to speed traffic between New York and Philadelphia. The 118-mile toll road will receive 2 billion tolls in its first 25 years.

Rabbi Menachem Mendel Schneerson assumes the leadership of Brooklyn's Lubavitcher Hasidic sect in Crown Heights February 4 (see 1950). Now 48, he has studied science at Leningrad, Berlin, and the Sorbonne at Paris but will now concentrate on religious teachings and multiply the sect's worldwide membership (see 1991).

Illinois-born New York Roman Catholic priest Fulton J. (John) Sheen, 56, begins a weekly television program under the title Life Is Worth Living and is appointed bishop. Named last year to head the Society for the Propagation of the Faith, Bishop Sheen will clash with Cardinal Spellman over the financial management of the Society and will not thereafter be asked to speak from the pulpit of St. Patrick's Cathedral.

City schoolchilden are issued "identification necklaces" as fears of a possible nuclear attack grow. The Bead Chain Manufacturing Co. produces the necklaces (it also makes army dog tags).

Pace College buys the old New York Times Building in Park Row (see 1946). Originally Pace Institute, it will move into its new quarters near the Brooklyn Bridge in 1953, receive authorization to grant bachelor degrees, offer MBA courses beginning in 1958, open a Pleasantville campus in 1962, complete the Pace Plaza building in lower Manhattan in 1970, and become a university in 1973 as it continues to broaden its academic curriculum.

Recording for the Blind has its beginnings in a two-room New York office opened by former American Red Cross Nurses' Aide Corps assistant director Anne MacDonald (née Thompson), 54. While working for the Women's Auxiliary of the New York Public Library, MacDonald has observed a program that provided recordings for blind veterans attending college on the G.I. Bill of Rights.

The Newsdealers Association of Greater New York votes to ban sales of the Communist Party's Daily Worker from licensed newsstands.

RCA broadcasts color television programs from the Empire State Building May 2, and they are picked up on black-and-white sets. CBS broadcasts color television programs on a regularly scheduled commercial basis beginning June 25 on a five-station East Coast network, but 10.5 million monochrome sets are in U.S. homes and viewers who want color must buy special sets (see RCA, 1954).

A new coaxial cable carries the first transcontinental U.S. television broadcast September 4.

William Randolph Hearst dies of a cerebral hemorrhage at Beverly Hills, Calif., August 14 at age 88, having spent his final years in virtual seclusion; former Jewish Daily Forward editor Abraham Cahan dies at Beth Israel Hospital August 31 at age 91; New Yorker magazine founder Harold W. Ross at Boston December 6 at age 59. Chicago-born staff member William Shawn (originally Chon), 44, has been with the magazine since 1933 and is promoted to succeed Ross, becoming the magazine's second editor. He will remain in the job until his death in 1987.

Nonfiction: A Walker in the City by Alfred Kazin, who writes of his boyhood in "Brunzvil," "In the last crazy afternoon light the neons over the delicatessens bathe all their wares in a cosmetic smile, but strip the streets of every personal shadow and concealment. The torches over the pushcarts hold in a single breath of yellow flame the acid smell of half-sour pickles and herring floating in their briny barrels. There is a dry rattle of loose newspaper sheets around the cracked skins of the 'chiney' oranges. Through the kitchen windows along every ground floor I can already see the containers of milk, the fresh round poppy-seed evening rolls. Time for supper, time to go home;" *Incredible New York: High Life and Low Life of the Last Hundred Years* by New York author Lloyd Morris, 57; *The Vicious Circle: The Story of the Algonquin Round Table* by Margaret Case Harriman; *God and Man at Yale—The Superstition of Academic Freedom* by New York-born 1950 graduate William F. (Frank) Buckley, 24, who has been working in Mexico for the CIA; *The Story of the New York Times; The First 100 Years, 1851-1951* by veteran *Times* reporter Meyer Berger, now 53.

Fiction: *The Catcher in the Rye* by J. D. Salinger, whose hero Holden Caulfield seeks the pure and the good, eschews the "phonies," and meets people under the clock in the Biltmore Hotel lobby.

Poetry: *The Mills of the Kavanaughs* by Robert Lowell; *Collected Poems* by Marianne Moore.

Painting: *Composition for Clarinets and Tin Horn* by Ben Shahn; *Little Giant Still Life* by Stuart Davis; *Black and White Painting* by Jackson Pollock. John F. Sloan dies at Hanover, N.H., September 7 at age 80.

Sculpture: *Hudson River Landscape* by David Smith.

Theater: *Second Threshold* by the late Philip Barry 1/2 at the Morosco Theater, with British actor Clive (originally Clifford) Brook, 59, German-born actress Betsy von Furstenberg, 18, 126 perfs.; *The Rose Tattoo* by Tennessee Williams 2/3 at the Martin Beck Theater, with Maureen Stapleton, Hollywood, Calif.-born actor Don Murray, 21, 306 perfs.; *The Autumn Garden* by Lillian Hellman 3/7 at the Coronet Theater, with Florence Eldridge, actor Kent Smith, 33, Campjaw, N.J.-born actress Jane Wyatt, 40, 101 perfs.; *The Four Poster* by Dutch playwright Jan de Hartog, 37, 10/24 at the Ethel Barrymore Theater, with Jessica Tandy, Canadian-born actor Hume Cronyn, 40, 632 perfs.; *I Am a Camera* by John Van Druten 11/28 at the Empire Theater, with Grosse Point, Mich.-born actress Julie Harris, 25, as Sally Bowles, Nichols, N.Y.-born actor William (LeRoy) Prince, 38, as Christopher Isherwood, 262 perfs.

Actor David Warfield dies at New York June 27 at age 84.

Films: Laslo Benedek's *Death of a Salesman* with Fredric March, Mildred Dunnock; Michael Gordon's *I Can Get It for You Wholesale* with Susan Hayward, Dan Dailey, Sam Jaffe, George Sanders; Sidney Lanfield's *The Lemon Drop Kid* with Bob Hope, Marilyn Maxwell, in a screenplay based on a story by the late Damon Runyon; Edgar G. Ulmer's *St. Benny the Dip* with Dick Haymes, Nina Foch, Roland Young, Lionel Stander.

Film musicals: Michael Curtiz's *I'll See You in My Dreams* with Danny Thomas as songwriter Gus Kahn, Doris Day, songs that include "Ain't We Got Fun" and "It Had to Be You;" David Butler's *Lullaby of Broadway* with Doris Day, Gene Nelson, Gladys George, S. Z. Sakall, Billy de Wolfe; James V. Kern's *Two Tickets to Broadway* with Tony Martin, Janet Leigh, Gloria De Haven, Eddie Bracken, Smith and Dale, dancer Ann Miller, score by Jule Styne and Leo Robin plus the Rodgers and Hart song "Manhattan."

Broadway musicals: *The King and I* 3/29 at the St. James Theater, with Gertrude Lawrence, Yul Brynner, Doretta Morrow, choreography by Jerome Robbins, music by Richard Rodgers, lyrics by Oscar Hammerstein II, songs that include "Getting to Know You," "Hello, Young Lovers," "We Kiss in a Shadow," "Shall We Dance," "Whistle a Happy Tune," 1,246 perfs.; *Make a Wish* 4/18 at the Winter Garden Theater, with Nanette Fabray, Helen Gallagher, dancer Harold Lang, choreography by Gower Champion, music and lyrics by Alabama-born composer-writer Hugh Martin, 37, book by Preston Sturges and Abe Burrows, sets and costumes by Raoul Pène Du Bois, 102 perfs.; *A Tree Grows in Brooklyn* 4/19 at the Alvin Theater, with Shirley Booth, Johnny Johnston, Herbert Ross, music by Arthur Schwartz, lyrics by Dorothy Fields, songs that include "Make the Man Love Me," "Look Who's Dancing," "I'll Buy You a Star," 267 perfs.; *Flahooley* 5/14 at the Broadway Theater, with Peruvian soprano Yma Sumac (Emperatrice Chavarri), 23, who appeared at the Hollywood Bowl 2 years ago, puppeteers Bil and Cora Baird, and Atlanta-born soprano Barbara (Nell) Cook, 23, music by Sammy Fain, lyrics by E. Y. Harburg, songs that include "Here's to Your Illusions," 40 perfs.; *Top Banana* 11/1 at the Winter Garden Theater, with Phil Silvers, Joey Faye, music and lyrics by Johnny Mercer, 350 perfs.; *Paint Your Wagon* 11/12 at the Shubert Theater, with James Barton, Brooklyn-born ingénue Olga San Juan, 24, New York-born ingénue Kay Medford (originally Maggie O'Regin), 31, music by Frederick Loewe, lyrics by Alan Jay Lerner, songs that include "They Call the Wind Maria," "I Talk to the Trees," "I Still See Elisa," 289 perfs.

Fanny Brice dies of a cerebral hemorrhage at her Hollywood, Calif., home May 29 at age 59; comedian Leon Errol at Hollywood October 12 at age 70; composer Sigmund Romberg of a cerebral hemorrhage at New York November 9 at age 64.

Opera: *Amahl and the Night Visitors* 12/24 on the NBC Television Opera Theater, with music by Gian-Carlo Menotti, who has written the first opera for television (NBC executive Robert W. Sarnoff, 33, has commissioned the work).

Ballet: *The Miraculous Mandarin* 9/6 at City Center, with Canadian ballerina Melissa Hayden (Mildred Herman), 28, Hugh Laing, music by the late Béla Bartók, choreography by Todd Bolender; *The Pied Piper* 12/4 at City Center, with Tanaquil LeClerq, Jerome Robbins, music by Aaron Copland, choreography by Robbins.

Charlie Parker records "My Little Suede Shoes" in March and scores a hit. He has been living since last year in a basement apartment at 151 Avenue B, between 7th and 10 streets, and will remain there with his wife, Chan Richardson, and their three children until 1954.

New York-born singer and vaudeville entertainer Sammy Davis, Jr., 25, makes his Carnegie Hall debut 3/31.

English-born U.S. jazz pianist-composer Marian Margaret McPartland (*née* Turner), 31, forms her own trio.

Pianist-orchestra leader Edwin Frank "Eddie" Duchin dies of leukemia at Memorial Hospital February 9 at age 41.

 A New York college basketball point-shaving scandal rocks the sports world (*see* 1949). Manhattan College sophomore center Junius Kellogg, 23, tells his coach Ken Norton in January that gamblers have approached him as the team's high scorer and offered him $1,000 to make sure Manhattan loses its game to DePaul at Madison Square Garden by 10 points or more (DePaul is a three-point favorite, but gamblers bet on point-margins, not just results). Henry Poppe, a co-captain of last year's Manhattan team, has put the deal to Kellogg, Coach Norton calls in college authorities, who notify police, who persuade Kellogg to co-operate, wiring him with a listening device to wear when he meets the gamblers at a neighborhood bar. They tell him to "throw hook shots over the basket" and "miss rebounds occasionally." A six-foot-eight Virginia-born scholarship student, Kellogg is too nervous to play for long, Norton puts in a substitute who sinks eight baskets,

and Manhattan upsets DePaul 62 to 59. Police arrest Poppe a few hours later and confront him with wire-tap evidence; he admits under questioning that he and his co-captain John A. Byrne have helped to throw 49 to 50 games, with each co-captain collecting $5,000 plus a salary of $40 per week. Also arrested are two bookmakers and a go-between. Three stars of last year's CCNY national championship team are arrested in February on charges that they accepted payoffs from gamblers to throw games (the most anyone collected was $4,650). Other arrests and indictments follow. Manhattan District Attorney Frank Hogan says that one gambler (who has served time for armed robbery) has bet $8,000 to $10,000 per day, winning about $300,000 betting on just 10 fixed games. Three stars of this year's LIU team are arrested, and the most prominent of them says, "This wouldn't have happened if basketball had been kept on the campus . . . It seems more of a business than a sport." The players turn over $23,540 in payoff money to the DA's office. A makeshift CCNY five beats Lafayette 67 to 48 in a half-empty Garden in March, and CCNY coach Nat Holman says, "The game has meant too much to the youth of the college, the nation, even the world to be affected by half a dozen kids who have a price." LIU trustees order basketball abandoned except for intramural sport, although the $50,000 produced by the game each year has funded other athletics. The Board of Higher Education rules April 30 that CCNY and the other three municipal colleges (Brooklyn College, Hunter, and Queens) may no longer play at Madison Square Garden or other commercially operated sports arenas or in any organized competition outside the regular school program, and there will be no recruitment of players or preferential treatment shown to athletes. LIU drops basketball entirely. The scandal brings demands that newspapers stop printing betting odds, that a basketball czar be appointed, and that the penalties under state law for fixing an athletic contest (a maximum of 5 years in prison and up to $10,000 in fines) be doubled. Junius Kellogg receives some threats along with letters of praise, he will be signed by the Harlem Globetrotters, but his spinal cord will be severed in a car accident at Pine Bluff, Ark., in April 1954. Not until the 1970s will a New York school (St. John's) gain a high national basketball ranking.

Frank Sedgman, 23, (Australia) wins in men's singles at Forest Hills, Maureen ("Little Mo") Connolly, 16, in women's singles.

Gov. Dewey replaces boxing commissioner Edward P. "Eddie" Eagan as chairman of the state athletic commission September 25, naming hotel executive Robert K. Christianberry to succeed him in the $9,378-per-year post.

Willie Mays joins the New York Giants lineup in center field. Former Dodgers manager Leo Durocher moved to the Giants in 1948 and has signed Alabama-born Willie Howard Mays, Jr., 20, who will play his first full season in 1954, win the National League's batting championship with a .345 average, continue with the Giants when they move from the Polo Grounds to San Francisco in 1957, and remain a stalwart of the team until 1972.

Mickey Mantle joins the New York Yankees at center field, playing alongside Joe DiMaggio, who handles left field (see 1936). Oklahoma-born Mickey Charles Mantle, 19, plays only 96 games and sets a league record of 111 strikeouts but shows he can hit the ball out of the park; he will be a Yankee star for 17 years beginning next season and his batting average in his 10 peak years will always be above .300.

"The Giants win the pennant! The Giants win the pennant!" shouts radio sportscaster Russ Hodges October 3 as Scottish-born third baseman Robert Brown "Bobby" Thomson, 27, hits a three-run homer off a pitch by Ralph Branca in the bottom of the ninth inning of the third playoff game of the National League pennant race to beat the Brooklyn Dodgers 5 to 4 before a Polo Grounds crowd that includes Jackie Gleason, J. Edgar Hoover, Toots Shor, and Frank Sinatra. Thompson has gone to bat with two on, one out, and the Giants trailing 4 to 2; "The shot heard round the world" wins it for the Giants, who have come from 13 games behind to tie the Dodgers and force the playoff.

The New York Yankees win the World Series, defeating the Giants 4 games to 2. Giant pitcher Dave Koslo (originally George Bernard Koslowski), 31, wins the first game, and Jim Hearn, 29, the third, but Eddie Lopat wins the second and fifth for the Yankees, Allie Reynolds the fourth, and Vic Raschi the sixth. Giant shortstop Alvin Dark, 29, gets 10 hits, including three doubles and a home run; first baseman Carroll Walter "Whitey" Lockman, 25, six hits, including a double and a home run; outfielder Monford Merrill "Monte" Irvin, 32, 11 hits, including a triple. Phil Rizzuto gets eight hits for the Yankees, including a home run; Joe DiMaggio six hits, including two doubles and a home run; infielder Gil McDougald, 23, six hits, including a double and a home run; first baseman Joe Collins, 29, four hits, including a home run; and outfielder Gene Woodling, 29, three hits, including a double, a triple, and a home run.

Yankee outfielder Joe DiMaggio retires at age 36 with career totals of 361 home runs and only 369 strikeouts. His underworld connections have set up a million-dollar pension fund for him at the Bowery Savings Bank.

The first April-in-Paris Ball is held at the Waldorf-Astoria Hotel. Elsa Maxwell has persuaded Waldorf manager Claude C. Philippe and the French consul-general to underwrite the ball that will continue each spring for some years.

New York designer Ann Fogarty (née Whitney), 32, wins the Fashion Critics' Award. She has perfected the New Look (see 1947) and will modify the Empire style with a "camise" look for young women sized 6 to 12.

Liberty Travel opens with one desk in a Times Square office to begin what will become America's largest privately owned leisure travel chain. Specializing initially in travel to the Catskills and Miami, Vienna-born entrepreneur Fred Kassner, 22, and his NYU classmate Gilbert Haroche will soon add Caribbean and Mexican destinations, expanding to cover Hawaii, Europe, Asia, and South America as they market vacation packages through 88 sales offices in 31 states, employing 2,500 people to serve more than 1 million customers per year.

The federal government files civil antitrust suits April 30 against five truck-owner organizations serving the city's garment district. The same five were charged in 1944 with the same activities and fined a total of $58,000, but this has evidently failed to stop them from monopolizing the delivery of dresses and women's and children's coats and suits in the area.

The body of waterfront racketeer Philip Mangano, 51, is found April 19 in a deserted marsh near Jamaica Bay south of Avenue Y near East 72nd Street in Brooklyn's Bergin Beach section. Mrs. Mary Gooch, a middle-aged fishing boat owner, has discovered the body lying face down and clad only in a white shirt, white undershorts, white shorts, black socks, and black tie with a gold tie-clip. An aide to waterfront boss Joe Adonis (who lives in Fort Lee, N.J.), Mangano has evidently been killed elsewhere with three bullets fired into the back of his head. Police grill gambler Frank Costello, Adonis, Umberto "Albert" Anastasia, and others, including Mangano's son Vincent, 22; they speculate that Mangano may have been killed because he had talked of leaving town and might have been trying to sever his connections with the Mafia hierarchy. His brother Vincent disappears shortly thereafter,

Anastasia is believed to have had the Mangano brothers killed, and he assumes control of the Genovese crime family with help from mobster Frank Scalise (see 1957; Sutton, 1952).

Federal agents arrest former bootlegger Waxey Gordon and three accomplices on a New York street August 2 when he tries to deliver a $6,300 package of heroin to an agent disguised as a burglar (see Gordon, 1933). Now 63, Gordon was convicted during the war of selling 10,000 pounds of sugar to an illegal distillery and served a year in jail; he renewed his involvement in the narcotics trade after the war, a General Sessions jury finds him guilty, he is a four-time offender, and the judge sentences him December 13 to a term of 25 years to life.

 The 41-year-old Ritz-Carlton Hotel comes down to the dismay of its many admirers, making way for a new Madison Avenue office building (see Goelet death, 1941; "new" Ritz-Carlton, 1983).

Manhattan House is completed in the block bounded by Second and Third avenues between 65th and 66th streets. Financed by New York Life Insurance Co., the 19-story apartment block of glazed pale gray brick replaces the car barn of the Third Avenue El and some other structures, it towers above the low-rise tenements in the area, it has been designed by Gordon Bunshaft of Skidmore, Owings & Merrill with an assist from Mayer & Whittlesey, its 582 units have working fireplaces, and air pressure in the hallways is higher than in the apartments to prevent cooking odors from circulating.

The four 14-story Lexington Houses are completed in May on a site extending from Park Avenue to Third between 98th and 99th streets. Built as a slum-clearance project, they have accommodations for 448 families.

Central Park's Wollman Ice-Skating Rink opens January 6 just north of the 59th Street entrance at the Avenue of the Americas (see 1858). Philanthropist Kate Wollman receives an award for raising the necessary funds (daughter of stockbroker William J. Wollman, she has donated $600,000), but critics complain that Parks Commissioner Moses has cannibalized the Park's five-acre Pond, reducing it to just three acres, to make room for the rink that skaters will enjoy until 1980 (see 1986).

A new Central Park carousel opens July 2, replacing one that burned last year (the old mechanical horses were moved in January to Bronx Beach Park for repairs). Mayor Impelliteri and Commissioner Moses take the first ride.

 Russian-born Manhattan food-store owner Louis Zabar dies of cancer, leaving his business to his sons Saul, 22; Stanley, 18; and Eli, 7. Saul cancels his plans to enter medical school and will keep the business going while Stanley goes through college and law school, keeping the store on the west side of Broadway between 80th and 81st streets but selling four other self-service Broadway food stores (at 91st, 92nd, 96th, and 110th streets). Russian refugee Murray Klein arrived last year without a dime and worked briefly as a bottle sorter at Louis Zabar's 110th Street store, has been assistant manager of the 96th Street store, and will eventually be brought in to manage the main store; he will save it from bankruptcy and turn it into an emporium for gourmet foods and kitchen tools, selling not only smoked fish, pickled herring, coffee beans, and a few cheeses but also caviar and a vast array of other delicacies not be found elsewhere (except at much higher prices), including a panoply of ready-to-eat dishes (see 1977; shopping bag, 1966; E.A.T. restaurant, 1973).

Contract talks between members of the Bagel Bakers of America, AFL, and the Bagel Bakers Association break off December 16; sales of smoked salmon plummet (New Yorkers consume 1.2 million bagels on an average weekend).

 New York (with suburban areas) has 12.3 million people, London 8.4 million, Paris 6.4, Tokyo 6.3, Shanghai 6.2, Chicago 5.

1952 The United Nations General Assembly meets in its new headquarters on the East River February 27 (see real estate, 1950). Each of the 2,070 seats in the new chamber is equipped with earphones that offer simultaneous translations in several languages. The Security Council holds its first meeting at the new site April 4.

The communist "witch hunt" continues, ruining many careers (see 1951). Comedian Zero Mostel, now 37, is among those blacklisted as a communist; to support his family he rents a studio in West 28th Street and takes up painting.

Puerto Rico adopts a new Constitution July 25 and becomes the first U.S. commonwealth. Many Puerto Ricans have family in New York, every Puerto Rican obtains all rights of U.S. citizenship except voting in federal elections and need not pay federal income taxes (see 1898; 1954; population, 1953).

Gen. Eisenhower tells an American Legion audience at New York August 25 that the United States should help other nations escape the "Red yoke." Nominated to head the Republican Party presidential ticket, he defeats Gov. Adlai E. Stevenson, 52, of Illinois, winning 55 percent of the popular vote (and 442 of the 531 electoral votes) with help from his campaign manager Herbert Brownell, Jr. and hard-sell television commercials created by Virginia-born New York advertising man Rosser Reeves, 41, of the 12-year-old Ted Bates agency, who has promoted Ike as if he were Anacin, Palmolive Soap, Wonder Bread, or some other brand of packaged goods.

$ Wall Street's Dow Jones Industrial Average closes December 31 at 292.90, up from 269.23 at the end of 1951.

The Transport Workers' Union (TWU) starts the year with a drivers' strike against five private bus lines, demanding a 40-hour week and a pay raise. Some 3.5 million riders are affected.

The United States Lines passenger ship S.S. *United States* leaves New York with 1,000 passengers July 3 on her first transatlantic voyage and sets a new speed record on her second day out by covering 801 nautical miles in 24 hours. Designed by naval architect-marine engineer William Francis Gibbs, now 66, she has been built with immense 240,000-horsepower steam turbines that can push her at 50 miles per hour and is convertible to a troopship that can transport 14,000 men. The $79 million, 53,000-ton vessel is 990 feet in length overall, 102 feet wide (slim enough to get through the Panama Canal), can carry 1,750 passengers, and makes the crossing of 2,949 nautical miles in 3 days, 10 hours, 40 minutes, averaging 35.59 knots per hour (more than 40 mph) to break the *Queen Mary*'s 14-year-old record by 10 hours, 2 minutes. Equipped with a gymnasium, swimming pool, two theaters, and three Meyer Davis orchestras, she breaks the record on her westward return voyage as well, averaging 34.51 knots.

Robert Moses proposes construction of a 48-foot roadway through Washington Square Park to link Fifth Avenue with West Broadway. The road would eliminate some playgrounds, and neighborhood women led by Chicago-born activist Shirley Hayes (née Zak), 40, mount an effort to oppose the idea; the issue becomes a cause célèbre that will continue for years (see 1959).

Eviction notices signed "Robert Moses, City Construction Coordinator" arrive December 4 in the East Tremont section of the Bronx, where Moses's plan for a Cross-Bronx Expressway calls for demolition of 54 six- and seven-story apartment houses along a mile-long strip. Deputy Mayor Henry Epstein has opposed the Moses plan, pointing out that the Expressway could just as easily be built two blocks away and require demolition of only six small brownstone tenements, but investigators hired by Moses have found out that Epstein has a mistress and Moses has blackmailed Epstein into endorsing a plan that requires displacing 60,000 middle-class rent-controlled tenants, most of them Jewish but many German and Irish as well, along with some blacks. All tenants are ordered to move within 90 days, although construction of the Expressway is not scheduled to begin for another 3 years (see 1963).

New York State reclaims Halloran General Hospital from the Veterans Administration and converts it into the Willowbrook State School (initially called the Richmond Complex of the Staten Island Developmental Center) (see 1942). The hospital has begun admitting children and other civilians who are mentally retarded or disabled, and state institutions will for the next 20 years send their most severely retarded children to Willowbrook (see 1963).

Mount Sinai Hospital's Magdalene and Charles Klingenstein Pavilion is completed to designs by Kahn & Jacobs (see 1904; Annenberg Building, 1976).

Malcolm X joins U.S. Black Muslim leader Elijah Mohammed following Malcom's release from prison after having served 6 years on a conviction of armed robbery (see 1931). Now 27, the Omaha-born disciple has educated himself in prison, read the teachings of Elijah Mohammed, adopted the new faith, changed his name from Malcolm Little, and will become the sect's first "national minister" in 1963 (see 1965).

Kindergarten pioneer Bessie Locke dies at New York April 9 at age 86; educator John Dewey of pneumonia at New York June 1 at age 92.

The city dismisses eight public-school teachers October 23 for alleged communist activities.

Mad magazine has its beginnings in the *Mad* comic book that appears in May with 32 pages in full color satirizing other comic books and even making fun of itself. New York-born founder-editor Harvey Kurtzman, 27, will develop a freckled, big-eared, cow-licked idiot boy character, comedian Ernie Kovaks will name the boy Melvin Cowznofski, and he will become infamous as Alfred E. Neuman ("What—Me Worry?") as circulation reaches a peak of 2.5 million. New York-born publisher William M. (Maxwell) Gaines, 32, will sell his E. C. (Entertaining Comics) Publications to Kinney National Service Corp. (later Warner Communications) but remain publisher.

The *National Enquirer* is taken over by Generoso Pope, Jr., 25, whose father made a fortune in sand and gravel and has published the New York Italian-language newspaper *Il Progresso*. Founded in 1926 by a former Hearst advertising executive, the *Enquirer* has become little more than a tout sheet, but Pope will emphasize crime, gore, miracle cures, gossip, and sex to build circulation that will pass 4 million per week by 1975 and will multiply his $75,000 investment hundreds of times over.

Advertising pioneer Albert D. Lasker dies at New York May 30 at age 72. In the last 10 years he has given away large sums of money through the Albert and Mary Lasker Foundation that his widow will continue.

The Duane Jones trial outcome October 28 discourages advertising agency account executives from taking accounts to start their own agencies. A Manhattan jury awards $300,000 plus any accumulated profits in the Scheideler, Beck and Werner agency to box-top king Duane Jones, 52, whose former executives are ruled to have conspired with executives of the Manhattan Soap Co. to move the account (industry rumor has it that Jones is rarely sober after 11 o'clock in the morning).

St. Martin's Press is founded at New York as the U.S. branch of the London-based Macmillan Co. (see Verlagsgruppe Georg von Holtzbrinck, 1995).

Nonfiction: *The Diary of George Templeton Strong* (edited by Allan Nevins and Milton Halsey Thomas, abridged by Thomas J. Presley); *As You Pass By* by New York author Kenneth Holcomb Dunshee traces the history of the city's infrastructure and pays tribute to its firefighters; *The Power of Positive Thinking* by Ohio-born clergyman Norman Vincent Peale, 54, of the Marble Collegiate Church; *A House Is Not a Home* by former New York madam Polly Adler, whose best-seller contains revelations that make her internationally famous; *Amy Vanderbilt's Complete Book of Etiquette* by former International News Service columnist Vanderbilt, 43, whose 700-page volume is illustrated by Pittsburgh-born artist Andy Warhol (originally Andrew Warhola), 14 (see Painting, 1960). It is a source of customs, mores, and manners by a relative of the late Commodore Vanderbilt (who had no manners at all).

Fiction: *The Natural* by Brooklyn-born New York novelist Bernard Malamud, 38; *The Groves of Academe* by Mary McCarthy; *Sibyl* by Louis Auchincloss, who has done some of his work at the New York Society Library; *Player Piano* by Indianapolis-born novelist Kurt Vonnegut, Jr., 29, who 5 years ago joined the public-relations staff of General Electric at Schenectady and has been inspired to write a science-fiction work on the technocratic tendencies of modern industrial society.

Juvenile: *Charlotte's Web* by E. B. White, illustrations by Garth Williams.

 Painting: *Red Painting* by Buffalo-born New York minimalist Adolf Frederick "Ad" Reinhardt, 38; *Woman and Bicycle* by Willem de Kooning; *Number Three* by Jackson Pollock; *Adam* and *Ulysses* by Barnett Newman; *Man* by Ben Shahn; *Mountains and Sea* by New York-born painter Helen Frankenthaler, 25, daughter of a State Supreme Court judge, who studied under Mexican painter Rufino Tamayo at the Dalton School, pursued her studies at Bennington College, was influenced by Jackson Pollock and Hans Hofmann, has developed a technique of applying very thin paint to unprimed canvas, allowing it to soak in and create atmospheric blots, and has begun a relationship with Bronx-born New York critic Clement Greenberg, now 43; Elaine de Kooning gives her first exhibition at the Stable Gallery. Now 32 and still married to Willem de Kooning, now 48, she will teach at Bard College, Cooper Union, and other colleges, but her career will not really take off until she and her husband separate in 1957.

 Theater: *The Shrike* by Philadelphia-born playwright Joseph Kramm, 44, 1/15 at the Cort Theater, with José Ferrer, Judith Evelyn, 161 perfs.; *The Fifth Season* by New York-born playwright Sylvia Regan, 44, 1/23 at the Cort Theater, with veteran Yiddish comedian Menasha Skulnik, now 61, Richard Whorf, 654 perfs.; *Jane* by S. N. Behrman 2/1 at the Coronet Theater with Edna Best, Basil Rathbone, 100 perfs.; *The Time of the Cuckoo* by Arthur Laurents 10/15 at the Empire Theater, with Shirley Booth, Italian-born actor Dino DiLuca, 49, New York-born actress Geraldine Brooks, 26, 263 perfs.; *The Seven-Year Itch* by New York-born playwright George Axelrod, 30, 11/20 at the Fulton Theater, with Kentucky-born actor Tom Ewell (originally Yewell Tomkins), 43, Vienna-born actress Vanessa Brown, 24, 1,141 perfs.

Playwright Ferenc Molnar dies at New York April 1 at age 74; actor Canada Lee of a heart attack at New York May 8 at age 45; Gertrude Lawrence of a liver ailment (aggravated by an injection for ivy poisoning) at New York September 6 at age 54.

Television: *The Today Show* 1/14 on NBC with former Chicago radio personality Dave Garroway, 38, serving as master of ceremonies for the 2-hour morning news and interview show developed by Pat Weaver.

Working out of a street-level studio with a window facing on Rockefeller Center street traffic, Garroway is soon joined by chimpanzee J. Fred Muggs, whose presence encourages children to turn on the TV set.

Films: Ray Ashley, Morris Engel, and Ruth Orkin's *Little Fugitive* with Richie Andrusco as a young child who thinks he has killed his brother and roams lost through Coney Island. Also: John Sturges's *The Girl in White* with June Allyson as Emily Dunning, the first woman to work as a physician in a New York public hospital; Alfred E. Green's *Invasion, U.S.A.* with Gerald Mohr, Peggie Castle, Dan O'Herlihy (New York City is threatened with nuclear annihilation); Joseph Pevney's *Meet Danny Wilson* with Frank Sinatra, Shelley Winters; Henry Hathaway, Howard Hawks, Henry King, Henry Koster, and Jean Negulesco's *O. Henry's Full House* with Charles Laughton, Marilyn Monroe, Anne Baxter, Gregory Ratoff, Richard Widmark, Jeanne Crain, and Farley Granger; Samuel Fuller's *Park Row* with Gene Evans, Mary Welch as rival newspaper owners in 1880s New York; Lewis Seiler's *The Winning Team* with Doris Day, Ronald Reagan (as St. Louis pitcher Grover Cleveland Alexander, who beat the Yankees to win the 1926 World Series).

Motion picture pioneer William Fox dies of a heart ailment at Doctors Hospital May 8 at age 73; actor John Garfield of a heart attack at New York May 21 at age 39 (he was blacklisted two years ago for refusing to name friends who might have been communists and has been living with his wife and two children at 88 Central Park West).

Film musicals: Charles Walters's *The Belle of New York* with Fred Astaire, Vera-Ellen, Marjorie Main, Keenan Wynn, Alice Pearce, songs that include "Let a Little Love Come In;" Henry Koster's *Stars and Stripes Forever* with Clifton Webb (as bandleader-composer John Philip Sousa), Robert Wagner, Ruth Hussey.

Broadway musicals: *New Faces* 5/16 at the Royale Theater, with South Carolina-born singer Eartha Kitt, 24, Missouri-born comedienne Alice (Margaret) Ghostley, 25, songs that include "Love Is a Simple Thing" by Jane Carroll, lyrics by Arthur Siegal, "Monotonous" by Arthur Siegal, lyrics by Jane Carroll, Nancy Graham, 365 perfs.; *Wish You Were Here* 6/25 at the Imperial Theater, with Richmond Hill-born actor John Edward Joseph "Jack" Cassidy, 25, Bronx-born actor Sidney Armus, 27, Houston, Texas-born actor Larry Blyden (originally Lawrence Blieden), 27, music and lyrics by Harold Rome, story set in the Catskills resort area, songs that include "Where Did the Night Go?" and the title song, 598 perfs.

Charlie Parker records "Autumn in New York" in January, appears on TV with Dizzy Gillespie 2/24, and appears with Paul Robeson at Rockland Place 9/26.

Dave Brubeck and his San Francisco quartet pioneer "modern" or "progressive" jazz. David Warren Brubeck, 31, makes his New York debut and begins a 15-year career of innovation that will give jazz music a new complexity of rhythm and counterpoint.

The Modern Jazz Quartet is founded at New York by pianist John Lewis, drummer Kenny Clarke (who will be replaced in 1955 by Connie Kay [originally Conrad Kirnon]), now 25, Detroit-born vibraphonist Milt Jackson, 30, and bassist Percy Heath. Members wear tailored suits, use powerfully subdued arrangements, and will continue (with some substitutions) until 1995, working to return jazz to the prestige it enjoyed before losing popularity to big bands and extending its appeal to a wider audience.

Popular song: "Lullaby of Birdland" by George Shearing, lyrics by B. Y. Forster.

Composer Percy Wenrich dies at New York March 18 at age 72; jazz pianist-bandleader Fletcher Henderson of a stroke at his Harlem home December 29 at age 54.

Frank Sedgman wins in men's singles at Forest Hills, Maureen Connolly in women's singles.

The New York Yankees win the World Series, defeating the Brooklyn Dodgers 4 games to 3. Pee Wee Reese gets 10 hits, including a home run; Duke Snider 10 hits that include two doubles and four home runs; Dodger third baseman Billy Cox, 33, eight hits, including two doubles; but Yankee first baseman Johnny Mize, 39, gets six hits, including a double and three home runs; Mickey Mantle's home run in the sixth inning of the seventh game puts the Yankees ahead (Mantle's 10 hits include a double, a triple, and three home runs); and Yankee reliever Bob Kuzava, 29, retires the last eight Brooklyn batters.

Bonnie Cashin Designs is founded by Oakland, Calif.-born New York fashion designer Cashin, 36, who has created costumes for Roxy Theater dancers, helped design uniforms for women in the armed services, and has won her first Coty Award for her casual, layered clothes. She introduces canvas raincoats this year, will use industrial zippers for jumpsuits in 1955, and make suede Indian dresses with fringes in 1957.

Bank robber Willie Sutton is recognized on a New York subway February 18, rearrested, and sentenced to 17 years in prison on charges of having held up a Queens bank in 1950. Asked why he robs banks, he says it's because "that's where the money is" and offers to sell his life story to the highest bidder; the money to be used to help discourage youngsters from criminal careers. Clothing salesman Arnold Schuster, 24, is credited with having pointed Sutton out to the police, rejects offers of police protection, and is shot dead near his Boro Park, Brooklyn, home the night of March 8 on orders from Murder, Inc. boss Albert Anastasia. Sutton has stolen an estimated $2 million over the years, will serve time at the Attica State Correctional Facility, be paroled in 1967, and will die in November 1980 at age 79.

Former New York bootlegger and drug dealer Waxey Gordon dies of a heart attack at Alcatraz Prison June 24 at age 64.

 The 32-story Kent Building (initially the Chrysler Building East) is completed at 161 East 42nd Street (666 Third Avenue) to designs by Reinhard, Hofmeister & Walquist.

A combination office building and parking garage is completed at 1120 Sixth Avenue, between 43rd and 44th streets, replacing the Hippodrome that opened in 1905. Kahn & Jacobs has designed the structure.

Lever House opens April 29 on Park Avenue between 53rd and 54th streets. Commissioned by Charles Luckman of Lever Brothers and designed in International Style by Gordon Bunshaft of Skidmore, Owings & Merrill, with an interior designed by Raymond Loewy, the 24-story glass-walled building takes up far less of its site than the law permits, critics hail its aesthetics (although some find it incongruous in a street of conventional buildings that are still mostly apartment houses), a traveling gondola suspended from its roof enables window cleaners to wash its 1,404 panes of heat-resistant blue-green glass, but the windows are sealed, the centrally air-conditioned building makes profligate use of energy, and it will be a model for energy-wasting architectural extravangazas that will be constructed throughout much of the world. It has a 63-car basement garage, and Lever Brothers (part of the multinational colossus Unilever) will maintain U.S. headquarters in the building until 1998.

The Yale architecture magazine *Perspecta* carries an article entitled "Monumental Architecture—Or the Art of Pleasing in Civic Design" by critic Henry Hope Reed, 37, who calls "clean and modern" architecture a fraud: "We have sacrificed the past, learning, the crafts, all the arts on the altar of 'honest functionalism.' In so doing we have given up . . . the very stuff which makes a city beautiful, the jewels in the civic designer's diadem."

Lever House went up on Park Avenue. Ninety-five apartment houses and hotels gave way to office towers. CHIE NISHIO

Architect C. P. H. Gilbert dies at Pelham Manor October 25 at age 92.

 The Penn Bar and Grill opens at the corner of Eighth Avenue and 31st Street, where it will continue for 46 years to serve longshoremen, merchant mariners, Penn Station commuters and, later, Madison Square Garden patrons.

The first Blarney Stone Bar and Grill opens on Third Avenue between 44th and 45th streets. Irish-born entrepreneur Daniel Flanagan, 46, arrived at New York in 1924 at age 18 and has worked for the A&P; by the 1960s he will have 23 Blarney Stones in Manhattan, each with a steam table where a workingman can eat a hearty meal of corned beef, brisket, or pastrami with beer at moderate prices.

Restaurateur James "Dinty" Moore dies of an embolism at his West 42nd Street restaurant December 25 at age 83, having served corned beef and cabbage, Irish stew, and other dishes for 38 years at the same address.

Congress passes the McCarran-Walter Immigration and Nationality Act over President Truman's veto and it becomes law June 27. It removes the ban on Asian and African immigrants to the United States and permits spouses and minor children to enter as nonquota immigrants, but it extends the national origins quota system set up by the Johnson-Reed Act of 1924. Critics point out that while Britain uses only half her quota of 65,000, Italy has a 20-year waiting list for her quota of 5,500 (emerging nations of Africa and Asia have token quotas of 100 each) (see 1955).

1953 Former mayor William O'Dwyer's position as U.S. ambassador to Mexico ends as a new Republican administration begins at Washington; his wife, Sloan, obtains a civil divorce in Mexico (see 1949; 1950). Publisher's wife and former playwright Clare Boothe Luce, now 49, has taken office March 3 as U.S. ambassador to Italy (but see 1954).

Ethel Rosenberg and her husband Julius are executed at Sing Sing June 19 for transmitting U.S. atomic secrets to Soviet agents although doubts persist that either of them gave the Russians anything of value (see 1951); a new series of U.S. atomic tests begins in the Nevada desert.

Korean hostilities end in an armistice signed July 27 at Panmunjom after a 3-year conflict that has cost 36,914 U.S. lives. New York lawyer Arthur (Hobson) Dean, 55, of Sullivan & Cromwell has negotiated for 7 weeks on behalf of the United States and UN at the Panmunjom talks.

Former U.S. senator Robert F. Wagner dies at New York May 5 at age 75 as his son and namesake campaigns for election as mayor; Sen. Robert A. Taft (R. Ohio) dies of cancer at New York July 31 at age 63 a few months after becoming Senate majority leader (see real estate, 1949); former Bronx political boss Edward J. Flynn sails with his wife and daughter on the Mauretania but dies of heart disease at a Dublin hospital August 18 at age 61.

Manhattan Borough President Robert F. Wagner, 43, wins the mayoralty election on the Democratic-Liberal-Fusion ticket, garnering 1,022,626 votes as compared with 661,591 for Republican Harold Riegelman, 467,104 for Liberal-Independent candidate Rudolph Halley. Manhattan Democratic Party boss Carmine (Gerard) De Sapio, 44, became a district leader in his native Greenwich Village at age 30 and has played a key role in securing Wagner's landslide victory.

The New York Police Department establishes a Civilian Complaint Review Board in response to charges that officers use excessive force against blacks and Puerto Ricans; the new departmental investigating arm is made up entirely of police officials (see 1966).

The Bureau of Labor Statistics reports that 30 percent of New York City's workforce is engaged in manufacturing, 21 percent in the wholesale and retail trade, 15 percent in service jobs, 11 percent in government jobs, and 10 percent in finance and real estate (see 1954).

The American Stock Exchange is created by a renaming of the New York Curb Exchange, whose members have not traded from curbs since 1921.

Wall Street's Dow Jones Industrial Average closes December 31 at 280.90, down from 291.90 at the end of 1952.

Bernard F. Gimbel retires as president of the family business, whose stores take in $286 million, up from $122 million in 1927, the year he took over management. Now 66 and chairman of the board, he continues to build a chain of Gimbels and Saks Fifth Avenue stores in New York suburbs and in other cities nationwide.

Italian leather-goods manufacturer Aldo Gucci, 48, and his brother Rodolfo open a New York store against the wishes of their father, Guccio, who opened a leather-goods shop at Florence in 1921 but has died this year at age 72. Gucci loafers with colorful fabric strips and double-G metal trim will become status symbols (but see crime, 1986).

A bill signed by Gov. Dewey March 20 provides for a New York City Transportation Authority (NYCTA) and it begins operations June 15. Dewey has pushed for the legislation, promising that it will make the subway "the greatest transit system in the world" and ensure "efficient management and the elimination of politics from its operation," but opponents have charged that it weakens the public commitment to rapid transit and—by giving highest priority to economy—takes away the taxing powers needed to put the system on a sound footing; it places the power to control transit fares in the hands of a political body with no responsibility to the electorate—a semi-independent public corporation run by a five-member board of directors (two members appointed by the governor, two by the mayor, and one chosen by the other appointees).

Technology and federal crackdown ended mob control of the docks. LIBRARY OF CONGRESS

their waterfronts into ghost ports. The walkout ends October 6, and tugboats escort 100 freighters into port. The states of New York and New Jersey establish a bistate Waterfront Commission to investigate the involvement of organized crime in activities that are driving business away from Brooklyn, Manhattan, Hoboken, and Jersey City piers. The American Federation of Labor expels the corrupt International Longshoremen's Association, whose New York boss Joseph Ryan is forced out after a 26-year career of corruption on the city's docks (*see* crime, 1950). Revelations of graft and embezzlement have brought Ryan down, but what will end criminal racketeering on Manhattan piers is their obsolescence; New Jersey piers using modern containership methods will take the shipping business away from New York (*see* containerships, 1956). Longshoremen immobilize the port once again December 1, striking in defiance of a federal injunction, and this time the strike will continue for 5 months.

 The Yeshiva University Medical School is renamed Albert Einstein Medical College March 15 (*see* 1955; Van Etten, 1954).

 Metromedia, Inc. is founded at New York under the direction of German-born broadcasting and advertising executive John W. (Werner) Kluge, 39, who

Transit fares rise 50 percent to 15¢ July 25 (*see* 1948) and the first subway tokens are introduced, replacing the nickels and dimes used since 1904 (the brass tokens have a Y cut into their centers and are about the size of a dime in order to limit the need for retooling turnstiles that are not equipped to handle two coins; about 48 million of them will be minted). Ridership drops by 10.4 percent in the first week, and revenues fall by $1,048,422. Subway trains in this decade will be lengthened to 10 cars, up from six in 1904, and platforms throughout the city will have to be lengthened to at least 525 feet, up from 310 in 1904, but ridership will decline by 33 percent in the next 23 years, and on Eighth Avenue-line trains such as the A Train it will decline by 42 percent as fares continue to rise and frequency of trains decreases (*see* 1966).

Omnibus Corp. sells its interests in the Fifth Avenue Coach Co. and New York City Omnibus Corp. It acquires the Hertz Drive-Ur-Self System from General Motors and will change its name in November of next year to Hertz Corp. The last of Fifth Avenue's double-decker buses go out of service after 46 years on the avenue (*see* 1944).

A dock strike begins October 1, idling longshoremen at New York and other East Coast cities and turning

Subways got fluorescent lighting (but not air conditioning) and tokens replaced coins. LIBRARY OF CONGRESS

heads the company's Foster & Kleiser outdoor advertising division as well as its metropolitan and worldwide broadcasting divisions.

TV Guide begins publication April 3 with pocket-size weekly program listings and has a circulation of 1.5 million by year's end. Publisher Walter H. Annenberg has merged his 9-year-old *Seventeen* magazine with his father's *Philadelphia Inquirer* and racing publications to create Triangle Publications; he combines small TV-list publishers at New York and other cities, creating 10 regional editions.

The Paris Review begins publication at New York with New York-born *Harvard Lampoon* alumnus George (Ames) Plimpton, 25, as editor. Plimpton and his Bisbee, Ariz.-born friend Harold L. "Doc" Humes and Peter Matthiessen got the idea for the "little magazine" last year while on holiday in Paris, and it will be the first to publish authors such as Philip Roth and Terry Southern.

New York public-relations man Howard J. Rubenstein, 21, gets his start with help from his journalist father, Sam, who covers Brooklyn police activities for the *New York Herald Tribune*, moonlighting as a PR man for a Brooklyn restaurant and, sometimes, for politicians. Sam teaches Harvard Law School dropout Howard how to write a press release and introduces him to people who can help. The younger Rubenstein will make himself a political power in the city.

Nonfiction: *Columbia Historical Portrait of New York* by Yonkers-born Columbia University historian John A. (Atlee) Kouwenhoven, 44; *Tomahawks to Textiles: The Fabulous Story of Worth Street* by Frank L. Walton; *The Age of the Moguls* by Vermont-born author Stewart H. Holbrook, 60; *The Honest Rainmaker* by A. J. Liebling is about James A. MacDonald, racing columnist for the *New York Enquirer*, who uses the pen name Col. John R. Stingo; *More in Anger: Some Opinions Uncensored and Unteleprompted of Marya Mannes* (essays) by New York novelist-critic-poet Marya Mannes, 48, a daughter of violinist-conductor David Mannes and pianist Clara Damrosch Mannes who served as a spy for the OSS in Spain during the war.

Fiction: *For Esme—With Love and Squalor* (nine stories) by J. D. Salinger, whose story "Teddy" appears in The *New Yorker* January 31; *The Adventures of Augie March* by Canadian-born novelist Saul Bellow, 40; *Go Tell It on the Mountain* by New York-born émigré novelist James Baldwin, 29, who has gone to Paris to escape U.S. prejudice against blacks and homosexuals; *Invisible Man* by Oklahoma City-born novelist

Ralph (Waldo) Ellison, 39, is about black identity; *Junkie: Confessions of an Unredeemed Drug Addict* by St. Louis-born novelist William Lee (William S. [Seward] Burroughs), 39. A grandson of the adding machine inventor, Burroughs has been a heroin addict since 1944 and will remain one until 1957. He killed his wife, Joan, at Mexico City in September 1951 while trying to shoot a glass off her head (he pleaded guilty to criminal negligence) and in 1953 shared an apartment with poet Allen Ginsberg at 206 East 7th Street; *The Subterraneans* by Jack Kerouac, whose character Julian Alexander is based on Greenwich Village painter-pianist-hipster (and heroin addict) Anton Rosenberg, 26, who runs a print shop in Christopher Street but hangs out at the San Remo Bar on the corner of Bleecker and Macdougal streets; *The Ill-Tempered Clavichord* by S. J. Perelman.

Doubleday Anchor Books are introduced by the 56-year-old New York publishing giant, whose quality paperbacks compete with lower-priced paperbacks.

Poetry: *Turandot and Other Poems* by Rochester-born New York advertising copywriter-poet John Ashbery, 26; *Poems* by Cincinnati-born New York poet Kenneth Koch, 27, who receives his Ph.D. from Columbia.

Poet-playwright Dylan Thomas collapses in his Chelsea Hotel room November 9 and dies of alcoholism at St. Vincent's Hospital at age 39.

Painting: *Blue Poles* by Jackson Pollock; *Washington Crossing the Delaware* by New York-born "beatnik" saxophonist-turned-painter Larry Rivers (originally Yizroch Loiza Grossberg), 29; *Open Wall* by Helen Frankenthaler; *City Vertical* (collage) and *The City* (collage) by Lee Krasner; *Second Allegory* and *Bookshop* by Ben Shahn. Everett Shinn dies at New York May 1 at age 79, the last surviving member of The Eight whose 1908 show shocked the art world; Bradley Walker Tomlin dies at New York May 11 at age 53; John Marin at Addison, Me., October 1 at age 82; sculptor James E. Fraser at Westport, Conn., October 11 at age 76 (the first major exhibition of his work was held only 2 years ago at New York).

Theater: *The Crucible* by Arthur Miller 1/22 at the Martin Beck Theater, with Jean Adair, Arthur Kennedy, Jennie Egan, Phillip Coolidge, E. G. Marshall, Walter Hampden in an account of the 1692 Salem witch trials intended as a parallel to the persecution of alleged communist sympathizers in the United States, 197 perfs.; *Picnic* by William Inge 2/19 at the Music Box Theater, with Minneapolis-born actor Ralph Meeker (originally Rathgerber), 32,

Ohio-born actress Janice Rule, 21, Cleveland-born actor Paul Newman, 28, New Mexico-born actress Kim Stanley (originally Patricia Kimberly Reid), 28, Columbus, Ohio-born actress Eileen Heckart, 33, 477 perfs.; *Camino Real* by Tennessee Williams 3/19 at the Martin Beck Theater, with New York-born actor Eli Wallach, 37, Kingston, Jamaica-born actor Frank Silvera, 37, Oakland, Calif.-born actress Jo Van Fleet, 31, Bronx-born actor Martin (Henry) Balsam, 33, Porterville, Calif.-born actress Barbara Baxley, 30, British actor Hurd Hatfield, 34, 60 perfs.; *Tea and Sympathy* by New York-born playwright Robert Anderson, 36, 9/30 at the Ethel Barrymore Theater, with Deborah Kerr, New York-born actor John Kerr, 21, 712 perfs.; *The Teahouse of the August Moon* by John Patrick 10/15 at the Martin Beck Theater, with Penn Grove, N.J.-born actor John Forsythe (originally John Freund), 35, David Wayne, 1,027 perfs.; *Sabrina Fair* by Samuel Taylor 11/11 at the National Theater, with Joseph Cotten, John Cromwell, Margaret Sullavan, Cathleen Nesbitt, scenic and lighting design by Donald Oenslager, 318 perfs.; *Oh, Men! Oh, Women!* by Edward Chodorov 12/17 at Henry Miller's Theater, with Larry Blyden, Peggy Cass, Anne Jackson, German-born ingénue Betsy von Furstenberg, 18, Gig Young, 382 perfs.; *In the Summer House* by New York-born novelist Jane (Sydney) Bowles (*née* Auer), 36, 12/29 at The Playhouse (Bowles and her husband have lived in Tangier since 1952), 55 perfs.; *The Remarkable Mr. Pennypacker* by New York-born playwright Liam O'Brien, 57, 12/30 at the Coronet Theater, with Burgess Meredith, Martha Scott, Glenn Anders, Una Merkel, 221 perfs.

The New York Shakespeare Festival is founded by Brooklyn-born theatrical impresario Joseph Papp (originally Yosl Papirofsky), 32, who will stage plays in a church beginning next year, present them free in the city parks in 1956 (initially in an amphitheater built in 1941 in East River Park, halfway between the Williamsburg and Manhattan bridges), and put them on in Central Park's Delacorte Theater beginning in 1962 with *The Merchant of Venice*.

Actress Maude Adams dies at Tannersville, N.Y., July 17 at age 80; playwright Eugene O'Neill of pneumonia at Boston November 27 at age 65 (a crippling disease has prevented him from writing for nearly a decade); Lee Shubert dies at New York December 25 at age 78.

Television: *Marty* by New York-born playwright Paddy (originally Sidney) Chayefsky, 30, 5/24 on NBC's Philco Playhouse, with Westhampton-born actor Rod Steiger, 28, Buffalo-born actress Nancy Marchand, 24; *The Big Deal* by Chayefsky 7/19 on NBC's Philco Playhouse with Anne Jackson, David Opatoshu; *The Bachelor Party* by Chayefsky 10/11 on NBC's Philco Playhouse, with Eddie Albert, Kathleen Maguire.

Films: Samuel Fuller's *Pickup on South Street* with Richard Widmark, Jean Peters. Also: Jean Negulesco's *How to Marry a Millionaire* with Marilyn Monroe, Betty Grable, Lauren Bacall, William Powell; George Marshall's *Money From Home* with Dean Martin, Jerry Lewis; Otto Preminger's *The Moon Is Blue* with William Holden, David Niven, Maggie McNamara; Don Weis's *Remains to Be Seen* with Van Johnson, June Allyson, Angela Lansbury, Louis Calhern, Dorothy Dandridge; Michael Curtiz's *Trouble Along the Way* with John Wayne (as a divorced father who returns to his old parish school on the Lower East Side to coach its football team), Donna Reed, Charles Coburn.

Actor Roland Young dies at his New York home June 5 at age 65.

Film musical: Vincente Minelli's *The Band Wagon* with Fred Astaire, Cyd Charisse, Oscar Levant, Jack Buchanan, Nanette Fabray, music and lyrics by Howard Dietz and Arthur Schwartz, songs that include "Shine On Your Shoes" and "That's Entertainment."

Broadway musicals: *Hazel Flagg* 2/11 at the Mark Hellinger Theater, with Helen Gallagher, choreography by Robert Alton, music by Jule Styne, lyrics by Bob Hilliard, songs that include "Every Street's a Boulevard in Old New York," 190 perfs.; *Wonderful Town* 2/25 at the Winter Garden Theater, with Rosalind Russell, Pennsylvania-born actress Edie Adams (originally Edith Elizabeth Enke), 25, music by Leonard Bernstein, book based on the 1940 stage play *My Sister Eileen*, lyrics by Betty Comden and Adolph Green, songs that include "Ohio," "A Quiet Girl," "Conga!," 559 perfs.; *Can Can* 5/7 at the Shubert Theater, with Los Angeles-born singer Gwen (originally Gwyneth Evelyn) Verdon, 28, Peter Cookson, book by Abe Burrows, music and lyrics by Cole Porter, songs that include "I Love Paris," "C'est Magnifique," "It's All Right with Me," 892 perfs.; *Me and Juliet* 5/28 at the Majestic Theater, with Isabel Bigley, Joan McCracken, choreography by Robert Alton, music by Richard Rodgers, lyrics by Oscar Hammerstein II, songs that include "No Other Love," 358 perfs.; *Comedy in Music* 10/2 at the John Golden Theater, with Danish pianist Victor Borge, 44, in a one-man show, 849 perfs.; *Kismet* 12/3 at the Ziegfeld Theater, with Alfred Drake, Chicago-born actor Richard Kiley, 31, Doretta Morrow, music based on the works of Aleksandr Borodin, lyrics by Robert Wright and George Forrest, songs that include "Baubles, Bangles and Beads," "Stranger in Paradise," "This Is My Beloved," 538 perfs.; *John Murray Anderson's Almanac, A Musical Harlequinade* 12/10 at the Imperial Theater, with singer Harry Belafonte, Knoxville, Ky.-born ingénue Polly Bergen (originally Nellie Paulina Burgin), 22, Wollaston, Mass.-born comedian Billy DeWolfe, 45, London-born comedienne Hermione Gingold, 55, Burlington, Vt.-born comedian Orson Bean (originally Dallas Burrows), 24, Alice Pearce, Kay Medford, New York-born ingénue Tina Louise, 17, Belgian-born ingénue Monique Van Vooren, 19, music and lyrics mostly by Richard Adler and Jerry Ross (originally Jerold Rosenberg), scenic design by Raoul Pène Du Bois, songs that include "Rags to Riches," 229 perfs.

Irene Bordoni dies of cancer at New York March 19 at age 59.

Opera: *The Harpies* 5/25 at New York, with music and lyrics by Marc Blitzstein (who wrote it in 1931).

The Merce Cunningham Dance Company founded late in the year by Cunningham, now 34, has its first season, performs to music by John Cage and David Tudor, will hire artist Robert Rauschenberg as resident designer next year, and will continue for more than half a century.

Violinist Albert Spalding dies at New York May 26 at age 64.

The 37-year-old David Mannes School of Music applies to the state Board of Regents, receives authorization to give courses leading to an academic degree, and becomes the Mannes College of Music; it will purchase an adjoining building next year and remain in East 74th Street until 1984.

 Marion Anthony "Tony" Trabert, 22, wins in men's tennis at Forest Hills, Maureen Connolly in women's singles (Connolly wins the "grand slam," taking the Australian, French, English, and U.S. women's singles championships).

Brooklyn Dodgers right fielder Carl Furillo, now 31, wins the National League batting title with a .344 average, despite having been sidelined for part of the season with a broken finger; Dodgers catcher Roy Campanella, now 31, is voted National League most valuable player (he received the award 2 years ago and will win it again in 1955). The New York Yankees win the World Series, defeating the Dodgers 4 games to 2 and gain the championship for

an unprecedented fifth consecutive time. Dodger pitcher Carl Erskine, 26, sets a Series record in the third game by striking out 14 men, and Duke Snider wins the fourth game by hitting two doubles and a home run, but Yankee second baseman Alfred Manuel "Billy" Martin, 25, gets 12 hits, including a double, two triples, and two home runs, and his hit in the bottom of the sixth game's ninth inning scores outfielder Hank Bauer, 31, to win the Series.

Brooklyn Dodgers radio sportscaster Red Barber quits after 14 years over a contract dispute at the end of the season and is hired by the Yankees. Now 45, he will remain with the Yankees until 1966, when he will be dismissed for telling listeners late in the season that only 413 fans have come out for a game.

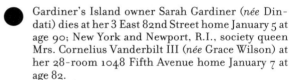 Gardiner's Island owner Sarah Gardiner (*née* Dindati) dies at her 3 East 82nd Street home January 5 at age 90; New York and Newport, R.I., society queen Mrs. Cornelius Vanderbilt III (*née* Grace Wilson) at her 28-room 1048 Fifth Avenue home January 7 at age 82.

The Utopia Lanes bowling alley opens in a basement at 188-08 Union Turnpike in Jamaica Estates, Queens, where the mom-and-pop establishment will be the neighborhood meeting place until 1997.

The first International Debutante Ball is held at the Plaza Hotel November 29 and introduces 23 young women from eight foreign countries (including Austria, Bolivia, Brazil, France, and Italy) and six states to society (*see* Cotillion, 1935). Founder Beatrice Dinsmore Joyce, 43, has read Consuelo Vanderbilt's new book *The Glitter and the Gold*, recognized the need for an international "coming out party," engaged Lester Lanin's orchestra, and inaugurated an event that will move to the Astor and then to the Waldorf-Astoria as the number of girls introduced grows as large as 65.

 The Republican-controlled state legislature at Albany grants landlords an across-the-board 15 percent rent increase on rent-controlled apartments (*see* rent control, 1944). Gov. Dewey has backed the measure.

Architect Rosario Candela dies at his suburban Mount Vernon home October 6 at age 63. An amateur cryptographer, he worked in military intelligence during World War II and gave classes on the subject to military personnel at Hunter College.

 The Internal Revenue Service rules that Irving and Murray Riese are, for tax purposes, not restaurateurs but actually real estate broker-dealers and cannot have their profits taxed as capital gains (*see*

1940). To be bona fide restaurateurs, says the IRS, they must hold a restaurant for at least 3 years, not just 6 months, but the Rieses have bought and sold so many restaurants since 1942 that it is hard to count them. By 1960 they will have virtual monopolies on eating places in Times Square, Grand Central Terminal, and Penn Station (*see* Childs, 1961).

The Newarker restaurant opens at the 24-year-old Newark Airport under the direction of Restaurant Associates, headed by New York-born restaurateur Jerome Brody, 25, who has hired Saratoga Springs-born Cornell University School of Hotel Management graduate Joseph Baum, 33, from a Florida hotel chain to help him. Brody's father-in-law, Abraham Wechsler of the Wechsler Coffee Co., supplies hotels and restaurants and a few years ago acquired half ownership of the Rikers coffee-shop chain in lieu of payment of overdue bills. He put Brody in charge, Brody upgraded the menus, and Riker's Corner House in East 57th Street soon featured beef in a burgundy wine sauce instead of ordinary hamburgers. The Newarker's kitchen is tiny, but Baum has retained Swiss chef Albert Stockli and dazzles patrons with oversize portions (e.g., seven oysters instead of the usual six and "three-clawed" lobsters); huge Absecon oysters (from an island off Atlantic City); flambéed dishes such as *shashlik* and steak chunks prepared tableside; and brandied coffee. The Newarker loses $25,000 its first year as three plane crashes force closings of the airport, but the place attracts a following of suburban New Jersey residents and launches Restaurant Associates on a path of success (*see* Forum of the Twelve Caesars, 1957).

 Puerto Rican immigration to New York peaks (*see* politics, 1952); Puerto Ricans represented less than 5 percent of the city's total population 3 years ago and were concentrated in East Harlem, but New York will have roughly 500,000 Puerto Ricans by 1955—twice the 1950 figure—and by 1956 more than 9 percent of the city's population will be Puerto Ricans, 20 to 25 percent of them black, with major communities in the South Bronx and parts of the upper West Side, notably the San Juan Hill section of the 60s west of Amsterdam Avenue.

1954 The March 5 CBS television program *See It Now* exposes the demagogy of Sen. Joseph McCarthy (R. Wis.), whose charges of communism within the U.S. government have been tearing the country apart (*see* 1951). Announcer Edward R. Murrow has produced the show with CBS executive Fred Friendly; they have used their own money to advertise the program in newspapers, omitting the CBS logo. The U.S. Sen-

ate votes 67 to 22 December 2 to condemn Sen. McCarthy for misconduct.

Former congressman and 1949 mayoral candidate Vito Marcantonio dies at New York August 8 at age 51.

Former diplomat and U.S. Secretary of Commerce W. Averell Harriman is elected governor of New York but will serve only one term. Now nearly 63, Democrat Harriman gets 2,560,738 votes to 2,549,613 for his Republican opponent, U.S. Sen. Irving M. (McNeil) Ives, 58. Mayor Impelliteri has appointed Brooklyn-born politician Arthur Levitt, 54, president of the Board of Education earlier in the year, and Levitt wins election as state comptroller, having replaced a candidate whose name was withdrawn following a scandal. He will serve as comptroller for a record 24 years, winning reelection five times as he and his staff turn out investigative reports probing the management and disbursal of public funds statewide.

President Eisenhower appoints Nelson A. Rockefeller special foreign policy aide December 16.

 The U.S. Supreme Court rules 9 to 0 May 17 in *Brown v. Board of Education* that racial segregation in public schools is unconstitutional. U.S. Attorney General Herbert Brownell, Jr., now 50, has submitted a brief to the court 6 months earlier contending that the court had the power to abolish segregation. Chief Justice Earl Warren orders Kansas and every other state to proceed "with all deliberate speed" to integrate educational facilities, but Harlem novelist Zora Neale Hurston criticizes the landmark decision on the grounds that pressure to integrate will be harmful to thriving black institutions.

Mayor Wagner issues an interim order recognizing the right of public employees to hold union membership (*see* 1958).

Civil rights lawyer Arthur Garfield Hays dies at New York December 14 at age 73.

Metropolitan Life Insurance Co. passes AT&T as the world's largest corporation February 22; it has $12 billion in assets.

The New York State Department of Commerce reports that New York City has 948,000 manufacturing jobs—more than in the next two cities combined, but a business downturn puts many out of work. Factory employment in New York has risen by 2 percent since 1947 (*see* 1953), so even though factory jobs in Manhattan have fallen by 6 percent jobs in the other boroughs have more than made up for the loss. Mayor Wagner announces that he is exploring ways to "prevail" on companies to stay in the city, and a change in the city charter introduced by the City Council in October grants the city's new commerce commissioner authority to investigate gross-receipts taxes and other encumbrances on business.

A New York taxpayer with an income of $100,000 may now pay more than $67,000 in federal income taxes, up from $16,000 or less in 1929, and the individual tax exemption is $600, down from $1,500 in 1929. Income taxes will be reduced slightly next year, but the average tax rate, including surtax, is just above 20 percent and taxpayers in top brackets pay 87 percent.

The 24-year-old magazine *Fortune* publishes its first Fortune "500" listings of the top U.S. companies. Two-thirds of the companies listed will either have disappeared by 1994 or be too small to make the list.

Financier Bernard J. Van Ingen dies at New York July 31 at age 65, having pioneered in floating public revenue bonds.

Chemical Bank and Trust Co. merges with the Corn Exchange Bank October 15, gaining many new branches (*see* 1929; 1959; Corn Exchange, 1853).

Wall Street's Dow Jones Industrial Average finally passes the 381.17 high of 1929 November 23 and closes December 31 at 404.39, up from 280.9 at the end of 1953 despite the year's business recession.

Ohrbach's takes over the 10-story James McCreery store at 7 West 34th Street and moves uptown from the 14th Street location where it began in 1923 (*see* 1987; McCreery's, 1837).

Wanamaker's closes December 18 after 58 years on Astor Place at the corner of Fourth Avenue and 10th Street (*see* fire, 1956).

New York longshoremen call off their 5-month dock strike April 2 after an ultimatum from the National Labor Relations Board (*see* 1953).

The city makes Seventh Avenue one-way southbound and Eighth Avenue one-way northbound (*see* 1951). Although traffic flow is speeded by 25 to 40 percent, the Fifth Avenue Coach Co. complains that it has lost customers on its Seventh and Eighth Avenue routes, and the Transport Workers Union opposes further one-way avenues (*but see* Broadway, 1956).

Chesapeake & Ohio chairman Robert Young resigns in January to comply with Interstate Commerce Commission rules against interlocking directorates (he has gained control of other roads) and becomes chairman of the New York Central in midyear after winning a proxy fight by sending agents door to door to solicit stockholders' votes (*see* 1946). The Central has reported a deficit of $2.5 million, and Young has demanded a seat on the board. Now 56, he names Alfred E. (Edward) Perlman, 51, of the Denver & Rio Grande Western chief executive officer of the Central, and Perlman, who received his degree from MIT at age 20, cuts the Central's workforce by some 15,000, bringing a new ruthlessness to management by skimping on car maintenance and ignoring commuters' complaints. The railroad claims to be losing $25 million per year on Grand Central Terminal and sells the 25-year-old New York Central Building (it becomes the New York General Building and later will become the Helmsley Building). Young announces in September that he will tear down the terminal and replace it with an 80-story office tower (*see* 1958; architecture, 1957).

A track opened October 30 between Brooklyn's Church Avenue and Ditmars Avenue stations establishes single-route subway service on the D Train between Coney Island and 205th Street in the Bronx.

The Bronx Municipal Hospital Center's Nathan B. Van Etten Hospital opens September 15 on Pelham Parkway and Eastchester Road, taking its name from former American Medical Association president Nathan Bristol Van Etten. A teaching affiliate of Yeshiva University's Albert Einstein College of Medicine, the hospital center has been created at the instigation of Commissioner of Hospitals Marcus Kogel; its first facility is initially for tuberculosis patients but will later be used for general care (*see* 1955).

Pioneer bacteriologist Anna W. Williams dies of heart failure at Westwood, N.J., November 20 at age 92.

The U.S. Supreme Court decision in *Brown v. Board of Education* begins a period of turmoil in New York City's public schools. Faced with new problems of overcrowding as more postwar "baby boomers" enter the system, the city's Board of Education has kept black and Hispanic pupils separate but must now cope with trying to integrate the schools.

Stern College opens at 245 Lexington Avenue in Manhattan's Murray Hill section as part of Yeshiva University, incorporated in 1946 (*see* 1929). Funded by Hartz Mountain pet-food millionaire Max Stern, now 55, the first women's liberal-arts college oper-

1954

ated by Orthodox Jews will grow to have 750 students, most of whom will study for a year in Israel.

The Yeshiva Chofetz Chaim acquires the 51-year-old former Isaac Rice mansion on Riverside Drive to use for its school (*see* 1988).

 FM radio inventor Major Edwin H. Armstrong takes his own life February 1, jumping out of his 13th-floor New York apartment at age 63.

The Morning Show debuts on CBS-TV March 16 with Walter Cronkite (the effort to compete with NBC's *Today Show* faces an uphill struggle). The *Tonight Show* debuts on NBC-TV November 1 with New York-born comedian Steve Allen, 32, as host; like the *Today Show*, it is a creation of NBC executive Sylvester "Pat" Weaver.

RCA introduces the first U.S. television receivers that can show both color and black-and-white (*see* 1951).

Forbes magazine founder B. C. Forbes dies in his New York office, pen still in hand, May 6 at age 73, leaving a debt-free publication to his sons Malcolm, Bruce C., Gordon B., and Wallace F.

Sports Illustrated begins publication August 16 at New York. The new Time-Life weekly will lose $26 million before it becomes profitable in 1964.

 American Heritage Publishing Co. is founded at New York by former Time-Life editor James Parton, 41, to publish magazines that will include *American Heritage*, *Horizon*, and *Americana* plus illustrated history books.

Nonfiction: *Manhattan and Me* by Greenwich Village-born writer Oriana Atkinson, wife of former *New York Times* drama critic Brooks Atkinson (with drawings by Al Hirschfeld); *Always in Vogue* (autobiography) by the magazine's editorial-board chair Edna Woolman Chase, now 77, and her actress daughter Ilka, now 51; *My Life and Loves in Greenwich Village* by the late poet-ladies' man Maxwell Bodenheim.

Maxwell Bodenheim is shot to death February 6 at age 61 in the room of a 97 Third Avenue flophouse that he has shared with two other alcoholics, one of them his wife, Ruth (*née* Fagan), who is killed with a knife by their companion, a former mental patient (the man will be committed to the Matteawan State Hospital for the Criminally Insane); Harcourt Brace cofounder Alfred Harcourt dies at Santa Barbara, Calif., June 20 at age 78.

Fiction: *The Blackboard Jungle* by New York novelist Evan Hunter (originally Salvatore Lombino), 28,

who graduated from high school at age 16, served in the navy, and has taught at Bronx Vocational High School; *Tunnel of Love* by Chicago-born comic novelist Peter De Vries, 44, who has been contributing to The *New Yorker* since 1944.

 Painting: *Colonial Cubism* by Stuart Davis; *Collection and Charlene* by Texas-born New York painter Robert Rauschenberg, 28; *Painting* by Philip Guston; *White Light* by Jackson Pollock; *Grand Street Brides* by Newark-born New York abstract expressionist Grace Hartigan, 32; *Blue Spot*, *Shattered Light* (both collages); *Forest #1* and *Forest #2* by Lee Krasner. Reginald Marsh dies of a heart attack outside Bennington, Vt., July 3 at age 56.

Sculpture: *The Caliph of Baghdad* by Joseph Cornell.

The André Emmerich Gallery opens at 41 East 57th Street under the direction of German-born art dealer and amateur archaeologist Emmerich, 30, who has worked for Time International, Life International, and the *New York Herald Tribune*.

Push Pin Studios is founded by New York graphic designers Milton Glaser, 25; Seymour Chwast, 23; and Jerome Snyder, 38.

 Photographs: *The Face of New York* by Andreas Feininger is a photographic collection.

Theater: *The Caine Mutiny Court-Martial* by Herman Wouk 1/2 at the Plymouth Theater, with San Francisco-born actor Lloyd Nolan, 51, as Lieut. Commander Philip Francis Queeg, Henry Fonda, Pittsburgh-born actor John Hodiak, 39, 415 perfs.; *King of Hearts* by Jean Kerr and Carson City, Nev.-born writer Eleanor Brooke, 48, 4/1 at the Lyceum Theater, with Des Moines-born actress Cloris Leachman, 27, Jackie Cooper, 279 perfs.; *The Tender Trap* by New York playwrights Robert Paul Smith and Max Shulman 10/13 at the Longacre Theater, with Newton Highlands, Mass.-born actor Robert Preston (originally R. P. Meservey), 36, Kim Hunter, Joey Faye, Philadelphia-born actor Ronny Graham (originally Ronald Montcrief Stringer), 35, 102 perfs.; *Ladies of the Corridor* by Dorothy Parker and Arnaud d'Usseau 10/21 at the Longacre Theater, with Betty Field, June Walker, Edna Best, Vera Allen, New York-born actor Walter Matthau (originally Matuschanskyayasky), 34, Shepperd Strudwick, 45 perfs.; *The Rainmaker* by Philadelphia-born playwright N. Richard Nash (originally Nathan Richard Nusbaum), 41, 10/28 at the Cort Theater, with Kirksville, Mo.-born actress Geraldine Page, 29, Short Hills, N.J.-born actor Richard Coogan, 40, Spokane-born actor Darren McGavin, 32, 125 perfs.; *The Bad Seed* by Maxwell Anderson (from the novel by William March) 12/8 at the 46th Street Theater, with Brooklyn-born ingénue Patty McCormack, 9, Nancy Kelly, Eileen Heckart, 334 perfs.

Television: *The Mother* by Paddy Chayefsky 4/4 on NBC's Philco Playhouse, with veteran English-born actress Cathleen Nesbitt, now 65, Troy-born actress Maureen Stapleton, 28; *Middle of the Night* by Chayevsky 8/9 on NBC's Philco Playhouse, with E. G. Marshall, Newark, N.J.-born actress Eva Marie Saint, 30; *Catch My Son* by Chayefsky 12/12 on NBC's Philco Playhouse, with Sylvia Sidney.

Films: George Cukor's *It Should Happen to You* with Judy Holliday (as wannabe Gladys Glover, who has come to New York from Binghamton and plasters her name across a billboard on Columbus Circle), Jack Lemmon, Peter Lawford; Elia Kazan's *On the Waterfront* with Marlon Brando as a former boxer ("I coulda been a contenduh"), Rod Steiger as his mobster brother, Eva Marie Saint, Karl Malden as the Rev. John M. Corridan (*see* crime, 1945); Alfred Hitchcock's *Rear Window* with James Stewart, Grace Kelly, Wendell Corey (set in a Greenwich Village apartment); Billy Wilder's *Sabrina* with Humphrey Bogart, Audrey Hepburn, William Holden. Also: George Seaton's *The Country Girl* with Bing Crosby, Grace Kelly, William Holden; Mark Robson's *Phfft!* with Judy Holliday, Jack Lemmon, Jack Oakie, Kim Novak; Jean Negulesco's *Woman's World* with June Allyson, Arlene Dahl, Lauren Bacall, Clifton Webb.

Film musical: Michael Curtiz's *The Jazz Singer* with Danny Thomas, Peggy Lee, Mildred Dunnock.

Broadway musicals: *The Girl in Pink Tights* 3/5 at the Mark Hellinger Theater, with a 52-member cast that includes New York-born dancer Gregory Hines, 18, 115 perfs.; *The Pajama Game* 5/13 at the St. James Theater, with John Raitt, Tacoma, Wash.-born singer Janis Paige, 31, music and lyrics by Richard Adler and Jerry Ross, book by Dubuque-born playwright (and tugboat operator) Richard (Pike) Bissell, 40, songs that include "Hey, There," "There Once Was a Man," "7-Cents," "Hernando's Hideaway," 1,063 perfs.; *Peter Pan* 10/20 at the Winter Garden Theater, with Mary Martin, Cyril Ritchard, now 55, Margalo Gilmore, music by Mark Charlap with additional music by Jule Styne, lyrics by New York-born writer Carolyn Leigh, 26, who began her career after graduation from NYU by writing announcements for WQXR and went on to write copy for ad agencies, additional lyrics by Betty Comden and Adolph Green, songs that include "I'm Flying," "Never Never Land," "Tender Shepherd," "I Won't Grow Up," "I've Gotta Crow," 152 perfs.; *Fanny* 11/4

at the Majestic Theater, with Ezio Pinza, William Tabbert, book by S. N. Behrman and Joshua Logan based on sketches by Marcel Pagnol, music and lyrics by Harold Rome, 888 perfs. (producer David Merrick will use publicity stunts to keep the show running); *House of Flowers* 12/30 at the Alvin Theater, with Pearl Bailey, Bronx-born ingénue Diahann Carroll (originally Carol Diahann Johnson), 19, Juanita Hall, Herbert Ross, music by Harold Arlen, lyrics by Arlen and Truman Capote, 165 perfs.

Producer John Murray Anderson dies of a heart attack at New York January 30 at age 67 but his *Almanac* musical continues until June 26 at the Imperial Theater; Fritzi Scheff dies at New York April 8 at age 74; comedian Joe Laurie, Jr. of a heart ailment at New York April 29 at age 62.

Opera: *The Threepenny Opera* 3/10 at the new Theatre de Lys at 121 Christopher Street in Greenwich Village, with Kurt Weill's Vienna-born widow, Lotte Lenya (née Karoline [Wilhelmine] Blamauer), now 55, who created the role of Jenny in the original 1928 Berlin production. Marc Blitzstein has written the new English-language version (former actress Lucille Lortel's husband, chemical engineer Louis Schweitzer, will buy the off-Broadway theater for her next year as a 24th-anniversary present, and it will be renamed the Lucille Lortel Theater in 1981. Now 53, Lortel (née Wadler) married Schweitzer in 1931, left the stage at his request in 1939, opened the White Barn Theater on her Westport, Conn., estate in 1947, and will be a theater patron for the next 40 years); *The Tender Land* 4/1 at the City Center Theater, with music by Aaron Copland (two-act version); *The Saint of Bleeker Street* 12/27 at the Broadway Theater, with music by Gian-Carlo Menotti.

The 69-year-old Boston Pops has its Carnegie Hall debut 10/19 under the direction of Arthur Fiedler.

Jazz trumpeter Oran "Hot Lips" Page dies of a heart attack at New York November 5 at age 46; musician-actor J. Rosamond Johnson at New York November 11 at age 81.

Heavyweight champion Rocky Marciano retains his title by defeating challenger Ezzard Charles in 15 rounds at New York June 17. He defeats Charles again September 17, this time with a knockout punch at New York. Floyd Patterson, 19, gains his first victory October 22 at New York, beating Joe Gannon.

Sportswriter Grantland Rice dies of a stroke at New York July 13 at age 73. Obituaries quote his verse, "When the Great Scorer comes/ To mark against your name,/ He'll write not 'won' or 'lost,'/ But how you played the game."

Vic Seixas wins in men's singles at Forest Hills, Doris Hart in women's singles.

The New York Giants win the World Series, defeating the Cleveland Indians 4 games to 0 for the first National League victory since 1946. Giant outfielder James Lamar "Dusty" Rhodes, 27, hits the team's only two home runs, and no Giant gets more than seven hits, but Giant manager Leo Durocher has said, "Nice guys finish last," and his pitchers Sal "The Barber" Maglie, 37, and Ruben Gomez, 27, are too much for the Indians.

Marilyn Monroe is married at San Francisco January 14 to former New York Yankees baseball star Joe DiMaggio. The marriage will be brief (see 1959).

The body of organized crime figure Jim Macri is found April 25 in the trunk of a parked car in the Bronx after what appears to be a gangland killing. Macri's brother Benedetto disappears, his blood-stained car is found, and he, too, is believed dead (see Scalice, 1957).

The New York Police Department's 25-year-old Aviation Unit retires its last plane and switches entirely to helicopters (see 1949). Turbine choppers will replace piston-driven machines in the 1960s and the unit will grow to have 33 pilots and 15 mechanics to fly and maintain six helicopters.

The Manufacturers Hanover Trust Co. branch-bank building (later to be a Chase Manhattan branch) is completed at 510 Fifth Avenue, southwest corner 43rd Street. Designed by Skidmore, Owings & Merrill, it is a glass box with the bank's giant safe on full display to passersby rather than hidden underground as at most banks.

A new federal housing act signed into law by President Eisenhower August 2 supplements the 1949 act, retaining Title I to provide funds for urban renewal.

A congressional investigation reveals that developers of a proposed "Manhattantown" housing project acquired six blocks of tenements—from 97th Street to 100th between Manhattan and Amsterdam avenues—from the city at reduced prices 5 years ago, promising to develop the area under Title I of the federal housing act, but instead of going ahead with their plans they have simply collected rents, avoided making repairs, and exploited the tenants in various ways. The scandal embarrasses former Parks Commissioner Robert Moses, whom Mayor Wagner has appointed head of a Slum Clearance Committee;

Moses has favored razing all the brownstones in a 20-block area and replacing them with modern high-rise buildings, but there is a deficit of 430,000 dwelling units and strong opposition to tearing down any building that can provide decent housing. Most of the sound brownstones will not be rehabilitated with Title I money until the late 1960s; meanwhile, the City Housing Authority will use federal funds to rebuild much of the densely populated Upper West Side with high-rise "project" housing (see Mitchell-Lama Act, 1955).

The Brevoort Hotel that has stood for a century on the eastern side of Fifth Avenue near 9th Street comes down to make way for an apartment house.

The beleaguered Pennsylvania Railroad sells an option in December for the air rights between Seventh and Eighth avenues, where Penn Station has stood since 1910. The buyer is William Zeckendorf's Webb & Knapp (see 1955).

Central Park's Loeb Boat House opens March 12 with ceremonies attended by Mayor Wagner, Park Commissioner Moses, and Borough President Hulan Jack. Investment banker Carl M. Loeb and his wife, Adeline (née Moses) have donated the facility to the city.

The Second Avenue Deli opens at 10th Street under the direction of Holocaust survivor Abe Lebewohl, 23, who arrived in New York from an Italian displaced persons camp in 1950 and will operate the delicatessen until his murder in 1996, developing a reputation for traditional kosher food including chopped liver, chicken soup with matzoh balls, and kasha varnishkes and cholent.

The restaurant-ice cream parlor Serendipity opens in a $550-per-month East 58th Street storefront (it will move in September 1959 to 225 East 60th Street) with six tables and 15 seats. Preston "Patch" Caradine, 29, has come up with the name, taken from the crossword puzzle in The Times of London, and southern family recipes from his native Arkansas); he and his partners Stephen Bruce and Calvin L. Holt, 29, have pooled $500 to start the place, serving Aunt Buba's sand tarts, pecan cookies, and other treats that will attract celebrities, tourists, and local residents, especially those with children. It will be best known for its frozen hot chocolate blend.

Ellis Island moves out its last detainee (a Norwegian seaman who has overstayed his leave) November 12; declared "excess federal property," it is boarded up. The facility has been used since 1932 as a detention center for deportees, a hospital for wounded servicemen, and a Coast Guard station (*see* 1965).

1955 The army positions radar-guided Nike Ajax missiles at launching sites on Hart Island, at Fort Tilden, near Rockaway Beach, and at 22 other sites in a "ring of steel" to protect the city from a possible Soviet air attack as cold-war tensions continue. Designed to intercept aircraft and explode with the force of one ton of TNT each, the 21-foot-long missiles can fly 65,000 feet high and have a range of nearly 300 miles, but although 23 are stored in underground magazines at the two Hart Island batteries and 46 in the four batteries at Fort Tilden, Moscow will test intercontinental ballistic missiles in 1957 and it will become apparent that no existing air-defense missiles can destroy missiles arriving from outer space. The Hart Island site will be closed in 1958, the Fort Tilden site in 1974.

Civil rights leader Walter F. White dies of a heart attack at New York March 21 at age 61. His autobiography *How Far the Promised Land* is published posthumously.

Philanthropist Kate Wollman dies at New York October 15 at age 85; philanthropist Archer M. Huntington at Bethel, Conn., December 11 at age 86.

$ Citibank (initially First National City Bank) is created March 30 by a merger of the 133-year-old National City Bank with the 92-year-old First National Bank of New York.

Chase Manhattan Bank is created March 31 by a merger of the 78-year-old Chase National Bank and the 156-year-old Bank of the Manhattan Co. to create a financial institution with assets rivaling those of Citibank and second in assets only to the Bank of America. Lithuanian-born investment banker Morris A. (Abraham) Shapiro, 62, has engineered the deal by recommending the two banks' stocks to rich clients and then asking them to pressure the banks' managements to merge (*see* Bank Holding Company Act, 1956).

Bankers Trust Co. retains its name after a merger with Public National Bank that makes 52-year-old Bankers Trust a rival to Chase Manhattan and First National City (*see* Chemical Corn Exchange, 1954; Morgan Guaranty, 1959).

The *New York Times* notes in a June 6 editorial that 500 manufacturing companies have left the city since World War II, as have 50,000 factory jobs, because of traffic congestion and rising costs, notably taxes, and while 47,000 other companies

remain the paper takes city officials to task for failing to find out "whether we are gaining or losing ground." A 10-part series, "Our Changing City," begins in the *Times* in July.

Investment banker Carl M. Loeb dies at New York January 3 at age 79; former National City Bank president Charles E. Mitchell at New York December 14 at age 78.

The Dreyfus Fund established by New York stockbroker Jack J. Dreyfus, Jr., 40, is a mutual fund that increases its holdings from $2.3 million to $5.6 million by year's end. Dreyfus has acquired the open-end Nesbett Fund and renamed it.

The New York Stock Exchange has its worst day thus far September 26, losing $44 million, but the Dow Jones Industrial Average closes December 30 at 488.50, up from 404.39 at the end of 1954.

Hearn's department store closes after more than a century in West 14th Street.

Tiffany & Co. hires Birmingham, Ala.-born window dresser Gene Moore, 55, as vice president for window display. He has developed a reputation for witty and fanciful ideas since 1935, beginning at the I. Miller shoe shop and moving on to Bergdorf Goodman and Bonwit Teller. In the next 39 years Moore will decorate some 5,000 Tiffany windows, enlisting the services of artists who will include Jasper Johns and Robert Rauschenberg (he will also design sets and costumes for the Paul Taylor dance group and others).

Dime-store magnate and philanthropist Samuel H. Kress dies at New York September 22 at age 92. His chain has grown since 1896 to have 264 stores but Kress has been bedridden since 1945, when he was felled by a paralytic stroke.

Consolidated Edison applies to the Atomic Energy Commission for permission to build and operate a private nuclear power plant, becoming one of the first utility companies to make such application. Space restrictions have made it much easier for Con Ed to repair old power stations than construct new ones, with the result that much of its physical plant is antiquated and inefficient (*see* 1962).

The 1.1-mile Queens-Midtown Expressway opens February 24 and is inadequate from the start for the volume of traffic. It is the first stretch of a projected Long Island (Brooklyn to Riverhead) Expressway.

New York installs "Walk/Don't Walk" signals at busy intersections beginning April 19, making it unnecessary for children to remember the rhyme "Cross at the green, not in between." Park Avenue is exempted, and agile New Yorkers quickly learn that if the light has just started flashing "Don't Walk" there is usually plenty of time to cross the street before it stops flashing. The city also institutes alternate side of the street parking regulations to facilitate street cleaning, and car owners often wait, double-parked, until they can move their cars back to a legal parking space. All major cities seek solutions to the problem of streets that are choked by trucks, buses, taxis, and private automobiles.

Manhattan's Third Avenue El makes its last run May 12 between Chatham Square and 149th Street after nearly 77 years of service. Its structure is razed, the avenue's cobblestone surface will be repaved, and its low buildings will gradually give way to high-rise office towers and apartment houses. The 35-year-old elevated line north of 149th Street in the Bronx will continue to operate until April 1973. City and state officials promise East Siders a Second Avenue subway to replace the El south of 149th Street, but although bonds will be issued for construction of the new subway it will not be built in this century and East Siders will have no rapid-transit line other than the Lexington Avenue line.

A connection opens December 1 between the 60th Street subway station in Long Island City and the Queens Boulevard line, linking the former BMT and IND lines.

 The Hospital for Special Surgery moves into a new building designed by Rogers & Butler at 535 East 70th Street, northwest corner FDR Drive and just north of the New York Hospital-Cornell Medical Center on the East River between 70th and 71st streets.

The Albert Einstein College of Medicine begins classes in the Bronx as part of Yeshiva University (see 1953). Emerson Radio cofounder Benjamin Abrams, now 62, has made a substantial contribution to the college. The Bronx Municipal Hospital Center's Abraham Jacobi Hospital opens November 1 on the same campus as the 1-year-old Nathan B. Van Etten Hospital (see 1954). The new facility will have 774 beds by 1994.

John Jay College of Criminal Justice has its beginnings in a police science program, given under the auspices of the Police Academy and the City College School of Business. It will soon be broadened to offer courses leading to bachelor's and master's degrees, and in 10 years will be taken over by a newly formed College of Police Science (see 1967).

Hunter College High School becomes part of the college's teacher-education program for intellectu-

ally gifted students, admitting girls from all five boroughs by competitive examination (see 1903). It has had grades seven through 12 since 1943, continues to be tuition free, and will begin admitting boys in the fall of 1974 (see 1977).

The *Brooklyn Eagle* suspends publication January 28 as Newspaper Guild employees strike the paper. Its assets are sold at auction March 16.

The *Village Voice* begins publication at New York in October. Daniel Wolf, 40, and Edward Fancher have started the 12-page 5¢ weekly with $15,000, its initial circulation is 2,500, but Wolf and Fancher will increase circulation to 56,000 by 1966 and have a readership of about 150,000 by 1970, when they will sell the *Voice* for $3 million.

The *National Review* begins publication at New York November 19. William F. Buckley, Jr., now 30, edits and publishes the bi-weekly journal of brash, erudite political opinion with help from Michigan-born author Russell (Amos) Kirk, 37, whose 1953 book *The Conservative Mind: From Burke to Santayana* has inspired it, but opinion makers in the aftermath of McCarthyism are using the word *conservative* to embrace reactionary ideas such as repealing the progressive income tax and New Deal programs (e.g., Social Security), positions that are anything but conservative. Contributors include Russian-born *Reader's Digest* editor Eugene Lyons, now 57, and Utica-born Hearst columnist George E. (Ephraim) Sokolsky, now 62.

The *Reader's Digest* abandons its 33-year-old position against running ads but will reject cigarette advertising and not sell ads on its back cover until 1997.

New York Times general manager Julius Ochs Adler dies at New York October 3 at age 62 after a 20-year career that has seen the *Times* become America's leading daily; publisher Bernarr MacFadden dies of jaundice after a 3-day fast at Jersey City October 12 at age 87; public-speaking teacher and author Dale Carnegie at New York November 1 at age 66. Some 50,000 people are enrolled in his classes nationwide, and his 1936 book *How to Win Friends and Influence People* has sold nearly 5 million copies; Ruthrauff & Ryan advertising agency cofounder Frederick B. Ryan dies at Fort Lauderdale, Fla., November 29 at age 72; Lennen & Newell ad agency cofounder Philip Lennen of heart disease at New York December 24 at age 68.

 Nonfiction: *Part of Our Time: Some Ruins and Monuments of the Thirties* by Baltimore-born *New York Post* columnist (James) Murray Kempton, 36, is about

U.S. communists and the McCarthy witch-hunt; *Let the Chips Fall: My Battle Against Corruption* by Newbold Morris (with Dana Lee Thomas); *Life with Fiorello* by East Rutherford, N.J.-born author Ernest L. Cuneo, 50; *Mr. New York: The Autobiography of Grover Whalen* by the city's former official greeter, now 69, who headed the mayor's reception committee from 1919 to 1953; *A Night to Remember* by Baltimore-born J. Walter Thompson copywriter Walter Lord, 37, is an account of the R.M.S. *Titanic* sinking in 1912; *Wall Street: Men and Money* by New York-born author Martin (Prager) Mayer, 27; *Auntie Mame* by Chicago-born *Foreign Affairs* magazine promotion manager Patrick Dennis (Edward Everett Tanner III), 34, whose story of a rich young orphan and his eccentric aunt has been rejected by 10 publishers.

Author Frederick Lewis Allen dies at New York February 13 at age 63. He retired as editor of *Harper's* magazine last year; author-screenwriter James Agee dies of heart disease at New York May 16 at age 45; Harcourt Brace cofounder Donald C. Brace at New York September 3 at age 73; author-critic Bernard De Voto of a heart attack at New York November 13 at age 58.

Fiction: *The Recognitions* by New York-born novelist William Gaddis, 33; *The Ginger Man* by Brooklyn-born Irish novelist J. P. (James Patrick) Donleavy, 29; *A Charmed Life* by Mary McCarthy; *Marjorie Morningstar* by Herman Wouk; *79 Park Avenue* by New York-born novelist Harold Robbins, 39.

Juvenile: *Eloise: A Book for Precocious Grown Ups* by St. Louis-born New York entertainer Kay Thompson (*née* Kitty Fink), 51 (approximate), whose ill-mannered, ill-tempered, ugly 6-year-old heroine lives at the Plaza Hotel (whose management will hang a portrait of the little imp in the lobby). Thompson came up with the idea for her precocious child impersonation during rehearsals of her act with the Williams Brothers, with whom she sang from 1947 to 1953, has used it since last year in a one-woman show at the Plaza's Persian Room, and has been introduced to illustrator Hillary Knight, whose pictures bring Eloise to life.

The Donnell Library branch of the New York Public Library opens December 13 in West 55th Street, between Fifth and Sixth avenues.

Painting: *Flag*, *Target with Four Faces* (painted assemblage), and *Target with Plaster Casts* by Augusta, Ga.-born New York painter Jasper Johns, 25, who has been helped by Robert Rauschenberg to survive by working as a window dresser for Bonwit

Teller and Tiffany's Gene Moore under the joint pseudonym Matson Jones; *Bed* and *Rebus* by Robert Rauschenberg; *Scent* by Jackson Pollock; *Double Portrait of Birdie* by Larry Rivers, who has painted two views of his mother-in-law in the nude; *Stretched Yellow*, *Milkweed*, *Desert Moon*, *Image on Green (Jungle)*, *Blue Level*, *Bald Eagle*, *Shooting Gull*, and *Porcelain* (all collages) by Lee Krasner; *City Landscape* by Chicago-born painter Joan Mitchell, 29, who has lived since 1950 on St. Marks Place but leaves for Paris, where she will live until her death in 1992.

Sculpture: *Portrait* (box construction) by Joseph Cornell; a bronze statue of Brazilian "patriarch of independence" José Bonifácio de Andrada e Silva by Brazilian sculptor José Lima, 21, is installed on the Avenue of the Americas near the northwest corner of Bryant Park.

The first annual Winter Antiques Show opens in January at the Seventh Regiment Armory on Park Avenue. The show benefits the East Side House Settlement in the South Bronx (*see* 1983).

Photographs: *The Family of Man* photographic exhibit opens January 23 at the Museum of Modern Art (MoMA) with 500 images from 68 countries. Arranged by Edward Steichen to convey the idea that mankind is universal, the most varied collection of pictures in the history of photography will tour America and much of the world. It includes notably *The Walk to Paradise Garden*, taken 8 years ago by Kansas-born LIFE magazine photojournalist W. Eugene Smith, then 28.

Theater: *Bus Stop* by William Inge 3/2 at the Music Box Theater, with Kim Stanley, Brooklyn-born actor Albert Salmi, 26, 478 perfs.; *Cat on a Hot Tin Roof* by Tennessee Williams 3/24 at the Morosco Theater, with Barbara Bel Geddes, New York-born actor Ben (originally Biagio Anthony) Gazzara, 34, Mildred Dunnock, Illinois-born folksinger Burl Ives (originally Burl Icle Ivanhoe), 46, as "Big Daddy," 694 perfs.; *Inherit the Wind* by Ohio-born playwrights Jerome Lawrence, 39, and Robert E. Lee, 37, 4/21 at the National Theater, with Paul Muni as Clarence Darrow, Ed Begley as William Jennings Bryan is based on the 1925 Scopes "monkey trial," 806 perfs.; *A View from the Bridge* by Arthur Miller 9/29 at the Coronet Theater, with J. Carrol Naish, Van Heflin, Eileen Heckart, Newark-born actor Jack Warden, 35, 149 perfs.; *The Diary of Anne Frank* by Frances Goodrich and Albert Hackett 10/5 at the Cort Theater, with Joseph Schildkraut, Susan Strasberg, 717 perfs.; *No Time for Sergeants* by New York playwright-novelist Ira Levin, 26, 10/20 at the Alvin Theater, with Mount Airy, N.C.-born actor Andrew Samuel

Marilyn Monroe in The Seven Year Itch *created a sensation.* AP/WIDE WORLD

"Andy" Griffith, 29, Morgantown, W. Va.-born actor Jesse Donald "Don" Knotts, 31, Santa Ana, Calif.-born actor Robert Webber, 31, 796 perfs.; *The Desk Set* by Allentown, Pa.-born playwright William Marchant, 32, 10/24 at the Broadhurst Theater, with Shirley Booth, Brooklyn-born ingénu Louis Gossett, Jr., 19, Joyce Van Patten, 296 perfs.; *The Chalk Garden* by English novelist-playwright Enid Bagnold, 66, 10/26 at the Ethel Barrymore Theater, with Irish actress Siobhan McKenna, 33, Pittsburgh-born actor Fritz (William) Weaver, 29, Betsy von Furstenberg, Gladys Cooper, New York-born actress Marian Seldes, 27 (daughter of the critic Gilbert Seldes and niece of the journalist George Seldes), 182 perfs. (it will have a run of 658 performances after it opens next May at London's Royal Court Theatre); *A Hatful of Rain* by New Jersey-born playwright Michael Gazzo, 32, 11/9 at the Lyceum Theater, with Ben Gazzara, Shelley Winters, Frank Silvera, New York (Little Italy)-born actor Anthony Franciosa (originally Anthony George Papaleo, Jr.), 27, is about drug addiction, 398 perfs.

Actress Ona Munson is found dead of a sleeping-pill overdose in her New York apartment February 11 at age 49; Broadway producer John Golden dies of a heart attack at Bayside June 13 at age 80; scene and costume designer Aline Bernstein of cancer at her native New York September 7 at age 72; actor Anthony Ross of a coronary thrombosis at New York October 25 at age 46; playwright Robert E. Sherwood of a heart attack at New York Hospital November 12 at age 59.

Films: Delbert Mann's *Marty* with Ernest Borgnine in an adaptation of the 1953 Paddy Chayefsky television script; Billy Wilder's *The Seven Year Itch* with Marilyn Monroe (whose white skirt blows up revealingly when she stands on a New York sidewalk subway grating), Tom Ewell, Evelyn Keyes (the novelty of an air-conditioned apartment is a major plot device); Charles Walters's *The Tender Trap* with Frank Sinatra, Debbie Reynolds, Celeste Holm, David Wayne. Also: Richard Fleisher's *The Girl in the Red Velvet Swing* with Ray Milland as Stanford White, Joan Collins as Evelyn Nesbit, Farley Granger as Harry K. Thaw; Russell Rouse's *New York Confidential* with Broderick Crawford, Richard Conte, Marilyn Maxwell, Anne Bancroft (originally Anna Maria Italiano), J. Carrol Naish.

Actress and dramatic coach Constance Collier dies of a heart attack at New York April 25 at age 75.

Film musicals: Jean Negulesco's *Daddy Long Legs* with Fred Astaire, Leslie Caron, Thelma Ritter, music by Johnny Mercer, songs that include "Something's Got to Give;" Joseph L. Mankiewicz's *Guys and Dolls* with Marlon Brando, Jean Simmons, Frank Sinatra, Vivian Blaine; Richard Quine's *My Sister Eileen* with Betty Garrett, Janet Leigh, Jack Lemmon; Melville Shavelson's *The Seven Little Foys* with Bob Hope, Milly Vitale, James Cagney (as George M. Cohan).

Broadway musicals: *Plain and Fancy* 1/27 at the Mark Hellinger Theater, with Barbara Cook and Minneapolis-born ingénue Nancy Andrews, 12, music by Berlin-born composer Albert Hague (originally Albert Marcuse), lyrics by Arnold Horwitt, scenic design and costumes by Raoul Pène Du Bois, 461 perfs.; *Silk Stockings* 2/24 at the Imperial Theater, with German actress Hildegarde Neff (originally Knef), 29, as Ninotchka, New York-born actor George Tobias, 53, Los Angeles-born ingénue Julie Newmar (originally Julie Newmeyer), 19, Bartlesville, Okla.-born ingénue Gretchen Wyler, 23, Kenosha, Wis.-born actor Don Ameche, 46, New York-born actor David Opatoshu, 37, music and lyrics by Cole Porter, songs that include "All of You," 478 perfs.; *Damn Yankees* 5/5 at the 46th Street Theater, with Gwen Verdon (as Lola), Maureen Stapleton, Laurel, Miss.-born actor Ray Walston, 40, music and lyrics by Richard Adler and Jerry Ross, songs that include "Whatever Lola Wants," "You've Got to Have Heart," "Two Lost Souls," 1,019 perfs. (George Abbott, now almost 68, has directed the production); *Pipe Dream* 11/3 at the Sam S. Shubert Theater, with Helen Traubel, now 56, Nancy Andrews, music by Richard Rodgers, lyrics by Oscar Hammerstein II based on the John Steinbeck novel *Sweet Thursday*, songs that include "All at Once You Love Her," 246 perfs.

Charlie Parker makes his final appearance at Birdland and dies of a heart attack March 12 at age 53 in the Fifth Avenue apartment of Baroness Nica Rothschild de Koenigswater; Tin Pan Alley lyricist Andrew B. Sterling dies at his Stamford, Conn., home in August at age 80.

 Tony Trabert wins in men's singles at Forest Hills, Doris Hart in women's singles.

Rocky Marciano retains his heavyweight title at New York September 21, knocking out challenger Archie Moore in the fifth round.

The Brooklyn Dodgers win their first World Series, defeating the New York Yankees 4 games to 3. Yogi Berra gets 10 hits, including a double and a home run, and home runs are credited also to Joe Collins, 22 (who hits two of them); Gil McDougald; Elston Howard, 26; Bob Cerv, 29; Mickey Mantle; and Bill "Moose" Skowron, 24; but Brooklyn pitcher Johnny Podres, 23, wins the third and seventh games, pitching all nine innings in each, and the Dodger pitching staff gets good support from Roy Campanella, Carl Furillo, and Duke Snider (who gets four home runs). First baseman Gil Hodges, 31, hits two RBIs in the seventh game, and Cuban-born outfielder Edmundo Isasi "Sandy" Amoros, 25, makes a spectacular running catch of a Berra fly ball to save the game.

Philip Morris chairman Joseph F. Cullman, Jr. dies at New York March 18 at age 72. His company has lagged behind American Tobacco Co., R. J. Reynolds, P. Lorillard, and Liggett & Myers but will overtake them in the next decade.

Russian-born financial manipulator Serge Rubinstein, 46, is found strangled to death January 27 in his town house (formerly the Jules S. Bache mansion) at 814 Fifth Avenue. The U.S. government imprisoned him for 2 years for draft evasion during World War II and for the past 11 years has been trying to deport him for having entered the country on a fraudulent Portuguese passport, but his death will remain a mystery.

Criminal lawyer Lloyd Paul Stryker falls into a coma at his 31 East 72nd Street apartment and dies of a cerebral hemorrhage at Doctors Hospital June 21 at age 70.

Long Island socialite Ann (Eden) Woodward (*née* Crowell), 33, shoots her banker-horsebreeder husband, William Woodward, Jr., 35, just after 2 o'clock on the morning of October 30 and tells police she mistook him for a prowler. Awakened by a sound downstairs, she has picked up a rifle and aimed at a moving shape in the night. Police find her bent over her husband's naked body; she is not prosecuted.

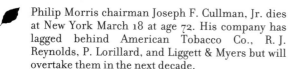 William Zeckendorf of Webb & Knapp signs an agreement in June with Pennsylvania Railroad president James Symes to buy the air rights over Penn Station and build a new station below street level (*see* 1954); the agreement is not made public (*see* 1960).

A 24-story structure at 415 Madison Avenue, northeast 48th Street, is the first office building erected by developer Lewis Rudin, 28, and his brother Jack, whose grandfather Louis Rudinsky came to the Lower East Side from his native Poland in 1883, prospered as a grocer, and in the 1920s bought an apartment house in 54th Street because he had heard that John D. Rockefeller owned property in the block. The Rudins will tear down the apartment house and put up a 32-story office building in its place.

Brooklyn-raised real estate developers Sol Goldman, 45, and Alex DiLorenzo, Jr., 38, buy their first piece of Manhattan property. Goldman left the family grocery business to a younger brother, dropped out of Brooklyn College after a few months, and has been in real estate since age 18, initially having bought foreclosed Brooklyn buildings for as little as $500 in cash and no mortgage. He has developed a reputation as an operator who will buy and sell properties over the telephone, leaving the management to his partner, DiLorenzo (*see* 1960).

The Helmsley-Spear real estate firm is founded by building owner Harry B. Helmsley, now 46, and Leon Spear (who manages buildings in the garment district); it will become the largest such firm in the city (*see* 1936).

The Mitchell-Lama Act (Limited Profit Corporations Act) signed into law by Gov. Harriman encourages construction of middle-income housing by authorizing mortgages backed by the state to cover 90 percent of the cost of eligible projects (*see* Public Housing Law, 1939). Named for State Senator MacNeill Mitchell of Manhattan and Assemblyman Alfred Lama of Brooklyn, passed with support from

Mayor Wagner, it grants builders partial tax exemptions for 20 years, limits their profits, places income limits on tenants, and will fund 259 developments with more than 105,000 apartments (*see* 1956).

The first 1,243 European refugees to be admitted under the 1953 McCarran-Walter Immigration Act arrive by ship at New York July 12 (*see* 1965).

1956 President Eisenhower wins reelection by a landslide, carrying New York State by a margin of more than 1.5 million votes and nearly carrying New York City, where political registration is heavily Democratic and most people have supported Adlai E. Stevenson in his second run for the presidency. Rep. Adam Clayton Powell, Jr. has broken with his party to endorse Eisenhower, saying that Ike is more likely than Gov. Stevenson to address civil-rights issues (the six-time elected Democratic congressman from Harlem has been the target of an ongoing income-tax investigation).

New York State Attorney General and former U.S. congressman Jacob K. Javits wins election to the U.S. Senate, where he will serve until 1981 (four terms). Now 52, Republican Javits defeats Mayor Robert F. Wagner by a margin of 460,000 votes, even though Wagner outpolls Democratic presidential candidate Adlai E. Stevenson by about 500,000 votes in the city.

A Hungarian patriot drapes his country's flag on the Statue of Liberty November 18; the United Nations demands a halt to mass deportations of Hungarians 3 days later, but Soviet tanks crush a revolt at Budapest November 23.

 The city asks banks February 13 to notify municipal authorities of business conditions in order to help retain and enhance existing businesses and attract new ones.

The Bank Holding Company Act signed into law with some reluctance by President Eisenhower May 9 bars bank mergers through acquisitions that tend to create monopolies. It extends the Clayton Act of 1914 by recognizing acquisitions to be a form of merger and will stem the concentration of banking (*see* 1955; *but see* Morgan Guaranty, 1959).

IBM signs a consent decree agreeing to sell its tabulating and computer machines as well as leasing them, thus ending a legal skirmish with the Department of Justice (*see* 1924). IBM board chairman Thomas J. Watson, Sr. dies of a heart attack at his New York home June 19 at age 82. He balked at going into the computer business, but by August IBM has sold 76 computers to Univac's 46, with orders for

193 machines versus 65 for Univac; while there are few intrinsic differences between the computers, IBM employs superior salesmanship and is far ahead of Remington Rand by year's end.

Merrill, Lynch founder Charles E. Merrill dies of heart disease at his Southampton, L.I., house October 6 at age 70, leaving $5.5 million to a philanthropic foundation.

Wall Street's Dow Jones Industrial Average closes above 500 for the first time March 12 and peaks at 521.05 September 20. It closes December 31 at 499.47, up from 488.40 at the end of 1955.

 The Wanamaker store opened by A. T. Stewart on Astor Place in 1862 burns down in a spectacular fire July 16, injuring 187 firefighters and disrupting subway service. The store has been closed since December 1954, when Wanamaker's moved its New York operations to Westchester, the fire has started during demolition work, and the old cast-iron building will be replaced by an apartment house.

Taxicab drivers go on strike again January 18 (*see* 1949). The Teamsters Union Local 826 has called a mass meeting to press for a union contract; the fifth union since 1934 to try to organize drivers, its major demands include letting drivers keep 50 percent of meter fares, eliminating the shape-up system for hiring, eliminating arbitrary firings, and increased vacation time. Some 3,500 drivers have attended the mass meeting with another 2,000 gathered outside, but while the one-day strike is marked by almost no violence it fails to achieve its goals. The transit system collects $18,000 more in fares than normal. It is announced that at least 50 air-conditioned cabs will be operating by summer, but the Police Department's Hack Bureau will not let them be marked as such lest they represent unfair competition. Police Commissioner Stephen P. Kennedy announces a plan that would allow drivers to refuse to pick up fares if they are returning to their garages with their off-duty signs lighted (*see* 1965).

Brooklyn's Fulton Street El comes to a complete stop April 29 after nearly 66 years of service (*see* 1940).

Subway service begins June 28 to Rockaway Wavecrest in Queens (*see* 1958).

The Major Deegan Expressway opens August 31 from the Bronx to Yonkers, taking its name from the late architect-political leader William F. Deegan, who served as city tenement house commissioner but died in 1932 at age 49. The Deegan feeds into the 20-year-old Triborough Bridge and is the final link in the 427-mile, $600 million New York-to-Buffalo

Thruway, whose first section opened in 1954. Tolls on the new Thruway average 1½¢ per mile between New York and Buffalo, it has no traffic lights, and the speed limit for passenger cars is 60 miles per hour (the limit for other vehicles is 50, as compared with 35 mph on multi-lane city highways, 25 mph for other city streets). Also inaugurated August 31 are the South Street Elevated Highway and ramps leading from the 73-year-old Brooklyn Bridge to the 14-year-old Franklin D. Roosevelt (East River) Drive, enabling cars and trucks to bypass the congested waterfront section in getting on and off the drive.

The city makes Broadway one-way southbound below 47th Street (*see* 1954; 1957).

The world's first containership port opens at Elizabeth, N.J., where the Port of New York Authority has paid $3.5 million to buy 40 acres for the new facility (*see* crime, 1953). The first containership is a converted tanker with simple trailer vans on her decks; containerships built as such will revolutionize cargo handling by reducing the need for longshoremen, Manhattan and Brooklyn commercial piers will disappear, Elizabeth will remain the world's leading containerport until it is overtaken by Hong Kong, and Norfolk, Va., will replace New York as the leading East Coast U.S. port because it has rail links to the entire North American continent whereas New York does not (*see* Red Hook Marine Terminal, 1981).

St. John's University opens a new campus on the site of the former Hillcrest Golf Club at Jamaica (*see* 1936; 1971).

A report by an outside librarian criticizes the 152-year-old New-York Historical Society for having a cataloguing backlog and no coherent policy with regard to acquisitions (*see* 1938; art, 1986).

Mayor Wagner opens City Hall to television cameras. Bronx-born journalist Gabe Pressman, 32, has outraged many of his colleagues in City Hall's Room 9 (the press room) by putting a radio microphone in front of the mayor and capturing voices on tape; he quickly becomes familiar to city TV viewers.

Onetime *PM* publisher Marshall Field III dies at New York October 22 at age 63 following surgery for a cerebral blood clot.

Collier's magazine ceases publication December 14 (*see* 1895; *Woman's Home Companion*, 1957).

Nonfiction: *Battle for Manhattan* by Los Angeles-born Bronx-raised writer Bruce Bliven, Jr., 40, who was in the D-Day invasion of Normandy 12 years ago and writes about George Washington's resistance to the British, relating events of the past to the city's present terrain. He notes, for example, that the area just south of 34th Street between Lexington and Park avenues was known as Sunfish Pond: "The fact that so much of the terrain is blanketed by buildings, asphalt, and macadam is surprisingly unimportant; if anything, it adds to the fun of seeing that the ground goes much as it did 180 years ago;" *Queen of the Golden Age: the fabulous story of Grace Wilson Vanderbilt* by Cornelius Vanderbilt, Jr. (IV), now 58, whose great-grandfather was the commodore. He writes that his mother's 33 servants, "imported from ducal and princely households abroad, kept her mansions on Fifth Avenue in New York and on Bellevue Avenue in Newport running to perfection . . . The number of her Fifth Avenue home, 640, was almost as well known on the Continent as 10 Downing Street is today . . . In a single year she entertained 37,000 guests. Her sway over society began in the gaslit red velvet parlors of the turn of the century and—outlasting two major wars, the Crash, bathtub gin, flappers, and café society—survived for fifty dazzling years;" *Mirror for Gotham* by Illinois-born NYU historian Bayrd Still, 50; *The Organization Man* by West Chester, Pa.-born *Fortune* editor William H. (Hollingsworth) Whyte, Jr., 39, argues that a new collective ethic has arisen from the bureaucratization of society and is replacing the old Protestant individualist code. "Belongingness" rather than personal fulfillment has become the ultimate need of the individual.

Hill & Wang publishers is founded at New York by former A. A. Wyn Inc. executives Lawrence Hill (who is sales manager) and Arthur Wang (editor-in-chief), who acquire 88 backlist titles from Wyn plus five outstanding contracts for future works. The firm starts off by publishing works of well-known British playwrights and in 1959 will purchase the rights to 26 American Century series titles (*see* 1971).

Doubleday-Doran cofounder George H. Doran dies at Toronto January 7 at age 86; writer John McNulty of a heart attack at West Wakefield, R.I., July 29 at age 60.

Fiction: *Seize the Day* by Saul Bellow is set in the "Hotel Gloriana," a fictionalized Ansonia that he describes as being "like a baroque palace from Prague or Munich enlarged a hundred times, with towers, domes, huge swells and bubbles of metal gone green from exposure, iron fretwork and festoons." Of the elderly people who live from the West 70s to the 90s, Bellow says, "Unless the weather is too cold or too wet they fill the benches about the tiny railed parks and along the subway gratings from

Verdi Square to Columbia University, they crowd the shops and cafeterias, the dime stores, the tearooms, the bakeries, the beauty parlors, the reading rooms and club rooms;" *Cop Hater* by Ed McBain (Evan Hunter), who will write dozens of thrillers about the "87th Precinct."

Novelist Michael Arlen dies of lung cancer at New York June 23 at age 62. He has lived at 812 Park Avenue.

Poetry: "Howl" by Alan Ginsberg, who apostrophizes New York as "Moloch, whose buildings are judgments!," a "sphinx of cement and aluminum" that devours its young, "too vast to know, too/ myriad windowed to govern."

Painting: *Easter Monday* and *July* by Willem de Kooning; *Eden* by Helen Frankenthaler; *Embrace* and *Birth* (both oil on canvas) by Lee Krasner, now 48, whose husband, Jackson Pollock, dies with a companion in an auto accident on eastern Long Island August 17 at age 44 while driving under the influence of alcohol. Lyonel Feininger has died at New York January 13 at age 84, survived by his photographer son Andreas, now 49.

Sculpture: a bronze seated figure of the 19th century Danish story writer Hans Christian Andersen is installed on the west bank of Central Park's Conservatory Pond near Fifth Avenue and 72nd Street. Created by St. Louis–born sculptor Georg Lober, 65, the $75,000 statue has been financed with funds raised by the Danish-American Women's Association and contributions from Danish and U.S. schoolchildren to commemorate the 150th anniversary of Andersen's birth.

The American Craft Museum opens at 40 West 53rd Street, where the American Craft Council will mount exhibits of handiwork, jewelry, textiles, and the like while building an extensive library for members.

Theater: *Auntie Mame* by Jerome Lawrence and Robert E. Lee (who have adapted last year's Patrick Dennis novel) 10/31 at the Broadhurst Theater, with Rosalind Russell, Boston-born actress Peggy Cass, 31, 634 perfs.; *Long Day's Journey into Night* by the late Eugene O'Neill 11/7 at the Helen Hayes Theater, with Fredric March, Florence Eldridge, Chicago-born actor Jason (Nelson) Robards, Jr., 34, San Francisco-born actor Bradford Dillman, 26, Hollywood, Calif.-born actress Katharine Ross, 12, in an autobiographical play about morphine addiction and alcoholism, 390 perfs.; *The Matchmaker* by Thornton Wilder 12/5 at the Royale Theatre, with Ruth Gordon, Saskatchewan-born actor Arthur Hill,

36, in a play that will be the basis of the 1964 musical *Hello, Dolly!*, 486 perfs.

Jujamcyn Theaters is founded to operate Broadway theaters, invest in Broadway shows, work with regional and resident theater groups to develop new works for Broadway, and work with the Broadway Alliance to produce dramas and comedies at reasonable prices. Minneapolis 3M heiress Virginia Binger (*née* McKnight), 40, and her husband, James, name the concern after their children—Judy, James, and Cynthia.

Comedian Fred Allen drops dead of a heart attack on a New York street March 17 at age 61; playwright Charles MacArthur dies of internal hemorrhaging at New York Hospital April 21 at age 60 with his wife, Helen Hayes, at his bedside (he has been hospitalized for nephritis and anemia); actor Jed Prouty dies at New York May 10 at age 77; actress Margaret Wycherly at New York June 6 at age 74; playwright Owen Davis at New York October 14 at age 82; monologist Ruth Draper of a heart attack at New York December 31 at age 72.

Television: *Twenty-One* (quiz show) 9/12 on NBC with two contestants in isolation booths competing under rules based on those of the card game popular at casinos (see Van Doren, 1958).

Broadway playwright Arthur Miller and Hollywood comedienne Marilyn Monroe, now 30, are married June 29 at White Plains (now nearly 41, he is her third husband) and move into a 13th-floor apartment at 444 East 57th Street, between First Avenue and Sutton Place, where they will remain together until 1961, when Miller will move back to the Chelsea Hotel and they get a divorce. It will still be Monroe's home when she takes her life at Los Angeles in August 1962.

Films: Richard Brooks's *The Catered Affair* with Bette Davis, Ernest Borgnine, Debbie Reynolds, Barry Fitzgerald; Rudolph Maté's *Miracle in the Rain* with Jane Wyman, Van Johnson; David Miller's *The Opposite Sex* with June Allyson, Jean Collins, Dolores Gray, Ann Sheridan in a remake of the 1939 film *The Women*; Fritz Lang's *While the City Sleeps* with Dana Andrews, Ida Lupino, Rhonda Fleming, George Sanders, Vincent Price, Thomas Mitchell.

Columbia Pictures cofounder Jack Cohn dies of a pulmonary embolism at New York December 8 at age 67.

Broadway musicals: *My Fair Lady* 3/15 at the Mark Hellinger Theater, with English-born singer Julie Andrews (originally Julia Elizabeth Wells), 20, as

Eliza Doolittle, Rex Harrison as Professor Higgins, book based on the 1914 Bernard Shaw play *Pygmalion*, sets by Oliver Smith, music by Frederick Loewe, lyrics by Alan Jay Lerner, songs that include "Why Can't the English Teach Their Children How to Speak," "The Rain in Spain," "The Street Where You Live," "I'm Getting Married in the Morning," "I've Grown Accustomed to Her Face," "I Could Have Danced All Night," 2,717 perfs.; *Mr. Wonderful* 3/22 at the Broadway Theater, with Sammy Davis, Jr. and Sr., Washington, D.C.-born actress Chita Rivera, 23, music by New Haven-born composer Jerrold Lewis "Jerry" Bock, 27, lyrics by Larry Holofcener and George Weiss, songs that include "Too Close for Comfort," 388 perfs.; *The Most Happy Fella* 5/3 at the Imperial Theater, with baritone Robert Weede, Art Lund, Jo Sullivan (Mrs. Frank Loesser), book based on the 1924 Sidney Howard play *They Knew What They Wanted*, music and lyrics by Frank Loesser, songs that include "Big D" and "Standing on the Corner," 676 perfs.; *Li'l Abner* 11/10 at the St. James Theater, with Peter Palmer as Abner Yokum, Edie Adams as Daisy Mae, Charlotte Rae as Mammy Yokum, Stubby Kaye as Marryin' Sam, Julie Newmar, New York-born actress Tina Louise (originally Tina Blacker), 22, as Appasionata von Climax, music by Gene de Paul, lyrics by Johnny Mercer, songs that include "Jubilation T. Cornpone," 693 perfs.; *Bells Are Ringing* 11/29 at the Sam S. Shubert Theater, with Judy Holliday, Jean Stapleton, music by Jule Styne, lyrics by Betty Comden and Adolph Green, songs that include "Just in Time," "The Party's Over," 924 perfs.; *Candide* 12/1 at the Martin Beck Theater, with Robert Rounseville in the title role, Irish-born actor Max Adrian (originally Max Bor), 53, as Dr. Pangloss, Barbara Cook as Gunegonde, Alberta-born actor Conrad Bain, 33, sets by Oliver Smith, music by Leonard Bernstein, book by Lillian Hellman based on the Voltaire classic, lyrics by the late John LaTouche, Dorothy Parker, and Richard Wilbur, 73 perfs.

Onetime Broadway musical star Elsie Janis dies at Hollywood February 26 at age 66; lyricist John LaTouche of a heart attack at his Calais, Vt., summer home August 7 at age 38.

Paris chanteuse Edith Piaf (originally Edith Giovanna Gassion), 40, makes her Carnegie Hall debut 1/4; Brooklyn-born soprano Beverly Sills (originally Belle Silverman), 26, her Carnegie Hall debut 2/3.

The Joffrey Ballet company is founded at New York by Seattle-born dancer-choreographer Robert Joffrey (originally Anver Bey Abdullah Jaffa Kahn), 27, with help from Staten Island-born balletomane Gerald Arpino, 33.

Conductor Arturo Toscanini dies at Riverdale in the South Bronx January 16 at age 89; bandmaster-composer Edwin Franko Goldman at his home in the Bronx February 21 at age 78; bandleader Tommy Dorsey chokes to death in his sleep at his Greenwich, Conn., home November 26 at age 51 (the coroner finds food lodged in his windpipe).

 Kenneth R. "Ken" Rosewall, 21, (Australia) wins in men's singles at Forest Hills, Shirley Fry, 29, in women's singles.

The New York Yankees win the World Series, defeating the Brooklyn Dodgers 4 games to 3 after losing last year's Series to the Dodgers by the same one-game margin. Brooklyn wins the first two games behind the pitching of Sal Maglie, Don Newcombe, and others, but Yankee outfielder Enos Slaughter, 40, hits a three-run homer to win the third, Yogi Berra and Mickey Mantle hit three home runs each (the Dodgers get no homers), and Don Larsen, 27, of the Yankees pitches the first "perfect" game in Series history, allowing no hits at all in the fifth game. Jackie Robinson hits a single in the tenth inning to win the sixth game (Slaughter misjudges the ball), and Hoboken-born pitcher Johnny Kucks, 23, allows no runs in the final game, which sees Bill "Moose" Skowrun hit a grand-slam home run after Berra has hit two 2-run homers and Elston Howard a one-run homer. There will not be another "subway series" until 2000.

The New York Giants win the National Football League championship December 30, beating the Chicago Bears 47 to 7 at New York.

 New York-born *Daily Mirror* and Hall Syndicate labor columnist Victor Riesel, 41, sustains eye injuries near Times Square April 5 when sulfuric acid is thrown in his face after he has conducted a radio program denouncing the leaders of Local 138 of the International Union of Operating Engineers, whose ex-president William C. DeKoning, Sr. has been sentenced to 18 months' imprisonment for extortion. Rewards totaling $45,000 are offered for the arrest of the perpetrators, Riesel is declared permanently blind May 4, FBI investigators say the assault was orchestrated by a group of garment workers, President Eisenhower sees Riesel interviewed on the television show *Meet the Press* and urges federal action against labor racketeers, Alex Rose of the Hat, Cap and Millinery Workers' Union proposes June 5 that the labor movement form a union with competent investigators, the Federal

Bureau of Investigation announces at New York August 17 that Riesel's acid-throwing attacker was Abraham Telvi, 22, who was found shot to death July 28. Mobster Joseph Peter Carlino, 33, allegedly paid Telvi $1,000 to throw the acid to keep Riesel from testifying before a grand jury investigating garment-industry labor racketeering, but John "Johnny Dio" Dioguardi, now 48, will eventually be convicted of ordering the hit.

 Webb & Knapp cofounder W. Seward Webb dies at Delray Beach, Fla., January 20 at age 68.

The 42-story Mobil Oil Building (initially the Socony-Mobil building) is completed at 150 East 42nd Street between Third and Lexington avenues as a construction boom begins on Third Avenue following removal of the elevated railway. Designed in International Style by Harrison & Abramovitz with John B. Peterkin, the structure is almost entirely covered with 7,000 embossed panels of stainless steel, contains 1.6 million square feet of floor space, and faces the 25-year-old Chrysler Building.

The Coliseum opens April 28 in Columbus Circle, where it replaces old offices, stores, and tenements that have been condemned by Robert Moses as a slum and acquired mostly with federal funds under Title I of the 1947 slum-clearance program. Built in 2 years by the Triborough Bridge and Tunnel Authority, championed by Moses as Exposition Capital of the World, the $35 million convention center has four exhibition floors with a total of 323,000 square feet—including an open, 150-foot-square three-story well—that enable it to accommodate six different shows independently (the International Automobile Show, National Photographic Show, and International Philatelic Exhibit all open April 28). Leon and Lionel Levy have designed the structure; it has been built to last, with steel trusses 120 feet long, 24 feet high, and decorated with four cast-aluminum plaques by sculptor Paul Manship depicting the seals of the United States, New York State, New York City, and the bridge authority. The windowless Coliseum replaces Grand Central Palace on Lexington Avenue, used since 1911 for boat shows, flower shows, and other traditional events as well as for commercial exhibitions, but it will be employed for such purposes for little more than 30 years and come down in 2000 (see Javits Center, 1986).

The city sells 3,593 properties, most of them in Brooklyn and Queens, bringing in nearly $17 million. The former Board of Education Building on Park Avenue at the southeast corner of 59th Street is sold for $2 million at public auction (it will stand until 1998) but most properties fetch far less. Nearly 2,000 families have been relocated from sites taken for Title I slum-clearance projects, bringing the total since 1952 to more than 10,000; about 3,200 families remain to be relocated.

Self-taught architect Lafayette A. Goldstone dies June 22 at age 80 after a heart attack at his 130 East End Avenue apartment; Ernest A. Van Vleck dies at St. Petersburg, Fla., August 8 at age 81.

 An artificial-flower factory at 4065 Third Avenue in the Bronx goes up in flames April 4, killing six firefighters.

 Mister Softee is founded at Runnemede, N.J., by entrepreneur James Conway and his brother William, whose ice-cream-truck business challenges Good Humor and will grow to have some 600 franchisees nationwide, with more than 30 routes in Manhattan alone.

Pasta maker Emanuele Ronzoni dies at his home at 35-05 166th Street, Flushing, Queens, August 25 at age 86; frozen-food pioneer Clarence Birdseye in his Gramercy Park Hotel suite October 7 at age 69.

 The population of the upper West Side east of Amsterdam Avenue above 86th Street is 14 percent Puerto Rican, and the percentage is increasing (see 1953).

1957 Congress denies Rep. Adam Clayton Powell, Jr. a subcommittee chairmanship in January as President Eisenhower begins a second term.

Former Tammany Hall leader James J. Hines dies at Long Beach, N.Y., March 26 at age 80; former Tammany boss John Francis Curry at Coral Gables, Fla., April 25 at age 83.

An Army Redstone ballistic missile is displayed at Grand Central Terminal July 7 as cold-war anxieties continue to mount in the city and nation.

FBI agents arrest English-born Soviet intelligence officer Rudolf Ivanovich Abel, 53, July 21; a search of his Brooklyn home uncovers a shortwave radio, transmitter, and receiver along with other spy equipment, and a federal district court at Brooklyn sentences Abel to a 30-year prison term October 25. Also known as Emil R. Golfus and William August Fisher, he will be returned to the Soviet Union in February 1962 in exchange for U.S. reconaissance pilot Francis Gary Powers.

Mayor Wagner wins reelection by a landslide. Running on the Democrat-Liberal-Fusion ticket, he defeats Republican Robert K. Christenberry, who receives only 585,768 votes as compared with 1,508,775 for the mayor. President of the Ambassador Hotel on Park Avenue, Christenberry has said the Police Department was corrupt and not enforcing the laws, whereupon police raided his hotel and found an illegal gambling operation.

$ Financier Carl H. Pforzheimer dies in his Manhattan apartment April 4 at age 78; traction heir and onetime mayoral aide Clendenin J. Ryan shoots himself in his 32 East 70th Street home September 12 at age 52 (once worth an estimated $40 million, he leaves a net estate of $690,000).

Wall Street's Dow Jones Industrial Average closes December 31 at 435.69, down from 499.47 at the end of 1956.

Macy's has the first $2 million day in department store history December 16.

Brooklyn Union Gas acquires the New York and Richmond Gas Co., which serves all of Staten Island, and Kings County Lighting Co., which serves Brooklyn's Bay Ridge section (see 1959; natural gas, 1950).

A Northeast Airlines DC-6A takes off from La Guardia Airport for Florida in a heavy snowstorm February 1 and crashes moments later on Riker's Island, burning 22 to death (72 survive).

The city's (and state's) last trolley car leaves Queensboro Plaza at 12:32 o'clock in the morning of April 7 and crosses the Queensboro Bridge into Manhattan as the Queensboro Bridge Railway Co. joins the rest of the traction companies that have gone out of business; motor buses have replaced streetcars in virtually all major U.S. cities, and most of the 125 passengers on the final run are teenagers and trolley enthusiasts.

The New York Central adds day coaches to the once glamorous *Twentieth-Century Limited* it has run between New York and Chicago since 1902. Hurt by the New York Thruway that was built with government subsidies, the railroad continues to hemorrhage money.

The Avenue of the Americas (Sixth Avenue) becomes one-way northbound, despite objections from the Fifth Avenue Coach Co. and the Transport Workers Union (see 1956; 1960).

The ocean liners *Britannic*, *Queen Mary*, *Mauretania*, *Flandre*, *Olympia*, *United States*, and *Independence* are berthed simultaneously at Hudson River terminals September 3, but the day of the transatlantic steamer is waning as more travelers choose to go by air. While 39 piers still compete for business from 13th Street north to the New York Central Yards in the West 60s, steamship passenger traffic and the

volume of cargo coming into and leaving Manhattan have declined and will continue to do so (see 1983).

Booth Memorial Hospital moves to Flushing, Queens, where it has 210 beds and provides general care as well as maternity care (see 1918). It will grow in the next 40 years to have 487 beds, treat more than 150,000 patients per year, and be a major teaching hospital affiliated with the New York University School of Medicine.

The Caspary Auditorium is completed to designs by Harrison & Abramovitz for the 56-year-old Rockefeller Institute just east of York Avenue (see 1906; President's House, 1958).

The New York University College of Dentistry moves into a new building of its own at the northwest corner of First Avenue and 24th Street (see 1925; 1978).

∞ North Carolina-born evangelist William Franklin "Billy" Graham, 37, opens a "crusade" at Madison Square Garden May 15. A farewell rally for Graham on Broadway September 1 attracts a crowd of 200,000.

Bronx Community College opens at the corner of 184th Street and Creston Avenue, a building used since 1938 by the Bronx High School of Science. A junior college of the City University of New York (CUNY), it will move in 1973 to an unused NYC campus at the corner of University Avenue and 181st Street, where the Hall of Fame of Great Americans was dedicated in 1901, and by 1991 will have 4,171 full-time and 2,561 part-time students enrolled in career training, liberal-arts, and adult education courses.

Bronx High School of Science relocates to a building at the corner of 205th Street and Jerome Avenue (see 1938). Former Haaren High School principal Alexander Taffel, 46, succeeds the now-legendary Morris Meister as principal of what has become one of three specialized high schools for gifted students in the city's public education system, with a curriculum that includes advanced college-placement courses in science and math; it also offers independent research programs, and by 1991 its enrollment will be about 2,700.

Museum of the American Indian founder George Gustav Heye dies at New York January 20 at age 82; former Horace Mann principal Virgil Prettyman at Fort Lauderdale, Fla., October 13 at age 83.

A new city aquarium opens June 6 at Seaside Heights, Coney Island, to replace the facility that opened in December 1896 at the Battery. Attendance at the old aquarium peaked at 3.4 million in

1927, Parks Commissioner Robert Moses closed it in 1942 and wanted it destroyed to make way for a bridge to Brooklyn, Eleanor Roosevelt led a movement to block its destruction, the Brooklyn-Battery Tunnel was built in lieu of the bridge, and attendance at the new aquarium, while initially slow (the old aquarium was free; this one charges admission), will grow to 23 million in 1989 and 34.7 million in 1995 as new attractions build enthusiasm (*see* 1993).

 The *Woman's Home Companion* folds January 4 after 85 years of monthly publication (*see Collier's*, 1956).

Public-relations pioneer Carl Byoir of 895 Park Avenue dies of cancer at New York Hospital February 3 at age 68; former *Vogue* editor Edna Woolman Chase at Sarasota, Fla., March 20 at age 80; ITT cofounder Carl Sosthenes Behn of heart disease at New York June 6 at age 75; former *New York Times* foreign correspondent Walter Duranty is married for a second time at Orlando, Fla., and dies there of a stomach ailment October 3 at age 73.

DuMont Broadcasting Corp. acquires radio station WNEW March 20 for $7.5 million—reportedly the highest price ever paid for a station.

The S. I. Newhouse newspaper chain acquires Condé Nast Publications (*see Vogue*, 1909; Newhouse, 1912, 1967).

Papert Koenig Lois advertising agency is founded at New York by former Young & Rubicam copy director Frederic (Stuart) Papert, 30 (who serves as president); former Doyle Dane Bernbach copywriter-turned-account executive Julian Koenig, 46; and former Doyle Dane Bernbach art director George Lois, 26 (who serves as creative director). Their agency will be the first in the industry to sell shares to the public, and will continue until 1967.

 Nonfiction: *La Guardia: A Salute and a Memoir* by Robert Moses; *New York, New York* by Stuart Hawkins; *Subways Are for Sleeping* by New York author Edmund G. Love is based on interviews with some of the social outcasts who live without money and without legal residences in the city; *Gypsy* (autobiography) by stripteaser Gypsy Rose Lee (*see* Broadway musicals, 1959).

Greenwich Village eccentric Joe Gould dies at Pilgrim State Hospital August 18 at age 67. A member of the Harvard Class of 1911, he has claimed for decades to be writing a gargantuan "oral history of the world," scribbling endlessly in notebooks, often at the Minetta Tavern, while cadging beer and smoking discarded cigarette butts. His "oral history" turns out to have existed mostly in his own mind.

Fiction: *On the Road* by poet-novelist Jack Kerouac, now 35, who in January 1951 moved with his second wife, Joan (*née* Haverty), into an apartment at 454 West 20th Street (a row house near Tenth Avenue), felt distracted by having to put fresh sheets of paper into his typewriter, began in early April to tape together 20-foot strips of Japanese drawing paper (teletype paper by some accounts) that could feed continously, had the work almost finished by April 25, split with Joan in June (she was pregnant with their daughter, Jan), and moved to a friend's apartment. Kerouac has spent more and more time in recent years with his mother in Queens. He gives a series of poetry readings at the Village Vanguard; *The Day the Money Stopped* by Brendan Gill; *The Road to Miltown, or, Under the Spreading Atrophy* by S. J. Perelman.

 Painting: *New York, N.Y.* by Newburgh-born abstract artist Ellsworth Kelly, 34,; *Black on Black* by Ad Reinhardt, who mixes subtle tones of olive, violet, and other deep colors in his blacks (he promulgates rules for what the artist should avoid, including texture, brushwork, drawing, forms, design, colors, light, space, time, size and scale, movement, and objects and symbols); *Painting with Red Letter 'S'* by Robert Rauschenberg; *1957D No. 1* by Clyfford Still; *Palisade* by Willem de Kooning; *Sunlight Reflections* by Milton Avery; *Billboard* by Grace Hartigan; *Music* by John Koch; *The Street* (casein on paper) by Jacob Lawrence.

Trieste-born art dealer Leo Castelli, 49, opens a gallery under his own name at 4 East 77th Street, where next year he will mount the first exhibitions of work by Jasper Johns and Robert Rauschenberg (*see* 1971).

Theater: *The Potting Shed* by English novelist-playwright Graham Greene, 52, 1/29 at the Bijou Theater, with Sybil Thorndike, Leueen MacGrath, New York-born ingénue Carol Lynley, 14, Frank Conroy, 157 perfs.; *Orpheus Descending* by Tennessee Williams 3/21 at the Martin Beck Theater, with Maureen Stapleton, La Jolla, Calif.-born actor Cliff Robertson, 32, Robert Webber, 68 perfs.; *A Moon for the Misbegotten* by the late Eugene O'Neill 5/2 at the Bijou Theater, with English-born actress Wendy Hiller, 44, Franchot Tone, Durban, South Africa-born Irish actor Cyril Cusack, 46, 68 perfs.; *The Rope Dancers* by Morton Wishengrad 11/20 at the Cort Theater, with Siobhan McKenna, Mount Vernon-born actor Art Carney, 40, Vienna-born actor Theodore Bikel, 34, 189 perfs.; *Look Homeward, Angel* 11/28 at the Ethel Barrymore Theater, with Jo Van Fleet, New York-born actor Anthony Perkins,

26, Arthur Hill is based on the 1929 Thomas Wolfe novel, 564 perfs.; *The Dark at the Top of the Stairs* by William Inge 12/5 at the Music Box Theater, with Denver-born actor Pat Hingle, 33, New York-born actress Teresa Wright, 39, Eileen Heckart, 468 perfs.

Actress Josephine Hull dies at New York after a series of paralytic strokes March 12 at age 70; drama critic Burton Rascoe of a heart attack at New York March 19 at age 64; former Orpheum Circuit head Marcus Heiman of a heart attack in his Sardi Building office September 9 at age 74.

Films: Walter Lang's *Desk Set* with Spencer Tracy, Katharine Hepburn, Gig Young, Joan Blondell; Martin Ritt's *Edge of the City* with John Cassavetes, Sidney Poitier, Jack Warden, Ruby Dee; Alexander Mackendrick's *Sweet Smell of Success* with Burt Lancaster as gossip columnist J. J. Hunsecker (based on Walter Winchell), who says, "I love this dirty town," Tony Curtis, script by Clifford Odets; Sidney Lumet's *12 Angry Men* with Henry Fonda, Lee J. Cobb, Ed Begley, E. G. Marshall, Jack Klugman, Jack Warden, Martin Balsam. Also: Melville Shavelson's *Beau James* with Bob Hope as Mayor Jimmy Walker; Vincente Minelli's *Designing Woman* with Gregory Peck, Lauren Bacall; Charles Chaplin's *A King in New York* with Chaplin, Dawn Addams in a satire of U.S. technology and communist witch-hunts (it will not be shown in the United States until 1973); Rudolph Maté's *Miracle in the Rain* with Jane Wyman, Van Johnson; Richard Quine's *The Solid Gold Cadillac* with Judy Holliday, Paul Douglas; Frank Tashlin's *Will Success Spoil Rock Hunter?* with Tony Randall, Jayne Mansfield, Betsy Drake, Joan Blondell; Alfred Hitchcock's *The Wrong Man* with Henry Fonda, Vera Miles, Anthony Quayle.

Actor Humphrey Bogart dies of esophageal cancer at Hollywood January 14 at age 56.

Film musical: Stanley Donen's *Funny Face* with Audrey Hepburn, Fred Astaire (as photographer Richard Avedon), Kay Thompson, Suzy Parker.

Broadway musicals: *The Ziegfeld Follies* 3/11 at the Winter Garden Theater, with Beatrice Lillie, Billy de Wolfe, Melrose Park, Ill.-born ingénue Carol Lawrence (originally Carol Maria Laraia), 22, in the 24th and final edition of the *Follies* 50 years after its first opening. Music by Sammy Fain, Jack Lawrence, Michael Myers, and others, lyrics by Howard Dietz, Carolyn Leigh, and others, 123 perfs.; *New Girl in Town* 5/14 at the 46th Street Theater, with Gwen Verdon, Thelma Ritter in a musical version of the 1921 Eugene O'Neill play *Anna Christie*, music and lyrics by Bob Merrill, songs that include "Sunshine Girl," 431 perfs.; *West Side Story* 9/26 at the Winter Garden Theater, with Carol Lawrence (as Maria) and 40 other players, book based on the 1595 Shakespeare tragedy *Romeo and Juliet*, sets by Oliver Smith, choreography by Jerome Robbins, music by Leonard Bernstein, lyrics by New York-born writer-musician Stephen Sondheim, 27, "juvenile delinquents" singing, "We're misunderstood . . . [we're] "depraved" because we're "deprived," "Goodness gracious, that's why I'm a mess," "deep down inside of us there's good," songs that include "Tonight," "Maria," 732 perfs.; *Jamaica* 10/31 at the Imperial Theater with Lena Horne, now 40, in her Broadway debut, Mexico City-born actor Ricardo Montalban, 36, Georgia-born actor Ossie Davis, 39, music by Harold Arlen, lyrics by E. Y. Harburg, 558 perfs.; *The Music Man* 12/19 at the Majestic Theater, with Robert Preston, music and lyrics by Meredith Willson, songs that include "Seventy-Six Trombones," "Gary, Indiana," "Till There Was You," 1,375 perfs.

Former *Ziegfeld Follies* lyricist Gene Buck dies at Manhasset, L.I., February 24 at age 71 (he was president of ASCAP from 1924 to 1941); bass-baritone Ezio Pinza dies in his sleep at his Stamford, Conn., home May 9 at age 64 following a series of strokes; former Ziegfeld girl Peggy Hopkins Joyce dies of throat cancer at New York June 12 at age 62.

Leonard Bernstein is appointed musical director of the New York Philharmonic November 19.

Grammy Awards are awarded for the first time by the new National Academy of Recording Arts and Sciences, founded by recording company executives who include Columbia Records president James B. Conkling, 42.

Bandleader Jimmy Dorsey dies of lung cancer at Doctors Hospital June 12 at age 53.

Althea Gibson, 29, (U.S.) wins in women's singles at Wimbledon (the first black American to be invited). Gibson receives a ticker-tape parade up Broadway July 11, Mayor Wagner tells her, "If we had more women like you the world would be a better place," and she goes on to win the singles title at Forest Hills. Malcolm James "Mal" Anderson, 22, wins in men's singles at Forest Hills.

Floyd Patterson retains his world heavyweight title July 29, defeating challenger Tommy Jackson in 10 rounds at New York.

Baseball diamonds with backstops are installed on Central Park's Great Lawn, between 79th and 86th streets, where boys have for decades played pickup games without such facilities.

Brooklyn's 43-year-old Ebbets Field closes September 24 as "Dem bums" prepare to move to Los Angeles. Fans go away with memories of devotee Hilda Chester ringing her cowbell and the Dodgers Sym-phony playing "Three Blind Mice" to greet umpires. The stadium will be razed (*see* real estate, 1960).

Giant fans chase the team into its clubhouse at the Polo Grounds after its last game in New York September 29 and steal souvenirs as the Giants prepare to move to San Francisco.

The New York Yankees win the American League pennant, but the Milwaukee Braves win the World Series, defeating the Yankees 4 games to 3. Hank Bauer and Tony Kubek each get eight hits, including two home runs (Bauer's second, in the bottom of the sixth game's ninth inning, ties the Series), but Milwaukee pitcher Selva Lewis "Lew" Burdette, 30, has shut out New York in the fifth game and does so again in the seventh, winning his third complete game with help from a third-inning error by Kubek that leads to four runs.

● Brooklyn woman Fannie Arms, 39, is critically injured June 16 when she falls from Coney Island's Cyclone roller coaster. She has squirmed out from behind a restraining bar to the top of a rear seat when the Cyclone was going 22 miles per hour and fallen from a height of 28 feet to a catwalk below, sustaining multiple fractures.

▥ Former Chicago gangster Johnny Torrio dies at Brooklyn April 16 at age 75.

A .32-caliber bullet grazes mobster Frank Costello's head May 2 in the lobby of the Majestic apartment house where he lives. His would-be assassin, Vincent "The Chin" Gigante, escapes, and Costello rushes to the emergency room of Roosevelt Hospital; he is not badly hurt, but police search his pockets and find a slip showing more than $1 million in winnings from his gambling casinos.

Two gunmen shoot Mafia lieutenant Frank (Don Cheech) Scalise, 55, four times in the head June 17 as he leaves a Bronx fruit stand at 2380 Arthur Avenue in the Crotona-Fordham section after buying 90¢ worth of fruits and vegetables. Scalise was a vice president of the Mario and Di Bon Plastering Co. of Corona, Queens, but was actually a henchman of onetime Murder, Inc. boss Umberto "Albert" Anastasia (*see* 1951), a onetime associate of Charles "Lucky" Luciano, and a reputed associate of Frank Costello. He is suspected of having been involved in an international narcotics smuggling ring and has been sought for more than a year by police for questioning in the 1954 murder of Jim Macri and the disappearance of Macri's brother Benedetto. He lived on City Island and his blue 1956 Cadillac is found parked in front of 630 Crescent Avenue, near a candy store run by his brother Jack.

Umberto "Albert" Anastasia is shot to death from behind October 25 at age 55 by two gunmen reputedly in the pay of Vito Genovese. The shooting takes place in the barbershop of the Park-Sheraton Hotel on Seventh Avenue (the same hotel where gambler Arnold Rothstein was killed in 1928 when it was still the Park Central). Anastasia has been arrested 10 times, five times for murder, but has generally gone free after witnesses disappeared or gave weakened testimony and served only 4 years in prison for murdering a fellow longshoreman in 1921. He has lived in recent years behind a seven-foot barbed-wire fence with Doberman pinschers at 75 Block Road in the Palisades section of Fort Lee, N.J. His killers, wearing scarves over the lower part of their faces, get away in the confusion after firing 10 shots. Anastasia, his brother Anthony "Tough Tony," and their underlings have been identified with extortion, gambling, pilfering, usury, wildcat strikes, and assaults and murders on the city's waterfront. They may also have had a hand in strong-arm rackets in the garment, laundry, shipping, and trucking industries. Carlo Gambino is believed to have been involved in Anastasia's murder; helped by mobsters Joe Biondo and Aniello Dellacroce, Gambino will remain boss until his death in 1976.

Apalachin, N.Y., makes headlines when police find 58 Mafia members from all over the United States gathered November 14 at the home of Joseph Barbara. Included are Vito Genovese, Joseph Bonanno, Carlo Gambino, Joseph Profaci, Jerry Catena, and Mike Miranda.

🏠 The 34-story 575 Lexington Avenue office building is completed at the northeast corner of 51st Street with 528,000 square feet of space. Designed by Sylvan Bien and his son Robert for Sam Minskoff & Sons, its exterior pioneers use of gold-finished extruded (or anodized) aluminum in New York. The Biens have specialized in apartment houses with white glazed-brick exteriors; 575 Lex has 100 square feet of the material rising above a base of gray graphite and stainless steel.

The 21-story 400 Park Avenue building is completed at the northwest corner of 54th Street. Designed by Emery Roth & Sons, it replaces a 48-

unit apartment house with a structure containing 225,000 square feet of office space.

The 32-story 425 Park Avenue office building is completed between 55th and 56th streets, replacing several four-story apartment houses put up by the late Robert Goelet in 1871. Kahn & Jacobs has designed the new structure.

Brooklyn's New York State Supreme Court Building is completed at 360 Adams Street, opposite Montague Street. Designed by Shreve, Lamb & Harmon, it is part of the borough's Civic Center, put up since the end of World War II, that has replaced 259 buildings and eliminated 8,200 industrial jobs.

The Coliseum Park apartment houses are completed at 345 West 58th Street and 30 West 60th Street—two 14-story buildings, separated by a large garden, on Ninth Avenue. Title I federal money has been used to acquire the land for the buildings; designed by Sylvan Bien, they have 575 rental units that will be offered as co-operatives beginning in 1985.

Park West Village (initially called West Park Apartments) opens its first buildings (see 1954). The former Manhattantown project has been taken over by Webb & Knapp Corp., whose William Zeckendorf is building it in partnership with Aluminum Co. of America (Alcoa). By the time the complex is finished in 1962 its seven buildings, each 17 to 20 stories high, will cover an area extending from 97th Street to 100th between Manhattan and Amsterdam avenues, with 2,700 middle-income units, tennis courts, and open-air parking spaces.

Architect-contractor Paul Starrett dies at Greenwich, Conn., July 5 at age 90; realtor-financier Robert Livingston Gerry at Delhi, N.Y., October 30 at age 80; his brother Peter Goelet Gerry at Providence, R.I., October 30 at age 78.

Levittown's first black family moves in August 16 under police guard (see 1947). The population of the community will reach 65,440 by 1970, but Levittown will remain 97.3 percent white in 1990 (137 blacks, 51,883 whites, 1,266 "other").

The Frederick Douglass Houses receive their first tenants in September, with each family paying $55 per month in rent. Part of the Upper West Side urban renewal area, the houses combine rehabilitated four-story structures with new 20-story high-rise buildings and will ultimately consist of 2,462 units in 29 buildings, covering a 12-block site from 100th Street to 104th, between Manhattan and Amsterdam avenues, with grassy lawns.

The Café Figaro opens in an Italian section of Greenwich Village at the corner of Bleecker and Macdougal streets with shellacked pages of the Paris newspaper on its walls. Started by Tom Ziegler and his wife, Royce Powell, the coffeehouse is lighted by Tiffany lamps, boasts a capuccino maker, and will become a favored hangout for counterculture artists, poets, authors, and entertainers who will include David Amram, Lenny Bruce, Jim Carroll, Gregory Corso, Bill Cosby, Salvador Dali, Bob Dylan, Alan Ginsberg, Jack Kerouac, and Larry Rivers.

Lindy's original restaurant closes in June after 46 years on Broadway when the eatery memorialized by the late Damon Runyon as "Mindy's" becomes uneconomic to operate because of its physical setup (see 1921). Founder Leo Lindeman dies of a heart ailment in his 25 Central Park West apartment September 24 at age 69; his second, larger restaurant will remain open for another few years, but although the Lindy's name will be acquired by other operators there will not be another Lindy's.

Le Pavillon restaurant moves to the Ritz Tower at 111 East 57th Street following a dispute with Columbia Pictures boss Harry Cohn, whose company owns the building at Fifth Avenue and 55th Street (see 1941; Côte Basque, 1958).

Diners Club founder Frank X. McNamara dies of a heart attack at Manhasset November 9 at age 40.

The Forum of the Twelve Caesars restaurant opens December 12 at 57 West 48th Street with a decor by designer William Pahlman, who for $6,000 has acquired 17th century paintings by Camilio Procaccini of the 12 Caesars from Julius to Domitian. Operated by Restaurant Associates of 1953 Newarker fame, it has tableware made in Milan, James Beard gives its waiters a course on wine, its chef Albert Stockli has read Apicius, its wines are cooled in centurion helmets, its four-page menu is bound with gold and a wax seal with a purple faille ribbon (see Four Seasons, 1959).

1958 U.S. Attorney General Herbert Brownell, Jr. resigns January 26 and returns to private law practice at New York. He has been outspoken in his opposition to communism while urging President Eisenhower to appoint judges who would enforce racial desegregation laws.

Judge Samuel Seabury dies at East Hampton May 7 at age 85. He forced the resignation of Mayor Jimmy Walker in 1932, pushed for the nomination of Fiorello H. La Guardia as a Fusion candidate for mayor in 1933, and will be memorialized in Manhat-

Harlem's voters repeatedly elected Rev. Adam Clayton Powell, Jr. to Congress. AP/WIDE WORLD

tan with a public playground at Lexington Avenue and 95th Street.

Rep. Adam Clayton Powell, Jr. is indicted May 8 on charges of tax fraud. The case has been pending for 2 years, and Powell's support of President Eisenhower in the 1956 election has alienated Tammany Hall boss Carmine G. De Sapio.

New York Shakespeare Festival founder Joseph Papp is called to testify before the House Un-American Activities Committee but refuses to divulge names of alleged communists he may have known.

The Committee for Democratic Voters is established at New York by citizens who include Eleanor Roosevelt, former governor Herbert H. Lehman, and lawyer Paul O'Dwyer to work for reform of the party in New York State.

Gov. Harriman loses his bid for reelection; despite a Democratic sweep in most contests, Republican Nelson A. Rockefeller, now 50, wins with a plurality of nearly 600,000 votes (he secures 3,126,929 votes to Harriman's 2,553,895). A grandson of the late oil magnate, Rockefeller was in the Eisenhower administration until 1956, when he left to work on a number of New York State boards and commissions. He has lived with his wife, Mary, in an apartment at 810 Fifth Avenue since 1931 but has campaigned for working-class votes with far more gusto than Harriman, touring the Lower East Side and other ethnic neighborhoods, kissing babies and eating blintzes, knishes, hot dogs, and the like. He bought a $5 salami wholesale for $3 in Rivington Street, where another customer was heard to say

about the delicatessen owner, "For a Rockefeller he gives discounts."

Rep. Adam Clayton Powell, Jr. wins reelection with help from the "Harlem Fox" J. Raymond Jones, now 60, who retired from politics in 1953 and has been working in a $12,000 patronage job as secretary to a judge. He has become Powell's campaign manager, and Powell, who has endorsed Gov. Harriman, easily defeats Tammany's primary candidate, winning by a three-to-one margin over Harvard-educated City Councilman Earl Brown, who writes a column for the *Amsterdam News*.

Tammany boss Carmine G. De Sapio comes under attack for mishandling the state Democratic convention. Democrats blame him not only for putting Gov. Harriman in a bad light but also for Manhattan District Attorney Frank Hogan's defeat in the U.S. Senate contest by Republican Kenneth B. Keating, 58.

A demented black woman stabs Alabama-born Southern Christian Leadership Conference (SCLC) president Rev. Martin Luther King, Jr., 29, in the chest with a letter opener September 20 as he autographs his book *Stride Toward Freedom: The Montgomery Story* at a white-owned Harlem department store. Gov. Harriman is by some accounts intent on making sure that King is treated by black physicians, and the civil-rights leader is rushed to Harlem Hospital, where surgeons crack his sternum with a hammer and chisel to remove the knife, whose blade has come close to his aorta. (An angry crowd begins to gather but violence is averted. Alfred Marrow, chairman of the Commission on Intergroup Relations, hears the facts in the case from Mayor Wagner's police commissioner and relays the information to black leaders.) The *New York Times* reports the next morning that if King had sneezed he would have drowned in his own blood; he remains hospitalized for 2 weeks. Many blacks share the view of King's assailant that appeals to the federal government are more effective than boycotts and protests.

Executive Order 49 grants unions in the public sector many of the bargaining rights enjoyed by workers in private industry and applies initially to 100,000 workers in departments directly responsible to the mayor. Issued March 30 by Mayor Wagner, it will be called the "Little Wagner Act," a reference to the National Labor Relations Act (Wagner-Connery Act) of 1935 (see 1954). By 1980 the city will have 450,000 public-sector jobs, most of them unionized. Wagner has scored so-called "right to work" laws, and he has issued the order to forestall action by major unions because his new budget makes no provision for pay increases. International Brotherhood of Teamsters president James R. Hoffa announces December 10 that his union plans to organize all city workers.

Moody's Investors Service founder and magazine publisher John Moody dies at La Jolla, Calif., February 16 at age 89, having moved to California last year.

Rising prices on the New York Stock Exchange push dividend yields below bond-market yields for the first time, beginning a trend that will continue for at least 40 years as investors come to realize that equities may appreciate in value and are potentially far more profitable (albeit riskier) long-term investments than fixed-income securities.

Wall Street's Dow Jones Industrial Average closes December 31 at a new high of 583.65, up from 435.69 at the end of 1957, but U.S. unemployment has reached a postwar high of more than 5.1 million, and a record 3.1 million Americans are receiving unemployment insurance benefits. Economic recession grips the nation with nearly one-third of major industrial centers classified as having "substantial" unemployment. A house that cost $47,409 in 1948 now sells for $59,558, a family size Chevrolet that sold for $1,255 sells for $2,081, a gallon of gasoline has climbed from 25.9¢ to 30.4¢, a pair of blue jeans that sold for $3.45 sells for $3.75, a pair of men's shoes that was $9.95 is now $11.95, a daily newspaper that cost 3¢ now costs 5¢, a year's tuition at Harvard that cost $455 costs $1,250, a hospital room that cost $13.09 per day costs $28.17, a ticket to a Broadway musical that cost $6.00 costs $8.05. Some prices have come down: a ranch mink coat that cost $4,200 in 1948 now costs $4,000, a round-trip flight between New York and London that cost $630 costs $453.60, a phone call from New York to Topeka, Kan., that cost $1.90 costs $1.80 (day rate), a pound of chicken that cost 61.2¢ has come down to 46.5¢.

American Express Co. introduces the American Express Card, charging an annual fee to "members" who use the plastic credit card for charging airfares, auto rentals, hotel and motel rooms, restaurant meals, and other expenses. American Express sets out to overtake Diners Club, whose card started the travel-and-entertainment card business in 1950.

Diamond dealer Harry Winston donates the 44.5-carat Hope Diamond to the Smithsonian Institution at Washington, D.C. Now 64, he sends it by registered mail as he sends all his jewelry (see 1932; 1960).

Subway service expands beginning January 16 to serve Far Rockaway in Queens (see 1956).

New York Central chairman Robert Young kills himself with a shotgun in the study of his Palm Beach mansion January 25 at age 60 (see 1951). The Interstate Commerce Commission has been insisting that the bankrupt New York, New Haven & Hartford be included in any merger, but neither the Central nor the Pennsy has wanted to take in the New Haven, whose position has been weakened by stock raiders and by the Connecticut Turnpike. Its commuter rail service to New York City is essential but unprofitable.

A Pan Am 707 takes off for Paris from New York's 11-year-old Idlewild Airport October 26, serving food from Maxim's, carrying 111 passengers to inaugurate transatlantic jet service. It reduces transatlantic flying time by one-half, and by the end of next year airlines will be carrying 63 percent of all cross-Atlantic traffic—more than 1.5 million air passengers versus 881,894 sea passengers, but European companies will continue to launch new passenger liners (see JFK, 1963).

Evangelist Billy Graham preaches at Yankee Stadium July 20; rallies by Jehovah's Witnesses August 3 attract 250,000 to Yankee Stadium and the Polo Grounds; Cardinal Spellman celebrates Mass at Yankee Stadium December 12.

The limestone-and-glass President's House for the 57-year-old Rockefeller Institute is completed to designs by Harrison & Abramovitz (see 1957; 1959).

Queensborough Community College is founded as part of the City University of New York (see 1978).

Polytechnic Institute of Brooklyn moves to a new site at 333 Jay Street (see 1935). The school has become coeducational but remains largely a male institution (see 1973).

The United Press and International News Service merge at New York May 24 to produce United Press International (UPI).

Nonfiction: *Al Smith and His America* by Brooklyn-born historian Oscar Handlin, 42; *Madison Avenue, USA* by Martin Mayer is about the advertising agency business; *Park Row: Turn of the Century Newspaper Days* by Flushing-born author Allen Churchill, 46.

Fiction: *Breakfast at Tiffany's* (stories) by Truman Capote, whose title story appears in the November issue of *Esquire* magazine; *The Oldest Confession* by New York-born novelist Richard (Thomas) Condon, 43; *The Best of Everything* by New York-born novelist

Rona Jaffe, 26, whose grandfather Moses Ginsberg put up the Carlyle Hotel in 1930.

Painting: *Three Flags* by Jasper Johns; *Four Darks on Red* by Mark Rothko; *Blue Sea, Red Sky* by Milton Avery.

Robert Rauschenberg pioneers "Pop Art" with four Coca-Cola bottles inserted in a semi-abstract hole.

Jazz Age illustrator John Held, Jr. dies at Belmar, N.J., March 2 at age 59; designer Norman Bel Geddes at New York May 8 at age 65.

Sculpture: *José Julian Marti* by sculptress Anna Hyatt Huntington, now 82, who donates the equestrian bronze statue of the Cuban hero to the city and pays for its installation on the north side of Central Park South at Sixth Avenue (*see* politics, 1895; 1960).

Photographs: *Once Upon a City* by former Museum of the City of New York photography curator Grace M. Mayer, 56, is based on turn-of-the-century photographs by the late Joseph and Percy Byron. Mayer joined the museum in 1930 when it was still in Gracie Mansion, built up its photo collection, and last year joined the Museum of Modern Art (MoMA), where she helped Edward Steichen organize a show; she will become curator of photography in 1962.

LIFE magazine runs a series of photographs under the title "Drama Beneath a City Window." Photojournalist W. Eugene Smith, now 39, has taken the pictures from his Sixth Avenue loft.

New York photographer Diane Arbus (*née* Nemerov), 35, begins 2 years of study with Austrian-born documentary photographer Lisette Model, now 51, who befriends her and will help Arbus get through her separation and divorce in the 1960s.

Theater: *The Garden District* (*Suddenly Last Summer* and *Something Unspoken*) by Tennessee Williams 1/7 at the York Theater, with Ocala, Fla.-born ingénue Elizabeth Ashley (originaly Elizabeth Ann Cole), 18, 31 perfs.; *Two for the Seesaw* by New York-born playwright William Gibson, 42, 1/16 at the Booth Theater, with Henry Fonda, Anne Bancroft (as Gittel Mosca), 750 perfs.; *Sunrise at Campobello* by Newark-born playwright (and former M-G-M production chief) Dore (originally Isadore) Schary, 52, 1/30 at the Cort Theater, with Ralph Bellamy as Franklin D. Roosevelt, Mary Fickett as Eleanor, 556 perfs.; *The Visit* by Swiss playwright Friedrich Durrenmätt 5/5 at the Lunt-Fontanne Theater (formerly the Globe), with Alfred Lunt, now 65, and Lynn Fontanne, now 70, in their final Broadway appearance, 189 perfs.; *A Touch of the Poet* by the late Eugene O'Neill 10/2 at the Helen Hayes Theater with Eric Portman, Helen Hayes, Kim Stanley, Betty Field, 284 perfs.; *The World of Suzie Wong* by Paul Osborn 10/14 at the Broadhurst Theater, with Marseilles-born ingénue France Nuyen (originally France Nguyen Vanaga), 19, Montreal-born actor William Shatner, 27, 508 perfs.; *The Pleasure of His Company* by Cornelia Otis Skinner and Samuel Taylor 10/22 at the Longacre Theater, with Skinner, Cyril Ritchard, Charles Ruggles, 474 perfs.; *The Disenchanted* by Budd Schulberg and Harvey Breit (based on Schulberg's novel) 12/3 at the Coronet Theater, with Jason Robards, Jr. (and Sr.), English-born actress Rosemary Harris, 28, Milwaukee-born actress Salome Jens, 23, North Carolina-born actor George Grizzard, 30, 189 perfs.; *The Cold Wind and the Warm* by S. N. Behrman 12/8 at the Morosco Theater, with Eli Wallach, Maureen Stapleton, Italian-born actor Vincent Gardenia (originally Scognamiglio), 37, Morris Carnovsky, New York-born ingénue Suzanne Pleshette, 21, 120 perfs.; *JB* by poet-playwright-statesman Archibald MacLeish, now 66, 12/11 at the ANTA Theater, with Raymond Massey, Christopher Plummer, Pat Hingle, 364 perfs.

Critic George Jean Nathan dies in his suite at the Hotel Royalton April 8 at age 76; playwright-composer-lyricist Clare Kummer at Carmel, Calif., April 22 at age 85; playwright F. Hugh Herbert at Hollywood May 17 at age 60; onetime showgirl Peggy Hopkins Joyce (*née* Upton) of throat cancer at Memorial Center for Cancer and Allied Diseases June 12 at age 63 with her sixth husband by her side; playwright-novelist Rachel Crowthers at Danbury, Conn., July 5 at age 75; critic Woollcott Gibbs of a heart attack at his Ocean Beach, Fire Island, summer home August 16 at age 56; playwright-novelist Zoë Akins of cancer at Hollywood October 29 at age 74.

Television: *The Ann Sothern Show* 10/6 on CBS with Sothern as the assistant manager of a New York hotel, Ernest Truex, Ann Tyrrall, Jack Mullaney (to 9/25/1961); *The Naked City* 9/30 on ABC with Missouri-born actor James Franciscus, 24, John McIntyre (to 9/11/1963).

Columbia University English instructor Charles Van Doren, 32, denies any wrongdoing when accused in August of having received answers in advance as a contestant on NBC's 2-year-old quiz show *Twenty-One*. Van Doren's salary at Columbia is $4,400 per year, his appearances on the show have brought him nearly $150,000, and he finally comes clean November 2; a grand jury indicts the show's producers (notably Dan Enright) for fraud; President Eisenhower calls the deception "a terrible thing to do to the American public;" NBC cancels *Twenty-One* November 2. The three networks take control of all programming out of the hands of advertising agencies, and a congressional committee will conduct hearings on the quiz-show fraud next year (*but see* 1999).

American Broadcasting Co. (ABC) founder (and Beech-Nut Life Savers board chairman) Edward J. Noble dies at his Greenwich, Conn., home December 28 at age 76.

Films: Morton DaCosta's *Auntie Mame* with Rosalind Russell, Forrest Tucker; Richard Quine's *Bell, Book and Candle* with James Stewart, Kim Novak, Jack Lemmon, Ernie Kovaks; Eugene Lourie's *The Colossus of New York* with John Baragrey, Mala Powers, Otto Kruger; Andrew L. Stone's *Cry Terror* with James Mason, Rod Steiger, Inger Stevens; Irving Rapper's *Marjorie Morningstar* with Gene Kelly, Natalie Wood; Sidney Lumet's *Stage Struck* with Henry Fonda, Susan Strasberg, Joan Greenwood, Christopher Plummer; George Seaton's *Teacher's Pet* with Clark Gable, Doris Day, Gig Young.

Broadway musicals: *Say, Darling* 4/3 at the ANTA Theater, with David Wayne, Vivian Blaine, Detroit-born actor Johnny Desmond (originally Giovanni Alberto de Simone), 38, Newton, Mass.-born comedian Robert Morse, 26, music and lyrics by Betty Comden, Adolph Green, and Jule Styne, book by Richard Bissell, his wife, Marian, and New York-born writer-director Abe Burrows, 47, in an adaptation of his 1957 novel (to the Martin Beck Theater 12/8), 332 perfs.; *Flower Drum Song* 12/1 at the St. James Theater, with California-born actress Pat (originally Chiyoko) Suzuki, 27, Juanita Hall, Hokkaido-born actress Miyoshi Umeki, 29 (as the mail-order bride Mei Li), Larry Blyden, music and lyrics by Richard Rodgers and Oscar Hammerstein II, 601 perfs.

Broadway producer Mike Todd is killed in the crash of his private plane near Grants, N.M., March 22 at age 48 while en route to New York for a banquet to be given in his honor at the Waldorf-Astoria (his wife, Elizabeth Taylor, has stayed home because of a cold); Broadway musical librettist Herbert Fields dies of a heart attack at Lenox Hill Hospital March 24 at age 60, survived by his sister Dorothy.

The Alvin Ailey American Dance Theater founded by Texas-born New York dancer-choreographer Ailey, 27, will perform works created not only by Ailey but also by choreographers such as Talley Beatty, John Butler, Ulysses Dove, Katherine Dunham, Lester Horton (one of Ailey's teachers), Bill T. Jones, Donald McKayle, Elisa Monte, and Pearl Primus. Ailey

will succeed in bringing black dancers into the mainstream of the performing arts (*see* Dance Theater of Harlem, 1969).

Tin Pan Alley songwriter Lew Brown dies of a heart attack at New York February 5 at age 64; Alfred Bryan at Morristown, N.J., April 1 at age 87; W. C. Handy of bronchial pneumonia at New York March 28 at age 84 (he has been blind since 1943); Maude Nugent dies at New York June 3 at age 85.

Esquire magazine art director Robert Benton decides to include photographs of jazz musicians for a special January 1959 issue, Bronx-born freelance art director-photographer Art Kane, 33, suggests that it be a group photograph, and 58 musicians turn up in mid-August outside a brownstone at 17 East 126th Street, between Fifth and Madison avenues (selected because it is close to the 125th Street subway entrance). Included are not only the famous Count Basie, Buck Clayton, Roy Eldridge, Art Farmer, Bud Freeman, Coleman Hawkins, Dizzy Gillespie, Max Kaminsky, Gene Krupa, bassist Charles Mingus, Oscar Pettiford, Jimmy Rushing, Pee Wee Russell, Zutty Singleton, Willie "the Lion" Smith (who wanders off to escape the heat and is not in the picture), George Wettling, and Lester Young but also the soon-to-be famous Art Blakey, Sonny Greer, Thelonious Sphere Monk, Gerry Mulligan, New York-born tenor saxophonist Sonny Rollins (at 27, the youngest), English pianist Marian McPartland, and teacher Mary Lou Williams (*see* Films, 1995).

 Ashley John Cooper, 21, (Australia) wins in men's singles at Forest Hills, Althea Gibson in women's singles.

The New York Road Runners Club is organized by a small group headed by Romanian-born enthusiast and promoter Fred Lebow (originally Fischl Lebowitz), 24 (*see* marathon, 1970).

An auto crash January 28 leaves Philadelphia-born Brooklyn Dodgers catcher Roy Campanella, 36, paralyzed from the waist down.

The Brooklyn Dodgers become the Los Angeles Dodgers and play their first season at Chavez Ravine. The New York Giants become the San Francisco Giants and play their first season at Candlestick Park.

The New York Yankees win the World Series, defeating the Milwaukee Braves 4 games to 3 after pitchers Warren Spahn and Lew Burdette have put the Braves ahead 2 games to 0. Pitcher Don Larsen shuts out Milwaukee in the third game with help from Wisconsin-born reliever Rinold George "Ryne"

Duren, 29, Spahn comes back in the fourth to shut out New York again, and the Yankees go on to become the first team since 1925 to win the Series after being down 3 games to 1. Yankee pitcher Bob Turley shuts out the Braves in the fifth, relieves reliever Ryne Duren to save the sixth, and relieves Don Larsen to win the seventh after Elston Howard has broken a tie in that game's eighth inning.

● The first Steuben Day parade steps off in September on Fifth Avenue at 63rd Street and marches to Yorkville in East 86th Street (*see* Steuben Society, 1919).

▦ The state legislature at Albany authorizes New York City Housing Authority police to carry weapons and make arrests. Youth gangs on the Lower East Side and elsewhere in the city battle over "turf" and have threatened to "take over" community facilities such as playgrounds and even settlement houses, but management moves against troublemakers lead to complaints about unjust evictions and demands for tenant boards of appeals. Housing Authority managers count 2,036 problem families in June and concede that the "behavior of problem families has become notorious . . . , [threatening] the reputation of the whole housing movement."

⌂ The Church of Our Saviour (Roman Catholic) is completed at 59 Park Avenue, southeast corner 38th Street, to Romanesque designs by Paul C. Reilly.

The eight-story Milliken Building (initially Deering Milliken) is completed at 1045 Sixth Avenue, northwest corner 39th Street, to designs by Carson & Lundin.

The Tishman Building is completed at 666 Fifth Avenue, between 52nd and 53rd streets. Designed in International Style by Carson & Lundin for developer David Tishman, now 68, the 38-story aluminum-clad office tower has 1 million square feet of floor space and a 40-foot-wide street-level "waterfall" fountain designed by California-born sculptor Isamu Noguchi, 53, plus other Noguchi works (the illuminated numerals 666 will be replaced on three façades by the blue-and-red Citigroup logotype in 2002).

The white-brick 475 Park Avenue apartment house is completed at the southeast corner of 58th Street, using as its framework the girders of a 1909 building that was one of the avenue's first co-ops. Aluminum Co. of America had intended to raze the structure and build a 30-story tower for its New York headquarters; unable to evict some legal tenants, it sold the property in 1950. Developer Henry Goelet engaged architects Charles N. and Selig Whinston to design a building with 14 stories plus penthouse that wraps around the 32-year-old Ritz Tower.

The "luxury decontrol" law enacted by the state legislature at Albany in March removes rent controls from vacant apartments that have rented for more than $416 per month. In the next 12 years more than 250,000 rental apartments in 8,000 buildings will be converted to co-operative ownership (*see* 1964).

The George Washington Carver Houses open in East Harlem, occupying most of the seven blocks between 99th and 106th streets from Madison Avenue to Park Avenue. Financed by the state as a slum-clearance project, the 13 buildings vary in height from six to 15 floors; 5 percent of the units are designed for the elderly, 1 percent for the handicapped (having, among other things, doorways without sills, mechanical openers for windows, nonslip ceramic tile in the bathroom, and grab bars along the wall by the tub and sink).

The first Mitchell-Lama housing units open (*see* 1955); by the 1970s nearly 140,000 subsidized units will have been built with mortgages guaranteed by the State of New York. Applicants must show the State Housing Commissioner that their incomes are no more than six or seven times the rental (or maintenance in the case of co-ops) charges (*see* 1985).

● The Elkins Co. building at 137 Wooster Street burns down February 14, killing two firefighters and four members of a fire patrol. The SGS Textile Printing Co. building at 623 Broadway burns down March 19, killing 24 people.

City police launch a campaign against "litterbugs" in an effort to keep streets and sidewalks clean.

♟ La Famille opens at 2017 Fifth Avenue near 125th Street with an upstairs dining room that boasts white linen tablecloths. Benjamin James and his sister Willette Crane Murray, both from South Carolina, have run a catering business and now offer specialties that include mushroom soup, cornbread, braised short ribs of beef, veal parmesan, fried chicken, black-eyed peas, and string beans.

La Côte Basque opens in October on the former site of Le Pavillon (*see* 1957). Bernard Lamotte has painted mural views of Saint-Jean-de-Luz, framed with actual shutters, awnings, and balustrades to create an illusion of being in France, and the cuisine rivals that of Le Pavillon. Henri Soulé runs both restaurants, the new place will change hands in 1962, it will fail under its new management, and Soulé will take over again in July 1965 (*see* 1966; Rachou, 1979).

1959 Cuban dictator Fulgencio Batista resigns January 1 after nearly 7 years in power, having sent his sons to New York at the end of December. He flees to Dominica and thence to Miami as rebel leader Fidel Castro, now 32, captures Santiago a day after taking the provincial capital of Santa Clara, roars into Havana January 3, and assumes office as premier February 16 after a 2-year rebellion. Many Cubans begin leaving the country to take up residence at Miami, New York, and in New Jersey (see 1960).

$ Real estate heir Vincent Astor suffers a heart attack at his 120 East End Avenue apartment February 3 and dies at age 67, leaving $62 million to his wife (Roberta) Brooke (née Russell), 57, whom he has appointed to administer the Vincent Astor Foundation that inherits assets worth $60 million. She will build the value of the holdings and by the time she liquidates the trust in 1997 Brooke Astor will have given grants of about $175 million to the city's cultural institutions, including most notably the New York Public Library (see 1985), the Metropolitan Museum of Art, the Bronx Zoo, and Rockefeller University (see 1996).

Chemical Bank acquires New York Trust Co. with its large wholesale banking network (see 1954). Like the Chase Manhattan merger of 1955, the deal has been engineered by investment banker Morris A. Shapiro, using the same technique he used to force the previous merger (see Security National, 1975).

The New York Stock Exchange reports June 15 that 13 million Americans own stock.

Donaldson, Lufkin and Jenrette is founded in December by New York investment bankers William Donaldson, 28, Dan W. Lufkin, 28, and Richard Hampton Jenrette, 30, who will profit by analyzing small companies with growth potential and develop into a major Wall Street banking house (see Alliance, 1962; Equitable Life, 1985).

Wall Street's Dow Jones Industrial Average closes December 31 at a new high of 679.36, up from 583.65 at the end of 1958.

⚡ Brooklyn Union Gas Co. acquires the Coney Island-based Brooklyn Borough Gas Co. (see 1957; 1970).

The city sells its rapid-transit power plants to Con Edison and the Port of New York Authority; the plants use Con Ed's network to supply power to the subways.

⚡ American Airlines begins the first coast-to-coast (New York-Los Angeles) jet service January 25, using Boeing 707s.

The new St. Lawrence & Great Lakes Waterway dedicated by Queen Elizabeth June 26 gives ocean-going vessels access to Great Lakes ports as far west as Duluth, some 2,342 miles from the Atlantic, and supplants the New York Barge Canal opened in 1918 (the canal will be used hereafter only for pleasure boats).

The 37,783-ton S.S. *Rotterdam* arrives from Rotterdam September 8 with accommodations for 665 first-class passengers, 801 in tourist class. Launched last year by the 87-year-old Holland-America Line, she bears the same name as the company's first transatlantic steamer (and some later HAL ships) but will end transatlantic service in 1969 and become a one-class cruise liner. Holland-America will become entirely a cruise line in 1971.

The Board of Estimate votes April 9 to eliminate buses and motorcars completely from Washington Square Park (see 1952). Responding to public opinion mobilized by Shirley Hayes and others, Tammany leader Carmine De Sapio has instructed his followers to block the roadway proposed by Robert Moses.

The city designates all of Manhattan below 96th Street a tow-away zone for illegally parked cars (see 1950; 1991).

New York has about 13,000 medallion taxicabs, down from 19,000 in 1933. Medallions now cost $17,000 to $20,000—about 10 times the cost of a vehicle; brokers obtain them from retiring fleet owners or owner-drivers and resell them. Fleet owners who bought medallions 20 years ago have become scandalously rich; drivers typically work for someone who has a medallion cab, or they lease medallions, or two drivers may pool their resources to get the $6,000 deposit needed to finance a medallion through a bank, each man working 12 hours per day to pay off the bank notes and clear $500 per month for himself.

A new Arthur Kill Bridge is completed to provide an improved rail link between Staten Island and Elizabeth, N.J. (see 1890). The world's longest and highest span of its kind, the steel vertical-lift structure carries a single track, has a 558-foot movable section suspended from two 215-foot-high towers, and can be raised 135 feet above the Arthur Kill (channel) to permit ships to pass below. The army approved a plan to span the Narrows in 1948 at the persuasion of Robert Moses, and ground is broken August 13 for a much larger bridge designed to carry vehicular traffic (see Verrazano-Narrows Bridge, 1964).

The Duane Reade drugstore chain has its beginnings in the spring, when entrepreneurs Eli, Jack, and Abraham Cohen of Flatbush, Brooklyn, lease a former dry cleaning shop at 299 Broadway, between Duane and Reade streets, and with a $20,000 investment open a shop selling pharmaceuticals, beauty aids, and the like in a 10-by-13-foot space. They open a second shop across the street at 290 Broadway a few months later (see 1992).

The 58-year-old Rockefeller Institute awards its first Ph.D. (see 1906). The Institute has been headed since 1953 by Detlev W. Bronk, who announced 3 years ago that it would become a graduate university with doctoral programs in the biological sciences (it will also award medical degrees and a joint M.D. and Ph.D. in co-operation with the Cornell University Medical College) (see 1965).

 New York Times columnist-author Meyer Berger has a gastrointestinal attack, suffers a stroke, and dies at his native New York February 8 at age 60.

John Hay Whitney assumes control of the *Herald Tribune* August 28 after 86 years of control by the Reid family (see 1924). He was persuaded last year to invest about $1.2 million in the paper. Circulation will reach a high of 400,000 by October 1962 (see strike, 1965).

The Clio Award for excellence in advertising is introduced by New York admen John P. Cunningham, David Ogilvy, and Wallace Ross.

 Atheneum publishers is founded by Simon Michael Bessie, Alfred A. Knopf, Jr., and Hiram Haydn, whose business will be acquired by Charles Scribner's Sons.

A federal district court at New York July 21 lifts a U.S. Post Office ban on distributing the 1928 D. H. Lawrence novel *Lady Chatterley's Lover* despite protests that the book uses such words as "fuck" and "cunt" and is explicit in its descriptions of the sex act (see *Ulysses*, 1933). Grove Press has distributed an unexpurgated version of the book, Postmaster General Arthur E. Summerfield has banned it from the mails, and Judge Frederick van Pelt Bryan, 55, rules in Grove's favor. His 30-page decision in *Roth v. the United States* says not only that the book is not obscene but also that the Postmaster General is neither qualified nor authorized to judge the obscenity of material to be sent through the mails; he is empowered only to halt delivery of matter already judged obscene.

Nonfiction: *New York Places and Pleasures: An Uncommon Guide* by Polish-born New York author Kate Simon (originally Kaila Grobsmith), 46; *The World Beneath the City* by New York author Robert Daly; *The Golden City* by architecture critic Henry Hope Reed, who bewails the replacement of beautiful older buildings with inferior modern works in the name of functionalism (see real estate, 1952); *For 2¢ Plain* (essays) by New York-born North Carolina humorist-social critic Harry (Lewis) Golden (originally Goldhurst), 57, who operated a stock brokerage in his 20s, pleaded guilty to a mail-fraud charge in 1928, served 4 years in prison, changed his name after his release, moved to North Carolina, and began publishing the *Carolina Israelite* in 1941. Golden lived as a child on the Lower East Side at 171 Eldridge Street, "a cold-water tenement house which must have been 30 years old in 1905. It is still full of tenants; originally the toilets were in the yard in back. Later on came the inside toilets, one to a floor, serving four families. And I want you to understand that I am talking about substantial families—father, mother, approximately five children, and three boarders. Examine the names on the mailboxes in the tenements of today and where once there were Rabinowitz, Cohen, there were now Perez and Amici;" *La Guardia in Congress* by New York-born historian Howard Zinn, 37; *La Guardia: A Fighter Against His Times* by Brooklyn-born historian Arthur Mann, 37; *The Newcomers: Negroes and Puerto Ricans in a Changing Metropolis* by Oscar Handlin; *Island in the City: The World of Spanish Harlem* by Indianapolis-born New York writer Dan Wakefield, 27; *The Years with Ross* by James Thurber is about his 24-year relationship with the late *New Yorker* magazine editor Harold Ross; *The Improper Bohemians: A Re-Creation of Greenwich Village in Its Heyday* by Allen Churchill is about the Village before and shortly after World War I.

Fiction: *Goodbye, Columbus* (stories) by Newark-born New York author Philip (Milton) Roth, 26; *The Little Disturbances of Man: Stories of Women and Men at Love* by New York-born writer Grace Paley (née Goodside), 36; *The Manchurian Candidate* by Richard Condon; *The Empire City* (collected novels) by New York-born novelist-poet-activist Paul Goodman, 48; *The Travels of Jaimie McPheeters* by Illinois-born *New Yorker* writer Robert Lewis Taylor, 49; *Advertisements for Myself* by Norman Mailer; *The Naked Lunch* by William Burroughs; *Pursuit of the Prodigal* by Louis Auchincloss; *A Cage for Lovers* by Dawn Powell, whose Greenwich Village apartment house in West 10th Street went co-op last year, forcing her and her husband, retired advertising executive Joseph Gousha, to move out of their duplex and find quarters in sublets and cheap hotels.

Painting: *Numbers in Color* by Jasper Johns; *Jill* by Malden, Mass.-born New York painter Frank Stella, 23; *Virginia Site* by Asheville, N.C.-born New York painter Kenneth (Clifton) Noland, 35; *Zinc Yellow* by Franz Kline; *Acres* by Helen Frankenthaler; *Boathouse by the Sea* by Milton Avery.

Sculpture: *White on White* by Russian-born New York sculptor Louise Nevelson (*née* Leah Berliawsky), 59, who emigrated with her family to America in 1905; *We Shall Beat Our Swords into Plowshares* (bronze) by Soviet sculptor Yevgeny Vuchetich, 51, is installed at the United Nations, a gift from the Soviet Union; a bronze statue of George M. Cohan by Georg Lober is installed at 46th Street in Times Square, his hat in one hand, his cane in the other; a bust of the late Sen. Robert F. Wagner by Georg Lober is installed at the corner of Second Avenue and 120th Street. Swedish-born sculptor Claes (Thure) Oldenburg, 30, has his first one-man show in May at the Judson Gallery in Greenwich Village (he moved to New York 3 years ago and rented an apartment in the East Village).

The Solomon R. Guggenheim Museum opens October 21 at 1071 Fifth Avenue, between 88th and 89th streets, to house the collection of the late copper magnate, whose mentor, Baroness Hilla Rebay, induced him to buy dozens of canvases by the late abstractionist Wassily Kandinsky. (The permanent collection will also include works by Marc Chagall, Robert Delaunay, Paul Klee, and Fernand Léger.) The spiral structure has taken 3 years to complete, Robert Moses has used his power to have the Zoning Board reverse its decision and allow the building's construction, and it has cost more than twice the $950,000 projected by its architect, the late Frank Lloyd Wright; collector Peggy Guggenheim calls the new museum, "My uncle's garage, that Frank Lloyd Wright thing on Fifth Avenue."

President Eisenhower breaks ground at New York May 14 for the Lincoln Center for the Performing Arts on a 14-acre site acquired with federal aid and built with contributions of $185 million, much of it from John D. Rockefeller, Jr. The cultural center owes its existence in large measure to Robert Moses, who proposed it as a replacement for existing five-story walk-up row houses and tenements as part of a West Side slum-clearance effort (*see* Philharmonic Hall, 1962).

Theater: *A Majority of One* by Brooklyn-born Hollywood screenwriter Leonard Spigelgass, 50, 2/16 at the Shubert Theater, with Gertrude Berg, Cedric Hardwicke, 558 perfs.; *Sweet Bird of Youth* by Tennessee Williams 3/10 at the Martin Beck Theater,

with Paul Newman, Geraldine Page, 378 perfs.; *Raisin in the Sun* by Chicago-born New York playwright Lorraine Hansberry, 29, 3/11 at the Ethel Barrymore Theater, with Sidney Poitier, Ruby Dee, Louis Gossett, Jr., Claudia McNeil, 530 perfs. (Hansberry has taken her title from a Langston Hughes poem containing the line, "What happens to a dream deferred?/ Does it dry up/ Like a raisin in the sun?"); *The Connection* by Chicago-born playwright Jack Gelber, 27, 7/5 at the off-Broadway Living Theater, with Leonard Hicks, Ira Lewis is about drug addiction, 722 perfs.; *The Miracle Worker* by William Gibson 10/19 at the Playhouse Theater, with New York-born actress Patty (originally Anna Maria) Duke, 12, as Helen Keller, Anne Bancroft as Annie Sullivan in a stage version of the 1957 *Playhouse 90* television drama, 702 perfs.; *The Tenth Man* by Paddy Chayefsky 11/5 at the Booth Theater, with Yiddish Art Theater founder Jacob Ben-Ami, now nearly 69, Brooklyn-born comedian Jack Gilford (originally Jacob Gellman), 51 (who appeared before the House Un-American Affairs Committee 3 years ago, refused to say whether he had ever been a communist, and cannot get work in films or on television), Toronto-born actor Lou Jacobi, 46, New York-born actor-director Gene Saks, 36, 623 perfs.; *The Andersonville Trial* by Hartford-born playwright Saul Levitt, 46, 12/29 at Henry Miller's Theater, with Virginia-born actor George C. Scott, 31, New York-born actor Albert Dekker, 54.

Playwright Maxwell Anderson dies of a stroke at Stamford, Conn., February 28 at age 70; actress Ethel Barrymore at Beverly Hills, Calif., June 18 at age 78.

The Second Avenue Theater and National Theater come down to make way for parking lots on Second Avenue; the Yiddish Art Theater and some other Yiddish theaters remain, but demographic changes have shrunk audiences.

Films: Douglas Sirk's *Imitation of Life* with Lana Turner, John Gavin, Sandra Dee; Alfred Hitchcock's *North by Northwest* with Cary Grant, Eva Marie Saint, James Mason; Michael Gordon's *Pillow Talk* with Doris Day, Rock Hudson, Tony Randall (who says to Day at one point, "Look out there: New York. People jostling, hurrying, struggling, milling, fighting for their lives. And you're part of it. In Texas there's nothing but a bunch of prairie dogs and stuff. Even the air out there: there's nothing in it but air. New York's got air you can sink your teeth into. It has character."). Also: Jean Negulesco's *The Best of Everything* with Hope Lange, Stephen Boyd, Suzy Parker, Joan Crawford; Walter Lang's *But Not For Me* with Clark Gable, Carroll Baker, Lili Palmer in a cinematic version of the 1934 Samson Raphaelson play *Accent on Youth*; Mervyn LeRoy's *The FBI Story* with James Stewart, Vera Miles; Daniel Mann's *The Last Angry Man* with Paul Muni as a Brooklyn doctor whose life is to be portrayed on TV; Charles Lederer's *Never Steal Anything Small* with James Cagney as a New York waterfront union racketeer; Robert Wise's *Odds Against Tomorrow* with Harry Belafonte, Robert Ryan, Shelley Winters.

Hotel operators Laurence and Robert Preston Tisch acquire the Loews theater chain from M-G-M; they will rename their parent company Loews, Inc. but their primary business will be tobacco.

Broadway musicals: *Once Upon a Mattress* 5/11 at the Phoenix Theater, with San Antonio-born comedienne Carol Burnett, 22, comedian Jack Gilford, music by New York-born composer Mary Rodgers, 28 (daughter of Richard Rodgers), lyrics by Marshall Barer, 458 perfs.; *Gypsy* 5/21 at the Broadway Theater, with Ethel Merman, Philadelphia-born actor Jack Klugman, 37, book by Arthur Laurents based on the life of striptease dancer Gypsy Rose Lee, music by Jule Styne, lyrics by Stephen Sondheim, songs that include "Small World," "Together Wherever We Go," "Everything's Coming Up Roses," 702 perfs.; *At the Drop of a Hat* 10/8 at the John Golden Theater, with English entertainers Michael Flanders and Donald Swann, music and lyrics by Flanders and Swann, 217 perfs.; *Take Me Along* 10/22 at the Shubert Theater, with comedian Jackie Gleason, Walter Pidgeon, Robert Morse, Una Merkel, St. Joseph, Mo.-born actress Ruth Warrick, 44, music and lyrics by Bob Merrill, 448 perfs.; *The Sound of Music* 11/16 at the Lunt-Fontanne Theater, with Mary Martin, Theodore Bikel, Kurt Kasznar, sets by Oliver Smith, music by Richard Rodgers, lyrics by Oscar Hammerstein II, songs that include "Climb Every Mountain," "Do-Re-Mi," "Edelweiss," "My Favorite Things," and the title song, 1,443 perfs.; *Fiorello!* 11/23 at the Broadhurst Theater, with Chicago-born actor-singer Tom Bosley, 32, as the late Mayor La Guardia, Howard Da Silva, Ellen Hanley, music by Jerry Bock, lyrics by Sheldon Harnick, songs that include "Politics and Poker," "The Name's La Guardia," "Little Tin Box," 796 perfs.

Tel Aviv-born New York violinist Itzhak Perelman, 23, appears on the Ed Sullivan TV show 2/15. Struck with polio at age 4, his legs are paralyzed and he can walk only with crutches.

Violinist-conductor David Mannes dies at New York April 24 at age 93.

Texas-born saxophonist-composer Ornette Coleman, 29, makes his New York debut in November at the Five Spot Café. Patrons give such a strong response that the management extends his engagement for 6 months.

Tenor saxophonist Lester Young dies at New York March 15 at age 49; jazz singer Billie Holiday ("Lady Day") of lung congestion and a heart ailment at New York July 17 at age 44 after a long struggle to overcome a heroin addiction.

Swedish prizefighter Ingemar Johansson, 26, wins the world heavyweight crown June 26 by knocking out Floyd Patterson in the third round of a title match at New York.

Neale Andrew Fraser, 25, (Australia) wins in men's singles at Forest Hills, Maria Bueno, 19, (Brazil) in women's singles.

Jamaica Racetrack closes August 1 after 56 years of operation (*see* 1945). Its facilities have deteriorated, and although the one-mile oval track is still well drained and very fast, other racetracks draw larger crowds.

Aqueduct Racetrack reopens September 14 with capacity for 80,000 racing fans (*see* 1894; 1944). The New York Racing Association has spent $33 million to renovate the track and clubhouse that are only 30 minutes from Times Square by express subway; by next year the Big A will be America's leading track in terms of betting, with a daily handle of as much as $2.7 million.

The American Football League awards franchises November 5 to eight cities, including New York. Founded by Dallas oilman Lamar Hunt and headed by sports announcer Harry Wismer, the new professional league names coaches December 18. The New York team is initially called the Titans (*see* Jets, 1963).

The Baltimore Colts win the National Football League title at Yankee Stadium December 28, defeating the Giants 23 to 17 in overtime. Led by quarterback Charlie Conerly, the Giants are ahead 17 to 14 with 7 seconds to go, Steve Myhra of the Colts kicks a field goal to tie the score, and Colts quarterback Johnny Unitas pushes his team downfield to let Alan Ameche score from the one-yard line. The Giants have played at the Stadium since 1956 and will do so through 1973.

Iowa-born Chicago hat designer Halston (Ray Halston Frowick), 27, arrives in New York to work for

Lilly Daché, is told by the reservations clerk at the Waldorf-Astoria that the only room available is a large suite, and uses it to hold a press conference with help from fashion publicist Eleanor Lambert, now 55 (*see* Bergdorf-Goodman, 1960).

Police Commissioner Stephen P. Kennedy announces August 31 that he is reassigning 1,400 officers to fight increasing youth crime.

Twenty alleged mob bosses are convicted of obstructing justice in a New York court December 18.

The first Wall Street area skyscraper in 25 years is completed at 2 Broadway, where it replaces the red terra-cotta and brick Produce Exchange built at Bowling Green in 1884. Uris Brothers had originally engaged architect William Lescaze to work with Kahn & Jacobs on the project, but then switched to Emery Roth & Sons, whose architects have designed an undistinguished 33-story air-conditioned Inter-national Style structure that makes maximum use of the building rights, has an area of 20,000 square feet for the Produce Exchange, and contains a two-level garage for 300 cars.

Fourth Avenue between 17th Street and 32nd is renamed Park Avenue South in the spring by a vote of the City Council (the change was suggested by an alderman 30 years ago). Only the six blocks between Astor Place and Union Square will hereafter be called Fourth Avenue.

Most of the West Side neighborhood known since 1881 as Hell's Kitchen is renamed Clinton following the killing of two children in a gang war. Named for De Witt Clinton Park, between 52nd and 54th streets west of Eleventh Avenue, it covers most of the area from Eighth Avenue west to the Hudson River between 42nd and 59th streets.

Architect Frank Lloyd Wright dies at Phoenix, Ariz., April 9 at age 89. His new Guggenheim Museum on Fifth Avenue opens in October after 16 years of design and construction changes made in response to building codes and objections from the Zoning Board, the museum's directors, and the general public; it has a domed skylight 92 feet high (fluorescent lighting will be added later) and an "organic" quarter-mile-long circular inner ramp employed by Wright earlier on a smaller scale in a Park Avenue automobile showroom; architect Sylvan Bien dies at his Croydon Hotel apartment May 12 at age 66; architect John Mead Howells at Kittery Point, Me., September 22 at age 91.

The Downtown-Lower Manhattan Association releases a plan October 14 for redeveloping that part of the city and the East River waterfront. Chase Manhattan Bank president David Rockefeller heads the association (*see* Battery Park City plan, 1966).

The 40-story Seagram Building is completed opposite the 41-year-old Racquet and Tennis Club on Park Avenue between 52nd and 53rd streets, where the Montana apartment house put up in 1913 was razed to make way for the structure. Seagram boss Samuel Bronfman's daughter Phyllis Lambert dissuaded her father from putting up a conventional building and enlisted the services of Ludwig Mies van de Rohe, now 73, who was assisted by Philip Johnson and Kahn & Jacobs; the bronze-clad International Style tower rises from a plaza landscaped with reflecting pools, fountains, and trees.

The Seagram Building on Park Avenue showed the world how handsome an office building could be. CHIE NISHIO

The 22-story 410 Park Avenue office building is completed at the southwest corner of 55th Street to designs by Emery Roth & Sons (a Chase Manhattan

Bank branch designed by Skidmore, Owings & Merrill occupies the first two floors).

A new 48-story Time-Life Building opens in December at 1271 Avenue of the Americas. Harrison, Abramovitz, and Harris has designed the International Style structure, and the 22-year-old 1 Rockefeller Plaza building now becomes the General Dynamics building.

The 26-story Steuben Glass (Corning Glass) Building is completed at 717 Fifth Avenue, southeast corner 56th Street, to International Style designs by Wallace K. Harrison of Harrison, Abramovitz & Abbe. The avenue's first glass-walled skyscraper, it replaces a four-story modernist fiberglass house built in 1948 to designs by Skidmore, Owings & Merrill.

The 19-story 700 Park Avenue apartment house is completed at the northwest corner of 69th Street, opposite the Union Club. Designed by Kahn & Jacobs with Paul Resnick and Harry F. Green, it replaces the Arthur Curtiss James mansion built in 1914 with a tower of gray glazed brick atop a two-story base of polished granite.

Real estate developers reply to complaints that rents have soared on the upper East Side with explanations that building sites sold for $40 to $75 per square foot in 1949 now fetch $100 to $225 per square foot, that wages of maintenance staffs have risen 44 percent, and that real estate taxes are 40 percent above 1945 levels.

The Franklin Houses (later the Franklin Plaza Cooperative) is completed for the City Housing Authority in the four-block area bounded by First and Third avenues between 106th and 108th streets. Holden, Egan, Wilson & Corser has designed the residential towers, whose plaza and play areas will be redesigned in 2 years by Mayer & Whittlesey.

Harry Golden's book *For 2¢ Plain* takes its title from that of a story he once wrote recalling "the joys and wonders of the Lower East Side of New York where even a hot-dog pushcart was an adventure." The entire East Side civilization, he recalls, was "addicted to seltzer [carbonated water]" and the great variety of sweet drinks mixed with seltzer. "You bought a drink from a man behind a marble counter at any of the hundreds of soda-water stands" in the area. "A small glass cost a penny—'Gimme a small plain,' no syrup. Syrup cost another penny. For a large glass you said, 'Gimme for 2 plain.'" Golden remembers saying casually as the man was filling his glass, "Put a little on the top." Meaning a little syrup. Of course he did not want to part with the extra penny, and

countermen soon got wise to his ruse, insisting that they be paid the two pennies before starting to fill the glass. "I know my customers," he quotes one counterman as saying.

Häagen-Dazs Ice Cream is introduced by Polish-born Bronx entrepreneur Reuben Mattus, 47, who since age 17 has been peddling his family's home-made ice cream to small candy stores and neighborhood restaurants, initially with a horse and wagon. Finding that most commercial ice cream has become cheaper, he puts more butterfat in his product than government standards require, uses less air filler, comes up with a Danish-sounding name (even though the umlaut does not exist in Danish), packs the ice cream in cartons adorned with maps of Scandinavia, creates a new category that will be called superpremium ice cream, and begins what will become a multimillion-dollar company (*see* 1983).

 The Four Seasons opens in July at 99 East 52nd Street in the new Seagram Building (375 Park Avenue) under the management of Restaurant Associates (*see* Forum of the Twelve Caesars, 1957). Joseph Baum will claim to have been inspired by reading *haiku* poetry in planning the new restaurant, it occupies 130,000 cubic feet of space, and its menu selections, plantings, flowers, banquette upholstery colors, table-linen colors, uniforms, graphics—even the colors of the typewriter ribbons—are changed four times per year. An original Picasso canvas acquired by Phyllis Lambert hangs in the corridor leading to the restaurant's main dining room (the pool room), metal sculptures by Richard Lippold hang over the bar in the grill room, anodized aluminum chains grace the huge windows, carpeting is hand loomed, a tank holds live trout for *truite bleu*, and the food prepared by Albert Stockli (with advice from James Beard) anticipates the nouvelle cuisine that will flourish beginning a decade hence, with emphasis on quality ingredients and on simplicity rather than rich, heavy sauces (*see* 1973). The Brasserie opens on the north side of the Seagram Building as a 24-hour French-style restaurant. Cost of The Four Seasons and the Brasserie total $12.5 million—$2 million over budget; The Four Seasons will never show a profit, but Restaurant Associates acquires Mama Leone's and will make more than enough money from that operation to defray its losses at The Four Seasons.

1960 Rep. Adam Clayton Powell, Jr. delivers a sermon from the pulpit of the Abyssinian Baptist Church January 10, saying, "I am stating one unchallengeable fact, that the Mafia and the syndicate are in complete control of Harlem." Now 51, Powell has delivered 10 weekly speeches on the floor of the House of Representatives, giving names and addresses of "numbers racket" operators, listing places where bets can be placed, and accusing the New York Police Department of involvement in protecting organized crime, especially the numbers racket in Harlem. Bettors on the "numbers," also known as "policy," place daily bets on a combination of three numbers: if the numbers correspond to three numbers appearing in the same order on a previously designated portion of the day's parimutuel betting total at a particular racetrack, the bettor wins, but the odds are usually about 600 to one. An estimated 1.3 million New Yorkers "play the numbers" each day, illegally betting as little as 5¢ or 10¢ per day at barbershops, bars, cafés, candy stores, newsstands, or with individual runners ("drops") and wagering a total of about $100 million per year. The city's police make no arrests, Powell says, because they are "on the pad," meaning they take bribes from organized crime, controlled by "Italians and Jews" who are squeezing out the local black operators (see Harry Gross, 1951). "This low-income community has drained from it between $3 million and $4 million per month," Powell charges, "and the first fact I wish to point out is that the numbers is pauperizing Harlem." The *New York Post* sends in its own investigators, who confirm virtually every charge Powell has made. Police officials deny any wrongdoing but arrest a number of low-level bookies, all black.

Rep. Adam Clayton Powell, Jr. says February 25 that a Harlem woman is extorting money from gamblers and acting as bagwoman for police officers; when he repeats the charge on television March 5, filling in for Sen. Hubert Humphrey on a New York talk show, Mrs. Esther James sues him for defamation of character, seeking $1 million. The station and its sponsors settle for $1,500. A 6-week trial of Rep. Powell on tax-fraud charges begins March 7; federal judge Frederick Van Pelt Bryan dismisses two counts but leaves the charge that he willfully defrauded the government on his 1951 tax return. The jury deliberates for 26 hours and takes 20 votes but cannot reach a verdict. Powell has been flagrantly unfaithful to his second wife, pianist Hazel Scott, she has divorced him, and he marries his Puerto Rican secretary Yvette Diago, 29, in November (see 1961).

A full-scale model of a do-it-yourself fallout shelter goes on display at a New York bank February 26 as fears of a nuclear attack continue to alarm residents. The shelter kit is priced at $105.

Mayor Wagner delivers his annual report on the state of the city to the City Council April 6 and demands that the state grant the city more home rule. New York City, he says, should "be free from the necessity of running to Albany for permission to proceed with a great variety of local matters. [We have] a right to govern ourselves with at least the powers of a small chartered city in California."

American Nazi Party leader George Lincoln Rockwell is mobbed outside the State Supreme Court Building in lower Manhattan June 22; Mayor Wagner promptly issues an order barring the American Nazi Party from holding a rally July 4 at Union Square, saying that its purpose is to incite a riot by preachng "race hatred and violence."

Cuba's president Fidel Castro arrives at New York September 18 to address the United Nations, is greeted by a cheering crowd of 2,000, moves from his hotel in Murray Hill to Harlem's Hotel Theresa September 20 and confers there with Soviet Premier Khrushchev (Rep. Adam Clayton Powell, Jr. attacks Castro for using Harlem as a political background), Castro confers the next day with Egypt's president Nasser, delivers a 4-hour speech at the General Assembly September 26 charging the United States with trying to punish Cuba for defying "monopolists," denies that his revolution is communist, and returns to Havana in a borrowed Soviet plane September 28.

Soviet Premier Nikita Khrushchev disrupts the UN October 12, banging on his desk with his shoe to protest a speech by a Filipino delegate who has accused the U.S.S.R. of "depriving" Eastern European nations of "political and civil rights." He warns that those nations will soon be "swallowed up" by the Soviet Union.

Sen. John Fitzgerald Kennedy (D. Mass.) holds a fourth debate with Vice President Nixon at New York October 21 and narrowly defeats Nixon in the November presidential election; now 43, he meets at his Georgetown, Washington, D.C., home with Rep. Adam Clayton Powell, Jr. to discuss legislative plans for the next congressional session with regard to educational aid and a minimum wage increase.

New York lawyer William Fitts Ryan, 38, wins election to Congress from Manhattan's West Side, becoming the city's first reform Democrat to gain public office. He will be a staunch defender of civil rights, social justice, and environmental protection.

$ Salomon Brothers and Hutzler cofounder and limited partner Percy S. Salomon dies at Lenox Hill Hospital April 8 at age 78. He has lived at 300 East 57th Street; philanthropist John D. Rockefeller, Jr. dies at Tucson, Ariz., May 27 at age 83.

The brokerage house Carter, Berlind, Potoma & Weill is founded by Wall Street stockbrokers who include Arthur L. Carter, 28, Roger Berlind, and Bensonhurst, Brooklyn-born broker Sanford I. Weill, 27, who began as a messenger with Bear, Stearns. Brooklyn-born *Time* magazine marketing department employee Arthur Levitt, Jr., 28 (son of the New York State comptroller) has taken a job selling cattle tax shelters for Oppenheimer Industries at Kansas City, Mo., but will come back to New York in 1963 and join the firm that will become Carter Berlind Weill Levitt; Levitt will become president in 1969, it will acquire Hayden Stone to become CBWL-Hayden Stone in 1970, change its name to Hayden Stone in 1972, become Shearson Hayden Stone in 1974 and Shearson Loeb Rhoades in 1979 after Levitt leaves in 1978 to become chairman and CEO of the American Stock Exchange (see 1981).

Wall Street's Dow Jones Industrial Average closes December 30 at 615.89, down from 679.36 at the end of 1959.

Ⓢ Harry Winston, Inc. moves into a handsome new six-story building at 718 Fifth Avenue, southwest corner 56th Street, with a plant for cutting, polishing, and setting diamonds in addition to offices and showrooms (see 1958).

Abraham & Straus chairman Walter N. Rothschild drops dead of a heart attack on the golf course at White Sulphur Springs, W. Va., October 8 at age 68. He joined the Brooklyn department store in 1913 and was president from 1937 to 1955.

Pennsylvania Railroad stockholders hear in May that Penn Station is in terrible condition and operating at a loss of $1.5 million per year (see real estate, 1955). Air and highway travel have reduced demand for passenger service, and while 64 long-distance trains still operate in and out of the facility, in addition to Long Island Rail Road commuter trains, Penn Station's location is no longer convenient to the center of the city. The number of redcaps has been cut nearly in half, and arriving passengers must now search for someone to help them with their bags. Because of "deferred maintenance" (the traditional railroad method of saving money), the majestic station's pink walls, once sparkling, are now covered with grime (see 1961).

The Erie Lackawanna Railroad is created October 15 by a merger of the 99-year-old Erie and slightly younger Delaware, Lackawanna and Western.

Chrysler halts production of the DeSoto, introduced in 1928 but used now mostly for taxicabs, especially New York's "Sky-Vue" cabs.

The city makes Third Avenue one-way northbound July 17 and Lexington Avenue one-way southbound, but merchants, the Fifth Avenue Coach Co. and the Transport Workers Union fight conversion of Fifth and Madison avenues to one-way traffic (see 1957; 1966).

Mass-transit ridership in the city falls to about 1.8 billion, down from about 2.4 billion in 1945, and rapid-transit ridership falls to 1.3 billion, down from 1.9 billion, as automobile ownership and use increases.

Bridge engineer David B. Steinman dies at his native New York August 21 at age 74, having designed more than 400 bridges worldwide. Construction began last year on the Verrazano Narrows Bridge, whose preliminary design was Steinman's (see 1964).

A United Airlines DC-8 collides with a TWA Super Constellation in a fog over the city December 16, killing 134 persons in the air and on the ground as wreckage falls in two boroughs. The United jet crashes in Brooklyn's Park Slope section, demolishing a church, and fuel from its tanks catches fire, setting much of the neighborhood ablaze. The TWA jet misses several houses by a few hundred feet as it crashes on Staten Island, 11 miles to the southeast. It is the world's worst aviation disaster to date.

☤ *Medical Tribune* begins biweekly publication at New York. Brooklyn-born entrepreneur and art collector Arthur M. Sackler, 47, joined the William Douglas McAdams ethical-drug advertising agency as a copywriter to finance his medical studies at New York University, became the agency's principal owner, acquired an interest in the Purdue-Frederick Drug Co. with his physician brothers Raymond and Mortimer, and 2 years ago founded the nonprofit Laboratories for Therapeutic Research at L.I.U.'s Brooklyn College of Pharmacy. Sackler will expand *Medical Tribune* into a worldwide operation with offices in 11 countries.

The United Federation of Teachers is created in March by a merger of the 2,000-member New York City Teachers Guild, headed by Lower East Side-born Bronx High School of Science teacher Charles Cogen (originally Cohen), 56, with the High School Teachers Association. The UFT asks the city's Board of Education to recognize it as the bargaining agent for the city's teachers, the board balks, and the UFT strikes November 7 in a 1-day job action involving 5,500 of the city's 44,000 public-school teachers. They challenge the Condon-Waldin Act that prohibits strikes by public employees, Mayor Wagner appoints a committee to investigate the dispute, the committee recommends an election, and the UFT beats out two rival unions to represent the teachers (*see* 1962).

Former columnist-humorist Franklin P. Adams ("F.P.A.") dies at New York March 23 at age 78.

Brooklyn-born *Commentary* magazine staff writer Norman Podhoretz, 30, is elevated to the position of editor, succeeding the late founding editor Elliot Cohen, whose secretary Midge Decter (*née* Rosenthal), now 33, Podhoretz married 4 years ago. After publishing articles critical of American life, the cold war, and U.S. involvement in Southeast Asia, Podhoretz will move the magazine's editorial position to the center and then strongly to the right.

Mayor Wagner orders a crackdown on sales of 50 "obscene" magazines. The "girly" magazines are confiscated and vendors who persist in carrying them are fined.

Former John Robert Powers model Candy Jones (originally Jessica Wilcox), now 35, takes over what remains of the 21-year-old Conover modeling agency at 52 Vanderbilt Avenue. Harry S. Conover bought her contract from Powers, changed her name, and promoted her, she became a pin-up girl in World War II (she was on the cover of 11 magazines in 1943), posed for WAC and WAVE recruitment posters, appeared in the Broadway musical *Mexican Hayride*, toured southwest Pacific military bases with a USO show, got malaria, and married Conover in July 1946 (he concealed his homosexuality and the marriage was not consummated for 5 months). Conover disappeared last year, having withdrawn all but $36 of the $100,000 in their joint checking account, and will serve 2 years in prison.

Interpublic Group of Companies has its beginnings as McCann-Erickson advertising agency president Marion Harper, Jr. starts acquiring other agencies that he joins with McCann in a horizontal conglomerate whose separate (and conflict-free) units share integrated collateral services (*see* 1948). Now 44, Harper has attracted clients that include Miles Laboratories (Alka-Seltzer), Coca-Cola, Cream of Wheat, Quaker Oats, Nestlé, and Westinghouse, McCann has been serving Chrysler Corp., Harper has been asked to make a proposal to General

Motors for the Buick account, he is loath to give up Chrysler, so he comes up with the idea of an umbrella organization whose various agencies can serve competing clients. Interpublic is the name of a research company owned by the H. K. McCann Co. of Germany, Harper uses it as the name for the first advertising agency holding company, he will bring under its umbrella such agencies as Erwin, Wasey; Marschalk Co.; and Jack Tinker & Partners, clients will have a choice between a large agency such as McCann-Erickson Worldwide or a small boutique shop, and by 1970 Interpublic will have 10 U.S. agencies with more than 100 offices worldwide, but its directors will have ousted Harper for his reckless spending (*see* 1967).

FM radio station WBAI goes on the air with no advertising but with listener-supported talk and music programming funded in part by the Pacifica Foundation, whose West Coast station has begun earlier.

New York Telephone Co. installs outdoor telephone booths with folding doors beginning in late April. The disappearance of candy and cigar stores since the 1940s has created a need for public phones, and the company sees an opportunity to profit from calls made on impulse by pedestrians, but the new booths will be vandalized, used as urinals, turned into shelters, and employed as offices by drug dealers; directories will be stolen, and beginning in the 1970s the company will replace the booths with simpler, doorless enclosures made by a St. Louis company, although a few booths will survive to the end of the century.

The Xerox 914 copier begins a revolution in paperwork reproduction (*see* 1950). The first production-line Xerox copier is called the 914 because it makes copies of up to nine by 14 inches on ordinary paper, but it is a 650-pound machine and costs $29,500.

Random House acquires Alfred A. Knopf and Vintage Books as the book publishing industry consolidates (*see* 1915; 1927; Newhouse, 1980).

Holt, Rinehart and Winston is created by a merger of the 94-year-old publishing house Henry Holt with the big textbook publishers Rinehart and Winston, founded, respectively, in 1929 and 1884 (*see* 1985).

Harcourt, Brace & World is created by a merger of the 41-year-old New York publishing house and the World Book Co. founded in 1905. Harcourt's Colorado-born president William Jovanovich, now 40, began with the company as a $50-per-week textbook salesman, took over at age 34 when it was worth only $8 million, and has engineered the merger. The company will become Harcourt, Brace Jovanovich in

1970 as Jovanovich attracts world-class authors and editors (*see* Harcourt General, 1991).

Time-Life Books is created by Time, Inc. to repackage editorial material developed by *Time* and LIFE.

Simon & Schuster cofounder Richard L. Simon dies at his North Stamford, Conn., country house July 29 at age 61 (he has another house at 4701 Grosvenor Avenue, Riverdale). Simon retired in 1957 after suffering two heart attacks.

Nonfiction: *Growing Up Absurd: Problems of Youth in the Organized System* by Paul Goodman is a study of youth and delinquency using materials from literature, psychology, and political theory; *Meyer Berger's New York* by the late *New York Times* reporter; "New York" by New Jersey-born *New York Times* writer Gay Talese, 29, whose essay in the July issue of *Esquire* magazine says, "New York is a city for eccentrics and a center for odd bits of information . . . On Broadway each evening a big, dark, 1948 Rolls-Royce pulls into Forty-sixth Street—and out hop two little ladies armed with Bibles and signs reading, 'The Damned Shall Perish;' "Moving Out" by John Cheever, whose essay in the July issue of *Esquire* magazine is a reminiscence of leaving for the suburbs after World War II; "Fifth Avenue, Uptown" by James Baldwin, whose essay in *Esquire* has been inspired by the sight of a housing project that has replaced his boyhood home; *The Bottom of the Harbor* by Joseph Mitchell.

Author and social arbiter Emily Post dies at her 39 East 79th Street apartment September 25 at age 86.

Fiction: *The House of Five Talents* by Louis Auchincloss; *The Mercenaries* by Brooklyn-born mystery novelist Donald E. (Edwin) Westlake, 27, who went to work last year as a reader for a literary agency, quit in April when his wife, Abby, announced that she was pregnant, and will turn out scores of mysteries under his own name and the pen name Richard Stark.

Poetry: *Salute* by Chicago-born New York poet James (Marcus) Schuyler, 36, who works at the Museum of Modern Art (MoMA).

Juvenile: *The Cricket in Times Square* by Hartford-born New York author George Selden (Thompson), 31, illustrations by Garth Williams; *The Thinking Book* by Birmingham, Ala.-born New York author Sandol Stoddard (Warburg), 32, illustrations by London-born New York designer Ivan Chermayeff, 28; *Little Blue and Little Yellow* by Dutch-born *Fortune* magazine art director Leo Lionni, 50, is the first of more than 30 children's books that Lionni will produce. In an effort to keep two grandchildren quiet on the train to his suburban Greenwich, Conn.,

home last year, Lionni took a copy of *LIFE* magazine from his briefcase, tore out small blue, green, and yellow circles from a page, made up a story about how "Little Blue" and "Little Yellow" hugged each other and became "Little Green." Noticing that other passengers had put down their newspapers and were listening, Lionni had "Little Green" go to the New York Stock Exchange, lose all his money, dissolve into yellow and blue tears, become "Little Blue" and "Little Yellow" once again, and recoup their money when their stock rises 12 points.

 Painting: *Door to the River* by Willem de Kooning; *Painted Bronze* (ale cans) by Jasper Johns; *Campbell's Soup Can* (*Tomato and Rice*) by pop artist Andy Warhol, now 32; *Islands #1* (oil and pencil on canvas), *The Ages* (oil on canvas), *Mountain* (ink on paper), and *Ocean Water* (ink on paper) by Agnes Martin; *Polar Stampede*, *The Eye is the First Circle*, and *Seated Nude* (charcoal on paper) by Lee Krasner. James Montgomery Flagg dies at New York May 27 at age 83.

Sculpture: the East Coast Memorial unveiled in Battery Park is dedicated to the 4,596 Americans who died in Atlantic coastal waters in World War II and whose bodies were never recovered. Sardinian-born sculptor Albino Manca, 62, has designed a stylized bronze eagle to accompany the granite slabs (designed by architects William Gehron and Gilbert Seltzer) inscribed with the names of the lost Americans; Central Park's Alice in Wonderland group is installed near Fifth Avenue and 76th Street. Created by Spanish-born New York sculptor José de Creeft, 76, in a setting landscaped by Hideo Sasaki, the work rises 11 feet high from a circular granite platform 16 feet in diameter and depicts characters from Lewis Carroll's 1865 work.

 Theater: *Toys in the Attic* by Lillian Hellman 2/25 at the Hudson Theater, with Maureen Stapleton, Jason Robards, Jr., 556 perfs.; *The Best Man* by West Point-born novelist-playwright Gore Vidal, 34, 3/31 at the Morosco Theater, with Melvyn Douglas, Atlanta-born actor Lee Tracy, 61, New York-born actor Frank Lovejoy, 45, 520 perfs.; *An Evening with Mike Nichols and Elaine May* 10/8 at the John Golden Theater, with Berlin-born improvisational comedian Nichols (originally Michael Igor Peschowsky), 28, and Philadelphia-born improvisational comedienne Elaine May (*née* Berlin), 27 (they met at Chicago 6 years ago and have staged their show earlier in that city), 306 perfs.; *Period of Adjustment* by Tennessee Williams 11/10 at the Helen Hayes Theater, with Nyack-born actor James Daly, 42, Barbara Baxley, Robert Webber, 132 perfs.; *All the Way Home* by Steubenville, Ohio-born playwright Tad Mosel,

38, 11/30 at the Belasco Theater, with Canadian actress Colleen Dewhurst, 34, Arthur Hill, Lillian Gish in a play based on the late James Agee's only novel, 334 perfs.

Margaret Sullavan dies of an accidental sleeping-pill overdose at New Haven January 1 at age 48; playwright Edwin Justus Mayer at New York September 11 at age 63; Sullavan's daughter Bridget Hayward of a deliberate sleeping-pill overdose at New York October 8 at age 21.

Back Stage begins publication from a small office in West 46th Street. New York-born *Show Business* advertising manager Ira Eaker, 38, has joined with Allen Zwerdling to start the theatrical newspaper that reports on forthcoming theater and film productions, reviews and previews for potential ticket buyers, and advice to actors on such matters as how to choose an agent. Eaker and Zwerdling will make their paper a must-read for actors seeking work and sell it to Billboard Publications in 1986.

San Francisco-born standup comedian Richard "Lord" Buckley makes his first New York café appearance in years at the Jazz Gallery, 80 St. Marks Place, in October, police suspend his cabaret license on grounds that he allegedly misstated some facts, he suffers a stroke at his 39 Gramercy Park West apartment November 13, and he dies at Columbus Hospital that night at age 54. Buckley has appeared frequently on the *Ed Sullivan Show* with hip monologues based on the classics, his death creates a furor over the issue of cabaret cards, entertainment unions ask Gov. Rockefeller to investigate, he asks Mayor Wagner for a report, Police Commissioner Kennedy sends in 1,000 police officers to inspect 2,478 places before Thanksgiving, it turns out that Joey Adams, Frank Sinatra, Sophie Tucker, and other prominent entertainers have been working without licenses, and the NYPD suspends the licenses of the Copacabana, El Morocco, the Stork Club, and other prominent nightspots, but those who can afford lawyers soon get them back.

Films: Billy Wilder's *The Apartment* with Jack Lemmon, Shirley MacLaine, Fred MacMurray; Daniel Mann's *Butterfield 8* with Elizabeth Taylor, Laurence Harvey, Eddie Fisher, Dina Merrill; Burt Balaban and Stuart Rosenberg's *Murder, Inc.* with Stuart Whitman, May Britt, Henry Morgan, Peter Falk, Morey Amsterdam, Sarah Vaughan; John Cassavetes's *Shadows* with Hugh Hurd, Lelia Goldoni.

Broadway and off-Broadway musicals: *A Thurber Carnival* (revue) 2/26 at the ANTA Playhouse, with Peggy Cass, Tom Ewell, Paul Ford, Alice Ghostley,

New York-born actor John McGiver, 47, book based on works by James Thurber, music by Somerville, N.J.-born composer Don Elliott, 33, and his quartet, 223 perfs.; *Bye Bye Birdie* 4/14 at the Martin Beck Theater, with Missouri-born comedian Dick Van Dyke, 34, Chita Rivera, Kay Medford, music and lyrics by Charles Strouse and Lee Adams, songs that include "Put on a Happy Face," 607 perfs.; *The Fantasticks* 5/3 at the 153-seat off-Broadway Sullivan Street Playhouse, with Bronx-born actor-singer Jerry Orbach, 24, as El Gallo, music by Harvey Schmidt, lyrics by Tom Jones, songs that include "Try to Remember," 17,162 perfs. (to 1/13/2002); *Tenderloin* 10/17 at the 46th Street Theater, with English actor Maurice Evans, 57, as the 1890s clergyman-reformer Charles H. Pankhurst, Evanston, Ill.-born actress Barbara Harris, 25, book by George Abbott based on a work by Samuel Hopkins Adams, music by Jerry Bock, lyrics by Sheldon Harnick, songs that include "How the Money Changes Hands," "My Gentle Young Johnny," "Little Old New York," "Artificial Flowers," "The Picture of Happiness," 216 perfs.; *The Unsinkable Molly Brown* 11/3 at the Winter Garden Theater, with Lynn, Mass.-born actress Tammy Grimes, 24, as the 1912 *Titanic* heroine, music and lyrics by Meredith Willson, 532 perfs.; *Camelot* 12/3 at the Majestic Theater, with Richard Burton, Julie Andrews, Lawrence, Mass.-born actor-singer Robert Goulet, 27, Knoxville, Tenn.-born actor-singer John Cullum, 30, sets by Oliver Smith, music by Frederick Loewe, lyrics by Alan Jay Lerner, songs that include "If Ever I Would Leave You," the title song, 873 perfs. (the new musical is based on Arthurian legend, President-elect Kennedy attends a performance, and his administration will be identified with the romance of Camelot); *Wildcat* 12/11 at the Alvin Theater, with Jamestown, N.Y.-born TV comedienne Lucille Ball, now 49, Ocean City, N.J.-born actor Keith Andes, 40, music by New York-born composer Cy Coleman (originally Seymour Kaufman), 31, lyrics by Carolyn Leigh, songs that include "Hey, Look Me Over," 171 perfs.; *Do Re Mi* 12/26 at the St. James Theater, with Phil Silvers, Nancy Walker, music by Jule Styne, lyrics by Betty Comden and Adolph Green, book by Garson Kanin, 400 perfs.

Comedian Bobby Clark dies at New York February 12 at age 71; Broadway composer Oscar Hammerstein II of stomach cancer at Doylestown, Pa., August 23 at age 65.

The city buys Carnegie Hall after violinist Isaac Stern persuades philanthropist Jacob M. Kaplan to help save it from demolition, although in some recent years it has turned a profit of roughly

$100,000 (*see* 1924). Stern and Kaplan lead a coalition of musicians, politicians, and civic figures in the drive to preserve the 69-year-old music hall (*see* 1986; Philharmonic Hall, 1962).

Russian pianist Sviatoslav Richter, 45, makes his Carnegie Hall debut 10/19, playing to a sold-out house.

Popular songs: "The Twist" by Hank Ballard is recorded by Ernest "Chubby Checker" Evans, 19, and launches an international dance craze. Checker performs at the small Peppermint Lounge bar off Times Square and moves on to the Copacabana night club. Discothèques where patrons dance to phonograph records blossom to cash in on the new teenage dance sensation; *Free Jazz* (album) by Ornette Coleman.

El Morocco moves to 307 East 54th Street after 29 years at 154 East 54th. Owner John Perona will die next year, and his successors will have trouble keeping the place popular.

 Floyd Patterson regains the world heavyweight boxing championship June 20 by knocking out Sweden's Ingemar Johansson in the fifth round of a title bout at New York.

Neale Fraser wins in men's singles at Forest Hills, Darlene Hard, 24, in women's singles.

The New York Yankees win the American League pennant, but the Pittsburgh Pirates win the World Series, defeating the Yankees 4 games to 3. Mickey Mantle gets 10 hits, including three home runs (his two homers and five RBIs in the second game help win it 16 to 3), Bill Skowron gets 12 hits and two home runs, pitcher Edward Charles "Whitey" Ford, 31, shuts out the Pirates in the third and sixth games, but the Yankees get a bad break from a Pittsburgh grounder in the seventh game and a home run by Pirate second baseman Bill Mazeroski, off Yankee pitcher Ralph Terry in the ninth inning of that game breaks the game and Series tie to win it for Pittsburgh. The Yankees let manager Casey Stengel go October 18.

The Madison Square Garden Corp. is organized and begins putting together plans for a new Garden to replace the one opened in 1925 on Eighth Avenue (*see* 1968).

 Hat designer Halston accepts an invitation by Bergdorf-Goodman to open a millinery department and soon has a clientele that will grow to include socialites and celebrities such as General Foods heiress Dina Merrill, Broadway hopeful Liza Minnelli, and film star Elizabeth Taylor (*see* 1959; 1966).

Publishing heir John (Burr) Fairchild, 33, returns from Paris to take over the 50-year-old *Women's Wear Daily* and reshape it. Determined to have the latest Paris sketches before anyone else, he features designs by Norman Norell, now 60, who will be Fairchild's favorite until early 1967.

Freedomland opens June 19 in the Bronx, where "the world's largest entertainment area" (bigger than Disneyland in California) occupies a 85 acres of a 200-acre site shaped like the United States at the nexus of the Hutchinson River Parkway and New England Thruway. A fire has destroyed some buildings before the opening, three gunmen have taken $28,000 from the amusement park's office in April and escaped by boat up the Hutchinson River before being apprehended, visitors to the theme park enjoy replicas of old New York, the 1871 Chicago fire, a Great Lakes stern-wheeler, a Kansas cornfield, southwestern stagecoaches, and the like, but Freedomland will survive only until 1964 (*see* real estate [Co-Op City], 1970).

 Brooklyn Mafia leaders Albert and Lawrence Gallo revolt from the Joseph Profaci organization and force Profaci to share more income with them.

Novelist Norman Mailer drunkenly stabs his second wife, Adele, with a three-inch penknife toward dawn on the morning of November 20 in their apartment at 73 Perry Street after a party attended by George Plimpton, Harold L. "Doc" Humes (who helped Plimpton start the *Paris Review* in 1952), poet Allen Ginsberg, actor Anthony Franciosa, critic C. Wright Mills, critic Norman Podhoretz, and writer Barbara Probst Solomon. He inflicts several wounds, but although she is hospitalized with a punctured cardiac sac and remains on the critical list for 3 weeks, Adele does not press charges; Mailer is arraigned on charges of felonious assault, is diagnosed as paranoid schizophrenic, and spends 17 days in Bellevue Hospital's psychiatric ward; the two then move with their baby daughter to a 12th-floor apartment at 250 West 94th Street (Plimpton shares an apartment on the 11th floor with John Train, who also helped with the *Paris Review*, and writer Peter Matthiessen).

 Architect William Adams Delano of Delano and Aldrich dies at his native New York January 12 at age 85 (Aldrich died in 1940).

Eleven new Manhattan office towers add 6.8 million square feet of rentable floor space.

Park Avenue continues its building boom with the 53-story Union Carbide Building (later Manufacturers Hanover Building, later Chase Manhattan International Headquarters), designed in International Style by Skidmore, Owings & Merrill at 270 Park, between 47th and 48th streets. It replaces the Marguery Hotel that stood with its large inner court-yard gardens from 1918 to 1957.

The 10-story Pepsi-Cola Building (later the Olivetti Building, later the Amro Bank Building) is completed at 500 Park Avenue, southwest corner 59th Street, to designs by Skidmore, Owings & Merrill.

Developers Sol Goldman and Alex DiLorenzo, Jr. acquire the 30-year-old Chrysler Building from the Zeckendorf interests on speculation and make it their flagship (see 1955; 1975).

Brooklyn's Ebbets Field stands come down beginning February 23 to make way for the 1,318-unit, middle-income Ebbets Field Apartments (later called the Jackie Robinson Apartments), covering an area bounded by McKeever Place, Bedford Avenue, Sullivan Place, and Montgomery Street (see sports, 1957).

The 21-story Kips Bay Plaza apartment house (south building) is completed in 30th Street between First and Second avenues, southwest of the United Nations. Put up by developer William Zeckendorf and designed by Chinese-born New York architect I. M. (Ieoh Ming) Pei, 44, it is the city's first exposed concrete apartment house (see north wing, 1965).

Wave Hill in Riverdale is deeded to the city at the persuasion of Robert Moses (see 1843). Now a 28-acre estate and public garden, it will be used as a nonprofit study center for nature and the arts.

Robert Moses announces his resignation as parks commissioner after more than 20 years in office, Newbold Morris is sworn in to replace him May 19, Moses steps down a few days later, and Morris will hold the post until 1966.

The Staten Island Botanic Garden has its beginnings in the Staten Island Arboretum. It will move in 1977 to an 80-acre site along Richmond Terrace at the Snug Harbor Cultural Center.

Hurricane Donna hits the city with 90-mile-per-hour winds September 12 after devastating Puerto Rico, Florida, and many Atlantic Coast communities. Called the worst such storm thus far on record, it creates flooding that delays subways, railroads, and other transit, knocks out 15,000 telephones, leaves more than 2,000 schoolchildren and scores of teachers stranded, and uproots 2,239 city trees. The Board of Estimate appropriates $200,000 to remove the trees.

The city bans use of lead-based paint on interior walls and ceilings (see National Lead Co., 1891). There have been thousands of cases of outright lead poisoning and impairment of learning ability among small children who have eaten chips of paint that have flaked off walls and ceilings, and cases will increase as 2 million city apartments deteriorate.

The U.S.S. *Constellation* catches fire December 19 while undergoing repairs at the Brooklyn Navy Yard, killing 50 people.

Grocer Pasquale D'Agostino dies of cancer at Memorial Hospital July 26 at age 55. Begun in 1932, his chain has grown to have seven large stores on Manhattan's East Side and will soon have some on the West Side as well.

La Caravelle opens at 33 West 55th Street in December with 35 tables and a table d'hôte dinner priced at $7.50 to $9.50 (with chateaubriand it is $11) and a $5.50 luncheon (extra if it includes food from the broiler). Proprietors Fred Decré and Robert Meyzen, formerly of Le Pavillon, have as their chef Roger Fessaguet, who will later become Meyzen's partner.

The city's population falls to 7,781,984 (about the same as London), down from 7,891,957 in 1950. Manhattan alone has lost 261,820 people; only Queens and Staten Island show increases. Some 900,000 whites have left the city (the Irish-born population has dropped to 114,008, down from 275,102 in 1900), about 800,000 blacks and Puerto Ricans have arrived, but contrary to all too common perceptions the departure of whites has far less to do with rising crime rates, a decline in public-school standards, or urban decay than simply the appeal of suburban living.

1961 Rep. Adam Clayton Powell, Jr. is sworn in as chairman of the House Committee on Education and Labor and honored with a banquet January 29 at the Commodore Hotel. He is the first black congressman to head a committee, and President Kennedy wires warm regards.

Two major Cuban opposition groups set up a revolutionary council at New York in late March with former premiere Jose Miro Cardona as president; he urges all Cubans to revolt against Fidel Castro, who has lead a revolution against the island's dictatorship and seized power (see 1962).

UN Secretary-General Dag Hammarskjöld is killed September 18 at age 56 when his plane crashes in the Congo en route to a meeting with the governor of Katanga Moise Tshombe, whose army is fighting UN forces attempting to disarm Katanga troops. Dag Hammarskjöld Plaza at Second Avenue and 47th Street in Manhattan will memorialize the late UN leader.

Police Commissioner Stephen P. Kennedy resigns in September after 6 years in the position. Now 54, he has demanded that police officers receive $600 per year more than firefighters, who are permitted to have second jobs while the police are not, but Mayor Wagner has turned him down.

Mayor Wagner handily defeats challenger Arthur Levitt in the Democratic Party primary and goes on to win a third term, receiving 1,237,421 votes as compared with 835,691 for Louis J. Lefkowitz, 321,604 for Lawrence E. Gerosa. Wagner has broken with Tammany boss Carmine G. De Sapio, now 54, and Tammany Hall will no longer be a power in city or state politics, having dominated the Democratic Party machine throughout the 19th century and much of the 20th. A reform movement led by former governor Herbert H. Lehman and former first lady Eleanor Roosevelt has depicted the boss system as corrupt and undemocratic, calling De Sapio a symbol of an outmoded system (De Sapio has worn tinted glasses since adolescence because of irisitis and they have not helped his image; see 1969).

Rep. Adam Clayton Powell, Jr. announces April 14 that he will withhold his anti-segregation amendment from school-aid legislation, as requested by President Kennedy, and if anyone else offers the amendment he will lead the opposition to it. "The Russian challenge to the United States in space," says Powell, "is now so great that no one can afford to do anything that would slow up federal aid to education at all levels." U.S. attorney Morton Robson tells a federal judge at New York April 14 that the Department of Justice will not pursue its tax case against Powell.

The 50-year-old National Urban League engages Kentucky-born Atlanta University dean of social work Whitney M. (Moore) Young, Jr., 40, as executive director. Working out of its New York headquarters, Young will try for the next decade to broaden the Urban League's program, calling for a "Marshall Plan" to help U.S. blacks catch up after generations of discrimination.

First National City Bank offers fixed-term certificates of deposit that pay a higher rate of interest than is permitted on savings accounts. It offers the CDs in denominations as low as $500, and other banks soon follow suit as depositors seek ways to keep inflation from eroding their savings.

Manufacturers Hanover Trust Co. is created by a merger of Manufacturers Trust, whose origins date to 1812, and Hanover Bank, founded in 1851 (see 1912; 1932). Manufacturers purchased Brooklyn Trust Co. in 1950; the U.S. Department of Justice has opposed the merger on antitrust grounds but it goes through nevertheless (see Chemical, 1992).

Lazard Frères & Co. at New York names Felix Rohatyn and Michel David-Weill partners (see 1977; Mayer, 1940).

Wall Street's Dow Jones Industrial Average closes December 29 at 731.14, up from 615.89 at the end of 1960; the U.S. Gross National Product has reached $521 billion, up 60 percent since World War II as measured in constant dollars.

The Throgs Neck Bridge opens to traffic January 11 to relieve congestion on the 22-year-old Bronx-Whitestone Bridge two miles to the west. Designed by Othmar H. Ammann and built by the Triborough Bridge and Tunnel Authority at a cost of $92 million (the new Clearview Expressway has cost another $32.5 million), the six-lane bridge spans the East River between Throgs Neck in the Bronx and Bayside in northern Queens with a main span of 1,800 feet and a total length of 13,410 feet (its name is derived from that of John Throckmorton; see 1642).

A coalition of Greenwich Village residents, Chinatown merchants, small manufacturers, and urban activists mobilizes to block implementation of the cross-Manhattan expressway proposed in 1929. Robert Moses envisions also a cross-Manhattan expressway at 34th Street and another at 125th Street, with any buildings in the way torn down to make way for "progress," but Scranton, Pa.-born Canadian social critic Jane Jacobs, 45, of 555 Hudson Street rallies opposition (see 1962).

The Pennsylvania Railroad announces in July that Penn Station will be replaced by a 29-story office tower and Madison Square Garden complex atop a new station using the original tracks and platforms (see 1960; real estate, 1962).

New York entrepreneur Saul Steinberg, 22, pioneers the computer-leasing business. When he finds that IBM has no interest in offering long-term leases on its machines, he uses certain accounting assumptions to calculate that computers will hold their value for at least several years, starts a company he calls Leasco, and shows immediate profits. Leasco stock will go public in 1965 and Steinberg will become a multi-millionaire (see commerce, 1968).

The Sciences begins bimonthly publication under the aegis of the 144-year-old New York Academy of Sciences.

The 112-year-old College of the City of New York (CCNY) joins with borough and community colleges to create the City University of New York (CUNY) (*see* 1876; SUNY, 1948). Board of Higher Education administrator Pearl Bernstein Max, now 57, has drafted the master plan and financing formula for CUNY, and it will grow within 40 years to have 11 senior colleges, six community colleges, a graduate division, a law school, and an affiliated medical school, with nearly 200,000 students working toward degrees plus 155,000 adult and continuing education students throughout the five boroughs.

The state legislature at Albany votes in a special session to remove the city's Board of Education, empowers Mayor Wagner to appoint a new board, and orders a revival of local school boards "to provide for effective participation by the people of the city in the government of their schools" (*see* 1896; 1968).

The United Federation of Teachers wins the right to represent all the city's public schoolteachers (*see* 1960). Contract talks have deadlocked, 22,000 teachers have walked out in a 1-day job action, and the UFT obtains the promise of a collective-bargaining agreement in the first comprehensive U.S. teachers' contract. Most of the union's members have Eastern European Jewish backgrounds and strong union convictions with regard to job security and academic freedom; their contract provides for a $1,000 salary increase, the establishment of a salary scale from $5,300 to $9,970, and a grievance procedure with binding arbitration. UFT leader Charles Cogen will obtain a new contract next year providing for a further wage increase, with the first limits ever on class size, and will be elected UFT president in 1964 (*see* 1962).

The 80-year-old New York Trade School takes the name Voorhees Technical Institute in honor of industrialist Enders M. Voorhees, who serves as a trustee. It moved in 1930 to a building on Second Avenue between 66th and 67th streets, added programs in air conditioning and lithography, saw its enrollment peak at 4,106 in 1949, and will move in 1963 to 450 West 41st Street (*see* 1971).

The IBM Selectric typewriter designed by Eliot F. (Fette) Noyes, 51, is introduced by International Business Machines (*see* computer, 1955). (IBM's chief designer since 1956, Noyes has helped Paul Rand design a new logotype for the company.) The Selectric has a moving "golf ball" cluster of interchangeable type, will be linked in 1964 to a magnetic tape recorder that permits automated, individually addressed original copies of any letter, and by 1975 will account for an estimated 70 to 80 percent of the electric typewriter market (*see* word processor, 1974).

Marvel Comics is founded by cartoonists who include Stan Lee and Jack Kirby. Their Spiderman will live in Forest Hills, Queens; their Fantastic Four in Manhattan's east midtown area; their Avengers in a mansion at "890" Fifth Avenue; their Daredevil in Hell's Kitchen; and their Doctor Strange, Earth's Sorcerer, at 177A Bleecker Street in Greenwich Village.

Harper & Row is created by a merger of the 144-year-old Harper Bros. with the Evanston, Ill., textbook publisher Row, Peterson & Co. (*see* 1969).

Macmillan publishers acquires the Free Press of Glencoe, Ill. (*see* 1934). It will go on in this decade to acquire Brentano bookstores, the Berlitz Language Schools, and the Katharine Gibbs secretarial schools (*see* 1973).

Nonfiction: *The La Guardia Years* by New York author Charles Garrett; *The New York I Know* (essays) by Marya Mannes; *Old Brooklyn Heights: New York's First Suburb* by Lexington, Ky.-born New York author Clay Lancaster, 54; *A Puerto Rican in New York, and Other Sketches* by Jesus Colón; *New York: A Serendipiter's Journey* by Gay Talese, who notes that the city has 10,000 bus drivers (who still make change), 38,000 taxi drivers, 650 apartment-house doormen, 325 hotel doormen (14 at the Waldorf-Astoria alone), 8,485 telephone operators, 1,364 Western Union messenger boys, 112 newspaper copyboys, 500 mediums (who "communicate" with the dead), 200 fortune-tellers, 200 chestnut vendors, 300,000 pigeons, 12,000 unionized cleaning ladies; *Reality in Advertising* by Ted Bates chairman Rosser Reeves, now 50, who creates a storm of controversy on Madison Avenue by insisting that the most effective way to promote products and ideas is with the hard-sell techniques used to promote Anacin, Colgate toothpaste, M & M candies, Wonder Bread, and Dwight D. Eisenhower; *Underfoot in Show Business* by Philadelphia-born New York playwright Helene Hanff, 45, who has never had one of her plays produced; *Megalopolis: the Urbanized Northeastern Seaboard of the United States* by French geographer Jean Gottman, who calls the 600-mile corridor between Boston and Washington, D.C., the "richest, best-educated, best-housed, and best-serviced" urbanized area in the world; *Robert Livingston, 1654–*

1728, and the Politics of Colonial New York by New York-born historian Lawrence H. Leder, 34; *The Schools* by Martin Mayer; *Out of My League* by George Plimpton.

Fiction: *The Pawnbroker* by New Haven-born novelist Edward Lewis Wallant, 35; *Catch-22* by Brooklyn-born novelist Joseph Heller, 38; *Franny and Zoey* by J. D. Salinger; *Seduction of the Minotaur* by Anaïs Nin; *The Rising Gorge* by S. J. Perelman.

Crime novelist Dashiell Hammett dies of lung cancer at New York January 10 at age 66; Jessie Redmon Fauset of heart disease at Philadelphia April 30 at age 77; Kenneth Fearing at New York June 26 at age 58; humorist-illustrator-playwright James Thurber at New York November 2 at age 66 soon after undergoing surgery for a blood clot on the brain.

 Painting: *New Madrid* by Frank Stella; *Delta Nu* by Baltimore-born New York painter Morris Louis (originally M. L. Bernstein), 49; *The Italians* by Lexington, Va.,-born New York painter Cy Twombly (Edwin Parker Twombley, Jr.), 33; *Switchsky's Syntax* by Stuart Davis; *Look Mickey, I've Hooked a Big One* by New York-born "pop" artist Roy Lichtenstein, 35, who has employed comic-strip techniques; *Words* (ink on paper mounted on canvas) and *Galleries* (ink on paper) by Agnes Martin. Max Weber dies at Great Neck, L.I., October 4 at age 80.

The Metropolitan Museum of Art pays $2.3 million to acquire the 17th century Rembrandt painting *Aristotle Contemplating the Bust of Homer*. No painting has ever before fetched such a high price.

Sculpture: *Man at a Table* by New York-born sculptor George Segal, 36, who has made plaster casts of friends and relatives to create life-size tableaux; *Cigarette* by South Orange, N.J.-born New York architect-turned-sculptor Anthony Peter "Tony" Smith, 49, who will establish a reputation with his minimalist style; animal sculptures by Paul Manship are installed on the gate of Central Park's Children's Zoo, north of the main zoo.

 Theater: *The American Dream* by Washington, D.C.-born playwright Edward (Franklin) Albee, 32 (grandson by adoption of the late theater owner), 1/24 at the off-Broadway York Theater, 370 perfs.; *Mary, Mary* by Jean Kerr 3/8 at the Helen Hayes Theater, with Barbara Bel Geddes, San Francisco-born actor Barry Nelson, 40, English actor Michael Rennie, 51, 1,572 perfs.; *Happy Days* by Irish-born French playwright Samuel Beckett, 55, 9/17 at the off-Broadway Cherry Lane Theater at 38 Commerce Street (founded in the 1920s by the late Edna St. Vincent Millay, who lived around the corner in Bed-

ford Street); *Purlie Victorious* by actor-playwright Ossie Davis 9/28 at the Cort Theater, with Davis, now 44, as Purlie Victorious Judson, Ruby Dee (his wife), New York-born actor-comedian Godfrey Cambridge, 28, New York-born actor Alan Alda (originally Alphonso Giuseppi Roberto d'Abruzzo), 25, 261 perfs.; *Gideon* by Paddy Chayefsky 11/9 at the Plymouth Theater, with Fredric March, New York-born actor George Segal, 27, 236 perfs.; *Sunday in New York* by Norman Krasna 11/27 at the Cort Theater (to John Golden Theater 1/1/1962), with Pat Harrington, his New York-born son Pat Harrington, Jr., 32, Santa Monica, Calif.-born actor Robert Redford, 24, Pat Stanley, 188 perfs.; *The Night of the Iguana* by Tennessee Williams 12/28 at the Royale Theater, with Ocala, Fla.-born actor Patrick O'Neal, 34, Bette Davis, Margaret Leighton, Alan Webb, 316 perfs.

Former Saks Fifth Avenue fashion designer Ellen Stewart, 41, rents a small basement in Greenwich Village and opens Café La Mama, an experimental theater club.

Playwright George S. Kaufman suffers a stroke and dies at New York June 2 at age 71; producer Guthrie McClintic dies of cancer at Sneeden's Landing on the Hudson October 29 at age 68, survived by his wife, Katherine Cornell; Ruth Chatterton dies at Norwalk, Conn., November 24 at age 67; playwright Moss Hart of a heart attack at Palm Springs, Calif., December 20 at age 57.

Television: *Car 54, Where Are You?* 9/17 on NBC with New York-born actor Fred Gwynne, 35, New York-born actor Joe E. Ross, 55, in a comedy series created by Nat Hiken (to 9/8/1963).

Films: Blake Edwards's *Breakfast at Tiffany's* with Audrey Hepburn, George Peppard, Patricia Neal; Shirley Clarke's *The Connection* with William Redfield, Warren Finnerty, Garry Goodrow; Delbert Mann's *Lover Come Back* with Rock Hudson, Doris Day, Tony Randall. Also: Burt Balaban's *Mad Dog Coll* with John Davis Chandler, Brooke Hayward, Kay Doubleday, Jerry Orbach, (Aristotle) Telly Savalas, Gene Hackman; Frank Capra's *Pocketful of Miracles* with Bette Davis, Glenn Ford, Hope Lange; Jack Garfein's *Something Wild* with Carroll Baker, Ralph Meeker, Mildred Dunnock.

Silent-film star Nita Naldi dies at New York February 17 at age 63; Charles Coburn of a heart attack at New York August 30 at age 84; Marion Davies of cancer at Los Angeles September 22 at age 64, leaving an estate worth upwards of $20 million, most of it invested in Manhattan real estate.

Broadway musicals: *Carnival* 4/13 at the Imperial Theater, with Italian-born singer Anna Maria Alberghetti, 24, Cleveland-born actress Kaye Ballard (originally Catherine Gloria Balotta), 34, actor Jerry Orbach, music and lyrics by Bob Merrill, 719 perfs.; *Milk and Honey* 10/10 at the Martin Beck Theater, with Robert Weede, onetime Metropolitan Opera soprano Mimi Benzell, now 40, veteran Yiddish Theater veteran Molly Picon, now 64, music and lyrics by Jerry Herman, 543 perfs.; *How to Succeed in Business Without Really Trying* 10/14 at the 46th Street Theater, with Robert Morse, Rudy Vallée, book by writer-director Abe Burrows, Jack Weinstock, and Willie Gilbert based on the novel by Shepherd Mead, music and lyrics by Frank Loesser, songs that include "I Believe in You," "Brotherhood of Man," 1,417 perfs.; *Subways Are for Sleeping* 12/27 at the St. James Theater, with Los Angeles-born actor Sydney Chaplin, 35, Carol Lawrence, comedian Orson Bean, Jersey City-born actress-writer Phyllis Newman, 28, Suffern-born ingénue Valerie Harper, 21, Buffalo-born ingénu Richard Bennett, 18, music by Jule Styne, lyrics by Betty Comden and Adolph Green, songs that include "Comes Once in a Lifetime," 205 perfs.

Frank Sinatra, now 45, makes his Carnegie Hall debut 1/27 singing, "My Way" and other favorites; Judy Garland, now 38, makes her Carnegie Hall debut 4/23.

Popular songs: "Talkin' New York" by Bob Dylan, who begins singing at Greenwich Village coffee-houses (he is the opening act in April for John Lee Hooker at Gerde's Folk City in MacDougal Street). Columbia Records vice-president John Hammond discovers him and releases his first album. Now 20, the Minnesotan has changed his name from Robert Zimmerman in honor of the late Welsh poet Dylan Thomas and will provide civil-rights demonstrators and student protest movements of the 1960s with their anthems "Blowin' in the Wind" and "The Times, They Are A-Changin';" *Sunday at The Village Vanguard* (album) is recorded live at New York June 25 by pianist Bill Evans, bassist Scott LaFaro, and drummer Paul Motian, whose 13 songs are released under the Riverside label.

U.S. Virgin Islands-born boxer Emile (Alphonse) Griffith, 23, wins the welterweight championship April 1, beating titleholder Benny "Kid" Paret with a 13th-round knockout punch, but Paret regains the title by decision at Madison Square Garden September 30 after a 15-round fight (*see* 1962).

Roy Emerson, 24, (Australia) wins in men's singles at Forest Hills, Darlene Hard in women's singles.

Roger Maris of the New York Yankees breaks Babe Ruth's home run record of 60 October 1 at Yankee Stadium, but purists maintain that the ball Ruth hit was heavier and Ruth set his record in a 154-game season while the October 1 game is the 162nd (and last) Yankee game for 1961.

The New York Yankees win the World Series, defeating the Cincinnati Reds 4 games to 1. Pitcher Whitey Ford shuts out the Reds in the first and fourth games (an ankle injury in the sixth inning forces him to retire after setting a Series record by pitching 32 scoreless innings in a row); home runs by Elston Howard, Bill Skowron, Johnny Blanchard, 28 (who gets two), Roger Maris (whose Series batting average is only .105), and Hector Lopez, 29, help overpower Cincinnati, and the Yankees might have done even better had Mickey Mantle and Yogi Berra not been sidelined with injuries.

Kinney Service Corp. is created by a merger of Kinney Parking & Rent-a-Car with the 35-year-old Riverside Memorial Chapel on Amsterdam Avenue at 76th Street, now headed by Edward Rosenthal, whose grandfather Louis Meyers started the family funeral business in 1897 (*see* Warner Communications, 1962).

The city's homicide rate will rise in the next 5 years to an unprecedented 7.6 per 100,000, up from 4.7 per 100,000 in the last 5 (*see* 1966).

A July 6 fight between a black woman and a Puerto Rican woman in West 84th Street between Columbus and Amsterdam avenues escalates into a riot; one rioter is blinded by lye thrown in his face, many others are injured, and although the block has been called the worst in New York it is actually little different from other blocks whose transient, unemployed black and Hispanic residents are obliged to occupy cramped and filthy quarters, making life difficult for their striving black and Hispanic neighbors. The *Herald Tribune* has been running a series by reporter Don Ross, who has written that the city has plans "to halt the flight of middle-class residents from the upper West Side to outlying parts of the city and suburbs." If the flight continues, Ross has said, "it is feared the area will deteriorate into a low-income ghetto like Harlem or East Harlem" (*see* 1962). The city deals summarily with the rioters and will bulldoze their tenements, replacing them with school buildings (the Louis D. Brandeis High School in 1965, P.S. 9 at about the same time) and playgrounds.

"I am overwhelmed by the lack of sensitivity among the planners in New York in their reshaping of Park

Avenue," Chicago architect Bertram Goldberg says in a February speech to the Chicago Real Estate Board. "These curtain walls are for me the eyes of the blind. Apartment buildings are being torn down and replaced by offices . . . This is the real estate man's answer to a need for additional income. Space, which as apartments, is returning $3 a square foot, is being replaced by space, which as offices, is returning $8 a square foot—a very simple arithmetic improvement." Goldberg has been even more appalled by the idea of "a 24-hour-a-day population . . . being replaced by a 7-hour-a-day population for a period of only a 5-day week . . . The 30-hour week is not too far from our present economic concepts. We therefore have to look at this expensive machine—Park Avenue—being developed for usage only 30 hours per week. Can our economy stand this kind of specialized development? Twenty years from now, it is conceivable that Park Avenue during half the week will look like Wall Street on Sunday . . . Our tax structure demands the two-shift central city."

The Death and Life of Great American Cities by Jane Jacobs observes that cities were safer and more pleasant when they consisted of neighborhood communities, where people lived in relatively low-priced buildings, knew their neighbors, and lived in the streets and on their doorsteps rather than in the depersonalized environment characteristic of modern cities. Critic Lewis Mumford, now 65, counters that congested 18th century cities were hardly safer or healthier. Noting that some areas of the city "go dead at night," Jacobs singles out "the stretch of new office buildings centering on Park Avenue between Grand Central Station and 59th Street, saying, "Many a once vital district, having lost in the past a mixture of primary uses which brought attraction, popularity and high economic value, has declined sadly . . . The new office stretch of . . . Park Avenue is far more standardized in content than Fifth Avenue. Park Avenue has the advantages of containing among its new office buildings several which, in themselves, are masterpieces of modern design." She praises Lever House and the Seagram, Pepsi-Cola, and Union Carbide buildings but argues that "homogeneity of use or homogeneity of age" does not help Park Avenue esthetically, that its office blocks are "wretchedly disorganized in appearance, and far more given than Fifth Avenue to a total effect of chaotic architectural wildness, overlaid on boredom."

New York adopts a new zoning resolution that permits buildings to contain a maximum of 12 times as much floor space as the area of the original site with special bonuses for enlightened land use (*see* 1916: the Equitable Life Assurance Society Building of 1915 contained nearly 30 times as much floor space as was contained in its land site). The new resolution's chief effect will be to encourage architects to set off their buildings with open plazas.

The 60-story Chase Manhattan Bank Building is completed in lower Manhattan to designs by Skidmore, Owings & Merrill; rising 813 feet high, the glass and aluminum tower gives the financial district its first open plaza (*see* Sculpture, 1972).

The 41-story Continental Can Building is completed at 633 Third Avenue, between 40th and 41st streets. Harrison & Abramovitz has designed the brick-clad skyscraper; the 32-story 235 East 42nd Street office building is completed at the northwest corner of Third Avenue. Designed by Emery Roth & Sons, it serves as world headquarters of Pfizer Inc.; the 25-story American Home Products Building is completed at 685 Third Avenue, between 43rd and 44th streets, to designs by Robert L. Bien; the 24-story Diamond National Building at 733 Third Avenue, southeast corner 46th Street, and the 20-story 850 Third Avenue office building between 51st and 52nd streets, both to designs by Emery Roth & Sons.

The PaineWebber Building (initially a new Equitable Life Assurance Society Building, later UBS) goes up at 1285 Avenue of the Americas, between 51st and 52nd streets. Skidmore, Owings & Merrill has designed the 38-story structure.

The First National City Bank Building is completed on the east side of Park Avenue between 53rd and 54th streets, extending east to Lexington Avenue. The bank acquired the site for the 39-story tower from the estate of the late Vincent Astor, who had intended to erect a building with an open plaza such as that of the Seagram building immediately to the south, but he was unable to obtain financing; Carson & Lundin has designed the structure in International Style with an assist from Kahn & Jacobs.

The Mayor's Committee for the Preservation of Structures of Historic and Esthetic Importance is set up by Mayor Wagner at the suggestion of City Planning Commission chairman James Felt.

The Dakota apartment house that opened in 1884 goes co-op at year's end, joining the ranks of buildings that have converted from rental to co-operative, although there are still a few rent-controlled tenants left over from World War II. Brooklyn-born real estate investor Louis J. Glickman, 56, bought the Dakota for $4.6 million at the end of last year (the Clark Foundation had been losing money on it for years), its parking lot (earlier the

Dakota's rose garden, generating plant, and tennis courts) was part of the deal, and Glickman has arranged for mortgage financing that enables Dakota tenants to buy individual apartments for a total of $4.8 million, giving him a $200,000 profit. Rents at the Dakota have risen only slightly since it opened: a 10-room apartment has been renting for $500 per month, and a tenant with 17 rooms, six baths, and eight working fireplaces has been paying $650. Lauren Bacall has recently moved in and buys her apartment overlooking Central Park for $53,340, a seven-room flat with two baths and three fireplaces may be had for $45,000, but some tenants cannot afford such prices, they move out, and the Dakota for the first time in its history advertises for buyers. One fairly large flat goes for only $5,000 (its buyer divides it and sells off half the space for $55,000). Another buyer pays $10,000 for an apartment and sells off its antique mahogany and marble mantelpiece for $35,000 (see Mayfair Towers, 1963).

The 21-story Summit Hotel opens at the southeast corner of Lexington Avenue and 51st Street, replacing a Loews movie theater. Preston Robert Tisch and Laurence Tisch have built the new hostelry, hailed as the city's first new transient hotel in 30 years and the first American hotel with a concierge, but few people have anything kind to say about its flamboyant design, bright lighting, and transparent plastic lobby furniture or its New York-raised architect Morris Lapidus, now 58, who studied architecture at Columbia and revolutionized retail-store design in the 1930s and 40s by introducing bold color, sweeping curves, and arresting storefronts. He has improved the interiors of various Miami Beach hotels, designed the $13 million 14-story Fontainebleau resort hotel that opened at Miami Beach in 1954, designed the Americana that opened at Bal Harbour in 1957, and has established a reputation for exuberant baroque ornamentation laid atop jazzed-up Modernist style with grand lobbies and curving "stairs that go nowhere" (see Americana, 1962).

The 22-story City Squire Hotel (later the Sheraton City Squire) opens at 790 Seventh Avenue (156 West 56th Street). Designed by Kahn & Jacobs, it replaces the Picadilly Theater.

A skating rink opens in Brooklyn's Prospect Park, where it has been built with funds raised by Kate Wollman (see Central Park, 1952). Like Central Park's rink, it is named for Wollman.

Cookbook: *The New York Times Cookbook* by Mississippi-born food expert Craig Claiborne, 41,

who has been the paper's food editor since 1957 and will retain that position until 1971.

Lutèce restaurant opens February 16 at 249 East 50th Street with two beautifully appointed rooms on the second floor that sparkle with flat silver by Christofle and Baccarat crystal. Local Francophile André Surmain (originally Andrew Sussman) has engaged Paris chef André Soltner, 28, of Chez Hansi to prepare the meals at the 29-table restaurant, whose name is the original name of Paris. Its kitchen is too small for grilling or frying, and although it offers a price-fixed lunch at $8.50 it will soon lower the price to $6.50 (dinner is entirely à la carte—soup, $2.25; first course, $4; main courses, $8.25; desserts, $2.75; wines $8.50 to $14, with a $1 cover charge). Lutèce's prices are generally considered outrageous and it will struggle for 2 years before gaining a reputation as the city's temple of traditional French cuisine.

The Harlem restaurant Sylvia's opens with four booths and a counter that seats 10. Using money her mother obtained by mortgaging the family farm, former South Carolina hairdresser Sylvia Wood, 36, serves patrons fried chicken, barbecued ribs, grits, black-eyed peas, collard greens, sweet potatoes, fresh corn bread, and sweet potato pie. Her husband, Herbert, 37, is a former taxi driver and helps in the operation. The Woods will move in the late 1960s to a larger place two doors away at 328 Lenox Avenue near 127th Street—a long, narrow, diner-like room with a larger counter and tables along one wall, but demand will force them to add a large new dining room with wood paneling on one side and an exposed brick wall on the other, expanding their capacity to more than 100 (see Sylvia's Foods, 1993).

The 73-year-old Childs restaurant chain is acquired by Irving and Murray Riese (see 1925; 1953). They will replace most of New York's Childs restaurants with fast-food operations such as Chock full o' Nuts (see 1981; Longchamps, 1969).

New York and its suburban environs have a population of 14.2 million, making it the most densely populated region in America.

1962 Opponents of what they call the "doctrinaire liberal philosophy of the welfare state at home and the collectivist ideology abroad" form the Conservative Party of New York State. Led by New York-born lawyer Kieran O'Doherty, 37, they dedicate themselves to preserving what they call "traditional American values of individual freedom, individual responsibility, and individual effort." The new party will espouse libertarian causes, fighting government

Fears of a nuclear attack led the city to establish fallout shelters as cold-war anxieties intensified.

regulation and taxation while resisting supporters of abortion rights.

Onetime official greeter Grover Whalen dies at New York April 20 at age 75; former Manhattan borough president Stanley M. Isaacs at New York July 12 at age 79.

Soviet Premier Nikita Khrushchev visits New York to address the United Nations and steps out on the second-floor balcony of his country's handsome red-brick consul general's house (formerly the Percy Rivington Pyne II mansion) at the northwest corner of Park Avenue at 68th Street September 21 to hold two impromptu press conferences.

The Cuban missile crisis in October brings a senseless rush to stock city fallout shelters with food and water as New Yorkers struggle with the realization that the city may be the target of nuclear warheads on long-range Soviet missiles based in Cuba. Aerial surveillance by U-2 spy planes has revealed the presence of offensive missile and bomber bases on the island, but President Kennedy resists pressures to invade Cuba, Premier Khrushchev agrees to dismantle the missiles, and they are removed from Cuba before month's end.

Former first lady and U.S. envoy to the United Nations Eleanor Roosevelt dies of anemia and a lung infection at her 55 East 74th Street house November 7 at age 78.

Gov. Rockefeller wins reelection, defeating U.S. District Attorney for Southern New York Robert M. (Morris) Morgenthau, 43, who has gained the Democratic Party nomination but receives only 2,552,418 votes to Rockefeller's 3,126,929. A grandson of the late businessman and philanthropist Henry Morgenthau, Sr., Morgenthau will try to get the Liberal Party nomination in 1970 but without success. He will remain D.A. into the 21st century. Kieran O'Doherty of the new Conservative Party runs for the Senate on Row F of the ballot and receives 43,000 votes.

City College of New York psychology professor Kenneth B. (Bancroft) Clark, 48, founds Harlem Youth Opportunities Unlimited (Haryou) to combat unemployment among youth in the New York ghetto and supplement local teaching facilities.

The *Herald Tribune* faces bankruptcy and gives up control of the 85-year-old Fresh Air Fund; the fund will become independent in 1967 and launch a farm training program for teenagers 9 years later.

East Brooklyn Savings Bank moves its headquarters from Bedford Avenue to Montague Street in Brooklyn Heights (*see* 1922; 1969).

Alliance Capital Management has its beginnings as the investment-management division of Donaldson, Lufkin & Jenrette (*see* 1959). It will merge in 1971 with Moody's Investors Service.

Wall Street's Dow Jones Industrial Average falls to a low of 535.76, down from a high of 734.91 late last year, and closes December 31 at 652.10, down from 731.14 at the end of 1961.

Consolidated Edison announces plans to build a million-kilowatt nuclear generating station at Ravenswood, Queens (*see* 1955). The Atomic Energy Commission rejects the proposal following a public outcry at the utility's seeming disregard of public safety, but the AEC approves construction of a plant 28 miles north of the city at Indian Point on the Hudson (*see* 1963; Big Allis, 1965).

The Board of Estimate holds a hearing February 4 on the proposed cross-Manhattan expressway (*see* 1961). Robert Moses dismisses opposition, saying critics never built anything, but Mayor Wagner announces that the Board has voted unanimously against the expressway.

The S.S. *France* arrives at New York February 8 on her maiden voyage from Le Havre. Launched last year by the Compagnie Générale Transatlantique, the $81.3 million 66,348-ton French Line ship measures 1,035.2 feet in overall length and is the longest (and last) of the great transatlantic passenger liners.

Bronx-Lebanon Hospital Center is created by a merger of the 51-year-old Bronx Hospital and the 69-year-old Lebanon Hospital.

A strike by the United Federation of Teachers brings 20,000 off the job April 12, violating the Condon-Walton Act (*see* 1960). The teachers' 1-day strike wins a wage increase, and their job action begins a series of strikes by public employees (*see* 1968).

Head Start has its beginnings in a pilot program for preschoolers from disadvantaged backgrounds started in Harlem by local educator Martin Deutsch, 37, and his wife, Cynthia, who 4 years ago founded the Institute for Developmental Studies at New York Medical College (the institute will later merge with NYU's School of Education) (the Head Start concept will also be credited in part to Vanderbilt University psychologist Susan W. Gray, now 48, who worked with poor children in Murfreesboro, Tenn., to develop an Early Training Project). Placing 3- and 4-year-olds in classes of 15 led by two teachers each, the program introduces children who have never held a pencil or seen themselves in a mirror to the world of art, books, and music through songs. Head Start will help kids achieve higher levels of health, nutrition, and preparedness for school (*see* 1965; human rights [Haryou], 1964).

Warner Communications has its beginnings as Brooklyn-born entrepreneur Steven J. Ross, 35, takes Kinney Services public, creating a $12.5 million (market value) company that will be sold in 1990 for $14 billion (*see* Kinney, 1961). Ross's father lost all his money in 1929 and changed his name from Rachnitz in order to find work during the Depression. When his father was dying, Ross will later say, he called his teenaged son to his bedside and told him, "There are those who work all day, those who dream all day, and those who spend an hour dreaming before setting to work to fulfill those dreams. Go into the third category because there's virtually no competition." Ross grew up in Flatbush, his wife's uncle provided limousines for funeral services but was losing money, so he asked young

Steven to look at his operation in the Bronx; seeing that the limousines were idle from 4:30 o'clock in the afternoon until 7:30 the next morning, Ross called Carey Limousine and proposed renting the vehicles to Carey for use at night. He started Abbey Rent-a-Car, added a parking company called Kinney, and then added an office-cleaning operation; he will purchase Ashley Famous Talent Agency in 1967, the ailing Warner Brothers-Seven Arts Studio for about $400 million in 1969 to enter the record business, pioneer in cable television in 1971, adopt the Warner Communications name in 1972, sell off the old Kinney businesses, put good people in charge of his media properties, acquire Atari for a song in 1976 but lose nearly $1 billion on it when sales of video games weaken (*see* 1990).

ABC begins color telecasts for 3½ hours per week beginning in September, 68 percent of NBC prime evening time programming is in color, but CBS confines itself to black and white after having transmitted in color earlier. All three networks will be transmitting entirely in color by 1967.

Channel 13 begins operations September 16 under the name WNDT with Edward R. Murrow of CBS saying, "This instrument can teach, it can illuminate, yes, and it can even inspire, but it can do so only to the extent that humans are determined to use it to those ends. Otherwise, it will be merely lights and wires in a box." The city's first public television station, 13 offers educational, instructional, and cultural programming that begins early in the morning (*see* 1967; *Sesame Street*, 1968).

Veteran *Harper's Bazaar* fashion editor Diana Vreeland joins *Vogue* as editor-in-chief (*see* 1937). Now 62, she will continue in the *Vogue* position until 1971, exercising great influence on what chic American women wear and becoming famous for pronouncing corduroy "cor du roi" and for such aphorisms as, "Pink is the navy blue of India" and "The bikini is the most important thing since the atomic bomb."

The International Typographical Union brings 20,000 workers off the job December 6, beginning a 4-month strike as typographers try to fight the inroads of technological advances that are eliminating jobs.

Right-wing journalist George E. Sokolsky dies at New York December 12 at age 69.

Nonfiction: *Fiorello La Guardia* by Polish-born New York author Bella Rodman (*née* Kashin), 58; *The Vanderbilts and Their Fortune* by Oregon-born Connecticut author Edwin Palmer Hoyt, 39; *The Great*

White Way: A Re-Creation of Broadway's Golden Era by Allen Churchill; *Sex and the Single Woman* by Arkansas-born New York advertising copywriter-turned-author Helen Gurley Brown, 40.

Fiction: *Portrait in Brownstone* by Louis Auchincloss; *The Golden Spur* by Dawn Powell.

Poetry: *The Lordly Hudson: Collected Poems* by Paul Goodman.

Juvenile: *James and the Giant Peach* by Roald Dahl; *A Wrinkle in Time* by New York-born Upper West Side author Madeleine L'Engle (Franklin), 44.

Author-artist Ludwig Bemelmans dies at New York October 1 at age 64.

 Painting: *100 Cans* (of Campbell's Beef Noodle Soup) and *Green Coca-Cola Bottles* by Andy Warhol, who has taken over an old New York Edison Co. sub-station at 19 East 32nd Street and 22 East 33rd, between Fifth and Madison avenues, and turned it into what he calls The Factory; *The Ring, Blam!* and *Head, Red and Yellow* by Roy Lichtenstein; *Silver Skies* by Grand Forks, N.D.-born New York painter James Rosenquist, 28; *Fool's House* and *Diver* by Jasper Johns; *Ace* by Robert Rauschenberg; *Cantabile* by Kenneth Noland; *Blue Flower* (oil, glue, nails, and canvas on canvas), *Little Sister* (oil on canvas), and *Starlight* (oil on canvas) by Agnes Martin; *Heron of Calvary No. 1* by Ben Shahn. Franz Kline dies at New York May 13 at age 51; Morris Louis of lung cancer at Washington, D.C., September 7 at age 50 (art critic Clement Greenberg "stretches" several hundred Louis canvases himself and helps the painter's widow sell them off at steadily mounting prices, keeping one for himself after each exhibition); banker-turned-art collector Chester Dale dies at his native New York December 16 at age 79, having served as a trustee of the Metropolitan Museum of Art since 1952 (but he has left the bulk of his collection to the National Gallery at Washington, D.C.).

 Theater: *The Funny House of a Negro* by Pittsburgh-born playwright Adrienne (Lita) Kennedy (*née* Hawkins), 29, 1/14 at the Circle-in-the-Square Theater; *Oh, Dad, Poor Dad, Mama's Hung You in the Closet and We're Feeling So Sad* by New York-born playwright Arthur (Lee) Kopit, 24, 2/26 at the off-Broadway Phoenix Theater, 454 perfs.; *A Thousand Clowns* by New York-born playwright-cartoonist Herbert "Herb" Gardner, 27, 4/5 at the Eugene O'Neill Theater, with Jason Robards, Jr., Hastings, Neb.-born actress Sandy (originally Sandra Dale) Dennis, 24, 428 perfs.; *Who's Afraid of Virginia Woolf?* by Edward Albee 10/13 at the Billy Rose Theater, with Arthur Hill as George, Uta Hagen as

Martha, 664 perfs.; *Lord Pengo* by S. N. Behrman 11/19 at the Royale Theater, with Charles Boyer, Agnes Moorehead, London-born actor Henry Daniell, 67, 175 perfs.

The Delacorte Theater opens in June south of the Great Lawn in Central Park with Shakespeare's *The Merchant of Venice* starring George C. Scott. Joseph Papp of the Public Theater has designed the outdoor amphitheater as a permanent summertime venue for the Mobile Theater he began in 1957, publisher-philanthropist George T. Delacorte, Jr. has provided funds for the theater, its productions will include at least one Shakespeare play each season, and it charges no admission, offering tickets on a first-come first-served basis beginning at 1 o'clock on the day of the performance.

Vaudeville veteran James Barton dies of a heart attack at Mineola February 19 at age 71; Lucile Watson at New York June 24 at age 83; Victor Moore following a stroke at an East Islip actors' home July 23 at age 86; Myron McCormick of cancer at New York July 30 at age 54; Frank Lovejoy is found dead of an apparent heart attack in his Warwick Hotel suite October 2 at age 50; philanthropist Vivian Beaumont (Allen) dies at New York October 10.

Films: H. Bruce Humberstone's *Madison Avenue* with Dana Andrews, Eleanor Parker, Jeanne Crain, Eddie Albert; Delbert Mann's *That Touch of Mink* with Cary Grant, Doris Day, Gig Young, Audrey Meadows (as an Automat worker); Robert Wise's *Two for the Seesaw* with Robert Mitchum, Shirley MacLaine; Sidney Lumet's *A View From the Bridge* with Raf Vallone, Maureen Stapleton, Carol Lawrence, Jean Sorel, Morris Carnovsky.

Times Square continues the descent into seediness that began during the Depression. Entrepreneur Martin J. Hodas puts pornographic films into nickeleodeon machines and the idea meets with such an enthusiastic response that Hodas will gain notoriety as "King of the Peeps" (and earn himself a fortune) (*see 1966*).

Broadway musicals: *No Strings* 3/15 at the 54th Street Theater, with Bronx-born actress-singer Diahann Carroll (originally Carol Diahann Johnson), 26, Richard Kiley, music and lyrics by Richard Rodgers, songs that include "The Sweetest Sounds," 580 perfs.; *I Can Get It For You Wholesale* 2/22 at the Shubert Theater, with Lillian Roth, dancer Harold Lang, Los Angeles-born actress Sheree North (originally Dawn Bethel), 29, Brooklyn-born singer Barbra (originally Barbara Joan) Streisand, 19, New York-born actor Elliott Gould (originally Elliot Goldstein), 23, Herbert Ross, music and lyrics by Harold Rome, book by Jerome Weidman, now 50, from his 1934 novel, 301 perfs.; *A Funny Thing Happened on the Way to the Forum* 5/8 at the Alvin Theater, with Zero Mostel, Jack Gilford, book by Burt Shevelove and Larry Gelbart, music and lyrics by Stephen Sondheim, songs that include "Comedy Tonight," 964 perfs.; *Little Me* 11/17 at the Lunt-Fontanne Theater, with Sid Caesar, Joey Faye, Virginia Martin, Nancy Andrews, book by Neil Simon, music by Cy Coleman, lyrics by Carolyn Leigh, songs that include "Real Live Girl," 257 perfs.; *Never Too Late* 11/27 at the Playhouse, with Paul Ford, Maureen O'Sullivan, Orson Bean, book by Sumner Arthur Long, 41, music by Kansas City–born composer John Kander, 36, lyrics by Jerry Bock and Chicago-born writer Sheldon Harnick, 38, songs that include the title cha-cha, 1,007 perfs.

Philharmonic Hall opens September 23 as part of the new Lincoln Center for the Performing Arts nearing completion on Columbus Avenue between 62nd and 66th streets (*see* 1959). Designed by Max Abramovitz and situated at the north end of a plaza, the $19.7 million, 2,863-seat concert hall becomes the new home of the New York Philharmonic after 69 years at Carnegie Hall; it will be renamed Avery Fisher Hall in 1973 (*see* Fisher, 1969), but its acoustics are so poor that it will undergo repeated guttings and redesigns (*see* Opera House, 1966).

New York–born singer Tony Bennett (originally Anthony Benedetto), now 35, makes his Carnegie Hall debut 3/18; the vocal group Peter, Paul and Mary its Carnegie Hall debut 11/24.

Popular songs: "On Broadway" by Barry Mann, Cynthia Weil, Jerry Lieber, and Mike Stoller; "In a Brownstone Mansion" by New York songwriters Sol Kaplan and Edward Eliscu.

Songwriter Maceo Pinkard dies at his 211 West 53rd Street apartment July 19 at age 65.

Warner Brothers releases the album *My Son, The Folk Singer* by Chicago-born New York gag writer Allan Sherman (originally Allan Copelon), 37, and it quickly becomes the fastest-selling album in Warner's history with parodies such as "Sarah Jackman" based on Jewish suburban humor. Carnegie Hall books Sherman for a concert, television programs vie for his appearances, and Warner Brothers quickly releases his second album *My Son, The Celebrity*.

New York disk jockey Alan Freed pleads guilty to two charges of commercial bribery and pays a $300 fine, having taken payola from record companies (*see*

1954). Freed has said that every disk jockey did it, and only New York and Pennsylvania have made it illegal, but the hard drinking, womanizing Freed's career is over.

 Emile Griffith regains the welterweight championship March 24 by knocking Benny "Kid" Paret senseless in the 12th round of a title bout at Madison Square Garden (*see* 1961). Paret dies April 3 at age 25 (*see* 1963).

Rod Laver wins in men's singles at Forest Hills (part of his "grand slam" victory in Australia, France, and Britain, as well as the United States); Margaret Smith, 19, (Australia) in women's singles.

The New York Mets play their first exhibition game March 10 at St. Petersburg, Fla., and go on to play their first season at the Polo Grounds, replacing the New York Giants, who moved to California in 1958. New York–born lawyer William Alfred Shea, 54, has obtained a new National League baseball franchise for New York by threatening to start a rival league and by getting political allies in Washington to threaten other team owners with restraint-of-trade hearings (*see* Shea Stadium, 1964). Managed by former Yankee manager Charles Dillon "Casey" Stengel, who turns 72 July 30, and owned principally by heiress Joan Whitney Payson, now 59 (she had been a major stockholder of the Giants), the Metropolitans win 40 games and lose 120, finishing at the bottom of the National League. Stengel has asked, "Can't anyone here play this game?" Nebraska-born outfielder Richie Ashburn, 35, finishes his playing career with a .306 batting average for the year, including seven home runs, is named Most Valuable Player (he has few rivals), and is given a 24-foot boat that sleeps six (docked at Ocean City, N.J., it sinks). The only Met pitcher who wins more games than he loses is former Milwaukee hurler Kenneth Purvis "Ken" Mackenzie, 28, a Canadian-born Yale graduate who wins five, loses four, but his earned run average is an unimpressive 4.95.

The New York Yankees win the World Series, defeating the San Francisco Giants 4 games to 3 with help from pitchers Ralph Terry, 26, and Whitey Ford. The Yankees go to the bottom of the ninth inning in the seventh game with a slim one-run lead, the Giants get two men on base with two outs, Willie McCovey, 24, hits a line drive that would win the Series for the Giants, but Bobby Richardson catches the ball to snuff out San Francisco's hopes.

 The New York Playboy Club opens in December at 5 East 59th Street, occupying a seven-story building used previously by the Savoy Art Galleries. Chicago publisher Hugh Hefner launched his *Playboy* magazine 9 years ago and has commissioned the architectural firm Oppenheimer, Brady & Lehrecke to remodel the structure, making it resemble a 1930s Hollywood movie set with a two-story entrance court and a cantilevered spiral staircase inside a glass cylinder. Women in scanty "bunny" costumes and three-inch heels serve businessmen seated at tables in interwoven balconies, mezzanines, and lounges decorated with LeRoy Neiman paintings. The place will continue in operation until 1982.

Former Mafia boss Charles "Lucky" Luciano dies of a heart attack at Naples airport January 26 at age 64; his body is flown to New York for burial in a Queens cemetery.

Architectural visionary Hugh Ferriss dies at New York January 29 at age 72; Skidmore, Owings & Merrill cofounder Louis Skidmore at Winter Haven, Fla., September 27 at age 69.

The Penn South apartment complex opens in May between Eighth and Ninth avenues from 23rd Street to 29th. Designed by Herman Jessor and sponsored by the International Ladies' Garment Workers' Union in co-operation with the United Housing Foundation, the 2,820-unit co-operative has been built as an urban renewal project. Prices are low, the waiting list for applicants is long, and it will effectively be closed in 1987, but tenants will have to fight to retain their community's nonprofit status.

The 33-story Tower East apartment house is completed at 190 East 72nd Street, southwest corner Third Avenue. The first residential building put up under the 1961 zoning resolution that encourages elimination of upper-floor setbacks, it has been designed by Emery Roth & Sons for Tishman Realty & Construction Co., has four apartments per floor (132 units in toto), and replaces the Loews 72nd Street movie theater of 1932 (although it does contain a 500-seat movie theater along with shops and a garage on its ground floor and basement).

A public hearing held in May by the City Planning Commission to discuss plans for West Side urban renewal erupts in a dispute between Jack E. Wood, housing secretary for the NAACP, and Aramis Gomez, leader of a Puerto Rican group (*see* riot, 1961). Wood says that to devise a plan providing low-rent housing for every low-income family to be relocated in the project area would be "to give municipal sanction for containment and economic balance." The NAACP does not condone all the city's relocation programs, Wood says, but he pleads for "the kind of racial and economic balance that complements the open city concept of New York." Gomez charges that the city's method for achieving a balanced community is "to get rid of the Negroes and Puerto Ricans and low income families from the area." He calls the project "a massive piece of deception" and "the biggest hoax perpetrated on the neighborhood and on the people of New York City."

A Planning Commission report seeks to reassure skeptics: "Old time New York residents still remember a quieter, more leisurely city: clean, attractive, good to look at, good to live in. That is essentially what the plan seeks to make out of these twenty crowded blocks with their rows of substandard houses and the squalid face of blight. When the plan has been carried out, new plazas will open unaccustomed stretches of sunlight and air. Traffic flow will be improved, trees planted . . ."

The state legislature at Albany approves a bill designed to prevent a landlord from evicting a tenant on public assistance for not paying rent if there are serious violations in the building. Assemblyman Samuel A. Spiegel has sponsored the measure, whose goal is to prevent taxpayers' money from being used to support landlords who permit hazardous conditions in their buildings, it will be known as the Spiegel defense, and although it will fall into disuse as lawyers argue about how it should be applied it will come back into favor in the late 1990s as Legal Services attorneys find it of value in parts of the city.

The 20-story Arthur H. Murphy Houses completed in the Bronx at 1800 Crotona Park North memorialize the borough's political boss who died in 1922.

The 25-story Sheraton Motor Inn opens at the northeast corner of Twelfth Avenue and 42nd Street. Designed by Morris Lapidus with Harle & Liebman, it is the city's tallest concrete-framed structure to date and has a rooftop swimming pool; it also has 10 ballrooms and five restaurants, and its 448 guest-room windows are angled to afford optimum views of river and midtown.

The 50-story Sheraton Centre (initiallly the Americana Hotel, later the Sheraton New York) opens September 24 at 811 Seventh Avenue, between 52nd and 53rd streets. Architect Morris Lapidus of Lapidus, Konbluth, Harle & Liebman has designed the 2,000-room hostelry for the late developer Erwin S. Wolfson, who has died at suburban Purchase June 26 at age 60 (*see* Summit, 1961).

Architects who belong to Action Group for Better Architecture in New York picket Pennsylvania Station in October to protest its announced demolition (*see* transportation, 1961). They carry signs reading, "Save Our Heritage," "Save Penn Station," and "Action Not Apathy" in the first concerted action to gain protection for city landmarks (*but see* 1963).

The circular East New York Savings Bank (later the Banco de Ponce) is completed at the corner of Kings Highway and Rockaway Parkway in Brooklyn's Brownsville to designs by architect Lester Tichy, who will replace Pennsylvania Station's main waiting room with a canopy.

Naturalist William Beebe of the New York Zoological Society dies in Trinidad June 4 at age 84.

A steam boiler explodes October 3 in a New York Telephone Co. building on Broadway at 213th Street in upper Manhattan's Inwood section. Weighing more than a ton, it rockets through the building's cafeteria, where about 100 employees, mostly women, are beginning to eat lunch; after striking the ceiling it bounces back down and smashes through the opposite wall, leaving 23 people dead and 95 injured.

The Sign of the Dove opens in a renovated brick tenement at 1110 Third Avenue (northwest corner 65th Street) with a decor that is initially more remarkable than the food served. Owner Joseph Santo will expand by acquiring adjacent buildings and will improve his kitchen; the place will survive until early 1998.

La Grenouille opens in December at 3 East 52nd Street. Proprietor Charles Masson came to New York in 1939 to work with Henri Soulé at the French Pavilion at the World's Fair and has worked as headwaiter on the S.S. *Independence*, traveling between New York, Cannes, Capri, and Naples. His wife, Gisèlle (his nickname for her is "Grenouille," meaning "frog"), has signed a lease for the ground floor of the house and cabled Masson aboard the *Independence*. When Masson dies unexpectedly in 1975 his son and namesake will drop out of Carnegie-Mellon University to help his mother, filling the place with fresh flowers every day as his father did (the restaurant will continue until 1993).

1963 A new city charter takes effect January 1. Approved by voters in November 1961, it vests more authority in the mayor, provides for a deputy mayor residing in each borough, reduces the power of borough presidents (who must now rely on personal persuasion to achieve their ends), and consolidates services separated heretofore by borough into citywide departments. Many sections of the charter have been amended by state law and local law since the voters approved changing what the Citizens' Budget Commission has called "the most dangerous and largest blank check ever authorized in municipal history." A new charter amendment is adopted in April, largely at the initiative of the Citizens Union, giving more time for public study of proposed capital expense budgets before public hearings by the Board of Estimate and the City Council.

Sen. John J. Williams (R. Del.) takes the floor of the Senate at Washington, D.C., February 5 to criticize Rep. Adam Clayton Powell, Jr., charging favoritism in awarding grants and loans to Powell. The congressman has gone to Europe, allegedly to investigate conditions of working women in the NATO countries, and has been photographed in popular nightclubs, attending theaters, dining at posh restaurants, and otherwise raising suspicions that the trip to Venice, Rome, and Athens was a pleasure junket, taken with two young female staff members at taxpayers' expense while the government was trying to collect back taxes from him. "This member of the House is a disgrace to Congress," Sen. Williams declares, and it comes out that Powell's third wife, Yvette, is living in Puerto Rico on a congressional salary of nearly $2,000 per month.

A Manhattan jury finds Rep. Powell guilty of defamation of character April 3, and a judge orders him to pay Mrs. Esther James $11,500 in compensatory damages plus $200,000 in punitive damages (*see* 1960). Powell has never appeared in court, a state court reduces the judgment to $46,500, and the congressman tries to laugh the matter off. He is given the ceremonial role of leading the congressional delegation to its reserved seats among the 200,000 people gathered for a march on Washington (*see* 1964).

Gov. Rockefeller is married May 4 at Pocantico to the former Mrs. Margaretta Murphy (*née* Fitler), 36, whose nickname is "Happy." (She has obtained a divorce in Idaho April 19 from Dr. James Slater Murphy, 40, a virologist at the Rockefeller Institute, on grounds of "mental anguish," the same grounds used by the former Mary Todhunter Clark to obtain a divorce from Rockefeller at Reno last year after 31 years of marriage.) Now 54, the governor moved out of his apartment at 810 Fifth Avenue in 1961 when he fell in love with Happy, and he has bought a large triplex at 812 Fifth Avenue. Many believe the divorce and remarriage will ruin any chance Rockefeller may have of winning the presidency.

The assassination of President Kennedy at Dallas November 22 shocks the city and the nation. Texas-born Vice President Lyndon Baines Johnson, 55, succeeds to the presidency.

Former governor Herbert H. Lehman dies at New York December 5 at age 85. Since leaving public life in 1956 he had led a reform movement that has broken Tammany Hall's hold on the city's Democratic Party.

$ The Paine, Webber, Jackson and Curtis brokerage house moves its headquarters from Boston to New York. Created by a 1942 merger of firms that date to 1880 (Paine, Webber) and 1879 (Jackson and Curtis), it will shorten its name simply to PaineWebber in 1974 (*see* Kidder, Peabody, 1995).

Wall Street's Dow Jones Industrial Average plummets 21 points in 30 minutes November 22 at news of President Kennedy's assassination but recovers to close December 31 at 762.95, up from 652.10 at the end of 1962.

⚡ Consolidated Edison opens a nuclear-powered electric power station on the Hudson River at Indian Point (*see* 1962), but the reactor's cost per kilowatt of capacity is two-and-a-half times that of a conventional generator, and there is a growing perception among New Yorkers that Con Ed is an inefficient utility. The company concedes that underutilized capacity is highly inefficient but says Manhattan has such a concentration of office workers that Con Ed must be prepared to generate a midday peak of electricity far greater than its 24-hour average, and that this obliges it to construct and maintain a generating capacity far greater than would otherwise be required. Its greatest expense is construction and upkeep, but it passes high taxes on to customers, so in effect it collects taxes on behalf of various city, state, and federal agencies. The law requires that most utility wires and pipes be laid underground, and Con Ed has more miles of underground wire than the rest of the nation's utilities combined (*see* 1965). The Indian Point plant is closer to a major center of population than any other U.S. nuclear facility and has been built over the protests of many experts.

⚡ The Cross-Bronx Expressway opens through the East Tremont and Crotona Park sections, traversing the Harlem River valley via a new Alexander Hamilton Bridge and linking the 32-year-old George Washington Bridge with the Major Deegan Expressway and Harlem River Drive completed in the 1950s. Extending for seven miles, the 225-foot-wide Expressway has cost $250 million (the original estimate by Robert Moses was $47 million; just one mile of the Cross-Bronx has cost $40 million), and its construction has entailed the displacement of 60,000 people (*see* 1952). A neighborhood that once was solidly middle class is cut in half, people in the southern half find it difficult to reach stores on East Tremont Avenue, rent-controlled tenants move out, welfare families move in, and the area will quickly deteriorate into a slum as middle-class families leave the Grand Concourse and Mott Haven. The Bruckner traffic circle at the Expressway's eastern end will not be finished for another decade.

The city charter that takes effect January 1 entrusts a new Highways Department and an extended Public Works Department with constructing and maintaining city streets and sewers, taking that authority away from borough presidents. The change affects some 3,376 former borough employees and involves transferring 633 pieces of motorized construction and maintenance equipment along with 75 vehicles. The new Highways Department commissioner says pointedly that he will enforce a full day's work for a day's pay. The new department centralizes mechanical service and purchasing and institutes standardized procedures, dispatching men and equipment across borough lines for the first time; 45 percent of city streets still lack permanent paving, and about one-third still lack sewers.

The 15-year-old Idlewild Airport in Queens is renamed John F. Kennedy (JFK) Airport in the wake of the president's assassination at Dallas in November.

⚕ Overcrowding at the Willowbrook State School on Staten Island brings demands for state intervention (*see* 1952). Designed for 4,200 patients and hospital personnel, the facility now has more than 6,000 and conditions have deteriorated (*see* 1972).

∞ Some 67,000 Jehovah's Witnesses from the United States, Canada, and Latin America pack Yankee Stadium July 7 and 8 for speeches and prayers.

▐▌ Newspapers in the city resume publication April 1 after a 114-day strike by the International Typographical Union that has displaced 14,000 employees (*see* 1962). The union permits use of new technology in return for a small wage increase, most morning papers (but not the *News* or *Mirror*) increase their newsstand price from 5¢ to 10¢.

New York Times publisher Orvil E. Dryfoos vacations in Puerto Rico, is hospitalized in a suburb of San Jose, is flown home and taken directly to Columbia Presbyterian Hospital's Harkness Pavilion, and dies there of a heart ailment May 25 at age 50 (he has been living at 1010 Fifth Avenue); *Newsday* publisher Alicia Guggenheim (*née* Patterson) dies of a stomach ailment at Doctors Hospital July 2 at age 56.

The Hearst Corp.'s financially weakened *New York Mirror* ceases publication after 39 years October 16 ("Valachi Sings Here Today," reads the headline on its final edition), having built up a circulation surpassed in the United States only by that of the *Daily News*. The *Mirror* has until recently been selling 800,000 papers per day and more than 1 million on Sunday but losing money; daily circulation of the *News* is more than 2 million, more than 3 million on Sunday, and the *News* acquires the *Mirror*'s goodwill and most of its assets, including Al Capp's comic strip "Li'l Abner" (but not the Walter Winchell column, which moves to the *Journal-American*). Having once published more than 30 papers, the Hearst Corp. now puts out only 10 and has been losing money since 1957; it pays over $3.5 million to jobless employees, including about 300 editorial staff members, but the closing leaves close to 1,500 out of work. Night editor Mort Ehrman has been with the *Mirror* since 1925; he leaves the offices at 235 East 45th Street at 1:25 A.M., saying, "Well, gentlemen, good night. And before you leave, be sure to kill the bottles." The loss of the *Mirror* reduces the number of daily papers in the city to six, down from 16 at the turn of the century (*see* 1966).

Nonfiction: *Beyond the Melting Pot: The Negroes, Puerto Ricans, Jews, Italians, and Irish of New York City* by New York-born Harvard sociologist Nathan Glazer, 40, and his New York-born colleague Daniel Patrick Moynihan, 36. "New York will very likely in the end be an integrated area," Glazer writes, but the authors will write in a foreword to a 1970 edition of their book that they never imagined that blacks would want to be treated as a separate ethnic group and are "saddened and frightened" by the implications of this choice; *The Man Who Rode the Tiger: The Life and Times of Judge Samuel Seabury* by New York-born *New York Times* editorial writer Herbert Mitgang, 43; *Herbert H. Lehman and His Era* by Columbia University historian Allan Nevins, now 73; *The Fire Next Time* (essays) by James Baldwin; *America's Case of Middle Age: Columns, 1950–62* by Murray Kempton, who leaves the *New York Post* to join the editorial staff of the *New Republic*; *Can't Anybody Here Play This Game?* (a question attributed to New York Mets manager Casey Stengel) by Jamaica, Queens-born *New York Journal-American* sportswriter James "Jimmy" Breslin, 32, who quits the Hearst paper to become a *Herald Tribune* columnist.

The *New York Review of Books* begins publication in February, a second issue appears in April, and it is published on a bi-weekly basis starting September 26 with a third issue that includes drawings by David Levine. Poet Robert Lowell and his novelist wife,

Elizabeth Hardwick, who live in a colossal duplex apartment at 15 West 67th Street, had dinner during the newspaper strike in the spring with Random House editor Jason Epstein and his wife, Barbara, at the Epsteins' similar apartment a few doors down the street; together, they developed the idea of a periodical that would carry literate book reviews like the ones that ran in the strikebound *New York Times* and *Herald Tribune*, and the first issue was laid out on the Lowells' dining room table.

The Farrar, Straus publishing house founded in 1946 becomes Farrar, Straus & Giroux as New Jersey-born editor Robert Giroux, 50, becomes a partner. A 1936 Columbia University honors graduate, he was a lieutenant commander in the navy during World War II and was editor-in-chief of trade books for Harcourt, Brace from 1948 to 1955 before joining Farrar, Straus as editor-in-chief and director.

Journalist-author Herbert Asbury dies of arteriosclerosis at New York February 24 at age 71; author and civil-rights leader W. E. B. Du Bois becomes a naturalized Ghanaian citizen and dies at Accra August 17 at age 95; Carl Van Vechten dies at New York December 21 at age 84; A. J. Liebling of bronchial pneumonia at Mount Sinai Hospital December 28 at age 59. He has lived at 45 West 10th Street and is survived by his writer wife, Jean Stafford.

Fiction: *V* by Oyster Bay-born novelist Thomas Pynchon, 26, who will spend some years in California before returning to New York; *The Benefactor* by New York-born novelist-critic Susan Sontag, 30; *The Group* by Mary McCarthy; *Textures of Life* by Hortense Calisher; *Powers of Attorney* by Louis Auchincloss.

Juvenile: *Where the Wild Things Are* by Brooklyn-born illustrator-writer Maurice (Bernard) Sendak, 35.

Painting: *Homage to the Square "Curious"* by German-born New York painter Josef Albers, now 75, who was a master at Weimar's Bauhaus for 10 years until 1933 and has been a major force on U.S. painters and architects ever since; *Jackie (The Week That Was)* (silkscreen) by Andy Warhol; *Nomad* by James Rosenquist; *Map* by Jasper Johns; *Bicycle* (oil and silkscreen collage) by Robert Rauschenberg; *Red, Blue, Green* by Ellsworth Kelly; *Whaam!* and *Hopeless* by Roy Lichtenstein.

The Pace Gallery opens at 32 East 57th Street. Duluth-born art dealer Arne (originally Arnold B.) Glimcher, 25, married Mildred "Millie" Cooper in December 1959, opened a Boston gallery under the name Pace in 1960, and will represent such artists as

Chuck Close, Jean Dubuffet, Adolph Gottlieb, Donald Judd, Sol Lewitt, Agnes Martin, Elizabeth Murray, Louise Nevelson, Isamu Noguchi, Claes Oldenburg, Robert Rauschenberg, Ad Reinhardt, Bridget Riley, Mark Rothko, Robert Ryman, and Saul Steinberg (*see* PaceWildenstein, 1993).

The Marlborough Gallery opens in the Fuller Building on Madison Avenue at 57th Street. Vienna-born art dealer Frank Lloyd (originally Franz Kurt Levai), 52, fled from the Nazis in 1938, opened his first gallery at London after the war, using the name Marlborough, dealt initially in Impressionists, Post-Impressionists, and French modern masters, but soon shifted to contemporary art. His austere new gallery will become the world's richest and most important, representing Abstract Impressionists such as Adolph Gottlieb, Philip Guston, Robert Motherwell, Mark Rothko, and David Smith, with branches at Montreal, Toronto, Rome, and Zurich as well as London (*see* Rothko, 1970).

Sculpture: *Cinema* by George Segal, who adds lighting and sound effects to his work.

Theater: *The Milk Train Doesn't Stop Here Anymore* by Tennessee Williams 1/16 at the Morosco Theater, with English actress Hermione Baddeley, now 56, Mildred Dunnock, 69 perfs.; *Barefoot in the Park* by Neil Simon 10/23 at the Biltmore Theater, with Ocala, Fla.-born ingénue Elizabeth Ashley (originally Elizabeth Cole), 22, Robert Redford, Mildred Natwick, Kurt Kasznar, 1,502 perfs.; *The Ballad of the Sad Cafe* by Edward Albee (who has adapted the novel by Carson McCullers) 10/30 at the Martin Beck Theater, with Colleen Dewhurst, Woodbury, N.J.-born actor Roscoe Lee Browne, 38, Jenny Egan, 123 perfs.

The Broadway season that ends in May is the most disastrous in recent memory, investors having lost more than $5.5 million (according to figures supplied by investor Roger L. Stevens; other estimates range as high as $7 million). The Pulitzer Prize committee refuses to award any prize for drama, causing *New York Evening Post* critic John Mason Brown, 64, and John Gassner to resign from the committee (they have recommended Edward Albee's *Who's Afraid of Virginia Woolf?*).

Theater critic-playwright-novelist Stark Young dies at a Fairfield, Conn., nursing home January 6 at age 81; actor Monty Woolley of kidney and heart ailments at Albany May 6 at age 74; playwright Clifford Odets of cancer at Los Angeles August 14 at age 57; J. J. Shubert—last of the famous Shubert brothers— of a cerebral hemorrhage in his apartment atop the Sardi Building December 26 at age 86; Theatre Guild founder Lawrence Langner of an apparent heart attack at New York December 26 at age 72.

Films: Bud Yorkin's *Come Blow Your Horn* with Frank Sinatra, Lee J. Cobb, Molly Picon, Barbara Rush, Jill St. John; Robert Mulligan's *Love With the Proper Stranger* with Natalie Wood, Steve McQueen; Peter Tewksbury's *Sunday in New York* with Jane Fonda, Rod Taylor, Cliff Robertson, Robert Culp, James Gilmore "Jim" Backus. Also: Shirley Clarke's *The Cool World* (filmed on the streets of Harlem, it tracks the life of a young man who rises, briefly, to the leadership of a juvenile gang); Don Weis's *Critic's Choice* with Bob Hope, Lucille Ball.

The first New York Film Festival opens September 10 at Lincoln Center's Philharmonic Hall and continues until September 19 with an emphasis on foreign films, e.g., Yasujiro Ozu's *An Autumn Afternoon* (*Samma No Aji*), Luis Buñuel's *The Exterminator Angel* (*El Angel Exterminador*), Ermanno Olmi's *The Fiancés* (*I Fillamzati*), Masuko Kobayoshi's *Harakiri*, Robert Enrico's *In the Midst of Life* (*Au Coeur de la Vie*), Roman Polanski's *Knife in the Water*, Alain Resnais's *Muriel*, Joseph Losey's *The Servant*, and Robert Bresson's *The Trial of Joan of Arc* (*Le Procès de Jeanne d'Arc*). Boston-born *cinéaste* Richard Roud, 33, has organized the festival as a New York counterpart to the London Film Festival that he cofounded with the British Film Institute 4 years ago.

Broadway musicals: *Tovarich* 3/18 at the Broadway Theater, with Vivien Leigh, Jean-Pierre Aumont, Alexander Scourby, music by Lee Pockriss, lyrics by Anne Crowell, choreography by Herbert Ross, 254 perfs.; *She Loves Me* 4/23 at the Eugene O'Neill Theater, with Barbara Cook, Jack Cassidy, music by Jerry Bock, lyrics by Sheldon Harnick, songs that include "Days Gone By," 301 perfs.

Broadway songwriter Otto Harbach dies at New York January 24 at age 84; John "Ole" Olsen of Olsen and Johnson fame after a kidney-stone operation at Albuquerque, N.M., January 26 at age 71; William Gaxton after a 4-month illness at New York February 2 at age 69; Lew Leslie of arteriosclerosis at Orangeburg, N.Y., March 10 at age 73; Dave Stamper at Poughkeepsie August 18 at age 79.

Violinist Itzhak Perelman, now 27, makes his professional debut at Carnegie Hall 3/5 playing with the National Orchestra Association.

Former Metropolitan Opera conductor Fritz Reiner dies at New York November 15 at age 74. Born at Budapest, he led the Met orchestra from 1948 to

1953 and was renowned for his interpretations of Strauss and Wagner.

Popular songs: "On Broadway" by The Drifters; "When You're Far Away From New York Town" by Arthur Schwartz, lyrics by Howard Dietz; *The Freewheelin' Bob Dylan* (album) by Dylan, who has been sharing an apartment with Susan Rotol, 19, at 161 West Fourth Street. His songs "Boots of Spanish Leather" and "Don't Think Twice, It's All Right" have by some accounts been inspired by her, although his songs "Blowin' in the Wind" and "A Hard Rain's A-Gonna Fall" will become far better known.

 The New York Titans professional football team files for bankruptcy February 6 (*see* 1959), a five-man syndicate buys the team for $1 million March 15, the new owners sign former Baltimore Colts NFL coach Wilbur "Weeb" Ewbank, 55, to a 3-year contract as general manager and coach, and they change the team's name to the New York Jets April 15. Heading the syndicate is David A. "Sonny" Werblin, a director of the Monmouth Park Race Track (*see* 1969).

Emile Griffith loses his welterweight boxing title to Luis Rodriguez at Los Angeles March 21 in a 15-round decision but regains it at Madison Square Garden June 8 by winning a 15-round decision over Rodriguez (*see* 1962; 1966).

Louisiana-born Grambling State basketball player Willis Reed, 22, joins the New York Knickerbockers as a second-round draft choice, averages 19.5 points per game in his first season, is named NBA Rookie of the Year, and will be a Knick star for 10 years.

Rafael Osuna, 24, (Mex.), wins in men's singles at Forest Hills, Maria Bueno in women's singles.

The New York Mets wind up in the bottom of their National League division, winning 51 games and losing 111.

The New York Yankees win the American League pennant, but the Los Angeles Dodgers win the World Series, defeating the Yankees 4 games to 0 behind the pitching of Brooklyn-born hurler Sanford "Sandy" Koufax, 27, who strikes out 15 men in the first game to set a Series record (Whitey Ford and two Yankee relief pitchers strike out 10 for an unprecedented Series total of 25 in a single game).

● The Princeton Club moves in February into new nine-story limestone clubhouse at 15 West 43rd Street, having leased rooms for the past few years in the Columbia University Club across the street (*see* 1922). By the end of the century the club will have a worldwide membership of about 7,000.

Montreal-born New York fashion designer Scaasi (originally Arnold Martin Isaacs), 32, opens a salon specializing in costly custom clothing. He has heretofore designed ready-to-wear fashions for men, women, and children, and his *haute couture* shop will for decades be the only one of its kind.

Society ball organizer Elsa Maxwell dies at New York November 1 at age 80; socialite Consuelo Vanderbilt (Mrs. Jacques Balsan) at Southampton, L.I., December 6 at age 88.

 Mob boss Anthony "Tough Tony" Anastasio dies of a heart attack at Brooklyn March 1 at age 57. He has been a vice president of the International Longshoremen's Association, AFL-CIO.

Newsweek copy girl Janice Wylie, 21, and her grade-school teacher roommate Emily Hoffert, 23, are brutally clubbed and stabbed to death August 28, apparently during an attempted burglary of their apartment at 57 East 88th Street. The perpetrator leaves no fingerprints or other physical clues and police are baffled (*see* 1964).

Bayonne, N.J., salad oil king Anthony De Angelis, 47, is indicted for fraud. His Allied Crude Vegetable Oil & Refining Corp. has rigged its tanks, using seawater in place of salad oil that served as collateral for warehouse receipts. The deficiency runs to 827,000 tons of oil valued at $175 million. De Angelis goes bankrupt and some investors are ruined.

 The 58-story Pan Am Building (Met Life Building beginning in 1991) is completed at 200 Park Avenue, between 44th and 45th streets, replacing the Grand Central Terminal Office Building. Designed by Emery Roth & Sons with help from architects Pietro Belluschi and Walter Gropius, the octagonal-shaped structure has a precast concrete curtain wall and 2.4 million square feet of floor space—more than the 30-year-old RCA Building (2.3 million), much more than the 32-year-old Empire State Building (1.8 million), and the highest square footage yet, making it the world's largest commercial office building. Pan American World Airways occupies 15 floors, but the building's size raises protests that it blocks the vista of Park Avenue.

The 32-story Bankers Trust Building is completed at 280 Park Avenue, between 48th and 49th streets. Industrial designer Henry Dreyfuss has drawn the plans for the International Style structure with help from Emery Roth & Sons (but the bank continues to use the pyramid of its 1912 building at 16 Wall Street as its logotype). A branch of Bankers Trust completed at the northeast corner of 66th Street and Columbus Avenue to designs by Oppenheimer,

Brady & Lehrecke will later become a branch of Bank Leumi.

The 38-story U.S. Plywood Building is completed at 777 Third Avenue, between 48th and 49th streets. Designed in International Style by William Lescaze, it replaces a row of tenements.

Twelve new Manhattan office buildings give the city 6.2 million square feet of additional floor space.

Demolition of Penn Station begins in October (*see* 1961). The City Planning Commission has held hearings in January on whether or not to grant a zoning variance for a sports arena to be built on the site, but the commission has no jurisdiction over the preservation of architecture, nor can it determine whether a company has the right to tear down its building and sell the land. "Any city gets what it admires, will pay for, and ultimately deserves," the *New York Times* editorializes October 10. "We want and deserve tin-can architecture in a tin-horn culture. And we will probably be judged not by the monuments we build but by those we have destroyed." A letter from the Pennsylvania Railroad's president responds by asking, "Does it make any sense to preserve a building merely as a monument?" Some 84 Doric columns, 17 million bricks, and 660,000 cubic feet of pink Milford granite, marble, travertine, and stone will be carted off to New Jersey's Meadowlands by the summer of 1966; 22 American eagles, carved in stone and weighing 5,700 pounds, will be given other homes, some in the Central Park Zoo, others as far west as Kansas City (*see* Landmarks Preservation Act, 1965).

Owners of some Manhattan luxury apartment houses "modify" rents early in the year in efforts to fill up their buildings—the first real cuts since the building boom began soon after World War II. The 21-story Parker Crescent at 225 East 36th Street now being built by Jack Parker cuts $23 to $33 off monthly rents of its 113 two-room and 2½-room units, making the rent $119 instead of $142 for the two-room apartments and $129 instead of $162 for the 2½-room apartments (neither has a separate bedroom). Rents for larger apartments range from $207 (one bedroom) to $258 (two bedrooms).

The 27-story Mayfair Towers apartment house is completed at 15 West 72nd Street, just west of the Dakota (*see* 1961). Investor Louis J. Glickman has put up the white-brick building that replaces the Dakota's gardens and tennis courts.

The 20-story Herbert H. Lehman Village (four buildings) dedicated in September occupies an East Harlem area bounded by Park and Madison avenues between 106th and 110th streets. The Kennedy administration has just launched a campaign to induce Congress to approve new funds for low-rent public housing; Robert C. Weaver, administrator of the Housing and Home Financing Agency, is the president's chief adviser on housing and warns that a halt in the program will mean "the continued shame of needless poverty and misery in the richest land the world has ever known."

The City Housing Authority begins converting run-down tenements in the West Side Renewal Area (*see* 1962). It takes four buildings at 48-54 West 94th Street and converts them into 40 new apartments that rent for between $43 and $79 per month, including utilities.

The Big Six towers go up in Woodside, Queens, where the seven 17- and 18-story co-operative apartment houses have been sponsored by the city's Typographical Union Local 6 and contain 975 units. The city-subsidized buildings cover an area bounded by Queens Boulevard and the Laurel Hill Boulevard access to the Brooklyn-Queens Expressway between 59th and 61st streets.

Trump Village is completed in Coney Island for builder Fred C. Trump, now 60, who adds 3,800 middle-income units to his portfolio. Architect Morris Lapidus has designed the 23-story complex with an initial 2,484 units. Trump often does his own exterminating to cut costs, and rather than pay $2 per bottle for floor cleaners he has had all the commercial floor-cleaning products analyzed, discovered their ingredients, and had his own cleaners made for him at 50¢ per bottle.

Real estate developer and builder Harry Lefrak dies at Doctors Hospital July 1 at age 78 (*see* Lefrak City, 1930). He has put up some 400 middle-income buildings in the metropolitan area and has lived with his family at 103-25 68th Avenue, Forest Hills. His son Samuel J. (Jayson) LeFrak (as written by a French-born physician on his birth certificate in 1918) took over the family business in 1948 and has been putting up clusters of six-story apartment houses close to schools, shopping, and subways. He has engaged architect Jack Brown to resume work on the Lefrak City complex alongside the Horace Harding Expressway, putting his name in huge orange letters atop the red-brick project and advertising it with a big rental sign that says "If We Lived Here, Daddy, You'd Be Home By Now." Lefrak City will grow to have 20,000 middle-class residents, making it the largest privately developed complex in the country; occupancy was initially all white but will be 25 percent black by 1972 and 70 percent black by 1976.

The 45-story New York Hilton opens on the west side of the Avenue of the Americas between 53rd and 54th streets. Designed in International Style by William B. Tabler, it has 2,200 rooms, a conference center, and a six-story Executive Tower.

The Regency Hotel opens at 540 Park Avenue, northwest corner 61st Street, with 20 floors plus penthouse containing 500 rooms (111 suites and 250 other luxury guest rooms). Built and operated by Loews Hotels, it will become known beginning in March 1966 for its "power breakfasts" but will also be popular with government leaders, business executives, and entertainment names (its California suite, occupying some 1,000 square feet, will always be in demand, and the hotel will sometimes be called "Hollywood East").

"You Don't Have to Be Jewish to Enjoy Levy's Real Jewish Rye," say headlines in advertisements for Levy's Bakery, whose facilities have moved to 115 Thames Street, Brooklyn (see 1888). Doyle, Dane, Bernbach copywriter Judith Protas and art director Bill Taubman have created the campaign.

Elaine's opens in April at 1703 Second Avenue. Restaurateur Elaine Kauffman, 35, will attract literati and other celebrities for more than 30 years.

Malachy's opens at the corner of Third Avenue and 64th Street under the management of bearded, Irish-raised bartender and raconteur Malachy McCourt, 31 (year approximate). His pioneer "singles bar" is an immediate success, attracting young women from the nearby Barbizon Hotel at 63rd Street and Lexington Avenue, whose beaux flock to the place. It is soon serving patrons from all over the city (see T.G.I. Friday's, 1965).

Nippon opens at 145 East 52nd Street—the first restaurant in the city to serve rigorously authentic Japanese fare not geared to American tastes. Head chef Eigiro Tanaka has been chef to the Japanese prime minister Shigeru Yoshida and will head Nippon's kitchen staff until his death in 1978. Nippon introduces the *sushi* bar to New York and will originate *negimayaki* (scallion-filled beef roll).

1964 The New York World's Fair opens April 22 in Flushing Meadow Park, site of the 1939–1940 fair, and attracts more than 27 million visitors by the time it closes its first season October 18. Denied sponsorship by the Bureau of International Expositions, the World's Fair Corp. headed by Robert Moses has leased the park from the city, issued $29.8 million in bonds to finance it, and borrowed $24 million in city funds that will never be repaid. Mayor Wagner last year appointed onetime newspaperman and public-relations executive Thomas J. Deegan, Jr., now 53, chairman of the fair, and Deegan has sold 28 million advance tickets for a gross revenue of $35 million (he persuaded Pope John XXIII that the Vatican should have a pavilion, and he has been instrumental in having the Vatican loan Michelangelo's 1501 sculpture *Pietà*, viewed by 14 million fairgoers). A Unisphere designed by Buckminster Fuller is the symbol of the new exposition, which has exhibits from 80 countries, the U.S. government, 24 states, New York City (whose pavilion includes a three-dimensional panorama showing every building in all five boroughs), and 50 corporations, including AT&T, Ford, General Electric, General Motors, IBM, Johnson's Wax, and Pepsi-Cola; its theme is "Peace Through Understanding," and the world is in a relatively peaceful state except for Brazil (where a military coup has overthrown the president) and Southeast Asia, but the Tonkin Gulf Resolution approved by Congress August 7 threatens to make Vietnam a new U.S. battleground.

Mayor Wagner's wife, Susan (*née* Edwards), dies of lung cancer at New York March 2 at age 54; Gen. Douglas MacArthur at Washington, D.C., April 5 at age 84. He has lived since 1951 in Suite 37A of the Waldorf Towers; former president Herbert C. Hoover dies at New York October 20 at age 90. He has made his home in Suite 31A of the Waldorf Towers.

Gov. Rockefeller's wife, Happy, gives birth to his son shortly before the June 2 California presidential primary; he had been heavily favored to win his

The city's third World's Fair proved a financial fiasco for Robert Moses but left Queens with a landmark.

party's nomination at the Republican Convention, but he is jeered by the crowd on the convention floor at San Francisco's Cow Palace while Happy looks on. Right-wing senator Barry M. Goldwater, 55, of Arizona narrowly defeats Rockefeller and receives the nomination after saying in a speech, "I would remind you that extremism in the defense of liberty is no vice. And . . . moderation in the pursuit of justice is no virtue." President Johnson wins election in his own right with the largest popular vote plurality in history, receiving 61 percent of the popular vote and 486 electoral votes in a landslide victory over Goldwater, who breaks the Democratic Party's control of the once "Solid" South. The Rockefellers return to their country house at Kykuit in Pocantico.

Rep. Adam Clayton Powell, Jr. wins election to an 11th term but is outpolled in Manhattan's 18th district by President Johnson.

Former mayor William O'Dwyer dies at New York November 24 at age 74.

Militant blacks stall their cars on roads approaching the World's Fair April 22 and tie up the subway system in an effort to dramatize the cause of civil rights. The Civil Rights Act signed by President Johnson July 2 not only prohibits racial discrimination in employment, places of public accommodation, publicly owned facilities, union membership, and federally funded programs but also, in Title VII, forbids sex discrimination in the workplace (see 1971).

Harlem has a race riot July 18 and violence erupts in an eight-block area between Eighth and Lenox avenues from 123rd Street to 127th. An apartment house super at 215 East 76th Street sprayed some black children with a watering hose; Robert F. Wagner, Jr. High School student James Powell, 15, chased him into the building, Powell emerged with a penknife in his hand, and police lieutenant Thomas Gilligan shot Powell three times (he will later say Powell advanced on him with the knife), and the youth dies. Rev. Nelson C. Dukes, pastor of a Baptist church at 158 West 126th Street, calls for a march down Seventh Avenue to the 123rd Street precinct house, demanding that Lieut. Gilligan be arrested on a murder charge. A crowd outside the police station chants, "Killer cops must go! Police brutality must go! Murphy [Police Commissioner Michael J. Murphy] must go!" Police fire at people throwing bricks and bottles at them from rooftops, the streets are covered with broken glass and overturned garbage cans, and at least 30 demonstrators are arrested. Says *Newsweek* magazine August 4, "Almost in a matter of minutes, Central Harlem was

aflame. Rioters raged madly through the streets, scattering as police counterattacked, regrouping to charge again. Rocks, bricks, and garbage can lids rained down on the cops. Bottles looped down from tenement rooftops, popping on the pavement . . . trashcans were set afire . . . Looters—some in organized gangs—smashed store windows, climbed inside, and crawled out with armloads of trophies: food, clothing, shoes, jewelry, radios—and rifles."

Philadelphia, Miss., makes headlines in early August with the discovery of the bodies of three civil-rights workers killed by white supremacists. James E. Chaney, 21; Michael H. Schwerner, 24; and New Yorker Andrew Goodman, 20, have been missing since June 21.

Haryou (Harlem Youth Unlimited)-ACT (Associated Community Teams) works to increase living standards in Manhattan's black community (see Head Start, 1962). Rep. Adam Clayton Powell, Jr. has persuaded the House Committee on Education and Labor to provide Kenneth B. Clark's Haryou with a grant of $230,000, the city has granted $100,000, and Haryou focuses on education, job training, and lobbying, but Clark resigns as director within a month, charging that Rep. Powell has "seized control of the organization to use for his own purposes;" ACT puts its emphasis on organizing neighborhood boards and staging rent strikes; both will continue those efforts until 1968.

Wall Street's Dow Jones Industrial Average closes December 31 at 874.13, up from 762.95 at the end of 1963.

Retailer Max Fortunoff and his wife, Clara, open a store at Westbury, L.I., selling fine jewelry and silverware (see 1922). Now 67 and 62, respectively, they have followed the advice of their son Alan M., 31, who received a bachelor's degree in business from New York University in 1953 and a degree from NYU's law school 9 years ago (see Fifth Avenue, 1979).

The Verrazano-Narrows Bridge opens across the harbor November 21 to link Brooklyn with Staten Island (see Brooklyn Bridge, 1883; Goethals and Outer Crossing bridges, 1928; George Washington Bridge, 1931; Bayonne Bridge, 1931). Designed by engineer Othmar H. Ammann, now 85, and built at a cost of $325 million (including the cost of land acquisition), the double-decked, 4,260-foot (1,298-meter) bridge carries a six-lane roadway as much as 228 feet above the harbor's mean high point; its four cables weigh nearly 10,000 tons each, they hang from towers that rise 690 feet into the air, and the world's largest single-span suspension bridge will remain the largest until 1981.

The Medicare Act signed by President Johnson July 30 at Independence, Mo., sets up the first government-operated health insurance program for Americans age 65 and over. The American Medical Association has opposed the amendment to the Social Security Act of 1935; funded by payroll deductions, federal subsidies, and (initially) $3 per month in individual premiums, Medicare covers 20 million seniors (mostly women, since they outlive men).

Methadone helps rehabilitate heroin addicts. Rockefeller Institute researcher Vincent P. Dole, 51, and psychiatrist Marie Nyswander employ a synthetic opiate invented by German chemists during World War II, some 1,000 addicts will be enrolled in methadone maintenance programs by 1968, nearly 10,000 will be on methadone by 1970, but heroin addiction will remain a source of crime in New York and other U.S. cities, where the need to support their costly habit will drive addicts to burglary, robbery, and prostitution (see 1974).

Unitarian minister-pacifist-NAACP and ACLU cofounder John Haynes Holmes dies at New York April 3 at age 84.

Civil rights leader Malcolm X makes a pilgrimage to Mecca and writes home April 17 describing crowds "of all colors, bowing in unison," saying that he was "not conscious of color [race] for the first time in my life." After returning from two trips to Africa and the Middle East he changes his name again, this time to El-Hajj Malik El-Shabazz (see human rights, 1965).

Roman Catholic churches throughout the city change their liturgy November 29 to include use of English in some prayers (the Vatican's Ecumenical Council voted in mid-October of last year to permit use of the vernacular in some sacraments, including confirmation, matrimony, and baptism; priests continue to say, after the given name of an infant, *"Te baptiso in nomine patris et filii et spiritus sancti,"* the entire mass will be in English by Easter 1970, but some priests will defy the Vatican and stick to Latin.

Trustees of the 45-year-old Dalton School hire New York-born Columbia University assistant dean (and author) Donald Barr, 43, as headmaster. A believer in rigid discipline and strong control by parents, Barr will move Dalton away from its original progressive-school philosophy. It will admit boys to its high school beginning in 1969 and by the 1990s will have an enrollment of 1,290 from kindergarten through grade 12 (see Nonfiction, 1971).

The U.S. Supreme Court rules unanimously May 9 that a public official cannot recover libel damages for criticism of his public performance without proving deliberate malice. The decision in *New York Times v. Sullivan* bolsters press freedom in America.

Newspaper publisher Roy W. Howard dies following a heart attack at his Park Avenue office November 20 at age 81.

Nonfiction: *The Story of New York* by local author Susan Elizabeth Lyman, 58; *At the Pleasure of the Mayor: Patronage and Power in New York City 1898–1958* by Alabama-born Cornell University historian Theodore Jay Lowi, 33; *New York Proclaimed* by English author V. S. (Victor Sawden) Pritchett, 64, with photographs by Evelyn Hofer; "New York at 6:30 P.M." by Dorothy Parker in the November issue of *Esquire* magazine is about painter John Koch.

Fiction: *Up the Down Staircase* by Russian-born New York schoolteacher-humorist Bel Kaufman, 53, who has expanded her magazine piece "From a Teacher's Wastebasket" that appeared last year. Her book will be translated into 16 languages, go through 47 printings in the next 35 years, and sell more than 6 million copies; *Last Exit to Brooklyn* by New York novelist Hubert Selby, 38 (a London court convicts Selby of obscenity but he wins reversal on appeal); *The Rector of Justin* by Louis Auchincloss.

Novelist Nella Larsen dies of heart failure at New York March 30 at age 72, having worked as a nurse in Manhattan hospitals for the past 20 years; Carl Van Vechten dies at New York December 21 at age 84.

Juvenile: *Charlie and the Chocolate Factory* by Roald Dahl.

Painting: *Retroactive I* by Robert Rauschenberg; *According to What* (oil on canvas with objects) and *Numbers, 1964* by Jasper Johns; *Fez* by Frank Stella; *Rising Moon* by Hans Hofmann; *Brillo Boxes* and *Shot Orange Marilyn* (silkscreen) by Andy Warhol. (A woman has walked into Warhol's Factory, taken off a pair of white gloves, pulled out a pistol, and shot a hole through a stack of four Marilyn Monroe paintings with various colored backgrounds—red, orange, light blue, and sage green. One with a turquoise background is not in the stack.) Lumber executive and modern art collector Anson Conger Goodyear dies at Old Westbury, L.I., April 24 at age 86; painter Stuart Davis at New York June 24 at age 69, a few months before his work appears on the first U.S. postage stamp with an abstract design.

Sculpture: *Homage to the 6,000,000* by Louise Nevelson. Sculptor Alexander Archipenko dies at New York February 25 at age 76.

Theater: *After the Fall* by Arthur Miller 1/23 at the ANTA Theater-Washington Square, with Jason Robards, Jr., Los Angeles-born actress Barbara (Ann) Loden, 26, David Wayne, Cleveland-born actor Hal Holbrook, 38, Salome Jens, Ralph Meeker, Ruth Attaway, Ocala, Fla.-born actress Faye Dunaway, 23, New York-born actress Zohra Lampert, 26, 208 perfs.; *Any Wednesday* by New York playwright Muriel Resnik 2/18 at the Music Box Theater, with Sandy Dennis, Gene Hackman, Rosemary Murphy, 982 perfs.; *But for Whom Charlie* by S. N. Behrman 3/12 at the ANTA Theater-Washington Square, with Salome Jens, Jason Robards, Jr., Barbara Loden, Ralph Meeker, David Wayne, 39 perfs.; *Dutchman* by Newark, N.J.-born playwright LeRoi Jones (Imanu Amiri Baraka), 29, 3/24 at the Cherry Lane Theater; *Benito Cereno* by poet-playwright Robert Lowell, now 47, 4/1 at the American Place Theater in St. Clements Church; *Blues for Mr. Charlie* by James Baldwin 4/23 at the ANTA Theater, with Pat Hingle, Texas-born actor Rip Torn (originally Elmore Rual Torn, Jr.), 33, Diana Sands, 148 perfs.; *The Subject Was Roses* by Bronx-born playwright Frank D. (Daniel) Gilroy, 39, 5/25 at the Royale Theater, with Dayton, Ohio-born actor Martin Sheen (originally Ramon Estevez), 23, Malden, Mass.-born actor Jack Albertson, 53, New York-born actress Irene Dailey, 43, 832 perfs.; *The Sign in Sidney Brustein's Window* by Lorraine Hansberry 10/15 at the Longacre Theater, with Barbados-born actor Gabriel Dell, 45, Rita Moreno, Alice Ghostley, New York-born actor Dolph Sweet, 44, 101 perfs.; *Slow Dance on the Killing Ground* by Ohio-born playwright William Hanley, 33, 11/3 at the Plymouth Theater, 88 perfs.; *Luv* by Brooklyn-born playwright Murray Schisgal, 37, 11/11 at the Booth Theater, with New York-born actor Alan Arkin (originally Roger Short), 30, Eli Wallach, Allegheny, Pa.-born actress Anne Jackson, 28, 901 perfs.; *Tiny Alice* by Edward Albee 12/30 at the Billy Rose Theater, with English actor John Gielgud, now 60, Irene Worth, 167 perfs.

New York State Theater opens in Lincoln Center April 23 with 2,729 seats. Philip Johnson has designed the house.

Actor Joseph Schildkraut dies at New York January 21 at age 68; Frank Conroy of a heart attack at Paramus, N.J., February 24 at age 73; playwright Ben Hecht of a heart attack at his New York apartment April 18 at age 70; Winifred Lenihan at Sea Cliff,

L.I., July 27 at age 65; Sir Cedric Hardwicke of emphysema at New York August 6 at age 71.

Films: Delbert Mann's *Dear Heart* with Glenn Ford, Geraldine Page; George Roy Hill's *The World of Henry Orient* with Peter Sellers, Tippy Walker, Merrie Spaeth, Paula Prentiss, Angela Lansbury.

The Beatles arrive at New York and perform to a sold-out audience at Carnegie Hall 2/12 with songs that include "I Want to Hold Your Hand." The Liverpool rock group includes songwriters John Lennon, 22, and Paul McCartney, 20, who are supported by George Harrison, 20, and drummer Ringo Starr (originally Richard Starkey), 24; The Rolling Stones who make their Carnegie Hall debut 6/20 are another English rock group. Taking their name from the Muddy Waters song "Rolling Stone Blues," they include leader Michael Philip "Mick" Jagger, 19, drummer Charlie Watts, and bass guitarist Bill Wyman.

Broadway musicals: *Hello, Dolly!* 1/16 at the St. James Theater with Carol Channing, sets by Oliver Smith, music and lyrics by Jerry Herman, 2,844 perfs.; *Funny Girl* 3/26 at the Winter Garden Theater, with Barbra Streisand as the late Fanny Brice, Kay Medford, music and lyrics by Jule Styne and Bob Merrill, songs that include "People," "Don't Rain on My Parade," 1,348 perfs.; *Fiddler on the Roof* 9/22 at the Imperial Theater, with Zero Mostel, choreography by Jerome Robbins, music by Jerry Bock, lyrics by Sheldon Harnick, songs that include "If I Were a Rich Man," "Tradition," "Matchmaker, Matchmaker," "Sunrise, Sunset," 3,242 perfs.

Carol Haney dies of pneumonia and diabetes complications at New York Hospital May 10 at age 30; composer Cole Porter following kidney-stone surgery at Santa Monica, Calif., October 16 at age 71.

Paris-born cello prodigy Yo-Yo Ma, 9, makes his Carnegie Hall debut 12/17. He has begun studies at Juilliard under cellist Leonard Rose.

Pianist-composer and Kodachrome co-inventor Leopold Damrosch Mannes dies on Martha's Vineyard August 11 at age 64.

Popular songs: "Don't Forget 127th Street" by New York composer Charles Adams, lyrics by Lee Strouse; "It Ain't Me, Babe" and "Mr. Tambourine Man" by Bob Dylan.

Songwriter Johnny Burke dies at New York February 25 at age 55.

English-born bridge expert Alan F. (Fraser) Truscott, 39, takes over the *New York Times* bridge column from Albert H. Morehead, who has written it since 1935. Truscott will continue the column into the 21st century.

The U.S. Olympic trials for the games at Tokyo are held at the World's Fair at the insistence of Robert Moses, who calls the fair an "Olympics of Progress."

Roy Emerson wins in men's singles at Forest Hills, Maria Bueno in women's singles.

Shea Stadium opens near the fairgrounds at Flushing, Queens, to replace the Polo Grounds and Ebbets Field. The 53,000-seat stadium for the 2-year-old Mets baseball team (and Jets football team) is named for lawyer William A. Shea, whose cronies receive food, beer, and parking franchises.

New York Yankees co-owner Dan Topping makes Ralph Houck general manager and Yogi Berra field manager; Topping and Del Webb sell their interest in the team to CBS for $12 million, Topping remains in command, and the Yankees win the American League pennant, but the St. Louis Cardinals win the World Series, defeating the Yankees 4 games to 3. Yankee rookie Mel Stottlemyre, 22, pitches all nine innings of the second game, wins it 8 to 0, and pitcher Jim Bouton, 25, wins the sixth, but St. Louis pitcher Bob Gibson, 28, is on the mound for a total of 26 innings, strikes out 31 men, and ninth-inning home runs by Mickey Mantle, third baseman Cletis Leroy "Clete" Boyer, 27, and shortstop Phil Linz, 25, fail to stop the Cards, even though Yankee second baseman Bobby Richardson has set a Series record with 13 hits. The Yankees will not win another pennant until 1977 (see 1972; Steinbrenner, 1973).

● *Vogue* magazine gives the miniskirt its imprimatur by showing it in its March issue.

Estée Lauder's Leonard Lauder launches a new line of cosmetics under the name Aramis (see 1946). Now 31, he aims the line at women but pulls it from the market when it fails to attract buyers and reintroduces it with great success as a fragrance for men (see Clinique, 1968).

▥ The Kitty Genovese case raises alarms about America's growing isolation, callousness, and inhumanity (see Jacobs book on cities, 1961). An attacker stalks Queens bar manager Catherine Genovese early in the morning of March 13; 38 of her Kew Gardens neighbors hear her wild calls for help; nobody interferes for fear of "getting involved," the neighbors watch from windows while Genovese is stabbed to death; nobody phones the police until half an hour later.

Brooklyn police arrest black delivery boy George Whitmore, 19, in April and say he has confessed to last August's murders of Janice Wylie and Emily Hoffert, but veteran Manhattan police detective Thomas J. Cavanagh, Jr., 50, notes that Whitmore has a low I.Q. but neither a police record nor a drug habit. "You have the wrong man," he says, and Whitmore later recants his confession amidst allegations of police beatings to force the confession. A jury will convict Richard Robles, a cat burglar and drug addict, and he will go to prison for life.

A Manhattan Grand Jury schedules a hearing for Mafia boss Joseph Bonanno October 21 but Bonanno disappears October 20 after having dinner with his lawyers. Now 59, he became a naturalized citizen in 1945 despite having entered the country illegally in 1924; his lawyers say he was kidnapped as he was entering the apartment house one of them occupied on Park Avenue at 36th Street (see 1966).

American Museum of Natural History attendant John Hoffman unlocks the heavy metal gate at the entrance to the Morgan Hall of Gems on the morning of October 30 and finds that thieves have broken into glass cases containing priceless gems. Among the missing stones is the world's largest blue star sapphire—the 563.35-carat Star of India. The thieves have also taken an 88-carat engraved emerald, a huge emerald "Easter egg" from 17th century Russia, some smaller emeralds, a 737-carat aquamarine, the 15-carat Eagle Diamond, and well over 100 other faceted and uncut diamonds. Los Angeles-born Miami beachboy-cat burglar Jack Roland "Murph the Surf" Murphy, 27, and his accomplices Allan D. Kuhn and Roger F. Clark checked out of their Stanhope Hotel room in early October, rented a large apartment in West 86th Street, and spent 10 days studying the museum's layout. While Clark waited outside in their white Cadillac on the night of October 29, Murphy and Kuhn scaled the rough granite wall to the fifth floor, swung down to a ledge outside the Hall of Gems on the fourth floor, and eluded the guards. An alarm battery had gone dead, the two men escaped with their loot, and they leave the next morning for Miami, but someone has overheard them say something in the elevator of their West 86th Street apartment and has told the police, Clark is arrested at New York, and FBI agents arrest the two others in Kuhn's Miami apartment (see 1965).

🏠 The 41-story 330 Madison Avenue office tower is completed at the northwest corner of 42nd Street to "modernistic" designs by Kahn & Jacobs for developer John J. Reynolds.

The 50-story 277 Park Avenue Building (initially the Chemical Bank–New York Trust Co. Building) is completed late in the year on the east side of the avenue between 47th and 48th streets, where it replaces the McKim, Mead & White-designed Heckscher Apartments that stood with their "acre of garden" from 1924 until late 1958. Stahl Equities Corp. has leased the block from the New York Central and New Haven railroads; Emery Roth & Sons has designed the structure in International Style.

The massive, windowless 21-story New York Telephone Co. Switching Center is completed at 811 Tenth Avenue, between 53rd and 54th streets, to International Style designs by Kahn & Jacobs (the floors are nearly double height so the building is as tall as the usual 40-story structure).

The City Council votes 27 to 7 February 18 to remove rent controls on luxury apartments renting for $250 or more per month (see 1958). It exempts those occupied by families of four or more. Landlords give assurances that they will exercise constraints in jacking up rents, but the initial increases in most buildings range from 25 percent to 100 percent, and the city will reinstitute a modified control plan in 1968 (see 1969).

The Condominium Ownership Law that takes effect March 2 gives legal status in New York State to a form of apartment ownership that has existed elsewhere in the country for decades (co-operatives have existed in the city since at least the 1880s and require no state authority since they are essentially business corporations created for the purpose of owning real estate on a co-operative basis). Condominium management boards, unlike co-op boards, will have little control over the quality of tenancy, making condominiums easier to buy and sell. Mayor Wagner has urged the legislature to extend the principle of condominium ownership to limited-profit projects developed by the city or state and to approve public loans to help individuals purchase condos.

The 24-story Chatham Towers co-operative apartment house is completed at 170 Park Row. Designed by Kelly & Gruzen for the Association for Middle Income Housing, the building has been financed under Title I of the Federal Housing Act for upper-middle-income families, it contains studios and one-, two- and three-bedroom units, windows are double-glazed with built-in venetian blinds, construction incorporates other measures for minimizing outside noise, and there is a 125-car garage in its basement.

The 35-story St. Tropez apartment house completed at 340 East 64th Street is the city's first major condominium residence. Put up between Second and First avenues at a time when the upper East Side has few high-rise buildings, it has 301 units; amenities include a concierge, full-service garage, roof deck, and health club with swimming pool.

The Polo Grounds stadium comes down to make way for apartment houses (built for the Giants in 1911, it has been used for football as well as baseball and for the past 2 years by the New York Mets baseball team).

A bill signed into law by President Johnson September 2 authorizes more than $1 billion in U.S. federal aid for housing and urban renewal through September 30 of next year (see 1963; HUD, 1965).

The Doral Park Avenue Hotel opens at 70 Park Avenue, northeast corner 38th Street. The 17-story, 204-room transient hotel, designed by Philip Birnbaum, has three penthouses, one of them for the owner, Alfred J. Kaskel, and his wife, Doris. They have owned the little Hotel 70 Park Avenue since the mid-1950s and have expanded by taking over the adjoining Dwight School building.

 The first Blimpie's fast-food restaurant opens April 4 at Hoboken, N.J. Entrepreneurs Anthony Conza, Peter DeCarlo, and Angelo Baldassere specialize in selling submarine sandwiches and are inspired by the sight of a lighter-than-air craft to name the place, whose first New York outlet will open at the corner of Eighth Avenue and 55th Street.

Le Périgord opens at 405 East 52nd Street. French-born owner Georges Briguet will attract not only East Side neighbors but also gastronomes from all over New York and other cities as well.

The Ginger Man (co-owner Patrick O'Neal has recently starred in a Broadway play of that name) opens in June in what was earlier a garage across from Lincoln Center at 51 West 64th Street, offering an à la carte menu that features omelettes at $2 and $2.50, hors d'oeuvres at 75¢ (with coquille $1.25), soups at 70¢, luncheon entrées at $2.75, dinner entrées at $4.25 (filet mignon is $4.50 at lunch or dinner), desserts mostly 75¢.

Benihana of Tokyo opens at 61 West 56th Street. The *teppinyaki-hibachi*-style steak, shrimp, mushroom, and bean sprouts restaurant operated by Japanese-born restaurateur Hiroaki "Rocky" Aoki, 25, meets with instant success and will be followed by Benihana (Red Flower) restaurants in other U.S. cities (see Benihana Palace, 1970). Aoki stopped at

New York en route to Rome 4 years ago as a member of Japan's Olympic wrestling team, ate at short-order hamburger grills, was struck with the idea that tabletop cooking as practiced in Tokyo's sukiyaki restaurants might appeal to Americans, obtained a degree in restaurant management at one of the city's community colleges, and has earned part of his initial investment by driving an ice-cream truck.

1965 The city observes Israel Independence Day May 7, beginning a tradition that will be marked in the future by scores of Jewish organizations marching in annual Salute to Israel Day parades up Fifth Avenue (*see* 1948).

A New York court convicts Robert S. Collier, 28, June 15 of having conspired to blow up national monuments, including the Statue of Liberty; he will serve 21 months of a 5-year sentence at Lewisburg Penitentiary.

Anti-war rallies October 15 draw crowds in four U.S. cities, but New York's demonstration attracts only about 400 participants outside the army induction center at 39 Whitehall Street; spectators jeer the speakers and one youth burns his draft card while federal agents look on. The Madison, Wis.-based National Coordinating Committee to End the War in Vietnam has organized the effort, and it has the support of Students for Democratic Action, Committee for Nonviolent Action, Socialist Workers Party, Youth Against War and Fascism, and the War Resisters League. State Supreme Court Justice Emilio Nuñez refuses to overrule a decision by Parks Commissioner Newbold Morris denying the New York chapter of the American Civil Liberties Union a permit for a protest rally in Central Park, but 600 City College students and faculty members stage a 2-hour rally preceded by a 4-hour silent vigil. Demonstrators estimated to number 10,000 to 20,000, most of them well dressed, parade down Fifth Avenue from 94th Street to 69th the next day (Saturday), carrying signs urging military withdrawal from Vietnam, and drawing cheers (along with sporadic physical attacks from about 1,000 hecklers, who tell the marchers to "support our boys in Vietnam," "bomb Hanoi," and "take a bath"); nearly 1,000 uniformed police officers and plainclothesmen prevent any escalation of the violence. Members of labor unions, the Students for a Democratic Society, the National Student Action Movement, the Women's Strike for Peace, and other groups, including scores of women wheeling perambulators, participate in the march, and many stay on into the evening to hear speeches by I. F. Stone and others urging negotiations to end the conflict in Indochina.

London-born New York lawyer Abraham (David) Beame, 59, wins the Democratic Party nomination for mayor, defeating Woodcliffe, N.J.-born City Council president Paul R. (Rogers) Screvane, 51, who at age 22 took a $35-per-week job driving a New York Sanitation Department truck and rose after serving heroically in World War II to become the department's youngest commissioner. Mayor Wagner has declined to run for a fourth term, Beame is the first Jewish mayoralty nominee since the city's consolidation in 1898, but he loses in the general election to Congressman John V. (Vliet) Lindsay, now 43, who runs on the Republican-Liberal-Independent Citizen lines. A handsome, six-foot-four-inch Yale graduate and Navy veteran who has backing from Gov. Rockefeller and Sen. Javits, Lindsay receives 1,149,106 votes to Beame's 1,046,699 (*see* 1966).

Malcolm X (El-Hajj Malik El-Shabazz) is shot dead February 21 at Harlem's Audubon Ballroom as he prepares to address a Sunday afternoon audience on the need for blacks and whites to coexist peacefully (*see* 1952). He broke relations with the Black Muslim sect last year and his modest 97th Street house in East Elmhurst, Queens, was fire-bombed earlier in February, endangering his pregnant wife, Betty Shabazz, and their four children. Three alleged assassins will be convicted next year of shooting the leader of the Organization of Afro-American Unity with a sawed-off shotgun, followed by a volley of .38- and .45-caliber bullets, but it will never be established whether or not they were members of the Black Muslim sect. Lenox Avenue will be renamed Malcolm X Boulevard in honor of the slain civil-rights leader.

The Social Service Employees Union brings 8,000 New York workers off the job from January 2 to February 1, winning salary increases, caseload reductions, a welfare fund for educational purposes, and an end to "midnight" raids on welfare recipients. New York City's welfare roll grows to 480,000. The number of welfare recipients will be 1.2 million by 1975, and the city's welfare agency will account for more than a quarter of the city's $12 billion budget with half the aid money reimbursed by the federal government.

Financier and sometime presidential adviser Bernard M. Baruch dies of a heart attack in his six-room apartment at 4 East 66th Street June 20 at age 94. He has lived in the apartment since giving up his Fifth Avenue mansion in 1946.

The New York World's Fair closes October 17 after a last-minute flurry of weekends when attendance soared to 500,000 per day, but in its second season the Fair has attracted only 17 million paying visitors, and critics blame Robert Moses for having lost millions of dollars through mismanagement.

Wall Street's Dow Jones Industrial Average closes December 31 at 969.26, up from 874.13 at the end of 1964.

Saks 34th Street closes in July on Herald Square and its three branches are turned into Gimbels stores (*see* Saks Fifth Avenue, 1924).

Alexander's department store opens south of Bloomingdale's at 731 Lexington Avenue, northeast corner 58th Street, and extends through to Third Avenue (*see* 1928). Emery Roth & Sons has designed the building for merchant George Farkas, now 63, and the store will sell at discount prices until it closes in 1992.

Macy's opens a Queens branch on Queens Boulevard between 55th and 56th streets. Designed by Skidmore, Owings & Merrill, the circular store is surrounded by a concentric parking garage.

New York retailers are hard hit by a 25-day newspaper strike in late summer and early fall.

The Diners Club of America founded at New York in 1950 reaches a membership of 1.3 million; American Express has 1.2 million after just 7 years, and major U.S. banks prepare to issue plastic credit cards (as opposed to the *charge* cards of Diners Club and American Express; *see* Franklin National Bank, 1951). Not only restaurants but also hotels, motels, airlines, travel agencies, car rental agencies, and many retail stores now honor the charge cards.

The Consolidated Edison plant that goes on line at Ravenswood, Queens, is powered by Big Allis—the largest electric generator in the world (*see* 1962). Made by Allis-Chalmers of Milwaukee, Wis., it uses conventional fuel sources and has a potential output of 1 million kilowatts—enough to supply nearly 2 million New York residents.

The worst power failure in history blacks out most of seven states and Ontario November 9, affecting 30 million people in an 80,000-square-mile area. New York's power fails at 5:27 o'clock in the afternoon, Brooklyn regains it at 2 the next morning, Queens at 4:20 in the morning, Manhattan at 6:58. Con Edison's revenues of $840 million make it the nation's largest utility, but its earnings have been growing at half the pace of a typical competitor. It assures the public that blackouts will not recur (*but see* 1977).

New York taxicab drivers strike March 24 (*see* 1956). The National Labor Relations Board supervises an election that results in victory for an AFL-CIO affiliate headed by Harry Van Arsdale, Jr., now 59, whose union will hereafter represent the drivers (*see* 1967). Taxicab pioneer Harry Nathaniel Allen dies at New York June 26 at age 88, having brought the first taximeter cabs to the city from Paris in 1907.

The New York Police Department adopts motor scooters to give its patrolmen greater mobility.

The S.S. *Michelangelo* and the S.S. *Raffaello* go into service for the Italian Line. The 45,911-ton sister ships are each 904 feet in length overall.

Bridge designer Othmar H. Ammann dies at suburban Rye September 22 at age 86.

The power blackout November 9 traps close to 800,000 subway riders below ground without lights for more than 12½ hours; thousands of others are trapped in office and apartment-house elevators.

A heliport opens late in the year on the roof of the 2-year-old Pan Am Building, despite protests that helicopters are too noisy, serve far too few people to justify the disturbance, and pose a safety hazard for midtown Manhattan. The helicopters provide service to Kennedy Airport, but the service will prove unprofitable and the facility will close in February 1968 (*see* 1977).

The 64-year-old Rockefeller Institute for Medical Research adopts the name Rockefeller University but continues to dedicate itself exclusively to graduate study, working with neighboring medical institutions (*see* 1959). Students pay no tuition, receiving annual stipends to pursue studies in cellular and molecular biology, biochemistry, genetics, immunology, neurobiology, mathematics, physics, and the behavioral sciences, with all activities centered about laboratory work.

The International Society for Krishna Consciousness is founded at New York by Calcutta chemist and Sanskrit scholar A. C. Bhaktivedanta, 59, whose followers call him Swami Prabhupada and regard him as the successor to an unbroken chain of Hindu spiritual teachers dating back 5,000 years. The swami has arrived in New York with $50 in rupees and a pair of cymbals, determined to spread the teachings of Lord Krishna, a supreme deity in Hindu mythology. He sits on a sidewalk in the East Village, begins the "Hare Krishna" chant that will soon become familiar throughout the world, offers young people a relatively ascetic life of devotion and proselytizing, an alternative to conventional society and drugs, and is soon holding religious classes in an empty storefront on Second Avenue, attracting youths who shave their heads, wear saffron-colored dhotis, and chant, "Hare Krishna . . ."

The Head Start program mandated by Congress begins May 18 to provide federally subsidized preschool preparation for needy children in New York and throughout the country (see 1962).

College and university enrollments swell as young New Yorkers take advantage of draft deferrals for students to escape the expanding war in Vietnam, but campuses are tense with unrest.

New York's first all-news radio programming begins April 19 on Westinghouse Broadcasting's WINS (see 1924). The station has been playing rock music with disc jockeys Alan Freed, Murray the K, and Cousin Brucie but has been losing market share. Other stations across the country will follow suit as radio becomes more specialized.

CBS News veteran Edward R. Murrow dies of lung and brain cancer at Pawling, N.Y., April 27 at age 57; radio news commentator H. V. Kaltenborn of a heart attack at Roosevelt Hospital June 14 at age 86; What's My Line panelist Dorothy Kilgallen appears on the TV show November 17 but is found dead at age 52 the next day in her town house off Park Avenue. A coroner's report blames a mixture of alcohol and sleeping pills. Buffalo-born Journal-American TV columnist John Dennis Patrick "Jack" O'Brien, 50, takes over Kilgallen's "Voice of Broadway" column, writing about couples headed for "splitsville" in the breezy style of his onetime mentor Walter Winchell; television pioneer Allen B. DuMont dies after a short illness at New York November 15 at age 64.

Cosmopolitan magazine names Helen Gurley Brown editor; she says its circulation has flagged because it has emphasized fiction, and beginning with the May issue she turns it into what some critics call an antifeminist equivalent of Playboy, with a monthly "Cosmopolitan Girl" photographed usually by Francesco Scavullo.

Model agency founder Harry S. Conover dies of a heart attack at New York July 21 at age 53, having created the term "cover girl."

New York's first automated newspaper vending machines are installed, in the Bronx. Within 15 years such machines will be seen everywhere in the city, putting pressure on newsstands.

The New York Post uses a computer June 24 to set stock quotations but is forced to suspend publication temporarily in a dispute with the International Typographers Union. Papers in other cities have used computers, but no New York paper has thus far dared to defy the ITU. Publisher Dorothy Schiff says the Post cannot survive without automation and pledges no loss of jobs, but she abandons her attempt August 24 after failing to reach agreement with the ITU. The American Newspaper Guild strikes the Times September 16, and the American Newspaper Publishers Association orders six other papers to close down. The Herald Tribune resigns from the ANPA for economic and other reasons and resumes publication September 26. The strike ends after 25 days as the Times unit of the Guild votes unanimously to accept a proposal by Theodore Kheel (the Times agrees to allow the Guild joint administration of an employee pension plan, guarantees jobs against automation and sub-contracting, and makes other concessions). The power blackout November 9 forces all New York newspapers except the Times to suspend publication (New Jersey has not lost power and the Times uses the facilities of the Newark Evening News across the river to get out a 10-page edition whose copy has been written by candlelight and lanterns). The National Labor Relations Board rules December 23 that seven of the city's papers have been guilty of unfair labor practices by refusing to bargain collectively with the ITU (see 1966).

Telephone companies maintain service during the power blackout November 9 and New York has a record 62 million phone calls in one day, nearly double the city's weekly average.

Nonfiction: The Autobiography of Malcolm X by the late Afro-American Unity leader and Ithaca-born writer Alex Haley, 43; Yes I Can by entertainer Sammy Davis, Jr., now 39, who lost an eye in an auto accident 11 years ago; Only One New York: The Unknown Worlds of the Great City by Brooklyn-born author Charles Samuels, illustrations by Belgian-born photographer Jan Yoor; Crossroads of the World (a history of Times Square) by New York author William Laas, 55; The Overreachers by Gay Talese is about New Yorkers, both "overreachers" and "underreachers;" La Guardia Comes to Power: 1933 by Arthur Mann; Boss Tweed's New York by Chicago-born University of Pennsylvania historian Seymour Mandelbaum, 29; Starting Out in the Thirties by Alfred Kazin; Joe Gould's Secret by Joseph Mitchell.

Fiction: Manchild in the Promised Land by Harlem author Claude Brown, 28, whose autobiographical novel chronicles the author's rise from a childhood of poverty and violent crime: "Throughout my childhood in Harlem, nothing was more strongly impressed upon me than the fact that you had to fight and that you should fight. Everybody would accept it if a person was scared to fight, but not if he was so scared that he didn't fight." The book will be translated into 14 languages and have sales of more than 4 million copies in Brown's lifetime; *An American Dream* by Norman Mailer, who moved from Manhattan to Brooklyn Heights in 1961; *The New York Ride* by New York-born novelist Anne Bernays (Kaplan), 34, daughter of the public-relations pioneer.

Novelist Dawn Powell dies of cancer at St. Luke's Hospital November 15 at age 67 and is interred in a mass grave on Hart Island, the city's potter's field. She has lived most recently in a Greenwich Village penthouse apartment at 95 Christopher Street, corner Bleecker Street that she could afford only with financial help from a friend.

Poetry: *The Old Glory* (three verse dramas based on stories by Herman Melville and Nathaniel Hawthorne) by Robert Lowell.

 Painting: *Campbell's Tomato Soup Can* and *'65 Liz* by Andy Warhol; "Op" art that creates optical illusions by using color, form, and perspective in bizarre ways becomes fashionable. Milton Avery dies at New York January 3 at age 71; Charles Sheeler at Dobbs Ferry May 7 at age 81 (a stroke ended his career 5 years ago).

Sculpture: *Woman Listening to Music* by George Segal; the Delacorte Musical Clock designed by Andrea Spadini and Edward C. Embury is installed outside the Central Park Zoo with bronze animals that move when the clock sounds the quarter hours.

The Huntington Hartford Gallery of Modern Art opens on the south side of Columbus Circle. Financed by the A&P supermarket heir and designed by Edward Durrell Stone, the $7.5 million pseudo-Venetian palazzo will fail as a museum (its representational art is generally of mediocre quality); Hartford will sell his collection for almost nothing in a depressed market and give the building away in 1969 to Fairleigh Dickinson University; the university will run it for 7 years as the New York Cultural Center, Gulf + Western will then buy it as a gift for the city, and it will become home to the New York City Department of Cultural Affairs and the Convention and Visitors' Bureau before finding other uses.

The Federal Aid to the Arts Act signed by President Johnson September 30 establishes a National Endowment for the Arts and Humanities funded by an initial 3-year appropriation of $63 million.

 Theater: *The Odd Couple* by Neil Simon 3/10 at the Plymouth Theater, with Walter Matthau as Oscar Madison, Art Carney as Felix Unger, 964 perfs.; *The*

Amen Corner by James Baldwin 4/15 at the Ethel Barrymore Theater, with Mississippi-born actress Beah Richards, 38, Juanita Hall, Frank Silvera, 84 perfs.; *Mrs. Dally Has a Lover* by William Hanley 9/22 at the John Golden Theater, with Arlene Francis, Ralph Meeker, Robert Foster, 52 perfs.; *Generation* by playwright William (Malcolm) Goodhart, 40, 10/6 at the Morosco Theater, with Henry Fonda, 299 perfs.; *Hogan's Goat* by playwright William Alfred, 43, 11/11 at the American Place Theater in St. Clements Church, with Ralph Waite, New York-born actor Cliff Gorman, 29, Faye Dunaway, 607 perfs.; *Cactus Flower* by Abe Burrows 12/8 at the Royale Theater, with Lauren Bacall, Barry Nelson, Brooklyn-born actress Brenda Vaccaro, 25, 1,234 perfs.

Playwright Lorraine Hansberry dies of cancer at New York January 12 at age 34; actor Pat Harrington, Sr., at New York September 2 at age 64.

The New York Public Library's Library of the Performing Arts opens on a partial basis in Lincoln Center July 15. Its Rodgers and Hammerstein Archives of Recorded Sound will contain 450,000 recordings of all kinds, its circulating collection will contain more than 150,000 books, scores, and recordings, and it will have an outstanding collection of reference books, manuscripts, photographs, scores, recordings, and videotapes related to cinema, music, dance, and the theater.

The Vivian Beaumont Theater opens in Lincoln Center October 21. Designed by the late Finnish-born architect Eero Saarinen, it has 1,140 seats. The Mitzi E. Newhouse Theater opens the same evening in Lincoln Center.

Films: Sidney Lumet's *The Pawnbroker* with Rod Steiger as Sol Nazerman, a survivor of Nazi prison camps who operates a Harlem pawnshop, Geraldine Fitzgerald, Brock Peters, Jaime Sanchez, Thelma Oliver, Juano Hernandez, Raymond St. Jacques, music by Quincy Jones; Fred Coe's *A Thousand Clowns* with Jason Robards, Jr., Barbara Harris, Barry Gordon, Martin Balsam, Gene Saks. Also: Richard Quine's *How to Murder Your Wife* with Jack Lemmon, Virna Lisi, Terry-Thomas.

Actress Judy Holliday dies of cancer at New York June 7 at age 42; Mary Boland at New York June 23 at age 83; Constance Bennett of a cerebral hemorrhage at a Fort Dix, N.J., hospital July 24 at age 61.

Broadway musicals: *Baker Street* 2/16 at the Broadway Theater, with Fritz Weaver as Sherlock Holmes, music and lyrics by Marian Grudeff and Raymond Jessel, 313 perfs.; *Flora the Red Menace* 5/11 at the

Alvin Theater, with Judy Garland's Los Angeles-born daughter Liza Minnelli, barely 19, in the title role (despite initial objections from producer George Abbott, now 77), music by John Kander, lyrics by New York-born writer Fred Ebb, 30, book by Abbott and Robert Russell based on Lester Atwell's novel *Love Is Just Around the Corner* (a spoof on the communist "peril" in America), songs that include "Express Yourself," "The Flame," "One Good Break," "A Quiet Thing," "Sing Happy," 87 perfs.; *The Roar of the Greasepaint—The Smell of the Crowd* 5/16 at the Shubert Theater, with London-born entertainer Anthony Newley, 33, Cyril Ritchard, book, music, and lyrics by Newley and London-born composer-lyricist Leslie Bricusse, 33, 231 perfs.; *Pickwick* 10/4 at the 46th Street Theater, with Welsh actor Harry Secombe, 44, in the title role, Charlotte Rae, music by Cyril Ornadel, lyrics by Leslie Bricusse, songs that include "If I Ruled the World," 56 perfs.; *Drat! The Cat!* 10/10 at the Martin Beck Theater, with New York-born actress-dancer Lesley Ann Warren, 19, Elliot Gould, music by Milton Schafer, lyrics by Ira Levin, songs that include "She (He) Touched Me," 8 perfs.; *On a Clear Day You Can See Forever* 10/17 at the Mark Hellinger Theater, with Barbara Harris, John Cullum, music by Burton Lane, lyrics by Alan Jay Lerner, songs that include the title song, 272 perfs.; *The Zulu and the Zayda* 11/10 at the Cort Theater, with Ossie Davis, Lou Gossett, Jr., Menasha Skulnik, music and lyrics by Harold Rome, 179 perfs.; *Skyscraper* 11/13 at the Lunt-Fontanne Theater, with Julie Harris as a brownstone owner who refuses to yield her property as a skyscraper goes up around her, book by Peter Stone (based on the 1945 Elmer Rice play *Street Scene*), music and lyrics by James Van Heusen and Sammy Cahn, 241 perfs.; *Man of La Mancha* 11/22 at the ANTA-Washington Square Theater, with Richard Kiley, Cleveland-born actress Joan Diener, Cincinnati-born actor Irving Jacobson, 67, Robert Rounseville, book by Wisconsin-born playwright Dale Wasserman, 48, based on the 1615 Cervantes novel *Don Quixote de la Mancha*, music by composer Mitch Leigh, 37, lyrics by New York-born writer Joe Darian, 54, songs that include "The Impossible Dream," "Dulcinea," and the title song, 2,329 perfs.

Vaudeville and musical-comedy veteran Eugene Howard dies at New York August 1 at age 84, survived by his brother Willie.

Ballet dancer-choreographer Twyla Tharp, 24, breaks with the Paul Taylor Dance Company after 3 years and becomes a freelance choreographer with her own modern-dance troupe.

An Evening with P.D.Q. Bach 4/24 at Town Hall features comedian-composer-conductor Prof. Peter Schickele, 30, who parodies classical composers and begins a New York holiday tradition that will continue for at least 32 years. Once a bassoonist with the Fargo Morehead Symphony Orchestra, Schickele has taught a Literature and Materials of Music course at the Juilliard School and been writing music since his own student days. He says, tongue in cheek, that P.D.Q. Bach (1807–1742) (sic) was the youngest son of Johannes, and his concert includes Bach's Piano Concerto in B flat (The Elivira Mulligan Concerto), the Gross Concerto for flute (S. 2), Symphonia Concertante (S. 98.6), a fully staged half-act of Bach's opera *The Stoned Guest*, and the Toot Suite in C minor. Schickele will perform at Carnegie Hall and (twice) at Philharmonic Hall in late December of next year with "newly discovered" works that include the Oratorio of the Seasonings (S.-tsp.), Echo Sonata for Two Unfriendly Groups of Instruments (a brass ensemble in the balcony opposes an onstage woodwind trio), and the Perücke Strücke Hair Piece from P.D.Q.'s only opera *The Civilian Barber* (S. V05). Later concerts will include the Chaconne à son gout (wherein Prof. Schickele will play the organ pedals manually while two assistants work the keyboards above and pull stops) and Concerto for Horn and Hardart (S. 27), containing a third movement entitled *Menuetto con Banna y Zucchero* (Minuet with Cream and Sugar), and the cantata *Iphigenia in Brooklyn*.

Seattle-born folk singer-guitarist-songwriter Judith Marjorie "Judy" Collins, 25, makes her Carnegie Hall debut 2/18 with songs that include "Wild Mountain Thyme."

Puerto Rico-born Lutheran clergyman John G. Gensel (originally Juan Garcia Velez), 48, asks for and receives special designation as Pastor of the Jazz Community in New York City. He came to the city in 1956 to assume duties at the Advent Lutheran Church, took a course in jazz history taught by Marshall Stearns at the New School for Social Research, has frequented Greenwich Village and Harlem nightclubs, and has become a close friend of musicians who include Duke Ellington and Billy Strayhorn. The Lutheran Board of American Missions lets Gensel devote half his time to ministering to the jazz community and half to his church duties (*see* 1970).

Popular songs: "The Sounds of Silence" by New York-born songwriters Paul Simon, 24, and Art Garfunkel, 25; "Like a Rolling Stone" by Bob Dylan.

Bandleader Emil Coleman dies of a kidney infection at New York January 26 at age 72; jazz pianist Nat

King Cole after surgery for removal of a lung at Santa Monica, Calif., February 15 at age 45; songwriter Harry Tierney of a heart attack at New York March 22 at age 74; bandleader Claude Thornhill of a heart attack at Caldwell, N.J., July 1 at age 55; composer Spencer Williams at Flushing, Queens, July 14 at age 75; jazz pianist-composer Clarence Williams of diabetes at New York November 6 at age 67.

 Louisiana-born Grambling State basketball star Willis Reed, 22, finishes his first season with the New York Knickerbockers (the Knicks acquired him as a second-round draft pick) and is named National Basketball Association rookie of the year, having averaged 19.5 points per game (see 1970).

Sports announcer Bill Slater dies at New Rochelle January 25 at age 62; Giants football team president John V. "Jack" Mara of cancer at New York June 29 at age 57.

Manuel Santana, 27, (Spain) wins in men's singles at Forest Hills, Margaret Smith in women's singles.

● Cosmetics queen Helena Rubinstein dies at New York April 1 at age 94.

 Police recover most of the jewels stolen last October from the American Museum of Natural History in January from a locker in Miami's Greyhound bus terminal (see 1964). Jewel thief Allan D. Kuhn has turned state's evidence, his two accomplices have also agreed to co-operate with authorities, all three men are sentenced April 6 to 3 years at the Rikers Island Correctional Facility, billionaire insurance man John D. MacArthur donates the $25,000 ransom demanded by "fences" holding the DeLong Star Ruby, the diamonds will never be recovered, and Jack "Murph the Surf" Murphy will wind up serving time for murder (he will not be released until December 1984).

Onetime New York gangster and nightclub owner Owen Vincent "Owney" Madden dies of emphysema at Hot Springs, Ark., April 24 at age 73.

Alice Crimmins tells police she gave her daughter Alice (Missy), 7, and her son Edmund, Jr., 4, a supper of manicotti and green beans at 7:30 on the evening of July 13, put them to bed at 9, found them well when she checked at midnight, but found them missing when she went to wake them in the morning. The 26-year-old cocktail waitress is estranged from her husband (a mechanic at Kennedy Airport) and occupies a garden apartment at 150-22 72nd Drive in Kew Gardens Hills, Queens. Her little boy's body, strangled by a pajama top, is discovered July 15 in Flushing. The decomposed body of her little girl

is found July 19 on an embankment overlooking the Van Wyck Expressway. New York City Medical Examiner Milton Helpern, 63, finds on autopsy that Missy died 2 hours after eating her manicotti and beans, his evidence raises doubts about the mother's testimony, and a court will eventually convict her of murder.

The City Council adopts landmarks preservation legislation pursuant to an enabling act passed by the state legislature (see Penn Station demolition, 1963). Signed by Mayor Wagner April 19, the law empowers a Landmarks Preservation Commission to designate a building a "landmark" on a particular "landmark site" and even to designate an entire area a "historic district." The Board of Estimate may thereafter modify or disapprove the designation, and the owner may seek judicial review of the final designation decision. Well-financed developers will battle in the courts against well-organized preservationists and neighborhood groups over proposed changes in the city's appearance (see 1966; Supreme Court decision, 1978).

Real estate developer William Zeckendorf's Webb & Knapp Co. files for bankruptcy May 6. Zeckendorf's willingness to take risks has led him to make some ill-considered moves, and his liabilities exceed his assets.

The Times Tower that has stood in Times Square since 1904 becomes the Allied Chemical Tower but continues to display headlines on the Zipper (the New York Times gave up control of the Zipper 2 years ago; see communications, 1997). Allied Chemical removes the tower's terra-cotta exterior and sheaths the structure in white marble.

The 38-story CBS Building is completed on the west side of the Avenue of the Americas (Sixth Avenue) at 52nd Street, replacing the structure put up in 1930. Designed by Eero Saarinen & Associates, "Black Rock" has floors that are mainly supported from a central core. The 45-story Crédit Lyonnais Building (initially the J. C. Penney Building) goes up at 1301 Avenue of the Americas, between 52nd and 53rd streets. It has been designed by Shreve, Lamb & Harmon Associates.

Developers rush apartment buildings to completion before a new zoning law takes effect, creating such a short-term glut of rental units that landlords offer deals that include waiving the first year's rent (see 1949). After the crisis is ended they will sharply increase rents, forcing many tenants to leave (see 1969).

The Kips Bay Plaza apartment complex is completed with a north wing (*see* 1960). Like the south wing, it has been financed by William Zeckendorf and designed by I. M. Pei. Chatham Towers, designed by Kelly & Gruzen, joins the complex, and it will be enhanced next year by Pei's University Plaza to give it a total of 1,118 condominium units.

The 20- and 34-story Dorchester Towers apartment house is completed at 155 West 68th Street, between Broadway and Amsterdam Avenue, with 684 units (a three-bedroom apartment rents for $500 per month). Designed by S. J. Kessler & Sons for developers Paul and Seymour Milstein, the white-brick structure extends to 69th Street and grossly exceeds the density normally allowed by the zoning rules; the chairman of the City Planning Commission files suit against another government agency for granting the Milsteins a variance, but the Milsteins will prevail and go on to build a total of nearly 2,000 apartment units in the Lincoln Center area. The Milsteins' father, Morris, founded a contracting company that installed the floors at Rockefeller Center and other buildings, he went on to start Mastic Tile Co., and Seymour became president of Mastic 10 years ago. Ruberoid Corp. acquired Mastic for $24 million in 1959, and Seymour, now 44, will join with his boisterous younger brother to become major players in the city's real estate and financial worlds.

The 19-story twin Stephen Wise Towers designed by Knappe & Johnson are completed with 398 units at 124 West 91st Street, between Columbus and Amsterdam avenues, as part of the upper West Side urban renewal program. The 22-story Goddard Riverside Towers are completed with 168 units at 74 West 92nd Street. The Goddard Riverside Community Center has sponsored the new structure, designed by The Edelman Partnership.

The federally financed one-, nine-, and 18-story De Witt Clinton Houses (six buildings) are completed late in the year as part of an East Harlem slum-clearance program in an area bounded by Park and Madison avenues between 104th and 106th streets and 108th and 110th streets. Dividing the site are some sound apartment structures that are preserved. The 19-story city-financed Sen. Robert A. Taft Houses (nine buildings) are completed late in the year in an East Harlem area bounded by Park and Fifth avenues between 112th and 115th streets. They take their name from the late Ohio senator whose 1949 housing act provided federal funds for slum-clearance projects.

A U.S. Department of Housing and Urban Development (HUD) is inaugurated September 9.

The Vanderbilt Hotel that opened in 1912 closes for conversion into three floors of stores and offices and 18 floors containing 354 co-operative apartments.

A "French Provincial" town house with garage is completed for banker Paul Mellon at 125 East 70th Street, between Park and Lexington avenues. Mazza & Seccia has designed the residence; it replaces two century-old row houses.

A major drought in the northeastern states forces New York City to turn off air conditioning in sealed skyscrapers in order to conserve water. City fountains are stopped, lawn watering is forbidden, and signs appear reading, "Save water: shower with a friend."

 T.G.I. Friday's opens March 15 at the corner of First Avenue and 63rd Street, where Brooklyn-born bachelor perfume salesman Alan Stillman has acquired the Good Tavern with $5,000 borrowed from his mother, spent $15,000 to give the place an old-fashioned saloon décor with bentwood chairs and fake Tiffany lamps, added red-and-white striped awnings, and opened a "singles bar" that capitalizes on the success of Malachy's (*see* 1963). Police soon have to set up barricades to control the crowds of young executives, airline flight attendants, secretaries, and fashion models waiting to enter, the place earns $1 million its first year, it will spawn a host of other singles bars (*see* Maxwell's Plum, 1966), Stillman will sell the business in 1972, and T.G.I. Friday's will go on to become a chain of some 500 restaurants worldwide (*see* Smith and Wollensky, 1977).

The Shun Lee Dynasty restaurant opened by Chinese-born chef Tsung Ting Wang will be followed by the Shun Lee Palace (155 East 55th Street) in 1971 and the Shun Lee West (43 West 65th Street) in 1983.

The Stork Club closes October 4 after more than 30 years of providing food, drink, and dance music to café society (*see* 1933). Labor-management problems have plagued it in recent years, host Sherman Billingsley will die of a heart attack at age 66 in exactly 1 year, and the building will be razed in 1967 to make way for a vest-pocket park funded by CBS chairman William S. Paley.

A new U.S. immigration act signed into law by President Johnson October 3 at the Statue of Liberty abolishes the national origins quota system of 1952. The new law permits entry by any alien who meets qualifications of education and skill provided such entry will not jeopardize the job of an American. It imposes an overall limit of 120,000 visas per year for Western Hemisphere countries and 170,000 per year for the rest of the world; immediate relatives of U.S. citizens may enter without regard to these limits, but the end of the national origins quota will reduce the number of immigrants from Britain, France, Germany, Ireland, Italy, and other European countries while increasing the number from Asian countries. The National Park Service takes over Ellis Island, whose buildings have been vandalized, looted by thieves, and damaged by weather (*see* 1954); the Immigrant Receiving Station that opened in 1892 is designated a National Historic Landmark May 11. The same office that administers the Statue of Liberty is given responsibility for protecting the former immigrant receiving station, long since deserted (*see* 1982).

1966 Mayor John V. Lindsay is sworn in January 1 with great expectations that he can revitalize the city. The first Republican mayor since the late Fiorello H. La Guardia, Lindsay has good looks, charisma, and progressive ideas but will fail important tests of leadership. Former Bronx borough president James J. Lyons dies at New York January 7 at age 75.

A Brooklyn patrolman approaches detective Frank Serpico, 32, of Brooklyn's 90th Precinct in August and hands him an envelope containing $300 in tens and twenties—protection money from a local gambler (*see* Harry Gross, 1951). Serpico has observed other officers accepting such payoffs and seen fit to ignore it; this time he consults with a colleague who is also concerned about corruption and reports the incident to the commander of the Department of Investigation's detective squad. If Serpico pursues the case he will have to go before a grand jury, says the commander. "By the time it's over, they'll find you face down in the East River." Serpico asks for a transfer out of the precinct, winds up in the Seventh Division in the Bronx, and runs into the same situation. He speaks about it to an acquaintance with close connections to Mayor Lindsay but gets no satisfaction (*see* 1970).

Mayor Lindsay proposes that some civilians be placed on the Civilian Complaint Review Board to hear allegations of misconduct by police officers (*see* 1953). The Patrolmen's Benevolent Association has objected to the original plan of having only private citizens on the board, a court has rejected the PBA's plea, the PBA wins by a wide margin in a referendum on the issue, and despite its name the board continues to be composed entirely of police officials (*see* 1986).

Rep. Adam Clayton Powell, Jr. wins reelection to a 12th term but is convicted of contempt of court later

Mayor Lindsay brought charisma to Gracie Mansion and worked to allay racial tensions. AP/WIDE WORLD

in November for claiming congressional immunity and refusing to answer a subpoena in connection with the defamation of character suit brought against him in 1960 (*see* 1963). His arrogance has alienated many of Powell's white colleagues (NAACP, they joke, stands for, "Never Antagonize Adam Clayton Powell"); he responds to the contempt judgment by remaining outside New York City except on Sundays (when legal papers cannot be served), but a court order issued November 28 tells the city's 53 deputy sheriffs, "Without further process, take the body of Adam Clayton Powell, the defendant judgment debtor, and commit him to the civil jail—on any day of the week, including Sunday" (*see* 1967).

Gov. Rockefeller wins election to a third 4-year term, defeating Democrat Frank D. (Daniel) O'Connor, 56, with 2,690,626 votes to O'Connor's 2,298,363.

 A bill signed into law by Gov. Rockefeller April 27 is the first major revision of the state's divorce law. Adopted in 1787, the old law has made adultery virtually the only grounds for divorce; couples wishing to terminate their marriages have had to either go out of state (or to Mexico) or participate in elaborate and farcical arrangements whereby the husband or wife is photographed in bed with a member of the opposite sex in order to produce "evidence" of adultery. Slated to take effect September 1 of next year, the new New York State law specifies that a couple must have lived apart for at least 2 years before a divorce can be granted.

$ Mayor Lindsay declares March 3 that the city will be paralyzed for lack of money if more is not forthcoming and proposes tax legislation that will impose a city income tax not only on residents but also on commuters who earn income in the city, with the tax to be collected by the state but deductible from federal tax. He also proposes a 50 percent increase in the stock transfer tax. Waterloo, Iowa-born New York Stock Exchange President G. (George) Keith Funston, 55, has headed the NYSE since 1951 and denounces any rise in the stock-transfer tax, calling it discriminatory and inequable, the exchange's board of governors halts plans for a new building, and it orders a search for a new site outside of New York State. Lindsay concedes March 5 that if his entire tax package were enacted it would produce a surplus of $130 million, but he warns March 12 that drastic cuts in city services will be necessary without more revenue. Gov. Rockefeller warns April 4 that Lindsay's proposed business income tax could be "disastrous" for the city, defeating the state's efforts to attract more business, and business leaders oppose the proposed tax program, spurring Lindsay to criticize the banking and insurance interests for attacking the city when they should be giving it more support. City Council hearings on the tax proposal open April 20 and the mayor testifies that exempting commuters from the tax would speed the flight of middle- and upper-income families from the city. The Council approves the tax measure May 9, insisting that the 15¢ transit fare be maintained. Mayor Lindsay says in a radio interview May 22 that he would agree to halve the income tax for commuters but reiterates his opposition to payroll taxes, calling them a burden on the poor. The state legislature at Albany approves a 25 percent increase in the stock transfer tax, it approves a business income tax to replace the gross receipts tax, it defeats a proposed realty tax amendment, and Gov. Rockefeller June 9 orders the legislature, the mayor, and the City Council to remain in session until the tax problem is solved. Debate continues for another 3 weeks, and the tax bill signed by the governor July 1 calls for an income tax on residents, an earnings tax on commuters, a business income tax, and a rise in the

stock transfer tax; the City Council that day votes overwhelmingly in favor of the new tax measures. Albany announces July 20 that the city's 600,000 commuters cannot use the earnings tax as a deduction on their state income tax returns (see 1975).

Standard and Poor's is acquired by McGraw-Hill Co. (see 1941); the financial publisher and rating service becomes a McGraw subsidiary.

Wall Street's Dow Jones Industrial Average closes October 7 at 744.32 and closes December 30 at 785.69, down from 969.26 at the end of 1965. The Department of Labor's Bureau of Labor Statistics reported the largest year-to-year rise in the U.S. cost of living since 1958 April 21 and reported August 22 that the fiscal year ending June 30 was the most inflationary since 1957.

MasterCard has its beginnings in the Master Charge credit card introduced by New York's 116-year-old Marine Midland Bank at the urging of Buffalo banker Karl H. Hinke, 60 (see Franklin National Bank, 1951). Marine Midland will license other banks to issue the plastic card; it will be available to customers without charge and accepted by hotels, restaurants, auto rental agencies, and airlines as well as by retail merchants.

Merchant Bernard F. Gimbel dies in his suite at the Hotel Pierre September 28 at age 81 after an 18-month bout with cancer (see 1953). Gimbel served on the boards of the 1939 and 1964 world's fairs and supported construction of airports, the Coliseum, hospitals, river tunnels, and waterworks, saying, "Anyone that lives in this city and doesn't make a contribution to it is like a barnacle on a boat" (see 1973).

The Transportation Workers Union takes 35,000 transit workers off the job from January 1 to January 13, crippling the city; former mayor Wagner did nothing to avert the threatened strike in his final days in office, Mayor Lindsay lectures TWU leader Michael J. Quill on "civic responsibility," refusing to negotiate lest there be an appearance of a backroom deal, and Quill thunders that the new mayor is a "Coward! Pipsqueak! Ass!" He goes to jail for contempt of court. Lindsay says, "I still think it's a fun city," and *Herald Tribune* columnist Dick Schaap begins calling New York "fun city," using the term sarcastically. The 13-day strike costs the city $1.5 billion in lost productivity and wages as New Yorkers bike or walk to work or simply stay home (on the mayor's advice) before a settlement is worked out providing $52 million over the course of 2 years—twice the size of any pact negotiated by former mayor Wagner. Quill dies of a coronary occlusion at New York January 28 at age 59 as other union leaders demand wage increases matching those granted to the TWU.

The city makes Fifth Avenue one-way southbound and Madison Avenue one-way northbound beginning January 14 to ease congestion caused by the transit strike (see Third and Lexington avenues, 1960). Tiffany & Co. president Walter Hoving, now 68, has led opposition to the one-way traffic scheme and says Fifth Avenue is now a "superhighway." Mayor Lindsay gets rid of pothole inspectors to save money, and motorists complain.

The Brooklyn Navy Yard closes; it will be sold in 1968 to the city and turned into an industrial park that will attract some 200 businesses employing 3,000 people, but Brooklyn's waterfront has been in decline for more than a decade in the absence of cheap land for container storage and pier facilities for container ships (see 1956; Red Hook Marine Terminal, 1981).

New York Harbor has its worst disaster since the fire aboard the S.S. *General Slocum* in 1904. The freighter *Alva Cape* explodes at anchor in Gravesend Bay June 28, spilling her cargo of naphtha into the water, and collides with the tanker *Texaco Massachusetts* in the Kill van Kull; about 60 men swim through burning waters to safety, and the tugboats *Harriet Moran* and *Julia C. Moran* rescue many, but fatalities number at least 32, including the captain of the *Texaco Massachusetts*. The collision spurs Port Authority efforts to gain federal help for widening the Kill van Kull-Newark Bay intersection, where 23 accidents have occurred since 1953. Ambrose Channel is closed while the *Alva Cape* is sent through it, and she is then shelled by a U.S. Coast Guard cutter until she sinks at sea July 3.

City transit fares rise to 20¢ July 5; they have been 15¢ since 1953, but the wage increase granted to settle the January transit workers' strike has forced the fare increase; the token issued in 1953 remains in use (see 1970).

Brooklyn's St. Ann's Episcopal Church pays $350,000 to acquire the 60-year-old Crescent Athletic Club building for the St. Ann's School it started last year at 129 Pierrepont Street. The club filed for bankruptcy in 1939, and the 12-level building has been used since then for offices and stores. St. Ann's will become separate from the church in 1982, adopting what it will later call "an undisguised, confident, and possibly reactionary commitment to Western civilization" to serve its coeducational student body.

The *Herald Tribune, Journal-American,* and *World-Telegram & Sun* announce a merger March 21 after 2 months of fighting a Newspaper Guild charge of unfair labor practices by all three (see 1965). The *Trib* is to continue daily morning publication, the *World-Journal* to appear afternoons, and the *World-Journal & Tribune* to be a combined Sunday paper; the merger reduces the number of major city dailies to five, down from 12 in 1930. The Guild strikes April 23, the *Trib* puts out its final edition April 24 after 42 years of publication, and all three remaining daily papers (the *News,* the *Post,* and the *Times*) shut down for 140 days. The *World-Journal & Tribune* (New Yorkers quickly dub it the WIDGET) appears for the first time September 12 and quickly sells out its 930,000-copy press run, but the Department of Justice forces the new company to offer its 19 syndicated columns and features to other papers (see 1967).

Wells, Rich, Greene is founded by Youngstown, Ohio-born New York advertising copywriter Mary Wells (née Berg), 37, with Dick Rich and Stewart Greene, her former associates at Jack Tinker & Partners (she began her career as a Macy's copywriter). Braniff Airways president Harding Lawrence, 45, has persuaded Wells to start her own agency and soon leaves Tinker for WRG, he will divorce his wife next year to marry Wells, but the agency will subsequently drop the Braniff account to take the larger TWA account, and WRG will gain a reputation for its Alka-Seltzer, Benson & Hedges cigarette, and "I Love New York" campaigns (see 1977).

Nonfiction: *Behind Closed Doors: Politics in the Public Interest* by former New York County Democratic Committee chairman Edward (Nazar) Costikyan, 41, who has worked to eliminate Tammany Hall's control of municipal government and judicial appointments; *A Stripe of Tammany's Tiger* by Louis Eisenstein and Elliot Rosenberg; *The Tweed Ring* by Denver-born University of California, Santa Barbara, historian Alexander B. Callow, 40; *The Epic of New York City* by New York author Edward Robb Ellis, 56; *Portal to America: The Lower East Side, 1870–1925* by Cleveland-born art consultant and designer Allon Schoener, 41 (editor); *Harlem: The Making of a Ghetto* by Brooklyn-born author Gilbert Osofsky, 31; *The Great Merchants* by Texas-born author John Thomas "Tom" Mahoney, 60, and *New York Times* financial writer Leonard Sloane, 34; *The Working Press: Special to the New York Times* by *Times* editor Ruth Adler, 56; *Against Interpretation* by Susan Sontag.

Alfred Knopf president Blanche Knopf dies at New York June 4 at age 71; former *Herald Tribune* literary editor Irita Van Doren at New York Hospital December 18 at age 75 (she has lived at 15 West 77th Street).

Fiction: *The Fixer* by Bernard Malamud; *The Embezzler* by Louis Auchincloss; *To the Precipice* by New York-born novelist Judith Rossner (*née* Perelman), 31; *The Valley of the Dolls* by Philadelphia-born New York novelist Jacqueline Susann, 45, a former actress whose book comes under criticism for its profanity and explicit description of breast cancer.

New American Library cofounder Victor Weybright quits to start a new publishing house, Weybright & Talley (*see* 1947).

Painting: *Who's Afraid of Red, Yellow, Blue* by Barnett Newman; *Yellow and Red Brushstrokes* by Roy Lichtenstein; *Marlon* and *Flowers* (both silkscreens) by Andy Warhol; *Typists* (tempera and gouache on paper) by Jacob Lawrence; *Le triomph de la musique* by Russian-born painter Marc Chagall, 79, for the new Metropolitan Opera House. Hans Hofmann dies of a heart attack at New York February 17 at age 85; Maxfield Parrish at Plainfield, N.J., March 30 at age 95; former Cloisters director James J. Rorimer of a heart attack at New York May 11 at age 60.

Sculpture: *The Truck* by George Segal; *Alamo* (a 16-foot-high cube of Cor-Ten steel) by Illinois-born sculptor Bernard "Tony" Rosenthal, 51 (it is installed on Astor Place as a gift to the city from Rosenthal and Susan Morse Hilles). The 15-foot-high sectionalized metal cube will stand on one point for decades. Melvina Hoffman dies of a heart attack in her New York studio July 10 at age 81.

The Whitney Museum of American Art moves September 2 into a new building at the southeast corner of Madison Avenue and 75th Street (*see* 1931). Designed by Marcel Breuer, it has been built with money left by the late Gertrude Vanderbilt Whitney, who died in April 1942.

Photography: *Many Are Called* by Walker Evans, now 62, who left *Fortune* magazine last year to become a professor of graphic design at Yale. Among the pictures included in his new book is his 1938 photograph *Subway Riders, New York*.

Theater: *The Lion in Winter* by Chicago-born playwright James Goldman, 38, 3/3 at the Ambassador Theater, with Robert Preston as Henry II, Rosemary Harris as Eleanor of Aquitaine, 92 perfs.; *A Delicate Balance* by Edward Albee 9/22 at the Martin Beck Theater, with Jessica Tandy, Hume Cronyn, 132 perfs.; *America Hurrah* (trilogy: *Interview*, *TV*, and *Motel*) by Belgian-born playwright Jean-Claude van Itallie, 31, 11/7 at the off-Broadway Pocket Theater

(100 Third Avenue, at 13th Street), with New York-born actor James Coco, 38, Cynthia Harris, Revere, Mass.-born actor Bill Macy, 44, dolls constructed by Robert Wilson, 640 perfs.; *Don't Drink the Water* by Brooklyn-born actor-playwright Woody Allen (originally Allen Stewart Konigsberg), 30, 11/17 at the Morosco Theater, with Lou Jacobi, Kay Medford (to Ethel Barrymore Theater 1/22/1967, Belasco Theater 3/25/1968), 598 perfs.

The Roundabout Theater has its beginnings in the renovated basement of a supermarket in West 26th Street. It will declare bankruptcy in 1978, decide to close in 1983, move twice, and grow to become the second largest nonprofit theater in America (Lincoln Center being larger).

The Negro Ensemble Company is founded with a 299-seat theater at 424 West 55th Street to present black-oriented plays.

Actress Helen Menken dies of a heart attack at New York March 27 at age 64; playwright Russel Crouse of pneumonia at New York April 27 at age 73; double-talk comedian Al Kelly (Al Kalish) of a heart attack at New York September 7 at age 66; playwright Anne Nichols of a heart attack at Englewood Cliffs, N.J., September 15 at age 74; theater critic Ward Morehouse at New York December 8 at age 67.

Peep shows (nickelodeon machines showing pornographic films) begin to proliferate in the Times Square area after Martin J. Hodas installs one in a magazine shop at 259 West 42nd Street (*see* 1962; burlesque, 1940; Supreme Court decision, 1967; 42nd Street Development Corp., 1976).

Mayor Lindsay establishes the Mayor's Office of Film, Theatre & Broadcasting to provide liaison on policy and regulatory issues, promote use of city locations for shooting scenes, and serve as an advocate for the industry. Producers and directors up to now have had to go from one city office to another, paying off cops, police captains, and bureaucrats to obtain permits for lighting, parking, police protection, and the like; the new office lets them do it all with one stop at no charge. No other city, state, or country in the world will have such an agency to facilitate production of feature films, television series and specials, TV commercials, and music videos.

TV star Gertrude Berg dies of heart failure at New York September 14 at age 66.

Films: Francis Ford Coppola's *You're a Big Boy Now* with Peter Kastner, Elizabeth Hartman, Geraldine

Page, Julie Harris. Also: Robert Ellis Miller's *Any Wednesday* with Jane Fonda, Jason Robards, Jr.; Irvin Kershner's *A Fine Madness* with Sean Connery, Joanne Woodward, Jean Seberg, Patrick O'Neal, Colleen Dewhurst.

Film director Robert Rossen dies of a coronary occlusion following surgery at New York February 18 at age 57; actor Montgomery Clift of a heart ailment at New York July 23 at age 45.

Broadway musicals: *Sweet Charity* 1/29 at the Palace Theater, with Gwen Verdon, book by Neil Simon based on the 1957 Federico Fellini film *The Nights of Cabiria*, music by Cy Coleman, lyrics by Dorothy Fields, songs that include "Big Spender," "If My Friends Could See Me Now," 608 perfs.; *It's a Bird! It's a Plane! It's Superman!* 3/29 at the Alvin Theater, with Jack Cassidy, Portland, Me.-born actress Linda Lavin, 28, music by Charles Strouse, lyrics by Lee Adams, songs that include "You've Got Possibilities," "We Don't Matter at All," 75 perfs.; *Mame* 5/24 at the Winter Garden Theater, with Angela Lansbury, New York-born actress Bea Arthur (originally Beatrice Frankel), 43, music and lyrics by Jerry Herman, songs that include "If He Walked into My Life," "Open a New Window," "We Need a Little Christmas," 1,508 perfs.; *The Apple Tree* 10/18 at the Shubert Theater, with Barbara Harris, Larry Blyden, Alan Alda, music by Jerry Bock, lyrics by Sheldon Harnick, 463 perfs.; *Cabaret* 11/20 at the Broadhurst Theater, with English ingénue Jill Haworth, 21, as Sally Bowles, Jack Gilford, Lotte Lenya, now 68, Cleveland-born actor Joel Grey (originally Joel Katz), 34, book by Joe Masteroff based on Christopher Isherwood's *Berlin Stories*, music by John Kander, lyrics by Fred Ebb, songs that include

"Wilkommen," "The Money Song," and the title song, 1,165 perfs.; *I Do! I Do!* 12/5 at the 46th Street Theater, with Mary Martin, Robert Preston, music by Harvey Schmidt, lyrics by Tom Jones, songs that include "My Cup Runneth Over," 584 perfs.

Singer-actress Sophie Tucker dies at New York February 9 at age 82; Broadway songwriter-producer Billy Rose of lobar pneumonia in a nursing home at Montego Bay, Jamaica, BWI, February 10 at age 66; onetime "boop-boop-a-doop girl" Helen Kane of cancer at New York September 26 at age 62.

Opera: a new Metropolitan Opera House opens September 16 to replace the 83-year-old Met that will be razed next year. Designed by Abby Rockefeller's brother-in-law Wallace K. Harrison, the new $45.7 million Met has 3,788 seats (the old one had 3,625) and is the largest building in Lincoln Center, but its premiere of the opera *Antony and Cleopatra* with Leontyne Price, music by Samuel Barber, is a disaster.

Lewisohn Stadium founder Minnie Guggenheimer dies at New York May 23 at age 83; composer-critic Deems Taylor at his native New York July 3 at age 80.

Popular songs: "59th Street Bridge Song" and "Scarborough Fair—Canticle" by Paul Simon and Art Garfunkel; "Summer in the City" by John B. Sebastian, Mark Sebastian, Joe Butler; *A Man and His Music* (album) by Frank Sinatra, now 51, who marries Los Angeles-born actress Mia Farrow, 21 (they will be divorced in 1968); "Guantanamero" by Pete Seeger and Hector Angulo, lyrics from a poem by the 19th century Cuban patriot José Martí; "Society's Child" by New York-born songwriter-singer Janis Ian (Janis Eddy Fink), 15, is about a white girl and a black boy; *More Than a New Discovery* (album) by Bronx-born New York singer-songwriter Laura Nyro (originally Nigro), 19, who 2 years ago wrote "And When I Die" for Peter, Paul, and Mary.

The jazz club Max's Kansas City opens at 213 Bowery, where it will continue until 1974.

 Welterweight champion Emile Griffith wins the world middleweight boxing title April 25 in a 15-round decision over Dick Tiger at Madison Square Garden (*see* 1963). Since he is not allowed under U.S. rules to hold both championships, he gives up his welterweight title (*see* 1967).

Fred Stolle, 27 (Australia), wins in men's singles at Forest Hills, Maria Bueno in women's singles.

Bergdorf Goodman hat designer Halston persuades the store to let him create a line of ready-to-wear, the show he puts on June 28 does not impress

The Lincoln Center for the Performing Arts provided new venues for musical and theatrical events. CHIE NISHIO

Women's Wear Daily, Bergdorf closes his in-store boutique as hats go out of fashion, and he opens his own house (*see* 1960; 1968).

Cosmetics queen Elizabeth Arden dies of a heart attack at New York October 18 at age 81.

The Black & White Ball given by millionaire author Truman Capote at the Plaza Hotel November 28 ("a little masked ball for Kay Graham and all my friends," Capote calls it) brings out 540 prominent actors, business moguls, entertainers, film producers, painters, politicians, publishers, scientists, socialites, and writers to dance to Peter Duchin's orchestra and the Soul Brothers, a rock 'n' roll group. Capote has asked that the men wear dinner jackets and black masks, the women white dresses and white masks. Halston and dressmaker Adolfo have designed some of the masks, and the guest list includes celebrities of all kinds.

Mafia boss Joseph Bonanno resurfaces in May at the federal courthouse in Foley Square (*see* 1964). He tells the court he was kidnapped at gunpoint by a rival boss, authorities believe he refused to testify 2 years ago because he wanted to make a truce with other Mafia bosses, he abdicates his leadership of the Bonanno mob, and although he is indicted on a charge of failing to appear before the grand jury the indictment will be dropped in 1971. Bonanno will soon give up his Hempstead, L.I., house and 14-room farmhouse outside Middletown, N.Y., to live at Tucson, Ariz.; his sons Salvatore and Joseph C. will allegedly operate money-laundering rackets in California, he will be convicted for the first time at age 75 when a jury finds him guilty of trying to block a grand jury probe of their operations, he will serve a year in prison, and he will serve another 14 months in the mid-1980s for refusing to testify in a federal racketeering case in Manhattan against reputed leaders of the five New York Mafia families.

The city's homicide rate will take a sharp upturn in the next 5 years, rising from 7.6 per 100,000 in the last 5 years to 12.6 per 100,000, and will not fall to single digits again in this century (*see* 1971).

The "Battery Park City" plan announced by Gov. Rockefeller May 12 is followed June 22 by a somewhat different plan released by the city (*see* 1958). The plan calls for using a landfill in the Hudson River created by excavation for a World Trade Center (*see* 1967).

Groundbreaking ceremonies August 5 begin excavation for a World Trade Center to be built on a superblock bounded by Vesey, Liberty, Church, and West streets, about three blocks north of the New York Stock Exchange, where it will replace the old Washington Market, the petshop district, the radio district, and the religious-supply district on a 16-acre site. Chase Manhattan Bank president David Rockefeller, now 51, became chairman 10 years ago of the Chamber of Commerce Committee on Lower Manhattan Redevelopment (later the Downtown Manhattan Association) and has helped promote the idea of a world trade facility to be owned and operated by the Port Authority of New York and New Jersey. Engineers John Skilling and Leslie Robertson of Worthington, Skilling, Helle and Jackson have worked with Seattle-born Troy, Mich., architect Minoru Yamasaki, 52, and Emery Roth & Sons on plans for the complex, which is projected to cost $350 million; its construction requires excavating 70 feet down to bedrock and building a "bathtub" to keep the river out of the Hudson Tubes, subway connections, and sub-basement levels of the WTC (*see* 1968).

A graceless 29-story office tower designed by Charles Luckman Associates replaces Pennsylvania Station (*see* 1963). The station's 11 platforms and 21 tracks remain in place, but the 25-acre site above it will now contain a new 20,000-seat Madison Square Garden sports arena (*see* 1968), a 1,000-seat Felt Forum, a 500-seat movie theater, and a 48-lane bowling alley in addition to the office building.

The National Historic Preservation Act signed into law by President Johnson includes measures designed to encourage preservation of sites and structures of historic or cultural significance. City Hall is designated a New York City Landmark February 1, Trinity Church August 16, the Flatiron Building September 20, St. Patrick's Cathedral October 19 (*see* Carnegie Hill Historic District, 1974; Supreme Court decision, 1978).

The 30-story University Village apartment complex is completed in La Guardia Place between Bleecker and Houston streets. Designed by I. M. Pei to provide faculty housing for New York University, the three reinforced concrete buildings have units of between one and four bedrooms.

Mayor Lindsay proposes a waterside complex for the East River December 20. Based on a plan submitted by developer Richard Ravitch in 1961, it calls for replacing some abandoned piers between 25th and 28th streets with four apartment towers containing 1,470 rent-subsidized units for medium- and low-income residents, but it will take an act of Congress to declare the area non-navigable and a $73 million loan extended on the basis of the mayor's personal involvement in the project (*see* 1974; United Nations School, 1973).

The 860 and 870 United Nations Plaza apartment towers are completed on the east side of First Avenue between 48th and 49th streets. Designed by Harrison, Abramovitz & Harris, the twin 32-story steel-and-glass towers rise above an office block overlooking the UN and East River. Luxury apartments range in size from three-and-a-half rooms with one bath to nine rooms with six-and-a-half baths; those on the top two floors, served by private elevators, are duplexes with curving staircases and wood-burning fireplaces. Initial offering prices: $27,600 to $166,000.

The 35-story Pavillion apartment house is completed at 500 East 77th Street overlooking the East River. Designed by Philip Birnbaum, it has 852 units, making it the city's largest single apartment building.

The 48-story 985 Fifth Avenue co-operative apartment house is completed at the northeast corner of 79th Street. Designed by Paul Resnick and Harry F. Green, it replaces the Isaac Brokaw mansion of 1887. Its 16-room duplex penthouse is offered at $418,000, but many of the building's 43 tenant-owners will replace the gold-plated bathroom fixtures and bidets in their apartments.

Thomas P. F. Hoving, 35, is sworn in January 1 as parks commissioner, replacing Newbold Morris, who dies of stomach cancer at New York March 30 at age 64. Son of merchant Walter Hoving, the new commissioner bans motorcars from city parks on weekends and during non-rush hours, he applies in April for a federal Housing and Urban Development Corp. (HUD) grant to create pocket parks (they will open in the summer of 1968), and with encouragement from Mayor Lindsay he stages musical events and other "happenings" in the major parks to increase their use and safety (in numbers).

A task force report published May 9 charges that New York has the most polluted air of any major U.S. city and that its buses and municipal incinerators are the worst violators of its own anti-pollution laws.

A fire collapses the Hotel Bartholdi at 6 East 23rd Street October 17, taking the lives of 12 firefighters.

Parks Commissioner Hoving is sworn in November 21 as the first head of the new New York City Recreation and Cultural Affairs Administration, his salary rises from $25,000 to $35,000, but he is then appointed director of the Metropolitan Museum of Art, the position to begin in mid-April of next year (*see* 1967).

A Thanksgiving smog emergency creates a dangerous situation for city residents with heart, lung, or respiratory conditions. The upper East Side reportedly has the most coal-burning furnaces, the highest average levels of sulfur dioxide in the air, and the highest average particulate matter.

The Hudson River shad catch falls to 116,000 pounds; the Bureau of Commercial Fisheries in the Department of the Interior stops keeping records of Hudson River shad (the fish are in any case generally tainted with oil and other pollutants).

Food prices are higher in poor neighborhoods of New York and other cities than in better neighborhoods, according to a study. Ghetto food merchants charge more to compensate for "shrinkage."

Zabar's begins using distinctive shopping bags designed by local graphic designer Elliott Schneider, 30 (*see* 1951; 1977).

Restaurateur Henri Soulé of Le Pavillon dies of a heart attack at La Côte Basque January 27 at age 62. His coatroom operator Henriette Spalter, 66, takes over the Côte Basque and will run it with her son Albert.

Maxwell's Plum opens in April on First Avenue at 64th Street. Capitalizing on the success of T.G.I. Friday's (*see* 1965), the singles bar launched by restaurateur Warner LeRoy, 32 (son of Hollywood producer Mervyn LeRoy), has an overwhelming decor and will continue until July 1988 (*see* Tavern on the Green, 1976).

The Underground Gourmet by New York graphic designer Milton Glaser, now 37, of Push Pin Studios and *Scientific American* magazine's art director Jerome Snyder is a collection of 101 restaurant reviews, written originally for the *Herald Tribune* and focusing on cheap eating places. Included are Chez Brigitte at 77 Greenwich Avenue, La Focacceria at 195 First Avenue (founded in 1914), and La Taza de Oro, a Puerto Rican luncheonette at 96 Eighth Avenue, near 15th Street. Glaser and Snyder introduce readers to ethnic specialties such as *morcilla* (a garlicky sausage), *estómago* (sliced pig's stomach), Puerto Rican *cuchifritos*, Jewish knishes, Chinese *dim sum* (dumplings), and Japanese sushi.

New York assemblymen introduce a bill calling for reform of New York State's 19th century abortion law, responding to an appeal by Manhattan borough president Percy Sutton, who has seen the costs of illegal abortions in lives and maimings in the city's ghettos (*see* 1970).

1967 The Democratic Caucus of Congress at Washington, D.C., votes January 9 to give Rep. Adam Clayton Powell's committee chairmanship to Rep. Carl Perkins (D. Ky.) on grounds that Powell has misused campaign funds (*see 1966*). Powell has been in Bimini over the Christmas holidays, he accuses the House of "racial bigotry" in its own chamber, raises the issue of "a double standard," and says his behavior has been no different from that of many other congressmen, but his 22 years of seniority have come to nought. A subcommittee headed by Rep. Wayne Hayes issues a damaging report January 30, charging that Powell has misused $45,000 in public funds; Powell's third wife, Yvette, tells the subcommittee February 16 that she has done virtually no official work for her husband since 1965, has not seen him since September of that year, and has asked him many times to let her return to Washington or remove her from the payroll. Powell files suit in federal district court March 8, challenging his exclusion from Congress and claiming he has been the victim of a "Northern-style lynching;" although he does not return from Bimini to campaign in the special election to fill his vacancy April 11, he wins with an overwhelming 86.1 percent of the vote in the 18th congressional district but declines to take his seat (*see 1968*).

Bronx County Democratic Party leader Charles A. Buckley dies of lung cancer at New York January 22 at age 76.

Popular sentiment turns increasingly against the war in Vietnam as more troops are shipped overseas and casualties mount. Sen. Robert F. Kennedy (D. N.Y.) proposes that bombing of North Vietnam be halted so that troop withdrawal may be negotiated. The U.S. government is "the greatest purveyor of violence in the world," says Martin Luther King, Jr. April 4 in a talk at Riverside Church. He criticizes U.S. sales of weapons to foreign countries, encourages draft evasion, and proposes a merger between the anti-war and civil rights movements.

A "Peace Mobilization" anti-war demonstration April 15 at New York brings out upwards of 100,000 protesters, and 300,000 join in a march to the United Nations. Protests against the Vietnam War and the draft continue. Loyalty Day parades in Brooklyn and along Fifth Avenue April 29 bring out supporters of the war effort, but the number of marchers is estimated at only 8,000 for both boroughs. A "Support Our Boys in Vietnam" parade down Fifth Avenue from 95th and east on 92nd Street to Third Avenue May 13 brings out more than

Anti-Vietnam War demonstrations became vehement as the conflict in Southeast Asia intensified. CHIE NISHIO

70,000 people waving American flags—the third parade in a month.

The Taylor Act adopted by the state legislature in Albany and signed into law by Gov. Rockefeller takes effect September 1, superseding the 20-year-old Condon-Wadlin Act. Adopted in the wake of last year's transit strike and previous strikes, it grants public-sector employees the right to organize, requires public employers to negotiate and enter into agreements with such employees, establishes procedures for resolving collective-bargaining disputes in the event of impasses, but prohibits strikes by police, firefighters, sanitation workers, teachers, and other such employees. Philadelphia-born University of Pennsylvania professor and industrial-relations expert George W. (William) Taylor, 69, has chaired the governor's Committee on Public Employee Relations (*but see* education [teachers' strike], 1968).

Mayor Lindsay arrives in a helicopter at the Jerome Park Reservoir in the Bronx May 11 with his

Schenectady-born commissioner of water supply, gas, and electricity James (Lewis) Marcus, 36, to officiate at ceremonies marking the start of its refilling after 5 months' scrubbing and refurbishing (the reservoir provides water for the Bronx and part of Manhattan). A socially prominent onetime financial consultant whose wife, Lily (*née* Lodge), is the daughter of a former Connecticut governor, Marcus resigns under pressure December 12, acknowledging that he is the subject of an inquiry by New York District Attorney Frank Hogan. Police arrest Marcus December 18, and Mayor Lindsay says he betrayed the administration if he lied; emergency contracts will hereafter be carefully scrutinized, the mayor vows. Marcus granted an emergency contract to drain and clear the reservoir, Mayor Lindsay and the Board of Estimate accepted his reasons for avoiding the slow process of competitive bidding and giving the $835,000 job to just one reliable contractor (S. T. Grant, headed by Henry Fried, 60), but it turns out that Marcus received a 5 percent kickback. The amount—$16,000 out of a $40,000 total—is trifling compared to the graft taken by the Tweed Ring a century ago, but the case becomes a cause célèbre, tarnishing the Lindsay administration when it emerges that organized crime in the person of one Antonio "Tony Ducks" Corallo, 54, has been involved. The FBI has called Corallo an underboss of the Luchese crime family and says S. T. Grant has ties to the mob. U.S. District Attorney Robert M. Morgenthau indicts Marcus; says the *New York Times* December 20, "The facts of the indictment leave no doubt that organized and experienced criminals and labor racketeers moved in, found a mark, and tried to make a score." The *Times* notes that the Mafia and its acquiescent accomplices represent an "arrogant, wealthy, and entrenched criminal elite" whose "profits from such activities as narcotics, gambling, bootlegging, extortion, and prostitution are used to infiltrate New York's legitimate commercial life." Five "Mafia" families operate in and about New York, says the *Times*, and number about 5,000 men (*see* 1968).

Fordham faculty members and students vote five to one in early November to continue the school's policy of allowing recruitment for the military to proceed on its Rose Hill campus in the Bronx, but another anti-war and antidraft rally in Whitehall Street, Manhattan, December 5 brings out a crowd of 2,500; among the 264 demonstrators arrested are physician Benjamin Spock and poet Allen Ginsberg.

Race riots in June and July rock 127 U.S. cities, kill at least 77 people, and injure at least 4,000, but Mayor Lindsay walks the streets of Harlem in his shirt-sleeves at night, with only a single police detective accompanying him as he talks to people with his jacket tossed over his shoulder and his necktie askew. He is credited with keeping violence and looting to a minimum while other cities burn. Urban Coalitions are organized late in the year at New York and in 47 other metropolitan areas following an appeal by former Health, Education and Welfare secretary John W. Gardner. Gardner has resigned to become head of the National Urban Coalition, and that group will mobilize the private sector to join in social-action projects with representatives of the cities' dispossessed minorities.

The New York State Lottery is instituted to compete with illegal numbers games and raise money for education. Federal laws ban lottery ads in newspapers, magazines, radio, and TV, so the $1.5 million advertising campaign that launches the lottery is mostly on billboards; critics call the lottery regressive taxation, taking money from those least able to afford it.

The U.S. Bureau of Labor Statistics reports that the annual cost of "moderate" living for a family of four in the New York area rose last year to $10,195—more than half again as much as in 1959 and the highest in the continental United States. Housing and taxes account for most of the higher costs. U.S. wage rates will rise by 92 percent in the next 10 years, buying power by only 8 percent as inflation eats away at paychecks.

The Conference Board founded in 1916 issues its first Consumer Confidence Index. Its survey "Consumer Attitudes and Buying Plans" reports intentions to buy automobiles, homes, and major appliances.

Banker Thomas S. Lamont dies after open-heart surgery at New York April 10 at age 68.

Emigrant Savings Bank takes that name after 117 years as the Emigrant Industrial Savings Bank (*see* 1850). It will grow in the next 25 years to have 37 branches, most of them in Manhattan, Brooklyn, and Queens, with 303,000 depositors and assets of $6.5 billion.

Cleveland-born stockbroker Muriel Siebert, 35, pays a reported $445,000 to buy a seat on the New York Stock Exchange—the first time a woman has had her own seat. She began her career as a Wall Street research trainee in 1954, became a top airline stock analyst, and has earned an annual salary said to be above $500,000.

Wall Street's Dow Jones Industrial Average closes December 29 at 905.11, up from 785.69 at the end of 1966.

First National City Bank launches "The Everything Card" in the biggest charge-service program ever undertaken in a single metropolitan area. By October it has signed up thousands of merchants and half a million card-holding families, but the bank will soon give up the effort and offer national credit cards. Master Charge card holders number 5.7 million by year's end and have charged $312 million worth of purchases (see 1966). By 1976 there will be 40 million Master Charge card holders nationwide and they will run up bills of $13.5 billion.

Consolidated Edison appoints former U.S. undersecretary of the interior Charles F. Luce as chairman in mid-year; he will continue in the post until mid-1982 (see 1972).

Illegally parked cars in midtown Manhattan are physically towed away for the first time beginning in February under a new city law designed to facilitate street cleaning, but United Nations delegates assert their immunity from the law and will disregard parking tickets. Realtor Douglas L. Elliman, now 84, says, "It is my opinion that an effort should be made to keep private cars out of the city rather than to encourage any increase. The problem can best be solved by wholesale transportation from points to the periphery of the city." Car owners whose vehicles have been towed can reclaim them only by paying large fines at Pier 76 on the Hudson River at 38th Street.

The city orders all licensed taxicabs to be painted yellow (see 1965). The number of medallion cabs will fall by attrition to 11,300 by 1970, and the requirement that such cabs be more easily identifiable will further increase the value of the medallion that 30 years ago cost just $10. Bulletproof partitions are ordered to be installed between front and back seats of Manhattan cabs to protect drivers from thievery and the violent crime that is claiming more and more cabbies' lives (see 1971).

The 84-year-old Brooklyn Bridge is designated a New York City Landmark August 24.

The 27-year-old Cunard liner *Queen Elizabeth* bound for New York passes the 31-year-old *Queen Mary* out of New York on the North Atlantic shortly before dawn August 25, but the day of the great transatlantic passenger ships is ending as jet aircraft replace them.

Naval architect and marine engineer William F. Gibbs dies at New York September 6 at age 81. He designed the superliner *United States* that went into service 15 years ago.

The New York Central discontinues its crack *Twentieth Century Limited* December 2 after 65 years on the Chicago run (see 1968).

Phoenix House opens on the fifth floor of a West 85th Street tenement with five detoxified former drug addicts. All have been patients of the Morris Bernstein Institute, one of the few city hospitals that admit addicts. By 1970 the facility will have returned 150 graduates to society and established seminar rap session techniques that other rehab centers will follow.

New York lawyer John D. Banzhaf III, 27, quits the firm he has joined to organize Action on Smoking and Health (ASH) with support from prominent physicians. Banzhaf has filed a formal complaint against CBS-TV, whose officers are notified by the Federal Communications Commission that the network's programs dealing with the effects of smoking on health are not sufficient to offset the influence of the 5 to 10 minutes of cigarette commercials aired each day by its New York television station. The FCC does not agree with Banzhaf's request for equal time, but it does order that all radio and TV cigarette commercials carry a notice of possible danger in cigarette smoking and asks WCBS-TV to provide free each week "a significant amount of time for the other viewpoint . . ." Banzhaf will take credit for having the networks devote $200 million worth of air time to anti-smoking commercials.

Francis Cardinal Spellman dies of a stroke at New York December 2 at age 78; in his 28 years he has created 45 new parishes, devised a system of diocesan high schools, and spent nearly $600 million in expanding Catholic charitable and educational facilities (see Cooke, 1968).

The South Street Seaport Museum chartered April 28 by the New York State Board of Regents opens headquarters at 16 Fulton Street under the direction of Brooklyn-born National Maritime Historical Society administrator Peter Stanford, 40, who with his wife, Norma, organized Friends of the South Street Seaport Museum 5 months ago. The first Mayor's Cup schooner race is held October 21 under the co-sponsorship of the Museum and the city, whose Seaport will become a major retail center of shops and restaurants while preserving buildings and ships from the 19th century (see 1968).

John Jay College of Criminal Justice opens at 315 Park Avenue South, where it will remain in rented space until 1973 (*see* 1955; 1973).

The Lexington School for the Deaf located for close to a century on Lexington Avenue in the 60s moves into a new building in Queens designed by Pomerance & Breines near La Guardia Airport on 30th Avenue, between 73rd and 75th streets. The old building is torn down to provide space for additional Hunter College buildings.

 The *New York World-Journal & Tribune* ceases publication May 5 after less than 8 months, having suffered 18 work stoppages in that time (management says the unions have forced it to employ 500 more people than necessary). The combined circulation has been 700,000 daily, 900,000 Sundays, and although the *New York Times* and the *Washington Post* will continue the Paris edition of the *Herald Tribune*, the end of the *World-Journal & Tribune* (WIDGET) leaves New York with only three regular dailies—the *Times*, *News*, and *Post*.

The South Korean daily *Hangkook Ilbo* begins publishing a New York edition as the city's Korean population grows in the wake of the 1965 immigration law. Within 30 years there will be Korean-language New York editions of the Seoul papers *Joong Ang Ilbo*, *Chosun Ilbo*, and *Sae Gae Ilbo*, plus three weekly papers, three radio stations (including one operated by *Hangkook Ilbo*), and three TV stations (channels 25, 31, and 53) whose programming will include Korean news and entertainment shows.

The U.S. Supreme Court upholds pornography May 8 by throwing out three obscenity cases, one of them involving a clerk in a subway book-and-magazine store at 263 West 48th Street, who was given a suspended sentence after being convicted of selling two paperback books (*see* 1966). The 7-to-2 decision makes it clear that the high court will not permit suppression of publications on obscenity grounds except in special, extreme circumstances. Congress creates a Commission on Obscenity and Pornography, it will conclude that pornography does not contribute to crime or sexual deviation, and the high court's ruling lends support to operators of Times Square peep shows (*see* 1966; Billy Graham, 1969; Forty-Second Street Redevelopment Corp., 1976).

Seven Arts magazine cofounder and author Waldo Frank dies at White Plains January 9 at age 77; publisher Henry R. Luce of a heart attack at Phoenix, Ariz., February 28 at age 68; Emerson Radio cofounder and philanthropist Benjamin Abrams of a heart attack at White Plains June 23 at age 74; adver-

tising executive-author Bruce Barton at New York July 5 at age 80; science-fiction publisher and inventor Hugo Gernsback at New York August 19 at age 83.

The advertising agency Della Femina, Travisano, & Partners is founded by Brooklyn-born copywriter Jerry Della Femina, 31, and others.

Interpublic Group directors vote unanimously at their board meeting November 7 to dismiss chairman Marion Harper, Jr., now 51, who has brought the huge advertising-agency conglomerate to the brink of being taken over by the banks for nonpayment of $2 million in debts (*see* 1960). Having built a colossus with a reported 8,700 employees worldwide and billings of about $650 million, Harper has squandered money on a company-owned horse ranch-conference center near Montauk, two company planes, and other luxuries; he has gotten into trouble with the Internal Revenue Service over a cattle ranch he owns; he resigns his position as president and CEO to former McCann-Erickson executive Robert Healey, 63, who comes out of semiretirement and will reduce operating costs to return the agency to profitability.

The Public Broadcasting Act signed into law by President Johnson November 7 creates a Corporation for Public Broadcasting to broaden the scope of noncommercial radio and TV beyond its educational role (*see* Channel 13, 1962). Federal grants (plus funds from foundations, business, and private contributions) will within 3 years make National Public Radio (WNYC in New York) and Public Broadcasting Service effective rivals to NBC, CBS, and ABC (*see* Sesame Street, 1968).

Nonfiction: *Lost New York* by Columbia University assistant professor of architecture Nathan Silver, 27, whose book of photographs bemoans the loss of such treasures as the old Pennsylvania Station and the old Metropolitan Opera House; *"Our Crowd"—The Great Jewish Families of New York* by Connecticut-born New York advertising agency copywriter and novelist Stephen Birmingham, 35, who began his career writing copy for Gimbels; *Macy's, Gimbels, and Me* by Wisconsin-born retail advertising executive Bernice Fitzgibbon, 68, who created the Macy's slogan "It's Smart to Be Thrifty," was the highest-paid advertising woman in America by 1941, and gave Macy's biggest competitor the slogan, "Nobody But Nobody Beats Gimbels;" *What Have You Done for Me Lately? The Ins and Outs of New York City Politics* by Warren Moscow; *Tigers of Tammany: Nine Men Who Ran New York* by Michigan-born author Alfred Connable, 41, and Edward Silverfarb; *Aaron Burr:*

Portrait of an Ambitious Man by Herbert Parmet and New York-born author Marie B. Hecht (*née* Bergenfeld), 48; *Remember When: A Loving Look at Days Gone By* by Allen Churchill; *Central Park: A History and Guide* by architecture critic and park curator Henry Hope Reed and Sophia Duckworth; *Prospect Park Handbook* by Clay Lancaster; *The Lawyers* by Martin Mayer.

Fiction: *The Chosen* by New York-born novelist Chaim (originally Herman Harold) Potok, 38, is about hasids in Brooklyn; *The Free-Lance Pallbearers* by Chattanooga-born New York novelist-poet Ishmael Reed, 29, who cofounded the *East Village Other* 2 years ago; *Snow White* by Philadelphia-born New York novelist Donald Barthelme, 36; *Rosemary's Baby* by Ira Levin; *Tales of Manhattan* (stories) by Louis Auchincloss; *The Diary of a Mad Housewife* by New York novelist Sue Kaufman, 40.

Poet-author Langston Hughes dies of congestive heart failure at New York May 22 at age 65. He has lived since 1947 on the top floor of an 1869 Italianate brownstone at 20 East 127th Street.

Juvenile: *From the Mixed-Up Files of Mrs. Basil E. Frankweiler* by New York-born Pennsylvania-raised author E. L. Konigsburg (*née* Elaine Lobl), 37, whose teenage heroine leaves home with her younger brother and winds up living comfortably at the Metropolitan Museum of Art.

Painting: *Central Park Looking North* by John Koch, whose Central Park West apartment overlooks the park; *Three Folk Musicians* (collage) by Romare Bearden; *The Human Edge* by Helen Frankenthaler. Edward Hopper dies at New York May 15 at age 84; Ad Reinhardt of a heart attack at New York August 30 at age 53.

Sculpture: *Broken Obelisk* by Barnett Newman; *Henry Moore Bound to Fail* by Bruce Nauman; *Laundromat* by George Segal.

Artforum begins publication at New York after 3 years at San Francisco, where it was founded by printing salesman John Irwin with a 10 3/8" × 10 3/8" format. It was acquired 2 years ago by publishing heir Charles Cowles, then 22, who put up money to get it out of debt, worked on it as his senior project at Stanford, moved it to Los Angeles, where the intellectual, slick-paper art magazine's editor Philip Leider had gone, and has come to New York with Leider in June (*see* 1979).

The Serge Sabarsky gallery opens at 987 Madison Avenue under the direction of Vienna-born dealer Sabarsky, 55, who worked as a clown before immigrating to America in 1939 but has become an authority on Austrian and German Expressionist painting (*see* Neue Galerie, 2001).

Theater: *MacBird* by Brooklyn-born playwright Barbara Garson, 25, 2/22 at the off-Broadway Village Gate Theater, with Savannah-born actor Stacy Keach, 25, 386 perfs.; *Fortune and Men's Eyes* by Toronto-born dancer-playwright John Herbert (originally John Herbert Brundage), 40, 2/23 at the off-Broadway Actor's Playhouse, with Robert Christian, Victor Arnold, 382 perfs.; *You Know I Can't Hear You When the Water's Running* by Robert Anderson 3/13 at the Ambassador Theater, with North Carolina-born actor George Grizzard, 38, Eileen Heckart, Martin Balsam, 755 perfs.; *La Turista* by Fort Sheridan, Ill.-born playwright Sam Shepard (originally Samuel Shepard Rogers), 23, 4/2 at the off-Broadway American Place Theater; *Little Murders* by New York-born cartoonist-playwright Jules Feiffer, 38, 4/25 at the Broadhurst Theater, with Elliott Gould, Heywood Hale Broun, Barbara Cook, 7 perfs.

Veteran set designer and Theater Guild cofounder Lee Simonson dies at Yonkers January 23 at age 78; actress Judith Evelyn of cancer at Roosevelt Hospital May 7 at age 54; playwright Elmer Rice of pneumonia at Southampton, England, May 8 at age 74; playwright-wit Dorothy Parker is found dead of a heart attack in her Volney Hotel suite at 23 East 74th Street June 7 at age 73 (she has lived for weeks on little but alcohol; her gravestone will not bear the epitaph she once suggested: "Excuse my dust"); theater owner David T. Nederlander dies at Detroit October 14 at age 81; playwright Joseph Kesselring at Kingston, N.Y., November 5 at age 65; comedian Bert Lahr of an internal hemorrhage at New York December 4 at age 72.

Television: *N.Y.P.D.* 9/5 on ABC with Jack Warden, Robert Hooker, Frank Converse (to 1969). Producer David Susskind signed a contract 2/7 with Police Commissioner Howard R. Leary providing for co-operation in providing technical information but not opening the department's files to the TV producers.

TV puppeteer Cora Baird (*née* Burlar) dies of cancer at New York December 6 at age 54.

Films: Robert Mulligan's *Up the Down Staircase* with Sandy Dennis in a movie version of the 1964 Bel Kaufman novel. Also: Curtis Harrington's *Games* with Simone Signoret, James Caan, Katharine Ross; Larry Peerce's *The Incident* with Tony Musante, Martin Sheen, Beau Bridges, Jack Gilford, Thelma Ritter (about two drunken hoodlums who terrorize passengers aboard a graffiti-filled New York subway); Shirley Clarke's documentary *Portrait of Jason* (a 105-minute interview with a gay black male prostitute that has been filmed during a single 12-hour session in Clarke's apartment).

Actor Basil Rathbone dies of a heart attack at New York July 21 at age 75.

Film musical: David Swift's *How to Succeed in Business Without Really Trying* with Robert Morse, Michele Lee, Rudy Vallée.

Broadway and off-Broadway musicals: *You're a Good Man, Charlie Brown* 3/7 at the 179-seat Theater 80 St. Marks, with Connecticut-born TV actor Gary Burghoff, 24, Reva Rose, book based on Charles Schultz's 17-year-old comic strip *Peanuts*, music and lyrics by Augusta, Me.-born Princeton graduate Clark Gesner, 28, 1,579 perfs.; *Hair* 10/29 at the new off-Broadway Public Theater created by Joseph Papp, with Pittsburgh-born actor Gerome Ragni, 25, as Bezar, New York-born ingénue Melba Moore (originally Melba Hill), 21, music by Montreal-born composer Galt MacDermot, lyrics by Ragni and James Rado, 28, songs that include "Hare Krishna" and "Aquarius," 94 perfs. (plus 1,742 beginning 4/29/68 at the Biltmore Theater with some nudity); *How Now, Dow Jones* 12/7 at the Lunt-Fontanne Theater, with six-foot-six-inch Wichita Falls, Texas-born dancer-choreographer Tommy Tune, 30, Bedford Hills-born actor Barnard Hughes, 52, Brenda Vaccaro, New York-born actor Tony Roberts, 28, music by Elmer Bernstein, book by Max Shulman, lyrics by Carolyn Leigh, 220 perfs. (a critic calls it "Standard and Poor," but it has a good run).

The Opera Orchestra of New York is founded as a training group/workshop for apprentice orchestra musicians by New York-born conductor Eve Queler (*née* Rabin), 31.

Carnegie Hall is designated a New York City Landmark June 20.

The Grateful Dead gives its first New York concert (a free Thursday afternoon event) in Tompkins Square Park 6/1. Started at San Francisco 2 years ago by electric guitarist Jerry Garcia, then 24, with drummer Mickey Hart, Ron "Pigpen" McKernan, and others, the group will gain wide popularity among young New Yorkers and fans worldwide.

Singer-actress Barbra Streisand performs in Central Park's Sheep Meadow 6/17 and attracts a crowd estimated at 135,000 (250,000 by some accounts). Wearing a pink gown, Streisand sings such favorites as "Cry Me a River" and "Second Hand Rose," she

sips tea while telling the audience stories of her life and the ironies of her success, but although the event is considered a great success the crowd leaves the Sheep Meadow so littered with blankets, bottles, cans, clothing, paper, and other debris that a 30-man crew has to work overtime to clean up the mess. (Rheingold Beer has sponsored the concert and pays for the clean-up.)

Popular songs: "Chelsea Morning" by Canadian-born singer-guitarist-songwriter Joni Mitchell (originally Roberta Joan Anderson), 24, who lives in a ground-floor apartment at 41 West 16th Street; "New York Mining Disaster" by the Bee Gees—English rock composer Barry Gibb, 20, and his brothers Robin and Maurice, 17 (fraternal twins).

Pianist-songwriter Dave Dreyer dies at New York March 2 at age 72; Dixieland jazz trumpeter Henry "Red" Allen returns from a tour of Britain in early March and dies of pancreatic cancer at New York April 17 at age 60; jazz composer Billy Strayhorn dies of cancer at New York May 31 at age 51; jazz saxophonist John Coltrane of a liver ailment at Huntington, L.I., July 17 at age 41 (the Rev. John G. Gensel of St. Peter's Lutheran Church officiates at his funeral); disk jockey Martin Block of "Make Believe Ballroom" fame dies after surgery at Englewood, N.J., September 19 at age 64; bandleader Paul "Pops" Whiteman of a heart attack at Doylestown, Pa., December 29 at age 77. Once known as the "king of jazz," he made his final public appearance in 1962.

Middleweight boxing champion Emile Griffith, now 29, loses his title April 17 to Nino Benvenuti, who is awarded the championship on points after 15 rounds at Madison Square Garden (*see* 1966), but Griffith regains the title September 29 by outscoring Benvenuti in another 15-rounder (*see* 1968).

John Newcombe, 23 (Australia), wins in men's singles at Forest Hills, Billie Jean King in women's singles.

Mickey Mantle of the New York Yankees hits his 500th home run in league competition.

New York Knicks owner Ned Irish persuades his Manhattan-born scout William "Red" Holzman, 47, to take over as coach in December, replacing Dick McGuire, whose team is in last place. Holzman fines several players $10 each for showing up late at his first practice and begins a new career; his Knickerbocker teams will win 613 games (*see* NBA championship, 1970).

Former state athletic commission chairman Eddie Egan dies of a heart attack at New York June 14 at age

69; former sports announcer Harry Wismer of a fractured skull after suffering a fall at New York December 4 at age 56.

● *Women's Wear Daily*'s front page February 8 hails James Galanos "the leader of American fashion," displacing Norman Norell, who has been favored by publisher John B. Fairchild since 1960 and remains preeminent despite Fairchild's snub.

The city's first West Indian American Day Parade steps off in Harlem to celebrate carnival before Lent. The event will move next year to Labor Day and grow to be a bigger parade than St. Patrick's in Manhattan as costumed masqueraders ride or strut two miles down Brooklyn's Eastern Parkway from Utica Avenue in Crown Heights to Grand Army Plaza while as many as 2 million Caribbean immigrants (mostly from English-speaking islands) cluster behind police barricades to watch a pageant of costumed celebrants, listen and dance to steel bands playing Trinidadian calypso and soca, shimmy to reggae, compas, and salsa, buy souvenirs, eat roti, and drink mango juice and beer.

Massage parlors proliferate in Times Square and other parts of the city following the City Council's removal of licensing requirements. The parlors are thinly disguised venues for prostitution (*see* 42nd Street Development Corp., 1976).

▥ Organized crime leader Thomas Gaetano "Three-Finger Brown" Luchese dies at Lido Beach, N.Y., July 13 at age 67.

🏠 The city creates the Office of Lower Manhattan Development January 18 to implement the Lower Manhattan Plan released by the Lindsay administration last year, but political rivalries will delay any implementation of plans to build Battery Park City (*see* 1969).

The Jacob K. Javits Federal Office Building and Court of International Trade (Customs Court) is completed on the west side of Foley Square at 26 Federal Plaza, between Duane and Worth streets. Designed by Alfred Easton Poor and Kahn & Jacobs in co-operation with Eggers & Higgins, the granite and glass tower rises 41 stories in height.

The Marine Midland Bank Building is completed at 140 Broadway, between Liberty and Cedar streets, with its east side on Nassau Street. Gordon Bunshaft of Skidmore, Owings & Merrill has designed the 51-story structure.

The 12-story Ford Foundation Building is completed at 321 East 42nd Street (320 East 43rd), between First and Second avenues. Dublin-born architect Kevin Roche, now 45, and his Michigan-born partner John G. Dinkeloo, 49, of Kevin Roche, John Dinkeloo Associates have designed the structure, whose offices are in an L shape around a 130-foot glassed-in atrium garden that is lushly planted but will remain largely off limits to the public.

The New York Public Library at 42nd Street is designated a New York City Landmark January 11, the Metropolitan Museum of Art June 9, Grand Central Terminal September 21 (*see* 1966; 1968).

The 47-story 245 Park Avenue office tower (initially the American Tobacco Building) is completed in the block bounded by Park and Lexington avenues between 46th and 47th streets, replacing the 12-story Grand Central Palace opened in 1911 and the 20-story Park-Lexington Building (247 Park) completed in 1922. Designed by Shreve, Lamb & Harmon for Uris Brothers, the new structure occupies the entire block, rising on columns that go into bedrock about six feet below Grand Central Terminal's three levels at 47th Street. The builders have not only acquired the air rights above the New York Central tracks but have also rented the railroad's 100-ton crane and some of its flatcars and gondolas to haul materials into position; their engineers had to memorize train schedules in order not to sink a steel column at the same time the stationmaster was dispatching a local to White Plains; and their workers had to dig, weld, and rivet among the 40 railroad tracks, avoiding the live third rail. The engineers have used many of the old Grand Central Palace underpinnings, insulating the bases of the column supports in mats of lead and asbestos to eliminate the vibrations of the two tiers of trains passing below.

The 42-story Westvaco Building is completed for the former West Virginia Pulp and Paper Co. on the east side of Park Avenue between 48th and 49th streets, where the Park Lane Hotel stood for 41 years. Emery Roth & Sons has designed the structure.

The 220-unit Strykers Bay Houses (two buildings, one of 17 stories, one of 21) are completed at 689 Columbus Avenue and 66 West 94th Street as part of the Upper West Side urban renewal area; Holden, Egan, Wilson & Corser has designed the structures. The 27-story Columbus Park Towers are completed with 163 units at 100 West 94th Street on Columbus Avenue to designs by Ballard, Todd & Snibbe. The 27-story Goddard Towers are completed with 194 units at 711 Amsterdam Avenue, northeast corner 94th Street, to designs by The Edelman Partnership. The 14-story RNA Houses are completed with 208 units at 150 and 160 West 96th Street, between

Columbus and Amsterdam avenues; sponsored by the Riverside Neighborhood Association, they have been designed by Edelbaum & Webster.

The Bedford Stuyvesant Restoration Corp. is founded through bipartisan efforts by Sen. Robert F. Kennedy and Sen. Jacob K. Javits. The first U.S. nonprofit community development corporation, its aim is to improve the economy of the neighborhood and its quality of life; the corporation will work with public and private capital to build a 300,000-square-foot Restoration Plaza with 2,225 residential housing units and a major health-care facility. It will find employment for 25,000 persons, sponsor the 214-seat Billie Holiday Theater, the Skylight Gallery at the Center for Art and Culture, the Restoration Dance Theater, and—in a joint venture with Pathmark Stores—develop a 30,000-square-foot supermarket (*see* food, 1977).

East Harlem's Riverbend Houses are completed on Fifth Avenue between 138th and 142nd streets. Designed by Davis, Brody & Associates, the eight- and 10-story structures contain a total of 625 apartments with semiprivate terraces overlooking the Harlem River.

Parks Commissioner Thomas Hoving resigns in February after 1 year on the job to become director of the Metropolitan Museum of Art. Mayor Lindsay appoints August Heckscher, 53, to the post, and Heckscher (a grandson and namesake of the late real estate developer and philanthropist) is sworn in March 17, landing in a helicopter with the mayor at Harlem's six-acre Mount Morris Park for the ceremony, held in the auditorium of an adjacent school (the weather is bitter cold, and a snowstorm has delayed the start of the annual St. Patrick's Day Parade). Formerly chief editorial writer for the *Herald Tribune*, Heckscher has headed the Twentieth Century Fund and will remain as parks commissioner until 1972. He organizes a festival to mark the 150th anniversary of Frederick Law Olmsted's birth April 27, putting sheep back in Central Park's Sheep Meadow for the day and serving a cake more than 100 feet long baked by young artists in the shape of Central Park. New fluorescent lights are installed in early May to illuminate the park at night, making it safer (Olmsted closed it at night because it could not be policed adequately), but love-ins, be-ins, and various "happenings" in the park during this decade will leave it in sorry condition.

Paley Park (Samuel Paley Plaza) opens just east of Madison Avenue in 53rd Street on a $750,000 site formerly occupied by the Stork Club (*see* 1965). Built with a gift of $1 million from CBS chairman William S. Paley, who has funded the project as a memorial to his late father, the 40-by-100-square-foot vest-pocket park is leased to the Parks Department at $1 per year. Landscape architect Robert L. (Lewis) Zion, 46, has designed the space with a thunderous waterfall on its back wall to muffle the sound of city traffic. Visitors sit on white wire-framed chairs by Harry Bertoia as they chat, read, eat lunch, or simply contemplate the park's waterfall, ivy, and leafy trees.

Flushing Meadows-Corona Park is rededicated June 3 in Queens. Originally dedicated in 1932 as Flushing Meadow Park, the city's second-largest park occupies land used by the 1939–1940 World's Fair, by the United Nations from 1946 to 1950, and by the 1964–1965 World's Fair.

An anti-pollution law goes into effect requiring that substandard incinerators be shut down. Designed to improve the city's air quality, the new regulation increases the need for more refuse-disposal dumps.

The Hunt's Point Market opens in the Bronx March 21 with a wholesale produce facility to serve the city's retail grocers and restaurants. Agitation has persisted since the 1930s for a relocation of the Washington Market, a survivor from the early 19th century that will soon be replaced by twin skyscrapers.

1968 Former water commissioner James L. Marcus pleads guilty January 18 to federal charges of having accepted a bribe and a New York County grand jury indicts him January 26 on charges of bribery and perjury (*see* 1967). He pleads guilty again, is fined $10,000, draws a sentence of 15 months in federal prison, and begins serving time September 13.

Gov. Rockefeller strips Robert Moses of power March 1 by merging the Triborough Bridge and Tunnel Authority into a new Metropolitan Transportation Authority (MTA). Now 79, Moses has had a major influence in the state for 44 years, building Long Island beaches and creating parks that now benefit millions, but although he has overseen construction of public housing projects for 555,000 people, his highway and slum-clearance projects have caused the eviction of about the same number.

Rep. Adam Clayton Powell flies to Newark Airport March 22, is driven to the Manhattan apartment of Judge Arthur Markewich, is technically arrested but immediately granted a parole, and attends a Welcome Home rally in Harlem (*see* 1967). A court of appeals has ruled February 28 that he was not entitled to his seat, the House of Representatives has fined him $25,000 and denied him seniority and committee assignments, but he tells a wildly cheering crowd March 23, "They've never seen a scene like they're gonna have if they touch Big Daddy." Powell preaches at the Abyssinian Baptist Church that Sunday, surrounded by young bodyguards dressed in military attire (one carries a machete with a Bible impaled on it).

Opposition to the Vietnam War enables Sen. Eugene McCarthy, 52 (D. Wis.), to make a strong showing in the New Hampshire primary; his success persuades President Johnson to announce March 31 that he will not be a candidate for reelection. New York civil-rights lawyer and anti-war activist Allard K. Lowenstein, 39, has led the opposition to another term for Johnson.

Columbia University explodes in violence April 23 as students protest campus-related military research in the continuing Vietnam War.

Sen. Robert F. Kennedy (D. N.Y.) makes a bid for the U.S. presidency. Now 42, he captures 174 delegate votes (winning the Indiana, Nebraska, and California primaries, losing in Oregon), but is shot June 5 in a Los Angeles hotel kitchen pantry after leaving a victory celebration and dies June 6. His body is flown to New York, where it lies in state June 7 at St. Patrick's Cathedral; a line of mourners from all ranks of life, extending for more than a mile long, waits to view the closed casket, guarded by a constantly shifting group of six young men and boys. The Kennedy family maintains an all-night vigil, and members attend a private mass at Holy Family Church. An estimated 151,000 persons file past the bier in the 23 hours that the cathedral is open to the public, and the 2,300 who attend the funeral June 8 include President Johnson, Nelson Rockefeller, former vice president Richard Nixon, and Averell Harriman.

Democrats in convention at Chicago nominate Vice President Hubert Humphrey to succeed President Johnson. Richard Nixon wins the Republican nomination on the first ballot, having actively campaigned for G.O.P. candidates in 1966 and regained favor. He wins election by the narrowest margin since his own defeat by John F. Kennedy in 1960— 43.4 percent of the popular vote to Humphrey's 43 percent (but 302 electoral votes to Humphrey's 191).

Sen. Javits wins reelection, defeating his Democratic challenger, lawyer Paul O'Dwyer.

Manhattan's 14th Congressional District (the "Silk Stocking" District) on the upper East Side elects its first Democrat to Congress in 34 years: reformer Edward I. (Irving) Koch, 43, has twice defeated Tammany leader Carmine G. De Sapio in primary

elections for district leaderships and now wins the seat held by Mayor Lindsay from 1958 to 1965.

Brooklyn's 12th Congressional District elects local activist Shirley (Anita St. Hill) Chisholm, 43, to the House of Representatives, where she will be the first elected black woman. A Democrat, she will serve for seven terms.

Former New York police officer Mario Biaggi, 51, wins election to the House from the 10th District (Astoria and parts of the Bronx and Yonkers). He is the most highly decorated officer in the history of the force and will run for mayor (unsuccessfully) in 1973 (see 1987).

Rep. Adam Clayton Powell, Jr., now 59, regains his former congressional seat in the regular election. The U.S. Supreme Court agrees November 18 to hear his case, and the Department of Justice decides December 9 not to seek an indictment against him (see 1969).

Social reformer and perennial Socialist presidential candidate Norman Thomas dies at New York December 20 at age 84.

Pioneer labor organizer Jacob Panken dies at New York February 4 at age 89, having helped to start the ILGWU, Amalgamated Clothing Workers, and other unions.

Civil rights leader Martin Luther King, Jr. is shot dead April 4 at age 39 as he steps out on the balcony of his Memphis motel room. Race riots erupt at Newark, N.J., and in scores of other U.S. cities following the King assassination, but New York remains relatively calm as Mayor Lindsay walks into black communities wearing a trenchcoat. He assures people that whites as well as blacks are distressed by the murder, and his gesture is credited with helping to keep the city peaceful.

A U.S. Civil Rights Bill signed into law by President Johnson April 11 stresses open housing.

Columbia University's student war protest in late April quickly turns to anger against university policies that have since 1919 involved acquiring dozens of buildings in the Morningside Heights area and evicting thousands of tenants, many of them black and Hispanic. The acquisition program has accelerated as university administrators have become alarmed at the deterioration in parts of Morningside Heights and West Harlem that once comprised a middle-class community but is fast becoming a neighborhood marked by crime, unemployment, and widespread failure by landlords to maintain their buildings.

$ The Uniformed Sanitationmen's Association strikes from February 8 to 19, halting the city's garbage pickups for 9 days while more than 100,000 tons of waste pile up on the streets, creating a health hazard; Mayor Lindsay and Gov. Rockefeller disagree on how to resolve the situation; the 10,000 strikers have worked without a contract since June of last year, making $6,624 per year to start and $7,956 after 3 years; they seek wage increases of $600 per year, time and a half for Saturday work, double time for Sundays, and a 1-year contract; they obtain large wage increases and binding arbitration of labor disputes.

New York's unemployment rate falls to 3.1 percent—well below the national average and lower than any other major city except Detroit. Among blacks, the unemployment rate is 4 percent, about half the level elsewhere in America.

The Ford Foundation launches the Fund for the City of New York, an organization whose chief function is to work with government agencies, assessing performance and improving accountability. The Fund will make grants to advocacy groups and loans to nonprofit recipients of government contracts.

New York entrepreneur Saul Steinberg uses money raised from the sale of the highly overvalued stock in his Leasco computer-leasing company to acquire control of Reliance Insurance Co. (see technology, 1961). Now 29, Steinberg has taken over a company 10 times the size of Leasco, but when he tries to take over Chemical Bank next year his Leasco shares will plummet and the takeover bid will fail.

American Insurance Group (AIG) founder Cornelius van der Starr dies at New York December 20 at age 76 (see New York Hospital, 1986).

Depository Trust Co. (DTC) is founded at New York to create a central depository for security certificates, a facility that will eliminate much of the physical transfer of paper and apply to equities and non-Treasury bonds the same principle employed by the Federal Reserve in its book-entry system. The volume of trade on Wall Street has forced the exchanges to close early in order to catch up with backoffice paperwork, trades fail increasingly because of late delivery of certificates, and brokers have acted to reduce the need for physical delivery by installing computers that interface with DTC computers to record transfer of ownership simply by debiting and crediting accounts.

Wall Street's Dow Jones Industrial Average closes December 31 at 943.75, up from 905.11 at the end of 1967.

Madison Avenue's first designer boutique opens in a former Gristede's grocery store that French couturièr Yves Saint Laurent has taken over and renamed Rive Gauche.

Penn Central (The Pennsylvania New York Central Transportation Co.) is created February 14 by a merger of the Pennsylvania Railroad with the New York Central (actually a takeover of the latter by the former). Both are in financial trouble as a result of competition from trucks and automobiles that use publicly financed highways and airlines using publicly financed airports, they agree only reluctantly to include the beleaguered New Haven Railroad, and the U.S. Supreme Court rules against the Erie Lackawanna and six other railroads that have tried to block the merger. The new $5 billion corporation will be bankrupt within 2 years.

Pope Paul VI appoints New York-born bishop Terence J. Cooke, 47, March 8 to succeed the late Francis Cardinal Spellman as archbishop of the New York archdiocese, having elevated him over dozens of senior prelates. Cooke will be elected to the college of cardinals at Rome next year and become Terence Cardinal Cooke.

Covenant House is founded in the East Village to provide shelter for homeless and runaway youths. Franciscan friar Bruce Ritter, 41, has taken over two abandoned tenements to start his nonprofit charitable organization; it will open shelters throughout the city, including one in West 41st Street near Times Square that will remain open 24 hours per day, and an outreach center in West 44th Street (see 1989).

Militant Columbia University students shut down the school to protest building a gymnasium in Morningside Park, an area needed for low-cost housing. The protesters include members of the radical Students for a Democratic Society (SDS) and black activists H. Rap Brown and Stokely Carmichael. Columbia halts gym construction April 25, students take over five buildings including Columbia College's administrative center Hamilton Hall, and they occupy the office of President Grayson L. Kirk, 64, in a week-long sit-in; 1,000 helmeted police swarm onto the campus and storm the buildings April 30 after wanton destruction of property, and they make make 628 arrests. Classes are formally suspended May 5, President Kirk retires in August, and a fact-finding board (the Cox Commission) will criticize his administration for "unhealthy relations" with Columbia's surrounding community and its methods of expansion in that community.

The City Planning Commission gives approval May 15 for a South Street urban renewal area, the 1-year-old South Street Seaport Museum acquires the Ambrose Light Ship from the U.S. Coast Guard August 5, the schooner *Cavaire* arrives at the museum from Gloucester September 20, Schermerhorn Row near the Seaport is designated a New York City Landmark October 2, and the Board of Estimate upholds the landmark status December 15 (*see* 1969).

The Eugenio Maria de Hostos Community College opens at 475 Grand Concourse in the South Bronx, fulfilling a dream of Puerto Rican-born Borough President Herman Badillo, 39. A junior college in the CUNY system, it is the first branch of the university deliberately to be placed in an economically blighted area, and it will pioneer in bilingual education. The student body will be 80 percent Hispanic by the 1980s, and enrollment by 1990 will reach 4,315, with 3,875 full-time students, free day care, a strong health sciences program, and affiliations with several city hospitals (*but see* 1997).

Brooklyn Law School completes a 10-story facility at 250 Joralemon Street (*see* 1901). It will add an annex and by the 1990s will have an enrollment of about 1,400, including part-time students.

The Eugene M. Lang Foundation is established by Refac Technology Development Corp. founder Lang, 49. The foundation will endow Eugene Lang College at the New School for Social Research and make grants to more than six dozen other educational, cultural, and social organizations (it will also support medical care and research) (*see* 1981).

Rhody McCoy, 46, administrator of Brooklyn's Ocean Hill-Brownsville school district, removes 13 teachers, a principal, and five assistant principals in April, accusing them of sabotaging community control of public schools (*see* 1961). Ford Foundation president McGeorge Bundy has recommended that three demonstration school districts be set up with a good deal of independent authority and has provided some funds to pay for the experiment, but the Board of Education has been unwilling to cede to the locally elected governing board. McCoy has been strongly influenced by the anti-white teachings of the late Malcolm X, all but one of the teachers whom he fires are white, many are Jewish, and the confrontation has racial and anti-Semitic aspects. United Federation of Teachers president Albert Shanker, 39, has succeeded the retiring Charles Cogen and pushed for adequate teachers' pay plus increased authority to make decisions; he says McCoy's transfers are a violation of union contracts

and is upheld in the courts; Mayor Lindsay waffles on the issue of using police officers to escort teachers back into the schools, and Shanker takes 54,000 workers off the job September 9 in violation of the Taylor Law adopted last year. The strike continues for 55 days, closing the city's 900 schools until the state education commissioner suspends the Ocean Hill board; strike leaders are jailed, but not until mid-November are teachers allowed back into Ocean Hill-Brownsville classrooms, and pupils in schools throughout the city have had no schooling for more than 2 months (*see* 1969).

Bilingual education is introduced on an experimental basis in the city schools, beginning with Spanish at P.S. 25 in the southeastern Bronx, in an effort to educate immigrant children who cannot understand English. Previous generations of immigrants have had to learn English or receive no education, and the new program for 900 Hispanic children is intended only to ease the youngsters' entry into English-speaking classes and raise their self-esteem. By 1970 32 schools will have federally funded programs for 2,332 pupils (*see* 1972).

New York magazine begins publication in the spring under the direction of former *Herald Tribune* editor Clay S. Felker, 42, who was with *Esquire* until hired by the *Trib* to edit its Sunday magazine in 1963. Milton Glaser of Push Pin Studios is art director, a position he will hold until 1976. The new magazine carries an interview by Toledo, Ohio-born writer Gloria Steinem, 34, with the wife of former vice president Nixon.

Screw begins publication at New York in October. The pornographic weekly has been started by former insurance salesman Al Goldstein, 33, with his friend James Buckley, who will sell his interest to Goldstein for $500,000 as the tabloid gains wide readership with explicit photographs.

New Yorker magazine cartoonist Peter Arno dies of emphysema and lung cancer at Port Chester April 4 at age 64; "Katzenjammer Kids" cartoonist Rudolf Dirks at New York April 20 at age 91; Xerox inventor Chester F. Carlson at New York August 18 at age 62; *New York Times* publisher Arthur Hays Sulzberger at New York December 11 at age 79. He and his wife, Iphigene, have lived since 1952 at 1115 Fifth Avenue.

The 911 emergency telephone number is instituted at New York to summon emergency police, fire, or ambulance assistance—the first such system in the United States (Britain inaugurated a system in 1937). By 1977 some 600 U.S. localities with a total population of 38 million will have 911 systems.

Time, Inc., acquires Little, Brown, a Boston publisher that has been independent for 121 years.

Nonfiction: *Making It* by *Commentary* magazine editor Norman Podhoretz, now 38, whose memoir claims that the city's intellectuals have let ambition displace their sexual energies. Podhoretz and his wife, Midge Decter, will soon be leaders of the right-wing "neo-conservative" movement; *The Urban Prospects* by Lewis Mumford; *Harlem on My Mind: Cultural Capital of Black America* by Allon Schoener (editor); *Senator Robert F. Wagner and the Rise of Urban Liberalism* by Rutgers University historian J. Joseph Huthmacher, 38; *The Geology of New York City and Environs* by Museum of Natural History geology lecturer Christopher J. Schuberth, 35.

Fiction: *The Electric Kool-Aid Acid Test* by Richmond, Va.-born New York journalist-novelist Tom Wolfe (Thomas Kennerly Wolfe, Jr.), 37; *A State of Change* by English-born journalist-novelist Penelope Gilliatt (née Conner), 36, who joins the staff of The *New Yorker* and will remain until 1979.

Novelist Fannie Hurst dies at New York February 23 at age 78; novelist-playwright Edna Ferber at New York April 16 at age 82; Charles Jackson by his own hand at New York September 21 at age 65; John Steinbeck of a heart ailment at New York December 20 at age 66.

The Studio Museum in Harlem opens at 144 West 125th Street, between Lenox and Seventh avenues. A fine arts museum dedicated to showing the art and artifacts of black America and the African diaspora, it will develop a permanent collection beginning in 1979 with works by Romare Bearden, Jacob Lawrence, Faith Ringgold, and other prominent painters and sculptors, and it will become the only black museum accredited by the American Association of Museums. The custodian of New York State's collection of black and Latin American art will grow to have more than 10,000 items, including photographs and textiles.

Museum of Modern Art (MoMA) director René d'Harnoncourt retires July 1 after 19 years and dies August 13 at age 67 when hit by a drunken driver while walking near his summer home at New Suffolk, N.Y.

Sculpture: *Sentinel* (bronze) by Polish-born New York abstract sculptor Theodore Roszak, 61, is installed in front of a public research building near Bellevue Hospital on First Avenue at 28th Street; *The Parking Garage* and *Artist in His Studio* by George Segal.

Photographer Arthur Fellig (Weegee) dies of a brain tumor at Park West Hospital December 26 at age 69. He has been living at 451 West 47th Street.

Theater: *The Prime of Miss Jean Brodie* by Jay Allen (who has adapted the novel by Muriel Spark) 1/16 at the Helen Hayes Theater, with Australian actress Zoë Caldwell, 34, 378 perfs.; *The Indian Wants the Bronx* by New York playwright Israel Horovitz 1/17 at the Astor Place Theater; *I Never Sang for My Father* by Robert Anderson 1/25 at the Longacre Theater, with Hal Holbrook, Lillian Gish, Matt Crowley, Teresa Wright, 124 perfs.; *The Price* by Arthur Miller 2/7 at the Morosco Theater, with Pat Hingle, London-born actress Kate Reid, 37, Arthur Kennedy, 429 perfs.; *The Boys in the Band* by Mart Crowley 4/18 at the off-Broadway Theater Four, with New York-born actor Cliff Gorman, 31, 1,000 perfs.; *The Great White Hope* by New York-born playwright Howard (Oliver) Sackler, 39, 10/3 at the Alvin Theater, with Mississippi-born actor James Earl Jones, 37, Boston-born actress Jane Alexander (née Quigley), 28, 276 perfs.; *Forty Carats* by Jay Allen (who has adapted a French play) 12/26 at the Morosco Theater, with Julie Harris, Enid, Okla.-born actress Glenda Farrell, now 64, 780 perfs.

Playwright Howard Lindsay dies of leukemia at New York February 11 at age 78.

Films: Mel Brooks's *The Producers* with Zero Mostel, Gene Wilder; Roman Polanski's *Rosemary's Baby* with Mia Farrow, John Cassavetes, Ruth Gordon, Sidney Blackmer, Maurice Evans, Ralph Bellamy. Also: Sidney Lumet's *Bye Bye Braverman* with George Segal, Jack Warden, Joseph Wiseman; Don Siegel's *Coogan's Bluff* with Clint Eastwood, Lee J. Cobb; David Lowell Rich's *A Lovely Way to Die* with Kirk Douglas, Sylva Koscina, Eli Wallach; Jack Smight's *No Way to Treat a Lady* with Rod Steiger, George Segal, Lee Remick, Eileen Heckart; Gene Saks's *The Odd Couple* with Jack Lemmon as fussy photographer Oscar Madison, Walter Matthau as sportswriter Felix Unger, who share an apartment at 131 Riverside Drive; Alex March's *Paper Lion* with Alan Alda as writer George Plimpton; Ulu Grosbard's *The Subject Was Roses* with Patricia Neal, Jack Albertson, Martin Sheen; Martin Scorsese's *Who's That Knocking at My Door* with Zina Bethune, Harvey Keitel.

Onetime film star Kay Francis dies of cancer at her New York apartment August 26 at age 63; Franchot Tone of lung cancer at New York September 18 at age 62; producer Walter Wanger (originally Feuchtwanger) of a heart attack at New York November 18 at age 74; Tallulah Bankhead of pneumonia and emphysema at St. Luke's Hospital December 12 at age 66. She has lived since 1962 at 447 East 57th Street.

 Film musical: William Wyler's *Funny Girl* with Barbra Streisand, Omar Sharif, music by Bob Merrill and Jule Styne, songs that include "Don't Rain on My Parade."

Broadway and off-Broadway musicals: *Your Own Thing* 1/18 at the off-Broadway Orpheum Theater, with book based on Shakespeare's *Twelfth Night*, music and lyrics by Hal Hester and Daniel George "Danny" Apolinar, 32, 937 perfs. (the first rock musical); *George M!* 4/10 at the Palace, with Joel Grey, Ozone Park-born ingénue Bernadette Peters (originally Lazzara), 20, music and lyrics by the late George M. Cohan, 433 perfs.; *Zorba* 11/17 at the Imperial Theater, with New York-born actor Herschel Bernardi, 44, Hartford-born actress Maria Karnilova (originally Dovgolenko), 47, Auburn, N.Y.-born actor John Cunningham, 36, book by Joe Stein based on the Nikos Kazantzakis novel, music by John Kander, lyrics by Fred Ebb, songs that include "Life Is," "The First Time," "The Top of the Hill," "No Boom Boom," "The Bend of the Road," and "The Happy Time," 305 perfs.; *Promises, Promises* 12/1 at the Shubert Theater, with Jerry Orbach, book by Neil Simon based on Billy Wilder's film *The Apartment*, music by Kansas City-born composer Burt Bacharach, 39, lyrics by New York-born writer Hal David, 47, songs that include "Whoever You Are," "I'll Never Fall in Love Again," 1,281 perfs.

Illinois-born self-taught pianist-singer Robert W. "Bobby" Short, 42, appears in a joint concert with Mabel Mercer at Town Hall, cuts a record of the event, and opens at the Café Carlyle on Madison Avenue at 76th Street, where the onetime vaudeville prodigy will appear each spring for more than 33 years, performing favorites by Cole Porter and others.

Opera: Italian tenor Luciano Pavarotti, 32, makes his Metropolitan Opera debut 4/23 singing the role of Rodolfo in the 1896 Puccini opera *La Bohème*; New Orleans-born soprano Shirley Verrett, 37, makes her Met debut 9/21 singing the title role in the 1875 Bizet opera *Carmen*; Spanish tenor Plácido Domingo, 27, makes his formal Met debut 9/28 singing the role of Maurice de Saxe in the 1902 Cilea opera *Adriana Lecouvrer* (Domingo makes his Carnegie Hall debut 11/15).

The Boys Choir of Harlem is founded by Manhattan School of Music doctoral candidate Walter J. Turnbull, 23, a tenor who gathers 20 youths—most of them from single-parent households headed by women whose income is often below the poverty level—and rehearses them at the Ephesus Seventh Day Adventist Church in central Harlem, raising money from corporate sponsors to support the group with counseling and tutoring. The Boys Choir will grow into a tuition-free academy of 563 students (girls as well as boys), ranging in age from 8 to 18, with 1,500 children auditioning each year in hopes of being among the 100 4th graders admitted to a three-story school building on Madison Avenue at 127th Street. Concert receipts and album sales will grow to cover nearly half the academy's annual budget of $3.2 million as its 40-boy choirs (it will have seven training and concert choirs) sing in some 120 concerts per year worldwide.

The 64-year-old (technically 22-year-old) Juilliard School of Music leaves its home at 120 Claremont Avenue on Morningside Heights and moves into a five-story, $29.5 million Lincoln Center building on Broadway between 65th and 66th streets (a bridge over 65th Street connects it to a plaza behind Philharmonic Hall). Designed by Pietro Belluschi with Eduardo Catalano and Westermann & Miller, the structure replaces the Lincoln Square Arcade (*see* Manhattan School of Music, 1969).

Simon and Garfunkel make their Carnegie Hall debut 1/27. Folk-rock singers-composers Paul Simon and Art Garfunkel entertain the audience with numbers that include "The Sounds of Silence" and "59th Street Bridge Song."

Fillmore East opens 3/8 at the corner of 6th Street and Second Avenue in the East Village. Berlin-born promoter Bill Graham (originally Wolfgang Grajonca), now 36, escaped the Nazis as a youth by walking across Europe, went to school in the Bronx, held various jobs after winning a bronze star with the U.S. Army in the Korean War, opened his first Fillmore at San Francisco late in 1965, and has taken over the Village Theater, once a Yiddish playhouse and later the site of a John Coltrane concert; Graham turns it into a showcase for rock bands and other performers (*see* 1971).

The new Madison Square Garden opens February 11 with a salute to the United Service Organization (USO) featuring Bob Hope and Bing Crosby. It replaces the Garden put up on Eighth Avenue and 50th Street in 1925 (that Garden comes down and its site is turned into a large parking lot that will not be developed until the mid-1980s).

Middleweight champion Emile Griffith loses his title by decision once again March 4 in a 15-round match with Nino Benvunuti at Madison Square Garden. Griffith will retire from the ring in 1977.

Joe Frazier wins the world heavyweight boxing crown March 24 at age 24 by knocking out Buster Mathis in the 11th round of a title bout at New York nearly 10 months after the World Boxing Association took the title away from Muhammad Ali for refusing to accept induction into the U.S. Army.

Virginia-born tennis pro Arthur (Robert) Ashe, (Jr.), 25, wins in men's singles at Forest Hills (the first black to do so), Margaret Smith Court wins in women's singles. Ashe wins the first U.S. Open men's singles, (Sarah) Virginia Wade, 22, (Brit), the women's singles.

The New York Jets of the American Football League play the Oakland Raiders at Oakland, Calif., November 17 and lead 32 to 29 with 65 seconds left on the clock. NBC-TV cuts away at that point to show the made-for-television film *Heidi*, the Raiders score two touchdowns to win 43 to 32, and many New York viewers do not know the final score until they watch the 11 o'clock news.

Ralph Lauren is founded by Bronx-born fashion designer Lauren (originally Lifshitz), 29, whose "old money" and "old West" Polo brand looks will earn him a fortune.

Bronx-born fashion designer Calvin Klein, 25, shows his first collection. A firm believer in functional simplicity, he eschews the theatrical ruffles of most other designers and engages fashion publicist Eleanor Lambert, now 64, to promote his line.

Anne Klein & Co. is founded by New York fashion designer Klein, now 47 (or 63, or somewhere in between), and her second husband (see 1948); she will continue to design until her death in 1974.

Halston starts his own manufacturing company with design studios and offices at the corner of Madison Avenue and 68th Street (see 1966). Now 36, he puts on an innovative fashion show December 2 with just 25 pieces and wins acclaim for the simple, natural lines of the clothing he has created in rich fabrics (see 1972).

Estée Lauder launches a new line of cosmetics under the name Clinique (see Aramis, 1964). The company has grown to have sales of $30 million per year and has hired *Vogue* managing editor Carol Phillips to help it introduce the first allergy-tested products to be sold in department stores, but Clinique will lose $20 million over the next 4 years before breaking even.

The financially pressed new Penn Central Railroad enters (even before its formal creation) into a 50-year lease and sublease agreements January 22 with UGP Properties, headed by English developer Morris Saady. UGP contracts to put up an office tower over Grand Central Terminal's waiting room; it has engaged Marcel Breuer to design the structure and pledges itself to pay Penn Central $1 million per year while the building is under construction plus $3 million per year thereafter. The Landmarks Preservation Commission rejects plans for the tower, saying, "To protect a landmark one does not tear it down. To perpetuate its architectural features, one does not strip them off." Penn Central's predecessor companies opposed the Landmarks Preservation Law 3 years ago and it joins with UGP in a suit filed in state court, claiming that application of the landmarks law took their property without just compensation, a violation of the Fifth and Fourteenth amendments, and arbitrarily deprived them of their property without due process of law, another violation of the Fourteenth Amendment. The case will drag on for years (see 1977).

Steel construction on the World Trade Center begins in August (see 1966; 1972).

The 32-story 909 Third Avenue office tower is completed between 54th and 55th streets. Designed by Max O. Urbahn & Associates, it incorporates the Franklin D. Roosevelt Station of the U.S. Post Office.

A commission appointed to develop Welfare Island (formerly Blackwell's Island) in the East River holds its first meeting during the summer. The two-mile long, 600-foot wide, 147-acre island has been used to house imprisoned felons and the city's destitute, impoverished, and chronically ill. Some members of the commission favor delaying any development, one proposes using part of the land for a convention center, one for housing, one for a nuclear-power plant, one for recreational facilities (see 1971).

The 21-story Jefferson Towers apartment house is completed with 190 units at 700 Columbus Avenue, between 94th and 95th streets. Designed by Horace Ginsbern & Partners, it is part of the Upper West Side urban renewal area; the 27-story West Side Manor is completed with 246 units at 70 West 95th Street, perpendicular to Columbus Avenue. Gruzen & Partners has designed the building; the three 14-story Westgate Houses are completed with 417 units at 120, 140, and 160 West 97th Street to designs by Joseph Feingold.

Gov. Rockefeller recruits lawyer-city planner Edward J. Logue, 47, to head the state's Urban Development Corp. created in the wake of the riots that followed the assassination of Rev. Martin Luther King, Jr. Logue is credited with having built housing in New Haven in the 1950s and (after taking over that city's moribund Redevelopment Authority in 1960) cutting through red tape to build downtown Boston's Government Center and affordable housing in Charlestown and Roxbury. Before the Urban Development Corp. goes bankrupt in 1975 Logue will have built or started under its auspices at least 117 housing development projects in 49 communities, including the Jackie Robinson Houses in Brooklyn and the Shorter Houses in Coney Island (*see* 1978).

The South East Bronx Community Organization (SEBCO) is founded in the fall by leaders of the Hunts Point and Longwood North communities at the instigation of Roman Catholic priest Louis R. Gigante (brother of Genovese crime family boss Vincent Gigante) to halt the decline of an area that has been demoralized and devastated by crime (notably arson) and drugs. The pastor of St. Anastasius Church, Father Gigante will spearhead SEBCO's efforts, initially to rehabilitate existing housing and later to build new apartment houses plus 250 one- and two-family houses, using a combination of public and private funds.

A fire at 232-36 Johnson Street in Brooklyn January 8 kills 13 people; a fire at 111-15 Mexico Street in Queens July 18 kills 11.

Clement Clark Moore Park opens at the southeast corner of Tenth Avenue and 22nd Street in Chelsea. Coffey, Levine & Blumberg has designed the park.

The Queens Zoo (later the Queens Wildlife Center) opens on the grounds of the 1964 World's Fair in Flushing Meadows-Corona Park, using for its aviary the exposition's geodesic dome, designed by Buckminster Fuller.

The Pathmark supermarket chain is founded under the direction of food retailer Milton Perlmutter. Several members of the Wakefern Co-operative have operated under the Shop Rite name and break away to join with Perlmutter in starting the new chain, whose management encourages members to pay attention to local needs and get involved in their communities (*see* Bedford Stuyvesant, 1977).

The first Michelin Green guide to New York appears, with ratings of restaurants (*see* Zagat, 1979).

1969 The 91st Congress votes 252 to 160 January 3 to seat Rep. Adam Clayton Powell but strip him of his seniority and fine him $25,000 for the moneys wrongly paid out in salary to his wife, Yvette, and used for inappropriate travel funds (*see* 1968). It is stipulated that $1,150 shall be deducted each month from his congressional salary until the fine has been paid, he is sworn in as a freshman, and his roll-call attendance falls to a new low of 5 percent as he resumes preaching at the Abyssinian Baptist Church. The Supreme Court rules 7 to 1 June 16 that Powell's exclusion from the 90th Congress 2 years ago was unconstitutional, even though he had been spending most of his time in Bimini with his mistress.

A federal grand jury at New York indicts 21 members of the Black Panther Party April 2 on charges of planning to kill a police officer and dynamite what the Panthers call parts of the power structure: retail stores (Abercrombie & Fitch, Alexander's, Bloomingdale's, Macy's), a police station, and tracks of the New Haven branch of the Penn Central Railroad at six points north of 148th Street. Heavily armed police arrest 12 of the defendants at their homes or friends' homes. The chairman of Youth Against War and Fascism deplores the indictments and arrests, as does the head of the American Servicemen's Union.

The Young Lords is founded at New York by Puerto Rican activists to agitate against inadequate health care, infrequent trash collection, and police brutality. Helped by Fred Hampton and other Black Panther members, the quasi-military organization is initially a chapter of Chicago's Young Lords, advocating political revolution and self-help programs for the city's poor Hispanics; it organizes a boycott of public schools in February to make the Board of Education institute changes, takes over a Harlem church 6 days per week for classes, and starts a free-breakfast program; although it will disband in 1972, some of its members will remain active for at least 2 decades.

Quondam water commissioner James L. Marcus is released from federal prison in Florida August 11, having served nearly 11 months of his 15-month sentence (*see* 1968). He testifies in the trial of former Tammany Hall boss Carmine G. De Sapio that he never met De Sapio but took orders from him through an intermediary in awarding the contract on the Jerome Park Reservoir. De Sapio is found guilty December 13 in federal court of having conspired to bribe Marcus and extort contracts from Consolidated Edison Co. that would result in kickbacks. The assistant U.S. district attorney asks that

De Sapio be held in $25,000 bail for sentencing "in view of the perjury committed here during the trial." Judge Harold R. Tyler, Jr. denies the application, saying, "Mr. De Sapio is a part of New York City. I don't think he can fail to be around. This is his city." Facing a possible maximum sentence of 15 years in prison and a $30,000 fine, De Sapio will receive a 2-year sentence in February of next year.

Mayor Lindsay fails to obtain the Republican Party nomination but wins reelection as a Liberal-Independent, securing 1,012,633 votes against 831,772 for Democrat-Non-Partisan-Civil Service Independent candidate Mario Procaccino, 542,411 for Republican-Conservative John Joseph Marchi, 48, of the State Senate. City Comptroller Procaccino has defeated former mayor Wagner and three also-rans in a five-way Democratic primary race. Novelist Norman Mailer has run with journalist Jimmy Breslin on a secessionist platform calling for the city to become the 51st state; asked what he would do if elected, Mailer quipped, "Demand a recount."

A bomb explodes at Manhattan's Criminal Court building November 12—the eighth government or corporate building to be bombed since July 26. Police and FBI agents arrest four militant radicals, including Jane (Hale) Alpert, 24, hours later. They also seek Pat Swinton in connection with the bombings, but she will evade apprehension, and Alpert will jump bail (see 1974). Radicals who have broken with the Students for a Democratic Society and call themselves the Weathermen change their name to the Weather Underground. The original name came from the Bob Dylan song "Subterranean Homesick Blues," whose lyric contains the words, "You don't need a weatherman to know which way the wind blows." The Weather Underground will plant more bombs to protest the continuing war in Vietnam.

A motorcade of 100 vehicles flying American flags roars through Brooklyn and Manhattan December 13 to a rally in Times Square supporting President Nixon's position on Vietnam, but Mayor Lindsay addresses an audience of about 1,200 that day at the Ethical Culture Society in West 64th Street and says, "For the sake of our children, for the sake of our country, we must get out of this wretched war right now." (Lindsay was one of the first members of Congress to speak out against the war.) Rep. Edward I. Koch, now 45, says, "The greatest harm the war is doing is dehumanizing our people. We are using a chemical defoliant there that is banned in this country because it has been shown to cause cancer and genetic deformities in laboratory animals."

"The end of violence in Vietnam will help make the streets of New York safe, too," says a prominent psychiatrist. "Law and order, which we all want, can come without preaching and slogans if we change the larger atmosphere and devote our resources to improving the environment." A billboard on Times Square says, "War Is Over! If You Want It. Happy Christmas From John [Lennon] and Yoko [Ono]."

The Stonewall Inn riot launches a "gay rights" movement as homosexuals protest a police raid on a Greenwich Village dance club and bar at 53 Christopher Street June 27. Eight officers of the NYPD's Public Morals Section have entered the bar just after midnight with a warrant charging that it had no liquor license; employees and customers (including three in drag) with no identification papers have been taken to the precinct station for processing, and violence ensues, ending with the arrest of 13 individuals on charges of harassment, resisting arrest, disorderly conduct, and the like. Most of those arrested wear the obligatory "beatnik" or "bohemian" chinos, T-shirts, and penny loafers. Gay bars have received unwelcome police attention in the past, and homophobia has been rampant in the Village, with many shops displaying signs that read, "If You're Gay Stay Away," but a sign reading, "Support Gay Power" soon appears on the boarded-up window of the Stonewall Inn; the gay community will now forcibly resist discrimination (see 1971).

The Harlem-Dowling Children's Service is founded as an outgrowth of the Spence-Chapin Adoption Agency created in 1943.

The first landing of men on the moon July 21 inspires Parks Commissioner August Heckscher to hold a Moon Watch on Central Park's muddy Sheep Meadow. The Parks Department obtains network co-operation in setting up three giant television screens, placed in a triangle, and while the crowd waits for astronaut Neil Armstrong to step out of Apollo 11's lunar module it is entertained with "moon music," served with "moon food," and diverted by a hot-air balloon rising at the end of its tether. German-born rocket scientist Willie Ley has died of a heart attack at New York June 24 at age 62, having introduced Werner von Braun to rocketry and paved the way for the U.S. space program.

The U.S. Department of Justice files an antitrust suit against IBM as its last official act under the outgoing Johnson administration (see 1956). Largest antitrust action ever taken, the case will not come to trial until 1975, and by that time International Business Machines will be the world's largest company in terms of the value of its stock (worth more than the combined value of all the stock of all companies listed on the American Stock Exchange).

Chemical Bank installs New York's first cash dispenser. First Philadelphia Bank imported a one-way cash dispenser from Britain and installed it last year; Canton, Ohio, safe manufacturer Deibold & Co. has begun making automatic teller machines.

East Brooklyn Savings Bank renames itself Metropolitan Savings Bank (see 1962; 1978).

Investment banker James Paul Warburg dies of a heart attack at Greenwich, Conn., June 3 at age 72; investment banker Sidney J. Weinberg of Goldman, Sachs at New York July 23 at age 77; investment banker-art collector Robert Lehman at Sands Point August 9 at age 76.

Great Neck, L.I.-born entrepreneur Bruce Bent, 32, starts the first money-market mutual fund in August with help from his friend Henry Brown. A former analyst for the pension-fund management firm TIAA-CREF, Bent opened an investment firm 2 years ago under the name Brown & Bent. Interest rates have climbed to 8 percent—their highest level since the Civil War—and the high rate has discouraged borrowing; federal banking laws limit interest on deposits and certificates of deposit to 5½ percent, CDs paying higher rates are available only in denominations of $100,000, and in a conversation in their office at the corner of Sixth Avenue and 52nd Street Bent suggests to Brown that they buy high-interest CDs, put them in a mutual fund, and allow small investors to buy shares with the promise of daily dividends, same-day redemptions, and telephone redemptions. Told that such a fund is impossible, Bent studies the regulations and finds nothing to forbid it, he and Brown send brochures to 144 financial institutions, not one gives them any encouragement, and they go $250,000 into debt (see Reserve Fund, 1970).

A booming U.S. economy employs a record number of workers, unemployment falls to its lowest level in 15 years, the prime interest rate is 7 percent, the dollar is strong in world money markets, but Wall Street's Dow Jones Industrial Average closes December 31 at 800.36, down from 943.75 at the end of 1968.

Stern Brothers closes its doors in April after 58 years in 42nd Street near Sixth Avenue and abandons Manhattan after 102 years as a retail merchant, keeping only its suburban stores.

The 84-year-old A. De Pinna Co. closes April 16. Its 41-year-old store on Fifth Avenue at 52nd Street will be razed to make way for a skyscraper, and its Eastchester store will become a Brooks Brothers branch (De Pinna has since 1950 belonged to the retailing corporation Garfinckel-Brooks Brothers-Miller & Rhodes that acquired Brooks Brothers in 1946). Once primarily a store for boys' and men's clothing, De Pinna's sales in recent years have been 60 percent in women's and girls' apparel.

Merchant Adam Gimbel dies of pancreatitis at New York September 19 at age 75.

The United States Lines retires its passenger ship S.S. *United States* after 17 years of operation; competition from transatlantic air carriers and foreign-flag liners has made U.S. passenger vessels unprofitable.

The Cunard liner R.M.S. *Queen Elizabeth 2* (*QE 2*) arrives at New York on her maiden voyage May 7, replacing the 83,673-ton *Queen Elizabeth* that was launched in 1940 and went of service last year. The new 65,863-ton passenger liner is 963 feet in length overall, carries 1,815 passengers (she has a capacity of 2,025 passengers in two classes), 1,000 in crew, and has four swimming pools, 13 decks, 24 elevators, and a 531-seat theater. More than 150 ships greet the arrival of the new $70 million liner when she docks at 52nd Street after a 4-day, 16-hour, 35-minute crossing; she has averaged 28.02 knots from Le Havre to the Ambrose Light Tower, making no effort to beat the record set by the S.S. *United States* in 1952, although she did move at 32 knots for long periods.

Brooklyn's Myrtle Avenue El makes its last run October 4 after nearly 80 years of service (see 1940).

Bridge builder Ole Singstad dies at New York December 8 at age 87.

Harlem's Hale House has its beginnings when Lorraine Hale sees a young heroin addict nodding off in the street with a 2-month-old infant falling out of her arms. She suggests that the woman take her baby to "my mother," Clara Hale (née McBride), 64, who accepts the child and within 2 months has turned her three-bedroom apartment into a nursery with 20 drug-addicted infants in cribs. With help from Manhattan Borough President Percy Sutton, Clara Hale obtains a Harlem brownstone that will in the next 25 years care for more than 1,000 babies, many of them addicted since birth.

Pope John Paul II makes a second visit to New York and holds Mass at Yankee Stadium October 2.

Former Riverside Church pastor Harry Emerson Fosdick dies at suburban Bronxville October 5 at age 91. Fosdick retired in 1946, having used his pulpit and nationwide radio addresses to oppose what he called the "fossilizing" of Christian beliefs.

 Barnard College women stage a sleep-in March 9, moving into dormitory rooms vacated by male Columbia students in a bid to integrate the dorms. "When you isolate people you only accentuate the differences," one student says. "Psychologically and educationally, it's a more natural way to live," adds another.

Medgar Evers College is founded as part of the City University of New York (CUNY). Named for the civil rights leader who was ambushed and shot dead by Mississippi racists in 1963, it will admit its first students in 1971, with its main campus at 1650 Bedford Avenue, Brooklyn (another will be at 1150 Carroll Street). The only college in the CUNY system to work with a community council of citizens, faculty members, public officials, and students, it will establish a Middle College High School whose first class will be graduated in 1997, and by that time the college will have an enrollment of more than 5,300 full- and part-time students taking courses in business, education, the health sciences, the humanities, natural sciences and mathematics, and social sciences.

Lehman College is created in the Bronx as part of CUNY by separating it from Hunter College and using the 45-acre Hunter campus that opened in 1931. Named for former governor Herbert H. Lehman, it will add a Center for the Performing Arts and grow to have more than 10,000 full- and part-time undergraduate and graduate students by the fall of 1990.

A bill passed by the state legislature at Albany April 30 authorizes the creation of 30 to 33 New York City public school districts, with a school chancellor to replace the current superintendent of schools. Elected community school boards are to have power beginning next year to hire superintendents, who will be empowered to hire principals of elementary and junior high schools. Made in response to last year's teachers' strike, the decentralization move ends years of stifling bureaucratic rule from Board of Education headquarters at 110 Livingston Street, Brooklyn, but Rhody McCoy of Brooklyn's Ocean Hill-Brownsville school district sees the move as a union sellout that will never provide true community control (only teachers and principals licensed by the central board can be hired). The local school boards will founder in many cases, and their administration will often be marked by abuse of power, corruption, decision-making paralysis, and outright incompetence (see 1996).

The Board of Estimate approves the first South Street Seaport plan July 25 (see 1968; 1970).

 The Saturday Evening Post puts out its final weekly issue February 8 after 148 years of publication; it will resume in the summer of 1971 on a six-times-per-year basis and reach a circulation of 500,000.

Columnist Arthur "Bugs" Baer dies of cancer at New York May 17 at age 69 (he has been widely quoted for such quips as, "Europe is where they name a street after you one day and chase you down it the next;" "We must make the world pay for the last war to prevent it from affording the next one;" and "Alimony is like buying oats for a dead horse;" *New Yorker* magazine cofounder Raoul Fleischmann dies in his 955 Fifth Avenue apartment May 30 at age 83; former *Journal-American* society gossip columnist Baron George Wrangell (known to many as the man with the eyepatch in the Hathaway shirt ads) of a heart attack at New York June 8 at age 65; editor-author Floyd Dell at Bethesda, Md., July 23 at age 82.

Penthouse magazine begins publication at New York in September. Brooklyn-born publisher Robert Guccione, 38, started the magazine at London in March 1965; scorning use of an airbrush to eliminate pubic hair from nude photographs, he challenges Hugh Hefner's 16-year-old *Playboy*, whose newsstand sales he will overtake by 1975.

Nonfiction: *The Hudson River: A Natural and Unnatural History* by Brooklyn-born *Sports Illustrated* senior editor Robert H. Boyle, 41, who champions the cause against pollution of the great estuary; *New York: The Story of the World's Most Exciting City* by Bruce Bliven, Jr. and his wife, Naomi (née Horowitz); *The Teachers' Strike: New York, 1968* by Martin Mayer; *The Valachi Papers* by New York-born investigative reporter Peter Maas, 40, who has edited a 1,800-page manuscript written at the request of the Justice Department by racketeer and Mafia hitman Joseph Valachi and produced a bestseller; *The Kingdom and the Power* by Gay Talese is about the *New York Times*; *Architecture in New York: A Photographic History* by Wayne Andrews.

Fiction: *The Bluest Eye* by Ohio-born New York novelist Toni Morrison (originally Chloe Anthony Wofford), 38, who has written much of it on the E train while commuting between her Queens home and her job at a Manhattan publishing house; *Portnoy's Complaint* by Philip Roth; *The Godfather* by New York-born novelist Mario Puzo, 48, whose novel about the Mafia will be on the *New York Times* bestseller list for 67 weeks and have sales of 21 million copies worldwide; *Come Back If It Doesn't Get Better* (stories) by Penelope Gilliatt; *The Gang That Couldn't Shoot Straight* by Jimmy Breslin.

Novelist Josephine Herbst dies of lung cancer at New York January 29 at age 71; Modern Library (and Book of the Month Club) cofounder Charles Boni of cancer at New York February 14 at age 74; publisher Stanley M. Rinehart, Jr. of lung cancer at Miami April 26 at age 71; Book of the Month Club cofounder Harry Scherman of a heart ailment at New York November 12 at age 82.

Painting: *Orange Yellow Orange* by Mark Rothko; *Montauk* by Willem de Kooning; *City Limits* by Philip Guston, who breaks with abstract expressionism and adopts an allegorical, mock-childlike style; *Study According to What* (graphite pencil, graphite wash, and tempera on paper) by Jasper Johns; *Night Empire* (acrylic on canvas) by Chicago-born New York painter Elizabeth Murray, 29; *Richard Serra* by Monroe, Wash.-born New York painter Charles Thomas "Chuck" Close, 28, whose black-and-white image of the sculptor is deceptively photolike. Ben Shahn dies following cancer surgery at New York March 14 at age 70.

El Museo del Barrio opens in an East Harlem storefront to display works by Hispanic artists. It will later move to the Heckscher Building on Fifth Avenue, across from Central Park's Conservancy Gardens.

Sculpture: *One-Ton Prop* (a house of cards) by San Francisco-born New York sculptor Richard Serra, 29; *City Fountains* by Victor Scallo is installed at the northeast corner of the plaza outside 77 Water Street, *Helix* by Rudolph de Harak at the northwest corner, *Rejected Skin* by William Tarr at the southwest corner, *Month of June* by George Adamy at the southeast corner; *Triad* (bronze) by New Jersey-born painter-sculptor Irving Marantz, 57, is installed on the east side of Park Avenue between 31st and 32nd streets; *Rondo* (polished bronze disk) by Tony Rosenthal is installed in 58th Street between Lexington and Park avenues.

Photographs: Villanova, Pa.-born *Look* magazine editor Patricia (Theresa) Carbine, 38, accepts a suggestion from Philadelphia-born photographer Mary Ellen Mark, 29, that she do a picture story on Italian film director Federico Fellini making *Fellini Satyricon*.

Theater: *To Be Young Gifted and Black* by the late Lorraine Hansberry (adapted by Robert Nemiroff) 1/2 at the off-Broadway Cherry Lane Theater, with Barbara Baxley, New York-born actress Cicely Tyson,

29, 380 perfs.; *Ceremonies in Dark Old Men* by Americus, Ga.-born playwright Lonnie Elder III, 41, 2/4 at the off-Broadway St. Marks Playhouse; *Does a Tiger Wear a Necktie?* by Iowa-born playwright Don Petersen, 41, at the Alvin Theater, with Hal Holbrook, 29-year-old East Harlem-born actor Al (originally Alfredo) Pacino, 39 perfs.; *No Place to Be Somebody* by Cleveland-born playwright Charles Gordone, 41, 5/4 at the off-Broadway Public Theater; *Butterflies Are Free* by New York-born playwright-screenwriter Leonard Gershe, 47, 10/21 at the Booth Theater, with Cleveland-born actor Keir Dullea, 33, as the Scarsdale youth who overcame blindness to get a law degree from Harvard, Philadelphia-born actress Blythe Danner, 26, Eileen Heckart, 1,128 perfs.; *Last of the Red Hot Lovers* by Neil Simon 12/28 at the Eugene O'Neill Theater, with James Coco, Linda Lavin, 706 perfs.

Broadway producer Gilbert Miller dies in his sleep at his 12-room Park Avenue apartment January 2 at age 85; actress Thelma Ritter of an apparent heart attack at Queens February 4 at age 63; playwright Jack Kirkland of a heart ailment at New York February 22 at age 66; former *Post* drama critic John Mason Brown of pneumonia at New York March 16 at age 68.

Television: *Sesame Street* in November (daytime) on PBS begins a revolution in children's attitudes toward learning and adults' attitudes about what children are capable of learning. Designed by the Children's Television Workshop and funded by the Ford Foundation, Carnegie Corp., and U.S. Office of Education, *Sesame Street* teaches preschool children letters and numbers with the same techniques used in commercial television programs such as the 14-year-old *Captain Kangaroo* show, introducing characters such as Oscar the Grouch (developed by puppeteer Jim Henson and Jon Stone and based on an ill-tempered waiter who serves them lunch at the Third Avenue seafood restaurant Oscar's), Big Bird, the Cookie Monster, Ernie, and Grover.

Films: Larry Peerce's *Goodbye, Columbus* with New York-born actor Richard Benjamin, 32, Westchester-born actress Ali MacGraw, 31, Jack Klugman; Peter Yates's *John and Mary* with Dustin Hoffman, Mia Farrow; John Schlesinger's *Midnight Cowboy* with Dustin Hoffman, Yonkers-born actor Jon Voight, 30.

Film musicals: Gene Kelly's *Hello, Dolly!* with Barbra Streisand, Walter Matthau, Michael Crawford, Louis Armstrong; Bob Fosse's *Sweet Charity* with Shirley MacLaine, John McMartin, Ricardo Montalban.

Broadway and off-Broadway musicals: *Dear World* 2/6 at the Mark Hellinger Theater, with Angela Lansbury, Dublin-born actor Milo O'Shea, 42, in an adaptation of the 1945 Jean Giraudoux play *The Madwoman of Chaillot*, music and lyrics by Jerry Herman, 132 perfs.; *1776* 3/16 at the 46th Street Theater, with Howard da Silva as Benjamin Franklin, William Daniels as John Adams, Ken Howard as Thomas Jefferson, Fort Worth, Texas-singer Betty Lynn Buckley, 21, as Martha Jefferson, Ronald Holgate as Richard Henry Lee, book by Peter Stone, music and lyrics by Sherman Edwards, songs that include "He Plays the Violin," 1,217 perfs.; *Oh! Calcutta!* 6/17 at the off-Broadway Eden Theater, a revue devised by English critic Kenneth (Peacock) Tynan, 42, with contributions by Samuel Beckett, Jules Feiffer, Dan Greenberg, John Lennon, and others, music and lyrics by the Open Door, scenes that include frontal nudity and simulated sex acts, 5,959 perfs. (704 at the Eden, 610 more at the Belasco Theater beginning late in February 1971, and the rest at the off-Broadway Edison Theater); *Coco* 12/18 at the Mark Hellinger Theater, with Katharine Hepburn as the late Coco Chanel, New York-born actor René Auberjonois, 29, Buenos Aires-born actress-writer-choreographer-lyricist Graciela Daniele, 30, music by German-born U.S. composer-conductor André Previn, now 40, book and lyrics by Alan Jay Lerner, 332 perfs.

Sammy's Bowery Follies founder Sammy Fuchs dies of a heart attack in his Jamaica Estates, Queens, home at 84-16 188th Street April 1 at age 65; composer-lyricist Frank Loesser of lung cancer at his native New York July 28 at age 59; blues and folk singer Josh White following brain surgery at Manhasset September 5 at age 61.

The 52-year-old Manhattan School of Music moves from the upper East Side to 120 Claremont Avenue on Morningside Heights, taking over quarters occupied until last year by the Juilliard School (now at Lincoln Center). Directed since 1956 by baritone John Brownlee (who retires this year), the conservatory has developed programs in opera, accompaniment, and jazz, enrolling upwards of 800 students and granting degrees (bachelor's, master's, and doctoral) in composition and performance.

High-fidelity pioneer Avery Fisher sells his Fisher Radio Co. for $31 million (*see* 1937). Now 63, he is an ardent concert goer and will donate $10.5 million to Lincoln Center not only for the maintenance of Philharmonic Hall (*see* 1973) but also to fund the Avery Fisher Artist Program for young instrumentalists.

The Woodstock Music and Art Fair in the Catskill Mountains at Bethel draws 300,000 youths from all over America for 4 days in August to hear Jimi Hendrix, Joan Baez, Ritchie Havens, the Jefferson Airplane, the Who, the Grateful Dead, Carlos Santana, and other rock stars. Despite traffic jams, thunderstorms, and shortages of food, water, and medical facilities the gathering is orderly with a sense of loving and sharing, but thousands in the audience are stoned or tripping on marijuana ("grass," "pot," "maryjane"), hashish ("hash"), lysergic acid diethylamide (LSD), barbiturates ("downs"), amphetamines ("uppers"), mescaline, cocaine, and other drugs.

The Led Zeppelin makes its Carnegie Hall debut 10/17. An English rock group formed last year, it includes Jimmy Page, 24; John Paul Jones, 23; John Bonham, 22; and Robert Plant, 22.

Popular songs: *New York Tendaberry* (album) by Laura Nyro includes "Tom Cat Goodbye" and "Captain Saint Lucifer;" "Give Peace a Chance" by Japanese artist Yoko Ono and John Lennon of the Beatles, who have married in March; "Lay Lady Lay" by Bob Dylan.

The New York Jets beat the Baltimore Colts 16 to 7 January 12 at Miami to win Super Bowl III. Coached by former Colts coach Wilbur Charles "Weeb" Ewbank, 61, Pennsylvania-born Jets quarterback Joseph William "Broadway Joe" Namath, 25, is credited with having engineered the upset win over Don Shula's heavily favored Colts—the first AFL Super Bowl victory. The Jets will not win another division title until December 1998.

Stillman's Gymnasium founder Lou Stillman dies of a heart attack at Santa Barbara, Calif., August 19 at age 82.

Rod Laver, now 31, wins the "grand slam" in tennis for a second time; Margaret Smith Court wins in women's singles at Forest Hills.

Baseball's two major leagues split into eastern and western divisions with two new expansion teams each.

New York Mets center fielder Tommie Agee, 27, hits a prodigious home run April 10, California-born pitcher Frank E. "Tug" McGraw, 24, says "Ya Gotta Believe" (it will become a watchword for the team's fans), and the (Amazin') Mets go on to win the National League pennant and their first World Series, defeating the Baltimore Orioles 4 games to 1. Pitchers Jerry Koosman, 25, Tom Seaver, 24, and Gary Gentry, 23, hold the Orioles to 9 runs while the Mets score 15. Met first baseman Donn Clendenon, 34, gets five hits, including a double and three home runs; Baltimore-born Met outfielder Ron Swoboda, 25, six hits, including a double; New York-born first baseman Ed Kranepool, 24, four hits, including a double and a home run; second baseman Al Weiss, 31, five hits, including a home run; center fielder Tommie Agee three hits, including a home run; outfielder Cleon Jones, 27, three hits, including a double.

The Madison Square Garden (MSG) Network cablecasts the opening game of the New York Rangers against the Minnesota North Stars October 15, reaching an initial audience of 18,000 cable television subscribers in lower Manhattan. The network goes on to cablecast Knicks basketball games as well as Rangers hockey matches; by 1997 it will be providing 7 hours of programming per night (17 hours per day on weekends) reaching more than 5.35 million subscribers via more than 236 cable affiliates.

Former Mafia kingpin Vito Genovese dies of heart disease at a Springfield, Mo., medical center for federal prisoners February 14 at age 71.

Vice in Times Square becomes an issue in the New York mayoralty race. Evangelist Billy Graham denounces the self-proclaimed "crossroads of the world" and exhorts the candidates to stamp out pornography. Mayor Lindsay sets up a task force to address the issue and begins cracking down on peep shows and sex-oriented magazine shops (see 1976).

Heroin sales to New York schoolchildren have jumped as a result of the federal government's Operation Intercept program to restrict the flow of marijuana from Mexico, says an expert testifying before a joint legislative committee at Washington. The price of marijuana, he claims, has climbed so high that heroin sells at a competitive price.

The Board of Estimate gives approval October 9 to a special Battery Park District zoning (see 1969; 1974).

The 50-story Astor Plaza office tower is completed at 1515 Broadway, between 44th and 45th streets. Designed by Kahn & Jacobs, it replaces the Astor Hotel that opened in 1904 and makes use for the first time of a special Times Square Theater District zoning bonus that allows a developer to put up a building of greater than normal bulk in return for constructing a new legitimate theater.

The Alliance Capital Building (initially called Burlington House) goes up on the west side of the Avenue of the Americas between 54th and 55th streets. The 50-floor tower rises on a site formerly occupied by an apartment house and by the Ziegfeld Theater that opened in 1927.

Who woulda believed the Amazin' Mets could win the National League Pennant and the World Series?

A new General Motors Building is completed at 767 Fifth Avenue, between 58th and 59th streets, where it occupies a site used by the Savoy Plaza Hotel in 1927 and some smaller structures of little note. Architect-teachers Elliot Willensky and Norval White brought out their students to demonstrate against the razing of the hotel 4 years ago, but their signs ("Renege on Rampant Wrecking," "Landmarks Preservation Weak," etc.) had no effect. Designed by architect Edward Durrell Stone with an assist from Emery Roth & Sons, the 50-story tower has 2 million square feet of office space, a huge automobile showroom and toy store on its lobby floor, and a sunken plaza, one floor below street level, that disrupts the classic Grand Army Plaza (see Trump, 1998).

The 44-story Gulf + Western Building is completed at Columbus Circle on a site between Central Park West and Broadway once occupied by the American Chicle Building. Designed by Thomas E. Stanley, its peculiar aerodynamics produce blasts of air that batter pedestrian passersby (see Trump International Hotel and Tower, 1996).

The state legislature at Albany enacts a rent-stabilization law (see 1965; rent controls, 1943). Landlords of apartment houses erected between 1947 and 1961 may increase rents every 2 years but are limited as to how much those rents may be raised (see Local Law 30, 1970).

Westbeth opens at 155 Bank Street, where the buildings put up for Bell Laboratories have been converted to use as artists' loft dwellings with financing from the J. M. Kaplan Fund. Newark, N.J.-born architect Richard (Alan) Meier, 35, of Richard Meier & Associates has redesigned the 19th century structures designed by Cyrus L. W. Eidlitz and others (see 1897).

The Urban Development Corporation embarks on a program of building apartments for middle-class tenants rather than for the poor. Gov. Rockefeller has created the public authority in response to President Nixon's cuts in federal public-housing appropriations; the state government at Albany declares that UDC bonds have the state's moral backing, but they have no legal backing (see 1975).

Architect William Lescaze dies at New York February 9 at age 72; builder Anthony Campagna in his apartment at Delmonico's Hotel May 8 at age 84.

The Dakota apartment house is designated a New York City Landmark February 11, the Washington Arch April 29, the Plaza Hotel December 9.

The 40-story 45 East 89th Street apartment house is completed on the east side of Madison Avenue between 89th and 90th streets. Designed in red-brown brick with bronze trim by Thomas Lehrecke of Oppenheimer, Brady & Lehrecke with Philip Birnbaum, it has sound-resistant construction, two- and three-bedroom apartments, nine-foot ceilings, an electronic security system, a year-round swimming pool, sun deck, lounge, lockers, and saunas for both men and women.

A blizzard February 9 dumps 15 inches of snow on the city, stranding 6,000 travelers at Kennedy Airport (some stay overnight in grounded jet planes), preventing thousands from reaching their jobs, forcing the stock and commodity exchanges to close in the most paralyzing storm to hit the city in 8 years. At least 43 deaths in the city (plus some 50 elsewhere in the state) and 288 injuries are blamed on the storm; 1,000 citizen volunteers help clear the main thoroughfares, but large parts of Queens are still snowbound by February 11 and bitter residents charge Mayor Lindsay with having neglected their borough while clearing the streets of Manhattan. United Nations under-secretary Ralph Bunche, a Queens resident, wires Lindsay to complain, a city councilman asks Gov. Rockefeller to declare the city outside of Manhattan a disaster area, have national guardsmen help in snow removal, and temporarily suspend Lindsay pending a probe.

A fire in an architectural firm's office at 595 Fifth Avenue February 25 kills 11 people and leaves five gravely injured after tracing paper on a wall bursts into flame. A fire in an overcrowded house at 31 Covert Street December 18 kills 10, including seven children from the same immigrant family.

The Bronx Zoo opens its World of Darkness—the first major exhibit for nocturnal animals such as bats. The Vincent Astor Foundation and the city have financed the installation.

Zoologist and conservation authority Fairfield Osborne dies of a heart attack at New York September 16 at age 82. He has served as head of the Aquarium and Bronx Zoo.

 New York schoolchildren participate in the National School Lunch Program that provides hot meals for 21 million children nationwide. About 3.8 million American kids receive lunch free or at substantially reduced prices, and the figure soon will rise to 8 million.

 The Longchamps restaurant chain is acquired by Irving and Murray Riese, whose locations they will convert in many cases into Brew Burger and, later, T.G.I. Friday's fast-food outlets (see Childs, 1961; T.G.I. Friday's, 1965; Schrafft's, 1973).

Restaurateur Vincent Sardi dies of a respiratory ailment at Saranac Lake November 19 at age 83.

1970 An explosion in Greenwich Village March 6 completely wrecks a town house at 18 West 11th Street allegedly used by members of the Weather Underground to produce bombs. Police arrest Weather Underground activist Bernardine Dohrn, 27 (she will jump bail), and call in the FBI to help look for Kathy Boudin, 26, and Catherine Platt Wilkerson, 25, one of whom was reportedly naked and both of whom were bruised and lacerated. Wilkerson was a member of the SDS (Students for a Democratic Society) delegation to Hanoi in 1967 and has allegedly joined the ultramilitary Weathermen faction of SDS.

The *New York Times* publishes an exposé beginning April 25 alleging that city police have received millions of dollars per year in illicit payments from bookmakers, businessmen, drug dealers, and organized crime (see 1966). Police detective Frank Serpico has worked with a few colleagues since 1967 to compile evidence of such corruption and has turned to the *Times* after failing to obtain a hearing from City Hall. The Knapp Commission, created by Mayor Lindsay in May to study the corruption charges, is headed by Whitman Knapp, who, with his

Women's Lib activists marched on Fifth Avenue to protest inequality. CHIE NISHIO

Powell's poor attendance record and narrowly defeats Powell in the primary, winning by just 150 votes in a five-man race. Powell charges election fraud and goes to court, but Rangel wins 80 percent of the vote in the general election, takes Powell's seat, and will hold it into the 21st century; a federal court rules in December that Powell was late in filing his appeal.

Gov. Rockefeller wins election to a fourth term after three abortive efforts to win the U.S. presidency as leader of the Republican Party's liberal wing. Former U.S. Supreme Court justice and UN delegate Arthur (Joseph) Goldberg, 62, has run against him as the Democratic candidate but receives 2,421,426 votes to Rockefeller's 3,151,432 (*see* 1973).

Conservative Party candidate James L. Buckley, 47, wins election to the U.S. Senate with support from his brother William's 15-year-old *National Review*. The 8-year-old party gains its first major victory at the polls.

A group of civil rights leaders attacks the policy of "benign neglect" toward blacks advocated by presidential adviser Daniel Patrick Moynihan, now 43. They call the policy "a calculated, aggressive, and systematic" effort by the administration to "wipe out" gains made by the civil rights movement.

Feminists demonstrate to "liberate" the men's bar at the Biltmore Hotel. The 116-year-old McSorley's Old Ale House in East 7th Street admits its first woman patron August 10 after Mayor Lindsay signs a bill prohibiting sexual discrimination in public places (with a few exceptions such as Turkish baths) (*see* McSorley's, 1987).

A nationwide U.S. Women's Strike for Equality celebrates the 50th anniversary of suffrage; more than 10,000 people march down Fifth Avenue August 26 carrying placards with demands for "emancipation," and many hear speeches by Betty Friedan, Gloria Steinem, Rep. Bella Abzug (*née* Savitzky), 50 (the first Jewish woman elected to Congress), and Kate Millett, who call for more day-care centers, nonsexist advertising, and a revision of some Social Security laws. "Man is not the enemy," says Friedan; "man is a fellow victim."

Former International Ladies' Garment Workers' Union vice president Julius Hochman dies of a heart attack at New York March 17 at age 78. He has played a key role in making Seventh Avenue an international fashion center; former Amalgamated Clothing Workers vice president Bessie Abramowitz (Mrs. Sidney Hillman) dies at New York December 23 at age 81.

chief counsel Michael Armstrong, will hold hearings for the next 2 years (*see* 1971; Nonfiction, 1973).

Construction workers break up an anti-war rally in the Wall Street area May 8, force City Hall officials to raise the American flag to full staff (it had been lowered in memory of Kent State students shot dead by Ohio militia), and invade Pace College. But President Nixon holds his first press conference in 3 months and announces that U.S. troops will be out of Cambodia by mid-June.

Rep. Adam Clayton Powell, Jr. loses his bid for reelection (*see* 1969). Manhattan's 18th congressional district has been redrawn to add a 16-block area of middle-class whites on the Upper West Side. Mayor Lindsay, Percy Sutton, Jackie Robinson, Roy Campanella, David Dinkins, Jimmy Breslin, Paul O'Dwyer, and other prominent individuals endorse Harlem-born assemblyman Charles B. (Bernard) Rangel, 40, a Korean War veteran who points to

$ The *New York Times* runs a story January 7 about the money-market fund pioneered last year by Bruce Bent and Henry Brown. Their Reserve Fund receives $1 million in depositors' funds by February, it will have $100 million by the end of 1973, $500 million by 1974 (*see* Dreyfus, 1974). Bent will go on to develop five equity funds (Reserve Blue Chip Growth, Reserve Small-Cap Growth, Reserve Informed Investors Growth, Reserve International Equity, Reserve Large-Cap Value Equity), advising investors to avoid bonds.

Salomon Brothers and Hutzler moves its headquarters to the new 1 New York Plaza building near Battery Park City and changes its name to Salomon Brothers (*see* 1935). Headed since 1957 by William Salomon, now 56, the firm has in recent years made "block trades" involving huge amounts of stock (*see* Phibro, 1981).

Wall Street's Dow Jones Industrial Average bottoms out at 631 and jumps 32.04 points May 27 to close at 663.20—the largest 1-day advance thus far recorded. Daily volume on the New York Stock Exchange averages 11.6 million shares, up from 2.6 million in 1955, 3 million in 1960. Brokerage houses struggle to automate their back rooms to keep up with mounting paperwork. The Dow closes December 31 at 838.92, up from 800.36 at the end of 1969.

$ Best & Co. closes its doors on Fifth Avenue November 16 (*see* 1947). The McCrory Co. acquired Best's in 1966, but soaring rents and land values have made prime retail locations irresistibly attractive to developers of office buildings (*see* real estate [Olympic Tower], 1977).

⚡ The transcontinental pipeline company (Transco) begins curtailing deliveries of natural gas from Texas (*see* 1950); New York's Public Service Commission restricts new sales to all but existing customers and prohibits Con Edison, Brooklyn Union Gas, and Long Island Lighting Co. from promoting natural gas (*see* 1974).

⚡ City transit fares rise 50 percent to 30¢ January 4; the fare has been 20¢ since 1966 (a larger version of the token that was minted in 1953 is introduced, but it still has a Y cutout in its center) (*see* 1979).

The spray-painted graffito "Taki 183" appears on subway cars, buses, and walls throughout the city. A Greek-born Brooklyn teenager named Demetrius has scrawled his nickname and street address in hundreds of places, and other "graffiti artists" follow suit (*see* 1972).

The 2-year-old Penn Central enters reorganization proceedings under the federal bankrupty law June 23. The Rail Passenger Service Act signed into law by President Nixon creates the National Rail Passenger Corp. (Amtrak) to save passenger rail travel from extinction (*see* 1971).

🎓 City University of New York (CUNY) adopts an "open admissions" policy for its senior colleges in response to pressure from blacks, Hispanics, and community groups, lowering academic standards to admit students whose high-school records do not qualify them to become college freshmen under previous standards (*see* 1849). So many middle-class students enrolled in the 1960s when their academic records qualified them for private colleges that the system has become overwhelmingly white, and CUNY administrator David Newton, 48, headed a Task Force on Open Enrollment whose report last year called for 1.6 million square feet of additional space and 1,200 more faculty members just for remedial instruction (the Task Force estimated that 25 to 45 percent of open-admission students would need counseling, remedial classes, and financial aid); enrollment will swell in the next 6 years from 174,000 to 268,000, mostly black and Hispanic, the faculty will grow from 7,800 to 12,800, and academic standards—despite protestations to the contrary—will decline as the colleges admit students who are not adequately prepared (*see* tuition, 1976).

St. Joseph's College in Brooklyn goes co-ed, accepting men for the first time since its founding in 1916.

The Bank Street School outgrows its children's classrooms in Greenwich Village and moves uptown to 112th Street, where it will start a small infant program for children under age 3, a summer program, and after-school programs to supplement the regular curriculum (*see* 1919).

The steamboat *Mathilda*, donated by McAllister Brothers, arrives at the South Street Seaport Museum July 30, and the former British sailing ship *Wavertree*, purchased by the museum 2 years ago, arrives from Buenos Aires August 11 (*see* 1969). The schooner *Pioneer* from Gloucester arrives August 30, and the museum purchases the steam ferry *Major William H. Hart* from the Coast Guard September 19. More vessels will soon be added.

🙌 The United Federation of Postal Clerks and the National Postal Union take 57,000 New York postal employees (152,000 nationwide) off the job from March 18 to 25, the army is sent in to sort the mail, and the strikers win wage increases based on local conditions, full health benefits, amnesty for striking workers. A Postal Reorganization Act signed into law August 12 converts the Post Office Department into the patronage-free U.S. Postal Service.

Essence magazine begins publication at New York. Four black men who include Edward Lewis, 30, have started the magazine for black women, their first print-run is 50,000 copies, and by 1994 the circulation will have topped 1 million.

Black Enterprise magazine begins publication at New York under the direction of Brooklyn-born management consultant Earl G. (Gilbert) Graves, (Jr.), 35, who was an administrative assistant to the late Sen. Robert F. Kennedy from 1965 to 1968. Circulation will reach 230,000 by 1990 with revenues in excess of $15 million.

Time and *Newsweek* run cover stories on the women's movement. *Newsweek* pays 46 editorial workers to settle a sex-discrimination suit. The August issue of *The Ladies' Home Journal* carries a special supplement in response to a sit-in by 100 women in the magazine's office to protest its portrayal of women.

Viacom is created by CBS at New York to comply with federal regulations that prevent TV networks from owning cable television systems (*see* 1987).

The first urban TV cable systems begin operations in Manhattan. Despite criticism by consumer advocates who believe the business should be regulated as a public utility the city grants 20-year monopolies to two companies—Teleprompter (controlled by Howard Hughes and later called Manhattan Cable TV) and Sterling Manhattan (owned by Time, Inc., and later called Paragon Cable). By 1975 all of Manhattan will be wired for cable TV, and a third company, Staten Island Cable, will have wired Richmond County.

The *New York Times* inaugurates an Op-Ed page at the instigation of assistant managing editor Harrison E. Salisbury, now 61. The page that heretofore has been reserved for obituaries carries pieces by the paper's columnists and by outside contributors (who will receive $75 for each essay accepted, a rate that will be continued for decades).

Former New York critic-naturalist-author Joseph Wood Krutch dies at Tucson, Ariz., May 22 at age 76; former *Herald-Tribune* publisher Helen Rogers Reid of arteriosclerosis at New York July 28 at age 87; cartoonist Rube Goldberg of cancer at New York December 7 at age 87.

Nonfiction: *Will They Ever Finish Bruckner Boulevard?* by New York-born *New York Times* critic Ada Louise Huxtable (*née* Landman), 49; *Public Works: A Danger-*

ous Trade by Robert Moses; *The Upper Crust: An Informal History of New York's Highest Society* by Allen Churchill; *Sexual Politics* by St. Paul-born New York feminist Kate (Katherine Murray) Millett, 35; *How To Make It in a Man's World* by New York publishing execitve Letty Cottin Pogrebin, 31; *Unbought and Unbossed* (autobiography) by Shirley Chisholm, who writes, "Brownsville in the 1930s was a heavily Jewish neighborhood of run-down tenements, some up to ten stories tall with twenty or more apartments. Today we would probably call it a 'ghetto.' Its residents then would have laughed at the word. Some of them were first-generation Jews from central and eastern Europe, and they knew the difference. They had come from real ghettos;" *84 Charing Cross Road* by Helene Hanff, now 54, whose exchange of letters with the antiquarian London bookshop Marks & Co. produces her first real success; *Wallflower at the Orgy* (articles) by New York-born writer Nora Ephron, 39.

Fiction: *Time and Again* by New York science-fiction novelist Jack (Walter Braden) Finney, 59; *Mr. Sammler's Planet* by Saul Bellow, whose protagonist, Arthur Sammler, surveys the world that lies beyond his window curtain: "Brownstones, balustrades, bay windows, wrought iron. Like stamps in an album—the dun rose of buildings canceled by the heavy black of grilles, of corrugated rainspouts . . . Such was Sammler's eastward view, a soft asphalt belly rising, in which lay sewer navels. Spalled sidewalks with clusters of ash cans. Brownstones. The yellow brick of elevator buildings like his own. Little copses of television antennas;" *Such Good Friends* by New York-born novelist Lois Gould (*née* Regensburg), 38, whose first husband died 4 years ago after surgery leaving a coded diary whose accounts of extramarital affairs have provided the basis for her novel; *The Anderson Tapes* by Brooklyn-born crime novelist Lawrence Sanders, 51, who has based the work in part on police reports and tape transcripts obtained by means of sophisticated surveillance devices. His fictional New York detective Edward X. Delaney will appear in a number of his books.

The Mid-Manhattan Library branch of the New York Public Library opens October 26 in the former Arnold Constable store building, built in 1914 at the southeast corner of Fifth Avenue and 40th Street. The library's main branch at 42nd Street becomes strictly a research library, with its lending library and picture collection relocated to the new Mid-Manhattan branch.

Harper & Row acquires Basic Books (*see* 1962). The Minneapolis Star and Tribune Co. acquired a large interest in the company 4 years ago and John Cowles, Jr. is now its board chairman (*see* 1977).

Simon & Schuster cofounder Max Lincoln Schuster dies at New York December 20 at age 73.

 Painting: *Andy Warhol* by Alice Neel; *Patchwork Quilt* (collage) by Romare Bearden. Mark Rothko dies by his own hand February 25 in his studio at 157 East 69th Street in a fit of depression at age 66 (he left his family last year to live by himself in the studio, a converted carriage house with a skylight); Barnett Newman dies of a heart attack at New York July 3 at age 65.

Mark Rothko leaves behind 798 paintings on canvas and paper. His three executors sign a contract with art dealer Frank Lloyd of the 7-year-old Marlborough Gallery to dispose of the works (*see* 1971).

Sculpture: *Portrait of Sylvette* (sand-blasted concrete, more than 30 feet tall) by Pablo Picasso is installed in the plaza of the 4-year-old New York University Village apartments on the south side of Bleecker Street, between La Guardia Place and Mercer Street; *The Aerial View* by George Segal; *Unfinished, Untitled or Not Yet* (nine dyed fishnet bags with clear polyethylene, paper, sand, and cotton string) by Eva Hesse, who dies of a brain tumor at New York May 29 at age 34.

Art in America is acquired by Whitney Communications, whose management will make Brian O'Doherty editor next year (*see* 1941). He will refocus it to give more emphasis to the contemporary art scene.

The 74-year-old Parsons School of Design becomes a division of the New School for Social Research.

 Broadway and off-Broadway theaters respond to growing fears of late-evening street crime that is blamed for poor ticket sales: they raise their curtains at 7:30 instead of 8:30 as of Monday, January 3.

Theater: *Child's Play* by New York playwright Robert Marasco, 32, 2/17 at the Royale Theater, with Pat Hingle, Fritz Weaver, El Centro, Calif.-born actor Ken Howard, 25, sets and lighting by Jo Mielziner, 342 perfs.; *The Effect of Gamma Rays on Man-in-the-Moon Marigolds* by New York-born playwright Paul Zindel, 33, 4/7 at the off-Broadway Mercer O'Casey Theater, with Pamela Payton-Wright, Amy Levitt, Des Moines-born actress Sada Thompson, 40, Omaha-born actress Swoosie Kurtz, 26, 819 perfs.; *The Gingerbread Lady* by Neil Simon 12/13 at the Plymouth Theater, with Maureen Stapleton, Betsy von Furstenberg, 193 perfs.

Comedian Menasha Skulnik dies at New York June 4 at age 80; critic Gilbert V. Seldes at New York September 29 at age 77.

Television: *The Odd Couple* 9/24 on ABC with Tony Randall, now 50, as fussy photographer Felix Unger, recently divorced, who moves into the 1049 Park Avenue apartment of sportswriter-slob Oscar Madison, played by Jack Klugman (to 7/1975; 113 episodes, with Unger remarrying his ex-wife, Gloria, in the final episode).

Films: William Friedkin's *The Boys in the Band* with Kenneth Nelson, Pete White, Leonard Frey, Cliff Gorman, Frederick Combs, Laurence Luckinbill; Ossie Davis's *Cotton Comes to Harlem* with Godfrey Cambridge, Raymond St. Jacques, Calvin Lockhart; Frank Perry's *Diary of a Mad Housewife* with Richard Benjamin, Frank Langella, Carrie Snodgress; Arthur Allan Seidman's *Hercules in New York* with Arnold Strong (Arnold Schwarzenegger), Arnold Stang, Taina Elg; Gilbert Cates's *I Never Sang for My Father* with Melvyn Douglas, Gene Hackman, Dorothy Stickney, Estelle Parsons; Hal Ashby's *The Landlord* with Beau Bridges, Pearl Bailey, Diana Sands; Cy Howard's *Lovers and Other Strangers* with Gig Young, Bea Arthur, Bonnie Bedelia, Anne Jackson, Harry Guardino; Arthur Hiller's *The Out of Towners* with Jack Lemmon, Sandy Dennis; Herbert Ross's *The Owl and the Pussycat* with Barbra Streisand, George Segal, Robert Klein; Carl Reiner's *Where's Poppa?* with George Segal, Ruth Gordon, Trish Van Devere.

 Broadway and off-Broadway musicals: *The Last Sweet Days of Isaac* 1/26 at the Eastside Playhouse with Warren, Ohio-born actor Austin Pendleton, music by Nancy Ford, lyrics by Indiana-born writer Gretchen Cryer, 34, 465 perfs.; *Purlie* 3/15 at the Broadway Theater with Melba Moore, music by Paterson, N.J.-born composer Gary Geld, 34, lyrics by Peter Udell, songs that include "I Got Love," 688 perfs.; *Applause* 3/30 at the Palace with Lauren Bacall, music by Charles Strouse, lyrics by Lee Adams, book by Betty Comden and Adolph Green, 896 perfs.; *Company* 4/26 at the Alvin Theater with Detroit-born comic Elaine Stritch, 45, Baldwin, L.I.-born ingénue Susan Browning, 29, music and lyrics by Stephen Sondheim, 706 perfs.; *The Me Nobody Knows* 5/18 at the Orpheum Theater, with a cast of inner-city youngsters, music by Gary William Friedman, lyrics by Will Holt, 587 perfs.; *The Rothschilds* 10/19 at the Lunt-Fontanne Theater, with Bronx-born actor Hal Linden (originally Harold Lipschitz), 39, New York-born actress Jill Clayburgh, 26, Dallas-born actor Robby Benson (originally Robin David Segal), 14, music by Jerry Bock, lyrics by Sheldon Harnick, 507 perfs.; *Two by Two* 11/10 at the Imperial Theater, with Danny Kaye, music by Richard Rodgers, lyrics by New York-born actor-writer Martin (Jay) Charnin, 35, 352 perfs.

Don Carlo Opera Company founder Fortune Gallo dies at New York March 28 at age 91. He has worked to popularize grand opera; soprano Mimi Benzell dies of cancer at Manhasset, L.I., December 23 at age 47.

Lincoln Center has its first season of outdoor events through the efforts of Leonard de Paur, 55, who became director of community relations 2 years ago and works to broaden the audience with support from Con Edison. Born in Summit, N.J., de Paur has conducted his own popular choral groups, Broadway musicals, and symphony orchestras; he adds jazz and spirituals to Lincoln Center's repertoire of classical music.

The Dance Theater of Harlem is founded by New York-born dancer Arthur Mitchell, 35, who from 1955 to 1968 was the first full-time black member of the New York City Ballet (*see* Ailey, 1958). He will serve as artistic director for the company, it will take over an abandoned garage next year at 466 West 152nd Street, between St. Nicholas and Amsterdam avenues, give its debut performance at the Guggenheim Museum, and go on to perform throughout America and abroad, assembling a large repertory, often adapting classical works to novel settings, and training students at its West 152nd Street school.

The Rev. John G. Gensel holds an All-Nite Soul marathon that will become an annual concert at St. Peter's Lutheran Church (*see* 1965). He has begun conducting afternoon jazz vespers at St. Peter's beginning at 5 o'clock each Sunday; the marathon concert features 12 hours of gospel choirs, big-band jazz groups, quintets, and solos.

Popular songs: "I Wouldn't Live in New York (If They Gave Me the Whole Damn Place)" by Buck Owens; "Bridge Over Troubled Water" by Simon and Garfunkel (who will break up their partnership next year); *Self Portrait* (album) by Bob Dylan; *Yoko Ono/Plastic Ono Band* and *John Lennon/Plastic Ono Band* (albums); *Let It Be* (album) by John Lennon and Paul McCartney of the Beatles.

Alto saxophonist John Cornelius "Johnny" Hodges dies at New York May 11 at age 63.

Joe Frazier regains the world heavyweight boxing title February 16 by knocking out Jimmy Ellis in the fifth round of a championship bout at New York.

The New York Knickerbockers win the first National Basketball Association (NBA) title in their 24-year history May 8. Coached by Red Holzman and led by Walt Frazier, 27, and all-star center Willis Reed, now 27 (who has been hobbled by a leg injury but is still named the outstanding player of the playoffs), the Knicks beat the Los Angeles Lakers 113 to 99 at the new Madison Square Garden in the seventh and deciding game (*see* 1967). Reed earns the Most Valuable Player award for the regular season, the championships, and the All-Star game, a distinction never before given to any player in the same season (*see* 1973).

Rangers hockey goalie Terry Sawchuk dies at New York May 31 at age 40 from injuries suffered while horsing around with a teammate. His career record of 103 shutouts will stand until the mid-1980s.

Contract bridge inventor and veteran yachtsman Harold S. Vanderbilt dies at Newport, R.I., July 4 at age 85.

Ken Rosewall wins in men's singles at Forest Hills, Margaret Smith Court in women's singles.

The first New York Marathon September 23 attracts 126 starters, who run around Central Park four times. The 12-year-old New York Road Runners Club has sponsored the event, Far Rockaway fireman Gary Muhrcke, 30, wins it, and it will grow to involve more than 25,000 male and female runners who beginning in 1976 will start on Staten Island, go through all five boroughs, and finish in Central Park.

Onetime society beauty Thelma Morgan, Lady Furness, dies of a heart attack at New York January 29 at age 65.

Indiana-born fashion designer William Ralph "Bill" Blass, 48, buys control of Maurice Rentner, the New York company for which he has been designing since 1959. Having built a reputation for women's sports clothes of top-quality fabrics and workmanship with help from fashion publicist Eleanor Lambert, he ventured into menswear 3 years ago and will make Bill Blass Ltd. a rival to the best Paris houses of *haute couture*.

U.S. women balk at a new midiskirt decreed by fashion arbiters such as *Women's Wear Daily* publisher John Fairchild. Stores return unsold garments to manufacturers, women wear their skirts as long or short as they like, and slaves to fashion fade from the scene.

Mobster Meyer Lansky flees to Israel in order to escape prosecution by federal authorities. He has invested in legitimate enterprises that include golf courses, hotels, and a meat-packing plant, his money is mostly in Swiss banks, and he has a net worth estimated at $300 million (*see* 1973).

The Racketeer Influenced and Corrupt Organizations (RICO) Act signed by President Nixon October 15 will be used in the 1980s to prosecute both Mafia kingpins and white-collar criminals, notably Wall Street traders using privileged information.

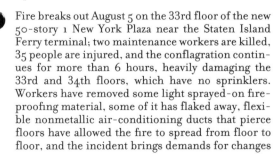 The 50-story 1 New York Plaza office tower is completed in Whitehall Street, between South and Water streets in lower Manhattan, to designs by Kahn & Jacobs with William Lescaze & Associates.

The 40-story 2 New York Plaza tower is completed at the northeast corner of Broad and South streets. Designed by Kahn & Jacobs, it adjoins the 2-year-old, 22-story 4 New York Plaza.

The 26-story 77 Water Street office tower is completed between Old Slip and Gouverneur Lane. Designed by Emery Roth & Sons with Corchia-de Harak Associates for developer Mel Kaufman, it has street-level decorative pools, bridges, and an arcade whose shops include an old-fashioned candy store.

The 35-story 475 Park Avenue office tower is completed at the southeast corner of 32nd Street. Shreve, Lamb & Harmon has designed the structure with details in dark metal, brick, and glass.

The 41-story 810 Seventh Avenue office tower is completed on the west side of Times Square between 52nd and 53rd streets. Designed by Kahn & Jacobs, it replaces the Broadway Rose Garden Theater.

The 39-story 540 Madison Avenue office tower is completed between 54th and 55th streets. Designed by Kahn & Jacobs and constructed by Diesel Construction Co., the building's brick wall has flaws on its east side, facing the avenue, where workers have failed to install corrugated metal strips into the mortar to secure the brickwork to the building's cinder-block wall, and it soon begins "to collapse, crack, spall, and otherwise deteriorate" (according to charges contained in a lawsuit that will be filed in 1973).

The 46-story 919 Third Avenue office tower is completed between 55th and 56th streets with a black metal-and-glass curtain wall. Skidmore, Owings & Merrill has designed the structure; it wraps around the 90-year-old P. J. Clarke bar and restaurant at the northeast corner of 55th Street.

The city adopts Local Law 30 governing rent increases for rent-controlled apartments, devising a formula to protect tenants from precipitous increases while recognizing the right of property owners to earn an annual return of about 8.5 percent on the market value of their investments (*see* rent stabilization, 1969). Based on an audit of about 74,000 buildings, the law establishes a Minimum Base Rent (MBR) for every rent-controlled apartment, but because this MBR is considerably higher than the rent being charged the law caps the annual increase at 7.5 per cent (the Maximum Collectible Rent, or MCR) (*see* 2001).

The 33-story East River Tower apartment house is completed at 1725 York Avenue, between 89th and 90th streets, to designs by Horace Ginsbern & Associates.

The 29-story Trinity House apartment house is completed with 200 units near the Trinity School at 100 West 92nd Street. Designed by Brown, Guenther, Battaglia, Seckler, it is part of the Upper West Side urban renewal area. The 22-story Eugenio Maria De Hostos Houses are completed with 223 units at 201 West 93rd Street to designs by Eggers & Higgins. The 33-story Columbus House is completed with 248 units at 386 Columbus Avenue, between 95th and 96th streets. Designed by Horace Ginsbern & Associates, it has balconies between deep protruding columns.

Co-Op City goes up in the northern Bronx. Financed by the state of New York under the Mitchell-Lama Act, the middle-income complex has been designed by architect Herman J. Jessor with landscaping by Zion & Breen. It will consist when completed of 35 towers, seven schools including a high school, a firehouse, a heating plant, an educational park, three retail centers (the Bay Plaza shopping center will not come until 1988), and eight parking garages. It occupies more than 300 acres between Interstate 95 (the New England Thruway) and the Hutchinson River Parkway, formerly the site of the Freedomland amusement park, and its 15,372 one- to three-bedroom apartments range in size from 750 to 1,400 square feet.

Fire breaks out August 5 on the 33rd floor of the new 50-story 1 New York Plaza near the Staten Island Ferry terminal; two maintenance workers are killed, 35 people are injured, and the conflagration continues for more than 6 hours, heavily damaging the 33rd and 34th floors, which have no sprinklers. Workers have removed some light sprayed-on fireproofing material, some of it has flaked away, flexible nonmetallic air-conditioning ducts that pierce floors have allowed the fire to spread from floor to floor, and the incident brings demands for changes in building standards. The demands will in many cases go unheeded.

A three-story building near City Hall explodes December 11 following a gas leak in the cellar of a storefront tavern. The explosion leaves nine dead, more than 60 injured.

 Broadway area restaurants serve dinner beginning as early as 4:30 in the afternoon in response to new theater hours. Many restaurateurs protest the new curtain time; Sardi's offers a choice of seven pre-theater mini-dinners: a main dish, such as chicken or canneloni, vegetables, dessert, and coffee, and it begins serving its after-theater supper at 9:30 instead of 10:30 as curtains fall just before 10 instead of just before 11.

Benihana Palace opens at 15 West 44th Street (*see* 1964).

Copeland's Restaurant opens at 549 West 145th Street. Calvin T. Copeland's eating place will survive into the 21st century as a Harlem institution.

 The most liberal abortion law in the United States goes into effect July 1 in New York State (*see* 1966). At least 147 women undergo abortions, more than 200 register at municipal hospitals for the procedure, bringing the application total to more than 1,200, and "Right to Life" groups continue to protest the new law.

New York City's population peaks at 7,894,862, up from 7,781,984 in 1960, but while the other boroughs show increases, Manhattan's population has dropped by more than 59,000, Brooklyn's by more than 25,000. Only 18 percent of the population is foreign-born, a 20th century low (it will rebound to 28.4 percent by 1990). The city's Puerto Rican population has grown to 817,712, up from 61,000 in 1940, and represents 10 percent of the total, up from just 1 percent (*see* 1950). The city's white population has fallen by about 1 million (the Irish have dwindled to 68,778, down from 114,008 in 1960), while its non-white population has increased 62 percent.

1971 The Patrolmen's Benevolent Association strikes from January 14 to 19; some 25,000 cops participate in an action that strengthens the city's police unions, wins salary increases, but brings prosecutions under the Taylor Law adopted in 1967.

Mayor Lindsay announces in August that he will leave the Republican Party and become a Democrat.

Former Tammany Hall boss Carmine G. De Sapio loses his post as Greenwich Village district leader in the Democratic Party (he is now serving time in fed-

The Police Benevolent Association demanded raises for New York's Finest. They deserved higher pay and got it.

eral prison on conspiracy charges; *see* 1969). The insurgent Village Independent Democrats win the district leadership with Rep. Edward I. Koch (*see* 1968; 1977).

Lawyer-diplomat Adolph A. Berle dies at New York February 17 at age 76; former governor (and two-time G.O.P. presidential candidate) Thomas E. Dewey at Bal Harbour, Fla., March 16 at age 68. He has lived since 1955 in an apartment at 141 East 72nd Street; former United Nations undersecretary and 1950 Nobel Peace Prize laureate Ralph J. Bunche dies at New York December 9 at age 67.

 A Gay Rights Bill introduced January 6 by City Councilmen Carter Burden and Eldon Clingan will be bottled up in committee. The first such bill ever proposed in America, it would prohibit discrimination in employment, housing, and public accommodations on the basis of sexual orientation (*see* 1974; Stonewall Inn riot, 1969).

Some 6,000 feminists stage a March for Equality up Fifth Avenue from 44th Street to Central Park's 72nd Street Mall August 26 carrying banners with slogans such as, "Crush Phallic Imperialism," "Pills for Men," "Woman Power," and "Sisterhood Is Powerful." Mayor Lindsay proclaims Women's Rights Day, greets the city's first woman police captain, meets for an hour and a half with feminist leaders, some of them in the city government, and reportedly agrees to a "substantial increase" in the number of women in top city jobs.

Attica Correctional Facility at Attica, N.Y., is the scene of the bloodiest 1-day encounter between Americans since the Indian massacres of the late 19th century. Inmates of the overcrowded prison discover inexplicable differences in sentences and parole decisions that appear to have a racial bias, outraged prisoners take over cell blocks beginning September 9 and kill several trusty guards, Gov. Rockefeller orders state police to move in September 13, and they retake the prison in 15 minutes, but only after killing 29 inmates and 10 hostages. More than 80 are wounded, the total death toll is 43, Rockefeller is called a murderer, and the Rockefellers come under the worst criticism since the Ludlow Massacre of 1914 (see 1972).

$ Wall Street's Over-the-Counter Market becomes NASDAQ (National Association of Securities Dealers Automated Quotation System) beginning February 8. Stocks not listed on either the New York Stock Exchange or American (formerly Curb) Exchange have been traded since the 1920s by telephone or in person, with mimeographed price sheets left on the doorstep of dealers as the only records of the previous day's trades. The NYSE and Amex use a single-specialist auction system, but the multitude of market makers in the O-T-C system has offered trading exposure that appealed to many newly emerging companies, especially technology companies. NASDAQ makes over-the-counter trades visible immediately on cathode-ray tubes and is not only more advanced than the mimeographed price sheets used up to now but also more advanced than the trading reports of the Big Board or Amex (see 1982).

The American Federation of State, County and Municipal Employees (AFSCME) brings 8,000 New York workers out on strike in June, winning nothing but public opposition. The union has violated the Taylor Law adopted in 1967 and is fined for its action.

Wall Street responds with enthusiasm to an economic message from President Nixon. The Dow Jones Industrial Average makes a record 1-day leap of 32.93 points August 16 on a record volume of 31.7 million shares, but the AFL-CIO says it has "absolutely no faith in the ability of President Nixon to successfully manage the economy of this nation" and refuses to co-operate in the president's wage freeze. The Dow closes December 31 at 890.20, up from 838.92 at the end of 1970.

Retailer J. C. Penney dies at New York February 12 at age 95, leaving an empire of 1,660 stores with annual sales of more than $4 billion—the largest nonfood retail enterprise after Sears, Roebuck.

Amtrak (the National Railroad Passenger Corp.) takes over virtually all U.S. passenger railroad operations including those of the Penn Central May 1 in a federally funded effort to halt the decline in rail passenger service (see 1970). By 1976 Penn Central will have turned its transportation assets over to the Consolidated Rail Corp., or Conrail, and will exist only as a real estate holding company, not a railroad.

The Taxi and Limousine Commission reports that so-called "gypsy" taxicabs such as those operated by Brooklyn's Black Pearl Livery Co. fill a real need in the inner city, employing nearly 13,000 drivers and providing service in areas shunned by the medallion cabs. About 58 percent of the gypsy cab drivers are blacks, 39 percent Hispanic.

The Hudson River Day Line steamboat *Alexander Hamilton* is retired in September after 47 years of service, ending the tradition of steamboat outings on the river (railroads made steamboats obsolete for purposes of travel as early as 1851).

More than 2,000 members of the Satmar hasidic sect celebrate their centennial June 1 in the grand ballroom of Brooklyn's St. George Hotel (see 1947). Most are bearded men wearing traditional black hats and long black coats. It was in 1871 that the Austro-Hungarian emperor Franz Josef II recognized Orthodox claims to represent the Jewish community, and the Satmars now number in the tens of thousands, most of them in Brooklyn.

St. John's University takes over the Notre Dame College of Staten Island and closes the downtown Brooklyn campus in Schermerhorn Street that it opened in 1929 (see 1956). Within 25 years St. John's will be offering degrees in more than 60 undergraduate and 30 graduate subjects; its 11 colleges and institutes will have a total enrollment of 21,000, making it the largest U.S. Roman Catholic university; and its tuitions will be lower than that of any other private university in New York State.

Fiorello H. La Guardia Community College opens in Long Island City. The 90-year-old Voorhees Technical Institute is absorbed into the New York City Community College of Applied Arts and Sciences, which will keep the institute's West 41st Street campus until 1987, when it will give the name Voorhees Hall to its engineering technology building at 186 Jay Street, Brooklyn.

Trinity School admits its first girl students after 133 years as an all-boys institution, taking them initially into the ninth grade. Trinity will not be totally coeducational until 1986.

The *Polish Daily News* (*Nowy Dziennik*) begins publication following the demise of the 52-year-old *Polish Morning Herald* (*Nowy Swiat*). Nearly 300,000 New Yorkers are of Polish birth and about 500,000 of Polish heritage, with 38 percent of them living in Brooklyn (Greenpoint has the largest concentration), 33 percent in Queens, 14 percent in Manhattan, 11 percent in the Bronx, and 4 percent in Staten Island.

The *New York Times* acquires *Family Circle* magazine and other Cowles Communications properties.

Look magazine ceases publication October 19 after competing with LIFE for 34 years; its circulation is 6.5 million, but rising postal rates and a fall-off in advertising have made it unprofitable. Other magazines shrink their formats to save postage in accordance with new postal regulations.

Diana Vreeland resigns under pressure as editor in chief of *Vogue*. Now over 70 she has promoted fashions that are considered too extreme to be marketable (*see* 1962; Metropolitan Museum of Art, 1973).

Mayor Lindsay cuts the budget for WNYC; the radio station is forced to lay off 55 workers.

Radio-television pioneer David Sarnoff of RCA dies December 12 at age 80 in his six-story, 30-room town house at 44 East 71st Street. His son Robert W., now 53, has been RCA chairman since last year and has recently written off its computer business for $490 million, giving up efforts to rival IBM; he will soon abandon the name Radio Corporation of America in favor of the RCA initials, will scrap use of the corporate symbol Nipper, the black-and-white terrier with its head cocked to "His Master's Voice" on the Victrola horn, and will be ousted in 1975 (*see* General Electric, 1985).

Nonfiction: *The Last of the Big-Time Bosses: The Life and Times of Carmine De Sapio and the Rise and Fall of Tammany Hall* by Warren Moscow; *The Black Minority in Early New York* by New York-born author David Kobrin, 30; *Irrational Ravings* by Brooklyn-born *New York Post* political columnist Pete Hamill, 36; *A Day in the Life of the Times* by Ruth Adler, whose 242-page book is an hour-by-hour account of what goes on at the paper on an ordinary day (February 28, 1969—a day chosen arbitrarily); *Out of My Time* (autobiography) by Marya Mannes, now 66; *Honor Thy Father* by

Gay Talese is about the Mafia; *The Literary Decade* by Allen Churchill is about Publishers Row in the 1920s; *The Wreck of the Penn Central* by Philadelphia-born author Joseph R. Daughen, 36, and Montclair-born author Peter (Husted) Binzen, 49.

New York bookseller Leonard Riggio, 30, buys the foundering Barnes & Noble bookstore and begins to build it into a chain (*see* 1931). Born in Mott Street in Little Italy, Riggio was raised in Bensonhurst, dropped out of NYU 6 years ago to open SBX (Student Book Exchange), has built up a chain of five SBX college bookstores in Manhattan, gained control of Barnes & Noble 2 years ago with help from his brother Stephen, sells Barnes & Noble's publishing division to Harper & Row, and concentrates on selling books at a discount (*see* 1979; B. Dalton, 1986).

The 25-year-old publishing house Farrar, Straus & Giroux acquires the 15-year-old firm Hill & Wang, whose sales manager and cofounder Lawrence Hill starts a firm under his own name while Arthur Wang remains as editor-in-chief of Farrar's Hill & Wang imprint (*see* Verlagsgruppe Georg von Holtzbrinck, 1994).

Publisher Bennett Cerf dies at his Mount Kisco home August 27 at age 73; fashion designer-author Elizabeth Hawes at New York October 6 at age 67.

Fiction: *Americana* by Bronx-born novelist Don DeLillo, 35, who has until recently been an advertising copywriter with Ogilvy, Benson & Mather; *The Tenants* by Bernard Malamud; *The Book of Daniel* by Bronx-born Sarah Lawrence College teacher E. L. (Edgar Lawrence) Doctorow, 39, is based on the 1951 Rosenberg trial (Doctorow grew up in a neighborhood near Mount Eden Avenue and the Grand Concourse); *Birds of America* by Mary McCarthy; *Queenie* by Hortense Calisher; *Angle of Repose* by Iowa-born novelist Wallace Stegner, 62, who writes of 1868, "The place was the Moses Beach house on Columbia Street in Brooklyn Heights, then a street inhabited by great merchant families—Thayers, Merritts, Walters, Havillands of 'the China Havillands.' The Beach house was all one great window on the water side and from its bluff overlooked the whole upper bay with its water-plug activity of tugs and ferries and barges. Governors Island as I imagine that last day of December would have floated like dirty ice out on the bay; the Jersey shore would have fumed with slow smokes. The view from Columbia Street I have seen but much obstructed and changed. As you saw it a hundred years ago there were no grimy warehouses thrusting out from the waterfront, there was no Brooklyn Bridge, no Statue of

Liberty, no New York skyline. In 1870 the tallest building in Manhattan was ten stories;" *Hail, Hail the Gang's All Here* by Ed McBain (Evan Hunter).

 Painting: *Amityville* by Willem de Kooning.

Art dealer Leo Castelli moves his gallery to 420 West Broadway in SoHo, where dozens of other galleries will open in the next few years (*see* 1957). Castelli has developed a reputation by displaying works by such artists as Donald Judd, Ellsworth Kelly, Roy Lichtenstein, Claes Oldenburg, James Rosenquist, Richard Serra, Cy Twombly, and Andy Warhol.

The late Mark Rothko's 20-year-old daughter Kate goes to court in November to have the three executors of her father's estate removed, beginning an 11-year legal battle that will end with a criminal trial (*see* 1970). Art dealer Frank Lloyd of the Marlborough Gallery and the executors have "wasted the assets" of the estate, Ms. Rothko charges, by obtaining her father's paintings for much less than their true value and under terms highly disadvantageous to the estate. The guardian of her brother Christopher joins in the suit, charging conflict of interest and seeking to cancel a contract that has enabled Marlborough to obtain 100 paintings for $1.8 million, payable in 12 years without interest, and a consignment of 698 other works for 12 years at a commission of 40 to 50 percent (*see* 1975).

The body of photographer Diane Arbus is found in her Westbeth apartment July 28. Dead at age 48, she has taken her own life after a career of photographing other people's traumatic experiences; Margaret Bourke-White dies of Parkinson's disease at her Connecticut home August 27 at age 65.

 Theater: *The House of Blue Leaves* by New York-born playwright John Guare, 33, 2/10 at the off-Broadway Truck and Warehouse Theater, with Brooklyn-born actress Anne Meara, 41, Galveston-born actress Katherine Helmond, 36, Schenectady-born actor Harold Gould, 47, 337 perfs.; *And Miss Reardon Drinks a Little* by Paul Zindel 2/25 at the Morosco Theater, with Estelle Parsons, Nancy Marchand, Julie Harris, 108 perfs.; *Where Has Tommy Flowers Gone?* by St. Petersburg, Fla.-born playwright Terrence McNally, 31, 10/7 at the off-Broadway Eastside Playhouse, 78 perfs.; *The Prisoner of Second Avenue* by Neil Simon 11/11 at the Eugene O'Neill Theater, with New York-born actor Peter Falk, 44, New York-born actress Lee Grant (originally Loyova Haskell Rosenthal), 39, Vincent Gardenia, 780 perfs.; a new American Place Theater opens 12/6 in the J. P. Stevens building at 111 West 46th Street.

The Ensemble Studio Theater is founded by Curt Dempster at 549 West 52nd Street to provide an artistic home for 20 member playwrights, directors, actors, technical personnel, and theater administrators whose numbers will grow in the next 20 years to more than 350.

Broadway producer Leland Hayward suffers a stroke February 9, returns from New York Hospital to his suburban Yorktown Heights home March 5, and dies there March 18 at age 68; nightclub comedian Joe E. Lewis collapses into a diabetic coma at his Warwick Hotel suite May 27 and dies at Roosevelt Hospital June 4 at age 54; actress Muriel Kirkland dies of emphysema at New York August 25 at age 68; playwright Samuel Spewack of blood cancer at New York October 14 at age 72.

Television: *All in the Family* 1/12 on CBS with New York-born actor Carroll O'Connor, 46, as Archie Bunker in a series devised by New Haven, Conn.-born writer-producer Norman Lear, 48 (who has adapted the British comedy *Till Death Do Us Part*). Co-starring Jean Stapleton as Bunker's wife, Edith (he calls her "The Dingbat," but she shows a certain intuitive wisdom and—in a sharp departure from the usual sitcom formulas—will go through menopause), Sally Struthers, 22, as his daughter Gloria (who will be the victim of an attempted rape in one episode and will have a miscarriage), Rob Reiner, 25, and Sherman Hemsley, 32, the show violates sacrosanct taboos against ethnic and bathroom humor (to 9/1979); *The Electric Company* in October (daytime) on PBS. Like *Sesame Street*, it is the product of Joan Ganz Cooney's Children's Television Workshop.

Films: Woody Allen's *Bananas* with Allen, Louise Lasser; William Friedkin's *The French Connection* with Gene Hackman, Fernando Rey, Roy Scheider; Alan J. Pakula's *Klute* with Jane Fonda as a New York call girl, Donald Sutherland; Alan Arkin's *Little Murders* with Elliott Gould, Marcia Rodd, Vincent Gardenia, Elizabeth Wilson; Jerry Schatzberg's *The Panic in Needle Park* with Al Pacino, Kitty Winn; Arthur Hiller's *Plaza Suite* with Walter Matthau, Maureen Stapleton, Barbara Harris, Lee Grant, Louise Sorel; Gordon Parks's *Shaft* with Richard Roundtree, Moses Gunn; James Goldstone's *The Gang That Couldn't Shoot Straight* with Jerry Orbach, Leigh Taylor-Young, Jo Van Fleet, Lionel Stander, Robert De Niro. Also: Ulu Grosbard's *Who Is Harry Kellerman and Why Is He Saying Those Terrible Things About Me?* with Dustin Hoffman, Barbara Harris, Jack Warden.

Greek-born film pioneer Spyros P. Skouras dies of an apparent heart attack at his Mamoroneck home August 16 at age 78.

 Broadway and off-Broadway musicals: *Follies* 4/14 at the Winter Garden Theater, with Gene Nelson, Vancouver, B.C.-born actress Yvonne De Carlo (originally Peggy Middleton), 48, Canadian-born actress Alexis Smith, 49, Canadian-born singer Dorothy Collins (originally Marjorie Chandler), 44, music and lyrics by Stephen Sondheim, book by James A. Goldman, songs that include "Broadway Baby," 521 perfs.; *Godspell* 5/17 at the Cherry Lane Theater (after opening at the Café LaMama), with music and lyrics by Stephen Schwartz based on the Gospel according to St. Matthew, songs that include "Day by Day," 2,605 perfs. (counting Promenade and Broadhurst Theaters); *Jesus Christ Superstar* 10/10 at the Mark Hellinger Theater, with Jeff Fenholt as Jesus of Nazareth, music by English composer Andrew Lloyd Webber, 23, lyrics by Tim Rice, book by Tom O'Horgan, 711 perfs.; *Ain't Supposed to Die a Natural Death* 10/20 at the Ethel Barrymore Theater, with an all-male cast of four that includes Avon Long, music and lyrics by Chicago-born songwriter Melvin Van Peebles, 39, 325 perfs.; *Two Gentlemen of Verona* 12/1 at the St. James Theater (after 14 performances at the off-Broadway Public Theater), with Puerto Rican-born actor Raul Julia, 27, Chicago-born actor-songwriter Clifton Davis, 26, Diana Davila, music by Galt MacDermot, lyrics by John Guare, 627 perfs.

Onetime actor and Broadway musical star Dennis King dies of a heart ailment at University Hospital May 22 at age 73. He has lived at 404 East 55th Street; former torch singer and Broadway musical star Libby Holman is found dead June 18 at age 67 in the front seat of her Rolls-Royce in the garage of her Connecticut mansion Treetops; former bandleader, comedian, and lyricist Ted Lewis dies at New York August 25 at age 80.

Fillmore East closes June 27 (*see* 1968). Bill Graham also closes his San Francisco Fillmore to concentrate on a single, larger West San Francisco musical performance venue.

Popular songs: "You'll Never Be Poor in New York" by Jule Styne; *Tapestry* (album) by Brooklyn-born singer-songwriter Carole King (originally Klein), 29, includes her songs "It's Too Late" and "You've Got a Friend" (it will have sales of more than 13 million copies by 1983); *Gonna Take a Miracle* (album) by Laura Nyro. Written in collaboration with the

rhythm and blues group LaBelle, it is a tribute to New York street music of an earlier era.

Jazz trumpeter Louis Armstrong dies at New York July 6 at age 71. He has lived since 1943 at 34-56 107th Street, between 34th and 37th avenues, in Corona, Queens. Peggy Lee sings The Lord's Prayer at his funeral; trumpeter-band leader Charlie Shavers dies at his native New York July 8 at age 54.

 New York State's Off-Track Betting Corp. (OTB) is created April 8 as legislation takes effect legalizing off-track betting in an effort to take business away from organized crime and produce revenues for the city and state. The legalized betting is, like the lottery, a form of regressive taxation, taking money from those least able to afford it, and the "numbers game" based on smaller bets will continue to flourish in the city, fattening the profits of underworld syndicates.

Stanley Roger "Stan" Smith, 24, (U.S.) wins in men's singles at Forest Hills, Billie Jean King in women's singles (she becomes the first woman in any sport to take home more than $100,000 in a single season).

The Big Apple gets that name as part of a publicity campaign organized by New York Convention and Visitors Bureau president Charles Gillett, who revives a nickname first popularized more than 40 years ago by *Morning Telegraph* reporter John J. Fitz Gerald (who had heard it used at New Orleans by black stablehands in reference to New York's racetracks). The name of a popular dance in the 1930s, it was used by jazz musicians of that era to mean New York City.

Police detective Frank Serpico is shot in the head at close range by a small-time heroin dealer February 3 while making a drug bust in Brooklyn's Williamsburg section (*see* politics, 1970); he survives but believes he was set up by fellow officers and resigns from the force to live on disability pay.

The city's 400-bed Women's Detention Center in Greenwich Village is closed June 13 for reasons of overcrowding. Arrests of women for major crimes have increased steeply all over America.

Hoodlum Joseph Gallo recruits blacks to replace the depleted ranks of the Mafia. Gallo has rebelled from the leadership of Joseph Colombo, who has attracted attention with public protests against insinuations in Mario Puzo's novel *The Godfather* that there is such a thing as the Mafia and hired pickets to demonstrate outside Manhattan FBI headquarters. Colombo helps organize an Italian-American Unity

Day parade June 28 at Columbus Circle and is shot three times by a black gunman and left crippled; an unidentified gunman immediately kills Colombo's assailant, but there is disagreement as to whether that assailant was in the pay of Joey Gallo, Mafia leader Carlo Gambino, or someone else.

New York's homicide rate will take another sharp upturn in the next 5 years, rising from 12.6 per 100,000 in the last 5 years to 21.7 per 100,000 (see 1976).

The city's Probation Department inaugurates an Alternative to Detention program for juvenile offenders, aged 12 to 16, who have been arrested and sent to Family Court on charges ranging from criminal possession of drugs to assault and robbery. The Family Court judge can place a youth in the program in lieu of setting him free pending trial, or sending him to Spofford, the city's major juvenile detention facility. Within 25 years the program will be taking about 1,100 of the 11,500 youths arrested each year and putting them in special classes, 8 hours per day, 5 days per week, in an effort to keep them from becoming hardened criminals. Only about 13 percent will wind up back in court.

The Standard Oil of New Jersey Building opens in September at 1271 Avenue of the Americas, between 49th and 50th streets. Harrison Abramovitz and Harris has designed the 54-story office tower that will soon be renamed the Exxon Building (see energy, 1972).

The state legislature at Albany gives the Urban Development Corporation a go-ahead to create a residential community in the center of Welfare Island (see 1968). Philip Johnson and Chicago-born architect John (Henry) Burgee, now 38, will create a master plan for the island that lies beneath the Queensboro Bridge, with the old Blackwell farmhouse of 1796–1804 to be restored, eight- to 10-story apartment houses to be built along a winding Main Street (no private cars permitted), with shops to serve residents, a megagarage to store residents' cars at the foot of a small lift bridge to Long Island City, a 3,100-foot-long overhead tramway to link what will now be called Roosevelt Island with Manhattan (see subway, 1989), and free buses to transport residents and visitors between tram or parking garage and apartment-house doors (see 1975).

The 42-story 1 Lincoln Plaza apartment house is completed on the east side of Broadway between 63rd and 64th streets, across from Lincoln Center on a site (formerly a 60,000-square-foot parking lot) purchased in December 1967 by developers Paul

and Seymour Milstein in partnership with their father, Morris. Architect Philip Birnbaum has designed the structure, whose 700 apartments range in size from two-and-a-half to six-and-a-half rooms and rent for between $400 per month (for a studio) and $1,160 (for a three-bedroom flat on a high floor with a dining room and three baths); the underground garage accommodates 300 cars, and there is a rooftop swimming pool and cabana club.

The 42-story 1 Sherman Square apartment house is completed at 202 West 70th Street, northwest corner Broadway. Designed by S. J. Kessler, it replaces the Sherman Square Hotel on what once was the Jacob Harsen homestead.

The 30-story 733 Park Avenue apartment house is completed at the southeast corner of 71st Street. Designed by Kahn & Jacobs with Harry F. Green, the red-brick tower rises on the site formerly occupied by Elihu Root's mansion and contains only 28 apartments. A typical unit consists of nine rooms, four-and-a-half baths, and sells for about $526,500 with monthly maintenance of about $3,145.

Bills signed into law by Gov. Rockefeller June 1 remove rent regulations on apartments as their tenants die or move out (see 1943; 1964); apartments in new buildings can be rented at market rates (developers may opt for rent stabilization in return for tax concessions), and rentals in older buildings can increase at a rate that has brought many of them up to market levels, but landlords have pressed for relief from regulation and real estate interests have lobbied hard for the new laws; regulations will be removed from more than 400,000 New York City apartments in the next 3 years, and many landlords will try to force tenants out; some will raise rents by 200 percent, 300 percent, and even more (see 1974).

The 27-story St. Martin's Tower apartment house is completed with 179 units at 65 West 90th Street, on the east side of Columbus Avenue, as part of the Upper West Side urban renewal program. Hill Johnson Hanchard has designed the structure; the 30-story Columbus Manor apartment house is completed at 70 West 93rd Street, along Columbus Avenue. Designed by Liebman & Liebman, it has 210 units; the 27-story New Amsterdam apartment house is completed with 228 units at 733 Amsterdam Avenue, between 95th and 96th streets. Designed by Gruzen & Partners, the buff brick structure has concrete balconies.

A new 44-story Park Lane Hotel opens at 36 Central Park South, between Fifth and Sixth avenues, with 640 rooms and a duplex penthouse cum swimming pool for real estate mogul Harry B. Helmsley, now 62, who will divorce his first wife next year after 32 years of marriage to wed his employee Leona Roberts (*née* Rosenthal), now 51.

Greenacre Park opens at 217-221 East 51st Street, between Second and Third avenues. Designed by landscape architects Sasaki, Dawson, Demay Associates in consultation with Goldstone, Dearborn & Hintz, the multi-level park is a gift from Mrs. Jean Mauzé, a daughter of the late John D. Rockefeller, Jr., and is wider than Paley Park with a less thunderous waterfall but with radiant heating concealed behind a trellis. Both vest-pocket parks are privately, and scrupulously, maintained by attendants who pick up litter.

The Forests and Wetlands of New York City by Texas-born New York city planner Elizabeth "Betsy" Barlow, 34, propels its author into prominence.

Gov. Rockefeller signs legislation May 26 repealing the 1912 law that has prohibited sales of oysters in the state from May 15 to August 31. The English oyster (*Ostrea edulis*) tastes gritty in the summer months because it keeps its young within its mantle cavity at that time of year, but the American oyster (*Crassostrea virginica*) discharges its eggs directly into the water. Pacific Coast oysters have always been sold all year round, and other states have dismissed the myth that oysters are only good in the "R" months. Modern refrigeration methods have long since made the 1912 law obsolete, and Long Island oysters have for years been shipped to buyers across the country during the months when they could not legally be sold within New York State borders.

1972 The Knapp Commission ends 2 years of Police Department investigations with findings of widespread corruption (*see* 1970; Gross trial, 1951). The department institutes sweeping organizational changes (*but see* Mollen Commission, 1992).

Former congressman Adam Clayton Powell, Jr. is flown from Bimini to Miami April 4 and dies in a hospital there that night at age 63 of complications following prostate surgery. The Rev. Samuel DeWitt Proctor, 50, succeeds him as senior pastor of Harlem's Abyssinian Baptist Church and delivers a eulogy, saying, "He gave us our first evidence that America's institutions were capable of any change at all. He gave us new basis for hope when our churches, colleges, unions, hotels—all were segregated. When my country, America, screamed at me, telling me I'm a nobody, he gave us all hope." Proctor will head the church until 1989.

Seven nuns are arrested April 30 in an anti-war protest at St. Patrick's Cathedral.

Congresswoman Bella Abzug (D. N.Y.) introduces a resolution May 9 calling for the impeachment of President Nixon following his decision to mine North Vietnamese harbors. Former congressman William F. Ryan wins renomination against Rep. Abzug, whose own congressional seat has been eliminated by redistricting; Ryan was one of the first elected officials to oppose the Vietnam War, but he dies at New York September 17 at age 50.

President Nixon wins reelection, easily defeating Sen. George S. McGovern, 49 (S.D.), who carries only Massachusetts with its 17 electoral votes (Mayor Lindsay had sought the Democratic Party nomination but found little national support). Nixon receives 47 million votes, 521 electoral votes, to 29 million for McGovern in the most one-sided presidential election since 1936.

Former Tammany leader Carmine G. De Sapio is released from federal prison at Allenwood, Pa., December 1 after serving his full 2-year sentence for bribery conspiracy (*see* 1969).

Skits at the annual Inner Circle dinner given by City Hall reporters at the New York Hilton April 15 include some that ridicule homosexuality, news of the proceedings reach the Gay Activist Alliance, members storm the room at about 11 o'clock, someone grabs the microphone and accuses everyone present of being a closet homosexual, and some of the 1,500 guests join with kitchen workers to drag the gay men out of the room and push them down the escalator. Michael J. Maye, 39, head of the Uniformed Firefighters Association and a former prizefighter, gets hold of prominent gay-rights leader Morty Manford, 21, as he is being led away by police, he begins kicking and stomping him, and the incident spurs efforts to have the city enact a gay-rights law (*see* 1969). Maye will go to work for the teamster's union and testify in 1982 before the City Council in behalf of gay rights (specifically for the union's president, Barry Feinstein) and develop cordial relationships with members of the Gay Activists Alliance (*see* 1973).

Former labor leader Rose Schneiderman dies August 11 at age 88 in the Jewish Home and Hospital at 120 West 106th Street where she has lived since December 1967.

A 470-page report by the McKay Commission investigating last year's Attica prison riot is issued in September and concludes that Gov. Rockefeller's action in sending in the state police was ill considered and far too harsh. The commission's chief counsel Arthur L. Liman, 39, of Paul, Weiss, Rifkind, Wharton & Garrison had Christmas dinner last year in the prison's cafeteria and made an effort to understand the inmates' grievances.

$ The 18-year-old New York securities firm Cantor Fitzgerald revolutionizes bond trading with the introduction of live market information displayed on computer screens in brokerage-house offices (see 1983).

Wall Street's Dow Jones Industrial Average closes at 1003.16 November 14, up 6.00 to cross the 1000 mark for the first time ever, but a front-page story in the *Wall Street Journal* says that "little market significance" should be attached to it; the Dow climbs to 1036.27 December 11, falls sharply December 18 at news of a breakdown in Vietnam peace talks, but closes December 29 at 1020.02, up from 890.20 at the end of 1971.

Merchant Nathan Ohrbach dies at New York November 19 at age 87.

Standard Oil of New Jersey renames itself Exxon November 1. It has become a worldwide petroleum colossus (its New York skyscraper, completed last year on the Avenue of the Americas, is renamed the Exxon Building).

Transit fares rise January 5 to 35¢, up from 30¢ (see 1970; 1975).

Construction begins on a proposed Second Avenue subway line for Manhattan's East Side; much wider than the Upper West Side, the East Side still has only the 55-year-old Lexington Avenue line whereas the West Side has two rapid-transit lines (Broadway and Central Park West) (see 1940). Gov. Rockefeller and Mayor Lindsay swing pickaxes and Sen. Javits wields a shovel at groundbreaking ceremonies for the new line that is to run between the Bronx and Wall Street. Crews begin work on tunnels along the avenue between 110th and 120th streets, 99th and 105th streets, and along a 700-foot section of the Bowery in Chinatown (*but see* 1975).

The Metropolitan Transportation Authority's budget for graffiti removal rises to $1 million, up from $250,000 in 1970 (see 1970). It costs the MTA $6,000 to remove graffiti from a subway car, and it tries various solvents without success. Bronx-born City Council President Sanford Garelik proposes a monthly "Anti-Graffiti Day" when New Yorkers may volunteer to clean up graffiti, Mayor Lindsay forms an anti-graffiti task force in October, he signs a bill in November making adults caught carrying open spray paint in public facilities liable to fines of up to $500 and prison terms of up to 3 months. CCNY sociology student Hugo Martinez organizes the United Graffiti Artists in November to promote graffiti as an art form, and members hold their first exhibition in December, but mainstream New Yorkers regard graffiti as vandalism, graffiti-covered cars add to the perception that the subways are unsafe, and ridership declines (see 1984).

Amtrak increases Metroliner service between New York and Washington to 14 daily round trips, up from six in 1969. (Eastern Airlines operates 16 daily shuttle flights between the two cities.)

Alarm about the neglect and filthy conditions at the overcrowded Willowbrook State School on Staten Island produces a class-action suit against Gov. Rockefeller (see 1963). New York-born WABC-TV reporter Geraldo (Miguel) Rivera, 23, has slipped into the facility and exposed the situation (see 1973).

An Office of Bilingual Education is created with a budget of $1 million to administer New York City's growing programs (see 1968). A lawsuit filed by the 11-year-old Puerto Rican group Aspira in conjunction with several other Puerto Rican groups has demanded that bilingual education be established as a right for every schoolchild not proficient in English (see 1974).

New York University's Tisch Hall is completed at 40 West 4th Street, between Washington Square East and Greene Street, to designs by Philip Johnson and Richard Foster. The Tisch family has contributed funds for the building. The university's Elmer Holmes Bobst Library is completed at 70 Washington Square South, between West Broadway and Washington Square East, to designs by Philip Johnson and Richard Foster. Donor Bobst, now 87, is a former Warner-Lambert Co. CEO who has given NYU more than $11 million for the new library.

Brooklyn Friends School moves to 375 Pearl Street, formerly the site of the Brooklyn Law School (see 1867).

Advertising agency founder Ted Bates dies while playing bridge with some friends at New York May 30 at age 70 (his agency has grown to have billings of about $425 million, but the self-effacing Bates has never given a speech, attended a convention, or had even a one-martini lunch); *New Yorker* magazine cartoonist Rea Irvin dies of a stroke at Frederiksted, Virgin Islands, May 28 at age 90.

Ms. magazine begins publication in July at New York with former *Look* editor Patricia Carbine as publisher, feminist writer Gloria Steinem, now 38, as editor. A spring preview issue has carried a column headed "What's a Ms.?" and answering it: "For more than 20 years, 'Ms.' has appeared in secretarial handbooks as the suggested form of address when a woman's marital status is unknown, a sort of neutral combination of 'Miss' and 'Mrs.' Now 'Ms.' is being adopted as a standard form of address by women who want to be recognized as individuals, rather than being identified by their relationship with a man. After all, if 'Mr.' is enough to identify 'male,' then 'Ms.' should be enough to identify 'female!' . . . The use of 'Ms.' isn't meant to protect either the married or the unmarried woman from social pressure—only to signify a female human being. It's symbolic and important. There's a lot in a name" (*see New York Times*, 1974).

Money magazine begins publication at New York in October. Launched by Time, Inc. with an initial circulation of 225,000, the journal of personal finance will grow to have a circulation larger than that of *Fortune*, *Forbes*, or any other financial magazine.

LIFE magazine suspends weekly publication December 29 after 36 years; more magazines shrink their formats to conform with new postal regulations.

 Nonfiction: *The Great Bridge* by Pittsburgh-born author David McCullough, 39, is a history of the Brooklyn Bridge; *Report from Engine Co. 82* by New York-born firefighter and author Dennis Smith, 32, whose book sells 1.5 million copies; *Bricks and Brownstone: The New York Row House, 1783–1929* by New York author Charles Lockwood; *Frederick Law Olmsted's New York* by Elizabeth "Betsy" Barlow; *Under the Guns: New York 1775–1776* by Bruce Bliven, Jr.; *The Happy Hooker* by Indonesian-born New York madam Xaviera Hollander, 29 (with Robin Moore and Yvonne Dunleavy); *Bella! Ms. Abzug Goes to Washington* (autobiography) by Rep. Abzug.

Fiction: *All Visitors Must Be Announced* by Washington, D.C.-born New York advertising copywriter-turned-novelist Helen Van Slyke, 53; *Sheila Levine Is Dead and Living in New York* by New York-born novelist Gail Parent (née Kostner), 32.

Poetry: *The Crystal Lithium* and *A Sun Cab* by James Schuyler.

Poet Marianne Craig Moore dies at her New York home February 5 at age 84; poet-author-activist Paul Goodman at North Stratford, N.H., August 3 at age 70.

Painting: *Mao* (silkscreen and paint on canvas) by Andy Warhol; *Madame Cézanne in Rocking Chair* by Elizabeth Murray.

The Queens Museum of Art is dedicated November 10 by Mayor Lindsay and Thomas Hoving. Occupying the New York City Building erected for the 1939-1940 New York World's Fair in Flushing Meadows-Corona Park, it contains the popular three-dimensional panoramic model of the city that was created for the fair (it will be changed as the city changes) but will also maintain a permanent art collection and present exhibitions of painting and sculpture from a wide variety of schools.

Sculpture: *Group of Four Trees* (aluminum, fiberglass, polyurethane) by French sculptor Jean Dubuffet, 70, is installed on the 11-year-old two-and-a-half-acre Chase Manhattan Plaza at the corner of William and Pine streets. The 25-ton work stands 43 feet tall; *Bachi 1972* (black granite) by Japanese-born sculptor Masayuki Nagare, 49, is installed under the second arch of World Trade Center's portico; *Skagerrak* by Illinois-born sculptor Antoni Milkowski, 37, is placed in Madison Square Park, a gift from the Association for a Better New York. Joseph Cornell dies at his Flushing, Queens, home December 29 at age 69.

 Theater: *Moonchildren* by New York-born playwright Michael Weller, 29, 2/21 at the Royale Theater, with New York-born actor Kevin Conway, 29, 16 perfs.; *Sticks and Bones* by Dubuque-born playwright David (William) Rabe, 31, 3/1 at the John Golden Theater (after 121 perfs. at the off-Broadway Public Theater), with Dayton, Ohio-born actor Tom Aldredge, 44, Elizabeth Wilson, 366 perfs. (total); *Small Craft Warnings* by Tennessee Williams 4/2 at the off-Broadway Truck and Warehouse Theater, 200 perfs.; *That Championship Season* by Scranton, Pa.-born playwright Jason Miller, 33, 9/14 at the Booth Theater (after 144 perfs. at the off-Broadway Public Theater), with Michael McGuire, Walter McGinn, Minnesota-born actor Richard Dysart, 43, 844 perfs. (total); *6 Rooms Riv Vu* by New York-born playwright Bob Randall (originally Stanley B. Goldstein), 35, 10/17 at the Helen Hayes Theater, with Jerry Orbach, Jane Alexander, 247 perfs.; *Not I* by Samuel Becket 11/22 at Lincoln Center; *The River Niger* by Washington, D.C.-born playwright Joseph A. Walker, 37, 12/5 at the St. Marks Playhouse (the play will move uptown next spring; 400 perfs. total); *The Sunshine Boys* by Neil Simon 12/20 at the Broadhurst Theater, with Jack Albertson, Sam Levene, now 67, Brooklyn-born actor Lewis J. Stadlen, 25, 538 perfs.

Broadway-Hollywood columnist Walter Winchell dies at Los Angeles February 20 at age 74.

The Irish Arts Center An Claidheamh Soluis is founded at 553 West 51st Street to give Irish performers their own venue.

The Manhattan Theater Club is founded at the City Center, 131 West 55th Street, where it will help develop new dramatic works for subscription audiences.

Films: Billy Wilder's *Avanti!* with Jack Lemmon, Juliet Mills, Clive Revill; Francis Ford Coppola's *The Godfather* with Marlon Brando, Al Pacino, James Caan, Diane Keaton; Peter Yates's *The Hot Rock* with Robert Redford, George Segal; Herbert Ross's *Play It Again, Sam* with Woody Allen, Diane Keaton; Gordon Parks, Jr.'s *Superfly* with Ron O'Neal in a film that is accused of glorifying Harlem drug pushers; Irvin Kershner's *Up the Sandbox* with Barbra Streisand; Melville Shavelson's *The War Between Men and Women* with Jack Lemmon, Barbara Harris, Jason Robards, Jr.

The Quad Cinema opens October 18 at 32 West 13th Street, where inventor Maurice Kanbar, 40, and his brother Elliott, 37, have converted a six-story loft building into New York's first cineplex—four theaters, each with 150 seats—on the premise that even a bad film attracts a certain audience. (Opening attractions: *The Gang's All Here* [1943]; *Play It Again, Sam* [1972]; *Butterflies Are Free* [1972]; *Slaughterhouse-Five* [1972]). The elder Kanbar bought the building in the 1960s with the idea of turning it into an off-Broadway theater; he will claim that he has noticed that most movie theaters have at least 300 seats but attract only about 80 patrons per showing (he has actually taken an idea pioneered in the late 1950s by Kansas City movie-theater operator Stanley H. Durwood, now 51). The Quad makes money right from the start, and its success will inspire larger exhibitors to chop up their theaters so that they may offer patrons a choice of films instead of just one.

Broadway musicals: *Sugar* 4/9 at the Majestic Theater, with Robert Morse, Cyril Ritchard, music by Jule Styne, lyrics by Bob Merrill, book from the 1959 film *Some Like It Hot*, 505 perfs.; *Don't Bother Me, I Can't Cope* 4/19 at the Playhouse, with Micki Grant (originally Minnie Perkins McCutcheon), 30, music and lyrics based on ballads, calypso songs, Gospel music, direction by Jamaican-born Urban Arts Corps founder Vinnette Carroll, 49, 1,065 perfs.; *Grease* 6/7 at the Broadhurst Theater (after 128 perfs. at the off-Broadway Martin Eden Theater), with

Sacramento-born actress Adrienne Barbeau, 26, San Mateo, Calif.-born actor Barry Bostwick, 26, music and lyrics by Jim Jacobs, book by Warren Casey, songs that include " 'Look at Me, I'm Sandra Dee," "We Go Together," "Alone at a Drive-In Movie," "Shakin' at the High School Hop," 3,388 perfs.; *Pippin* 10/23 at the Imperial Theater, with Beverly Hills, Calif.-born actor John Rubinstein, 25, Miami-born actor Benjamin Augustus "Ben" Vereen, Jill Clayburgh, book about 8th century English politics, music and lyrics by Stephen Schwartz, 1,944 perfs.; *Via Galactica* 11/28 at the new 1,870-seat Uris Theater (to be renamed the Gershwin in 1983) below ground level in the Uris Building at 1633 Broadway (50th Street), with Raul Julia, music by Galt McDermot, lyrics by Christopher Gore, 7 perfs.

The Kitchen Center for Video Music & Dance opens in May at the Broadway Central Hotel in Mercer Street, where the nonprofit experimental theater, supported largely by grants, will offer avant-garde performance space to artists such as Laurie Anderson, choreographer Trisha Brown, Eric Bogosian, composer Philip Glass, choreographer Meredith Monk, and director Robert Wilson. It will move to Broome Street and, in 1986, to a three-story building at 512 19th Street, between Tenth and Eleventh avenues.

The Rolling Stones concert at Madison Square Garden July 24 attracts a crowd of 20,000; John Lennon and Yoko Ono draw a similar crowd at the Garden when they perform there August 30.

The 40-year-old Radio City Music Hall stages its first pop music act November 2, featuring Boston-born folk-rock vocalist-songwriter James Taylor, 24, but the hall's films have drawn meager crowds and it continues to hemorrhage money (*see* 1978).

Popular songs: *Some Time in New York City* (album) by Yoko Ono and John Lennon includes their song "Woman Is the Nigger of the World" and Lennon's "New York City;" *Anticipation* (album) by New York-born rock singer-composer Carly Simon, 27.

Dancer-choreographer José Limón dies at Flemington, N.J., December 2 at age 64.

The new Long Island National Hockey League team announces February 15 that it has hired former Oakland Seals executive Bill Torrey as general manager and will call itself the Islanders. The team's home games will be at the Nassau Coliseum and its first season will end in May of next year with a 12-60 won-lost record, the worst in the NHL.

The Board of Estimate agrees March 23 to buy Yankee Stadium from Rice Institute and the Knights of Columbus (who own the land) and improve it at whatever cost (the latest estimate has been $24 million). CBS executive Michael Burke serves as Yankee president and expresses jubilation at the 30-year lease, whose terms commit the city to renovate the stadium beginning in 1974 while the Yankees play in Shea Stadium, but critics say the stadium is obsolete and the funds should be used for essential city services (*see* Steinbrenner, 1973). A strike by major league players has delayed the opening of the regular season; it begins at the Stadium April 15 without making up any of the 86 missed games.

Former Brooklyn Dodgers first baseman Gil Hodges dies of a heart attack at West Palm Beach, Fla., April 2 at age 47; former Dodgers second baseman-outfielder Jackie Robinson is honored at Cincinnati October 4 at the opening of the World Series to mark the 25th anniversary of his entry into major league baseball, but Robinson dies suddenly at Stamford, Conn., October 24 at age 53.

Ring magazine founder Nat Fleischer dies at his native New York June 25 at age 84, having continued to list Muhammad Ali as champion even after he was stripped of his title but referring to him always as Cassius Clay.

Ilie Nastase, 26 (Romania), wins in men's singles at Forest Hills, Billie Jean King in women's singles.

● Fashion designer Halston makes the cover of *Newsweek* August 21 as he expands his line to include sheets and other household furnishings as well as ready-to-wear.

Fashion designer Norman Norell suffers a stroke at his Amster Yard apartment in mid-October on the eve of a 50-year retrospective fashion show to be held at the Metropolitan Museum (he has fought throat cancer since 1961), and he dies at Lenox Hill Hospital October 25 at age 72.

▦ A robbery at the Hotel Pierre January 2 nets an estimated $3 million to $10 million in cash and jewelry for Bobby Comfort and Sorecho "Sammy the Arab" Nalo. They have pulled up in a limousine at 4 o'clock in the morning wearing dinner jackets and carrying luggage, the night guard admits them, and with three accomplices they proceed to round up 22 employees and guests, who are handcuffed, blindfolded, and locked in an office while the robbers crack the hotel's vault, open its safe-deposit boxes, and fill four suitcases. FBI agents catch Comfort in a Manhattan hotel January 7 and arrest Nalo in his Bronx apartment (the other three men are not identified);

Comfort and Nalo are convicted and receive 4-year sentences.

Reputed Mafia leader Joseph "Crazy Joe" Gallo is gunned down April 7 during a birthday party at Umberto's Clam House in Little Italy. Six other men with alleged gangland connections meet with violent deaths in 11 days; reputed Mafia leader Thomas "Tommy Ryan" Eboli is found dead July 10 on a Brooklyn sidewalk. He has been shot five times in the head.

Heroin kingpin Christian David, 41, pleads guilty in a New York court December 1, risking 80 years' imprisonment rather than accepting extradition to his native France, where he would be guillotined. David and a partner have handled about 10 percent of the world market; he is immediately sentenced to 20 years without parole and could receive another 60 on other charges. Police report December 20 that 300 pounds of seized narcotics have been stolen in the past week.

🏠 Two World Trade Center opens in January (One WTC opened just to the north in December 1970 while still incomplete, and the twin 110-story stainless-steel-and-glass office towers will be formally dedicated April 4 of next year). Under construction since 1968 and soaring 118 feet higher than the 1,250-foot Empire State Building of 1931, they have been built in International Style of heretofore unavailable high-strength steel that makes their outer walls into an exterior skeleton system instead of just being curtain walls, wind-tunnel tests have shown that these outer walls can withstand winds of 150 miles per hour, and engineers say a Boeing 707 flying into the buildings would not produce significant damage. Load-bearing exterior piers provide column-free floor space, the towers will have 43,600 narrow windows, and passengers from 23 express elevators will transfer to 72 local elevators at sky lobbies. The Port of New York Authority's offices since 1932 have been at 111 Eighth Avenue in Chelsea, but it moves them into the new Trade Center, whose second tower will be completed in 1976 after the expenditure of an estimated $800 million (its total cost may actually be closer to $1.5 billion, and it will escape bankruptcy only with help from a standing $100 million city-tax abatement and because Gov. Rockefeller will rent space for state agencies). The world's largest commercial complex, the WTC absorbs much of the downtown office market and will be augmented by three additional (low-rise) buildings, providing 10 million square feet of office floor space to accommodate 50,000 workers plus 80,000 visitors per day. Architectural critics generally find the WTC sterile and ugly; a five-acre plaza will connect the buildings, which will remain the world's tallest only until 1974 (and stand only until September 11, 2001).

The 55-story 55 Water Street skyscraper is completed between Coenties Slip and Old Slip with a terrace over South Street. Designed in International Style by Emery Roth & Sons for the Toronto-based firm Olympia & York, it is the largest privately owned U.S. building (only Chicago's Sears Tower will be larger), with 3.68 million square feet of floor space and 70 elevators (*see* crime, 1993).

The 57-story One Penn Plaza office tower is completed north of the new Penn Station. Designed in International Style by Kahn & Jacobs for developer Harry B. Helmsley of Mid City Associates, it covers an entire block bounded by Seventh and Eighth avenues between 33rd and 34th streets, rising 774 feet above a complex of low-rise shops and restaurants. Bisected by a pedestrian walkway, the structure has 14 entrances, 44 elevators grouped in seven banks, 695 underground parking spots, and direct access to the station.

The 48-story Uris Building (Paramount Plaza Building) is completed at 1633 Broadway, between 50th and 51st streets. Designed by Kahn & Jacobs, it replaces the Capitol Theater movie house.

The 32-story Franklin National Bank Building is completed at 450 Park Avenue, southwest corner 57th Street. Having acquired some neighboring properties, fashion designer Florence Lustig purchased the American Bible Society's handsome six-story red-brick building at the corner in 1965, thereby obtaining one of the most valuable sites in the city; the bronze-sheathed tower designed by Emery Roth & Sons fronts on both the avenue and 57th Street.

Real estate mogul Douglas L. Elliman of 485 Park Avenue dies at New York February 13 at age 89; architect Ely Jacques Kahn at New York September 5 at age 88.

Real estate mogul Harry Helmsley buys the 23-year-old Fresh Meadows housing development in Queens, paying New York Life Insurance Co. $53 million. A tenants' association will soon charge that Helmsley has reduced services and is planning to build on the open spaces that remain undeveloped, and although tenants and owners will reach an amicable settlement in 1982 the NAACP Legal Defense Fund will file a discrimination suit in 1983, and the community will come to have more Asian, black, and Native American residents in its 6,100 privately owned houses and 7,750 rental units.

The Bronx Zoo's Lila Acheson Wallace World of Birds installation opens June 16.

Congress establishes Gateway National Park; it includes Raritan Bay on Staten Island, Breezy Point in Rockaway, Queens, and—most importantly—the 9,155-acre Jamaica Bay Wildlife Refuge created in the 1950s.

Consolidated Edison Co. chairman Charles F. Luce agrees to halt the use of coal for generating electric power. Fuel oil produces fewer environmental contaminants, and by the fall of next year it will account for 85 percent of Con Ed's generating capacity (*but see* energy, 1973).

Snapple Fruit Juices are introduced at New York by Unadulterated Food Products (it will be renamed Snapple Beverage Co.), founded by local entrepreneurs Hyman Golden and Leonard Marsh, both 40, in partnership with Arnold Greenberg, 50, who has been operating a health-food store in St. Marks Place (brothers-in-law Golden and Marsh have had a window-washing business). Promoting itself with help from Wendy Kaufman, the brassy, boisterous "Snapple lady" with the "Noo Yawk" accent, the company will grow in the next 20 years to have 26 plants bottling nearly 60 all-natural Snapple varieties, carbonated and noncarbonated, many containing 100 percent real fruit juice, for distribution nationwide (*see* iced tea, 1987).

Balducci's in Greenwich Village moves into larger quarters diagonally across the street to 424 Avenue of the Americas (*see* 1948). Still owned by the Balducci family and still open 7 days a week, it ceases 24-hour operations but now offers fresh fruits (including *feijoa*) and vegetables (such as cardone, red Japanese eggplant, and purple asparagus), cheeses, coffees, meats, seafood, fresh pastas, sauces, and prepared dishes. It will survive until 2003 (*see* Fairway, 1975; Grace's Marketplace, 1985).

1973 Former president Lyndon B. Johnson dies on his Texas ranch January 23 at age 64. A cease-fire in Vietnam 5 days later ends direct involvement of U.S. ground troops in Indochinese hostilities. America's combat death toll has reached 45,958; the last U.S. troops leave South Vietnam March 29.

Lawyer and political adviser Samuel Rosenman dies at New York June 24 at age 77.

Democrat Abraham D. Beame wins the mayoralty election by an overwhelming margin, garnering

961,130 votes as compared to 276,575 for Republican John J. Marchi, 265,297 for Liberal Albert H. Blumenthal, and 189,986 for Congressman Mario Biaggi, who has run as a Conservative. Now 67, Beame will be the city's first Jewish mayor.

Gov. Rockefeller resigns December 18 after 15 years in office to head the National Commission on Critical Choices for Americans. Disappointed in his hopes for higher political office, Rockefeller has spent record amounts of state and federal money on new buildings, highways, parks, and other public developments. He has been the first governor to establish a permanent office in New York City, and the office at 22 West 55th Street has been his headquarters except during legislative sessions at Albany. His lieutenant governor Malcolm E. Wilson, 59, will be the state's chief executive through the end of next year.

The New York Commission on Human Rights decides that public accommodations must be open to all without regard to gender but makes an exception for hotels such as the 45-year-old Barbizon for Women, whose guests are mostly permanent (*see* Barbizon, 1985).

The National Gay and Lesbian Task Force is founded at New York to combat homophobia. Parents, Families and Friends of Lesbians and Gays (P-Flag) has its beginnings in Parents of Gays, founded by activists who include Queens mother Jeanne Manford, 52, whose homosexual son Morty was beaten last April by the head of the Uniformed Firefighters' Association. Mrs. Manford's three-story colonial house in Flushing will for more than 20 years be a meeting place and support center for distraught parents, their children, and gay-rights advocates.

Asian Americans for Equality has its beginnings in Asian Americans for Equal Employment, whose members stage Chinatown's first demonstration of its kind, protesting the exclusion of Asian workers from the federally financed Confucius Plaza apartment complex just south of the Manhattan Bridge (*see* 1975).

The oil shock and soaring grain prices precipitate a world monetary crisis and then a worldwide economic recession, the worst since the Great Depression of the 1930s.

The Soros Fund Management firm founded in August by Budapest-born New York investor George Soros (originally Schwartz), 43, and his Alabama-born, Yale-educated partner Jim Rogers, 31, opens a two-room office in Columbus Circle (Soros lives two blocks away at 25 Central Park West). Soros hired

Rogers as an analyst 5 years ago to help him at Arnhold & S. Bleichroder; their small, secretive partnership is chartered in Curaçao and manages investments for very rich overseas clients, purchasing some stocks and foreign currencies while selling others short (*see* Quantum Fund, 1979).

The Equity Funding Co. scandal makes headlines: 22 officers of the New York financial institution are indicted on charges of having created $100 million in non-existing assets by creating 64,000 fictitious life insurance policies, forging death certificates, and counterfeiting bonds.

Wall Street's Dow Jones Industrial Average closes December 31 at 850.86, down from 1020.02 at the end of 1972. Much worse is to come (*see* 1974).

Queens gets its first enclosed shopping mall September 12 on Queens Boulevard between Rego Park and Elmhurst. Abraham & Straus, Ohrbach's, and 70 specialty shops occupy the three-story mall, designed by Gruen Associates with 1.4 million square feet of space and built at a cost of $60 million. Some 2.1 million people live within seven miles of the new mall, whose managers project sales of $140 million in its first year.

Bloomingdale's introduces a Big Brown Bag designed by Massimo Vignelli to carry the oversize pillows sold in the store's linen department. The Little Brown Bag will follow next year, the Medium Brown Bag in 1992.

The Gimbel family sells its 36 Gimbels and Saks Fifth Avenue store chains to the British tobacco conglomerate B.A.T. Industries (*see* 1966; 1986).

An energy crisis grips the world; an oil embargo by OPEC in the fall exacerbates the problem, doubling the price of crude oil and putting pressure on utility companies such as Consolidated Edison (*see* environment, 1972). Con Ed cannot pass on the higher costs to consumers for 4 months, and the company is in the midst of a construction program to increase its capacity (*see* 1974).

The remaining section of the El in the Bronx along Third and Webster avenues between 149th Street and Gun Hill Road shuts down April 29 after 53 years of service.

The freighter *Sea Witch* suffers a rudder failure in New York Harbor June 2 and collides with the tanker *Esso Brussels*, killing 16 men. New York this year leads the nation in seafaring fatalities.

Manhattan's 43-year-old West Side Highway (Miller Elevated Highway) collapses near the Gansevoort Market December 15 under the weight of an asphalt-laden truck and an automobile (*see* Westway, 1974).

Federal Judge Orrin G. Judd of the Eastern District of New York issues an order April 30 requiring that the patient population of the Willowbrook State School on Staten Island be reduced forthwith to 250 with the remaining residents transferred to less confining environments such as group homes (*see* 1972). A bureaucratic struggle will result in the closing of Willowbrook, whose campus the City University of New York (CUNY) will acquire in 1989 to use for the College of Staten Island.

Empire Blue Cross and Blue Shield is created by a merger of the 38-year-old Associated Hospital Service (Blue Cross) and the 28-year-old United Medical Service (Blue Shield). It will soon establish a health maintenance organization (HMO) under the name Health Net, competing with HIP (*see* 1944), and implement a hospital reimbursement program mandated by the state to contain costs of in-patient care.

John Jay College of Criminal Justice moves to 59th Street, between Ninth and Tenth avenues (*see* 1967). While enrollment heretofore has come almost entirely from police and fire department personnel seeking advancement, the college will attract a growing number of local high school graduates, and by 1991 it will have 8,416 students, more than half of them women (*see* 1988).

Polytechnic Institute of Brooklyn merges with New York University's School of Science and Engineering (*see* 1958). Severe financial limitations have made it difficult for Polytech to retain faculty members and attract new students, but as Polytechnic Institute of New York it will receive more state aid and be able to strengthen its faculty (*see* Polytech University, 1985).

Dalton School founder Helen Parkhurst dies at a New Milford, Conn., hospital June 1 at age 86.

Nonfiction: *Briar Patch: The People of the State of New York versus Lumumba Shakur, et. al.* by Murray Kempton is about the Black Panther plot to blow up a city police station and the New York Botanical Garden; *Serpico* by Peter Maas recounts detective Frank Serpico's fight against police department corruption (*see* crime, 1971; Knapp Commission, 1970; 1972); *Real Lace: America's Irish Rich* by Stephen Birmingham; *The City and the Theatre: New York Playhouses from Bowling Green to Times Square* by Newark, N.J.-born author Mary C. Henderson (*née* Malanga), 45; *Pentimento* (autobiography) by Lillian Hellman.

Fiction: *Great Jones Street* by Don DeLillo; *World Without End, Amen* by Jimmy Breslin; *A Fairy Tale of New York* by J. P. Donleavy; *Once Is Not Enough* by Jacqueline Susann.

Macmillan Publishing Co. becomes the publishing subsidiary of Macmillan, whose name has been shortened (*see* 1961). The firm moved its headquarters in 1966 to 833 Third Avenue (*see* Scribner, 1984).

 Painting: *Wave Painting* by Elizabeth Murray.

Former *Vogue* editor-in-chief Diana Vreeland becomes fashion consultant to the Metropolitan Museum of Art (*see* 1971; Costume Institute, 1946); she mounts a retrospective show of clothes by Balanciaga from his first collection in 1938 to the design of a wedding dress that he will make next year for the granddaughter of Spanish dictator Gen. Francisco Franco.

Sculpture: *Ideogram* (polished stainless-steel bars) by Pennsylvania-born sculptor James Rosati, 61, is installed on the plaza between the twin towers of the new World Trade Center; *Bachi 1973* (black granite) by Masayuki Nagare is installed under the Trade Center's fourth portico; *Cube* by Isamu Noguchi, now 68, is installed on the plaza of the 6-year-old Marine Midland Bank Building at 140 Broadway; *Cubed Curve* (blue-painted steel) by New York-born sculptor William Crovello, 44, is installed in front of the Time & Life Building on 46th Street at the northwest corner of 50th Street; a memorial to the late Martin Luther King, Jr. is installed in front of the new high school named in his honor at the corner of Amsterdam Avenue and 66th Street. The dark-brown cube of welded steel has been created by New York sculptor William Tarr, 48.

 Photographer Edward Steichen dies at West Redding, Conn., March 25 at age 93.

Theater: *Finishing Touches* by Jean Kerr 2/8 at the Plymouth Theater, with Barbara Bel Geddes, San Diego-born actor Robert Lansing, 44, 164 perfs.; *The Hot l Baltimore* by Missouri-born playwright Lanford Wilson, 35, 3/22 at the Circle-in-the-Square Theater; *When You Comin' Back, Red Ryder* by Illinois-born playwright Mark (Howard) Medoff, 33, 11/4 at the Circle Repertory Theater, with Kevin Quinn, Robin Goodman, Addison Powell, James Kierman, 302 perfs.; *The Good Doctor* by Neil Simon 11/27 at the Eugene O'Neill Theater, with English actor Christopher Plummer, 45, Marsha Mason, 208 perfs.

The discount tkts booth opens June 25 on Broadway at 47th Street in Duffy Square, offering Broadway tickets at prices 25 to 50 percent below box-office prices plus a service charge that is used to develop new plays and increase audiences. John C. Schiff and Robert Mayers of Mayers & Schiff have designed the red trusswork frame and its canvas panels with the six-foot-high orange letters tkts on a budget of $5,000. Sponsored by the Theater Development Fund, the booth sells tickets for Broadway and off-Broadway theater seats that in many cases would otherwise go empty. After selling 155 tickets on opening day and 6,961 in its first week, waiting lines will become commonplace, by July 1999 it will have sold 36.5 million tickets, and the Development Fund will have opened another tkts booth in the financial district.

Sir Noël Coward dies after a heart attack at his villa on Jamaica's north coast March 26 at age 73; playwright S. N. Behrman of heart failure at his New York home September 9 at age 80.

Television Kojak 10/24 on CBS with Telly Savalas, now 49, as bald New York detective Theo Kojak in a series inspired by the career of detective Thomas J. Cavanaugh, 51 (to 1978).

Radio personality Martha Dean (Marian Young Taylor) dies of cancer at New York December 9 at age 65 (a former Scripps-Howard journalist, she took over the show in 1941 as the third "Martha Dean").

Films: Martin Scorsese's Mean Streets (set in Little Italy) with Robert De Niro, Harvey Keitel. Also: Aram Avakian's Cops and Robbers with Cliff Gorman, Joseph Bologna; William Friedkin's The Exorcist with Ellen Burstyn, Max von Sydow, Linda Blair; Milton Katselas's 40 Carats with Liv Ullmann, Gene Kelly, Edward Albert, Binnie Barnes; Ralph Bakshi's animated feature Heavy Traffic; John Frankenheimer's The Iceman Cometh with Lee Marvin, Fredric March, Robert Ryan, Jeff Bridges; Sidney Lumet's Serpico with Al Pacino as the police officer who exposed systemic bribe taking in the NYPD; Philip D'Antoni's The Seven-Ups with Roy Scheider, Tony LoBianco; Richard Fleischer's Soylent Green with Charlton Heston, Edward G. Robinson, Leigh Taylor-Young is about an overpopulated 2022 Manhattan.

♪♪ Broadway and off-Broadway musicals: El Grande de Coca-Cola 2/13 at the Mercer Arts Center, with Ron House, Diz White, music and lyrics by the cast, 1,114 perfs.; A Little Night Music 2/25 at the Shubert Theater, with Canadian-born actor Len Cariou, 33, Hermione Gingold, now 75, Pretoria-born actress Glynis Johns, 49, music and lyrics by Stephen Sond-

heim, book from the 1955 Ingmar Bergman film Smiles of a Summer Night, songs that include "Send In the Clowns," 600 perfs.; Irene 3/13 at the new 1,621-seat Minskoff Theater in the new 55-story Astor Plaza that has replaced the Astor Hotel on the west side of Broadway between 44th and 45th streets, with Debbie Reynolds, now 40, her Beverly Hills, Calif.-born daughter Carrie Fisher, 16, Ruth Warrick in a revival of the 1919 musical, 594 perfs. (named for developer Jerry Minskoff, the theater has been included to allow 20 percent more rental space under terms of the city's zoning laws); Seesaw 3/18 at the Uris Theater, with Los Angeles-born actress Michele Lee (originally Michele Lee Dusiak), 30 (who has replaced New York-born singer Lainie Kazan [originally Lainie Levine], 32, in previews), Ken Howard, dancer Tommy Tune, music by Cy Coleman, lyrics by Dorothy Fields, book by Buffalo-born choreographer Michael Bennett (originally Michael Di Figlia), 29, from the 1958 William Gibson play Two for the Seesaw, 296 perfs.; Raisin 10/18 at the 46th Street Theater, with New York-born actor Joe Morton, 26, St. Louis-born stage veteran Helen Martin, now 64, music by Judd Woldon, lyrics by Robert Britten, book from the 1959 Lorraine Hansberry play Raisin in the Sun, 847 perfs.

Lincoln Center renames its 11-year-old Philharmonic Hall Avery Fisher Hall to honor philanthropist Avery Fisher, now 67 (see 1969).

Michigan-born singer-composer Stevie Wonder (originally Stevland Morris), 22, makes his Carnegie Hall debut 2/27.

Popular songs: "You're in New York Now" by Dean Fuller, lyrics by Matt Dubey; "I Shot the Sheriff" by Jamaican reggai composer-performer Robert Nesta "Bob" Marley, 28.

CBGB opens on the Lower East Side at 315 Bowery, near Bleecker Street. Holly Kristal has started the place as a venue for country, bluegrass, and blues musicians, but it will have little success as such and next year will be turned into a rock club that will gain worldwide renown with performances by punk rock and new wave performers.

Jazz pianist Willie "the Lion" Smith dies after a short illness at University Hospital April 18 at age 79; jazz rhythm-guitarist Eddie Condon at New York August 4 at age 67; drummer Gene Krupa of leukemia at his Yonkers home October 16 at age 64; singer-comedian Allan Sherman of a respiratory ailment related to his obesity in California November 21 at age 48.

The New York Knicks win their second National Basketball Association (NBA) title May 10, beating Wilt Chamberlain, Jerry West, and Elgin Baylor of the Los Angeles Lakers 102 to 93 with help from coach Red Holzman. Center Willis Reed is named most valuable player after the five-game series.

John Newcombe wins in men's singles at Forest Hills, Margaret Smith Court in women's singles. The United States Tennis Association has announced July 19 that the U.S. Open will award equal prize money to women and men.

CBS announces January 3 that it is selling the New York Yankees for $10 million in cash to a 12-man syndicate headed by Cleveland shipbuilder George M. Steinbrenner 3d, 42, who is co-owner of a fleet of Manhattan limousines (see 1972). CBS paid $12 million for the franchise in 1964, and Michael Burke, now 54, will continue to direct the team. "We plan absentee ownership," says Steinbrenner, who acknowledges that $10 million was a bargain price and promises to improve the area around Yankee Stadium. Steinbrenner and Burke announce a week later that Cleveland Indians manager Gabe Paul, 63, and two more men are in the syndicate, whose other members include General Motors vice president John De Lorean, 47; lawyers for Steinbrenner's company, American Ship Building; Broadway theater owner James Nederlander, 50; Dallas oil heir Nelson Bunker Hunt, 46; Chicago real estate baron Lester Crown, 47. Steinbrenner made illegal contributions last year to President Nixon's reelection campaign and will be convicted of felony in that connection.

Baseball's American League permits teams to field a tenth player—a "designated hitter" to bat in place of the pitcher.

The New York Mets win the National League Pennant but lose the World Series to the Oakland A's, 4 games to 3. New York wins the second game in 12 innings (after nearly 4 hours of play) with help from pitcher Frank Edwin "Tug" McGraw, 29, and home runs by Cleon Jones, now 34, and third baseman Wayne Garrett, 26, who hits two; New York wins the fourth game behind the pitching of Jon Matlack, 24, with the help of three singles and a three-run homer by outfielder Daniel Joseph "Rusty" Staub, 30; Jerry Koosman shuts out the As in the fifth game, but Oakland comes back in the last two games, getting its first two home runs of the Series in the final game.

 Gangster Frank Costello dies of a heart attack at New York February 18 at age 82.

Mobster Meyer Lansky is convicted of income tax evasion and grand jury contempt but allowed to go free on bail (see 1970). He has been extradited from Israel to face trial.

New drug legislation signed by Gov. Rockefeller May 8 mandates prison sentences of 15 years to life for possession of more than four ounces—or sale of more than two ounces—of heroin or cocaine (possession of more than two ounces or sale of more than half an ounce can bring 3 years to life, with lower penalties for smaller amounts). The purpose of the tough new law is to discourage buyers and mid-level dealers, and to induce plea bargaining that will bring in drug kingpins, but big-time dealers will learn to avoid the sentences by using addicts and even children to carry drugs for them, and the law's effect will be to fill up state prisons with tens of thousands of low-level, nonviolent, non-predatory drug users, who will be confined at great cost for excessively long periods. Political leaders who try to repeal the law will risk being called "soft on crime," and the law will remain on the books into the 21st century, giving judges little or no discretion in sentencing.

Schoolteacher Roseann Quinn, 27, goes to the singles bar H. M. Tweed's at 250 West 72nd Street New Year's Eve, meets John Wayne Wilson, takes him home, and has sex with him. He strangles and knifes her to death, will be apprehended, confess, and commit suicide in the Tombs while awaiting trial. The case will be memorialized in the 1975 novel and 1977 film *Looking for Mr. Goodbar.*

The 32-story 88 Pine Street Building (later called Wall Street Plaza) is completed in Water Street between Pine Street and Maiden Lane to International Style designs by James Ingo Freed of I. M. Pei & Associates. Owned by Hong Kong shipowner Moley Cho, the building shares a plaza with 100 Wall Street.

A 38-story office building cum bookstore for Harper & Row (later HarperCollins) is completed at 10 East 53rd Street to plans by Smotrich & Platt, with design assistance from Chermayeff & Geismar.

The 44-story 1166 Avenue of the Americas skyscraper is completed between 45th and 46th streets to modernist designs by Skidmore, Owings & Merrill, who have given it a vest-pocket park that extends through the block.

The 45-story 1211 Avenue of the Americas skyscraper (initially the Celanese Building, later the NewsCorp Building) is completed between 47th and 48th streets. Designed in International Style by Harrison, Abramovitz & Harris, it is the southernmost of the Rockefeller Center Extension buildings and contains 1.8 million square feet of rentable floor space.

The Harlem State Office Building is completed at 163 West 125th Street, northeast corner Seventh Avenue, to designs by Hill Johnson Hanchard. Community residents demonstrated in opposition to the project, demanding that the site be used instead for a new high school, but Gov. Rockefeller persuaded the state legislature to construct a monumental structure resembling the colossal buildings he had built at Albany; it looms over Harlem as a symbol of state power and authority.

Architect Ralph T. Walker of Walker & Gillette dies at Chappequa January 17 at age 83.

SoHo is designated a Historic District by the City Landmarks Commission. Artists in the area SOuth of HOuston Street, north of Canal, between Crosby Street and Sixth Avenue, have long since converted warehouses—vacated decades ago in anticipation of an expressway whose construction was thwarted—into galleries, studios, and living spaces in defiance of zoning restrictions; the artists joined with other residents to have the city change its zoning laws with regard to the warehouses, and the area is beginning to sprout bars, restaurants, boutiques, and performance centers.

The Seward Park Houses Extension is completed at 64-66 Essex Street and 145-156 Broome Street on the Lower East Side. Designed by William F. Pedersen to supplement the original Seward Park Houses designed by Herman Jessor and built in 1960, the 22-story towers are two blocks apart.

The 30-story Lincoln Plaza Tower apartment house is completed at 44 West 62nd Street, southeast corner Columbus Avenue, to designs by Horace Ginsbern & Associates.

The six-story Lambert Houses are completed on the Boston Road between Bronx Park South and East Tremont Avenue in the Bronx. Financed by the nonprofit Phipps fund, they have been designed by Davis, Brody with a shopping mall and parking garage.

The Kitano Hotel opens at 66 Park Avenue, southwest corner 38th Street, where a Japanese construction firm has taken over the 18-story Murray apartment house built in 1926 and turned it into a 112-room transient hotel with a Japanese restaurant. Two suites are equipped with deep Japanese-style soaking tubs and living rooms whose floors are covered with tatami mats.

 A gas tank explosion on Staten Island February 10 kills 40 people; a fire at a Bronx social club October 24 kills 25.

 The Ninth Avenue Association sponsors the first Ninth Avenue International Food Festival in May, closing off the avenue between 42nd and 57th streets, attracting 250,000 visitors, and inaugurating an event that will continue for more than 25 years, growing larger each year as its length is extended to 37th Street.

General Foods cofounder Marjorie Merriweather Post dies at her Washington, D.C. Hillwood estate September 12 at age 86, leaving a fortune in excess of $200 million.

 Pet Incorporated announces an agreement June 20 to sell 22 of its 35 money-losing Schrafft's restaurants to veteran New York restaurateurs Irving and Murray Riese, who are more concerned with real estate values than food, although they operate some 200 eating places in the metropolitan area, including Luchow's and several Longchamps (see 1969). They will also acquire the Chock full o' Nuts luncheonette chain (see 1932) but will wind up closing Luchow's plus all of the Schrafft's, Longchamps, and Chock full o' Nuts restaurants (see 1974).

The Four Seasons restaurant that opened in 1959 is acquired by Hungarian-born restaurateurs Paul Kovi (a graduate of the University of Transylvania), 51, and Tom Margittai, who have worked at the Waldorf-Astoria and Sherry-Netherland hotels and at Restaurant Associates; Seppi Ranggli has been with RA since 1966 and is Kovi and Margittai's executive chef; their initial efforts disappoint longtime patrons, but they will rejuvenate the lavish eating place, emphasizing regional American cookery.

The food shop and restaurant E.A.T. opens at 867 Madison Avenue (corner 72nd Street). Launched by Eli Zabar and his wife, Abbie, it will move to 1084 Madison, near 80th Street, and feature bread and rolls baked to meet the owners' exacting standards (some of the city's best restaurants will buy their bread from E.A.T.). Zabar, now 29, is a younger brother of Saul and Stanley, who own the Upper West Side food and cooking-utensil shop along with Murray Klein.

Junior's cheesecake wins a contest sponsored by *New York* magazine (see 1950). Originated at the 23-year-old Brooklyn restaurant, it is made with softened cream cheese, graham cracker crumbs, sugar, cornstarch, eggs, heavy (whipping) cream, and vanilla extract. The cheesecake served by fast-talking waiters has become Junior's signature dish.

Gray's Papaya opens at the corner of 8th Street and the Avenue of the Americas in Greenwich Village and at the southeast corner of Amsterdam Avenue and 72nd Street under the direction of entrepreneur Nicholas A. B. Gray, 36, to serve fruit drinks of various kinds.

Mac Kriendler of the "21" Club is hospitalized with cancer and dies of pneumonia at New York August 7 at age 65.

1974 Conservative Party stalwart and former Nixon supporter Sen. James Buckley of New York urges President Nixon to resign March 19, saying it would be "an act at once noble and heartbreaking, at once serving the greater interest of the presidency, and the stated goals for which he successfully campaigned." Nixon nixes the proposal, saying it would be "bad statesmanship."

Longtime Manhattan district attorney Frank S. Hogan of 404 Riverside Drive dies at Lenox Hill Hospital April 2 at age 72. He served for 32 years but suffered a stroke last year and was operated on for removal of a lung tumor.

President Nixon resigns in disgrace August 9—the first U.S. chief of state ever to quit office. President Gerald R. Ford is sworn in August 9 and says, "The long nightmare is over." Freshman representatives Elizabeth Holtzman, 32 (D. N.Y.), and Charles Rangel (D. N.Y.) have played leading roles in the bipartisan House Judiciary Committee hearings that have ended with a decision to impeach the president.

Brooklyn-born congressman Hugh L. Carey, 55, wins election as governor, running on the Democratic Party ticket. He secures 3,028,503 votes to Lieut. Gov. Malcolm Wilson's 2,219,667, ending 20 years of Republican control.

Former governor Nelson A. Rockefeller is sworn in as President Ford's vice president December 19. He has survived a contentious Senate confirmation hearing and been forced to disclose his family's combined wealth ($1.3 billion—far less than had been thought). Right-wing Republicans will force Rockefeller off the ticket late next year and he will retire from public life.

The City Council defeats a Gay Rights Bill—the first bill in its history to be voted down by the full council after being reported out of committee (see 1971; 1986).

Federation of Jewish Philanthropies and the United Jewish Appeal combine their fund-raising activities (see Federation, 1917; UJA, 1939).

Dreyfus Liquid Assets is launched at New York in February—the first money-market fund to be advertised to the public (see Reserve Fund, 1970). It permits small investors to enjoy the same high rates of interest heretofore available only to individuals and institutions rich enough to buy financial instruments in denominations of $100,000 and more. Investors can write checks on their money-market funds, and there will be more than 100 such funds by 1980.

Vanguard Group has its beginnings in a mutual fund started by New York investment manager John C. Bogle, 44, who has been sacked as chief executive officer of Wellington Management. As a senior at Princeton in 1951, Bogle wrote a thesis positing the idea of a mutual fund that could be purchased without a sales commission and managed with low overhead. Vanguard is a fund distribution company mutually owned by shareholders and built on the ideas Bogle advanced 23 years ago; based at Valley Forge, Pa., it will grow in the next 30 years or so to become larger than Boston-based Fidelity Investments.

Quick & Reilly is founded by New York stockbroker Leslie C. (Charles) Quick, Jr., 48, and Kevin Reilly. When Wall Street abolishes fixed-rate commissions next year Quick will begin offering steep discounts, big brokerage houses will hoot at the idea and call the firm "Quick & Dirty," Reilly will quit in 1976, but other firms will join in discounting commissions, and Fleet Financial Services will acquire Quick & Reilly for $1.6 billion in Fleet stock (the Quick family's stake will be valued at $680 million).

Franklin National Bank is declared insolvent September 8—the biggest bank failure in U.S. history (many larger banks receive no interest on outstanding loans). Italian financier Michele Sindona, 53, is a director of the New York bank's parent company (see 1980). European American Bank (EAB) will take over Franklin branches (and Citibank will take over EAB in 2001).

New York banks begin bailing out of New York City bonds in the wake of Gov. Wilson's defeat at the polls. Mayor Beame confides to developer Lewis Rudin that the city is in dire financial shape because the federal government has turned down his request for a loan. Rudin persuades other property owners and executives from Con Edison, New York Telephone Co., and Rockefeller Center to pay their real estate taxes ahead of schedule and thereby keep the city afloat.

Former New York Stock Exchange president Richard Whitney dies at Short Hills, N.J., December 5 at age 85.

Wall Street's Dow Jones Industrial Average bottoms out December 9 at 570.01, down from 1020.16 at the end of 1972, and closes December 31 at 616.24, down from 850.86 at the end of 1973. Economic recession has deepened following last year's hike in oil prices by major petroleum producers; inflation, meanwhile, raises prices in most of the free world.

Peck & Peck and its parent company Brooks Industries, Inc. file for bankruptcy July 22. A credit crunch has prevented the 70-year-old chain from obtaining sufficient fall inventories of the classic girls' and women's apparel that have long been its stock in trade, and critics note that while sportswear has come back into fashion the Peck & Peck line has lost its distinction.

Brooklyn Union Gas completes a synthetic natural gas plant at Greenpoint in November (see 1970). Liquefied natural gas from Algeria has helped ease the shortage of natural gas from Texas (see 1976).

Consolidated Edison chairman Charles F. Luce withholds dividends in the first quarter, an unprecedented step taken to conserve cash critically needed for Con Ed's expansion program. Oil prices have escalated in the wake of last year's action by the Organization of Petroleum Exporting Countries (OPEC crude oil prices reach $11.25 per barrel by year's end, up from $2.50 at the beginning of 1973). Luce draws sharp criticism from stockholders and other utilities but persuades the state of New York to buy two of the company's generating plants now under construction, receiving $612 million in cash. Additional power needed by the city is bought back from the state.

A proposal to replace 4.2 miles of the West Side Highway with a Westway Project begins a controversy that will continue for more than decade (see highway collapse, 1973). Proponents include the Army Corps of Engineers; they envision developing 242 acres along (and in) the Hudson River, using 169 acres of new river landfill plus 73 acres of shoreline for commercial and residential real estate development and a public park (see environment, 1982).

Aviation pioneer Alexander P. de Seversky dies at New York August 24 at age 80; Charles A. Lindbergh on the Hawaiian island of Maui August 26 at age 72.

Bellevue Hospital gets a massive new building on the FDR Drive between 27th and 28th streets. Designed by Katz, Waisman, Weber, Strauss, Joseph Blumenkrantz, Pomerance & Breines, and Feld & Timoney, the 22-story beige structure has 20 elevators and an acre and a half of space per floor for clinics, laboratories, and patient beds.

The City Council votes to cede the air rights over the FDR Drive between 63rd and 71st streets to Rockefeller University, New York Hospital, and the Hospital for Special Surgery. Former governor Nelson Rockefeller arranged last year to transfer the air rights over the boulevard section between 62nd and 71st streets; the Council establishes a cut-off date of 2003 for new construction utilizing the air rights.

The 31-story Annenberg Building completed for the Mount Sinai School of Medicine on Madison Avenue between 99th and 100th streets contains a 600-seat auditorium and incorporates a range of school and research facilities. Roy O. Allen of Skidmore, Owings & Merrill has designed the structure, whose rusting Cor-ten steel sheathing is similar to that of the Ford Foundation building in 42nd Street.

The city's acting chief medical examiner reports March 19 that more New Yorkers died of methadone poisoning in the first half of last year than died of heroin overdoses (see 1964; 1998).

The city's Board of Health receives 37,000 reports of dog bites and 6,000 other complaints against dogs.

Boricua College opens in an Audubon Terrace building at 3755 Broadway formerly used by the American Geographical Society. Oriented towards Puerto Ricans and other Hispanic population groups, the private, nonprofit institution is the first in the nation to offer bilingual education, will become fully accredited in 1980, will open Brooklyn campuses at 9 Graham Avenue and 186 North 6th Street, and by 1990 will have about 1,100 students, four-fifths of them women, working towards associate and bachelor's degrees in business administration, elementary education, inter-American studies, the liberal arts, and social service casework.

The lawsuit filed 2 years ago by Aspira and other Hispanic community organizations ends with a consent decree that establishes bilingual education entitlement standards. Within 20 years more than 143,000 city schoolchildren will be entitled to receive special-language services, not only in Spanish but in 10 other languages, including Arabic, Bengali, Chinese, French, Greek, Haitian-Creole, Korean, Russian, Urdu, and Vietnamese. (Other languages spoken by at least 100 children each are Albanian, Dari-Farsi, Filipino, Gujarati, Hebrew, Hindi, Italian, Japanese, Khmer, Maylayalam, Pashto, Polish, Portuguese, Punjabi, Romanian, Serbo-Croatian, Thai, and Turkish.) Most students who fail a standard English-proficiency test at age 5 or 6, when they could most quickly and easily learn English, will be placed automatically in bilingual classes, where they will study math and social studies in their native languages, and some will remain in such classes for 6 years and more while they gradually (in theory) learn English. Critics of bilingual education will allege that bureaucrats seek out limited English proficient (LEP) students, and that funding for the programs will mean fewer resources for books, school modernization, and other educational needs.

The Great School Boards, New York City: 1805–1973 by local activist Diane Ravitch (*née* Silvers), 36, says that city schools have always had trouble educating the children of poor immigrants, and that schools cannot solve all the problems of society. While good schools can provide a pathway "from the gutter to the university" for the talented few, they can do little to ensure that no Americans will live under conditions that can be called "the gutter."

The South Street Seaport Museum opens a restoration of the Bowne & Co. print shop in October (*see* 1775).

 Some 50 women's groups from the tri-state area picket the *New York Times* March 4, protesting the paper's refusal to use the designation "Ms." when so requested, employ terms such as "spokesperson" and "chairperson," or give more than sporadic coverage to women's news except on the Family/Style page or in the back pages. The *Times* will not begin using "Ms." until the mid-1980s—long after other major papers have done so.

People magazine begins publication March 4 at New York. Time, Inc. has started the new 35¢ weekly in a bid to recoup circulation lost when LIFE ceased weekly publication late in 1972.

Word processors with cathode-ray tube displays and speedy printers begin to replace typewriters as the economic recession encourages business managers to automate offices. By 1976 impact printers with bidirectional "daisy wheels" will be printing documents at 30 to 55 characters per second, versus 15 for the typing ball on a power typewriter, while secretaries key in material for other documents.

Former *New York Times* Washington Bureau chief Arthur Krock dies at Washington, D.C. April 12 at age 86; NBC-TV newscaster Frank McGee of pneumonia while being treated for bone-marrow cancer at New York April 17 at age 52; journalist-author Walter Lippmann at New York December 14 at age 85; journalist-author Amy Vanderbilt at New York

December 27 at age 66 of injuries suffered in a fall from a second-floor window.

Nonfiction: *The Power Broker: Robert Moses and the Fall of New York* by New York-born writer Robert A. Caro, 38, whose book is highly critical of the long-time parks commissioner and master planner, now 85; *History Preserved: A Guide to New York City Landmarks and Historic Districts* by architect Harmon H. Goldstone, now 63, and Jean Dalrymple; *All Aboard with E. M. Frimbo* by veteran *New Yorker* editor and railroad buff Rogers E. M. Whitaker, now 75, who joined the magazine in 1926, established its fact-checking department soon afterward, wrote "Talk of the Town" pieces under the name "The Old Curmudgeon," reviewed nightclub entertainers in articles signed "Popsie," signed his football commentaries "J.W.L.," and has covered 2,748,636.81 miles by rail gathering material for his pieces about train travel (a publication party is held aboard a private railcar in Pennsylvania Station); *Gramercy Park: An Illustrated History* by Stephen Garvey; *South Street: A Photographic Guide to New York City's Historic Seaport* by Ellen Fletcher Rosebrock, photographs by Edmund V. Gillon, Jr.; *Alive in the City: Memoir of an Ex-Commissioner* by former parks commissioner August Heckscher, who writes that "in the long run it is the amenities of city life that will save the city—and save the souls of its inhabitants. If people are not enjoying the place where they live, they perish slowly; and they bring down the temple with them . . . [The] future does not belong to those who seduce and manipulate. It belongs to the men of faith who speak of the whole city—the city where they live and the large city of man; who bring the citizens to see their needs and interests in relation to those of others; and who work the healing of trust. The life of the city is this awareness of one another; and to be alive in it is to have one's sympathies fully awake;" *Gentleman Jimmy Walker: Mayor of the Jazz Age* by New York-born writer George (William) Walsh, 43; *A Writer's Capital* by novelist Louis Auchincloss, who writes of the 1920s, "With other children I took the anti-Semitism which then characterized the Protestant society of New York for granted. Most of the schools and clubs admitted no Jews at all unless they were converted or unless they had married Christians. Brearly was considered 'liberal' because it took one Jewish girl per class, yet I can never recall thinking that my parents or their friends had any particular animus against Jews . . . The same may be said about the prejudice against Roman Catholics. This certainly existed, though, like the anti-Semitism it was snobbish rather than religious in nature. Catholicism was associated in our minds with the poor, ignorant Irish maids who worked such long hours and slept in often unheated areas on the top of brownstone houses. So far as blacks were concerned, however, there was no prejudice at all, because blacks did not exist for us. Nobody that I knew had a black servant. They lived up in Harlem, presumably because they liked it, and our paths never crossed."

Fiction: *The Wanderers* by New York-born novelist Richard Price, 24, is about teenage gang members in a North Bronx housing project.

Novelist Jacqueline Susann dies of cancer at New York September 21 at age 53.

Painting: *Corpse and Mirror* (oil, encaustic, collage on canvas) by Jasper Johns; *Dancers* by Roy Lichtenstein; *Robert/104, 072* by Chuck Close; *The Builders* (screenprint on woven paper) by Jacob Lawrence. Moses Soyer dies at New York September 3 at age 74.

An October 18 auction at Sotheby's of works by Jasper Johns, Robert Rauschenberg, James Rosenquist, and Andy Warhol fetches $2.2 million for New York collector Robert Scull (originally Sokolnikoff), 59. Born on the Lower East Side, Scull built up a fleet of 130 taxicabs operated by 400 drivers; he and his wife, Ethel (*née* Redner), have been collecting modern art with encouragement from dealer Leo Castelli. Sotheby's sold some of the Scull collection in October 1965 (*see* 1986).

Sculpture: *5 in 1* by Tony Rosenthal is installed in the new Police Plaza east of the Municipal Building on Park Row. Commissioned by the city 3 years ago, the $80,000 work contains five interlocking steel disks, each weighing 15,000 pounds, and is 20 feet in diameter, 10 inches thick; it has cost $20,000 to install.

Theater: *Short Eyes* by Puerto Rico-born New York playwright Miguel Piñero, 27, 1/3 at the Riverside Church Theater, 102 perfs. (Piñero was arrested on burglary charges 10 years ago, convicted, and has spent most of the time since then in the correctional system for petty crimes related to drug addiction. His play is related to prison life); *Thieves* by Herb Gardner 4/7 at the Broadhurst Theater, with Dick Van Patten, Marlo Thomas, New York-born actor "Professor" Irwin Corey, now 61, 312 perfs.; *Bad Habits* by Terrence McNally 5/5 at the Booth Theater (after 96 perfs. at the Astor Place Theater), with Cynthia Harris, Doris Rafelo, Emory Bass, J. Frank Luca, 273 perfs.; *All Over Town* by Murray Schisgal 12/29 at the Booth Theater, with Bedford Hills-born actor Barnard Hughes, 59, Oklahoma-born actor Cleavon Little, 35, 233 perfs.

Actress Patricia Collinge dies at New York April 10 at age 81; Katherine Cornell at Vineyard Haven, Mass., June 8 at age 81; playwright George Kelly at Bryn Mawr, Pa., June 18 at age 87.

Television: *Rhoda* 9/9 on CBS with Valerie Harper (formerly of the *Mary Tyler Moore Show*) as Bronx window dresser Rhoda Morgenstern, David Groh as Joe Girard (whom Rhoda marries 10/28 but will divorce in 1976), Julie Kavner as Rhoda's sister Brenda, Nancy Walker as Mama Ida Morgenstern (to 1978).

Former NBC producer Dan Golenpaul of *Information Please* fame dies at New York February 23 at age 73; CBS-TV program director Hubbell Robinson of lung cancer at New York September 4 at age 68; Ed Sullivan at New York October 13 at age 73.

Films: Francis Ford Coppola's *The Godfather (Part Two)* with Al Pacino, Robert Duvall, Diane Keaton; Gordon Parks's *The Super Cops* with Ron Leibman, David Selby, Sheila Frazier, Pat Hingle; Joseph Sargent's *The Taking of Pelham One, Two, Three* with Walter Matthau, Robert Shaw, Martin Balsam. Also: Carlo Lizzati's *Crazy Joe* with Peter Boyle (as Mafioso Joe Gallo), Rip Torn, Eli Wallach, Paula Prentiss, Luther Adler; Michael Winner's *Death Wish* with Charles Bronson, Hope Lange, Vincent Gardenia; Peter Yates's *For Pete's Sake* with Barbra Streisand, Michael Sarazin, Estelle Parsons; Paul Mazursky's *Harry and Tonto* with Art Carney, Ellen Burstyn; Ivan Passer's *Law and Disorder* with Carroll O'Connor, Ernest Borgnine, Anne Wedgeworth; Stephen F. Verna's *The Lords of Flatbush* with Martin Davidson, Perry King, Sylvester Stallone, Henry Winkler.

Broadway and off-Broadway musicals: *Let My People Come* 1/8 at the Village Gate, with music and lyrics by Earl Wilson, Jr., 31, songs that include "Dirty Words," "Give It to Me," and "Whatever Turns You On." The sexually oriented show will move uptown to the Morosco Theater 7/27/1976, 1,167 perfs.; *Lorelei* 1/27 at the Palace, with Carol Channing, Columbus, Ohio-born stage veteran Dody Goodman, now 57, in a revised version of the 1949 musical *Gentlemen Prefer Blondes*, music by Jule Styne, lyrics by Betty Comden and Adolph Green, 321 perfs.; *The Magic Show* 5/28 at the Cort Theater, with Manitoba-born illusionist Doug Henning, 27, music and lyrics by Stephen Schwartz, 1,859 perfs.

Broadway impresario Sol Hurok dies of a heart attack March 5 at age 85 in the office of Chase Manhattan Bank president David Rockefeller following a visit to guitarist Andres Segovia; baritone William

Tabbert dies of a heart attack at New York October 19 at age 53 while rehearsing for a nightclub act.

Popular songs: "The Way We Were" by New York-born composer Marvin Hamlisch, 30, lyrics by Brooklyn-born writer Alan Bergman, 48, and his wife, Marilyn (*née* Keith), 44 (title song for film).

Composer Duke Ellington dies at Columbia-Presbyterian Medical Center May 24 at age 75. He has been hospitalized with lung cancer since early April, and his close friend John G. Gensel of St. Peter's Lutheran Church officiates at his funeral (*see* Duke Ellington Boulevard, 1977).

The New York Nets win the American Basketball Association (ABA) championship May 10, beating the Utah Stars 111 to 100. Nets forward Julius "Dr. J." Erving, 24, is named most valuable player (the Nets acquired him from the Virginia Squares in the off season).

St. Louis-born tennis ace James Scott "Jimmy" Connors, 21, wins in men's singles at Forest Hills, Billie Jean King in women's singles. *A Long Way, Baby: Behind the Scenes in Women's Pro Tennis* by New York journalist Grace Lichtenstein (*née* Rosenthal), 32, is an exposé.

Former world heavyweight champion James J. Braddock dies at his North Bergen, N.J., home November 29 at age 68.

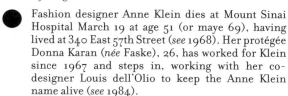

Fashion designer Anne Klein dies at Mount Sinai Hospital March 19 at age 51 (or maye 69), having lived at 340 East 57th Street (*see* 1968). Her protégée Donna Karan (*née* Faske), 26, has worked for Klein since 1967 and steps in, working with her co-designer Louis dell'Olio to keep the Anne Klein name alive (*see* 1984).

French daredevil Philippe Petit, 24, secretly stretches a cable between the twin towers of the new World Trade Center and walks across it August 7, electrifying spectators for nearly an hour. In the next 25 years he will make 70 other high-wire walks in various parts of the world (*see* Willig, 1977).

The city has 140 kennels, 750 pet shops, and nearly 100 grooming shops.

The Dial-a-Joke line introduced by New York Telephone Co. features Henny Youngman, now 68, as its first comedian. The line receives 3,331,638 calls in its opening month from people who hear 30 seconds of Youngman one-liners.

Greenwich Village holds a Halloween parade October 31 with 200 costumed marchers who include a man in a seven-foot lobster suit borrowed from a Sam Shepard play, a two-headed pig monster, and a lizard. The participants stage a mock battle between good and evil on the steps of the Washington Square Methodist Church, proceed across to the park, and initiate an event that will become a city tradition (drag queens and overtly homosexual elements will not be noticeable for several years).

The 54-story U.S. Steel Building is completed at 1 Liberty Plaza on a site bounded by Broadway, Liberty, Church, Cortlandt, and Church streets. Designed in International Style by Roy Allen of Skidmore, Owings & Merrill, the massive monolith replaces Ernest Flagg's 46-story Singer Tower of 1908 that was once the tallest in the world but was razed in 1968. Big Steel will later sell the building and it will become simply One Liberty Plaza.

The 40-story 1 Bankers Trust Plaza skyscraper is completed south of the World Trade Center at 130 Liberty Street to International Style designs by Shreve, Lamb & Harmon, who have given it a façade of black, anodized aluminum and darkened glass.

The nearly windowless AT&T Long Lines Building is completed at 33 Thomas Street in Tribeca to designs by California-born architect John Carl Warnecke, 57. The tall concrete slab sheathed in pink Swedish granite rises 29 stories high, but each floor is nearly twice the height of ordinary office floors.

The 42-story New York Merchandise Mart is completed at 41 Madison Avenue, northeast corner 26th Street, with 23 floors devoted to showcasing the wares of tenants engaged in manufacturing and/or selling decorations and tableware. Emery Roth & Sons has designed the tall, narrow, glass-walled structure.

The 40-story New York Telephone Co. Building (initially the W. T. Grant Building) is completed at 1095 Avenue of the Americas, southwest corner 42nd Street, to International Style designs by Kahn & Jacobs. Its top floors contain telecommunications equipment.

Architect Louis I. Kahn dies of a heart attack at Pennsylvania Station March 17 at age 73.

The 50-story W. R. Grace Building at 41 West 42nd Street and 1114 Avenue of the Americas, southeast corner 43rd Street, is completed with a large, vacant plaza that owes its existence to the misguided 1961 zoning law that allows extra height to builders who provide such spaces. Designed by Gordon Bunshaft of Skidmore, Owings & Merrill, the skyscraper occupies the former site of Stern's department store and has a swooping curvature copied from some Chicago buildings.

The 50-story 9 West 57th Street skyscraper is completed between Fifth and Sixth avenues for builder Sheldon H. (Henry) Solow, 46, to designs by Gordon Bunshaft of Skidmore, Owings & Merrill. Like the Grace Building, it has a bell-bottomed, vertically curved façade; a tomato-red steel "9" designed by Ivan Chermayeff identifies the building (standing 10 feet high and five feet wide, the six-ton numeral occupies about 50 square feet of sidewalk space, rented from the city for $1,000 per year).

The state legislature at Albany repeals its vacancy decontrol rent law in the spring following release of a report by the Stein Commission, appointed by former governor Rockefeller last year to study the results of the law (see 1971). Rents in New York City have increased by an average of 52 percent, the amount of money spent on renovation has decreased by 30 percent, and political reaction has brought pressure on legislators to change the law. Headed by Assemblyman Andrew J. Stein, 29 (son of investor, publisher, and Rockefeller ally Jerry Finkelstein), the commission has reported, "Decontrol has neither stimulated new building construction, stopped abandonment, spurred renovation, nor has it brought substantial new money into the city's housing stock." Full-scale rent regulation is reimposed, but landlords will make repeated efforts to revive vacancy decontrol and even total abolishment of controls (see 1997).

The five- and six-story West Village Houses open July 22 in Washington Street between 10th and Bank streets and along Christopher and Morton streets. Designed by Perkins & Will, built at a cost of $25 million, and financed under the Mitchel-Lama program, the low-rise walk-ups with 420 co-op units have been championed by critic Jane Jacobs over the opposition of Robert Moses and developer William Zeckendorf, who favored an urban renewal plan that called for high-rise buildings.

A groundbreaking ceremony September 20 begins work on Battery Park City (see 1969).

Wall Street's falling security prices depress New York co-operative apartment prices: the triplex of the late Fannie Hurst at the Hotel des Artistes sells for only $170,000.

The East Midtown Plaza apartment complex is completed from First Avenue to Second between 23rd and 25th streets. Davis, Brody & Associates has designed the six brown brick buildings, some of which opened in 1972 (the tallest, in 24th Street, has 28 floors; one on Second Avenue has 27; one on First Avenue has 22; two in 23rd Street have 11 each; one in 25th Street has nine).

The fourth 37-story Waterside apartment building is completed east of the FDR Drive between 25th and 28th streets (see 1966; United Nations School, 1973). Designed by Davis, Brody & Associates for developer Richard Ravitch (the north building has been built with Mitchell-Lama funds), the complex has 1,470 units (including some in town houses), a pedestrian plaza, a health club with swimming pool, and its own bank branch, restaurants, and shops.

The 30-story Nevada apartment house is completed on a triangular site at 2025 Broadway, between 69th and 70th streets. Designed by Philip Birnbaum, it replaces an earlier Nevada.

The 41- and 38-story Tracey Towers are completed in the Bronx at 20 and 40 West Mosholu Parkway, southwest corner Jerome Avenue, to designs by architect Paul Rudolph. They are the tallest structures in the borough; the Boulevard Manor apartment houses are completed in the Bronx at 2001 and 2045 Story Avenue, between Pugsley and Olmstead avenues in the Castle Hill section, to designs by Gruzen & Partners.

Central Park is designated a New York City Landmark April 16.

Brooklyn's Park Slope Food Co-operative is founded to help residents buy good, wholesome food at prices lower than those charged by supermarkets. Similar co-operatives have opened in other parts of the city, with members volunteering their labor (see 1997).

The Schrafft's restaurant in the Chrysler Building closes March 29 after 44 years in business (see 1973). There were once more than 50 Schrafft's restaurants in the city, and at least one will survive into the 1980s, but Irving and Murray Riese, now 65 and 63, respectively, have grown rich from escalating real estate values and continue to convert money-losing restaurants into fast-food outlets (see Martini's, 1994).

Le Cirque opens in late March at 58 East 65th Street with a three-course luncheon at $12.75. Chef Jean Vergnes has known owner-manager Sirio Maccioni since both worked at the Colony (he has more recently been chef at Maxwell's Plum). Dinner entrées average about $9, and the new eating place in the Mayfair House that opened in 1925 will attract the fashion crowd and others (Oleg Cassini, Jacqueline Onassis, Beverly Sills, Barbara Walters) for more than 20 years as the prix-fixe luncheon climbs to $29.95 (by 1994) (*see* 1997).

Il Monello opens at 1460 Second Avenue (between 76th and 77th streets). Owner Adi Giovannetti, 30, worked as a scullion for Frank Giambelli after arriving at New York from his native Lucca 16 years ago; his Genoese chef Luigi Strazzuli, also a veteran of Giambelli's, prepares *osso bucco*; rolled veal (at $6.20); Livornese fish stew (at $7, with other entrées at $5.50 to $9); and pastas of all sorts (at $4.40 to $5).

The Oyster Bar and Restaurant at Grand Central Terminal closes July 31 after 62 years but reopens in September under the management of Restaurant Associates cofounder Jerome Brody, who has left RA and is also proprietor of the Rainbow Room and Gallagher's Steak House. Brody leases the premises from the Metropolitan Transportation Authority and promises to restore the Oyster Bar's policy of serving only fresh fish and shellfish, cooked to order, with salmon and brook trout smoked on the premises.

Jack Dempsey's Restaurant closes on the west side of Broadway between 49th and 50th streets. Former heavyweight champion Dempsey and his wife donate to the Smithsonian Institution at Washington the six-by-eighteen-foot James Montgomery Flagg painting commissioned by Dempsey in 1944 to commemorate his July 4, 1919, third-round knockout of then titleholder Jess Willard.

Planned Parenthood Federation of America President Alan F. Guttmacher dies at New York March 18 at age 75.

1975 A terrorist bomb explodes in an annex to the dining room of Fraunces Tavern at 54 Pearl Street January 24, killing two and injuring 56. Authorities blame the Puerto Rican nationalist group Fuerzas Armadas de Liberación (FALN) for the incident.

A bomb explosion at La Guardia Airport December 29 kills 14 and leaves 70 injured. The device has been planted in the baggage-claim area of the main terminal.

Police beat up Chinese-born student Peter Yew, the 1-year-old Asian Americans for Equality brings out 20,000 protesters to picket City Hall May 19, and the developers of Confucius Plaza in Chinatown hire 27 minority workers; the AAFE draws criticism by adopting what opponents call Maoist tactics, but the organization will renounce violence in 1979 and devote itself to social service work in Chinatown (*see* rezoning fight, 1981).

The Urban Development Corp. created by former governor Nelson A. Rockefeller in 1969 defaults in January on $100 million worth of notes in the biggest default of any government agency since the Great Depression of the 1930s. Large influxes of poverty-level blacks and Hispanics have raised welfare costs, banks have stopped loaning the city money, Albany has not been forthcoming with aid, the federal government has rejected appeals for financial help, and the default depresses prices of New York City bonds as investors stop buying them. Barred from access to the credit markets, the city has a budget crisis.

Wall Street's fixed commission rate ends May 1 by order of the Securities and Exchange Commission. Institutional investors (bank trust departments, insurance companies, and the like) begin negotiating lower rates, some will enjoy rates up to 90 percent lower than those paid at fixed rates, many brokers and dealers will be forced out of business in the next two years or will survive only by merging, and the change will encourage more individual investors to buy mutual funds. The reduction in the cost of doing business will make more money available for investment purposes. Brokerage houses will cut back on services to compensate for the loss in revenue.

Baruch College business-school professor Donna Shalala, 34, serves as director and treasurer of the Municipal Assistance Corp. (MAC), a separate borrowing authority created by the state in June in an effort to deal with the fiscal crisis by giving the city access to credit. The 65-year-old investment banking house Salomon Brothers underwrites more than $1 billion worth of bonds for the Municipal Assistance Corp.

The state of New York takes formal control of the city's finances in September, using the powers of the Emergency Financial Control Board, and begins collecting city income taxes on the city's behalf (*see* 1966). Gov. Carey's State of the State message January 8 has contained an implied promise to take over the function, as Mayor Beame has often requested. Theodore R. Morell has urged July 1 that the state implement its plan, saying it will save the city $3.5 million per year in administrative costs, and the mayor has detailed ways he would use that money. Gov. Cary has said that efforts are being made to work out a solution to city-state fiscal problems. Increased revenues from income taxes, sales taxes, and taxes on automobiles, gross payrolls, hotel rooms, theater tickets, and the like have reduced the proportion of the burden borne by property taxes to 55 percent, down from 70 percent in the 1950s (*see* 1982).

Trustees of the New York City Teacher Retirement System balk October 16 at having their pension funds used to bail out the city, whose other sources of funds have run dry. United Federation of Teachers president Albert Shanker has seen an opportunity to increase his power.

The city's fiscal crisis forces it to curtail essential services such as police and fire protection, and it narrowly avoids defaulting on its bonds. "FORD TO CITY: DROP DEAD," says the front page of the *Daily News* October 30 (the headline was written by Bill Brink, whose subhead reads, "Vows He'll Veto Any Bail-Out"). Stocks plummet on the news, the price of gold skyrockets, and the value of the dollar declines in foreign exchange markets. Albert Shanker is finally persuaded to release funds that provide temporary relief, and the president soon has a change of heart: legislation passed by the House of Representatives 275 to 130 December 15 and signed by Ford December 18 includes a special federal loan guarantee of nearly $2 billion for the city.

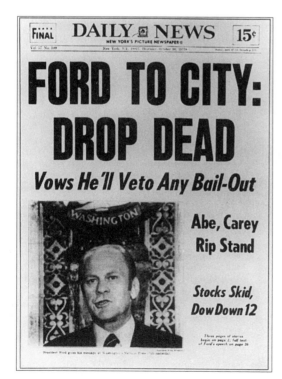

President Ford refused to help the city out of its financial difficulties but later relented. DAILY NEWS

Sen. Javits establishes the Citizens Committee for New York City to stimulate and support self-help and civic action aimed at improving the city's quality of life, with special regard to crime, disaffected youth, drugs, environmental hazards, and poverty. The Committee will work to strengthen more than 11,000 block, neighborhood, youth, and other grassroots volunteer organizations through hands-on assistance, small grants, self-help publications, and training.

Chemical Bank acquires Long Island's Security National Bank as it continues to expand into retail banking (*see* 1959).

Detroit-born restaurateur's son Ivan F. (Frederick) Boesky, 38, uses money from his wife, Seema, to open a New York risk-arbitrage firm under his own name (her father, Ben Silberstein, is a real estate magnate). Buying up shares in a company that is being taken over and speculating that he can exchange them at a profit when the deal is done, sleeping little more than 3 hours per night, the dapper workaholic will soon have a marble office on Fifth Avenue and a 300-line telephone console plus three lines in his car as he trades openly, accumulating large positions that often go beyond the 5 percent limit that requires reporting to the Securities and Exchange Commission, raising money by establishing limited partnerships that he will often dissolve and reestablish to bring in additional investors (who may be assigned 45 percent of the profits and 95 percent of the losses but still average annual returns of 43 percent on their capital; *see* 1985).

Financier-industrialist-lawyer Charles A. Dana dies at Wilton, Conn., November 27 at age 94.

Wall Street's Dow Jones Industrial Average closes December 31 at 852.41, up from 616.24 at the end of 1974. Economic recovery has begun in much of the world despite continued high unemployment and a new 10 percent increase in OPEC prices.

S. Klein closes in August after 63 years on Union Square (*see* 1931). McCrory's has taken over the store and failed to make it pay.

City transit fares rise from 35¢ to 50¢ September 1 (*see* 1972; 1980).

"Kneeling" buses go into service on Metropolitan Transportation Authority lines beginning in September. Made by General Motors, their front ends can be lowered to accommodate passengers not spry enough to climb aboard otherwise.

The Second Avenue subway project begun in 1972 is abandoned for lack of funds after the city has spent

$87 million to build an East River Tunnel at 63rd Street, excavate a stretch of 20 blocks, and install three-section shells at 120th Street, 110th Street, and Canal Street. Much of the money is thought to have been diverted to corrupt politicians, and Manhattan's East Side is left with only one (Lexington Avenue) rapid-transit line (*see* 2000).

Lyme disease is identified at Lyme, Conn. Transmitted primarily by the bite of a tick found on white-tailed deer, white-footed field mice, and other animals, the bacterial infection can lead to serious neurological, cardiac, or arthritic complications. It will spread quickly throughout most of Westchester, the northern Bronx, Long Island, and much of the entire country.

Korean evangelist Sun Myung Moon, 45, pays $1.2 million to acquire the 75-year-old Columbia University Club building at 4 West 43rd Street, between Fifth and Sixth avenues, for use as headquarters of his Unification Church and pays more than $2 million September 8 to acquire the Manhattan Center. Moon founded the church in 1954, claiming to have received a vision at age 16 that gave him the "key to righteousness and restoration of the Kingdom of Heaven on Earth." He has developed a theology based on platitudes, rabid anticommunism, and pop history, supported by bits of astrology, numerology, and Scientology. His supporters claim that the Bible is written in code, and that only Moon has broken the code (*see* 1976).

The Museum of Television and Radio has its beginnings in the Museum of Broadcasting, opened by CBS founder William S. Paley off Madison Avenue in East 52nd Street (*see* 1991).

Fire sweeps through the New York Telephone Co.'s central office in lower Manhattan February 27, knocking out more than 170,000 phones, but service is restored within 22 days (*see* AT&T break-up, 1982).

New York taxis begin in the summer to display elongated, backlighted, pyramid-like, plasticized billboards on their roofs. Local outdoor advertising executive J. Rembrandt George, 51, has persuaded the Metropolitan Taxicab Board of Trade to endorse the idea, the Board has convinced Mayor Beame that objections are unwarranted, George has joined with Vincent Van Beuren to found Vango Media, and by 1995 some 3,500 of the city's 11,800 medallion cabs will be carrying the signs, with the city receiving $50 per year from each of the 3,500 (cab owners pledge

25 percent of their receipts to the New York City Taxi Drivers Union).

Radio station WNYC holds its first fund-raising drive; the city's straitened finances have forced it to cut back on funding for the station, and listeners contribute $75,000 to keep it on the air (*see* 1997).

The New York Public Library receives a $10 million grant from Vincent Astor Foundation head Brooke Astor, now 82. Iranian-born library president Vartan Gregorian, now 40, will say that she "has given equal attention to janitors and guards as to the librarians and curators and the rich and famous."

Nonfiction: *Toward an Urban Vision: Ideas and Institutions in Nineteenth-Century America* by San Mateo, Calif.-born NYU historian Thomas Bender, 31; *Colonial New York: A History* by Rochester-born Cornell University historian Michael Gedaliah Kammen, 38; *City on Two Rivers: Profiles of New York— Yesterday and Today* by New York-born author Stephen Longstreet, 68; *Rails under the Mighty Hudson: The Story of the Hudson Tubes, the Pennsy Tunnels, and Manhattan Transfer* by Brooklyn-born author Brian J. (James) Cudahy, 39; *Apartments for the Affluent: A Historical Survey of Buildings in New York* by local architectural writer Andrew Alpern, 36; *Stubborn for Liberty: The Dutch in New York* by Alice B. Kenney; *Being With Children* by Jamaica, Queens-born author Phillip Lopate, 31, who has taught creative writing in the city's public schools since 1968; *The Chase, The Capture: Collecting at the Metropolitan* by Thomas Hoving; *On Photography* by Susan Sontag; *All Around the Town: A Walking Guide to Outdoor Sculpture in New York City* by Joseph Lederer, photographs by Arley Bondarin.

Fiction: *Ragtime* by E. L. Doctorow (*see* Films, 1981); *Looking for Mr. Goodbar* by Judith Rossner (*see* crime, 1973; Films, 1977); *A Dove of the East and Other Stories* by New York writer Mark Helprin, 28; *Legs* by former Albany journalist William Kennedy, 35, is based on the Prohibition-era gangster Jack "Legs" Diamond; *The First to Know* and *Growing Up Rich* by Anne Bernays; *Where Are the Children?* by Bronx-born novelist Mary Higgins Clark, 43, a barkeeper's daughter who became an airline stewardess, married a sweetheart from her old neighborhood at age 20, was widowed at age 32 with five children, got a job writing radio scripts, and worked on novels and stories from 5 o'clock to 7 each morning.

The Metropolitan Museum of Art completes a 7-year redesign involving its front stairs, decorative pools, a new Lehman Wing, and renovations to its Great Hall. Kevin Roche/John Dinkeloo and Associates has

been responsible for the architectural work and will continue to be the museum's architects for at least 15 years.

Painting: *Weeping Women*, *The Barber's Tree*, and five other encaustic cross-hatched works by Jasper Johns; *Whose Name Was Writ in Water* by Willem de Kooning; *Cubist Still Life with Lemons*, a "commercialized" reinterpretation of Picasso, by Roy Lichtenstein; *Morro Da Viuva II*, *Montenegro*, and other brightly colored aluminum reliefs by Frank Stella; *The Magnet and Blue Light* by Philip Guston.

Judge Millard L. Midonick of New York County Surrogate Court in Manhattan rules March 8 that the executors of the late Mark Rothko were guilty of conflicts of interest and imposes damages and fines totaling $9.25 million against the executors, art dealer Frank Lloyd, and the Marlborough Gallery (*see* 1971). Lloyd has taken up residence on Paradise Island in the Bahamas. The State Appeals Court upholds the ruling March 28 (*see* 1977).

Representational painter Fairfield Porter dies at Southampton, L.I., September 18 at age 68.

The International Center of Photography is founded at New York by Budapest-born photographer Cornell Capa, 56, whose late brother Robert was a cofounder of Magnum Photos 8 years ago. The ICP occupies the neo-Georgian red-brick house at the northeast corner of Fifth Avenue and 94th Street built for the Willard Straights in 1914 and subsequently used by the National Audubon Society; it will remain in the house until 2000.

Theater: *The Ritz* by Terrence McNally 1/20 at the Longacre Theater, with Rita Moreno, Jerry Stoller, 406 perfs.; *Seascape* by Edward Albee 1/26 at the Shubert Theater, with Deborah Kerr, Barry Nelson, Frank Langella, 63 perfs.; *Same Time, Next Year* by Canadian playwright Bernard Slade, 44, 3/13 at the Brooks Atkinson Theater, with Ellen Burstyn, Pittsburgh-born actor Charles Grodin, 39, 1,444 perfs.; *The Taking of Miss Janie* by Philadelphia-born playwright Ed Bullins, 39, 5/4 at the Mitzi E. Newhouse Theater, with Hilary Jean Beane, Diane Oyama Dixon, 42 perfs.

Broadway scenic designer Donald Oenslager dies at his summer home near suburban Bedford June 21 at age 73; playwright-novelist Thornton Wilder of a heart attack at his Hamden, Conn. home December 7 at age 78.

Television: *Barney Miller* 1/23 on ABC with Hal Linden, now 43, and New York-born actor Abe Vigoda, 53, as police detectives in Greenwich Village (all

action takes place inside the 12th Precinct squad room) (to 9/1982); *Welcome Back, Kotter* 9/9 on ABC with Gabe Kaplan (who grew up in Crown Heights near Ebbets Field) as history teacher Gabe Kotter at Brooklyn's "James Buchanan" Remedial High School (actually New Utrecht High), John Travolta, 21, Ron Pallilo, 21, Lawrence-Hilton Jacobs, Robert Hegyes, 24 (to 1979); *NBC's Saturday Night Live* 10/11 with New York-born actor Chevy Chase, 32, John Belushi, 26, comedienne Gilda Radner, 31, Bill Murray, 25, Dan Aykroyd, 23.

Films: Sidney Lumet's *Dog Day Afternoon* with Al Pacino; Joan Micklin Silver's *Hester Street* with Steven Keats, Carol Kane; Melvin Frank's *The Prisoner of Second Avenue* with Jack Lemmon, Anne Bancroft (the protagonist's apartment house is the 9-year-old high-rise at 247 East 87th Street); Herbert Ross's *The Sunshine Boys* with Walter Matthau, George Burns, Richard Benjamin, and the Hotel Ansonia; Sidney Pollack's *Three Days of the Condor* with Robert Redford, Faye Dunaway, Cliff Robertson. Also: Sidney J. Furie's *Sheila Levine Is Dead and Living in New York* with Jeannie Berlin, Roy Scheider.

Silent-film "vamp" Dagmar Godowsky dies at New York February 13 at age 78; Arthur Treacher of a heart ailment at Manhasset December 14 at age 81.

Film musical: Herbert Ross's *Funny Lady* with Barbra Streisand, James Caan (as Billy Rose), Omar Sharif.

Broadway musicals: *The Wiz* 1/5 at the Majestic Theater, with Trinidadian actor and costume designer Geoffrey Holder, 44, Mississippi-born ingénue Stephanie Mills, 17, music and lyrics by Charlie Smalls, songs that include "Ease on Down the Road," book based on L. Frank Baum's *The Wizard of Oz*, 1,666 perfs.; *Shenandoah* 1/7 at the Alvin Theater (to Mark Hellinger Theater 3/30/1977), with John Cullum, music by Gary Geld, lyrics by Peter Udell, 1,050 perfs.; *Chicago* 6/3 at the Forty-Sixth Street Theater, with Chita Rivera, Gwen Verdon, Jerry Orbach, music by John Kander, lyrics by Fred Ebb, songs that include "Razzle Dazzle" and "We Both Reached for the Gun," 922 perfs.; *A Chorus Line* 10/19 at the Shubert Theater (after 101 perfs. at the off-Broadway Public Theater), with music by Marvin Hamlisch, lyrics by Edward Kleban, 36, 6,137 perfs. (a record that will stand until 1997).

Opera: the Metropolitan Opera appoints Cincinnati-born conductor James (Lawrence) "Jimmy" Levine, 32, musical director. He has been the Met's principal conductor since 1973 and in 1986 will be made artistic director.

Discothèques enjoy a resurgence unequaled since the early 1960s in New York and other major world cities. Highly formula-conforming disco records by Van McCoy, Donna Summer, the Bee Gees, and others will dominate popular music until 1979.

Popular songs: "New York State of Mind" by Billy Joel; *Blood on the Tracks* (album) and "Tangled Up in Blue" by Bob Dylan; *Born to Run* (album) by New Jersey-born singer-composer Bruce Springsteen, 26, whose energetic anthems to his blue-collar background will make him one of the decade's most influential rock stylists; *Smile* (album) by Laura Nyro.

Composer Leroy Anderson dies of lung cancer at his Woodbridge, Conn., home May 18 at age 66; jazz drummer Arthur James "Zutty" Singleton at New York July 14 at age 77; songwriter Joseph A. McCarthy of cancer at New York November 7 at age 53.

 Manuel Orantes, 26 (Spain), wins in men's singles at Forest Hills, Christine Marie "Chris" Evert, 20, in women's singles.

Former Mets manager Casey Stengel dies at Glendale, Calif., September 30 at age 85; former Mets owner Joan Whitney Payson at New York October 4 at age 72.

A baseball arbitration panel that made pitcher James Augustus "Catfish" Hunter a free agent last year rules December 23 that Montreal Expos pitcher Dave McNally, 33, and Los Angeles Dodger pitcher Andy Messersmith, 30, are no longer bound by their contracts and are free to negotiate with other teams. Baseball's reserve clause has allowed a team owner to renew contracts unilaterally on a yearly basis and has prevented a player who rejected the contract from playing for any other team; the panel's ruling strikes at that clause (*see* 1976). Hunter signs a 5-year contract with the Yankees at $200,000 per year plus $2.5 million in bonuses, insurance, and lawyer fees.

 Revlon's Charles Revson dies of cancer at New York August 24 at age 68.

The Doubles Club holds a gala preview party December 17 at the Sherry Netherland Hotel, where it will formally open next year as a supper club and continue into the next century as a nonprofit English-style family dining club for the city's Old Guard. Named for the doubling cube used in backgammon betting, it has about 800 charter members, who have paid $1,000 initiation fees plus $200 per year in dues, and will grow in 25 years to have 2,300 members despite initiation fees that will rise to $6,000 and dues that will rise to $920 (lower for younger members). Prix-fixe lunches next year will be $7,

dinner $10, and by 2001 will be $23 and about $40, respectively.

 United Fruit Co. president Eli M. Black throws himself through the window of his office in the Pan Am Building February 3 and plummets 44 floors to his death at age 53. United Fruit has lost its leadership in the banana business to Castle & Cook, earnings have declined, and company executives who have not quit have been fomenting an insurrection against Black. Improper payments by United Fruit to foreign governments will come to light, helping to explain Black's suicide.

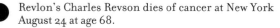 Developers Lewis and Jack Rudin complete 1 Battery Park City to designs by Emery Roth & Sons. Located between Bridge and Pearl streets, its address is 24 State Street. Lewis joins with PR man Howard J. Rubenstein, Preston Robert Tisch, Alan V. Tishman, and other midtown property owners to form the Association for a Better New York; it will hand out Polished Apple awards to worthy merchants and Rotten Apple awards to shop owners who do not pick up litter outside their storefront and otherwise fail to measure up.

Developers Sol Goldman and Alex DiLorenzo, Jr. lose scores of properties from their bloated portfolio as interest rates soar and real estate values collapse. DiLorenzo dies of a heart attack in his Chrysler Building office at age 58; Goldman remains the city's largest (and probably least popular) private landlord, controlling more than 400 buildings with assessed valuations of $450 million, and will rebuild his empire by pledging his equity in old investments in order to take on new ones (*see* 1987).

The Philippine government acquires the former M. Knoedler & Co. building at 556 Fifth Avenue, southwest corner 46th Street, for use by its consulate, its mission to the United Nations, and as a tourist office and trade board. It commissions architect Augusto Camacho to give the five-story structure a new façade; he eliminates all windows above the ground floor, giving that floor a new façade of soft, native Philippine rock with a projecting wooden gable evocative of western Pacific architecture. *New York Times* architectural critic Ada Louise Huxtable next year will describe the new Philippine Center in an article headlined, "The Trashing of Fifth Avenue," saying it is "slip-covered in pre-cast panels with ethnic hut details."

Roosevelt Island's Rivercross apartment houses are completed at 505, 513, and 541 Main Street, opposite Rockefeller Institute (*see* 1971). Johansen & Bhavnani has designed the buildings, whose units are offered as co-operative apartments; Roosevelt Island's Island House apartment building is completed at 551, 575, and 595 Main Street, across the river from the New York Hospital-Cornell Medical Center. Johansen & Bhavnani has designed the rental structure, whose skylight-enclosed indoor swimming pool faces on the river. It is just north of the Good Shepherd Community Ecumenical Center, built in 1889 as the Chapel of the Good Shepherd (Episcopalian) and restored by architect Giorgio Cavaglieri; Roosevelt Island's two initial apartment complexes rise 20 stories high, more than twice the height proposed in the original Johnson-Burgee master plan, but contain only 2,138 units, less than half the number originally contemplated (a "critical mass" of 18,000 residents is considered necessary to sustain a community with entertainment facilities, a hotel, restaurants, and more than a bare minimum of shops, but by 1998 Roosevelt Island will still have just 3,200 apartments with 8,400 residents. Owned by the city but leased to the state until the year 2068, it will be considered part of Manhattan but receive police and fire services from Queens).

The 17-story Christodora House on Avenue B at 9th Street is sold at public auction for $62,500 (see 1928). The old settlement house fell into disrepair in the late 1940s, the city acquired it and used it for 20 years to house community groups, but a fire destroyed its electrical system, the building was sealed, and it will remain idle until the mid-1980s, when it will be converted to use for luxury condominiums, raising objections by local activists that it is contributing to unwanted gentrification.

Manhattan's 54-story Galleria apartment house is completed at 119 East 57th Street, between Park and Lexington avenues, to designs by David Kenneth Specter in association with Philip Birnbaum. Its below-grade floor contains shops, its eight lower floors offices; the quadruplex penthouse atop its 47 residential floors has outdoor terraces and an indoor swimming pool for millionaire owner Stewart Mott (who was evicted from his 800 Park Avenue apartment building for turning its roof into a vegetable garden and will soon give up his "biosphere" project).

The 32-story Glen Gardens apartment house is completed at 175 West 87th Street, northeast corner Amsterdam Avenue, to designs by Seymour Joseph. Built to provide affordable housing under the Mitchell-Lama program instituted in 1955, its developers have received low-cost mortgages and tax breaks; state and federal agencies set rents, but owners have the option to buy out of the program after 20 years and the owners of Glen Gardens will exercise that option in 2002.

The Jacob Ruppert Brewery housing project is completed on a four-block site extending from 90th Street to 94th between Second and Third avenues. The brewery operated from 1867 to 1965, 91st Street has been closed to traffic and paved with cobblestones to provide a plaza-like thoroughfare, and the southeastern part of the site is a public park and playground for residents of the project's three red-brick towers, all designed by Davis, Brody & Associates: Yorkville Towers (32 to 42 stories) is at Third Avenue and 92nd Street (710 units); Ruppert Towers (24 to 34 stories) at Third Avenue and 90th Street (549 units); Knickerbocker Plaza (40 stories) at Second Avenue and 92nd Street (578 units, 70 percent of them for subsidized seniors, 20 percent for low-income tenants).

The 32-story 1199 Plaza apartment complex is completed in an area bounded by the FDR Drive and First Avenue between 107th and 110th streets, with an extension along the Drive to 111th Street. Sponsored by District 1199 of the National Union of Hospital and Health Care Employees, AFL-CIO, the four U-shaped red-brick towers and their six-, eight-, and 10-story wings of duplexes have been designed by the Minneapolis firm Hodney/Stageberg Partners with landscaping by Herb Baldwin.

The 35-story Arthur A. Schomburg Plaza apartment house is completed with twin towers at Frawley Circle, the south tower at 1295 Fifth Avenue, corner 110th Street, and the north tower at 1309 Fifth Avenue (there is also an 11-story building on the Madison Avenue side of the site with a landscaped, multi-level plaza). Gruzen & Partners has designed the buildings with Castro-Blanco, Piscioneri & Feder (see fire, 1987).

Brooklyn's sprawling Bedford Gardens apartments are completed with 639 units in a Williamsburg area bounded by Wythe Avenue, Ross Street, and the Brooklyn-Queens Expressway. The precast concrete project has been built with federal money as part of an effort to stimulate building with factory-made modules rather than traditional on-site construction methods.

Consolidated Edison stops covering every one of its underground steam pipes with asbestos for insulation following studies that show the fiber causes cancer, but Manhattan has 103 miles of steam line crisscrossing the avenues below 96th Street, and 15 years from now more than 90 percent of them will still be covered with asbestos.

Central Park falls into sorry shape as the city's fiscal crisis brings cuts in maintenance budgets (*see* Central Park Conservancy, 1980).

The Bronx has 13,000 fires in the course of the year. Many if not most are of suspicious origin (landlords have in some cases hired arsonists to torch their buildings in order to collect insurance), and they cause devastation over an area of 12 square miles.

A backstage fire December 18 at the Blue Angel nightclub, 123 East 54th Street, kills seven persons (employees have tried for nearly 30 minutes to extinguish the flames with glasses of water and milk before calling the fire department). Inspectors discover that the club has been operating without a permit of assembly or a certificate of occupancy, and furniture blocks exits. The City Council will enact a so-called "Blue Angel" law requiring display of well-lighted signs indicating that occupancy by more than a certain number of people (one per 12 square feet) is "dangerous and unlawful."

Fairway Market opens at 2127 Broadway (between 74th and 75th streets) in competition with Balducci's (*see* 1972) and Korean greengrocers, many of them emigré professionals who cannot practice law or medicine in America. Howard Glickberg's grandfather opened a grocery store on the site in the 1920s and turned it into a supermarket, Howard forms a partnership with his brothers-in-law Harold Seybert and David Sneddon, they sell fresh produce from the Hunt's Point market, buy direct from three farmers in Long Island and Pennsylvania, undercut the competition, and will soon be serving an estimated 30,000 customers per week from 3,700 square feet of space (it will expand to more than 5,000 square feet as demand grows for its fresh fruit and vegetables, baked goods, imported butters, cheeses, cold cuts, fish, coffees, and nuts) (*see* 1995).

The Café des Artistes at 1 West 67th Street closes after 58 years and its proprietor makes off with half the Howard Chandler Christy murals that have graced it since 1934. Hungarian-born New York restaurateur George Lang, 51, replaces the missing murals with mirrors that brighten up the place, brings in Breton chef André Guillou, and reopens with an innovative menu. Lang came to America as a violinist in 1946, was assistant to Claude Philippe at the Waldorf-Astoria in the 1950s, ran the Four Seasons restaurant for a few years in the 1960s, and developed some Restaurant Associates locations.

Ellis Island is made part of the Statue of Liberty national monument (*see* 1965); it has been practically unused since 1954 (*see* 1984).

1976 New York celebrates the bicentennial of the Declaration of Independence July 4 with Operation Sail, attracting ships from many nations. Empire State Building owner Harry B. Helmsley decides to honor the occasion by illuminating the building's tower in red, white, and blue, a gesture that requires sliding colored plastic discs over most of the 1,336 light fixtures on three levels from the 72nd floor to the 102nd (the 200-foot mast is illuminated by fluorescent bulbs); the job takes six electricians a full day. In future the top of the building will be lighted in red, white, and blue for Presidents Day, Armed Forces Day, Memorial Day, Flag Day, Independence Day, Labor Day, and Veterans Day, with other colors used for more than 15 other days and weeks (companies and even individuals will be able to buy special lighting until 1997).

Onetime Democratic Party political boss James A. Farley dies of cardiac arrest in his New York hotel suite July 9 at age 88. The Democratic Party holds its convention at Madison Square Garden and selects former Georgia governor James Earl "Jimmy" Carter, Jr., 52, as its presidential candidate.

City Councilman Matthew H. Troy, Jr., 47, resigns September 3 as chairman of the Council's finance committee. He has pleaded guilty in Brooklyn Federal Court July 1 of filing fraudulent income tax returns for 1972; a judge suspends all but 2 months

Fires in the South Bronx and elsewhere kept uniformed firefighters busy as arsonists torched insured buildings.

The city celebrated America's bicentennial with an international Sail-In that filled the harbor. AP/WIDE WORLD

head Eleanor Holmes Norton, 39, to head the U.S. Equal Employment Opportunity Commission, its first woman chair.

The New York Stock Exchange has a record 44.5-million-share day February 20 and the Dow Jones Industrial Average peaks at 1014.79 September 21, short of the 1051.70 high reached January 11, 1973, but a high that will not be seen again for 6 years.

Kohlberg Kravis Roberts is created at New York by bankers Jerome Kohlberg, Jr., 51, Henry Kravis, 32, and Kravis's cousin George Roberts, 32. The investment banking firm will concentrate on mergers and acquisitions.

Drexel Burnham Lambert is founded at New York through a merger. The investment banking firm will soon concentrate on high-yield "junk" bonds to finance corporate takeovers.

Former New York Stock Exchange chairman Gustave L. Levy dies of a stroke at New York November 3 at age 66.

Wall Street's Dow Jones Industrial Average closes December 31 at 1004.65, up from 852.41 at the end of 1975, having gained nearly 18 percent for the year, most of the rise coming in a big January spurt with volume averaging 40 million shares per day. Daily volume for the year averages 21 million.

The first annual Third Avenue Fair opens in September. The Third Avenue Merchants' Association has organized the event, and police bar traffic for 20 blocks to create a shopping mall. Other avenues and streets have, or will inaugurate, similar fairs, with the same people offering virtually the same merchandise and virtually the same food and beverages at every one.

The Public Service Commission restores the selling rights of Con Edison and Brooklyn Union Gas in all their markets as supply problems ease (*see* 1974; 1989; blackout, 1977).

A $6.4 billion Railroad Revitalization and Reform Act signed by President Ford February 5 is followed March 30 by a $2.14 billion measure designed to improve rail service on the Boston-New York-Washington, D.C. line (*see* Amtrak, 1970).

Roosevelt Island's Aerial Tramway Station opens north of the Queensboro Bridge. Designed by Prentice & Chan, it connects the island with Second Avenue in Manhattan and will be the only point of entry and departure for pedestrians until the opening of a subway station in 1989. The tramway's two synchronized cable cars weigh 18,300 pounds each, reach a peak altitude of 250 feet, and are taken out of

of his 2-year prison term, but he is fined $5,000, obliged to pay taxes on the $37,000 that he failed to report, and goes to jail October 22.

Jimmy Carter wins the presidential election with 297 electoral votes to 240 for President Ford, having capitalized on the widespread distrust of Republicans in the wake of the Watergate affair. New York State gives Carter a 276,000-vote plurality (3,335,433 votes as compared to 3,059,154 for Ford; Carter receives 1,367,537 votes in New York City, Ford 692,066). Every borough goes for Carter except Richmond (Staten Island), where Ford gets 55,572 votes to Carter's 45,849.

Former congresswoman Bella Abzug seeks her party's nomination for the U.S. Senate but loses narrowly to Harvard political science (government) professor Daniel Patrick Moynihan, now 49, the onetime U.S. delegate to the United Nations; he defeats Conservative Party incumbent Sen. James L. Buckley with a 574,000-vote plurality (54 percent of the vote).

Liberal Party founder Alex Rose dies of cancer at New York December 28 at age 78.

President-elect Carter appoints New York City's Washington, D.C.-born Human Rights Commission

service during electrical storms or when north-south winds gust above 40 miles per hour.

Conrail (Consolidated Rail Corp.) begins operations May 1 with 88,000 freight workers as the federal government attempts to maintain service on lines served by now-bankrupt roads such as Penn Central. Railroads now carry less than 37 percent of U.S. freight. Until 1981 Conrail will carry New York area commuters in addition to freight.

The NYC Passenger Ship Terminal is completed along Twelfth Avenue at 48th, 50th, and 52nd streets to provide piers for modern transatlantic liners, but the Port Authority's terminal will soon be used mostly by cruise-line companies as more and more travelers opt for air transportation (see 1984).

∞ Britain's *Elizabeth II* visits Trinity Church and is presented with symbolic back rents of 279 peppercorns, one for each year of the church's existence (see 1697).

Korean evangelist Sun Myung Moon's Unification Church pays more than $5 million May 12 to acquire the 41-story, 2,000-room Hotel New Yorker that opened in 1930 and closed in 1972. Moon holds a "God Bless America" rally at Yankee Stadium June 1 (see 1975); his New York property holdings have an assessed value of $16 to $17 million (he also has estates in Dutchess and Westchester counties and a 600-acre farm in California), but the Internal Revenue Service conducts an investigation into his church's tax-exempt status. Moon moves his headquarters to the newly acquired hotel and turns it into the World Mission Center (see real estate, 1994).

The multicollege City University of New York (CUNY) levies tuitions for the first time (see open enrollment, 1970). Budget cuts will reduce enrollment to 172,000 by 1980, the faculty will be cut by some 3,000, and in 20 years only 10.2 percent of students will be white (38.3 percent black, 31 percent Hispanic, 15.4 percent Asian), although admission will still require a high-school average of 80 (1,000 students who meet financial criteria and have academic averages of 70 or more will be admitted through the SEEK program). CUNY will draw students from 90 different countries, three out of four entering freshmen will be assigned to at least one remedial or English-as-a-second-language class, and the tuition will rise in 20 years to $3,200 per year, with 70 percent of students receiving financial aid (20 percent will work full time, 20 percent will be raising children). Academic standards will inevitably be compromised (see 1991).

Norman Thomas High School (formerly the Central Commercial High School) moves from 214 East 42nd Street to occupy the first nine floors of a 42-story skyscraper at 3 Park Avenue, between 33rd and 34th streets.

Brooklyn's Boys High School moves to 1700 Fulton Street, begins accepting girls, and takes the name Boys and Girls High School (see 1878). Its Madison Street building was designated a city landmark last year (designed in Romanesque Revival style by the late James W. Naughton, it opened in 1892) and will house the Street Academy, an alternative high school. By 1991 Boys and Girls High will have an enrollment of 3,409—the oldest high school in the city to have started as a public school.

The 77-year-old Brooklyn Children's Museum moves into a new building at the entrance to Brower Park. Designed by Italian-born British architect Hugh (Gelston) Hardy, 44, of Hardy Holzman Pfeiffer Associates, it replaces the two mansions that originally housed the museum.

The 79-year-old Cooper-Hewitt National Design Museum moves into the Andrew Carnegie mansion built in 1901 on Fifth Avenue between 91st and 92nd streets.

Word processors made by Wang Laboratories begin to revolutionize New York offices with workstations that share central computers (see 1974).

Fax (facsimile transmission) machines gain ground as second-generation technology cuts transmission time from 6 minutes per page to 3. The devices translate a printed page or graphics into electronic signals, transmit them over telephone lines, and print out signals received from other fax machines thousands of miles (or one block) away. Government offices, law enforcement agencies, news agencies, publishers, and banks are the major users. Prices fall for machines, but quality remains poor (see 1982).

Manhattan's fountains flow in red, white, and blue to celebrate the bicentennial and the Democratic National Convention. Electrical sign impresario Douglas Leigh, now 69, has illuminated the fountains and created other effects in his role as official decorator for the convention.

The Greek-language morning daily *Proini* begins publication, competing with the *Ethnikos Kerux* (*National Herald*) (see 1915).

The *New York Post* is acquired in November by Australian-born publisher (Keith) Rupert Murdoch, 45, who has built up a worldwide empire of 83 newspapers and 11 magazines with strong emphasis on scandals, sex, crime, and sports. His lurid tabloid weekly *The Star* competes with *The National Enquirer* (*see* 1952) and is his most lucrative property. The city's oldest continuously published daily, the *Post* has been New York's only afternoon paper since 1967, but owner Dorothy Schiff, now 73, has grown tired of losing money on it. Murdoch's (second) wife, Anna, tells him that if he puts topless women on page three she will leave him because she does not want her children to see it, so Murdoch contents himself with giving the paper a more right-wing editorial tone, replacing one-quarter of its staff with reporters previously employed on his other tabloids, and although he will rehire veteran left-wing columnist Murray Kempton next year (Kempton was a *Post* columnist from 1949 to 1963 and again from 1966 to 1969, writing in the interim for the *World-Telegram and Sun*), Kempton will move in 1981 to the more politically mature *Newsday*.

Nonfiction: *World of Our Fathers* by New York-born Hunter College English professor Irving Howe (originally Horenstein), 56, a onetime Trotskyite activist whose account of Jewish life in New York City is a best-seller; *Tammany Hall and the New Immigrants: The Progressive Years* by Thomas M. Henderson; *Kicked a Building Lately?* by Ada Louise Huxtable; *Seeing New York* by New York-born author John Tauranac, 37, who began his career as an advertising agency copywriter and since 1974 has been the Metropolitan Transportation Authority's chief designer of maps; *Manhattan Moves Uptown: An Illustrated History* by Charles Lockwood; *Uptown, Downtown* by New York author Stan Fischler, 44, is a history of streetcars, elevated trains, and—especially—subways; *A Place Called Home* by English-born Nova Scotia architect Anthony Jackson, 49, is a history of the New York tenement; *The Statue of Liberty* by Tulsa-born architectural historian Marvin (Lawrence) Trachtenberg, 37; *Literary New York* by New York-born authors Susan Edmiston (*née* Szekely), 36, and Linda D. Cirino (*née* Davis), 35; *City Lives* by Lansing, Mich.-born New York writer-photographer James Wagenvoord, 39; *Patience and Fortitude: Fiorello La Guardia: A Biography* by Pennsylvania-born prizefighter-turned-author William Manners (originally Rosenberg), 70, whose title comes from the names bestowed by La Guardia in jest on the stone lions in front of the Public Library.

Humorist-author Edward Streeter dies at New York March 7 at age 84; author Patrick Dennis (Edward E. Tanner III) of cancer at New York November 6 at age 55.

George T. Delacorte, Jr. sells his 55-year-old Delacorte Press to Doubleday for $35 million; now 82, he sets up a fund to build and maintain public monuments in the city, with special attention to Central Park.

Painting: *Skull* (silkscreen) by Andy Warhol; *Portrait of Andy* (Warhol) by Andrew Wyeth; *Corpse and Mirror* by Jasper Johns; *Imperfect Indicative* (collage of charcoal and paper on linen) and *Imperative* (collage of oil and paper on panel) by Lee Krasner; *Falcon Avenue, Seaside Walk, Dwight Street, Jarvis Street, Greene Street* (baked enamel on silkscreen grid) by California-born New York artist Jennifer Bartlett (*née* Losch), 35; *Beginning* by Elizabeth Murray, who was Bartlett's best friend at Mills College in the early 1960s. Josef Albers dies at New Haven March 24 at age 88; sculptor Alexander Calder of a heart attack at New York November 11 at age 78.

A cartoon depiction of the United States as seen from a provincial New York vantage by architect-artist-cartoonist Saul Steinberg, now 61, appears in the March 29 issue of The *New Yorker* and will be widely reproduced for more than 25 years.

Push Pin Studio cofounder Jerome Snyder dies of a heart attack at New York May 2 at age 60.

Photographs: *Old New York in Early Photographs: 196 Prints, 1853–1901* by New York editor Mary Black. Photographer Paul Strand dies at his home in the village of Oregeval west of Paris March 31 at age 85.

Theater: *American Buffalo* by Chicago-born playwright David Mamet, 28, 1/26 at the off-Broadway St. Clement's Theater, 135 perfs.; *Knock Knock* by Jules Feiffer 2/24 at the Biltmore Theater, with English actress Lynn Redgrave, 32, John Heffernan, 38 perfs.; *Streamers* by David Rabe 4/2 at the off-Broadway Mitzi E. Newhouse Theater, 478 perfs.; *The Runner Stumbles* by Detroit-born playwright Milan Stitt, 34, 5/18 at the off-Broadway Little Theater, 191 perfs.; *California Suite* by Neil Simon 6/10 at the Eugene O'Neill Theater, with Tammy Grimes, North Carolina-born actor George Grizzard, 48, Chicago-born actress Barbara Barrie, 45, Jack Weston, 445 perfs.; *For Colored Girls Who Have Considered Suicide/When the Rainbow Is Enuf* by Trenton, N.J.-born playwright Ntozake Shange (*née* Paulette Williams), 27, 9/15 at the Booth Theater (after 120 perfs. at the Public Theater), with Trazana Beverly, Laurie Carlos, Rise Collins, Aku Kadogo, June League, Paul Moss, and Shange, 867 perfs. (total); *A Texas Trilogy* (*Lu Ann Hampton Laverty Oberlander, The Oldest Living Graduate*, and *The Last Meeting of the Knights of the White Magnolia*) by Albuquerque, N.M.-born playwright Preston Jones, 40, 9/22 at the Broadhurst Theater, with Mississippi-born actress Diane Ladd, now 43, 21 perfs. in repertory.

Actor-producer-writer-lyricist Eddie Dowling dies at Smithfield, R.I., February 18 at age 86; stage designer Jo Mielziner of a stroke while returning to his apartment at the Dakota March 15 at age 74; Broadway producer Kermit Bloomgarden of a brain tumor at his New York apartment September 20 at age 73; Broadway columnist Leonard Lyons of Parkinson's disease at his New York apartment October 7 at age 70.

Television: *The Muppet Show* in September (daytime) on PBS with combination marionettes and puppets devised by Greenville, Miss.-born puppeteer James Maury "Jim" Henson, 29, whose Kermit the Frog and the Cookie Monster have appeared on *Sesame Street* since 1968. English-born puppeteer Frank Oz (originally Oznowicz), 32, creates Miss Piggy for the new show, she will attract a wide following, and the programs will reach 235 million viewers in 100 countries.

Films: Martin Ritt's *The Front* with Woody Allen, Zero Mostel (about black listing of alleged communists in the 1950s); John Schlesinger's *Marathon Man* with Dustin Hoffman, Laurence Olivier, Roy Scheider; Sidney Lumet's *Network* with Faye Dunaway, Peter Finch ("I'm mad as hell and I'm not going to take this anymore"), William Holden, Robert Duvall; John G. Avildsen's *Rocky* with Sylvester Stallone; Martin Scorsese's *Taxi Driver* with Robert De Niro, Cybill Shepherd, Harvey Keitel; Roman Polanski's *The Tenant* with Polanski, Isabelle Adjani. Also: Paul Mazursky's *Next Stop, Greenwich Village* with Lenny Baker, Shelley Winters, Ellen Greene; Richard Lester's *The Ritz* with Jack Weston, Rita Moreno, Brooklyn-born comedian Jerry Stiller, 47, Kaye Ballard.

Broadway musicals: *Pacific Overtures* 1/11 at the Winter Garden Theater, with Kobe-born actress Mako (Makoto Iwamatori), 42, book by John Weidman based on the opening of Japan in 1853, music and lyrics by Stephen Sondheim, 193 perfs.; *Bubblin' Brown Sugar* 3/2 at the ANTA Theater, with Avon Long, music and lyrics by Danny Holgate, Emme Kemp, and Lillian Lopez plus old songs by Duke Ellington, Noble Sissle, Eubie Blake, Andy Razaf, Fats Waller, and others, 766 perfs.; *Your Arms Too Short to Box with God: A Soaring Celebration in Song and Dance* 12/22 at the Lyceum Theater, with 21 performers directed by Vinnette Carroll, music and lyrics by Alex Bradford, additional music and lyrics by Micki Grant, 429 perfs.

Popular songs: *Ramones* (album) by the 2-year-old group founded by Virginia-born Queens punk rocker Dee Dee Ramone (originally Douglas Glen Colvin), 24, and three companions who perform at CBGB's and Max's Kansas City, developing a new wave rock whose back-to-basics approach is gaining favor among England's working-class youth with its highly amplified, politically rebellious style; *Smile* (album) by Laura Nyro.

The disco nightclub Regine's opens at 502 Park Avenue, where it will continue until 1991.

Paul Robeson dies at Philadelphia January 23 at age 77 (he suffered a stroke in December); society bandleader Meyer Davis dies of cancer at New York April 5 at age 83; singer Connee Boswell of stomach cancer at New York October 10 at age 68.

 The New York Nets win their second American Basketball Association (ABA) championship May 13, beating the Denver Nuggets 112 to 104 before a capacity crowd at the Nassau Coliseum in Uniondale, but they lose Julius "Dr. J." Erving to the NBA's Philadelphia 76ers as the two leagues merge before the start of the 1976–1977 season.

Jimmy Connors wins in men's singles at Forest Hills, Chris Evert in women's singles.

A U.S. District Court judge at Kansas City upholds last year's arbitration panel ruling on free agents February 4, a three-judge panel of the U.S. Court of Appeals at St. Louis upholds the federal judge's ruling March 9, and the first draft of free agents is held November 4 at New York's Plaza Hotel.

The New York Yankees win the American League Pennant, beating the Kansas City Royals with a lead-off home run by first baseman Chris Chambliss, 27, in the bottom of the ninth inning in the fifth game at the Stadium, but the Cincinnati Reds field one of the greatest squads in baseball history and shut out the Yankees in the World Series, winning 4 games to zip. Although Baseball Commissioner Bowie Kuhn and NBC come under fire for permitting the second and third games to be played on bitter cold evenings, the weather has little to do with the outcome. Shortstop pinchhitter Jim Mason, 26, gets the only New York home run in his one Series at-bat in the third game.

Professional football's New York Giants move to a new stadium in the New Jersey Meadowlands after years of playing in the Polo Grounds, Yankee Stadium, and Shea Stadium. Jets president Philip Iselin dies of an apparent heart attack at New York December 28 at age 74.

 Liz Claiborne fashions are introduced January 19 by New York fashion designer Elisabeth Claiborne, 46, and her husband, Arthur Ortenberg (they have two other partners), whose affordable, casual, mix-and-match sportswear separates for working women will break new ground. Born and raised in Brussels (her father was a banker from New Orleans), Claiborne returned with her family to the United States before the Nazis invaded Belgium in 1940, studied art in Europe after the war, worked on Seventh Avenue for designer Tina Lesser beginning in 1950, had a series of other bosses, and has been a top dress designer since the 1960s, but has waited until her son and two stepchildren finished college before introducing her own label. The Ortenbergs will build a company with 3,400 employees before they retire from active management in June 1989 with stock valued at nearly $100 million.

The .44-caliber killer claims his first victim early in the morning of July 29. A man who will prove to be David Berkowitz, 24, of Yonkers approaches an Oldsmobile double-parked in front of a Bronx apartment house and opens fire with a .44-caliber Bulldog revolver on medical technician Donna Lauria, 18, who has just returned from a Manhattan discothèque with her friend Jody Valenti, 19, a nurse; Berkowitz will terrorize the city for 12 months, killing five women and one man, leaving seven persons wounded (see 1977).

A new Mayor's Office of Midtown Enforcement cracks down on vice in the Times Square area, notorious for massage parlors, pornographic movie houses, prostitution, topless bars, and other sex-related businesses (see 1977).

Crime boss Carlo Gambino dies of cancer (by some accounts of a heart attack) at his Long Island summer home October 15 at age 74. He has lived with his family in a modest house at 2230 Ocean Avenue, Brooklyn; his wife, Catherine, died of cancer in 1971; and he has gratified his vanity only to the extent of having a CG-1 license plate on his gray Oldsmobile. Although Gambino has developed 25 groups whose 800 men steal cargo from New York airports, infiltrate the truckers' union to profit from almost every garment sold on Seventh Avenue, keep construction costs high by rigging prices on the cement used in buildings, and control dozens of other rackets, including loan sharking, numbers running, and prostitution, Gambino himself has never served a day in prison. His funeral attracts people from all over the country, and the low-profile "don" is succeeded as head of the Gambino crime family by his first cousin (and brother-in-law) Paul Castellano, 61, a Brooklyn-born butcher's son who has interests in legitimate meat businesses but gets most of his income from the rackets (see 1985).

Former underworld boxing "boss" Paul John "Frankie" Carbo dies of diabetes at Miami Beach November 9 at age 72.

New York's homicide rate will rise to 23.5 per 100,000 in the next 5 years, up from 21.7 in the last 5.

Landfill operations for Battery Park City are completed after nearly 2 years' work that have seen 65 acres of new land added to the 24.7 acres created by excavations for the World Trade Center (see 1974). Implementing plans by foundation engineer Robert C. Johnston, 67, millions of cubic yards of sand have been dredged up from the bottom of Lower New York Bay, carried to the site in barges, and pumped in behind a new bulkhead that is supported by piers driven into the bedrock 70 feet down, but fiscal problems delay development of the project, whose acreage will grow to 92 as it embraces two parks, a school, and about 24 apartment and office buildings along a two-mile stretch of the Hudson River (see 1980).

The 42-story 3 Park Avenue office tower is completed between 33rd and 34th streets, replacing the 71st Regiment Armory of 1891. Designed by Shreve, Lamb & Harmon Associates and set at an angle to the street, the brick tower has been financed by the Educational Construction Fund and incorporates the Norman Thomas High School on its first nine floors (the school will later take over two additional floors).

The private, nonprofit Forty-Second Street Development Corp. is founded by former advertising agency executive Fred Papert with support from Jacqueline Kennedy Onassis and former Lindsay administration officials "to rescue West Forty-second Street from four decades of misuse and neglect . . . to reverse Forty-second Street's fall from grace . . . creating in time a river-to-river grand boulevard that would become a magnet for private investment, visitors, jobs and tax revenues, and have a major impact on the economy of New York City and the tristate region." Papert gets a start-up grant of $150,000 from the Ford Foundation, whose headquarters building is in East 42nd Street; it acquires the Crossroads Building at the intersection of Broadway, Seventh Avenue, and 42nd Street, a 65-year-old cinderblock tower whose peep show it replaces with a 24-hour Police Department substation and information center, engaging artist Richard Haas to paint a trompe l'oeil mural on the structure's old advertising tower, but concentrates initially on the block between Ninth and Tenth avenues, where massage parlors such as the French Palace and the Body Rub Institute are keeping away more desirable tenants and depressing property values (*see* Manhattan Plaza, 1977).

The 25-story Lincoln-Amsterdam House is completed on West End Avenue between 64th and 65th streets. Designed by David Todd & Associates the high-rise co-operative with 88 units has been built by Starrett Corp. with Mitchell-Lama financing in co-operation with the Lincoln Square Community Council, sponsor of the project.

Roosevelt Island's Eastwood apartments are completed at 510, 516, 536, 546, 566, 576, and 580 Main Street (*see* 1975). Designed by Sert, Jackson & Associates, their 1,000 units face Consolidated Edison's "Big Allis" (for Allis-Chalmers) electric generating plant and are for low-, middle-, and moderate-income tenants; Roosevelt Island's Westview apartments are completed at 595 and 625 Main Street, opposite Manhattan's Hospital for Special Surgery. Sert, Jackson & Associates has designed the buildings for more affluent tenants. Residential construction on the island will cease for more than a decade, but by that time Roosevelt Island will have more than 5,100 residents, 46 percent of them minorities, with hundreds of United Nations diplomats from various foreign countries (*see* transportation, 1989).

Brooklyn's Starrett City is completed in an area bounded by Flatlands Avenue and Shore Parkway between Seaview and Louisiana avenues. Designed by Herman Jessor for Starrett Corp., the nation's largest federally subsidized housing complex has 5,881 apartments, its own schools, churches, synagogues, and shopping center, generates its own heat, light, and power, and institutes an affirmative-action policy in an effort to keep the development racially mixed. It has a quota of 30 percent for minorities, some critics call it "a monument to fear," but Starrett Corp. is close to bankruptcy and needs to make a profit, white politicians in the district are fearful of losing their voter base, and the city worries about losing its middle-class tax base (*see* human rights, 1984).

Coney Island's Sea Rise I apartment house is completed for the Urban Development Corp. on Neptune and Canal avenues between 33rd and 37th streets to designs by Hoberman & Wasserman.

The Riverside Park apartment houses are completed at 3333 Broadway, between 133rd and 135th streets. Designed by Richard Dattner & Associates, Henri A. LeGendre & Associates, and Max Wechsler Associates, the five buildings range in size from 11 to 35 stories (two have 29 stories and one 20) and have

been financed by the New York City Educational Construction Fund; they include the Roberto Clemente School (I.S. 195) at 625 West 133rd Street, between Broadway and 12th Avenue.

Changes in the city's J-51 tax abatement law take effect, giving substantial benefits to anyone converting a commercial building into a residential building. The change spurs conversion of loft buildings that have a 25 percent vacancy rate and older office buildings into apartment houses and hotels.

Real estate developer William Zeckendorf dies of a stroke at New York September 30 at age 71. His son William, Jr. will be a prominent developer in the 1980s.

The United Nations Plaza Hotel/office tower opens at the northwest corner of First Avenue and 44th Street with offices on the lower 26 floors. Designed by Kevin Roche, John Dinkeloo & Associates, the structure's 13-story hotel has a health club with glass-walled swimming pool on the 27th floor, the only Manhattan hotel tennis court on the 39th, and 247 guest rooms, a number that will be expanded to 427 rooms when a second tower is completed in 1983. The city and the 8-year-old United Nations Development Corp. share ownership, but Millennium Hotels will buy the hotel in 1999, renovate it, and reopen it 2 years later as the Millennium Hotel New York, UN Plaza.

Hilton Hotel Corp. agrees in October to buy the Waldorf-Astoria for $35 million from the bankrupt Penn Central Transportation Co. that owns the land. New York City opposes the sale, claiming that $9.75 million in real estate taxes are due on the property and must be paid in full, but a federal court at Philadelphia approves the sale and a federal district judge in that city of brotherly love orders trustees of the Penn Central to pay New York $2.5 million.

A fire in a six-story tenement at 311 West 94th Street near Riverside Drive February 3 leaves 10 dead and one missing. A fire the same day in the city's oldest commercial building burns for nearly 30 hours at 273 Water Street in the South Street Seaport district before it can be brought under control and suffers severe damage. Its first two buildings were erected by a sea captain in 1772; two additional stories were added in 1804.

The U.S. Department of Transportation issues an order November 18 requiring airlines to muffle 1,000 noisy plane engines that exceed noise limits established after they were built. New Yorkers living near La Guardia and Kennedy airports continue to suffer from excessive noise produced by aircraft.

Liebmann Brewing Co. announces in mid-January that it is closing its Brooklyn plant after 121 years in what once was America's second largest city; F. & M. Schaefer Brewing Co. chairman Robert W. Lear announces January 22 that the company is closing the Brooklyn plant that it opened in 1916 and moving operations to its far more modern facility at Lehigh Valley, Pa., built in 1972. The closings leave New York and Brooklyn without a single producing brewery.

The nonprofit Council on the Environment opens an outdoor market on Union Square, launching a greenmarkets program that will grow to have 20 outdoor food markets selling direct from producer to consumer. Most will be open on weekends from May through December, but the Union Square market will have winter hours beginning in January 1984.

 Windows on the World opens on the top (107th) floor of the 3-year-old south tower of the World Trade Center with views of the Statue of Liberty, Staten Island Ferry, and other sights far below. Architect Hugh Hardy and designer Milton Glaser have designed the place for Joseph Baum; he heads up the entire food-service operation at the World Trade Center, whose 22 places to eat and drink occupy 120,000 square feet of floor space. Windows offers drinks at the City Lights Bar, snacks at the Hors D'Oeuvrerie (where breakfast is served from 7:30 o'clock to 10:30 in the morning, tea and cocktails beginning at 3 in the afternoon), wine at the Cellar in the Sky, and meals at the Restaurant. A Wall Street luncheon club during the week, Windows will be better known for its views than for its cuisine but will nevertheless be among the four top-grossing restaurants in the world.

The Tavern on the Green reopens August 31 in Central Park under the management of Warner LeRoy, now 42, who opened Maxwell's Plum fame in 1966 and now offers $2.85 hamburgers, chicken sandwiches on potato bread for $2.50, rack of lamb for $24.50, or steak châteaubriand. Opened originally in 1934 on the site of the park's former sheepfold, Tavern on the Green was run for a few years in the 1960s by Restaurant Associates (until executives called it Tavern in the Red), $2.5 million has been spent to refurbish it, and 600 invited guests, including James Beard, file past a buffet table, helping themselves to cold salmon, lamb stew, and turkey in aspic. Critics question the parks commissioner for permitting LeRoy to encroach on park land, but the park stands to make $60,000 (5.5 percent of gross receipts) per year from the new Tavern on the Green, where it only received $25,000 from the previous concessionaire. LeRoy will add more and more glitz to the place in the next 18 years as the Tavern on the Green becomes a major tourist attraction and the country's most profitable restaurant.

Mortimer's restaurant opens at the corner of Lexington Avenue and 75th Street, where its 19 small tables will draw a crowd of socialites, politicians, and other celebrities attracted less by the food (chicken hash, twin burgers, mashed potatoes, lemon meringue pie, rice pudding) and undistinguished decor than by the need to see and be seen. Philadelphia-born entrepreneur Glenn Bernbaum, 54, has started the place after 16 years of running the Custom Shop that he will continue to run until 1980.

 The Statue of Liberty that has welcomed so many immigrants to America since 1886 is designated a New York City Landmark September 14.

1977 A revision in the city charter provides for the creation of 59 community boards staffed and funded by the city. They will act as ombudsmen but have little real power.

Gov. Carey encourages his Queens-born secretary of state Mario (Matthew) Cuomo, 45, to seek the New

Rep. Ed Koch was elected to be mayor of what some said was an ungovernable city. LIBRARY OF CONGRESS

York mayoralty, but Cuomo loses in a Democratic primary runoff to bachelor congressman Edward I. Koch, now 52, who says he would have called out the National Guard to prevent rioting in July's power outage. Koch goes on to win the general election, campaigning on the slogan, "After eight years of charisma [a reference to Lindsay, who has declined to run for a third term] and four years of the clubhouse [a reference to Beame], why not try competence?" Koch also favors the death penalty and garners 717,376 votes as compared to 522,942 for Cuomo, who has run on the Liberal ticket. State Senator Roy M. Goodman runs as a Republican and receives 58,606 votes.

The U.S. Supreme Court upholds racial quotas used in reapportioning legislative districts to comply with the Voting Rights Act of 1964. It hands down the 7-to-1 decision March 1 in *United Jewish Organizations of Williamsburg, N.Y. v. Carey.*

Kohlberg Kravis Roberts pioneers the leveraged buyout April 7, using mostly commercial bank loans to buy a small maker of truck suspensions (*see* 1976). KKR will employ high-yield "junk" bonds to finance future LBOs.

The 105-year-old New York Mercantile Exchange moves its operations into the 4-year-old World Trade Center (*see* 1941; 1978).

The Securities and Exchange Commission (SEC) concludes that Lazard Frères advised its clients ITT and Mediobanca on improper transactions in order to avoid taxes. The Foreign Corrupt Practices Act passed by Congress December 7 provides for a fine of up to $1 million for any U.S. corporation found to have paid a bribe to a foreign government, political party official, or political candidate. A corporate official or employee is subject to imprisonment for up to 5 years and a $10,000 fine if convicted of involvement in such a bribe.

Wall Street's Dow Jones Industrial Average falls below 900 May 27, closes December 20 at 806.22, and closes December 31 at 831.17, down from 1004.65 at the end of 1976.

Barney's begins selling women's apparel after 54 years as a men's retail store on Seventh Avenue at 17th Street (*see* 1923; 1991).

Franklin Simon closes after 75 years on Fifth Avenue.

Bond Stores closes its Times Square location. Robert Hall Clothes padlocks all of its 366 stores June 29; the menswear chain is owned by United Merchants and Manufacturers, and its unionized retail clerks charge a lockout.

Gov. Carey vetoes a bill August 12 that would restore a ban on Sunday sales. A growing number of New York City retailers, including major department stores, now remain open on Sundays. The governor signs a bill August 12 that allows the city to impose a new tax on Nassau Street mall stores in order to provide special services and maintenance to the area.

The S. H. Kress store on the west side of Fifth Avenue at 39th Street closes after 42 years.

Macy's announces September 19 that it will close its Jamaica, Queens, branch.

Abercrombie & Fitch files for bankruptcy and closes its 60-year-old Madison Avenue sporting-goods and clothing store along with eight branch stores. Houston-based Oshman's Sporting Goods will buy the company name next year, open a shop at the South Street Seaport in 1984 appealing to teenaged customers, and sell out to the Limited in 1988. By the mid-1990s there will be 40 Abercrombie & Fitch shops, including two in New York, and the company will be doing a large catalogue business.

A power failure even worse than that of 1965 blacks out all five New York boroughs and Westchester County July 13 and continues for 25 hours during a heat wave as four lightning strikes north of the city knock out lines that feed into the Consolidated Edison power grid. The first lightning strike comes at 8:37 o'clock in the evening, air conditioners and elevators stop running as temperatures soar into the 90s, neighbors help each other cope (young people climb endless stairs to keep elderly and disabled fellow-tenants supplied with food), but looters in ghetto areas of Brooklyn, Harlem, and the South Bronx break into shops, stealing clothes, furniture, and TV sets (50 cars are stolen from a dealership in the Bronx); 1,037 fires break out and firefighters respond to 1,700 false alarms; police make 3,776 arrests but are overwhelmed, business losses from theft and property damage come to nearly $150 million. Con Edison calls the blackout an "act of God" but will be found guilty of negligence.

Commercial helicopter flights from the top of the Pan Am Building resume February 1 after a 9-year suspension (*see* 1965). New York Airways uses 50-foot-long Sikorsky S-61 choppers that carry 30 passengers each, whisking them to and from Kennedy Airport in 10 minutes or less for $22.15 ($15 for passengers holding tickets on flights of Pan Am or other airlines). But New York Airways Flight 972 arrives from Kennedy just after 5 o'clock on the afternoon of May 16, sets down on the landing pad at the northeast corner of the building's roof, its 20 passengers deplane, 12 of the 21 passengers booked for the next flight board, and the rest await boarding when the craft's right front landing gear suddenly collapses. One of its four 20-foot rotor blades, idling at 1,000 revolutions per minute, snaps off, slashes four people to death on the roof, plunges over the side, smashes into a window on the 36th floor, and breaks in two. A shower of glass descends upon rush-hour pedestrians in Vanderbilt and Madison avenues, and part of the rotor blade falls to earth on Madison Avenue, killing a woman at 43rd Street. Severed limbs are found on the roof, and helicopter flights from the building will not be resumed.

∞ Roman Catholic missionary James G. Keller dies of Parkinson's disease at New York February 7 at age 76. Keller founded the Christophers, an informal ecumenical movement that has stressed individual action; its motto has been, "Better to light one candle than to curse the darkness."

A new St. Peter's Lutheran Church opens in the new Citicorp Center at the southeast corner of Lexington Avenue and 54th Street (its previous building was razed to permit construction of the skyscraper).

Hunter College High School and Hunter College Elementary School move to 94th Street between Park and Madison avenues, taking over the former Squadron A armory building that has been rebuilt for its new use (see 1955). Within 20 years the high school will have an enrollment of some 1,250 male and female students, and its high educational standards combined with free tuition will make it the favored choice of parents with intellectually gifted children.

The 11-year-old Wells, Rich, Greene advertising agency comes up with the slogan "I Love New York" to promote the financially ailing city. The logo and musical tag gain worldwide currency.

Public-relations pioneer John W. Hill of Hill & Knowlton dies of a brain tumor at his 50 East 77th Street home March 17 at age 86. His firm has grown to have 560 employees in 36 U.S. offices and 18 offices abroad to serve clients who include the Business Roundtable, Procter & Gamble, Texaco, and Warner Lambert; Young & Rubicam cofounder Raymond Rubicam dies at Scottsdale, Ariz., May 8 at age 85; NBC radio announcer Ben Grauer of a heart ailment at New York May 31 at age 68; New York Times correspondent Herbert L. Matthews at Adelaide, Australia, July 30 at age 77; model agency founder John

R. Powers at Glendale, Calif., July 19 at age 84; former New Yorker magazine fiction editor Katherine S. White at North Brooklin, Me., July 20 at age 84; former New York Daily News cartoonist C. D. (Charles Daniel) Batchelor at Deep River, Conn., September 5 at age 89; New Yorker writer Geoffrey T. Hellman of cancer at New York September 26 at age 70; former New York Times Sunday editor Lester Markel of cancer at his native New York October 23 at age 83 (he has lived at 135 Central Park West).

The American Lawyer begins publication at New York. Far Rockaway-born lawyer-journalist Steven Brill, 28, has negotiated the deal to start the magazine, whose material he edits. It will spawn a cable television channel (Court TV) that Brill will sell along with the magazine in 1997 to Time Warner for $20 million.

Nonfiction: Tweed's New York: Another Look by New York-born author Leo Hershkowitz, 53, who writes, "Tweed's concepts about urbanization and accommodation, while not philosophically formalized, were years beyond their time . . . Twenty or thirty years later, such programs were adopted by reformers and urban planners. Tweed was a pioneer spokesman for an emerging New York, one of the few who spoke for its interests, one of the very few who could have his voice heard in Albany. Tweed grew with the city; his death was a tragedy for the future metropolis . . . His life in the end was wasted, not so much by what he did but by what was done to him, his work in the city being relegated to the garbage heap, both branded by the same indelible iron. He became a club with which to beat New York, really the ultimate goal of the blessed reformers;" The Golden Door: Italian and Jewish Immigrant Mobility in New York City, 1880–1915 by German-born New School for Social Research historian Thomas Kessner, 30; Grand Central, The World's Greatest Railway Terminal by William D. Middleton, 49.

Author Louis Untermeyer dies of cancer at Newton, Conn., December 18 at age 92.

Fiction: The Professor of Desire by Philip Roth; Ackroyd by Jules Feiffer; Refiner's Fire: The Life and Adventures of Marshal Pearl, a Foundling by Mark Helprin; Long Time No See by Ed McBain (Evan Hunter).

Poetry: The Duplications by Kenneth Koch.

Poet Robert Lowell dies of a heart attack in a taxi en route from JFK Airport to Manhattan September 12 at age 60.

Harper & Row acquires the 101-year-old publisher Thomas Y. Crowell and next year will acquire the venerable Philadelphia publisher J. B. Lippincott as the industry continues to consolidate (*see* 1969). Harper's moved in 1972 to 10 East 53rd Street, it sustained a 17-day strike 2 years later by 320 of its New York employees—the first such strike in modern book publishing history—and this year 240 of its workers strike for a week (*see* Murdoch, 1987).

 The Frick Collection that opened in 1935 starts charging a $1 entrance fee January 4 (50¢ for children) and expands to the east along 70th Street, using an alteration designed by Harry Van Dyke, John Barrington Bayley, and G. Frederick Poehler to house some of its works.

Painting: *Self-Portrait* by Chuck Close, who has painted a photograph taken with a wide aperture and with the focus on the eyes; *New York Dawn*, *Searchin'*, and *Spring Point* by Elizabeth Murray; *392 Broadway* (baked enamel on silkscreen grid) and *17 White Street* (baked enamel on silkscreen, enamel on steel plates, 80 plates) by Jennifer Bartlett. William Gropper dies at Manhasset January 6 at age 79.

Erie, Pa.-born art dealer Mary Boone, 26, opens her own tiny gallery at 420 West Broadway, in SoHo, just below the gallery opened by Leo Castelli in 1971. Boone came to New York at age 19, the Bykert Gallery where she worked closed last year despite her vigrous efforts to have collectors pay their bills, she will champion the works of artists who will include Brooklyn-born, Texas-raised Julian Schnabel, whom other dealers have scorned, and her success will enable her to open a second larger gallery across the street at 417 West Broadway.

The New York State Court of Appeals unanimously upholds the 1975 Surrogate Court's ruling against the executors of the late Mark Rothko, the Marlborough Gallery, and Frank Lloyd, calling their conduct "manifestly wrongful and indeed shocking." A Manhattan grand jury returns an indictment against Lloyd for tampering with evidence presented at the trial, but Lloyd is a British subject, vacationing at his home in the Bahamas, and will not return to stand trial until 1983.

Sculpture: a statue of the late Dag Hammarskjöld by sculptor Tony Rosenthal is unveiled November 24 at Dag Hammarskjöld Plaza (*see* 1961; apartment house, 1984).

 Theater: *The Shadow Box* by White Horse, N.J.-born playwright Michael Cristofer (originally Procaccino), 32, 3/31 at the Morosco Theater, with Fort Smith, Ark.-born actor Laurence Luckinbill, 36, as a terminal cancer patient, Dublin-born actress Geraldine Fitzgerald, 63, Chicago-born actor

Mandy (originally Mandel Bruce) Patinkin, 24, 315 perfs.; *The Basic Training of Pavlo Hummel* by David Rabe 4/24 at the Longacre Theater, with Al Pacino, 117 perfs. (originally produced by Joseph Papp's New York Shakespeare Festival); *Gemini* by New York playwright and opera commentator Albert Innaurato, 28, 5/21 at the Little Theater, with New York-born actor Danny Aiello, 43, 1,789 perfs.; *The Gin Game* by East Baltimore-born playwright D. L. (Donald Lee) Coburn, 36, 10/6 at the John Golden Theater, with Hume Cronyn, Jessica Tandy, 518 perfs.; *A Life in the Theater* by David Mamet 10/20 at Lucille Lortel's off-Broadway Theater de Lys, with Ellis Rabb, Peter Evans, 288 perfs.; *Dracula* by the late Irish writer Hamilton Deane, who adapted the screenplay by the late John L. Balderston 10/20 at the Martin Beck Theater, with Frank Langella, 925 perfs.; *Chapter Two* by Neil Simon 12/4 at the Imperial Theater, with Cliff Gorman, Baltimore-born actress Anita Gillette, 41, Judd Hirsch, Abilene, Tex.-born actress Ann Wedgeworth, 42, 857 perfs.; *Cold Storage* by New York-born playwright Ronald Ribman, 45, 12/29 at the Lyceum Theater, with Martin Balsam, Len Cariou, 227 perfs. (including 47 at the off-Broadway American Place Theater).

Playwright Richard Bissell dies at his native Dubuque May 4 at age 63; Jewish Art Theater founder Jacob Ben-Ami at New York July 22 at age 86; actor Alfred Lunt at Chicago August 3 at age 85.

The Big Apple Circus gives its first performance in a modest-sized ring at Battery Park City. The nonprofit one-ring show will move to Damrosch Park behind Lincoln Center and become a fixture in the city's entertainment scene, touring the country and offering outreach programs that will run in local hospitals and schools.

Films: Woody Allen's *Annie Hall* with Allen, Diane Keaton, Shelley Duvall; Herbert Ross's *The Goodbye Girl* with Richard Dreyfuss, Marsha Mason; Robert Benton's *The Late Show* with Art Carney, Lily Tomlin; Richard Brooks's *Looking for Mr. Goodbar* with Diane Keaton, Richard Gere, William Atherton, Tuesday Weld (Susan Ker), Richard Kiley (*see* crime, 1973); James Ivory's *Roseland* with Teresa Wright, Lou Jacobi, Geraldine Chaplin, Helen Gallagher, Joan Copeland, Christopher Walken; John Badham's *Saturday Night Fever* with John Travolta as Bay Ridge youth Tony Manero, who leaves Brooklyn for a new life in Manhattan.

Joan Crawford dies of a heart attack in her 158 East 68th Street apartment February 14 at age 68.

Film musical: Martin Scorsese's *New York, New York* with Robert De Niro, Liza Minnelli, Lionel Stander, title song by John Kander and Fred Ebb. Frank Sinatra records the song, helping to make "Start spreading the news . . ." almost an anthem for the city.

Broadway musicals: *Side by Side by Sondheim* 4/18 at the Music Box Theater, with a seven-member cast, music and lyrics by Stephen Sondheim, 384 perfs.; *Annie* 4/21 at the Alvin Theater, with Philadelphia-born actress Andrea McArdle, 13, as the cartoon character "Little Orphan Annie" (*see* communications, 1924), Salem, Ore.-born actor Reid Shelton, 52, as Oliver "Daddy" Warbucks, Boston-born actress Dorothy Loudon, 43, as Miss Hannigan, music by Charles Strouse, lyrics by Martin Charnin, songs that include "N.Y.C." ("N.Y.C., what is it about you? You're big, you're loud, you're tough. N.Y.C., I go years without you, then I can't get enough. Enough of cabdrivers answering back in language far from pure. Enough of frankfurters answering back . . . You snap, you fizz, the best there is for you, is N.Y.C.," 2,377 perfs.

The New York, New York disco nightclub opens at 33 West 52nd Street, where it will continue until 1981.

Studio 54 opens April 26 at 254 West 54th Street, where Brooklyn-born entrepreneur Stephen "Steve" Rubell, 33, and his Syracuse University friend Ian Schrager have remodeled what once was the Gallo Theater, an opera house. Admitting patrons on a selective basis at the door, the discothèque will attract crowds of celebrities and café society people until December 1979, when federal agents will arrest Rubell and Schrager on charges of having evaded taxes on more than $2.5 million skimmed from club receipts (*see* 1981).

Harlem's Apollo Theater reopens May 5 after a shutdown of nearly 2 years for renovations. Police and security guards usher in a crowd that includes politicians, athletes, models, and musicians, who file past television cameras and microphones.

Former Latin Quarter owner Lou Walters dies of a heart attack at Miami August 18 at age 81, survived by his TV journalist daughter Barbara.

Popular songs: *Blondie* (album) and *Plastic Letters* (album) by the New York new wave rock group Blondie (Miami-born singer-songwriter Debbie [Deborah] Harry, 32, guitarist Chris Stein, 28, drummer Clem Burke, bass guitarist Nigel Harrison, guitarist Frank Infante, keyboardist Jimmy Destri); *Rumours* (album) by Fleetwood Mac becomes the largest-selling pop album thus far,

indicating a dramatic increase in record sales that will continue until 1979.

West 106th Street between Riverside Drive and Central Park West is renamed Duke Ellington Boulevard October 7 in honor of the late composer-pianist-bandleader, who died in 1974. The "Duke" owned a Riverside Drive mansion at 106th Street.

Metropolitan Opera conductor Thomas Schippers dies of lung cancer at New York December 16 at age 47.

Guillermo Villas, 25 (Argentina), wins in U.S. Open men's singles, Chris Evert in women's singles.

The New York Yankees win their first World Series since 1962, defeating the Los Angeles Dodgers 4 games to 2 behind the pitching of Mike Torrez, 31 (who plays all nine innings of the third and sixth games), Ron Guidry, 27, and Albert Walker "Sparky" Lyle, 33. Outfielder Reggie Jackson, 31, gets nine hits, including a double and five home runs; catcher Thurman Munson, 30, eight hits, including two doubles and a home run; second baseman Willie Randolph, 23, four hits, including two doubles and a home run; first baseman Chris Chambliss seven hits, including a double and a home run.

Surveys show that the number of U.S. adults under age 35 living alone has more than doubled since 1970. Analysts ascribe the growing trend toward leaving home early and marrying late to such factors as easier credit, an increased wariness about marriage, and greater career opportunities for young women. Perhaps especially in New York, more and more married couples now live apart, usually to pursue independent careers, and often see each other only on weekends.

Queens toy designer and amateur mountain climber George Willig, 27, climbs to the top of the World Trade Center May 26 wearing suction cups on the soles of his shoes to scale the 110-foot tower (*see* Petit, 1974). The ascent takes him 3 hours, and he is fined $1.10—one penny per floor.

Fashion designer Halston earns nearly $3 million, spends $75,000 on orchids, dances the nights away at the new Studio 54 disco, but still leaves for the office at 7 o'clock each morning (*see* 1972). Norton Simon Industries acquires Halston's firm (*see* 1978).

The .44-caliber killer continues his murders (*see* 1976). He kills Wall Street clerk Christine Freud, 25, January 29 as she sits with her boyfriend in his car in Ridgewood, Queens. He shoots Virginia Voskerichain, 19, in the face at point-blank range

March 8 less than 100 yards from the Freund shooting. He shoots Bronx student Valentine Suriani, 18, and her boyfriend Alexander Esau, 20, of Manhattan in a parked car April 17 a few blocks from last year's Lauria murder. He shoots Bronx student Judy Placido, 17, and her boyfriend Sal Lupo, 20, of Brooklyn June 26 in a parked car outside a Bayside, Queens, discothèque, but both survive. Flatbush, Brooklyn, woman Stacy Moscowitz, 20, and her Bensonhurst boyfriend Robert Violante, 20, are shot July 31; she dies after extensive brain surgery, and he is blinded. Psychotic Yonkers postal worker David Berkowitz, 24, is arrested August 10 and claims he has acted on orders from the dog of his neighbor Sam Carr, 64, who does not know him.

A Nuisance Abatement Law takes effect in the summer, making it much easier to close down illegal sex businesses in Times Square and other venues (*see* 1976). By 1986 the number of massage parlors in central Manhattan will have fallen to 44, down from 147 in 1975 (*see* 1996).

A rally outside Grand Central Terminal in April enlists demonstrators who include Jacqueline Kennedy Onassis and arouses public opposition to a proposed 59-story skyscraper that would be built above the terminal's waiting room (*see* 1968). The New York Court of Appeals reviews the lower court's decision and concludes that the landmarks law did not transfer control of the property to the city but merely restricted exploitation of it; there was no "taking" of property without due process of law because the same use of the terminal was permitted as before; the appellants did not show that they could not earn a reasonable return on their investment from the terminal itself; even if the terminal itself could never operate at a reasonable profit, some of the income from Penn Central's real estate holdings in the area must realistically be imputed to the terminal; and because development rights above the terminal are transferable to numerous sites in the vicinity this provides significant compensation for any loss of rights above the terminal itself. The U.S. Supreme Court agrees in September to hear the case (*see* 1978).

The 59-story Citicorp Center (later the Citigroup Center) is completed in the block bounded by Lexington and Third avenues between 53rd and 54th streets. The Lutheran church of St. Peter's sold its site at the southeast corner of 54th Street to First National City Bank in 1970, and the bank bought up other properties in the block through intermediaries. Designed in International Style by Alabama-born Boston architect Hugh (Asher) Stubbins, 65, of

Hugh Stubbins & Associates with Emery Roth & Sons, the aluminum-and-glass tower rises 915 feet high, incorporates the church in its former location at 619 Lexington Avenue, contains 1.65 million square feet of office space, and includes a seven-story central atrium illuminated by skylights with shops and restaurants; the steeply sloped roof on the building's southern side gives the Midtown skyline a distinctive new silhouette.

The Bronx Development Center is completed to designs by Richard Meier, now 43, whose four-story aluminum-skinned mental-health center is hailed as a milestone of modernism. Built for the State Department of Mental Hygiene in Waters Place between Eastchester Road and the Hutchinson River Parkway, it will come down early in 2002 to make way for a more conventional building.

The Manhattan Plaza apartment complex opens with a 45-story building on Ninth Avenue and a 46-story building on Tenth between 42nd and 43rd streets. Designed by David Todd & Associates and built as a Mitchell-Lama project, it is reserved entirely for performing artists, who pay no more than 30 percent of their gross incomes for rent (the federal Housing Preservation and Development Agency pays the rest); the red-brick buildings contain 1,688 units, making this the largest U.S. housing project for people in the performing arts; by attracting such tenants it will help the new Forty-Second Street Development Corp. achieve its objective of converting massage parlors and such into classrooms, rehearsal studios, restaurants, and 99-seat theaters.

The 51-story Olympic Tower condominium apartment and office building is completed at 641 and 645 Fifth Avenue, just north of St. Patrick's Cathedral, where Best & Co. stood from 1947 to 1970. Designed by Skidmore, Owings & Merrill for Arlen Realty and Development Corp. and Victory Development Corp. (owned by millionaire shipowner Aristotle Onassis), it is sheathed in brown-tinted glass and has a concierge, maid and valet service, restaurant, wine cellar, barbershop, hairdressing salon, health club, and international newsstand, stock quotation board, and internal telephone system for the 225 apartments that occupy its top 29 floors. The two top floors contain large duplex apartments, while lower residential floors have eight apartments per floor. The public shopping arcade designed by Chermayeff, Geismar & Associates, Zion & Breen, and Levien, Deliso & White will open on the ground floor next year between 51st and 52nd streets.

The Confucius Plaza complex opens in Chinatown at the corner of Bowery and Division streets. Designed by Horowitz & Chun, its 44-story eastern part faces the Manhattan Bridge, its 19-story western portion the Bowery and Chatham Square. P.S. 124 and a day-care center share ground-floor areas with shops and a community center above an underground garage; upper floors of the brown brick-covered structure contain 762 apartments, and a statue of the philosopher Confucius by sculptor Liu Shih is on the plaza in front.

The Metropolitan Museum Historic District is established along Fifth Avenue between 78th and 86th streets with irregular boundaries that reach Madison Avenue at only two points.

President Carter visits Charlotte Street in the rubble-strewn South Bronx October 5 and promises to revive urban renewal after 8 years of Republican neglect, but a $500 million program for the South Bronx, unveiled in April of next year, will take years to implement. Meanwhile, the section will remain a disaster area of arson-gutted buildings (*see* Logue, 1978; Charlotte Gardens, 1983; 1997).

The Bronx Zoo opens its Wild Asia exhibit, with snow leopards from the Himalayan Highlands, Indian rhinos, and other species from Asia's tropical forests, including tigers and gaur. The Vincent Astor Foundation has financed the 39-acre installation; the "Bengali Express" monorail allows visitors to tour it.

Pathmark signs an agreement with the Bedford Stuyvesant Restoration Corp. to build a supermarket in one of Brooklyn's most economically depressed areas (*see* 1968). Residents of inner-city neighborhoods have been obliged to pay premium prices for food at small retail shops because no large supermarkets have been willing to open in such areas (*see* 1978).

The Dean and DeLuca food emporium opens in August at 121 Prince Street in SoHo. Former publishing-house employee Joel Dean has teamed up with former schoolteacher and cheese-store owner Giorgio DeLuca to offer cheeses, smoked fish, quail eggs, 30 kinds of charcuterie, 15 types of pâté, bread loaves, fruit in and out of season, Italian honey, raspberry and blueberry vinegars, coffee beans, jams, preserves, and kitchen equipment. It will pride itself on having certain delicacies before anyone else and will grow to have several additional locations in the city.

Zabar's buys the entire four-story pseudo-English half-timbered building where it has leased space for nearly 40 years (*see* 1951). The food store begins to expand from its original 2,500-square-foot space

and by 1980 will be doing $12 million worth of business per year (*see* 1985).

Restaurateur Toots Shor dies of cancer at New York January 22 at age 73.

The steakhouse Smith and Wollensky opens at the northeast corner of Third Avenue and 49th Street, where The Restaurant Group headed by Alan Stillman of 1965 T.G.I. Friday's fame has acquired the premises of another steakhouse, Manny Wolf's (Stillman has picked the names Smith and Wollensky at random from the telephone directory).

The River Café opens in July on a Brooklyn barge in the East River with a spectacular view of the Manhattan skyline. Proprietor Michael O'Keefe has run several restaurants, including Puddings on Lexington Avenue at 90th Street, and his first cook, Jean Deli-Pizzi, will be succeeded by such outstanding chefs as Larry Forgione (who will refuse to cook anything not French until O'Keefe insists that he cook American), Charles Palmer, Rick Stefan, and George Morone, all of whom will go on in the next decade to have fine restaurants of their own, either in New York or in other cities.

1978 The Manhattan Institute founded by local lawyer William J. (Joseph) Casey, 65, is a nonprofit research and education group that promotes controversial ideas that include privatizing municipal services, reducing local business taxes, limiting multiculturalism, taking a tough attitude toward homeless drug addicts, and supporting private as well as public education. Some of the city and state's Republican political leaders will adopt such ideas; Casey will become head of the CIA in 1981.

Opponents of nuclear weapons gather at Dag Hammerskjöld Plaza May 27; protesters from around the world march to Central Park carrying signs and voicing their anger at world leaders.

The interracial Flames basketball team is founded in Brooklyn's racially troubled Bensonhurst section. Gerard Papa, 24, has started the group in the gymnasium of the Most Precious Blood Church, the Brooklyn Diocese will expel the Flames from the Catholic Youth Organization following a personality clash in 1997, but women in the community will come up with funds to keep the team alive.

The federal government stabilizes New York City's finances with a $1.65 billion loan-guarantee package (*see* 1975).

Loeb, Rhoades merges in January with the century-old firm Hornblower Weekes, Noyes and Trask as Wall Street brokerage houses continue to sustain losses in the bear market that began in 1974 (*see* 1938); Loeb, Rhoades has a staff of more than 2,000 and clears more trading volume than any other Wall Street firm except Merrill Lynch, but it has been losing more than $1 million per month (*see* 1979).

Forstmann Little is founded by Greenwich, Conn.-born woollens heir and investment banker Theodore J. Forstmann, 38, whose firm will provide venture capital to fund mergers and acquisitions.

Metropolitan (formerly East Brooklyn) Savings Bank acquires Fulton Savings Bank (*see* 1969; 1981).

Former Commerce Clearing House chairman Oakley L. Thorne dies of cancer at New York February 15 at age 68; banker E. Roland Harriman at Arden, N.Y., February 16 at age 82; former city comptroller Joseph D. McGoldrick of cancer at Savannah, Ga., April 5 at age 77; Bear Stearns senior partner Salim L. Lewis suffers a stroke at the Harmonie Club April 27 and dies at Mount Sinai Hospital 2 days later at age 69; philanthropist John D. Rockefeller III dies in an automobile accident at Pocantico Hills July 10 at age 72.

Inflation pressures force President Carter to act. He announces a program of voluntary wage-price guidelines October 24, resisting demands that he impose mandatory controls and raising fears that inflation will worsen. Wall Street's Dow Jones Industrial Average nevertheless leaps a record 35.4 points November 1; the Dow closes December 29 at 805.61, down from 831.17 at the end of 1977, having fallen below 800 January 6.

Lerner Stores cofounder Michael Lerner dies of cancer at Miami April 17 at age 86 (the chain has grown to have 470 women's apparel shops, all owned by Rapid-American Corp.); gem dealer Harry Winston dies of a heart attack at New York December 8 at age 82.

The New York Mercantile Exchange begins trading in heating-oil futures. It is now in the World Trade Center (*see* 1977), and energy futures will dominate its activities in the next decade.

Former Port Authority executive director Austin J. Tobin dies of cancer at New York February 8 at age 74.

The Firefighters Skin Bank opened March 28 at the New York Hospital-Cornell Medical Center is the city's first facility designed to freeze and store skin tissue from people who have just died, thus ensuring a ready source of skin covering for badly burned patients.

The Roman Catholic Archdiocese of New York takes over Flower Fifth Avenue Hospital and the New York Medical College (*see* 1938). The hospital will be converted next year from an acute-care facility into the Terence Cardinal Cooke Nursing Home.

The New York State Department of Human Services licenses the Salvation Army's 65-year-old Booth House at 275 Bowery to take care of people with mental health problems. It will continue as a shelter for the mentally ill until 1994, providing shelter and food for 370 residents.

The New York University College of Dentistry adds the 11-story Arnold and Marie Schwartz Hall of Dental Sciences to its Weissman Clinical Science Building (*see* 1957); its expanded facility enables its faculty and students to treat as many as 1,200 patients daily (its students come from many parts of the world as well as from all over the United States and work under the close supervision of experienced dentists, who often perform the more difficult procedures themselves) (*see* 1987).

Former Warner-Lambert president Elmer Holmes Bobst dies at New York August 2 at age 93.

Mayor Koch appoints Brooklyn-born lawyer and political scientist Frank J. (Joseph) Macchiarola, 37, schools chancellor to succeed Irving Anker.

The Revisionists Revised: A Critique of the Radical Attack on Schools (essays) by Diane Ravitch is a polemic refuting recent suggestions that teaching in public schools reflects a conspiracy against the proletariat or an assault upon human spontaneity. Education has meant different things to different people over the years, she says, but the poorest Americans have consistently placed their hopes for their children in formal education, and with good reason.

Queensborough Community College moves to a new 34-acre campus completed at 222-05 56th Avenue, corner Springfield Boulevard, in a residential neighborhood of Bayside that was formerly the grounds of the Oakland Golf Course (*see* 1958). A junior college of the City University of New York, it has had to use classrooms in various locations as enrollment grew, and by 1991 it will have 4,823 full-time and 7,423 part-time students taking courses in such subjects as laser and fiber optics, with a conference-call program of External Education for the Homebound.

Self magazine begins publication at New York in January as Condé Nast expands.

Working Woman magazine begins publication at New York in March.

Liz Smith begins her own column at the *New York Daily News* and becomes an overnight success. Texas-born journalist Smith, 55, grew up in Fort Worth reading Walter Winchell and dreaming about the Stork Club, came to New York with $50 in her purse, has worked for Igor Cassini (whose society gossip column was signed "Cholly Knickerbocker"), *Candid Camera* host Allen Funt, CBS newsman Mike Wallace, and *Cosmopolitan* editor Helen Gurley Brown. When strikers close the *News* down along with the city's other papers in August, Smith appears on WNBC-TV's *Live at Five* newscast; her column will be syndicated, within a decade she will be earning $350,000, and she will remain at the *News* until 1991 before moving her column to *Newsday* and, later, the *Post*.

The *New York Times* prints its last edition from hot type as Linotype machines invented in 1884 give way to computers for typesetting (*see* Typographers Association, 1911). New York newspapers resume publication November 6 after an 88-day strike by 10 unions representing some 11,000 workers. Automation was the underlying issue, but Newspaper Guild employees have been the last to settle, voting 225 to 121 early in the morning of November 6 to accept an agreement.

The New York advertising agency Backer and Spielvogel is founded by former McCann-Erickson creative director and songwriter ("I'd Like to Teach the World to Sing") William (Montague) Backer, 53, and McCann-Erickson account executive (and one-time *New York Times* advertising columnist) Carl Spielvogel, 50.

Irish Echo publisher Patrick Grimes dies at a Scarsdale nursing home June 19 at age 88; public-relations pioneer Benjamin Sonnenberg of a heart attack at New York September 6 at age 77. He has described himself as "a cabinetmaker who fashions pedestals for small statues," and his clients have included CBS, Federated Department Stores, Samuel Goldwyn, Robert Lehman, Lever Brothers, William S. Paley, Pan American World Airways, and David O. Selznick; former *New Yorker* magazine Paris correspondent Janet Flanner dies of a heart attack at New York November 7 at age 86.

Nonfiction: *When LaGuardia Was Mayor: New York's Legendary Years* by August Heckscher, now 65 (with his former Parks Department aide Phyllis Robinson). Heckscher's previous book spelled the former mayor's name correctly (La Guardia), but this one for some reason does not; *Open Spaces: The Life of American Cities* by August Heckscher; *Fifth Avenue: A Very Social History* by Kate Simon; *New York Jew* by Alfred Kazin; *The Last Bull Market: Wall Street in the 1960s* by Robert Sobel; *The Street Book: An Encyclopedia of Manhattan's Street Names and Their Origins* by Henry Moscow; *The City of New York: A History Illustrated from the Collections of the Museum of the City of New York* by Fort Worth-born gallery executive Jerry E. (Eugene) Patterson, 46, is a catalogue of the museum's permanent collection; *Metropolitan Life* (essays) by New York writer Fran (Frances Ann) Lebowitz, 27, who champions smoking and other increasingly unpopular practices while opposing such things as shirts with messages on them; *In Search of History* by Theodore H. White, who recalls that when he and his wife returned to New York in October 1953 after 5 years in Europe they were warned Manhattan's West Side was in a state of transition: "Obviously that meant that blacks and Puerto Ricans were moving in . . . [We] believed in integration, would have felt like traitors to join 'white flight,' if the term had been coined then, and wanted to live on the West Side." The Whites moved into a Central Park West apartment with a view of the park at the corner of 84th Street, obtaining a foyer, living room, dining room, study, three bedrooms, two maid's rooms, and modern kitchen for $300 per month. But, writing about himself in the third person, White says, "He could not send his children to school here . . . For the first time in all his life—in Irish Boston, in warlord China, in darkling Germany—he was afraid to walk the street outside his own house at night; . . . his children were not safe going to play in Central Park just below the window of his apartment house . . . The problem was one of compression—two kinds of culture contesting in the pressure of closed city apartment blocks. It took White no more than six months from homecoming to pass through his particular adjustment to the confrontation. First, the blindness to the problem; then the bravado-disdain of the reality; then discomfort, and finally fear." Half a mile to the north, White notes, birds being raised in apartment house courtyards for illegal cockfights were making their presence known each morning. A movie theater on Broadway near 103rd Street began showing only Spanish-language films (*see* population, 1953). The Whites left after 1 year for what they called the "perfumed stockade" of the East Side.

Former Columbia University linguistics teacher Mario Pei dies of a a heart attack at Glen Ridge, N.J., March 2 at age 77; publisher Victor Weybright of cancer at New York November 3 at age 75; anthropologist-author Margaret Mead of cancer at New York November 15 at age 76.

Poet Phyllis McGinley dies at New York February 22 at age 72. When she turned 70 in 1976 she wrote, "Seventy is wormwood/ Seventy is gall/ But it's better to be 70/ Than not alive at all."

 Painting: *Children Meeting* by Elizabeth Murray; *Self-Portrait* by Andy Warhol; *Diptych* (collage of charcoal and paper on canvas) by Lee Krasner. Realist painter John Koch dies of a stroke at New York April 19 at age 69; illustrator Norman Rockwell at Stockbridge, Mass., November 13 at age 84.

Sculpture: *Hot Dog Stand* (plaster of paris) by George Segal; *Throwback* by Tony Smith.

The Metropolitan Museum of Art appoints its first paid president May 25: former U.S. ambassador to Turkey William B. Macomber, Jr., 57, is also named chief executive officer, C. Douglas Dillon is moved up to board chairman, and the board immediately appoints Paris-born art curator Guy-Philippe Lannes de Montebello, 42, director to succeed Thomas Hoving, who retired in July of last year. In the next 20 years, the imperious de Montebello will increase attendance (to 5.5 million in 1996–1997), boost membership dues, secure hundreds of millions of dollars in bequests and contributions, and raise revenues from admission fees and merchandise sales, thereby restoring the Met's financial solvency despite cutbacks in city and state support.

Theater: *Deathtrap* by Ira Levin 2/26 at the Music Box Theater, with John Wood, Marian Seldes, Canadian-born actor Victor Garber, 28, 1,793 perfs.; *Tribute* by Bernard Slade 6/1 at the Brooks Atkinson Theater with Jack Lemmon, 212 perfs.; *Buried Child* by Sam Shepard 12/5 at Lucille Lortel's off-Broadway Theater de Lys, with Richard Hamilton, Mary McDonnell, Tom Noonan, Jacqueline Brooks, 152 perfs.

Broadway producer Max Gordon dies of a heart attack at New York November 2 at age 86.

Television: *Taxi* 9/12 on ABC with Judd Hirsch, Danny De Vito, 33, New York-born actor Andy Kaufman, 29, Jeff Conway (to 7/27/1983); *Diff'rent Strokes* 11/3 on NBC with Gary Coleman, 20, comedienne Dody Goodman, 49, Conrad Bain (to 8/30/1986).

Radio City Music Hall draws a capacity crowd April 12 for what has been billed as its final show (*see* 1972). It has exhibited nothing racier than G-rated films that have often attracted no more than a few hundred patrons, leaving most of its nearly 6,000 seats empty, and has been losing money at a phenomenal rate. Rockefeller Center management has announced the closing of the great music hall, but the Rockettes have worked the streets to get signatures on a petition to keep it open, management meets that night at the Rainbow Room to discuss the Music Hall's fate, and it is announced April 13 that it will remain open, not as a movie house but with stage shows featuring celebrity performers (and the famed Rockettes).

Films: Floyd Mutrux's *American Hot Wax* with Tim McIntyre as 1950s disk jockey Alan Freed, Fran Drescher, comedian Jay Leno; Paul Mazursky's *An Unmarried Woman* with Jill Clayburgh, Alan Bates. Also: Irvin Kirshner's *The Eyes of Laura Mars* with Faye Dunaway, Tommy Lee Jones; Robert Zemeckis's *I Wanna Hold Your Hand* with Nancy Allen, Bobby DiCicco; Woody Allen's *Interiors* with Kristin Griffith, Mary Beth Hurt, Diane Keaton; John Korty's *Oliver's Story* with Ryan O'Neal, Candice Bergen; Sylvester Stallone's *Paradise Alley* with Stallone, Lee Canalito, Armand Assante, screenplay based on a Damon Runyon story.

Actress Maggie McNamara dies of a sleeping-pill overdose at New York February 18 at age 48 (she has not appeared on stage or screen in 15 years and has worked as a typist); actor Gig Young dies by his own hand at New York October 19 at age 60 (apparently after fatally shooting his bride of 3 weeks).

 Broadway musicals: *On the Twentieth Century* 2/19 at the St. James Theater, with Imogene Coca, St. Louis-born actor Kevin Kline, 30, John Cullum, Boston-born actress Madeline Kahn, 35, music by Cy Coleman, book and lyrics by Betty Comden and Adolph Green, 453 perfs.; *Dancin'* 3/27 at the Broadhurst Theater, with 18 dancers, choreography by Bob Fosse, music by 25 composers from J. S. Bach to Neil Diamond, 1,774 perfs.; *Ain't Misbehavin'* 5/9 at the Longacre Theater, with Ken Page, Amelia McQueen, André De Shields, Charlotte Woodward, music and lyrics mostly by the late Thomas Wright "Fats" Waller, songs that include "Honeysuckle Rose," "Mean to Me," "The Joint Is Jumpin'," and the title song, 1,604 perfs.; *Runaways* 5/13 at the Plymouth Theater (after 76 perfs. at the Public/Cabaret Theater), with a 33-member cast that includes guitarist Elizabeth Swados, 27, music and lyrics by Swados, 274 perfs.; *The Best Little Whorehouse in Texas* 6/19 at the 46th Street Theater, with Missouri-born actor Henderson Forsythe, 60, music and lyrics by Carol Hall, choreography by dancer Tommy Tune, now 39, in a production financed by Universal Pictures, book by Putnam, Tex.-born journalist Larry L. King, 49, and Houston-born writer Peter Masterson, 44, based on King's *Playboy* magazine story about the closing of the "Chicken Ranch" at La Grange,

Texas, 1,584 perfs.; *The Act* 10/9 at the Majestic Theater, with Liza Minnelli, music by John Kander, lyrics by Fred Ebb, 233 perfs.; *Ballroom* 12/14 at the Majestic Theater, with Dorothy Loudon, Vincent Gardenia, music by Billy Goldenberg, lyrics by Alan Bergman and his wife, Marilyn, directed by Michael Bennett, 116 perfs.

Popular songs: "Just the Way You Are" by Bronx-born composer-piano bar performer William Martin "Billy" Joel, 29; "Three Times a Lady" by Tuskegee, Ala.-born songwriter Lionel Richie, 28, and the soul group The Commodores (Richie, Walter Orange, 31; Thomas McClary, 28; Ronald La Pread, 28; William King, 29; and Milan Williams, 29).

 Jimmy Connors wins in men's singles at the new USTA stadium in Flushing Meadow, Chris Evert in women's singles.

Yankee manager Billy Martin resigns in tears July 25 under pressure from principal owner George Steinbrenner after feuding with slugger Reggie Jackson and is succeeded by former Cleveland Indians pitcher Robert Granville "Bob" Lemon, 57, who was fired as manager of the Chicago White Sox June 30. The Yankees have trailed the Boston Red Sox by 14 games since mid-July but will win 48 of their next 68 games; Lemon will last less than a year, however, before being fired and replaced by Martin, who will manage the team until October 1980.

Yankee Stadium cannot bar female reporters from locker rooms under a ruling handed down in September by federal judge Constance Baker Motley in a case filed last year by *Sports Illustrated* reporter Melissa Lincoln (*née* Ludtke).

The Yankees beat the Boston Red Sox 5 to 4 in a one-game playoff for the American League eastern division title (a renovated Yankee Stadium draws a record crowd of 165,080 for the game), beat Kansas City 3 games to 1 to win the league pennant, and go on to win their 22nd World Series, defeating the Los Angeles Dodgers 4 games to 2 behind the pitching of Jim "Catfish" Hunter, now 32, Ron Guidry, Jim Beattie, 24, and reliever Rich Gossage, 27. Designated hitter Reggie Jackson gets nine hits, including a double and two home runs.

Norton Simon Industries moves fashion designer Halston into new quarters on the 22nd floor of the new Olympic Tower overlooking St. Patrick's Cathedral (*see* 1977). Halston designs a perfume and other products that are sold under the Halston name with considerable success (*see* 1982).

Longtime (1933–1955) *New York Times* fashion editor Virginia Pope dies at her 419 East 57th Street home January 16 at age 92; B. H. Wragge designer Sidney Wragge (originally Goldstein) of bone-marrow cancer at Boca Raton, Fla., March 23 at age 70; socialite Barbara Cushing "Babs" Paley of cancer at New York July 6 at age 63.

Reputed Mafia leader Joseph Columbo, Sr. dies of cardiac arrest at Newburgh, N.Y., May 22 at age 54. He has been paralyzed and semi-comatose since sustaining bullet injuries in 1971.

A precision robbery December 11 at the Lufthansa cargo terminal of JFK Airport nets more than $5 million in unmarked currency and $850,000 in jewelry for six or seven bandits.

Mayor Koch and Deputy Mayor Herman Badillo hire former State Urban Development Corp. chief executive Edward J. Logue to head the South Bronx Development Organization and address the problems exposed by President Carter's visit last year to Charlotte Street, where arson, drugs, and crime have blighted neigborhood after neighborhood. President Carter has pledged $1.5 billion to rebuild the area but is unable to deliver on his promise.

The U.S. Supreme Court rules 6 to 3 June 26 that the application of the landmarks law to Grand Central Terminal's real estate holdings did not constitute a "taking" of the property "within the meaning of the Fifth Amendment as made applicable to the States by the Fourteenth Amendment" (*see* 1977). The Municipal Art Society has appealed last year's lower court decision. "In a wide variety of contexts," says the majority opinion (written by Justice William J. Brennan, Jr.), "the government may execute laws or programs that adversely affect recognized economic values without its action constituting a 'taking' . . . That the Landmarks Law affects some landowners more severely than others does not itself result in 'taking,' for that is often the case with general welfare and zoning legislation . . . Landmarks cannot be divorced from aesthetics—particularly when the setting is dramatic and integral part of the original concept. The terminal in its setting is a great example of urban design. Such examples are not so plentiful in New York City that we can afford to lose any of the few we have, and we must preserve them in a meaningful way—with alterations and additions of such character, scale and materials and mass as will enhance, protect and perpetuate the original design rather than overwhelm it."

The dean of the Cathedral of St. John the Divine inaugurates a stone-cutting apprentice program for the cathedral's unfinished south tower and announces a design competition for the south transept (*see* 1941; 1982).

Delirious New York: A Retroactive Manifesto for Manhattan by Dutch architect Rem Koolhaas, 33, reinterprets the city from a contemporary point of view at a time when some architects are prepared to dismiss the modern movement as a conspiracy to replace everything with glass boxes. Koolhaas has been a Visiting Fellow of New York's Institute for Architecture and Urban Studies since 1973.

Architect Edward Durrell Stone dies at New York August 6 at age 76.

The 48-year-old Chrysler Building is designated a New York City Landmark September 12.

AIA Guide to New York City by New York-born architect-teacher Norval (Crawford) White, 52, and Brooklyn-born architect preservationist Elliot Willensky, 45, is the first comprehensive architectural guide to any U.S. city. Along with architectural descriptions of buildings, it includes maps, walking tours, and illustrations.

The 35-story Piaget Building is completed at 650 Fifth Avenue, southwest corner 52nd Street. Designed by John Carl Warnecke for the Shah of Iran's Pahlavi Foundation, it occupies a site formerly used by the De Pinna store and will remain vacant for some years before Piaget takes over office space.

The 34-story 800 Fifth Avenue apartment house designed by Wechsler & Schimenti is completed at the northeast corner of 61st Street, opposite the Hotel Pierre, on a site formerly occupied by the Geraldine R. Dodge mansion (the late Mrs. Marcellus Hartley Dodge [*née* Rockefeller] lived in New Jersey and rarely used the house).

The 33-story 30 Lincoln Plaza apartment house is completed at 1844-96 Broadway, northeast corner 62nd Street, to designs by Philip Birnbaum. Its plaza contains a waterfall, pool, and lawn, with a complex of movie theaters below ground.

The 46-story 265 East 66th Street apartment house is completed at the northwest corner of Second Avenue with 301 rental units. Designed by William Wilson of Gruzen Sampton Steinglass for developer Sheldon Solow, the bronze-glass tower fills the west side of the block between 66th and 67th streets.

 The City Council enacts a "Pooper Scooper" law following a campaign waged largely by activist Fran Lee (Mrs. Samuel Weiss), 68, a former actress and one-time kindergarten teacher. The city has 500,000 dogs, according to an estimate by the Society for the Prevention of Cruelty to Animals (SPCA), and only a fraction of them are licensed. Dog owners are required by the law to clean up the mess left when they walk their animals, peer pressure makes most owners co-operate, and the Sanitation Department estimates that 60 percent comply with the law.

A Waldbaum's supermarket in Brooklyn's Sheepshead Bay section goes up in flames August 2, six firefighters are killed when a roof collapses, and others are brought to Coney Island Hospital in critical condition.

Mayor Koch opens the 30,000-square-foot Pathmark supermarket in Brooklyn's Bedford-Stuyvesant February 18 (*see* 1977). Pathmark has been opening 24-hour-per-day stores throughout the New York-New Jersey-Philadelphia metropolitan area since its founding by Herb Brody, Milton Perlmutter, and Alex Aidekman 10 years ago; its newest is the largest such store to have been built in Bed-Stuy in more than 20 years.

All remaining Automats except one at 200 East 42nd Street are converted to Burger King outlets (*see* 1912). Labor problems have been squeezing Automat profits; the chain's blue-collar clientele has gone to the suburbs; and unemployed and homeless people who nurse cups of coffee for hours while smoking endless endless cigarettes have discouraged other patrons, as has the declining quality of the chicken pot pie and creamed spinach and the disappearance of such favorites as warm apple pie with vanilla sauce. The 20-year-old Automat that remains (at the southeast corner of 42nd Street and Third Avenue) will survive until 1991, mostly as a venue for upscale parties.

Legislation signed by Gov. Carey May 11 ends the ban on using the word "saloon" for an establishment selling alcoholic beverages, a holdover from Prohibition days.

Waldorf-Astoria maitre d' Philippe of the Waldorf (Claudius C. Philippe) dies of heart failure at New York December 25 at age 68.

1979 Former vice president and New York governor Nelson A. Rockefeller suffers a fatal heart attack January 26 at age 70. It is initially reported that a security guard found him dead at his desk in his RCA Building office where he had been editing an art book, but it then comes to light that he was making love with a young woman aide at his 13 West 54th Street town house. Rockefeller and his second wife, Happy, have lived since their 1963 marriage in the triplex at 812 Fifth Avenue.

Iran's Riza Shah Pahlevi is permitted entry to the United States October 22 at the insistence of former secretary of state Henry A. Kissinger and Chase Manhattan president David Rockefeller despite warnings from the U.S. ambassador in Teheran. Terminally ill with cancer, the shah is admitted to New York Hospital for removal of his gall bladder, and Iranian terrorists seize the U.S. embassy at Teheran November 4, taking 66 hostages and demanding extradition of the shah; he departs for Panama via Texas December 16.

Civil war breaks out in El Salvador, prompting a mass migration of Salvadorans, many as illegal aliens, to New York City, whose population now includes fewer than 7,000 people from the tiny Central American country, most of them middle-class.

Some of New York's Korean dry cleaners, fishmongers, grocers, and other businessmen come under attack from a few organizations, predominantly black, whose members fear losing business to the immigrants and picket their stores (see 1988).

Civil rights leader A. Philip Randolph dies at New York May 16 at age 90; union leader Jacob S. Potofsky of cancer at New York August 5 at age 84.

Loeb Rhoades Hornblower becomes Shearson Loeb Rhoades in May after being acquired by Shearson Hayden Stone, headed by Sanford I. Weill (see 1978; 1981; Hayden Stone, 1906; Weill, 1960). John M. Loeb, now 77, and his family retain their arbitrage, investment banking, real estate, and venture capital operations and will continue to operate under the name Loeb Partners (see 1981).

Former Dillon Read chairman Clarence Dillon dies at his Far Hills, N.J., home April 14 at age 96, leaving a vast estate that includes the Château Haut-Brion Bordeaux vineyards and large pieces of choice New Jersey property; ready-to-wear coat and suit maker Ben Zuckerman dies at Palm Beach, Fla., August 10 at age 89.

Gold prices top $300 per ounce for the first time in history July 18, President Carter appoints New York banker Paul A. Volcker, 52, chairman of the Federal Reserve Board in August, gold prices top $400 per ounce September 27 as world financial markets react to inflation worries.

The New York Cocoa Exchange merges with the Coffee and Sugar Exchange.

Lazard Frères chairman-philanthropist-art collector André Meyer dies of pneumonia and other ill-nesses at Lausanne, Switzerland, September 19 at age 81, having headed the firm since 1943. He leaves a fortune of at least $250 million (and possibly twice that much); Paris-born Michel (Alexandre) David-Weill, 46, succeeds Meyer as chairman of the family-owned firm and with help from deal maker Felix Rohatyn will continue Lazard's preeminence in mergers and acquisitions.

Paul Volcker announces October 6 that he is imposing a 1 percent increase in the discount interest rate that Federal Reserve banks charge member institutions. The move to halt inflation sends stock prices sharply lower and begins a short recession. Double- and even triple-digit inflation plagues much of the world. U.S. prices increase 13.3 percent for the year, largest jump in 33 years, and the Federal Reserve Board's move in October to tighten the money supply sparks a jump in loan rates that will continue for 6 months. Banks raise their prime loan rate to 14.5 percent October 9, Wall Street's Dow Jones Industrial Average falls 26.48 points that day, and the New York Stock Exchange has a record 81.6 million share day October 10 as small investors panic. The U.S. Gross National Product has risen by more than a third in constant dollars since 1969, and unemployment has averaged less than 6 percent (it topped 9 percent in only one calendar year, versus a peak of 25 percent in the 1930s when the GNP rose by only 4 percent and when stock prices declined by only 31 percent as compared to 42 percent in the 1970s).

Funds manager George Soros splits with his partner Jim Rogers late in the year and renames the Soros Fund the Quantum Fund (see 1973); he has quietly gained a reputation for wizardry in money management and borrows a term from physics with an allusion to work by the late German physicist Werner Heisenberg, who postulated the idea in 1927 that it is impossible to predict accurately the speed or velocity of an atomic particle; Soros will use his wits to predict future movements in currency-exchange rates and make himself a billionaire (see Plaza Accord, 1985).

Wall Street's Dow Jones Industrial Average closes November 7 at 976.67, falls sharply in the weeks that follow, but closes December 31 at 838.74, up from 805.51 at the end of 1978.

Fortunoff Fine Jewelry and Silverware opens a Fifth Avenue store in October (see 1964).

Iran's new government announces February 17 that oil exports will resume March 5 at a price about 30 percent higher than that set by the OPEC nations in December 1978. Iranian production averages only

3.4 million barrels per day for the year, down from 5.4 million last year. Since the 900,000 barrels of Iranian crude imported daily by the United States last year supplied 6 percent of U.S. consumption, the drop in Iranian imports creates genuine fuel shortages in many states. The New York City Rent Guidelines Board votes April 4 to let landlords levy fuel-cost surcharges retroactive to March 1 of 2.5 percent to 8.5 percent on tenants of rent-stabilized apartments. New York motorists line up at filling stations from spring through summer and are often unable to obtain more than a few gallons at a time.

The Board of Estimate gives unanimous approval January 11 to a bill awarding a 10-year contract to the Convention and Safety Corp. to erect and maintain 4,100 bus shelters, beginning with structures in Brooklyn, Queens, and Staten Island. Busstop Shelter, Inc. has pioneered the idea with 500 shelters in Manhattan and the Bronx, defraying its costs by selling advertising space.

The city wins a lawsuit against Pullman, Inc. and Rockwell International in a case involving 754 defective subway cars. Arthur L. Liman of Paul, Weiss, Rifkind, Wharton & Garrison represents the city and asks how it can be that Rockwell, a key player in the Apollo space program, was able to put a man on the moon but could not transport a man from 34th Street to 42nd. The court awards the city a judgment of $72 million.

The Metropolitan Transportation Authority introduces a "diamond jubilee" token October 12 to mark the 75th anniversary of the subway system. It features a picture of the original subway kiosk and the phrase, "People Moving People;" 5.8 million of the tokens are minted.

New York taxi-fleet owners gain the right to impose a 50¢ surcharge on rides between 8 o'clock in the evening and 6 o'clock in the morning. Independent owner-drivers soon win the same right.

St. Luke's-Roosevelt Hospital Center is created October 1 by a merger of St. Luke's Hospital, opened in 1858, and Roosevelt Hospital, opened in 1871. It is the largest merger thus far of nonprofit teaching hospitals.

The New York Infirmary for Indigent Women and Children merges with Downtown Hospital, having become a gender-neutral facility in the 1960s (see 1857; New York Hospital, 1991).

Hasidic Satmar leader Rabbi Joel Teitelbaum dies of a heart attack at New York August 19 at age 93.

Pope John Paul II visits New York for a third time and appears at Yankee Stadium October 7. Archbishop Fulton J. Sheen dies of heart disease at New York December 9 at age 84.

Business Week magazine founder Malcolm Muir dies of bronchial pneumonia at New York January 30 at age 93; New York Times assistant managing editor and English language authority Theodore M. Bernstein of cancer at New York June 27 at age 74; publisher Samuel I. Newhouse of a stroke at New York August 29 at age 84; Time magazine publisher Roy E. Larsen at Fairfield, Conn., September 10 at age 80.

Mayor Koch orders the city's municipal radio station WNYC to broadcast the names of men convicted of patronizing prostitutes, but the so-called "John Hour" airs only once. The mayor promises not to interfere with the station hereafter.

Nonfiction: The Powers That Be by New York-born journalist David Halberstam, 45, is about the media; The Streets Were Paved with Gold by New York-born New Yorker magazine and New York Daily News writer Ken Auletta, 37; Essential New York by John Tauranac; The City Observed by New York Times architectural critic Paul Goldberger, 29; How We Lived: A Documentary History of Immigrant Jews in America by Irving Howe and Kenneth Libo; New York by Scranton, Pa.-born New York Times promotion copywriter William F. Harris, Jr., 45; Life at the Dakota by Stephen Birmingham; Under the Sidewalks of New York: The Story of the Greatest Subway System in the World by Brian J. Cudahy (revised editions will appear in 1988 and 1995).

Barnes & Noble's Leonard Riggio buys six Marboro Books stores and a mail-order operation in October as he expands his discount book chain (see 1971; B. Dalton, 1986).

Humorist S. J. Perelman dies at New York October 17 at age 75; author Richard H. Rovere of emphysema at Poughkeepsie November 23 at age 64.

Fiction: The Ghost Writer by Philip Roth; Good as Gold by Joseph Heller; Sleepless Nights by Elizabeth Hardwick; The Subway to New York by English novelist-poet Philip (Kenneth) Callow, 54.

Novelist Helen Van Slyke dies of cancer at New York July 3 at age 59; James T. Farrell of a heart attack at New York August 22 at age 75.

The Metropolitan Museum of Art's Sackler Wing is completed to house the Temple of Dendur, moved from Egypt and donated (along with the wing) by

Medical Tribune publisher Arthur Sackler and his brothers. Kevin Roche John Dinkeloo & Associates has designed the wing with a glass wall facing Central Park to the north.

Artforum is acquired from Charles Cowles in October by a group headed by Anthony Korner (*see* 1967). Korner and his associate publisher Amy Baker (later Amy Sandback) will improve the magazine's paper stock and color, give it a perfect binding, employ clearer typography, and work to make its writing more accessible.

Portrait photographer Philippe Halsman dies at New York June 25 at age 73.

Theater: *Wings* by Arthur Kopit 1/28 at the Lyceum Theater, with Constance Cummings, now 68, as a woman who has suffered a stroke, 113 perfs.; *On Golden Pond* by Bellows Falls, Vt.-born playwright (Richard) Ernest Thompson, 29, 2/28 at the New Apollo Theater, with Tom Aldredge, Washington, D.C.-born actress Frances Sternhagen, 38, 126 perfs.; *Knockout* by Hoboken-born playwright Louis LaRusso II, 43, 5/6 at the Helen Hayes Theater, with Danny Aiello, 154 perfs.; *Loose Ends* by Michael Weller 6/7 at the Circle in the Square Theater, with Kevin Kline, Trenton, N.J.-born actress Roxanne Hart, 26, 270 perfs.; *Romantic Comedy* by Bernard Slade 11/8 at the Ethel Barrymore Theater, with Anthony Perkins, Mia Farrow, 396 perfs.; *Bent* by Philadelphia-born playwright Martin Sherman, 40, 12/2 at the New Apollo Theater, with Richard Gere, San Francisco-born actor David Dukes, 34, Westport, Conn.-born ingénu David Marshall Grant, 24, 241 perfs.

Broadway producer-director Herman Shumlin dies of heart failure at New York June 14 at age 80; actress-author Cornelia Otis Skinner of a cerebral hemorrhage at New York July 9 at age 78; producer Jed Harris at New York November 15 at age 79.

Films: Ira Wohl's documentary *Best Boy* with Philly Wohl, Zero Mostel; Robert Benton's *Kramer vs. Kramer* with Dustin Hoffman, Meryl Streep; Woody Allen's *Manhattan* with Allen, Mariel Hemingway, Diane Keaton, Marshall Brickman; Leon Ichaso and Orlando Jiminez-Leal's *El Super* with Raymundo Hidalgo-Gato, Zully Montero (probably the first Spanish-language film to be shot in New York); Philip Kaufman's *The Wanderers* with Ken Wahl, John Friedrich; Walter Hill's *The Warriors* with Michael Beck, James Remar, Thomas Waites in a drama about New York street gangs. Also: Robert Moore's *Chapter Two* with James Caan, Marsha Mason; David Helpern's *Something Short of Paradise*

with Susan Sarandon (originally Susan Abigail Tomalin), David Steinberg, Jean-Pierre Aumont.

Director Nicholas Ray dies of cancer at New York June 16 at age 67.

Broadway and off-Broadway musicals: *They're Playing Our Song* 2/11 at the Imperial Theater, with Hollywood-born ingénue Lucie Arnaz, 19, New York-born comedian Robert Klein, 36, book by Neil Simon, music by Marvin Hamlisch, lyrics by Carole Bayer Sager, 1,082 perfs.; *Sweeny Todd* 3/1 at the Uris Theater, with Len Cariou as the "demon barber of Fleet Street," Angela Lansbury, music and lyrics by Stephen Sondheim, songs that include "Pretty Women," 558 perfs.; *Scrambled Feet* (revue) 6/11 at the Village Gate, with Jeffrey Haddon, 31, John Driver, 32, Evalyn Barron, Roger Neil, skits and songs by Haddon and Driver; *Evita* 9/25 at the Broadway Theater (it opened at London's Prince Edward Theater 6/21/78) with Northport, N.Y.-born actress Patti LuPone, 30, as Eva Perón, music by Andrew Lloyd Webber, lyrics by Tim Rice, songs that include "Don't Cry For Me, Argentina," 1,566 perfs.; *Sugar Babies* 10/8 at the Mark Hellinger Theater, with Ann Miller, Mickey Rooney, songs by Jimmy McHugh, additional lyrics by Arthur Malvin, scenic design and costumes by Raoul Pène Du Bois, 1,208 perfs.; *One Mo' Time* by New Orleans-born actor-singer-dancer-playwright Vernel Bagneris, 30, 10/22 at the Village Gate Downstairs, with Bagneris, 1,372 perfs.

Broadway writer-lyricist Guy Bolton dies at London September 5 at age 94; comedian Zero Mostel at Philadelphia September 8 at age 62; composer Richard Rodgers of throat cancer at New York December 30 at age 77.

English punk rock star Sid Vicious (originally John Simon Ritchie), 21, of the Sex Pistols is released on bail at New York February 1 after being charged with fatally stabbing his former girlfriend at the Chelsea Hotel in October of last year; he celebrates with a party in another girl's Greenwich Village apartment and dies of a heroin overdose February 2 (*see* Films, 1986).

Liza Minnelli makes her Carnegie Hall debut 4/4 at age 33 and dazzles the audience as her late mother, Judy Garland, did at age 38 in 1961.

Rock singer James Taylor, now 31, gives a concert in Central Park's Sheep Meadow 7/31 and attracts a crowd estimated to number 250,000.

Metropolitan Opera Guild founder and society grandame Eleanor Robson (Mrs. August) Belmont dies at New York October 24 at age 100.

Popular songs: *52nd Street* (album) by Billy Joel; "Do Ya Think I'm Sexy?" by Rod Stewart.

The Walkman casette player introduced by Sony Corp. is a $200 pocket stereo with two pairs of earphones, making it possible to hear high-fidelity sound in any location without disturbing one's neighbors. It is the brainchild of Sony chairman Akio Morita, now 58, and will soon have an FM radio version, but some New Yorkers will continue to use "boom boxes" and "ghetto blasters."

The Underground disco nightclub opens at 860 Broadway on Union Square, where it will continue until 1991.

 Douglaston, Queens, player John McEnroe, 20, wins in men's singles at Forest Hills, Tracy Ann Austin, 16, (U.S.) in women's singles.

Yankee catcher Thurman Munson crashes his private jet near Canton, Ohio, August 2 and dies at age 32; Dodgers owner Walter F. O'Malley dies of emphysema at Rochester, Minn., August 9 at age 75.

 The Guardian Angels volunteer crime-fighting group has its beginnings in the Magnificent Thirteen Subway Safety Patrol formed in February. New York-born founder Curtis Sliwa, 24, and his comrades ride the subways wearing T-shirts and red berets, make citizen's arrests, rename themselves in September, and will eventually have more than 1,000 members, but many question the vigilante aspects of the group.

Blonde, blue-eyed schoolboy Etan Patz leaves his family's loft at 113 Prince Street May 25 to walk to his school bus alone for the first time; the 6-year-old will never be seen again, and his disappearance will remain a mystery despite extensive police investigation.

Hitmen hired by an underworld rival gun down Mafia boss Carmine Galante, 69, as he eats lunch at a Brooklyn café July 12. Head of a 200-member "family" formerly led by Joseph Bonanno, Sr., Galante had hoped to succeed the late Carlo Gambino as the "boss of bosses;" police say he has been marked for execution for more than a year.

A New York State law that takes effect September 1 modifies the severe penalties (mandatory life sentences for anyone convicted of selling any amount of heroin, cocaine, morphine, or other "hard" drug) of the law put through by former governor Nelson Rockefeller in 1973. Hundreds of persons are serving longer terms for selling or possessing small amounts of drugs than for rape or robbery, the old

The Guardian Angels vigilante group took it upon itself to police the city's graffiti-covered subways. CHIE NISHIO

law has not helped to control the drug traffic, and state courts are backlogged with cases of people standing trial rather than working out plea bargains, but the 1973 law will remain on the books into the 21st century.

 A 24-story limestone apartment house is completed opposite the Metropolitan Museum of Art at 1001 Fifth Avenue, between 81st and 82nd streets. Replacing two old town houses that had stood between a Beaux Arts apartment house dating to 1903 and a tall McKim, Mead & White town house dating to 1911, it has been designed in International Style by Philip Birnbaum with a limestone façade by Philip Johnson and John Burgee.

The 35-story Taino Towers apartment complex is completed in a block bounded by 122nd and 123rd streets and Second and Third avenues. Silverman & Cika has designed the complex for the East Harlem Tenants' Committee. Built at a cost of $48.5 million with pre-cast concrete, concrete cast on the spot, rounded corners and landscaped plazas, its first six floors are occupied by rent-paying community services (there are 225,000 square feet of commercial space); the four glass towers contain generous-sized apartments with huge picture windows, and some have glass walls from floor to ceiling, but although there is central air conditioning, a swimming pool, a health-care center, a theater, the city's first vacuum garbage-disposal system, and other upscale amenities, the place will remain largely unoccupied until the mid-1980s.

Mayor Koch approves the appointment of Central Park's first administrator: city planner Elizabeth "Betsy" Barlow, now 43, has played a prominent role in private efforts to protect the park during the city's fiscal crisis, working with the Central Park Community Fund, the Central Park Task Force, Friends of Central Park, and the Parks Council. Parks Commissioner Gordon Davis is a former City Planning Commission member and has recommended the appointment, placing responsibility for the park's maintenance and quotidian operations in the hands of one person for the first time since Frederick Law Olmsted's dismissal in 1878 (see Central Park Conservancy, 1980).

Central Park's 15-acre Sheep Meadow closes for a renovation that will take 2 years to complete. Used for concerts, ball fields, and the like, its grass has been destroyed, leaving it a dust bowl (see 1981).

La Côte Basque at 5 East 55th Street is acquired by Jean-Jacques Rachou, who revitalizes its kitchen and (in 1983) will enlarge its premises.

Le Chanterelle opens at 89 Grand Street, corner Green Street, in SoHo. Proprietress Karen Waltuck has brought in Hollywood set designer Bill Katz to design the place; her husband, David, is the chef, and it buys its cheeses at the nearby Dean and DeLuca shop (see 1989).

The *Zagat New York City Restaurant Survey* is introduced by local corporate lawyer Timothy Zagat, 40, and his lawyer wife, Nina, who like to eat out and have rated restaurants according to "customer satisfaction" as determined by 150 friends and acquaintances. The burgundy-covered, pocket-sized Zagat Surveys will grow to cover more than 30 major U.S. and foreign cities with some 75,000 unpaid survey participants, most of them amateur critics who fill out extensive questionnaires, and by 1994 the Zagats will be grossing $7 million, netting about $1.5 million after paying 25 full-time employees and covering other costs.

1980 Former state comptroller Arthur Levitt dies of a heart attack at his Lincoln Savings Bank desk May 6 at age 79, having declined to run for reelection in 1978 and supported Republican nominee Edward V. Regan in his successful campaign because he deplored Democrat Harrison J. Goldin's inclination to use state pension funds to relieve the city's fiscal crisis.

Voters turn President Carter out of office and elect former California governor (and former film actor) Ronald (Wilson) Reagan, now 69, who campaigns with slick television commercials and wins 489 electoral votes to Carter's 149, with 51 percent of the popular vote (43.2 million) vs. 42.5 percent (34.9 million) for Carter (whose New York City vote is much larger than Reagan's except in Staten Island, where Republican Reagan wins).

Nassau County Republican Alfonse M. D'Amato, 43, of Hempstead wins election to the U.S. Senate, succeeding Sen. Javits, now 76, whose age and health became big issues in D'Amato's campaign. Running on the Republican, Conservative, and Right to Life Party tickets, D'Amato receives 2,532,925 votes, narrowly defeating Brooklyn congresswoman Liz Holtzman, now 39, who has defeated former mayor Lindsay and another contender in the Democratic primary, is supported by the United Federation of Teachers, and receives 2,459,639 votes. Liberal Party candidate Javits has the support of violinist Isaac Stern but trails badly with 611,163.

Representatives of the neighborhood-based East Brooklyn Congregations give Borough President Howard Golden their resignations from local community boards and demand a meeting with Democratic Party county leader Meade Esposito to discuss the absence of city services in their district. By the time of the 1984 elections, EBC will have registered 10,000 new voters, 70 percent of them black.

Bensonhurst, Brooklyn, welder Ralph Tarrantino, 29, dies August 24 after what neighbors describe as a police beating following a dispute. He has swung an iron pipe at a neighbor and an autopsy shows that Tarrantino's blood contains the street drug phencyclidine, known as "angel dust," that sometimes causes users to become violent; the autopsy report says Tarrantino died of "cardiac arrest" during a hospital procedure when a tube was introduced into his chest to relieve pressure.

A federal jury at New York convicts Italian financier Michele Sindona March 27 on 65 counts of fraud, conspiracy, false statements, and perjury in connection with the 1974 failure of Franklin National Bank, the 20th largest U.S. bank; it sentences him June 13 to 25 years in prison (see 1984).

Swingline Inc. founder Jack Linsky dies at a West Palm Beach, Fla., hospital June 3 at age 83; he sold his stapler company to American Brands for $210 million 10 years ago and remained chairman until he retired in 1975.

Wall Street's Dow Jones Industrial Average closes April 21 at 759.13 but closes December 31 at 963.99, up from 838.74 at the end of 1979. Gold falls to $600 per ounce by year's end, having peaked at $875 in January amidst predictions of $2,000 as double-digit inflation continues, with prices rising 12.4 percent by year's end as compared to 13.3 percent last year, fueling opposition to President Carter. A recession in the second quarter has cut real output by 9.9 percent; the economy is on the rise again by fall.

A water leak at the Consolidated Edison nuclear reactor at Indian Point October 3 and subsequent leaks force a temporary shutdown of the facility. Con Ed announces at month's end that it will add about 10 percent to customers' bills to make up for the extra $800,000 per day it has been forced to pay for oil.

A city transit strike ends April 11 after 35,000 workers have stopped the city's 6,400 subway cars and 4,550 buses for 11 days, forcing 5.4 million people to walk, bike, or find other means of transportation. The archaic, crime-ridden, graffiti-defaced subways remain dirty and dangerous; the Metropolitan Transportation Authority issues a solid brass token June 28 with a Y engraved in its center but not cut out as in earlier tokens (see fare rise, 1981).

The West Side High Line that opened in 1934 runs its last train, carrying a load of frozen turkeys. The demise of industry in the area has made the line an anachronism, and its right-of-way will soon be covered with grass and weeds.

Reformer and journalist Dorothy Day dies of cancer November 29 at age 83, having spent her final days in her beachfront bungalow on Staten Island. The monthly Catholic Worker she cofounded in 1933 still sells for 1¢ per copy and still has a circulation of about 85,000.

Random House publishers is acquired for $60 million from RCA by Newhouse Publications, whose owners diversify into book publishing and change their company name to Advance Publications (see Bertelsmann, 1998).

Nonfiction: New York in the Nineteenth Century by New York writer John Grafton; The Villard Houses: Life Story of a Landmark by NYU architectural histo-

rian Mosette Broderick (née Glaser), 35 (with William Shopsin); Public Enemies: The Mayor, the Mob, and the Crime That Was by George Walsh.

Author and New Yorker magazine contributor St. Clair McKelway dies at New York January 10 at age 74.

Fiction: So Long, See You Tomorrow by former New Yorker magazine writer-editor William Maxwell, now 71; Loon Lake by E. L. Doctorow; Green Monday by New York-born Metropolitan Museum of Art curator-turned Lehman Brothers investment banker-turned novelist Michael M. (Mackenzie) Thomas, 44.

Poetry: Satan Says by San Francisco-born New York poet Sharon Olds, 37.

Poet Muriel Rukeyeser dies of a heart attack at New York February 12 at age 66.

Painting: Dancers on a Plane (oil and acrylic on canvas with painted bronze frame) by Jasper Johns; Joined and Breaking (both oil on two canvases) by Elizabeth Murray; Crisis Moment (collage of oil and paper) and Vernal Yellow (collage of oil and paper on canvas) by Lee Krasner. Philip Guston dies at Woodstock, N.Y., June 7 at age 66.

Sculpture: Gay Liberation by George Segal. Sculptor Tony Smith dies of congestive heart failure at New York Hospital December 26 at age 68.

The Fun Gallery opens on 10th Street in the East Village—the first commercial venture in the hybrid of punk rock and visual art. The area will soon have close to 50 art galleries, many of them operated out of private residences, with names like the Civilian Warfare Gallery, the Gracie Mansion Gallery, and the International with Monument Gallery.

The Metropolitan Museum of Art's American wing is completed to designs by Kevin Roche/John Dinkeloo and Associates.

The Sotheby's art auction house founded at London in 1744 opens as the Sotheby, Parke-Bernet York Avenue Gallery at 1334 York Avenue, between 71st and 72nd streets. Lundquist & Stonehill has converted a 51-year-old Eastman Kodak Co. office building; it will be expanded in 9 years by Michael Graves as Sotheby's becomes the city's major venue for selling works of art.

Photography: New York by Bridgeport, Conn.-born architectural photographer Philip Trager, 45, with text by author Louis Auchincloss.

Theater: The Lady from Dubuque by Edward Albee 1/31 at the Morosco Theater, with Irene Worth, 12 perfs.; *Talley's Folly* by Lanford Wilson 2/10 at the Brooks Atkinson Theater, with Judd Hirsch, Trish Hawkins, 279 perfs.; *Children of a Lesser God* by Mark Medoff 3/30 at the Longacre Theater, with John Rubinstein as the speech therapist for hearing-impaired students, North Dakota-born actress Phyllis Frelich, 36 (totally deaf since birth), as the student he marries, 854 perfs.; *I Ought to Be in Pictures* by Neil Simon 4/3 at the Eugene O'Neill Theater, with New York-born actor Ron Leibman, 42, New York-born ingénue Dinah Manoff, 22 (daughter of Lee Grant), Joyce Van Patten, 324 perfs.; *Home* by North Carolina-born actor-playwright Samm-Art (Samuel Arthur) Williams, 33, 5/7 at the Cort Theater, with Charles Brown, 56, L. Scott Caldwell, Michelle Shay, 278 perfs.; *The Fifth of July* by Lanford Wilson 11/3 at the New Apollo Theater, with New York-born actor Christopher Reeve, 28, Swoosie Kurtz, 511 perfs.; *True West* by Sam Shepard 12/23 at the Public Theater, with Peter Boyle, Tommy Lee Jones, 52 perfs.

Yiddish theater veteran Ida Kaminska dies of a heart ailment at New York May 21 at age 80; actor-writer Donald Ogden Stewart at London August 2 at age 85; actor-playwright Elliott Nugent at New York August 9 at age 83; director-producer Harold Clurman of cancer at New York September 9 at age 78; playwright Marc Connelly at New York December 21 at age 90; actor Sam Levene of a heart attack in his St. Moritz Hotel apartment December 26 at age 75.

Television: *Bosom Buddies* 11/29 on ABC with Tom Hanks, 24, Peter Scolari, 26 (to 9/15/1984).

Films: Martin Scorsese's *Raging Bull* with Robert De Niro as middleweight boxer Jake La Motta. Also: Brian G. Hutton's *The First Deadly Sin* with Frank Sinatra as a New York City police officer, Faye Dunaway; Colin Higgins's *9 to 5* with Jane Fonda, Lily Tomlin, and country singer-actress Dolly Parton as New York secretaries with a sexist boss.

Actress Lillian Roth dies of cancer at New York May 12 at age 69; actress-politician Helen Gahagan Douglas of cancer at New York June 28 at age 71; producer-playwright Dore Schary of cancer at New York July 7 at age 74.

Film musical: Alan Parker's *Fame* with Bronx-born actress-singer Irene Cara, 21, Lee Curreri, Eddie Barth, Brooklyn-born actress-comedienne Anne Meara, 51, music by Michael Gore, lyrics by Dean Pitchford, story line about the aspirations, dreams, struggles, and failures of students at the High School for the Performing Arts.

Broadway musicals: *Barnum* 4/20 at the St. James Theater, with English-born actor-singer-songwriter Jim Dale, 41, as P. T. Barnum, music by Cy Coleman, lyrics by Michael Stewart, 854 perfs.; *42nd Street* 8/25 at the Winter Garden Theater, with Jerry Orbach (as Julian Marsh), Wanda Richert, Tammy Grimes, Peggy Cass, music and lyrics from the 1933 Hollywood musical (plus others by Harry Warren and Al Dubin), direction and choreography by Gower Champion (who dies opening night at age 61 of a rare blood cancer), 3,486 perfs.

Former Broadway musical star Kay Medford dies of cancer at her native New York April 10 at age 59.

The Mark Morris Dance Group is founded at New York by Seattle-born dancer-choreographer Morris, 24 (*see* 1990).

English-born rock star Elton John (originally Reginald Kenneth Dwight), 33, gives a concert on Central Park's Great Lawn 9/13 and attracts a crowd estimated to number 300,000.

Popular songs: *Double Fantasy* (album) by John Lennon and Yoko Ono (who sees her husband shot to death).

Jazz pianist Bill Evans dies of a bleeding ulcer and bronchial pneumonia at New York September 15 at age 51.

The 8-year-old New York Islanders hockey team wins its first Stanley Cup May 24, beating the Philadelphia Flyers 5 to 4 in overtime on home ice at the Nassau Coliseum in Uniondale. Islanders right wing Bob Nystrom scores the winning goal, but center Bryan Trottier, who has scored (or assisted in scoring) 29 points in the playoffs, receives the Conn Smythe Trophy awarded to the most valuable player. Having no Broadway, Fifth Avenue, or Main Street for their victory parade, the Islanders celebrate with a motorcade that goes around and around the Nassau Coliseum's parking lot.

Swedish tennis player Björn Borg, 24, defeats John McEnroe to win his fifth consecutive Wimbledon singles, but McEnroe defeats Borg to win in U.S. men's singles; Chris Evert-Lloyd wins in U.S. women's singles.

Former congressman Allard K. Lowenstein is mortally wounded March 14 at age 51 in his Rockefeller Center law office by New London, Conn., carpenter Dennis Sweeney, 37. A former associate in the civil rights movement, Sweeney walks out of the inner office, places a semi-automatic pistol on a secretary's desk, and waits for police to arrive. Lowenstein has been struck in the diaphragm and heart, he is rushed to the hospital, but he dies 6 hours later after surgery. Sweeney will be judged criminally insane in February of next year.

John Lennon of Beatles fame is shot to death December 8 outside the Dakota apartment building. Lennon's death at age 40 increases demands for gun control laws, but President-elect Reagan says more effective laws would not have prevented Lennon's shooting by a deranged fan.

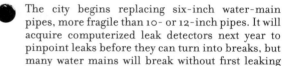 The Façade Bill signed into law February 27 requires building owners to have their structures examined by experts and to submit reports to the Buildings Department. Prompted by the death last year of a Barnard College freshman who was hit by a piece of masonry that fell from a Columbia University building, the law amends Chapter 27, Section 129 of the New York Administrative Code. Preservationists fear that some owners will strip their buildings of ornamentation rather than repair them, but this will happen only in a minority of cases.

Mayor Koch rejects a proposal to transform Times Square into an enclosed World's Fair environment that would be financed by rents from a "fashion mart" and big office towers that would be erected on the four corners of 42nd Street. Architects, designers, former city officials, and philanthropists have drawn up the plan, major foundations have supported it, but Koch finds it Disneyesque and says New York wants "seltzer instead of orange juice."

Metropolitan Life Insurance Co. makes a preliminary agreement in late July to buy the 17-year-old Pan Am Building at 200 Park Avenue for $400 million—the highest amount paid to date for any single building. It will be renamed the Met Life Building.

The Toronto-based developer Olympia & York is designated November 13 to undertake the entire commercial development of Battery Park City, the work to begin in 1981 and be completed by 1985 (see 1976; 1981).

The Milford Plaza Hotel opens on Eighth Avenue between 44th and 45th streets in late July with 1,310 rooms. Developer Paul Milstein and his brother Seymour have wangled a 20-year real estate tax abatement that has made it financially attractive to refurbish the old 28-story Lincoln Hotel.

Workmen with jackhammers destroy architectural features of the Biltmore Hotel's Palm Court in order to thwart efforts to have the room landmarked. The men act on orders from developer Paul Milstein.

The Grand Hyatt Hotel opens September 25 with 1,400 rooms. Designed by Der Scutt of Gruzen Samp-

ton Steinglass on the skeleton of the 1919 Commodore Hotel, the 30-story hotel has a mirrored glass façade and an atrium four stories high. The Commodore had been losing money for years and defaulting on its taxes when Queens developer Donald Trump, now 34, bought it in 1974 from the bankrupt Penn Central on condition that the city give him a huge tax break. Trump has been living in a three-bedroom apartment at the Phoenix apartment house, 160 East 65th Street.

The New York Palace Hotel (initially the Helmsley Palace Hotel) opens at 457 Madison Avenue between 50th and 51st streets. Designed by Emery Roth & Sons, the 55-story vertical shaft has 963 guest rooms, retaining the six landmarked brownstone Villard houses of 1884 to frame its avenue entrance: the south wing's Gold Room occupies the former offices of the New York diocese that sold its buildings to a developer in 1974 and is used by the hotel for a cocktail lounge (see restaurant, 1997); the north wing formerly used by Random House publishers becomes an Urban Center containing a bookstore plus offices for architectural groups that include the Municipal Art Society.

The city begins replacing six-inch water-main pipes, more fragile than 10- or 12-inch pipes. It will acquire computerized leak detectors next year to pinpoint leaks before they can turn into breaks, but many water mains will break without first leaking (see 1982).

The Bryant Park Restoration Corp. is founded to rescue the 96-year-old park from drug dealers and vagabonds who have discouraged its use by other citizens (see 1934). Set up by former LIFE magazine publisher Andrew W. Heiskell with seed money from the Rockefeller Brothers, the corporation hires as its executive director Daniel A. Biederman, 26, who has chaired Community Board 5 (see 1992).

The 85-year-old New York Zoological Society signs a contract with the city April 22 to operate the Central Park Zoo that opened in 1934. A Society design team headed by William Conway and Richard Lattis sets out to redesign the outdated facility (see 1988).

The Central Park Conservancy holds its first board meeting December 4 (see 1979); created at the urging of Park Administrator Betsy Barlow and headed by S&H trading stamp millionaire William Beinecke, the privately funded group will implement a 2-year-old plan to renew the park over a 10-year span at a cost of $100 million (the estimate will later rise to $150 million, the time span to 17 years, and by the end of fiscal year 1988 upwards of $84 million will have been spent, more than $60 million of it by the city, $21 million by the conservancy, more than $13 million by the New York Zoological Society.

✕ *Gourmet* magazine editor-publisher Earle McAusland dies on Nantucket Island June 4 at 89. Condé Nast will acquire the magazine, increasing its circulation and advertising.

The Odeon opens October 14 at 145 West Broadway, corner of Thomas Street, in TriBeCa (Triangle Below Canal). London-born brothers Keith and Brian McNally have started the restaurant with Lynn Wagenknecht (who will later marry Keith) and 300-pound, Brooklyn-born chef Patrick Clark, 25 (who has worked at Michel Guérard's restaurant in France but specializes in American cuisine). Clark and Brian McNally will move on to work at other places, leaving Lynn and Keith to run The Odeon with Clark's protégé Tony Sheck in charge of the kitchen.

New York's population falls to 7,071,639—its lowest level since 1930, with declines in every borough except Richmond (Staten Island). Brooklyn's Brownsville section was once mostly Jewish and second only to Manhattan's Lower East Side as a Jewish enclave but has now become almost completely black.

1981 New York has a ticker-tape parade January 30 to celebrate the release of U.S. hostages by Iran's fundamentalist Islamic regime established in 1979. Former congressman Emmanuel Celler has died at his Brooklyn home January 15 at age 92; onetime parks commissioner and power broker Robert Moses dies at East Islip, L.I., July 29 at age 92.

Mayor Koch crushes his Unity Party challenger Frank J. Barbaro to win reelection, piling up 912,622 votes to Barbaro's 162,719, but Koch has alienated his former Harlem supporters, including Puerto Rican-born Herman Badillo, now 52 (who was Bronx borough president before serving 2 years in Congress), Basil Patterson, and others.

Civil libertarian Roger Baldwin dies at his native New York August 26 at age 97.

$ Metropolitan (formerly East Brooklyn) Savings Bank acquires Greenwich Savings Bank and becomes a federal mutual savings bank (*see* 1978). It will change its name to Cross Land Savings Bank in 1983 and be the city's largest thrift by 1988, with assets of more than $15 billion (*see* 1992).

Shearson Loeb Rhoades merges with American Express Co. and becomes Shearson/American Express (*see* 1979). Sanford I. Weill has engineered the merger in hopes of going "beyond Wall Street to build a great American institution," but he will not be able to work out his differences with AmEx chairman James D. Robinson, III and will leave in August 1985 (*see* Commercial Credit, 1986).

The 71-year-old investment banking house Salomon Brothers becomes Phibro Salomon following a $550 million merger with the commodities firm Phibro Corp., founded at New York by Julius and Oscar Philipp in 1892 (*see* 1970). New York-born financier John Gutfreund, 52, has headed Salomon since William Salomon's retirement in 1978 and oversees the merger that will provide Salomon with enough capital to become the largest securities underwriting firm by the mid-1980s (Salomon Brothers will become simply Salomon in 1987; *see* 1991).

Bloomberg Financial Markets has its beginnings in a four-person midtown Manhattan office opened by Medford, Mass.-born 15-year Salomon Brothers veteran Michael R. (Rubens) Bloomberg, 39, who rose from a job as clerk sorting securities by hand to become a general partner (a block equity trader and computer-data designer) before Salomon merged with Phibro and dismissed Bloomberg with a $10 million golden parachute (*see* 1990).

Wall Street's Dow Jones Industrial Average closes January 6 at 1004.69 but closes December 31 at 875, down from 963.99 at the end of 1980. The prime interest rate has reached 21.5 percent, highest since the Civil War, double-digit inflation and high unemployment plague the economy, and President Reagan has signed a bill August 13 mandating the deepest tax and budget cuts in U.S. history. It follows "supply-side" economic theories that reject Keynesian ideas popular since the 1930s. Supply-siders led by California economist Arthur Laffer, 40, have claimed that reducing taxes will encourage business and the rich to invest in taxable activities rather than parking income in nonproductive tax shelters and will thus help the overall economy. While "Reaganomics" will be credited with producing the longest peacetime boom in history, it will also lead to neglect of cities like New York, deterioration of infrastructure, and massive deficits financed by foreign borrowing.

The Red Hook Marine Terminal opens on the Brooklyn waterfront to load and unload cargo containers (*see* 1956), but after some initial success its volume of cargo business will fall drastically and it will have to be subsidized to generate new business (*see* 1996).

Transit fares rise to 75¢ July 3, up from 60¢; the Metropolitan Transportation Authority has issued a new "bulls-eye" token April 21 with a steel center designed to combat counterfeiting (*see* 1980; 1984).

Pan American World Airways founder Juan Trippe dies at New York April 3 at age 81.

Air service out of La Guardia, Newark, JFK, and other U.S. airports drops 25 percent. President Reagan has signaled a tough new policy toward organized labor August 6 by dismissing air traffic controllers who have defied his return-to-work order. Patco (Professional Air Traffic Controllers Organization) has struck August 3, demanding a 4-day week and a $10,000-per-year raise. New air traffic controllers are trained to supplement the 2,000 remaining Patco workers plus 2,500 nonunion workers and military personnel; Patco is decertified as the bargaining body for air traffic controllers in October and files for bankruptcy in November.

IBM introduces its first personal computer August 12 and soon has 75 percent of the market. Its PC uses a Microsoft disk-operating system (MS-DOS); competitors quickly introduce lower-priced "clones."

AIDS (Acquired Immune Deficiency Syndrome) begins taking a worldwide toll that will be compared to that of the Black Death in the 14th century. New York and San Francisco physicians report that a few dozen previously healthy homosexual men have died of Kaposi's sarcoma, a form of cancer endemic in Africa but rare in the rest of the world. The men have suffered abnormalities of the immune system. St. Luke's-Roosevelt Hospital physicians diagnosed one of the first cases of an AIDS-related illness on the East Coast 2 years ago, and other New York doctors realize they have seen a number of similar cases in the past few years, all unexplained. More cases appear each month. Drug addicts, mostly black and Hispanic, in New York, Newark, and other northeastern cities begin dying of a previously rare pneumonia and other diseases brought on by a collapse of the body's disease-fighting ability. Invariably fatal, AIDS will be diagnosed in more than 32,000 Americans by early 1987, and nearly 60 percent will have died. Spread by exchange of bodily fluids containing a retrovirus, AIDS finds its victims almost exclusively among homosexual males, drug addicts using contaminated needles, people given prophylactic medical shots with such needles, or given transfusions of contaminated blood (*see* Gay Men's Health Crisis, 1982).

Acquired Immune Deficiency Syndrome began to exact a toll, especially in the art, fashion, music, and theater circles.

The Asia Society opens to the public in October at 725 Park Avenue, northeast corner 70th Street (formerly the site of the Gerrish Milliken house). The late John D. Rockefeller III founded the society in 1956, he donated about one-quarter of the $21 million that the new eight-story building has cost, Edward Larrabee Barnes has designed it, and it contains an auditorium and two galleries in addition to its reference library and offices.

Industrialist-philanthropist Eugene M. Lang, now 61, surprises 61 sixth graders in the auditorium of Harlem's P.S. 121 by promising them that if they obtain high-school diplomas he will make sure that they have a chance to attend college (*see* 1968). The Eugene M. Lang Foundation will provide scholarships for dozens of teenagers (*see* 1989).

CBS newsman Walter Cronkite, 64, goes off the air March 6 after 19 years as top U.S. "anchorman." Texas-born announcer Dan Rather, 49, succeeds him. Former newsman Lowell Thomas dies in his sleep of a heart attack at his Pawling, N.Y., home August 29 at age 89.

Reader's Digest co-founder DeWitt Wallace dies of pneumonia at suburban Mt. Kisco March 30 at age 91; former *Daily News* editorial writer Reuben Maury at a Norwalk, Conn., hospital April 22 at age 81.

Chicago's Tribune Co. announces December 18 that it plans to sell the *New York Daily News*, whose circulation and advertising have suffered sharp drops and is losing money at the rate of $11 million per year (*but see* 1982).

The $3.7 million Schomburg Center for Research in Black Culture opens at 515 Lenox Avenue in Harlem (*see* 1948). The New York Public Library has obtained federal, state, city, and private financing to help construct the new building that has space for lectures and educational programs, replacing the Countee Cullen branch in 135th Street as a research center. Jean Blackwell Hutson took over the collection in 1948 and has lobbied Albany and Washington for funds to construct the five-story, red-brick and glass, climate-controlled building; she retired as the Schomburg's chief last year at age 66 to take an administrative job at the Library's 42nd Street offices. By the time she dies early in 1998 the Schomburg Collection will have grown to hold 150,000 volumes, 3.5 million manuscripts, valuable artifacts, and the world's largest collection of photographs documenting black life.

Nonfiction: *When Harlem Was in Vogue* by Little Rock-born historian David Levering Lewis, 45; *Mornings on Horseback* by David McCullough is a biography of Theodore Roosevelt containing a good deal of New York history; *New York: A History* by Bruce Bliven, Jr., now 65, who deals with the entire state; *The New Metropolis: New York City, 1840–1857* by Fairlawn, N.J.-born Indiana State University history professor Edward K. (Kenneth) Spann, 50.

Author, railroad buff, and former *New Yorker* editor Roger E. M. Whitaker ("E. M. Frimbo") dies of cancer at New York May 11 at age 82.

Fiction: *Ellis Island and Other Stories* by Mark Helprin; *Women's Work* by New York-born advertising copywriter-turned-novelist Anne Tolstoi Wallach, 52; *The Further Adventures of Halley's Comet* by Bryn Mawr, Pa.-born New York novelist John Calvin Batchelor, 33.

 Painting: *Self-Portrait* by Alice Neel, now 81, who shows herself in her armchair wearing only her eyeglasses; *Artist with Painting and Model* (collage) by Romare Bearden; *Brush's Shadow, Heart and Mind*, and *Just in Time* (all oil on two canvases), *Painter's Progress* (oil on 19 canvases), and *Walk* (pastel drawing on paper) by Elizabeth Murray; *Twelve Hour Crossing, March Twenty-First* and *Between Two Appearances* (both collages of oil and paper on canvas) by Lee Krasner.

New York artist Frank Moore and the advocacy group Visual Aids invents the first version of the AIDS ribbon that will soon appear as a symbol of the loss, suffering, and anger related not only to the disease that now begins to take a heavy toll of the arts community but also of breast cancer and runaway children. Otherwise naked men will wear the AIDS ribbon as a thong in parades, a string of rubies will be made as a Tiffany version, and the ribbon will gain worldwide recognition.

Sculpture: *Tilted Arc* (rusting industrial Cor-ten steel) by Richard Serra is installed in Federal Plaza (the General Services Administration commissioned the work 2 years ago and has paid Serra $175,000, but the 12-foot-high, 120-foot-long wall obliges pedestrians to walk around it when they enter the Federal Building and it meets with almost immediate public scorn; *see* 1989).

Art scholar Alfred H. Barr, Jr. dies at Salisbury, Conn., August 15 at age 79, having served as first director of the Museum of Modern Art (MoMA) from 1929 to 1943.

The Metropolitan Museum of Art's Michael C. Rockefeller Wing for Primitive Art, André Meyer Galleries for European Paintings, and Dillon Galleries for Far East Art are completed to designs by Kevin Roche/John Dinkeloo and Associates.

Otto L. Bettmann, now 78, sells his 46-year-old Bettmann Archive to the Kraus-Thomson Organization. It has grown to include 5 million cartoons, photographs, prints, posters, woodcuts, and other images, and in 1990 will acquire another 11.5 million photographic images, mostly from United Press International and Reuters. Microsoft cofounder Bill Gates will acquire the archive through his Corbis Corp. in October 1995, by which time it will have grown to hold some 16 million images, including 11.5 million photographs.

 Theater: *Key Exchange* by Hollywood screenwriter-playwright Kevin Wade, 27, 7/14 at the off-Broadway Orpheum Theater, with Brooke Adams, 32, Mark Blum, Ben Masters; *A Talent for Murder* by Jerome Chodorov and Norman Panama 10/1 at the Biltmore Theater, with Claudette Colbert, now 76, Jean-Pierre Aumont, now 72, 77 perfs.; *Sister Mary Ignatius Explains It All For You* by Montclair, N.J.-born playwright Christopher Durang, 32, 10/16 at the Playwrights Horizons Theater, with Palo Alto, Calif.-born actress Polly Draper, 32, Akron, Ohio-born actress Elizabeth Franz, 40, 947 perfs.; *Torch Song Trilogy* by Brooklyn-born actor-playwright

Harvey (Forbes) Fierstein, 27, 10/16 at the off-off-Broadway Richard Allen Center, with Fierstein as the drag queen Arnold, 117 perfs.; *Crimes of the Heart* by Jackson, Miss.-born playwright Beth Henley, 29, 11/4 at the John Golden Theater, with Mia Dillon, Georgia-born actress Holly Hunter, 23, Lizbeth Mackay, Dallas-born actor Peter MacNicol, 27, 535 perfs.; *A Soldier's Play* by Philadelphia-born playwright Charles H. Fuller, Jr. 42, 11/5 at the off-Broadway Theater Four, 468 perfs.; *Mass Appeal* by New York-born playwright Bill C. Davis, 30, 11/12 at the Booth Theater, with Dublin-born actor Milo O'Shea, 55, Larchmont-born actor Michael O'Keefe, 26, 212 perfs.; *The West Side Waltz* by Ernest Thompson 11/10 at the Ethel Barrymore Theater, with Katharine Hepburn, Dorothy Loudon, 126 perfs.

Drama critic Richard Watts dies of cardiac arrest at New York January 2 at age 82; former *New York Times* critic Bosley Crowther of heart failure at suburban Mount Kisco March 7 at age 71; actress Madge Evans of cancer at her Oakland, N.J., home April 26 at age 71; playwright Paddy Chayefsky of cancer at New York August 1 at age 58; burlesque veteran Georgia Sothern of cancer at New York October 14 at age 61.

Films: Paul Kagan's *The Chosen* with Maximilian Schell, Rod Steiger, Robby Benson, Barry Miller; John Carpenter's *Escape from New York* with Kurt Russell; Peter Yates's *Eyewitness* with William Hurt, Sigourney Weaver; Daniel Petrie's *Fort Apache, The Bronx* with Paul Newman, Edward Asner, Ken Wahl, Danny Aiello; Bruce Malmuth's *Nighthawks* with Sylvester Stallone, New York-born actor Billy Dee Williams, 44, Lindsay Wagner; Glenn Jordan's *Only When I Laugh* with Marsha Mason, Kristy McNichol, James Coco, New York-born actress Joan Hackett, 47, script by Neil Simon based on his 1970 play *The Gingerbread Lady*; Sidney Lumet's *Prince of the City* with Treat Williams, Jerry Orbach as cops in a New York special investigations unit (Williams tries to redeem himself by turning in his crooked friends); Milos Forman's *Ragtime* with James Cagney, Elizabeth McGovern, Howard E. Rollins, Jr., Mary Steenburgen; Andrew Bergman's *So Fine* with Ryan O'Neal, Jack Warden; Michael Wadleigh's *Wolfen* with actor Albert Finney, Diane Venora.

Actor Melvyn Douglas dies of cancer at Sloan-Kettering Hospital August 4 at age 80; author Anita Loos of a heart attack at Doctors Hospital August 18 at age 88; actor Robert Montgomery of cancer at New York September 27 at age 77.

♪♪ Simon and Garfunkel give a concert on Central Park's Great Lawn 9/19 and attract a crowd estimated to number 400,000.

Broadway musicals: *Sophisticated Ladies* 2/1 at the Lunt-Fontanne Theater, with dancer Gregory Hines, Pittsburgh-born, Philadelphia-raised singer Phyllis Hyman, 30, P. J. Benjamin, music by the late Duke Ellington, 767 perfs.; *Marry Me a Little* 3/12 at the Actor's Playhouse, with Atlanta-born actor Craig Lucas, 30, songs by Stephen Sondheim that include "Can That Boy Foxtrot!" "Happily Ever After," and "There Won't Be Trumpets," 96 perfs.; *Woman of the Year* 3/29 at the Palace, with Lauren Bacall, now 56, Harry Guardino, now 55, music and lyrics by John Kander and Fred Ebb, songs that include "The Grass Is Always Greener," book by Peter Stone based on a screenplay by Ring Lardner, Jr. and Michael Kanin, 770 perfs.; *March of the Falsettos* 4/19 at the Playwrights Horizons Theater, with Michael Rupert, Stephen Bogardus, 27, Natick, Mass.-born actress Alison Fraser, 30, music and lyrics by Boston-born composer-playwright William (Alan) Finn, 29, 170 perfs.; *Dreamgirls* 12/21 at the Imperial Theater, with Texas-born singer-actress Jennifer Holliday, 21, music by Henry Krieger, book and lyrics by Ohio-born writer Tom Eyen, 40, directed by Michael Bennett, 1,522 perfs.

Joe Smith of Smith and Dale vaudeville fame dies at the Actors Fund home in Englewood, N.J., February 17 at age 97 (his partner Charley Dale died in 1971); Broadway songwriter E. Y. "Yip" Harburg dies in an auto accident near Hollywood, Calif., March 5 at age 84; dancer Vera-Ellen of cancer at Los Angeles August 30 at age 60; actress-singer Lotte Lenya at New York November 27 at age 83 (she has been living in an apartment at 404 East 55th Street).

Popular songs: "Boy From New York City" by the rock group Manhattan Transfer; "Not a Day Goes By" by Stephen Sondheim (for his short-lived musical *Merrily We Roll Along*).

Reggae singer Bob Marley dies of brain cancer at a Miami hospital May 11 at age 36; songwriter Frank McHugh at Greenwich, Conn., September 11 at age 83; pianist-arranger Hazel Scott of cancer at New York October 2 at age 61.

MTV (Music Television) goes out to cable TV subscribers from New York beginning August 1 with visual presentations of pop hits.

Studio 54 reopens (*see* 1977). Founders Steve Rubell and Ian Schrager were sentenced to 3½-years in prison for tax evasion, their sentences were reduced, each has served 13 months, they have sold the discothèque to Mark Fleishman, and it will continue until 1988 while Rubell and Schrager join with other partners to create a real estate syndicate that will acquire and renovate luxury hotels and other properties (*see* Palladium nightclub, 1985).

The New York Islanders retain the Stanley Cup, beating the Minnesota North Stars 5 to 1 May 21 at the Nassau Coliseum. Bryan Trottier has suffered a partial shoulder separation in the fourth game but coach Al Arbour lets him play enough to score at least one point in 25 consecutive games (a record), Denis Potvin scores 25 points in the playoffs (a record for a defenseman), but center Butch Goring is awarded the Conn Smythe Trophy as most valuable player.

John McEnroe wins the British and U.S. men's singles titles, Tracy Austin the U.S. women's title.

The New York Yankees win the American League pennant, but the Los Angeles Dodgers win the World Series, defeating the Yankees 4 games to 2 after a season interrupted by a 7-week players' strike. Los Angeles-born Yankee first baseman Bob Watson, 35, gets a three-run homer to help Louisiana-born pitcher Ron Guidry, 31, win the first game; Indiana-born Yankee pitcher Tommy John, 38, and Colorado-born reliever Rich "Goose" Gossage, 30, shut out the Dodgers in the second, but the Dodgers then go on to win four games, although they take the third, fourth, and fifth only by one-run margins. The Mets, piloted by manager Joe Torre, finish near the bottom of their division (only the Chicago Cubs do worse), winning 41 games and losing 62.

An effort to free convicted cocaine dealer Robert Wyler, 43, from a New York City correctional facility fails January 25 when a helicopter commandeered by an armed man and woman is unable to break through the wire mesh on the roof of the facility. Inmates on the roof have overpowered a guard and locked him in a washroom, the hijackers have dropped a pistol to them, but the inmates soon realize that escape is impossible and surrender to police.

Ada Louise Huxtable in the *New York Times* May 24 extols the plan for Battery Park City as "a new Rockefeller Center" (*see* 1980). The "city" will grow to have office buildings with more than 30,000 employees and apartment houses with more than 7,000 residents (*see* 1982).

The 50-year-old Empire State Building is designated a New York City Landmark May 19 and a National Historical Landmark October 23.

The 48-story 101 Park Avenue office building is completed at the northeast corner of 40th Street. Designed by Eli Attia, the glass tower replaces the Architects Building of 1912.

The stainless steel arches and triangular windows of the 51-year-old Chrysler Building at 405 Lexington Avenue are illuminated by bright white lights specified in the original plan by architect William Van Alen but not installed until now.

The 44-story Park Avenue Plaza office tower is completed just west of the Racquet & Tennis Club on Madison Avenue between 52nd and 53rd streets. The club has sold its air rights to a developer, and Skidmore, Owings & Merrill has designed the green glass tower in International Style with help from Raul De Armas.

A rezoning of Chinatown to encourage luxury housing results in a lawsuit by the 8-year-old Asian Americans for Equality, whose members succeed in having the zoning plan modified (*see* 1986).

The 38-story Rivertower apartment house is completed at 420 East 54th Street, east of First Avenue, to designs by Schuman, Lichtenstein, Claman & Efron (with help from Rudolph de Harak).

The 22-story Vista International Hotel opens with 820 rooms at 3 World Trade Center. Designed by Skidmore, Owings & Merrill, it will later become the Marriott World Trade Hotel (*see* 1993).

The 42-story Hotel Parker Meridien opens at 118 West 57th Street, on a site formerly occupied by the Great Northern Hotel. Designed by the office of Philip Birnbaum with a four-story atrium, the structure is mostly in 56th Street but has a two-story vaulted entranceway in 57th.

Developer Donald Trump acquires the 42-story Barbizon-Plaza Hotel opened in 1930 at the northwest corner of Sixth Avenue and 58th Street; he also buys the 14-story 101 Central Park South apartment house that opened in 1918 with the idea of razing it. He will convert the hotel into a condominium called Trump Parc, and when rental tenants in the apartment house (including designer Arnold Scaasi) refuse to move, Trump will threaten to make some of its 80 units available to house the homeless (Mayor Koch will quash the idea next year); litigation will continue until March 1998, when the apartment house, camouflaged to look like part of Trump Parc, will become a condominium.

Architect H. I. Feldman dies at his Riverside Drive home January 7 at age 84; John G. Dinkeloo of a heart attack at Fredericksburg, Va., June 15 at age 63; Wallace K. Harrison at New York December 2 at age 86.

Fire destroys the 159-year-old Church of St. Luke-in-the-Fields at 485 Hudson Street, whose interior

The privately funded Central Park Conservancy rehabilitated the Sheep Meadow. CHIE NISHIO

was remodeled in 1875 and 1886. It will be restored and expanded in 1986 to designs by Hardy Holzman Pfeiffer Associates.

Central Park's Sheep Meadow reopens in the spring (*see* 1979). Now a lush, grassy lawn (carpeted with squares of sod), it is surrounded by a wire fence to protect the grass by keeping people out during the winter months, and signs are posted to outlaw ball playing, bicycles, dogs, and loud music; the meadow becomes a tranquil haven for sunbathers and frisbee tossers.

Flying Foods International is founded at New York by entrepreneur Walter F. Martin II, who initially works out of his apartment, bringing in small quantities of fresh Dover sole by cargo jet from the Netherlands for sale to New York restaurants. Martin takes advantage of the fact that JFK is the world's largest air-cargo port. Paul Morates and Andrew Udelson soon join him, they acquire a riverfront warehouse in Long Island City, and André Soltner of Lutèce is one of their first customers, providing useful advice as the firm expands. The partners will sell out in 1987, having grown to supply 750 restaurants nationwide, about half of them in New York City (*see* Gourmet Garage, 1992).

Citymeals-on-Wheels is founded by cookbook writers James Beard, Gael Greene, and Barbara Kafka in co-operation with New York restaurateurs to supplement the federal Meals-on-Wheels program. Supervised by the city's Department for the Aging, the privately funded charitable organization provides five hot meals per week to elderly New Yorkers who cannot get out of their homes to shop for food; it will raise $4 million per year to keep seniors well nourished on weekends, holidays, and in emergencies, and within a decade will be serving close to 9,000 people who are unable to fend for themselves.

Felidia Ristorante opens at 243 East 58th Street under the direction of Italian-born chef Lidia Bastianach (*née* Mattichio), 35, and her husband, Felice, a fellow Istrian, with whom she has operated two restaurants in Queens.

Irving and Murray Riese acquire the five-story Childs restaurant building of 1925 at 604 Fifth Avenue and turn the restaurant space into a combination Roy Rogers and Pizza Hut fast-food outlet.

1982 The retiring comptroller of the Parking Violations Bureau goes to the Department of Investigation February 4 with allegations of irregularities in contracts awarded by the bureau. The department receives other such allegations from "another source," and department officials open the case April 9, assigning it to Sally Michaels, a lawyer new to the department. Michaels will later resign and the issue will erupt into a major political scandal for the Koch administration (*see* 1986).

A rally against the nuclear arms race brings 600,000 (some estimates say 800,000) demonstrators to Central Park's Great Lawn June 12. A cynical sign on a low floor of the Century apartment house north of Columbus Circle reads, "Dupes," but the No-Nukes Rally will long be remembered.

Mayor Koch runs in the state gubernatorial primary (Gov. Carey has decided in January that he would not seek reelection) but speaks disparagingly of upstate New York in an interview and loses to Lieut. Gov. Mario Cuomo, who wins the governorship that he will hold for the next 12 years. Now 50, Cuomo receives 2,617,752 votes as compared with 2,452,881 for his Harrisburg, Pa.-born Republican opponent Lewis E. (Edward) Lehrman, 44, who has been president and CEO of Rite-Aid Corp.

The Howard Beach community of Queens has a series of robberies perpetrated by blacks against the mostly Irish and Italian residents, whose prejudice against blacks is exacerbated by the incidents (*see* 1986).

Investor, sportsman, diplomat and newspaper publisher John Hay "Jock" Whitney dies of congestive heart failure at Manhasset, L.I., February 8 at age 77, having amassed a fortune of $250 million.

The NASDAQ system begun early in 1971 creates a National Market System in April to provide detailed, up-to-the-minute information on the most actively traded issues in response to a Securities and Exchange Commission directive that the public be provided with more information. By May 1983 there will be 184 stocks on the National Market System, with terminals showing trades 90 seconds after they occur; the terminals show the bid and offering prices, the high and low of the last trade, and the volume. The maximum one-time fee required for a company to have its stock listed on the NASDAQ is $5,000, as compared with $15,000 on the AMEX and $29,350 on the Big Board. At least 220 companies, and possibly as many as 600, prefer to have their stock traded on the NASDAQ, even though their earnings and stockholder distribution qualify them for AMEX or NYSE listing, and trading volume on the NASDAQ has mushroomed (it will grow on many days to surpass that on the NYSE).

A U.S. tax reform measure approved by Congress August 19 cuts back on the tax reductions enacted last year, raises taxes on cigarettes, and tightens loopholes that have permitted rich people to avoid taxes. Critics call it the end of the "supply-side" economic experiment. The state legislature at Albany enacts a law establishing four classes of property for purposes of taxation: one-, two-, and three-family houses, apartment buildings (chiefly co-operatives and condominiums), utilities, and commercial property. The ratio of assessed valuation to market value is different for each class, a system that benefits homeowners in outlying boroughs (see 1975; 1995).

Wall Street stages a rally on the strength of lower inflation and lower interest rates. The Dow Jones Industrial Average sets a record high of 1072.55 December 27, up from 776.92 August 12, after trading a record 147.1 million shares October 7, and the bull market will continue for at least 18 years. The Dow closes December 31 at 1046.54, up from 875 at the end of 1981, but recession continues throughout most of the world, international trade declines, unemployment in the United States has reached 10.8 percent in November—the highest since 1940— and the number of Americans living below the poverty line is the highest in 17 years.

The Herald Center opens south of Macy's on Sixth Avenue between 33rd and 34th streets. Financed by President Ferdinand E. Marcos of the Philippines and his wife, Imelda, the vertical shopping center is wrapped in dark, mirrored glass and replaces the former Saks 34th Street store; it leases space to tenants who initially include Brookstone, Alfred Dunhill of London, and Ann Taylor but will soon change to a discount mall with more downscale retailers such as Daffy's, Payless Shoes, and Toys "R" Us.

The city embarks on a $6.3 billion program to rehabilitate the subways, with most of the financing to come from a state bond issue.

The Checker taxi assembly line at Kalamazoo, Mich., closes in July after 60 years of production (see 1932). New York's taxi fleet still contains thousands of the capacious cabs (rear leg-room: 46.3 inches, rear head-room: 34.5 inches), but they get only 11 miles per gallon as compared to 17 for the stock-model Chevrolets and Fords that have begun to replace them (rear leg-room: 39.5 and 39.6 inches, rear head-room: 37.9 and 38 inches). By 1993 only 10 Checkers will still be picking up fares in New York; and by March 1997, there will be only one licensed Checker in the city's fleet of 12,053 yellow cabs.

The Gay Men's Health Crisis (GMHC) is founded in early January by Bridgeport, Conn.-born activist Larry Kramer, 43, who assembles a group of successful gay men in his apartment overlooking Washington Square Park (see AIDS, 1981). The disease that has begun to kill sexually active gays still has no name (some call it GRID, for gay-related immune deficiency), but GMHC sets up the world's first hot line of its kind; it will support men, women, and children stricken with AIDS or infected with the retrovirus HIV, lobby for more government services, and distribute condoms and educational materials in bars. The specter of AIDS will lead to an increased use of condoms that provide some protection (see 1983).

The New York Hospital-Cornell Medical Center receives a bequest of $15 million in October from the estate of the late John Hay Whitney, whose name will be memorialized in the hospital's Whitney Pavilion. His gifts to the hospital have totaled $21 million; his late sister Joan Whitney Payson (who died in 1975 and whose name will be memorialized in Payson Pavilion) gave another $8.3 million; their children continue the family's tradition of supporting the medical center.

Woodhull Medical & Health Center opens November 4 in northern Brooklyn, replacing Greenpoint and Cumberland hospitals. It is the first municipal hospital to provide its own medical care rather than contracting it out to a medical school or affiliated teaching hospital, but the opening has been delayed for 6 years and critics say the new 10-story, 610-bed facility is already outmoded.

The Intrepid Sea, Air, Space Museum opens in August at Pier 86 on the Hudson River in the 40-year-old aircraft carrier U.S.S. *Intrepid*. She was scheduled to be scrapped in 1976 but has been decommissioned and converted through the efforts of a foundation organized in 1978 by builder-philanthropist Zachary Fisher, now 70. The 900-foot ship that once carried 3,000 men and more than 100 fighter planes now displays jets as well as propeller planes and contains exhibits recounting the vessel's history through three wars.

 American Telephone & Telegraph agrees January 8 to be broken up in settlement of an antitrust suit filed in 1974. AT&T will retain its long-distance lines, its Western Electric manufacturing arm, and Bell Laboratories, spinning off its 22 regional and local companies (*see* 1984). Independent companies begin installing outdoor telephones on the sides of buildings, and advertising begins to appear on the New York Telephone Co.'s outdoor phone enclosures (*see* 1997).

Chicago's Tribune Co. changes its mind in May and decides not to sell the *New York Daily News*, even though the *News* continues to lose money (*see* 1981). The company warns union leaders, however, that costs will have to be cut severely (*see* 1990).

SoHo News ceases publication May 15 after 8½ years on the newsstands (*see* 1973). Owned from 1978 to 1980 by the publishers of the *London Daily Mail*, it has piled up losses totaling $6 million.

USA Today begins publication September 15. Keeping stories brief and making wide use of color, the Gannett paper is the only national daily except for the *Christian Science Monitor* and *Wall Street Journal* (although the *New York Times* prints editions in several cities and has worldwide distribution).

"Electronic mail" via fax machines gains popularity as third-generation Japanese technology cuts transmission time to 20 seconds per page, down from 6 minutes with first-generation machines, and thus reduces telephone charges from $4 per page to less than $1 (*see* 1976), but e-mail over the Internet will soon make fax transmissions seem old-fashioned.

Grey Advertising cofounder Lawrence Valenstein dies at his Scarsdale home September 12 at age 83; advertising pioneer William Bernbach of leukemia at New York October 2 at age 71.

Nonfiction: *Sketches from Life* by Lewis Mumford, now 87. Born in 1895 to a serving girl who had been seduced by an East Side bachelor, Mumford spent his early years in his grandmother's West 65th Street brownstone and recalls the days "before the High School of Commerce was built across the way and long before the Lincoln Arcade—which still later became a refuge for penurious artists—was razed to make way for Lincoln Center." The new subway, he remembers, tore up "Boss Tweed's tree-lined Boulevard . . . as Broadway above 59th Street was called," and where it formerly had been "a quite

respectable" street it later turned into a "sordid red-light area." North of 65th Street, Broadway was lined with "vacant lots, with visible chickens and market gardens, genuine beer gardens like Unter den Linden, and even more rural areas." The brownstone used for the rowhouses in the immediate area of his younger days, he says, had been very popular in the third quarter of the 19th century—an ugly chocolate-colored sandstone from the quarries around Hartford [that] had displaced the warm reddish-brown sandstone from Belleville, New Jersey, which one may still find on Brooklyn Heights," and those brownstone houses were "giving way to a more variegated type of domestic architecture;" *Bronx Primitive: Portraits of a Childhood* by Kate Simon, now 69, who grew up in the area of Lafontaine Avenue and 178th Street; *Power and Society: New York at the Turn of the Century* by Coulee Dam, Wash.-born Case Western Reserve historian David C. (Conrad) Hammack.

Fiction: *Prizzi's Honor* by Richard Condon; *Other People's Money* by Michael M. Thomas.

Novelist Djuna Barnes dies of cancer in her tiny Patchin Place apartment June 19 at age 90.

 Painting: *Keyhole*, *Beam* (oil on three canvases), *Yikes* (oil on two canvases), *Popeye* (pastel and charcoal on eight sheets of cut and pasted paper), *Hear* (pastel on two sheets of paper), and *Last Night* (pastel on eight sheets of paper) by Elizabeth Murray.

 Theater: *Pump Boys and Dinettes* by Middletown, Ohio-born actress-playwright Debra Monk, 32, in collaboration with John Foley, Mark Hardwick, Cass Morgan, John Schwind, and Tim Warner 2/4 at the off-Broadway Princess Theater, 573 perfs.; *The Dining Room* by Buffalo-born playwright (and MIT literature professor) A. R. (Albert Ramsdell) Gurney, Jr., 42, 2/11 at the Playwrights Horizons Theater, with New Hampshire-born actor John Shea, 32, 607 perfs.; *Agnes of God* by Altoona, Pa.-born playwright John Pielmeier, 33, 3/30 at the Music Box Theater, with Elizabeth Ashley, Geraldine Page, New York-born actress Amanda Plummer, 25, 599 perfs.; *"Master Harold" . . . and the Boys* by South African playwright Athol Fugard, 49, 5/4 at the Lyceum Theater with Zakes Mokae, Lonny Price, 344 perfs.; *True West* by Sam Shepard 10/17 at the off-Broadway Cherry Lane Theater, with Illinois-born actor John Malkovich, 28, 762 perfs.; *Foxfire* by English-born writer Susan Cooper, 47, and actor Hume Cronyn 11/10 at the Ethel Barrymore Theater, with Cronyn, Jessica Tandy, 213 perfs.; *Extremities* by Trenton, N.J.-born playwright William Mastrosimone, 35, 12/22 at the off-Broadway West Side Arts Theater, with Susan Sarandon, James Russo, 317 perfs.; *Whodunnit*

by Anthony Shaffer 12/30 at the Biltmore Theater, with St. Louis-born actor George Hearn, 48, Barbara Baxley, 157 perfs.

Director Lee Strasberg of the Actors Studio dies of a heart attack at New York February 17 at age 80; Ellen Burstyn and Al Pacino assume leadership of the 35-year-old studio, whose artistic director beginning in 1988 will be Frank Corsaro.

Bulldozers knock down the 76-year-old Astor, 73-year-old Victoria (formerly the Gaiety), 71-year-old Helen Hayes (originally the Folies Bergère, later the Fulton), and 65-year-old Bijou and Morosco theaters to make way for a new hotel in Times Square. Only three of the six have remained legitimate theaters. The theater community has protested, prominent actors and playwrights have demonstrated against the destruction of the houses, but to no avail (*see* real estate [Marriott Marquis Hotel], 1985).

Television: *Cagney and Lacey* 3/25 on CBS with Meg Foster, 33 (later Sharon Gless), as New York detective Christine Cagney, Tyne Daley, 36, as her partner Mary Beth Lacey (to 8/16/1988).

Veteran radio talk-show host Ed Fitzgerald dies in his apartment at 40 Central Park South March 22 at age 89 after 44 years on WOR. His widow, Pegeen (*née* Worrall), continues on the air without him; radio comedian Goodman Ace dies in his Ritz Tower apartment July 18 at age 83.

Films: Sydney Pollack's *Tootsie* with Dustin Hoffman, Jessica Lange, Geena Davis. Also: Arthur Hiller's *Author! Author!* with Al Pacino, Dyan Cannon, Tuesday Weld; Richard Benjamin's *My Favorite Year* with Peter O'Toole, Mark Linn-Baker; Susan Seidelman's *Smithereens* with Susan Berman; Paul Mazursky's *Tempest* with John Cassavetes, Gena Rowlands, Susan Sarandon; Jane Morrison's *The Two Worlds of Angelita* with Marien Perez Riera, Rosalba Rolon is about a family that moves from Puerto Rico to a New York barrio; Charlie Ahearn's *Wild Style* with graffiti artists "Lee" Quinones, Sandra "Pink" Fabara; George Roy Hill's *The World According to Garp* with Robin Williams, Mary Beth Hurt, Glenn Close.

Film musical: John Huston's *Annie* with Albert Finney, Aileen Quinn, Carol Burnett.

Broadway and off-Broadway musicals: *Forbidden Broadway* (revue) 1/15 at the off-Broadway Palsson's Upstairs Supper Club, with Gerard Alessandrini and his friends Nora Mae Lyng, Fred Barton, and Wendee Winter (who is replaced in April by comedienne Chloe Webb), music from various sources,

and parody lyrics by Alessandrini, 2,332 perfs.; *Nine* 5/9 at the 46th Street Theater with Puerto Rico-born singer-dancer Raul Julia (originally Raul Rafael Carlos Julia y Arcelay), 42, New York-born actress Karen Akers, 36, Finnish-born performer Taina Elg, 51, music and lyrics by Maury Yeston, book by Arthur Kopit based on the 1963 Fellini film *8-*, directed by Tommy Tune, 739 perfs.; *Little Shop of Horrors* 7/27 at the off-Broadway Orpheum Theater, with Brooklyn-born actress Ellen Greene, 32, music by New Rochelle-born composer Alan Menken, 33, book and lyrics by Baltimore-born writer Howard Ashman, 31, 2,209 perfs.; *Cats* 10/7 at the Winter Garden Theater (it opened 5/11/1981 at London's New London Theater), with a cast of 26 headed by Betty Lynn Buckley, now 35, as Grizabella and German-born actor Harry Groener, 31, music by Andrew Lloyd Webber, lyrics by the late T. S. Eliot, songs that include "Memory," 7,485 perfs. (a new record; it will run until 5/25/2000).

Dancer Eleanor Powell dies at Beverly Hills, Calif., February 11 at age 71; director Burt Shevelove at his London apartment April 8 at age 66.

The Joyce Theater opens 6/2 at 175 Eighth Avenue, southwest corner 19th Street, with a performance by the Feld Ballet. Eliot Feld has arranged to have a 41-year-old Art Deco structure (originally the Elgin movie theater) converted to a dance theater by architect Hugh Hardy of Hardy Holzman Pfeiffer Associates.

Juilliard-trained New York trumpet virtuoso Wynton Marsalis, 20, makes his Carnegie Hall debut 6/30.

Popular songs: *The Nylon Curtain* (album) by Billy Joel; *Tug of War* (album) by Paul McCartney with his memorial to John Lennon "Here Today;" "That's What Friends Are For" by Carol Bayer Sager and Burt Bacharach.

Jazz pianist-composer Thelonious Sphere Monk dies of a stroke at Englewood, N.J., February 16 at age 64.

The Club A disco nightclub opens at 333 East 60th Street, where it will continue until 1987 (*see* Scores, 1991).

Sportswriter Red Smith dies at Stamford, Conn., January 15 at age 76.

The New York Islanders win their third National Hockey League championship May 16, retaining the Stanley Cup by defeating the Vancouver Canucks 3 to 1 in the fourth and final game. Right wing Mike Bossy, who has gained 27 points on 17 goals and 10 assists, is awarded the Conn Smythe Trophy as most valuable player.

Jimmy Connors wins his fourth U.S. Open singles title, Chris Evert-Lloyd wins in women's singles.

Brooklyn-born shoe designer Kenneth Cole, 36, rents a broken-down trailer and opens for business selling a line of women's footwear that includes an $84 pair of stonewashed-denim boots. He will introduce a line of sportswear in 1998 and by 1999 his company will have estimated sales of $300 million, with 41 retail stores from Atlanta to Amsterdam.

Fashion designer Halston agrees to design a collection for J. C. Penney, the mass-market retailer (*see* 1978; 1983).

Former toy maker Louis Marx dies at White Plains Hospital February 5 at age 85; Hartz Mountain Industries founder Max Stern at his Manhattan home May 20 at age 83 (his son Leonard, now 44, joined the company in 1959 and has been expanding it with real estate acquisitions).

The 40 Broad Street office building is completed between Exchange Place and Beaver Street to designs by Gruzen & Partners.

The 28-story 875 Third Avenue office tower is completed between 52nd and 53rd streets to designs by the Chicago office of Skidmore, Owings & Merrill.

The New York Landmarks Preservation Commission grants landmark status to the 20-year-old Lever House on Park Avenue. Mayor Koch has appointed Kent L. Barwick, 45, head of the commission, and Barwick has declared the building a landmark (he will become president of the Municipal Art Society next year and serve until 1995); the Fisher Brothers own Lever House and have sought to block the landmark designation by appealing to the Board of Estimate. Manhattan Borough President Andrew Stein, now 37, has sided with them, but Jacqueline Kennedy Onassis has visited City Comptroller Harrison "Jay" Goldin, now 46, and Goldin's two votes have carried the day.

Builder Harold D. Uris of Uris Brothers dies at Palm Beach, Fla., March 28 at age 76.

The first of Battery Park City's three 34-story Gateway Plaza towers opens in June with 1,712 apartments and the first residents move in at 345, 355, 365, 375, 385, and 395 South End Avenue (*see* 1981). Architects Jack Brown and Irving E. Gershon have designed the buildings, whose lines are relieved by an interior green plaza with enclosed swimming pool (*see* Esplanade, 1983).

The Maria Lopez Plaza apartments in the South Bronx are completed at 635 Morris Avenue, north-

west corner 151st Street. John Ciardullo Associates has designed the white-columned structure with half-cylindrical balconies and a grassy interior courtyard.

The city opens barracks-style shelters to house the homeless in armories and other venues.

Construction on the south tower of the Cathedral of St. John the Divine resumes September 29 after a 4-year hiatus (*see* 1978). The winning design for the south transept will not be implemented, and construction of the south tower will be halted in 1992 after it has been built to a height of 50 feet.

 A 48-inch water main breaks February 27 at 40th Street and Broadway, halting service on several subway lines and disrupting water service in a 24-block area.

A U.S. district court at New York bars construction of the Westway Project, saying that the Army Corps of Engineers has failed to present an adequate environmental impact statement with regard to the striped bass that normally inhabit the Hudson River area that developers want to fill with land (*see* transportation, 1974; 1985). A federal appeals court will uphold the decision.

 Citarella changes hands as entrepreneur Joe Gurrera takes over (*see* 1940). He will expand the seafood shop enormously in the next 20 years, offering meat, game, poultry, and a wide variety of foods, including ready-to-serve dishes, as he enlarges the store to occupy the corner site at 75th Street (*see* East Side store, 1997).

 The Water Club restaurant opens in November on a converted lumber barge in the East River at 30th Street and the Franklin D. Roosevelt Drive. Michael O'Keeffe of 1977 River Cafe fame has hired Toulouse chef Guy Peuch.

The Reagan administration announces formation of the Statue of Liberty/Ellis Island Centennial Commission to raise funds for the restoration of the two landmarks in time for the statue's 100th birthday celebration in 1986 (*see* 1975). The commission is also to counsel the Department of the Interior and National Park Service on establishing a monument to the immigrants who have come through Ellis Island, whose facilities have deteriorated in 28 years of desuetude (*see* 1983).

1983 Terrence Cardinal Cooke creates a controversy at the St. Patrick's Day Parade March 17 by refusing to greet its grand marshal, who has been associated with the Irish Republican Army.

New Yorkers observe the bicentennial of Evacuation Day November 25. Its proximity to Thanksgiving and a rise in friendship toward Britain have discouraged observance of the day since World War I.

A committee of U.S. congressmen headed by Rep. John Conyers, Jr. (D. Mich.) reports that racism is a major factor in police misconduct in New York City (see 1953; Bumpers, 1984).

Dollar Dry Dock Savings Bank is created February 5 by a merger of the 135-year-old Dry Dock and the 93-year-old Dollar savings banks.

Apple Bank for Savings is adopted in May as the name for the 120-year-old Harlem Savings Bank.

The 39-year-old securities firm Cantor Fitzgerald becomes the first company to offer worldwide computer-screen brokerage services for trading U.S. government securities (see 1972). It will soon have offices at Boston, Chicago, Dallas, Los Angeles, Toronto, London, Paris, and Tokyo as well as at New York, where its offices are near the top of the World Trade Center.

Los Angeles-born Drexel Burnham Lambert executive Michael (Robert) Milken, 37, suggests in November that high-yield "junk" bonds be used to facilitate both friendly and hostile takeovers, and for buy-outs of companies "going private" (buying up publicly owned stock). Assets of a target company are pledged to repay the principal of the junk bonds that yield 13 to 30 percent and are bought by many insurance and savings & loan companies.

Economic recovery sends Wall Street's Dow Jones Industrial Average to new heights (it closes the year at 1258.64, up from 1046.54 at the end of 1982). Inflation remains low, unemployment begins to drop, but the Census Bureau reports that 35.3 million Americans live in poverty—the highest rate in 19 years.

Metro-North is created by the Metropolitan Transportation Authority to take over the remnants of New York Central and New Haven Railroad suburban rail lines. Onetime brakeman Donald N. Nelson, 37, is vice president for operations (he will later be president) and in 25 years will increase ridership 34 percent—from 47 million to 63 million—while reducing costs from $12.52 per passenger to $7.36.

The Taxi and Limousine Commission inaugurates a mandatory orientation program for taxi drivers, many of whom are recent arrivals in New York and unlike London cabbies have never been required to pass geography tests. New drivers must spend 20 hours in classrooms to acquaint themselves with the city's streets, avenues, and major destination points, and even though the test is an open-book exam many will fail (see 1992).

The weekly New York newspaper *Native* carries a front-page article March 14 under the title "1,112 and Counting." Written by gay activist Larry Kramer, it accuses Mayor Koch and other local politicians of refusing to acknowledge the growing danger of the AIDS epidemic (see Gay Men's Health Crisis, 1982), leveling the same charge at Memorial Sloan-Kettering Cancer Center physicians, officials of the Centers for Disease Control at Atlanta, and researchers at the National Institutes of Health in Washington: "How many of us have to die before you get scared off your ass and into action? Aren't 195 dead New Yorkers enough?" Warning readers against the anonymous and promiscuous sex in which gay men have been engaging along North River piers, in bathhouses, on Fire Island, and elsewhere, Kramer runs into a wall of denial and hostility, but within 20 years AIDS will have killed some 75,000 New Yorkers; 20 percent of all U.S. AIDS victims will be New Yorkers (see Act Up, 1987).

New York Hospital installs Magnetic Resonance Imaging (MRI) equipment to give its physicians a better diagnostic tool. It is the first of its kind in the city for patient use, and the hospital works in co-operation with Memorial-Sloan Kettering across York Avenue this year to be the first in the city to use Positron Emission Tomography (PET).

Terrence Cardinal Cooke dies at New York October 6 at age 62 after 25 years as head of the New York archdiocese; he will be succeeded beginning next year by Philadelphia-born Scranton bishop John Joseph O'Connor, now 63, who will be elected to the college of cardinals at Rome in 1985 and head the diocese until his death in 2000.

De Witt Clinton High School in the Bronx becomes coeducational after 86 years as a boys' school (see 1929); it has been the city's last public high school to remain open only to boys.

Vanity Fair (the fourth magazine to bear that name) begins publication at New York in March under the aegis of Condé Nast and its parent company Advance Publications, headed by S. I. Newhouse, Jr.

Nonfiction: *From Colonia to Community: The History of Puerto Ricans in New York City, 1917–1948* by New York-born author Virginia Sánchez-Korrol, 47; *New York 1900* by local architect Robert A. M. Stern, 44, with Gregory Gilmartin and John Massengale; *Little Flower: The Life and Times of Fiorello La Guardia* by Brooklyn-born *Reader's Digest* writer Lawrence

Elliott (originally Edelstein), 59; *New York: A Guide to the Metropolis. Walking Tours of Architecture and History* by New York author Gerard R. Wolf; *Blue Guide, New York* by Carol von Pressentin Wright includes a good deal of the city's physical history; *NYC Access* by Philadelphia-born architect-graphic designer-travel writer Richard Saul Wurman, 48, is an idiosyncratic guide to the city.

Fiction: *Winter's Tale* by Mark Helprin; *Our House in the Last World* by New York-born novelist Oscar Hijuelos, 32; *Ironweed* by William Kennedy, now 53; *The Anatomy Lesson* by Philip Roth; *Heartburn* by Nora Ephron; *August* by Judith Rossner; *The Auerbach Inheritance* by Stephen Birmingham.

Juvenile: *The Little Fire Engine That Saved the City* by Dennis Smith.

Painting: *Racing Thoughts* (encaustic and collage on canvas) by Jasper Johns; *Table Turning* and *Deeper than D.* (both oil on two canvases), *Sail Baby* (oil on three canvases), *More Than You Know* (oil on nine canvases), and *Sophie Last Summer* (charcoal and pastel on five sheets of paper) by Elizabeth Murray. Lee Krasner, now 75, has a retrospective exhibition of her work at the Museum of Modern Art (MoMA).

Marlborough Gallery owner Frank Lloyd, now 72, returns to Manhattan to stand trial (*see* 1977). A jury convicts him January 6 of tampering with evidence in the lawsuit brought by the Mark Rothko estate, Supreme Court Justice Herbert I. Altman orders him to establish a scholarship fund and present a series of art lectures and private showings for city high-school students in lieu of a possible 4-year prison sentence. Lloyd asserts his innocence, but he concedes that the sentence is "a fair, humane, and socially useful conclusion to the Rothko litigation." The Pace Gallery will hereafter handle the Rothko estate, Knoedler will handle Gottlieb, Motherwell, and the David Smith estate, but Marlborough will continue under the direction of Lloyd's nephew Pierre Levai.

The first annual Spring Armory Antiques Show, organized by Sanford L. Smith, opens in the Seventh Regiment Armory on Park Avenue, where the Winter Antiques Show has been held since 1955.

Providence, R.I.-born art dealer Pat Hearn, 28, opens her first gallery in November, locating it at Avenue B and 6th Street as she begins a 17-year career. She will soon move it to larger quarters in 9th Street near Avenue D where she will have plenty of space and polished wood floors, and in 1988 will move to the southwest corner of SoHo in Wooster Street near Grand, attracting other galleries to that area as she shares new artists and ideas with other dealers (*see* 1995).

Kodachrome co-inventor Leopold Godowsky II dies of a heart attack at his native New York February 18 at age 82; photographer Lisette Model at New York March 30 at age 82.

Theater: *Painting Churches* by New York-born playwright Tina Howe, 45, 2/8 at the off-Broadway South Street Theater, with Marian Seldes, English-born actor Donald Moffatt, 51, Frances Conroy, 206 perfs.; *Brighton Beach Memoirs* by Neil Simon 3/27 at the Alvin Theater (renamed the Neil Simon Theater 6/29), with New York-born ingénu Matthew Broderick, 21, Buffalo-born actor Peter Michael Goetz, 41, Elizabeth Franz, Joyce Van Patten (to 46th Street Theater 2/26/85), 1,530 perfs.; *'night, Mother* by Louisville, Ky.-born playwright Marsha Norman, 35, 3/31 at the Golden Theater, with Memphis-born actress Kathy Bates, 34, Anne Pitoniak, 380 perfs.; *Fool for Love* by Sam Shepard 11/30 at the off-Broadway Douglas Fairbanks Theater, with Englewood, N.J.-born actor Ed Harris, 33, 1,000 perfs.; *Isn't It Romantic* by New York-born playwright Wendy Wasserstein, 33, 12/15 at the Playwrights Horizons Theater, with Lisa Banes, 28, Betty Comden, Chip Zien, 233 perfs.

Playwright Tennessee Williams chokes to death on a bottle cap at New York February 25 at age 71 (he has been living at the Hotel Elysée in East 54th Street); Samson Raphaelson dies in his West 67th Street apartment July 16 at age 89 (he has taught his craft at Columbia right to the end).

Films: Martin Scorsese's *The King of Comedy* with Robert De Niro, Jerry Lewis. Also: Roberto Faenza's *Corrupt* with Harvey Keitel, Nicole Garcia, Leonard Mann; Sidney Lumet's *Daniel* with Timothy Hutton, Mandy Patinkin, Lindsay Crouse, Edward Asner, Ellen Barkin in a screen version of the 1971 E. L. Doctorow novel about the children of Ethel and Julius Rosenberg; John Landis's *Trading Places* with Dan Aykroyd, comedian Eddie Murphy, Ralph Bellamy, Don Ameche (some of the action is shot in the former East River Savings Bank branch completed in 1935 in Church Street between Cortlandt and Dey streets).

Gloria Swanson dies of a heart ailment at New York Hospital April 4 at age 84 (her chief residence since 1938 has been a large apartment at 920 Fifth Avenue).

Broadway and off-Broadway musicals: *Merlin* 2/13 at the Mark Hellinger Theater, with Doug Henning, Chita Rivera, Jersey City-born comedian Nathan

Lane (originally Joseph Lane), 27, music by New York-born Hollywood composer Elmer Bernstein, now 60, book and lyrics by Philadelphia-born writers Richard Levinson and William Link, both 48, 199 perfs.; *Mama, I Want to Sing* 3/25 at the 667-seat off-Broadway Heckscher Theater, with Tisha Campbell, 14, gospel music by Rudolph V. Hawkins, book and lyrics by Vy Higginsen and Ken Wydro, 2,213 perfs.; *My One and Only* 5/1 at the St. James Theater, with Tommy Tune, English model Twiggy (Lesley Hornby), 35, Roscoe Lee Brown, now 57, dancer Charles "Honi" Coles, now 72, music from old Gershwin musicals, 767 perfs.; *La Cage aux Folles* 8/21 at the Palace, with George Hearn, New York-born actor Gene Barry (originally Eugene Klass), now 64, music and lyrics by Jerry Herman, 1,761 perfs.; *The Gospel at Colonus* 11/8 at the Brooklyn Academy of Music's Carey Playhouse, with music by Bob Telson, lyrics by Sophocles and New York playwright Lee Breuer, 46, (who has taken the Sophocles play *Oedipus at Colonus* and recast it as sermons set in a black Pentecostal church), 61 perfs.; *Baby* 12/4 at the Ethel Barrymore Theater, with a cast of 17 that includes Chicago-born actor-stage manager Philip Hoffman, 29, Beth Fowler, Chicago-born ingénue Liz Callaway, 22, music by Buffalo-born composer David Shire, 46, lyrics by director Richard Maltby, Jr., 241 perfs.; *The Tap Dance Kid* 12/21 at the Broadhurst Theater, with German-born dancer Hinton Battle, 28, 699 perfs.

Tower Records opens June 22 in Greenwich Village. Started by 35-year-old entrepreneur Russell Solomon 23 years ago at Sacramento, Calif., the record-store has never before had an East Coast outlet and will soon open a second New York store on Broadway near Lincoln Center.

Detroit-born soul singer Diana Ross, 33, of the Supremes is scheduled to give a concert on Central Park's Great Lawn 7/21, attracts a crowd estimated to number 300,000, is rained out, and performs the following evening to a crowd equally large.

Ballet impresario George Balanchine dies of the very rare Creutzfeldt-Jakob disease (a devastating mental disorder) at New York April 30 at age 79; lyricist Howard Dietz of Parkinson's disease at his native New York July 30 at age 86; lyricist Carolyn Leigh at her native New York November 19 at age 57.

Popular songs: "Uptown Girl" by Billy Joel; "I Hate New York" by Louisiana-born country singer Hank Williams, Jr., 34; "I'm Never Going Back to New York City" by Bruce Donnelly, Joey Harris; *She's So Unusual* (album) by Queens-born rock singer Cyndi Lauper, 30, includes "Girls Just Want to Have Fun."

The Area disco nightclub opens at 157 Hudson Street, where it will continue until 1987; the Limelight disco nightclub opens with a party thrown by artist Andy Warhol in the former Church of the Holy Communion that opened in 1846 at the corner of 20th Street and Sixth Avenue. Peter Gatien has converted the church's sanctuary into a dance floor, and his club will enjoy enormous popularity until it is closed in 1996; the World disco nightclub opens at 254 East 2nd Street, where it will continue until 1990; the Surf Club disco opens at 415 East 91st Street, where it will continue until 1991.

The New York Islanders win their fourth consecutive National Hockey League (NHL) title, retaining possession of the Stanley Cup by beating the Edmonton Oilers 4 to 3 May 17 at the Nassau Coliseum. Islander goalie Billy Smith has slashed Edmonton superstar Wayne Gretzky in the second game; Islanders Mike Bossy, Bob Morrow, Duane and Brent Sutter, John Tonelli, and Bryan Trottier all contribute to the victory, but it is Smith who limits Gretzky to 4 goals and who is awarded the Conn Smythe Trophy as most valuable player.

Jimmy Connors wins in U.S. Open men's singles at Flushing Meadow, Martina Navratilova, 26 (Czech.), in women's singles.

Fashion designer Halston presents his line of moderately priced ready-to-wear for J. C. Penney June 7 (*see* 1982). Critics hail the collection, but Bergdorf Goodman abruptly stops selling Halston-designed clothing. Norton Simon will be acquired by another company next year, Beatrice Foods will acquire that company, and Halston himself, now 50, will be laid off and not permitted to use the Halston name.

 Mobster Meyer Lansky dies of lung cancer at Miami Beach January 15 at age 80.

 The 70-year-old Woolworth Building is designated a New York City Landmark April 12.

Battery Park City's Esplanade opens officially June 29; Cooper Eckstut and Hanna Olin have designed the walkway, and although it is still incomplete, and isolated by construction activities and the West Side Highway, it becomes an instant attraction.

The 34-story Seaport Plaza building is completed at 199 Water Street near the South Street Seaport to designs for developer Jack Resnick & Sons. Swanke Hayden Connell & Partners has designed the structure that extends to Front Street between John and Fulton streets with 1 million square feet of office space.

The 29-story 85 Broad Street Building is completed next to the Fraunces Tavern Historic Block with a brownstone façade. Skidmore, Owings & Merrill has designed the structure in International Style, and its chief tenant will for years be the Goldman, Sachs investment bank.

The 41-story Continental Center is completed at 180 Maiden Lane. Designed in International Style for Continental Insurance Co. by architect Der Scutt, the octagonal structure is bounded by Pine, Front, and South streets.

The 30-story National Westminster Bank USA Building is completed near the East River at 175 Water Street to International Style designs by Fox & Fowle, who have created a plan calling for twin glass-walled cylinders that rise from a rectangle covered in brownstone with horizontal bands of glass.

The 26-story Philip Morris Building is completed at 120 Park Avenue, between 41st and 42nd streets, to International Style designs by Ulrich Franzen & Associates. Occupying the site used from 1906 to 1931 by the old Belmont Hotel, and by the Airlines Terminal Building beginning in 1940, it contains a 5,000-square-foot Whitney Museum Gallery that is open to the public (and is soon taken over by vagrants).

The 36-story 900 Third Avenue office tower is completed at the northwest corner of 54th Street for Argentine developer Jacobo Finkielstain. Argentine-born architect Cesar Pelli, now 57, and Rafael Viñoly have designed the structure with help from Emery Roth & Sons.

The 35-story American Telephone and Telegraph Building (later the SONY Building) is completed at 550 Madison Avenue, between 55th and 56th streets, to designs by John Burgee and Philip Johnson. Popularly called the "Chippendale" Building because of its unusual superstructure, it has a lobby containing the 24-foot-high "Golden Boy" statue that surmounted the old AT&T building at 195 Broadway in 1917, but the statue will be removed when AT&T gives up the new building in 1992 and moves downtown to 32 Avenue of the Americas, off Walker Street.

The 42-story IBM Building designed by Edward Larrabee Barnes is completed at 590 Madison Avenue, between 56th and 57th streets, with an atrium on its south side containing giant fern trees (landscape architect Robert L. Zion has designed it) and a subterranean art gallery. IBM will sell the building to developer Edward Minskoff, who will lease the gallery space to the Arlington, Va.-based Freedom Forum for its Media Studies Center, now at Columbia University.

Trump Tower is completed at 725 Fifth Avenue, northeast corner 56th Street. Developer Donald Trump has razed the Art Deco Bonwit Teller store and engaged architect Der Scutt of Swanke Hayden Connell to design a 68-story structure whose mirrored black glass exterior sheaths a complex of apartments, including a triplex penthouse, that rise above an atrium filled with upscale shops. Trump has reneged on his promise to give Bonwit Teller's bas-reliefs to the Metropolitan Museum of Art, saying (after they were shattered) that it was too expensive to save them.

Manhattan residential construction increases after falling last year to the lowest point since World War II: the number of units completed rises to 2,558, up from last year's 1,812, and will rise next year to 3,952 as the economy improves.

The first Charlotte Gardens single-family, suburban-style ranch houses are completed in the South Bronx, an area that has for years been notorious for crime and urban decay (see 1977). Built almost entirely with city money, the last of the 89 houses in the development will be sold in 1986 at prices ranging from $49,500 to $60,000, depending on extra features such as carports (see 1997).

A "new" Ritz-Carlton Hotel opens at 112 Central Park South (its developer has gutted the 25-story Navarro Hotel that opened in 1927, provided its rooms with built-in air conditioners, added a noisy restaurant exhaust system, and boosted room rates). It will become the Westin Hotel in 1998 and the Inter-Continental 2 years later.

A 68-year-old, 12-inch water main break at Seventh Avenue and 34th Street August 10 floods an underground Consolidated Edison substation, plunges the garment district into a 3-day blackout, forces the shutdown of about 1,000 business firms, interrupts service for 7 hours on the Lexington Avenue IRT subway between Grand Central and the Brooklyn Bridge (service on the BMT from 57th Street to City Hall is interrupted for 6 hours). Another 68-year-old water main breaks August 24 beneath a section of Broadway north of 23rd Street near the intersection with Fifth Avenue; it sends hundreds of thousands of gallons gushing through the streets, snarls morning rush-hour traffic, knocks out major subway lines, disrupts water and telephone service for hours, and forces the Metropolitan Life Insurance Company at 1 Madison Avenue to send home 5,000 workers before they can enter the building. The city spends about $6 million per year on water-main replacements, but 60 percent of the pipes were installed before 1900, many are well over a century old, their sizes range from six inches in diameter to 72 inches, vibrations from surface and subway traffic have loosened the earth that supports Manhattan's 6,000 miles of mains, and breaks occur at the rate of about 10 per week (the rate was highest in 1979 following the fiscal crisis that forced a halt in water-main repairs), although most are not important enough to make headlines.

La Réserve opens February 11 at 4 West 49th Street, formerly the Swiss Pavilion. Managing owner Jean-Louis Missud's chef André Gaillard will die young in 1990 and be succeeded by Dominique Payradeau.

Parioli Romanissimo moves after 11 years on First Avenue at 76th Street into the ground floor of a neo-Renaissance town house at 24 East 81st Street. The proprietor is Rubrio Rossi.

An American Place opens in October with 50 seats at 969 Lexington Avenue between 70th and 71st streets (formerly the premises of Le Plaisir), taking its name from that of Alfred Stieglitz's art gallery early in the century. Former River Café chef Lawrence P. Forgione, 31, offers a prix-fixe dinner at $45 per person plus cocktails, wine, tips, and taxes (see 1989).

Il Cantinori opens at 32 East 10th Street serving Tuscan dishes. Florence-born restaurateur Pino Luongo, 30, arrived in New York 3 years ago to pursue a career as an actor (and escape Italy's military draft), found work as a busboy at the Greenwich Village Tuscan restaurant Don Sylvano, worked his way up to become manager, and has gone into partnership with Greek-born restaurateurs Steve Tzolis, 44, and Nicola Kotsoni, 36, to start Il Cantinori.

The Hard Rock Café opens at 221 West 57th Street, between Seventh Avenue and Broadway, with the tail section of a 1959 Cadillac impaled above its door. An offshoot of a London establishment, the place specializes in hamburgers, loud music, and memorabilia that is sold in its gift shop, attracting hordes of tourists. Similar establishments will open nearby in the early 90s.

The 40-year-old Bavarian Inn at 232 East 86th Street closes in December. Yorkville's "German Broadway" has begun to lose its ethnic character.

Workers erect scaffolding around the Statue of Liberty as restoration work begins to give the statue a new torch, new stainless-steel supports, a glass-walled hydraulic elevator, and improved visitor facilities. The Centennial Commission formed last year has set a fund-raising goal of $230 million to spruce up not only the statue but also Ellis Island, where walls and other structures installed after 1924 are to be removed, the main building repaired, and historic areas—especially the Registry—restored (see 1984).

1984 Brooklyn-born Department of Corrections commissioner Benjamin Ward, 57, takes office as the city's first black police commissioner. Appointed by Mayor Koch, Ward began his career as a white-gloved traffic officer on First Avenue and will serve until 1989, commanding the city's efforts against the crack epidemic and its related crime wave. Says Ward at a press conference, "Many people make the mistake of thinking that black people are liberal because they are black. I'm very, very liberal when it comes to race relations, but when it comes to law enforcement, I am very, very conservative. I certainly believe bad guys belong in jail."

President Reagan wins reelection with 525 electoral votes to 13 for former vice president Walter Mondale, 56, who has run with Queens congresswoman Geraldine Ferraro, 48, but carries only the District of Columbia and his home state of Minnesota. Now 73, Reagan receives 59 percent of the popular vote.

Brooklyn's Starrett City wins a federal district court decision upholding its race-based occupancy controls (see real estate, 1976). The limit on minorities has been raised to 40 percent, but the black plaintiffs appeal the decision, the appeal will succeed, and although Starrett City will be obliged to admit applicants without regard to race it will remain racially integrated.

The City Council enacts legislation (Local Law 63) banning discrimination in clubs that have more than 400 members, provide regular meal service, and regularly receive "payment for dues, fees, use of space, facilities, services, meals or beverages directly from or on behalf of non-members for the furtherance of trade or business." The law is designed in part to protect professional and business women, who have been excluded from clubs such as the Union League, University, Athletic, and Century Association where men often conduct business. Dues payment by employers makes a club subject to the law (see 1988).

Police officers try to evict Eleanor Bumpers, 66, from her Bronx apartment for nonpayment of rent October 29, she slashes at a cop with a butcher knife, other cops shoot her dead with two shotgun blasts, and the incident produces charges of racism (Bumpers was black) and brutality. Commissioner Ward defends the officer who shot Bumpers, saying he followed the laws and guidelines on use of force, but the Police Department revises its policies with regard to restraining emotionally disturbed persons.

$ Italian authorities extradite financier Michele Sindona from New York to Milan September 25 to face charges of bank fraud and a possible connection with the 1979 murder of lawyer Giorgio Ambrosoli (see 1974). Now serving a 25-year sentence at New York, Sindona is alleged to have ties to Mafia crime families; a Milan court will sentence him next year to a 15-year prison term for bank fraud.

Wall Street's Dow Jones Industrial Average closes December 31 at 1211.57, down from 1258.64 at the end of 1983. Economic growth has risen at a 6.8 percent rate, highest since 1951; the inflation rate (3.7 percent) is the lowest since 1967, but budget and trade deficits have risen to record levels; the Department of Housing and Urban Development has reported May 1 that 250,000 to 350,000 Americans—thousands of them in New York City—are homeless.

Transit fares rise January 2 from 75¢ to 90¢ (see 1981; 1986).

Metropolitan Transportation Authority boss David L. Gunn hires Massachusetts Bay Transit executive A. Richardson Goodlatte, 45, and makes him responsible for cleaning and repairing the city's fleet of 6,000 subway cars that are not only filthy, smelly, and covered with graffiti but also average fewer than 6,000 miles before breaking down. On-time performance has fallen to 70 percent, down from 90 percent in the 1930s and 40s. Despite some labor-union opposition, Goodlatte will revolutionize the MTA's maintenance operations, heretofore based on a piecemeal approach with cars being sent to the barn for a faulty motor, a broken hose, or some other defect: henceforth, every car sent to the barn will be gutted and totally refitted with new or rebuilt equipment. Goodlatte will also clean up the cars, stationing crews at each terminal and ordering them to remove graffiti from each car as it comes in (trains with major graffiti problems are taken out of service and sent to the yard for more thorough cleaning). A graffiti artist whose work is promptly removed will become discouraged and quit, Goodlatte argues, and his initial success with cars on the No. 7 Flushing line will be followed on other lines; by 1989 the cars will be free of graffiti and soon thereafter will be averaging 66,000 miles between repairs.

The New York Times publishes its "Shipping/Mails" column for the last time April 15. While New York and New Jersey piers continue to handle more cargo than any other U.S. port, passenger volume in the port has dwindled to 400,000, down from 900,000 in 1960, and most of the arrivals and departures are cruise ships (see terminal, 1976). Jet planes have almost completely supplanted transatlantic passenger liners. "Fainter Toots From Atlantic Liners" (Op-Ed piece) by White Plains-born New York author James Trager, 59, in the New York Times April 20 notes the decline of Manhattan piers.

The Port Authority adopts a rule capping at 1,500 the number of miles that planes out of La Guardia Airport may fly, thereby forcing planes bound for the West Coast, Europe, Asia, and Latin America to use Newark or JFK airports.

The Avenue of the Americas that got its name in 1943 receives supplementary street signs identifying it as Sixth Avenue.

Bennington College freshman Libby Zion, 18, is brought to the emergency room of New York Hospital March 4 dehydrated and suffering from the chills and fever that physicians call "rigors." She is given 25 mgs. of Demerol but thrashes about so violently that nurses strap her to her bed to keep her from falling out; Zion dies 4 hours later, evidently from adverse drug reactions, and her father, New York Times writer Sidney Zion, 49, will sue the hospital and its staff members for malpractice and pain and suffering. Litigation will continue until February 1995, juries will find no evidence of malpractice, administering such a small amount of Demerol will be ruled out as having contributed to the girl's death, but the case will lead to legislation limiting the number of hours that hospital interns and residents can work without rest (see 1998).

The New York Hospital-Cornell Medical Center installs the city's first lithotripter for treating kidney stones (see laser, 1989).

Stanley H. Kaplan Educational Centers generate $35 million in revenues (see 1947). S.A.T. preparation pioneer Kaplan sells the business to the Washington Post, under whose management revenues will increase by 1999 to $151 million.

American Telephone & Telegraph Co. divests itself January 1 of its 22 Bell operating companies pursuant to a federal court order (see 1982). AT&T remains in the long-distance telephone business, and Ma Bell retains its Bell Laboratories research facilities and Western Electric manufacturing facilities. Regional holding companies—Ameritech, Bell

Atlantic, BellSouth, NYNEX, Pacific Telesis, Southwestern Bell, and USWest—take over 22 Bell units and thrive as local telephone rates go up across the country and service deteriorates (*see* 1997).

Former Ted Bates ad agency chairman Rosser Reeves dies of a heart attack at Chapel Hill, N.C., January 24 at age 73; *Reader's Digest* cofounder Lila Acheson Wallace of heart failure at suburban Mount Kisco May 8 at age 94. Her philanthropic contributions are estimated to have exceeded $60 million.

A two-and-a-half-story high snowflake containing 3,000 lights goes up above Fifth Avenue at 57th Street near Tiffany & Co. Electrical sign impresario Douglas Leigh, now 77, has created the new spectacular that will be put up before Christmas every year.

Nonfiction: *Mayor* by Mayor Ed Koch (with his Indianapolis-born aide William Rauch, 34); *The World According to Breslin* by columnist Jimmy Breslin, whose wife, Rosemary (*née* Dattolico), died of cancer in June 1981, leaving him with six children. He was married 2 years ago to Ronnie Eldridge, a widow with three children, who had been a top aide to Mayor Lindsay; *A City in the Republic: Antebellum New York and the Origins of Machine Politics* by Amy Bridges; *Living It Up: A Guide to the Names of Apartment Houses of New York* by Massachusetts-born historian Thomas Elliott Norton, 41, and Fort Worth-born gallery executive Jerry E. (Eugene) Patterson, 52; *Holdout!* by real estate developer Seymour B. Durst and architect-writer Andrew Alpern, who detail cases where property owners thwarted developers, singling out examples such as P. J. Clark's saloon, that remained standing when other buildings were razed to make way for 919 Third Avenue, and a Chock full o' Nuts coffee shop that tied up development at 135 Broadway from 1965 to 1980; *Top Drawer: American High Society from the Gilded Age to the Roaring Twenties* by Cleveland-born author Mary Cable, 64; *Scenes from the Life of a City: Corruption and Conscience in Old New York* by Philadelphia-born author Eric (Ross) Homberger, 42; *New York City's Gracie Mansion: A History of the Mayor's House* by Pittsfield, Mass.-born New-York Historical Society curator Mary Black (*née* Childs), 62 (with Joan R. Olshansky); *History in Asphalt: The Origin of Bronx Street and Place Names* by New York author John McNamara.

Publisher Alfred A. Knopf dies of congestive heart failure at suburban Purchase August 11 at age 91 (his wife, Blanche, died in June 1966 and he remarried 10 months later).

Painting: *Polestar* by Andy Warhol, French-born painter Jean-Michel Basquiat, 24, and Italian-born painter Francesco Clemente, 32; *History of Matzo: The Story of the Jews Part III* by Larry Rivers; *Can You Hear Me?* (oil on four canvases), *Her Story* (oil on three canvases), *Both Hands* (charcoal and pastel with clay on two sheets of paper), and *Sleep* (oil on canvas) by Elizabeth Murray. Lee Krasner (Pollock) dies at New York June 19 at age 75; Alice Neel of cancer at New York October 13 at age 84.

The Museum of Modern Art (MoMA) opens a new (west) wing that more than doubles its gallery space (*see* 1939). Architect Cesar Pelli & Associates has designed the structure in association with Edward Durrell Stone Associates (*see* 2002).

Theater: *The Miss Firecracker Contest* by Beth Henley 5/27 at the off-Broadway Manhattan Theater Club, with Holly Hunter, Mark Linn-Baker, 113 perfs.; *Hurlyburly* by David Rabe 8/7 at the Ethel Barrymore Theater, with William Hurt, Harvey Keitel, Christopher Walken, Jerry Stiller, Sigourney Weaver, 343 perfs.; *Balm in Gilead* by Lanford Wilson 9/6 at the off-Broadway Minetta Lane Theater, with Steven Bauer, Glenn Headley, Laurie Metcalf, 143 perfs. (originally presented 1/26/1965 at Ellen Stewart's Café La Mama experimental theater club); *Ma Rainey's Black Bottom* by Pittsburgh-born playwright August Wilson (Frederick Wilson Kittel), 38, 10/11 at the Cort Theater, with Newport News, Va.-born Theresa Merritt, 61, Baltimore-born actor Charles Dutton, 33, 225 perfs.; *The Foreigner* by New Orleans-born Chicago-raised actor-playwright Larry Shue, 38, 11/1 at the Astor Place Theater, with Shue, New Rochelle-born actor Anthony Heald, 40, in a play about American xenophobia, 686 perfs.

Former *New York Times* drama critic (and foreign correspondent) Brooks Atkinson dies of pneumonia at Huntsville, Ala., January 13 at age 89 (he was at the *Times* for 31 years); playwright Lillian Hellman dies of a heart attack on Martha's Vineyard June 30 age 74; playwright-screenwriter Norman Krasna of a heart attack at Los Angeles November 7 at age 74.

Television: *Night Court* 1/4 on NBC with Gail Strickland, Henry Anderson, Karen Austin, John Larroquette, 36, Selma Diamond, 62 (to 5/31/1992); *Kate and Allie* 3/19 on CBS with Susan Saint James (originally Susan Miller), 36, and Jane Curtin, 35, as divorced women with children who share a Greenwich Village apartment, Kelsey Grammer, 29 (to 9/11/1989); *The Cosby Show* 9/20 on NBC with comedian Bill Cosby, now 47, as Brooklyn obstetrician Cliff Huxtable of "10 Stigwood Avenue" (the episodes are filmed in Brooklyn's Midwood section with exterior shots of a Greenwich Village house at 10 St. Luke's Place), Phylicia Rashad, 35, Lisa Bonet, 15 (to 9/17/1992).

The black-and-white comic book *Teen-Age Mutant Ninja Turtles* created in May by New York freelance artists Kevin Eastman and Peter Laird features the turtles Donatello, Leonardo, Michelangelo, and Raphael, who were transformed by a radioactive "mutigant" and now live in New York's sewers. The comic book has little success until a UPI reporter writes a syndicated story that attracts the attention of licensers, Eastman and Laird sign a contract, and by the end of 1990 about $1 billion worth of Teen-Age Mutant Ninja Turtle T-shirts, buttons, comic books, toys, video games, breakfast cereals, and other merchandise will have been sold in 30 countries. The TMNT cartoon show will be the highest-rated CBS morning show in CBS history, and the first TMNT film will earn $250 million.

Films: Stan Lathan's *Beat Street* with Rae Dawn Chong, Guy Davis; Francis Ford Coppola's *The Cotton Club* with Richard Gere, dancer-actor Gregory Hines, Diane Lane; Ulu Grosbard's *Falling in Love* with Robert De Niro, Meryl Streep, Harvey Keitel; the documentary *In Our Hands* shows scenes of the 1982 Central Park anti-nuclear rally with appearances, performances, and speeches by Ellen Burstyn, Helen Caldicott, Jill Clayburgh, Holly Near, Peter, Paul & Mary, Roy Scheider, Pete Seeger, Benjamin Spock, Orson Welles, and dozens of others; Ivan Reitman's *Ghostbusters* with Bill Murray, Dan Aykroyd; Arthur Hiller's *The Lonely Guy* with comedian Steve Martin, Charles Grodin, Judith Ivey; Paul Mazursky's *Moscow on the Hudson* with Robin Williams, Maria Conchita Alonso; Frank Oz's *The Muppets Take Manhattan* with Kermit the Frog, Miss Piggy, Fozzie Bear, and the Muppets (Jim Henson, Frank Oz, Jerry Nelson, Richard Hunt, Dave Goelz); Marisa Silver's *Old Enough* with Sarah Boyd, Rainbow Harvest, Neil Barry, Danny Aiello; Sergio Leone's *Once Upon a Time in America* with Robert De Niro, James Woods, Elizabeth McGovern, Tuesday Weld, William Forsyth, Danny Aiello, Joe Pesci; Menachem Golan's *Over the Brooklyn Bridge* with Elliott Gould, Margaux Hemingway, Sid Caesar; Ron Howard's *Splash* with Daryl Hannah, Tom Hanks, John Candy.

Broadway musicals: *The Rink* 2/9 at the Martin Beck Theater, with Liza Minnelli, Chita Rivera, Newark-born actor Jason Alexander, 34, music by John Kander, lyrics by Fred Ebb, book by Terrence McNally, 204 perfs.; *Sunday in the Park with George* 5/2 at the Booth Theater, with Mandy Patinkin as painter Georges Seurat, Bernadette Peters, now 36, as his mistress Dot, music and lyrics by Stephen Sondheim, 604 perfs.

Ethel Merman is found dead in her 20 East 76th Street apartment at the Surrey February 15 at age 76—10 months after undergoing surgery for a brain tumor; actor-dancer Avon Long dies at New York February 15 at age 73; composer Arthur Schwartz of a stroke at Kintnersville, Pa., September 3 at age 83; lyricist Leo Robin at Woodland Hills, Calif., December 29 at age 84.

The 68-year-old Mannes College of Music moves in February from East 74th Street to 150 West 84th Street, occupying a handsome red-brick building put up in 1926. It will become an independent division of the New School for Social Research in 1989 and grow to have an enrollment of about 200.

Popular songs: *Born in the U.S.A.* (album) Bruce Springsteen; *A Mother's Spiritual* (album) by Laura Nyro.

Former émigrée nightclub owner-cabaret singer Bricktop (Ada Beatrice Queen Victoria Louise Virginia Smith) dies at New York January 31 at age 89, having helped to launch the careers of Josephine Baker, Mabel Mercer, Duke Ellington, and others; songwriter Eubie Blake dies at his Brooklyn home February 12 at age 100; blues singer Alberta Hunter at New York October 17 at age 89.

Trumpet virtuoso Wynton Marsalis, now 22, wins Grammy awards in both the jazz and classical music categories.

Former heavyweight champion Jack Dempsey dies of a heart ailment at New York May 31 at age 87, having closed his restaurant in 1974.

John McEnroe wins both the U.S. and British men's singles titles, Martina Navratilova the women's titles.

Donna Karan mounts her first show as an independent designer (*see* 1974). She and her partner launched Anne Klein II last year and gained quick success, but the Japanese conglomerate that owns a majority stake in Anne Klein has urged Karan to start her own label. She has resisted, Takiyho has sacked her while agreeing at the same time to back her new company, and she breaks all records at a special sale for customers of Bergdorf Goodman, now the top U.S. fashion retailer.

The "Mayflower Madam" makes headlines following an October 11 raid by officers of the Manhattan North Public Morals District on a small, first-story apartment at 307 West 74th Street and, 1 hour later, the arrest of a young woman in a $300-per-night room at the Parker Meridien Hotel, where she has been entertaining a "John" (actually an undercover cop). Three young women at the West 74th Street apartment have been shredding documents, but police find records linking them to a $1 million-per-year ring of 20 or 30 call girls working for one "Sheila Devlin." She turns out to be Sidney Biddle Barrows, 32, who surrenders October 16 to the Manhattan district attorney. The landlord of her West 80th Street apartment has been trying to evict her for alleged "business use" offenses and excessive "traffic," but Barrows is listed in the Social Register and is a descendant (on the Barrows side) of two Pilgrims who landed at Plymouth in 1620 (she attended the annual party of the Mayflower Society in March). Barrows has trained her "girls" to behave as if they, like she, attended finishing school; she has forbade them to use condoms, instructed them to kiss clients on the lips, discouraged them from using drugs or alcohol, urged them to be "romantic" and "loving," used the telephone directory's yellow pages and the *Village Voice* to advertise for recruits, and advertised "escort services" under the names Cachet, Elan, and Finesse, each with a different address, in the classified telephone directory. After plea bargaining, Barrows is let off with a $5,000 fine; she is permitted to keep more than $150,000 in profits, and her list of 3,000 clients (said to include company presidents, lawyers, physicians, and Arab sheiks who paid $200 to $400 per hour or $1,150 for the night) is not made public. Women Against Pornography estimates that the city has some 25,000 prostitutes.

A "subway vigilante" shoots four black youths December 22, climbs off the train, and disappears into a tunnel after telling a motorman that the teenagers had tried to rob him. Crime has been rampant in the subways, and public support rallies at first behind the unknown gunman, especially when his victims all turn out to have criminal records. Engineer Bernhard Hugo Goetz, 37, will surrender to New Hampshire police early in January and confess to the shootings that have left one youth paralyzed from the waist down. A Manhattan grand jury will indict Goetz only on charges of illegal weapon possession (he will be convicted and serve 8 months). A second grand jury will indict Goetz for attempted murder, but he will be acquitted.

The 49-story Wang Building is completed at 780 Third Avenue, between 48th and 49th streets, to International Style designs by Skidmore, Owings & Merrill. Its exterior is sheathed in polished red Bal-moral granite from Finland, its plaza is paved in red brick and granite, a row of trees separates it from the avenue, and its conference center includes a 154-seat auditorium.

The glass-sheathed 28-story Banque de Paris Building is completed at 499 Park Avenue, southeast corner 59th Street, to designs by I. M. Pei & Partners.

Two-story, single-family Nehemiah Plan houses go up on formerly city-owned land in Brownsville and East New York. Retired commercial builder and former City Club president I. D. Robbins, 69, has persuaded the East Brooklyn Congregations—a nonprofit, community-based coalition of mostly black churches—to back his plan for working-class and low-income row houses (the name comes from the Old Testament prophet who rebuilt Jerusalem). The subsidized houses cost only $59,000 to build and sell for $49,000 with a no-interest loan repayable when the house is resold. By April 1989 there will be 1,250 Nehemiah Plan houses in Brooklyn with 250 under construction (*see* 1991).

Dag Hammarskjöld Tower is completed at 240 East 47th Street, southwest corner Second Avenue. Designed in International Style by Gruzen & Partners and erected beside the Dag Hammarskjöld Plaza opened in 1974, the 43-story structure has 133 apartments with a health club and swimming pool. It is sheathed in brown brick, has corner balconies containing prefabricated elements, and extends through to 46th Street.

The 40-story 500 Park Tower is completed just west of the former Pepsi-Cola building opened in 1959 at the southwest corner of Park Avenue and 59th Street. Designed by James Stewart Polshek & Partners, it has condominium apartments on floors 12 through 40 (offices occupy the lower floors).

Trump Plaza is completed at 167 East 61st Street, northwest corner Third Avenue. Designed by Philip Birnbaum & Associates for developer Donald Trump, the 40-story apartment tower extends to 62nd Street.

The 40-story Kingsley apartment house is completed with rounded balconies at 400 East 70th Street, southeast corner First Avenue, to designs by Stephen B. Jacobs & Associates.

The 40-story Saratoga apartment house is completed at 330 East 75th Street, between First and Second avenues. Schuman, Lichtenstein, Claman & Efron has designed the building with a sidewalk clock.

The 31-story Columbia apartment house is completed at the northwest corner of Broadway and 96th Street. Designed by Liebman Williams & Ellis, it occupies a site once earmarked for an uptown branch of Gimbels department store.

The 32-story Novotel opens on the west side of Broadway at 52nd Street with 470 rooms.

A spokesman for the state's Urban Development Corp. dismisses an 1,100-page environmental statement issued August 20 about a $1.6 billion plan to rebuild Times Square. Consultants to the city and the corporation say the project is likely not only to lead to more crowded buses and subway trains than was previously predicted, and higher rents in surrounding areas, but also will cast deep shadows on 42nd Street, especially when the sun is high in summer. The spokesman says the redevelopment plan will still be "overwhelmingly advantageous" to the vast majority of New Yorkers.

City Council President Carol Bellamy releases a study July 2 showing that the city had 20 percent fewer supermarkets last year than in 1981 even though the population grew by 1 percent. The exodus of stores from the city, she says, has meant higher prices and fewer jobs, especially for the poor, aged, and disabled.

Au Bon Pain opens its first New York shop in Rockefeller Center. The Boston-based chain moves outside the Boston area for the first time and will add muffins and sandwiches to its stores' menus in 1986.

The Manhattan Ocean Club opens at 57 West 58th Street. The New York Restaurant Group headed by Alan N. Stillman soon employs New Jersey-born chef Steve Mellina, who has studied at the Cordon Bleu in Paris and under Michel Guérard in the south of France.

Petrossian opens in September at 182 West 58th Street on the ground floor of the 75-year-old Alwyn Court apartment house. An offshoot of the Paris Petrossian, it features caviar (the sturgeon roes beluga, osetra, and sevruga plus salmon roe and smoked cod roe), Périgord goose and duck foie gras, champagne, and vodka by the glass or bottle. Prix-fixe luncheon is $27, dinner $42, $59, and $98.

Arcadia opens in December at 21 East 62nd Street, where Ken Aretsky and chef Anne Rosenzweig, 27, offer a variety of imaginative dishes, many of them only seasonally, that will establish Rosenzweig's reputation. Originally an anthropologist, she learned about food in Africa, returned to New York in 1980, and apprenticed to be a chef. The prix-fixe

dinner is $45 with surcharges for a few dishes (such as the "chimney-smoked" lobster); luncheon service is à la carte.

Ellis Island closes for renovation (see 1983). Looters landing from small boats have vandalized the facility, ripping out copper piping and anything else of value (see museum, 1990).

1985 The city's chief medical examiner Elliot M. Gross, 50, comes under fire beginning January 27 with a series of New York Times articles by Philip Shenon charging that he has supplied false autopsy reports on police-custody deaths. Gross has headed the office since 1979, pathologists in other cities are quoted as saying the Medical Examiner's Office—once the best in the country—has lost credibility, and Gross's colleagues are quoted as saying that he has "weaseled" his reports. Mayor Koch appoints Arthur L. Liman of Paul, Weiss, Rifkind, Wharton & Garrison to head a commission investigating charges that Gross has leaned over backwards to favor the police. The commission finds evidence of serious misconduct but concludes that no crimes were committed. (The State Health Department will later find enough irregularities to charge Gross with gross negligence and incompetence.)

Mayor Koch wins a third term in a runaway election, asking voters, "How'm I doing?" City Council President Carol Bellamy runs on the Liberal ticket and receives 113,471 votes; Republican-Conservative candidate Diane McGrath gets 101,668, and the incumbent receives 862,226, but his final term will be marred by economic troubles, racial strife, and a scandal in the Parking Violations Bureau.

 More than two dozen Queens police officials are removed following allegations that officers in the 106th Precinct used stun guns to torture suspects in drug cases. Some officers are convicted on various charges after victims of the abuses show marks on their bodies caused by electric prods.

An elderly, homeless woman identified only as "Mama Doe" dies of pneumonia December 25 after Metro-North guards at Grand Central Terminal allow her to move back into the waiting room at dawn. Nearly all the benches have been removed from the waiting room to discourage loitering, and the terminal's 300 lockers have been removed; Metro-North has barred a fast-food chain from distributing unsold doughnuts at the terminal lest it attract more hungry people, the authority has forbidden shaving and laundering in the men's room, janitors have mopped the ramp leading to the 42nd Street entrance with a strong ammonia mixture, and they have chained the 42nd Street doors open even in 10° F. cold. Vigils will be held each Christmas to commemorate the death of "Mama Doe."

$ Equitable Life Assurance Society acquires the 26-year-old Wall Street investment banking house Donaldson, Lufkin and Jenrette in January for $440 million.

Chemical Bank introduces New York's first major automated cash machine network—New York Cash Exchange (NYCE) (*see* Chase merger, 1992).

Merrill Lynch at New York receives a letter May 25 alleging insider trading in its Caracas, Venezuela, office; typed in broken English, the one-page letter sparks an internal inquiry that leads to a bank in Nassau and thence to Dennis B. Levine, 32, a managing director of acquisitions for Drexel Burnham Lambert in New York. It will turn out that Levine has been feeding inside information to stock trader Ivan F. Boesky, now 48, whose book *Merger Mania* is published by CBS-owned Holt Rinehart & Winston (CBS sues Boesky in connection with his effort to take over the network) (*see* 1986; Boesky, 1975).

The Plaza Accord signed at the Plaza Hotel September 22 commits the finance ministers and central bank governors of Britain, France, Germany, Japan, and the United States to pursue a vigorous policy of disinflation, lower taxes by curbing public expenditures, resist protectionism, and take other measures designed to improve the world economic environment. Quantum Fund manager George Soros has been accumulating Japanese yen (*see* 1979), he recognizes that the ministers will work to bring down the value of the overvalued dollar, some of his traders have taken profits by selling yen, he orders them to increase their yen holdings, and by year's end the value of the fund has grown 122.2 percent.

Wall Street's Dow Jones Industrial Average hits a record high of 1955.57 December 2 and closes December 31 at 1895.95, up 27.6 percent from its 1984 closing of 1211.57. The NASDAQ closes at 325.16, up 31.3 percent.

$ Henri Bendel is acquired by The Limited, a Columbus, Ohio-based retail chain (*see* 1959). Founded in 1963 by Leslie Wexner, The Limited opens in August at 691 Madison Avenue, northeast corner 62nd Street (a site once occupied by a Louis Sherry's store designed by McKim, Mead & White), where it has put up a low-rise glass store, designed by Beyer Blinder Belle, that will later become a Hermès store (*see* Bendel, 1986).

Macy's chairman Edward Finkelstein, 60, announces October 21 that he will lead a leveraged buyout to transfer control of the retail giant from its stockholders to Macy's 350 top executives (*see* 1986; *but see also* 1992).

The Army Corps of Engineers grants a landfill permit for the proposed Westway Project February 25 (*see* environment, 1982), U.S. District Judge Thomas P. Griesa says August 7 that the Corps acted improperly, and he announces August 7 that he is continuing his 3-year-old injunction barring construction of Westway in lower Manhattan. Cost estimates for the project range between $4 billion and $10 billion, with 90 percent of the funding to come from the federal government. "It is the court's conclusion that two failures to justify the Westway landfill and federal funding under the applicable legal standards should bring the matter to an end," Judge Griesa says, noting that "transportation needs can be satisfied by the existing roadway improved at a cost of $50 billion," but Governor Cuomo and Mayor Koch say the fight is not over. It would be "a gross error" to drop Westway at this point, says Koch.

The city receives 8,000 formal complaints about taxi service, 22 percent of them from people who say drivers have refused to pick them up or take them where they wanted to go. An administrative law judge hears such complaints, and drivers convicted of three refusals in 24 months may have their licenses revoked.

The United Federation of Teachers elects Sandra Feldman, 46, president January 9; she criticizes the city's public school system, saying it is managed from the top down with the teacher remaining "low man on the totem pole." Feldman succeeds Albert Shanker, who resigns January 21 after 21 years in the job (he wants to devote more time to the American Federation of Teachers), and she is only the third person (and the first woman) to head the 25-year-old teachers' union.

The U.S. Supreme Court rules in June that New York City may no longer send public school teachers into parochial schools to provide federally mandated remedial reading and mathematics education. Mayor Koch puts in a telephone call July to Msgr. Vincent D. Breen, vicar for education of the Archdiocese of Brooklyn, who says that while it may be an unconstitutional mixing of Church and State to have the teachers in religious schools the Court did not rule out having the remedial classes off site. Says Koch, "How about a van?" Within 10 years the city will have 114 mobile classrooms with drivers, serving 22,000 students outside 250 religious and private schools, supported by $15 million per year in federal antipoverty funds under a program known as Title I (*see* 1997).

The State Board of Regents acts October 18 to rename Polytechnic Institute of New York, making it Polytechnic University (*see* 1973). The 131-year-old school now has campuses on Long Island and in Westchester as well as in Brooklyn and Manhattan.

A libel suit brought against CBS by the right-wing Fairness in Media group in behalf of Gen. William Westmoreland is settled February 18, Atlanta broadcaster Ted Turner tries to buy the network, CBS president Thomas H. Wyman, 54, replaced founder William S. Paley as CEO 5 years ago and borrows heavily to fend off Turner's bid, the company's growing debt forces it to lay off 125 of 1,250 CBS News employees September 19, morale sags, Loews Corp. chairman Laurence A. Tisch becomes the largest single shareholder in the $3.5 billion broadcasting giant, and Wyman invites him to become a member of the board (*see* 1986).

Capital Cities Communications buys American Broadcasting Co. for $3.5 billion in March (*see* 1995).

Twentieth Century-Fox Film Corp. agrees May 6 to buy Metromedia's seven independent television stations in a deal valued at $2 billion ($650 million in cash plus assumption of $1.3 billion in debt) (*see* Multimedia, 1984). Publisher Rupert Murdoch has owned 50 percent of Fox since March in partnership with Denver oil investor Marvin Davis and has been negotiating since the end of last year with Metromedia's John W. Kluge, who retains the Metromedia name and will continue to develop interests in television and radio broadcasting, telecommunications, outdoor advertising, entertainment (the Ice Capades, Harlem Globetrotters, music publishing companies, Orion Pictures). An FCC regulation bars foreign citizens from owning U.S. television stations, but Murdoch has announced May 3 that he would become a U.S. citizen (*see* 1986; *Post*, 1988).

General Electric agrees December 11 to acquire RCA and its National Broadcasting Co. for $6.3 billion in a deal engineered by RCA chairman (and former Atlantic Richfield president) Thornton F. Bradshaw, now 68, who since his appointment in 1981 has succeeded in restoring NBC to first place in terms of ratings. Analysts call it the largest acquisition thus far in history outside of the oil business (*see* Thomson S.A., 1987; CNBC, 1989).

The Newhouse family's Advance Publications acquires the 60-year-old *New Yorker* magazine from the Fleischmann family March 8 for $168 million. The magazine has been losing money for years and will continue to operate at a deficit for more than a decade (*see* Gottlieb, 1987). Former *New Yorker* "Talk of the Town" essayist and author E. B. White dies of Alzheimer's disease at North Brooklin, Me., October 1 at age 86.

Murdoch Magazines and Hachette Publications bring out a U.S. version of the 44-year-old French fashion magazine *Elle*, making *Vogue* look a little dowdy. *Elle*'s circulation will quickly reach 825,000, knocking *Harper's Bazaar* to third place among U.S. fashion magazines. Media magnate Rupert Murdoch, now 54, becomes a U.S. citizen, although his News Corp. continues to be based at Sydney, Australia.

Nonfiction: *The Rise and Fall of New York City* by former Housing and Development Administration commissioner Roger Starr, 67; *Canarsie: The Jews and Italians of Brooklyn against Liberalism* by Yale sociologist Jonathan Rieder; *Elegant New York: The Builders and the Buildings* by John Tauranac and Christopher Little; *The Late, Great Pennsylvania Station* by New York-born author Lorraine B. Diehl (*née* Bascaglia), 45; *Ellis Island: A Pictorial History* by New York author Barbara Benton.

Author Stuart Chase dies at Redding, Conn., November 16 at age 97.

Fiction: *American Falls* by John Calvin Batchelor deals in large part with events that occurred in the city during Civil War days; *City of Glass* by Newark-born New York novelist Paul Auster, 38; *World's Fair* by E. L. Doctorow; *Zuckerman Bound* by Philip Roth; *White Noise* by Don DeLillo; *Hard Money* by Michael M. Thomas; *Queer* by William S. Burroughs, now 71.

CBS sells the trade division of its Holt Rinehart & Winston publishing house December 3 to the German media conglomerate Verlagsgruppe Georg von Holtzbrinck, whose management retains the name Henry Holt (*see* Farrar, Straus, 1994). CBS will sell Holt Rinehart's textbook operation for $500 million next year to Harcourt Brace Jovanovich, now based at Orlando, Fla.

Painting: *Van Heusen* (Ronald Reagan, silkscreen) by Andy Warhol; *Kitchen Painting* (oil on two canvases) and *Open Book* (oil on five canvases) by Elizabeth Murray; *Fanny/Fingerpainting* by Chuck Close (who has created the photolike portrait of his grandmother-in-law from thousands of his own fingerprints); *Elands and Bull* (acrylic on canvas), *Purple Wall* (oil on canvas), and *Green-gold Wall* (acrylic on canvas) by Elaine de Kooning, who has been inspired by the paleolithic cave paintings at

Lescaux in France and Altamira in Spain that she finds close in spirit to 20th century art.

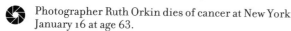 Photographer Ruth Orkin dies of cancer at New York January 16 at age 63.

Theater: *Biloxi Blues* by Neil Simon 3/28 at the Neil Simon Theater, with Matthew Broderick, Los Angeles-born ingénu Barry Miller, 27, Los Angeles-born ingénue Penelope Ann Miller, 21, 524 perfs.; *As Is* by New York-born playwright William M. (Moses) Hoffman, 46, 5/1 at the Lyceum Theater, with Jonathan Hadary and Jonathan Hogan, is about homosexuals and AIDS, 285 perfs.; *Doubles* by Lincoln, Neb.-born writer David Wiltse, 44, 5/8 at the Ritz Theater, with John Cullum, Ron Leibman, Austin Pendleton, Tony Roberts, 277 perfs.; *I'm Not Rappaport* by Herb Gardner 11/19 at the Booth Theater, with Judd Hirsch, Cleavon Little, 1,071 perfs.; *A Lie of the Mind* by Sam Shepard 12/5 at the Promenade Theater, 185 perfs.

Actor-playwright Larry Shue is killed in the crash of a commuter airplane in Virginia's Blue Ridge Mountains September 23 at age 39.

Television: *The Equalizer* 9/25 on CBS with Edward Woodward, 55, as a former CIA agent turned New York vigilante, Tammy Grimes (to 8/24/1989).

Films: Martin Scorsese's *After Hours* with Griffin Dunne, Rosanna Arquette; Susan Seidelman's *Desperately Seeking Susan* with Rosanna Arquette, singer-actress Madonna (originally Louise Ciccone), Aidan Quinn, Mark Blum; Amos Kolleck's *Goodbye, New York* with Julie Hagerty, Kolleck, David Topaz; Michael Dinner's *Heaven Help Us* with Donald Sutherland, John Heard; Jud Taylor's *Out of the Darkness* with Martin Sheen as Eddie Zigo, the New York police officer who broke the Son of Sam murders in the late 1970s; Woody Allen's *Purple Rose of Cairo* with Allen, Mia Farrow.

Actress Ruth Gordon dies at Edgartown, Mass., August 28 at age 88; Yul Brynner of lung cancer at New York Hospital October 9 at age 65 (he has been smoking since age 12); Anne Baxter at Lenox Hill Hospital December 12 at age 62 following a stroke.

Broadway musicals: *Big River* 4/25 at the Eugene O'Neill Theater, with René Auberjonois, Susan Browning, book based on Mark Twain's *Huckleberry Finn*, music and lyrics by Fort Worth-born composer-writer Roger Miller, 49, 1,005 perfs.; *The Mystery of Edwin Drood* 12/2 at the Imperial Theater, with English actor George Rose, 65, Betty Buckley, English jazz singer Cleo Laine, 58, Los Angeles-born actor Howard McGillin, 32, music and lyrics by

English-born songwriter Rupert Holmes, 39, songs that include "Perfect Strangers," "Don't Quit While You're Ahead," "Moonfall," book based on the unfinished Dickens novel, 608 perfs.

Scenery and costume designer Raoul Pène Du Bois dies at New York January 1 at age 72.

Radio City Music Hall is designated a New York City Landmark April 23 (its interior was given landmark status in March 1978).

The Palladium opens at 126 East 14th Street. Created by Steve Rubell and Ian Schrager of Studio 54 notoriety, who have converted the old Academy of Music into a posh multi-media nightclub, it will continue until 1997.

Compact discs and CD players are introduced with superior sound qualities. Music lovers hail the improvement and shift to the new technology.

Jazz drummer Jonathan "Jo" Jones dies of pneumonia at New York September 3 at age 73; jazz trumpeter Charles M. "Cootie" Williams at New York September 15 at age 77 (approximate).

The New York Knicks win a nationally televised National Basketball Association lottery and choose Georgetown University center Patrick Ewing, 21, as their number one college draft pick. The Knickerbockers will build successful, defense-oriented teams around Ewing but will fail to win an NBA championship in an era dominated by Michael Jordan and the Chicago Bulls.

Ivan Lendl, 25 (Czech.), wins in U.S. men's singles at Flushing Meadow, Hana Mandlikova, 23 (Czech.), in women's singles.

Police officer Lee Van Houten, 24, checks Cornell University sophomore Jonah Perry, 19, for possible car thefts at the corner of Morningside Drive and 113th Street at the rear of St. Luke's Hospital June 12, Perry allegedly attacks him, he shoots Perry dead, and he arrests his 17-year-old brother Edmund, who has just graduated from the Philips Exeter Academy in New Hampshire, started a summer job at Kidder, Peabody in Wall Street, and is scheduled to enter Stanford University in the fall. Neither has any criminal record, and the incident creates a furor in the city's black community.

Mafia boss Paul Castellano and his bodyguard Thomas Bibotti are shot dead outside Sparks Steak House in East 46th Street December 16 while Castellano is on trial with nine others for auto-theft conspiracy. Castellano has lived in a mansion atop Todd Hill in Staten Island and consorted with legitimate businessmen while letting his blue-collar underlings carry on the rackets organized by his late cousin (and brother-in-law), Carlo Gambino (*see* 1976). Bronx-born John J. Gotti, 45, has served time for manslaughter and is facing trials on racketeering and assault charges; he is suspected of having had the 71-year-old Castellano rubbed out so that he can seize control of the Gambino organized-crime family, doing so with help from his Bensonhurst-born henchman Salvatore "Sammy the Bull" Gravano, 40 (*see* 1992).

The 44-story 7 World Trade Center (Tishman Center) is completed to International Style designs by Emery Roth & Sons.

The 40-story 1 World Financial Center (Dow Jones & Co. Building and Oppenheimer & Co. Tower) is completed in West Street opposite Cedar Street in Battery Park City, and 3 World Financial Center (American Express Headquarters) at the southwest corner of West Street and Vesey Street, both to designs by Cesar Pelli and Adamson Associates. A third building (No. 4; Merrill Lynch World Headquarters, North Tower) will open next year at the southeast corner of Vesey Street and North End Avenue, a fourth (No. 2; Merrill Lynch World Headquarters, South Tower) in 1987 in West Street between Liberty and Vesey streets, and a fifth (No. 5) in 1992 in Vesey Street between West Street and North End Avenue (Pelli will have an assist from Haines Lundberg Waehler on all but the first) (*see* Wintergarden, 1988).

The turreted 27-story 33 Maiden Lane office tower is completed opposite the Federal Reserve Building. Designed by Philip Johnson and John Burgee, its street-level brick archways echo the Renaissance design of the Fed, and its space (570,000 square feet) is shared initially by Chase Manhattan Bank and IBM, with a branch of the Whitney Museum (later closed) reached through a sunken plaza. The address will be changed to 2 Federal Plaza and some 800 Fed employees will occupy the space beginning early in 1999.

Columbia University sells the land under Rockefeller Center to the Rockefeller family, receiving $400 million. It has owned the land since 1814 and received annual rent on it since 1929, the rent has been $11.1 million per year, giving it a yield of only 2.8 percent, and Columbia wants to use the proceeds of the sale to increase its $863 million endowment fund, diversify its investment portfolio, and gain more flexibility in its financial affairs. The sale announced early in the year follows 42 years of negotiations. The Rockefellers have charged low rents and provided more service than do most landlords, they have never derived much profit from the eight square blocks of real estate, and fifth-generation Rockefellers, many of them in need of cash, later in the year offer a 60 percent interest in Rockefeller Center to the public for $1.1 billion, raising fears that new owners will try to maximize the return on their investment by building additional floors atop smaller structures such as the Eastern Airlines Building (*see* 1989).

Rockefeller Center is designated a New York City Landmark April 23 (it will be designated a National Historic Landmark in 1987); the New York Stock Exchange building receives the designation July 9; the 54-year-old Eldorado apartment house is designated a landmark, having gone co-op 3 years ago.

Mayor Koch suspends further conversions of single-room-occupancy hotels as of January 8. The number of such hotel units has fallen to 45,000, down from an estimated 145,000 in the late 1970s, and those that remain often have whole families living in a single room, kitchens are almost non-existent, beds are often in hallways, drug dealers and prostitutes may work the corridors, and the buildings are poorly maintained. Owners—most of them absentee landlords interested only in collecting rents—have converted their buildings into luxury apartment houses, forcing previous occupants to relocate (thousands have become homeless). The moratorium is intended to give the city time to study ways to protect the remaining SRO hotels, but developer Harry Macklowe, 47, has his contractors demolish the Hotel Lennox, an SRO hotel at 143–151 West 44th Street, and three small adjoining buildings, on the night of January 7. (Criminal indictments are handed down against Macklowe's vice president for construction and against the contractor who did the actual demolition, but criminal intent cannot be shown in Macklowe's case. He bought the property for commercial office construction but will be barred from building on it until 1987.)

The city's year-round homeless population has risen to 4,000, up from 1,000 just a few years ago, reports Robert Jorgen, 60, who 8 years ago was named head of Crisis Intervention Services in the Welfare Department and worked with the Red Cross 2 years ago to set up the first municipal shelter system exclusively for displaced families, obtaining additional support from nonprofit agencies. Gentrification has forced many families out of their homes, and critics say Jorgen has dealt with welfare hotel owners who exploit the homeless at taxpayers' expense. "The policy of the city," Jorgen says, "is to allow no family to sleep in the streets."

Landlords protest in July when the City Council enacts a modification of the mayor's SRO proposal into law. Says one, "The moratorium is not an appropriate way to deal with the problems of the homeless. Solving it is the responsibility of the community and the local government. Dumping it into the laps of the landlords may have a short-term political impact, but it's not going to solve anything . . . There are landlords who own SROs with not a single occupied room; because of the moratorium they can't make any sort of conversion. That's not helping the homeless or anyone else" (see 1986).

Residents of Mitchell-Lama housing units must now show that their incomes are no more than seven or eight times the rent or maintenance charges (see 1958). No more units have been built since 1978, when it became impossible to float bonds at low interest rates.

The 52-story Museum Tower apartment house is completed at 15 West 53rd Street. Designed in International Style by Cesar Pelli & Associates and built at a cost of $55 million, it has an opaque blue-green glass façade with recessed terraces at the top, its 263 condominium apartments have teakwood floors and microwave ovens, it has manned elevators, a one-bedroom unit with 1,164 square feet is offered at $350,000, a two-bedroom with 1,917 square feet at $770,000. The Museum of Modern Art (MoMA) uses the building's first six floors.

The 46-story Marriott Marquis Hotel opens as part of a Times Square redevelopment program. Designed in International Style by South Carolina-born architect John (Calvin) Portman, Jr., 60, the 876-room structure has a 35-story main atrium rising from its 13th-floor lobby, 1,946 rooms, 56 suites, a revolving bar, glass-bubble elevators, and a 1,050-seat theater, but the new Marquis Theater does not begin to replace the Astor, Bijou, Victoria (originally Gaiety), Helen Hayes, and Morosco theaters that were razed to make way for the hotel. Portman has acted as co-developer of the project and obtained at least 90 percent of the necessary financial backing.

The worst drought to affect the city in 20 years drops levels in New York's reservoirs to 59 percent capacity in late February (they are usually 96 percent full at this time of year). Mayor Koch declares a drought warning April 3 and asks voluntary restraints on water use; he declares a drought emergency April 26, imposing mandatory restrictions on water use by business firms and residents. Leaks in the city account for losses estimated at 50 million or more gallons per day, and inspectors redouble efforts to find such leaks. Hurricane Gloria in late September drops 2.3 inches of rain over the city's watershed, adding 25.3 billion gallons to the reservoirs, but although they are now at 49.1 percent capacity, versus 44.4 before the storm, they are still well below the 75.1 normal for late September. A city law takes effect October 1 banning showerheads that use more than three gallons of water per minute; the law will create a bonanza for plumbing-fixture manufacturers and suppliers, but although violations carry a fine of $100, officials concede that compliance will depend on voluntary cooperation.

The Bronx Zoo's Jungle World opens June 21. It has been funded with a gift from publishing heiress Enid Haupt.

Central Park's Strawberry Fields opens October 9. John Lennon's widow, Yoko Ono, has given the park $1 million to landscape the hillside opposite the 101-year-old Dakota apartment house where she lives, and the gardens are opened to the public on what would have been Lennon's 45th birthday (see crime, 1980). Henry J. Stern proposed the project in 1981 while a member of the City Council, Republican members proposed dedicating the three-acre site at 72nd Street to the less politically controversial Bing Crosby, but Stern prevailed, and a memorial at the crest of the hill (a circular black-and-white mosaic) bears the word *Imagine*—the title of one of Lennon's best-known songs.

 God's Love We Deliver serves two meals per day to victims of AIDS. Founded by philanthropists at New York, GLWD will be serving 750 men, women, and children per day by 1994.

Cookbook author James Beard dies at New York January 23 at age 81 and is hailed as the father of American gastronomy (he has written thousands of syndicated newspaper columns and numerous magazine articles as well as cookbooks, and he hosted one of the first television cooking shows). At Julia Child's suggestion his Greenwich Village home at 167 West 12th Street is turned into the home of the Beard Foundation and made the site of cooking classes and almost nightly events related to food and its preparation.

Zabar's does $25 million worth of business, up from $12 million in 1980, with nearly $5 million of it in cheese (it carries nearly 400 varieties and sells 10 tons per week) (see 1977). The store has 160 employees, not counting its agents abroad.

Grace's Marketplace opens on the upper East Side. Grace Balducci Doria and her husband, Joseph, have quit Balducci's in Greenwich Village after a rancorous dispute and started a high-end grocery at 1237 Third Avenue, corner 71st Street. Her brother Andrew has sued Grace to stop her from using the famiy name for her new store.

The storefront Soup Kitchen International opens at 259A West 55th Street under the management of entrepreneur Al Yeganeh, whose brusque service will not discourage patrons from lining up to buy his innovative soups in six to 10 varieties per day, including corn-and-seafood chowder and Cuban black bean, with complimentary bread, fruit (apple, banana, or grapes), and a chocolate mint.

Montrachet opens at 239 West Broadway, between White and Water Streets in TriBeCa. Proprietor Drew Nieporent's Connecticut-born, French-trained chef, David Bouley, 33, will be dismissed next year, replaced by another man, and then by Debra Ponzek, who will remain until 1994, building a reputation (*see* Bouley, 1987).

The Union Square Café opens at 21 East 16th Street. Proprietor Danny Meyer, 27, will succeed by offering good food at affordable prices.

1986 Queens Borough President Donald R. Manes, 51, is found in his car near Shea Stadium January 11 in a dazed condition and bleeding heavily from knife wounds to his left wrist. A close ally of Mayor Koch, he concocts a fable about having been assaulted and kidnapped; the police conclude that he has attempted suicide with the knife found on the seat beside him, and it develops that he has been operating a bribery scam out of the Parking Violations Bureau and has heard that the FBI was investigating. Manes resigns, succeeds in his suicide attempt March 13 at his Jamaica Estates home, and is succeeded by his deputy Claire Shulman, 60, pending election by the voters in November.

Labor leader Harry Van Arsdale, Jr. dies in Queens February 16 at age 80; former senator Jacob K. Javits at Palm Beach, Fla., March 7 at age 83.

Liberty Weekend July 5 brings a crowd to Central Park's Great Lawn that is estimated to number 500,000.

Former governor W. Averell Harriman dies at Yorktown, N.Y., July 26 at age 94.

Mayor Koch signs a bill changing the composition of the Civilian Complaint Review Board to make half of its members private citizens (*see* 1966). Civilians will be appointed to the board next year, but investi-gations will continue to be conducted entirely by police officers (*see* 1993; Tompkins Square, 1988).

Mayor Koch expresses shock and outrage September 5 at a 63-page report detailing how the Department of Investigation repeatedly botched its inquiries into the Parking Violations Bureau case of 1982, passing allegations of wrongdoing from one office to another without taking action.

Gov. Cuomo wins reelection by a landslide, defeating Westchester County Executive Andrew P. O'Rourke, 53, with a 1.3 million-vote plurality—seven times his 1982 plurality—and 65 percent of the total vote, a record for any New York State gubernatorial race. O'Rourke wins in only one of the state's 62 counties.

Claire Shulman wins election in her own right to the $80,000-per-year post of Queens Borough president, defeating her 54-year-old rival, Republican district leader Estelle Cooper of Forest Hills, who has claimed that Shulman should have known about the Parking Violations Bureau scam used by her late predecessor Donald R. Manes to extort bribes from city contractors in the scandal for which Bronx Democratic Party leader Stanley J. Friedman now faces federal charges at New Haven.

The City Council finally passes a Gay Rights Bill March 20 (*see* 1974). The council has approved the measure by a vote of 21 to 15, and Mayor Koch signs it into law April 2.

The death of Brooklynite Michael Griffith, 23, on the Belt Parkway at Howard Beach, Queens, December 20 sets off weeks of protest demonstrations. Griffith and two companions have been walking through the predominantly white community after their car broke down; a group of white teenagers (who have been watching a female stripper at a party) confront the trio, shouting racial epithets; the white youths chase Griffith onto the parkway, where he is struck by a car and killed. Civil rights activist Rev. Alfred Charles "Al" Sharpton, Jr., 33, leads a black protest march and will play a conspicuous role in the city's politics into the next century.

Former American Express executive Sanford I. Weill buys a controlling interest in the consumer-loan company Commercial Credit Corp. after a failed attempt to buy Bank of America (*see* 1981). The computer maker Control Data has sold most of the stock in Commercial Credit to the public and Weill will buy the rest of it next year (*see* Primerica, 1988).

Real estate developer Seymour Milstein and his brother Paul acquire control of the financially failing Emigrant Savings Bank; they will pump $90 million into the 156-year-old institution as they increase their ownership to 91 percent.

General Electric Co. announces April 24 that it has agreed to pay $602 million to acquire an 80 percent interest in Kidder, Peabody & Co. and will distribute the remaining 20 percent among current partners in a move designed to retain Kidder's most valuable employees (see 1994). Other leading Wall Street firms have recently made public offerings or been sold to public corporations in order to acquire new capital (Kidder's $464 million in capital has paled beside that of Merrill Lynch's $2.6 billion).

The Securities and Exchange Commission accuses Drexel Burnham Lambert acquisitions director Dennis B. Levine May 12 of making $12.6 million by trading on non-public information; he cuts a deal, pleading guilty to felony charges and agreeing to co-operate with government investigators (he will serve only 18 months of a 2-year sentence). Arbitrageur Ivan F. Boesky pleads guilty and agrees after the close of the market November 14 to pay a record $100 million in penalties after admitting to being tipped off about forthcoming merger bids and then buying huge blocks of stock. Boesky will be sentenced to 3 years in a light-security California prison but given 19 months to wind up his business. While claiming that he picked stocks on the basis of careful research, he has reportedly devoted close to 20 hours per day to work, working his telephone to obtain information from thousands of Wall Street contacts, tape recording conversations in recent months as part of an agreement with the SEC (see Drexel, 1988).

Wall Street's Dow Jones Industrial Average soars nearly 350 points. The financial district's recovery creates hundreds of thousands of jobs, midlevel clerical workers earn $75,000 to $80,000 in salaries and bonuses, secretaries who work past 6:30 in the evening receive overtime pay, dinner money, and a driver to take them home, and the prosperity in the district provides more work for lawyers, accountants, printers, limousine drivers, office temps, building maintenance workers, and the like. The Dow closes at a record 1955.57 December 2 and closes December 31 at 1895.95, up 27.6 percent from its 1985 close of 1546.67. The NASDAQ closes at 325.16, up 31.3 percent.

The Discover Card introduced by Sears, Roebuck in January through its Dean Witter Financial Services division competes with American Express and bank-issued credit cards.

Former Gucci Shops Ltd. chairman Aldo Gucci pleads guilty January 20 in federal court at New York to two charges of tax evasion and one charge of conspiracy to defraud the federal government (see 1951). Now 80, Gucci admits that he has not reported $11.9 million diverted fraudulently from the company's income between 1977 and 1982, thereby evading payment of some $7.4 million in taxes. He agrees under a plea-bargain agreement to pay the $7.4 million prior to sentencing.

F. A. O. Schwarz announces April 4 that it sold its unexpired lease last year to the space it has occupied since 1930 at 745 Fifth Avenue and will move a block north to the new General Motors Building.

The Ralph Lauren retail store opens in April at 867 Madison Avenue, southeast corner 72nd Street, where the haberdasher has taken over the 88-year-old Gertrude Rhinelander Waldo mansion and turned it into a boutique. Major department stores in the city have leased Ralph Lauren departments and sell merchandise with Ralph Lauren labels in their other departments.

Gimbels in Greeley Square and on Lexington Avenue at 86th Street close June 19 and the 144-year-old Gimbels department-store chain is dissolved (see 1973). B.A.T. Industries has sold its properties to real-estate developers, and the Greeley Square store, a shopping institution since 1910, holds a liquidation sale in September, slashing prices by as much as 80 percent on its final day (see Manhattan Mall, 1989). Abraham & Straus acquires the Gimbels store at Valley Stream.

R. H. Macy chairman Edward Finkelstein completes a $3.7 billion leveraged buyout July 15—the largest management-led buyout ever (the group making the buyout includes 500 Macy executives). Macy's will borrow another $1 billion to acquire more stores, including Federated's Bullocks, Bullocks-Wilshire, and I. Magnin divisions (see 1988).

Associated Dry Goods Corp. agrees July 16 to accept a stock-swap offer valued at $2.7 billion from May Department Stores Co. Included are Lord & Taylor and the discount chains Caldor and Loehmann's.

Campeau Corp. buys Allied Stores for $3.6 billion, most of it borrowed by issuing high-yield "junk" bonds. Self-made Canadian real estate developer Robert Campeau, 63, sets his sights on building a retail empire and acquires stores that include Brooks Brothers (see Federated, 1988).

Barney's unveils a new women's clothing store September 1 after 2 years of delays and expenditures of more than $25 million.

The 37-year-old Pottery Barn chain is acquired by California-based Williams-Sonoma, whose management will expand the chain with catalog sales and out-of-state locations.

Henri Bendel announces that it will move in 1988 after 74 years in West 57th Street to a new location on Fifth Avenue, between 55th and 56th streets, where it will occupy premises four times as large (see 1912). The store has been owned since last year by The Limited (see 1991).

The lease on the 46-year-old Essex Street Retail Market expires (see 1940); a private developer takes over, evicts some of the market's merchants, and raises rents for most of the others.

City transit fares rise 33.3 percent January 1 from 75¢ to $1 (see 1984). The Metropolitan Transportation Authority continues efforts to rid subway cars of graffiti, install air conditioning, and make other improvements (see 1990).

New York Hospital's $120 million C. V. Starr Pavilion for Ambulatory Care, Diagnosis, and Treatment is completed in East 70th Street between York Avenue and the FDR Drive. Perkins & Will has designed the nine-story structure with 200,000 square feet—the hospital's first major expansion in 50 years. It has been financed by a tax-exempt New York State Dormitory Authority bond issue and, in part, by a grant from the Starr Foundation, established by the late Cornelius Vander Starr, who founded the American International Group (AIG) insurance organization (see commerce, 1926) and died in 1968. The building's atrium is named for AIG's CEO Maurice Raymond "Hank" Greenberg, 64, who chairs the hospital's board of governors.

The Brooklyn Museum is finally completed to designs by Arata Isosaki & Associates and James Stewart Polshek & Partners (see 1955). Only 300,000 of the 1.5 million square feet originally allotted have been used up to now, and the new Post Modern design provides 680,000 square feet of space.

Washington Irving High School in Manhattan's Irving Place admits boys for the first time in the fall after 84 years as a girls-only school (the last single-sex public school in the city) and changes its emphasis from child care, nursing, and secretarial skills to foreign languages and international studies.

Loews Corp. acquires a large block of CBS Inc. stock August 11, raising its interest in the company to just under 25 percent (see 1985). Loews chairman Laurence A. Tisch, now 63, has refused to sign a standstill agreement committing Loews to buy no more than 25 percent, Thomas H. Wyman resigns as chairman and president September 10 after a 7-hour board meeting in which he has revealed secret talks with Coca-Cola Co. about a possible friendly takeover, Tisch becomes acting CEO, founder William S. Paley, now 84, assumes the post of acting chairman, and the Federal Communications Commission (FCC) rules 4 to 0 October 16 that Loews has not gained control of CBS and that Tisch does not "dominate" its board of directors (see 1995).

Publisher Rupert Murdoch acquires Metromedia's New York television station WNEW-TV and renames it WNYW (see 1955; 20th Century Fox, 1985). Murdoch also acquires five other U.S. television stations from Metromedia, establishing the basis for what will become the Fox TV network (see Post, 1988).

DDB Needham Worldwide is created by a merger of the 37-year-old Doyle Dane Bernbach advertising agency with Needham and Harper Worldwide.

Former advertising agency head Chester Bowles dies at Sussex, Conn., May 25 at age 85 (he served as federal price administrator in 1943, directed the Office of Economic Stabilization in 1946, was elected governor of Connecticut in 1948, served as ambassador to India, and later worked for the UN). D'Arcy Masius Benton and Bowles is created by a merger of Benton and Bowles with D'Arcy MacManus Masius of Detroit.

Nonfiction: *When Brooklyn Was the World: 1920–1957* by Elliot Willensky; *Mansions in the Clouds: The Skyscraper Palazzi of Emery Roth* by Denver-born architectural historian Steve Ruttenbaum, 41; *Cities and the Wealth of Nations* by Jane Jacobs; *Tales of Times Square* by New York author Josh Alan Friedman; *The New York Public Library: Its Architecture and Decoration* by Henry Hope Reed.

Random House cofounder Donald S. Klopfer dies of a cerebral hemorrhage at Lenox Hill Hospital May 30 at age 84; educator-editor-author John A. Kouwenhoven of heart failure at Manchester, Vt., November 1 at age 80.

Barnes & Noble acquires the B. Dalton bookstore chain in November (see 1971). Leonard Riggio, now 45, uses junk-bond financing to purchase B. Dalton's 796 stores and gains nationwide distribution (see Doubleday, 1990).

Novelist Laura Z. Hobson dies of cancer at her native New York February 28 at age 85; Bernard Malamud at his native New York March 18 at age 71.

Painting: *Mural with Blue Brushstroke* by Roy Lichtenstein (for the five-story lobby of the new Equitable Center); *Chain Gang* (oil on four canvases) by Elizabeth Murray; *Rose Bison, Gold Grotto, Blue Bison, Morning Wall*, and *Red Bison Blue Horse* by Elaine de Kooning.

Former art collector-taxi owner Robert Scull dies of diabetes complications at his Warren, Conn., home January 1 at age 70. A sale of his collection at Sotheby's November 11 fetches $7.8 million.

Conditions at the New-York Historical Society's warehouse for art and artifacts are the most blatantly shocking" he has ever seen, says an outside consultant (*see* 1956; 1993).

The Metropolitan Museum of Art's Wallace Galleries for 20th Century Art are completed to designs by Kevin Roche John Dinkeloo & Associates.

Theater: *Coastal Disturbances* by Tina Howe 11/19 at the off-Broadway Second Stage Theater, with Topeka, Kan.-born actress Annette Bening, 28, Timothy Daly, Rosemary Murphy, Addison Powell, 350 perfs.; *Broadway Bound* by Neil Simon 12/4 at the Broadhurst Theater, with Los Angeles-born actor Jonathan Silverman, 20, Linda Lavin, Jersey City-born actress Phyllis Newman, 51, Jason Alexander, New York-born actor John Randolph, 71, Philip Sterling, 756 perfs.

Actor-director-producer-playwright Howard da Silva dies of a lymphoma at suburban Ossining February 16 at age 76.

The Lucille Lortel Awards are established by the League of Off-Broadway Theaters and Producers to honor outstanding achievements in the Off-Broadway theater.

Films: Woody Allen's *Hannah and Her Sisters* with Allen, Michael Caine, Mia Farrow, Maureen O'Sullivan (Farrow's mother), Diane Wiest. Also: Gene Saks's *Brighton Beach Memoirs* with Blythe Danner, Bob Dishy, Jonathan Silverman; John Hughes's *Ferris Buhler's Day Off* with Matthew Broderick; Robert Mandel's *F/X* with Bryan Brown, Brian Dennehy; Ivan Reitman's *Legal Eagles* with Robert Redford, Debra Winger, Daryl Hannah; Fielder Cook's *Seize the Day* with Robin Williams, Joseph Wiseman, Jerry Stiller; Alex Cox's *Sid and Nancy* with Gary Oldman as the late Sid Vicious of the Sex Pistols, Chloe Webb as groupie Nancy Spungen (*see* music, 1979); Jonathan Demme's *Something Wild* with Jeff Daniels,

Melanie Griffith; Joe Roth's *Streets of Gold* with Klaus Maria Brandauer, Adrian Pasdar, Wesley Snipes.

The RKO Keith's movie theater on Main Street in Flushing closes on Labor Day. The 3,000-seat theater was carved into a triplex, drug dealers have been using the place openly for sales, the ticket lobby has smelled of urine, and attendance has fallen off.

Carnegie Hall closes May 17 for a comprehensive, 7-month $60 million renovation and restoration to plans by the architectural firm James Stewart Polshek & Partners (*see* 1960). To help ensure the 95-year-old hall's financial stability, an adjacent lot in 57th Street acquired by Andrew Carnegie in 1903 is subleased to the Rockrose Development Corp. for construction of a 60-story office tower (*see* real estate, 1990).

Composer-arranger-pianist Harold Arlen dies at New York April 21 at age 80; clarinetist-bandleader Benny Goodman of a heart attack in his Manhattan House apartment at 200 East 66th Street June 13 at age 77; Broadway musical composer Alan Jay Lerner of lung cancer at his native New York June 14 at age 67; jazz pianist Teddy Wilson of cancer at New Britain, Conn., August 1 at age 73.

Ivan Lendl wins in U.S. men's singles at Flushing Meadow, Martina Navratilova in women's singles.

The New York Mets win the World Series, beating the Boston Red Sox 4 games to 3 with help from two home runs by California-born catcher Gary Carter, 32, two by California-born outfielder Len Dykstra, 23, one by Connecticut-born second baseman Tim Teufel, 28, and one by California-born outfielder Daryl Strawberry, 24. Boston wins the first two games, the Mets rally to win the next two, Boston wins the fifth, New York the sixth with a dramatic comeback in the bottom of the tenth inning as California-born relief pitcher Rick Aguilera, 24, retires the Rex Sox batters, and Georgia-born third baseman Charles Ray Knight, 34, hits a leadoff homer in the seventh inning of the seventh game to overcome a 3-to-0 deficit.

The *New York Times* reports May 22 that Central Park's 35-year-old Wollman Ice-Skating Rink will have to be rebuilt from scratch. Closed for renovations since June 1980, it has been the victim of labor disputes, engineering snafus, and general incompetence. Developer Donald Trump's 3-year-old Trump Tower skyscraper on Fifth Avenue overlooks Central Park and he writes to Mayor Koch May 28, offering to build a new Wollman Rink at his own expense, have it ready by November, lease it to the city at a fair market rental, and run it. Koch replies that the city will not let Trump operate the rink but will be happy to accept a $3 million donation for its rebuilding and Trump's supervision of the project. The new Wollman Rink is ready by mid-October, the work has cost less than $2.25 million, and even Trump's critics are bound to admire his efficient handling of a matter that the city has bungled. Admission fees are lower than at private rinks in the city, all profits go to charity and to the Parks Department, and Trump receives permission to use the rest of the allotted construction money to renovate the rink's skatehouse and restaurant.

The partially nude and bruised body of New York barfly Jennifer (Dawn) Levin, 18, is found behind the Metropolitan Museum in Central Park August 26 and police arrest "preppy" Robert E. Chambers, Jr., 19, shortly afterward. The six-foot-four Chambers makes a videotaped confession that he met Levin in Dorrian's Red Hand at 300 East 84th Street, went with her to the park, and engaged in rough sex play; when she tied his hands with her panties and squeezed his testicles so painfully that he reacted in a "frenzy," he locked his arm around her neck, killing her accidentally. He is indicted September 10 on two counts of second-degree murder (see 1988).

The Chinatown gang Born to Kill (B.T.K.) begins terrorizing local merchants. Founded by Vietnamese immigrant David Thai, the gang profits from extortion and murder to attract followers (see 1991).

Sen. Alfonse D'Amato dons army fatigues and sunglasses, goes to Washington Heights with cameramen and federal prosecutor Rudolph W. Giuliani (wearing a Hell's Angels vest decorated with swastikas), and buys crack cocaine as part of his successful reelection campaign, publicizing the ease with which drugs can be purchased in northern Manhattan.

Mafia crime family bosses go on trial at Federal District Court in Manhattan September 9. A team of State Organized Crime Task Force investigators led by Vermont-born crime fighter Richard F. Tennien, then 46, slipped a recording device inside the dashboard of the black Jaguar sedan used to chauffeur Luchese family Mafia boss Anthony "Tony Ducks" Corallo on his daily rounds. After 6 months the federal investigators had a record of Corallo's conversations and private musings; they also wiretapped him talking with Anthony "Fat Tony" Salerno of the Genovese family and Carmine "Junior" Persico of the Colombo family; prosecutors use the self-incriminating evidence to link Corallo with labor racketeering in the private trash-hauling business and major construction projects. The trial ends in November with convictions that severely damage the five major crime families: now 73, Corallo is sentenced to a 100-year prison term.

More than a dozen officers of Brooklyn's 77th Precinct are charged with a variety of thefts and other felonies in a major corruption case. Honolulu-born Newsday police reporter Mike McAlary, 29, persuades several officers to talk to him, and one of them, Brian O'Regan, kills himself a few hours later; a copy of McAlary's article is beside him when O'Regan's body is discovered.

The Jacob K. Javits Convention Center opens in April with 1.8 million square feet of space in four blocks between Eleventh and Twelfth avenues, from 34th Street to 37th, replacing the much smaller, 30-year-old Coliseum at Columbus Circle (whose facilities will remain in use to some extent for more than a decade). James Ingo Freed of I. M. Pei & Partners has designed it with help from Lewis Turner Associates, but the Javits Center is plagued from the start with crime and excessive labor costs that discourage many groups from using it.

The 29-story Republic National Bank Tower (later the HSBC Tower) is completed at 452 Fifth Avenue, between 39th and 40th streets. Designed by Attia & Perkins with an entrance in 40th Street, it wraps around the 84-year-old Knox Hat Building.

The 54-story Equitable Center Tower West is completed at 787 Fifth Avenue, between 51st and 52nd streets, for the Equitable Life Assurance Society that owns the block. Designed in International Style by Edward Larrabee Barnes, it rises 752 feet high with two setbacks, has access to the underground concourse that connects it to Rockefeller Center buildings, and incorporates a 100-seat auditorium, a fitness club, and restaurants.

The 34-story 885 Third Avenue office building is completed between 53rd and 54th streets. Designed by John Burgee and Philip Johnson with easy access to the IND Lexington Avenue subway concourse, its telescoping tiers and elliptical shape of red-brown and pink quickly have people calling it the "Lipstick Building."

The city provides shelter for 4,500 homeless families and 4,000 single men and women by early November. Experts predict that the numbers will grow, and the city announces the inauguration of a 10-year, $2.4 billion program to rehabilitate the apartment buildings it owns to help meet a severe shortage of low- and middle-income housing. Concerned that rooms for single adults with low incomes are being lost at an alarming rate and thus adding to homelessness despite last year's moratorium on conversion of single-room occupancy hotels, the City Council enacts an "anti-warehousing" law that makes it illegal for owners of such hotels to hold rooms vacant for more than 30 days. Many SROs are in neighborhoods that are being upgraded; they have been emptied, remodeled, and rented or sold to upscale tenants or razed to make way for new projects, some of which have been aborted because the moratorium has frustrated developers' plans.

The Hudson Tower apartment house is completed at the southeast corner of Albany Street and the Esplanade of the developing Battery Park City in lower Manhattan (see Esplanade, 1983). Davis, Brody & Associates has designed the 15-story structure and also the six five-story Albany Street town houses completed just to the east; Battery Park City's new Rector Place apartments add 2,200 units on ten parcels of land south of the Gateway Plaza opened in 1982: the Parc Place apartments are completed at 225 Rector Place, southeast corner South End Avenue, to designs by Gruzen Samton Steinglass. Rents range from $1,390 per month for one-bedroom units, two bedrooms $2,175. The River Rose apartments are completed at 333 Rector Place, northeast corner South End Avenue, to designs by Charles Moore and Rothzeid, Kaiserman, Thomson & Bee. The Liberty House apartments are completed at 377 Rector Place on the Esplanade to designs by James Stewart Polshek & Partners for Paul and Seymour Milstein.

Tower 67 is completed at 145 West 67th Street. Designed by Philip Birnbaum & Associates for developer Amir Manocherian and his brother Eskandar, the 48-story building contains 450 rental units—most of them one- and two-bedroom suites renting for between $1,440 and $3,550 per month; 33 studios on the lower floors are for low-income tenants chosen by lottery from among existing residents of the Community Board 7 district. The city had condemned the block to make way for a public garage, and when Manocherian Brothers bought the land from the city in 1980 they were required as a condition of the purchase to provide a certain amount of subsidized housing. Plans for the building were approved before passage in 1984 of the R10a zoning law that superseded a 1980 law and forbade construction of buildings with the density of Tower 67 and Park South Tower; in any case, zoning laws are not strictly enforced and it remains all too easy for developers to obtain variances.

The 27-story Broadway apartment house is completed at 1991 Broadway, between 67th and 68th streets. Designed by John Harding, it has three to four condominium apartments per floor and rises above a three-story glass-enclosed plaza. Studios sell initially for $171,200 and up, one-bedroom units for $191,000 and up, two-bedroom units from $485,600, duplex penthouses from $775,000.

The 30-story Copley apartment house is completed at 2000 Broadway, northeast corner 68th Street. Davis Brody & Associates has designed it.

The 31-story 188 East 70th Street apartment house (initially called the Trafalgar) is completed at the southwest corner of Third Avenue to Post Modern designs by Kohn Pedersen Fox Associates.

The 25-story Forum apartment house is completed at 343 East 74th Street, running through to 75th, between First and Second avenues. Designed by the Vilkas Group, it employs air rights from two churches on either side of it. Midblock downzoning has gone into effect between 59th and 96th streets while the building was under construction, and it will be difficult hereafter to build such tall structures in the area. Initial offering prices range from $177,400 for a one-bedroom unit and $316,400 for two bedrooms to duplex and triplex penthouses from $717,900.

The 23-story Bromley apartment house is completed at 225 West 83rd Street on the east side of Broadway between 83rd and 84th Streets. Burundi-born architect Costas (Andrew) Kondylis, 46, of Philip Birnbaum Associates has designed the 306-unit structure that rises above the Loews 84th Street six movie-theater complex. Studios are offered at $200,000 and up, a duplex penthouse for $1.2 million.

The 26-story Montana apartment house is completed at 247 West 87th Street, northeast corner Broadway. Designed by Gruzen Sampton Steinglass, it extends to 88th Street.

The 23-story New West apartment house is completed at 2431-39 Broadway, southwest corner 90th Street. Designed by Philip Birnbaum & Associates, it replaces a supermarket that had, in turn, replaced a movie theater.

A new U.S. tax law will lead to depressed prices in New York's housing market by eliminating tax shelters, although interest on mortgages and home-equity loans remains tax-deductible. Prices will rebound.

Chinatown's Park Street is bulldozed to expand the Columbus Park playground in a joint "asphalt reclamation" effort by the Department of Transportation and the Parks and Recreation Department to take over unnecessary streets and add them to existing park space. Sheridan Square in Greenwich Village was reclaimed in 1983, when space used for parking trucks was replaced with a garden. Babi-Yar Triangle has been created this way with trees and benches in Brooklyn's Brighton Beach section and Federoff Triangle in Rego Park, Queens. Says Parks Commissioner Henry J. Stern, "A lot of New York was paved over when it was fashionable to do so; now we are retrieving extra large streets, extra large squares, and giant paved spaces in the city." The southeast corner of Madison Square Park was shaved off years ago to ease traffic flow but will be restored as parkland, Stern promises.

Le Bernardin opens in the new Equitable Center at 155 West 51st Street with Parisian chef Gilbert Le Coze, 41, preparing seafood dishes that quickly gain accolades. Le Coze and his sister Maguy will go on to open the Brasserie Le Coze in Miami's Coconut Grove section and also in Atlanta, leaving the New York kitchen increasingly in the hands of chef Eric Ripert (see 1994).

The centennial of the Statue of Liberty is observed "Liberty Weekend" (July 4) with fireworks displays in the harbor; flotillas of visiting naval vessels and pleasure boats crowd the waterway.

Congress enacts sweeping revisions in the U.S. immigration law. The Simpson-Mazzoli Act signed into law by President Reagan November 7 permits millions of illegal immigrants to remain in the country legally and imposes criminal sanctions on employers who hire undocumented workers.

1987 Former Brooklyn political leader Meade Esposito, now 80, is indicted on charges of having made an illegal gift to Congressman Mario Biaggi, now 69, who is convicted of having accepted bribes from Coastal Dry Dock Co., whose officers received nearly $500 million in U.S. navy shipbuilding contracts and gave nearly $2 million per year in insurance premiums to a company owned by Esposito. Biaggi has used the bribes to vacation with his mistress while his wife lay dying. Convicted by a jury, Esposito is sentenced to a 2-year prison term (suspended) and fined $500,000.

Parking Violations Bureau hearings officer George Aronwald, 78, is shot to death gangland style in a Long Island City laundry March 20. His son is a defense lawyer and former Manhattan district attor-

ney who represents a government informer whose Chicago undercover work led to revelations of corruption in the bureau.

Former Sullivan & Cromwell senior partner and U.S. presidential adviser Arthur H. Dean dies of pneumonia at Glen Cove, L.I., November 30 at age 89.

A criminal investigation into last year's Howard Beach killing of Michael Griffith polarizes the city's black and white communities. The case is turned over to District Attorney Charles Hynes and a special prosecutor; nine people will be convicted for their roles in the attack, three of them for manslaughter, the other six on lesser charges for which they will be sentenced only to community service or, in one case, to 6 months in jail.

The Catholic archdiocese of New York bans a Mass for homosexuals at the Church of St. Francis Xavier in Chelsea. The Rev. Michael E. Donahue, a pastor at the church, openly criticizes the decision, and within a few years his church will be welcoming gay worshipers and running AIDS support groups.

ACT-UP (AIDS Coalition to Unleash Power) is founded at New York to advocate stronger measures against AIDS and stages a demonstration in Wall Street in March; 250 people protest drug-company profiteering. The coalition has been founded by Greenwich Village activist Larry Kramer, who formed the Gay Men's Health Crisis (GMHC) 6 years ago; its purpose is to defend those afflicted with the disease that is devastating significant parts of the city's art, music, and theater worlds. It will direct its confrontational approach against federal, state, and local governments, the medical profession, and pharmaceutical companies (see 1989).

Civil rights activist Bayard Rustin dies of cardiac arrest after surgery for a ruptured appendix at New York August 24 at age 75. He has been open about his sexual orientation.

McSorley's Old Ale House installs a woman's lavatory (see 1970). The 133-year-old bar's slogan before 1970 was, "Good Ale, Raw Onions, and No Ladies," but times have changed.

Police enter the Greenwich Village brownstone apartment of book editor Joel Steinberg, 45, and his lawyer companion Hedda Nussbaum, 34, November 2 and find their 6-year-old daughter Lisa dying on the floor with their urine-soaked toddler Mitchell tethered to his playpen. Nussbaum, battered almost beyond recognition and delusional, is arrested along with Steinberg for child abuse, and it turns out that she has been a victim of cocaine and sadism.

The case focuses public attention on child and spousal abuse. Nussbaum will waive immunity and agree to testify against Steinberg in a marathon TV trial next year, she will spend a year at a Westchester psychiatric hospital, he will be convicted of first-degree manslaughter and given a prison sentence of 8 1/3 to 25 years.

Philanthropist Jacob M. Kaplan dies at New York July 18 at age 95, leaving his daughter Joan K. Davidson to head the 40-year-old J. M. Kaplan Fund that she has managed for the past 10 years.

Three Wall Street traders are charged February 12 with illegal "insider" trading that has given them millions in profits (see 1986). Ivan F. Boesky is sentenced December 18 to 3 years in prison for conspiring to falsify stock trading records connected with insider deals, half of his $100 million fine is tax-deductible, and he is spared a heavier sentence because he has named others who have profited from insider trading (see 1988).

Citicorp, Manufacturers Hanover Trust, and Bankers Trust report major losses July 21, blaming nonpayment of foreign debts.

The U.S. Senate votes 91 to 2 August 3 to confirm President Reagan's choice of New York-born economist Alan Greenspan, 51, as chairman of the Federal Reserve Board. He succeeds Paul Volcker, who has resigned, and although Greenspan sharply disagrees with Volcker on the subject of bank deregulation he promises to be just as aggressive in fighting inflation.

Wall Street's Dow Jones Industrial Average starts the year at 1895.95, closes above 2000 for the first time January 8, peaks at 2722.42 August 25, falls to 2346 the third week of October (after rising a record 75.23 points September 22), then plunges 508 points—22.61 percent—October 19 to 1738.74, a drop matching that of October 19, 1929, as volume on the New York Stock Exchange exceeds 604 million shares. Pundits blame computerized trading programs, the U.S. trade and budget deficits, and other factors. It closes December 31 at 1938.33, but by August 24, 1989, the Dow will have topped its 1987 highs.

Value Line founder Arnold Bernhard dies at New York December 22 at age 86. His 50-year-old concern has become the world's largest investment advisory service, with well over 250,000 private and institutional subscribers and fund shareholders. Bernhard's daughter Jean Bernhard Buttner, 53, succeeds him as CEO.

Ohrbach's store in West 34th Street closes in February after nearly 63 years in business (see 1954). It has developed a reputation for offering moderate-priced copies of Paris couturière originals and for fashion and advertising savvy, but the Dutch retail holding company Breninkmeyer that bought the Ohrbach's chain in 1962 has been losing money on it.

NY Waterway is founded by New Jersey trucking company owner Arthur Imperatore to provide ferry service for commuters. Other operators will introduce services of their own, and within 10 years there will be dozens of ferries linking Brooklyn, Manhattan, New Jersey, and Queens.

Medical Tribune founder (and art collector) Arthur M. Sackler dies of a heart attack at Columbia-Presbyterian Medical Center May 26 at age 73. He is credited with having pioneered the use of ultrasound in diagnostic medicine.

The New York University College of Dentistry dedicates its new David B. Kriser Dental Center on First Avenue between 24th and 25th streets (see 1978). The school's enrollment has grown to more than 1,200 pre- and postdoctoral students as well as students in dental hygiene. Since 1984 it has co-operated with WABC-TV in sponsoring a free dental-screening week, a program that will grow to attract upwards of 6,000 New Yorkers. More than 700 clinicians and researchers work at the college on a full- or part-time basis, and many of them have pioneered in implant dentistry, pain control, dental sealants, adult orthodontics, and other areas.

Random House book editor Robert A. Gottlieb, 55, is appointed editor of The *New Yorker* January 12, succeeding William Shawn (see Newhouse, 1985). Staff members protest the announcement by Advance Publications chairman S. I. Newhouse, Jr., but Gottlieb will remain in the post for 4 years, and while circulation will increase, advertising will continue to decline (see Tina Brown, 1992).

The Metropolitan Transportation Authority demolishes 42 of the city's 97 subway newsstands, citing safety factors. The stands impede crowd movement and obstruct the vision of police officers, say MTA officials. Within a decade, the city will have only 329 licensed newsstands above and below ground, down from 1,580 in 1940.

The closing of Ohrbach's on top of last year's closing of Gimbels deals a severe blow to advertising revenues of the *Daily News* and *Post* (the *Times* is affected to a lesser degree).

The *New York Observer* begins weekly publication September 22 on paper that is either orange, pink, salmon, or peach, depending on who is talking. Financed by former investment banker Arthur L. Carter, now 55, it is initially distributed free and will grow in 10 years to have an in-house staff of 25 full-time people whose work is supplemented by several dozen regular freelance writers.

The Viacom firm started by CBS-TV in 1970 is acquired in March by National Amusements, a movie-theater chain owned by investor Sumner Redstone. Viacom has acquired radio and television stations plus cable systems that include MTV, Nickelodeon, and Showtime (*see* 1994).

Radio station WFAN begins broadcasting at New York July 1 at 1,050 kilohertz—the world's first 24-hour sports station. It will buy the license of WNBC in October of next year and move to 660 kHz, offering play-by-play accounts of baseball, basketball, football, and hockey games along with call-in programs.

Nonfiction: *New York Intellect: A History of Intellectual Life in New York City from 1750 to the Beginnings of Our Own Time* by California-born author Thomas Bender, 43, who writes, "We cannot fully understand ourselves as intellectuals, as Americans, until we grasp the special character of New York—both its possibilities and its limitations—as a place of intellect;" *Gramercy Park: An American Bloomsbury* by New York-born Greenwich Village author-teacher Carole Klein (*née* Doreen Honig), 52; *New York 1930* by architect Robert A. M. Stern with Gregory Gilmartin and Thomas Mellins; *New York: A Physical History* by Norval White, now 61; *West of Fifth: The Rise and Fall and Rise of Manhattan's West Side* by James Trager; *New York's Fabulous Luxury Apartments* by Andrew Alpern; *Trump: The Art of the Deal* by Donald Trump with Tony Schwartz; *Manhattan Water-Bound: Planning and Developing Manhattan's Waterfront from the Seventeenth Century to the Present* by Washington, D.C.-born New York city planner Ann Buttenwieser (*née* Lubin), 51.

Fiction: *The Bonfire of the Vanities* by Tom Wolfe, whose protagonist Sherman McCoy calls his fictional apartment house at "816 Park Avenue" "one of the great ones built just before the first World War! Back then it was still not entirely proper for a good family to live in an apartment (instead of a house). So the apartments were built like mansions, with eleven-, twelve-, thirteen-foot ceilings, vast entry galleries, staircases, servants' wings, herringbone parquet floors, interior walls a foot thick, exterior walls as thick as a fort's, and fireplaces, fireplaces, fireplaces, even though the buildings were all built with central heating. A mansion!—except that you arrived at the front door via an elevator (opening upon your own private vestibule) instead of the street" (McCoy takes a wrong turn in the Bronx and finds himself threatened by what he considers a hostile world he has never known.); *Wall Street* by New York-born lawyer-investment banker Kenneth Lipper, 46, who has been a partner at both Lehman Brothers and Salomon Brothers, served as deputy mayor from 1983 to 1985, and now starts a money-management firm that will grow by 1993 to have $2 billion in fixed-income investments under its management.

Rupert Murdoch's News Corp. acquires Harper & Row (*see* 1977). Harper will take over the Chicago-based textbook publisher Scott, Foresman in 1989 (*see* HarperCollins, 1990).

Painting: *The Hunger Artist* by Elizabeth Murray; *Lucas II* by Chuck Close, who has painted Lucas Samaras. Andy Warhol dies after gallbladder surgery at New York Hospital February 23 at age 58 (he has lived since 1974 in a town house at 57 East 66th Street); Raphael Soyer dies of cancer at New York November 4 at age 87 (his twin brother, Moses, died in 1974, his younger brother Isaac in 1981).

Theater: *Fences* by August Wilson 3/26 at the 46th Street Theater, with James Earl Jones, Indianola, Miss.-born actress Mary Alice, 45, Miami, Fla.-born actor Ray Aranha, 47, Detroit-born actor Courtney B. Vance, 27, 526 perfs.; *Driving Miss Daisy* by Atlanta-born playwright Alfred Uhry, 51, 4/15 at the Playwrights Horizons Theater, with Atlanta-born actress Dana Ivey, 44, Memphis-born actor Morgan Freeman, 49, Ray Gill, 80 perfs.; *Frankie and Johnny in the Clair de Lune* by Terrence McNally 6/2 at the Manhattan Theater Club, with Memphis-born actress Kathy Bates, 38, Pittsburgh-born actor F. Murray Abraham; *Burn This* by Lanford Wilson 10/15 at the Plymouth Theater, with John Malkovich, Illinois-born actress Joan Allen, 31, 437 perfs.

Actor James Coco dies of a heart attack at New York February 25 at age 56; Broadway producer Alfred De Liagre, Jr. of lung cancer at New York March 5 at age 82; burlesque producer Morton Minsky (last of the four Minsky brothers) of cancer at New York March 25 at age 85; actor Walter Abel at Essex, Conn., March 26 at age 88; Hermione Gingold at New York May 24 at age 89; Geraldine Page of a heart attack at New York June 13 at age 62; playwright (and political figure) Clare Boothe Luce of cancer at Washington, D.C., October 9 at age 84.

Television puppeteer Bil Baird dies at New York March 18 at age 82 of pneumonia brought on by bone-marrow cancer.

Films: Yurek Bogayevicz's *Anna* with Sally Kirkland, Paulina Porizkova; Charles Shyer's *Baby Boom* with Diane Keaton, Harold Ramis, Sam Shepard, Sam Wanamaker; John Schlesinger's *The Believers* with Martin Sheen, Helen Shaver (about a young widow and her son who move to New York and get involved in the Santeria religious cult); David Jones's *84 Charing Cross Road* with Anne Bancroft, Anthony Perkins; Adrian Lyne's *Fatal Attraction* with Michael Douglas, Glenn Close, Anne Archer; Norman Jewison's *Moonstruck* with Cher (originally Cherilyn Sarkisian LaPiere), Nicolas Cage (originally Nicholas Coppola), Vincent Gardenia, Olympia Dukakis, Danny Aiello (parts of it are set in the 68-year-old Cammareri Brothers Bakery in Carroll Gardens, Brooklyn); Woody Allen's *Radio Days* with Allen, Mia Farrow is about growing up in Queens in the 1940s and has been shot in the old Astoria Studio that next year will be turned into the Museum of the Moving Image; Herbert Ross's *The Secret of My Success* with Michael J. Fox; Ridley Scott's *Someone to Watch Over Me* with Tom Berenger, Mimi Rogers, Lorraine Bracco, Jerry Orbach; Jerry Schatzberg's *Street Smart* with Christopher Reeve, Kathy Baker, Morgan Freeman; Oliver Stone's *Wall Street* with Michael Douglas (as a stockbroker [modeled on Ivan F. Boesky] whose shibboleth is "Greed Is Good" and who has his clothes made by Sills), Charlie Sheen, Daryl Hannah, Hal Holbrook, Martin Sheen, script based on the novel by Kenneth Lipper.

Broadway musicals: *Les Misérables* 3/12 at the Imperial Theater (it opened 10/8/1985 at London's Palace Theater), with Dublin-born actor Colin Wilkinson, 42, Kentucky-born actor Terrence Mann, 35, Brooklyn-born actor Randy Graff, 31, Valparaiso, Ind.-born actress Jennifer Butt, 28, Louisville, Ky.-born actor Leo Burmester, 43, New York-born singer Judy Kuhn, 28, music by Claude-Michel Schonberg, lyrics by Alain Boubil and Herbert Kretzmer, 6,680 perfs.; *Into the Woods* 11/5 at the Martin Beck Theater, with Bernadette Peters, Winnipeg-born actress Joanna Gleason, 37, Philip Hoffman, book by James Lapine, music and lyrics by Stephen Sondheim, 764 perfs.

Former Broadway leading man Robert Preston dies of lung cancer at Santa Barbara, Calif., March 21 at age 68; director Michael Bennett of AIDS-related lymphoma at Tucson, Ariz., July 2 at age 44; jazz and blues afficianado John Hammond at New York July 10 at age 76, having "discovered" Count Basie, Benny Goodman, Billy Holiday, and Bessie Smith. He is credited with having signed Bob Dylan, Aretha Franklin, and Bruce Springsteen to Columbia Records contracts.

The New York Giants beat Denver 39 to 20 at Pasadena January 25 in Super Bowl XXI. Coached by Bill Parcells, 46, the Giants have linebacker Lawrence Taylor to lead the defense against Broncos quarterback John Elway; Giants quarterback Phil Simms, 32, completes 22 of his 25 passes to gain 268 yards, three touchdowns, and the most valuable player award.

Ivan Lendl wins in U.S. men's singles at Flushing Meadow, Martina Navratilova in women's singles.

Pizza Connection defendant Pietro Alfano is shot in the back three times with a .38 caliber revolver February 11 after shopping at Balducci's on Sixth Avenue as a mob war rages in the city over control of the narcotics business. A member of the Sicilian Mafia whose uncle Gaetano Badalamenti, 64, is an international heroin kingpin, Alfano was arrested with Badalamenti 2 years ago in Spain and brought back to Manhattan to be tried with 20 other defendants, all charged with having brought $1.6 billion worth of heroin into the country and distributing it through East Coast and Midwestern pizzerias between 1979 and 1984. The trial has cost $50 million and has been going on for more than 16 months—the longest federal jury criminal trial in history. Alfano is left paralyzed from the waist down, pleads guilty to narcotics conspiracy, and is given a 15-year prison sentence. Of the 19 defendants present at the end of the trial, 18 are found guilty; Badalamenti is given a 45-year sentence and fined $125,000, Bonanno family number-two man Salvatore Catalano a 45-year sentence and fined $1.15 million.

Federal agents announce March 10 that they have broken an elaborate cocaine-smuggling ring of airline workers who have smuggled nearly $1.5 billion worth of the drug into Kennedy International Airport aboard Pan American World Airways flights from Brazil. Crack-cocaine gangs operate throughout much of the city, wreaking havoc mostly in minority communities. One of the most notorious gangs is the Supreme Team, whose members sell crack in and about the Baisley Park Houses in southeastern Queens, taking in $250,000 per week and ruthlessly liquidating anyone who gets in their way.

The New York Police Department announces March 23 that reported murders have soared by 50 percent or more in 21 of the city's 75 police precincts, reflecting the impact of drug-related crime on neighborhoods.

Millionaire con man and loan shark Irwin Schiff, 50, is shot to death gangland style August 8 while having dinner with a model at the Bravo Sergio restaurant on Second Avenue between 75th and 76th streets. Schiff weighs more than 350 pounds, he was convicted of income-tax evasion in the 1970s and more recently of check fraud, authorities link him to $70 million in fraudulent financial transactions, his bodyguard is absent, and he has evidently been killed on orders from the capo of a Jersey City Genovese crime family. By October fully 10 gangland-style murders in Brooklyn will have been linked to rivalry between the Bonanno and Columbo crime families, most of the victims being low-level figures involved in a wide range of criminal activities (*see* 1991).

Former trial lawyer William H. Suddugh, 77, is found bludgeoned to death in his upper East Side apartment August 9. He helped hundreds of World War II refugees settle in America.

Former advertising executive John Goodwillie, 77, is found beaten and strangled to death on the floor of a bedroom in his 1185 Park Avenue apartment December 29. The apartment had belonged to his late wife, and the last person to have seen him alive was evidently her son-in-law Jonathan de Sola Mendes, 65, a retired marine corps captain who has an office in the Seagram Building, works as an investment counselor, and will not be prosecuted.

The city acquires two British prison barges and two ferry boats, formerly used on the Staten Island run, to house prison inmates, mostly drug offenders, whose numbers have outgrown the facilities at Riker's Island (*see* 1884), on Staten Island (whose facilities have a combined capacity of 3,137), a work camp on Hart Island, and prison wards at Bellevue, Elmhurst, and Kings County hospitals. Within 4 years the city will be holding about 21,000 prisoners, up from 10,000 in 1980.

The 37-story 1 Financial Square building is completed on the East River at 32 Old Slip, extending to South Street at the intersection of Gouverneur Slip and replacing the U.S. Assay Building that opened in 1930. Designed by Edward Durrell Stone Associates, it has 1 million square feet of office space.

Zeckendorf Towers is completed at 1 Irving Place on the east side of Union Square between 14th and 15th streets, occupying the site used until 1975 by the retailer S. Klein on the Square (and before that by the Union Square Hotel). Designed by Davis, Brody & Associates, whose experience heretofore has been mostly in publicly assisted housing, the 27-story structure is a combination apartment house and office building.

The UNICEF Building is completed at 3 United Nations Plaza (44th Street, between First and Second avenues). Kevin Roche/John Dinkeloo and Associates has designed it for the United Nations International Children's Emergency Fund.

Park Avenue Tower is completed at 65 East 55th Street, between Madison and Park avenues. Designed by Nuremberg-born Chicago architect Helmut Jahn, 47, of Murphy/Jahn, the 36-story office complex is just west of 430 Park and has 550,894 square feet of space.

The 26-story Heron Tower is completed at 70 East 55th Street. Designed by Kohn Pedersen Fox, the office building has a gray granite façade decorated with rock-face blocks.

The Liberty Court apartment house is completed at 200 Rector Place, southwest corner West Street, as Battery Park City grows; architect Ulrich Franzen has designed the structure. The Soundings apartment house is completed at 280 Rector Place, southeast corner South End Avenue, to designs by Bond Ryder James. The Battery Pointe apartment house is completed at 300 Rector Place, southwest corner South End Avenue, to designs by Bond Ryder James. The Hudson View East apartment house is completed at 250 South End Avenue, southeast corner Albany Street; the architectural firm Mitchell-Giurgola has designed the structure. Hudson View West is completed at 300 Albany Street, southwest corner South End Avenue, to designs by Conklin & Rossant.

The 57-story Corinthian apartment house is completed at 645 First Avenue, between 37th and 38th streets, to designs by Der Scutt with help from Michael Schimenti.

The 36-story Cosmopolitan apartment house is completed at 145 East 48th Street, between Lexington and Third avenues, to Post Modern designs by Gruzen Sampton Steinglass.

The building that once housed the United Nations School on First Avenue at 51st Street is converted in the spring for use as a 180-bed shelter for homeless women, many of them mentally ill. It will remain as such until 1997, operated by the Salvation Army under contract for the city.

The 72-story CitySpire completed at 150 West 56th Street, between Sixth and Seventh avenues, rises

814 feet high and has 355 condominium apartments atop more than 300,000 square feet of office space, but a design flaw at its top allows the wind to blow through a vent, creating a whistle that can be heard for a mile in every direction (the Department of Environmental Protection will not locate the source of the disturbance for years). Designed by Helmut Jahn of Murphy/Jahn for developer Bruce Jay Eichner, New York's tallest mixed-use building uses air rights obtained from the City Center and has won approval from the City Planning Commission by a vote of seven to four after Eichner promised to give the City Center $5.5 million for renovations.

The Metropolitan Tower completed at 140 West 57th Street is a combination condominium apartment house and office building. Developer Harry Macklowe has hired Schuman, Lichtenstein, Claman & Efron to draw up plans for the 68-story (he claims 78) glass structure that rises 716 feet high, but Macklowe claims the design is his own creation.

Real estate developer Sol Goldman dies at Lenox Hill Hospital October 18 at age 70, leaving a large fortune and an estranged wife. He has reportedly controlled close to 600 properties, including an estimated 400 in the city, and in recent years has been paying cash for properties that other investors would be able to buy only with mortgages.

The 40-story Evansview apartment house (initially called Memphis Uptown) is completed at 305 East 60th Street, between First and Second avenues, extending to 61st Street. Designed by Abraham Rothenberg and Gruzen Sampton Steinglass, the tower has a balcony for virtually every apartment.

The 42-story Royale apartment house is completed at 188 East 64th Street, southwest corner Third Avenue. Designed by Schuman Lichtenstein Claman & Efron with Alfredo De Vido Associates, it has a grand staircase that leads from the lobby to three special rooms where tenants can entertain.

The 50-story 200 East 65th Street apartment house is completed at the southeast corner of Third Avenue. Designed by Ulrich Franzen & Associates for developers Paul Milstein and Robert Olnick, the controversial "Milro Tower" has five-sided corner windows.

The 53-story Bristol Plaza apartment house is completed at 210 East 65th Street between Third and Second avenues. It has 380 condominium units and offers tenants amenities that include a garden, health club, swimming pool, roof deck, and full-service garage.

The 40-story Rio apartment house is completed at 304 East 65th Street, southeast corner Second Avenue, to designs by Gruzen Samton Steinglass.

The 23-story Le Chambord apartment house is completed at 350 East 72nd Street, between First and Second avenues. Designed by Costas Kondylis of Philip Birnbaum & Associates, it replaces a Trans-Lux movie theater.

The 49-story 525 East 72nd Street apartment house is completed between York Avenue and FDR Drive, running through to 73rd Street with nine rental apartments per floor. Davis, Brody & Associates has designed the structure.

The 39-story Promenade apartment house is completed at 530 East 76th Street, southwest corner FDR Drive. Costas Kondylis of Philip Birnbaum & Associates has designed the condominium structure that wraps around the 14-year-old Town School building and utilizes its air rights.

The 27-story 45 East 80th Street apartment house is completed at the northeast corner of Madison Avenue to designs by Liebman, Liebman & Associates.

The 36-story America apartment house is completed at 300 East 85th Street, southeast corner Second Avenue, to designs by Helmut Jahn of Murphy/Jahn.

The 40-story Channel Club Condominiums apartment house is completed at 451 East 86th Street and 1637–1639 York Avenue. Wechsler, Grasso & Menziuso has designed the tower.

The 13-story-plus-penthouse 60 East 88th Street apartment house is completed between Madison and Park avenues to designs by Beyer Blinder Belle.

The 48-story Waterford apartment house is completed at 300 East 93rd Street, southeast corner Second Avenue, to designs by Beyer Blinder Belle with an assist from Vinjay Kale. It has four to five condominium apartments per floor.

Building permits for the city fall to 1,200, down from 9,900 in 1985.

The North River Sewage Treatment Plant goes into operation at the edge of the Hudson River between 137th and 145th streets at Hamilton Heights and another begins operating on Newtown Creek in Brooklyn's Red Hook section. The 13th and 14th such plants built since 1937, they are soon operating at full capacity, enabling the city to process the nearly 1.6 billion gallons of sewage carried each day through 6,200 miles of pipe. The North River plant will make the Hudson safe for sailing, kayaking, fishing, and even swimming by 1997 (only marine researchers and River Project volunteers will be permitted to swim), but residents of West Harlem and Red Hook complain that the plants are far from odorless, as the city had promised, final-stage sewage precipitate will continue to be dumped at sea until 1992, and storm drains will still dump garbage into the water after heavy rains.

Central Park's Belvedere Lake is renamed the Turtle Pond.

Snapple ready-to-drink bottled iced tea is introduced by the 15-year-old Snapple Beverage Co., virtually creating a new category of soft drink that will grow in 6 years to have 14 Snapple tea flavors, including lemon, mint, orange, peach, raspberry (and four diet varieties)—and some high-powered competitors.

The Union Square farmers' market opens along 17th Street between Broadway and Park Avenue South. Architect-city planner Barry Benepe has proposed and pushed for the open-air plaza where farmers can sell directly to consumers.

Brooklyn-born entrepreneur Howard Schultz, 33, buys Starbucks—originally a Seattle coffee-bean business—and starts building an empire of coffee bars to supplement the Starbucks wholesale and mail-order operations. Within 8 years he will have 470 coffee bars nationwide, dozens of them in New York, with 8,000 employees and annual sales of nearly $300 million.

Bouley opens August 6 at 165 Duane Street and will soon be ranked as the city's finest restaurant (it will move in 1996 to a new location nearby). David Bouley trained under Gaston LeNôtre, Roger Verget, Paul Bocuse, Paul Haeberlin, Joël Robuchon, and Freddy Girardet before becoming chef at the nearby Montrachet (see 1985); he offers a $65 menu dégustation of eight small courses, while first courses are normally $6 to $16, main courses $20 to $27, desserts about $7.

Periyali opens at 35 West 20th Street. Steve Tzolis and Nicola Kotsoni have created the upscale Greek restaurant.

1988 Congressman Mario Biaggi loses the 10th District's primary election (Elliott Engel defeats him and goes on to win the general election) and is convicted of having helped the Bronx-based defense contractor Wedtech obtain city-owned property in violation of the law (see 1987). Now 71, Biaggi will serve 21

months in federal prison at Fort Worth, Tex. (see 1992).

Vice President George Herbert Walker Bush, 64, wins the presidential election with 53 percent of the popular vote to 46 percent for Massachusetts Governor Michael Dukakis, 54, who takes 10 states, including New York, winning 52 percent of the state's popular vote to Bush's 48 percent. Republican Bush is the first sitting vice president to win election since 1836. Sen. Moynihan is elected to a third term with more than two-thirds of the vote, defeating Garden City, L.I., lawyer Robert R. McMillen to win the largest plurality for a senator in the state's history.

The U.S. Supreme Court rules unanimously June 20 in *New York State Club Association, Inc., v. The City of New York* that the city's 1984 law banning discrimination against women and minorities in private clubs with more than 400 members does not violate First Amendment rights. The ruling supports the city's human rights law and will affect clubs in every other U.S. city. Lawyers for the New York State Club Association have argued that Local Law 63 violated "the fundamental right of our citizens . . . to choose who their friends will be," and although the high court has rejected their pleas, the law leaves untouched those "distinctly private clubs" like the Colony, Racquet, and Union clubs that do not obtain revenues from nonmembers "for the furtherance of trade or business."

The Tompkins Square riot August 6 brings charges of police brutality. Homeless squatters (the city's homeless population has reached an unprecedented 17,800 in January) have erected makeshift dwellings in the park, neighbors have complained, and the police have used force to drive the squatters out. Charges of police misconduct are referred to the 22-year-old Civilian Complaint Review Board (see 1986; 1993).

A black boycott drives a Korean grocer in Brooklyn out of business (see 1979). Koreans have developed a major presence in Elmhurst, Flushing, Jackson Heights, Sunnyside, and other Queens communities and are gaining dominance in such businesses as beauty parlors, costume jewelry, delicatessens, and small grocery shops (see 1990).

The U.S. Supreme Court rules 5 to 4 April 20 that Congress may tax interest on municipal bonds issued by states and local governments, a decision that upsets owners of—and dealers in—New York State, New York City, Triborough Bridge Authority, and other such bonds.

Sanford I. Weill of Commercial Credit Corp. acquires Primerica, Inc. and its Smith, Barney brokerage business (*see* 1986; Travelers, 1992).

The Securities and Exchange Commission accuses Drexel Burnham Lambert September 7 of having a secret agreement to defraud clients by trading on inside information (*see* 1987). The firm's high-yield "junk" bond expert Michael Milken in Beverly Hills has been instrumental in effecting scores of mergers and acquisitions, Drexel pleads guilty in December to 6 felony charges, agrees to pay a record $650 million in fines, and says it will withhold $200 million due Milken for 1988 under terms of his employment contract (*see* 1989).

Chase Manhattan Bank receives a package of tax incentives equal to $51,000 per employee to remain in Manhattan.

The 204-year-old Bank of New York receives approval from the Federal Reserve Board November 28 to acquire Irving Bank Corp., whose 137-year-old Irving Trust Co. has retail branches in desirable locations throughout Manhattan. Irving has resisted the hostile offer that has escalated to $1.5 billion.

MacArthur Foundation chairman and former Atlantic Richfield president and RCA chairman Thornton F. Bradshaw dies of a heart attack at New York December 6 at age 71.

The state legislature at Albany votes unanimously December 15 to adopt a measure making takeovers of New York State corporations much more difficult by allowing them to issue shareholder rights ("poison pills"). The absorption of Irving Trust by the Bank of New York is believed to have prompted the action.

Wall Street's Dow Jones Industrial Average closes December 30 at 2168.57, up 229.74 (11.8 percent) from its 1987 close of 1938.83. The New York Stock Exchange has announced February 4 that it would curb use of its electronic trading system when the Dow rose or fell more than 50 points in a day. The NASDAQ closes at 381.38, up 15.4 percent on the year.

Campeau Corp. outbids R. H. Macy and pays $6.6 billion to acquire Federated Department Stores, whose properties include Bloomingdale's and A&S (*see* Allied 1986). Campeau sells off Brooks Brothers to Marks & Spencer for $770 million (the price will be trimmed to $750 million) and sells Bonwit Teller to reduce its staggering $11 billion debt, but its losses outpace its profits (*see* 1990; A&S, 1989; Macy's, 1992).

The Metropolitan Transportation Authority terminates its extra-fare "Train-to-the-Plane" subway service between the Sixth Avenue and 57th Street station and the Howard Beach station on the Rockaway line, a short bus ride (included in the fare) from JFK International Airport. The A Train continues to serve Howard Beach and is much cheaper but makes far more stops. A new two-level subway spur opens in December under Archer Avenue in the Jamaica section of Queens, making it easier for riders to transfer to and from the Long Island Rail Road; new stations are opened at Archer Avenue, Parson, and Jamaica Center. The MTA issues a special Archer Avenue token December 11 to mark the openings.

John Jay College of Criminal Justice moves into the 82-year-old former DeWitt Clinton High School building at 899 Tenth Avenue, between 58th and 59th streets (*see* 1973). The structure's interior has been rebuilt and expanded to plans by architect Rafael Viñoly.

Barnard College's 20-story Sulzberger Hall is completed to designs by James Stewart Polshek & Partners, creating a new residential quadrangle with a café, student lounge, and accommodations for 400 students.

The Lower East Side Tenement Museum receives a charter "to promote tolerance and historical perspective through the presentation and interpretation of the variety of immigrant experiences on Manhattan's Lower East Side, a gateway to America." The new museum occupies an 1863 building at 97 Orchard Street.

The Yeshiva Ketana takes over the now-landmarked 1903 Isaac Rice mansion on Riverside Drive (*see* 1954).

The Italian-language newspaper *Il Progresso Italo-Americano* ceases publication after 108 years, but *America Oggi* begins publication in New Jersey to take up the readership (and advertisers) that remain.

New York Post publisher Rupert Murdoch sells the paper to real estate developer Peter S. (Stephen) Kalikow following a court ruling that a company may not own both a newspaper and a television station in the same market (*see* 1986; 1993).

Vogue magazine names London-born editor Anna Wintour, 38, to its top job in July. Wintour's career at *House & Garden* and, before that, at British *Vogue* has been unremarkable, but she will be credited with raising *Vogue*'s influence in the $110 billion

1988

fashion industry in the next 10 years and boosting the magazine's revenues.

New Yorker cartoonist Charles Addams dies of a heart attack at New York September 29 at age 76.

 Nonfiction: *City for Sale: Ed Koch and the Betrayal of New York* by *Daily News* deputy city editor Jack Newfield, 49, and *Village Voice* staff writer Wayne Barrett; *Imperial City: New York* by English author Geoffrey Moorhouse, 57; *Rediscovering the Center* by William H. Whyte; *The City That Never Was* by New York author Rebecca Read Shannor; *The Battle of St. Bart's: A Tale of the Material and Spiritual* by Indiana-born New York author Brent Cruse Brolin, 47; *The Landmarks of New York* by New York author Barbara-lee Diamonstein (*née* Dworkin); *The Blizzard of '88* by Mary Cable.

Author Allen Churchill dies of pancreatic cancer at New York January 16 at age 76.

Fiction: *Libra* by Don DeLillo; *Steely Blue* by Dennis Smith, who retired from the Fire Department in 1981.

The Italian-based Benetton clothing chain purchases the former Scribner Building at 597 Fifth Avenue, owned by the Italian-based publishing firm Rizzoli since 1984, and beginning in November 1996 will use the magnificent Scribner's Book Store of 1913 as a United Colors of Benetton retail shop instead of a bookstore.

Novelist-playwright Rose Franken dies at Tucson, Ariz., June 24 at age 92.

 The Metropolitan Museum of Art's Tisch Galleries are completed to designs by Kevin Roche/John Dinkeloo and Associates.

Painter Romare Bearden dies of bone cancer at New York March 12 at age 75; sculptor Louise Nevelson of lung cancer at New York April 17 at age 88; painter Jean-Michel Basquiat of a drug overdose at New York August 12 at age 27; sculptor Isamu Noguchi of heart failure at New York December 30 at age 84.

Theater: *M. Butterfly* by Hong Kong-born playwright David Henry Hwang, 30, 3/20 at the Eugene O'Neill Theater with Rochester-born actor John Lithgow, 42, B. D. Wong, John Getz, San Francisco-born actress Kathleen Chalfant (originally Kathleen Palmer), 43, 777 perfs.; *The Heidi Chronicles* by Wendy Wasserstein 4/15 at the off-Broadway Playwrights Horizons Theater, with John Allen, Peter Friedman, Boyd Gaines, 621 perfs.; *Speed-the-Plow* by David Mamet 5/2 at the Royale Theater with Madonna, Joe Montegna, New York-born actor Ron Silver, 41, 278 perfs.; *Rumors* by Neil Simon 11/17 at

the Broadhurst Theater, with Joyce Van Patten, André Gregory, Ken Howard, Ron Leibman, 531 perfs.

Playwright Paul Osborn dies at New York May 12 at age 86; Miguel Pinero of cirrhosis of the liver at New York June 16 at age 41; director Joshua Logan of supranuclear palsy at New York July 12 at age 79 (he has used lithium to control his manic depression since 1969).

Films: Woody Allen's *Another Woman* with Gena Rowlands, Mia Farrow, Ian Holm, Blythe Danner, Gene Hackman; Jim Abrahams's *Big Business* with Bette Midler, Lily Tomlin; Roger Donaldson's *Cocktail* with Tom Cruise Bryan Brown, Elisabeth Shue; John Landis's *Coming to America* with Eddie Murphy, Arsenio Hall, James Earl Jones; Joan Micklin Silver's *Crossing Delancey* with Amy Irving, Reizl Bozyk, Peter Riegert, Jeroen Krabbe, Sylvia Miles; Tony Bill's *Five Corners* with Jodie Foster, Tim Robbins, Todd Graff, John Turturro; Peter Yates's *The House on Carroll Street* with Kelly McGillis, Jeff Daniels, Mandy Patinkin; Jonathan Demme's *Married to the Mob* with Michelle Pfeiffer, Matthew Modine, Dean Stockwell, Queens-born actress Mercedes Ruehl, 40, Alec Baldwin; James Glickenhaus's *Shakedown* with Peter Weller, Sam Elliott, Patricia Charbonneau; Paul Morrissey's *Spike of Bensonhurst* with Sasha Mitchell, Ernest Borgnine; Charlotte Zwerin's documentary *Thelonious Monk: Straight No Chaser*; Mike Nichols's *Working Girl* with Melanie Griffith, Sigourney Weaver, Harrison Ford.

 Broadway musical: *The Phantom of the Opera* 1/26 at the Majestic Theater (it opened 10/9/1985 at Her Majesty's Theatre, London), with a cast of 35 headed by English actor Michael Crawford, 46, in the title role, London-born actress Sarah Brightman, 26, book based on the 1911 Gaston Leroux novel, music by Andrew Lloyd Webber, lyrics by Charles Hart, directed by Harold Prince, 6,075+ perfs.

Former Broadway composer Frederick Loewe dies at Palm Springs, Calif., February 14 at age 86; former Broadway musical star Irene Rich at California's Hope Ranch April 22 at age 96; former Broadway musical star Hazel Dawn at New York August 26 at age 97.

Popular songs: *Simple Pleasures* (album) by New York-born musician Bobby McFerrin, 38, includes the single "Don't Worry, Be Happy."

Irving Berlin declines to attend his 100th birthday celebration at Carnegie Hall May 11. He has written the scores for 23 Broadway shows and 18 films, published more than 1,000 songs (more than 100 have become standards), and enjoys an enormous income from royalties (the most valuable copyright in the history of the music business is Berlin's copyright on "White Christmas").

Atlantic Records celebrates its 40th anniversary May 14 with an 11-hour Madison Square Garden concert featuring performers who include Phil Collins, Crosby, Stills, Nash & Young, Peter Townshend of the Who, Mick Jagger of the Rolling Stones, and rhythm-and-blues singer La Vern Baker, now 56, who has been running a nightclub at Subic Bay in the Philippines since 1969. Atlantic announces that proceeds will go to charity and that it is recalculating its past royalty payments to give more to the rhythm & blues performers who brought it early fame and success.

Singer-actor Lancelot Patrick "Lanny" Ross dies of heart failure at New York April 25 at age 82; jazz composer-arranger-trumpeter Sy (Melvin James) Oliver of lung cancer at New York May 27 at age 77; former Café Society nightclub proprietor Barney Josephson of internal bleeding at New York September 29 at age 86, having launched the careers of singers Billie Holiday, Lena Horne, and Sara Vaughan.

Choreographer Robert Joffrey dies of liver, renal, and respiratory failure at New York March 25 at age 57; dancer Hugh Laing of cancer at New York May 10 at age 77.

A concert by Plácido Domingo, Linda Ronstadt, Gloria Estefan, and Rosario Andrade on Central Park's Great Lawn 7/11 attracts a crowd estimated to number 150,000.

 Steffi Graf, 19, (W. Ger.) wins tennis's first "grand slam" since Margaret Court of England did it in 1970. Mats Wilander, 23, wins at Flushing Meadow and becomes the first Swede to win the U.S. singles.

▥ "Preppy" murder suspect Robert E. Chambers, Jr. pleads guilty March 25 to first-degree manslaughter in the 1986 killing of Jennifer Levin after a 13-week trial; his lawyers have tried to depict his victim as a tramp but he admits in a plea-bargaining arrangement on the 9th day of jury deliberations that he intended to injure Levin seriously and "thereby caused her death." Sentenced to 5 to 15 years' imprisonment for manslaughter and burglary, Chambers says August 10 that he will not contest a $25 million wrongful death suit filed against him by Levin's parents. He will be confined until March 2003.

 Real estate developer Irwin Chanin dies at New York February 24 at age 96.

The 32-story 135 East 57th Street office building is completed at the northwest corner of Lexington Avenue to designs by Kohn Pedersen Fox Associates. Built by developer Robert Gladstone and his family, it has a sweeping concave façade that rises to the building's full height and wraps around a plaza containing a 30-foot-high circle of classical columns and a fountain. It combines shops, offices, and apartments.

The Capital Cities/ABC Inc. headquarters building is completed at 55 West 66th Street, between Central Park West and Columbus Avenue, to designs by Kohn Pedersen Fox Associates.

The 44-story Horizon apartment house is completed at 415 East 37th Street, between First Avenue and FDR Drive. Costas Kondylis of Philip Birnbaum Associates has designed the structure; it has 411 condominium units and includes two private clubs, a jogging track, club lounge, business center, and conference room.

The 56-story Central Park Place apartment house is completed at 301 West 57th Street, northwest corner Eighth Avenue. Davis, Brody & Associates has designed the structure.

The 40-story 52–54 East End Avenue apartment house is completed on a 4,000-square-foot lot at the southwest corner of 82nd Street to designs by Michael Lynn Associates.

The city establishes an SRO Loan Program to help nonprofit sponsors renovate or construct single-room occupancy units (see 1985). Created out of growing alarm about the increasing numbers of people living in the streets, the program will provide more than $175 million to more than 100 agencies in the next 8 years, most of the money going to organizations that gear their efforts toward poor single adults and provide an array of social services, including drug and alcohol treatment (see 1991).

The 83-year-old Gotham Hotel at the southwest corner of Fifth Avenue and 55th Street becomes the Peninsula, having been acquired by Hong Kong & Shanghai Hotels, Ltd. (the Peninsula Group), whose management converts it from a 400-room residential hotel to a 241-room transient hotel with 42 suites that include a 2,500-square-foot presidential suite. Swiss hotel owner René Hatt took over the hotel 9 years ago, closed it for a long renovation that cost $200 million, and gave it a rooftop health club and pool (see 1998).

The Central Park Zoo reopens August 8 as the Central Park Wildlife Center under the management of the New York Zoological Society (*see* 1980). Gone are the elephants, lions, and all other large mammals except polar bears and seals; gone, too, are the monkey house and reptile house; architects Kevin Roche/John Dinkeloo and Associates have redesigned the 5-acre facility, open 365 days of the year with a tropical rain forest, a temperate area, and a polar theme area exhibiting 626 animals of 102 species, including colobus and snow monkeys, red pandas, chinstrap and gentoo penguins, puffins, Asian water dragons, and poison dart frogs.

The 45,000-square-foot Winter Garden opens in October to serve as a grand public space for the World Financial Center. It has a 10-story, 145-foot high atrium skylight, 2,000 panes of tempered safety glass, and 16 *Washingtonia robusta* palm trees brought in on flatbed trucks from Arizona's Sonora Valley (or California's Anza-Borrego Desert; accounts vary). Initially 35 feet tall, they will grow another 15 to 20 feet under the 120-foot-high, glass-barrel vault of the Winter Garden, designed by Cesar Pelli with landscaping by M. Paul Friedberg & Partners. A marble staircase leads to 1 World Trade Center, a theatrical stage faces the Hudson River, and a food court will serve 100,000 lunches per week. The grand staircase helps make the Winter Garden a public space comparable to the concourse of the Grand Central Terminal that opened in 1913.

The City Council enacts a law in April requiring restaurants with 50 seats or more to provide separate sections for smokers and nonsmokers. Many restaurants predict a slump in business, but their dire outlook will prove unfounded (*see* 1995).

San Domenico opens at 240 Central Park South, near Columbus Circle. Restaurateur Tony May has started the place with Bolognese banker Gian Luigi Morini, who about 18 years ago opened another San Domenico in his 15th-century house at the town of Immola, near Bologna. A full-time expert from Italy prepares fresh pasta daily.

Aureole opens in November at 34 East 61st Street. Charles Palmer of the River Café has gained backing from Steve Tzolis and Nicola Kotsoni of Peryali to start the new restaurant. Prix-fixe dinner is $50.

Illegal immigrants flood agency offices prior to May 4, expiration date for the amnesty program set up under the 1986 Immigration Control and Reform Act.

1989 The U.S. Supreme Court rules unanimously March 22 that New York City's powerful Board of Estimate is unconstitutional because it violates the one-person/one-vote principle. The five borough presidents on the Board have equal votes even though the boroughs vary greatly in population. Mayor Koch appoints F. A. O. Schwarz, Jr. to head a commission charged with creating a charter-revision referendum in time for the November election.

City voters give narrow (5 to 4) approval to the most sweeping revision in the city charter since 1898, shaking up the power structure by increasing the size of the City Council to give more representation to minority groups and small political parties (*see* 1990).

New York elects its first black mayor. A patronage scandal has tarnished the image of Mayor Koch, who has lost the Democratic Party primary to New Jersey-born Manhattan Borough President David (Norman) Dinkins, 63, who calls New York a "gorgeous mosaic" and narrowly defeats his Republican

The homeless forced the city to take steps that some called heartless; it had little choice. CHIE NISHIO

rival, associate U.S. attorney general Rudolph W. Giuliani, now 45. Dinkins receives 917,544 votes to 870,464 for Giuliani (who beats Dinkins in Queens and Staten Island). Conservative Party candidate Ronald S. (Stephen) Lauder, 45, of the Estée Lauder cosmetics family (he left the company in 1983 to join NATO) served as U.S. ambassador to Austria from 1986 to 1987 and has spent a lot of money on his campaign but voices unpopular views and fares poorly at the polls.

Hecklers boo Mayor Koch June 1 when he proclaims June to be Lesbian and Gay Pride Month in New York. More than 1,500 people march from Greenwich Village to Central Park without a police permit June 24, marking the 20th anniversary of the Stonewall Inn riot that began the gay rights movement in the city, and thousands march down Fifth Avenue June 25. An impromptu march through Greenwich Village that day protests two recent killings of gay men and reenacts the events of 1969.

Seven white youths attack four black youths visiting a Bensonhurst (Brooklyn) neighborhood August 23 to look at a used car (see Howard Beach, 1986); Yusef K. Hawkins, 16, is shot dead in a racial incident that plays a role in the mayoral election contest. Rev. Al Sharpton leads a group of black teenagers through Bensonhurst August 26 to express outrage while white youths wave watermelons to taunt them, but Sharpton has made no effort to work with local community leaders who wanted to join the march.

The state court of appeals rules July 6 in *Braschi v. Stahl Associates* that the longtime partner of a gay man who has died is entitled to the same right of succession to a rent-controlled apartment as would a legal spouse.

Seven members of ACT-UP interrupt trading on the New York Stock Exchange in September to protest lack of investment in finding a cure for, or vaccine against, AIDS (see 1987). Some 4,500 people converge on St. Patrick's Cathedral December 10 and disrupt a sermon by John Cardinal O'Connor to protest church opposition to legal abortion and safer-sex education. Police arrest 111, including 43 inside the cathedral.

Astoria Federal Savings and Loan Association moves its headquarters from Long Island City to the Bulova Corporate Center at Jackson Heights (see 1937). It opened branches in Ditmars, Forest Hills, and Flushing beginning in the late 1950s, merged with Metropolitan Federal Savings and Loan of Middle Village in 1973, bought Citizens Savings and Loan of Woodside in 1979, celebrated its centennial last

year, and next year will buy Whitestone Savings and Loan. By 1991 Astoria will have 13 branches, and its assets of more than $3 billion will make it the city's sixth largest thrift institution.

Former Drexel Burnham Lambert "junk" bond guru Michael Milken is indicted March 29 along with his brother Lowell, 40, and a 31-year-old former colleague on 98 counts of conspiracy, stock manipulation, racketeering, and securities fraud (see 1988). The government estimates that Milken's salary and bonuses for 1984–1986 came to $554 million, and that he was paid $550 million in 1987 (more than $150 billion worth of the bonds have been issued by year's end). Prominent New York business leaders rise to Milken's defense (see 1990).

The National Debt Clock begins flashing near the northwest corner of 42nd Street and the Avenue of the Americas to show "Our National Debt" growing second by second plus the growing share of the debt borne by each U.S. household. Real estate developer Seymour B. Durst, now 75, owns the property, he makes a practice of buying lots and erecting one-story "taxpayer" retail stores to produce income until he can develop or resell, and although many prominent economists insist that the national debt is not excessive given the size of the nation's economy he has engaged Artkraft Strauss to create a sign that will continue to flash numbers until September 2000, by which time the national debt will be declining (the sign will be revived in 2002 when the debt increases).

Wall Street's Dow Jones Industrial Average drops 190.58 points Friday, October 13, as confidence weakens in "junk" bond financing of mergers and acquisitions, but prices rebound the following week and the Dow closes the year at 2753, up 584.63 from its close at the end of 1988.

The Manhattan Mall (initially called A&S Plaza) opens on Greeley Square in mid-September, replacing Gimbels (see 1986; Abraham & Straus, 1893; Gimbels, 1910). Converted at a cost of $450 million and located just south of the Herald Center that opened in 1982, it is the city's largest shopping mall. Federated Department Stores will merge with Macy's in 1994, and by March 2001 the vertical shopping center will have grown to include some 80 small retail establishments built around an atrium with a food court on the seventh level, but Campeau Corp., its owner, battles creditors and puts the 17-store Bloomingdale's chain up for sale (see 1988; 1990).

The British conglomerate B.A.T. Industries announces in October that it will sell its U.S. retailing operations that include 46 Saks Fifth Avenue stores (see 1990).

B. Altman & Co. on Fifth Avenue holds going-out-of-business sales beginning November 22 (see 1917). Sales at the 83-year-old store have been declining for a decade, and a 1985 change in the tax laws requires nonprofit foundations to divest themselves of certain profit-making entities, forcing the Altman Foundation to sell its buildings to a real estate group and its retail activities to another group. The 124-year-old enterprise has been losing between $800,000 and $1 million per day, its Australian-based owner (who also controls Bonwit Teller) has suffered other reversals and filed for bankruptcy in August, no acceptable bid for it has been received in the past month, and bankruptcy judge Tina Brozman has ruled November 17 in favor of the owner's plea for protection from creditors. The demise of the store is a calamity to Altman's 1,700 employees (hundreds of them in New Jersey, Pennsylvania, and elsewhere) and many thousands of customers (see 1990).

Growing use of natural gas in the New York area threatens to put pressure on supplies once again (see 1970; 1976). Electric utility companies have begun using natural gas to generate electricity; Brooklyn Union Gas supplies 75 percent of one- and two-family residences in its area, and 33 percent of apartments; other companies have made similar gains (see Consolidated Edison, 1990).

The market price of a New York taxicab medallion reaches $136,000, up from $10 in 1937. A survey shows that while owner-drivers average $40,000 per year in tips and commissions, drivers who lease their cabs earn just $21,000 to $31,000, but only 30 percent of drivers work full time.

The Metropolitan Transportation Authority introduces new sign-display guidelines as part of a program to standardize graphics and reduce "visual clutter" in the subways.

The subway's last graffiti-covered train is taken out of service May 12 on the C line (see 1984). The city has spent by some estimates $250 million to wipe out the "writings," making it a priority to take back the trains while other needs went unfunded. Vandals will continue to deface the system's more than 5,800 cars, mindlessly scratching windows and other surfaces with keys, coins, razor blades, and the like.

A new subway tunnel opens under the East River October 29 to link Manhattan (at East 63rd Street) with Long Island City; a station on Roosevelt Island provides an option to the aerial tramway that has been that community's only direct link with Manhattan since its opening in 1976 (see 1994).

The 36-story Helmsley Medical Tower is dedicated February 14 at New York Hospital. Made possible by a $33 million gift from billionaire real estate mogul Harry B. Helmsley and his wife, Leona, the structure has 519 apartments for nurses and other hospital staff, 142 short-term housing units for out-of-town patients and their families, plus medical and administrative offices.

The New York Hospital-Cornell Medical Center installs the city's first lasertripter for treating kidney and urinary stones (see 1984).

Rev. Samuel Proctor retires from the leadership of the Abyssinian Baptist Church that he inherited from the late Adam Clayton Powell, Jr. in 1972 and is succeeded by New York-born clergyman Calvin O. (Otis) Butts III, 40, who has voiced his disapproval of police brutality.

Two men accuse Covenant House founder Rev. Bruce Ritter in December of having had sexual relations with them when they were teenagers (see 1969). Now 62, he is then accused of having misused Covenant House money but denies both charges. Manhattan District Attorney Robert Morgenthau will announce that he lacks sufficient evidence of financial misconduct to bring criminal charges, but Ritter will resign in February of next year.

The Eugene M. Lang Foundation offers to pay the college tuition of every sixth grader at P.S. 121 in East Harlem (see 1981). By January of next year more than 20 other New York philanthropists will have followed the foundation's example. Started in 1968, the foundation also pays for tutoring and other student aid, making annual contributions averaging $2 million (total foundation assets by 1991 will be nearly $27.5 million).

The Children's Museum of Manhattan opens October 15 at 212 West 83rd Street, between Amsterdam Avenue and Broadway, with five floors of attractions funded by the Tisch Foundation, Time Warner, and other corporate sponsors.

Veteran radio talk-show personality Pegeen Fitzgerald dies of breast cancer at New York January 30 at age 78. In recent years she has been appearing on Leonard Lopate's WNYC show *New York & Com-*

pany, speaking from her apartment at 40 Central Park South.

The Museum of Broadcasting opens at 23 West 52nd Street. Built on land donated by CBS founder William S. Paley, it has been designed by John Burgee with Philip Johnson and replaces an earlier facility with the same name at 1 East 53rd Street.

Time Warner is created July 24 through a $14 billion takeover of Warner Communications by Time, Inc., whose founder Henry R. Luce died in 1967. Warner Communications CEO Steven J. Ross, now 62, becomes head of the new corporation and receives $78.2 million, more than any other executive of a publicly owned company, including a one-time payment of $74.9 million for his interest in Warner Communications (605 staff workers in Time's publishing division were laid off last year, Ross makes one-and-a-half times as much as the combined salaries of the laid-off workers, and he is widely hated). Time secured a controlling interest in the cable television service Sterling Communications in 1970, launched Home Box Office (HBO) in November 1972 to make the service more profitable, and now provides cable TV service to the southern half of Manhattan. Magazines accounted for less than 40 percent of Time's $4.5 billion in revenues last year, with cable TV accounting for 41 percent and book publishing 20 percent. Warner Communications owns MTV and Nickelodeon; Time Warner sets up a new cable TV entity that takes over Brooklyn Queens Cable customers, giving it a total of 700,000 subscribers, but it labors under the burden of an enormous $11.8 billion debt and loses more than $150 million per year (*see* AOL Time Warner, 2000).

Puerto Rican-born publisher Carlos D. Ramírez, 42, leads a partnership that buys *El Diario/La Prensa* for $20 million from the Gannett Co. that bought it for $9 million. Ramírez will be credited with building circulation of the 7-day-per-week paper from less than 40,000 to 68,000.

Former *Harper's Bazaar* (1939–1962) and *Vogue* (1961–1971) editor and fashion arbiter Diana Vreeland dies of a heart attack at New York August 22 at age 88 (approximate); former *New York Post* publisher Dorothy Schiff dies at her native New York August 30 at age 86; former McCann-Erickson president (and Interpublic chairman) Marion Harper, Jr. of a heart attack at his Oklahoma City home October 25 at age 73.

Street News begins publication in November, giving homeless New Yorkers an opportunity to help themselves by offering a product to people instead of just begging for help. The publication will lead to the housing of hundreds of former street people and will be imitated in other cities across the country and worldwide.

Nonfiction: *Fiorello H. La Guardia and the Making of Modern New York* by Thomas Kessner; *The Living City* by New York architectural critic Roberta Brandes Gratz; *You Must Remember This: An Oral History of Manhattan from the 1890s to World War II* by local journalist Jeff Kisseloff; *Upper West Side Story: A History and Guide* by New York author Peter Salwen, 57; *In Transit: The Transport Workers' Union in New York City* by Philadelphia-born Columbia University assistant professor Joshua B. Freeman, 40; *The Vanderbilt Era: Profiles of a Gilded Age* by lawyer-novelist Louis Auchincloss, now 72, who married a Vanderbilt; *Manhattan for Rent: 1785–1850* by New York historian Elizabeth Blackmar, 39; *The New Crowd: The Changing of the Jewish Guard on Wall Street* by Judith Ramsey Ehrlich and New York-born author Barry J. Rehfeld, 43, who say of Salomon Brothers senior partner John Gutfreund, "the kind of money required to put his bride and himself on the social map was buried in the Salomon Brothers' partnership." (Gutfreund's second wife, Susan, was a Pan Am flight attendant before he married her in 1981.)

Gotham Book Mart proprietor Frances "Fanny" Steloff dies of pneumonia at Mount Sinai Medical Center April 15 at age 101 but her shop in West 47th Street continues as it has since 1920.

Fiction: *The Mambo Kings Play Songs of Love* by Oscar Hijuelos; *Billy Bathgate* by E. L. Doctorow.

 Painting: *Elizabeth* by Chuck Close, who was left nearly quadriplegic in December of last year by a blood clot in his spinal artery but has gone back to work with help from his wife, Leslie, after 7 months of rehabilitation at the Rusk Institute. Elaine de Kooning dies of lung cancer at Southampton (N.Y.) Hospital February 1 at age 68; Manhattan-born *New Yorker* magazine artist Barney Tobey at New York March 27 at age 82.

The controversial Pathfinder Mural is completed on the wall of a six-story Greenwich Village building at the corner of West and Charles streets after more than 2 years of work by 80 volunteer artists from 20 countries. Featuring portraits of Fidel Castro, Che Guevara, Mother Jones, Karl Marx, Leon Trotsky, and Malcolm X, the work has cost $100,000, and although only $500 came from New York State Council on the Arts (private donors contributed the rest) the *Daily News* criticizes use of public funds for what it calls a "colorful, cheery celebration of mass political murder, slavery, repression and human misery."

Sculptor Richard Serra's 1981 work *Tilted Arc* is removed from Federal Plaza March 17 amidst much controversy (Serra has argued in court that the stark, site-specific work would almost cease to exist if moved). The General Services Administration will store it in three stacked sections in an outdoor government parking lot at the corner of Third Avenue and 29th Street, Brooklyn, until September 1999, when it will be moved by flatbed truck at a cost of $36,000 to a storage building at Middle River, Md.

Theater: *Love Letters* by A. R. Gurney 10/31 at the Edison Theater, with a rotating cast of two (Jason Robards, Jr. and Colleen Dewhurst, New York-born actor Richard (Earl) Thomas, 38, and Swoosie Kurtz), 96 perfs.; *A Few Good Men* by New York-born playwright Aaron Sorkin, 28, 11/15 at the Music Box Theater, with Wisconsin-born actor Tom Hulce, 36, Reading, Pa.-born actress Megan Gallagher, 29, Roxanne Hart, 497 perfs.

Films: Woody Allen's *Crimes and Misdemeanors* with Allen, Martin Landau, Mia Farrow, Anjelica Huston; Spike Lee's *Do the Right Thing* with Danny Aiello, Ossie Davis, Ruby Dee; Paul Mazursky's *Enemies, A Love Story* with Anjelica Huston, Ron Silver; Harold Becker's *Sea of Love* with Al Pacino, Ellen Barkin, John Goodman; Rob Reiner's *When Harry Met Sally* with Billy Crystal, Meg Ryan, Carrie Fisher. Also: Howard Zieff's *The Dream Team* with Michael Keaton, Christopher Lloyd, Peter Boyle; Ivan Reitman's *Ghostbusters II* with Bill Murray, Dan Aykroyd (the firehouse in the film is that of Ladder No. 8 at the corner of North Moore and Varick streets); Eddie Murphy's *Harlem Nights* with Murphy, Richard Pryor, Redd Foxx, Danny Aiello; Uli Edel's *Last Exit to Brooklyn* with Stephen Lang, Jennifer Jason Leigh; Henry Jaglom's *New Year's Day* with Jaglom, Melanie Winter, Gwen Welles, Maggie Jakobson; Martin Scorsese, Francis Ford Coppola, and Woody Allen's *New York Stories* with Nick Nolte, Rosanna Arquette, Deborah Harry, Talia Shire (originally Talia Rose Coppola), Allen, Mia Farrow, Mayor Koch; Michael Roemer's *The Plot Against Harry* with Martin Priest, Ben Lang, Maxine Woods; Charles Lane's *Sidewalk Stories* with Lane as a homeless man struggling for survival in Greenwich Village; James Ivory's *Slaves of New York* with Bernadette Peters, Adam Coleman; Joseph Ruben's *True Believer* with James Woods, Robert Downey, Jr.; Nancy Savoka's *True Love* with Annabella Sciorra, Ron Eldard, Aida Turturro.

Broadway musicals: Claudio Segovia and Héctor Orezzolio's *Black and Blue* 1/26 at the Minskoff Theater, with soul singer Ruth Brown, now nearly 61, dancer Savion Glover, music and lyrics from various sources, 829 perfs.; *Dangerous Games* 10/19 at the Nederlander Theater, with a 17-member cast directed by Buenos Aires-born Graciela Daniele, 49, tango music by Astor Piazzolla, lyrics by William Finn, 4 perfs. (after 12 previews); *Grand Hotel* 11/12 at the Martin Beck Theater, with a 33-member cast headed by Karen Akers, Tennessee-born actor Michael Jeter, 37, directed by Tommy Tune, music and lyrics by Robert Wright, George Forrest, and Maury Yeston (to George Gershwin Theater beginning 2/3/1992), 1,017 perfs.; *City of Angels* 12/7 at the Virginia Theater, with a 27-member cast that includes Middletown, Conn.-born actor James Naughton, 42, René Auberjonois, Chicago-born actor Gregg Edelman, 31, book by Larry Gelbart, music by Cy Coleman, lyrics by David Zippel, 35, 879 perfs.

The 70-year-old St. Thomas Church Choir School moves into a 14-story structure at 202 West 58th Street built as a boarding school for 50 students with faculty.

Composer-critic Virgil Thomson dies at his New York home September 30 at age 92; piano virtuoso Vladimir Horowitz of an apparent heart attack at his New York home November 5 at age 86; dancer-choreographer Alvin Ailey of a blood disorder at a New York hospital December 1 at age 58.

Popular songs: *Life at the Bottom Line* (album) by Laura Nyro, now 42, includes "The Wild World" and "Japanese Restaurant;" *Queen Mary* (album) by St. Croix-born New York jazz drummer Denis Charles, 55, is based on Caribbean folk songs. A member of the city's jazz underground, Charles arrived in Harlem with his two brothers in 1945 and from 1955 to 1960 used his hand-drumming style with pianist Cecil Taylor before moving on to play with other groups.

The Blue Note jazz recording label celebrates its 50th anniversary with a June 30 concert at Carnegie Hall as part of the JVC Jazz Festival.

Village Vanguard founder Max Gordon dies at a New York hospital May 11 at age 86, having helped to promote the careers of many jazz greats and comedians (his 54-year-old, 123-seat nightclub continues under the direction of his widow, Lorraine, now 67, whose first husband was Blue Notes record founder Alfred Lion); Atlantic Records cofounder Neshuhi Ertegun dies following cancer surgery at New York

July 15 at age 71 (components of the new Time Warner conglomerate include Warner Bros. records and Atlantic records); Studio 54 discothèque founder Steve Rubell dies of complications from hepatitis and septic shock at Beth Israel Medical Center July 25 at age 45; songwriter Irving Berlin at age 101 September 22 at the 17 Beekman Place town house where he has lived since 1948. His wife, Ellin, died of a stroke last year at age 85.

Boris Becker and Steffi Graff win the U.S. Open singles titles at Flushing Meadow.

Yankee owner George Steinbrenner gives up control of the team on orders issued July 30 by Baseball Commissioner Fay Vincent, who cites Steinbrenner's relationship with "known gambler" Howard Spira (Spira has claimed that he received $40,000 from Steinbrenner for providing information intended to damage former Yankee Dave Winfield). Vincent's ruling requires Steinbrenner to give up his position as general partner by August 20 and reduce his 53 percent interest in the team to less than 50 percent within a year, but Steinbrenner will retain a major interest.

Former New York Giants first baseman Bill Terry (the last National League player to bat .400) dies at Jacksonville, Fla., January 9 at age 90; former Brooklyn Dodgers right fielder Carl Furillo of an apparent heart attack at his Stony Creek Mills, Pa., home January 21 at age 66; Yankee manager Billy Martin December 25 at age 61 from injuries suffered in an auto accident near his home at Binghamton.

The first Crunch health club opens in Manhattan under the direction of former stockbroker Doug Levine, 30, who competes with the Vertical Club and others; he will have five New York gyms by 1997, charging about $800 per year in membership fees, and the Crunch exercise program will be broadcast twice per day on the cable station ESPN2.

Commercial property owners in midtown Manhattan finance a force of 29 uniformed but unarmed security guards to patrol a 50-block area around Grand Central Terminal and Bryant Park to discourage crime. The Midtown South police precinct's anticrime squad stakes out Times Square with hidden surveillance posts to discourage pickpockets who steal credit cards. State Supreme Court chief justice Sol Wachtler announces emergency measures April 17 to keep up with arrests for crack-related crime, setting up makeshift courts on Rikers Island to sentence prisoners, but violent crime rages out of control.

A 29-year-old investment banker jogging in Central Park is raped April 19 and left for dead. Police arrest a band of black and Hispanic youths who are indicted.

A jury convicts hotel operator Leona Helmsley, now 69, August 30 on 33 counts of income tax evasion and massive tax fraud (she and her husband, Harry, have used company funds to decorate their own house and apartment) but acquits her of the more serious charge of scheming to extort kickbacks from contractors and suppliers; the Helmsleys have cheated the government of $1.2 million, a former housekeeper has testified that Mrs. Helmsley told her, "Only the little people pay taxes," and the "queen of mean" draws a 4-year prison term plus a $7.1 million fine.

Arnulfo Williams, Jr., 19, is shot dead December 2 while trying to protect his younger brother from some thugs at a south Jamaica bus stop. Like dozens of other such killings (four innocent bystanders are killed in 4 days beginning December 21 in unrelated incidents), crimes committed by blacks against other blacks draw little attention; black militants, clergymen, and civil rights lawyers do not speak out against them, nor do white activists.

The 47-story Morgan Building is completed at 60 Wall Street, between Nassau and William streets (its north side faces Pine Street). Designed by Kevin Roche, the stucture contains 1.7 million square feet of floor space, and J. P. Morgan & Co. relocates from the building it has occupied since 1913 at 23 Wall Street, but a glut of office space, combined with the business recession that has persisted since the stock-market collapse of October 1987, forces many real estate owners to offer rental contracts calling for no rents at all to be paid for 10 years or more. Entire buildings stand empty for lack of tenants willing to take space even on the most liberal terms.

The 42-story 1585 Broadway office building is completed at the southwest corner of 48th Street in Times Square. Designed by Gwathmey Siegel Associates with Emery Roth & Sons, it replaces the Strand movie theater of 1914 that was later cut up into smaller theaters and has 1.3 million square feet of space that is occupied mainly by Morgan Stanley.

1 Worldwide Plaza opens May 15 at 880 Eighth Avenue in the block bounded by Eighth and Ninth avenues between 49th and 50th streets, where a parking lot has for more than 20 years occupied the site of Tex Rickard's 1925 Madison Square Garden in what used to be Hell's Kitchen. Capped with a glazed pyramid that houses a beacon, it has been

built by World Wide Holdings (a partnership that includes Moroccan-born architect-entrepreneur Victor Elmaleh, now 70, and Frank Stanton, 68, who have made fortunes as Volkswagen distributors) with William Zeckendorf, Jr., Arthur Cohen Realty, and the Japanese construction company Kumagai Gumi; the $550 million complex combines a 49-story office tower designed by David Childs of Skidmore, Owings & Merrill (its 1.5 million square feet of rentable space exceeds that of the Empire State Building) with 650 condominium apartment units designed by Frank Williams (also included are town houses, movie theaters, restaurants, and shops). Cement for the 778-foot-high structure has cost twice as much as it costs in New Jersey (a crime family still controls the city's cement industry), and pressure from the Clinton Community Board has forced the developers to give away 32 renovated apartments at a cost of $12 million. Condominium units are priced from $135,000, one-bedroom apartments from $180,000, two bedrooms from $300,000, but rents from the commercial tenants will for some years fall short of the developers' interest payments.

The 35-story 1675 Broadway office building is completed on the west side of Broadway between 52nd and 53rd streets. Designed by Fox & Fowle with a façade of gray granite and green windows, it replaces the Alvin Hotel.

The 48-story Citicorp office building is completed across the Queensboro Bridge from Manhattan in Hunters Point, replacing St. John's Hospital on a site bounded by 44th Drive, 45th Avenue, and Jackson Avenue. Designed by Skidmore, Owings & Merrill, it is the tallest New York structure outside of Manhattan.

The Rockefeller Group announces October 30 that Mitsubishi Estate Co. of Tokyo has bought a 51 percent interest in Rockefeller Center for $1.5 billion, including $846 million in cash (see 1985). Made to diversify the group's holdings, the sale involves the 14 original buildings, the skating rink, and Radio City Music Hall. The money is to go into a philanthropic trust set up by the late John D. Rockefeller, Jr. in 1934 (some of the 22 members of the family's fourth generation, ranging in age from 22 to 61, have been pressuring the administrators of the trust to diversify). The buildings are 98.4 percent occupied, as compared with 88 to 89 percent in most midtown Manhattan office buildings, and rents are said to be nearly as high as in other buildings (although many tenants pay far less) (see 1995).

The Belair apartment house is completed at 525–535 East 71st Street, between York Avenue and the FDR Drive. Designed by Frank Williams & Associates, the 38-story tower replaces a five-story garage.

The 21-story Boulevard apartment house is completed at 2373 Broadway. Designed by architect Alexander Cooper for developer Bruce Eichner, the "condop" extends up the west side of what was once called "the Boulevard" between 86th and 87th streets with 354 apartments plus medical offices and retail space.

The 46-story Crowne Plaza Hotel opens at 1601 Broadway, between 48th and 49th streets. Designed for Marriott Corp. by architect Alan Lapidus (son and sometime partner of Morris), the hotel has 770 rooms and will become a Holiday Inn. William Zeckendorf, Jr. has built the structure in partnership with Victor Elmaleh and Frank Stanton of World Wide Holdings.

The City Council adopts a law requiring that at least 25 percent of residential trash be recycled by July 1996; included are newspapers, magazines, telephone directories, glass, metal, plastic containers, and Christmas trees (see 1997).

The 140-acre area surrounding Brooklyn's historic Floyd Bennett Field is cleared of dense underbrush to provide a grassy biopreserve for grassland birds such as grasshopper sparrows, meadowlarks, short-eared owls, and upland sandpipers. Audubon Society volunteers join with Park Service rangers of the new Gateway National Recreation Area in the New York area's first "prescription burn." Bluestem grass will grow waist high within a few years, providing a habitat also for barn owls, box turtles, hog-nosed snakes, opossums, rabbits, and ring-necked pheasants.

Consolidated Edison spends several million dollars to remove the asbestos from 1,000 of its 1,700 Manhattan manhole covers (see 1975), but rather than remove the asbestos from all its underground steam pipes it opts to replace such insulation in routine maintenance or in cleaning up after accidents.

Alison on Dominick Street in TriBeCa (Triangle South of Canal Street) opens in an old brick house at No. 38 (Dominick is a two-block thoroughfare between Sixth Avenue and Hudson Street). Restaurateur Alison Price (née Becker) has a résumé that includes a stint at the Gotham Bar and Grill, and she works with chef Thomas Valenti. First courses are $5 to $12, main courses $17 to $26, desserts $5 to $9.

The 10-year-old restaurant Le Chanterelle moves to 2 Harrison Street, near Hudson Street, where it occupies what was once the lunch room of the Mercantile Exchange, built in 1884 for traders who dealt originally in grain, butter and eggs, and Maine potatoes (operations were relocated to the World Trade Center in 1977).

Le Madri opens at 168 West 18th Street, southeast corner Seventh Avenue. Restaurateur Pino Luongo has obtained backing from the Pressman family that owns the building (and the clothing store Barney's one block to the south) (see Cocopazzo, 1990).

An American Place moves late in the year into larger premises at 2 Park Avenue, with an entrance in East 32nd Street (see 1983).

1990 The Board of Estimate that has been such a power in New York City's governance since 1901 holds its final hearing August 16 following last year's U.S. Supreme Court ruling that it is unconstitutional. The U.S. Department of Justice has given approval to the sweeping charter revisions approved by the city's voters last November, the City Council expands from 35 members to 51; Mayor Dinkins, City Comptroller Elizabeth Holtzman, and other prominent officials make a rare appearance at the hearing; the terms of the charter revisions are implemented gradually over the course of the year, but complaints will grow that the revised charter unfairly favors the mayor's office at the expense of the City Council, especially in matters relating to budget matters and land-use policy.

The political assassination of Brooklyn-born Israeli extremist Meir (originally Martin David) Kahane at age 58 by a gunman at a midtown Manhattan hotel November 5 exacerbates Israeli-Palestinian animosities. Rabbi Kahane founded the Jewish Defense

Ellis Island got a makeover, becoming a tourist attraction for immigrants and their descendants. CHIE NISHIO

League in 1968, moved to Israel in 1971, and has stirred up anger against Arabs. A drive-past shooting on the West Bank November 6 kills a 65-year-old Palestinian man and a 61-year-old woman in what is evidently an act of retaliation.

Gov. Cuomo wins election to a third term, but turnout (53 percent of registered voters) is the lowest in at least 50 years. The governor receives 2,029,125 votes, Republican Pierre Rinfret 801,503; NYU faculty member Herbert (Ira) London, 51, runs on the Conservative Party line and receives 778,700.

 A January boycott of two Korean grocery stores on Brooklyn's Church Avenue attracts national attention (see 1988).

Tenured CCNY black studies professor Leonard Jeffries, Jr., 53, and tenured CCNY philosophy professor Michael Levin, 46, draw criticism for their allegedly "racist" teachings. Levin cites various controversial "authorities" for his statements that blacks are significantly less intelligent than whites, while Jeffries calls people of European ancestry "ice people" who are fundamentally "materialistic, greedy, and intent on domination," while those of African descent, the "sun people," are essentially humanistic and communal. Rich Jews, says Jeffries, financed the development of Europe and also financed the slave trade, the Holocaust was not the only such example of genocide, and blacks have been deliberately miseducated from a false white, European point of view to make them "Afropeans." "Levin is not the problem," he says. "Many people hold the same beliefs. They teach out of contempt. The problem is racism—insidious in our society and built into our culture." Raised in Newark, Jeffries has taught at City College since 1969, has made 51 visits to Africa, and affects African-style clothing (see 1991).

The Americans with Disabilities Act signed by President Bush July 26 bans discrimination in employment, public accommodations, transportation, and telecommunications against the nation's 43 million disabled persons. The law provides new protection for workers with AIDS and will not only force New York's Metropolitan Transportation Authority to accommodate wheelchair passengers on its buses, but also require many of the city's property owners to make their buildings accessible to people in wheelchairs.

$ "Junk bond" king Michael Milken pleads guilty to insider trading April 24 at Federal District Court in New York (see 1989). He agrees to pay a record $600 in fines and restitution and is sentenced November

21 to 10 years in prison. The sentence will be reduced to 3 years.

Bloomberg Business News is created by Bloomberg Financial Markets to provide round-the-clock monitoring of markets worldwide (*see* 1981); Bloomberg's 24-hour financial news-gathering service is becoming a major source of market information, competing with Reuters and Dow Jones and making Michael R. Bloomberg a billionaire (*see* politics, 2001).

The 83-year-old North Fork Bank completes its acquisition August 1 of the 130-year-old Southold Savings Bank, oldest thrift institution in Suffolk County (*see* 1991).

The Federal Reserve Board acts September 20 to authorize J. P. Morgan & Co. to underwrite stocks, the first time a bank has had that power since the 1933 Glass-Steagall Act. Critics will attack Fed chairman Alan Greenspan for reopening the door to possible conflicts of interest.

Mayor Dinkins imposes a 5 percent pay cut on himself and 700 other senior city officials October 22 and cuts salaries of 3,800 managerial employees to demonstrate belt-tightening and save $4.5 million for the fiscal year. Union leaders call it a "gimmick" to strengthen the city's hand in stalled contract talks.

A seat on the New York Stock Exchange sells for a high of $450,000, up from $85,000 in 1939 but still well below the $625,000 peak of 1929.

America's record 8-year economic boom ends in July as the country goes into recession.

Wall Street's Dow Jones Industrial Average closes at 2999.75 July 16 and 17, falls to 2365.10 in October, and ends the year at 2633.66, down 4.3 percent since the end of 1989.

B. Altman & Co. files for bankruptcy in January (*see* 1989; library, 1996).

The U.S. retailing operations of Campeau Corp. file for Chapter 11 bankruptcy court protection January 15 (*see* 1988). Bloomingdale's, A&S, and other Federated Department Store properties are put up for sale, as are Allied Stores that include Lord & Taylor, but are allowed to remain operating under court supervision (*see* 1994).

Britain's BAT Industries sells Saks Fifth Avenue and its 45 stores nationwide to Bahrain-based Investcorp for $1.5 billion April 25 (*see* 1989; 1998).

New York City limits the number of licenses granted to street vendors selling general merchandise to 853 (plus those granted automatically to military veterans). The waiting list for such licenses is 710 (*see* 1994).

Consolidated Edison launches a $4.2 billion campaign to modernize its existing plants, make alliances with independent power producers, and encourage conservation in energy use, setting its sights on the year 2008 with the goal of having customers reduce their use of electricity by 15 percent by that date as compared to what usage would be without a conservation program.

City transit fares rise January 1 to $1.15, but the subways are now graffiti-free, and 94 percent of the 6,200 cars in the system are air-conditioned (*see* 1984; 1995).

The Metropolitan Transportation Authority hires American Express credit-analyst trainer Stephen Vidal, 35, to revamp the training of city bus drivers. An in-house investigation has shown a 30 percent increase in accidents (to 9,500 per year) from 1985 to 1988, jeopardizing the safety of bus riders and pedestrians alike. Transit Workers Union Local 100 surface transportation management director Edwin Melendez, also 35, initially opposes Vidal, who wants to get bad drivers off the road (Melendez wants to preserve jobs), but the two compromise their differences and together develop a new program for hiring and training (or retraining) drivers. Every driver is given a 2-day refresher course so that bad drivers will not be singled out; accidents will be cut in half over the next 5 years.

A survey of the city's taxi industry shows that high turnover of drivers and higher automobile prices are putting pressure on profits, as is competition from radio-equipped limousines. Independent drivers pay up to $75 per day plus the cost of gasoline to lease their vehicles, and many are discouraged by the threat of armed robbery and even murder (*see* 1993).

The bilingual cartoon strip "Decision/La Decisión" debuts on car cards in city subways to make straphangers more aware of AIDS and the need to practice safe sex. Cartoonist Jerry Gonzalez draws the strip, whose cliff-hanger episodes feature Marisol and her friends in a series sponsored by the city Health Department; its team of writers works to create new episodes that will continue until 1995 and resume in 1997.

The Museum of the Jewish Heritage opens in an apartment tower at Battery Place, west of First Place, in the new Battery Park City. The museum and tower have been designed by James Stewart Polshek & Partners.

Tuition at Columbia, Barnard, NYU, and other top U.S. colleges tops $14,000 per year, total expenses exceed $20,000, but 80 percent of undergraduates attend public universities, where tuition averages less than $2,000 per year, another 16 percent go to private colleges, where tuition is below $10,000, scarcely 4 percent pay more, and up to two-thirds of these receive scholarships, subsidized loans, or both.

New York-born educator Joseph A. Fernandez, Jr., 54, accepts the position of public schools chancellor with a mandate to address the system's problems of dropouts, crime, teenage pregnancy, and the like. Texas-born educator Ramon C. Cortines, 58, leaves a job in Florida's Dade County to accept a position under Fernandez. Cortines will work to reform one of the nation's most troubled school systems with aggressive measures that will often put him at odds with the Board of Education and the mayor.

Entertainment Weekly begins publication at New York February 12. Time Warner spends $150 million to launch its first new magazine since *People* in 1974.

A *Time* magazine telephone poll published in its September 17 issue reports that 75 percent of respondents said, "Pushy," when asked to describe people living in New York; 64 percent said, "Arrogant," 60 percent "Sophisticated."

Daily News workers go on strike October 25 following a confrontation at the paper's Brooklyn printing plant (*see* 1982). Nine of the paper's 10 unions walk off the job after months of stalled negotiations, the *News* uses replacement workers to keep publishing, but circulation will plummet in the next 5 months (*see* 1991).

Nonfiction: *A New York Life: Of Friends and Others* by Brendan Gill; *Our New York* by Alfred Kazin; *On Broadway: A Journey Uptown over Time* by *New York Times* real-estate reporter David N. Dunlap; *The Civil War and New York City* by SUNY Maritime College teacher Ernest A. McKay; *The House of Morgan: An American Banking Dynasty and the Rise of Modern Finance* by Brooklyn-born author Ron Chernow, 41; *The Greatest Ever Bank Robbery: The Collapse of the Savings and Loan Industry* by Martin Mayer; *Too Good to be True: the Outlandish Story of Wedtech* by New York journalist James Traub, 36, whose father is chairman of Bloomingdale's; *The Closest of Strangers: Liberalism and the Politics of Race in New York* by Boston-born *New York Newsday* editor Jim Sleeper, 43, who writes that its real estate industry "is to New

York City what big oil is to Houston, a remarkable agglomeration of bankers, investors, developers, builders, owners, managers, and brokers who speculate frenetically on the sites of the great enterprises and headquarters and on the neighborhoods where their owners, managers, workers, clients, and customers might live. These key players in the real-estate game have a culture and subcultures all their own; they sluice the currents of neighborhood investment and disinvestment that are so swift and unsparing. As they try to profit from various communities' emergence, stabilization, upgrading, or decline, they stamp the perceptions and preferences of New Yorkers, whose standing in the real-estate market is determined by income and tastes derivative of their relationships to the larger, nonspatial networks of the city;" *The Westies: Inside the Hell's Kitchen Irish Mob* by New York writer T. J. English; *New York's Jewish Jews: The Orthodox Community in the Interwar Years* by YIVO Institute scholar Jenna Weissman Joselit; *Central Park: The Birth, Decline, and Renewal of a National Treasure* by former *New Yorker* writer Eugene Kinkead, now 83; *Bridges of Central Park* by Henry Hope Reed, Robert M. McGee, and Esther Mipaas; *Park Avenue: Street of Dreams* by James Trager.

Author Kate Simon dies at New York February 4 at age 77; Marya Mannes suffers a stroke at San Francisco and dies there September 13 at age 85; Crown Publishers founder Nathan "Nat" Wartels dies of pneumonia at a New York hospital February 7 at age 88. He sold his company to Random House 2 years ago.

HarperCollins takes that name in June following a merger of Harper & Row with the British publisher William Collins, owned—as is Harper & Row—by Rupert Murdoch's News Corp. (*see* 1987).

Barnes & Noble acquires the Doubleday Book Shops chain, consisting of more than three dozen retail outlets (*see* B. Dalton, 1986). It will soon be operating some 800 B. Dalton bookshops, 200 Barnes & Noble college stores, and 50 Barnes & Noble retail stores nationwide.

Fiction: *American Psycho* by Los Angeles-born novelist Bret Easton Ellis, 26, is about a serial killer in Wall Street; *Hanover Place* by Michael M. Thomas.

Painter Keith Haring dies of AIDS at New York February 16 at age 31, having begun as a graffiti artist.

Theater: the 65-year-old 46th Street Theater is renamed the Richard Rodgers Theater in March; *Prelude to a Kiss* by actor-turned-playwright Craig Lucas, now 38, 5/1 at the Helen Hayes Theater, with Barnard Hughes, Fort Jackson, S.C.-born actress

Mary-Louise Parker, 25, Malibu, Calif.-born actor Timothy Hutton, 29, Concord, Calif.-born actor Larry Bryggman, 51, Debra Monk, is (fancifully) about AIDS, 440 perfs.; *Six Degrees of Separation* by John Guare 6/14 at the Mitzi E. Newhouse Theater, with Washington, D.C.-born actor James McDaniel, 32, New York-born actress Stockard Channing (originally Susan Stockard), 46, John Cunningham, Courtney B. Vance: "I read somewhere that everybody on this planet is separated by only six other people. Six degrees of separation. Between us and everybody else on this planet. The president of the United States. A gondolier in Venice. Fill in the names . . . [But] you have to find the right six people to make the connection;" 485 perfs.

Playwright Arnaud d'Usseau dies of complications from stomach cancer surgery at New York January 29 at age 73. Blacklisted for refusing to answer questions related to Communist Party membership in the 1950s, he has taught writing at NYU and the School for Visual Arts since his return from self-imposed exile in Europe; actor Albert Salmi commits suicide at Spokane, Wash., April 23 at age 62.

Public Theater director Joseph Papp rejects a National Endowment for the Arts grant to protest an anti-obscenity clause in the NEA's charter.

Television: *Seinfeld* 5/31 on NBC with New York stand-up comic Jerry Seinfeld, 36, Julia Louis-Dreyfus, Michael Richards, Jason Alexander (to 5/14/1998); *Law & Order* 9/13 on ABC with German-born actor George Dzundza, 45, as New York detective Max Greevey, Madison, Wis.-born actor Christopher Noth, 35, as his partner Mike Logan, Bronx-born actor Michael Moriarty, 49, as Assistant D.A. Ben Stone, Seattle-born actor Steven Hill (originally Solomon Krakovsky), 68, as D.A. Adam Schiff (to 5/25/1999).

Muppets creator Jim Henson dies of streptococcal pneumonia at New York May 16 at age 53.

Films: Woody Allen's *Alice* with Mia Farrow, Alec Baldwin, Blythe Danner, Judy Davis, William Hurt, Keye Luke, Joe Mantagna, Bernadette Peters, Cybill Shepherd, Gwen Verdon, Patrick O'Neal; Larry Cohen's *The Ambulance* with Eric Roberts, James Earl Jones; Penny Marshall's *Awakenings* with Robert De Niro, Robin Williams is about a Bronx chronic-care hospital; Joseph B. Vasquez's *The Bronx War* with Vasquez, Fabio Urena, Charmaine Cruz; Andrew Bergman's *The Freshman* with Marlon Brando, Matthew Broderick, Maximilian Schell; Peter Weir's *Green Card* with Gerard Dépardieu, Andie MacDowell; Abel Ferrara's *King of New York*

with Christopher Walken, David Caruso, Larry Fishburne, Victor Argo, Wesley Snipes; Norman René's *Longtime Companion* with Stephen Caffrey, Patrick Cassidy, Brian Cousins, Bruce Davison is about the AIDS epidemic; Whit Stillman's *Metropolitan* with Edward Clements, Carolyn Farina; Sidney Lumet's *Q & A* with Nick Nolte as a rogue NYPD detective, Timothy Hutton as a prosecutor; Howard Franklin's *Quick Change* with Bill Murray, Geena Davis, Randy Quaid, Jason Robards; Alan J. Pakula's *See You in the Morning* with Jeff Bridges, Alice Krige, Farah Fawcett, Linda Lavin, Drew Barrymore; Ian Egleson's *A Shock to the System* with Michael Caine, Elizabeth McGovern; Phil Joanou's *State of Grace* with Sean Penn, Ed Harris, Gary Oldman is about Irish-American hoods in Hell's Kitchen.

Greta Garbo dies at New York Hospital April 15 at age 84 (she has not made a film since 1941); comedian Jack Gilford dies of stomach cancer at his New York home June 4 at age 82; Joan Bennett of a heart attack at Scarsdale December 7 at age 80.

Broadway musical: *Once on This Island* 10/18 at the Booth Theater, with a cast of 11 headed by La Chanze and Jerry Dixon, music by Pittsburgh-born composer Stephen Flaherty, book and lyrics by New York-born writer Lynn Ahrens, 42, based on a novel by Trinidadian author Rosa Guy (who adapted Hans Christian Andersen's story "The Little Mermaid"), choreography by Graciela Daniele, 469 perfs.

The White Oak Dance Project is founded by Mark Morris (see 1980) and Mikhail Baryshnikov. Morris has won a MacArthur Award and worked since 1988 at the Théâtre de la Monnaie, Brussels, but will return to New York next year and gain a reputation for his iconoclastic choreography and musicality.

Actress-singer Pearl Bailey dies of an apparent heart attack at Philadelphia August 17 at age 72; drummer-bandleader Art Blakey (Abdullah Ibn Buhaina) of lung cancer at a New York hospital October 16 at age 71; composer Aaron Copland of respiratory failure at a North Tarrytown hospital December 2 at age 90.

Pete Sampras, 19, wins in U.S. Open men's singles at Flushing Meadow, Gabriela Sabatini, 20, (Arg.) in women's singles.

New York-born fashion designer Vera Wang, 41, opens her own boutique on Madison Avenue. After attending Sarah Lawrence College and the Sorbonne, the onetime figure-skating competitor worked for 16 years as an editor at *Vogue* and for 2 as design director for Ralph Lauren. She will specialize in wedding gowns but will also design skating outfits, evening wear, and ready-to-wear.

Former New York fashion designer Halston dies of AIDS in a San Francisco hospital March 26 at age 57.

 An illegal social club in the Bronx goes up in flames March 25, killing 87 in the worst New York conflagration since the Triangle Shirtwaist Factory fire of March 25, 1911. The club's hatcheck girl has rejected a Cuban immigrant's advances and he has set the fire in retaliation; he is charged with 87 counts of murder, but by 1997 half a dozen other illegal social clubs will be operating in the same area.

The city has 2,262 homicides, a new record. A shift away from crack cocaine, increased incarceration, and innovative police strategies will bring a sharp reduction in the homicide rate by 1998.

Police arrest Mafia boss John Gotti, Sr. December 11 along with three aides identified with the Gambino crime family at the Ravenite Social Club, 247 Mulberry Street, between Prince and Spring streets, in Little Italy. Now 50, Gotti has swaggered about the city in $2,000 Brioni suits, surrounded by bodyguards and dining at elegant nightclubs and restaurants while his organization grossed an estimated $500 million per year from gambling, loan sharking, stock fraud, stealing gasoline excise taxes, and extorting money from garment makers, food suppliers, and garbage-carting companies. FBI agents observed Gotti meeting with narcotics traffickers and have taped him plotting in one of the 16 apartments of the 19th century row house and recorded his confession to murder, bribery, obstruction of justice, and other crimes (*see* 1992).

Vacant office space in midtown Manhattan totals 28.5 million square feet—more than the total combined office space in Portland, Ore., Seattle, and Tampa, Fla. It will be 8 years before the real estate market recovers.

Architect Gordon Bunshaft dies of cardiovascular arrest at his New York home August 6 at age 81.

Battery Park City is completed on a 92-acre parcel of land built up from excavating earth in Lower Manhattan for the World Trade Center 20 years ago. Its apartments have been designed by Paul Segal Associates and Costas Kondylis of Philip Birnbaum Associates, James Stewart Polshek & Partners, and Gruzen Sampton Steinglass. Architect Stanton Eckstut of Cooper, Eckstut Associates has designed its Esplanade (1.2 miles long, 75 feet wide) with help from landscapers Hanna/Oltin, Ltd.

The 53-story TriBeCa Tower is completed at 105 Duane Street, between Broadway and Church Street, with eight to 10 apartments per floor.

Moderate-priced housing remains scarce in New York. Stuyvesant Town, now 43 years old, has a waiting list of nearly 8,000 applicants. The city has lost 70,000 single-room-occupancy hotel units to upscale conversions in this decade, forcing low-income residents into the streets.

The City Landmarks Preservation Commission gives landmark status in April to a complex of 14 buildings in Manhattan's Yorkville section that were originally built in a privately financed experiment to provide housing for the poor. Landmarking them deals a major blow to developer Peter S. Kalikow, who owns the property and has planned to raze the low-rise buildings in order to raise an 80-story apartment tower on the site. Kalikow says he will appeal.

The 31-year-old Guggenheim Museum is designated a New York City Landmark August 14.

The City Landmarks Preservation Commission confers historic district status on a large section of about 2,000 buildings on the Upper West Side, built between 1901 and 1913 just west of Central Park. Included are 13 model tenements with more than 1,300 apartments—the largest low-income housing in the world until the 1930s.

The 19-story Coronado apartment house is completed at 2040-52 Broadway, northeast corner 70th Street. Schuman, Lichtenstein, Claman & Efron has designed the structure; the 25-story Alexandria apartment house is completed at 2081-89 Broadway, northwest corner 72nd Street. Designed by Frank Williams & Associates with Skidmore, Owings & Merrill, it replaces the two-story Embassy Theater Building and Embassy movie theater, put up in 1938.

The 23-story 279 Central Park West apartment house is completed at the northwest corner of 88th Street to designs by Costas Kondylis.

Doubletree Guest Suites opens in the fall in 47th Street on Times Square. Designed by A. Van Beuren, the 43-story Art Deco tower contains 460 units; its lobby is on the third floor.

The 54-story Rihga Royal Hotel opens October 24 at 151 West 54th Street, off Seventh Avenue, with 496 rooms. Architect Frank Williams designed it for developer William Zeckendorf, Jr., who sold it last year to the Japanese-owned Royal International Hotel Group & Associates, but Zeckendorf remained responsible for completing construction, costs ran wild, especially for plumbing and electrical work, and the cost overruns have wiped out his profit.

The last of the city's 22 municipal incinerators ceases operations (see 1885). Steep operating costs, ash-disposal problems, and air-quality concerns have made incineration undesirable, but some apartment buildings will continue legally to burn waste in their incinerators until they are shut down by city regulation in 1993 (see 1996).

The Tom Cat Bakery opens in September in Long Island City to bake bread and rolls for city's restaurant trade. Proprietor Noel Comess, 29, has bought an oven for $500 at auction, spent $20,000 to refurbish space in a 150-year-old building (originally a foundry), and produces white bread, baguettes, sourdough loaves, and rolls for restaurants such as Aradia, Le Cirque, Lutèce, and the Union Square Café and stores such as Balducci's and Dean and DeLuca. Comess will soon relocate to a larger room in the building (formerly an ice cream factory).

The U.S. Census reveals that New York has more than 350,000 men and women over age 65 living by themselves.

The New York area has 14 million people, with a population density of 23,670 per square mile. The city's population reaches 7,322,564, up from its 50-year low of 7,071,639 in 1980, with gains in every borough (only one New Yorker in five lives in Manhattan), but while the Irish still dominate the construction trades their total numbers have fallen to less than half what they were in 1970. Immigration accounts for almost all of the increase (28.4 percent of the city's population is foreign born, up from 23.6 percent in 1980 and the highest since 1940 as Dominicans, Russians, Chinese, Jamaicans, Guayanans, and Indians pour in; the native language of 3 million New Yorkers is something other than English). The city's Korean population reaches 69,718, according to the federal census, with another 64,462 in the metropolitan area (the Korean Foreign Ministry puts the total at 210,000). Some 100,000 native New Yorkers will leave the city each year in the next decade but will be replaced each year by some 100,000 newcomers, most of them from East Asia, Southwest Asia, and Latin America.

Ellis Island reopens in September as a museum, with a token list of 400,000 immigrant names chiseled into a wall to represent the millions who were processed at the receiving station between 1892 and 1932. The facility has been restored with $150 million in private donations raised in a drive led by for-

mer Detroit auto executive Lee Iacocca, who is himself the son of immigrants (see Supreme Court ruling, 1998).

1991 Operation Desert Storm begins February 24 and ends in 100 hours with Iraqi forces defeated with minimum U.S. casualties. President Bush has spurned the advice of Gen. Colin Powell, 53, chairman of the Joint Chiefs of Staff, to give economic sanctions more time to work and make Iraq's dictator Saddam Hussein withdraw from Kuwait. Former mayor Robert F. Wagner has died at New York February 12 at age 80 amidst anti-war demonstrations. Former Carver Democratic Club leader J. Raymond Jones dies at New York June 9 at age 92, having been called the "Harlem Fox."

The Roman Catholic archdiocese denies gays and lesbians permission to march as such in the annual St. Patrick's Day parade on Fifth Avenue March 17. A U.S. Supreme Court ruling in 1995 will uphold the right of parade organizers to include or exclude anyone they choose, but the homosexual community will continue to protest its exclusion.

Brooklyn's Crown Heights section has a race riot following the August 19 vehicular homicide of 7-year-old Gavin Cato near the corner of Utica Avenue and President Street. The Lubavitcher Rebbe Menachem M. Schneerson has been visiting his late wife's grave, a car driven in his motorcade hits Cato, Australian Hasidic scholar Yankel Rosenbaum, 29, is stabbed 3 hours later by one or more of 10 to 15 black youths in apparent retaliation for Cato's death, Rosenbaum dies August 20 from a wound undetected in the emergency room, violence continues to August 22, and efforts to convict Rosenbaum's assailant or assailants will go on for years as rela-

Crown Heights riots triggered by the accidental killing of a 7-year-old boy heightened tensions. CHIE NISHIO

tions deteriorate between the Lubavitchers and their black neighbors (most are Caribbean immigrants) (*see* 1997; Lapine, 1992).

The board of the City University of New York (CUNY) votes 10 to 4 October 28 to retain Professor Leonard Jeffries, Jr. as chairman of CCNY's Afro-American Studies Department for another 8 months while officials continue to assess his performance (*see* 1990). Flagrantly anti-Semitic remarks have been attributed to Jeffries (*see* 1992).

$ The city's fiscal crunch begins to show itself by January in dirtier and bumpier streets, broken street lights, higher city university tuitions, shorter library hours, and the like, but Standard & Poor's removes its "credit watch" in early February on the city's bonds and reaffirms its A-bond rating, previously in jeopardy, as the city confronts its fiscal policies.

Wall Street's NASDAQ closes above 500 for the first time April 12 and the Dow Jones Industrial Average closes above 3000 for the first time April 17 in anticipation of an early recovery from the 9-month recession, but the Dow has trouble holding above 3000 amidst forecasts that the recession is not about to end. Executives and professionals feel the pinch as well as blue-collar workers. Inflation moderates in the United States, but rents are 35 percent above the 1982–1984 average, electricity 28 percent higher, medical care 56 percent higher, food 34 percent higher, entertainment 28 percent higher.

The Bank of Commerce and Credit International (BCCI) is indicted at New York July 29 on criminal charges of fraud, theft, and money laundering. New York State seeks extradition of Aga Hassan Abedi, 68, a former Pakistani banker who founded BCCI in 1972, and Swaleh Naqvi of Abu Dhabi, the bank's former chief operating officer.

Top Salomon executives who include 38-year veteran John Gutfreund, now 61, resign following revelations of illegal auction bids made for U.S. Treasury bonds (*see* 1981). Gutfreund's legal bills and related costs will amount to more than $11 million, he will be forced to sell his Salomon stock, and he will fail to recover more than $15 million in vested stock options and pension benefits but will retain his 16-room Fifth Avenue apartment and his Paris pied-à-terre. Billionaire Omaha investor Warren Buffet assumes control of Salomon to protect his investment in the firm, which has $109 billion in assets; Wall Street, he says, is a place where people arrive in Rolls-Royces to seek advice from people who come by subway (*see* Salomon Smith Barney, 1997).

Citicorp suspends dividend payments October 15 and will not resume them until 1994. Citicorp common stock falls to a low of $8.50 per share. Saudi Prince Alwaleed Bin Talal Bin Abdulaziz Al Saud, 34, seizes the opportunity and buys $590 million worth of new convertible preferred stock, an investment that will grow to more than $8 billion within 7 years.

Chemical Banking Corp. merges with the ailing Manufacturers Hanover Corp. December 31 (*see* Chemical, 1985; Manufacturers Hanover, 1961). Chemical has grown through previous mergers to have 297 banks in New York State plus 140 in New Jersey, 120 in Texas, and 20 overseas. Manufacturers Hanover becomes a division of Chemical (*see* 1961; Chase, 1995).

Wall Street's Dow Jones Industrial Average closes December 31 at 3168.83, up 535.17 (20.3 percent) for the year despite the Gulf War in February and the ongoing recession. The NASDAQ has 4 record-high days and closes at 586.34, up 212.50 (56.8 percent) from its 1990 close.

 The Concourse Plaza shopping center opens May 19 in the South Bronx.

Alexander's department stores close in Manhattan, Brooklyn, and the Bronx, leaving vacant the building on Lexington and Third avenues between 58th and 59th streets, the 341,000 square feet it has occupied in Brooklyn's Kings Plaza shopping mall, and other locations (*see* 1992). Developer Donald Trump owns more than 27 percent of Alexander's stock and is more interested in the company's real estate potential than in its retail operations.

Brooks Brothers closes its factory in Brooklyn, begins farming out its suit production to contractors, and gives up its bespoke (custom-tailored) department as Ralph Lauren copies his ex-employer's styles.

Henri Bendel moves after a long delay from 57th Street to a building at 712 Fifth Avenue with three-story windows designed by the French glass designer René Lalique (*see* 1986).

The Eddie Bauer retail chain opens a Manhattan store on Third Avenue in May. Founded at Seattle in 1920, it is now owned by the Chicago-based mail-order firm Spiegel Bros. and will soon have additional Manhattan stores.

Retailer Barney Pressman dies in a Miami hospital August 24 at age 96 (*see* 1977). He founded Barney's in 1923, retired in 1975, but until recently has continued to phone New York collect every day to inquire about the store that now sells suits ranging in price from $450 to $2,000, ties as much as $125, plus women's apparel, cosmetics, and gift items (*see* 1993).

 Eastern Airlines ceases operations January 18 after 62 years of operation following a 22-month strike by machinists. Pan Am ceases operations December 4 after 68 years, partly as a result of bad publicity related to a 1988 terrorist explosion over Lockerbie, Scotland.

The 78-year-old Grand Central Terminal becomes strictly a commuter terminal April 7 as the last Amtrak train leaves for Montreal. Amtrak reroutes its remaining long-distance trains (to Albany, Montreal, Toronto, Schenectady, Niagara Falls, Buffalo, and Chicago). They now leave from Penn Station and move up the West Side to the Spuyten Duyvil Bridge or to Queens and across the the Hell Gate Bridge that opened in 1917, but Amtrak has not fenced off the tracks in some areas of the upper West Side, where many homeless people live, and 3-year-old James Rodriguez is struck and killed when he wanders away from his mother and runs onto the track extending alongside Riverside Park. Workers begin installing temporary fences alongside the tracks on Washington Heights and state bureaucrats are blamed for not allocating $1 million for proper fencing out of the total $96 million spent on the project.

The city stops cleaning streets on Wednesdays and Saturdays, citing budget constraints (*see* 1959). Fines for illegal parking violations have reached $35, cars are towed away and held until fines are paid, and parking violations bring more than $100 million per year into the city's coffers. The Alternate Side Parking Rules will be renamed the Street Cleaning Rules next year (*see* 1994).

New York Double Decker Tours is founded by entrepreneur Alexander Garzon, who imports British-made buses to Manhattan and launches a business that attracts tourists and competition. By 1997 he will have 12 such tour buses in operation (*see* Apple Tours, 1992).

The New York Transit Museum holds a 2-day seminar on subway history in May, attracting participants from all over the country. The museum occupies an unused subway station adjacent to Brooklyn's Borough Hall.

The subway system has its worst accident in 63 years August 28 when a Brooklyn-bound train on the IRT Lexington Avenue line derails early in the morning under Union Square, killing five, injuring as many as 200, and causing so much damage that service must be suspended for 6 days until repairs can be made, forcing 500,000 riders to find alternative transportation. Motorman Robert Ray walks away unhurt, police pick him up near his home in the Bronx 5 hours later, they charge him with drunkenness (he says he had a few beers after the accident), an empty vial with traces of crack cocaine is found in his cab, he has allegedly been running the train erratically and been warned by an off-duty transit worker that he was driving too fast; Ray admits he was going 35 to 40 miles per hour—four times the speed limit at that point—and is indicted on murder charges. The Metropolitan Transportation Authority announces that it will begin random drug and alcohol testing of bus drivers and subway crews, the Transport Workers Union drops its objection to such testing, and the MTA implements new safety procedures that include closer monitoring of conductors and motormen and automatic brake systems that stop any train traveling too fast.

 Health authorities begin handing out free condoms to New York public high-school students in a pioneering effort aimed at slowing the spread of sexually transmitted diseases, including the HIV virus that produces AIDS, and reducing teenage pregnancies. Opponents decry the move, charging that it will increase sexual activity among teenagers, but a study released in 1997 will show that while the teenagers may not always use the condoms their free availability does not increase their sexual activity.

The New York Infirmary for Women and Children that opened in 1857 becomes part of the New York Hospital-Cornell Medical Center (*see* 1979).

Mount Sinai Hospital's North Pavilion is completed to designs by I. M. Pei.

 The Mosque of New York of the Islamic Center of New York opens in September at the corner of Third Avenue and 97th Street. Designed by Michael A. McCarthy of Skidmore, Owings & Merrill with Mustafa K. Abadan and built largely with Kuwaiti financing, it combines a dome and a minaret with modern features and is the largest of the city's 60 mosques; like every mosque in the world, it is oriented toward the Qiblah in the direction of the ancient Kaaba shrine within the Grand Mosque at Mecca in Saudi Arabia. By the mid-1990s New York will have an estimated 400,000 to 600,000 Muslims, the great majority of them Sunnis, 25 to 40 percent of them black, most of them from India or Pakistan.

 The City University of New York (CUNY) imposes new course requirements that will keep students from graduating unless they demonstrate that they can meet standards equal to those set by the state for its best high-school graduates. The move is partly to put pressure on city high schools to give their students, especially minority students, better preparation for college (see 1976). Higher tuitions draw protests from students, who barricade themselves inside CCNY's largest building in early April, keeping 75 percent of students from attending classes. The protest movement convulses 21 campuses; protesters take over buildings at Manhattan Community, Bronx Community, Lehman, and Hunter College demanding elimination of a $500 tuition increase and reversal of state budget cuts; CUNY suspends at least 37 students; faculty members and students who want classes resumed put an end to the Manhattan Community College takeover April 25 by storming the building, breaking a glass door, and angrily confronting the protesters. Students fearful of losing a semester's work put pressure on the protesters, and police in a late night raid April 24 retake Bronx Community College. The demonstrations end May 2 as students surrender buildings at City College (see 1992).

The 16-year-old Museum of Broadcasting moves to a new building at 23 West 52nd Street, beside the "21" Club restaurant, and becomes the Museum of Television and Radio.

Czech.-born London publisher Robert Maxwell (originally Ludvik Hoch), 68, buys the strike-bound New York Daily News for $40 million March 15 and settles with union leaders March 31, ending the 5-month strike and enabling him to lay off 35 management workers (see 1990). Maxwell disappears mysteriously from his luxury yacht November 5 off the Canary Islands, his publishing empire collapses, and the Daily News files for bankruptcy protection in December (see 1992).

Nonfiction: New York New York by Cambridge, Mass.-born New York author Oliver E. Allen, 69; "Or Does It Explode?" Black Harlem in the Great Depression by Massachusetts-born Trinity College, Hartford, assistant professor Cheryl (Lynn) Greenberg, 33; Adam Clayton Powell, Jr.: The Political Biography of an American Dilemma by Oklahoma-born Columbia University political science professor Charles Vernon Hamilton, 70; The Promised Land: The Great Black Migration and How It Changed America by New Orleans-born journalist Nicholas Lemann, 37; Low Life: Lures and Snares of Old New York by Belgian-born New York writer Luc Sante, 37; Damon Runyon by Jimmy Breslin.

Journalist-author Warren Moscow dies at Putnam Valley, N.Y., September 20 at age 84.

Fiction: Object Lessons by New York Times syndicated columnist Anna Quindlen, 38; Tar Beach by Brooklyn-born novelist Richard Elman, 57.

Poetry: Flow Chart by John Ashbery.

Poet James Schuyler dies of a stroke at New York April 12 at age 67.

Publisher-philanthropist George T. Delacorte dies at New York May 4 at age 97.

Painting: Self-Portrait by Chuck Close. Robert Motherwell dies of a stroke on Cape Cod July 17 at age 76.

Sculpture: American Merchant Marine Memorial by the sculptor Marisol is installed on a breakwater south of Pier A in Battery Park. Sponsored by the American Merchant Mariners' Memorial Committee, the bronze-and-stainless-steel work tells the story of seven seamen who survived the sinking of a U.S. ship by a German U-boat in World War II but died on their raft.

Theater: Lost in Yonkers by Neil Simon 2/21 at the Richard Rodgers Theater, with Irene Worth, Queens-born actress Mercedes Ruehl, 42, South Orange, N.J.-born actor Kevin Spacey, 31, Newark-born actor Mark Blum, 40, 780 perfs.; The Substance of Fire by Los Angeles-born playwright Jon Robin Baitz, 29, 3/17 at the Playwrights Horizon Theater, with Ohio-born actress Sarah Jessica Parker, 25, Patrick Breen, Ron Rifkin; Park Your Car in Harvard Yard by Wakefield, Mass.-born playwright Israel Horovitz, 52, 11/7 at the Music Box Theater, with Jason Robards, Jr., Judith Ivey, 124 perfs.

Eva Le Gallienne dies of heart failure at her Weston, Conn., home June 3 at age 92; Colleen Dewhurst of cancer at her suburban South Salem home August 21 at age 67; New York Public Theater founder Joseph Papp of prostate cancer at New York October 31 at age 70.

Television: Brooklyn Bridge 9/20 on CBS with Mount Vernon-born actor Danny Gerard (originally Daniel Gerard Lanzetta), 14, as postal worker's son Alan, Minnesota-born actress Marion Ross, 62, as his immigrant grandmother (to 6/8/1993).

Films: Robert Benton's Billy Bathgate with Dustin Hoffman, Nicole Kidman, Loren Dean, Bruce Willis; Terry Gilliam's The Fisher King with Robin Williams, Jeff Bridges, Amanda Plummer; Garry Marshall's Frankie and Johnny with Al Pacino, Michelle Pfeiffer; Spike Lee's Jungle Fever with Wesley Snipes, Annabella Sciorra, Lee, Ossie Davis, Ruby Dee; David Cronenberg's Naked Lunch with Peter Weller, Judy Davis, Ian Holm, Julian Sands; Mario Van Peebles's *New Jack City* with Wesley Snipes, rap artist Ice T (originally Tracy Morrow), 33; Heywood Gould's *One Good Cop* with Michael Keaton, Rene Russo; Steve Rash's *Queens Logic* with Kevin Bacon, Linda Fiorentino, John Malkovich, Joe Mantegna, Jamie Lee Curtis; Bill Duke's *A Rage in Harlem* with Forrest Whitaker, Gregory Hines, Robin Givens, Danny Glover; Matty Rich's *Straight Out of Brooklyn* with George T. Odom, Ann D. Sanders, Lawrence Gilliard, Jr.; Rod Daniel's *The Super* with Joe Pesci, Vincent Gardenia, Madolyn Smith-Osborne, Ruben Blades; George Gallo's *29th Street* with Danny Aiello, Anthony LaPaglia, Lainie Kazan (originally Lainie Levine), Frank Pesce.

♪♪ Broadway musicals: *The Will Rogers Follies: A Life in Revue* 3/31 at the Palace Theater, with a cast of about 37 headed by San Mateo, Calif.-born actor Keith Carradine, 40, in the title role, music by Cy Coleman, lyrics by Betty Comden and Adolph Green, direction and choreography by Tommy Tune, 981 perfs.; *Miss Saigon* 4/11 at the Broadway Theater (it opened 9/20/1989 at London's Theatre Royal Drury Lane), with a 45-member cast headed by Welsh-born actor Jonathan Pryce, 43, Manila-born ingénue Lea Salonga, 20, Liz Callaway, dancer Hinton Battle, book and music by Alan Boubil and Claude-Michel Schönberg, lyrics by Richard Maltby, Jr., 4,092 perfs.; *The Secret Garden* 4/25 at the St. James Theater, with a 26-member cast headed by Brooklyn-born ingénue Daisy Eagan, 12, Mandy Patinkin, music by Lucy Simon, book and lyrics by Marsha Norman based on the 1903 Burnett story, 709 perfs.

Lyricist Howard Ashman dies of AIDS at New York March 14 at age 39; dancer-choreographer Martha Graham of cardiac arrest at her New York home April 1 at age 96; writer-lyricist Gerome Ragni of cancer at New York July 19 at age 48.

A concert by Paul Simon with African performers on Central Park's Great Lawn 8/15 attracts a record crowd estimated to number 600,000.

Jazz cornetist Jimmy McPartland dies of lung cancer at Port Washington March 13 at age 83; record-store magnate Sam Goody (originally Samuel Gutowitz) of heart failure at a Queens hospital August 8 at age 87 (his Sam Goody chain has grown to have 320 outlets across the country); veteran jazz trumpeter Buck Clayton dies at New York December 8 at age 80.

🏃 The New York Giants win their second Super Bowl title, upsetting a favored Buffalo Bills team 21 to 19 at Tampa January 27 in Super Bowl XXV. Coached by Bill Parcells, the Giants keep possession of the ball for more than 40 minutes; their regular starting quarterback Phil Simms has been sidelined with a foot injury, but quarterback Jeff Hostetler completes 20 of 32 passes to gain 222 yards, running back Otis J. (O. J.) Anderson, 34 (the oldest running back in the league), gains 102 yards on 21 carries, the Bills miss a 47-yard field goal attempt in the closing seconds, and Anderson receives the most valuable player award.

Stefan Edberg wins the U.S. Open in men's singles at Flushing Meadow, Monica Seles, 17, (Yugo.) in women's singles.

Manhattan College leases Gaelic Park following disputes between the O'Donnell family and the Gaelic Athletic Association (*see* 1941).

Eight young people are trampled and crushed to death outside a CCNY gymnasium December 28 and 29 others are injured, many seriously and one fatally. Attracted by heavy radio advertising to a benefit for AIDS charities, an estimated 5,000 young people have lined up on 138th Street for the Heavy D and Puff Daddy Celebrity Charity Basketball Game-rap music event; the Police Department has stationed 66 officers outside the gym, City College has provided 30 security officers, and the promoters have hired an additional 20 security workers, but the crowd passes through two sets of doors, files down a short flight of stairs, and tries to surge through one entrance to the 2,730-seat gym. More than 5,000 tickets may have been sold for the charity event that has been promoted by rap artist Puffy Combs, 22.

● Developer Donald Trump's wife, Ivana, obtains a $25 million divorce settlement March 20 from "the Donald," who has been blatantly unfaithful. Now 41, she wins $14 million plus the couple's New York apartment, their Connecticut estate, and custody of their three children (she will marry an Italian businessman in November 1995 at New York's Mayfair Hotel). Now 45, Trump calls a TV show July 3 to announce his engagement to Georgia-born showgirl Marla Maples, 27 (*see* 1993).

Scores New York Sports Cabaret opens October 31 at 333 East 60th Street, between First and Second avenues in the shadow of the Queensboro Bridge, with a restaurant and several private V.I.P. rooms in the rear (*see* Club A, 1982). Patrons enjoy steaks, cigars, current sports events on TV monitors, and striptease shows whose performers can earn as much as $100,000 per year. Although a beer costs $8, plus tip and cover charge, the place quickly draws crowds of athletes, businessmen, Hollywood celebrities, Wall Street brokers, and U.N. diplomats in expensive suits who come to ogle the 100 athletic women who dance topless for their entertainment each night and make Scores the hottest club in town (organized crime figures allegedly begin trying to take over, getting kickbacks from hatcheck girls, parking attendants, and others; *see* crime, 1998).

 A Chinatown merchant who has co-operated with police in identifying members of the 5-year-old Born to Kill (B.T.K) gang is killed March 10. Agents of the federal Alcohol Tobacco and Firearms division of the Treasury Department arrest B.T.K. founder David Thai at his Long Island home in August, find illegal firearms, and raid a B.T.K. Brooklyn safehouse, where they find other incriminating evidence. Seven members of the gang will be convicted next year on murder and racketeering charges; Thai and his top lieutenant will be sentenced to life imprisonment without parole.

Gunmen shoot mobster Rosario Nastasi to death December 5 in a Brooklyn social club; mobster Vincent Fusaro, 30, is shot to death outside his Bath Beach, Brooklyn, home December 6 while fastening a Christmas wreath to his front door (he has been night manager of the diner Venus II, a Mafia hangout). Police say the gangland shootings, like four others since June, are related to a struggle for control of the Colombo crime family, whose members have been involved in narcotics distribution, extortion, gambling, and other activities (*see* 1987); 28 reputed associates of the family show up with their lawyers in the grand jury room of Brooklyn's State Supreme Court December 16 and a prosecutor questions them about the murders and other violence.

Southern Manhattan's real estate market slumps after a period more than 12 years that has seen the area become a model of how to mix housing with commercial buildings and open a neglected waterfront to recreational use. Office vacancies rise and residential construction comes to a standstill as the effects of the 1987 stock market fall persist. The Regional Planning Commission estimates in September that there are 60 million square feet of vacant office space in Manhattan (*see* 1990).

Citibank negotiates the sale of a vacant 42-story office building at 1540 Broadway on Times Square to the German publishing giant Bertelsmann AG. The bank holds a $250 million mortgage on the structure that it took over in a foreclosure but accepts a much lower price as demand for office space collapses.

The Times Square Business Improvement District is established by property owners under the chairmanship of *New York Times* publisher Arthur Sulzberger, Jr. They engage Staten Island-born, Philadelphia-raised former school teacher and foundation executive Gretchen Dykstra, 42, to manage the district; financed by $6 million per year in assessments, she will employ sanitation workers (who will pick up more than 100 pounds of discarded cigarettes per day in a "Can Your Butt" campaign), security guards, counselors for homeless people, and city planners and will be credited with cleaning up an area that has become a national symbol of crime and urban decay.

The 60-story Carnegie Hall Tower is completed at 152 West 57th Street, east of Seventh Avenue. Designed by Cesar Pelli & Associates, the office skyscraper rises 757 feet high, replaces the Rembrandt Studio building of 1881 and is in a style consistent with the century-old Carnegie Hall immediately to its west.

The Nippon Club that moved to 145 West 57th Street in 1963 erects a 21-story tower on the site, using the first seven floors as its clubhouse.

The Corporation for Supportive Housing provides seed money for creating single-room-occupancy units (*see* 1988). Occupants of the new "supportive" S.R.O.s qualify for state and federal benefits that help pay their rents, and the units provide economic benefits to the city (it costs an estimated $12,500 per year to house an individual in a supportive S.R.O., including the cost of renovating a building and providing social services, as compared to $20,000 in a shelter, $60,000 in a jail cell, and $113,000 in a psychiatric ward) (*see* 1994).

The last of 2,200 Nehemiah Project houses is completed after 7 years of construction in East New York and Brownsville under the supervision of I. D. Robbins, now 80 (*see* 1984). By next year there will be upwards of 2,500, and South Bronx Churches, Inc. will be planning 540 more. Kitchens of the single-family, pitched-roof houses are placed in the front on the premise that homeowners spend much of their time in the kitchen and will tend to keep neighborhoods safer if prospective miscreants know that people are looking out their windows (*see* Jacobs book, 1961).

The Marriott Corp. takes over the 67-year-old Shelton Towers Hotel on Lexington Avenue between 48th and 49th streets and renames it the Marriott East.

A Carnegie Hall benefit concert September 24 celebrates the reopening of the 60-year-old Essex House Hotel after a 2-year renovation that has cost the Japan-based Nikko Hotel company $175 million.

Where originally it had 1,286 rooms, the hotel now offers 595 guest rooms and 77 suites, each unit having its own serving pantry with stove and refrigerator.

New York hotel occupancy rates drop to a low of 67.6 percent, down from more than 90 percent in October 1979.

 The last Automat closes April 9 at 200 East 42nd Street, a location that did not open until 1958 and has been charging high prices for what used to be bargains (see 1978). Former (and future) Parks Commissioner Henry J. Stern stopped at other Automats (there once were 30 of them) for lemon meringue pie between deliveries when he was a young Western Union bicycle messenger and says of the Automat, "It was equivalent to the Woolworth Building and Macy's windows. It was the most public place in town." Municipal Art Society president Kent L. Barwick says, "Automats were right up there with the Statue of Liberty."

The TriBeCa Grill opens at 375 Greenwich Street, near Franklin Street, in a onetime coffee warehouse that has been turned into the TriBeCa Film Center by screen actor Robert De Niro and others. De Niro has engaged Drew Nieporent of the nearby Restaurant Montrachet to manage the place whose long bar, formerly used at Maxwell's Plum on Second Avenue, was purchased at an auction of that restaurant's fixtures. Paintings, prints, and drawings on the wall are by Robert De Niro, Sr. Chef Don Pintabona has worked for La Régence at the Plaza-Athenée and Aureole.

Lespinasse opens in September at 2 East 55th Street in the 87-year-old St. Regis Hotel, refurbished at a cost of more than $100 million. Named for Julie de Lespinasse, one of the great Parisian salon leaders in the reign of Louis XV, the restaurant has a kitchen headed by Swiss-born chef Gray Kunz. The prix-fixe lunch is $38, dinner $50, and a five-course dinner with a sampling of desserts $64.

1992 Suffolk County police arrest six New York City officers on narcotics charges. Mayor Dinkins appoints deputy mayor and former judge Milton Mollen, 66, in July to head a commission of inquiry to probe allegations of corruption in the police department (see Knapp Commission, 1972). The Mollen Commission will uncover evidence that the nation's largest police force has tolerated widespread illegalities, and while less pervasive than the bribery unearthed by the Knapp Commission, they are far more serious: groups of officers will turn out to have assisted and protected drug traffickers, engaged themselves in drug trafficking and robberies, con-

ducted unlawful searches and seizures, committed perjury, and falsified records. The commission will call for an independent oversight agency (see 1995).

Sol Wachtler resigns in disgrace from his seat as chief justice of the State Court of Appeals at Albany in November after being arrested and charged by federal prosecutors with trying to extort money from his former lover, Joy Silverman, a married woman. Now 63, Wachtler will plead guilty to a felony count of threatening to kidnap Silverman's 14-year-old daughter and after some wrangling about his mental condition will serve nearly a year of a 15-month sentence in federal prison.

Former congressman Mario Biaggi makes an unsuccessful bid to regain his seat from Rep. Elliot Engel (see 1988). Now 75, Biaggi has been released from federal prison for reasons of health.

Voters elect Arkansas governor William Jefferson Blythe "Bill" Clinton, 46, to the presidency, rejecting George Bush's reelection bid as economic recession shows few signs of abating. New York is among the 32 states that go for Clinton.

 Crown Heights, Brooklyn, Hasidic housewife Phyllis Lapine, 38, is stabbed to death as she returns home from shopping February 6 and apparently interrupts a robber. Thousands of Jewish demonstrators crowd the streets February 7 in a protest march through the neighborhood, but city officials join with black and Jewish community leaders to prevent the march from escalating into a repetition of last August's racial confrontations.

Trustees of City College (CCNY) vote March 23 to replace Leonard Jeffries as head of the college's black studies department after months of controversy stemming from Jeffries' racially charged teachings (see 1991). Edmund W. Gordon has headed Yale's black studies program and is brought in to replace Jeffries, recruit new faculty, and reorganize the department. Jeffries remains as a tenured professor and says he will sue, predicting that his colleagues will not accept Gordon as chairman.

Federal authorities seize control in January of Cross Land Savings Bank, whose officers have invested heavily in junk bonds and leveraged buyouts while they made real estate loans that are not paying interest (see 1981). The government renames the bank Crossland Federal Savings and will sell off many of the housing projects it has bankrolled.

Former New York Stock Exchange president G. Keith Funston dies of a heart attack at his Greenwich, Conn., summer home May 15 at age 81.

The Securities and Exchange Commission files a civil lawsuit at New York June 4 charging socially prominent figures such as former Bear Stearns director Edward R. Downe, Jr., 62 (husband of automobile heiress Charlotte Ford), with insider trading, alleging that they exchanged information at poker games and other gatherings, both at Southampton, L.I., and at Caribbean resorts.

Sanford I. Weill begins acquiring Travelers Insurance Co., whose finances are reeling from bad real estate investments (*see* 1988). His personal compensation for the year as head of Primerica exceeds $100 million, well below that of currency speculator George Soros ($850 million, according to an estimate by *Financial World* magazine) but far above that of New York-born Goldman, Sachs co-chairman Robert Rubin, now 54 ($28.5 million) (*see* Weill, 1993).

North Fork Bancorp merges its subsidiaries October 1 to create a state-chartered commercial bank (*see* 1990). It will acquire Bayside Federal Savings in 1994, Bank of Great Neck in 1995, open its first Manhattan Branch in 37th Street the following year, make further acquisitions, and by 2002 have assets of $17 billion with 168 branches in the Bronx, Brooklyn, Manhattan, Queens, Nassau and Suffolk counties, Rockland and Westchester counties, and Connecticut.

Wall Street's Dow Jones Industrial Average closes December 31 at 3301.11, up 132.28 (4.2 percent) since the end of 1991. The NASDAQ closes at 676.95, up 90.61 (15.5 percent), but the U.S. national debt tops $3 trillion, up from $735 billion in January 1981.

R. H. Macy Co. files for bankruptcy in January (*see* 1986). Chairman and CEO Edward S. Finkelstein, now 67, resigns April 27, having acquired a reputation in his 12-year career as a merchandising genius (but not a financial wizard), and Macy's enters Chapter 11 protection to avoid paying creditors' bills (*see* 1994).

Alexander's files for bankruptcy in May, having closed its 11 retail outlets throughout the city (*see* 1991).

The city's 33-year-old Duane Reade drugstore chain changes hands in a deal valued at more than $200 million. Eli, Jack, and Abraham Cohen have opened 37 stores, most of them in Manhattan, selling food and a wide variety of goods in addition to pharmaceuticals; by 1997 there will be more than 60 Duane Reade stores and by 2002 Manhattan alone will have 88, Brooklyn 18, the Bronx eight, Queens 17, and Staten Island two, with two in New Jersey, eight in Nassau County, and five in Westchester.

A Bed Bath and Beyond superstore opens in the former Siegel-Cooper department store building on the east side of Sixth Avenue between 18th and 19th streets as the onetime "Ladies Mile" revives.

The Taxi and Limousine Commission reports that 42.8 percent of applicants for professional driving licenses last year were from South Asia (notably India and Pakistan), 11.2 percent from Africa, 7.6 percent from the Caribbean, 7 percent from the Middle East, 6.8 percent from Russia, only 10.5 percent being native-born Americans (*see* 1983).

New York Apple Tours is founded with two British-made double-decker buses that compete with the Double Decker Tours launched last year. By 1997 Apple will have 38 such buses in operation (*see* Gray Line, 1994).

Billionaire shipping magnate and industrialist Daniel K. Ludwig dies of heart failure at his Fifth Avenue apartment August 27 at age 95.

Two new experimental subway trains are unveiled in a ceremony November 19 and begin operational tests: one, built in Japan by Kawasaki, is intended for service on the former IRT lines (identified by numbers); the second, built in Canada by Bombardier, is for former BMT and IND lines (identified by letters) that can carry slightly larger and wider cars. Fare beaters cost the subway system an estimated $80 million per year, spurring the Metropolitan Transportation Authority to seek more sneak-proof turnstile equipment and find other ways to frustrate fare beaters (*see* 1997).

City University of New York (CUNY) announces major tuition increases April 14 but makes an effort to prevent dropouts by promising that the final semester for seniors will be tuition free (*see* 1991). Tuitions for freshmen would rise $600 to $2,450 and that class would be the first to have a free semester. CUNY announces April 27 that it will increase academic standards without giving up open admissions.

Stuyvesant High School moves in September into a $150 million building in Chambers Street near the West Side Highway (*see* 1907). The 88-year-old public school has been coeducational since 1969 and now has 2,700 students, 51 percent of them Asian, and more than 100 teachers. Its new building has 12 science labs, an 850-seat auditorium, five gyms, and a swimming pool. Its admission test—"Examination for the Specialized Science High

Schools"—is the same one given to applicants to Bronx High School of Science and Brooklyn Technical High School (only one out of eight is accepted). By 1997 fewer than half of Stuyvesant students will be Asian, partly because of increased immigration from Russia and Eastern Europe.

The *New York Times* announces February 4 that it will buy the Metropolitan News Co. and Newark News-dealers Supply Co., whose trucks distribute nearly half of the papers sold in the metropolitan area. The deal will give the *Times* a voice in newspaper wholesalers' labor talks with the Newspaper and Mail Deliverers' Union, whose members have worked to delay opening of the paper's $450 million color printing plant at Edison, N.J., a facility designed to operate more efficiently and flexibly. Two drivers' unions clash with the Newspaper and Mail Deliverers' Union, whose 2,100 truck drivers bundle editions of the *Times*, *Daily News*, and *Post*; it is the only union with enough power to halt deliveries during a strike. A settlement of the 12-day-old dispute is announced May 17, but the bitter controversy continues until May 28, when the unions agree to a far-reaching settlement that promises to bring labor peace until at least the year 2000.

A bankruptcy judge declares October 28 that a new owner will not be bound by an 18-year-old agreement to give printers lifetime job guarantees at the *Daily News*, since the paper is in bankruptcy (*see* 1991); she thus clears the way for purchase of the paper by the brash, flamboyant, Canadian-born Boston real estate developer and publisher Mortimer Zuckerman, now 55, who has acquired the *Atlantic Monthly* and *U.S. News and World Report*. The Newspaper Guild and National Typographers' Union have opposed Zuckerman's bid, and an appeals court judge overturns the lower court's decision December 3, ruling that a new buyer cannot strip the typographers of their lifetime job guarantees (*but see* 1993).

Manhattan District Attorney Robert M. Morgenthau charges November 23 that corrupt labor officials and the Mafia have controlled the Newspaper and Mail Deliverers' Union of New York for decades; he says he will seek the appointment of independent trustees to run the union, the first time that state prosecutors have used the law against organized crime to seek a takeover of a union.

Former *El Diario-La Prensa* editor-in-chief Manuel de Dios Unanue is shot to death in a Jackson Heights restaurant March 11. Publisher at his death of the Spanish-language magazine *Cambio 21*, he has been well known for his crusading editorials against drug trafficking and has received death threats from anti-Castro Cuban groups; *Mad* magazine founder William M. Maxwell dies at his native New York June 3 at age 70; *New York Post* columnist and author Max Lerner at New York June 5 at age 89, having written his last column in May.

British-born magazine editor Christina Hambley "Tina" Brown, 39, becomes editor of the 68-year-old *New Yorker* June 30 (*see* Newhouse, 1985); she took over the ailing *Vanity Fair* early in 1984, made it thrive, and beginning with the October 5 issue puts bylines at the tops of *New Yorker* articles and stories, increases the use of color, and makes controversial design changes calculated to stem the magazine's mounting losses. Condé Nast president Steven T. Florio, now 43, will raise the cover price from $1.75 to $3, newsstand sales will double and advertising revenues increase, circulation will rise by 28.6 percent to 807,935 as of December 1997, but the magazine will lose $30 million next year (much of it from severance pay and other reorganization expenses) and will still be losing close to $1 million per month by 1998.

Former *New Yorker* magazine editor William Shawn dies in his upper East Side apartment December 8 at age 85, taking to his grave the fact that he has for 40 years carried on an extra-marital affair with writer Lillian Ross, now in her 70s. He and Ross (no relation to the late Harold Ross) set up house 10 blocks south of the Shawn apartment and jointly raised her adopted son, Erik, while Shawn and his wife, Cecille, raised their son, Wallace.

The first New York bus in "full wrap" advertising appears on city streets, its 1,000-square-foot surface covered by as many as 90 vinyl sheets (produced by the Supergraphics Co. of Sunnyvale, Calif.), making its exterior seem opaque (passengers can see out, albeit dimly). By mid-1997 the Bronx-based New York Bus Service and the Queens Surface Bus Lines (but not the Metropolitan Transportation Authority) will have a dozen such buses, with an advertiser paying about $8,000 per month to have a bus wrapped with its message.

New York 1 News goes out to Time Warner cable TV subscribers beginning September 8. Former deputy mayor (under John Lindsay) Richard Aurelio of Time Warner uses his company's 3,500 miles of fiber-optic and coaxial cable to launch 24-hour news-and-weather coverage on Channel 1.

Time Warner CEO Steven J. Ross dies of prostate cancer at Los Angeles December 20 at age 65 and is succeeded by his hand-picked heir Gerald M. Levin,

52, who has edged out his rival Nicholas J. Nicholas and been acting CEO since June. Time Warner's properties include not only *Time*, *Fortune*, *People*, *Entertainment Weekly*, and *Sports Illustrated* magazines but also D.C. Comics, Little, Brown and other book publishing assets; the Warner Brothers studio; the Asylum, Atlantic, Electra, and Warner record companies; Home Box Office (HBO); and some of the nation's largest cable television systems (*see* AOL Time Warner, 2000).

Nonfiction: *Changing New York: The Architectural Scene* by Christopher Gray, whose weekly "Streetscapes" column has appeared in the Sunday *New York Times* since 1997. *Citizen Koch: An Autobiography* by former mayor Ed Koch (with Daniel Paisner); *New York in the 50s* by Dan Wakefield; *Stealing the Market: How the Giant Brokerage Firms, with Help from the SEC, Stole the Stock Market from Investors* by Martin Mayer; *The Park and the People: A History of Central Park* by New York-born George Mason University history professor Roy Rosenzweig, 42, and Columbia University history professor Elizabeth Blackmar.

Fiction: *Dreaming in Cuban* by Havana-born *Time* magazine correspondent Christina Garcia, 34, who writes, "Dad feels kind of lost here in Brooklyn. I think he stays in his workshop most of the day because he'd get too depressed or crazy otherwise;" *Clockers* by Richard Price; *Leviathan* by Paul Auster.

Sculpture: *The Yearling* by Chicago-born Sag Harbor sculptor Donald G. Lipski, 44, whose fiberglass representation of a full-size horse atop a 20-foot-high red school chair has been commissioned for P.S. 48 in Washington Heights. The work is removed after a school official expresses disapproval; Lipski will create *La Guardia Suite* for installation at the Fiorello H. La Guardia High School of Music and Art and Performing Arts at Lincoln Center.

Theater: *Two Shakespearean Actors* by Chicago-born playwright Richard Nelson, 41, 1/16 at the Cort Theater, with Victor Garber as Edwin Forrest, Brian Bedford as William Macready (*see* 1849 Astor Place riot), 29 perfs.; *The Baltimore Waltz* by Washington, D.C.-born Greenwich Village playwright Paula (Anne) Vogel, 40, 2/1 at the Circle Repertory Theater, with Paris, Tenn.-born actress Cherry Jones, 35, as a schoolteacher, Richard Thompson as her HIV-positive librarian brother, Joe Mantello; *Jake's Women* by Neil Simon 3/24 at the Neil Simon Theater, with Alan Alda, Brenda Vaccaro, Joyce Van Patten, 245 perfs.; *Conversations With My Father* by Herb Gardner 3/29 at the Royale Theater, with Judd Hirsch, 402 perfs.; *Two Trains Running* by August Wilson 4/13 at the Walter Kerr Theater, with Larry

Fishburne, Roscoe Lee Browne, now 67, 160 perfs.; *Fires in the Mirror: Crown Heights, Brooklyn, and Other Identities* by Baltimore-born playwright-actress Anna Deavere Smith, 42, 5/14 at the Public Theater; *The Sisters Rosensweig* by Wendy Wasserstein 10/22 at the Mitzie E. Newhouse Theater, with Jane Alexander, Madeline Kahn, Illinois-born actress Frances McDormand, 35, comedian Robert Klein, John Cunningham, 556 perfs.

Actress Molly Picon dies at Lancaster, Pa., April 5 at age 93; Sandy Dennis of cancer at her Westport, Conn., home March 2 at age 54; Shirley Booth at her Chatham, Mass., home October 16 at age 94; acting teacher Stella Adler at Los Angeles December 21 at age 91.

Films: Woody Allen's *Husbands and Wives* with Allen, Blythe Danner, Judy Davis, Mia Farrow (with whom Allen has a nasty and highly publicized legal battle over his relations with their adopted daughter and custody of their son, Satchel, whose name will be changed to Sean); Martin Brest's *Scent of a Woman* with Al Pacino, Chris O'Donnell. Also: Arthur Hiller's *The Babe* with John Goodman (as Babe Ruth), Kelly McGillis; Abel Ferrera's *Bad Lieutenant* with Harvey Keitel; Chris Columbus's *Home Alone 2: Lost in New York* with Macaulay Culkin, 12, Joe Pesci, Daniel Stern; Alexandre Rockwell's *In the Soup* with Steve Buscemi, Seymour Casell, Jennifer Beals; Paul Schrader's *Light Sleeper* with Willem Dafoe, Susan Sarandon; Spike Lee's *Malcolm X* with Mount Vernon-born actor Danzel Washington, 37; Kenny Ortega's *Newsies* with Christian Bale, Bill Pullman, Robert Duvall deals with the 1899 newsboy strike; Irwin Winkler's *Night and the City* with Robert De Niro, Jessica Lange, Cliff Gorman, Alan King, Jack Warden, Eli Wallach; Howard Franklin's *The Public Eye* with Joe Pesci as the late photographer WeeGee, Barbara Hershey, Stanley Tucci; Barbet Schroder's *Single White Female* with Bridget Fonda, Jennifer Jason Leigh; Sidney Lumet's *A Stranger Among Us* with Melanie Griffith as a New York City police officer who goes to live in a Brooklyn Hasidic community to find a murderer among its members.

New York State takes over the 90-year-old Republic Theater (originally the Victory) in West 42nd Street. It has been showing pornographic films, but architect Hugh Hardy, now 60, will redesign its interior; refurbished at a cost of $11.5 million, it will reopen in December 1995 as a legitimate theater.

Broadway musicals: *Crazy For You* 2/19 at the Shubert Theater, with a 32-member cast headed by Harry Groener, now 40, Rockford, Ill.-born soprano Jodi Benson, 30, old Gershwin songs, book by Ken Ludwig, 1,622 perfs.; *Jelly's Last Jam* 4/26 at the Virginia

Theater, with Gregory Hines as the late "Jelly Roll" Morton, Savion Glover, music by Morton, lyrics by Susan Birkenhead, 569 perfs.; *Falsettos* 4/29 at the John Golden Theater, with Michael Rupert, Stephen Bogardus, Philip Hoffman, Chip Zien, music and lyrics by William Finn, book by Finn and James Lapine, 487 perfs.

Actor-singer Alfred Drake dies at his native New York July 25 at age 77; tap dancer Charles "Honi" Coles at New York November 12 at age 81; onetime Broadway musical star Vivienne Segal at Beverly Hills, Calif., December 29 at age 95.

Composer John Cage dies at New York August 12 at age 79; dancer Hanya Holm at New York November 3 at age 94.

Stefan Edberg wins the U.S. Open men's singles title at Flushing Meadow, Monica Seles the women's.

Former Brooklyn Dodgers (and, later, New York Yankees) radio sportscaster Walter Lanier "Red" Barber dies following abdominal surgery at Tallahassee, Fla., October 22 at age 84.

Mafia boss John Gotti, Sr. draws a life sentence without parole June 23 after being convicted April 2 of murder (*see* 1990); Salvatore "Sammy the Bull" Gravano has associated him with six murders, including those of Paul Castellano and Thomas Bilotti in 1985, and he will be confined to a seven-by-eight-foot cell in a federal prison at Marion, Ill. John Gotti, Jr. takes over as acting boss, with help from Nicholas Corozzo, and the Gambino crime family tries to find a new, less conspicuous boss (*see* 1997).

Manhattan District Attorney Robert M. Morgenthau begins an investigation of bid rigging in the city's construction industry. Previous probes have involved payoffs to corrupt union officials or mobsters; this one focuses on architects, interior designers, contractors, project managers, and real estate brokers who allegedly give or receive kickbacks and payoffs that inflate building costs by as much as 20 percent.

The national waste-hauling company Browning-Ferris tries to move into the New York area, where the mob controls waste disposal; one of the company's managers finds a dog's head on the lawn of his Rockland County home with a note reading "Welcome to New York" stuffed into the dog's mouth (*see* 1993).

Robbers get into an armored car warehouse in Brooklyn's Greenpoint section December 27 and take $8.3 million.

Project Jericho announces plans to convert a commercial single-room occupancy hotel at 2013 Adam Clayton Powell, Jr. Boulevard (at 121st Street) into supportive housing units (*see* 1991). The agency runs supportive S.R.O.s on Manhattan's Upper West Side and in the South Bronx as well as in Harlem but encounters resistance from neighbors, who fear that the building will be turned into a drug-treatment center. When the new units open it becomes clear that the supportive S.R.O. can help people rise out of the depths of prostitution and substance abuse; many of those who opposed it will become members of its board (*see* 1994).

The city has 855,923 registered rent-stabilized apartments—half of the total rental units. Rent-stabilization laws allow landlords to raise rents by 7 percent every 2 years, so rents of many apartments have climbed to market rates.

A three-story mansion for Tishman-Speyer Real Estate Properties president Jerry I. Speyer is completed at 174—176 72nd Street, between Lexington and Third avenues. Designed by Peter Claman of Schuman, Lichtenstein, Claman & Efron, the 7,900-square-foot house replaces two Victorian brownstones; it is 33 feet wide and has four bedrooms, a 46' × 12' basement swimming pool, and other amenities. Speyer has been living in a glass-walled town house at 209 East 71st Street, between Second and Third avenues.

Bryant Park reopens April 21 after a restoration program financed by commercial firms in the park's Business Improvement District (*see* 1980). Andrew W. Heiskell has raised $1.6 million in private money to finance the project, the state legislature at Albany has passed a $20 million bond issue, construction workers have blasted a hole 30 feet deep, and landscape architect Laurie Olin has created a new park based in large part on the ideas of urbanist-author William H. Whyte with an eye to safety. New stacks for the Public Library extend beneath the park's grassy lawn, and restaurants overlook that lawn from its east end.

Central Park birders sight a pair of red-tailed hawks, a rare occurrence even in what has been ranked among the 14 best bird-watching sites in the United States (*see* 1995).

 Amy's Breads opens June 20 at 672 Ninth Avenue, between 46th and 47th streets. Minneapolis-born entrepreneur Amy Scherber, 32, came to New York 8 years ago for a marketing job, went on to study baking in France, and produces a line of specialty breads that will grow to include baguettes, semolina and fennel rolls and twists, raisin and fennel rolls and twists, black olive twists, parmesan cheese twists, and prosciutto and black pepper twists for use at upscale restaurants and for sale at stores such as Balducci's, Citarella, Fairway, and Grace's Market. Scherber will open a second location in 1996 in the Chelsea Market at 75 Ninth Avenue, between 15th and 16th streets.

The City Council votes unanimously September 19 to override Mayor Dinkins's veto of a bill that would require price stickers on items sold in supermarkets. The state pricing law expired in June, the mayor has maintained that initial fines of $1,000 for noncompliance with the law were too low, and the vote signals Council President Peter Vallone's determination to establish the council as a governing body with powers equal to those of the mayor.

The Gourmet Garage opens at 47 Wooster Street in SoHo. Founded by entrepreneurs who include former Flying Foods partner Andrew Arons (see 1981), it sells specialty foods wholesale from 2 o'clock in the morning until 9 and opens for retail customers at 10, offering exotic vegetables, free-range chickens, and other items not readily obtainable elsewhere, some at bargain prices, some at prices higher than anywhere else.

1993 A bomb explosion at the World Trade Center February 26 kills six people and starts a fire that sends black smoke through the 110-story twin towers, injuring hundreds and forcing 100,000 to evacuate the premises. Illegal Jordanian immigrant Mohammed A. Salameh, 25, is arrested in Jersey City March 4 and proves to be a follower of self-exiled Islamic fundamentalist Sheik Omar Abdel Rahman, 55, who is wanted by Egypt for inciting anti-government riots in 1989. FBI agents make further arrests and in June seize Arab terrorists accused of plotting to blow up the United Nations headquarters and the Holland and Lincoln tunnels. Agents arrest Rahman and imprison him 72 miles northwest of New York on suspicion of complicity in the World Trade Center bombing; Egyptian authorities request extradition of the blind, diabetic cleric; his Islamic supporters threaten retaliation if he is extradited.

Mayor Dinkins loses his bid for reelection. Rudolph W. Giuliani secures both the Republican and Liberal party nominations, promises to be tougher on crime, privatize some city services, and reduce business taxes (proposals advanced for some time by the 15-year-old Manhattan Institute), and garners 930,236 of the 2,889,003 votes cast

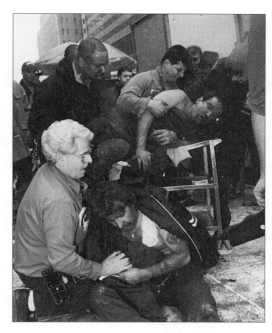

Mideastern terrorists planted a bomb that severely damaged the World Trade Center. AP/WIDE WORLD

(Dinkins receives 876,896). Giuliani becomes the first Republican to win the mayoralty in 28 years.

Mayor-elect Giuliani names Boston-born New York transit police head William S. Bratton, 46, to head the city's police department December 3. The new commissioner, who replaces Lee Brown, has antagonized Mayor Dinkins, Brown, and others by demanding that officers be equipped with 9-millimeter semiautomatic pistols in place of the .38 specials they have carried for years; he prepares to move into a Central Park South apartment and will take credit for reducing incidence of crime in the city (see 1996).

The City Council acts at the urging of Mayor Dinkins to pass a bill changing the composition of the city's Civilian Complaint Review Board (see 1986; Tompkins Square Riot, 1988; Mollen Commission, 1992). All members of the board are to be civilians, with five appointed by the mayor, five by the City Council, three by the police commissioner (see Mollen Commission, 1994).

The city's official unemployment rate reaches 13.4 percent in January, one of the highest in the nation and nearly double the national average of 7.1 percent; it is only about half the rate experienced in the Depression years of 1933 and 1934, and it falls to 11.3 percent in February, but the Department of Employment Commissioner argued last year that the real unemployment rate would be 28.7 percent if it included workers discouraged from looking for jobs and part-timers who wanted full-time work.

IBM announces in January that it lost $4.6 billion last year, the largest operating loss of any company in history. Competitors have taken away the popular personal computer market, leaving Big Blue dominant only in larger, costlier computers that are in less demand. Thomas J. Watson, Jr., who was responsible for getting IBM into the PC business, suffers a stroke and dies at Greenwich, Conn., December 31 at age 79.

CS First Boston adopts that name in September (*see* 1934). First Boston received capital from Credit Suisse following the stock market crash of October 1987, and in December 1988 it became a privately held subsidiary of an international investment bank controlled by Credit Suisse, whose holding company will increase its share in CS First Boston from 44.5 percent to 69 percent.

Sanford I. Weill of Primerica completes his acquisition of Travelers Insurance Co. in December (*see* 1992), pays $1.1 billion to buy back the Shearson retail brokerage that he merged into American Express Co. in 1981, and combines its activities with those of the Smith, Barney brokerage he acquired in 1988. He drops the name Primerica and calls his new combination Travelers Group (*see* Salomon Brothers, 1997).

Advisers to Mayor-elect Giuliani announce December 27 that the city faces a budget deficit of more than $2.2 billion for the fiscal year beginning July 1, 1994. A financial panel appointed by Mayor Dinkins December 2 has issued a report predicting a shortfall of just under $2.2 billion, but there has been an unexpected decline in assessed property values. The Dinkins panel proposed increases in sales and property taxes, fees for garbage collection, and a 14 percent reduction in the city's workforce; Giuliani's spokesmen rule out any tax increases and focus attention on the $32 billion budgeted for government services.

Wall Street's Dow Jones Industrial Average closes December 30 at 3834.44, up a mere 80.5 points (2.1 percent) from the end of 1992. The NASDAQ reaches a record high of 487.89 but closes the year at 477.15, down 3.2 percent.

Barney's opens a 200,000-square-foot uptown store on Madison Avenue at 61st Street, following the lead of Ralph Lauren 7 years ago, and enters a joint venture with Isetan, Japan's sixth largest retail chain, that would open Barney's outlets across the country and worldwide (*but see* 1996). Madison Avenue north of 59th Street will soon be a veritable upscale shopping mall lined with retail outlets featuring clothes by individual designers.

The *New Yorker* magazine cover for December 13 is an illustration by Edward Sorel depicting a crowd of ghostly shoppers in angels' wings crowding a street whose buildings wear the signs of departed retail establishments that include Arnold Constable, B. Altman, Best & Co., Bonwit Teller, Franklin Simon, McCreery's, Peck & Peck, and John Wanamaker.

Thousands of taxi drivers snarl Manhattan traffic October 26, driving slowly in mass formation on major thoroughfares to protest armed robberies and the murders that by year's end will have taken the lives of four yellow-cab and 41 "gypsy" cab drivers in the course of 1 year.

Roosevelt Hospital's new 13-story building opens in January at the northeast corner of Tenth Avenue and 59th Street. Designed by Skidmore, Owings & Merrill, it replaces older buildings on Ninth Avenue that have been sold to developer Harold Brodky.

Former Marble Collegiate Church minister Norman Vincent Peale suffers a stroke and dies at Pawling, N.Y., December 24 at age 95.

Mortimer B. Zuckerman takes over the *Daily News* January 8 in partnership with Fred Drasner and begins firing 175 of the Newspaper Guild's 540 members, some of whom have worked for the *News* for decades (*see* 1992). The paper has been losing $7 million per year, and Zuckerman says he hopes to make it profitable beginning in his first year of ownership by cutting labor costs and achieving other savings. Guild members stage an angry protest outside the News building as it develops that Zuckerman is not only cutting one-third of all unionized jobs but reducing the salaries of the people he retains. The paper's nine other unions have reached an agreement with him and have refused to support any Guild strike; envisioning the *News* as a saucier version of the upscale tabloid *London Daily Mail*, Zuckerman visits the paper's printing plant in Brooklyn and tries to dissipate some of the anger over lost jobs.

The *New York Post* says it will suspend publication as early as Monday, January 25, unless its 720 employees take a 20 percent temporary pay cut (*see* 1988).

The *Daily News* lures away top *Post* editors, the *Post* files suit in February to stem the exodus. Collection agency head and real estate developer Steven Hoffenberg, 48, of the Towers Financial Corp. proposes to take over the failing *Post* from publisher Peter S. Kalikow, who has sought personal bankruptcy protection, a federal bankruptcy court judge approves the sale to Hoffenberg February 19, but the deal falls apart in March as financial experts examine Hoffenberg's ledgers and question his accounting methods. Hoffenberg has a criminal record; he has enriched himself with a giant pyramid scheme to build a financial-services conglomerate and will plead guilty in 1995 to securities and mail fraud after bilking investors of $475 million. The *Post*'s staff headed by Pete Hamill revolts in March upon hearing that 272 people—one-third of the paper's work force—will be dismissed immediately, the March 15 edition is scrapped as union members and top managers resist a court-approved bid by Polish-born developer and parking-garage magnate Abraham Jacob "Abe" Hirschfeld, 73, to take control. Hirschfeld puts out an edition that hurls insults at owner Kalikow. The paper seeks bankruptcy protection, former owner Rupert Murdoch offers to operate the *Post* for 60 days, and the bankruptcy court judge rules March 29 that he can start printing the *Post* immediately. Murdoch says it will cost $1.5 million to take over the paper, plus $3 million to pay off debts incurred by Peter Kalikow, and $200,000 per week to cover operating losses until he obtains ownership of the paper, whose liabilities total at least $20 million. He then says the situation is far worse than he had thought, and that weekly operating losses are $350,000; he halts publication July 9 after failing to secure major concessions from unions. Locked out by Murdoch, the unions agree to $6.2 million in concessions July 12 and return to work. The bankruptcy court approves Murdoch's takeover September 13, but the Newspaper Guild goes on strike 2 weeks later, production unions refuse to cross Guild picket lines, and Murdoch threatens to pull out of his agreement to buy the *Post*. The production unions capitulate after publication is suspended September 27, the city's only remaining afternoon daily returns to newsstands September 30 as some workers opt for job security under Murdoch's control, and Murdoch formally buys the *Post* October 1, despite the ongoing Guild strike. Guild members, he says, will have to reapply for their jobs.

Former *New York Times* editor Harrison E. Salisbury dies outside Providence, R.I., July 5 at age 84. The *Times* acquires the *Boston Globe* October 1 for $1.1 billion.

AT&T announces August 16 that it will pay $12.6 billion to acquire McCaw Cellular Communications, the nation's largest cellular telephone company. The move raises possibilities that as wireless phones replace wired lines AT&T will be able to bypass the regional telephone companies, thus avoiding fees that amount to billions of dollars per year. Pocket-size cellular phones become commonplace in New York and other cities. Telephone and media companies work to structure multi-billion-dollar megadeals with a view to creating a huge information superhighway offering on-demand video, telephone calls on cable, and TV programming on phone lines.

 Nonfiction: *New York Days* by former *Harper's* magazine editor-in-chief Willie Morris, now 57; *The Fifties* by David Halberstam; *The Tiger: The Rise and Fall of Tammany Hall* by Oliver E. Allen; *The New York Approach: Robert Moses, Urban Liberals, and Redevelopment of the Inner City* by Montclair State College history professor Joel Schwartz, 51; *To Be Mayor of New York: Ethnic Politics in the City* by New York author Chris McNickle; *The Assassination of New York* by CUNY sociologist Robert Fitch who savages the real estate industry; *The Warburgs: The Twentieth-Century Odyssey of a Remarkable Jewish Family* by Ron Chernow; *Nightmare on Wall Street: Salomon Brothers and the Corruption of the Marketplace* by Martin Mayer; *722 Miles: The Building of the Subways and How They Transformed New York* by Hobart and William Smith Colleges historian Clifton Hood; *Behind the Times: Inside the New York Times* by NYU journalism professor Edwin Diamond, whose column on the media has appeared in *New York* magazine since 1985; *New York, New York: How the Apartment House Transformed the Life of the City (1869–1930)* by former *New Yorker* staff writer Elizabeth Hawes, 53; *New York Landmarks: A Collection of Architecture and Historical Details* by New York author Charles J. Ziga; *Luxury Apartment Houses of Manhattan: An Illustrated History* by Andrew Alpern.

Fiction: *The Fourteen Sisters of Emilio Montez O'Brien* by Oscar Hijuelos; *Operation Shylock: A Confession* by Philip Roth; *Carriage Trade* by Stephen Birmingham.

 PaceWildenstein is created through a joint venture by Arne Glimcher's Pace Gallery and the 90-year-old Wildenstein to represent contemporary artists as well as the estates of some major modern artists.

Sculpture: *Intersection II* (hot-rolled steel) by Richard Serra.

The Municipal Art Society celebrates its centennial October 29 with a dance in the 80-year-old Grand

Central Terminal that it helped to save from the wrecking ball and that will soon be more resplendent even than it was in 1913.

Theater: *Redwood Curtain* by Lanford Wilson 3/30 at the Brooks Atkinson Theater, with Chelsea, Miss.-born actor Jeff Daniels, 38, Debra Monk, Seoul-born ingénue Sung Yun Cho, 21, 40 perfs.; *Angels in America: Millennium Approaches, a Gay Fantasia on National Themes* by Tony Kushner 5/4 at the Walter Kerr Theater, with Kathleen Chalfant, David Marshall Grant, Ron Leibman, 367 perfs.; *Playboy of the West Indies* by Trinidadian playwright Mustapha Matura 5/9 at the Mitzi E. Newhouse Theater; *A Perfect Ganesh* by Terrence McNally 6/27 at the Manhattan Theater Club, with Frances Sternhagen, Zoë Caldwell.

Actress Helen Hayes dies at Nyack March 17 at age 92; Kate Reid of cancer at Stratford, Ont., March 27 at age 62; Eugenia Leontovich at New York April 2 at age 93; costume designer Irene Sharaff at New York August 16 at age 83.

Indianapolis-born NBC comedian David Letterman, 46, moves to CBS and stars in a *Late Show* after the 11 o'clock news opposite Jay Leno, who has succeeded veteran host Johnny Carson on NBC's *Tonight Show*. CBS renovates the old Ed Sullivan Theater on Broadway at 53rd Street for Letterman's show, which will continue for more than a decade to entertain viewers nationwide.

Television: *The Nanny* 11/3 on CBS with Fran Drescher as a door-to-door cosmetics saleswoman who becomes governess for New York widower Maxfield Sheffield (Charles Shaughnessy) (to 1999).

Films: Robert De Niro's *A Bronx Tale* with De Niro, Calogero Lorenzo "Chazz" Palminteri, Lillo Brancato, Joe Pesci (shot in Brooklyn and Queens in an effort to re-create the Bronx of the 1950s); Brian De Palma's *Carlito's Way* with Al Pacino, Sean Penn; Barry Sonnenfeld's *For Love or Money* with Michael J. Fox, Gabrielle Anwar; Nancy Savoka's *Household Saints* with Tracey Ullman, Vincent D'Onofrio, Lili Taylor; Leslie Harris's *Just Another Girl on the I.R.T.* with Ariyan Johnson, Kevin Thigpen; Amir Naderi's *Manhattan by Numbers* with John Wojda, Branislav Tomich, Mary Chang Faulk; Woody Allen's *Manhattan Murder Mystery* with Allen, Diane Keaton, Alan Alda, Anjelica Huston; Anthony Minghella's *Mr. Wonderful* with actor Matt Dillon, Annabella Sciorra, Mary-Louise Parker; Warren Light's *The Night We Never Met* with Matthew Broderick, Annabella Sciorra, Kevin Anderson; Tim Hunter's *The Saint of Fort Washington* with Matt Dillon, Danny Glover; Fred Schepsi's *Six Degrees of Separation* with Stockard Channing, Will Smith, Donald Sutherland, Ian McKellen; Nora Ephron's *Sleepless in Seattle* with Tom Hanks, Meg Ryan; Philip Noyce's *Sliver* with Sharon Stone, William Baldwin, Tom Berenger; Ang Lee's *The Wedding Banquet* with Winston Chao, May Chin, Mitchell Lichtenstein.

Actress Lillian Gish dies of heart failure at Nyack February 28 at age 99; Myrna Loy while undergoing surgery for cancer at New York December 14 at age 88.

The number of sex-oriented businesses in the city rises to 177 by year's end, up 35 percent from 131 in 1984 (see 1977). The number of video stores and peep shows has tripled, topless bars have increased by 26 percent, but the number of theaters showing pornographic films has fallen by more than 50 percent, mostly because such material can be bought at bargain prices in video stores.

Broadway musicals: *The Who's Tommy* 4/23 at the St. James Theater, with Bethesda, Md.-born actor Michael Cerveris, 32, music by Peter Townshend, who has recycled songs from a 1969 rock opera by the Who, 899 perfs.; *Kiss of the Spider Woman* 5/3 at the Broadhurst Theater (it first opened in October of last year at London's Shaftsbury Theater), with Canadian-born actor Brent Carver, 41 (as Molina), Milwaukee-born actor Anthony Crivello, 37 (as Valentin), Chita Rivera, now 60, who sings and dances in the title role despite a recent auto accident that left her with a smashed leg, book by Terrence McNally based on the 1976 novel by the late Manuel Puig, music and lyrics by John Kander and Fred Ebb, songs that include "The Day After That" (the American Foundation for AIDS research will adopt it as its official anthem), 904 perfs.

Onetime Broadway musical dancer-actress Ruby Keeler dies of cancer at her Palm Springs, Calif., home February 28 at age 82.

A concert by Luciano Pavarotti on Central Park's Great Lawn 6/26 draws a crowd estimated to number 250,000.

Choreographer Agnes de Mille dies of a stroke in her Greenwich Village apartment October 7 at age 88 (a stroke in 1975 nearly ended her career).

Popular songs: *River of Dreams* (album) by Billy Joel; *Walk the Dog and Light the Light* (album) by Laura Nyro.

Jazz trumpeter-composer Dizzy Gillespie dies of pancreatic cancer at an Englewood, N.J., hospital January 6 at age 75. The Rev. John G. Gensel of St. Peter's Lutheran Church in Manhattan officiates at Gillespie's funeral but Gensel himself turns 75 later in the year and announces his retirement at year's end; lyricist Mitchell Parish dies at a New York hospital March 31 following a stroke at age 92.

The New York Rangers win their first National Hockey League championship since 1940, beating the Vancouver Canucks 3 to 2 at Madison Square Garden June 14 in the seventh game (carried live on the ESPN cable television channel and watched by more people than ever before watched a hockey game on cable). Rangers center Mark Messier, 33, has led the attack, but defenseman Brian Leetch, 26, who has been helped by fellow goalie Mike Richter, 27, is awarded the Conn Smythe Trophy as most valuable player in the playoffs—the first U.S.-born player to be thus honored.

Former Brooklyn Dodgers catcher Roy Campanella dies at his Woodland Hills, Calif., home June 26 at age 71, having been paralyzed from the chest down since a January 1958 automobile accident; former Brooklyn (and L.A.) Dodgers pitcher Don Drysdale dies of a heart attack at Montreal July 3 at age 56.

Tennis great Arthur Ashe dies of AIDS-related pneumonia at a New York hospital February 6 at age 49, having started tennis programs for inner-city youths in cities nationwide (see Memorial Stadium, 1997).

Pete Sampras wins in men's singles at Flushing Meadow, Steffi Graf in women's singles (Monica Seles has been stabbed in mid-match April 30 by a fanatical Graf supporter at Hamburg).

Developer Donald Trump is married December 20 to Marla Maples who has borne him a daughter, Tiffany (see 1991). The new marriage will be brief.

The failing Canadian developer Olympia & York sells its 21-year-old 55 Water Street office tower, now only 60 percent occupied, to Alabama's state pension fund, whose chief executive officer David G. Bronner embarks on a $150 million renovation program. Bronner finds that since the building's completion it has been paying the Mafia-controlled cartel V. Ponte & Sons about $1.2 million per year to haul away recyclable waste that the cartel has then sold (see 1992). In a scheme developed with help from his Manhattan district attorney friend Robert M. Morgenthau, Bronner employs city detective Harry Bridgwood, 47, who goes to work October 3 as the building's manager, wearing one of three Moe Ginsburg suits bought for him by the D.A.'s office and using the pseudonym "Paul Vassil." Bridgwood will obtain wiretape evidence against Angelo Ponte, 67, whose firm is part of the 34-company cartel allegedly run by the Gambino and Genovese crime

families; it is said to have been overcharging clients $500 million per year (see 1995).

The "Brady Bill" signed by President Clinton November 30 requires a 5-day waiting period for handgun purchases (it is named for former President Reagan's press secretary James Brady who was so severely wounded by a would-be presidential assassin in early 1981 that he was left a paraplegic). Demands increase for federal licensing of handguns, steep taxes on ammunition, and other measures after a gunman massacres passengers aboard a Long Island Rail Road commuter train December 7, killing five and wounding 18. Police arrest Jamaican-born gunman Colin Ferguson, 35, and charge him with the murders.

More than 1,500 New Yorkers die of gunshot wounds, up from 44 in 1943.

The bombing of the World Trade Center February 26 displaces 350 tenant companies with 40,000 employees, and restoration of the world's largest office complex will cost the Port Authority of New York and New Jersey more than $1 billion: $300 million in repairs and cleanup (2,700 people go to work round the clock for 2 weeks at a cost of $20 million), $250 million in loss of business ($1 million per day in rental income for every day the towers are closed), $220 million in extra security personnel and equipment, $200 million in backup power for electrical and other systems (the 200-foot-wide hole left by the bomb has knocked out the main electrical system, an air-conditioning engine room, and a central command station for both towers), $110 million in higher insurance premiums and deductibles, and $5 million for new office locks and keys.

General Electric Co. donates its 50-story Art Deco building at 570 Lexington Avenue to Columbia University in June as a real estate slump makes it cheaper to give buildings away than to maintain them. Minneapolis investors Miles and Shirley Fiterman donate their 15-story building at 30 West Broadway to City University as their sole tenant, Morgan Guaranty Trust Co., prepares to leave. Some commercial landlords offer Manhattan office space on terms that allow free rent for 10 years in efforts to fill up "see-through" buildings.

The bombing of the World Trade Center February 26 leaves the underground area of the 12-year-old Vista Hotel heavily damaged (but see 1994).

The Four Seasons Hotel opens in June at 57 East 57th Street, between Madison and Park avenues. Designed by I. M. Pei, the 52-story, 367-room hostelry is the city's tallest, its guest rooms average 600 square feet (25 to 40 percent larger than is typical at other hotels) and about half of them have full views of Central Park and the skyline. Lower floors average 12 guest rooms each, floors between the 30th and 49th average only six, the 50th has four, the 51st two grand suites with outdoor terraces, and the 52nd a presidential suite with 360-degree views. Room rates range from $440 per night for a single to $7,000 for the presidential suite, but although the hotel has cost $477 million to develop, its owners will soon sell it for $190 million.

The New York Zoological Society becomes the Wildlife Conservation Society in February (see 1899). Having added the Central Park Zoo to its Bronx Zoo responsibilities, it opens the Sea Cliffs marine animal center at the Coney Island aquarium April 22 with penguins, seals, sea otters, walruses, and various fish species in a 300-foot re-creation of rocky Pacific coastal habitat. Brooklyn's 12-acre Prospect Park Zoo reopens at 450 Flatbush Avenue October 5 as the Prospect Park Wildlife Center after a $37 million redesign. Aimed primarily at children, the center houses 400 animals from 80 species in a complex that comprises a World of Animals, Animal Lifestyles, and Animals in Our Lives.

The 88-year-old National Audubon Society acquires the 102-year-old Schermerhorn Building at 700 Broadway, just north of 4th Street, where its offices will occupy all but two floors of the nine-story structure.

The Food Network begins on cable television August 19 from studios in 33rd Street. Created by CNN founder Reese Schoenfeld, it will grow in 5 years to reach 32 million U.S. and Canadian homes with half-hour programs featuring chefs, cookbook authors, and other culinary authorities.

Sylvia's Food Products introduces a line of canned soul food based on the menu of the famous Harlem restaurant, now headed by the founder's son, Van D. Woods (see 1961).

The restaurant Daniel opens June 4 in the Surrey Hotel at 20 East 76th Street and soon rivals Bouley as the city's finest. Chef-owner Daniel Boulod, 37, has for 6 years been chef at Le Cirque (see 1999).

U.S. immigration authorities try to stem the influx of illegal aliens, including potential terrorists. Chinese smuggling gangs cram would-be émigrés into freighter holds and try to get them into the United States; most are from Fujian province and some die June 6 when 200 jump into the water after the freighter *Golden Venture* runs aground off Rockaway Peninsula in Queens (the survivors are arrested, and some will remain in prison until 1997, among them the Indonesian skipper Amir Humuntal Lumban Tobing, 43).

1994 The driver of a car crossing Brooklyn Bridge March 1 fires through his own window at a van full of Lubavitcher Hasidic students and wounds four of them, one fatally. Police arrest Lebanese livery driver Rashad Baz, 28, the next day and charge him with the assault. Israeli-Palestinian peace talks halted after a Brooklyn-born Jewish extremist walked into a Hebron mosque February 25 and opened fire with an automatic rifle on hundreds of praying Muslims.

Former president Richard M. Nixon dies of a stroke at New York Hospital April 22 at age 81; former State Department official George W. Ball of abdominal cancer at New York May 26 at age 84.

A confidential report prepared for the Securities and Exchange Commission reveals that Sen. Alfonse M. D'Amato (R. N.Y.) last year made a profit of $37,125 in one day after a Long Island brokerage house allowed him to buy 4,500 units of an initial public offering that was not available to ordinary investors. D'Amato is the ranking Republican on the Senate Banking Committee that oversees the SEC; the brokerage firm (Stratton Oakmont) was under investigation by the SEC last year for allegedly cheating customers, it has generally required clients to have a net worth of at least $500,000 just to open an account, D'Amato's net worth was only $70,000 last year, but when the SEC report is made public in June 1996 he will call it "old news" floated by people "trying to embarrass" him.

Gov. Cuomo loses his bid for election to a fourth term. State Senator George E. (Elmer) Pataki, 49, has campaigned on promises to reduce state income taxes by 25 percent in 4 years and restore the death penalty for capital crimes; he wins 2,488,631 votes to Cuomo's 2,292,332, and many credit his victory to Sen. Alfonse D'Amato, now 57, who has made Mayor Giuliani's outspoken support of Gov. Cuomo a major issue in the campaign. A native of Peekskill who has run as both a Republican and Conservative, Pataki is the first Republican to win the gubernatorial race since 1970 and the first governor-elect in many decades without any New York City roots. Since the city depends on state financial aid, Mayor Giuliani tries to mend fences with the state's new Republican Party leadership, but the governor-elect does not see him until November 30, when they meet at the Union League Club.

Mayor Rudolph Giuliani cracked down on street crime and introduced "workfare." LAURENCE MASLON

The Mollen Commission that has been investigating charges of police corruption since 1992 uncovers evidence of organized police "crews" that terrorize minority neighborhoods (*see* Review Board, 1993). The Commission publishes its report in July, concluding that corruption and brutality are inextricably linked; it urges revisions in the screening, recruiting, and training of officers (*see* 1996).

Police officer Francis X. Livoti, 35, is indicted on charges of negligent homicide in connection with the death of Anthony Baez. Visiting his boyhood home in the University Heights section of the Bronx December 22, Florida resident Baez, 29, was tossing a football with his three brothers, the ball hit Livoti's patrol car, Livoti arrested one of the brothers, and when Anthony intervened Livoti applied an illegal choke hold that proved fatal (*see* 1996).

New York State auditors examining the books at Bankers Trust early in the year find that unclaimed customers funds amounting to millions of dollars have dwindled. They ask for additional documents from the bank, but although they will repeat the request it will go unheeded for the next 2 years (*see* 1996).

General Electric discloses in its annual report that its cumulative investment in Kidder, Peabody totals $1.2 billion, but a bond-trading scandal rocks Kidder and it announces April 14 that it has dismissed its chief government-bond trader and temporarily reassigned six other people in his division. Joseph Jett, 36, has allegedly reported "phantom" trades for more than a year, inflating the firm's profits by as much as $350 million; he has received huge bonuses but lives modestly and denies any wrongdoing. GE sells most of its Kidder assets to PaineWebber in October for $670 million in common and preferred stock, thereby obtaining a 23 percent interest in PaineWebber (*see* 1995).

Former Securities and Exchange Commission chairman John S. R. Shad dies following heart surgery at New York July 7 at age 71, having helped Drexel Burnham Lambert settle its fines and criminal penalties; investment banker Charles Allen, Jr. of Allen & Co. dies at his Sherry-Netherland Hotel apartment July 15 at age 91 (*see* 1933). Having amassed a fortune of roughly $1 billion, he has contented himself with getting about Manhattan by taxi while members of his family went in chauffeur-driven Rolls-Royces.

Wall Street's Dow Jones Industrial Average closes at a record high of 3794.33 December 29 and closes December 31 at 3754.09, up 452.98 (13.7 percent) from the end of 1993. The NASDAQ closes at a record 787.42 October 15 and closes December 31 at 777.13, up 16.3 percent for the year.

R. H. Macy & Co. directors agree in principle July 14 to a merger with Federated Department Stores, ending a 6-month battle for control of Macy's and creating the largest U.S. department-store company, with more than 450 stores employing nearly 120,000 people and annual sales of nearly $14 billion. Federated emerges from 4 years of bankruptcy and takes over Macy's, which has itself been in bankruptcy since January 1992 (*see* 1995).

Mayor Giuliani begins clearing 125th Street of licensed sidewalk vendors selling everything from baseball cards, batteries, and imitation gold watches to expensive leather briefcases and T-shirts, but more and more such vendors—mostly immigrants from Africa, the Caribbean, and Latin America—crowd onto the sidewalks of Canal Street, 14th Street, and other venues, selling umbrellas at the first sign of rain and generally competing with retail merchants who pay high rents and fume at the competition that pays none. *Fortune* magazine estimated in 1990 that sales from street vendor carts in the city totaled more than $1 billion; depending on location, a cart may generate revenues of $250,000 or more per year, and a well-located food cart will average $750 in sales per day, with about one-third of that being net profit (*see* food vendors, 1995).

Retailer Milton J. Petrie dies of lung and kidney ailments at his Manhattan home November 6 at age 92.

The city begins reducing street cleaning in residential areas to 90 minutes, down from 3 hours, and to 30 minutes in commercial areas, down from 1 hour, but restores cleaning on Wednesdays and Saturdays (*see* 1991). The change eases parking restrictions for car owners.

Ground is broken in September for a tunnel connecting the 10th East River subway tunnel that opened in 1989 with the IND Queens Boulevard line; by 1998 about 2,500 of Roosevelt Island's 8,000 residents will be commuting each day by the Q train to and from Manhattan (about 1,500 will continue to ride the tramway in each direction on a daily basis; Queens Surface Corp. buses connect the island with Queensboro Plaza and Astoria).

Gray Line New York Tours enters the double-decker tour-bus business launched by New York Double Decker in 1991. Long the city's largest operator of conventional tour buses, Gray Line will have 33 double-deckers in service by 1997 and (counting a small fourth competitor) there will be 80 such buses plying the streets of Manhattan from Battery Park to 125th Street, adding to traffic congestion and air-quality problems.

Hasidic Jewish leader Menachem Mendel Schneerson dies at New York June 12 at age 93. Seventh in a line of so-called "grand rebbes," Rabbi Schneerson took over the small Lubavitch sect in 1951 and built it into an international organization with considerable political influence. His followers thought he might reveal himself as the Messiah before his death; he did not, and his passing leaves the sect without a leader.

YIVO Institute acquires the former American Foundation for the Blind headquarters in 16th Street, between Fifth and Sixth avenues, taking over two four-story neo-Georgian structures (*see* 1940). YIVO last year sold its 1048 Fifth Avenue mansion at 86th Street and it will be turned into an art museum (*see* 2001).

The Museum of the American Indian moves in October from Audubon Terrace to the former U.S. Customs House near Battery Park and becomes the George Gustav Heye Center of the National Museum of the American Indian (*see* 1922). When Heye died in 1957 he left a will requiring that the museum's holdings remain in New York.

P.S. 200 in Harlem begins encouraging every pupil to wear a school "uniform"—pressed navy-blue slacks or navy skirt, black shoes, crisp white shirt, and a clip-on navy-blue necktie. Pupils have been showing up in baggy pants, short shorts, sneakers, and other costumes; some continue defiantly to make "fashion statements" that are at odds with a school policy designed to concentrate attention on learning (*see* 1998).

Viacom acquires Paramount Communications (formerly Gulf + Western Industries) in March (*see* 1987). The acquisition brings with it the book publishing houses Macmillan and Simon & Schuster plus the Madison Square Garden sports complex (Viacom resells the Garden to Cablevision Inc. in August for $1.1 billion).

WABC TALKRADIO 77 AM becomes the most listened-to radio station in North America. It added syndicated right-wing talk-show host Rush Limbaugh's program in 1988 and right-wing host Bob Grant in 1989; by airing former mayor Ed Koch and other talk-show hosts, it has built up a huge following.

Mayor Giuliani suggests in public that the city's municipal radio station WNYC hire Guardian Angels founder Curtis Sliwa, whose program on WABC has been canceled. WNYC puts Sliwa on the air despite widespread protests, but he soon quits his call-in show; like most other such shows it attracts calls from ill-informed listeners who like to sound off.

NBC-TV launches Chopper 4 with gyroscopically stabilized TV cameras to transmit clear pictures as the peacock-emblazoned helicopter swoops and hovers over scenes of breaking news events. NBC news anchors Chuck Scarborough and Sue Simmons compete with ABC-TV's Bill Beutel and Diana Williams, while CBS tries to keep up with fewer resources (Pittsburgh-born Charles Bishop Scarborough III, now 50, has been at NBC since 1974; Cleveland-born William Charles Beutel, now 63, has been at NBC since 1962).

In Style magazine begins publication in June at New York. The new Time, Inc. publication is a virtual catalogue of designer dresses, fashion accessories, cosmetics, home furnishings, restaurants, and vacation spots but will have a paid circulation of more than 700,000 by December of next year and in 4 years will have a circulation of 1,151,024.

The investment firm Forstmann-Little & Co. agrees October 27 to pay $1.4 billion for most of the 67-year-old Ziff-Davis publishing firm that has sold off many of its earlier magazines and become the leading publisher of computer-related periodicals, including *PC Magazine*, *PC Week*, and *Computer Shopper*.

The Stuttgart-based media conglomerate Verlagsgruppe Georg von Holtzbrinck acquires a controlling interest in the 48-year-old New York publishing house Farrar, Straus & Giroux (*see* Henry Holt, 1985). FS&G's imprints have included L. C. Page since 1957, Hill & Wang since 1971, and North Point Press since 1991 (*see* St. Martin's Press, 1995).

Viacom boss Sumner Redstone abruptly fires Simon & Schuster chief executive Richard E. Snyder, who in 2 years will obtain backing from Barry Diller and Warburg Pincus Ventures to buy a controlling interest in Western Publishing; he will rename it Golden Books Family Entertainment as he receives financial help from Hallmark Cards of Kansas City to revitalize his venerable line of children's books.

Entry-level jobs in book publishing generally pay between $15,000 and $24,000 per year, and editors in higher-level jobs are usually too young to retire; most would-be editors with talent look for employment elsewhere.

Nonfiction: *Rebellions, Perversions and Main Events* by Murray Kempton, now 76; *The View from Mt. Morris: A Harlem Boyhood* by historian and novelist John Sanford, now 90; *City on a Hill: Testing the American Dream at City College* by journalist (and Harvard graduate) James Traub, who writes that students are "sometimes dreadfully prepared," not true in CCNY's past, but that people in the school's upper echelons "have every reason to feel good about the education they're getting, and that's overlooked;" *The Historical Atlas of New York City: A Visual Celebration of Nearly 400 Years of New York City's History* by Eric Homberger; *Nellie Bly: Daredevil, Reporter, Feminist* by Kansas City-born former *New York Newsday* reporter-editor Brooke Kroeger, 45; *Gay New York* by University of Chicago history professor George Chauncey, who writes, "In the half-century between 1890 and the beginning of the Second World War, a highly visible, remarkably complex, and continually

changing gay male world took shape in New York City. That world included several gay neighborhood enclaves, widely publicized dances and other social events, and a host of commercial establishments where gay men gathered, ranging from saloons, speakeasies, and bars to cheap cafeterias and elegant restaurants. The men who participated in that world forged a distinctive culture with its own language and customs, its own traditions and folk histories, its own heroes and heroines."

Fiction: *The Waterworks* by E. L. Doctorow; *The Alienist* by New York military historian-novelist Caleb Carr, 39, who writes about New York in the 1890s. Carr's father, Lucien, was imprisoned for murder nearly 50 years ago (*see* crime, 1945); *One True Thing* by Anna Quindlen, who resigns from the *New York Times* to become a full-time novelist.

 Missouri-born sculptor Donald Judd dies at New York February 12 at age 65; art critic Clement Greenberg of emphysema at Lenox Hill Hospital May 7 at 85.

 Theater: *Three Tall Women* by Edward Albee 4/5 at the Promenade Theater (after opening downtown at the Vineyard Theater), with Chicago-born actress Myra Carter, Marian Seldes, Jordan Baker, David Dukes; *Broken Glass* by Arthur Miller 4/24 at the Booth Theater, with Amy Irving, New York-born actor Ron Rifkin, 54, 73 perfs.

Actress Jessica Tandy dies of cancer at her Easton, Conn., home September 11 at age 85.

Television: *Ellen* (initially titled *These Friends of Mine*) 3/29 on ABC with Ellen DeGeneres, Arye Gross, 33 (to 5/13/1998); *NYPD Blue* 9/21 on ABC with David Caruso, Dennis Franz, Nicholas Turturro, James McDaniel, Amy Brenneman in another police show created by Steven Bochco, now 50 (opening credits for each episode include a shot of the Ninth Precinct station at 321 East 5th Street); *New York Undercover* 9/22 on Fox with Malik Yoba as detective J. C. Williams, Michael DeLorenzo as Eddie Torres in a series created by Dick Wolf, now 49 (6/25/98); *Friends* 9/22 on NBC with Courteney Cox, Jennifer Aniston, David Schwimmer, Lisa Kudrow, Matt LeBlanc, Matthew Perry (to 5/17/2001).

Radio satirist Henry Morgan dies of lung cancer at New York May 19 at age 79.

Films: Jeff Pollack's *Above the Rim* with Duane Martin, Leon, rap artist Tupac Shakur, 23; Martha Coolidge's *Angie* with Geena Davis, Stephen Rae, James Gandolfini, Aida Turturro; Woody Allen's *Bullets*

Over Broadway with John Cusack, Dianne Wiest; Bill Fishman's *Car 54, Where Are You?* with David Johansen, John C. McGinley, Al Lewis; Spike Lee's *Crooklyn* with Alfred Woodard, Delroy Lindo, David Patrick Kelly; Terry Zwigoff's documentary *Crumb* about underground comic-book artist Robert Crumb; Joel Coen's *The Hudsucker Proxy* with Tim Robbins, Jennifer Jason Leigh, Paul Newman; Darnell Martin's *I Like It Like That* with Lauren Velez, Jon Seda, Tomas Melly; Alan Rudolph's *Mrs. Parker and the Vicious Circle* with Jennifer Jason Leigh (as Dorothy Parker), Campbell Scott, Matthew Broderick; Michael Almereyda's *Nadja* with Elene Lowensoh, Peter Fonda, Suzy Amis; Dan Algrant's *Naked in New York* with Eric Stoltz, Mary-Louise Parker, Ralph Macchio, Kathleen Turner, Tony Curtis, Timothy Dalton, Jill Clayburgh, Roscoe Lee Brown; Ron Howard's *The Paper* with Michael Keaton, Glenn Close, Robert Duvall; Robert Redford's *Quiz Show* with Ralph Fiennes, John Turturro, Rob Morrow, David Paymer; Heywood Gould's *Trial by Jury* with Joanne Whalley-Kilmer, Armand Asante.

The Sony Theater Lincoln Square Complex opens with 13 screens and a 3D Imax theater on Broadway at 67th Street.

 Former sound-equipment manufacturer and Lincoln Center philanthropist Avery Fisher dies at New Milford, Conn., February 26 at age 87.

Broadway musicals: *Beauty and the Beast* 4/18 at the Palace, with Seal Beach, Calif.-born actress Susan Egan, 24, Terrence Mann, Tom Aldredge, Tom Bosley, music by Alan Menken, lyrics by the late Howard Ashman and Tim Rice (to Lunt-Fontanne Theater 11/11/99), 3,325+ perfs.; *Passion* 5/9 at the Plymouth Theater, with Donna Murphy, Rockford, Ill.-born actress Marin Mazzie, 33, music and lyrics by Stephen Sondheim, 280 perfs.

Set designer Oliver Smith dies at New York January 23 at age 75; musical-comedy actor Raul Julia at a Manhasset hospital October 24 at age 54 following a stroke.

Popular song: *MTV Unplugged in New York* by the Seattle rock group Nirvana.

Composer-producer Jule Styne dies at New York September 20 at age 88; dancer Pearl Primus at her New Rochelle home October 30 at age 74; singer-bandleader Cab Calloway at Hockessin, Del., November 18 at age 86; jazz drummer Connie Kay of cardiac arrest at his New York home November 30 at age 67.

 Andre Agassi, 24, wins the U.S. Open men's singles title at Flushing Meadow, Arantxa Sánchez Vicario, 22 (Sp.), the women's.

Major league baseball players go on strike August 12, protesting a decision by owners to impose salary caps (the average player now earns $1.2 million per year, the minimum is $109,000, and some earn as much as $7.29 million). The two sides fail to reach agreement by September 9 and the remainder of the season is canceled. There is no World Series for the first time in 90 years.

Marathon organizer Fred Lebow dies at his New York home October 9 at age 62 (see 1958). His New York Road Runners Club has grown to have a membership of more than 28,000, and although he ran in the 1992 marathon when his brain cancer was in remission it has finally taken its toll; Lebow will be memorialized with a statue outside the Tavern on the Green in Central Park.

 Former first lady Jacqueline Kennedy Onassis dies of lymphoma at her 1040 Fifth Avenue apartment May 19 at age 64 and is buried beside her first husband May 23 in Arlington Cemetery at Washington, D.C. Mourners include her longtime companion Maurice Tempelsman, 64, a Polish-born Orthodox Jew whose financial advice helped "Jackie O" quadruple her fortune (see auction, 1996).

Mayor Giuliani takes action immediately upon assuming office January 1 to reduce low-level crime. Uniformed police officers and undercover men remove "squeegee men" who have hassled motorists at stoplights and smeared their windshields, chase drug peddlers out of Central Park entrances and other conspicuous locations, and drive out prostitutes from many areas. Giuliani has the help of a police force enlarged by 6,000 new cops hired by former mayor David Dinkins, and cars parked on city streets soon have fewer signs in their windows reading, "No Radio," "No Nothing," and "Everything Stolen." Giuliani proposes in September that comprehensive zoning regulations be instituted to bar adult video stores, X-rated theaters, and topless bars from operating within 500 feet of residences, houses of worship, schools, or one another.

 Levittown developer William Levitt dies of kidney disease at Manhasset, L.I., January 28 at age 86. He sold Levitt & Sons to International Telephone & Telegraph for $92 million in 1968 but has lost most of the money.

A consortium led by the Hong Kong-based New World Development Corp. buys the 75-acre waterfront property (formerly the Penn Central rail yards) between 59th and 72nd streets and agrees to finance Donald Trump's $2.5 billion Riverside South apartment and office complex. Chase Manhattan Bank has sold its $250 million mortgage on the land for $88 million, and the deal allows Trump to remain as developer and receive a 30 percent interest in the project after development costs. A coalition of civic groups led by the Municipal Art Society has come up with an alternative to Trump's original plan: instead of having a skyscraper that would be the world's largest it calls for 16 apartment houses with 5,700 units, a 21.5-acre public park, and 1.8 million square feet of new office space (see 1998).

The new Giuliani administration cuts property taxes for co-op and condominium apartment owners.

The Belnord apartment house of 1909 is sold for $15 million in late October, ending a rent strike that has continued for 20 years. Tenants have charged the octagenarian owner Lilian Seril with failure to maintain the premises, and nearly half of them have been putting their rents in an escrow account.

The Hotel New Yorker that opened in 1930 reopens as a transient hotel (see religion, 1976). The Ramada Inn chain has acquired and refurbished it.

The city's hotel-room occupancy tax drops in September from 6 percent to 5 percent (it has been as high as 21.25 percent, making it the highest in the country), but hotel bills remain subject to the 8.25 percent city sales tax and a flat fee of $2 per night).

The Vista Hotel reopens November 1 near the World Trade Center (see 1993). Nine floors had been renovated before last year's explosion, and the entire building has been redone to create what will be renamed the Marriott Trade Hotel.

The Common Ground Community completes renovation of the Times Square Hotel into 650 studio apartments, each with a bath and some with kitchenettes, in a once-elegant building that had become a crime- and rodent-infested "hell for the homeless." Rents—generally subsidized by state and federal programs—are between $300 and $500 per month, and social and medical services are available in the building (see 1992; Euclid Hall, 1995). The federal Department of Health and Human Services issues a study showing that 85 percent of those living in supportive housing, people who were formerly mentally ill and homeless, become productive members of the community, but poverty is so persistent in much of the city that for every government-financed S.R.O. unit there are scores of illegal rooms being created in available spaces,

including basements and attics, in the city's more residential areas.

Martini's opens March 17 on Seventh Avenue at 53rd Street. Restauranteur Irving Riese has died; Murray Riese will soon follow him, Murray's son Dennis, 44, now heads the Riese Organization (whose collection of New York eating places includes some franchised Charley O's, Dunkin' Donuts, Houlihan's, Kentucky Fried Chicken, Nathan's, Pizza Hut, and T.G.I. Friday's outlets), and he has hired California-born chef Richard Krause from the Silverado restaurant to head the kitchen staff of a new 200-seat, white-tablecloth, sidewalk dining establishment that Dennis intends to represent a departure from the Riese family tradition of second- or third-rate food and first-rate real estate investment potential.

The Gramercy Tavern opens in early July at 40 East 20th Street, where Union Square Café proprietor Danny Meyer, now 36, has joined forces with Tom Colicchio, chef at Mondrian, to lease the entire ground floor and basement of a building whose neighbors are now tenanted with ad agencies and magazine and book publishers; the restaurant's 140 seats are soon filled both at lunch and dinner.

Chef-restaurateur Gilbert Le Coze dies of a heart attack at his health club July 28 at age 49. His executive chef Eric Ripert, now 29, carries on the quality of Le Bernardin (see 1986).

Lutèce's chef-owner André Soltner, now 62, sells a majority interest in his 33-year-old restaurant October 11 to Ark, a company that owns or manages 30 restaurants, most of them in the Northeast, none of any gastronomic distinction. Eberhard Mueller, a chef at Le Bernardin, comes in as chef of Lutèce, and while Soltner and his staff of 42 remain, at least for the time being, longtime patrons fret that they may no longer count on enjoying their favorite Alsatian dishes.

1995 The United Nations celebrates its 50th anniversary at New York October 24 with a gathering of more than 140 heads of state (the largest such gathering in world history). While most people recognize the value of the UN in many areas some groups foment fears that U.S. sovereignty may in the future be subordinated to that of a "world government."

 Mayor Giuliani launches a "workfare" program, assigning welfare recipients to menial jobs in city offices, hospital wards, and parks. In the next 3 years some 200,000 people will go through what will become the nation's largest such program. No other city will move large numbers of single mothers into workfare; such mothers find it difficult if not impossible to obtain safe child care. New York's welfare rolls will shrink by 31 percent—from 1.16 million to 797,000 by March 1998 (partly because workfare will force out recipients who worked secretly while getting public assistance), but workfare participants will receive few if any marketable skills and little or no help in finding permanant work (*see* federal law, 1996).

Civil rights lawyer William Kunstler dies of cardiac arrest at New York September 4 at age 76.

The death of 6-year-old Elisa Izquierdo shocks New Yorkers into demanding reforms in the city's Child Welfare Administration, whose $1.2 billion budget has been cut by city, state, and federal legislators. The CWA first heard about the child having been abused in February 1989; school officials alerted case workers in September that the little girl's body was covered with bruises, but the CWA failed to act promptly and her body is found on the Lower East Side November 22. An autopsy shows that she has been sexually abused and suffered a brain hemorrhage. Her mother, Awilda Lopez, 29, is found in a drunken stupor; she was a crack addict when the child was born but had been reported free of drugs. Her other five children are taken from her and she is charged with second-degree murder. Mourners at Elisa's funeral are told by the Rev. Gianni Agostinelli that "Elisa was not killed only by the hand of a sick individual, but by the impotence of silence of many, by the neglect of child welfare institutions and the moral mediocrity that has intoxicated our neighborhoods." Elisa is buried at Cypress Hills Cemetery, Queens, and *Time* magazine pictures her on the cover of its December 11 issue, calling hers "a shameful death" that "symbolizes America's failure to protect its children."

$ New York homeowners own 32.5 percent of the city's property but pay only 11.5 percent of its property taxes (co-op and condominium apartment owners pay far more). Of the more than $18 billion raised in taxes, 43 percent is derived from property taxes, 19 percent from income taxes that range from 2.51 percent to 4.6 percent, 13 percent from sales taxes, 6 percent from corporate taxes, 19 percent from all other taxes.

Grace & Co. chairman J. Peter Grace, Jr., dies of cancer at New York April 19 at age 81.

PaineWebber acquires the balance of the 140-year-old Kidder, Peabody investment banking house (*see* 1993; UBS, 2000).

Wall Street's Dow Jones Industrial Average closes above 4000 February 23, up from 2000 in early 1987 and 3000 in mid-April 1991, as a slowdown in the U.S. economy suggests that the Federal Reserve Board may stop raising interest rates, but while the U.S. unemployment rate in September is only 5.7 percent, paychecks have barely managed to keep up with inflation.

Chase Manhattan and Chemical banks announce a $10 billion merger August 28, creating the largest U.S. bank and the world's fourth largest (*see* Manufacturers Hanover, 1992). The new entity retains the name Chase (although it is actually a takeover of Chase by Chemical); the merger follows five other mergers by major U.S. banks earlier in the year. A study by a major accounting firm has predicted that within 10 years half the nation's 50,000 bank branches will have closed, eliminating 450,000 of the nation's 2.8 million banking jobs (*see* J. P. Morgan Chase, 2000).

Wall Street's Dow Jones Industrial Average tops 5000 November 21 (and closes December 29 at 5117.12—up 33.5 percent from its December 31, 1994, closing) as low inflation combines with high corporate profits to give investors confidence.

$ Federated Department Stores merges with Macy's and folds Abraham & Straus into the latter (*see* 1994). The A&S Plaza on Greeley Square, formerly Gimbels, becomes the Manhattan Mall, but sales will be disappointing.

Upper Madison Avenue continues to sprout new retail stores and boutiques. The 30-year-old Chicago-based Crate & Barrel opens a huge New York branch in March at 650 Madison, northwest corner 59th Street; designer Calvin Klein opens a minimalist store in September at 654 Madison in the former Morgan Guaranty Trust building at the corner of 60th Street (*see* 1996; The Limited, 1985; Lauren, 1986; Barney's, 1993).

Amtrak discontinues the *Broadway Limited* September 10 to cut costs, ending more than 93 years of daily rail service between New York and Chicago. Passengers must now change trains at Pittsburgh and lay over there for nearly 2 hours.

New York City transit fares rise to $1.50 November 12, up from $1.25, and the Transit Authority issues a small "five borough" token with a hole punched in its center. The fare has increased 30-fold since 1947, while bridge and tunnel tolls have risen only four-fold; if motorists had to pay 30 times as much as they did in 1947 to cross into Manhattan via the George Washington or Triborough bridge or the

Holland or Lincoln tunnel, the toll would be about $15 each way, and the discrepancy suggests that straphangers are subsidizing automobile owners. Some 3.4 million men and women commute to and from the city's central business district each weekday; two-thirds of them use the tunnels, mostly subway tunnels.

∞ Pope John Paul II arrives at Newark Airport October 4, visits the UN October 5, celebrates Mass and delivers a homily at Giants Stadium in the New Jersey Meadowlands, celebrates Mass and delivers a homily at Aqueduct Race Track October 6, attracts 350,000 Roman Catholics (plus other curious observers) to Central Park's Great Lawn October 7 for a third Papal Mass, meets with John Cardinal O'Connor at St. Patrick's Cathedral, recites the Rosary at St. Patrick's, blesses the offices of the Holy See Mission to the United Nations, meets with regional bishops at the cardinal's residence, and meets there also with Jewish leaders.

Tacoma, Wash., school administrator Rudy Crew, 45, is selected as city schools chancellor October 16, replacing Raymond Cortines, now 51, in the Board of Education Building at 110 Livingston Street, Brooklyn. Mayor Giuliani has had no power to dismiss Cortines, with whom he has feuded, but has humiliated him in public and hounded him out of office.

The *New York Daily News* leaves its 65-year-old building at 220 East 42nd Street May 4 and moves to cheaper offices at 450 West 33rd Street (*see* 1993; 1999).

George magazine begins publication at New York with a cover photograph of model Cindy Crawford dressed as George Washington. Developed by John F. Kennedy, Jr., 35, and Michael J. Berman, 38, the consumer-oriented publication about politics has financial backing from Hachette Filipacchi Magazines and projects a circulation of about 250,000, but within 18 months will have a rate base of 400,000 (versus 101,000 for the *New Republic*, 196,000 for the *National Review*).

Syndicated newspaper columnist Victor Riesel dies of a heart attack at his New York apartment January 4 at age 81; *New Yorker* cartoonist George Price at an Englewood, N.J., hospital January 12 at age 93; journalist-author George Seldes at a Windsor, Vt., hospital July 2 at age 104; former *New York Times* Washington correspondent James B. "Scotty" Reston, Jr. of cancer at his Washington, D.C., home December 6 at age 86. He retired in 1989 after 50 years at the *Times*.

Westinghouse Electric Co. makes a $5.4 billion offer for CBS. Originally a producer of air brakes for trains, Westinghouse has been involved in radio since 1920 and in television since 1923; it made the first color TV broadcast in 1939 from a CBS transmitter atop the Chrysler Building, and it will expand that part of its business in the next 2 years (*see* 1997).

Verlagsgruppe Georg von Holtzbrinck acquires the 43-year-old St. Martin's Press, formerly the U.S. branch of London-based Macmillan & Co. (*see* FS&G, 1994). Founder's son Dieter von Holtzbrinck has taken over *Scientific American* magazine and two other New York book publishers as part of a drive to develop a worldwide media empire.

The New York Public Library begins in November to offer Internet services in all of its 87 libraries. The Internet is soon being used for 150,000 searches per month.

Nonfiction: *The Encyclopedia of New York City* by Memphis-born Columbia University history professor Kenneth C. Jackson, 56 (editor); *New York 1960* by Robert A. M. Stern, Thomas Mellins, and David Fishman; *Shaping the City: New York and the Municipal Art Society* by Gregory F. Gilmartin; *Terrible Honesty: Mongrel Manhattan in the 1920s* by Morristown, N.J.-born Columbia University English professor Ann Douglas, 53; *Remarkable, Unspeakable New York: A Literary History* by University of Massachusetts, Boston, professor Shaun O'Connell, whose title is a quote from Henry James; *Guilty: The Collapse of Criminal Justice* by veteran New York State Supreme Court Justice Harold Rothwax, 65, who began as a criminal-defense attorney for the poor but has become increasingly reactionary; *New York: The Metropolis of the American Dream* by Martin Mayer (who has moved to Washington, D.C.) and Christopher Ouellette, 33; *Manhattan When I Was Young* by *New York Times* editorial board writer Mary Cantwell, 64, who has lived for decades in Greenwich Village: "I have never lived anyplace else. I do not want to. That is not because of what the Village is but because of what I have made it, and what I have made of it depends on who I am at the time. The Village is amorphous; I can shape it into any place. The rest of Manhattan is rectilinear, its grid an order, a single definition, that I dislike. But the Village is a collection of cowpaths and landfill and subterranean rivers, visible, if you know about them, because they are traced by streets paved to mask them. If some areas have a certain architectural unity, it is not because an architect had a grand scheme but because row houses with common walls were put up hastily for people fleeing a yellow fever epidemic downtown;" *The Empire State Building: The Making of a Landmark* by John Tauranac; *Historic Manhattan Apartment Houses* by Andrew Alpern.

Fiction: *The Ring of Brightest Angels around Heaven* (novella and stories) by New York-born editor-novelist Hiram F. "Rick" Moody III, 34, is about AIDS, drugs, despair, rock music, and artistic ambitions in the bohemian East Village; *Sabbath's Theater* by Philip Roth; *Mr. Ives' Christmas* by Oscar Hijuelos; *From Time to Time* by Jack Finney.

 Art dealer Pat Hearn opens a new gallery in February in West 22nd Street (*see* 1983). Now 40, she is joined the same evening by two other galleries that open in the block—the Matthew Mark Gallery and the Morris-Healy Gallery—to begin a flowering that will see nearly 150 new galleries in the Chelsea area.

 Theater: *Love! Valour! Compassion!* by Terrence McNally 2/14 at the Walter Kerr Theater (after a run at the Manhattan Theater Club), with comedian Nathan Lane, Stephen Bogardus, Salisbury, Md.-born actor John Glover, 50, New Rochelle-born actor Anthony Heald, 50, in another play about the AIDS epidemic, 248 perfs.; *Defending the Caveman* by San Jose, Calif.-born comedian Rob Becker, 38, 3/26 at the Helen Hayes Theater, with Becker in what began as a stand-up act at San Francisco's Improv, 674 perfs.; *The Food Chain* by New York playwright Nicky Silver, 35, 8/24 at the Westside Theater Upstairs, with Hope Davis, Jersey City-born actress Phyllis Newman, 60, Rudolf Martin, Patrick Fabian, and Tom McGowan; *Moon Over Buffalo* by Ken Ludwig 10/1 at the Martin Beck Theater, with Carol Burnett, Jersey City-born actor Philip Bosco, 65, 309 perfs.; *Mrs. Klein* by Cape Town-born London playwright Nicholas Wright 10/24 at the off-Broadway Lucille Lortel Theater, with Uta Hagen, now 76, as psychoanalyst Melanie Klein; *Riff Raff* by actor-playwright Laurence Fishburne, now 32, 11/1 at the Circle-in-the-Square Downtown; *Master Class* by Terrence McNally 11/5 at the Golden Theater, with Zoë Caldwell as the late diva Maria Callas, 598 perfs.

Broadway legend George Abbott dies at his Miami Beach home January 31 at age 107; playwright Sidney Kingsley of a stroke at his Oakland, N.J., home March 20 at age 88; playwright John Patrick is found dead at his Delray Beach, Fla., nursing home November 7 at age 90, apparently a suicide; playwright Charles Gordone dies of cancer at his College Station, Texas, home November 17 at age 70.

Television: *NewsRadio* 3/21 on NBC with David Foley, Phil Hartman (to 1999); *Caroline in the City* 9/21 on NBC with Lea Thompson, Eric Lutes, Malcolm Gets, Amy Pietz (to 4/26/99); *The City* 11/13 on ABC with Amelia Heinie (to 3/1997).

Films: Spike Lee's *Clockers* with Harvey Keitel, John Turturro; John McTiernan's *Die Hard with a Vengeance* with Bruce Willis, Jeremy Irons; Jean Bach's documentary *A Great Day in Harlem* about the jazz musicians photographed by Art Kane for *Esquire* magazine in August 1958; James Gray's *Little Odessa* with Tim Roth, Edward Furlong, Maximilian Schell, Vanessa Redgrave; Woody Allen's *Mighty Aphrodite* with F. Murray Abraham, Allen, Claire Bloom, Helena Bonham-Carter; Daisy von Scherler Mayer's *Party Girl* with Parker Posey, Sasha von Scherler; Wayne Wang's *Smoke* with William Hurt, Harvey Keitel, Stockard Channing; Douglas Keeve's documentary *Unzipped* about New York fashion designer Issac Mizrahi; Wes Craven's *Vampire in Brooklyn* with Eddie Murphy, Angela Bassett.

 Broadway musicals: *Smokey Joe's Cafe* (revue) 3/2 at the Virginia Theater, with a nine-member cast, music and lyrics by Jerry Leiber and Mike Stoller, now both 61, 2,037 perfs.; *Victor/Victoria* 11/17 at the Marquis Theater, with Julie Andrews, now 60, Tony Roberts, 734 perfs.

Onetime musical-comedy star David Wayne dies at Santa Monica, Calif., February 9 at age 81; Vivian Blaine of congestive heart failure at Beth Israel Medical Center North December 9 at age 74.

The Empire State Building displays two rows of blue lights December 12 to celebrate the 80th birthday of Frank Sinatra ("Ol' Blue Eyes"), who is famous for singing, "If I can make it here I can make it anywhere,/ It's up to you, New York, New York."

New York-born basketball legend Nat Holman dies in a city nursing home February 12 at age 98. He coached the CCNY team for 40 years after retiring in 1927 from the Boston Celtics; sports commentator Howard Cosell dies of a coronary embolism at New York April 23 at age 77.

Baseball resumes major-league play April 26 following a truce between team owners and players that has ended a 234-day player strike, but the season is abbreviated from 162 games to 144, making it impossible for anyone to set a record, and outstanding issues remain unresolved. Ballpark attendance drops sharply, and TV viewer ratings slip.

Pete Sampras wins in men's singles at Flushing Meadow, Steffi Graf in women's (Graf wins her third successive grand slam event).

The Reebok Sports Club/NY opens at the northwest corner of Columbus Avenue and 67th Street with a 140,000-square-foot gym. The city's most expensive health club, it has an initiation fee of $3,000 that includes 1 year's dues.

The City Council enacts a zoning law sponsored by Walter L. McCaffrey of Woodside, Queens, banning topless bars and other such "supper clubs" from residential neighborhoods (see Scores, 1993). The Paradise Club at the corner of Fifth Avenue and 33rd Street is unaffected, as is Flashdancers at Broadway and 52nd Street, but Dolls in the financial district, the VIP Club in the Flatiron District, Ten's World Class Cabaret at the corner of Madison Avenue and 21st Street are among the places that will be closed down when the Giuliani administration begins enforcing the law in 1998.

New Yorkers Against Gun Violence files suit in January against the handgun industry. Headed by Barbara Hohlt, 51, and headquartered in a small downtown Manhattan office, the volunteer gun-control group has acted in response to the accidental shooting in 1993 of Brooklyn teenager Njuzi Ray Hamilton, whose mother, Freddie, 51, is a social-services administrator and says the bullet that killed her son was intended for somebody else (see 1999).

Federal authorities indict 29 leaders of the Latin Kings gang July 6 on charges of attempted murder, murder, racketeering, cocaine and heroin trafficking, and other crimes. The organization has chapters in five states with an estimated 3,000 members in the New York area. The murder charges stem from street shootings of bystanders in shootouts with rival gangs.

An indictment unsealed in June names 17 executives from 23 carting companies and four trade associations as conspirators in a decades-old scheme to control private garbage-hauling in the metropolitan area (see 1993). The Giuliani administration creates the Trade Waste Commission to regulate private carting, allegedly controlled by the Mafia, and Browning-Ferris is awarded the 55 Water Street waste-hauling contract at $120,000 per year—one-tenth of what V. Ponte & Sons charged (see 1997).

The Port of New York Authority appoints Peekskill construction industry entrepreneur Robert Eugene Boyle, 58, chief executive of the troubled Jacob K. Javits Convention Center. "I can't wait to prove the skeptics wrong," Boyle tells the press, and he will make good on his promise to eliminate the mismanagement, labor problems, and mob corruption that have plagued the state-run facility, lowering costs for exhibitors (who need no longer slip $50 bills to workers in order to have them unload trucks) and generally improving service.

Transit police begin arresting subway turnstile-jumpers; 5 percent of those caught are found to be carrying weapons, and the police claim that stopping low-level crime helps reduce the rate of more serious crime.

New York State's capital-punishment law goes into effect in September, with lethal injection to be used rather than the electric chair; legal experts predict that 15 to 20 percent of murder cases each year will be "death-eligible," but in practice only 5 percent will be found to satisfy the law's requirements (the law requires proof, for example, that the defendant intended to kill his victim), the state's prosecutors will seek the death penalty in less than 1 percent of cases, and defendants will avoid execution by pleading guilty, making their maximum sentence life imprisonment without parole (see 1998).

The body of a Central Park jogger is found September 17 and later proves to be that of Brazilian shoe-store employee Maria Isabel Pinto Monteiro Alves, 44. Police are stymied, but the city's crime rate is markedly lower than in recent years.

Freddy's clothing store in 125th Street is torched and shot up December 8 in a racial incident that leaves eight dead, most of them young Hispanic and black women, and four wounded. Street vendor Roland J. Smith, Jr. is among the dead; he reportedly walked into the shop with a handgun, a container of flammable liquid, and a book of matches. "It's on now. All blacks out," he reportedly shouted, whereupon he doused piles of shirts and jeans, fired every round in his gun, and set the clothing ablaze.

Real estate developer Seymour B. Durst suffers a stroke May 12 and dies at New York Hospital May 19 at age 81 without having regained consciousness (see 1927; Nonfiction, 1984; National Debt Clock, 1989). In the 1980s he went to court in an effort to block the state Urban Development Corporation from taking any land for the Times Square Redevelopment Project, and he has decried the decline in private housing development in the city since 1975, blaming "irrational" zoning regulations that set aside so much land for manufacturing when there was little likelihood of it ever being used for that purpose.

The 34-story Mutual of America Building is completed at 320 Park Avenue to designs by Swanke Hayden Connell.

The Rockefeller Group Inc. partnership that holds title to Rockefeller Center and is owned 80 percent by Japan's Mitsubishi Estate Co. files for bankruptcy protection May 11, saying it will halt mortgage payments to the real estate investment trust (REIT) Rockefeller Properties Inc. A consortium headed by Polish-born Chicago investor Samuel Zell, 54, submits a bid August 16 (the group includes Walt Disney Co. and General Electric), Tishman Speyer Properties submits a bid August 17, both want to share ownership with Rockefeller Properties, Mitsubishi drops its efforts to retain title to the center September 11, a bidding war ensues for the 22-acre site and its complex of buildings, Zell raises his group's bid October 27, offering $1.16 billion for the center's mortgages, the board of Rockefeller Properties rejects the offer October 30, and it announces November 7 that it has agreed to accept a bid worth nearly $1.2 billion from a group headed by Goldman, Sachs & Co. that has agreed to pay $306.1 million in cash and assume debts of between $830 million and $900 million. Goldman's group includes David Rockefeller, Tishman Speyer Properties president Jerry Speyer, the investing branch of Italy's Agnelli Group, and a holding company controlled by Greek shipping magnate Stavros Niarchos (see Radio City, 1997; Zell, 2000).

The six-story, 37-room town house of the late Benjamin Sonnenberg at Gramercy Park South and Irving Place is sold in late June to fashion designer Richard Tyler and his wife, Lisa Trafficante.

The Roosevelt Hotel that opened in 1924 closes for renovation in July. Now owned by PIA Investments, a division of Pakistan International Airline, the 1,070-room structure will undergo a $55 million reconstruction and reopen as the Radisson-Roosevelt.

The Euclid Hotel on the west side of Broadway at 86th Street reopens in the fall as a supportive single-room occupancy housing structure with programs that help residents turn their lives around (see 1994). The city will have 54,894 single-occupancy units by next year, up from 45,000 in 1985, but the Giuliani administration comes under attack from the Coalition for the Homeless and other groups for not doing enough to create permanent housing for the poor.

The red-tailed hawks sighted in Central Park 3 years ago produce chicks on a sheltered ledge above a 12th-story window on a Fifth Avenue apartment house at 74th Street. Passers-by and tourists watch and marvel as the birds catch prey in the park and teach their young how to fly and hunt.

Walt Disney Productions uses Central Park's Great Lawn for the premiere of its film *Pocahantas* June 10. The Great Lawn's grassy cover has long since been worn away by ballplayers and concertgoers, the Disney event makes matters worse, and the Disney organization pledges a multi-million-dollar contribution to restore the area (see Sheep Meadow, 1981). The Central Park Conservancy and the city make plans in October for a complete resodding of the 55-acre lawn (see 1996).

An uptown Fairway Market opens in December at the corner of 133rd Street and 12th Avenue, where owners of the Fairway at 74th and Broadway have joined forces with Joseph Fedele to launch a warehouse-sized supermarket with parking space (see 1975). Fedele owns 40 percent of the venture and will soon have a falling out with Harold Seybert, David Sneddon, and Harold Glickberg, who each own 20 percent and divide their time between the two locations.

Nobu restaurant opens at 105 Hudson Street. Actor Robert De Niro, restaurateur Drew Nierporent of Tribeca Grill fame, and Japanese sushi chef Nobuyuki Matsuhisa, 47, have formed a partnership with another investor to create the place, whose cuisine combines South American specialties such as *ceviche* with Nobu's new-style Japanese dishes.

No-smoking rules take effect April 10 in New York restaurants seating 35 or more; most restaurateurs and patrons obey the new city ordinance that allows smoking only in some separate bar areas.

The City Council enacts a law allowing only one food vendor permit "per individual, corporation, partnership, or other business entity" (see retailers, 1994). Permits up to now have been monopolized by a few powerful individuals, who have rented them—illegally—at outrageous rates to distributors lacking permits. Previous holders of multiple permits work behind the scenes to have the law revised, enabling each of them to regain as many as 180 of the 3,000 available permits.

Planet Hollywood's Official All Star Cafe opens in December at Broadway and 45th Street with a sports theme.

1996 Police Commissioner William S. Bratton resigns under pressure in April amidst what critics call a personal tiff with Mayor Giuliani, who has allegedly taken umbrage at the praise given to the "commish" and fears that Bratton will become a political rival (*see* 1993). Hizzoner appoints Howard Safir, 54, to the position, and during Safir's 4 years in office the city's crime rate will decline, albeit in the face of allegations about racial profiling and civil-rights abuse.

President Clinton wins reelection, defeating former Senate Majority Leader Robert Joseph "Bob" Dole, 73, of Kansas. Now 50, Clinton wins nearly 80 percent of the New York City vote; Richmond County (Staten Island) gives the Democrat a majority for the first time since its voters rejected Barry Goldwater's bid in 1964.

Mexican-born New York garment worker Aurora Blancas, 28, loses her job in July after asking for a wage increase and bringing the attention of her union to conditions at New Young Fashions, the 14th-floor Eighth Avenue sweatshop that has employed her. Her South Korean-born employer Kim Young Han has his mostly female Hispanic employees toil for up to 60 hours per week at sewing machines and presses in a poorly ventilated room with no fire exits, pays them wages below the $4.25-per-hour minimum (paying in cash to avoid taxes), arbitrarily cuts workers' pay or delays paying when he is short of cash, fines workers $30 in addition to docking them their pay if they miss a day's work for any reason, has dismissed at least one new employee for yawning on the job, and generally abuses workers. Koreans own up to 40 percent of the roughly 4,000 contract and sub-contract sewing shops in the city, Chinese immigrants own most of the rest, both hire illegal aliens who are afraid to complain lest they be deported, and their shops produce garments that are ultimately sold at stores such as J. C. Penney, Sears, and Wal-Mart. Union and U.S. Department of Labor officials say that labor costs typically account for only 3 percent of the retail price of garments made in domestic sweatshops, and scarcely one-half of 1 percent of clothing made in Asian and Central American sweatshops (*see* 1997).

Amnesty International issues a report on the New York Police Department that alleges a pattern of "ill treatment of suspects, deaths in custody, and unjustified shootings by officers" (*see* Mollen Commission report, 1994). Most of the abuses occur in black, Hispanic, and Asian neighborhoods, according to the report (*see* 1997). Police officer Francis X. Livoti is acquitted in October on charges of negligent homicide in connection with the choking of Anthony Baez in December 1994, but he will be dismissed from the force in February of next year, found guilty 8 months later of having slapped and choked a teenager while on patrol in 1993, and given a prison sentence of 7½ years (*see* 1998).

The state court of appeals at Albany rules November 19 that people can seek money damages in suing the state for violating their rights under the state constitution. Lower courts have ruled for years that the state government is immune from civil damage suits accusing state agencies of breaching constitutional protections.

Mayor Giuliani and the City Council reach an agreement June 26 on an anti-begging law designed to crack down on "aggressive" panhandlers, including so-called "squeegee men" (who often ignore traffic tickets and police summonses) and others who are insistent and menacing. The Giuliani administration announces in August that it will no longer automatically offer shelter to homeless New Yorkers who have doubled up with friends and relatives, but State Supreme Court Justice Helen E. Freedman rules November 27 that the Emergency Assistance Unit in the Bronx cannot deny people places in its shelter system without conducting "adequate investigation."

AT&T Chairman Robert E. Allen, 61, announces in January that his company will eliminate up to 50,000 of its 300,000 jobs in the next 3 years as it implements a "force management program" aimed at reducing an "imbalance of forces or skills" (*see* breakup plan, 1995). Corporate downsizing continues at many other large companies as they try to maximize profits, and while some economists insist that public perception inflates the size of layoffs, especially among white-collar workers, when layoffs as a percentage of employment (measured by initial claims for unemployment insurance) are actually near a 50-year low, they concede that anxiety about job security has increased, that women have replaced older men in many jobs, and that living standards have shown painfully slow growth.

A group of 50 local corporations and business executives announce June 28 that they have raised $50 million to start the New York City Investment Fund, a privately run economic development authority designed not for profit but solely to create jobs and promote economic development. Financier Henry R. Kravis heads the group, hoping to attract another 50 contributors of $1 million each.

President Clinton signs legislation August 20 raising the minimum wage from $4.25 to $4.75 beginning October 1 and—11 months thereafter—to $5.15.

A welfare reform act signed into law August 22 ends the federal AFDC (Aid to Families with Dependent

Children) provisions of the 1935 Social Security Act, leaves it up to the states to provide for needy families, limits the amount of time that anyone can receive welfare checks without working, and bans most forms of public assistance and social services for legal immigrants who have not become citizens (*see* New York's "workfare," 1995). President Clinton campaigned in 1992 with a promise to "end welfare as we know it," he vetoed a welfare bill in January, saying it would undermine efforts to bring people out of poverty, the new Personal Responsibility and Work Opportunity Reconciliation Act is less harsh, but critics warn that the law will still put 1 million children into poverty. New York State has 1.4 million people dependent for survival on the federal welfare program; the new law's work requirements and aid cutoffs pose severe challenges in an environment of shrinking job opportunities for unskilled workers. Gov. George Pataki faces a state budget deficit of $3 billion produced in large part by tax cuts, he proposes to reduce monthly welfare payments from $577 to $317 by 2002—a cut that amounts to 45 percent when inflation is factored in, and he prepares drastic changes in the state's Home Relief program for childless adults. The state instituted its own welfare program in 1993 and has substantially reduced its public-assistance rolls, although far more people in the city remain on welfare than in 1990 (*see* 1998).

New York City's unemployment rate reaches 9.9 percent—the highest of the 20 largest U.S. urban centers. The city creates 44,500 jobs, up from 27,000 in 1995 and its best showing since the 1980s, as it benefits from the boom in Wall Street, which has generated huge salaries and bonuses, but the gross city product (based on total jobs and income) rises only 1.9 percent for the year, as compared with a national growth rate of 2.5 percent. The financial sector creates only 12,500 jobs despite the boom in stock prices, and by year's end Wall Street is actually cutting jobs. The city has 2.8 million private-sector jobs, down from 3.2 million in 1969, and critics blame it on the city's high taxes. The Giuliani administration has eliminated commercial rent taxes except in Manhattan south of 96th Street, where the tax rate has been cut from 6 percent to 4.5 percent, and has made minor reductions in some other taxes, but net taxes on individuals and business firms have actually increased.

Securities firm founder B. Gerald Cantor dies of cancer at Los Angeles July 3 at age 79, having made Cantor Fitzgerald the world's largest broker of U.S. government securities, Eurobonds, and sovereign debt.

Wall Street's Dow Jones Industrial Average closes at 6010 October 14, crossing the 6000 mark less than 11 months after passing 5000. Aides to Mayor Giuliani say November 13 that rising profits in Wall Street means the city will take in $450 million more in taxes this fiscal year than was projected. The Dow falls more than 100 points December 31 on news of a strong economy but ends the year at 6448.75, up 26 percent since the end of 1995. Wall Street firms employ 12,000 fewer people than in 1987 but have record pretax profits totaling $11.3 billion, and the city taxes on those profits fuel many social programs. Mid-level earnings for brokers, analysts, and investment bankers range from $150,000 to $300,000 per year, while managers pull down $600,000 or more, sometimes much more (top traders take home millions). Just 151,000 people pay enough in taxes to provide 14 percent of the city's revenues.

Barney's files for Chapter 11 bankruptcy protection from creditors in January (*see* 1993); it will close its store on Seventh Avenue at 17th Street late next year after 74 years at the location. Loehmann's opens a Manhattan store in October on Seventh Avenue between 16th and 17th streets in a building previously used exclusively by Barney's, whose entrance is moved to the side street (*see* 1920).

The Virgin Megastore opens on Times Square at the corner of Broadway and 45th Street. British record producer and airline mogul Richard Branson, 45, has opened 122 Virgin stores in 13 countries.

NikeTown opens in East 57th Street to sell sneakers and other athletic equipment, taking the space just east of Tiffany & Co. occupied earlier by Bonwit Teller.

Emporio Armani opens in September at 601 Madison Avenue, Valentino in September at 747 Madison, and Giorgio Armani in September at 760 Madison as the avenue continues its growth as an upscale retail shopping thoroughfare (Italian-made Giorgio Armani suits can cost more than $2,000 each). More than 25 new shops open on the avenue between 57th and 72nd streets, despite the fact that ground-floor space rents for $325 to $400 per square foot below 72nd Street and $175 between 72nd and 86th streets (some retailers pay as much as $2 million more to buy out leases).

Mayor Giuliani comes under fire for favoring developers who want to build large superstores that will compete with smaller merchants. The mayor announced support 2 years ago for zoning-law changes that would permit "big box" warehouse-style megastores in manufacturing areas, but leaders in some communities have fought to keep big Home Depot, Pathmark, and Wal-Mart stores out of their neighborhoods, and the mayor's proposal dies in the City Council in early December.

The Atlantic Center opens in November on a long-vacant site at the intersection of Atlantic and Flatbush avenues in downtown Brooklyn; a 380,000-square-foot shopping mall, it puts pressure on the 26-year-old Kings Plaza Shopping Center. Within a year it will have 263 stores on three floors, employing about 1,500, many if not most of them in part-time, minimum-wage, non-union jobs with no benefits, but while Pathmark, Old Navy, Office Max, and other retailers will do well at the new mall, the 44,000-square-foot Sports Authority store will close early in 1999 and the Norwalk, Conn.-based Caldor discount chain will close its 130,000-square-foot store in May 1999.

The city's Economic Development Corp. announces a deal to provide two shipping companies with incentives to keep them from leaving the Brooklyn waterfront for New Jersey (see Red Hook Marine Terminal, 1981).

A new Taxi and Limousine Commission order takes effect in March requiring that all taxis be air conditioned and equipped to provide passengers with receipts (owners will in many cases install makeshift air conditioners that pretend to cool interiors but are actually ineffectual); another order that takes effect in November after months of court battles prohibits any vehicle more than 5 years old from being used as a taxicab (owners complain that the Fords and Chevrolets they buy now cost upwards of $20,000, an amount difficult to amortize in just 5 years) (see 1997).

Injuries from taxicab accidents soar by 59 percent to 19,958, up from 12,536 in 1990 (injuries from accidents that do *not* involve taxis have dropped in that period from 102,182 to 97,893); 29 people are killed in taxi accidents, down from a high of 46 in 1990 but up from 27 in 1992.

The St. Luke's-Roosevelt Hospital Center and Beth Israel Medical Center announce an agreement December 10 to create a single parent corporation with an integrated system that will have 2,732 beds (including some in Westchester and Rockland counties), more than 3,200 physicians and dentists, a workforce of more than 14,000, and an annual operating budget of $1.35 billion.

A Board of Education report completed in February shows that one in five city schools is in such poor physical condition as to pose a hazard for students and teachers. Citing 237 schools where bricks or concrete are falling from weak exterior walls, windows falling from rotten moldings, and the like, it suggests that correcting the problems will cost as much as $500 million.

Mayor Giuliani presents a plan in November to spend $70 million on textbooks for the public schools, many of them struggling as they have for years with worn-out and outdated books. Enrollment in the city's public schools has increased in the past 10 years from 850,000 to 1.06 million, and the system has 134,875 students who have entered the United States in the past 3 years; high schools are filled to nearly 140 percent of capacity, and schools are forced to hold classes in spaces carved out of auditoriums, in locker rooms, and wherever else possible.

The most exhaustive accounting in the history of the city's school system is released in mid-November: it shows that elementary and middle schools receive a higher percentage of education dollars than do public high schools that receive on average $6,831 per student but can spread their costs over more students (elementary schools average $7,229 per pupil, junior high schools $7,591).

The state legislature at Albany votes in a special session December 17 to overhaul New York City's public school system, giving Schools Chancellor Rudy Crew more control over hiring and increasing his authority at the expense of the city's 32 community school boards; some have been so plagued with corruption, incompetence, patronage, and scandal in the past 26 years that schools have not been able to teach students to read or calculate effectively (see 1969). One provision of the new 24-page law gives borough presidents power to create new borough-level deputies in the school administration. Critics of the return to centralized control say that centralized bureaucrats will be insensitive to the special ethnic, social, and political nuances of particular neighborhoods (see DeGrasse, 2001).

Bloomberg Television News begins transmitting on a 24-hour basis October 10, using a city-run cable channel over the objections of Time Warner, whose cable subscribers receive the Bloomberg station over Channel 71. Cablevision Systems blocks the Bloomberg channel at about 10:55 P.M.—5 minutes after it goes on the air, and Bloomberg will later be moved to Channel 31 as Channel 71 reverts to use for horse race coverage and other events.

The New York Public Library opens a Science, Business and Industry Library May 2 in part of the old B. Altman department store building on Fifth Avenue between 34th and 35th streets.

Nonfiction: *The Rain on Macy's Parade: How Greed, Ambition and Folly Ruined America's Greatest Store* by *Wall Street Journal* reporter Jeffrey A. Trachtenberg; *Manhattan Gateway: New York's Pennsylvania Station* by William D. Middleton, now 68; *Great American Railroad Stations* by U.S. author Janet Potter (*née* Goldstein); *Infamous Manhattan: A Colorful Walking History of New York's Most Notorious Crime Sites* by Berlin author Andrew Roth; *Angela's Ashes* by Brooklyn-born Stuyvesant High School English teacher Frank McCourt, 66; *New York Jews and the Great Depression* by University of Pennsylvania historian Beth W. Wenger; *The Architecture of Literacy: The Carnegie Libraries of New York City* by architectural preservation consultant Mary B. Dierickx; *Rise of the New York Skyscraper, 1865–1913* by Sarah Bradford Landau, 61, and Carl W. Condit.

Former *New York Times* book critic Orville Prescott dies at New Canaan, Conn., April 28 at age 89; author Joseph Mitchell at New York May 24 at age 87; former *Wall Street Journal* editorial writer-author Vermont Royster at Raleigh, N.C., July 22 at age 82; Diana Trilling at New York October 23 at age 91.

Fiction: *Manhattan Nocturne* by New York-born novelist Colin Harrison, 35; *New York, New York* (stories) by New York writer Layle Silbert; *Emerald City and Other Stories* by Chicago-born novelist Jennifer Egan, 34, who compares New York in her title story to the glittering city of Oz in the L. Frank Baum story.

The Historical Landmarks Preservation Center places a plaque to honor the late Jack Kerouac October 23 at 133-01 Cross Bay Boulevard in Ozone Park, Queens (*see* Fiction, 1957). Kerouac died in Florida of alcoholism-related disease in 1969 at age 47.

The Ann Arbor, Mich.-based Borders Books and Music chain opens a superstore October 25 in the Ritz Tower at 461 Park Avenue with 42,600 square feet on four levels, larger than the three-level Borders shop at the World Trade Center.

Sculpture: *Eleanor Roosevelt* by sculptor Penelope Jencks, whose eight-foot-high bronze has been commissioned by the Eleanor Roosevelt Monument Fund and is installed in Riverside Park at 72nd Street.

Graphic designer Paul Rand dies of cancer at his Norwalk, Conn., home November 26 at age 82 as an exhibition of his work continues at Cooper Union.

Theater: *Seven Guitars* by August Wilson 3/28 at the Walter Kerr Theater, with Harlem-born actor Keith David, 41, South Carolina-born actress Viola Davis, 19, 188 perfs.

Drama critic-playwright Walter Kerr dies at Dobbs Ferry October 9 at age 83.

Films: Donald Petrie's *The Associate* with Whoopi Goldberg (originally Caryn E. Johnson) as the owner of a Brooklyn Heights apartment house whose tenants cannot pay their rents, Tim Daly (Tyne's brother) as a corporate lawyer; Michael Goldenberg's *Bed of Roses* with Christian Slater, Mary Stuart Masterson; Harold Becker's *City Hall* with Al Pacino, John Cusack, Bridget Fonda, Danny Aiello; Chantal Akerman's *A Couch in New York* with Juliette Binoche, William Hurt; John Carpenter's *Daylight* with Sylvester Stallone (several truckloads of toxic waste headed for New Jersey blow up in the "Manhattan" Tunnel); John Walsh's *Ed's Next Move* with Matt Ross, Callie Thorne; Woody Allen's *Everyone Says I Love You* with Allen, Goldie Hawn, Alan Alda, Julia Roberts; Herb Gardner's *I'm Not Rappaport* with Walter Matthau, Ossie Davis; Todd Solonde's *Welcome to the Dollhouse* with Heather Matarazzo, 14, Brendan Sexton, Jr., 16, Doris Kalininia, Matthew Faber. Also: Roland Emmerich's *Independence Day* with Will Smith, Bill Pullman, Jeff Goldblum, 44 (an alien spaceship 15 miles across turns Manhattan into a firestorm); Barbra Streisand's *The Mirror Has Two Faces* with Streisand, Jeff Bridges, Lauren Bacall; Angel Muñiz's *Nueba Yol* with Dominican comedian Luisito Marti as Orodoto Balbuena, the protagonist of a 15-year-old Dominican television comedy series *The Noon Show*, whose schemes to get to New York are forever being frustrated (the film has been shot both in the Dominican Republic, where New York is generally mispronounced "Nueba Yol," and in Manhattan); Michael Hoffman's *One Fine Day* with Michelle Pfeiffer, George Clooney, Robert Klein; Penny Marshall's *The Preacher's Wife* with Denzel Washington, Gregory Hines, singer-actress Whitney Houston; Ron Howard's *Ransom* with Mel Gibson; Stanley Tong's *Rumble in the Bronx* with Hong Kong-born martial-arts expert Jackie Chan; Edward Burns's *She's the One* with Burns, Cameron Diaz, Jennifer Aniston, John Mahoney; Belgrade-born director Goran Paskaljevici's *Someone Else's America* with Tom Conti, Maria Casares; Nicole Holofcener's *Walking and Talking* with Catherine Keener, Liev Schreiber, Todd Field, Kevin Corrigan.

Pioneer film animator Shamus Culhane dies at his Manhattan home February 2 at age 87; director Peter Glenville at a friend's Manhattan home June 3 at age 82; actress Jo Van Fleet at Jamaica Hospital, Queens, June 10 at age 81; Claudette Colbert at her home in the Barbados July 30 at age 92.

A Blockbuster Video store opens in 125th Street in an area that has had no good videotape rental or purchase outlets, and some 1,500 people buy membership cards in the new store's first 2 weeks. Many New Yorkers prefer to see films in the privacy and safety of their own homes rather than at theaters, where rising ticket prices discourage attendance.

Film musical: Woody Allen's *Everyone Says I Love You* with Edward Norton, Drew Barrymore, Goldie Hawn, Alan Alda, Woody Allen.

Broadway musicals: *Bring In 'Da Noise Bring In 'Da Funk: A Tap/Rap Discourse on the Staying Power of the Beat* 4/25 at the Ambassador Theater (after a run at the Public Theater), with tap dancers (Newark-born Savion Glover, 22, Washington, D.C.-born Baakari Wilder, 19, Orange, N.J.-born Dulé Hill, Jimmy Tate, Vincent Bingham), former street musicians Jared Crawford, 20, Raymond King, 21, 1,135 perfs.; *Rent* 4/29 at the Nederlander Theater (after a sold-out run at the 150-seat off-Broadway Theater Workshop) with Anthony Rapp, 24, Adam Pascal, book (based on a tenant-landlord dispute) derived from the 1896 Puccini opera *La Bohème*, rock music and AIDS-oriented lyrics by Jonathan Larson (who has died of an aortic aneurism January 25 at age 35).

Ballet producer Lincoln Kirstein dies at his New York home January 5 at age 88; composer-conductor Morton Gould at an Orlando, Fla., hotel February 21 at age 82.

Popular songs: *Tidal* (album) by New York singer-songwriter Fiona Apple, 18, includes "The First Taste," "Sullen Girl," and "Tidal."

Jazz innovator Gerry Mulligan dies at his Darien, Conn., home January 20 at age 68; dancer Paul Draper of emphysema at his Woodstock, N.Y., home September 20 at age 86; Broadway composer-lyricist Harold Rome at New York October 26 at age 88; songwriter Irving Caesar at Mount Sinai Hospital December 17 at age 101.

Pete Sampras wins his fourth U.S. Open at Flushing Meadow, Steffi Graf her fifth.

Former Yankees radio and TV announcer Mel Allen dies at his Greenwich, Conn., home June 16 at age 83.

The New York Yankees win their first American League pennant since 1981, beating the Baltimore Orioles with help from Yankee fan Jeffrey Maier, 12, who reaches into playing territory to snatch a long fly ball; no interference is called, the play is ruled a home run for the Yankees, and the Bronx Bombers go on to win their first World Series since 1978, defeating the Atlanta Braves 4 games to 2 after losing the first two. Pitching by David Cone, 33, and Andy Pettite, 24, in the third and fifth games, and a game-tying three-run homer by catcher Jim Leyritz, 32, in the eighth inning of the fourth game, combine to give Brooklyn-born manager Joe Torre, now 56, his first Series victory in a 37-year major-league career (it is his first year with the Yankees). The city celebrates with a ticker-tape parade October 29.

The Sports Center at Chelsea Piers opens on a restored pier (Pier 59 at West 20th Street) that juts about 300 yards into the Hudson with a quarter-mile indoor track, an ice-skating rink, an indoor sand beach for volleyball games, a six-lane swimming pool, a boxing ring, kayaks, and other attractions. Film producer Roland W. Betts, 50, and other investors have financed the complex that has 150,000 square feet of gymnasium space.

A zoning restriction enacted by the City Council last year takes effect October 25, requiring that adult-entertainment establishments (peep shows, topless bars, video parlors, and such) close or relocate, but most of the city's 180 X-rated businesses have joined the American Civil Liberties Union in a suit to block the new law on First Amendment grounds, and although Times Square and West 42nd Street have seen a marked diminution in porno shops, many operators of such places remain in business.

Sotheby's auction house puts the estate of the late Jacqueline Kennedy Onassis up for sale in April and buyers pay $34.5 million for commonplace items that include a footstool ($33,350), a cigar humidor ($547,500), a set of MacGregor golf woods and bag ($772,500), a leather desk set ($189,500), and a rocking horse ($85,000).

The city has a record 30.3 million visitors, up from 28.8 million in 1994, with U.S. vacation travelers accounting for about 16.3 million of the total, up 1.1 million from last year. More than half are overnight visitors, not day-trippers. The increase in tourism makes hotel rooms, theater tickets, restaurant reservations, and the like harder to get and boosts business for the city's 21 licensed tour companies and 1,152 licensed tour guides (many are unlicensed and misinformation abounds).

Federal grand juries in Brooklyn and Manhattan investigate whether the industry-financed Council for Tobacco Research has fraudulently maintained its nonprofit status and whether Manhattan companies defrauded shareholders by failing to acknowledge the addictiveness of nicotine and the harmfulness of smoking.

William F. Buckley's *National Review* says February 12 that the war against drugs has been a failure and calls for decriminalization.

Second Avenue Deli owner Abe Lebewohl, now 64, is gunned down March 4 in a daylight robbery as he tries to deposit $13,000 in receipts at a bank near his restaurant. His killer will elude capture despite the posting of a $100,000 reward for information leading to his arrest. Lebewohl's brother Jack, 47, takes over and will operate the famed deli with Abe's daughter Sharon, 36.

New York City's crime rate falls for the third consecutive year, dropping to a point 16 percent below 1995's figure, 39 percent below 1993's figure. The number of homicides is the lowest since 1968 (the city's murder toll falls to 985, down from 2,005 in 1992), and the decline in major felonies (assault, auto theft, burglary, grand larceny, murder, rape, and robbery) is the sharpest since the end of Prohibition in 1933. Even Brooklyn's notorious Brownsville section has only 33 murders, down 57 percent from 77 in 1993, and 1,025 robberies, down 54 percent from 2,252 in 1993. Mayor Giuliani and the police department point to new strategies, such as arresting people for misdemeanors (e.g., graffiti vandalism, loud radios, and public drunkenness), that were instituted in 1994, but criminologists also credit such factors as a decline in crack use, an aging population, and changing patterns of behavior among teenagers (many younger brothers have seen their siblings succumb to crack-cocaine or go to prison).

Federal prosecutors announce November 21 that they have arrested 29 people in the city's largest tax fraud case. Among those seized are three present or past city employees, including the former chief tax collector in Brooklyn, who are charged with having accepted bribes from property owners to make it appear that taxes were paid when they were not, cheating the city of $20 million, including $13 million in real estate taxes that were erased from the Finance Department computers. More arrests follow.

Federal agents arrest reputed Gambino crime family head Nicholas Corozzo, 56, in Florida December 18 on charges of attempted murder, loan sharking, and racketeering (*see* 1992). Corozzo has been the capo (captain) of a Canarsie underworld unit known as the crew and is believed to have succeeded John Gotti (now confined to a federal penitentiary at Marion, Ill.) as godfather of the crime syndicate; eight other men identified as Gambino soldiers are also arrested (*see* 1997).

The vacancy rate in midtown Manhattan office buildings falls to 11.8 percent, down from 17.2 percent in 1992, and in downtown buildings it falls to 15.2 percent, down from 20.2 percent.

The SoHo Grand Hotel opens in August on West Broadway between Canal and Grand streets. Designed by Helpern Architects and William Sofield, the 375-room hotel is the first in the area in more than 125 years.

Manhattan hotel occupancy rates rise 14.2 percent above 1991 levels and visitor spending increases 29.3 percent over 1991.

The Blizzard of '96 that hits the eastern United States January 7 to 8 is the worst since 1947; the Nor'easter is followed 2 weeks later by devastating floods in much of New York and some other states.

The Henry Luce Nature Observatory in Central Park's Belvedere Castle opens in May. Created by the Central Park Conservancy with a 5-year matching grant of $1.5 million from the Henry Luce Foundation, it features hands-on exhibits of the animals and plants that exist in the park.

Legislation signed by Gov. Pataki June 9 quashes city plans to build new and larger incinerators (*see* 1990) and requires that Staten Island's Fresh Kills garbage-disposal site be closed by December 31, 2001. The closing of Edgemere Landfill in Queens 5 years ago has left Fresh Kills as the city's only remaining landfill, its 650 employees use 700 pieces of equipment (bulldozers, compressors, cranes, skimmer boats, and tractors) to bury more than 10,000 tons of waste per day, they truck in 675,000 cubic yards of soil each year to cover the waste, the dump produces 5 million pounds of methane gas per year, but Fresh Kills is home to only 40,000 seagulls, down from 155,000 in 1989 (it has 40,000 other birds, including barn owls, mallards, and sparrows). Waste-disposal companies buy up cheap land in Virginia and other states to use as dumps.

The Central Park Conservancy's 3-year Wonder of New York campaign ends in June with contributions of nearly $77.2 million (the goal was $71.5 million). Corporations, foundations, and individuals have given money to complete the park's major landscape restoration by the end of the century, but maintenance of the 1.577-mile oval track around the Reservoir (officially named after Jacqueline Kennedy Onassis since 1994) has declined, the crushed-bluestone surface of the potholed track is used by more than 5,000 joggers and walkers per day and is nearly as hard as concrete, and drainage is a problem after even minor rainstorms. Central Park's Great Lawn is sodded with Kentucky blue grass in October and new baseball diamonds are installed as work continues on renovations of the Turtle Pond (formerly Belvedere Lake) (see 1995; 1997).

Noise complaints account for 54 percent of calls to a quality-of-life hotline (888 677-LIFE) instituted by the city's Police Department in late August. A poll published in the *Daily News* March 24 put excessive noise at the top of the list when New Yorkers were asked what feature of urban life they found most annoying. Vibrations from stereo systems of inconsiderate neighbors, jackhammers, sanitation trucks, car alarms, shrieking subways, low-flying aircraft, unmuffled motorcycles, thudding pile drivers, music from bars and restaurants, exhaust system compressors, and mechanical systems all came in for criticism. New York has one of the toughest noise-control codes of any U.S. city, and some tenants have been able to obtain substantial rent rebates after litigation, but the Department of Environmental Protection lacks the staff needed to enforce the code (see 1997).

 The 70-year-old Kleine Konditorei Cafe and Restaurant at 234 East 86th Street closes April 13 following a fire, leaving Yorkville without a German restaurant (see Bavarian Inn, 1983).

Windows on the World reopens June 27 on the 107th floor of the World Trade Center with 240 seats (its six banquet rooms on the 106th floor have opened in May). Closed since the bombing of the building in January 1993, it has been refurbished by architect Hugh Hardy at a cost of $25 million—more than three times its original cost in 1976.

Brooklyn's Gage & Tollner reopens after a hiatus, as does Lundy's in Sheepshead Bay.

Union Pacific restaurant opens in September at 111 East 22nd Street under the direction of Queens-born chef and co-owner Rocco DiSpirito, 31, who helped Gray Kunz open Lespinasse 5 years ago.

The restaurant Patroon opens November 4 at 160 East 46th Street, formerly the site of Christ Cella's (see 1948). Restaurateur Ken Aretsky of Arcadia fame has taken over the place, gutted it, given it a more upscale, club-like atmosphere, and hired former Four Seasons chef Frank Delatrain to head its kitchen staff. Patroon features pasta dishes in addition to porterhouse steaks for two, chops, seafood, and the traditional creamed spinach of Christ Cella's.

 A new U.S. immigration law requires that residents of foreign birth earn 125 percent of the minimum wage to obtain green cards for members of their families who want to enter the country. The new law will cut by more than half the number of New York's legal immigrants from the Dominican Republic, the city's largest source of immigration since 1965.

1997 Palestinian tourist Ali Abu Kamal, 69, opens fire with a .380-caliber semi-automatic Beretta handgun atop the Empire State Building February 23, killing one man and wounding six others, some seriously, before turning the weapon on himself (see 1993). Metal detectors are promptly installed on the observation platform. Brooklyn police conduct a raid July 30 on a squalid apartment in a shack behind a store at 248 Fourth Avenue, between President and Carroll streets at the edge of Park Slope. Acting on a tip, they find two illegal Palestinian immigrants making pipe bombs with evident intentions to bomb the Atlantic Avenue subway station and other stations in a terrorist campaign aimed at derailing the Israeli peace process. Ghazi Ibrahim Abu Maizar, 23, is shot twice in the right leg; Lafi Khalil, 22, receives five wounds; both are taken to Kings County Hospital and arraigned in their beds (see 2001).

A 25-year-old police officer in Brooklyn's 70th Precinct station house is arrested August 13 and charged with having assaulted and brutalized Haitian immigrant Abner Louima, 33, subjecting him to racial slurs, jamming the wooden handle of a toilet plunger up his rectum (causing severe internal injuries) and then into his mouth. A private security guard, Louima was allegedly arrested ouside a Flatbush club early in the morning of August 9; his treatment produces major protests and demonstrations against police brutality. Further arrests follow, and the incident becomes a cause célèbre. Says Mayor Giuliani, "If you really are a police officer of the City of New York, if you really understand what it means to be a police officer, . . . what it means to protect the lives of other people, then you will be among the most revulsed and repulsed by what happened here. If you don't understand that, then you really should leave the Police Department." Thousands march across the Brooklyn Bridge from the heart of Brooklyn to City Hall August 29 to protest police brutality, and former detective Frank Serpico writes in a *New York Times* op-ed piece that "nothing about police culture has significantly changed since I left the force in 1972."

Mayor Giuliani wins his bid for reelection as the city rides a wave of apparent prosperity without inflation and with markedly lowered crime rates, but the city's unemployment rate has reached 10 percent in June (the highest of the nation's 20 largest cities) and falls only to 9 percent by election day, housing costs have increased, the number of people living in homeless shelters has increased 15 percent since 1994, public schools are severely overcrowded, and complaints of police misconduct have increased. Manhattan Borough President Ruth W. Messinger, 56, has won the Democratic Party primary and receives 540,075 votes (41 percent) to Republican Giuliani's 757,564 (57 percent).

A federal court convicts Lemrick Nelson, Jr. and Charles Price of civil rights violations in February in connection with the fatal 1991 stabbing of Hasidic student Yankel Rosenbaum in Crown Heights. Nelson, now 21, was acquitted in 1992 in a state trial but Attorney General Janet Reno ordered a federal investigation and Price, now 43, was indicted for agitating the incident (he has a long record of minor crimes and drug addiction) (*see* 1998).

Four deaf and mute Mexicans walk into a Jackson Heights precinct station before dawn July 19, announce that they are indentured workers, and lead police to two nearby apartments where 62 men, women, and children sleep on bunk beds, mattresses, and sleeping bags. Police arrest seven people, most of them illegal immigrants, on charges of running a smuggling ring that has sneaked scores of deaf Mexicans across the border, kept them in California safe houses, flown them to New York, and forced them by threats of physical abuse to peddle trinkets in the subways. Immigration authorities take over the Westway Motor Inn at Astoria, Queens, to provide shelter for 50 Mexican adults and 10 children, keeping them under armed guard; 18 men and women will plead guilty in the case and either be sentenced to prison or deported to Mexico (*see* 1998).

U.S. Secretary of Labor Alexis Herman tells a news conference October 16 that 63 percent of the city's garment-industry companies violate overtime or minimum-wage laws (*see* 1996). In the first compliance survey conducted by federal investigators, 59 of the 94 garment makers, chosen at random from 4,000, have been found to be in violation, and in Chinatown 90 percent have been in violation. Of the 20 shops where workers are represented by the Los Angeles-based Union of Needle-trades, Industrial and Textile Employees (Unite), 75 percent are in violation as compared with 63 percent overall. Joanna Cheng, director of Manhattan's Garment Workers' Justice Center, hails the report for focusing on what she calls a worsening problem; largely eliminated in the 1950s and 60s, sweatshops have crept back since the 1970s as immigrant labor has poured into the city. Federal investigators report December 12 that two Chinatown clothing factories—MSL Sportswear and Laura & Sarah Sportswear, both at 446 Broadway and both owned by Lai Fong Yuen—supply Wal-Mart, Kmart, Nordstrom, and the Limited with goods made by employees who work at piece rates, often earning less than the minimum wage ($5.15 per hour) and less than time-and-a-half for overtime (the factories keep two sets of books, one with false numbers showing compliance with wage and working-hour laws).

The death of 9-year-old Sabrina Green in November brings new charges of neglect against the city's school system and child welfare agency. The hyperactive daughter of a Harlem drug addict who died when she was a toddler, the little girl has stumbled to school (P.S. 112) in shoes two sizes too large, she was not given her medication, and her body was found in her half-sister Yvette's four-bedroom Bronx apartment at 4034 Laconia Avenue November 8 from untreated burns, gangrene, and blows to the head. Yvette, 32, has 10 children of her own, eight of them by her live-in boyfriend, and has been receiving $2,189 per month in welfare payments and food stamps. No one from Sabrina's school has investigated the child's absences.

Unemployment in the city falls to 9.0 percent by October, down from 11.5 percent in 1992, but in the Bronx it is 11.3 percent (down from 14.1), in Brooklyn 10.3 percent (down from 12.6). In Manhattan it is 7.8 percent, down from 9.7, but a study released in mid-December shows that New York State has the widest income gap between rich and poor in the nation: the top fifth of families with children averages $132,390 versus $6,787 for the bottom fifth. Largely because the finance industry has seen such huge salary increases and bonuses, New York is the only state where 20 percent of families receive more than 50 percent of all earned income, and the gap has been growing. The city adds 54,800 net new jobs, up 69 percent from the 32,500 added in 1996 and the best 1-year performance since 1984, when 77,700 net new jobs were added.

Investment banker Herbert Allen dies at his Manhattan apartment January 18 at age 88; lawyer Arthur L. Liman of bladder cancer at his Fifth Avenue apartment July 17 at age 64.

Morgan Stanley and Dean Witter announce an $8.8 billion (later increased to $10.2 billion) merger February 5 that creates the world's largest investment banking house, exceeding even Merrill Lynch in size. Salaries in the securities industry are up 42 percent over 1989 levels, while ordinary wages have risen only 3.8 percent since 1989.

Standard & Poor's raises its rating of New York State general obligation bonds from A- to A, making them tied with Louisiana bonds in terms of credit worthiness instead of below Louisiana's, but a spokesperson for S&P warns that recent tax and spending measures signed by Gov. Pataki "do pose some risks in the years 2000 and beyond, and that's still a concern of ours." Standard & Poor's agrees April 24 to keep its 2,057 employees in New York through the year 2019 in exchange for a package of tax incentives and energy discounts worth $23.7 million. S&P had received a more lucrative bid from New Jersey.

Swiss Bank announces May 15 that it will acquire Dillon, Read & Co. for about $600 million (see 1921). Dillon, Read has grown to have more than 700 employees; Swiss Bank acquired the London firm S. G. Warburg 2 years ago and says it will be incorporated into SBC Warburg Dillon Read.

Travelers Group announces September 24 that it will acquire Salomon Brothers for more than $9 billion in stock and add its financial services to those of Smith Barney to create Salomon Smith Barney (see 1993; Salomon, 1991; Citigroup, 1998).

Wall Street's Dow Jones Industrial Average closes at 7022.44 February 13, breaking through the 7000 mark for the first time as inflation remains low and industry continues to improve productivity. Trading in sixteenths begins on the NASDAQ June 2 and on the New York Stock Exchange a few days later, theoretically giving small investors better prices. The Dow closes at 8038.88 July 16 and rises above 8100 in early August, but it plunges 554.26 points (7.18 percent) October 27 in the worst point drop ever as markets worldwide react to problems in Asia, New York exchanges close early; the Dow rallies 337.17 points October 28, the largest point gain ever, on a day that sees nearly 1.2 billion shares change hands, the highest volume ever, and prices continue to gyrate wildly. The Dow closes December 31 at 7708.25—up 22.6 percent from the end of 1996.

F. A. O. Schwarz expands September 27 from 40,000 square feet to 60,000 as it takes over ground-floor and basement space in the General Motors Building that has been vacated by J. P. Morgan & Co. Now a subsidiary of the Dutch retailer KBB, Schwarz operates 37 stores in the United States (see 2001).

The city's Department of Consumer Affairs conducts a sweep of 21 electronics stores and announces December 3 that it has found 671 violations. Marquis Galleries of 519 Lexington Avenue has 75 violations (e.g., it priced a Sony camcorder at $1,699 without revealing that the suggested list price was $699); other major violators include Loco John at 2960 Third Avenue in the Bronx; 54th Street Photo at 840 Seventh Avenue in Manhattan; Top USA Electrical Appliances at 164-18 Jamaica Avenue, Queens; and A&S Stereo at 920 Flatbush Avenue, Brooklyn.

Manhattan retailers pay the highest commercial rents in America: space on Fifth Avenue averages $48.33 per month per square foot, on East 57th Street between Fifth and Madison it is only slightly less, on Madison Avenue between 57th and 69th streets it is just over $31, in Rockefeller Plaza $20.

Consolidated Edison agrees September 10 to roll back electric rates 10 percent across the board, break up into several parts, and open the door to competition in a market that Con Ed has monopolized for decades. The city's electric rates have been among the highest in the nation, the rate rollback is the largest since 1948, and the state's Public Service Commission announces its intention to break up each of the seven regional electric monopolies statewide.

A Taxi and Limousine Commission order takes effect April 1 requiring that any fleet-owned taxi more than 3 years old, or any individually owned taxi more than 5 years old, must be replaced with a new vehicle (see 1996). Owners have succeeded in delaying implementation of the order but could not block it. Tapes recorded by celebrities (actor Judd Hirsch, singer Eartha Kitt, comedian Jackie Mason, comedian Joan Rivers, Yankees manager Joe Torre) urge passengers to fasten their seat belts when they get in, ask the driver for a receipt, and not forget their belongings when they leave (the repetition is hard on drivers and the tapes will be discontinued in 2003).

The Metropolitan Transportation Authority permits MetroCard holders to transfer from buses to subways and vice versa at no extra fare beginning July 4, although transfers must be made within 2 hours (and a round trip requires only one fare if the return begins within 2 hours). The MTA has invested $700 million in the MetroCard system, and nearly one-third of all passengers (close to 1 million rides) now use the 4-year-old MetroCard instead of tokens, up from one-sixth (less than 400,000 rides) late last year, as the MTA completes the job of equipping all 468 subway stations to accept the cards that can now be purchased at grocery stores and from special vans as well as at subway stations. Users deposit up to $80 and the fare is deducted by computer each time the electronic fare card is "swiped" through a scanner, the MetroCard boosts ridership and revenues by about 10 percent, prompting demands that fares be lowered, and although naysayers warn that the new system will make it easier to raise fares, most of the tokens used in various sizes since 1953 will soon be retired and sold for scrap.

A new Times Square subway entrance opens July 15 at the southeast corner of Seventh Avenue and 42nd Street with street-level turnstiles and escalators for the 11 lines (A, C, E, N, R, S, 1, 2, 3, 7, and 9) and 500,000 daily passengers that the station serves. New turnstile equipment at the subway system's 750-odd entrances make it harder to get into stations without paying fares (see 1992), and arrests for fare beating decline sharply (fewer than 1 percent of riders pay no fare in October for the first time since record keeping began in 1989), partly because police check every fare beater they catch for outstanding warrants and prior arrests.

E-Z Pass electronic toll collection begins on the 66-year-old George Washington Bridge July 28, and E-Z Pass users get a 10 percent discount against the reg-

The MetroCard introduced computer technology that enabled riders to transfer freely from bus to subway.

ular $4 toll, charged only on northbound crossings. The system goes into effect at Hudson River tunnels October 28. Drivers use transponders the size of casette tapes to have tolls deducted from amounts they have deposited (see 1998).

New York Hospital's 11-story Maurice R. and Corinne P. Greenberg Pavilion admits semi-private patients July 11. Dedicated April 8, it has opened for private patients in May and provides more modern and comfortable patient rooms than those used since 1932 in the other pavilions, converted now for use as offices, laboratories, and such (rooms in the new pavilion contain no more than two beds each, with private showers and toilet facilities but no bathtubs). The pavilion has 776 beds in 850,000 square feet of space, three banks of elevators (one for patients only, one for visitors, one for service) plus two trauma elevators connecting intensive-care units with emergency rooms and operating rooms, but the elevators are badly located, the building is not wired for fiber optics, the nurses' stations on each floor are cramped, and there are no food-preparation facilities in the new $760 million pavilion. The structure has been constructed on a platform over the FDR Drive between 68th and 70th streets, and completed ahead of schedule and under budget; most of its financing has come from federally guaranteed bonds, but some has come in the form of grants from prominent contributors who include the chairman emeritus of American Insurance Group (AIG) (see Starr Pavilion, 1989).

The city begins hiring up to 100 private rodent exterminators in August as rat populations proliferate. The budget for the Bureau of Pest Control was cut nearly in half in 1992 and 1993, an increase in asthma in the South Bronx and other areas has been linked to rats, the Health Department spends about $5.6 million per year on rat control, and the new initiative is expected to add another $2.5 million to $3 million.

The Allen African Methodist Episcopal Church opens a $23 million, 2,500-seat cathedral in Jamaica, Queens, in late July (only Brooklyn's Concord Baptist Church is larger among the city's churches with predominantly black congregations). Rep. Floyd H. Flake, 52, announces July 31 that he will give up his congressional seat before year's end to devote full time to his position as Allen A. M. E.'s pastor.

Longtime United Federation of Teachers president Albert Shanker dies of bladder cancer at Memorial-

Sloan Kettering Cancer Center February 22 at age 68. He is succeeded by Sandra Feldman.

The New-York Historical Society signs an agreement in May with New York University to have NYU catalogue the Society's manuscripts, books, prints, photographs, architectural records, and other holdings (see 1993). Only about 30 percent of the 2 million manuscripts, 650,000 books, 15,000 maps and atlases, and 10,000 newspapers are catalogued at all, and the system used has been antiquated.

The Eugenio Maria de Hostos Community College that opened in the South Bronx in 1968 makes headlines in early June by holding up the degrees of graduates who have failed to pass a newly instituted English proficiency examination (only 23 pass out of 125). Critics note that "proficiency" does not mean fluency or mastery and question whether so-called "bilingual" education is preparing students for life in a predominantly English-speaking country (77 percent of Hostos students are of Hispanic background; many are recent immigrants). "If you can't express yourself in English, you shouldn't graduate," says Herman Badillo, who is now the college's leading critic. Bilingual education works, even at the college level, he insists, but "people" have "corrupted the process." (At Boricua College in upper Manhattan, all classes are in English; faculty members and administrators must be bilingual, but only to help students who have language problems.)

The U.S. Supreme Court rules June 23 in *Agostini v. Felton* that public school teachers may teach remedial classes at religious schools, thus overturning its 1985 decision that this would violate the Constitution's strict separation of Church and State. New York City's mobile classrooms for such classes become a thing of the past (see 1985), but civil libertarians worry that the Court is on a slippery slope while religious groups view the decision as a possible opening to more taxpayer aid for their schools.

The city's public schools open September 3 with many newly hired aides to help control overcrowding. Gov. Pataki vetoes a bill September 3 that would have allowed thousands of the city's most experienced teachers to retire at age 55 with full pensions; Mayor Giuliani and Schools Chancellor Rudy Crew have opposed the measure that has been supported by the teachers' union (see DeGrasse, 2000).

The Museum of Jewish Heritage opens its core exhibition September 15 at 18 First Place in Battery Park City. Former mayor Ed Koch first proposed the museum some 16 years ago; it contains exhibits chronicling the rich life of European Jews before

Adolf Hitler came to power in Germany in 1933, the Holocaust that began 5 years later, and the rebuilding of Jewish life since 1945. Kevin Roche has designed the three-story hexagonal granite building.

The city privatizes its 74-year-old radio station WNYC January 7, transferring ownership to the not-for-profit WNYC Foundation that has been running the station (820 AM, 93.9 FM) for some time. Contributions from listeners will by year's end have paid off half the $20 million owed to the city, but cost-cutting measures will dismay many longtime supporters.

The State Public Service Commission issues an order February 12 requiring NYNEX to refund $109.6 million to telephone customers for what it calls shoddy service and improper business practices between 1984 and 1996. Refunds average at least $8.70 per customer. The PSC gives qualified approval March 20 to a $22 billion merger of NYNEX with Bell Atlantic, but only on condition that NYNEX invest in its aging telephone network and improve its customer service. The PSC announces November 25 that beginning in mid-1998 new Manhattan telephone numbers will have the area code 646 instead of 212, and that even when calls are made within Manhattan to 212 numbers the caller will have to precede the area code with a 1.

Former RCA chairman Robert W. Sarnoff dies at Lenox Hill Hospital February 22 at age 78.

ABC announces in March that Roone Arledge, now 65, will become chairman of the news division, giving up the presidency of the division that he has held for nearly 20 years. Television-network group president David Westin, 44, has had no news experience but replaces Arledge, who hired David Brinkley, Diane Sawyer, and Chris Wallace away from competing networks, created *Nightline*, *20/20*, and *Prime Time Live*, and made ABC the leading U.S. television news source.

New rules signed into law by Mayor Giuliani May 16 increase annual fees charged to the city's 330 newsstand vendors from $538 to as much as $5,000, depending on location; scheduled to take effect January 1, 1998, the rules call for putting 100 more stands out for competitive bids, and current renters will have 5 years before the city decides whether to continue renting the stands or to seek bids on them. The new rules threaten to put 50 to 100 of the city's 330 sidewalk newsdealers out of business. Blind newsdealers have operated sidewalk stands since the 1850s, but fewer than a dozen still work every day.

The *New York Times* moves production to a new $350 million, five-press printing plant at College Point, Queens, June 15 after 93 years on Times Square (it has used a $450 million six-press plant at Edison, N.J., since 1983). The city has given the *Times* $21.5 million in tax credits, grants, and purchase options for the new plant that frees Times Square of traffic jams caused by huge tractor-trailers delivering newsprint or picking up cargoes from the 43rd Street loading bays. The paper's weekday circulation is 1.1 million, Sunday circulation is 1.64 million, Times Square remains Times Square, but the paper stops delivering "bulldog editions" before midnight and begins using colored ink in daily papers in September as the "Good Gray Times" follows the example set by *USA Today* 15 years ago.

The "Zipper" on what once was the Times Tower in Times Square is replaced during the summer with a new, brighter, faster-moving sign installed by Artkraft Strauss. Dow, Jones & Co. acquired the "Zipper" in 1995; its news bulletins can be set at variable speeds but its letters generally go by at the rate of nine per second, relaying headlines illuminated with 235,000 orange-colored diodes in place of the 12,400 30-watt incandescent bulbs used since 1928.

"Possibly the only good thing in New York Rudy hasn't taken credit for," says a *New York* magazine advertisement on city buses in November. Mayor Giuliani objects, calling the ad a violation of his rights to privacy and to protect his name from commercial exploitation. The ads are removed, a federal judge rules December 1 that a mayor who is in the headlines every day and has appeared in drag on national television "cannot avoid the limelight of publicity—good and bad," and a federal appeals judge the next day stays the case.

The 111-year-old Westinghouse Electric Corp. changes its name to CBS Corp. December 1 and moves its headquarters from Pittsburgh to New York (*see* 1995). It will sell its remaining assets outside of the broadcasting realm next year.

The Democratic-controlled City Council persuades Mayor Giuliani June 4 to include $16 million in new aid to the city's libraries as part of the $33.4 billion municipal budget.

Nonfiction: *The Future Once Happened Here: New York, D.C., L.A., and the Fate of America's Big Cities* by Gloversville, N.Y.-born political consultant and urbanologist Fred Siegel, 56, who examines political developments since the 1960s, when "riot psychology" took root among community leaders (his title is a quote from former governor Mario Cuomo); *Writing New York: A Literary Anthology* by Phillip Lopate (editor); *The Empire City: New York and Its People, 1624—1996* by New York-born Baruch College historian emerita Selma Cantor Berrol, 72; *Touring Historic Harlem: Four Walks in Northern Manhattan* by Columbia University architectural historian Andrew S. Dolkart; *Bloomberg by Bloomberg* by financial news billionaire Michael Bloomberg; *The New York Waterfront: Evolution and Building Culture of the Port and Harbor* by Kevin Bone (editor), who has collected essays and historical illustrations; *Battery Park City: Politics and Planning on the New York Waterfront* by Canadian urban and regional planning professor David L. A. Gordon; *Trump: The Art of the Comeback* by developer Donald Trump (with Kate Bohner) reveals how he acquired the 72-story 40 Wall Street skyscraper for only $1 million; *Underboss: Sammy the Bull Gravano's Story of Life in the Mafia* by Peter Maas; *The Gay Metropolis 1940—1996* by Charles Kaiser.

Fiction: *Underworld* by Don DeLillo; *Snow in August* by Pete Hamill, who loses his job as *Daily News* editor September 4 after 8 months (average weekday circulation in March dropped to 728,000, down from 758,000 in March 1996, and owner Mortimer Zuckerman has blamed Hamill. Zuckerman hires English-born Random House boss Harold Evans, 69, November 25 and makes him editorial director of all Zuckerman publications, including the *News*); *The Angel of Darkness* by Caleb Carr is about the pursuit of a kidnapper in turn-of-the-century New York.

Novelist-language expert Leo Rosten dies at New York February 19 at age 88.

Poet Allen Ginsberg dies of liver cancer at New York April 5 at age 70.

Juvenile: *Nothing Ever Happens on 90th Street* by Roni Schotter.

 Painting: *Self-Portrait* by Chuck Close. Willem de Kooning dies at his East Hampton, L.I., home March 19 at age 92; pop painter Roy Lichtenstein of pneumonia at New York University Medical Center September 29 at age 73 after completing a 57-foot *Times Square Mural* in porcelain enamel for installation in the subway station.

Christie's auction of the Victor and Sally Ganz modern and contemporary art collection November 10 brings in $206.5 million, a record for any single-owner sale, with Picasso's 1932 painting *The Dream* fetching $48.4 million (Victor paid $7,500 for it in 1941). The couple collected not only Picassos but also works by Jasper Johns, Frank Stella, and Eva Hesse over the course of 50 years, paying less than

$2 million. Victor died in 1987, Sally has died earlier this year, and their four children have put the collection up for sale.

 Theater: *How I Learned to Drive* by Providence, R.I., playwright Paula Vogel, now 45, 3/10 at the off-Broadway Vineyard Theater, with Mary-Louise Parker as 18-year-old L'il Bit, Beverly, Mass.-born actor David Morse, 43, as her pedophilic uncle, 450 perfs.; *An American Daughter* by Wendy Wasserstein 4/12 at the Cort Theater, with Kate Nelligan, New York-born actor Peter Riegert, 49, Joliet, Ill.-born actress Lynne Thigpen (originally Lynne Redmond), now 48, Hal Holbrook, Texas-born actor Bruce Norris, 36, 89 perfs.; *As Bees in Honey Drown* by New York playwright Douglas Carter Beane 7/15 at the off-Broadway Lucille Lortel Theater (after an earlier opening at the Greenwich House Theater), Louisville, Ky.-born actress J. Smith-Cameron (originally Jeannie Smith), Bo Foxworth; *The Old Neighborhood* by David Mamet 11/19 at the Booth Theater, with Peter Riegert, Patti LuPone, 197 perfs.

Actor-director-teacher Sanford Meisner dies at his Sherman Oaks, Calif., home February 2 at age 91; theatrical lighting expert Abe Feder at his Manhattan home April 24 at age 87; burlesque comic Joey Faye at the Actors' Home in Englewood, N.J., April 26 at age 87, having gained fame long ago for his routine that began, "Slowly I turned . . ."

Films: James Brooks's *As Good as It Gets* with Jack Nicholson, Helen Hunt, Greg Kinnear. Also: Griffin Dunne's *Addicted to Love* with Meg Ryan, Matthew Broderick; Alex Sichel's *All Over Me* with Allison Folland, Tara Subkoff, Wilson Cruz; Richard Donner's *Conspiracy Theory* with Mel Gibson as New York taxi driver Jerry Fletcher, Julia Roberts; Greg Mottola's *The Daytrippers* with Hope Davis, Stanley Tucci, Anne Meara, Pat McNamara, Parker Posey; Woody Allen's *Deconstructing Harry* with Allen, now 62 (who marries Mia Farrow's adopted daughter Soon-Yi Previn, 27, at Venice December 24; she has been his mistress for 6 years and is his third wife. "She's too old for him," says actor Tony Randall, now 77, whose wife, Heather, is 27 and the mother of Randall's son); Taylor Hackford's *The Devil's Advocate* with Al Pacino, Keanu Reeves; Mike Newell's *Donnie Brasco* with Al Pacino, Johnny Depp as a New York gangland father and his surrogate son (who is actually an FBI undercover agent); Luc Besson's *The Fifth Element* with Bruce Willis; Salvatore Stabile's *Gravesend* with Tony Tucci, Michael Parducci, Tom Malloy, Thomas Brandise; Bill Duke's *Hoodlum* with Laurence Fishburne, Tim Roth (as Dutch Schultz), Andy Garcia (as Lucky Luciano) (the script grossly distorts the role

of the late Thomas E. Dewey in fighting the mob as Manhattan district attorney in the 1930s); Joe Mantello's *Love! Valour! Compassion!* with Jason Alexander, Randy Becker, Stephen Bogardus; Barry Sonnenfeld's *Men in Black* with Tommy Lee Jones; Sidney Lumet's *Night Falls on Manhattan* with Andy Garcia, Ian Holm, Ron Leibman, Richard Dreyfuss; Mimi Leder's *The Peacemaker* with George Clooney, Nicole Kidman in a story about a possible terrorist attack on the UN; Jonathan Nossiter's *Sunday* with David Suchet, Lisa Harrow, Jared Harris; Agnieszkwa Holland's *Washington Square* with Jennifer Jason Leigh, Helena Bonham-Carter, Albert Finney, Ben Chaplin, Dame Maggie Smith, Charlotte Rampling, Alison Elliott.

 Broadway and off-Broadway musicals: *Violet* 3/11 at the Playwright Horizons Theater with Lauren Ward, Amanda Posner, Stephen Lee Anderson, music by Jeanine Tesori, book and lyrics by Brian Crawley based on Doris Betts's novel *The Ugliest Pilgrim*; *Dream: The Johnny Mercer Musical* 4/3 at the Royale Theater, with a 22-member cast that includes New York-born actress-dancer Lesley Ann Warren, 50, John Pizzarelli, Margaret Whiting, now 72, music by composers who include the late Harold Arlen, Hoagy Carmichael, Jerome Kern, Henry Mancini, Harry Warren, and Richard A. Whiting, lyrics by the late Mercer, 109 perfs.; *Titanic* 4/23 at the Lunt-Fontanne Theater, with a 42-member cast that includes John Cunningham as the ship's captain, Michael Cerveris as her builder, Long Branch, N.J.-actor David Garrison, 44, as Lord Ismay, book by Peter Stone, music and lyrics by Maury Yeston, songs that include "How Did They Build Titanic?", 804 perfs.; *Steel Pier* 4/24 at the Richard Rodgers Theater, with Dublin-born actor Daniel McDonald, Joel Blum, Debra Monk, Ohio-born actress Karen Ziemba, 41, music and lyrics by John Kander and Fred Ebb, songs that include "Leave the World Behind" and "Second Chance," 76 perfs.; *The Life* 4/26 at the Barrymore Theater, with Vernel Bagneris, Brooklyn-born actress Lillias White, 45, Cleveland-born actor Chuck Cooper, 42, music by Cy Coleman, lyrics by Ira Gasman, 466 perfs.; *Jekyll and Hyde* 4/28 at the Plymouth Theater with Robert Cuccioli, music by New York-born composer Frank Wildhorn, 38, book and lyrics by Leslie Bricusse, songs that include "This Is the Moment," "Once Upon a Dream," 1,543 perfs.; *King David* 5/18 at the newly restored New Amsterdam Theater (architect Hugh Hardy has designed the restoration), with Marcus Lovett in the title role, Judy Kuhn as Michal, music by Alan Menken, lyrics by Tim Rice, 6 perfs.; *Forever Tango* 6/19 at the Walter Kerr Theater, with

Argentinian singer Carlos Morel and 17 dancer-choreographers, 332 perfs.; *Side Show* 10/10 at the Richard Rodgers Theater, with Ken Jennings, Alice Ripley and Emily Skinner as the Siamese Twins Daisy and Violet, music by Henry Krieger, book and lyrics by Bill Russell, 84 perfs.; *The Scarlet Pimpernel* 11/9 at the Minskoff Theater, with Terrence Mann, Douglas Sills, 37, Camden, N.J.-born actress Christine Andreas, Philip Hoffman, music by Frank Wildhorn, book and lyrics by Nan Knighton, 772 perfs.; *The Lion King* 11/13 at the New Amsterdam Theater, with John Vickery as Scar, Samuel E. Wright as Mufasa, Jason Raize as Simba, Scott Irby-Ranniar as Young Simba, music and lyrics by Elton John and Tim Rice, additional music and lyrics by Lebo M. Mark Mancina, Jay Rifkin, Julie Taymor (who directs), and Hans Zimmer, 2,500+ perfs.; *Ragtime* 12/26 (preview) at the new $30 million, 1,821-seat Ford Center for the Performing Arts (second in size only to the 1,933-seat Gershwin) built on a site bounded by 42nd and 43rd streets between Broadway and Eighth Avenue. Beyer Blinder Belle and Kofman Engineering has designed the center for a Toronto firm that has leased the site from the nonprofit New 42nd Street Inc. and torn down the Lyric Theater of 1903 and the Apollo Theater of 1920.

Songwriter Burton Lane dies at his Manhattan home January 6 at age 84; rhythm-and-blues singer La Vern Baker of heart complications at St. Luke's-Roosevelt Hospital March 10 at age 67 (a diabetic, her legs were amputated in 1995 but she returned to performing last year); 280-pound Brooklyn-born rap star Christopher G. Wallace (known variously as Biggie Smalls and the Notorious B.I.G.), 24, is killed in a drive-by shooting near Beverly Hills, Calif., March 9 and given a funeral procession March 18 from Fort Greene through Bedford-Stuyvesant; Laura Nyro dies of ovarian cancer at her Danbury, Conn., home April 8 at age 49; jazz singer Thelma Carpenter at her native New York May 5 at age 77.

The 25-foot Duke Ellington Memorial by California-based sculptor Robert Graham is unveiled July 1 at Duke Ellington Circle (formerly Frawley Circle) at the northeast corner of Central Park, with ceremonies that include Ellington music, a performance by Wynton Marsalis, and speeches by notables who include pianist-singer Bobby Short (he organized a Duke Ellington Memorial Fund in 1979, 5 years after the legendary composer's death).

Oklahoma-born country singer Garth Brooks, 35, gives a free concert in Central Park's North Meadow 8/7 and attracts a crowd estimated to number per-haps 250,000. HBO has sponsored the event for its TV audience, whose numbers are far greater.

Former Metropolitan Opera general manager Sir Rudolf Bing dies of Alzheimer's disease at a Yonkers nursing home September 2 at age 95.

Cablevision Systems Corp. leases Radio City Music Hall in early December from Rockefeller Center's majority owner Tishman Speyer Properties (*see* 1995). Cablevision is also a co-owner of Madison Square Garden and says it will spend $25 million to renovate the 65-year-old Music Hall and install a new television production studio.

 The IBM computer Deep Blue (RS/6000SP) defeats chess grandmaster Garry Kasparov, 34, at the Equitable Center in midtown Manhattan in May, winning 3-games to Kasparov's 2-(three ended in draws). Kasparov retains the title he has held since 1985, but it is the first time a computer has beaten a human.

New York Mets pitcher Dave Mlicki shuts out the world-champion New York Yankees 6 to 0 in the June 16 opener of the city's first regular-season interleague series, but the Yankees win the final two games (each game has attracted more than 56,000 fans to Yankee Stadium, suggesting a renewal of interest in what was once called the national pastime).

The Arthur Ashe Memorial Stadium opens at Flushing Meadow August 25 for the start of the U.S. Open tennis matches, displacing Louis Armstrong Stadium as the Open's main arena, but Mayor Giuliani does not attend, registering his protest against a deal requiring the city to pay a fine every time a plane from nearby La Guardia Airport flies over the new $254 million National Tennis Center; corporations have paid up to $100,000 per box to reserve all the best seats, antagonizing longtime tennis fans, but the city receives higher profits from tennis than from baseball. Patrick Rafter, 24 (Australia) wins in men's singles, Czech-born Swiss prodigy Martina Hingis, 16, in women's.

The New York Liberty basketball team of the new Women's National Basketball Association (WNBA) plays its first (10-week) season at Madison Square Garden and opposition teams' courts, drawing an average attendance of 11,400 per game (many of them televised). Its regular 28-game season ends August 24 at the Garden with 18,051 fans on their feet to cheer the Liberty's victory over the Cleveland Rockers.

 The New York-New York Hotel Casino opens at Las Vegas, Nev., January 3 with 12 hotel towers on an 18-acre site. Former mayor Ed Koch attended a start-of-construction party on the site in 1995, the $460 million complex has a 50-foot-high replica of the Brooklyn Bridge 200 feet in length, its 200-foot-high roller coaster is called the Manhattan Express, and its hotels range in height from 26 stories to 47, the tallest being a scaled-down replica of the Empire State Building, the shortest a replica of the AT&T Building, with replicas of Lever House, the Municipal Building, the Chrysler Building, the Seagram Building, and other New York landmarks in between, plus replicas of Grand Central Terminal, Times Square, Greenwich Village, the UN Assembly Hall, the Soldiers and Sailors Monument, Central Park, the Ellis Island Immigrant Receiving Station, and other familiar sights.

New York for the first time bans the use of firecrackers to celebrate the lunar new year in Chinatown, saying they pose a safety hazard. Local merchants and community groups protest, saying the traditional fireworks have attracted tourists to the area's narrow streets; the city also cracks down on Fourth of July fireworks, ending a tradition in many neighborhoods.

The city ends a 35-year ban on tattoo parlors March 27. Fears of hepatitis and other disease outbreaks have not materialized despite widespread illegal tattooing, and 200 licenses will be issued to tattooers in the next 12 months. Lasers have made it possible to remove most tattoos and do it with less pain than previous methods that caused scarring, but the procedure is costly.

High winds on Thanksgiving Day create problems for balloon handlers at the annual Macy's parade: the six-story-high Cat in the Hat balloon hits a light pole on Central Park West at 72nd Street, a piece of the pole falls on some spectators, and Kathleen Caronna, 34, remains in a coma 1 week later.

A deal reached June 20 requires tobacco companies to pay nearly $370 billion over 25 years, abandon advertising (including the Marlboro Man and Joe Camel) that glamorizes smoking, and allow the FDA to regulate nicotine as a drug. The City Council agrees December 2 to weaken slightly a bill prohibiting tobacco advertising within four blocks of schools, playgrounds, day-care centers, youth centers, and amusement arcades in order to ensure that the bill can withstand challenges from tobacco and advertising companies (*but see* 1998).

Ten of the 17 men indicted in June 1995 on conspiracy charges related to trash hauling plead guilty to bribery and bid rigging in violation of the state's Organized Crime Control Act and are sentenced to 1 to 6 years (*see* 1995). More than 100 hours of wiretap evidence suggest that the Mafia-run cartel has for decades collected $400 million to $500 million per year by inflating garbage-removal bills for virtually every business in the city, using arson and violence to keep honest companies from competing for carting contracts and extorting $790,000 from Chambers Papers Fibres Corp., whose officers tried to defy the cartel. The Greater New York Waste Paper Association, largest of the carters' trade groups in the metropolitan area, has as its executive director one Joseph Francolino, 59, who has been videotaped meeting in the early 1990s with John Gotti, former boss of the Gambino crime family; prosecutors identify the executive secretary of the association Frank Giovinco, 30, as a soldier in the Genovese crime family. Angelo Ponte, now 71, begins serving his sentence in mid-April at a correctional facility in Sullivan County; his son Vincent will get 5 years' probation in a plea bargain. The other seven men face sentences of up to 25 years (*see* 1998). Three national companies now compete for the city's private carting business, the Trade Waste Commission has ordered cuts in maximum prices, and the result is supposed to save more than $300 million per year for some 200,000 customers, most of them hotels, restaurants, office buildings, private hospitals, and universities.

A *New York Times* editorial April 12 congratulates the city for its progress in combating organized crime in commercial garbage collection, Fulton Fish Market operations, and other mob-influenced places of business; it urges the City Council to enact legislation that would expand the city's ability to remove corrupt businesses and unions from the big meat and produce markets where kickbacks and extortion are endemic. Some union leaders, the *Times* charges, are trying to block such legislation or water it down, but the City Council and the Giuliani administration agree April 15 on a bill that would give the city sweeping new power to crack down on organized crime in five major food markets. It will be able to expel union members suspected of having Mafia connections.

Genovese crime family boss Vincenzo "Chin" Gigante, now 69, is convicted in July of racketeering and conspiring to kill former Gambino crime family leader John Gotti. Bronx capo Dominick V. Cirillo, 67, known as the "Quiet Dom," succeeds Gigante as "godfather" of America's largest and richest crime family, according to law enforcement officials, after decades of maintaining a low profile in the mob. The family allegedly takes in hundreds of millions of dollars per year from illegal gambling, loan-sharking, and extortion but crackdowns and indictments have weakened its grip on the construction trades, garbage-removal industry, Feast of San Gennaro, Fulton Fish Market, and Jacob K. Javits Convention Center.

Gambino crime family underboss Nicholas Corozzo pleads guilty August 22 to charges of racketeering, loan sharking, and trafficking in stolen goods (*see* 1996). He will be sentenced to 10 years in prison (*see* 1998).

Taft High School English teacher Jonathan M. Levin, 31, is found shot to death in his modest Upper West Side apartment June 2. Son of Time Warner CEO Gerald M. Levin, his feet have been bound and he has been stabbed in the chest.

The city has a total of 770 homicides, down from 2,154 in 1992, down 20 percent from last year, and the lowest number in 30 years (murders are down in other major cities as well, but New York's 64.3 percent decline is the highest; the total number of crimes in the city falls to 355,893, down 43.2 percent from the 626,182 in 1992, and that, too, is a greater reduction than elsewhere).

🏠 Billionaire real estate mogul Harry B. Helmsley of Helmsley-Spear dies of pneumonia at a Scottsdale, Ariz., hospital January 4 at age 87, leaving a real estate empire that stretches from the garment district to Central Park South, to say nothing of properties in Chicago, Newark, and Texas. He has been ill since about 1988, his diminished mental capacity was disclosed in 1991, and his widow, Leona, is soon squabbling with Helmsley's former partners and associates, who include millionaires Peter Malin, Irving Schneider, and Alvin Schwartz.

The 25-story 667 Madison Avenue building is completed at the southeast corner of 61st Street. Designed for Hartz Mountain Industries by Helpern Architects with a granite façade enhanced by decorative limestone trim, it has 236,000 square feet of office space, replaces a 10-story apartment house put up in 1902; its limestone-clad lobby rises 40 feet high, and an 18th century Gobelin tapestry hangs behind the concierge's lobby desk.

The Trump International Hotel and Tower opens in January at Columbus Circle, where developer Donald Trump has taken over the 44-story Gulf + Western Building of 1969, converted 17 floors into 168 transient hotel rooms and suites, and turned the rest into condominium residences. Apartments range in price from $915,000 to $3.1 million, with penthouses priced from $5.4 million to $8.375 million.

The death of four Polish immigrants in a fire at Maspeth, Queens, April 20 exposes widespread illegal conversions of properties into low-cost apartments, especially in Queens but also in other boroughs. A shortage of available middle-income housing has encouraged the illegal conversions.

Rent regulation ends in New York State at midnight June 15 as landlords gain the right to raise rents on vacated apartments, but legislators at Albany approve bills June 19 that keep the existing system in place for another 6 years while allowing landlords much larger increases for vacant apartments. A group of New York City property owners has contributed $578,000 to Republican political campaigns since 1994, but the most concerted effort by landlords in years to end rent controls completely has met with strong resistance from tenants of the city's 1.1 million rent-controlled or rent-stabilized apartments (the average rent for a one-bedroom apartment in the city has risen above $700, and more than half of New Yorkers pay over one-third of their incomes on rent, where in earlier years the normal figure was 25 percent). A temporary agreement reached June 16 prevents landlords from hiking rents, and under terms of the final bills the rent limits are lifted only on some high-rent units occupied by some high-income tenants; landlords receive the right to require payment of rents during court disputes. The City Council revises the formula for recalculating Maximum Base Rent increases (Local Law 73), but the system adopted in 1971 remains substantially unchanged, despite questionable arguments that it is unfair to younger people, has led to abandonment of buildings, favors the rich, has discouraged new construction, and hastens the decay of existing apartment houses (*see* 2000).

New York real estate investor Jacob A. Frydman, 39, agrees in late June to buy Starrett Corp., whose subsidiaries include HRH Construction, Grenadier Realty, and Levitt Corp. (Grenadier oversees 20,000 residential units in buildings that include Brooklyn's Starrett City.) The family of Paul and Seymour Millstein controls about a third of Starrett and persuades the other stockholders to accept Frydman's $80.4 million offer.

Architect Paul Rudolph dies of mesothelemia (asbestos cancer) at a New York hospital August 8 at age 78. He has lived since the 1960s at 23 Beekman Place, a house overlooking the East River between 50th and 51st streets that was formerly occupied by actress Katharine Cornell and her director husband, Guthrie McClintic; Rudolph added four stories to the five-story house to create two simplex and two duplex rental units, both in Modernist style with extensive use of mirrors on walls, floors, and ceilings.

The 42-story Citylights co-op apartment house is completed near the East River in Queens with 521 units (70 are reserved for households with incomes below $57,000 per year).

A 33-story rental apartment house is completed at 530 West 43rd Street, between Tenth and Eleventh avenues, with 375 units ranging in size from 400-square-foot studios to 950-square-foot two-bedroom apartments. Designed by Schuman Lichtenstein Claman & Efron, it rises in Clinton (known until 1959 as Hell's Kitchen) on a site that was once a piano factory and extends through to 42nd Street; 20 percent of its units are for tenants whose annual incomes are between $14,000 and $24,500.

President Clinton visits the South Bronx December 10 and finds Charlotte Gardens a model community of suburban-style houses in tree-shaded streets (see 1983); the houses fetch prices as high as $185,000 but few of the police dispatchers, secretaries, truck drivers, and other owners are willing to sell. Although Charlotte Street itself remains a bleak, drug-infested, crime-ridden wasteland, some 30,000 housing units have been built or renovated in the South Bronx since 1987. Addressing an audience at the Madison Square Boys and Girls Club in the South Bronx, Clinton says, "If you can do it, everybody else can do it," and he announces that he will release $96 million to New York through the Department of Housing and Urban Development's Innovative Homes Program for more housing construction. The president cites empowerment zones, the federal tax credit for low-income housing, and the Community Reinvestment Act as examples of his urban policy.

A State Supreme Court justice rules January 16 that the city is in violation of its own 1989 recycling law (see 1989). He agrees with arguments of environmental groups that only 14 percent of residential trash, about 2,200 tons per day, is recycled rather than the 25 percent required by year. Mayor Giuliani cut the city's recycling budget by $25 million last year ($6 million was restored late in the year), eliminated weekly recycling pickups in many neighborhoods, and ended the recycling program for mixed paper that has included junk mail, cereal boxes, and milk cartons. City lawyers contend that construction debris is recycled, since it is ground up into gravel and used to create roads at the Fresh Kills landfill (scheduled to close in 2001), and that this easily

brings the city into compliance; critics say this is not residential trash and cannot be counted. A cast-iron water main laid down in the 1870s breaks at 3 o'clock in the morning of January 24 under Seventh Avenue south of 16th Street, flooding Chelsea with millions of gallons of water before work crews can shut off the flow (see 1983). Subway service is halted for 10 hours, surface transit is affected throughout much of Manhattan, business firms are crippled between 14th and 18th streets, and residents of the area are left for several days without steam heat, electricity, or water.

The city begins January 22 to spend $660 million on a 5-year program to cut the flow of pollution into its reservoirs, avoiding the need for a $4 billion filtration plant, but the U.S. Department of Justice files suit against the city April 24 for failing to build a $600 million filtration plant to clean drinking water from reservoirs in the Croton watershed east of the Hudson, many of them polluted but still producing about 10 percent of the city's water supply. Money shortages and location disputes have delayed completion of the plant for 20 years, and the city has since June 1993 been in violation of the federal Safe Drinking Water Act. The alternative $660 million program, created under an agreement worked out among city, state, and federal environmental officials with a coalition of small watershed communities, provides for the money to be given to the communities to support economic development projects in the Catskills and combat pollution by buying thousands of acres of land around reservoirs and upgrade more than 100 aging sewage-treatment plants. It will increase a typical city water bill in steps from $400 to $435 by the year 2002.

Sandhogs working on a third water tunnel for the city link up January 31, breaking through the bedrock between two sections more than 600 feet beneath Maspeth, Queens (see 1937). Begun in 1970, the tunnel's first phase—a 13.5-mile section from the Hillview Reservoir in Yonkers through the Bronx and Manhattan and under the East River to Astoria, Queens—was completed in 1993; the second phase has been progressing from Hicks and Nelson streets in Brooklyn's Red Hook section with help from a $12 million, British-made tunnel borer that chips out a cylinder 20 feet in diameter. Completion of the 60-mile-long third tunnel under four boroughs is not expected until 2020 at the earliest and is projected to cost at least $6 billion (see 1998).

Parks Department employees cut down hundreds of beetle-infested Norway maples, horse chestnut, and other hardwood shade trees at Greenpoint, Brooklyn, in early March before the dormant beetles' larvae can hatch. Asian long-horned beetles native to China, Japan, and the Korean peninsula can be up to an inch and a half long, some arrived last year in solid wood packing material from China, they pose a threat to old or ailing trees throughout much of the northeast, Parks Commissioner Henry J. Stern assures Greenpoint residents that the city will replace the felled trees by fall with more than 1,000 new trees, each 10 to 20 feet tall, but the black-bodied, white-spotted beetles will show up in two Central Park maples early in 2002, raising fears that they may spread to rural woods and forests.

Former parks commissioner August Heckscher dies of heart failure at New York April 5 at age 83.

A new Central Park Children's Zoo opens September 17 with an admission fee of $2.50 for adults, 50¢ for children. Formally named the Tisch Children's Zoo (philanthropists Henry and Edith Everett revoked their gift of $3 million in April and the Tisch Foundation has replaced that sum and added another $1.5 million), it occupies just over half an acre, has domestic animals, its Enchanted Forest accounts for about three-quarters of its space and contains small animals and birds, and it is the only facility in the country designed for children too young to read.

Central Park's 45-acre Great Lawn between 79th and 86th streets reopens to the public October 10 after a face-lift that has cost $18.2 million (see 1996); the lush blue-grass covering of its 14-acre Great Oval has taken firm root, it has been engineered for irrigation and drainage, and it is surrounded by a six-gated six-foot fence that will remain for at least a year, with 270 automatic sprinklers and strict taboos against dogs and cricket players.

The City Council votes October 14 to double and triple fines for repeated violations of the city's noise code (see 1996). "New York is never going to be a sleepy town where you hear the crickets chirping, but I think we can make it a little quieter, a little saner," says Councilman A. Gifford Miller, who drafted the new legislation. Third offenses under the new law can bring fines as high as $525 for animals (barking dogs most commonly), $750 for car alarms, $1,050 for radios, $2,625 for car horns, $4,200 for motorcycles, air conditioners, or jackhammers, and $24,000 for bars. No mention is made of sanitation trucks, whose hydraulic compression disturbs the sleep of so many New Yorkers, and implementation of the new law remains problematical, given the paucity of Environmental Protection Department investigators and the limitations on their powers.

A bitter struggle threatens in January to tear apart the 23-year-old Park Slope, Brooklyn, Food Cooperative that has grown to have 5,200 members. Three of six board members are accused of letting six full-time coordinators run the operation without oversight and packing the monthly meetings with their supporters.

The C. Y. Bravo supermarket opens in early February on Fifth Avenue at 126th Street, becoming the first black-owned supermarket in Harlem. Guyanese immigrant Wellton Skeefers and his partner Leon Woo plan to get a Small Business Administration-guaranteed loan for minority-group members.

Citarella continues expansion with the opening of new departments that cater to take-out meal buyers (see 1982). It opens an East Side store near the southeast corner of Third Avenue and 75th Street, and in 2003 will take over Balduccci's (see restaurant, 1999). Fairway Market on the Upper West Side and Jefferson Market in Greenwich Village expand considerably by taking over adjoining space. Korean-born grocers in Flatbush, Brooklyn, begin learning some Creole to please Haitian customers and hire more non-Koreans in an effort to bridge cultural differences that have discouraged shopping by Caribbean-born patrons.

More than half of the city's green markets remain open through the winter, selling apples, baked goods, cheeses, potatoes, and other items. Newspaper delivery services in the city offer customers milk, cheese, bread, and bagels as well as papers.

The Grill Room opens at the Wintergarden of 2 World Financial Center in lower Manhattan under the direction of restaurateur Larry Forgione to serve affluent patrons with good food and stunning views of yachts (belonging for the most part to brokers, not customers) on the lower Hudson.

The elegant French restaurant Jean-Georges opens in March at the Trump International Hotel, 1 Central Park West, under the direction of Alsatian-born chef-restaurateur Jean-Georges Vongerichten, 40, who has been in America since 1985. His new restaurant seats 68 and aims to compete with Lutèce, Michael, and one or two others as the best in the city.

Le Cirque 2000 opens May 1 in part of the landmarked 1884 Villard houses at the 17-year-old Palace Hotel off Madison Avenue, now owned by the royal family of Brunei (it will be extensively redecorated and refurbished next year under the direction of architects Hardy Holzman Pfeiffer).

The New York State Court of Appeals at Albany over-turns a February 1996 decision and rules unanimously June 17 that Mayor Giuliani can bar sidewalk food vendors from congested midtown Manhattan and downtown Brooklyn streets. The Giuliani administration implements a plan to enforce the new restrictions and drive out vendors from more than 20 midtown streets in order to ease crowding.

1998 President Clinton appoints New York-born diplomat-investment banker Richard C. A. Holbrooke, 57, chief U.S. representative at the United Nations June 17. Holbrooke negotiated the Bosnia peace agreement at Dayton, Ohio, 3 years ago and continues to live with his family in their Central Park West apartment, using the official $27,000-per-month residence atop the Waldorf Towers only for official functions.

Former congresswoman Bella Abzug dies of complications following heart surgery at Columbia-Presbyterian Hospital March 31 at age 77; former City Council president Paul O'Dwyer at his Goshen, N.Y., home June 23 at age 90.

Gov. Pataki wins easy reelection, defeating City Council President Peter Vallone with a margin of more than 1 million votes in the largest landslide for a Republican governor in the state's history (he receives 348,272 votes on the Conservative Party line), but voters oust three-term U.S. Sen. Alfonse "Al" D'Amato, now 61, and elect Democratic congressman Charles "Chuck" Schumer, 47, of Brooklyn. Sen. Daniel Patrick Moynihan, now 71, announces that he will not seek reelection, making it certain that the state will have no one with seniority rights in the U.S. Senate.

Federal District Court Judge David G. Trager gives Lemrich Nelson, Jr., now 22, the maximum 19-year prison sentence March 31 for the fatal stabbing of Hasidic student Yankel Rosenbaum in the 1991 Crown Heights riots (see 1997). Nelson insists he is innocent and has been made a scapegoat. Mayor Giuliani apologizes on behalf of the city for the riots April 2 (former Mayor Dinkins takes issue with Giuliani's characterization of the police department's response to the riots), and he awards $1.5 million to the Lubavitcher community. (Nelson's conviction will be overturned on appeal in 2002.)

A federal jury convicts former police officer Francis X. Livoti June 26 of willful assault that caused "bodily injury" in the 1994 choking of Anthony Baez (see 1996). U.S. Attorney Mary Jo White says the verdict in the case "shows that police officers who commit acts of brutality can be prosecuted and convicted, even, as the government states in its summation, when other officers fabricate testimony or cover up the truth." The city agrees October 1 to pay the Baez family $2.94 million, believed to be the largest settlement ever made in a case of wrongful death arising from police misconduct (the family had sought $48 million).

Immigration authorities free more than 40 of the deaf Mexicans they have held since August of last year, give them work permits July 17, and provide them with good housing in a renovated East New York, Brooklyn, shelter where lights flash when someone is at the door and beds are fitted with devices that make them shake when children cry at night (13 adults and four children chose earlier in the week to return to Mexico). The city pays for interpreters, social workers, mental health workers, and teachers.

More than 4,000 demonstrators march down Fifth Avenue October 19 in a rally to protest the homophobic killing of 22-year-old student Matthew Shepard in Wyoming 7 days earlier. They carry a pine coffin and signs that read, "Where Is Your Rage?" (against gay-bashing) but have no permit for the march; police in riot gear, some of them on horseback, make nearly 100 arrests as scuffles break out and several people sustain slight injuries. The event ends with a candlelight vigil.

A New York State survey released in March finds that only 29 percent of New York City welfare recipients found full-time or part-time jobs in the first several months after they were dropped from public assistance between July 1996 and April 1, 1997. While it does not take into account people who work off the books, or are self-employed, or whose employers do not report wage data promptly, the study raises doubts that cutting off aid will put people to work.

Citicorp chairman John S. Reed and Sanford I. Weill of Travelers Group stun the financial community April 6 with the announcement that they will merge to create Citigroup, a $50.4 billion combination that will be the world's largest financial institution, offering corporate banking, private banking, consumer finance, credit cards, life insurance, property and casualty insurance, and investment services on a global basis. Reed, now 59, and Weill, now 65, know the merger may violate the Glass-Steagall Act of 1933, but the Federal Reserve Board approves it in September.

Goldman, Sachs partners vote in mid-June to sell up to 17 percent of the 129-year-old investment bank's shares to the public beginning in August, but the plan is aborted in late September as markets gyrate. Goldman remains the last major private partnership in Wall Street.

More than 20,000 construction workers stage a rally outside Metropolitan Transportation Authority headquarters on Madison Avenue at 54th Street June 30 to protest use of a non-union contractor on a site at Ninth Avenue and 54th Street. The rally paralyzes traffic on Madison and Fifth avenues, and 21 people, 18 of them police officers, are hurt in clashes with mounted police dispatched to control the crowd.

The city's Department of Business Services announces July 29 that it will not renew the contract of the 10-year-old Grand Central Partnership, thus stopping the business improvement district from collecting fees from property owners for services that include garbage pickups, security, and street beautification (fees will still be collected to service an accumulated debt of $32 million held by bond owners). The BDI's president Daniel A. Biederman, now 44, and his board have not complied with regulations or cooperated with officials, says the department, and it threatens to disband Biederman's 34th Street Partnership and Bryant Park Restoration Corp. as well (his combined salary has been $335,000 plus $30,000 in health benefits).

The 128-year-old Frankfurt-based Deutsche Bank and New York's Bankers Trust announce finalization November 30 of a $9.7 billion merger that creates the world's largest financial-services firm (as measured by assets). The eighth largest U.S. bank, Bankers Trust has lost heavily in the global financial turmoil of recent months.

Wall Street's Dow Jones Industrial Average closes at 9033.23 April 6, crossing the 9000 mark for the first time, and closes at 9333.97 July 17; it drops nearly 2,000 points in the next 6 weeks before recovering to set new highs, but only 41 percent of U.S. households (1995 figures) own any equities (mostly through mutual funds), and although that represents an increase from 32 percent in 1989 and 37 percent in 1992, the gap between rich and poor is widening.

NASDAQ (National Association of Securities Dealers) chairman Frank G. Zarb acquires the American Stock Exchange in late October and works with city and state officials to obtain a $200 million subsidy package that will enable it to build a new joint headquarters, probably in a 40-story structure that developer Douglas Durst plans to build on the west side of Sixth Avenue between 42nd and 43rd streets.

Wall Street's Dow Jones Industrial Average roars back to set a new high of 9374.27 November 23, and closes the year at 9181.43 (the NASDAQ closes at a record 2192.70, helped in large part by gains in stocks of Internet-related companies).

The real estate firm Cushman & Wakefield reports in November that Madison Avenue between 57th and 72nd streets has become the world's costliest retail shopping space, with monthly rents averaging more than $43 per square foot.

Former Tiffany & Co. window dresser Gene Moore dies at his Manhattan home November 23 at age 88. Tiffany's draws the curtains on its five window displays November 25 in tribute.

The E-Z Pass speeds bridge, highway, and tunnel traffic in and about the city (see 1997): five Northeastern toll authorities have signed a $4.88 million contract in March with Omaha-based MFS Network Technologies, a motorist prepays a minimum of $25 to obtain the pass, an electronic device at the toll plaza "reads" the pass, there is no need to roll down a window, and the motorist receives regular statements.

Yellow-cab taxi drivers stage demonstrations in May to protest Giuliani administration rules that make it difficult for them to make a living. Drivers typically clear about $80 per day, enjoy no union protection, and have no health insurance or pensions; the owners of the city's 12,187 medallioned cabs are often middlemen who profit most from a system that encourages reckless driving by the hard-pressed drivers.

The 2-year-old Danish container ship *Regina Maersk* passes under the Bayonne Bridge July 22 and negotiates the Kill van Kull with help from two seasoned New York Harbor pilots, but the ship carries only 20 percent of a full load. While Congress has authorized spending $35 million to deepen the major channels of the harbor, the pace of dredging by the Army Corps of Engineers has been slow, and major shipping companies have said they may move their cargo-handling operations to another East Coast port with lower rents and deeper channels.

Grand Central Terminal is rededicated October 1 after a massive 2-year, $197 million restoration job by the architectural firm of Beyer Blinder Belle. A new eastern stairway has been added, increasing access to the concourse balconies; a low deck that has covered the east ramp to the Oyster Bar since 1927 is gone, permitting light from the terminal's skylights to reach the concourse; the blue-green ceiling has been repainted and improved with a fiber-optic lighting system that employs hundreds of light bulbs; the terminal's chandeliers have been cleaned and repaired to sparkle as they did in 1913; and a plaque on a wall of the 42nd Street waiting room pays tribute to the late Jacqueline Kennedy Onassis, who helped save the terminal from destruction in the 1970s.

A new rail-freight link opens on the Harlem River in the Bronx October 12 in an effort to reduce the number of tractor-trailers on local highways, decrease diesel-fume pollution, allow freight trains to bypass commuter tracks (the derailment of a Conrail train September 18 stopped traffic for a day on Metro-North's Hudson River line) and (among other things) permit produce from New Jersey to arrive at the Hunt's Point Market by rail instead of truck. Less than two miles long, the Oak Point Link occupies a 28-acre intermodal yard, has taken 1 year to complete, and cost the State Department of Transportation $100 million per mile, but it is expected to attract businesses to the Bronx, Brooklyn, and Bay Shore from parts of New Jersey where they moved in the 1970s to be closer to rail yards.

State health inspectors make unannounced visits to Columbia-Presbyterian, New York, and St. Lukes-Roosevelt hospitals in March, demanding documents and charts to enforce 10-year-old regulations that bar emergency-room physicians from working more than 12 straight hours, medical-ward residents from working more than 24 straight hours, and surgery residents from working without a 16-hour break between 24-hour-plus shifts (see Libby Zion, 1984).

Gov. Pataki uses his line-item veto April 26 to block $5.25 million for AIDS and H.I.V. programs, $17.2 million for a 2.5 percent cost-of-living adjustment in the pay of mental health employees of nonprofit providers, and $1 million to help create the first U.S. cancer map.

Mount Sinai and New York University Medical Centers merge July 17, creating the Mount Sinai-NYU Hospitals/Health System and bringing their medical schools under one institutional umbrella.

Mayor Giuliani attacks methadone treatment for heroin addicts July 20, calling it an exchange of one chemical dependency for another (see 1964); he proposes a plan in August to wean former heroin addicts away from methadone. Most experts protest the idea, noting that 20 to 45 patients in methadone-to-abstinence programs typically relapse within 1 year, even when highly motivated, and that little research exists to show who might benefit from such programs. Retired Rockefeller University professor Vincent P. Dole, now 85, calls the plan "a radical experiment with no research or background and certainly not with the informed consent of any of the subjects."

Brooklyn's 113-year-old Salem Evangelical Lutheran Church becomes the Salam Arabic Lutheran Church. It applied to the New York Synod of the Evangelical Church in America for an Arab pastor in August 1992.

Borough Park Orthodox rabbi Moshe Sherer dies in Manhattan May 17 at age 76. He has built up his Congregation Agudath Israel in Brooklyn and transformed its lobbying group, headquartered at 84 William Street in Manhattan, into a powerful right-wing political force with branches nationwide and a claimed membership of 100,000; Hungarian-born Satmar Hasidic leader Rabbi Leibish Lefkowitz dies of pneumonia at Mount Sinai Medical Center August 1 at age 78.

The Board of Education votes unanimously March 18 to require public elementary-school pupils to wear uniforms beginning in the fall of 1999 (see 1994). Individual schools may opt out of the program, as may parents of individual pupils, but many parents complain that while the measure is ostensibly designed to focus attention on learning rather than on fashion statements it does not begin to address the more basic needs to improve school buildings, reduce class sizes, and devote more resources to public education.

Schools Chancellor Rudy Crew vows April 20 that beginning in the spring of 2000 he will hold back fourth and seventh graders who fail to meet minimum standards for their grade level, but he says that he hopes to have more opportunities for summer school and longer hours for teaching in the regular school year. Crew makes no comment in November when he releases the results of a state benchmark reading test, given in the spring that show significant declines in reading ability among third- and sixth-grade pupils in at least 30 of 33 school districts across the city (scores among eighth graders remain virtually unchanged).

Gov. Pataki vetoes a $500 million school construction fund April 26 because it is not specific about how the money would be used, there is plenty of unspent money in the pipeline, and the measure would have been funded largely by borrowing. His line-item veto also nixes $77.5 million in teacher support aid, a $13 million increase in base aid for SUNY's community colleges, money to provide SUNY and CUNY students with $65 each per year for textbooks, $5.4 million for new CUNY faculty members, and $2.5 million for new SUNY faculty members.

City University trustees vote May 26 to phase out "remediation" in the system's 11 4-year colleges. The new policy will prevent freshmen and transfer students from enrolling unless they have passed a set of placement examinations in reading, writing, and mathematics, making the colleges much more selective than they have been since the adoption of an "open admissions" policy in 1970. Proponents of the measure say it will increase the value of a CUNY degree and the university is obligated to find ways to help students pass the tests quickly; opponents estimate that ending open admissions will have an adverse effect on 46 percent of black students, 51 percent of Asians, 55 percent of Hispanics, and 38 percent of whites.

New Yorker editor Tina Brown, now 44, announces July 8 that she is resigning after 6 years to start a new venture. Advance Publications chairman S. I. Newhouse, Jr. announces July 13 that 6-year *New Yorker* veteran and Pulitzer prize-winning author David Remnick, 39, will succeed Brown, becoming the fifth editor in the magazine's 73-year history.

The Spanish-language daily *Hoy* begins publication in October in slick-paper tabloid form with pages devoted to Colombian, Cuban, Dominican, Ecuadorian, Mexican, Puerto Rican, and other Hispanic groups. *Newsday* has formed a joint venture with New Jersey-based A1 Holding Co. to pursue a proposal by Cuban-born *Newsday* senior vice president Louis Sito, 52, who has observed a sharp decline in circulation of that paper in Spanish-speaking neighborhoods and seen an opportunity to challenge *El Diario-La Prensa*. That 50¢ paper has remained focused on the Puerto Rican community, but Puerto Ricans have declined as a percentage of the city's 2 million Hispanics while other groups have increased. *Hoy* sells on newsstands for only 25¢ and within 3 years will have overtaken its long-established competitor.

Former CBS news president Fred Friendly dies at his Riverdale home March 4 at age 82 following a series of strokes; publisher Theodore "Ted" Newhouse dies at New York November 28 at age 95; *Daily News* police reporter Mike McAlary of colon cancer at Columbia-Presbyterian Medical Center December 25 at age 41.

 The 163-year-old German media giant Bertelsmann A.G. buys Random House from the Newhouse family in late March for an estimated $1.4 billion and merges it with its Bantam Doubleday Dell unit (Bertelsmann also publishes *Family Circle* and *McCall's* magazines). The acquisition makes Bertelsmann larger than Simon & Schuster, whose educational division Viacom sells in mid-May to Britain's Pearson PLC in a $4.6 billion deal involving the Texas-based firm Muse, Tate & Furst that controls 450 radio stations and buys S&S's reference, business, and professional divisions (Viacom retain's S&S's trade division).

The New York Public Library main branch at 42nd Street reopens its third-floor reading room November 16 after more than 18 months' work to restore it to its 1911 splendor and equip it for Internet access plus more connections for laptop computers.

Nonfiction: *Gotham: A History of New York City to 1898* by Brooklyn College history professor Edwin G. Burrows and John Jay College of Criminal Justice history professor Mike Wallace; *American Metropolis: A History of New York City* by New York-born Bronx Community College history professor emeritus George J. (John) Lankevich, 58; *New York: An Illustrated History of the People* by Allon Schoener; *TITAN: The Life of John D. Rockefeller, Sr.* by Ron Chernow; *On the Outside Looking In: A Year in an Inner-City High School* by New York author Christina Rathbone; *The Lord Cornbury Scandal: The Politics of Reputation in British America* by NYU professor of history emerita Patricia U. Bonomi, who refutes suggestions that Cornbury was a transvestite; *The Murder of Helen Jewett: The Life and Death of a Prostitute in 19th Century New York* by New York author Patricia Cline Cohen is about the 1836 crime; *Fifth Avenue: The Best Address* by Jerry E. Patterson; *Brooklyn's Best* by Alfred Gingold and Helen Rogan; *Red-Tails in Love: A Wildlife Drama in Central Park* by *Wall Street Journal* nature columnist and veteran birder Marie Winn details the story of the hawks that appeared in 1992 and have been producing broods since 1995.

Author Cary Reich dies at New York March 3 at age 48; Alfred Kazin of prostate and bone cancer in his upper West Side home June 5 at age 83; Edward Robb Ellis at St. Vincent's Hospital September 7 at age 87.

Fiction: *The Treatment* by Random House editor-novelist Daniel Menaker, 57; *Charming Billy* by Brooklyn-born novelist Alice McDermott, now 45, is about lower-class Irish-American life in the Bronx; *Black and Blue* by Anna Quindlen.

"Eloise" creator Kay Thompson dies at New York July 2 at age 94 (approximate); novelist-playwright

Jerome Weidman at his Manhattan apartment October 6 at age 85.

Photographs: *Invisible New York: The Hidden Infrastructure of the City* by Stanley Greenberg. German-born photographer Ilse Bing dies at St. Luke's-Roosevelt Hospital March 10 at age 98. She was awarded the first Gold Medal for photography by the National Arts Club 5 years ago; picture archivist Otto L. Bettmann dies of kidney failure at Boca Raton, Fla., May 1 at age 94.

Theater: *The Beauty Queen of Leenane* by London-born playwright Martin McDonagh, 27, at the off-Broadway 165-seat Atlantic Theater in Chelsea 2/26 and 4/22 at the 949-seat Walter Kerr Theater, with Anna Manahan, Marie Mullen, Tom Murphy, Brian F. O'Byrne (it first opened in February 1996 at Galway's 400-seat Town Hall and had a run last year at London's 586-seat Royal Court Theater), 365 perfs.; *Golden Child* by David Henry Hwang 4/2 at the Longacre Theater, with Julyana Soelistyo, Randall Duk Kim, Tsai Chin, 69 perfs.; *Power Plays* by Elaine May (*The Way of All Fish* and *In and Out of the Light*) and Alan Arkin (*Virtual Reality*) 5/21 at the Promenade Theater, with May (now 66), Arkin (now 63), Jeannie Berlin, Anthony Arkin; *Side Man* by playwright Warren Leight 6/25 at the Criterion Center Stage Right (1530 Broadway), with Robert Sella, Wendy Makkena, Angelica Torn, Frank Wood, Michael Mastro; *Corpus Christi* by Terrence McNally 10/13 at the Manhattan Theater Club in the City Center arouses protests by portraying Jesus and his apostles as gay men in modern-day Corpus Christi, Texas.

Comedian Henny Youngman is hospitalized with pneumonia January 2 and dies at Mount Sinai Medical Center February 24 at age 91. He has been living in West 55th Street.

Television: *The King of Queens* 9/21 on CBS with Jerry Stiller, stand-up comedian Kevin James; *Felicity* 9/29 on WB cable TV with former Mouseketeer Keri Russell, now 22, as Felicity Porter, a California teenager who comes to New York as an NYU freshman (the show glamourizes New York, spurring student applications to NYU) (to 9/22/2002).

Ten prime-time TV series are filmed in New York, up from six in 1994.

Films: Harold Ramiris's *Analyze This* with Billy Crystal, Robert De Niro; Nora Ephron's *You've Got Mail* with Tom Hanks, Meg Ryan. Also: Bennett Miller's *The Cruise* with tour-bus guide Timothy "Speed" Levitch; Alex Proyas's *Dark City* with Rufus Sewell, Kiefer Sutherland, Jennifer Connelly; Roland Emmerich's *Godzilla* with Matthew Broder-

ick, Jean Reno, and a monster (designed by Patrick Tatopoulos) that creates havoc in New York; Spike Lee's *He Got Game* with Milwaukee Bucks basketball star Ray Allen, Denzel Washington; Hal Hartley's *Henry Fool* with Thomas Jay Ryan, James Urbaniak, Parker Posey; Erica Spellman-Silverman's *Hi-Life* with Katrin Carlidge, Charles Durning, Daryl Hannah; Boaz Yakin's *A Price Above Rubies* with Renée Zellweger, Glenn Fitzgerald; Tom DiCillo's *The Real Blonde* with Elizabeth Berkley, Matthew Modine; Lynda Obst's *The Siege* with Denzel Washington, Annette Bening, Bruce Willis.

Filmmakers shoot a record 221 pictures in New York, up from 69 in 1993, generating $2.57 billion in economic activity for the city (it is the fifth record-breaking year, and the number of days when films are shot is up 50 percent over 1994).

Broadway musicals: *Ragtime* 1/18 at the new Ford Center for the Performing Arts with Brian Stokes Mitchell, 39, as Coalhouse Walker, German-born actress Audra McDonald, 27, New York-born actor Peter Friedman, 48, book by Terrence McNally based on the 1975 E. L. Doctorow novel, music by Stephen Flaherty, lyrics by Lynn Ahrens, 834 perfs.; *Capeman* 1/29 at the Marquis Theater, with Ruben Blades, Marc Anthony, Ednita Nazario, music by Paul Simon, book by Simon and poet Derek Walcott based on a 1959 murder in Manhattan's Latino community, 68 perfs.; *Parade* 12/16 at the Vivian Beaumont Theater, with Brent Carver as Leo Frank, Carolee Carmelo as his wife, music and lyrics by Jason Robert Brown, 28, book by Alfred Uhry based on an anti-Semitic 1915 Georgia lynching, 85 perfs.

Actress-singer Theresa Merritt dies of skin cancer at Calvary Hospital in the Bronx June 12 at age 75; producer Jean Dalrymple at her West 55th Street apartment opposite the City Center November 15 at age 96.

Choreographer Jerome Robbins dies following a stroke in Manhattan July 29 at age 79.

Frank Sinatra dies of a heart attack at Los Angeles May 14 at age 82 (New York City Council speaker and gubernatorial hopeful Peter F. Vallone proposes that Sinatra's version of the 1977 Fred Ebb-John Kander song "New York, New York" be made the city's official anthem).

Baseball's opening day at the 75-year-old Yankee Stadium is delayed after a 500-pound chunk of steel crushes Seat 7 in Section 22 April 13; cynics say the accident has been staged by principal owner George Steinbrenner to bring pressure on the city to build a new stadium on Manhattan's West Side or risk having him move to a new stadium promised by New Jersey's governor. California-born Yankee pitcher David Wells hurls a perfect game May 17 at the stadium, retiring 27 Minnesota Twins batters to record the 15th perfect game in major league history. The Yankees go on to have their best season since the legendary 1927 season of Babe Ruth and Lou Gehrig, winning 114 of their 160 games to set a new American League record. They win the World Series, defeating the San Diego Padres 4 games to o.

Patrick Rafter wins in men's singles tennis at the U.S. Open, Lindsay Davenport, 22 (U.S.), in women's.

The New York Jets win their first American Football Conference (AFC) division title in 29 years December 19, defeating the Buffalo Bills 17 to 10 at Orchard Park, N.Y., with help from two touchdown passes thrown by quarterback Vinny Testaverde, 35. Coached by Bill Parcells, now 57, they have remained in contention despite a questionable ruling in an earlier game.

Former Columbia football star Sid Luckman dies at Aventura, Fla., July 5 at age 81; onetime fight announcer Don Dunphy at a suburban Roslyn hospital July 21 at age 90; former Manhattan College basketball star Junius Kellogg of respiratory failure at the Kingsbridge Veteran Affairs Medical Center in the Bronx September 16 at age 71 (he has been confined to a wheelchair since 1954); former Knicks basketball coach Red Holzman of complications from leukemia at Long Island Jewish Hospital November 13 at age 78.

● The Giuliani administration cracks down on adult-entertainment clubs beginning in July, enforcing a restrictive new zoning law that limits to 40 percent the space in a store or club and its stock in trade devoted to adult entertainment. The crackdown forces strip joints, some video stores, and clubs featuring topless dancers to close, a Supreme Court judge rules August 6 that public health laws justify the closings, but critics protest and more serious threats to the city's quality of life (car alarms, noisy sanitation trucks, and the like) go unchallenged.

The city's fashion industry goes into shock October 1 at news that Chanel, Inc. will no longer bankroll designer Isaac Mizrahi, whose firm has had retail sales of between $20 million and $30 million per year but has been losing money. Two other houses have gone out of business earlier in the year, the owners of Anne Klein put it up for sale, and the industry wonders who else will fall. Tommy Hilfiger, Donna Karan, Ralph Lauren, and a few other big names dominate the fashion scene. "It's very sad," *Harper's Bazaar* editor-in-chief Liz Tilberis tells a *New York Times* reporter, "[and] the saddest part is we are heading toward a kind of mediocrity . . . We have to have commercial clothes in the stores. But we must have a little madness." Many houses cancel their appearances at the industry's showcase of women's wear collections in Bryant Park in early November.

▥ Three gunmen get past security at 1 World Trade Center January 13, intercept two Brink's guards delivering six bags of cash to an 11th floor Bank of America currency exchange center, and escape with $1.6 million.

Federal agents arrest Gambino crime family acting boss John Gotti, Jr. January 21 and a judge indicts him on various charges, including telecommunications and construction fraud, labor racketeering, loansharking, and extortion of money from the 7-year-old topless club Scores at 330 East 60th Street; operators of the "sports cabaret" were implicated 2 years ago in an unrelated $400 million Florida fraud case and have been cooperating secretly with federal authorities investigating the Gambino family's extortion of more than $1 million from club officials and employees. John Gotti, Sr., now 57, is serving a life sentence without parole but remains in touch with his capo, John D'Amico, 63, who reportedly has homes on the upper East Side and at Hillsdale, N.J. Gotti, Sr. lived in a modest house in the Howard Beach section of Queens, Gotti, Jr. has been living in a $700,000 house in Oyster Bay, he has alienated other Gambino associates with his arrogance, and he is held without bail pending trial. Law-enforcement authorities say the power of the Mafia has waned, partly because of murderous family disputes, turncoats, and convictions; Gotti, Jr. is released on bail in late September. Scores files for bankruptcy protection October 30.

Uniformed firefighters attend a ceremony at City Hall June 3 to honor acts of bravery, 50 to 100 of them gather later at the Bryant Park Grill's outdoor café behind the public library, heavy drinking ensues, the men refuse to leave, some of them get into a bloody brawl, and three are disciplined June 12.

Federal authorities file kidnapping, extortion, and robbery charges July 7 against 28 members of the violent Asian gang Tung On, which has preyed on Chinatown since 1994. Tung On is one of four well-established Chinatown gangs (others include the Fukienese Flying Dragons) that victimize illegal immigrants and are under investigation by the FBI, the U.S. Immigration and Naturalization Service, and the city Police Department. Tung On leader Chen Kevin, 31, is among those charged in the 51-page racketeering indictment but remains at large with 12 other defendants.

The New York State Court of Appeals rules unanimously December 22 that most of the state's 1995 death-penalty law's plea-bargaining provisions are unconstitutional. The law has said that defendants who plead guilty to murder cannot be executed; the maximum penalty on a guilty plea has been imprisonment for life. The high court, however, says this arrangement places an unfair burden on defendants who opt to exercise their constitutional right to a trial; it limits the circumstances under which defendants may negotiate plea bargains.

The city ends the year with only 620 homicides, down from a peak of 2,262 in 1990 and even lower than the 1964 total of 636. Although the city's population is much larger than that of Chicago, that city now has more homicides, and out of 200 U.S. cities with populations of 200,000 or more, New York ranks 163rd in per-capita crime.

The General Motors Building on Fifth Avenue is acquired in May for $800 million by Donald Trump and the Carmel, Ind.-based insurance company Conseco (Trump will cover most of the building's ill-conceived sunken plaza and lease part of the ground floor to CBS); the Woolworth Building is acquired in late June for $155 million by the Witcoff Group development firm.

The first two buildings of Donald Trump's Riverside South begin advertising for tenants in June on the former Penn Central rail yards along the Hudson River (see 1994). Designed by Skidmore, Owings & Merrill with façades by Philip Johnson, now 92, and apartments designed by Costas Kondylis, they comprise a 40-story building at 180 Riverside Boulevard, between 68th and 69th streets with 412 rental units, and a 46-story tower at 200 Riverside Boulevard with 377 one-, two-, three-, and four-bedroom condominium units priced at between $315,000 (for a 663-square-foot one-bedroom) and $1.975 million (for a 2,200-square-foot four-bedroom). Rentals range from $1,900 per month for a studio to $7,800 for a two-bedroom, two-and-a-half-bath penthouse, with two-bedroom terraced flats fetching up to $8,500, but 104 apartments are rented at more reasonable rates ($728 per month for a two-bedroom flat) to moderate-income tenants under the state's 421a Affordable Housing Program. Owners of Lincoln Towers apartments facing west lose their views, and values of what once were river-view apartments decline somewhat in value.

Brooklyn's first large new hotel in 68 years opens July 7 near the Brooklyn Bridge: put up beside the Metrotech office and university complex completed in the 1960s as an urban-renewal project, the 376-room Marriott fills the lower seven floors of a new 32-story building whose higher floors provide office space for the borough's district attorney and business firms that include an insurance company (the St. George that opened in 1930 has been turned into a cooperative apartment house).

The Peninsula New York Hotel (originally the Gotham) reopens in November after a $45 million renovation that has involved gutting its 241 guest rooms and rebuilding them with ISDN telephone lines (for faster Internet access) and large bathrooms that have color television screens over their tubs (see 1988). A single master console on the bedside table controls lights, messages, temperature, and TV.

The first 13.5-mile section of the city's third water tunnel begins operating August 13 after 28 years of work in which 24 sandhogs have lost their lives (see 1997); a ceremony in Central Park includes the restarting of a giant fountain in the reservoir, 400 feet above the new tunnel. America's largest public works project, the tunnel is 14 feet in diameter and permits temporary closing of the tunnels that opened in 1917 and 1937 for their first inspections.

A study released in August by City Comptroller Alan G. Hevesi finds that the city will have to spend more than $90 billion in the next decade to make needed repairs on water mains, bridges, schools, and subways to keep them in safe working order; the ciy had budgeted $52 billion for such work, but Hevesi says more must be spent now on repairs and maintenance or conditions will deteriorate and it will be more expensive to do the work later.

A five-alarm fire August 28 leaves the 126-year-old Central Synagogue heavily damaged. Raging out of control for 3 hours at 652 Lexington Avenue, southwest corner 55th Street, the fire sends heavy clouds of smoke over much of the city.

A December 23 fire on the 19th floor of the 12-year-old high-rise Park South Towers leaves three women and a man dead in a stairwell. The fire had broken out in two apartments occupied by the family of child actor Macaulay Culkin. The lower 10 floors of the building have a sprinkler system, but city regulations do not require sprinkler systems for upper residential floors.

The 64-year-old Rainbow Room atop the General Electric Building closes to the general public

December 19 and will be open henceforth only for private functions (except for Friday evenings and Sunday brunch, beginning in February of next year). Tishman Speyer Properties has acquired Rockefeller Center and raised the annual rent on the space from $3 million to $4 million, B. E. Rock has not renewed its lease after 11 years of managing the restaurant along with its Rainbow & Stars cabaret and Promenade Bar; the Cipriani family of Venice has acquired the lease.

Mortimer's restaurant founder Glenn Bernbaum dies at New York the night of September 7 at age 76; restaurateur Joseph H. Baum of prostate cancer at his Manhattan apartment October 5 at age 78.

The U.S. Supreme Court rules 6 to 3 May 26 that New Jersey has sovereignty over the landfill area that represents nearly 90 percent of Ellis Island (*see* 1990). The ruling's chief effect is to let New Jersey receive the tax revenues from souvenirs sold on the island through which millions of immigrants arrived in America.

1999 Federal Judge William H. Pauley III rules January 25 that the Giuliani administration has violated federal law in its zeal to overhaul welfare; it is overlooking the "urgent needs of the poor," says Judge Pauley, and he bars the city from expanding its tough new "workfare" policies until it can guarantee prompt access to food stamps and Medicaid applications. Training and procedures must be revised, he says, and his decision puts at least a temporary stop to conversion of welfare offices into "job centers."

The shooting of West African immigrant street vendor Amadou Diallo, 22, at the entrance to his Bronx apartment house February 4 raises new charges of police racism and brutality. Four plainclothes officers of the elite street crimes unit fire 41 bullets at Diallo, who is unarmed, and he is hit by 19 of them. Demonstrations protest the excesses of the 380-member unit, which last year frisked 27,061 people for weapons, up from 18,023 in 1997, and made 4,647 arrests. Dispatched each night into neighborhoods considered dangerous with instructions to apprehend muggers, dangerous fugitives, and rapists, the officers are credited with having seized 40 percent of all the illegal guns confiscated in the city, but critics charge that they violate civil rights by singling out blacks and Hispanics (*see* 2000).

Mayor Giuliani issues orders in November for police to arrest homeless persons if they refuse to move on or accept a ride to a shelter. The crackdown begins November 23, more than 220 people are arrested within 3 weeks, but the state supreme court issues a restraining order to prevent implementation December 12 of the mayor's order that able-bodied shelter residents who refuse to accept jobs be evicted, and if they are parents that their children be taken away on grounds of negligence. Cities nationwide have taken punitive measures to reduce homelessness, but the city with America's strongest constitutionally based right to shelter has tried to implement the nation's harshest sanctions against the homeless, and critics accuse the mayor of "criminalizing" homelessness.

Former International Rescue Committee chairman Leo Cherne dies at Mount Sinai Medical Center January 12 at age 86; philanthropist Paul Mellon of cancer at his Upperville, Va., home February 1 at age 91.

Legislation signed by Gov. Pataki ends the commuter tax that has been levied in varying forms since 1966, costing more than 800,000 people who work in the city 0.4 percent of their income; the city has been deriving $210 million per year from about 480,000 suburban Long Island, Rockland County, and Westchester commuters, the state stops collecting the tax from their paychecks July 1, but 340,000 New Jersey and Connecticut commuters remain subject to the tax, which has been producing $150 million in revenues. Mayor Giuliani has protested the law, insisting that suburbanites who enjoy police and fire-department protection and other city services have a duty to help support those services; repeal of the law, he has said, was a product of politics "out of control," blaming it on the legislator "who panders to the people in Rockland County and doesn't accomplish anything for them" (*see* 2000).

The Swingline stapler company relocates to Nogales, Mexico, in May after more than 50 years in Long Island City, taking 450 jobs and leaving a 285,000-square-foot plant at 32-00 Skillman Avenue plus a 140,000-square-foot annex across Queens Boulevard at 45-20 43rd Street (*see* MoMA, 2002).

Wall Street's Dow Jones Industrial Average closes at 10006.84 March 29, having broken through the 10000 mark earlier on an interday basis. It closes at 11014 May 3, breaking through 11000 for the first time. The NASDAQ average closes at 3028.51 November 3, breaking through the 3000 mark as investors continue their demand for technology stocks.

The Financial Services Modernization Act signed into law by President Clinton November 12 repeals parts of the 1933 Glass-Steagall Act, allowing the merger of banks, securities firms, and insurance companies.

Beirut-born international banker Edmond J. Safra dies in a fire set by two intruders at his Monaco penthouse December 3 at age 67 while he negotiates a deal to sell his Republic National Bank of New York for $9.9 billion. HSBC (Hong Kong and Shanghai Banking Corp.) acquires Republic and will transform its branches into HSBC branches.

Wall Street's Dow Jones Industrial Average closes at 11497.12 December 31, up 25.2 percent for the year; the NASDAQ at 4069.31, up 85.59 percent since the end of 1998.

A Fifth Avenue Brooks Brothers store opens May 3 at the southwest corner of 53rd Street, where the two-story premises occupy part of the 666 Fifth Avenue office tower to supplement the 84-year-old main store on Madison Avenue at 44th Street.

MetroCard machines are installed beginning January 25 at subway stations, initially at the 68th Street Lexington Avenue station and at Columbus Circle, under a program that will employ roughly 2,500 vending machines in place of token-booth clerks. The machines cost $50,000 each; they accept cash, credit cards, or debit cards, offer audio or print instructions in six languages, and will be installed in public buildings and at other sites outside the subway system. The aim of the program is to reassign token-booth clerks to work as attendants and service representatives.

The city's last Checker taxi fails to meet inspection tests and goes out of service July 26, but some Japanese minivans have been introduced as an alternative to the Fords and Chevrolets that have long held dominance in taxi fleets.

An outbreak of encephalitis in late August is the first in the city's history. More than a dozen cases have been identified by mid-September, three elderly people have died, and the Public Health Department sprays all the boroughs with malathion in an effort to kill the mosquitoes that transmit the disease from birds to humans. Four more people in the metropolitan area die, a total of 62 are infected, and the illness is traced to the West Nile virus, first recognized in 1937 but never before seen in America (*see* 2000).

Gov. Pataki appoints former deputy mayor and former City University of New York trustee Herman Badillo, now 69, chairman of CUNY May 30. Badillo is a longtime critic of CUNY, which he has accused of grade inflation and low standards for graduation.

Schools Chancellor Rudy Crew announces an overhaul of the school system June 23, using expanded powers granted to him under a state law enacted in December 1996; he dismisses three superintendents outright, closes 13 schools, takes direct control of 43 others, and holds back thousands of failing students. Results of a fourth-grade math test and eighth-grade math and language-skills tests released by the State Education Department in the fall show that about two-thirds of city eighth graders failed the English language test, about three-quarters failed the math test, and half the fourth graders failed the math test. Critics blame the poor showing on low academic standards, a surfeit of uncertified teachers, and unfair testing, but the figures for New York are similar to those nationwide, and more sophisticated analyses suggest that the problem is related less to the schools themselves than to environmental factors related to poverty and peer pressure that supports poor academic performance. Crew resigns under pressure at Christmas after feuding with Mayor Giuliani; he will be succeeded by New York-born businessman Harold O. Levy, 48, a former Citigroup executive who will be elected unanimously May 17 of next year after demonstrating as interim chancellor that he has a grasp of the problems facing the city's failing public school system.

Daily News truck drivers receive large wage increases following arbitration March 8 (*see* 1995). Members of the paper's craft unions are entitled to the same raises under terms of a clause in their contracts; owner Mortimer Zuckerman has invested heavily in newsroom computerization, extra reporters, and Balkan war coverage, but despite price cutting and repeated editor replacements the paper's circulation has declined since 1995, advertising revenues have dropped accordingly, and there are doubts about how long the *News* can survive.

Former Grey Advertising CEO Arthur C. Fatt dies at his Delray Beach, Fla., winter home January 12 at age 94; *El Diario/La Prensa* publisher Carlos D. Ramírez of pancreatic cancer at a Manhattan hospital July 11 at age 52; *George* magazine cofounder John F. Kennedy, Jr., in the crash of his Piper Saratoga plane en route to Martha's Vineyard July 16 at age 38; advertising pioneer David Ogilvy dies at his Château Touffou home near Bonnes in the Loire Valley July 21 at age 88; *New Yorker* cartoonist Whitney Darrow, Jr. at Burlington, Vt., August 10 at age 89; electrical billboard impresario Douglas Leigh at a Manhattan hospital December 14 at age 92.

Nonfiction: *Divided We Stand: A Biography of New York's World Trade Center* by New York-born author Eric Darton, 49; *The Great Game: The Emergence of Wall Street as a World Power 1653–2000* by New York-born author John Steele Gordon, 55; *New York: An Illustrated History* by Ric Burns and James Sanders; *Once Upon a Time in New York: Jimmy Walker, Franklin Roosevelt and the Last Great Battle of the Jazz Age* by Herbert Mitgang, now 79; *New York 1880: Architecture and Urbanism in the Gilded Age* by Robert A. M. Stern, Thomas Mellins, and David Fishman; *The Creative Destruction of Manhattan, 1900–1940* by Yale historian Max Page, 33, who writes, "Contrary to the popular sense of New York as an ahistorical city, the past—as recalled, invented, and manipulated by powerful New Yorkers—was, in fact, at the heart of defining how the city would henceforth be built. Indeed, all of the diverse city-building efforts New Yorkers took part in and witnessed were shaped by the use and invention of collective memories. Collective memories were fashioned and used with abandon by the city's builders in complex and sometimes contradictory ways: by real estate developers hoping to enhance the prestige of Fifth Avenue; by historic preservation advocates seeking moral inspiration and assimilationist lessons through the preservation of historic landmarks; by tenement reformers eager to expunge deplorable memories of slums; and by street tree advocates who saw in nature a link to a more stable pace of change that would serve as a palliative for the ills of the modern city;" *Cities Back from the Edge: New Life for Downtown* by journalist-urban critic Roberta Brandes Gratz and downtown revitalization consultant Norman Mintz; *Vampires, Dragons, and Egyptian Kings: Youth Gangs in Postwar New York* by Eric C. Schneider, who suggests that lack of economic opportunity is what led many working-class youths to join gangs; *Urban Castles: Tenement Housing and Landlord Activism in New York City, 1890–1943* by Jared N. Day.

Author William H. Whyte dies at Lenox Hill Hospital January 13 at age 81; business historian Robert Sobel of brain cancer at his Long Beach, L.I., home June 2 at age 68.

Fiction: *The Night Inspector* by Brooklyn-born novelist Frederick Busch, 58; *Geographies of Home* by New York novelist Loida Maritz Pérez; *Dreamland* by Englewood, N.J.,-born novelist Kevin (Breen) Baker, 41, is about Coney Island and early 20th century city crime and politics; *The Big Bad City* by Ed McBain (Evan Hunter) (his 49th Ed McBain novel).

Novelist Mario Puzo dies of heart failure at his Bay Shore home July 2 at age 78.

HarperCollins acquires William Morrow as consolidation continues in the book-publishing industry.

 Mayor Giuliani threatens September 2 to cut off all city funding of the Brooklyn Museum unless it cancels an exhibition of art scheduled to open October 2. The collection of London advertising man and contemporary arts patron Charles Saatchi, 56, of Saatchi & Saatchi includes a portrait of a black Virgin Mary stained with elephant dung, a bust of a man made from his own frozen blood, and a shark suspended in a tank of formaldehyde. Art critics praise the work (the mayor has only seen the catalogue but calls the works "sick stuff"), and Giuliani comes under fire for trying to censor legitimate expressions of talent.

Artist-cartoonist Saul Steinberg dies at his Manhattan home May 12 at age 84; art dealer Leo Castelli at his Manhattan home August 21 at age 91.

 Theater: *Voices in the Dark* by John Pielmeier 8/12 at the Longacre Theater, with Judith Ivey, 68 perfs.; *Epic Proportions* by Larry Coen and David Crane 9/30 at the Helen Hayes Theater, with Tom Beckett, Kristin Chenoweth, 92 perfs.; *Waiting in the Wings* by the late Noël Coward 12/16 at the Walter Kerr Theater with Rosemary Harris, Rosemary Murphy, Elizabeth Wilson, Lauren Bacall (to Eugene O'Neill Theater, 2/15/2000), 144 perfs.

Actress Susan Strasberg dies of cancer at her Manhattan home January 21 at age 60; Circle in the Square cofounder José Quintero at New York February 26 at age 74; comedienne Peggy Cass at New York March 8 at age 73; playwright-director Garson Kanin at his Manhattan apartment March 13 at age 86; theater patron Lucille Lortel at New York Presbyterian Hospital April 4 at age 98; comedian Joey Adams at St. Vincent's Hospital December 2 at age 88, survived by his gossip-columnist wife, Cindy (née Heller).

Television: Ric Burns's documentary *New York* 11/14 on PBS (five episodes, with a sixth scheduled for January 2000).

Films: Martin Scorsese's *Bringing Out the Dead* with Nicolas Cage, Patricia Arquette; Tim Robbins's *Cradle Will Rock* with Rubén Blades, John Carpenter, John Cusack, Bill Murray, Susan Sarandon, John Turturro, Emily Watson; Joel Schumacher's *Flawless* with Robert De Niro, Philip Seymour Hoffmann; Richard Wenk's *Just the Ticket* with Andie MacDowell, Andy Garcia, Elizabeth Ashley, Abe Vigoda, Bill Irwin, Mayor Giuliani's wife, Donna Hanover; Wes Craven's *Music of the Heart* with Meryl Streep, Aidan Quinn, Angela Bassett, Gloria Estefan; Bruno de Almeida's *On the Run* with Richard Imperiolo, John Ventiniglia, Drena De Niro; Rob Minkoff's *Stuart Little* with Sony Pictures Imageworks animation, voices of Michael J. Fox, Geena Davis, Jonathan Lipnicki, Julia Sweeney, Nathan Lane; Spike Lee's *Summer of Sam* with John Leguizamo, Adrien Brody, Mira Sorvino, Jennifer Esposito; John McTiernan's *The Thomas Crown Affair* with Pierce Brosnan, Rene Russo, Denis Leary, Ben Gazzara.

Actress Sylvia Sidney dies at Lenox Hill Hospital July 1 at age 88.

Broadway musicals: *Contact* 10/7 at the Mitzi E. Newhouse Theater, with dancer-actors Boyd Gaines, Jack Hayes, Deborah Yates, book by John Weidman, choreography by Susan Stroman, 1,110 perfs.; *Saturday Night Fever* 10/21 at the Minskoff Theater, with a cast of 42, stage adaptation by Nan Knighton of the 1977 film, songs by the Bee Gees, 500 perfs.

Radio City Music Hall reopens October 4 after a 7-month, $70 million restoration supervised by architect Hugh Hardy of Hardy Holzman Pfeiffer Associates.

Jazz vibraphonist Milt Jackson of Modern Jazz Quartet fame dies of liver cancer at St. Luke's-Roosevelt Hospital October 29 at age 76.

Yankee right-hander David Cone pitches a perfect game July 18, holding the Montreal Expos hitless through nine innings at the stadium in 98° F. heat as a crowd of 41,930 that includes veteran Don Larsen looks on.

Former Yankee All-Star Joe DiMaggio dies of lung cancer and pneumonia at his Hollywood, Fla., home March 8 at age 84; former Dodgers shortstop Pee Wee Reese of lung cancer at Louisville, Ky., August 14 at age 81; former Yankee pitcher Jim "Catfish" Hunter of amytrophic lateral sclerosis (Lou Gehrig's disease) at his Hertford, N.C., home September 9 at age 53.

The New York Mets win their division title but lose to the Atlanta Braves in the National League playoffs. The New York Yankees win the American League pennant, narrowly defeating the Boston Red Sox after a series of wrong calls by umpires that went against the Sox, and the Yankees go on to win their 25th World Series (no other team has won more than nine), defeating the Atlanta Braves 4 games to 0.

Andre Agassi, now 29, wins in men's singles at the U.S. Open, Serena Williams, 17, in women's singles.

Times Square 2000 celebrates New Year's Eve as if it were the end of the millennium, with a televised extravaganza beginning at 6:30 o'clock in the morning of December 31 and continuing for 24 hours (to mark the new year as it begins in various countries around the world), parades from 42nd Street to 48th, a Waterford crystal ball six feet in diameter and weighing 1,070 pounds, a 16-foot Father Time, and a crowd estimated to number 1.5 million, but the annual International Debutante Ball is canceled because so many people want to avoid the traffic congestion attendant to the celebration.

All remaining U.S. cigarette billboards come down by midnight April 21 as part of the $206 billion agreement reached last year between tobacco companies and 40 states. Anti-smoking billboards take their place in many states, some of them suggesting that smoking saps a man's sexual powers, but New York State drags its feet, raising criticisms that tobacco companies are using political muscle to resist implementation of effective anti-smoking efforts (23 percent of adults in the state continued to smoke in 1996, as compared with 18 percent in California). A city law banning most outdoor advertisements for tobacco products and restricting such ads in stores has taken effect in January, but a group of grocery stores has filed suit against the city on First Amendment grounds, and Judge Deborah Batts of the U.S. District Court strikes down the law December 15 on grounds that federal labeling laws bar

The Yankees had their most successful season since 1927, recalling the glory years when they seemed unbeatable.

cities and states from imposing further restrictions on cigarette advertising.

 Federal authorities announce October 27 that eight U.S. Department of Agriculture food inspectors at the Hunts Point Terminal Market in the Bronx have been arrested on charges of having participated in a bribery and kickback scheme that allowed wholesalers to cheat their suppliers, declaring food to be of lower quality and thereby letting the wholesalers pay less for fruits and vegetables. The eight have had salaries of between $40,000 and $50,000 per year but have allegedly taken as much as $100,000 each per year in illegal payoffs; they include seven of the 14 USDA inspectors currently assigned to Hunts Point plus one no longer having that assignment, and 13 employees of wholesalers are also charged. The market has become so corrupt that some growers have told authorities they no longer wish to sell their produce in New York, and a 2-year undercover investigation ("Operation Forbidden Fruit") has brought the racket to light.

The 48-story Condé Nast Building is completed in August at 4 Times Square, northeast corner Broadway and 42nd Street, to designs by Robert Fox & Bruce Fowle of Fox & Fowle, who have used the various façades of the building for advertising spectaculars. John Burgee and Philip Johnson had designed four granite shafts with mansard roofs for the four corners of Times Square in the 1980s, intending them as a businesslike rebuke to the sleaziness that dominated the area at the time, but the Empire State Development Corp. engaged planner Rebecca Robertson to study the situation, she hired architect Robert A. M. Stern and graphic designer Tibor Kalman's M & Co. to codify what she called the "honky tonk" aesthetic into rules that architects and developers could follow, the environment had changed, and the Fox & Fowle design was judged more appropriate. Photovoltaics and hydrogen-powered fuel cells produce nearly 10 percent of the building's electricity.

The 23-story LVMH Tower opens in December at 19 East 57th Street between Fifth and Madison avenues to designs by French architect Christian de Portzamparc, who employs French glass sand-blasted in Canada and assembled at Miami. Completed after 4 years of construction delays and complicated real estate deals, it will serve as U.S. headquarters for the French firm LVMH Moët Hennessy Louis Vuitton.

The 42-story Tribeca Pointe apartment house is completed in January at Battery Park City with 342 rental units ranging in size from 555 to 1,214 square feet (monthly rents range from $1,820 to $5,370).

The 16-story 145 East 76th Street apartment house is completed between Park and Lexington avenues. Designed by Hardy Holzman Pfeiffer Associates and Schuman Lichtenstein Claman & Efron for the Macklowe Organization, it has 22 units ranging in size from 2,800 to 6,000 square feet, with a private dining and reception space at which a resident can entertain as many as 250 guests at a sit-down dinner.

The city's population has grown by 350,000 since 1981 but it has added only 42,000 rental apartments, median rents have increased 33 percent since 1975 while median incomes (adjusted for inflation) have risen only 3 percent, the Census Bureau says that one in four New York households spends more than half its monthly income on rent, apartment vacancy rates are negligible, the waiting list for public housing has risen to 130,000, the list for rent vouchers has reached 215,000, the stock of apartments renting for $500 per month and less has shrunk by 55 percent since 1991, the inflation-adjusted value of welfare's housing allowance has fallen by more than 50 percent since 1975, poor immigrants often live in illegal attic, basement, and garage apartments, city shelters typically house nearly 5,000 families and 7,000 single people per night, and the average price of a Manhattan co-op or condominium south of Harlem is more than $700,000.

Builder Zachary Fisher dies at Memorial Sloan-Kettering Cancer Center June 4 at age 88; real estate investor Louis J. Glickman at New York Hospital June 18 at age 94; builder Fred C. Trump of Alzheimer's disease at a Queens hospital June 25 at age 93.

The city's last incinerator is demolished May 5 (see 1996). Opened in 1993, the medical-waste incinerator at the corner of East 138th Street and Locust Avenue in the Bronx was operated until 1997 by Browning-Ferris Industries for the Bronx-Lebanon Hospital Center and 12 other hospitals, but community leaders, environmental activists, and church groups fought to have it shut down and dismantled.

The Bronx Zoo's Congo Gorilla Forest opens June 25 with a half-mile trail that takes visitors through a 6-acre tract of central African rain forest.

Hurricane Floyd hits the city September 16, dumping more than 13 inches of rain in some areas and producing winds of up to 62 miles per hour that cause considerable damage to trees.

Grand Central Market opens October 14 at Grand Central Terminal, where a 7,400-square-foot arcade lined with small shops has been built of brushed metal and honeyed wood from Lexington Avenue and 43rd Street to the upper level of the terminal. Five of the 16 shops are not ready for the opening but soon will be.

A new Daniel restaurant opens in May at 60 East 65th Street, occupying premises in the Mayfair Hotel previously used by Le Cirque (restaurateur Daniel Boulud worked at Le Cirque before starting his own restaurant in 1994). A two-course prix-fixe lunch is $35, a three-course $42, a five-course tasting menu $69, a five-course chef's tasting menu $99.

Hurley's restaurant and bar at the northeast corner of Sixth Avenue and 49th Street closes in September after some 129 years in which it has grown to occupy all four floors of a town house on the site. Tishman Speyer Properties is part of the partnership that owns Rockefeller Center and last year suggested to Joe Gurrera of Citarella that he take over the 8,000-square-foot space (see Citarella, 1997). Gurrera has signed a 25-year lease and will open a 150-seat restaurant in 2001.

The Campbell Apartment cocktail lounge opens in September off a vestibule to the right of Grand Central Terminal's Vanderbilt Avenue entrance after a $2 million renovation of the late financier John W. Campbell's private pied-à-terre.

The Russian Tea Room reopens October 11 under the direction of Warner LeRoy, who had a falling out with chef David Bouley last year and has engaged French-trained former San Francisco chef Fabrice Canelle, 38, to revitalize its dishes (see 1945). The Tea Room has been closed for nearly 4 years, and LeRoy's additions include a bear-shaped aquarium housing five sturgeon on the second floor plus a gold-spangled ballroom with etched mirrors and a stained-glass ceiling on the third, but the food does not impress critics and the RTR will close in 2002.

2000 Mayor Giuliani announces in May that he has prostate cancer and will not be a candidate for the U.S. Senate seat being vacated by Daniel Patrick Moynihan. The mayor later announces that he is divorcing his wife, TV journalist Donna Hanover. The Republicans nominate Long Island congressman Rick Lazio to run for the Senate, the Democrats nominate Hillary Rodham Clinton, the first lady campaigns hard upstate and wins with 55 percent of the popular vote, but the presidential election ends in confusion and consternation, even though 60 percent of New York State voters cast their ballots

for Vice President Al Gore. Republican governor of Texas George W. Bush wins only 35 percent (he gets barely 16 to 17 percent of New York City's vote), and he loses the nationwide popular vote to Gore, who wins by a landslide in the city, getting 86 percent of the vote in the Bronx, 80 in Brooklyn, 79 in Manhattan, 74 in Queens, and 52 in Staten Island. But Bush's vote in Florida tops Gore's by a few hundred, and with the electoral count divided almost 50-50 the outcome remains in doubt pending recounts as required by Florida law in the closest national election since 1876. A 5-to-4 ruling by the U.S. Supreme Court December 12 aborts the recount and Gov. Bush is declared the winner.

Former mayor John V. Lindsay dies of Parkinson's disease and pneumonia at Hilton Head, S.C., December 19 at age 79.

Albany jurors acquit all four officers involved in last year's shooting of Amadou Diallo February 25. Rev. Al Sharpton has brought busloads of supporters up from New York to witness their trial and leads a protest march of thousands in the streets of New York February 26.

The fatal March 16 police shooting of unarmed security guard Patrick M. Dorismond, 26, creates another scandal as Mayor Giuliani releases the victim's sealed juvenile record to show that he had a felony record. Approaching the Haitian immigrant at about 12:30 in the morning outside the Wakamba Cocktail Lounge on Eighth Avenue near 37th Street, undercover detective Anthony Vasquez reportedly asked Dorismond if he had any marijuana to sell, Dorismond reportedly became belligerent and grabbed for Vasquez's gun, the gun allegedly went off, and Dorismond was pronounced dead at St. Clare's Hospital. He is the fourth unarmed civilian to have been killed by police in 13 months, his death outrages black activists, they demand Mayor Giuliani's resignation, and Rev. Al Sharpton demands a federal investigation.

Wall Street's Dow Jones Industrial Average rises 140.55 January 14 to close at an all-time high of 11722.98, falls 60.50 March 7 to close at 9796.03, rises a record 499.19 March 16 to close at 10630.39, but plummets a record 617.78 points (5.66 percent) April 14 to close at 10305.77 following news of a 0.7 percent increase in the U.S. Consumer Price Index for March; a "bubble" of speculation in technology stocks has driven the NASDAQ to a peak of 5048.62 March 10 but it plunges 355.49 points (9.7 percent) to 3321.29 April 14, another record drop.

The State Court of Appeals at Albany rules unanimously April 4 that the city's tax on commuters who live outside the state is illegal and must be eliminated (*see* 1999).

Chase Manhattan agrees in September to pay $36 billion for the 139-year-old investment banking house J. P. Morgan and changes its name to JP Morgan Chase while continuing to operate under the Chase Manhattan, J. P. Morgan, and Morgan Guaranty names (*see* Chemical, 1995).

Wall Street's Dow Jones Industrial Average closes December 31 at 10786.84, down 6.2 percent for the year, and holders of 401(k) plans see the value of their portfolios decline for the first time since such plans were instituted in 1978. The NASDAQ ends the year at 2470.52, down 54 percent from its March 10 peak and down 39.3 percent from its close at the end of 1999.

Retailer Alan M. Fortunoff dies of liver cancer at his Old Westbury home July 4 at age 67.

The city's subway trains cover 118,064 miles per day (1,058,993 revenue car miles) on average from Monday through Friday—the equivalent of nearly 20 round trips to California. The Metropolitan Transportation Authority (MTA) allocates $1.05 billion in its 2000–2004 capital budget for construction of a Second Avenue subway (*see* 1975). The plan is to restart the work that was halted 25 years ago, but state voters in November reject a transportation bond that includes an additional $1 billion for the project (*see* 2001).

The Metropolitan Transportation Authority (MTA) introduces articulated buses on crosstown 23rd, 79th, and 86th Street routes; 20 feet longer than other MTA buses, they hold 50 percent more passengers, and despite angry protests from riders the MTA insists that the new buses are more cost effective and will run them on First, Second, and Lexington avenue routes beginning in the fall of 2002.

Taxi fares for the year top $1 billion; the average fare is about $6, and drivers average 30 fares per 12-hour shift, covering 180 miles per shift. More than 1 million people take taxis at least once per day; complaints against yellow-cab drivers total about 13,000 for the year.

The Hayden Planetarium that opened in October 1935 reopens February 19 after a complete makeover that includes the Rose Center for Earth and Space. The Polshek Partnership headed by architect James Stewart Polshek has designed a glass cube surmounted by a sphere.

The West Nile virus that killed seven New Yorkers last year and infected 62 reappears in July, killing birds; the city sprays wide areas with the relatively costly insecticide pyrethroid to destroy mosquitoes carrying the virus, but by 2002 it will be taking human lives in nearly a dozen other states nationwide.

Archbishop John Cardinal O'Connor dies of brain cancer at his Manhattan residence May 3 at age 80 after a 16-year term in which he has defended the poor and working class among the 2.37 million Roman Catholics in his archdiocese while opposing abortion and homosexuality. He is succeeded by Bridgeport bishop Edward Michael Egan, 68, whose views are similar.

America Online and Time Warner announce January 10 that AOL will acquire Time Warner for about $162 billion in a deal that eclipses all previous mergers and acquisitions. AOL has only 12,000 employees and less than $5 billion in annual revenues, while Time Warner has 70,000 employees with nearly $27 billion in revenues, but AOL stock has been worth twice that of Time Warner, whose CEO Gerald M. Levin, now 60, removes his necktie for the announcement and becomes CEO of AOL Time Warner. The new company commands a large share of the world's Internet, TV cable, and publishing industries (aol.com, Netscape, CompuServe, MovieFone, Instant Messenger, Time Warner Cable, HBO, WB network, Warner Bros. Pictures, Warner Music Group, 33 magazines including *Time*, *People*, *Sports Illustrated*, and *Fortune*, Warner Books, Little, Brown). Stephen M. Case, now 41, puts on a necktie and becomes chairman of the new behemoth (the merger receives Federal Trade Commission approval December 14 subject to strict

A redesigned Hayden Planetarium gave the city a spectacular new landmark. CHIE NISHIO

conditions intended to ensure competition in providing Internet services).

Verizon Communications Inc. is created at New York June 30 through a merger of Bell Atlantic Corp. and GTE Corp., providing local and long-distance telephone service.

Nonfiction: *American Moderns: Bohemian New York and the Creation of a New Century* by Princeton historian Christine Stansell, who writes of Greenwich Village, Mabel Dodge, Emma Goldman, Georgia O'Keeffe, John Reed, Margaret Sanger, and Alfred Stieglitz; *Working-Class New York: Life and Labor since World War II* by Joshua B. Freeman; *The Black New Yorkers: The Schomburg Illustrated Chronology* by Howard Dodson, Christopher Moore, and Roberta Yancy; *Lower East Side Memories: A Jewish Place in America* by Milwaukee-born NYU historian Hasia R. (Rena) Diner, 54; *Bronx Accent: A Literary and Pictorial History of the Borough* by the late Lloyd Ultan (who died in 1998 at age 69) and New York-born fiction writer Barbara Unger (née Frankel), 68; *NYPD: A City and Its Police* by journalist James Lardner and Citizens Crime Commission president Thomas Repetto; *Twin Towers* by Bryn Mawr, Pa.-born Rutgers University professor Angus (Kress) Gillespie, 58; *Privately-Owned Public Space: The New York City Experience* by New York-born Harvard city planner Jerold S. Kayden, 47, in cooperation with the Municipal Arts Society and the Department of Planning (Kayden notes that "incentive zoning" has enabled developers to build about 20 million square feet of extra floor space—as much as 14 feet to one of extra public space—at a cost one-fifth the cost that they would otherwise have born, but commercial tenants have been allowed to occupy much of the "public" space); *Water for Gotham: A History* by New York-born journalist Gerard T. Koeppel, 42; *Fat of the Land: Garbage of New York, the Last 200 Years* by Connecticut-born scholar Benjamin Miller, 86; *Celluloid Skyline: New York and the Movies* by New York-born architect-author James Sanders; *Stork Club: America's Most Famous Nightspot and the Lost World of Café Society* by Ralph Blumenthal; *Gilded City: Scandal and Sensation in Turn-of-the-Century New York* by Iowa State University historian M. H. (Mary Helen) Dunlop, 59; *From Ellis Island to JFK: America's Two Great Waves of Integration* by New York-born University of New York, Purchase, anthropologist Nancy Foner, 54; *Manhattan Block by Block: A Street Atlas* by John Tauranac.

Author and *New York Times* editorial writer Mary Cantwell dies of cancer at NYU Medical Center February 1 at age 69; Dover Publications cofounder Hayward Cirker at a Roslyn hospital March 8 at age 82.

Fiction: *City of God* by E. L. Doctorow.

Author, novelist, short-story writer, and longtime *New Yorker* staff writer William Maxwell dies at New York July 31 at age 91.

New York has a "cow parade" beginning in June, with artists of all kinds painting and otherwise decorating 500 fiberglass cows—standing (head up), grazing (head down), or supine—that are then placed in strategic locations throughout the city. Each horned, uddered, 100-pound cow is sponsored by a corporation, community organization, individual, or business which has paid $7,500 and chosen an artist to paint its cow or selected a design from among the many submitted earlier in the year during an open call for artists (suburban Stamford, Conn., and West Orange, N.J., also have cow parades). Zürich had the first such "cow parade" in 1998, with 800 cows.

Painting: *Fashion and the Fish* by Larry Rivers. Art dealer Pat Hearn dies of liver cancer at her Provincetown, Mass., summer home August 18 at age 45.

Theater: *Dirty Blonde* by Brooklyn-born actress-playwright Claudia Shear 5/1 at the Helen Hayes Theater, with Shear (as the late Mae West), Bob Stillman, Kevin Chamberlin, 352 perfs.; *Proof* by Chicago-born playwright David Auburn, 31, 10/24 at the Walter Kerr Theater, with Mary-Louise Parker, Larry Bryggman, Bethesda, Md.-born actor Ben Shenkman, 32, 917 perfs.

Broadway producer Alexander H. Cohen dies of respiratory failure at New York April 22 at age 79; Broadway producer David Merrick at London April 26 at age 88; former *New York Times* theater and film critic Vincent Canby at New York October 15 at age 76; playwright-novelist N. Richard Nash at New York December 11 at age 87.

Tourists account for 56 percent of all New York theater ticket sales, 63 percent of the Broadway audience is female, the average age of a theater goer is 42 (although nearly 1.4 million are under 18), 81 percent are Caucasian, ticket prices are more than most people can afford, and the average household income of a theater goer is $92,900 (source: Research Department of the League of American Theatres and Producers). Most Broadway offerings are long-running musicals or revivals of old stage plays and musicals.

Films: Joan Chen's *Autumn in New York* with Richard Gere, Winona Ryder; Chuck Russell's *Bless the Child* with Kim Basinger, Jimmy Smits, Holliston Coleman; Gus Van Sant's *Finding Forrester* with Sean Connery as a reclusive writer, Rob Brown as his gifted protégé from the South Bronx; Laurence Fisburne's *Once in the Life* with Fishburne, Eamon Walker, Gregory Hines, Michael Paul Chan; Jim McKay's *Our Song* with Ray Anthony Thomas, Kerry Washington, Anna Simpson (about Crown Heights in the summer of 1991); Curtis Hanson's *Wonder Boys* with Michael Douglas, Toby Maguire; James Gray's *The Yards* with Leo Handler, James Caan, Ellen Burstyn.

Actor Douglas Fairbanks, Jr. dies at Mount Sinai Medical Center May 7 at age 90.

♪♪ Broadway musical: *Seussical* 11/30 at the Richard Rodgers Theater, with David Shiner as The Cat in the Hat, Kevin Chamberlin as Horton the Elephant, music by Sephen Flaherty, lyrics by Lynn Ahrens, 197 perfs.

Dancer Harold Nicholas dies of heart failure following surgery at New York July 3 at age 79; choreographer Peter Gennaro at New York September 28 at age 80; dancer Gwen Verdon at Woodstock, Vt., October 18 at age 75; dancer José Greco at his Lancaster, Pa., home December 31 at age 82.

🏃 Marat Safin, 20, wins in men's singles at the U.S. Open to become the first Russian title holder, Venus Williams wins in women's singles.

Former Yankee manager Bob Lemon dies at a Long Beach, Calif., nursing home January 11 at age 79. The Yankees win their third consecutive World Series, beating the New York Mets 4 games to 1 in the first "Subway Series" since 1956 (but the subway that then cost 15¢ now costs $1.50, and a box seat that cost $5 now costs $160). Pitcher Mike Stanton wins two games for the Yankees, Roger Clemens and Jeff Nelson one each with help from outstanding relief pitching by Mariano Rivera, pitcher John Franco gets the only Met victory, each team hits four home runs, Pequannock, N.J.-born Yankee shortstop Derek Jeter, 26, gets two, bats .409 (Yankee third baseman Scott Brosius gets one and bats .308, center fielder Bernie Williams gets one but bats only .111, right fielder Paul O'Neil gets none but bats .474 and matches Jeter with nine hits, including two doubles and two triples). Jeter is voted most valuable player.

● Fashion designer Bonnie Cashin dies February 3 at age 84 following open-heart surgery at NYU Medical Center.

🏛 Former city tax assessor Joseph Marino, 71, pleads guilty in April to having accepted $4.1 million in bribes from owners of Manhattan skyscrapers, factories, warehouses, and apartment houses who want lower assessments to reduce their property tax obligations. An ongoing grand jury investigation probes allegations that bribe taking has been routine among assessors.

The city's annual Puerto Rican Day parade ends June 11 with an ugly incident in Central Park: 10 amateur videotapes show as many as 50 drunken black, white, and Hispanic youths spraying women with water, tearing off their clothes, groping and fondling them, while police stand by without intervening. Police identify many of the perpetrators and arrest them; some of the police blame the lack of response on a shortage of radios that prevented communication of the outrage to officers who would have rushed to the scene had they known what was happening.

Former Luchese crime family boss Anthony Corallo dies in a federal prison at Springfield, Mo., August 23 at age 87, having been sentenced in November 1986 to a 100-year sentence for Mafia labor racketeering.

Vehicle thefts in the city fall to 35,673, down from 147,123 in 1990 (Police Department figures); car alarms proliferate, as do anti-theft devices, and windshield signs reading "No Radio" and the like to discourage thieves grow scarce.

🏠 Chicago billionaire Samuel Zell acquires New York-based Beacon Properties for $4 billion (*see* 1995). Now 59, he has become one of the world's richest men with hundreds of office buildings, millions of square feet of office space, and hundreds of thousands of residential units.

A lease signed October 13 by the accounting firm Arthur Andersen with Boston Properties permits the developer to build a fourth office tower on Times Square. Designed by David M. Childs of Skidmore, Owings & Merrill, the 47-story skyscraper on the island bounded by Broadway, Seventh Avenue, 41st Street, and 42nd Street is to have 1.2 million square feet of space (Andersen is to occupy more than 500,000), cost $600 million, and replace the Times Square Brewery and a nearly vacant office building. The vacancy rate in midtown office buildings has fallen to 3 percent, and rents have gone through the roof.

Supreme Court justice Leland DeGrasse, 54, rules in Manhattan April 6 that rent increases for rent-controlled tenants going back to January 1, 1996, will remain at the rates temporarily used by the Division of Housing & Community Renewal (*see* 1997). Landlords have sought a 32.4 percent increase, and annual increases of 7 percent, but the judge's decision protects the bi-yearly 3.8 percent increase in minimum basic rents. The average price of a Manhattan co-op or condominium apartment south of Harlem exceeds $850,000 by August; 40 percent of the city's residents have annual incomes of $20,000 or less.

The 40-story 1 River Place apartment house opens in July in 42nd Street between 11th and 12th avenues with 921 rental units ranging in size from 360-square-foot studios to 1,202-square-foot two-bedroom flats. Studios rent for $1,650 per month and up, one-bedroom flats from $2,100, two-bedrooms from $3,200, but the city has given developer Larry Silverstein a 20-year tax abatement in return for which he has set aside 20 percent of the units for tenants with maximum incomes of $25,545 to $47,770, depending on family size, and these moderate-income units rent for between $639 and $822. Designed by Costas Kondylis, the $225 million brick-and-glass tower has ribbon windows that afford good city and river views.

The 42-story 515 Park Avenue apartment house is completed at the southeast corner of 60th Street with just 38 condominium apartments that include 26 full-floor units, 12 floors of two units each, and a 6,514-square-foot, five-bedroom duplex on the 15th and 16th floors with a 1,500-square-foot terrace; the other units range in size from five to 12 oversize rooms each, with 10-foot ceilings and formal entrance foyers. Designed by Frank Williams for Zeckendorf Realty, its units are priced at between $2.65 million (for 2,200 square feet) and $14 million.

The Bridge Tower Place apartment house opens at 401 East 60th Street with a 38-story tower containing 127 one- to four-bedroom condominium units ranging in price from $635,000 to more than $2 million, plus a 10-story wing with 91 one- and two-bedroom units priced from slightly over $400,000 to $1 million. Architect Costas Kondylis has designed the bronze and glass tower, its lobby has been designed by David Rockwell, and the $155 million project has 95,000 square feet of retail space at its base (shops and restaurants in the new 98,000 Bridgemarket plaza have attracted business to the area in the shadow of the 91-year-old Queensboro Bridge).

The 34-story Chatham apartment house is completed at 181 East 65th Street with 94 units. Designed by architect Robert A. M. Stern, it has two apartments per floor beginning at the 24th floor, each with 10-foot ceilings, three to four bedrooms, his and her baths for the master bedroom suite, formal dining room, library, separate maid's room. Prices range from $600,000 to more than $6 million.

The hotel occupancy rate in the city is 89.1 percent in April, the highest in 20 years.

The Embassy Suites Hotel opens in June at 102 North End Avenue (between Vesey and Murray streets) with 463 nearly identical suites, some overlooking the Hudson. Its 14-story atrium begins one-floor above ground level and has a restaurant, the Broker's Loft.

The 29-story Sofitel Hotel opens July 14 at 44 West 44th Street with 400 guest rooms ($350 per night), including 51 suites ($450 per night). Designed by Yann LeRoy of Brennan Beer Gorman and built at a cost of $100 million for French developers who also own the Novotel and Motel 6 chains, its entrance is close to those of the Algonquin, the Royalton, the New York Yacht Club, and the Harvard Club. It has a 130-seat brasserie restaurant, a 2,500-square-foot grand ballroom, and seven other meeting rooms.

The Metropolitan Transportation Authority strikes a deal with the state legislature at Albany to clean up the emissions of the city's 4,500 buses. The MTA decides in the fall to switch to a special low-sulfur diesel fuel (it buys 42 million gallons per year and fuel companies increase production to meet the demand), engineers and maintenance workers at a huge garage on Zerega Avenue in the Bronx will rebuild the oldest and most polluting diesel buses (at a cost of about $85,000 per bus), and the combination of less polluting fuel, custom-made engines that weigh 1,100 pounds each, electronic emission controls, and powerful filters on exhaust pipes will reduce particle emissions, making the diesel buses nearly as clean as buses powered by natural gas (the city will soon have 650 such buses, which emit carbon dioxide and nitrogen oxide but are generally considered less polluting than diesel buses).

Former *New York Times* food critic and cookbook author Craig Claiborne dies at St. Luke's-Roosevelt Hospital January 22 at age 79; former sturgeon king Murray Bernstein of Murray's Sturgeon Shop at a Lauderdale, Fla., nursing home February 21 at age 87.

The Brooklyn restaurant Junior's opens a 60-seat branch at Grand Central Terminal May 2, serving its cheesecake and other specialties.

The Census Bureau reports in late July that a survey taken last year of 15,417 households showed that 40 percent of New Yorkers were born abroad, up from 28 percent in 1990 and the highest percentage since 1910. Had it not been for immigration the city's population would have shrunk, whereas it actually rose by about 130,000 last year to an estimated 7.4 million. Sen. Daniel Patrick Moynihan tells a *New York Times* reporter, "Boy, that is some number—wow, wow! It's an enriching experience for us. It's wonderful—I mean, we have to think of it that way. If we think of it any other way, it won't be." When released in March of next year the census will show that the city's population has gained 456,000 people since 1990, reaching 8,008,278 to top 8 million for the first time, with Staten Island up 15 percent over 1990, Queens up 11 percent, the Bronx 7 percent, Brooklyn 4 percent, Manhatttan unchanged.

21st CENTURY

2001 ✕ Mideastern terrorists hijack commercial airliners September 11 and use them as missiles to destroy the World Trade Center, killing themselves and all aboard plus nearly 2,900 in the twin towers (initial estimates are much higher). A Los Angeles-bound Boeing 767 (American Airlines Flight 11 out of Boston) carrying 81 passengers and 11 crew hits the North Tower of the Trade Center at 8:48 o'clock in the morning; a Los Angeles-bound 767 (American Airlines Flight 175 out of Boston) carrying 54 passengers and 11 crew hits the South Tower at 9:03; both planes are loaded with highly inflammable jet fuel, which explodes in flames, both towers subsequently collapse as temperatures of close to 2,000° F. destroy their steel girders. New York firefighters and police perform heroically (343 firefighters lose their lives, the previous record having been 12 in a 1966 fire in East 23rd Street, 23 police are killed in line of duty), the death toll is the highest in U.S. history since the Battle of Antietam in 1862, and civilians impress the world with their courage. Even those who have been critical of Mayor Giuliani acclaim his performance in the city's darkest hour, he loses some support when he tries to extend his term in office, but Britain's Elizabeth II confers honorary knighthood upon him.

Billionaire Michael R. "Mike" Bloomberg wins the mayoralty election November 6, defeating Consumer Advocate Mark Green, now 56. Worth an estimated $4 billion, the 59-year-old Bloomberg has switched from Democrat to Republican and spent nearly $69 million of his own money on his campaign, claiming that his business experience qualifies him for the unenviable job of dealing with a massive shortfall of revenues related to the looming recession and the events of September 11. Giuliani has endorsed Bloomberg in the final weeks, Rev. Al Sharpton supported Bronx Borough President Fernando Ferrer in the primaries, Democrats have failed to unite, Hispanic voters do not turn out in

9/11 became a worldwide term for fanatical terrorism against innocent civilians. DOUG MILLS, AP/WIDE WORLD

large numbers for Green, and their absence costs him the election. Former mayor Abraham Beame has died at New York University Medical Center February 10 at age 94, having served during the city's great fiscal crisis of the mid-1970s. Former mayor Ed Koch says Beame was "the last of the clubhouse mayors."

$ President Bush promises massive financial aid to help the city rebuild; the $20 billion he has pledged is soon cut to about $6 billion, but the figure will be raised.

Quick & Reilly discount brokerage pioneer Leslie C. Quick dies of cancer at Boston March 8 at age 75; mutual funds manager David Alger is killed along with all 35 employees in the collapse of the World Trade Center September 11 at age 57.

U.S. exchanges do not open September 11 following the attack on the World Trade Center and remain closed until September 17, the first such shutdown since the oubreak of World War I in 1914. Wall Street's Dow Jones Industrial Average closes at a new low for the year September 17, falling a record 684 points (7.1 percent) to 8920, despite a cut in the fed funds rate from 3.5 percent to 3 percent. Heavy selling continues all week, and by Friday's close the Dow has sustained its worst one-week fall since July 1933, dropping 14.26 percent and losing $1.4 trillion in value.

The 76-year-old municipal-bond house Lebenthal & Co. announces in early October that the family company will be acquired for $25 million by the Hartford, Conn.-based Advest Group, subsidiary of the Mutual of New York (MONY) insurance company. CEO Alexandra Lebenthal succeeded her father, Jim, as president in 1995 and remains CEO, with Jim continuing as chairman emeritus. His brother-in-law and former company president H. Gerard Bissinger II dies of leukemia October 27 at age 75, having made the firm's operations profitable while Jim's advertising helped raise the total amount of client funds under Lebenthal management to $5.1 billion (Advest's client assets total about $30 billion).

The Treasury Department announces October 31 that it will discontinue the 30-year "long" bond, equity prices rebound, and the Dow Jones Industrial Average closes December 31 at 10021.50, down from 10876.84 at the end of 2000. The NASDAQ closes at 1950.40, down from 5000 in March of last year as the new economy "bubble" bursts.

The 102-year-old Chicago-based Hartmarx Corp. opens its Hickey Freeman menswear store in September at 666 Fifth Avenue, just south of the Brooks Brothers store that opened in 1999. The company justifies paying an "astronomical" rent for the sake of visibility that cannot be attained through advertising or promotion and hopes merely to break even on the store.

Marks & Spencer puts its money-losing Brooks Brothers store chain up for sale in March, having paid $750 million for it in 1988. The Italian-controlled Retail Brand Alliance Inc. agrees in November to buy the chain for about $225 million.

Toys "R" Us opens a new four-level Times Square store November 17 on Broadway between 44th and 45th streets with a 60-foot-high Ferris wheel, 700 employees, and 110,000 square feet of space offering almost everything sold at F.A.O. Schwarz but at lower prices; the Calabasas, Calif.-based children's retailer Right Start Inc. agrees November 19 to buy the New York F.A.O. Schwarz store and 23 of the

other 41 Schwarz toy stores for about $51 million in stock and debt assumption. The Dutch retailer Royal Vendex KBB bought Schwarz in 1989 and receives a 15 percent stake in Right Start, which has 70 stores nationwide.

The two-story Prada shoe store opens December 15 at the corner of Broadway and Prince Street in SoHo. Designed by Rem Koolhaas for the Milan-based fashion colossus and built at an estimated cost of $40 million, the store extends through a full block to Mercer Street and has a cylindrical glass elevator to the basement, where most of the merchandise is displayed.

New York area airports shut down in the wake of the September 11 attack on the World Trade Center, overseas flights to New York are diverted to Canadian airports, and when U.S. airports reopen there is much tighter security. American Airlines Flight 587 takes off from JFK for Santo Domingo at 9:14 o'clock in the morning November 12 and crashes 3 minutes later into the Belle Harbor residential neighborhood of Queens 5 miles from JFK, killing all 251 passengers and nine crew members aboard the A300 Airbus plus five people on the ground. Most of the passengers are Dominicans who had lived in Washington Heights, that community is devastated, and while the accident is not related to terrorism it strikes a heavy blow to the Rockaway community that lost many men in the World Trade Center collapse 2 months earlier. It is the worst such disaster since a United Airlines jet fell on Park Slope, Brooklyn, in 1960 and takes far more lives.

Former Metropolitan Transportation Authority chairman David L. Yunich dies at his Scarsdale home September 19 at age 84. The MTA unveils a blueprint late in the year for a two-track Second Avenue subway line that would run eight miles from 125th Street in East Harlem to the southern tip of the financial district, with stations roughly every 10 blocks and transfers available at many stations to link the new line with the Lexington Avenue line and Metro-North trains (see 2000). The estimated cost of the project (at least $10 billion) looms as a stumbling block.

Anthrax creates a scare in the city as cases of the deadly disease are diagnosed in October. Envelopes contaminated with anthrax spores turn up in various locations, including a New York post office facility, the office of NBC news anchor Tom Brokaw, and the *New York Post*; Vietnamese-born Manhattan Eye, Ear, and Throat Hospital storeroom worker Kathy T. Nguyen is admitted to Lenox Hill Hospital the night of October 28 so ill that investigators cannot question her and dies of inhalation anthrax 3 days later at age 61, no spores turn up in her Bronx apartment or in the hospital where she worked, but although it is clear that at least one terrorist is planting anthrax spores neither the Police Department nor the FBI is able to determine whether the perpetrator is a foreign or domestic terrorist.

State Supreme Court Justice Leland DeGrasse rules January 10 that the state's school-funding system is unconstitutional, saying the "education provided New York City students is so deficient that it falls below the constitutional floor set by the education article in the New York State Constitution." The judge orders state officials to devise a system that will help the city acquire more books, computers, and supplies, hire more qualified teachers, improve physical conditions in the schools, relieve overcrowding, and reduce class size. "The majority of the city's public-school students leave high school unprepared for more than low-paying work, unprepared for college and unprepared for the duties placed on them by a democratic society," he says. "The schools have broken a covenant with students, and with society" (see 2002)

Public-school teachers near the collapsing World Trade Center towers in Lower Manhattan evacuate 8,000 pupils to safety on the third day of the school year (one child sees burning bodies falling from one tower and cries out, "Look, teacher, the birds are on fire!"). Carrying some on their shoulders, the teachers send many youngsters by ferry to Staten Island and Jersey City, they walk others north through debris-strewn streets for 40 minutes to the safety of Greenwich Village schools, and some kids go home with the teachers, staying with them until their parents can be reached by telephone.

City University (CUNY) launches a generous new honors program to raise the academic prestige of its colleges by attracting outstanding students. Chancellor Matthew Goldstein initiated the idea 2 years ago, and it attracts 1,400 applicants not only from Bronx Science, Stuyvesant, and other top city high schools but also many from other states and foreign countries who score high on Scholastic Aptitude Tests (SATs); each of the 200 selected receives free tuition, a $7,500 academic expense account, a laptop computer, tickets to museums and theaters, personal academic counseling, and invitations to special seminars. The program will expand next year to admit 325 students (from 2,500 applicants), and some will select one of the five CUNY colleges (Baruch, Brooklyn, CCNY, Hunter, Queens) in the program rather than Stanford or one of the Ivy League colleges (Lehman and the College of Staten Island will be added in 2003).

The 81-year-old Hewitt School agrees in early December to pay $11 million for a town house at 3 East 76th Street, close to its main building at 45 East 75th Street but nearly twice as large and in an area zoned for non-residential use. Hewitt agreed in late August to buy a slightly smaller house at 10 East 75th Street for $7.95 million and has found a buyer willing to pay just over $8 million for it.

Interpublic announces March 19 that it has agreed to pay $2.1 billion for Chicago-based True North Communications (parent company of Foote Cone & Belding and the Bozell Group), outbidding France's Havas Advertising and Britain's WPP Group to become the world's largest ad agency, incorporating McCann-Erickson WorldGroup and Lowe Group.

The *New York Times* runs obituaries with pictures of virtually every individual who died in the collapse of the World Trade Center (or leapt from one of the burning twin towers before it fell). The careful documentation puts a human face on what otherwise would be mind-numbing numbers.

Nonfiction: *The Ungovernable City: John Lindsay and His Struggle to Save New York* by Hudson Institute adjunct fellow Vincent J. Cannato; *Rudy! An Investigative Biography of Rudolph Giuliani* by *Village Voice* reporter Wayne Barrett; *Rudy Giuliani: Emperor of the City* by New York-born journalist Andrew Kirtzman, 40, who since 1992 has been host of "Inside City Hall" on New York 1 News; *Times Square Roulette: Remaking the City Icon* by Flushing-born author Lynne B. Sagalyn (*née* Beyer), 53, who directs the MBA real estate program at Columbia University's business school; *Five Points: The 19th-Century New York City Neighborhood That Invented Tap Dance, Stole Elections, and Became the World's Most Notorious Slum* by Cambridge, Mass.-born University of Wyoming historian Tyler (Gregory) Anbinder, 38; *Mambo Montage: The Latinization of New York City* by Augustin Laó-Montes and Arlene Davis (editors); *23rd Precinct: The Job* by Bronx-born sportswriter and photojournalist Arlene Schulman, 40; *The New York Apartment Houses of Rosario Candela and James Carpenter* by Andrew Alpern; *The Post's New York: Celebrating 200 Years of New York City through the Pages and Pictures of the New York Post* compiled by Antonia Felix and editors of the paper; *New York Year by Year: A Chronology of the Great Metropolis* by College of Staten Island CUNY librarian Jeffrey A. Kroessler; *New York September 11: As Seen by Magnum Photographers* with text by David Halberstam.

The British-Dutch scientific journal publisher Reed Elsevier agrees in July to buy Harcourt General (formerly Harcourt Brace Jovanovich) for $5.7 billion.

Publisher Clarkson N. Potter dies of a heart attack at his Jamestown, R.I., home June 24 at age 73; author Peter Maas at Mount Sinai Hospital August 23 at age 72; Roger Starr of pneumonia at Easton, Pa., September 10 at age 83, having suffered a debilitating stroke in May; publisher William Jovanovich dies of a heart attack at his San Diego home December 4 at age 81; journalist-author Dick Schaap of acute respiratory distress syndrome following hip-replacement surgery at Lenox Hill Hospital December 21 at age 67.

Fiction: *City of Dreams: A Novel of Nieuw Amsterdam and Early Manhattan* by New York novelist Beverly Swerling; *Look at Me* by Jennifer Egan; *Lit Life* by Kurt Wenzel; *The Mystery of Mary Rogers* by Rick Geary; *The Two Chinatowns* by Dan Mahoney; *The Nanny Chronicles* by former Park Avenue "nannies" Nicola Kraus and Emma McLaughlin.

The Neue Gallerie New York opens November 16 in the 87-year-old 1048 Fifth Avenue mansion at the southeast corner of 86th Street, acquired from the YIVO Institute of Jewish Research 7 years ago by former U.S. ambassador to Austria Ronald S. Lauder, now 57, of the Estée Lauder cosmetics family and restored to its 1914 condition by architect Annabelle Selldorf. Chairman of the Museum of Modern Art (MoMA), Lauder began buying German and Austrian art at age 13, he received help from the late Madison Avenue gallery operator Serge Sabarsky (who died in 1996 at age 83), and their collection includes pre-World War II works by Gustav Klimt, Oskar Kokoschka, Egon Schiele, Max Beckmann, George Grosz, Kurt Schwitter, and lesser known artists plus furniture and objets d'art.

The American Folk Art Museum opens December 1 in a new building designed by Tod Williams and Billie Tsien. Located in West 53rd Street next door to the Museum of Modern Art (MoMA), it is far more spacious than the museum's previous quarters.

Theater: *If You Ever Leave Me . . . I'm Going With You* by Joseph Bologna and Renée Taylor 8/6 at the Cort Theater, 53 perfs.; *45 Seconds From Broadway* by Neil Simon 11/11 at the Richard Rodgers Theater with Marian Seldes, 73 perfs.

Television: *100 Centre Street* 1/22 on A&E with Alan Arkin as Judge Joe Rifkind (to 3/5/2002).

Comedienne Imogene Coca dies at Westport, Conn., June 2 at age 92.

Films: James Mangold's *Kate & Leopold* with Meg Ryan, Hugh Jackman; Frank Prinzi's *Sidewalks of New York* with Heather Graham, Brittany Murphy, Rosario Dawson, Edward Burns, Dennis Farina, Stanley Tucci; Peter Chelsom's *Town & Country* with Warren Beatty, Diane Keaton, Goldie Hawn, Garry Shandling, Andie MacDowell, Nastassja Kinski; Cameron Crowe's *Vanilla Sky* with Tom Cruise, Penélope Cruz, Cameron Diaz.

Film critic Pauline Kael dies at her Great Barrington, Mass., home September 3 at age 82.

Broadway musicals: *The Producers* 4/19 at the St. James Theater, with Nathan Lane, Matthew Broderick, Cady Huffman, music and lyrics by Mel Brooks, choreography by Susan Stroman (most tickets go for $100 each, but the theater begins selling some at $480 each in October to frustrate scalpers, who sometimes resell tickets for $1,000 and more); *Urinetown* 9/20 at the Henry Miller Theater, with John Cullum, now 71, Nancy Opel, Jeff McCarthy, Spencer Kayden, book by George Kotis, music by Mark Hollman, lyrics by Kotis and Hollman.

Former Broadway dancer Larry Adler dies at London August 6 at age 87; veteran actor-choreographer-director Herbert Ross at New York October 9 at age 74.

Violinist Isaac Stern dies of heart failure at a New York hospital September 21 at age 81.

Lleyton Hewitt, 20 (Australia) wins in U.S. Open men's singles play at Arthur Ashe Stadium, Venus Williams in women's.

The New York Yankees win their fourth consecutive American League pennant but lose the World Series to the 5-year-old Arizona Diamondbacks 4 games to 3 after coming from a two-game deficit to lead the Diamondbacks by one game.

Crime fighter Richard F. Tennien suffers a heart attack and dies at a Mineola hospital April 23 at age 65, having put Mafia boss Anthony "Tony Ducks" Corallo behind bars in the 1980s.

The collapse of the World Trade Center and adjacent structures September 11 removes more than 20 million square feet of prime office space, fully 30 percent of the total downtown market of 82.4 million square feet becomes unavailable, and the shortage drives up commercial rents. The city has 9 million square feet of office space under construction, including 2.5 million in Queens, 1 million in Brooklyn. American Express, Lehman Brothers, Merrill Lynch, and other major companies move operations to Stamford, Jersey City, Long Island City, and elsewhere but most say they will return to Lower Manhattan when buildings there reopen or new buildings are completed. Developer Larry A. Silverstein, now 70, has signed a lease obliging him to pay rent on the property for 99 years and vows to rebuild on the site. Debris exploding from the WTC has knocked out a major load-bearing column in the 40-story Bankers Trust Building completed in 1974 at 130 Liberty Street, its value plummets from $170 million to $70 million, black mold soon infests its walls and ventilating systems, and its owner (Deutsche Bank) debates whether to tear the deserted structure down or try to restore it.

The Lower Manhattan Redevelopment Corp. created in November is a subsidiary of the Empire State Development Corp. Gov. Pataki appoints seven of its 11 directors (who include New York Stock Exchange chairman Richard A. Grasso), and its chairman is former Goldman Sachs co-chairman John C. Whitehead, now 79.

The 32-story Reuters Tower is completed at 3 Times Square, northwest corner 42nd Street and Seventh Avenue, to designs by Fox & Fowle. The 150-year-old London-based news organization Reuters Holding PLC received a tax break worth up to $62.9 million late in 1997 from the city and state to finance the $400 million building, and the Rudin Organization stands to gain additional tax benefits as its developer. Some 34,000 square feet of electric signs covers much of the tower's exterior, while inside there is a Financial News television studio.

The 72-story Trump World Tower opens at 845 United Nations Plaza with 371 condominium apartments averaging 1,900 square feet in size with ceilings 10 to 16 feet high. Rising 861 feet above the United Nations, it is the world's tallest residential tower (Trump claims it has 90 floors), and boasts an 11,000-square-foot health club with a 60-foot swimming pool; its duplex penthouse has sold for a record $38 million.

The Renaissance co-op apartment house opens in early July on the east side of Lenox Avenue between 116th and 117th Streets in Harlem. Designed by Greenberg Farrow Architecture and built with $60 million in public and private funds, including money from the Malcolm Shabazz Mosque across 117th Street, the 11-story structure has 240 one- to three-bedroom units ranging in size from 675 to 1,100 square feet and ranging in price from $113,000 to $381,831 (chosen by lottery from 3,500 applicants whose annual incomes are between $31,500 and $147,750, buyers must put up $4,533 to

$15,393 in cash, depending on size and location of the unit purchased).

Architect Harmon Goldstone dies at his upper East Side home February 21 at age 89; real estate developer Lewis Rudin of bladder cancer at his Manhattan home September 20 at age 74; developer Seymour Milstein of pneumonia at New York Presbyterian Hospital October 2 at age 81.

The State Court of Appeals rules 5 to 1 December 20 that landlords may not calculate rent increases in a way that would have required more than 30,000 rent-controlled tenants to pay thousands of dollars in additional rents, retroactively and going forward (*see* Local Law 30, 1970). The case has been in court since 1997 and affects mostly tenants of housing built before February 1947 who have occupied their apartments since before July 1971. More than a million households occupy rent-stabilized apartments and are not affected by the ruling.

The Bryant Park Hotel opens February 14 in the 77-year-old Radiator Building at 40 West 40th Street between Fifth and Sixth avenues, with 129 rooms (including 24 suites). Room rates initially run to about $550 per night at a time when the average rate in the city's hotels is $232.04 but will drop sharply.

Developer Donald Trump agrees November 28 to buy the 72-year-old Delmonico Hotel on Park Avenue at 58th Street for $115 million from the estate of the late Sarah Korein, who died in 1998. She bought it from William Zeckendorf, Jr. in 1984 for $32 million and converted it into a luxury apartment house.

Restaurateur Warner LeRoy dies of complications from lymphoma at New York Hospital February 22 at age 65 (he leaves behind a $48 million estate that includes a 16-room, 8,200-square-foot duplex apartment comprising five condominiums combined into a unit with eight bedrooms, gym, and screening room). LeRoy's 22-year-old daughter Jennifer takes over as CEO of the Russian Tea Room but it will close next year; restaurateur Jerome Brody dies of lung disease at his Miami, Fla., home May 17 at age 78; restaurateur Gino Circiello at his Manhattan apartment November 30 at age 89; "21" Club cofounder H. Peter Kriendler at his upper East Side apartment December 21 at age 95.

2002 Gov. Pataki wins election to a third term, winning 49 percent of the popular vote as compared to 34 percent for his Democratic challenger H. Carl McCall, 67, and 15 percent for billionaire Independence Party candidate Thomas Golisano after the costliest campaign in the state's history (the three major candidates have spent a total of more than $131 million, about half of it Golisano's own money). Former police commissioner Benjamin Ward has died in a Queens hospital June 10 at age 75, having suffered from asthma most of his life.

$ Times Square Business Improvement District (BID) founder Gretchen Dykstra takes office in February as commissioner of the New York City Department of Consumer Affairs. Now 53, she moved to California 4 years ago but has returned to her favorite city.

Mayor Bloomberg struggles to close the city's $4.8 billion budget deficit, pledging to reduce his own staff by 20 percent, proposing tolls on East River bridges, suspending waste-recycling programs, raising cigarette taxes, and antagonizing unions by suggesting personnel reductions across the board. He announces May 15 that his administration has plans to provide extensive job training, child care, and other programs to help welfare recipients find jobs and become self-supporting, but he promises to continue former mayor Giuliani's requirements that recipients be fingerprinted, that most work for their welfare checks, and that the number of people on public assistance be kept to a minimum. The city faces a $6.4 billion revenue shortfall in the fiscal year that begins July 1 of next year, state law requires that it have a balanced budget, Bloomberg's administration agrees to restore $50 million in budget cuts on condition that property taxes be raised, a City Council bill adopted November 25 by a vote of 41 to 6 and signed into law December 2 raises property taxes by a whopping 18.5 percent (the first increase in more than a decade), and an imminent rise in transit fares threatens a further increase in the cost of living.

Merrill Lynch announces May 21 that it has agreed to pay $100 million in penalties to New York and other states, averting possible criminal charges by New York's attorney general Eliot L. Spitzer, who has accused Merrill of promoting stocks in companies whose investment-banking business Merrill covets.

Wall Street's Dow Jones Industrial Average closes December 31 at 8341.63, down from 10021.50 at the end of 2001. The NASDAQ closes at 1335.51, down from 1950.40 at the end of 2001.

Amtrak verges on bankruptcy in June after more than 30 years of mismanagement, raising fears that such a move will affect the Long Island Rail Road (Amtrak's largest source of traffic flow) and New Jersey Transit System. Both lease tracks and tunnels from the federal rail-passenger system, and the LIRR alone moves 550 trains per day carrying 235,000 people in and out of Penn Station, employ-

ing its own dispatchers, electricians, and track workers while the Jersey system pays Amtrak a fee to operate its routes.

∞ Archbishop Edward Cardinal Egan shrugs off criticisms in March that he mishandled cases of pedophilic child abuse by priests during the 12 years he served as bishop of Bridgeport, Conn. The issue has roiled the Church from Boston to the Vatican as sealed court documents dating back for decades continue to surface, raising hopes for reform.

Mayor Bloomberg says at a news conference March 18 that he intends to use the old Tweed Courthouse just north of City Hall for Board of Education offices and a model school. The building would house most of the 800 employees now at 110 Livingston Street, Brooklyn, which would be sold. Former mayor Rudolph Giuliani promised to let the Museum of the City of New York have the 126-year-old building, and at least $89 million has been spent to renovate it for that purpose, but Bloomberg says it will cost "next to nothing" to create bullpen-style open offices like his own at City Hall and that he will help find other quarters for the museum that has been on Fifth Avenue in East Harlem since 1932.

Mayor Bloomberg and legislative leaders at Albany reach a tentative agreement June 6 to strip the city's local school boards of their last major power; legislation signed by Gov. Pataki June 12 gives the mayor direct control of the city's public schools, whose management reverts to the centralized authority it had before the legislature decentralized it in 1969 (see DeGrasse ruling, 2001). The nation's largest public-school system, New York's system has 1.1 million pupils, 80,000 teachers, and an annual budget of nearly $12 billion, but test scores have been low. Wasteful rules and regulations, inhibiting labor contracts, and Board of Education politics have stymied efforts to stem drop-out rates and energize teacher recruitment.

Mayor Bloomberg announces July 29 that he has appointed New York-born lawyer Joel I. (Irwin) Klein, 55, schools chancellor, replacing Harold O. Levy. Klein has gained a reputation as deputy White House Counsel in the Clinton administration, a Justice Department prosecutor of Microsoft, and most recently CEO of Bertelsmann Inc.

Former Hearst newspapers gossip columnist Igor Cassini dies at New York January 5 at age 86, having once claimed a readership of nearly 20 million for his "Cholly Knickerbocker" columns.

The New York Sun that ceased publication as such early in 1950 reappears as a broadsheet on newsstands April 16 at 50¢ per copy, making coverage of the metropolitan area its chief priority. The New York Times Co. and Tribune Co. agree to distribute it, the 5-day-per-week paper cuts its price in half November 4, and it begins to develop a readership.

"The New York Miracle" public service television spots produced by BBDO Worldwide promote Big Apple tourism with Yogi Berra conducting the Philharmonic, Henry Kissinger playing for the Yankees, Barbara Walters singing on Broadway, and the like, but veteran BBDO creative director Phil Dusenberry, 65, announces in March that he will retire effective May 31.

The New York Public Library cuts back operations of its research branches to 5 days per week (Tuesday through Saturday) after Labor Day for budgetary reasons. The Donnell Library in West 53rd Street remains open 7 days.

Nonfiction: *The Unfinished City: New York and the Metropolitan Idea* by Thomas Bender; *Empire City: New York Through the Centuries* by Kenneth T. Jackson and David S. Dunbar (editors); *Cityscapes* by Howard B. Rock (editor) and New York-born Vassar religion historian Deborah Dash Moore, 56; *Report From Ground Zero: The Story of the Rescue Efforts at the World Trade Center* by 18-year Fire Department veteran Dennis Smith, now 61; *Firehouse* by David Halberstam (more than 150 other books about 9/11/2001 are published); *Divided Loyalties: How the American Revolution Came to New York* by Pittsburgh-born author Richard M. (Malcolm) Ketchum, 80; *The Battle for New York: The City at the Heart of the American Revolution* by New York sculptor-turned-author Barnet Schecter, 43; *How Harlem Nearly Killed King: The 1958 Stabbing of Dr. Martin Luther King, Jr.* by Hugh Pearson; *Harlem Lost and Found* by Akron, Ohio-born historian Michael Henry Adams, 46; *Mrs. Astor's New York* by Eric Homberger; *Naming New York: Manhattan Places and How They Got Their Names* by Sanna Feirstein; *New York City Trees: A Field Guide for the Metropolitan Area* by Edward Sibley Barnard.

Author Bruce Bliven, Jr. dies at his Manhattan home January 2 at age 85; Claude Brown of 1965 *Manchild in the Promised Land* fame of lung complications in Manhattan February 2 at age 64; Walter Lord at his Manhattan apartment May 19 at age 84.

Fiction: *Paradise Alley* by Englewood, N.J.-born novelist Kevin (Breen) Baker, 34, is about the city's 1863 draft riots; *Violence, Nudity, Adult Content* by New York novelist Vince Passaro; *Social Crimes* by

upper East Side novelist Jane Stanton Hitchcock, 55; *The Good People of New York* by Thisbe Nissen.

Novelist Lois Gould dies at Memorial Sloan-Kettering Cancer Center May 29 at age 70.

Poet Kenneth Koch dies of leukemia at his Manhattan apartment July 6 at age 77.

The Museum of Modern Art (MoMA) closes May 22 in west 53rd Street (it will be torn down after 63 years and reopen in 2005 with a large new building). MoMA Queens (QNS) opens June 29 in the former Swingline staple factory at 33rd Street and Queens Boulevard in Long Island City, which is just across the street from a No. 7 subway station; the 160,000-square-foot plant has been painted bright blue and reconfigured for its new, temporary role but will be closed Tuesdays and Wednesdays.

Painter Larry Rivers dies of liver cancer at his Southampton, L.I. home August 14 at age 78.

Sculpture: The Irish Hunger Memorial opens July 16 in Battery Park City on the Hudson River, where New York sculptor Brian Tolle, 38, has replicated a 96 × 170-foot field on a giant concrete slab that rises up and tilts to a height of 25 feet. Containing 62 plants native to County Mayo and dotted with stones from each of Ireland's 32 counties, it includes a roofless stone cottage and texts evoking the horrors of the famine that devastated Ireland from 1845 to 1852.

Theater: *Metamorphoses* by Mary Zimmerman 3/4 at the Circle in the Square Theater with a 27-foot-wide pool of water providing a background for mythical gods and goddesses from Ovid's poems to disport themselves; *The Graduate* by Terry Johnson (who has adapted the 1967 film) 4/4 at the Plymouth Theater, with Pompton Plains, N.J.-born actor Jason Biggs, 23, Kathleen Turner, now 47, as Elaine Robinson; *The Goat, or Who Is Sylvia?* by Edward Albee 3/10 at the John Golden Theater, with Bill Pullman, Mercedes Ruehl; *Top Dog/Underdog* by Suzan-Lori Parks 4/7 at the Ambassador Theater. Now 38, Parks becomes the first black woman to win a Pulitzer Prize for drama; *A Few Stout Individuals* by John Guare 5/12 at the off-Broadway Signature Theater in West 42nd Street, with Donald Moffat as Ulysses S. Grant in his dying days; *Frankie and Johnny in the Clair de Lune* by Terrence McNally 8/8 at the Belasco Theater, with Edie Falco, Stanley Tucci.

Actress Irene Worth suffers a stroke at a post office near her West Side apartment and dies in a hospital March 10 at age 85; producer Robert Whitehead at his suburban Pound Ridge home June 15 at age 85; actress Kim Hunter of a heart attack at her Manhattan apartment above the Cherry Lane Theater September 11 at age 69.

Television: *The Shield* 3/12 on Fox's FX cable channel, with Michael Chiklin as undercover New York detective Vic Mackey, who sometimes takes the law into his own hands.

Former NBC TV executive Sylvester "Pat" Weaver dies at his Santa Barbara, Calif., home March 15 at age 93, having created the *Today* and *Tonight* shows half a century ago; comedian Milton Berle dies of colon cancer at his Los Angeles home March 27 at age 93; former ABC TV news executive Roone Arledge of cancer in Manhattan December 5 at age 71.

Films: Martin Scorsese's *Gangs of New York* with Daniel Day-Lewis, Leonardo DiCaprio. Also: Roger Michell's *Changing Lanes* with Ben Affleck, Samuel L. Jackson; Wayne Wang's *Maid in Manhattan* with superstar Jennifer Lopez, now 32, Ralph Fiennes; David Fincher's *Panic Room* with Jodie Foster, Kristen Stewart, Forest Whitaker; Sam Raimi's *Spider-Man* with Tobey Maguire, Willem Dafoe, Kirsten Dunst; Adrian Lyne's *Unfaithful* with Richard Gere, Diane Lane.

The Thalia movie theater that attracted film buffs to West 95th Street from 1932 until it closed in 1993 reopens April 13 as the Leonard Nimoy Thalia, having been rebuilt as part of the $12 million makeover of Symphony Space.

Actor Rod Steiger dies at Los Angeles July 9 at age 77.

 Broadway and off-Broadway musicals: *Sweet Smell of Success* 3/14 at the Martin Beck Theater, with John Lithgow as gossip columnist J. J. Hunsecker (based on the late Walter Winchell), music by Marvin Hamlisch, lyrics by Craig Carmela, book by John Guare, 109 perfs.; *Thoroughly Modern Millie* 4/18 at the Marquis Theater, with Sutton Foster as the Kansas girl who comes to New York in 1922, three Elmer Bernstein songs from George Roy Hill's 1967 film of the same name, four 1920s standards, 11 new songs by Jeanine Tesori, lyrics by Dick Scanlan; *Harlem Song* 8/6 at the newly refurbished Apollo Theater, with a 14-member cast that includes B. J. Crosby, Queen Esther, Randy André Davis, Delandis McClam, and Keith Thomas, some original music by Daryl Waters and Zane Mark, period songs, new lyrics for some by director-producer George C. Wolfe, now 47; *Hairspray* 8/15 at the Neil Simon Theater, with Harvey Fierstein, Marissa Jaret Winokur, Dick Latessa, music by Marc Shaiman, lyrics by Scott Wittman and Shaiman, songs that include "I'm a Big Girl Now;" *Movin' Out* 10/24 at the Richard Rodgers Theatre, with music and lyrics by Billy Joel; *Dance of the Vampires*

12/9 at the Minskoff Theater, with Michael Crawford, music and lyrics by Jim Steinman, 56 perfs.

Composer-lyricist Clark Gesner of 1967 *Charlie Brown* fame dies of a heart attack on a visit to the Princeton Club July 23 at age 64; vibraphonist Lionel Hampton dies of heart failure at Mount Sinai Medical Center August 31 at age 94; lyricist Adolph Green at his Manhattan home October 24 at age 87.

 Pete Sampras wins in men's singles at the U.S. Open, Serena Williams in women's.

 Fashion designer Pauline Trigère dies at her upper East Side home February 13 at age 93; designer Bill Blass of throat cancer at his New Preston, Conn., home June 12 at age 79.

 Smokers in the city pay $7.50 per pack of cigarettes beginning July 1 as the tax rises $1.42 from 8¢ to $1.50. Health authorities say higher prices will discourage smoking and save 50,000 lives per year, 33,000 of them among young children; critics call the tax regressive, smokers with Internet access pay about $30 per carton, housing-project residents buy "loosies" in violation of the law, paying $1 for two or three cigarettes or roll their own, buying loose tobacco that is not covered by the new tax.

 Mafia boss Joseph Bonanno dies at Tucson May 11 at age 97; John Gotti, Sr. of cancer at a federal prison in Springfield, Mo., June 10 at age 61.

Removal of debris from the 16-acre site of the World Trade Center ends May 30 with ceremonies to mark the occasion (*see* politics, 2001). The 12-story pile of rubble (some 1.8 million tons) has been taken away but controversy continues as to what should rise in place of the twin towers.

The 44-story Bear Stearns World Headquarters building is completed at 383 Madison Avenue between 44th and 45th streets. Designed by Skidmore, Owings & Merrill with state-of-the-art systems from trading floors to conference centers, it replaces the Zeckendorf Building.

The 24-story Austrian Cultural Forum opens April 18 at 11 East 52nd Street. Austrian-born New York architect Raimund Abraham, 68, gave up his Austrian citizenship March 1, having designed the narrow concrete, glass, and steel film, music, dance, visual arts, and design center for the Austrian Ministry for Foreign Affairs.

The 45-story Victory apartment house is completed at 501 West 41st Street to designs by Schuman, Lichtenstein, Claman & Efron.

The 70-story Park Imperial apartment house is completed at 230 West 56th Street, southwest corner Broadway, with 110 condominium units on floors 48 through 70 atop 46 floors of commercial space (the Imperial Club on the 47th floor is a business, entertainment, and exercise facility reserved exclusively for residents). Skidmore, Owings & Merrill has designed the 684-foot structure, whose apartments range in size from 811 to 2,975 square feet, have 10-foot ceilings, and offer views of Central Park, the Hudson River, and the Manhattan skyline.

The Ritz-Carlton apartment house opens in March at 50 Central Park West, where the 35-story St. Moritz Hotel of 1930 has been converted into luxury condominiums that in some cases occupy two entire floors.

The 504-room Marriott Financial Center Hotel reopens January 7 two blocks south of the World Trade Center site with views of ground zero.

The 14-story Ritz-Carlton Battery Park Hotel opens February 1 with nearly 300 rooms as part of a 39-story condominium complex with a gym, spa, and 14th-floor restaurant.

The 45-story Westin Hotel opens in October on Eighth Avenue between 42nd and 43rd streets. Designed with Latin-American styling by the Miami firm Arquitectron for the 104-year-old Tishman Realty and Construction Co., the 800-room hotel (part of the Times Square Redevelopment Program) rises above a four-story entertainment complex.

Architect Robert L. Bien dies of a heart attack at his home near Stuyvesant Square May 25 at age 78.

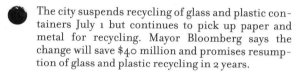

The city suspends recycling of glass and plastic containers July 1 but continues to pick up paper and metal for recycling. Mayor Bloomberg says the change will save $40 million and promises resumption of glass and plastic recycling in 2 years.

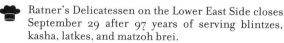

Ratner's Delicatessen on the Lower East Side closes September 29 after 97 years of serving blintzes, kasha, latkes, and matzoh brei.

Index

Note: with some exceptions, all **ad agencies**, **airports**, **apartment houses**, **architects**, **art galleries**, **banks** and financial institutions, **bridges**, major **Broadway and off-Broadway musicals**, **churches** (plus mosques and synagogues), **clubs** and **nightclubs**, **fashion industry** names, **hospitals**, **hotels**, **insurance companies**, **libraries**, **movie theaters**, **museums**, **parks**, **public relations firms**, (book) **publishers stations**, **radio**, **restaurants**, **retail merchants**, **schools**, **skyscrapers**, **steamships**, **theaters** (legitimate), and **tunnels** are listed alphabetically under these headings and not individually.

A&P, 122, 134, 156, 371, 448, 500
  Woman's Day in, 502
Abbott, Berenice, 483, 502
Abbott, George, 406, 414, 420, 490, 605, 631, 661, 832
Abbott, Lyman, 216
Abel, Rudolf, 610
Abel, Walter, 788
Abeles, Edward, 273, 296, 301, 375, 380
abortion, 84, 165, 670, 699
  Mme. Restell and, 188
  patent medicine abortifacients and, 151
Abraham, Raimund, 878
Abramowitz, Bessie, 693
Abrams, Charles, 499
Abzug, Bella, 693, 705, 707, 729, 853
Academy of Music, 108, 215
Ace, Goodman, 461, 763
Ackerman, Frederick L., 409, 493, 512
Actors' Equity, 346, 380, 536
Actors Studio, 559
ACT-UP, 797
Adair, Janet, 387, 396
Adair, Jean, 437
Adams, Brooke, 757
Adams, Cindy, 862
Adams, Edie, 609
Adams Express, 80
Adams, Franklin P., 380, 510, 629
Adams, Herbert, 332
Adams, Joey, 529, 631, 862
Adams, John, 31, 33
Adams, Lee, 631, 668, 696

Adams, Maude, 248, 254, 313, 374, 594
Adams, Michael Henry, 877
Adamson, Harold, 452, 461, 566
Adamy, George, 689
Addams, Charles, 794
Addams, Jane, 316
Ade, George, 284, 291, 320, 346
Adelson, Abe N., 454
Adler, Felix, 180, 183, 227, 275, 475
Adler, Jacob P., 420
Adler, Julius Ochs, 602
Adler, Larry, 470, 568, 874
Adler, Polly, 408, 492, 543, 588
Adler, Richard, 595, 599, 605
Adler, Ruth, 666, 791
Adler, Stella, 460, 490, 570, 817
Adonis, Joe, 462, 585
advertising agencies, 146, 154, 228, 235, 272
  Audit Bureau of Circulation and, 351
  Backer and Spielvogel, 743
  Bates, Ted, 522, 587
  Batten, Barton, Durstine & Osborn (BBDO), 436
  Benton & Bowles, 443, 782
  Biow, Milton, 367, 479
  D'Arcy Masius Benton and Bowles, 782
  DDB Needham Worldwide, 782
  Della Femina, Travisano, 674
  Doyle Dane Bernbach, 569, 651, 782
  Duane Jones, 588

  Foote, Cone and Belding, 541, 873
  George Batten Co., 436
  Grey, 367, 412
  Interpublic, 629, 674, 873
  Lennen & Newell, 602
  Lord & Thomas, 541
  McCann-Erickson, 331, 451, 569, 629, 674
  Ogilvy & Mather, 564
  Papert Koenig Lois, 612
  Ruthrauff & Ryan, 415, 602
  Scheideler, Beck and Werner, 588
  Thompson, J. Walter, 150, 187, 436
  Wells, Rich, Greene, 666, 737
  William Douglas McAdams, 628
  Young & Rubicam, 419, 737
AFL-CIO, 213, 592, 701
AFSCME, 701
Agassi, Andre, 828, 863
Agee, James, 603, 631
Agee, Tommie, 691
Aguilera, Rick, 783
Ahrens, Lynn, 806, 857, 868
AIDS, 756, 757, 765, 786, 797, 803, 804, 810
  God's Love We Deliver and, 779
Aiello, Danny, 738, 749, 758, 772, 789, 800, 812, 838
Ailanthus tree, 156
Ailey, Alvin, 619, 800
air conditioning, 334, 397, 414, 499, 512, 557, 590, 604

  store, 521
  subways, 782, 804
  theaters, 491
air pollution, 47, 465, 670
airports,
  Floyd Bennett Field, 459, 802
  Idlewild (JFK), 564, 617
  JFK, 646, 745
  La Guardia, 515, 770
    bomb explosion at, 722
  Newark, 442
Air Traffic Controllers strike, 756
Akers, Karen, 763, 800
Akins, Zöe, 380, 396, 450, 490, 618
Albany Convention, 26
Albany Post Road, 57
Albany Regency, 60, 67, 93
Albany Times Union, 112
Albee, Edward, 636, 642, 648, 654, 667, 725, 752, 827, 877
Albee, Edward F., 202, 215, 346, 451
Albers, Josef, 647, 731
Albert Einstein Medical College, 592
Albert, Eddie, 496, 503, 511, 594
Albertson, Jack, 654, 707
Albion, Robert G., 516
Alcoholics Anonymous, 493, 532
Alcott, Louisa May, 154
Alda, Alan, 636, 668, 682, 817, 822, 839
aldermen, 256
Aldredge, Tom, 828

Aldrich, Winthrop W., 449
Aleichem, Sholom, 361
Alexander, Jane, 682, 707, 817
Alexander, Jason, 772, 783
Alexander, Magnus W., 349,
    356, 466
Alfred, William, 660
Alger, Horatio, 146, 154, 164, 278
Algonquin Round Table, 380,
    472
Alien Registration Act (Smith
    Act), 519
Allen, Fred, 396, 444, 452, 608
Allen, Frederick Lewis, 489,
    570, 603
Allen, Harry Nathaniel, 306,
    312, 318, 658
Allen, Joel E., 195
Allen, Mel, 525, 839
Allen, Oliver E., 811, 821
Allen, Red, 478, 676
Allen, Viola, 196
Allen, Woody, 667, 702, 708,
    732, 738, 744, 749, 777,
    783, 789, 794, 800, 817,
    822, 827, 832, 839, 847
Allison, Wilmer, 492
Allyson, June, 517, 530, 546, 555
almshouses, 58
Alonso, Alicia, 551, 566
Alpern, Andrew, 724, 771, 788,
    821, 832, 873
Alpert, Jane, 686
Althof, Herman, 150
Alton, Robert, 484, 511, 517, 518,
    524, 536, 594
Amalgamated Clothing Workers,
    384, 466, 500
Amalgamated Housing Corp.,
    423, 432
Amazing Stories magazine, 418
Ambrose, John Wolfe, 496
American Academy of Dramatic
    Arts, 208
American Airlines, 488, 621
American Anti-Slavery Society,
    70, 80
American Ballet Theater, 524
American Bank Note Co., 117
American Beet Sugar Co., 264
American Bible Society, 58, 710
American Birth Control League,
    393, 403
American Broadcasting Co.
    (ABC), 541, 641, 776
American Cancer Society, 344
American Chicle Co., 262
American Civil Liberties Union,
    (ACLU), 383, 657, 839
American Express Co., 102, 755
    credit card, 617, 658
    Travelers Cheque, 227

American Federation of
    Musicians, 391
American Female Guardian
    Society, 275
American Geographical Society,
    300
American Heritage, 598
American Home Products
    (Wyeth),
    building, 638
American Horse Exchange, 195
American Ice Co., 305
American Institute of Architects
    (AIA), 116, 547
American Jewish Committee,
    299
American Labor party, 544
American Library Association,
    193
American Magazine, 301
American Medical Assn., 92, 653
American Nazi Party, 627
American Newspaper Guild,
    476, 659, 743
American Newspaper Publishers
    Assn (ANPA), 235, 659
American Numismatic Society,
    300
American Red Cross, 458
American Society of Civil
    Engineers, 255
American Stock Exchange, 591,
    854 (see also Curb
    Exchange)
American Sugar Refining Co.,
    230, 234, 264, 311
American Telephone &
    Telegraph Co., 307, 394,
    762, 770, 821, 831, 835
    buildings, 370
    Western Union and, 325
American Tobacco Co., 225, 333,
    362, 445
American Vitagraph, 257
Ames, Winthrop, 338
Ammann, Othmar H., 459, 514,
    634, 652, 658
Amon, Will Rice, 505
Amoros, Sandy, 605
Amro Bank Building, 633
Amsterdam Avenue, 199
Amsterdam News, 319
Amtrak, 694, 700, 706, 830
    LIRR and, 876
Anastasia, Albert, 462, 531, 548,
    585, 590, 614
Anastasio, Tony, 649
Anbinder, Tyler, 873
Ancient Order of Hibernians, 75
An Claidheamh Soluis, 708
Anders, Glenn, 406, 437, 444
Andersen, Hans Christian, 608

Anderson, John Murray, 387,
    396, 400, 407, 478, 491,
    492, 599
Anderson, Judith, 437, 490, 516,
    559
Anderson, Leroy, 726
Anderson, Mal, 613
Anderson, Marian, 437, 526
Anderson, Maxwell, 406, 428,
    436, 477, 490, 503, 511,
    517, 529, 535, 555, 565,
    571, 598, 623
Anderson, O.J., 812
Anderson, Robt., 594, 675, 682
Andrada e Silva, José Bonifácio
    de, 603
Andrade, Rosario, 795
André, Maj. John, 37
Andrews, F.M., 340
Andrews, Julie, 608, 631, 832
Andrews, Nancy, 604, 605, 643
Andrews, Wayne, 528, 688
Andros, Edmund, 12–14, 20
Angell, Edward L., 223
Annenberg, Moses, 395
Annenberg, Walter, 545, 593
Anspacher, Louis, 357
Anthony, C.L. (Dodie Smith),
    541
Anthony, Susan B., 144, 150,
    152, 157, 160, 162, 166,
    170
anthrax, 872
Antiques Show, 603
anti-Semitism, 217, 231, 275,
    500
    Gentleman's Agreement novel
    and, 559
Aoki, Hiroaki "Rocky," 656
AOL Time Warner, 866
Apalachin, N.Y., 614
apartment houses, 155
    10 Park Avenue, 463
    10th Street Studio Bldg., 115
    120 East End Avenue, 464
    23 East 83rd Street, 512
    240 Central Park South, 531
    40 Central Park South, 525
    475 Park Avenue, 620
    565 West End Avenue, 505
    625 Park Avenue, 464
    700 Park Avenue, 626
    710 Park Avenue, 568
    Abraham Lincoln Houses, 568
    Alexandria, 807
    Alhambra (Bklyn), 226
    Alhambra Gardens (Bronx),
    432
    Alwyn Court, 321, 327, 512
    America, 791
    Ansonia, 292, 320, 607
    Apthorp, 315

Ardsley, 464
Arthur H. Murphy Houses,
    644
Astor Apartments, 297
Astor Court, 363
Astral (Bklyn), 215
Barcelona, 203
Battery Pointe, 790
Beach Haven, 579
Beaux-Arts, 455
Bedford Gardens, 727
Beekman Tower, 440
Belair, 802
Belnord, 321, 829
Benedick, 190
Beresford, 447
Big Six towers, 650
Boulevard, 802
Boulevard Manor (Bronx), 721
Bromley, 785
Bryant Park Studios, 274
1 Lincoln Plaza, 704
1 Sherman Square, 704
1001 Fifth Avenue, 750
1199 Plaza, 727
265 East 66th Street, 746
49 East 89th Street, 692
733 Park Avenue, 704
800 Fifth Avenue, 746
980 Fifth Avenue, 670
Bridge Tower Place, 869
Bristol Plaza, 791
Carver, George Washington,
    620
Castle Village, 512
Central Park Mews, 237
Century, 464
Channel Club Condominiums,
    791
Chatham Towers, 656, 663
Chatsworth, 292
Citylights, 851
Clarendon, 315, 505
Cliff Dwellers', 363
Clinton, DeWitt, Houses, 663
Coliseum Park, 615
Colonnade, 327
Columbia, 774
Columbus House, 698
Columbus Manor, 704
Columbus Park Towers, 677
Confucius Plaza, 740
Co-Op City, 698
co-operative apartments, 656
Copley, 785
Cordova, 203
Corinthian, 790
Coronado, 807
Cosmopolitan, 790
Dag Hammarskjöld Tower,
    773
Dakota, 209, 638, 650, 692

INDEX

apartment houses (*continued*)
De Witt Clinton Houses, 663
Dorchester Towers, 663
Dorilton, 279
Dunbar Apartments, 439
East Midtown Plaza, 721
East River Houses, 531
East River Tower, 698
Eastwood (Roosevelt Island), 734
Edgecombe Avenue, 371
Eldorado, 464, 778
Elliott Houses, 562
Euclid Hall, 268
Evanston, 334
Evansview, 791
First Houses, 493, 499
Flagg Court, 499
Fort Greene Houses, 547
Forum, 785
Franklin Houses, 626
Franklin Plaza, 626
Frederick Douglass, 615
Gainsborough Studios, 315
Galleria, 727
Gateway Plaza, 764
Glen Gardens, 727
Goddard Riverside Towers, 663
Goddard Towers, 677
Graham Court, 274, 315
Gramercy, 203
Grenada, 203
Hampshire, 203
Hampshire House, 505
Harlem River, 505, 519
Heckscher Apartments, 656
Hendrik Hudson, 310
Hostos, Eugenia Maria De, Houses, 698
Hotel des Artistes, 371, 446, 721
Hudson Tower, 785
Hudson View East, 790
Hudson View Gardens, 408
Hudson View West, 790
Horizon, 795
Island House (Roosevelt Island), 727
Jackie Robinson Apts., 633
Jefferson Towers, 684
Johnson, James Weldon, Houses, 568
Kenilworth, 315
Kew Bolmer, 358
Kingsley, 773
Kips Bay Plaza, 633, 663
Knickerbocker Village, 486
Kortwright, 293
Lambert Houses, 715
Langham, 310
Le Chambord, 791

Lefrak City, 455
Lehman, Herbert H., Village, 650
Leverich Towers, 432
Lexington Houses, 586
Liberty Court, 790
Liberty House, 785
Lincoln Plaza Tower, 715
Lincoln-Amsterdam House, 734
Lisbon, 203
London Terrace, 454
Lucania, 327
Lucerne, 293
Madrid, 203
Manhattan, 194
Manhattan House, 586
Manhattan Plaza, 740
Manhattantown, 600, 615
Master Apartments, 443
Mayfair House, 417
Mayfair Regent, 417
Mayfair Towers, 650
Metropolitan Tower, 791
Milan House, 464
Montana, 785
Multiple Dwellings Law and, 446
Muriel Arms, 397
Museum Tower, 779
Nathan Hale Memorial, 409
Nevada, 721
New Amsterdam, 704
New West, 785
Normandy, 519
Oliver Cromwell, 440
Olympic Tower, 740
Osborne, 211
Parc Place, 785
Parc Vendome, 464
Park Imperial, 879
Park South Tower, 785
Park South Towers, 859
Park West Village, 615
Parkchester, 525
Paterno, 327
Pavilion, 670
Penn South, 644
Peter Cooper Village, 562
Phipps Garden, 440
Phipps houses, 310
Portsmouth, 203
Prasada, 310, 406
Promenade, 791
Queensbridge Houses, 519
Queensview, 579
Red Hook Houses, 519
Red House, 292
Rembrandt Studios, 194
Rio, 791
Ritz Tower, 423
Riverbend Houses, 678

Rivercross (Roosevelt Island), 726
River House, 463
River Rose, 785
Riverside Park, 734
Riverside South, 829, 859
Rivertower, 759
RNA Houses, 678
Rockefeller Apartments, 499
Rodin Studios, 370
Royale, 791
Ruppert Brewery houses, 727
Salamanca, 203
San Remo, 455
Saratoga, 773
Schomburg Plaza, 727
Schwab House, 567
Sea Rise I, 734
Seward Park Houses, 715
Sherwood Studios, 194
Shore Haven, 572
Soundings, 790
Spanish Flats, 203, 204
St. Martin's Tower, 704
St. Tropez, 656
St. Urban, 292
Starrett City, 734, 769
Stephen Wise Towers, 663
Strykers Bay Houses, 677
Stuyvesant, 155
Stuyvesant Town, 562, 581, 807
Taft, Sen. Robert A., Houses, 663
Taino Towers, 750
Thomas Garden, 440
Tolosa, 203
Tower (Bklyn), 185
Tower East, 644
Tower 67, 785
Tracey Towers, 721
Tribeca Pointe, 864
TriBeCa Tower, 807
Trinity House, 698
Trump International, 850
Trump Parc, 456, 759
Trump Plaza, 773
Trump Tower, 875
Trump Village, 650
Tudor City, 439
Turrets, 268
Umbria, 354
United Nations Plaza, 670
University Plaza, 663
University Village, 669
Valencia, 203
Van Corlear, 191
Vaux and, 116
Verona, 321
Victory, 878
Waterside, 721
West Side Manor, 684

West Village Houses, 721
Westbeth, 692
Westgate Houses, 684
Westview (Roosevelt Island), 734
Williamsburg Houses, 512
Windermere, 200
Windsor Park, 579
Worldwide Plaza, 801
Wyoming, 304
Young, Sarah Gilman, and, 197
1 Central Park Place, 795
1 River Place, 869
145 East 76th Street, 864
180 East 70th Street, 785
181 East 65th Street, 869
1991 Broadway, 785
200 East 65th Street, 791
279 Central Park West, 807
401 East 60th Street, 869
45 East 80th Street, 791
500 Park Tower, 773
515 Park Avenue, 869
52–54 East End Avenue, 795
525 East 72nd Street, 791
121 Madison Avenue, 203
10th Street Studio, 115
322 East 57th Street, 455
1 Lexington Avenue, 327
1 Sutton Place South, 431
1000 Park Avenue, 363
1030 Fifth Avenue, 417
1040 Fifth Avenue, 455
1040 Park Avenue, 424
1050 Park Avenue, 402
1088 Park Avenue, 424
1105 Park Avenue, 402
1107 Fifth Avenue, 424
1111 Park Avenue, 417
1115 Fifth Avenue, 424
1155 Park Avenue, 358
1172 Park Avenue, 424
1175 Park Avenue, 447
1185 Park Avenue, 447
1192 Park Avenue, 447
1215 Fifth Avenue, 455
130 West 57th Street, 315
140 West 57th Street, 315
140 West 58th Street, 370
173–175 Riverside Drive, 432
2 East 88th Street, 455
30 Sutton Place South, 439
322 East 57th Street, 455
39 East 79th Street, 423
4 East 66th Street, 388
40 West 55th Street, 408
417 Park Avenue, 370
45 East 66th Street, 315
550 Park Avenue, 371
563 Park Avenue, 327
570 Park Avenue, 362

580 Park Avenue, 402
600 West End Avenue, 354
630 Park Avenue, 363
635 Park Avenue, 340
660 Park Avenue, 431
67th Street Studios, 287
720 Park Avenue, 447
730 Park Avenue, 447
740 Park Avenue, 455
765–775 Park Avenue, 432
810 Fifth Avenue, 423
812 Park Avenue, 432
817 Fifth Avenue, 416
820 Fifth Avenue, 362
820 Park Avenue, 423
838 West End Avenue, 354
845 Fifth Avenue, 388
860 Park Avenue, 416
863 Park Avenue, 315
903 Park Avenue, 354
907 Fifth Avenue, 363
927 Fifth Avenue, 371
956 Fifth Avenue, 402
960 Fifth Avenue, 455
960 Park Avenue, 340
998 Fifth Avenue, 334
Apollo Theater, 352, 484
Appellate Courthouse, 268
Apple, Fiona, 839
April-in-Paris Ball, 585
Apthorp, Charles W., 27, 38, 124
Aquarium, 247, 611
Aqueduct Racetrack, 254, 547, 624
Aranha, Ray, 788
Arbour, Al Arbour, 759
Arbuckle, Fatty, 478
Arbuckle, John, 165, 250, 275, 341
Arbus, Diane, 618, 702
arc lighting, 186, 189
Archer, William, 390
Archipenko, Alexander, 654
architects,
    Abraham, Raimund, 878
    Abramovitz, Max, 643
    Abramson, Louis, 463
    Ackerman, F.L., 493, 512
    Adamson Associates, 778
    Ahlschlager, Walter, 429, 437
    Aiken, William Martin, 303
    Ajello, Gaetan, 327
    Aldrich, Chester Holmes, 287, 525
    Alfredo De Vido Associates, 791
    Allen & Collens, 325, 354, 397, 450
    Allen, Ingalls & Hoffman, 374
    Amon, Will Rice, 505
    Andrews, F.M., 340
    Angell, Edward L., 223
    Arquitectron, 879

Atterbury, Grosvenor, 310
Attia & Perkins, 784
Attia, Eli, 759
Babb, Cook and Willard, 274
Bacon, Henry, 345
Badger, Daniel, 116
Ballard, Todd & Snibbe, 677
Barnes, Edw. Larrabee, 756, 768, 784
Baum, Dwight J., 454
Bayley, John Barrington, 738
Belluschi, Pietro, 649, 683
Benepe, Barry, 792
Beyer Blinder Belle, 775, 791, 848, 854
Bien, Robert L., 614, 638, 879
Bien & Prince, 456
Bien, Sylvan, 456, 567, 568, 614, 615, 625
Birge, Charles E., 315
Birnbaum, Philip, 656, 670, 692, 704, 721, 727, 746, 750, 759, 773, 785, 791, 807
Blesch & Eidlitz, 112
Blum, George and Edward, 334, 348, 354
Blumenkrantz, Joseph, 717
Boehm, George and Henry, 337, 370
Bogardus, James, 96, 105, 116, 119, 129
Bolton, Charles W., 399
Bond Ryder James, 790
Boring, Wm. A., 269
Bosworth, Welles, 370
Bottomley, Wagner & White, 463
Breuer, Marcel, 667, 684
Brown, Archibald Manning, 505, 562
Brown, Guenther, Battaglia, Seckler, 698
Brown, Jack, 650, 764
Brunner, Arnold W., 303
Buchman & Kahn, 424
Buckham, Charles W., 315
Buckley, Richard W., 505
Bulfinch, Charles, 51
Bunshaft, Gordon, 590, 677, 720, 721, 802
Bunting, Charles T., 124
Burgee, John, 704, 750, 768, 778, 784, 799, 864
Burnham, Daniel H., 279, 282, 324, 339
Butler, Charles, 454
Cady, J.C., 228
Cady, Berg & See, 276
Candela, Rosario, 402, 408, 424, 431, 439, 447, 455, 491, 505, 595

Carpenter, J.E.R., 340, 363, 371, 388, 402, 417, 423, 424, 432, 439, 453, 464, 472
Carrère & Hastings, 208, 249, 268, 269, 290, 318, 326, 331, 340, 348, 355, 392, 416, 423
Carrère, John M., 208, 383
Carson & Lundin, 562, 620, 638
Carstensen, Georg J.B., 104
Castro-Blanco, Piscioneri & Feder, 727
Catalano, Eduardo, 683
Caughey & Evans, 455, 505
Cavaglieri, Giorgio, 727
Chambers, Walter B., 249, 327
Chanin, Irwin S., 407, 414, 420, 428, 429, 446, 464, 795
Chermayeff & Geismar, 740
Childs, David M., 802, 868
Churchill, Henry, 519
Ciardullo, John, Assocs., 764
Claman, Peter, 818
Clarke, Gilmore D., 486, 562
Clavan, Irwin, 562
Clawson, Harry M., 455
Clinton & Russell, 229, 274, 279, 297, 310, 315, 321, 463
Clinton, Charles W., 194, 327
Clinton & Russell, Holton & George, 471
Cobb, Henry Ives, 327
Coffey, Levine & Blumberg, 685
Colt, Stockton B., 249
Conklin & Rossant, 790
Cooper, Alexander, 802
Cooper, Eckstut Assocs., 807
Corbett, Harvey Wiley, 370, 397
Corbett Harrison & MacMurray, 479
Cory, Russell G. and Walter M., 463
Cram, Ralph Adams, 209, 334
Cram, Goodhue & Ferguson, 340, 354
Crane, C. Howard, 391
Cross & Cross, 363, 416, 431, 447, 463, 493, 521
Cross, Eliot, 425
da Cunha, G.W., 203
Dattner, Richard, 734
Davis, Alexander Jackson, 79, 80, 84
Davis, Brody & Assocs., 678, 715, 721, 727, 785, 790, 791, 795
Debevoise, George, 261

Delamarre, Jacques, 464
Delano & Aldrich, 286, 358, 365, 388, 402, 424, 464, 479
Delano, Wm. Adams, 287, 632
De Lemos & Cordes, 246, 276
Dinkeloo, John G., 677, 759
D'Oench & Yost, 333
Doran, John, 73
Dreyfuss, Henry, 649
Duboy, Paul, 278, 292
Dudley & Diaper, 134
Duncan, John H., 255, 258
Eberson, John, 451, 470
Eckstut, Stanton, 807
Edelbaum & Webster, 677
Edelman Partnership, 663, 677
Eggers & Higgins, 527, 677, 698
Eidlitz, Cyrus L.W., 112, 249, 254, 255, 392
Eidlitz, Leopold, 112, 116, 151, 314
Eidlitz and McKenzie, 292
Elett, Thomas H., 472
Embury, Aymar, II, 495
Farrar & Watmaugh, 433, 454
Feingold, Joseph, 684
Feld & Timoney, 717
Feldman, H.I., 505, 759
Fenischel, Irving, 472
Ferguson, Frank W., 334
Fernbach, Henry, 169
Ferriss, Hugh, 397, 446, 644
Flagg, Ernest, 237, 246, 249, 255, 292, 314, 340, 345, 355, 499, 567
Flagg & Chambers, 263
Forster, Frank J., 505
Foster, George W., Jr., 417
Foster, Richard, 706
Fouilhoux, André, 408, 453
Fox & Fowle, 768, 802, 864, 875
Franzen, Ulrich, 768, 790, 791
Freed, James Ingo, 714, 784
Freeman, Frank, 233, 304
French, Fred F., 439
Friedlander, Joseph H., 468, 486
Frost, Frederick G., 519
Fuller, Charles F., 505, 758
Gage, S. Edson, 358
Gaynor, John P., 116
Gehron, Wm., & Andrew J. Thomas, 531
Gershon, Irving E., 764
Gibson, Robert W., 237, 241
Gilbert, Bradford L., 205, 223, 257
Gilbert, C.P.H., 263, 279, 297, 315, 376, 590

INDEX

architects (*continued*)

Gilbert, Cass, 309, 347, 370, 439, 459, 471, 486, 498
Gildemeister, Charles, 104
Giles, James H., 170
Gilman, Arthur D., 161, 172
Giná, Francis X., & Assocs., 621
Ginsbern, Horace, 505, 684, 698, 715
Goldberg, Bertram, 638
Goldner & Goldner, 433
Goldstone, Harmon H., 519, 718, 875
Goldstone, Dearborn & Hintz, 705
Goldstone, Lafayette A., 423, 447, 453, 610
Goldwin Starrett, 279
Goodhue, Bertram G., 354, 370, 375, 376, 408, 454
Grad, Frank, 465
Graham, Anderson, Probst & White, 358
Graves, Michael, 752
Green, Harry F., 626, 670, 704
Griffin, Percy, 348
Gronenberg & Leuchtag, 432
Gropius, Walter, 649
Gruzen & Partners, 684, 704, 721, 727, 764, 773
Gruzen Sampton Steinglass, 746, 754, 785, 790, 791
Guastavino, Rafael, y Esposito, 322
Guastavino, Rafael, y Morano, 322
Gwathmey Siegel Assocs., 801
Haight, Charles C., 214, 370
Haines Lundberg Waehler, 778
Hale & Rogers, 309
Halsey, McCormack and Helmer, 446
Harde & Short, 292, 315, 321, 348
Hardenbergh, H.J., 191, 203, 209, 237, 255, 257, 274, 286, 293, 310, 347, 375
Harding, John, 785
Hardy Holzman Pfeiffer, 730, 760, 763, 852, 864
Hardy, Hugh, 730, 735, 763, 817, 841, 847, 863
Harmon, Arthur Loomis, 409, 455
Harney, George E., 173
Harrison & Abramovitz, 610, 617, 638
Harrison, Abramovitz, and Harris, 626, 670, 704, 714

Harrison & Fouilhoux, 499, 513, 522
Harrison, Wallace K., 578, 626, 668, 759
Hastings, Thomas, 208, 331, 332, 352, 383, 392, 406, 446
Hausle, Max, 486
Hebert, Maurice, 303
Heins, George L., 233, 289
Helmle, Corbett & Harrison, 443, 463
Helpern Architects, 840, 850
Herter Brothers, 217
Herts & Tallant, 284
Herts, Henry B., 346
Hill Johnson Hanchard, 704, 715
Hiss and Weekes, 321
Hoberman & Wasserman, 734
Hodney/Stageberg Partners, 727
Hoffman, F. Burrall, Jr., 447
Holden, Egan, Wilson & Corser, 626, 677
Holten & George, 463
Hood & Fouilhoux, 408, 479
Hood, Godley & Fouilhoux, 455
Hood, Raymond M., 408, 453, 455, 463, 486
Horowitz & Chun, 741
Howells, John Mead, 251, 310, 427, 440, 453, 625
Howells & Stokes, 251
Hubert, Philip G., 194, 203, 209, 233, 237
Hubert, Pirsson & Co., 203, 217
Hubert, Pirsson and Hoddick, 233
Huckel, Samuel, Jr., 265
Hunt, Richard Morris, 115, 116, 167, 183, 204, 214, 244, 257, 287
Huntington, Charles Pratt, 300
Ingalls & Hoffman, 338
Isosaki, Arata, & Assocs., 782
Israels, Charles, 317
Ives, H. Douglas, 431, 439
Jacobs, Harry Allan, 392, 423
Jacobs, Robert Allan, 567
Jacobs, Stephen B., & Assocs., 773
Jahn, Helmut, 790, 791
Janes and Leo, 279
Jardine, D. and J., 182
Jardine, Hill & Murdock, 362
Jessor, Herman J., 644, 698, 734
Johansen & Bhavnani, 726, 727

Johnson, Philip, 625, 654, 704, 706, 750, 768, 778, 784, 799, 859, 864
Joseph, Seymour, 727
Kahn & Jacobs, 434, 567, 579, 587, 590, 615, 625, 626, 639, 655, 656, 677, 691, 698, 704, 710, 720
Kahn, Ely Jacques, 431, 453, 567, 710
Kahn, Louis I., 720
Kale, Vinjay, 791
Katz, Waisman, Weber, Strauss, 717
Keely, Patrick Charles, 72
Keister, George, 241, 308, 352, 461
Kellum, John, 116, 137, 156
Kelly & Gruzen, 656, 663
Kendall, Edward H., 161
Kendall, Wm. Mitchell, 354
Kessler, S.J., 663, 704
Kevin Roche John Dinkeloo & Assocs., 677, 724, 734, 749, 752, 757, 783, 790, 794, 796
Kiehler, E. George, 391
Kimball & Thompson, 259
Kimball, Francis H., 199, 217, 229, 297, 321, 383
King & Kellum, 116
King, Gamaliel, 94
Kirchhoff & Rose, 346
Knapp, Herbert J., 465
Knappe & Johnson, 663
Koehler, V. Hugo, 338
Kohn, Robert D., 324, 454
Kohn Pederson Fox, 785, 790, 795
Kondylis, Costas, 785, 791, 795, 807, 859, 869
Koolhaas, Rem, 746, 872
Krapp, Herbert J., 368, 391, 407, 414, 420, 428, 429
Kroehl, Julius, 110
La Farge, Christopher G., 233, 289
Lafever, Minard, 68, 109
Lamb, Hugh, 286
Lamb & Harmon, 471
Lamb & Rich, 200, 215, 216
Lamb, Thomas W., 338, 339, 347, 352, 361, 368, 381, 386, 415, 431, 440, 451, 470, 491
Lapidus, Konbluth, Harle & Liebman, 644
Lapidus, Alan, 802
Lapidus, Morris, 639, 644, 650
Lansburgh, C. Albert, 407
Lauritzen & Voss, 229

Lawrence, James Crommelin, 29
Le Brun, Napoleon, 237, 241, 244, 274, 321
Le Corbusier, 578
LeGendre, Henri A., 734
Lescaze, Wm., 486, 512, 531, 562, 650, 692, 698
Levien, Deliso & White, 740
Levy, Leon and Lionel, 610
Liebman & Liebman, 704
Liebman, Liebman & Assocs., 791
Liebman Williams & Ellis, 774
Lindsay & Warren, 409
Lindsey, Edward D., 161
Livingston, Goodhue, 249, 416, 488
Lord, James Brown, 229, 268, 279
Lowell, Guy, 287, 422
Lucas, Herbert, 327
Luce, Clarence S., 229
Luckman, Charles, 590, 669
Ludlow & Peabody, 431
Lund & Gayler, 388
Lundquist & Stonehill, 752
Lynn, Michael, Assocs., 795
Lyons, Robert L., 292, 354, 358
Magonigle, H. Van Buren, 345
Mangin, Joseph F., 54, 56
Margon & Holder, 464
Marvin & Davis, 304
Matsui, Yasuo, 439, 453, 463
Mayer & Whittlesey, 586, 626
Mayer, Whittlesey and Glass, 525, 531
Mayers & Schiff, 713
Mayers, Murray & Philip, 446
Maynicke & Franke, 417
Mazza & Seccia, 663
McCarthy, Michael A., 810
McComb, John, Jr., 50–52, 54, 61, 105
McKenzie, Voorhees & Gmelin, 423
McKim, Charles F., 191, 253, 263, 322
McKim, Mead & Bigelow, 190
McKim, Mead & White, 191, 203, 217, 229, 239, 241, 244, 253, 294, 301, 304, 324, 334, 347, 354, 376, 391, 413, 433, 439
Mead, William R., 191, 439
Meier, Richard, 692, 740
Mellen, Nicholas Clark, 249
Mies van de Rohe, Ludwig, 625
Mitchell-Giurgola, 790
Morris, Benj. Wistar, 392, 439, 454, 547

Morris, Montrose W., 226
Mould, Jacob Wrey, 116, 156, 193
Mowbray, William E., 321
Moyer, Charles F., 446
Murchison, Kenneth, 424, 455
Murgatroyd & Ogden, 424, 447, 456
Murphy/Jahn, 791
O'Donnell, James, 60
Ogden, S.B., 268
Ohm, Philip H., 348
Oppenheimer, Brady & Lehrecke, 644, 650, 692
O'Rourke, Jeremiah, 181
Peabody, Wilson & Brown, 297
Pedersen, William F., 715
Pei, I.M., 633, 663, 669, 714, 773, 784, 810, 823
Pelham, George F., 287, 424, 506
Pelham, George F. II, 409, 512
Pelli, Cesar, 768, 771, 778, 779, 796, 813
Pelton, Henry C., 397, 45
Pennington & Lewis, 455
Pennington, Lewis & Mills, 493
Perkins & Will, 721, 782
Peterkin, John B., 610
Peterson, Frederick A., 121
Pfeiffer, Carl, 177
Pilcher & Tachau, 370
Pirsson, James L., 194
Platt, Charles A., 303, 315, 363, 464, 480
Poehler, G. Frederick, 738
Pollard, Calvin, 94
Pollard & Steinam, 303, 315
Pollard, George Mort, 371
Polshek, James Stewart, 773, 782, 783, 785, 793, 805, 866
Pomerance & Breines, 674, 717
Poor, Alfred Easton, 519, 531, 677
Pope, John Russell, 340, 446, 456, 506
Portman, John, 779
Portzamparc, Christian de, 864
Post, George B., 177, 183, 192, 208, 211, 223, 226, 258, 286, 307, 348, 410, 416, 440, 447
Potter, William A., 259
Prentice & Chan, 729
Price, Bruce, 229, 244, 286, 304, 395

Prince, Harry M., 568
Putnam, J. Pickering, 185
Ramsey & Sleeper, 512
Rapp & Rapp, 421, 423, 451
Rapuano, Michael, 505
Reed & Stem, 321
Reilly, Paul C., 620
Reilly, Robert J., 568
Reinhard and Hofmeister, 479
Reinhard, Hofmeister & Walquist, 590
Renwick, James, Jr., 91, 109, 112, 116, 121, 134, 138, 190, 244
Renwick, Aspinwall & Tucker, 315
Resnick, Paul, 626, 670
Rich & Mathesius, 382
Rich, Charles A., 274
Richardson, Henry H., 155
Richardson, W.S., 334
Ritch, John W., 110
Robertson, R.H., 209, 244, 263
Robinson, Canby, 467
Roche, Kevin, 677, 801, 845
Roche, Kevin, John Dinkeloo & Assocs., 790
Rogers & Butler, 602
Rogers, Isaiah, 84
Rogers, James Gamble, 333, 358, 482, 508, 567
Romeyn, Charles, 310
Rosenfeld, Isador, 440
Roth, Emery, 287, 362, 363, 370, 417, 423, 424, 433, 440, 447, 455, 456, 464, 519, 567
& Sons, 567, 579, 614, 625, 638, 644, 649, 656, 658, 669, 677, 691, 698, 710, 720, 726, 740, 754, 768, 778, 801
Rothenberg, Abraham, 791
Rothzeid, Kaiserman, Thomson & Bee, 785
Rouse & Goldstone, 423, 424
Rouse & Sloan, 304
Rouse, William L., 310, 423
Rudolph, Paul, 721, 850
Russell, Wm. Hamilton, 310
Saarinen, Eero, 660, 662
Sacchetti & Siegel, 512
Saeltzer, Alexander, 96
Sanger, John B., 479
Schickel, William, 206, 207, 246
Schimenti, Michael, 790
Schlanger & Irrera, 470
Schlarsmith, John E., 292
Schlusing, C.W., 531

Schmidt, Mott B., 424, 432, 505
Schulman & Soloway, 579
Schultze & Weaver, 409, 424, 455, 456, 463, 465
Schuman Lichtenstein Claman & Efron, 759, 773, 791, 807, 818, 851, 864, 878
Schwartz & Gross, 327, 370, 371, 417, 440, 447
Scutt, Der, 754, 768, 790
Segal, Paul, Associates, 807
Sert, Jackson & Assocs., 734
Severance, H. Craig, 425, 431, 446, 453, 463, 531
Shampan & Shampan, 392
Shapter, R.S., 402
Shepley, Henry R., 467
Shreve & Lamb, 416, 439
Shreve, Lamb & Harmon, 392, 439, 463, 522, 615, 662, 677, 698, 720, 733
Shreve, Richmond H., 512
Silliman & Farnsworth, 193, 203
Silliman, Benjamin, Jr., 203
Silverman & Cika, 750
Simon, Lewis A., 493
Skidmore, Owings & Merrill, 586, 590, 600, 626, 633, 638, 658, 677, 698, 714, 717, 720, 721, 740, 759, 764, 768, 773, 802, 807, 820, 859, 868, 878, 879
Skidmore, Louis, 644
Sloan & Robertson, 431, 446, 447
Sloan, John, 397
Smith, Henry Atterbury, 464
Smotrich & Platt, 714
Snook, John B., 90, 103, 119, 163, 274
Snyder, Charles B.J., 261, 300, 344
Specter, David Kenneth, 727
Springsteen & Goldhammer, 432
Stanley, Thomas E., 691
Starrett & Van Vleck, 350, 362, 404, 408, 432, 454, 462
Starrett, Paul, 615
Stein, Clarence, 409, 454
Stenhouse, J. Armstrong, 376
Stent, Edward J. Neville, 241
Stern, Robert A.M., 864, 869
Stillman, Leo, 568
Stokes, I.N. Phelps, 251, 310, 370, 402, 436, 516, 547
Stone, Edward Durrell, 516, 660, 691, 746, 771, 790

Stoughton & Stoughton, 314
Stoughton, Arthur A., 278
Stubbins, Hugh, 740
Sturgis, Russell, 322
Sugarman & Berger, 443, 453, 456
Sullivan, Louis H., 263
Swanke Hayden Connell, 767, 768, 834
Swartwout, Egerton, 254, 552
Tabler, William B., 651
Tachau, William, 401
Thomas, Andrew J., 409, 439, 440, 464, 531
Thomas, Griffith, 152, 172
Thomas, John R., 244, 333
Thompson, Martin E., 63, 94
Tichy, Lester, 645
Tillion and Tillion, 456
Tilton, Edward Lippincott, 269
Todd, David, 734, 740
Town, Ithiel, 84
Townsend, Ralph S., 203, 315
Townsend, Steinle & Haskell, 310, 315
Tracy & Swartwout, 268
Tracy, Evarts, 254, 358, 431
Trench & Snook, 90, 103
Trowbridge, S.B.P., 249
Trowbridge, Colt & Livingston, 249
Trowbridge & Livingston, 286, 293, 334, 339, 350, 354, 370, 416, 422, 488
Trumbauer, Horace, 340, 439, 469
Tsien, Billie, 874
Tubby, William, 247
Turner, Burnett C., 519
Turner, Lewis, Assocs., 784
Tuthill, William B., 229, 275, 322
Upjohn, Richard, 82, 91, 116, 143, 188, 286
Urbahn, Max O., & Assocs., 684
Urban, Joseph, 425, 429, 439, 477
Van Alen, William, 417, 453, 759
Van Beuren, A., 807
Van Dyke, Harry, 738
Van Vleck, Ernest A., 404, 610
Van Wart & Ackerman, 486
Van Wart & Wein, 402
Vaux, Calvert, 103, 116, 121, 143, 147, 155, 156, 173, 179, 184, 193, 209, 244, 425
Vilkas Group, 785

architects (*continued*)
Viñoly, Rafael, 768, 793
Voorhees, Gmelin & Walker, 471
Voorhees, Walker, Foley and Smith, 531
Wagner, Albert and Herman, 215
Waid, D. Everett, 340
Walker & Gillette, 370, 392, 431, 446, 472, 493, 509
Walker, Ralph T., 423, 471, 715
Ware, James E., 190, 211, 263
Warnecke, John Carl, 720, 746
Warner, Samuel A., 109
Warren & Wetmore, 274, 287, 297, 304, 321, 333, 340, 348, 354, 371, 382, 397, 416, 428, 446, 455
Warren, Whitney, 274, 297, 552
Washburn, William, 122
Wechsler & Schimenti, 746
Wechsler, Grasso & Menziuso, 791
Wechsler, Max, & Assocs., 734
Weekes, H. Hobart, 297, 321
Wells, James C., 96
Wells, James Hollis, 321
Werner & Windolph, 303
Westermann & Miller, 683
Wetmore, Charles D., 274, 327, 531
Whinston, Charles N. and Selig, 620
White, Stanford, 191, 196, 211, 220, 221, 225, 233, 237, 244, 254, 257–259, 261, 274, 286, 291, 293, 294, 303, 304, 309, 376
Whitfield and King, 334
Whittlesey, Julian, 568
Willauer, Shape & Bready, 339
Williams, Frank, 802, 807, 869
Williams, Tod, 874
Wilson, John L., 505
Withers, F.C., 98, 184
Wright, Frank Lloyd, 623, 625
Wright, Henry, 409
Yamasaki, Minoru, 669
York & Sawyer, 283, 300, 313, 370, 402, 408, 416, 418, 431, 439, 454, 512
Zion & Breen, 740
Zucker, Alfred, 263
Arden, Elizabeth (*see* Elizabeth Arden)
Arden, Eve, 484, 497, 517, 524, 530, 560, 566

Argosy magazine, 247
Arkin, Alan, 654
Arledge, Roone, 845, 878
Arlen, Harold, 451, 470, 484, 517, 536, 546, 555, 599, 613, 783
Arlen, Michael, 414
Arliss, George, 291, 301, 332, 390
armories, 229, 244, 733
Kingsbridge, 370, 401
Seventh Regiment, 194
369th Regiment, 402
69th Regiment, 303, 345
Armory Show, 345
Armstrong, Edwin H., 598
Armstrong, Louis, 444, 703
Armstrong, Paul, 291, 296, 313, 319, 325, 332, 338, 357
Arnaz, Desi, 517
Arno, Peter, 412, 452, 523, 681
Arnold, Benedict, 35, 37
Arnold, Dorothy, 326
Arnold, Edward, 491, 550
Arnstein, Nick, 445
Aronwald, George, 786
Arpino, Gerald, 609
Arsenal, 94, 184
Art Digest, 420
art galleries, 752
André Emmerich, 598
Duveen, Joseph, 348
Fun, 752
Hartford, Huntington, Gallery of Modern Art, 660
Hearn, Pat, 766, 832, 867
Knoedler, M., & Co., 90, 338, 413
Leo Castelli, 612, 702, 719, 738
Marlborough, 648, 696, 725, 738, 766
Mary Boone, 738
Neue Gallerie, 874
Pace, 647
PaceWildenstein, 821
Peggy Guggenheim, 541
Safani, 554
Serge Sabarsky, 675
Stable, 588
Tibor de Nagy, 576
Wildenstein, 283, 469
Artforum, 675
Art in America, 345, 528, 696
ARTnews, 278, 291, 390, 490, 528
Art Students League, 176, 257, 450
Arthur, Bea, 668
Arthur, Chester A., 166, 191, 195, 201
statue of, 261
Arthur, Jean, 491

Arthur Andersen, 868
Artkraft Strauss, 253, 489, 528, 797, 846
asbestos, 727, 802
ASCAP, 353, 369, 517, 525
Asbury, Herbert, 428, 647
Ashbery, John, 593, 811
Ashcan School of U.S. art, 313
Ashcroft, Peggy, 503
Ashe, Arthur, 684, 823
Ashley, Elizabeth, 648, 762
Ashman, Howard, 763, 812, 828
Asian Americans for Equality, 711, 722, 759
Asia Society, 756
Asner, Edward, 758, 766
aspartame, 760
Aspinwall, Henry, 104
Aspinwall, William H., 94, 137, 151, 175
Aspira, 717
Assn. for a Better New York, 726
Associated Press, 94, 197, 266
Association for Improving the Condition of the Poor, 85, 117, 513
Association for the Relief of Respectable Aged Females, 57, 78, 204
Association of Catholic Charities, 277
Astaire, Adele, 461
Astaire, Fred, 369, 375, 381, 407, 452 461, 470, 503, 517, 566, 570, 594
Astor, Brooke, 452, 621, 724
Astor, John Jacob, 49, 69, 72, 76, 77, 86, 94, 102
II, 139, 165, 206
III, 92
IV, 214, 255, 293, 304, 336, 339
Astor, Mrs. (Caroline Schermerhorn), 105, 168, 203, 220, 314
Astor, Vincent, 339, 363, 432, 447, 464, 493, 502, 621, 638
Astor, William B., 86, 91, 94, 96, 102, 105, 124, 127, 133
Astor, William Waldorf, 1st Viscount, 92, 255, 293, 297, 315, 336, 383
Astor Place Opera House, 92
Astor Place, 122
Astoria, 156
Elevated Railway, 366
Astoria Studio, 381, 429, 536, 789
Atkinson, Brooks, 413, 503, 598, 598

Atkinson, Oriana, 598
Atlantic Cable, 118, 119, 154, 202
Atlantic Center, 837
Atlantic Records, 561, 795
atomic energy,
Con Edison and, 640, 646
Atomic Energy Commission, 640
Attaway, Ruth, 654
Atteridge, Harold, 339, 347, 352, 357, 361, 362, 368, 375, 381, 387, 396, 400, 407
Auberjonois, René, 690, 777, 800
Auburn, David, 867
Auburndale, 274
Auchincloss, Louis, 576, 588, 622, 630, 642, 647, 653, 667, 675, 718, 752, 799
Audit Bureau of Circulation, 351
Audubon, John James, 82, 84, 102, 134
Audubon Society, 269, 298, 358, 802, 824
Audubon Terrace, 300, 717
Audubon Theater, 339
Auletta, Ken, 748
Aumont, Jean-Pierre, 757
Aurelio, Richard, 816
Aurelio, Thomas A., 539
Auster, Paul, 716, 817
Austin, Tracy, 750, 759
Austrian Cultural Forum, 878
Austrians, 269
automobiles, 261, 514, 521, 673
Avedon, Richard, 613
Avenue of the Americas, 549, 611, 770
Avery Fisher Hall, 643
Avery, Milton, 545, 612, 618, 623, 660
aviation,
transatlantic flights, 515
Avon Books, 528
Avon Products, 215, 445
awnings, 447, 537
Ayer, Harriet Hubbard, 292
Aykroyd, Dan, 725

Bacall, Lauren, 594, 599, 639, 660, 696, 758, 862
Bacharach, Burt, 683, 763
Bache, Jules S., 263, 544
Back Stage, 631
Backer, George, 447, 515
Bacon, Henry, 345
Baddeley, Hermione, 648
Badillo, Herman, 681, 745, 845, 861
Baehr, Dr. George, 545
Baer, Arthur "Bugs," 688

Baer, Max, 485, 492
Baerer, Henry, 207
Baez, Anthony, 825, 835, 853
Baez, Joan, 690
bagels, 586
Bagneris, Vernel, 749
Bagnold, Enid, 604
Bailey, James A., 220
Bailey, Pearl, 555, 599, 806
Bain, Conrad, 609, 744
Baird, Bil, 583, 789
Baird, Cora, 583, 675
Baitz, Jon Robin, 811
Baker, George F., 203, 231, 305, 337, 343, 409, 458, 464
Baker, George Pierce, 491
Baker, Jordan, 827
Baker, Josephine, 391, 497
Baker, Kevin, 862, 877
Baker, La Vern, 795, 848
Baker, Sara Josephine, 272, 283, 549
baking, 9, 25, 259
  Amy's Breads, 818
  Levy's, 221
Balanchine, George, 484, 537, 556, 567, 767
Balducci's, 568, 710, 780
Baldwin, James, 568, 593, 630, 647, 654, 660
Baldwin, Roger, 755
Baldwin, Simeon, 104
Ball, George W., 824
Ball, Lucille, 631
Ball, Thomas, 180
Ballantine, Ian, 549
Ballard, Kaye, 637
Ballet Theater, 524
ballpoint pen, 549
Balsam, Martin, 594, 613, 660, 675, 719, 738
Baltimore & Ohio, 182, 224, 446
bananas, 726
Bancroft, Anne, 604, 618, 623, 725
Bancroft, George, 138
Bank Holding Company Act, 606
Bankers' Agreement, 474, 481
Bankhead, Tallulah, 390, 496, 516, 535, 682
banks, brokers, financial
  institutions,
  Alger, David, 871
  Allen & Co., 474, 825
  Allen, Charles, Jr., 825
  Allen, Herbert, 843
  Alliance Capital, 640
    building, 691
  Amalgamated, 398
  Apple Savings, 133, 439, 765
  Astoria Federal S&L, 218, 501, 797

Bache & Co., 231
Banco de Ponce, 645
Bank of Commerce and Credit
  Internatl. (BCCI), 809
Bank of Manhattan, 372
Bank of New York, 38, 138, 793
  building, 439
Bank of the Manhattan Co.,
  48, 453, 601
  building, 453
Bank of the United States, 43,
  63, 343, 449
Bankers Trust, 282, 453, 601,
  787, 825, 854
  buildings, 339, 649
Bear, Stearns, 398
  building, 878
Belmont, 242
Bowery Savings, 70, 402, 456
Brooklyn Trust Co., 201, 634
Brown Brothers, 62, 73, 85,
  98, 107, 182, 458
Brown Brothers Harriman,
  317, 458
Cantor Fitzgerald, 544, 706
Carver Federal Savings, 574
Central Savings, 439
Chase Manhattan, 48, 182,
  449, 453, 474, 601, 626,
  638, 793, 829, 830
  Morgan, J.P., and 866
Chase National, 182, 481, 601
  building, 439
Chatham and Phenix, 466
Chemical, 61, 97, 113, 175,
  218, 384, 441, 597, 621,
  687, 723, 775, 809, 830
Citibank, 55, 68, 133, 138, 271,
  305, 434, 601, 634, 638,
  787, 813
  building, 638
  Everything Card of, 673
  travelers checks, 288
Citicorp, 787, 809, 853
  building (Queens), 802
  Center, 740
Citigroup, 853
City Bank of New York, 55
Corn Exchange, 104, 597
Cross Land Savings, 123, 393,
  640, 687, 742, 755, 814
CS First Boston, 481, 820
Dean Witter Reynolds, 458
Depository Trust Co. (DTC),
  680
Dillon Read, 389, 747, 843
Dollar Dry Dock Savings, 765
Dollar Savings, 223, 765
Donaldson, Lufkin and
  Jenrette, 621, 640, 775
Drexel Burnham Lambert,
  729, 765, 775, 781, 793

Dreyfus Fund, 601
Dreyfus Liquid Assets, 716
Dry Dock Savings, 94, 512,
  765
Dunbar National, 439
East Brooklyn Savings, 123,
  393, 640, 687, 742, 755
East New York Savings, 645
East River Savings, 94, 431,
  493
Emigrant Savings, 98, 672,
  781
European American, 716
Fahnestock & Co., 195
Federal Reserve, 343, 408,
  747
Fiduciary Trust, 458
First Boston, 481, 820
First National, 133, 305, 601
First National City, 601, 634
  building, 638
Forstmann-Little, 827
Franklin National, 716,751
  building, 710
Fulton Savings, 742
German Savings, 439
Goldman, Sachs, 152, 251,
  288, 365, 434, 441, 540,
  540, 768, 853
Greater New York Savings, 251
Green Point Savings, 152, 305,
  458
Greenwich Savings, 70, 755
Guaranty Trust, 136
Hanover, 100, 336, 634
Harlem Savings, 133, 765
Harriman, W. A., & Co., 425
Hayden Stone, 299
Home Savings, 458
HSBC, 861
Hutton, E.F., 288
Independence Savings, 97
Irving Trust, 100, 299, 471, 793
  building, 471
Jarmulovsky's, 350
Kidder, Peabody, 781, 825,
  830
Knickerbocker Trust, 205,
  305, 312
Kohlberg Kravis Roberts, 729,
  736
Kuhn, Loeb, 144, 175, 251
Lazard Frères, 192, 205, 520,
  634, 736
Lebenthal & Co., 410, 501, 872
Lehman Brothers, 117, 158
Leumi, 650
Loeb, Rhoades, 507, 741, 747
Loeb Rhoades Hornblower,
  747
Manhattan Savings, 97, 187,
  533

Manufacturers Hanover Trust,
  634, 787, 809
  building, 600
Manufacturers Trust, 55, 466,
  634
Marine Midland, 97, 665
  building, 677
Merchants, 50
Merrill Lynch, 350, 527, 757
Metropolitan Savings, 144,
  687, 742, 755
Morgan, J.P., & Co., 242, 350,
  356, 384, 474, 801, 804
  Chase Manhattan and, 866
Morgan Stanley, 474, 488
National Bank of the City of
  NY (National City), 69,
  138, 305, 336, 372, 434,
  601
New York Bank for Savings,
  60
New York Trust, 621
North Fork, 293, 804, 815
North Side Savings, 294, 501
  of the Metropolis, 163, 286,
  372
PaineWebber, 645, 830
  building, 638
  GE and, 825
  Kidder, Peabody and, 825
Primerica, 793
Public National, 601
Quick & Reilly, 716
Republic National, 861
Reynolds & Co., 458
Salomon Bros., 323, 378, 434,
  488, 628, 694, 722, 755,
  799, 809, 843
Salomon, Arthur K., 434
Salomon, Percy S., 628
Seligman, J.& W., 136
Shearson/American Express,
  755
Shearson Hayden Stone, 747
Shearson Loeb Rhoades, 747,
  755
Smith, Barney, 793
South Brooklyn Savings, 97
Spencer Trask, 158, 239, 252,
  264, 301, 317
Stabile, 139
Tradesmen's, 66
United States Trust, 104
Vanguard Group, 716
Williamsburgh Savings, 100,
  446
Banzhaf, John, 673
Bara, Theda, 357
Baraka, Imanu Amiri, 654
Bar Association, 158, 162
  building, 249
Barbaro, Frank J., 755

Barbeau, Adrienne, 708
Barbella, Maria, 244, 249
Barber, Red, 518, 534, 595, 818
Barber, Samuel, 556, 668
Barbour, Joyce, 437, 444
Barck, Oscar T., 460
Bard, Dr. John, 26
Bard, Samuel, 41
Bard, William, 67, 105
Barkin, Ellen, 766
Barlow, Betsy, 705, 707, 751, 754
Barnard College, 222, 558, 688, 805
   Greek Games at, 286
   Sulzberger Hall at, 793
Barnard, Edward Sibley, 877
Barnard, George G., 510
Barnes & Noble, 171, 367, 460, 701, 748, 782, 805
Barnes, Djuna, 496, 762
Barney, Charles T., 205, 226, 305
Barnum & Bailey, 196, 278, 302, 308
Barnum, P.T., 82, 84, 87, 99, 134, 164, 173, 200, 202, 229, 249
Baron de Hirsch Fund, 227
Barr, Alfred H., Jr., 444, 576, 757
Barr, Donald, 653
barrel murder, 286
Barrett, Lawrence, 115
Barrett, Wayne, 794, 873
Barrie, Barbara, 731
Barrie, James M., 254, 313, 374
Barron, Clarence W., 276
Barrows, Sidney Biddle, 773
Barry, Gene, 767
Barry, Philip, 390, 399, 406, 414, 428, 437, 460, 469, 510, 516, 535, 570, 583
Barrymore, Ethel, 248, 273, 284, 296, 374, 380, 390, 437, 623
Barrymore, John, 284, 296, 319, 390, 421, 523
Barrymore, Lionel, 284, 296
Barrymore, Maurice, 296
Barsotti, Carlo, 233
Bartell, Dick, 498
Barthelme, Donald, 675
Bartholdi, F.A., 164, 180
Bartlett, Jennifer, 731, 738
Bartlett, Paul, 286, 331, 406
Bartók, Bela, 584
Barton, Bruce, 379, 436, 674
Barton, James, 381, 407, 555, 583, 642
Bartow, John, 18
Baruch, Bernard M., 221, 282, 316, 365, 401, 519, 657
Baruch, Simon, 206

Barwick, Kent L., 764, 814
Baryshnikov, Mikhail, 806
Barzini, Luigi, Jr., 460
baseball, 90, 161, 278, 285, 291, 302, 391, 397, 401, 470, 511, 530, 589
   (see also Brooklyn Dodgers, Ebbets Field, New York Giants, New York Mets, New York Yankees, Polo Grounds, Shea Stadium, Yankee Stadium)
   American League, 273
   curve ball, 146
   designated hitter in, 714
   expansion, 619, 643, 690
   free agents in, 726, 732
   Ladies' Day and, 146, 203
   player strike, 828
   World Series (in which New York teams play; * denotes a Dodgers, Giants, Mets, or Yankees win), 285, 297, 333, 339, 347, 362, 369, 391*, 397*, 401*, 408, 422, 430*, 438*, 470*, 479*, 498*, 504*, 511*, 518*, 530*, 537, 543*, 561*, 571*, 578*, 585*, 589*, 595*, 600*, 605*, 609*, 614, 619*, 632, 637*, 643*, 649*, 655*, 690*, 714, 732, 739*, 745*, 759, 783*, 839*, 858*, 863*, 868*, 874
   cancellation of, 291, 828
Basie, Count, 511
basketball, 285, 396, 485, 511, 556, 567, 578, 697, 714, 720, 732, 777, 848 (see also New York Knicks)
   gambling scandals in, 551, 571, 584
Basquiat, Jean-Michel, 771, 794
Bassett, Angela, 862
Bastianach, Lidia, 760
Batchelor, C.D., 737
Batchelor, John Calvin, 757, 776
Bates, Blanche, 273, 278, 325, 529
Bates, Kathy, 766
bathhouses, 44, 85, 96, 254, 314, 354
baths, 140
Batista, Fulgencio, 621
Battery, 16, 23, 37, 156
Battery Park City, 625, 669, 677, 691, 721, 733, 754, 759, 764, 778, 785, 790, 807, 864
   Esplanade of, 767

Battle, Hinton, 767, 812
Bauer, Hank, 595, 614
Baum, Dwight J., 454
Baum, Joseph, 596, 626, 735, 860
Baxley, Barbara, 594, 630, 689, 763
Baxter, Anne, 777
Baxter, Warner, 368
Bayard, Nicholas, 14, 15, 17, 18
Bayard, William, 22
Bayes, Nora, 314, 320, 438
Bayley, Dr. Richard, 40, 45–47, 49
Bayonne Bridge, 459
Bay Ridge, 7, 105, 499
Beach, Alfred E., 158, 171
Beach, Moses Yale, 78, 86
Beach, Rex, 319
beaches,
   Jones,
   Orchard, 493
Beacon Theater, 437
Beame, Abraham D., 657, 710, 716, 722, 871
Bean, Orson, 595, 637, 643
Beard, James, 525, 615, 626, 760, 779
Beard, William Holbrook, 190
Bearden, Romare, 386, 545, 675, 696, 757, 794
Beatles, 654
Beattie, Jim, 745
Beaumont, Vivian, 642
Beauregard, Pierre, 125
Beck, Martin, 346, 392, 524
Becker, Boris, 801
Becker, Charles, 335
Becker, Rob, 832
Beckett, Samuel, 636, 690, 707
Beckmann, Max, 576
Bedford, Brian, 817
Bedford Stuyvesant, 741
   Pathmark supermarket in, 746
   Restoration Corp., 678
Bedloe Island,
   pest house on, 46
Beebe, Charles William, 263
Beebe, Lucius, 443, 475
Beebe, William, 645
Beecher, Catharine, 162, 177
Beecher, Henry Ward, 96, 111, 122, 162, 169, 177, 216
Beekman, Gerardus, 20, 21
Beekman, Henry Rutgers, 212, 213, 217, 218
Beekman, James Wm., 71, 97
Beekman, William, 8, 14, 56
Beer, Frederick, 210
Beery, Wallace, 308, 408
Begley, Ed, 559, 603, 613

Behn, Carl Sosthenes, 612
Behrman, S.N., 428, 443, 469, 478, 484, 496, 516, 588, 599, 618, 654, 713
Beiderbecke, Bix, 409, 462
Beinecke, William, 754
Belafonte, Harry, 595
Belasco, David, 190, 199, 207, 236, 243, 267, 278, 296, 302, 308, 332, 380, 460
Bel Geddes, Barbara, 566, 603, 636, 712
Bel Geddes, Norman, 504
Bell Laboratories, 254, 307, 427, 762, 770
Bell Telephone, 184, 189
Bell, Agrippa Nelson, 111
Bell, Alexander Graham, 184, 356
Bellamy, Carol, 774
Bellamy, Ralph, 541, 550, 570, 618
Bellerose, 255
Bellow, Saul, 593, 607, 695
Bellows, George, 307, 313, 319, 406, 413
Bellows, Henry W., 135
Belmont, August, 77, 116, 117, 123, 124, 139, 143, 165, 185, 188, 224, 242, 277
   II, 224, 265, 287, 290, 300, 304, 326, 334, 351, 403
Belmont, Eleanor Robson, 326, 749
Belt Parkway, 449, 521
Belushi, John, 725
Bemelmans, Ludwig, 516, 642
Ben-Ami, Jacob, 406, 623, 738
Benchley, Robert, 380, 396, 408, 550
Bender, Thomas, 724, 788, 877
Bendix, William, 517
Benepe, Barry, 792
Benét, Stephen Vincent, 428, 541
Bening, Annette, 783
Benjamin, Richard, 725
Bennett Building, 172
Bennett, Constance, 660
Bennett, Floyd, 417, 435
Bennett, James Gordon, 73, 75, 82, 127, 142, 146, 155, 168, 172, 174, 203
   Jr., 146, 151, 162, 202, 373
Bennett, Joan, 806
Bennett, John J., Jr., 533
Bennett, Michael, 713, 745, 758, 789
Bennett, Richard, 284, 301, 406, 490, 637
Bennett, Tony, 643
Benson, Jodi, 817

Benson, Robby, 696
Bensonhurst, 6, 10, 741, 797
Bent, Bruce, 687, 694
Bentley, Jack, 408
Benton, Barbara, 776
Benton, Robert, 738
Benzell, Mimi, 637, 697
Berg, Gertrude, 444, 623, 667
Berg, Molly, 570
Bergen, Polly, 595
Berger, Meyer, 535, 583, 622, 630
Bergh, Henry, 172, 218
Bergman, Alan and Marilyn, 720
Bergman, Ingrid, 555
Bergner, Elisabeth, 541
Berkeley, Busby, 429, 437
Berkman, Alexander, 298
Berle, Adolph A., 465, 700
Berle, Milton, 451, 470, 542, 566, 878
Berlin, Irving, 308, 332, 339, 352, 353, 357, 362, 375, 381, 382, 387, 391, 400, 407, 415, 422, 429, 438, 470, 478, 524, 536, 555, 566, 571, 577, 794, 801
Berlind, Roger, 628
Berliner, Emile, 184
Bernays, Anne, 660, 724
Bernays, Edward L., 379, 445
Bernbach, William, 569, 762
Bernbaum, Glenn, 735, 860
Bernhard, Arnold, 458, 501, 574, 787
Bernhardt, Sarah, 338, 346
Berns, Charlie, 457
Bernstein, Aline, 484, 516, 576, 604
Bernstein, Leonard, 542, 546, 570, 578, 594, 609, 613
Bernstein, Pearl, 509, 635
Bernstein, Theodore M., 748
Berra, Yogi, 578, 605, 609, 637
Berrol, Selma Cantor, 846
Berwind, Edward J., 249, 494
Best, Edna, 469, 588, 598
Bethlehem Steel, 293
Bethune, Joanne, 51, 65
Bettmann Archive, 489, 757
Bettmann, Otto L., 489, 857
Betz, Pauline, 537, 543, 547
Beutel, Bill, 826
Biaggi, Mario, 679, 711, 786, 792, 814
Bickmore, Albert, 153, 195
bicycles, 258
Biederman, Daniel A., 754, 854
Bierce, Ambrose, 301
Bierstadt, Albert, 137, 197, 278
B.I.G., 848
Big Apple Circus, 738

Big Apple, 703
Bigard, Barney, 461
Biggers, Earl Derr, 346
Biggs, Hermann M., 232, 239, 373, 399
Biggs, Jason, 877
Bigley, Isabel, 594
Bikel, Theodore, 612, 624
Billboard magazine, 240, 497
Billings, C.K.G., 287, 493
Billings, John Shaw, 272, 331, 345
Billingsley, Sherman, 448, 480, 663
Bilotti, Thomas, 818
Bing & Bing, 340, 354, 362, 363, 370, 433
Bing, Ilse, 523
Bing, Rudolf, 577, 848
Bingham, Amelia, 429
Binney, Constance, 375
Biograph Co., 243, 339
Biondo, Joe, 614
Biow, Milton, 367, 479
Bird, Robert M., 69
Birdland, 605
Birdseye, Clarence, 371, 610
Birge, Charles E., 315
Birkenhead, Susan, 818
Birmingham, Stephen, 674, 712, 748, 766, 821
Bissel, Israel, 31
Bissell, George E., 225, 248, 261
Bissell, Richard, 738
Bitter, Karl, 268, 345, 352, 357
Bjurstedt (Mallory), Molla, 422
Black, Eli M., 726
Black, Frank S., 245
Black, Mary, 731, 771
Black Enterprise magazine, 695
Black Panthers, 685
Blackmar, Elizabeth, 799, 817
blacks, 40, 59, 60, 64, 81, 103, 110, 117, 269, 526, 652, 680
Black Tom explosion, 359
Blackwell, Elizabeth, 95, 114, 137
Blackwell, Emily, 114
Blackwell's Island, 12, 66, 169, 390, 684
   asylum on, 216
   Bellevue Hospital and, 173
   hospitals on, 80, 112, 121
   insane asylum on, 216
Blades, Ruben, 812
Blaeser, Gustav, 154
Blaine, James G., 178, 205
Blaine, Vivian, 604
Blair, Mary, 396

Blake, Eubie, 391, 452, 772
Blakey, Art, 806
Blanchard, Johnny, 637
Blatch, Harriet Eaton, 305
Blavatsky, Helena, 176, 207
Bleakley, William F., 493
Bledsoe, Jules, 420
Bleecker, Jan Jansen, 8, 14, 23
Bleecker, John, 23
Bleecker, Rutger, 23
Blimpie's, 656
Blind, New York Assn. for, 290, 344
Blind, Recording for the, 582
blindness, 356, 845
Bliss, Cornelius N., 218
Bliss, Henry H., 260
Blitzstein, Marc, 504, 595, 599
Bliven, Bruce, Jr., 607, 688, 707, 757, 877
blizzards, 218–220, 563, 692, 840
Bloch, Paul, 466
Block, Martin, 676
Bloomberg Business News, 804
Bloomberg Financial Markets, 755
Bloomberg TV News, 837
Bloomberg, Michael R., 755, 804, 846, 871, 876
Bloomgarden, Kermit, 732
Bloomingdale Asylum, 60, 239
Bloomingdale Road, 19, 152
Bloomingdale village, 124
Bloomingdale's, 213, 289, 442, 458, 558, 711, 782, 793, 804
Blossom, Henry, 296, 302, 352, 357, 362, 381
blue laws, 57
Blue Note jazz records, 518, 800
Blum, Mark, 811
Blumberg, Julius, 215
Blumenthal, Albert H., 711
Blumenthal, George, 334, 527
Blumenthal, Ralph, 867
Bly, Nellie, 216, 222, 224, 394
Blyden, Larry, 619, 668
Blyth, Ann, 529
BMI, 517
B'nai B'rith, 85
Board of Education (see education)
Board of Estimate, 270, 403, 662, 803
Board of Health, 159, 171, 190, 245
Bobst, Elmer H., 706, 742
Bochco, Steven, 827
Bock, Jerry, 609, 624, 631, 643, 648, 654, 668, 696

Bodenheim, Maxwell, 374, 385, 395, 399, 406, 413, 419, 443, 476, 598
Boehm, George, 337
Boesky, Ivan F., 723, 775, 781, 787
Bogardus, Dominie Everardus, 5
Bogart, Humphrey, 428, 444, 510, 535, 599, 613
Bogle, John C., 716
Boland, Mary, 380, 470, 491, 660
Bolender, Todd, 537, 556, 584
Bolger, Ray, 461, 484, 497, 536, 566
Bolton, Charles W., 399
Bolton, Guy, 362, 368, 369, 375, 380, 391, 415, 437, 484, 546, 749
Bonanno, Joseph, 408, 462, 614, 655, 669, 750, 878
Bondarin, Arley, 724
Bondi, Beulah, 428
Bone, Kevin, 846
Bonfanti, Marie, 142
Bonner, Hugh, 268
Bonner, Robert, 101, 261
Bonomi, Patricia U., 856
Book-Of-The-Month Club, 419
booksellers, 359
Booksellers Row, 236, 406, 523
Boomer, Lucius M., 340, 433
Booth, Edwin, 361, 374, 137, 154, 201, 220, 236
Booth, John Wilkes, 137
Booth, Shirley, 490, 516, 524, 541, 576, 583, 588, 604, 817
Borden, Gail, 102, 106, 111, 112, 117, 119, 128, 174
Borden, John Gail, 174
Borders, 838
Bordoni, Irene, 368, 414, 438, 524, 595
Borg, Björn, 739
Borge, Victor, 594
Borglum, Gutzon, 374
Borgnine, Ernest, 604, 719, 794
Boricua College, 717, 845
Bosley, Tom, 624, 828
Bossy, Mike, 763, 767
Boston Properties, 868
Boston Post Road, 12, 61
Bostwick, Barry, 708
Boswell, Connee, 732
Boswell, Peyton, 390
Botanical Garden, New York, 229
botanical gardens, 49
botany, 60, 159
Boucicault, Dion, 115, 119, 121, 124, 225
Bouck, William C., 86, 95

INDEX

Boudin, Kathy, 692
Boulanger, Nadia, 414
Boulevard, The, 152, 153
Bouley, David, 780, 792, 865
Boulud, Daniel, 865
Bourke-White, Margaret, 495, 702
Boutwell, George S., 152
Bowery B'hoys, 97, 132
Bowery, 186, 411
   theaters in, 64
"Bowery, The," 236
Bowes, Major Edward J., 381, 491, 555
Bowker, Richard R., 190, 192, 207
Bowles, Chester, 443, 782
Bowles, Jane, 594
bowling alleys
   Utopia Lanes, 595
Bowling Green, 23, 25, 30, 32, 248
Bowman, John McEntee, 304
Bowne & Co., 31, 718
Bowne, John, 10
Boyer, Charles, 642
Boyer, Clete, 655
Boyle, Peter, 753
Boyle, Robert E., 833
Boyle, Robert H., 688
Boys Choir of Harlem, 683
boxing, 362, 369, 387, 391, 422, 430, 556
Brace, Charles Loring, 104, 106, 168, 223
Bracken, Eddie, 510, 517, 570
Braddock, James J., 492, 720
Bradford, Roark, 450
Bradford, William, 20, 23
Bradshaw, Thornton F., 776, 793
Brady, Alice, 460, 517
Brady Bill, 823
Brady, "Diamond Jim," 280, 365
Brady, Matthew B., 99, 112, 122, 128, 248
Brady, William A., 332, 338, 576
Brady, William V., 91, 93, 105
Braham, David, 200, 208, 215, 225
Brando, Marlon, 546, 559, 570, 599, 604, 708, 806
Branson, Richard, 836
brassieres, 353
   Maiden Form and, 401
Bratton, William S., 819, 834
breadlines, 457
Breakstone's, 221, 264, 376, 544
Brent, Romney, 414, 421, 444
Breuer, Lee, 767
Brevoort, Henrick Van, 20
Brevoort, Henry, 55, 73, 91
   Jr., 73

brewing, 60, 111, 144, 230, 328, 383, 480, 735
   lager, 85
   Rheingold, 111
   Ruppert, 147, 174, 472, 480, 493
   Schaefer, F. & M., 85, 230, 363, 376, 383, 480, 735
Bricken, Abraham, 447
Breslin, Jimmy, 647, 686, 689, 712, 771, 811
Brice, Fanny, 326, 347, 352, 362, 368, 381, 386, 391, 400, 445, 452, 461, 484, 497, 584
Bricktop, 772
Bricusse, Leslie, 661, 847
bridge, contract, 416, 445, 654
bridges,
   Alexander Hamilton, 646
   Arthur Kill, 366, 621
   Bayonne, 459
   Bronx-Whitestone, 514, 634
   Brooklyn, 201, 215, 251, 450, 544
   George Washington, 459, 844
   Goethals, 435
   Hell Gate, 366
   Henry Hudson, 495
   Kings Bridge, 16, 33, 35
   Kosciuszko, 514
   Manhattan, 318
   Outerbridge Crossing, 435
   Queensboro, 318
   Sputen Duyvil, 810
   steel arch, 459
   suspension, 109, 283, 313, 459
   Third Avenue, 271
   Throgs Neck, 634
   Triborough, 495
   Verrazano-Narrows, 628
   Williamsburg, 283, 313, 330
   Willis Avenue, 271
Bridges, Amy, 771
Brighton Beach,
   Babi Yar Triangle in, 786
Briguet, Georges, 656
Brill Building, 462
Brill, Steven, 737
Brisbane, Arthur, 216, 253, 423, 440, 455, 482, 496
Broad Street, 17
Broadhead, Charles C., 57
Broadway, 4, 57, 222, 607
   trolley line, 553
Broadway and off-Bwy musicals,
   Ain't Misbehavin', 744
   Annie, 739
   Annie Get Your Gun, 555
   Anything Goes, 484
   Apple Blossoms, 381

Applause, 696
As the Girls Go, 566
As Thousands Cheer, 478
Babes in Arms, 504
Babes in Toyland, 285
Band Wagon, The, 461
Barnum, 753
Beauty and the Beast, 828
Bells Are Ringing, 609
Best Foot Forward, 530
Best Little Whorehouse in Texas, The, 744
Big Boy, 414
Big River, 777
Black and Blue, 800
Black Crook, The, 142
Bloomer Girl, 546
Blossom Time, 391
Blue Paradise, The, 357
Bombo, 391
Boys from Syracuse, The, 511
Brigadoon, 560
Bring in da' Noise, 839
Bubblin' Brown Sugar, 732
By Jupiter, 536
Bye Bye Birdie, 631
Cabaret, 668
Cabin in the Sky, 524
Call Me Madam, 577
Call Me Mister, 555
Camelot, 631
Can Can, 594
Captain Jinks of the Horse Marines, 273
Carmen Jones, 542
Carousel, 551
Cat and the Fiddle, The, 461
Cats, 763
Chicago, 725
Chin-Chin, 352
Chinese Honeymoon, A, 278
Chorus Line, A, 725
City of Angels, 800
Cocoanuts, The, 415
Company, 696
Connecticut Yankee, A, 429
Contact, 863
Countess Maritza, 421
Cradle Will Rock, The, 504
Crazy for You, 817
Damn Yankees, 604
Dancin', 744
Dearest Enemy, 414
Desert Song, The, 421
Don't Bother Me, I Can't Cope, 708
Dreamgirls, 758
Du Barry Was a Lady, 517
El Grande de Coca-Cola, 713
Eternal Road, The, 504
Evita, 749
Fanny, 599

Fantasticks, The, 631
Fiddler on the Roof, 654
Fifty Million Frenchmen, 445
Finian's Rainbow, 560
Fiorello!, 624
Flahooley, 583
Flower Drum Song, 619
Follow the Girls, 546
Follow Thru, 444
Forbidden Broadway, 763
Forty-Five Minutes from Broadway, 302
42nd Street, 753
Funny Face, 429
Funny Girl, 654
Funny Thing Happened, A, 643
Gay Divorce, 470
Gentlemen Prefer Blondes, 571
Gingham Girl, The, 396
Girl Crazy, 451
Girl Friend, The, 421
Girl From Utah, The, 352
Godspell, 703
Going Up, 369
Good Boy, 437
Good News, 429
Grand Hotel, 800
Grease, 708
Guys and Dolls, 577
Gypsy, 624
Hair, 676
Hats Off to Ice, 546
Hello, Dolly!, 654
Helzapoppin, 510
High Button Shoes, 560
Hit the Deck, 429
Hold Everything, 438
Honeymoon Lane, 421
Hot Chocolates, 444
House of Flowers, 599
How to Succeed in Business, 637
I'd Rather Be Right, 504
I Married an Angel, 510
In Dahomey, 284
Into the Woods, 789
Irene, 381
Jekyll and Hyde, 847
Jelly's Last Jam, 817
Jesus Christ Superstar, 703
Jumbo, 491
June Moon, 445
Kid Boots, 400
Kiki, 391
King and I, The, 583
Kismet, 594
Kiss Me Kate, 566
Kiss of the Spider Woman, 822
Knickerbocker Holiday, 511
La Cage aux Folles, 767
Lady Be Good, 407

Lady in the Dark, 529
Leave It to Me, 511
Lend an Ear, 566
Les Misérables, 789
Let My People Come, 719
Let's Face It, 530
Li'l Abner, 609
Life Begins at 8:40, 484
Lion King, The, 848
Little Nellie Kelly, 396
Little Night Music, A, 713
Little Shop of Horrors, 763
Little Show, The, 444
Lost in the Stars, 571
Louisiana Purchase, 524
Madame Sherry, 326
Magic Show, The, 719
Mama, I Want to Sing, 767
Mame, 668
Man of La Mancha, 661
Maytime, 368
Me Nobody Knows, The, 696
Mexican Hayride, 546
Miss Saigon, 812
Mlle. Modiste, 296
Most Happy Fella, The, 609
Music Man, The, 613
My Fair Lady, 608
My One and Only, 767
Mystery of Edwin Drood, The, 777
Naughty Marietta, 326
Never Too Late, 643
New Moon, The, 437
New Yorkers, The, 452
Nine, 763
No Strings, 642
Of Thee I Sing, 461
Oh, Boy!, 368
Oh! Calcutta!, 690
Oh, Kay, 421
Oklahoma!, 542
On the Town, 546
On Your Toes, 497
One Mo' Time, 749
One Touch of Venus, 542
Paint Your Wagon, 583
Pajama Game, The, 599
Pal Joey, 524
Panama Hattie, 524
Peggy-Ann, 421
Peter Pan, 599
Phantom of the Opera, The, 794
Pink Lady, The, 332
Pins and Needles, 504
Pippin, 708
Plain and Fancy, 604
Producers, The, 874
Promises, Promises, 683
Purlie, 696
Ragtime, 857

Raisin, 713
Red Mill, The, 302
Rent, 839
Rio Rita, 429
Roberta, 478
Rosalie, 437
Rose Marie, 407
Sally, 387
Scarlet Pimpernel, The, 848
Secret Garden, The, 812
1776, 690
Shenandoah, 725
Show Boat, 430
Shuffle Along, 391
Silk Stockings, 604
Smoky Joe's Cafe, 832
Something for the Boys, 542
Song of Norway, The, 546
Sons O'Fun, 530
Sophisticated Ladies, 758
South Pacific, 571
Star and Garter, 536
Strike Up the Band, 451
Student Prince, The, 407
Sound of Music, The, 624
Subways Are for Sleeping, 637
Sugar Babies, 749
Sugar, 708
Sunday in the Park with George, 772
Sunny, 414
Sweeny Todd, 749
Sweet Adeline, 445
Sweet Charity, 668
Tap Dance Kid, The, 767
They're Playing Our Song, 749
Three Musketeers, The, 437
Titanic, 847
Too Many Girls, 517
Trip to Chinatown, A, 236
Unsinkable Molly Brown, The, 631
Up in Central Park, 551
Urinetown, 874
Vagabond King, The, 414
Very Good Eddie, 357
Victor/Victoria, 832
West Side Story, 613
Where's Charley, 566
Whoopee, 438
Who's Tommy, The, 822
Will Rogers Follies, The, 812
Wish You Were Here, 589
Wizard of Oz, The, 284
Wiz, The, 725
Woman of the Year, 758
Wonderful Town, 594
You're a Good Man, Charlie Brown, 676
Your Own Thing, 683
Brockholles, Anthony, 13
Broderick, Helen, 414

Broderick, Matthew, 766, 777, 806, 828, 874
Broderick, Mosette, 752
Brodie, Steve, 215
Brody, Jerome, 596, 722, 875
Brolin, Brent C., 794
Bronck, Jonas, 5
Bronfman, Samuel, 625
Bronson-Howard, George, 319
Bronx, 5, 172, 466, 473
    Am. Female Guardian Society in, 275
    apartments in, 397, 409, 423, 432, 440, 526, 587, 644, 646, 685, 698, 715, 721, 741, 745, 764, 851
    Bartow, John, in, 18
    Botanical Garden in, 229
    Charlotte Gardens in, 851
    Community College, 611
    County Building, 486
    county of, 348
    Cross-Bronx Expressway and, 587, 646
    Development Center, 740
    East Tremont, 587
    elevated railways in, 215, 246, 373, 384, 602, 711
    fires in, 728
    Gaelic Park in, 422, 530, 812
    Grand Concourse in, 232
    Home News, 307, 394, 549, 564
    Jerome Avenue in, 133
    Kingsbridge in, 16
    Kingsbridge Armory in, 370
    Lehman College in, 688
    Loews Paradise in, 451
    Mosholu Parkway in, 219
    Mott Haven in, 99, 215
    Mount Eden in, 58, 60
    NYU in, 239
    Orchard Beach in, 493
    Parkchester in, 525
    parks in, 204
    Pelham Bay Park, 220, 498
    Pelham Bay Golf Course, 353
    Pelham Parkway in, 330
    Pondiac Democratic Club in, 390
    population of, 259 (1898), 580 (1950), 870 (2000)
    Puerto Ricans in, 596
    River, 5
    Riverdale in, 6
    social club fire in, 807
    SEBCO in, 685
    South, 685, 741, 745
    Split Rock golf course, 498
    subways and, 290, 312, 467, 597
    Yankee Stadium in, 401, 857

    Throgs Neck in, 5
    University Heights in, 239
    West Farms in, 90
    Westchester Square, 8
    Woodlawn in, 172
    Zoo, 263, 299, 531, 621
Bronx cocktail, 305
Bronx River Parkway, 411
Brook, Clive, 583
Brooklyn, 4
    Atlantic Center in, 837
    Battle of, 33
    Bay Ridge in, 7, 105
    Borough Hall in, 94
    Botanic Garden, 328
        Japanese Garden in, 358
    Brownsville in, 377, 451
    Bush Terminal in, 226
    Bushwick in, 10, 48, 106
    Canarsie in, 13
    Catholic diocese of, 105
    churches in, 96, 482
    Civic Center in, 615
    crime in, 818
    Crown Heights in, 173, 522, 549, 814
    Eastern Parkway in, 153, 173
    Ebbets Field in, 347, 511, 614
    education in, 40, 186, 214, 216, 235, 247
    elevated railways in, 210, 235, 246, 521, 575, 606, 687
    fires in, 94
    Flatbush in, 233
    gas lighting in, 63, 92, 118, 189
    Grand Army Plaza in, 258
    Gravesend in, 6
    Green-Wood Cemetery in, 81, 185, 386
    horsecars in, 175
    hotels in, 859
    housing in, 184
    Jackie Robinson Apartments in, 633
    Kings Plaza Shopping Center in, 837
    Lefferts Homestead in, 39
    Loews Kings movie theater in, 451
    Lubavitchers in, 808
    mayors of, 71, 85
    merchants in, 234
    Montauk Club in, 229
    Norwegians in, 64
    Ocean Parkway in, 153, 179
    parks in, 147
    Park Slope in, 224, 229
    Paramount movie theater in, 451
    Polytechnic Institute, 107, 153, 224, 272, 488, 617, 712

Brooklyn (*continued*)
population of, 17 (1698), 48
(1800), 259 (1898)
Prospect Park in, 122, 143,
169, 258, 639
Public Library, 528
Red Hook, 5
riots in, 808, 814
Satmar in, 580, 700, 748
Starrett City in, 734, 769
subways and, 290, 299, 312,
373, 467, 475, 597
transit in, 235
trolley cars in, 582
Wallabout district, 5
wards in, 103
Williamsburgh in, 48, 106
Wyckoff House in, 7
Brooklyn Academy of Music
(BAM), 314
Brooklyn Benevolent Society, 93
Brooklyn Botanic Garden, 328
Brooklyn Bridge, 201, 215, 251,
450, 544, 673
Brooklyn Bushwicks, 375
Brooklyn College, 325, 418, 450,
502, 515
basketball at, 551
Brooklyn Conservatory of Music,
254
Brooklyn Dodgers, 258, 262,
268, 362, 387, 530, 585,
605, 609, 614, 619
Brooklyn Eagle, 82, 250
Brooklyn Edison Co., 411
Brooklyn Elevated Railroad, 202
Brooklyn, Flatbush & Coney
Island RR, 186
Brooklyn Heights, 56, 94
Brooklyn Historical Society, 134,
192
Brooklyn Howard Orphan
Asylum, 141
Brooklyn Institute of Arts and
Sciences, 60, 63
Brooklyn Law School, 272, 681
Brooklyn Municipal Building,
422
Brooklyn-Manhattan Transit
Corp. (BMT), 398
Brooklyn Navy Yard, 48, 51, 127,
539, 544, 666
Brooklyn Rapid Transit Co., 398
Brooklyn Sanitary Fair, 135
Brooklyn Tech, 475
Brooklyn Theater fire, 180
Brooklyn Union Gas, 242, 299,
410, 418, 434, 488, 549,
574, 611, 621, 694, 717,
729, 798
Brooks Brothers, 59, 67, 70, 98,
127, 132, 173, 246, 256,

317, 356, 503, 553, 781,
793, 809, 861, 872
button-down collar and, 246
seersucker suit and, 67
Brooks, Garth, 848
Brooks, Mel, 577, 874
Broome, John, 34
Brough, Althea, 561
Broun, Heywood, 380, 419, 427,
476, 516
Brown, Anne Wiggins, 492
Brown, Charles Brockden, 48
Brown, Claude, 877
Brown, Edwin G., 856
Brown, H. Rap, 680
Brown, Helen Gurley, 642, 659
Brown, Henry, 687, 694
Brown, Henry Kirke, 112, 150
Brown v. Board of Ed., 596
Brown, John Crosby, 325
Brown, John Mason, 648, 689
Brown, Lew, 414, 415, 421, 429,
437, 438, 444, 461, 478,
504, 619
Brown, Nacio Herb, 470
Brown, Tina, 816, 856
Browne, Junius Henri, 154
Browne, Roscoe Lee, 648, 767,
817
Brownell, Herbert, Jr., 533, 544,
587, 596, 615
Browning, "Peaches," 430
Browning, Susan, 696
brownstone, 91, 102, 194
Brownsville, 377, 451, 695, 755
Brubeck, Dave, 589
Bruce, Carol, 524, 571
Bruce, Nigel, 460
Bruckner traffic circle, 646
Bruckner, Henry, 466
Brumidi, Constantino, 109
Brunel, I.K., 78, 123
Brunel, Marc Isambard, 44
Brush arc lighting, 192
Bryan, Alfred, 326, 619
Bryan, Vincent P., 296
Bryan, William Jennings, 245,
287, 311
Bryant, William Cullen, 84, 87,
91, 116, 122, 138, 164,
178, 187, 332
Bryant Park, 486, 818
Restoration Corp., 754
Bryant's Minstrels, 121
Bryggman, Larry, 806, 867
Brynner, Yul, 555, 583, 777
bubonic plague scare, 540
Buchalter, "Lepke," 519, 527,
531, 547
Buchanan, Jack, 407, 414, 445,
504, 594
Buchanan, James, 111, 118

Buck, Gene, 352, 357, 381, 387,
396, 400, 613
bucket shops, 265
Buckley, Betty, 763, 777
Buckley, Betty Lynn, 690
Buckley, Charles A., 671
Buckley, James L., 693, 716, 729
Buckley, Richard "Lord," 631
Buckley, William F., 583, 840
Buckner, Emory R., 433
Budge, Don, 504, 511
Bueno, Maria, 624, 649, 655,
668
building codes, 131, 147, 211
Building Congress, 392
Buitoni Foods, 532
Bulkley, Henry D., 75
Bullins, Ed, 725
Bullock, William A., 139, 160
Bunche, Ralph J., 692, 700
Buntline, Ned, 96, 106
Burden, Carter, 700
Burden, Henry, 88
Burden, I. Townsend, 358
Burden, James A., Jr., 297
Burden, William A.M., 324
Burdette, Lew, 614, 619
Bureau of Labor Statistics, 494
Bureau of Municipal Research,
305
Burghoff, Gary, 676
Burgoyne, Gen. John, 35
Burjstedt Mallory, Molla, 396
Burke, Billie, 570
Burke, Johnny, 654
burlesque, 503, 536
Burnet, William, 21, 22
Burnett, Carol, 624, 832
Burns, George, 725
Burns, Ric, 862
Burr, Aaron, 47, 51, 53, 55
Burroughs, Wm. S., 551, 593,
622, 776
Burrows, Abe, 594, 619, 637,
660
Burstyn, Ellen, 713, 725, 763, 772
Burton, Richard, 631
Busch, Frederick, 862
buses, 306, 356, 494, 553, 575,
592, 611, 804, 869
articulated, 866
double-decker, 544
full-wrap advertising on, 816
kneeling, 723
shelters, 748
strike on, 587
Bush, George H.W., 792, 803
Bush Terminal, 226
Bush, Irving T., 226, 370
Bush, Joe, 401
Bushnell, David, 34
Bushwick Democratic Club, 233

Bushwick, 10, 48, 106
Business Improvement
Districts, 818
Business Week, 443, 748
Butler, Mother Marie Joseph,
495
Butler, Nicholas Murray, 216,
222, 228, 277, 559
Buttenwieser, Ann, 788
Buttenwieser, Joseph, 365
Butterfield, Gen. Daniel, 374
Butterick, Ebenezer, 137, 146,
155, 285
Butterworth, Charles, 421, 429,
437, 445, 470
Butts, Calvin O., 798
B.V.D.s, 181
Byington, Spring, 406, 450
Byoir, Carl, 337, 468, 482, 520,
612
Byrd, Richard E., 417
Byrnes, Thomas F., 203, 326
Byron, Arthur, 396
Byron, A.S., 248
Byron, Joseph and Percy, 618

Cable Building, 237
cable cars, 149, 222, 237, 243
Cable, Mary, 771, 794
Cablevision Inc., 826
Cabrini Boulevard, 508
Caesar, Irving, 375, 381, 396,
400, 407, 430, 445, 839
Caesar, Sid, 577, 643
Cage, John, 561, 595, 818
Cagney, James, 510, 517, 524,
604, 624
Cahan, Abraham, 247, 252, 257,
367, 582
Cahill, Marie, 278, 284
Cahn, Sammy, 560, 661
Cain, Auguste, 146
Caine, Georgia, 396
cakewalk, 184
Calder, Alexander Stirling, 244
Calder, Alexander, 731
Caldwell, Zoë, 682, 822, 832
Calhern, Louis, 414
Calhoun, Catherine, 386, 428,
460
Calisher, Hortense, 647, 701
Callahan, J. Will, 375
Callaway, Liz, 812
Callow, Alexander B., 666
Callow, Philip, 748
Calloway, Cab, 451, 462, 478, 828
Cambria Heights, 403
Cameron, Hugh, 368
CAMI Hall, 370
Cambridge, Godfrey, 636
Camilli, Dolf, 530

Campagna, Anthony, 327, 424, 432, 455, 569, 692
Campanella, Roy, 571, 605, 619, 823
Campbell, Alan, 198
Campbell, Frank E., 258, 478, 485, 504
Campeau Corp., 793, 797
Campeau, Robert, 781
Canal Ring, 172
canals, 10
Canarsee (Canarsie) tribe, 4, 11, 13
Canby, Vincent, 867
Canelle, Fabrice, 865
Canfield, Richard, 263, 273
Cannato, Vincent J., 873
Canova, Judy, 497
Cantor, Eddie, 368, 375, 381, 400, 429, 438, 451, 508, 526
Cantor, B. Gerald, 544, 836
Cantor Fitzgerald, 765, 836
Cantwell, Mary, 831, 867
Capa, Cornell, 725
Cape Cod Ship Canal, 351
Capek, Josef, 396
Capek, Karel, 396
Capital Cities/ABC, 795
capital punishment, 226, 833, 859
Caples, John, 415
Capone, Al, 408
Capote, Truman, 570, 599, 617, 669
Carbine, Patricia, 689, 706
Carbo, Frankie, 561, 733
Carey, Hugh L., 716, 722, 735, 746, 760
Carey, Joyce, 414
Carillo, Leo, 361, 368, 406
Cariou, Len, 713, 738, 749
Carlino, Joseph P., 610
Carlson, Chester F., 681
Carmichael, Hoagy, 497
Carmichael, Stokely, 680
Carnegie Corp., 331, 689
Carnegie Hall, 229, 236, 407, 631, 676, 783
Carnegie, Andrew, 221, 229, 270, 274, 287, 294, 295, 297, 331, 377
    philanthropies of, 272
Carnegie, Dale, 419, 496
Carnera, Primo, 478, 485
Carney, Art, 612, 660, 738
Carnovsky, Morris, 400, 477, 490, 510, 524, 618
Caro, Robert A., 718
Carpenter, Thelma, 848
carpenters, 195
Carpentier, Georges, 391
Carr, Caleb, 827

Carr, Lucien, 551
Carradine, Keith, 812
Carrier, Willis H., 280, 334,
Carroll, Earl, 368, 407
Carroll, Diahann, 599, 642
Carroll, Paul Vincent, 510, 516
Carroll, Vinnette, 708, 732
Carstensen, Georg J.B., 104
cartage, 13, 15, 42, 60, 62, 66, 833
Carter, Arthur L., 628, 788
Carter, Benny, 547
Carter, Gary, 783
Carter, Jimmy, 729, 741, 742, 747
Carter, Mrs. Leslie, 243
Carter, Myra, 827
Cartier's, 365
Caruso, David, 806
Caruso, Enrico, 284
Carver, Victor, 817
Caryll, Ivan, 240, 285, 332, 352
Case, Stephen M., 866
Casey, William, 741
Casino Theater, 199
Cass, Peggy, 571, 594, 608, 631, 753, 862
Cassidy, Jack, 589, 668
Cassatt, Alexander, 271, 324
Cassini, Igor, 743, 876
Castellano, Paul, 733, 777, 818
cast iron building fronts, 96, 116
Castle Clinton, 53, 60, 61, 363, 557
Castle Garden, 61, 99, 212, 217, 247
    immigrant receiving station at, 111
Castle, Irene, 332, 347, 352
Castle, Vernon, 302, 308, 320, 332, 339, 347, 352, 375
Castoria, Fletcher's, 168
Castro, Fidel, 621, 627
Catalano, Eduardo, 683
Catalano, Salvatore, 789
cat shows, 244
Cather, Willa, 345, 559
Catholic Charities, 277, 384
Catholic Protectory, 104
Catholic Worker, The, 476
Catholic World, 139
Catholics, Roman, 52, 53, 57, 58, 63, 64, 72, 83, 95, 190, 515, 554, 653, 673, 680, 764, 765, 808
Catholic Archdiocese, 742
Catholic Industrial Conference, 474
Cato, Gavin, 808
Catskills, 64, 371, 499
Cautley, Marjorie, 409
Cavanagh, Thomas J., Jr., 655
Cawthorn, Joseph, 262, 296, 326

CBS, 436, 641, 756, 776, 782, 846
    buildings, 453, 662
CCNY (see City College)
Celler, Emmanuel, 574, 755
Celler-Kefauver Amendment, 574
cemeteries,
    Green-Wood, 81, 185, 386
    Woodlawn, 134, 514
Central Park, 87, 102, 106, 116, 117, 119, 122, 134, 164, 181, 188, 226, 410, 433, 486, 721, 728
    bandshell in, 401
    barracks in, 125
    Belvedere Castle in, 156, 383, 840
    Bethesda Fountain in, 171
    bird watching in, 818, 834
    carousel in, 165, 401, 586
    Children's Zoo in, 852
    Cleopatra's Needle in, 193, 196
    concerts in, 676, 749, 753, 758, 767, 795, 812, 822, 848
    Delacorte and, 731
    Great Lawn in, 486, 613, 753, 758, 760, 767, 780, 795, 812, 822, 831, 834, 841
    Henry Luce Nature Observatory in, 840
    Hooverville in, 479
    joggers in, 801, 833
    lawn bowling in, 422
    Loeb Boat House in, 600
    Metropolitan Museum in, 193, 355
    Olmsted Festival in, 678
    Ramble in, 156
    reservoir in, 131
    restaurants in, 188
    sculpture in, 121, 146, 154, 160, 164, 171, 180, 184, 187, 193, 202, 207, 210, 413, 428, 559, 608, 630
    Sheep Meadow in, 138, 676, 686, 749, 751, 760
    Strawberry Fields in, 779
    transverse roads, 121
    Turtle Pond in, 792
    Wollman Rink in, 586, 783
    World War II and, 527
    Zoo, 138, 486, 754, 796, 824
        sculpture in, 660
Central Park Casino, 425
Central Park Conservancy, 841
Central Park Wildlife Center, 796
Central Park West, 199, 435
Century Illustrated Monthly, 160, 450

Century Magazine, 192
certificates of deposit, 634, 687
Cerv, Bob, 605
Chabas, Paul, 345
Chadbourne, Thomas L., 434
Chagall, Marc, 667
Chalif, Louis, 370
Chalfant, Kathleen, 794, 822
Chamber of Commerce, 29, 30, 135, 239, 249, 312
    building, 279
Chambers, Whittaker, 563, 572
Chambliss, Chris, 732, 739
Champion, Gower, 583, 753
Champlain, Lake, 35
Champlain, Samuel de, 1
Chandler, Charles F., 171
Chandler, Spud, 543
Chanin, Irwin S., 407, 414, 420, 428, 429, 446, 464, 795
Chanler, Lewis Stuyvesant, 311
Channing, Carol, 571, 654, 719
Channing, Stockard, 806
Chapin Nursery, 323
Chaplin, Charles, 325, 346, 352, 613
Charisse, Cyd, 570, 594
Charity Organization Society, 198, 274, 513
Charles, Denis, 800
Charles, Ezzard, 599
Charles II of England, 12
Charlick, Oliver, 134, 145, 158
Charlot, André, 400
Charlotte Street, 741
Charnin, Martin, 697, 739
Chase, Chevy, 725
Chase, Edna Woolman, 319, 462, 468, 598, 612
Chase, Ilka, 469, 484, 496, 598
Chase, Mary Coyle, 546
Chase, Salmon P., 136
Chase, Stuart, 413, 776
Chase, W. Parker, 468
Chase, Wm. Merritt, 115, 177, 248
Chasen, Dave, 451
Chatterton, Ruth, 352, 636
Chauncey, George, 827
Chayefsky, Paddy, 594, 599, 604, 623, 636, 758
Cheatham, Doc, 438, 462
Checker taxicabs, 467, 761, 861
"cheesecake," 339
Cheever, John, 516, 630
Chelsea, 63, 93, 124, 454
    Cushman and, 67, 81
Chenault, Lawrence R., 509
Chermayeff, Ivan, 630, 721
Cherne, Leo, 488, 581, 860
Chernow, Ron, 805, 821, 856
Chesbro, Jack, 285

Chesebrough Mfg. Co., 158
Chesebrough-Pond's, 605
chess, (Morphy), 115
chestnuts, American, 293
Chevalier, Maurice, 452
chewing gum, 165, 262
Chickering Hall, 177
childbirth, 52
Child, Julia, 779
child labor, 311
    Natl. Consumers League and, 264
child welfare, 24, 46, 52, 75, 175, 260, 544, 786, 830, 842
Children, Society for Prevention of Cruelty to (SPCC), 172
Children's Aid Society, 104, 168, 223
Chinatown, 93, 148, 175, 193, 259, 711, 722, 759
    Columbus Park in, 786
    Confucius Plaza complex in, 740
    crime in, 784, 813, 858
    new year celebration in, 849
    sweatshops in, 842
    Tongs in, 408, 416, 445
Chinese Exclusion Act, 200
Chinese Hand Laundry Alliance, 473
Chinese, 313, 500
Chisholm, Shirley, 679, 695
Choate, Joseph H., 162, 239, 242, 365
Chock full 'o Nuts, 425
Chodorov, Edward, 546, 594
Chodorov, Jerome, 524, 529, 757
Chofetz Chaim Yeshiva, 598
cholera, 69, 95, 98, 107, 141, 176, 232
Cholly Knickerbocker, 876
Christenberry, Robert K., 610
Christians, Mady, 529, 546
Christie, Audrey, 496, 535, 541
Christie's, 846
Christman, Elizabeth, 281
Christodora House, 251, 434, 727
Christmas, 61, 66, 130, 142, 172, 173, 198, 252, 253, 330, 350, 462, 551
    bird count, 269
Christy, Edwin P., 131
Christy, Howard Chandler, 728
Chrysler, Walter P., 453, 521
Chrysler Building, 746, 759
Church, Frederick E., 92, 115, 137, 194, 267
Church, George, 497
Church Missions House, 241
churches, mosques, synagogues
    Abyssynian Baptist, 399, 507, 527, 705, 798

African Methodist Episcopal Zion, 59
Allen A.M.E., 844
A.M.E. Zion, 417
Anglican, 16
Anshe Chesed, 67, 88, 96, 180
Assemblies of God, 307
Beth Hamedrash Hagodol, 103
Bialystoker, 294
B'nai Jeshurum, 63
Brick, 512
Calvary, 91
Central Presbyterian, 397
Central Synagogue, 169, 859
Christ (Episcopal) (Riverdale), 143
Christ Scientist, Third of, 402
Dutch Reformed, 2, 9
East Brooklyn Congregations, 751
Eldridge Street Synagogue, 217
Emmanuel Baptist, 217
Fifth Avenue Presbyterian, 52, 120, 177
First Presbyterian, 21, 378
Flatbush Reformed, 46
German Lutheran, 289
Grace Episcopal, 91, 134
John Street Methodist, 29, 82
Judson Memorial, 233
Marble Collegiate, 109, 820
Methodist Episcopal, 94
Mosque of New York, 810
of Our Lady of Esperanza, 300
of Our Lady of Mount Carmel, 207
of Our Lady of Pompeii, 238
of Our Saviour (R.C.), 620
of the Ascension, 82, 87, 223
of the Heavenly Rest, 446
of the Holy Communion, 90, 91
of the Holy Cross, 468
of the Holy Name of Jesus, 431
of the Intercession (Episcopal), 354
of the Transfiguration (Little Church Around the Corner), 98, 159
Park Avenue Christian, 340
Plymouth, 96, 150, 482
Reformed Protestant Dutch, 13
Riverdale Presbyterian, 134
Riverside, 450, 687
Rodeph Shalom, 88, 105
Sacred Heart of Jesus, 232
St. Ann's, 39, 147
St. Bartholomew's, 375
St. Clement's, 161, 654, 660
St. Francis Xavier, 551, 786

St. George's, 112
St. James (Episcopal) (Bronx), 134
St. James Episcopal (Manh.), 208
St. John the Divine, Cathedral of, 233, 322, 334, 363, 417, 569, 579, 745, 764
St. Joseph's, 72, 73
St. Luke-in-the-Fields, 63
St. Mark's in-the-Bowery, 12, 48
St. Mark's, 43
St. Mary's (Manhattan), 72
St. Nicholas, 71, 83
St. Patrick's Cathedral, 56, 116, 190, 669
St. Paul the Apostle, 181
St. Paul's Chapel, 29
St. Paul's, 74
St. Peter's Protestant Episcopal, 79
St. Peter's Lutheran, 697, 737
St. Stephen's, 109
St. Thomas, 354, 381
St. Vincent Ferrer, 375
Salam Arabic Lutheran, 855
Salem Evangelical Lutheran, 855
Sea and Land, 58
Second Presbyterian, 42
Shearith Israel, 8, 22, 73
Temple Beth El (Brooklyn), 392
Temple Emanu-El, 88, 151, 324, 454
Trinity, 16, 17, 19, 26, 35, 42, 43, 80, 91, 378, 730
Universalist, 259
West End Collegiate, 237
Willett Street, 294
Zion English Lutheran, 49
Churchill, Allen, 617, 622, 642, 675, 695, 701, 794
Churchill, Henry, 519
Churchill, Jennie (Jerome), Lady Randolph, 174
Churchill, Winston, 552
Chwast, Seymour, 598
CIA, 533
cigarettes, 220 (see also smoking, tobacco)
    Chesterfield, 416
    Duke and, 208
    English Ovals, 279
    L&M, 595
    Lucky Strike, 362, 416, 438
    Marlboro, 279
    Murad, 416
    Old Gold, 416
    Philip Morris, 479
        building, 768

cigars,
    General Cigar Co., 303
    White Owl, 369
Circle Line, 551
circus, 164, 196, 308
Cirillo, Dominick V., 849
Cirino, Linda D., 731
Cirker, Hayward, 528, 867
Cisco, John J., 136
Citarella, 425, 525, 764, 852
Citizens Mutual Gas Co., 139
Citizens' Association of New York, 133
Citizens' Budget Commission, 645
Citizens Committee for NYC, 723
Citizens Union, 250, 328, 481, 645
City and Suburban Homes Co., 348
City Center, 542
city charters, 494, 645, 646, 735
    charter revisions, 803
City Club, 481
City College (CCNY), 95, 142, 307, 312, 375, 635, 803, 827
    basketball, 578, 584
    fatal stampede at, 812
City Council, 494, 506
City Hall, 17, 55, 72, 119, 237, 669
city halls, 5, 56
City Housing Authority, 486, 493, 600, 620, 650
Citymeals-on-Wheels, 760
city planning, 233, 423, 638
City Planning Commission, 494, 499, 512, 644, 650
City Reform League, 104
City University of New York (CUNY), 635, 688, 694, 730, 809, 810, 815, 856, 861, 873 (see also City College)
    College of Staten Island, 712
    Medgar Evers College, 688
Civil Rights acts, 652, 679
Civil Service Commission, 201
Civil Service Reform Assn., 242
Civil War, 125, 138
Claflin, Tennessee, 157, 160, 169, 182
Claiborne, Craig, 639
Claire, Ina, 362, 380, 396, 451, 469, 472, 496
Claremont Stables, 222
Clark, Aaron, 76, 78, 79
Clark, Alfred Corning, 209
Clark, Alonzo, 75
Clark, Bobby, 396, 400, 451, 470, 484, 497, 517, 536, 546, 566, 631

Clark, Edward S., 101, 129, 191, 209
Clark, Grenville, 458
Clark, Kenneth B., 640, 652
Clark, Mary Higgins, 724
Clark, Myron Holley, 106, 111
Clark, Susan Vanderpoel, 334
Clark, William A., 275, 455
Clarke, George, 24, 25
Clawson, Harry M., 455
Clay, Henry, 68, 97
Clayburgh, Jill, 696, 708
Clayton Act, 350
Clayton, Buck, 812
Clayton, Jan, 551
clearing house, bank, 104
Clearview Expressway, 634
Clemente, Francesco, 771
Cleveland, Grover, 205, 215, 218, 231
Clews, Henry, 136, 313
Clift, Montgomery, 491, 523, 535, 546, 668
Clingan, Eldon, 700
Clinton, 625 (see also Hell's Kitchen)
Clinton, Bill, 814, 835, 851
Clinton, Charles, 194
Clinton, Charles W., 327
Clinton, De Witt, 49–51, 53, 55, 57, 58, 60, 62–64, 66
Clinton, George, 35–37, 41, 44, 45, 50, 55
Clinton, George, Admiral, 25
Clinton, Henry, Gen. Sir, 33, 36, 37
Clinton, Hillary Rodham, 865
Clio Award, 622
clipper ships, 56, 86, 88, 95, 100, 103, 114
Cloisters, 509
Close, Chuck, 689, 719, 738, 788, 799, 811, 846
clubs, 792
 American Woman's, 454
 Army & Navy, 268
 Boys' Club of New York, 179
 Calumet, 217, 274
 Cavendish, 416
 Century Association, 91, 155, 229, 769
 Century Road Club, 258
 Chemists' Club, 258
 City Club, 230, 481
 Colony, 286, 309, 792
 Columbia University, 268
 Commonwealth, 212
 Communist, 113
 Cosmopolitan, 193, 472
 Crescent Athletic, 304
 Doubles, 726

 Downtown Athletic, 422, 454, 492
 Explorers, 291
 Friars, 291, 332
 Grolier, 207, 370
 Harmonie, 103, 304
 Harvard, 140, 241
 Knickerbocker, 165, 358
 Lambs, 173, 291
 Links, 363
 Lotos, 161, 562
 Madison Square Boys' and Girls', 205
 Metropolitan, 229, 237
 Montauk, 229
 National Arts, 301
 New York Athletic, 143, 456, 769
  building, 454
  Winged Foot, 401
 New York Reform, 215
 New York Yacht, 87, 274
 Nippon, 297, 340, 533, 813
 Northeasterners, The, 452
 Players, 220
 Princeton, 262, 309, 397, 649
 Racquet & Tennis, 225, 376, 398, 759, 792
 River, 463
 Salmagundi, 160
 Union League, 150, 151, 197, 231, 454, 769
 Union, 75, 110, 229, 286, 431, 479, 558, 792
 University, 140, 263
 West Side Tennis, 232, 278, 314
 Women's City, 317, 356
 Yale, 254, 358
Clurman, Harold, 406, 490, 576, 753
coal, 130
Coalition for the Homeless, 834
Coast Guard Memorial, 565
Cobb, Lee J., 503, 523, 570, 613
Cobb, Henry Ives, 327
Coburn, Charles, 636
Coburn, D.L., 738
Coca, Imogene, 452, 470, 577, 744, 874
cocaine, 206, 750, 784, 789
Cochet, Henri, 438
cocktails,
 Bronx, 305
 Jack Rose, 341
Coco, James, 758, 788
coffee,
 Martinson's, 259
 rationing, 538
 Starbucks, 792
 vacuum-packed, 259
coffeehouses, 16
Cogen, Charles, 628, 635, 681

Cohan, George M., 273, 291, 302, 304, 308, 314, 319, 325, 332, 346, 352, 369, 381, 396, 400, 428, 437, 477, 504, 536, 623, 683
Cohen, Alexander H., 867
Cohen, Arthur, Realty, 802
Cohen, Benjamin V., 398
Cohen, Patricia Cline, 856
Colbert, Claudette, 444, 757, 839
Colden, Cadwallader, 21, 22, 27–29, 34
cold war, 610
Cole, Kenneth, 764
Cole, Nat King, 525, 662
Cole, Thomas, 64, 65, 72, 75, 79, 87, 94
Coleman, Cy, 631, 643, 668, 713, 744, 753, 800, 812
Coleman, Emil, 661
Coleman, Gary, 744
Coleman, Ornette, 624, 632
Coler, Bird S., 275, 300
Coles, Charles "Honi," 571, 767, 818
Colgate, William, 51, 58, 113
Colgate-Palmolive, 51
Coliseum, 610, 784
Coll, Vincent, 471
College Entrance Board, 266, 418
College Point Gas Co., 141
College Point, Queens, 107
Collegiate Chorale, 559
Collier, Constance, 469, 604
Collier, Peter F., 219, 319
Collier, Robert F., 266
Collier, Robert J., 374
Collier, Wm., 273, 278, 313, 339
Collier's magazine, 243, 266, 319, 379, 412, 607
Collinge, Patricia, 332, 352, 386, 469, 516, 555, 719
Collins, E.K., 98, 107, 186
Collins, Joe, 585, 605
Collins, Judy, 661
Collison, Wilson, 380, 390, 529
Collyer brothers, 562
Colombo, Joseph, 703
Colón, Jesus, 635
Colonnade Row, 72
Colonial Sand and Gravel, 436
Colored Orphan Asylum, 75, 132, 144, 305
Coltrane, John, 547, 676, 683
Columbia Spectator, 184
Columbia University, 16, 27, 39, 57, 63, 66, 114, 118, 192, 227, 228, 239, 246, 277, 463, 559, 564, 679, 680, 778, 805
 Alma Mater statue at, 284
 Butler Library of, 482

 Club, 268, 724
 football, 168, 485, 561
 Low Library at, 253
 Rockefeller Center and, 439
 Saint Paul's Chapel of, 310
 School of Journalism, 344, 352
Columbo, Joseph, 745
Columbus Avenue, 199
Columbus Circle, 233, 294, 691
Columbus Day parade, 316
Comden, Betty, 546, 551, 570, 594, 599, 609, 619, 631, 637, 696, 719, 744, 766, 812
comic books, 523, 635
comic strips,
 "Barnaby and Mr. O'Malley," 522
 "Bringing Up Father," 344
 "Buster Brown," 277
 "Captain and the Kids, The," 367
 "Katzenjammer Kids," 253, 367
 "Krazy Kat," 361
 "Little Nemo," 295
 "Little Orphan Annie," 405
 "Winnie Winkle," 385
 "Yellow Kid, The," 247, 252
Commentary magazine, 549, 629
Commercial Cable, 202
Commissioners' Plan, 55, 69, 106
Commission on Intergroup Relations, 616
Common Ground Community, 829
Commonwealth Fund, 520
Commonwealth & Southern Corp., 442
Communists, 425, 440, 448
community boards, 735
community councils, 734
Community Service Society, 513
commuter tax, 860
Como, Perry, 409
compact disc, 777
Compton, Betty, 421, 429, 438, 445, 492, 546
comptrollers, 49
computers,
 IBM, 756
 Univac, 606
Comstock, Anthony, 169, 171, 188, 240, 296, 345, 359
condominiums, 656
condoms, 810
Condon, Eddie, 713
Condon, Richard, 617, 622, 762
Cone, David, 863
Con Edison (see Consolidated Edison)

Coney Island, 147, 183, 208, 254, 333, 353, 430
  beaches, 181
  Boardwalk, 401
  Cyclone roller coaster at, 614
  Dreamland in, 291
  housing in, 734
  Luna Park in, 286, 339
  Nathan's at, 363, 371
  Parachute Jump at, 530
  roller coasters, 309, 422, 614
  Steeplechase Park in, 309, 530
Conference Board, 356, 359
  Consumer Confidence Index of, 672
Congdon-Wadlin Act, 557
Conklin, Peggy, 444, 503
Conkling, Roscoe, 111, 144, 166, 178, 192, 194, 197, 201, 204, 218, 221
  statue of, 236
Connable, Alfred, 674
Connelly, Marc, 380, 390, 395, 400, 406, 450, 464, 753
Connolly, Bishop John, 57, 58, 63
Connolly, Maureen, 584, 589
Connolly, Richard B., 162
Connors, Jimmy, 720, 732, 745, 767
Conrad, Con, 400
Conrail, 730, 756
Conroy, Frank, 654
Conservative Party, 639, 693, 853
Consolidated Edison, 198, 494, 574, 601, 640, 646, 658, 673, 685, 694, 697, 710, 711, 717, 727, 729, 736, 752, 802, 804
  power failures, 658, 736
  subways and, 621
Consolidated Gas Co., 206, 224, 271, 289, 299, 318, 418, 494
constitution, New York State, 60
Constitution, U.S., 40, 83, 157, 342, 383, 384, 480
  Schechter case and, 487
construction industry, 91, 99, 102, 140, 147, 190, 211, 223, 233, 237, 279, 387, 392, 402, 423, 446, 447, 454, 455, 463, 494, 499, 505, 533, 543, 556, 587, 605, 662, 693, 698, 721, 733, 768, 778, 785, 802, 808, 818
Consumer Affairs, Dept. of, 843
Consumers' League of New York, 329
container ships, 607, 755, 854

contraception,
  Comstock and, 169, 174, 188
  Sanger and, 355, 363
Coogan's Bluff, 229
Cook, Barbara, 583, 609, 648, 675
Cook, Elisha, Jr., 477
Cook, George Cram, 361
Cook, Joe, 407, 451
Cooke, Jay, 136, 170
Cooke, Sarah Palfrey, 530, 551
Cooke, Terence Cardinal, 680, 764, 765
Cookson, Peter, 555, 594
Cooney, Joan Ganz, 702
Cooper Union, 114, 121, 122, 316, 317, 335, 399
Cooper, Ashley, 619
Cooper, Edward, 127, 185, 193
Cooper, Gladys, 604
Cooper, Jackie, 598
Cooper, James Fenimore, 59, 61, 64, 81, 82, 84, 102
Cooper, Peter, 59, 104, 114, 119, 142, 178, 201
  statue of, 253
Cooper, Melville, 491
Cooper, William, 45
Coote, Richard, earl of Bellomont, 17, 18
Coots, J. Fred, 414
Copeland, Royal S., 393, 500
Copland, Aaron, 414, 536, 584, 599, 806
Coplon, Judith, 572
Coppola, Francis Ford, 800
copyright laws, 112, 254
Corallo, "Tony Ducks," 784, 868
Corbett, James J., 478
Corbett, Leonora, 555
Corbin, Austin, 185
Corcoran, Thomas G., 493
Corey, Irwin, 719
Corey, Wendell, 550
Corlear, Jacob van, 4
Cornbury, E.H., Viscount, 18–20
Cornell University, 139, 173
  Medical College, 257, 266, 290, 337, 427
  women and, 168
Cornell, Alonzo B., 166, 178, 188
Cornell, Ezra, 86, 112, 139, 166, 173, 178
Cornell, Joseph, 469, 550, 598, 603, 707
Cornell, Katherine, 390, 414, 477, 516, 541, 719
Cornell, Thomas, 77
Cornwallis, Gen. Charles, 34
Corona, Queens, 109, 519
Corozzo, Nicholas, 818, 840, 850
Corridan, Rev. John M., 551

Corrigan, Michael Archbishop, 210, 213, 277
Corrigan, "Wrong-Way," 508
Corsaro, Frank, 763
Corsi, Edward, 574
Cortelyou, George B., 281, 287, 305, 318
Cortelyou, Jacques, 8, 9
Cortines, Ramon C., 805
Corwin, Norman, 545
Cosby, Bill, 771
Cosby, Gerry, 511
Cosby, William, 23, 24
Cosell, Howard, 832
cosmetics,
  Avon, 215, 258, 445
  Ayer, Harriet Hubbard, 292
  Estée Lauder, 556, 655, 684
  Revlon, 471, 571
Cosmopolitan magazine, 217, 235, 242, 257, 295, 412, 659
Costello, Frank, 525, 537, 539, 547, 580, 614, 714
Costikyan, Edward, 666
Cotten, Joseph, 516, 594
Cotting, Amos, 191
Cotton Exchange, 211
Coulouris, George, 516, 529
Council on Foreign Relations, 388
Court of Appeals, 91, 814
Coutan, Jules A., 348
Couwenhoven, W.G. van, 4
Covenant House, 680, 798
Cowan, Jerome, 477, 490
Coward, Noël, 415, 461, 477, 490, 496, 713, 862
Cowl, Jane, 414, 428, 484, 524, 576
Cowles, Gardner, 502
Cowley, Malcolm, 483
Cox, Billy, 589
Cox, Samuel Sullivan, 228
crack cocaine, 784, 789
Cracker Jack, 314
Crain, Thomas C.T., 479
Crane, Hart, 419, 445, 450, 469
Crane, Stephen, 235, 266
Crater, Judge, 452
Craven, Frank, 352, 369, 386, 428, 510
Crawford, Broderick, 490
Crawford, Cheryl, 555, 559
Crawford, Joan, 451, 738
Crawford, Michael, 878
credit cards, 617
  American Express, 658
  Discover, 781
  Mastercard, 665, 673
Crédit Lyonnais Building, 662
Crédit Mobilier, 145, 167

Creeft, José de, 630
Crew, Rudy, 831, 837, 845, 855, 861
Crews, Laura Hope, 420, 536
cricket, 26
crime, 110, 446, 692, 801, 818, 840 (see also homicide)
Crimmins, Alice, 662
crinoline, 112
Crisis, The 325
Crittenden, Florence, 224
Croker, Richard, 181, 212, 250, 251, 257, 264, 270, 281, 393
Croly, Herbert D., 351
Cromwell, William N., 280, 281
Cronkhite, Walter, 598, 756
Cronyn, Hume, 583, 667, 738
Cropsey, Jaspar, 92, 186, 267
Crosby, Caresse (Polly Jacob), 353, 445
Crosby, Howard, 187
Crosetti, Frankie, 511
Cross-Bronx Expressway, 587, 646
Cross-County Parkway, 467
crossword puzzles, 344, 535
  book, 405
Crothers, Rachel, 301, 390, 460, 503
Croton Aqueduct, 77, 85, 226, 331
Croton water, 310
Crouse, Russel, 484, 497, 517, 550, 667
Crovello, William, 712
Crowley, Matt, 535
Crown, Henry, 552
Crown Building, 397
Crown Heights, 173, 522, 549, 808, 814, 842
  riots in, 853
Crowninshield, Frank, 380, 489, 528
Crowther, Bosley, 758
Crowthers, Rachel, 618
Cruger, John, 24, 43
  Jr., 26, 28, 29
Crystal, Billy, 800
Crystal Palace, 119
Cuba, 242, 621
Cudahy, Brian J., 724, 748
Cuddihy, Robert J., 424
Culbertson, Ely, 416, 445
Culhane, Shamus, 414, 839
Cullen, Countee, 413, 419, 428, 440, 443, 555, 559
Cullman, Joseph F., 605
Cullum, John, 631, 661, 725, 744, 777, 874
Cummings, Constance, 484, 749
Cummings, Robert, 400

Cunard, Samuel, 81
Cuneo, Ernest, 603
Cunningham, John, 817
Cunningham, Merce, 518, 595
Cuomo, Mario, 735, 760, 775, 780, 803, 824
Curb Exchange, 390, 591 (*see also* American Stock Exchange)
Curran, Henry H., 335
Currier & Ives, 115, 219
Curry, John F., 433, 441, 465, 466, 610
Curtis, George W., 178, 205, 290
Curtiss, Glenn, 324
Cusack, Cyril, 612
Cushman, Don Alonzo, 81, 177
Cushman-Wakefield, 81, 177, 552, 854
Customs House, 42, 84, 129, 309
Cutting, R. Fulton, 250, 264, 275, 305
Cutting, W. Bayard, 264
Cutting, William, 57, 102
Cuyler, Abraham, 23

da Cunha, G.W., 203
D'Agostino's, 472, 633
D'Amato, Alfonse, 751, 784, 824
Dahl, Arlene, 599
Dahl, Roald, 642, 653
Dailey, Dan, 504
Daily News Record, 325
Daily Worker, The, 582
Dale, Chester, 444, 642
Dale, Jim, 753
Dalrymple, Jean, 543, 718, 857
Daly, Augustin, 146, 154, 165, 171, 190
Daly, James, 630
Daly, Kay, 571
Daly, Robert, 622
Damrosch, Clara, 262
Damrosch, Leopold, 171, 187, 211
Damrosch, Walter, 211, 229, 296, 438, 578
Dana, Charles A., 150, 167, 216, 230, 231, 252
Dana Corp., 350
Dana, Charles A., 309, 350
Dance Theater of Harlem, 697
Dane, Clemence, 390
Daniele, Graciela, 690, 806
Daniell, Henry, 642
Daniels, Jeff, 822
Danner, Blythe, 689, 817
Dannon Yogurt, 538
Dante Park, 388
Dark, Alvin, 585
Darton, Eric, 861
Darnell, Linda, 527

Darrow, Whitney, Jr., 475, 861
da Silva, Howard, 504, 624, 690, 783
David, Hal, 683
Davidson, Jo, 568
David-Weill, Michel, 634, 747
Davies, Marion, 362, 368, 440, 636
Davis, Benny, 368
Davis, Bette, 451, 636
Davis, Bill C., 758
Davis, Elmer, 390
Davis, Owen, 399, 414, 608
Davis, Stuart, 345, 460, 469, 509, 528, 583, 598, 636, 653
Davis, Eddie "Lockjaw," 511
Davis, Gordon, 751
Davis, Marvin, 776
Davis, Meyer, 732
Davis, Miles, 511, 547, 561
Davis, Ossie, 613, 636, 661, 800, 838
Davis, Sammy, Jr., 584, 609, 659
Davison, Henry P., 370
Dawn, Hazel, 362, 380, 390, 794
Day, The, 351
Day, Benjamin H., 223
Day, Benjamin, 72, 78
Day, Clarence, 468, 489, 502, 517, 523
Day, Doris, 496
Day, Dorothy, 367, 404, 476, 752
Day, Jared N., 862
day-care centers, 544, 563
Dean, Arthur H., 591, 786
Dean and DeLuca, 741
D-Day, 544
DDT, 519
Dean, Martha, 713
De Angelis, Anthony, 649
death rate, 176, 232
De Carlo, Yvonne, 703
Declaration of Independence, 33
Decter, Midge, 629, 682
Dee, Ruby, 546, 623, 636, 800
Deegan, Thomas J., Jr., 651
Deegan, Major, 606
Deering, Milliken, 139
building, 620
Deering, William, 139
De Forest, Lee, 394
DeForest, William H., 191
De Francisi, Anthony, 420
DeGrasse, Leland, 868, 873
De Groot, Albert, 348
de Harak, Rudolph, 759
de Kay, Charles, 301
Dekker, Albert, 623
de Kooning, Elaine, 554, 588, 776, 783, 799

de Kooning, Willem, 541, 545, 554, 565, 570, 576, 588, 608, 612, 630, 689, 702, 725, 788, 846
De Koven, Reginald, 320, 340
de Kruif, Paul, 484
Delacorte, George T., Jr., 385, 390, 535, 642, 731, 811
Delafield, John, 38
De Lamar mansion, 297
Delamater, Cornelius H., 85, 129
de Lancey, James, 21–23, 25–27
de Lancey, Oliver, 25
de Lancey, Stephen, 14, 21
Delanoy, Peter, 15
Delaware & Hudson Canal, 66
Delaware River, 80
Delaware, Lackawanna & Western, 136
De Liagre, Alfred, Jr., 788
DeLillo, Don, 701, 712, 776, 794, 846
Dell, Floyd, 344, 374, 419, 541, 688
Dellacroce, Aniello, 614
Delmonico, Lorenzo, 78, 89, 131, 174, 181, 197
Demarest, William, 461
de Mille, Agnes, 536, 542, 566, 822
De Mille, Cecil B., 346
Deming, Horace E., 191, 198, 205, 212, 215, 319, 449
Demorest, Ellen Curtis, 258
Demorest, Nell, 123
Dempsey, Jack, 391, 401, 422, 430, 722, 772
De Niro, Robert, 702, 732, 739, 753, 766, 772, 814, 822, 862
Dennett, Mary Ware, 393
Dennis, Patrick, 603, 731
Dennis, Sandy, 642, 654, 696, 817
Denny, Reginald, 381
dentistry, 266
Dentyne chewing gum, 262
department stores (*see* retail merchants)
de Paur, Leonard, 697
Depew, Chauncey M., 260, 276, 434
De Peyster, Abraham, 15, 17, 22
De Peyster, John Watts, 225
Depression, 449
dermatology, 75
De Sapio, Carmine G., 580, 591, 616, 621, 634, 679, 685, 700, 705
Deskey, Donald, 470
DeSylva, B.G., 387, 391, 396, 400, 407, 414, 421, 429,

437, 438, 444, 470, 478, 518, 524
Deutsch, Martin, 641
Devery, William, 260
De Vinne, Theodore L., 207, 350
De Vito, Danny, 744
De Vries, Peter, 598
Dewey, John, 316, 587
Dewey, Melvil, 192
Dewey, Thomas E., 479, 492, 493, 500, 506, 513, 519, 520, 533, 544, 552, 563, 574, 591, 595, 700
Dewhurst, Colleen, 631, 648, 800, 811
de Wilde, Brandon, 576
DeWolfe, Billy, 595
de Wolfe, Elsie (Lady Mendl), 273, 284, 309, 422, 576
Dexter, Henry, 313, 325
Dial, The, 192, 406, 443
Diallo, Amadou, 860
diamond district, 527
Diamond National Bldg., 638
Diamond, Edwin, 821
Diamond, "Legs," 408, 438, 462
Diamonstein, Barbaralee, 794
Dickens, Charles, 84, 146
Dickey, Bill, 498, 518, 543
Dickson, Dorothy, 368, 375, 381
Diehl, Lorraine B., 776
Dierickx, Mary B., 838
Dies Committee, 573
Diesel Construction Co., 556
Dietz, Howard, 421, 444, 452, 461, 470, 491, 504, 594, 613, 649, 767
Digges, Dudley, 386, 400, 444, 503, 510, 546, 555, 560
Dillingham, Charles B., 248, 326, 491
Dillman, Bradford, 608
Dillon, Clarence, 389
Dillon, C. Douglas, 744
DiLorenzo, Alex, Jr., 605, 663, 726
Dingley Tariff Act, 251
Dilworth, J. Richardson, 783
DiMaggio, Joe, 498, 504, 511, 518, 530, 561, 571, 578, 585, 600, 863
Diner, Hasia R., 867
Diners Club, 579, 615, 658
Dinkins, David N., 796, 814, 819, 828, 853
Dioguardi, John, 610
diphtheria, 228, 239
in Alaska, 413
Disabilities Act, 803
discothèques, 726 (*see also* nightclubs)

DiSpirito, Rocco, 841
Ditmars, Raymond, 263
divorce law, 240, 664
Dix, John A., 93, 125, 131, 166, 167, 171, 172
Dix, John Alden, 323
"Dixie," 121, 128
Dixon, Mort, 461
Dobbs hats, 312
docks, 13, 95, 548, 592
    strike on, 597
Doctorow, E.L., 701, 724, 752, 766, 776, 799, 827, 867
Dodge, Geraldine R., 308
Dodge, Mabel, 337
Dodge, Marcellus Hartley, 295, 308, 402
Dodge-Morse divorce, 297
Dodge, William C., 473
Dodge, William E., 137, 166, 201
    statue of, 210
Doeg, John, 452
dogs, 717, 720, 746
Doherty, Henry L., 471, 514
Dokoudovsky, Vladimir, 524
Dolkart, Andrew S., 846
Dolin, Anton, 451
Dolly Sisters, 332
Dolly, Rozsika, 352
domestic help, 161, 387, 487, 488, 507, 538
Domingo, Plácido, 683, 795
Dominican Republic,
    immigration from, 841
Dominicans, 872
Donahue, Jack, 414, 437
Donahue, Rev. Michael E., 786
Donaldson, Walter, 375, 396, 438, 452, 461
Donen, Stanley, 570
Dongan, Thomas, 13, 14, 21
Donleavy, J.P., 603, 712
Donlevy, Brian, 406, 484
Donnelly, Bruce, 767
Donnelly, Dorothy, 352, 391, 400, 407
Donovan, William J., 364, 466, 532
Dooley, Ray, 407, 484
Dorsey, Jimmy, 451, 461, 613
Dorsey, Tommy, 461, 518
Dos Passos, John, 413, 496
Dos Passos, John R., 166, 413, 496
Doubleday, Nelson, 278, 483, 570
Douglas, Ann, 831
Douglas, Helen Gahagan, 753
Douglas, Melvyn, 630, 758
Douglas, Paul, 554
Douglass, David, 29
Douglass, Frederick, 97, 152, 166

Douglaston, 8, 23, 58, 74, 141
Dove, Arthur, 325, 338, 345, 390, 406, 413, 428, 437, 444, 450, 460, 477, 489, 496, 502, 509, 523, 528, 535, 541, 545, 554
Dow, Charles H., 276
Dow Jones & Co., 199, 222, 276
    Industrial Average, 245
    Times Square Zipper and, 846
Dowling, Eddie, 381, 421, 430, 510, 517, 550, 732
Downing, Andrew J., 82, 102, 103
Downing, John J., Stadium, 511
Drake, Alfred, 504, 524, 542, 555, 566, 594, 818
Drake, Joseph Rodman, 72
Drama Critics Circle Awards, 490
Draper, Andrew S., 214, 247, 290
Draper, John W., 80, 81
Draper, Paul, 568, 839
Draper, Polly, 757
Draper, Ruth, 608
Dreier, Katherine S., 386
Dreier, Mary E., 356
Dreiser, Theodore, 262, 267, 338, 399
Dresser, Louise, 302, 308, 368, 407
Dresser, Paul, 262
Dressler, Marie, 291, 326, 362, 387
dress patterns,
    Butterick, 137, 146, 155
    Demorest and, 123
    Simplicity Pattern Co., 430
    Vogue, 318
Drew, Daniel, 100, 136, 141, 149, 188
Drew, John, 124, 199, 236, 248
Drexel, Anthony J., 163
Drexel, J.R., 203
Dreyer Dave, 676
Dreyfuss, Henry, 649
drought, 197, 663
drug abuse, 673, 691, 756
drunkenness, 217
Dryfoos, Orvil E., 646
Drysdale, Don, 823
Duane, James, 68
Dubin, Al, 415, 478, 492, 517, 551
Dubinsky, David, 432, 466, 500, 544
DuBois, W.E.B., 283, 316, 325, 365, 380, 436, 440, 647
DuBois, Bishop John, 64, 78, 83
Du Bois, Raoul Pène, 484, 511, 517, 518, 583, 595, 604, 749, 777

Dubuffet, Jean, 707
Duchamp, Marcel, 345, 386
Duchin, Eddie, 584
Duer, William, 39, 44, 48
Duffy, Francis P., 366, 468, 502
Duke, Doris, 416, 452
Duke, James B., 208, 225, 333, 340, 416
Duke, Patty, 623
Duke, Vernon, 452, 470, 484, 497, 504, 543
Duke, Washington B., 220
Dukes, David, 749
Dullea, Keir, 689
DuMont Broadcasting Corp., 612
Du Mont, Allen B., 515, 659
Dumont, Margaret, 415, 438
Dun & Bradstreet, 82, 107, 109, 120, 474
Dun, R.G., & Co., 81
Dunaway, Faye, 654, 660, 725, 732, 753
Dunbar, David S., 877
Dunbar, Paul Laurence, 243, 248, 284
Duncan, Isadora, 371
Duncan, Todd, 492, 524, 571
Dundy, Elmer "Skip," 296, 339
Dunham, Katherine, 524
Dunlap, David N., 805
Dunlap, William, 42
Dunlop, M.H., 867
Dunmore, J. Murray, earl of, 30, 54
Dunne, Finley Peter, 363
Dunnock, Mildred, 555, 570, 584, 603, 648
Dunphy, Don, 858
du Pont, T. Coleman, 340, 347, 433
Durand, Asher, 59, 75, 79, 80, 86, 96, 214
Durand-Ruel, Paul, 214
Durang, Christopher, 757
Durante, Jimmy, 401, 445, 451, 452, 478, 484, 491, 497, 525, 555, 560
Duranty, Walter, 612
Durbin, Deanna, 566
Duren, Ryne, 620
Durocher, Leo, 530, 585, 600
Durst, Douglas, 854
Durst, Joseph, 431
Durst, Seymour B., 431, 771, 797, 833
Duryée, Abram, 96, 125, 170, 172, 223
d'Usseau, Arnaud, 541, 598, 806
Dutch Reformed Church, 2, 13
Dutch West India Company, 4
Dutton, Charles S., 771
Duval, H. Gordon, 397, 435

Duval, Shelley, 738
Duvergier de Hauranne, E., 137
Duyckinck, Evert A., 92
Dvořák, Antonin, 236
Dyckman House, 39
Dyckman, Jan, 10
Dykstra, Gretchen, 813, 876
Dykstra, Len, 783
Dylan, Bob, 637, 649, 654, 661, 686, 690, 697, 726
Dysart, Richard, 707

Eagels, Jeanne, 396, 444
Eakins, Thomas, 308
Eames, Clare, 380, 390
Eastman, Annis Ford, 317
Eastman, Crystal, 317, 323, 349, 377, 434
Eastman, Max, 317, 331, 337, 344, 395
Earl Carroll's Vanities, 461, 470
East Coast Memorial, 630
East River (FDR) Drive, 495, 534
Eastman Kodak,
    Colorama, 575
    Kodachrome, 490, 496
earthquakes, 10, 209
East India Company, Dutch, 1
East River,
    bathing in, 161
    piers, 7
East Village,
    art galleries in, 752
East Side Association, 151
Eastern Airlines, 706, 810
Ebb, Fred, 661, 668, 683, 725, 739, 745, 758, 772, 822, 847
Ebbets Field, 347, 614, 633
Ebbets, Charles, 258, 347
Eboli, Tommy Ryan, 709
Ebsen, Buddy, 470, 484
Eckstine, Billy, 546
Edberg, Stefan, 812, 818
Edelman, Gregg, 800
Eddinger, Wallace, 346, 357
Ederle, Gertrude, 415
Edison Electric Light Co., 195, 206, 257
Edison, Thomas A., 176, 186, 195, 198, 206, 231, 248, 459
    incandescent bulb of, 189, 192
    Kinetoscope and, 236
Edman, Irwin, 509
Edmiston, Susan, 731
Edson, Franklin, 198
education, bilingual, 681, 706, 717, 845
Education, Board of, 83, 635, 681, 837, 855, 861, 873, 876 (see also schools)

Educational Alliance, 222
Ed Sullivan Show (TV), 566
Edwards, Gus, 296, 320, 326, 517, 551
Egan, Eddie, 676
Egan, Edward Cardinal, 876
Egan, Jennifer, 648, 838, 874
egg cream, 547
Eggleston, Edward, 164
Ehret, George, 144, 174, 447
Ehrlich, Judith Ramsey, 799
Eichner, Bruce Jay, 791, 802
Eight, The, 313
Eighth Avenue, 597
Einstein, Albert, 473
    College of Medicine, 602
Einstein, Louis, 666
Eisenhower, Dwight D., 544, 548, 564, 606, 610, 618
El Barrio, 526, 580
Elchanan, Isaac, 252
Elder, Lonnie, 689
El Diario/La Prensa, 564, 799, 816
Eldridge, Florence, 395, 516, 535, 583, 608
Eldridge, Ronnie, 771
electric
    chair, 226
    Christmas tree lights, 198
    elevator, 223
    fan, 198
    flatiron, 200
    steam, 422
    locomotives, 271
    sewing machine, 222
    signs, 366
    streetcars, 173
    taxicabs, 251
electricity, 198, 257
    Edison and, 186
    Tesla and, 210, 218
    Westinghouse and, 210
Elett, Thomas Harlan, 472
elevated railways, 149, 167, 186, 189, 192, 210, 213, 227, 235, 246, 260, 265, 271, 277, 290, 294, 313, 343, 366, 373, 384, 389, 404, 508, 514, 521, 534, 540, 544, 553, 558, 575, 602, 606, 687, 711
    Brooklyn, 202
    Third Avenue, 213, 215
elevators, 161, 375, 549
    hydraulic, 259
    electric, 223
    Otis and, 103, 108, 116, 128, 223, 423
    Westinghouse, 423
Elg, Taina, 763
Eliot, T.S., 576

Elizabeth Arden (see Graham, Florence Nightingale)
Elizabeth Arden beauty salons, 326, 353
Elle magazine, 554, 776
Elliman, Douglas L., 334, 673, 710
Ellington, Duke, 430, 445, 452, 461, 478, 542, 551, 555, 720, 848
    Boulevard, 739
Elliott, Don, 631
Elliott, Lawrence, 766
Elliott, Maxine, 524
Ellis, Bret Easton, 805
Ellis, Edward Robb, 666, 856
Ellis Island, 234, 256, 269, 275, 311, 334, 359, 363, 376, 383, 388, 393, 398, 457, 472, 600, 664, 728, 764, 774, 808, 860
    Japanese on in World War II, 533
Ellison, Ralph, 593
Ellsworth, Elmer, 125
Elmaleh, Victor, 802
Elman, Richard, 811
Elmhurst, 7, 249
    shopping mall in, 711
Eltinge, Julian, 332, 338, 352, 529
Ely, Smith, Jr., 179
Emancipation Proclamation, 129
Embargo Act, 51
Emergency Financial Control Board, 722
Emerson Radio, 394
Emerson, Roy, 637, 655
Emmett, Daniel Decatur, 86, 128, 121
Emmy Awards, 570
Empire Blue Cross/Blue Shield, 712
Empire City Subway Co., 229
Empire State Building, 463, 468, 469, 549 728, 759
    killings on, 841
    TV transmitters on, 460
encephalytis, 861
Engel, Elliot, 792, 814
Engel, Lehman, 504
Englander, Ludwig, 240, 262, 278, 285
Englis, John, 127
English, T.J., 805
Eno, Amos R., 122
Enright, Richard E., 371
Ensemble Studio Theater, 702
Entertainment Weekly, 805
Environmental Protection, Dept. of, 841

Ephron, Nora, 695, 766, 857
Episcopal Missionary Society, 241
Epstein, Barbara, 647
Epstein, Jason, 647
Equal Employment Opportunity Commission, 729
Equal Rights Party, 73
Equity Funding scandal, 711
Ericsson, John, 129, 236
Erie Canal, 54, 57–59, 63, 158, 198, 372
Erie RR, 69, 85, 100, 134, 136, 148, 149, 166, 167, 175, 182, 235, 628, 634
Erie Lackawanna, 628, 634, 680
Erlanger, A.L., 220, 248, 267, 296, 451
Errol, Leon, 332, 339, 347, 352, 362, 368, 387, 584
Ernst, Morris L., 482
Erskine, Carl, 595
Ertegun, Ahmed, 561
Ertegun, Nesuhi, 800
Erving, Julius, 720, 732
escalator, 233
Esopus tribe, 9
Esposito, Giovanni, Pork Shop, 259
Esposito, Meade, 751, 786
Esquire magazine, 476, 619
Essence magazine, 695
Essex Street Market, 59, 521, 782
Esso, 330
    building, 562
Estefan, Gloria, 795, 862
Eternal Light Memorial, 406
Ethical Culture Society, 180, 183, 290, 324, 435, 475
Etting, Ruth, 429, 451, 461
Eugene M. Lang Foundation, 681, 798
Europe, James Reese, 339, 377, 382
Evacuation Day, 765
Evan-Picone, 571
Evans, Bill, 637, 753
Evans, George H., 86
Evans, Madge, 478, 510, 541, 758
Evans, Walker, 510, 667
Evelyn, Judith, 529, 588, 675
Evarts, William M., 147, 158, 162, 177
Everlast Sports Mfg. Co., 369, 391, 511
Evert (Lloyd), Chris, 726, 739, 745, 753, 764
Ewbank, Weeb, 649, 690
Ewell, Tom, 496, 588, 631
Ewing, Patrick, 777

explosions, 99, 124, 359, 384, 645, 666, 686, 692, 699, 715, 722
    Black Tom, 359
    Staten Island ferry, 163
    World Trade Center, 819
Exxon, 330, 706
    building, 704, 706
Eyssell, Gus, 478
E-Z Pass, 854

Faber, Eberhard, 96, 128, 189
Fabray, Nanette, 530, 536, 546, 560, 594
Façade Law, 754
Fadiman, Clifton, 510
Fahnestock, William, 195
Fain, Sammy, 430, 504, 511, 517, 524, 530, 556, 583, 613
Fairbanks, Douglas, 352
Fairchild Publications, 325
Fair Employment Practice Committee (FEPC), 527
Fair Labor Standards Act, 506
Fairchild, John B., 632, 677
Fairway Market, 728, 834, 852
Falco, Edie, 788, 877
Falk, Peter, 702
FALN, 722
Family Court, 263
Family Circle magazine, 468, 554
Family of Man photos, 603
Famous Players-Lasky, 346, 429
Farberware, 269, 572
Farley, James A., 493, 520, 728
Farley, John Cardinal, 277, 331, 373
Farrar, John C., 443
Farrar, Margaret P., 405, 535
Farrell, Frank, 285
Farrell, Glenda, 682
Farrell, James T., 748
Far Rockaway, 187
    hurricane and, 238
Farrow, Mia, 668, 749, 777, 789, 800, 817
fashion industry, 402, 537, 556, 693, 794, 858
    Adolfo, 669
    Blass, Bill, 697, 878
    Carnegie, Hattie, 320, 382, 530, 537
    Cashin, Bonnie, 589
    Chapman, Ceil, 556
    Claiborne, Liz, 732
    Coty awards, 537
    Daché, Lilly, 408, 458, 462
    Fashion Group Internatl., 462
    Fogarty, Anne, 458, 585
    Furstenberg, Betsy von, 604

fashion industry (*continued*)
 Galanos, James, 677
 Halston, 624, 632, 668, 669, 684, 709, 739, 745, 764, 767, 807
 Hannah Troy, 567
 hoopskirts, 177
 Karan, Donna, 720, 772
 Klein, Anne, 567, 684, 720, 858
 Klein, Calvin, 684, 830
 Lambert, Eleanor, 445, 537, 625, 684, 697
 Lauren, Ralph, 684, 781, 809
 McCardell, Claire, 458, 462, 512, 530, 537
 Mainbocher, 452, 537
 midiskirt, 697
 miniskirt, 655
 Mizrahi, Isaac, 832, 858
 Norell, Norman, 530, 537, 632, 677, 709
 Roman Catholic Church and, 585
 Scaasi, Arnold, 649, 759
 Simpson, Adele, 462
 Trigère, Pauline, 458, 505, 537, 878
 Wang, Vera, 806
Fashion Institute of Technology, 545
Father Divine, 360
Fatt, Arthur C., 412, 861
Fauset, Jessie Redmon, 380, 406, 636
fax machines, 730, 762
Fay, Frank, 375, 400, 429, 546
Faye, Alice, 484, 491
Faye, Joey, 560, 583, 598, 643, 847
FBI, 383, 533, 572
FCC, 541
FDR Drive, 534
Fearing, Kenneth, 443, 489, 541, 554, 565, 636
Feder, Abe, 504, 847
Feder, Joseph, 519
Federal Hall, 129, 363
Federalist Papers, 40
Federalists, 46
Federal Reserve System, 747, 804
Federation of Jewish Philanthropies, 365, 716
Feiffer, Jules, 675, 690, 731, 737
Feininger, Andreas, 565, 570, 598
Feininger, Lyonel, 608
Feirstein, Sanna, 877
Feld, Eliot, 763
Feldman, Sandra, 775, 845
Felker, Clay, 681

Felt Forum, 669
Felt, James, 638
Feltman, Charles, 147, 174, 177, 328
Fenton, Reuben E., 132, 140, 148
Ferber, Edna, 380, 406, 430, 469, 496, 682
Ferguson, Colin, 823
Fernandez, Joseph A., 805
Fernbach, Henry, 169
Ferrara's, 234
Ferraro, Geraldine, 769
Ferrer, José, 496, 517, 588
Ferrick, Tom, 578
ferries, 4, 8, 10, 55, 57, 75, 90, 107, 167, 283, 312, 553, 787
 East River, 145
Fessaguet, Roger, 633
Fiedler, Arthur, 599
Field, Betty, 503, 510, 550, 598, 618
Field, Cyrus W., 83, 118, 142, 154, 203, 231
Field, David Dudley, 93
Field, Marshall, III, 522, 607
Field, Stephen Dudley, 173
Fields, Dorothy, 429, 437, 451, 542, 546, 551, 583, 619, 668, 713
Fields, Herbert, 414, 619
Fields, Lew, 258, 339, 517
Fields, W.C., 346, 357, 362, 368, 375, 381, 387, 396, 400, 407
Fierstein, Harvey, 758, 878
Fifth Avenue Association, 310, 378, 384, 394, 411, 417
Fifth Avenue Coach Co., 246, 356, 494, 544, 592, 597, 628
Fifth Avenue, 61, 67, 73, 130, 519, 628, 666
Fillmore, Millard, 97
Fillmore East, 683, 703
Film, Theatre & Broadcasting, Mayor's Office of, 667
financial panics, 43, 77, 113, 136, 152, 206, 228, 271, 305, 441
Finkelstein, Jerry, 721
Finegan, James E., 476
Finn, William, 758, 800, 818
Finney, Jack, 695, 832
fire alarm boxes, 188
firecrackers, 849
Fire Department, 10, 140, 161, 238, 634, 871
fire escapes, 147, 268
firefighters, 74, 316, 670, 871
Fire!! magazine, 419

fires, 24, 35, 41, 51, 73, 74, 80, 89, 94, 106, 109, 119, 122, 132, 180, 200, 230, 233, 263, 275, 280, 289, 327, 328, 340, 359, 397, 534, 543, 553, 557, 610, 620, 633, 670, 685, 692, 728, 734, 871
 Central Synagogue, 859
 1 New York Plaza, 698
 Waldbaum's, 746
Firpo, Luis, 401
First Avenue, 582
Fischer, Carl, 400
Fischler, Stan, 731
Fish, Hamilton, 82, 93, 100, 102, 139, 151, 157, 234
Fish, Preserved, 57, 66
Fish, Stuyvesant, 51, 89, 476
Fishburne, Laurence, 806, 817, 832
Fisher, Avery, 504, 690, 828
Fisher, Carrie, 713, 800
Fisher, Dorothea Canfield, 419
Fisher, Eddie, 631
Fisher, Fred, 326, 357, 537
Fisher, Irving, 441
Fisher, Rudolph, 436, 496
Fisher, Zachary, 761, 864
Fisk, James, 136, 141, 143, 149, 150, 152, 162, 166
Fiske, Harrison Grey, 225, 273, 535
Fiske, Minnie Maddern, 199, 225, 273, 313, 291, 301, 332, 469
Fitch, Clyde, 225, 261, 273, 278, 284, 296, 319
Fitch, Robert, 821
Fitzgerald, Barry, 516
Fitzgerald, Ed, 763
Fitzgerald, Ella, 485, 525, 561
Fitzgerald, F. Scott, 385, 395, 413, 483
Fitzgerald, Geraldine, 738
Fitzgerald, Pegeen, 763, 798
Fitzgibbon, Bernice, 674
Fitzsimmons, Bob, 262
Five Points House of Industry, 107
Five Points Mission, 94
Five Points, 143, 225
Flagg, James Montgomery, 367, 630, 722
Flagler, H.M., 219
Flaherty, Stephen, 857, 868
Flake, Floyd H., 844
Flames basketball team, 741
Flanner, Janet, 412, 743
Flatbush, 48, 186, 233
 agriculture in, 161
Flatiron Building, 279, 669

Flatlands, 48
Fleeson, Neville, 396
Fleetwood Mac, 739
Fleischer, Max, 326
Fleischer, Nat, 397, 709
Fleischmann, Raoul, 411, 688
Fletcher, Benjamin, 15, 16
Fletcher, Charles H., 168, 394
Fletcher, Isaac D., 263
Fletcher's Castoria, 168
Flexner, Ann Crawford, 273
Flint, Austin, 127
floating baths, 161, 353
Flower, Roswell P., 227
Flower Show, 355
Flushing and North Side RR, 153
Flushing Gas Light Co., 109
Flushing Remonstrance, 9
Flushing, 31
Flying Foods International, 760
Flynn, Edward J., 390, 393, 410, 433, 466, 473, 474, 493, 520, 559, 591
Flynn, Helen Gurley, 337
Fokine, Michel, 537
Foley Square, 422
Foley, Thomas, 281
Folger, Charles J., 197
Folks, Homer, 234, 390
Fonda, Henry, 565, 598, 613, 660
Fonda, Jane, 668, 702, 753
Foner, Nancy, 867
Fontanne, Glenn, 437
Fontanne, Lynn, 428, 477, 490, 496, 523, 554, 618
food cooperatives, 721
Food Network (TV), 824
football, 168, 438, 492, 561, 624
 college, 485
 professional, 732
Forbes magazine, 367, 598
Forbes, B.C., 367, 598
Ford, Edsel, 540
Ford, Eileen, 554
Ford, Gerald R., 716, 723, 729
Ford, Helen, 414, 421
Ford, Henry, 557
Ford, Paul, 643
Ford, Whitey, 578, 632, 637, 643, 649
Ford Foundation, 540, 557, 680, 689, 733
 building, 677
Fordham University, 82, 295, 672
Fordham, Manor of, 40
Foreign Corrupt Practices Act, 736
Forest Hills, 304, 495
Forgione, Larry, 741, 769, 852
Forrest, Edwin, 67, 69, 96
Forster, Frank J., 505

Forstmann, Theodore J., 742
Forsythe, Henderson, 744
Fort Amsterdam, 4
Fort Hamilton, 8
Fort Stanwix, Treaty of, 29
Fort Totten, 113, 364, 527
Fortune magazine, 450, 515
Fortunoff, Alan M., 866
.44-caliber killer, 733, 739
42nd Street Development Corp.,
    733, 740
Fosdick, Charles B., 210
Fosdick, Harry Emerson, 378,
    394, 450, 687
Fosse, Bob, 744
Foster, George G., 98
Foster, George W., Jr., 417
Foster, Stephen C., 137
foundlings, 139, 153
fountain pen, 207
Fowler, Gene, 570
Fox, William, 339, 357, 429, 589
Foxx, Redd, 800
Foy, Eddie, 291, 438
    Jr., 284, 339, 452, 461, 491
Franciosa, Anthony, 604, 632
Francis, John Wakefield, 92
Francis, Arlene, 496, 577, 660
Francis, Kay, 682
Franconi's Hippodrome, 108
Frank, Waldo, 674
Franken, Rose, 469, 794
Frankenthaler, Helen, 588, 593,
    608, 623, 675
Frankfurter, Alfred, 490, 528
Frankfurter, Felix, 326, 383
frankfurters (bangers, hot dogs,
    wieners), 304
    Chock Full 'o Nuts, 472
    Hebrew National, 298
    kosher, 298
    Nathan's Famous, 363, 371
    Nedick's 348
Franklin Square, 41
Franklin, Benjamin, 33, 168
Franz, Elizabeth, 757, 766
Fraser, James E., 278, 495, 593
Fraser, Neale, 624, 632
Fraser, Simon, 36
Fraunces Tavern, 27, 29, 311, 722
Frazee, H.H., 346
Frazee, John, 84
Frazier, Joe, 684, 697
Frazier, Walt, 697
Fredericksz, Cryn, 2, 4
Freed, Alan, 643
Freedley, Vinton, 396
Freedom Forum, 768
Freedomland, 632
free lunch bars, 388
Freeman, Joshua B., 799, 867
Freeman, Morgan, 788

Freeman's Journal, 65
Freemasons, 24, 40, 42, 59, 177,
    193
Frelich, Phyllis, 753
Frémont, John C., 111
French Ball, 143, 236
French, Daniel Chester, 257,
    263, 268, 284, 376
French, Fred F., 431, 439, 486
French Institute/Alliance
    Française, 258
Fresh Air Fund, 182, 640
Fresh Kills Landfill, 552, 568,
    840
Fresh Meadows, 557, 572, 710
Freund, Gisèle, 559
Frick, Henry Clay, 348, 378, 490
Friedan, Betty, 693
Friedman, Josh Alan, 782
Friedman, Leo, 320
Friedman, Stanley J., 780
Friend, Cliff, 445
Friendly, Fred, 596, 856
Friends Seminary, 40, 64, 124
Frimbo, E.M., 757
Friml, Rudolf, 339, 347, 375,
    400, 437, 407, 414
Frisch, Frankie, 397, 408
Frohman, Charles, 220, 236,
    248, 267, 338, 355
Frohman, Daniel, 220, 284
Froman, Jane, 484, 542
Frost, Frederick G., 570
frozen foods, Birdseye and, 371
Frydman, Jacob A., 850
Fuchs, Daniel, 483
Fugard, Athol, 762
Fugitive Slave Acts, 44, 97, 100
Fulbright, J. William, 539
Fuller, Buckminster, 651, 685
Fuller Construction Co., 446
Fuller, George A., 321, 424, 463,
    464
Fulton Market, 60, 156, 194, 311,
    519
Fulton, Robert, 52, 55, 57, 61
fun city, 665
Fund for the City of NY, 680
Funston, G. Keith, 665, 814
fur trade, 1, 72
Furber, Douglas, 407
Furillo, Carl, 561, 595, 605, 801
Furman, Gabriel, 46

Gable, Clark, 437
Gabor, Eva, 576
Gaddis, William, 603
Gaelic Athletic Association, 353,
    422, 812
Gaelic Park, 422, 530, 812
Gage, S. Edson, 358

Gaines, William M., 587
Galante, Carmine, 538, 750
Gale, Zona, 386
Gallagher, Ed, 396
Gallagher, Helen, 480, 546, 560,
    571, 583, 594, 738
Gallagher, Megan, 800
Gallagher and Shean, 445
Gallatin, Albert, 69, 77, 95
Gallatin, James, 139, 148
Gallico, Paul, 430
Gallo, Fortune, 697
Gallo, Joey, 704, 709
Gambino, Carlo, 392, 537, 614,
    704, 733
    crime family, 807, 840
gambling, 102, 148, 169, 193,
    211, 240, 273, 335, 371,
    531, 539, 573, 580, 624,
    627
Gannett Co., 762
Ganz, Victor and Sally, 846
garbage disposal, 8, 486, 547,
    552, 840
Garbo, Greta, 414, 451, 461, 806
Garcia, Jerry, 676
Garden City, L.I., 156
Gardenia, Vincent, 618, 702,
    745, 789, 812
Gardiner, Asa Bird, 263
Gardiner's Island, 5
Gardiner, Sarah Dindati, 595
Gardner, Ava, 570
Gardner, Herb, 642, 719, 777,
    817, 838
Gardner, John W., 672
Garelik, Sanford, 706
Garfield, James A., 191, 195
Garfield, John, 490, 503, 524,
    560, 566, 589
Garfunkel, Art, 661, 668, 697
Gargan, William, 469
Garibaldi Guard, 125
Garibaldi, Giuseppe, 97, 220,
    349
Garland, Judy, 517, 524, 566,
    637, 749
garment industry, 101, 585, 835
    (see also fashion)
Garrett, Betty, 555, 570
Garrett, Charles, 635
Garrett, Wayne, 714
Garrison, Wm. Lloyd, 80, 97, 188
Garroway, Dave, 588
Garson, Barbara, 675
Garvey, Marcus, 359, 383, 403
Garvey, Stephen, 718
gas lighting, 60, 63, 65, 67, 83,
    92, 133, 141, 158, 163,
    189, 398, 410
    Welsbach mantle and, 210
Gashouse Gang, 181

gasoline, 617, 809
    price of, 569
    rationing, 534, 549
Gates, Gen. Horatio, 35, 51
Gates, John W., 296, 330
Gatti-Casazza, Giulio, 314
Gaunt, Percy, 232, 236
Gaxton, William, 396, 429, 445,
    461, 478, 484, 524, 648
Gaynor, Charles J., 322
Gaynor, William J., 316, 317, 335
Gay Activist Alliance, 705
Gay Men's Health Crisis, 761
Gay Rights Bill, 700, 716, 780
gay rights, 686, 705, 711, 780,
    786, 797, 853
Gazzara, Ben, 604
Gazzo, Michael, 604
Geddes, James, 54, 57, 78
Geddes, Norman Bel, 375, 618
gefilte fish, 298
Gehrig, Lou, 375, 415, 422, 430,
    471, 498, 505, 518, 530
Gelbart, Larry, 643, 800
Gelber, Jack, 623
Geld, Gary, 696
Gellers, Irving, 524
Gellis, Isaac, 217
General Electric, 232, 245, 823
    buildings, 463, 479
    fluorescent lighting, 508
    Kidder, Peabody and, 781, 825
    PaineWebber and, 825
    RCA and, 776
General Motors, 442
    buses and, 494
    Futurama at World's Fair, 514
General Post Office, 347
General Theological Seminary,
    57, 64
General Trades' Union (GTU),
    70
Gennaro, Peter, 868
Genovese, Kitty, 655
Genovese, Vito, 408, 462, 614,
    691
Gensel, John G., 661, 676, 697,
    720, 822
gentrification, 778
George magazine, 831
George Washington Bridge, 459,
    844
George White's Scandals, 381,
    386, 391, 396, 400, 407,
    421, 445
George, Henry, 188, 212, 250
Gerard, James W., 519
Gere, Richard, 749
German-American Bund, 500
Germans, 125, 241, 269, 289,
    538, 620
Gernsbach, Hugo, 674

Gerosa, Lawrence E., 634
Gerry, Elbridge T., 172, 203
Gerry, Peter Goelet, 615
Gerry, Robert L., 615
Gershe, Leonard, 689
Gershwin, George, 375, 381, 386, 391, 396, 400, 407, 415, 421, 429, 437, 438, 445, 451, 461, 478, 492, 497, 503, 504
Gershwin, Ira, 391, 396, 407, 415, 421, 429, 437, 438, 445, 451, 452, 478, 484, 492, 497, 503, 529, 555
Gesner, Clark, 676, 878
Getchell, Margaret, 123, 152
Getty, J. Paul, 512
Geva, Tamara, 470, 478, 497
Ghostley, Alice, 589, 631, 654
G.I. Bill, 545, 547
Gibb, Barry, 676
Gibbons v. Ogden, 61
Gibbons, Thomas, 67
Gibbs, Wolcott, 576
Gibbs, Woollcott, 618
Gibson, Althea, 613, 619
Gibson, Bob, 655
Gibson Girl, 225
Gibson, Charles Dana, 225, 248, 278, 293, 374, 546
Gibson, William, 618, 623
Gideonse, Harry D., 515
Gielgud, John, 559, 654
Gigante, Louis R., 685
Gigante, Vincent, 573, 685, 849
Gilbert and Sullivan, 190
Gilbert, Rufus H., 167, 210
Giles, James H., 170
Gilford, Jack, 623, 624, 643, 668, 675, 806
Gill, Brendan, 576, 612, 805
Gillespie, Angus, 867
Gillespie, Dizzy, 511, 547, 589, 822
Gillette, Wm. H., 196, 214, 220, 236, 240, 248, 261, 368
Gilliatt, Penelope, 682, 689
Gilmartin, Gregory, 765, 788, 831
Gilmore, Patrick S., 173
Gilmore, Margalo, 420, 428, 444, 496, 516, 599
Gilpin, Charles S., 338, 386, 451
Gilroy, Frank D., 654
Gilroy, Thomas F., 230, 237
Gingold, Alfred, 856
Gingold, Hermione, 595, 708, 713
Ginsberg, Alan, 608
Ginsberg, Allen, 551, 593, 632, 672, 846
Ginsberg, Moses, 456

Giroux, Robert, 647
Gisborne, Frederick N., 118
Gish, Dorothy, 517
Gish, Lillian, 357, 631, 682, 822
Giuliani, Rudolph W., 784, 819, 824–826, 828, 836, 837, 840–842, 845, 846, 862, 865
Glackens, William, 295, 308, 313, 509
Glad Tidings Tabernacle, 307
Glamour magazine, 515
Glaser, Milton, 598, 670, 681, 735
Glaspell, Susan, 361
Glass-Steagall Act, 474, 804, 860
Glass-Owen Currency Act, 343
Glazer, Nathan, 647
Gleason, James, 413
Gleason, Jackie, 542, 546, 571, 624
Gleason, Joanna, 789
Glendale, 156, 235
Glickberg, Howard, 728
Glickman, Louis J., 638, 650, 864
Glimcher, Arne, 647
Glover, Savion, 818
Godfrey, Arthur, 550
Godkin, E.L., 139, 178, 185, 196, 202, 205
God's Love We Deliver, 779
Godowsky, Dagmar, 725
Godowsky, Leopold, 490
Jr., 766
Godwin, Parke, 97
Goelet Building, 217
Goelet, Francis, 12
Goelet, Jacobus, 12
Goelet, Ogden, 203, 217
Goelet, Robert, 217
Goelet, Robert W., 327, 376, 531
Goethals, George W., 435
Goetz, Bernhard, 773
Goetz, Peter Michael, 766
Goetz, E. Ray, 339, 368, 396, 400, 438, 452
Gold and Stock Telegraph Co., 144, 164
gold rush, 93
gold, 133, 136
Morgan and, 242
price of, 747, 751
Goldberg, Arthur J., 693
Goldberg, Rube, 307, 695
Goldberger, Paul, 748
Golden, Harry, 622, 626
Golden, John, 339, 604
Golden Gloves boxing, 430
Golden Venture freighter, 824
Goldfaden, Avram, 232, 420

Goldin, Harrison J., 751, 764
Goldman, Edwin Franko, 332, 396, 609
Goldman, Emma, 234, 270, 298, 316, 337, 364, 460
Goldman, James A., 703
Goldman, Sol, 605, 633, 726, 791
Goldmark, Peter, 522, 567
Goldstein, Al, 681
Goldstein, Jonah J., 548
Goldwyn, Samuel, 346
Golenpaul, Dan, 510, 719
golf, 36, 401
    Pelham Bay Golf Course, 353
    public course, 249
    Split Rock course, 498
    U.S. Open, 240
    Van Cortland Park course, 249
Gomez, Lefty, 504, 511
Gomez, Ruben, 600
Gompers, Samuel, 182, 185, 213, 317
Gonzalez, Pancho, 567, 571
Goodhart, William, 660
Goodlatte, A. Richardson, 770
Goodman, Andrew, 652
Goodman, Benny, 451, 452, 511, 537, 546, 783
Goodman, Dody, 744
Goodman, Paul, 622, 630, 642, 707
Goodman, Roy M., 736
Goodrich, Arthur F., 420
Goodwin, Philip S., 516
Goody, Sam, 812
Goodyear, A. Conger, 444, 516, 653
Goodyear, Charles, 124
Gordon, David L. A., 846
Gordon, Joe, 511, 543
Gordon, John Steele, 862
Gordon, Leon, 400
Gordon, Mack, 452
Gordon, Max, 744, 800
Gordon, Ruth, 428, 608, 777
Gordon, Waxey, 479, 586, 590
Gordone, Charles, 689, 832
Gorham Building, 203
Goring, Butch, 759
Gorky, Arshile, 523, 565
Gorman, Cliff, 660, 682, 738
Gorney, Jay, 571
Gorringe, Henry H., 193
Gossage, Rich, 745, 759
Gossett, Louis, Jr., 604, 623, 661
Gotham, 52
Gotti, John, 778, 807, 818, 840, 878
    Jr., 818, 858
Gottlieb, Robert A., 787
Gottman, Jean, 635

Gould, Elliott, 642, 675, 702
Gould, George, 231
Gould, Jay, 136, 148–150, 152, 166–168, 196, 197, 202, 203, 231
Gould, Joe, 612
Gould, Lois, 695, 877
Gould, Morton, 470, 551, 566, 839
Goulet, Robert, 631
Gourmet Garage, 819
Gourmet magazine, 531, 755
Governors Island, 2, 23, 60, 274, 575
    Admiral's House on, 86
    incinerator on, 212
Gowanus Canal, 88, 212, 238, 334
Gowanus Parkway, 527
Goya Foods, 500
Grace Church, 91
Grace, J. Peter, Jr., 830
Grace, W.R., 141, 191, 205
    building, 720
Grace's Marketplace, 780
Gracie Mansion, 47, 66, 399, 532, 572
Gracie, Archibald, 47, 49, 50, 52, 66
Graf, Steffi, 795, 801, 823, 833
graffiti, 694, 706, 770, 798
Grafton, John, 752
Graham, Benjamin, 481
Graham, Billy, 611, 617, 691
Graham, David, 68
Graham, Florence N., 326
Graham, Martha, 400, 421, 484, 518, 556, 592
Graham, Ronny, 598
Gramercy Park, 68, 70
Grammy Awards, 613
Grand Army Plaza, 352
Grand Central Depot, 257, 265
Grand Central Palace, 333, 355, 367, 610, 677
Grand Central Parkway, 475, 495
Grand Central Station (radio), 503
Grand Central Post Office, 321
Grand Central Terminal, 282, 300, 343, 348, 366, 330, 418, 553, 569, 597, 677, 740, 745, 810, 822, 854, 865
    Colorama in, 575
Grand Central Partnership, 854
Grand Central Viaduct, 384, 389, 398, 426, 435
Grand Concourse, 232
Grant, Bob, 826
Grant, Cary, 642
Grant, David Marshall, 749, 822

Grant, Hugh J., 205, 218, 223, 230, 238, 323
Grant, Jane, 411
Grant, Lawrence, 352, 396
Grant, Lee, 570, 702
Grant, Micki, 708, 732
Grant's Tomb, 255, 363
Grant, Ulysses S., 129, 143, 148, 151, 165, 166, 178, 195, 206, 210
Grasso, Richard A., 875
Gratz, Roberta B., 799, 862
Grateful Dead, The, 676, 690
Grauer, Ben, 737
Gravano, Salvatore, 778, 818
Graves, Earl G., 695
Gravesend, 6, 48, 218
Gray, Asa, 116
Graybar Building, 431
Gray, Susan, 641
Gray's Papaya, 716
Grayson, Kathryn, 555, 560
Graziano, Rocky, 556, 561
Greater New York, 250, 256
Greco, José, 868
Greeks, 239, 730
Greeley Square, 168
Greeley, Horace, 82, 116, 157, 165, 168
    statues of, 225
Green Book, The, 374
Green, Adolph, 546, 551, 570, 594, 599, 609, 619, 631, 637, 696, 719, 744, 812, 878
Green, Andrew H., 140, 147, 152, 162, 250, 281
Green, Harry F., 626, 670, 704
Green, Hetty, 360
Green, Johnny, 452
Green, Mark, 871
Green, Mitzi, 504, 551
Green, Paul, 460
Green, Paul Eliot, 420, 529
Green, Sabrina, 842
Greenacre Park, 705
Greenberg, Cheryl, 811
Greenberg, Clement, 588, 642, 827
Greenberg, Maurice R., 782, 844
Greenberg, Stanley, 857
Greene, Ellen, 732
Greene, Gael, 760
Greene, Graham, 612
Greene, Gen. Nathanael, 33, 34
Greenglass, David, 573
Greengrass, Barney, 448
green markets, 735, 852
Greenspan, Alan, 787, 804
Greenstreet, Sydney, 478, 523
Greenwich Street, 4

Greenwich Village, 60, 184, 721
    Cantwell on, 831
    fire in, 71
    Halloween parade in, 720
    Sheridan Square in, 786
Greenwich House, 275, 365
Green-Wood Cemetery, 386
Greenwood, Charlotte, 339, 347, 396
Greer, Seth, 72
Gregg, John R., 569
Gregorian, Vartan, 724
Gregory, André, 794
Grey, Joel, 668, 683
Grey, Clifford, 414, 429, 437, 452
Greyhound, 442
grid plan, 140
Griffith, Andy, 604
Griffith, D.W., 308, 346, 357
Griffith, Emile, 637, 643, 649, 668, 683
Griffith, Michael, 780, 786
Griffiths, John W., 88, 198
Grimes, Patrick, 436, 743
Grimes, Tammy, 631, 731, 753
Grinnell, Henry, 104
Grinnell, Joseph, 57
Grinnell, Moses H., 125, 178
Gristede's, 230
Griswold, John A., 148
Grit, 202
Grizzard, George, 618, 675, 731
Grodin, Charles, 725
Groener, Harry, 763, 817
Grofé, Ferde, 407
Groh, Heinie, 397
Groot, Benjamin de, 168
Gropper, William, 738
Gross, Elliot, 774
Gross, Harry, 531, 580, 581
Grosz, George, 545
Group Theater, 460
Guardian Angels, 750
Guardino, Harry, 758
Guare, John, 702, 703, 806, 877
Gubitchev, Valentin A., 572
Guccione, Robert, 688
Guérard, Michel, 774
Guggenheim Foundation, Daniel and Florence, 396
Guggenheim, Daniel, 320, 449
Guggenheim, Meyer, 294
Guggenheim family, 522
Guggenheim, Peggy, 535, 541, 623
Guggenheim, Solomon R., 623
Guggenheimer, Minnie, 374, 668
Guidry, Ron, 739, 745, 759
Guild Theater, 510
Guinan, "Texas," 396, 480
Gulick, Luther H., 285

Gumpertz, Samuel, 333
Gunn, David L., 770
Gunther, C. Godfrey, 126, 133, 138
Gunther, Carl Gottfried, 149
Gurney, A.R., 762, 800
Guston, Philip, 598, 689, 725, 752
Gutfreund, John, 755, 799, 809
Guttmacher, Alan F., 722
Gwenn, Edmund, 560
Gwynne, Fred, 636

Häagen-Dazs, 626
Hackett, James H., 64, 96, 165
Hackett, Joan, 758
Hackman, Gene, 636, 654, 702
Hadassah, 334
Hadley, Bump, 518
Hagen, Uta, 517, 576, 642, 832
Haines, William, 559
Halberstam, David, 748, 821, 873, 877
Hale House, 687
Hale, Nathan, 34, 284
Haley, Alex, 659
Haley, Jack, 444, 470, 524, 536
halftones, 252
Hall, A. Oakey, 148, 151, 155, 157, 174, 256
Hall, Bettina, 444, 461
Hall, George A., 71
Hall, Juanita, 571, 599, 619, 660
Hall of Records, 333
Halleck, Fitz-Greene, 55, 60, 69, 184
Halley, Rudolph, 573–575, 579, 591
Halliday, Robert, 415, 421, 437
Halloween, 720
Halper, Albert, 476
Halpern, Moyshe-Leyb, 380
Halsey, Adm. Wm. F., Jr., 548
Halsman, Philippe, 749
Halsted, William S., 206
Hamersley, L. Gordon, 417
Hamill, Pete, 701, 821, 846
Hamilton Grange, 48, 50, 191, 363, 409
Hamilton, Alexander, 30, 31, 35, 37, 39–41, 43–45, 48–51
    statue of, 313
Hamilton, Charles V., 811
Hamilton, Margaret, 469
Hamilton, Mary Agnes, 468
Hamilton, William Peter, 276, 441, 443
Hamlisch, Marvin, 720, 725, 749
Hammack, David C., 762
Hammarskjöld, Dag, 633
    Plaza, 738

Hammerstein, Oscar, 223, 236, 243, 267, 302, 314, 381
    II, 381, 400, 407, 414, 421, 429, 430, 438, 445, 470, 497, 517, 542, 551, 561, 571, 583, 594, 605, 619, 624, 631
Hammett, Dashiell, 443, 483, 484, 581, 636
Hammond, John, 637, 789
Hammond, Ruth, 428
Hampden, Walter, 319, 361, 420, 593
Hampton, Lionel, 878
Hand, Learned, 316
handguns, 833
Handlin, Oscar, 617, 622
Haney, Carol, 654
Handwerker, Nathan, 363, 371
Hanff, Helene, 635, 695
Hanks, Tom, 857
Hanley, James F., 381, 391, 421, 484
Hanley, William, 654, 660
Hansberry, Lorraine, 654, 660, 689, 623
hansom cabs, 227
Hapgood, Hutchins, 277
Harak, Rudolph de, 689
Harbach, Otto, 314, 326, 339, 347, 369, 380, 407, 414, 421, 429, 461, 478, 542, 648
Harburg, E.Y., 452, 461, 470, 484, 517, 546, 560, 583, 613, 758
Hard, Darlene, 632, 637
Hardesty, Shortridge, 435
Harding, Warren G., 383
Hard Rock Café, 769
Hardwick, Elizabeth, 647, 748
Hardwicke, Cedric, 510, 623, 654
Hardy, Charles, 26, 27
Haring, Keith, 805
Harkness, Edward S., 309, 519, 520
Harlan, John M., 433
Harlem, 9, 274, 293, 679
    Apollo Theater in, 352, 484, 739
    Boys Choir of, 683
    Bravo supermarket in, 852
    Dance Theater of, 697
    East, 505, 521, 568, 580
    Hale House in, 687
    health statistics for (1929), 442
    Hotel Theresa in, 348
    housing projects in, 505, 519, 531, 663
    Kortwright apartments in, 293
    Lafayette Theater in, 338

INDEX

Harlem (*continued*)
Music Settlement in, 326
numbers racket in, 627
Opera House, 223
parks in, 80
race riots in, 487, 539, 652
racial violence in, 833
Renaissance Center in, 396
Renaissance, 395, 405
Savoy Ballroom in, 421
Schomburg Center in, 757
slum clearance in, 663
Smalls' Paradise in, 415
Smith photographs and, 483
Strivers' Row in, 229
Studio Museum in, 682
Harlem Equal Rights League, 293
Harlem Gas Light Co., 109
Harlem Globetrotters, 776
Harlem River Ship Canal, 243
Harlem Speedway, 258
Harlem State Office Building, 715
Harlem Youth Opportunities, 640
Harlem-Dowling Children's Service, 686
Harlow, Alvin F., 460
Harnden, William F., 80
Harnett, William M., 187, 232
Harnick, Sheldon, 624, 631, 643, 648, 654, 668, 697
Harnoncourt, René d', 576, 682
Harper, James, 86, 88, 104
Harper, Marion, Jr., 569, 674, 799
Harper, Valerie, 637
Harper's Bazaar, 344, 468, 502, 776
Harper's Monthly, 98
Harper's Weekly, 112, 153, 160
Harpur, Robert, 27, 35, 39, 63
Harrigan & Hart, 184, 190m, 200, 202, 203, 208, 215, 225
Harrigan, Ned, 225
Harriman, Edward H., 179, 251, 271, 305, 312, 317
Harriman, E. Roland, 742
Harriman, Margaret Case, 583
Harriman, W. Averell, 458, 502, 596, 616, 780
Harrington, Pat, 524, 536, 636, 660
Harrington, Virginia D., 489
Harris, Barbara, 661, 668
Harris, Bill, 748
Harris, Ed, 766
Harris, Elisha, 159
Harris, Jed, 749
Harris, Julie, 576, 583, 682, 702

Harris, Rosemary, 618, 667, 862
Harris, Sam H., 529
Harris, Townsend, 95, 185
Harris, Winifred, 381
Harrison Drug Act, 362
Harrison, Benjamin, 218, 231
Harrison, Colin, 838
Harrison, Rex, 565, 576, 609
Harry, Debbie, 739
Hart, Doris, 600, 605
Hart, Lorenz, 414, 421, 422, 429, 437, 444, 451, 461, 478, 491, 504, 510, 511, 517, 524, 536, 542
Hart, Marvin, 262
Hart, Moss, 428, 450, 478, 484, 496, 510, 516, 524, 546, 636
Hart, Roxanne, 800
Hart, William S., 296
Hartford, George Huntington, 122, 156, 371
Hartigan, Grace, 598, 612
Hartley, Jonathan Scott, 236
Hartley, Marcellus, 247
Hartley, Robert M., 85
Hartman, Grace, Paul, 561
Hartz Mountain Industries, 471, 850
Haryou Act, 652
Hassam, Childe, 257, 261, 315, 345, 489
Hastings, John Russel, 405
Hatton, Frederick, 338, 361, 368
Hauerbach, Otto, 332
Hauptmann, Bruno, 486, 498
Havemeyer, Frederick C., 51
Havemeyer, H.O., 217, 230, 234, 242, 311
Havemeyer, Henry, 134, 188
Havemeyer, Townsend, 117
Havemeyer, Wm. F., 51, 88, 93, 120, 162, 166, 172, 217
Havoc, June, 524, 546
Hawes, Elizabeth, 512, 701, 821
Hawkins, Coleman, 547
Hawkins, Erskine, 485, 524
Hawkins, Stuart, 612
Hawkins, Yusef, 797
Hawley, James, 430
Hay, John, 280
Hayden, Charles, 299, 488, 501
Hayden Planetarium, 488, 866
Hayden, Melissa, 584
Haydon, Julie, 510, 517, 550
Hayes, Helen, 320, 380, 437, 529, 541, 559, 618, 822
Hayes, Patrick Cardinal, 378, 384, 404, 474, 476, 509
Hayes, Rutherford B., 178, 182, 183
Hayes, Shirley, 587, 621

Hays, Arthur Garfield, 383, 596
Hays, Jacob, 50
Hays, Will, 421
Hayward, Brooke, 636
Hayward, Leland, 702
Head, Edith, 462
Head Start, 641, 659
Heald, Anthony, 771
health clubs, 801, 833, 839
Health Department, 564 (*see also* Board of Health)
Hearn, George, 763, 767
Hearn, Jim, 585
Hearst, Wm. Randolph, 243, 245, 252, 253, 256, 257, 270, 275, 289, 293, 295, 298, 301, 315, 316, 344, 351, 362, 364, 390, 405, 439, 440, 502, 528, 529, 582
Mrs., 505
Heathcote, Caleb, 16, 18, 20, 21
Hebrew Actors Union, 380, 420, 451
Hebrew Benevolent Society, 60
Hebrew Immigrant Aid Society, 322
Hebrew National Foods, 298
Hebrew Orphan Asylum, 533
Hecht, Ben, 380, 437, 477, 478, 546, 654
Hecht, Marie B., 675
Heckart, Eileen, 594, 599, 603, 613, 675, 689
Hecker, Isaac T., 101, 118, 219
Heckscher, August, 144, 205, 292, 362, 390, 397, 448, 531
II, 678, 686, 718, 743, 852
Heckscher State Park, 448
Hedges, Job Elmer, 335
Heeney, Cornelius, 58, 93, 116
Heflin, Van, 496, 516, 570, 603
Heggen, Thomas, 565
Heifetz, Jascha, 368
Heiman, Marcus, 613
Heiskell, Andrew W., 754
Heisman Trophy, 492
Held, Anna, 248, 291, 308, 320, 375
Held, John, Jr., 395, 618
helicopters, 572, 600, 658, 736
Heller, Joseph, 636, 748
Hellinger, Mark, 450
Hellman, Geoffrey T., 737
Hellman, Lillian, 484, 516, 529, 546, 555, 583, 630, 712, 771
Hellmann's Mayonnaise, 341
Hell's Gate Bridge, 810
Hell's Kitchen, 197, 251, 625, 801, 851 (*see also* Clinton)

Helmsley, Harry B., 499, 605, 705, 710, 728, 798, 850
Helmsley, Leona, 705, 798, 801, 850
Helmsley-Spear, 605, 638
Helpern, Milton, 662
Helprin, Mark, 724, 737, 757
Hemingway, Ernest, 523
Hemingway, Mariel, 749
Hemsley, Sherman, 702
Henderson Place, 200
Henderson, Mary C., 712
Henderson, Fletcher, 387, 421, 509
Henderson, Ray, 414, 421, 429, 437, 438, 444, 461, 478, 491, 542
Henderson, Thomas M., 731
Henrich, Tommy, 530, 561
Hendrix, Jimi, 690
Henley, Beth, 758, 771
Henning, Doug, 719, 766
Henri, Robert, 307, 308, 319, 361, 444
Henry, O., 290, 325
Henry Street Settlement, 234, 264, 356, 545
Neighborhood Playhouse of, 357
Henson, Jim, 732, 772, 806
Henson, Matthew A., 440
Hepburn, Audrey, 599
Hepburn, Katharine, 477, 503, 516, 535, 542, 690, 758
Herald Square, 244, 274, 276, 404
Herbert, F. Hugh, 618
Herbert, John, 675
Herbert, Joseph, 302
Herbert, Victor, 258, 262, 285, 296, 302, 320, 326, 339, 347, 352, 353, 357, 362, 368, 369, 381, 387, 396, 400, 407, 428
Herbst, Josephine, 436, 689
Herman, Billie, 530
Herman, Jerry, 637, 654, 668, 690, 767
Herne, Chrystal, 261, 267, 413
Herne, James A., 190, 225, 236, 261, 267, 273
Herne, Katharine Corcoran, 190, 220, 225, 261, 541
heroin, 653, 691, 709, 717, 750, 789
Herrick, D. Cady, 288
Herriman, George, 428
Hershkowitz, Leo, 737
Herter Brothers, 217
Herter, Christian, 161, 204
Hertz Corp., 592
Hess, Thomas, 528

Hesse, Eva, 696
Hevesi, Alan G., 859
Hewitt, Abram S., 127, 212, 218, 219
Hewitt, Lleyton, 874
Heye, George G., 394, 611, 826
Heyman, Edward, 452, 470, 478
Heyward, DuBose, 428, 492
Hichens, Robert S., 332
Higbe, Kirby, 530
Higgins, Charles M., 386
Higgins, Frank W., 288, 298
High Bridge Water Tower, 169, 226
High Line, 482, 752
Hijuelos, Oscar, 766, 799, 821, 832
Hiken, Nat, 571
Hill, Arthur, 608, 613, 631, 642
Hill, Billy, 484
Hill, D.B., 210, 218, 238
Hill, G. Washington, 416, 438
Hill, James J., 271
Hill, Ureli C., 84, 177
Hiller, Wendy, 555, 612
Hilliard, Bob, 561, 594
Hillman, Sidney, 500, 553
Hindemith, Paul, 537, 556
Hine, Lewis W., 311, 368, 460, 469, 523
Hines, Gregory, 599, 758
Hines, James J., 441, 513, 610
Hingle, Pat, 613, 618, 654, 682, 696, 719
Hippodrome, 295, 301, 517, 590
Hirsch, Judd, 738, 744, 753, 777, 817
Hirsch, Louis A., 339, 357, 362, 369, 375, 381, 396, 400
Hirschfeld, Abe, 821
Hirschfeld, Al, 407, 542, 598
Hiss, Alger, 563, 572, 580
Hitchcock, Jane Stanton, 877
Hitchcock, Raymond, 308, 314, 319, 368, 387, 391
Hitler, Adolf, 513
Hobart, George V., 278, 320, 326, 339, 380, 381, 396, 420
Hobson, Laura Z., 559, 783
Hochman, Julius, 693
hockey, ice, 369, 438, 478, 525, 708, 753, 759, 763, 767, 823
Hodges, Gil, 571, 605, 709
Hodges, Johnny, 697
Hodgins, Eric, 554
Hodiak, John, 598
Hoe, Richard M., 90, 160, 176
Hoffa, Portland, 444
Hoffenberg, Steven, 821
Hoffert, Emily, 649, 655

Hoffman, Dustin, 689, 732, 763, 811
Hoffman, John T., 138, 140, 144, 148, 157, 158, 162, 218
Hoffman, Malvina, 446, 667
Hoffman, Philip, 789, 767, 818, 848
Hoffman, William F., 777
Hofmann, Hans, 653, 667
Hofstadter, Samuel H., 457, 466
Hog Island, 238
Hogan, Frank S., 573, 584, 616, 716
Hokinson, Helen, 412, 569
Holbrook, Hal, 654, 682
Holbrook, Stewart H., 593
Holbrooke, Richard, 853
Holden, William, 599
Holiday, Billie, 525, 624, 795
Holland, George, 159
Holland, Josiah G., 196
Holland Tunnel, 426, 467
Hollander, Xaviera, 707
Holliday, Jennifer, 758
Holliday, Judy, 554, 609, 660
Hollins, Harry B., 274
Holloway, Sterling, 414, 421, 452
Hollywood Black List, 557
Holm, Celeste, 517, 542, 546, 576
Holm, Hanya, 818
Holm, John Cecil, 490
Holman, Libby, 429, 444, 452, 703
Holman, Nat, 584, 832
Holmes, John Haynes, 316, 481, 653
Holmes, Rupert, 777
Holt, Winifred, 290, 344, 356
Holtz, Lou, 386, 391
Holtzman, Elizabeth, 716, 751
Holzman, Red, 676, 697, 714, 858
Homberger, Eric, 771, 827, 877
Homer, Winslow, 115, 142, 168, 191
home rule, 40, 627
homelessness, 321, 342, 479, 579, 764, 770, 774, 778, 779, 784, 785, 790, 795, 799, 807, 829, 834, 835
homicide rate, 165, 181, 229, 249, 273, 303, 362, 422, 531, 556, 637, 669, 714, 733, 807, 840, 850
Homolka, Oscar, 546
Hone, Philip, 48, 63, 72, 77, 87, 101
Honest Ballot Association, 316
Hood, Clifton, 821
Hooker, Isabella Beecher, 162, 177

hoopskirts, 112
Hoover, Herbert, 433, 434, 449, 458, 463, 466, 651
Hoover, J. Edgar, 573
Hoovervilles, 479
Hoover Village, 472
Hope, Bob, 452, 478, 497, 604, 613
Hopkins, Harry L., 350
Hopper, De Wolf, 249, 267, 368
Hopper, Edward, 345, 428, 444, 450, 469, 516, 535, 541, 675
Hopwood, Avery, 325, 380, 386, 390, 406, 414, 437
Horn, Joseph B., 341
Hornaday, William T., 263
Horne, Lena, 525, 546, 561, 613, 795
Horovitz, Israel, 682, 811
Horowitz, Vladimir, 437, 800
horsecars, 67, 69, 72, 98, 173, 306, 366
  Brooklyn, 175
horseracing, 59, 61, 258, 547
  Aqueduct, 254, 547, 624
  Belmont Stakes, 146
  Freehold, N.J., 105
  Jamaica, 285, 551, 624
  Jockey Club, 146
  Wood Memorial, 415
horses, 244, 366, 397
Horticultural Society, 355
Hosack, David, 49, 50
Hoschna, Karl, 313, 326
hospitals, 855
  Bellevue, 24, 45, 46, 55, 69, 75, 92, 95, 101, 114, 127, 141, 145, 159, 164, 171, 173, 179, 183, 186, 278, 717
  Bellevue Medical College, 127
  Beth Israel, 228, 837
  Booth Memorial, 373, 611
  Bronx-Lebanon, 641
  Bronx Municipal, 330, 468, 597, 602, 641
  Columbia Presbyterian, 411, 435
    Harkness Pavilion at, 520
  Creedmore, 337
  Downstate, 575
  East Harlem, 390
  Emigrant Refuge and Hospital, 92
  Eye and Ear Infirmary, 58
  Flower Fifth Avenue, 508, 742
  Foundling, 153
  Halloran General, 534, 587
  Harlem, 183, 216, 307, 616
  Jamaica, 228, 360
  Kings County, 69, 459

Lebanon, 235, 468, 641
Lenox Hill, 114, 127, 149, 176, 199, 272, 373
Lying-In, 384, 467
  Memorial, 206
  Memorial Sloan-Kettering, 508, 765
  mental, 13, 60
  Methodist, 195
  Metropolitan, 80
  Montefiore, 206, 344
  Mount Sinai, 103, 110, 141, 167, 290, 587, 810
  Mount Sinai-NYU, 855
  New York, 30, 34, 40, 43, 44, 46, 48, 52, 58, 61, 82, 110, 141, 183, 214, 227, 330, 337, 365, 366, 404, 427, 467, 545, 717, 742, 761, 765, 770, 782, 798, 810, 844
  New York Cancer, 214
  New York Downtown, 114, 492, 748
  New York Infirmary, 114, 492, 748, 810
  Presbyterian, 167
  Roosevelt, 164, 183, 206, 232, 366, 545, 820
  Smallpox, 112
  St. Luke's, 90, 110, 118, 183, 246, 545
  St. Luke's-Roosevelt, 756, 837
  St. Vincent's, 95, 111, 549
  Special Surgery, 602, 717
  Stuyvesant Polyclinic, 206
  University, 554
  Veterans Admin., 394, 558
  Woman's, 110
  Woodhull, 761
Hostetler, Jeff, 812
Hostos Community College, 681, 845
hotel-room occupancy tax, 829
hotels,
  Alamac, 417
  Albert, 203
  Alden, 424
  Algonquin, 279, 380, 472
  Americana, 644
  Ashland House, 151
  Astor, 293, 691
  Astor House, 76, 105
  Astoria, 255
  Barbizon, 424, 711
  Barbizon-Plaza, 456, 759
  Barclay, 425
  Belleclaire, 287
  Belmont, 304, 456
  Biltmore, 354, 583, 693, 754
  Brevoort, 109, 280, 378, 600
  Bryant Park, 875

hotels (*continued*)
Buckingham, 417
Burnham's, 124
Carlyle, 456
Carter, 456
Chelsea, 209, 608
City Squire, 639
Clarendon, 91, 105, 106
Commodore, 382, 754
Crowne Plaza, 802
Delmonico, 433, 875
Delmonico's, 392
Dixie, 456
Doral Park Avenue, 656
Doubletree Guest Suites, 807
Drake, 433
Edison, 465
Embassy Suites, 869
Empire (Radisson), 397
Endicott, 223
Essex House, 464, 813
Euclid, 834
Everett House, 105
Fifth Avenue, 108, 122, 424
Four Seasons, 823
Gilsey House, 165
Girard, 241
Gotham, 297, 795 (Peninsula)
Governor Clinton, 447
Gramercy Park, 417
Grand, 151
Grand Hyatt, 754
Grand Union, 174, 354
Greenwich, 255
Hartford, 76
Helmsley Palace, 754
Henry Hudson, 531
Hilton, 651
Holiday Inn, 802
Holland House, 230
Imperial, 226, 230
Inter-Continental, 425
Kitano, 715
Knickerbocker, 304
Lafarge House, 135
Lafayette, 378, 572
Lincoln, 440, 754
Loews Hotels, 651
Lombardy, 433
Lovejoy's, 135
Lucerne, 293
Manhattan Beach, 185
Manhattan Towers, 456
Marriott (Brooklyn), 859
Marriott East, 409, 813
Marriott Financial Center, 879
Marriott Marquis, 763, 779
Marriott World Trade, 759
Martinique, 255
Mayflower, 424
McAlpin, 340

Metropole, 335
Metropolitan, 103, 134, 135
Milford Plaza, 440, 754
Millennium U.N. Plaza, 734
Murray Hill, 579
New Netherland, 237
New Yorker, 456, 730, 829
Novotel, 774
Oliver Cromwell, 440
1-2-3, 241
Pabst, 263, 292
Palace, 852
Panhellenic, 440
Paramount, 440
Paris, 465
Park Avenue, 187, 240
Park Central, 432
Park Lane, 409, 704
Park Royal, 424
Park-Sheraton, 543
Park Wald, 237
Parker Meridien, 759
Peninsula, 297, 795, 859
Pennsylvania, 382
Pierre, 456, 512
robbery, 709
Plaza, 310, 311, 369, 577, 603, 692
Regency, 651
Renaissance, 268
Rihga Royal, 807
Ritz-Carlton, 327, 586, 768
Ritz-Carlton Battery Park, 879
Roosevelt, 409, 834
Royal, 233
Royalton, 254
Russell, 543
Salisbury, 456
Savoy-Plaza, 433
Sevillia, 237
Shelton Towers, 409, 813
Sheraton Centre, 644
Sheraton City Squire, 639
Sheraton hotels, 543
Sheraton Motor Inn, 644
Sheraton New York, 644
Sherry-Netherland, 424, 521, 726
single-room occupancy, 795, 807, 813, 818, 829, 834
Sofitel, 869
SoHo Grand, 840
St. George, 212, 447
St. James, 135
St. Moritz, 456
St. Nicholas, 105, 128, 132, 135
St. Regis, 293, 304, 447, 814
Stanhope, 424
Stevens House, 392
Sweets, 89
Taft, 425

Theresa, 348
Times Square, 409, 829
Trump International, 691, 850
United Nations Plaza, 734
Vanderbilt, 340, 663
Vista International, 759, 823
Waldorf, 237, 238
Waldorf-Astoria, 255, 465, 487, 572, 585, 734
Wales, 293
Warwick, 440
Westin, 768, 879
Windsor, 172, 263
Woman's, 110
Woodward, 287
Houdini, Harry, 240, 338, 346, 374, 421
House and Garden magazine, 356
House, Col. Edward M., 335
house finch, 525
House of Refuge, 63, 79
House Un-American Activities Committee, 557, 561, 563, 573
Houseman, John, 484, 504, 534
housing, 110, 131, 134, 140, 147, 194, 268, 387, 446, 486, 493, 512, 519, 531, 557, 562, 600, 610, 644, 650, 704, 734, 784, 807, 850
Mitchell-Lama, 620, 727, 779
Housing and Urban Development (HUD), Dept. of, 663
Hoving, Thomas, 670, 678, 707, 724
Hoving, Walter, 666
Howard Beach, 760, 780, 786
Howard, Bronson, 161, 187, 190, 199, 210, 217
Howard, Elston, 605, 609, 620
Howard, Eugene, 339, 352, 375, 387, 396, 437, 484, 491, 517, 661
Howard, Ken, 713, 794
Howard, Leslie, 386, 396, 406, 414, 444, 469
Howard, Roy W., 307, 411, 459, 575, 653
Howard, Sidney, 390, 406, 414, 420, 477, 484
Howard, Willie, 339, 352, 375, 387, 396, 437, 445, 461, 484, 491, 517, 571
Howe, Elias, 145
Howe, Irving, 731, 748
Howe, Richard, Admiral, 32, 33, 36
Howe, Tina, 766, 783
Howe, William, Gen., 32–34

Howe & Hummel, 169, 171, 172, 181, 187, 196, 197, 208, 219, 220, 233, 236, 240, 242, 279, 285, 291, 297, 302, 308, 309, 314
Howell, James, 250
Howells, Wm. Dean, 225, 243, 248, 315, 385
Howland, G. G., 56, 72, 94, 100
Howland, S. S., 56, 72, 94, 105
Hoy, 856
Hoyt, Charles, 232, 236
Hoyt, Edwin P., 641
Hoyt, John Sherman, 370
Hoyt, Waite "Schoolboy," 392, 430
HRH Construction, 850
Hubbard, Gardiner, 184
Hubbell, Carl, 479, 504
Hubbell, Raymond, 296, 302, 352, 357, 368, 407
Hudson Guild settlement house, 242
Hudson River Day Line, 69, 404, 700
Hudson River RR, 95, 100, 109, 136, 145, 153
Hudson & Manhattan RR, 289, 300, 312, 318, 321, 324
Hudson Terminal Building, 321
Hudson River, 1, 32, 36, 60
bathing in, 161
Erie Canal and, 63
ferries on, 55
steamboats on, 52, 55, 67, 100, 127, 272, 343, 404
sturgeon in, 255
tunnels, 289, 312, 426
Hudson, Henry, 1
Hughes, Barnard, 719, 805
Hughes, Charles Evans, 298, 311, 322, 359
Hughes, Ellen, 90, 95
Hughes, Hatcher, 406
Hughes, Howard R., 508
Hughes, John Archbishop, 78, 80–83, 86, 98, 104, 104, 132, 137
Hughes, Langston, 406, 419, 428, 469, 477, 483, 541, 565, 576, 612, 623, 675
Hulce, Tom, 800
Hull, Dorothy, 450
Hull, Henry, 395, 406, 450, 477, 503
Hull, Josephine, 496, 529, 613
Hull, Lytle, 542
Hume, William H., 182
Humes, Harold L. "Doc," 632
Hummel, Abraham, 219, 236, 240, 279, 285, 291, 297, 302, 308, 309, 314, 422

Hungarian Legion, 125
Hunt, Joseph, 543
Hunt, Walter, 69, 96, 121
Hunt, Washington, 97, 102
Hunter, Alberta, 401, 772
Hunter College, 153, 344, 351,
    459, 522, 674
    UN and, 552
Hunter, Evan, 598, 608, 702,
    737, 862
Hunter, Glenn, 444
Hunter, Holly, 758, 771
Hunter, Jim "Catfish," 726, 745,
    863
Hunter, Kim, 559, 598, 877
Hunter, Robert, 21
Hunter's Point, 156, 802
Huntington, Anna Hyatt, 618
Huntington, Archer M., 300,
    368, 601
Huntington, Collis P., 145,
    203
Hunt's Point Market, 678, 864
Hupfeld, Herman, 461, 470
Hurok, Sol, 719
hurricanes, 238
    Donna, 633
    Floyd, 864
Hurst, Fannie, 357, 371, 374,
    395, 721
Hurston, Zora Neale, 419, 502,
    596
Hurt, William, 771
Huston, Anjelica, 800
Huston, John, 529
Huston, Walter, 406, 437, 511
Hutchinson, Anne, 6
Huthmacher, J. Joseph, 682
Hutson, Jean Blackwell, 564,
    757
Hutton, Barbara, 452
Hutton, Betty, 524
Hutton, Timothy, 806
Huxtable, Ada Louise, 695, 726,
    731, 759
Hwang, David Henry, 794, 857
Hyatt, Anna Vaughn, 357
Hyde, James Clarence, 278
Hylan, John F., 364, 371, 374,
    377, 389, 390, 411, 467
Hyman, Phyllis, 758
Hynes, Charles, 786

Iacocca, Lee, 808
Ian, Janis, 668
IBM, 403, 475, 606, 635, 686,
    756, 820, 830
    building, 768
ice, 200, 250
Ice Capades, 776
Ice Trust, 250, 270

ice cream,
    Häagen-Dazs, 626
    Louis Sherry, 392
ice skating, 249
Ickes, Harold L., 495
Ideal Toy Co., 279
Il Corriere d'America, 493
Il Progresso Italo-Americano,
    196, 319, 436, 493, 527,
    793
immigration, 64, 93, 102, 174,
    197, 200, 212, 215, 217,
    223, 227, 230, 238, 241,
    256, 280, 293, 311, 334,
    359, 371, 376, 383, 388,
    389, 393, 398, 410, 526,
    591, 606, 663, 786, 796,
    808, 824, 841
    Castle Garden and, 111
    Dillingham Act, 393
Impellieri, Vincent R., 573, 574,
    580, 586
incandescent bulb, 189, 192
incinerators, 212, 678, 808, 840,
    864
income tax, 129, 133, 166, 238,
    242, 342, 431, 527, 540,
    597, 665, 722
Independents exhibition, 367
Index Medicus, 189
Industrial Workers of the World
    (IWW), 328
In fact, 522, 575
infanticide, 150
inflation, 9, 127, 553, 617, 717,
    742, 747, 752, 755, 765,
    770, 809
Inge, William, 576, 593, 603,
    613
Ingersoll, Raymond V., 473,
    519
Ingersoll, Robert G., 178
Ingoldesby, Richard, 15, 20
Ingram, Rex, 524
Inman, Henry, 72, 90
Innaurato, Albert, 738
Institute of Public
    Administration, 305
In Style magazine, 827
Insull, Samuel, 198
insurance companies,
    American International
        Group (AIG), 417, 782
    Atlantic Mutual, 83
    Continental, 105
    Eagle, 51
    Equitable Life, 120, 129, 293,
        295, 638, 775
        buildings, 161, 340, 347,
            358
    Guardian Life, 123
        building, 333

Health Insurance Plan (HIP),
    545
Home, 104
Home Life, 123
    building, 241
Johnson & Higgins, 88, 107
Manhattan Life, 98, 241
Metropolitan Life, 148, 189,
    237, 321, 409, 423, 505,
    525, 562, 581, 596, 754
    tower, 321
Mutual of America,
    building, 834
National Reinsurance, 51
New Amsterdam Casualty Co.,
    463
New York Life, 67, 439, 557,
    586, 710
Prudential, 175
Travelers Group, 820, 843, 853
Travelers Insurance, 815, 820
United Insurance, 40
United States Life, 98
Interborough Rapid Transit Co.
    (IRT), 277
Interborough Parkway, 495
International Center of
    Photography, 358, 725
International Debutante Ball,
    595
International House, 409
Internatl. Ladies' Garment
    Workers' Union
    (ILGWU), 264, 311, 317,
    323, 336, 342, 359, 466,
    504, 644
International Longshoremen's
    Assn., 578, 592
International News Service
    (INS), 301
International Rescue
    Committee, 473, 581
Internet, 831
Ireland, 355
    agriculture in, 135
    "Black and Tans" in, 383
    emigration from, 135
    Sinn Fein in, 383
Irish Echo, 436
Irish Emigrant Society, 82, 98
Irish World and Industrial
    Liberator, 160
Irish, 17, 38, 53, 58, 66, 67, 72,
    75, 89, 93, 101, 106, 111,
    156, 157, 196, 224, 269,
    359, 633, 699, 808
    crime among, 110
    death rate among, 103
Irish Arts Center, 708
Irish, Ned, 485
Irish Hunger Memorial, 877
Iroquois, 1, 10, 17, 29, 49

Irvin, Monte, 585
Irvin, Rea, 706
Irving, Amy, 827
Irving, Washington, 52, 54, 60,
    84, 116, 121, 164, 210
Irwin, Elisabeth, 390, 468, 534
Irwin, May, 248
Irwin, Will, 301, 313, 564
Isaacs, Stanley M., 446, 454,
    521, 563
Iselin, Adrian, 203
Iselin, Philip, 732
Islanders hockey team, 708
Ismay, Thomas H., 149
Israeli-Palestinian conflict, 824
Israel, 657
Italian consulate, 370
Italian Cultural Institute, 376
Italians, 125, 139, 159, 174, 269,
    349, 388, 412, 487, 793
ITT, 436, 612
Ives, Burl, 603
Ives, Irving M., 596
Ivey, Dana, 788
Ivey, Judith, 811, 862
Izquierdo, Elisa, 830
Ivins, William M., 293

Jack Rose cocktail, 341
Jackson Heights, 348, 366, 464
    Bulova Corporate Center in,
        797
Jackson, Anne, 565, 594, 654
Jackson, Anthony, 731
Jackson, Arthur, 386
Jackson, Charles, 545, 682
Jackson, Kenneth C., 831
Jackson, Kenneth T., 877
Jackson, Mahalia, 578
Jackson, Milt, 589, 863
Jackson, Reggie, 739, 745
Jacob, Polly, 353 (see also
    Crosby, Caresse)
Jacobi, Abraham, 124, 149, 168,
    602
Jacobi, Lou, 667
Jacobi, Mary Putnam, 168
Jacobi, Victor, 381
Jacobs, Harry Allan, 392, 423
Jacobs, Helen Hull, 470, 478,
    485, 492
Jacobs, Jane, 634, 638, 721, 782
Jacobs, Robert Allan, 567
Jaffe, Rona, 618
Jaffe, Sam, 450, 504
Jagger, Mick, 654
jails, 2, 5, 27, 32, 47, 58, 63, 69,
    76, 79, 99, 208, 790
Jamaica Bay, 360
Jamaica Bay Wildlife Refuge, 710
Jamaica Racetrack, 285, 551, 624

James, Arthur Curtiss, 205, 334, 354, 370, 434
James, D. Willis, 325
James, Harry, 518
James, Henry, 176, 196
Jarmulovsky, Meyer, 338
Jarmulowsky, Sandor, 217
Janis, Byron, 571
Janis, Elsie, 302, 320, 339, 362, 414, 492, 609
Japanese, 533, 755
Japanese American Assn., 349
Jarvis, John, 81
Jauncey, William, 38
Javits, Jacob K., 552, 606, 678, 679, 706, 723, 751, 780
   Convention Center, 784, 833
   Federal Office Bldg., 677
Jay, John, 35, 36, 39–42, 44–47, 49, 66
Jay's Treaty, 45
jay walking, 343
   La Guardia on, 495
jazz, 369, 546, 589
Jeffers, Robinson, 559
Jefferson, Joseph, 124, 159
Jefferson, Thomas, 42, 51–53
   statue of, 352
Jefferson Courthouse Market, 184, 448, 852
Jeffries, Leonard, Jr., 803, 809
Jehovah's Witnesses, 617, 646
Jencks, Penelope, 838
Jencks, Francis M., 226
Jenkins, Gordon, 556, 571
Jennings, Louis, 162
Jennings, Oliver Gould, 263
Jens, Salome, 618, 654
Jerome Avenue, 133
Jerome Park Racetrack, 143
Jerome, Jerome K., 261
Jerome, Leonard W., 133, 136, 143, 174, 185, 227
Jerome, William, 240
Jerome, Wm Travers, 270, 273, 278, 279, 286, 291, 296, 297, 301, 302, 308, 309, 480
Jerries, James J., 262
Jervis, John B., 78, 85, 169
Jessel, George, 400, 414, 452, 536
Jesup, Morris K., 195, 228, 312, 313
Jessye, Eva, 492
jet aircraft, 621
Jeter, Derek, 868
Jeter, Michael, 800
Jett, Joseph, 825
Jewett murder, 75
Jewish Child Care Assn., 60, 533

Jewish Daily Forward, 252, 337, 423, 515
Jews, 8, 22, 64, 88, 98, 103, 174, 195, 197, 217, 252, 254, 275, 283, 367, 506, 563, 657, 695, 748, 814 (see also Lubavitchers, Satmars)
Jewish Board of Guardians, 390
Joan of Arc statue, 357
Joel, Billy, 726, 745, 750, 763, 767, 822, 878
Joffrey, Robert, 609, 795
Joffrey Ballet, 609
Johansson, Ingemar, 624, 632
John, Elton, 753
John, Tommy, 759
John Jay College of Criminal Justice, 602, 674, 712, 793
John Street, 22
Johns, Glynis, 713
Johns, Jasper, 603, 612, 618, 623, 630, 642, 647, 653, 689, 719, 725, 731, 752, 766
Johns Manville, 119
Johnson, Alvin S., 394
Johnson, Andrew, 147
Johnson, Billy, 561
Johnson, Eastman, 119, 261, 301
Johnson, Howard E., 357, 391, 530
Johnson, J. Rosamond, 262
Johnson, James Weldon, 262, 338, 365, 395
Johnson, John Taylor, 112
Johnson, Lyndon B., 645, 652, 653, 660, 663, 669, 679, 710
Johnson, Nunnally, 555
Johnson-Reed Act, 410
Johnson, (Wm.) Samuel, 27
Johnson, Van, 517, 550
Johnson, Sir William, 24–26, 29, 31
Johnston, James Boorman, 115
Johnston, Mary, 319
Johnston, Moffat, 395, 437, 477
Johnston, Robert C., 733
Jolson, Al, 332, 361, 375, 381, 382, 391, 414, 429, 445, 478, 577
Jones Beach, 442
Jones, Candy, 629
Jones, Cleon, 691, 714
Jones, George, 205
Jones, Henry Arthur, 301
Jones, Isham, 369
Jones, James Earl, 682, 788
Jones, J. Raymond, 616, 808
Jones, Jonathan "Jo," 777
Jones, LeRoi, 654
Jones, Margo, 550, 555

Jones, Preston, 731
Jones, Tom, 631, 668
Jones, Tommy Lee, 753
Joplin, Scott, 308, 369
Jorgen, Robert, 778
Jorgensen, Spider, 561
Joselit, Jenna Weissman, 805
Joseph, Rabbi Jacob, 275
Josephson, Barney, 511, 525, 561, 795
Journal of Commerce, 65, 128
Jovanovich, William, 629, 874
Joyce, James, 476
Joyce, Peggy Hopkins, 613, 618
Joyce Theater, 763
Judd, Donald, 827
Judge magazine, 196
Judson, E.Z.C. "Ned Buntline," 168, 215
Julia, Raul, 703, 763
Juilliard, Augustus D., 170, 231, 377
Juilliard Quartet, 556
Juilliard School of Music, 296, 306, 683
Jumbo, 200
Jumel, Stephen, 53
Junior League, 268, 432, 446
junk bonds, 765
Juvenile Court, 263
juvenile crime, 704

Kael, Pauline, 874
Kafka, Barbara, 760
Kahal, Irving, 430, 511, 530
Kahane, Meir, 803
Kahn, Gus, 362, 391, 396, 438, 445, 583
Kahn, Madeline, 744, 817
Kahn, Otto, 251, 375, 376, 450, 464, 475, 481, 482
Kaiser, Charles, 846
Kalikow, Peter S., 793, 807, 821
Kalman, Emmerich, 362, 429
Kalman, Tibor, 864
Kalmar, Bert, 400, 437, 438
Kaltenborn, H.V., 443, 506, 659
Kaminska, Ida, 753
Kander, John, 643, 661, 668, 683, 725, 739, 745, 758, 772, 822, 847
Kane, Art, 619
Kane, Helen, 437, 668
Kanin, Garson, 490, 554, 631, 862
Kaplan, J.M., Fund, 557, 787
Kaplan, Jacob M., 480, 631, 787
Kaplan, Stanley H., 558, 770
Karloff, Boris, 529
Kassner, Fred, 585
Kasznar, Kurt, 624, 648

Katharine House, 327
Katz's Delicatessen, 221, 538
Kauff, Benny, 369
Kauffman, Elaine, 651
Kaufman, Andy, 744
Kaufman, Bel, 653
Kaufman, George S., 380, 390, 395, 400, 406, 408, 414, 415, 428, 438, 445, 450, 451, 469, 472, 478, 484, 496, 503, 504, 510, 516, 524, 546, 555, 636
Kaufman, Irving R., 581
Kaufman, Mel, 698
Kaufman, Sue, 675
Kay, Connie, 589, 828
Kayden, Jerold S., 867
Kaye, Danny, 529, 530, 555, 697
Kaye, Stubby, 609
Kazan, Elia, 477, 503, 559, 560, 599
Kazan, Lainie, 713, 812
Kazin, Alfred, 528, 582, 659, 743, 805, 856
Keach, Stacy, 675
Keane, Doris, 301, 406
Keating, Kenneth B., 616
Keaton, Diane, 708, 738, 744, 749, 822
Keck, Charles, 502, 565, 576
Keeler, Ruby, 444, 445, 478, 822
Keeler, Wee Willie, 262, 268, 285, 401
Keely, Patrick Charles, 72
Keene, Laura, 110, 112, 171
Kefauver Committee, 580
Kefauver, Estes, 574
Keitel, Harvey, 732, 771
Keith, B.F., 196, 202, 215, 346
Keller, Charlie, 518, 537
Kelley, Forence, 264
Kellogg, Junius, 858
Kelly, Al, 667
Kelly, Ellsworth, 612, 647
Kelly, Gene, 517, 524, 570
Kelly, George, 406, 414, 496, 719
Kelly, John, 106, 148, 162, 179
Kelly, Kitty, 400, 428
Kelly, Nancy, 503, 576
Kelly, Paul, 559, 576
Kelly, Patsy, 429
Kelso, James J., 162
Kempton, Murray, 602, 647, 712, 731, 827
Kemys, Edward, 202
Kendall, Messmore, 381
Kennedy, Adrienne, 642
Kennedy, Arthur, 570, 593, 682
Kennedy, John F., 627, 631, 633, 645
   Jr. 861

Kennedy, Joseph P., 481, 547
Kennedy, Robert F., 671, 678, 679
Kennedy, Stephen P., 606, 625, 634
Kennedy, William, 766
Kenney, Alice B., 724
Kensett, John F., 92, 160, 168
Kent, William, 400, 451
Kenyon, Doris, 357
Kern, Jerome, 332, 352, 353, 357, 362, 368, 369, 375, 387, 396, 407, 414, 430, 445, 461, 470, 478, 517, 551
Kernan, Francis, 166, 178
kerosene, 109
Kerouac, Jack, 551, 565, 593, 612, 838
Kerr, Deborah, 594, 725
Kerr, Jean, 571, 598, 636, 712
Kerr, Walter, 571, 838
Kerrigan, J.M., 406
Kesselring, Joseph, 529, 675
Kessner, Thomas, 737, 799
Ketana Yeshiva, 793
Ketchum, Richard M., 877
Keteltas, William, 46
Kew Gardens, 327, 358, 495
    Grand Central Parkway and, 475
kewpie doll, 320
Key Food, 506
Keystone Kops, 352
Kheel, Theodore, 564
Khrushchev, Nikita, 627
Kidd, William, 15–18
Kieft, Willem, 4–6
Kiehl's, 101
Kiley, Richard, 595, 642, 661, 738
Kilgallen, Dorothy, 494, 577, 659
Kilgour, Joseph, 319
kindergartens, 65, 318
King George's War, 25
King, Billie Jean, 676, 703, 720
King, Carole, 703
King, David H., Jr., 229
King, Dennis, 395, 407, 414, 437, 510, 703
King, John Alsop, 111, 113, 144
King, Martin Luther, Jr., 616, 671, 679, 685
    memorial sculpture, 712
King, Moses, 248
King, Rufus, 42, 45, 66
Kingsbridge Armory, 370
Kings County, 13
Kingsland House, 31
Kingsland, Ambrose C., 97, 98, 185

Kingsley, Sidney, 477, 490, 541, 570, 832
Kingsley, William M., 205
Kings Plaza Shopping Center, 837
Kingston, 36
Kinkead, Eugene, 805
Kinney Services, 637, 641
Kirby, Rollin, 466
Kirk, Grayson L., 680
Kirk, Lisa, 560
Kirk, Russell, 602
Kirkland, Jack, 689
Kirkland, Muriel, 437, 444, 450, 702
Kirkwood, James, 396
Kirstein, Lincoln, 484, 556, 839
Kirtzman, Andrew, 873
Kisseloff, Jeff, 799
Kissinger, Henry, 747
Kitchen, The, 708
Kitt, Eartha, 589
Klaw & Erlanger, 220, 284
Klaw, Marc, 220, 248, 267, 497
Klein, Carole, 788
Klein, Joel I., 876
Klein, Murray, 586, 715
Klein, Robert, 817
Kline, Adolph L., 342
Kline, Franz, 576, 623, 642
Kline, Kevin, 744, 749
Kluge, John W., 592, 776
Klugman, Jack, 613, 624
Knapp Commission, 692, 705
Knapp, Joseph F., 301, 331
Knickerbocker Ice Co., 110, 200, 250, 472
    fire, 557
Knickerbocker Laundry Building, 472
Knickerbocker magazine, 72
Knight, Sarah Kemble, 19
Knight, Charles, 783
Knights of Labor, 215, 218
knishes, 328
Knoblock, Edward, 332
Know-Nothing Party, 106
Knox Hat Co., 78, 276, 312
Knox, Philander C., 276, 342
Kober, Arthur, 503
Kobrin, David, 701
Koch, Edward I., 679, 686, 700, 736, 745, 748, 754 755, 760, 764, 769, 771, 774, 775, 780, 783, 796, 797, 800, 817, 826, 845, 871
Koch, Howard, 510, 529
Koch, John, 612, 675, 744
Koch, Kenneth, 593, 737, 877
Koehler, Ted, 451, 470
Koehler, V. Hugo, 338
Koeppel, Gerard T., 867

Kohlmann, Anthony, 52
Kollmar, Richard, 511
Konigsburg, E.L., 675
Koosman, Jerry, 690, 714
Kopit, Arthur, 642, 749, 763
Koreans, 385, 674, 728, 747, 792, 803, 808, 835
Korean War, 573
Korein, Sarah, 875
Kosciuszko, Thaddeus, 35
kosher foods,
    Hebrew National and, 298
    Ratner's and, 298
    Schechter case and, 487
Koslo, Dave, 585
Kotsoni, Nicola, 769
Koufax, Sandy, 649
Kouwenhoven, John A., 593, 782
Kovaks, Ernie, 587
Kovi, Paul, 715
Kramer, Jack, 556, 561
Kramer, Larry, 765, 786
Kramm, Joseph, 496
Kranepool, Ed, 691
Krasna, Norman, 546, 771
Krasner, Lee, 450, 523, 559, 593, 598, 603, 608, 630, 731, 744, 752, 757, 766, 771
Kraus, Nicola, 874
Kravis, Henry R., 729, 835
Krehbiel, Henry E., 193, 400
Kreisler, Fritz, 381
Kriendler, H. Peter, 563, 875
Kriendler, Jack, 457, 563
Krishna Consciousness, 658
Kriza, John, 566
Krock, Arthur, 718
Kroeger, Brooke, 827
Kroessler, Jeffrey A., 873
Kruger, Otto, 357, 414, 428
Krupa, Gene, 713
Krutch, Joseph Wood, 695
Kubek, Tony, 614
Kuhn, Fritz, 538
Ku Klux Klan, 406, 410
Kummer, Clare, 285, 361, 368, 618
Kunhardt, Rudolph, 183
Kunstler, William, 830
Kunz, Gray, 814
Kurtz, Swoosie, 696, 753, 800
Kurtzman, Harvey, 587
Kushner, Tony, 822

Laas, William, 659
labor, 68, 70, 97, 113, 261, 328, 336, 359, 482, 548, 562, 616, 641, 657, 680, 701
Labor Day, 198
labor disputes, 50
Lachaise, Gaston, 345, 489

Kohlmann, LaCoste, René, 422, 430, 438
Ladies' Home Journal, 318, 695
Ladies' Mile, 175, 186
Laemmle, Carl, 319, 339
La Farge, Christopher, 289
La Farge, John, 115, 128, 160, 191, 223, 325
Lafayette, marquis de, 38, 61, 63, 67
Laffer, Arthur, 755
La Grange Terrace, 72
La Guardia, Fiorello H., 372, 425, 440, 466, 473, 481, 482, 486, 487, 493–495, 499–501, 503, 505, 506–509, 513, 518, 521, 526, 532–534, 537–540, 542, 544, 545, 547, 549, 553, 557, 562, 615
    slot machines and, 485
La Guardia Community College, 700
Lahr, Bert, 429, 438, 484, 491, 517, 518, 546, 675
Laing, Hugh, 536, 546, 551, 584, 795
Lake Erie, Battle of, 55
Lake George, Battle of, 26
Lake Shore & Michigan Southern, 171, 145
Lamb, Arthur J., 268
Lamont, Thomas W., 392, 540, 545, 563, 672
LaMotta, Jake, 561
Lancaster, Clay, 635, 675
Landau, Martin, 800
Landau, Sarah Bradford, 838
Landis, Kennesaw Mountain, 397
Landmarks Preservation, 662, 677, 764, 807
Lane, Burton, 461, 530, 560, 661, 848
Lane, Nathan, 767, 874
Lang, Eugene M., 681, 756, 798
Lang, George, 728
Lang, Harold, 566, 583
Langella, Frank, 725, 738
Langner, Lawrence, 648
Langtry, Lillie, 200
Lankevich, George J., 856
Lansbury, Angela, 654, 668, 690, 749
Lansky, Meyer, 375, 382, 438, 479, 493, 537, 697, 714, 767
Lantz, Walter, 326
Lapine, James, 789, 818
La Prensa, 344, 564
Larchmont, 18
Lardner, James, 867

Lardner, Ring, 396, 437, 445, 477
Jr., 758
Larimore, Earle, 420, 428, 437, 469, 484, 560
Larrimore, Francine, 390
Larsen, Arthur, 578
Larsen, Don, 609, 619, 620
Larsen, Nella, 436, 443, 653
Larsen, Roy E., 748
LaRusso, Louis, II, 749
Lascoff, J. Leon, & Son, 261
Lasker, Albert D., 541, 588
Lasky, Jesse L., 346
Lasser, Louise, 702
Las Vegas casino, 848
Latin Kings, 833
Latham, Hope, 319
LaTouche, John, 524, 555, 609
Latting Observatory, 108
Lauder, Estée, 556
Lauder, Leonard, 556, 655, 797
Lauper, Cyndi, 767
Laurelton Parkway, 495
Laurents, Arthur, 550, 588, 624
Laurie, Joe, Jr., 599
Lavagetto, Cookie, 530
Laver, Rod, 643, 690
Lavezzo, Daniel H., Jr., 579
Lavin, Linda, 668, 689, 783
Law & Order (TV), 806
Lawes, Lewis E., 382, 562
Lawrence, Carol, 613, 637
Lawrence, Cornelius Van Wyck, 71, 73–75
Lawrence, Gertrude, 414, 421, 438, 451, 503, 516, 529, 583, 588
Lawrence, Jacob, 528, 612, 667, 719
Lawrence, James, 55
Lawrence, Jerome, 608
Lawrie, Lee, 483
Lawson, John Howard, 413
Lawson, Louise, 228
Lazarus, Emma, 146, 215
Lazarus, Moses, 165
Lazio, Rick, 865
Lazzeri, Tony, 422, 471, 498
Leachman, Cloris, 598
lead-based paint, 227
Leaf, William H., 252
Lear, Norman, 702
Lebowitz, Fran, 743
Lebewohl, Abe, 600, 840
Lebewohl, Jack, 840
Lebow, Fred, 619, 828
LeClerq, Tanaquil, 536, 556, 567, 584
Le Coze, Gilbert, 786
Led Zeppelin, 690
Leder, Lawrence H., 636

Lederer, Joseph, 724
Lee, Basil, 541
Lee, Canada, 529, 546, 555, 588
Lee, Fran, 746
Lee, Gideon, 70, 71
Lee, Gypsy Rose, 536, 612, 624
Lee, Ivy, 351, 483
Lee, James T., 409
Lee, Michele, 713
Lee, Richard Henry, 31
Lee, Spike, 800, 817, 828, 857, 863
Leetch, Brian, 823
Lederer, Francis, 469
Lefcourt, Abraham E., 462, 472, 439, 446
Lefferts Homestead, 39
Lefkowitz, Louis J., 634
Lefrak, Harry, 650
LeFrak, Sam, 650
Legal Aid Society, 179
Le Gallienne, Eva, 374, 420, 555, 609
Leggett, William, 73
Lehman, Arthur, 365
Lehman, Herbert H., 440, 466, 473, 475, 480, 493, 506, 513, 521, 533, 634, 646, 616
Lehman College, 688
Village, 650
Lehman, Irving, 466
Lehman, Robert, 687
Lehn & Fink, 207
Lehrman, Lewis E., 760
Leibman, Ron, 753, 777, 794, 822
Leigh, Carolyn, 599, 613, 631, 643, 676, 767
Leigh, Douglas, 476, 528, 564, 730, 771, 861
Leigh, Mitch, 661
Leighton, Margaret, 636
Leisler, Jacob, 14, 18, 226
Lemlich, Clara, 317
Lemann, Nicholas, 811
Lemmon, Jack, 599, 604, 631, 631, 696, 708, 725, 744
Lemon, Bob, 745, 868
Lenape, 2
Lendl, Ivan, 777, 783, 789
L'Engle, Madeleine, 642
Lenihan, Winifred, 374, 400, 654
Lennon, John, 654, 686, 690, 697, 708, 753, 754, 779
Leno, Jay, 744
Lenox Hill, 37, 80
Lenox, James, 80, 160, 167
Lenox, Robert, 37, 80
Lenya, Lotte, 504, 529, 599, 668, 758
Leonard, Benny, 369, 561
Leonard, Eddie, 530

Leontovich, Eugenie, 450, 477, 541, 822
Lerner, Alan Jay, 560, 583, 609, 631, 661, 690, 783
Lerner, Max, 816
Lerner, Michael, 366, 742
LeRoy, Warner, 670, 735, 865, 875
LeRoy, Mervyn, 469, 570
Leslie, Frank, 107, 164, 180, 192
Leslie's Illustrated, 107, 110, 117, 124
Leslie, Lew, 648
Letterman, David, 822
Leutze, Emanuel, 137
Levant, Oscar, 570, 594
Levene, Sam, 469, 484, 490, 503, 542, 707, 753
Lever House, 590, 764
Levi, Maurice, 314, 320
Levin, Gerald M., 816, 850, 866
Levin, Ira, 603, 675, 744
Levin, Jennifer, 784, 795
Levin, Jonathan M., 850
Levin, Michael, 803
Levine, Dennis B., 775, 781
Levine, James, 725
Levitt, Arthur, 634, 751
Jr., 628
Levitt, Saul, 623
Levitt, William, 563, 828
Levittown, 563, 615
Levy, Gustave L., 729
Levy's Bakery, 221, 651
Lewis, Alfred Henry, 273
Lewis, David Levering, 757
Lewis, Augusta, 148, 152, 163, 185
Lewis, Edna, 568
Lewis, Francis, 29
Lewis, Joe E., 702
Lewis, Morgan, 50, 55, 59
Lewis, Robert, 559
Lewis, Salim L., 742
Lewis, Sam M., 375
Lewis, Sinclair, 380
Lewis, Ted, 381, 391, 703
Lewisohn Stadium, 374
Lewisohn, Adolph, 172, 374, 507
Lewisohn, Irene, 502
Lewisohn, Leonard, 357
Lexington Avenue, 75, 628
Lexington School for Deaf, 674
Lexow Committee, 241
Leypoldt, Frederick, 142, 168, 189, 192, 207
Liberty Weekend, 780
Liberal Party, 544, 729
Liberty League, 481
Liberty Travel, 585
libraries, 5, 22, 26, 27, 46, 214, 247, 846

Astor, 94, 108
Brooklyn Public, 253, 295
Carnegie and, 272
Free Circulating, 207, 272
Lenox, 243, 348
Mercantile, 60, 67, 108, 160, 476
Morgan, Pierpont, 301, 405
New York Public, 207, 272, 243, 331, 677, 695, 724, 818, 838, 856, 877
Internet and, 831
Library of the Performing Arts, 660
Mid-Manhattan, 695
Schomburg Center, 413, 419
Society, 26, 46, 101, 502, 588
Tilden, 214, 243
Lichtenstein, Grace, 720
Lichtenstein, Roy, 636, 647, 667, 719, 725, 783, 846
Lie, Trygve, 552
Lieber, Jerry, 643
Liebling, A.J., 509, 593, 647
Liebmann, Samuel, 111
life insurance, 148 (see also insurance)
Life magazine, 202
LIFE magazine, 495, 707
Life Savers, 519
Lighthouse, The, 344
Lillie, Beatrice, 407, 414, 461, 469, 470, 491, 546, 613
Lima, José, 603
Liman, Arthur L., 706, 748, 774, 843
Limbaugh, Rush, 826
Limon, José, 561, 708
Limpus, Lowell L., 509, 516
Lincoln, Abraham, 122, 129, 135, 150, 316, 453
statue of, 565
Lincoln, Mary Todd, 135
Lincoln Building, 439
Lincoln Square, 304
Lincoln Square Community Council, 734
Lincoln Center, 623, 643, 660, 683, 697
Avery Fisher Hall, 713
New York State Theater, 654
Lincoln Tunnel, 501
Lind, Jenny, 99, 164
Lindbergh, Charles A., 426, 486, 526, 717
Linden, Hal, 696, 725
Lindenthal, Gustav, 318, 366, 488
Lindsay, Howard, 484, 497, 517, 550, 682

Lindsay, John V., 657, 664, 665, 671, 672, 678–681, 686, 691–693, 699, 700, 701, 705, 706, 736, 751, 865
Linn-Baker, Mark, 771
Linotype machine, 207, 214, 331, 743
Linsky, Jack, 416, 556, 752
Linz, Phil, 655
Lionel trains, 268
Lionni, Leo, 630
Lipper, Kenneth, 788, 789
Lippmann, Walter, 337, 351, 718
Lipski, Donald, 817
Lipstick Building, 784
Litchfield, Edwin C., 143, 212
Litchfield, Edwin, 88
Litchfield, Electus, 212
Literary Guild, 427, 483
Lithgow, John, 794
lithography, 60
litterbugs, 620
Little, Christopher, 776
Little, Cleavon, 719, 777
Little Egypt, 249
Little Red Lighthouse, 389, 535
Livermore, Jesse L., 299, 306, 312, 410, 441, 481, 521
Livingston, Edward, 51, 74
Livingston, Peter V., 31
Livingston, Philip, 31
Livingston, Robert R., 28, 31, 61
2nd, 31, 35, 41, 42, 45, 52, 55
Livingston, Robert, 13–15, 19, 21, 22
Livingston, William, 26
Livoti, Francis X., 825, 835, 853
Lizana, Anita, 504
Lloyd, Harold, 421
Lober, Georg, 608, 623
Locke, Bessie, 318, 587
Lockhart, Gene, 477
Lockman, Whitey, 585
Lockwood, Charles, 707, 731
Lockwood, Sarah M., 419
Loco-Focos, 73, 75, 76, 86
Loden, Barbara, 654, 753
Loeb, Carl M., 458, 600, 601
Loeb, John Jacob, 543
Loeb, John L., 458
Loeb, John M., 747
Loehmann, Frieda M., 384
Loesser, Frank, 566, 577, 609, 637, 690
Loew, Marcus, 380, 407, 429
Loew, William G., 472
Loewe, Frederick, 560, 583, 609, 631, 794
Loews Corp., 380, 624
Loewy, Raymond, 428, 590

Logan, Ella, 503, 517, 530, 536, 560
Logan, Joshua, 565, 599, 794
Logue, Edward J., 685, 745
Lois, George, 612
Lombardo, Carmen, 543
Lombardo, Guy, 445
London, Herbert I., 803
Lonergan, Lenore, 529, 546
Long, Avon, 555, 703, 732, 772
Long, John Luther, 278
Long, Sumner Arthur, 643
Longman, Evelyn Beatrice, 370
Long Island City, 156, 366, 409, 579
Long Island Expressway, 601
Long Island Lighting Co., 574
Long Island Rail Road, 69, 134, 143, 145, 149, 158, 192, 266, 294, 324, 366, 418, 440, 553, 793
    Amtrak and, 876
    shooting on, 823
Long Island University (LIU), 418
longshoremen, 215, 548, 578, 592
Longworth, Alice Roosevelt, 204, 303, 544
Look magazine, 502, 701
    building, 579
Loomis, Arphaxed, 93
Loomis, Alfred Lee, 442
Loos, Anita, 559, 758
Lopat, Eddie, 571, 585
Lopate, Leonard, 798
Lopate, Phillip, 724, 846
Lopez, Hector, 637
Lopez, Jennifer, 878
Lorca, Federico García, 523
Lord, Pauline, 390, 406, 577
Lord, Walter, 603, 877
Lorillard, P., 42, 333, 416
Lorraine, Lillian, 320, 326, 339, 352
Lortel, Lucille, 599, 738, 744, 862
Lossing, Benson J., 205, 207
lottery, 27, 672
Loudon, Dorothy, 745, 758
Louis, Joe, 497, 518, 525, 556
Louis, Morris, 636
Louise, Tina, 595
Love, Edmund G., 612
Lovejoy, Frank, 642
Lovelace, Sir Francis, 12
Lovelace, John, Lord, 19
Low, A.A., 80, 86, 95, 119, 123, 133, 140, 145, 148, 234, 253
Low, Seth, 198, 222, 228, 234, 250, 251, 253, 270, 275, 281, 359

Lowell, Josephine Shaw, 179, 198, 207, 210, 213, 218, 223, 238, 242
Lowell, Robert, 554, 583, 647, 654, 660, 737
Lowenstein, Allard K., 679, 753
Lower East Side, 67, 96, 105, 194, 218, 225, 245, 268, 269, 274, 283, 298, 456, 457, 486, 499, 521, 620, 715
Lowi, Theodore, 653
Loy, Myrna, 484, 497, 822
Lubavitchers, 522, 549, 575, 582, 824, 826
Lucas, Craig, 805
Luce, Clare Boothe, 510, 517, 520, 591, 788
Luce, Henry R., 399, 450, 496, 674, 799
Luchese, Thomas, 677
Luciano, "Lucky," 462, 479, 493, 498, 537, 556, 644
Luckman, Sid, 498, 512, 858
Ludlow, Thomas W., 88, 94, 95, 185
Ludlow massacre, 349
Ludwig, Daniel K., 494, 815
Ludwig, Ken, 817, 832
Lukeman, Augustus, 358
Lukemeyer, Henry, 172
Luks, George, 307, 477
Lumbard, J. Edward, 433
Lunt, Alfred, 380, 428, 738
Lukas, Paul, 529
Lumet, Sidney, 504, 613
Lund, John, 550
Lunt, Alfred, 477, 490, 496, 523, 554, 618
Luongo, Pino, 769, 803
Lustig, Florence, 710
Lyle, Sparky, 739
Lyman, Susan Elizabeth, 653
Lyme Disease, 724
Lynch, Walter A., 574
Lyons, Eugene, 602
Lyons, James J., 473, 664
Lyons, Leonard, 732
Lynch, Denis Tilden, 428
Lysol, 337

Ma, Yo-Yo, 654
Maas, Peter, 688, 712, 846, 874
MacArthur, Charles, 380, 437, 477, 608
MacArthur, Gen. Douglas, 580, 581, 651
MacAusland, Earle, 531
Macchiarola, Frank J., 742
Maccioni, Sirio, 721

MacDonald, Anne, 582
MacDonald, Ballard, 381, 400, 492
MacDonald, Jeanette, 415, 437
MacDonald, J. Wilson, 164, 184, 228
Macdonough, Thomas, 55
MacDowell, Edward, 208
Macfadden, Bernarr, 269, 379, 405, 602
Mack, Edward C., 570
Mack, Cecil, 400
Mackay, Clarence H., 435, 509
Mackay, J.W., 202, 214
Mackaye, Milton, 483
Mackaye, Steele, 240
Mackintosh, Millicent C., 558
MacLeish, Archibald, 618
Macklowe, Harry, 778, 791
MacMonnies, Frederick, 236, 258, 284, 304, 331, 395, 502
MacNeil, Herman A., 244
Macready, William C., 96
Macri, Jim, 600, 614
Macy's, 117, 123, 133, 141, 145, 152, 170, 173, 183, 218, 274, 265, 276, 343, 362, 393, 404, 426, 459, 501, 611, 775, 815, 825, 830, 849
    and Federated, 825
Mad magazine, 587
Madden, Owney, 401, 430, 48, 471, 478, 526, 662
Mademoiselle magazine, 515
Madison Avenue, 75, 628, 666
Madison Square, 79
    Eternal Light in, 406
    Park, 786
    Farragut statue in, 196
    sculpture in, 707
Madison Square Garden, 173, 184, 190, 208, 225, 233, 259, 266, 305, 353, 377, 415, 430, 634, 669, 683, 826
    concerts at, 708
    fire, 275
    gambling at, 584
Madison, James, 40, 41, 43, 52, 54, 55
Madonna, 794
Mafia, 408, 462, 537, 585, 590, 614, 626, 632, 691, 703, 709, 745, 750, 770, 778, 784, 789, 790, 813, 816, 823, 849, 868
Magnes, Judah L., 324
Maglie, Sal, 600
Magnum Photos, 559, 873

magnetic resonance imaging (MRI), 765
Mahican tribe, 5
mah-jongg, 396
Mahoney, Jeremiah T., 500
Mahoney, Tom, 666
Mailer, Norman, 565, 622, 632
Main, Marjorie, 496
Maine Memorial, 334
Major Deegan Expressway, 606
Makemie, Francis, 19, 21
Malamud, Bernard, 588, 667, 701, 783
Malcolm X, 587, 653, 657, 659
    Boulevard, 657
Malden, Karl, 503, 559, 599
Malkiel, Theresa, 325
Malkovich, John, 762, 788
Mallory, Molla Bjurstedt, 391
Malone, Dudley Field, 363
Malone, Maud, 293
Mamet, David, 731, 738, 794, 847
Manca, Albino, 630
Mandel, Henry, 370, 397, 416, 433, 454, 464, 537
Mandelbaum, Seymour, 659
Mandlikova, Hana, 777
Manes, Donald R., 780
Mangano, Philip, 585
Mangano, Vincent, 585
Manhattan, 1, 2
    population of, 259 (1898)
    street numbering in, 78
Manhattan Beach, 185
Manhattan Cable TV, 695
Manhattan Center, 724
Manhattan College, 105, 399, 812
    basketball and, 571, 584
Manhattan Company, 47, 48
Manhattan Elevated Railway, 197
Manhattan Institute, 741, 819
Manhattan Mall, 797, 830
Manhattan Opera House, 302
Manhattan Schist, 49, 69, 106, 209, 376
Manhattan Theater Club, 708
Manhattan Transfer (rock group), 758
Manhattanville College, 82
Mann, Arthur, 622, 659
Mann, Barry, 643
Mann, Horace, 216
Manners, J. Hartley, 313, 338
Manners, William, 731
Mannes College of Music, 381, 490, 595, 772
Mannes, David, 187, 262, 326, 361, 381, 624
Mannes, Leopold D., 490
Mannes, Leopold Damrosch, 654

Mannes, Marya, 593, 701, 805
Manning, Bishop, 390, 569
Manocherian, Amir, 785
Manocherian, Eskandar, 785
Manoff, Dinah, 753
Man Ray, 386
Mansfield, Richard, 225, 254, 308
Manship, Paul, 483, 610, 636
Mantle, Burns, 565
Mantle, Mickey, 585, 589, 605, 609, 632, 637, 655, 676
Manumission Society, 38
Maples, Marla, 823
Mara, Jack, 662
Marantz, Irving, 689
Marbe, Fay, 381
Marble, Alice, 498, 511, 518, 525
Marcantonio, Vito, 568, 596
March of Dimes, 508
March for Equality, 700
March, Fredric, 451, 516, 535, 583, 608, 636, 713
Marchi, John J., 686, 711
Marchant, William, 604
Marciano, Rocky, 599, 605
Marcus, James L., 672, 685
Marcus, Peter, 390
Marcy, Wm. L., 68, 69, 76, 78, 100, 113
Margittai, Tom, 715
marijuana, 505
Marin, John, 319, 338, 345, 593
Maris, Roger, 637
Marisol, 811
Mark, Mary Ellen, 689
Markel, Lester, 399, 737
Markey, Enid, 380, 496
Marley, Bob, 713, 758
Marlowe, Julia, 261, 319, 577
Marquard, Rube, 333, 339
Marqueta, La, 521
Marquis, Don, 428
marriage, 320, 739
Married Women's Property Act, 93
Marrow, Alfred, 616
Marsalis, Wynton, 763, 772
Marsh, Mae, 346
Marsh, Reginald, 450, 460, 469, 496, 545, 598
Marshall, E.G., 593, 599, 613
Marshall, Herbert, 460, 469
Marshall, Louis, 275, 299, 323
Martí, Jose, 221, 242
Martin, Agnes, 630, 636, 642
Martin, Billy, 595, 745, 801
Martin, Hugh, 583
Martin, Mary, 511, 517, 529, 542, 555, 571, 599, 624, 668
Martin, James J., 241
Martinson's Coffee, 259

Martiny, Philip, 308, 390
Marvel Comics, 635
Marx Brothers, 415, 438
Marx, Karl, 113, 115
Mary Celeste, 167
Marymount Manhattan College, 495
Mason, James, 570
Masseria, Joe, 462
Massey, Raymond, 510, 618
Mason jar, 119
Mason, Cyrus, 89
Mason, Jim, 732
Mason, John L., 119
Mason, Marsha, 712, 758
Maspeth,
    fertilizer factory in, 172
Masses, The, 331
massage parlors, 677
Massengale, John, 765
Masson, Charles, 645
Masson, Gisèlle, 645
Masterson, Bat, 277, 390
Maternity Center Association of
    New York, 373
Mathewson, Christy, 268, 273, 285, 297, 333, 339, 347, 415
Matlack, Jon, 714
Matthau, Walter, 598, 660, 719, 725, 838
Matthews, David, 32
Matthews, Herbert L., 737
Matthiessen, Peter, 632
Matura, Mustapha, 822
Maugham, W. Somerset, 396, 420
Maurer, Alfred H., 406, 469
Maurin, Peter, 404
Maury, Reuben, 756
Mauzé, Mrs. Jean, 705
Maxwell, Elsa, 585, 649
Maxwell, Robert, 811
Maxwell, William, 502, 752
Maxwell, William H., 247, 257, 290, 385
Maxwell, William M., 816, 867
May Co., 781
May, Cornelis Jacobsen, 2
May, Elaine, 630, 857
Mayer, Edwin Justus, 450, 631
Mayer, Martin, 603, 617, 636, 675, 688, 805, 817, 821, 831
Mayflower Madam, 772
Mayor's Committee for Historic
    Preservation, 638
Mayor's Office of Film, Theatre
    & Broadcasting, 667
Mays, Carl, 392
Mays, Willie, 585

Mazet Committee, 260
Mazursky, Paul, 732
McAdoo, William Gibbs, 289, 300, 318, 321, 324, 350
McAlary, Mike, 784, 856
McAllister, Ward, 169, 203, 220
McAllister Bros., 136, 404, 694
McAneny, George, 513
McAvoy, John V., 404
McBain, Ed, 608, 702, 737, 862
McBurney, Charles, 232
McCall's magazine, 180
McCarran-Walter Act, 591
McCarthy, Eugene, 679
McCarthy, Joseph, 375, 381, 387, 400, 429, 543, 726
McCarthy, Sen. Joseph, 581
McCarthy, Mary, 535, 588, 603, 647, 701
McCartney, Paul, 697, 763
McCay, Winsor, 295, 483
McClellan, George B., Jr., 281, 289, 293, 305
McClendon, Rose, 460, 477
McClintic, Guthrie, 346
McCloskey, John Cardinal, 72, 82, 137, 176, 190, 211
McClure, S.S., 253, 569
McClure's magazine, 235, 253, 450
McComas, Carroll, 386
McClintic, Guthrie, 636
McCormick, Myron, 550, 571, 642
McCourt, Frank, 838
McCourt, Malachy, 651
McCoy, Rhody, 681, 688
McCracken, Joan, 551, 594
McCree, Junie, 278, 326, 375
McCullers, Carson, 576
McCullogh, David, 707, 757
McCutcheon, George Barr, 301, 436
McDermot, Galt, 676, 703, 708
McDermott, Alice, 856
McDormand, Frances, 817
McDougald, Gil, 585, 605
McEnroe, John, 750, 753, 759, 772
McFarland, Albert, 157
McFerrin, Bobby, 794
McGavin, Darren, 598
McGee, Frank, 718
McGill, Ralph, 619
McGillin, Howard, 777
McGinley, Phyllis, 744
McGiver, John, 631
McGoldrick, Joseph D., 742
McGrath, Diane, 774
McGraw, John J., 278, 291, 485
McGraw, Tug, 690, 714

McGraw-Hill, 219, 443, 665
  building, 463
McGuire, Michael, 707
McHugh, Frank, 758
McHugh, Jimmy, 429, 437, 451, 517, 566, 749
McKane, John Y., 218, 254
McKay, Claude, 386, 395, 436, 443, 565
McKay, Donald, 100, 103, 105
McKay, Ernest A., 805
McKay, Richard C., 483
McKee, Joseph V., 466
McKelway, St. Clair, 250, 523, 752
McKenna, Siobhan, 604, 612
McKesson & Robbins, 70
McKinley Tariff Act, 224
McKinley, William, 245, 256, 264, 270
McLaughlin, Emma, 874
McManus, George, 509
McNally, Terrence, 702, 719, 725, 772, 832, 822, 877
McNamara, Ed, 444
McNamara, Frank X., 579, 615
McNamara, John, 771
McNaughton, Harry, 400, 407, 429
McNaughton, Tom, 326
McNeil, Claudia, 623
McNeil, Donald, 525
McNickle, Chris, 821
McNulty, John, 607
McPartland, Jimmy, 812
McPartland, Marian, 584
McPhail, Larry, 551
McSorley's Old Ale House, 109, 693, 786
Mead, Margaret, 743
Meagher, Thomas F., 126, 131
Meara, Anne, 702, 753
Mechanics and Tradesmen, Society of, 258
Medford, Kay, 583, 595, 654, 667, 753
Medgar Evers College, 688
Medical College for Women, 130
Medical Society of State of New York, 52
Medicare, 653
Medina, Harold, 568
Medoff, Mark, 712, 753
Medwick, Joe, 530
Meek, Donald, 369
Meeker, Ralph, 593, 654
Meisner, Sanford, 406, 437, 491, 847
Mellins, Thomas, 788, 831, 862
Mellon, Paul, 663, 860

Melville, Herman, 90, 92, 101, 103, 105, 112, 115, 134, 142, 253
Menaker, Daniel, 856
Menken, Adah, 131
Menken, Alan, 763, 828
Menken, Helen, 490, 667
Menotti, Gian-Carlo, 555, 561, 584, 599
mental disease, 44, 52
Menuhin, Yehudi, 429
Mercer, Johnny, 452, 518, 555, 583, 604, 609
Merchant's Exchange, 84
merchants' exchange, 12
Mergenthaler, Ottmar, 207
Meredith, Burgess, 490, 503, 594
Merkel, Una, 594, 624
Merman, Ethel, 451, 461, 470, 484, 497, 518, 524, 542, 555, 577, 624, 772
Merrick, David, 523, 599, 867
Merrill, Bob, 613, 624, 637, 654, 683, 708
Merrill, Charles E., 350, 441
Merrill, Dina, 631
Merrill, Gary, 554
Merrill Lynch, 350, 441, 527, 606, 775, 876
Merritt Parkway, 514
Merritt, Theresa, 771, 857
Messier, Mark, 823
Messinger, Ruth, 842
methadone, 653, 717, 855
Merzbacher, Leo, 85, 88
Mesta, Perle, 425
Methodists, 143
MetroCard, 843
Metro-Goldwyn-Mayer, 407
Metroliner, 706
Metromedia, 592, 782
Metro-North, 765
Metropolitan Museum, 757, 783, 794
Metropolitan Opera, 202, 203, 215, 314, 375, 577, 668, 848
  Guild, 492
Metropolitan Transportation Authority, 591, 678, 706, 722, 723, 748, 752, 756, 765, 770, 793, 803, 804, 810, 815, 843, 866, 869
Metzger, Juan, 538
Meucci, Antonio, 97
Mexican War, 89
Meyer, André, 520, 747
Meyer, Annie Nathan, 222
Meyer, Cord, 172, 249
  II, 304
Meyer, Danny, 780

Meyer, Grace M., 618
Meylin, Cornelius, 2
Michaëlius, Rev. Jonas, 2, 4
Michelin guide, 685
Michener, James, 571
Mickle, Andrew H., 90
Microsoft, 756, 831
Middleton, Ray, 478, 555
Middleton, William D., 737, 838
Mielziner, Jo, 469, 696, 732
midwifery, 21
Milbank, Jeremiah, 117, 431
Milholland, Inez, 336
milk, 85, 277
  adulteration of, 112
  bottled, 191
  condensed, 102, 106, 111, 112, 117, 119, 128
  pasteurized, 233
  price of, 569
  railcars for, 85
Milken, Michael, 765, 793, 797, 803
Milkowski, Antoni, 707
Millais, John Everett, 200
Millay, Edna St. Vincent, 380, 385, 390, 399, 436, 483, 576, 637
Mill Basin, 11
Miller, Ann, 517, 566, 570, 749
Miller, Arthur, 559, 570, 593, 603, 608, 654, 682, 827
Miller, Barry, 777
Miller, Benjamin, 867
Miller, Gilbert, 420, 689
Miller, Glenn, 451, 511
Miller, Henry J., 225, 346, 374, 420
Miller, Jason, 707
Miller, Julius, 435
Miller, Marilyn, 352, 357, 375, 381, 387, 414, 437, 452, 478, 497
Miller, Nathan L., 383, 393
Miller, Penelope Ann, 777
Miller, Warner, 218
Miller, William Starr, 355
Millett, Kate, 693, 695
Milliken, Seth, 139
millionaires, 94, 158, 231
Millrose Games, 353
Mills, C. Wright, 632
Mills, Darius Ogden, 203, 255
Mills, Irving, 461, 478
Mills, Ogden L., 417, 501
Milstein, Morris, 704
Milstein, Paul, 663, 704, 754, 781, 785, 791, 850
Milstein, Seymour, 663, 704, 754, 781, 785, 860, 875
minimum wage laws, 410, 494, 507, 568, 835

Minnelli, Liza, 661, 739, 745, 749, 772
Minskoff, Edward, 768
Minskoff, Jerry, 713
Minskoff, Sam, 397, 409, 579
  & Sons, 568, 614
Minsky brothers, 338, 396, 400, 407, 461, 503, 571, 788
minstrel shows, 70, 86, 121
Minton, Henry, 511
Mintz, Norman, 862
Minuit, Pieter, 2, 4
Miramova, Elena, 541
Miranda, Carmen, 517, 530, 546
Mister Softee, 610
Mitchel, John Purroy, 342, 348, 351, 364
Mitchell, Arthur, 697
Mitchell, Charles E., 601
Mitchell, Grant, 296, 338
Mitchell, Joan, 603
Mitchell, John, 275
Mitchell, John Ames, 202
Mitchell, Joni, 676
Mitchell, Joseph, 541, 565, 630, 659, 838
Mitchell, Langdon Elwyn, 301
Mitchell, Lucy Sprague, 360, 379, 405
Mitchell-Lama housing, 620, 727, 779
Mitgang, Herbert, 647, 862
Mitzi E. Newhouse Theater, 660
Mizner, Addison, 308
Mizner, Wilson, 302, 308, 319, 325, 332, 338, 477
Mobil Oil, 330
Model, Lisette, 523, 618
modeling agencies,
  Conover, 515, 629, 659
  Ford, 554
  Powers, John Robert, 419
Modern Jazz Quartet, 589
Mohawk tribe, 6, 24
Moisseff, Leon, 318
Moley, Raymond, 465
Mollen Commission, 814, 825
Mollen, Milton, 814
Molnar, Ferenc, 588
Monckton, Lionel, 326
Monckton, Robert, 27
Mondrian, Piet, 541, 546
Money magazine, 707
money-market funds, 687, 694, 716
Monk, Debra, 806, 822
Monk, Thelonious Sphere, 511, 763
Monongahela decision, 237
Monroe, James, 67, 74
Monroe, Marilyn, 577, 589, 594, 600, 604, 608

Montalban, Ricardo, 613
Montebello, Philippe de, 744
Montegna, Joe, 794
Montez, Lola, 128
Montgomerie, John, 22
Montgomery, Dave, 273, 284, 302, 339
Montgomery, Robert, 758
Moody, Deborah, Lady, 6
Moody, John, 264, 617
Moody, Rick, 832
Moody, William Vaughn, 301
Moody's, 640
moon landing, 686
Moon, Sun Myung, 724
Moore, Archie, 605
Moore, Charles, 785
Moore, Clement Clarke, 57, 61, 63, 79, 89, 134, 454
   park, 685
Moore, Deborah Dash, 877
Moore, Frank, 757
Moore, Gene, 601, 603, 854
Moore, Grace, 387, 400
Moore, Sir Henry, 28, 29
Moore, Marianne, 406, 583, 707
Moore, Melba, 676, 696
Moore, Victor, 302, 308, 414, 421, 429, 438, 461, 478, 484, 524, 642
Moorehead, Agnes, 643
Moorhouse, Geoffrey, 794
Moran and Mack, 387, 491, 571
Moran, Edward S., 514
Moran Towing Co., 124, 133, 299, 366, 404, 534, 545
Moran, Thomas, 184
Morehead v. New York, 494
Morehouse, Ward, 494, 667
Moreno, Rita, 654, 725
Morgan, Anne, 317, 454
Morgan, Edwin D., 98, 117, 122, 132, 179, 201, 207
Morgan, Frank, 437
Morgan, Helen, 415, 430, 445, 461, 530
Morgan, Henry, 827
Morgan, J. Pierpont, 126, 149, 163, 186, 198, 204, 206, 217, 225, 229, 231, 232, 237, 242, 265, 343
   Jr., 384, 409, 488, 539
Morgan, Thelma, Lady Furness, 697
Morgen Zhornal, 272
Morgenthau, Henry, 335, 552
Morgenthau, Robert M., 640, 672, 798, 816, 818, 823
Moriarty, Michael, 806
Morley, Christopher, 380, 419
Morningside Heights, 679
Morning Telegraph, 80, 395

Morris, Andrew, 116
Morris, George Pope, 67, 90
Morris, Gouverneur, 34, 35, 37, 56
Morris, Howard, 577
Morris, Lewis, 19, 21
   II, 23, 24
Morris, Lewis Gouverneur, 355
Morris, Mark, 753, 806
Morris, Montrose W., 226
Morris, Newbold, 500, 506, 542, 548, 568, 603, 633, 657, 670
Morris, Robert H., 80–82, 85
Morris, Wm. Lewis, 86
Morris, William, 469
Morris, Willie, 821
Morris-Jumel mansion, 28, 53, 283
Morrison, Toni, 688
Morrisania, 12, 172
Morrissey, John, 169
Morrow, Doretta, 566, 583, 595
Morrow, Dwight W., 350, 458
Morse, Charles F., 270, 326
Morse, Charles W., 250, 264, 270, 277, 285, 369
Morse, Dolly, 391
Morse, Robert, 624, 637, 708
Morse, Samuel F.B., 64, 65, 69, 75, 77, 81, 84, 86, 121, 164, 168, 193
Morton, Levi P., 238, 384
Moscow, Henry, 743
Moscow, Warren, 565, 674, 701, 743, 811
Mosel, Tad, 630
Moses, Robert, 410, 442, 448, 449, 472, 475, 480, 486, 493, 495, 527, 532, 548, 549, 552, 553, 562, 563, 565, 586, 587, 600, 610, 612, 621, 623, 633, 634, 640, 646, 651, 655, 658, 678, 695, 721, 755
Mosholu Parkway, 219
Moskowitz, Belle, 317, 329, 349, 356, 372, 473
Moskowitz, Henry, 316, 329, 349
Mortimer, Lee, 561
Moss, Frank, 253
Most, Johann J., 210
Mostel, Zero, 525, 555, 586, 643, 654, 732, 749
Motherwell, Robert, 565, 811
motion pictures, 243, 248, 258, 319, 338
   cartoons, 325
   double features, 461
   Kinetoscope and, 236
   Kinetoscope parlor, 240
   sound and, 421, 429

Motley, Constance Baker, 745
Mott, Lucretia, 93
Mott, Stewart, 727
Mott Haven, 99, 215
Mott, Dr. Valentine, 114, 139
Mott, Valentine, 92, 95
Mount Eden, 60
Mount Sinai School of Medicine, Annenberg Building of, 717
movies (see motion pictures)
movie theaters,
   Beacon, 437
   Brooklyn Paramount, 451
   Capitol, 381, 386
   Guild, 510
   Little Carnegie, 791
   Loew's 175th Street, 451
   Loews Kings, 451
   Loews Paradise, 451
   Loews Pitkin, 451
   Loews 72nd Street, 470
   Loews State, 386
   Loews Valencia, 451
   Paramount, 421
   Radio City Music Hall, 470
   Rialto, 491
   Rivoli, 368
   Roxy, 429
   Sony Theaters, 828
   Strand, 352
   Thalia, 470
moving day, 69
Mowatt, Anna, 89
Mowbray, William E., 321
Moyer, Charles F., 446
Moynihan, Daniel Patrick, 647, 693, 729, , 792, 853, 865, 870
M'Robert, Patrick, 31
Ms. magazine, 706
MTV, 758
Muhlenberg, William A., 164
Muir, Malcolm, 748
Mulberry Bend, 218, 225
Mullaly, John, 204
Mulligan, Gerry, 839
Multiple Dwellings Act, 454
Mumford, Lewis, 405, 409, 431, 460, 509, 572, 638, 682, 762
Muni, Paul, 460, 517, 603
Municipal Art Society, 236, 565, 745, 754, 764, 821, 829
Municipal Assistance Corp., 722
municipal bonds, 410, 501, 792, 872
Municipal Building, 354
Municipal Ownership League, 289
Muñoz Marin, Luis, 520
Munsee tribe, 6

Munsey, Frank, 199, 228, 235, 47, 337, 338, 361, 379, 385, 399, 404, 412
Munshin, Jules, 570
Munson, Ona, 604
Munson, Thurman, 739, 750
Murdoch, Rupert, 730, 776, 782, 793, 805, 821
Murphy, Arthur H., 393
Murphy, Charles F., 264, 281, 298, 316, 328, 335, 341, 342, 372, 393, 420, 441
Murphy, Eddie, 800
Murphy, George, 478
Murphy, Gerald, 483
Murphy, Jack "Murph the Surf," 655, 662
Murphy, Michael J., 652
Murphy, Rosemary, 862
Murphy, Thomas F., 574
Murphy, Timothy, 36
Murray, Arthur, 415
Murray, Bill, 725
Murray, Don, 583
Murray, Elizabeth, 689, 707, 712, 731, 738, 744, 752, 757, 762, 766, 771, 776, 783, 788
Murray, Kathryn, 415
Murray Hill, 21, 33
Murray, Mary Lindley, 33
Murray, Robert, 33
Murray, Thomas E., 376
Murray's Sturgeon Shop, 552, 869
Murrow, Edward R., 516, 596, 641, 659
museums,
   American Craft Museum, 608
   American Folk Art Museum, 874
   American Museum of Natural History, 153, 183, 195, 228, 313, 488
      jewel robbery at, 655, 662
   Brooklyn, 63, 78, 86, 225, 228, 253, 413, 782
   Brooklyn Children's, 261, 730
   Children's of Manhattan, 798
   Cooper-Hewitt, 253, 730
   Frick Collection, 490, 738
   Guggenheim, 623, 625, 807
   Hispanic, 300
   Intrepid Sea, Air, Space Museum, 761
   Jewish, 315, 558
   Lower East Side Tenement, 793
   Metropolitan Museum of Art, 160, 168, 193, 219, 355, 460, 495, 621, 636, 670, 677, 724, 744
      American Wing, 752

Cloisters of, 509
Costume Institute of, 502, 559, 570
Hayden Planetarium of, 488
Historic District, 741
Sackler Wing, 748
Morris-Jumel mansion, 283
Museo del Barrio, 689
Neue Gallerie, 874
New York Transit, 810
of the American Indian, 300, 394, 611, 826
of Broadcasting, 724, 799, 811
of the City of New York, 399, 468, 503, 618, 743, 876
of Jewish Heritage, 804, 845
of Modern Art (MoMA), 444, 450, 469, 516, 576, 682, 771, 779, 877
of the Moving Image, 789
of Television and Radio, 724, 811
Queens Museum of Art, 707
Roerich, 443
Studio (Harlem), 682
Whitney, 460, 667, 768
Musical Mutual Protective Union, 296, 361, 391
Muslims, 810
Mutual Broadcasting, 482
Muzak, 525
Myers, Gustavus, 266, 273, 325
Myers, Margaret G., 460

NAACP, 316, 323, 365, 372, 513, 644, 710
Nagare, Masayuki, 707, 712
Naish, J. Carrol, 603, 604
Naldi, Nita, 636
Namath, Joe, 690
narcotics, 362
Naumburg Bandshell, 401
NASDAQ, 701, 760
and American Stock Exchange, 854
Nash, N. Richard, 598, 867
Nash, Ogden, 450, 542
Nast, Condé, 266, 318, 344, 356, 424, 468, 489, 535, 612, 742, 755, 765
Nast, Thomas, 128, 130, 142, 153, 160, 178, 197, 277
Nastase, Ilie, 709
Nathan, George Jean, 618
Nathan, Maud, 223
Nathan's Famous, 363, 829
Nation, The, 139, 196, 373
National Academy of Design, 65, 134, 176
National Assn. of Manufacturers, 360

National Audubon Society, 725
Natl. Cash Register, 282, 312
National Conference of Christians and Jews, 434
National Consumers League, 264
National Debt Clock, 797
national debt, 815
Natl. Endowment for the Arts, 660, 806
National Enquirer, 588
National Gay and Lesbian Task Force, 711
National Horse Show, 208
Natl. Industrial Recovery Act (NIRA), 487
National Inst. of Arts and Letters, 300
Natl. Labor Relations Act, 487
National Lead Co., 227
National Park Service, 363
National Reform Assn., 86
National Review, 602, 840
National Rifle Assn., 165
National Urban Coalition, 672
National Urban League, 299, 329, 405, 634
natural gas, 574, 694, 717, 798
Natwick, Mildred, 484, 496, 648
Naughton, James, 800
Nauman, Bruce, 675
Navigation Acts, 10, 16
Navratilova, Martina, 772
Nazimova, Alla, 460
NBC, 419, 427, 450, 460, 504, 641
NCAA, 302
Neagle, Anna, 414
Neal, Patricia, 555, 682
Nearing, Scott, 372
Nederlander, David, 675
Nederlander, James, 714
Nedick's, 348
Neel, Alice, 523, 696, 757, 771
Neff, Hildegarde, 604
Negro Ensemble Company, 667
Nehemiah houses, 773, 813
Neighborhood Playhouse, 357, 491
Neighborhood School of Theater, 437
Nelson, Barry, 636, 660, 725
Nelson, Richard, 817
Nesbit, Evelyn, 273, 303, 309, 357
Nesbitt, Cathleen, 576, 594, 599
Nestor, Agnes, 281
Netherlands Legion, 125
Nevelson, Louise, 623, 654, 794
Nevins, Alan, 565, 647
New Amsterdam (see Nieuw Amsterdam)
Newark, N.J., 11

Newcombe, John, 676, 714
Newfield, Jack, 794
Newhouse Publications, 752
Newhouse, S.I., 337, 612, 748, 776
Jr., 765, 787, 856
Newhouse, Ted, 856
New Jersey Turnpike, 582
Newley, Anthony, 661
Newman, Barnett, 554, 570, 588, 667, 675, 696
Newman, Paul, 594, 623, 758
Newman, Phyllis, 637, 783
Newmar, Julie, 604, 609
New Netherland, 11, 12
New Republic magazine, 351
New Year's Eve, 292, 445
newsboys, 106
Newsday, 646
Newspaper Guild, 602
newspapers, early, 24, 92
newspaper strikes, 646, 743
newspaper vending machines, 659
newsstands, 261, 344, 582, 629, 659, 787, 845
Newsweek, 475, 502, 636
Newton, David, 694
New Utrecht, 6–8, 13, 48
New York Academy of Medicine, 46, 92, 418
New York Academy of Sciences, 57, 635
New York Airways, 736
New York American, 243, 405
building, 431
New York & Harlem RR, 69, 70, 72, 77, 80, 82, 86, 94, 95, 114, 163
New York & Long Island RR, 277
New York & Queens County Railway, 283
New York & Sea Beach Rwy., 183, 251
New York Assn. for Improving the Condition of the Poor, 110, 117, 147
New York Barge Canal, 621
New York Bible Society, 54
New York Botanical Garden, conservatory in, 280
New York Central, 105, 153, 175, 182, 183, 210, 219, 227, 235, 260, 276, 282, 300, 330, 343, 382, 472, 482, 515, 597, 611, 617, 680
building, 446
commutation ticket fares, 563
grain elevator, 185
Twentieth Century Limited, 277, 673
Vanderbilt and, 145, 153

West Side terminal of, 183
Yale Club and, 358
New York Charities Commission, 179
New York City Ballet, 567
New York City Investment Fund, 835
New York City Opera, 542
New York City Transit Authority (NYCTA), 591
New York Clearing House, 104, 449
New York Cocoa Exchange, 747
New York Coffee and Sugar Exchange, 747
New York Commission on Human Rights, 711
New York Convention & Visitors Bureau, 492
New York Cotton Exchange, 158
New York County Court House, 422
New York Curb Exchange, 527
(see also American Stock Exchange)
New York Daily Mirror, 405, 482, 647
New York Daily News, 379, 385, 405, 500, 559, 647, 666, 757, 762, 805, 811, 820, 831, 846, 861
building, 453
WPIX, 569
New York Edison Co., 271, 289
New York Evening Mail, 404
New York Film Festival, 648
New York Gazette, 21, 22, 25
New York Genealogical Society, 155
New York Giants baseball, 278, 285, 291, 333, 339, 347, 369, 391, 397, 401, 408, 479, 498, 504, 585, 600, 619
New York Giants football, 415, 445, 485, 609, 789, 812
New York Graphic, 405
New York Harbor, 16, 215, 269, 666, 854
New York Herald, 73, 76, 82, 88, 124, 127, 155, 373, 385, 405
New York Herald Tribune, 405, 420, 551, 622, 640, 659, 666, 674
New-York Historical Society, 51, 65, 134, 192, 193, 313, 399, 509, 607, 783, 845
New York Infant Asylum, 138
New York Islanders, 753, 759, 763, 767
New York Jets, 643, 690, 732, 858

INDEX

New York Journal, 243, 252, 253, 257, 270
  building, 431
  Journal-American, 666
New York Knicks, 556, 567, 578, 676, 697, 714, 777
New York Lawn Bowling Club, 422
New York Law School, 228, 558
New York Ledger, 101, 261
New York Loan & Improvement Co., 226
New York Lung Association, 272
New York magazine, 681, 846
New York Marathon, 697
New York Marble Cemetery, 74, 80, 135
New York Mercantile Exchange, 166, 198, 527, 736, 742
New York Mets, 643, 649, 656, 690, 714, 759, 783
New York Nets, 720, 732
New York, New Haven & Hartford, 86, 94, 114, 163, 167, 276, 343, 617, 680
New York Observer, 788
New York Philharmonic, 84, 139, 211, 236, 258, 551, 613
New York Police (see Police Department)
New York Post, 25, 49, 73, 196, 202, 253, 373, 374, 515, 564, 659, 666, 730, 793, 821
  building, 438
New York Produce Exchange, 128
New York Public Library, 207, 331, 621, 677, 695, 724, 818, 838, 856, 877
  Donnell, 603
  Internet and, 831
  Library of the Performing Arts, 660
  Mid-Manhattan, 695
  Schomburg Center, 413, 419, 757
New York Rangers, 438, 478, 525, 823
New York Review of Books, 647
New York Road Runners Club, 619, 697
New York State,
  Australian ballot in, 221
  in Civil War, 132
  Supreme Court, 15
  Thruway, 607
  Urban Development Corp., 685
New York State Club Assn. v. City of NY, 792

New York Steam Co., 198, 494
New York Stock Exchange, 44, 58, 68, 125, 133, 134, 138, 242, 245, 305, 350, 425, 665, 729, 778, 804, 843
  building, 286
New York Sun, 78, 150, 199, 216, 253, 379, 399, 876 (new)
New York Sunday News, 390
New York Symphony Society, 262
New York Telegram, 146, 253, 373, 385, 404, 427
New York Telephone Co., 247, 301, 645, 720, 724
  building, 720
  Switching Center, 656
New York Thruway, 611
New York Times, 101, 128, 252, 292, 295, 344, 348, 399, 489, 500, 659, 666, 674, 695, 743, 770, 816, 821, 846
  Book Review, 331, 395
  Neediest Cases Fund, 330
  use of "Ms." and, 718
  v. Sullivan, 653
New York Titans, 624, 649
New York Tribune, 82, 98, 115, 168, 182, 193, 214, 252, 337, 400, 405
New York University (NYU), 69, 239, 246, 554, 712
  Bobst Library at, 706
  College of Dentistry, 139, 411, 611, 742, 787
  Gould Memorial Library of, 261
  Institute of Fine Arts, 340
  School of Medicine, 80, 611
  Tisch Hall at, 706
New York World, 124, 197, 202, 212, 214, 215, 226, 235, 247, 253, 295, 324, 331, 344
  fire, 200
New York World-Journal & Tribune, 674
New York World-Telegram, 459, 575
New York World-Telegram & Sun, 666
New York Yankees, 285, 347, 357, 387, 391, 397, 401, 422, 430, 438, 470, 498, 504, 511, 518, 530, 537, 543, 578, 585, 589, 595, 605, 609, 614, 619, 637, 643, 649, 655, 732, 739, 745, 759, 839
New York Zoological Society, 247, 263, 299, 313, 754, 755, 824

New Yorker, The, 411, 450, 516, 535, 576, 593, 668, 776, 787, 816
New Yorker Staats-Zeitung, 73, 272
New Yorkers Against Gun Violence, 833
Niagara Falls, 109
Niblo's Garden, 67, 131
Nicholas, Harold, 868
Nicholas Brothers, 497
Nichols, Anne, 396, 667
Nichols, Mike, 630, 794
Nichols, Red, 451
Nicoll, De Lancy, 230
Nicoll, William, 14
Nicolls, Mathias, 10–12 14
Nicolls, Richard, 11, 12
Niebuhr, Reinhold, 474, 581
Nieporent, Drew, 780
Niesen, Gertrude, 497, 546
Nieuw Amsterdam, 2, 7, 9, 10
  inflation in, 9
Nieuw Netherlands, 1
nightclubs, 401, 430
  Area, 767
  Billy Rose's Diamond Horseshoe, 492
  Blue Angel, 728
  CBGB, 713
  Club A disco, 763
  Café Society, 511, 525, 561
  Copacabana, 525, 631
  Cotton Club, 401, 430, 478, 497
  El Morocco, 462, 631, 632
  Latin Quarter, 536
  Limelight, 767
  Max's Kansas City, 668
  New York, New York, 739
  Nick's, 497
  Palladium, 777
  Regine's, 732
  Stork Club, 448, 480, 631, 663
  Studio 54, 739, 758
  Surf Club, 767
  Underground, 750
  Village Vanguard, 492, 612
  World, 767
Nimitz, Chester W., 548
Nin, Anaïs, 554, 636
92nd Street Y, 173
Ninth Avenue Food Festival, 715
Nissen, Thisbe, 877
Nixon, Richard M., 679, 701, 705, 716, 824
Noble, Edward J., 619
Noble, Ray, 461
Noeggerath, Emil, 149
Noguchi, Isamu, 620, 712, 794
noise pollution, 734, 841, 852
Noland, Kenneth, 623, 642

Norman, Dorothy, 428
Norman, Edward A., 428 551
Norman, Marsha, 766
Normand, Mabel, 346, 352
Norris-La Guardia Act, 466
Northern State Parkway, 475
North River Sewage Treatment, 791
Norton, Eleanor Holmes, 729
Norton, Thomas E., 771
Norwegians, 201
Norworth, Jack, 302, 314, 320, 510
NRA, 474
Nugent, Elliott, 523, 535, 541, 753
Nugent, Maude, 619
numbers racket, 627
nursing,
  Wald, Lillian, and, 234, 235
Nussbaum, Hedda, 786
Nuthall, Betty, 452
NY Waterway, 787
NYCE, 775
Nynex, 771, 845
Nyro, Laura, 668, 690, 703, 726, 732, 772, 800, 822, 848
Nystrom, Bob, 753

O'Brien, Jack, 659
O'Brien, John P., 466, 473
O'Brien, William T., 573, 574
O'Connor, Andrew, 496
O'Connell, Shaun, 831
O'Connor, Carroll, 702, 719
O'Connor, Frank, 664
O'Connor, John Cardinal, 765, 866
O'Donovan Rossa, Jeremiah, 157, 196, 355
O'Dwyer, Paul, 581, 616, 679, 853
O'Dwyer, Wm., 527, 531, 548, 557, 564, 568, 571, 573, 575, 580, 591
O'Hanlon, Virginia, 252
O'Hara, John, 483, 524
O'Hara, Maureen, 560
O'Keeffe, Georgia, 413, 420, 428, 444, 554
O'Keeffe, Michael, 758, 764
O'Malley, Walter F., 750
O'Neal, Patrick, 636, 656
O'Neill, Eugene,
  All God's Chillun Got Wings, 406
  Anna Christie, 390
  Beyond the Horizon, 386
  Bound East for Cardiff, 361
  Desire Under the Elms, 406
  Diff'rent, 390

Dynamo, 444
Emperor Jones, The, 386
Great God Brown, The, 420
Hairy Ape, The, 396
In the Zone, 368
Long Day's Journey into
    Night, 608
Long Voyage Home, The, 368
Marco Millions, 437
Moon of the Caribbees, The,
    374
Moon for the Misbegotten, A,
    612
Strange Interlude, 437
Welded, 406
O'Neill, James, 386
O'Neill, Rose Cecil, 320
O'Reilly, Leonora, 316
O'Rourke, Andrew P., 780
O'Shea, Milo, 690, 758
O'Sullivan, Maureen, 643
O'Sullivan, Timothy, 128
Ocean Hill-Brownsville schools,
    681
Ochs, Adolph S., 247, 252, 292,
    295, 330, 489
Odell, Benjamin B., 264, 275
Odell, George C.D., 428, 570
Odets, Clifford, 460, 477, 490,
    491, 503, 510, 576, 648
Oenslager, Donald, 496, 497,
    555, 594, 725
office vacancy rates, 840
Office of Price Administration
    (OPA), 527, 533, 537
Office of Strategic Services
    (OSS), 532
Off-Track Betting Corp. (OTB),
    703
Ogden, Aaron, 61
Ogilvy, David, 622, 861
Olcott, Chauncey, 262, 339
Oldenburg, Claes, 623
Olds, Sharon, 752
Oliver, Edna May, 368
Oliver, Sy, 795
Olivier, Laurence, 516
Olmo, Luis, 571
Olmsted, Frederick Law, 116,
    119, 121, 135, 143, 147,
    156, 173, 178, 179, 188,
    194, 287, 493, 678
Olnick, Robert, 791
Olsen and Johnson, 396, 510,
    530, 648
Olson, Ivy, 362
Olvany, George W., 457
Olympia & York, 710, 754, 823
Onassis, Aristotle, 740
Onassis, Jacqueline Kennedy,
    733, 740, 764, 828, 839,
    841, 855

Oneida, 35
one-way streets, 294, 360, 373,
    404, 426
Ono, Yoko, 686, 690, 697, 708,
    753, 779
Op Art, 660
Opatoshu, David, 594, 604
Opdyke, George, 120, 126, 132,
    133, 191
OPEC, 717, 748
Opera News, 492
ophthalmology, 207
opium, 148, 175, 193
    U.S. law and, 362
Orantes, Manuel, 726
Oratorio Society, 171, 229
Orbach, Jerry, 631, 636, 637,
    683, 702, 707, 725, 753,
    758
Orchard Beach, 493
Original Dixieland Jazz Band,
    369
Orkin, Ruth, 565, 570, 589, 777
Orlob, Harold, 430
orphan asylums, 111, 141
Orphan Asylum Society, 46, 51,
    52, 75, 260
Orteig, Raymond, 227, 280, 378,
    426
Osato, Sono, 536, 546
Osborn, Fairfield, 228, 263, 313,
    692
Osborn, Paul, 510, 517, 618, 794
Osborne, Danvers, 26
Osborne duPont, Margaret, 567,
    571, 578
Oscar of the Waldorf, 465
Osofsky, Gilbert, 666
Ostrowski, Stanislaw, 559
Osuna, Rafael, 649
Otis, Elisha G., 103, 108, 116, 128
Ott, Mel, 479, 498, 505
Ottendorfer, Anna, 127, 199
Ottendorfer, Oswald, 123, 127,
    206, 207
Ottinger, Albert, 433
Oullette, Christopher, 831
Outcault, Richard F., 239, 277,
    436
Outerbridge, Eugenius H., 389,
    435
Ovington, Mary White, 316, 581
Owen, Mickey, 530
Owen, Reginald, 437, 576
Owens, Buck, 697
oysters, 13, 99, 156, 340
Oz, Frank, 732

P-Flag, 711
Pace University, 300, 488, 558,
    582, 693

Pacino, Al, 689, 708, 713, 725,
    738, 763, 817, 822
Page, Geraldine, 598, 623, 762,
    788
Page, "Hot Lips," 599
Page, Joe, 561, 571
Page, Max, 862
Pahlman, William, 615
Paige, Satchel, 375
Paine, Thomas, 54
Paley, Barbara Cushing, 745
Paley, Grace, 622
Paley Park, 678
Paley, William S., 436, 663, 679,
    724, 782, 799
Palisades, 493
Palmer, Charles, 796
Palmer, Fanny Bond, 115
Pan Am, 398, 411, 426, 515, 516,
    810
    building, 649, 658, 736
Panama, Norman, 757
Panama Canal, 280, 311, 351
panhandlers, 835
Panken, Jacob, 679
paperback books, 516, 528, 535,
    549, 593
Papert, Fred, 612, 733
Papp, Joseph, 594, 616, 642,
    676, 806, 811
Parachute Jump, 518, 530
parades, 67 (see also ticker-tape
    parades)
    Columbus Day, 316
    Pulaski Day, 505
    St. Patrick's Day, 38, 103, 359,
        808
    Salute to Israel Day, 657
    Steuben Day, 620
    Thanksgiving Day, 558
    West Indian Day, 677
Paramount Pictures, 346, 381,
    429, 436
Parcells, Bill, 789, 858
Parent, Gail, 707
Parish, Mitchell, 478, 823
Park Avenue, 219, 300, 303, 336,
    398
    Association, 397
    Christmas trees on, 551
    food markets on, 521
    office buildings on, 567, 590,
        625, 633, 638, 649, 656,
        677, 698, 710, 733, 759,
        764, 768
    Social Review, 397
    traffic on, 426, 435
Park Avenue South, 625
Park Slope Food Cooperative,
    852
Park West Chapels, 485
Parker, Alton B., 287

Parker, Charlie, 511, 547, 561,
    578, 584, 589, 605
Parker, Dorothy, 380, 419, 454,
    460, 516, 598, 609, 653,
    675
Parker, Frank, 547, 551
Parker, Louis Napoleon, 248,
    325, 332
Parker, Mary-Louise, 806, 867
Parker, Painless, 252, 266
Parker, Suzy, 571
Parker, Willard, Dr. 139
Parkhurst, Charles H., 205, 230,
    399, 475
Parkhurst, Helen, 379, 712
parking, 673
    alternate-side parking, 575
    meters, 575
    Parking Violations Bureau
        scandal, 760, 780
    regulations, 621, 810, 826
parks, 80, 786
    Battery, 357
    sculpture in, 236, 319, 496,
        565, 630
    Bowling Green, 23
    Bryant, 93, 209, 486, 754, 818
    Carl Schurz, 181, 334
    Central (see Central Park)
    Clement Clark Moore, 685
    Clove Lakes, 425
    Columbus, 245
    dancing in, 518
    Flushing Meadow, 472, 519
    Flushing Meadows-Corona,
        678
    Fort Greene, 147, 311
    Fort Tryon, 493, 509
    Gateway National, 710, 802
    Gramercy, 68, 70
    Hamilton Fish, 268, 269
    Jacob Riis, 298, 506
    John Jay, 314
    Marcus Garvey Memorial, 80
    Mount Morris, 80, 110
    Pelham Bay, 220, 493, 498
    Prospect (see Prospect Park)
    Riverside (see Riverside Park)
    Seward,
        Pig Market in, 271
    St. John's, 52
    Straus, 358
    Stuyvesant, 77
    Tompkins Square, 54, 73, 172
    Van Cortlandt, 223
        golf course in, 249
    Washington Square, 47, 67,
        244, 587, 621
Parks, Suzan-Lori, 877
Parmet, Herbert, 675
Parrish, Maxfield, 667
Parsons School of Design, 696

Parsons, Wm. Barclay, 265, 277
Partridge, Wm. Ordway, 313, 352
Passaro, Vince, 877
Pastor, Tony, 139, 314
Pataki, George, 824, 836, 840, 845, 853, 855, 861, 876
Patco strike, 756
Patent Office, U.S., 43
Paterno, Charles V., 432
Paterno, Joseph, 432, 439
Paterno, Michael E., 424, 432
Pathfinder Mural, 799
Patinkin, Mandy, 738, 766, 772, 794, 812
Patrick, John, 550, 594, 832
Patrick, Saint, 27
Patrolmen's Benevolent Assn., 664, 699
Patterson, Alicia, 411, 522
Patterson, Floyd, 599, 613, 624, 632
Patterson, Jerry E., 743, 771, 856
Patterson, John H., 282, 312
Patterson, Joseph Medill, 379, 411, 453, 526, 554
Patti, Adelina, 121, 284, 285
Paulding, James Kirke, 52, 69
Paulding, William, Jr., 61, 79
Paulist Fathers, 118, 181, 219
paving, 9, 13, 20, 40, 42, 179, 206, 224
Pavonia Massacre, 5
Payne, John Howard, 55
Payne, Oliver Hazard, 206, 257, 303, 305, 333, 337, 365
Pavarotti, Luciano, 683, 822
Payson, Joan Whitney, 427, 444, 643, 726, 761
Payton, Philip A., Jr., 293
Peale, Norman Vincent, 588, 820
Pearce, Alice, 546, 566, 570, 571, 595
Pearl Harbor, 527
Pearl Street, 4
Pearson, Fred S., 235, 246
Pearson, Hugh, 877
Pearson, Monte, 511, 518
Pecora, Ferdinand, 574
peddlers, 7
Pegler, Westbrook, 568
Pei, Mario, 743
Pelham Manor, 11, 13
Pelham Parkway, 330
Pell, John, 11, 13
Pemberton, Brock, 576
Pender, John, 142
Pendleton Act, 201
Pendleton, Austin, 777
Penn Central, 680, 684, 694, 700
    yards, 829

Pennington, Ann, 347, 352, 357, 362, 381, 386, 391, 421, 437, 452, 461
Pennock, Herb, 401
Pennsylvania RR, 163, 182, 198, 266, 271, 324, 366, 515, 600, 628, 634, 680
    Broadway Limited, 277
Pennsylvania Station, 324, 366, 418, 553, 600, 605, 628, 634, 644, 645, 650, 669, 810
People magazine, 718
Pepsi-Cola Building, 633
Pereira, I. (Irene) Rice, 523
Perelman, Itzhak, 624, 648
Perelman, S.J., 443, 502, 542, 545, 576, 593, 612, 636, 748
Pérez, Loida Maritz, 862
Perkins, Anthony, 612, 749
Perkins, Frances, 329, 356, 473
Perkins, Maxwell, 443
Perkins, Osgood, 406, 437, 460, 496
Perlman, Alfred, 597
Perry, Antoinette, 308, 444, 555, 560
Perry, Fred, 478, 485, 555, 560
Perry, Jonah, 777
Perry, Matthew C., 117
Perry, Oliver Hazard, 55
Pershing Square, 377
Pershing, John J., 364, 371, 377
Pesce, Frank, 812
Pesci, Joe, 772, 812, 822
Peter, Paul & Mary, 643, 772
Peters, Bernadette, 683, 772, 789
Petersen, Don, 689
Petit, Phillipe, 720
Petrie, Milton J., 826
petroleum, 121, 133, 163
    Rockefeller and, 127
Petrosino, Joseph, 286, 320
Peyster, Abraham de, 248
Pfeiffer, Carl, 144, 177
Pfizer Inc., 95, 638
Pforzheimer, Carl H., 276, 611
Phelps, Dodge, 70, 105, 166, 201
Phelps, Elizabeth Wooster, 103
Philadelphia, Miss., 652
Philharmonic Hall, 643
Philip Morris, 279, 479
Philippe of the Waldorf, 746
Philippine Center, 726
Philipse Manor, 36, 147, 492
Philipse, Adolph, 18, 25
Philipse, Frederick, 10, 12, 16, 18
    II, 18, 23, 26 .
Phillips, David Graham, 319
Phillips, John S., 235

Phillips Milk of Magnesia, 176
Phipps, Henry Clay, 310, 334, 431, 449
Phoenix House, 673
Phoenix, J.P., 81, 82
phonograph records, 567
photoengraving, 177
photography, 81
    Abbott and, 502
    Brady and, 99, 112, 128
    halftones and, 193, 252
    International Center of, 358, 725
    Magnum Photos and, 559
    portrait, 177
Phyfe, Duncan, 44, 108
Physical Culture magazine, 379
Piaf, Edith, 609
pianos,
    Steinway and, 121
Picasso, Pablo, 696
Piccirilli, Attilio, 334, 345
Pickford, Mary, 319
Picon, Molly, 566, 637, 817
Pidgeon, Walter, 414, 624
Piel, Gerard, 554
Pike's Opera House, 150
pinball machines, 537
Piñero, Miguel, 719, 794
Pinkard, Maceo, 643
Pintard, John, 41, 51, 58
Pinza, Ezio, 524, 571, 599, 613
Pitcher, Nathaniel, 66
pizza, 245, 298, 410, 448, 480
Pizza Connection heroin case, 789
Planetarium, 584, 866
Planned Parenthood, 722
Plant, Morton F., 365
Plassman, Ernst, 168
plastic,
    credit card, 581, 617
    phonograph record, 567
Platt, Thomas C., 191, 194, 204, 218, 230, 238, 250, 264, 322
Playbill, The, 207
Playboy Club, 643
Plaza Accord, 775
Plaza Hotel, 310, 311, 369, 577, 603, 692
    Black & White Ball at, 669
Pleshette, Suzanne, 618
Plimpton, George, 593, 632, 636, 682
plumbing, 99
Plummer, Christopher, 618, 712
Plunkitt, George W., 281, 295, 403
Podhoretz, Norman, 629, 632, 682

Podres, Johnny, 605
Poe, Edgar Allan, 82, 84, 86, 88
Pogrebin, Letty Cotton, 695
Poitier, Sidney, 623
Poles, 125, 701
Police Department, 66, 87, 88, 91, 104, 113, 218, 241, 260, 298, 329, 349, 486, 580, 634, 664, 686, 692, 699, 703, 705, 765, 770, 774, 814, 825, 828, 835, 840–842, 853
    Aviation Unit, 572, 600
    Civilian Review Board, 591, 664, 780, 792, 819
    Harbor Patrol, 119
    Mollen Commission and, 814
    motor scooters of, 658
    Mounted Unit, 165
    numbers racket and, 627
    taxis and, 398, 411
Police Athletic League (PAL), 349
Police Gazette, 88
poliomyelitis, 360, 389, 482
    March of Dimes and, 508
Polish Legion, 125
polka, 87
Pollack, Lew, 415
Pollard, Calvin, 94
Pollia, Joseph, 496
Pollock v. Farmers' Loan, 242
Pollock, Channing, 396, 555
Pollock, Jackson, 541, 554, 559, 565, 570, 583, 588, 593, 598, 603, 608
Polo Grounds, 181, 229, 333, 347, 387, 656
Polytechnic University, 107, 153, 224, 272, 488, 617, 712, 776
Pomerantz, Sidney I., 509
Pondiac Democratic Club, 390
Ponselle, Rosa, 408
Ponte, Lorenzo da, 63–65, 72, 79
Poole, William "Butcher Boy," 110
Pooper Scooper law, 746
Poor, Anna Louise, 334
Poor, Henry Varnum, 144
poorhouses, 8
Pop Art, 618, 630, 636
Pope, Generoso, 436, 493, 527, 575
    Jr., 588
Pope, Virginia, 462, 745
Poppenhusen, Conrad, 107, 148, 150, 153, 159, 201
population, 11, 17, 19, 23, 28 (1765), 30, 35 (1776), 38, 43 (1790), 49 (1801), 55 (1811), 60 (1820), 67

(1827), 81 (1840), 92
(1847), 100 (1850), 124
(1860), 132 (1862), 194
(1880), 256 (1898), 269
(1900), 328 (1910), 388
(1920), 417 (1925), 457
(1930), 526 (1940), 580
(1950), 586 (1951), 633
(1960), 639 (1961), 699
(1970), 755 (1980), 808
(1990), 870 (2000)
Populist Party, 231
pornography, 674, 839
Porter, Cole, 339, 407, 438, 445,
452, 470, 484, 491, 497,
511, 517, 518, 524, 530,
542, 546, 566, 577, 594,
604, 654
Porter, Edwin S., 273, 278, 284,
308, 529
Porter, Fairfield, 725
Porter, Katherine Ann, 489
Porter, William Sydney (O.
Henry), 301, 307, 313,
319, 325
Port of New York, 61, 158, 265
Port of New York Authority, 389,
435, 450, 459, 607, 666,
709, 730, 770, 823, 833
and World Trade Center, 669
building, 471
bus terminal, 575
Porters, Sleeping Car, 410
Portman, Eric, 618
Post, Emily, 395, 424, 630
Post, Langdon W., 486
Post, Marjorie Merriwether,
424, 452, 531, 715
Post, Wiley, 459
Post, Wright, 40
Postal Life Building, 370
postal service, 695
Postal Telegraph, 214, 509
Potofsky, Jacob S., 747
Potok, Chaim, 675
Potter, Henry Codman, 219, 233,
313, 345
Potter, Howard, 104
Potter, Janet, 838
Potvin, Denis, 759
Pound, Arthur, 489
Powell, Adam Clayton, 633
Jr., 507, 527, 544, 606, 610,
616, 626, 627 633, 634,
645, 652, 664, 678, 679,
685, 693, 705
Powell, Charles Underhill, 358
Powell, Colin, 808
Powell, Dawn, 436, 483, 496,
523, 535, 622, 642, 660
Powell, Eleanor, 484, 497, 560,
763

power failures, 658, 736
Powers, John R., 737
Pratt Institute, 216, 427
Free Library, 247
Pratt, Charles, 163, 215–217, 227
Pratt, Harold I., 388
Preminger, Otto, 517
Prendergast, Maurice, 313
Prendergast, William, 360
Prentiss, Paula, 654
Presbyterians, 19, 21
Prescott, Orville, 838
Press, The, 207, 337
Pressman, Gabe, 607
Preston, James, 667
Preston, Robert, 529, 598, 613,
668, 789
Prettyman, Virgil, 611
Previn, André, 690
Prial, Frank J., 481
price fixing laws, 581
Price, George, 831
Price, Leontyne, 668
Price, Richard, 719, 817
Price, Vincent, 529
Primus, Pearl, 828
Prince, Harold, 794
Printer's Ink, 219
printing trade, 16
rotary press and, 90, 139,
160
prisons, 58 (see also Sing Sing)
Prison Ship Martyrs'
Monument, 311
Spofford, 704
The Tombs, 79
Pritchett, V.S., 653
prizefighting, 556
Procaccino, Mario, 686
Proctor, Samuel, 798
Produce Exchange, 208, 625
Profaci, Joseph, 614
Prohibition, 106, 111, 383, 388,
398, 403, 408, 425, 433,
457, 472, 480
crime in, 430
Prospect Park, 122, 143, 169
Botanic Garden in, 358
sculpture in, 164
skating rink in, 639
zoo in, 238, 824
prostitution, 31, 76, 84, 97, 122,
126, 131, 143, 155, 208,
240, 270, 408, 492, 543,
677, 748, 773
Prouty, Jed, 326, 352, 381, 608
Provident Loan Society, 238, 314
Provincetown Players, 361
Provoost, Samuel, 40
Pryce, Jonathan, 812
Pryor, Roger, 428, 469
public baths, 251, 268, 303

Public Broadcasting, 674, 689,
702
Public Education Assn., 239
public health, 18, 45, 46, 60, 95,
118, 130, 139, 141, 150,
159, 176, 228, 232, 245,
283, 372, 373, 390, 465,
530, 653
Public Housing Law, 519
public relations
Bernays, Edward, 379, 445
Byoir, Carl, 468, 482, 520, 612
Hill & Knowlton, 483, 737
Lee, Ivy, 351
Rubenstein, Howard, 593
Sonnenberg, Benj., 476, 743
Public School Athletic League,
285
public transit, 105
Public Works Administration,
512
publishers (book),
American Heritage, 598
Appleton, D., 79
Appleton-Century, 476
Atheneum, 622
Avon Books, 528
Bantam Books, 549
Bantam Doubleday Dell, 856
Barnes & Noble, 460
Bertelsmann AG, 813
Boni, Charles, 689
Century Co., 192
Cerf, Bennett, 413, 427, 577,
701
Crowell, Thomas Y., 180, 737
Crowell-Collier, 483
Crown, 805
Delacorte Press, 390, 731
Dell, 390
Dial Press, 405
Dodd, Mead, 160
Doran, George H., 313, 607
Doubleday & Co., 253, 267,
428, 483, 593, 731
Doubleday Anchor, 593
Doubleday, Doran, 428, 483
Doubleday, Frank Nelson, 483
Dover Publications, 528
Farrar and Rinehart, 443
Farrar, Straus, 554
Farrar, Straus & Giroux, 647,
701, 827
Funk & Wagnalls, 184
Golden Books, 827
Harcourt Brace, 379, 603, 630
Harcourt, Alfred, 598
Harcourt General, 874
Harper Bros., 57, 106, 154,
160, 176, 184, 635
Harper & Row, 635, 695, 701,
714, 737, 788, 805

HarperCollins, 805, 862
and Morrow, 862
Henry Holt, 142, 188, 379,
419, 629, 776
Holt, Rinehart and Winston,
629
Holtzbrinck, Verlagsgruppe
Georg von, 776, 827, 831
Hill & Wang, 607, 701
Klopfer, Donald S., 782
Knopf, Alfred A., 356, 629,
666, 771
Little, Brown, 682
Macmillan, 154, 257, 483,
635, 712, 826
McGraw-Hill, 319
Modern Library, 413, 427
New American Library, 559
Norton, W.W., 399, 419
Pantheon, 535
Pocket Books, 516
Popular Library, 535
Potter, Clarkson N., 874
Prentice-Hall, 345
Putnam, G.P., 75, 142
Random House, 427, 547,
629, 752, 754, 856
Scribner's, 90, 160, 164, 340,
345
Simon & Schuster, 405, 630,
696, 826, 827
St. Martin's Press, 588, 831
Street & Smith, 119
Viking Press, 413
Vintage Books, 629
Weybright & Talley, 667
Weybright, Victor, 667, 743
Western Publishing, 827
Wiley & Putnam, 92
Wiley, John, & Sons, 52, 75
William Morrow, 862
Workman, 674
Publishers Weekly, 168, 189,
207
Puck magazine, 180
building, 215
Puente, Tito, 561
Puerto Ricans, 526, 580, 596,
699, 717
Puerto Rico, 520, 586
Jones Act and, 364
labor in, 507
Pujo Committee, 342
Pulaski Skyway, 467, 488
Pulaski, Kazimierz, 505
Pulitzer, Joseph, 150, 202, 212,
214, 215, 222, 224, 231,
235, 238, 245, 247, 253
283, 293, 295, 324, 331,
344, 352, 459
fountain, 352
prizes, 283, 374

Pullman, Bill, 877
Pullman, George M., 118, 219
punk rock, 732
Purple, Samuel S., 92, 155
pushcarts, 251, 299
Push Pin Studios, 598
Putnam, Israel, 33
Puzo, Mario, 688, 862
Pynchon, Thomas, 647
Pythias, Knights of, 431

Quakers, 9, 10, 40, 64, 146
Quantum Fund, 711, 747, 775
Queen Anne's War, 20
Queens,
    Auburndale in, 274
    blizzard and, 692
    Cambria Heights in, 403
    Douglaston in, 8, 23, 58, 74,
        141
    Elmhurst Shopping Mall in,
        711
    Els in, 366
    Forest Hills in, 304, 495
    Fresh Meadows in, 557, 572,
        710
    house numbering in, 358
    Jackson Heights in, 348, 366
    Kew Gardens in, 327, 358, 495
    Lefrak City in, 455
    Macy's in, 658
    parks in, 472, 519, 678
    parkways in, 475
    Rego Park in, 402, 440, 495,
        568
    subways and, 306, 356, 366,
        467, 495, 501, 602, 606,
        617, 793, 798, 826
    Sunnyside in, 409
    Woodside in, 366
    parks in, 678
    zoo, 685
Queens Borough Hall, 531
Queens College, 502
Queens-Midtown Tunnel, 514,
    521
Queensborough Community
    College, 617, 742
Queler, Eve, 676
Quill, Michael J., 488, 564, 665,
    666
Quinn, Aidan, 862
Quinn, Edmond T., 361, 374,
    428
Quinn, Roseann, 714
Quindlen, Anna, 811, 827, 856
Quintero, José, 862

Rabe, David, 707, 731, 771, 738
Racing Form, 395

radio (wireless), 427, 788
    all-news programming, 659
    commercials, 394
    Sarnoff and, 337
    Tesla and, 219
    U.S. set ownership, 405
    WABC TalkRadio, 826
    WBAI, 629
    WEAF, 394, 405, 419
    WEVD, 427
    WFAN, 788
    WINS, 405, 659
    WJZ, 392, 394
    WNBC, 405
    WNEW, 612
    WNYC, 411, 482, 509, 522,
        534, 549, 701, 724, 748,
        826, 845
    WQXR, 497
Radio City Music Hall, 470, 477,
    478, 708, 744, 777, 802,
    848, 863
Radner, Gilda, 725
Raesly, Ellis S., 549
Ragni, Gerome, 812
ragtime, 332
Ragú Sauce, 506
railroads, 86, 94, 114, 855
Raines Law, 298
Rainger, Ralph, 444, 537
Raitt, John, 551, 599
Ramírez, Carlos D., 799, 861
Ramone, Dee Dee, 732
Rand, Paul, 489, 635, 838
Randall, Bob, 707
Randall, Robert R., 49
    statue of, 202
Randall, Thomas, 49
Randall, Tony, 613, 847
Randalls Island, 4, 39, 99, 153,
    511
Randolph, A. Philip, 410, 440,
    527, 747
Randolph, Willie, 739
Ranelagh Garden tavern, 28
Rangel, Charles B., 693, 716
Ranhofer, Charles, 131, 174
Raphaelson, Samson, 414, 484,
    516, 766
Raritan tribe, 5
Raschi, Vic, 571, 578, 585
Rascoe, Burton, 613
Raskob, John J., 463, 481
Rathbone, Basil, 555, 588
Rathbone, Christina, 856
Rather, Dan, 756
rats, 844
Rattigan, Terence, 554
Rauschenberg, Robert, 595, 598,
    603, 612, 618, 642, 647,
    653
Ravenswood, 519, 640, 658

Ravitch, Diane, 718, 742
Ravitch, Richard, 721
Ravitch, Saul, 455
Raymond, Henry J., 104, 128,
    154
Razaf, Andy, 444, 452
RCA, 379, 598, 701
    GE and, 379, 776
Reader's Digest, 394, 602
Readers' Guide, 367
Reagan, Ronald, 560, 570, 751,
    754, 756, 769, 786
Real Estate Board, 249
Rebay, Hilla, 623
recycling, 879
Red Channels, 573
Redford, Robert, 636, 648, 725
Red Hook, 212
    Marine Terminal, 755
Redman, Joyce, 565
Redpath, James, 106
Reed, Florence, 319
Reed, Henry Hope, 590, 622,
    675, 782, 805
Reed, John, 337
Reed, John S., 853
Reed, Willis, 649, 662, 697, 714
Reese, Pee Wee, 530, 561, 571,
    589, 863
Reeve, Christopher, 753
Reeves, Rosser, 569, 587, 635,
    771
Regents, Board of, 39, 283
Regional Plan Association, 442
Regan, Sylvia, 588
Rego Park, 402, 440, 495, 568
    Alexander's store in, 621
    Federoff Triangle in, 786
Rehan, Ada, 171, 190, 199, 262,
    361
Rehfeld, Barry J., 799
Reich, Cary, 856
Reid, Carl Benton, 516, 555
Reid, Helen Rogers, 695
Reid, Kate, 682, 822
Reid, Ogden Mills, 337, 405,
    564
Reid, Rose Marie, 458
Reid, Whitelaw, 168, 188, 193,
    209, 337
Reilly, Frank V., 493
Reiner, Carl, 577
Reiner, Fritz, 648
Reiner, Rob, 702
Reinhardt, Ad, 588, 612, 675
Reinhardt, Max, 504, 541
Reiser, Pete, 530
Reles, "Kid Twist," 531
Remington, Frederic, 257
Remnick, David, 856
Rensselaer, Kiliaen van, 2, 4
rent control, 402

rent regulation, 387, 423, 440,
    537, 543, 572, 595, 620,
    656, 691, 698, 721, 818,
    850, 868, 875
Rentschler, Gordon, 519
Repetto, Thomas, 867
Research Institute of America,
    488
reservoir system, 85, 671
    Ashokan, 340
    Croton Aqueduct, 331
Resnick, Jack, 767
restaurants,
    Alison on Dominick Street,
        802
    An American Place, 769,
        803
    Angelo's, 280
    Arcadia, 774
    Au Bon Pain chain, 774
    Aureole, 796
    Automats, 341, 746, 814
    Bavarian Inn, 769
    Benihana, 656, 699
    Bouley, 792
    Brasserie, The, 626
    Burger King, 746
    Bustanoby's, 280
    Café des Artistes, 371, 728
    Café Figaro, 615
    Café Lafayette, 280, 572
    Café Martin, 280
    Café Nicholson, 568
    Carolina, 769
    Chez Brigitte, 670
    Childs, 221, 417, 639
    Chock full o' Nuts, 472, 715
    Christ Cella, 425, 563, 841
    Clarke's, P.J., 194, 552, 579
    Colony, 398
    Copeland's, 699
    Daniel, 824, 865
    Delmonico's, 66, 70, 76, 78,
        89, 150, 172, 181, 194,
        226, 256, 388, 403
    Dinty Moore's, 355
    E.A.T., 715
    Elaine's, 651
    El Morocco nightclub, 462,
        631, 632
    Exchange Buffet, 212
    Felidia, 760
    Forum of the Twelve Caesars,
        615
    Four Seasons, The, 626, 715
    Fraunces Tavern, 27, 29, 311,
        722
    Gage & Tollner's, 191, 841
    Gallagher's, 480, 722
    Ginger Man, The, 656
    Gino, 552
    Gramercy Tavern, The, 829

Grand Central Oyster Bar, 341, 722
Grill Room, The, 852
Hard Rock Café, 769
Horn & Hardart Automats, 341, 746, 814
Houlihan's, 829
Il Cantinori, 769
Il Monello, 722
Jack Dempsey's, 722
Jean-Georges, 852
Junior's, 579, 715, 869
Katz's Delicatessen, 221, 538
Keen's English Chop House, 212
Kleine Konditorei Cafe, 841
La Caravelle, 633
La Côte Basque, 620, 751
La Famille, 620
La Focacceria, 670
La Grenouille, 645
Landmark Tavern, 151
La Réserve, 769
La Taza de Oro, 670
Le Bernardin, 786, 829
Le Chanterelle, 751, 803
Le Cirque, 721, 852
Le Madri, 803
Le Pavillon, 532, 615, 620, 670
Le Périgord, 656
Lespinasse, 814
Lindy's, 392, 615, 692
Longchamps, 383, 692, 715
Louis Sherry, 227, 259, 287, 383, 392
Luchow's, 200, 480, 715
Lundy's, 388, 841
Lutèce, 639, 829
Malachy's, 651
Mama Leone's, 355, 626
Manhattan Ocean Club, 774
Manny Wolf's, 741
Martini's, 829
Maxwell's Plum, 670, 735
Montrachet, 780
Mortimer's, 735
Nathan's, 829
Newarker, 596
Nippon, 651
Nobu, 834
Odeon, 755
Official All Star Cafe, 834
Old Homestead Steak House, 151
Palm, The, 425
Parioli Romanissimo, 769
Patroon, 841
Patsy's, 547
Penn Bar and Grill, 590
Periyali, 792

Pete's Tavern, 67, 138
Peter Luger, 217
Petrossian, 774
P.J. Clarke's (see Clarke's)
Planet Hollywood, 834
Puddings, 741
Rainbow Room, 487, 538, 579, 722, 859
Ratner's, 298, 376, 879
Rector's, 264
Reuben's, 341
River Café, 741
Rosoff's, 335
Russian Tea Room, 433, 552, 865, 875
San Domenico, 796
Sardi's, 692, 699
Schrafft's, 255, 259, 305, 417, 506, 715, 721
Scores Sports Cabaret, 812
Serendipity, 600
Shanley's, 264, 388
Sherry (see Louis Sherry)
Shun Lee Dynasty, 663
Shun Lee Palace, 663
Shun Lee West, 663
Sign of the Dove, 645
Smith and Wollensky, 741
smoking in, 796, 834
Stork Club, 448, 480, 631, 663
Sylvia's, 639, 824
Tavern on the Green, 735
T.G.I. Friday's, 663, 692
theater hours and, 699
Toots Shor's, 526, 741
TriBeCa Grill, 814
"21" Club, 457, 563, 716
Union Pacific, 841
Union Square Café, 780
Voisin, 348
Waldorf Men's Bar, 487
Water Club, 764
White Horse Tavern, 194
Windows on the World, 735, 841
Restell, Mme., 188
Reston, James B., Jr., 831
retail merchants 514
ABC Carpet, 251
Abercrombie & Fitch, 231, 288, 366, 736
Abraham & Straus, 234, 441, 501, 628, 711, 781, 793, 797, 804, 830
Alexander's, 434, 621, 658, 809, 815
Allied Stores, 488, 781
Altman, B., 139, 179, 182, 231, 299, 343, 350, 362, 798
Argosy Book Store, 406, 460
Armani, Giorgio, 836

Arnold Constable, 66, 83, 111, 136, 152, 350, 362
Barnes & Noble, 171, 367, 460, 701, 748, 782, 805
Barney's, 403, 736, 782, 809, 820, 836
Bed Bath and Beyond, 815
Bendel, Henri, 246, 336, 621, 775, 782, 809
Benetton, 794
Bergdorf Goodman, 282, 434, 668, 767, 772
Best & Co., 189, 558, 694
Bloomingdale's, 213, 289, 442, 458, 558, 711, 782, 793, 804
Bond Stores, 564, 736
Bonwit Teller, 257, 449, 768, 793, 798
Borders Bookstores, 838
Brentano Bookstores, 105, 635
Brooks Brothers, 59, 67, 70, 98, 127, 132, 173, 246, 256, 317, 356, 503, 553, 781, 793, 809, 861, 872
Caldor, 781
Cartier, 365
Caswell Massey, 150
Concourse Plaza shopping center, 809
Crate & Barrel, 830
Crouch and Fitzgerald, 79
Custom Shop Shirtmakers, 505
De Pinna, 210, 330, 360, 434, 687
Dobbs hats, 434
Doubleday Book Shops, 805
Duane Reade, 622, 815
Eddie Bauer, 809
Federated Department Stores, 441, 793, 825
Filene's, 441
Finkelstein, Edward S., 775, 815
Fortunoff's, 393, 652, 747
Franklin Simon, 276, 736
Genovese drugstores, 404
Gimbel, Adam, 687
Gimbel, Bernard F., 323, 404, 426, 591, 665
Gimbels, 323, 362, 405, 591, 658, 665, 687, 711, 781
Gorham, 294
Gotham Book Mart, 386, 799
Grande Maison de Blanc, 434
Gucci, 591, 781
Hammacher Schlemmer, 418
Hearn's, 83, 276, 601
Herald Center, 761
Hermès, 775

Hickey Freeman, 872
Howard Stores, 360
Klein, S., 336, 458, 476, 723
Knox Hat Co., 78, 276
Kress, Samuel H., 265, 601, 736
Lane Bryant, 288, 582
Lerner Stores, 366, 742
Lilliputian Bazaar, 189
Limited, The, 775, 809
Loehmann's, 384, 781, 836
Loeser, Frederick, & Co., 152, 216
Lord & Taylor, 64, 78, 123, 145, 170, 265, 276, 343, 350, 362, 393, 458, 488, 501, 781, 804
Macy's, 117, 123, 133, 141, 145, 152, 170, 173, 183, 218, 274, 265, 276, 343, 362, 393, 404, 426, 459, 501, 525, 611, 658, 736, 815
    Federated and, 825
    Jamaica, 736
    Queens, 658
    Thanksgiving Day parades, 558
Mark Cross & Co., 459
McCreery, James T., 77, 201, 257, 597
McCrory Co., 694
Mme. Demorest's, 123
Modell's, 152
NikeTown, 836
Ohrbach's, 398, 597, 707, 711, 787
Ohrbach, Nathan, 398, 706
O'Neill's, Hugh, 175
Paul Stuart, 507
Peck & Peck, 282, 324, 717
Penney, J.C., 701
    building, 662
Pottery Barn, 574, 782
Prada, 872
Rive Gauche, 680
Saks 34th Street, 276, 362, 658
Saks Fifth Avenue, 404, 591, 711, 788, 804
Saks, Andrew, 276, 404
Saks, Horace, 404
Schwarz, F.A.O., 158, 449, 781, 843
Scribner Book Store, 345, 794
Sears, Roebuck, 781
Siegel-Cooper, 245, 356
Sloane, W. & J., 86, 246
Stern's, 145, 186, 330, 687
Stewart, A.T., 60, 86, 90, 125, 129, 133, 135, 155, 156, 162, 179, 187
Strand Bookshop, 436

retail merchants (*continued*)
Straus, Isidor, 170, 218, 231,
    246, 276, 336, 358
Straus, Jesse, 447
Straus, Nathan, 170, 218, 233,
    238, 246, 276, 336, 343
Tiffany & Co., 77, 145, 184,
    186, 213, 276, 294, 521,
    601, 854
Tower Records, 767
Toys 'R Us, 872
Traub, Marvin, 805
Valentino, 836
Van Cleef & Arpels, 434
Virgin Megastore, 836
Wanamaker's, 179, 245, 282,
    312, 597, 606
Winston, Harry, 467, 617,
    628, 742
Woolworth, F.W., 189, 246,
    274, 369, 378
Revlon, 471, 571, 726
Revson, Charles, 464, 471,
    726
Reynolds, Allie, 561, 571, 578,
    585
Reynolds, Debbie, 713
Reynolds, R.J., 225, 333
Reynolds, William J., 453
Rheingold Beer, 111
Rhinelander, Wm., 203, 217
Rhodes, Dusty, 600
Rice, Elmer, 352, 399, 437, 444,
    460, 550, 675
Rice, Grantland, 599
Rice, Isaac L., 274
Rice, Thomas Dartmouth, 70,
    124
Rice, Tim, 703, 828
Rich, Irene, 566, 794
Richards, Beah, 660
Richardson, Bobby, 643, 655
Richardson, James, 157
Richie, Lionel, 745
Richman, Charles, 261
Richardson, W.S., 334
Richman, Arthur, 396
Richman, Harry, 437, 451, 461
Richmond Hill, 147
Richter, Mike, 823
Richter, Sviatoslav, 632
Rickard, Tex, 303, 362, 391, 415,
    430, 438
RICO Act, 698
Ridder, Herman, 272, 356
Ridge, Lola, 374, 385, 489,
    528
Ridgewood, 241, 304
Rieder, Jonathan, 776
Riegelmann, Edward, 401
Riegelman, Harold, 591
Riese, Dennis, 829

Riese, Irving, Murray, 526, 595,
    639, 692, 715, 721, 760,
    829
Riesel, Victor, 609, 831
Rifkin, Ron, 827
Riggio, Leonard, 701, 748
Riggs, Bobby, 518, 530
Riis, Jacob, 218, 224, 235, 242,
    253, 274, 277, 283, 351
Riker's Island, 208, 572
Rinehart, Mary Roberts, 319, 386
Rinehart, Stanley M., 443, 689
Rinfret, Pierre, 803
Ring, The, 396
Ringling Bros., 308
Riordon, William L., 295
riots, 45, 48, 71, 72, 132, 323,
    371, 637
    Astor Place, 96
    Attica prison, 701, 705
    mug-house, 21
    Orange, 162
    police, 113
    Tompkins Square, 792
Ripert, Eric, 786
Ripley, George, 192
Ripley, Robert L., 374, 569
Ritch, John W., 110
Ritchard, Cyril, 414, 599, 618,
    661, 708
Ritt, Martin, 535
Ritter, Bruce, 798
Ritter, Thelma, 613, 675, 689
Ritter, Victor F., 507
Rivera, Chita, 609, 631, 725,
    766, 772, 822
Rivera, Diego, 477
Rivera, Geraldo, 706
Riverdale, 6
    Wave Hill in, 91, 633
Rivers, Larry, 593, 603, 771, 867,
    877
Riverside Church, 687
Riverside Drive, 140, 191, 210,
    368, 278, 312
Riverside funeral home, 254,
    485, 637
Riverside Neighborhood Assn.,
    678
Riverside Park, 194
Rivington, James, 30, 31, 36, 38
Rizzuto, Phil, 537, 571, 585
Roach, Max, 561
Robards, Jason, Jr., 608, 618,
    630, 642, 654, 660, 668,
    708, 800, 811
Robb, James Hampden, 259
Robbins, Harold, 603
Robbins, I.D., 773
Robbins, Jerome, 536, 546, 551,
    560, 571, 577, 578, 583,
    584, 613, 654, 857

Robert Shaw Chorale, 567
Roberts, Tony, 777, 832
Robertson, Archibald, 45
Robertson, Cliff, 612
Robertson, Dave, 369
Robertson, Rebecca, 864
Robeson, Paul, 406, 430, 440,
    589, 732
Robin, Leo, 429, 571, 772
Robinson, Bill "Bojangles," 437,
    440, 451, 517, 571
Robinson, Edward G., 400,
    546
Robinson, Edwin Arlington,
    248, 253, 265, 278, 390,
    406, 428, 489
Robinson, Hubbell, 719
Robinson, Jackie, 375, 561, 577,
    609, 709
Robinson, Lucius, 179
Robinson-Patman Act, 494
Robinson, Phyllis, 743
Robson, May, 296
Rochambeau, Comte de, 37
Rock, Howard B., 817, 877
Rockefeller Center, 439, 463,
    479, 493, 505, 778, 802,
    834, 848
    Christmas tree, 462
    Guild Theater in, 510
    Prometheus statue in, 483
    skating rink, 498
Rockefeller, David, 625, 669,
    719, 747, 834
Rockefeller, Nelson A., 477, 516,
    576, 596, 616, 640, 645,
    664, 678, 680, 692, 693,
    701, 704–706, 711, 716,
    746, 750
    drug laws and, 714
Rockefeller Foundation, 342
Rockefeller Institute, 271, 277,
    283, 300, 622, 658
Rockefeller University, 271, 283,
    611, 617, 621, 622, 658,
    717
Rockefeller, Abby Aldrich,
    444
Rockefeller, John D., 127, 198,
    221, 226, 231, 271, 300,
    330, 342, 351, 501
    Jr., 271, 344, 349, 351, 388,
    397, 439, 450, 455, 463,
    478, 487, 493, 499, 509,
    532, 545, 552, 578, 623,
    628, 802
    III, 742, 756
Rockefeller, William, 203,
    231
Rockwell, George Lincoln,
    627
Rockwell, Norman, 361, 744

Rodman, Bella, 641
Rodgers, Mary, 624
Rodgers, Richard, 414, 421, 422,
    429, 437, 444, 451, 461,
    478, 491, 497, 504, 510,
    511, 517, 524, 536, 542,
    551, 561, 571, 583, 594,
    605, 619, 624, 642, 697,
    749
Roe, Preacher, 571
Roebling, J.A., 109, 153, 201
Roebling, Washington A., 153,
    201, 418
Roelantsen, Adam, 4
Roerich, Nicholas, 443
Rogan, Helen, 856
Rogers, Charles F., 315
Rogers, Ginger, 497, 503, 517,
    550, 570
Rogers, Henry H., 163, 318
Rogers, Jim, 747
Rogers, John S., 370
Rogers, Moses, 54
Rogers, Randolph, 180
Rogers, Will, 332, 368, 375, 381,
    395, 396, 407
Rohatyn, Felix, 634, 747
Rolfe, Red, 505
roller coasters, 208, 430
roller skates, 134
Rolling Stones, 654
Romberg, Sigmund, 332, 347,
    352, 361, 362, 368, 369,
    375, 381, 391, 400, 407,
    421, 429, 437, 438, 551,
    584
Rome, Harold, 504, 542, 555,
    589, 599, 643, 661, 839
Ronstadt, Linda, 795
Ronzoni, Emanuele, 376, 610
Rooney, Mickey, 749
Roosevelt Island, 4, 12, 66, 390,
    684, 704, 726, 727, 734,
    798, 826
    tramway and, 729
Roosevelt, Eleanor, 297, 315,
    356, 473, 493, 515, 548,
    569, 616, 634, 640, 838
Roosevelt, Franklin D., 297, 315,
    366, 383, 389, 417, 433,
    446, 449, 452, 454 457,
    463, 465, 466, 473, 474,
    495, 506, 514, 520, 544,
    547
Roosevelt, James Henry, 164
Roosevelt, Nicholas J., 52, 57,
    107
Roosevelt, Theodore (Sr.), 104,
    178, 185
Roosevelt, Theodore, 185, 197,
    201, 204, 212, 228, 241,
    250, 256, 259, 264, 275,

276, 278, 279, 287, 297,
303, 305, 311, 316, 335,
376, 495
Jr., 403
Root, Elihu, 250, 334, 458, 501
Rorimer, James J., 667
Rosati, James, 712
Rose, Alex, 544, 609, 729
Rose, Billy, 400, 415, 445, 452,
461, 472, 491, 492, 520,
668
Rose, Ernestine L., 93
Rosebrock, Ellen Fletcher, 718
Rose Hill, 40
Roseland Ballroom, 382
Rosenbaum, Yankel, 808, 842,
853
Rosenberg, Anton, 593
Rosenberg, Elliot, 666
Rosenberg, Ethel, Julius, 573,
581, 591
Rosenman, Samuel, 402, 433,
465, 466, 473, 493, 710
Rosenquist, James, 642
Rosenthal, Herman, 334
Rosenthal, Ida, 401
Rosenthal, Tony, 667, 689, 719,
738
Rosenwach Tank Co., 143
Rosenzweig, Anne, 774
Rosenzweig, Roy, 817
Rosewall, Ken, 609, 697
Rosie the Riveter, 533
Ross, Anthony, 529, 604
Ross, Diana, 767
Ross, Don, 637
Ross, Harold, 411, 569, 582, 622
Ross, Herbert, 555, 583, 599,
643, 874
Ross, Jerry, 595, 599, 605
Ross, Lanny, 795
Ross, Lillian, 352, 374, 816
Ross, Steven J., 641, 816
Rossen, Robert, 668
Rossner, Judith, 667, 724, 766
Rosten, Leo, 502, 846
Roszak, Theodore, 682
rotary press, 90, 160
color, 235
Roth, Andrew, 838
Roth, Henry, 483
Roth, Lillian, 461, 753
Roth, Philip, 622, 688, 737, 748,
766, 776, 821, 832
Rothafel, S.L. "Roxy," 352, 361,
361, 386, 429, 470, 491
Rothko, Mark, 554, 618, 689,
696, 702, 725, 738, 766
Rothschild, Walter N., 628
Rothstein, Arnold, 382, 408,
438, 479
Rothwax, Harold, 831

Roundabout Theater, 667
Rounseville, Robert, 504, 609
Rountree, Martha, 550
Rouss loft building, 263
Rouss, Charles, 263
Rouverol, Aurania, 437, 444
Rovere, Richard H., 559, 748
Rowell, George P., 146
rowing, 143
Rowland, Henry, 186
Rowson, Susanna H., 45
Royster, Vermont, 838
Rubell, Steve, 739, 758, 777, 801
Rubenstein, Howard J., 593, 726
Rubin, Robert, 815
Rubinstein, Helena, 353, 462,
464, 662
Rubinstein, John, 708, 753
Rubinstein, Serge, 605
Ruby, Harry, 400, 437, 438
Rudel, Julius, 542
Rudin, Jack, 605, 726
Rudin, Lewis, 605, 716, 726, 875
Rudin Organization, 875
Ruehl, Mercedes, 811, 877
Ruffing, Red, 498, 511, 518, 537
Ruggles, Charles, 368, 375, 380,
386, 400, 618
Ruggles, Samuel B., 68, 70, 73,
75
Rukeyeser, Muriel, 752
Rule, Janice, 594
Ruml, Beardsley, 540
running, 353, 619
Runyon, Damon, 391, 460, 477,
480, 484, 495, 555, 583
Ruppert, Col. Jacob, 260, 357,
387, 388, 401, 472, 493,
518
Ruppert, Jacob, 147, 174, 231
Russell, Keri, 857
Russell, Lillian, 193, 197, 236,
262, 267, 278, 313, 339
Russell, Rosalind, 452, 594, 608
Russo, Gaetano, 233
Rustin, Bayard, 786
Rutgers, Anthony, 28
Rutgers, Henry, 68
Ruth, Babe, 362, 375, 387, 391,
401, 422, 430, 470, 535,
567
Ruttenbaum, Steve, 782
Ruyter, Michiel de, 11
Ryan, Clendenin J., 434, 473,
611
Ryan, Joseph, 578, 592
Ryan, Meg, 857
Ryan, Rosy, 408
Ryan, Thomas Fortune, 214, 225,
231, 293, 295, 299, 302,
305, 333, 335, 434
Ryan, William F., 627, 705

Ryder, Albert Pinkham, 191,
345, 367
Ryskind, Morrie, 438, 478

Saady, Morris, 684
Sabatini, Gabriela, 806
Sackler, Arthur M., 628, 749,
787
safety pin, 96
Safir, Howard, 835
Safra, Edmond J., 861
Sagalyn, Lynne B., 873
Sag Harbor, 42, 43, 158
Sage, Abby, 157
Sager, Carol Bayer, 749, 763
Sailors' Snug Harbor, 49, 68
Saint, Eva Marie, 599
Saint-Gaudens, A., 196, 202,
232, 253, 291
Saks, Gene, 623, 660
Sale, Chic, 381
Salinger, J.D., 576, 583, 636
Salisbury, Harrison, 695, 821
Salmi, Albert, 806
Salomon, Haym, 34, 36
Salonga, Lea, 812
saloons, 131, 746
Salvadorans, 747
Salvation Army, 192, 259, 342,
406, 742, 790
Booth Memorial Hospital of,
373
Salwen, Peter, 799
Sammy's Bowery Follies, 484,
557, 690
Sampras, Pete, 806, 823, 833,
839, 878
Samuels, Charles, 659
Sánchez Korrol, Virginia, 765
Sánchez Vicario, Arantxa, 828
Sanders, James, 867
Sanders, Lawrence, 695
Sands, Diana, 654
Sanford, John, 827
Sanger, Margaret, 337, 355, 363,
393, 403, 448
Sanitary Commission, 135
sanitation, 9, 139
Sanitation, Dept. of, 568, 579
pooper scooper law and, 746
San Juan Hill, 310, 596
San Juan, Olga, 583
Santana, Manuel, 662
Santa Anna, Antonio de, 165
Santa Claus, 54, 61, 130, 142,
252
Sante, Luc, 811
Santo, Joseph, 645
Sarandon, Susan, 762
Saratoga, Battles of, 35
Sardi, Vincent, 692

Sarnoff, David, 337, 394, 419,
427, 701
Sarnoff, Dorothy, 536
Sarnoff, Robert W., 584, 701, 845
Saroyan, William, 516, 517
Sasaki, Dawson, Demay Assocs.,
705
Satmars, 580, 700, 748
SAT scores, 418
Saturday Evening Post, 361, 688
Savalas, Telly, 636, 713
savings banks, 60 (see also
banks)
savings & loan companies, 765
Savoy Ballroom, 421
Savoy, Bert, 387, 396, 400
Sawchuk, Terry, 697
Saypol, Irving, 580
Sayre, Lewis A., 127
Scalamandré, Franco, 552
Scalise, Frank, 586, 614
Scallo, Victor, 689
Scarborough, Chuck, 826
scarlet fever, 141
Scarsdale, 18, 21
Scavullo, Francesco, 659
Schaap, Dick, 665, 874
Schary, Dore, 618, 753
Schechter v. U.S., 487
Schecter, Barnet, 877
Scheff, Fritzi, 285, 296, 599
Schell, August, 185
Schenck, Joseph, 381, 421
Schenck, Nicholas, 381, 429
Schenectady, 12
Schermerhorn Row, 56, 681
Schermerhorn, Peter, 56
Schermerhorn, Richard, Jr.,
298
Schickele, Peter, 661
Schiff, Jacob H., 172, 175, 206,
251, 271, 303, 384
Schirmer, Gustav, 128, 236
Schiff, Dorothy, 515, 549, 659,
731, 799
Schiff, Irwin, 790
Schildkraut, Joseph, 603, 654
Schinasi Brothers, 274
Schinasi, Morris, 322
Schippers, Thomas, 739
Schisgal, Murray, 654, 719
Schmeling, Max, 452, 470, 497,
511
Schmidt, Harvey, 631, 668
Schnabel, Julian, 738
Schneersohn, Joseph I., 575
Schneerson, Menachem, 575,
582, 808, 826
Schneider, Eric C., 862
Schneiderman, Rose, 288, 317,
323, 329, 335, 342, 365,
466, 705

INDEX

Schoenberg, Arnold, 536
Schoener, Allon, 666, 682, 856
Schomburg Center, 757
Scholastic Aptitude Test
 (S.A.T.), 418
School Lunch Program, 692
schools,
 African Free School, 40
 Alexander Robertson, 42
 Bank Street, 360, 379, 694
 Board of Regents and, 39
 Boys and Girls High, 186, 730
 Brearley, 207, 443, 558
 Bronx Science, 509, 611
 Brooklyn Friends, 146, 706
 Brooklyn Polyprep, 107, 153,
  224, 272
 Brooklyn Tech, 394, 475
 Cardinal Hayes Memorial, 527
 Chapin, 272, 435
 Choir School of St. Thomas,
  381, 800
 Collegiate, 4, 61, 232
 Columbia Grammar School,
  27, 307
 Cooper Union, 114, 121, 122,
  316, 317, 335, 399
 Convent of the Sacred Heart,
  482
 Curtis High, 290
 Dalton, 379, 443, 515, 653
 De Witt Clinton High, 252,
  300, 442, 765
 Elisabeth Irwin, 527
 Erasmus Hall High, 40, 247
 Ethical Culture, 243, 475
 Fashion Inst. of Technology
  (FIT), 545
 Fieldston, 435, 475
 Girls' High, Bklyn, 214
 Haaren High, 442
 Hewitt, 385, 873
 High School for the
  Performing Arts, 753
 Horace Mann, 216, 222, 228,
  239, 272, 351, 611
 Hunter College High, 153,
  283, 602, 737
 Katharine Gibbs, 367, 635
 Lexington School for Deaf,
  146
 Little Red School House, 390,
  468, 527
 Louis D. Brandeis, 637
 Loyola High, 266
 Lycée Français, 456, 488, 611
 Manhattan Day, 540
 Marymount, 279
 New School for Social
  Research, 378, 394
  Mannes College of Music
   and, 772

 Parsons School of Design
  and, 696
 Nightingale-Bamford, 300,
  385, 443
 Norman Thomas High, 730,
  733
 parochial, 78, 83, 351, 527, 775
 Parsons School of Design, 248
 Poppenhusen Institute, 150
 Professional Children's, 351
 public, 81, 83, 86, 142, 146,
  157, 176, 186, 214, 247,
  257, 261, 277, 290, 300,
  313, 351, 360, 385, 390,
  442, 569, 597, 629, 635,
  637, 688, 730, 765, 782,
  815, 826, 837, 845, 855,
  861, 873, 876
 Regis High, 351
 Riverdale Country, 307, 489
 Roberto Clemente I.S. 195,
  734
 Sacred Heart of Jesus, 232
 School of Visual Arts, 559
 Spence, 232, 242, 443
 St. Ann's, 666
 St. Bernard's, 290
 Stuyvesant High, 290, 307,
  815
 Town, 791
 Trinity, 20, 78, 222, 243, 701
 United Nations International,
  558
 Voorhees Technical Institute,
  635, 700
 Washington Irving High, 277,
  782
 Xavier High, 98
Schotter, Roni, 846
Schrager, Ian, 739, 758, 777
Schriftgeisser, Karl, 541
Schroeder, Ted, 537
Schulberg, Budd, 618
Schulman, Arlene, 873
Schulz, Dutch, 408
Schuman, William, 551, 556
Schumer, Charles, 853
Schurman, Jacob Gould, 266
Schurz, Carl, 150, 165, 178, 179,
  182, 196, 202, 205, 298,
  334
 statue of, 345
Schuyler, James, 630, 707, 811
Schuyler, Louisa Lee, 126, 157,
  159, 171, 234, 356, 417
Schuyler, Montgomery, 201
Schuyler, Peter, 21
Schuyler, Philip J., 35, 39, 44,
  50
Schuyler, Robert, 108

Schwab, Charles M., 265, 270,
  293, 303, 513
Schwartz, Arthur, 444, 452, 461,
  491, 504, 555, 583, 594,
  649, 772
Schwartz, Delmore, 541, 565
Schwartz, Jean, 278, 291, 296,
  302, 308, 332, 347, 375,
  387, 400, 407, 437
Schwartz, Joel, 821
Schwartz, Stephen, 703, 708, 719
Schwartz, Tony, 788
Schwarz, F.A.O., 781, 843
Schwed, Fred, Jr., 523
Scientific American, 88, 554
Scores, 858
Scorsese, Martin, 732, 739, 766,
  800, 862
Scott, George C., Jr., 623
Scott, Hazel, 627, 758
Scott, Martha, 510, 594
Scott, Raymond, 555
Scott, Winfield, 93, 102
Scotto, Vincent, 308
Scourby, Alexander, 570
Screvane, Paul R., 657
Scribner's Monthly, 160
Scripps, Edward W., 307
Scripps-Howard papers, 411
Scull, Robert, 719, 783
Seabury, Judge Samuel, 289,
  359, 465, 466, 615
Sea Gate, 233
Seaman, Dr. Valentine, 171
Seagram, 486
Seagram Building, 625
Sears, Zelda, 284, 296, 352
Second Avenue Deli, 600, 840
Securities and Exchange
 Commission (SEC), 481,
  722, 793
Sedgman, Frank, 584, 589
Seeger, Pete, 567, 668, 772
Seeley, Blossom, 381
Segal, George (sculptor), 636,
  675, 744, 752
Segal, George, 648, 660, 667,
  682, 696
Segal, Paul, 807
Segal, Vivienne, 357, 375, 407,
  421, 437, 510, 524, 818
Seidl, Anton, 211, 258
Seinfeld, Jerry, 806
Seixas, Gershon Mendes, 29, 39,
  40, 58
Seixas, Vic, 600
Selby, Hubert, 653
Seldes, George, 522, 575, 831
Seldes, Gilbert, 405, 443, 483,
  696
Seldes, Marian, 604, 744, 766,
  827, 874

Seles, Monica, 812, 818, 823
Self magazine, 742
Seligman, Edwin R.A., 192
Seligman, Joseph, 123, 162, 192
Seligman, Theodore, 231
Selkirk, George, 498
Sendak, Maurice, 647
Seneca tribe, 49
Seneca Village, 116
Sennett, Mack, 333, 346, 352
Serkin, Rudolf, 497
Serpico, Frank, 664, 692, 703,
  842
Serra, Richard, 689, 757, 800,
  821
settlement houses, 213, 218, 242,
  227, 251, 275
Seuss, Dr., 502
Seventeen magazine, 545
Seventh Avenue, 597, 693 (see
  also fashion industry)
Seven Years' War, 27
Seventh Regiment, 51, 96, 113,
  125, 132, 364
 monument, 428
Seward, William H., 67, 78, 80,
  81, 93, 97, 100, 106, 132,
  166
 statue of, 180
sewer system, 46, 97, 280, 323,
  506
sewing machine, 145
 electric, 222
 Hunt and, 69
 Singer and, 127, 129, 222
sex-discrimination suits, 695
Seymour, Horatio, 79, 83, 88,
  97, 102, 129, 131, 132,
  135, 148, 166
Seymour, Mary Foot, 189
Shad, John S.R., 825
shad, 2, 223, 670
Shadgren, Joseph, 513
Shahn, Ben, 469, 509, 516, 541,
  576, 583, 588, 593, 642,
  689
Shaffer, Anthony, 763
Shakespeare Festival, 594
Shalala, Donna, 722
Shange, Ntozake, 731
Shanker, Albert, 681, 723, 775,
  844
Shannon, Effie, 338
Shannor, Rebecca Read, 794
Shapiro, Morris A., 601, 621
Sharaff, Irene, 822
Sharkey, Jack, 430, 452, 470,
  478
Sharpton, Al, 780, 797, 871
Shatner, William, 618
Shattuck, Frank G., 255, 259, 506
Shaver, Dorothy, 458, 501

Shavers, Charlie, 703
Shaw, Irwin, 496
Shaw, Robert L., 530, 567, 719
Shawkey, Bob, 401
Shawn, William, 582, 816
Shea, Spec, 561
Shea Stadium, 655
Shea, William A., 643, 655
Shean, Al, 357, 396, 422, 470, 571
Shearing, George, 589
Shearman and Sterling, 177
Sheeler, Charles, 345, 391, 399, 444, 509, 660
Sheen, Archbishop Fulton J., 582, 748
Sheen, Martin, 654
Sheldon, Edward, 313, 345, 352, 555
Sheldon, Edward, 555
Shelley v. Kramer, 563
Shelley, Gladys, 524
shellfish, 355
Shenkman, Ben, 867
Shepard, Sam, 744, 753, 762, 766, 777
Shepp, James W. and Daniel B., 239
Sherer, Moshe, 855
Sherman, Allan, 643, 713
Sherman Anti-Trust Act, 224, 242
Sherman, Frederic Fairchild, 528
Sherman, Lowell, 396
Sherman Square, 227
Sherman, Wm. Tecumseh, 215
Sherwood, Robert, 380, 428, 490, 496, 510, 523, 534, 604
Shevelove, Burt, 643, 763
Shimmel's Knish Bakery, 328
Shinn, Everett, 261, 308, 313, 593
Shinnecock tribe, 5
shipping, 495, 730
Short, Bobby, 683, 848
Shubert brothers, 267, 648
Shubert, J.J., 296, 301
Shubert, Lee, 296, 301, 594
Shubert, S.S., 296
Shue, Larry, 771
Shulman, Claire, 780
Shulman, Max, 598
Shumlin, Herman, 749
Sibley, Hiram, 86, 112
Sickles, Daniel E., 106, 120, 125, 131, 334, 337, 347, 349
"Sidewalks of New York, The," 240
Sidney, Sylvia, 461, 599, 863
Siebert, Muriel, 672

Siegel, Bugsy, 382, 462
Siegel, Fred, 846
Sigman, Carl, 561
Silbert, Layle, 838
Sille, Nicasius de, 7, 8
Sills, Beverly, 609
Silver, Nathan, 674
Silver, Nicky, 832
Silver, Ron, 794
Silvera, Frank, 594, 604, 660
Silverfarb, Edward, 674
Silverman, Sid, 576
Silvers, Phil, 560, 583, 631
Silvers, Sid, 470
Silverstein, Larry A., 875
Simenon, Georges, 559
Simkovitch, Mary, 275, 486, 499
Simms, Phil, 789, 812
Simon and Garfunkel, 683, 758
Simon, Carly, 708
Simon, Kate, 622, 762
Simon, Neil, 577, 643, 648, 660, 668, 689, 696, 702, 707, 712, 731, 738, 749, 753, 758, 766, 777, 783, 794, 811, 817, 874
Simon, Paul, 661, 668, 697, 812, 857
Simon, Sol, 304
Simonson, Lee, 380, 675
Simplicity Pattern Co., 430
Simpson, Lusby, 486
Simpson, Rev. Matthew, 143
Simpson-Mazzoli Act, 786
Sims, J. Marion, 98, 110, 206
Sinatra, Frank, 518, 525, 537, 546, 547, 560, 570, 589, 604, 631, 637, 668, 739, 753, 832, 857
Sindona, Michele, 716, 751, 770
Singer loft building, 292
Singer Sewing Machine, 101, 170
Singer, Isaac Merrit, 101, 127, 129
singles bars, 651, 670, 714
Singleton, "Zutty," 726
Sing Sing Prison, 66, 68, 244, 289, 325, 335, 382, 430, 507, 539, 547
Singstad, Ole, 687
Sissle, Noble, 391
Sisters of Charity of Mount St. Vincent, 90, 95
Sivaji, 12
69th Regiment, 100, 126, 364, 365
Sixth Avenue, 514, 549
skeleton construction, 233
Skinner, Cornelia Otis, 546, 618, 749
Skinner, Otis, 190, 332, 535
Skouras, Spyros P., 703

Skowron, Bill, 605, 632
Skulnik, Menasha, 588, 661, 696
skyscrapers,
    Astor Plaza, 691
    AT&T Long Distance Building, 471
    AT&T Long Lines Building, 720
    American Tel & Tel Bldg., 768
    Bankers Trust Building, 339, 875
    Bank of the Manhattan Bldg., 453
    Banque de Paris Building, 773
    Barclay-Vesey Building, 423
    Bayard Building, 263
    Bear Stearns, 878
    Broadway-Cortlandt Building, 321
    Burlington House, 691
    Bush Terminal Bldg., 370
    Candler Building, 339
    Carnegie Hall Tower, 813
    CBS Building, 662
    Celanese Building, 714
    Central Park Place, 795
    Chanin Building, 446
    Chase Natl. Bank Bldg., 439
    Chase Manhattan Building, 638
    Chrysler Bldg., 453, 633, 746, 759
    Citibank Building, 638
    Citicorp Bldg. (Queens), 802
    Citicorp Center, 737, 740
    Citigroup Center, 740
    City Investing Co. Bldg., 321
    CitySpire, 790
    Condé Nast Building, 864
    Condict Building, 263
    Consolidated Gas Bldg., 347
    Continental Can Building, 638
    Continental Center, 768
    Crédit Lyonnais Building, 662
    Cunard Building, 392
    Daily News Building, 453
    Downtown Athletic Club, 454
    Equitable Life Building, 358
    Empire Building, 259
    Empire State Building, 463, 468, 469, 549, 728, 759
        TV transmitters on, 460
    Equitable Center, 784
    Equitable Life building, 638
    Esso Building, 562
    Exxon Building, 704, 706
    Fisk Building, 392
    Flatiron Building, 279
        23-Skidoo and, 279
    Ford Foundation Building, 677
    French, Fred F., Building, 431
    Fuller Building, 446

    Galleria apartments, 727
    General Electric buildings, 463, 479
    General Motors buildings, 439, 691, 859
    Grace, W.R., Building, 720
    Graybar Building, 431
    Gulf + Western Bldg., 691
    Heckscher Building, 362
    Helmsley Building, 446, 597
    Helmsley Palace Hotel, 754
    Heron Tower, 790
    Horizon apt. house, 795
    HSBC Tower, 784
    Hudson Terminal Building, 321
    IBM Building, 768
    International Building, 493
    J.C. Penney Building, 662
    Kent Building, 590
    Lefcourt National Bldg., 439
    Lever House, 590
    Liberty Tower, 327
    Lincoln Building, 439
    Manhattan Plaza apartments, 740
    McGraw-Hill buildings, 463
    Met Life Building, 649, 754
    Metropolitan Life Tower, 321
    Metropolitan Tower, 791
    Mobil Oil Building, 610
    Morgan Building, 801
    Morse Building, 193
    Municipal Building, 354
    National Westminster Bank USA, 768
    Navarre Building, 453
    Nelson Tower, 463
    News Corp. Building, 714
    New York Life Building, 439
    New York Merchandise Mart, 720
    New York Times Bldg., 223
    Olympic Tower, 740
    One Liberty Plaza, 720
    One Penn Plaza, 710
    PaineWebber Building, 638
    Pan Am Building, 649
    Paramount Building, 423
    Park Avenue Tower, 790
    Park Row Building, 263
    Pershing Square Building, 397
    Piaget Building, 746
    Postum Building, 416
    Pulitzer Building, 226
    Radiator Building, 408, 875
    RCA Building, 479
    Republic National Bank Tower, 784
    Reuters Tower, 875
    Seagram Building, 625
    Seaport Plaza, 767

skyscrapers (*continued*)
setback law and, 402
Singer Tower, 314, 375
Socony-Mobil Building, 610
Squibb Building, 453
St. Paul Building, 258
Standard Oil Building, 416
Steuben Glass Building, 626
Telephone Co. buildings, 423,
720
Time-Life Building, 626
Times Tower, 292, 662
Tishman Building, 620
Tower Building, 223
Tower 67, 785
Transportation Building, 439
TriBeCa Tower, 807
Tribune Building, 177
Trinity Building, 297
Trump Tower, 768
Union Carbide Building, 632
Uris Building, 710
U.S. Rubber Co. Building, 340
U.S. Steel Building, 720
Wang Building, 773
West Street Building, 309
Western Union Building, 177
Westvaco Building, 677
Whitehall Building, 286
Williamsburgh Savings Bank
Tower, 446
Woolworth Building, 347, 767,
859
World Building, 226
World Trade Center, 709, 823
terrorist bombing of, 819
terrorist destruction of,
871
Worldwide Plaza, 801
Zeckendorf Towers, 790
100 Broadway, 244
150 Nassau Street, 244
120 Wall Street, 453
19 Rector, 453
2 Park Avenue, 431
225 Broadway, 439
26 Broadway, 416
27 Cedar Street, 339
295 Madison Avenue, 446
39 Broadway, 439
44 Wall Street, 422
50 Broadway, 431
512 Seventh Avenue, 453
52 Wall Street, 439
67 Broad Street, 439
80 Maiden Lane, 339
1 Wall Street, 471
116 John Street, 463
150 William Street, 463
2 Broadway, 625
22 William Street, 463
450 Seventh Avenue, 463

500 Fifth Avenue, 463
575 Lexington Avenue, 614
60 John Street, 463
70 Pine Street, 471
1 Bankers Trust Plaza, 720
1 Battery Park City, 726
1 New York Plaza, 698
1166 Avenue of the Americas,
714
2 New York Plaza, 698
245 Park Avenue, 677
277 Park Avenue, 656
3 Park Avenue, 733
330 Madison Avenue, 655
475 Park Avenue, 698
540 Madison Avenue, 698
55 Water Street, 710
9 West 57th Street, 721
909 Third Avenue, 684
1 Financial Square, 790
1585 Broadway, 801
200 East 65th Street apt.
house, 791
33 Maiden Lane, 778
52–54 East End Avenue, 795
55 Water Street, 823
667 Madison Avenue, 850
7 World Trade Center, 778
85 Broad Street, 768
875 Third Avenue, 764
885 Third Avenue, 784
900 Third Avenue, 768
77 Water Street, 698
Slade, Bernard, 725, 744, 749
Slater, Bill, 662
slaughterhouses, 13, 141, 552
slavery, 2, 6, 8, 10, 16, 17, 20, 22,
25, 26, 38, 54, 65, 66, 70,
80, 97, 129
abolitionism and, 72
Sleeper, Jim, 805
sleeping car, 118, 145
Slezak, Walter, 470
Sliwa, Curtis, 750, 826
Sloan, John French, 307, 313,
338, 352, 397, 437, 583
Sloan, Samuel, 109, 136
Sloane, Emily Thorn, 376
Sloane, Everett, 490
Sloane, Henry T., 249
Sloane, John H.H., 287
Sloane, Leonard, 666
Sloane, W. and J., 86, 246, 304
Sloane, William D., 376
Slocum, Henry W., 125
slot machines, 263, 485
Sloughter, Henry, 15
slum clearance, 610
smallpox, 18, 22, 130, 139, 141,
159, 176, 564
Smalls' Paradise, 415
Smith and Dale, 583, 758

Smith, Alfred E., 281, 328, 329,
341, 349, 355, 372, 376,
383, 387, 393, 403, 404,
410, 411, 417, 426, 433,
434, 440, 448, 463, 473,
481, 499, 500, 544, 576
Dinner, 549
Smith, Bessie, 401
Smith, Betty, 541
Smith, Billy, 767
Smith, Buffalo Bob, 566
Smith, David, 583
Smith, Dennis, 707, 766, 877
Smith, Edgar, 267, 291, 320,
326, 339, 357, 361
Smith, Gerrit, 80, 172
Smith, Harry B., 258, 262, 278,
285, 314, 320, 326, 332,
357, 368, 421, 429
Smith, Junius, 78, 105
Smith, Kate, 421, 461, 503, 511,
526
Smith, Kent, 524, 583
Smith, Liz, 743
Smith (Court), Margaret, 643,
684, 690, 714
Smith, Oliver, 536, 546, 560,
571, 609, 613, 624, 631,
654, 828
Smith, Red, 551, 763
Smith, Robert B., 347
Smith, Robert Paul, 598
Smith, Stan, 703
Smith, Stephen, Dr., 141, 159,
176
Smith, Tony, 636, 752
Smith, W. Eugene, 603, 618
Smith, Willie "the Lion," 713
Smith, Winchell, 301, 313, 319,
357, 374, 477
Smithers Alcoholism Center,
472
smoking, 8, 314, 796, 834 (*see
also* cigarettes, cigars,
tobacco)
Sullivan Ordinance and, 314
Smoot-Hawley Tariff, 449
Snapple Beverage Co., 710
bottled iced tea and, 792
Snider, Duke, 589, 595, 605
Snow, Carmel, 319, 462, 468,
512
Snow, George P., 512
Snyder-Gray case, 430, 437
Snyder, Jerome, 598, 670, 731
Sobel, Robert, 743, 862
Sobell, Morton, 581
Sobol, Louis, 471
Social Register, 217
Social Security, 487, 520
Social Service Employees Union,
657

Society for Prevention of Cruelty
to Animals (SPCA), 141,
746
Society for the Prevention of
Cruelty to Children, 390
Society for Prevention of Crime,
187, 230
Society for Reformation of
Juvenile Delinquents, 99
SoHo, 6, 122, 702, 715, 738
furniture making in, 170
Sokolsky, George E., 602, 641
Soldiers and Sailors Monument,
279
Solomon, Barbara Probst, 632
Solow, Sheldon H., 721, 746
Soltner, André, 639, 760, 829
Sondheim, Stephen, 613, 624,
643, 696, 703, 713, 732,
739, 749, 758, 772, 789,
828
Sonnenberg, Benjamin, 476,
743, 834
Sons of Liberty, 28–30
Sontag, Susan, 647, 666, 724
SONY, 750
building, 768
Sorkin, Aaron, 800
Soros, George, 711, 747, 775, 815
Sotheby's, 752
Sothern, Ann, 461
Sothern, Edward H., 477
Sothern, Georgia, 536, 758
Soulé, Henri, 532, 620, 645,
670
Soup Kitchen International,
780
Sousa, John Philip, 249, 353
South Brooklyn Railway, 265
South East Bronx Community
Organization (SEBCO),
685
South Side RR, 145, 149, 153,
159, 167
South Street Seaport, 673, 681,
688, 694, 718
Southern State Parkway, 442
Soyer, Moses, 719
Soyer, Raphael, 409, 788
Spaak, Paul Henri, 552
Spacey, Kevin, 811
Spahn, Warren, 619
Spalding, Albert, 314, 526, 595
Spalding, James Reed, 124
Spalding, Lyman, 58
Spanish-American War, 256,
257
Spann, Edward K., 757
Spellman, Francis Cardinal, 515,
536, 549, 554, 569,
580–582, 617, 673
Spelvin, George, 301

Spence-Chapin Adoption Agency, 242, 539
Spewack, Bella, 490
Spewack, Samuel, 490, 702
Speyer, Jerry I., 818, 834
Spigelgass, Leonard, 623
Spingarn, Joel E., 316, 349, 379, 513
Spirit of the Times, 70
spiritualists, 152, 157, 207
Spivak, Lawrence E., 550, 560
Spock, Benjamin, 672, 772
spoils system, 68
Sports Center at Chelsea Piers, 839
Sports Illustrated, 598
spousal abuse, 787
Sprague, Frank J., 482
Sprague, Joseph, 85
Spring Antiques Show, 766
Springsteen, Bruce, 726, 772
Squadron A Armory, 244
squeegee men, 828, 835
Squibb, E.R., 118, 266
St. Albans, 258
St. Denis, Ruth, 421
St. John the Divine, Cathedral of, 233, 322, 334, 363, 417, 569, 579, 745, 764
St. John's University, 160, 300, 495, 531, 569, 607, 700
St. Joseph's College, 360, 694
St. Lawrence Seaway, 621
St. Nicholas Arena, 249
St. Nicholas Avenue, 271
St. Patrick's Day, 38, 103, 764
Stafford, Jean, 647
Stafford, Jo, 530
stagecoaches, 12
Stallone, Sylvester, 719, 732
Stallings, Laurence, 406
Stamp Act, 28
Stamper, Dave, 352, 357, 362, 368, 381, 396, 400, 407, 461, 648
Stanchfield, J.B., 264
Standard and Poor's, 144, 343, 527, 665, 843
Standard Oil Co., 163, 198
Stander, Lionel, 702, 739
Stanlaws, Penrhyn, 382
Stanley, Kim, 594, 603, 618
Stanley, Thomas E., 691
Stansell, Christine, 867
Stanton, Edwin M., 147
Stanton, Elizabeth Cady, 93, 122, 130, 144, 148, 150, 157, 160, 162, 275
Stanton, Frank, 802
Stanton, Henry Brewster, 144
Stanwyck, Barbara, 570
Stapleton, Jean, 609, 702

Stapleton, Maureen, 570, 583, 599, 604, 612, 618, 630, 696
Starbucks, 792
Starin, John H., 121, 141, 318
starlings, 226
Starr, Cornelius van der, 417, 680, 782
Starr, Roger, 776, 874
Starrett Corp., 734, 850
Starrett-Lehigh Bldg., 463
State Charities Aid Assn., 157, 159, 234
State University of New York (SUNY), 564
Staten Island, 2, 10, 13, 30, 43, 48, 835
Billopp House on, 33
Botanic Garden, 633
bridges and, 224
cable TV and, 695
Clove Lakes Park in, 425
education in, 290
Fresh Kills landfill on, 552, 568, 840
gas tank explosion, 715
immigrant medical inspection on, 111
Moravian Cemetery in, 183
pauper farm colonies on, 469
population of, (1898) 259
quarantine station, 111, 118
Wagner College in, 373
Staten Island Ferry, fire, 553
Statler, E. M., 382
Statue of Liberty, 212, 215, 363, 606, 735, 764, 769, 786
Staub, Rusty, 714
steamboats, 42, 43, 50, 54, 57, 60, 67, 69, 100, 127, 404, 700
Cornell and, 77
Fall River Line, 306, 351
Fulton and, 52, 55
General Slocum, 289
Gibbons v. Ogden and, 61
Stevens and, 52
Westfield, 163
steamships, 78, 127, 235, 252
Berengaria, S.S., 343
Bremen, S.S., 442, 515
Collins and, 98, 102, 107, 102
Cunard Line, 81, 94, 135, 159, 216, 239, 306, 324, 350, 482, 687
Aquitania, S.S. 350
Ile de France, S.S., 426
Leviathan, 350, 378
Lusitania, 306, 355
Majestic, 350, 378
Mauretania, S.S. 324, 488

Olympic, 330
QE2, 687
Queen Elizabeth, 673
Queen Mary, 494, 673
Cunard-White Star Line, 482, 494
French Line, 136
France, S.S., 641
Normandie, 488, 534
Fugazy and, 159
Hamburg-Amerika Line, 92, 252, 350
Kaiserin Auguste Victoria, 299
Amerika, S.S., 294
Holland-America Line, 167
Rotterdam, S.S., 621
Italian Line,
Michelangelo, S.S., 658
Raffaello, S.S., 658
Rex, S.S., 474
Luckenbach and, 98
Mauretania, 488
Morro Castle, 482
North German-Lloyd Line, 289, 442
Bremen, S.S. 118
Europa, S.S., 474
United States, S.S., 587, 687
White Star Line, 149, 224, 239, 271, 330, 336
Titanic, R.M.S., 336
Stearns, John, Dr., 52
Stebbins, Emma, 171
Steell, John, 193
Steffens, Lincoln, 290, 316, 337, 460
Stegner, Wallace, 701
Steichen, Edward, 295, 618, 712
Steiger, Rod, 594, 599, 660, 758, 878
Stein, Andrew J., 721, 764
Stein, Clarence S., 409, 454
Stein, Gertrude, 561
Steinbeck, John, 503, 682
Steinberg, Joel, Lisa, 786
Steinberg, Saul (entrepreneur), 634, 680
Steinberg, Saul, 529, 731, 862
Steinbrenner, George, 714, 745, 801, 857
Steinem, Gloria, 681, 693, 707
Steinetz, William, 268
Steinman, David B., 366, 459, 628
Steinway & Sons, 124
Steinway Hall, 142, 146, 150, 416
Steinway, Henry E., 165, 249
Steinway, Theodore, 165
Steinway, William, 156, 165, 306
Stella D'Oro Biscuit Co., 457
Stella, Frank, 623, 636, 653, 725

Stella, Joseph, 345, 399, 516, 554
Steloff, Frances, 477, 799
Stengel, Casey, 401, 632, 643, 647, 726
stenography, 189
stenotypy, 180
Stephens, John Lloyd, 95
Sterling, Andrew B., 308, 605
Stern, Henry J., 779, 786, 814
Stern, Isaac, 542, 631, 751, 874
Stern, Max, 471, 764
Stern College, 597
Stern, Leonard, 764
Stern, Robert A.M., 765, 788, 831, 862, 864
Sternhagen, Frances, 749, 822
Steuben, Baron von, 38, 41, 42
Steuben Glass, 284
Steuben Society, 382
Steuer, Max, 314, 329, 449, 520
Stevens, Edwin A., 149
Stevens, Harry M., 241, 304
Stevens, J.P., 260
Stevens, John, 42, 43, 50, 52, 54, 55, 78
Stevens, Paran, Col., 122
Stevens, Risë, 550
Stevenson, Adlai E., 587, 606
Stewart, Donald Ogden, 380, 437, 451, 753
Stewart, Ellen, 636
Stewart, Rod, 750
Stewart, Wm. Rhinelander, 244
Stickney, Dorothy, 437, 469, 510, 517
Stieglitz, Alfred, 240, 295, 319, 325, 332, 337, 368, 413, 444, 554
Still, Bayrd, 607
Still, Clyfford, 559, 612
Stiller, Jerry, 771, 783
Stillman, Alan, 663, 741, 774
Stillman, James, 249, 271, 305, 343, 372, 544
Stillman, Whit, 806
Stillman's Gymnasium, 391, 690
Stimson, Henry C., 152
Stimson, Henry L., 323, 326, 574
Stimson, Lewis A., 152, 266, 296, 323, 337
Stitt, Milan, 731
stock ticker, 144
Stockli, Albert, 596, 615, 626
Stoddard, Lothrop, 516
Stoddard, Sandol, 630
Stokes, Anson Phelps, 343
Stokes, W.E.D., 226, 292
Stolle, Fred, 668
Stoller, Mike, 643
Stone, Fred, 273, 284, 302, 339
Stone, I.F., 509, 657
Stone, John A., 67

Stone, Melville E., 266, 443
Stonewall Inn, 686
Stony Point, 36
Storrs, Frank Vance, 243
Storrs, Richard Salter, 250
Story magazine, 460
Stowe, Harriet Beecher, 103, 162, 177
Straight, Willard, 298, 351, 358
Strand, Paul, 368, 391, 731
Strange, Michael, 390, 577
Strasberg, Lee, 460, 490, 560, 763
Strasberg, Susan, 603, 862
Straus, Nathan, 459
Straus, Oscar S., 335
Stravinsky, Igor, 567
Strawberry, Daryl, 783
Strayhorn, Billy, 530, 676
Streep, Meryl, 862
streetcars, 173, 241, 304 (see also trolleys)
street cleaning, 245, 575
Street News, 799
street paving, 105, 141
street vendors, 251, 804, 825, 834
Streeter, Edward, 374, 731
Streisand, Barbra, 642, 676, 683
Stritch, Elaine, 561, 696
Stromberg, John, 244, 278, 291, 339
Strong, George Templeton, 102, 107, 116, 122, 141, 176, 588
Strong, William L., 238, 241, 247
Strouse, Charles, 631, 668, 696, 739
Strudwick, Shepperd, 477, 496, 576, 598
Strunk, William, Jr., 374
Struthers, Sally, 702
Stryker, Gerrit, 38
Stryker, Lloyd P., 513, 563, 605
Stuart, Robert L., 184
Students for a Democratic Society (SDS), 680, 686, 692
sturgeon, 255
    Greengrass and, 448
    Murray's and, 552, 869
Sturges, Preston, 444, 583
Stuyvesant-Fish house, 51, 89, 476
Stuyvesant Square, 114, 124
    Episcopal church on, 112
    Park, 76
Stuyvesant, Peter, 6–10, 12, 496
    statue of, 357
Stuyvesant, Rutherford, 155
Styne, Jule, 560, 571, 594, 599, 609, 619, 624, 631, 637,

654, 683, 703, 708, 719, 828
submarine, 34
suburbs, 86, 538, 540, 547, 633
subways, 158, 171, 239, 265 283, 289, 299, 312, 343, 356, 389, 404, 411, 467, 475, 521, 540, 553, 558, 592, 602, 606, 628, 706, 723, 748, 752, 761, 770, 793, 798, 804, 810, 815, 826, 843, 844
    accidents on, 373, 394, 435
    air conditioning in, 782, 804
    BMT, 398
    Con Edison and, 621
    crime in, 773
    D train, 597
    distance traveled each day, 866
    fare beating on, 815
    graffiti and, 798
    IND, 435
    IRT, 277
    Lexington Avenue, 373
    newsstands in, 787
    Queens, 366, 495, 501, 617
    Second Avenue, 866, 872
    turnstile-jumpers, 833
subway vigilante, 773
Suddugh, William H., 790
sugar,
    price of, 480
    rationing of, 538
sugar refining, 22, 27, 51, 60, 117, 169, 172
    Domino brand, 334
    Havemeyer and, 217, 230, 234, 242
Sullavan, Margaret, 496, 529, 541, 594, 631
Sullivan, Ed, 566, 719
Sullivan, James E., 192, 220, 223
Sullivan, John, Gen. 34
Sullivan, John L., 208
Sullivan Law, 333
Sullivan, Tim, 230, 240, 329, 333, 341
Sulzberger, Arthur H., 489, 681 Jr., 813
Sulzberger, Iphigene Ochs, 489
Sulzer, William, 335, 341, 342
Sumac, Yma, 583
Summer, Donna, 726
Sunnyside, Queens, 409
supermarkets, 500
    Bravo, 852
    D'Agostino's, 472, 633
    Key Food, 506
    King Kullen, 457
    Pathmark, 685, 741, 746, 837

supply-side economics, 755, 761
Surmain, André, 639
Surrogate's Court bldg., 333
Susann, Jacqueline, 667, 712, 719
Susman, Karen, 643
Sutton, Percy, 670, 687
Sutton, Willie, 471, 567, 578, 589
Suzuki, Pat, 619
Swanson, Gloria, 766
Swartwout, Samuel, 79
sweatshops, 281, 311, 317, 323, 835, 842
Swedish consular residence, 562
Swerling, Beverly, 874
Swift, Kay, 444, 451
swimming pools, 334, 498
Swingline Inc., 416, 556, 752, 860
Swoboda, Ron, 691
Swope, Gerard, 457
Swope, Herbert Bayard, 335
Synanon, 617
Sylvia's Food Products, soul food, 824

Tabbart, Bill, 546, 551
Tabbert, William, 599, 720
Tabler, William B., 651
Tachau, William, 401
Taft, Robert A., 520, 572, 591
Taft-Hartley Act, 557
Taft, Wm. Howard, 311, 337
Takamine, Jokichi, 271, 394
Talbot, Howard, 278, 326, 438
Talese, Gay, 630, 635, 659, 688, 701
Tallchief, Maria, 566
Tammany Hall, 41, 55, 58, 69–71, 73, 74, 79, 131, 137, 162, 270, 281, 298, 359, 403, 446, 457, 465, 466, 468, 473, 500, 580, 634, 646
    Lexow Committee and, 241
Tandy, Jessica, 516, 559, 583, 667, 738, 762, 827
Tanguay, Eva, 273, 285, 320
Tappan, Arthur, 65, 70, 75, 80
Tappan, Lewis, 65, 72, 80, 81, 107, 170
Tappen, Frederick D., 148
Tarkington, Booth, 313, 380
Tarr, William, 689, 712
tattoo parlors, 849
Tatum, Art, 543
Tauranac, John, 731, 748, 776, 832, 867

taverns, 7
taxes, 7, 49, 120, 211, 227, 245, 474 (see also income tax)
    business, 481
    commuter, 860
    property, 722, 761
    sales, 481
taxis, 306, 312, 318, 394, 398, 411, 450, 467, 482, 514, 553, 569, 606, 621, 628, 658, 673, 700, 748, 761, 765, 798, 804, 820, 837, 866
    Checker, 861
    electric, 251
    medallions for, 501
    rooftop advertising on, 724
    strikes, 312, 318, 482, 501, 508, 514, 569, 606, 658
Tayler, John, 58
Taylor Law, 671, 681, 699
Taylor, Deems, 668
Taylor, Elizabeth, 631
Taylor, Estelle, 461
Taylor, James, 749
Taylor, Laurette, 338, 414, 550, 555
Taylor, Lawrence, 789
Taylor, Moses, 69, 86, 104, 109, 126, 198
Taylor, Robert Lewis, 622
Taylor, Samuel, 576, 594
Taylor, Tell, 369
Taylor, Tom, 119, 199
Taylor, Zachary, 93, 95
Tchaikovsky, Petr Ilich, 229
Teachers College, 216, 228, 239
Teagarden, Jack, 451, 452
Teasdale, Sara, 357
Teddy Bear, 279
Teen-Age Mutant Ninja Turtles, 772
Teitelbaum, Joel, 748
telegraph, 77, 86, 90, 94, 121
    Field and, 142
    Gooch and, 142
    Morse and, 69, 84
    Pender and, 142
    Postal, 214
    Western Union, 112, 142
telephones, 184, 232, 243, 247, 301, 356, 443, 629, 845
    cellular, 821
    classified directory, 436
    directory listings, 186, 217
    in blizzard of '88, 219
    911 emergency number, 681
    public, 541
    switchboard, 189
    transatlantic, 427

television, 427, 450, 460, 515, 528
  baseball and, 518
  basketball and, 525
  Beard, James, and 779
  cable, 695, 758, 816
  coaxial cable, 582
  color, 522, 569, 582, 598
  Home Box Office (HBO), 799
  New York 1 News, 816
Tell, Alma, 380
Templeton, Fay, 278, 302, 339, 478
Temple Court office building, 203
Templeton, Fay, 258, 267
Tenderloin area, 181, 323, 324
tenements, 63, 99, 134, 137, 140, 147, 190, 194, 237, 245, 268, 440, 446, 499, 580
  rental rates in, 322
Tennien, Richard F., 784, 874
tennis, lawn, 173
  Forest Hills, 407
  USLTA, 407
  U.S. Open, 684
  West Side Tennis Club, 232, 278, 314
Terry, Bill, 408, 479, 801
Terry, Paul, 326
Terry, Ralph, 632, 643
Terry, Ruth, 380
Tesla, Nikola, 210, 218, 540
Tettrazini, Luisa, 314
Tetzel, Joan, 546
Teufel, Tim, 783
Texaco, 524
Textile Building, 274
Thanksgiving Day, 404, 514 (see also parades)
Tharp, Twyla, 661
Thaw, Harry K., 303, 309, 320, 347, 357
theaters, legitimate, 23
  Alvin, 429
  Ambassador, 391
  American Place, 654
  ANTA, 414
  Bijou, 368
  Booth, 346
  Broadhurst, 368
  Broadway, 407
  Candler, 352
  Century, 391
  Cort, 338
  Delacorte, 642
  Empire, 236, 338
  Eugene O'Neill, 414
  46th Street, 407
  Fulton, 332
  Gaiety, 319
  Garrick, 225

George M. Cohan's, 332
  Guild, 414
  Harris, 352
  Helen Hayes, 332, 338
  Henry Miller's, 374
  Imperial, 400
  John Golden, 428
  Jujamcyn, 608
  Lafayette, 338
  Longacre, 346
  Lucille Lortel, 599
  Lunt-Fontanne, 326
  Lyceum, 284
  Majestic, 429
  Mansfield, 420
  Mark Hellinger, 450
  Martin Beck, 407
  Music Box, 391
  Nederlander, 390
  Neil Simon, 429
  Palace, 345
  Park, 47, 52
  Plymouth, 368
  Rialto, 361
  Richard Rodgers, 407
  Royale, 429
  Second Avenue, 623
  Selwyn, 374
  Shubert, 346
  St. James, 392, 428
  Stuyvesant, 308
  Theatre de Lys, 599
  Vanderbilt, 375
  Virginia, 414
  Vivian Beaumont, 660
  Walter Kerr, 390
  Winter Garden, 332
  Yiddish Art, 420
Theater Development Fund, 713
Theatre Guild, 380
theater hours, 696
Theater Program Corp., 243
Theosophical Society, 176
Third Avenue, 602, 628
  fair, 729
This Week, 489
Thomas, Andrew J., 464, 531
Thomas, Augustus, 273, 284, 308, 491
Thomas, Danny, 583
Thomas, Dylan, 593
Thomas, John Charles, 357
Thomas, John R., 333
Thomas, Lowell, 756
Thomas, Marlo, 719
Thomas, Michael M., 752, 762, 776, 805
Thomas, Norman, 383, 565, 679
  High School, 730, 733
Thomas' English Muffins, 194
Thomas, Richard, 800
Thomashefsky, Boris, 199, 517

Thompson, Bobby, 585
Thompson Starrett Co., 339, 447, 455, 465
Thompson, Dorothy, 548
Thompson, Ernest, 749, 758
Thompson, Fred, 286, 296, 339, 380
Thompson, John, 133, 182
Thompson, Kay, 603, 613, 856
Thompson, Martin E., 63, 94
Thompson, Sada, 696
Thomson, Virgil, 561, 800
Thorndike, Sybil, 484, 612
Thorne, Jonathan, 279
Thorne, Oakley L., 742
Thornhill, Claude, 524, 662
Three Stooges, 517
Throop, Enos T., 66, 67
Thurber, James, 380, 412, 476, 516, 523, 535, 622, 631, 636
Thurman, Wallace, 443, 444
TIAA-CREF, 294, 373
Tichy, Lester, 645
ticker-tape parades, 221, 398, 422, 426, 435, 459, 508, 548, 552, 580, 755
Ticonderoga, Fort, 35
Tiemann, Daniel F., 113
Tierney, Gene, 523
Tierney, Harry, 381, 387, 400, 407, 429, 662
Tiffany, Charles L., 77, 145, 211, 231
Tiffany, Louis Comfort, 187, 240, 284, 477
Tilden, Bill, 391, 396, 401, 408, 415, 445
Tilden, Samuel J., 151, 162, 172, 178, 182, 209, 212, 214, 301
Tillich, Paul, 475
Tilyou, George C., 286, 309, 353
Tilzer, Albert von, 314, 326
Tilyou, George C., 254
Time-Life buildings, 505, 626
Time magazine, 399, 805
Time Warner, 737, 798, 799, 801, 805, 816, 837, 866
Time, Inc., 682, 799, 827
Times Square, 272, 292–295, 318, 352, 368, 381, 386, 421, 429, 435, 491, 495, 532, 540–542, 548, 564, 642, 662, 667, 674, 677, 691, 733, 736, 740, 754, 774, 779, 807, 813, 836, 839, 844, 846, 863, 864, 868, 875
  Astor Hotel and, 293
  Cohan statue in, 623
  Father Duffy statue in, 502

  recruiting office in, 552
  spectaculars, 528
  Times Tower in, 293
  TKTS booth in, 713
  Zipper in, 435
Tin Pan Alley, 285
Tisch Children's Zoo, 852
Tisch Foundation, 798, 852
Tisch, Laurence A., 624, 639, 776, 782
Tisch, Preston Robert, 639, 726
Tishman Brothers, 567
Tishman, David, 620
Tishman, Alan V., 726
Tishman Speyer Properties, 834, 848
Titanic Memorial Lighthouse, 344
Titanic, R.M.S., 336, 337
TKTS booth, 713
tobacco, 42, 333
  colonial American export of, 28
  Liggett & Myers, 333, 416
  Philip Morris, 279, 479
Tobey, Barney, 799
Tobias, Charles, 511
Tobias, George, 496, 604
Tobin, Austin J., 742
Todd, Mike, 536, 577, 619
Todd Shipyards, 360
Toler, Sidney, 285, 444
Toller, Ernst, 517
Tombs, The, 79
Tom Cat Bakery, 808
Tompkins Square "Massacre," 172
Tompkins Square riots, 792
Tompkins, Daniel D., 51, 55–58, 63, 234
Tomlin, Bradley W., 576, 593
Tomlin, Lily, 738, 753
Tom Thumb (Charles Stratton), 84, 134
Tone, Franchot, 460, 523, 612, 682
Tony Awards, 560
Tooker, George, 576
topless bars, 833
Toretzka, Ludmilla, 541
Torn, Rip, 654
Torre, Joe, 759
Torrey, John, 57, 159, 171
Torrey, William, 89
Torrez, Mike, 739
Torrio, Johnny, 614
Toscanini, Arturo, 504, 609
tour buses, 810, 815, 826
Town & Country magazine, 90
Town Hall, 391, 393
Townsend, James Bliss, 390

Trabert, Tony, 595, 605
Tracy, Lee, 406, 420, 437, 630
Trachtenberg, Jeffrey A., 838
Trachtenberg, Marvin, 731
traffic, vehicular, 411, 426, 495, 549, 582, 597, 602, 607, 628, 666
cops, 312, 318, 324, 378
signals, 378, 404
Trager, James, 770, 788, 805
Trager, Philip, 752
Train, Arthur, 291, 301, 313, 319, 322, 385, 390, 395, 428, 483, 550
Train, George F., 115, 144, 150, 160, 171
Train, John, 632
transcontinental pipeline, 694
transcontinental railroad, 153, 156, 158
Transit Authority, 770
transit fares, 213, 289, 389, 563, 592, 666, 694, 706, 723, 756, 770, 782, 804, 830
transit strikes, 213, 288, 752
Transport Workers Union (TWU), 488, 501, 527, 587, 597, 628, 665
trash baskets, 579
Traub, James, 805, 827
Traubel, Helen, 605
Travers, William R., 143
Travolta, John, 738
Treacher, Arthur, 524, 775
Treadwell, Adam, 56
Treadwell, Sophie, 437
Tresca, Carlos, 349, 538
Triangle Shirtwaist Co., 311
fire, 328
Triborough Bridge and Tunnel Authority, 553
Triborough Bridge, 495, 606
Trilling, Diana, 838
Trinity Cemetery, 84
Trinity Church, 16, 17, 19, 26, 27, 35, 42, 43, 80, 91, 378, 730
Trippe, Juan, 398, 756
trolleys, 210, 219, 235, 265, 300, 318, 494, 553, 554, 582, 611
Trollope, Frances, 69
Trotsky, Leon, 364
Trottier, Bryan, 753, 759, 767
Trowbridge, John, 186
Troy, Matthew H., 728
Truex, Ernest, 313, 461, 524
True Story magazine, 379
Truman, Harry S., 553, 557, 563, 591
Trumbull, Edward, 446
Trumbull, Jonathan, 51, 86

Trump, Donald, 754, 768, 773, 783, 788, 809, 812, 823, 829, 846, 859, 875
Trump, Fred C., 572, 579, 650, 864
Trump, Ivana, 812
Truscott, Alan F., 654
Tryon, William, 30, 31, 33
Tschirky, Oscar, 238, 465, 580
tuberculosis, 114, 232, 272, 499
Tucci, Stanley, 788, 877
Tucker, Sophie, 320, 401, 407, 415, 511, 631, 668
Tudor, Antony, 536, 551
tugboats, 124, 133, 404, 534, 545, (see also McAllister, Moran)
Tugwell, Rexford Guy, 465, 499, 520
Tune, Tommy, 676, 713, 744, 763, 767, 812
Tunnel Authority, 495, 553
tunnels, 300, 318
Brooklyn-Battery, 574
Holland (see Holland Tunnel)
Lincoln, 501
Moses, Robert, and, 495
Queens-Midtown, 521
Steinway, 277, 306, 356
Tunney, Gene, 422, 430
Turini, Giovanni, 187, 220
Turk, Roy, 407
Turkey Trot, 332, 347
Turley, Bob, 620
Turner Construction Co., 279
Turner, Kathleen, 877
Tuscarora, 35
Tuttle, Charles M., 449
tuxedo, 215
TV Guide, 593
Twain, Mark, 146, 159, 210, 214
Tweed, W. M. "Boss," 100, 109, 126, 127, 131, 133, 137, 143, 144, 148, 149, 151, 154, 157, 160–162, 166, 169, 174, 178, 181, 185, 737
courthouse, 137, 876
Twentieth Century-Fox, 776
Twiggy, 767
Twiller, Wouter van, 4
Twist, The, 632
2¢ plain, 626
Twombly, Cy, 636
Twombly, Hamilton McK., 183, 324
Tyler, John, 81, 87
Tyler, Royall, 40
Tynan, Kenneth, 690

typewriters, 173, 184, 187, 189, 202
IBM, 475
L.C. Smith, 295
Remington, 176, 176, 187
Royal, 295
Underwood, 243
Typhoid Mary, 283, 306, 508
typhoid fever, 141
typhus, 101, 127, 139, 141
typographers, 641, 646
Typographers Association, 331
typography,
Fotosetter, 569
Linotype and, 207
Tyson, Cicely, 689
Tzolis, Steve, 769, 796

Uhl, Anna Behr, 88
Uhl, Jakob, 88, 127
Uhry, Alfred, 788
Ulric, Lenore, 380, 391, 406
Ultan, Lloyd, 867
Umeki, Miyoshi, 619
Uncle Sam, 367
Underwood-Simmons Tariff, 346
unemployment, 819, 842
Unger, Barbara, 867
UNICEF Building, 790
Unification Church, 724, 730
Uniformed Sanitationmen's Assn., 680
Union College, 55
Union Pacific RR, 145, 271
Union Square, 54, 70, 112, 333
farmers' market in, 792
Union Theological Seminary, 75, 80, 207, 325, 475
United Artists, 421
United Brotherhood of Carpenters, 195
United Federation of Teachers, 628, 635, 681, 723, 775
United Fruit Co., 726
United Hebrew Charities, 172
United Hebrew Trades union, 311
United Hospital Fund, 189
United Jewish Appeal (UJA), 513, 716
United Mine Workers, 275, 349
United Nations, 539, 552, 568, 578, 579, 633, 734, 790, 829, 853
car parking and, 673
UNRRA, 539
United Negro College Fund, 545
United Press, 307
United Press International, 617
United States Steel, 270, 305

Universal Pictures, 339
building, 567
University Settlement, 238
Untermeyer, Louis, 577, 737
Untermyer, Samuel, 520
Urban Center, 754
Urban Development Corp., 692, 704, 722, 734
Uris Brothers, 456, 579, 625, 677, 764
U.S. Courthouse, 498
U.S. Customs Service, 42
U.S. Pharmaeopoeia, 58
U.S. v. E. C. Knight Co., 242
U.S.S. Maine, 256
Utopia, 298

Vaccaro, Brenda, 660, 676, 817
Vail, Alfred L., 77, 121
Vail, Theodore N., 325
Valenstein, Lawrence, 367, 412, 762
Valentine, Lewis J., 486, 559
Valentino, Rudolph, 371, 421
Vallée, Rudy, 409, 438, 461, 484, 491, 637
Vallone, Peter, 819, 853
Value Line, 458, 501, 574, 787
Van Alstyne, Egbert, 284, 326, 362
Van Anda, Carr, 295
Van and Schenck, 381, 387
Van Arsdale, Harry, Jr., 658, 780
Van Beuren, A., 807
Van Buren, Martin, 60, 62, 66, 68, 74, 80, 93, 129
Van Buren, William H., 95
van Corlear, P.A., 2, 5
Van Cortlandt Mansion, 25, 223
Van Cortlandt, Jacobus, 19
van Cortlandt, Oloff S., 4
Van Cortlandt, Philip, 35, 37, 38, 68
Van Cortlandt, Pierre, 37
Van Cortlandt, Stephanus, 13–15, 17
Van Dam, Rip, 22, 23, 26
van der Donck, Adriaen, 6, 8
Van Doren, Carl, 405, 427
Van Doren, Charles, 618
Van Doren, Irita B., 420, 667
Van Druten, John, 469, 484, 524, 541, 546, 576, 583
Van Dyke, Dick, 504, 631
Van Etten, Nathan B., 597
Van Fleet, Jo, 594, 612, 839
Van Ingen, Bernard J., 597
van Itallie, Jean-Claude, 667
Van Patten, Brenda, 817
Van Patten, Dick, 719

Van Patten, Joyce, 604, 753, 766, 794
Van Peebles, Melvin, 703
Van Rensselaer, Stephen, 38, 63, 79, 86
Van Schaick, Myndert, 95
Van Slyke, Helen, 707
Van Vechten, Carl, 647, 653
Van Wyck, Robert A., 251, 264, 270
Van Wyck, Theodorus, 54
Van Zandt, Peter, 56
Van Zandt, Wyant, 58
Vance, Courtney B., 788, 806
Vandenheuvel, John Cornelius, 38
Vanderbeeck, Rem Jansen, 5
Vanderbilt, Alfred Gwynne, 340, 355
Vanderbilt, Alice Gwynne, 310
Vanderbilt, Alva (Mrs. William K.), 177, 203, 317
Vanderbilt, Amy, 588, 718
Vanderbilt, Consuelo, 595, 649
Vanderbilt, Cornelius, 59, 67, 72, 86, 105, 129, 133, 136, 145, 149, 152, 153, 155, 157, 160, 170, 183
II, 205, 241, 260, 310, 312
III, 238, 519, 525, 534
IV, 450, 489
Jr., 607
Vanderbilt, Grace (Mrs. Cornelius II), 607
Vanderbilt, Frederick W., 350
Vanderbilt, George W., 216, 239
Vanderbilt, Virginia G. Fair, 456
Vanderbilt, Harold S., 416, 425, 445, 697
Vanderbilt, William H., 136, 182, 183, 196, 199, 204, 206, 211, 376
Vanderbilt, William K., 190, 195, 203, 204, 260, 285, 384
Vanderbilt, Mrs. William K., Jr., 456
Vander Meer, Johnny, 511
VanDerZee, James, 361
Vane, Sutton, 406
Vanity Fair magazine, 344, 765, 816
Varela, Felix, 65, 75
Varian, Isaac L., 74, 78, 79, 82, 135
Varick, James, 59
Varick, Richard, 41, 49, 67
Variety, 296, 325, 491
Vaseline petroleum jelly, 177
vaudeville, 190, 196, 202, 215, 389, 470
Vaughan, Sarah, 525, 547, 795
Vechten, Carl Van, 337

Veiller, Lawrence, 268, 299
Vera-Ellen, 517, 524, 555, 570, 758
Verdi Park, 439
Verdon, Gwen, 594, 604, 613, 668, 725, 868
Vereen, Ben, 708
Verhulst, Willem, 2
Verizon Communications, 867
Verneuil, Louis, 576
Verplanck, Gulian Crommelin, 71
Verrazano, Giovanni da, 1, 319
Verrazano-Narrows Bridge, 621, 628
Verrett, Shirley, 683
Viacom, 695, 788, 826, 827
Vicious, Sid, 749
Victory Gardens, 538
Vidal, Gore, 630
Vidal, Stephen, 804
videos, 839
Viele, Gen. Egbert L., 174, 191, 194
Vietnam War, 657, 671, 679, 686, 705, 710
Villa Julia, 274
Village Voice, 602
Villard houses, 209, 547
Villard, Henry, 195, 196, 206, 209, 232, 253, 266
Villard, Oswald Garrison, 266, 316, 373, 569
Villas, Guillermo, 739
Vines, Ellsworth, 462, 470
Virginia Minstrels, 86
Visiting Nurse Service, 392, 545
vodka, 715
Vogel, Paula, 817
Vogue magazine, 318, 655, 701, 776, 793
Voice of America, 534
Volcker, Paul, 747, 787
Volstead Act, 383
Volunteers of America, 245
von Furstenberg, Betsy, 583, 594
von Tilzer, Albert, 396
Von Tilzer, Harry, 268, 285, 308, 556
Vonnegut, Kurt, 588
Vorse, Mary Heaton, 332, 361
voting machines, 231
Voting Rights Act, 736
Vreeland, Diana, 502, 641, 701, 712, 799
Vuchetich, Yevgeny, 623

Wachtler, Sol, 814
WACS, 537
Wade, Virginia, 684
waffles,
    Dutch colonists and, 2

Wagenvoord, James, 731
Wagner College, 373
Wagner, Robert F., 473, 591, 600, 606, 610, 613, 627, 629, 634, 635, 638, 651, 662, 808
    Jr., 596, 616, 657, 686
    Sen. Robert F., 505, 591
    bust of, 623
Wagner-Steagall Act, 505
Wagner, Webster, 145
Wainwright, Jonathan M., 548
Waite, Ralph, 660
Wakefield, Dan, 622, 817
Wald, Lillian D., 234, 235, 299, 356, 520
Waldo, Gertrude Rhinelander, 259
Waldo, Rhinelander, 322
Waldorf-Astoria, 465, 487, 572, 585
    Alfred E. Smith Dinner at, 549
    debutante balls at, 492, 595
Waldorf salad, 238
Waldron, Charles, 390
Walk/Don't Walk signals, 601
Walken, Christopher, 771
Walker, C.J., Mme., 382
Walker, Dixie, 530, 561
Walker, Elisha, 334
Walker, James J., 296, 387, 417, 425, 435, 438, 440, 446, 457, 463, 467, 469, 492, 508, 552, 613
Walker, John Brisben, 217, 235, 242, 257, 295
Walker, Joseph A., 707
Walker, June, 374, 460
Walker, Nancy, 530, 546, 566, 571, 631
Walker, Stanley, 483
Walkman casette player, 750
Wall Street Journal, 222, 276
Wall Street, 8
Wall, E. Berry, 225
Wallace, Christopher G., 848
Wallace, De Witt, 394, 756
Wallace, Lila Bell Acheson, 394, 771
Wallace, Mike, 856
Wallach, Anne Tolstoi, 757
Wallach, Eli, 594, 618
Wallant, Edward Lewis, 636
Waller, Fats, 543, 744
Wallack, James W., 92, 110, 128, 137
Wallack, Lester, 92, 128, 137, 199, 220
Walling, George W., 113
Walling, William English, 311, 316

Walsh, George, 752
Walston, Ray, 604
Walter, Eugene, 319, 529
Walters, Charles, 570
Walters, Lou, 536, 739
Walthall, Henry B., 346
Walton, Frank L., 593
Wanamaker, John, 179, 245, 282, 337
Wanamaker, Rodman, 410
Wanamaker, Sam, 555
Wanger, Walter, 682, 654
Wang Labs, 730
Wantagh Causeway, 442
Wappinger tribe, 6
war bonds, 527
Warburg, Felix M., 315, 365, 501, 558
Warburg, James, 451, 466
Warburg, Paul, 441
Ward, Benjamin, 769, 770, 876
Ward, Ferdinand, 195, 206
Ward, J.Q.A., 154, 160, 210, 214, 225, 236, 286, 325
Warden, Jack, 603, 613
Wards Island, 4, 92, 99
Warfield, David, 267, 308, 332, 583
Warhol, Andy, 588, 630, 642, 647, 653, 660, 667, 707, 731, 744, 767, 771, 776, 788
Waring, George E., Jr., 116, 245, 259
Warner Brothers corsets, 353
Warner Communications, 641
Warren, Earl, 596
Warren, Harry, 452, 461, 478, 492
Warren, Adm. Sir Peter, 25
Warren, Lavinia, 134
Warrick, Ruth, 624, 713
Wartels, Nat, 805
Washington Arch, 244, 692
Washington, Booker T., 316
Washington, George, 30, 31, 33–35, 37, 41, 42, 221
    statue of, 214
Washington Heights, 289, 299, 451
Washington Market, 547, 678
Washington Square Park, 587, 621
Wasserstein, Wendy, 766, 794, 817, 847
waste disposal, 212, 808, 864
water system, 47, 48, 69, 77, 85, 226, 310, 371, 499, 754, 764, 768, 851, 859
waterfront, 495
    Commission, 592
Waterman fountain pen, 207

Waterman, Lewis E., 272
Waters, Ethel, 452, 478, 491, 524, 576
Watson, Bob, 759
Watson, Elkanah, 44
Watson, Lucile, 278, 399, 503, 642
Watson, Thomas A., 184
Watson, Thomas J., 282, 312, 403, 528, 606
Jr., 820
Watts, John, 225
Watts, Richard, 758
Wave Hill, 86, 633
Wavecrest, 187
WAVES, 537
Wayne, Anthony, 36
Wayne, David, 560, 565, 594, 654, 832
Weather Underground, 686
Weathermen, 692
Weaver, Fritz, 604, 660, 696
Weaver, Robert C., 650
Weaver, Sigourney, 771, 794
Weaver, Sylvester "Pat," 577, 588, 598, 878
Webb & Knapp, 610, 662
Webb, Clifton, 368, 414, 438, 444, 452, 470, 478, 546, 589, 599
Webb, J. Seward, Jr., 425
Webb, William H., 75, 153, 261
Webber, Andrew Lloyd, 763, 794
Webber, Robert, 604, 612, 630
Weber and Fields, 202, 249, 267, 285, 536
Weber, Joe, 258, 339
Weber, Max, 332, 450, 636
Webster, Daniel, 56, 61, 180
Webster, Jean, 352
Webster, Margaret, 555, 565
Wechsler Coffee Co., 596
Wedtech, 792
Weed, Thurlow, 67, 78, 80, 93, 100, 132, 135
Weegee, 550, 566, 682, 817
Weidman, Jerome, 483, 643, 857
Weil, Cynthia, 643
Weill, Kurt, 504, 511, 529, 542, 571, 577
Weill, Sanford I., 628, 747, 780, 793, 815, 820, 853
Weinberg, Sidney J., 540, 687
Weiner, August, 516
Weinman, Adolf A., 354
Weiss, Al, 691
Welch, William H., 186
Weld, Tuesday, 738, 772
welfare, 472, 657, 722, 836, 853, 876
Welfare Island, 12, 390, 684, 704

Weller, Michael, 707, 749
Welles, Orson, 490, 504, 510, 529, 772
Wells, Fargo, 102
Wells, David, 858
Wells, James N., 63
Wenger, Beth S., 838
Wenrich, Percy, 391, 589
Werfel, Franz, 504
Werner, Morris R., 436
Wertenbaker, Thomas J., 565
Wesendonck, Hugo, 123
West, Dorothy, 483
West, Mae, 375
West, Nathanael, 460, 476
West End Avenue, 194
West Side Association, 143, 191, 194
West Side Highway, 449, 501, 711
West Side Renewal Area, 650
Westbrook, T.R., 197
Westchester, 18
parkways in, 467
Westcott, Edward N., 257
Western Union, 112, 142, 164, 178, 184, 195, 197, 325
Building, 177
Westervelt, Jacob A., 102
Westinghouse, 210, 831
bankruptcy of, 312
building, 408
elevators, 423
Westinghouse, George, 149, 210, 226, 350
air brake, 149
Westminster Kennel Club, 184
Weston, William, 44
West End Avenue, 354
West Nile virus, 861, 866
Western Electric, 770
Westlake, Donald E., 630
Westley, Helen, 386, 400, 460
Westmoreland, Wm. C., 776
Weston, Jack, 576, 731
Westway, 717, 764, 775
Whalen, Grover, 377, 474, 513, 580, 603, 640
Wharton, Edith, 267, 295, 345, 385, 405, 443, 483
Wheatena, 191
Wheatley, William, 131
Whitaker, Rogers E.M., 718, 757
White Plains, 18
Battle of, 34
Whitestone, 156
white wings, 245
White, Alfred Tredway, 184, 392
White, Andrew D., 205
White, Andrew J., 139
White, E.B., 412, 550, 569, 588, 776

White, George, 332, 357, 381, 386, 484, 491
White, Josh, 690
White, Katherine S., 737
White, Norval, 746
White, Stanford, 191, 196, 211, 220, 221, 225, 229, 233, 237, 244, 254, 257–259, 261, 273, 274, 284, 286, 291, 293, 294, 303, 304, 309, 376
White, Theodore H., 743
White, Walter F., 372, 601
Whitehead, John C., 875
Whitehead, Robert, 576, 877
Whitelaw, Edward A., 254
Whiteman, Paul, 387, 396, 400, 407, 676
Whiteside, Walker, 319
Whiting, George, 543
Whiting, Jack, 438, 517
Whiting, Richard, 381, 470
Whitman, Charles S., 298, 316, 335, 349, 359, 372, 557
Whitman, Walt, 110, 112, 147
Whitmore, James, 559
Whitney, George, 539
Whitney, Gertrude Vanderbilt, 249, 320, 395, 449, 460, 496, 519, 535
Whitney, Harry Payne, 249, 288, 320, 449
Whitney, John Hay "Jock," 427, 622, 760, 761
Whitney, Payne, 288, 303, 404, 427
Whitney, Richard, 441, 507, 716
Whitney, Wm. C., 162, 174, 203, 205, 214, 225, 226, 288
Who, The, 690
Whorf, Richard, 576, 588
Whyte, William H., 607, 794, 818
Wickersham, George W., 494
Wickes, Forsyth, 489
Wickham, William C., 172
Wiechquaesgeck tribe, 5, 8
Wilander, Mats, 795
Wilbur, Richard, 609
Wilde, Cornel, 503
Wilder, Billy, 599, 604
Wilder, Thornton, 510, 535, 608, 725
Wildhorn, Frank, 847
Wildlife Conservation Society, 263, 824
Wilgus, William J., 260, 265, 282, 330
Wilkerson, Catherine, 692
Willard, Frances, 224
Willard, Jess, 362
Willard, John, 380, 395

Willensky, Elliot, 746, 782
Willett, Marinus, 59
Willett, Thomas, 11
Williams, Anna W., 228, 239, 294, 597
Williams, Alexander "Clubber," 181
Williams, Bert, 332, 381, 396
Williams, Clarence, 662
Williams, Cootie, 445, 777
Williams, Garth, 550, 588
Williams, Hank, Jr., 767
Williams, Harry H., 284
Williams, Hope, 428, 437, 452, 469, 478
Williams, Jesse Lynch, 368, 374
Williams, Robin, 783
Williams, Samm-Art, 753
Williams, Serena, 863, 878
Williams, Spencer, 662
Williams, Tennessee, 550, 559, 565, 583, 594, 603, 612, 618, 623, 630, 636, 648, 707, 766
Williamsburg, 48, 283
fires, 359
Satmars in, 558, 700, 748
Willig, George, 739
Willis, Nathaniel Parker, 90, 110
Willkie, Wendell L., 442, 474, 520, 544
Willowbrook, 587, 646, 706, 712
Wills Moody, Helen, 401, 415, 462, 511
Willson, Meredith, 613, 631
Wilson, August, 771, 788, 817, 838
Wilson, Bill, 493
Wilson, Earl, 535
Wilson, Edmund, 443, 554
Wilson, Elizabeth, 862
Wilson, H.W., Co., 367
Wilson, James, 40
Wilson-Gorman Tariff Act, 238
Wilson, Lanford, 712, 753, 771, 788, 822
Wilson, Malcolm E., 711, 716
Wilson, Teddy, 783
Wilson, Woodrow, 305, 335, 359, 362, 365, 371, 383
Wiltse, David, 777
Winchell, Walter, 469, 471, 480, 503, 561, 581, 647, 708
Windels, Paul, 450, 480
Winfield, Dave, 801
Winkle, Matt, 398
Winkler, Henry, 719
Winn, Marie, 856
Winninger, Charles, 381
Winters, Shelley, 732
Wintour, Anna, 793

Wise, Rabbi Stephen S., 316, 329, 481
Wiseman, Joseph, 570, 783
Wismer, Harry, 677
Witt, Johan de, 11
Wodehouse, P.G., 368, 375, 437, 484
Wolf, Dick, 827
Wolf, Gerard R., 766
Wolfe, George C., 878
Wolfe, Thomas, 443, 484, 489, 516
Wolfe, Tom, 682, 788
Wolfert, Ira, 541
Wolff, Kurt, 535
Wolfson, Erwin S., 556, 644
Wolheim, Louis, 396, 406
Wollman Rink, 586
Wollman, Kate, 586, 601
wolves, 14
Woman's Day, 502
Woman's Home Companion, 607, 612
Woman Teachers' Association, 235
Women Against Pornography, 773
Women's Detention Center, 703
Women's Medical Association, 168
Women's Medical College, 137
Women's Political Union, 305
women's rights, 93, 122, 141, 144, 157, 293, 311, 317, 329, 365, 377, 384, 693, 700
Women's Strike for Equality, 693
Women's Wear Daily, 325, 632, 677, 697
Wonder, Stevie, 713
Wood, Alfred M., 135
Wood, Fernando, 97, 106, 109, 111, 113, 114, 120, 125, 126, 144
Wood, Herbert, 639
Wood, James R., 92, 114
Wood, Maxine, 555
Wood, Peggy, 352, 357, 368, 381
Wood, Sylvia, 639
Woodford, Stewart L., 157
Woodhaven, 59
    Dexter Park in, 211
Woodhull & Claflin's Weekly, 160, 166, 169, 171, 172
Woodhull, Caleb S., 95–98
Woodhull, Nathaniel, 31, 32

Woodhull, Victoria C., 152, 157, 160, 162, 166, 169, 182, 425
Woodlawn Cemetery, 134, 253, 330, 364, 378, 390
Woodlawn, 172
Woodling, Gene, 585
Woods, Arthur, 349
Woodside, 147, 269, 366
    Dexter Park in, 375
Woodstock, 690
Woodward, Ann, 605
Woodward, Helen Rosen, 419
Woollcott, Alexander, 380, 517, 541
Woolley, Monty, 517, 648
Woolworth Building, 347
Wooster, Boots, 352, 399
word processors, 718, 730
workers' comp, 323
workfare, 829
Working Girls' Vacation Society, 201
Workingman's Movement, 66
Workingmen's Home, 110, 147
Working Woman, 742
World Almanac, 150
World Book, 629
world's fairs, 104, 512, 514, 515, 519, 651, 657
World Financial Center, 778
World Trade Center, 669, 684, 709, 720, 735, 736, 739, 819, 871
World War I, 349, 355, 359, 363, 371
    II, 513, 527, 533, 538, 544, 547, 548
World Wide Holdings, 802
Worth, Irene, 541, 576, 654, 752, 811, 877
Worth Monument, 115
Wouk, Herman, 559, 565, 598, 603
WPA, 489, 495, 516, 544
Wrangell, Baron George, 564, 688
Wray, Fay, 478, 503
Wragge, Sidney, 745
Wright, Benjamin, 55, 57
Wright, Carol von P., 766
Wright, Richard, 523, 529, 549
Wright, Silas, 76, 86, 89
Wright, Teresa, 613, 682
Wurman, Saul, 766
Wurster, Frederick W., 242
Wyatt, Jane, 583
Wyatt, Whit, 530

Wycherly, Margaret, 469, 608
Wyeth, Andrew, 731
Wyler, Gretchen, 604
Wylie, Janice, 649, 655
Wynn, Ed, 346, 352, 357, 362, 391, 451, 461
Wynn, Keenan, 524, 550

Xerox copier, 509, 629
Ximenes, Ettore, 319

yachting,
    transatlantic race, 151
Yale, Frankie, 430
Yankee Stadium, 511, 556, 624, 709, 745, 857
Yates, Abraham, Jr., 31
Yates, Joseph C., 60
Yellen, Jack, 391, 415, 491, 517, 524, 530, 542
yellow fever, 18, 25, 44–47, 49, 50, 60, 111, 118, 141
yellow journalism, 253
Yorkville, 769, 807
Yunich, David L., 872
Yerkes, Charles T., 163, 294, 338, 357
Yeshiva University, 214, 597
Yezierska, Anzia, 385, 395, 413
Yiddish Art Theater, 420
Yiddish theater, 199, 232, 420, 623
Yiddishe Tageblatt, 210
YIVO Institute, 522, 826
YMCA, 103, 114, 142, 154, 184, 205, 409, 454
YM-YWHA, 173, 277
Yonkers, 12, 16
Yoor, Jan, 659
Yordan, Philip, 546
Yorkville, 77, 289
York Avenue, 435
Youmans, Vincent, 391, 429, 452, 470
Young, Art, 235, 331, 344, 374, 541
Young, Gig, 594, 744
Young, Joe, 375, 461
Young, John, 89, 95
Young, Lester, 624
Young Lords, 685
Young, Owen D., 379
Young, Rida Johnson, 326, 369, 386
Young, Robert R., 553, 597, 617
Young, Roland, 361, 381, 594

Young, Sarah Gilman, 197
Young, Stark, 406, 483, 648
Young, Whitney M., Jr., 634
Youngman, Henny, 503, 720, 857

Zabar, Eli, 586, 715
Zabar, Louis, 586
Zabar, Saul, 586, 715
Zabar, Stanley, 586, 715
Zabar's, 586, 715, 779
Zackrzewska, Marie E., 114
Zagat, Timothy, 751
Zale, Tony, 556, 561
Zangwill, Israel, 319
Zeckendorf, William, 552, 600, 605, 633, 662, 663, 721, 734
    Jr., 734, 802, 807, 875
Zeisloft, E.I., 261
Zell, Samuel, 834, 868
Zenger, John Peter, 23, 25
Ziegfeld, Florenz, 248, 308, 320, 326, 381, 429, 470
Ziegfeld Follies, 308, 314, 320, 326, 332, 347, 352, 357, 362, 368, 375, 381, 386, 391, 396, 400, 407, 429
Ziff-Davis, 427, 827
Ziga, Charles J., 821
Zimmerman, Heinie, 369
Zindel, Paul, 696, 702
Zinn, Howard, 622
Zion, Libby, 770
Zion, Robert L., 678, 768
Zion, Sidney, 770
zoning regulations, 362, 638, 644, 650, 662, 663, 691, 713, 715, 720, 745, 785, 833
zoos,
    Bronx, 263, 531, 692, 741, 824
    Congo Gorilla Forest in, 864
    Jungle World at, 779
    World of Birds at, 710
    Central Park, 138, 486, 754, 796, 824
    Prospect Park, 238, 824
Zorina, Vera, 510, 525
Zouaves, 125
Zuckerman, Ben, 747
Zuckerman, Mortimer B., 820, 846, 861
Zukor, Adolph, 338, 436